TO THE STUDENT

Could you use a little help? A Student Workbook for this textbook is available through your college bookstore under the title *Student Workbook for use with Business Law and the Regulatory Environment: Concepts and Cases, Ninth Edition.* The workbook, prepared by Michael J. Phillips and Arlen W. Langvardt, can help you test your understanding of the concepts covered in the textbook and learn how to study business law.

If the Student Workbook is not on the bookshelf, ask your bookstore manager to order a copy for you.

Michael B. Metzger is currently Associate Dean of Academics at the Indiana University School of Business. Before joining the faculty at Indiana, he held several positions, including Deputy Securities Commissioner, state of Indiana; Senior Legislative Analyst, Indiana Legislative Council; and partner in a private law firm. Metzger has served as the Senior Staff Editor for the *American Business Law Journal*. He has received three "Best Article" awards from the *Journal*, and also has earned 12 undergraduate and graduate teaching awards at Indiana University. Metzger received his B.A. from Indiana University and his J.D. from Indiana University's School of Law.

Jane P. Mallor has taught business law at Indiana University since 1976. During that time, she has received several teaching awards, including the Student Alumni Council Senior Faculty Award, the Faculty Colloquium for Excellence in Teaching, and the Amoco Foundation Award for Distinguished Teaching. Mallor received her B.A. from Indiana University and her J.D from Indiana University School of Law.

A. James Barnes currently is Dean and Professor of Public and Environmental Affairs at Indiana University, as well as Director of the Long Island Lighting Company. He previously won a distinguished teaching award from Indiana University's School of Business. Barnes's government positions include Deputy Administrator of EPA, General Counsel of EPA, General Counsel of the Department of Agriculture, and trial attorney in the Department of Justice. Barnes received his B.A. with honors from Michigan State University and J.D. Cum Laude from Harvard Law School.

Thomas Bowers joined the faculty of Indiana University's School of Business after working for the Brooklyn District Attorney and the Enforcement Division of the United States Securities and Exchange Commission in New York City. He has received 10 outstanding teaching awards at Indiana, and is the only two-time recipient of the Indiana University Student Choice Award for outstanding teaching. Bowers graduated Summa Cum Laude from the Ohio State University and earned his J.D. at New York University.

Michael J. Phillips has been teaching business law at Indiana University's School of Business since 1977. During that period, he has won eight best article or comment awards from the *American Business Law Journal*. After filling various editorial board positions, Phillips also served as editor-in-chief of the *Journal* from 1988 to 1990. In addition, he has twice chaired the business law department at Indiana University's School of Business. Phillips received his B.A. from Johns Hopkins University, earned a J.D. from Columbia University, and received L.L.M. and S.J.D. degrees from George Washington University.

Arlen W. Langvardt currently Associate Professor of Business Law, joined the Indiana University Graduate School of Business after private practice as a trial attorney involved in a variety of legal areas. Langvardt has received several teaching awards at both the undergraduate and M.B.A. levels, and in 1989, he received the Holmes/Cardozo Award from the Academy of Legal Studies in Business. He has published 15 articles in law and business journals and delivered the 1992 Boal Memorial Lecture at Georgetown University Law Center. Langvardt received his B.A. with highest honors from Hastings College and J.D. with distinction from the University of Nebraska.

Business Law and the Regulatory Environment

Concepts and Cases

Ninth Edition

Michael B. Metzger
Jane P. Mallor
A. James Barnes
Thomas Bowers
Michael J. Phillips
Arlen Langvardt
all of
Indiana University

IRWIN

Chicago • Bogota • Boston • Buenos Aires • Caracas
London • Madrid • Mexico City • Sydney • Toronto

Senior sponsoring editor: *Craig Beytien*
Associate editor: *Karen Mellon*
Marketing manager: *Cindy Ledwith*
Project editor: *Ethel Shiell*
Production manager: *Laurie Kersch*
Interior designer: *Sailer & Cooke Design Services*
Cover designer: *Andrew Curtis*
Art coordinator: *Mark Malloy*
Compositor: *Carlisle Communications, Ltd.*
Typeface: *10/12 Times Roman*
Printer: *Von Hoffmann Press*

Library of Congress Cataloging-in-Publication Data

Business law and the regulatory environment : concepts and cases /
    Michael B. Metzger . . . [et al.].—9th ed.
        p.   cm.—(Irwin legal studies in business series)
        Includes index.
        ISBN 0-256-14103-7.—ISBN 0-256-17191-2 (instructor's ed.)
        1. Commercial law—United States—Cases.   2. Commercial law—United
States.   I. Metzger, Michael B.   II. Series.
    KF888.B8   1995
    346.73′07—dc20
    [347.3067]   94–12503

Printed in the United States of America

2 3 4 5 6 7 8 9 0 VH 1 0 9 8 7 6 5

PREFACE

This is the ninth UCC edition (and the sixteenth edition overall) of a text that first appeared in 1935. Throughout its 60-odd years of existence, this text has been a leader in the fields of business law and the legal environment of business. To us, there are two major reasons for the book's continuing success. The first is its lucid and comprehensive treatment of the many legal topics that concern business-people and that comprise the traditional business law curriculum. The second is its responsiveness both to changes in those traditional subjects and to new views about that curriculum. This edition, we believe, continues to nurture each of these strengths.

IMPORTANT CHANGES IN THIS EDITION

Chapter Changes

This edition's lineup of chapters remains much the same as the eighth edition's lineup. However, relevant materials from the eighth edition's computer law chapter have been relocated in other chapters throughout the book. Replacing the computer law chapter as Chapter 53 is a new insurance chapter that focuses primarily on fire and casualty insurance.

Substantive Changes within Chapters

This text has always excelled in keeping readers up-to-date about changes in the many legal areas it covers. This edition continues in that tradition. In addition to the extensive checking and updating that always accompany a text's revision, the following changes deserve special mention.

- Chapter 2's expanded discussion of alternative dispute resolution.

- Chapter 4 (the ethics, corporate social responsibility, and corporate control chapter) has been rewritten and reorganized to emphasize business ethics and corporate social responsibility more than previously.

- Chapter 5, Crimes, contains an expanded discussion of the constitutional aspects of criminal law, including recent Supreme Court decisions on various constitutional issues. The chapter also expands its discussion of RICO, in the process including major recent Supreme Court decisions. Finally, the chapter now contains discussions of the Federal Sentencing Guidelines and of computer crimes.

- Chapter 8 now contains a case on the amended version of Lanham Act section 43(a).

- The Uniform Probate Code is integrated into Chapter 26, Estates and Trusts.

- Chapters 30 to 33, the commercial paper chapters, have been completely revised to incorporate Revised Article 3 of the Uniform Commercial Code and the concomitant amendments to Articles 1 and 4 of the UCC. The revision and the amendments have now been adopted by a majority of the states. The revised UCC is presented in full in Appendix B.

- Material on an important new business form, the Limited Liability Company, has been added to Chapters 36 and 39. The latter chapter now bears the title "Limited Partnerships and Limited Liability Companies."

- Material on another new business form, the Limited Liability Partnership, has been added to Chapters 36 to 38.

- Chapters 48 and 49, the antitrust chapters, discuss some recent Supreme Court decisions on attempted monopolization and predatory pricing.

- Chapter 50, Employment Law, now includes the Family Medical and Leave Act of 1993. Also, the chapter's employment discrimination discussion has been significantly revised to reflect the changes made by the Civil Rights Act of 1991 and Supreme Court decisions of 1992 and 1993. Finally, the chapter now contains an Americans with Disabilities Act case.
- Chapter 52, The Legal Environment for International Business, has updated material on GATT and European economic unification.
- As noted earlier, relevant aspects of Chapter 53's computer law discussion have been moved to other chapters. Chapter 53 now is an insurance chapter that emphasizes fire and casualty insurance.

CONTINUING STRENGTHS

This edition naturally continues the following basic features that have made its predecessors successful.

The Previous Edition's Major Changes

This edition continues the two major changes that marked the previous edition: (1) an increased emphasis on ethics, and (2) new pedagogy. Thus, we continue to offer a chapter (Chapter 4) on business ethics, corporate social responsibility, and corporate control. To develop the ethical implications of conventional legal topics, moreover, we continue to present "Ethical and Public Policy Concerns" at the end of each chapter except Chapter 4. As for pedagogy, we continue to make extensive use of figures, charts, concept reviews, and other visual aids.

Comprehensive Coverage

Above all things, we take pride in our thorough and up-to-date coverage of business law. The text continues to excel both in the number of topics it addresses and in the coverage it provides within each topic. This is true both of the basic business law subjects that comprise the core of the text and

also of the regulatory and other areas that commonly are said to constitute the "legal environment" curriculum.

Style and Presentation

We continue to think—and users and reviewers continue to confirm—that this text is written in a style that is at once direct, lucid, and organized, yet also relatively relaxed and conversational. For this reason, we have often been able to cover certain topics by assigning them as reading without lecturing on them. As always, we continue to employ italics and boldface to emphasize key points and terms, to use numbered paragraphs to state the elements of a legal claim or the applications of a legal concept, and to make liberal use of examples. Also aiding students' comprehension of difficult subjects are the charts, figures, and concept summaries mentioned earlier.

Case Selection

We make great efforts to find cases that clearly illustrate important points made in the text. We also try to select cases that are of interest to students and are fun to teach. Except where older decisions are landmarks or best illustrate particular concepts, we try to select recent cases. Our collective in-class experience with recent editions has helped us determine which cases best meet all these criteria. As a result, we think, the average quality of our cases is increasing with each edition.

AACSB Curricular Standards

This text also is well suited to advance the relevant AACSB curricular standards pertaining to business law, the legal environment, and allied areas. The AACSB's April 1991 standards, as revised in April of 1993, say that both undergraduate and MBA curricula should include: ethical and global issues; the influence of political, social, legal, regulatory, environmental, and technological issues; and the impact of demographic diversity on organizations.

Like all business law texts, this book obviously focuses on legal issues, but it helps satisfy the AACSB's standards in other ways as well. Its emphasis on ethics and ethical issues has already been mentioned. In addition, the book provides detailed coverage of the regulatory matters—including environmental law—that usually are central to legal environment courses. It also reflects the AACSB's emphasis on global concerns by containing a full chapter on the legal environment for international business. Furthermore, several of this text's chapters enhance students' understanding of the influence of political and social issues on business and the law. For example, the chapters on the introduction to contracts, product liability, and employment law discuss how the tremendous changes in those areas from the 19th century to the present day reflect the equally great changes in American society over that period. Finally, although we wonder whether business law or any other subject in the business curriculum effectively examines demographic diversity, Chapter 50's discussion of employment discrimination certainly is relevant here.

THE PACKAGE

The ninth edition of this book is complemented by the most extensive, innovative package material in its history. New video and computerized supplements provide methods of applying, updating, and maximizing text materials as never before. Traditional support materials for both students and instructors enhance day-to-day classroom instruction and foster learning. This is truly *the* package for business law education today.

New Teaching and Updating Aids

Irwin's Legal Studies in Business Video Series
Adopters of the ninth edition can obtain Irwin's new case videos for classroom use. These videos, which number 20 in all, are contemporary dramatizations that portray recurrent business law issues. Some of the videos concern an issue or tightly focused group of issues that fit within a single chapter. Most, however, raise multiple issues spanning two or more chapters.

Portions of the case videos are integrated as problem cases in many of this book's chapters. They are designated by a video cassette icon—📼—and the term *Video Case*. The title of the video in question follows immediately.

Supplementary Video Case Notes, prepared by Richard Finkley of Governors State University, outline the facts, issues, and decision for each video segment. In most instances, there are several issues within each dramatization. You will also note that with each identified issue, there is an annotation directing you to the appropriate chapter in this text.

IrwinLink
An innovative new electronic bulletin board service—IrwinLink: Legal Studies—is available to all adopters of the ninth edition. This modem-driven system allows access to the text at its most fundamental levels. "Authors Forum" and "Editors Message" features allow adopters to leave notes for this book's authors and editors. "Instructors Forum" allows interaction among IrwinLink users.

The IrwinLink system will be updated, on-line, by the authors and editors of this book. This electronic format will allow for expeditious responses to queries, requests for updated case information, and suggestions for text revisions. This new service will replace the annual updates that have appeared with previous editions of the text.

Student and Instructor Support Material

Student Workbook
The student workbook, prepared by Michael J. Phillips and Arlen W. Langvardt, is structured by text chapter. Each chapter contains a complete chapter outline, plus true-false, multiple-choice, and short essay questions. For the first time, there is also a section for the student entitled "How to Study Business Law."

Instructor's Manual

We have prepared the instructor's manual for this text. Each chapter in the manual contains outlined suggestions for structuring presentation of the corresponding text chapter material, provides additional material and examples not mentioned in the text, and discusses each text case, providing points for its discussion with students. Each instructor's manual chapter also contains suggested answers to the chapter's ethical and public policy concerns and provides answers to the problems and problem cases. There is also an answer key for questions presented in the student workbook.

Test Bank

The test bank, prepared by Thomas Bowers and Frona Powell of Indiana University, contains true-false, multiple-choice, and short essay questions.

Computest 4

A computerized version of the book's test bank is available. It allows instructors to generate random tests and to add their own questions.

ACKNOWLEDGMENTS

We would like to recognize and thank the many people who have assisted in the preparation of this text. Of particular importance are the able and industrious external reviewers who provided innumerable suggestions for improving the text:

Wayne Anderson, *Southwest Missouri State University*
Rodolfo Camacho, *Oregon State University*
Frank Chong, *Southeast Missouri State University*
Theodore Dinges, *Longview Community College*
William Elliott, *Saginaw Valley State University*
Michael Engber, *Ball State University*

Gene Marsh, *The University of Alabama*
Cary Mills, *Florida Atlantic University*
Gregory Naples, *Marquette University*
Rick Orsinger, *College of DuPage*
Dennis Pappas, *Columbus State Community College*
Robert Peace, *North Carolina State University*
Carol Rasnic, *Virginia Commonwealth University*
Linda Samuels, *George Mason University*
Daphne Sipes, *University of Texas at San Antonio*

We would like to recognize Pam Davis of Indiana University who assisted in the preparation of the manuscript.

Last but not least, we also extend our thanks to Craig Beytien, Karen Mellon, Ethel Shiell, and Jerry Saykes of Richard D. Irwin, Inc.

Michael B. Metzger
Jane P. Mallor
A. James Barnes
Thomas Bowers
Michael J. Phillips
Arlen W. Langvardt

CONTENTS IN BRIEF

CONTENTS

PART 2

CRIMES AND TORTS

P A R T
4

SALES

PART 7

COMMERCIAL PAPER

PART 8

AGENCY LAW

35   THIRD–PARTY RELATIONS OF THE PRINCIPAL AND THE AGENT   *733*

PARTNERSHIP LAW

36   INTRODUCTION TO FORMS OF BUSINESS AND FORMATION OF PARTNERSHIPS   *752*

37   OPERATION OF PARTNERSHIP AND RELATED FORMS   *771*

PART 10

CORPORATIONS

PART
11

REGULATION OF BUSINESS

47   THE FEDERAL TRADE COMMISSION ACT AND CONSUMER PROTECTION LAWS   *1001*

48   ANTITRUST: THE SHERMAN ACT   *1018*

49   THE CLAYTON ACT, THE ROBINSON–PATMAN ACT, AND ANTITRUST EXEMPTIONS AND IMMUNITIES   *1047*

PART   12

Special Topics

List of Cases

FOUNDATIONS

OF

AMERICAN

LAW

CHAPTER 1

THE NATURE OF LAW

INTRODUCTION

Today, businesspeople confront the law at every turn. For example, business firms continually utilize the law of property, contract, and agency. Indeed, business could hardly function without these and other basic bodies of law. In addition to facilitating business activity, the legal system restricts it as well. Today, government regulates most aspects of a firm's operations—for example, advertising, product safety, employee relations, the issuance of securities, and behavior toward competitors.

Thus, businesspeople constantly use, rely on, react to, plan around—and sometimes violate—innumerable legal rules or "laws." For this reason, managers should have a general knowledge of the legal system and the most important legal rules affecting their firms. This text discusses many such rules, often in detail. But your ability to use and apply the legal rules affecting business is incomplete unless you also understand law's general nature, its functions, and how judges interpret it. This understanding could go some way toward reducing business complaints about the law and lawyers.

FOUR PERSPECTIVES ON LAW

This chapter examines law's nature from four different angles. First, it describes, classifies, and ranks the various kinds of rules that are regarded as law in the United States—the *types* of law. This discussion, however, only partly conveys law's general nature. Thus, the chapter's second section discusses a subject known as *jurisprudence* or legal philosophy. Jurisprudence tries to establish a general definition of law, and each of the competing definitions we examine highlights an important facet of law's many-sided nature. Shifting from the theoretical to the pragmatic, this chapter's third section examines some of the *functions* law serves—what it *does*. The chapter concludes by discussing *legal reasoning*, the set of techniques judges use when interpreting legal rules. This discussion should help dispel the common misconception that the law consists of clear and precise commands that judges merely look up and then mechanically apply.

TYPES AND CLASSIFICATIONS OF LAW

The Types of Law

Constitutions   **Constitutions,** which exist at the state and federal levels, have two general functions.[1] First, they establish the structure of government for the political unit they control (a state or the federal government). This involves stating the branches and subdivisions of the government and the powers given and denied to each. Through its **separation of powers,** for example, the U.S. Constitution establishes a Congress and gives it power to legislate or *make* law in certain areas, provides for a chief executive (the president) whose function is to execute or *enforce* the laws, and helps create a federal judiciary to *interpret* the laws. The U.S. Constitution also structures the relationship between the federal government and the states. In the process, it respects the principle of **federalism** by recognizing the states' power to make law in certain areas.

The second function of constitutions is to prevent other units of government from taking certain actions or passing certain laws. Constitutions do so mainly by prohibiting government action that restricts certain individual rights. The Bill of Rights to the U.S. Constitution is an example.

Statutes   **Statutes** are laws created by Congress or a state legislature. They are stated in an authoritative form in statute books or codes. As you will see, however, their interpretation and application are often difficult.

Throughout this text, you encounter state statutes that were originally drafted as **uniform acts.** Uniform acts basically are model statutes drafted by private bodies of lawyers and/or scholars. They do not become law until they are enacted by a legislature. Their aim is to produce state-by-state uniformity on the subjects they address. Examples include the Uniform Commercial Code (which deals with a wide range of commercial law subjects), the Uniform Partnership Act, the Revised Uniform Limited Partnership Act, and the Revised Model Business Corporation Act.

Common Law   The **common law** (also called judge-made law or case law) is that law made and applied by judges as they decide cases not governed by statutes or other types of law. In theory, it exists at the state level only. The common law originated in medieval England. It developed from the decisions of judges in settling disputes. Over time, judges began to follow the decisions of other judges in similar cases. This practice became formalized in the doctrine of *stare decisis* (let the decision stand). As discussed later in this chapter, *stare decisis* has enabled the common law to evolve to meet changing social conditions. Thus, the common law rules in force today often differ considerably from the common law rules of earlier times.

The common law came to America with the first English settlers and was applied by courts during the colonial period.[2] It continued to be used after the Revolution and the adoption of the Constitution, and still governs many cases today. For example, the rules of tort, contract, and agency discussed in this text are mainly common law rules. However, the states have codified (enacted into statute) some parts of the common law. They have also passed statutes superseding judge-made law in certain situations. As discussed in Chapter 9, for example, the states have established special rules for contract cases involving the sale of goods by enacting Article 2 of the Uniform Commercial Code.

This text's torts, contracts, and agency chapters often refer to the *Restatement* (or *Restatement (Second)*) rule on a particular subject. The *Restatements* are collections of common law (and occasionally statutory) rules covering various areas of the law. Because they are promulgated by the American Law Institute rather than by courts, the *Restatements* are not law and do not bind courts. However, state courts often find *Restatement* rules persuasive and adopt them as common law rules within their states. Usually, the *Restatement* rules are the rules actually followed by a majority of the states. Occasionally, however, the *Restatements* stimulate changes in the common law by stating new rules that the courts later decide to follow.

---

[1]Chapter 3 contains more detail on how the U.S. Constitution performs these functions.

[2]However, Louisiana adopted the Code Napoléon, which was based on Roman law.

Equity   The body of law called **equity** has traditionally tried to do discretionary rough justice in situations where common law rules would produce unfair results. In medieval England, common law rules were technical and rigid and the remedies available in common law courts were too few. This meant that some deserving parties could not obtain adequate relief in the common law courts. As a result, the chancellor, the king's most powerful executive officer, began to hear cases that the common law courts could not resolve fairly.

Eventually, separate equity courts emerged to handle the cases heard by the chancellor. These courts took control of a case only when there was no adequate remedy in a regular common law court. In equity courts, procedures were flexible, and rigid rules of law were de-emphasized in favor of general moral maxims. Equity courts also provided several remedies not available in the common law courts (which generally awarded only money damages or the recovery of property). Perhaps the most important of these *equitable remedies* is the **injunction,** a court order forbidding a party to do some act or commanding him to perform some act. Others include the contract remedies of **specific performance** (whereby a party is ordered to perform according to the terms of her contract), **reformation** (in which the court rewrites the contract's terms to reflect the parties' real intentions), and **rescission** (a cancellation of a contract in which the parties are often returned to their precontractual position).

Like the common law, equity principles and practices were brought to the American colonies by the English settlers. They continued to be used after the Revolution and the adoption of the Constitution. Over time, however, the once-sharp line between law and equity has become blurred. Most states have abolished separate equity courts, now allowing one court to handle both legal and equitable claims. Also, equitable principles have been blended together with common law rules, and some traditional equity doctrines have been restated as common law or statutory rules. An example is the doctrine of unconscionability discussed in Chapter 15. Finally, courts sometimes combine an award of money damages with an equitable remedy.

Administrative Regulations and Decisions

Throughout this century, the *administrative agencies* established by Congress and the state legislatures and discussed in Chapter 46 have acquired considerable power, importance, and influence over business. A major reason for the rise of administrative agencies was the myriad of social and economic problems created by the industrialization of the United States that began late in the 19th century. Because legislatures generally lacked the time and expertise to deal with these problems on a continuing basis, the creation of specialized, expert agencies was almost inevitable.

Administrative agencies get the ability to make law through a *delegation* (or handing over) of power from the legislature. Agencies normally are created by a statute that specifies the areas in which the agency can make law and the scope of its power in each area. Often, these statutory delegations are worded so broadly that the legislature has, in effect, merely pointed to a problem and given the agency wide-ranging powers to deal with it.

The two kinds of law made by administrative agencies are **administrative regulations** and **agency decisions.** Like statutes, administrative regulations appear in a precise form in one authoritative source. However, they differ from statutes in that the body enacting them is an agency, not the legislature. In addition, some agencies have an internal court structure that enables them to hear cases arising under the statutes and regulations they enforce. The resulting agency decisions are another kind of law.

Treaties   According to the U.S. Constitution, **treaties** made by the president with foreign governments and approved by two thirds of the U.S. Senate are "the supreme Law of the Land." As we note shortly, treaties invalidate inconsistent state (and occasionally federal) laws.

Ordinances   State governments have subordinate units that exercise certain functions. Some of these units, such as school districts, have limited powers. Others, such as counties, municipalities, and townships, exercise a number of governmental functions. The enactments of municipalities are called **ordinances;** zoning ordinances are an example. The enactments of other political subdivisions may also be referred to as ordinances.

Executive Orders   In theory, the president or a state's governor is a chief executive who enforces the laws but has no lawmaking powers. However, these officials sometimes have the power to issue laws called **executive orders.** This power normally results from a legislative delegation.

Priority Rules

Because the different types of law conflict, rules for determining which type takes priority are necessary. Here, we briefly describe the most important priority rules.

1. According to the principle of **federal supremacy,** the U.S. Constitution, federal laws enacted pursuant to it, and treaties are the supreme law of the land. This means that federal law defeats conflicting state law.

2. Constitutions defeat other types of law within their domain. Thus, a state constitution defeats all other state laws inconsistent with it, and the U.S. Constitution defeats inconsistent federal laws.

3. When a treaty conflicts with a federal statute over a purely domestic matter, the measure that is latest in time usually prevails.

4. Within either the state or the federal domain, statutes defeat conflicting laws that depend on a legislative delegation for their validity. For example, a state statute defeats an inconsistent state administrative regulation.

5. State statutes and any laws derived from them by delegation defeat inconsistent common law rules. For example, either a statute or a state administrative regulation defeats a conflicting common law rule.

CONCEPT REVIEW

THE TYPES OF LAW COMPARED

	Who Enacts?	State and/or Federal?	Stated in One Authoritative Form?	Remarks
Constitutions	U.S. Constitution originally ratified by states; complex amendment process. States may vary.	Both	Yes, but see Chapter 3 on constitutional decision making	Defeat other forms of positive law within sphere (federal or state)
Statutes	Legislatures	Both	Yes, but see this chapter's discussion of statutory interpretation	Normally defeat other forms of positive law within sphere (federal or state) except constitutions
Common Law	Courts	In theory, state only	No. See this chapter's discussion of legal reasoning	Law of tort, contract, and agency mainly common law
Equity	Formerly, equity courts; now usually courts in general	In theory, state only. But equitable principles pervade federal law as well.	No	Traditional separation of law and equity now virtually gone
Administrative Regulations	Administrative agencies	Both	Yes	See Chapter 46

	Who Enacts?	State and/or Federal?	Stated in One Authoritative Form?	Remarks
Administrative Decisions	Administrative agencies	Both	No	See Chapter 46
Treaties	President plus two thirds of Senate	Federal	Yes	Defeat inconsistent state law
Ordinances	Usually, local government bodies	State (mainly local)	Yes	
Executive Orders	Chief executives	Both	Yes	Usually based on delegation from legislature

Classifications of Law

Cutting across the different types of law are three common *classifications* of law. These classifications involve distinctions between: (1) criminal law and civil law, (2) substantive law and procedural law, and (3) public law and private law. One type of law might be classified in each of these ways. For example, a state statute might be criminal, substantive, and public.

Criminal and Civil Law

Criminal law is the law applied when the government prosecutes someone for the commission of a crime. **Civil law** is the law applied when one party sues another party because the other did not meet a legal duty owed to the first party. Civil lawsuits usually involve private parties, but the government may be a party to a civil suit (as, for instance, where a city sues, or is sued by, a construction contractor). Criminal penalties (e.g., imprisonment or fines) differ from civil remedies (e.g., money damages or equitable relief). Although most of the legal rules in this text are civil law rules, Chapter 5 deals specifically with the criminal law, and criminal provisions may appear in other chapters.

Even though the civil law and the criminal law are distinct bodies of law, the same behavior can violate both. For instance, if due to A's careless driving his car hits and injures B, A may face both a criminal prosecution by the state and B's civil suit for damages.

Substantive Law and Procedural Law

Substantive law sets the rights and duties of people as they act in society. **Procedural law** controls the behavior of government bodies (mainly courts) as they establish and enforce rules of substantive law. A statute making murder a crime, for example, is a rule of substantive law. But the rules describing the proper conduct of a criminal trial are procedural. This text mainly discusses substantive law. Chapters 2 and 5, however, examine some of the procedural rules governing civil and criminal cases, respectively.

Public and Private Law

Public law concerns the powers of government and the relations between government and private parties. Examples include constitutional law, administrative law, and criminal law. **Private law** establishes a framework of legal rules that enable private parties to set the rights and duties they owe each other. Examples include the rules of contract, property, and agency.

JURISPRUDENCE

The types of law are sometimes collectively referred to as *positive law*. Positive law comprises the rules that have been laid down (or posited) by a recognized political authority. Knowing the types of positive law is essential for understanding the American legal system and the business law topics discussed in this text. But defining *law* by listing

---

FIGURE 1   **A Brief Sketch of the Jurisprudential Schools**

	Definition of Law	Relation between Law and Morality	Practical Tendency
Legal Positivism	Command of a recognized political authority	Separate questions: "law is law, just or not"	Valid positive law should be enforced and obeyed, just or not
Natural Law	All commands of recognized political authorities that are not unjust	"Unjust law is not law"	Unjust positive laws should not be enforced and obeyed
American Legal Realism	What public decisionmakers actually do	Unclear	"Law in action" often more important than "law in the books"
Sociological Jurisprudence	Process of social ordering in accordance with dominant social values and interests	Although moral values influence positive law, no way to say whether this is right or wrong	Law inevitably does (and should?) follow dominant social values and interests

---

these different kinds of positive law is much like defining the word *automobile* by describing all the vehicles going by that name. To define law properly, we need a general description that captures its essence.

The field known as **jurisprudence** or legal philosophy tries to provide such a description. Over time, different schools of jurisprudence have emerged, each with its own distinctive view of law. The differences among these schools are not merely academic matters. As Figure 1 suggests, their conceptions of law often affect their approach toward real-life issues.

Legal Positivism

One feature common to all types of positive law is their enactment by a recognized political authority such as a legislature or an administrative agency. This common feature underlies the definition of law adopted by the school of jurisprudence called **legal positivism**. Legal positivists define law as the *command of a recognized political authority*. To the British political philosopher Thomas Hobbes, for instance, "Law properly, is the word of him, that by right hath command over others."

The commands made by recognized political authorities can be good, bad, or indifferent in moral terms. But as Figure 2 demonstrates, to legal positivists such commands are valid law regardless of their goodness or badness. For positivists, in other words, legal validity and moral validity are different questions. Sometimes this view is expressed by the slogan: "Law is law, just or not." For this reason, some (but not all) positivists say that every properly enacted positive law should be enforced and obeyed, whether just or not. Similarly, positivist judges usually try to enforce the law as written, excluding their own moral views from the process.

Natural Law

At first glance, legal positivism's "law is law, just or not" approach may seem like perfect common sense. But it presents a problem, for it could mean that *any* positive law (no matter how unjust) is valid law and should be enforced and obeyed so long as some recognized political authority (no matter how wicked) enacted it. Here, the school of jurisprudence known as **natural law** takes issue with legal positivism by rejecting the positivist separation of law and morality.

The basic idea behind most systems of natural law is that some higher law or set of universal moral rules binds all human beings in all times and places. The Roman statesman Marcus Cicero described

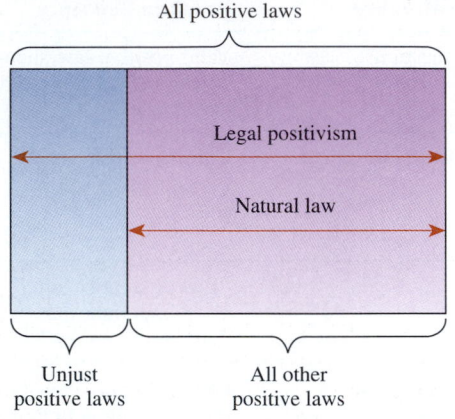

FIGURE 2   The Positivist and Natural Law Definitions of Law

All positive laws

Legal positivism

Natural law

Unjust
positive laws

All other
positive laws

natural law as "the highest reason, implanted in nature, which commands what ought to be done and forbids the opposite." Because this higher law determines what is ultimately good and ultimately bad, it is a criterion for evaluating positive law. To Saint Thomas Aquinas, for example, "every human law has just so much of the nature of law, as it is derived from the law of nature." To be genuine law, in other words, positive law must resemble the law of nature by being good—or at least by not being bad. This suggests the practical natural law definition of law depicted in Figures 1 and 2—that natural law equals *those commands of recognized political authorities that do not offend the higher law by being unjust.*

Unjust positive laws, on the other hand, simply are not law. As Cicero put it: "What of the many deadly, the many pestilential statutes which are imposed on peoples? These no more deserve to be called laws than the rules a band of robbers might pass in their assembly." This view is sometimes expressed by the slogan: "An unjust law is not law." Because unjust positive laws are not truly law, many natural law thinkers conclude that they should not be enforced or obeyed.

As compared with positivist judges, therefore, judges influenced by natural law ideas are more likely to read constitutional provisions broadly to invalidate positive laws they regard as unjust. They also are more likely to let morality influence their interpretation of the law. Of course, neither judges nor natural law thinkers always agree on morality's *content*, and this is a major difficulty for the natural law position. This

difficulty allows legal positivists to claim that only by keeping legal and moral questions separate can we get any stability and predictability in the law.

American Legal Realism

To some people, the debate between natural law and legal positivism seems unreal. Not only is natural law pie-in-the-sky, such people might say, but sometimes positive law does not mean much either. For example, juries often pay little attention to the legal rules that are supposed to guide their decisions, and prosecutors frequently have discretion whether or not to enforce criminal statutes. In some legal proceedings, moreover, the background, biases, and values of the judge—and not the positive law—determine the result. As the joke goes, justice sometimes is what the judge ate for breakfast.

Remarks like these typify the school of jurisprudence known as **American legal realism.** Legal realists regard the positivist law-in-the-books as less important than the *law in action*—the conduct of those who enforce and interpret the positive law. Thus, American legal realism defines law as the *behavior of public officials (mainly judges) as they deal with matters before the legal system.* Because the actions of such decisionmakers—and not the rules in the books—really affect people's lives, the realists say, this behavior is what counts and what deserves to be called law.

It is doubtful whether the legal realists have ever developed a common position on the relation between law and morality or the duty to obey positive law. But they have been quick to tell judges how to behave. Many realists feel that the modern judge should be a kind of social engineer who weighs all relevant values and considers social science findings when deciding a case. Such a judge would make the positive law only one factor in her decision. Because judges inevitably base their decisions on personal considerations, the realists seem to say, they should at least do this honestly and intelligently. To promote this kind of decisionmaking, the realists have sometimes favored fuzzy, discretionary rules that allow judges to decide each case according to its unique facts.

Sociological Jurisprudence

The term **sociological jurisprudence** is a general label uniting several diverse jurisprudential approaches whose common aim is to examine law within its social context. Their outlook is captured by the following quotation from Justice Oliver Wendell Holmes:

The life of the law has not been logic: it has been experience. The felt necessities of the time, the prevalent moral and political theories, intuitions of public policy, avowed or unconscious, even the prejudices which judges share with their fellow-men, have had a good deal more to do than the syllogism in determining the rules by which men should be governed. The law embodies the story of a nation's development through many centuries, and it cannot be dealt with as if it contained only the axioms and corollaries of a book of mathematics.[3]

Despite this common outlook, there is no distinctive sociological definition of law. If one were attempted, it might go as follows: *Law is a process of social ordering reflecting society's dominant interests and values.*

Different Sociological Approaches   By examining a few examples of sociological legal thinking, we can put some flesh on the definition just offered. The "dominant interests" portion of the definition is exemplified by the writings of Roscoe Pound, an influential 20th-century American legal philosopher. Pound developed a detailed catalog of the social interests that press on government and the legal system and thus shape positive law. During his life, Pound's catalog changed along with changes in American society. An example of the definition's "dominant values" component is the *historical school* of jurisprudence identified with the 19th-century German legal philosopher Friedrich Karl von Savigny. Savigny saw law as an unplanned, almost unconscious, reflection of the collective spirit (*Volksgeist*) of a particular society. In his view, legal change could only be explained historically, as a slow response to social change.

By emphasizing the influence of dominant social interests and values, Pound and Savigny undermine the legal positivist view that law is nothing more than the command of some political authority. The early 20th-century Austrian legal philosopher Eugen Ehrlich went even further in rejecting positivism. He did so by distinguishing two different "processes of social ordering" contained within our definition of sociological jurisprudence. The first of these is "state law," or positive law. The second is the "living law," informal social controls such as customs, family ties, and business practices. By regarding both as law, Ehrlich blurred the line between positive law and other kinds of social ordering. In the process, he stimulated people to recognize that positive law is only one element within a spectrum of social controls.

The Implications of Sociological Jurisprudence
Because its definition of law includes social values, sociological jurisprudence seems to resemble natural law. But most sociological thinkers are only concerned with the *fact* that moral values influence the law and not with the goodness or badness of those values. In Chapter 9, for instance, we note that laissez-faire economic values were widely shared in 19th-century America and strongly influenced the contract law of that period. But we do not say whether this was good or bad. Thus, it might seem that sociological jurisprudence gives no practical advice to those who must enforce and obey positive law.

However, sociological jurisprudence has at least one practical implication—a tendency to urge that the law must change to meet changing social conditions and values. This is basically the familiar notion that the law should keep up with the times. Some might stick to this view even when society's values are changing for the worse. To Holmes, for example, "[t]he first requirement of a sound body of law is, that it should correspond with the actual feelings and demands of the community, *whether right or wrong*."[4]

Comparing the Schools

The following *Rochin* case helps illustrate the differences among the schools of jurisprudence. To highlight those differences, consider the following questions about *Rochin*. Despite Justice Frankfurter's denial, doesn't the Supreme Court's reasoning in *Rochin* resemble natural law's unjust-law-is-not-law approach? What *observation* would almost any American legal realist make about this case? Would most legal positivists approve of the *Rochin* decision? With the benefit of hindsight, it looks as if *Rochin* was a precursor of the many liberal criminal procedure decisions of the 1960s—decisions that probably had their roots in changed social values. If so, what might an exponent of sociological jurisprudence say about *Rochin*?

---

[3]Holmes, *The Common Law* (1881).

[4]The italics have been added for emphasis.

ROCHIN v. CALIFORNIA[5]
342 U.S. 165 (U.S. Sup. Ct. 1952)

In 1949, three Los Angeles County deputy sheriffs heard that Antonio Rochin was selling narcotics. In search of evidence, they entered Rochin's home one morning and forced open the door to his bedroom. They spotted two capsules on a nightstand beside the bed on which the half-clad Rochin was sitting. After the deputies asked, "Whose stuff is this?" Rochin quickly put the capsules in his mouth. The deputies then jumped Rochin and tried to force the capsules from his mouth. When this proved unsuccessful, they handcuffed Rochin and took him to a hospital. Over Rochin's opposition, they had a doctor insert a tube into his stomach and force an emetic (vomit-inducing) solution through the tube. This stomach pumping caused Rochin to vomit. Within the material he disgorged were two capsules containing morphine.

Rochin then was tried and convicted for possessing a morphine preparation in violation of California law. The two morphine capsules were the main evidence against him, and the trial court admitted this evidence over Rochin's objection. An intermediate appellate court and the California Supreme Court affirmed the conviction. Rochin then appealed to the U.S. Supreme Court. The main issue before the Court was whether the methods by which the deputies obtained the capsules violated the Due Process Clause of the U.S. Constitution's Fourteenth Amendment, which states that "No state shall . . . deprive any person of life, liberty, or property, without due process of law."

Note: At the time this case was decided, evidence obtained through a forced stomach pumping probably was admissible in a majority of the states that had considered the question. Also, the Supreme Court did not then require that state courts exclude evidence obtained through an illegal search or seizure.

Frankfurter, Justice   The requirements of due process impose upon this Court an exercise of judgment upon the proceedings resulting in a conviction to ascertain whether they offend those canons of decency and fairness which express the notions of justice of English-speaking peoples even toward those charged with the most heinous offenses. These standards of justice are not authoritatively formulated anywhere as though they were specifics. Due process of law is a summarized guarantee of respect for those personal immunities so rooted in the traditions and conscience of our people as to be fundamental, or implicit in the concept of ordered liberty.

The vague contours of the due process clause do not leave judges at large. We may not draw upon our merely personal and private notions and disregard the limits that bind judges. These limits are derived from considerations that are fused in the whole nature of our judicial process. These are considerations deeply rooted in reason and in the compelling traditions of the legal profession. The due process clause places upon this Court the duty of exercising a judgment upon interests of society pushing in opposite directions. Due process thus conceived is not to be derided as a resort to the revival of "natural law."

Applying these general considerations to the present case, we conclude that the proceedings by which this conviction was obtained do more than offend some fastidious squeamishness or private sentimentalism about combatting crime too energetically. This is conduct that shocks the conscience. Illegally breaking into the privacy of Rochin, the struggle to open his mouth and remove what was there, the forcible extraction of his stomach's contents—this course of proceeding is bound to offend even hardened sensibilities. They are methods too close to the rack and the screw to permit of constitutional differentiation.

Judgment reversed in favor of Rochin.

---

[5]At this point, you may want to examine this chapter's appendix on the reading and briefing of cases.

THE FUNCTIONS OF LAW

In traditional societies, people often viewed law as a set of unchanging rules that deserved obedience because they were part of the natural order of things. By now, however, most lawmakers treat law as a flexible *tool* or *instrument* for the accomplishment of chosen purposes. For example, the law of negotiable instruments, discussed later in this text, is designed to stimulate commercial activity by promoting the free movement of money substitutes such as promissory notes, checks, and drafts. Throughout the text, moreover, you will see courts manipulating existing legal rules to get the results they desire. One strength of this *instrumentalist* attitude is its willingness to adapt the law to further the social good. One weakness is the legal instability and uncertainty those adaptations often produce.

Just as individual legal rules advance specific purposes, *law as a whole* serves many general social functions. Among the most important of those functions are:

1. *Peacekeeping.* The criminal law rules discussed in Chapter 5 best further this basic function of any legal system. Also, as Chapter 2 suggests, one major function of the civil law is the resolution of private disputes.

2. *Checking government power and thereby promoting personal freedom.* Obvious examples are the constitutional restrictions on government regulation in Chapter 3.

3. *Facilitating planning and the realization of reasonable expectations.* The rules of contract law discussed in Chapters 9–18 help fulfill this function of law.

4. *Promoting economic growth through free competition.* The antitrust laws discussed in Chapters 48 and 49 are among the many legal rules that help perform this function.

5. *Promoting social justice.* Throughout this century, government has intervened in private social and economic affairs to correct perceived injustices and give all citizens equal access to life's basic goods. One example is the collection of employer-employee regulations treated in Chapter 50.

6. *Protecting the environment.* The most important federal environmental statutes are discussed in Chapter 51.

Obviously, the law's various functions can conflict. The familiar clash between economic growth and environmental protection is an example. The *Rochin* case illustrates the equally familiar conflict between effective law enforcement and the preservation of personal rights. Only rarely does the law achieve one end without sacrificing others to some degree. In law, as in life, there is generally no such thing as a free lunch. Where the law's ends conflict, lawmakers can only try to strike the best possible balance among those ends. This suggests limits on the law's usefulness as a device for promoting particular social goals.

LEGAL REASONING

This text's main aim is to describe the most important legal rules affecting business. Like virtually every other business law text, it states those rules in what lawyers call "black letter form," using precise sentences saying that certain legal consequences will occur if certain events happen. Although it enables a clear statement of the law's commands, this black letter approach can be misleading. It suggests definiteness, certainty, permanence, and predictability—attributes the law frequently lacks. To illustrate this and to give you some idea how lawyers think, we now discuss the two most important kinds of legal reasoning: **case law reasoning** and **statutory interpretation.**[6] However, we first must examine legal reasoning in general.

Legal reasoning is basically deductive, or syllogistic. The legal rule is the major premise, the facts are the minor premise, and the result is the product of combining the two. Suppose that a state statute says that a driver operating an automobile between 55 and 70 miles per hour must pay a $50 fine (the rule or major premise) and that Jim Smith drives his car at 65 miles per hour (the facts or minor premise). If Jim is arrested, and if the necessary facts can be proved, he will be required to pay the $50 fine. As you will now see, however, legal reasoning is often more difficult than this example would suggest.

---

[6] The reasoning courts employ in constitutional cases resembles that used in common law cases, but it is often somewhat looser. For the way courts decide constitutional cases, see Chapter 3.

Case Law Reasoning

In cases governed by the common law, courts find the appropriate legal rules in prior cases or *precedents*. The standard for choosing and applying prior cases to decide present cases is the doctrine of *stare decisis*, which states that like cases should be decided alike.[7] That is, the present case should be decided in the same way as past cases presenting the same facts and legal issues. If a court decides that an alleged precedent is not like the present case and should not control the decision in that case, it *distinguishes* the prior case.[8]

Because every present case differs from the precedents in *some* respect, it is always theoretically possible to distinguish those precedents. For example, one *could* distinguish a prior case because both parties in that case had black hair, while one party in the present case has brown hair. Of course, such distinctions are usually ridiculous because the differences they identify are insignificant in moral or social policy terms. In other words, a good distinction of a prior case involves a widely accepted policy reason for treating the present case differently from its predecessor. Because people disagree about moral ideas, public policies, and the degree to which they are accepted, and because all these factors change over time, judges may differ on the wisdom of distinguishing a prior case. This is a significant source of uncertainty in the common law. But it

also gives the common law the flexibility to adapt to changing social conditions.

The following *MacPherson* case illustrates the common law's ability to change over time. In the series of New York cases *MacPherson* discusses, the **plaintiff** (the party suing) claimed that the **defendant** (the party being sued) had been negligent in manufacturing or inspecting some product, thus injuring the plaintiff, who later purchased or used the product.[9] In the mid-19th century, such suits often failed due to the general rule that a seller or manufacturer was not liable for negligence unless there was *privity of contract* between the defendant and the plaintiff. Privity of contract is the existence of a direct contractual relationship between two parties. Thus, the no-liability-outside-privity rule prevented injured plaintiffs from recovering against a seller or manufacturer who had sold the product to a dealer who in turn sold it to the plaintiff. Over time, however, courts began to allow injured plaintiffs to recover from sellers or manufacturers with whom they had not directly dealt. These courts were creating *exceptions* to the general rule; that is, they were distinguishing prior cases announcing the rule and creating new rules to govern the situations they distinguished. *MacPherson* describes the gradual enlargement of such an exception in New York. Eventually, the exception "consumed the rule" by covering so many situations that the original rule became relatively insignificant.[10]

---

[7]*Stare decisis* should be distinguished from the doctrine of *res judicata*, which says that a final judicial decision on the merits conclusively settles the rights of *the parties to the case.*

[8]Also, while they exercise the power infrequently, courts sometimes completely *overrule* their prior decisions.

---

[9]Negligence law is discussed in Chapter 7.

[10]The present status of the old no-liability-outside-privity rule in sale-of-goods cases is discussed in Chapter 20.

MacPherson v. Buick Motor Co.
111 N.E. 1050 (N.Y. Ct. App. 1916)

One wheel of an automobile manufactured by the Buick Motor Company was made of defective wood. Buick could have discovered the defect had it made a reasonable inspection after it purchased the wheel from another manufacturer. Buick sold the car to a retail dealer, who then sold it to MacPherson. While MacPherson was driving his new Buick, the defective wheel collapsed and he was thrown from the vehicle. He sued Buick for his injuries in a New York trial court, alleging that it had negligently failed to inspect the wheel. Buick's main defense was that it had not dealt directly with MacPherson and thus owed no duty to him. Following trial and appellate court judgments in MacPherson's favor, Buick appealed to the New York Court of Appeals, the state's highest court.

———————◼———————

Cardozo, Justice   The foundations of this branch of the law were laid in *Thomas v. Winchester* (1852). A poison was falsely labeled. The sale was made to a druggist, who sold to a customer. The customer recovered damages from the seller who affixed the label. The defendant's negligence, it was said, put human life in imminent danger. A poison, falsely labeled, is likely to injure anyone who gets it. Because the danger is to be foreseen, there is a duty to avoid the injury. *Thomas v. Winchester* became quickly a landmark of the law. In the application of its principle there may, at times, have been uncertainty or even error. There has never been doubt or disavowal of the principle itself.

The chief cases are well known. *Loop v. Litchfield* (1870) was the case of a defect in a small balance wheel used on a circular saw. The manufacturer pointed out the defect to the buyer. The risk can hardly have been an imminent one, for the wheel lasted five years before it broke. In the meanwhile the buyer had made a lease of the machinery. It was held that the manufacturer was not answerable to the lessee. *Loop v. Litchfield* was followed by *Losee v. Clute* (1873), the case of the explosion of a steam boiler. That decision must be confined to its special facts. It was put upon the ground that the risk of injury was too remote. The buyer had not only accepted the boiler, but had tested it. The manufacturer knew that his own test was not the final one. The finality of the test has a bearing on the measure of diligence owing to persons other than the purchaser.

These early cases suggest a narrow construction of the rule. Later cases evince a more liberal spirit. In *Devlin v. Smith* (1882), the defendant contractor built a scaffold for a painter. The painter's workmen were injured. The contractor was held liable. He knew that the scaffold, if improperly constructed, was a most dangerous trap. He knew that it was to be used by the workmen. Building it for their use, he owed them a duty to build it with care. From *Devlin v. Smith* we turn to *Statler v. Ray Manufacturing Co.* (1909). The defendant manufactured a large coffee urn. It was installed in a restaurant. The urn exploded and injured the plaintiff. We held that the manufacturer was liable.

We said that the urn was of such a character that it was liable to become a source of great danger if not carefully and properly constructed.

It may be that *Devlin v. Smith* and *Statler v. Ray Manufacturing Co.* have extended the rule of *Thomas v. Winchester*. If so, this court is committed to the extension. The defendant argues that things imminently dangerous to human life are poisons, explosives, deadly weapons—things whose normal function is to injure or destroy. But whatever the rule in *Thomas v. Winchester* may once have been, it no longer has that restricted meaning. A scaffold is not inherently a destructive instrument. No one thinks of [a coffee urn] as an implement whose normal function is destruction.

We hold, then, that the principle of *Thomas v. Winchester* is not limited to things which are implements of destruction. If the nature of a thing is such that it is reasonably certain to place life and limb in peril when negligently made, it is a thing of danger. If to the element of danger there is added knowledge that the thing will be used by persons other than the purchaser, then, irrespective of contract, the manufacturer is under a duty to make it carefully.

The nature of an automobile gives warning of probable danger if its construction is defective. This automobile was designed to go 50 miles an hour. Unless its wheels were sound and strong, injury was almost certain. The defendant knew the danger. It knew that the car would be used by persons other than the buyer, a dealer in cars. The dealer was indeed the one person of whom it might be said with some certainty that by him the car would not be used. Yet the defendant would have us say that he was the one person it was under a legal duty to protect. The law does not lead us to so inconsequent a conclusion. Precedents drawn from the age of travel by stagecoach do not fit the conditions of travel today. The principle that the danger must be imminent does not change, but the things subject to the principle do change. They are whatever the needs of life in a developing civilization require them to be.

Judgment for MacPherson affirmed.

FIGURE 3 **The Steps in a Statute's Passage and the Techniques of Statutory Interpretation**

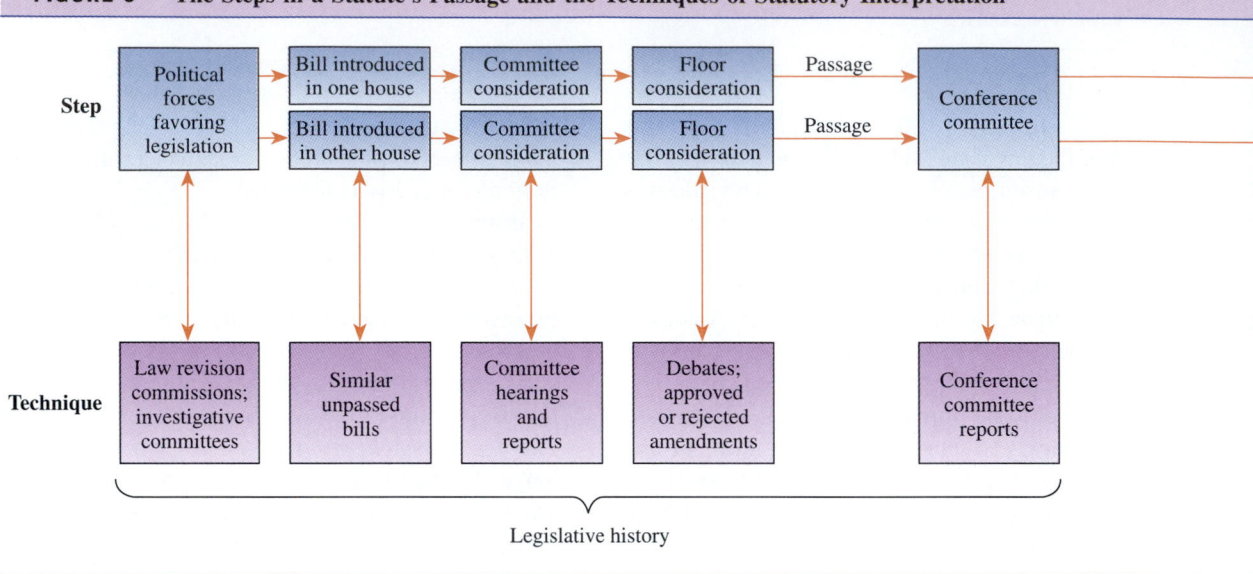

Legislative history

Statutory Interpretation

Because statutes are written in one authoritative form, their interpretation might seem easier than case law reasoning. However, this is not so. One reason courts face difficulties when interpreting statutes is the natural ambiguity of language. This is especially true when statutory words are applied to situations the legislature did not foresee. Also, legislators may deliberately use ambiguous language when they are unwilling or unable to deal specifically with each situation the statute was enacted to regulate. When this happens, the legislature expects courts and/or administrative agencies to fill in the details on a case-by-case basis. Other reasons for deliberate ambiguity include the need for legislative compromise and legislators' desire to avoid taking controversial positions.

Due to problems like these, courts need and use various techniques of statutory interpretation. Figure 3 states the most common of these techniques, relating them to the steps in the passage of a statute. As you will see shortly, different techniques can dictate different results in a particular case. Moreover, judges sometimes employ the techniques in an instrumentalist or result-oriented fashion, emphasizing the technique that will produce the result they want and downplaying the others. Thus, it is unclear which technique should control when different techniques yield different results. Although there are some "rules" on this subject, courts often ignore them.

Plain Meaning   Courts begin their interpretation of a statute with its actual language. Where the statute's words have a clear, common, accepted meaning, some courts employ the *plain meaning rule*. This rule states that in such cases, the court should simply apply the statute according to the plain, accepted meaning of its words, and should not concern itself with anything else.

Legislative History   Some courts, like the Supreme Court in the following *Weber* case, refuse to follow a statute's plain meaning when its legislative history suggests a different result. And almost all courts resort to legislative history when the statute's language is ambiguous. A statute's legislative history includes the following sources: the reports of investigative committees or law revision commissions that led to the legislation, the hearings of the legislative committee(s) originally considering the legislation, any reports issued by such a committee, legislative debates, the report of a conference committee reconciling two houses' conflicting versions of the law, amendments or defeated amendments to the legislation, other bills not passed by the legislature but proposing similar legislation, and discrepancies between a bill passed by one house and the final version of the statute.

Sometimes a statute's legislative history provides no information or conflicting information about its

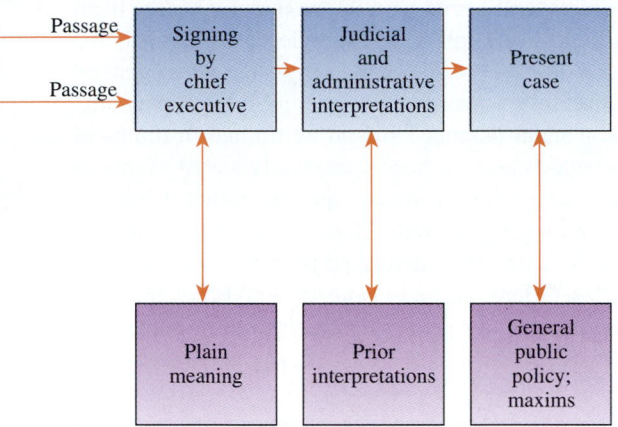

meaning, its scope, or its purposes. Also, some sources are more authoritative than others. The worth of debates, for instance, may depend on which legislator (e.g., the sponsor of the bill or an uninformed blowhard) is quoted. Some sources are useful only in particular situations; prior unpassed bills and amendments or defeated amendments are examples. To illustrate those sources, consider whether mopeds are covered by an air pollution statute applying to "automobiles, trucks, buses, and other motorized passenger or cargo vehicles." If the statute's original version included mopeds but this reference was removed by amendment, it is unlikely that the legislature wanted mopeds to be covered. The same might be true if six similar unpassed bills had included mopeds but the bill that was eventually passed did not, or if one house had passed a bill including mopeds but mopeds did not appear in the final version of the legislation.

Courts use legislative history in two overlapping but distinguishable ways. They may use it to determine what the legislature thought about the specific meaning of statutory language. They may also use it to determine the overall aim, end, or goal of the legislation. In this second case, they then ask whether a particular interpretation of the statute is consistent with this purpose. To illustrate the difference between these two uses of legislative history, suppose that a court is considering whether the pollution statute's "other motorized passenger or cargo vehicles" language includes battery-powered vehicles. The court might scan the legislative history for specific references to battery-powered vehicles or other indications of what the legislature thought about their inclusion. However, the court might also use the same history to determine the overall aims of the statute and then ask whether including battery-powered vehicles is consistent with those aims. Because the history probably would reveal that the statute's purpose was to reduce air pollution from internal combustion engines, the court might well conclude that battery-powered vehicles should not be covered.

General Public Purpose   Occasionally, courts construe statutory language in the light of various *general public purposes*. These purposes are not the purposes underlying the statute in question; rather, they are widely accepted general notions of public policy. In one case, for example, the U.S. Supreme Court used the general public policy against racial discrimination in education as one argument for denying tax-exempt status to a private university that discriminated on the basis of race.[11]

Prior Interpretations   Courts sometimes follow prior cases (and administrative decisions) interpret-

---

[11]*Bob Jones University v. United States,* 461 U.S. 574 (1983).

ing a statute regardless of the statute's plain meaning or its legislative history. The main argument for following these *prior interpretations* is to promote stability and certainty by preventing each successive court that considers a statute from adopting its own interpretation. The courts' willingness to follow a prior interpretation depends on such factors as the number of past courts adopting the interpretation, the authoritativeness of those courts, and the number of years that the interpretation has been followed. Note that in *Weber* the Supreme Court arguably did not follow one of its own prior interpretations.

Maxims   Maxims are general rules of thumb employed in statutory interpretation. There are many maxims, and courts tend to use them or ignore them at their discretion. One example of a maxim is the *ejusdem generis* rule, which says that when general words follow words of a specific, limited meaning, the general language should be limited to things of the same class as those specifically stated. Suppose that the pollution statute quoted earlier listed 32 types of gas-powered vehicles and ended with the words "and other motorized passenger or cargo vehicles." Here, *ejusdem generis* would probably dictate that battery-powered vehicles not be included.

United Steelworkers v. Weber
443 U.S. 193 (U.S. Sup. Ct. 1979)

As part of its collective bargaining agreement with the United Steelworkers of America, the Kaiser Aluminum and Chemical Company established a new on-the-job craft training program at its Gramercy, Louisiana, plant. The selection of trainees for the program was based on seniority, but at least 50 percent of the new trainees had to be black until the percentage of black skilled craft workers in the plant approximated the percentage of blacks in the local labor force.

Brian Weber was a rejected white applicant who would have qualified for the program had the racial preference not existed. He sued Kaiser and the union in federal district court, arguing that the racial preference violated Title VII of the 1964 Civil Rights Act. Section 703(a) of the act states: "It shall be an unlawful employment practice for an employer . . . to discriminate against any individual with respect to his compensation, terms, conditions, or privileges of employment, because of such individual's race, color, religion, sex, or national origin." Section 703(d) has a similar provision specifically forbidding racial discrimination in admission to apprenticeship or other training programs. Weber's suit was successful, and the federal court of appeals affirmed. Kaiser and the union appealed to the U.S. Supreme Court.

Brennan, Justice   The only question before us is whether Title VII forbids private employers and unions from voluntarily agreeing upon bona fide affirmative action plans that accord racial preferences in the manner and for the purpose provided in the Kaiser-USWA plan. That question was expressly left open in *McDonald v. Santa Fe Trail Transp. Co.* (1976), which held, in a case not involving affirmative action, that Title VII protects whites as well as blacks from racial discrimination.

Weber argues that Congress intended in Title VII to prohibit all race-conscious affirmative action plans. His argument rests upon a literal interpretation of sections 703(a) and (d) of the act. Those sections make it unlawful to discriminate because of race in the selection of apprentices for training programs. Since, the argument runs, *McDonald* settled that Title VII forbids discrimination against whites as well as blacks, and since the Kaiser-USWA plan discriminated against white employees solely because they are white, it follows that the plan violates Title VII.

Weber's argument is not without force. But it overlooks the fact that the Kaiser-USWA plan is an affirmative action plan voluntarily adopted by private parties to eliminate traditional patterns of racial segregation. It is a familiar rule, that a thing may be within the letter of the statute and yet not within the statute, because not within its spirit. Sections 703(a) and (d) must therefore be read against the background of the legislative history of Title VII and the historical context from which the act arose. Examination of these sources makes clear that an interpretation that forbade all race-conscious affirmative action would bring about an end completely at variance with the purpose of the statute and must be rejected.

Congress's primary concern in enacting the prohibition against racial discrimination in Title VII was the plight of the Negro in our economy. Before 1964, blacks were largely relegated to unskilled and semi-skilled jobs. Because of automation the number of such jobs was rapidly decreasing. As a consequence the relative position of the Negro worker was steadily worsening. Congress feared that the goal of the Civil Rights Act—the integration of blacks into the mainstream of American society—could not be achieved unless this trend were reversed. Accordingly, it was clear to Congress

that the crux of the problem was to open employment opportunities for Negroes in occupations which have traditionally been closed to them, and it was to this problem that Title VII's prohibition against racial discrimination in employment was primarily addressed.

Given this legislative history, we cannot agree with Weber that Congress intended to prohibit the private sector from taking effective steps to accomplish the goal that Congress designed Title VII to achieve. It would be ironic indeed if a law triggered by a nation's concern over centuries of racial injustice and intended to improve the lot of those who had been excluded from the American dream for so long, constituted the first legislative prohibition of all voluntary, private, race-conscious efforts to abolish traditional patterns of racial segregation and hierarchy.

Judgment reversed in favor of Kaiser and the union.

Limits on the Power of Courts

By now, you may think that anything goes when courts decide common law cases or interpret statutes. However, many factors discourage courts from adopting a completely freewheeling approach. Due to their legal training and mental makeup, judges tend to respect established precedents and the will of the legislature. Many courts issue written opinions, which expose judges to academic and professional criticism. Lower court judges may be discouraged from innovation by the fear of being overruled by a higher court. Finally, certain political factors inhibit judges. For example, some judges are elected, and even judges with lifetime tenure can sometimes be removed.

An even more fundamental limit on the power of courts is that they cannot make law until some parties present them with a case to decide. In addition, any such case must be a *real dispute;* that is, courts generally limit themselves to genuine, existing "cases or controversies" between real parties with tangible opposing interests in the lawsuit. Thus, courts generally do not issue *advisory opinions* on abstract legal questions unrelated to a

genuine dispute. Nor do they decide *feigned controversies* that parties concoct to get answers to such questions. Also, courts may refuse to decide suits that are insufficiently *ripe* to have matured into a genuine controversy, or that are *moot* because there no longer is a real dispute between the parties. Expressing similar ideas is the doctrine of **standing to sue**, which generally requires that the plaintiff have some direct, tangible, and substantial stake in the outcome of the suit.

Nonetheless, state and federal **declaratory judgment** statutes allow parties to determine their rights and duties even though their controversy has not advanced to the point where harm has occurred and legal relief may be necessary. This enables them to determine their legal position without taking action that could expose them to liability. For example, if Joan thinks that she is not obligated to perform her contract to Jim, she may seek a declaratory judgment on the question rather than risk Jim's lawsuit by breaking the contract. Usually, though, a declaratory judgment is awarded only when the parties' dispute is sufficiently advanced to constitute a real case or controversy.

ETHICAL AND PUBLIC POLICY CONCERNS

1. What might be troubling about the result in this chapter's *Rochin* case? *Hint:* Today, what aspect of the case is commonly regarded as one of the country's most serious problems? As discussed in Chapter 4, moral philosophers sometimes distinguish *deontological* ethical theories from *consequentialist* (or teleological) ethical theories. Strict or extreme deontological theories say that certain actions are right or wrong and should be pursued or avoided, *no matter what the consequences of doing so*. Consequentialist theories, on the other hand, assess the moral worth of actions by looking to their consequences. Which of these approaches best describes the Supreme Court's decision in *Rochin*?

2. Earlier in this chapter, we quoted Justice Holmes's statement that "[t]he first requirement of a sound body of law is, that it should correspond with the actual feelings and demands of the community, whether right or wrong." This statement may mean that the law should reflect prevailing moral views, whatever they happen to be. What is good about such an approach to the law and to lawmaking? What is bad about it?

3. Legal positivists often say that even morally bad laws are still law and that such laws (or some of them, at least) should still be enforced and obeyed. What *moral* arguments can you make for this position?

APPENDIX

READING AND BRIEFING CASES

Throughout this text, you encounter cases—the judicial opinions accompanying court decisions. These cases are highly edited versions of their much longer originals. What follows are explanations of the format of the cases presented in this book, plus some pointers to assist you in studying these cases.

1. Each case has a *case name* that includes at least some of the parties to the case. Because the order of the parties may change when a case is appealed, do not assume that the first party listed is the plaintiff (the party suing) and the second the defendant (the party being sued). Also, because some cases have many plaintiffs and/or many defendants, the parties discussed in the court's opinion sometimes differ from those found in the case name.

2. Each case also has a *citation*, which includes the volume and page number of the legal reporter in which the full case appears, plus the year the case was decided. *United Steelworkers v. Weber*, for instance, begins on page 193 of volume 443 of the United States Reports (the official reporter for U.S. Supreme Court decisions) and was decided in 1979. (Each of the many different legal reporters has its own abbreviation, and they are too numerous to include here.) In the parenthesis accompanying the date, we also give you some information about the court that decided the case. For example: "U.S. Sup. Ct." is the United States Supreme Court, "3d Cir." is the U.S. Court of Appeals for the Third Circuit, "S.D.N.Y." is the U.S. District Court for the Southern District of New York, "Minn. Sup. Ct." is the Minnesota Supreme Court, and "Mich. Ct. App." is the Michigan Court of Appeals (a Michigan intermediate appellate court). Chapter 2 describes the various kinds of courts.

3. At the beginning of each case, there is a *statement of facts* containing the most important facts that gave rise to the case.

4. Immediately after the statement of facts, we give you the case's *procedural history*. (Chapter 2 discusses civil procedure and Chapter 5 discusses criminal procedure.) Basically, this history tells you what courts previously handled the case you are reading, and how they dealt with it.

5. Next comes your major concern: the *body of the court's opinion*. Here, the court typically determines the applicable law and applies it to the facts to reach a conclusion. The court's discussion of the relevant law may be elaborate; it can include prior cases, legislative history, applicable public policies, and more. The court's application of the law to the facts usually occurs after it has arrived at the applicable legal rule or rules, but it may also be intertwined with its legal discussion.

6. At the very end of the case, we complete the procedural history by stating the court's *decision*. For example, "Judgment reversed in favor of Smith" says that a lower court judgment *against* Smith was reversed on appeal, which means that Smith's appeal was successful and Smith wins.

7. The cases' main function is to provide concrete examples of rules stated in the text. (Frequently, the text tells you what point the case illustrates.) In studying law, it is easy to conclude that your task is finished once you have memorized a black letter rule. In real life, however, legal problems rarely present themselves as abstract questions of law; instead, they are implicit in particular situations you encounter or particular actions you take. Without some sense of a legal rule's concrete application, therefore, your knowledge of that rule is incomplete. The cases help provide this sense.

8. You may find it helpful to *brief* the cases. There is no one correct way to brief a case, but most good briefs contain the following elements: (1) a short statement of the relevant facts, (2) the case's prior history, (3) the question(s) or issue(s) the court had to decide, (4) the answer(s) to those question(s), (5) the reasoning the court used to justify its decision, and (6) the final result. Using "P" and "D" for the plaintiff and the defendant, a brief of the *Weber* case might look like this:

United Steelworkers v. Weber (p. 16)

Facts   The Ds were a private employer and a union that had voluntarily established a craft training program through a collective bargaining agreement. The procedures for selecting the program's trainees favored black workers over white workers by establishing an effective 50 percent quota for the former. P, a white worker who was denied access to the program, would have qualified had the racial preference not existed.

History   P sued the Ds under Title VII of the 1964 Civil Rights Act, which forbids employment discrimination on the basis of race. He won in federal district court and the court of appeals affirmed. The Ds appealed to the U.S. Supreme Court.

Issue   Does this voluntary racial preference favoring blacks violate Title VII's ban on racial discrimination in employment?

Answer   No.

Reasoning   Even though Title VII's plain meaning favors P and a prior interpretation holds that Title VII forbids racial discrimination against both whites and blacks, neither point is decisive. The reason is that holding for P would frustrate Title VII's purpose. Title VII's legislative history and its historical context make clear that its aim was to integrate blacks into the American mainstream. This was especially true in the area of employment, an area in which blacks were falling behind. The Ds' preference helped further this purpose because it helped blacks get better jobs, and declaring the preference illegal would have frustrated the purpose.

Result   Court of appeals decision reversed; Ds win.

PROBLEMS AND PROBLEM CASES

1. In which way do administrative regulations resemble statutes? In which way do they differ from statutes?

2. Suppose that Congress passes a federal statute that conflicts with a state constitutional provision. The state argues that the constitutional provision should prevail over the statute because constitutions are a higher, more authoritative kind of law than statutes. Is this argument correct? Why or why not?

3. Suppose that someone objects to the president's promulgation of an executive order by claiming that the U.S. Constitution only gives the president the power to *execute* the laws, not the power to make them. What concept explains the president's power to make law through executive orders? Explain its meaning.

4. State A passes a statute declaring that those who sell heroin are to receive a mandatory 30-year prison sentence. Describe this statute in terms of the three classifications of law stated in the text—criminal/civil, substantive/procedural, and public/private.

5. Nation X is a dictatorship in which one ruler has the ultimate lawmaking power. The ruler issues a statute declaring that certain religious minorities are to be exterminated. An international convocation of jurisprudential scholars meets to discuss the question, "Is Nation X's extermination statute truly law?" What would be the typical natural law answer to this question? What would be the typical legal positivist response? Assume that all of those present at the convocation think that Nation X's statute is morally wrong.

6. Nation Y has enacted positive laws forbidding all abnormal sexual relations between consenting adults. However, the police of Nation Y rarely enforce these laws, and even when they do, prosecutors never bring charges against violators. What observation would American legal realists make about this situation? In order to determine what a believer in natural law would think about these laws, what else would you have to know?

7. Many states and localities used to have so-called Sunday Closing laws—statutes or ordinances forbidding the conduct of certain business on Sunday. A few may still do so. Often, these laws have not been obeyed or enforced. What would an extreme legal positivist tend to think about the duty to enforce and obey such laws? What would a natural law exponent who strongly believes in economic freedom tend to think about this question? What about a natural law adherent who is a Christian religious traditionalist? What *observation* would almost any American legal realist make about Sunday Closing laws? Looking at these laws from a sociological perspective, finally, what social factors help explain their original passage, their relative lack of enforcement today, and their continuance on the books despite their lack of enforcement?

8. The Supreme Court of State X is about to decide on the constitutionality of a statute restricting some controversial activity. Three of the court's justices—Justices A, B, and C—are taking the coming decision very seriously. In an effort to determine the true rule of law that governs the case, Justice A is reading and rereading all the relevant precedents and legislative history. In order to determine what result is morally right, Justice B is reading books on moral philosophy. To determine what the public thinks, finally, Justice C is reading every available public opinion poll on the behavior at issue in the case. Which jurisprudential schools do Justices A, B, and C most nearly exemplify?

9. Although you would not know this from reading the *MacPherson* case in this chapter, two of the cases mentioned there distinguished *Thomas v. Winchester* (the case involving the falsely labeled poison) in a certain way. The courts in *Loop v. Litchfield* (the circular saw case) and *Losee v. Clute* (the steam boiler case) both distinguished *Thomas v. Winchester* because in *Thomas*, the thing that caused the injury—a poison—was *by its nature intended to cause harm*. In other words, these courts held that a poison should be treated differently from a circular saw that flies apart or an exploding steam boiler. If the relevant public policy here is to allow recovery for injuries caused by highly dangerous products, does this distinction make any sense?

10. In 1910, the White Slave Traffic Act (usually known as the Mann Act) went into effect. Congress passed the act in response to an alleged white slave traffic in which gangs of certain nationalities were said to be forcing or luring American women into prostitution. One portion of the act stated that "any person who shall knowingly transport or cause to be transported . . . any woman or girl for the purpose of prostitution or debauchery, or for any other immoral purpose, . . . shall be deemed guilty of a felony." In 1913, F. Drew Caminetti was indicted for transporting a woman from Sacramento, California, to Reno, Nevada, to be his mistress. Which technique of statutory interpretation would you use in arguing that Caminetti is guilty under the Mann Act? Which technique would you use to argue that Caminetti should not be guilty under the act?

THE RESOLUTION

OF

PRIVATE DISPUTES

INTRODUCTION

Most business law consists of substantive legal rules. The courts apply such rules when they decide civil cases.[1] Because courts play such an important role in formulating and enforcing substantive rules, your understanding of business law is incomplete unless you know something about the various kinds of courts, the cases they decide, and the procedures under which they operate in civil suits.

The United States has 52 court systems—a federal system, plus a system for each state and the District of Columbia. This chapter first describes the various state and federal courts. Included in this discussion is the jurisdiction *of these courts—their power to decide certain kinds of cases. Then the chapter examines the* procedures *courts follow in civil cases. Because private disputes are increasingly being resolved outside the formal court system, the chapter concludes by discussing* alternative dispute resolution.

STATE COURTS AND THEIR JURISDICTION

Courts of Limited Jurisdiction

Minor criminal matters and civil disputes involving small amounts of money are frequently decided in *courts of limited jurisdiction* (also called courts of inferior or special jurisdiction). Examples include municipal courts, justice of the peace courts, and small claims courts. Such courts often handle a large number of cases. Their procedures may be informal, the presiding judicial officer may not be a lawyer, and the parties may argue their own cases. Also, courts of limited jurisdiction are usually not courts of record; that is, they ordinarily do not keep a transcript of the testimony and proceedings. Thus, appeals from their decisions require a new trial (a trial *de novo*) in a trial court.

---

[1]See Chapter 1 for the distinctions between civil law and criminal law and between procedural law and substantive law.

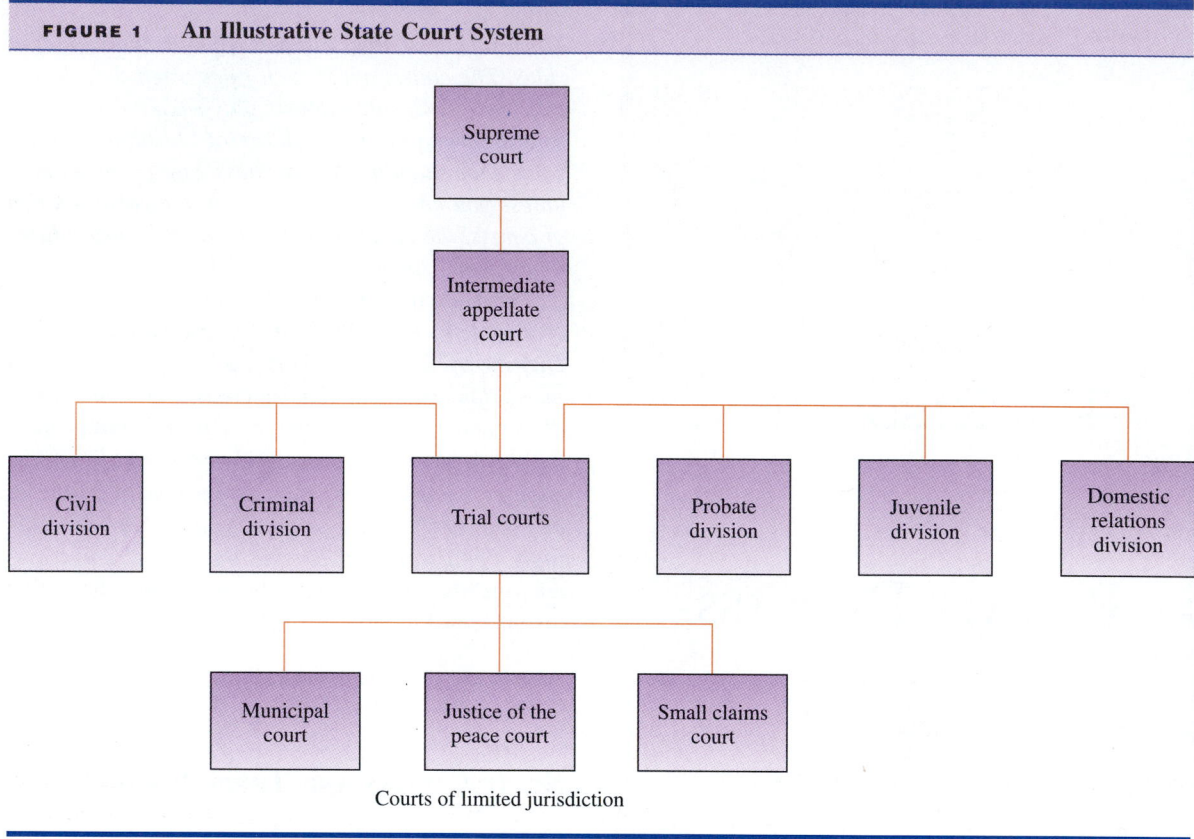

FIGURE 1   An Illustrative State Court System

Courts of limited jurisdiction

Trial Courts

Courts of limited jurisdiction find the relevant facts, identify the appropriate rule(s) of law, and combine the facts and the law to reach a decision. State trial courts do the same, but they differ from inferior courts in at least three ways. First, they are not governed by the limits on civil damages or criminal penalties that govern courts of limited jurisdiction. Thus, cases involving significant dollar amounts or major criminal penalties usually begin at the trial court level. Second, trial courts are courts of record that keep detailed records of their proceedings. Third, the trial court judge almost always is a lawyer. The trial court's fact-finding function may be handled by the judge or by a jury. Determination of the applicable law is the judge's responsibility.

States usually have one trial court for each county. It may be called a circuit, superior, district, county, or common pleas court. Trial courts often have civil and criminal divisions. They may also contain divisions set up to hear particular matters—for example, domestic relations courts, probate courts, and juvenile courts.

State Appeals Courts

In general, state appeals (or appellate) courts only decide *legal* questions. Their judges do not make factual findings and they have no jury. Thus, although appellate courts can correct legal errors made by the trial judge, they generally accept the trial court's findings of fact. Appellate courts may also hear appeals from state administrative agency decisions. Some states have only one appeals court (usually called the supreme court), while others also have an intermediate appellate court. The U.S. Supreme Court sometimes hears appeals from decisions of the state's highest court.

FIGURE 2 **State Court Jurisdiction**

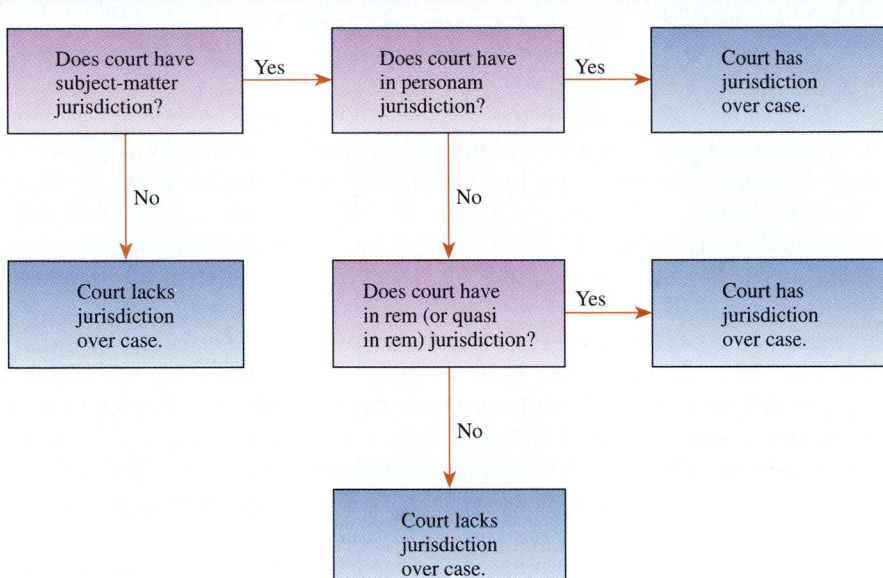

State Court Jurisdiction and Venue

The party who sues in a civil case (the plaintiff) cannot sue the defendant (the party being sued) in any court he chooses. Instead, the chosen court must have **jurisdiction** over the case. Jurisdiction is a court's power to hear a case and to issue a decision binding on the parties. As Figure 2 indicates, in order to render a binding decision in a civil case, a state court must have *both*: (1) subject-matter jurisdiction, and (2) *either* in personam jurisdiction *or* in rem jurisdiction. Even if a court has jurisdiction, it also must meet the state's **venue** requirements in order for the suit to proceed there.

Subject-Matter Jurisdiction   **Subject-matter jurisdiction** is a court's power to decide the *type* of dispute involved in the case. Criminal courts, for example, cannot hear civil matters, and a $500,000 suit for breach of contract cannot proceed in a small claims court.

In Personam Jurisdiction   Even a court with subject-matter jurisdiction cannot decide a civil case unless it also has either **in personam jurisdiction** or **in rem jurisdiction.** In personam jurisdiction is

based on the residence, location, or activities of the defendant. A state court has in personam jurisdiction over defendants who are citizens or residents of the state (even if situated out of state), who are within the state's borders when process is served against them (even if nonresidents),[2] or who consent to the suit (for instance, by entering the state to defend against it).[3]

In addition, many states have enacted "long-arm" statutes that give their courts in personam jurisdiction over certain out-of-state defendants. Under these statutes, nonresident individuals and businesses may become subject to the state's jurisdiction by doing business within the state, contracting to supply goods or services within the state, or committing a tort (a civil wrong) within the state. As the following *Knowles* case indicates, a state's assertion of in personam jurisdiction over an out-of-state defendant is subject to federal due process standards.

---

[2]Service of process is discussed later in this chapter.

[3]In some states, however, out-of-state defendants may make a *special appearance* to challenge the court's jurisdiction without consenting to that jurisdiction.

KNOWLES V. MODGLIN
553 So. 2d 563 (Ala. Sup. Ct. 1989)

Albert Knowles, an Alabama truck driver, died of natural causes in California while hauling produce from Alabama to California. After Knowles's body was discovered inside his truck, it was taken to Hems Brothers Mortuaries, where an autopsy was performed by Damon Reference Laboratories at the request of the local coroner. Both Hems and Damon did business in California. After a request from an Alabama funeral home, Hems prepared Knowles's body for shipment and arranged for it to be flown to his hometown. Hems billed the Alabama funeral home for these services and for the price of a casket; it also mailed a statement to Knowles's wife.

Mrs. Knowles did not view her husband's body after its return to Alabama and before its burial, and no one positively identified the body as that of Mr. Knowles during this period. After the burial, Mrs. Knowles received an autopsy report from Damon describing a body that was different from her husband's body. As a result, she had the buried body exhumed and personally viewed it to verify that it was her husband's body—which it was. However, Mrs. Knowles also found that the body had been buried nude, had been packed in cotton in a "disaster pouch," was terribly discolored, and was lying in an awkward position. She described it as looking like "a monster."

Mrs. Knowles then sued Hems and Damon in an Alabama trial court for the wrongful mishandling of her husband's body. Both Damon and Hems had no contacts with Alabama other than those just described, and each moved to dismiss the claim because the court lacked in personam jurisdiction. After the court granted Damon's motion but denied Hems's motion, both Mrs. Knowles and Hems appealed to the Alabama Supreme Court.

Houston, Justice   The issue is whether, consistent with the Due Process Clause of the Fourteenth Amendment to the United States Constitution, the defendants have sufficient contacts with this state to make it fair and reasonable to require them to come here to defend against the present action. Due process requires that to subject a defendant to a judgment in personam, he have certain minimum contacts with it such that the maintenance of the suit does not offend traditional notions of fair play and substantive justice. Alabama's long-arm statute has been interpreted to extend the jurisdiction of Alabama courts to the permissible limits of due process.

A relevant factor in a due process analysis is whether the defendant should have reasonably anticipated that he would be sued in the forum state. In determining [this question], it is essential that there be some act by which the defendant purposefully avails itself of the privilege of conducting activities within the forum state, thus invoking the benefits and protections of its laws. Other relevant factors include the burden placed on the defendant, the interest of the forum state in adjudicating the dispute, the plaintiff's interest in obtaining convenient

and effective relief, and the interstate judicial system's interest in obtaining the most efficient resolution of the controversy.

The trial court did not err in dismissing Damon for lack of in personam jurisdiction. It does not appear that Damon ever had any contacts with Alabama, with the exception of mailing the autopsy report to Mrs. Knowles. Damon could not have reasonably anticipated that Mr. Knowles's body would make its way to Alabama, that it would not be positively identified by anyone before burial, and that, thereafter, Damon would be haled into an Alabama court to defend against a suit based on a misdescription contained in the autopsy report.

However, Hems established significant contacts with this state by agreeing to prepare and ship Mr. Knowles's body here. In addition, Hems sold Mrs. Knowles a casket, and later solicited payment by mail in Alabama. Hems purposefully availed itself of the privilege of conducting business in Alabama [and] should have reasonably anticipated being summoned to an Alabama court to answer any charges of misconduct in the handling and shipment of Mr. Knowles's body. Furthermore, given the progress in communications and transportation in recent years, we cannot say that it would be unduly burdensome for Hems to defend against the suit in an Alabama court. Considering the nature of Hems's activity, the resultant foreseeability of its being required to defend an action in Alabama, the obvious interest of the plaintiff in obtaining convenient and effective relief, and the relative lack of inconvenience that would be incurred by Hems in appearing and defending, it is fair and reasonable to require Hems to defend against this action in Alabama.

Trial court decision dismissing Mrs. Knowles's suit against Damon for lack of jurisdiction and finding jurisdiction over Hems affirmed.

In Rem Jurisdiction   **In rem jurisdiction** is based on the presence of *property* within the state. It empowers state courts to determine rights in that property even if the persons whose rights are affected are outside the state's in personam jurisdiction. For example, a state court's decision regarding title to land within the state is said to bind the world.[4]

Venue   Even where a court has jurisdiction, it may be unable to decide the case because **venue** requirements have not been met. In general, a court has venue if it is a territorially fair and convenient forum in which to hear the case. Venue requirements are typically set by state statutes, which normally determine the county in which suit must be brought. For instance, the statute might say that a suit concerning land must be brought in the county where the land is located, and that other suits must be brought in the county where the defendant resides or is doing business. In certain cases where justice so requires, the defendant may obtain a *change of venue*. This can occur when, for example, a fair trial is impossible within a particular county.

---

[4]Another form of jurisdiction, *quasi in rem jurisdiction* or *attachment jurisdiction,* is also based on the presence of property within the state. Unlike cases based on in rem jurisdiction, cases based on quasi in rem jurisdiction do not necessarily determine rights in the property itself. Instead, the property is regarded as an extension of the out-of-state defendant, which enables the court to decide claims unrelated to the property. For example, a plaintiff might attach the defendant's bank account in the state where the bank is located, sue the defendant on a tort or contract claim unrelated to the bank account, and recover the amount of the judgment from the account if the suit is successful.

FEDERAL COURTS AND THEIR JURISDICTION

Federal District Courts

In the federal system, lawsuits usually begin in the federal district courts, which basically are federal trial courts. Like state trial courts, the federal district courts determine both the relevant facts and the applicable law. The fact-finding function may be entrusted to either the judge or a jury, but determining the law is the judge's responsibility. Each state has at least one district court, and each district court has at least one judge.

District Court Jurisdiction and Venue   There are many bases of federal district court civil jurisdiction. The two most important are **diversity jurisdiction** and **federal question jurisdiction.** Diversity jurisdiction exists when: (1) the suit is between citizens of different states, and (2) the amount in controversy exceeds $50,000. Diversity jurisdiction also exists in certain suits between citizens of a state and citizens or governments of foreign nations where the amount in controversy exceeds $50,000. Under diversity jurisdiction, a corporation is normally a citizen of both the state where it has been incorporated and the state where it has its principal place of business.

Federal question jurisdiction exists when the case arises under the Constitution, laws, or treaties of the United States. The "arises under" requirement normally is met when a right created by federal law is a basic part of the plaintiff's case. There is no amount-in-controversy requirement for federal question jurisdiction.

A district court's diversity or federal question jurisdiction usually includes only those defendants who would be subject to the in personam jurisdiction of the state where the district court sits. Further limiting the plaintiff's choice of federal district courts are the federal system's complex venue requirements. These requirements, which have recently been amended by Congress, are beyond the scope of this text.

Concurrent Jurisdiction and Removal The federal district courts have *exclusive jurisdiction* over some matters—for example, patent and copyright cases. This means that such cases *must* be heard in federal district court. Often, however, the district courts have *concurrent jurisdiction* with state courts; here, both state and federal courts have jurisdiction over the case. For example, a plaintiff might assert state court in personam jurisdiction over an out-of-state defendant or might sue in a federal district court under that court's diversity jurisdiction. Also, a state court may decide a case involving a federal question if it has jurisdiction over that case. Where concurrent jurisdiction exists and the plaintiff opts for a state court, the defendant sometimes can *remove* the case to a federal district court.

Specialized Courts

The federal court system also includes certain specialized federal courts, including the Claims Court (which hears claims against the United States), the Court of International Trade (which is concerned with tariff, customs, import, and other trade matters), the Bankruptcy Courts (which operate as adjuncts of the district courts), and the Tax Court (which reviews certain IRS determinations). Usually, the decisions of these courts can be appealed to one or more of the federal courts of appeals.

Courts of Appeals

Like state intermediate appellate courts, the U.S. courts of appeals do not have a fact-finding function, and review only the legal conclusions reached by lower federal courts. As Figure 3 on the next page illustrates, there are 13 federal courts of appeals: 11 organized territorially into circuits covering several states each, one for the District of Columbia, and the Court of Appeals for the Federal Circuit.

Except for the Court of Appeals for the Federal Circuit, the most important function of the U.S. courts of appeals is to hear appeals from decisions of the federal district courts. Appeals from a district court

ordinarily proceed to the Court of Appeals for that district court's region. Appeals from the District Court for the Southern District of New York, for example, go to the Second Circuit Court of Appeals. The courts of appeals also hear appeals from the Tax Court, from many administrative agency decisions, and (via appellate panels they appoint) from some Bankruptcy Court decisions. The Court of Appeals for the Federal Circuit hears a wide variety of specialized appeals, including some patent and trademark matters, Claims Court decisions, and decisions by the Court of International Trade.

The U.S. Supreme Court

The United States Supreme Court is mainly an appellate court. Thus, it only considers questions of law when it decides appeals. Most of the appeals handled by the Supreme Court come from the federal courts of appeals and the highest state courts.[5] Today, most appealable decisions from these courts fall within the Supreme Court's *certiorari* jurisdiction, under which the Court has discretion whether or not to hear the appeal. The Court hears only a small percentage of the many appeals it receives through its certiorari jurisdiction.

Virtually all appeals from the federal courts of appeals are within the Court's discretionary certiorari jurisdiction. Appeals from the highest state courts are within the certiorari jurisdiction when: (1) the validity of any treaty or federal statute has been questioned; (2) the validity of any state statute is questioned because it is repugnant to federal law; or (3) any title, right, privilege, or immunity is claimed under federal law. The Supreme Court generally defers to the highest state courts on questions of state law, and normally does not hear appeals from those courts if the case only involves such questions.

In certain rare situations, finally, the U.S. Supreme Court has **original jurisdiction,** which means that it acts as a trial court. The Supreme Court has *original and exclusive* jurisdiction over all controversies between two or more states. It has *original,* but not exclusive, jurisdiction over cases involving foreign ambassadors, ministers, and like

---

[5]There are, however, situations in which the Supreme Court will hear appeals directly from the federal district courts.

FIGURE 3   The Thirteen Federal Judicial Circuits

First Circuit (*Boston, Mass.*) Maine, Massachusetts, New Hampshire, Puerto Rico, Rhode Island

Second Circuit (*New York, N.Y.*) Connecticut, New York, Vermont

Third Circuit (*Philadelphia, Pa.*) Delaware, New Jersey, Pennsylvania, Virgin Islands

Fourth Circuit (*Richmond, Va.*) Maryland, North Carolina, South Carolina, Virginia, West Virginia

Fifth Circuit (*New Orleans, La.*) Louisiana, Mississippi, Texas

Sixth Circuit (*Cincinnati, Ohio*) Kentucky, Michigan, Ohio, Tennessee

Seventh Circuit (*Chicago, Ill.*) Illinois, Indiana, Wisconsin

Eighth Circuit (*St. Louis, Mo.*) Arkansas, Iowa, Minnesota, Missouri, Nebraska, North Dakota, South Dakota

Ninth Circuit (*San Francisco, Calif.*) Alaska, Arizona, California, Guam, Hawaii, Idaho, Montana, Nevada, Northern Mariana Islands, Oregon, Washington

Tenth Circuit (*Denver, Colo.*) Colorado, Kansas, New Mexico, Oklahoma, Utah, Wyoming

Eleventh Circuit (*Atlanta, Ga.*) Alabama, Florida, Georgia

District of Columbia Circuit (*Washington, D.C.*)

Federal Circuit (*Washington, D.C.*)

---

parties; controversies between the United States and a state; and cases where a state proceeds against citizens of another state or against aliens.

Figure 4 on the following page combines the state and federal court systems.

CIVIL PROCEDURE

Civil procedure is the set of legal rules governing the conduct of a trial court case between private parties.[6] Because this law sometimes varies with the jurisdiction in question,[7] the following presentation is only a summary of the most widely accepted rules governing civil cases in state trial courts and the federal district courts. Knowing about these basic

procedural matters is useful if you become involved in a civil lawsuit. Such knowledge also helps you understand the cases in this text. Figure 5 on page 29 presents the major steps through which a civil case normally proceeds and the most significant motions the parties (or *litigants*) can make at each step.

The Adversary System

In any civil case, the *adversary system* is at work. Through their attorneys, the litigants present contrary positions of fact or law before a theoretically impartial judge and possibly a jury. To win a civil case, the plaintiff must prove each element of his claim by a *preponderance of the evidence*.[8] That is, the plaintiff must show that the greater weight of the evidence—by *credibility,* not quantity—supports the

---

[6]Criminal procedure is discussed in Chapter 5, and the procedures used before administrative agencies in Chapter 46.

[7]In the following discussion, the term *jurisdiction* refers to 1 of the 50 states, the District of Columbia, or the federal government.

[8]However, in a criminal case the government must prove the elements of the alleged crime *beyond a reasonable doubt.*

FIGURE 4   **A Simplified Model of the State and Federal Court Systems**

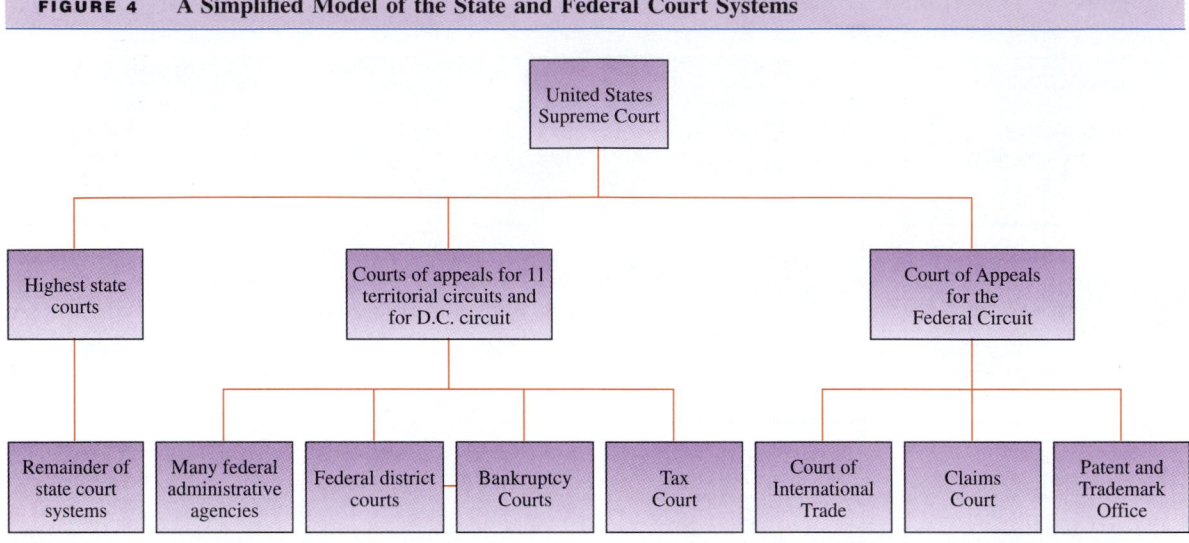

---

existence of each element. In other words, the plaintiff must convince the fact finder that the existence of each factual element is more probable than its nonexistence. Thus, the lawyers for each party present their clients' version of the facts, try to convince the judge or jury that this version is true, and attempt to rebut conflicting factual allegations by the other party. Each attorney also seeks to persuade the judge that her reading of the law is correct.

Supporters of the adversary system believe that allowing the litigants to make competing arguments of fact and law gives the judge and jury the best chance of making accurate determinations because it enables the presentation and criticism of all relevant arguments. The system's critics contend that rather than promoting the disinterested search for truth, it encourages the parties to employ incomplete, distorted, and even false arguments whenever such arguments seem useful. Defenders of the adversary system reply that attacks from the other party and the rulings of an impartial judge should weed out such arguments. This weeding-out process, however, may proceed unequally if one party has superior resources and thus can obtain better representation.

Service of the Summons

The function of the **summons** is to notify the defendant that he is being sued. The summons typically names the plaintiff and states the time within which

the defendant must enter an *appearance* in court (usually through her attorney). In most jurisdictions, the summons is accompanied by a copy of the plaintiff's complaint (which is described below).

The summons is usually delivered, or served, to the defendant by an appropriate public official after the plaintiff has filed his complaint with the court. To ensure that the defendant is properly notified of the suit, statutes, court rules, and constitutional due process guarantees set standards for proper service of the summons in particular cases. For example, personal delivery of the summons to the defendant almost always meets these standards, and many jurisdictions also permit the summons to be left at the defendant's home or place of business. Service to corporations often may be accomplished by delivery of the summons to the firm's general or managing agent. Many state long-arm statutes permit out-of-state defendants to be served by registered mail. Although inadequate service of process may sometimes defeat the plaintiff's claim, in most jurisdictions the defendant must make his objection early or it will be waived.

The Pleadings

The **pleadings** are the documents the parties file with the court when they first state their respective cases. They include the **complaint**, the **answer**, and (in some jurisdictions) the **reply.**

FIGURE 5   The Most Important Stages and Motions in Civil Litigation (Appeals Assumed)

Stage   Motion   Appealability*

*As discussed later in the chapter, many other trial court rulings also are appealable.

The Complaint   The complaint states the plaintiff's claim in separate, numbered paragraphs. It must contain sufficient facts to show that the plaintiff is entitled to legal relief and to give the defendant reasonable notice of the nature of the plaintiff's claim. The complaint also must state the remedy requested by the plaintiff.

The Answer   Within a designated time after the complaint has been served, the defendant normally files an answer to the plaintiff's complaint. The answer responds to the complaint paragraph by paragraph. Usually, it admits the allegations of each paragraph, denies them, or states that the defendant lacks the information to assess the truth or falsity of the allegations (which has much the same effect as a denial).

The answer may also include an **affirmative defense** to the claim asserted in the complaint. A successful affirmative defense would enable the defendant to win the case even if all the allegations in the complaint are true and, by themselves, entitle the plaintiff to recover. For example, suppose that the plaintiff bases her suit on a contract that she alleges the defendant has breached (broken). The defendant's answer may admit or deny the existence of the contract or the assertion that the defendant breached it. In addition, the answer may make assertions that, if proven, would show that the defendant has an affirmative defense because the plaintiff's fraud induced the defendant to enter the contract.

The answer may also contain a **counterclaim.** A counterclaim is a *new* claim by the defendant arising from the matters stated in the complaint. Unlike an affirmative defense, it is not merely an attack on the plaintiff's claim but is the *defendant's* attempt to obtain legal relief. In addition to using fraud as an affirmative defense to a plaintiff's contract claim, for example, a defendant might counterclaim for damages caused by that fraud.

The Reply   In some jurisdictions, the plaintiff is allowed or required to respond to an affirmative defense or a counterclaim by making a reply. The reply is the plaintiff's point-by-point response (a kind of answer) to the allegations in the affirmative defense or counterclaim. However, many jurisdictions do not allow a reply to an affirmative defense; instead, the defendant's new allegations are automatically denied. Usually, though, a plaintiff who wishes to contest a counterclaim must reply to it.

The Functions of the Pleadings   Traditionally, the main function of the pleadings has been to define and limit the questions to be decided at later stages of the case. Only those issues raised in the pleadings have been considered part of the case; points omitted from the pleadings have been excluded from further consideration; and few, if any, amendments to the pleadings have been permitted. Also, litigants usually have been bound to allegations admitted in the pleadings; only those allegations that have not been admitted have been regarded as in dispute. Many jurisdictions retain some of these rules. Over time, however, the main purpose behind pleading rules has shifted from defining and limiting the questions to be resolved in the case to affording the parties notice of each other's claims. Accompanying this shift have been a greater tendency to decide cases on their merits, a more relaxed attitude toward technical defects in the pleadings, and a greater tendency to permit amendments to the pleadings.

Motion to Dismiss

Sometimes it is evident from the complaint or the pleadings that the plaintiff has no case. Here, it is wasteful for the suit to proceed further, and it is useful to have a procedural device for ending it. This device has various names, but it is commonly called the **motion to dismiss.** This motion is often made after the plaintiff has filed his complaint. A similar motion allowed by some jurisdictions, the **motion for judgment on the pleadings,** normally occurs after the pleadings have been completed. A successful motion to dismiss means that the defendant wins the case; if the motion fails, the case proceeds further.

The motion to dismiss may be made on various grounds—for example, inadequate service of process or lack of jurisdiction. The most important type of motion to dismiss, however, is the motion to dismiss for failure to state a claim upon which relief can be granted, sometimes called the **demurrer.** This motion basically says "So what?" to the factual allegations in the complaint. It asserts that the plaintiff cannot recover even if all these allegations are true because no rule of law entitles him to win on those facts. Suppose that Potter sues Davis on the theory that Davis's bad breath is a form of "olfactory pollution" entitling Potter to recover damages. Potter's complaint describes Davis's breath and the distress it causes Potter in great detail. Even if all of Potter's factual allegations are true, Davis's motion to dismiss almost certainly will succeed. Thus, Davis will win the case, for there is no rule of law allowing a civil recovery for bad breath.

Discovery

Litigants sometimes lack the factual information to prove their cases when the suit begins. To help them prepare their arguments and to narrow and clarify the issues for trial, all jurisdictions permit the parties to undertake extensive **discovery** of relevant information. The most common kinds of discovery are **depositions** (oral examinations of a party or a party's witness by the other party's attorney), **interrogatories** (written questions directed to a party, answered in writing, and signed under oath), **requests for admissions** (one party's written demand that the other party agree to certain statements of fact or law), **requests for documents and other evidence**, and

physical and mental examinations. The permissible limits of discovery are set by the trial judge, whose rulings are controlled by the procedural law of the jurisdiction. In an effort to make civil litigation less of a battle of wits or a sporting event and more of a disinterested search for the truth, many jurisdictions have liberalized their discovery rules to give parties freer access to all relevant facts.

The jurisdiction's law of evidence determines whether or when discovery findings are admissible trial evidence. However, almost all jurisdictions allow some discovery findings to be employed at trial for certain purposes. Depositions, for instance, may sometimes be used as "paper testimony" from dead or distant witnesses, or to attack the credibility of a witness whose trial testimony differs from statements she made at the deposition.

Summary Judgment

The proceeding accompanying a motion for **summary judgment** has been described as a trial by affidavit. The summary judgment is a device for disposing of relatively clear cases without a trial. It differs from a demurrer because it involves factual determinations. To prevail, the party moving for a summary judgment must show that: (1) there is no genuine issue of material (legally significant) fact, and (2) he is entitled to judgment as a matter of law. A moving party satisfies the first element of the test by using the pleadings, discovery information, and affidavits (signed and sworn statements regarding matters of fact) to show that there is no real question about any significant fact. She satisfies the second element by showing that, given the established facts, the applicable law directs that she win.

Either or both parties may move for a summary judgment. If the court rules in favor of either party, that party wins the case. If no party's motion for summary judgment is granted, the case proceeds to trial. The judge may also grant a partial summary judgment, which settles some issues in the case but leaves the others to be decided at trial.

The Pretrial Conference

Depending on the jurisdiction, a **pretrial conference** is either mandatory or at the discretion of the trial judge. At this conference, the judge meets informally with the attorneys for both litigants. The judge may try to get the attorneys to *stipulate,* or agree to, the resolution of certain issues to simplify the trial. He may also encourage them to get their clients to *settle* the case by coming to an agreement that eliminates the need for a trial.[9] If the case is not settled, the judge enters a pretrial order including the attorneys' stipulations and any other agreements. Ordinarily, this order binds the parties throughout the remainder of the case.

The Trial

Once the case has been through discovery and has survived any pretrial motions, it is set for trial. The trial may be before a judge alone, in which case the judge makes separate findings of fact and law before issuing the court's judgment. But if the right to a jury trial exists and either party demands one, the jury handles the fact-finding function, with the resolution of legal questions still entrusted to the judge.[10] At a pretrial jury screening process known as *voir dire,* most jurisdictions: (1) allow biased potential jurors to be removed *for cause,* and (2) give the attorney for each party a certain number of *peremptory challenges,* which allow each attorney to remove potential jurors without *any* cause.

The Basic Scenario   At either a judge or a jury trial, the attorneys for each side typically begin by making opening statements explaining what they intend to prove. After this, the plaintiff's witnesses and other evidence are introduced, and these witnesses are cross-examined by the defendant's attorney. This may be followed by the plaintiff's redirect examination of his witnesses, and perhaps by the defendant's recross-examination of those same witnesses. Then, using the same procedures, the defendant's evidence is presented. Throughout each side's presentation, the opposing attorney may object to the admission of certain evidence. Using the law of evidence, the judge then decides whether the challenged proof is admissible. After the plaintiff and defendant have completed their initial presentations of evidence, each is allowed to offer evidence

---

[9]Settlement of a civil case is discussed in more detail later in this chapter.

[10]The rules governing availability of a jury trial are largely beyond the scope of this text. The U.S. Constitution guarantees a jury trial in federal court suits "at common law" whose amount exceeds $20, and most of the states have similar constitutional provisions. Also, Congress and the state legislatures may allow jury trials in various other cases.

rebutting the other's evidence. Once all the evidence has been presented, each attorney makes a closing argument summarizing her position. In nonjury trials, the judge then makes findings of fact and law, renders judgment, and states the relief to which the plaintiff is entitled if the plaintiff is victorious.

Jury Trials   At the end of a jury trial, the judge issues a **charge** or **instruction** to the jury. The charge sets out the law applicable to the case. The judge may also summarize the evidence for the jury. Then the jury is supposed to make the necessary factual determinations, apply the law to these, and arrive at a **verdict** on which the court's **judgment** is based.

The most common verdict is the **general verdict,** which only requires that the jury declare which party wins and the relief (if any) awarded. Because the jury need not state its factual findings or its application of the law to those findings, the general verdict gives the jury freedom to ignore the judge's charge and follow its own inclinations. Arguably, this freedom allows the jury to soften the law's rigors by bringing common sense and community values to bear on the case, but it also weakens the rule of law and allows juries to commit injustices. The **special verdict** is one response to this problem. Here, the jury only makes specific findings of fact, and the judge then applies the law to these findings. The decision whether to utilize a special verdict is usually within the trial judge's discretion.

Directed Verdict   Although the general verdict gives the jury considerable power, the American legal system also establishes devices for limiting that power. The special verdict is one of these devices. Another, the **directed verdict,** essentially takes the case away from the jury and gives a judgment to one party before the jury gets a chance to decide. The motion for a directed verdict can be made by either party; it usually occurs after the other (nonmoving) party has presented her evidence. The moving party basically asserts that, even when read most favorably to the other party, the evidence leads to only one result and need not be considered by the jury. Courts differ on the test governing a motion for a directed verdict: Some deny the motion if there is *any* evidence favoring the nonmoving party, while others deny the motion only if there is *substantial* evidence favoring the nonmoving party.

Judgment Notwithstanding the Verdict   On occasion, the case is taken away from the jury and one party wins a judgment even *after* the jury has reached a verdict *against* that party. The device for doing so is the **judgment notwithstanding the verdict** (also known as the judgment *non obstante veredicto* or judgment n.o.v.). Some jurisdictions require that, in order to make a motion for judgment n.o.v, the moving party must previously have moved for a directed verdict. In any event, the standard used to decide the motion for judgment n.o.v. is usually the same standard the jurisdiction uses to decide the motion for a directed verdict.

Motion for New Trial   In a wide range of situations that vary among jurisdictions, the losing party can successfully move for a new trial. Acceptable reasons for granting a new trial include errors by the judge during the trial, jury or attorney misconduct, new evidence, or an award of excessive damages to the plaintiff.

CONCEPT REVIEW

THE MAJOR CIVIL MOTIONS COMPARED

Motion	When Typically Made	By Whom Typically Made	Typical Test	Typical Effect if Successful
To Dismiss or for Judgment on the Pleadings	After complaint or pleadings	Defendant	Assuming the facts in the complaint are true, can plaintiff win as a matter of law?	Defendant wins case

Motion	When Typically Made	By Whom Typically Made	Typical Test	Typical Effect if Successful
For Summary Judgment	Varies; often after discovery	Either party	No genuine issue of material fact, and moving party entitled to judgment as a matter of law	Moving party wins case; partial summary judgment also possible
For Directed Verdict	After other party has presented evidence at trial	Either party	Two versions. Moving party loses if: (1) *any* evidence favoring nonmoving party; or (2) *substantial* evidence favoring nonmoving party	Moving party wins case
For Judgment Notwithstanding Verdict	After adverse jury verdict	Losing party	Same test jurisdiction uses for directed verdict	Moving party wins case
For New Trial	After adverse judgment or jury verdict	Losing party	Wide range of possible grounds	New trial ordered

Appeal

Appellate courts normally consider only alleged errors of law made by the trial court. As Figure 5 indicated earlier in the chapter, among the matters ordinarily considered "legal" and thus appealable are the trial judge's decisions on a motion to dismiss or a motion for judgment on the pleadings, the scope of discovery, a motion for summary judgment, a motion for a directed verdict or for judgment notwithstanding the verdict, and a motion for a new trial. Other matters typically considered appealable include any trial court rulings on service of process, its rulings on the admission of evidence at trial, its legal findings in a nonjury trial, its instruction to the jury in a jury trial, and the damages or other relief awarded.

Appellate courts may, among other things, *affirm* the trial court's decision, *reverse* it, or affirm one part of the decision and reverse another part. As Figure 5 also suggests, one of three things ordinarily results from the appellate courts' disposition of the appeal: (1) the plaintiff wins the case; (2) the defendant wins the case; or (3) if the case is reversed in whole or in part, it is *remanded* (returned) to the trial court for further proceedings. For example, if the plaintiff appeals a trial court decision granting the defendant's motion to dismiss and the appellate court(s) affirm that decision, the plaintiff loses. On the other hand, where an appellate court reverses a trial court verdict and judgment in the defendant's favor, the plaintiff might win outright, or the case might be returned to the trial court for further proceedings not inconsistent with the appellate decision.

Enforcing a Judgment

In this text, you occasionally see cases where someone was not sued even though he appeared to be liable to the plaintiff, and where another party was sued instead. One explanation is that the first party was "judgment-proof"—so lacking in assets as to make a civil suit for damages impractical. The other party's financial condition also affects a winning plaintiff's ability to actually recover whatever damages she has been awarded.

When the defendant fails to pay as required after losing a civil suit, the winning plaintiff must enforce the judgment. Ordinarily, the plaintiff will obtain a *writ of execution* enabling the sheriff to seize designated property of the defendant and sell it at a judicial sale to satisfy the judgment. A judgment winner may also use a procedure known as *garnishment* to seize property, money, or wages of the defendant that are in the hands of a third party. If the property needed to satisfy the judgment is located in another state, the plaintiff must use that state's execution or garnishment procedures. Under the U.S. Constitution, the second state must give "full faith and credit" to the judgment of the state where the plaintiff originally sued. Finally, when the court has awarded an equitable remedy such as an injunction, the defendant may be found in contempt of court and subjected to a fine or imprisonment if he fails to obey the court's order.

Class Actions

So far, our civil procedure discussion has proceeded as if the plaintiff and the defendant each were a single party. Actually, several plaintiffs and/or defendants can be parties to one lawsuit. Also, each jurisdiction has procedural rules stating when other parties can be *joined* to a suit that begins without them.

One special type of multiparty suit, the **class action,** allows one or more persons to sue on behalf of themselves and all others who have suffered similar harm from substantially the same wrong. Class action suits by consumers, environmentalists, women, minorities, and other groups are now common events. The usual justifications for the class action are that: (1) it allows legal wrongs causing losses to a large number of widely dispersed parties to be fully compensated, and (2) it promotes economy of judicial effort by combining many similar claims into one suit.

The requirements for a class action vary among jurisdictions. The issues addressed by class action statutes include the following: whether there are questions of law and fact common to all members of the alleged class, whether the class is small enough to allow all of its members to join the case as parties rather than use a class action, and whether the plaintiff(s) and their attorney(s) can competently represent the class without conflicts of interest or other forms of unfairness. To protect the individual class member's right to be heard, some jurisdictions have required that unnamed or absent class members be given notice of the suit if this is reasonably possible. The damages awarded in a successful class action usually are apportioned among the entire class. Establishing the total recovery and distributing it to the class, however, pose problems when the class is large, the class members' injuries are indefinite, or some members cannot be identified.

ALTERNATIVE DISPUTE RESOLUTION

Courts are not the only devices for resolving civil disputes. Nor are they always the best means of doing so. Settling private disputes through the courts can be a cumbersome, lengthy, and expensive process for litigants. With the advent of a litigious society and the increasing caseloads it has produced, handling disputes in this fashion also imposes ever-greater *social* costs. For these and other reasons, the various forms of **alternative dispute resolution (ADR)** have assumed increasing importance in recent years.

Common Forms of ADR

Settlement   The settlement of a civil suit is not everyone's idea of an alternative dispute resolution mechanism. But it is an important means of avoiding protracted litigation, one that is often a sensible compromise for the parties. Many cases settle at some stage in the civil proceedings described previously. The typical settlement agreement is a contract whereby the defendant agrees to pay the plaintiff a sum of money, in exchange for the plaintiff's promise to release the defendant from liability on the claims in his suit. Although courts are predisposed to enforce settlement agreements, such agreements still must satisfy the requirements of contract law discussed later in this text. In some cases, moreover, the court must approve the settlement in order for it to be enforceable. Examples include class actions and litigation involving minors.

Arbitration   Arbitration is the submission of a dispute to a neutral, nonjudicial third party (the *arbitrator*) who issues a binding decision resolving that dispute. Arbitration usually results from the parties' agreement. That agreement is normally made before the dispute arises (most often through an *arbitration clause* in a contract), but it can occur after the dispute begins. Arbitration may also be compelled by statute. One example is the *compulsory arbitration* many states require as part of the collective bargaining process for certain public employees.

Arbitration is normally less formal than regular court proceedings. The arbitrator need not be an attorney; often, she is a professional who may be expert in the subject matter of the dispute. Although arbitration hearings often resemble civil trials in their broad outlines, the applicable procedures, the rules for admission of evidence, and the record-keeping requirements typically are not as rigorous as those governing courts. Also, arbitrators have some freedom to ignore rules of substantive law that would bind a court.

The arbitrator's decision, called an *award,* is filed with a court, which will enforce it if necessary. The losing party may object to the arbitrator's award, but the courts' review of arbitration proceedings is limited. Possible grounds for overturning an arbitration award include: (1) its procurement by fraud, (2) the arbitrator's partiality or corruption, and (3) other misconduct by the arbitrator (e.g., refusing to hear relevant evidence).

Court-Annexed Arbitration

In court-annexed arbitration, certain types of civil lawsuits basically are diverted into arbitration. One example might be cases where less than a specified dollar amount is at issue. Most often, court-annexed arbitration is mandatory and is ordered by the judge, but some jurisdictions merely offer litigants the option of arbitration. The losing party in a court-annexed arbitration still has the right to a regular trial.

Mediation

In mediation, a neutral third party called a *mediator* helps the parties reach an agreeable, cooperative resolution of their dispute by facilitating communication between them, clarifying their areas of agreement and disagreement, helping them to see each other's viewpoints, suggesting settlement options, and so forth. Unlike arbitrators, mediators cannot make decisions that bind the parties. Instead, a successful mediation process typically results in a *mediation agreement*. Such agreements normally are enforced under regular contract law principles.

Mediation is used in a wide range of situations, including labor, commercial, family, and environmental disputes. It may occur by agreement of the parties after a dispute has arisen. It may also result from a previous contractual agreement by the parties. Increasingly, moreover, court-annexed mediation is either compelled or made available by courts in certain cases.

Summary Jury Trial

Sometimes settlement of civil litigation is impeded because the litigants have different perceptions of the merits of their cases. In such cases, the summary jury trial may give either or both parties a needed dose of reality. As its name suggests, the summary jury trial is an abbreviated, nonpublic mock jury trial that does not bind the parties. Often, this "trial" occurs before a real judge, with jurors chosen from the regular pool of jurors. If the parties do not settle after completion of the summary jury trial, they are still entitled to a regular court trial. Also, there is some disagreement over whether courts can compel the parties to undergo a summary jury trial in the first place.

Minitrial

A minitrial is an informal, abbreviated private "trial" whose aim is to promote settlement of disputes. Normally, it arises out of a private agreement, which also describes the procedures to be followed. In the typical minitrial, counsel for each party present their cases to a panel composed of senior management from each side. Sometimes a neutral adviser such as an attorney or a retired judge presides. This party may also offer an opinion about the case's likely outcome in court. After the presentations, the managers try to negotiate a settlement.

Other ADR Devices

Other ADR devices include: (1) *med/arb* (a hybrid of mediation and arbitration in which the third party first acts as a mediator, and then as an arbitrator); (2) the appointment of *magistrates* and *special masters* to perform various tasks during complex litigation in the federal courts; (3) *early neutral evaluation* (ENE) (a court-annexed procedure involving early, objective evaluation of the case by a neutral private attorney with experience in its subject matter); (4) *private judging* (in which litigants hire a private referee to issue a decision that may be binding but that usually does not preclude some recourse to the courts); and (5) *private panels* instituted by an industry or an organization to handle claims of certain kinds (e.g., the Better Business Bureau). Also, some formally legal processes are sometimes called ADR devices;

examples include small claims courts and the administrative procedures used to handle claims for veterans' benefits or social security benefits.

The Pros and Cons of ADR

Taken collectively, the various forms of ADR have many advantages over litigation before a court. These advantages include:

1. *Quicker resolution of disputes.* This is due mainly to the relative informality of most ADR proceedings and their ability to promote settlement of the case.
2. *Lower costs in time, money, and aggravation for the parties.* Again, these benefits flow mainly from the relative informality and speed of many ADR procedures, and from their ability to spur a settlement.
3. *Reduced strains on an overloaded court system.*
4. *The possible availability of expert decisionmakers.* For example, arbitrators may possess special expertise in the subject matter of the disputes they handle.
5. *Flexibility and consensus-building.* Mediation, for instance, often avoids the adversarial climate and tendency toward either/or decisions that characterize formal litigation. Thus, it can promote consensus and compromise solutions by the parties themselves.

However, ADR also has a number of possible disadvantages. These include:

1. *A tendency to undermine the rule of law.* At its best, the civil law states general norms that apply uniformly to all the private disputes they cover. ADR decisions, on the other hand, sometimes are ad hoc affairs in which rules of substantive law play little role and precedent even less. Thus, the widespread use of ADR tends to undermine the *uniformity* and *predictability* associated with the rule of law.
2. *Inaccurate or biased decisionmaking processes.* One reason for the complexity of the rules of civil procedure and evidence is that they try to give each party the utmost in procedural protection and to ensure that factual determinations are as accurate as possible. The relatively relaxed procedures and evidentiary

rules—not to mention the occasional absence of lawyers—in some ADR proceedings may mean that these ends are less likely to be served under ADR.

3. *Second-class justice for the relatively powerless in their disputes with the powerful?* Sometimes, agreements to submit disputes to alternative dispute resolution are buried in complex standard-form contracts drafted by a party with superior knowledge and business sophistication and are unknowingly agreed to by less knowledgeable parties. Sometimes, too, such clauses compel ADR proceedings before decisionmakers who may be biased in favor of the stronger party. Occasionally, courts strike down arbitration clauses for these reasons.

ETHICAL AND PUBLIC POLICY CONCERNS

1. As you might expect, the preceding arguments against ADR often come from the legal profession. Are these self-serving arguments? Who stands to lose money and influence if ADR becomes more popular? Assuming that these arguments are self-serving, is this fact alone enough to rebut them?

2. The *Knowles* case presented earlier in this chapter used a style of legal reasoning different from the simple deductive model presented in Chapter 1. This style, which might be called *factor-based balancing,* appears from time to time in this text. Courts using this style of reasoning typically consider several factors (values or policy goals) when deciding. They assess a particular result in light of each factor, trying to determine whether that result advances or frustrates the values embodied in each factor. Then, they try to assess the overall desirability of that result by weighing its positive and negative effects against each other and determining whether the result has a positive or negative effect on balance. Such determinations naturally vary depending on the facts of the case. In *Knowles,* the decision was easy, because almost all the factors the court considered pulled in the same direction. What is good about this kind of legal decisionmaking? What is bad about it?

3. As noted in Chapter 4, debates in the ethics and business ethics literature have sometimes involved clashes between *utilitarian* ethical theories

and *deontological rights-based* ethical theories. Utilitarians normally say that we should maximize aggregate satisfaction, and they tend to approve measures that disadvantage particular individuals so long as those measures actually produce maximum *total* satisfaction. Such theories occasionally use social wealth maximization as a rough measure of total satisfaction. Deontological rights-based theories generally urge that some rights are so important that they can only be overridden by certain other rights, and *not* by maximum aggregate utility.

Speaking generally, into which category would many foes of ADR fit? Assume that these people oppose ADR because they feel that due to the sloppiness of its procedures, it causes injustices to individuals—injustices that could be avoided were normal court procedures used. Although the use of such procedures costs more money than ADR, they assert, this is of no consequence because basic issues of *justice* are involved.

Speaking generally, into which category would many proponents of ADR fit? Assume that these people stress the social and economic costs created by the court system and argue that the widespread use of ADR would free money and resources for other purposes, thus making people wealthier and happier. This increased wealth and happiness, they would add, easily outweigh the personal suffering caused by whatever injustices ADR permits.

PROBLEMS AND PROBLEM CASES

1. Peters sues Davis. At trial, Peters's lawyer attempts to introduce certain evidence to help make his case. Davis's attorney objects, and the trial judge refuses to allow the evidence to be admitted. Peters eventually loses the case at the trial court level. He appeals, his attorney arguing that the trial judge's decision not to admit the evidence was erroneous. Davis's attorney argues that the appellate court cannot consider this question, because appellate courts only review errors of *law* (not fact) at the trial court level. Is Davis's attorney correct? Why or why not?

2. Phillips sues Dilks for $500,000 in a state small claims court set up to handle cases where the amount in controversy does not exceed $5,000. The court clearly does not have jurisdiction over the case. What *kind* of jurisdiction is absent here?

3. Dial, a resident of Indiana, vandalizes a parked car in Columbus, Ohio. This action results in harm to the car and also prevents the owner from using it for a period of time. In the meantime, Dial has fled to Indiana and remains there. The owner, an Ohio resident, plans to sue Dial for trespass to personal property, a tort described in Chapter 6. He claims $5,000 in damages and wants to sue either in an Ohio trial court or in a federal district court. Do each of these courts have jurisdiction over the case? Why or why not? Assume for purposes of this problem that: (a) subject-matter jurisdiction is present, (b) Dial has had no other contacts with the state of Ohio, and (c) Ohio has a long-arm statute with all the features described in the chapter.

4. State *two* differences between the motion to dismiss for failure to state a claim upon which relief can be granted (or demurrer) and the motion for summary judgment.

5. In a suit by Pierce against Dodge, the jury has rendered a verdict in favor of Dodge. Pierce and her attorney think that the evidence was overwhelmingly in Pierce's favor. They also have reason to believe that the jury was bribed by someone connected with Dodge. What *two* motions can Pierce's attorney make in an attempt to overturn the jury's verdict?

6. While driving to work one day, Dember runs over Pearson, causing him severe injuries. Pearson sues Dember in a state trial court. His complaint alleges that Dember's negligent driving caused his injuries. The law of the state declares that if the plaintiff's own negligence contributed to his injury, the defendant has a complete defense and the plaintiff cannot recover. Dember wants to argue that whether he was negligent or not, Pearson's own negligence helped cause his injuries and that Pearson therefore has no case. In order to be *sure* of his ability to raise this argument at trial, what should Dember's attorney do in response to Pearson's complaint?

7. What is the main difference between a motion for a directed verdict and a motion for judgment notwithstanding the verdict?

8. The state of Mississippi is planning to sue the state of Massachusetts. Mississippi's attorney general wants to sue in an appropriate federal district court. Do the federal district courts have jurisdiction over this case? If not, which federal court does have jurisdiction? You can assume that Mississippi's suit involves issues of federal law, and that the amount in controversy exceeds $50,000.

9. Jackson was born in Texas but has had absolutely no contact with that state for 20 years. Jackson's father dies, and a Texas court interprets his will so that Jackson receives none of his father's property, which is located in Texas. Assume that the court had jurisdiction to make this decision. What *kinds* of jurisdiction did it have?

10. Pike sues Dillon, alleging that his parked car was destroyed due to Dillon's negligent driving. After the pleadings and discovery have been com-pleted, Pike's attorney concludes that the case is an obvious winner on both the facts and the law. What motion should the attorney make in an attempt to win the case without having to go to trial?

11. Does ADR really resolve disputes without any help from the courts? Give two examples of ADR processes that depend on courts for their operation or their effectiveness, and state how they depend on the courts.

BUSINESS AND
THE CONSTITUTION

INTRODUCTION

Constitutions serve two general functions. They set up the structure of government, allocating power among its various branches and subdivisions. Constitutions also prevent government from taking certain actions—especially actions that restrict individual rights. As the following overview of its provisions suggests, the U.S. Constitution performs both these functions.[1]

A BRIEF OVERVIEW OF THE U.S. CONSTITUTION

The U.S. Constitution embodies the principle of **separation of powers** by giving distinct powers to Congress, the president, and the federal courts. Thus, Article I of the Constitution establishes a Congress composed of a Senate and a House of Representatives, gives it sole power to *legislate* at the federal level, and sets out rules for the passage of legislation. Also, Article I, section 8 defines when Congress can make law by stating its *legislative powers*. Three of those powers—Congress's commerce, tax, and spending powers—are discussed later in this chapter.

Article II of the Constitution gives the president the *executive power*—the power to execute or enforce the laws passed by Congress. Section 2 of that article lists some other presidential powers, including the powers to command the nation's armed forces and to make treaties. Article III gives the *judicial power* of the United States to the Supreme Court and the other federal courts later established by Congress. Article III also sets the kinds of cases the federal courts can decide.

In addition to instituting a separation of powers, Articles I, II, and III of the Constitution also create a system of **checks and balances** among Congress, the president, and the courts. For example, Article I, section 7 gives the president the power to veto legislation passed by Congress, and also allows Congress to override such a veto by a two-thirds vote of each House. Article I, section 3 and Article II, section 4 provide that the president, the vice

---

[1]Appendix A to this book contains the text of the U.S. Constitution.

president, and other federal officials may be impeached by a two-thirds vote of the Senate. Article II, section 2 says that treaties made by the president must be approved by a two-thirds vote of the Senate. Article III, section 2 gives Congress some control over the Supreme Court's appellate jurisdiction.

Sometimes, the U.S. Constitution also recognizes the principle of **federalism** in the way it structures power relations between the federal government and the states. Article I, section 9 lists certain powers that Congress cannot exercise. The Tenth Amendment provides that those powers the Constitution neither gives to the federal government nor denies to the states are reserved to the states or the people.

Article VI, however, makes the Constitution, laws, and treaties of the United States supreme over state law. As discussed later in this chapter, this means that where the Constitution gives Congress the power to legislate, this principle of **federal supremacy** allows federal statutes to *preempt* inconsistent state laws. The U.S. Constitution also puts specific limits on the states' lawmaking powers. One example from this chapter is Article I, section 10's command that no state shall pass any law impairing the obligation of contracts.

Article V sets the procedures for amending the Constitution. By now, the Constitution has been amended 27 times. The first 10 of these amendments comprise the Bill of Rights. Although the rights stated in the first 10 amendments once applied to the federal government alone, most of them now apply to the states as well. As you will learn, this is due to their *incorporation* within the Due Process Clause of the Fourteenth Amendment, which applies to the states. This application of federal constitutional rights to the states is another reason why the Constitution gives only partial support to the principle of federalism.

THE EVOLUTION OF THE CONSTITUTION AND THE ROLE OF THE SUPREME COURT

According to Chapter 1's legal realists, written "book law" is less important than what public decisionmakers *actually do*. Using this approach, we discover a Constitution that differs from the written Constitution just described. For example, the actual powers of today's presidency far exceed anything you would expect from reading Article II.

As you will see throughout the chapter, moreover, some constitutional provisions now have a different practical meaning than they did when first enacted. American constitutional law is much more *evolving* than static.

Many of these changes have resulted from the way one public decisionmaker—the U.S. Supreme Court—has interpreted the Constitution over time. In theory, constitutional change can be accomplished through the formal amendment process. Because this process is fairly difficult to use, however, amendments to the Constitution have been relatively infrequent. For better or worse, the Supreme Court has been the Constitution's main amender. Many factors help explain the Supreme Court's ability and willingness to play this role. Due to their vagueness, some key constitutional provisions invite diverse interpretations; "due process of law" and "equal protection of the laws" are examples. Also, the history surrounding the enactment of constitutional provisions is sometimes sketchy, confused, or contradictory. Probably more important, however, is the perceived need to adapt the Constitution to changing social conditions. As the old saying goes, Supreme Court decisions tend to follow the election returns.

Under the power of **judicial review,** courts can declare the actions of other governmental bodies unconstitutional. How courts exercise this power depends on how they choose to read the Constitution. This means that courts—especially the Supreme Court—have *political power*. Indeed, the Supreme Court's nine justices basically are *public policymakers*. Thus, their beliefs are quite important in determining how America is governed. This is why the justices' nomination and confirmation often involve so much political controversy.

But even though the Constitution is often what the Supreme Court says it is, the Court's power to shape the Constitution has limits. Most of these limits spring from the tension between modern judicial review and democratic theory. As you have seen, unelected judges sometimes exercise political power by declaring the actions of more representative government bodies unconstitutional under standards that are largely of the judiciary's own devising. This naturally leads to charges that courts are undemocratic, elitist institutions, and those charges put political constraints on courts. Those constraints exist because the Supreme Court and other courts

	Law Does Not Conflict with Any Independent Check	**Law Conflicts with an Independent Check**
Law Is within Congress's Enumerated Powers	Law is constitutional	Law is unconstitutional
Law Is Not within Congress's Enumerated Powers	Law is unconstitutional	Law is unconstitutional

depend on the other branches of government—and ultimately on public belief in judges' fidelity to the rule of law—to make their decisions effective. Thus, federal judges may be inhibited from declaring federal statutes unconstitutional because they are wary of power struggles with a more representative body such as Congress. Because judges tend to believe in majority rule, the charge that courts are undemocratic also puts self-imposed moral constraints on them. Thus, judges often feel obligated to limit their power by following their own past decisions. They may also feel bound to follow constitutional language or the history behind a constitutional provision where these clearly command a particular result.

The Coverage and Structure of This Chapter

This chapter examines certain constitutional provisions that are important to business; it does not discuss constitutional law in its entirety. These provisions help define *federal and state power to regulate the economy*. The U.S. Constitution limits government regulatory power in two general ways. First, it restricts *federal* legislative authority by listing the powers Congress can exercise and restricting it to these **enumerated powers.** To be constitutional, in other words, federal legislation must be based on a power specifically stated in the Constitution. Second, the U.S. Constitution limits both *state* and *federal* power by placing certain **independent checks** in the path of each. In effect, the independent checks declare that even if Congress has an enumerated power to act in a particular area or a state constitution authorizes a state to act in a certain way, there are still certain protected spheres into which neither can reach.

As Figure 1 suggests, therefore, a federal law must meet two general tests in order to be constitutional: (1) it must be based on an enumerated power of Congress, and (2) it must not collide with any of the independent checks. For example, Congress has the power to regulate commerce among the states. By itself, this power might allow Congress to pass legislation forbidding certain racial minorities from crossing state lines to buy or sell goods. But such a law, although arguably based on an enumerated power, would surely be unconstitutional. The reason is that it conflicts with an independent check: the equal protection guarantee discussed later in this chapter. Today, the independent checks are the main limitations on congressional power. The most important reason for the decline of the enumerated powers limitation is the perceived need for active federal regulation of economic and social life.

This chapter begins by discussing the most important state and federal powers to regulate economic matters. Next, the chapter examines certain independent checks that apply to both the federal government and the states. After this, it discusses some independent checks affecting the states alone. The chapter concludes by considering a provision—the Takings Clause of the Fifth Amendment—that both recognizes a governmental power and limits its exercise.

State and Federal Power to Regulate

State Regulatory Power

Although *state constitutions* may do so, the U.S. Constitution does not list the powers state legislatures can exercise. However, the U.S. Constitution does place certain independent checks in the path of state lawmaking. It also declares that certain powers (e.g., creating currency and taxing imports) can only be exercised by Congress. In many other areas, though, Congress and the state legislatures have *concurrent powers.* Within those areas, both can make law unless Congress preempts state regulation under the Supremacy Clause. A very important state legislative power that operates concurrently with many congressional powers is the **police power.** The police power is a broad state power to regulate for the public health, safety, morals, and welfare.

Federal Regulatory Power

Article I, section 8 of the U.S. Constitution states a number of business-related areas in which Congress can legislate. For example, it empowers Congress to coin and borrow money, regulate commerce with foreign nations, establish uniform laws regarding bankruptcies, create post offices, and regulate copyrights and patents. However, the most important business-related congressional powers contained in Article I, section 8 are the powers to regulate commerce among the states, to lay and collect taxes, and to spend for the general welfare. Because they are now read so broadly, these three powers are the main constitutional bases for today's extensive federal social and economic regulation.

The Commerce Power   Article I, section 8 states that "The Congress shall have Power . . . To regulate Commerce . . . among the several States." The original reason for giving Congress this power to regulate *interstate commerce* was to block the protectionist state restrictions on interstate trade that were common after the Revolution and thus to nationalize economic life. This *Commerce Clause* has two major thrusts. First, as discussed later in this chapter, it is an independent check on state regulation that unduly restricts interstate commerce. Our present concern is the second aspect of the Commerce Clause—its role as a source of congressional regulatory power.

By its literal language, the Commerce Clause simply gives Congress power to regulate *commerce* that occurs *among the states.* Today, the clause is basically an all-purpose federal police power en-

abling Congress to regulate most activities within a state's borders (*intrastate* matters). How has this transformation occurred?

One step in the transformation was the Supreme Court's conclusion that the power to regulate *interstate* commerce includes the power to regulate *intrastate* activities that affect interstate commerce. For example, in the *Shreveport Rate Cases* (1914), the Supreme Court upheld the Interstate Commerce Commission's regulation of railroad rates within Texas (an intrastate matter outside the language of the Commerce Clause) because those rates affected rail traffic between Texas and Louisiana (an interstate matter within the clause's language). A second step in the Commerce Clause's transformation was the Supreme Court's increasing willingness to let Congress use the clause for noncommercial "police power" ends. Originally, the Court did so by upholding federal legislation that restricted the interstate movement of disfavored people or commodities. For instance, Congress was allowed to attack sexual immorality, gambling, and food poisoning by limiting the interstate movement of prostitutes, lottery tickets, and impure food, respectively. Here, Congress was acting within the literal language of the Commerce Clause but was using it for purposes different from its original purpose of cracking down on state economic protectionism.

Eventually, these two expansions of the Commerce Clause merged into one general doctrine: *Congress can regulate intrastate police matters that have some effect on interstate commerce.* About 30 years ago, for example, the Supreme Court upheld the application of the 1964 Civil Rights Act's "public accommodations" section to a family-owned restaurant in Birmingham, Alabama. It did so because the restaurant's racial discrimination affected interstate commerce by: (1) reducing the restaurant's business and limiting its purchases of out-of-state meat, and (2) restricting the ability of blacks to travel among the states. As this example suggests, Congress now can regulate intrastate activities even though they have relatively little impact on commerce among the states. In our highly interdependent society, almost all intrastate activities have *some* effect on interstate commerce. Thus, as the following *Wickard* case illustrates, few intrastate matters are outside the reach of the commerce power today.

WICKARD V. FILBURN
317 U.S. 111 (U.S. Sup. Ct. 1942)

Congress enacted the Agricultural Adjustment Act of 1938 to stabilize agricultural production and thus to give farmers reasonable minimum prices. The act empowered the secretary of agriculture to proclaim a yearly national acreage allotment for the coming wheat crop. This was apportioned among the states and their counties, and then among individual farms. Filburn was an Ohio farmer who raised a small acreage of winter wheat, some of which was sold but much of which was used on his farm. Filburn's permitted allotment for 1941 was 11.1 acres. However, he sowed and harvested 23 acres. For this, he was assessed a penalty of $117.11.

Filburn sued the secretary of agriculture (Wickard) for an injunction against enforcement of the penalty. A three-judge district court found in Filburn's favor, and the government appealed to the U.S. Supreme Court.

Jackson, Justice   It is urged that under the Commerce Clause Congress does not possess the power it has in this instance sought to exercise. The question would merit little consideration, except that this Act extends federal regulation to production not intended in any part for commerce but wholly for consumption on the farm. Such activities are, Filburn urges, beyond the reach of congressional power under the Commerce Clause, since they are local in character.

For nearly a century, decisions of this Court dealt rarely with questions of what Congress might do under the Clause, and almost entirely with the permissibility of state activity which discriminated against or burdened interstate commerce. During this period there was perhaps little occasion for the affirmative exercise of the commerce power, and the influence of the clause on American life and law was a negative one, resulting almost wholly from its restraint upon the powers of the states. It was not until 1887, with the enactment of the Interstate Commerce Act, that the commerce power began to exert positive influence in American law and life. This was followed in 1890 by the Sherman Anti-Trust Act and, thereafter, by many others.

When it first dealt with this new legislation, the Court allowed but little scope to the power of Congress. However, other cases called forth broader interpretations of the Commerce Clause destined to supersede the earlier ones. It was soon demonstrated that the effects of many kinds of intrastate activity upon interstate commerce were such as to make them a proper subject of federal regulation. [Thus,] even if Filburn's activity be local, it may still be reached by Congress if it exerts a substantial economic effect on interstate commerce.

The effect of consumption of home-grown wheat on interstate commerce is due to the fact that it constitutes the most variable factor in the disappearance of the wheat crop. Consumption on the farm where grown appears to vary in an amount greater than 20 percent of average production. That Filburn's own contribution to the demand for wheat may be trivial by itself is not enough to remove him from the scope of federal regulation where, as here, his contribution, taken together with that of many others similarly situated, is far from trivial.

The power to regulate commerce includes the power to regulate the prices at which commodities in that commerce are dealt and practices affecting such prices. One of the primary purposes of the Act was to increase the market price of wheat, and to that end to limit the volume thereof that could affect the market. It can hardly be denied that a factor of such volume and variability as home-consumed wheat would have a substantial influence on price and market conditions. This may arise because such wheat overhangs the market and, if induced by rising prices, tends to flow into the market and check price increases. But if we assume that it is never marketed, it supplies a need of the man who grew it which would otherwise be reflected by purchases in the open market. Congress may properly have considered that wheat consumed on the farm where grown, if wholly outside the scheme of regulation, would have a substantial effect in defeating its purpose to stimulate trade therein at increased prices.

Judgment reversed in favor of Wickard.

The Taxing Power   Article I, section 8 of the Constitution also states that "The Congress shall have Power To lay and collect Taxes, Duties, Imposts and Excises." The main purpose behind this *taxing power* is to raise revenue for the federal government.[2] But the taxing power can also serve as a regulatory device. Because the power to tax is the power to destroy, Congress can regulate by imposing a heavy tax on a disfavored activity. Although some past regulatory taxes have been struck down, today the reach of the taxing power, while poorly defined, is still very broad. Sometimes it is said that a regulatory tax is constitutional if its purpose could be furthered by one of Congress's *other* powers. Due to the broad scope of the commerce power, this may mean that the taxing power has few limits.

The Spending Power   If taxing power regulation uses a federal club, congressional *spending power* regulation employs a federal carrot. After stating the taxing power, Article I, section 8 gives Congress a broad ability to spend for the general welfare. By basing the receipt of federal money on the performance of certain conditions, Congress can use the spending power to advance specific regulatory ends. Conditional federal grants to the states, for instance, are common.

Over the past 50 years, congressional spending power regulation invariably has been upheld. Still, there are limits on its use. First, an exercise of the spending power must serve *general* public purposes and not particular interests. Second, when Congress conditions the receipt of federal money on certain conditions, it must do so unambiguously. Third, the condition must be reasonably related to the purpose behind the federal expenditure. For example, Congress probably cannot condition a state's receipt of federal highway money on the state's adoption of a one-house legislature.

INDEPENDENT CHECKS ON THE FEDERAL GOVERNMENT AND THE STATES

Even if a regulation is within Congress's enumerated powers or a state's police power, it is still unconstitutional if it collides with one of the Constitution's *independent checks*. In examining the major independent checks affecting government regulation of the economy, we first discuss three checks that limit both the federal government and the states. These are freedom of speech, due process, and equal protection. Before discussing these guarantees, however, it is necessary to consider three preliminary matters.

Incorporation

The Fifth Amendment prevents the federal government from depriving any person "of life, liberty, or property, without due process of law," and the Fourteenth Amendment does the same to the states. The First Amendment, however, applies only to the federal government. And the Fourteenth Amendment merely says that no *state* shall "deny to any person . . . the equal protection of the laws." Thus, while due process clearly applies to both the federal government and the states, the First Amendment seems to apply only to the federal government and the Equal Protection Clause only to the states. But the First Amendment's free speech guarantee has been included within the "liberty" protected by Fourteenth Amendment due process, and thus made applicable to the states. This is part of the process of *incorporation* by which almost all Bill of Rights provisions now apply to the states. The Fourteenth Amendment's Equal Protection Clause, on the other

---

[2] The Constitution imposes some restrictions on the types of taxes that may be used to raise revenue, but these restrictions are beyond the scope of this text.

FIGURE 2 **Why Certain Individual Rights Guarantees Apply to Both the Federal Government and the States**

Guarantee	Why Applicable to States	Why Applicable to Federal Government
Due Process	Text of Fourteenth Amendment	Text of Fifth Amendment
First Amendment	Incorporation within Fourteenth Amendment	Text of First Amendment
Equal Protection	Text of Fourteenth Amendment	Incorporation within Fifth Amendment

---

hand, has been made applicable to the federal government by incorporating it within the Fifth Amendment's due process guarantee. Figure 2 summarizes all these points.

Government Action

People often talk as if the Constitution protects them against *all* parties who might threaten their rights. However, most of the Constitution's individual rights provisions only block the actions of *government* bodies, state and federal.[3] Private behavior that denies individual rights, while perhaps forbidden by statute, is not supposed to be a constitutional matter. This **government action** or **state action** requirement forces courts to distinguish between governmental behavior and private behavior. Their approach to this problem has varied over time.

Before World War II, only formal organs of government such as legislatures, administrative agencies, municipalities, courts, prosecutors, and state universities were deemed state actors. But after the war, the scope of government action increased considerably, with all sorts of traditionally private behavior being subjected to individual rights limitations. In *Marsh v. Alabama* (1946), the Supreme Court treated a privately owned company town's restriction of free expression as government action under the *public function* theory because the town

was like a regular municipality in most respects. Also, in *Shelley v. Kraemer* (1948), the Court held that state court enforcement of certain white homeowners' private agreement not to sell their homes to blacks was unconstitutional state action under the Equal Protection Clause. Later, in *Burton v. Wilmington Parking Authority* (1961), the Court concluded that racial discrimination by a privately owned restaurant located in a state-owned and state-operated parking garage was unconstitutional state action, in part because the garage and the restaurant were intertwined in a mutually beneficial "symbiotic" relationship. Among the other factors leading courts to find state action during the 1960s and 1970s were extensive government regulation of private activity and government financial aid to a private actor.

Due mainly to the changed composition of the Supreme Court, however, the reach of state action was limited considerably in the 1970s and 1980s. Now, the Court usually treats private behavior as state action only when a regular unit of government is directly *responsible* for the challenged private behavior because it has coerced or encouraged such behavior. Also, the public function doctrine has been limited to situations where a private entity exercises powers that have *traditionally* been *exclusively* reserved to the state; private police protection is a possible example. In addition, government regulation and government funding now are relatively unimportant factors in state action determinations. Despite all these changes, however, state action doctrine probably has not returned to its narrow pre–World War II definition, and much uncertainty remains in this area.

---

[3]However, the Thirteenth Amendment, which bans slavery and involuntary servitude throughout the United States, does not have a state action requirement. Also, some state constitutions have individual rights provisions that lack a state action requirement.

To illustrate the Supreme Court's state action cutback, consider its 1982 decision in *Rendell-Baker v. Cohn*, where it rejected various constitutional challenges to the firing of teachers and counselors at a private school for maladjusted high school students because no state action was present. Although the school was extensively regulated by the state, this did not matter because no state regulation compelled or even influenced the challenged firings. Even though the school depended heavily on state funding, this was not sufficient for state action either. The Court also rejected a "symbiosis" argument without much discussion. Finally, it found the public function doctrine inapplicable because the education of maladjusted high school students, while public in nature, is not *exclusively* a state function.

Means-Ends Tests

Throughout this chapter, you will see tests of constitutionality that seem strange at first glance. One example is the test for determining whether laws that discriminate on the basis of sex violate the Equal Protection Clause. This test says that to be constitutional, such laws must be substantially related to the achievement of an important government purpose. The Equal Protection Clause does not contain such language. It simply states that "No State shall ... deny to any person ... the equal protection of the laws." What is going on here?

The sex discrimination test just stated is a **means-ends test.** Courts create such tests because no constitutional right is absolute; therefore, judges must weigh individual rights against the social purposes served by laws that restrict those rights. In other words, means-ends tests determine how courts strike the *balance* between individual rights and the social needs that may justify their suppression. The "ends" component of a means-ends test specifies how *significant* a social purpose must be in order to justify the restriction of a right. The "means" component states how *effectively* the challenged law must promote that purpose in order to be constitutional. In our sex discrimination test, for example, the challenged law must serve an "important" government purpose (the significance of the end) and must be "substantially" related to the achievement of that purpose (the effectiveness of the means).

Because some constitutional rights are deemed more important than others, courts use tougher tests of constitutionality in such cases and more lenient tests in other situations. Sometimes these tests are long, wordy, and complicated. Throughout the chapter, therefore, we simplify by employing three general kinds of means-ends tests:

1. *The rational basis test.* This is a very relaxed test of constitutionality that challenged laws usually pass with ease. A typical formulation of the rational basis test might say that government action need only have a *reasonable* relation to the achievement of a *legitimate* government purpose to be constitutional.

2. *Intermediate scrutiny.* This comes in many forms; the sex discrimination test we have been discussing is an example.

3. *Full Strict Scrutiny.* Here, the court might say that the challenged law must be *necessary* to the fulfillment of a *compelling* government purpose. Government action that is subjected to this rigorous test of constitutionality almost always is struck down.

Business and the First Amendment

Introduction   The First Amendment says that "Congress shall make no law ... abridging the freedom of speech." Despite its absolute language ("*no* law"), the First Amendment does not prohibit every law that restricts speech. As Justice Oliver Wendell Holmes once remarked, the First Amendment does not protect someone who falsely shouts "Fire!" in a crowded theater. But while the First Amendment's free speech guarantee is not absolute, government action restricting speech usually receives very strict judicial scrutiny. The justifications for this high level of protection vary, but perhaps the most important is the "marketplace" rationale. In this view, the free competition of ideas is the surest means of attaining truth, and the marketplace of ideas best serves this end when restrictions on speech are kept to a minimum and all viewpoints can be considered.

This chapter does not consider most of the situations in which the First Amendment's free speech guarantee has been applied during the 20th century. Nor does it examine *corporate political speech*, which generally receives full First Amendment protection. Instead, we discuss one First Amendment issue of considerable concern to business—the government's power to regulate *commercial speech*.

Commercial Speech   Commercial speech is expression proposing a commercial transaction; commercial advertising is the most common example. In addition, an ad with some noncommercial content may constitute commercial speech if it refers to a specific product and if the advertising firm had an economic motive for issuing it.

In 1942, the Supreme Court ruled that commercial speech was outside the First Amendment's protection, but the Court reversed its position during the 1970s. Now, restrictions on commercial speech receive an *intermediate* level of means-ends scrutiny that is less rigorous than the full strict scrutiny given laws that restrict corporate political speech. However, this intermediate test does not apply to commercial speech that is false, deceptive,

or misleading. Such expression can be freely regulated.

The usual justification for protecting commercial speech is to promote informed consumer choice by removing barriers to the flow of commercial information. The Supreme Court's decisions striking down state restrictions on advertising by groups such as pharmacists and lawyers, restrictions that arguably promoted price-fixing within these professions, seem consistent with this marketplace rationale. However, the commercial speech doctrine could also benefit business interests if, for example, government regulators ever decide to mount a serious attack on advertising that is not false or misleading but that attempts to manipulate consumers by appealing to irrational drives of all sorts.[4]

---

[4]As footnote 6 in Chapter 47 observes, the FTC's regulation of advertising can be challenged as an unconstitutional restriction of commercial speech. However, such challenges usually have little effect.

CITY OF CINCINNATI V. DISCOVERY NETWORK, INC.
113 S. Ct. 1505 (U.S. Sup. Ct. 1993)

Discovery Network, Inc. provides adult educational, recreational, and social programs in the Cincinnati area. It advertises those programs in a free magazine that is distributed in that area. Harmon Publishing Company, Inc. publishes and distributes in the Cincinnati area a free magazine containing real estate advertisements. In 1989, the city of Cincinnati authorized Discovery's placement of 38 newsracks on public property for the distribution of its magazine, and also authorized Harmon's placement of 24 newsracks on public property for the same purpose.

In March of 1990, however, the city revoked Discovery's and Harmon's permits. It did so pursuant to a municipal ordinance prohibiting the distribution of "commercial handbills" on public property. The motive for the revocation was the city's desire to improve the safety and appearance of its streets and sidewalks. However, the city's action did not affect some 1,500 to 2,000 other newsracks containing noncommercial publications such as regular newspapers.

Discovery and Harmon challenged the city's action in federal district court, claiming that it was an unconstitutional regulation of commercial speech. The district court agreed, and the court of appeals affirmed. The city appealed to the U.S. Supreme Court.

Stevens, Justice   There is no claim that there is anything unlawful or misleading about the contents of Discovery's and Harmon's publications. Moreover, Discovery and Harmon do not challenge their characterization as commercial speech. Nor do they question the substantiality of the city's interest in safety and aesthetics.

It was the city's burden to establish a reasonable fit between its legitimate interests in safety and aesthetics and its limited and selective prohibition of newsracks as the means chosen to serve those interests. There is ample support in the record for the conclusion that the city did not establish the reasonable fit we require. The ordinance on which it relied was an outdated prohibition against the distribution of any commercial handbills on public property. It was enacted long before any concern about newsracks developed. Its apparent purpose was to prevent the kind of visual blight caused by littering, rather than any harm associated with permanent, freestanding dispensing devices.

The fact that the city failed to address its recently developed concern about newsracks by regulating their size, shape, appearance, or number indicates that it has not carefully calculated the costs and benefits associated with the burden on speech imposed by its prohibition. The benefit to be derived from the removal of 62 newsracks while about 1,500–2,000 remain in place was considered "minute" by the district court and "paltry" by the court of appeals. We share their evaluation of the fit between the city's goal and its method of achieving it.

Court of appeals decision in Discovery's and Harmon's favor affirmed.

Due Process

Procedural Due Process

The Fifth and Fourteenth Amendments require that the federal government and the states observe **due process** when they deprive a person of life, liberty, or property. The traditional conception of due process, called **procedural due process**, establishes the *procedures* that government must follow when it takes life, liberty, or property. Although the requirements of procedural due process vary from situation to situation, their core idea is that people are entitled to adequate *notice* of the government action to be taken against them and to some sort of *fair trial or hearing* before that action can occur.

In order to trigger due process protections, the government must deprive a person of life, liberty, or property. Due process *liberty* includes a very broad and poorly defined range of freedoms. It even includes certain interests in personal reputation. For example, the firing of a government employee might require some kind of due process hearing if it is publicized, the fired employee's reputation is sufficiently damaged, and her future employment opportunities are restricted. The Supreme Court has said that due process *property* is not created by the Constitution but by existing rules and understandings that stem from an independent source such as state law. These rules and understandings must give a person a *legitimate claim of entitlement* to a benefit, not merely some need, desire, or expectation for it. This definition includes almost all of the usual forms of property. It also includes the job rights of tenured public employees who can be discharged only for cause, but not the rights of untenured or probationary employees.

The following *Doehr* case obviously involves property. One issue in the case is whether the challenged government action *deprived* the property owner of his property sufficiently to trigger due process protection. Another issue is whether the *procedures* accompanying the deprivation were adequate to protect the property owner's interests and to satisfy due process. Both questions arose in a familiar due process context: a state law permitting prejudgment attachment of the defendant's property in civil litigation.

CONNECTICUT V. DOEHR
501 U.S. 1 (U.S. Sup. Ct. 1991)

John DiGiovanni was about to sue Brian Doehr for assault and battery in a Connecticut trial court. In order to ensure that funds would be available to satisfy a judgment, DiGiovanni applied for a $75,000 prejudgment attachment on Doehr's home. He did so under a state statute permitting prejudgment attachments on real estate without notice or a hearing if there is probable cause to sustain the plaintiff's claim. Basing its judgment on five one-sentence paragraphs in the affidavit accompanying DiGiovanni's application, the court found probable cause and ordered the requested attachment on Doehr's home.

Shortly thereafter, and before he was served with DiGiovanni's complaint for assault and battery, Doehr received his first notice of the attachment. As required by the statute, he was also informed of his right to a postattachment hearing to challenge the attachment. Rather than pursuing this option, however, Doehr challenged the attachment statute's constitutionality in federal district court, arguing that it violated due process. The district court rejected Doehr's challenge, but the court of appeals reversed, and the case eventually came before the U.S. Supreme Court.

White, Justice   We return to the question of what process must be afforded by a state statute enabling an individual to deprive another of his or her property by means of the prejudgment attachment or similar procedure. . . . For this type of case, the relevant inquiry requires first, consideration of the private interest that will be affected by the prejudgment measure; second, an examination of the risk of erroneous deprivation through the procedures under attack; and third, attention to the interests of the party seeking the prejudgment remedy.

The property interests that the attachment affects are significant. For a property owner like Doehr, attachment ordinarily clouds title; impairs the ability to sell or otherwise alienate the property; taints any credit rating; reduces the chance of obtaining a home equity loan or additional mortgage; and can even place an existing mortgage in technical default where there is an insecurity clause. The state correctly points out that these effects do not amount to a complete, physical, or permanent deprivation of real property. But even the temporary or partial impairments to property rights that attachments, liens, and similar encumbrances entail are sufficient to merit due process protection.

The risk of erroneous deprivation that the state permits here is substantial. For attachments before judgment, Connecticut asks whether there is probable cause to sustain the validity of the plaintiff's claim. What probable cause means in this context, however, remains obscure. If the statute demands inquiry into the sufficiency of the complaint, or, still less, the plaintiff's good-faith belief that the complaint is sufficient, requirement of a complaint and a factual affidavit would permit a court to make these minimal determinations. But neither inquiry adequately reduces the risk of erroneous deprivation. The potential for unwarranted attachment in these situations is self-evident. Even if the provision requires probable cause to believe that judgment will be rendered in favor of the plaintiff, the risk of error was substantial in this case. Only a skeletal affidavit need be and was filed. The judge normally reviews the complaint as well, but the complaint may also be conclusory. The judge could make no realistic assessment concerning the likelihood of an action's success based upon these one-sided, self-serving, and conclusory submissions.

Connecticut points out that the statute provides an expeditious post-attachment adversary hearing [to reduce the risk of incorrect probable cause determinations]. But this would not cure the temporary deprivation that an earlier hearing might have prevented. Any significant taking of property by the state is within the due process clause.

Finally, the interests in favor of an attachment, particularly the interests of the plaintiff, are too minimal here. DiGiovanni had no existing interest in Doehr's real estate when he sought the attachment. His only interest in attaching the property was to ensure the availability of assets to satisfy his judgment if he prevailed on the merits. Yet there was no allegation that Doehr was about to transfer or encumber his real estate or take any other action during the pendency of the action that would render his real estate unavailable to satisfy a judgment. . . . A survey of state attachment provisions reveals that nearly every state requires either a preattachment hearing, a showing of some exigent circumstance, or both, before permitting an attachment to take place. . . .

Because Connecticut's prejudgment remedy provision violates the requirements of due process by authorizing prejudgment attachment without prior notice or a hearing, the judgment of the court of appeals is affirmed.

Judgment in Doehr's favor affirmed.

Substantive Due Process   Procedural due process does not challenge rules of *substantive law*—the rules that set standards of behavior for organized social life. For example, imagine that State X makes adultery a crime and allows people to be convicted of adultery without a trial. Arguments that adultery should not be a crime go to the substance of the statute, while objections to the lack of a trial are procedural in nature.

Sometimes, the Due Process Clauses have been used to attack the substance of government action. For our purposes, the most important example of this **substantive due process** occurred early in the 20th century, when courts struck down various kinds of social legislation as denying due process. They did so mainly by reading freedom of contract and other economic rights into the liberty protected by the Fifth and Fourteenth Amendments, and then interpreting "due process of law" to require that laws denying such rights be subjected to means-ends scrutiny. The best-known example is the Supreme Court's 1905 decision in *Lochner v. New York*, where it struck down a state law setting maximum hours of work for bakery employees because the statute limited freedom of contract and did not directly advance the legitimate state goal of promoting worker health.

This "economic" form of substantive due process has been criticized as giving probusiness courts a powerful tool for striking down social and economic regulations designed to protect the powerless. After 1937, the doctrine ceased to be a significant check on government regulation of social and economic matters. Today, substantive due process attacks on such regulations trigger only a lenient kind of rational basis review and have little chance of success. In the 1970s and 1980s, however, substantive due process became increasingly important as a device for protecting *noneconomic* rights—most importantly, the constitutional right of privacy. But such applications of substantive due process are beyond this chapter's scope.

Equal Protection

The Fourteenth Amendment's Equal Protection Clause says that "[n]o State shall . . . deny to any person . . . the equal protection of the laws." Because it has been incorporated within Fifth Amendment due process, the clause also applies to the federal government. As currently interpreted, the equal protection guarantee applies to all situations in which government *classifies* or *distinguishes* people. The law inevitably makes distinctions among people, benefiting or burdening some groups but not others. The equal protection guarantee sets the standards such distinctions must meet to be constitutional.

The Rational Basis Test   The basic equal protection standard is the *rational basis* test described earlier. This is the standard usually applied to social and economic regulations that are challenged as denying equal protection. Although formulations of the rational basis test vary, here it generally means that the government's classification must be *reasonably* related to the accomplishment of a *legitimate* public purpose. As the following *Stanglin* case indicates, this lenient test usually does not impede state and federal regulation of social and economic matters.

CITY OF DALLAS V. STANGLIN
490 U.S. 19 (U.S. Sup. Ct. 1989)

The city of Dallas, Texas, adopted an ordinance restricting admission to so-called "Class E" dance halls to persons between the ages of 14 and 18. However, it did not impose similar age limitations on most other establishments where teenagers might congregate—for example, skating rinks. Charles Stanglin, who in one building operated both a Class E dance hall and a roller-skating rink, sued for an injunction against enforcement of the ordinance in a Texas trial court. One of his arguments was that the ordinance denied the equal protection of the laws because its distinction between Class E dance halls and other establishments for teenagers was irrational. The Texas trial court upheld the ordinance, but a higher Texas court struck down its age restriction. The city appealed to the U.S. Supreme Court.

Rehnquist, Chief Justice The Dallas ordinance implicates no suspect class. The question remaining is whether the classification survives rational basis scrutiny under the Equal Protection Clause. The city has chosen to impose a rule that separates 14- to 18-year-olds from what may be the corrupting influences of older teenagers and young adults. An urban planner for the city testified: "Older kids can access drugs and alcohol, and they have more mature sexual attitudes, more liberal sexual attitudes in general. . . . And we're concerned about mixing up these individuals with youngsters [who] have not fully matured."

Stanglin claims that this restriction has no real connection with the city's stated objectives. Except for saloons and teenage dance halls, he argues, teenagers and adults in Dallas may associate with each other, including at the skating area of his rink. We think Stanglin's arguments misapprehend the nature of rational basis scrutiny, which is the most relaxed and tolerant form of judicial scrutiny under the Equal Protection Clause. If the classification has some reasonable basis, it does not offend the Constitution simply because the classification is not made with mathematical nicety or because in practice it results in some inequality. The rational basis standard is true to the principle that the Fourteenth Amendment gives the federal courts no power to impose upon the states their views of what constitutes wise economic or social policy.

In the local economic sphere, it is only the invidious discrimination, the wholly arbitrary act, which cannot stand consistently with the Fourteenth Amendment. The city could reasonably conclude that teenagers might be susceptible to corrupting influences if permitted to frequent a dance hall with older persons [and that] limiting dance hall contacts between juveniles and adults would make less likely illicit or undesirable juvenile involvement with alcohol, illegal drugs, and promiscuous sex. It is true that the city allows teenagers and adults to roller-skate together, but skating involves less physical contact than dancing. The differences between the two activities may not be striking, but differentiations need not be striking in order to survive rational basis scrutiny.

Texas court decision striking down the age limitation reversed.

The rational basis test is the basic equal protection standard. Some classifications, however, get tougher means-ends scrutiny. Specifically, laws that discriminate regarding **fundamental rights** or involve **suspect classifications** now receive more rigorous review. This is a development that mainly began after World War II and that greatly accelerated during the 1960s and 1970s.

Fundamental Rights The list of rights regarded as "fundamental" for equal protection purposes is not completely clear, but it includes voting, interstate travel, and certain criminal procedure protections. Laws creating unequal enjoyment of these rights receive something resembling *full strict scrutiny*. In 1969, for instance, the Supreme Court struck down the District of Columbia's one-year residency requirement for receiving welfare benefits because that requirement unequally and impermissibly restricted the right of interstate travel.

Suspect Classifications Certain "suspect" bases of classification also trigger more rigorous equal protection review. As of mid-1993, these **suspect classifications** and the level of scrutiny they attract are as follows:

1. *Race and national origin.* Classifications disadvantaging racial or national minorities receive the strictest kind of strict scrutiny and are almost never constitutional. Still, the Supreme Court often has upheld so-called reverse racial discrimination—government action that benefits racial minorities and disadvantages whites. In 1989, however, a majority of the Court concluded that discrimination of this kind should receive the same full strict scrutiny as discrimination *against* racial or national minorities. But in 1990 the Court held that minority preferences enacted *by Congress* should be reviewed under the *sex discrimination* test described below, which is generally regarded as a form of *intermediate scrutiny.*

2. *Alienage.* Classifications based on one's status as an alien also receive strict scrutiny of some kind, but it is doubtful whether this standard is as tough as the full strict scrutiny normally used in race discrimination cases. Under the "political function" exception, moreover, laws restricting aliens from employment in positions that are intimately related to democratic self-government only receive *rational basis review.* This exception has been read broadly to uphold laws excluding aliens from being state troopers, public school teachers, and probation officers.

3. *Sex.* Although sex has never formally been declared a suspect classification, for nearly 20 years

laws discriminating on the basis of gender have been subjected to *intermediate scrutiny.* Specifically, such laws must be *substantially* related to the furtherance of an *important* government purpose. Under this test, measures discriminating against women have almost always been struck down. The Supreme Court has said that laws disadvantaging men get the same scrutiny as those disadvantaging women, but this has not prevented the Court from upholding men-only draft registration and a law making statutory rape a crime for men alone.

4. *Illegitimacy.* Classifications based on one's illegitimate birth receive a form of *intermediate scrutiny* that is probably less strict than the scrutiny given gender-based classifications. Under this vague standard, the Court has struck down state laws discriminating against illegitimates in areas such as recovery for wrongful death, workers' compensation benefits, social security payments, inheritance, and child support.

CONCEPT REVIEW

THE LEVELS OF EQUAL PROTECTION REVIEW: A ROUGH SUMMARY

Rational Basis Review	1. Most general social and economic regulations 2. Laws discriminating against aliens under the political function exception
Intermediate Scrutiny	1. Sex discrimination against both men and women 2. Discrimination against illegitimates 3. Minority preferences enacted by Congress
Full or Nearly Full Strict Scrutiny	1. Discrimination regarding fundamental rights 2. Most discrimination against aliens 3. Most race and national origin discrimination

---

INDEPENDENT CHECKS APPLYING ONLY TO THE STATES

The Contract Clause

Article I, section 10 of the Constitution says: "No State shall . . . pass any . . . Law impairing the Obligation of Contracts." This *Contract Clause* applies to state laws that change the parties' performance obligations under an *existing* contract *after* that contract has been made.[5] The original purpose behind the Contract Clause was to strike down the many

debtor relief statutes passed by the states after the Revolution. These statutes impaired the obligations of existing private contracts by relieving debtors of the obligations they owed to contract creditors. Early in the 19th century, however, the Contract Clause was also held to protect the obligations of *governmental* contracts, charters, and grants.

---

[5]Also, under the Fifth Amendment's Due Process Clause, standards similar to those described in this section apply to the federal government.

The Contract Clause was probably the most important constitutional check on state regulation of the economy in the 19th century. Beginning in the latter part of that century, though, the clause gradually became subordinate to legislation based on the states' police powers. By the mid-20th century, most observers treated the clause as a constitutional dead letter. In 1977, however, the Supreme Court gave the Contract Clause new life by announcing a fairly strict constitutional test governing situations where a state impairs *its own* contracts, charters, and grants. Such impairments, it said, must be "reasonable and necessary to serve an important public purpose." With one exception in 1978, however, the Court has continued its deference toward state regulations that impair the obligations of *private* contracts. The following *Exxon* case is an example.

EXXON CORPORATION V. EAGERTON
462 U.S. 176 (U.S. Sup. Ct. 1983)

For years, the Exxon Corporation paid a severance tax on the oil and gas it drilled in Alabama. Under the sales contracts that Exxon made with purchasers of its oil and gas, it was able to pass on any tax increase to the purchasers. In 1979, Alabama raised the severance tax from 4 percent to 6 percent and forbade producers of oil and gas from passing on the increase to purchasers.

Exxon sued the Alabama commissioner of revenue in an Alabama trial court, seeking a ruling that the pass-on restriction was unconstitutional under the Contract Clause. The trial court found for Exxon, but the Alabama Supreme Court reversed. Exxon appealed to the U.S. Supreme Court.

Marshall, Justice   By barring Exxon from passing the tax increase through to its purchasers, the pass-through prohibition nullified the purchasers' contractual obligations to reimburse Exxon for any severance taxes. While the prohibition thus affects contractual obligations, it does not follow that the prohibition constituted a "Law impairing the Obligation of Contracts" within the meaning of the Contract Clause. Although the language of the Clause is facially absolute, its prohibition must be accommodated to the inherent police power of the state to safeguard the vital interests of its people. If the law were otherwise, one would be able to obtain immunity from state regulation by making private contractual arrangements.

The Contract Clause does not deprive the states of their broad power to adopt general regulatory measures without being concerned that private contracts will be impaired, or even destroyed, as a result. Thus, a state prohibition law may be applied to contracts for the sale of beer that were valid when entered into, a law barring lotteries may be applied to lottery tickets that were valid when issued, and a workmen's compensation law may be applied to employers and employees operating under preexisting contracts of employment that made no provision for work-related injuries.

Like the laws upheld in these cases, the pass-through prohibition did not prescribe a rule limited in effect to contractual obligations or remedies, but instead imposed a generally applicable rule of conduct designed to advance a broad societal interest, protecting consumers from excessive prices. The prohibition applied to all oil and gas producers, regardless of whether they happened to be parties to sale contracts permitting them to pass tax increases through to their purchasers. The effect of the pass-through prohibition on existing contracts that did contain such a provision was incidental to its main effect of shielding consumers from the burden of the tax increase.

Judgment for the commissioner affirmed on the Contract Clause issue. Case returned to the Alabama Supreme Court for consideration of other questions.

Burden on Interstate Commerce

In addition to empowering Congress to regulate interstate commerce, the Commerce Clause also limits the states' ability to *burden* such commerce. This limitation is not expressly stated in the Constitution. Instead, it arises by implication from the Commerce Clause and reflects that clause's original purpose of blocking state protectionism and assuring free interstate trade. This *burden-on-commerce* limitation operates independently of congressional legislation under the commerce power or other federal powers. If relevant federal regulation is present, the preemption questions discussed in the next section may also arise.

Many different state laws can raise burden-on-commerce problems. For example, state regulation of transportation (e.g., limits on train or truck lengths) have been a prolific source of litigation. The same is true of state restrictions on the importation of goods or resources—for example, laws forbidding the sale of out-of-state food products unless they meet certain standards. Such restrictions sometimes benefit local economic interests and reflect their political influence. Burden-on-commerce issues also arise when states try to aid their own residents by blocking the exportation of scarce or valuable products, thus denying out-of-state buyers access to those products.

Due in part to the many different regulations it has had to consider, the Supreme Court has not adhered to one consistent test for determining when such regulations impermissibly burden interstate commerce. According to a 1986 case, however, state laws are *almost always unconstitutional* under the Commerce Clause when they do one of the following:

1. *Directly regulate interstate commerce.* This can occur, for example, when state price regulations require firms to post the prices at which they will sell within the state and to promise that they will not sell below those prices in other states. Because they affect prices in other states, such regulations directly regulate interstate commerce and are usually unconstitutional.

2. *Discriminate against interstate commerce.* This generally occurs when state laws treat local and interstate commerce unequally on their face. In 1992, for example, the Supreme Court considered a 1986 Oklahoma statute that required Oklahoma coal-fired electric generating plants producing power for sale in Oklahoma to burn at least 10 percent Oklahoma-mined coal. The Court said that because this measure treated Oklahoma coal more favorably than out-of-state coal, it clearly discriminated against interstate commerce. For this reason, any attempted justification of the statute would receive very strict scrutiny. Because it suspected that the Oklahoma statute had protectionist motivations and because the alleged justifications for it were weak, the Court found the measure unconstitutional.

3. *Favor in-state economic interests over out-of-state interests.* State laws can have this effect even though they do not discriminate against interstate commerce on their face. In one case, for example, the Supreme Court considered a North Carolina statute requiring all closed containers of apples sold within the state to bear only the applicable U.S. grade or standard. Washington State, the nation's largest apple producer, had its own inspection and grading system for Washington apples, a system that generally was regarded as superior to the federal system. The Court struck down the North Carolina statute because it benefited local apple producers by forcing Washington sellers to regrade apples sold in North Carolina (thus raising their costs of doing business) and by undermining the competitive advantage provided by Washington's superior grading system.

Finally, state laws that *regulate evenhandedly and have only incidental effects on interstate commerce* are *constitutional* if they serve legitimate state interests and their local benefits exceed the burden they place on interstate commerce. There is no sharp line between such regulations and those that are almost always unconstitutional under the tests discussed above. In a 1981 Supreme Court case, a state truck-length limitation that differed from the limitations imposed by neighboring states failed to satisfy these tests. First, the Court concluded that the measure did not further the state's legitimate interest in highway safety because the trucks the state banned generally were as safe as those it allowed. Second, whatever marginal safety advantage the law provided was outweighed by the numerous problems it posed for interstate trucking companies.

Federal Preemption

The constitutional principle of **federal supremacy** dictates that where state law conflicts with valid federal law, the federal law is supreme. Where a state law conflicts with a federal statute, the state law is said to be *preempted* by the federal regulation. The central question in most federal preemption cases is Congress's intent. Thus, such cases often present questions of statutory interpretation[6] that can be complex and that are decided on a case-by-case basis.

As the following *Mortier* case suggests, federal preemption of state law generally occurs for one or more of four reasons.

1. *There is a literal conflict between the state and federal measures, so that it is impossible to follow both simultaneously.*

2. *The federal law specifically states that it will preempt state regulation in certain areas.* Similar statements may also appear in the federal statute's legislative history, and courts may find such statements persuasive.

3. *The federal regulation is pervasive.* The fact that Congress has "occupied the field" by regulating a subject in great breadth and/or in considerable detail suggests its intent to displace state regulation of that subject. This may be especially true where Congress has given an administrative agency broad regulatory power in a particular area.

4. *The state regulation is an obstacle to fulfilling the purposes of the federal law.* Here, the party challenging the state law's constitutionality typically claims that the state law interferes with the purposes she attributes to the federal measure (purposes usually found in its legislative history).

[6]Chapter 1 discusses statutory interpretation.

WISCONSIN PUBLIC INTERVENOR v. MORTIER
111 S. Ct. 2476 (U.S. Sup. Ct. 1991)

The small town of Casey in rural Wisconsin adopted an ordinance that regulated the use of pesticides. The ordinance required a permit for applications of pesticides to public lands, private lands subject to public use, and private lands by air. Ralph Mortier applied for a permit to spray a portion of his land from the air. The town granted him a permit, but it refused to let him spray by air and also restricted the areas in which Mortier could spray.

Mortier sued for a declaratory judgment against the ordinance in a state trial court, arguing that it was preempted by the Federal Insecticide, Fungicide, and Rodenticide Act (FIFRA). The Wisconsin Public Intervenor, an assistant attorney general charged with the protection of environmental rights, was admitted as a defendant in Mortier's suit. The trial court decided in Mortier's favor, and the Wisconsin Supreme Court affirmed. The state intervenor appealed to the U.S. Supreme Court.

White, Justice Under the Supremacy Clause, state laws that interfere with, or are contrary to, the laws of Congress are invalid. The ways in which federal law may preempt state law are well established. Congress's intent to supplant state authority in a particular field may be express in the terms of the statute. Absent explicit preemptive language, Congress's intent to supersede state law may none-theless be implicit if a scheme of federal regulation is so pervasive as to make reasonable the inference that Congress left no room for the states to supplement it. Even when Congress has not chosen to occupy a particular field, preemption may occur to the extent that state and federal law actually conflict. Such a conflict arises when compliance with both federal and state regulations is a physical impossibility, or when a state law stands as an obstacle to the accomplishment and execution of the full purposes and objectives of Congress.

Applying these principles, we conclude that FIFRA does not preempt the town's ordinance either explicitly, implicitly, or by virtue of an actual conflict. FIFRA nowhere expressly supersedes local regulation of pesticide use. . . . Likewise, FIFRA fails to provide any clear and manifest indication that Congress sought to supplant local authority over pesticide regulation impliedly. While [its] 1972 amendments turned FIFRA into a comprehensive regulatory statute, the resulting scheme was not so pervasive as to make reasonable the inference that Congress left no room for the states to supplement it. FIFRA addresses numerous aspects of pesticide control in considerable detail, in particular: registration and classification, applicator certification, inspection of pesticide production facilities, and the possible ban and seizure of pesticides that are misbranded or that otherwise fail to meet federal requirements. FIFRA nonetheless leaves substantial portions of the field vacant, including the area at issue in this case. FIFRA

nowhere seeks to establish an affirmative permit scheme for the actual use of pesticides. It certainly does not equate registration and labeling requirements with a general approval to apply pesticides throughout the nation without regard to regional and local factors like climate, population, geography, and water supply.

Finally, we discern no actual conflict either between FIFRA and the ordinance before us or between FIFRA and local regulation generally. Mortier does not rely, nor could he, on the theory that compliance with the ordinance and FIFRA is a physical impossibility. Instead, he urges that the town's ordinance stands as an obstacle to the statute's goals of promoting pesticide regulation that is coordinated solely on the federal and state levels, that rests upon some degree of technical expertise, and that does not unduly burden interstate commerce. Each one of these assertions rests on little more than snippets of legislative history and policy speculations. None of them is convincing.

Judgment reversed in favor of the Wisconsin intervenor.

THE TAKINGS CLAUSE

The Fifth Amendment provides that "private property [shall not] be taken for public use, without just compensation." This Takings Clause has been incorporated within Fourteenth Amendment due process and thus applies to the states. Traditionally, it has often come into play when the government formally condemns land through its power of **eminent domain,**[7] but it has many other applications as well.

The Takings Clause recognizes government's power to take private property and also limits the exercise of that power. It does so by requiring that when *property* is subjected to a governmental *taking*, the taking must be for a *public use* and the property owner must receive *just compensation*. We

now consider these four aspects of the Takings Clause in turn. Figure 3 describes how they interact.

1. *Property.* The Takings Clause protects other property interests besides land and interests in land. Although its full scope is unclear, the clause has been held to cover takings of personal property, liens, trade secrets, and contract rights.

2. *Taking.* Due to the range of property interests it may cover, the Takings Clause potentially has a broad scope. Another reason for the clause's wide possible application is the range of government activities that may be considered takings. Of course, the government's use of formal *condemnation procedures* to acquire private property almost always is a taking. There is also a taking when the government *physically invades* private property or allows someone else to do so. The following *Lucas* case describes this type of taking.

---

[7]Eminent domain and the Takings Clause's application to land use problems are discussed in Chapter 24.

FIGURE 3   Analyzing a Takings Clause Case

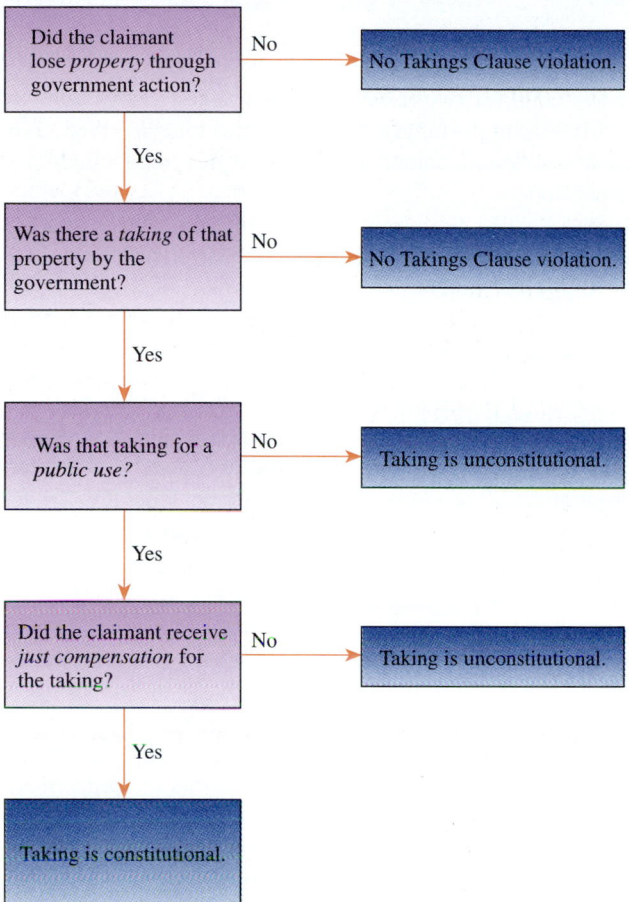

In addition, it has long been recognized that government *regulation* may so diminish the value of property or the owner's enjoyment of it as to constitute a taking. Land use regulation such as zoning is an example. Among the factors courts consider in such "regulatory taking" cases are the degree to which government deprives the owner of free possession, use, and disposition of his property; the overall economic impact of the regulation on the owner; and how much the regulation interferes with the owner's reasonable investment-backed expectations regarding the future use of the property. As *Lucas* declares, there is an automatic taking where the government denies the owner *all* economically beneficial uses of the land. Where this is not the case, courts occasionally apply some form of means-ends scrutiny in determining whether a regulatory taking has occurred.

3. *Public Use.* Once a taking of property has occurred, it is unconstitutional unless it is for a public use. Because courts now apply a relaxed version of the rational basis test to resolve "public use" questions, that test is very easy to meet.

4. *Just compensation.* Even if a taking of property is for a public use, it is still unconstitutional if the property owner does not receive just compensation. Although the standards for determining just compensation vary with the circumstances, the basic test is the fair market value of the property at the time of the taking.

LUCAS V. SOUTH CAROLINA COASTAL COUNCIL
112 S. Ct. 2886 (U.S. Sup. Ct. 1992)

In 1986, David Lucas paid $975,000 for two residential lots on the Isle of Palms in Charleston County, South Carolina. His intent was to build single-family homes on the lots. In 1988, however, the South Carolina legislature enacted the Beachfront Management Act. The act prevented Lucas from erecting any permanent habitable structures on the two lots.

Lucas then sued in a South Carolina trial court, arguing that the state had taken his property without just compensation. The trial court held in his favor, but the South Carolina Supreme Court reversed that decision. Lucas appealed to the U.S. Supreme Court.

Scalia, Justice   Prior to Justice Holmes's exposition in *Pennsylvania Coal Co. v. Mahon* (1922), it was generally thought that the Takings Clause reached only a direct appropriation of property, or the functional equivalent of a practical ouster of the owner's possession. That case [gave birth to] the oft-cited maxim that while property may be regulated to a certain extent, if regulation goes too far it will be recognized as a taking. *Mahon* offered little insight into when a given regulation would be seen as going "too far." In the 70-odd years of succeeding "regulatory takings" jurisprudence, we have generally eschewed any set formula for determining how far is too far, preferring to engage in essentially ad hoc factual inquiries.

We have, however, described at least two categories of regulatory action as compensable without case-specific inquiry into the public interest advanced in support of the restraint. The first encompasses regulations that compel the property owner to suffer a physical invasion of his property. In general, no matter how minute the intrusion, and no matter how weighty the public purpose behind it, we have required compensation. For example, in *Loretto v. Teleprompter Manhattan CATV Corp.* (1982), we determined that New York's law requiring landlords to allow television cable companies to emplace cable facilities in their apartment buildings constituted a taking, even though the facilities occupied at most only 1½ cubic feet of the landlords' property. The second situation in which we have found categorical treatment appropriate is where the regulation denies all economically beneficial or productive use of land. . . . [W]hen the owner of real property has been called upon to sacrifice *all* eco-

nomically beneficial uses in the name of the common good, he has suffered a taking. The trial court found Lucas's two beachfront lots to have been rendered valueless by [the state's] enforcement of the coastal-zone construction ban. Under Lucas's theory of the case, which rested upon our "no economically viable use" statements, that finding entitled him to compensation. . . .

Where the state seeks to sustain regulation that deprives land of all economically beneficial use, it may resist compensation only if the logically antecedent inquiry into the nature of the owner's estate shows that the proscribed use interests were not part of his title to begin with. . . . Any limitation so severe [as a regulation that prohibits all economically viable uses of land] cannot be newly legislated (without compensation), but must inhere in the title itself, in the restrictions that background principles of the state's law of property and nuisance already place upon land ownership. A law or decree with such an effect must, in other words, do no more than duplicate the result that could have been achieved in the courts. . . . When, however, a regulation that declares off-limits all economically productive or beneficial uses of land goes beyond what the relevant background principles would dictate, compensation must be paid to sustain it. . . .

It seems unlikely that common-law principles would have prevented the erection of any habitable or productive improvements on Lucas's land. The question, however, is one of state law to be dealt with on remand. [To win,] South Carolina must identify background principles of nuisance and property law that prohibit the uses Lucas now intends in the circumstances in which the property is presently found. Only on this showing can the state fairly claim that, in proscribing all such beneficial uses, the Beachfront Management Act is taking nothing.

South Carolina Supreme Court's judgment against Lucas reversed; case returned to the South Carolina courts for proceedings not inconsistent with the Supreme Court's opinion.

ETHICAL AND PUBLIC POLICY CONCERNS

1. Throughout history, the main threat to individual rights of all kinds arguably has come from kings, oligarchs, dictators, and other unrepresentative rulers. Is this true of the rights discussed in this chapter? In the American system of government, who is the main threat to these rights?

2. Courts sometimes state which rights are fundamental and protect those rights by imposing tough means-ends scrutiny on laws that restrict them. What fundamental ethical objection almost always applies to such actions by the courts? *Hint:* Look at the section on the evolution of the Constitution and the role of the Supreme Court.

3. As Chapter 4 makes clear, recent discussions of ethical theory often distinguish between *consequentialist* ethical theories (which judge the rightness of actions by their consequences) and *deontological* theories (which say that some actions are morally obligatory regardless of their consequences). Which theory best justifies the means-ends tests discussed in this chapter?

4. Although this chapter is mainly concerned with economic rights, one of the great generalizations about modern American constitutional law is that since 1937, the Supreme Court has shifted from protecting economic rights to protecting personal rights. One example of the Court's former solicitude for economic rights is the doctrine of economic substantive due process mentioned earlier in this chapter. The most important aspect of modern substantive due process, on the other hand, is the constitutional right of privacy. Today, social and economic regulations that are challenged on substantive due process grounds usually get very light means-ends review, while strict scrutiny still applies to some laws that violate privacy rights.

With all of the above in mind, consider the following groups of questions. Throughout, we assume for the sake of argument that it is desirable for courts to give great protection to personal rights.

a. Why are personal rights intrinsically more important than economic rights? Why, for example, is the right to an abortion more important than freedom of contract? Or consider the distinction between a right protected by the old-time substantive due process—the right to pursue a trade, occupation, or profession—and freedom of speech. To ordinary people, which right really matters the most in their daily lives? Finally, aren't freedom of contract and the right to pursue a chosen occupation "personal" rights too?

b. What are the possible consequences of giving greater protection to economic rights? Would this imperil social and economic regulations intended to protect the poor and the powerless? In considering this question, examine the text's discussion of the Supreme Court's 1905 *Lochner* decision. Even if such regulations would be jeopardized, is this a decisive objection to giving greater protection to economic rights?

On the other hand, would greater constitutional protection for economic rights increase productivity and thereby benefit both rich and poor? Many free-market economists believe that this would happen. But the U.S. economy has grown spectacularly over the last 50 years even though economic rights have received little constitutional protection during that time.

c. If courts ever give economic rights greater protection, could they make intelligent decisions on the questions this would force them to consider? This would require that courts apply tougher means-ends scrutiny to social and economic regulations. This, in turn, probably means that they would have to decide with some precision how well particular statutes advance their purposes. Are courts likely to do a good job if they try this? How much do most lawyers know about these matters?

On the other hand, don't courts sometimes have to consider complex questions of social policy when they apply tough scrutiny to laws that restrict *personal* rights? If so, does this mean that courts can also handle issues related to economic rights?

PROBLEMS AND PROBLEM CASES

1. In 1984, Congress passed a statute directing the Secretary of Transportation to withhold a percentage of the federal highway funds due to a state if the state allowed the purchase or possession of alcoholic beverages by those under 21 years of age. South Dakota, which permitted those 19 or older to buy 3.2 beer, sued to have the statute declared unconstitutional. On what enumerated power is this federal law based? Is it a constitutional exercise of that power? If the statute is constitutional, does this mean that South Dakota cannot permit the purchase or consumption of alcoholic beverages by those under 21?

2. The United States Olympic Committee (USOC) is a federally chartered private corporation. Under the Amateur Sports Act, it has broad powers to handle U.S. participation in international athletic competition and to promote amateur athletics within this country. In addition to granting the USOC its charter, Congress imposed certain regulatory requirements on it and also gave it some funding. Congress also gave the USOC near-exclusive rights in the commercial and promotional use of the term *Olympic*. When the USOC sued to protect those rights, the defendant argued that its discriminatory enforcement of them violated the Equal Protection Clause.

Suppose that you are an attorney for the defendant in this case. Based on the discussion in the text, what arguments would you make for the proposition that the USOC's enforcement of its rights was state action? Do you think that those arguments will succeed today? Why or why not?

3. The Consolidated Edison Company (Con Ed), a privately owned corporation that is a regulated public utility, placed written inserts touting nuclear power in the bills it sent to its customers. Then the New York Public Service Commission prohibited state utilities from using bill inserts to discuss controversial public policy issues such as the desirability of nuclear power. Con Ed challenged this regulation as an unconstitutional restriction of freedom of speech under the First Amendment. What kind of speech is at issue here? What level of scrutiny does such speech receive when laws restricting it are examined by the courts?

4. The Youngs Drug Products Company planned a marketing campaign for its condoms. The campaign involved the unsolicited mass mailing of advertising fliers and other materials to the general public. The mailings were to include: (1) fliers promoting a range of products available in drugstores (including condoms), (2) fliers specifically promoting condoms, and (3) informational pamphlets discussing the usefulness of condoms in preventing venereal disease and aiding family planning. Are Youngs's *fliers* commercial speech? What about the *informational pamphlets?*

5. Alfred Jean Moore bought some real property on credit from the Mennonite Board of Missions (MBM). MBM took a mortgage on the property to secure Moore's payment of the purchase price. Under the sales agreement, Moore was responsible for paying all property taxes, but she failed to do so. Eventually, a local government body began proceedings for the sale of Moore's property to satisfy the tax debt. State law required that mortgagees such as MBM receive posted and published notice of those proceedings. MBM, however, challenged those notice procedures, arguing that they failed to satisfy due process. What *kind* of due process claim was MBM making?

6. In 1968, David Roth became an assistant professor of political science at Wisconsin State University-Oshkosh. He did not have academic tenure; indeed, his contract ran for only one year. At the end of that year, Roth was fired without receiving a statement of reasons and a hearing at which to challenge those reasons. Roth later sued the state's Board of Regents, arguing that his firing was unconstitutional because it deprived him of liberty and property without due process of law. Was Roth deprived of liberty or property here? Assume that the firing was not publicized and that Roth's reputation in the community was not damaged to any significant extent.

7. One provision of the federal Deficit Reduction Act of 1984 established a 15-month freeze on the fees certain physicians could charge medicare patients. A group of physicians challenged the constitutionality of this provision, alleging that it restricted freedom of contract in violation of the Fifth Amendment's Due Process Clause. What *kind* of due process attack is this? Will it succeed?

8. The Minnesota legislature passed a statute banning the sale of milk in plastic nonrefillable, nonreusable containers. However, it allowed sales of milk in other nonrefillable, nonreusable containers such as paperboard cartons. One of the justifications for this ban on plastic jugs was that it would ease the state's solid waste disposal problems because plastic jugs occupy more space in landfills than other nonreturnable milk containers. A group of dairy businesses challenged the statute, arguing that its distinction between plastic containers and other containers was unconstitutional under the Equal Protection Clause. What means-ends test or level of scrutiny applies in this case? Under that test, is easing the state's solid waste disposal problems a sufficiently important *end?* Also is there a sufficiently close fit between the classification and that end to make the statutory *means* constitutional? In answering the last question, assume for the sake of argument that there were better ways of alleviating the solid waste disposal problem than banning plastic jugs while allowing paperboard cartons.

9. Oklahoma statutes set the age for drinking 3.2 beer at 21 for men and 18 for women. The asserted purpose behind the statutes (and the sex-based classification that they established) was traffic safety. The statutes were challenged as a denial of equal protection by male residents of Oklahoma. What level of scrutiny would this measure receive if *women* had been denied the right to drink 3.2 beer until they were 21 but men had been allowed to consume it at age 18? Should this standard change because the measure discriminates against *men?* Is the male challenge to the statute likely to be successful?

10. In 1984, Ohio enacted a gasoline tax credit for each gallon of ethanol (ethyl alcohol) sold as a gasohol component by Ohio fuel dealers. However, this tax credit was denied to ethanol coming from states that did not grant a similar tax credit to ethanol made in Ohio. What category of burden-on-commerce analysis does this statute involve? Is it most likely constitutional or unconstitutional?

11. After nine years and eight months of service, Perry McClendon was fired from his sales job with the Ingersoll-Rand Company. Believing that Ingersoll-Rand fired him to avoid pension obligations that would have arisen after 10 years of service, McClendon sued the firm for wrongful discharge. During the litigation, Ingersoll-Rand argued that McClendon's common law claim was preempted by the Employee Retirement Income Security Act (ERISA). ERISA has a provision stating that: "[T]he provisions of this subchapter and subchapter III of this chapter shall supersede any and all State laws insofar as they may now or hereafter relate to any employee benefit plan [covered by relevant ERISA provisions]." Assuming that ERISA covers his pension plan, does this language preempt McClendon's claim?

CHAPTER 4

BUSINESS ETHICS, CORPORATE SOCIAL RESPONSIBILITY, AND THE CONTROL AND GOVERNANCE OF CORPORATIONS

INTRODUCTION

Ethics is becoming an increasingly important part of the business curriculum. Ethics courses are a response to socially irresponsible business behavior—businesspeople's failure to meet basic ethical standards in the course of their work. Ordinarily, the result of such failures is harm to society or to specific third parties. Business ethics courses usually proceed on the theory that such harm can be reduced, and socially responsible business behavior increased, if tomorrow's managers are instructed in their ethical obligations.

THE DEBATE OVER THE LARGE CORPORATION

Business ethics instruction is a relatively recent phenomenon. But it is only the latest stage in a century-long struggle to control corporate misbehavior.[1] In America, large corporations first appeared when the country began its rapid industrialization late in the 19th century. Ever since, such firms have been villains to some and heroes to others. Hostility to big business was one theme in the populist movement of the late 19th century, and the control of large corporations preoccupied the progressive movement of the early 20th century. The perceived need to check abuses of business power was a major force behind both the New Deal statutes of the 1930s and the many new federal regulations enacted during the 1960s and 1970s. Much the same motives underlie modern calls for more business ethics instruction.

Common Criticisms of the Corporation

Over the past 30 years, critics of corporations probably have been more vocal than their defenders. By now, the critics' litany of complaints is very familiar. In the single-minded pursuit of profits, the critics say, corporations despoil the environment, mistreat employees, fire loyal workers at will, abandon local communities without warning, market shoddy and dangerous products, and corrupt the

---

[1]Of course, many of this chapter's observations apply to other business forms besides corporations.

political process. Underlying these criticisms are some general perceptions about modern business. Large corporations, it is observed, perform such essential national economic functions as raw materials extraction, energy production, the provision of transportation and communications, and military production—functions that many countries entrust to government bodies. How corporations perform these functions is critical to the nation's well-being. Despite their importance, however, corporations are not nearly so accountable to the public as the formal organs of government. For example, the public has little to say about the appointment of their officers and directors. This lack of accountability is made all the more serious, critics maintain, by the tremendous power big corporations wield in many spheres of American life.

Proposed Remedies

These criticisms and perceptions have naturally generated calls for changes in the ways corporations decide and behave. Throughout the 20th century, the law has been the main device for checking corporate misdeeds. However, some observers have come to feel that legal regulation, while an important element in any corporate control scheme, is insufficient by itself. To supplement regulation, they urge that business be led to adhere to standards of ethical or socially responsible behavior higher than those imposed by existing law. One example is the *stakeholder theory* of corporate social responsibility, which says that rather than striving only to maximize profits for shareholders, a business firm should balance shareholder interests against the interests of other stakeholders such as employees, managers, suppliers, customers, and local community residents. To promote such behavior, some corporate critics have proposed significant changes in the internal governance of corporations. Others have argued that the business community's own resources be brought to bear. It is within the latter context that the move toward ethics instruction has arisen.

Defenses of the Corporation

Despite all the concern about abuses of its power, big business has contributed mightily to the unprecedented material abundance that America has experienced over the last century. In part for this reason,

the debate about the modern corporation has not been totally dominated by its critics. In opposition to the critics, defenders of business argue that profit maximization should be its main goal and that the only ethical norms firms must follow are those embodied in the law. In short, they say that the only social responsibility of corporations is to maximize profits within the bounds set by the law.

Unlike stakeholder theory, therefore, this traditional view of corporate social responsibility stresses the interests of the firm's shareholders. Its main justification is economic. When corporations maximize profits under genuinely competitive conditions, their defenders insist, they use scarce economic resources efficiently and thereby maximize productivity. Because "ethical" firms recognize moral duties other than profit maximization and try to serve other constituencies besides shareholders, they are not likely to maximize profits. Thus, they should be less efficient and less productive than firms that worry only about the bottom line.

The corporation's defenders also disagree with its critics on a number of specific points raised above. In their view, corporate size is not the issue; what is critical is that firms efficiently *compete*. Because truly competitive markets and other private forces such as unfavorable publicity go some way toward controlling business misbehavior, they add, corporate accountability is not a big problem. Where markets and other private forces fail to curb socially irresponsible conduct, moreover, the law can do the job. Indeed, sometimes the law does that job too well. In the corporate defenders' view of things, business is often hamstrung by a maze of regulations that deter socially valuable profit-seeking without producing comparable benefits.

Chapter Organization

To some degree, the disagreement between the corporation's critics and its defenders reflects differences over factual issues—for example, how well the law and markets control corporate misbehavior. Largely, though, the disagreement is *ethical*. In other words, the corporation's critics and its defenders tend to disagree about how things *ought to be*.

For this reason, the chapter begins by discussing some ethical theories that are relevant to the debate over corporate social responsibility. Then it examines those theories' implications for that debate.

After this, the chapter criticizes an assumption often made by the corporation's defenders—that the law, markets, and other private forces adequately check corporate misbehavior. Then the chapter turns its fire on some assumptions commonly made by the corporation's critics—that ethics instruction and other ethics initiatives from within the business community will significantly reduce corporate misconduct; and that where they fail, changes in corporate governance will do the job at little cost to efficiency and organizational effectiveness. The chapter's last section tries to state some tentative conclusions about the subjects the chapter addresses.

The Relevance of the Debate

From the preceding discussion, it should be obvious that the debate over the large corporation is important as a matter of social policy. But why should it concern *you* personally? For one thing, your life is affected directly and indirectly by the decisions of corporate managers. Those decisions can influence the safety of the car you drive, your job security and working conditions, and the quality of the environment in which you live. More importantly, the issues discussed in this chapter will concern you if you become a corporate manager. In that event, *your* decisions may affect the health, physical security, livelihood, and lifestyle of employees, consumers, and many others.

SOME ETHICAL BACKGROUND

What is ethical or socially responsible corporate behavior? This question requires another: What is moral or ethical behavior generally? Of course, a full consideration of moral philosophy is far beyond the scope of this text. Nonetheless, two well-known ethical views have implications for the corporate social responsibility debate. The first of these views is **rights theory**; the other is **utilitarianism.** Before discussing these two views, however, we must consider the difference between **deontological** ethical theories and **consequentialist** (or teleological) theories.

Deontological and Consequentialist Ethical Theories

Suppose that by breaking a contract with another party you could make yourself richer without harming that party in any way. Is it morally right for you to break the contract under these circumstances? Moral philosophers called *consequentialists* generally would answer this question in the affirmative. The rightness or wrongness of an action, consequentialists say, depends on its *consequences.* Here, the consequences of breaking the contract clearly seem favorable: You are better off and the other party is no worse off. Because a consequentialist has to consider *all* of an action's likely consequences, however, he might conclude that you should perform the contract. For example, by breaking your contract, you might encourage other people to break theirs when it would be harmful for them to do so.

Note that by breaking the contract you are breaking the *promise* contained in that contract. To some moral philosophers, promises are sacred (or nearly so). This attitude is an example of *deontological* moral thinking. Extreme (or strict) deontologists say that certain actions are absolutely right or wrong *in themselves*—irrespective of their consequences. Thus, a strict deontologist who believes in the sanctity of promises would say that you should never break your contracts, no matter what. Of course, a person can be a deontologist without thinking that promises should always be kept. For example, someone might believe that it is always wrong to take human life, or that people should always tell the truth, but not that promises are sacred.

Few moral philosophers have been strict deontologists. One possible exception, however, was the German philosopher Immanuel Kant (1724–1804). Kant apparently believed that certain moral rules apply universally, irrespective of their consequences. The key to determining these rules was his famous **categorical imperative.** One major formulation of the categorical imperative says: "Act only according to that maxim by which you can at the same time will that it should become a universal law."[2] Suppose you want to borrow some money even though you know that you will never be able to repay the loan. To justify this action, you affirm the following maxim, rule, or principle: "When I believe myself to be in need of money, I will borrow money and promise to repay it, although I know I shall never be able to do so." According to Kant, you would *not* will that this maxim become a

---

[2]This quotation and those that follow can be found in Kant, *Foundations of the Metaphysics of Morals,* 2d ed. (MacMillan/Library of Liberal Arts paperback, 1990), pp. 38–39, 46–47.

universal law. If it did become a universal law, no one would believe in promises to repay debts, and you would be unable to borrow the money you want. Thus, your maxim fails to satisfy the categorical imperative. Unless there is an alternative maxim that justifies such behavior and that can be universalized, it is wrong to falsely promise that you will repay a loan.

Kant also had a second major formulation of the categorical imperative: "Act so that you treat humanity, whether in your own person or in that of another, always as an end and never as a means only." One application of this statement is that we should not use or manipulate other people to serve our own purposes, but instead should appeal to their reason when trying to influence their behavior. In Kant's eyes, if you falsely promise a lender that you will repay the money she lends you, you are *using* that person, because she would not rationally agree to the loan if she knew all the facts.

Strict deontological views like Kant's face an obvious problem—the absolute nature of the duties they assert. Such theories essentially say that we should *always* tell the truth, *never* lie, or *never* kill; and such positions are difficult for most morally reflective people to maintain. Responding to this difficulty, some philosophers have advocated what we will call *mixed deontological theories.* One example emphasizes the notion of **prima facie duties.**[3] Prima facie duties are moral rules that bind us unless they conflict with another, more compelling prima facie duty. In such cases, our *actual duty* is to obey the moral rule that is stronger under the circumstances. For example, your duty to preserve human life probably overrides your duty to tell the truth where lying is necessary to prevent someone from being killed.

Rights Theories

Modern rights theories normally are mixed deontological theories that emphasize rights rather than duties. Such theories usually identify certain fundamental rights, try to justify them and establish their relative importance, and assert that such rights should be honored unless doing so would compromise a more important right. These rights may be

---

[3]The notion of prima facie duties comes from W. D. Ross, *The Right and the Good* (1930), pp. 18–34.

FIGURE 1	The Various Categories of Rights—Some Examples	
Categories	**Economic**	**Noneconomic**
Negative	Property rights Freedom of contract	Freedom of speech Freedom of religion
Positive	Unemployment compensation Old-age assistance	Guaranteed medical care Public education

either *negative* or *positive.* Negative rights such as freedom of expression or the right of privacy are claims that the community should not interfere with certain personal choices. Positive or "welfare" rights such as rights to old-age assistance or unemployment compensation are claims that the community should provide people with certain goods or services. Note that negative and positive rights differ in *what they require of other people.* Negative rights basically obligate us to leave the rightholder alone when she undertakes certain activities, while positive rights obligate us to do something for the rightholder.

Rights also may be *economic* or *noneconomic.* Economic rights generally involve money or the production, consumption, and distribution of valuable material things. Two important examples are property rights and freedom of contract. Noneconomic rights cover all other kinds of rights. Examples include freedom of religion, freedom of speech, and freedom of association. Economic and noneconomic rights each can be either positive or negative. Figure 1 states some likely examples.

The distinction between economic rights and noneconomic rights breaks down at some point. For example, claimed rights to engage in advertising or prostitution may not clearly fit either category. As the prostitution example suggests, moreover, there is much disagreement about which claimed rights really deserve respect. For example, people may agree that the asserted right to smoke marijuana would be a negative noneconomic right, but they disagree about whether it ought to be recognized. However, while rights theorists differ in the rights they favor, they often agree on two general points:

1. *Where rights-based claims conflict, the right that is stronger under the circumstances wins out.* Thus, Justice Oliver Wendell Holmes's famous statement that no one has the right to shout "Fire!" in a crowded theater basically says that in some cases, the rights to life and physical safety overcome free speech rights. Of course, there is often disagreement over the relative strength or importance of competing rights. Whether it is justified or not, however, since the 1930s there has been a strong tendency for philosophers and legal scholars to favor noneconomic rights over economic rights. Another problem, one suggested by the words "under the circumstances," is that our decision to favor one right over another often depends on the *degree* to which each is involved in the case before us. Even though someone *might* be hurt as a result, for example, most people would agree that someone has a moral right to scream "Fire!" at an outdoor fraternity party.

2. *Rights-based claims overcome utilitarian claims where the two conflict.* Rights, it is frequently said, are "trumps" that defeat arguments based on utility. This is because rights theories are deontological, which means that rights claims defeat the moral claims generated by consequences such as utility. However, some rights theorists say that utility can be considered where no rights are at stake. But what is a utilitarian claim, and what is utility?

Utilitarianism

Utilitarianism says that the moral worth of actions depends on *their tendency to maximize utility.*[4] Thus, utilitarianism is a consequentialist ethical theory. In general, to maximize utility is to achieve the greatest overall balance of satisfactions over dissatisfactions. The British utilitarian Jeremy Bentham (1748–1832) limited these satisfactions and dissatisfactions to pleasure and pain. Believing Bentham's approach too narrowly hedonistic, later utilitarians such as John Stuart Mill (1806–1873) broadened the notion of utility to include satisfac-

tions such as health, knowledge, friendship, and aesthetic delights. Some modern utilitarians have urged that actions should be judged by their ability to promote the greatest net satisfaction of actual human preferences, whatever their nature. But no matter what the definition used, the aim generally is to maximize *total* or *aggregate* utility,[5] not the individual actor's *own* utility.

Utilitarianism has encountered many criticisms over time. One common objection is that there is no reliable method for measuring utility, however defined. Another is that utilitarianism is indifferent to the manner in which utility is realized. To a committed utilitarian, for example, satisfying sick or perverted desires is more important than satisfying healthy ones if the former would generate more utility. So long as total utility is maximized, moreover, utilitarianism seems indifferent to inequalities in its distribution among society's members. Finally, utilitarianism tends to sacrifice personal rights and interests to the maximization of collective utility. If enough Romans congregate to watch the lion devour the Christian, their collective pleasure will outweigh the pain of the Christian, however intense.[6] Similarly, utilitarian calculations might justify evils such as slavery, religious intolerance, infanticide, and the extermination of despised minorities—so long as total net satisfaction is maximized thereby.

Trying to Accommodate Rights Theory and Utilitarianism

As the preceding discussion should suggest, rights theory and utilitarianism clearly can conflict. Rights theorists say that rights-based claims always overcome claims based on total utility. Utilitarians, on the other hand, assert that total utility is all that counts. For example, imagine that Firm X's manufacturing processes discharge a harmful, but legally permissible, amount of pollutants into the atmosphere. The measures needed to eliminate such pollution would increase X's manufacturing costs, make it less efficient, and thereby cost someone (e.g., X's shareholders or its customers) some money and the utility it could purchase. If that utility exceeds the utility lost by the people whom

---

[4]This is *act-utilitarianism.* Another form of utilitarianism, called *rule-utilitarianism,* says that we should follow the *rule* that would maximize utility if it were consistently followed in like cases. For example, a rule-utilitarian might say that we should never break our promises because if we follow an absolute rule to this effect, we will generate more utility than if we try to make case-by-case judgments.

---

[5]Some utilitarians, however, say that the standard should be *average* utility per capita, not total utility.

[6]M. Sandel, ed., *Liberalism and Its Critics* (1984), p. 2.

FIGURE 2   A Utilitarian Argument for Profit Maximization

the pollution harms, a utilitarian would say that the pollution should continue. A rights theorist, on the other hand, might argue that the pollution is sufficiently great to violate a positive right to breathe clean air. Because rights-based claims "trump" claims based on aggregate utility, the critic would declare the pollution unethical even if the necessary pollution controls would mean less total utility.

However, rights theory and utilitarianism are not always opposed. First, much depends on how the rights in question are defined. For example, many rights theorists might agree that highly efficient manufacturing methods that create considerable wealth and utility but pose only a minor threat to worker safety are permissible because workers merely have a right to *reasonably safe* working conditions. Recall that in such cases, some rights theorists would consider utility because no right is involved. Second, some of the positive rights embraced by rights theorists seem to embody utilitarian values. For instance, positive rights to old-age assistance and unemployment compensation presumably increase their recipients' utility.

Also, generations of utilitarians have argued that long-run utility is maximized when society respects rights of both an economic and a noneconomic nature. Their basic point, one arguably supported by history, is that a free economy in which basic civil liberties are recognized generates the most wealth over time. Rights theorists, however, find such arguments troubling because they subordinate rights to utility maximization by making the former merely means to achievement of the latter. Where total utility can be increased by denying cherished rights, they add, utilitarians will not respect those rights.

Conceivably, all these problems would disappear if there were some way to directly weigh rights against utility while respecting the moral worth of each. Because it is often regarded as utilitarian, cost-benefit analysis probably cannot do the job.

Some mixed deontological theories that emphasize prima facie duties, however, seem to recognize a duty to maximize utility.[7] Perhaps this duty could be weighed against our various duties to respect other people's positive and negative rights. Most likely, however, this would have to be accomplished by intuition, and people's intuitions differ.

ETHICAL THEORY AND THE CORPORATE SOCIAL RESPONSIBILITY DEBATE

Defenders of the corporation generally say that business's only moral obligations are to maximize profits and to obey the law. The corporation's critics, on the other hand, assert that business has other moral obligations as well—obligations that may conflict with profit maximization. Assuming that there is a moral duty to obey the law, what does ethical theory have to say about the remaining claims?

Ethical Supports for Profit Maximization

Utilitarianism   Our utilitarian argument for profit maximization assumes that material things usually provide utility to their possessors and that material abundance is a reasonably good source of utility. The argument also assumes that the efficient allocation and use of society's scarce resources contribute powerfully to material abundance. Finally, the argument assumes that profit maximization under genuinely competitive conditions results in such an allocation and use of society's resources. Figure 2 summarizes the steps in the argument.

Why is there a relationship between profit maximization and efficiency? Firms that efficiently use resources can generally undersell their competitors.

---

[7]For example, Ross, *The Right and the Good*, p. 21, asserted a *duty of beneficence* that can be regarded as a duty to maximize utility.

As a result, they gain greater sales and reap higher profits. For this reason, they can often outbid less efficient resource users. Hence, scarce resources are allocated efficiently; they flow to the users and uses most highly valued by consumers and best able to give them a maximum return on their expenditures. If corporate managers pursue goals other than profit maximization, resources will not be put to their most efficient uses and society's total wealth will be reduced by the resulting allocational inefficiencies. In other words, corporate social responsibility generally does not come free.

To illustrate the last point, assume for simplicity's sake that there is no foreign competition in the American steel industry and that all domestic steelmakers spontaneously decide to observe pollution standards stricter than those imposed by law. Also, assume that the firms know that their buyers may not be willing to pay extra for "responsibly" produced steel. Because such socially responsible behavior costs money, the firms face a dilemma. They can try to pass on the increased costs to buyers in the form of higher prices, thus reducing the buyers' return per dollar spent and, most likely, their ability to make other purchases and their overall utility. Higher prices also might cause some buyers to seek substitutes for steel, with obvious effects on the steel firms' profits and their shareholders' utility. Or the firms might decide to retain existing customers by refusing to increase prices despite the higher costs they face. In this case, the firms almost certainly would have to accept lower profits. If profits fall, dividends and salaries might be reduced, with corresponding utility losses for shareholders and employees. In addition, the firms' ability to bid for scarce resources such as iron ore also might suffer. The likely result is a flow of employees, investment funds, and resources away from those firms. This, in turn, may mean lower steel production, which may also mean lower societal utility. If all these various possible losses in utility exceed the utility gains from reduced pollution, the steel firms' "socially responsible" behavior is wrong from a utilitarian point of view.

As Figure 2 suggests, however, the utilitarian argument for profit maximization depends on at least two further assumptions:

1. *Profit maximization occurs under conditions of genuine competition.* As Adam Smith observed in his *The Wealth of Nations* over 200 years ago, people in the same business seldom converse, even on social occasions, without the conversation ending in a conspiracy against the public or in some scheme to raise prices. In other words, competitors often try to thwart the market and maximize their profits by engaging in the various anticompetitive practices described in Chapters 48 and 49 or by using government to restrict competition. To the extent that they succeed, they weaken the link between profit-seeking and allocational efficiency, thereby reducing utility.

For example, firms that get government to give them tariff protection or members of professions who establish government-backed occupational licensing schemes often gain significant protection from competition. This may allow them to restrict output, raise prices, and/or offer lower-quality products or services. To illustrate the point, consider the extreme case in which one firm has a monopoly in a certain product. Economists say that such a firm can maximize its sales revenues and reap monopoly profits by restricting output and raising prices. This results in inefficiencies because the total amount of goods or services is reduced and purchasers of those goods or services do not receive a maximum return for the higher prices they pay. Outright monopolization is illegal under section 2 of the Sherman Act. But economists often argue that tacit price-fixing agreements among firms in *oligopolistic* industries have similar, if less serious, effects, and the antitrust laws have done relatively little to curb oligopolistic price-fixing.[8] This is one example of a theme we stress later in this chapter—the law's limits as a corporate control device.

2. *The disutility resulting from profit maximization does not exceed the utility it produces.* This assumption is illustrated by our earlier steel industry example. In that example, it would be difficult to defend profit maximization on utilitarian grounds if the utility gained from reduced pollution exceeds the utility lost due to reduced efficiency. The point is that competitive profit maximization

---

[8]See Chapter 48. An oligopolistic industry is one dominated by a few large sellers.

often has social costs, and sometimes those costs outweigh the material benefits it provides.

Negative Economic Rights

If they exist and are strong enough to outweigh other moral concerns, negative economic rights such as freedom of contract and property rights also support profit maximization. They do so mainly by protecting the activities through which profits are made.

For example, suppose that in order to maximize profits, the XYZ Corporation does not provide health insurance for its employees. If XYZ is criticized for failing to respect its employees' alleged positive right to decent health care, it can claim that its employees freely contracted to work on this basis, and that freedom of contract outweighs any right to decent health care. However, this argument faces difficulties if XYZ has greater bargaining power than its employees. To take another example, suppose that the ABC Corporation closes an inefficient plant to improve its profit picture. If employees or members of the affected local community object, ABC might defend its action by saying that it has an absolute or near-absolute right to dispose of its property as it sees fit. Because the plant is its property, ABC could continue, it is morally entitled to shut down that plant whenever it desires.

Ethical Supports for the Critics' Position

The preceding arguments depended on the assumptions that negative economic rights are very important and that there are no competing moral concerns strong enough to override them. But what if negative economic rights are less important than positive rights of all kinds? First, this would undermine an important defense of profit maximization. Second, it would powerfully justify the view that business has other ethical responsibilities besides maximizing profits. To be sure, some of these positive rights might diminish economic efficiency and productivity. But to a rights theorist, rights trump utility-based claims.

As our steel industry example suggests, sometimes utilitarianism can justify responsible business behavior that subordinates profits to other concerns. But the same results can probably be reached more directly if people have certain positive rights. Thus, if people have strong positive rights to clean air and clean water, those rights would justify the "responsible" steel firms' behavior. Also, if employees have

a positive right to be discharged only for just cause, it would be wrong to arbitrarily fire them.[9] Similarly, employees might have positive rights to safe working conditions, to a decent wage, and to medical care or medical insurance. These rights would create corresponding duties for business—duties that probably conflict with profit maximization.

Both rights theory and Kant's categorical imperative also might justify the stakeholder theory of corporate social responsibility mentioned at the beginning of this chapter.[10] Suppose that, consistent with the second major formulation of Kant's categorical imperative, certain stakeholders have a right to be treated as ends in themselves, and not merely as means. This could mean that they should not be treated as objects to be used for corporate profit and discarded when they cease to be useful. If so, it might be wrong for a corporation to fire workers once their services are no longer required, or to suddenly leave a community with which it has had a long relationship. As discussed earlier, another implication of the categorical imperative is that we should appeal to people's rational nature when trying to influence them or when taking action that affects their interests. This could mean that affected stakeholders should be allowed to participate in corporate governance, or at least be consulted and have their views taken into account before any adverse action against them can occur. Later in this chapter, we will examine proposals for stakeholder participation in corporate governance.

PRACTICAL PROBLEMS WITH THE DEFENDERS' POSITION

Although there are genuine ethical differences between the corporation's critics and its defenders, no one thinks that business should maximize profits to the exclusion of everything else. According to the corporation's defenders, business's other (nonprofit-related) responsibilities can be met by obeying the law. This position is plausible only if the law is very effective in controlling corporate misbehavior. Also,

---

[9]Unless an exception applies, such firings would be legal under the doctrine of employment at will discussed in Chapter 50.

[10]For an argument resembling the one made in this paragraph, see W. Evan and R. Freeman, "A Stakeholder Theory of the Modern Corporation: Kantian Capitalism," in *Ethical Theory and Business,* ed. T. Beauchamp and N. Bowie, 3rd ed., (1988), pp. 97–106.

FIGURE 3   The Major Points Argued by Defenders of the Corporation

Overall Position	Business's only moral responsibility is to maximize profits within the bounds set by the law
Preferred Moral Theories	Utilitarianism and rights theories stressing negative economic rights
Other Arguments	1. Markets and other private forces such as protests, publicity, and public opinion are significant checks on business misconduct 2. The law is a very effective (perhaps *too* effective) constraint on business

the position becomes more plausible if such private forces as the market and unfavorable public opinion are significant checks on business misconduct. In fact, the corporation's defenders tend to assert—or assume—the truth of both these contentions. Thus, they could say, it is safe to let managers concentrate on profit maximization because the law, the market, and various other private forces do so good a job keeping them in line. Figure 3 summarizes the defenders' major positions. Of course, not every defender of business embraces every one of Figure 3's propositions.

In reality, however, the defenders' contentions are questionable. Market forces and other private checks, while sometimes effective, offer very incomplete protection against business misconduct. The law's ability to control such misbehavior also has its limits. Thus, it may not be enough for firms to simply seek profits and obey the law. Even if you were persuaded by the moral arguments for profit maximization, therefore, you may still want business to have other ethical responsibilities besides simply following the law.

Markets and Other Private Forces

Defenders of the corporation tend to argue or assume that market forces and free private activity force corporations to behave in a socially respon-

sible fashion. For such reasons, the corporation's defenders sometimes conclude, there is little need for managers to abandon their profit orientation and the utility it generates. Unfortunately, however, market checks and other forms of private behavior have definite limits as corporate control devices. As a rule, the former only check certain kinds of corporate misbehavior. In addition, many practical obstacles stand in the way of the latter's success.

Market Checks   Market forces clearly can influence corporate behavior for the better. Sooner or later, firms that market defective and/or dangerous products are likely to lose business. This possibility naturally stimulates corporate managers to avoid this form of corporate irresponsibility. But are market checks well equipped to stop other forms of real or alleged corporate misbehavior such as overseas bribery, environmental degradation, and poor working conditions? In these cases, consumers of the offending firm's products may not be directly harmed by the firm's wrongdoing, and thus may lack strong incentives to act against it. Indeed, they may not even know about the misconduct.

These considerations suggest that while market forces impel firms to offer safe and trouble-free products and services, they are much less effective against corporate irresponsibility that does not involve those products and services. In fact, market forces are not always effective even in the former case. One reason is that people who are injured or otherwise disadvantaged by defective products may not be aware of the harm at the time it occurs. In the past, for instance, many cigarette smokers did not know that cigarette smoking helps cause lung cancer. In some cases, even the manufacturer itself is unaware of these "unknown harms." In all these situations, some people will be harmed before the problem is discovered and corrective action taken. A second reason why market forces do not always curb product-related harms, one discussed later in this section, is that business organizations sometimes do not respond rationally to external pressures. This can prevent them from acting quickly on negative information about defective products.

Protest, Publicity, and Public Opinion   Thus, market forces seem to be fairly effective against certain forms of corporate misbehavior, but not against the full range of such misbehaviors. However, other kinds of private activity appear not to have this limitation. Citizens angered by corporate misconduct can organize boycotts (which might be regarded as a market check), initiate letter-writing campaigns, engage in picketing, and stage demonstrations against the offending firm. Such activities may attract media attention. Or the media itself may uncover and publicize irresponsible corporate behavior. All these forms of private action can provoke government regulation, hurt the firm's image, and expose managers to criticism in their nonbusiness lives. The prospect of such happenings can force managers to change their ways for the better.

Thus, protests, publicity, and public opinion obviously *can* influence business conduct in responsible directions. But how often? Clearly, they cannot work where the offender is unaware of the misbehavior, or where knowledge of the misbehavior stays within the offender's confines. Even if the information becomes public, moreover, how many people will find out? Of those people, how many will view the information negatively? Within that group, how great is the level of concern? For those who are significantly concerned, what are the costs of taking action and the obstacles to organizing for collective action? Finally, how effectively can the offending firm counter any bad publicity that emerges? These questions suggest that a series of conditions must normally be met before protests, publicity, and public opinion can threaten a firm's well-being and thus change its behavior for the better.

The Law

Even the most ardent defender of the corporation would probably admit that markets and free private activity have limitations as corporate control devices. However, he would be less inclined to concede that the law has any such weaknesses. In fact, he might well think that it puts *excessive* restrictions on business, thereby deterring valuable profit-seeking activity.

Throughout this century, legal checks have been the main means of controlling corporate misdeeds. Lawmakers usually assume that corporations are rational actors that can be deterred from misbehavior by the threats the law presents. Those threats are the sanctions (e.g., fines, civil damages) the law imposes on those who violate its rules. For deterrence to work effectively, corporate decisionmakers must understand when the law's penalties will be imposed, must fear the costs those penalties create, and must act rationally to avoid them.

Unfortunately, the law's ability to control irresponsible corporate behavior, while significant, has limits. Some of the reasons for this are discussed below. To the extent that these arguments are valid, the profit-maximizers' insistence that legal checks are sufficient to control corporate misbehavior is weakened. If so, then it may make sense to say that business has moral duties that go beyond those stated in the law and to seek additional ways to make firms live up to those duties.

Corporate Influence on the Content of the Law
One reason the law is an imperfect corporate control device, some argue, is that business has a significant voice in determining its content. Thus, the law sometimes reflects corporate interests. This may allow corporations to engage in unethical behavior that nonetheless is perfectly legal.

The political influence exerted by large corporations is a familiar subject. Because of their size, resources, and sophistication, they have (or can purchase) the ability to influence legislation through methods such as lobbying and contributions to business-oriented political action committees. Even if Congress or a state legislature passes hostile regulation, moreover, business sometimes can blunt its impact. It may use its political influence to reduce the funding received by the agency enforcing the legislation. Over time, business may co-opt the agency by inducing it to take a probusiness view of its functions. One way this occurs is through the continuous exchange of personnel between the agency and the industry it is supposed to regulate in the public interest. Also, an agency, the industry it regulates, and the congressional subcommittee controlling the agency may form a mutually beneficial relationship that is relatively impervious to outside influence (the so-called Iron Triangle).

By now, however, critics of the corporation have also become adept at playing the political game, and on some occasions they are able to counteract corporate political power. Consumer groups and environmental groups are but two examples. More importantly, what is the implication of the previous arguments? That business should have *no* say in determining the rules by which it is governed? Although this prospect might make the corporation's critics happy and increase their influence, it is not clear that they have a monopoly on wisdom, virtue, and objectivity either.

Unknown Harms   As noted earlier, for market forces to control corporate behavior, consumers must know that they are being harmed at the time the harm occurs. Reliance on the law involves a similar assumption—that legislators and regulators possess such knowledge. Legal action to control harmful corporate behavior will not be forthcoming until the need for such action is apparent. Yet lawmakers generally learn about previously unknown harms even later than the business producing those harms or the people suffering them. This means that, in some cases, legal action to correct those harms will occur only after they have already taken place. Such situations involve almost inevitable limits on the law's effectiveness as a control device.

Are Corporations Always Rational Actors? Another argument against the law's ability to control corporations is that much of their irresponsible behavior results from an *inability to respond sensibly* to legal threats. The law's ability to affect business behavior depends on managers' clear perception of the penalties for illegal actions and their rational response to the resulting risk. To the extent that corporations fail these tests of clear perception and rational response, the law's ability to control them suffers.

As a rule, people are not especially perceptive and clearheaded. Everyone blocks out certain aspects of the external world, and this tendency is especially noticeable when the excluded information is troubling. In this way, corporate managers planning a highly profitable venture may discount potential legal problems that would render the venture less attractive. By combining the abilities of many people, though, organizations should be able to overcome these individual deficiencies. But while this is often true, there are also certain features of organizational life that make clear perception and rational response *less* likely.

Social psychologists and students of organizational behavior, for instance, have long been aware of a phenomenon called *risky shift*. This means that a group of people who must reach consensus on an acceptable level of risk often choose a level *higher* than the level they would accept as individuals.

Thus, decisions made by a team of managers may create greater legal problems than decisions made by an isolated manager. Also relevant here is the familiar phenomenon of *groupthink*—the tendency for members of a group to internalize the group's values and perceptions and to suppress critical thought. Thus, if our team of managers is planning a highly profitable venture to which the success of each team member is tied, each may minimize the venture's legal problems because these conflict with the group's goals.

Somewhat similar to groupthink is another familiar feature of organizational life—the tendency for *bad news not to get to the top*. When subordinates know that top managers are strongly committed to a particular course of action, they may not report problems for fear of provoking their superiors' disapproval. Ideally, of course, managers should want to be fully apprised of potential legal risks, but occasionally their response is to penalize the bearer of bad news instead. Also, subordinates may distort the information they present to their superiors in order to make their own performance look better than it actually is. Finally, the complex and unwieldy organizational structures of some modern corporations sometimes diminish their capacity for rational and effective response to legal problems. For example, they may worsen the tendency for bad news not to reach top managers. They also may make it difficult for top managers to ensure that their decisions are fully implemented at lower levels.

Conscious Lawbreaking   Throughout this chapter, we assume that business firms have a moral obligation to obey the law. Yet no discussion of the law's limits can ignore the fact that businesses sometimes ignore the law's commands. Unlike the corporate irrationality just discussed, here we have disobedience that is knowing, thought-out, and deliberate. Corporations may conclude that breaking the law poses acceptable risks if the potential benefits are great, the penalties for violation are relatively light, and/or the chances of being sued or prosecuted are low. Sometimes, for example, it may make sense for a firm to continue to market a defect-ridden product rather than redesign it, if competitors' products are no better and the costs of paying product liability claims or of procuring product liability insurance are sufficiently low that they can be passed on to consumers.

Other factors increase the likelihood that corporations will engage in conscious lawbreaking. The let's-take-the-risk mentality may be reinforced when the law is (or is perceived to be) uncertain. Corporate or industry norms may regard a measure of illegal (or borderline) behavior as morally acceptable. This is especially likely where corporate managers regard the relevant legal rules as misguided.

The tendency toward conscious lawbreaking could be reduced, many argue, by stiffer penalties and increased enforcement efforts. But corporate political influence may prevent either from occurring. As noted above, corporations sometimes try to blunt politically popular legislation by devoting their efforts to such less visible matters as agency funding. State and federal prosecutors are usually either elected or politically appointed. Finally, the public is not always willing to fund increased enforcement efforts.

Problems with the Criminal Sanction   The existence of conscious corporate lawbreaking leads naturally to a related subject—the effectiveness of the criminal sanction in the corporate context. As discussed in Chapter 5, both the corporate entity and individual corporation members can be liable for crimes committed in the course of the corporation's business. However, there are reasons to ask how well such liability checks corporate misconduct.

Criminal penalties directed at the corporation itself are a problematical control device. Such penalties work by deterring future misbehavior. But deterrence requires rationality, and as we have seen, corporate behavior is not always rational. Moreover, the main criminal penalty for corporations is the fine, and many observers believe that the fines now imposed on corporations are too small for effective deterrence. Although bigger fines might better deter corporate misbehavior, corporate political influence could prevent them from ever being enacted or imposed. In addition, such fines involve possible injustices. In all likelihood, the costs they impose will ultimately be passed on to the firm's customers in the form of higher prices—or will fall on its shareholders (as lower dividends) or employees (as lower wages). Usually, these parties were unable to prevent the wrongdoing that gave rise to criminal liability and did not benefit from it. The managers responsible for the crime, on the other hand, may escape any significant financial penalty.

Such problems have led some observers to advocate greater *individual* criminal liability to control corporate misbehavior. Because managers with the power to order or prevent criminal activity would know that *they* will suffer if the activity is detected and a prosecution results, individual sanctions promise significant deterrence of corporate misconduct. In addition, this deterrence could be achieved without unjustly penalizing customers, shareholders, and innocent employees. Despite its apparent attractiveness, however, individual criminal liability suffers from serious problems. Due to the diffused, collective nature of corporate decisionmaking, it often is difficult to pinpoint people with the necessary culpability for criminal liability. Where a guilty party can be identified, moreover, she may not be a high-level executive. Because bad news tends not to reach the top and because those at the top consciously avoid knowing too much, individual criminal liability often falls on middle-level managers instead. Juries may be unwilling to convict such people if they appear to be scapegoats for someone higher up. Even where either a middle- or high-level manager is convicted, moreover, imprisonment may not occur. Instead, the guilty individual may merely be fined and then may be indemnified by the corporation. Even where the convicted party does jail time, he is likely to receive a short sentence in a "country club" institution where early parole is a possibility.

PRACTICAL PROBLEMS WITH THE CRITICS' POSITION

The preceding section concluded that markets and other private forces are useful but imperfect checks on corporate misbehavior, and that despite its great importance as a corporate control device, the law is not as effective as many people believe. This suggests that if business misconduct is to be adequately controlled, corporations have to assume other moral duties besides maximizing profits and obeying the law. But how can they be led to do so? As Figure 4 states, critics of the corporation often say that ethics instruction and other ethical initiatives from within the business community can play a significant role in producing such behavior.[11] Where these methods

---

[11]These methods, of course, have often attracted significant support within the business community as well. Because they are generally consistent with the critics' agenda, however, we include them here.

FIGURE 4 Major Points Argued by Critics of the Corporation	
Overall Position	Business has moral obligations that go beyond—and may conflict with—the duty to maximize profits
Preferred Moral Theories	Rights theories emphasizing positive rights; Kantianism
Other Arguments	1. Ethics instruction and other ethical initiatives from within the business community can significantly reduce corporate irresponsibility 2. Where these methods fail, changes in the internal governance of corporations will cause them to behave responsibly

fail, critics often add, certain changes in the corporation's internal governance can cause it to behave more responsibly. However, all these corporate control tactics face significant objections. Worse yet, some of the critics' proposed changes could negatively affect both the corporation's internal functioning and its profitability.

Responses from within the Business Community

Ethics Instruction   In a sense, greater ethical awareness and more ethical behavior by business managers are *the* solutions to corporate irresponsibility. If all corporate decisionmakers possess such traits, business misbehavior should fall sharply, and the need for other control devices should diminish appreciably. In recent years, business schools have increasingly attempted to advance this goal by injecting ethical considerations into their curricula and executive education programs. Such efforts are attempts to generate socially responsible corporate behavior by changing the outlook of existing and future managers.

Despite its promise, however, ethics instruction faces significant theoretical and practical problems. One concerns the substance of the instruction: Which moral theories and which values should receive emphasis? As this chapter's brief ethics discussion suggests, there is considerable disagreement on these questions. Even if there is consensus on content, can ethics instruction really instill the chosen values and make them stick after the educational process is completed? Such instruction is directed at people whose character—or lack thereof—has largely been formed by the time the instruction occurs. Although ethics instruction should increase the moral awareness of those who are predisposed to listen, its effect on the basically self-interested, indifferent, or unethical is questionable. Even those who are positively influenced by ethics instruction, moreover, may still behave irresponsibly if their careers or their livelihoods require them to act in their employer's financial interest. For the firm itself, ethical behavior may be economically injurious unless all the firm's competitors follow suit. And for people employed by companies with a strong profit orientation, the thoughtways acquired in a business ethics course may not survive the tendency for organizations to socialize their members to accept the group's goals as paramount.

Corporate or Industry Codes of Ethical Conduct
Over time, many large corporations and several industries have adopted codes of conduct to guide managerial and/or employee decisionmaking. For example, an industry code might define as unethical certain types of advertising or certain hiring practices. Or a corporate code of conduct might prohibit employees from accepting gifts from suppliers of the corporation.

There are two popular views of such codes. One sees them as genuine efforts to foster ethical behavior within a firm or an industry. The other regards them as thinly disguised attempts to make the firm function better, mislead the public into believing that business behaves ethically, forestall legislation that would impose stricter constraints on business, and/or limit competition under the veil of ethical standards. Even where the first view is correct, moreover, ethical codes do not address all possible forms of corporate misbehavior. As the previous examples suggest, they tend to emphasize either the behavior required for the firm's effective internal functioning or the relations between competitors within a particular industry—and not corporate misbehavior that affects society generally.

The Corporate Stewardship Argument   Earlier in the chapter, we suggested that some large, entrenched corporations in oligopolistic industries try to avoid competition by fixing prices and otherwise collaborating among themselves. Such behavior is bad for efficiency and probably for total utility. For certain observers of years past, however, it had great promise for promoting more responsible corporate behavior. Their argument was that once corporations become economically secure, they would be free to behave in a more ethical manner. One proponent of this position, which we call the corporate stewardship argument, contended that modern corporate managers have come to resemble a professional civil service more than a group of property-owning entrepreneurs.[12]

Although corporate stewardship is a *possible* consequence of oligopolistic corporations' anticompetitive behavior, it is hardly a *necessary* result of such behavior. Rather than behaving ethically, such firms might simply strive to maximize their return to shareholders, or instead might funnel money toward executive salaries and perquisites, a pleasant work environment, and so forth. Also, large, oligopolistic firms arguably are less accountable to outside forces than smaller businesses in competitive markets. Thus, the incentives for irresponsible behavior may *increase* because large, secure firms can indulge in such behavior with relative impunity.

Stakeholder Theory Revisited   One way for an enlightened "corporate steward" to behave is to follow the stakeholder theory described earlier in the chapter. In other words, such a person might define ethical corporate behavior as the effort to act in the interests of the corporation's various constituencies. If our criticisms of the corporate stewardship argument are valid, it is questionable whether entrenched corporations in oligopolistic industries will behave in this way. But this

definition of corporate social responsibility suffers from other problems as well. First, the interests of the relevant constituencies may conflict. For instance, consumers' interest in lower prices may conflict with employees' interest in higher wages and perhaps with the surrounding community's interest in environmental protection. From an ethical point of view, moreover, why should a corporation's immediate constituencies be favored over the larger society? For example, firms or industries that corrupt the national political processes to get unjustified tax breaks may well be *helping* their various stakeholders.

The Corporate Governance Agenda

Despite the problems they face, ethics instruction and other efforts from within the business community may eventually generate more responsible corporate conduct. But corporate critics of the 1960s and 1970s chose to encourage it in a more direct fashion. They did so by making various proposals for altering the *internal governance* of corporations. The general aim of such proposals was to give representation to the firm's stakeholders and to make corporations more sensitive to their interests.

Chapters 42 and 43 discuss some of these internal governance proposals, and this chapter's remarks supplement that discussion. Although a few such proposals have occasionally been adopted in modified form, public interest in them has diminished since the 1970s. However, they may again become popular if the political and attitudinal winds shift. Here, we discuss three such recommendations—and the problems they present—in general terms. First, however, we must say a few words about intracorporate power relations.

As Chapter 42 relates, corporation law gives a corporation's shareholders the power to elect directors who are empowered to manage the corporation. The directors, in turn, typically delegate this power to the corporation's officers while retaining general supervisory powers over them. This formal legal model suggests that the directors have more authority over corporate policy than management, and that corporate policy ultimately is set by the shareholders as they elect the directors. Yet for much of the 20th century, it has been widely agreed that man-

---

[12]A. Berle, *Power without Property* (1959), p. 113.

agement really runs the show within most large corporations, that directors tend to ratify managerial decisions, and that shareholders have little effective control over such decisions. The many reasons for this famous *separation of ownership from control* are beyond the scope of this chapter. Chief among these reasons, however, are the complexity of corporate decisionmaking and the limited time and expertise directors and shareholders can bring to bear on such matters.

Greater Shareholder Power   Some proposals for changing internal corporate governance say that shareholders should have a greater voice in shaping corporate policy. Specific recommendations include giving shareholders greater power to nominate directors and the ability to adopt resolutions binding the directors.

Of the various corporate governance proposals, granting greater power to shareholders has the least to recommend it. For one thing, such proposals seem unrealistic when we consider the facts of intracorporate life noted above. Of particular importance here is a matter discussed in Chapters 42 and 43—management's tendency to get its way on corporate policy decisions by dominating the proxy machinery through which shareholders often vote. If shareholders somehow were to exercise greater power, moreover, effective corporate decisionmaking could be impaired as this relatively uninformed group issues edicts to management.

From a corporate control perspective, however, the real problem with giving greater power to shareholders concerns the values they are likely to advance. Although it is conceivable that some corporate managers do not make profit maximization their first priority, the orientation of shareholders is almost always completely pecuniary. For this reason, shareholders are unlikely to initiate or approve corporate actions hostile to profit maximization. The same is generally true of institutional investors such as pension funds and mutual funds, which own significant blocks of stock in many corporations. Such investors tend to follow the "Wall Street Rule," under which they either support management or sell their shares.

Changing the Composition of the Board   Despite the tendency for corporate management to dominate the board of directors, the board's formal

legal powers are still considerable. Recognizing this, critics of the corporation have made innumerable recommendations for changing the board's composition to make corporations more representative and more responsible. Some of the recommendations have been fairly modest—for example, creating nominating committees composed of outside directors, requiring that there be more such directors and fewer insiders, and limiting the number of corporate boards on which one individual can serve.[13] More extreme proposals include recommendations that constituencies of all sorts (e.g., labor, government, creditors, local communities, minorities, environmentalists) be represented, that certain directors be assigned special areas of concern (e.g., consumer protection, environmental affairs), and that special committees of the board be given similar functions. By giving the firm's constituencies a voice in corporate governance, the first set of proposals implements stakeholder theory and enables corporations to treat stakeholders as ends rather than means.

From a corporate social responsibility perspective, the basic problem with all such proposals is that they fail to confront the main reason for management's domination of the board—the limited time, information, and expertise that directors can bring to bear when considering corporate affairs. One solution to this problem is to give outside or constituency directors a full-time staff with the power to dig for information within the corporation. Doing so, however, effectively creates another—perhaps competing—layer of management within the corporate organizational structure. Although this could curtail certain corporate misdeeds, it could also lessen firms' ability to innovate and respond to changing developments, with negative implications for their profitability and the utility they can generate.

Another, more down-to-earth, set of problems with some of these proposals concerns the details of their implementation. Which constituencies deserve representation? How many directors should each constituency have? Within each constituency, what

---

[13]Inside directors are generally defined as either present or former managers of the firm on whose board they serve; normally, all other directors are regarded as outside directors.

criteria should govern the choice of directors? For example, is it desirable or undesirable that they have business experience?

Finally, in addition to complicating the management structure, these proposals might make the board less cohesive and render it incapable of coherent action. Conflicts among constituency representatives or between insiders and outsiders are entirely possible. In fact, the addition of constituency directors might simply mean the intrusion of broader social conflicts into corporate boardrooms. The board, that is, could be divided by disputes among consumers who want lower prices, workers who want higher wages and job security, environmentalists who want pollution to cease, and communities that want to preserve jobs and their tax bases. This could render the board incapable of pushing management in responsible directions.

Changes in Management Structure   As noted above, one of the great commonplaces about large 20th-century corporations is the separation of ownership from control—the shift of power away from shareholders and directors to the corporation's managers. Because this is where true power resides, some corporate reformers argue, the best way to produce more responsible corporate behavior is to change the corporation's *management structure.*

The main proponent of this view, Christopher Stone, has made several recommendations for such changes.[14] These include the establishment of: (1) specified offices within certain corporations (e.g., offices for environmental affairs, worker safety, and product safety); (2) requirements for holding certain corporate positions (e.g., educational requirements for safety engineers); (3) offices for ensuring that relevant external information (e.g., data from auto repair shops for car manufacturers or data from doctors for drug companies) is received by the corporation; and (4) internal information flow procedures for ensuring that relevant external information gets to the proper corporate departments (to guarantee, for instance, that bad news gets to the top). Stone and others have also

recommended that corporations be required to make internal findings before undertaking certain activities. For example, drug companies might be required to produce a document resembling an environmental impact statement before marketing a new product.

These proposed requirements are procedural in the sense that they do not dictate what decisions the corporation should make. Their general aim is to ensure that corporations can anticipate problems before they arise so that timely responses are possible. Such requirements probably would do little to deter a strongly profit-oriented corporation from taking irresponsible actions. It is also possible that corporate personnel responsible for implementing these requirements could be influenced by a strong internal profit orientation or frozen out of the final decisionmaking process.

In cases where irresponsible corporate behavior results less from profit-seeking than from failed perceptions, however, Stone's proposals could have an impact. For example, they may be especially effective in addressing the unknown-harms problem discussed earlier. But such benefits would probably be obtained only at the cost of further organizational complexity, with a consequent reduction in the corporation's ability to make quick responses to changing business conditions.

CONCLUSIONS

Critics of the corporation say that business should be held to a standard of socially responsible behavior higher than that imposed by law. Ethics instruction and other ethical initiatives from within business, they continue, can do much to make responsible corporate behavior a reality. And where these fail, changes in internal corporate governance can finish the job. The corporation's defenders, on the other hand, say that the firm's only moral responsibility is to maximize profits within the bounds set by the law. Because the law, markets, and other private forces adequately restrain corporations, they add, this stance will not threaten society.

As the chapter has revealed, neither the corporation's critics nor its defenders have convincingly made their case. To be sure, each position finds some support in ethical theory. Positive rights of either an economic or a noneconomic nature help

---

[14]C. Stone, *Where the Law Ends: The Social Control of Corporate Behavior,* Chapters 17–19 (1975).

justify the critics' position, while negative economic rights and utilitarianism support the defenders' stance. But philosophers disagree about the relative merits of these theories (and others). In addition, the more or less factual arguments made by each side have problems. At best, ethics instruction and ethics initiatives from within business can only supplement the other means of controlling corporate misconduct. Worse yet, the critics' proposed changes in corporate governance are likely either to adversely affect organizational functioning or to be ineffective—or both. As for the defenders' factual arguments, markets and such other private checks, while important constraints on corporate misconduct, have limited scope. Although the law has long been the main force by which society tries to check business misbehavior, it is far from a perfect control device.

What, then, can safely be said about the social responsibilities of business and the control of corporate misconduct? The three following generalizations strike us as valid.

1. *Competitive profit maximization is an extremely important—perhaps the most important— social responsibility of business.* Although the corporation's critics downplay competitive profit maximization and sometimes subordinate it to other values, they do not really deny this point. The reason is the economic efficiency and material abundance profit-maximizing economic competition generally produces. For this reason, it finds ready support in utilitarianism. And it also contributes to the realization of certain positive economic rights. Without economic abundance, how likely are positive rights such as the rights to a decent living wage, unemployment compensation, old-age assistance, and adequate health care to be realized?

2. *Competitive profit maximization does not exhaust business's social responsibilities.* In other words, business has other moral obligations in addition to profit maximization. If the law, the market, and other private forces were as effective as the corporation's defenders sometimes seem to think, perhaps society could safely limit business's social responsibilities to profit maximization. In fact, however, they are imperfect control devices. To be sure, this does not directly establish that business has other moral responsibilities besides competitive profit maximization; for that, a moral argument is needed. But the necessary arguments are readily available. As we have seen, positive rights clearly support such duties. In cases where profit-maximizing behavior's disutility exceeds its utility, utilitarianism supports those duties as well.

3. *For all its flaws, the law is—and probably will remain—the most important means by which society controls business misconduct.* This chapter's catalog of the law's imperfections reminds us of the old debate concerning whether a glass filled to its halfway mark is half empty or half full. Overall, the law is probably the best—or the least bad—of the control devices discussed in this chapter. Of these devices, only the law and the various private controls impose real penalties for corporate misbehavior. Although legal norms have no special claim to moral correctness, at least they are arrived at through a fairly open political process in which competing arguments may be weighed and evaluated. This cannot be said about the intuitions of some "responsible" businessperson, the edicts of some "public interest" group, or the theories of some academic economist or philosopher. As a general rule, finally, the law's commands should have less adverse effect on corporations' internal functioning than many of the corporate reform proposals.

More importantly, the law has a track record as a corporate control device, and that record contains a number of real accomplishments. For example, although the antitrust laws discussed in Chapters 48–49 remain controversial, they have at least eliminated some of the worst anticompetitive abuses that were common before their enactment. If nothing else, similarly, the federal securities regulations examined in Chapters 44–45 have prevented the shady practices that, some contend, led to the stock market crash of the late 1920s. Although environmentalists often demand more regulation, virtually everyone agrees that the environmental laws treated in Chapter 51 have appreciably improved the quality of our air and water and reduced our exposure to toxic substances. Finally, the various employment regulations discussed in Chapter 50—especially those forbidding employment discrimination—have worked enormous changes in the American workplace over the course of this century.

CONCEPT REVIEW

The Corporate Control Devices Compared: A Tentative Box Score

Device	Likely Effectiveness in Curbing Corporate Irresponsibility	Possible Costs in Efficiency and in Ineffective Corporate Decisionmaking	Remarks
Ethical Instruction	Will it take? Will it stick? Which values?	Disunity within corporation? Adverse effects on efficiency?	Effects probably long term
Codes of Conduct	Questionable, due to limited scope	Could be anticompetitive	A sham?
Corporate Stewardship	Questionable at best	By hypothesis, firms in question are inefficient oligopolists	Has this really happened? Would such firms necessarily behave ethically?
Advancing Stakeholder Interests	Interests of stakeholders may conflict	Occasional adverse effects on efficiency?	Are interests of stakeholders necessarily congruent with larger social good?
Market Forces and Private Action	Should vary with type of corporate misbehavior	Fairly low. Market forces tend to *promote* efficiency	Fine where they work
Greater Shareholder Power	Poor, due to pecuniary orientation of shareholders	Less coherent decisionmaking?	Maybe the weakest of the bunch
Packing the Board	Likely to be minimal unless the causes of board's subservience are overcome	Could adversely affect corporate decisionmaking and efficiency	Which constituencies and interests deserve representation?
Changing the Internal Management Structure	Probably most effective for unknown harms	Could complicate corporate decisionmaking	Focus on *management* structure an advantage
The Law	Despite limits on effectiveness, has a respectable track record	Can have adverse impact on efficiency	The best of a flawed group?

PROBLEMS AND PROBLEM CASES

1. Defenders of the corporation often argue that the principal moral obligation of corporations is to maximize profits within the law. But are the law's commands necessarily moral? And is there an ethical obligation to obey morally bad laws? What do the *natural law* and *legal positivist* schools of

jurisprudence discussed in Chapter 1 say about these questions?

2. The law's ability to control corporate misbehavior depends heavily on the assumption that corporations are rational actors that will respond sensibly to the threats the law imposes. Suppose for the sake of argument that corporations do *not* behave rationally, generally speaking. This would tend to undermine a position sometimes taken by defenders of the corporation—that legal threats effectively counter most kinds of irresponsible corporate behavior. But the assumption that corporations behave irrationally might undermine *another* argument typically made by the corporation's defenders. What is this argument, and how would corporate irrationality weaken it? *Hint:* Do irrational people and businesses generally make money?

3. Is the right to obtain an abortion a negative or a positive right? How about the asserted right to have one's abortion funded by the federal government or the states?

4. Suppose that by keeping your promise to A, you would give her 1,000 units of utility. However, by breaking your promise to A and performing the promised act for B, you would give B 1,001 units of utility. You have not promised B anything, however. Assume that it is impossible to perform for both A and B.

What course of action would utilitarianism dictate here? (The question refers to act-utilitarianism; see footnote 4 in this chapter.) What would a person who is a strict deontologist about promises recommend? What about a mixed deontologist who thinks that keeping promises is important, but who also recognizes a duty to maximize utility? Which, if any, of your answers would change if, instead of giving B 1,001 units of utility, breaking the promise to A would give B one million units of utility? Here, again assume that keeping the promise to A would give A only 1,000 units of utility.

5. The ABC Corporation declares itself a "socially responsible" firm, and defines socially responsible behavior as behavior that maximizes the well-being of its various stakeholders. ABC identifies the following stakeholders to which it feels responsible: its workers, consumers of its products, its shareholders, and the communities where its plants are situated. There are many possibilities, but identify three situations where the interests of two or more of these stakeholders might clash. Feel free to assume whatever facts are necessary to create such conflicting interests.

6. One particular problem discussed in this chapter negatively affects both the ability of markets to control corporate misconduct and the law's ability to control such misconduct. What is that problem? Which of the corporate control devices

discussed in this chapter is probably best equipped to address this problem?

7. Unknown to most Americans, the XYZ Corporation, which markets soft drinks, routinely bribes the officials of foreign nations in order to make sales there. Suppose that you are a critic of business who thinks that American firms' overseas bribery is clearly immoral. Which of the following corporate control techniques has the *best* (or least bad) chance of stopping XYZ's overseas bribery? The choices are: (1) market pressure from XYZ's American consumers, (2) XYZ's adoption of the stakeholder theory of corporate social responsibility, (3) giving greater power to XYZ's shareholders, and (4) legal penalties against American firms that engage in overseas bribery. Why are the three options you did *not* pick likely to be inadequate?

8. You are president and CEO of a small, publicly held company. Your national sales manager (and best friend), Frank Wilson, started out with you 20 years ago when you founded the company. His hard work, dedication, and good advice played a major role in your success. However, as a result of family problems and executive burnout, Frank has developed a drinking problem. At first, you tried to ignore Frank's problem, but by now other employees are clearly aware of it. In addition, you have lost some important accounts due to Frank's ineffectiveness. You've tried to gently discuss the matter with Frank, but he denies that he has a problem, and he is obviously hurt by the discussion. Your executive vice president has urged you to fire Frank, saying: "We can get a young comer in here who'll do a better job for half what we're paying that drunken bum." You know that this is true, and you know that Frank's behavior cannot be tolerated for much longer. But you also know that Frank will be personally and financially devastated if he is fired, and he will probably not be able to find another job. From a *utilitarian* perspective, what should you do?

9. You have recently been appointed CEO of Pureco Pharmaceutical Corporation. While being briefed on company operations by your vice president for sales, you ask him about the seemingly high volume of business the company is doing in the sale of amphetamines. The vice president reluctantly admits that about 70 percent of Pureco's amphetamine sales are made to small pharmacies in Mexico. When asked why Mexican pharmacies should purchase such high quantities of amphet-amines, the vice president says: "Well, I guess they buy them to resell in quantity." "You mean to drug dealers, don't you?" you respond. "Yeah, I guess so," he admits. "This means that a lot of this stuff is probably being smuggled back across the border and sold illegally in the U.S., doesn't it?" you ask. "Yeah, probably," he replies, "but let me set you straight on a few things before you get too critical. First, this is a *very* profitable line of business for us, and the last thing you probably want to do as a new CEO is to take action that will negatively affect earnings. Second, we are violating no U.S. or Mexican law when we make these sales. Third, every other major U.S. pharmaceutical firm does the same thing. Fourth, if we stopped tomorrow, that would simply encourage the entry of illicit suppliers who might put *anything* in their drugs. Finally, due to the high R&D costs in this industry, losing the profits from these sales could impair our ability to develop new drugs that could do a lot of good." Should Pureco continue the Mexican sales?

10. Virginia Parker, a new MBA, has recently been hired by the First Planetary Bank. She has received an overseas assignment as assistant direc-tor of lending in the bank's office in Chauvinaria. Virginia's boss, Thomas Paine, seems friendly and professional, and appears to go out of his way to make her feel welcome in her new position. During their first joint interview with an important local client, however, Tom treats Virginia in an obviously patronizing and demeaning manner, making her get coffee for the men and excluding her from their conversation. After the interview is over, Virginia angrily demands an explanation. Tom appears genu-inely surprised and says: "Gee, I'm sorry, but I thought you knew the score here. Chauvinarians just have these archaic attitudes toward women. In fact, we're taking a risk even bringing female managers out here. None of our competitors do, and we'd be committing suicide in a very lucrative market if the Chauvinarians perceived us as treating women like complete equals. Personally, I think their attitudes are nonsense, but business is business. 'When in Rome' and all that, you know." Assume that Tom is being honest about his reasons for treating Virginia as he did. Is Tom's position ethically justified?

CRIMES

AND

TORTS

CRIMES

INTRODUCTION

When one lists legal topics relevant to business, criminal law may come to mind less readily than contracts, torts, agency, corporations, and various other subjects dealt with in this text. Today, however, business owners (whether sole proprietors or corporate) and their employees are more likely than ever before to experience unpleasant contact with the criminal justice system. A working understanding of major criminal law concepts therefore has become essential to a manager's education.

THE CRIMINAL LAW

This century has witnessed society's increasing tendency to use the criminal law as a major device for controlling corporate behavior. Many regulatory statutes establish criminal and civil penalties for statutory violations. The criminal penalties often apply to individual employees as well as to their employers.

Advocates of using the criminal law in this way typically argue that doing so achieves a deterrence level superior to that produced by damage awards and other civil remedies. Corporations may be inclined to treat damage awards as simply a business cost and to violate regulatory provisions when doing so makes economic "sense." Criminal prosecutions, however, threaten corporations with the stigma of a criminal conviction. In some cases, the criminal law allows society to penalize corporate employees who would not be directly affected by a civil judgment against their employer. Moreover, by alerting private parties to a violation that could also give rise to a civil damage suit, criminal prosecutions may increase the likelihood that a corporation will bear the full costs of its actions.

Whatever the merit of these arguments, the threat of criminal prosecution plays an undeniable role in today's legal environment of business. Accordingly, this chapter begins by examining the nature and essential components of the criminal law. It then considers various problems encountered in applying the criminal law to the corporate setting.

Nature of Crime

Crimes are *public wrongs*—acts prohibited by the state or federal government. Criminal prosecutions are initiated by a prosecutor (an elected or appointed government employee) in the name of the state or the United States, whichever is appropriate. Persons convicted of crimes bear the *stigma* of a criminal conviction—the social condemnation resulting from being found guilty of a crime. Convicted offenders also face the uniquely coercive force of the *criminal sanction*, society's punishment of those who violate its most important rules. This punishment may be a fine, imprisonment, or, in extreme cases, execution.

Our legal system also contemplates noncriminal consequences for violations of legal duties. For example, the next two chapters deal with *torts*, private wrongs for which the wrongdoer must pay money damages to compensate the harmed "victim." In some tort cases, the court may also assess punitive damages in order to punish the wrongdoer. Only the criminal sanction, however, combines the threat to life or liberty with the stigma of conviction. This potent combination makes the criminal sanction "the law's ultimate threat."[1]

Crimes are typically classified as felonies or misdemeanors. A **felony** is a serious crime such as murder, rape, arson, illicit drug-dealing, or a theft offense of sufficient magnitude. Most felonies involve significant moral culpability on the offender's part. Felonies are punishable by lengthy confinement of the convicted offender to a penitentiary, as well as by a fine. A person convicted of a felony may experience other adverse consequences, such as *disenfranchisement* (loss of voting rights) and disqualification from the practice of certain professions (e.g., law or medicine). A **misdemeanor**, on the other hand, is a lesser offense such as disorderly conduct or battery resulting in minor physical harm to the victim. Misdemeanor offenses usually involve less—sometimes much less—moral culpability than felony offenses. As such, misdemeanors are punishable by lesser fines and/or limited confinement in jail. Depending on their seriousness and potential for harm to the public, traffic violations are classified either as misdemeanors or as less serious

infractions. Really only quasi-criminal, infractions usually are punishable by fines but not by confinement in jail.

It is a social question whether to classify a given act as criminal. As our social values have changed over time, so have our definitions of criminal conduct. Many observers argue that the criminal sanction should be reserved for behavior involving serious moral culpability. As this chapter will reveal, however, we have criminalized a wide variety of behavior that has very little moral content.

Purpose of the Criminal Sanction

Much of the disagreement about when the criminal sanction should be employed stems from a dispute over the criminal sanction's purpose. Persons accepting the *utilitarian* view of the criminal sanction believe that *prevention* of socially undesirable behavior is the only proper purpose of criminal penalties. This prevention goal includes three major components: deterrence, rehabilitation, and incapacitation.

Deterrence theorists hold that the threat or imposition of punishment deters the commission of crimes in two different ways. The first, *special deterrence*, occurs when punishment of a convicted offender deters him from committing further crimes. The second, *general deterrence*, results when punishment of a convicted wrongdoer deters other persons from committing a similar offense. Factors influencing the probable effectiveness of deterrence include the respective likelihoods that the crime will be detected, that detection will be followed by prosecution, and that prosecution will result in a conviction. The severity of the probable punishment (should there be a conviction) serves as another key factor. In economic terms, effective deterrence requires that the penalty imposed for an offense, discounted by the likelihood of apprehension and conviction, must equal or exceed the gains to the offender from committing the offense.

A fundamental problem attends deterrence theories: we cannot be certain whether deterrence works because we can never know what the crime rate would be in the absence of punishment. For example, high levels of crime and *recidivism* (repeat offenses by previously punished offenders) may indicate only that sufficiently severe and certain criminal sanctions have not been employed, not that

---

[1] H. Packer, *The Limits of the Criminal Sanction,* 250 (Stanford, Calif.: Stanford University Press, 1968).

FIGURE 1   **A Note on State and Federal Approaches to Sentencing of Convicted Offenders**

As a general rule, state laws on criminal punishments seek to further the deterrence, rehabilitation, and incapacitation purposes discussed in the text. State statutes usually set forth ranges of sentences (e.g., minimum and maximum amounts of fines and imprisonment) for each crime established by law. The court sets the convicted offender's sentence within the appropriate range unless the court places the defendant on probation.

Probation is effectively a conditional sentence that suspends the usual imprisonment and/or fine if the offender "toes the line" and meets other judicially imposed conditions for the period specified by the court. It is sometimes granted to first-time offenders and other convicted defendants deemed suitable candidates by the court. In deciding whether to order probation or what is the appropriate sentence within the statutory range, the court normally places considerable reliance on a presentence investigation conducted by the state probation office. Relevant information revealed in this investigation, coupled with evidence of the offender's prior criminal history, will influence the court in deciding at what point within the statutory range a particular offender's punishment should fall.

The federal approach to sentencing was essentially the same until very recent years, when the Federal Sentencing Guidelines set by the U.S. Sentencing Commission took effect. In the Sentencing Reform Act of 1984, Congress created the Sentencing Commission and authorized it to develop sentencing guidelines. Congress thereby sought to reduce judicial discretion in sentencing and to minimize disparities among sentences imposed by judges on similar offenders. The Sentencing Guidelines, which are binding on federal courts and have been criticized by some judges, contain a table with more than 40 levels of seriousness of offense. Where a particular offender's crime and corresponding sentence are listed on the table depends on various factors associated with the offense and on the offender's prior criminal history. The court normally must sentence the defendant to what the table shows, although departures are allowed in the event of exceptional circumstances specified by the court.

For various crimes, the Federal Sentencing Guidelines appear to have led to the imposition of more severe—sometimes much more severe—sentences than had previously been the case. Although the prospect of probation for certain offenses still exists, an increased use of incarceration of individuals convicted of serious offenses also appears to have resulted from the Sentencing Guidelines. As for what purposes incarceration should serve, the Sentencing Reform Act specifically rejected rehabilitation as one of them. Instead, the statute stated that the goals of punishment should be education, deterrence, and incapacitation.

---

criminal sanctions in general cannot effectively deter. Deterrence theory's other major problem is its assumption that potential offenders are rational beings who consciously weigh the threat of punishment against the benefits derived from an offense. The threat of punishment, however, may not deter the commission of criminal offenses produced by irrational or unconscious drives.

Rehabilitation of convicted offenders—changing their attitudes or values so that they are not inclined to commit future offenses—serves as another way to prevent undesirable behavior. Critics of rehabilitation commonly point to high rates of recidivism as evidence of the general failure of rehabilitation efforts to date. Even if rehabilitation efforts fail, however, *incapacitation* of convicted offenders results from their incarceration and thus contributes to the goal of prevention. While imprisoned, offenders have much less ability to commit other crimes.

Prevention is not the only goal advanced for the criminal sanction. Some persons see *retribution*—the infliction of deserved suffering on violators of

society's most fundamental rules—as the central focus of criminal punishment. Under this theory, punishment satisfies community and individual desires for revenge, and reinforces important social values. A retributionist therefore is unlikely to see prevention as a sufficient reason to criminalize socially undesirable but morally neutral behavior. When serious moral culpability is present, however, a retributionist is likely to favor punishment even if convinced that punishment would not prevent future offenses.

Figure 1 contains a general discussion of how state and federal law approach the proper determination of a convicted offender's punishment.

Essentials of Crime

To convict a defendant of a crime, the state ordinarily must: (1) demonstrate that his alleged acts violated a criminal statute; (2) prove beyond a reasonable doubt that he committed those acts; and (3) prove that he had the capacity to form a criminal intent.

Prior Statutory Prohibition Crimes are *statutory* offenses. A given behavior is not a crime unless Congress or a state legislature has criminalized it.[2] The U.S. Constitution prohibits *ex post facto* criminal laws. This means that a defendant's act must have been prohibited by statute at the time she committed it and that the penalty imposed must be the one provided for at the time of her offense.

The Constitution places other limits on legislative power to criminalize behavior. If behavior is constitutionally protected, it cannot be deemed criminal. For example, the right of privacy held implicit in the Constitution caused the Supreme Court, in *Griswold v. Connecticut,* to strike down state statutes that prohibited the use of contraceptive devices and the counseling or assisting of others in the use of such devices.[3] This decision provided the constitutional basis for the Court's historic *Roe v. Wade* decision, which limited the states' power to criminalize abortions.[4]

By prohibiting laws that unreasonably restrict freedom of expression, the First Amendment to the Constitution also plays a major role in limiting legislative power to criminalize behavior. Legislative attempts to hold persons criminally liable for the content of their written or spoken statements are usually suspect under the First Amendment. Various times during the past several years, the Supreme Court has considered the extent to which so-called expressive conduct—an action that expresses a point of view or message regardless of whether written or spoken words accompany the action—merits First Amendment protection against government attempts to criminalize it. Figure 2 contains a discussion of the Court's recent expressive conduct decisions.

Besides limiting the sorts of behavior that may be made criminal, the Constitution limits the manner in which behavior may be criminalized. The Due Process Clauses of the Fifth and Fourteenth Amendments require that criminal statutes define the prohibited behavior precisely enough that an ordinary person can understand which behavior violates the law.[5] Statutes that fail to provide such fair notice may be challenged as unconstitutionally vague. The Fourteenth Amendment's Equal Protection Clause[6] prohibits criminal statutes that discriminatorily treat certain persons of the same class or arbitrarily discriminate among different classes of persons.[7] Legislatures usually are extended considerable latitude in making statutory classifications if the classifications have a rational basis. "Suspect" classifications, such as those based on race, are subjected to much closer judicial scrutiny, however.

Finally, the Constitution limits the type of punishment imposed on convicted offenders. The Eighth Amendment forbids "cruel and unusual punishments." This prohibition furnishes, for example, the constitutional basis for judicial decisions establishing limits on the imposition of the death penalty.[8] Although various Supreme Court cases indicate that the Eighth Amendment may bar a sentence whose harshness is disproportionate to the seriousness of the defendant's offense, the Court recently signaled that any Eighth Amendment concerns along these lines are unlikely to be triggered unless the sentence-crime disproportionality is exceedingly gross.[9] In another recent decision revealing a different potential application of the guarantee against cruel and unusual punishment, the Court held that the Eighth Amendment may sometimes be implicated by prison officials' confinement of a nonsmoking inmate in the same cell with an inmate who smokes heavily and thereby exposes the nonsmoker to the potentially harmful effects of secondhand smoke.[10]

[2]Infractions of a minor criminal or quasi-criminal nature (such as traffic offenses) are often established by city or county ordinances but will not be considered here. For discussion of ordinances as a type of law, see Chapter 1.

[3]381 U.S. 479 (U.S. Sup. Ct. 1965).

[4]410 U.S. 113 (U.S. Sup. Ct. 1973).

[5]Chapter 3 discusses due process in greater detail.

[6]Chapter 3 discusses equal protection in greater detail.

[7]For an example, see *McLaughlin v. Florida,* 379 U.S. 1984 (U.S. Sup. Ct. 1964), where the Court struck down a Florida statute forbidding cohabitation between black males and white females on the ground that no valid statutory purpose justified prohibiting only interracial cohabitation.

[8]See, for example, *Thompson v. Oklahoma,* 487 U.S. 815 (U.S. Sup. Ct. 1988), where the Court held that the Eighth Amendment bars the execution of a defendant who was under 16 years of age at the time of his offense.

[9]See *Harmelin v. Michigan,* 111 S. Ct. 2680 (U.S. Sup. Ct. 1991), where the Court upheld, against an Eighth Amendment–based attack, a statutorily mandated sentence of life imprisonment without parole for persons convicted of possessing 650 or more grams of cocaine.

[10]*Helling v. McKinney,* 113 S. Ct. 2475 (U.S. Sup. Ct. 1993).

FIGURE 2   Recent Supreme Court Decisions Exploring First Amendment Limits on Legislative Power to Criminalize Expressive Conduct

In the controversial case of *Texas v. Johnson,* 491 U.S. 397 (U.S. Sup. Ct. 1989), the Court held that Gregory Johnson's burning an American flag during a protest demonstration was protected expressive conduct. The Court reasoned that regardless of the presence or absence of spoken or written words, certain conduct such as flag-burning may be "sufficiently imbued with elements of communication" to come under the First Amendment umbrella. In view of the considerable First Amendment protection extended to political speech—to which Johnson's expressive conduct surely was equivalent—Johnson could not constitutionally be convicted of violating a Texas statute that prohibited the "desecration of a venerated object." A year later, in *U.S. v. Eichman,* 496 U.S. 310 (U.S. Sup. Ct. 1990), the Court used the *Johnson* rationale to strike down a federal statute that criminalized flag-burning.

As if the flag-burning decisions somehow were not "hot" enough, the Court's expressive conduct focus then turned to nonobscene nude dancing. In *Barnes v. Glen Theatre, Inc.,* 111 S. Ct. 2456 (U.S. Sup. Ct. 1991), the Court noted that such dancing is expressive conduct "marginally" within the First Amendment's protective scope. Nevertheless, in a plurality decision that did not produce a controlling rationale, the Court concluded that the First Amendment was not violated by Indiana's application of a public indecency statute to nude dancing.

R.A.V. v. City of St. Paul, 112 S. Ct. 2538 (U.S. Sup. Ct. 1992) was a different story, however. There, the Court considered the city's hate-crimes ordinance, which prohibited placing on public or private property "a burning cross" or other symbol "which one knows or has reasonable grounds to know arouses anger, alarm or resentment in others on the basis of race, color, creed, religion or gender." The Court held that the ordinance was an impermissible content-based and viewpoint-based restriction on expressive conduct. The First Amendment thus protected the cross-burning defendants from being convicted of violating the ordinance, even though their behavior was, as the Court acknowledged, "reprehensible."

Although some observers assumed that *R.A.V.* would dictate a similar outcome in *Wisconsin v. Mitchell,* 113 S. Ct. 2766 (U.S. Sup. Ct. 1993), it did not. Mitchell was convicted of aggravated battery for severely beating a child. On the basis of a Wisconsin statute that authorized the imposition of an enhanced maximum penalty when the offender selected his victim on the basis of the victim's race, Mitchell received a stiffer sentence than otherwise would have been allowed under the law. Rejecting Mitchell's argument that *R.A.V.* controlled and that the enhanced penalty he received was an unconstitutional criminalization of thought and expression, the Court upheld the imposition of the greater sentence. It distinguished *R.A.V.* by observing that the ordinance at issue there was obviously directed at expression, whereas the Wisconsin penalty-enhancement statute under which Mitchell was sentenced was nothing more than a permissible regulation of nonexpressive conduct.

Proof Beyond a Reasonable Doubt   The serious matters at stake in a criminal case—the life and liberty of the accused—justify our legal system's placement of significant limits on the government's power to convict a person of a crime. One of the most fundamental safeguards is the presumption of innocence; defendants in criminal cases are presumed innocent until proven guilty. The Due Process Clauses require the government to overcome this presumption by proving beyond a reasonable doubt every element of the offense charged against the defendant.[11] Requiring the government to meet this stern burden of proof minimizes the risk of

erroneous criminal convictions. It also reflects a strong belief shared by all common law jurisdictions about the proper way to enforce laws and administer justice.

Defendant's Criminal Intent and Capacity
Most serious crimes require *mens rea,* or criminal intent, as an element. The level of fault required for a given criminal violation depends on the wording of the statute in question. Many criminal statutes require proof of intentional wrongdoing. Others impose liability for reckless conduct or sometimes mere negligence. In the criminal context, recklessness generally means that the accused consciously disregarded a substantial risk that the harm prohibited by the statute would result from her actions. Negligence, in criminal cases, means that the accused failed to perceive a substantial risk of harm that a reasonable person would have perceived.

---

[11]The beyond a reasonable doubt standard required of the government in criminal cases contemplates a stronger and more convincing showing than that required of plaintiffs in civil cases. As explained in Chapter 2, plaintiffs in civil cases need only prove the elements of their claims by a preponderance of the evidence.

Criminal intent may be inferred from an accused's behavior, because a person is normally held to have intended the natural and probable consequences of her acts. The criminal intent requirement furthers the criminal law's general goal of punishing conscious wrongdoers. Accordingly, proof that the defendant had the capacity to form the required intent is a traditional prerequisite of criminal responsibility. The criminal law recognizes three general types of incapacity: *intoxication, infancy,* and *insanity.*

Voluntary intoxication, although not a complete defense to criminal liability, may sometimes diminish the degree of a defendant's liability. This is so because a highly intoxicated person may be incapable of forming the specific criminal intent required for certain crimes. For example, many first-degree murder statutes require proof of *premeditation,* a conscious decision to kill. One who kills while highly intoxicated may be incapable of premeditation—meaning that he would not be guilty of first-degree murder. He may be convicted, however, of another homicide offense that does not require proof of premeditation. Involuntary intoxication may be a complete defense to criminal liability.

The common law usually presumed that children younger than 14 years of age could not form a criminal intent. Today, most states treat juvenile offenders below a certain statutory age (usually 16 or 17) differently from adult offenders, with special juvenile court systems and separate detention facilities. Current juvenile law emphasizes rehabilitation rather than capacity issues. Repeat offenders or offenders charged with very serious offenses, however, may sometimes be treated as adults.

A criminal defendant's insanity may affect a criminal prosecution in various ways. Insanity rendering a defendant incapable of assisting in her defense will delay her trial until she regains sanity. Insanity manifesting itself after conviction, but before sentencing, can delay sentencing until sanity returns. If a condemned prisoner becomes insane while awaiting execution, the Eighth Amendment's prohibition of cruel and unusual punishment serves to bar the execution.[12]

In addition, an accused's insanity at the time the charged act was committed may constitute a complete defense to liability. This possible effect of insanity has generated expressions of public dissatisfaction with the insanity defense, as well as disagreements over the proper basis on which to determine insanity. Courts have adopted various insanity tests in an effort to achieve consistency with the goal of punishing conscious wrongdoers.[13]

The primary common law test for insanity is the *M'Naghten* rule: A criminal defendant is not responsible if, at the time of the offense, he did not know the nature and quality of his act, or, if he did know this, he did not know his act was wrong.[14] Some states have replaced or supplemented this test with the *irresistible impulse* rule, which absolves a defendant of responsibility if mental disease rendered her incapable of controlling her behavior and resisting the impulse to commit a crime. Many jurisdictions apply the American Law Institute's insanity test. Under this test, a defendant is not responsible if, at the time the act was committed, mental disease or defect caused him to lack the substantial capacity to appreciate the wrongfulness of his act or to conform his conduct to the law's requirements.

Public reaction to highly publicized cases in which insanity defenses were raised, however, has spurred two significant trends in recent years. One is a tendency to return to the narrower *M'Naghten* standard or something closely resembling it. Congress took such action in the Comprehensive Crime Control Act of 1984, which provides the insanity standard applicable in federal criminal cases. The other recent trend is the creation of procedural rules that make it more difficult for defendants to succeed with an insanity defense. Criminal defendants are presumed to be sane. Traditionally, once an accused introduced evidence tending to prove insanity, the government was expected to prove her sanity beyond a reasonable doubt. Today, however, many states and the federal government treat insanity as an affirmative defense under which the defendant bears the burden of proving insanity. In addition, some states have instituted a "guilty, but mentally ill" verdict as an alternative to the traditional "not guilty by reason of insanity" verdict. This alterna-

---

[12]*Ford v. Wainwright,* 477 U.S. 399 (U.S. Sup. Ct. 1986).

[13]These tests are *legal* tests, not medical tests. A defendant who was medically insane at the time of the criminal act may still be legally responsible.

[14]This rule is derived from *Daniel M'Naghten's Case,* 8 Eng. Reprint 718 (House of Lords 1843).

FIGURE 3	**Essentials of Crime Checklist**

- Did the accused violate an existing statute?

- Is the statute constitutionally valid?
Does it prohibit constitutionally protected behavior?
Does it clearly define the prohibited behavior?

- Did the accused have the required criminal intent?
Did he have the capacity to form the required intent?
Can the necessary level of intent be inferred from his actions?

- Did the state prove each element of the crime beyond a reasonable doubt?

tive allows jurors to convict (rather than acquit) mentally ill defendants, with the assurance that they will receive postconviction treatment.

Figure 3 summarizes the essential components of criminal liability under our legal system.

CRIMINAL PROCEDURE

Criminal Prosecutions

Persons arrested for allegedly committing a crime are taken to the police station and booked. **Booking** is an administrative procedure for recording the suspect's arrest and the alleged offenses involved. In some states, temporary release on bail may be available at this stage. After booking, the police file an arrest report with the prosecutor, who decides whether to charge the suspect with an offense. If she decides to prosecute, the prosecutor prepares a complaint identifying the accused and detailing the charges. Most states require that arrested suspects be taken promptly before a magistrate or other judicial officer (such as a justice of the peace or judge whose court is of limited jurisdiction) for an **initial appearance**. During this appearance, the magistrate informs the accused of the charges against him and outlines the accused's constitutional rights. In misdemeanor cases in which the accused pleads guilty, the sentence may be (but need not be) imposed without a later hearing. If the accused pleads not guilty to the misdemeanor charge, the case is set for trial. In felony cases, as well as misdemeanor cases in which the accused pleads not guilty, the magistrate sets the amount of bail.

In many states, defendants in felony cases are protected against unjustified prosecutions by an additional procedural step, the **preliminary hearing**. The prosecutor must introduce enough evidence at this hearing to persuade a magistrate that there is **probable cause** to believe the accused committed a felony.[15] If persuaded that probable cause exists, the magistrate binds over the defendant for trial in the appropriate court.

After a bindover, the formal charge against the defendant is filed with the trial court. The formal charge consists of either an **information** filed by the prosecutor or an **indictment** returned by a grand jury. Roughly half of the states require that a grand jury approve the decision to prosecute a person for a felony. Grand juries are bodies of citizens selected in the same manner as the members of a trial (petit) jury; often, they are chosen through random drawings from a list of registered voters. Grand juries traditionally included 23 members, with a majority vote being necessary for an indictment. Today, many states have reduced the size of the grand jury. There is also significant variation in the number of votes required for an indictment. Indictment of an accused prior to a preliminary hearing normally eliminates the need for a preliminary hearing because the indictment serves essentially the same function as a magistrate's probable cause determination.

The remainder of the states allow felony defendants to be charged by either indictment or information, at the prosecutor's discretion. An **information** is a formal charge signed by the prosecutor outlining the facts supporting the charges against the defendant. In states allowing felony prosecution by information, prosecutors elect the information method in the vast majority of felony cases. Misdemeanor cases are prosecuted by information in virtually all states.[16]

Once an information or indictment has been filed with a trial court, an *arraignment* occurs. The defendant is brought before the court, informed of

---

[15]The state need not satisfy the beyond a reasonable doubt standard of proof at the preliminary hearing stage. The prosecutor sufficiently establishes probable cause by causing the magistrate to believe it is more likely than not that the defendant committed the felony alleged.

[16]As for federal crimes, a prosecutor in the relevant U.S. Attorney's office files an information to institute the case if the offense involved carries a penalty of not more than one year of imprisonment. Federal prosecutions for more serious crimes with potentially more severe penalties are commenced by means of a grand jury indictment.

the charges, and asked to enter a plea. The defendant may plead guilty, not guilty, or nolo contendere. Although technically not an admission of guilt, nolo contendere pleas indicate that the defendant does not contest the charges. This decision by the defendant will lead to a finding of guilt. Unlike evidence of a guilty plea, however, evidence of a defendant's nolo plea is inadmissible in later civil suits against that defendant based on the same conduct amounting to the criminal violation. Individuals and corporate defendants therefore may find nolo pleas attractive when their chances of mounting a successful defense to the criminal prosecution are poor and the prospect of later civil suits is likely.

At or shortly after the arraignment, the defendant who pleads not guilty chooses the type of trial that will take place. Persons accused of serious crimes for which incarceration for more than six months is possible have a constitutional right to be tried by a jury of their peers. The accused, however, generally may waive this right and opt for a bench trial (i.e., before a judge only).

Constitutional Safeguards

The preceding pages referred to several procedural devices designed to protect persons accused of crime. The Bill of Rights, which consists of the first 10 amendments to the U.S. Constitution, sets forth other rights of criminal defendants. These rights guard against unjustified or erroneous criminal convictions and serve as reminders of government's proper role in the administration of justice in a democratic society. Justice Oliver Wendell Holmes aptly addressed this latter point when he said, "I think it less evil that some criminals should escape than that the government should play an ignoble part." Although the specific language of the Bill of Rights refers only to federal government actions, the U.S. Supreme Court has applied the most important Bill of Rights guarantees to state government actions by "selectively incorporating" those guarantees into the Fourteenth Amendment's Due Process Clause. Once a particular safeguard has been found to be "implicit in the concept of ordered liberty" or "fundamental to the American scheme of justice," it has been applied equally in state and federal criminal trials. This has occurred with the constitutional protections examined earlier in this chapter as well as with the Fourth, Fifth, and Sixth Amendment guarantees discussed in the following pages.

The Fourth Amendment   The Fourth Amendment protects persons against arbitrary and unreasonable governmental violations of their privacy rights. It states:

The right of the people to be secure in their persons, houses, papers, and effects, against unreasonable searches and seizures, shall not be violated, and no Warrants shall issue, but upon probable cause, supported by Oath or affirmation, and particularly describing the place to be searched, and the persons or things to be seized.

Both the language of the amendment and the judicial interpretations it has generated reflect the difficulties inherent in properly balancing citizens' legitimate expectations of privacy and government's legitimate interest in securing evidence of wrongdoing. Citizens are not protected against all searches and seizures—only against unreasonable ones. Because the Fourth Amendment safeguards reasonable privacy expectations, the Supreme Court has extended the amendment's protection to such places or items as private dwellings and immediately surrounding areas (often called the *curtilage*), telephone booths, sealed containers, and first-class mail. The Court has denied protection to places, items, or matters as to which it found no reasonable expectations of privacy, such as open fields, personal bank records, and voluntary conversations between criminal defendants and government informants.

Even when plainly protected areas or items are involved, not every governmental action is deemed sufficiently intrusive to constitute a search or seizure for Fourth Amendment purposes. Thus, for example, the Court held that exposing an airline traveler's luggage to a narcotics detection dog in a public place was not a search, considering the minimally intrusive nature of the intrusion and the narrow scope of information it revealed.[17] No seizure occurred, according to the Court in *Florida v. Bostick,* when police boarded a bus at a regular stop and asked a passenger for permission to search his luggage.[18] In the *Dow Chemical* case, which follows shortly, the Court refused to hold that aerial photographs of an industrial complex violated the Fourth Amendment.

---

[17]*United States v. Place,* 426 U.S. 696 (U.S. Sup. Ct. 1983). In this case, however, the Court also held that the warrantless detention of the defendant's luggage for 90 minutes was unlawful, given the fact that the agents in question had several hours' advance notice of the defendant's arrival.

[18]111 S. Ct. 2382 (1991).

In its treatment of the Fourth Amendment's Warrant Clause, the Supreme Court has engaged in similar balancing of individual and governmental interests. The warrant requirement further protects privacy interests by mandating that a judge or magistrate authorize and define the scope of intrusive governmental action. As a general rule, the Court has held that searches carried out without a proper warrant are unreasonable. Nonetheless, the Court has upheld warrantless searches of the area within the immediate control of an arrestee, of premises police enter in hot pursuit of an armed suspect, and of automobiles and containers located therein under certain circumstances (due to automo-

biles' mobile nature). Warrantless seizures of contraband items in the plain view of officers acting lawfully have likewise been upheld. The Court has also authorized customs searches, stop-and-frisk searches for weapons, inventory searches of property in an arrestee's possession, and consensual searches, despite the absence of a warrant in each of these instances. Finally, the Court has upheld warrantless administrative inspections of closely regulated businesses.[19]

---

[19]See, e.g., *New York v. Burger,* 482 U.S. 691 (U.S. Sup. Ct. 1987).

DOW CHEMICAL CO. V. UNITED STATES
476 U.S. 227 (U.S. Sup. Ct. 1986)

Dow Chemical Company operates a 2,000-acre chemical manufacturing facility at Midland, Michigan. The facility consists of numerous covered buildings, with manufacturing equipment and piping conduits between various buildings plainly visible from the air. At all times, Dow maintained elaborate security around the perimeter of the complex barring ground-level public views of these areas. It also investigated any low-level flights by aircraft over the facility. Dow did not, however, attempt to conceal all manufacturing equipment within the complex from aerial views because the cost was prohibitive.

In early 1978, enforcement officials of the Environmental Protection Agency (EPA) made an on-site inspection of two power plants in this complex with Dow's consent. When a subsequent request for a second inspection was denied, EPA did not thereafter seek an administrative search warrant. Instead, EPA employed a commercial aerial photographer, using a standard floor-mounted, precision aerial mapping camera to take photographs of the facility from altitudes of 12,000, 3,000, and 1,200 feet. At all times, the aircraft was lawfully within navigable airspace.

EPA did not inform Dow of this aerial photography. When Dow became aware of it, the company brought suit, alleging that EPA's action violated the Fourth Amendment. In granting Dow's motion for summary judgment, the District Court permanently enjoined EPA from taking aerial photographs of Dow's premises and from disseminating, releasing, or copying the photos already taken. When the Sixth Circuit Court of Appeals reversed, Dow appealed.

Burger, Chief Justice   Dow claims that the EPA's use of aerial photography was a "search" of an area that was within an "industrial curtilage" rather than an "open field," and that it had a reasonable expectation of privacy from such photography protected by the Fourth Amendment. In making this contention, however, Dow concedes that a simple flyover with naked-eye observation, or the taking of a photograph from a nearby hillside

overlooking such a facility, would give rise to no Fourth Amendment problem.

In *California v. Ciraolo,* decided today, we hold that naked-eye aerial observation from an altitude of 1,000 feet of a backyard within the curtilage of a home does not constitute a search under the Fourth Amendment. The curtilage area immediately surrounding a private house has long been given protection as a place where the occupants have a reasonable and legitimate expectation of privacy that society is prepared to accept.

As the curtilage doctrine evolved to protect much the same kind of privacy as that covering the interior of a structure, the contrasting "open fields" doctrine evolved as well. From *Hester v. United States* (1924) to *Oliver v. United States* (1984), the Court has drawn a line as to what expectations are reasonable in the open areas beyond the curtilage of a dwelling; open fields do not provide the setting for those intimate activities that the Fourth Amendment is intended to shelter from governmental interference or surveillance. In *Oliver,* we held that "an individual may not legitimately demand privacy for activities out of doors in fields, except in the area immediately surrounding the home." To fall within the open fields doctrine, the area need be neither "open" nor a "field" as those terms are used in common speech.

Dow plainly has a reasonable, legitimate, and objective expectation of privacy within the interior of its covered buildings. Moreover, it could hardly be expected that Dow would erect a huge cover over a 2,000-acre tract. Dow argues that its exposed manufacturing facilities are analogous to the curtilage surrounding a home because it has taken every possible step to bar access from ground level. In *Oliver,* the Court described the curtilage of a dwelling as "the area to which extends the intimate activity associated with the sanctity of a man's home and the privacies of life." The intimate activities associated with family privacy and the home and its curtilage simply do not reach the outdoor areas of spaces between structures and buildings of a manufacturing plant.

Admittedly, Dow's enclosed plant complex does not fall precisely within the "open fields" doctrine. The area at issue here can perhaps be seen as falling somewhere between "open fields" and curtilage, but lacking some of the critical characteristics of both. Dow's inner manufacturing areas are elaborately secured to ensure they are not open or exposed to the public from the ground. Any actual physical entry by EPA into any enclosed area would raise significantly different questions, because the businessman, like the occupant of a residence, has a constitutional right to go about his business free from unreasonable official entries upon his private commercial property. The narrow issue raised by Dow's claim of search and seizure, however, concerns aerial observation of a 2,000-acre outdoor manufacturing facility without physical entry. The Government has greater latitude to conduct warrantless inspections of commercial property because the expectation of privacy that the owner of commercial property enjoys in such property differs significantly from the sanctity accorded an individual's home. Unlike a homeowner's interest in his dwelling, the interest of the owner of commercial property is not one in being free from any inspections. With regard to regulatory inspections, we have held that what is observable by the public is observable without a warrant, by the Government inspector as well.

Oliver recognized that in the open field context, "the public and police lawfully may survey lands from the air." Here, the EPA was not employing some unique sensory device that, for example, could penetrate the walls of buildings and record conversations in Dow's plants, offices, or laboratories, but rather a conventional, albeit precise, commercial camera commonly used in mapmaking. The Government asserts it has not yet enlarged the photographs to any significant degree, but Dow points out that simple magnification permits identification of objects such as wires as small as one-half inch diameter. It may well be that surveillance of private property by using highly sophisticated surveillance equipment not generally available to the public, such as satellite technology, might be constitutionally proscribed absent a warrant. But the photographs here are not so revealing of intimate details as to raise constitutional concerns. The mere fact that human vision is enhanced somewhat, at least to the degree here, does not give rise to constitutional problems.

We conclude that the open areas of an industrial plant complex with numerous plant structures spread over an area of 2,000 acres are not analogous to the curtilage of a dwelling for purposes of aerial surveillance; such an industrial complex is more comparable to an open field and as such it is open to the view and observation of persons in aircraft lawfully in the public airspace immediately above or sufficiently near the area for the reach of cameras.

We hold that the taking of aerial photographs of an industrial plant complex from navigable airspace is not a search prohibited by the Fourth Amendment.

Judgment for the EPA affirmed.

The exclusionary rule serves as the basic remedial device in cases of Fourth Amendment violations. Under this judicially crafted rule, evidence seized in illegal searches cannot be used in a subsequent trial against an accused whose constitutional rights were violated.[20] Because the exclusionary rule may result in suppression of convincing evidence of crime, it has generated considerable controversy. The rule's supporters regard it as necessary to deter police from violating citizens' constitutional rights. The rule's opponents assert that it has no deterrent effect on police who believed they were acting lawfully. A loudly voiced complaint in some quarters has been that "because of a policeman's error, a criminal goes free."

In recent years, the Court has responded to such criticism by rendering decisions restricting the operation of the exclusionary rule. For example, in *Nix v. Williams,* the Court held that illegally obtained evidence may be introduced at trial if the prosecution convinces the trial judge that the evidence would inevitably have been obtained anyway by lawful means.[21] In *United States v. Leon,* the Court created a "good faith" exception to the exclusionary rule. This exception allows the use of evidence seized by police officers who acted pursuant to a search warrant later held invalid if the officers reasonably believed that the warrant was valid.[22] Although the Court has not extended the good faith exception to the warrantless search setting, it did expand the exception's scope to include searches made in reliance on a statute that is later declared invalid.[23]

The Fifth Amendment   The Fifth Amendment's Due Process Clause guarantees basic procedural and substantive fairness to criminal defendants. In another significant provision, the Fifth Amendment protects against *compelled testimonial self-incrimination* by establishing that "[n]o person . . . shall be compelled in any criminal case to be a witness against himself." This provision prevents the government from coercing a defendant into making incriminating statements and thereby assisting in his own prosecution.

In *Miranda v. Arizona,* the Supreme Court established procedural requirements—the now-familiar *Miranda* warnings—to safeguard this Fifth Amendment right and other constitutional guarantees. The Court did so by requiring police to inform criminal suspects, before commencing custodial interrogation of them, that they have the right to remain silent, that any statements they make may be used as evidence against them, and that they have the right to the presence and assistance of a retained or court-appointed attorney (with court appointment occurring when suspects lack the financial ability to retain counsel).[24] Incriminating statements that the accused makes without first having been given the *Miranda* warnings are inadmissible at trial. If the suspect invokes her right to silence, custodial interrogation must cease. If, on the other hand, the suspect knowingly and voluntarily waives her right to silence after being given the *Miranda* warnings, her statements will be admissible.

The right to silence is limited, however, in various ways. For example, the traditional view that the Fifth Amendment applies only to *testimonial* admissions serves as the basis for allowing the police to compel an accused to furnish nontestimonial evidence such as fingerprints, samples of body fluids, and hair. Recent Supreme Court decisions have recognized further significant limitations on the right to silence. For instance, a longstanding view holds that the right includes a corresponding implicit prohibition of prosecutorial comments at trial about the accused's failure to speak in his own defense. Although Supreme Court decisions still support this prohibition as a general rule, the Court has sometimes allowed prosecutors to use the defendant's pretrial silence to impeach his trial testimony. For example, the Court has held that the Fifth Amendment is not violated by prosecutorial use of a defendant's silence (either prearrest or postarrest, but in advance of any *Miranda* warnings) to discredit his trial testimony that he killed the victim in self-defense.[25]

---

[20]The Supreme Court initially authorized application of the exclusionary rule in federal criminal cases only. In *Mapp v. Ohio,* 367 U.S. 643 (U.S. Sup. Ct. 1961), the Court made the exclusionary rule applicable to state criminal cases as well.

[21]467 U.S. 431 (U.S. Sup. Ct. 1984).

[22]468 U.S. 897 (U.S. Sup. Ct. 1984).

[23]*Illinois v. Krull,* 480 U.S. 340 (U.S. Sup. Ct. 1987).

[24]384 U.S. 436 (U.S. Sup. Ct. 1966). The portions of the *Miranda* warnings dealing with the right to an attorney further Sixth Amendment interests. The Sixth Amendment is discussed later in this chapter.

[25]*Fletcher v. Weir,* 455 U.S. 603 (U.S. Sup. Ct. 1982); *Jenkins v. Anderson,* 447 U.S. 231 (U.S. Sup. Ct. 1980).

A similar inclination to narrow *Miranda*'s applicability and effect has also been displayed by the Supreme Court during the past decade. In *Moran v. Burbine,* for instance, the Court upheld a suspect's waiver of his *Miranda* rights and approved the use of his confession at trial, despite the police's failure to notify the suspect that an attorney retained for him by a family member was seeking to contact him.[26] As another example, *Illinois v. Perkins* established that an undercover police officer posing as a fellow inmate need not give a jailed suspect the *Miranda* warnings before asking questions that could lead to incriminating admissions.[27]

The preceding discussion of the privilege against self-incrimination applies to criminal defendants in general. The Fifth Amendment's scope, however, has long been of particular concern to businesspersons charged with crimes. Documentary evidence often is quite important to the government's case in many white-collar crime prosecutions. To what extent does the Fifth Amendment protect business records? More than a century ago, the Supreme Court held, in *Boyd v. United States,* that the Fifth Amendment protects individuals against compelled production of their private papers.[28]

In more recent years, however, the Court has drastically limited the scope of the protection contemplated by *Boyd.* The Court has held various times that the private papers privilege is personal and thus cannot be asserted by a corporation, partnership, or other "collective entity." Because such entities have no Fifth Amendment rights, the Court has held, moreover, that when an organization's individual officer or agent has custody of organization records, the officer or agent cannot assert any personal privilege to prevent their disclosure. This rule holds even if the contents of the records incriminate her personally. Finally, various decisions allow the government to require business proprietors to keep certain records relevant to transactions that are appropriate subjects for government regulation. These "required records" are not entitled to private papers protection. They may be subpoenaed and used against the record-keeper in prosecutions for regulatory violations.

The Court's most recent business records decisions cast further doubt on the future of the private papers doctrine. Instead of focusing on whether subpoenaed records are private in nature, the Court now considers whether the *act of producing* the records would be sufficiently testimonial to trigger the privilege against self-incrimination. In *Fisher v. United States,* the Court held that an individual subpoenaed to produce personal documents may assert his Fifth Amendment privilege only if the act of producing the documents would involve incriminating testimonial admissions.[29] This is likely when the individual producing the records is in effect certifying the records' authenticity or admitting the existence of records previously unknown to the government (demonstrating that she had access to the records and, therefore, possible knowledge of any incriminating contents).

In *United States v. Doe,* the Court extended the act-of-production privilege to a sole proprietor whose proprietorship records were subpoenaed.[30] The Court, however, held that normal business records were not themselves protected by the Fifth Amendment because they were voluntarily prepared and thus not the product of compulsion. In view of *Doe*'s emphasis on the testimonial and potentially incriminating nature of the act of producing business records, some observers thought that officers of collective entities under government investigation might be able to assert their personal privileges against self-incrimination as a way to avoid producing incriminating business records. *Braswell v. United States,* however, dashed such hopes, as the Court refused to extend its *Doe* holding to cover a corporation's sole shareholder who acted in his capacity as custodian of corporate records.[31] The Court held that Braswell (the sole shareholder), having chosen to operate his business under the corporate form, was bound by the rule that corporations and similar entities have no Fifth Amendment privilege. Because Braswell acted in a representative capacity in producing the requested records, the government could not make evidentiary use of his act of production. The government, however, was free to use the contents of the records against Braswell and the corporation.

[26]475 U.S. 412 (U.S. Sup. Ct. 1986).

[27]496 U.S. 292 (U.S. Sup. Ct. 1990).

[28]116 U.S. 616 (U.S. Sup. Ct. 1886).

[29]425 U.S. 391 (U.S. Sup. Ct. 1976).

[30]463 U.S. 605 (U.S. Sup. Ct. 1984).

[31]487 U.S. 99 (U.S. Sup. Ct. 1988).

In the following *In re Grand Jury Subpoenas* decision, the Second Circuit Court of Appeals relied heavily on *Braswell* in rejecting a corporate president's Fifth Amendment–based attempt to avoid production of records pertaining to telephone lines listed in the president's name but paid for by the corporation.

IN RE GRAND JURY SUBPOENAS DATED OCTOBER 22, 1991, AND NOVEMBER 1, 1991 (U.S. v. DOE)
959 F.2d 1158 (2d Cir. 1992)

A federal grand jury was investigating "John Doe," president and sole shareholder of the corporation "XYZ," concerning possible violations of federal securities and money-laundering statutes. During the investigation, the government learned that XYZ had paid the bills for various telephone lines, including those used by Doe in his homes and car. Grand jury subpoenas duces tecum (i.e., subpoenas calling for production of documents) were then served on the custodian of XYZ's corporate records, on Doe, and on the law firm Paul, Weiss, Rifkind, Wharton & Garrison (Paul-Weiss), which represented Doe. These subpoenas sought production of telephone bills, records, and statements of account regarding certain telephone numbers (including the numbers of the telephone lines in Doe's homes and car).

Paul-Weiss possessed copies of these documents because it had received them from its client, Doe. Paul-Weiss refused, however, to comply with the subpoena. To justify this refusal, Paul-Weiss asserted that any copies of records in its possession were exempted from production due to (1) Doe's Fifth Amendment privilege against self-incrimination, and (2) the attorney-client and attorney-work-product privileges. Contending that the subpoenaed documents amounted to corporate records of XYZ rather than records belonging to or created by Doe, the government maintained that the asserted privileges were inapplicable. The government therefore filed a motion asking the district court to order Paul-Weiss to provide the subpoenaed documents. Doe, who was permitted to intervene in the proceeding, raised the same arguments made by Paul-Weiss in its refusal to comply with the subpoena.

After an evidentiary hearing on the government's motion, the district court determined that the records and documents at issue were those of XYZ rather than Doe. Concluding that requiring Paul-Weiss or Doe to produce the subpoenaed material would not violate Doe's Fifth Amendment rights, the attorney-client privilege, or the attorney-work-product privilege, the district court granted the government's motion and entered an order compelling Paul-Weiss to produce the subpoenaed material. Doe appealed.

Kearse, Circuit Judge   Doe contends that enforcement of the subpoena served on Paul-Weiss would violate his Fifth Amendment privilege principally because the act of producing the documents would tend to incriminate him. Preliminarily, we note that when documents have been transferred by a client to his attorney for the purpose of obtaining legal advice and the client claims attorney-client privilege, the attorney may refuse to produce the documents if the client, had he retained possession of them, would have had a Fifth Amendment privilege to refuse production. Accordingly, though Paul-Weiss was in possession of the subpoenaed records, we examine Doe's Fifth Amendment arguments as if Doe himself were the custodian.

The district court found that the subpoenaed records were not Doe's personal records but rather XYZ records. Artificial entities are not protected by the Fifth Amendment's prohibition against compelled self-incrimination. A corporation thus may not claim the privilege for the contents of its subpoenaed corporate records. Moreover, the custodian of corporate records is not entitled to refuse to produce those records on the ground that their contents may incriminate him personally, because they are not his personal records, and hence any incrimination would not be self-incrimination. This is so whether the subpoena for the corporate records is addressed to the corporation or to the custodian. Accordingly, Doe as custodian of XYZ's records is not entitled to prevent compliance with a subpoena calling for those records by asserting that the contents of those records would tend to incriminate him.

Further, the custodian of corporate records has no Fifth Amendment privilege to refuse to produce those records on the ground that the act of production itself would tend to incriminate him. This is the rule because, as pointed out by the Supreme Court in *Braswell v. United States,* "the custodian's act of production is not deemed a personal act, but rather an act of the corporation. Any claim of Fifth Amendment privilege asserted by the agent would be tantamount to a claim of privilege by the corporation—which of course possesses no such privilege." The policy reason for this limitation on the custodian's claim of privilege is that if not for this limitation, governmental efforts to investigate and prosecute white-collar crime by corporations and their agents would be seriously impaired. The fact that the custodian of corporate records is not entitled to assert an individual Fifth Amendment privilege to avoid producing the documents does not mean, however, that the custodian's act of production may be used against him. *Braswell* establishes that the government cannot make evidentiary use of the custodian's act of production.

Doe argues, however, that the above principles do not apply to him because, he contends, the subpoenaed documents are not in fact XYZ corporate records. Doe instead maintains that the records are his, either because they pertain to his personal telephone lines or because he obtained copies of the records from XYZ's files or from the telephone company for his own personal use. We disagree with Doe's characterization of the records. It is superficial for Doe to assert that the original records belonged to him because they pertained to his personal telephone lines. Although the lines may have been listed in his name, there was evidence that XYZ paid all of the bills, that Doe did not reimburse XYZ for these payments, that XYZ deducted the payments on its income tax returns, and

that the telephone bills and statements had been stored in corporate files on corporate premises. The district court found that the documents were in fact XYZ corporate records. That finding was amply supported by the evidence.

We also reject Doe's assertion that he owns the subpoenaed records because all that remain in existence are copies. Copies of corporate records do not become the personal property of an individual merely because he caused the copies to be made. Allowing a corporate officer to obtain copies of corporate records and secure for them greater protection than could be enjoyed for the originals would create a rule ripe for abuse.

Further, even if we construed the copies of the telephone company records as papers belonging to Doe, compelled production of those papers would not violate Doe's privilege against self-incrimination. The Fifth Amendment does not proscribe the compelled production of every sort of incriminating evidence. It applies only when the accused is compelled to make a *testimonial* communication that is incriminating. When, as is the case here, the documents sought by the government were not prepared by the person subpoenaed and contain no testimonial declarations by him, a subpoena duces tecum does not compel self-incrimination.

Neither would the act of producing copies of the telephone company statements and bills cause Doe to incriminate himself. The subpoenaed documents were prepared and sent by the telephone company in the ordinary course of its business. There is no dispute that the bills were received or that the bills were paid by XYZ. The mere fact that Doe has or produces the copies of the records will not constitute testimonial self-incrimination.

We conclude that the district court correctly ruled that Doe's Fifth Amendment privilege does not entitle him to prevent Paul-Weiss from complying with the subpoena.

Order compelling Paul-Weiss to produce subpoenaed documents affirmed.

Note: In a later portion of the opinion not set forth here, the Second Circuit concluded that the district court correctly rejected Doe's and Paul-Weiss's attorney-client privilege and attorney-work-product privilege arguments.

Another Fifth Amendment provision worthy of note is the **Double Jeopardy Clause**. This provision protects criminal defendants from multiple prosecutions for the same offense. It prevents an accused from being charged with more than one count of the same statutory violation for one offense, such as being charged with two robbery violations for a one-time robbery of one individual. This clause also prevents a second prosecution for the same offense after the defendant has been acquitted or convicted of that offense. Moreover, it bars the imposition of multiple punishments for the same offense.

The Double Jeopardy Clause does not, however, preclude the possibility that a single criminal act may lead to more than one criminal prosecution. One criminal act may produce several statutory violations, all of which may give rise to prosecution. For example, a defendant who commits rape may also be prosecuted for battery, assault with a deadly weapon, and kidnapping if the facts of the case indicate that the relevant statutes were violated. In addition, the Supreme Court has long used a "same elements" test to determine what constitutes the same offense.[32] This means that a single criminal act with multiple victims (e.g., a restaurant robbery in which several patrons are robbed) could result in several prosecutions because the identity of each victim would be an additional fact or element of proof in each case. Finally, the Double Jeopardy Clause does not protect against multiple prosecutions by different sovereigns. A conviction or acquittal in a state prosecution does not prevent a subsequent federal prosecution for a federal offense arising out of the same event, or vice versa. This principle was illustrated recently by the prosecutions stemming from the highly publicized beating of motorist Rodney King at the hands of Los Angeles police officers. After the officers were found not guilty in state prosecutions stemming from the beating, two of them were found guilty in federal prosecutions for violations of King's civil rights.

The Sixth Amendment   The Sixth Amendment contains several provisions applicable to criminal cases. It entitles criminal defendants to a speedy trial by an impartial jury, and guarantees them the right to confront and cross-examine the witnesses against them. The Sixth Amendment also gives the accused in a criminal case the right "to have the assistance of counsel" in her defense. This provision has been interpreted to mean not only that the accused may employ her own attorney but also that an indigent criminal defendant is entitled to court-appointed counsel.[33] The police must inform the accused of his right to counsel before custodial interrogation begins.[34] Once the accused has requested the assistance of counsel, he may not as a general rule be interrogated further unless he voluntarily initiates further conversations with the authorities.[35] In *McNeil v. Wisconsin,* however, the Supreme Court held that if a defendant has made an in-court request for an attorney's assistance regarding a crime with which he has been formally charged, that request does not preclude police interrogation of him—in the absence of counsel—regarding another unrelated crime.[36]

Finally, an accused is entitled to *effective* assistance of counsel. This means that the accused is entitled to representation at a point in the proceedings when an attorney may effectively assist him,[37] and to reasonably competent representation by that attorney. Inadequate assistance of counsel can be a proper basis for setting aside a conviction and ordering a new trial.[38]

Figure 4 summarizes the major procedural safeguards enjoyed by defendants under our criminal justice system.

WHITE-COLLAR CRIMES AND THE DILEMMAS OF CORPORATE CONTROL

Introduction

White-collar crime is the term broadly used to describe a wide variety of nonviolent criminal offenses committed by businesspersons and business

---

[32]*United States v. Dixon,* 113 S. Ct. 2849 (U.S. Sup. Ct. 1993); *Blockburger v. United States,* 284 U.S. 299 (U.S. Sup. Ct. 1932).

[33]*Gideon v. Wainwright,* 372 U.S. 335 (U.S. Sup. Ct. 1963).

[34]This is included in the previously discussed warnings required by *Miranda v. Arizona,* 384 U.S. 436 (U.S. Sup. Ct. 1966).

[35]*Edwards v. Arizona,* 451 U.S. 477 (U.S. Sup. Ct. 1981).

[36]111 S. Ct. 2204 (U.S. Sup. Ct. 1991).

[37]*Powell v. Alabama,* 287 U.S. 45 (U.S. Sup. Ct. 1932).

[38]In *Strickland v. Washington,* 446 U.S. 668 (U.S. Sup. Ct. 1984), the Court held that a defendant's conviction would not be set aside unless his attorney's performance fell below an objective standard of reasonableness and so prejudiced him as to result in the denial of a fair trial. As applied, this standard makes ineffective assistance of counsel claims rather difficult ones for convicted defendants to invoke successfully.

| FIGURE 4 | **Major Procedural Safeguards** |

Fourth Amendment

- Prohibits unreasonable searches and seizures

Fifth Amendment

- Due Process Clause
  Presumption of innocence
  Prohibits vague criminal statutes
  Requires basic procedural and substantive
  fairness

- Right to silence
  Double Jeopardy Clause

Sixth Amendment

- Speedy trial
- Impartial jury
- Confront and cross-examine prosecution's
  witnesses
- Right to counsel

Eighth Amendment

- Forbids cruel and unusual punishments

organizations. Although this term often includes offenses committed by employees against their employers (such as theft, embezzlement, or accepting a bribe), our discussion will focus on criminal offenses committed by corporate employers and employees against society. Each year, corporate crime costs consumers billions of dollars. It takes various forms, from consumer fraud, securities fraud, and tax evasion to price-fixing, environmental pollution, and other regulatory violations. Corporate crime presents our legal system with a variety of problems—problems we have failed to resolve satisfactorily.

Corporations form the backbone of the most successful economic system in history. They dominate the international economic scene and provide us with substantial benefits in the forms of efficiently produced goods and services. Yet these same corporations may pollute the environment, swindle their customers, produce dangerously defective products, and conspire with others to injure or destroy competition. How are we to achieve effective control over these large organizations so important to our existence? Increasingly, we have come to rely on the criminal law as a major corporate control instrument. The criminal law, however, was developed with individual wrongdoers in mind. Who is at fault when a large organization causes social harm? Corporate crime is *organizational* in nature. Any given corporate action may be the product of the combined actions of many individuals acting within the corporate hierarchy. It may be that no individual had sufficient knowledge to possess the *mens rea* necessary for criminal responsibility under traditional criminal law principles. Moreover, criminally penalizing corporations raises special problems in view of the obvious inability to apply standard sanctions such as imprisonment to legal entities.

Evolution of Corporate Criminal Liability

The common law initially rejected the notion that corporations could be criminally responsible for their employees' actions. Early corporations, small in size and number, had little impact on public life. Their small size made it relatively easy to pinpoint individual wrongdoers within the corporation and thereby avoid the above-mentioned conceptual difficulties associated with criminal liability.

As corporations grew in size and power, however, the social need to control their activities grew accordingly. Not coincidentally, the rules governing corporate criminal liability also began to change. Legislatures enacted statutes creating *public welfare offenses* of which corporations were convicted.[39] These regulatory offenses did not require proof of *mens rea.* By the turn of this century, American courts had begun to impose criminal liability on corporations for general criminal offenses that required proof of *mens rea.* This expansion of corporate criminal liability involved imputing the criminal intent of corporate employees to the corporation

---

[39]These statutes followed the lead of early corporate criminal liability cases in which criminal liability was imposed on public corporations such as municipalities—initially the most common type of corporation—for failures to perform such public duties as road and bridge repair.

in a fashion similar to the imposition of tort or contract liability on corporations under the *respondeat superior* doctrine.[40]

Corporations now may face criminal liability for almost any criminal offense if the statute in question indicates a legislative intent to hold corporations responsible. This legislative intent requirement is sometimes problematic. Many state criminal statutes are based on common law crimes and may contain language suggesting an intent to hold only humans liable. For example, state manslaughter statutes often define the offense as "the killing of one human being by the act of another." When statutes are framed, however, in more general terms—such as by referring to "persons"—courts are generally willing to apply them to corporate defendants.

Corporate Criminal Liability Today

Under the modern rule on corporate criminal liability, a corporation may be held liable for criminal offenses committed by employees who *acted within the scope of their employment and for the benefit of the corporation.* A major corporate criminal liability issue centers around the classes of corporate employees whose intent can be imputed to the corporation. Some commentators argue that a corporation should be criminally responsible only for offenses committed by high corporate officials or those linked to them by authorization or acquiescence. (Virtually all courts impose criminal liability on a corporation under such circumstances.) Such arguments reflect fairness notions, for if any group of corporate employees can fairly be said to constitute a corporation's mind, that group is its top officers and directors.

The problem with imposing corporate liability only on the basis of top corporate officers' actions or knowledge is that such a policy often insulates the corporation from liability. Many corporate offenses may be directly traceable only to middle managers or more subordinate corporate employees. It may be impossible to demonstrate that any higher-level corporate official had sufficient knowledge to constitute *mens rea.* Recognizing this problem, the

federal courts have adopted a general rule that a corporation can be criminally liable for the actions of any of its agents, regardless of whether any link between the agents and higher-level corporate officials can be demonstrated.

Problems with Corporate Criminal Liability

Despite the legal theories that justify corporate criminal liability, the punishment of corporations remains problematic. Does a criminal conviction stigmatize a corporation in the same way it stigmatizes an individual? The idea of viewing a corporation as a criminal may be difficult for many people to embrace. Perhaps the only stigma resulting from a corporate criminal conviction is felt by corporate employees, many of whom are entirely innocent of any wrongdoing. Is it just to punish the innocent in an attempt to punish the guilty?

And what of the cash fine, the primary punishment imposed on convicted corporations? Most critics of contemporary corporate control strategies maintain that fines imposed on convicted corporations tend to be too small to provide effective deterrence. These critics urge the use of fines keyed in some fashion to the corporate defendant's wealth, such as a percentage of the defendant's income or total capital. As explained in Chapter 4, Business Ethics, Corporate Social Responsibility, and the Control and Governance of Corporations, however, larger fines may lead to undesirable results if the corporate defendant ultimately passes along the fines to its customers (through higher prices), shareholders (through lower dividends or no dividends), or employees (through lower wages). Moreover, fines large enough to threaten corporate solvency may harm corporate employees and those economically dependent on the corporation's financial well-being. Most of these persons, however, neither had the power to prevent the violation nor derived any benefit from it. The managers responsible for a violation may avoid the imposition of direct burdens on them when the fine is assessed against the corporation. Given the randomness inherent in criminal fines, legislatures may be unwilling to authorize—and courts reluctant to impose—fines large enough to produce deterrence.

Still other deficiencies make fines less-than-adequate corporate control devices. Fine strategies assume that all corporations are rationally acting profit-maximizers. Fines of sufficient size, it is argued, will erode the profit drive underlying most

---

[40]Chapter 35 discusses *respondeat superior* in detail. For an early landmark case on this subject, see *New York Central & Hudson River R.R. v. United States,* 212 U.S. 481 (U.S. Sup. Ct. 1909).

corporate violations. Numerous studies of actual corporate behavior, however, suggest that many corporations are neither profit-maximizers nor rational actors. Mature firms with well-established market shares may embrace goals other than profit maximization, such as technological prominence, increased market share, or higher employee salaries. In addition, the interests of managers who make corporate decisions and establish corporate policies may not coincide with the long-range economic interests of their corporate employers. The prospect that their employer could have to pay a substantial fine at some future point may not trouble top managers, who tend to have relatively short terms in office and are often compensated in part by large bonuses keyed to year-end profitability.

Individual Liability for Corporate Crime

Individuals committing criminal offenses while acting in corporate capacities have always been personally subjected to criminal liability. Most European nations reject corporate criminal liability and rely exclusively on individual criminal responsibility. In view of the problems associated with imposing criminal liability on corporations, individual liability may seem a more attractive control device. Besides being more consistent with traditional criminal law notions about the personal nature of guilt, individual liability may provide better deterrence than corporate liability if it enables society to use the criminal punishment threat against the persons who make important corporate decisions. The prospect of personal liability may cause individuals to resist corporate pressures to violate the law. If guilty individuals are identified and punished, the criminal law's purposes may be achieved without harm to innocent employees, shareholders, and consumers.

Problems with Individual Liability   Attractive as it may sound, individual liability also poses significant problems when applied to corporate acts. Identifying responsible individuals within the corporate hierarchy becomes difficult—and frequently impossible—if we follow traditional notions and require proof of criminal intent. Business decisions leading to corporate wrongs often result from the collective actions of numerous corporate employees, none of whom had complete knowledge or specific criminal intent. Other corporate crimes are

structural in the sense that they result from internal bureaucratic failures rather than the conscious actions of any individual or group.

Proving culpability on the part of high-level executives may be particularly difficult. Bad news sometimes does not reach them; other times, they consciously avoid knowledge that would lead to criminal responsibility. It therefore may be possible to demonstrate culpability only on the part of middle-level managers. As noted in Chapter 4, however, juries may be unwilling to convict such individuals if they seem to be scapegoats for their unindicted superiors. Even when a culpable individual is identified, significant problems can prevent meaningful application of the criminal sanction. The individual in question may have died, retired, or been transferred to another post outside the jurisdiction where the offense occurred. If convicted, white-collar defendants usually are either not imprisoned or imprisoned for a short period of time. This phenomenon is generally attributed to public doubts about the moral culpability involved in certain white-collar offenses and to the positive image that such offenders—often well-educated, well-spoken community leaders—may possess. Most convicted white-collar offenders receive fines that may be small in comparison to their wealth.

These difficulties in imposing criminal penalties on individual corporate employees have led to the creation of regulatory offenses imposing strict or vicarious liability on corporate officers. Strict liability offenses dispense with the requirement of proof of criminal intent on the defendant's part, but ordinarily require proof that the defendant committed some wrongful act. Vicarious liability offenses impose criminal liability on a defendant for the acts of third parties (normally employees under the defendant's personal supervision), but may require proof of some form of *mens rea,* such as the defendant's negligent or reckless failure to supervise. Statutes often combine these two approaches by making corporate executives liable for the acts or omissions of corporate employees without requiring proof of criminal intent on the part of the employees. *United States v. Park,* discussed in Figure 5, is a famous example of such a prosecution.

Critics of strict liability offenses often argue that *mens rea* is a basic principle in our legal system and that it is unjust to stigmatize with a criminal conviction persons who are not morally culpable. In addition, critics commonly doubt that strict liability

---

FIGURE 5   **A Note on *United States v. Park*, 421 U.S. 658 (U.S. Sup. Ct. 1975)**

John R. Park was CEO of Acme Markets, Inc., a national retail food chain with approximately 36,000 employees, 874 retail outlets, and 16 warehouses. Acme and Park were charged with five counts of violating the federal Food, Drug, and Cosmetic Act (the Act) by storing food shipped in interstate commerce in warehouses where it was exposed to rodent contamination. The violations were detected during Food and Drug Administration (FDA) inspections of Acme's Baltimore warehouse. Inspectors saw evidence of rodent infestation and unsanitary conditions, such as mouse droppings on the floor of the hanging meat room and alongside bales of lime Jell-O, and a hole chewed by a rodent in a bale of Jell-O. The FDA notified Park by letter of these findings.

Upon checking with Acme's vice president for legal affairs, Park learned that the Baltimore division vice president "was investigating the situation immediately and would be taking corrective action." An FDA inspection three months after the first one disclosed continued rodent contamination at the Baltimore warehouse despite improved sanitation there. The criminal charges were then filed against Acme and Park. Acme pleaded guilty; Park refused to do so. Park was convicted on each count, but the court of appeals overturned the conviction.

The Supreme Court, however, reversed. In sustaining Park's conviction, the Court noted that in view of the substantial public interest in purity of food, the Act did not require awareness of wrongdoing as an element of criminal conduct. This did not mean, however, that a person "remotely entangled in the proscribed shipment" was at risk of being criminally convicted. Instead, the defendant must be shown to have had "a responsible share" in the violation, such as by failing to exercise authority and supervisory responsibility. The Court emphasized that the Act imposes on supervisory personnel the "highest standard of foresight and vigilance." This includes a duty to seek out and remedy violations when they occur, and a duty to implement measures to prevent violations from occurring.

Although one who was "powerless" to prevent or correct the violation cannot be held criminally responsible under the Act, the Court emphasized that Park was hardly powerless. He had the authority and responsibility to prevent or correct the prohibited condition. The evidence showed that prior to the Baltimore warehouse inspections giving rise to the criminal charges, Park was advised by the FDA of unsanitary conditions in another Acme warehouse. According to the Court, Park thus acquired notice—prior to the time that the Baltimore warehouse violations were discovered—that he could not rely on his previously employed system of delegation to subordinates to prevent or correct unsanitary conditions at company warehouses. Despite evidence indicating Park's prior awareness of this system's deficiencies well before the Baltimore violations were discovered, Park had not instituted any new procedures designed to prevent violations of the Act. The Court therefore concluded that his conviction should stand.

---

statutes produce the deterrence sought by their proponents. Such statutes may reduce the moral impact of the criminal sanction if they apply it to relatively trivial offenses. Moreover, they may not result in enough convictions or sufficiently severe penalties to produce deterrence because juries and judges are unwilling to convict or punish defendants who may not be morally culpable. Although statutes creating strict liability offenses are generally held constitutional, they are disfavored by courts. Most courts require a clear indication of a legislative intent to dispense with the *mens rea* element.[41]

Strict liability offenses are also criticized on the ground that even if responsible individuals within the corporation are convicted and punished appropriately, individual liability unaccompanied by corporate liability is unlikely to achieve effective corporate control. If immune from criminal liability, corporations could benefit financially from employees' violations

of the law. Individual liability, unlike a corporate fine, does not force a corporation to give up the profits flowing from a violation. Thus, the corporation would have no incentive to avoid future violations. Incarcerated offenders would merely be replaced by others who might eventually yield to the pressures that produced the violations in the first place. Corporate liability, however, may sometimes encourage corporate efforts to prevent future violations. When an offense has occurred but no identifiable individual is sufficiently culpable to justify an individual prosecution of him or her, corporate liability is uniquely appropriate.

New Directions

The preceding discussion suggests that future efforts at corporate control are likely to include both corporate and individual criminal liability. It also suggests, however, that new approaches are necessary if society is to gain more effective control over corporate activities.

---

[41]See, for example, *United States v. U.S. Gypsum Co.,* 425 U.S. 422 (U.S. Sup. Ct. 1978).

Various novel criminal penalties have been suggested in the individual liability setting. For example, white-collar offenders could be deprived of leisure time or sentenced to render public service rather than being incarcerated or fined. Some have even suggested the licensing of managers, with license suspensions as a penalty for offenders. The common thread in these and other similar approaches is an attempt to create penalties which are meaningful yet not so severe that judges and juries are unwilling to impose them.

A promising recent suggestion regarding corporate liability involves imaginative judicial use of corporate probation for convicted corporate offenders. For example, courts could require convicted corporations to do, or hire independent consultants to do, self-studies identifying the source of a violation and proposing appropriate steps to prevent future violations. If bureaucratic failures caused the violation, the court could order a limited restructuring of the corporation's internal decisionmaking processes as a condition of obtaining probation or avoiding a penalty. Possible orders might include requiring the collection and monitoring of the data necessary to discover or prevent future violations and mandating the creation of new executive positions to monitor such data. Restructuring would minimize the previously discussed harm to innocent persons that often accompanies corporate financial penalties. In addition, restructuring could be a more effective way to achieve corporate rehabilitation than relying exclusively on a corporation's desire to avoid future fines as an incentive to police itself. Because restructuring would represent a new form of governmental intrusion into the private sector, however, it should be applied sparingly and with discretion.

The Federal Sentencing Guidelines, discussed earlier in this chapter in Figure 1, contain good reasons for corporations to institute measures to prevent regulatory violations. Under the guidelines, organizations convicted of violating federal law may face greatly increased penalties for certain offenses, with some crimes carrying fines as high as $290 million. The penalty imposed on an organization depends on its "culpability score," which increases (thus calling for a more severe penalty) if, for example, high-level corporate officers were involved in the offense or the organization had a history of such offenses. Even apart from the potentially severe penalties, however, the Sentencing Guidelines provide an incentive for corporations to adopt compliance programs designed "to prevent and detect violations of the law." The presence of an effective compliance program can reduce the corporation's culpability score for sentencing purposes. Prior to the time the Sentencing Guidelines took effect, courts generally concluded that the existence of a compliance program should not operate as a mitigating factor in the sentencing of a convicted organization.

IMPORTANT WHITE–COLLAR CRIMES

Regulatory Offenses

Numerous state and federal regulatory statutes on a wide range of subjects prescribe criminal as well as civil liability for violations. The Food, Drug, and Cosmetic Act, at issue in the case discussed in Figure 5, is an example of such a statute. Several other major federal regulatory offenses are discussed in detail in later chapters. These include violations of the Sherman Antitrust Act, the Securities Act of 1933, the Securities Exchange Act of 1934, the Clean Waters Act of 1972, the Resource Conservation and Recovery Act, and the Electronic Funds Transfer Act.

Fraudulent Acts

Many business crimes involve some fraudulent conduct. In most states, it is a crime to obtain money or property by fraudulent pretenses, issue fraudulent checks, make false credit statements, or give short weights or measures. Certain forms of fraud in bankruptcy proceedings, such as false claims by creditors or fraudulent concealment or transfer of a debtor's assets, are federal criminal offenses.[42] In addition, federal mail fraud and wire fraud statutes make criminal the use of the mail, telephone, or telegrams to accomplish a fraudulent scheme. The Travel Act of 1961 makes it a federal offense to travel or otherwise use facilities in interstate commerce in order to commit criminal acts.

Bribery

State and federal law have long made it a crime to offer public officials gifts, favors, or anything of value to influence official decisions for private

---

[42]Chapter 29 discusses bankruptcy in detail.

benefit. In 1977, Congress passed the Foreign Corrupt Practices Act, which criminalized giving anything of value to officials of foreign governments in an attempt to influence their official actions.[43] Most states also have enacted commercial bribery statutes that outlaw offering kickbacks and payoffs to private individuals to secure some commercial advantage.

RICO

When Congress passed the Racketeer Influenced and Corrupt Organizations Act (RICO) as part of the Organized Crime Control Act of 1970, lawmakers were primarily concerned about organized crime's increasing entry into legitimate business enterprises. RICO's broad language, however, allows the statute to be applied in a wide variety of cases having nothing to do with organized crime. As a result, RICO has become one of the most controversial pieces of legislation affecting business in our legal history. Supporters of RICO argue that it is an effective and much-needed tool for attacking a broad range of unethical business practices. Its critics, however, see RICO as an overbroad statute that needlessly taints business reputations. Critics also argue that RICO has operated unduly to favor plaintiffs in civil litigation rather than serving as an aid to law enforcement.

Criminal RICO   Under RICO, it is a federal crime to: (1) use income derived from a "pattern of racketeering activity" to acquire an interest in an enterprise, (2) acquire or maintain an interest in an enterprise through a pattern of racketeering activity, (3) conduct or participate in the affairs of an enterprise through a pattern of racketeering activity, or (4) conspire to do any of the preceding acts. RICO is a compound statute because it requires proof of "predicate" criminal offenses that constitute the necessary pattern of racketeering activity.

Racketeering activity includes the commission of any of more than 30 state or federal criminal offenses. Although most offenses that qualify (e.g., arson, gambling, extortion) have no relation to normal business transactions, such offenses as mail and wire fraud, securities fraud, and bribery are also included. Thus, almost any business fraud may be alleged to be a racketeering activity. To show a *pattern* of such activity, the prosecution must first prove the defendant's commission of at least two acts of racketeering activity within a 10-year period. The pattern requirement also calls for proof that these acts are related and amount to (or pose the threat of) continuing racketeering activity. Most courts have interpreted the statutory term *enterprise* broadly to include partnerships and unincorporated associations as well as corporations.

Individuals found guilty of RICO violations are subject to substantial fines and imprisonment for up to 20 years. In addition, RICO violators risk the forfeiture of any interest gained in any enterprise as a result of a violation. To prevent defendants from hiding assets that may be forfeitable upon conviction, federal prosecutors may seek pretrial orders freezing a defendant's assets. Some RICO critics argue that the harm such a freeze may work on a defendant's ability to conduct business, coupled with the threat of forfeiture of most or all of the business upon conviction, has led some defendants to make plea bargains rather than risk all by fighting prosecutions they believe to be unjustified.

Civil RICO   Under RICO, the government may also seek various civil penalties for violations. These include divestiture of a defendant's interest in an enterprise, the dissolution or reorganization of the enterprise, and injunctions against future racketeering activities by the defendant.

RICO's most controversial sections, however, are those allowing private individuals to recover treble damages (three times their actual loss) and attorney's fees for injuries caused by a statutory violation. To qualify for recovery under RICO, a plaintiff must prove that the defendant violated RICO's provisions (as set forth in the above subsection Criminal Rico) and that the plaintiff was "injured in his business or property" as a result. Aided by the Supreme Court's refusal, in *Sedima, S.P.R.L. v. Imrex Co.,*[44] to give a narrowing construction to the broadly phrased RICO, private plaintiffs have brought a large number of civil RICO cases in recent years. In *Sedima,* the Court rejected, as an erroneous statutory interpretation, some lower federal courts' approach of requiring civil RICO plaintiffs to prove that the defendant had actually been criminally

---

[43]Chapter 44 discusses the Foreign Corrupt Practices Act in detail.

[44]473 U.S. 479 (U.S. Sup. Ct. 1985).

convicted of a predicate offense. In addition, the Court rejected the argument that civil RICO plaintiffs should be expected to prove a "distinct racketeering injury" as a precondition of recovery. The Court acknowledged lower courts' concern about RICO's breadth and noted the fact that most civil RICO suits are filed against legitimate businesses rather than against "the archetypal, intimidating mobster." Nevertheless, the Court observed that "[t]his defect—if defect it is—is inherent in the statute as written, and its correction must lie with Congress."

The *Northwestern Bell* case, which follows, focuses on the necessary "pattern of racketeering activity" element of a RICO claim.

H. J. Inc. v. Northwestern Bell Telephone Co.

492 U.S. 229 (U.S. Sup. Ct. 1989)

Customers of Northwestern Bell Telephone Company filed a class action suit alleging violations of RICO based on allegations that between 1980 and 1986 Northwestern Bell sought to influence members of the Minnesota Public Utilities Commission (MPUC) to approve rates for Northwestern in excess of a fair and reasonable amount. They alleged that Northwestern made cash payments to commissioners, negotiated with them regarding future employment, and paid for parties and meals, tickets to sporting events, and airline tickets. These acts, they alleged, were in violation of the state bribery statute and state common law prohibiting bribery. The district court dismissed their civil RICO claims because the complaint failed to allege the "multiple illegal schemes" that the Eighth Circuit Court of Appeals had previously held were necessary to establish a "pattern of racketeering activity" under RICO.

Brennan, Justice   In *Sedima, S.P.R.L. v. Imrex Co.,* we acknowledged concern in some quarters over civil RICO's use against "legitimate" businesses, as well as "mobsters and organized criminals." But we suggested that RICO's expansive uses "appear to be primarily the result of the breadth of the predicate offenses, and the failure of Congress and the courts to develop a meaningful concept of 'pattern.'" Congress has done nothing in the interim to illuminate RICO's key requirement of a pattern of racketeering activity, and developing a meaningful concept of "pattern" within the existing statutory framework has proved to be no easy task.

It is, nevertheless, a task we must undertake in order to decide this case. Our guides must be the text of the statute and its legislative history. We find no support in those sources for the proposition that predicate acts of racketeering may form a pattern only when they are a part of separate illegal schemes. Nor can we agree with those courts that have suggested that a pattern is established by proving two predicate acts, or with *amici* in this case who argue that the word "pattern" refers only to predicates that are indicative of a perpetrator involved in organized crime.

As we remarked in *Sedima,* the section of the statute headed "definitions," section 1961, does not so much define a pattern of racketeering activity as state a minimum necessary condition for the existence of such a pattern. Unlike other provisions in section 1961 that tell us what various concepts used in the Act "mean," section 1961(5) says of the phrase "pattern of racketeering activity" only that it "requires at least two acts of racketeering activity, one of which occurred after October 15, 1970 and the last of which occurred within ten years after the commission of a prior act of racketeering activity."

Section 1961(5) does indicate that Congress envisioned circumstances in which no more than two predicates would be necessary to establish a pattern. But the statement that a pattern "requires at least" two predicates implies that while two acts are necessary, they may not be sufficient. Section 1961(5) concerns only the minimum *number* of predicates necessary to establish a pattern; and it assumes that there is something to a RICO pattern *beyond* simply the number of predicate acts involved. The legislative history bears out this interpretation, for the principal sponsor of the Senate bill expressly indicated that "proof of two acts of racketeering activity, without more, does not establish a pattern." Section 1961(5) does not identify, though, these additional prerequisites for establishing the existence of a RICO pattern.

In normal usage, the word "pattern" here would be taken to require more than just a multiplicity of racketeering predicates. A "pattern" is an "arrangement or order of things or activity," 11 Oxford English Dictionary 357 (2d ed. 1989). It is not the number of predicates but the relationship that they bear to each other or to some external organizing principle that renders them "ordered" or "arranged."

RICO's legislative history reveals Congress' intent that to prove a pattern of racketeering activity a plaintiff or prosecutor must show that the racketeering predicates are related, *and* that they amount to or pose a threat of continued criminal activity. In the Organized Crime Control Act of 1970, Congress defined a pattern requirement solely in terms of the *relationship* of the defendant's criminal acts one to another: "criminal conduct forms a pattern if it embraces criminal acts that have the same or similar purposes, results, participants, victims, or methods of commission, or otherwise are interrelated by distinguishing characteristics and are not isolated events." We have no reason to suppose that Congress had in mind for RICO's pattern component any more constrained a notion of the relationships between predicates that would suffice.

RICO's legislative history also tells us, however, that the relatedness of racketeering activities is not alone enough to satisfy the pattern element. It must also be shown that the predicates themselves amount to, or that they otherwise constitute a threat of, *continuing* racketeering activity. It is this aspect of RICO's pattern element that has spawned the "multiple scheme" test adopted by the Court of Appeals in this case. But although proof that a defendant has been involved in multiple criminal schemes would certainly be highly relevant to the inquiry into the continuity of the defendant's racketeering activity, it is implausible to suppose that Congress thought continuity might be shown *only* by proof of multiple schemes. We adopt a less inflexible approach that seems to us to derive from a common-sense, everyday understanding of RICO's language and Congress' gloss on it. What a plaintiff or prosecutor must prove is continuity of racketeering activity, or its threat.

A party alleging a RICO violation may demonstrate continuity over a closed period by proving a series of related predicates extending over a substantial period of time. Predicate acts extending over a few weeks or months and threatening no future criminal conduct do not satisfy this requirement: Congress was concerned in RICO with long-term criminal conduct. Often a RICO action will be brought before continuity can be established in this way. In such cases, liability depends on whether the *threat* of continuity is demonstrated.

The threat of continuity is sufficiently established where the predicates can be attributed to a defendant operating as part of a long-term association that exists for criminal purposes. Such associations include, but extend well beyond, those traditionally grouped under the phrase "organized crime." The continuity requirement is likewise satisfied where it is shown that the predicates are a regular way of conducting defendant's ongoing legitimate business, or of conducting or participating in an ongoing legitimate RICO "enterprise."

Plaintiffs' complaint alleges that at different times over the course of at least a 6-year period the defendants gave five members of the MPUC numerous bribes, in several different forms, with the objective—in which they were allegedly successful—of causing these Commissioners to approve unfair and unreasonable rates. RICO defines bribery as a racketeering activity, so plaintiffs have alleged multiple predicate acts. They may be able to prove that the multiple predicates alleged constitute a "pattern of racketeering activity," in that they satisfy the requirements of relationship and continuity. The acts of bribery alleged are said to be related to a common purpose, to influence Commissioners to win approval of unfairly high rates for Northwestern Bell. Furthermore, the racketeering predicates allegedly occurred over at least a 6-year period, which may be sufficient to satisfy the continuity requirement. Alternatively, a threat of continuity might be established at trial by showing that the alleged bribes were a regular way of conducting or participating in the conduct of the alleged and ongoing RICO enterprise, the MPUC. The Court of Appeals thus erred in affirming the District Court's dismissal of plaintiff's complaint for failure to plead "a pattern of racketeering activity."

Judgment reversed in favor of plaintiffs; case remanded for trial.

FIGURE 6 **Recent Civil RICO Decisions of the Supreme Court**

In *Holmes v. Securities Investor Protection Corp.,* 112 S. Ct. 1311 (U.S. Sup. Ct. 1992), the Court held that plaintiffs in treble damages cases under RICO must demonstrate that the harm they experienced was directly and proximately caused by the defendants' wrongful conduct. Plaintiffs whose injury was only an indirect result of the defendants' actions do not have legal standing to sue.

The defendant in *Holmes* allegedly engaged in fraudulent stock-manipulation schemes that caused certain broker-dealers to become insolvent and unable to meet their obligations to customers. When the broker-dealers collapsed financially, Securities Investor Protection Corp. (SIPC), a private corporation authorized by federal law, fulfilled its legal obligation to provide funds to satisfy the claims of customers of the insolvent broker-dealers. SIPC then brought a treble damages action under RICO against defendant Holmes on the theory that SIPC, having supplied the funds to pay the customers of the failed broker-dealers, stood in the shoes of the customers in terms of collecting losses caused by Holmes's alleged stock-manipulation schemes. The Court noted that even if SIPC stood in the customers' shoes, any loss being alleged by SIPC was too indirect to support a RICO claim against Holmes. The harm necessary to support a RICO claim would instead have been that experienced by the broker-dealers, whose financial demise presumably stemmed directly from Holmes's actions.

In recent years, the highly attractive treble damages and attorney's fee provisions in RICO have led to the frequent use of RICO by plaintiffs in commercial fraud cases. Stockbrokers, banks, insurance companies, and accounting firms have been typical targets of such civil suits. In *Reves v. Ernst & Young,* 113 S. Ct. 1163 (U.S. Sup. Ct. 1993), however, the Court limited plaintiffs' ability to use civil RICO against "outside" professionals such as accounting firms when financial institutions involved in fraudulent activities fail. The Court held that accounting firms and "other" outside professionals who performed work for such a financial institution are potentially liable under RICO only if they "participate[d] in the management or operation of the enterprise." Merely providing auditing services to the financial institution, without more, would not be sufficient to constitute participation in the management or operation of the enterprise.

Over the past decade, RICO reform proposals have been unsuccessfully introduced in Congress. Although the Supreme Court has generally continued to interpret RICO expansively in the absence of congressional action, it recently handed down two decisions that critics of frequent uses of civil RICO have found encouraging. Those decisions are discussed in Figure 6.

COMPUTER CRIME

As computers have come to play an increasingly important role in our society, new opportunities for crime have resulted. In some instances, computers may be used to accomplish "traditional" crimes such as theft, embezzlement, espionage, and fraud. In others, computers or the information stored there may be targets of crimes such as unauthorized access, vandalism, tampering, or theft of services. The law's response to computer crimes has evolved with this new technology. For example, computer hacking—once viewed by some as a mischievous but clever activity—can now lead to significant prison sentences and fines.

The technical nature of computer crime tends to complicate its detection and prosecution. Traditional criminal statutes have often proven inadequate because they tend not to address explicitly the types of crime associated with the use of computers. Assume, for example, that a general statute on theft defines the offense in terms of stealing "property," and that the defendant is charged with violating the statute by taking and using computer data without authorization. The court could decide to dismiss this case if categorizing data stored in a computer as "property" strikes the court as a strained interpretation of the statute. Although some courts have interpreted existing criminal laws narrowly so as to exclude instances of computer abuse, other courts have construed them more broadly. In light of the uncertainties attending statutory interpretation, legislatures on the state and federal levels have become increasingly aware of the need to revise their criminal codes to be certain that they explicitly cover computer crime.

Almost all states have now enacted criminal statutes specifically outlawing certain abuses of computers. Common provisions prohibit such acts as obtaining access to a computer system without authorization, tampering with files or causing damage to a system (e.g., by spreading a virus or deleting files), invading the privacy of others, using a computer to commit fraud or theft, and trafficking in passwords or access codes.

On the federal level, computer crime has been prosecuted with some success under existing federal statutes, primarily those forbidding mail fraud, wire fraud, transportation of stolen property, and thefts of property. As has been true at the state level, successful prosecution of these cases often depends on broad interpretation of the statutory prerequisites. The Computer Fraud and Abuse Act, enacted by Congress in 1984 and amended in 1986, outlaws certain improper uses of computers. Among the crimes covered by this federal statute are intentionally gaining unauthorized access to a computer used by or for the U.S. government, trafficking in passwords and other access devices, and using a computer to obtain government information that is protected from disclosure.

ETHICAL AND PUBLIC POLICY CONCERNS

1. Few issues have managed to provoke more prolonged, heated controversy than the death penalty. Many of the arguments both for and against the death penalty are, at base, ethical arguments. Identify and briefly discuss some fundamental arguments on both sides of the issue.

2. Are strict and vicarious liability ethically defensible? Who would be more likely to support such liability, utilitarians or rights theorists? Which form of liability would rights theorists find more palatable?

3. Business opponents of RICO argue that federal prosecutors sometimes use the threat of asset forfeitures under the RICO statute to coerce business defendants to enter plea agreements that they would not otherwise enter. Assuming that these allegations are true, are such prosecutorial practices defensible?

PROBLEMS AND PROBLEM CASES

1. Two police officers on patrol observed Dickerson leaving an apartment building that the police department considered to be a "crack house," in view of the various drug-related complaints made to the police about the building. Dickerson began walking in the opposite direction after seeing the police car and the officers. Based on Dickerson's behavior and the fact that he had just left a building suspected of being a site of drug traffic, the officers decided to stop Dickerson and investigate further. The officers ordered Dickerson to stop and submit to a patdown search. Although the patdown search revealed no weapons, the officer who conducted the search noted a small lump in a pocket of Dickerson's jacket. The officer knew immediately that the lump was not a weapon but did not know what the lump was on the basis of initially touching it. After probing the lump further, the officer concluded that it could be contraband. The officer removed the "lump," which proved to be a plastic bag containing crack cocaine. Dickerson was arrested and later charged with possession of cocaine. Dickerson moved to suppress (i.e., exclude evidence of) the cocaine, on the ground that his Fourth Amendment rights were violated by the warrantless search and seizure. The trial court denied the motion to suppress, and Dickerson was found guilty. Did the trial court err in concluding that Dickerson's Fourth Amendment rights were not violated and in denying the motion to suppress?

2. Dixon was arrested and indicted for possession of cocaine with intent to distribute. He was then convicted of criminal contempt of court for violating a condition of his release on an unrelated offense. This condition of release had forbidden him from committing any criminal offense. After the conviction of criminal contempt, the trial court dismissed the cocaine indictment on double jeopardy grounds. Was the trial court correct in doing so?

3. Johnny Paul Penry was convicted of murder and sentenced to death after a jury rejected his insanity defense. His defense had presented evidence that due to organic brain damage, he had the intelligence of a six-year-old child. Penry challenged his conviction on a number of grounds, including the argument that the Eighth Amendment forbids execution of the retarded. Was he correct?

4. Police officers who suspected Billy Greenwood of dealing in drugs asked trash collectors to pick up and turn over plastic garbage bags that Greenwood left at the curb. The officers found drug-related items in the bags and used them to secure a search warrant for Greenwood's home. The search revealed narcotics. Greenwood was arrested on felony narcotics charges. A California Superior Court dismissed the charges against Greenwood on the ground that the warrantless search of his trash was in violation of the Fourth Amendment. Was the dismissal proper?

5. Doe, the target of a federal grand jury investigation, was subpoenaed to produce records of his accounts in banks in the Cayman Islands and Bermuda. He produced some records, testified that he had no other records in his possession or control, and invoked the Fifth Amendment when asked to reveal the existence or location of other records. The U.S. branches of Doe's banks cited their nations' bank secrecy laws and refused to comply with subpoenas ordering them to produce records of his accounts. At the government's request, the district court then ordered Doe to sign a consent directive authorizing the banks to turn over records of any and all accounts over which he had a right of withdrawal. The ordered consent directive, however, was to be structured so that it would not be an identification or acknowledgment by Doe of the existence of any such accounts. When Doe refused to obey the court's order, the court found him in contempt. Would being forced to sign the consent directive violate Doe's Fifth Amendment rights?

6. Reckmeyer was charged with running a massive drug importation and distribution scheme alleged to be a continuing criminal enterprise (CCE) in violation of the federal CCE statute. Relying on a portion of the CCE statute authorizing forfeiture to the government of property acquired as a result of drug violations, the indictment sought forfeiture of specified assets in Reckmeyer's possession. The district court entered a restraining order forbidding Reckmeyer from transferring any of the potentially forfeitable assets, but Reckmeyer nonetheless transferred $25,000 to Caplin & Drysdale, a law firm, for preindictment legal services. The firm placed the money in escrow and continued to represent Reckmeyer after he was indicted. Reckmeyer subsequently reached a plea agreement with the government in which he entered a guilty plea to the CCE charge and agreed to forfeit all the assets listed in the indictment. A forfeiture order was entered by the district court when Reckmeyer was sentenced. Caplin & Drysdale filed a petition challenging the order, claiming an interest in $170,000 of Reckmeyer's assets for expenses incurred in conducting his defense, seeking the $25,000 held in escrow, and

arguing that forfeiture of attorney's fees under the CCE statute would violate Reckmeyer's Sixth Amendment right to counsel. Was their argument correct?

7. The Internal Revenue Service filed a claim in the Chapter 11 bankruptcy proceeding of American Biomaterials Corp. (ABC) in an effort to collect unpaid taxes and penalties from ABC. The bankruptcy court and district court disallowed the penalty portion, which exceeded $120,000. Both courts concluded that ABC's failure to comply with the tax code was the result of embezzlement by two ABC officers. This caused the bankruptcy and district courts to rule that ABC's noncompliance with the tax code was due to reasonable cause rather than willful neglect. On appeal to the Third Circuit Court of Appeals, however, the IRS argued that ABC should be held accountable on a vicarious basis for the actions of its wrongdoing officers, and that the penalties therefore should be assessed against ABC. Was the IRS correct in this argument?

8. Muniz was arrested on a charge of driving under the influence of alcohol. He was taken to a booking center, where he was asked several questions by a police officer without first being given the *Miranda* warnings. Videotape (which included an audio portion) was used to record the questions and Muniz's answers. The officer asked Muniz his name, address, height, weight, eye color, date of birth, and current age. Muniz stumbled over answers to two of these questions. The officer then asked Muniz the date of his sixth birthday, but Muniz did not give the correct date. At a later point, Muniz was read the *Miranda* warnings for the first time. He was later convicted of the charged offense, with the trial court denying his motion to exclude the videotape (both video and audio portions) from evidence. Assume that the video portion of the tape violated neither the Fifth Amendment nor *Miranda.* Should all or any part of the audio portion of the tape (which contained Muniz's stumbling responses to two questions plus his incorrect answer to the sixth birthday date question) have been excluded as a violation of either the Fifth Amendment or *Miranda?*

9. Riggs, a Georgia resident, used his home computer to gain unlawful access to a Bell South Telephone Company computer file. He then downloaded the file and transferred it via an interstate computer data network to an Illinois computer bulletin board. Neidorf, who lived in Missouri, downloaded the file, revised it to conceal how it had been acquired, and uploaded it back to the bulletin board. Riggs and Neidorf were later charged with various violations of federal criminal law, including interstate transportation of stolen property. They challenged the applicability of the interstate transportation of stolen property statute, asserting that the electronic impulses which crossed state lines were not "goods, wares, or merchandise" within the meaning of the statute and that the "thing" transferred never took the tangible form contemplated by the statute. Should the trial court have dismissed the interstate transportation of stolen property charge on the grounds asserted by Riggs and Neidorf?

10. Ferris J. Alexander owned various businesses that dealt in sexually explicit materials. He was convicted on various counts of violating federal obscenity laws and the RICO statute. The obscenity convictions served as the predicates for the RICO convictions. Besides sentencing Alexander to a prison term and a fine, the district court ordered Alexander, as punishment for the RICO violations, to forfeit his businesses and approximately $9 million acquired through racketeering activity. The court of appeals affirmed the forfeiture order. In doing so, it rejected Alexander's argument that his businesses were expression-oriented and that the forfeiture order thus violated the First Amendment. Was Alexander's argument correct?

11. In December 1983, a grand jury indicted Automated Medical Laboratories, Inc. (AML), Richmond Plasma Corporation (RPC) (a wholly owned AML subsidiary), and three former RPC managers for engaging in a conspiracy that included falsification of logbooks and records required to be maintained by businesses producing blood plasma. The falsification was designed to conceal from the Food and Drug Administration (FDA) various violations of federal regulations governing the plasmapheresis process and facilities. The evidence introduced at trial indicated that the managers and several other members of the team charged with ensuring compliance with FDA regulations had actively participated in record falsification. AML was convicted and appealed on the ground that there was no evidence that any officer or director of AML knowingly or willfully participated in or authorized the unlawful practices at RPC. Was AML's conviction in the absence of such proof proper?

INTENTIONAL TORTS

INTRODUCTION

Torts are private (civil) wrongs against persons or their property. The basis of tort liability is a breach of a legal duty owed to another person resulting in some legally recognizable harm to that person. The primary aim of tort law is to compensate injured persons for such harms.

NATURE AND FUNCTION OF TORT LAW

Persons injured by the tortious act of another may file a civil suit for the *actual (compensatory) damages* that they have suffered as a result of a tort. Depending on the facts of the particular case, these damages may be for direct and immediate harms, such as physical injuries, medical expenses, and lost pay and benefits, or for harms as intangible as loss of privacy, injury to reputation, or emotional distress.

In cases where the behavior of the person committing a tort is particularly reprehensible, injured victims may also be able to recover an award of *punitive damages.* Punitive damages are not intended to compensate tort victims for their losses. Instead, they are designed to punish flagrant wrongdoers and to deter them and others from engaging in similar conduct in the future. Accordingly, they are theoretically reserved for only the most egregious forms of wrongdoing. Punitive damages have always been controversial, but they have grown more so in recent years because of the size of some punitive damage awards and the perception that juries are awarding them in cases where they are not justified.

The punishment function of punitive damage awards is obviously similar to the deterrent function in criminal law. Some kinds of behavior can give rise to both criminal and tort liability. For example, a rapist may be criminally liable for rape and also liable for the torts of assault, battery, false imprisonment, and intentional infliction of mental distress. However, since tort suits are civil rather than criminal, the plaintiff's burden of proof in a tort case is the *preponderance of the evidence,* rather than the more stringent beyond a reasonable doubt standard that applies to criminal cases. This means that the greater weight of the evidence introduced at the trial

FIGURE 1	Crimes and Intentional Torts	
	Crimes	**Intentional Torts**
Nature	Criminal	Civil
Elements	1. Violation of a statute 2. Intent	1. Harm to another person or property 2. Intent
Actors	Prosecutor versus defendant	Plaintiff (victim) versus defendant (tortfeasor)
Burden	Prosecutor must establish the defendant's guilt beyond a reasonable doubt	Plaintiff must establish the defendant's liability by a preponderance of the evidence
Punishment	Fines, imprisonment, execution	Defendant may have to pay the plaintiff compensatory and punitive damages

must support the plaintiff's position on every element of the case. Figure 1 summarizes the important differences between criminal and tort liability.

In tort law, society is engaged in a constant balancing of competing social interests. Excessive protection of some people's physical integrity, for example, may unduly impair other people's freedom of movement. Likewise, undue protection of peace of mind, privacy, and personal reputation may inordinately restrict constitutionally protected freedoms of speech and of the press. Over time, our tort law has demonstrated a tendency to protect an increasingly broad range of personal interests. Some commentators have explained this tendency by saying it demonstrates the courts' growing sensitivity to the nature of life in an increasingly interdependent urban industrialized society. Whatever its origins, this and the next chapter demonstrate that, although the range of the human interests that tort law protects is expanding, the courts have remained mindful of the fact that the protection of any given interest necessarily involves a trade-off in the form of limitations placed on other competing social interests.

Torts are generally classified according to the level of fault exhibited by the wrongdoer's behavior. This chapter deals with **intentional torts**—behavior that indicates either the wrongdoer's conscious desire to cause harm to a legally protected interest or the wrongdoer's knowledge that such harm is substantially certain to result from his actions. The following chapter discusses tort liability founded on principles of *negligence* and *strict liability*, neither of which require proof of any intentional wrongdoing by a defendant.

INTERFERENCE WITH PERSONAL RIGHTS

Battery

The tort of *battery* protects a fundamental personal interest—the right to be free from harmful or offensive bodily contacts. Battery is the *intentional, harmful* or *offensive touching of another without his consent.* A contact is *harmful* if it produces any bodily injury. As the following *England* case illustrates, even nonharmful contacts may be considered battery if they are *offensive*—that is, calculated to offend a reasonable sense of personal dignity. Direct contact between a wrongdoer's body and the body of another is not necessary for a battery to result. For example, if Delano throws a rock at Stevens or places a harmful or offensive substance in her food, Delano has committed a battery if Stevens is hit by the rock or if she eats the food. Nor is it necessary that the wrongdoer actually intend to produce the contact if contact in fact results and the wrongdoer's intent was merely to threaten the victim with contact. So, if Delano threatens to shoot Stevens with a gun he mistakenly believes is unloaded, and ends up shooting Stevens, Delano would be liable for battery.

Also, the person who suffers the harmful or offensive touching does not have to be the person whom the wrongdoer intended to injure for liability for battery to occur. Under a general intentional tort concept called the doctrine of *transferred intent,* a wrongdoer who intends to injure one person, but injures another, is nonetheless liable to the person injured, despite the absence of any specific intent to injure him. So, if Walters is hit by the rock thrown at Stevens, or if he eats Stevens's food, Delano would be liable to Walters for battery. Finally, touching anything connected with a person's body in a harmful or offensive manner can also create liability for battery. So, if Johnson snatches Martin's purse, or kicks her dog while she is walking her dog on a leash, he may be liable for battery even though he has not touched her body.

Some of the most interesting battery cases involve the nature of the *consent* that is necessary to avoid liability for battery. As a general rule, consent must be *freely* and *intelligently* given to be a defense to battery. In some cases, consent may be inferred from a person's voluntary participation in an activity. Such consent is ordinarily limited, however, to contacts that are considered a normal consequence of the activity in question. For example, Joe Frazier would be unable to win a battery suit against Muhammad Ali for injuries he suffered during their famous "Thrilla in Manila" title fight. However, the quarterback who is knifed on the 50-yard line during a game has a valid battery claim.

Assault

The tort of **assault** protects the personal interest in freedom from the *apprehension* of battery. Any *attempt* to cause a harmful or offensive contact with another, or any *offer* to cause such a contact, is an assault if it causes a *well-grounded apprehension of imminent (immediate) battery* in the mind of the person threatened with contact. Whether the threatened contact actually occurs is irrelevant.

Because assault is limited to threats of *imminent* battery, threats of *future* battery do not create liability for assault. Likewise, because assault focuses on the apprehension in the mind of the victim, the threats in question must create a reasonable apprehension of battery in the victim's mind. Therefore, threatening words, unaccompanied by any other acts or circumstances indicating an intent to carry out the threat, do not amount to an assault. Finally, the elements of assault require that the victim must actually experience an apprehension of imminent battery before liability results. Therefore, if Markham fires a rifle at Thomas from a great distance and misses him, and Thomas learns of the attempt on his life only at a later date, Markham is not liable to Thomas for the tort of assault.

ENGLAND v. S & M FOODS, INC.
511 So.2d 1313 (La. Ct. App. 1987)

Betty England worked at a Dairy Queen restaurant owned by S & M Foods in Tallulah, Louisiana. One day while she was at work, her manager, Larry Garley, became upset when several incorrectly prepared hamburgers were returned by a customer. Garley allegedly expressed his dissatisfaction by using profane language and throwing a hamburger that hit England on the leg. England filed a battery suit against Garley and S & M and won a $1,000 judgment. Garley and S & M appealed.

Jones, Judge   Defendants contend no battery was committed because Garley did not intend to inflict bodily harm upon England. They argue Garley was disgusted about the returned hamburgers and threw one toward the trash can and it inadver- tently splattered on her and Alcie Rash, another employee. They contend that England's embarrassment was caused as much by her overreaction to the situation as by Garley's conduct.

England said that Garley used profane language when he told her to prepare the hamburgers correctly. She said Garley, while looking straight at her, then threw the hamburger which hit her on the leg. She testified that she argued with Garley about the matter and that several patrons observed the incident which caused her to cry and become emotionally upset.

Rash said that she did not see Garley throw the hamburger, but observed it hit the floor and splatter mayonnaise and mustard on her and England.

A battery is any intentional and unpermitted contact with the plaintiff's person or anything attached to it. In the area of intentional torts, intent means the defendant either desired to bring about the physical results of his act or believed they were substantially certain to follow from what he did. Mental distress and humiliation in connection with a battery are compensable items of damage.

The totality of the evidence provided a substantial basis for the trial judge to conclude Garley must have been substantially certain the hamburger would hit England or splatter on her when he threw it toward her. His contact with her was, therefore, intentional and unpermitted and constituted a battery.

Judgment for England affirmed.

False Imprisonment

The tort of **false imprisonment** protects the personal interest in freedom from *confinement*. False imprisonment is the intentional *confinement of another* for an *appreciable time* (a few minutes is enough) *without his consent*. Confinement may result from physical barriers to the plaintiff's freedom of movement, such as locking a person in a room with no other doors or windows, or the use of physical force or the threat to use physical force against the plaintiff. Confinement also results from the assertion of legal authority to detain the plaintiff, or the detention of the plaintiff's property—for example, a purse containing a large sum of money. Likewise, a threat to harm another, such as the plaintiff's spouse or child, can also be confinement if it prevents the plaintiff from moving.

The confinement required for false imprisonment must be *complete*. Partial confinement of another by blocking her path or by depriving her of one means of escape where several exist, such as locking one door of a building having other, unlocked doors, does not amount to false imprisonment. The fact that a means of escape exists, however, does not render a confinement partial if the plaintiff cannot reasonably be expected to know of its existence. The same is true if it involves some unreasonable risk of harm to the plaintiff, such as walking a tightrope or climbing out of a second-story window, or some affront to his sense of personal dignity (e.g., Jones steals Smith's clothes while Smith is swimming in the nude).

The personal interest in freedom from confinement protected by false imprisonment involves a mental element—knowledge of confinement—as well as a physical element—freedom of movement. Therefore, courts generally hold that the plaintiff must have *knowledge* of his confinement before liability for false imprisonment arises. Similarly, liability for false imprisonment does not arise in cases where the person has *consented* to his confinement. Such consent, however, must be freely given. Consent in the face of an implied or actual threat of force or an assertion of legal authority by the confiner is not freely given.

As the following *Speight* case indicates, many contemporary false imprisonment cases involve shoplifting. The common law held store owners liable for any torts committed while detaining a suspected shoplifter if subsequent investigation revealed that the detainee was innocent of any wrongdoing. In an attempt to accommodate the legitimate interests of store owners in preventing theft of their property, most states have passed statutes giving store owners a *conditional privilege* to stop persons who they reasonably believe are shoplifting. However, the owner must act in a reasonable manner and only detain the suspect for a reasonable length of time. Store owners who act within the scope of such a statute are not liable for any torts committed in the process of detaining a suspected shoplifter.

J.H. Harvey Co. v. Speight
344 S.E.2d 701 (Ga. Ct. App. 1986)

Acting on information that someone had just stolen several cartons of cigarettes from the store, the manager of Harvey's Supermarket stepped outside and approached Speight, who had himself walked out of the store only moments earlier. Upon being asked by the manager if he had anything that did not belong to him, Speight answered, "No, do you want to see?" He then briefly held the sides of his jacket open and let them close, at which point the manager parted the jacket with his hands to see if anything was concealed there. Simultaneously, Speight pointed to another person in the immediate vicinity and said, "I think that is the man you are looking for." The manager then left Speight to pursue this other person. Speight subsequently filed suit against Harvey's for false imprisonment and assault and battery. When a jury awarded him $2,500 in compensatory damages and $30,000 in punitive damages, Harvey's appealed.

Banke, Chief Judge   Speight testified that the store manager had not been rude to him but stated that he did not consider the manager's conduct in looking inside his jacket as courteous. He admitted that he had invited this search and that the manager had not cursed him nor spoken loudly to him; however, he testified that he felt the manager was angry because of the look in his eyes and the fact that several people had followed the manager out of the store. At trial, Speight testified that the entire encounter had lasted about 45 seconds, whereas during an earlier deposition he had testified that the encounter lasted between 15 and 30 seconds.

According to *Prosser, Law of Torts* (4th ed.), in false imprisonment:

[T]he imprisonment need not be for more than an appreciable length of time, and . . . it is not necessary that any damage result from it other than the confinement itself, since the tort is complete with even a brief restraint of the plaintiff's freedom. . . . It is essential, however, that the restraint be against the plaintiff's will, and if he agrees of his own free choice to surrender his freedom of motion, as by remaining in a room or accompanying the defendant voluntarily, to clear himself of suspicion or to accommodate the desires of another, rather than yielding to the constraint of a threat, then there is no imprisonment.

Speight's testimony in this case fails to establish any involuntary restraint by Harvey's store manager or employees. Although a person need not make an effort to escape or await application of open force before he can recover, there must be restraint whether by force or fear. With regard to the second count of the complaint, Speight admitted that any touching of his person had been invited by him; and such invitation is inconsistent with the torts of assault and battery. The evidence was consequently insufficient to support any recovery.

Judgment reversed in favor of Harvey's.

Defamation

The tort of *defamation* protects the individual's interest in his *reputation*. It recognizes the value that society places on reputation, concerning not only the individual's personal dignity but also the value that a good reputation has in the individual's business dealings with others. Defamation is ordinarily defined as the unprivileged *publication of false and defamatory statements* concerning another. A defamatory statement is one that harms the reputation of another by injuring his community's estimation of him or by deterring others from associating or dealing with him. Whether a given statement is defamatory is ordinarily decided by a jury.

Because the primary focus of defamation is to protect the *individual's* right to reputation, an essential element of defamation is that the alleged defamatory statement must be "of and concerning" the plaintiff. That is, the statement must harm the particular plaintiff's reputation. This causes several problems. What about allegedly fictional accounts such as those found in novels and short stories? Do they amount to defamation if the fictional characters bear a substantial resemblance to real persons? Most courts that have dealt with the issue say they do, if a reasonable reader would identify the plaintiff as the subject of the story. Similarly, humorous or satirical accounts do not ordinarily amount to defamation unless a reasonable reader would believe that they purport to describe real events. Likewise, statements of personal opinion traditionally have been thought not to be a proper ground for defamation because they are not statements of fact concerning the plaintiff, unless such statements imply the existence of undisclosed facts that are false and defamatory. Thus, the statement that "Smedley is a lousy governor" would probably not be actionable. But, the statement "I think Irving must be a thief" may be defamatory because a jury may believe that the statement implies that its maker knows facts that justify this opinion.

What about defamatory statements concerning particular groups of persons? The courts generally hold that an individual member of a defamed group cannot recover for damage to her personal reputation unless the group is so small that the statement can reasonably be understood as referring to specific members. This is also true when the circumstances in which the statement is made are such that it is reasonable to conclude that a particular group member is being referred to. So, the statement that "all Germans are thieves," standing alone, would not provide the basis for a defamation suit by any person of German descent. However, if Schmidt, a person of German origin, is being considered for a controller's position in her employer's company and a fellow employee makes the same statement in response to a question concerning Schmidt's qualifications for the job, the statement would probably be a proper basis for a defamation suit.

Finally, the courts have placed some limits on the persons or entities that can suffer injury to reputation. For example, it is generally held that no liability attaches to defamatory statements concerning the dead. Corporations and other business entities have a limited right to reputation and can file suit for defamatory statements that harm them in conducting their business or deter others from dealing with them. As a general rule, statements about a corporation's officers, employees, or shareholders do not amount to defamation of the corporation unless such statements also reflect on the manner in which the corporation conducts its business. Statements concerning the quality of a corporation's products or the quality of its title to land or other property may be the basis of an *injurious falsehood* suit.[1]

Publication   The elements of the tort of defamation require *publication* of a defamatory statement before liability for defamation arises. This requirement can be misleading because, as a general rule, no widespread communication of a defamatory statement is required for publication. Communication of the defamatory statement to *one person* other than the person defamed is ordinarily sufficient for publication. Making a defamatory statement about a person in a personal conversation with him or in a private letter sent to him therefore does not satisfy the publication requirement. In addition, the courts generally hold that one who repeats or republishes a defamatory statement is liable for defamation, regardless of whether he identifies the source of the statement.

Libel and Slander   The courts have divided the tort of defamation into two categories, libel and slander, depending on the medium used to communicate the defamatory statement. **Libel** refers to written or printed defamations or to those that have a physical form, such as a defamatory picture or statue. **Slander** refers to oral defamation. The advent of radio and television initially resulted in some judicial confusion concerning the proper classification of defamatory statements communicated by these new media. Today, the great majority of courts treat broadcast defamations as libel. The distinction between libel and slander is important because the courts have traditionally held that libel,

---

[1]Chapter 8 discusses injurious falsehood in detail.

due to its more permanent nature and the seriousness that we tend to attach to the written word, is actionable without any proof of special damage (the loss of anything of monetary value) to the plaintiff. Slander, however, is generally not actionable without proof of special damage, unless the nature of the slanderous statement is so serious that it can be classified as *slander per se.* In slander per se, injury to the plaintiff's reputation is presumed. Four defamatory statements ordinarily qualify for per se treatment: allegations that the plaintiff (1) has committed a crime involving moral turpitude or potential imprisonment, (2) has a loathsome disease (usually a venereal disease or leprosy), (3) is professionally incompetent or guilty of professional misconduct, or (4) is guilty of serious sexual misconduct.

Defamation and the Constitution   Nowhere is the social balancing task of tort law more obvious than in cases of defamation. Overzealous protection of individual reputation could result in an infringement of our constitutionally protected freedoms of speech and of the press, which could thereby inhibit the free flow of information necessary to a free society. In recent years, the Supreme Court has balanced these conflicting social interests in a series of important cases that define the amount of protection the Constitution affords to otherwise defamatory statements. Under the common law, defendants were strictly liable (liable without fault) for defamatory statements. In *New York Times v. Sullivan,* however, the Court held that *public officials* seeking to recover for defamatory statements relating to performance of their official duties must prove *actual malice* (knowledge of falsity or reckless disregard for the truth) on the part of a media defendant to recover any damages.[2] This significant limitation on public officials' right to reputation was justified largely by the public interest in "free and unfettered debate" on important social issues.

For similar reasons, the Court subsequently extended the actual malice test to *public figures,* persons in the public eye because of their celebrity status or because they have voluntarily involved themselves in matters of public controversy.[3] Then,

in *Gertz v. Robert Welch, Inc.,* the Court refused to extend the actual malice test to media defamation of private citizens who involuntarily become involved in matters of public concern.[4] Instead, the Court held that to recover compensatory damages, such persons must prove some degree of fault at least amounting to negligence on the part of the defendant; to recover punitive damages, they must prove actual malice. Most recent was *Dun & Bradstreet, Inc. v. Greenmoss Builders, Inc.,* a case involving a private figure plaintiff—a construction contractor—and defamatory speech about a matter of purely private concern—a false credit report.[5] The Court refused to apply the *Gertz* standard and upheld a recovery based on the common law strict liability standard.

The amount of protection the Constitution affords to otherwise defamatory statements appears to depend on two factors: whether the plaintiff is a public figure or official or a private person and whether the subject matter of the speech at issue is a matter of public concern or private concern. The Court has yet to speak definitively on the standard that it will apply to cases involving defamatory statements about private matters concerning public figures and officials. Its decisions to date, however, suggest that the *Gertz* test is likely to be applied to such cases.

Defenses to Defamation   *Truth* is an absolute defense to defamation. The tort of defamation requires that a statement serving as the basis of a defamation suit be *false* as well as defamatory.

Even where defamatory statements are false, a defense of *privilege* may serve to prevent liability in some cases. The idea of privilege recognizes the fact that, in some circumstances, other social interests may be more important than an individual's right to reputation. Privileges are either *absolute* or *conditional.* Absolute privileges shield the author of a defamatory statement regardless of her knowledge, motive, or intent. Absolutely privileged statements include those made by participants in judicial proceedings, legislators or

---

[2]376 U.S. 254 (U.S. Sup. Ct. 1964).

[3]*Curtis Publishing Co. v. Butts,* 388 U.S. 130 (U.S. Sup. Ct. 1967).

[4]418 U.S. 323 (U.S. Sup. Ct. 1974).

[5]472 U.S. 749 (U.S. Sup. Ct. 1985).

witnesses in the course of legislative proceedings, certain executive officials in the course of their official duties, and between spouses in private.

Conditional privileges are conditioned on their proper use. One who *abuses* a conditional privilege by making a defamatory statement with the knowledge that it is false, or in reckless disregard of the truth, loses the protection afforded by the privilege. Conditional privileges are abused when the author of a defamatory statement acts with an improper motive, such as a purpose other than protecting the interests justifying the privilege. The author can also exceed the scope of the privilege by communicating the defamation unnecessarily to third persons who do not share his interests. Conditional privileges are often recognized when the author of a defamatory statement acts to protect her own legitimate interests or those of a third person with whom she shares some interest or to whom she owes some duty. Many intracorporate communications enjoy such a conditional privilege.

In recent years, the courts have also begun to recognize a conditional privilege of "fair comment." This privilege protects fair and accurate media reports of defamatory matter in reports or proceedings of official action or originating from public meetings. The privilege is justified by the public's right to know what occurs in such proceedings and meetings. The conditional privilege most important to business, however, is the traditional privilege enjoyed by employers who provide prospective employers with reference letters about former employees. Despite this privilege, employers in recent years have faced a growing number of defamation claims from disgruntled former employees. As a result, many companies, as a matter of policy, refuse to divulge any information about former employees other than to confirm that they did work for the company at one time and the duration of their employment. However, as the following *Lewis* case indicates, even such a policy does not always shield employers from liability.

LEWIS V. EQUITABLE LIFE ASSURANCE SOCIETY
389 N.W. 2d 876 (Minn. Sup. Ct. 1986)

Carole Lewis, Mary Smith, Michelle Rafferty, and Suzanne Loizeaux were employed as dental claim approvers in the St. Paul, Minnesota, office of the Equitable Life Assurance Society of the United States. In October 1980, they were sent to assist in Equitable's Pittsburgh office. None of the women had ever traveled on company business before, and they departed for Pittsburgh without being given copies of Equitable's travel expense policies or being told that expense reports would have to be filed. Instead, they were verbally given information on Equitable's daily meal and maid tip allowances and told to keep receipts for hotel bills and airfare. In addition, each was given a $1,400 travel allowance which, having no instruction to the contrary, they spent in full.

When they returned to St. Paul, each of the women received a personal letter from management commending her on her job performance in Pittsburgh. Each was also told for the first time that she would have to submit expense reports detailing her daily expenses in Pittsburgh. This they did, but a dispute subsequently arose over the amount of allowable expenses because Equitable's written guidelines differed from the instructions they had received prior to departure. After first changing their reports with respect to maid tips, they were asked to change their reports again, the net effect of which would have been to obligate each employee to return approximately $200 to Equitable. They refused to do this, arguing that the expenses shown on their reports were honestly incurred, a claim that Equitable never disputed. Subsequently, the women were fired for "gross insubordination."

In seeking new jobs, each woman was asked by prospective employers why she had left Equitable, and each said she had been terminated. When asked in interviews to explain their terminations, each stated that she had been terminated for gross insubordination and attempted to explain the situation. Only one of the women found a new job by being forthright with a prospective employer about her termination from Equitable. The others had various difficulties finding new jobs. They filed a defamation suit against Equitable, and when a jury ruled in their favor, Equitable appealed.

Amdahl, Chief Justice   In order for a statement to be considered defamatory, it must be communicated to someone other than the plaintiff, it must be false, and it must tend to harm the plaintiff's reputation. Generally, there is no publication where a defendant communicates a statement directly to a plaintiff, who then communicates it to a third person. Plaintiffs themselves informed prospective employers that they had been terminated for gross insubordination. They did so because prospective employers inquired why they had left their previous employment. The question raised is whether a defendant can ever be held liable for defamation when the statement in question was published to a third person only by the plaintiff.

We have not previously been presented with the question of defamation by means of "self-publication." Courts that have considered the question, however, have recognized a narrow exception to the general rule that communication of a defamatory statement to a third person by the person defamed is not actionable. These courts have recognized that if a defamed person was in some way compelled to communicate the defamatory statement to a third person, and if it was foreseeable to the defendant that the defamed person would be so compelled, then the defendant could be held liable for the defamation.

Several courts have specifically recognized this exception for compelled self-publication in the context of employment discharges. The trend of modern authority persuades us that Minnesota law should recognize the doctrine. Compelled self-publication does no more than hold the originator of the defamatory statement liable for damages caused by the statement where the originator knows, or should know, of circumstances whereby the defamed person has no reasonable means of avoiding publication of the statement or avoiding the resulting damages. In such circumstances, the damages are fairly viewed as the direct result of the originator's actions.

The St. Paul office manager admitted that it was foreseeable that plaintiffs would be asked by prospective employers to identify the reason that they were discharged. Their only choice would be to tell them "gross insubordination" or to lie. Fabrication, however, is an unacceptable alternative.

Finding that there was a publication, we next turn to the issue of truth. True statements, however disparaging, are not actionable. The company contends the relevant statement to consider when analyzing the defense of truth is the one that plaintiffs made to their prospective employers, that is, that they had been fired for gross insubordination. Plaintiffs counter that it is the truth or falsity of the underlying statement—that they engaged in gross insubordination—that is relevant.

Requiring that truth as a defense go to the underlying implication of the statement, at least where the statement involves more than a simple allegation, appears to be the better view. Here, the company's charges against plaintiffs went beyond accusations and were conclusory statements that plaintiffs had engaged in gross insubordination. The record amply supports the jury verdict that the charge of gross insubordination was false.

Even though an untrue defamatory statement has been published, the originator of the statement will not be held liable if the statement is published under circumstances that make it conditionally privileged and if privilege is not abused. The doctrine of privileged communication rests upon public policy considerations. The existence of a privilege results from the court's determination that statements made in particular contexts or on certain occasions should be encouraged despite the risk that the statements might be defamatory.

In the context of employment recommendations, the law generally recognizes a qualified privilege between former and prospective employers as long as the statements are made in good faith and for a legitimate purpose. Plaintiffs argue that a self-publication case does not properly fit within the qualified privilege doctrine, but the logic of imposing liability upon a former employer in a self-publication case appears to compel recognition of a qualified privilege. A former employer in a compelled self-publication case may be held liable as if it had actually published the defamatory statement directly to prospective employers. Where an employer would be entitled to a privilege if it had actually published the statement, it makes little sense to deny the privilege where the identical communication is made to identical third parties with the only difference being the mode of publication. Finally, recognition of a qualified privilege seems to be the only effective means of addressing the concern that every time an employer states the reason for discharging an employee it will subject itself to potential liability for defamation. It is in the public interest that information regarding an employee's discharge be readily available to the discharged employee and to prospective employers, and we are concerned that, unless a significant privilege is recognized by the courts, employers will decline to inform employees of reasons for discharges.

This conclusion does not necessarily determine that the company's statements were privileged. A qualified privilege is abused and therefore lost if the plaintiff demonstrates that the defendant acted with actual malice. The jury found that the company's statements were "actuated by actual malice."

Judgment for the plaintiffs affirmed.

Invasion of Privacy

The recognition of a personal *right of privacy* is a relatively recent development in tort law. At present, four distinct behaviors provide a proper basis for an invasion of privacy suit: (1) intrusion on a person's solitude or seclusion, (2) public disclosure of private facts concerning a person, (3) publicity placing a person in a false light in the public eye, and (4) appropriation of a person's name or likeness for commercial purposes. The thread tying these different behaviors together is that they all infringe on a person's "right to be let alone."

Intrusion on Solitude   Any intentional intrusion on the solitude or seclusion of another constitutes an invasion of privacy if that intrusion would be highly offensive to a reasonable individual. The intrusion in question may be physical, such as illegal searches of a person's home or body or the opening of his mail. It may also be a nonphysical intrusion such as tapping his telephone, examining his bank account, or subjecting him to harassing telephone calls. As a general rule, no liability attaches to examining public records concerning a person, or observing or photographing him in a public place, because a person does not have a reasonable expectation of privacy in these instances.

Publicity Concerning Private Facts   Publicizing facts concerning a person's private life can be an invasion of privacy if their publicity would be highly offensive to a reasonable person. The idea is that the public has no legitimate right to know certain aspects of a person's private life. Thus, publicity concerning a person's failure to pay his debts, humiliating illnesses that he has suffered, and details concerning his sex life constitute an invasion of privacy. Truth is *not* a defense to this type of invasion of privacy because the essence of the tort is giving unjustified publicity to purely private matters. Publicity in this context means a widespread dissemination of private details.

This variant of invasion of privacy, similar to the tort of defamation, represents a potential source of conflict with the constitutionally protected freedoms of the press and of speech. The courts have attempted to accommodate these conflicting social interests in several ways. First, no liability ordinarily attaches to publicity concerning matters of public record or of legitimate public interest. Second, public figures and public officials have no right of privacy concerning information that is reasonably related to their public lives.

False Light   Publicity that places a person in a *false light* in the public eye can be an invasion of privacy if that false light would be highly offensive to a reasonable person. This variant of invasion of privacy may in some cases also involve defamation. As in defamation cases, truth is an absolute defense to liability. For liability for invasion of privacy to arise, however, it is not necessary that a person be defamed by the false light in which he is placed. All that is required is unreasonable and highly objectionable publicity attributing to a person characteristics that he does not possess or beliefs that he does not hold. Signing a person's name to a public telegram or letter without her consent or attributing authorship of an inferior scholarly or artistic work to her are examples of this form of invasion of privacy. Because of the overlap between this form of invasion of privacy and defamation and the obvious First Amendment issues at stake, defendants in false light cases enjoy constitutional protection similar to that enjoyed by defamation defendants.

Appropriation of Name or Likeness   Some of the earliest invasion of privacy cases involved the appropriation of a person's name or likeness for commercial purposes without his consent. Liability for invasion of privacy can be created by using a person's name or image in an advertisement to imply his endorsement of a product or service or a nonexistent connection with the person or business placing the ad. This variant of invasion of privacy differs markedly from those previously discussed in that it recognizes the personal property right connected with a person's identity and that he has the exclusive right to its control.

The potential for conflict between this property right and the freedoms of speech and of the press has been illustrated in recent years by cases involving public figures' *right of publicity,* such as the following *White* case. To what extent do public persons have the right to control the use of their names, likenesses, or other matters associated with their identities? For example, should a well-known movie star have the right to prevent the writing of a book about her life or the televising of a docudrama about her? At this point, the scope of a public person's right of publicity varies greatly from state to state; considerable disagreement exists concerning such issues as its duration and inheritability.

Other Limitations   In addition to the various limitations on the right of privacy discussed earlier, two further limits are applicable to invasion of privacy actions. First, with the exception in some states of cases involving the appropriation of a person's name or likeness, the right of privacy is a purely *personal* right. This means that only living individuals whose personal privacy has been invaded can bring suit for invasion of privacy. Therefore, family members of a person exposed to publicity ordinarily cannot maintain an invasion of privacy action unless their personal privacy has also been violated. Second, corporations and other business organizations generally have no personal right of privacy. They do, however, have limited rights associated with the use of their names and identities. These rights are protected by the law of unfair competition.[6]

_____

[6]Chapter 8 discusses this subject in detail.

WHITE V. SAMSUNG ELECTRONICS AMERICA, INC.
971 F.2d 1395 (9th Cir. 1992)

Samsung Electronics America ran a series of advertisements prepared by David Deutsch Associates, Inc., in a number of national publications. The ads were set in the 21st century and depicted a current item from the popular culture and a Samsung electronic product. The basic message conveyed was that the Samsung products would still be in use at that time in the future. By hypothesizing outrageous future outcomes for the cultural items, the ads created humorous effects.

One of the ads depicted a robot dressed in a wig, gown, and jewelry that Deutsch consciously selected to resemble Vanna White, the hostess of the "Wheel of Fortune" game show. The robot was posed next to a game board that was instantly recognizable as the Wheel of Fortune set, in a stance for which White is famous. The caption of the ad read: "Longest-running game show. 2012 A.D." Deutsch and Samsung referred to the ad as the "Vanna White" ad. White, who had not consented to the ad, filed suit against Deutsch and Samsung, alleging, among other things, violation of her common law right of publicity. When the district court granted the defendants' summary judgment motion, White appealed.

———————— ■ ————————

Goodwin, Circuit Judge   In *Eastwood v. Superior Court* (1983), the California Court of Appeal stated that the common law right of publicity cause of action "may be pleaded by alleging (1) the defendant's use of the plaintiff's identity; (2) the appropriation of plaintiff's name or likeness to defendant's advantage, commercially or otherwise; (3) lack of consent; and (4) resulting injury." The district court dismissed White's claim for failure to satisfy *Eastwood's* second prong, reasoning that the defendants had not appropriated White's "name or likeness" with their robot ad. We agree that the robot ad did not make use of White's name or likeness. However, the common law right of publicity is not so confined.

The "name or likeness" formulation referred to in *Eastwood* originated not as an element of the right of publicity cause of action, but as a description of the types of cases in which the cause of action had been recognized. The source of this formulation is Prosser, *Privacy*, 48 Cal. L. Rev. 383 (1960), one of the earliest and most enduring articulations of the right of publicity cause of action. Even though Prosser focused on appropriations of name or likeness in discussing the right of publicity, he noted that "[i]t is not impossible that there might be appropriation of the plaintiff's identity, as by impersonation, without the use of either his name or his likeness." At the time Prosser wrote, he noted, however, that "no such case appears to have arisen."

Since Prosser's early formulation, the case law has borne out his insight that the right of publicity is not limited to the appropriation of name or likeness. In *Motschenbacher v. R. J. Reynolds Tobacco Co.* (1974), the defendant used a photo of the plaintiff's race car in a television commercial. Even though the defendant had not appropriated the plaintiff's name or likeness, this court held that Motschenbacher's right of publicity claim should reach the jury. In *Carson v. Here's Johnny Portable Toilets, Inc.* (1983), the defendant marketed portable toilets under the brand name "Here's Johnny"—Johnny Carson's signature "Tonight Show" introduction—without Carson's permission.

The district court dismissed Carson's right of publicity claim because the defendants had not used Carson's "name or likeness." In reversing, the sixth circuit found "the district court's conception of the right of publicity . . . too narrow" and held that the right was implicated because the defendant had appropriated Carson's identity by using the phrase "Here's Johnny."

Although the defendants in these cases avoided the most obvious means of appropriating the plaintiffs' identities, each of their actions directly implicated the commercial interests which the right of publicity is designed to protect. As the *Carson* court explained:

The right of publicity has developed to protect the commercial interest of celebrities in their identities. The theory of the right is that a celebrity's identity can be valuable in the promotion of products, and the celebrity has an interest that may be protected from the unauthorized commercial exploitation of that identity. If the celebrity's identity is commercially exploited, there has been an invasion of his right whether or not his "name or likeness" is used.

Motschenbacher and *Carson* teach the impossibility of treating the right of publicity as guarding only against a laundry list of specific means of appropriating identity. A rule which says that the right of publicity can be infringed only through the use of nine different methods of appropriating identity merely challenges the clever advertising strategist to come up with the tenth. If we treated the means of appropriation as dispositive in our analysis of the right of publicity, we would not only weaken the right but effectively eviscerate it. The right would fail to protect those plaintiffs most in need of its protection. The identities of the most popular celebrities are not only the most attractive for advertisers, but also the easiest to evoke without resorting to obvious means such as name, likeness, or voice.

Viewed separately, the individual aspects of the ad in the present case say little. Viewed together, they leave little doubt about the celebrity the ad is meant to depict. Indeed, the defendants themselves referred to their ad as the "Vanna White" ad. We decline Samsung and Deutsch's invitation to permit the evisceration of the right of publicity through means as facile as those in this case. Because White has alleged facts showing that Samsung and Deutsch appropriated her identity, the district court erred by rejecting her right of publicity claim.

Summary judgment reversed in White's favor; case remanded for trial.

Infliction of Emotional Distress

For many years, the courts refused to allow recovery for purely emotional injuries in the absence of some other tort. Thus, victims of such torts as assault, battery, and false imprisonment could recover for the emotional injuries resulting from these torts, but the courts were unwilling to recognize an independent tort of infliction of emotional distress. The reasons for this judicial reluctance included a fear of spurious or trivial claims, concerns about the difficulty in proving purely emotional harms, and uncertainty concerning the proper boundaries of an independent tort of intentional infliction of emotional distress. Recent advances in medical knowledge concerning emotional injuries, however, have helped to overcome some of these judicial impediments. Today, most courts allow recovery for *severe* emotional distress regardless of whether the elements of any other tort are proven.

The courts are not, however, in complete agreement on the elements of this new tort. All courts require that a wrongdoer's conduct must be *outrageous* before liability for emotional distress arises. The *Restatement (Second) of Torts* speaks of conduct "so outrageous in character, and so extreme in degree as to go beyond all possible bounds of decency, and to be regarded as atrocious and utterly intolerable in a civilized community."[7] Some courts, however, still fear fictitious claims and require proof of some bodily harm resulting from the victim's emotional distress. The courts also differ in the extent to which they allow recovery for emotional distress suffered as a result of witnessing outrageous conduct directed at persons other than the plaintiff. The *Restatement (Second) of Torts* suggests that persons be allowed to recover for severe emotional distress resulting from witnessing outrageous behavior toward a member of their immediate family.[8] Where the third person is not a member of the plaintiff's immediate family, the *Restatement (Second)* restricts liability to severe emotional distress that results in some bodily harm.[9]

The tendency to expand the circumstances in which recovery for intentional infliction of emotional distress will be allowed is a matter of growing concern for business because, as the *Monsanto* case that follows indicates, recent years have witnessed a growing number of emotional distress claims filed by employees. These include suits by employees who have been discharged or required to take drug tests. Sexual harassment cases have also been a fertile source of emotional distress claims.

---

[7]*Restatement (Second) of Torts* § 46, comment *d* (1965).
[8]*Restatement (Second) of Torts* § 46(2)(a) (1965).
[9]*Restatement (Second) of Torts* § 46(2)(b) (1965).

White v. Monsanto
585 So.2d 1205 (La. Sup. Ct. 1991)

Irma White, a church-going woman in her late 40s, worked in the labor pool at Monsanto's refinery. In the spring of 1986, she was assigned to the canning department for several weeks. While there, she and three other employees were told to transfer a chemical from a large container into smaller containers. When they noticed that the large container was marked "hazardous—corrosive," they asked for rubber gloves and goggles. After a supervisor sent for the equipment, White began cleaning up the work area and one of the other employees went to another area to do some work. The other two employees sat around waiting for the safety equipment, contrary to a work rule requiring employees to busy themselves in such situations.

Someone informed Gary McDermott, the canning department foreman, that the group was idle. McDermott became angry and went to the work station where he launched into a profane tirade at White and the other two workers present, calling them "motherf-----s," accusing them of sitting on their "f-----g asses," and threatening to "show them to the gate." The tirade lasted for about a minute, and then McDermott left the area. White was upset and began to experience pain in her chest, pounding in her head, and had difficulty breathing. The company nurse suggested she see a doctor. Her family physician met her at the hospital where he admitted her, fearing that she was having a heart attack. She was later diagnosed as having had an acute anxiety reaction. White was discharged after three days and returned to work within a week. Monsanto paid her regular wages while she was off work and the company health plan covered her medical expenses. White later sued McDermott and Monsanto for intentional infliction of emotional distress. When a jury awarded her $60,000, Monsanto and McDermott appealed.

Hall, Justice   LSA-R.S. 23:1032 makes worker's compensation an employee's exclusive remedy for a work-related injury caused by a co-employee, except for a suit based on an intentional tort. The particular intentional tort alleged in this case is the intentional infliction of emotional distress. Most states now recognize intentional infliction of emotional distress as an independent tort, not "parasitic" to a physical injury or a traditional tort such as assault, battery, false imprisonment or the like.

The *Restatement (Second) of Torts*, section 46(1) provides:

One who by extreme and outrageous conduct intentionally or recklessly causes severe emotional distress to another is subject to liability for such emotional distress, and if bodily harm to the other results from it, for such bodily harm.

Several Louisiana court of appeal decisions have recognized and defined the tort, generally in accordance with the *Restatement*. We affirm the viability in Louisiana of a cause of action for intentional infliction of emotional distress with the legal precepts set forth in the *Restatement*. Thus, in order to recover for intentional infliction of emotional distress, a plaintiff must establish (1) that the conduct of the defendant was extreme and outrageous; (2) that the emotional distress suffered by the plaintiff was severe; and (3) that the defendant desired to inflict severe emotional distress or knew that severe emotional distress would be certain or substantially certain to result from his conduct.

The conduct must be so outrageous in character, and so extreme in degree, as to go beyond all possible bounds of decency, and to be regarded as atrocious and utterly intolerable in a civilized community. The extreme and outrageous character of the conduct may arise from an abuse by the actor of a position, or a relation with the other, which gives him actual or apparent authority over the other, or power to affect his interests. Thus, many of the cases have involved circumstances arising in the workplace. A plaintiff's status as an employee may entitle him to a greater degree of protection from insult and outrage by a supervisor with authority over him than if he were a stranger.

On the other hand, conduct which may otherwise be extreme and outrageous may be privileged under the circumstances. Liability does not attach where the actor has done no more than insist upon his legal rights in a permissible way, even though he is aware that such insistence is certain to cause emotional distress. Thus, disciplinary action and conflict in a pressure-packed workplace environment, although calculated to cause some degree of mental anguish, is not ordinarily actionable.

Applying these precepts to the facts of the instant case, we find that White has failed to establish her right to recover from the defendants for an intentional tort. The one-minute outburst of profanity directed at three employees by a supervisor in the course of dressing them down for not working as he thought they should does not amount to such extreme and outrageous conduct as to give rise to recovery for intentional infliction of emotional distress. Such conduct, although crude, rough and uncalled for, was not tortious. The brief, isolated instance of improper behavior by the supervisor who lost his temper was the kind of unpleasant experience persons must expect to endure from time to time. The conduct was not more than a person of ordinary sensibilities can be expected to endure. The tirade was directed to all three employees and not just to White. Although White was a decent person and a diligent employee who would not condone the use of vulgar language and who would be upset at being unjustifiably called down at her place of work, there was no evidence that she was particularly susceptible to emotional

distress, or that McDermott had knowledge of any such susceptibility.

The duty here was not to engage in extreme or outrageous conduct intended or calculated to cause severe emotional distress. The duty was not breached because the conduct was not extreme or outrageous to a degree calculated to cause severe emotional distress to a person of ordinary sensibilities and the supervisor did not intend to inflict emotional distress of a severe nature, nor did he believe such a result was substantially certain to follow from his conduct.

Judgment reversed in favor of McDermott and Monsanto.

Misuse of Legal Proceedings

Three intentional tort theories protect persons against the harm that can result from wrongfully instituted legal proceedings. **Malicious prosecution** affords a remedy for the financial and emotional harm, and the injury to reputation, that can result when *criminal* proceedings are wrongfully brought against a person. This tort balances society's interest in efficient enforcement of the criminal law against the individual's interest in freedom from unjustified criminal prosecutions. A plaintiff seeking to recover for malicious prosecution must prove *both* that the defendant *acted maliciously*—that is, without probable cause to believe that an offense had been committed and for an improper purpose—and that the criminal proceedings were *terminated in the plaintiff's favor.* As a general rule, proof that the defendant acted in good faith on the advice of legal counsel, after fully disclosing the relevant facts, conclusively establishes probable cause. Also, proof of the plaintiff's guilt is generally held to be a complete defense to liability, and the issue of his guilt can be retried in the malicious prosecution suit, despite his acquittal in the criminal proceedings. Proof of the plaintiff's innocence, however, cannot support a malicious prosecution action if the criminal proceedings were not terminated in his favor.

The tort of **wrongful use of civil proceedings** is similar to malicious prosecution, but it is designed to protect persons from wrongfully instituted *civil*

suits. Its elements are very similar to those of malicious prosecution: It requires proof that the civil proceedings were initiated without probable cause and for an improper purpose and proof that the suit was terminated in favor of the person sued.

The tort of **abuse of process** imposes liability on those who initiate legal proceedings for a primary purpose other than the one for which such proceedings are designed. Abuse of process cases normally involve situations in which the legal proceedings compel the other person to take some action unrelated to the subject of the suit. For example, Rogers wishes to buy Herbert's property, but Herbert refuses to sell. To pressure him into selling, Rogers files a nuisance suit against Herbert, contending that Herbert's activities on his land interfere with Rogers' use and enjoyment of his adjoining property. Rogers may be liable to Herbert for abuse of process despite the fact that he had probable cause to file the suit and regardless of whether he wins the suit.

Deceit (Fraud)

Deceit is the formal name of the tort action for damages that is available to victims of knowing misrepresentation, often called **fraud.** The elements of deceit are a false statement of material fact, knowingly made by the defendant, with the intent to induce reliance by the plaintiff, justifiable reliance by the plaintiff, and harm to the plaintiff due to his reliance. The second element, technically called *scienter,* separates deceit from other forms of misrepresentation. Scienter is present only when the maker of a statement believes it is untrue, doesn't believe it is the truth, or recklessly disregards its truth. So, neither negligent nor innocent misrepresentations can serve as the basis for a deceit action.[10] Because most deceit actions arise in a contractual setting, and because a tort action for deceit is only one of the remedies available to a victim of fraud, a fuller discussion of this topic is deferred until Chapter 13, Reality of Consent.

INTERFERENCE WITH PROPERTY RIGHTS

Nature of Property Rights

The rights associated with the acquisition and use of property have traditionally occupied an important position in our legal system. Tortious interference with property rights is generally treated as an offense against the right to *possession*. Therefore, where the party entitled to possession is not the same as the owner of the property in question (e.g., a tenant leasing property from its owner), the party entitled to possession is ordinarily the proper person to file suit for interference with his possessory rights. If the interference also results in lasting damage to the property, however, its owner may also have a right to recover for such damage.

Trespass to Land

A person is liable for *trespass* if he: (1) intentionally and unlawfully enters land in the possession of another, (2) unlawfully remains on such land after entering lawfully, such as a tenant who refuses to move at the end of the lease, (3) unlawfully causes anything to enter such land, or (4) fails to remove anything that he has a duty to remove from such land. In general, no actual harm to the land is required for liability for intentional trespasses, but actual harm is required for liability for reckless or negligent trespasses. Recently, some courts have required plaintiffs to prove actual harm when seeking to recover for trespasses resulting from invisible airborne particulants entering onto their property. Such cases straddle the border between trespass theory and nuisance theory.

It is important to note that a person can be liable for trespass even though the trespass resulted from his mistaken belief that his entry was legally justified. This could arise from a belief that he had a right to possess the land, had the consent of the party entitled to possession, or had some other legal right or privilege entitling him to enter.

Nuisance

Unlawful and unreasonable interferences with another person's right to the use or enjoyment of his land are called *nuisances.* Nuisance suits, unlike trespass actions, do not necessarily involve any physical invasion of a person's property. Noise, vibration, and unpleasant odors are all examples of things that could be nuisances but would not justify a trespass action. In nuisance suits, the courts attempt to balance the competing interests of landowners to use their land as they see fit. Nuisance law recognizes an unfortunate fact of life: to preserve freedom, it must be limited. Put another way, my free use of my property may destroy your enjoyment of yours. For example, should I be able to open a solid waste disposal plant next to your restaurant? The law of nuisance attempts to resolve such perplexing issues.[11]

Trespass to Personal Property

Any intentional intermeddling with personal property in the possession of another is a trespass if it: (1) results in harm to that property (e.g., Franks strikes Goode's dog or throws paint on his car); or (2) deprives the party entitled to possession of its use for an appreciable time (e.g., Franks hides Goode's car and Goode cannot find it for several hours).

Conversion

Conversion is the intentional exercise of dominion or control over another's personal property. To amount to conversion, the defendant's actions must

---

[10]Chapter 45 discusses negligent misrepresentation as an important basis of professional liability for accountants. Innocent misrepresentations can sometimes serve as a defense to the enforcement of a contract. Chapter 13 discusses this aspect of misrepresentation in detail.

[11]Chapter 24 discusses nuisances in detail.

be such a serious interference with another's right to control the property that they justify requiring the defendant to pay damages for the full value of the property. The difference between conversion and trespass to personal property is based on the *degree* of interference with another's property rights. In considering whether an interference with another's property amounts to its conversion, the courts consider such factors as the extent of the harm done to the property, the extent and duration of the interference with the other's right to control the property, and whether the defendant acted in good faith. For example, Sharp goes to Friendly Motors and asks to test-drive a new Ford Thunderbird. If Sharp either wrecks the car, causing major damage, or drives it across the United States, he is probably liable for conversion and obligated to pay Friendly Motors the reasonable value of the car. On the other hand, if Sharp is merely involved in a fender bender, or keeps the car for eight hours, he is probably only liable for trespass. Therefore, he is only obligated to pay damages to compensate Friendly for the loss in value of the car or for its loss of use of the car.

Evolving Concepts of Tort Liability

Recent developments indicate a continuing tendency to expand the scope of tort law as society recognizes an increasing range of personal interests that deserve legal protection. For example, recent cases have recognized the right of fired employees to recover against their employers for a new tort of *wrongful or abusive discharge*.[12] Also, some courts have allowed plaintiffs to recover punitive damages in tort suits arising out of a defendant's bad faith breach of contract,[13] and employee drug-testing programs have spawned a number of claims against employers on intentional tort theories such as defamation, intentional infliction of emotional distress, and invasion of privacy.

Finally, plaintiffs in so-called toxic tort suits, mass actions seeking to recover for a variety of injuries resulting from exposure to toxic substances, are currently attempting to employ novel tort theories to support their claims. Should persons exposed to carcinogenic substances be able to recover for the emotional distress caused by the fear that they may

contract cancer in the future? Should employees whose employers knowingly expose them to such substances in the workplace be allowed to sue their employers for damages in tort that would not be recoverable under their state's workers' compensation statute? All of these examples illustrate the dynamic nature of our legal system in general and of tort law in particular. Given the historical development of tort law, one can reasonably expect that as growing technical knowledge or changing social circumstances create the need to protect new personal interests, tort law will evolve to satisfy that need.

Business Torts

Figure 2 summarizes the many and varied interests protected by the intentional tort theories we have discussed in this chapter. Today, courts also recognize a variety of tort actions designed to protect various economic interests. Chapter 8, Unfair Competition, discusses these torts in detail.

ETHICAL AND PUBLIC POLICY CONCERNS

1. Tort law attempts to protect various individual interests by giving persons whose rights are violated by others the right to sue for money damages. Can monetary awards, however, ever truly compensate persons who have suffered harms such as an invasion of privacy or emotional distress? If not, how do we justify such awards?

2. Safeco Plastics Corporation owns a plant upstream from Morrison's farm. Safeco periodically discharges large amounts of water into the stream, a practice which occasionally results in the flooding of Morrison's property. Assuming that it is cheaper for Safeco to pay damages to Morrison for trespass than it is to take corrective steps to prevent the flooding, is it ethically proper for Safeco to continue to flood Morrison's land?

3. Maxwell is defamed by an article in a local newspaper as a result of careless reporting. When confronted with its error, the paper promptly apologizes and runs an article retracting the defamatory statement. Maxwell has noticed no negative effects from the article, but his lawyer advises him that he would have no trouble proving defamation by the

---

[12]Chapter 50 discusses this subject in detail.

[13]Chapter 18 discusses this subject in detail.

FIGURE 2	Interests Protected by Tort Law

Interest	Tort Theory
Freedom from harmful or offensive contacts	Battery
Freedom from apprehension of battery	Assault
Freedom from confinement	False imprisonment
Right to reputation	Defamation
Right of privacy	Invasion of privacy
Freedom from disagreeable emotions	Intentional infliction of emotional distress
Freedom from improper criminal proceedings	Malicious prosecution
Freedom from improper civil proceedings	Wrongful use of civil proceedings and abuse of process
Possession and enjoyment of personal property	Trespass and conversion
Possession and enjoyment of real property	Trespass and nuisance
Freedom from knowing misstatements	Deceit

paper and that, as a result, the paper's liability insurance company would probably be eager to settle in the event that Maxwell files suit. Should Maxwell sue?

PROBLEMS AND PROBLEM CASES

1. While shopping in a Publix Supermarket, Anthony Gatto was accosted by Publix employees who believed that he had shoplifted some paperback books. Gatto alleged that in the process of trying to get the books from him, Harold Stepp, the store manager, touched "either part of my palm or my wrist or my arms." Gatto later filed suit against Publix for assault, battery, and false imprisonment. At trial, Gatto admitted that he was never prevented from leaving and at all times considered himself free to leave the premises. Was the trial court's directed verdict in favor of Publix on all three tort theories correct?

2. In 1985, Ford Motor Company and its ad agency, Young & Rubicam, Inc., ran a series of 19 television commercials aimed at making an emotional connection with Yuppies, bringing back memories of their college days. Seventies pop songs were sung in each commercial, and the agency tried to get the original artists to sing the songs. One of the songs selected was "Do You Want to Dance," a song from a 1973 Bette Midler album. The agency acquired a license from the copyright holder to use the song, but Midler refused to do the commercial. The agency then hired a former backup singer for Midler to record it, instructing her to "sound as much as possible like the Bette Midler record." After the commercial was aired, a number of people told Midler that it "sounded exactly" like her recording. Midler filed suit against Ford and Young & Rubicam. The trial judge granted summary judgment for the defendants because he believed no legal principle prevented the imitation of Midler's voice. Was the trial judge's decision correct?

3. On April 14, 1984, during the "Saturday Night News" segment of NBC's "Saturday Night Live" program, a skit was presented as the "Fast Frank Feature." A performer was introduced to the audience as Maurice Frank, a tax consultant. The performer bore a noticeable physical resemblance to Maurice Frank, a resident of Westchester County, New York, who was engaged in business as an accountant, tax consultant, and financial planner. The performer proceeded to give "ludicrously inappropriate" tax advice, suggesting, among other things, that viewers claim houseplants as dependents and write off acne medicine under an oil depletion allowance, and guaranteeing that taxpayers who used his service would receive refunds in excess of their earnings. The real Maurice Frank filed a defamation suit against the network. Was he defamed by the skit?

4. In February 1986, Lois Grimsley, a 46-year-old security inspector, unexpectedly gave birth in her home less than two days after doctors had told her that her stomach pains were nothing more than a urinary tract infection and a case of hemorrhoids. A reporter from a local newspaper interviewed Grimsley about the birth, and Grimsley provided details about it and posed for a picture with the child. The story appeared in the local paper the following day, was subsequently picked up by the Associated Press, and also appeared in several other newspapers. In July 1986, a synopsis of the article (including a photo of Grimsley and her son) appeared in the "Hard Times" section of *Penthouse* magazine (a section that the magazine describes as "a compendium of bizarre, idiotic, lurid, and ofttimes witless driblets of information culled from the nation's press") under the heading "Birth of a Hemorrhoid." Grimsley filed suit against *Penthouse* for defamation, invasion of privacy, and intentional infliction of mental distress. Should her suit succeed?

5. In September 1987, *The National Enquirer* ran an article reporting Henry Dempsey's harrowing escape from injury or death when he fell out of a small airplane while in flight but clung to the open boarding ladder of the plane, surviving his copilot's landing with only a few scratches. Dempsey had refused to be interviewed for the article, despite repeated attempts by an *Enquirer* reporter to gain an interview. The reporter allegedly came to his home twice, repeatedly drove past his home for three quarters of an hour after the first refusal, and followed him to a restaurant where she attempted to photograph him and again requested an interview. After the article appeared, Dempsey filed suit against the *Enquirer* for invasion of privacy and intentional infliction of emotional distress. Should Dempsey's suit succeed?

6. Dorothy Yu, an employee of Northwest Pipeline Corporation, was found to have in her possession a confidential personnel document that she was not authorized to possess. She admitted possession and identified Enser, who worked in the records department, as the source of the document. Both Yu and Enser were terminated for violating Northwest's confidentiality policy. Northwest then informed the Utah Job Services that Yu had been fired for this reason and therefore was ineligible for unemployment compensation. Selected nonsupervisory Northwest employees were also informed of the reasons for Yu's termination. Yu filed a defamation suit against Northwest. Should Northwest's motion for summary judgment be granted?

7. Leta Fay Ford's supervisor at Revlon, Inc., Karl Braun, made numerous sexual advances toward her. At a Revlon picnic on May 3, 1980, Braun grabbed Ford, restrained her in a chokehold with his right arm, and ran his hand over her breasts, stomach, and crotch. Later in May, Ford began meeting with various members of Revlon management about Braun, who continued to harass her verbally. Revlon failed to act until nine months after Ford's first complaint, when Braun was called in and confronted, and Ford was told that he would be closely monitored. Three months later, Revlon's personnel director submitted a report confirming Ford's charges and recommending that Braun be censured. One month later, Revlon gave Braun a letter of censure. Due to the harassment, Ford developed high blood pressure, a nervous tic in her left eye, chest pains, rapid breathing, and other symptoms of emotional stress. Four months after Braun's censure, she attempted suicide. Later, Ford filed suit against Revlon for intentional infliction of emotional distress. Was the jury correct in ruling in her favor?

8. The Blanks purchased a lot in the Indian Fork subdivision next to a lot owned by Gary Rawson. When Rawson built his home, he located a basketball goal and dog pen immediately next to the property separating the two lots. The Blanks complained to the subdivision developer that Rawson was violating the minimum setback restrictions applicable to the subdivision and were told that Rawson had received permission from the developer to do so. They then filed a nuisance suit against Rawson. At the trial, they alleged that the sound of the basketball hitting the backboard when Rawson's son played was offensive and that when he missed, the ball could come into their yard. They also stated that the dog was a large one and that the pen was not cleaned regularly, with the result that offensive odors continued to reach their property despite the

10-foot privacy fence Rawson had erected between their properties shortly after their complaint against him was filed. Was the trial judge's order forcing Rawson to remove or relocate the goal and the dog pen proper?

9. Moore was receiving treatment for hairy-cell leukemia at a university hospital. After his spleen was removed as part of that treatment, the treating physician and another university employee determined that his cells were unique. Without Moore's knowledge or consent, they applied genetic engineering techniques to his cells, producing a cell line that they patented and marketed very successfully through agreements with a pharmaceutical company and a biotechnology firm. To further their research, they continued to monitor him and take tissue samples from him for almost seven years after his spleen was removed. When Moore discovered the truth, he filed a conversion suit against the university, which moved to dismiss his claim, arguing that he had no property right in his spleen and that, in any event, his cells were worthless without their subsequent modifications to them. Should Moore's suit survive their motion to dismiss?

10. The Bradleys owned land on Vashon Island in King County, Washington, about four miles north of American Smelting and Refining Company's copper smelter in Ruston, Washington. They sued American on trespass and nuisance theories, arguing that invisible arsenic and cadmium particles emitted by American's smelter had been carried by the wind and deposited on their property. American sought summary judgment on the trespass claim on the grounds that the Bradleys had incurred no actual damages. Even assuming that particles of arsenic and cadmium emitted from American's smelter had settled onto the Bradleys' land, American argued that these materials are innocuous in the tiny concentrations in which they actually had been found in the Bradleys' soil. Assuming American's statements are factually correct, should its motion for summary judgment be granted?

CHAPTER 7

NEGLIGENCE AND STRICT LIABILITY

INTRODUCTION

The Industrial Revolution that changed the face of 19th-century America created serious problems for the law of torts. Railroads, machinery, and other newly developing technologies contributed to a growing number of injuries to persons and their property. These injuries did not fit within the intentional torts framework, however, because most of them were unintended. Some injuries were simply the unavoidable consequences of life in a high-speed, technologically advanced, modern society. Holding infant industries totally responsible for all of the harms they caused could have seriously impeded the process of industrial development. To avoid such a result, new tort rules were needed. In response to these growing social pressures, the courts created the law of negligence.

ELEMENTS OF NEGLIGENCE

Negligence focuses on conduct that falls below the legal standards that the law has established to protect members of society against unreasonable risks of harm. Negligence essentially involves an unintentional breach of a legal duty owed to another that results in some legally recognizable injury to the other's person or property. A plaintiff in a negligence suit must prove several things to recover: (1) that the defendant had a *duty* not to injure him, (2) that the defendant *breached* that duty, and (3) that the defendant's breach of duty was the *actual* and *legal (proximate) cause* of his *injury*. To be successful, a plaintiff must also overcome any *defenses* to negligence liability that are raised by the defendant. Most of these defenses involve behavior by the plaintiff that may have originally contributed to his injury.

Duty

The basic idea of negligence is that each member of society has a duty to conduct her affairs in a way that avoids an unreasonable risk of harm to others. The law of negligence holds each of us up to an *objective,* yet *flexible,* standard of conduct—that of a "reasonable person of ordinary prudence in similar circumstances." This standard is objective because the reasonable person is a hypothetical person who is always thoughtful and cautious and never unreasonably endangers others. It is flexible because it allows consideration of all the circumstances surrounding a particular injury. For example, the law does not require the same level of caution and deliberation of a person confronted with an emergency requiring rapid decisions and action as it does of a person in circumstances allowing for calm reflection and deliberate action. Likewise, to a limited extent, the law considers the personal characteristics of the particular defendant whose conduct is being judged. For example, children are generally required to act as a reasonable person of similar age, intelligence, and experience would act under similar circumstances. Persons with physical disabilities are required to act as would a reasonable person with the same disability. Mental deficiencies, however, ordinarily do not relieve a person from the duty to conform to the reasonable person standard.

Special Duties   The question of whether a particular duty exists is entirely a question of law. Does the law recognize a duty of the defendant to protect the interests of this particular plaintiff from harm? Legal duties can originate from several sources. A *contractual relationship* between the plaintiff and the defendant can give rise to a variety of duties that might not exist otherwise. For example, most professional malpractice cases are based on claims that professionals negligently breached professional duties owed to their clients or to third persons who rely on their competent performance of professional tasks.[1]

Other *special relationships* between the parties have long been recognized as the source of special legal duties. For example, common carriers and innkeepers have long been held virtually strictly liable for damaging or losing the property of their customers. In recent years, many courts have extended this duty to include an affirmative duty to protect passengers or guests against the foreseeable wrongful acts of third persons. This has happened despite the fact that the law has long refused to recognize any general duty to aid and protect others

from third-party wrongdoing unless a defendant's actions foreseeably increased the risk of such wrongdoing. Some recent decisions have imposed a similar duty on landlords to protect their tenants against the foreseeable criminal acts of others.

The relationship between the parties can also affect the *level* of duty that one person owes to another. For example, the common law has long held that the level of duty that a person in possession of land owes to other persons who enter on the land depends on whether such persons were invitees, licensees, or trespassers. **Invitees** are members of the public who are lawfully on public land, such as a park, swimming pool, or government office; they are also customers, delivery persons, or paying boarders who are on private premises for a purpose connected with the business interests of the possessor of the land. **Licensees** are those whose privilege to enter on the land depends entirely on the possessor's consent. Licensees include persons who are on the land solely for their own purposes, such as someone soliciting money for charity, members of the possessor's household, and social guests. **Trespassers** are persons who enter or remain on another's land without any legal right or privilege to do so.

At common law, a possessor of land owed invitees a duty to exercise reasonable care to keep the premises in reasonably safe condition for their use. He also had a duty to protect invitees against dangerous conditions on the premises that he knew about or reasonably should have discovered, and that they were unlikely to discover. He only owed licensees a duty to warn them of known dangerous conditions that they were unlikely to discover. The possessor of land owed no duty to trespassers to maintain his premises in a safe condition, and only a duty not to willfully and wantonly injure them once their presence was known. As the following *Hopkins* case indicates, recent years have seen a marked tendency to erode these common law distinctions. Many courts no longer distinguish between licensees and invitees, holding that the possessor of land owes the same duties to licensees that he owes to invitees. Also, the courts have made numerous exceptions to the minimal duties that possessors of land owe to trespassers. For example, a higher level of duty is ordinarily owed to trespassers who the possessor of land knows are constantly entering the land (e.g., using a well-worn path across the land)

---

[1]Chapter 45 discusses this subject in detail.

and greater duties are ordinarily owed to protect children if the possessor of land knows that they are likely to trespass.

Finally, *statutes* can create legal duties that can be the source of a negligence action. The doctrine of **negligence per se** provides that one who violates a statute is guilty of negligent conduct if a harm that the statute was designed to prevent results to a person whom the statute was intended to protect. The defendant who has violated a statute may still seek to avoid liability by arguing that his violation was not the legal cause of the plaintiff's injury or by asserting some other general defense to liability, but the statutory violation is generally held to be conclusive evidence of breach of duty.

HOPKINS V. FOX & LAZO REALTORS
625 A.2d 1110 (N.J. Sup. Ct. 1993)

On April 26, 1987, Emily Hopkins accompanied her son and daughter-in-law to an open house in Plainsboro, New Jersey, to which they had been invited by a salesperson employed by Fox & Lazo Realtors. When they first arrived, they were not greeted by a realtor, so they started to tour the house on their own. When they reached the kitchen, they were greeted by a Fox & Lazo representative, who left them free to inspect the house unaccompanied. The house's kitchen led up to a family room that was slightly elevated from the front portion of the house, which also contained a powder room and laundry room. Mrs. Hopkins waited on the upper level in the family room while her family viewed the patio and grounds.

When Mrs. Hopkins heard her son and daughter-in-law reenter the house, she sought to join them in the foyer, where the staircase to the second floor was located. She went down the hallway from the laundry room toward the foyer, unaware that a step led down from the hallway into the foyer. The floors on both levels and the step were covered with the same pattern vinyl, causing Mrs. Hopkins to fail to see the step. She fell, fracturing her ankle. She sued Fox & Lazo, arguing that they had a duty to warn her of any known risks inside the house or any risks that a reasonable inspection would have revealed. When the trial court dismissed her complaint on the ground that the broker had no such duty, she appealed.

Handler, Justice   The traditional common law approach to landowner tort liability toward a person who has been injured because of a dangerous condition on private property is predicated on the status of the person on the property at the time of the injury. Historically, the duty of the owner to such a person is gauged by the right of that person to be on the land. Only to the invitee does a landowner owe a duty of reasonable care to guard against any dangerous conditions on his or her property that the owner either knows about or should have discovered.

Initially, we question whether we should resort to the common law doctrine of premises liability to determine if a real-estate broker owes a duty of care to prospective potential purchasers who are inspecting the owner's home on an open-house tour. The rules of the common law embody underlying principles of public policy and perceptions of social values. Because public policy and social values evolve over time, so does the common law. The traditional common law doctrine governing premises liability is no exception. The historical classifications of the degrees of care owing to visitors upon land are undergoing gradual change in favor of a broadening application of a general tort obligation to exercise reasonable care against foreseeable harm to others.

The common law doctrine is rooted in early nineteenth century notions of private property. With the development of a more urbanized, heterogenous, and complex society, the status of persons in relation to the use of property could no longer be adequately accommodated by traditional classifications of the common law. California was the first jurisdiction to eliminate the common law boundaries between premises-liability classifications in its landmark decision *Rowland v. Christian* (1971). Approximately fourteen jurisdictions have also eliminated the hierarchical scheme defining a landowner's duty toward persons who came on to their land. Many other jurisdictions have eliminated the distinction between licensees and invitees.

The inquiry should be not what common law classification most closely characterizes the relationship of the parties, but whether in the light of the actual relationship between the parties under all of the surrounding circumstances the imposition on the broker of a general duty to exercise reasonable care in preventing foreseeable harm to its open-house customers is fair and just.

A real-estate broker, in many situations, manages or directs an open-house inspection of the premises. The broker is responsible for advertising the open house, posting signs, and ultimately inviting customers onto the premises. A broker frequently suggests conducting such an event to a homeowner. The owner is often absent from the premises for the duration of the open house. In this case, defendant extended a personal invitation to Hopkins and her family. One may reasonably assume in this context that a customer acts on the broker's invitation to come on to the property. The customer may reasonably expect to be able to rely on and use the services proffered by the broker in connection with an examination of the premises.

The broker receives very tangible economic benefits from the relationship with the potential buyers who visit the home. The open house enables the broker to sell the house and earn a commission. Also, an open house presents a broker with an opportunity to meet and cultivate future clients. More generally, the broker can discuss other listings with visitors and thus promote his or her individual business interests. Thus, the economic benefit that a broker obtains from staging an open house extends beyond the potential sale of the particular property. We conclude that implicit in the broker's invitation to customers is some commensurate degree of responsibility for their safety while visiting the premises.

In determining the scope of a broker's duty in these circumstances, one must analyze the extent of the invitation, the risk involved in the activity, and the fairness of imposing a duty to avoid that risk. It is highly foreseeable that visitors to an open house could be injured by dangerous conditions during the course of wandering through an unfamiliar house. In many cases, the customer may reasonably expect that the broker will be familiar with the premises and would rely on the broker's presumed familiarity with the house, including a knowledge of all of its important features and physical characteristics. Nevertheless, not all brokers are actually familiar with all of the houses that they may show to potential buyers. Some brokers will not have had the opportunity to inspect the house before the open house commences.

We thus determine that a broker is under a duty to conduct a reasonable broker's inspection when such an inspection would comport with the customary standards governing the responsibilities and functions of real-estate brokers with respect to open-house tours. Such inspection should consist of an examination of the premises to ascertain the obvious physical characteristics that are material to its salability, as well as those features that a prospective purchaser would routinely examine during a "walk through" of the premises. That inspection would impose on the broker the duty to warn of any such discoverable physical features or conditions of the property that pose a hazard or danger to visitors. That duty, however, would not require the broker to warn against any dangers that are not otherwise known to the broker or would not be revealed during the course of such a reasonable broker's inspection.

As a point of comparison, we underscore the fact that a broker's duty does not replicate the more comprehensive duty owed by homeowners towards their invitees. The homeowner's duty to the business guest will be in most circumstances much broader than a broker's duty toward the customer. We further emphasize that the existence of a duty by no means resolves the legal dispute between the parties. Although we are satisfied that a sufficient basis exists for finding that a broker has a duty for the safety of its customers who are visitors at an open-house tour, the trier of fact must ultimately determine whether under the circumstances of this case the broker breached a duty to Mrs. Hopkins.

Judgment in favor of Hopkins; case remanded for further proceedings.

Breach

A person is guilty of breach of duty if she exposes another to an *unreasonable, foreseeable* risk of harm. Negligence consists of doing something that a reasonable person would not have done under the circumstances, or failing to do something that a reasonable person would have done under the same circumstances. If a person guards against all foreseeable risks and exercises reasonable care, but harm to others nonetheless occurs, no liability for negligence ordinarily results. For example, if Wilson is carefully driving his car within the speed limit and has a heart attack that causes him to lose control and crash into a car driven by Thomas, Wilson would ordinarily not be liable to Thomas for his injuries. As another member of the public using the highways, Wilson owed Thomas a duty to exercise reasonable care while driving. However, the accident was not the result of any breach of that duty because it was unforeseeable. If, on the other hand, Wilson's doctor had advised him that he had a heart condition that made driving dangerous, his failure to heed his doctor's warning would probably amount to a breach of duty because he was plainly exposing others to a foreseeable risk of harm by driving.

Of course, many behaviors involve some risk of harm to others, but the risk must be an *unreasonable* one before that behavior amounts to a breach of duty. In deciding the reasonableness of the risk, the courts balance the social utility of a person's conduct and the ease of avoiding or minimizing the risk against the likelihood that harm will result and the probable seriousness of that harm. As the risk of serious harm to others increases, so does the duty to take steps to avoid that harm. The following *Culli* case illustrates the steps a court follows in deciding whether a business has breached its duty to an invitee.

CULLI V. MARATHON PETROLEUM CO.
862 F.2d 119 (7th Cir. 1988)

On Saturday, August 4, 1984, Elizabeth Culli stopped at a 24-hour self-service gas station operated by Marathon Petroleum in Mt. Vernon, Illinois. She filled her gas tank and then picked up five eight-pack cartons of soda that were featured as part of a special soda sale the station was running that day. After paying for the gas, she headed back toward her car. Before she reached her car, however, she slipped and fell on what an ambulance attendant who was called to the scene later described as a "clearish" slippery substance in a pool approximately 8 to 10 inches in width and length. Culli suffered a compound fracture of her ankle and had to use a wheelchair and walker for several months thereafter.

At the trial of her suit against Marathon, the evidence indicated that the station was typically staffed by one person, who would primarily stay inside and run the cash register and was also responsible for replenishing supplies of the other items sold at the station, such as milk, candy, hot food, and sandwiches. The station lot was normally swept once a day during the night shift, but the attendant on duty the evening prior to the accident could not recall whether or not he had swept that night. There was also testimony that spills in general occurred once or twice each day, and that one employee had asked the station manager to hire more help because the station was understaffed, a request that he relayed to his superiors but which went unheeded. When a jury awarded Culli $87,500, Marathon appealed.

Will, Senior District Judge The defendant owed the plaintiff invitee the duty of maintaining its property in a reasonably safe condition. This includes a duty to inspect and repair dangerous conditions on the property or give adequate warnings to prevent injury.

To be liable, Marathon must have had actual or constructive notice of the dangerous condition. Both parties agree that Marathon did not have actual notice.

Constructive notice can be established under Illinois law under two alternative theories: (1) the dangerous condition existed for a sufficient amount of time so that it would have been discovered by the exercise of ordinary care, or (2) the dangerous condition was part of a pattern of conduct or a recurring incident.

In *Hresil v. Sears, Roebuck & Co.* (1980), plaintiff sought damages for injuries she suffered when she slipped on a "gob" of phlegm in the defendant's self-service store. At the time of her accident, there were few customers in the store and, due to the inactivity in the store at the place where she fell, the foreign substance could have been on the floor for at least 10 minutes. The court found that, as a matter of law, 10 minutes was not long enough to give Sears constructive notice of the gob, and "to charge the store with constructive notice would place upon the store the unfair requirement of the constant patrolling of its aisles."

Because of the lack of testimony establishing how long the substance in this case was present, we do not know if it was present for a period of time which would have placed Marathon on constructive notice of it. It could have been present for a few minutes or several hours. Under the first constructive notice theory evidence establishing how long the particular substance was present is necessary.

Under the second constructive notice theory what is needed is a pattern of dangerous conditions which were not attended to within a reasonable time. There was substantial evidence presented at trial establishing that there were spills on a daily basis in the pump area and that the volume of sales on the day in question made it unreasonable for Marathon to sweep the lot only at night and operate for most of the day with only one attendant who was primarily confined to the cash register. The evidence is sufficient to support the jury's verdict that Marathon's maintenance of its property was unreasonable and proximately caused Culli's injury.

Judgment for Culli affirmed.

Causation

Even if a person breaches a duty that he owes to another person, no liability for negligence results unless the breach of duty was the *actual cause,* or the cause in fact, of injury to the other person. To determine the existence of actual cause, many courts employ a *but for* test: A defendant's conduct is the actual cause of a plaintiff's injury if that injury would not have occurred *but for* the defendant's breach of duty. In some cases, however, a person's negligent conduct may combine with the negligent conduct of another to cause a plaintiff's injury. For example, on a windy day, Allen negligently starts a fire by using gasoline to start his charcoal grill. The fire started by Allen spreads and joins forces with another fire started by Baker, who was burning brush on his property but who failed to take any precautions to prevent the fire from spreading. The combined fires burn Clark's home to the ground. Clark sues both Allen and Baker for negligence. In such a case, the court would ask whether each defendant's conduct was a *substantial factor* in bringing about Clark's loss. If the evidence indi-

cates that Clark's house would have been destroyed by either fire in the absence of the other, both Allen and Baker are liable for Clark's loss.

Proximate Cause   Holding persons guilty of negligent conduct responsible for all of the harms that actually result from their negligence could, in some cases, expose them to potentially catastrophic liability. Although the law has long said that those who are guilty of intentional wrongdoing are liable for all of the direct consequences of their acts, however bizarre or unforeseeable, the courts have also recognized that a person who was merely negligent should not necessarily be responsible for every injury actually caused by her negligence. This idea of placing some legal limit on a negligent defendant's liability for the consequences of her actions is called **proximate cause.** Courts often say that a negligent defendant is liable only for the *proximate* results of her conduct. Thus, although a defendant's conduct may have been the *actual cause* of a particular plaintiff's injury, she is liable only if her conduct was also the *proximate (legal) cause* of that injury.

The courts have not, however, reached any substantial agreement on the test that should be employed for proximate cause. In reality, the proximate cause question is one of social policy. In deciding which test to adopt, a court must weigh the possibility that negligent persons can be exposed to catastrophic liability by a lenient test for proximate cause against the fact that a restrictive test inevitably prevents some innocent victims from recovering any compensation for their losses. Courts have responded in a variety of ways to this difficult choice.

Some courts have said that a negligent person is liable only for the "natural and probable consequences" of his actions. Others have limited a negligent person's liability for unforeseeable injuries by saying that he is liable only to plaintiffs who are within the "scope of the foreseeable risk." Thus, such courts hold that if the defendant could not have reasonably foreseen *some* injury to the plaintiff as a result of his actions, he is not liable to the plaintiff for any injury that in fact results from his negligence. Although this rule is often characterized as a rule of causation, in reality it is a rule limiting the defendant's *duty,* because courts adopting the rule hold that a defendant owes *no duty* to those to whom he cannot foresee any injury. On the other hand, such courts commonly hold that a defendant may be liable even for unforeseeable injuries to persons whom he has exposed to a foreseeable risk of harm.[2] The *Restatement (Second) of Torts* suggests that a defendant's negligence is not the legal cause of a plaintiff's injury if, looking back after the harm, it appears "highly extraordinary" to the court that the defendant's negligence should have brought about the plaintiff's injury.[3]

In the following *Republic of France* case, the defendant is able to avoid tremendous liability for the actual consequences of its negligence because the court refuses to hold it legally responsible due to the unforeseeable nature of those consequences.

---

[2]The most famous case adopting this approach is *Palsgraf v. Long Island Railroad Co.,* 12 N.E. 99 (N.Y. Ct. App. 1928).

[3]*Restatement (Second) of Torts* § 435(2) (1965).

REPUBLIC OF FRANCE v. UNITED STATES
290 F.2d 395 (5th Cir. 1961)

On April 16, 1947, the SS *Grandchamp,* a cargo ship owned by the Republic of France and operated by the French Line, which was also 80 percent owned by the Republic of France, was loading a cargo of Fertilizer Grade Ammonium Nitrate (FGAN) at Texas City, Texas. A fire began on board the ship, apparently as a result of a cigarette or match carelessly discarded by a longshoreman in one of the ship's holds. Despite attempts to put it out, the fire spread quickly. A little over an hour after the fire was first discovered, the *Grandchamp* exploded with tremendous force. Fire and burning debris spread throughout the waterfront, touching off accompanying fires and explosions in other ships, refineries, gasoline storage tanks, and chemical plants that were not brought under complete control for days. When the conflagration was over, 500 people had been killed and more than 3,000 had been injured.

The evidence indicated that despite the fact that ammonium nitrate was known throughout the transportation industry as an oxidizing agent and as a fire hazard, no one aboard the *Grandchamp* made any attempt to prevent smoking in the ship's holds. Numerous lawsuits were filed after the incident, many of them against the United States because the FGAN had been manufactured in army ordnance plants. After the United States was found not liable, Congress passed the Texas City Relief Act in 1955. The act left insurance underwriters to bear their own losses but allowed those with uninsured claims to recover up to $25,000 per claim. The U.S. government paid out approximately $16 million to victims of the disaster, obtaining in return assignments of their claims for death, personal injuries, and property damage totaling approximately $70 million. The U.S. government sought to recover the full $70 million. The Republic of France and the French Line argued that they should not be liable for claims arising out of the explosion because FGAN was not known to be capable of exploding under such circumstances. When the trial court rejected their petition for limitation of liability, they appealed.

———————————————— ■ ————————————————

Rives, Circuit Judge In Texas, as elsewhere, not only proximate causal connection but also the very existence of a duty depends upon reasonable foreseeability of consequences. The test of whether a negligent act or omission is a proximate cause of an injury is whether the wrongdoer might by the exercise of ordinary care have foreseen that *some similar injury* might result from the negligence.

The United States argues with much force that the district court found that fault or negligence of the owners caused the fire and permitted it to increase in intensity, and that the fire caused the disastrous explosion. It insists that that causal connection is sufficient. The fallacy in that chain of argument is that it is only the operation of natural forces theretofore recognized as normal which one is charged with foreseeing.

The district court found it "undoubtedly true that the force and devastating effects of this explosion shocked and surprised the scientific field as well as the transportation industry." The court further found as to ammonium nitrate, which constituted approximately 95 percent of the FGAN, and which, with the benefit of hindsight, we now know to be the explosive part of the mixture:

Despite its use as a principal ingredient of high explosives, at the time of the disaster ammonium nitrate was not, and is not now, classified as an "explosive" for transportation purposes by the Interstate Commerce Commission or the Coast Guard. This is true because it was considered that to cause the detonation of ammonium nitrate, an initial shock or "booster" of considerable magnitude was required. The chances of such an initial or booster detonation being encountered in normal conditions of transportation has always been considered so remote as to be negligible.

Substantially all of the evidence is to the effect that the explosion, as distinguished from the fire, could not reasonably have been foreseen.

It would be ironic indeed if the United States were permitted to impose liability for these claims on the Republic of France and the French Line by claiming now that, unlike the officials and employees of the United States, the officials and employees of the French Government and the master of the *Grandchamp* should have known that FGAN was a dangerous explosive and that an explosion from fire should reasonably have been anticipated.

Judgment reversed in favor of the Republic of France.

───

Superseding Causes In some cases, an *intervening force* occurring after a defendant's negligence may play a significant role in bringing about a particular plaintiff's injury. For example, a high wind may spring up that causes a fire set by Davis to spread and damage Parker's property, or after Davis negligently runs Parker down with his car, a thief may steal Parker's wallet while he is lying unconscious in the street. Such cases present difficult problems for the courts, which must decide when an intervening force should relieve a negligent defendant from liability. As the following *Rowe* case indicates, if the intervening force is a *foreseeable* one, either because it frequently occurs in the ordinary course of human events or because the defendant's

negligence substantially increases the risk of its occurrence, it will *not* relieve the defendant from liability. So, in the first example given above, if high winds are a reasonably common occurrence in the locality in question, Davis may be liable for the damage to Parker's property even though his fire would not have spread that far under the wind conditions that existed when he started it. Likewise, in our second example, Davis may be responsible for the theft of Parker's wallet if the theft is foreseeable, given the time and location of the accident.

On the other hand, if the intervening force that contributes to the plaintiff's injury is unforeseeable, most courts hold that it is a **superseding** or **intervening cause** that absolves the defendant of any liability for negligence. For example, Dalton negligently starts a fire that causes injury to several persons. The driver of an ambulance summoned to the scene to aid the injured has been drinking on duty and, as a result, loses control of his ambulance and runs up onto a sidewalk, injuring several pedestrians. Most courts would not hold Dalton responsible for the pedestrians' injuries. One important exception to this general rule, however, concerns intervening forces that produce a harm

identical to the harm risked by the defendant's negligence. For example, the owners of a concert hall fail to install the number of emergency exits required by law for the protection of patrons. A negligently operated aircraft crashes into the hall during a concert, and many patrons are burned to death in the ensuing fire because the few available exits are jammed by panicked patrons trying to escape. Most courts would probably find that the owners of the hall were liable for the patrons' deaths.

ROWE V. STATE BANK OF LOMBARD
531 N.E.2d 1358 (Ill. Sup. Ct. 1988)

In the early morning hours of April 24, 1978, Lori Rowe and Bonnie Serpico were shot by an intruder while working at the offices of their employer, J-Mar Enterprises, in the Glen Hill Office Park in Glen Ellyn, Illinois. Serpico died and Rowe was seriously injured. The intruder was later identified as James Free, a former construction laborer for the park's developer. Free was arrested, convicted, and sentenced to death.

Rowe's and Serpico's estates filed suit against the Paramount Group, Inc., the beneficial owner and manager of the office park; Todd Fennessey, Paramount's managing agent; and the State Bank of Lombard, which held title to the property and served as trustee. The complaint alleged that the defendants were negligent for failing to warn tenants that master keys to the complex were outstanding and unaccounted for; failing to properly maintain the locks and doors on J-Mar's offices; failing to warn of numerous criminal incidents that had been reported at the park; and failing to provide adequate security on the premises. The trial court granted the defendants' motion for summary judgment on the ground that they had no duty as a matter of law to protect Rowe and Serpico from the criminal actions of Free.

Ward, Justice   Generally, there is no duty requiring a landowner to protect others from criminal activity by third persons on his property absent a "special relationship" between the parties. A special relationship has been recognized where the parties are in a position of innkeeper and guest, or business invitor and invitee, but this court has repeatedly held that the simple relationship between a landlord and tenant, or a landlord and those on the premises with the tenant's consent, is not a "special" one imposing a duty to protect against the criminal acts of others. Although there are courts that have placed a duty upon a landlord to protect tenants from foreseeable criminal acts committed by third parties on the premises, the overwhelming majority of courts have not.

A landlord may be held liable for the criminal acts of third parties when it voluntarily undertakes to provide security measures, but performs the undertaking negligently, if the negligence is the proximate cause of injury to the plaintiff. The plaintiffs have not shown that Paramount or Fennessey did anything which can be reasonably considered as a voluntary assumption of protecting Rowe and Serpico from the criminal acts of third persons on the premises. On the contrary, in the lease Paramount specifically disclaims responsibility for protecting its tenants or their property from criminal acts.

There is no evidence in the record that Paramount or its agents were negligent in failing to maintain proper control over the master keys which possibly enabled Free to gain access to a key. They were aware, nonetheless, of the risk posed by the outstanding master keys, having been informed that keys were outstanding and that they were unaccounted for. Under these circumstances we consider that they had a duty either to warn those rightfully on the premises of the danger or to take reasonable precautions to prevent foreseeable unauthorized entries by those with a master key. Having failed to do so, they breached their duty and can be held responsible for the reasonably foreseeable criminal acts of third persons which are proximately caused by their negligence.

Paramount and Fennessey argue that even if they were negligent the criminal acts constituted an "independent intervening cause" of the plaintiff's injuries. Generally, where between the defendant's negligence and the plaintiff's injury an independent, illegal act of a third person has intervened which causes the plaintiff's injury, and without which it would not have occurred, the criminal act is a superseding cause of injury relieving the originally negligent party of liability. There is an exception where the defendant's acts or omissions create a condition conducive to a foreseeable intervening criminal act. If the criminal act is reasonably foreseeable at the time of the negligence, the causal chain is not necessarily broken by the intervention of such an act.

From the record it is a reasonable inference that Free's entry into J-Mar's office was facilitated by the failure to take precautions to guard against unauthorized entries by those with master keys. It is Paramount and Fennessey's contention that although they might have had notice that master keys were outstanding, it was not foreseeable that an individual would use one and enter a tenant's office and assault those present, particularly in light of the fact that there had not been any violent crimes at the office park in the past. On the record the contention

is not convincing. There were 17 incidents of criminal activity at the complex in the preceding two years. Though most were minor thefts from the parking lot area, several of the incidents involved burglaries from offices where there were no signs of forced entry. Even though there had not been previous crimes of violence at the office park, where a plaintiff's injury results from the same risk, the existence of which required the exercise of greater care, unforeseeability of what exactly could develop and the extent of the injury or loss will not limit liability. Under the circumstances here the crimes were within the scope of the foreseeable risk created by the inadequate control of the master keys.

Providing adequate security measures would have been relatively inexpensive. The office space in the park could have been secured simply by "rekeying" the locks, which would cost $2,500. The risk of unauthorized entry could also have been avoided by notifying those on the premises of the danger. In light of the risks created, it would not have been an unreasonable burden for Paramount to assume. The circumstances here create a triable issue of fact as to whether the danger of criminal conduct by individuals possessing passkeys was sufficiently probable and predictable to create a duty upon the defendants to take reasonable precautionary measures, and whether their failure to do so was a proximate cause of the plaintiffs' damages. The trial court erred in granting Paramount and Fennessey summary judgment.

Judgment reversed in favor of Rowe and Serpico; case remanded for trial.

Generally Accepted Causation Rules   Whatever test for proximate cause a court says it adopts, most courts generally agree on certain basic principles of causation. One such basic principle is that persons guilty of negligence "take their victims as they find them." This means that a negligent defendant is liable for the full extent of his victim's injuries even if those injuries are aggravated by some preexisting physical characteristic of the victim. Similarly, negligent defendants are normally held liable for diseases contracted by their victims

while in a weakened state caused by their injuries. They are *jointly* liable—along with the attending physician—for negligent medical care that their victims receive for their injuries.

Negligent defendants are also commonly held responsible for injuries sustained by persons seeking to avoid being injured by the defendant's negligence. For example, Peters swerves to avoid being hit by Denning's negligently driven car and in the process loses control of her own car and is injured. Denning is liable for Peters's injuries. Finally, it is commonly said that "danger invites rescue." This means that negligent persons are liable to those injured in attempting to rescue the victims of their negligence. One corollary of this rescue rule is that the claim of a would-be rescuer ordinarily is not defeated by contributory fault on the part of the rescuer so long as he is not reckless in making the rescue attempt.

Res Ipsa Loquitur

In some cases, negligence may be difficult to prove because the defendant has superior knowledge of the circumstances surrounding the plaintiff's injury. Thus, it may not be in the defendant's best interests to disclose those circumstances if they point to liability on his part. The classic example of this is *Byrne v. Boadle,* where a pedestrian was hit on the head by a barrel of flour that fell from a warehouse owned by the defendant.[4] The victim had no way of knowing what caused the barrel to fall; he merely knew he had been injured. The only persons likely to know the relevant facts were the owners of the warehouse and their employees, but the odds were that they were the ones responsible for the accident. The English court observed: "A barrel could not roll out of a warehouse without some negligence" and held that it was up to the defendant owner to show that he was not at fault. Out of this case grew the doctrine of ***res ipsa loquitur*** ("the thing speaks for itself"). *Res ipsa* applies when: (1) the defendant has *exclusive control* of the instrumentality of harm (and therefore probable knowledge of, and responsibility for, the cause of the harm), (2) the harm that occurred *would not ordinarily occur* in the absence of negligence, and (3) the plaintiff was in no way responsible for his own injury. When these elements are present, most states hold that an *inference* may arise that the defendant was negligent and that her negligence was the cause of the plaintiff's injury. Practically speaking, this may force the defendant to come forward with evidence to rebut the inference that she is responsible. If she fails to do so, a court or jury *may* choose to impose liability on her. Some courts, however, give *res ipsa* much greater effect, holding that it creates a *presumption* of negligence

that requires a directed verdict for the plaintiff in the absence of proof by the defendant rebutting the presumption.

Injury

The plaintiff in a negligence case must prove not only that the defendant breached a duty owed to the plaintiff and that the breach of duty was the legal cause of her injury, but also that the resulting injury was to an interest that the law seeks to protect. Ordinarily, purely physical injuries to a person or her property present no problem in this respect because the law has long protected such interests. Serious problems arise, however, when injuries are purely *emotional* in nature. As you learned in Chapter 6, Intentional Torts, the law has long demonstrated a considerable reluctance to afford recovery for purely emotional harms. The courts' reluctance is due, among other things, to the danger of spurious claims and the difficulty inherent in placing a monetary value on emotional injuries. Given our great reluctance to impose liability for purely emotional harms caused by intentional wrongs, one might correctly assume that an even greater reluctance would exist when the conduct producing an emotional injury was merely negligent.

Negligent Infliction of Emotional Distress
Until fairly recently, most courts would not allow a plaintiff to recover for emotional injuries resulting from a defendant's negligent behavior in the absence of some impact or contact with the plaintiff's person. Today, many courts have abandoned the impact rule and allow recovery for foreseeable emotional injuries standing alone. A large number of such courts, however, still require, as a precondition of recovery, proof that some serious physical injury or symptoms resulted from the plaintiff's emotional distress. Nonetheless, a growing number of courts have dispensed with the injury requirement where the plaintiff has suffered serious emotional distress as a foreseeable consequence of the defendant's negligent conduct.

Third-Party Emotional Distress   In recent years, more and more negligence cases have involved claims by third persons for emotional injuries that they suffered by witnessing a negligently caused harm to another person, usually a spouse or

---

[4]2 H. & C. 722 (Eng. 1863).

child. For example, Mr. Porter has a heart attack after seeing Mrs. Porter run down by a car negligently driven by Denton. Is Denton liable for Mr. Porter's injury? Until fairly recently, most courts would have denied Mr. Porter any recovery on the ground that he had suffered no impact as a result of Denton's negligence. In recent years, however, many courts have abandoned the impact rule in third-party cases in favor of the "zone of danger" test. This test allows third parties who are themselves in the zone of danger created by a defendant's negligence to recover for emotional injuries resulting from the threat of harm to them, regardless of whether any impact ever occurred. Courts following this rule would, therefore, allow Mr. Porter to recover if he was close enough to his wife to be in danger of being hit by Denton's car. Some courts would insist, in addition, that Mr. Porter prove that he suffered some physical injury as a result of his emotional distress.

Today, some courts have abandoned the zone of danger requirement entirely and allow recovery for emotional injuries suffered by third parties, regardless of whether there was any threat of injury to them. However, most courts that have taken this step still attempt to limit recovery in a variety of ways. For example, such courts commonly require that a close personal relationship exist between the third-party plaintiff and the direct victim of the defendant's negligence and that the third party's emotional distress result from actually witnessing the injury to the direct victim. Also, they commonly impose a requirement that the third party demonstrate some physical "injury" resulting from his emotional distress. This area of the law is undergoing rapid development, however, and some recent cases may be found that dispense with the injury requirement or allow recovery for emotional distress suffered as a result of seeing the direct victim in an injured state shortly after the injury occurred.

Defenses to Negligence

The common law traditionally recognized two defenses to negligence: **contributory negligence** and **assumption of risk.** Both of these defenses are based on the idea of *contributory fault:* If a plaintiff's own behavior contributed in some way to his injury, this fact should relieve the defendant from liability. As the following paragraphs indicate, however, the contributory fault idea often produced harsh results, and recent years have witnessed a significant erosion of its impact in negligence cases.

Contributory Negligence   The doctrine of **contributory negligence** provides that plaintiffs who *fail to exercise reasonable care for their own safety* are totally barred from any recovery if their contributory negligence is a *substantial factor* in producing their injury. So, if Parker steps into the path of Dworkin's speeding car without first checking to see whether any cars are coming, Parker would be denied any recovery against Dworkin because of the clear causal relationship between his injury and his failure to exercise reasonable care for his own safety. On the other hand, if Parker is injured one night when his speeding car crashes into a large, unmarked hole in the street caused by a city street repair project, and the facts indicate that the accident would have occurred even if Parker had been driving at a legal speed, he is not barred from recovering damages from the city for its negligence.

In some cases, a contributorily negligent plaintiff may be able to overcome an otherwise valid contributory negligence defense by arguing that the defendant had the **last clear chance** to avoid harm. The doctrine of last clear chance focuses on who was *last* at fault *in time.* Therefore, if, despite the plaintiff's contributory negligence, the harm could have been avoided if the defendant had exercised reasonable care, the defendant's *superior opportunity* to avoid the accident makes him more at fault. For example, Durban pulls into the path of Preston's speeding car without looking, causing an accident. When Preston files suit to recover for the damage, Durban argues that the fact that Preston was speeding amounts to contributory negligence. If Preston can convince the court that the accident could have been avoided if Durban had looked before pulling onto the highway, she has a good chance of overcoming Durban's contributory negligence defense.

Comparative Negligence   Contributory negligence can sometimes produce harsh results because it may operate to prevent slightly negligent persons from recovering any compensation for their losses. In reaction to this potential unfairness, most of the states have adopted **comparative negligence** systems either by statute or by judicial decision. The details of these systems vary by state, but the principle underlying them is essentially the same: Courts seek to determine the *relative fault* of the

---

FIGURE 1	Plaintiff's Recovery under Contributory and Comparative Negligence Systems

Plaintiff's Relative Fault	Contributory Negligence	Comparative Negligence (Pure)	Comparative Negligence (Mixed)
0%	100%	100%	100%
10	0	90	90
60	0	40	0
90	0	10	0

---

parties to a negligence action and to award damages in proportion to the degree of fault determined. For a simple example, assume that Dunne negligently injures Porter and Porter suffers $10,000 in damages. A jury, however, determines that Porter was 20 percent at fault. Under a comparative negligence system, Porter could recover only $8,000 from Dunne. But what if Porter is determined to be 60 percent at fault? Here, the results vary depending on whether the state in question has adopted a *pure* or a *mixed* comparative fault system. Under a pure comparative fault system, plaintiffs are allowed to recover a portion of their damages even if they are more at fault than the defendant, so Porter could recover $4,000. Under a mixed system, plaintiffs who are as much at fault as,

or, in some states, more at fault than, the defendant are denied any recovery. Such a state refuses Porter any recovery, just as though contributory negligence principles still applied (see, for example, Figure 1).

The full extent of the impact that comparative fault systems will have on tort law is as yet undetermined. What is clear, however, is that comparative fault is affecting other tort doctrines besides contributory negligence. For example, as the following *Roggow* case indicates, many comparative negligence states have discarded the doctrine of last clear chance. In addition, some states now apply comparative fault principles to recklessness and strict liability cases, as well as to negligence cases.

ROGGOW V. MINERAL PROCESSING CORP.
698 F. Supp. 1441 (S.D. Ind. 1988)

Charles Roggow, a long-distance truck driver out of Buffalo, New York, made a delivery of scrap aluminum to a processing plant located in Needmore, Indiana, and owned by Mineral Processing Corporation— Needmore Division (Needmore). After making delivery, Roggow was to pick up an unloaded trailer. Because Needmore's employees had failed to secure the header bar of the trailer (the part that secures the sides of the trailer to prevent damaging vibration), Roggow had to fasten the bar before leaving Needmore's plant. The bar had to be set in place at the very top of the trailer, but Needmore had no ladder available for Roggow's use. Consequently, Tracy Phillips, a Needmore employee, offered to assist Roggow by placing him in the bucket of a highloader and raising him high enough to set the bar in place.

Roggow accepted the offer and succeeded in fastening the header bar, but as Phillips was lowering him to the ground, Phillips's sleeve caught the highloader's dump lever, causing the bucket to overturn and dump Roggow approximately 9 feet onto a concrete floor. As a result of the fall, Roggow fractured both wrists and suffered two compressed vertebrae. He filed suit against Needmore. The jury found Roggow's damages to be $80,000 but reduced his award to $48,000 because they found him to be 40 percent at fault. Roggow filed a motion for a new trial, arguing, among other things, that the trial court erred in refusing to instruct the jury on the doctrine of last clear chance.

Endsley, U.S. Magistrate   This matter was tried under Indiana's Comparative Fault Act (the Act). Prior to the enactment of comparative fault, Indiana followed the common law rule of contributory negligence. This antiquated "all-or-nothing" rule totally bars a plaintiff from recovering damages for injuries if he is guilty of negligence, albeit slight. During the twentieth century, common law doctrines were developed to alleviate the harsh results of contributory negligence. Last clear chance was one of those doctrines. Roggow now invites the Court to determine the applicability of this exception to contributory negligence under the Act even though the statute is silent and no Indiana court of review has yet passed on these issues.

Because no Indiana court has addressed this issue, this federal court must determine how the highest court in Indiana would decide this issue if it were presented with the question. Under the Act, assumption of risk is not available as an absolute defense for the defendant. Specifically, "assumption of risk not constituting an enforceable express consent" is a factor to be considered by the fact finder when weighing the fault attributable to the individual actors. Similarly, by its definition in the Act, "fault" necessarily includes the factors which make up last clear chance. The Indiana legislature defined fault as "any act or omission that is negligent, willful, wanton, or reckless toward the person or property of the actor or others." Consequently, just as assumed risk is no longer available to completely excuse the negligence of the defendant, so too, this Court believes, is the doctrine of last clear chance no longer available to completely excuse the negligence of the plaintiff. This conclusion is in accord with the holdings and statutes of a majority of states which have addressed the issue. Consequently, failure to give Roggow's tendered instruction was not error in this case.

Motion for new trial denied.

Assumption of Risk   In some cases, a plaintiff has *voluntarily* exposed herself to a *known danger* created by the defendant's negligence. Such plaintiffs are said to have *assumed the risk* of their injury and ordinarily are denied any recovery for it. The idea here is that the plaintiff *impliedly* consented to accept the risk, thereby relieving the defendant of the duty to protect him against it. For example, Stevens voluntarily goes for a ride in Markley's car, even though Markley has told him that her brakes are not working properly. Stevens has assumed the risk of injury as a result of the car's defective brakes. A person must fully understand the nature and extent of the risk, however, to be held to have assumed it. A plaintiff can also assume the risk of injury *expressly* by entering a contract containing a provision purporting to relieve the defendant of a duty of care that he would otherwise owe to the plaintiff. Such contract provisions are called *exculpatory clauses*. Chapter 15, Illegality, discusses in detail exculpatory clauses and the numerous limitations that courts have imposed on their enforceability. As the *Roggow* case indicated, some states that have adopted comparative negligence systems have done away with the assumption of risk defense in negligence cases and treat all forms of contributory fault under their comparative negligence scheme. The following *Hull* case, however, proves that assumption of risk remains a viable defense in some jurisdictions.

HULL v. MERCK & Co., Inc.
758 F.2d 1474 (11th Cir. 1985)

On September 4, 1980, Augusta Fiberglass Coatings (AFC) began replacing fiberglass sewer lines at three adjacent Albany, Georgia, chemical plants operated by Merck & Co., Inc. The lines delivered waste chemicals into a 1 million gallon neutralizing pool. Merck warned AFC that it intended to continue in operation throughout the replacement activity and that bypass pipes and various safety equipment would be necessary to the work. AFC relayed Merck's warnings to its employees and provided them with rubber boots, pants, coats, and gloves, as well as goggles and masks.

Jim Dale Hull was AFC's supervisor on the job at Merck. Although Hull had long experience working with chemicals, he quit wearing any of the safety gear after a few days on the job. Hull spent four hours each day in the trench dug to expose the pipelines. He regularly breathed gases and allowed liquid to spill on his clothing and body. He noted at the time that the chemical fumes in and around the pipes were a health hazard. On September 22, 1980, Hull stuck his head inside a 20-inch connecting pipe which, due to an accidental spill in the factories, contained an 80 to 85 percent solution of toluene, rather than the 2 percent solution the pipes were supposed to carry. He became dizzy and nauseous and was given oxygen at the plant infirmary.

Within a year after completion of the Merck contract, Hull suffered bone marrow depression, followed by leukemia. Hull sued Merck for $2.5 million plus punitive damages, alleging that: (1) Merck had negligently failed to disclose the nature and health dangers of the waste chemicals carried by the pipelines; (2) Merck had negligently failed to inform him adequately of the necessity for wearing protective gear during construction; (3) the intermittent discharge without warning of high-concentration spills into the pipelines resulted from the negligent operation of the factories; and (4) Merck's decision to continue plant operations and consequently the flow of waste chemicals during the pipeline replacement project amounted to negligence. After being charged by the trial judge that assumption of risk on Hull's part would bar his recovery under Georgia's comparative fault law, the jury ruled in favor of Merck. Hull appealed.

━━━━━━━━━━━━ ■ ━━━━━━━━━━━━

Per Curiam   Under Georgia law, a plaintiff assumes the risk when he "deliberately chooses an obviously perilous course of conduct and fully appreciates the danger involved." The plaintiff must do so voluntarily, "without restriction from his freedom of choice either by the circumstances or by coercion." Georgia typically applies assumption of risk to situations where the plaintiff races to beat a train at a crossing, drag races, or walks onto a pond covered with thin ice. Although assumption of the risk presupposes awareness of the nature and extent of the threat posed, perfect knowledge is not necessary. But Georgia law offers little guidance as to the depth of knowledge a plaintiff must possess to assume the sometimes very subtle risks posed by chemical exposure.

There was ample evidence to justify the charge in this case, especially as it pertained to Hull's allegation that Merck negligently decided to operate the factories during the replacement of the pipelines. Hull knew before he ever entered the plant grounds that Merck and AFC planned for operations to continue, with waste chemicals to be expelled via a bypass system of hoses assembled by AFC workers. Although Hull might or might not have had knowledge of any specific carcinogenic risk posed by toluene, he knew from long experi-ence that the handling of waste chemicals war-ranted protective measures, and that coping with a continued flow of waste warranted an even greater degree of caution.

He also knew Merck and AFC were supplying adequate safety gear, which he used only for the first few days, but which many of his coworkers wore throughout the project without hampering their work. The gear remained available for his use at all times. He testified that while he was working he concluded the fumes were dangerous to good health. Finally, his severe exposure on September 22, 1980, forcefully brought home the risk posed by Merck's operations, yet he voluntarily re-mained, exposing himself for another month or more. The evidence at the trial left the jury free to conclude that Hull's leukemia was caused by post-September 22nd exposure, and Hull's remain-ing after that date might be construed as a knowing assumption of all four of the risks arising from Merck's alleged negligence. In any case, there was more than enough evidence to warrant the jury finding that Hull assumed the risk posed by working around a continuing flow of waste chemicals during the replacement of the pipes.

Judgment for Merck affirmed.

FIGURE 2   **Elements of Negligence**

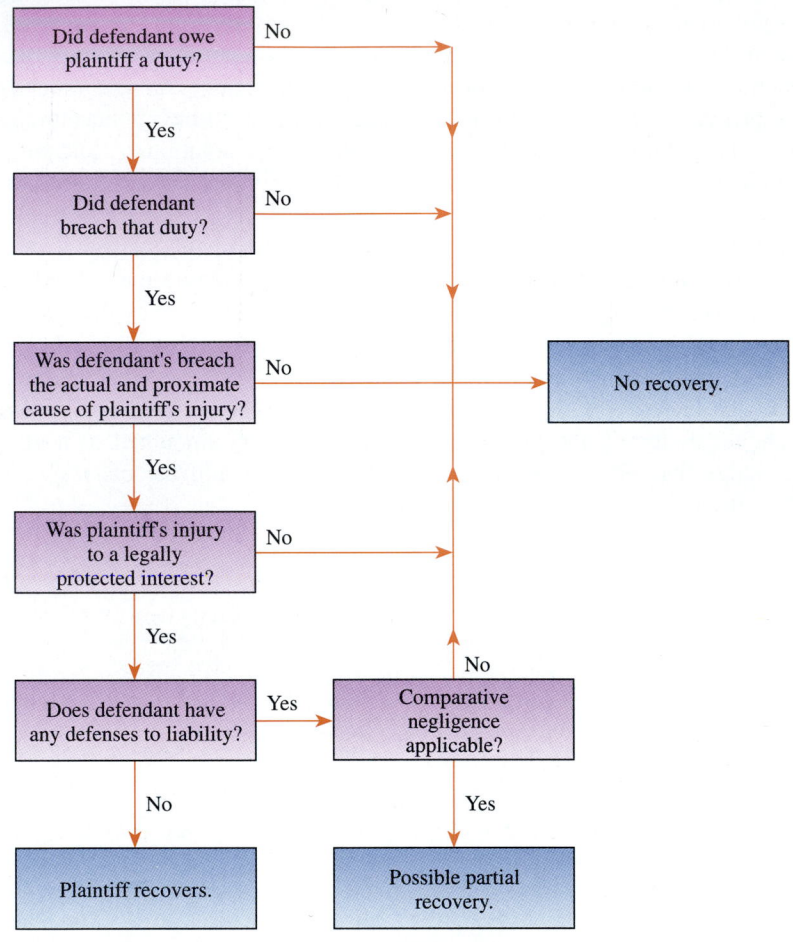

Figure 2 shows all of the elements of a successful negligence case.

STRICT LIABILITY

Introduction

In addition to intentional wrongdoing and negligence, the third fundamental basis of tort liability is **strict liability.** Strict liability means that defendants who participate in certain harm-producing activities may be held *strictly liable* for any harm that results to others, even though they did not intend to cause the harm and did everything in their power to prevent it. Also, defendants in strict liability cases traditionally have fewer defenses to liability than do defendants in negligence cases. This is because most courts hold that contributory negligence is *not* a defense to strict liability, although assumption of risk is a good defense. The imposition of strict liability represents a social policy decision that the risk associated with an activity should be borne by those who pursue it, rather than by wholly innocent persons who are exposed to that risk.

Such liability has been justified either by the defendant's voluntary decision to engage in a particularly risky activity or, more recently, by the defendant's superior ability to bear losses. Thus, corporations are often said to be superior to individuals as risk bearers due to their ability to pass the costs of liability on to consumers in the form of higher prices for goods or services. The owners of trespassing livestock and the keepers of naturally dangerous wild animals were among the first classes of defendants on whom the courts imposed strict liability. Today, the two most important activities subject to judicially imposed strict liability are *abnormally dangerous (or ultrahazardous) activities* and the *manufacture or sale of defective and unreasonably dangerous products*. Chapter 20, Product Liability, discusses the product liability dimension of strict liability in detail.

Abnormally Dangerous Activities

Abnormally dangerous activities are activities that *necessarily involve a risk of harm to others that cannot be eliminated by the exercise of reasonable care*. Activities that have been classed as abnormally dangerous include blasting, crop dusting, stunt flying, and, in one case, the transportation of large quantities of gasoline by truck. The following *Klein* case discusses the numerous factors that courts must consider before deciding whether a particular activity should be classified as abnormally dangerous.

KLEIN V. PYRODYNE CORPORATION
810 P.2d 917 (Wash. Sup. Ct. 1991)

Pyrodyne Corporation was hired to display the fireworks at the Western Washington State Fairgrounds in Puyallup, Washington, on July 4, 1987. During the display, one of the 5-inch mortars was knocked into a horizontal position, from which position a rocket inside ignited and flew 500 feet parallel to the earth, exploding near the crowd of onlookers. Danny and Marion Klein were injured by the explosion. They filed a strict liability suit against Pyrodyne, arguing that Pyrodyne failed to carry out a number of the statutory and regulatory requirements in preparing for and setting off the fireworks. Pyrodyne argued that the accident was caused by a rocket detonating in its mortar tube without ever leaving the ground, causing another rocket to be knocked over, ignited, and set off horizontally. Pyrodyne moved for summary judgment on the ground that negligence principles should be applied to the case. When the trial court denied its motion and found it strictly liable, Pyrodyne appealed.

Guy, Justice   The modern doctrine of strict liability for abnormally dangerous activities derives from *Rylands v. Fletcher* (Eng. 1866), in which the defendant's reservoir flooded mine shafts on the plaintiff's adjoining land. *Rylands v. Fletcher* has come to stand for the rule that "the defendant will be liable when he damages another by a thing or activity unduly dangerous and inappropriate to the place where it is maintained, in the light of the character of that place and its surroundings." *Prosser and Keeton on Torts* (1984).

The basic principle of *Rylands v. Fletcher* has been accepted by the *Restatement (Second) of Torts* (1977). Section 519 of the *Restatement* provides that any party carrying on an "abnormally dangerous activity" is strictly liable for the ensuing damages. Section 520 of the *Restatement*

lists six factors that are to be considered in determining whether an activity is "abnormally dangerous":

a. existence of a high degree of risk of some harm to the person, land or chattels of others;

b. likelihood that the harm that results from it will be great;

c. inability to eliminate the risk by the exercise of reasonable care;

d. extent to which the activity is not a matter of common usage;

e. inappropriateness of the activity to the place where it is carried on; and

f. extent to which its value to the community is outweighed by its dangerous attributes.

The comments to section 520 explain how these factors should be evaluated:

Any one of them is not necessarily sufficient of itself in a particular case, and ordinarily several of them will be required for strict liability. On the other hand, it is not necessary that each of them be present, especially if others weigh heavily. The essential question is whether the risk created is so unusual, either because of its magnitude or because of the circumstances surrounding it, as to justify the imposition of strict liability for the harm that results from it, even though it is carried on with all reasonable care.

We find that the factors stated in clauses (a), (b), and (c) are all present in the case of fireworks displays. Any time a person ignites rockets with the intention of sending them aloft to explode in the presence of large crowds of people, a high risk of serious personal injury or property damage is created. That risk arises because of the possibility that a rocket will malfunction or be misdirected. Furthermore, no matter how much care pyrotechnicians exercise, they cannot entirely eliminate the high risk inherent in setting off powerful explosives near crowds.

Pyrodyne argues that the factor stated in clause (d) is not met because fireworks are a common way to celebrate the 4th of July. Although fireworks are frequently and regularly enjoyed by the public, few persons set off special fireworks displays. Indeed, anyone wishing to do so must first obtain a license.

The Puyallup Fairgrounds is an appropriate place for the fireworks show because the audience can be seated at a reasonable distance from the display. Therefore, the clause (e) factor is not present in this case. The factor in clause (f) requires analysis of the extent to which the value of the fireworks to the community outweighs its dangerous attributes. This country has a long-standing tradition of fireworks on the 4th of July. That tradition suggests that we have decided that the value of fireworks on the day celebrating our national independence and unity outweighs the risks of injuries and damage.

In sum, we find that setting off public fireworks displays satisfies four of the six conditions under the *Restatement* test. We therefore hold that conducting public fireworks displays is an abnormally dangerous activity justifying the imposition of strict liability.

Judgment for the Kleins affirmed.

Statutory Strict Liability

Strict liability is not an exclusive creation of the courts. Strict liability principles are also embodied in modern legislation. The most important examples of this phenomenon are the *Workers' Compensation Acts* passed by most states in the early decades of this century. Such statutes allow employees to recover statutorily limited amounts from their employers despite the absence of any fault on the part of the employer or the presence of contributory fault on the part of the employee. Employers participate in a compulsory liability insurance system and are expected to pass the costs of the system on to consumers, who then become the ultimate bearers of the human costs of industrial production. Other examples of statutory strict liability include the Dram Shop statutes of some states, which impose liability on sellers of alcoholic beverages without proof of any negligence when third parties are harmed due to a buyer's intoxication. Also included is the statutory liability without proof of fault that some states impose on the operators of aircraft for ground damage resulting from aviation accidents.

TORT REFORM

By 1990, most states had enacted some form of tort reform legislation. The primary beneficiaries of such legislation were physicians, local governments, and manufacturers. The main driving force behind the tort reform movement is the "crisis" in the liability insurance system. In recent years, the insurance system has been characterized by outright refusals of coverage, reductions in coverage, and dramatically escalating premiums when coverage remains available. The supporters of tort reform argue that the main factors underlying the insurance crisis are the trend toward strict liability for various harms and escalating damage awards. Observers often attribute this latter factor to the increased frequency with which punitive damages are awarded and to a tendency toward more frequent damage awards for noneconomic harms such as pain and suffering in tort cases.

Tort reform advocates also argue that large jury awards contribute to inflation because, where market conditions permit, those who initially bear the cost of liability insurance will pass such costs on to their customers in the form of higher prices. Supporters of tort reform also argue that the threat of huge jury awards impedes the development of new products and technologies.

States have enacted a variety of devices in the name of tort reform. Statutes that limit the amounts recoverable for noneconomic harms are now fairly common, as are statutes that limit the liability of social hosts or businesses for the damage caused by intoxicated persons to whom they serve alcohol. Local governments in many states now enjoy statutory limits on their liability for negligence, affording them partial relief from the negligence claims for improper maintenance of streets and traffic signals; such claims now routinely accompany many automobile accident cases. Likewise, physicians in a number of states have received some relief from spiraling liability costs by reform devices such as caps on the amount recoverable in liability suits and mandatory pretrial mediation of all claims over a prescribed threshold. Finally, statutory ceilings on punitive damage awards or rules making such damages more difficult to recover are also common reform measures.

Critics of the tort reform movement argue that the liability insurance crisis is largely the fault of the insurance industry. Some have argued that insurers have manufactured the crisis to get unjustified premium increases and to divert attention from insurer mismanagement of invested premium income. Others argue that insurers are raising premiums to offset income losses resulting from the drop in interest rates in recent years. Whatever the truth of such allegations, it is becoming increasingly common for state legislatures to couple tort reform legislation with increased regulation of insurers, something that is understandably dulling the insurance industry's enthusiasm for tort reform. For example, Florida forced a rate rollback as a price of tort reform. Other common reform devices include requiring prior approval of rate increases and placing closer restraints on insurer policy cancellation and nonrenewal practices.

The battle for tort reform is far from over, however. Tort reform opponents who lost the fight against tort reform in the legislature have continued it in the courts. Thus, tort reform statutes have been challenged by arguments that statutes capping damage awards violate state constitutional provisions guaranteeing jury trials because they limit jury discretion in setting damages, and by arguments that reform measures targeted at certain types of cases (e.g., medical malpractice cases) violate equal protection guaranties by unjustifiably discriminating against plaintiffs in such cases. Such challenges have succeeded in some states and have been rebuffed in others. Whatever the outcome of the current struggle, the tort reform debate highlights the perennial dilemma facing tort law—how to fashion a system adequately compensating the victims of civil wrongs in an economically efficient manner that does not impose undue burdens on business or society as a whole.

ETHICAL AND PUBLIC POLICY CONCERNS

1. In the famous *Palsgraf* case cited in footnote 2 in this chapter, the plaintiff was injured when a late-boarding train passenger dropped a package of fireworks he was carrying as he attempted to board a train that was pulling out of the station. Two employees of the railroad were trying to help him board, one pulling and one pushing. The package was jostled loose and exploded on impact. The concussion from the explosion caused some scales to fall on the victim, who was standing several feet away from the action. The defendant railroad escaped liability to the victim because the court found it had no duty to her because its employees could not reasonably have foreseen that they were endangering her by their actions. Yet, plainly the harm to her would not have occurred had the railroad's employees refused to allow the passenger to try to board a moving train. Even if the railroad had no legal duty to Palsgraf, did it have any ethical duty to her?

2. Implicit in the idea of proximate cause is the fact that a negligent defendant can be the actual cause of some plaintiffs' injuries but avoid any liability for those injuries because his negligence was not the proximate cause of such injuries. Is the doctrine of proximate cause ethically justifiable?

3. While the doctrine of proximate cause allows defendants to avoid responsibility for some consequences of their negligence, the doctrine of strict liability imposes liability on persons who participate in abnormally dangerous activities even though they exercised all possible care to avoid injuring anyone. Can such liability be ethically justified?

PROBLEMS AND PROBLEM CASES

1. On September 5, 1984, the Citizens for Bob Olexo Campaign Committee rented three tanks of helium from James Dawes Company. The helium was to be used to fill balloons that were to be handed out to the public during the Belmont County Fair. Although the agreement with Dawes called for the Committee to return the used cylinders, they were left at the fairgrounds leaning up against a commercial building. On September 28, Philip C. Jeffers III, age 14, attended a football game at the fairgrounds, where he and some friends discovered the tanks. Despite the warning on the tanks, which stated "CAUTION! HIGH PRESSURE GAS. CAN CAUSE RAPID SUFFOCATION," Jeffers inhaled some helium from one of the tanks, collapsed, and died. Jeffers's father sued the Dawes Company, which moved for a summary judgment on a number of grounds, among which was the argument that it owed no duty to Jeffers. Should Dawes's motion be granted?

2. On August 7, 1981, a young man abducted R.M.V., age 10, from the sidewalk in front of her home and dragged her across the street to a vacant apartment at the Chalmette Apartments. He raped her, put her in the closet, told her not to leave, and disappeared. The apartment in question was described by the police officer called to the scene as "empty, filthy, dirty, and full of debris." Glass was broken from its windows and the front door was off its hinges. In the two years prior to the attack on R.M.V., Dallas police had investigated numerous crimes committed at the Chalmette Apartments complex, including 1 attempted murder, 2 robberies,

2 aggravated assaults, 16 apartment burglaries, 4 vehicle burglaries, 4 cases of theft, and 5 cases of criminal mischief. A Dallas City Ordinance established minimum standards for property owners, requiring them, among other things, to "keep the doors and windows of a vacant structure or vacant portion of a structure securely closed to prevent unauthorized entry." Gaile Nixon, R.M.V.'s mother, filed a negligence suit against the Chalmette's owner and Mr. Property Management Company, Inc., the manager of the complex. Were the defendants correct in arguing that they owed no duty to R.M.V.?

3. On September 3, 1984, Valerie Jones, a lab technician at Kelco's chemical plant in Okmulgee, Oklahoma, stole a cupful of sulfuric acid from the plant. After work, she drove to the home of her sister-in-law, Gwendolyn Henry. After a brief verbal altercation with Henry over the fact that Henry, who had been baby-sitting Jones's 2-year-old son, had trimmed the child's hair, she threw the acid in Henry's face. Henry suffered severe and permanent injuries, and Jones was ultimately sentenced to 7 years in prison for the attack. Henry filed a negligence suit against Kelco, and a jury awarded her $450,000. Kelco appealed, arguing that it owed no duty to Henry and that, in any event, Jones's act was an intervening cause that relieved it of liability. The evidence at trial indicated that Jones had been a model employee who had to have access to the chemical storage area to perform her duties. Should the jury's verdict be reversed?

4. On August 12, 1980, while riding her bike in the residential area near her home. 14-year-old Mumtaz Mazzagatti was struck and fatally injured by a car driven by Ricky Everingham. At the time of the accident her mother, Jane Mazzagatti, was at work, approximately one mile away. She received a telephone call immediately after the collision informing her that her daughter had been involved in an automobile accident. She arrived on the scene a few minutes later and saw her daughter lying in the road. She later filed a negligent infliction of emotional distress suit against Everingham. In her complaint she alleged that she "became hysterical, unnerved, and emotionally shattered" at the sight of her injured daughter, that as a result of the observation she suffered shock to her nervous system, and grievous mental pain and suffering, resulting in severe depression and an acute nervous condition.

Was the trial court's decision to grant a summary judgment in favor of Everingham justified?

5. In July 1980, Higgins and some friends went to a night baseball game at Comiskey Park in Chicago. Near the end of the game, Higgins went to the men's room. On his way back to his seat, he walked down a corridor that ran past a concession stand. As he passed the stand, the door to the front of the stand (a 4 by 6-foot sheet of plywood attached to the top of the stand and hooked to an eyelet in the ceiling when opened) fell from its open position and struck him on the head, causing permanent head and neck injuries. None of the eyewitnesses to the incident saw anyone touch either the door or the hook securing it or do anything that might have caused the door to fall. There was, however, testimony that, just before the door fell, the crowd in the stadium was screaming and stamping, and that one "could feel the place tremble." Higgins filed suit against the Chicago White Sox, owners of the stadium, arguing that *res ipsa loquitur* should be applied to the case. Was he right?

6. At 6:45 A.M. on July 25, 1982, Simone Waters was walking on a public street where she was accosted by a knife-wielding man who forced her to walk with him to a building around the corner. Once inside the building, which was unlocked, the man forced her to the roof and, after taking her money, sodomized her. The building was owned by the New York Housing Authority. The evidence at the trial indicated that the front door locks on the building had been either broken or missing for at least two years before Simone was attacked, that several tenants had complained about the condition over that two-year period, and that there had been at least five criminal incidents in the building involving outsiders. The Housing Authority argued that it owed no duty to Waters to protect her against the criminal acts of third persons. Was the trial court's decision to grant a summary judgment in favor of the Housing Authority correct?

7. Jenkins, an employee of Acme Paper Stock Company, was riding on a freight elevator in Acme's plant when the elevator cable broke. As a result, the hoist motor fell on Jenkins, fatally injuring him. The hoist motor and lifting cables had been installed by Edwards Transfer Company. The evidence at trial indicated that Edwards used steel cables to mount the hoist from an I-beam that ran along the ceiling of Acme's plant, but failed to use "softeners" to protect the cables against the sharp edges of the beam. The evidence also indicated that Acme had warned employees that the elevator was only to be used for freight and was not safe for use as a personnel elevator and that Jenkins himself had told an Edwards employee prior to the accident that the hoist was improperly secured. Jenkins's heirs filed a negligence suit against Edwards. The trial judge refused to instruct the jury on contributory negligence on the ground that Jenkins could not reasonably have foreseen that he could be injured by the falling hoist motor. Was this refusal proper?

8. On April 25, 1984, Allen Beckett, a fourth-year player on his high school baseball team, was injured when he collided with another player during outfielder practice. The accident occurred after the coach conducting the practice hit a fly ball to Beckett. Beckett called for the ball, but the wind was blowing so hard that neither the coach nor the other players heard him. The coach called for another player to catch the ball, and that player and Beckett collided head-on. Beckett's jaw was broken, and he filed suit against the school, arguing that it had failed to warn him of the danger of such collisions, failed to adequately supervise the practice, and had conducted the practice in an unreasonably dangerous manner. At one point in his testimony, Beckett denied that he had ever heard of baseball players colliding and said that he had no knowledge of any accidents happening on baseball fields. Under cross-examination, however, he admitted that his coaches had repeatedly stressed communication among players to avoid accidents, that it was possible on such a windy day for his voice to have gotten lost in the wind, and that the same type of thing could have happened in a game. Was the trial court summary judgment in favor of the school proper?

9. Lee Ann Laird, age 12, was injured when her bicycle was hit by a car driven by Larry Kostman. Lee Ann was in the process of pulling into the street from a driveway, and she emerged from behind a van parked at the curb. At the trial, Kostman testified that he hit his brakes as soon as he saw the bicycle. His passenger testified that Laird "came out of nowhere," and that he didn't see her until the moment of impact. Laird testified that she saw Kostman's car turn onto the street from an intersection more than 200 feet from the point of impact, that no more than two feet of her bicycle extended into the street from behind the parked van, and that when she tried to move the bike back to avoid the collision, the brakes locked. After the trial judge refused to instruct the jury on the doctrine of last clear chance, the jury ruled in favor of Kostman. Was the trial judge's refusal proper?

10. On January 9, 1979, a railroad car leased by American Cyanamid (American) and containing 20,000 gallons of acrylonitrile manufactured by American began leaking. At the time, the car was sitting just south of Chicago in the Blue Island yard of the Indiana Harbor Belt Railroad (Indiana) awaiting switching to Conrail for delivery to its final destination. Indiana's employees stopped the leak but were uncertain about how much of the car's contents had escaped. Because acrylonitrile is flam-mable, highly toxic, and possibly carcinogenic, Illinois authorities ordered homes near the yard temporarily evacuated. Later, it was discovered that only about a quarter of the car's contents had leaked, but the Illinois Department of Environmental Protection, fearing that the soil and water had been contaminated, ordered Indiana to take decontamination measures costing $981,000. Indiana filed suit against American on negligence and strict liability theories seeking to recover its expenses. Evidence introduced at the trial included a list of 125 hazardous materials that are shipped in highest volume on the nation's railroads. Acrylonitrile was the 53rd most hazardous on the list. Was the trial court's entry of summary judgment for Indiana on the strict liability claim proper?

UNFAIR COMPETITION

INTRODUCTION

This chapter discusses certain legal rules that limit free competition by allowing civil recoveries for abuses of that freedom. These abuses are: (1) patent, copyright, and trademark infringement; (2) the misappropriation of trade secrets; (3) the intentional torts of injurious falsehood, interference with contractual relations, and interference with prospective advantage; and (4) the many forms of unfair competition attacked by section 43(a) of the Lanham Act. Indeed, the term unfair competition describes the whole chapter. In general, competition is deemed unfair because: (1) it discourages creative endeavor by robbing creative people of the fruits of their innovations, or (2) it renders commercial life too uncivilized and indecent for the law to tolerate.

PATENT, COPYRIGHT, AND TRADEMARK INFRINGEMENT

Patents

A patent can be regarded as an agreement between an inventor and the federal government. Under that agreement, the inventor gets the exclusive right to make, use, and sell his invention, in return for making the invention public by giving the government certain information about it. The patent holder's (or **patentee's**) monopoly encourages the creation and disclosure of inventions by stopping third parties from appropriating them once they become public. However, third parties may develop the invention in ways that do not interfere with the patentee's rights.

What Is Patentable?   An inventor may patent: (1) a *process* (as described in the following *Diamond* case), (2) a *machine*, (3) a *manufacture* or product, (4) a *composition of matter* (a combination of elements with qualities not present in the elements taken individually, such as a new chemical compound), (5) an *improvement* of any of the above, (6) an *ornamental design* for a product, and (7) a *plant* produced by asexual reproduction. Naturally occurring things (e.g., a new wild plant) and new business methods (e.g., an innovative accounting technique) are not patentable. In addition, as

Diamond states, abstract ideas, scientific laws, and other mental concepts are not patentable, although their practical applications often are. As *Diamond* also reveals, a computer program may be patentable if it is part of a patentable process. However, it is unclear whether a program that stands alone and that is not part of a patentable process is patentable.[1]

Even though an invention fits within one of the above categories, it is not patentable if it lacks novelty, is obvious, has no utility, was not created by the patent applicant, or was abandoned by him.[2] One example of the *novelty* requirement is the rule that no patent should be issued where *before the invention's creation* it has been: (1) known or used in the United States, (2) patented in the United States or a foreign country, or (3) described in a printed publication in the United States or a foreign country. Another example is the requirement that no patent should be issued if more than one year before the *patent application* the invention was: (1) patented in the United States or a foreign country, (2) described in a printed publication in the United States or a foreign country, or (3) in public use or on sale in the United States. Also, there can be no patent if the invention would have been *obvious* to a person having ordinary skill in the area. Furthermore, a patentable invention must have *utility,* or usefulness. Finally, there can be no patent if the party seeking it did not create the invention in question, or if she abandoned the invention. *Creation* problems frequently arise where several people allegedly contributed to the invention. *Abandonment* can be by express statement, such as publicly devoting an invention to humanity, or by implication from conduct, such as delaying for an unreasonable length of time before making a patent application.

Obtaining a Patent   The Patent and Trademark Office of the Department of Commerce handles patent applications. The application must include a *specification* describing the invention with sufficient detail and clarity to enable any person skilled in the area to make and use it. The application must also contain a *drawing* where this is necessary for understanding the subject matter to be patented. The Patent Office then determines whether the invention meets the various tests for patentability. If the application is rejected, the applicant may resubmit it. Once any of the applicant's claims has been twice rejected, the applicant may appeal to the Office's Board of Patent Appeals and Interferences. Subsequent appeals to the federal courts also are possible.

---

[1]As discussed later in this chapter, however, computer programs do get copyright and trade secrets protection.

[2]Plant and design patents are subject to slightly different requirements than those stated here.

DIAMOND V. DIEHR
450 U.S. 175 (U.S. Sup. Ct. 1981)

Diehr and Lutton attempted to obtain a patent covering a process for molding raw, uncured synthetic rubber into cured precision products. The process used a mold for shaping the uncured rubber under heat and pressure and then curing it in the mold. Previous efforts at curing and molding synthetic rubber had suffered from an inability to measure the temperature inside the molding press and thus to determine a precise curing time. Diehr and Lutton's invention involved a process for constantly measuring the temperature inside the mold, feeding this information to a computer that constantly recalculated the curing time, and enabling the computer to signal the molding press to open at the correct instant.

The patent examiner rejected Diehr and Lutton's patent application. The Patent and Trademark Office Board of Appeals (now the Board of Patent Appeals and Interferences) agreed with the examiner, but the now-defunct Court of Customs and Patent Appeals reversed. The patent office appealed to the U.S. Supreme Court.

Rehnquist, Justice   In defining the nature of a patentable process, this Court has stated:

A process is a mode of treatment of certain materials to produce a given result. It is an act, or a series of acts, performed upon the subject matter to be transformed and reduced to a different state or thing. If new and useful, it is just as patentable as is a piece of machinery. The machinery pointed out as suitable to perform the process may or may not be new or patentable; whilst the process itself may be altogether new and produce an entirely new result.

Recently, we repeated the above definition, adding:

Transformation and reduction of an article to a different state or thing is the clue to the patentability of a process claim that does not include particular machines.

That Diehr and Lutton's claims involve the transformation of an article, raw uncured synthetic rubber, into a different state or thing cannot be disputed. Industrial processes such as this have historically been eligible to receive the protection of our patent laws.

Excluded from patent protection are laws of nature, physical phenomena, and abstract ideas. Only last Term, we explained:

A new mineral discovered in the earth or a new plant found in the wild is not patentable subject matter.

Likewise, Einstein could not patent his celebrated law that $E = mc^2$; nor could Newton have patented the law of gravity. Such discoveries are manifestations of nature, free to all men and reserved exclusively to none.

Diehr and Lutton do not seek to patent a mathematical formula. Instead, they seek patent protection for a process of curing synthetic rubber. Their process employs a well-known mathematical equation, but they do not seek to preempt the use of that equation. They seek only to foreclose from others the use of that equation in conjunction with all the other steps in their process. It is now a commonplace that an *application* of a law of nature or mathematical formula to a known structure or process may be deserving of patent protection.

It may later be determined that the process is not deserving of patent protection because it fails to satisfy the statutory conditions of novelty or nonobviousness. A rejection on either of these grounds does not affect the determination that Diehr and Lutton's claims recited subject matter which was eligible for patent protection.

Judgment for Diehr and Lutton affirmed.

Ownership and Transfer of Patent Rights   A patent normally gives the patentee exclusive rights to make, use, and sell the patented invention for a 17-year period. Design patents, however, extend for only 14 years. The patentee can transfer title to all or part of his patent rights by *assigning* them, or may retain title and *license* them.

Usually, the party who created the invention is the patent holder. But what happens when the creator of the invention is an employee and her employer seeks rights in her invention? If the invention was developed by an employee *hired to do inventive or creative work,* she must use the invention solely for the employer's benefit and must assign any patents she obtains to the employer. But if the employee was hired for purposes *other than invention or creation,* she owns any patent she acquires. Regardless of the purpose for which the employee was hired, finally, the *shop right* doctrine gives the employer a nonex-clusive, royalty-free *license* to use the employee's invention if it was created on company time and through company facilities. Any patent the employee might retain is still effective against parties other than the employer.

Patent Infringement   A *direct* patent infringement occurs when a party makes, uses, or sells a patented invention without the patentee's authorization. It is easy to establish a direct infringement where the subject matter made, used, or sold clearly is within the language of a successful patent application. Courts also find direct infringement where this subject matter is *substantially equivalent* to the protected invention. Here, the test is whether the alleged offender's subject matter performs substantially the same function as the protected invention in substantially the same way to produce substantially the same result.

Also, one who *actively induces* another's infringement of a patent is liable as an infringer if he knows and intends that the infringement occur. For example, if Isaac directly infringes Pinder's patent on a machine and Dailey knowingly sells Isaac an instruction manual for the machine, Daily may be liable as an infringer. Finally, if one knowingly sells a direct patent infringer a component of a patented invention or something useful in employing a patented process, the seller may be liable for *contributory infringement*. Here, the thing sold must be a material part of the invention and must not be a staple article of commerce with some other significant use. For example, suppose that Ireland directly infringes Potter's patent for a radio by selling virtually identical radios. If Davis sells Ireland sophisticated circuitry for the radios with knowledge of Ireland's infringement, Davis may be liable for contributory infringement if the circuitry is an important component of the radios and has no other significant uses.

The basic recovery for patent infringement is damages adequate to compensate for the infringement, plus court costs and interest. The damages cannot be less than a reasonable royalty for the use made of the invention by the infringer. Also, the court may in its discretion award damages of up to three times those actually suffered. Finally, injunctive relief is sometimes available, and attorney's fees may be awarded in exceptional cases.

Defenses to Patent Infringement   One defense to a patent infringement suit is that the subject matter of the alleged infringement is neither within the literal scope of the patent nor substantially equivalent to the patented invention. Also, the alleged infringer may defend by attacking the validity of the patent. Despite their approval by the Patent and Trademark Office, many patents are declared invalid when challenged in court.

Further, the defendant can sometimes assert that the patentee has committed *patent misuse*. This is behavior that unjustifiably exploits the patent monopoly. For example, the patentee may require the purchaser of a license on his patent to buy his unpatented goods, or may tie the obtaining of a license on one of his patented inventions to the purchase of a license on another.[3] One who refuses

the patentee's terms and later infringes the patent may escape liability by arguing that the patentee misused his monopoly position.

Copyrights

Copyright law gives creative people certain exclusive rights to their intellectual endeavors. Thus, it prevents others from using their work, gives them an incentive to innovate, and thereby benefits society. But copyright law also tries to balance these purposes against the equally compelling public interest in the free movement of ideas, information, and commerce. It does so mainly by limiting the intellectual products it protects and by allowing the fair use defense described later.

Coverage   Federal copyright law protects a wide range of creative works, including books, periodical articles, dramatic and musical compositions, works of art, motion pictures, sound recordings, lectures, computer programs, and architectural plans. To merit copyright protection, such works must be *fixed*—set out in a tangible medium of expression from which they can be perceived, reproduced, or communicated. They also must be *original* (the author's own work), but unlike the inventions protected by patent law, they need not be novel.

Copyright protection does not extend to ideas, procedures, processes, systems, methods of operation, concepts, principles, or discoveries *as such*. However, it may protect the *form in which they are expressed*. The story line of a play, for instance, probably is protected, but the ideas, themes, or messages underlying it probably are not. Although there is no copyright in facts as such, nonfiction works and compilations of fact are protectible if their creation involved originality. The following *Narell* case discusses the protection of phrases and expressions within a copyrighted work.

Computer programs involve their own special problems. It is fairly well settled that copyright law protects a program's *object code* (program instructions that are machine-readable but not intelligible to humans) and *source code* (instructions intelligible to humans). But there is less agreement about the copyrightability of a program's nonliteral elements such as its organization, its structure, and its presentation of information on the screen. Most of the courts that have considered the issue hold that

---

[3]Some forms of patent misuse may be antitrust violations. Chapter 49 discusses the interaction between patent law and antitrust law.

nonliteral elements can be protected by copyright law, but courts differ about the extent of this protection.

Creation and Notice

A copyright comes into existence upon the creation and fixing of a protected work. For works created in 1978 and thereafter, the copyright usually lasts for *the life of the author plus 50 years.* Although a copyright owner may register the copyright with the Copyright Office of the Library of Congress, registration is not necessary for the copyright to exist. However, registration often *is* necessary before the owner can begin a suit for copyright infringement.

Even though it is not required, copyright owners often provide *notice* of the copyright. Federal law authorizes various forms of notice for different copyrighted works. A book, for example, might include the term *Copyright,* the year of its first publication, and the name of the copyright owner in a location likely to give reasonable notice to readers.

Ownership Rights

A copyright owner has exclusive rights to: (1) reproduce the copyrighted work, (2) prepare derivative works based on it (e.g., a movie version of a novel), (3) distribute copies of the work by sale or otherwise, and (4) perform or display it publicly. Copyright ownership initially resides in the creator of the copyrighted work, but the copyright may be transferred to another party. Also, the owner may individually transfer each of the listed rights, or a portion of each, without losing ownership of the remaining rights. Most transfers of copyright ownership require a writing signed by the owner or his agent. The owner may also retain ownership while licensing the copyrighted work or a portion of it.

Infringement

Those who violate any of the copyright owner's exclusive rights may be liable for *copyright infringement.* Infringement is easily proven where direct evidence of copying exists; verbatim copying of protected material is an example. But as *Narell* states, infringement usually is proven by showing that the defendant had *access* to the copyrighted work and that there is *substantial similarity* between that work and the allegedly infringing work. Access can be proven circumstantially—for example, by wide circulation of the copyrighted work. Determining substantial similarity necessarily involves discretionary case-by-case judgments.

The basic recovery for copyright infringement is the owner's actual damages plus the profits received by the infringer. However, the plaintiff may elect to receive statutory damages— which fall within certain defined ranges—in lieu of the basic remedy. Injunctive relief, awards of costs and attorney's fees, and criminal penalties are possible in certain cases.

The Fair Use Defense

The fair use defense to a copyright infringement suit requires the weighing of several factors whose application varies from case to case. These factors are: (1) the purpose and character of the use, (2) the nature of the copyrighted work, (3) the amount and substantiality of the portion used in relation to the copyrighted work as a whole, and (4) the effect of the use on the potential market for the copyrighted work or on its value. *Narell* discusses and applies these factors.

NARELL V. FREEMAN

872 F.2d 907 (9th Cir. 1989)

Irena Narell wrote a social history of the Bay area Jewish community entitled *Our City: The Jews of San Francisco.* After its publication in 1981, her book sold fewer than 5,000 copies. In 1986, Narell repurchased the copyright and the remaining inventory from the publisher.

Illusions of Love, a novel by Cynthia Freeman, was published in hardcover in 1984 and in paperback in 1986, selling approximately 1 million copies. *Illusions* told a fictional story about the heir of a large, wealthy Jewish family who had to choose between his family and a lover from a vastly different background. Freeman consulted and used *Our City* in writing *Illusions,* and portions of *Illusions* were based on historical events described in *Our City*. Also, *Illusions* contained several instances of verbatim copying from *Our City;* these totaled about 300 words. On several more occasions, Freeman paraphrased passages from Narell's book.

Narell sued Freeman and her publishers for copyright infringement in federal district court. The court granted the defendants' motion for summary judgment and Narell appealed.

Farris, Circuit Judge   To establish a successful copyright infringement claim, Narell must show that she owns the copyright and that Freeman copied protected elements of the work. Because in most copyright cases direct evidence of copying is not available, a plaintiff may establish copying by showing that the infringer had access to the work and that the two works are substantially similar. Narell's ownership of the copyright and Freeman's access to Narell's work are not in dispute.

The [first] question is whether Freeman's admitted takings— several instances of identical phrases and the more numerous paraphrases—were of protected material. Copyright law protects only an author's expression. Facts and ideas within a work are not protected. Freeman largely took unprotected factual information from *Our City*.

Freeman did copy a few phrases from Narell. Ordinary phrases [and] phrases and expressions conveying an idea typically expressed in a limited number of stereotyped fashions are not subject to copyright protection. Most of the phrases Freeman copied are commonly-used expressions, such as describing a muddy street as a "cow path." The appropriation of expressive elements is minimal. The more numerous paraphrasings cited by Narell [also] cannot be said to take the expressive elements of her work. Instead, unprotected factual details are taken, although in some cases commonly-used expressions are echoed, such as "mosquitos ravished his flesh" versus "mosquitos feasted on his flesh." Freeman's borrowings did not take a sequence of creative expression, as opposed to an ordinary phrase, and therefore were not infringing.

The arguments of the parties and the decision of the district court focused on the issues of substantial similarity and fair use. Viewed as a whole, the two works have slight resemblance to each other. *Illusions* is a romantic novel. *Our City* is a historical treatment of the Bay area Jewish community. The similarities between the two works are neither quantitatively nor qualitatively significant. Quantitatively insignificant infringement may be substantial only if the material is qualitatively important to either work. The passages at issue are a small part of Narell's book. The material taken is not qualitatively important to either book. Because of the fundamental differences between the works and the insubstantial nature of the copied passages, no reasonable reader could conclude that the works are substantially similar.

The doctrine of fair use allows [one] to use copyrighted material in a reasonable manner without the consent of the copyright owner. The copyright act sets out four factors for evaluating whether a use is a fair use.

Purpose and Character of the Use—The first factor strongly weighs against Freeman, because commercial use of copyrighted material is presumptively unfair. Freeman's use is admittedly commercial.

Nature of the Copyrighted Work—The scope of permissible fair use is greater with an informational work than a creative work. Although this factor weighs slightly in Freeman's favor, Narell's work contains enough creative expression that any use of it is not presumptively fair.

Amount and Substantiality of Portions Used—This factor essentially repeats the analysis of the substantial similarity test. As explained above, no reasonable juror could conclude that *Illusions* is substantially similar to *Our City*. This factor weighs strongly in Freeman's favor.

Effect on the Market—This is the single most important element of fair use. The publication of *Illusions* has not had, and is not likely to have, any effect on the value or marketability of *Our City*. The works are directed to fundamentally different purposes. Readers interested in Narell's book are highly unlikely to find historical romance novels an acceptable substitute.

In sum, the first factor weighs strongly in Narell's favor and the second factor slightly favors Freeman. However, the third and final factors strongly favor Freeman. Because of the predominant role of the market factor, the district court's grant of summary judgment on the fair use defense should be affirmed.

Summary judgment for Freeman affirmed.

Trademarks

Trademarks help purchasers identify favored products and services. For this reason, they also give sellers and manufacturers an incentive to innovate and to strive for quality. However, both these ends would be defeated if competitors were free to appropriate each other's trademarks. Thus, the federal Lanham Act protects trademark owners against certain uses of their marks by third parties.[4]

Protected Marks   The Lanham Act recognizes four kinds of marks. It defines a **trademark** as any word, name, symbol, device, or combination thereof used by a manufacturer or seller to identify its products and to distinguish them from the products of competitors. On occasion, federal trademark protection has been extended to colors, pictures, label and package designs, slogans, sounds, arrangements of numbers and/or letters (e.g., "7-Eleven"), and shapes of goods or their containers (e.g., Coca-Cola bottles). **Service marks** resemble trademarks but identify and distinguish services.

Certification marks certify the origin, materials, quality, method of manufacture, and other aspects of goods and services. Here, the user of the mark and its owner are distinct parties. A retailer, for example, may sell products bearing the Good Housekeeping Seal of Approval. **Collective marks** are trademarks or service marks used by organizations to identify themselves as the source of goods or services. Trade union and trade association marks fall into this category. Although all four kinds of marks receive federal protection, this chapter focuses on trademarks and service marks, using the terms *mark* or *trademark* to refer to both.

Distinctiveness   Because their purpose is to help consumers identify products and services, trademarks must be *distinctive* to merit maximum Lanham Act protection. Marks fall into four general categories of distinctiveness:

1. *Arbitrary or fanciful marks.* These marks are the most distinctive—and the most likely to be protected—because they do not describe or suggest the qualities of the product or service they identify. The "Exxon" trademark is an example.

2. *Suggestive marks.* These marks convey the nature of a product or service only through imagination, thought, and perception. A "Dietene" trademark for a dietary food supplement is an example. Although not as secure as arbitrary or fanciful marks, suggestive marks still are good candidates for protection.

3. *Descriptive marks.* These marks directly describe the product or service they identify—for example, "Exquisite" wearing apparel. Descriptive marks usually are not protected unless they acquire a *secondary meaning.* This occurs when their identification with particular goods or services has become firmly established in the minds of a substantial number of buyers. Among the factors considered in secondary-meaning determinations are the length of time the mark has been used, the volume of sales associated with that use, and the nature of the advertising employing the mark. When applied to a package delivery service, for instance, the term *overnight* is usually just descriptive and thus not protectible. But it may come to deserve trademark protection through long use by a single firm that advertised it extensively and made many sales while doing so.

4. *Generic marks.* Generic marks (e.g., "diamond" or "truck") simply refer to the general class of which the particular product or service is one example. Because any seller has the right to call a product or service by its common name, generic marks are quite unlikely to receive Lanham Act protection.

---

[4]In addition, the owner of a trademark may enjoy legal protection under common law trademark doctrines and state trademark statutes.

Federal Registration   Once the seller of a product or service uses a mark in commerce or forms a bona fide intention to do so, she may try to register the mark with the U.S. Patent and Trademark Office. The office reviews applications for distinctiveness. Its decision to deny or grant the application may normally be contested either by the applicant or by a party who feels that he would be injured by registration of the mark. Such challenges may eventually reach the federal courts.

Trademarks of sufficient distinctiveness are placed on the Principal Register of the Patent and Trademark Office. A mark's inclusion in the Principal Register: (1) is prima facie evidence of the mark's ownership, validity, and registration (which is useful in trademark infringement suits); (2) gives nationwide constructive notice of the owner's claim of ownership (thus eliminating the need to show that the defendant in an infringement suit had notice of the mark); and (3) helps make the mark incontestable after five years (as described later).

Regardless of their distinctiveness, however, some kinds of marks are denied placement on the Principal Register. Examples include marks that: (1) consist of the flags or other insignia of governments; (2) consist of the name, portrait, or signature of a living person; (3) are immoral, deceptive, or scandalous; or (4) are likely to cause confusion or deceive because they resemble a mark previously registered or used in the United States. Certain other marks are not placed on the Principal Register unless they have acquired a secondary meaning. Examples include marks that: (1) are deceptively misdescriptive (such as "Dura-Skin" plastic gloves); (2) are geographically descriptive (e.g., "Nationwide" Life Insurance); or (3) are primarily a surname (because everyone should have the right to use his own name in connection with his business).

Transfer of Rights   Due to the purposes underlying trademark law, transferring trademark rights is more difficult than transferring copyright or patent interests. A trademark owner may license the use of the mark, but only if the licensee is a related company through which the owner can control the nature and quality of the goods or services identified by the mark. An uncontrolled "naked license" would allow the sale of goods or services bearing the mark but lacking the qualities formerly associated with it, and could confuse purchasers. Trademark rights may also be assigned or sold, but only along with the sale of the goodwill of the business originally using the mark.

Losing Federal Trademark Protection   Federal registration of a trademark lasts for 10 years, with renewals for additional 10-year periods possible. However, trademark protection may be lost before the period expires. The government must cancel a registration six years after its date, unless the registrant files with the Patent and Trademark Office an affidavit detailing that the mark is in use or explaining its nonuse and does so within the fifth and sixth years following the registration date.

Also, any person who believes that he is or will be damaged by a mark's registration may petition the Patent and Trademark Office to cancel that registration. Normally, the petition must be filed within five years of the mark's registration or the mark becomes *incontestable* as regards goods or services with which it has continuously been used for five consecutive years after the registration.[5] A mark's incontestability means that the permissible grounds for canceling its registration are limited. Even an incontestable mark, however, may be canceled *at any time* if, among other things, it was obtained by fraud, has been abandoned, or has become the generic name for the goods or services it identifies. *Abandonment* can occur through an express statement or agreement to abandon, through the mark's losing its significance as an indication of origin, or through the owner's failure to use it. A mark acquires a *generic meaning* when it comes to refer to a class of products or services rather than a particular product or service. For example, this has happened to such once-protected marks as aspirin and cellophane.

Trademark Infringement   A registered trademark is infringed when, without the registrant's consent, another party uses a substantially similar mark in connection with the advertisement or sale of goods or services and this is likely to cause confusion, mistake, or deception regarding their origin. The following *Nikon* case discusses many of the factors courts sift and weigh when determining

---

[5]The Lanham Act's incontestability provision also imposes on the owner an affidavit requirement resembling the cancellation affidavit requirement just stated.

whether the use is likely to cause confusion, mistake, or deception. A trademark owner who wins an infringement suit can obtain an injunction against uses of the mark that are likely to cause confusion. In certain circumstances, the owner can also obtain money damages for provable injury resulting from the infringement and for profits realized by the defendant from the sale of infringing products or services.

NIKON, INC. V. IKON CORP.
987 F.2d 91 (2d Cir. 1993)

In 1986, Jack Elo founded Ikon Photographic Corporation (IPC) to market inexpensive 35 mm and 110 mm pocket cameras. Later, IPC applied to register the "Ikon" trademark and its logo but failed to get it on the Principal Register. Still later, IPC managed to register a separate "Ikon" mark with a stylized "I" logo. Eventually, Nikon, Inc., sued IPC for infringement of its "Nikon" trademark in federal district court. Nikon mainly manufactures more expensive and complicated cameras than those made by IPC, but it also had been making point-and-shoot cameras similar to IPC's offerings. After the court found IPC liable and issued an injunction recalling all of its outstanding products and enjoining it from using the "Ikon" mark, IPC appealed.

Timbers, Circuit Judge   On this appeal from a permanent injunction, our function is limited to a review for abuse of discretion. Abuse of discretion can be found if the district court relied on a clearly erroneous finding of fact or incorrectly applied the law. The Lanham Act prohibits trademark infringement. The key issue in [such] cases is whether an appreciable number of consumers are likely to be misled or confused about the source of the product in question. It is well settled that in cases involving a claim under the Lanham Act the trier of fact must consider and balance [certain] factors to determine the likelihood of confusion. This list, however, is not exhaustive, nor is any one factor determinative.

1. *Strength of the Nikon Mark.* There is no dispute over the strength of the Nikon mark. It deserves broad protection against infringement.

2. *Similarity Between the Marks.* Although one of IPC's marks uses a stylized "I" and is not visually very similar to the Nikon mark, the stylized "I" is not used on all of IPC's cameras or packaging. In several contexts, therefore, the marks are similar. Further, the sounds of both marks are extremely similar, differing by only one letter. That letter is easily obscured in statements such as "This is an Ikon," and "This is a Nikon." There [also] was similarity in the appearance of the cameras.

3. *Proximity of the Products.* This factor focuses on whether the products compete. If the products serve the same purposes, fall within the same class, or are used for similar purposes, the likelihood of confusion is greater. While the parties have cameras at the opposite ends of the spectrum, there is a substantial overlap of Nikon's low-end cameras with IPC's high-end cameras. These lines produce a substantial percentage of the respective companies' sales. Further, both Nikon and IPC market these products through similar channels of trade and to similar types of customers.

4. *Bridging the Gap.* While this factor turns on the likelihood of whether the senior user will enter the market of the junior user, the court was correct in finding that, if there already is an overlap in the market, the likelihood of confusion is greater. There [indeed] already is a market overlap, increasing the likelihood of confusion.

5. *Sophistication of Consumers.* The more sophisticated and careful the average consumer of a product, the less likely it is that similarities in trademarks will result in confusion concerning the source of the product. Although the purchasers of Nikon's upper-end cameras generally are sophisticated in this area, the purchasers of the lower-end line often are amateur photographers, not unlike the purchasers of IPC cameras. While purchasers of these cameras are not impulsive, less sophisticated consumers could be confused about an affiliation between the products.

6. *Quality of Junior User's Product.* We have taken two approaches about the quality of the junior user's product: (1) an inferior quality product injures the senior user's reputation because people may think they come from the same source, or (2) a product of equal quality promotes confusion that they come from the same source. While IPC's quality is good for its price, IPC does not have the same quality controls as Nikon. This factor [weighs] in favor of Nikon.

7. *Actual Confusion.* [There is] very limited evidence to support a claim of actual confusion. Thus, this factor [tips] toward IPC.

8. *Bad Faith.* IPC claims the name "Ikon" was chosen after Elo saw this spelling of the word in an encyclopedia and thought it would be familiar because of the pictorial religious connotations associated with it. Elo's twenty years of experience in the camera business make it unlikely that he did not realize there was a significant resemblance between this name and Nikon. There also is evidence that he rejected the advice of his counsel to adopt a mark with a word other than Ikon as the dominant part. Elo did not disclose to his counsel his intent to market 35 mm cameras similar to Nikon's. There [is] sufficient evidence that IPC acted in bad faith.

9. *Balancing the Factors.* Each factor, with the exception of actual confusion, weighs heavily in favor of Nikon. We hold that the situation taken as a whole clearly tips in favor of Nikon and supports the finding of a likelihood of confusion and trademark infringement.

District court judgment in Nikon's favor affirmed.

CONCEPT REVIEW

THE THREE FORMS OF INTELLECTUAL PROPERTY COMPARED

	Patent	Copyright	Trademark
What Is Protected?	Process, machine, product, composition of matter, improvement, ornamental design, plant produced by asexual reproduction, if *novel, nonobvious,* and *useful*	Wide range of creative works that are *fixed* and *original*	Trademarks, service marks, certification marks, and collective marks of sufficient distinctiveness
Registration Needed?	Yes	Although copyright exists in the absence of registration, registration often necessary for infringement suit	Necessary for infringement suit under Lanham Act section 32(1). Unregistered marks protected under Lanham Act section 43(a).
Duration	17 years (14 years for design patents)	Life of author plus 50 years	10 years, with 10-year renewals possible
Transferability	By assignment or license	By assignment or license	Limited
How Infringed	Making, using, or selling patented invention or its substantial equivalent	Violation of owner's exclusive rights to reproduce, prepare derivative works, distribute copies, perform, or display. But *fair use* defense available.	Use of mark in connection with advertisement or sale that is likely to cause confusion, mistake, or deception regarding origin

FIGURE 1	Patent and Trade Secrets Protection Compared	

Factor	Patent Law	Trade Secrets Law
Range of Protected Matter?	Probably narrower than trade secrets law	Probably broader than patent law
Need to Register?	Yes	No
Burden of Maintaining Secrecy?	No	Yes
Duration	Usually 17 years	So long as secrecy maintained?
Transferability	Fairly easy	Fairly easy
Ability to Keep Knowledge Secret?	No	Yes, if secrecy really maintained
Effective Monopoly over Protected Matter?	Yes	No, because discovery/use by proper means is permissible

TRADE SECRETS

The law provides at least two means of protecting creative inventions. Owners of such inventions may go public and obtain monopoly patent rights. Or they may keep the invention secret and rely on trade secrets law to protect it. Figure 1 sketches some of the advantages and disadvantages of each alternative.

The policies underlying patent protection and trade secrets protection differ. The general aim of patent law is to encourage the creation and disclosure of inventions by granting the patentee a temporary monopoly in the patented invention in exchange for his making it public. Trade secrets, however, are nonpublic by definition. Although protecting trade secrets may stimulate creative activity, it also keeps the information from becoming public knowledge. Thus, the main justification for trade secrets protection is simply to preserve certain standards of commercial morality.

Definition of a Trade Secret

A trade secret can be defined as any secret formula, pattern, process, program, device, method, technique, or compilation of information that is used in the owner's business and that gives its owner an advantage over competitors who do not know it or use it.[6] Examples include chemical formulas, computer software, manufacturing processes, designs for machines, and customer lists. To be protectible, a trade secret must usually have sufficient value or originality to provide an actual or potential competitive advantage. But it need not possess the novelty required for patent protection.

The following *Mason* case considers some factors courts may examine when determining whether a trade secret exists. As several of those factors suggest, a trade secret must actually be *secret*. A substantial measure of secrecy is necessary, but it need not be absolute. Thus, information that becomes public knowledge or becomes generally known in the industry cannot be a trade secret. Also, information that is reasonably discoverable by proper means may not be protected. "Proper means" include independent invention of the secret, observation of a publicly displayed product, the owner's advertising, published literature, product analysis, and reverse engineering (starting with a legitimately acquired product and working backward to discover how it was developed).

In addition, a firm claiming a trade secret must usually show that it took *reasonable measures to assure secrecy*. Examples include advising employees about the secret's secrecy, limiting access to the

---

[6]This definition comes mainly from *Restatement of Torts* section 757, comment b (1939), with some additions from *Uniform Trade Secrets Act* section 1(4) (1985). Many states have adopted the Uniform Trade Secrets Act (UTSA) in some form. The discussion in this chapter is a composite of the *Restatement's* and the UTSA's rules.

secret on a need-to-know basis, requiring those given access to sign a nondisclosure agreement, disclosing the secret only on a confidential basis, and controlling access to an office or plant. Computer software licensing agreements commonly forbid the licensee to copy the program except for backup and archival purposes, require the licensee and its employees to sign confidentiality agreements, require those employees to use the program only in the course of their jobs, and require the licensee to use the program only in a central processing unit. Because the owner must only make *reasonable* efforts to ensure secrecy, however, she need not adopt extreme measures to block every ingenious form of industrial espionage.

Ownership and Transfer of Trade Secrets

The owner of a trade secret is usually the person who developed it or the business under whose auspices it was generated. But establishing the ownership of a trade secret can pose problems where an employee develops a secret in the course of her employment. In such cases, courts often find the *employer* to be the owner if: (1) the employee was hired to do creative work related to the secret, (2) the employee agreed not to divulge or use trade secrets, or (3) other employees contributed to the development of the secret. Even where the employee owns the secret, the employer still may obtain a royalty-free license to use it through the shop right doctrine discussed in the section on patents.

The owner of a trade secret can transfer rights in the secret to third parties. This can occur by assignment (in which case the owner loses title) or by license (in which case the owner retains title but allows the transferee certain uses of the secret).

Misappropriation of Trade Secrets

Misappropriation of a trade secret can occur in various ways, most of which involve *disclosure or use* of the secret. For example, misappropriation liability occurs when the secret is disclosed or used by one who did one of the following:

1. Acquired it by *improper means.* Improper means include theft, trespass, wiretapping, spying, bugging, bribery, fraud, impersonation, and eavesdropping.

2. Acquired it from a party who *is known or should be known* to have obtained it by improper means. For example, a free-lance industrial spy might obtain one firm's trade secrets by improper means and sell them to the firm's competitors. If those competitors know or have reason to know that the spy obtained the secrets by improper means, they are liable for misappropriation along with the spy.

3. *Breached a duty of confidentiality regarding the secret.* Where an employer owns a trade secret, for example, an employee is generally bound not to use or disclose it during his employment or thereafter.[7] The employee may, however, utilize general knowledge and skills acquired during her employment.

Remedies for misappropriation of a trade secret include damages, which might involve both the actual loss caused by the misappropriation and/or the defendant's unjust enrichment. In some states, punitive damages are awarded for willful and malicious misappropriations. Also, an injunction may be issued against actual or threatened misappropriations.

---

[7]This is an application of the agent's duty of loyalty, which is discussed in Chapter 34.

Mason v. Jack Daniel Distillery
518 So. 2d 130 (Ala. Civ. App. 1987)

Tony Mason created a mixed drink that he named "Lynchburg Lemonade." The drink consisted of Jack Daniel's whiskey, Triple Sec, sweet and sour mix, and 7-Up. Mason served the drink at his restaurant and lounge, where it became very popular. Later, Winston Randle, a sales representative for Jack Daniel Distillery, drank Lynchburg Lemonade while in Mason's restaurant and lounge. Although the source of his information is unclear, he also learned the recipe for the drink at this time. Randle informed his superiors about Lynchburg Lemonade and its recipe, and about one year later Jack Daniel was developing a national promotion campaign for the drink.

Mason, who never received any compensation for this use of Lynchburg Lemonade, sued Jack Daniel and Winston for misappropriation of a trade secret. Mason won a trial court jury verdict, and the defendants appealed the trial court's refusal to grant their motion for a directed verdict.

Holmes, Judge   The defendants contend that Mason's recipe for Lynchburg Lemonade was not a trade secret. The *Restatement* provides in pertinent part:

A trade secret may consist of any formula, pattern, device, or compilation of information which is used in one's business, and which gives him an opportunity to obtain an advantage over competitors who do not know or use it. . . .

An exact definition of a trade secret is not possible. Some factors to be considered in determining whether given information is one's trade secret are: (1) the extent to which the information is known outside of his business; (2) the extent to which it is known by employees and others involved in his business; (3) the extent of measures taken by him to guard the secrecy of his information; (4) the value of the information to him and to his competitors; (5) the amount of effort or money expended by him in developing the information; (6) the ease or difficulty with which the information could be properly acquired or duplicated by others.

Applying these factors to this case, we find that some support and some negate the conclusion that Lynchburg Lemonade was Mason's trade secret.

Mason apparently spent little time, effort, or money in concocting the recipe for Lynchburg Lemonade. He seems to have created the beverage one evening to ease a sore throat. However, he put much effort into making the beverage an exclusive specialty of his restaurant and lounge. Mason testified that Lynchburg Lemonade comprised about a third of his total sales of alcoholic drinks. Obviously, the exclusive sale of Lynchburg Lemonade was of great value to Mason. The beverage could also have been valuable to his competitors in the area.

Mason [also] testified that he told only a few of his employees the recipe. He stated that each one was specifically instructed not to tell anyone the recipe. To prevent customers from learning the recipe, the beverage was mixed in the back of the restaurant and lounge. Mason's efforts to keep the recipe a secret were apparently successful until Randle learned the recipe. It appears that one could not order a Lynchburg Lemonade in any establishment other than that of the plaintiff. Absolute secrecy is not required for the recipe to constitute a trade secret—a substantial element of secrecy is all that is necessary.

The defendants contend that Mason's recipe was not a trade secret because it could be easily duplicated by others. The defendants' [expert] testimony characterized Lynchburg Lemonade as a member of the Collins family of drinks, of which there are dozens, if not hundreds, with essentially the same elements. At least one witness testified that he could duplicate the recipe after tasting a Lynchburg Lemonade. Certainly, this testimony is a strong factor against the conclusion that Mason's recipe was a trade secret. We do not think, however, that this evidence in and of itself could prevent such a conclusion. Rather, this evidence should be weighed and considered along with the evidence tending to show the existence of a trade secret. Courts have protected information as a trade secret despite evidence that it could easily be duplicated by others competent in the given field.

A motion for directed verdict should not be granted if there is a scintilla of evidence supporting an element essential to the plaintiff's claim. Our review of the record indicates that Mason did present a scintilla of evidence that his recipe, or formula, for Lynchburg Lemonade was a trade secret.

Trial court's refusal to grant the defendant's motion for a directed verdict affirmed.

COMMERCIAL TORTS

In addition to the intentional torts discussed in Chapter 6, certain other intentional torts involve business or commercial competition. Like the rules discussed thus far in this chapter, they are means by which the law polices commercial life. These torts may help promote innovation by protecting creative businesses against certain competitive abuses. But their main aim is simply to uphold certain minimum standards of commercial morality.

Injurious Falsehood

Injurious falsehood also goes by names such as product disparagement, slander of title, and trade libel. This tort involves the publication of false statements that disparage another's business, property, or title to property, and thus harm her economic interests. One common kind of injurious falsehood involves false statements that disparage either a person's *property rights* in land, things, or intangibles, or their *quality*. The property rights in question include virtually all legally protected property interests that can be sold; examples include leases, mineral rights, trademarks, copyrights, and corporate stock. As the following *Atlas* case indicates, injurious falsehood also includes false statements that harm another's economic interests even though they do not disparage property or property rights as such.

Elements and Damages

In injurious falsehood cases, the plaintiff must prove that the defendant made a statement of the sort just described, the statement's falsity, and its communication to a third party. The degree of fault required for liability is unclear. Sources often say that the standard is malice, but formulations of this differ. The *Restatement* requires either knowledge that the statement is false, or reckless disregard as to its truth or falsity. There is usually no liability for false statements that are made negligently and in good faith.

The plaintiff must also prove that the false statement played a substantial part in causing him to suffer *special damages*. These may include: losses resulting from the diminished value of disparaged property, the expense of measures for counteracting the false statement (e.g., advertising or litigation expenses), losses resulting from the breach of an existing contract by a third party, and the loss of prospective business. In cases involving the loss of prospective business, the plaintiff is usually required to show that some specific person or persons refused to buy because of the disparagement. But as *Atlas* states, this rule is often relaxed where these losses are difficult to prove.

The special damages that the plaintiff is required to prove are his usual—and virtually his only—remedy in injurious falsehood cases. Damages for personal injury or emotional distress, for instance, are generally not recoverable. However, punitive damages and injunctive relief are sometimes obtainable.

Injurious Falsehood and Defamation

Injurious falsehood may or may not overlap with the tort of defamation discussed in Chapter 6. Statements impugning a businessperson's character or conduct are probably only defamatory. If the false statement is limited to the plaintiff's business, property, or property rights, on the other hand, his normal claim is for injurious falsehood. Both claims are possible where the injurious falsehood implies something about the plaintiff's character and affects his overall reputation. An example is a defendant's false allegation that the plaintiff knowingly sells dangerous products to children.

Defamation law's absolute and conditional privileges generally apply in injurious falsehood cases.[8] Certain other privileges protect defendants who are sued for injurious falsehood. For example, a rival claimant may in good faith disparage another's property rights by asserting his own competing rights. Similarly, one may make a good faith allegation that a competitor is infringing one's patent, copyright, or trademark. Finally, a person may sometimes make unfavorable comparisons between her own property and that of a competitor. This privilege is generally limited to sales talk asserting the superiority of one's property and does not cover unfavorable statements about a competitor's property.

---

[8]Chapter 6 discusses those privileges.

CHARLES ATLAS, LTD. v. TIME-LIFE BOOKS, INC.

570 F. Supp. 150 (S.D.N.Y. 1983)

Time-Life Books published a book entitled *Exercising for Fitness*. The book contained a reproduction of the famous Charles Atlas advertisement in which a 97-pound weakling uses Atlas's Dynamic Tension body-building program to become a real man after a bully kicks sand in his face and the face of his girlfriend. The caption accompanying the reproduction told the book's readers that Atlas's program is a system of isometric exercises. On the same page, the book warned readers about the extreme dangers of isometric exercises.

Charles Atlas, Ltd. sued Time-Life in federal district court for product disparagement (injurious falsehood). It basically alleged that the book's caption was false because Atlas's method was not isometric, and that this falsehood, coupled with the warning about the dangers of isometric exercises, caused it to suffer economic loss. Time-Life moved to dismiss Atlas's complaint. The question before the court was whether the facts in the complaint were sufficient to state a claim upon which relief could be granted.

Goettel, District Judge   This court cannot say as a matter of law that the alleged misstatements are not reasonably susceptible to a defamatory meaning and that no reasonable reader could conclude that the statements [concern] the plaintiff's product. When the caption is read in conjunction with the text, a reasonable reader could conclude that Atlas markets an isometric exercise program, that isometric exercises are dangerous, and that therefore Atlas's exercise program is dangerous. Whether the trier of fact will conclude that a defamatory connotation was indeed conveyed will have to await trial.

Malice is pleaded adequately. It is extremely questionable whether the plaintiff must show common-law malice to state a claim for product disparagement. Rather, it appears that the plaintiff must show knowledge of the alleged false statement or reckless disregard as to the truth of the statement [citing the *Restatement*]. Atlas alleges that the allegedly false statements were known by Time-Life to be false when they were made, or were made with recklessness, malice, and intent to injure Atlas.

Finally, Atlas has pleaded special damages adequately. According to Atlas, the alleged disparagement has caused it to lose $30,323 in sales and revenues and to expend $14,000 in special advertising expenses and $16,687 in legal expenses to counteract the alleged disparagement. Special damage is the pecuniary loss resulting directly from the effect of a defendant's allegedly wrongful conduct. Among the losses deemed to constitute special damages are the expenses necessary to counteract the alleged wrongful conduct. Thus, Atlas can recover at least the spe-

cial advertising expenses incurred to counteract the alleged product disparagement, and the pleading of these expenses is sufficient to support the claim at this stage of the litigation.

Loss of sales is also a proper item of special damages. However, Time-Life argues that Atlas has failed to plead this adequately because it has failed to identify lost customers. Adopting such a rule would be grossly unfair in this case. Atlas sells only through mail orders. It is, therefore, virtually impossible to identify those who did not order Atlas's product because of *Exercising for Fitness*. As Dean Prosser has noted: "[A] more liberal rule has been applied, requiring the plaintiff to be particular only where it is reasonable to expect him to do so. It is probably still the law everywhere that he must either offer the names of those who have failed to purchase or explain why it is impossible for him to do so; but where he cannot, the matter is dealt with by analogy to the proof of lost profits resulting from breach of contract."

Whether legal fees expended to prosecute a claim for product disparagement can be recovered as an item of special damages is an interesting issue. It can be argued that the expenses incurred in bringing the lawsuit are similar to other expenses necessary to counteract the alleged wrongful conduct. Be that as it may, the court need not resolve the question at this time because it has already determined that Atlas has stated a claim for product disparagement.

Time-Life's motion to dismiss denied; Atlas's case continues.

Interference with Contractual Relations

In a suit for intentional interference with contractual relations, one party to a contract claims that the defendant's interference with the other party's per-

formance of the contract wrongly caused the plaintiff to lose the benefit of that performance. One can interfere with the performance of a contract by causing a party to repudiate it, or by wholly or partly preventing that party's performance. The means of interference can range from mere persuasion to threatened or actual violence. The agreement whose performance is checked, however, must be an *existing* contract. This includes contracts that are voidable, unenforceable, or subject to contract defenses, but *not* void bargains, contracts that are illegal on public policy grounds, or contracts to marry. Finally, the defendant must have *intended* to cause the breach; there is usually no liability for negligent contract interferences.

Even if the plaintiff proves these threshold requirements, the defendant is liable only if his behavior was *improper.* The following *RAN* case lists the factors the *Restatement* uses to decide this question. Despite the flexible, case-by-case nature of such determinations, a few generalizations about improper interference are possible.

1. Where the contract's performance was blocked by such clearly improper means as threats of physical violence, misrepresentations, defamatory statements, bribery, harassment, or bad-faith civil or criminal actions, the defendant usually is liable. Liability is also likely where the interference was motivated *solely* by malice, spite, or a simple desire to meddle.

2. If his means and motives are legitimate, a defendant generally escapes liability when his contract interference is in the *public interest*—for example, when he informs an airport that an air traffic controller is a habitual user of hallucinogenic drugs. The same is true where the defendant acts to *protect a person for whose welfare she is responsible*—for example, where a mother induces a private school to discharge a diseased student who could infect her children.

3. A contract interference resulting from the defendant's good faith effort to protect her own *existing* legal or economic interests usually does not create liability so long as appropriate means are used. For example, a landowner can probably induce his tenant to breach a sublease to a party whose business detracts from the land's value. However, business parties generally cannot interfere with existing contract rights merely to further some *prospective* competitive advantage. For example, a seller cannot entice its competitors' customers to break existing contracts with those competitors. Is the *RAN* case completely consistent with these rules?

4. Finally, competitors are unlikely to incur liability where, as is still often true of employment contracts, the agreement interfered with is *terminable at will.*[9] The reason is that in such cases, the plaintiff has only an expectancy that the contract will continue, and not a right to have it continued. Thus, a firm that hires away its competitors' at-will employees usually escapes liability.

The basic measure of damages for intentional interference with contractual relations is the value of the lost contract performance. Some courts also award compensatory damages reasonably linked to the interference (including emotional distress and damage to reputation). Sometimes the plaintiff may obtain an injunction prohibiting further interferences.

Interference with Prospective Advantage

The rules and remedies for intentional interference with prospective advantage parallel those for interference with contractual relations. The main difference is that the former tort involves interferences with *prospective* relations rather than existing contracts. The protected future relations are mainly potential contractual relations of a business or commercial sort. Liability for interference with such relations requires intent; negligence usually does not suffice.

The "improper interference" factors weighed in interference-with-contract cases generally apply to interference with prospective advantage as well. One difference, however, is that interference with prospective advantage can be justified if: (1) the plaintiff and the defendant are in competition for the prospective relation with which the defendant interferes; (2) the defendant's purpose is at least partly competitive; (3) the defendant does not use such improper means as physical threats, misrepresentations, and bad faith lawsuits; and (4) the defendant's behavior does not create an unlawful restraint of trade under the antitrust laws or other regulations. Thus, a competitor ordinarily can win customers by offering lower prices and attract suppliers by offering higher prices. Unless this is otherwise illegal, he can also refuse to deal with suppliers or buyers who also deal with his competitors.

---

[9]Chapter 50 discusses terminable-at-will employment contracts.

RAN CORPORATION V. HUDESMAN
823 P.2d 646 (Alaska Sup. Ct. 1991)

David Hudesman leased commercial property housing the Red Dog Saloon to Don Harris, the saloon's owner and operator. The lease said that Harris could assign it to any subtenant or assignee who was financially responsible and would properly care for the premises. It also required that Hudesman consent to such an assignment, but added that this consent could not be withheld unreasonably. After Harris decided to relocate his business, he was contacted by Richard Stone, president of the RAN Corporation. Stone wanted to use the property for an artifacts gallery. Harris and Stone agreed that Harris would assign the lease for $15,000, conditional on Hudesman's approval.

About this time, a politically influential man named Jerry Reinwand contacted Hudesman about the property. In exchange for Reinwand's promise to help Hudesman secure government leases for a large building Hudesman owned, Hudesman promised Reinwand that if Harris relocated his business, Reinwand would be assigned the property. Then Hudesman told Harris that he would not consent to Harris's assignment of the lease to RAN, and that Harris would be "looking at litigation" if he tried to assign the lease to Stone. Thus, Harris told Stone that the deal was off, returned his $15,000 deposit, and assigned the lease to Reinwand for $15,000.

RAN then sued for an injunction to invalidate Reinwand's lease and to enforce its assignment contract with Harris, and also for damages. After RAN settled with several defendants, its main remaining claims were interference with contractual relations and interference with prospective advantage claims against Hudesman. Both parties then moved for summary judgment, and the trial court held for Hudesman. RAN appealed.

Matthews, Justice   The elements of intentional interference with contractual relations are: (1) a contract existed, (2) the defendant knew of the contract and intended to induce a breach, (3) the contract was breached, (4) the defendant's wrongful conduct engendered the breach, (5) the breach caused the plaintiff's damages, and (6) the defendant's conduct was not privileged or justified. The fourth, fifth, and sixth elements also apply to the related tort of intentional interference with prospective economic advantage. As our analysis applies equally to either tort, we will refer to them collectively.

The sixth element is troublingly vague. The *Restatement (Second) of Torts* section 767 speaks not in terms of "privilege," but requires that the actor's conduct not be "improper." Other authorities used the catch word "malice." Regardless of the phrase used, the critical question is what conduct is not "privileged" or "improper" or "malicious." The *Restatement* lists seven factors for consideration: (1) the nature of the actor's conduct, (2) the actor's motive, (3) the interests of the other with which the actor's conduct interferes, (4) the interests sought to be advanced by the actor, (5) the social interests in protecting the freedom of action of the actor and the contractual interests of the other, (6) the proximity or remoteness of the actor's conduct to the interference, and (7) the relations between the parties. While these factors are relevant in some or all incarnations of the interference tort, they are hard to apply in any sort of predictive way.

Instead of relying on the *Restatement* factors, we [have] adopted a test of privilege which hold[s] that where an actor has a direct financial interest, he is privileged to interfere with a contract for economic reasons, but not where he is motivated by spite, malice, or some other improper motive. In our view, this rule applies to this case. A number of other cases have recognized that a landlord has a sufficient interest to interfere with a prospective or actual lease assignment. The right to intervene has also been recognized in the analogous setting of transfers of distributorships.

It seems beyond reasonable argument that an owner of property has a financial interest in the assignment of a lease of the property he owns. An effective lease assignment makes the assignee the tenant of the owner. The tenant has an obligation to pay rent directly to the owner, and the use, or abuse, of the property by the assignee may affect its value to the owner. Further, the owner may know of another potential assignee who will pay more rent than the prospective assignee. Moreover, the owner may wish to terminate the lease based on knowledge of a more profitable use for the property.

Since Hudesman had a direct financial interest in the proposed assignment of the lease, the essential question in determining if interference is justified is whether Hudesman's conduct is motivated by a desire to protect his economic interest, or whether it is motivated by spite, malice, or some other improper objective. As there is no evidence of spite, malice, or other improper objective—Hudesman did not even know RAN Corporation's principals—and since it is clear that Hudesman refused to approve the assignment because he believed that he would receive a

greater economic benefit from a tenancy by Reinwand, the interference was justified.

Hudesman's threat of litigation does not seem relevant to RAN's claim for interference. RAN's assignment agreement with Harris was explicitly conditional on Hudesman's approval. When Hudesman disapproved of the assignment, the interference was complete. Hudesman's disapproval may have been a breach of the Hudesman/Harris lease, but it was privileged from a tort standpoint because of Hudesman's preexisting interest as a property owner-lessor. The threat of litigation may, at worst, have been another breach of the Hudesman/Harris lease. However, it too was not tortious and it was, in any case, superfluous to the interference, because RAN's prospective economic relationship was terminated by Hudesman's disapproval, not by his threat to sue.

Lower court judgment in favor of Hudesman affirmed.

Lanham Act Section 43(a)

Section 43(a) of the Lanham Act basically creates a federal law of unfair competition. Section 43(a) is not a consumer remedy; it is normally available only to commercial parties, who usually are the defendant's competitors. The section creates civil liability for a wide range of false, misleading, confusing, or deceptive descriptions of fact made in connection with goods or services. Section 43(a)'s many applications include:

1. *Common law tort suits for "palming off" or "passing off."* This tort involves false representations that are likely to induce third parties to believe that the defendant's goods or services are those of the plaintiff. Such representations include imitations of the plaintiff's trademarks, trade names, packages, labels, containers, employee uniforms, and place of business.

2. *Trade dress infringement claims.* These claims resemble palming-off claims. A product's trade dress is its overall appearance and sales image. Section 43(a) prohibits a party from passing off its goods or services as those of a competitor by employing a sub-

stantially similar trade dress that is likely to confuse consumers as to the source of its products or services. For example, a competitor that sells antifreeze in jugs that are similar in size, shape, and color to a well-known competitor's jugs may face section 43(a) liability.

3. *The infringement of both registered and unregistered trademarks.*

4. *Some cases involving a form of invasion of privacy discussed in Chapter 6—the appropriation of another's name or likeness for commercial purposes.*

5. *Commercial advertising that misrepresents the nature of goods or services.* This important application of section 43(a) includes ads that misrepresent the nature or origin of either the *advertiser's* products and services or a *competitor's* products and services. As the following *Castrol* case asserts, this includes ads that are likely to deceive buyers even if they are not clearly false on their face. Section 43(a) probably applies to ads containing certain deceptive *omissions* as well.

CASTROL, INC. V. QUAKER STATE CORP.
977 F.2d 57 (2d Cir. 1992)

A Quaker State Corporation television commercial asserted that "tests prove" that: "At start up Quaker State 10W-30 protects better than any other leading 10W-30 motor oil." The commercial also depicted an engine, superimposed over which were bottles of Quaker State oil and four competing motor oils, including Castrol GTX 10W-30. Nearby was a bar graph displaying the superior speed with which Quaker State oil flowed to engine components once the engine is started.

Castrol, Inc., sued Quaker State for false advertising under Lanham Act section 43(a). As part of that suit, it sought a preliminary injunction against Quaker State's airing the commercial. The evidence at trial indicated that while Quaker State's oil indeed did reach engine parts faster than its competitors at start-up, this had no discernible effect on engine wear. The apparent reason is that the "residual oil" remaining from prior engine starts protects the engine until new oil arrives. The district court granted Castrol's requested preliminary injunction, and Quaker State appealed.

Walker, Circuit Judge   A party seeking preliminary injunctive relief must show: (a) that it will suffer irreparable harm if relief is denied, and (b) either (1) a likelihood of success on the merits or (2) sufficiently serious questions going to the merits to make them fair ground for litigation and a balance of hardships tipping decidedly in plaintiff's favor. We presume irreparable harm where plaintiff demonstrates a likelihood of success in showing literally false defendant's comparative advertisement which mentions plaintiff's product by name.

To succeed under section 43(a), a plaintiff must demonstrate that an advertisement is either literally false, or that an advertisement, though literally true, is likely to mislead and confuse consumers. Where the advertising claim is shown to be literally false, the court may enjoin the use of the claim without reference to the advertisement's impact on the buying public. Here, Castrol contends that the challenged advertisement is literally false. It bears the burden of proving this to a "likelihood of success" standard.

Plaintiff bears a different burden in proving literally false the advertised claim that tests prove defendant's product superior, than it does in proving the falsity of a superiority claim which makes no mention of tests. Where the defendant's advertisement claims that its product is superior, plaintiff must affirmatively prove defendant's product equal or inferior. Where, as in the current case, defendant's ad represents that tests or studies prove its

product superior, plaintiff satisfies its burden by showing that the tests did not establish the proposition for which they were cited. A plaintiff can meet this burden by demonstrating that the tests were not sufficiently reliable to permit a conclusion that the product is superior. If the plaintiff can show that the tests, even if reliable, do not establish the proposition asserted by the defendant, the plaintiff [also] has met its burden. The district court held that Castrol had met this latter burden. We will reverse the district court's order of preliminary injunctive relief only upon a showing that it abused its discretion, which may occur when a court bases its decision on clearly erroneous findings of fact or on errors as to applicable law.

Quaker State asserts that the district court's factual findings as to the role of residual oil are clearly erroneous. We disagree. If the district court's account of the evidence is plausible in light of the record viewed in its entirety, the court of appeals may not reverse it even though convinced that had it been sitting as the trier of fact, it would have weighed the evidence differently. We owe particularly strong deference where the district court premises its findings on credibility determinations. In this case, the district court heard five days of expert testimony. Its credibility determinations in favor of Castrol's experts support its finding that residual oil holds the fort. This finding also receives support from [a] videotape of residual oil in the engine and [the tests'] failure to demonstrate reduced engine wear. Nothing in the record convincingly contradicts the district court's conclusion.

District court preliminary injunction against Quaker State affirmed.

ETHICAL AND PUBLIC POLICY CONCERNS

1. An ethical theory known as *utilitarianism* says that the test for the moral worth of actions is their ability to produce the greatest degree of aggregate net satisfaction throughout society. Some utilitarians say that satisfaction is maximized when people are best able to realize their individual preferences. Some say that one measure of satisfaction is the creation of economic wealth. Look at the purposes said to underlie trademark law. Are these generally utilitarian? Why or why not?

2. Legal reasoning is sometimes deductive or syllogistic. In such cases, the court states a general rule as a major premise, treats the facts as a minor premise, and applies the rule to the facts to generate a result. But another style of legal reasoning called *factor-based balancing* proceeds differently. In cases of this kind, the court states various factors that are relevant to its decision and decides by weighing these factors against one another under the facts before it. Which cases in this chapter use this method in whole or in part? Based on those cases, what is good about this style of legal reasoning? Are sensible decisions possible in any other way? On the other hand, what is bad about this decisionmaking process? In answering this last question, consider whether or how well this process enables business parties to predict the legal consequences of their behavior.

3. Take another look at the *Narell* case earlier in the chapter. Even though Narell's copyright infringement suit failed, isn't Freeman morally obligated to give Narell *something* for the portions of Narell's book that Freeman used? After all, this material probably helped sell Freeman's book. On the other hand, what would be likely to happen if everyone in a similar situation has such a moral obligation and acts on it? Would this result be consistent with the purposes underlying copyright law? *Hint:* If Freeman had to pay Narell for whatever she used, would Freeman be likely to use Narell's information? Who loses out if Freeman doesn't use that information in her book?

PROBLEM CASES

1. Huey J. Rivet patented an "amphibious marsh craft" for hauling loads and laying pipeline in swamps. Rivet's model could "walk" over stumps for extended periods while carrying heavy loads. Later, Robert Wilson, who had once worked for Rivet as a welder, began marketing a similar craft. The craft sold by Wilson differed from the craft described in the specification accompanying Rivet's patent application in several respects. Overall, though, the Wilson boat performed much the same functions about as effectively as the Rivet craft, and used much the same engineering techniques and concepts to do so. Has Wilson infringed Rivet's patent?

2. Lorna Nelson, half-sister of the rock star Prince, sued Prince for copyright infringement. She alleged that Prince's hit "U Got the look" infringed her copyrighted song "What's Cooking in this Book." Lorna's song, to which Prince had access, had six verses totaling 35 lines and 176 words. "U Got the look" had eight verses totaling 47 lines and 242 words. The alleged infringements concerned the following verses and words from the two songs:
a. *Lorna's verse 2:* "I glanced up and saw you, a smile so pretty." *Prince's verses 2 and 7:* "I woke up, I've never seen such a pretty girl."
b. *Lorna's verse 3:* "Makeup was rolling down my face." *Prince's verse 5:* "A whole hour just to make up your face."
c. *Lorna's verse 6:* "What's cooking in this book, what's cooking in . . ." *Prince's verses 4 and 6:* "U sho 'nuf do be cooking in my book."

d. *Lorna's verses 1 and 6:* "Take a look, Take another look." *Prince's verses 1 and 7:* "U got the look."

The main issue in the case was whether there was substantial similarity between the lyrics just quoted. Although you cannot answer this question from the chapter, do you think that these lyrics are sufficiently similar to justify imposing liability on Prince?

3. In 1970–71, James Doran, a student at Iowa State University, helped produce a 28-minute film biography of Dan Gable, an Iowa State wrestler who eventually won a gold medal at the 1972 Olympics. Iowa State obtained a valid statutory copyright to the film. In 1972, when Doran was employed by the American Broadcasting Company, he helped arrange for ABC to use a 2½ minute segment of the film for the network's broadcasts of the 1972 Olympics. He did so without Iowa State's knowledge or consent. Is the fact that ABC only used about 9 percent of the film sufficient by itself to give ABC a fair use defense in a copyright infringement suit by Iowa State?

4. Accuride International, Inc., is a wholly owned subsidiary of Standard Precision, Inc., a leading producer of drawer slide mechanisms. Standard Precision and Accuride market drawer slide mechanisms under the "ACCURIDE" trademark. Is this mark arbitrary or fanciful, suggestive, descriptive, or generic?

5. Levi Strauss & Co. makes Levi jeans. Each pair of Levi jeans has a striking and original back pocket stitching pattern consisting of two intersecting arcs that roughly bisect both pockets. In terms of distinctiveness, what kind of trademark is this? Should such a mark receive strong protection or relatively little protection if Levi Strauss sues another jeans manufacturer for trademark infringement?

6. E. I. du Pont de Nemours & Co., was building a plant to develop a highly secret unpatented process for producing methanol. During the construction, some of its trade secrets were exposed to view from the air because the plant in which they were contained did not yet have a roof. These secrets were photographed from an airplane by two photographers who were hired by persons unknown to take pictures of the new construction. Did this action amount to a misappropriation of Du Pont's trade secrets?

7. Frank and Frances Gardner sued Sailboat Key, Inc., to prevent it from constructing certain improvements pursuant to building permits issued by the city of Miami. Sailboat Key later sued the Gardners for injurious falsehood. It alleged that false statements contained in the Gardners' pleadings in the earlier case caused it to lose its interest in the land where the construction was to occur because it could not obtain financing. The Gardners claimed that defamation law's absolute privilege for statements made in the course of judicial proceedings also applied to this injurious falsehood action, and thus protected them from liability. Are the Gardners correct?

8. Joanna Wells and Paula Snyder visited the Brownsville Golden Age Nursing Home in connection with their interest in placing a relative in a nursing home. Appalled at the conditions they found there, Wells and Snyder communicated their concerns to a variety of sources, including the governor of Pennsylvania, President Ronald Reagan, CBS News, and the television show "60 Minutes." Their various communications eventually caused Golden Age to lose its state operating license due to various violations of state regulations. Golden Age sued Wells and Snyder for intentional interference with its contractual relations. Did Golden Age win? Why or why not?

9. The New Mexico and Arizona Land Company owned a sizable tract of land in Arizona. It leased a portion of this land, which contained water for grazing, to the Bar J Bar Cattle Company. New Mexico had the right to cancel the lease upon 30 days' notice once it sold the land. Malcolm Pace, who owned a ranch adjoining the Bar J Bar ranch and wanted its water rights, bought the land leased by Bar J Bar from New Mexico. Shortly thereafter, New Mexico gave Bar J Bar 30 days' notice of termination. Bar J Bar sued Pace for intentional interference with contractual relations. One feature of the Bar J Bar lease weakens its chances of recovery against Pace. What is that feature of the lease? *Hint*: The answer requires that you make an analogy to a subject discussed in this chapter's discussion of intentional interference with contractual relations.

10. After retiring from professional football, ex–Notre Dame and Green Bay Packer star Paul Hornung began a career as a television sports announcer. From the mid-1960s until 1980, he worked as a play-by-play announcer and color commentator at both college and professional games. In 1981 or

1982, the Atlanta television station WTBS contracted with the NCAA to telecast 19 college football games during the 1982 and 1983 seasons. The contract gave the NCAA the right to approve or disapprove any announcer or color commentator used on the broadcasts. When WTBS proposed Hornung as a color analyst for the games, the NCAA rejected him. The stated reasons for Hornung's rejection were his close association with professional football, his suspension for gambling while an NFL player, and his participation in Miller Lite beer commercials. The NCAA, however, itself accepted advertising revenue from the Miller Brewing Company.

Hornung sued the NCAA for intentional interference with prospective advantage. Did he win? Why or why not?

11. Tracy-Locke, Inc., the ad agency for Frito-Lay, Inc., used a 1976 Tom Waits song called "Step Right Up" in an advertisement for a new Frito-Lay product called "SalsaRio Doritas." Tracy-Locke got Stephen Carter, a professional singer and musician, to sing "Step Right Up" in the commercial. Carter did a near-perfect imitation of Waits's distinctive singing voice and style. After the ad containing Carter's imitation was disseminated to the public, Waits found out about it. As a result, he wanted to sue Frito-Lay. Of the various statutory provisions and common law rules discussed in this chapter, which is Waits's best bet?

CONTRACTS

INTRODUCTION TO CONTRACTS

INTRODUCTION

Scholars and courts have formulated numerous definitions of the term contract. *The* Restatement (Second) of Contracts *defines a contract as "a promise or set of promises for the breach of which the law gives a remedy, or the performance of which the law in some way recognizes as a duty."[1] The essence of this definition for our purposes is that a contract is a* legally enforceable promise or set of promises. *In other words, parties to contracts are entitled to call on the state to force those with whom they have contracted to honor their promises. However, not all of the promises that people make attain the status of contracts. We have all made and broken numerous promises without fear of being sued by those to whom our promises were made. If you promise to take a friend out to dinner but fail to do so, you do not expect to be sued for breaching your promise. What separates such social promises from legally enforceable contracts?*

THE NATURE OF CONTRACTS

Over the years, the common law courts have developed several basic tests that a promise must meet before it is treated as a contract. These tests comprise the basic elements of contract. Contracts are *agreements* (an *offer,* made and *accepted*) that are *voluntarily* created by persons with the *capacity* to contract. The objectives of the agreement must be *legal* and, in most cases, the agreement must be supported by some *consideration* (a bargained-for exchange of legal value). Finally, the law requires *written* evidence of the existence of some agreements before enforcing them (see Figure 1). The following chapters discuss each of these elements and other points that are necessary to enable you to distinguish contracts from unenforceable, social promises.

THE SOCIAL UTILITY OF CONTRACT

Contracts enable persons acting in their own interests to enlist the support of the law in furthering their personal objectives. Contracts enable us to enter into agreements with others with the confi-

[1]*Restatement (Second) of Contracts* § 1 (1981).

FIGURE 1   **Getting to Contract**

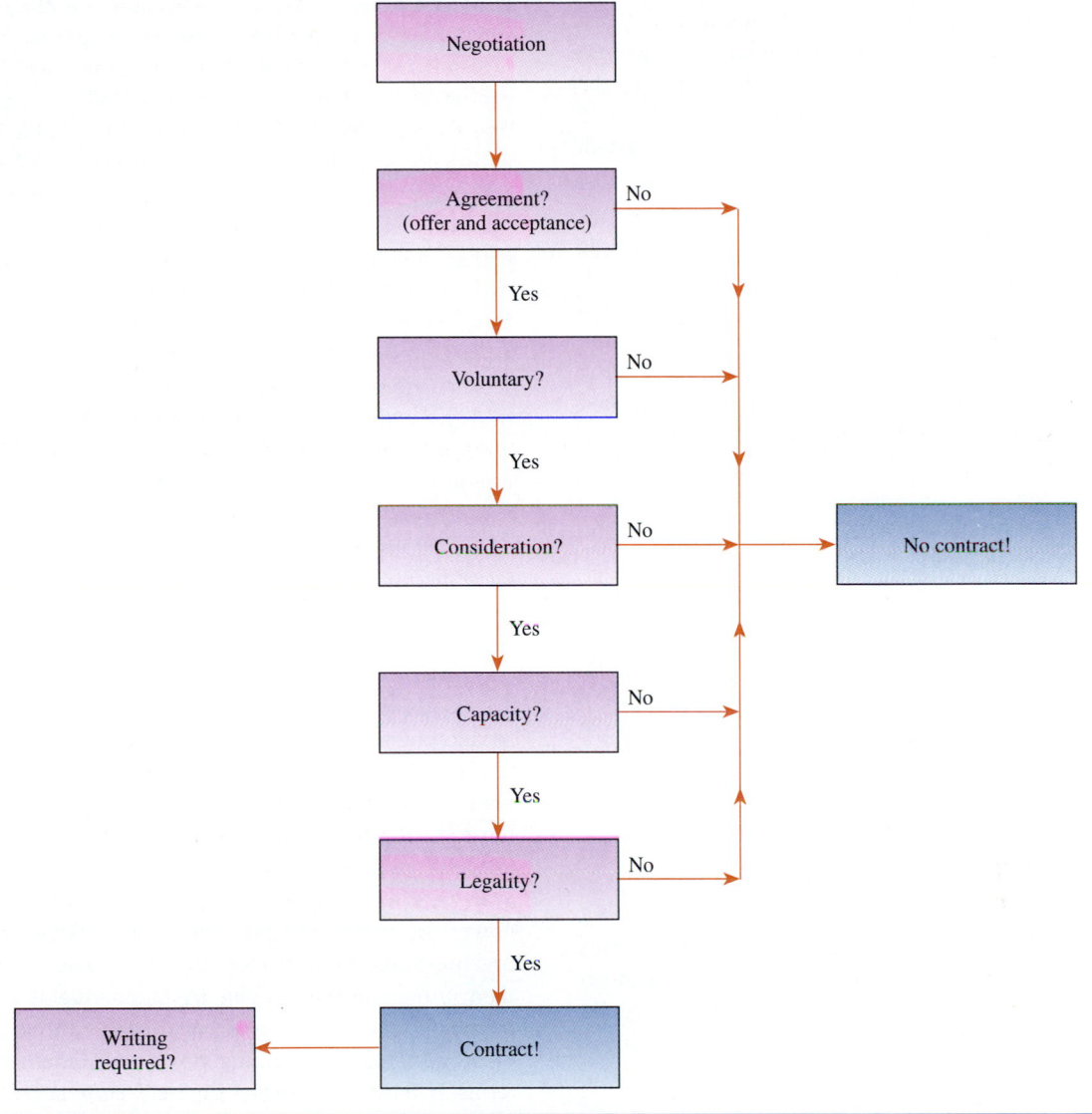

dence that we may call on the law, and not merely the good faith of the other party, to ensure that those agreements will be honored. Within broad limits defined by contract doctrine and public policy, the contract device enables us to create the private law that governs our relations with others—the terms of the agreements we make.

Contracts facilitate the private planning that is necessary in a modern, industrialized society. Few people would invest in a business enterprise if they could not rely on the builders and suppliers of their facilities and equipment, the suppliers of the raw materials necessary to manufacture products, and the customers who agree to purchase those products to honor their commitments. How could we make loans, sell goods on credit, or rent property unless loan agreements, conditional sales agreements, and leases were backed by the force of the law? Contract, then, is an inescapable and valuable part of the world as we know it. Like that world, its particulars tend to change over time, while its general characteristics remain largely stable.

THE EVOLUTION OF CONTRACT LAW

Classical Contract Law

The contract idea is ancient. Thousands of years ago, Egyptians and Mesopotamians recognized devices like contracts; by the 15th century, the common law courts of England had developed a variety of theories to justify enforcing certain promises. Contract law did not, however, assume major importance in our legal system until the 19th century, when numerous social factors combined to shape the common law of contract. Laissez-faire (free market) economic ideas had a profound influence on public policy thinking during this period, and the Industrial Revolution created a perceived need for private planning and certainty in commercial transactions. The typical contract situation in the early decades of the 19th century involved face-to-face transactions between parties with relatively equal bargaining power who dealt with relatively simple goods.

The contract law that emerged from this period was strongly influenced by these factors. Its central tenet was *freedom of contract*: Contracts should be enforced because they are the products of the free wills of their creators, who should, within broad limits, be free to determine the extent of their obligations. The proper role of the courts in such a system of contract was to enforce these freely made bargains but otherwise to adopt a hands-off stance. Contractual liability should not be imposed unless the parties clearly agreed to assume it, but once an agreement had been made, liability was near absolute. The fact that the items exchanged were of unequal value was usually legally irrelevant. The freedom to make good deals carried with it the risk of making bad deals. As long as a person voluntarily entered a contract, it would generally be enforced against him, even if the result was grossly unfair. And since equal bargaining power tended to be assumed, the courts were usually unwilling to hear defenses based on unequal bargaining power. This judicial posture allowed the courts to formulate a pure contract law consisting of precise, clear, and technical rules that were capable of general, almost mechanical, application. Such a law of contract met the needs of the marketplace by affording the predictable and consistent results necessary to facilitate private planning.

Modern Contract Law Development

As long as most contracts resembled the typical transaction envisioned by 19th-century contract law, such rules made perfect sense. If the parties dealt face-to-face, they were likely to know each other personally or at least to know each other's reputation for fair dealing. Face-to-face deals enabled the parties to inspect the goods in advance of the sale, and since the subject matter of most contracts was relatively simple, the odds were great that the parties had relatively equal knowledge about the items they bought and sold. If the parties also had equal bargaining power, it was probably fair to assume that they were capable of protecting themselves and negotiating an agreement that seemed fair at the time. Given the truth of these assumptions, there was arguably no good reason for judicial interference with private contracts.

America's Industrial Revolution, however, undermined many of these assumptions. Regional, and later national, markets produced longer chains of distribution. This fact, combined with more efficient means of communication, meant that people often contracted with persons whom they did not know for goods that they had never seen. And rapidly developing technology meant that those goods were becoming increasingly complex. Thus, sellers often knew far more about their products than did the buyers with whom they dealt. Finally, the emergence of large business organizations after the Civil War produced obvious disparities of bargaining power in many contract situations. These large organizations found it more efficient to standardize their numerous transactions by employing standard form contracts, which could also be used to exploit disproportionate bargaining power by dictating the terms of their agreements. Figure 2 summarizes the factors that shaped modern contract law.

The upshot of all this is that many contracts today no longer resemble the stereotypical agreements envisioned by the common law of contract. It has been estimated that over 90 percent of all contracts today are form contracts.[2] How should courts respond to contracts where the terms have been dictated by one party to another party who may not have read or understood them, and who, in

---

[2]Slawson, "Standard Form Contracts and Democratic Control of Lawmaking Power," 84 *Harv. L. Rev.* 529 (1971).

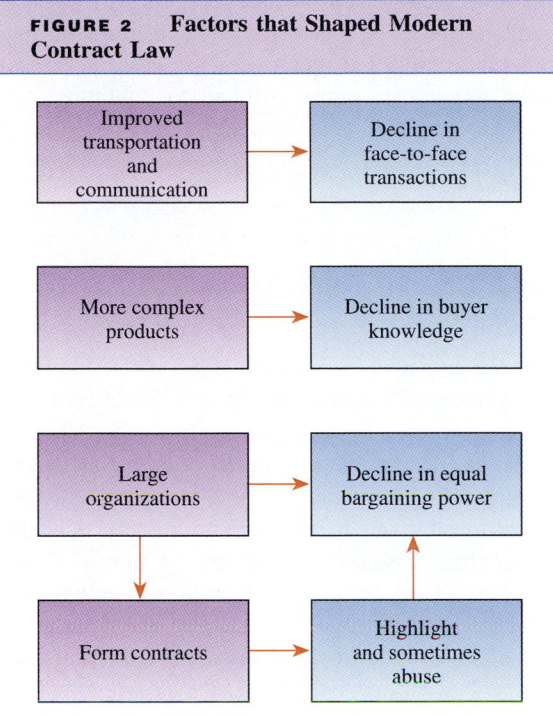

FIGURE 2   Factors that Shaped Modern Contract Law

Improved transportation and communication → Decline in face-to-face transactions

More complex products → Decline in buyer knowledge

Large organizations → Decline in equal bargaining power

Form contracts → Highlight and sometimes abuse

increasingly hands-on posture by courts that often feel compelled to intervene in private contractual relationships to protect weaker parties. In the name of avoiding injustice, some modern contract doctrines impose contractual liability, or something quite like it, in situations where traditional contract rules would have denied liability. Similarly, other modern contract doctrines allow parties to avoid contract liability in cases where traditional common law rules would have recognized a binding agreement and imposed liability.

In the process of evolving to accommodate changing social circumstances, the basic nature of contract rules is changing. The precise, technical rules that characterized traditional common law contract are giving way to broader, imprecise standards such as good faith, injustice, reasonableness, and unconscionability. The reason for such standards is clear. If courts are increasingly called on to intervene in private contracts in the name of fairness, it is necessary to fashion rules that afford the degree of judicial discretion required to reach just decisions in the increasingly complex and varied situations where intervention is needed.

This heightened emphasis on fairness, like every other choice made by law, carries with it some cost. Imprecise, discretionary modern contract rules do not produce the same measure of certainty and predictability that their precise and abstract predecessors afforded. And because modern contract rules often impose liability in the absence of the clear consent required by traditional common law contract rules, one price of increased fairness in contract cases has been a diminished ability of private parties to control the nature and extent of their contractual obligations.

This change in the nature of contract law is far from complete, however. The idea that a contract is an agreement freely entered into by the parties still lies at the heart of contract law today, and contract cases may be found that differ very little in their spirit or ultimate resolution from their 19th-century predecessors. It is probably fair to say, however, that these are most likely to be cases where 19th-century assumptions about the nature of contracts are still largely valid. Thus, these cases involve contracts between parties with relatively equal bargaining power and relatively equal knowledge about the subject of the contract. Despite the existence of such cases, it is evident that contract law is in the process

any event, may have lacked the power to bargain for better terms? Contract law is changing to reflect these changes in social reality. The 20th century has witnessed a dramatic increase in public intervention into private contractual relationships. Think of all the statutes governing the terms of what were once purely private contractual relationships. Legislatures commonly dictate many of the basic terms of insurance contracts. Employment contracts are governed by a host of laws concerning maximum hours worked, minimum wages paid, employer liability for on-the-job injuries, unemployment compensation, and retirement benefits. In some circumstances, product liability statutes impose liability on the manufacturers and sellers of products regardless of the terms of their sales contracts. The avowed purpose of much of this public intervention has been to protect persons who lack sufficient bargaining power to protect themselves.

Nor have the legislatures been the only source of public supervision of private agreements. Twentieth-century courts have been increasingly concerned with creating contract rules that produce just results. The result of this concern has been an of significant change. Subsequent chapters high-lighting the differences between modern contract rules and their traditional common law forebears render this conclusion inescapable. Before discussing particular examples of this new thrust in contract law, however, we should familiarize ourselves with the basic contract terminology that is used throughout the text.

BASIC CONTRACT CONCEPTS AND TYPES

Bilateral and Unilateral Contracts

Contracts have traditionally been classified as **bilateral** or **unilateral,** depending on whether one or both of the parties has made a promise. In unilateral contracts, only one party makes a promise. For example, if a homeowner says to a painter, "I will pay you $1,000 if you paint my house," the homeowner has made an offer for a unilateral contract, a contract that will be created only if and when the painter paints the house. If the homeowner instead says to the painter, "If you promise to paint my house, I will promise to pay you $1,000," he has asked the painter to commit to painting the house rather than just to perform the act of painting. This offer contemplates the formation of a bilateral contract. If the painter makes the requested promise to paint the house, a bilateral contract is created at that point.

In succeeding chapters, you will learn that unilateral contracts cause some particular problems related to offer and acceptance and to mutuality of obligation. These problems have caused many commentators to argue that the unilateral-bilateral contract distinction should be abandoned. The *Restatement (Second) of Contracts* and the Uniform Commercial Code, both of which are discussed later in this chapter, do not expressly use unilateral-bilateral terminology. However, both of these important sources of modern contract principles contain provisions for dealing with typical unilateral contract problems. Despite this evidence of disfavor, the courts continue to use unilateral contract terminology, in part because it enables them to do justice in some cases by imposing contractual liability on one party without the necessity of finding a return promise of the other party. For example, many recent employment cases have used unilateral contract analyses to hold employers liable for promises relating to pension rights, bonuses or incentive pay, and profit-sharing benefits, though the employees in question did not make any clear return promise to continue their employment for any specified time or to do anything else in exchange for the employer's promise.[3]

Valid, Unenforceable, Voidable, and Void Contracts

A **valid contract** is one that meets all of the legal requirements for a binding contract. Valid contracts are, therefore, enforceable in court.

An **unenforceable contract** is one that meets the basic legal requirements for a contract but may not be enforceable due to some other legal rule. Chapter 16, Writing, discusses the statute of frauds, which requires written evidence of certain contracts. An otherwise valid oral contract that the statute of frauds requires to be in writing, for example, may be unenforceable due to the parties' failure to reduce the contract to written form. Another example of an unenforceable contract is an otherwise valid contract whose enforcement is barred by the applicable contract statute of limitations.

Voidable contracts are those in which one or more of the parties have the legal right to cancel their obligations under the contract. They are enforceable against both parties unless a party with the power to void the contract has exercised that power. Chapter 13, Reality of Consent, for example, states that contracts induced by misrepresentation, fraud, duress, or undue influence are voidable at the election of the injured party.

Void contracts are agreements that create no legal obligations because they fail to contain one or more of the basic elements required for enforceability. A void contract is, in a sense, a contradiction in terms. It would be more accurate to say that no contract was created in such cases. Chapter 15, Illegality, for example, mentions that a contract to commit a crime, such as an agreement for the sale of cocaine, does not create a binding legal obligation. Nonetheless, practical constraints may some-

---

[3]See Petit, "Modern Unilateral Contracts," 63 *B.U.L. Rev.* 551 (1983).

times encourage a party to such a contract to perform his agreement rather than raise an illegality defense.

Express and Implied Contracts

In an **express contract,** the parties have directly stated the terms of their contract orally or in writing at the time the contract was formed. As the following *Cook v. Cook* case illustrates, however, the mutual agreement necessary to create a contract may also be demonstrated by the conduct of the parties. When the surrounding facts and circumstances indicate that an agreement has in fact been reached, an **implied contract** (also called a contract implied in fact) has been created. When you go to a doctor for treatment, for example, you do not ordinarily state the terms of your agreement in advance, although it is clear that you do, in fact, have an agreement. A court would infer a promise by your doctor to use reasonable care and skill in treating you and a return promise on your part to pay a reasonable fee for her services.

Executed and Executory Contracts

A contract is **executed** when all of the parties have fully performed their contractual duties, and it is **executory** until such duties have been fully performed.

Any contract may be described using one or more of the above terms. For example, Eurocars, Inc., orders five new Mercedes-Benz 500 SLs from Mercedes. Mercedes sends Eurocars its standard acknowledgment form accepting the order. The parties have a *valid, express, bilateral* contract that will be *executory* until Mercedes delivers the cars and Eurocars pays for them.

COOK V. COOK
691 P.2d 664 (Ariz. Sup. Ct. 1984)

Intending to marry as soon as Donald's divorce became final, Rose Elsten and Donald Cook moved to Tucson in 1969 and lived there together until 1981. Although they did not marry, Rose used Donald's last name and they represented themselves to the community as husband and wife. Both parties worked throughout most of the relationship, pooling their income in two joint accounts and acquiring a house, two cars, and a number of shares of stock, all owned as joint tenants with right of survivorship. Rose left Donald in 1981. Of their joint assets, she received only one car and a few hundred dollars; Donald retained the balance.

Rose filed suit against Donald, arguing that he had breached their agreement to share their assets equally. In her deposition she said: "[E]verything we did and purchased, whether it be a vacuum cleaner or a car, was together as husband and wife. It was just something *that we agreed on,* that is how we were going to do it." When the trial court ruled against her, she appealed.

Feldman, Justice   The *sine qua non* of any contract is the exchange of promises. From this exchange flows the obligation of one party to another. Although it is most apparent that two parties have exchanged promises when their words express a spoken or written statement of promissory intention, mutual promises need not be express in order to create an enforceable contract. Indeed, a promise "may be inferred wholly or partly from conduct," and "there is no distinction in the effect of the promise whether it is expressed in writing, or orally, or in acts, or partly in one of these ways and partly in others." *Restatement (Second) of Contracts.*

Thus, two parties may by their course of conduct express their agreement, though no words are ever spoken. From their conduct alone the finder of fact can determine the existence of an agreement. Although isolated acts of joint participation such as cohabitation or the opening of a joint account may not suffice to create a contract, the fact finder may infer an exchange of promises, and the existence of the contract, from the entire course of conduct between the parties.

The conduct of the parties certainly demonstrates such an agreement and intent. Rose and Donald maintained two joint accounts, a checking account and a credit union savings account, in the names of "Rose and Don Cook" and held them as joint tenants with right of survivorship. Neither Rose nor Donald maintained a separate account. Both deposited portions of their paychecks into the accounts and used the funds to pay for household expenses and various assets they purchased. In addition, Rose and Donald held jointly a number of shares of Southwest Gas stock purchased with funds from the credit union account. In 1972 they purchased a house, taking the deed as husband and wife in joint tenancy with right of survivorship. Both signed the mortgage, incurring liability for the full purchase price of the house, and payments on the mortgage were made out of the joint checking account. There is ample evidence to support a finding that Rose and Donald agreed to pool their resources and share equally in certain accumulations; their course of conduct may be seen as consistently demonstrating the existence of such an agreement.

Judgment reversed in favor of Rose; case remanded for further proceedings.

QUASI–CONTRACT

The traditional common law insistence on the presence of all the elements required for a binding contract before contractual obligation is imposed can cause injustice in some cases. One person may have provided goods or services to another person who benefited from them but has no contractual obligation to pay for them because no facts exist that would justify a court in implying a promise to pay for them. Such a situation can also arise in cases where the parties contemplated entering into a binding contract but some legal defense exists that prevents the enforcement of the agreement. Consider the following examples:

1. Jones paints Smith's house by mistake, thinking it belongs to Reed. Smith knows that Jones is painting his house but does not inform him of his error. There are no facts from which a court can infer that Jones and Smith have a contract, because the parties have had no prior discussions or dealings.

2. Thomas Products fraudulently induces Perkins to buy a household products franchise by grossly misstating the average revenues of its franchisees. Perkins discovers the misrepresentation after he has resold some products that he has received but before he has paid Thomas for them. Perkins elects to rescind (cancel) the franchise contract on the basis of the fraud.

In the preceding examples, both Smith and Perkins have good defenses to contract liability; however, enabling Smith to get a free paint job and Perkins to avoid paying for the goods he resold would *unjustly enrich* them at the expense of Jones and Thomas. To deal with such cases and to prevent such unjust enrichment, the courts imply *as a matter of law* a promise by the benefited party to pay the *reasonable value* of the benefits he received. This idea is called **quasi-contract** (or contract implied in law) because it represents an obligation imposed by law to avoid injustice, not a contractual obligation created by voluntary consent. Quasi-contract liability has been imposed in situations too numerous and varied to detail. In general, however, quasi-contract liability is imposed when one party *confers a benefit* on another who *knowingly accepts it* and *retains it* under circumstances that make it *unjust* to do so without paying for it. So, if Jones painted Smith's house while Smith was away on vacation, Smith would probably not be liable for the reasonable value of the paint job because he did *not* knowingly accept it and because he has no way to return it to Jones. The following *Corrado* case highlights the centrality of the unjust enrichment idea to quasi-contract liability.

ANTHONY CORRADO, INC. v. MENARD & CO.
589 A.2d 1201 (R.I. Sup. Ct. 1991)

Hart Engineering Company (Hart) was the general contractor for the construction of the Fields Point Waste Water Treatment Facility. Hart posted the necessary bond for the project, and Seaboard Surety Company (Seaboard) wrote the bond. Hart subcontracted with Menard & Co. Building Contractors (Menard) to do the masonry work. Menard purchased certain building materials for the project from Corrado, who supplied the materials but was never paid by either Menard or Hart. Corrado later sued Hart, Seaboard, and Menard. He won a summary judgment against Menard, but the trial court granted summary judgments in favor of Seaboard and Hart because Menard, not Hart or Seaboard, had ordered the materials. Corrado appealed.

Per Curiam   Corrado argues that under quasi-contract, he had a cause of action against Hart and Seaboard for unjust enrichment. In order to recover under quasi-contract, a plaintiff is required to prove three elements: (1) a benefit must be conferred upon the defendant by the plaintiff, (2) there must be appreciation by the defendant of such a benefit, and (3) there must be an acceptance of such benefit in such circumstances that it would be inequitable for a defendant to retain the benefit without paying the value thereof.

In reviewing a motion for summary judgment, a trial justice must determine, after an examination of the pleadings, affidavits, admissions, and answers to interrogatories, viewed in the light most favorable to the opposing party, whether there is a genuine issue regarding any material fact that must be resolved.

In his affidavit Frank Rampone, president of Hart, avers that from time to time Menard would submit an application for payment and that periodic payments were made to Menard. He further averred that Hart had no contractual relationship with Corrado and that it was Menard's obligation to pay Corrado directly from the periodic payments made to it. Hart never agreed to pay Corrado directly.

It is obvious from the record that there is no genuine issue regarding any material fact that must be resolved. No conflicting evidence was introduced to establish that Menard was not paid in full by Hart. Moreover, there was no evidence that would establish that Hart received any unjust enrichment from Corrado's building materials since Hart made periodic payments to Menard.

Judgment for Hart and Seaboard affirmed.

PROMISSORY ESTOPPEL

Another very important idea that 20th-century courts have developed to deal with the unfairness that would sometimes result from the strict application of traditional contract principles is the doctrine of **promissory estoppel.** In numerous situations, one person may *rely* on a promise made by another even though the promise and surrounding circumstances are not sufficient to justify the conclusion that a contract has been created because one or more of the required elements is missing.

To allow the person who made such a promise (the promisor) to argue that no contract was created would sometimes work an injustice on the person who relied on the promise (the promisee). For example, in *Ricketts v. Scothorn,* a grandfather's promise to pay his granddaughter interest on a demand note he gave her so that she would not have to work was enforced against him after she had quit her job in reliance on his promise.[4] The

---

[4]57 Neb. 51, 77 N.W. 365 (1898).

Nebraska Supreme Court acknowledged that such promises were traditionally unenforceable because they were gratuitous and not supported by any consideration, but held that the granddaughter's reliance prevented her grandfather from raising his lack of consideration defense. In the early decades of this century, many courts began to extend similar protection to relying promisees. They said that persons who made promises that produced such reliance were *estopped,* or equitably prevented, from raising any defense they had to the enforcement of their promise. Out of such cases grew the doctrine of promissory estoppel. Section 90 of the *Restatement (Second) of Contracts* states:

A promise which the promisor should reasonably expect to induce action or forbearance on the part of the promisee or a third person and which does induce such action or forbearance is binding if injustice can be avoided only by enforcement of the promise. The remedy granted for breach may be limited as justice requires.

Thus, the elements of promissory estoppel are a *promise* that the *promisor should foresee is likely to induce reliance, reliance* on the promise by the promisee, and *injustice* as a result of that reliance.

When you consider these elements, it is obvious that promissory estoppel is fundamentally different from traditional contract principles. Contract is traditionally thought of as protecting *agreements* or bargains. Promissory estoppel, on the other hand, protects *reliance.* Early promissory estoppel cases applied the doctrine only to donative or gift promises. As subsequent chapters demonstrate, however, promissory estoppel is now being used by the courts to prevent offerors from revoking their offers, to enforce indefinite promises, and to enforce oral promises that would ordinarily have to be in writing. Given the basic conceptual differences between estoppel and contract, and the judicial tendency to use promissory estoppel to compensate for the absence of the traditional elements of contract, its growth as a new device for enforcing promises is one of the most important developments in modern contract law. Figure 3 summarizes the ways in which contract differs from quasi-contract and promissory estoppel.

| FIGURE 3 | Contract and Contractlike Theories of Recovery |
| | | |

Theory	Key Concept	Remedy
Contract	Voluntary agreement	Enforce promise
Quasi-Contract	Unjust enrichment	Reasonable value of services
Promissory Estoppel	Foreseeable reliance	Enforce promise or recover reliance losses

THE UNIFORM COMMERCIAL CODE

Origins and Purposes of the Code

The Uniform Commercial Code (UCC) was created by the American Law Institute and the National Conference of Commissioners on Uniform State Laws. All of the states have adopted it except Louisiana, which has adopted only part of the Code. The drafters of the Code had several purposes in mind, the most obvious of which was to establish a uniform set of rules to govern commercial transactions, which are often conducted across state lines in today's national markets. Despite the Code's almost national adoption, however, complete uniformity has not been achieved. Many states have varied or amended the Code's language in specific instances, and some Code provisions were drafted in alternative ways, giving the states more than one version of particular Code provisions to choose from. Also, the various state courts have reached different conclusions about the meaning of particular Code sections. Work is currently under way to revise many basic sections of the Code, so uniformity will continue to be a problem as states adopt the revised sections at different rates and to different degrees.

In addition to promoting uniformity, the drafters of the Code sought to create a body of rules that would realistically and fairly solve the common problems occurring in everyday commercial transactions. Finally, the drafters tried to formulate rules that would promote fair dealing and higher standards in the marketplace.

Scope of the Code

The Code contains nine substantive articles, most of which are discussed in detail in Parts 4, 6, and 7 of this book. The most important Code article for our present purposes is Article 2, the Sales article of the Code.

Nature of Article 2

Many of the provisions of Article 2 exhibit the basic tendencies of modern contract law discussed earlier in this chapter. Accordingly, they differ from traditional contract law rules in a variety of important ways. The Code is more concerned with rewarding people's legitimate expectations than with technical rules, so it is generally more flexible than contract law. A court that applies the Code is more likely to find that the parties had a contract than is a court that applies contract law [2–204] (the numbers in brackets refer to specific Code sections). In some cases, the Code gives less weight than does contract law to technical requirements such as consideration [2–205 and 2–209].

The drafters of the Code sought to create practical rules to deal with what people actually do in today's marketplace. We live in the day of the form contract, so some of the Code's rules try to deal fairly with that fact [2–205, 2–207, 2–209(2), and 2–302]. The words *reasonable, commercially reasonable,* and *seasonably* (within a reasonable time) are found throughout the Code. This reasonableness standard is different from the hypothetical reasonable person standard in tort law. A court that tries to decide what is reasonable under the Code is more likely to be concerned with what people really do in the marketplace than with what a nonexistent reasonable person would do.

The drafters of the Code wanted to promote fair dealing and higher standards in the marketplace, so they imposed a **duty of good faith** [1–203] in the performance and enforcement of every contract under the Code. Good faith means "honesty in fact," which is required of all parties to sales

contracts [1–201(19)]. In addition, merchants are required to observe "reasonable commercial standards of fair dealing" [2–103(1)(b)]. The parties cannot alter this duty of good faith by agreement [1–102(3)]. Finally, the Code expressly recognizes the concept of an **unconscionable contract,** one that is grossly unfair or one-sided, and it gives the courts broad discretionary powers to deal fairly with such contracts [2–302].[5]

The Code also recognizes that buyers tend to place more reliance on professional sellers and that professionals are generally more knowledgeable and better able to protect themselves than nonprofessionals. So, the Code distinguishes between **merchants** and nonmerchants by holding merchants to a higher standard in some cases [2–201(2), 2–205, and 2–207(2)]. The Code defines the term *merchant* [2–104(1)] on a case-by-case basis. If a person regularly deals in the kind of goods being sold, or pretends to have some special knowledge about the goods, or employed an agent in the sale who fits either of these two descriptions, that person is a merchant for the purposes of the contract in question. So, if you buy a used car from a used-car dealer, the dealer is a merchant for the purposes of your contract. But, if you buy a refrigerator from a used-car dealer, the dealer is probably not a merchant.

Application of the Code

Article 2 expressly applies only to *contracts for the sale of goods* [2–102]. The Code contains a somewhat complicated definition of *goods* [2–105], but the essence of the definition is that *goods* are *tangible, movable, personal property.* So, contracts for the sale of such items as motor vehicles, books, appliances, and clothing are covered by Article 2. But Article 2 does *not* apply to contracts for the sale of real estate, stocks and bonds, or other intangibles. Article 2 also does not apply to *service* contracts. This can cause confusion because, although contracts of employment or other personal services are clearly not covered by Article 2, many contracts involve elements of both goods and services. As the

---

[5]Chapter 15 discusses unconscionability in detail.

following *Advent* case illustrates, the test that the courts most frequently use to determine whether Article 2 applies to such a contract is to ask which element, goods or services, *predominates* in the contract. Is the major purpose or thrust of the agreement the rendering of a service, or is it the sale of goods, with any services involved being merely incidental to that sale? This means that contracts calling for services that involve significant elements of personal skill or judgment in addition to goods probably are not governed by Article 2. Construction contracts, remodeling contracts, and auto repair contracts are all examples of mixed goods and services contracts that may be considered outside the scope of the Code.

Two other important qualifications must be made concerning the application of Code contract principles. First, the Code does not change *all* of the traditional contract rules. Where no specific Code rule exists, traditional contract law rules apply to contracts for the sale of goods. Second, and ultimately far more important, the courts have demonstrated a significant tendency to apply Code contract concepts by analogy to contracts not specifically covered by Article 2. For example, the Code concepts of good faith dealing and unconscionability have enjoyed wide application in cases that are technically outside the scope of Article 2. Thus, the Code is an important influence in shaping the evolution of contract law in general, and if this trend toward broader application of Code principles continues, the time may come when the dichotomy between Code principles and traditional contract rules is a thing of the past.

ADVENT SYSTEMS LTD. v. UNISYS CORPORATION
925 F.2d 670 (3d Cir. 1991)

Advent Systems Limited (Advent), a British company engaged primarily in the production of computer software, developed an electronic document management system (EDMS), a process for transforming engineering drawings and similar documents into a computer database. Unisys Corporation (Unisys), an American computer manufacturer, decided to market Advent's EDMS in the United States. In 1987, Advent and Unisys signed two documents, one labeled "Heads of Agreement" and the other "Distribution Agreement," in which Advent agreed to provide the software and hardware making up the EDMS, as well as sales and marketing material and the technical personnel to work with Unisys employees in building and installing the document systems. The agreement was to continue for two years, subject to automatic renewal or termination on notice.

During the summer of 1987, Unisys attempted to sell the document system to a large oil company but was unsuccessful. Nevertheless, progress on the sales and training programs in the United States was satisfactory. But Unisys, then in the throes of restructuring, decided it would be better off developing its own document system, and in December 1987, it told Advent that the agreement was ended. Advent filed suit, alleging breach of contract, among other things. Unisys argued that the agreement with Advent was covered by the UCC and that it failed to contain an express quantity provision that the UCC statute of frauds requires. The trial court ruled, however, that the agreements were not covered by the Code because their services aspect predominated. When the jury awarded Advent $4,550,000 for breach of contract, Unisys appealed.

Weis, Circuit Judge As the district court appraised the transaction, provisions for services outweighed those for products and, consequently, the arrangement was not predominantly one for the sale of goods. The agreements provided that Advent was to modify its software and hardware interfaces to run initially on equipment not manufactured by Unisys but eventually on Unisys hardware. "In so far as Advent has successfully completed [some of the processing] of software and hardware interfaces," Unisys promised to reimburse Advent to the extent of $150,000 derived from a "surcharge" on products purchased.

Advent agreed to provide twelve man-weeks of marketing manpower, but with Unisys bearing certain expenses. Advent also undertook to furnish an experienced systems builder to work with Unisys personnel at Advent's prevailing rates, and to provide sales and support training for Unisys staff as well as its customers.

The Distribution Agreement begins with the statement "Unisys desires to purchase, and Advent desires to sell, on a nonexclusive basis, certain of Advent hardware products and software licenses for resale worldwide." Following a heading "Subject Matter of Sales," appears this sentence, "Advent agrees to sell hardware and license software to Unisys, and Unisys agrees to buy from Advent the products listed in Schedule A." Schedule A lists twenty products, such as computer cards, plotters, imagers, scanners and designer systems.

Because software was a major portion of the "products" described in the agreement, this matter requires some discussion. Computer systems consist of "hardware" and "software." Hardware is the computer machinery, its electronic circuitry and peripheral items such as keyboards, readers, scanners and printers. Software is a more elusive concept. Generally speaking, "software" refers to the medium that stores input and output data as well as computer programs. The medium includes hard disks, floppy disks, and magnetic tapes.

In simplistic terms, programs are codes prepared by a programmer that instruct the computer to perform certain functions. When the program is transposed onto a medium compatible with the computer's needs, it becomes software. The increasing frequency of computer products as subjects of commercial litigation has led to controversy over whether software is a "good" or intellectual property. The Code does not specifically mention software.

In the absence of express legislative guidance, courts interpret the Code in the light of commercial and technological developments. The Code is designed "to permit the continued expansion of commercial practices" [1–102(2)(b)]. The Code applies to "transactions in goods" [2–102], which are defined as "all things (including specially manufactured goods) which are moveable at the time of the identification for sale" [2–105(1)].

Our Court has addressed computer package sales in other cases, but has not been required to consider whether the UCC applied to software per se. Computer programs are the product of an intellectual process, but once implanted in a medium are widely distributed to computer owners. An analogy can be drawn to a compact disc recording of an orchestral rendition. The music is produced by the artistry of musicians and in itself is not a "good," but when transferred to a laser-readable disc becomes a readily merchantable commodity. Similarly, when a professor delivers a lecture, it is not a good, but, when transcribed as a book, it becomes a good.

That a computer program may be copyrightable as intellectual property does not alter the fact that once in the form of a floppy disc or other medium, the program is tangible, moveable and available in the marketplace. The fact that some programs may be tailored for specific purposes need not alter their status as "goods" because the Code definition includes "specially manufactured goods." The topic has stimulated academic commentary with the majority espousing the view that software fits with the definition of a "good" in the UCC.

The relationship at issue here is a typical mixed goods and services arrangement. The services are not substantially different from those generally accompanying package sales of computer systems consisting of hardware and software. Although determining the applicability of the UCC to a contract by examining the predominance of goods or services has been criticized, we see no reason to depart from that practice here. We consider the purpose or essence of the contract. Comparing the relative costs of the materials supplied with the costs of the labor may be helpful in this analysis, but not dispositive. In this case the contract's main objective was to transfer "products." The specific provisions for training of Unisys personnel by Advent were but a small part of the parties' contemplated relationship.

The compensation structure of the agreement also focuses on "goods." The projected sales figures introduced during the trial demonstrate that in the contemplation of the parties the sale of goods clearly predominated. The payment provision of $150,000 for developmental work which Advent had previously completed was to be made through individual purchases of software and hardware rather than through the fees for services and is further evidence that the intellectual work was to be subsumed into tangible items for sale.

Applying the UCC to computer software transactions offers substantial benefits to litigants and the courts. The Code offers a uniform body of law on a wide range of questions likely to arise in computer software disputes: implied warranties, consequential damages, disclaimers of liability, the statute of limitations, to name a few. The importance of software to the commercial world and the advantages to be gained by the uniformity inherent in the UCC are strong policy arguments favoring inclusion. The contrary arguments are not persuasive, and we hold that software is a "good" within the definition of the Code.

Judgment reversed and remanded for further proceedings consistent with the Court's opinion.

Figure 4 illustrates when the Uniform Commercial Code applies.

RESTATEMENT (SECOND) OF CONTRACTS

Nature and Origins

In 1932, the American Law Institute published the first *Restatement of Contracts,*[6] an attempt to codify and systematize the soundest principles of contract law gleaned from thousands of often conflicting judicial decisions. As the product of a private organization, the *Restatement* did not have the force of law, but as the considered judgment of some of the leading scholars of the legal profession, it was highly influential in shaping the evolution of contract law. The *Restatement (Second) of Contracts,* issued in 1979, is an attempt to reflect the significant changes that have occurred in contract law in the years following the birth of the first *Restatement of Contracts.* The tone of the *Restatement (Second) of Contracts* differs dramatically from that of the first *Restatement,* which is often characterized as a positivist attempt to formulate a system of black letter rules of contract law. The *Restatement (Second),* in contrast, reflects the "shift from rules to standards" in modern contract law—the shift from precise, technical rules to broader, discretionary principles that produce just results.[7] The *Restatement (Second)* plainly bears the mark of the legal realists, discussed in Chapter 1, and has been heavily influenced by the

---

[6]See Chapter 1 for a general discussion of the *Restatement* phenomenon.

[7]Speidel, "Restatement Second: Omitted Terms and Contract Method," 67 *Cornell L. Rev.* 785, 786 (1982).

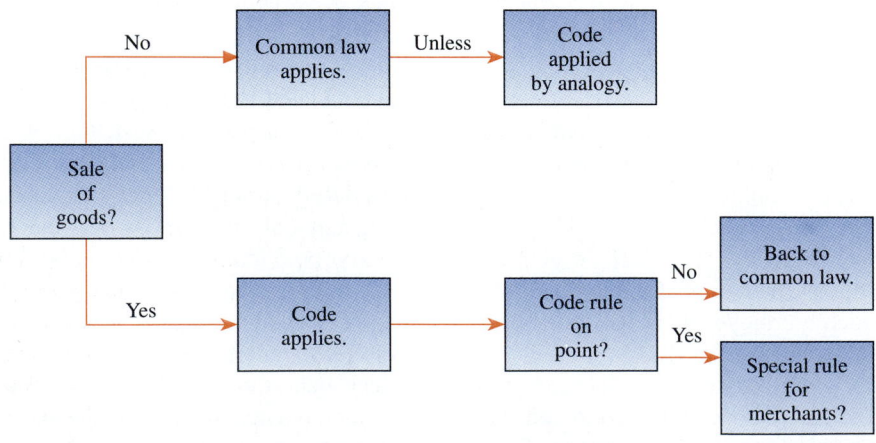

FIGURE 4   When the Uniform Commercial Code Applies

UCC. In fact, many *Restatement (Second) of Contracts* provisions are virtually identical to their Code analogues. For example, the *Restatement (Second)* has explicitly embraced the Code concepts of *good faith*[8] and *unconscionability*.[9]

Impact

The *Restatement (Second) of Contracts,* like its predecessor, does not have the force of law, and its relative newness prevents any accurate assessment of its impact on contemporary contract cases. Nonetheless, given the influential role played by the first *Restatement* and the previously mentioned tendency of the courts to employ Code principles by analogy in contract cases, it seems fair to assume that the *Restatement (Second)* will serve as a major inspiration for contract developments in the decades to come. For this reason, we give significant attention to the *Restatement (Second) of Contracts* in the following chapters.

ETHICAL AND PUBLIC POLICY CONCERNS

1. Compare and contrast the ethical values at the heart of classical contract law with those at the heart of modern contract law. If all contracts today fit the typical model assumed by classical contract law, would we necessarily feel ethically compelled to treat them differently than they were treated under classical contract law?

2. Do a brief social cost-benefit analysis of the "shift from rules to standards" that has occurred in modern contract law. Do a contrasting cost-benefit analysis of the rule-oriented approach of classical contract law.

3. The idea that contracts should be enforced because they are voluntary agreements can obviously be justified on ethical grounds. What ethical justifications, if any, can you give for departing from the notion of voluntary agreement in quasi-contract and promissory estoppel cases?

---

[8] *Restatement (Second) of Contracts* § 205 (1981).

[9] *Restatement (Second) of Contracts* § 208 (1981).

PROBLEMS AND PROBLEM CASES

1. In 1973, Baker and Ratzlaff entered a contract requiring Ratzlaff to grow 380 acres of popcorn and Baker to buy it at $4.75 per hundredweight. The contract gave Ratzlaff the right to terminate if Baker failed to pay for any of the popcorn on delivery. Early in 1974, Ratzlaff made the first two deliveries under the contract to Baker's plant. Baker's plant manager gave Ratzlaff weight tickets acknowledging receipt of the popcorn. Ratzlaff was not given payment and did not ask for it. Nor did he stop by Baker's business office, which was on a direct route between his farm and Baker's plant, to ask for payment. When Baker called to ask for further deliveries, Ratzlaff offered excuses, but did not mention payment. Ratzlaff later told Baker he was terminating due to Baker's failure to pay upon delivery, selling the remaining 1.6 million pounds of popcorn elsewhere for $8.00 per hundredweight. After hearing evidence that Baker's normal practice was to make payments at its office on the basis of copies of weight tickets sent from the plant, and that Baker would have paid promptly had Ratzlaff requested payment, the trial court ruled that Ratzlaff's termination was a breach of his duty to act in good faith. Was this ruling proper?

2. In April 1988, Reifschneider, a farmer since 1957, orally agreed to sell Grain Company 12,500 bushels of corn for $2.25 per bushel. The corn was to be delivered as harvested in October 1988. Shortly thereafter, Grain Company mailed Reifschneider a written confirmation of the oral agreement, with instructions to sign it and return the original. Reifschneider neither signed nor returned the confirmation, and in late June he told Grain Company that he felt no contract existed and would not deliver the corn. Reifschneider continued to refuse to acknowledge the contract, and ultimately sold his crop elsewhere. To cover his default, Grain Company bought 12,500 bushels of corn from another farmer, paying $8,425 more for it than it had agreed to pay Reifschneider. When Grain Company sued Reifschneider for breach of contract, he raised the Code statute of frauds [2–201] as a defense, arguing that his failure to sign the confirmation meant that it could not satisfy the writing requirement against him. Grain Company countered by arguing that he was a merchant, and pointing to Code section 2–201(2), which says that merchants who fail to object in writing to written confirmations they receive from other merchants within 10 days of receipt lose their statute of frauds defense. Was the trial court justified in ruling in favor of Grain Company?

3. When Thomas and Sandra Cole were divorced in 1983, Sandra received a judgment against Thomas of $36,556. In May and June 1985, Thomas incurred a hospital bill of $5,985. After discussing the matter with him, Sandra paid the bill with her own funds even though he still owed her $11,884 on the marriage dissolution judgment. When Thomas died in April 1986, Sandra filed claims against his estate for the balance due her under the marriage dissolution judgment and for the hospital bill. The estate challenged Sandra's claim for the hospital payment, arguing that she had paid it voluntarily and had no contractual right to recover the amount she paid. Was the trial court right in ruling in Sandra's favor?

4. First National Bank filed suit against Jessie Ordoyne and Patricia Ordoyne Bordelon for failure to pay sums due on a Visa card account. Ordoyne argued that he did not know that the account existed until the bank called him to inquire about his failure to make payments. He then told the bank that he and Patricia were divorced and that she must have forged his signature to the account application form. The bank argued that he was nonetheless liable on a quasi-contractual basis, although it failed to prove that he had received any of the merchandise charged to the card. Was the trial court's decision in Jessie's favor correct?

5. Chow arranged through a travel agent to fly from Indianapolis to Singapore on June 27, 1986. Singapore Airlines gave him a round-trip ticket that included a TWA flight to Los Angeles. Shortly before the trip, Chow's flight was rerouted so that he had to fly to St. Louis first and then to San Francisco. During the St. Louis stopover, the flight developed engine trouble, causing a substantial delay. TWA personnel assured Chow that if he missed his connecting flight, TWA would arrange for him to take the next Singapore flight out of San Francisco. After the engine problem was fixed, TWA delayed the flight's departure an additional two hours to board additional passengers. Chow was again assured that if he missed his scheduled flight, TWA would make arrangements for him. Chow missed his Singapore flight by minutes, and was housed overnight at TWA's expense in San Francisco after once more being assured that TWA would make arrangements to get him on the next Singapore flight. When he called Singapore Airlines the next morning to see whether TWA had made him a reservation, Chow was told that no arrangements had been made. When he contacted TWA, he was told TWA would make the arrangements immediately. After waiting several hours, Chow learned TWA had still not made the arrangements and was told that TWA could no longer help him. Because Singapore Airlines no longer had economy class seats available, Chow had to buy a business class seat at an additional cost of $928. When he filed suit against TWA for that amount, TWA argued that the Conditions of Contract printed on Chow's ticket disclaimed any liability for failure to make connections. Did Chow have a valid claim against TWA?

6. Commercial Cornice, a subcontractor, entered a contract with Camel Construction, a general contractor, to furnish labor and materials for a construction project owned by Malarkey's, Inc. Commercial completed its obligations under the contract but only received $78,000 of the $177,773. When Commercial filed suit against Camel and Malarkey's for the remaining $99,773, Malarkey's moved to dismiss Commercial's claims against it on the ground that Commercial's only contract was with Camel. The trial court granted Malarkey's motion, despite the fact that the evidence indicated that Malarkey's had never paid Camel for the work. Was the dismissal of Commercial's claim against Malarkey's proper?

7. Early in 1986, Gray Communications contacted various television tower builders concerning the manufacture and erection of a television tower. After several discussions with Kline Iron & Steel, Gray received a signed written proposal from Kline to build and install the tower for $1,485,368. The proposal said that it could be revoked or modified by Kline prior to acceptance by Gray, and it required Kline's approval after acceptance by Gray. Gray refused to sign the proposal after Kline would not lower its bid to meet a competitor's lower bid, and Kline filed suit for breach of contract. At trial, Gray argued that no contract existed, and that even if a contract existed it was unenforceable because Gray had never signed the writing the UCC requires for all contracts for $500 or more. Kline argued that the contract was not covered by the UCC because it was a services contract. The evidence at trial indicated that the service component of the agreement amounted at most to 26 percent of the total cost. Should the court apply the UCC?

8. Dr. Monteleone, a neurologist, entered into a lease-purchase agreement for a turnkey computer system from Neilson Business Equipment Center, Inc. The system included both hardware and software recommended by Neilson after two Neilson representatives studied Dr. Monteleone's manual billing system. When the computer was delivered in July 1982, serious problems immediately developed. Neilson's attempts to modify the software, which it had acquired elsewhere and renamed the "Neilson Medical Office Management System," were unsuccessful. Dr. Monteleone notified Neilson that he was terminating the lease for cause and later filed suit against Neilson. The trial court awarded him $34,983.42 in damages for breaches of the implied warranties of merchantability and fitness for a particular purpose. Did the trial court err in holding that the case was governed by the UCC?

9. Stephen Gall and his family became ill after drinking contaminated water supplied to their home by the McKeesport Municipal Water Authority. They filed suit against the utility, arguing, among other things, that the utility had breached the UCC implied warranty of merchantability when it sold them contaminated water. The utility moved to dismiss their complaint, arguing that since water was not "goods," the UCC did not apply. Should the Galls' complaint be dismissed?

10. In February of 1981, Salamon, a builder, entered into written agreements to buy two lots owned by Terra for $9,000 each. The agreement provided that Salamon would take possession of the lots by April 15, 1981, but would not have to pay the bulk of the purchase price ($8,500 per lot) until delivery of the deeds in August 1981. Salamon intended to build a house on each lot and then sell the houses to third parties, paying off Terra with the proceeds of the house sales. Salamon partially completed the two houses but was unable either to obtain financing to complete them or to find purchasers for them. Terra extended the date of performance under the purchase agreements by several months, but because Salamon was never able to pay for the lots, he retained ownership of them. Salamon filed a quasi-contract suit against Terra to recover the value of the partially completed houses. The trial judge ruled that Terra had been unjustly enriched in the amount of $15,000. Had Terra been unjustly enriched?

11. *Video Case.* See "Car Deals." Jeff went to look at a car owned by Acme Motors. He wanted to buy the car and tentatively agreed on a price with Marx, but he asked if he could wait until his wife could see the car that evening. Acme agreed, promising in writing not to sell the car to anyone else in the interim. When Jeff and his wife returned to Acme that evening, however, they found that Acme had sold the car to another buyer. Jeff filed a breach of contract suit against Acme, pointing to a section of the UCC that provides that merchants can't revoke signed written offers. Should Jeff win?

THE AGREEMENT:

OFFER

INTRODUCTION

The concept of mutual agreement lies at the heart of traditional contract law. Courts faced with deciding whether two or more persons entered into a contract look first for an agreement *between the parties. Because the formation of an agreement is normally a two-step process by which one party makes a proposal and the other responds to the proposal, it is customary to analyze the agreement in two parts: offer and acceptance. This chapter, which concerns itself with the offer, and the next chapter, which covers acceptance, focus on the tools used by courts to determine whether the parties have reached the kind of agreement that becomes the foundation of a contract.*

THE OBJECTIVE THEORY OF CONTRACT

At the outset, it is important to clarify one aspect of what is meant by the word *agreement.* In determining whether the parties reached an agreement, should courts look at what each party actually, in his own mind (*subjectively*) intended? Or should an agreement be dependent on the impression that each party has given to the rest of the world through words, acts, and circumstances that *objectively* indicate that intent? Early American courts took a subjective approach to contract formation, asking whether there was truly a "meeting of the minds" between the parties. This subjective standard, however, created uncertainty in the enforcement of contracts because it left every contract vulnerable to disputes about actual intent. The desire to meet the needs of the marketplace by affording predictable and consistent results in contracts cases dictated a shift toward an *objective theory of contracts.* By the middle of the 19th century, the objective approach to contract formation, which judges agreement by looking at the parties' outward manifestations of intent, was firmly established in American law. Judge Learned Hand once described the effect of the objective contract theory as follows:

A contract has, strictly speaking, nothing to do with the personal, or individual, intent of the parties. A contract is an obligation attached by the mere force of law to certain acts of the parties, usually words, which ordinarily accompany and represent a known intent. If however, it were proved by twenty bishops that either party when he used the words intended something else than the usual meaning which the law imposes on them, he would still be held, unless there were mutual mistake or something else of that sort.[1]

What Is an Offer?

The *Restatement (Second) of Contracts* defines an **offer** as "the manifestation of willingness to enter into a bargain, so made as to justify another person in understanding that his assent to that bargain is invited and will conclude it."[2] An offer says, in effect, "This is it—if you agree to these terms, we have a contract." An offer is a critically important first step in the contract formation process. The person who makes an offer (the **offeror**) gives the person to whom she makes the offer (the **offeree**) the power to bind her to a contract simply by accepting the offer. If no offer was ever made, however, there was nothing to accept and no contract results.

Traditional contract law rules on contract formation are designed to ensure that persons are never bound to contracts unless they clearly intend to be bound. Therefore, the basic thing that the courts require for the creation of an offer is some objective indication of a *present intent to contract* on the part of the offeror. Two of the most important things from which courts infer an intent to contract are the *definiteness* of the alleged offer and the fact that it has been *communicated to the offeree.*

----

[1]*Hotchkiss v. National City Bank*, 200 F. 287, 293 (S.D.N.Y. 1911).

[2]*Restatement (Second) of Contracts* § 24 (1981).

Definiteness of Terms

If Smith says to Ford, "I'd like to buy your house," and Ford responds, "You've got a deal," has a contract been formed? An obvious problem here is the parties' lack of specificity. A proposal that fails to state specifically what the offeror is willing to do and what he asks in return for his performance is unlikely to be considered an offer. One reason for the requirement of definiteness is that definiteness and specificity in an offer tend to indicate an intent to contract, whereas indefiniteness and lack of specificity tend to indicate that the parties are still negotiating and have not yet reached agreement. In the conversation between Smith and Ford, Smith's statement that he'd like to buy Ford's house is merely an invitation to offer or an invitation to negotiate. It indicates a willingness to contract in the future if the parties can reach agreement on mutually acceptable terms, but not a present intent to contract. If, however, Smith sends Ford a detailed and specific written document stating all of the material terms and conditions on which he is willing to buy the house and Ford writes back agreeing to Smith's terms, the parties' intent to contract would be objectively indicated and a contract would probably be created.

A second reason definiteness is important is that courts need to know the terms on which the parties agreed in order to determine if a breach of contract has occurred and calculate a remedy if it has. Keep in mind that the offer often contains all the terms of the parties' contract. This is so because all that an offeree is allowed to do in most cases is to accept or reject the terms of the offer. If an agreement is too indefinite, a court would not have a basis for giving a remedy if one of the parties alleged that the "contract" was breached. The following case, *Vian v. Carey,* presents an example of a situation in which the terms of the alleged contract were too indefinite.

Vian v. Carey
1993 U.S. Dist. LEXIS 5460 (U.S. Dist. Ct. S.D.N.Y. 1993)

Mariah Carey is a famous, successful, and apparently wealthy entertainer. Joseph Vian, Carey's stepfather before she achieved stardom, was in the business of designing, producing, and marketing gift and novelty items. He claimed that Carey agreed orally to give him a license to produce "Mariah dolls," which would be statuettes of the singer that would play her most popular songs. Vian asserted that this right was given in exchange for his financial and emotional support of Carey, including picking her up from late-night recording sessions, providing her with the use of a car, paying for dental care, allowing her to use his boat for business meetings and rehearsals, and giving her various items to help furnish her apartment. Vian based his claim of an oral contract on three conversations, twice in the family car and once on Vian's boat. Vian said to Carey, "Don't forget about the Mariah dolls," and "I get the Mariah dolls." According to Vian, on one occasion, Carey responded "Okay"; on other occasions, she merely smiled and nodded. Although Carey admits that Vian mentioned the dolls two or three times, she testified that she thought it was a joke. Claiming that Carey breached the contract to license dolls in her likeness, Vian brought this action for breach of contract. Carey moved for summary judgment.

Mukasey, District Judge   An oral contract can form a binding contract. However, the prerequisites to contract formation must be satisfied. In determining whether a contract exists, what matters are the parties' expressed intentions, the words and deeds which constitute objective signs in a given set of circumstances. The issue is whether the objective circumstances indicate that the parties intended to form a contract. Without such an intent, neither a contract nor a preliminary agreement to negotiate in good faith can exist. In making such a determination, a court may look at whether the terms of the contract have been finally resolved. In addition, a court may consider the context of the negotiations. Vian has adduced no evidence that Carey ever intended by a nod of her head or the expression "okay" to enter into a complex commercial licensing agreement involving dolls in her likeness playing her copyrighted songs. The context in which this contract between an 18-year-old girl and her stepfather allegedly was made was an informal family setting, either in the car or on Vian's boat, while others were present. Vian's own version of events leads to the conclusion that there was no reason for Carey to think Vian was entirely serious, let alone that he intended to bind her to an agreement at that time.

There can be no meetings of the minds, required for the formation of a contract, where essential material terms are missing. Thus, even if the parties both believe themselves to be bound, there is no contract when the terms of the agreement are so vague and indefinite that there is no basis or standard for deciding whether the agreement had been kept or broken, or to fashion a remedy, and no means by which such terms may be made certain. As the New York Court of Appeals has held, "definiteness as to material matters is of the very essence of contract law. Impenetrable vagueness and uncertainty will not do."

Licensing contracts such as the one Vian claims a right to exploit normally are intricate business. They involve details. Even if the agreement was merely to agree on terms at some future time, under New York law, a mere agreement to agree, in which a material term is left for future negotiations, is unenforceable. The word "license" was not even used. As Carey points out, no price nor royalty term was mentioned, nor was the duration or geographic scope of the license, nor was Carey's right to approve the dolls. Vian has not raised a triable issue of fact as to the existence of a contract.

Summary judgment granted in favor of Carey.

Definiteness: Traditional Approach   Classical contract law took the position that courts are contract enforcers, not contract makers. The prospect of enforcing an agreement in which the parties had omitted terms or left terms open for later agreement was unthinkable to courts that took a traditional, hands-off approach to contracts. Traditionally, contract law required a relatively high standard of definiteness for offers, requiring that all the essential terms of a proposed contract be stated in the offer. The traditional insistence on definiteness can serve useful ends. It can prevent a person from being held to an agreement when none was reached or from being bound by a contract term to which he never assented. Sometimes, however, it can operate to frustrate the expectations of parties who intend to contract but, for whatever reason, fail to procure an agreement that specifies all the terms of the contract. Although vague agreements such as the one alleged in the *Vian* case are too indefinite to constitute a contract, the trend of modern contract law is to tolerate a lower degree of specificity in agreements than did classical contract law.

Definiteness and Modern Contract Law

Modern contract principles, with their increased emphasis on furthering peoples' justifiable expectations and their encouragement of a hands-on approach by the courts, often create contractual liability in situations where no contract would have resulted at common law. Perhaps no part of the Code better illustrates this basic difference between modern contract principles and their classical counterparts than does the basic Code section on contract formation [2–204]. Sales contracts under Article 2 can be created "in any manner sufficient to show agreement, including conduct which recognizes the existence of a contract" [2–204(1)]. So, if the parties are acting as though they have a contract by delivering or accepting goods or payment, for example, this may be enough to create a binding contract, even if it is impossible to point to a particular moment in time when the contract was created [2–204(2)]. The fact that the parties left open one or more terms of their agreement does not necessarily mean that their agreement is too indefinite to enforce. A sales contract is created if the court finds that the parties intended to make a contract and that their agreement is complete enough to allow the court to reach a fair settlement of their dispute ("a reasonably certain basis for giving an appropriate remedy" [2–204(3)]). The Code contains a series of gap-filling rules to enable courts to fill in the blanks on matters of price [2–305], quantity [2–306], delivery [2–307, 2–308, and 2–309(1)], and time for payment [2–310] when such terms have been left open by the parties.[3] Of course, if a term was left out because the parties were *unable* to reach agreement about it, this would indicate that the intent to contract was absent and no contract would result, even under the Code's more liberal rules. Intention is still at the heart of these modern contract rules;

the difference is that courts applying Code principles seek to further the parties' *underlying* intent to contract even though the parties have failed to express their intention about specific aspects of their agreement.

The *Restatement (Second) of Contracts* takes an approach to the definiteness question that is quite similar to the Code approach. It seeks to further the intent of the parties and, where intent to contract is indicated but some essential terms are left open, "a term which is reasonable in the circumstances is supplied by the court."[4] Unlike the Code, however, the *Restatement (Second)* indicates that a party's reliance on an indefinite agreement may justify its full or partial enforcement.[5] This provision highlights one of the most intriguing recent developments in contract law—the use of **promissory estoppel** to enforce indefinite agreements.[6]

Promissory Estoppel and Indefinite Agreements

It has long been the rule that promissory estoppel could not be used to enforce indefinite agreements because their indefiniteness meant that the court was left with no promise capable of being enforced. Sometimes people do, however, act in reliance on indefinite agreements, and to protect that reliance a few courts have deviated from the general rule. In such cases, it is common for courts to overcome the indefiniteness problem by awarding damages based on the promisee's losses due to reliance rather than by attempting to enforce the indefinite agreement.

Hoffman v. Red Owl Stores, Inc., is probably the most famous case of this type.[7] Hoffman wanted to acquire a Red Owl franchised convenience store and, in reliance on Red Owl's promises during their negotiations, sold his bakery at a loss, bought a small grocery to gain experience, moved his family, and bought an option on a proposed site for the franchised store. The negotiations fell through, and when Hoffman sued, Red Owl argued that no contract resulted because the parties had never reached agreement on the essential terms governing their relationship. The Supreme Court of Wisconsin agreed, but nonetheless allowed Hoffman to recover

---

[3]Chapter 19 discusses these Code provisions in detail.

[4]*Restatement (Second) of Contracts* § 204 (1981).

[5]*Restatement (Second) of Contracts* § 34(3) (1981).

[6]See the general discussion of promissory estoppel in Chapter 9.

[7]26 Wis.2d 683, 133 N.W.2d 267 (Wis. Sup. Ct. 1965).

his reliance losses on the basis of promissory estoppel. In doing so, the court noted that nothing in the language of section 90 of the *Restatement* required that a promise serving as the basis of promissory estoppel be "so comprehensive in scope as to meet the requirements of an offer." Another example of both modern standards regarding definiteness and the use of promissory estoppel is seen in the following *Arok Construction Co. v. Indian Construction Services* case.

AROK CONSTRUCTION CO. v. INDIAN CONSTRUCTION SERVICES
848 P.2d 870 (Ariz. Ct. App. 1993)

Indian Construction Services (ICS) is a general contractor. AROK Construction Co. is a drywall and stucco contractor. AROK and the principal owners of ICS had entered into contracts on three occasions prior to this case, using in all three situations identical standard form contracts.

In 1985, Window Rock Unified School District solicited bids for the services of a general contractor on its construction project. ICS submitted a bid to act as the general contractor, listing AROK in its bid as subcontractor for the drywall and stucco portions of the project. AROK had first submitted its bid over the telephone to ICS for $1.549 million. Before bid closing, however, ICS asked AROK to reduce its bid to $1.42 million. AROK's president told ICS's project manager that AROK would reduce its bid even further to $1.4 million if, as a result, ICS would agree to contract with AROK if the school district awarded the job to ICS. ICS's project manager stated that in exchange for AROK's further reduction to $1.4 million, "If [ICS] gets the job, [AROK] gets a job." AROK sent a letter to ICS confirming the $1.4 million quote and enclosed a detailed bid confirmation. The school district awarded the contract to ICS. After receiving notice to proceed with the project from the school district, ICS requested that AROK perform "value engineering" services with regard to its bid. (Value engineering involves changing the bid structure to lower the overall bid price without changing the profit structure for either the general contractor or the subcontractor). AROK complied and worked approximately 8 to 10 hours further reducing the subcontract price. Several months later, a dispute arose between ICS and AROK over the amount of the contract price, and ICS entered into subcontracts with two other companies to perform the drywall and stucco work. AROK brought suit for breach of contract. The trial court granted summary judgment in favor of ICS, and AROK appealed.

Lankford, Judge   The old "formalist" view limited the agreement to written terms and emphasized rules of contract, such as the requirement that the agreement include all material terms. This has long since given way to the "realist" approach exemplified by the Uniform Commercial Code and the Second Restatement of Contracts. The latter emphasizes standards rather than rules, and assigns to courts the task of upholding the agreements parties intended to make.

ICS concedes for purposes of this appeal that its conditional promise, "If we get the job, you get the job," is an acceptance of AROK's promise to perform the work for a reduced price. ICS contends, however, that the parties failed to specify other terms essential to indicate their intent to be bound: the manner and time of payments, penalty provisions, time for completion, and bonding. ICS argues that as a result of the missing terms, no enforceable contract exists as a matter of law.

Is the agreement too uncertain to enforce? *Restatement (Second) of Contracts* section 33 establishes "reasonable certainty" as the standard for enforcement. The Restatement rule exemplifies the policy of the law to uphold agreements. Courts are never eager to undo agreements. Only when courts ensure that promises create obligations do promises have real meaning. Only then can those in the marketplace rely on their bargains to allocate their resources and plan for the future. For example, AROK presented evidence that it did not bid for other jobs because it had a contract with ICS. If that contract is not enforced, and AROK's resources were idled as a result of ICS's promise and breach, then one of the goals of contract law—economic efficiency—would be thwarted.

The enforcement of incomplete agreements is a necessary fact of economic life. Business people are not soothsayers, and can neither provide in advance for every unforeseen contingency nor answer every unasked question regarding a commercial agreement. This is especially so with a complex contract for a major construction project. Nor are entrepreneurs perfect at drafting legal documents. Finally, parties may want to bind themselves and at the same time desire to leave some matters open for future resolution in order to maintain flexibility. Thus, courts are often presented with incomplete bargains when the parties intend and desire to be bound. Refusing the enforcement of obligations the parties intended to create and that marketplace transactions require hardly seems the solution.

The standard for contract enforceability is not whether the agreement included a resolution of every matter and anticipated every contingency. "The terms of a contract are reasonably certain if they provide a basis for determining the existence of a breach and for giving an appropriate basis for determining the existence of a breach and for giving an appropriate remedy." *Restatement (Second) of Contracts* section 33(2). If a court can determine the existence of a breach by ICS and fashion an appropriate remedy for AROK, then the terms of their agreement are reasonably certain and enforceable. Thus, "gaps" or omitted terms, or vague and indefinite terms, are not invariably fatal to the rights of the parties to obtain enforcement of their bargain.

The terms of this contract are sufficiently certain for two independent reasons. First, ICS breached the contract at a point when the only terms necessary to determine the existence of the breach (scope of the work) and for giving an appropriate remedy (agreed-upon price) were present. Second, there was evidence of a course of dealing involving a standard form contract which could be used to supply any missing terms. We hold that the agreement is sufficiently definite to be enforceable.

AROK also claims that it is entitled to relief based upon promissory estoppel. We hold that this is a proper claim for relief as an alternative to the contract claim. If AROK can show that it acted or detrimentally relied upon ICS's promise to award the contract, then promissory estoppel is available. For example, AROK performed "value engineering" allegedly in reliance upon ICS's promise. AROK may also have forgone other work because it anticipated employing its resources in performing this contract. *Restatement (Second) of Contracts* section 90(1) states:

A promise which the promisor should reasonably expect to induce action or forbearance on the part of the promisee or a third person and which does induce such action or forbearance is binding if injustice can be avoided only by enforcement of the promise.

However, the remedy under this theory may be more limited than damages for breach of contract. In particular, relief may sometimes be limited to restitution or to damages or specific relief measured by the extent of the promisee's reliance rather than by the terms of the promise. Thus, AROK may be entitled to recover only the value of its work in "value engineering" unless it can show greater loss due to its reliance.

Reversed and remanded in favor of AROK.

Communication to Offeree

When an offeror communicates the terms of an offer to an offeree, he objectively indicates an intent to be bound by those terms. The fact that an offer has *not* been communicated, on the other hand, may be evidence that the offeror has not yet decided to enter into a binding agreement. For example, assume that Stevens and Meyer have been negotiating over the sale of Meyer's restaurant. Stevens confides in his friend, Reilly, that he plans to offer Meyer $150,000 for the restaurant. Reilly goes to Meyer and tells Meyer that Stevens has decided to offer him $150,000 for the restaurant and has drawn up a written offer to that effect. After learning the details of the offer from Reilly, Meyer telephones Stevens and says, "I accept your offer." Is Stevens now contractually obligated to buy the restaurant? No. Since *Stevens* did not communicate the proposal to Meyer, there was no offer for Meyer to accept.

SPECIAL OFFER PROBLEM AREAS

Advertisements

Generally speaking, advertisements for the sale of goods at specified prices are *not* considered to be offers. Rather, they are treated as being invitations to offer or negotiate. The same rule is generally applied to signs, handbills, catalogs, price lists, and price quotations. This rule is based on the presumed intent of the sellers involved. It is not reasonable to conclude that a seller who has a limited number of items to sell intends to give every person who sees her ad, sign, or catalog the power to bind her to contract. Thus, if Customer sees Retailer's advertisement of Whizbang XL laptop computers for $2,000 and goes to Retailer's store indicating his intent to buy the computer, Customer is making an offer, which Retailer is free to accept or reject. This is so because Customer is manifesting a present intent to contract on the definite terms of the ad.

In some cases, however, particular ads have been held to amount to offers. Such ads are usually highly specific about the nature and number of items offered for sale and what is requested in return. This specificity precludes the possibility that the offeror could become contractually bound to an infinite number of offerees. In addition, many of the ads treated as offers have required some special performance by would-be buyers or have in some other way clearly indicated that immediate action by the buyer creates a binding agreement. The potential for unfairness to those who attempt to accept such ads and their fundamental difference from ordinary ads justify treating them as offers. *Jackson v. Investment Corporation of Palm Beach* presents an example of an advertisement that was held to constitute an offer.

JACKSON V. INVESTMENT CORP. OF PALM BEACH
585 So.2d 949 (Fla. Ct. App. 1991)

John Jackson read an ad in the *Miami Herald* stating that the Pic-6 Jackpot for the last evening of the dog track racing season would be $825,000. Jackson went to the track on that date, picked the winner in the six designated races, and won the jackpot. However, Investment Corporation of Palm Beach, the owner of the dog track, contended that it should not have to pay more than $25,000 because it had intended the amount of the jackpot to be $25,000, not $825,000. The mix-up occurred when Investment submitted to the newspaper a prior ad with the following words written on the face of it: "Guaranteed Jackpot $25,000 must go tonight," and the newspaper employee who prepared the final draft of the ad mistook the dollar sign with only one slash-mark to be the number 8. Investment paid Jackson $25,000 on the night of the races, but Jackson later brought suit to claim the balance. At trial, the judge instructed the jury that it should find for Investment unless the evidence supported the claim that Investment intended by its newspaper advertisement to make an offer to pay a guaranteed jackpot of $825,000. The jury returned a verdict in favor of Investment and the trial judge entered judgment on the verdict. Jackson appealed, claiming that this instruction to the jury was erroneous.

Downey, Judge　　There was no evidence adduced that Investment intended the jackpot to be $825,000. Jackson concedes that Investment never intended the jackpot to be the larger amount. The point is that Investment's subjective intent was not material in determining what the contract was between the parties. As the Florida Supreme Court said in

Gendzier v. Bielecki, quoting from Justice Oliver Wendell Holmes:

The making of a contract depends not on the agreement of two minds in one intention, but on the agreement of two sets of external signs—not on the parties having meant the same thing but on their having said the same thing.

Professor Williston, in his work on Contracts, describes the test as:

[T]he test of the true interpretation of an offer or acceptance is not what the party making it thought it meant or intended it to mean, but what a reasonable person in the position of the parties would have thought it meant. 1 *Williston on Contracts* sec. 94, 339–40.

It appears to us that the law, applicable to offers of a reward, is also applicable to the type of advertisement involved in this case. The offer is a mere proposal or conditional promise which, if accepted before it is revoked, creates a binding contract. We have given due consideration to Investment's argument regarding the advertisement as an "invitation to bargain," but find it inapposite here. The "invitation to bargain" rule appears to be applied in advertising wherein:

Neither the advertiser nor the reader of his notice understands that the latter is empowered to close the deal without further expression by the former. Such advertisements are understood to be mere requests to consider and examine and negotiate; and no one can reasonably regard them otherwise unless the circumstances are exceptional and the words used are very plain and clear. 1 *Corbin on Contracts* sec. 25 (1963).

Here there are no further negotiations indicated. If a member of the public buys a winning ticket on six races, he has accepted the offer and the parties have a contract. We thus hold that the trial court erred in instructing the jury as it did and we reverse the judgment appealed from and remand the cause for a new trial.

Judgment reversed in favor of Jackson.

Rewards

Advertisements offering rewards for lost property, for information, or for the capture of criminals are generally treated as offers for unilateral contracts. To accept the offer and be entitled to the stated reward, offerees must perform the requested act—return the lost property, supply the requested information, or capture the wanted criminal. Some courts have held that only offerees who started performance with knowledge of the offer are entitled to the reward. Other courts, however, have indicated the only requirement is that the offeree know of the reward before completing performance. In reality, the result in most such cases probably reflects the court's perception of the equities of the particular case at hand.

Auctions

Sellers at auctions are generally treated as making an invitation to offer. Those who bid on offered goods are, therefore, treated as making offers that the owner of the goods may accept or reject. Acceptance occurs only when the auctioneer strikes the goods off to the highest bidder; the auctioneer may withdraw the goods at any time before acceptance. However, when an auction is advertised as being "without reserve," the seller is treated as having made an offer to sell the goods to the highest bidder and the goods cannot be withdrawn after a call for bids has been made unless no bids are made within a reasonable time.[8]

Bids

The bidding process is a fertile source of contract disputes. Advertisements for bids are generally treated as invitations to offer. Those who submit bids are treated as offerors. According to general contract principles, bidders can withdraw their bids at any time prior to acceptance by the offeree inviting the bids, and the offeree is free to accept or reject any bid. The previously announced terms of the bidding may alter these rules, however. For example, if the advertisement for bids unconditionally states that the contract will be awarded to the lowest responsible bidder, this will be treated as an offer that is accepted by the lowest bidder. Only proof by the offeror that the lowest bidder is not responsible can prevent the formation of a contract.

---

[8]These rules and others concerned with the sale of goods by auction are contained in § 2–328 of the UCC.

Also, under some circumstances discussed later in this chapter, promissory estoppel may operate to prevent bidders from withdrawing their bids.

Bids for governmental contracts are generally covered by specific statutes rather than by general contract principles. Such statutes ordinarily establish the rules governing the bidding process, often require that the contract be awarded to the lowest bidder, and frequently establish special rules or penalties governing the withdrawal of bids.

WHICH TERMS ARE INCLUDED IN THE OFFER?

After making a determination that an offer existed, a court must decide which terms were included in the offer so that it can determine the terms of the parties' contract. Put another way, which terms of the offer are binding on the offeree who accepts it? Should offerees, for example, be bound by fine print clauses or by clauses on the back of the contract? Originally, the courts tended to hold that offerees were bound by all the terms of the offer on the theory that every person had a duty to protect himself by reading agreements carefully before signing them.

In today's world of lengthy, complex form contracts, however, people often sign agreements that they have not fully read or do not fully understand. Modern courts tend to recognize this fact by saying that offerees are bound only by terms of which they had actual or reasonable notice. If the offeree actually read the term in question, or if a reasonable person should have been aware of it, it will probably become part of the parties' contract. A fine-print provision on the back of a theater ticket would probably not be binding on a theater patron, however, because a reasonable person would not expect such a ticket to contain contractual terms. By contrast, the terms printed on a multipage airline or steamship ticket might well be considered binding on the purchaser if such documents would be expected to contain terms of the contract.

This modern approach to deciding the terms of a contract gives courts an indirect, but effective, way of promoting fair dealing by refusing to enforce unfair contract terms on the ground that the offeree lacked reasonable notice of them. Disclaimers and exculpatory clauses (contract provisions that seek to relieve offerors of some legal duty that they would otherwise owe to offerees) are particularly likely to be subjected to close judicial scrutiny. Additional ways of analyzing unexpected and unfair contract terms are discussed in Chapter 15.

TERMINATION OF OFFERS

After a court has determined the existence and content of an offer, it must determine the duration of the offer. Was the offer still in existence when the offeree attempted to accept it? If not, no contract was created and the offeree is treated as having made an offer that the original offeror is free to accept or reject. This is so because, by attempting to accept an offer that has terminated, the offeree has indicated a present intent to contract on the terms of the original offer though he lacks the power to bind the offeror to a contract due to the original offer's termination.

Terms of the Offer

The offeror is often said to be "the master of the offer." This means that offerors have the power to determine the terms and conditions under which they are bound to a contract. As the following *Newman* case indicates, an offeror may include terms in the offer that limit its effective life. These may be specific terms, such as "you must accept by December 5, 1994" or "this offer is good for five days," or more general terms, such as "for immediate acceptance," "prompt wire acceptance," or "by return mail." General time limitation language in an offer can raise difficult problems of interpretation for courts trying to decide whether an offeree accepted before the offer terminated. Even more specific language, such as "this offer is good for five days," can cause problems if the offer does not specify whether the five-day period begins when the offer is sent or when the offeree receives it. Not all courts agree on such questions, so wise offerors should be as specific as possible in stating when their offers terminate.

NEWMAN V. SCHIFF
778 F.2d 460 (8th Cir. 1985)

Irwin Schiff, a self-styled tax rebel who had made a career out of his tax protest activities, appeared live on the February 7, 1983, CBS News "Nightwatch" program. During the course of the program, which had a viewer participation format, Schiff repeated his longstanding position that "there is nothing in the Internal Revenue Code which says anyone is legally required to pay the tax." Later in the program, Schiff stated: "If anybody calls this show and cites any section of this Code that says an individual is required to file a tax return, I will pay them $100,000."

Attorney John Newman failed to see Schiff live on "Nightwatch," but saw a two-minute taped segment of the original "Nightwatch" interview several hours later on the "CBS Morning News." Certain that Schiff's statements were incorrect, Newman telephoned and wrote "CBS Morning News," attempting to accept Schiff's offer by citing Internal Revenue Code provisions requiring individuals to pay federal income tax. CBS forwarded Newman's letter to Schiff, who refused to pay on the ground that Newman had not properly accepted his offer. Newman sued Schiff for breach of contract. The trial court ruled in Schiff's favor, and Newman appealed.

Bright, Senior Circuit Judge   It is a basic legal principle that mutual assent is necessary for the formation of a contract. Courts determine whether the parties expressed their assent to a contract by analyzing their agreement process in terms of offer and acceptance. An offer is the "manifestation of willingness to enter into a bargain, so made as to justify another person in understanding that his assent to that bargain is invited and will conclude it." *Restatement (Second) of Contracts* § 24 (1981). Schiff's statement on "Nightwatch" that he would pay $100,000 to anyone who called the show and cited any section of the Internal Revenue Code "that says an individual is required to file a tax return" constituted a valid offer for a reward. If anyone had called the show and cited the code sections that Newman produced, a contract would have been formed and Schiff would have been obligated to pay the $100,000 reward.

Newman, however, never saw the live CBS "Nightwatch" program on which Schiff appeared and this lawsuit is not predicated on Schiff's "Nightwatch" offer. Newman saw the "CBS Morning News" rebroadcast of Schiff's "Nightwatch" appearance. This rebroadcast served not to renew or extend Schiff's offer, but rather only to inform viewers that Schiff had made an offer on "Nightwatch." An offeror is the master of his offer and it is clear that Schiff by his words, "If anybody calls this show," limited his offer in time to remain open only until the conclusion of the live "Nightwatch" broadcast. A reasonable person listening to the news rebroadcast could not conclude that the above language constituted a new offer rather than what it actually was, a news report of the offer previously made, which had already expired.

Although Newman has not "won" his lawsuit in the traditional sense of recovering a reward that he sought, he has accomplished an important goal in the public interest of unmasking the "blatant nonsense" dispensed by Schiff. For that he deserves great commendation from the public. Perhaps now CBS and other communication media who have given Schiff's mistaken views widespread publicity will give John Newman equal time in the public interest.

Judgment for Schiff affirmed.

Lapse of Time

Offers that fail to provide a specific time for acceptance are valid for a reasonable time. What constitutes a reasonable time depends on the circumstances surrounding the offer. How long would a reasonable person in the offeree's position believe she had to accept the offer? Offers involving things subject to rapid fluctuations in value, such as stocks, bonds, or commodities futures, have a very brief duration. The same is true for offers involving goods that may spoil, such as produce.

The context of the parties' negotiations is another factor relevant to determining the duration of an offer. For example, most courts hold that when parties bargain face-to-face or over the telephone, the normal time for acceptance does not extend past the conclusion of their conversation unless the offeror indicates a contrary intention. Where negotiations are carried out by mail or telegram, the time for acceptance would ordinarily include at least the normal time for communicating the offer and a prompt response by the offeree. Finally, in cases where the parties have dealt with each other on a regular basis in the past, the timing of their prior transactions would be highly relevant in measuring the reasonable time for acceptance.

Revocation

General Rule: Offers are Revocable As the masters of their offers, offerors can give offerees the power to bind them to contracts by making offers. They can also terminate that power by revoking their offers. The general common law rule on revocations is that offerors may revoke their offers at any time prior to acceptance, *even if they have promised to hold the offer open for a stated period of time*. In the following situations (summarized in Figure 1), however, offerors are *not* free to revoke their offers.

1. *Options.* An **option** is a separate contract in which an offeror agrees not to revoke her offer for a stated time in exchange for some valuable consideration.[9] You can think of it as a contract in which an offeror sells her right to revoke her offer. For example, Jones, in exchange for $5,000, agrees to give Dewey Development Co. a six-month option to

purchase her farm for $550,000. In this situation, Jones would not be free to revoke the offer during the six-month period of the option. The offeree, Dewey Development, has no obligation to accept Jones's offer. In effect, it has merely purchased the right to consider the offer for the stated time without fear that Jones will revoke it. The traditional common law rule on options requires the actual payment of the agreed-on consideration before an option contract becomes enforceable. Therefore, in the above example, if Dewey Development never, in fact, paid the $5,000, no option was created and Jones could revoke her offer at any time prior to its acceptance by Dewey Development.

2. *Firm offers for the sale of goods.* The Code makes a major change in the common law rules governing the revocability of offers by recognizing the concept of a **firm offer** [2–205]. Like an option, a firm offer is irrevocable for a period of time. In contrast to an option, however, a firm offer does not require consideration to be given in exchange for the offeror's promise to keep the offer open. Not all offers to buy or sell goods qualify as firm offers, however. To be a firm offer, an offer must:

· Be made by an offeror who is a *merchant.*
· Be contained in a signed[10] writing.
· Give assurances that the offer will be kept open.

An offer to buy or sell goods that fails to satisfy these three requirements is governed by the general common law rule and is revocable at any time prior to acceptance. If an offer *does* meet the requirements of a firm offer, however, it will be irrevocable for the time stated in the offer. If no specific time is stated in the offer, it will be irrevocable for a *reasonable* time. Regardless of the terms of the firm offer, the outer limit on a firm offer's irrevocability is *three* months. For example, if Worldwide Widgets makes an offer in a signed writing in which it proposes to sell a quantity of its XL7 Turbo Widgets to Howell Hardware and gives assurances that the offer will be kept open for a year, the offer is a firm offer, but it can be revoked after three months if Howell Hardware has not yet accepted it.

---

[9]Chapter 12 discusses consideration in detail.

[10]Under UCC § 1–201(39), the word *signed* includes any symbol that a person makes or adopts with the intent to authenticate a writing.

In some cases, however, offerees are the true originators of an assurance term in an offer. When offerees have effective control of the terms of the offer by providing their customers with preprinted purchase order forms or order blanks, they may be tempted to take advantage of their merchant customers by placing an assurance term in their order forms. This would allow offerees to await market developments before deciding whether to fill the order, while their merchant customers, who may have signed the order without reading all of its terms, would be powerless to revoke. To prevent such unfairness, the Code requires that assurance terms on forms provided by offerees be separately signed by the offeror to effect a firm offer. For example, if Fashionable Mfg. Co. supplies its customer, Retailer, with preprinted order forms that contain a fine-print provision giving assurances that the customer's offer to purchase goods will be held open for one month, the purported promise to keep the offer open would not be enforceable unless Retailer separately signed that provision.

3. *Offers for unilateral contracts.* Suppose Franklin makes the following offer for a unilateral contract to Waters: "If you mow my lawn, I'll pay you $25." Given that an offeree in a unilateral contract must fully perform the requested act to accept the offer, can Franklin wait until Waters is almost finished mowing the lawn and then say "I revoke!"? Obviously, the application of the general rule that offerors can revoke at any time before acceptance creates the potential for injustice when applied to offers for unilateral contracts because it would allow an offeror to revoke after the offeree has begun performance but before he has had a chance to complete it. To prevent injustice to offerees who rely on such offers by beginning performance, two basic approaches are available to modern courts.

Some courts have held that once the offeree has begun to perform, the offeror's power to revoke is suspended for the amount of time reasonably necessary for the offeree to complete performance. Section 45 of the *Restatement (Second)* takes a similar approach for offers that unequivocally require acceptance by performance by stating that once the offeree begins performance, an option contract is created. The offeror's duty to perform his side of the bargain is conditional on full performance by the offeree.

FIGURE 1	**When Offerors Cannot Revoke**
Options	Offeror has promised to hold offer open and has received consideration for that promise
Firm Offers	Merchant offeror makes written offer to buy or sell goods, giving assurances offer will be held open
Unilateral Contract Offers	Offeree has started to perform requested act before offeror revokes
Promissory Estoppel	Offeree foreseeably and reasonably relies on offer being held open, and will suffer injustice if it is revoked

Another approach to the unilateral contract dilemma is to hold that a bilateral contract is created once the offeree begins performance. This is essentially the position taken by section 62 of the *Restatement (Second),* which states that when the offer invites acceptance either by a return promise or performance, the beginning of performance operates as an acceptance and a promise by the offeree to render complete performance.

4. *Promissory estoppel.* In some cases in which the offeree *relies* on the offer being kept open, the doctrine of promissory estoppel can operate to prevent offerors from revoking their offers prior to acceptance. Section 87(2) of the *Restatement (Second)* says:

An offer which the offeror should reasonably expect to induce action or forbearance of a substantial character on the part of the offeree before acceptance and which does induce such action or forbearance is binding as an option contract to the extent necessary to avoid injustice.

Many of the cases in which promissory estoppel has been used successfully to prevent revocation of offers involve the bidding process. For example, Gigantic General Contractor seeks to get the general contract to build a new high school gymnasium for Shadyside School District. It receives bids from subcontractors. Pliny Electric submits the lowest bid to perform the electrical work on the job, and Gigantic uses Pliny's bid in preparing its bid for the general contract. Here, Pliny has made an offer to

Gigantic, but Gigantic cannot accept that offer until it knows whether it has gotten the general contract. The school district awards the general contract to Gigantic. Before Gigantic can accept Pliny's offer, however, Pliny attempts to revoke it. In this situation, a court could use the doctrine of promissory estoppel to hold that the offer could not be revoked.

Effectiveness of Revocations   The question of *when* a revocation is effective to terminate an offer is often a critical issue in the contract formation process. For example, Davis offers to landscape Winter's property for $1,500. Two days after making the offer, Davis changes his mind and mails Winter a letter revoking the offer. The next day, Winter, who has not received Davis's letter, telephones Davis and attempts to accept. Contract? Yes. As the following *Lyon* case indicates, the general rule on this point is that revocations are effective only when they are actually *received* by the offeree.

The basic idea behind this rule is that the offeree is justified in relying on the intent to contract manifested by the offeror's offer until she actually knows that the offeror has changed his mind. This explains why many courts have also held that if the offeree receives reliable information indicating that the offeror has taken action inconsistent with an intent to enter the contract proposed by the offer, such as selling the property that was the subject of the offer to someone else, this terminates the offer. In such circumstances, the offeree would be unjustified in believing that the offer could still be accepted.

The only major exception to the general rule on effectiveness of revocations concerns offers to the general public. Because it would be impossible in most cases to reach every offeree with a revocation, it is generally held that a revocation made in the same manner as the offer is effective when published, without proof of communication to the offeree.

LYON v. ADGRAPHICS
540 A.2d 398 (Conn. Ct. App. 1988)

Edward Sherman engaged V. R. Brokers as listing agent for the sale of Adgraphics, his business. On December 5, 1985, William Lyon made a written offer to purchase the business for $75,000 and attached certain conditions to the offer. Later the same day, Sherman signed a written counteroffer offering to sell for $80,000 and rejecting two of the conditions contained in Lyon's offer. On December 7, at 11:35 A.M., Lyon signed the counteroffer before a notary public and then brought it to the office of V. R. Brokers around noon on that day. Before Lyon could hand the signed counteroffer to Robert Renault, the principal of V. R. Brokers, Renault told him that Sherman wanted to cancel his counteroffer. Lyon filed a breach of contract suit, and, when the trial court ruled in his favor, Sherman appealed.

■

Borden, Judge   It is a basic principle of contract law that in order to form a binding contract there must be an offer and acceptance based on a mutual understanding of the parties. The counteroffer by Sherman created a power of acceptance in Lyon. That counteroffer, however, was revocable by Sherman at any time prior to acceptance by Lyon.

The trial court's conclusion that Lyon's acceptance of the counteroffer was effective when he signed it was contrary to our law. Revocation of an offer in order to be effectual must be received by the offeree before he has exercised his power of creating a contract by acceptance of the offer. Acceptance is operative, if transmitted by means which the offeror has authorized, as soon as its transmission begins and it is put out of the offeree's possession. Lyon's act of signing the written counteroffer failed to communicate the acceptance to Sherman or his agent and failed to put the acceptance out of Lyon's possession. It was, therefore, ineffective to create a contract.

When Sherman, through his agent, informed Lyon that the counteroffer was withdrawn, Lyon's power to accept the counteroffer no longer existed. This was done before Lyon had properly accepted the counteroffer by transmitting the signed counteroffer to Renault. Accordingly, no enforceable contract between the parties was ever created. **Judgment reversed in favor of Sherman.**

Rejection

An offeree may expressly reject an offer by indicating that he is unwilling to accept it. He may also impliedly reject it by making a counteroffer, an offer to contract on terms materially different from the terms of the offer.[11] As a general rule, either form of rejection by the offeree terminates his power to accept the offer. This is so because an offeror who receives a rejection may rely on the offeree's expressed desire not to accept the offer by making another offer to a different offeree.

One exception to the general rule that rejections terminate offers concerns offers that are the subject of an option contract. Some courts hold that a rejection does not terminate an option contract and that the offeree who rejects still has the power to accept the offer later, so long as the acceptance is effective within the option period.[12]

Effectiveness of Rejections   As a general rule, rejections, like revocations, are effective only when actually received by the offeror. This is because there is no possibility that the offeror can rely on a rejection by making another offer to a different offeree until she actually has notice of the rejection. Therefore, an offeree who has mailed a rejection could still change her mind and accept if she communicates the acceptance before the offeror receives the rejection.[13]

Death or Insanity of Either Party

The death or insanity of either party to an offer automatically terminates the offer without notice. A meeting of the minds is obviously impossible when one of the parties has died or become insane.[14]

Destruction of Subject Matter

If, prior to an acceptance of an offer, the subject matter of a proposed contract is destroyed without the knowledge or fault of either party, the offer is terminated.[15] So, if Marks offers to sell Wiggins his lakeside cottage and the cottage is destroyed by fire before Wiggins accepts, the offer was terminated on the destruction of the cottage. Subsequent acceptance by Wiggins would not create a contract.

Intervening Illegality

An offer is terminated if the performance of the contract it proposes becomes illegal before the offer is accepted. So, if a computer manufacturer offered to sell sophisticated computer equipment to another country, but two days later, before the offer was accepted, Congress placed an embargo on all sales to that country, the offer was terminated by the embargo.[16]

---

[11]Chapter 11 discusses counteroffers in detail.

[12]Section 37 of the *Restatement (Second) of Contracts* adopts this rule.

[13]Chapter 11 discusses this subject in detail.

[14]Death or insanity of a party that occurs after a contract has been formed can excuse performance in contracts that call for personal services to be performed by the person who has died or become insane. This is discussed in Chapter 18.

[15]In some circumstances, destruction of the subject matter can also serve as a legal excuse for a party's failure to perform his obligations under an existing contract. Chapter 18 discusses this subject.

[16]In some circumstances, intervening illegality can also serve as a legal excuse for a party's failure to perform his obligations under an existing contract. Chapter 18 discusses this subject.

CONCEPT REVIEW

WHAT TERMINATES OFFERS?

- Their own terms
- Lapse of time
- Revocation
- Rejection
- Death or insanity of offeror or offeree
- Destruction of subject matter
- Intervening illegality

ETHICAL AND PUBLIC POLICY CONCERNS

1. Classical contract theory has traditionally found strong ethical justification in the notion of voluntary consent. To parties who want out of their contracts and ask why they should be held to them, the law has often responded: "Because you agreed to them." How does this ethical justification square with the objective theory of contract, which can in some cases result in holding people to agreements that are inconsistent with their subjective intent? Is there some other ethical justification for holding people to the objective manifestations of consent, regardless of their actual or subjective intent?

2. Compare and contrast the underlying ethical justifications of the classical and modern contract positions on what terms are included in offers. Is it ethical for businesses that deal with consumers or other unsophisticated parties to "hide" contract terms under misleading headings, in small print, or on the reverse side of contracts? What about putting form contracts in complex, technical language that consumers are unlikely to understand?

3. As you learned earlier in this chapter, there are now a number of exceptions to the traditional rule that offerors can revoke at any time prior to acceptance, even if they have promised not to. Is there an ethical basis for each of these exceptions? If so, what is it?

PROBLEMS AND PROBLEM CASES

1. In 1989, the New Jersey Highway Authority increased its tolls from 25 cents to 35 cents. In connection with this increase, it authorized the sale of tokens for a discounted price—$10 for a roll of 40 tokens, a savings of $4 per roll for customers—for a limited time. The authority advertised this sale through several media, including signs on the parkway itself. Shortly after the discount sale began, complaints were made that the tokens were not available. The authority explained that the shortage probably resulted from an unanticipated demand for the tokens resulting from purchasers hoarding them. The authority then began limiting the sales to certain days of the week, but even with that limitation, the demand could not be satisfied. Schlictman, a motorist who used the toll roads, sued the authority for breach of contract after trying unsuccessfully, on five different occasions within the authorized sale dates and times, to buy the discounted tokens. What should the result be?

2. In 1985, First Colonial Savings Bank ran a newspaper advertisement that stated in part:

You Win 2 Ways

WITH FIRST COLONIAL'S

Savings Certificates

1 Great Gifts   2 & High Interest

Saving at First Colonial is a very rewarding experience. In appreciation for your business we have Great Gifts for you to enjoy **NOW**—and when your investment matures you get your entire principal back **PLUS GREAT INTEREST.**

Plan B: 3½ Year Investment

Deposit $14,000 and receive two gifts: a Remington Shotgun and GE CB Radio, OR an RCA 20" Color-Trac TV, and $20,136.12 upon maturity in 3½ years.

Relying on this ad, the Changs deposited $14,000 with First Colonial on January 3, 1986. They received a color television that day from First Colonial and expected to receive the sum of $20,136.12 upon maturity of the deposit in three and one-half years. First Colonial also gave the Changs a certificate of deposit when they made their deposit. When the Changs returned to liquidate the certificate of deposit upon its maturity, they were informed that the advertisement contained a typographical error and that they should have deposited $15,000 in order to receive the sum of $20,136.12 upon maturity of the certificate of deposit. First Colonial did not inform the Changs, nor were the Changs aware, that the advertisement contained an error until after the certificate of deposit had matured. First Colonial did display in its lobby pamphlets that contained the correct figures when the Changs made their deposit. The Changs sued First Colonial to recover the $1,312.19 difference between the $20,136.12 amount in the advertisement and the $18,823.93 that First Colonial actually paid to the Changs. Should they prevail?

3. On August 4, 1980, Normile made a written offer to buy property owned by Miller. Miller signed and returned the offer after making several substantial changes in its terms and initialing those changes. The executed form was delivered to Normile by Byer, the real estate agent who had shown him the property. In the early afternoon of August 5, 1980, Miller accepted an offer by Segal to buy her property on terms similar to those in the modified offer she had returned to Normile. At 2:00 P.M. that day, Byer told Normile: "You snooze, you lose; the property has been sold." Shortly thereafter, Normile attempted to accept Miller's proposal. Was the trial court correct in ruling that Normile and Miller had no contract?

4. In April 1981, Action Ads, Inc., hired Judes as a salesperson. The employment contract provided that: "Sixty days from your date of hire, Action Ads will provide a medical insurance program for you and your dependents." Judes was not very successful as a salesperson for Action, earning only $580.09 in commissions during the entire tenure of his employment with the company. Action never provided the promised medical insurance, a fact Judes learned when he inquired about whether he was covered in August of 1981. Judes did little or no solicitation for Action after August, and the last order he placed with Action was in October 1981. During the period in which he was purportedly working for Action, Judes held himself out as unemployed, collecting $2,448 in unemployment benefits. In November 1981, Judes was seriously burned in a gas explosion at a mobile home. He filed suit against Action to recover his medical expenses, arguing that Action had breached the employment contract by failing to provide insurance coverage for him. Action Ads asserted that the agreement to provide "a medical insurance program" was too indefinite to be enforceable because the parties' agreement did not cover anything specific about the nature of the insurance coverage. What should be the result?

5. Less than an hour before his estranged wife underwent emergency surgery for an ectopic pregnancy caused by another man, McAdoo was asked to sign a standard form contract prepared by St. John's Episcopal Hospital. McAdoo testified that at the time he signed the form his wife's physical appearance and declared mental state convinced him that she was near death. Further, he stated that, under such circumstances, it did not occur to him to read carefully or question the implications of the papers he was being asked to sign. The form contained a provision that read as follows:

ASSIGNMENT OF INSURANCE BENEFITS: I hereby authorize payment directly to the above named hospital of the hospital expense benefits otherwise payable to me but not to exceed the hospital's regular charges for this period of hospitalization. I understand that I am financially responsible to the hospital for the charges not covered by my group insurance plan.

McAdoo's wife survived and was discharged from St. John's eight days later. McAdoo did not visit her after the day of the operation and had not had any further contact with her when the hospital filed suit against him to collect her hospital bill. Should St. John's be able to enforce the agreement against McAdoo?

6. Phyllis Chaplin filed a class action suit against Consolidated Edison (Con Ed) for allegedly discriminating against epileptics in violation of the Rehabilitation Act of 1973. In August 1981, Con Ed's lawyer sent Chaplin's lawyer a settlement offer. Chaplin's lawyer replied by saying that Chaplin had "objections" to the proposed settlement. On September 16, 1981, Con Ed's lawyer replied, saying: "Any further negotiation is an impossibility; if this agreement is not satisfactory to your client in its present form, I must withdraw all offers of settlement." In a letter dated September 17, 1981, Chaplin's lawyer answered that "after careful consideration" Chaplin still had "objections" to Con Ed's offer. Later on September 17, a federal appellate court ruled that private suits such as Chaplin's were not allowed under the Rehabilitation Act. On September 30, 1981, Chaplin's lawyer told Con Ed's lawyer that Chaplin had had "a change of heart" and was accepting the settlement offer. Con Ed's lawyer replied that the settlement was no longer acceptable. Was Con Ed bound by the settlement offer?

7. In October 1981, Christy and Andrus were involved in an automobile accident. On November 8, 1982, Aetna Casualty and Surety Company, Andrus's insurer, sent a letter to Christy and his insurer, The Travelers Insurance Company, offering to settle Christy's claim against Andrus for $8,507. Neither Christy nor The Travelers responded to this letter until February 4, 1984, when an attorney for The Travelers sent Aetna a letter attempting to accept the settlement offer. Aetna then responded that any claim Christy had against Andrus was barred by the state's two-year statute of limitations and that The Travelers' attempt to accept was not timely. Christy filed suit against Andrus and Aetna, arguing that they were bound by the settlement. At trial, Aetna introduced uncontradicted testimony that customary practice in the insurance industry was to respond to settlement offers within a few weeks. Was the trial court decision in Aetna's favor correct?

8. In March 1985, Cagle, a potato farmer, entered into a written agreement to buy seed potatoes from H. C. Schmieding Produce Company. The terms of the contract obligated Cagle to pay a portion of the purchase price immediately, with the balance to be paid when the crop to be raised from the seed potatoes was harvested. Cagle paid the preharvest portion of the price and proceeded to cultivate the potatoes. He failed to harvest most of the resulting crop, however, or to pay Schmieding the postharvest portion of the purchase price. When Schmieding sued him for breach of contract, Cagle filed a counterclaim arguing that Schmieding had breached a second contract, which obligated him to purchase Cagle's crop. According to Cagle, this second contract resulted from two telephone conversations with Schmieding's employees, occurring in late February 1985 and in May 1985. Cagle introduced evidence to show that Schmieding had agreed in those conversations to pay him $5.50 per bag for approximately 10,000 bags of white potatoes and to pay him market price at harvest time for all of his red potatoes grown on 30 acres of land. Cagle also introduced a letter from Schmieding, dated May 26, 1985, which said: "We are looking forward to working with you on the shipment of your crop," and asked him to "give us a week notice before you are ready to ship, in order for us to prepare our sales orders." Was this contract sufficiently definite to be enforceable?

9. In June 1973, Berryman signed an agreement giving Kmoch, a real estate broker, a 120-day option to purchase 960 acres of Berryman's land in exchange for "$10.00 and other valuable consideration," which was never paid. Kmoch hired two agricultural consultants to produce a report that he intended to use in order to interest other investors in joining him to exercise the option. In late July 1973, Berryman telephoned Kmoch and asked to be released from the option agreement. Nothing definite was agreed to, and Berryman later sold the land to another person. In August, Kmoch decided to exercise the option and contacted the local Federal Land Bank representative to make arrangements to buy the land. After being told by the representative that Berryman had sold the property, Kmoch sent Berryman a letter attempting to exercise the option. Kmoch argued that the option was still in effect and that, in any event, Berryman was estopped from revoking it. Was Kmoch right?

10. Warner Electric, an electrical subcontractor, submitted a bid to the Utah Subcontractors Bid Depository Service for the electrical subcontract on the construction of the General Services Administration (GSA) Metallurgy Research Center in Salt Lake City, Utah. Warner based its bid on specifications and bid forms supplied by the GSA. John Price Associates, a general contractor, used Warner's subcontract bid, which was the lowest submitted, in preparing its bid for the general contract. Price was the lowest bidder and was awarded the contract for the project. A few days after Price had signed a contract with the GSA, Warner told Price that it had a problem with its subcontract bid because the bid did not include certain laboratory work described in section 11600 of the GSA plans, work which Warner had thought would be performed by the general contractor. Warner refused to sign the subcontract without a promise of additional payment for the section 11600 work. Price notified Warner by mailgram that it was accepting Warner's bid. Later that day, Warner's attorney delivered a letter to Price withdrawing Warner's bid. Price then contacted the other subcontractors and ultimately hired another subcontractor for $94,845 more than Warner's bid price. Was Warner free to revoke its offer?

11. 🔲 *Video Case.* See "Too Good to Be True." A couple read three advertisements: The first was a newspaper ad for a new Mark 12 Luxury

Automobile for $9,999. Although they thought the ad might be a typographical mistake, there was no fine print in the ad and the two decided to go to the dealership and see if it would "make good on the offer." Once there, they learned that the price of the car was $29,999, not $9,999. The salesperson stated that the advertised price was an obvious typo. Is the dealership obligated to sell the car for $9,999?

The second was a flyer from a supermarket inviting customers to "Come celebrate good old-fashioned values for our 25th anniversary." The flyer advertised New York strip steak for $.99 per pound. Upon arrival at the store, however, the couple learned that the ad was an error and the price was intended to be $7.99 per found, not $.99. The employee pointed to a memo posted in the store that announced that the ad was an error. Was the ad an offer? If it had been an offer, would the memo posted in the store be a valid revocation?

The third ad was a flyer from an electronics superstore that stated, "Dear Preferred Customer: special close-out of Ubachi VCRs. Only three available at this unbelievable price, first come, first served, no rain checks." The couple camped outside the store all night to be first in line, but the store refused to sell the advertised item and tried to sell them a different, higher-priced model instead. Was this ad an offer?

12.   **[▣]**   *Video Case.*   See "Roof Repair." Roofer had submitted a bid to resurface a roof on the Bobco factory in Industrial Park. He had gotten encouraging signals about getting the job and was just about to get a signed contract to do the work when the Bobco factory burned to the ground. What is the status of Roofer's offer to resurface the roof?

See also "Car Deals" and "Martin Manufacturing."

CHAPTER
11

THE AGREEMENT:
ACCEPTANCE

INTRODUCTION

The preceding chapter discussed the circumstances under which a proposal would constitute the first stage of formation of an agreement: the offer. This chapter focuses on the final stage of forming an agreement: the acceptance. The acceptance is vitally important because it is with the acceptance that the contract is formed. This chapter discusses the requirements for making a valid acceptance as well as the rules concerning the time at which a contract comes into being.

WHAT IS AN ACCEPTANCE?

An **acceptance** is "a manifestation of assent to the terms [of the offer] made by the offeree in the manner invited or required by the offer."[1] In determining if an offeree accepted an offer, thus creating a contract, a court will look for evidence that the offeree intended to enter the contract on the terms proposed by the offeror and that he communicated his acceptance to the offeror.

Intention to Accept

In determining whether an offeree accepted an offer, the court is looking for the same *present intent to contract* on the part of the offeree that it found on the part of the offeror. The difference is that the offeree must objectively indicate a present intent to contract on the terms of the offer before a contract results. As the master of the offer, the offeror may specify in detail what behavior is required of the offeree to bind him to a contract. If the offeror does so, the offeree must ordinarily comply with all the terms of the offer before a contract results.

Intent and Acceptance on the Offeror's Terms

Traditional Mirror Image Rule   The traditional contract law rule is that an acceptance must be the *mirror image* of the offer. As the following *Benya* case indicates, attempts by offerees to change the terms of the offer or to add new terms to it are

---

[1]*Restatement (Second) of Contracts* § 50(1) (1981).

treated as counteroffers because they impliedly indicate an intent by the offeree to reject the offer instead of being bound by its terms. However, if an offeree merely asks about the terms of the offer without indicating its rejection (an *inquiry regarding terms*), or accepts the offer's terms while complaining about them (a *grumbling acceptance*), no rejection is implied. Also, recent years have witnessed a judicial tendency to apply the mirror image rule in a more liberal fashion by holding that only *material* (important) variances between an offer and a purported acceptance result in an implied rejection of the offer. Distinguishing among a counteroffer, an inquiry regarding terms, and a grumbling acceptance is often a difficult task. The fundamental issue, however, remains the same: Did the offeree objectively indicate a present intent to be bound by the terms of the offer?

BENYA V. STEVENS AND THOMPSON PAPER CO.

468 A.2d 929 (Vt. Sup. Ct. 1983)

On September 24, 1979, Vincent Benya's agent presented Stevens and Thompson Paper Company (S&T) with a sales agreement to purchase 5,243 acres of timber land owned by S&T for $605,366.50. S&T's lawyer made several modifications to the agreement, raising the cash to be paid at closing from $5,000 to $10,000, raising the interest rate on the mortgage S&T would hold on the property until it was fully paid for from 9 percent to 10 percent, providing for quarterly rather than annual payments on the mortgage, and changing the deed S&T was to provide from a warranty to a special warranty deed. S&T's vice president then initialed each change and signed the document, which was mailed back to Benya's agent. In early November, S&T received a new sales agreement from Benya, which differed from the two previous versions in a number of ways. S&T neither signed this agreement nor responded to it in any way. On November 7, S&T sold the property to someone else. Benya filed suit for breach of contract, and, when the trial court ruled in his favor, S&T appealed.

Billings, Chief Justice   The trial court found that the September 24th sales agreement constituted a binding contract as both parties had signed it. The court concluded that the changes made by S&T to Benya's sales agreement were minor since the purchase price, closing date and deposit were substantially the same, and therefore did not constitute a counteroffer.

The law relative to contract formation has long been well settled in Vermont and elsewhere. For an acceptance of an offer to be valid, it must substantially comply with the terms of the offer. An acceptance that modifies or includes new terms is not an acceptance of the original offer; it is a counteroffer by the offeree that must be accepted or rejected by the original offeror. The offeror's acceptance of the offeree's counteroffer may be accomplished either expressly or by conduct.

On the record before us it is clear that the September 24th purchase and sales agreement was an offer from Benya to S&T that S&T never accepted. Instead, S&T significantly altered the terms of Benya's offer. These changes were not, as characterized by the trial court, minor and therefore of no effect on Benya's offer. Taken together, they constitute S&T's proposal for a new deal, or, more precisely, a counteroffer. Also clear from the record is that Benya never accepted, either expressly or otherwise, S&T's counteroffer. After Benya and his agent discussed S&T's counteroffer, the decision was made to draft a third proposal, which in turn altered the deposit and time of payment terms of S&T's counteroffer. S&T never signed or in any other way expressed its assent to this proposal. Additionally, the conduct of the parties demonstrates their understanding that agreement had not yet been reached.

Judgment reversed in favor of S&T.

FIGURE 1   The "Battle of the Forms"—A Section 2–207 Flowchart

The UCC and the "Battle of the Forms"

Strictly applying the mirror image rule to modern commercial transactions, most of which are carried out by using preprinted form contracts, would often result in frustrating the parties' true intent. Offerors use standard order forms prepared by their lawyers, and offerees use standard acceptance or acknowledgment forms drafted by their counsel. The odds that these forms will agree in every detail are slight, as are the odds that the parties will read each other's forms in their entirety. Instead, the parties to such transactions are likely to read only crucial provisions concerning the goods ordered, the price, and the delivery date called for, and if these terms are agreeable, believe that they have a contract.

If a dispute arose before the parties started to perform, a court strictly applying the mirror image rule would hold that no contract resulted because the offer and acceptance forms did not match exactly. If a dispute arose after performance had commenced, the court would probably hold that the offeror had impliedly accepted the offeree's counteroffer and was bound by its terms.

Because neither of these results is very satisfactory, the Code, in a very controversial provision often called the "Battle of the Forms" section [2–207] (see Figure 1), has changed the mirror image rule for contracts involving the sale of goods. As you will see in the following *Union Carbide* case, section 2–207 allows the formation of a contract even when there is some variance between the terms of the offer and the terms of the acceptance. It also makes it possible, under *some* circumstances, for a term contained in the acceptance form to become part of the contract. The Code provides that a *definite and timely expression of acceptance* creates a contract, even if it includes terms that are *different from those stated in the offer* or even if it states *additional terms* that the offer did not address [2–207(1)]. An attempted acceptance that *was expressly conditioned* on the offeror's agreement to the offeree's terms would *not* be a valid acceptance, however [2–207(1)].

What are the terms of a contract created by the exchange of standardized forms? The *additional terms* contained in the offeree's form are treated as "proposals for addition to the contract." If the parties are both *merchants*, the additional terms become part of the contract *unless*:

1. The offer *expressly limits acceptance* to its own terms,
2. The new terms would *materially alter* the offer, or
3. The offeror gives notice of objection to the new terms within a reasonable time after receiving the acceptance [2–207(2)].

The *Union Carbide* case shows how courts analyze whether a term contained in the acceptance has become part of the contract.

When the offeree has made his acceptance expressly conditional on the offeror's agreement to the new terms or when the offeree's response to the offer is clearly not "an expression of acceptance" (e.g., an express rejection), no contract is created under section 2–207(1). A contract will only result in such cases if the parties engage in conduct that "recognizes the existence of a contract," such as an exchange of performance. Unlike his counterpart under traditional contract principles, however, the offeror who accepts performance in the face of an express rejection or expressly conditional acceptance is not thereby bound to all of the terms contained in the offeree's response. Instead, the Code provides that the terms of a contract created by such performance are those on which the parties' writings *agree*, supplemented by appropriate gap-filling provisions from the Code [2–207(3)].

UNION CARBIDE CORP. V. OSCAR MAYER FOODS CORP.
947 F.2d 1333 (7th Cir. 1991)

Union Carbide sold Oscar Mayer plastic casings that Oscar Mayer uses in manufacturing sausages. The prices in Union Carbide's invoices to Oscar Mayer included two 1 percent sales taxes that are applicable to sales that originate in Chicago. In 1980, another one of Oscar Mayer's suppliers of plastic sausage casings began charging a price that was 1 percent lower than Union Carbide's. This supplier had begun accepting orders at an office outside of Chicago and had decided that therefore it did not have to pay one of the sales taxes. When Oscar Mayer informed Union Carbide of this, Union Carbide instructed its customers to send their orders to an address outside Chicago, too, and it stopped paying both sales taxes and therefore deleted them from the invoices it sent Oscar Mayer. Thus Union Carbide had met and indeed beat the other supplier's discount by lowering its price 2 percent compared to the other supplier's reduction of 1 percent.

In 1988, the Illinois tax authorities decided that the two sales taxes were due notwithstanding the change of address and assessed Union Carbide $88,000 in back taxes on sales to Oscar Mayer and $55,000 in interest on those sales. Union Carbide paid this and then brought this suit to recover what it had paid from Oscar Mayer, claiming that Oscar Mayer had agreed to indemnify it for all sales tax liability. It relied on the following provision printed on the back of its invoices to Oscar Mayer and also in a "price book" that it sent its customers:

In addition to the purchase price, Buyer shall pay Seller the amount of all governmental taxes . . . that Seller may be required to pay with respect to the production, sale or transportation of any materials delivered hereunder.

The trial court granted a summary judgment in favor of Oscar Mayer, and Union Carbide appealed.

Posner, Circuit Judge The common law rule was that if the purported acceptance of an offer was not identical to the offer, the acceptance was a fresh offer and had to be expressly accepted by the original offeror for the parties to have a contract. This "mirror image" rule was widely believed to take insufficient account of the incorrigible fallibility of human beings engaged in commercial as in other dealings, and is changed by the Uniform Commercial Code, which allows an acceptance to make a contract even if it adds terms to the offer. Moreover, if it is a contract between "merchants" (in the sense of "pros," UCC section 2–104(1)—as Union Carbide and Oscar Mayer are), the additional terms become part of the contract. But not any additional terms; only those to which the offeror would be unlikely to object, because they fill out the contract in an expectable fashion, and hence do not alter it materially. If a term added by the offeree in his acceptance works a material alteration of the offer, the acceptance is still effective, but the term is not; that is, the contract is enforceable minus the term the offeree tried to add. An alteration is material if consent to it cannot be presumed. What is expectable, hence unsurprising, is okay; what is unexpected, hence surprising, is not.

This is not the end of the analysis, however. Even if the alteration is material, the other party can, of course, decide to accept it. Put differently, consent can be inferred from other things beside the unsurprising character of the new term: even from silence, in the face of a course of dealings that makes it reasonable for the other party to infer consent from a failure to object. An offeror can protect himself against additional terms, material or not, by expressly limiting acceptance to the terms of the offer.

The record does not reveal the origins of Union Carbide's dealings with Oscar Mayer. All we know is that in 1980 the parties' method of dealing was as follows. Oscar Mayer would from time to time send large purchase orders to Union Carbide which would not be filled immediately but instead would be filed for future reference. When Oscar Mayer actually needed casings it would phone Union Carbide and tell it how many it needed and Union Carbide would ship the casings the next day. After the casings arrived Oscar Mayer would send Union Carbide a purchase order for the shipment on the same form used for the standing orders. These "release orders," as the specific purchase orders were called, were like checks written against a bank account—only this was a sausage-casings account. At about the same time that Oscar Mayer sent Union Carbide a release order, Union Carbide would send Oscar Mayer an invoice for the shipment—and the so-called indemnity clause was

on the back of the invoice and also in a price book that Union Carbide sent its customers from time to time. So every actual purchase of sausage casings involved an exchange of four documents: the standing order, the price book, the release order, the invoice. Such a pattern of sequential exchange of documents governing a single sale is a prototypical situation for the application of UCC section 2–207. Union Carbide does not question that for purposes of our decision the purchase orders by Oscar Mayer are the offers and Union Carbide's invoices are the acceptances, and that the price book, if it be assumed to be an offer, was never accepted. So the indemnity clause was binding on Oscar Mayer only if the clause did not work a material alteration of the terms in the purchase orders.

Those orders don't exactly *discuss* taxes, but they contain a space for sales tax to be added into the purchase price, and Union Carbide points out that, consistent with this indication of willingness to pay sales tax, Oscar Mayer paid uncomplainingly all sales taxes that appeared on Union Carbide's invoices. If the sales tax rates had risen, Oscar Mayer would have had to pay the higher rates. What difference does it make, asks Union Carbide, if the increase took the form of an assessment of back taxes? It makes a big difference, amounting to a material alteration to which Oscar Mayer did not consent either explicitly or implicitly. If a tax increase showed up on an invoice, Oscar Mayer would have to pay but might then decide to cease buying casings from Union Carbide, as it had every right to do; it did not have a requirements contract with Union Carbide but could switch at will to other suppliers some of whom might not be subject to the tax. To assume responsibility for taxes shown on an individual invoice is quite different from assuming an open-ended, indeed incalculable, liability for back taxes. The tax clause altered the contract materially; and since the clause was at best ambiguous, this is not a case where consent can realistically be inferred from Oscar Mayer's silence in the face of a succession of acceptances (Union Carbide's invoices) containing the new term. There was no breach of contract.

Judgment affirmed in favor of Oscar Mayer.

Acceptance in Unilateral Contracts

A unilateral contract involves the exchange of a promise for an act. To accept an offer to enter such a contract, the offeree must perform the requested act. As you learned in the last chapter, however, courts applying modern contract rules may prevent an offeror from revoking such an offer once the offeree has begun performance. This is achieved by holding either that a bilateral contract is created by the beginning of performance or that the offeror's power to revoke is suspended for the period of time reasonably necessary for the offeree to complete performance.

Acceptance in Bilateral Contracts

A bilateral contract involves the exchange of a promise for a promise. As a general rule, to accept an offer to enter such a contract, an offeree must *make the promise requested by the offer.* This may be done in a variety of ways. For example, Wallace sends Stevens a detailed offer for the purchase of Stevens's business. Within the time period prescribed by the offer, Stevens sends Wallace a letter that says, "I accept your offer." Stevens has *expressly* accepted Wallace's offer, creating a contract on the terms of the offer. Acceptance, however, can be *implied* as well as express. Offerees who take action that objectively indicates agreement risk the formation of a contract. For example, offerees who act in a manner that is inconsistent with an offeror's ownership of offered property are commonly held to have accepted the offeror's terms. So, if Arnold, a farmer, leaves 10 bushels of corn with Porter, the owner of a grocery store, saying, "Look this corn over. If you want it, it's $5 a bushel," and Porter sells the corn, he has impliedly accepted Arnold's offer. But what if Porter just let the corn sit and, when Arnold returned a week later, Porter told Arnold that he did not want it? Could Porter's failure to act ever amount to an acceptance?

Silence as Acceptance   Since contract law generally requires some objective indication that an offeree intends to contract, the general rule is that an offeree's silence, without more, is *not* an acceptance. In addition, it is generally held that an offeror cannot impose on the offeree a duty to respond to the offer. So, even if Arnold made an offer to sell

corn to Porter and said, "If I don't hear from you in three days, I'll assume you're buying the corn," Porter's silence would still not amount to acceptance.

On the other hand, the circumstances of a case sometimes impose a duty on the offeree to reject the offer affirmatively or be bound by its terms. These are cases in which the offeree's silence objectively indicates an intent to accept. Customary trade practice or prior dealings between the parties may indicate that silence signals acceptance. So, if Arnold and Porter had dealt with each other on numerous occasions and Porter had always promptly returned items that he did not want, Porter's silent retention of the goods for a week would probably constitute an acceptance. Likewise, an offeree's silence can also operate as an acceptance if the offeree has indicated that it will. For example, Porter (the *offeree*) tells Arnold, "If you don't hear from me in three days, I accept."

Finally, it is generally held that offerees who accept an offeror's performance knowing what the offeror expects in return for his performance have impliedly accepted the offeror's terms. So, if Apex Paving Corporation offers to do the paving work on a new subdivision being developed by Majestic Homes Corporation, and Majestic fails to respond to Apex's offer but allows Apex to do the work, most courts would hold that Majestic is bound by the terms of Apex's offer.

Acceptance When a Writing Is Anticipated
Frequently, the parties to a contract intend to prepare a written draft of their agreement for both parties to sign. This is a good idea not only because the law requires written evidence of some contracts,[2] but also because it provides written evidence of the terms of the agreement if a dispute arises at a later date. If a dispute arises before such a writing has been prepared or signed, however, a question may arise concerning whether the signing of the agreement was a necessary condition to the creation of a contract. A party to the agreement who now wants out of the deal may argue that the parties did not intend to be bound until both parties signed the writing. As the following *Texaco* case indicates, a clear expression of such an intent by the parties

---

[2]Chapter 16 discusses this subject in detail.

during the negotiation process prevents the formation of a contract until both parties have signed. However, in the absence of such a clear expression of intent, the courts ask whether a reasonable person familiar with all the circumstances of the parties' negotiations would conclude that the parties intended to be bound only when a formal agreement was signed. If it appears that the parties had concluded their negotiations and reached agreement on all the essential aspects of the transaction, most courts would probably find a contract at the time agreement was reached, even though no formal agreement had been signed.

TEXACO, INC. V. PENNZOIL CO.
729 S.W.2d 768 (Tex. Ct. App. 1987)

On December 28, 1983, in the wake of well-publicized dissension between the board of directors of Getty Oil Company and Gordon Getty, Pennzoil announced an unsolicited, public tender offer for 16 million shares of Getty Oil at $100 each. Gordon Getty was a director of Getty Oil and the owner, as trustee of the Sarah C. Getty Trust, of 40.2 percent of the 79.1 million outstanding shares of Getty Oil. Shortly thereafter, Pennzoil contacted both Gordon Getty and a representative of the J. Paul Getty Museum, which held 11.8 percent of the shares of Getty Oil, to discuss the tender offer and the possible purchase of Getty Oil.

The parties drafted and signed a Memorandum of Agreement providing that Pennzoil and the Trust (with Gordon Getty as trustee) were to become partners on a 3/7ths to 4/7ths basis, respectively, in owning and operating Getty Oil. The museum was to receive $110 per share for its 11.8 percent ownership, and all other outstanding public shares were to be cashed in by the company at $110 per share. The memorandum provided that it was subject to the approval of Getty Oil's board. On January 2, 1984, the board voted to reject the memorandum price as too low and made a counterproposal to Pennzoil of $110 per share plus a $10 debenture. On January 3, the board received a revised Pennzoil proposal of $110 per share plus a $3 "stub" that was to be paid after the sale of a Getty Oil subsidiary. After discussion, the board voted 15 to 1 to accept Pennzoil's proposal if the stub price was raised to $5. This counteroffer was accepted by Pennzoil later the same day. On January 4, Getty Oil and Pennzoil issued identical press releases announcing an agreement in principle on the terms of the Memorandum of Agreement. Pennzoil's lawyers began working on a formal transaction agreement describing the deal in more detail than the outline of terms contained in the Memorandum of Agreement and press release.

On January 5, the board of Texaco, which had been in contact with Getty Oil's investment banker, authorized its officers to make an offer for 100 percent of Getty Oil's stock. Texaco first contacted the Getty Museum, which, after discussion, agreed to sell its shares to Texaco. Later that evening, Gordon Getty accepted Texaco's offer of $125 per share. On January 6, the Getty Board voted to withdraw its previous counteroffer to Pennzoil and to accept Texaco's offer. Pennzoil later filed suit against Texaco for tortious interference with its contract with the Getty entities. At trial, Texaco argued, among other things, that no contract had existed between Pennzoil and the Getty entities. The jury disagreed, awarding Pennzoil $7.53 billion in actual damages and $3 billion in punitive damages. Texaco appealed.

Warren, Justice   Texaco contends that there was insufficient evidence to support the jury's finding that at the end of the Getty Oil board meeting on January 3, the Getty entities intended to bind themselves to an agreement with Pennzoil. Pennzoil contends that the evidence showed that the parties intended to be bound to the terms in the Memorandum of Agreement plus a price term of $110 plus a $5 stub, even though the parties may have contemplated a later, more formal document to memorialize the agreement already reached.

If parties do not intend to be bound to an agreement until it is reduced to writing and signed by both parties, then there is no contract until that event occurs. If there is no understanding that a signed writing is necessary before the parties will be bound, and the parties have agreed upon all substantial terms, then an informal agreement can be binding, even though the parties contemplated evidencing their agreement in a formal document later. It is the parties' expressed intent that controls which rule of contract formation applies. Only the outward expressions of intent are considered—secret or subjective intent is immaterial to the question of whether the parties were bound.

Several factors have been articulated to help determine whether the parties intended to be bound only by a formal, signed writing: (1) whether a party expressly reserved the right to be bound only when a written agreement is signed; (2) whether there was any partial performance by one party that the party disclaiming the contract accepted; (3) whether all essential terms of the alleged contract had been agreed upon; and (4) whether the complexity or magnitude of the transaction was such that a formal, executed writing would normally be expected.

Any intent of the parties not to be bound before signing a formal document is not so clearly expressed in the press release to establish, as a matter of law, that there was no contract at that time. The press release does refer to an agreement "in principle" and states that the "transaction" is subject to execution of a definitive merger agreement. But the release as a whole is worded in indicative terms, not in subjunctive or hypothetical ones. The press release describes what shareholders will receive, what Pennzoil will contribute, that Pennzoil will be granted an option, etc.

We find little relevant partial performance in this case that might show that the parties believed that they were bound by a contract. However, the absence of relevant part performance in this short period of time does not compel the conclusion that no contract existed.

There was sufficient evidence for the jury to conclude that the parties had reached agreement on all essential terms of the transaction with only the mechanics and details left to be supplied by the parties' attorneys. Although there may have been many specific items relating to the transaction agreement draft that had yet to be put in final form, there is sufficient evidence to support a conclusion by the jury that the parties did not consider any of Texaco's asserted "open items" significant obstacles precluding an intent to be bound.

Although the magnitude of the transaction here was such that normally a signed writing would be expected, there was sufficient evidence to support an inference by the jury that that expectation was satisfied here initially by the Memorandum of Agreement, signed by a majority of shareholders of Getty Oil and approved by the board with a higher price, and by the transaction agreement in progress that had been intended to memorialize the agreement previously reached.

Judgment for Pennzoil affirmed.

Note: The court's decision was contingent on a reduction in the punitive damages awarded by the jury from $3 billion to $1 billion. Texaco ultimately sought reorganization under the protection of the Bankruptcy Court and the parties finally settled the case for $3 billion.

Acceptance of Ambiguous Offers

Although offerors have the power to specify the manner in which their offers can be accepted by requiring that the offeree make a return promise (a bilateral contract) or perform a specific act (a unilateral contract), often an offer is unclear about which form of acceptance is necessary to create a contract. In such a case, both the Code [2–206(1)(a)] and the *Restatement (Second)*[3] sug-

gest that the offer may be accepted in any manner that is *reasonable* in light of the circumstances surrounding the offer. Thus, either a promise to perform or performance, if reasonable, creates a contract.

Acceptance by Shipment   The Code specifically elaborates on the rule stated in the preceding section by stating that an order requesting prompt or current shipment of goods may be accepted either by a *prompt promise to ship* or by a *prompt or current shipment* of the goods [2–206(1)(b)]. So, if

---

[3]*Restatement (Second) of Contracts* § 30(2) (1981).

Ampex Corporation orders 500 IBM personal computers from Marks Office Supply, to be shipped immediately, Marks could accept either by promptly promising to ship the goods or by promptly shipping them. If Marks accepts by shipping, any subsequent attempt by Ampex to revoke the order will be ineffective.

What if Marks did not have 500 IBMs in stock and Marks knew that Ampex desperately needed the goods? Marks might be tempted to ship another brand of computers (that is, *nonconforming goods*—goods different from what the buyer ordered), hoping that Ampex would be forced by its circumstances to accept them because by the time they arrived it would be too late to get the correct goods elsewhere. Marks would argue that by shipping the wrong goods it had made a counteroffer because it had not performed the act requested by Ampex's order. If Ampex accepts the goods, Marks could argue that Ampex has impliedly accepted the counteroffer. If Ampex rejects the goods, Marks would arguably have no liability since it did not accept the order.

The Code prevents such a result by providing that prompt shipment of either conforming goods (what the order asked for) or nonconforming goods (something else) operates as an acceptance of the order [2–206(1)(b)]. This protects buyers such as Ampex because sellers who ship the wrong goods have simultaneously accepted their offers and breached the contract by sending the wrong merchandise.[4]

But what if Marks is an honest seller merely trying to help out a customer that has placed a rush order? Must Marks expose itself to liability for breach of contract in the process? The Code prevents such a result by providing that no contract is created if the seller notifies the buyer within a reasonable time that the shipment of nonconforming goods is intended as an accommodation (an attempt to help the buyer) [2–206(1)(b)]. In this case, the shipment is merely a counteroffer that the buyer is free to accept or reject and the seller's notification gives the buyer the opportunity to seek the goods he needs elsewhere.

Who Can Accept an Offer?

As the masters of their offers, offerees have the right to determine who can bind them to a contract. So, the only person with the legal power to accept an offer and create a contract is the *original offeree.* An attempt to accept by anyone other than the offeree is treated as an offer, because the party attempting to accept is indicating a present intent to contract on the original offer's terms. For example, Price offers to sell his car to Waterhouse for $5,000. Berk learns of the offer, calls Price, and attempts to accept. Berk has made an offer that Price is free to accept or reject.

COMMUNICATION OF ACCEPTANCE

Communication Required for Valid Acceptance

To accept an offer for a bilateral contract, the offeree must make the promise requested by the offer. In the Offer chapter, you learned that an offeror must communicate the terms of his proposal to the offeree before an offer results. This is so because communication is a necessary component of the present intent to contract required for the creation of an offer. For similar reasons, it is generally held that an offeree must communicate his intent to be bound by the offer before a contract can be created. To accept an offer for a unilateral contract, however, the offeree must perform the requested act. The traditional contract law rule on this point assumes that the offeror will learn of the offeree's performance and holds that no further notice from the offeree is necessary to create a contract unless the offeror specifically requests notice. The traditional rule can sometimes cause hardship to offerors who may not, in fact, know that the offeree has commenced performance. Neither the Code [section 2–206(2)] nor the *Restatement (Second)* will enforce such a contract against an offeror who has no way of learning of the offeree's performance with reasonable promptness and certainty.[5]

Manner of Communication

The offeror, as the master of the offer, has the power to specify the precise time, place, and manner in which acceptance must be communicated. This is called a *stipulation.* If the offeror stipulates a particular manner of acceptance, the offeree must respond in this way to form a valid acceptance. Suppose Prompt Printing makes an offer to Jackson

---

[4]Chapter 21 discusses the rights and responsibilities of the buyer and seller following the shipment of nonconforming goods.

[5]*Restatement (Second) of Contract* § 54 (2) (1981).

and the offer states that Jackson must respond by certified mail. If Jackson deviates from the offer's instructions in any significant way, no contract results unless Prompt Printing indicates a willingness to be bound by the deviating acceptance. If, however, the offer merely *suggests* a method or place of communication or is *silent* on such matters, the offeree may accept within a *reasonable time* by *any reasonable means* of communication. So, if Prompt Printing's offer did not *require* any particular manner of accepting the offer, Jackson could accept the offer by any reasonable manner of communication within a reasonable time.

When Is Acceptance Communicated?

Acceptances by Instantaneous Forms of Communication When the parties are dealing face-to-face, by telephone, or by other means of communication that are virtually instantaneous, there are few problems determining when the acceptance was communicated. As soon as the offeree says, "I accept," or words to that effect, a contract is created, assuming that the offer was still in existence at that time.

Acceptances by Noninstantaneous Forms of Communication Suppose the circumstances under which the offer was made reasonably lead the offeree to believe that acceptance by some noninstantaneous form of communication is acceptable, and the offeree responds by using mail, telegraph, or some other means of communication that creates a time lag between the dispatching of the acceptance and its actual receipt by the offeror. The practical problems involving the timing of acceptance multiply in such transactions. The offeror may be attempting to revoke the offer while the offeree is attempting to accept it. An acceptance may get lost and never be received by the offeror. The time limit for accepting the offer may be rapidly approaching. Was the offer accepted before a revocation was received or before the offer expired? Does a lost acceptance create a contract when it is dispatched, or is it totally ineffective?

Under the so-called "mailbox rule," properly addressed and dispatched acceptances can become effective when they are *dispatched*, even if they are lost and never received by the offeror. The mailbox rule, which is discussed further in the following *Casto v. State Farm Mutual Insurance Co.* case,

protects the offeree's reasonable belief that a binding contract was created when the acceptance was dispatched. By the same token, it exposes the offeror to the risk of being bound by an acceptance that she has never received. The offeror, however, has the ability to minimize this risk by stipulating in her offer that she must actually receive the acceptance for it to be effective. Offerors who do this maximize the time that they have to revoke their offers and ensure that they will never be bound by an acceptance that they have not received.

Operation of the Mailbox Rule: Traditional Rules Under traditional contract law, the mailbox rule makes acceptances effective upon dispatch when the offeree used a manner of communication that was expressly or impliedly **authorized** (invited) by the offeror. Any manner of communication *suggested* by the offeror (e.g., "You may respond by mail") would be *expressly* authorized, resulting in an acceptance sent by the suggested means being effective on dispatch. Unless circumstances indicated to the contrary, a manner of communication *used by the offeror in making the offer* would be *impliedly* authorized (e.g., an offer sent by mail would impliedly authorize an acceptance by mail), as would a manner of communication common in the parties' trade or business (e.g., a trade usage in the parties' business that offers are made by mail and accepted by telegram would authorize an acceptance by telegram). Conversely, an improperly dispatched acceptance or one that was sent by some means of communication that was *nonauthorized* would be effective when *received*, assuming that the offer was still open at that time. This placed on the offeree the risk of the offer being revoked or the acceptance being lost.

Operation of the Mailbox Rule: Modern Rules Under both the UCC and the *Restatement (Second) of Contracts*, an offer that does not indicate otherwise is considered to invite acceptance by *any reasonable means* of communication, and a properly dispatched acceptance sent by a reasonable means of communication within a reasonable time is effective on dispatch. What is reasonable depends on the circumstances in which the offer was made. These include the speed and reliability of the means used by the offeree, the nature of the transaction (e.g., does the agreement involve goods subject to rapid price fluctuations?), the existence of any trade usage governing the transaction, and the existence of prior dealings between the parties (e.g., has the offeree previously used the mail to accept telegraphed offers from the offeror?). So, under proper circumstances, a mailed response to a telegraphed offer or a telegraphed response to a mailed offer might be considered reasonable and therefore effective on dispatch.

What if an offeree attempts to accept the offer by some means that is *unreasonable* under the circumstances or if the acceptance is not properly addressed or dispatched (e.g., misaddressed or accompanied by insufficient postage)? Modern contract law rejects the traditional rule that such acceptances cannot be effective until received. Under both the Code [1–201(38)] and section 67 of the *Restatement (Second)*, an acceptance sent by an unreasonable means would be effective on dispatch *if* it is received within the time that an acceptance by a reasonable means would normally have arrived. The *Casto* case shows what happens when an improperly dispatched acceptance is not received within the time that a properly dispatched acceptance would have been.

CASTO V. STATE FARM MUTUAL INSURANCE CO.
594 N.E.2d 1004 (Ct. App. Ohio 1991)

In 1985, State Farm issued Deborah Casto an automobile insurance policy on her Jaguar. Casto also insured a second car, a Porsche, with State Farm. Sometime in September or early October 1987, Casto received two renewal notices, indicating that the next premium was due on October 10, 1987. State Farm sent a notice of cancellation on October 16, indicating that the policy would be canceled on October 29. Casto denied having received this notice. On October 20, Casto placed two checks, one for the Jaguar and one for the Porsche, in two preaddressed envelopes that had been supplied by State Farm. She gave these envelopes to Donald Dick, who mailed them on the same day. The envelope containing the Porsche payment was timely delivered to State Farm, but State Farm never received the Jaguar payment, and that policy was canceled.

Casto was involved in an accident on November 20 while driving the Jaguar. When she made a claim with State Farm, she learned that the policy had been canceled. After the accident, the envelope containing the Jaguar payment was returned to her stamped "Returned for postage." Casto brought this declaratory judgment action seeking a declaration that her insurance policy was in effect as of the date of the accident. The trial court rendered a judgment for State Farm and Casto appealed.

Reilly, Presiding Judge   The facts indicate that while the payment was mailed before October 29, it was not received by the insurance company. The issue then is whether the insurance premium is effectively paid on the day it was mailed or the day it is received by the company.

An insurance policy is a contract and the relationship between the insurer and its insured is contractual in nature. The renewal of an insurance policy is generally considered a new contract of insurance to which the requirements of offer and acceptance apply. The well-established general rule of contract formation is that an acceptance transmitted in a form invited by the offer is operative as soon as it is put out of the offeree's possession, regardless of whether it ever reaches the offeror. This is the so-called "mailbox rule" which states that in the absence of any limitation to the contrary in the offer, an acceptance is effective when mailed. One of the parties must bear the risk of loss. As the offeror has the power to condition acceptance of the offer on actual receipt, the courts have uniformly held that, in the absence of language to the contrary, an acceptance is effective when mailed.

To be effective upon mailing, however, the acceptance must be properly dispatched. The offeree must properly address the acceptance and take whatever other precautions as are ordinarily observed in the transmission of similar messages. It is undisputed that State Farm provided Casto with pre-addressed envelopes and thus authorized her to mail her premium payments. Furthermore, the renewal notices contain no language requiring actual receipt before payment is deemed effective. Finally, Casto and Donald Dick testified in their depositions that the Jaguar and Porsche payments were mailed on October 20, 1987, nine days before the cancellation date. Their testimony is further supported by the fact that the Porsche payment was actually received by State Farm before the cancellation date. Thus, the only remaining question is whether the payment was properly dispatched.

Casto testified that the check and renewal notice were placed in a pre-addressed and stamped envelope. Donald Dick also testified that both envelopes were stamped when he mailed them. Nevertheless, the envelope did not bear any postage when it was returned to Casto. Casto bore the burden of proving that the envelope was stamped when it was mailed. When the findings of fact leave some material fact undetermined, a reviewing court will presume that the issue of fact was not proved by the party having the burden of proof. We thus presume that the trial court concluded that the envelope was not stamped when mailed, and there is sufficient evidence in the record to support such a finding. As the envelope was not properly dispatched, the payment was not effective upon mailing under the facts of this case.

Judgment affirmed in favor of State Farm.

Stipulated Means of Communication As we discussed earlier, an offer may stipulate the means of communication that the offeree must use to accept by saying, in effect: "You must accept by mail." An acceptance by the stipulated means of communication is effective on dispatch, just like an acceptance by any other reasonable or authorized means of communication (see Figure 2). The difference

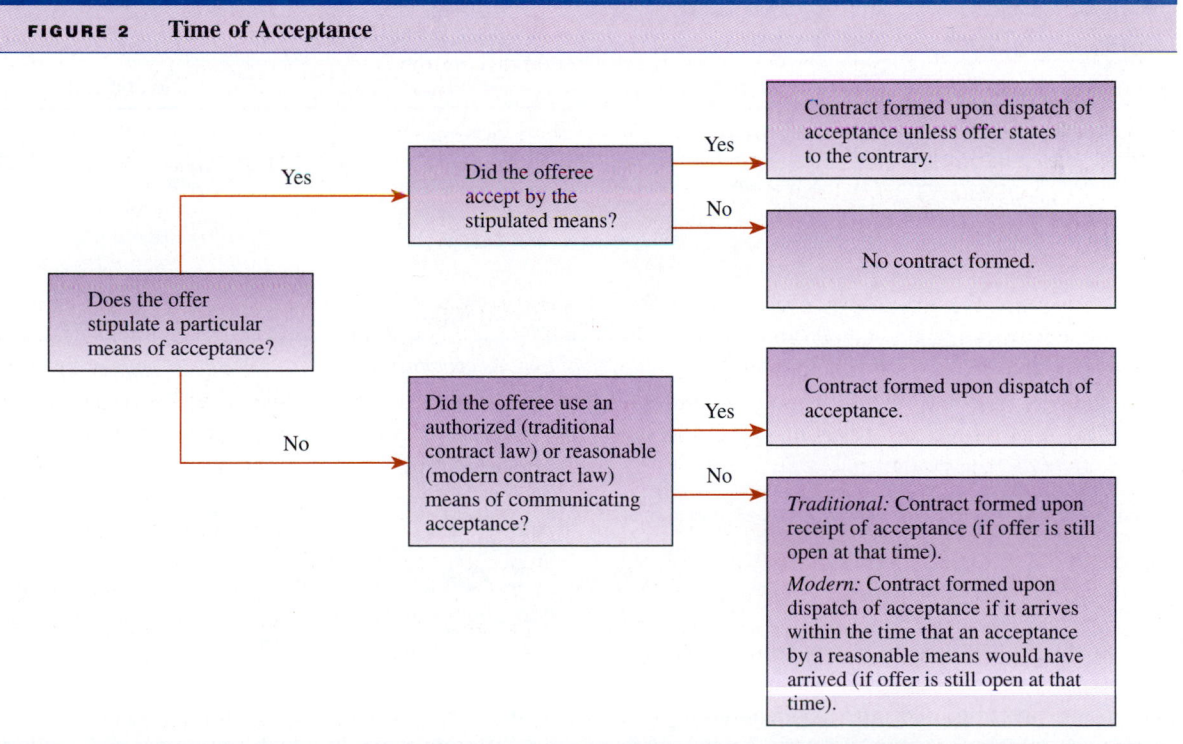

FIGURE 2   Time of Acceptance

Does the offer stipulate a particular means of acceptance?

Yes → Did the offeree accept by the stipulated means?

- Yes → Contract formed upon dispatch of acceptance unless offer states to the contrary.
- No → No contract formed.

No → Did the offeree use an authorized (traditional contract law) or reasonable (modern contract law) means of communicating acceptance?

- Yes → Contract formed upon dispatch of acceptance.
- No → *Traditional:* Contract formed upon receipt of acceptance (if offer is still open at that time).

  Modern: Contract formed upon dispatch of acceptance if it arrives within the time that an acceptance by a reasonable means would have arrived (if offer is still open at that time).

is that an acceptance by other than the stipulated means does not create a contract because it is an acceptance at variance with the terms of the offer.

Contradictory Offeree Responses   How do these rules work when the offeree sends mixed signals to the offeror? Suppose Case mails a counteroffer to White, impliedly rejecting an offer that White has made to him, and then, before White receives the rejection, Case mails a letter of acceptance. Is a contract formed? In the last chapter, you learned that Case's counteroffer (that is, rejection) would not be effective to terminate White's offer until White actually *receives* it. If we applied the normal rules of offer and acceptance to these facts, we might conclude that the parties had a contract because Case's acceptance by mail was effective on dispatch. White, however, might receive Case's counteroffer and sell the house to a third party before he receives Case's acceptance. To prevent

such an unfair result, most courts hold that when an offeree dispatches an acceptance after first dispatching a rejection, the acceptance does not create a contract unless it is received before the rejection. Therefore, if White receives the counteroffer before he receives the acceptance, no contract results. If, on the other hand, he receives the acceptance before receiving the counteroffer, a contract results.

What is the result if Case had first mailed White an acceptance, then changed his mind and shortly thereafter mailed White a rejection? Applying normal offer and acceptance rules to these facts, we would conclude that Case's acceptance was effective on dispatch and that Case no longer had the power to reject the offer. But the application of these rules would result in unfairness if White received Case's rejection first and relied on it by selling to someone else. In such a situation, Case would be *estopped* from enforcing the contract due to White's reliance.

CONCEPT REVIEW

CONTRADICTORY OFFEREE RESPONSES

Offeree Sends First	Offeree Sends Second	Offeror Receives First	Result
Rejection	Acceptance	Rejection	No contract
Rejection	Acceptance	Acceptance	Contract
Acceptance	Rejection	Rejection	If offeror relied on rejection, offeree is estopped from enforcing the contract
Acceptance	Rejection	Acceptance	Contract

ETHICAL AND PUBLIC POLICY CONCERNS

1. It should be apparent to you from the discussion of section 2–207 of the Code, the "Battle of the Forms" section, that the application of that section can sometimes result in a party being held to

a contract term to which she has not actually consented. How can this be justified?

2. Compare the ethical standards underlying the traditional contract law approach to the seller who ships nonconforming goods with the ethical standards reflected by section 2–206(1)(b) of the Code.

3. Compare the public policy stances implicit in the different ways in which traditional and modern contract law treat offeree attempts to accept by an nonauthorized or unreasonable means of communication.

1. Since 1974, Lone Star Donut Company had placed orders for its sugar requirements with Great Western Sugar Co. (GWS) through a sugar broker. In October 1980, GWS adopted a new policy of requiring a letter agreement for each order. The first such letter was forwarded from GWS to Lone Star by the broker on October 9, 1980. It concluded with the following language:

This letter is a written confirmation of our agreement, and unless it is signed by the buyer and returned to Great Western within 15 days of the date hereof, the agreement shall be deemed breached by Buyer and automatically terminated. Please sign and return to me the enclosed counterpart of this letter signalling your acceptance of the above agreement.

Lone Star signed and returned this letter. On December 2, Lone Star again ordered sugar. GWS initially neglected to send a letter agreement, finally doing so in late January 1981, in response to prodding by the broker. This letter concluded as follows:

This letter is a written confirmation of our agreement. Please sign and return to me the enclosed counterpart of this letter signalling your acceptance of the above agreement.

Lone Star, angered over the delay, refused to sign and subsequently refused to purchase sugar. Was a contract formed?

2. First Texas Savings Association promoted a "$5,000 Scoreboard Challenge" contest. Contestants who completed an entry form and deposited it with First Texas were eligible for a random drawing. The winner was to receive an $80 savings account with First Texas, plus four tickets to a Dallas Mavericks home basketball game chosen by First Texas. If the Mavericks held their opponent in the chosen game to 89 or fewer points, the winner was to receive an additional $5,000 money market certificate. In October 1982, Jergins deposited a completed entry form with First Texas. On November 1, 1982, First Texas tried to amend the contest rules by posting notice at its branches that the Mavericks would have to hold their opponent to 85 or fewer points before the contest winner would receive the $5,000. In late December, Jergins was notified that she had won the $80 savings account and tickets to the January 22, 1983, game against the Utah Jazz. The notice contained the revised contest terms. The Mavericks held the Jazz to 88 points. Was Jergins entitled to the $5,000?

3. In April 1973, in response to a request from Mobil Chemical for a bid on a two-sided precoater, Egan Machinery submitted a "quotation" describing the components of the precoater and the details of its operation. The quotation stated a price for the precoater but did not contain conditions of sale. In May 1973, Mobil sent Egan a purchase order for the precoater. The purchase order contained the following language:

Important—this order expressly limits acceptance to terms stated herein, and any additional or different terms proposed by the seller are rejected unless expressly agreed to in writing.

Egan responded with an order acknowledgment in May 1973, which provided that:

This order is accepted on the condition that our Standard Conditions of Sale, which are attached hereto and made a part hereof, are accepted by you, notwithstanding any modifying or additive conditions contained on your purchase order. Receipt of this acknowledgment by you without prompt written objection thereto shall constitute an acceptance of these terms and conditions.

One of the terms included in Egan's Standard Conditions required Mobil to indemnify Egan against any liability Egan might incur to persons injured by the precoater if the injury resulted from Mobil's failure to require its employees to follow safety procedures and/or use safety devices while operating it. When a Mobil employee who was injured while operating the precoater later won a $75,000 judgment against Egan, Egan filed suit against Mobil seeking indemnity. Did the indemnity clause become part of the contract?

4. Atwood bought a new pickup truck from Best Buick. When he took it home, his wife objected to the purchase. Atwood returned the car to Best, which agreed to take the truck back as a trade-in on another vehicle. Atwood traded for a new station wagon, which he registered and insured and sought to title in his name. When he took the car home, however, his wife objected to the color of its interior. Atwood returned the car to Best, but refused to accept any of the numerous other vehicles Best made available to him. He also refused to sign an application that would allow Best to retrieve the title to the car so it could sell it to someone else. Best then told him that unless he removed the car from its premises it would charge him a $5 per day storage fee. The Atwoods later sued Best for the return of the purchase price. Best counterclaimed for the storage fee. Should the Atwoods prevail?

5. Western Tire, Inc., had a lease on a building owned by the Skredes that was due to expire on April 30, 1978. The lease gave Western the right to renew the lease for an additional five-year term if the Skredes were given written notice of Western's intent to renew at least 30 days prior to the expiration date. It also specifically provided that notice would only be effective when it was deposited in a U.S. Post Office by registered or certified mail. On February 27, Western's attorney sent the Skredes a notice of Western's intent to renew by ordinary mail, which the Skredes did not receive until after April 1, 1978. On April 5, 1978, Western's lawyer, discovering his mistake, sent a second notice by certified mail. On April 14, 1978, the Skredes told Western that the lease was canceled. Did they have the right to cancel?

6. On January 16, 1987, Koop, an employee of Professional Search, Inc., called Renner, the director of systems software for Northwest Airlines, to inquire about possible job openings in Renner's department. Koop explained to Renner that if Northwest Airlines hired a candidate recommended by Professional Search, Professional Search would be entitled to charge Northwest Airlines 30 percent of the candidate's starting salary. Renner told Koop that a systems analyst position was open and described the job. Renner also stated that Northwest Airlines was not currently interviewing for that position and that Koop should direct further inquiries to Northwest Airlines's human resources department. Later, Koop and Wawrzyniak discussed Wawrzyniak's desire to be placed as a systems analyst and Wawrzyniak signed a placement contract. On January 20, 1987, Koop sent Wawrzyniak's résumé to Renner. Koop later called Renner, who told him the résumé "looked good." On February 19,

Wawrzyniak filled out an application for a systems position with Northwest Airlines, claiming he heard of the opening through a friend. On April 13, Northwest Airlines hired Wawrzyniak. Professional Search claimed that a placement contract had been formed between it and Northwest Airlines, and sought to recover its $12,000 commission. Will Professional Search prevail?

7. In 1986, Mercy Memorial Hospital decided to open an outpatient family practice clinic in Petersburg. It retained a recruiter to identify a private family practitioner. The recruiter brought the hospital and Dr. Kamalnath together. In June 1986, Iacoangeli, the hospital's director of planning and development, wrote Dr. Kamalnath a letter in which he made an offer to her that proposed terms regarding salary, office rental, line of credit for professional and operational expenses, home relocation, and other matters. Dr. Kamalnath did not accept this written offer. Instead, she suggested various changes and additions, principally an increase in the term of employment to three years and a provision that the hospital handle marketing. On June 30, Iacoangeli sent Dr. Kamalnath a second letter incorporating the longer period of employment, subject to annual performance reviews, and proposing other terms. Iacoangeli also prepared several drafts of a proposed contract, but none of these proved satisfactory to Dr. Kamalnath. Dr. Kamalnath nevertheless moved to Petersburg and began work, although she had no signed contract, the parties still differed as to some contractual duties such as the responsibility for certain major expenses, and the clinic was not yet complete. The Petersburg clinic was not as successful as the parties had hoped. Relations between them deteriorated, and the hospital notified Dr. Kamalnath to vacate the clinic in November 1987. Was there a contract between the hospital and Dr. Kamalnath?

8. On March 30, Cushing, a member of an antinuclear protest group, applied to the New Hampshire adjutant general's office for permission to hold a dance in the Portsmouth armory. On March 31, the adjutant general mailed a signed contract offer agreeing to rent the armory to the group. The agreement required Cushing to accept by signing a copy of the agreement and returning it to the adjutant general within five days after its receipt. On April 3, Cushing received the offer and signed it.

At 6:30 P.M. on April 4, Cushing received a call from the adjutant general attempting to revoke the offer. Cushing told the adjutant general that he had signed the contract and placed it in the office outbox on April 3, customary office practice being to collect all mail from outboxes at the end of the day and deposit it in the U.S. mail. On April 6, the adjutant general's office received the signed contract in the mail, dated April 3 and postmarked April 5. Assuming Cushing was telling the truth, did the parties have a contract?

9. Krack Corporation bought steel tubing from Metal-Matic for 10 years. The parties' usual practice was for Krack to send Metal-Matic purchase orders to which Metal-Matic would respond by sending an acknowledgment form and shipping the requested tubing. Metal-Matic's form provided that its acceptance was "expressly made" conditional on Krack's assent to the acknowledgment's terms, which included a clause limiting Metal-Matic's liability for consequential damages due to breach of warranty. Krack sold a cooling unit it had made with Metal-Matic's tubing to Diamond Fruit. The tubing was defective, causing losses to Diamond's fruit. When Diamond sued Krack, Krack sought indemnity from Metal-Matic. Metal-Matic argued that it was not responsible, citing the consequential damages clause in its acknowledgment. Was that clause part of the contract between Krack and Metal-Matic?

10. Soldau was fired by Organon, Inc. He received a letter from Organon offering to pay him double the normal severance pay if he would sign a release giving up all claims against the company. The letter incorporated the proposed release, which Soldau signed, dated, and deposited in a mailbox outside a post office. When he returned home, Soldau found that he had received a check from Organon in the amount of the increased severance pay. He returned to the post office and persuaded a postal employee to open the mailbox and retrieve the release. Soldau cashed Organon's check and subsequently filed an age discrimination suit against Organon. Was Soldau bound by the release?

CHAPTER

12

CONSIDERATION

INTRODUCTION

One of the things that separates a contract from an unenforceable social promise is that a contract requires voluntary agreement by two or more parties. Not all agreements, however, are enforceable contracts. At a fairly early point in the development of classical contract law, the common law courts decided not to enforce gratuitous (free) promises. Instead, only promises supported by consideration were enforceable in a court of law. This was consistent with the notion that the purpose of contract law was to enforce freely made bargains. As one 19th-century work on contracts put it: "The common law . . . gives effect only to contracts that are founded on the mutual exigencies of men, and does not compel the performance of any merely gratuitous agreements."[1] The concept of consideration distinguishes agreements that the law will enforce from gratuitous promises, which are normally unenforceable. This chapter focuses on the concept of consideration.

THE IDEA OF CONSIDERATION

A common definition of **consideration** is *legal value, bargained for and given in exchange for an act or a promise.* Thus, a promise generally cannot be enforced against the person who made it (the *promisor*) unless the person to whom the promise was made (the *promisee*) has given up something of legal value in exchange for the promise. In effect, the requirement of consideration means that a promisee must pay the price that the promisor asked to gain the right to enforce the promisor's promise. So, if the promisor did not ask for anything in exchange for making her promise or if what the promisor asked for did not have legal value (e.g., because it was something to which she was already entitled), her promise is not enforceable against her because it is not supported by consideration. Figure 1 graphically illustrates the elements of consideration.

Consider the early case of *Thorne v. Deas*, in which the part owner of a sailing ship named the *Sea Nymph* promised his co-owners that he would insure the ship for an upcoming voyage.[2] He failed

---

[1] T. Metcalf, *Principles of the Law of Contracts* (1874), p. 161.
[2] 4 Johns. 84 (N.Y. 1809).

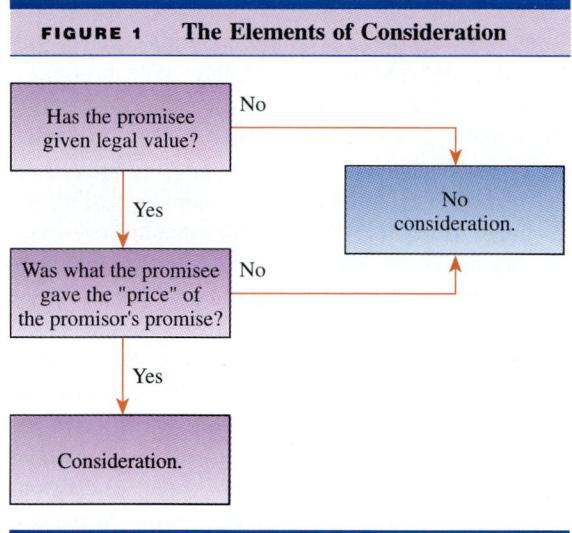

FIGURE 1   The Elements of Consideration

to do so, and when the ship was lost at sea, the court found that he was not liable to his co-owners for breaching his promise to insure the ship. Why? Because his promise was purely gratuitous; he had neither asked for nor received anything in exchange for making it. Therefore, it was unenforceable because it was not supported by consideration.

This early example illustrates two important aspects of the consideration requirement. First, the requirement *tended to limit the scope of a promisor's liability for his promises* by insulating him from liability for gratuitous promises and by protecting him against liability for reliance on such promises. Second, the mechanical application of the requirement *often produced unfair results*. This potential for unfairness has produced considerable dissatisfaction with the consideration concept. As the rest of this chapter indicates, the relative importance of consideration in modern contract law has been somewhat eroded by numerous exceptions to the consideration requirement and by judicial applications of consideration principles designed to produce fair results.

LEGAL VALUE

Consideration can be an act in the case of a unilateral contract or a promise in the case of a bilateral contract. An act or a promise can have legal value in one of two ways. If, in exchange for the promisor's promise, the promisee does, or agrees to

do, something he had no prior legal duty to do, that provides legal value. If, in exchange for the promisor's promise, the promisee refrains from doing, or agrees not to do, something she has a legal right to do, that also provides legal value. Note that this definition does not require that an act or a promise have monetary (economic) value to amount to consideration. Thus, in a famous 19th-century case, *Hamer v. Sidway*,[3] an uncle's promise to pay his nephew $5,000 if he refrained from using tobacco, drinking, swearing, and playing cards or billiards for money until his 21st birthday was held to be supported by consideration. Indeed, the nephew had refrained from doing any of these acts, even though he may have benefited from so refraining. He had a legal right to indulge in such activities, yet he had refrained from doing so at his uncle's request and in exchange for his uncle's promise. This was all that was required for consideration. *Lyon v. Reames Foods, Inc.*, which appears later in this chapter, elaborates on the different forms that legal value can take.

Adequacy of Consideration

The point that the legal value requirement is not concerned with actual value is further borne out by the fact that the courts generally will not concern themselves with questions regarding the adequacy of the consideration that the promisee gave. This means that as long as the promisee's act or promise satisfies the legal value test, the courts do not ask whether that act or promise was worth what the promisor gave, or promised to give, in return for it. This rule on adequacy of consideration reflects the laissez-faire assumptions underlying classical contract law. Freedom of contract includes the freedom to make bad bargains as well as good ones, so promisors' promises are enforceable if they got what they asked for in exchange for making their promises, even if what they asked for was not nearly so valuable in worldly terms as what they promised in return. Also, a court taking a hands-off stance concerning private contracts would be reluctant to step in and second-guess the parties by setting aside a transaction that both parties at one time considered satisfactory. Finally, the rule against considering the adequacy of consideration can promote certainty and predictability in commercial transactions by

[3]27 N.E. 256 (N.Y. Ct. App. 1891).

denying legal effect to what would otherwise be a possible basis for challenging the enforceability of a contract—the inequality of the exchange.

Several qualifications must be made concerning the general rule on adequacy of consideration. First, if the inadequacy of consideration is apparent on the face of the agreement, most courts conclude that the agreement was a disguised gift rather than an enforceable bargain. Thus, an agreement calling for an unequal exchange of money (e.g., $500 for $1,000) or identical goods (20 business law textbooks for 40 identical business law textbooks) and containing no other terms would probably be unenforceable. Gross inadequacy of consideration may also give rise to an inference of fraud, duress,[4] lack of capacity,[5] unconscionability,[6] or some other independent basis for setting aside a contract. However, inadequacy of consideration, standing alone, is never sufficient to prove lack of true consent or contractual capacity. Although gross inadequacy of consideration is not, by itself, ordinarily a sufficient reason to set aside a contract, the courts may refuse to grant specific performance or other equitable remedies to persons seeking to enforce unfair bargains.

Finally, some agreements recite "$1," or "$1 and other valuable consideration," or some other small amount as consideration for a promise. If no other consideration is actually exchanged, this is called *nominal consideration*. Often, such agreements are attempts to make gratuitous promises look like true bargains by reciting a nonexistent consideration. Most courts refuse to enforce such agreements unless they find that the stated consideration was truly bargained for.

Illusory Promises

For a promise to serve as consideration in a bilateral contract, the promisee must have promised to do, or to refrain from doing, something at the promisor's request. It seems obvious, therefore, that if the promisee's promise is illusory because it really does not bind the promisee to do or refrain from doing anything, such a promise could not serve as consideration. Such agreements are often said to lack the

mutuality of obligation required for an agreement to be enforceable. So, a promisee's promise to buy "all the sugar that I want" or to "paint your house if I feel like it" would not be sufficient consideration for a promisor's return promise to sell sugar or hire a painter. In neither case has the promisee given the promisor anything of legal value in exchange for the promisor's promise. Remember, though: So long as the promisee has given legal value, the agreement will be enforceable even though what the promisee gave is worth substantially less than what the promisor promised in return.

Cancellation or Termination Clauses   The fact that an agreement allows one or both of the parties to cancel or terminate their contractual obligations does not necessarily mean that the party (or parties) with the power to cancel has given an illusory promise. Such provisions are a common and necessary part of many business relationships. The central issue in such cases concerns whether a promise subject to cancellation or termination actually represents a binding obligation. A right to cancel or terminate at any time, for any reason, and without any notice would clearly render illusory any other promise by the party possessing such a right. However, limits on the circumstances under which cancellation may occur, such as a dealer's failure to live up to dealership obligations, or the time in which cancellation may occur (such as no cancellations for the first 90 days), or a requirement of advance notice of cancellation (such as a 30-day notice requirement) would all effectively remove a promise from the illusory category. This is so because in each case the party making such a promise has bound himself to do *something* in exchange for the other party's promise.

Of course, some parties to agreements may not want their agreements to amount to binding contracts. For example, a manufacturer selling through a system of independent retail dealers may want to retain maximum flexibility by giving itself a unilateral right to terminate a dealer at any time, for any reason, without notice. Such an "intentional no contract" strategy relies on the fact that the manufacturer's greater bargaining power may allow it to impose such terms on its dealers. This kind of business strategy is very difficult, if not impossible, to pursue today, however, given the numerous "dealer day in court" statutes that past abuses have

---

[4] Fraud and duress are discussed in Chapter 13.

[5] Lack of capacity is discussed in Chapter 14.

[6] Chapter 15 discusses unconscionability in detail.

produced and the fact that many courts have stricken down unilateral cancellation clauses as unconscionable. As you will see in the following *Lyon* case, a party's duty of good faith and fair dealing can limit the right to terminate and prevent its promise from being considered illusory.

LYON v. REAMES FOODS, INC.
1992 U.S. Dist. LEXIS 4184 (U.S. Dist. Ct. Kan. 1992)

William Reames, president and sole shareholder of Reames Foods, recruited and hired Donald Lyon to be a salesperson for the company. Before joining Reames Foods, Lyon had been employed by and was a part owner in the Certified Meat Company. Lyon claims that when Reames approached him about joining the company, he had been concerned about the possibility that Reames might decide to sell the company in the future. Lyon did not want to help build the company's sales over time and then be subject to termination by a new owner after the company was sold. Lyon claimed that he received from Reames and Reames Foods an oral agreement guaranteeing him employment for five years after a change in ownership of the company, but the existence of such an agreement was denied by Reames Foods. Lyon asserted that, in reliance on this oral contract, he sold his ownership interest in the Certified Meat Company, quit his old job, and joined Reames Foods in April 1976.

Lyon attempted to get the terms of the alleged oral contract with Reames Foods reduced to writing, but Reames continually put off his requests. Finally, at a meeting in November 1977, after several discussions between Reames and Lyon, Reames handed to Lyon a copy of a document entitled "Work Agreement." This document, which Lyon claims sets forth the terms of the earlier oral agreement, was typed on Reames Foods's letterhead, and was signed by Reames as president and agent of Reames Foods. The document provided in part that:

it is agreed that in event of the sale of the company . . . we of REAMES FOODS, INC. do guarantee and assure Donald F. Lyon of five (5) years continued employment at a minimum of his current salary effective at such time. . . . Donald Lyon agrees that he will, during such period of time, maintain all of his efforts in working for the company and will be employed by no other party during said period of time and said employment may be discontinued at any time if said Donald F. Lyon fails to perform his work in a manner satisfactory to the Board of Directors.

The document was signed by Reames, but was not signed by Lyon. Reames and Reames Foods claim that this document was merely one of many proposals and counterproposals considered by Lyon and Reames, and that it does not amount to an enforceable contract in itself.

Reames sold Reames Foods to the T. Marzetti Company in October 1989. In December 1989, Lyon was terminated. Lyon sued Reames and Reames Foods for breach of contract, among other claims. Lyon sought summary judgment asking the court to determine whether there was an enforceable contract and whether various defenses asserted by the defendants, including lack of consideration, could be maintained.

Lungstrom, District Judge   It is elementary that, as a general rule, in order for a promise to be legally enforceable as a contract there must be consideration. Consideration can be either a benefit given or to be given to the promisee, a forbearance experienced or to be experienced by the promisor, or mutual promises. Reames Foods contends that the agreement did not require Lyon to give anything of value to Reames Foods in consideration for his alleged employment guarantee. Yet, assuming that an agreement between the parties was reached, the written memorialization, signed by William Reames, requires that Lyon give up his right to work for another employer during the five years that his employment would be guaranteed. If the condition contained in the agreement occurred, i.e., if Reames Foods was sold, Lyon promised to work exclusively for that company in exchange for

Reames Foods's promise to assure Lyon of a job for five years. Lyon's promised forbearance would be consideration for Reames Foods's promised employment. In addition, however, Lyon gave up a job and an ownership interest in his former employer in order to join Reames Foods. Therefore, Reames Foods's contention that any alleged agreement was not supported by sufficient consideration is unfounded.

Reames Foods argues that, even if the alleged agreement was supported by consideration, it is unenforceable because it is illusory. According to Reames Foods, it could have terminated Lyon just before a sale of the company was finalized and thereby avoided all liability to him. If a promise is illusory it cannot be sufficient consideration to support a contract. Professor Farnsworth has recognized that promises which allow the promisor to terminate its rights and duties at any time will, without more, have been held to be illusory. He notes, however, that when the promisor retains the power to terminate, but only within a period of time after which it loses this power, the promise is not illusory "if the period expires without either party manifesting an intention not to be bound." E. Farnsworth, Contracts, section 2.14, at 81 (2d ed. 1990). This is exactly the case here. Although Reames Foods may have had the ability to terminate the alleged contract before ownership of the company was transferred, it failed to do so. After this triggering event came and passed without Reames Foods exercising its option to fire Lyon, it became bound to fulfill its obligations under the contract.

Moreover, it also appears that the promise was not illusory from its original making. Lyon argues that Reames Foods was not free to fire him at any time before the company was sold. The court agrees. Iowa law recognizes an implied obligation in all contracts requiring that the party for whom performance will be done will not obstruct, hinder, or delay the other party to the contract from completing his or her obligations under the contract. The current trend among courts is to read such obligations into allegedly illusory promises in order to make them enforceable. Contrary to its assertion, Reames Foods did not possess an unbridled right to terminate Lyon before a sale of the company in order to avoid liability to him. There were sufficient legal constraints on Reames Foods's ability to fire Lyon that this alleged agreement is not illusory.

Reames Foods contends that Lyon never signed [the written document] or otherwise manifested the intention to accept it. It is obvious that genuine issues of fact remain regarding whether the written document delivered to Lyon constitutes an enforceable contract. Resolution should be by the trier of fact, not by the court on a motion for summary judgment. If the trier of fact determines that the parties intended to enter into a contract and that sufficient assent was manifested, the agreement between the parties would be enforceable.

Summary judgment granted in part in favor of Lyon and denied in part.

Note: The case was tried several months later, and the court found in favor of Lyon, awarding him $234,144.82 in damages.

Output and Requirements Contracts   Contracts in which one party to the agreement agrees to buy all of the other party's production of a particular commodity (*output* contracts) or to supply all of another party's needs for a particular commodity (*requirements* contracts) are common business transactions that serve legitimate business purposes. They can reduce a seller's selling costs and provide buyers with a secure source of supply. Prior to the enactment of the UCC, however, many common law courts used to refuse to enforce such agreements on the ground that their failure to specify the quantity of goods to be produced or purchased rendered them illusory. The courts also feared that a party to such an agreement might be tempted to exploit the other party. For example, subsequent market conditions could make it profitable for the seller in an output contract or the buyer in a requirements contract to demand that the other party buy or provide more of the particular commodity than the other party had actually intended to buy or sell. The Code legitimizes requirements and output contracts. It addresses the concern about the potential for exploitation by limiting a party's demands to those quantity needs that occur in *good faith* and are not unreasonably disproportionate to any quantity estimate contained in the contract, or to any normal prior output or requirements if no estimate is stated [2–306(1)]. Chapter 19, Formation and Terms of Sales Contracts, discusses this subject in greater detail.

Exclusive Dealing Contracts

When a manufacturer of goods enters an agreement giving a distributor the exclusive right to sell the manufacturer's products in a particular territory, does such an agreement impose sufficient obligations on both parties to meet the legal value test? Put another way, does the distributor have any duty to sell the manufacturer's products and does the manufacturer have any duty to supply any particular number of products? Such agreements are commonly encountered in today's business world, and they can serve the legitimate interests of both parties. The Code recognizes this fact by providing that, unless the parties agree to the contrary, an exclusive dealing contract imposes a duty on the distributor to use her best efforts to sell the goods and imposes a reciprocal duty on the manufacturer to use his best efforts to supply the goods [2–306(2)].

Preexisting Duties

The legal value component of our consideration definition requires that promisees do, or promise to do, something in exchange for a promisor's promise that they had no prior legal duty to do. Thus, as a general rule, performing or agreeing to perform a preexisting duty is not consideration. This seems fair because the promisor in such a case has effectively made a gratuitous promise, since she was already entitled to the promisee's performance.

Preexisting Public Duties

Every member of society has a duty to obey the law and refrain from committing crimes or torts. Therefore, a promisee's promise not to commit such an act can never be consideration. So, Thomas's promise to pay Brown $100 a year in exchange for Brown's promise not to burn Thomas's barn would not be enforceable against Thomas. Since Brown has a preexisting duty not to burn Thomas's barn, his promise lacks legal value.

Similarly, public officials, by virtue of their offices, have a preexisting legal duty to perform their public responsibilities. For example, Smith, the owner of a liquor store, promises to pay Fawcett, a police officer whose beat includes Smith's store, $50 a week to keep an eye on the store while walking her beat. Smith's promise is unenforceable because Fawcett has agreed to do something that she already has a duty to do.

Preexisting Contractual Duties

The most important preexisting duty cases are those involving preexisting *contractual* duties. These cases generally occur when the parties to an existing contract agree to *modify* that contract. As the *Gross* case (which follows shortly) indicates, the general common law rule on contract modification holds that an agreement to modify an existing contract requires some *new consideration* to be binding.

For example, Turner enters into a contract with Acme Construction Company for the construction of a new office building for $350,000. When the construction is partially completed, Acme tells Turner that due to rising labor and materials costs it will stop construction unless Turner agrees to pay an extra $50,000. Turner, having already entered into contracts to lease office space in the new building, promises to pay the extra amount. When the construction is finished, Turner refuses to pay more than $350,000. Is Turner's promise to pay the extra $50,000 enforceable against him? No. All Acme has done in exchange for Turner's promise to pay more is build the building, something that Acme had a preexisting contractual duty to do. Therefore, Acme's performance is not consideration for Turner's promise to pay more.

Although the result in the preceding example seems fair (why should Turner have to pay $400,000 for something he had a right to receive for $350,000?) and is consistent with consideration theory, the application of the preexisting duty rule to contract modifications has generated a great deal of criticism. Plainly, the rule can protect a party to a contract such as Turner from being pressured into paying more because the other party to the contract is trying to take advantage of his situation by demanding an additional amount for performance. However, mechanical application of the rule could also produce unfair results when the parties have freely agreed to a fair modification of their contract. Some critics argue that the purpose of contract modification law should be to enforce freely made modifications of existing contracts and to deny enforcement to coerced modifications. Such critics commonly suggest that general principles such as good faith and unconscionability, rather than technical consideration rules, should be used to police contract modifications.

Other observers argue that most courts in fact apply the preexisting duty rule in a manner calculated to reach fair results, because several exceptions to the rule can be used to enforce a fair modification agreement. For example, any new consideration furnished by the promisee provides sufficient consideration to support a promise to modify an existing contract. So, if Acme had promised to finish construction a week before the completion date called for in the original contract, or had promised to make some change in the original contract specifications such as to install a better grade of carpet, Acme would have done something that it had no legal duty to do in exchange for Turner's new promise. Turner's promise to pay more would then be enforceable because it would be supported by new consideration.

Many courts also enforce an agreement to modify an existing contract if the modification resulted from *unforeseen circumstances* that a party could not reasonably be expected to have foreseen, and which made that party's performance far more difficult than the parties originally anticipated. For example, if Acme had requested the extra payment because abnormal subsurface rock formations made excavation on the construction site far more costly and time-consuming than could have been reasonably expected, many courts would enforce Turner's promise to pay more.

Courts can also enforce fair modification agreements by holding that the parties mutually agreed to terminate their original contract and then entered a new one. Because contracts are created by the will of the parties, they can be terminated in the same fashion. Each party agrees to release the other party from his contractual obligations in exchange for the other party's promise to do the same. Because such a mutual agreement terminates all duties owed under the original agreement, any subsequent agreement by the parties would not be subject to the preexisting duty rule. A court is likely to take this approach, however, only when it is convinced that the modification agreement was fair and free from coercion.

GROSS v. DIEHL SPECIALTIES INTERNATIONAL
776 S.W.2d 879 (Mo. Ct. App. 1989)

In 1977, Dairy Specialties, Inc. (Dairy), hired George Gross to develop nondairy products for customers allergic to milk and to serve as general manager. The employment contract was for a term of 15 years and provided for annual wages of $14,400 plus cost-of-living increases. It also provided that when 10 percent of Dairy's gross profits exceeded Gross's annual salary, he would receive the difference between the two figures. In addition, Gross would receive a royalty of 1 percent of the selling price of all products Dairy produced using one or more of Gross's inventions or formulae. This royalty increased to 2 percent after the expiration of the agreement, at which time ownership of the inventions and formulae (which were jointly held during the term of the agreement) would revert to Gross.

In 1982, Dairy was bought from its original owner by the Diehl family. The Diehls insisted on renegotiation of Gross's contract with Dairy as a condition of the purchase. Although he was not a party to the sale and received nothing tangible from it, Gross agreed to a new contract that had the same expiration date as the first one but that eliminated his cost-of-living increases, gave Dairy exclusive ownership of his inventions and formulae during and after the term of the agreement, and eliminated his right to royalties after the agreement expired. After the sale, Gross was given additional duties but no additional compensation. In 1984, after a business downturn, Gross was fired. He filed suit, arguing that his termination benefits should be calculated under his original contract. When the trial court ruled in the company's favor, he appealed.

Smith, Presiding Judge A modification of a contract constitutes the making of a new contract and such new contract must be supported by consideration. Where a contract has not been fully performed at the time of the new agreement, the substitution of a new provision, resulting in a modification of the obligation of both sides, for a provision in the old contract still unperformed is sufficient consideration for the new contract. A promise to carry out an existing contractual duty does not constitute consideration.

Under the 1982 agreement the company undertook no greater obligations than it already had. Gross on the other hand received less than he had under the original contract. His base pay was reduced back to its 1977 amount despite the provision in the 1977 contract calling for cost of living adjustments. He lost his equal ownership in his formulae during the term of the agreement and his exclusive ownership after the termination of the agreement. He lost all royalties after termination of the agreement. In exchange for nothing, the company acquired exclusive ownership of the formulae during and after the agreement, eliminated royalties after the agreement terminated, and achieved a reduction in Gross's base salary. The company did no more than promise to carry out an already existing contractual duty. There was no consideration for the 1982 agreement.

Judgment reversed in favor of Gross; case remanded for recalculation of damages.

Code Contract Modification The drafters of the Code sought to avoid many of the problems caused by the consideration requirement by dispensing with it in two important situations: As discussed in the Offer chapter, the Code does not require consideration for firm offers [2–205]. The Code also provides that an agreement to modify a contract for the sale of goods needs *no consideration* to be binding [2–209(1)]. For example, Electronics World orders 200 XYZ televisions at $150 per unit from XYZ Corp. Electronics World later seeks to cancel its order, but XYZ refuses to agree to cancellation. Instead, XYZ seeks to mollify a valued customer by offering to reduce the price to $100 per unit. Electronics World agrees, but when the televisions arrive, XYZ bills Electronics World for $150 per unit. Under classical contract principles, XYZ's promise to reduce the price of the goods would not be enforceable because Electronics World has furnished no new consideration in exchange for XYZ's promise. Under the Code, no new consideration is necessary and the agreement to modify the contract is enforceable.

Several things should be made clear about the operation of this Code rule. First, XYZ had no duty to agree to a modification and could have insisted on payment of $150 per unit. Second, as the following *Roth Steel Products* case illustrates, modification agreements under the Code are still subject to scrutiny under the general Code principles of good faith and unconscionability, so unfair agreements or agreements that are the product of coercion are unlikely to be enforced. Finally, the Code contains two provisions to protect people from fictitious claims that an agreement has been modified. If the original agreement requires any modification to be in writing, an oral modification is unenforceable [2–209(2)]. Regardless of what the original agreement says, if the price of the goods in the modified contract is $500 or more, the modification is unenforceable unless the requirements of the Code's statute of frauds section [2–201] are satisfied [2–209(3)].[7]

---

[7]Chapter 16 discusses § 2–201 of the Code in detail.

ROTH STEEL PRODUCTS v. SHARON STEEL CORPORATION
705 F.2d 134 (6th Cir. 1983)

In November 1972, when conditions in the steel industry were highly competitive and the industry was operating at about 70 percent of its capacity, Sharon Steel Corporation agreed to sell Roth Steel Products several types of steel at prices well below Sharon's published book prices for such steel. These prices were to be effective from January 1 until December 31, 1973.

In early 1973, however, several factors changed the market for steel. Federal price controls simultaneously discouraged foreign steel imports and encouraged domestic steel producers to export a substantial portion of their production to avoid domestic price controls, sharply reducing the domestic steel supply. In addition, the steel industry experienced substantial increases in labor, raw material, and energy costs, compelling steel producers to increase prices. The increased domestic demand for steel and the attractive export market caused the entire industry to operate at full capacity; as a consequence, nearly every domestic steel producer experienced substantial delays in delivery.

On March 23, 1973, Sharon notified Roth that it was discontinuing all price discounts. Roth protested, and Sharon agreed to continue to sell at the discount price until June 30, 1973, but refused to sell thereafter unless Roth agreed to pay a modified price that was higher than that agreed to the previous November but still lower than the book prices Sharon was charging other customers. Because Roth was unable to purchase enough steel elsewhere to meet its production requirements, it agreed to pay the increased prices. When a subsequent dispute arose between the parties over late deliveries and unfilled orders by Sharon in 1974, Roth filed a breach of contract suit against Sharon, arguing, among other things, that the 1973 modification agreement was unenforceable. When the trial court ruled in favor of Roth, Sharon appealed.

Celebrezze, Senior Circuit Judge   The ability of a party to modify a contract which is subject to Article Two of the UCC is broader than common law, primarily because the modification needs no consideration to be binding. [UCC Sec. 2–209(1)]. A party's ability to modify an agreement is limited only by Article Two's general obligation of good faith. In determining whether a particular modification was obtained in good faith, a court must make two distinct inquiries: whether the party's conduct is consistent with "reasonable commercial standards of fair dealing in the trade," and whether the parties were in fact motivated to seek modification by an honest desire to compensate for commercial exigencies.

The first inquiry is relatively straightforward; the party asserting the modification must demonstrate that his decision to seek modification was the result of a factor, such as increased costs, which would cause an ordinary merchant to seek a modification of the contract. The second inquiry, regarding the subjective honesty of the parties, is less clearly defined. Essentially, this requires the party asserting the modification to demonstrate that he was, in fact, motivated by a legitimate commercial reason and that such a reason is not offered merely as a pretext. Moreover, the trier of fact must determine whether the means used to obtain the modification are an impermissible attempt to obtain a modification by extortion or overreaching.

The single most important consideration in determining whether the decision to seek a modification is justified is whether, because of changes in the market or other unforeseeable conditions, performance of the contract has come to involve a loss. In this case, the district court found that Sharon suffered substantial losses by performing the contract as modified. We are convinced that unforeseen economic exigencies existed which would prompt an ordinary merchant to seek a modification to avoid a loss on the contract.

The second part of the analysis, honesty in fact, is pivotal. The district court found that Sharon "threatened not to sell Roth any steel if Roth refused to pay increased prices after July 1, 1973" and, consequently, that Sharon acted wrongfully. We believe that the district court's conclusion that

Sharon acted in bad faith by using coercive conduct to extract the price modification is not clearly erroneous. Therefore, we hold that Sharon's attempt to modify the November 1972 contract, in order to compensate for increased costs which made performance come to involve a loss, is ineffective because

Sharon did not act in a manner consistent with Article Two's requirement of honesty in fact when it refused to perform its remaining obligations under the contract at 1972 prices.

Judgment affirmed in favor of Roth.

Debt Settlement Agreements

One special variant of the preexisting duty rule that causes considerable confusion occurs when a debtor offers to pay a creditor a sum less than the creditor is demanding in exchange for the creditor's promise to accept the part payment as full payment of the debt. If the creditor later sues for the balance of the debt, is the creditor's promise to take less enforceable? The answer depends on the nature of the debt and on the circumstances of the debtor's payment.

Liquidated Debts   A **liquidated debt** is a debt that is both due and certain; that is, the parties have no good faith dispute about either the existence or the amount of the original debt. If a debtor does nothing more than pay less than an amount he clearly owes, how could this be consideration for a creditor's promise to take less? Such a debtor has actually done less than he had a preexisting legal duty to do—namely, to pay the full amount of the debt. For this reason, the creditor's promise to discharge a liquidated debt for part payment of the debt at or after its due date is *unenforceable* for lack of consideration.

For example, Connor borrows $10,000 from Friendly Finance Company, payable in one year. On the day payment is due, Connor sends Friendly a check for $9,000 marked: "Payment in full for all claims Friendly Finance has against me." Friendly cashes Connor's check, thus impliedly promising to accept it as full payment by cashing it, and later sues Connor for $1,000. Friendly is entitled to the $1,000 because Connor has given no consideration to support Friendly's implied promise to accept $9,000 as full payment.

However, had Connor done something he had no preexisting duty to do in exchange for Friendly's promise to settle for part payment, he could enforce Friendly's promise and avoid paying the $1,000. For

example, if Connor had paid early, before the loan contract called for payment, or in a different medium of exchange than that called for in the loan contract (such as $4,000 in cash and a car worth $5,000), he would have given consideration for Friendly's promise to accept early or different payment as full payment.

Unliquidated Debts   A good faith dispute about either the existence or the amount of a debt makes the debt an **unliquidated debt**. The settlement of an unliquidated debt is called an **accord and satisfaction**.[8] When an accord and satisfaction has occurred, the creditor cannot maintain an action to recover the remainder of the debt that he alleges is due. For example, Computer Corner, a retailer, orders 50 personal computers and associated software packages from Computech for $75,000. After receiving the goods, Computer Corner refuses to pay Computech the full $75,000, arguing that some of the computers were defective and that some of the software it received did not conform to its order. Computer Corner sends Computech a check for $60,000 marked: "Payment in full for all goods received from Computech." A creditor in Computech's position obviously faces a real dilemma. If Computech cashes Computer Corner's check, it will be held to have impliedly promised to accept $60,000 as full payment. Computech's promise to accept part payment as full payment would be enforceable because Computer Corner has given consideration to support it: Computer Corner has given up its right to have a court determine the amount it owes Computech. This is something that Computer Corner had no duty to do; by giving up this right and the $60,000 in exchange for Computech's implied promise, the consideration require-

---

[8]Accord and satisfaction is also discussed in Chapter 18.

ment is satisfied. The result in this case is supported not only by consideration theory but also by a strong public policy in favor of encouraging parties to settle their disputes out of court. Who would bother to settle disputed claims out of court if settlement agreements were unenforceable?

Computech could refuse to accept Computer Corner's settlement offer and sue for the full $75,000, but doing so involves several risks. A court may decide that Computer Corner's arguments are valid and award Computech less than $60,000. Even if Computech is successful, it may take years to resolve the case in the courts through the expensive and time-consuming litigation process. In addition, there is always the chance that Computer Corner may file for bankruptcy before any judgment can be collected. Faced with such risks, Computech may feel that it has no practical alternative other than to cash Computer Corner's check.[9]

UCC Section 1–207 and Accord and Satisfaction

In some states, a creditor such as Computech has a third, and much more desirable, alternative course of action to either returning the debtor's full-payment check or cashing it and entering an accord and satisfaction. The original version of section 1–207 of the UCC states that:

A party who with explicit reservation of rights assents to performance in a manner offered by the other party does not thereby prejudice the rights reserved. Such words as "without prejudice," "under protest" or the like are sufficient.

Some state courts have interpreted this language to mean that the Code has changed the common law accord and satisfaction rule by allowing a creditor to accept a full-payment check "under protest" or "without prejudice" without giving up any rights to sue for the balance due under the contract. However, the majority of courts that have considered the issue have held that 1–207 does *not* supersede accord and satisfaction rules. In addition, a recent

revision of 1–207 that has been enacted in a growing number of states specifically provides that 1–207 does not apply to accord and satisfaction.

Composition Agreements   Composition agreements are agreements between a debtor and two or more creditors who agree to accept as full payment a stated percentage of their liquidated claims against the debtor at or after the date on which those claims are payable. Composition agreements are generally enforced by the courts despite the fact that enforcement appears to be contrary to the general rule on part payment of liquidated debts. Many courts have justified enforcing composition agreements on the ground that the creditors' mutual agreement to accept less than the amount due them provides the necessary consideration. The main reason why creditors agree to compositions is that they fear that their failure to do so may force the debtor into bankruptcy proceedings, in which case they might ultimately recover a smaller percentage of their claims than that agreed to in the composition.

Forbearance to Sue

An agreement by a promisee to refrain, or forbear, from pursuing a legal claim against a promisor can be valid consideration to support a return promise—usually to pay a sum of money—by a promisor. The promisee has agreed not to file suit, something that she has a legal right to do, in exchange for the promisor's promise. The courts do not wish to sanction extortion by allowing people to threaten to file spurious claims against others in the hope that those threatened will agree to some payment to avoid the expense or embarrassment associated with defending a lawsuit. On the other hand, we have a strong public policy favoring private settlement of disputes. Therefore, it is generally said that the promisee must have a good faith belief in the validity of his or her claim before forbearance amounts to consideration.

Bargained–For Exchange

Up to this point, we have focused on the legal value component of our consideration definition. But the fact that a promisee's act or promise provides legal value is not, in itself, a sufficient basis for finding that it amounted to consideration. In addition, the promisee's act or promise must have been bargained

---

[9]A new provision of Article 3 of the Uniform Commercial Code, section 3–311, covers accord and satisfaction by use of an instrument such as a "full payment" check. With a few exceptions, the basic provisions of section 3–311 parallel the common law rules regarding accord and satisfaction that are described in this chapter and Chapter 18.

for and given in exchange for the promisor's promise. In effect, it must be the price that the promisor asked for in exchange for making his promise. Over a hundred years ago, Oliver Wendell Holmes, one of our most renowned jurists, expressed this idea when he said, "It is the essence of a consideration that, by the terms of the agreement, it is given and accepted as the motive or inducement of the promise."[10]

Past Consideration

Past consideration—despite its name—is not consideration at all. Past consideration is an act or other benefit given in the past that was *not* given in exchange for the promise in question. Because the past act was not given in exchange for the present promise, it cannot be consideration. Consider again the facts of the famous case of *Hamer v. Sidway*, discussed earlier in this chapter. There, an uncle's promise to pay his nephew $5,000 for refraining from smoking, drinking, swearing, and other delightful pastimes until his 21st birthday was supported by consideration because the nephew had given legal value by refraining from participating in the prohibited activities. However, what if the uncle

---

[10]O. W. Holmes, *The Common Law*, p. 239 (1881).

had said to his nephew on the eve of his 21st birthday: "Your mother tells me you've been a good lad and abstained from tobacco, hard drink, foul language, and gambling. Such goodness should be rewarded. Tomorrow, I'll give you a check for $5,000." Should the uncle's promise be enforceable against him? Clearly not, because although his nephew's behavior still passes the legal value test, in this case it was not bargained for and given in exchange for the uncle's promise.

Moral Obligation

As a general rule, promises made to satisfy a preexisting moral obligation are unenforceable for lack of consideration. The fact that a promisor or some member of the promisor's family, for example, has received some benefit from the promisee in the past (e.g., food and lodging, or emergency care) would not constitute consideration for a promisor's promise to pay for that benefit, due to the absence of the bargain element. Some courts find this result distressing and enforce such promises despite the absence of consideration. In addition, a few states have passed statutes making promises to pay for past benefits enforceable if such a promise is contained in a writing that clearly expresses the promisor's intent to be bound.

CONCEPT REVIEW

CONSIDERATION

Consideration*	Not Consideration
Doing something you had no preexisting duty to do	Doing something you had a preexisting duty to do
Promising to do something you had no preexisting duty to do	Promising to do something you had a preexisting duty to do
Paying part of a liquidated debt prior to the date the debt is due	Nominal consideration (unless actually bargained for)
Paying a liquidated debt in a different medium of exchange than originally agreed to	Paying part of a liquidated debt at or after the date the debt is due
Agreeing to settle an unliquidated debt	Making an illusory promise
Agreeing not to file suit when you have a good faith belief in your claim's validity	Past consideration
	Preexisting moral obligation

*Assuming bargained for.

EXCEPTIONS TO THE CONSIDERATION REQUIREMENT

The consideration requirement is a classic example of a traditional contract law rule. It is precise, abstract, and capable of almost mechanical application. It can also, in some instances, result in significant injustice. Modern courts and legislatures have responded to this potential for injustice by carving out numerous exceptions to the requirement of consideration. Some of these exceptions (for example, the Code firm offer and contract modification rules) have already been discussed in this and preceding chapters. In the remaining portion of this chapter, we focus on several other important exceptions to the consideration requirement.

Promissory Estoppel

As discussed in Chapter 9, Introduction to Contracts, the doctrine of promissory estoppel first emerged from attempts by courts around the turn of this century to reach just results in donative (gift) promise cases. Classical contract consideration principles did not recognize a promisee's reliance on a donative promise as a sufficient basis for enforcing the promise against the promisor. Instead, donative promises were unenforceable because they were not supported by consideration. In fact, the essence of a donative promise is that it does not seek or require any bargained-for exchange. Yet people continued to act in reliance on donative promises, often to their considerable disadvantage.

Refer to the facts of *Thorne v. Deas*, discussed earlier in this chapter. The co-owners of the *Sea Nymph* clearly relied to their injury on their fellow co-owner's promise to get insurance for the ship. Some courts in the early years of this century began to protect such relying promisees by *estopping* promisors from raising the defense that their promises were not supported by consideration. In a wide variety of cases involving gratuitous agency promises (as in *Thorne v. Deas*), promises of bonuses or pensions made to employees, and promises of gifts of land, courts began to use a promisee's detrimental (harmful) reliance on a donative promise as, in effect, a *substitute for* consideration.

In 1932, the first *Restatement of Contracts* legitimized these cases by expressly recognizing promissory estoppel in section 90. The elements of promissory estoppel were then essentially the same as they are today: a *promise* that the promisor should reasonably expect to induce reliance, *reliance* on the promise by the promisee, and *injustice* to the promisee as a result of that reliance. As the following *Niehaus* case illustrates, promissory estoppel is now widely used as a consideration substitute, not only in donative promise cases but also in cases involving commercial promises contemplating a bargained-for exchange. The construction contract bid cases discussed in Chapter 10 are another example of this expansion of promissory estoppel's reach. In fact, although promissory estoppel has expanded far beyond its initial role as a consideration substitute into other areas of contract law, it is probably fair to say that it is still most widely accepted in the consideration context.

NIEHAUS V. DELAWARE VALLEY MEDICAL CENTER
631 A.2d 1314 (Super. Ct. Pa. 1993)

Patricia Niehaus was an employee of Delaware Valley Medical Center. The medical center distributed an employee handbook that stated that if an employee were granted an approved leave of absence, that employee, at the end of the leave, would be guaranteed the same position or one similar to the position occupied prior to the leave of absence. The handbook also stated, however, that the provisions in the handbook were not to be interpreted as a contract of employment and that either party could terminate the employment relationship at any time. Niehaus made a written request for a nine months' leave, and her request was approved. At the end of her leave, however, Delaware Valley refused to rehire Niehaus for any position. Niehaus sued the medical center for breach of contract and promissory estoppel, and the trial court dismissed her complaint. Niehaus appealed.

Wieand, Judge   The presumption under Pennsylvania law is that all employment is at will and, therefore, an employee may be discharged for any reason or no reason. The medical center contends in this case that because Niehaus was an employee at will, she could be terminated for any reason or no reason, and that it would be absurd to require a rehiring of Niehaus when she could thereafter be discharged immediately. In any event, suggests the employer, there was no consideration for an agreement to rehire Niehaus following an approved leave of absence. It is argued, therefore, that the provision in the handbook is unenforceable.

In the instant case, whether or not there was consideration, the employer's promise is enforceable under principles of promissory estoppel. "A promise which the promisor should expect to induce action or forbearance on the part of the promisee or a third person and which does induce such action or forbearance is binding if injustice can be avoided only by enforcement of the promise." *Restatement (Second) of Contracts* section 90(1). Where an employer expects, if not demands, that its employees abide by a policy expressed with particularity in an employee handbook, an employee may justifiably rely thereon and expect justifiably that the employer will do the same.

Here, the medical center, by its handbook, had guaranteed its employees that if a leave of absence were requested and approved by the employer, then the employee could return at the end of the leave of absence and would be restored to the same or similar position as that occupied by the employee prior to the leave of absence. Under this policy, the employer had a right to expect a stable work force, where employees would take leave of absence only with the employer's consent and approval. An employee who was granted an approved leave of absence, however, could also rely upon the employer's promise that the employee would be rehired. The employer's promise was not illusory. When the employee was induced in fact to seek and obtain an approved leave of absence without pay on the assurance that she could return to the same or similar employment at the expiration of her leave, enforcement of the promise was essential to avoid injustice.

The medical center argues, however, that a cause of action for breach of contract of employment cannot be based on the provisions of the handbook where other language disclaims an intent to form a contract. In this case, Niehaus was initially employed at will. When the employee requested a leave of absence without pay, the employer could have refused to approve it or, indeed, could have revoked its promise of renewed employment at the end of the leave of absence. This it did not do. Instead, it approved the leave of absence in accordance with its handbook promise. It is this approval which thereupon gave rise to an implied contract and not the mere language in the handbook.

We conclude that the trial court erred when it summarily dismissed Niehaus's amended complaint. The complaint is sufficient to allege a cause of action for breach of a contract to rehire.

Reversed in favor of Niehaus and remanded for further proceedings.

Debts Barred by Statutes of Limitations

Statutes of limitations set an express statutory time limit on a person's ability to pursue any legal claim. A creditor who fails to file suit to collect a debt within the time prescribed by the appropriate statute of limitations loses the right to collect it. Many states, however, enforce a new promise by a debtor to pay such a debt, even though technically such promises are not supported by consideration because the creditor has given nothing in exchange for the new promise. Most states afford debtors some protection in such cases, however, by requiring that the new promise be in writing to be enforceable.

Debts Barred by Bankruptcy Discharge

Once a bankrupt debtor is granted a discharge,[11] creditors no longer have the legal right to collect discharged debts. Most states enforce a new promise by the debtor to pay (reaffirm) the debt regardless of whether the creditor has given any consideration to support it. To reduce creditor attempts to pressure debtors to reaffirm, the Bankruptcy Reform Act of 1978 made it much more difficult for debtors to reaffirm debts discharged in bankruptcy proceedings.

---

[11]Chapter 29 discusses bankruptcy in detail.

The act requires that a reaffirmation promise be made prior to the date of the discharge and gives the debtor the right to revoke his promise within 30 days after it becomes enforceable. This act also requires the Bankruptcy Court to counsel individual (as opposed to corporate) debtors about the legal effects of reaffirmation and requires Bankruptcy Court approval of reaffirmations by individual debtors. In addition, a few states require reaffirmation promises to be in writing to be enforceable.

Charitable Subscriptions

Promises to make gifts for charitable or educational purposes are often enforced, despite the absence of consideration, when the institution or organization to which the promise was made has acted in reliance on the promised gift. This result is usually justified on the basis of either promissory estoppel or public policy.

ETHICAL AND PUBLIC POLICY CONCERNS

1. In this chapter, you learned the general rule that the law does not enforce promises that are not supported by consideration. Are there ethical arguments that one could make to support the proposition that people should generally honor their promises to others regardless of whether they are legally required to do so? What might those arguments be? Do any of them help to explain the doctrine of promissory estoppel as an exception to the consideration requirement?

2. Discuss the public policy behind the rule that courts will not inquire into the adequacy of consideration. What social benefits are purchased by such a rule and at what price?

3. Discuss the ethical dimensions of offers by debtors to satisfy a liquidated debt by part payment before the due date. Are such offers ever ethical? What factors would be relevant in determining whether such an offer was ethical?

PROBLEMS AND PROBLEM CASES

1. Grouse, a recently graduated pharmacist who was working as a retail pharmacist for Richter Drug, applied for a job with Group Health Plan, Inc.

Grouse was interviewed at Group Health by Elliott, chief pharmacist, and Shoberg, general manager. On December 4, 1975, Elliott telephoned Grouse at work and offered him a job as a pharmacist at Group Health's St. Louis Park Clinic. Grouse accepted, informing Elliott that he would give Richter two weeks' notice. That afternoon, Grouse received an offer from a Veterans Administration Hospital in Virginia, which he declined because of Group Health's offer. Elliott called back to confirm that Grouse had resigned. Sometime in the next few days, Elliott mentioned to Shoberg that he had hired, or was thinking of hiring, Grouse. Shoberg told him that company hiring requirements included a favorable written reference, a background check, and approval of the general manager. Elliott contacted two faculty members at the University of Minnesota School of Pharmacy, who declined to give references. He also contacted an internship employer and several pharmacies where Grouse had done relief work. Their responses were that they had not had enough exposure to Grouse's work to form a judgment about his capabilities. Because Elliott was unable to supply a favorable reference for Grouse, Shoberg hired another person to fill the position. On December 15, 1975, Grouse called Group Health and reported that he was free to begin work. Elliott informed Grouse that someone else had been hired. Grouse had difficulty regaining full-time employment and suffered wage loss as a result. Does he have any recourse against Group Health?

2. Omni Group, Inc., signed an earnest money agreement offering Mr. and Mrs. John Clark $2,000 per acre for a piece of property the Clarks owned, which was thought to contain about 59 acres. The agreement provided that Omni's obligation was subject to receipt of a satisfactory engineer's and architect's feasibility report assessing the property's development potential. The Clarks signed the earnest money agreement, but later refused to proceed with the sale. When Omni filed suit for breach of contract, the Clarks argued that their promise to sell was unenforceable because Omni's promise to buy was illusory due to the fact that it was conditioned on a satisfactory feasibility report. Was Omni's promise illusory?

3. When Nancy and Gerald Harrington were divorced in 1981, they executed a property settlement agreement giving him ownership of their farm.

In return, he agreed to pay her $150,000; a $10,000 down payment and 15 annual payments. He gave her two mortgages on the farm to secure the debt. Gerald paid Nancy the initial $10,000, but was able to pay her only $3,000 in subsequent payments due to financial difficulties. Late in 1981, Gerald asked Nancy to execute satisfactions of the two mortgages so he could obtain refinancing of previous bank loans, which lenders were unwilling to provide as long as the farm was encumbered by the mortgages she held. At that time Nancy and Gerald's son, Ronn, was farming the land with Gerald. Nancy was afraid that Ronn would not inherit the farm because Gerald had remarried and his wife had become pregnant. In exchange for Gerald's promise to will the farm to Ronn, Nancy promised to execute satisfactions of the mortgages and to release Gerald from liability on his debt to her under their original agreement. Gerald subsequently made a will leaving his land to Ronn, but Nancy did not execute satisfactions of the mortgages. Instead, in 1983, she filed a foreclosure suit against Gerald. She asserted that her promise to execute satisfactions of the mortgages was unenforceable for lack of consideration. Is she correct?

4. In November 1981, C. F. Wooding Co. (Wooding) ordered a number of metal doors and door frames from County Fire Door Corporation (County) for a construction project Wooding was working on. After County was allegedly late in delivering the goods to the work site, Wooding told County that it would only pay $416.88 of the $2,618.88 that County claimed was the balance due because the delays in delivery caused Wooding additional installation expenses. County denied the validity of Wooding's claim and insisted that the full amount was due. Wooding then sent County a check for $416.88. On its face was a notation stating that it was final payment for the project, and on its reverse side the check stated: "By its endorsement, the payee accepts this check in full satisfaction of all claims against the C. F. Wooding Co. arising out of or relating to Purchase Order #3302, dated 11/17/81." County cashed the check, but only after crossing out the conditional language on the reverse side and adding the following language: "This check is accepted under protest and with full reservation of rights to collect the unpaid balance for which this check is offered in settlement." County filed suit against Wooding for the unpaid balance. In a state

that follows the majority view about the effect of UCC section 1–207 on the common law doctrine of accord and satisfaction, can County prevail?

5. Roland and Leslie lived together for four years and had a child together. In June 1983, Roland filed suit to evict Leslie from his house in Duxbury, Massachusetts, and to obtain custody of their child. Leslie then filed a breach of contract action against Roland arguing that she had a right to a share of the property. In September 1983, Leslie and Roland agreed to settle both actions. She and his child were to return to live with him and he was to support them. Roland also promised to pay her legal fees from both actions. Roland and Leslie later separated again, and he refused to pay her legal fees, arguing that his promise was not supported by consideration because Massachusetts does not recognize "palimony" actions by unmarried cohabitants. Is Roland right?

6. Marna Balin, who had suffered two automobile accidents in 1972, hired Norman Kallen, an attorney, to represent her. Kallen did not do much work on the cases and urged Balin to settle for $25,000. She became dissatisfied with his representation, and in 1974 she asked Samuel Delug, another attorney, to take over the cases and get her files from Kallen. Delug wrote and called Kallen several times, but Kallen refused to forward the files or sign a Substitution of Attorney form (things he was obligated to do by the California rules of professional conduct) because he was afraid Balin would not pay him for the work he had done. Only when Delug promised to give him 40 percent of his attorney's fee did Kallen forward the files and sign the form. Delug negotiated a settlement of $810,000, and the attorney's fees amounted to $324,000. When he refused to pay Kallen 40 percent, Kallen filed suit. Is Delug's promise enforceable?

7. The Larabees owned a farm in Dearborn County, Indiana, subject to a life estate held by Mrs. Larabee's mother. In the autumn 1971, the Larabees gave their friends, the Booths, permission to build a summer cottage on the farm. Construction began in the spring of 1972. Shortly thereafter, the Booths asked if they could build a permanent home there, and Mrs. Larabee agreed. In September 1972, she and her husband signed an agreement promising to convey a piece of the farm to the Booths on the expiration of Mrs. Larabee's mother's life estate.

The agreement specifically provided that the land was to be conveyed for "no consideration." When the house was completed and Mrs. Larabee's mother had died, however, the Larabees refused to convey the land as promised. Is their promise to convey enforceable?

8. Passander was executive vice president of Spickelmier Industries. Because Spickelmier was facing financial difficulties, a committee of creditors had been formed to oversee its operations. In November 1971, the committee projected a small profit for the year and recommended that bonuses be given to certain key employees if the profit materialized. This recommendation was adopted by Spickelmier's board of directors in late December, and Passander was promised a $1,500 bonus. In January 1972, however, the board's executive committee discovered that the earlier profit estimates had been overly optimistic and that insufficient funds were available to pay the bonuses. Instead of taking the board's recommendation that the bonuses not be paid, the chairman of the board negotiated a compromise whereby one half of the originally specified bonus would be paid as planned, with the balance to be paid when funds were available. Passander accepted the half bonus, and later in the month his contract with Spickelmier was renegotiated to provide for a 25 percent salary increase and guaranteed quarterly bonuses of $500. In June 1972, Passander quit his job, later filing suit against Spickelmier for the remaining half of his 1971 bonus. Can he recover it?

9. Kaufmann was employed by Fiduciary Management, Inc. (FMI). In September 1988, Lanier, president and sole shareholder of FMI, signed and gave a letter to Kaufmann, which stated in part:

If your employment is terminated without cause before July 1, 1990, Fiduciary Management, Inc. agrees that within one month of the date on which your full salary ceases to be paid you will receive an additional payment of $150,000.

The context of this letter was that several projects serviced by FMI were experiencing financial difficulties and Lanier's sons advised him that Kaufmann was distracted, that he may have been considering leaving FMI, and that he needed to focus on his work. The letter was intended to help him focus on his work, presumably by giving him a sense of job security. After receiving the letter, Kaufmann undertook a secret and systematic search for another job. In January 1990, Kaufmann's employment with FMI ceased. He was not paid the $150,000 that had been promised in the letter, and he sued Lanier and FMI to recover the money. Was Lanier's promise to pay $150,000 enforceable?

10. 🎞️   *Video Case.* See "California Dreaming." Jensen offered Judy, a resident of Chicago, a position in a company in Los Angeles. Jensen gave Judy an employee handbook, extolled the low turnover of his firm's work force, and told her that there was a "no-cut policy." Jensen told Judy that if she decided to relocate within a year, the job was hers. After deciding to accept the job, Judy called Jensen and informed him. She also told him that she did not know how long it would take to sell her house in Chicago, but Jensen told her to give him a call as soon as she arrived in Los Angeles and said, "We're really looking forward to having you on board." Six months later, Judy and her husband quit their jobs, sold their house in Chicago, and moved to Los Angeles. When Judy called Jensen, however, he said that the position they had discussed was not available and the company had no openings. Was the company's promise to hire Judy enforceable?

11. 🎞️   *Video Case.* See "A Christmas Story." Tinker Construction had a contract with Scroge to build a factory addition for Scroge by a particular date. The contract contained a penalty clause exacting daily penalties for late performance, and Tinker was working hard to complete the building on time. Because prompt completion of the addition was so important to Scroge, however, Scroge offered Tinker a bonus if it completed the factory addition on time. Scroge also learned that the supplier of parts for machinery that he had contracted for had called and said that it could not deliver the parts on Scroge's schedule for the price it had agreed to. Because there was no other supplier, Scroge promised to pay the requested higher price. The factory addition was completed on time and the parts arrived on time. Scroge then refused to pay both the bonus to Tinker and the higher price for the parts. Were these promises enforceable?

See also "The Stock Option" and "A Bedtime Story."

REALITY OF CONSENT

INTRODUCTION

In a complex economy that depends on planning for the future, it is crucial that the law can be counted on to enforce contracts. In some situations, however, there are compelling reasons for permitting people to escape or avoid *their contracts. An agreement obtained by force, trickery, unfair persuasion, or error is not the product of mutual and voluntary consent. A person who has made an agreement under these circumstances will be able to avoid it, because his consent was not* real.

This chapter discusses five doctrines that permit people to avoid their contracts because of the absence of real consent: misrepresentation, fraud, mistake, duress, and undue influence. Doctrines that involve similar considerations will be discussed in Chapter 14, Capacity to Contract, and Chapter 15, Illegality.

EFFECT OF DOCTRINES DISCUSSED IN THIS CHAPTER

Contracts induced by misrepresentation, fraud, duress, mistake, or undue influence are generally considered to be **voidable**. This means that the person whose consent was not real has the power to **rescind** (cancel) the contract. A person who rescinds a contract is entitled to the return of anything he gave the other party. By the same token, he must offer to return anything he has received from the other party.

Necessity for Prompt and Unequivocal Rescission Suppose Johnson, who recently bought a car from Sims Motors, learns that Sims Motors made fraudulent statements to her to induce her to buy the car. She believes the contract was induced by fraud and wants to rescind it. How does she act to protect her rights? To rescind a contract based on fraud or any of the other doctrines discussed in this chapter, she must act promptly and unequivocally. She must object promptly upon learning the facts that give her the right to rescind and must clearly express her intent to cancel the contract. She must also avoid any behavior that would suggest that she affirms or **ratifies** the contract. (Ratification of a voidable contract means that a person who had the right to rescind has elected not to do so. Ratification ends the right to rescind.) This means that she should avoid unreasonable delay in notifying the other party of her rescission, because unreasonable delay communicates that she has ratified the contract. She should also avoid any conduct that would send a "mixed message," such as continuing to accept benefits from the other party or behaving in any other way that is inconsistent with her expressed intent to rescind.

MISREPRESENTATION AND FRAUD

Nature of Misrepresentation

A misrepresentation is an assertion that is not in accord with the truth. When a person enters a contract because of his justifiable reliance on a misrepresentation about some important fact, the contract is voidable.

It is not necessary that the misrepresentation be intentionally deceptive. Misrepresentations can be either *innocent* (not intentionally deceptive) or *fraudulent* (made with knowledge of falsity and intent to deceive). A contract may be voidable even if the person making the misrepresentation believes in good faith that what he says is true. Either innocent misrepresentation or fraud gives the complaining party the right to rescind a contract.

Nature of Fraud

Fraud is the type of misrepresentation that is committed knowingly, with the intent to deceive. The legal term for this knowledge of falsity, which distinguishes fraud from innocent misrepresentation, is **scienter**. A person making a misrepresentation would be considered to do so "knowingly" if she knew that her statement was false, if she knew that she did not have a basis for making the statement, or even if she just made the statement without being confident that it was true. The intent to deceive can be inferred from the fact that the defendant knowingly made a misstatement of fact to a person who was likely to rely on it.

As is true for innocent misrepresentation, the contract remedy for fraudulent misrepresentation is rescission. The tort liability of a person who commits fraud is different from that of a person who commits innocent misrepresentation, however. A person who commits fraud may be liable for dam-

ages, possibly including punitive damages, for the tort of **deceit**.[1] As you will learn in following sections, innocent misrepresentation and fraud share a common core of elements.

Election of Remedies   In some states, a person injured by fraud cannot rescind the contract *and* sue for damages for deceit; he must elect (choose) between these remedies. In other states, however, an injured party may pursue both rescission and damage remedies and does not have to elect between them.[2]

REQUIREMENTS FOR RESCISSION ON THE GROUND OF MISREPRESENTATION

The fact that one of the parties has made an untrue assertion does not in itself make the contract voidable. Courts do not want to permit people who have exercised poor business judgment or poor common sense to avoid their contractual obligations, nor do they want to grant rescission of a contract when there have been only minor and unintentional misstatements of relatively unimportant details. A drastic remedy such as rescission should be used only when a person has been seriously misled about a fact important to the contract by someone he had the right to rely on. A person seeking to rescind a contract on the ground of innocent or fraudulent misrepresentation must be able to establish each of the following elements:

1. An untrue assertion of fact was made.
2. The fact asserted was material *or* the assertion was fraudulent.
3. The complaining party entered the contract because of his reliance on the assertion.
4. The reliance of the complaining party was reasonable.

In tort actions in which the plaintiff is seeking to recover damages for deceit, the plaintiff would have to establish a *fifth* element: injury. He would have to prove that he had suffered actual economic injury because of his reliance on the fraudulent assertion.

---

[1]The tort of deceit is discussed in Chapter 6.

[2]Under every state's law, however, a person injured by fraud in a contract for the *sale of goods* can both rescind the contract and sue for damages. This is made clear by section 2–721 of the Uniform Commercial Code, which specifically states that no election of remedies is required in contracts for the sale of goods.

In cases in which the injured person seeks only rescission of the contract, however, proof of economic injury is usually not required.

Untrue Assertion of Fact

To have misrepresentation, one of the parties must have made an untrue assertion of fact or engaged in some conduct that is the equivalent of an untrue assertion of fact. The fact asserted must be a *past or existing fact*, as distinguished from a promise or prediction about some future happening.

The **concealment** of a fact through some active conduct intended to prevent the other party from discovering the fact is considered to be the equivalent of an assertion. Like a false statement of fact, concealment can be the basis for a claim of misrepresentation or fraud. For example, if Summers is offering his house for sale and paints the ceilings to conceal the fact that the roof leaks, his active concealment constitutes an assertion of fact. Under some circumstances, **nondisclosure** also can be the equivalent of an assertion of fact. Nondisclosure differs from concealment in that concealment involves the active hiding of a fact, while nondisclosure is the failure to offer information.

Problem Area: Nondisclosure   Suppose you are a prospective home buyer who inspects a house for possible purchase. The seller of the house knows that there is a hidden but serious structural defect in the house that will cost approximately $30,000 to correct, but does not mention this to you. Neither you nor the professional inspector you hire to examine the house for defects observes any evidence of structural defects, and you contract to purchase the house based on your assumption that it is in good condition. You later learn about the existence of this defect. Do you have the right to rescind the contract? The issue raised by this problem is whether the seller's silence about the defect was misrepresentation. In other words, was his nondisclosure the equivalent of an assertion that the structural defect did not exist?

Under traditional contract law, the answer to this question would probably have been no. Under the traditional view of nondisclosure, the circumstances under which the law required disclosure were very limited. (These are the first three circumstances described in the next section.) Mere silence on the part of a contracting party generally did not amount

to misrepresentation. One reason for this treatment of nondisclosure was that unlike concealment and outright statements of fact, which are active forms of misconduct, nondisclosure is passive. Fundamentally, though, the traditional view of nondisclosure expressed the highly individualistic philosophy expressed in the well-known phrase *caveat emptor* ("let the buyer beware"): Each contracting party is responsible for taking care of himself and is not his "brother's keeper."

In recent years, however, courts and legislatures have expanded the circumstances under which a person has the duty to take affirmative steps to disclose relevant information. This is consistent with modern contract law's emphasis on influencing ethical standards of conduct and achieving fair results. Some duties of disclosure have been created by statutes, such as the Truth in Lending Act[3] and the federal securities laws,[4] but courts also have been increasingly active in expanding the duty to disclose. In addition to the circumstances in which federal or state statutes would require a contracting party to disclose facts, there are four circumstances in which most courts today require disclosure. In these situations, the person's failure to disclose a fact would be the equivalent of an assertion that the fact did not exist.

1. *Fiduciary relationship.* If a fiduciary relationship (a relationship of trust and confidence) exists between the parties to the contract, a party who knows of an important fact that the other person does not know about would have the duty to disclose it. This makes sense, because a person who has good reason to believe that the other party is looking out for his welfare will not approach the contract with the same degree of vigilance as the person who is dealing at arm's length with a stranger. This sort of duty to disclose would not apply to ordinary contracting parties who are bargaining at arm's length.

2. *Correcting "half-truths."* When a person makes a statement about a situation, he has the duty to disclose any facts that would be necessary to correct a half-truth. For example, Carlson, a car salesperson who is trying to sell a used car, knows that the previous owner of the car used it exclusively for drag racing on Sundays. If Carlson tells a

---

[3]See Chapter 27 for a discussion of the Truth in Lending Act.
[4]These laws are discussed in Chapter 44.

customer that the previous owner of the car "drove it only on Sundays," he would have the legal duty to disclose the additional material fact that the car had been used exclusively for drag racing.

3. *Correcting statements made false by later events.* A person has the duty to disclose information that will be necessary to correct a previous statement that may have been true when made but that has become false because of later events. For example, White, who wants to sell her house, tells a prospective purchaser truthfully that the roof of the house has never leaked. Several days later, the roof leaks after a heavy storm. White has the legal duty to make the disclosure that is necessary to correct her previous statement.

4. *Good faith and fair dealing require disclosure.* In the hypothetical case with which we began this discussion of nondisclosure—the case of the seller who failed to disclose the existence of a hidden structural defect in the house he was selling—the home buyer entered into the contract under the mistaken assumption that the house was free of structural defects. The *Restatement (Second) of Contracts* provides for a duty to disclose that would be applicable in this situation. Under section 161 of the *Restatement (Second)*, a person must disclose facts necessary to correct the other party's mistake about a basic assumption of the contract when nondisclosure amounts to a failure to act in good faith and in accordance with reasonable stan-

dards of fair dealing. Most states today apply a duty to disclose along these lines.

Note that this sort of duty to disclose has broader application than the first three circumstances described above because it can apply even when the parties are dealing at arm's length and no partial disclosures have been made. Note also that this duty to disclose is intertwined with concepts of good faith and fair dealing. The *Restatement (Second)* does *not* say that a person who possesses information always has the obligation to educate the other party. Rather, the duty to speak arises only when failing to do so would constitute a failure to behave in a way that is in accord with prevailing concepts of good faith and reasonable standards of dealing. Nondisclosure is most likely to constitute a failure to act reasonably and in good faith when a party has access to information that is not readily available to the other party. In addition, sellers are more likely to be required to disclose information than are buyers.

Transactions involving the sale of real estate are among the most common situations in which this duty to disclose arises. Most states now hold that a seller who knows about a latent (hidden) defect that materially affects the value of the property he is selling has the obligation to speak up about this defect. *Stambovsky v. Ackley*, which follows, involves an interesting application of the duty to disclose in the context of a sale of real estate.

STAMBOVSKY V. ACKLEY
572 N.Y.S.2d 672 (N.Y. Sup. Ct., App. Div. 1991)

Jeffrey Stambovsky, a resident of New York City, contracted to purchase a house in the Village of Nyack, New York, from Helen Ackley. The house was widely reputed to be possessed by poltergeists, which Ackley and members of her family had reportedly seen. Ackley did not tell Stambovsky about the poltergeists before he bought the house. When Stambovsky learned of the house's reputation, however, he promptly commenced this action for rescission. The trial court dismissed his complaint, and Stambovsky appealed.

Rubin, Justice   The unusual facts of this case clearly warrant a grant of equitable relief to the buyer who, as a resident of New York City, cannot be expected to have any familiarity with the folklore of the Village of Nyack. Not being a "local,"

Stambovsky could not readily learn that the home he had contracted to purchase is haunted. Whether the source of the spectral apparitions seen by Ackley are parapsychic or psychogenic, having reported their presence in both a national publication

("Readers' Digest") and the local press (in 1977 and 1982, respectively), Ackley is estopped to deny their existence and, as a matter of law, the house is haunted. More to the point, however, no divination is required to conclude that it is Ackley's promotional efforts in publicizing her close encounters with these spirits which fostered the home's reputation in the community. In 1989, the house was included in a five-home walking tour of Nyack and described in a November 27th newspaper article as a "riverfront Victorian (with ghost)." The impact of the reputation thus created goes to the very essence of the bargain between the parties, greatly impairing both the value of the property and its potential for resale.

[*The court discussed the fact that New York law does not recognize a remedy for damages incurred as a result of the seller's mere silence, applying instead the doctrine of caveat emptor. The court then proceeded to discuss the availability of rescission.*]

From the perspective of a person in the position of the plaintiff, a very practical problem arises with respect to the discovery of a paranormal phenomenon: "Who you gonna call?" as the title song to the movie "Ghostbusters" asks. Applying the strict rule of *caveat emptor* to a contract involving a house possessed by poltergeists conjures up visions of a psychic or medium routinely accompanying the structural engineer and Terminix man on an inspection of every home subject to a contract of sale. The doctrine of *caveat emptor* requires that a buyer act prudently to assess the fitness and value of his purchase. It should be apparent, however, that the most meticulous inspection and the search would not reveal the presence of poltergeists at the premises or unearth the property's ghoulish reputation in the community. Therefore, there is no sound policy reason to deny Stambovsky relief for failing to discover a state of affairs which the most prudent purchaser would not be expected to even contemplate.

Where a condition which has been created by the seller materially impairs the value of the contract and is peculiarly within the knowledge of the seller or unlikely to be discovered by a prudent purchaser exercising due care, nondisclosure constitutes a basis for rescission as a matter of equity. Any other outcome places upon the buyer not merely the obligation to exercise care in his purchase but rather to be omniscient with respect to any fact which may affect the bargain. No practical purpose is served by imposing such a burden upon a purchaser. To the contrary, it encourages predatory business practice and offends the principle that equity will suffer no wrong to be without a remedy.

In the case at bar, Ackley deliberately fostered the public belief that her home was possessed. Having undertaken to inform the public at large, to whom she has no legal relationship, about the supernatural occurrences on her property, she may be said to owe no less a duty to her contract vendee. Application of the remedy of rescission is entirely appropriate to relieve the unwitting purchaser from the consequences of a most unnatural bargain.

Judgment modified in favor of Stambovsky, reinstating his action seeking rescission of the contract.

Problem Area: Statements of Opinion   In holding that only untrue statements of *fact* give a relying person the right to rescind a contract, contract law traditionally has distinguished between assertions of *fact* and assertions of *opinion*. Although it can be difficult to separate fact from opinion, there is an important distinction between a statement that communicates a person's knowledge and a statement that communicates only his uncertain belief about a fact or his personal judgment about such matters as quality or value. The latter sort of statement usually cannot be the basis of a misrepresentation claim because the person to whom such a statement of opinion is made is not justified in relying on it. This is especially true when the statement relates to something about which the parties have relatively equal knowledge and peoples' points of view are likely to differ. In such a case, each party is expected to form his own opinion. A classic example of this sort of statement of opinion is a seller's "puff" (salestalk or general praise of an item being sold), such as "This suit will look terrific on you."

Even when the statement is clearly one of opinion, there are three situations in which the statement of opinion can be the basis of a misrepresentation claim because reliance is justifiable under the circumstances.[5] These include:

1. *Relationship of trust and confidence.* A person can be justified in relying on a statement of opinion if it is reasonable to do so because of a relationship of trust and confidence between him and the speaker. For example, if Madison, the long-time financial adviser of the elderly Holden, persuades Holden to invest her money in Madison's failing business by telling her that it is a wise investment, Holden would be justified in relying on Madison's statement of opinion.

2. *Relying party is unusually susceptible.* Reliance on a statement of opinion can be justifiable when the relying party is someone who is particularly susceptible to the particular type of misrepresentation involved. This sort of case would be likely to involve relying parties who are vulnerable to being misled because of some obvious disadvantage such as illiteracy or lack of intelligence or experience.

3. *Reliance on person who has superior skill or judgment.* Reliance on an assertion of opinion can also be justifiable when the relying party reasonably believes that the person on whose opinion he is relying has superior skill or judgment about the subject matter of the contract. This would apply when the opinion relates to some matter about which superior training or experience is necessary to form the opinion. For example, Buyer, who knows that Salesperson is an experienced auto mechanic, would be justified in relying on Salesperson's statement that a particular used car is "in A-1 condition."

Materiality

If the misrepresentation was innocent, the person seeking to rescind the contract must establish that the fact asserted was **material**. A fact will be considered to be material if it is likely to play a

significant role in inducing a reasonable person to enter the contract or if the person asserting the fact knows that the other person is likely to rely on the fact. For example, Rogers, who is trying to sell his car to Ferguson and knows that Ferguson idolizes professional bowlers, tells Ferguson that a professional bowler once rode in the car. Relying on that representation, Ferguson buys the car. Although the fact Rogers asserted might not be important to most people, it would be material here because Rogers knew that his representation would be likely to induce Ferguson to enter the contract.

Even if the fact asserted was not material, the contract may be rescinded if the misrepresentation was *fraudulent*. The rationale for this rule is that a person who fraudulently misrepresents a fact, even one that is not material under the standards previously discussed, should not be able to profit from his intentionally deceptive conduct.

Actual Reliance

Reliance means that a person pursues some course of action because of his faith in an assertion made to him. For misrepresentation to exist, there must have been a causal connection between the assertion and the complaining party's decision to enter the contract. If the complaining party knew that the assertion was false or was not aware that an assertion had been made, there has been no reliance.

Justifiable Reliance

Courts also scrutinize the reasonableness of the behavior of the complaining party by requiring that his reliance be *justifiable*. A person does not act justifiably if he relies on an assertion that is obviously false or not to be taken seriously.

Problem Area: The Relying Party's Failure to Investigate the Accuracy of an Assertion　One problem involving the justifiable reliance element is determining the extent to which the relying party is responsible for investigating the accuracy of the statement on which he relies. Classical contract law held that a person who did not attempt to discover readily discoverable facts was generally not justified in relying on the other party's statements about them. For example, under traditional law, a person would not be entitled to rely on the other party's

---

[5]*Restatement (Second) of Contracts* § 169.

assertions about facts that are a matter of public record or that could be discovered through a reasonable inspection of available documents or records.

The extent of the responsibility placed on a relying party to conduct an independent investigation has declined in modern contract law, however. For example, section 172 of the *Restatement* states that the complaining party's fault in not knowing or discovering facts before entering the contract does not make his reliance unjustifiable unless the degree

of his fault was so extreme as to amount to a failure to act in good faith and in accordance with reasonable standards of fair dealing. Recognizing that the traditional rule operated to encourage misrepresentation, courts in recent years have tended to decrease the responsibility of the relying party and to place a greater degree of accountability on the person who makes the assertion. The case of *Cousineau v. Walker*, which follows, is an excellent example of this trend.

Cosineau v. Walker
613 P.2d 608 (Alaska Sup. Ct. 1980)

Devin and Joan Walker owned property in Eagle River, Alaska. In 1976, they listed the property for sale with a real estate broker. They signed a multiple listing agreement that described the property as having 580 feet of highway frontage and stated, "ENGINEER REPORT SAYS OVER 1 MILLION IN GRAVEL ON PROP." A later listing contract signed with the same broker described the property as having 580 feet of highway frontage, but listed the gravel content as "minimum 80,000 cubic yds of gravel." An appraisal prepared to determine the property's value stated that it did not take any gravel into account but described the ground as "all good gravel base."

Wayne Cousineau, a contractor who was also in the gravel extraction business, became aware of the property when he saw the multiple listing. After visiting the property with his real estate broker and discussing gravel extraction with Mr. Walker, Cousineau offered to purchase the property. He then attempted to determine the lot's road frontage, but was unsuccessful because the property was covered with snow. He was also unsuccessful in obtaining the engineer's report allegedly showing "over 1 million in gravel." Walker admitted at trial that he had never seen a copy of the report, either. Nevertheless, the parties signed and consummated a contract of sale for the purchase price of $385,000. There was no reference to the amount of highway frontage in the purchase agreement.

After the sale was completed, Cousineau began developing the property and removing gravel. Cousineau learned that the description of highway frontage contained in the real estate listing was incorrect when a neighbor threatened to sue him for removing gravel from the neighbor's adjacent lot. A subsequent survey revealed that the highway frontage was 410 feet—not 580 feet, as advertised. At about the same time, the gravel ran out after Cousineau had removed only 6,000 cubic yards.

Cousineau stopped making payments and informed the Walkers of his intention to rescind the contract. Cousineau brought an action against the Walkers, seeking the return of his money. The trial court found for the Walkers, and Cousineau appealed.

Boochever, Justice An innocent misrepresentation may be the basis for rescinding a contract. There is no question that the statements made by Walker and his real estate agent in the multiple listing were false.

The bulk of the Walkers' brief is devoted to the argument that Cousineau's unquestioning reliance on Walker and his real estate agent was imprudent and unreasonable. Cousineau failed to obtain and review the engineer's report. He failed to obtain a survey or examine the plat available at the recorder's office. He failed to make calculations that would have revealed the true frontage of the lot. Although the property was covered with snow, the buyer, according to Walker, had ample time to inspect it. The buyer was an experienced businessman who frequently bought and sold real estate. Discrepancies existed in the various property descriptions which should have alerted Cousineau to potential problems. In short, the Walkers urge that the doctrine of *caveat emptor* precludes recovery.

There is a split of authority regarding a buyer's duty to investigate a vendor's fraudulent statements, but the prevailing trend is toward placing a minimal duty on a buyer. The recent draft of the *Restatement of Contracts* allows rescission for an innocent material misrepresentation unless a buyer's fault was so negligent as to amount to "a failure to act in good faith and in accordance with reasonable standards of fair dealing." We conclude that a purchaser of land may rely on material representations made by the seller and is not obligated to ascertain whether such representations are truthful. A buyer of land, relying on an innocent misrepresentation, is barred from recovery only if the buyer's acts in failing to discover defects were wholly irrational, preposterous, or in bad faith.

Although Cousineau's actions may well have exhibited poor judgment for an experienced businessman, they were not so unreasonable or preposterous in view of Walker's description of the property that recovery should be denied.

Judgment reversed in favor of Cousineau.

CONCEPT REVIEW

MISREPRESENTATION AND FRAUD

	Innocent Misrepresentation	**Fraud**
Remedy	Rescission	Rescission *and/or* tort action for damages
Elements	1. Untrue assertion of fact (or equivalent) 2. Assertion relates to material fact 3. Actual reliance 4. Justifiable reliance	1. Untrue assertion of fact (or equivalent) 2. Assertion made with knowledge of falsity (scienter) and intent to deceive 3. Actual reliance 4. Justifiable reliance 5. Economic loss (in a tort action for damages)

MISTAKE

Nature of Mistake

Anyone who enters a contract does so on the basis of his understanding of the facts that are relevant to the contract. His decision about what he is willing to exchange with the other party is based on this understanding. If the parties are wrong about an important fact, the exchange that they make is likely to be quite different than what they contemplated when they entered the contract, and this difference is due to simple error rather than to any external events such as an increase in market price. For example, Fox contracts to sell to Ward a half-carat stone, which both believe to be a tourmaline, at a price of $65. If they are wrong and the stone is actually a diamond worth at least $2,500, Fox will have suffered an unexpected loss and Ward will have reaped an unexpected gain. The contract would not have been made at a price of $65 if the parties' belief about the nature of the stone had been in accord with the facts. In such cases, the person adversely affected by the mistake can avoid the contract under the doctrine of mistake. The purpose of the doctrine of mistake is to prevent unexpected and unbargained for losses that result when the parties are mistaken about a fact central to their contract.

What Is a Mistake? In ordinary conversation, we may use the term *mistake* to mean an error in judgment or an unfortunate act. In contract law, however, a mistake is a *belief* about a fact that is *not in accord with the truth.*[6] The mistake must relate to facts as they exist at the time the contract is created. An erroneous belief or prediction about facts that might occur in the future would not qualify as a mistake.

_____

[6]*Restatement (Second) of Contracts* § 151.

As in misrepresentation cases, the complaining party in a mistake case enters a contract because of a belief that is at variance with the actual facts. Mistake is unlike misrepresentation, however, in that the erroneous belief is not the result of the other party's untrue statements.

The *Wilkin v. 1st Source Bank* case, which follows, illustrates the concept and effect of mistake in contract law.

WILKIN V. 1ST SOURCE BANK
548 N.E.2d 170 (Ind. Ct. App. 1990)

Olga Mestrovic, the widow of internationally known sculptor and artist Ivan Mestrovic, owned a large number of works of art created by her late husband. Mrs. Mestrovic died, leaving a will in which she directed that all the works of art created by her husband were to be sold and the proceeds distributed to surviving members of the Mestrovic family. Mrs. Mestrovic also owned real estate at the time of her death. 1st Source Bank, as the personal representative of Mrs. Mestrovic's estate, entered into a contract to sell this real estate to Terrence and Antoinette Wilkin. The purchase agreement provided that certain personal property on the premises would be sold to the Wilkins, too: specifically, the stove, refrigerator, dishwasher, drapes, curtains, sconces, and French doors in the attic.

After taking possession of the property, the Wilkins complained to the bank that the property was left in a cluttered condition and would require substantial cleaning effort. The trust officer of the bank offered the Wilkins two options: Either the bank would obtain a rubbish removal service to clean the property, or the Wilkins could clean the property and keep any items of personal property they wanted. The Wilkins opted to clean the property themselves. At the time these arrangements were made, neither the bank nor the Wilkins suspected that any works of art remained on the premises.

During the clean-up efforts, the Wilkins found eight drawings apparently created by Ivan Mestrovic. They also found a plaster sculpture of the figure of Christ with three small children. The Wilkins claimed ownership of these works of art by virtue of their agreement with the bank. The probate court ruled that there was no agreement for the purchase of the artwork, and the Wilkins appealed.

Hoffman, Judge   Mutual assent is a prerequisite to the creation of a contract. Where both parties share a common assumption about a vital fact upon which they based their bargain, and that assumption is false, the transaction may be avoided if because of the mistake a quite different exchange of values occurs from the exchange of values contemplated by the parties. *J. Calamari & J. Perillo, The Law of Contracts* section 9-26 (1987).

The necessity of mutual assent is illustrated in the classic case of *Sherwood v. Walker* (1887). The owners of a blooded cow indicated to the purchaser that the cow was barren. The purchaser appeared to believe that the cow was barren. Consequently, a

bargain was made to sell at a price per pound at which the cow would have brought approximately $80.00. Before delivery, it was discovered that the cow was with calf and that she was, therefore, worth from $750.00 to $1,000.00 The court ruled that the transaction was voidable: "[T]he mistake . . . went to the very nature of the thing. A barren cow is substantially a different creature than a breeding one."

Like the parties in *Sherwood*, the parties in the instant case shared a common presupposition as to the existence of certain facts which proved false. The bank and the Wilkins considered the real estate which the Wilkins had purchased to be cluttered with items of personal property variously characterized as "junk," "stuff," or "trash." Neither party suspected that works of art created by Ivan Mestrovic remained on the premises.

As in *Sherwood*, one party experienced an unexpected, unbargained-for gain while the other experienced an unexpected, unbargained-for loss. Because the bank and the Wilkins did not know that the eight drawings and the plaster sculpture were included in the items of personalty that cluttered the real property, the discovery of those works of art by the Wilkins was unexpected. The resultant gain to the Wilkins and loss to the Bank were not contemplated by the parties when the bank agreed that the Wilkins could clean the premises and keep such personal property as they wished.

The following commentary on *Sherwood* is equally applicable to the case at bar:

"Here the buyer sought to retain a gain that was produced, not by a subsequent change in circumstances, nor by the favorable resolution of known uncertainties when the contract was made, but by the presence of facts quite different from those on which the parties based their bargain." *Palmer, Mistake and Unjust Enrichment* 16–17 (1962).

The probate court properly concluded that there was no agreement for the purchase, sale, or other disposition of the eight drawings and plaster sculpture.

Judgment for 1st Source Bank affirmed.

Mistakes of Law

A number of the older mistake cases state that mistake about a principle of law will not justify rescission. The rationale for this view was that everyone was presumed to know the law. More modern cases, however, have granted relief even when the mistake is an erroneous belief about some aspect of law.

Negligence and the Right to Avoid for Mistake

Although courts sometimes state that relief will not be granted when a person's mistake was caused by his own negligence, they have often granted rescission even when the mistaken party was somewhat negligent. Section 157 of the *Restatement (Second) of Contracts* focuses on the *degree* of a party's negligence in making the mistake. It states that a person's fault in failing to know or discover facts before entering the contract will not bar relief unless his fault amounted to a failure to act in good faith.

Effect of Mistake

The mere fact that the contracting parties have made a mistake is not, standing alone, a sufficient ground for avoidance of the contract. The right to avoid a contract because of mistake depends on several factors that are discussed in following sections. One important factor that affects the right to avoid is whether the mistake was made by just one of the parties (**unilateral mistake**) or by both parties (**mutual mistake**).

Mutual Mistake

A mutual mistake exists when both parties to the contract have erroneous assumptions about the same fact. When *both* parties are mistaken, the resulting contract can be avoided if the three following elements are present:

1. The mistake relates to a basic assumption on which the contract was made.
2. The mistake has a material effect on the agreed-on exchange.
3. The party adversely affected by the mistake does not bear the risk of the mistake.[7]

Mistake about a Basic Assumption   Even if the mistake is mutual, the adversely affected party will not have the right to avoid the contract unless the mistake concerns a basic assumption on which the contract was based. Assumptions about the identity, existence, quality, or quantity of the subject matter of the contract are among the basic assumptions on which contracts typically are founded. It is not

---

[7]*Restatement (Second) of Contracts* § 152.

necessary that the parties be consciously aware of the assumption; an assumption may be so basic that they take it for granted. For example, if Peterson contracts to buy a house from Tharp, it is likely that both of them assume at the time of contracting that the house is in existence and that it is legally permissible for the house to be used as a residence.

An assumption would not be considered a basic assumption if it concerns a matter that bears an indirect or collateral relationship to the subject matter of the contract. For example, mistakes about matters such as a party's financial ability or market conditions usually would not give rise to avoidance of the contract.

Material Effect on Agreed-On Exchange   It is not enough for a person claiming mistake to show that the exchange is something different from what he expected. He must show that the imbalance caused by the mistake is so severe that it would be unfair for the law to require him to perform the contract. He will have a better chance of establishing this element if he can show not only that the contract is *less* desirable for him because of the mistake, but also that the other party has received an unbargained-for advantage.

Adversely Affected Party Does Not Bear the Risk of Mistake   Even if the first two elements are present, the person who is adversely affected by the mistake cannot avoid the contract if he is considered to bear the risk of mistake.[8] Courts have the power to allocate the risk of a mistake to the adversely affected person whenever it is reasonable under the circumstances to do so.

One situation in which an adversely affected person would bear the risk of mistake is when he has expressly contracted to do so. For example, if Buyer contracted to accept property "as is," he may be considered to have accepted the risk that his assumption about the quality of the property may be erroneous.

The adversely affected party also bears the risk of mistake when he contracts with *conscious awareness* that he is ignorant or has limited information

about a fact—in other words, he *knows that he does not know* the true state of affairs about a particular fact, but he binds himself to perform anyway. Suppose someone gives you an old, locked safe. Without trying to open it, you sell it and "all of its contents" to one of your friends for $25. When your friend succeeds in opening the safe, he finds $10,000 in cash. In this case, you would not be able to rescind the contract because, in essence, you gambled on your limited knowledge . . . and lost.

Mutual Mistakes in Drafting Writings

Sometimes, mutual mistake takes the form of erroneous *expression* of an agreement, frequently caused by a clerical error in drafting or typing a contract, deed, or other document. In such cases, the remedy is *reformation* of the writing rather than avoidance of the contract. Reformation means modification of the written instrument to express the agreement that the parties made but failed to express correctly. Suppose Arnold agrees to sell Barber a vacant lot next to Arnold's home. The vacant lot is "Lot 3, block 1;" Arnold's home is on "Lot 2, block 1." The person typing the contract strikes the wrong key, and the contract reads, "Lot 2, block 1." Neither Arnold nor Barber notices this error when they read and sign the contract, yet clearly they did not intend to have Arnold sell the lot on which his house stands. In such a case, a court will reform the contract to conform to Arnold and Barber's true agreement.

Unilateral Mistake

A unilateral mistake exists when only one of the parties makes a mistake about a basic assumption on which he made the contract. For example, Plummer contracts to buy from Taylor 25 shares of Worthright Enterprises, Inc., mistakenly believing that he is buying 25 shares of the much more valuable Worthwrite Industries. Taylor knows that the contract is for the sale of shares of Worthright. Taylor (the nonmistaken party) is correct in his belief about the identity of the stock he is selling; only Plummer (the mistaken party) is mistaken in his assumption about the identity of the stock. Does Plummer's unilateral mistake give him the right to avoid the contract? Courts are more

---

[8]*Restatement (Second) of Contracts* § 154.

likely to allow avoidance of a contract when both parties are mistaken than when only one is mistaken. The rationale for this tendency is that in cases of unilateral mistake, at least one party's assumption about the facts was correct, and allowing avoidance disappoints the reasonable expectations of that nonmistaken party.

It is possible to avoid contracts for unilateral mistake, but to do so, proving the elements necessary for mutual mistake is just a starting point. *In addition to* proving the elements of mistake discussed earlier, a person trying to avoid on the ground of unilateral mistake must show *either* one of the following:

1. *The nonmistaken party caused or had reason to know of the mistake.* Courts permit avoidance in cases of unilateral mistake if the nonmistaken party caused the mistake, knew of the mistake, or even if the mistake was so obvious that the nonmistaken party had reason to realize that a mistake had been made.[9] For example, Ace Electrical Company makes an error when preparing a bid that it submits to Gorge General Contracting. If the mistake in Ace's bid was so obvious that Gorge knew about it when it accepted Ace's offer, Ace could avoid the contract even though Ace is the only party who was mistaken.

The reasoning behind this rule is that the nonmistaken person could have prevented the loss by acting in good faith and informing the person in error that he had made a mistake. It also reflects the judgment that people should not take advantage of the mistakes of others or

2. *It would be unconscionable to enforce the contract.* A court could also permit avoidance because of unilateral mistake when the effect of the mistake was such that it would be unconscionable to enforce the contract. To show that it would be unconscionable to enforce the contract, the mistaken party would have to show that the consequences of the mistake were severe enough that it would be unreasonably harsh or oppressive to enforce the contract.[10] In the example above, Ace Electrical Company made an error when preparing a bid that it submits to Gorge General Contracting. Suppose that Gorge had no reason to realize that a mistake had been made, and accepted the bid. Ace might show that it would be unconscionable to enforce the contract by showing that not only will its profit margin not be what Ace contemplated when it made its offer, but also that it would suffer a grave loss by having to perform at the mistaken price.

---

[9] *Restatement (Second) of Contracts* § 153.

[10] The concept of unconscionability is developed more fully in Chapter 15.

CONCEPT REVIEW

AVOIDANCE ON THE GROUND OF MISTAKE

	Mutual Mistake	Unilateral Mistake
Description	Both parties mistaken about same fact	Only one party mistaken about a fact
Needed for Avoidance	Elements of mistake: 1. Mistake about basic assumption on which contract was made 2. Material effect on agreed exchange 3. Person adversely affected by mistake does not bear the risk of the mistake	Same elements as mutual mistake *Plus* *a.* Nonmistaken party caused mistake or had reason to know of mistake *Or* *b.* Effect of mistake is to make it unconscionable to enforce contract

DURESS

Nature of Duress

Duress is wrongful coercion that induces a person to enter or modify a contract. One kind of duress is physical compulsion to enter a contract. For example, Thorp overpowers Grimes, grasps his hand, and forces him to sign a contract. This kind of duress is rare, but when it occurs, a court would find that the contract was *void*. A far more common type of duress occurs when a person is induced to enter a contract by a *threat* of physical, emotional, or economic harm. In these cases, the contract is considered *voidable* at the option of the victimized person. This is the form of duress addressed in this chapter.

The elements of duress have undergone dramatic changes. Classical contract law took a very narrow view of the type of coercion that constituted duress, limiting duress to threats of imprisonment or serious physical harm. Today, however, courts take a much broader view of the types of coercion that will constitute duress. For example, modern courts recognize that threats to a person's economic interests can be duress.

Elements of Duress

To rescind a contract because of duress, one must be able to establish both of the following elements:

1. The contract was induced by an improper threat.
2. The victim had no reasonable alternative but to enter the contract.[11]

Improper Threat   It would not be desirable for courts to hold that every kind of threat constituted duress. If they did, the enforceability of all contracts would be in question, because every contract negotiation involves at least the implied threat that a person will not enter into the transaction unless her demands are met. What degree of wrongfulness, then, is required for a threat to constitute duress? Traditionally, a person would have to threaten to do something she was not legally entitled to do—such as threaten to commit a crime or a tort—for that threat to be duress. Many courts today follow the *Restatement (Second)* position that, to be duress, the

threat need not be wrongful or illegal but must be *improper*— that is, improper to use as leverage to induce a contract.

Under some circumstances, threats to institute legal actions can be considered improper threats that will constitute duress. A threat to file either a civil or a criminal suit without a legal basis for doing so would clearly be improper. What of a threat to file a well-founded lawsuit or prosecution? Generally, if there is a good faith dispute over a matter, a person's threat to file a lawsuit to resolve that dispute is *not* considered to be improper. Otherwise, every person who settled a suit out of court could later claim duress. However, if the threat to sue is made in bad faith and for a purpose unrelated to the issues in the lawsuit, the threat can be considered improper. In one case, for example, duress was found when a husband who was in the process of divorcing his wife threatened to sue for custody of their children—something he had the right to do— unless the wife transferred to him stock that she owned in his company.[12]

The *Restatement (Second)* takes the position that a threat to institute a criminal prosecution is always impermissible pressure to induce a contract, even if the person making the threat has good reason to believe that the other person has committed a crime. It also provides that it is improper for a contracting party to make a threat that would constitute a breach of the duty of good faith and fair dealing under his contract with the person who is the recipient of the threat.[13] This provision is relevant to the many duress cases that arise in the context of coerced modifications of existing contracts or settlements of existing debts.

Victim Had No Reasonable Alternative   The person complaining of duress must be able to prove that the coercive nature of the improper threat was such that he had no reasonable alternative but to enter or modify the contract. Classical contract law applied an objective standard of coercion, which required that the degree of coercion exercised had to be sufficient to overcome the will of a person of ordinary courage. The more modern standard for coercion focuses on the alternatives open to the

---

[11]*Restatement (Second) of Contracts* § 175.

[12]*Link v. Link*, 179 S.E.2d 697 (1971).
[13]*Restatement (Second) of Contracts* § 176.

complaining party. For example, Barry, a traveling salesperson, takes his car to Cheatum Motors for repair. Barry pays Cheatum the full amount previously agreed on for the repair, but Cheatum refuses to return Barry's car to him unless Barry agrees to pay substantially more than the contract price for the repair. Because of his urgent need for the return of his car, Barry agrees to do this. In this case, Barry technically had the alternative of filing a legal action to recover his car. However, this would not be a *reasonable alternative* for someone who needs the car urgently because of the time, expense, and uncertainty involved in pursuing a lawsuit. Thus, Barry could avoid his agreement to pay more money under a theory of duress.

Problem Area: Economic Duress   Today, the doctrine of duress is often applied in a business context. *Economic duress*, or *business compulsion*, are terms commonly used to describe situations in which one person induces the formation or modification of a contract by threatening another person's economic interests. A common coercive strategy is to threaten to breach the contract unless the other party agrees to modify its terms. For example, Moore, who has contracted to sell goods to

Stephens, knows that Stephens needs timely delivery of the goods. Moore threatens to withhold delivery unless Stephens agrees to pay a higher price. Another common situation involving economic duress occurs when one of the parties offers a disproportionately small amount of money in settlement of a debt and refuses to pay more. Such a strategy exerts great economic pressure on a creditor who is in a desperate financial situation to accept the settlement because he cannot afford the time and expense of bringing a lawsuit.

Classical contract law did not recognize economic duress because this type of hard bargaining was considered neither improper nor coercive. After all, the victim of the sorts of economic pressure described above had at least the theoretical right to file a lawsuit to enforce his rights under the contract. Modern courts recognize that improper economic pressure can prevent a resulting contract or contract modification from being truly voluntary, and the concept of economic duress is well-accepted today. Even in recent cases, however, it is not always clear how much hard bargaining is tolerated. *Eulrich v. Snap-On Tools Corp.*, which follows, presents an example of hard bargaining that a court found to have gone too far.

EULRICH V. SNAP-ON TOOLS CORP.
853 p.2d 1350 (Or. Ct. App. 1993)

Snap-On manufactures and sells hand tools to a nationwide network of dealers, each of whom is assigned a marketing territory. The dealers, in turn, resell the tools to professional mechanics. Dan Eulrich, an auto body mechanic who had never before operated a business, entered into a dealership agreement and became a Snap-On dealer in 1986. Eulrich initially invested $22,000 from his savings and promised to pay a balance of $22,500 from the sale of inventory. The dealership agreement included a provision allowing termination of the dealership by either party. It further provided that upon termination, if Snap-On consented, Eulrich could resell to Snap-On any new tools remaining in his possession.

From the very beginning, Eulrich's dealership was not profitable. In early 1987, he tried to get a more profitable territory because his territory was not supporting him, but he was told to work the territory harder. Eulrich's supervisors, Tim Kash and Ray Park, insisted that anyone could succeed as a dealer by following Snap-On's sales program. (However, there was evidence that Snap-On's marketing system was designed to provide a maximum number of potential dealers and profit for Snap-On, while providing inadequate revenue to support dealers. As a result, dealers quickly failed and were replaced by new recruits.) By the spring of 1987, Eulrich was financially ruined and informed Kash and Park that he wanted to exercise his rights under the dealership agreement and terminate his dealership.

Beginning in April, he attempted to get Kash and Park to "check in" his truck, which he understood would allow him to receive a refund for the tools and the equity in his van. He needed this money to pay his household bills because his dealership had depleted his personal finances. Kash and Park repeatedly put off this check-in until June 1. By that time, as they knew, Eulrich was in serious financial difficulty and could not pay his living expenses, a situation that was aggravated by the fact that Eulrich's wife was ill and required hospitalization but had no medical insurance.

On the day of the check-in, after having worked five or six hours to unload the van under trying circumstances, Kash and Park had Eulrich come into Park's office to "do paperwork." Eulrich was physically tired and emotionally drained. In the office, Kash and Park berated Eulrich for his poor business practices. They also presented Eulrich with a number of documents, none of which had been sent to him in advance to review, and told him to sign them. Kash told Eulrich that he would have to sign the papers before he could get any money. When he asked when he would get a check, Park told him that there would be no checks until the inventory was done and all of the papers were signed. Eulrich signed the papers.

Included in the papers that he signed was a "Termination Agreement," which included an agreement by Snap-On to repurchase Eulrich's tool inventory at current dealer cost. Also included in the document was a release of claims which provided that "each party to this Agreement waives any and all claims it may have against the other arising out of the Dealership terminated by this Agreement. . . ." Eulrich was not aware that a release was included in the Termination Agreement, nor was he aware that he had any legal claims against Snap-On.

Eulrich later filed a lawsuit against Snap-On, Kash, Park, and another Snap-On supervisor to recover damages for fraud, breach of good faith and fair dealing, and breach of contract arising out of the original dealership contract. The defendants asserted that the release barred these claims. Eulrich sought to rescind the release on a number of grounds, including economic duress. The trial judge allowed the rescission and the jury awarded general and punitive damages to Eulrich on his damage claims in the amount of $8,912,000. Snap-On appealed.

Riggs, Judge   Eulrich acknowledges that, if the release is not rescinded, all of his claims for damages are barred. He asserts that the release should be rescinded because it was executed under economic duress. The gravamen of a claim of economic duress is that, as a result of some wrongful act by one party, the other party is deprived of free will in entering in the agreement.

Defendants argue that we should look only at their threat not to repurchase the tools and that, because the dealership agreement did not require defendants to buy back Eulrich's tools, there was nothing legally wrongful in that conduct. That inquiry is too narrow. Even if we look only at defendants' acts at the time that the termination agreement was executed, requiring Eulrich to sign the termination agreement in order to receive payment for the tools was a wrongful act. The contract conditioned repurchase of the tools on Snap-On's consent, but defendants' performance of that contract term is subject to the duty of good faith and fair dealing. A threat may be a breach of the duty of good faith and fair dealing under the contract even if the threatened act is not itself a breach of the contract. "In the context of duress, an act or threat

is wrongful if it is 'an abuse of the powers of the party making the threat; that is, any threat the purpose of which was not to achieve the end for which the right, power, or privilege was given.' " *Calamari & Perillo, Contracts section 9-3 (3d ed. 1987).* Defendants had no right to abuse their power to consent under the contract by threatening to withhold consent unless Eulrich executed another contract releasing all claims.

In determining whether there was economic duress, a court must consider all surrounding factors and circumstances. Here, there was evidence that defendants' actions, up to the time the termination agreement was signed, were fraudulent and caused Eulrich's economic distress. Defendants knowingly engaged in an ongoing scheme to induce Eulrich into the business, to deny him an adequate sales territory to support his business, to browbeat and demoralize him into believing that the failure of the business was his fault rather than that of the inadequate design of the marketing system, and by depleting all of his financial resources. Defendants knew that their ongoing scheme was causing Eulrich financial distress, resulting in a lack of resources to meet daily household needs and his wife's medical needs. Despite this knowledge, and the provision in the dealer agreement that allowed either party to terminate the agreement on written notification, and despite Eulrich's numerous attempts to return the van and tools for a refund, defendants made Eulrich wait six or seven weeks to terminate the agreement. In the light of all the circumstances leading to the signing of the termination agreement, we conclude that defendants' conduct was wrongful.

Nevertheless, defendants argue that there was no economic duress because Eulrich had reasonable alternatives to signing the release. They contend that, under the dealership agreement, Eulrich had the option of keeping the inventory and selling it outside the dealership, which would have allowed him to recoup his inventory investment, or that he could have refused to sign the agreement, reserving his rights, or could have taken the termination agreement home with him and sought legal advice before he signed it. Under the coercive circumstances present here, those were not reasonable alternatives.

Eulrich had tried in vain for nearly two months to check in his van and tools and obtain the refund that defendants had promised for the tools. During that time, his poor financial situation deteriorated further. Selling Snap-On's product was a losing proposition; it would not have been a reasonable alterna-

tive for him to continue that course as a way of recouping his investment. Neither was refusing to sign the termination agreement and seeking a legal remedy a reasonable alternative. By the time defendants finally allowed Eulrich to check in the tools for the promised refund, Eulrich needed money immediately, and defendants knew it. For a legal remedy to be a reasonable alternative, it must be an "immediate and adequate remedy" and [this] is tested by a practical standard that takes into consideration the exigencies of the situation. Refusing to sign defendants' termination agreement and commencing legal action against them was not a reasonable alternative, because such a course would have taken time and Eulrich's financial condition was perilous. Faced with the choice between complying with defendants' demand and receiving the badly needed funds, or refusing to sign and facing financial disaster, Eulrich had no reasonable alternative and thus found himself deprived of the exercise of his free will. Accordingly, we conclude that his agreement to the release was a result of economic duress and that the trial court did not err in allowing the rescission.

Judgment allowing rescission affirmed in favor of Eulrich. [The case was also remanded for the correction of an error in the damages awarded to Eulrich.]

Undue Influence

Nature of Undue Influence

Undue influence is unfair persuasion. Like duress, undue influence involves wrongful pressure exerted on a person during the bargaining process. In undue influence, however, the pressure is exerted through *persuasion* rather than through coercion. The doctrine of undue influence was developed to give relief to persons who are unfairly persuaded to enter a contract while in a position of weakness that makes them particularly vulnerable to being preyed on by those they trust or fear. A large proportion of undue influence cases arise after the death of the person who has been the subject of undue influence, when his relatives seek to set aside that person's contracts or wills.

Determining Undue Influence   All contracts are based on persuasion. There is no precise dividing line between permissible persuasion and impermissible persuasion. Nevertheless, several hallmarks of undue influence cases can be identified. Undue influence cases normally involve both of the following elements:

1. The relationship between the parties is either one of trust and confidence or one in which the person exercising the persuasion dominates the person being persuaded.
2. The persuasion is unfair.[14]

---

[14]*Restatement (Second) of Contracts* § 177.

Relation between the Parties   Undue influence cases involve people who, though they have capacity to enter a contract, are in a position of particular vulnerability in relationship to the other party to the contract. This relationship can be one of trust and confidence, in which the person being influenced justifiably believes that the other party is looking out for his interests, or at least that he would not do anything contrary to his welfare. Examples of such relationships would include parent and child, husband and wife, or lawyer and client.

The relationship can also be one in which one of the parties holds dominant psychological power that is not derived from a confidential relationship. For example, Royce, an elderly man, is dependent on his housekeeper, Smith, to care for him. Smith persuades Royce to withdraw most of his life savings from the bank and make an interest-free loan to her. If the persuasion Smith used was unfair, the transaction could be avoided because of undue influence.

Unfair Persuasion   The mere existence of a close or dependent relationship between the parties that results in economic advantage to one of them is not sufficient for undue influence. It must also appear that the weaker person entered the contract because he was subjected to unfair methods of persuasion. In determining this, a court will look at all of the surrounding facts and circumstances. Was the person isolated and rushed into the contract, or did he have access to outsiders for advice and time to consider his alternatives? Was the contract discussed and consummated in the usual time and place that would be expected for such a transaction, or was it discussed or consummated at an unusual time or in an unusual place? Was the contract a reasonably fair one that a person might have entered voluntarily, or was it so lopsided and unfair that one could infer that he probably would not have entered it unless he had been unduly influenced by the other party? The answers to these and similar questions help determine whether the line between permissible and impermissible persuasion has been crossed.

CONCEPT REVIEW

WRONGFUL PRESSURE IN THE BARGAINING PROCESS

	Duress	Undue Influence
Nature of Pressure	Coercion	Unfair persuasion of susceptible individual
Elements	1. Contract induced by improper threat 2. Threat leaves party no reasonable alternative but to enter or modify contract	1. Relationship of trust and confidence or dominance 2. Unfair persuasion

ETHICAL AND PUBLIC POLICY CONCERNS

1. You read that modern contract law has expanded the circumstances under which a contracting party has the duty to disclose facts material to the contract. Keep in mind that the facts that he is required to disclose would almost always harm his bargaining position—otherwise, he would have been only too happy to have volunteered the information. What are some ethical and public policy justifications for requiring an individual to volunteer information that is contrary to his interests?

2. Do you think the legal rules applied today regarding misrepresentation and duress encourage a higher standard of ethical dealing than did the legal rules applicable under classical contract law?

3. In this chapter, you learned a few of the circumstances under which a contracting party owes a higher duty of conduct to someone with whom she is in a relationship of trust and confidence than she would owe to individuals with whom she stood in an arm's-length relationship. What is the justification for requiring a higher standard of ethical dealing in such relationships? Would you favor the law's imposing the same high standards of conduct in relation to the rest of the world? Why or why not?

PROBLEMS AND PROBLEM CASES

1. King Chevrolet provided a 1982 Chevrolet Cavalier to one of its salespeople, Stein. During the eight months Stein drove the car, it was repaired or adjusted 10 times. There were repairs to the carburetor, choke, speedometer, door moldings, seat belt buzzer alarm, and spark plugs as well as a complete paint job. Of the 36 demonstrators Stein had driven over the years as a car salesperson, this was the worst. Stein finally complained to the service department about the car, and asked Lewis, King Chevrolet's sales manager, if he could have another demonstrator because his car was so unreliable. Not long afterward, Muzelak, who had purchased her previous car from Lewis, contacted Lewis about buying a new car. Lewis told her that the "right car for her" was the 1982 Chevrolet Cavalier demonstrator that Stein had used. Lewis did tell Muzelak that the car was a demonstrator, but he did not mention any of the previous repair problems with the car. (Stein later testified that Lewis told him it took someone with his sales ability to "get rid of" that car.) Muzelak bought the car. Over the course of the next eight months, Muzelak's car was in King Chevrolet's service department for repairs 13 times. Some of the problems were never corrected. The car was so unreliable that Muzelak did not drive it after the first eight months of use. Does Muzelak have grounds for an action for fraud?

2. On May 17, Cobaugh was playing in the East End Open Golf Tournament. When he arrived at the ninth tee, he found a new Chevrolet Beretta, together with signs which proclaimed: "HOLE-IN-ONE Wins this 1988 Chevrolet Beretta GT Courtesy of KLICK-LEWIS Buick Chevy Pontiac $49.00 OVER FACTORY INVOICE in Palmyra." Cobaugh aced the ninth hole and attempted to claim his prize. Klick-Lewis refused to deliver the car,

however. Klick-Lewis had offered the car as a prize for a charity golf tournament sponsored by the Hershey-Palmyra Sertoma Club two days earlier and had neglected to remove the car and signs prior to Cobaugh's hole-in-one. Cobaugh sued to compel delivery of the car. Would the doctrine of mistake provide a ground for Klick-Lewis to avoid the contract?

3. West Branch Land Co. owned a tract of land, which it listed for sale. The listing that was published in the local Multiple Listing Service listing sheet and distributed to all subscribing real estate agencies described the property as being "zoned multi for 35 townhouses" when in fact it was really zoned for only 30. Acleson, a licensed real estate broker, received a copy of the listing and, after calculating the costs per unit on the basis of 35 units, submitted an offer to purchase the property. The parties ultimately contracted for the sale of the property for $65,000. The final contract made no mention of the acreage of the land or of its zoning status. Acleson could have determined the true acreage and zoning status by checking the plat map that was available at the local city planner's office. Almost two years after the sale, Acleson learned that the property was really zoned for only 30 units. Will Acleson's failure to investigate the zoning of the land prevent him from obtaining a remedy for misrepresentation or fraud?

4. Odorizzi, an elementary school teacher, was arrested on criminal charges involving illegal sexual activity. After having been arrested, questioned by police, booked, and released on bail, and going 40 hours without sleep, he was visited in his home by the superintendent of the school district and the principal of his school. They told him that they were trying to help him and that they had his best interests at heart. They advised him to resign immediately, stating that there was no time to consult an attorney. They said that if he did not resign immediately, the district would dismiss him and publicize the proceedings, but that if he resigned at once, the incident would not be publicized and would not jeopardize his chances of securing employment as a teacher elsewhere. Odorizzi gave them a written letter of resignation, which they accepted. The criminal charges against Odorizzi were later dismissed, and he sought to resume his employment. When the school district refused to reinstate him, Odorizzi attempted to rescind his letter of resignation on several grounds, including undue influence. (He also alleged duress, but the facts of his case did not constitute duress under applicable state law.) Can Odorizzi avoid the contract on the ground of undue influence?

5. The O'Connors entered into a contract with the Kings in 1986 to lease their townhouse to the Kings with an option to purchase. Prior to leasing the townhouse, Mr. King noticed a crack in a retaining wall near the house's driveway, and Mr. O'Connor showed him an area along the east foundation wall where there was a separation of the earth and foundation. The O'Connors agreed to pay for dirt to be brought in and placed along the east foundation. Both parties believed this would eliminate potential water problems in the basement. At some point prior to the time the Kings leased the townhouse, water seeped into the basement of the townhouse, but the O'Connors did not tell the Kings about this because there was no apparent water damage. Furthermore, when Ms. King explicitly questioned the O'Connors about the existence of water in the basement, the O'Connors denied any existence of water in the basement. The Kings exercised their option to purchase the townhouse in June of 1987. By the fall of that year, the Kings began experiencing problems with doors sticking and interior walls cracking. They later discovered that the retaining wall crack had widened and that there was water damage in the basement bathroom. When the O'Connors refused their demand to pay for the repairs, the Kings moved out of the townhouse. The O'Connors sued the Kings for breach of contract, and the Kings counterclaimed for rescission of the contract. Can the Kings rescind the contract?

6. Boskett, a part-time coin dealer, paid $450 for a dime purportedly minted in 1916 at Denver and two additional coins of relatively small value. After carefully examining the dime, Beachcomber Coins, a retail coin dealer, bought the coin from Boskett for $500. Beachcomber then received an offer from a third party to purchase the dime for $700, subject to certification of its genuineness from the American Numismatic Society. That organization labeled the coin a counterfeit. Can Beachcomber rescind the contract with Boskett on the ground of mistake?

7. Robert & Wendy Pfister asked Foster & Marshall, a stock brokerage firm, to evaluate some stocks that they owned, including 100 shares of Tracor Computing Corporation. The stock was no longer traded on the New York Stock Exchange. The Pfisters did not know the value of the stock, but they believed it to be of little value. They were surprised when Foster & Marshall told them that the stock was trading at $49.50 under its new name, Continuum Co., Inc., so that the value of the Pfisters' stock was $4,950. They asked Foster & Marshall to recheck the figures and brought their stock certificates in for verification. Based on Foster & Marshall's reassurances that they owned 100 shares of Continuum and that these were worth $4,950, the Pfisters sold the stock to Foster & Marshall. As a result of receiving this money for the stock, the Pfisters made a commitment to build a new home, which before the sale had been a "borderline decision." A year after the transaction, Foster & Marshall discovered that the Tracor Computing stock had been exchanged for Continuum stock at a 10-to-1 ratio and that the Pfisters had owned only 10 shares of Continuum. Foster & Marshall claimed relief under the doctrine of mistake and sued the Pfisters to recover the $4,466.25 it had overpaid them. Will Foster & Marshall win?

8. Mrs. Gossinger slipped and fell on soapy water that had flooded the bathroom floor of the apartment that she and her husband rented from Sutherland, a member of the Apartment Owners Association of the Regency of Ala Wai. She immediately drove herself to the hospital, where the physician examined her, performed tests, and concluded that she had suffered a back strain, which he advised her "would take a long time to heal." He advised her to have a follow-up examination at the beginning of the following week—or sooner if her condition worsened. The next day, the Gossingers wrote to the Association demanding compensation for personal injury and property damage caused by the flooding incident. Three days later, an insurance adjuster for State Farm Insurance Company met with the Gossingers to settle their claims. As a result of the meeting, the Gossingers settled their claims for $1,100 and signed a release that purported to discharge the Association and all other persons who might be liable for her injuries from all liability for any personal injury or property damage resulting from her fall. Approximately one year after signing the release, Mrs. Gossinger's back pain had not subsided. Upon examination by a physician, she was diagnosed as suffering from a herniated disc, requiring surgery and leading to more than $20,000 in medical expenses. The Gossingers filed a negligence suit against Sutherland and the Association. The Gossingers asserted that the release is invalid because of unilateral or mutual mistake. Was it?

9. Ashton Development hired Rich & Whillock, Inc., to do grading and excavating work on a construction project. The contract specified that removal of any rock encountered would be considered an "extra." After a month's work, Rich & Whillock encountered rock on the project site. Ashton agreed that the rock would have to be blasted and that this would involve extra costs. It directed Rich & Whillock to go ahead with the blasting and bill for the extra cost. Rich & Whillock did so, submitting separate invoices for the regular contract work and the extra blasting work and receiving payment every two weeks. After completing the work, Rich & Whillock submitted a final billing for an additional $72,286.45. This time Ashton refused to pay. Rich & Whillock communicated that it would "go broke" without this final payment because it was a new business with rented equipment and had numerous subcontractors waiting to be paid. Ashton replied that it would pay $50,000 or nothing. Stating, "I have a check for you, and just take it or leave it, this is all you get. If you don't want this, you have got to sue me," Ashton's agent presented Rich & Whillock with an agreement for a final compromise payment of $50,000. Rich & Whillock signed the settlement agreement and received a $25,000 check after communicating that the agreement was "blackmail" and that it was signing the agreement only because it was necessary in order to survive. Rich & Whillock later signed a release form and received a second check for $25,000. Several months afterward, however, Rich & Whillock sued Ashton for breach of contract, maintaining that the settlement agreement and release should not be enforced. Are the settlement agreement and release voidable?

10. Reed purchased a house from King. Neither King nor his real estate agents told Reed before the sale that a woman and her four children had been murdered there 10 years earlier. Reed learned of the gruesome episode from a neighbor after the sale. She sued King and his real estate agents, seeking rescission and damages on the ground that King should have disclosed the history of the house to her. Can Reed rescind the contract?

11. ▣   *Video Case.* See "In the Cards." Johnson owned a new baseball card store that had been very busy during its first week of operation. Not wanting to close the store while he went out for dinner, he got a temporary clerk who knew nothing about baseball cards to staff the store in his absence. He instructed the clerk that the prices on the cards were marked and if anyone wanted to negotiate for the more expensive cards in the glass case, she was to tell them to return and talk to Johnson. While Johnson was out, a boy came in and asked to look at the Ernie Banks rookie card, which was in the glass case. The card was marked "1200." The boy asked whether the card was really worth $12 and the clerk replied, "Yeah, I guess it is" and sold the card to him for $12. When Johnson returned and looked through the sales, he saw that the card had been sold for $12, when its true price was $1,200. Is the contract voidable on the ground of any reality of consent doctrine?

12. ▣   *Video Case.* See "The Stock Option." As part of an employee benefit plan, Famco gave stock options to its employees. There were two restrictions on the sale of stock to employees, however. First, if the employee terminated employment for any reason, Famco had the right to buy the stock at book value (often less than market value). Second, if an employee wanted to sell the stock while employed, Famco had a right of first refusal. Famco's CEO called a meeting with three employees who had purchased stock. During this meeting, the CEO reminded the employees that if their employment terminated, the company could repurchase the stock at book value. The employees felt that they had to sell their stock back to Famco or they would lose their jobs, in which case they would have to sell their stock anyway. Two employees agreed to resell the stock to Famco. Were these agreements to sell the stock to Famco voidable?

See also "Car Deals."

Capacity to Contract

INTRODUCTION

One of the major justifications for enforcing a contract is that the parties voluntarily consented *to be bound by it. It follows, then, that a person must have the* ability *to give consent before he can be legally bound to an agreement. For truly voluntary agreements to exist, this ability to give consent must involve more than the mere physical ability to say yes or shake hands or sign one's name. Rather, the person's maturity and mental ability must be such that it is fair to presume that he is capable of representing his own interests effectively. This concept is embodied in the legal term* capacity.

LACK OF CAPACITY

Capacity means the ability to incur legal obligations and acquire legal rights. Today, the primary classes of people who are considered to lack capacity are minors (who, in legal terms, are known as *infants*), persons suffering from mental illnesses or defects, and intoxicated persons.[1] Contract law gives them the right to *avoid* (escape) contracts that they enter during incapacity. This rule provides a means of protecting people who, because of mental impairment, intoxication, or youth and inexperience, are disadvantaged in the normal give and take of the bargaining process.

Usually, lack of capacity to contract comes up in court in one of two ways. In some cases, it is asserted by a plaintiff as the basis of a lawsuit for the money or other benefits that he gave the other party under their contract. In others, it arises as a defense to the enforcement of a contract when the defendant is the party who lacked capacity. The responsibility for alleging and proving incapacity is placed on the person who bases his claim or defense on his lack of capacity.

Effect of Lack of Capacity

Normally, a contract in which one or both parties lacks capacity because of infancy, mental impairment, or intoxication is considered to be voidable.

---

[1] In times past, married women, convicts, and aliens were also among the classes of persons who lacked capacity to contract. These limitations on capacity have been removed by statute and court rule, however.

People whose capacity is impaired in any of these ways are able to enter a contract and enforce it if they wish, but they also have the right to avoid the contract. There are, however, some individuals whose capacity is so impaired that they do not have the ability to form even a voidable contract. A bargain is considered to be void if, at the time of formation of the bargain, a court had already **adjudicated** (adjudged or decreed) one or more of the parties to be mentally incompetent or one or more of the parties was so impaired that he could not even manifest assent (for example, he was comatose or unconscious).

Minors' Contracts

Minors' Right to Disaffirm

Courts have long recognized that minors are in a vulnerable position in their dealings with adults. Courts granted minors the right to avoid contracts as a means of protecting against their own improvidence and against overreaching by adults. The exercise of this right to avoid a contract is called **disaffirmance**. The right to disaffirm is personal to the minor. That is, only the minor or a legal representative such as a guardian may disaffirm the contract. No formal act or written statement is required to make a valid disaffirmance. Any words or acts that effectively communicate the minor's desire to cancel the contract can constitute disaffirmance.

If, on the other hand, the minor wishes to enforce the contract instead of disaffirming it, the adult party must perform. You can see that the minor's right to disaffirm puts any adult contracting with a minor in an undesirable position: He is bound on the contract unless it is to the minor's advantage to disaffirm it. The right to disaffirm has the effect of discouraging adults from dealing with minors.

Exceptions to the Minor's Right to Disaffirm

Not every contract involving a minor is voidable, however. State law often creates statutory exceptions to the minor's right to disaffirm. These statutes prevent minors from disaffirming such transactions as marriage, agreements to support their children, educational loans, life and medical insurance contracts, contracts for transportation by common carriers, and certain types of contracts approved by a court (such as contracts to employ a child actor).

Period of Minority

At common law, the age of majority was 21. However, the ratification in 1971 of the 26th Amendment to the Constitution giving 18-year-olds the right to vote stimulated a trend toward reducing the age of majority. The age of majority has been lowered by 49 states. In almost all of these states, the age of majority for contracting purposes is now 18.

Emancipation

Emancipation is the termination of a parent's right to control a child and receive services and wages from him. There are no formal requirements for emancipation. It can occur by the parent's express or implied consent or by the occurrence of some events such as the marriage of the child. In most states, the mere fact that a minor is emancipated does *not* give him capacity to contract. A person younger than the legal age of majority is generally held to lack capacity to enter a contract, even if he is married and employed full time.

Time of Disaffirmance

Contracts entered during minority that affect title to *real estate* cannot be disaffirmed until majority. This rule is apparently based on the special importance of real estate and on the need to protect a minor from improvidently disaffirming a transaction (such as a mortgage or conveyance) involving real estate. All other contracts entered during minority may be disaffirmed as soon as the contract is formed. The minor's power to avoid his contracts does not end on the day he reaches the age of majority. It continues for a period of time after he reaches majority.

How long after reaching majority does a person retain the right to disaffirm the contracts he made while a minor? A few states have statutes that prescribe a definite time limit on the power of avoidance. In Oklahoma, for example, a person who wishes to disaffirm a contract must do so within one year after reaching majority.[2] In most states, however, there is no set limit on the time during which a person may disaffirm after reaching majority. In determining whether a person has the right to

---

[2]Okla. Stat. Ann. tit. 15 sec. 18 (1983).

FIGURE 1   **Time Line Showing Effect of Ratification**

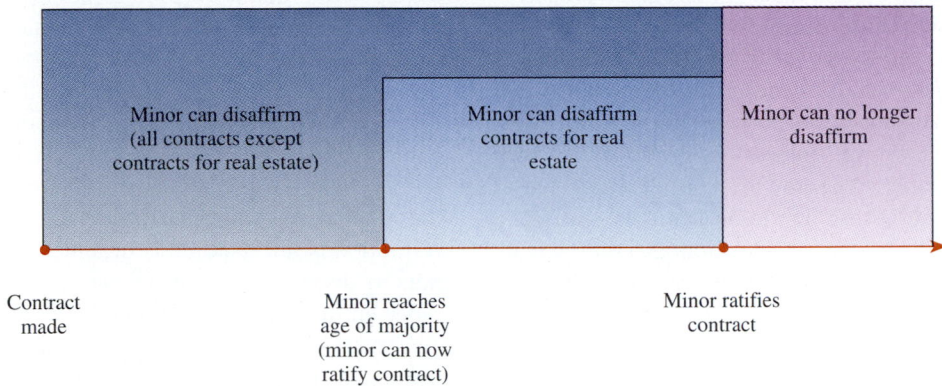

disaffirm, a major factor that courts consider is whether the adult has rendered performance under the contract or relied on the contract. If the adult has relied on the contract or has given something of value to the minor, the minor must disaffirm within a reasonable time after reaching majority. If he delays longer than a period of time that is considered to be reasonable under the circumstances, he will run the risk of *ratifying* (affirming) the contract. (The concept and consequences of ratification are discussed in the next section.) If the adult has neither performed nor relied on the contract, however, the former minor is likely to be accorded a longer period of time in which to disaffirm, sometimes even years after he has reached majority.

Ratification

Though a person has the right to disaffirm contracts made during minority, this right can be given up after the person reaches the age of majority. When a person who has reached majority indicates that he intends to be bound by a contract that he made while still a minor, he surrenders his right to disaffirm. This act of affirming the contract and surrendering the right to avoid the contract is known as **ratification**. Ratification makes a contract valid from its inception. Because ratification represents the former minor's election to be bound by the contract, he cannot later disaffirm. Ratification can be done effectively only after the minor reaches

majority. Otherwise, it would be as voidable as the initial contract. The effect of ratification is illustrated in Figure 1.

There are no formal requirements for ratification. Any of the former minor's words or acts after reaching majority that indicate with reasonable clarity his intent to be bound by the contract are sufficient. Ratification can be *expressed* in an oral or written statement, or, as is more often the case, it can be *implied* by conduct on the part of the former minor. Naturally, ratification is clearest when the former minor has made some express statement of his intent to be bound. Predicting whether a court will determine that a contract has been ratified is a bit more difficult when the only evidence of the alleged ratification is the conduct of the minor. A former minor's acceptance or retention of benefits given by the other party for an unreasonable time after he has reached majority can constitute ratification. Also, a former minor's continued performance of his part of the contract after reaching majority has been held to imply his intent to ratify the contract.

Duty to Return Consideration upon Disaffirmance

If neither party has performed his part of the contract, the parties' relationship will simply be canceled by the disaffirmance. Since neither party has given anything to the other party, no further adjustments are necessary. But what about the situation where, as is often the case, the minor has paid money to the adult and the adult has given property to the minor? Upon disaffirmance, each party has the duty to return to the other any consideration that the other has given. This means that the minor must return any consideration given to him by the adult that remains in his possession. However, if the minor is unable to return the consideration, most states will still permit him to disaffirm the contract.

The duty to return consideration also means that the minor has the right to recover any consideration he has given to the adult party. He even has the right to recover some property that has been transferred to third parties. One exception to the minor's right to recover property from third parties is found in section 2–403 of the Uniform Commercial Code, however. Under this section, a minor cannot recover *goods* that have been transferred to a good faith purchaser. For example, Simpson, a minor, sells a 1980 Ford to Mort's Car Lot. Mort's then sells the car to Vane, a good faith purchaser. If Simpson disaffirmed the contract with Mort's, he would *not* have the right to recover the Ford from Vane.

Must the Disaffirming Minor Make Restitution? A Split of Authority

If the consideration given by the adult party has been lost, damaged, destroyed, or simply has depreciated in value, is the minor required to make restitution to the adult for the loss? The traditional rule is that the minor who cannot fully return the consideration that was given to her is *not* obligated to pay the adult for the benefits she has received or to compensate the adult for loss or depreciation of the consideration. Some states still follow this traditional rule. (As you will read in the next section, however, a minor's misrepresentation of age can, even in some of these states, make her responsible for reimbursing the other party upon disaffirmance). The rule that restitution is not required is designed to protect minors by discouraging adults from dealing with them. After all, if an adult knew that he might be able to demand the return of anything that he transferred to a minor, he would have little incentive to refrain from entering into contracts with minors.

The traditional rule, however, can work harsh results for innocent adults who have dealt fairly with minors. It strikes many people as unprincipled that a doctrine intended to protect against unfair exploitation of one class of people can be used to unfairly exploit another class of people. As courts sometimes say, the minor's right to disaffirm was designed to be used as a "shield rather than as a sword." For these reasons, a growing number of states have rejected the traditional rule. The courts and legislatures of these states have adopted rules that require minors who disaffirm their contracts and seek refunds of purchase price to reimburse adults for the use or depreciation of their property. The following case, *Dodson v. Shrader*, follows this approach.

DODSON V. SHRADER
824 S.W.2d 545 (Tenn. Sup. Ct. 1992)

Joseph Dodson, age 16, bought a 1984 Chevrolet truck from Burns and Mary Shrader, owners of Shrader's Auto Sales, for $4,900 cash. At the time, Burns Shrader, believing Dodson to be 18 or 19, did not ask Dodson's age and Dodson did not volunteer it. Dodson drove the truck for about eight months, when he learned from an auto mechanic that there was a burned valve in the engine. Dodson did not have the money for the repairs, so he continued to drive the truck without repair for another month until the engine "blew up" and stopped operating. He parked the car in the front yard of his parents' house. He then contacted the Shraders, rescinding the purchase of the truck and requesting a full refund. The Shraders refused to accept the truck or to give Dodson a refund. Dodson then filed an action seeking to rescind the contract and recover the amount paid for the truck. Before the court could hear the case, a hit-and-run driver struck Dodson's parked truck, damaging its left front fender. At the time of the circuit court trial, the truck was worth only $500. The Shraders argued that Dodson should be responsible for paying the difference between the present value of the truck and the

$4,900 purchase price. The trial court found in Dodson's favor, ordering the Shraders to refund the $4,900 purchase price upon delivery of the truck. The Tennessee Court of Appeals affirmed this judgment, and the Shraders appealed.

O'Brien, Justice   The law on the subject of the protection of infants' rights has been slow to evolve. The underlying purpose of the "infancy doctrine" is to protect minors from their lack of judgment and from squandering their wealth through improvident contracts with crafty adults who would take advantage of them in the marketplace.

There is, however, a modern trend among the states, either by judicial action or by statute, in the approach to the problem of balancing the rights of minors against those of innocent merchants. As a result, two minority rules have developed which allow the other party to a contract with a minor to refund less than the full consideration paid in the event of rescission. The first of these minority rules is called the "Benefit Rule." This rule holds that, upon rescission, recovery of the full purchase price is subject to a deduction for the minor's use of the merchandise. This rule recognizes that the traditional rule in regard to necessaries has been extended so far as to hold an infant bound by his contracts, where he failed to restore what he has received under them to the extent of the benefit actually derived by him from what he has received from the other party to the transaction. The other minority rule holds that the minor's recovery of the full purchase price is subject to a deduction for the minor's "use" of the consideration he or she received under the contract, or for the "depreciation" or "deterioration" of the consideration in his or her possession.

We are impressed by the statement made by the Court of Appeals of Ohio:

At a time when we see young persons between 18 and 21 years of age demanding and assuming more responsibilities in their daily lives; when we see such persons charged with the responsibility for committing crimes; when we see such persons being sued in tort claims for acts of negligence; when we see such persons subject to military service; when we see such persons engaged in business and acting in almost all other respects as an adult, it seems timely to re-examine the case law pertaining to contractual rights and responsibilities of infants to see if the law as pronounced and applied by the courts should be redefined.

We state the rule to be followed hereafter, in reference to a contract of a minor, to be where the minor has not been overreached in any way, and there has been no undue influence, and the contract is a fair and reasonable one, and the minor has actually paid money on the purchase price, and taken and used the article purchased, that he ought not to be permitted to recover the amount actually paid, without allowing the vendor of the goods reasonable compensation for the use of, depreciation, and willful or negligent damage to the article purchased, while in his hands. If there has been any fraud or imposition on the part of the seller or if the contract is unfair, or any unfair advantage has been taken of the minor inducing him to make the purchase, then the rule does not apply. This rule will fully and fairly protect the minor against injustice or imposition, and at the same time it will be fair to a business person who has dealt with such minor in good faith.

This rule is best adapted to modern conditions under which minors are permitted to, and do in fact, transact a great deal of business for themselves, long before they have reached the age of legal majority. Many young people work and earn money and collect it and spend it oftentimes without any oversight or restriction. The law does not question their right to buy if they have the money to pay for their purchases. It seems intolerably burdensome of everyone concerned if merchants cannot deal with them safely, in a fair and reasonable way. Further, it does not appear consistent with practice of proper moral influence upon young people, tend to encourage honesty and integrity, or lead them to a good and useful business future if they are taught that they can make purchases with their own money, for their own benefit, and after paying for them, and using them until they are worn out and destroyed, go back and compel the vendor to return to them what they have paid upon the purchase price. Such a doctrine can only lead to the corruption of principles and encourage young people in habits of trickery and dishonesty.

Reversed and remanded in favor of the Shraders.

Effect of Misrepresentation of Age

It is not unheard of for a minor to occasionally pretend to be older than he is. The normal rules dealing with the minor's right to disaffirm and his duties upon disaffirmance can be affected by a minor's misrepresentation of his age.[3] Suppose, for example, that Jones, age 17, wants to lease a car from Acme Auto Rentals, but knows that Acme rents only to people who are at least 18. Jones induces Acme to lease a car to him by showing a false identification that represents his age to be 18. Acme relies on the misrepresentation. Jones wrecks the car, attempts to disaffirm the contract, and asks for the return of his money. What is the effect of Jones's misrepresentation? State law is not uniform on this point.

The traditional rule was that a minor's misrepresentation about his age did not affect his right to disaffirm and did not create any obligation to reimburse the adult for damages or pay for benefits received. The theory behind this rule is that one who lacks capacity cannot acquire it merely by claiming to be of legal age. As you can imagine, this traditional approach does not "sit well" with modern courts, at least in those cases in which the adult has dealt with the minor fairly and in good faith, because it creates severe hardship for innocent adults who have relied on minors' misrepresentations of age.

State law today is fairly evenly divided among those states that take the position that the minor who misrepresents his age will be *estopped* (prevented) from asserting his infancy as a defense and those that will allow a minor to disaffirm regardless of his misrepresentation of age. Among the states that allow disaffirmance despite the minor's misrepresentation, most hold the disaffirming minor responsible for the losses suffered by the adult, either by allowing the adult to counterclaim against the minor for the tort of deceit or by requiring the minor to reimburse the adult for use or depreciation of his property.

---

[3]You might want to refer back to Chapter 13 to review the elements of misrepresentation.

Minors' Obligation to Pay Reasonable Value of Necessaries

Though the law regarding minors' contracts is designed to discourage adults from dealing with (and possibly taking advantage of) minors, it would be undesirable for the law to discourage adults from selling minors the items that they need for basic survival. For this reason, disaffirming minors are required to pay the reasonable value of items that have been furnished to them that are classified as **necessaries.** A necessary is something that is essential for the minor's continued existence and general welfare that has not been provided by the minor's parents or guardian. Examples of necessaries include food, clothing, shelter, medical care, tools of the minor's trade, and basic educational or vocational training.

A minor's liability for necessaries supplied to him is **quasi contractual**. That is, the minor is liable for the *reasonable value* of the necessaries that she actually receives. She is not liable for the entire price agreed on if that price exceeds the actual value of the necessaries, and she is not liable for necessaries that she contracted for but did not receive. For example, Joy Jones, a minor, signs a one-year lease for an apartment in Mountain Park at a rent of $300 per month. After living in the apartment for three months, Joy breaks her lease and moves out. Because she is a minor, Joy has the right to disaffirm the lease. If shelter is a necessary in this case, however, she must pay the reasonable value of what she has actually received—three months' rent. If she can establish that the actual value of what she has received is less than $300 per month, she will be bound to pay only that lesser amount. Furthermore, she will not be obligated to pay for the remaining nine months' rent, because she has not received any benefits from the remainder of the lease.

Whether a given item is considered a necessary depends on the facts of a particular case. The minor's age, station in life, and personal circumstances are all relevant to this issue. As is emphasized in the *Webster Street Partnership* case, which follows, an item sold to a minor is not considered a necessary if the minor's parent or guardian has already supplied him with similar items. For this reason, the range of items that will be considered necessaries is broader for married minors and other emancipated minors than it is for unemancipated minors.

WEBSTER STREET PARTNERSHIP V. SHERIDAN
368 N.W.2d 439 (S. Ct. Neb. 1985)

Webster Street owns real estate in Omaha, Nebraska. On September 18, 1982, Webster Street entered into a written contract to lease an apartment to Matthew Sheridan and Pat Wilwerding for one year at a rental of $250 per month. Although Webster Street did not know this, both Sheridan and Wilwerding were younger than the age of majority (which was 19) when the lease was signed.

Sheridan and Wilwerding paid $150 as a security deposit and rent for the remainder of September and the month of October, for a total of $500. They failed to pay their November rent on time, however, and Webster Street notified them that they would be required to move out unless they paid immediately. Unable to pay rent, Sheridan and Wilwerding moved out of the apartment on November 12. Webster Street later demanded that they pay the expenses it incurred in attempting to rerent the property, rent for the months of November and December (apparently the two months it took to find a new tenant), and assorted damages and fees, amounting to $630.94. Sheridan and Wilwerding refused to pay any of the amount demanded on the ground of minority, and demanded the return of their security deposit. Webster Street then filed this lawsuit. The district court found that the apartment was a necessary and that Sheridan and Wilwerding were liable for the 12 days in November in which they had actually possessed the apartment without paying rent, but that they were entitled to the return of their security deposit. Webster Street appealed from this ruling.

Krivosha, Chief Justice   The privilege of infancy will not enable an infant to escape liability under all circumstances. For example, it is well established that an infant is liable for the value of necessaries furnished him. Just what are necessaries, however, has no exact definition. The term is flexible and varies according to the facts of each individual case. A number of factors must be considered before a court can conclude whether a particular product or service is a necessary. The articles must be useful and suitable. To be necessaries the articles must supply the infant's personal needs, either those of his body or those of his mind. However, the term "necessaries" is not confined to merely such things as are required for bare subsistence. What may be considered necessary for one infant may not be necessaries for another infant whose state is different as to rank, social position, fortune, health, or other circumstances. To enable an infant to contract for articles as necessaries, he must have been in actual need of them, and obliged to procure them for himself. They are not necessaries as to him, however necessary they may be in their nature, if he was already supplied with sufficient articles of the kind, or if he had a parent or guardian who was able and willing to supply them. The

burden of proof is on the plaintiff to show that the infant was destitute of the articles and had no way of procuring them except by his own contract.

The undisputed testimony is that both tenants were living away from home, apparently with the understanding that they could return home at any time. It would appear that neither Sheridan nor Wilwerding was in need of shelter but, rather, had chosen to voluntarily leave home, with the understanding that they could return whenever they desired. One may at first blush believe that such a rule is unfair. Yet, on further consideration, the wisdom of such a rule is apparent. If landlords may not contract with minors, except at their peril, they may refuse to do so. In that event, minors who voluntarily leave home but who are free to return will be compelled to return to their parents' home—a result which is desirable. We therefore hold that the district court erred in finding that the apartment was a necessary.

Because the rental of the apartment was not a necessary, the minors had the right to avoid the contract, either during their minority or within a reasonable time after reaching their majority. Disaffirmance by an infant completely puts an end to the contract's existence both as to him and as to the adult with whom he contracted. Because the parties then stand as if no contract had ever existed, the infant can recover payments made to the adult, and the adult is entitled to the return of whatever was received by the infant.

The record shows that Wilwerding clearly disaffirmed the contract during his minority. Moreover, when Webster Street ordered the minors out for failure to pay rent and they vacated the premises, Sheridan likewise disaffirmed the contract. The record indicates that Sheridan reached majority on November 5. To suggest that a lapse of 7 days was not disaffirmance within a reasonable time would be foolish. Once disaffirmed, no contract existed between the parties and the minors were entitled to recover all of the moneys which they paid and to be relieved of any further obligation under the contract. The judgment of the district court is therefore reversed and the cause remanded with directions to vacate the judgment in favor of Webster Street and to enter a judgment in favor of Matthew Sheridan and Pat Wilwerding in the amount of $500, representing September rent in the amount of $100, October rent in the amount of $250, and the security deposit in the amount of $150.

Judgment reversed in favor of Sheridan and Wilwerding.

CAPACITY OF MENTALLY IMPAIRED PERSONS

Theory of Incapacity

Like minors, people who suffer from a mental illness or defect are at a disadvantage in their ability to protect their own interests in the bargaining process. Contract law makes their contracts either void or voidable to protect them from the results of their own impaired perceptions and judgment and from others who might take advantage of them.

Test for Mental Incapacity

Incapacity on grounds of mental illness or defect, which is often referred to in cases and texts as "insanity," encompasses a broad range of causes of impaired mental functioning, such as mental illness, brain damage, mental retardation, or senility. The mere fact that a person suffers from some mental illness or defect does not necessarily mean that he lacks capacity to contract, however. He could still have full capacity unless the defect or illness affects the particular transaction in question.

The usual test for mental incapacity is a *cognitive* one; that is, courts ask whether the person had sufficient mental capacity to understand the nature and effect of the contract. Some courts have criticized the traditional test as unscientific because it does not take into account the fact that a person suffering from a mental illness or defect might be unable to *control* his conduct. Section 15 of the *Restatement (Second) of Contracts* provides that a person's contracts are voidable if he is unable to *act* in a reasonable manner in relation to the transaction and the other party has reason to know of his condition. Where the other party has reason to know of the condition of the mentally impaired person, the *Restatement (Second)* standard would provide protection to people who understood the transaction but, because of some mental defect or illness, were unable to exercise appropriate judgment or to control their conduct effectively. This standard is employed by the court in the following case, *Farnum v. Silvano*.

FARNUM V. SILVANO
540 N.E.2d 202 (App. Ct. of Mass. 1989)

Viola Farnum was 90 years old when she sold her real estate in South Yarmouth to Joseph Silvano, age 24. Farnum knew and trusted Silvano because he had done mowing and landscape work on her property. Although the fair market value of Farnum's property was $115,000 at the time of the sale, she agreed to sell it as well as the furniture and other furnishings in the house for $64,900. Silvano had reason to know of the inadequacy of the purchase price. Farnum's nephew had warned Silvano not to proceed with the sale. In addition, Silvano was able to get a mortgage for $65,000 from the bank to finance the purchase.

Farnum's mental competence had begun to fail seriously three years before the sale to Silvano. She began to engage in aberrant conduct such as lamenting not hearing from her sisters, who were dead, and she would wonder where the people upstairs in her house had gone, when there was no upstairs to her house. She offered to sell her house to a neighbor for $35,000. She became abnormally forgetful, locking herself out of her house and breaking into it rather than calling on a neighbor with whom she had left a key. She hid her cat to protect it from "the cops." She would express the desire to return to Cape Cod although she was on Cape Cod. She easily became lost. Her sister and nephew had to pay her bills and balance her checkbook. She was hospitalized several times during the three-year period preceding the sale to Silvano. Medical tests revealed organic brain disease.

During the transaction in question, Farnum was represented by a lawyer selected and paid by Silvano. That lawyer and a lawyer for the bank that was making a loan to Silvano attended the closing at Farnum's house. At the closing, Farnum was cheerful, engaged in pleasantries, and made instant coffee for those present. After the transaction, however, Farnum insisted to others, including her sister and nephew, that she still owned the property. Six months after the conveyance, Farnum was admitted to the hospital for treatment of dementia and seizure disorder. She was discharged to a nursing home.

Farnum's nephew, who was ultimately appointed her guardian, brought this suit on Farnum's behalf to rescind the sale on the ground of Farnum's mental impairment. The trial judge concluded that Farnum had been "aware of what was going on," and denied the rescission. Farnum appealed.

Kass, Judge   On the basis of a finding that Farnum enjoyed a lucid interval when she conveyed her house to Silvano, for approximately half its market value, a Probate Court judge decided that Farnum had capacity to execute the deed. A different test measures competence to enter into a contract and we, therefore, reverse the judgment.

Competence to enter into a contract presupposes something more than a transient surge of lucidity. It involves not merely comprehension of what is "going on," but an ability to comprehend the nature and quality of the transaction, together with an understanding of its significance and consequences. In the act of entering into a contract there are reciprocal obligations, and it is appropriate, when mental incapacity, as here, is manifest, to require a baseline of reasonableness.

In *Krasner v. Berk*, the court cited with approval the synthesis of those principles now appearing in the *Restatement (Second) of Contracts* section 15(1), which regards as voidable a transaction entered into with a person who, "by reason of mental illness or defect (a) . . . is unable to understand in a reasonable manner the nature and consequences of the transaction, or (b) . . . is unable to act in a reasonable manner in relation to the transaction and the other party has reason to know of [the] condition."

Applied to the case at hand, Farnum could be aware that she was selling her house to Silvano for much less than it was worth, while failing to understand the unreasonableness of doing so at a time when she faced serious cash demands for rent, home care, or nursing care charges. That difference between awareness of the surface of a transaction, *i.e.*, that it was happening, and failure to comprehend the unreasonableness and consequences of the transaction by a mentally impaired person was recognized and discussed in *Ortolere v. Teachers' Retirement Bd.* In the Ortolere case, a teacher who was enrolled in a retirement plan suffered a psychotic break. Her age was sixty and she also suffered from cerebral arteriosclerosis. While thus afflicted, Grace Ortolere changed her selection of benefit to choose the maximum retirement allowance during her lifetime with nothing payable after her death—this in the face of severely diminished life expectancy and her husband having given up his employment to care for her full time. The court observed that her selection was so unwise and foolhardy that a fact finder might conclude that it was explainable only as a product of psychosis.

We think Farnum did not possess the requisite contextual understanding. She suffered mental disease which had manifested itself in erratic and irrational conduct and was confirmed by diagnostic test. Her physician did not think she was competent to live alone. Relatively soon after the transaction, Farnum's mental deficits grew so grave that it became necessary to hospitalize her. The man to whom she sold her property for less than its value was not a member of her family or someone who had cared for her for long duration. Farnum was not represented by a lawyer who knew her and considered her overall interests as a primary concern. The mission of the lawyer secured by Silvano, and paid by him, was to effect the transaction. As we have observed, Farnum was faced with growing cash demands for her maintenance, and, in her circumstances, it was not rational to part with a major asset for a cut-rate price.

The decisive factor which we think makes Farnum's delivery of her deed to Silvano voidable was his awareness of Farnum's inability to act in a reasonable manner. Silvano knew or had reason to know of Farnum's impaired condition from her conduct, which at the times material caused concern to her relatives, her neighbors, and her physician. Silvano was aware that he was buying the house for about half its value. He had been specifically warned by Farnum's nephew about the unfairness of the transaction and Farnum's mental disability.

Farnum is entitled to rescission of the conveyance.

Judgment reversed in favor of Farnum.

The Effect of Incapacity Caused by Mental Impairment

The contracts of people who are suffering from a mental defect at the time of contracting are usually considered to be *voidable*. In some situations, however, severe mental or physical impairment may prevent a person from even being able to manifest consent. In such a case, no contract could be formed.

As mentioned at the beginning of this chapter, contract law makes a distinction between a contract involving a person who has been *adjudicated* (judged by a court) incompetent at the time the contract was made and a contract involving a person who was suffering from some mental impairment at the time the contract was entered but whose incompetency was not established until *after* the contract was formed. If a person is under guardianship at the time the contract is formed—that is, if a court has found a person mentally incompetent after holding a hearing on his mental competency and has appointed a guardian for him—the contract is considered *void*. On the other hand, if *after* a contract has been formed, a court finds that the person who manifested consent lacked capacity on grounds of mental illness or defect, the contract is usually considered *voidable* at the election of the party who lacked capacity (or his guardian or personal representative).

The Right to Disaffirm

If a contract is found to be voidable on the ground of mental impairment, the person who lacked capacity at the time the contract was made has the right to disaffirm the contract. A person formerly incapacitated by mental impairment can ratify a contract if he regains his capacity. Thus, if he regains capacity, he must disaffirm the contract unequivocally within a reasonable time, or he will be deemed to have ratified it.

As is true of a disaffirming minor, a person disaffirming on the ground of mental impairment must return any consideration given by the other party that remains in his possession. A person under this type of mental incapacity is liable for the reasonable value of necessaries in the same manner as are minors. Must the incapacitated party reimburse the other party for loss, damage, or depreciation of non-necessaries given to him? This is generally said to depend on whether the contract was basically fair and on whether the other party had reason to be aware of his impairment. If the contract is fair, bargained for in good faith, and the other party had no reasonable cause to know of the incapacity, the contract cannot be disaffirmed unless the other party is placed in *status quo* (the position she was in before the creation of the contract). However, if the other party had reason to know of the incapacity, the incapacitated party is allowed to disaffirm without placing the other party in status quo. This distinction discourages people from attempting to take advantage of mentally impaired people, but it spares those who are dealing in good faith and have no such intent.

CONTRACTS OF INTOXICATED PERSONS

Intoxication and Capacity

Intoxication (either from alcohol or the use of drugs) can deprive a person of capacity to contract. The mere fact that a party to a contract had been drinking when the contract was formed would *not* normally affect his capacity to contract, however. Intoxication is a ground for lack of capacity only when it is so extreme that the person is unable to understand the nature of the business at hand. Section 16 of the *Restatement (Second) of Contracts* further provides that intoxication is a ground for lack of capacity only if *the other party has reason to know* that the affected person is so intoxicated that he cannot understand or act reasonably in relation to the transaction.

The rules governing the capacity of intoxicated persons are very similar to those applied to the capacity of people who are mentally impaired. The basic right to disaffirm contracts made during incapacity, the duties upon disaffirmance, and the possibility of ratification upon regaining capacity are the same for an intoxicated person as for a person under a mental impairment. In practice, however, courts traditionally have been less sympathetic with a person who was intoxicated at the time of contracting than with minors or those suffering from a mental impairment. It is rare for a person to actually escape his contractual obligations on the ground of intoxication. A person incapacitated by intoxication at the time of contracting might nevertheless be bound to his contract if he fails to disaffirm in a timely manner.

ETHICAL AND PUBLIC POLICY CONCERNS

1. You read that the age of majority for contracting purposes is 18 in almost all states today. We all know that maturity at a given age varies greatly from individual to individual. Does it make sense for the law to *presume* that a person is sufficiently mature to be responsible for his agreements merely because he has reached the age of 18? Would public policy be better served if the maturity of contracting parties were determined on a case-by-case basis in the same way that we now determine the capacity of those who are mentally impaired or intoxicated? Why or why not?

2. In *Dodson v. Shrader*, the court rejected the traditional view that minors who no longer have the consideration in their possession can disaffirm their contracts without reimbursing the adult party for use or depreciation of the adult's property. Which rule, the traditional rule or the rule applied in *Dodson*, makes the most sense? Was Judge O'Brien correct in his remark that the traditional rule is inconsistent with "proper moral influence upon young people?" Discuss.

3. In recent years, there has been growing public concern over alcohol and drug abuse. Through legal developments such as vigorous enforcement of drunken driving laws and the imposition of tort liability on the part of alcohol suppliers, the law encourages moderation in the use of alcohol. Yet, the law also makes it possible for a person who is so intoxicated that he does not appreciate the business at hand to escape his contractual obligations. Is this rule about the capacity of intoxicated persons out of step with sound public policy?

PROBLEMS AND PROBLEM CASES

1. Smith, age 17, purchased a car from Bobby Floars Toyota, signing an agreement to pay the balance of the purchase price in 30 monthly installments. Ten months after he reached majority (which was 18 in that state), Smith voluntarily returned the car to Floars and stopped making payments. At this point, he had made 11 monthly payments, 10 of which were made after his 18th birthday. Floars sold the car at public auction and sued Smith for the remaining debt. Will Smith be required to pay?

2. Robertson, while a minor, contracted to borrow money from his father for a college education. His father mortgaged his home and took out loans against his life insurance policies to get some of the money he lent to Robertson, who ultimately graduated from dental school. Two years after Robertson's graduation, his father asked him to begin paying back the amount of $30,000 at $400 per month. Robertson agreed to pay $24,000 at $100 per month. He did this for three years before stopping the payments. His father sued for the balance of the debt. Could Robertson disaffirm the contract?

3. Green, age 16, contracted to buy a Camaro from Star Chevrolet. Green lived about six miles from school and one mile from his job, and used the Camaro to go back and forth to school and work. When he did not have the car, he used a car pool to get to school and work. Several months later, the car became inoperable due to a blown head gasket, and Green gave notice of disaffirmance to Star Chevrolet. Star Chevrolet refused to refund the purchase price, claiming, in part, that the car was a necessary. Was it?

4. Clardy had suffered from a manic depressive condition for 15 years, for which he took medication. On April 1, 1989, Clardy first spoke to Shoals Ford about the purchase of a truck and filled out the initial papers. On that same day, while visiting his daughter, he had become agitated and out of control, throwing his medicine into a burning pile of leaves. On April 3, he signed the necessary documents, but was advised that, because of a poor credit rating, a down payment of $10,500 would be required rather than the $5,000 down payment that had been previously discussed. Early in the morning of April 5, Clardy banged on the doors and windows of his daughter's household until he awakened everyone there. He threatened their lives and forced his daughter to write him a check for $500. After Clardy left, his daughter went to her attorney's office and asked that he prepare a petition to have Clardy involuntarily committed. She then called Shoals Ford to notify it that Clardy would be coming in to purchase a particular truck and to tell it of his condition. Clardy's wife also spoke with Shoals Ford's sales representatives and told them that Clardy was not working, that he was ill and would be committed, that "buying sprees" were a symptom of his disease, and that the truck could not be insured. She asked them not to sell the truck to him. Shoals Ford's representative merely stated that if Clardy had the money to buy the truck it was "none of her concern." That same day, Clardy returned to Shoals Ford with the down payment and picked up the truck. Clardy was admitted to the

hospital later that night. The psychiatrist who saw him the next day found him to be incompetent and testified that he could not visualize Clardy being otherwise on April 5. A month later, his wife was appointed conservator and guardian for him. She brought an action to set aside the purchase on the ground of lack of capacity and recover the money that Clardy had paid Shoals Ford. Will she win?

5. At a time when the age of majority in Ohio was 21, Lee, age 20, contracted to buy a 1964 Plymouth Fury for $1,552 from Haydocy Pontiac. Lee represented herself to be 21 when entering the contract. She paid for the car by trading in another car worth $150 and financing the balance. Immediately following delivery of the car to her, Lee permitted one John Roberts to take possession of it. Roberts delivered the car to someone else, and it was never recovered. Lee failed to make payments on the car, and Haydocy Pontiac sued her to recover the car or the amount due on the contract. Lee repudiated the contract on the ground that she was a minor at the time of purchase. Can Lee disaffirm the contract without reimbursing Haydocy Pontiac for the value of the car?

6. In 1955, the Probate Court of Franklin County adjudged Beard to be mentally incompetent and appointed a guardian for him. Thereafter, in 1978, a successor guardian was appointed for Beard. On February 22, 1989, while still under guardianship, Beard executed a promissory note for $10,254.60 to Huntington National Bank in order to finance the purchase of a 1987 Nissan pickup truck. The flexible interest rate for the note was to be paid over a five-year period, with monthly installments of $170.91. Beard made only a few payments on the note before dying on July 31, 1989. In the four- or five-year period prior to his death, Beard had had several dealings with the bank, including the financing of two other truck purchases. He had maintained a sparkling credit rating, fully repaying his previous loans. Toland was appointed administrator of Beard's estate. When she learned of the outstanding debt to the bank, she returned the car to the bank. The bank sold it and sought to have the estate pay the outstanding debt left after crediting the proceeds of the car and Beard's payments. Toland rejected the bank's claim, contending that the promissory note was invalid because of Beard's lack of capacity. Is she right?

7. Randy Hyland owed money to the First State Bank of Sinai on two promissory notes that had already become due. The bank agreed to extend the time of payment if Randy's father, Mervin, acted as a cosigner. Mervin had executed approximately 60 promissory notes with the bank and was a good customer. A new note was prepared for Mervin's signature. Buck, the bank employee with whom Randy dealt, knew that Mervin drank, but later testified that he was unaware of any alcohol-related problems. Mervin had been drinking heavily from late summer through the early winter of 1981. During this period, his wife and son managed the farm, and Mervin was weak, unconcerned with family and business matters, uncooperative, and uncommunicative. When he was drinking, he spent most of his time at home, in bed. He was involuntarily committed to hospitals twice during this period. He was released from his first commitment on September 19 and again committed on November 20. Between the periods of his commitments, he did transact some business himself, such as paying for farm goods and services, hauling his grain to storage elevators, and making decisions concerning when grain was to be sold. When Randy brought this note home, Mervin was drunk and in bed. On October 20 or 21, he rose from the bed, walked into the kitchen, and signed the note. Later, Randy returned to the bank with the note, which Mervin had properly signed, and added his own signature. The due date on this note was April 20, 1982. On April 20, the note was unpaid. Buck notified Randy of the overdue note, and on May 5, Randy brought to the bank a blank check signed by Mervin with which the interest on the note was to be paid. Randy filled in the check for the amount of interest owing. No further payments were made on the note, and Randy filed for bankruptcy in June 1982. After unsuccessfully demanding the note's payment from Mervin, the bank ultimately filed suit against Mervin. Mervin asserted incapacity on the ground of intoxication, claiming that he had no recollection of seeing the note, discussing it with his son, or signing it. Can Mervin now avoid the contract?

8. In 1984, when Kavovit was 12 years old, he and his parents entered into a contract with Scott Eden Management whereby Scott Eden became the exclusive personal manager to supervise and promote Kavovit's career in the entertainment industry. This agreement ran from February 8, 1984 to February 8, 1986, with an extension for another three years. It entitled Scott Eden to receive a 15 percent commission on Kavovit's gross compensation. It specifically provided that, with respect to contracts entered by Kavovit during the term of the agreement, Scott Eden was entitled to its "commission from the residuals or royalties of such contracts, the full term of such contracts, including all extensions or renewals thereof, notwithstanding earlier termination of this agreement." In 1986, Kavovit signed an agency contract with the Andreadis Agency, a licensed agent selected by Scott Eden pursuant to industry requirements. Thereafter, Kavovit signed several contracts for his services. The most important contract secured a role for him on "As the World Turns." Income from this contract began in 1987 and continued through 1990 with a possibility of renewal. In February 1989, one week before Kavovit's contract with Scott Eden was to expire, Kavovit's attorney notified Scott Eden that Kavovit was disaffirming the contract on the ground of infancy. Scott Eden sued Kavovit to recover its commissions for Kavovit's performances prior to the date of disaffirmance and its commissions on Kavovit's contracts in the entertainment or promotion fields that were executed during the term of the agreement between Scott Eden and Kavovit. Must Kavovit pay these commissions even though he disaffirmed the contract?

9. 🔲 *Video Case.* See "In the Cards." A boy bought an Ernie Banks rookie card for $12 from an inexperienced clerk in a baseball card store owned by Johnson. The card had been marked "1200," and Johnson, who had been away from the store at the time of the sale, had intended the card to be sold for $1,200, not $12. Can Johnson get the card back by asserting the boy's lack of capacity?

ILLEGALITY

INTRODUCTION

Although the public interest normally favors the enforcement of contracts, there are times when the interests that usually favor the enforcement of an agreement are subordinated to conflicting social concerns. As you read in Chapter 13, Reality of Consent, and Chapter 14, Capacity to Contract, for example, people who did not truly consent to a contract or who lacked the capacity to contract have the power to cancel their contracts. In these situations, concerns about protecting disadvantaged persons and preserving the integrity of the bargaining process outweigh the usual public interest in enforcing private agreements. Similarly, when an agreement involves an act or promise that violates some legislative or court-made rule, the public interests threatened by the agreement outweigh the interests that favor its enforcement. Such an agreement will be denied enforcement on the ground of illegality, *even if there is voluntary consent between two parties who have capacity to contract.*

MEANING OF ILLEGALITY

When a court says that an agreement is illegal, it does not necessarily mean that the agreement violates a criminal law, although an agreement to commit a crime is one type of illegal agreement. Rather, an agreement is illegal either because the legislature has declared that particular type of contract to be unenforceable or void or because the agreement violates a **public policy** that has been developed by courts or that has been manifested in constitutions, statutes, administrative regulations, or other sources of law.

The term *public policy* is impossible to define precisely. Generally, it is taken to mean a widely shared view about what ideas, interests, institutions, or freedoms promote public welfare. For example, in our society, there are strong public policies favoring the protection of human life and health, free competition, and private property. Judges' and legislators' perceptions of desirable public policy influence the decisions they make about the resolution of cases or the enactment of statutes. Public policy may be based on a prevailing moral code, on an economic philosophy, or on the need to protect a valued social institution such as the family or the judicial system. If the enforcement of an agreement would create a threat to a public policy, a court may determine that it is illegal.

Determining Whether an Agreement Is Illegal

If a statute states that a particular type of agreement is unenforceable or void, courts will apply the statute and refuse to enforce the agreement. Relatively few such statutes exist, however. More frequently, a legislature will forbid certain conduct but will not address the enforceability of contracts that involve the forbidden conduct. In such cases, courts must determine whether the importance of the public policy that underlies the statute in question and the degree of interference with that policy are sufficiently great to outweigh any interests that favor enforcement of the agreement.

In some cases, it is relatively easy to predict that an agreement will be held to be illegal. For example, an agreement to commit a serious crime is certain to be illegal. However, the many laws enacted by legislatures are of differing degrees of importance to the public welfare. The determination of **illegality** would not be so clear if the agreement violated a statute that was of relatively small importance to the public welfare. For example, in one Illinois case,[1] a seller of fertilizer failed to comply with an Illinois statute requiring that a descriptive statement accompany the delivery of the fertilizer. The sellers prepared the statements and offered them to the buyers but did not give them to the buyers at the time of delivery. The court enforced the contract despite the sellers' technical violation of the law because the contract was not seriously injurious to public welfare.

Similarly, the public policies developed by courts are rarely absolute; they, too, depend on a balancing of several factors. In determining whether to hold an agreement illegal, a court will consider the importance of the public policy involved and the extent to which enforcement of the agreement would interfere with that policy. They will also consider the seriousness of any wrongdoing involved in the agreement and how directly that wrongdoing was connected with the agreement.

For purposes of our discussion, illegal agreements will be classified into three main categories: (1) agreements that violate statutes, (2) agreements that violate public policy developed by courts, and (3) unconscionable agreements and contracts of adhesion.

AGREEMENTS IN VIOLATION OF STATUTE

Agreements Declared Illegal by Statute

State legislatures occasionally enact statutes that declare certain types of agreements unenforceable, void, or voidable. In a case in which a legislature has specifically stated that a particular type of contract is void, a court need only interpret and apply the statute. These statutes differ from state to state. Some are relatively uncommon. For example, an Indiana statute declares surrogate birth contracts to be void.[2] Others, such as *usury statutes* and *wagering statutes*, are common.

Usury Statutes   Federal law and the law of most states set limits on the amount of interest that can be charged for a loan or forbearance (refraining from making a demand for money that is already due). *Usury* means obtaining interest beyond the amount that is authorized by law for these transactions. The statutes that define usury and set the maximum permissible limit for interest are not uniform in their prohibitions or their penalties. When a transaction is covered by usury laws and the rate of interest charged for the use of money exceeds the statutory limit, the contract to pay that interest rate is unenforceable.

Wagering Statutes   All states either prohibit or regulate wagering, or gambling. There is a thin line separating wagering, which is illegal, from well-accepted, lawful transactions in which a person will profit from the happening of an uncertain event. The hallmark of a wager is that neither party has any financial stake or interest in the uncertain event except for the stake that he has created by making the bet. The person making a wager *creates* the risk that he may lose the money or property wagered upon the happening of an uncertain event. Suppose Ames bets Baker $20 that the Cubs will win the pennant this year. Ames has no financial interest in a

---

[1]*Amoco Oil Co. v. Toppert*, 56 Ill. App. 3d 1294 (Ill. Ct. App. 1978).

[2]Ind. Code 31-8-2-2 (1988).

Cubs victory other than that which he has created through his bet. Rather, he has created the risk of losing $20 for the sole purpose of bearing that risk. If, however, people make an agreement about who shall bear an existing risk in which one of them has an actual stake or interest, that is a legal, risk-shifting agreement. Property insurance contracts are classic examples of risk-shifting agreements. The owner of the property pays the insurance company a fee (premium) in return for the company's agreement to bear the risk of the uncertain event that the property will be damaged or destroyed. If, however, the person who takes out the policy had no legitimate economic interest in the insured property (called an **insurable interest** in insurance law), the agreement is an illegal wager.

Agreements that Violate the Public Policy of a Statute

As stated earlier, an agreement can be illegal even if no statute specifically states that that particular sort of agreement is illegal. Legislatures enact statutes in an effort to resolve some particular problem. If courts enforced agreements that involve the violation of a statute, they would frustrate the purpose for which the legislature passed the statute. They would also promote disobedience of the law and disrespect for the courts.

Agreements to Commit a Crime
For the reasons stated above, contracts that require the violation of a criminal statute are illegal. If Grimes promises to pay Judge John Doe a bribe of $5,000 to dismiss a criminal case against Grimes, for example, the agreement is illegal. Sometimes the very formation of a certain type of contract is a crime, even if the acts agreed on are never carried out. An example of this is an agreement to murder another person. Naturally, such agreements are considered illegal under contract law as well as under criminal law.

Agreements that Promote Violations of Statutes
Sometimes a contract of a type that is usually perfectly legal—say, a contract to sell goods—is deemed to be illegal under the circumstances of the case because it promotes or facilitates the violation of a statute. Suppose Davis sells Sims goods on credit. Sims uses the goods in some illegal manner and then refuses to pay Davis for the goods. Can Davis recover the price of the goods from Sims? The answer depends on whether Davis knew of the illegal purpose and whether he intended the sale to further that illegal purpose. Generally speaking, such agreements will be legal unless there is a direct connection between the illegal conduct and the agreement in the form of active, intentional participation in or facilitation of the illegal act. Knowledge of the other party's illegal purpose, standing alone, is generally not sufficient to render an agreement illegal. When a person is aware of the other's illegal purpose *and* actively helps to accomplish that purpose, an otherwise legal agreement—such as a sale of goods—might be labeled illegal.

Licensing Laws: Agreement to Perform an Act for Which a Party Is Not Properly Licensed
Congress and the state legislatures have enacted a variety of statutes that regulate professions and businesses. A common type of regulatory statute is one that requires a person to obtain a license, permit, or registration before engaging in a certain business or profession. For example, state statutes require lawyers, physicians, dentists, teachers, and other professionals to be licensed to practice their professions. In order to obtain the required license, they must meet specified requirements such as attaining a certain educational degree and passing an examination. Real estate brokers, stockbrokers, insurance agents, sellers of liquor and tobacco, pawnbrokers, electricians, barbers, and others too numerous to mention are also often required by state statute to meet licensing requirements to perform services or sell regulated commodities to members of the public.

What is the status of an agreement in which one of the parties agrees to perform an act regulated by state law for which she is not properly licensed? This will often be determined by looking at the purpose of the legislation that the unlicensed party has violated. If the statute is **regulatory**—that is, the purpose of the legislation is to protect the public against dishonest or incompetent practitioners—an agreement by an unlicensed person is generally held to be unenforceable. For example, if Spencer, a first-year law student, agrees to draft a will for Rowen for a fee of $150, Spencer could not enforce the agreement and collect a fee from Rowen for drafting the will because she is not licensed to practice law. This result makes sense, even though it imposes a hardship on Spencer. The public interest in ensuring that people on whose legal advice others rely have an appropriate educational background and proficiency in the subject matter outweighs any interest in seeing that Spencer receives what she bargained for.

On the other hand, where the licensing statute was intended primarily as a **revenue-raising** measure— that is, as a means of collecting money rather than as a means of protecting the public—an agreement to pay a person for performing an act for which she is not licensed will generally be enforced. For example, suppose that in the example used above, Spencer is a lawyer who is licensed to practice law in her state and who met all of her state's educational, testing, and character requirements but neglected to pay her annual registration fee. In this situation, there is no com-

pelling public interest that would justify the harsh measure of refusing enforcement and possibly inflicting forfeiture on the unlicensed person.

Whether a statute is a regulatory statute or a revenue-raising statute depends on the intent of the legislature, which may not always be expressed clearly. Generally, statutes that require proof of character and skill and impose penalties for violation are considered to be regulatory in nature. Their requirements indicate that they were intended for the protection of the public. Those that impose a significant license fee and allow anyone who pays the fee to obtain a license are usually classified as revenue raising. The fact that no requirement other than the payment of the fee is imposed indicates that the purpose of the law is to raise money rather than to protect the public. Because such a statute is not designed for the protection of the public, a violation of the statute is not as threatening to the public interest as is a violation of a regulatory statute.

CONCEPT REVIEW

CONTRACTS THAT VIOLATE A LICENSING STATUTE

Type of Licensing Statute	Regulatory	Revenue Raising
Purpose of Statute	Protect the public welfare	Provide source of revenue
Typical Characteristics of Statute	Require proof of character, skill, and training, and impose penalties for violation	Impose fee with no or few other requirements
Status of Contracts that Violate Statute	Contracts violating statute usually illegal	Contracts violating statute still legal (validity of contract not affected by statute)

It would be misleading to imply that cases involving unlicensed parties always follow such a mechanical test. In some cases, courts may grant recovery to an unlicensed party even where a regulatory statute is violated. If the public policy promoted by the statute is relatively trivial in relation to the amount that would be forfeited by the unlicensed person and the unlicensed person is neither dishonest nor incompetent, a court may conclude that the statutory penalty for violation of the regulatory statute is sufficient to protect the public

interest and that enforcement of the agreement is appropriate. Under section 181 of the *Restatement (Second) of Contracts*, an agreement to pay an unlicensed person for doing an act for which a license is required is unenforceable only if the licensing statute has a regulatory purpose *and* if the interest in enforcement of the promise is clearly outweighed by the public policy behind the statute.

The following case, *Ransburg v. Haase*, shows how courts treat contracts that violate licensing statutes designed to protect the public interest.

RANSBURG V. HAASE
586 N.E.2d 1295 (Ill. Ct. App. 1992)

David and Alexandra Ransburg, residents of Peoria, Illinois, orally hired David William Haase Associates, a Peoria business that designs and decorates houses, to act as the architect, construction manager, designer, and decorator of a house that the Ransburgs wanted to have built in Vail, Colorado. The parties discussed this project both in Peoria and in Colorado. The parties agreed that Haase would provide budgetary control and monitor every aspect of the design, construction, and furnishing of the house. They also agreed to a construction budget of $838,000 and a furnishing budget of $107,500, for a total project cost of $949,500. The scheduled completion date was December 18, 1988. Haase was to receive $80,000, including travel and other expenses, as compensation for his services. The Ransburgs ultimately sued Haase, alleging that he failed to complete the project on time, failed to ensure compliance with applicable building codes and easements, and failed to control the budget so that the total cost of the project exceeded $1.2 million. Count II of this suit stated an alternative cause of action in which the Ransburgs alleged that Haase had held himself out as an architect but is not a registered architect in Illinois or any other state. Claiming that the contract for architectural services was against public policy, they sought recovery of the fees paid to Haase. The trial court dismissed this count, and the Ransburgs appealed.

Barry, Justice   The initial question is whether Haase acted in violation of the Illinois Architecture Act when he represented to the Ransburgs that he is an architect and undertook to provide architectural services in connection with the construction of a residence in Colorado. The allegations in the complaint plainly charge Haase with offering professional services as an architect in Peoria where he operated a design and decorating business. Regardless of where the services were ultimately furnished, holding himself out to the Ransburgs as an architect in Illinois was a violation of the Illinois Architecture Act.

As a general rule, courts will not enforce a contract involving a party who does not have a license called for by legislation that expressly prohibits the carrying on of the particular activity without a license where the legislation was enacted for the protection of the public, not as a revenue measure. In other words, a person practicing a profession without a license cannot recover fees for services rendered. The purposes of the Illinois statute prohibiting the practice of architecture without the required registration has long been held to be for the protection of the public. In *Hattis Associates, Inc. v. Metro Sports Inc.*, the court said:

The statute was not intended to protect architects by limiting the work to licensed architects. Rather, its real purpose was to protect the public from damage caused by the work of incompetent and unlicensed architects.

Applying the general rule to the case before us, it does not appear that the contract would be enforceable.

Do Illinois courts recognize a cause of action to recover money previously paid to defendant for architectural services which have been rendered but for which defendant was not licensed? Although it is a general rule that parties to a void contract will be left where they have placed themselves with no recovery of money paid for illegal services, exceptions to that rule have been recognized under two different rationales: (1) that the person who paid for the services is not in *pari delicto* [equally at fault] with the unlicensed person, and (2) that the law in question was passed for the protection of the person who paid and it appears that the purposes of the law would be better effectuated by granting relief than by denying it.

We believe the public policy of Illinois to be better served by recognizing a cause of action here. To allow the unlicensed architect to retain the fees paid is to allow him to practice architecture in the state of Illinois without a license and to reap the rewards thereof. The purpose of the Illinois licensing act can best be effectuated by recognizing the Ransbergs' right to recovery.

Dismissal of Count II reversed in favor of the Ransburgs, and case remanded for further proceedings.

Agreements in Violation of Public Policy Articulated by Courts

Courts have broad discretion to articulate public policy and to decline to lend their powers of enforcement to an agreement that would contravene what they deem to be in the best interests of society. There is no simple rule for determining when a particular agreement is contrary to public policy. Public policy may change with the times; changing social and economic conditions may make behavior that was acceptable in an earlier time unacceptable today, or vice versa. The following are examples of agreements that are frequently considered vulnerable to attack on public policy grounds.

Agreements in Restraint of Competition

The policy against restrictions on competition is one of the oldest public policies declared by the common law. This same policy is also the basis of federal and state antitrust statutes. The policy against restraints on competition is based on the economic judgment that the public interest is best served by free competition. Nevertheless, courts have long recognized that some contractual restrictions on competition serve legitimate business interests and should be enforced. Therefore, agreements that limit competition are scrutinized very closely by the courts to determine whether the restraint imposed is in violation of public policy.

If the *sole* purpose of an agreement is to restrain competition, it violates public policy and is illegal. For example, if Martin and Bloom, who own competing businesses, enter an agreement whereby each agrees not to solicit or sell to the other's customers, such an agreement would be unenforceable. Where the restriction on competition was part of (*ancillary to*) an otherwise legal contract, the result may be different because the parties may have a legitimate interest to be protected by the restriction on competition.

For example, if Martin had *purchased* Bloom's business, the goodwill of the business was part of what she paid for. She has a legitimate interest in making sure that Bloom does not open a competing business soon after the sale and attract away the very customers whose goodwill she paid for. Or suppose that Martin hired Walker to work as a salesperson in her business. She wants to assure herself that she does not disclose trade secrets, confidential information, or lists of regular customers to Walker only to have Walker quit and enter a competing business.

To protect herself, the buyer or the employer in the above examples might bargain for a contractual clause that would provide that the seller or employee agrees not to engage in a particular competing activity in a specified *geographic area* for a specified *time* after the sale of the business or the termination of employment. This type of clause is called an **ancillary covenant not to compete**, or as it is more commonly known, a **non-competition clause**. They most frequently appear in *employment contracts, contracts for the sale of a business, partnership agreements*, and *small-business buy-sell agreements*. In an employment contract, the non-competition clause might be the only part of the contract that the parties put in writing.

Enforceability of Non-Competition Clauses Although non-competition clauses restrict competition and thereby affect the public policy favoring free competition, courts enforce them if they meet the following three criteria.

1. *Clause must serve a legitimate business purpose.* This means that the person protected by the clause must have some justifiable interest—such as an interest in protecting goodwill or trade secrets—that is to be protected by the non-competition clause. It also means that the clause must be *ancillary* to, or part of, an otherwise valid contract. For example, a non-competition clause that is one term of an existing employment contract would be ancillary to that contract. By contrast, a promise not to compete would not be enforced if the employee made the promise *after* he had already resigned his job, because the promise not to compete was not ancillary to any existing contract.

2. *The restriction on competition must be reasonable in time, geographic area, and scope.* Another way of stating this is that the restrictions must not be any greater than necessary to protect a legitimate interest. It would be unreasonable for an employer or buyer of a business to restrain the other party from engaging in some activity that is not a competing activity or from doing business in a territory in which the employer or buyer does not do business, because this would not threaten his legitimate interests.

3. *The non-competition clause should not impose an undue hardship.* A court will not enforce a non-competition clause if its restraints are unduly burdensome either on the public or on the party whose ability to compete would be restrained. In one case, for example, the court refused to enforce a non-competition clause against a gastroenterologist because of evidence that the restriction would have imposed a hardship on patients and other physicians requiring his services.[3] Non-competition clauses in employment contracts that have the practical effect of preventing the restrained person from earning a livelihood are unlikely to be enforced as well. This is discussed further in the next section.

Non-Competition Clauses in Employment Contracts   Restrictions on competition work a greater hardship on an employee than on a person who has sold a business. For this reason, courts tend to judge non-competition clauses contained in employment contracts by a stricter standard than they judge similar clauses contained in contracts for the sale of a business. In some states, statutes limit or

---

[3]*Iredell Digestive Disease Clinic, P.A. v. Petrozza*, 373 S.E.2d 449 (N.C. Ct. App. 1988).

even prohibit non-competition clauses in employment contracts. In others, there is a trend toward refusing enforcement of these clauses in employment contracts unless the employer can bring forth very good evidence that he has a protectible interest that compels enforcement of the clause. The employer can do this by showing that he has entrusted the employee with trade secrets or confidential information, or that his goodwill with "near-permanent" customers is threatened. In the absence of this kind of proof, a court might conclude that the employer is just trying to avoid competition with a more efficient competitor and refuse enforcement because there is no legitimate business interest that requires protection. You will see this approach in the case of *Steamatic of Kansas City, Inc. v. Rhea*, which follows.

Furthermore, many courts refuse to enforce non-competition clauses if they restrict employees from engaging in a "common calling." A common calling is an occupation that does not require extensive or highly sophisticated training but instead involves relatively simple, repetitive tasks. Under this common calling restriction, various courts have refused to enforce non-competition clauses against salespersons, a barber, and an auto trim repairperson.

STEAMATIC OF KANSAS CITY, INC. v. RHEA
763 S.W.2d 190 (Mo. Ct. App. 1988)

Steamatic of Kansas City, Inc., specialized in cleaning and restoring property damaged by fire, smoke, water, or other elements. It employed Samuel Rhea as a marketing representative. His duties included soliciting customers, preparing cost estimates, supervising restoration work, and conducting seminars. At the time of his employment, Rhea signed a non-competition agreement prohibiting him from entering into a business in competition with Steamatic within six counties of the Kansas City area for a period of two years after the termination of his employment with Steamatic.

Late in 1987, Rhea decided to leave Steamatic. In contemplation of the move, he secretly extracted the agreement restricting his postemployment activity from the company's files and destroyed it. Steamatic learned of this and discharged Rhea. Steamatic filed suit against Rhea to enforce the non-competition agreement when it learned that he was entering a competing business. The trial court enforced the non-competition agreement and granted an injunction against Rhea. Rhea appealed.

Clark, Presiding Judge   Covenants not to compete restrain commerce and limit the freedom of an employee to pursue his trade. Enforcement of such

agreements is, therefore, carefully restricted. An employer cannot extract a restrictive covenant from an employee merely to protect himself from competition but a limited time and geographical restraint may be deemed reasonable and enforceable if a legitimate protectible interest of the employer is served. An employer has a protectible and proprietary right in his "stock of customers" and their good will.

In the present case, before Steamatic may claim to enforce the agreement prohibiting Rhea from engaging in a competing business, it must appear that Steamatic has a stock of customers who regularly deal with Steamatic. A customer in this sense is one who repeatedly has business dealings with a particular tradesman or business. Unless the proponent of the restrictive covenant has a trade following, that is, a group of customers who regularly patronize the business of the particular employer, there can be no stock of customers and no protectible interest.

In this case the facts showed that disaster victims engaged Steamatic to provide restoration services only on a single occasion after the event of a fire or other casualty. The only possible repeat business which Steamatic could anticipate would be in those rare instances when a second casualty befell the same victim. No evidence was adduced to show that such had occurred in the past, or, indeed, that Steamatic enjoyed any repeat business at all. Steamatic was not shown to have had any contact with the customer before the casualty gave rise to a need for restoration services. After the services were performed, there was no repeat business. Prospects for restoration services were not contacted and solicited through any confidential or privileged source, but merely upon knowledge generally available to the public at large that a casualty had

occurred. There was, therefore, no ongoing customer relationship between Steamatic and any identifiable persons or companies.

The evidence did show that Rhea was careful to maintain a good reputation for Steamatic with the [insurance] adjustors as a company which "got the job done" and satisfied the insured. The purpose was to procure a favorable recommendation for Steamatic by the adjustor if the latter's advice were sought by a disaster victim. The evidence was that the owner of the damaged property decided whether to employ Steamatic, or some other company, and it was the owner's responsibility to pay the charges even though the proceeds of an insurance claim would defray the expense in whole or in part. The insurance companies were not Steamatic customers and therefore Steamatic had no protectible interest in the good will of the adjustors.

It is apparent Rhea set about to enter employment competitive with Steamatic under the impression that he would be in violation of his agreement. His conduct in surreptitiously removing and destroying the agreements leads to this conclusion. Guilty conduct, however, is not the test by which the availability of injunctive relief is measured. The question is whether Steamatic had a protectible interest in a stock of customers. It did not and therefore Rhea's conduct in removing his papers from Steamatic's files is not relevant. The trial court erred when it enjoined Rhea from engaging in the damage restoration business.

Judgment reversed in favor of Rhea.

The Effect of Overly Broad Non-Competition Clauses

The courts of different states treat unreasonably broad non-competition clauses in different ways. Some courts will strike the entire restriction if they find it to be unreasonable and will refuse to grant the buyer or employer any protection. Others will refuse to enforce the restraint as written, but will adjust the clause and impose such restraints as would be reasonable. In case of breach of an enforceable non-competition clause, the person ben-

efited by the clause may seek damages or an injunction (a court order preventing the promisor from violating the covenant).

Exculpatory Clauses

An **exculpatory clause** is a provision in a contract that purports to relieve one of the parties from tort liability. Exculpatory clauses are suspect on public policy grounds for two reasons. First, courts are concerned that a party who can contract away his liability for negligence will not have the incentive to use care to avoid hurting others. Second, courts are concerned that an agreement that accords one party such a powerful advantage might have been the result of the abuse of superior bargaining power rather than truly voluntary choice. Although exculpatory agreements are often said to be "disfavored" in the law, courts do not want to prevent parties who are dealing on a fair and voluntary basis from determining how the risks of their transaction shall be borne if their agreement does not threaten public health or safety.

Courts enforce exculpatory clauses in some cases and refuse to enforce them in others, depending on the circumstances of the case, the identity and relationship of the parties, and the language of the agreement. A few ground rules can be stated. First, an exculpatory clause cannot protect a party from liability for any wrongdoing greater than negligence. One that purports to relieve a person from liability for fraud or some other willful tort will be considered to be against public policy. In some cases, in fact, exculpatory clauses have been invalidated on this ground because of broad language stating that one of the parties was relieved of "all liability." Second, exculpatory clauses will not be effective to exclude tort liability on the part of a party who owes a duty to the public (such as an airline) because this would present an obvious threat to the public health and safety.

A third possible limitation on the enforceability of exculpatory clauses arises from the increasing array of statutes and common law rules that impose certain obligations on one party to a contract for the benefit of the other party to the contract. Workers' compensation statutes and laws requiring landlords to maintain leased property in a habitable condition are examples of such laws. Sometimes the person on whom such an obligation is placed will attempt to escape it by inserting an exculpatory or waiver provision in a contract. Such clauses are often—though not always—found to be against public policy because, if enforced, they would frustrate the very purpose of imposing the duty in question. For example, an employee's agreement to relieve her employer from workers' compensation liability is likely to be held illegal as a violation of public policy.

Even if a clause is not against public policy on any of the above three grounds, a court may still refuse to enforce it if a court finds that the clause was **unconscionable**, a **contract of adhesion**, or some other product of abuse of superior bargaining power. (Unconscionability and contracts of adhesion are discussed later in this chapter.) This determination depends on all of the facts of the case. Facts that tend to show that the exculpatory clause was the product of *knowing* consent will increase the likelihood that it will be enforced. For example, a clause that is written in clear language and conspicuous print is more likely to be enforced than one written in "legalese" and presented in fine print. Facts that tend to show that the exculpatory clause was the product of *voluntary* consent increase the likelihood of enforcement of the clause. For example, a clause contained in a contract for a frivolous or unnecessary activity, such as the Ironman Decathlon in *Milligan v. Big Valley Corporation*, is more likely to be enforced than is an exculpatory clause contained in a contract for a necessary activity such as medical care.

Milligan v. Big Valley Corporation
754 P.2d 1063 (Sup. Ct. Wyo. 1988)

Dean Griffin, an expert skier and certified ski instructor, entered the Ironman Decathlon held at the Grand Targhee ski resort, which was owned and operated by Big Valley Corporation. The decathlon was held for fun rather than profit. It consisted of several events, including swimming five pool laps, bowling one line, drinking a quart of beer, throwing darts, and skiing in both downhill and cross-country races. The downhill ski race was the first event in the decathlon. It was held early in the morning before the resort was opened to the public. Prior to the race, Griffin and all of the other downhill contestants were required to sign a document entitled "General Release of Claim." This provided in part:

In consideration of my being allowed to participate in IRONMAN DECATHLON at Targhee Resort, Alta, Wyoming, I irrevocably and forever hereby release and discharge any and all of the employees, agents, or servants and owners of Targhee Resort and the other sponsors of IRONMAN DECATHLON officially connected with this event of and from any and all legal claims or legal liability of any kind involving bodily injury or death sustained by me during my stay at Targhee Resort. I hereby personally assume all risks in connection with said event and I further release the aforementioned resort, its agents, and operators, for any harm which might befall me as a participant in this event, whether foreseen or unforeseen and further save and hold harmless said resort and persons from any claim by me or my family, estate, heirs or assigns. /s/ Dean Griffin 4/13/84

About 10 minutes after the race began, Griffin was found unconscious approximately three quarters of the way down the mountain. He died a few hours later. No one witnessed the incident that caused his death, but it was speculated that he lost control of his skis and hit a tree.

Elizabeth Milligan, as personal representative for Griffin's estate, filed this wrongful death action against Big Valley on behalf of Griffin's son. The trial court granted a summary judgment in favor of Big Valley on the ground that the exculpatory agreement signed by Griffin released Big Valley from all liability. Milligan appealed.

Cardine, Justice   Exculpatory agreements releasing parties from negligence liability for damages or injury are valid and enforceable in Wyoming if they do not violate public policy. Generally, agreements absolving participants and proprietors from negligence liability during hazardous recreational activities are enforceable, subject to willful misconduct limitations.

To determine whether this type of release is valid and enforceable, we consider:

1. Whether there exists a duty to the public;
2. The nature of the service performed;
3. Whether the contract was fairly entered into;
4. Whether the intention of the parties is expressed in clear and unambiguous language.

A duty to the public exists if the nature of the business or service affects the public interest and the service performed is considered an essential service. Types of services thought to be subject to public regulation and therefore demanding a public duty or considered essential have included common carriers, hospitals and doctors, public utilities, innkeepers, public warehousemen, employers, and services involving extra-hazardous activities. Generally, a private recreational business does not qualify as a service demanding a special duty to the public, nor are its services of a special, highly necessary or essential nature. The Ironman Decathlon can best be labeled a recreational type of activity of no great public import.

The agreement in question does not involve severe disparity of bargaining power. A disparity of bargaining power will be found when a contracting party with little or no bargaining strength has no reasonable alternative to entering the contract at the mercy of the other's negligence. For example, a member of the public contracting with a public utility, common carrier, hospital, or employer often has no real choice or alternative and is, therefore, at the mercy of the other. Such is not the case here. Grand Targhee did not force Griffin to ski in the race. Skiing in the race was not a matter of practical necessity for the public, and putting on the race was not an essential service. Thus, no decisive bargaining advantage existed. No evidence suggests that Griffin was unfairly pressured into signing the agreement or that he was deprived of an opportunity to understand its implications.

Milligan argues that the release was entered into unfairly because it contained boilerplate language prepared solely by the resort and was an adhesive contract. The argument is without merit. The mere fact that a contract is on a printed form prepared by one party and offered on a "take it or leave it" basis does not automatically establish it as an adhesive contract. There must be a showing that the parties were greatly disparate in bargaining power and that there was no opportunity for negotiation for services which could not be obtained elsewhere. Here no such showing was made. Indeed, the evidence is to the contrary. The release was fairly executed and satisfies the first three criteria.

The final factor requires us to determine whether the release agreement evidences the parties' intent to release Big Valley from liability for negligent acts in clear and unambiguous language. The language could not be clearer. Examining the release in light of the purpose of the contract, it is clear that the parties intended to release the ski resort and all those involved in the Ironman Decathlon from liability. It is clear that the intent was to release Big Valley from

negligence liability. The absence of the word "negligence" is not fatal to an exculpatory clause if the terms of the contract clearly show intent to extinguish liability.

We conclude that the release is not void as a matter of public policy and that Big Valley was entitled to judgment as a matter of law.

Judgment for Big Valley affirmed.

Family Relationships and Public Policy   In view of the central position of the family as a valued social institution, it is not surprising that an agreement that unreasonably tends to interfere with family relationships will be considered illegal. Examples of this type of contract include agreements whereby one of the parties agrees to divorce a spouse or agrees not to marry.

In recent years, courts have been presented with an increasing number of agreements between unmarried cohabitants that purport to agree upon the manner in which the parties' property will be shared or divided upon separation. It used to be widely held that contracts between unmarried cohabitants were against public policy because they were based on an immoral relationship. As unmarried cohabitation has become more widespread, however, the law concerning the enforceability of agreements between unmarried couples has changed. For example, in the 1976 case of *Marvin v. Marvin*, the California Supreme Court held that an agreement between an unmarried couple to pool income and share property could be enforceable.[4] Today, most courts hold that agreements between unmarried couples are not against public policy unless they are explicitly based on illegal sexual relations as the consideration for the contract or unless one or more of the parties is married to someone else.

---

[4]134 Cal. Rptr. 815 (1976).

Unfairness in Agreements: Contracts of Adhesion and Unconscionable Contracts

Under classical contract law, courts were reluctant to inquire into the fairness of an agreement. Because the prevailing social attitudes and economic philosophy strongly favored freedom of contract, American courts took the position that so long as there had been no fraud, duress, misrepresentation, mistake, or undue influence in the bargaining process, unfairness in an agreement entered into by competent adults did not render it unenforceable.

As the changing nature of our society produced many contract situations in which the bargaining positions of the parties were grossly unequal, the classical contract assumption that each party was capable of protecting himself was no longer persuasive. The increasing use of standardized contracts (preprinted contracts) enabled parties with superior bargaining power and business sophistication to virtually dictate contract terms to weaker and less sophisticated parties.

Legislatures responded to this problem by enacting a variety of statutory measures to protect individuals against the abuse of superior bargaining power in specific situations. Examples of such legislation include minimum wage laws and rent control ordinances. Courts became more sensitive to the fact that superior bargaining power often led to **contracts of adhesion** (contracts in which a stronger party is able to determine the terms of a contract, leaving the weaker party no practical choice but to "adhere" to the terms). Some courts responded by borrowing a doctrine that had been developed and used for a long time in courts of equity,[5] the doctrine of **unconscionability**. Under this doctrine, courts would refuse to grant the equitable remedy of specific performance for breach of a contract if they found the contract to be oppressively unfair. Courts today can use the concepts of unconscionability or adhesion to analyze contracts that are alleged to be so unfair that they should not be enforced.

UNCONSCIONABILITY

One of the most far-reaching efforts to correct abuses of superior bargaining power was the enactment of section 2–302 of the Uniform Commercial Code, which gives courts the power to refuse to enforce all or part of a contract for the sale of goods or to modify such a contract if it is found to be unconscionable. By virtue of its inclusion in Article 2 of the Uniform Commercial Code, the prohibition against unconscionable terms applies to every contract for the sale of goods. The concept of unconscionability is not confined to contracts for the sale of goods, however. Section 208 of the *Restatement (Second) of Contracts,* which closely resembles the unconscionability section of the UCC, provides that courts may decline to enforce unconscionable terms or contracts. The prohibition of unconscionability has been adopted as part of the public policy of many states by courts in cases that did not involve the sale of goods, such as banking transactions and contracts for the sale or rental of real estate. It is therefore fair to state that the concept of unconscionability has become part of the general body of contract law.

Consequences of Unconscionability

The UCC and the *Restatement* (Second) sections on unconscionability give courts the power to manipulate a contract containing an unconscionable provision so as to reach a just result. If a court finds that a contract or a term in a contract is unconscionable, it can do one of three things: it can refuse to enforce the entire agreement; it can refuse to enforce the unconscionable provision but enforce the rest of the contract; or it can "limit the application of the unconscionable clause so as to

avoid any unconscionable result." This last alternative has been taken by courts to mean that they can make adjustments in the terms of the contract.

Meaning of Unconscionability

Neither the UCC nor the *Restatement (Second) of Contracts* attempts to define the term *unconscionability.* Though the concept is impossible to define with precision, unconscionability is generally taken to mean the *absence of meaningful choice* together with *terms unreasonably advantageous* to one of the parties.

The facts of each individual case are crucial to determining whether a contract term is unconscionable. Courts will scrutinize the process by which the contract was reached to see if the agreement was reached by fair methods and whether it can fairly be said to be the product of knowing and voluntary consent.

Procedural Unconscionability   Courts and writers often refer to unfairness in the bargaining process as *procedural unconscionability*. Some facts that may point to procedural unconscionability include the use of fine print or inconspicuously placed terms, complex, legalistic language, and high-pressure sales tactics. One of the most significant facts pointing to procedural unconscionability is the lack of voluntariness as shown by a marked imbalance in the parties' bargaining positions, particularly where the weaker party is unable to negotiate more favorable terms because of economic need, lack of time, or market factors. In fact, in most contracts that have been found to be unconscionable, there has been a serious inequality of bargaining power between the parties. It is important to note, however, that the mere existence of unequal bargaining power does not make a contract unconscionable. If it did, every consumer's contract with the telephone company or the electric company would be unenforceable. Rather, in an unconscionable contract, the party with the stronger bargaining power *exploits* that power by driving a bargain containing a term or terms that are so unfair that they "shock the conscience of the court." You will see several examples of procedural unconscionability in the following case, *John Deere Leasing Company v. Blubaugh.*

---

[5]Chapter 1 discusses courts of equity.

John Deere Leasing Company v. Blubaugh
636 F. Supp. 1569 (U.S. Dist. Ct., D. Kan. 1986)

Reuben Blubaugh, a farmer, leased a Model 6620 combine from John Deere Leasing (JDL). The lease, which was printed on very lightweight paper, provided that Blubaugh would pay four annual rentals of $15,991.37 and at the end of the lease term would have the option to purchase the equipment for $27,191.25. On the reverse side of the lease, printed in light-colored fine print, were several terms that spelled out what JDL's remedies would be if Blubaugh failed to make a rental payment. These provisions gave JDL the right to repossess the combine, sell it, and keep the proceeds of such a sale. Even though Blubaugh was only agreeing to rent the combine rather than to buy it, these default provisions also made Blubaugh responsible for an additional amount of money that represented the difference between the "termination value" of the combine (as defined in a complicated formula on the reverse side of the lease) and any money received by JDL if it repossessed and sold the combine.

Blubaugh read and signed the front of the contract but did not read the back. His understanding was that he had entered a basic lease with an option to purchase arrangement. His potential liability under the lease was not explained to him by anyone from JDL. Blubaugh paid $30,939.16 toward the first two rental payments, then made no further payments. JDL repossessed the combine and sold it for $42,000. JDL then sued Blubaugh for an additional $12,054.63, which was the amount due under the default clauses on the reverse side of the lease. Blubaugh defended on the ground that the default clauses were unconscionable.

Kelly, District Judge   Before turning to the discussion of the legal principles which are controlling in this case, the court makes the following observations. The terms in question herein are on the back of the lease, and are written in such fine, light print as to be nearly illegible. In fact, the print is so light that neither party was able to obtain a satisfactory photocopy. The court was required to use a magnifying glass to read the reverse side. The court found the wording to be unreasonably complex. It is as if the scrivener intended to conceal the thrust of the agreement in the convoluted language and fine print. The term which provides for the addition of the option price to the lessee's liability on default is a term quite outside the norm. JDL's contention that Blubaugh had a duty to ascertain the meaning of all terms, in the face of the near concealment of this unusually harsh remedy, is inexcusably inadequate and need not be tolerated by any court. This court is surprised that a reputable company such as Deere would stoop to this.

The term "unconscionability" is not defined in the UCC. Courts, in attempting to define "unconscionability" under UCC 2–302, have distinguished between "procedural" and "substantive" unconscionability. An illustrative case is *Bank of Indiana, N.A. v. Holyfield*, wherein the court stated:

The indicators of procedural unconscionability generally fall into two areas: (1) lack of knowledge, and (2) lack of voluntariness. A lack of knowledge is demonstrated by a lack of understanding of the contract terms arising from inconspicuous print or the use of complex, legalistic language, disparity in sophistication of parties, and lack of opportunity to study the contract and inquire about contract terms. A lack of voluntariness is demonstrated in contracts of adhesion when there is a great imbalance in the parties' relative bargaining power, the stronger party's terms are unnegotiable, and the weaker party is prevented by market factors, timing or other pressures from being able to contract with another party on more favorable terms or to refrain from contracting at all.

Substantive unconscionability is found when the terms of the contract are of such an oppressive character as to be unconscionable. It is present when there is a one-sided agreement whereby one party is deprived of all the benefits of the agreement or left without a remedy for another party's nonperformance or breach, a large disparity between the cost and price or a price far in excess of that prevailing in the market price, or terms which bear no reasonable relationship to business risks assumed by the parties.

In the case at bar, *both* procedural and substantive unconscionability are present. First, the lease was procedurally unconscionable because Blubaugh agreed to terms of which he had no knowledge, and his agreement was not "voluntary." While it is true that Blubaugh failed to read the back of the lease, he probably did not read it because he did not see it. On the first try here the court did not! Moreover, the court is convinced that even if he had read it, he would not have understood it. The lease was preprinted and so complex by virtue of its legalistic language that a party with no training in law or finance could not possibly decipher the potential for disadvantage. Further, there was clearly a disparity in sophistication between JDL and Blubaugh, a farmer. Therefore, Blubaugh lacked knowledge of his risk of liability when he signed the lease.

Additionally, the surrounding circumstances indicate Blubaugh's agreement to the detrimental term was not voluntary. The lease was an "adhesion" contract that was obviously drafted by JDL for its benefit and presented to Blubaugh in a manner that did not leave room for negotiations. JDL was clearly in a superior bargaining position. Because Blubaugh lacked knowledge and voluntariness, the contract was procedurally unconscionable.

The clause was also substantively unconscionable in that it exacted a penalty on Blubaugh for terminating the lease. In this case, the lessor's remedies allowed JDL to add the "purchase option" amount to the rental deficiency, and then to set this amount off against the sale proceeds. Here, however, no binding contract of sale existed. Allowing JDL to recoup the option to purchase price from Blubaugh is a penalty and would allow JDL to reap a windfall. Accordingly, the court finds the provision to be substantively unconscionable.

Judgment entered in favor of Blubaugh.

Substantive Unconscionability

In addition to looking at facts that might indicate procedural unconscionability, courts will scrutinize the contract terms themselves to determine whether they are oppressive, unreasonably one-sided, or unjustifiably harsh. This aspect of unconscionability is often referred to as *substantive unconscionability*. Examples include situations in which a party to the contract bears a disproportionate amount of the risk or other negative aspects of the transaction and situations in which a party is deprived of a remedy for the other party's breach. In some cases, unconscionability has been found in situations in which the contract provides for a price that is greatly in excess of the usual market price.

There is no mechanical test for determining whether a clause is unconscionable. Generally, in cases in which courts have found a contract term to be unconscionable, there are elements of *both* procedural and substantive unconscionability. Though courts have broad discretion to determine what contracts will be deemed to be unconscionable, it must be remembered that the doctrine of unconscionability is designed to prevent oppression and unfair surprise—not to relieve people of the effects of bad bargains.

The cases concerning unconscionability are quite diverse. Some courts, such as the court in the following case, *Murphy v. McNamara*, have found unconscionability in contracts involving grossly unfair sales prices. Although the doctrine of unconscionability has been raised primarily by victimized consumers, there have been cases in which businesspeople in an inherently weak bargaining position have been successful in asserting unconscionability.

MURPHY v. MCNAMARA
416 A.2d 170 (Conn. Super. Ct. 1979)

Carolyn Murphy, a welfare recipient with four minor children, saw an advertisement in the local newspaper that had been placed by Brian McNamara, a television and stereo dealer. It stated the following:

Why buy when you can rent? Color TV and stereos. *Rent to own!* Use our Rent-to-own plan and let TV Rentals deliver either of these models to your home. *We feature*—Never a repair bill—No deposit—No credit needed—No long term obligation—Weekly or monthly rates available—Order by phone—Call today—Watch color TV tonight.

As a result of this advertisement, Murphy leased a 25-inch Philco color console television set from McNamara under the ''Rent to Own'' plan. The lease agreement provided that Murphy would pay a $20 delivery charge and 78 weekly payments of $16. At the end of this period, Murphy would own the set. The agreement also provided that the customer could return the set at any time and terminate the lease as long as all rental payments had been made up to the return date. Murphy entered the lease because she believed that she could acquire ownership of a television set without first establishing credit, as was stressed in McNamara's ads. At no time did McNamara inform Murphy that the terms of the lease required her to pay a total of $1,268 for the set. The retail sales price for the same set was $499.

After making $436 in payments over a period of about six months, Murphy read a newspaper article criticizing the lease plan and realized the amount that the agreement required her to pay. She stopped making payments, and McNamara sought to repossess the set, threatening to file a criminal complaint against her if she failed to return it. Murphy, claiming that the agreement was unconscionable, filed suit for an injunction barring McNamara from repossessing the TV set or filing charges against her.

———————————————————■———————————————————

Berdon, Judge   An excessive price charged a consumer with unequal bargaining power can constitute a violation of 2–302 of the Uniform Commercial Code. In the case of *Jones v. Star Credit Corp.*, the plaintiffs, welfare recipients, purchased a home freezer unit for $900.00. The freezer had a retail value of approximately $300.00. The court held the contract was unconscionable under 2–302 of the Uniform Commercial Code and reformed the contract by excusing further payments over the $600.00 already paid by the plaintiffs. There have been similar holdings by other courts. The failure on the part of McNamara to advise Murphy of the total price she would be required to pay under the terms of the contract further compounded the unfairness of his trade practices.

In sum, an agreement for the sale of consumer goods entered into with a consumer having unequal bargaining power and which calls for an unconscionable purchase price, constitutes an unfair trade practice. By unequal bargaining power, the court means that at the time the contract was made there was such an inequality of bargaining power (for example, be-

cause of the consumer's need for credit) that the merchant could insist on the inclusion of unconscionable terms in the contract which were not justifiable on the grounds of commercial necessity. The intent of this rule is not to erase the doctrine of freedom of contract, but to make realistic the assumption of the law that the agreement has resulted from real bargaining between parties who had freedom of choice and understanding and ability to negotiate in a meaningful fashion. Viewed in that sense, freedom to contract survives but the marketers of consumer goods are brought to an awareness that the restraint of unconscionability is always hovering over their operations and that courts will employ it to balance the interests of the consumer public and those of the seller.

Injunction granted, prohibiting McNamara from repossessing the TV set, using harassing collection techniques, or filing criminal charges against Murphy, but permitting McNamara to file suit for the difference between the amount Murphy paid and the value of the set.

CONTRACTS OF ADHESION

A contract of adhesion is a contract, usually on a standardized form, offered by a party who is in a superior bargaining position on a ''take it or leave it'' basis. The person presented with such a contract has no opportunity to negotiate the terms of the contract; they are imposed on him if he wants to receive the goods or services offered by the

stronger party. In addition to not having a ''say'' about the terms of the contract, the person who signs a standardized contract of adhesion may not even know or understand the terms of the contract that he is signing. When these factors are present, the objective theory of contracts and the normal duty to read contracts before signing them may be modified.

All of us have probably entered contracts of adhesion at one time or another. The mere fact that a contract is a contract of adhesion does not, in and of itself, mean that the contract is unenforceable. Courts will not refuse enforcement to such a contract unless the term complained of is either unconscionable or is a term that the adhering party could not reasonably expect to be included in the form that he was signing.

Unenforceable contracts of adhesion can take different forms. The first is seen when the contract of adhesion contains a term that is harsh or oppressive. In this kind of case, the party offering the contract of adhesion has used his superior bargaining power to dictate unfair terms. Here the concepts of unconscionability and adhesion overlap. A court—as you saw in the *Blubaugh* case—may use the word adhesion when describing procedural unconscionability.

The second situation in which contracts of adhesion are refused enforcement occurs when a contract of adhesion contains a term that, while it may not be harsh or oppressive, is a term that the adhering party could *not* be expected to have been aware that he was agreeing to. This type of case relates to the fundamental concept of agreement in an era in which lengthy, complex, standardized contracts are common. If a consumer presented with a contract of adhesion has no opportunity to negotiate terms and signs the contract without knowing or fully understanding what he is signing, is it fair to conclude that he has consented to the terms? It is reasonable to conclude that he has consented at least to the terms that he could have expected to be in the contract, but *not* to any terms that he could not have expected to be contained in the contract. The following case, *Broemmer v. Abortion Services, Inc.*, presents an example of a contract of adhesion that was held to be unenforceable.

BROEMMER V. ABORTION SERVICES OF PHOENIX, LTD.
840 P.2d 1013 (Sup. Ct. Ariz. 1992)

In December 1986, Melinda Broemmer was 21 years old, unmarried, and 16 or 17 weeks pregnant. She was a high school graduate earning less than $100 a week and had no medical benefits. The father-to-be insisted that she have an abortion, but her parents advised against it. Broemmer later described the time as one of considerable confusion and turmoil for her. Broemmer's mother contacted Abortion Services of Phoenix and made an appointment for Broemmer for December 29, 1986. When they arrived at the clinic, Broemmer was escorted into an adjoining room and asked to complete three forms: a consent to treatment form, a questionnaire asking for a detailed medical history, and an agreement to arbitrate. The agreement to arbitrate stated that "any dispute arising between the Parties as a result of the fees and/or services" would be settled by binding arbitration and that "any arbitrators appointed by the AAA [American Arbitration Association] shall be licensed medical doctors who specialize in obstetrics/gynecology." No one made any effort to explain this to Broemmer and she was not provided with a copy of the agreement. She completed all three forms in less than five minutes. After Broemmer returned the forms to the front desk, she was taken into an examination room where preoperation procedures were performed. She was then instructed to return at 7:00 A.M. the next morning. She returned the following day and a physician performed the abortion. As a result of this procedure, Broemmer suffered a punctured uterus, which required medical treatment. Broemmer later filed a malpractice lawsuit against Abortion Services. Abortion Services moved to dismiss the suit on the ground that arbitration was required under the agreement. The trial court granted a summary judgment to Abortion Services. Although the Court of Appeals found that the agreement to arbitrate was a contract of adhesion, it still affirmed the trial court's judgment because the arbitration agreement was neither unconscionable nor beyond Broemmer's reasonable expectations. Broemmer appealed.

Moeller, Justice   The enforceability of the agreement to arbitrate is determined by principles of general contract law. Under those principles, the contract in this case was one of adhesion. An adhesion contract is typically a standardized form offered to consumers of goods and services on essentially a "take it or leave it" basis without affording the consumer a realistic opportunity to bargain and under such conditions that the consumer cannot obtain the desired product or services except by acquiescing in the form contract.

The printed form agreement signed by Broemmer in this case possesses all the characteristics of a contract of adhesion. The form is a standardized contract offered to Broemmer on a "take it or leave it" basis. In addition to removing from the courts any potential dispute concerning fees or services, the drafter inserted additional terms potentially advantageous to itself requiring that any arbitrator appointed by the American Arbitration Association be a licensed medical doctor specializing in obstetrics/gynecology. The contract was not negotiated but was, instead, prepared by Abortion Services and presented to Broemmer as a condition of treatment. Staff at the clinic neither explained its terms to Broemmer nor indicated that she was free to refuse to sign the form; they merely represented that she had to complete three forms. Applying general contract law to the undisputed facts, the court of appeals correctly held that the contract was one of adhesion.

Our conclusion that the contract was one of adhesion is not, of itself, determinative of its enforceability. To determine whether this contract of adhesion is enforceable, we look to two factors: the reasonable expectations of the adhering party and whether the contract is unconscionable. As the court stated in *Graham v. Scissor-Tail, Inc.*:

Generally speaking, there are two judicially imposed limitations on the enforcement of adhesion contracts. The first is that such a contract or provision which does not fall within the reasonable expectations of the weaker or "adhering" party will not be enforced against him. The second is that a contract or provision, even if consistent with the reasonable expectations of the parties, will be denied enforcement if, considered in its context, it is unduly oppressive or "unconscionable."

Clearly, the issues of knowing consent and reasonable expectations are closely related and intertwined. Although customers typically adhere to standardized agreements and are bound by them without even appearing to know the standard terms in detail, they are not bound to unknown terms which are beyond the range of reasonable expectation. The *Restatement* focuses our attention on whether it was beyond plaintiff's reasonable expectations to expect to arbitrate her medical malpractice claims, which includes waiving her right to a jury trial, as part of the filling out of the three forms. Clearly, there was no conspicuous or explicit waiver of the fundamental right to a jury trial or any evidence that such rights were knowingly, voluntarily, and intelligently waived. The only evidence presented compels a finding that waiver of such fundamental rights was beyond the reasonable expectations of Broemmer. In this case failure to explain to Broemmer that the agreement required all potential disputes, including malpractice disputes, to be heard only by an arbitrator who was a licensed obstetrician/gynecologist requires us to view the "bargaining process" with suspicion. It would be unreasonable to enforce such a critical term against Broemmer when it is not a negotiated term and Abortion Services failed to explain it to her or call her attention to it.

Broemmer was under a great deal of emotional stress, had only a high school education, was not experienced in commercial matters, and is still not sure "what arbitration is." The contract fell outside Broemmer's reasonable expectations and is, therefore, unenforceable. Because of this holding, it is unnecessary for us to determine whether the contract is also unconscionable.

Judgment reversed in favor of Broemmer.

Effect of Illegality

General Rule

As a general rule, courts will refuse to give any remedy for the breach of an illegal agreement. A court will refuse to enforce an illegal agreement and will also refuse to permit a party who has fully or partially performed her part of the agreement to recover what she has parted with. The reason for this rule is to serve the public interest, not to punish the parties.

In some cases, the public interest is best served by allowing some recovery to one or both of the parties. Such cases constitute exceptions to the "hands off" rule. The following discussion concerns the most common situations in which courts will grant some remedy even though they find the agreement to be illegal.

Excusable Ignorance of Facts or Legislation

Though it is often said that ignorance of the law is no excuse, courts will, under certain circumstances, permit a party to an illegal agreement who was excusably ignorant of facts or legislation that rendered the agreement illegal to recover damages for breach of the agreement. This exception is used where only *one* of the parties acted in ignorance of the illegality of the agreement and the other party was aware that the agreement was illegal. For this exception to apply, the facts or legislation of which the person claiming damages was ignorant must be of a relatively minor character—that is, it must not involve an immoral act or a serious threat to the public welfare. Finally, the person who is claiming damages cannot recover damages for anything that he does after learning of the illegality. For example, Warren enters a contract to perform in a play at Craig's theater. Warren does not know that Craig does not have the license to operate a theater as required by statute. Warren can recover the wages agreed on in the parties' contract for work that he performed before learning of the illegality.

When *both* of the parties are ignorant of facts or legislation of a relatively minor character, courts will not permit them to enforce the agreement and receive what they had bargained for, but they will permit the parties to recover what they have parted with.

Rights of Parties Not Equally in the Wrong

The courts will often permit a party who is not equally in the wrong (in technical legal terms, not *in pari delicto*) to recover what she has parted with under an illegal agreement. One of the most common situations in which this exception is used involves the rights of "protected parties"—people who were intended to be protected by a regulatory statute—who contract with parties who are not properly licensed under that statute. Most regulatory statutes are intended to protect the public. As a general rule, if a person guilty of violating a regulatory statute enters into an agreement with another person for whose protection the statute was adopted,

the agreement will be enforceable by the party whom the legislature intended to protect. You saw an example of this in *Ransburg v. Haase*, which appeared earlier in this chapter.

Another common situation in which courts will grant a remedy to a party who is not equally in the wrong is one in which the less guilty party has been induced to enter the agreement by misrepresentation, fraud, duress, or undue influence.

Rescission before Performance of Illegal Act

Obviously, public policy is best served by any rule that encourages people not to commit illegal acts. People who have fully or partially performed their part of an illegal contract have little incentive to raise the question of illegality if they know that they will be unable to recover what they have given because of the courts' hands-off approach to illegal agreements. To encourage people to cancel illegal contracts, courts will allow a person who rescinds such a contract before any illegal act has been performed to recover any consideration that he has given. For example, Dixon, the owner of a restaurant, pays O'Leary, an employee of a competitor's restaurant, $1,000 to obtain some of the competitor's recipes. If Dixon has second thoughts and tells O'Leary the deal is off before receiving any recipes, he can recover the $1,000 he paid O'Leary.

Divisible Contracts

If part of an agreement is legal and part is illegal, the courts will enforce the legal part so long as it is possible to separate the two parts. A contract is said to be *divisible*—that is, the legal part can be separated from the illegal part—if the contract consists of several promises or acts by one party, each of which corresponds with an act or a promise by the other party. In other words, there must be a separate consideration for each promise or act for a contract to be considered divisible.

Where no separate consideration is exchanged for the legal and illegal parts of an agreement, the agreement is said to be *indivisible*. As a general rule, an indivisible contract that contains an illegal part will be entirely unenforceable unless it comes within one of the exceptions discussed above. However, if the major portion of a contract is legal, but the contract contains an illegal provision that does

FIGURE 1   **Effect of Illegality**

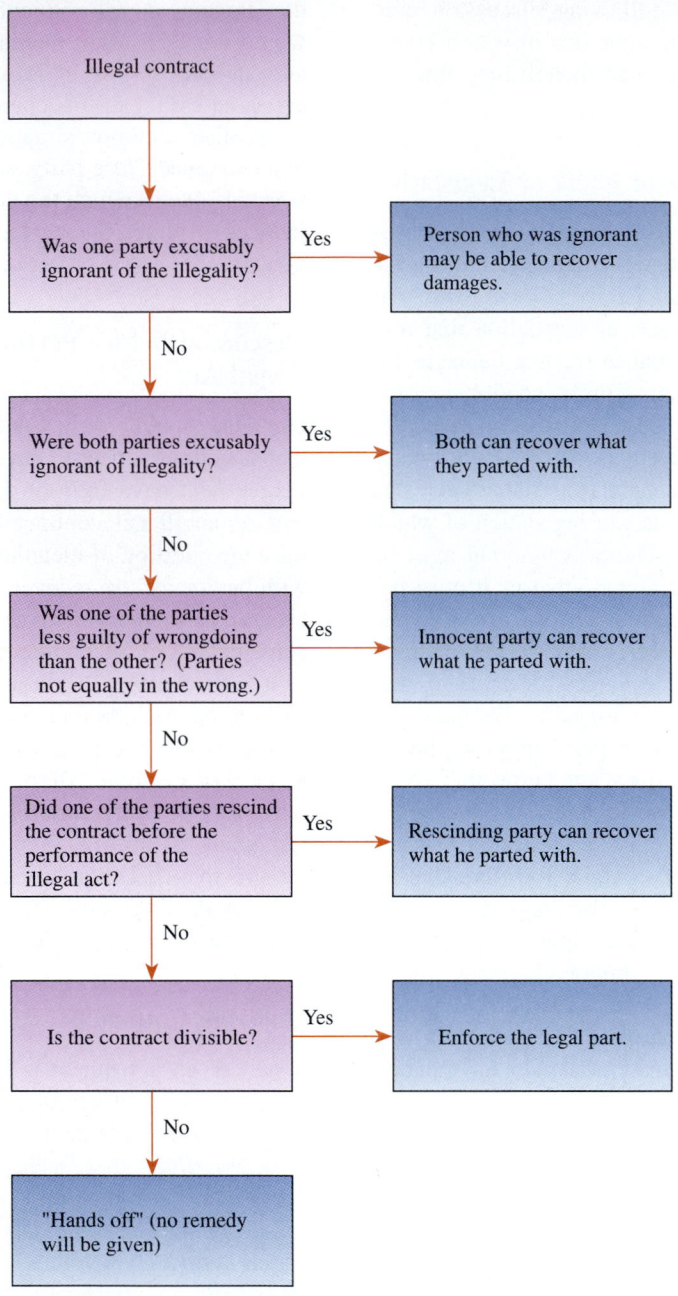

not affect the primary, legal portion, courts will often enforce the legal part of the agreement and simply decline to enforce the illegal part. For example, suppose Alberts sells his barbershop to Bates. The contract of sale provides that Alberts will not engage in barbering anywhere in the world for the rest of his life.

The major portion of the contract—the sale of the business—is perfectly legal. A provision of the contract—the ancillary covenant not to compete—is overly restrictive, and thus illegal. A court would enforce the sale of the business but modify or refuse to enforce the restraint provision. See Figure 1.

ETHICAL AND PUBLIC POLICY CONCERNS

1. In the *Steamatic* case, the court refused to enforce a non-competition clause in an employment contract despite the fact that the employee had secretly extracted the contract from company files and destroyed it in contemplation of leaving the company. How can this decision be justified?

2. You read that the law makes a distinction between contracts that violate regulatory statutes and contracts that violate revenue-raising statutes. What is the rationale for this distinction? Would it be better for the law simply to hold that *any* contract that violates *any* statute would be illegal? Why or why not?

3. What are some ethical justifications for the decisions that the courts reached in the *Murphy* and *Blubaugh* cases? In both cases, the contracts in question were held to be unconscionable even though the individuals who signed the contracts *could have* read them and figured out their obligations. Who should have the responsibility to make sure that the person signing a contract understands his obligations, the person who drafts and offers the contract or the person who signs it?

PROBLEMS AND PROBLEM CASES

1. Isokappacase, a product manufactured by PTX Corp., is used as a starter medium and bacteriophage preventative medium in the production of cheese. Because of its high protein content, Isokappacase can also be used as a yield enhancer by adding it directly into cheese milk. When the product is used in this way, however, federal law requires that the resulting product be labeled as an imitation cheese and that the label list the ingredients in the end product to reflect the characteristics of imitation cheese. Podell, a salesman for Blossom Farm Products, was the sole U.S. distributor of Isokappacase. Over the course of three years, Blossom sold a large volume of Isokappacase to Kasson Cheese. Kasson used Isokappacase as a yield enhancer, introducing it

directly into cheese milk to enhance cheese yields from the milk, but it did not label its final product as imitation cheese as required by federal standards. Had Kasson labeled its end product as an imitation cheese, it would have been able to sell the end product for only $.70 per pound rather than the $1.40 per pound it received for selling it as real cheese. Blossom was aware of the fact that Kasson's extremely large volume purchases of the product could only be accounted for by Kasson's use of Isokappacase as a yield enhancer. Podell acknowledged that once he recognized that Kasson was ordering about 100 times more Isokappacase than would be needed if it were using the products as a starter medium, he realized that such large volume orders could only mean that Kasson was using the product as a yield enhancer. Blossom also tacitly knew that Kasson was mislabeling its product. Both Kasson and Blossom benefited economically from this volume purchase and use. Kasson failed to pay Blossom $138,306 for its last order of Isokappacase, and Blossom brought suit to collect the money. Kasson defended on the ground that the contract was illegal. Was it? Must Kasson pay for the Isokappacase?

2. Moorehead & Associates is an "heir locating" business. In 1987, Arkules, Moorehead's brother, was doing a random review of probate files for Moorehead & Associates, when he discovered the estate of Yelverton, who had died apparently leaving no known heirs. After some genealogical research and a tip from a third party, the existence of Landi, the son of Yelverton, eventually became known to Moorehead & Associates. It located Landi and entered into a contract with him to do "all things necessary to obtain the inheritance" in exchange for 40 percent of the inheritance. The contract provided that Moorehead would retain an attorney and pay the expenses for researching and proving the validity of Landi's claim of inheritance, including attorney's fees. Moorehead's father, a licensed attorney, later contacted Landi by telephone and agreed to send him genealogical materials. He also sent a letter to Landi on his legal stationery in which he provided Landi with Yelverton's family history and gave Landi advice regarding probating the Yelverton estate. Landi later hired his own attorney and filed an action to rescind or reform the heir locator agreement, claiming that the agreement was illegal because a state statute limits fees charged for assistance in recovering escheated property (property going to the state because the deceased died without heirs) to 30 percent of the value of the property and because the defendants were acting as private investigators without first having obtained a private investigator license. Will the agreement be upheld?

3. Stern and Whitehead entered into a surrogacy contract in New Jersey. The contract provided that in exchange for $10,000, Whitehead would become pregnant through artificial insemination using Stern's sperm, carry the child to term, bear it, and surrender her parental rights to the child so that the child could be adopted by Stern's wife. A New Jersey criminal statute prohibits paying or accepting money in connection with any placement of a child for adoption. New Jersey also has a comprehensive statutory scheme regulating the termination of parental rights. This law provides that parental rights can be terminated only in cases of voluntary, written surrender of a child to an approved agency or where there has been a showing of parental abandonment or unfitness.

Whitehead did become pregnant with Stern's child and carried it to term. After the child's birth, however, she resisted surrendering the child. Stern sued to enforce the surrogacy contract, but Whitehead asserted that it was illegal. Should the surrogacy contract be enforced?

4. Strickland attempted to bribe Judge Sylvania Woods to show leniency toward one of Strickland's friends who had a case pending before the judge. Judge Woods immediately reported this to the state's attorney and was asked to play along with Strickland until the actual payment of money occurred. Strickland gave $2,500 to the judge, who promptly turned it over to the state's attorney's office. Strickland was indicted for bribery, pled guilty, and was sentenced to a four-year prison term. Three months after the criminal trial, Strickland filed a motion for the return of his $2,500. Will the court order the return of his money?

5. Sadri, a California resident, incurred $22,000 in gambling debts over a two-day period in 1991 while gambling at Caesar's Tahoe casino in Nevada, where gambling is legal. On January 13 and 14, he wrote the casino two personal checks for $10,000 and $2,000. On January 14, he executed two memoranda of indebtedness for $5,000 each. In exchange for the checks and memoranda, Sadri received chips, which

he lost playing baccarat. Sadri later stopped payment on the checks and memoranda, which had been drawn on his bank in California. Caesar's Tahoe could have sought a judgment in Nevada courts, where gambling debts may legally be recovered. Instead, it assigned its claim to Metropolitan Creditors Service (MCS) for collection. MCS sued Sadri in a California trial court to collect the gambling debts. California courts historically have refused to enforce gambling debts—even those incurred in a state in which gambling was legal—on the public policy ground that gambling is contrary to good morals. California also has a strong public policy against gambling on credit. In recent years, California has demonstrated increasing tolerance of gambling by enacting a state lottery and allowing forms of gambling such as pari-mutuel horse racing, draw poker clubs, and charitable bingo games. Will the California court allow MCS to recover the gambling debt from Sadri?

6. Ben Lee Wilson had been licensed to practice architecture in the state of Hawaii, but his license lapsed in 1971 because he failed to pay a required $15 renewal fee. A Hawaii statute provides that any person who practices architecture without having been registered and "without having a valid unexpired certificate of registration . . . shall be fined not more than $500 or imprisoned not more than one year, or both." In 1972, Wilson performed architectural and engineering services for Kealakekua Ranch, for which he billed the Ranch $33,994.36. When the Ranch failed to pay Wilson's fee, he brought an action for breach of contract. What will the result be?

7. Ralph contracted to purchase a business, American Horse Enterprises, from Bovard. He executed promissory notes to Bovard in connection with this purchase. American Horse Enterprises was primarily in the business of manufacturing drug paraphernalia such as "roach clips" and "bongs" used to smoke marijuana. At the time of the sale of American Horse Enterprises, the manufacture of drug paraphernalia was not itself illegal, but state criminal statutes made it illegal to possess, use, and transfer marijuana. Both Ralph and Bovard knew that the products produced by American Horse Enterprises were used for illegal purposes. Ralph defaulted on the promissory notes and Bovard sued to recover on them. Ralph defends on the ground that the sale of the business was illegal. Was it?

8. Dr. Ellis, an orthopedic surgeon, entered into a contract of employment with the Elko Clinic.

Among other provisions, the contract of employment contained a non-competition clause in which Dr. Ellis agreed not to practice medicine within a distance of five miles from the city limits of Elko, Nevada, for a period of two years from the termination date of his employment. During Dr. Ellis's employment, he treated patients who would otherwise have had to travel to Reno, Salt Lake City, or elsewhere to seek the services of an orthopedic surgeon. At the expiration of his employment contract, Dr. Ellis gave notice to the Clinic that he intended to establish his own office in Elko for the practice of his specialty. The Clinic sued Dr. Ellis to enforce the non-competition clause. Should the non-competition clause be enforced as written?

9. Hohe, a 15-year-old student at Mission Bay High School, was injured during an annual campus hypnotism show sponsored by the PTSA (Parent, Teacher, and Student Association) as a fundraiser. Hohe was one of 18 or 20 subjects selected at random from a group of many volunteers. Her participation in the "Magic of the Mind Show" was conditioned on signing two release forms. Hohe's father signed a form entitled "Mission Bay High School PTSA Presents Dr. Karl Santo," which stated that he waived "all liability" against the PTSA, high school, and school district. Hohe and her father both signed a second form entitled "KARL SANTO HYPNOTIST," in which they agreed to "indemnify and hold you and any third parties harmless from any and all liability, loss or damage . . . caused by or arising in any manner from my participation in the Magic of the Mind Show." During the course of the show, Hohe was injured when she slid from her chair and also fell to the floor about six times. Hohe sued the school district and the PTSA for her injuries. She argues that the releases she and her father signed are contrary to public policy. Are they?

10. Gianni Sport was a New York manufacturer and distributor of women's clothing. Gantos was a clothing retailer headquartered in Grand Rapids, Michigan. In 1980, Gantos's sales total was 20 times greater than Gianni Sport's, and in this industry, buyers were "in the driver's seat." In June 1980, Gantos submitted to Gianni Sport a purchase order for women's holiday clothing to be delivered on October 10, 1980. The purchase order contained the following clause:

Buyer reserves the right to terminate by notice to Seller all or any part of this Purchase Order with respect to Goods that have not actually been shipped by Seller or as to Goods which are not timely delivered for any reason whatsoever.

Gianni Sport made the goods in question especially for Gantos. This holiday order comprised 20 to 22 percent of Gianni Sport's business. In late September 1980, before the goods were shipped, Gantos canceled the order. Was the cancellation clause unconscionable?

11. On September 29, 1987, Guido, a practicing lawyer, visited Koopman's Academy of Equestrian Arts to inquire about taking horseback riding lessons. At that time, she signed an agreement stating that she agreed to release the owners and managers of the Academy for liability for any injury, loss, or damage that she might suffer as a result of negligence by any of them. Prior to signing, Koopman told Guido that the form "didn't mean anything. It is something that I need to have you sign, because my insurance company won't let me give lessons unless I have people sign this. . . ." Guido went ahead and signed the form without reading it because she did not think it was enforceable. Guido took lessons from Koopman as often as twice a week until June 1988, when she was thrown from one of Koopman's horses and injured. Guido sued Koopman for negligence and Koopman asserted the release as a defense. Guido claimed that the release is illegal and unenforceable. Was it?

12. Kansas City Community Center (KCCC), a not-for-profit provider of drug and alcohol rehabilitation services, contracted with Heritage Industries, a manufacturer of prefabricated modular housing, to plan, design, and construct KCCC's new rehabilitation facility for $477,300. As part of its contract, Heritage agreed to complete architectural plans and engineering work for the facility. KCCC paid Heritage $9,546 to begin architectural drawing and site engineering. Soon after Heritage began designing the facility, however, KCCC learned that Heritage lacked a corporate certificate of authority to practice either architecture or engineering in the state of Missouri. KCCC filed suit to terminate the contract and get restitution of the $9,546 that it had paid Heritage as a down payment. Heritage argued that rather than voiding the entire contract, the court should treat as unenforceable only the provisions dealing with architectural and engineering services. Is this a good argument?

WRITING

INTRODUCTION

Your study of contract law so far has focused on the requirements for the formation of a valid contract. You should be aware, however, that even when all the elements of a valid contract exist, the enforceability of the contract and the nature of the parties' obligations can be greatly affected by the form in which the contract is set out and by the language that is used to express the agreement. An otherwise valid contract can become unenforceable if it does not comply with the formalities required by state law. A person may be unable to offer evidence about promises and agreements made in preliminary negotiations because the parties later adopted a written contract that did not contain those terms. And, of course, the legal effect of any contract is determined in large part by the way in which a court interprets the language it contains. This chapter discusses the ways in which the enforceability of a contract and the scope of contractual obligations can be affected by the manner in which people express their agreements.

THE STATUTE OF FRAUDS

Despite what many people believe, there is no general requirement that contracts be in writing. In most situations, oral contracts are legally enforceable, assuming that they can be proven. Still, oral contracts are less desirable than written contracts in many ways. They are more easily misunderstood or forgotten than written contracts. They are also more subject to the danger that a person might fabricate terms or fraudulently claim to have made an oral contract where none exists.

In 17th-century England, the dangers inherent in oral contracts were exacerbated by a legal rule that prohibited parties to a lawsuit from testifying in their own cases. Since the parties to an oral contract could not give testimony, the only way they could prove the existence of the contract was through the testimony of third parties. As you might expect, third parties were sometimes persuaded to offer false testimony about the existence of contracts. In an attempt to stop the widespread fraud and perjury that resulted, Parliament enacted the Statute of Frauds in 1677. It required written evidence before certain classes of contracts would be enforced.

Although the possibility of fraud exists in every contract, the statute focused on contracts in which the potential for fraud was great or the consequences of fraud were especially serious. The legislatures of American states adopted very similar statutes, also known as statutes of frauds. These statutes, which require certain kinds of contracts to be evidenced by a signed writing, are exceptions to the general rule that oral contracts are enforceable.

Statutes of frauds have produced a great deal of litigation, due in part to the public's ignorance of their provisions. It is difficult to imagine an aspect of contract law that is more practical for businesspeople to know about than the circumstances under which an oral contract will not suffice.

EFFECT OF FAILURE TO COMPLY WITH THE STATUTE OF FRAUDS

The statute of frauds applies only to executory contracts. If an oral contract has been completely performed by both parties, the fact that it did not comply with the statute of frauds would not be a ground for rescission of the contract.

What happens if an executory contract is within the statute of frauds but has not been evidenced by the type of writing required by the statute? It is not treated as an illegal contract because the statute of frauds is more of a formal rule than a rule of substantive law. Rather, the contract that fails to comply with the statute of frauds is *unenforceable*. Although the contract will not be enforced, a person who has conferred some benefit on the other party pursuant to the contract can recover the reasonable value of his performance in an action based on *quasi-contract*.

CONTRACTS WITHIN THE STATUTE OF FRAUDS

A contract is said to be "within" the statute of frauds if the statute requires that sort of contract to be evidenced by a writing. In almost all states, the following types of contracts are within the statute of frauds:

1. Collateral contracts in which a person promises to perform the obligation of another person.
2. Contracts for the sale of an interest in real estate.
3. Bilateral contracts that cannot be performed within a year from the date of their formation.
4. Contracts for the sale of goods for a price of $500 or more.
5. Contracts in which an executor or administrator promises to be personally liable for the debt of an estate.
6. Contracts in which marriage is the consideration.

Of this list, the first four sorts of contracts have the most significance today, and our discussion will focus primarily on them.

The statutes of frauds of the various states are not uniform. Some states require written evidence of other contracts in addition to those listed above. For example, a number of states require written evidence of contracts to pay a commission for the sale of real estate. Others require written evidence of ratifications of infants' promises or promises to pay debts that have been barred by the statute of limitations or discharged by bankruptcy.

The following discussion examines in greater detail the sorts of contracts that are within most states' statute of frauds.

Collateral Contracts

A **collateral contract** is one in which one person (the *guarantor*) agrees to pay the debt or obligation that a second person (the *principal debtor*) owes to a third person (the *obligee*) if the principal debtor fails to perform. For example, Cohn, who wants to help Davis establish a business, promises First Bank that he will repay the loan that First Bank makes to Davis if Davis fails to pay it. Here, Cohn is the guarantor, Davis is the principal debtor, and First Bank is the obligee. Cohn's promise to First Bank must be in writing to be enforceable.

Figure 1 shows that a collateral contract involves at least three parties and at least two promises to perform (a promise by the principal debtor to pay the obligee and a promise by the guarantor to pay the obligee). In a collateral contract, the guarantor promises to pay *only if the principal debtor fails to do so*. As you will read in the following case, *Crozier and Gudsnuk, P.C. v. Valentine,* the essence of the collateral contract is that the debt or obligation is owed primarily by the principal debtor and the guarantor's debt is *secondary*. Thus, not all three-party transactions are collateral contracts.

FIGURE 1   Collateral Contract

When a person undertakes an obligation that is *not* conditioned on the default of another person, and the debt is his own rather than that of another person, his obligation is said to be *original,* not collateral. For example, when Timmons calls Johnson Florist Company and says, "Send flowers to Elrod," Timmons is undertaking an obligation to pay *her own*—not someone else's—debt.

CROZIER AND GUDSNUK, P.C. v. VALENTINE
1992 Conn. Super. LEXIS 1179 (Super. Ct. Conn. 1992) No. CV-91-0036504

Michael Valentine, Jr., an adult over the age of 18, was charged with criminal assault. His parents, Lorraine and Michael Valentine, Sr., contacted the law firm of Crozier and Gudsnuk about representing their son in the criminal action. In October 1990, attorney Barbara DeGennaro, an associate in the law firm, agreed to represent Valentine. The law firm claims that Valentine's parents orally agreed to guarantee payment for the legal fees incurred by their son. Approximately 10 days after DeGennaro had agreed to represent Valentine, Mrs. Valentine paid the firm's retainer by signing a check for $250. The law firm represented Valentine in the criminal assault charge until February 25, 1991, when its representation ended at the request of the Valentines. The law firm claims that the reasonable value of the legal services it performed was $4,200. It brought suit against Valentine's parents to recover the legal fees owed to the firm. It asked the court for a prejudgment attachment of the Valentines' home. A hearing was held on this issue.

Jones, Judge   The present case involves an alleged oral contract made between a law firm and the parents of an adult child charged in a criminal action. The Statute of Frauds provides that:

No civil action may be maintained in the following cases unless the agreement, or a memorandum of the agreement, is made in writing and signed by the party, or the agent of the party, to be charged . . . (2) against any person upon any special promise to answer for the debt, default or miscarriage of another.

The Valentines have raised the Statute of Frauds as a defense, claiming that the oral agreement of guarantee made between the parents and the law firm was a separate, collateral undertaking independent of the law firm's representation of Michael Valentine, Jr. In *Adamowicz v. Stevens,* the court held:

The statute is not a defense if the promise was an original undertaking. Fundamentally the distinction between a contract which falls within the condemnation of the statute of frauds and one which does not is that the former is a collateral undertaking to answer in case of a default on the part of the obligor in the contract, upon whom still rests the primary liability to perform; whereas, in the latter, the obligation assumed is a primary one that the contract shall be performed.

Further, an undertaking by a party not before liable, for the purpose of securing the performance of a duty for which the party for whom the undertaking is made continues liable, is a special promise to answer for the debt, default or miscarriage of another and is within the statute of frauds.

In the present case, only the adult son of the Valentines was legally represented by the law firm.

The parents were not charged in any criminal action and received no material benefit from the law firm's representation of Michael Valentine, Jr. If the oral agreement between the parents and the law firm was in fact a separate, collateral undertaking, then the agreement will be within the statute of frauds. From the facts before this court, the parents cannot be seen as principal parties in the legal services agreement between the law firm and their adult son. The record indicates that the oral agreement to guarantee payment for legal fees constitutes a separate and collateral undertaking and as such, it falls within the statute of frauds.

For the foregoing reasons, this Court denies the plaintiff's application for prejudgment remedy. The Court notes in passing that [the statute of frauds] was adopted by the legislature in order to encourage certain contracting parties to put their agreements into writing so as to avoid certain pitfalls.

Plaintiff's application denied in favor of the Valentines.

Exception: Main Purpose or Leading Object Rule   There are some situations in which a contract that is technically collateral is treated like an original contract because the person promising to pay the debt of another does so for the primary purpose of securing some personal benefit. Under the **main purpose** or **leading object** rule, no writing is required where the guarantor makes a collateral promise for the main purpose of obtaining some personal economic advantage. When the consideration given in exchange for the collateral promise is something the guarantor seeks primarily for his own benefit rather than for the benefit of the primary debtor, the contract is outside the statute of frauds and does not have to be in writing. Suppose, for example, that Penn is a major creditor of Widgetmart, a retailer. To help keep Widgetmart afloat and increase the chances that Widgetmart will repay the debt it owes him, Penn orally promises Rex Industries, one of the Widgetmart's suppliers, that he will guarantee Widgetmart's payment for goods that Rex sells to Widgetmart. In this situation, Penn's oral agreement could be enforced under the main purpose rule if the court finds that Penn was acting for his own personal financial benefit.

Interest in Land

Any contract that creates or transfers an interest in land is within the statute of frauds. The inclusion of real estate contracts in the statute of frauds reflects the values of an earlier, agrarian society in which land was the primary basis of wealth. Our legal system historically has treated land as being more important than other forms of property. Courts have interpreted the land provision of the statute of frauds broadly to require written evidence of any transaction that will affect the ownership of an interest in land. Thus, a contract to sell or mortgage real estate must be evidenced by a writing, as must an option to purchase real estate or a contract to grant an easement or permit the mining and removal of minerals on land. A lease is also a transfer of an interest in land, but most states' statutes of frauds do not require leases to be in writing unless they are long-term leases, usually those for one year or more. On the other hand, a contract to erect a building or to insure a building would not be within the real estate provision of the statute of frauds because such contracts do not involve the transfer of interests in land.[1]

Exception: Full Performance by the Vendor   An oral contract for the sale of land that has been completely performed by the vendor (seller) is "taken out of the statute of frauds"—that is, is enforceable without a writing. For example, Peterson and Lincoln enter into an oral contract for the sale of Peterson's farm at an agreed-on price and Peterson, the vendor, delivers a deed to the farm to Lincoln. In this situation, the vendor has completely performed and most states would treat the oral contract as being enforceable.

Exception: Part Performance (Action in Reliance) by the Vendee   When the vendee (purchaser of land) does an act in clear reliance on an oral contract for the sale of land, an equitable

---

[1]Note, however, that a writing might be required under state insurance statutes.

doctrine commonly known as the "part performance doctrine" permits the vendee to enforce the contract notwithstanding the fact that it was oral. The part performance doctrine is based on both evidentiary and reliance considerations. The doctrine recognizes that a person's conduct can "speak louder than words" and can indicate the existence of a contract almost as well as a writing can. The part performance doctrine is also based on the desire to avoid the injustice that would otherwise result if the contract were repudiated after the vendee's reliance.

Under section 129 of the *Restatement (Second) of Contracts,* a contract for the transfer of an interest in land can be enforced even without a writing if the person seeking enforcement:

1. Has *reasonably relied* on the contract and on the other party's assent.
2. Has changed his position to such an extent that *enforcement of the contract is the only way to prevent injustice.*

In other words, the vendee must have done some act in reliance on the contract and the nature of the act must be such that restitution (returning his money) would not be an adequate remedy. The part performance doctrine will not permit the vendee to collect damages for breach of contract, but it will permit him to obtain the equitable remedy of **specific performance,** a remedy whereby the court orders the breaching party to perform his contract.[2]

A vendee's reliance on an oral contract could be shown in many ways. Traditionally, many states have required that the vendee pay part or all of the purchase price and either make substantial improvements on the property or take possession of it. For example, Contreras and Miller orally enter into a contract for the sale of Contreras's land. If Miller pays Contreras a substantial part of the purchase price and either takes possession of the land or begins to make improvements on it, the contract would be enforceable without a writing under the part performance doctrine. These are not the only sorts of acts in reliance that would make an oral contract enforceable, however. Under the *Restatement (Second)* approach, if the promise to transfer land is clearly proven or is admitted by the breaching party, it is not necessary that the act of reliance

include making payment, taking possession, or making improvements.[3] It still is necessary, however, that the reliance be such that restitution would not be an adequate remedy. For this reason, a vendee's payment of the purchase price, standing alone, is usually *not* sufficient for the part performance doctrine.

Contracts that Cannot Be Performed within One Year

A bilateral, executory contract that cannot be performed within one year from the day on which it comes into existence is within the statute of frauds and must be evidenced by a writing. The apparent purpose of this provision is to guard against the risk of faulty or willfully inaccurate recollection of long-term contracts. Courts have tended to construe it very narrowly.

One aspect of this narrow construction is that most states hold that a contract that has been fully performed by *one* of the parties is "taken out of the statute of frauds" and is enforceable without a writing. For example, Nash enters into an oral contract to perform services for Thomas for 13 months. If Nash has already fully performed his part of the contract, Thomas will be required to pay him the contract price.

In addition, this provision of the statute has been held to apply only when the terms of the contract make it impossible for the contract to be completed within one year. If the contract is for an indefinite period of time, it is not within the statute of frauds. This is true even if, in retrospect, the contract was not completed within a year. Thus, Weinberg's agreement to work for Wolf for an indefinite period of time would not have to be evidenced by a writing, even if Weinberg eventually works for Wolf for many years. As demonstrated by *Hodge v. Evans Financial Corporation,* which follows, the mere fact that performance is unlikely to be completed in one year does not bring the contract within the statute of frauds. In most states, a contract "for life" is not within the statute of frauds because it is possible—since death is an uncertain event—for the contract to be performed within a year. In a few states such as New York, contracts for life are within the statute of frauds.

---

[2]Specific performance is discussed in more detail in Chapter 18.

[3]*Restatement (Second) of Contracts* § 129, comment *d.*

HODGE V. EVANS FINANCIAL CORPORATION
823 F.2d 559 (D.C. Cir. 1987)

On two occasions in 1980, Albert Hodge met with John Tilley, president and chief operating officer of Evans Financial Corporation, to discuss Hodge's possible employment by Evans. Hodge was 54 years old at that time and was assistant counsel and assistant secretary of Mellon National Corporation and Mellon Bank of Pittsburgh. During these discussions, Tilley asked Hodge what his conditions were for accepting employment with Evans, and Hodge replied, "No. 1, the job must be permanent. Because of my age, I have a great fear about going back into the marketplace again. I want to be here until I retire." Tilley allegedly responded, "I accept that condition." Regarding his retirement plans, Hodge later testified, "I really questioned whether I was going to go much beyond 65." Hodge subsequently accepted Evans's offer of employment as vice president and general counsel. He moved from Pittsburgh to Washington, D.C., in September 1980 and worked for Evans from that time until he was fired by Tilley on May 7, 1981.

Hodge brought a breach of contract suit against Evans. The case was tried before a jury, which rendered a verdict in favor of Hodge for $175,000. Evans appeals.

Wald, Chief Justice   Evans argues that the oral employment agreement between Evans and Hodge is unenforceable under the statute of frauds. Because the agreement here contemplated long-term employment for a number of years, Evans argues that the statute requires it to have been in writing in order to be enforceable.

Despite its sweeping terms, the one-year provision of the statute has long been construed narrowly and literally. Under prevailing interpretation, the enforceability of a contract under the statute does not depend on the actual course of subsequent events or on the expectations of the parties. Instead, the statute applies only to those contracts whose performance could not possibly or conceivably be completed within one year. The statute of frauds is thus inapplicable if, at the time the contract is formed, any contingent event could complete the terms of the contract within one year.

Hodge argues that, under this interpretation of the statute of frauds, a permanent or lifetime employment contract does not fall within the statute because it is capable of full performance within one year if the employee were to die within the period. Hodge's view of the statute's application to lifetime or permanent employment contracts has, in fact, been accepted by an overwhelming majority of courts and commentators.

The employment contract in this case cannot reasonably be interpreted as a contract for a specified period of time. Hodge unequivocally alleged a contract for permanent employment, not a contract until he reached age sixty-five or for any other stated period of time. The fact that Hodge expected to retire at some point does not mean that his contract could not possibly be performed within one year. All employment contracts of permanent, lifetime, or indefinite duration undoubtedly contemplate retirement; such contracts certainly do not mean that employees are bound to work until the moment they drop dead. Hodge's permanent employment contract with Evans could therefore be fully performed, according to its terms, upon Hodge's retirement or upon his death. Under the conventional view the latter possibility is sufficient to take the contract out of the statute. That Hodge expected to retire before he died is completely irrelevant to this case so long as the contract was legally susceptible of performance within one year. The applicability of the statute of frauds does not depend on the expectations of the parties.

We recognize that the conventional view of the statute is somewhat "legalistic." Yet the statute of frauds itself is widely understood as a formal device that shields promise breakers from the consequences of otherwise enforceable agreements. The conventional, narrowing interpretation overwhelmingly adopted by courts and commentators is designed to mollify the often harsh and unintended consequences of the statute. Here the jury concluded, despite Evans's vigorous defense, that Hodge was promised permanent employment and that he was nonetheless fired without cause. Under the traditional, narrow view of the statute, the statute of frauds does not bar the enforcement of such jury verdicts.

Judgment for Hodge affirmed.

Computing Time   In determining whether a contract is within the one-year provision, courts begin counting time on the day when the contract comes into existence. If, under the terms of the contract, it is possible to perform it within one year from this date, the contract does not fall within the statute of frauds and does not have to be in writing. If, however, the terms of the contract make it impossible to complete performance of the contract (without breaching it) within one year from the date on which the contract came into existence, the contract falls within the statute and must meet its requirements to be enforceable. Thus, if Hammer Co. and McCrea agree on August 1, 1993, that McCrea will work for Hammer Co. for one year, beginning October 1, 1993, the terms of the contract dictate that it is not possible to complete performance until October 1, 1994. Because that date is more than one year from the date on which the contract came into existence, the contract falls within the statute of frauds and must be evidenced by a writing to be enforceable.

Sale of Goods for $500 or More

The original English Statute of Frauds required a writing for contracts for the sale of goods for a price of 10 pounds sterling or more. In the United States today, the writing requirement for the sale of goods is governed by section 2–201 of the Uniform Commercial Code. This section provides that contracts for the sale of goods for the price of $500 or more are not enforceable without a writing or other specified evidence that a contract was made. There are a number of alternative ways of satisfying the requirements of section 2–201. These will be explained later in this chapter.

Modifications of Existing Sales Contracts   Just as some contracts to extend the time for performance fall within the one-year provision of the statute of frauds, agreements to modify existing sales contracts can fall within the statute of frauds if the contract as modified is for a price of $500 or more.[4] UCC section 2–209(3) provides that the requirements of the statute of frauds must be satisfied if the contract as modified is within its provisions. For example, if Carroll and Kestler enter into a contract for the sale of goods at a price of $490, the original contract does *not* fall within the statute of frauds. However, if they later modify the contract by increasing the contract price to $510, the modification falls within the statute of frauds and must meet its requirements to be enforceable.

Promise of Executor or Administrator to Pay a Decedent's Debt Personally

When a person dies, a personal representative is appointed to administer his estate. One of the important tasks of this personal representative, who is called an executor if the person dies leaving a will or an administrator if the person dies without a will, is to pay the debts owed by the decedent. No writing is required when an executor or administrator—acting in his representative capacity—promises to pay the decedent's debts from the funds of the decedent's estate. The statute of frauds requires a writing, however, if the executor, acting in her capacity as a private individual rather than in her representative capacity, promises to pay one of the decedent's debts out of her own (the executor's) funds. For example, Thomas, who has been appointed executor of his Uncle Max's estate, is presented with a bill for $10,500 for medical services rendered to Uncle Max during his last illness by the family doctor, Dr. Barnes. Feeling bad that there are not adequate funds in the estate to compensate Dr. Barnes for his services, Thomas promises to pay Dr. Barnes from his own funds. Thomas's promise would have to be evidenced by a writing to be enforceable.

---

[4]Modifications of sales contracts are discussed in greater detail in Chapter 12.

Contract in which Marriage Is the Consideration

The statute of frauds also requires a writing when marriage is the consideration to support a contract. The marriage provision has been interpreted to be inapplicable to agreements that involve only mutual promises to marry. It can apply to any other contract in which one party's promise is given in exchange for marriage or the promise to marry on the part of the other party. This is true whether the promisor is one of the parties to the marriage or a third party. For example, if Hicks promises to deed his ranch to Everett in exchange for Everett's agreement to marry Hicks's son, Everett could not enforce Hicks's promise without written evidence of the promise.

Prenuptial (or antenuptial) agreements present a common contemporary application of the marriage provision of the statute of frauds. These are agreements between couples who contemplate marriage. They usually involve such matters as transfers of property, division of property upon divorce or death, and various lifestyle issues. Assuming that marriage or the promise to marry is the consideration supporting these agreements, they are within the statute of frauds and must be evidenced by a writing.[5]

---

[5]Note, however, that "nonmarital" agreements between unmarried cohabitants who do not plan marriage are not within the marriage provision of the statute of frauds, even though the agreement may concern the same sorts of matters that are typically covered in a prenuptial agreement. The legality of agreements between unmarried cohabitants is discussed in Chapter 15.

CONCEPT REVIEW

CONTRACTS WITHIN THE STATUTE OF FRAUDS

Provision	Description	Exceptions (situations in which contract does not require a writing)
Marriage	Contracts, other than mutual promises to marry, where marriage is the consideration	—
Year	Bilateral contracts that, *by their terms,* cannot be performed within one year from the date on which the contract was formed	Full (complete) performance by one of the parties
Land	Contracts that create or transfer an ownership interest in real property	1. Full performance by vendor (vendor deeds property to vendees) or 2. "Part performance" doctrine: Vendee relies on oral contract—for example, by: a. Paying substantial part of purchase price, and b. Taking possession or making improvements
Executor's Promise	Executor promises to pay estate's debt out of his own funds	—
Sale of Goods at Price of $500 or More (UCC § 2–201)	Contracts for the sale of goods for a contract price of $500 or more; also applies to modifications of contracts for goods where price as modified is $500 or more	See alternative ways of satisfying statute of frauds under UCC
Collateral Contracts, Guaranty	Contracts where promisor promises to pay the debt of another if the primary debtor fails to pay	"Main purpose" or "leading object" exception: Guarantor makes promise primarily for her own economic benefit

MEETING THE REQUIREMENTS OF THE STATUTE OF FRAUDS

Nature of the Writing Required

The statutes of frauds of the various states are not uniform in their formal requirements. However, most states require only a *memorandum* of the parties' agreement; they do not require that the entire contract be in writing. The memorandum must provide written evidence that a contract was made, but it need not have been created with the intent that the memorandum itself would be binding.

In fact, in some cases, written offers that were accepted orally have been held sufficient to satisfy the writing requirement. As you will see in the following *Putt v. City of Corinth* case, a memorandum may be in any form. Typical examples include letters, telegrams, receipts, or any other writing indicating that the parties had a contract. The memorandum need not be made at the same time the contract comes into being; in fact, the memorandum may be made at any time before suit is filed. If a memorandum of the parties' agreement is lost, its loss and its contents may be proven by oral testimony.

PUTT V. CITY OF CORINTH
579 So. 2d 534 (Sup. Ct. Miss. 1991)

John Putt owned commercial real estate known as the King Tractor Building, which was located in Corinth, Mississippi. Putt had most recently used it to operate a used car business. In the fall of 1984, the Corinth Gas and Water Department, which is an arm of the City of Corinth, was seeking a building suitable for housing its maintenance department and storing equipment and spare parts. Putt learned about this and approached Wayne McGee, department manager, and Dennis Coleman, a department employee, telling them his building was for sale for $100,000. McGee appeared at the regular monthly meeting of the Utilities Commission and reported his conversation with Putt. The commission authorized the inspection of Putt's building and, after receiving a favorable inspection report, authorized commissioner Leland Martin to negotiate a purchase agreement with Putt. There was a metal shed or building on the property that the commission saw no use for. Putt agreed to remove it and reduce the purchase price to $95,000. The parties then reached an agreement for the purchase of the building for $95,000. On March 11, 1985, the commission formally approved the purchase as evidenced by the following minute entry:

WAREHOUSE: Commissioner Martin reported that they had obtained the agreement of John Putt to sell the building on Old Highway 45 (Tate Street) to the City for $95,000.00 with him to retain the shed immediately north of the building. After discussion, the Commission found that the appraisal by Lou Miller was $100,000.00 and that the shed would be of little value to the Gas and Water Department and that the reasonable market value of the property was $95,000.00 and should be purchased for the use of the Water and Gas Departments. The purchase to be made with funds from the Gas Department and the Water Department to pay rent on the building.

These minutes were signed by the chairman of the commission and attested by the secretary of the commission.

Putt removed the shed from the land and moved his used car business to another location. He also terminated the tenancy of some at-will renters on the property from whom he had been receiving $250 and $450 a month, respectively. He also cleaned up the warehouse in preparation for the closing. A dispute arose between Putt and the City about matters involved in the closing of the sale and the City refused to purchase Putt's property. In July 1985, the City purchased other property. Putt sued the City for breach of contract. The City moved for summary judgment on the ground that the contract did not comply with the statute of frauds, and the trial court granted a summary judgment in favor of the City and dismissed Putt's complaint. Putt appealed.

Robertson, Justice   People are able to contract for the purchase and sale of real property and have their contracts given effect because the law allows such. As with the other facilities our law affords persons for realizing their wishes, land sales contracts are attended by certain formalities which, if not met, may leave the agreement a nullity and legally unenforceable. As a general rule, Mississippi law does not require that contracts be made in writing. Put otherwise, oral contracts are ordinarily no less enforceable than others.

The legislature has enacted an exception to this general rule, to the end of reducing the risk that persons will be held to contracts they did not make. This exception performs an evidentiary function, and provides, in the present context, that

An action shall not be brought whereby to charge a defendant . . . upon any contract for the sale of lands . . . unless the promise or agreement upon which such action may be brought, *or some memorandum or note thereof,* shall be in writing, and signed by the party to be charged therewith.

It is commonly known as the statute of frauds.

What is central to our inquiry today is whether there is in fact an otherwise legally enforceable contract of sale between Putt and the City. Nothing in the statute of frauds requires that the contract itself be in writing. The statute is satisfied so long as there is "some memorandum or note thereof." For the prevention of frauds, the statute merely prescribes the form a part of the evidence must take. Oral testimony regarding the fact is admissible as well. The "memorandum or note" serves but to show a basis for believing that the offered oral evidence rests on a real transaction. *Gulf Refining Company v. Travis* suggests the memorandum "must contain words appropriate to, and indicating an intention thereby, to convey or lease land, must identify the land, [and] set forth the purchase price."

The minutes of the Utilities Commission unmistakably authorized an intent to buy, identify the land, set out the purchase price and otherwise meet *Gulf Refining's* indicia. These minutes are signed by the President and Secretary of the Utilities Commission and were, in fact, approved at a subsequent meeting. We hold that these minutes are a "memorandum or note" satisfying the statute. Beyond this, the present record provides an evidentiary basis upon which we may find that Putt and the City entered a valid and enforceable contract of sale.

Reversed and remanded in favor of Putt.

Contents of the Memorandum   Although there is a general trend away from requiring complete writings to satisfy the statute of frauds, an adequate memorandum must still contain several things. Generally, the essential terms of the contract must be indicated in the memorandum, although states differ in their requirements concerning how specifically the terms must be stated. The identity of the parties must be indicated in some way, and the subject matter of the contract must be identified with reasonable certainty. This last requirement causes particular problems in contracts for the sale of land, since many statutes require a detailed description of the property to be sold.

Contents of Memorandum under the UCC The standard for determining the sufficiency of the contents of a memorandum is more flexible in cases concerning contracts for the sale of goods. This looser standard is created by the language of UCC section 2–201, which states that the writing must be sufficient to indicate that a contract for sale has been made between the parties, but a writing can be sufficient even if it omits or incorrectly states a term agreed on. However, the memorandum is not enforceable for more than the quantity of goods stated in the memorandum. Thus, a writing that does not indicate the *quantity* of goods to be sold would not satisfy the Code's writing requirement.

Signature Requirement   The memorandum must be signed by the *party to be charged* or his authorized agent. (The party to be charged is the person using the statute of frauds as a defense— generally the defendant unless the statute of frauds is asserted as a defense to a counterclaim.) This means that it is not necessary for purposes of meeting the statute of frauds for both parties' signatures to appear on the document. It is, however, in the best interests of both parties for both signatures to appear on the writing; otherwise, the contract evidenced by the writing is enforceable only against the signing party. Unless the statute expressly provides that the memorandum or contract must be signed at the end, the signature may appear any place on the memorandum. Any writing, mark, initials, stamp, engraving, or other symbol placed or printed on a memorandum will suffice as a signature, as long as the party to be charged intended it to authenticate (indicate the genuineness of) the writing.

Memorandum Consisting of Several Writings

In many situations, the elements required for a memorandum are divided among several documents. For example, Wayman and Allen enter into a contract for the sale of real estate, intending to memorialize their agreement in a formal written document later. While final drafts of a written contract are being prepared, Wayman repudiates the contract. Allen has a copy of an unsigned preliminary draft of the contract that identifies the parties and contains all of the material terms of the parties' agreement, an unsigned note written by Wayman that contains the legal description of the property, and a letter signed by Wayman that refers to the contract and to the other two documents. None of these documents, standing alone, would be sufficient to satisfy the statute of frauds. However, Allen can combine them to meet the requirements of the statute, provided that they all relate to the same agreement. This can be shown by physical attachment, as where the documents are stapled or bound together, or by references in the documents themselves that indicate that they all apply to the same transaction. In some cases, it has also been shown by the fact that the various documents were executed at the same time.

ALTERNATIVE MEANS OF SATISFYING THE STATUTE OF FRAUDS IN SALE OF GOODS CONTRACTS

As you have learned, the basic requirement of the UCC statute of frauds [2–201] is that a contract for the sale of goods for the purchase price of $500 or more must be evidenced by a written memorandum that indicates the existence of the contract, states the quantity of goods to be sold, and is signed by the party to be charged. Recognizing that the underlying purpose of the statute of frauds is to provide more evidence of the existence of a contract than the mere oral testimony of one of the parties, however, the Code also permits the statute of frauds to be satisfied by any of four other types of evidence. These different methods of satisfying the UCC statute of frauds are depicted in Figure 2. Under the UCC, then, a contract for the sale of goods for a purchase price of $500 or more for which there is no written memorandum signed by the party to be charged can meet the requirements of the statute of frauds in any of the following ways:

1. *Confirmatory memorandum between merchants.* Suppose Gardner and Roth enter into a contract over the telephone for the sale of goods at a price of $5,000. Gardner then sends a memorandum to Roth confirming the deal they made orally. If Roth receives the memo and does not object to it, it would be fair to say that the parties' conduct provides some evidence that a contract exists. Under some circumstances, the UCC permits such confirmatory memoranda to satisfy the statute of frauds even though the writing is signed by the party who is seeking to enforce the contract rather than the party against whom enforcement is sought [2–201(2)]. This exception applies only when *both* of the parties to a contract are *merchants.* Furthermore, the memo must be sent within a reasonable time after the contract is made and must be sufficient to bind the person who sent it if enforcement were sought against him (that is, it must indicate that a contract was made, state a quantity, and be signed by the sender). If the party against whom enforcement is sought receives the memo, has reason to know its contents, and yet fails to give written notice of objection to the contents of the memo within 10 days after receiving it, the memo can be introduced to meet the requirements of the statute of frauds.

2. *Part payment or part delivery.* Suppose Rice and Cooper enter a contract for the sale of 1,000 units of goods at $1 each. After Rice has paid $600, Cooper refuses to deliver the goods and asserts the statute of frauds as a defense to enforcement of the contract. The Code permits part payment or part delivery to satisfy the statute of frauds, but only for the quantity of goods that have been delivered or paid for [2–201(3)(c)]. Thus, Cooper would be required to deliver only 600 units rather than the 1,000 units Rice alleges that he agreed to sell.

FIGURE 2   **Satisfying the Statute of Frauds for a Contract for the Sale of Goods for a Price of $500 or More**

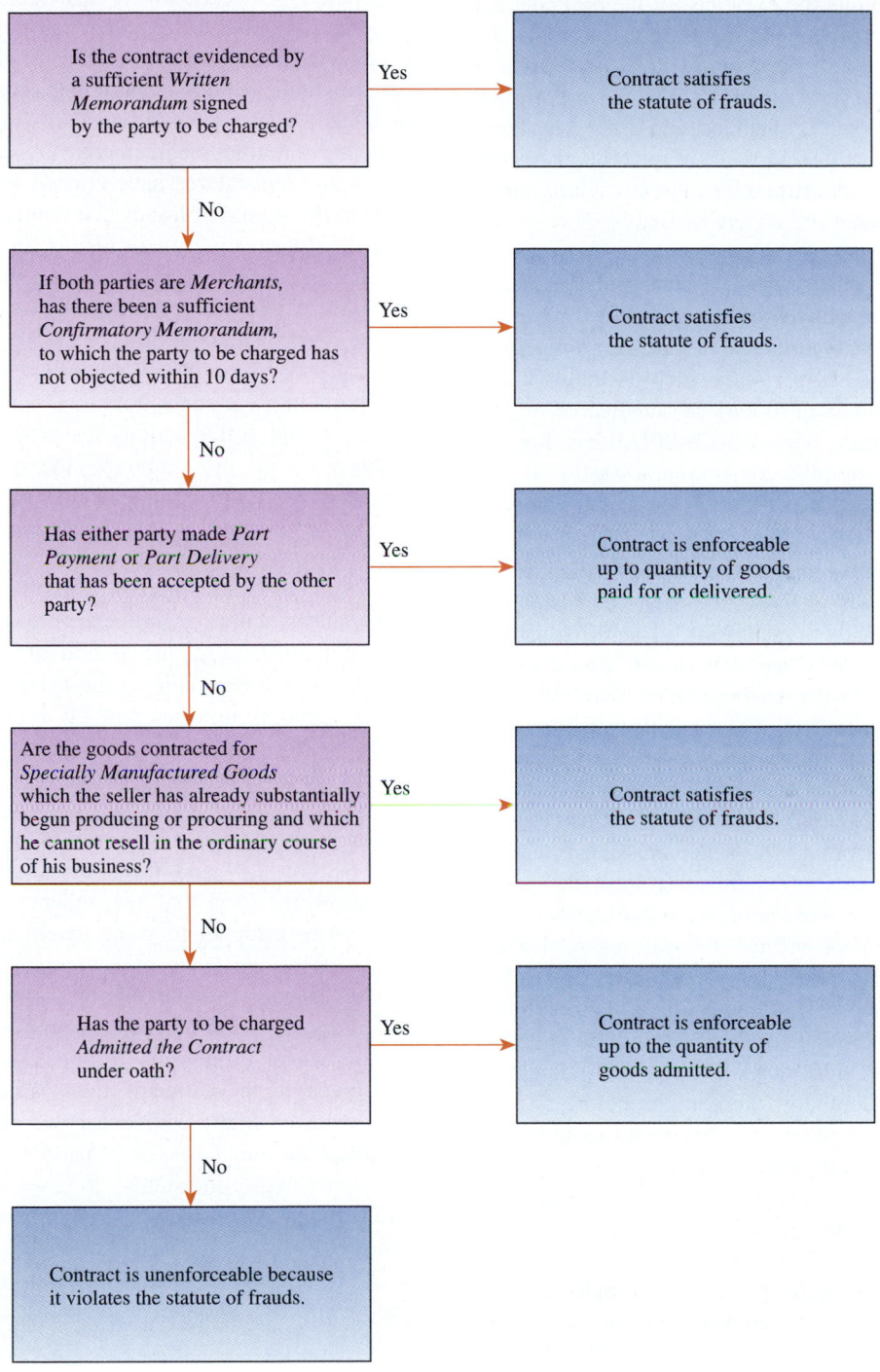

3. *Admission in pleadings or court.* Another situation in which the UCC statute of frauds can be satisfied without a writing occurs when the party being sued admits the existence of the oral contract in his trial testimony or in any document that he files with the court. For example, Nelson refuses to perform an oral contract he made with Smith for the sale of $2,000 worth of goods, and Smith sues him. If Nelson admits the existence of the oral contract in pleadings or in court proceedings, his admission is sufficient to meet the statute of frauds. This exception is justified by the strong evidence that such an admission provides. After all, what better evidence of a contract can there be than is provided when the party being sued admits under penalty of perjury that a contract exists? When such an admission is made, the statute of frauds is satisfied as to the quantity of goods admitted [2–201(3)(b)]. For example, if Nelson only admits contracting for $1,000 worth of goods, the contract is enforceable only to that extent.

4. *Specially manufactured goods.* Finally, an oral contract within the UCC statute of frauds can be enforced without a writing in some situations involving the sale of specially manufactured goods. This exception to the writing requirement will apply only if the nature of the specially manufactured goods is such that they are not suitable for sale in the ordinary course of the seller's business. Completely executory oral contracts are not enforceable under this exception. The seller must have made a substantial beginning in manufacturing the goods for the buyer, or must have made commitments for their procurement, before receiving notice that the buyer was repudiating the sale [2–201(3)(a)]. For example, Bennett Co. has an oral contract with Stevenson for the sale of $2,500 worth of calendars imprinted with Bennett Co.'s name and address. If Bennett Co. repudiates the contract before Stevenson has made a substantial beginning in manufacturing the calendars, the contract will be unenforceable under the statute of frauds. If, however, Bennett Co. repudiated the contract after Stevenson had made a substantial beginning, the oral contract would be enforceable. The specially manufactured goods provision is based both on the evidentiary value of the seller's conduct and on the need to avoid the injustice that would otherwise result from the seller's reliance.

PROMISSORY ESTOPPEL AND THE STATUTE OF FRAUDS

The statute of frauds, which was created to prevent fraud and perjury, has often been criticized because it can create unjust results. One of the troubling features of the statute is that it can as easily be used to defeat a contract that was actually made as it can to defeat a fictitious agreement. As you have seen, courts and legislatures have created several exceptions to the statute of frauds that reduce the statute's potential for creating unfair results. In recent years, courts in some states have allowed the use of the doctrine of **promissory estoppel**[6] to enable some parties to recover under oral contracts that the statute of frauds would ordinarily render unenforceable.

Courts in these states hold that, when one of the parties would suffer serious losses because of her reliance on an oral contract, the other party is estopped from raising the statute of frauds as a defense. This position has been approved in the *Restatement (Second) of Contracts.* Section 139 of the *Restatement (Second)* provides that a promise that induces action or forbearance can be enforceable notwithstanding the statute of frauds if the reliance was foreseeable to the person making the promise and if injustice can be avoided only by enforcing the promise. The idea behind this section and the cases employing promissory estoppel is that the statute of frauds, which is designed to prevent injustice, should not be allowed to work an injustice. Section 139 and these cases also impliedly recognize the fact that the reliance required by promissory estoppel to some extent provides evidence of the existence of a contract between the parties, since it is unlikely that a person would materially rely on a nonexistent promise.

The use of promissory estoppel as a means of circumventing the statute of frauds is still controversial, however. Many courts fear that enforcing oral contracts on the basis of a party's reliance will essentially negate the statute. In cases involving the UCC statute of frauds, an additional source of concern involves the interpretation of section 2–201. Some courts have construed the provisions listing specific alternative methods of satisfying

---

[6]The doctrine of promissory estoppel is discussed in Chapters 9 and 12.

section 2–201's formal requirements to be *exclusive,* precluding the creation of any further exceptions by courts.

THE PAROL EVIDENCE RULE

Explanation of the Rule

In many situations, contracting parties prefer to express their agreements in writing even when they are not required to do so by the statute of frauds. Written contracts rarely come into being without some prior discussions or negotiations between the parties, however. Various promises, proposals, or representations are usually made by one or both of the parties before the execution of a written contract. What happens when one of those prior promises, proposals, or representations is not included in the terms of the written contract? For example, suppose that Jackson wants to buy Stone's house. During the course of negotiations, Stone states that he will pay for any major repairs that the house needs for the first year that Jackson owns it. The written contract that the parties ultimately sign, however, does not say anything about Stone paying for repairs, and, in fact, states that Jackson will take the house "as is." The furnace breaks down three months after the sale, and Stone refuses to pay for its repair. What is the status of Stone's promise to pay for repairs? The basic problem is one of defining the boundaries of the parties' agreement. Are all the promises made in the process of negotiation part of the contract, or do the terms of the written document that the parties signed supersede any preliminary agreements?

The **parol evidence rule** provides the answer to this question. The term *parol evidence* means written or spoken statements that are *not contained in the written contract.* The parol evidence rule provides that, when parties enter a *written contract* that they intend as a complete **integration** (a complete and final statement of their agreement), a court will not permit the use of evidence of *prior* or *contemporaneous* statements to add to, alter, or contradict the terms of the written contract. This rule is based on the presumption that when people enter into a written contract, the best evidence of their agreement is the written contract itself. It also reflects the idea that later expressions of intent are presumed to prevail over earlier expressions of intent. In the hypothetical case involving Stone and Jackson, assuming that they intended the written contract to be the final integration of their agreement, Jackson would not be able to introduce evidence of Stone's promise to pay for repairs. The effect of excluding preliminary promises or statements from consideration is, of course, to confine the parties' contract to the terms of the written agreement. The lesson to be learned from this example is that people who put their agreements in writing should make sure that all the terms of their agreement are included in the writing. The following case, *Slivinsky v. Watkins-Johnson Company,* illustrates the application of the parol evidence rule.

SLIVINSKY V. WATKINS-JOHNSON COMPANY
270 Cal. Rptr. 585 (Cal Ct. App. 1990)

In July 1984, Sandra Slivinsky applied for a job as a materials scientist with Watkins-Johnson Company, a large aerospace manufacturer. Directly above the signature line on the application she signed was the statement: "I understand that employment by WATKINS-JOHNSON COMPANY is conditional upon . . . execution of an Employment Agreement. . . . I further understand that if I become employed by Watkins-Johnson Company, there will be no agreement, expressed or implied, between the company and me for any specific period of employment, nor for continuing or long-term employment." Over the next several months, Watkins-Johnson contacted Slivinsky's references, requested her transcripts, and set up a series of interviews. Slivinsky claims that at these interviews she was promised "long-term," "indefinite," and "permanent" employment, not dependent on business cycles, and subject to termination only for cause. Finally, Watkins-Johnson made a verbal offer of employment to Slivinsky and she accepted. On January 7, 1985, which was Slivinsky's first day at work, Slivinsky signed the employee agreement that had been referred to in her employment application. Set apart in bold type, the last paragraph of this agreement provided that there was no express or implied agreement between the parties regarding the duration of her employment and that the employment could be terminated at any time with or without cause.

As a result of the space shuttle *Challenger* disaster in January 1986, Watkins-Johnson experienced significant business losses and government contract cancellations. The management decided that employee cutbacks were essential to cope with the loss of business. Ultimately, 24 employees, including Slivinsky, were selected for the reduction in force program. Watkins-Johnson terminated her employment in June 1986.

Slivinsky brought suit against Watkins-Johnson for breach of the employment contract, asserting that she had been terminated without cause in violation of the parties' express and implied agreement. She also claimed that the reasons given for her termination were pretextual and that she was really fired for other reasons, such as her supervisor disliking her. The trial court granted Watkins-Johnson's motion for summary judgment, and Slivinsky appealed.

Cottle, Associate Justice   Slivinsky claims that the parties' employment agreement includes factors such as oral assurances of job security and Watkins-Johnson's personnel policies and practices not to terminate employees except for good cause. Watkins-Johnson [argues] that it is limited to the parties' express written contract defining the employment as at-will.

The dispositive issue, therefore, is whether we can look beyond the four corners of the parties' written agreements to ascertain the complete agreement of the parties. The answer to that question involves application of the parol evidence rule, a rule of substantive law precluding the introduction of evidence which varies or contradicts the terms of an integrated written instrument. If the parties intended that the Application and Employment Agreement constituted an integration, i.e., the final expression of their agreement with respect to grounds for termination, then those agreements may not be contradicted by evidence of any prior agreement or of a contemporaneous oral agreement. No particular form is required for an integrated agreement. When only part of the agreement is integrated, the parol evidence rule applies to that part.

Applying these standards, we conclude that the contract was integrated with respect to the grounds for termination. Slivinsky's employment application specifically conditioned employment upon execution of an employment agreement. It further provided that if Slivinsky were to become employed by Watkins-Johnson, there "will be no agreement, ex-

pressed or implied, . . . for any specific period of employment, nor for continuing or long-term employment." When Slivinsky executed the Employee Agreement, she acknowledged "that there is no agreement, express or implied, between employee and the Company for any specific period of employment, nor for continuing or long-term employment. Employee and the Company each have a right to terminate employment, with or without cause." Reading these documents together, the only reasonable conclusion that can be drawn is that the parties intended that there would be no other agreement regarding termination other than that set forth in the Employee Agreement. Consequently, evidence of an implied agreement which contradicts the terms of the written agreement is not admissible. There cannot be a valid express contract and an implied contract, each embracing the same subject, but requiring different results.

Because we hold that the contract is a contract for employment terminable at will, we do not reach the issues regarding whether good cause existed for Slivinsky's termination based on Watkins-Johnson's decision to reduce its work force. Even if the reduction in force were a pretextual ground for terminating Slivinsky's employment, it would not be actionable with an at-will employment contract unless the employer's motivation for a discharge contravenes some significant public policy principle. No such public policy violation is alleged here.

Judgment for Watkins-Johnson affirmed.

Scope of the Parol Evidence Rule

The parol evidence rule is relevant only in cases in which the parties have expressed their agreement in a written contract. Thus, it would not apply to a case involving an oral contract or to a case in which writings existed that were not intended to embody the final statement of at least part of the parties' contract. The parol evidence rule has been made a part of the law of sales in the Uniform Commercial Code [2–202], so it is applicable to contracts for the sale of goods as well as to contracts governed by the common law of contracts. Furthermore, the rule excludes only evidence of statements made *prior to* or *during* the signing of the written contract. It does not apply to statements made after the signing of the contract. Thus, evidence of subsequent statements is freely admissible.

Admissible Parol Evidence

In some situations, evidence of statements made outside the written contract is admissible notwithstanding the parol evidence rule. Parol evidence is permitted in the situations discussed below either because the writing is not the best evidence of the contract or because the evidence is offered, not to contradict the terms of the writing, but to explain the writing or to challenge the underlying contractual obligation that the writing represents.

1. *Additional terms in partially integrated contracts.* In many instances, parties will desire to introduce evidence of statements or agreements that would supplement rather than contradict the written contract. Whether they can do this depends on whether the written contract is characterized as *completely integrated* or *partially integrated*. A completely integrated contract is one that the parties intend as a *complete and exclusive statement* of their entire agreement. A partially integrated contract is one that expresses the parties' final agreement as to some but not all of the terms of their contract. When a contract is only partially integrated, the parties are permitted to use parol evidence to prove the *additional* terms of their agreement. Such evidence cannot, however, be used to contradict the written terms of the contract. To determine whether a contract is completely or partially integrated, a court must determine the parties' intent. A court judges intent by looking at the language of the contract, the

apparent completeness of the writing, and all the surrounding circumstances. It will also consider whether the contract contains a **merger clause** (also known as an **integration clause**). These clauses, which are very common in form contracts and commercial contracts, provide that the written contract is the complete integration of the parties' agreement. They are designed to prevent a party from giving testimony about prior statements or agreements and are generally effective in indicating that the writing was a complete integration. Even though a contract contains a merger clause, parol evidence could be admissible under one of the following exceptions.

2. *Explaining ambiguities.* Parol evidence can be offered to explain an ambiguity in the written contract. Suppose a written contract between Lowen and Matthews provides that Lowen will buy "Matthews's truck," but Matthews has two trucks. The parties could offer evidence of negotiations, statements, and other circumstances preceding the creation of the written contract to identify the truck to which the writing refers. Used in this way, parol evidence helps the court interpret the contract. It does not contradict the written contract.

3. *Circumstances invalidating contract.* Any circumstances that would be relevant to show that a contract is not valid can be proven by parol evidence. For example, evidence that Holden pointed a gun at Dickson and said, "Sign this contract, or I'll kill you," would be admissible to show that the contract was voidable because of duress. Likewise, parol evidence would be admissible to show that a contract was illegal or was induced by fraud, misrepresentation, undue influence, or mistake.

4. *Existence of condition.* It is also permissible to use parol evidence to show that a writing was executed with the understanding that it was *not to take effect until the occurrence of a condition* (a future, uncertain event that creates a duty to perform). Suppose Farnsworth signs a contract to purchase a car with the agreement that the contract is not to be effective unless and until Farnsworth gets a new job. If the written contract is silent about any conditions that must occur before it becomes effective, Farnsworth could introduce parol evidence to prove the existence of the condition. Such proof merely elaborates on, but does not contradict, the terms of the writing.

5. *Subsequent agreements.* As you read earlier, the parol evidence rule does not forbid parties to introduce proof of *subsequent agreements.* This is true even if the terms of the later agreement cancel, subtract from, or add to the obligations stated in the written contract. The idea here is that when a writing is followed by a later statement or agreement, the writing is no longer the best evidence of the agreement. You should be aware, however, that subsequent modifications of contracts may sometimes be unenforceable due to lack of consideration or failure to comply with the statute of frauds. In addition, contracts sometimes expressly provide that modifications must be written. In this situation, an oral modification would be unenforceable.

CONCEPT REVIEW

PAROL EVIDENCE RULE

Parol Evidence Rule	Applies when:	Provides that:
	Parties create a writing intended as a final and complete integration of at least part of the parties' contract.	Evidence of statements or promises made before or during the creation of the writing cannot be used to supplement, change, or contradict the terms of the written contract.
But Parol Evidence *Can* Be Used to	1. Prove consistent, additional terms when the contract is *partially integrated.* 2. Explain an ambiguity in the written contract. 3. Prove that the contract is void, voidable, or unenforceable. 4. Prove that the contract was subject to a condition. 5. Prove that the parties subsequently modified the contract or made a new agreement.	

INTERPRETATION OF CONTRACTS

Once a court has decided what promises are included in a contract, it is faced with *interpreting* the contract to determine the *meaning* and *legal effect* of the terms used by the parties. Courts have adopted broad, basic standards of interpretation that guide them in the interpretation process.

The court will first attempt to determine the parties' *principal objective.* Every clause will then be determined in the light of this principal objective. Ordinary words will be given their usual meaning and technical words (such as those that have a special meaning in the parties' trade or business) will be given their technical meaning, unless a different meaning was clearly intended.

Guidelines grounded in common sense are also used to determine the relationship of the various terms of the contract. Specific terms that follow general terms are presumed to qualify those general terms. Suppose that a provision that states that the subject of the contract is "guaranteed for one year" is followed by a provision describing the "one-year guarantee against defects in workmanship." Here, it is fair to conclude that the more specific term qualifies the more general term and that the guarantee described in the contract is a guarantee of workmanship only, and not of parts and materials.

Sometimes, there is internal conflict in the terms of an agreement and courts must determine which term should prevail. When the parties use a form contract or some other type of contract that is partially printed and partially handwritten, the handwritten provisions will prevail. If the contract was drafted by one of the parties, any ambiguities will be resolved against the party who drafted the contract.

If both parties to the contract are members of a trade, profession, or community in which certain words are commonly given a particular meaning (this is called a *usage*), the courts will presume that the parties intended the meaning that the usage gives to the terms they use. For example, if the word dozen in the bakery business means 13 rather than 12, a contract between two bakers for the purchase of 10 dozen loaves of bread will be presumed to mean 130 loaves of bread rather than 120. Usages can also add provisions to the parties' agreement. If the court finds that a certain practice is a matter of common usage in the parties' trade, it will assume that the parties intended to include that practice in their agreement. If contracting parties are members of the same trade, business, or community but do not intend to be bound by usage, they should specifically say so in their agreement.

ETHICAL AND PUBLIC POLICY CONCERNS

1. The statute of frauds requires written evidence of some, but not all, contracts. Is this defensible from a public policy standpoint? Would it be preferable for the law to simply require that all contracts be evidenced by a writing?

2. What ethical problem was the statute of frauds designed to prevent, and what ethical problem does the statute of frauds create? Is the "cure worse than the disease"?

3. Under the law of some states, the doctrine of promissory estoppel permits the enforcement of promises that induce reliance, even when those promises do not comply with the statute of frauds. Should all states adopt this position? What effect would this have on the statute of frauds?

4. For those parties who draft and proffer standardized form contracts, the parol evidence rule can be a powerful ally because it has the effect of limiting the scope of an integrated, written contract to the terms of the writing. Although statements and promises made to a person before he signs a contract might be highly influential in persuading him to enter the contract, the parol evidence rule effectively prevents these precontract communications from being legally enforceable. Consider also that standardized form contracts are usually drafted for the benefit of and proffered by the more sophisticated and powerful party in a contract (e.g., the insurance company rather than the insured, the automobile dealer rather than the customer, the landlord rather than the tenant). Considering all of this, do you believe that the parol evidence rule promotes ethical behavior?

PROBLEMS AND PROBLEM CASES

1. Golomb allegedly orally agreed to sell to Lee for $275,000 the Ferrari once owned by King Leopold of Belgium. Golomb ultimately refused to sell the car and Lee sued him. At trial, Golomb denied ever promising to sell the car to Lee. Can Lee enforce this alleged promise?

2. Boyd-Scarp, a building contractor, was building a new home for Rathmann. Rathmann paid Boyd-Scarp for appliances for the new home and Boyd-Scarp contracted with Al Booth's, an appliance supplier, for the purchase of the appliances. Al Booth's had heard that Boyd-Scarp was having financial problems. Before delivering the appliances to the Rathmanns' new home, it contacted Rathmann and asked him to guarantee payment. Al Booth's alleges that Rathmann orally promised to pay for the appliances if Boyd-Scarp failed to pay. Al Booth's then delivered the appliances. Boyd-Scarp became insolvent and did not pay Al Booth's for the appliances. Al Booth's turned to Rathmann for payment. Rathmann asserted the statute of frauds as a defense. Will he be successful in using this defense?

3. In January 1980, Mayer entered into an oral contract of employment with King Cola for a three-year term. Mayer moved from Chattanooga to St. Louis and began working. King Cola paid his moving expenses. In accordance with the parties' negotiations, Mayer awaited a written contract, but none was ever executed. The employment relationship soon began to deteriorate, and after several months King Cola's president told Mayer that he was not going to be given a contract. In May 1980, King Cola discharged Mayer. In a state that does not recognize the doctrine of promissory estoppel as an exception to the statute of frauds, will Mayer be able to enforce the contract?

4. Green owns a lot (Lot S) in the Manomet section of Plymouth, Massachusetts. In July 1980, she advertised it for sale. On July 11 and 12, the Hickeys discussed with Green purchasing Lot S and orally agreed to a sale for $15,000. On July 12, Green accepted the Hickeys' check for $500. Hickey had left the payee line of the deposit check blank, because of uncertainty whether Green or her brother was to receive the check. Hickey asked Green to fill in the appropriate name. Green, however, held the check, did not fill in the payee's name, and neither cashed nor indorsed it. Hickey told Green that his intention was to sell his home and build on the lot he was buying from Green. Relying on the arrangements with Green, the Hickeys advertised their house in newspapers for three days in July. They found a purchaser quickly. Within a short time, they contracted with a purchaser for the sale of their house and accepted the purchaser's deposit check. On the back of this check, above the Hickeys' signatures indorsing the check, was noted: "Deposit on purchase of property at Sachem Rd. and First St., Manomet, Ma. Sale price, $44,000." On July 24, Green told Hickey that she no longer intended to sell her property to him and instead had decided to sell it to someone else for $16,000. Hickey offered to pay Green $16,000 for the lot, but she refused this offer. The Hickeys then filed a complaint against Green seeking specific performance. Green asserted that relief was barred by the statute of frauds. Is this correct?

5. In June 1976, Moore went to First National Bank and requested the president of the bank to allow his sons, Rocky and Mike, to open an account in the name of Texas Continental Express, Inc. Moore promised to bring his own business to the bank and orally agreed to make good any losses that the bank might incur from receiving dishonored checks from Texas Continental. The bank then furnished regular checking account and bank draft services to Texas Continental. Several years later, Texas Continental wrote checks totaling $448,942.05 that were returned for insufficient funds. Texas Continental did not cover the checks, and the bank turned to Moore for payment. When Moore refused to pay, the bank sued him. Does Moore have a good statute of frauds defense?

6. Mark and Barney Brownlee were farmers who, as a partnership doing business as Brownlee Brothers, grew and sold crops. In addition to farming, Barney Brownlee owned a gas station. On July 22, 1983, Barney Brownlee allegedly telephoned Goldkist and, after checking on the current price of soybeans, allegedly agreed to deliver 5,000 bushels of soybeans to Goldkist between August 22 and September 22, at $6.88 per pound. Although no written agreement signed by either of the Brownlees was created, Goldkist did send the Brownlees a written memorandum dated July 22, which confirmed the agreement to sell 5,000 bushels of soybeans on the terms described above. The Brownlees

received the memorandum but did not respond to it. They also did not deliver the soybeans, and Goldkist was forced to "cover" the contract (buy soybeans from another source). Goldkist then brought this action to recover its losses arising out of the necessity to cover. The Brownlees asserted as a defense the fact that there was no writing signed by either of them as required by UCC section 2–201. Is this a good argument?

7. Dyer purchased a used Ford from Walt Bennett Ford for $5,895. She signed a written contract, which showed that no taxes were included in the sales price. Dyer contended, however, that the salesperson who negotiated the purchase with her told her both before and after her signing of the contract that the sales tax on the automobile had been paid. The contract Dyer signed contained the following language:

The above comprises the entire agreement pertaining to this purchase and no other agreement of any kind, verbal understanding, representation, or promise whatsoever will be recognized.

It also stated:

This contract constitutes the entire agreement between the parties and no modification hereof shall be valid in any event and Buyer expressly waives the right to rely thereon, unless made in writing, signed by Seller.

Later, when Dyer attempted to license the automobile, she discovered that the Arkansas sales tax had not been paid on it. She paid the sales tax and sued Bennett for breach of contract. What result?

8. Starry is a general contractor in the business of asphalt road construction. Murphy was one of its suppliers. In March 1990, a Murphy sales manager orally promised to sell Starry 20,000 tons of asphalt cement oil for $90 per ton. That agreement was confirmed with a written acknowledgment form that specifically stated that causes beyond the control of either party would be an excuse for delay or failure to perform if notice were given promptly. In April 1990, Starry determined that it would need more asphalt cement oil. It contacted Murphy and requested an additional 5,000 tons. Several days later, Murphy's sales manager orally agreed to sell the additional oil on the same terms and conditions as those initially agreed to. Starry neglected to send a confirmatory memorandum of this oral modification. In August 1990, due to the war in the Persian

Gulf, Murphy began experiencing an unprecedented demand for asphalt cement oil. Starry employees became concerned that Murphy might not supply the additional oil and contacted Murphy to request a written confirmation of the modification. Murphy's sales manager allegedly responded, "Don't worry about it. I'll take care of you. I've never cheated you in the past. You are a good customer, and I treat our good customers right." This sales manager, however, was subsequently promoted and replaced by another Murphy employee. In September, the new sales manager informed Starry that because of the oil crisis, Murphy would be forced to allocate its supply. Believing that Murphy would ultimately deliver the additional oil, Starry did not approach other suppliers until late September. At that time, it made arrangements to purchase the additional oil from other suppliers at a higher price. In October 1990, Starry sent a letter to Murphy discussing the agreement between it and Murphy for the sale of 25,000 tons of oil. Murphy was unable to deliver the additional oil and denied that the agreement was ever modified to include an additional 5,000 tons of oil. Starry sued it for breach of contract. Will Starry be able to enforce an agreement to sell the additional quantity of oil?

9. Lovely was living in Ann Arbor, Michigan, and working at two jobs there when Dierkes offered Lovely employment with the Real Food Company in Jackson, Michigan. Dierkes promised Lovely a three-year employment contract, a salary of $400 per week, and a percentage interest in Real Food. He also promised that Lovely would not be discharged without good cause. Lovely relocated his family to Jackson in reliance on Dierkes's promise. He began performing under the agreement and requested several times that Dierkes reduce the contract to writing. Dierkes allegedly assured Lovely that a writing was forthcoming. After two months of employment, Dierkes discharged Lovely. Lovely sued Dierkes and Real Food for breach of contract. Dierkes claims that the contract is unenforceable because of the statute of frauds. Can Lovely enforce this contract?

10. In 1981, Goodman was living in Oklahoma with her husband, who was suffering from a termi-

nal illness. She and her husband traveled to the Connecticut home of her mother, Mayer, to discuss whether Goodman should return to Connecticut. Goodman and Mayer reached an oral agreement providing that Goodman would live in Mayer's house, would make certain refurbishments, and care for Mayer in return for which Mayer would convey the house to Goodman. Goodman also agreed to pay one half the value of the house to her sister, Savoy, upon the death of Goodman's husband. The Goodmans sold their Oklahoma home and moved to Connecticut. They contracted for renovations, which were paid from the proceeds of the Oklahoma house. In September 1981, Goodman and Mayer had an argument, after which the Goodmans vacated Mayer's house at her request. Shortly thereafter, Mayer changed her will, which had left one-half of her estate to each of her two daughters, and disinherited Goodman, leaving her entire estate on her death to Savoy. Mayer sued her mother's estate, claiming the existence of an enforceable oral contract. Will she prevail?

11. 🎞️ *Video Case.* See "Car Deals." Acme Used Cars Sales and Service sold a used car to Jones. Prior to the signing of a written purchase contract, Acme's salesperson told Jones that he "wouldn't find a car like this at any price" and "this car is a crown jewel." However, the purchase order that Jones signed stated that the car was being sold "as is" and that "no warranties or representations concerning the car have been made or given except as contained" in the contract. Jones later discovered that the brakes were defective and needed to be rebuilt. If Jones sued Acme, would the parol evidence rule prevent the admission of testimony about the salesperson's statements?

12. 🎞️ *Video Case.* See "Sour Grapes." Fred, a jelly manufacturer in Chicago, ordered grapes by telephone for a price of $800 from Gus, a grape grower in California. Gus sent a written purchase order confirmation. He also shipped the grapes, but they were spoiled when they arrived. Would the statute of frauds prevent this contract from being enforced?

See also "Software Horror Story" and "A Christmas Story."

RIGHTS OF

THIRD PARTIES

INTRODUCTION

In preceding chapters, we have emphasized the way in which an agreement between two or more people creates legal rights and duties on the part of the contracting parties. Since a contract is founded on the consent of the contracting parties, it might seem to follow that they are the only ones who have rights and duties under the contract. Although this is generally true, there are two situations in which people who were not parties to a contract have legally enforceable rights under it: when a contract has been assigned *(transferred) to a third party and when a contract is* intended to benefit a third person *(a* third-party beneficiary*). This chapter discusses the circumstances in which third parties have rights under a contract.*

ASSIGNMENT OF CONTRACTS

Contracts give people both rights and duties. If Murphy buys Wagner's motorcycle and promises to pay him $1,000 for it, Wagner has the *right* to receive Murphy's promised performance (the payment of the $1,000) and Murphy has the *duty* to perform the promise by paying $1,000. In most situations, contract rights can be transferred to a third person and contract duties can be delegated to a third person. The transfer of a *right* under a contract is called an **assignment.** The appointment of another person to perform a *duty* under a contract is called a **delegation.**

Nature of Assignment of Rights

A person who owes a duty to perform under a contract is called an **obligor.** The person to whom he owes the duty is called the **obligee.** For example, Samson borrows $500 from Jordan, promising to repay Jordan in six months. Samson, who owes the duty to pay the money, is the obligor, and Jordan, who has the right to receive the money, is the obligee. An assignment occurs when the obligee transfers his right to receive the obligor's performance to a third person. When there has been an assignment, the person making the assignment—the original obligee—is then called the **assignor.** The person to whom the right has been transferred is called the **assignee.** Figure 1 summarizes these key terms.

FIGURE 1	**Assignment: Key Terms**			
Obligor	**Obligee**	**Assignment**	**Assignor**	**Assignee**
Person who owes the duty to perform	Person who has the right to receive obligor's performance	Transfer of the right to receive obligor's performance	Obligee who transfers the right to receive obligor's performance	Person to whom the right to receive obligor's performance is transferred

FIGURE 2   **Assignment**

Before assignment — Owes duty to perform — Obligor → Obligee

Assignment — Transfers right to receive obligor's performance — Obligee (Assignor) → Assignee

Result of assignment — Owes duty to perform — Obligor → Assignee

Suppose that Jordan, the obligee in the example above, assigns his right to receive Samson's payment to Kane. Here, Jordan is the assignor and Kane is the assignee. The relationship between the three parties is represented in Figure 2. Notice that the assignment is a separate transaction; it occurs after the formation of the original contract.

The effect of the assignment is to extinguish the assignor's right to receive performance and to transfer that right to the assignee. In the above example, Kane now owns the right to collect payment from Samson. If Samson fails to pay, Kane, as an assignee, now has the right to file suit against Samson to collect the debt.

People assign rights for a variety of reasons. A person might assign a right to a third party to satisfy a debt that he owes. For example, Jordan, the assignor in the above example, owes money to Kane, so he assigns to Kane the right to receive the $500 that Samson owes him. A person might also sell or pledge the rights owed to him to obtain financing. In the case of a business, the money owed to a business by customers and clients is called *accounts receivable*. A business's accounts receivable are an asset to the business that can be used to raise money in several ways. For example, the business may pledge its accounts receivable as collateral for a loan. Suppose Ace Tree Trimming Co. wants to borrow money from First Bank and gives First Bank a security interest (an interest in the debtor's property that secures the debtor's performance of an obligation) in its accounts receivable.[1] If Ace defaults in its payments to First Bank, First Bank will acquire Ace's rights to collect the accounts receivable. A person might also make an assignment of a contract right as a gift. For example, Lansing owes $2,000 to Father. Father assigns the right to receive Lansing's performance to Son as a graduation gift.

Evolution of the Law Regarding Assignments
Contract rights have not always been transferable. Early common law refused to permit assignment or delegation because debts were considered to be too personal to transfer. A debtor who failed to pay an honest debt was subject to severe penalties, including imprisonment, because such a failure to pay was viewed as the equivalent of theft. The identity of the creditor was of great importance to the debtor, since one creditor might be more lenient than another.

---

[1]Security interests in accounts and other property are discussed in Chapter 28.

Courts also feared that the assignment of debts would stir up unwanted litigation. In an economy that was primarily land-based, the extension of credit was of relatively small importance. As trade increased and became more complex, however, the practice of extending credit became more common. The needs of an increasingly commercial society demanded that people be able to trade freely in intangible assets such as debts. Consequently, the rules of law regarding the assignment of contracts gradually became more liberal. Today, public policy favors free assignability of contracts.

Sources of Assignment Law Today Legal principles regarding assignment are found not only in the common law of contracts but also in Articles 2 and 9 of the Uniform Commercial Code. Section 2–210 of Article 2 contains principles applicable to assignments of rights under a contract for the sale of *goods*. Article 9 governs security interests in accounts and other contract rights as well as the outright sale of accounts. Article 9's treatment of assignments will be discussed in more detail in Chapter 28, Security Interests in Personal Property, but some provisions of Article 9 relating to assignments will be discussed in this chapter.

Creating an Assignment

An assignment can be made in any way that is sufficient to show the assignor's intent to assign. No formal language is required, and a writing is not necessary unless required by a provision of the statute of frauds or some other statute. Many states do have statutes requiring certain types of assignments to be evidenced by a writing, however. Additionally, an assignment for the purposes of security must meet Article 9's formal requirements for security interests.[2]

It is not necessary that the assignee give any consideration to the assignor in exchange for the assignment. Gratuitous assignments (those for which the assignee gives no value) are generally revocable until such time as the obligor satisfies the obligation, however. They can be revoked by the

---

[2]These requirements are discussed in Chapter 28.

assignor's death or incapacity or by notification of revocation given by the assignor to the assignee.

Assignability of Rights

Most, but not all, contract rights are assignable. Although the free assignability of contract rights performs a valuable function in our modern credit-based economy, assignment is undesirable if it would adversely affect some important public policy or if it would materially vary the bargained-for expectations of the parties. There are several basic limitations on the assignability of contract rights.

First, an assignment will not be effective if it is *contrary to public policy*. For example, most states have enacted statutes that prohibit or regulate a wage earner's assignment of future wages. These statutes are designed to protect people against unwisely impoverishing themselves by signing away their future incomes.

Second, an assignment will not be effective if it *adversely affects the obligor* in some significant way. An assignment is ineffective if it materially changes the obligor's duty or increases the burden or risk on the obligor. Naturally, any assignment will change an obligor's duty to some extent. The obligor will have to pay money or deliver goods or render some other performance to one party instead of to another. These changes are not considered to be sufficiently material to render an assignment ineffective. Thus, a right to receive money or goods or land is generally assignable. In addition, covenants not to compete are generally considered to be assignable to buyers of businesses. For example, Jefferson sells RX Drugstore to Waldman, including in the contract of sale a covenant whereby Jefferson promises not to operate a competing drugstore within a 30-mile radius of RX for 10 years after the sale. Waldman later sells RX to Tharp. Here, Tharp could enforce the covenant not to compete against Jefferson. The reason for permitting assignment of covenants not to compete is that the purpose of such covenants is to protect an asset of the business—goodwill—for which the buyer has paid.

An assignment could be ineffective because of its variation of the obligor's duty, however, if the contract right involved a *personal relationship* or an element of *personal skill, judgment,* or *character.* For this reason, contracts of employment in which an employee works under the direct and personal supervision of an employer cannot be assigned to a new employer. An employer could assign a contract of employment, however, if the assignee-employer could perform the contract without adversely affecting the interests of the employee, such as would be the case when an employment relationship does not involve personal supervision by an individual employer. This point is illustrated by the following case, *Special Products Manufacturing, Inc. v. Douglass.*

A purported assignment is ineffective if it significantly increases the burden of the obligor's performance. For example, if Walker contracts to sell Dwyer all of its requirements of wheat, a purported assignment of Dwyer's rights to a corporation that has much greater requirements of wheat would probably be ineffective because it would significantly increase the burden on Walker.

Special Products Manufacturing, Inc. v. Douglass
553 N.Y.S.2d 506 (N.Y. S. Ct., App. Div. 1990)

Thaddeus Douglass was a highly trained servicer of hardness-testing machinery who was employed by Page-Wilson Corporation. In August and April 1983, Douglass signed two employment agreements governing the terms and conditions of his employment with Page-Wilson. The first agreement prohibited Douglass, while he was working for Page-Wilson and for one year after the termination of his employment, from using, to Page-Wilson's detriment, any of its customer lists or other intellectual property acquired from his job there. The second agreement, which applied to the same time period, prohibited Douglass from accepting employment from or serving as a consultant to any business that was in competition with Page-Wilson. In April 1987, Canrad Corporation purchased all assets and contractual rights of Page-Wilson, including Douglass's two employment contracts. Special Products Manufacturing (Special Products), a wholly owned subsidiary of Canrad, assumed plant operations. Douglass worked for Special Products until his resignation in February 1988.

Shortly after that, Special Products filed this lawsuit against Douglass, alleging that Douglass had affixed his name and home telephone number to the machines he serviced, so that the ensuing maintenance calls would reach him personally. It also alleged that, following his resignation, Douglass established a competing business and actively solicited Special Products's clientele. Douglass did not answer the complaint in a timely manner, and, after a long delay, the trial judge entered a default judgment in favor of Special Products. Douglass appealed this order, arguing in part that Special Products did not have the right to enforce the agreements not to compete.

Yesawich, Justice   We perceive no merit in the contention that because Douglass entered into the agreements with Page-Wilson, they are unenforceable by Special Products. In an uncontroverted affidavit based upon personal knowledge, Special Products's vice-president of sales avows that Special Products acquired all of Page-Wilson's contract rights, including Douglass's. Douglass's consent was not required to effectuate this transfer. When the original parties to an agreement so intend, a covenant not to compete is freely assignable. Here, such intent is unmistakably evident in the first employment agreement which expressly "inure[s] to the benefit of the successors and assigns of Page-Wilson." And, while the second document contains no similar provision, neither does it specifically forbid assignment. Because executory contracts, which do not involve exceptional personal skills on the part of the assignor and which the assignee can perform without adversely affecting the rights and interests of the adverse party, are freely assignable absent a contractual, statutory or public policy prohibition, a clear and unambiguous prohibition is essential to effectively prevent assignment. Accordingly, the assignment to Special Products perpetuated the restrictive covenant provision, the very terms of which Douglass violated without justification.

Order in favor of Special Products affirmed.

Contract Clauses Prohibiting Assignment A contract right may also be nonassignable because the original contract expressly forbids assignment. For example, leases often contain provisions forbidding assignment or requiring the tenant to obtain the landlord's permission for assignment.[3]

Antiassignment clauses in contracts are generally enforceable. Because of the strong public policy favoring assignability, however, such clauses are often interpreted narrowly. For example, a court might view an assignment made in violation of an antiassignment clause as a breach of contract for which damages may be recovered, but not as an invalidation of the assignment. Another tactic is to interpret a contractual ban on assignment as prohibiting only the delegation of duties.

The UCC takes this latter position. Under section 2–210(2), general language prohibiting assignment of "the contract" or "all my rights under the contract" is interpreted as forbidding only the delegation of duties, unless the circumstances indicate to the contrary. Section 2–210 also states that a right to damages for breach of a whole sales contract or a right arising out of the assignor's performance of his entire obligation may be assigned even if a provision of the original sales contract prohibited assignment. In addition, UCC section 9–318(4) invalidates contract terms that prohibit (or require the debtor's consent to) an assignment of an account or creation of a security interest in a right to receive money that is now due or that will become due.

Nature of Assignee's Rights

When an assignment occurs, the assignee is said to "step into the shoes of his assignor." This means that the assignee acquires all of the rights that his assignor had under the contract. The assignee has the right to receive the obligor's performance, and if performance is not forthcoming, the assignee has the right to sue in his own name for breach of the obligation. By the same token, the assignee acquires no greater rights than those possessed by the assignor.

Because the assignee has no greater rights than did the assignor, the obligor may assert any defense or claim against the assignee that he could have asserted against the assignor, subject to certain time limitations discussed below. A contract that is void, voidable, or unenforceable as between the original parties does not become enforceable just because it has been assigned to a third party. For example, if Richards induces Dillman's consent to a contract by duress and subsequently assigns his rights under the contract to Keith, Dillman can assert the doctrine of duress against Keith as a ground for avoiding the contract.

Importance of Notifying the Obligor An assignee should promptly notify the obligor of the assignment. Although notification of the obligor is not necessary for the assignment to be valid, such notice is of great practical importance. One reason notice is important is that an obligor who does not have reason to know of the assignment could render performance to the assignor and claim that his obligation had been discharged by performance. An obligor who renders performance to the assignor without notice of the assignment has no further liability under the contract. For example, McKay borrows $500 from Goodheart, promising to repay the debt by June 1. Goodheart assigns the debt to Rogers, but no one informs McKay of the assignment, and McKay pays the $500 to Goodheart, the assignor. In this case, McKay is not liable for any further payment. But if Rogers had immediately notified McKay of the assignment and, after receiving notice, McKay had mistakenly paid the debt to Goodheart, McKay would still have the legal obligation to pay $500 to Rogers. Having been given adequate notice of the assignment, he may remain liable to the assignee even if he later renders performance to the assignor.

An assignor who accepts performance from the obligor after the assignment holds any benefits that he receives as a trustee for the assignee. If the assignor fails to pay those benefits to the assignee, however, an obligor who has been notified of the assignment and renders performance to the wrong person may have to pay the same debt twice.

An obligor who receives notice of an assignment from the assignee will want to assure himself that the assignment has in fact occurred. He may ask for written evidence of the assignment or contact the assignee and ask for verification of the assignment. Under UCC section 9–318(3), a notification of assignment is ineffective unless it reasonably identifies the rights assigned. If requested by the account debtor (an obligor who owes money for goods sold

---

[3]The assignment of leases is discussed further in Chapter 25.

or leased or services rendered), the assignee must furnish reasonable proof that the assignment has been made, and, unless he does so, the account debtor may disregard the notice and pay the assignor.

Defenses against the Assignee   An assignee's rights in an assignment are subject to the defenses that the obligor could have asserted against the assignor. Keep in mind that the assignee's rights are limited by the terms of the underlying contract between the assignor and the obligor. When defenses arise from the terms or performance of that contract, they can be asserted against the assignee even if they arise after the obligor receives notice of the assignment. For example, on June 1, Worldwide Widgets assigns to First Bank its rights under a contract with Widgetech, Inc. This contract obligates Worldwide Widgets to deliver a quantity of widgets to Widgetech by September 1, in return for which Widgetech is obligated to pay a stated purchase price. First Bank gives prompt notice of the assignment to Widgetech. Worldwide Widget fails to deliver the widgets and Widgetech refuses to pay. If First Bank brought an action against Widgetech to recover the purchase price of the widgets, Widgetech could assert Worldwide Widget's breach as a defense, even though the breach occurred after Widgetech received notice of the assignment.[4]

In determining what other defenses can be asserted against the assignee, the time of notification plays an important role. After notification, as we discussed earlier, payment by the obligor to the assignor will not discharge the obligor.

Subsequent Assignments

An assignee may "reassign" a right to a third party, who would be called a **subassignee.** The subassignee then acquires the rights held by the prior assignee. He should give the obligor prompt notice of the subsequent assignment, because he takes his

interest subject to the same principles discussed above regarding the claims and defenses that can be asserted against him.

Successive Assignments

Notice to the obligor may be important in one other situation. If an assignor assigns the same right to two assignees in succession, both of whom pay for the assignment, a question of priority results. An assignor who assigns the same right to different people will be held liable to the assignee who acquires no rights against the obligor, but which assignee is entitled to the obligor's performance? Which assignee will have recourse only against the assignor? There are several views on this point.

In states that follow the "American rule," the first assignee has the better right. This view is based on the rule of property law that a person cannot transfer greater rights in property than he owns. In states that follow the "English rule," however, the assignee who first gives notice of the assignment to the obligor, without knowledge of the other assignee's claim, has the better right. The *Restatement (Second) of Contracts* takes a third position. Section 342 of the *Restatement (Second)* provides that the first assignee has priority unless the subsequent assignee gives value (pays for the assignment) and, without having reason to know of the other assignee's claim, does one of the following: obtains payment of the obligation, gets a judgment against the obligor, obtains a new contract with the obligor by novation, or possesses a writing of a type customarily accepted as a symbol or evidence of the right assigned (such as a passbook for a savings account).

Assignor's Warranty Liability to Assignee

Suppose that Ross, a 16-year-old boy, contracts to buy a used car for $2,000 from Donaldson. Ross pays Donaldson $500 as a down payment and agrees to pay the balance in equal monthly installments. Donaldson assigns his right to receive the balance of the purchase price to Beckman, who pays $1,000 in cash for the assignment. When Beckman later attempts to enforce the contract, however, Ross disaffirms the contract on grounds of lack of capacity. Thus, Beckman has paid $1,000 for a worthless claim. Does Beckman have any recourse against

---

[4]Similarly, if the assignor's rights were subject to discharge because of other factors such as the nonoccurrence of a condition, impossibility, impracticability, or public policy, this can be asserted as a defense against the assignee even if the event occurs after the obligor receives notice of assignment. See *Restatement (Second) of Contracts* § 336(3). The doctrines relating to discharge from performance are explained in Chapter 18.

FIGURE 3	**Delegation: Key Terms**			
Obligor	**Obligee**	**Delegation**	**Delegator**	**Delegatee**
Person who owes the duty to perform	Person who has the right to receive obligor's performance	Appointment of another person to perform the obligor's duty to the obligee	Obligor who appoints another to perform his duty to obligee	Person who is appointed to perform the obligor's duty to the obligee

Donaldson? When an assignor is paid for making an assignment, the assignor is held to have made certain implied warranties about the claim assigned.

The assignor impliedly warrants that the claim assigned is valid. This means that the obligor has capacity to contract, the contract is not illegal, the contract is not voidable for any other reason known to the assignor (such as fraud or duress), and the contract has not been discharged prior to assignment. The assignor also warrants that he has good title to the rights assigned and that any written instrument representing the assigned claim is genuine. In addition, the assignor impliedly agrees that he will not do anything to impair the value of the assignment. These guarantees are imposed by law unless the assignment agreement clearly indicates to the contrary. One important aspect of the assigned right that the assignor does not impliedly warrant, however, is that the obligor is solvent.

DELEGATION OF DUTIES

Nature of Delegation

A **delegation** of duties occurs when an obligor indicates his intent to appoint another person to perform his duties under a contract. For example, White owns a furniture store. He has numerous existing contracts to deliver furniture to customers, including a contract to deliver a sofa to Coombs. White is the *obligor* of the duty to deliver the sofa and Coombs is the *obligee*. White decides to sell his business to Rosen. As a part of the sale of the business, White assigns the rights in the existing contracts to Rosen and delegates to him the performance of those contracts, including the duty to deliver the sofa to Coombs. Here, White is the *delegator* and Rosen is the *delegatee*. White is

appointing Rosen to carry out his duties to the obligee, Coombs. Figure 3 summarizes the key terms regarding delegation.

In contrast to an assignment of a right, which extinguishes the assignor's right and transfers it to the assignee, the delegation of a *duty* does *not* extinguish the duty owed by the delegator. This point is made in *Rosenberg v. Son, Inc.,* which follows this discussion. The delegator remains liable to the obligee unless the obligee agrees to substitute the delegatee's promise for that of the delegator (this is called *a novation,* and will be discussed in greater detail later in this chapter). This makes sense because, if it were possible for a person to escape his duties under a contract by merely delegating them to another, any party to a contract could avoid liability by delegating duties to an insolvent acquaintance. The significance of an effective delegation is that performance by the delegatee will discharge the delegator. In addition, if the duty is a delegable one, the obligee cannot insist on performance by the delegator; he must accept the performance of the delegatee. The relationship between the parties in a delegation is shown in Figure 4.

Delegable Duties

A duty that can be performed fully by a number of different persons is delegable. Not all duties are delegable, however. The grounds for finding a duty to be nondelegable resemble closely the grounds for finding a right to be nonassignable. A duty is nondelegable if delegation would violate public policy or if the original contract between the parties forbids delegation. In addition, both section 2–210(1) of the UCC and section 318(2) of the *Restatement (Second) of Contracts* take the position that a party to a contract may delegate his duty to

FIGURE 4   **Delegation**

Before delegation	Delegation	Result of delegation
Owes duty to perform	Appoints delegatee to perform his duty to obligee	Performs obligor's duty
Obligor → Obligee	Delegator* (Obligor) → Delegatee	Delegatee → Obligee

*Delegator retains duty to obligee until performance is rendered by delegatee.

perform to another person unless the parties have agreed to the contrary or unless the other party has a *substantial interest* in having the original obligor perform the acts required by the contract. The key factor used in determining whether the obligee has such a substantial interest is the degree to which performance is dependent on the individual traits, skill, or judgment of the person who owes the duty to perform. For example, if Jansen hires Skelton, an artist, to paint her portrait, Skelton could not effectively delegate the duty to paint the portrait to another artist. Similarly, an employee could not normally delegate her duties under an employment contract to some third person, because employment contracts are made with the understanding that the person the employer hires will perform the work. The situation in which a person hires a general contractor to perform specific work is distinguishable, however. In that situation, the person hiring the general contractor would normally understand that at least part of the work would be delegated to subcontractors.

Language Creating a Delegation

No special, formal language is necessary to create an effective delegation of duties. In fact, since parties frequently confuse the terms *assignment* and *delegation,* one of the problems frequently presented to courts is determining whether the parties intended an assignment only or both an assignment and a delegation. Unless the agreement indicates a contrary intent, courts tend to interpret assignments as including a delegation of the assignor's duties. Both the UCC 2–210(4) and section 328 of the *Restatement*

(Second) of Contracts provide that, unless the language or the circumstances indicate to the contrary, general language of assignment such as language indicating an assignment of "the contract" or of "all my rights under the contract" is to be interpreted as creating *both* an assignment and a delegation.

Assumption of Duties by Delegatee

A delegation gives the delegatee the right to perform the duties of the delegator. The mere fact that duties have been delegated does not always place legal responsibility on the delegatee to perform. The delegatee who fails to perform will not be liable to either the delegator or the obligee unless the delegatee has assumed the duty by expressly or impliedly undertaking the obligation to perform. However, both section 2–210(4) of the UCC and section 328 of the *Restatement (Second)* provide that an assignee's acceptance of an assignment is to be construed as a promise by him to perform the duties under the contract, unless the language of the assignment or the circumstances indicate to the contrary. Frequently, a term of the contract between the delegator and the delegatee provides that the delegatee assumes responsibility for performance. A common example of this is the assumption of an existing mortgage debt by a purchaser of real estate. Suppose Morgan buys a house from Friedman, agreeing to assume the outstanding mortgage on the property held by First Bank. By this assumption, Morgan undertakes personal liability to both Friedman and First Bank. If Morgan fails to make the mortgage payments, First Bank has a cause of action against Morgan personally. An assumption does *not* release the delegator from liability, however. Rather, it creates a situation in which both the delegator and the assuming delegatee owe duties to the obligee. If the assuming delegatee fails to pay, the delegator can be held liable. Thus, in the example described above, if Morgan fails to make mortgage payments and First Bank is unable to collect the debt from Morgan, Friedman would have secondary liability. Friedman, of course, would have an action against Morgan for breach of their contract.

Discharge of Delegator by Novation

As you have seen, the mere delegation of duties—even when the delegatee assumes those duties—does not release the delegator from his legal obligation to the obligee. A delegator can, however, be discharged from performance by **novation.**

A novation is a particular type of substituted contract in which the obligee agrees to discharge the original obligor and to substitute a new obligor in his place. The effects of a novation are that the original obligor has no further obligation under the contract and the obligee has the right to look to the new obligor for fulfillment of the contract. A novation requires more than the obligee's consent to having the delegatee perform the duties. In the example used above, the mere fact that First Bank accepted mortgage payments from Morgan would not create a novation. Rather, there must be some evidence that the obligee agrees to discharge the old obligor and substitute a new obligor. As you will see in the following *Rosenberg* case, this can be inferred from language of a contract or such other factors as the obligee's conduct or the surrounding circumstances.

Rosenberg v. Son, Inc.
491 N.W.2d 71 (Sup. Ct. N.D. 1992)

In February 1980, Mary Pratt entered into a contract to buy a Dairy Queen restaurant located in Grand Forks's City Center Mall from Harold and Gladys Rosenberg. The terms of the contract for the franchise, inventory, and equipment were a purchase price totaling $62,000, a $10,000 down payment, and $52,000 due in quarterly payments at 10 percent interest over a 15-year period. The sales contract also contained a provision denying the buyer a right of prepayment for the first five years of the contract. In October 1982, Pratt assigned her rights and delegated her duties under this contract to Son, Inc. The assignment between Pratt and Son contained a "Consent to Assignment" clause, which was signed by the Rosenbergs. It also contained a "save harmless" clause, in which Son promised to indemnify Pratt for any claims, demands, or actions that might result from Son's failure to perform the agreement. After this transaction, Pratt moved to Arizona and had no further knowledge of or involvement with the Dairy Queen business. Also following the assignment, the Dairy Queen was moved from the mall to a different location in Grand Forks.

Son assigned the contract to Merit Corporation in June 1984. This assignment did not include a consent clause, but the Rosenbergs knew of the assignment and apparently acquiesced in it. They accepted a large prepayment from Merit, reducing the principal balance to $25,000. After the assignment, Merit pledged the inventory and equipment of the Dairy Queen as collateral for a loan from Valley Bank and Trust. Payments from Merit to the Rosenbergs continued until June 1988, at which time the payments ceased, leaving an unpaid principal balance of $17,326.24 plus interest. The Rosenbergs attempted collection of the balance from Merit, but Merit filed bankruptcy. The business assets pledged as collateral for the loan from Valley Bank and Trust were repossessed. The Rosenbergs brought this action for collection of the outstanding debt against Son and Pratt. The trial court granted summary judgment in favor of Son and Pratt and against the Rosenbergs, and the Rosenbergs appealed.

Erickstad, Chief Justice   It is a well-established principle in the law of contracts that a contracting party cannot escape its liability on the contract by merely assigning its duties and rights under the contract to a third party. This rule of law applies to all categories of contracts, including contracts for the sale of goods, which is present in the facts of this case.

Thus, when Pratt entered into the "assignment agreement" with Son, a simple assignment alone was insufficient to release her from any further liability on the contract. It is not, however, a legal impossibility for a contracting party to rid itself of an obligation under a contract. It may seek the approval of the other original party for release, and substitute a new party in its place. In such an instance, the transaction is no longer called an assignment; instead, it is called a novation. If a novation occurs in this manner, it must be clear from the terms of the agreement that a novation is intended by all parties involved. Both original parties to the contract must intend and mutually assent to the discharge of the obligor from any further liability on the original contract.

It is evident from the express language of the assignment agreement between Pratt and Son that only an assignment was intended, not a novation. The agreement made no mention of discharging Pratt from any further liability on the contract. To the contrary, the latter part of the agreement contained an indemnity clause holding Pratt harmless in the event of a breach by Son. Thus, it is apparent that Pratt contemplated being held ultimately responsible for performance of the obligation. Furthermore, the agreement was between Pratt and Son; they were the parties signing the agreement, not the Rosenbergs. An agreement between Pratt and Son cannot unilaterally affect the Rosenbergs' rights under the contract. The Rosenbergs did sign a consent to the assignment at the bottom of the agreement. However, by merely consenting to the assignment the Rosenbergs did not consent to a discharge of the principal obligor—Pratt. Nothing in the language of the consent clause supports such an allegation. A creditor is free to consent to an assignment without releasing the original obligor. Thus, the express language of the agreement and intent of the parties at the time the assignment was made did not contemplate a novation by releasing Pratt and substituting Son in her stead.

The inquiry as to Pratt's liability does not end at this juncture. The trial court released Pratt from any liability on the contract due to the changes or alterations which took place following her assignment to Son. While it is true that Pratt cannot be forced to answer on the contract irrespective of events occurring subsequent to her assignment, it is also true that she cannot be exonerated for every type of alteration or change that may develop.

The buyer can assign his right to the goods or land and can delegate performance of his duty to pay that price. But observe that he remains bound "as before"; the assignee and the seller cannot, by agreement or by waiver, make it the assignor's duty to pay a different price or on different conditions. If the seller is willing to make such a change, he must trust to the assignee alone.

4 *Corbin on Contracts* section 866 at 458–59.

The trial court decided that any alteration in the underlying obligation resulted in a release of Pratt on the contract. It appears that not every type of alteration is sufficient to warrant discharge of the assignor. As suggested by Professor Corbin in the language highlighted above, the alteration must "prejudice the position of the assignor." 4 *Corbin on Contracts* section 866 at 459.

If the changes in the obligation prejudicially affect the assignor, a new agreement has been formed between the assignee and the other original contracting party. More concisely, a novation has occurred and the assignor's original obligation has been discharged. Although we have previously determined that the terms of the assignment agreement between Pratt and Son did not contemplate a novation, there are additional methods of making a novation besides doing so in the express terms of an agreement. The question of whether or not there has been a novation is a question of fact. The trial court should not have granted summary judgment. There are questions of fact remaining as to the result of the changes in the contract. Thus, we reverse the summary judgment and remand for further proceedings.

Reversed and remanded in favor of the Rosenbergs.

FIGURE 5   Third-Party Beneficiaries

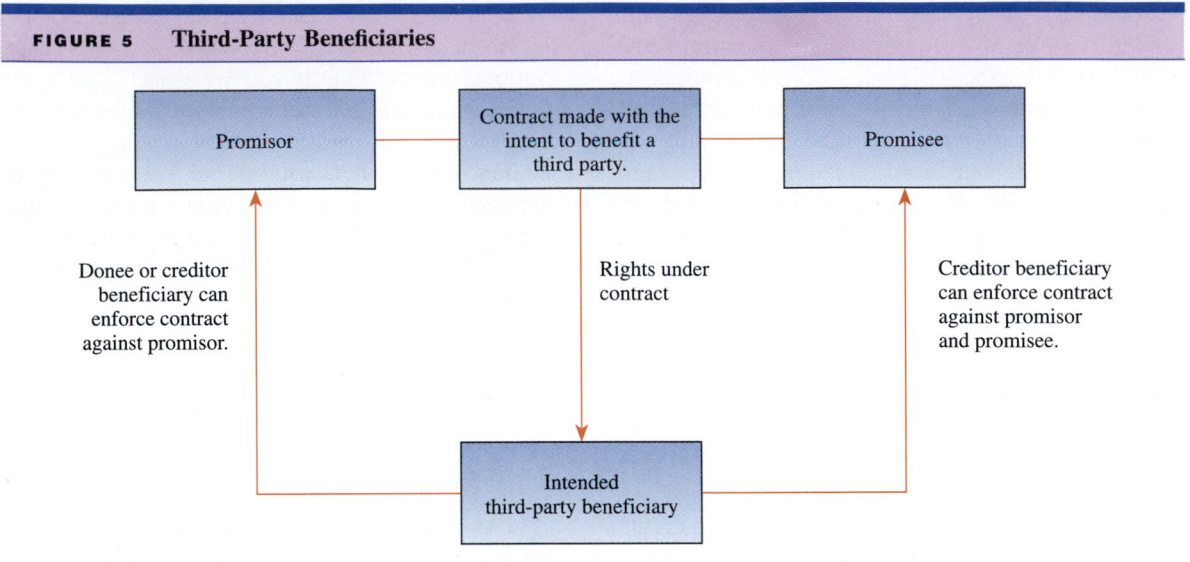

THIRD–PARTY BENEFICIARIES

There are many situations in which the performance of a contract would constitute some benefit to a person who was not a party to the contract. Despite the fact that a nonparty may expect to derive advantage from the performance of a contract, the general rule is that no one but the parties to a contract or their assignees can enforce it. In some situations, however, parties contract for the purpose of benefiting some third person. In such cases, the benefit to the third person is an essential part of the contract, not just an incidental result of a contract that was really designed to benefit the parties. Where the parties to a contract *intended* to benefit a third party, courts will give effect to their intent and permit the third party to enforce the contract. Such third parties are called **third-party beneficiaries.** Figure 5 illustrates the relationship of third-party beneficiaries to the contracting parties.

Intended Beneficiaries versus Incidental Beneficiaries

For a third person (other than an assignee) to have the right to enforce a contract, she must be able to establish that the contract was made with the intent to benefit her. A few courts have required that both parties must have intended to benefit the third party. Most courts, however, have found it to be sufficient

if the person to whom the promise to perform was made (the *promisee*) intended to benefit the third party. In ascertaining intent to benefit the third party, a court will look at the language used by the parties and all the surrounding circumstances. One factor that is frequently important in determining intent to benefit is whether the party making the promise to perform (the *promisor*) was to render performance directly to the third party. For example, if Allison contracts with Jones Florist to deliver flowers to Kirsch, the fact that performance was to be rendered to Kirsch would be good evidence that the parties intended to benefit Kirsch. This factor is not conclusive, however. There are some cases in which intent to benefit a third party has been found even though performance was to be rendered to the promisee rather than to the third party. Intended beneficiaries are often classified as either *creditor* or *donee beneficiaries.* These classifications are discussed in greater detail below.

A third party who is unable to establish that the contract was made with the intent to benefit her is called an *incidental beneficiary.* A third party is classified as an incidental beneficiary when the benefit derived by that third party was merely an unintended by-product of a contract that was created for the benefit of those who were parties to it. Incidental beneficiaries acquire no rights under a contract. For example, Hutton contracts with Long

Construction Company to build a valuable structure on his land. The performance of the contract would constitute a benefit to Keller, Hutton's next-door neighbor, by increasing the value of Keller's land. The contract between Hutton and Long was made for the purpose of benefiting themselves, however. Any advantage derived by Keller is purely incidental to their primary purpose. Thus, Keller could not sue and recover damages if either Hutton or Long breaches the contract.

As a general rule, members of the public are held to be incidental beneficiaries of contracts entered into by their municipalities or other governmental units in the regular course of carrying on governmental functions. A member of the public cannot recover a judgment in a suit against a promisor of such a contract, even though all taxpayers will suffer some injury from nonperformance. A different result may be reached, however, if a party contracting with a governmental unit agrees to reimburse members of the public for damages or if the party undertakes to perform some duty for individual members of the public.

Creditor Beneficiaries If the promisor's performance is intended to satisfy a legal duty that the promisee owes to a third party, the third party is a **creditor beneficiary.** The creditor beneficiary has rights against both the promisee (because of the original obligation) and the promisor. For example, Smith buys a car on credit from Jones Auto Sales. Smith later sells the car to Carmichael, who agrees to pay the balance due on the car to Jones Auto Sales. (Note that Smith is delegating his duty to pay to Carmichael, and Carmichael is assuming the personal obligation to do so.) In this case, Jones Auto Sales is a creditor beneficiary of the contract between Smith and Carmichael. It has rights against both Carmichael and Smith if Carmichael does not perform.

Donee Beneficiaries If the promisee's primary purpose in contracting is to make a gift of the agreed-on performance to a third party, that third party is classified as a *donee beneficiary.* If the contract is breached, the donee beneficiary will have a cause of action against the promisor, but not against the promisee (donor). For example, Miller contracts with Perpetual Life Insurance Company, agreeing to pay premiums in return for which Perpetual agrees to pay $100,000 to Miller's husband when Miller dies. Miller's husband is a donee beneficiary and can bring suit and recover judgment against Perpetual if Miller dies and Perpetual does not pay. The following case, *Warren v. Monahan Beaches Jewelry Center, Inc.,* provides another example of a donee beneficiary. It also demonstrates the implications of a person's status as an intended beneficiary.

Warren v. Monahan Beaches Jewelry Center, Inc.
548 So. 2d 870 (Fla. Ct. App. 1989)

Jay Andreson went to Monahan Beaches Jewelry Center (Monahan) to shop for a diamond engagement ring for his fiancée, Laneya Warren. Andreson told Monahan that the ring was to be given to Warren. Andreson and a salesperson discussed several aspects of the size, type, and style of the ring, and the salesperson made suggestions about what would be likely to be pleasing to Warren. Shortly before Christmas, Monahan sold Andreson a ring, which Monahan represented as being a diamond ring, for $3,974.25. Andreson gave the ring to Warren for Christmas as a symbol of their engagement. Warren soon noticed a small chip in the stone under the setting. She returned the ring to Monahan shortly after the Christmas holidays, and Monahan agreed to replace the stone with one of equal or greater value at no charge to Warren. After making this agreement, Warren took the ring to another jeweler to have it appraised. There she learned for the first time that the alleged diamond that Monahan sold to Andreson was in fact nothing more than cut glass or cubic zirconia.

Warren filed suit against Monahan on several counts, including breach of contract and violation of the Florida Deceptive and Unfair Trade Practices Act. The trial court dismissed her complaint and Warren appealed.

Booth, Judge   The law is that a person not party to a contract may sue for breach of contract where the parties' dealings clearly express the parties' intent to create a right primarily and directly benefiting a third party. In the present case, the precontract dealings between Andreson and Monahan, and the subsequent dealings between Warren and Monahan, clearly establish Warren as an intended third party beneficiary of the contract at issue. The complaint properly alleges that Monahan breached the contract when he failed to deliver a diamond ring to Andreson. The alleged breach of contract deprived Warren of the benefit of owning a diamond ring, which was the purpose of the sale. Warren has a valid cause of action for breach of contract as an intended third party beneficiary.

The trial court also erred in dismissing Warren's claim brought pursuant to [the Florida Deceptive and Unfair Trade Practices Act]. One of the purposes of Florida's Deceptive and Unfair Trade Practices Act is to protect consumers from suppliers who commit deceptive and unfair trade practices. Nothing in the statute or case law limits causes of action to the immediate purchaser. The issue of whether the intended beneficiary of a gift may be classified as a "consumer" appears to be an issue of first impression in this state. We hold that [the Act] applies and that Warren, as the beneficiary of the consumer transaction is a "consumer" in her own right and entitled to the remedies afforded.

Judgment reversed in favor of Warren and case remanded for further proceedings.

Vesting of Beneficiary's Rights

Another possible threat to the interests of the third-party beneficiary is that the promisor and the promisee might modify or discharge their contract so as to extinguish or alter the beneficiary's rights. For example, Gates, who owes $500 to Sorenson, enters into a contract with Connor whereby Connor agrees to pay the $500 to Sorenson. What happens if, before Sorenson is paid, Connor pays the money to Gates and Gates accepts it or Connor and Gates otherwise modify the contract? Courts have held that there is a point at which the rights of the beneficiary vest—that is, the beneficiary's rights cannot be lost by modification or discharge. A modification or discharge that occurs after the beneficiary's rights have vested cannot be asserted as a defense to a suit brought by the beneficiary. The exact time at which the beneficiary's rights vest differs from jurisdiction to jurisdiction. Some courts have held that vesting occurs when the contract is formed, while others hold that vesting does not occur until the beneficiary learns of the contract and consents to it or does some act in reliance on the promise.

The contracting parties' ability to vary the rights of the third-party beneficiary can also be affected by the terms of their agreement. A provision of the contract between the promisor and the promisee stating that the duty to the beneficiary cannot be modified would be effective to prevent modification. Likewise, a contract provision in which the parties specifically reserved the right to change beneficiaries or modify the duty to the beneficiary would be enforced. For example, provisions reserving the right to change beneficiaries are very common in insurance contracts.

ETHICAL AND PUBLIC POLICY CONCERNS

1. You learned that an assignor's rights are extinguished as soon as he assigns them. Should a delegator's duties be extinguished by his delegation of them?

2. Why does public policy favor allowing third parties to enforce contracts made for their benefit? Should incidental beneficiaries have a right to enforce contracts? Why or why not?

PROBLEMS AND PROBLEM CASES

1. In 1974, Spiklevitz loaned money to Vincent and Geraldine Heron. The Herons signed a promissory note agreeing to repay the debt by January 15, 1975. In April 1980, the Herons sold their business to Markmil Corp. At that time, $3,510 of their debt to Spiklevitz remained unpaid. Markmil executed an "Assumption of Obligation," which stated that as part of the purchase price of the Herons' business, Markmil agreed to pay the list of debts written on an attached sheet of paper labeled "Exhibit A." Spiklevitz was listed as a creditor in Exhibit A for the balance owed to him. In June 1981, Spiklevitz sued Markmil to recover the amount remaining due on the note. Is Markmil obligated to pay?

2. Peterson was employed by Post–Newsweek as a newscaster-anchorman on station WTOP–TV (Channel 9) under a three-year employment contract that was to end June 30, 1980, and could be extended for two additional one-year terms at the option of Post–Newsweek. In June 1978, Post–Newsweek sold its operating license to the Evening News Association (Evening News), and Channel 9 was then designated as WDVM–TV. The contract of sale between Post–Newsweek and Evening News provided for the assignment of all contracts, including Peterson's employment contract. Peterson continued working for the station for more than a year after the change of ownership and received all of the compensation and benefits provided by his contract with Post–Newsweek. In early August 1979, he negotiated a new contract with a competing television station and tendered his resignation to Evening News. Evening News sued Peterson. Peterson defended on the ground that his employment contract was not assignable. Is he correct?

3. In May 1978, John and Judith Brooks contracted with Hayes to construct a Windsor Home (a packaged, predesigned, and precut home) on a lot that they owned. Hayes was primarily a real estate broker but also sold Windsor Homes. The construction contract required Hayes to "provide all necessary labor and materials and perform all work of every nature whatsoever to be done in the erection of a residence for" the Brookses. The Brookses and Hayes contemplated that Hayes would hire subcontractors to perform much of the home construction work and Hayes, who had no personal experience in construction, would not control the method of construction. During the construction, the Brookses requested that a "heatilator" be installed as an extra to increase the efficiency of the fireplace. Marr, the mason hired by Hayes to do the fireplace and other masonry work, installed the heatilator. The Brookses moved into the house in the winter of 1978.

When they used the fireplace, they smelled smoke in areas of the house remote from the fireplace. Both the Brookses and Hayes hired several masons to inspect the fireplace system, but none of the masons was able to discover the cause of the problem. The Brookses used the fireplace with some frequency until November 1980, when a fire in the home caused structural damage around the fireplace and smoke damage to the house and the couple's personal property. It was discovered that Marr's negligence in installing the heatilator had caused the fire. The Brookses sued both Marr and Hayes. The case against Marr was dismissed because Marr went bankrupt. Is Hayes liable to the Brookses?

4. On April 20, Chapman-Harkey Company ordered a quantity of toys known as hang-ups from A. G. Bond Company, at a total cost of $13,378.56. Under the agreement between Chapman-Harkey and A. G. Bond, the hang-ups were sold on a "guaranteed-sale" basis—that is, Chapman-Harkey could return to A. G. Bond any hang-ups that it could not sell and receive a credit. On May 17, Chapman-Harkey received notice that A. G. Bond had assigned the account for this sale to Equitable Factors. In a letter dated May 19, Chapman-Harkey received written confirmation from A. G. Bond's agent that the goods were being sold on a guaranteed-sale basis. Chapman-Harkey failed to pay for the hang-ups, and Equitable Factors brought suit against it to recover the purchase price of the goods sold. At this point, Chapman-Harkey still had in its possession $5,753.78 worth of hang-ups, which it had been unable to sell. Can the guaranteed-sale term be raised as a defense against Equitable Factors, even though the defense did not become available until after notification of the assignment?

5. Jones paid Sullivan, the chief of the Addison Police Department, $6,400 in exchange for Sullivan's cooperation in allowing Jones and others to bring marijuana by airplane into the Addison airport without police intervention. Instead of performing the requested service, Sullivan arrested Jones. The $6,400 was turned over to the district attorney's office and was introduced into evidence in the subsequent trial in which Jones was tried for and convicted of bribery. After his conviction, Jones assigned his alleged claim to the $6,400 to Melvyn Bruder. Based on the assignment, Bruder brought suit against the state of Texas to obtain possession of the money. Will he be successful?

6. Post, Lumber, and Samson were construction-related businesses owned and operated by DiPietro. In May 1984, Boynton contracted with DiPietro personally and with Post for the lease of Boynton's property, which contained a sawmill. Lumber and Samson used the millsite along with Post in related businesses. At the same time, Boynton entered into a separate contract with Post, giving it a one-year option to purchase the millsite for $60,000. This option provided that on payment of $6,000 at the time of exercising the option, Boynton would transfer title to the property, and the balance would be financed in a specified way. In October 1984, Post assigned its rights in the option agreement to Lumber. In January 1985, Lumber attempted to exercise the option by sending a $6,000 check to Boynton with a letter expressing its readiness to execute the agreement and advising Boynton that the payment of rent would stop. Boynton cashed Lumber's check but did not respond to the letter. Lumber sent Boynton two more letters seeking to exercise the option before it lapsed, but Boynton did not respond. In later litigation, Boynton contended that the assignment of the option agreement was invalid because he was not notified of it. Is this a good argument?

7. Jay Beard Trucks entered into a franchise Dealer Sales and Service Agreement with General Motors (GMC). The agreement contained a provision limiting the possible future transfer of ownership of the dealership. These provisions required Beard to give notice to GMC of any proposed sale of the dealership and gave GMC the right to select each successor and replacement dealer. The contract also provided that GMC "shall not arbitrarily refuse to agree to such proposed change or sale" and that, in determining whether the proposal is acceptable to it, "GMC will take into account the qualifications, personal and business reputation, and financial standing of the proposed dealer operator and owners." Noller, the owner-operator of a Ford dealership and a Toyota dealership and one of the top 100 Ford dealers in the country, entered into negotiations to purchase Beard's dealership. The parties worked out a proposed buy-sell agreement and submitted it to GMC. GMC never contacted Noller, sent dealership transfer applications to him, obtained any documentation or additional information from him, or made inquiries to Beard about Noller's qualifications. Without doing an investiga-

tion about these matters, GMC refused to grant the franchise to Noller, apparently because he was also a Ford dealer. As a result, the contract between Noller and Beard fell through and Beard sold the dealership to a third party. Noller brought suit against GMC, asserting that he was an intended beneficiary of the Dealer Sales and Service Agreement between GMC and Beard, wherein GMC had agreed to specifically consider the proposed dealer's qualifications, personal and business reputation, and financial standing. Was he an intended beneficiary?

8. Yellow Cab contracted with the Birmingham Board of Education to transport physically handicapped students in the Birmingham school system. The contract provided that Yellow Cab would furnish all necessary vehicles and personnel as well as perform maintenance and make all repairs so as to keep the equipment in a safe and efficient operating condition at all times. Yellow Cab subcontracted with Metro Limousine and Leasing to provide the transportation called for by its contract with the Board. Thereafter, Metro purchased two buses from Yellow Cab to use in transporting the students. DuPont, an employee of Metro, was injured when the brakes on the bus that he was driving failed, causing the bus to collide with a tree. DuPont sued Yellow Cab for breach of contract, alleging that Yellow Cab breached a nondelegable duty to properly maintain the bus and that that duty flowed to DuPont as a third-party beneficiary of the contract between Yellow Cab and the Board. Should DuPont win?

9. Mercantile-Safe Deposit & Trust Company frequently advised its long-time customer, Chaplin, about the planning of her estate. Merrick, Chaplin's former son-in-law, maintained a close relationship with Chaplin, and this relationship was reflected in the wills that Chaplin executed. At Chaplin's request, one of Mercantile's trust officers visited her at her home to discuss making certain changes in her will. Without first consulting with Mercantile's attorneys or other estate planning personnel about the appropriateness of these changes, the trust officer instructed Chaplin's attorney to draft a new will reflecting the changes that Chaplin requested. Merrick would have benefited under this will. The will was executed and Chaplin died in 1981. Because of a technical problem overlooked by Mercantile's trust officer, the will provision benefiting

Merrick and his children was held to be ineffective and Merrick lost the bequest that he would have had otherwise. Merrick brought suit against Mercantile because of its failure to advise Chaplin properly. Does Merrick have any rights under the contract between Chaplin and Mercantile?

10. [cassette icon] *Video Case.* See "Roof Repairs." Roofer contracted with Driscoll Industries to do a roofing job. The job was too big for Roofer to handle, so he delegated his duties under the contract to another company that claimed to do that kind of roofing work all the time. However, the other company did such a poor job that it damaged the heating and cooling systems of the building. Is Roofer liable to Driscoll for the damage done by its delegatee?

See also "TV Repair" and "The Student Loan."

CHAPTER

18

PERFORMANCE AND REMEDIES

INTRODUCTION

Contracts are generally formed before either of the parties renders any actual performance to the other. A person may be content to bargain for and receive the other person's promise at the formation stage of a contract because this permits him to plan for the future. Ultimately, however, all parties bargain for the performance *of the promises that have been made to them.*

In most contracts, each party carries out his promise and is discharged *(released from all of his obligations under the contract) when his performance is complete. Sometimes, however, a party fails to perform or performs in an unsatisfactory manner. In such cases, courts are often called on to determine the respective rights and duties of the parties. This frequently involves deciding such questions as whether performance was due, whether the contract was breached, to what extent it was breached, and whether performance was excused. This task is made more difficult by the fact that contracts often fail to specify the consequences of nonperformance or defective performance. In deciding questions involving the performance of contracts and remedies for breach of contract, courts draw on a variety of legal principles that attempt to do justice, prevent forfeiture and unjust enrichment, and effectuate the parties' presumed intent.*

This chapter presents an overview of the legal concepts that are used to resolve disputes arising in the performance stage of contracting. It describes how courts determine whether performance is due and what kind of performance is due, the consequences of contract breach, and the excuses for a party's failure to perform. It also includes a discussion of the remedies that are used when a court determines that a contract has been breached.

CONDITIONS

Nature of Conditions

One issue that frequently arises in the performance stage of a contract is whether a party has the duty to perform. Some duties are *unconditional* or *absolute*—that is, the duty to perform does not depend on the occurrence of any further event other than the passage of time. For example, if Root promises to pay Downing $100, Root's duty is unconditional. When a party's duty is unconditional, he has the duty to perform unless his performance is excused. (The various excuses for nonperformance will be discussed later in this chapter.) When a duty is unconditional, the promisor's failure to perform constitutes a *breach of contract.*

In many situations, however, a promisor's duty to perform depends on the occurrence of some event that is called a **condition.** A condition is an uncertain, future event that affects a party's duty to perform. For example, if Melman contracts to buy Lance's house on condition that First Bank approve Melman's application for a mortgage loan by January 10, Melman's duty to buy Lance's house is *conditioned* on the bank's approving his loan application by January 10. When a promisor's duty is conditional, his duty to perform is affected by the occurrence of the condition. In this case, if the condition does not occur, Melman has no duty to buy the house. His failure to buy it because of the nonoccurrence of the condition will *not* constitute a breach of contract. Rather, he is discharged from further obligation under the contract.

Almost any event can be a condition. Some conditions are beyond the control of either party, such as when Morehead promises to buy Pratt's business if the prime rate drops by a specified amount. Others are within the control of a party, such as when one party's performance of a duty under the contract is a condition of the other party's duty to perform.

Types of Conditions

There are two ways of classifying conditions. One way of classifying conditions focuses on the effect of the condition on the duty to perform. The other way focuses on the way in which the condition is created.

Classifications of Conditions Based on Their Effect on the Duty to Perform   As Figure 1 illustrates, conditions vary in their effects on the duty to perform.

1. *Condition precedent.* A condition precedent is a future, uncertain event that creates the duty to perform. If the condition does not occur, performance does not become due. If the condition does

occur, the duty to perform arises. The condition at issue in *Beverly Way Associates v. Barham,* which follows this discussion, is an example of a condition precedent.

2. *Concurrent condition.* When the contract calls for the parties to perform at the same time, each person's performance is conditioned on the performance or tender of performance (offer of performance) by the other. Such conditions are called **concurrent conditions.** For example, if Martin promises to buy Johnson's car for $5,000, the parties' respective duties to perform are subject to a concurrent condition. Martin does not have the duty to perform unless Johnson tenders his performance, and vice versa.

3. *Condition subsequent.* A **condition subsequent** is a future, uncertain event that **discharges** the duty to perform. When a duty is subject to a condition subsequent, the duty to perform arises but is discharged if the future, uncertain event occurs. For example, Wilkinson and Jones agree that Wilkinson will begin paying Jones $2,000 per month, but that if XYZ Corporation dissolves, Wilkinson's obligation to pay will cease. In this case, Wilkinson's duty to pay is subject to being discharged by a condition subsequent. The major significance of the distinction between conditions precedent and conditions subsequent is that the plaintiff bears the burden of proving the occurrence of a condition precedent, while the defendant bears the burden of proving the occurrence of a condition subsequent.

Classifications of Conditions Based on the Way in which They Were Created   Another way of classifying conditions is to focus on the means by which the condition was created.

1. *Express condition.* An **express condition** is a condition that is specified in the language of the parties' contract. For example, if Grant promises to sell his regular season football tickets to Carson on condition that Indiana University wins the Rose Bowl, Indiana's winning the Rose Bowl is an express condition of Grant's duty to sell the tickets.

When the contract expressly provides that a party's duty is subject to a condition, courts take it very seriously. When a duty is subject to an express condition, that condition must be strictly complied with in order to give rise to the duty to perform.

FIGURE 1   Effect of Conditions

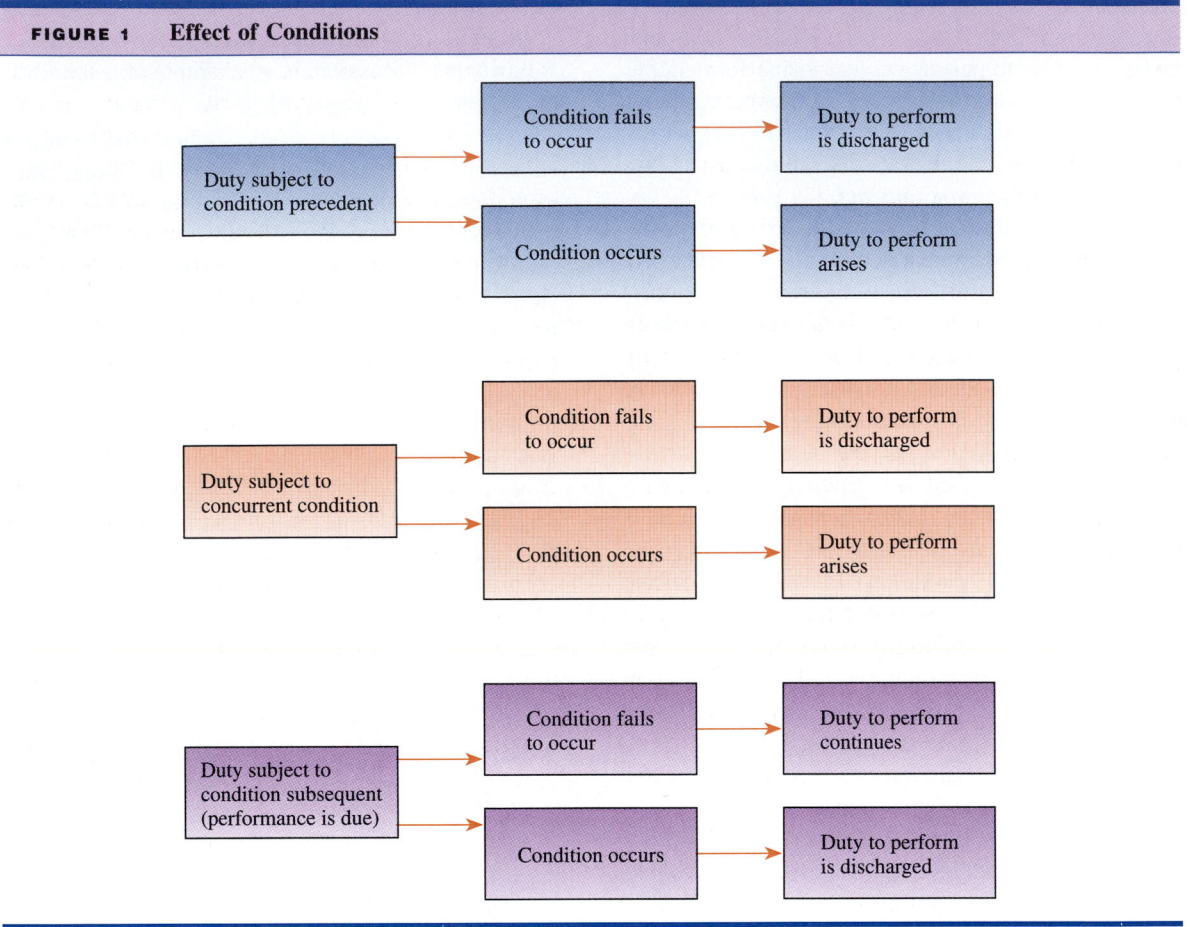

2. *Implied-in-fact condition.* An **implied-in-fact condition** is one that is not specifically stated by the parties but is *implied* by the nature of the parties' promises. For example, if Summers promises to unload cargo from Knight's ship, the ship's arrival in port would be an implied-in-fact condition of Summer's duty to unload the cargo.

3. *Constructive condition.* **Constructive conditions** (also known as *implied-in-law conditions*) are conditions that are imposed by law rather than by the agreement of the parties. The law imposes constructive conditions to do justice between the parties. In contracts in which one of the parties is expected to perform before the other, the law normally infers that that performance is a constructive condition of the other party's duty to perform. For example, if Thomas promises to build a house for King, and the parties' understanding is that King will pay Thomas an agreed-on price when the house is built, King's duty to pay is subject to the constructive condition that Thomas complete the house. Without such a constructive condition, a person who did not receive the performance promised him would still have to render his own performance.

Creation of Express Conditions

Although no particular language is required to create an express condition, the conditional nature of promises is usually indicated by such words as *provided that, subject to, on condition that, if, when, while, after,* and *as soon as.* The process of determining the meaning of conditions is not a mechanical one. Courts look at the parties' overall intent as indicated in language of the entire contract.

The following discussion explores two common types of express conditions.

Example of Express Condition: Satisfaction of Third Parties

It is common for building and construction contracts to provide that the property owner's duty to pay is conditioned on the builder's production of certificates to be issued by a specific architect or engineer. These certificates indicate the satisfaction of the architect or engineer with the builder's work. They are often issued at each stage of completion, after the architect or engineer has inspected the work done.

The standard usually used to determine whether the condition has occurred is a *good faith* standard. As a general rule, if the architect or engineer is acting honestly and has some good faith reason for withholding a certificate, the builder cannot recover payments due. In legal terms, the condition that will create the owner's duty to pay has not occurred.

If the builder can prove that the withholding of the certificate was fraudulent or done in bad faith (as a result of collusion with the owner, for example), the court may order that payment be made despite the absence of the certificate. In addition, production of the certificate may be excused by the death, insanity, or incapacitating illness of the named architect or engineer.

Example of Express Condition: Personal Satisfaction

Contracts sometimes provide that a promisee's duty to perform is conditioned on his personal satisfaction with the promisee's performance. For example, Moore commissions Allen to paint a portrait of Moore's wife, but the contract provides that Moore's duty to pay is conditioned on his personal satisfaction with the portrait.

How does a court determine whether the condition of personal satisfaction has occurred? If the court applies a standard of actual, subjective satisfaction and Moore asserts that he is not satisfied, it would be very difficult for Allen to prove that the condition has occurred. If, on the other hand, the court applies an objective, "reasonable person" standard of satisfaction, Allen stands a better chance of proving that the condition has occurred.

In determining which standard of satisfaction to apply, courts distinguish between cases in which the performance bargained for involves personal taste and comfort and cases that involve mechanical fitness or suitability for a particular purpose. If personal taste and comfort are involved, as they would be in the hypothetical case described above, a promisor who is honestly dissatisfied with the promisee's performance has the right to reject the performance without being liable to the promisee. If, however, the performance involves mechanical fitness or suitability, the court will apply a reasonable person test. If the court finds that a reasonable person would be satisfied with the performance, the condition of personal satisfaction has been met and the promisor must accept the performance and pay the contract price. For example, Kitt Manufacturing Company hires Pace to design a conveyor belt system for use in its factory, conditioning its duty to pay on its personal satisfaction with the system. A court would be likely to find that this is a contract involving mechanical fitness and suitability for which an objective test of satisfaction could be used. These standards are illustrated in Figure 2 (see page 339). Because the "honest satisfaction" standard involves a danger of forfeiture by the performing party, courts prefer the objective test of satisfaction when objective evaluation is feasible. The following *Beverly Way Associates v. Barham* case discusses a further implication of personal satisfaction conditions.

BEVERLY WAY ASSOCIATES V. BARHAM
276 Cal. Rptr. 240 (Ct. App. Cal. 1990)

On July 7, 1988, Phyllis Barham entered into a contract to sell her residential building in Long Beach, California, to Beverly Way Associates (Beverly Way) for $3.9 million. The contract provided for the opening of escrow (the procedure by which the sale would be consummated) and a closing within 60 days of that time. It also provided that Beverly Way's obligation to purchase the property "shall be conditioned upon" its approval of a number of specified inspections and documents and delivery of clear title. One of these items was a certified survey of the property that would show all improvements to the property and the location of all exceptions to the title. The contract gave Beverly Way 28 business days in which to inspect and approve documents after having been furnished them by Barham. On November 15, 1988, Barham furnished the material that Beverly Way required, and on December 2, Beverly Way wrote to Barham stating, "We reluctantly disapprove of the matters disclosed on the Survey and relating to the Property." This letter described in detail the reasons for its rejection. The letter expressed the hope that the parties could "keep the deal alive" and proposed two alternatives that would have changed the parties' arrangement substantially. There was no further communication between the parties until February 1989, when Beverly Way sent a second letter stating that it was prepared to waive its objections to the survey and to proceed to close the deal. Barham refused to sell the property and Beverly Way sued for specific performance. The trial court sustained a demurrer in favor of Barham, and Beverly Way appealed.

Epstein, Judge   Both sides to this appeal treat the buyer's right of approval under the contract as a condition precedent in favor of the buyer. They are quite correct in that characterization. "A condition is an event, not certain to occur, which must occur, unless its non-occurrence is excused, before performance under a contract becomes due." (*Rest. 2d, Contracts,* section 224).

We turn to an examination of the nature of the buyer's power to approve the condition precedent and to the effect of its disapproval. Most of the textual and case material on "satisfaction" conditions precedent turns on whether an objective or subjective standard is to be used in reviewing the reasonableness of its exercise. Neither party questions the reasonableness of the buyer's exercise of its approval authority in the December 2, 1988, letter.

The effect of a buyer's power to approve documentation required in a contract for the purchase of real estate "is to give the buyer an option not to consummate the purchase if it fails to meet the condition," at least so long as the buyer acts reasonably and in the exercise of good faith. Stated another way, the contract gives the buyer the power and privilege of termination in the event that it reasonably concludes that the condition has not been fulfilled. Except for the judicial gloss that the power of rejection must be exercised reasonably, the party having the power to approve or reject is in the same position as a contract offeree. It is hornbook law that an unequivocal rejection by an offeree, communicated to the offeror, terminates the offer; even if the offeror does no further act, the offeree cannot later purport to accept the offer and thereby create enforceable contractual rights against the offeror. There can be no question but that Beverly Way exercised its power of disapproval in this case. The December 2, 1988, letter said so expressly. This rejection, communicated to Barham, terminated the contract. It left Beverly Way with no power to create obligations against Barham by a late "waiver" of its objections and acceptance of the proffered documentation.

The fact that Beverly Way considered the existing contract to be at an end is reflected also by its effort to keep the "deal alive" by proposing two entirely new formulations that were novel to the agreement of the parties. It may be inferred that Beverly Way was hoping to find a way to acquire the property, but it cannot be doubted that it was unwilling to do so on the basis of what had been presented by Barham.

Affirmed in favor of Barham.

Excuse of Conditions

In most situations involving conditional duties, the promisor does not have the duty to perform unless and until the condition occurs. There are, however, a variety of situations in which the occurrence of a condition will be excused. In such a case, the person whose duty is conditional will have to perform even though the condition has not occurred.

One ground for excusing a condition is that the occurrence of the condition has been *prevented* or *hindered* by the party who is benefited by the condition. For example, Connor hires Ingle to construct a garage on Connor's land, but when Ingle

FIGURE 2   **Duty to Perform Conditioned on "Personal Satisfaction" (a form of express condition precedent)**

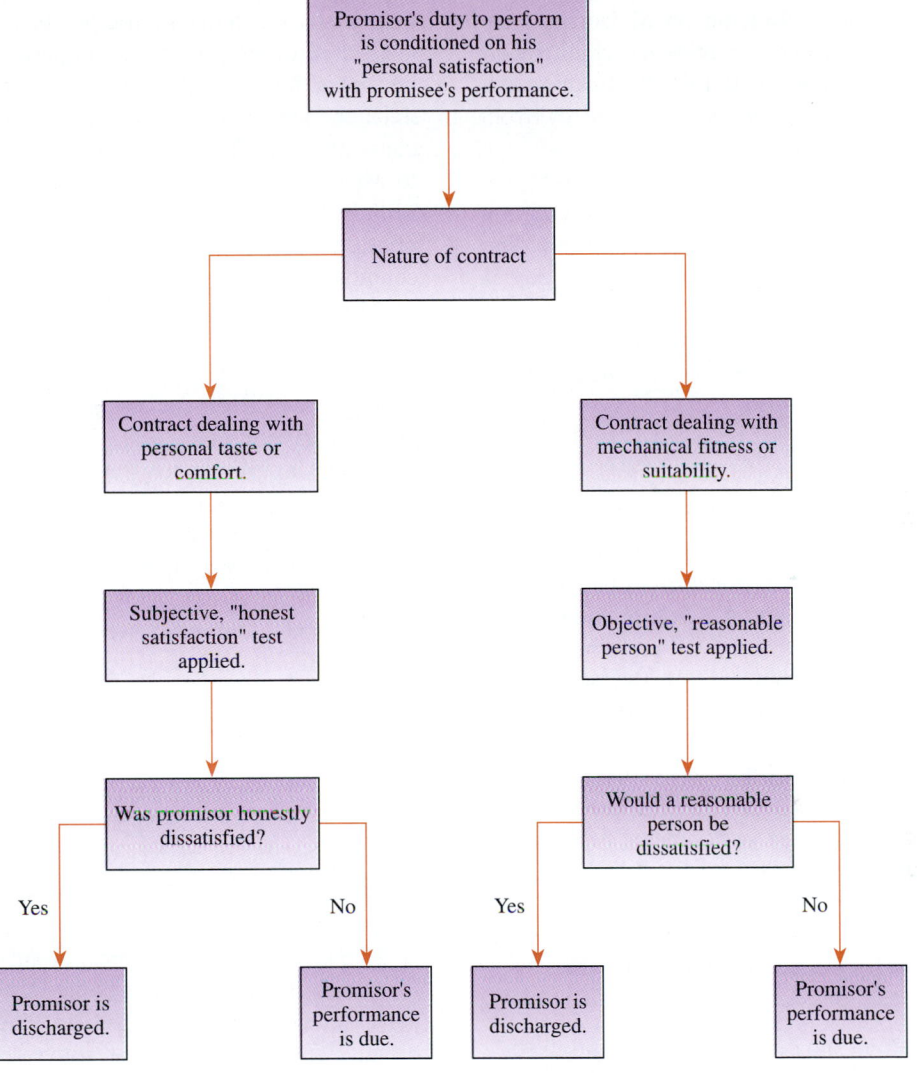

attempts to begin construction, Connor refuses to allow Ingle access to the land. In this case, Connor's duty to pay would normally be subject to a constructive condition that Ingle build the garage. However, since Connor prevented the occurrence of the condition, the condition will be excused, and Ingle can sue Connor for damages for breach of contract even though the condition has not occurred.

Other grounds for excuse of a condition include **waiver** and **estoppel.** When a person whose duty is conditional voluntarily gives up his right to the oc-

currence of the condition (waiver), the condition will be excused. Suppose that Buchman contracts to sell his car to Fox on condition that Fox pay him $2,000 by June 14. Fox fails to pay on June 14, but, when he tenders payment on June 20, Buchman accepts and cashes the check without reservation. Buchman has thereby *waived* the condition of payment by June 14.

When a person whose duty is conditional leads the other party to rely on his noninsistence on the condition, the condition will be excused because of estoppel. For example, McDonald agrees to sell his business to Brown on condition that Brown provide a credit report and personal financial statement by July 17. On July 5, McDonald tells Brown that he can have until the end of the month to provide the necessary documents. Relying on McDonald's assurances, Brown does not provide the credit report and financial statement until July 29. In this case, McDonald would be *estopped* (precluded) from claiming that the condition did not occur.

A condition may also be excused when performance of the act that constitutes the condition becomes *impossible*. For example, if a building contract provides that the owner's duty to pay is conditioned on the production of a certificate from a named architect, the condition would be excused if the named architect died or became incapacitated before issuing the certificate.

PERFORMANCE OF CONTRACTS

When a promisor has performed his duties under a contract, he is discharged. Because his performance constitutes the occurrence of a constructive condition, the other party's duty to perform is also triggered, and the person who has performed has the right to receive the other party's performance. In determining whether a promisor is discharged by performance and whether the constructive condition of his performance has been fulfilled, courts must consider the standard of performance expected of him.

Level of Performance Expected of the Promisor

In some situations, no deviation from the promisor's promised performance is tolerated; in others, less-than-perfect performance will be sufficient to discharge the promisor and give him the right to recover under the contract.

1. *Strict performance standard.* A **strict performance** standard is a standard of performance that requires virtually perfect compliance with the contract terms. Remember that, when a party's duty is subject to an express condition, that condition must be strictly and completely complied with in order to give rise to a duty of performance. Thus, when a promisor's performance is an express condition of the promisee's duty to perform, that performance

must strictly and completely comply with the contract in order to give rise to the other promisee's duty to perform. For example, if McMillan agrees to pay Jester $500 for painting his house "on condition that" Jester finish the job no later than June 1, 1994, a standard of strict or complete performance would be applied to Jester's performance. If Jester does not finish the job by June 1, his breach will have several consequences. First, since the condition precedent to McMillan's duty to pay has not occurred, Mc-Millan does not have a duty to pay the contract price. Second, since it is now too late for the condition to occur, McMillan is discharged. Third, McMillan can sue Jester for breach of contract. The law's commitment to freedom of contract justifies such results in cases in which the parties have expressly bargained for strict compliance with the terms of the contract.

The strict performance standard is also applied to contractual obligations that can be performed either exactly or to a high degree of perfection. Examples of this type of obligation include promises to pay money, deliver deeds, and, generally, promises to deliver goods. A promisor who performs such promises completely and in strict compliance with the contract is entitled to receive the entire contract price. The promisor whose performance deviates from perfection is not entitled to receive the other party's performance if he does not render perfect performance within an appropriate time. He may, however, be able to recover the value of any benefits that he has conferred on the other party under a theory of quasi-contract.

2. *Substantial performance.* A **substantial performance** standard is a somewhat lower standard of performance that is applied to duties that are difficult to perform without some deviation from perfection *if* performance of those duties is *not* an express condition. A common example of this type of obligation is a promise to erect a building. Other examples include promises to construct roads, to cultivate crops, and to render some types of personal or professional services. Substantial performance is performance that falls short of complete performance in minor respects. As you will see in *Reale v. Linder,* it does not apply when a contracting party has been deprived of a material part of the consideration he bargained for. When a substantial performance standard is applied, the promisor who has substantially performed is discharged. His substantial performance triggers the other party's duty to pay the contract price less any damages resulting from the defects in his performance. The obvious purpose behind the doctrine of substantial performance is to prevent

forfeiture by a promisor who has given the injured party most of what he bargained for. Substantial performance is generally held to be inapplicable to a situation in which the breach of contract has been *willful,* however.

REALE V. LINDER

514 N.Y.S.2d 1004 (N.Y. Dist. Ct. 1987)

Thomas Linder hired Orlando Reale to build a 12 foot by 12 foot extension on his house with a raised wooden deck, sliding glass doors, and a gas-fired barbeque. Their written contract made no provision regarding obtaining a building permit or compliance with building codes, although it did contain a notation stating "plairs (sic) and permit $500 Dep." The agreed price for these improvements was $22,560.

It became evident that several features of the finished addition deviated from the state building code and the building plans that had been approved by the town. Reale had built the crawl space beneath the addition some 4 to 7 inches less than the 18 inches mandated by the state building code, which prevented inspection underneath the addition for structural defects. In addition, Reale sealed the framing of the addition, where substantial problems existed, without a prior inspection by the city building department or his own architect. Serious defects existed in the roof, and the plumbing work was not done by a licensed plumber, although it was later corrected. Improper or incomplete materials were used for the gas line for the barbeque, which caused a gas leak that had to be corrected. The steps leading down from the main dwelling to the addition are each 4 inches high rather than the 6 and 8 inches each that appear in the plan. In addition, Reale did no grade survey of the property before building, although expert witnesses testified that a grade survey was necessary to build the addition properly. The city building department initially denied a certificate of occupancy because the construction had been "closed up" and could not be inspected. It was issued only after Reale procured an architect's affidavit stating that he had inspected the location and that the work had been done in conformity with the approved plans and the state fire and building code, but this was apparently based on false information that Reale gave to the architect.

Linder made partial payment under the contract but withheld $5,855. Reale sued Linder to collect the unpaid balance. A trial was held and this is the trial court's opinion.

Mogil, Judge   The crux of Reale's argument in support of his complaint is that he substantially performed the contract. In order for a building contractor to be able to take advantage of the doctrine of substantial performance, he must not be guilty of a willful or intentional departure from the terms of his contract. This doctrine, however, permits compensation for all defects caused by the contractor's performance. Under this rule the party sued is protected as to any damages he may suffer due to the contractor's failure to strictly perform. The contractor must prove that the defects or omissions were insubstantial. This he has not done. Although the written agreement does

not expressly provide that the contract be performed in conformance with state and local fire prevention and building code regulations, it must be presumed that the parties intended that the contract be performed in accordance with state and local laws. In every home improvement contract, the contractor has an implied duty to perform the contract in accordance with fire prevention and building code requirements. The consumer homeowner relies upon the contractor's skill and expertise to perform the improvements. Reale's failure to construct the extension to code requirements renders the alterations illegal and frustrates the purpose of the contract.

The doctrine of substantial performance is an equitable one intended to prevent injustice where a contractor inadvertently caused trivial, minor, non-essential deficiencies which may be easily and inexpensively remedied. Where the defect cannot be corrected without partially reconstructing the building, the doctrine of substantial performance does not apply. It has been shown that any request for a new or currently revised certificate of occupancy will be denied unless the defect of an improper crawl space is corrected. To correct the defect, the floor of the extension must be removed, the walls braced, excavations undertaken to remove additional earth, and the concrete and floor rebuilt. These corrections are tantamount to reconstructing the addition. Reale has not therefore shown either complete or substantial performance.

Judgment entered in favor of Linder.

CONCEPT REVIEW

SUBSTANTIAL PERFORMANCE

Definition	Application	Effects	Limitation
Performance that falls short of complete performance in some minor respect but that does not deprive the other party of a material part of the consideration for which he bargained	Applies to performance that (1) is *not* an express condition of the other party's duty to perform and (2) is difficult to do perfectly	Triggers other party's duty to perform; requires other party to pay the contract price minus any damages caused by defects in performance	Breach cannot have been willful

Good Faith Performance

One of the most significant trends in modern contract law is that courts and legislatures have created a duty to perform in good faith in an expanding range of contracts.[1] The Uniform Commercial Code specifically imposes a duty of good faith in every contract within the scope of any of the articles of the Code [1–203]. A growing number of courts have applied the duty to use good faith in transactions between lenders and their customers as well as insurance contracts, employment contracts, and contracts for the sale of real property.

This obligation to carry out a contract in good faith is usually called the **implied covenant of good faith and fair dealing.** It is a broad and flexible duty that is imposed by law rather than by the agreement of the parties. It is generally taken to mean that neither party to a contract will do any-thing to prevent the other from obtaining the benefits that he has the right to expect from the parties' agreement or their contractual relationship. The law's purpose in imposing such a term in contracts is to prevent abuses of power and encourage ethical behavior.

Breach of the implied covenant of good faith gives rise to a contract remedy. In some states, it can also constitute a tort, depending on the severity of the breach. A tort action for breach of the implied covenant of good faith is more likely to be recognized in situations in which a contract involves a special relationship of dependency and trust between the parties or where the public interest is adversely affected by a contracting party's practices. Numerous cases exist, for example, in which insurance companies' bad faith refusal to settle claims or perform duties to their insured and lenders' failure to exercise good faith in their dealings with their customers have led to large damage verdicts. Likewise, in states in which the implied duty of good

---

[1]This trend is discussed in Chapter 9.

faith has been held applicable to contracts of employment, employers who discharge employees in bad faith have been held liable for damages.[2]

BREACH OF CONTRACT

When a person's performance is due, any failure to perform that is not excused is a breach of contract. Not all breaches of contract are of equal seriousness, however. Some are relatively minor deviations, whereas others are so extreme that they deprive the promisee of the essence of what he bargained for. The legal consequences of a given breach depend on the extent of the breach.

At a minimum, a party's breach of contract gives the nonbreaching party the right to sue and recover for any damages caused by that breach. When the breach is serious enough to be called a **material breach,** further legal consequences ensue.

Effect of Material Breach

A material breach occurs when the promisor's performance fails to reach the level of performance that the promisee is justified in expecting under the circumstances. In a situation in which the promisor's performance is judged by a substantial performance standard, saying that he failed to give substantial performance is the same thing as saying that he materially breached the contract.

The party who is injured by a material breach has the right to withhold his own performance. He is discharged from further obligations under the contract and may cancel it. He also has the right to sue for damages for total breach of contract.

Effect of Nonmaterial Breach   By contrast, when the breach is not serious enough to be material, the nonbreaching party may sue for only those damages caused by the particular breach. In addition, he does not have the right to cancel the contract, although a nonmaterial breach can give him the right to suspend his performance until the breach is remedied. Once the breach is remedied, however, the nonbreaching party must go ahead and render his performance, minus any damages caused by the breach.

---

[2]This is discussed in Chapter 50.

Determining the Materiality of the Breach
The standard for determining materiality is a flexible one that takes into account the facts of each individual case. The key question is whether the breach deprives the injured party of the benefits that he reasonably expected. For example, Norman, who is running for mayor, orders campaign literature from Prompt Press, to be delivered in September. Prompt Press's failure to deliver the literature until after the election in November deprives Norman of the essence of what he bargained for and would be considered a material breach.

In determining materiality, courts take into account the extent to which the breaching party will suffer forfeiture if the breach is held to be material. They also consider the magnitude (amount) of the breach and the willfulness or good faith exercised by the breaching party. The timing of the breach can also be important. A breach that occurs early on in the parties' relationship is more likely to be viewed as material than is one that occurs after an extended period of performance. Courts also consider the extent to which the injured party can be adequately compensated by the payment of damages.

Time for Performance   A party's failure to perform on time is a breach of contract that may be serious enough to constitute a material breach, or it may be relatively trivial under the circumstances.

At the outset, it is necessary to determine when performance is due. Some contracts specifically state the time for performance, which makes it easy to determine the time for performance. In some contracts that do not specifically state the time for performance, such a time can be inferred from the circumstances surrounding the contract. In the Norman and Prompt Press hypothetical example, the circumstances surrounding the contract probably would have implied that the time for performance was some time before the election, even if the parties had not specified the time for performance. In still other contracts, no time for performance is either stated or implied. When no time for performance is stated or implied, performance must be completed within a "reasonable time," as judged by the circumstances of each case.

Consequences of Late Performance   After a court determines when performance was due, it must determine the consequences of late performance. In some contracts, the parties expressly state that "time is of the essence" or that timely performance is "vital." This means that each party's timely performance by a specific date is an express condition of the other party's duty to perform. Thus, in a contract that contains a time is of the essence provision, any delay by either party normally constitutes a material breach. You will see an example of this in *F. J. Miceli and Slonim Development Corporation v. Dierberg,* which follows. Sometimes, courts will imply such a term even when the language of the contract does not state that time is of the essence. A court would be likely to do this if late performance is of little or no value to the promisee. For example, Schrader contracts with the local newspaper to run an advertisement for Christ-mas trees from December 15, 1994, to December 24, 1994, but the newspaper does not run the ad until December 26, 1994. In this case, the time for performance is an essential part of the contract and the newspaper has committed a material breach.

When a contract does not contain language indicating that time is of the essence and a court determines that the time for performance is not a particularly important part of the contract, the promisee must accept late performance rendered within a reasonable time after performance was due. The promisee is then entitled to deduct or set off from the contract price any losses caused by the delay. Late performance is not a material breach in such cases unless it is unreasonably late.

F. J. Miceli and Slonim Development Corporation v. Dierberg
773 S.W.2d 154 (Mo. Ct. App. 1989)

Joanne and Louis Basso contracted with Mary Dierberg to purchase her property for $1,310,000. One term of the contract stated "The sale under this contract shall be closed . . . at the office of Community Title Company . . . on May 16, 1988 at 10:00 A.M. . . . . Time is of the essence of this contract." After forming this contract, the Bassos assigned their right to purchase Dierberg's property to F. J. Miceli and Slonim Development Corporation.

At 10:00 A.M. on May 16, 1988, Dierberg appeared at Community Title Company for closing. No representative of Miceli and Slonim was there, nor did anyone from Miceli and Slonim inform Dierberg that there would be any delay in the closing. At 10:20 A.M., Dierberg declared the contract null and void because the closing did not take place as agreed, and she left the title company office shortly thereafter. Dierberg had intended to use the purchase money to close another contract to purchase real estate later in the day. At about 10:30 A.M., a representative of Miceli and Slonim appeared at Community Title Company to begin the closing procedures, but the representative did not have the funds for payment until 1:30 P.M. Dierberg refused to return to the title company to close, stating that Miceli and Slonim had breached the contract by failing to tender payment on time. She had already made alternative arrangements to finance her purchase of other real estate to meet her obligation under that contract.

Miceli and Slonim sued Dierberg for specific performance of the contract, claiming that the contract did not require closing exactly at 10:00 A.M., but rather some time on the day of May 16. Dierberg filed a motion for summary judgment, and the trial court granted it. Miceli and Slonim appealed.

———————— ■ ————————

Karohl, Judge   Parties to a contract may provide that time is of the essence. A clause specifying time is of the essence ordinarily means a specific contractual provision fixing the time of performance is to be regarded as a vital element of the contract. If a contract specifies a certain time for performance, the contract must be performed at that time, even if time is specified by the hour. Custom will not alter express agreement of the parties.

Here, the contract clearly and precisely stated closing was to occur at 10:00 A.M. on May 16, 1988. Time and date were specifically referred to in three separate sections of the contract. It was agreed time was of the essence of the contract. This provision would relate to all three times and dates. Dierberg was obligated to close under another contract to purchase real estate later the same day. She relied on receiving the proceeds of her sale at 10:00 A.M. Because closing did not occur as agreed, Dierberg was required to make other arrangements to meet her obligation. These facts lend meaning to the judgment of the trial court that "10:00 A.M." was the agreement of Bassos and Dierberg, not a mere guideline.

When there is no ambiguity in a contract, it is the duty of the court to state its clear meaning. Here, the court found there was no ambiguity in the contract and that the contract required closing at or reasonably near 10:00 A.M. We find no error in the judgment. Miceli and Slonim's failure to tender payment until 1:30 P.M. combined with its failure to inform Dierberg of the delay in closing, was a breach of contract. On undisputed facts, summary judgment was proper.

Summary judgment for Dierberg affirmed.

CONCEPT REVIEW

TIME FOR PERFORMANCE

Contract Language	Time for Performance	Consequences of Late Performance
"Time is of the essence" or similar language	The time stated in the contract	Material breach
Specific time is stated in or implied by the contract and late performance would have little or no value	The time stated in or implied by the contract	Material breach
Specific time is stated in or implied by the contract, but the time for performance is a relatively unimportant part of the contract	The time stated in or implied by the contract	Not a material breach unless performance is unreasonably late
No time for performance is stated in or implied by the contract	Within a reasonable time	Not material breach unless performance is unreasonably late

Anticipatory Repudiation   One type of breach of contract occurs when the promisor indicates before the time for his performance that he is unwilling or unable to carry out the contract. This is called **anticipatory repudiation** or **anticipatory breach.** Anticipatory breach generally constitutes a material breach of contract that discharges the promisee from all further obligation under the contract.

In determining what constitutes anticipatory repudiation, courts look for some unequivocal statement or voluntary act that clearly indicates that the promisor cannot or will not perform his duties under the contract. This may take the form of an express statement by the promisor. The promisor's intent not to perform could also be implied from actions of the promisor such as selling to a third party the property that the promisor was obligated to sell to the promisee. For example, if Ross, who is obligated to convey real estate to Davis, conveys the property to some third person instead, Ross has repudiated the contract.

When anticipatory repudiation occurs, the promisee is faced with several choices. For example, Marsh and Davis enter a contract in which Davis agrees to deliver a quantity of bricks to Marsh on

September 1, 1994, and Marsh agrees to pay Davis a sum of money in two installments. The agreement specifies that Marsh will pay 50 percent of the purchase price on July 15, 1994, and 50 percent of the purchase price within 30 days after delivery. On July 1, 1994, Davis writes Marsh and unequivocally states that he will not deliver the bricks. Must Marsh go ahead and send the payment that is due on July 15? Must he wait until September 1 to bring suit for total breach of contract? The answer to both questions is no.

When anticipatory repudiation occurs, the nonbreaching party is justified in withholding his own performance and suing for damages right away, without waiting for the time for performance to arrive.[3] If he can show that he was ready, willing, and able to perform his part of the contract, he can recover damages for total breach of the contract. The nonbreaching party is not obligated to do this, however. If he chooses, he may wait until the time for performance in case the other party changes his mind and decides to perform.

Recovery by a Party Who Has Committed Material Breach

A party who has materially breached the contract (that is, has not substantially performed) does not have the right to recover the contract price. If a promisor who has given some performance to the promisee cannot recover under the contract, however, the promisor will face forfeiture and the promisee will have obtained an unearned gain. There are two possible avenues for a party who has committed material breach to obtain some compensation for the performance he has conferred on the nonbreaching party.

1. *Quasi-contract.* A party who has materially breached a contract might recover the reasonable value of any benefits he has conferred on the promisee by bringing an action under quasi-contract.[4] This would enable him to obtain compensation for the value of any performance he has given that has benefited the nonbreaching party. Some

courts take the position that a person in material breach should not be able to recover for benefits he has conferred, however.

2. *Partial performance of a divisible contract.* Some contracts are divisible; that is, each party's performance can be divided in two or more parts and each part is exchanged for some corresponding consideration from the other party. For example, if Johnson agrees to mow Peterson's lawn for $20 and clean Peterson's gutters for $50, the contract is divisible. When a promisor performs one part of the contract but materially breaches another part, he can recover at the contract price for the part that he did perform. For example, if Johnson breached his duty to clean the gutters but fully performed his obligation to mow the lawn, he could recover at the contract price for the lawn-mowing part of the contract.

EXCUSES FOR NONPERFORMANCE

Although nonperformance of a duty that has become due will ordinarily constitute a breach of contract, there are some situations in which nonperformance is excused because of factors that arise after the formation of the contract. When this occurs, the person whose performance is made impossible or impracticable by these factors is discharged from further obligation under the contract. The following discussion concerns the most common grounds for excuse of nonperformance.

Impossibility

When performance of a contractual duty becomes impossible after the formation of the contract, the duty will be discharged on grounds of **impossibility.** This does not mean that a person can be discharged merely because he has contracted to do something that he is simply unable to do or that causes him hardship or difficulty. Impossibility in the legal sense of the word means "it cannot be done by anyone" rather than "I cannot do it." Thus, promisors who find that they have agreed to perform duties that are beyond their capabilities or that turn out to be unprofitable or burdensome are generally not excused from performance of their duties. Impossibility will provide an excuse for nonperformance, however, when some unexpected event arises after the formation of the contract and renders

---

[3]Uniform Commercial Code rules regarding anticipatory repudiation in contracts for the sale of goods are discussed in Chapter 21.

[4]Quasi-contract is discussed in Chapter 9. It involves the use of the remedy of restitution, which is discussed later in this chapter.

performance objectively impossible. The event that causes the impossibility need not have been entirely unforeseeable. Normally, however, the event will be one that the parties would not have reasonably thought of as a real possibility that would affect performance.

There are a variety of situations in which a person's duty to perform may be discharged on grounds of impossibility. The three most common situations involve illness or death of the promisor, supervening illegality, and destruction of the subject matter of the contract.

Illness or Death of Promisor   Incapacitating illness or death of the promisor excuses nonperformance when the promisor has contracted to perform personal services. For example, if Pauling, a college professor who has a contract with State University to teach for an academic year, dies before the completion of the contract, her estate will not be liable for breach of contract. The promisor's death or illness does not, however, excuse the nonperformance of duties that can be delegated to another, such as the duty to deliver goods, pay money, or convey real estate. For example, if Odell had contracted to convey real estate to Ruskin and died before the closing date, Ruskin could enforce the contract against Odell's estate.

Supervening Illegality   If a statute or governmental regulation enacted after the creation of a contract makes performance of a party's duties illegal, the promisor is excused from performing. Statutes or regulations that merely make performance more difficult or less profitable do not, however, excuse nonperformance. You will see an example of this form of impossibility in the following case, *Centex Corporation v. Dalton.*

Centex Corporation v. Dalton
840 S.W.2d 952 (Sup. Ct. Tex. 1992)

Centex is a company engaged in residential and commercial construction and related financial services. John Dalton was an executive of a Texas thrift institution. In 1988, because the flagging Texas economy adversely affected the state's thrift institutions, the Federal Home Loan Bank Board (Bank Board) and other regulatory agencies decided to close, merge, liquidate, or sell several large thrift institutions. This plan was called the "Southwest Plan." In November 1988, Centex contacted Dalton to request that he help Centex acquire certain thrifts made available through the Southwest Plan. A few weeks later, Dalton traveled to Washington, D.C., where he made an unsuccessful bid to acquire a group of thrifts for Centex. While there, Dalton learned about the availability of four central Texas thrifts known as the "Lamb Package." Dalton informed Centex about this, and in December 1988, Centex entered into a letter agreement with Dalton in which it promised to pay Dalton $750,000 over a three-year period if Centex were successful in acquiring the Lamb Package. Before the parties signed this agreement, Centex met with the Bank Board and told it of its intention to pay fees to Dalton on completion of the purchase of the Lamb Package. The Bank Board told Centex that this would be acceptable as long as Centex—rather than any of the thrift institutions in the Lamb Package or any entity formed to acquire the Lamb Package—made the payment to Dalton. Arrangements were made to acquire the Lamb Package, but on December 28, 1988, the night before Centex's acquisition of the Lamb Package was to be finalized, Centex's representative learned that the Bank Board probably would not permit payment of the fees to Dalton. Centex nevertheless went ahead and finalized the purchase of the Lamb Package, forming a wholly owned subsidiary, Texas Trust Savings Bank, as the acquiring entity. At a meeting on December 28, 1988, the Bank Board approved the acquisition of the Lamb Package, conditioned on a prohibition against Texas Trust's direct or indirect payment of finder's fees. The transcript of the meeting shows that members of the Bank Board discussed Texas Trust's planned payment of fees to Dalton, made specific objection to the payment, and requested its general counsel to prepare an amendment to clarify that its prohibition against the payment of fees extended to affiliates of Texas Trust. On January 31, 1989, the Bank Board adopted the amendment proposed by its counsel.

Dalton performed the services required of him under the letter agreement, but Centex did not pay him because of the prohibition imposed by the Bank Board. Dalton brought suit against Centex for breach of contract. The trial court granted a summary judgment in favor of Dalton, awarding him $750,000 in damages plus interest, costs, and attorney's fees. Centex appealed, and the court of appeals affirmed the summary judgment. Centex appealed to the Texas Supreme Court. (In August 1989, while the case was on appeal, a federal statute called the Financial Institutions Reform Recovery and Enforcement Act became effective. This statute abolished the Bank Board, created the Office of Thrift Supervision (OTS), and gave OTS the powers formerly vested in the Bank Board. On December 11, 1990, OTS issued a cease-and-desist order to prevent Centex or Texas Trust from paying any fees to Dalton under the letter agreement.)

Gammage, Justice   Centex argues that, because its performance under the letter agreement has been made impracticable by having to comply with the Bank Board's order, its duty to render that performance is discharged. Congress gave the Bank Board power to regulate the acquisition and control of federally-insured thrifts by savings and loan holding companies. As a result, the Bank Board's prohibition makes it illegal for Centex to perform under the letter agreement. "Where a party's performance is made impracticable by the occurrence of an event the non-occurrence of which was a basic assumption on which the contract was made, his duty to render that performance is discharged." *Restatement (Second) of Contracts* section 261 (1981). A governmental regulation or order that makes impracticable the performance of a duty "is an event the non-occurrence of which was made a basic assumption on which the contract was made." Consequently, to avoid inconsistency with the Bank Board's prohibition and conflict with federal regulatory law, we must hold that Centex is excused from performance by the doctrine of impossibility.

When courts are asked to excuse a party's performance due to supervening circumstances which made performance impracticable or impossible, they sometimes attempt to allocate the burden of risk and decide who must pay for the unanticipated occurrence. Foreseeability is one factor used to decide which party assumed the risk of supervening impossibility. The foreseeability factor has, however, gradually decreased in importance. Here, one party,

Centex, cannot be required to pay, regardless of the foreseeability of the Bank Board's prohibition.

The court of appeals reasoned that the Bank Board's prohibition applied only to Texas Trust and not to Centex. We note, however, that the prohibition forbids not only the direct payment of finder's fees by Centex, which is an affiliate of Texas Trust, but also the indirect payments of such fees. We also note the court of appeals reasoned that, because the obligation of Centex to pay Dalton arose when the letter agreement was signed on December 23, 1988, before the Bank Board's adoption of its prohibition on December 29, 1988, the prohibition did not apply to the letter agreement. The court of appeals' reasoning was incorrect because the letter agreement is premised on a condition precedent. By the terms of the letter agreement, Dalton's right to enforce it could not accrue until the Bank Board approved the acquisition. Because the Bank Board, in approving the acquisition, prohibited the payment of the finder's fees, thereby invalidating the letter agreement, Dalton's right to enforce the letter agreement never accrued.

The Bank Board's order prohibits Centex's performance under the letter agreement, which otherwise would be enforceable under state contract law. Centex cannot pay Dalton and obey the governmental regulation, which has prohibited the proposed payment. Centex's duty to perform under the letter agreement is excused.

Reversed in favor of Centex.

Destruction of the Subject Matter of the Contract   If something that is essential to the promisor's performance is destroyed after the formation of the contract through no fault of the promisor, the promisor is excused from performing. For example, Woolridge contracts to sell his car to Rivkin. If an explosion destroys the car after the contract has been formed but before Woolridge has made delivery,

Woolridge's nonperformance will be excused. The destruction of nonessential items that the promisor intended to use in performing does not excuse nonperformance if substitutes are available, even though securing them makes performance more difficult or less profitable. Suppose that Ace Construction Company had planned to use a particular piece of machinery in fulfilling a contract to build a building for Worldwide Widgets Company. If the piece of machinery is destroyed but substitutes are available, destruction of the machinery before the contract is performed would *not* give Ace an excuse for failing to perform.

Frustration of Venture

Closely associated with impossibility is the doctrine of **frustration of venture** (also known as **commercial frustration** or **frustration of purpose**). This doctrine provides an excuse for nonperformance when events that occur after the formation of the contract would deprive the promisor of the benefit of return performance. Although courts often include frustration cases within the general terminology of impossibility, frustration can be distinguished from impossibility and impracticability by the fact that the promisor in a frustration case is not necessarily prevented from performing. Rather, in frustration cases, the promisor is excused because the return performance by the other party has become worthless to him. For example, Boyd signs a contract for a one-year membership in an Eden Exercise Salon, for which he agrees to pay $50 per month. One week after signing the contract, Boyd is involved in a serious automobile accident and suffers injuries that cause him to be bedridden for a year. In such a case, the automobile accident and Boyd's resulting injuries did not prevent him from performing his duties under the contract (paying money each month), but this unexpected event does deprive Boyd of the benefit of receiving Eden's return performance. In such a case, a court might excuse Boyd's performance on the ground of frustration of venture.

Commercial Impracticability

Section 2–615 of the Uniform Commercial Code has extended the scope of the common law doctrine of impossibility to cases in which unforeseen developments make performance by the promisor highly impracticable, unreasonably expensive, or of little value to the promisee. Rather than using a standard of impossibility, then, the Code uses the more relaxed standard of **impracticability.** Despite the less stringent standard applied, cases actually excusing nonperformance on grounds of impracticability are relatively rare. To be successful in claiming excuse based on impracticability, a promisor must be able to establish that the event that makes performance impracticable occurred without his fault and that the contract was made with the basic assumption that this event would not occur. This basically means that the event was beyond the scope of the risks that the parties contemplated at the time of contracting and that the promisor did not expressly or impliedly assume the risk that the event would occur.

Case law and official comments to UCC section 2–615 indicate that neither increased cost nor collapse of a market for particular goods is sufficient to excuse nonperformance, because those are the types of business risks that every promisor assumes. However, drastic price increases or severe shortages of goods resulting from unforeseen circumstances such as wars and crop failures can give rise to impracticability.

If the event causing impracticability affects only a part of the seller's capacity to perform, the seller must allocate production and deliveries among customers in a "fair and reasonable" manner and must notify them of any delay or any limited allocation of the goods. You can read more about commercial impracticability in Chapter 21, Performance of Sales Contracts.

The impracticability standard has been adopted in section 261 of the *Restatement (Second) of Contracts,* which closely resembles the provisions of section 2–615 of the UCC. States that follow the *Restatement (Second)* approach apply the impracticability standard to all types of contracts, not just those for the sale of goods.

OTHER GROUNDS FOR DISCHARGE

Earlier in this chapter, you learned about several situations in which a party's duty to perform could be discharged even though that party had not himself performed. These include the nonoccurrence of a condition precedent or concurrent condition, the occurrence of a condition subsequent, material breach by the other party, and excuse from performance by impossibility, impracticability, or frustration. The following discussion deals with additional ways in which a discharge can occur.

Discharge by Mutual Agreement

Just as contracts are created by mutual agreement, they can also be discharged by *mutual agreement.* An agreement to discharge a contract must be supported by consideration to be enforceable.

Discharge by Accord and Satisfaction

An **accord** is an agreement whereby a promisee who has an existing claim agrees with the promisor that he will accept some performance different from that which was originally agreed on. When the promisor performs the accord, that is called a **satisfaction.**[5] When an accord and satisfaction occurs, the parties are discharged. For example, Root contracts with May to build a garage on May's property for $30,000. After Root has performed his part of the bargain, the parties then agree that instead of paying money, May will transfer a one-year-old Porsche to Root instead. When this is done, both parties are discharged.

Discharge by Waiver

A party to a contract may voluntarily relinquish any right he has under a contract, including the right to receive return performance. Such a relinquishment of rights is known as a **waiver.** If one party tenders an incomplete or defective performance and the other party accepts that performance without objection, knowing that the defects will not be remedied, the party to whom performance was due will have discharged the other party from his duty of performance. For example, a real estate lease requires Long, the tenant, to pay a $5 late charge for late payments of rent. Long pays his rent late each month for five months, but the landlord accepts it without objection and without assessing the late charge. In this situation, the landlord has probably waived his right to collect the late charge.

To avoid waiving rights, a person who has received defective performance should give the other party prompt notice that she expects complete performance and will seek damages if the defects are not corrected.

Discharge by Alteration

If the contract is represented by a *written* instrument, and one of the parties intentionally makes a material alteration in the instrument without the other's consent, the alteration acts as a discharge of the other party. If the other party consents to the alteration or does not object to it when he learns of it, he is not discharged. Alteration by a third party without the knowledge or consent of the contracting parties does not affect the parties' rights.

Discharge by Statute of Limitations

Courts have long refused to grant a remedy to a person who delays bringing a lawsuit for an unreasonable time. All of the states have enacted statutes known as **statutes of limitation,** which specify the period of time in which a person can bring a lawsuit.

The time period for bringing a contract action varies from state to state, and many states prescribe time periods for cases concerning oral contracts that are different from those for cases concerning written contracts. Section 2–725 of the Uniform Commercial Code provides for a four-year statute of limitations for contracts involving the sale of goods.

The statutory period ordinarily begins to run from the date of the breach. It may be delayed if the party who has the right to sue is under some incapacity at that time (such as minority or insanity) or is beyond the jurisdiction of the state. A person who has breached a contractual duty is discharged from liability for breach if no lawsuit is brought before the statutory period elapses.

Discharge by Decree of Bankruptcy

The contractual obligations of a debtor are generally discharged by a decree of bankruptcy. Bankruptcy is discussed in Chapter 29.

REMEDIES FOR BREACH OF CONTRACT

Our discussion of the performance stage of contracts so far has focused on the circumstances under which a party has the duty to perform or is excused

---

[5]Accord and satisfaction is also discussed in Chapter 12.

from performing. In situations in which a person is injured by a breach of contract and is unable to obtain compensation by a settlement out of court, a further important issue remains: What remedy will a court fashion to compensate for breach of contract?

Contract law seeks to encourage people to rely on the promises made to them by others. Contract remedies focus on the economic loss caused by breach of contract, not on the moral obligation to perform a promise. The objective of granting a remedy in a case of breach of contract is simply to compensate the injured party.

Types of Contract Remedies

There are a variety of ways in which this can be done. The basic categories of contract remedies include:

1. Legal remedies (money damages).
2. Equitable remedies.
3. Restitution.

The usual remedy is an award of money damages that will compensate the injured party for his losses. This is called a **legal remedy** or **remedy at law,** because the imposition of money damages in our legal system originated in courts of law. Less frequently used but still important are **equitable remedies** such as specific performance. Equitable remedies are those remedies that had their origins in courts of equity rather than in courts of law.[6] Today, they are available at the discretion of the judge. A final possible remedy is **restitution,** which requires the defendant to pay the value of the benefits that the plaintiff has conferred on him.

Interests Protected by Contract Remedies

Remedies for breach of contract protect one or more of the following interests that a promisee may have:[7]

1. *Expectation interest.* A promisee's **expectation interest** is his interest in obtaining the objective or opportunity for gain that he bargained for and "expected." Courts attempt to protect this interest by formulating a remedy that will place the promisee in the position he would have been in if the contract had been performed as promised.

2. *Reliance interest.* A promisee's **reliance interest** is his interest in being compensated for losses that he has suffered by changing his position in reliance on the other party's promise. In some cases, such as when a promisee is unable to prove his expectation interest with reasonable certainty, the promisee may seek a remedy to compensate for the loss suffered as a result of relying on the promisor's promise rather than for the expectation of profit.

3. *Restitution interest.* A **restitution interest** is a party's interest in recovering the amount by which he has enriched or benefited the other. Both the reliance and restitution interests involve promisees who have changed their position. The difference between the two is that the reliance interest involves a loss to the promisee that does not benefit the promisor, whereas the restitution interest involves a loss to the promisee that does constitute an unjust enrichment to the promisor. A remedy based on restitution enables a party who has performed or partially performed her contract and has benefited the other party to obtain compensation for the value of the benefits that she has conferred.

LEGAL REMEDIES (DAMAGES)

Limitations on Recovery of Damages in Contract Cases

An injured party's ability to recover damages in a contract action is limited by three principles:

1. *A party can recover damages only for those losses that he can prove with reasonable certainty.* Losses that are purely speculative are not recoverable. Thus, if Jones Publishing Company breaches a contract to publish Powell's memoirs, Powell may not be able to recover damages for lost royalties (her expectation interest), since she may be unable to establish, beyond speculation, how much money she would have earned in royalties if the book had been published. (Note, however, that Powell's reliance interest might be protected here; she could be allowed to recover provable losses incurred in reliance on the contract.)

2. *A breaching party is responsible for paying only those losses that were foreseeable to him at the time of contracting.* A loss is foreseeable if it would

---

[6]The nature of equitable remedies is also discussed in Chapter 1.

[7]*Restatement (Second) of Contracts* § 344.

ordinarily be expected to result from a breach or if the breaching party had reason to know of particular circumstances that would make the loss likely. For example, if Prince Manufacturing Company renders late performance in a contract to deliver parts to Cheatum Motors without knowing that Cheatum is shut down waiting for the parts, Prince will not have to pay the business losses that result from Cheatum's having to close its operation.

3. *Plaintiffs injured by a breach of contract have the duty to mitigate (avoid or minimize) damages.* A party cannot recover for losses that he could have avoided without undue risk, burden, or humiliation. For example, an employee who has been wrongfully fired would be entitled to damages equal to his wages for the remainder of the employment period. The employee, however, has the duty to minimize the damages by making reasonable efforts to seek a similar job elsewhere.

Compensatory Damages

Subject to the limitations discussed above, a person who has been injured by a breach of contract is entitled to recover **compensatory damages.** In calculating the compensatory remedy, a court will attempt to protect the expectation interest of the injured party by giving him the "benefit of his bargain" (placing him in the position he would have been in *had the contract been performed as promised*). To do this, the court must compensate the injured person for the provable losses he has suffered as well as for the provable gains that he has been prevented from realizing by the breach of contract. Normally, compensatory damages include one or more of three possible items: loss in value, any allowable consequential damages, and any allowable incidental damages.

1. *Loss in value.* The starting point in calculating compensatory damages is to determine the **loss in value** of the performance that the plaintiff had the right to expect. This is a way of measuring the expectation interest. The calculation of the loss in value experienced by an injured party differs according to the sort of contract involved and the circumstances of the breach. In contracts involving nonperformance of the sale of real estate, for example, courts normally measure loss in value by the difference between the contract price and the market price of the property. Thus, if Willis repudiates a

contract with Renfrew whereby Renfrew was to purchase land worth $20,000 from Willis for $10,000, Renfrew's loss in value was $10,000. Where a seller has failed to perform a contract for the sale of goods, courts may measure loss in value by the difference between the contract price and the price that the buyer had to pay to procure substitute goods.[8] In cases in which a party breaches by rendering defective performance—say, by breaching a warranty in the sale of goods—the loss in value would be measured by the difference between the value of the goods if they had been in the condition warranted by the seller and the value of the goods in their defective condition.[9]

2. *Consequential damages.* **Consequential damages** (also called **special damages**) compensate for losses that occur as a consequence of the breach of contract. Consequential losses occur because of some special or unusual circumstances of the particular contractual relationship of the parties. For example, Apex Trucking Company buys a computer system from ABC Computers. The system fails to operate properly, and Apex is forced to pay its employees to perform the tasks manually, spending $10,000 in overtime pay. In this situation, Apex might seek to recover the $10,000 in overtime pay in addition to the loss of value that it has experienced.

Lost profits flowing from a breach of contract can be recovered as consequential damages if they are foreseeable and can be proven with reasonable certainty. It is important to remember, however, that the recovery of consequential damages is subject to the limitations on damage recovery discussed earlier.

3. *Incidental damages.* **Incidental damages** compensate for reasonable costs that the injured party incurs after the breach in an effort to avoid further loss. For example, if Smith Construction Company breaches an employment contract with Brice, Brice could recover as incidental damages those reasonable expenses he must incur in attempting to procure substitute employment, such as long-distance telephone tolls or the cost of printing new résumés.

---

[8]Remedies under Article 2 of the Uniform Commercial Code are discussed in detail in Chapter 22.

[9]See Chapter 20 for further discussion of the damages for breach of warranty in the sale of goods.

Alternative Measures of Damages The foregoing discussion has focused on the most common formulation of damage remedies in contracts cases. The normal measure of compensatory damages is not appropriate in every case, however. When it is not appropriate, a court may use an alternative measure of damages. For example, where a party has suffered losses by performing or preparing to perform, he might seek damages based on his *reliance interest* instead of his expectation interest. In such a case, he would be compensated for the provable losses he suffered by relying on the other party's promise. This measure of damages is often used in cases in which a promise is enforceable under promissory estoppel.[10]

Nominal Damages

Nominal damages are very small damage awards that are given when a technical breach of contract has occurred without causing any actual or provable economic loss. The sums awarded as nominal damages typically vary from 2 cents to a dollar.

Liquidated Damages

The parties to a contract may expressly provide in their contract that a specific sum shall be recoverable if the contract is breached. Such provisions are

---

[10]Promissory estoppel is discussed in Chapters 9 and 12.

called **liquidated damages** provisions. For example, Murchison rents space in a shopping mall in which she plans to operate a retail clothing store. She must make improvements in the space before opening the store, and it is very important to her to have the store opened for the Christmas shopping season. She hires Ace Construction Company to construct the improvements. The parties agree to include in the contract a liquidated damages provision stating that, if Ace is late in completing the construction, Murchison will be able to recover a specified sum for each day of delay. Such a provision is highly desirable from Murchison's point of view because, without a liquidated damages provision, she would have a difficult time in establishing the precise losses that would result from delay. Courts scrutinize these agreed-on damages carefully, however.

If the amount specified in a liquidated damages provision is reasonable and if the nature of the contract is such that actual damages would be difficult to determine, a court will enforce the provision. When liquidated damages provisions are enforced, the amount of damages agreed on will be the injured party's exclusive damage remedy. If the amount specified is unreasonably great in relation to the probable loss or injury, however, or if the amount of damages could be readily determined in the event of breach, the courts will declare the provision to be a penalty and will refuse to enforce it. The issue of reasonableness of liquidated damages is presented in the *Luminous Neon, Inc. v. Parscale* case, which follows.

LUMINOUS NEON, INC. V. PARSCALE
836 P.2d 1201 (Ct. App. Kan. 1992)

Rita Parscale, the owner of a restaurant, entered into negotiations to acquire outdoor advertising signs for her business from Luminous Neon. At the outset of the negotiations, Luminous Neon had offered to sell the signs to Parscale for $5,600 plus tax, but Parscale ultimately leased them. Under the terms of the lease, Parscale paid a rental of $191.75 plus tax per month for a term of five years. The lease also contained a liquidated damages clause that required Parscale, in the event of breach, to pay damages equal to 80 percent of the remaining payments due. That 80 percent represented Luminous Neon's expenses incurred in manufacturing, financing, and installing the signs, as well as profit. The 20 percent of the remaining payments that was not included as liquidated damages was for maintenance and service expenses that would not be incurred due to Parscale's breach.

Sometime after Parscale leased the signs, the City of Topeka began construction on a street that limited access to Parscale's business. That construction had an adverse effect on Parscale's business, and it ultimately closed. Parscale stopped making payments on the signs after making a total of 19 payments. Forty-one monthly payments of $191.75 remained due and payable, resulting in liquidated damages, including tax, of $6,651.04. Luminous Neon removed the signs from Parscale's business at her request. The removal added another $300 to the damages. Luminous Neon ultimately sued Parscale to collect this money. The trial court granted Luminous Neon's motion for summary judgment and awarded it $6,951.04. Parscale appealed.

Bullock, Judge   Parscale contends the court erred in granting summary judgment because a material fact existed relating to the liquidated damages claim of Luminous Neon. She argues that Luminous Neon's offer to sell the signs for $5,600 plus tax reveals that the liquidated damages were unreasonable. The contention that only the original sale price of the signs constitutes reasonable damages is not persuasive. There are advantages to be weighed when one considers leasing rather than purchasing an item. However, when one chooses to lease an item and then breaches that lease, it is unreasonable to believe damages should be based upon values attendant to a purchase of that item. By leasing rather than purchasing, Parscale avoided financing charges, insurance, repair, and maintenance expenses. Luminous Neon agreed to maintain the signs during the term of the lease.

The general rule is that courts will "refuse to enforce a liquidated damage provision which fixes damages in an amount grossly disproportionate to the harm actually sustained or likely to be sustained, and under certain circumstances indicative of gross proportion," such a provision will be deemed a penalty. 22 *Am. Jur. 2d, Damages* section 701, p. 758.

Luminous Neon custom designed the signs specifically for Parscale, and, notwithstanding her argument to the contrary, we are not persuaded that the signs are of particular value to Luminous Neon. Moreover, the trial court awarded the signs to Parscale. The damage clause of the lease was not a penalty, and the award did not unjustly enrich Luminous Neon.

Judgment affirmed in favor of Luminous Neon.

Punitive Damages

Punitive damages are damages awarded in addition to the compensatory remedy that are designed to punish a defendant for particularly reprehensible behavior and to deter the defendant and others from committing similar behavior in the future. The traditional rule is that punitive damages are not recoverable in contracts cases unless a specific statutory provision (such as some consumer protection statutes) allows them or the defendant has committed *fraud* or some other independent tort. A few states will permit the use of punitive damages in contracts cases in which the defendant's conduct, though not technically a tort, was malicious, oppressive, or tortious in nature.

Punitive damages have also been awarded in many of the cases involving breach of the implied covenant of good faith. In such cases, courts usually circumvent the traditional rule against awarding punitive damages in contracts cases by holding that breach of the duty of good faith is an independent tort. The availability of punitive damages in such cases operates to deter a contracting party from deliberately disregarding the other party's rights. Insurance companies have been the most frequent target for punitive damages awards in bad faith cases, but employers and banks have also been subjected to punitive damages verdicts.

EQUITABLE REMEDIES

In exceptional cases in which money damages alone are not adequate to fully compensate for a party's injuries, a court may grant an **equitable remedy** either alone or in combination with a legal remedy. Equitable relief is subject to several limitations, however, and will be granted only when justice is served by doing so. The primary equitable remedies for breach of contract are specific performance and injunction.[11]

---

[11]Another equitable remedy, *reformation,* allows a court to reform or "rewrite" a written contract when the parties have made an error in expressing their agreement. Reformation is discussed, along with the doctrine of mistake, in Chapter 13.

Specific Performance

Specific performance is an equitable remedy whereby the court orders the breaching party to perform his contractual duties as promised. For example, if Barnes breached a contract to sell a tract of land to Metzger and a court granted specific performance of the contract, the court would require Barnes to deed the land to Metzger. (Metzger, of course, must pay the purchase price.) This remedy can be advantageous to the injured party because he is not faced with the complexities of proving damages, he does not have to worry about whether he can actually collect the damages, and he gets exactly what he bargained for. However, the availability of this remedy is subject to the limitations discussed below.

The Availability of Specific Performance

Specific performance, like other equitable remedies, is available only when the injured party has no adequate remedy at law—in other words, when money damages do not adequately compensate the injured party. This generally requires a showing that the subject of the contract is unique or at least that no substitutes are available. Even if this requirement is met, a court will withhold specific performance if the injured party has acted in bad faith, if he unreasonably delayed in asserting his rights, or if specific performance would require an excessive amount of supervision by the court.

Contracts for the sale of real estate are the most common subjects of specific performance decrees because every tract of real estate is considered to be unique. Specific performance is rarely granted for breach of a contract for the sale of goods because the injured party can usually procure substitute goods. However, there are situations involving sales of goods contracts in which specific performance is given. These cases involve goods that are unique or goods for which no substitute can be found. Examples include antiques, heirlooms, works of art, and objects of purely sentimental value.[12] Specific performance is not available for the breach of a promise to perform a personal service (such as a contract for employment, artistic performance, or consulting services). A decree requiring a person to specifi-cally perform a personal-services contract would probably be ineffective in giving the injured party what he bargained for. It would also require a great deal of supervision by the court. In addition, an application of specific performance in such cases would amount to a form of involuntary servitude.

Injunction

Injunction is an equitable remedy that is employed in many different contexts and is sometimes used as a remedy for breach of contract. An **injunction** is a court order requiring a person to do something (**mandatory injunction**) or ordering a person to refrain from doing something (**negative injunction**). Unlike legal remedies that apply only when the breach has already occurred, the equitable remedy of injunction can be invoked when a breach has merely been *threatened*. Injunctions are available only when the breach or threatened breach is likely to cause *irreparable injury*.

In the contract context, specific performance is a form of mandatory injunction. Negative injunctions are appropriately used in several situations, such as contract cases in which a party whose duty under the contract is forbearance threatens to breach the contract. For example, Norris sells his restaurant in Gas City, Indiana, to Ford. A term of the contract of sale provides that Norris agrees not to own, operate, or be employed in any restaurant within 30 miles of Gas City for a period of two years after the sale.[13] If Norris threatens to open a new restaurant in Gas City several months after the sale is consummated, a court could *enjoin* Norris from opening the new restaurant.

RESTITUTION

Restitution is a remedy that can be obtained either at law or in equity. Restitution applies when one party's performance or reliance has conferred a benefit on the other. A party's restitution interest is protected by compensating him for the value of benefits he has conferred on the other person.[14] This can be done through **specific restitution,** in

---

[12]Specific performance under § 2–716(1) of the UCC is discussed in Chapter 22.

[13]Ancillary covenants not to compete, or noncompetition agreements, are discussed in detail in Chapter 15.

[14]Quasi-contract is discussed in detail in Chapter 9.

which the defendant is required to return the exact property conferred on him by the plaintiff, or **substitutionary restitution,** in which a court awards the plaintiff a sum of money that reflects the amount by which he benefited the defendant. In an action for damages based on quasi-contract, substitutionary restitution would be the remedy.

Restitution can be used in a number of circumstances. Sometimes, parties injured by breach of contract seek restitution as an alternative remedy instead of damages that focus on their expectation interest. In other situations, a *breaching party* who has partially performed seeks restitution for the value of benefits he conferred in excess of the losses he caused. In addition, restitution often applies in cases in which a person rescinds a contract on the grounds of lack of capacity, misrepresentation, fraud, duress, undue influence, or mistake. Upon rescission, each party who has been benefited by the other's performance must compensate the other for the value of the benefit conferred. Another application of restitution occurs when a party to a contract that violates the statute of frauds confers a benefit on the other party. For example, Boyer gives Blake a $10,000 down payment on an oral contract for the sale of a farm. Although the contract is unenforceable (that is, Boyer could not get compensation for his expectation interest), the court would give Boyer restitution of his down payment.

ETHICAL AND PUBLIC POLICY CONCERNS

1. Is it good public policy for a party who has materially breached a contract to be able to obtain restitution for the benefits he has conferred on the nonbreaching party?

2. How does the duty of good faith and fair dealing encourage ethical dealings? Do you see any problems with such a duty?

3. You have seen that contract remedies focus solely on the economic effect of contract breaches rather than on the moral implications of such breaches or the emotional harms that might result from a breach of contract. As a result, contract remedies are much more limited than are remedies in tort cases. Is this sound public policy? Explain.

PROBLEMS AND PROBLEM CASES

1. In October 1984, the Gildeas put their house on the market. Kapenis met with the Gildeas' realtor, Murphy, to talk about making a bid on the Gildea home. Murphy prepared several purchase offers and, after some negotiation, both Kapenis and the Gildeas agreed to a contract that contained a clause stating that the contract was "subject to buyer obtaining suitable financing interest rate no greater than 12¾%." Kapenis and Murphy then began a search for financing. When Kapenis talked with an officer of First Federal Savings & Loan, he learned that under this mortgage his interest rate could be adjusted twice a year and that 2 percentage points could be added to the adjusted rate after the two-year fixed period. He was dissatisfied with this and asked that Murphy find additional forms of financing. Murphy continued to inform Kapenis about various loan programs, but Kapenis rejected them because the monthly payments were too high. Another broker located a loan program of a 15-year term at 12½ percent interest with monthly payments of $419, but Kapenis stated that the monthly payments would be too high and not assumable and that these terms were unsatisfactory. Kapenis then informed the Gildeas that he could not find suitable financing and that he was withdrawing his offer. Is he legally entitled to do this?

2. Asphalt International chartered a tanker, the *Oswego Tarmac,* from Enterprise Shipping. The contract provided that Enterprise was obligated to maintain the vessel in good order but that it was absolved of responsibility for any loss or damage resulting from a collision and that, if the vessel should be lost, the contract would cease. While loading cargo alongside a pier, the *Oswego Tarmac* was rammed amidships by the bow of the motor vessel *Elektra* with such heavy impact that four of its tanks ruptured and heated asphalt spewed across the harbor. Expert appraisers estimated the cost of repair at not less than $1.5 million. The fair market value of the *Oswego Tarmac* prior to the collision was $750,000. Enterprise advised Asphalt International that the *Oswego Tarmac* was a complete loss. It refused Asphalt International's request to repair the vehicle. Asphalt International brought suit against Enterprise for breach of contract. Will it be successful?

3. Light contracted to build a house for the Mullers. After the job was completed, the Mullers refused to pay Light the balance they owed him under the contract, claiming that he had done some of the work in an unworkmanlike manner. When Light sued for the money, the Mullers counterclaimed for $5,700 damages for delay under a liquidated damages clause in the contract. The clause provided that Light must pay $100 per day for every day of delay in completion of the construction. The evidence indicated that the rental value of the home was between $400 and $415 per month. Should the liquidated damages provision be enforced?

4. The Warrens hired Denison, a building contractor, to build a house on their property. They executed a written contract in which the Warrens agreed to pay $73,400 for the construction. Denison's construction deviated somewhat from the specifications for the project. These deviations were presumably unintentional, and the cost of repairing them was $1,961.50. The finished house had a market value somewhat higher than the market value would have been without the deviations. The Warrens failed to pay the $48,400 balance due under the contract, alleging that Denison had used poor workmanship in constructing the house and that they were under no obligation to perform further duties under the contract. Are they correct?

5. Forman made a written offer to buy real estate from Benson under terms whereby Forman would pay the purchase price over a 10-year period. Benson did not know Forman and was concerned about his creditworthiness, so Forman's real estate agent suggested a term stating that the contract was "subject to seller's approving buyer's credit report." This term was agreed to by both parties and was inserted in the contract before it was signed. Forman then gave Benson a credit report and a personal financial statement. Benson said that the report "looks real good" and that he would have his attorney review it and begin the title work on the property. Over the course of the next six weeks, however, Benson met with Forman three times. During these meetings, he attempted to negotiate for a higher purchase price and interest rate. He also requested more financial information. Finally, Benson informed Forman that he rejected Forman's credit rating. Forman brought suit to enforce the contract. Will he prevail?

6. Kim, a homeowner, entered into a contract with Kilianek, an experienced contractor, to add an additional room onto his home. The architectural work in designing the room was to be done by Park & Associates. One provision of the contract between Kim and Kilianek stated that "Final payment . . . shall be paid by the Owner to the Contractor when the work has been completed, the contract fully performed, and a final Certificate for Payment has been issued by the Architect." Kim made periodic payments for a total of $14,100 toward the costs of construction. Although no final certificate for payment was issued by the architect, Kilianek demanded a final payment of $2,739. Is Kim obligated to make this payment?

7. Wolf Trap, an organization for the advancement of the performing arts, sponsors operas and other artistic programs at the Filene Center. The Filene Center is located in the Wolf Trap National Park, a national park owned by the U.S. government and operated by the National Park Service. The Center, which consists of a main stage tower, an auditorium, and an open lawn, provides both covered and uncovered seating for approximately 6,500 people. The park provides the parking space, which is separated from the Center and accessible by a number of pathways. Wolf Trap entered into a contract with the Opera Company of Boston whereby it agreed to pay the Opera Company $272,000 to perform four operas at the Filene Center on the nights of June 12, 13, 14, and 15, 1980. Among Wolf Trap's duties under the contract was the duty to provide lighting equipment as specified by the Opera Company's lighting designer. All four performances were sold out. Both parties performed their obligations for the first three performances. On June 15, the day of the last performance, however, there was a severe thunderstorm, which caused an electrical power outage that blacked out all electrical service in the park, its roadways, parking area, pathways, and auditorium. Representatives of the National Park Service and Wolf Trap held several conferences to decide what to do about the performance. The public utility advised that electrical service would not be resumed in the park until 11:00 P.M. or perhaps not even until the next morning. Various alternatives for supplying power were considered but none was regarded as being sufficient to resolve the problem. The Park Service was concerned about the safety of the 3,000 people who were already in the park; 3,500 more were expected before 8:00 P.M. The Park Service recommended the immediate cancellation of the performance and advised Wolf Trap that it disclaimed responsibility for the safety of the people who were to attend the performance. Wolf Trap agreed and the performance was canceled. A representative of the Opera Company was present at this meeting, but she neither took part in the decision nor voiced objection to the decision. Since the performance was canceled, Wolf Trap did not make the final payment called for in the contract to the Opera Company. The Opera Company sued Wolf Trap to recover the balance due under the contract. Was Wolf Trap's performance excused?

8. Shirley MacLaine Parker entered into a contract with Twentieth Century-Fox to play the female lead in Fox's contemplated production of a movie entitled *Bloomer Girl*. The contract provided that Fox would pay Parker a minimum "guaranteed compensation" of $53,571.42 per week for 14 weeks, beginning May 23, 1966, for a total of $750,000. Fox decided not to produce the movie, and in a letter dated April 4, 1966, it notified Parker that it would not "comply with our obligations to you under" the written contract. In the same letter, with the professed purpose "to avoid any damage to you," Fox instead offered to employ Parker as the leading actress in another movie, tentatively entitled *Big Country, Big Man*. The compensation offered was identical. Unlike *Bloomer Girl,* however, which was to have been a musical production, *Big Country* was to be a dramatic "western type" movie. *Bloomer Girl* was to have been filmed in California;

Big Country was to be produced in Australia. Certain other terms of the substitute contract varied from those of the original. Parker was given one week within which to accept. She did not, and the offer lapsed. Parker then filed suit against Fox for recovery of the agreed-on guaranteed compensation. Will she prevail?

9. Richmond Medical Supply (RMS) occupied commercial space that it leased from Clifton. When the lease was renewed, the parties included an addendum that required Clifton to make certain repairs, including "replacement and make in good working order the rear overhead door on or before the commencement of this lease, August 1, 1983." RMS continued in possession of the property even though Clifton failed to repair or replace the door. On November 8, 1983, thieves broke into the leased property by knocking out a wooden panel in the overhead door and removed cases, equipment, and inventory valued by RMS at $60,000, none of which was ever recovered. RMS brought an action for breach of contract, alleging that its loss was the direct consequence of Clifton's breach of his express promise to replace the door. Will Clifton be held liable for this loss?

10. 🎞 *Video Case.* See "Roof Repair." Roofer had a contract to repair the roof on the Seaside Hotel. After the formation of the contract, however, extensive flood damage caused the hotel to be condemned. Are the parties' duties under the contract discharged?

See also "Sour Grapes" and "California Dreaming."

SALES

FORMATION AND TERMS OF SALES CONTRACTS

INTRODUCTION

In Part 3, Contracts, we introduced the common law rules that govern the creation and performance of contracts generally. Throughout much of history, special rules, known as the law merchant, *were developed to control mercantile transactions in goods. Because transactions in goods commonly involve buyers and sellers located in different states—and even different countries—a common body of law to control these transactions can facilitate the smooth flow of commerce. To address this need, a Uniform Sales Act was drafted in the early 1900s and adopted by about two thirds of the states. Subsequently, the Uniform Commercial Code (UCC or Code) was prepared to simplify and modernize the rules of law governing commercial transactions.*

This chapter reviews some Code rules that govern the formation of sales contracts previously discussed. It also covers some key terms in sales contracts, such as delivery terms, title, and risk of loss. Finally, it discusses the rules governing sales on trial, such as sales on approval and consignments.

SALE OF GOODS

The **sale of goods** is the transfer of ownership to tangible personal property in exchange for money, other goods, or the performance of services. The law of sales of goods is codified in Article 2 of the Uniform Commercial Code. While the law of sales is based on the fundamental principles of contract and personal property, it has been modified to accommodate current practices of merchants. In large measure, the Code discarded many technical requirements of earlier law that did not serve any useful purpose in the marketplace and replaced them with rules that are consistent with commercial expectations.

Article 2 of the Code applies only to *transactions in goods.* Thus, it does not cover contracts to provide services or to sell real property. However, some courts have applied the principles set out in the Code to such transactions. When a contract appears to call for the furnishing of both goods and services, a question may arise as to whether the Code applies. For example, the operator of a beauty parlor may use a commercial permanent solution intended to be used safely on humans that causes injury to a person's head. The injured person then might bring a lawsuit claiming that there was a breach of the Code's warranty of the suitability of the permanent solution. In such cases, the courts commonly assess whether the sale of goods is the *predominant* part of the transaction or merely an *incidental* part; where the sale of goods predominates, courts normally apply Article 2. The *Advent Systems Ltd. v. Unisys Corp.* case, which follows, illustrates the type of analysis courts use to determine whether a particular contract should be governed by the Code.

ADVENT SYSTEMS LTD. V. UNISYS CORP.
925 F.2d 670 (3rd Cir. 1991)

Advent Systems Ltd. is a British company engaged primarily in the production of software for computers. As a result of its research and development efforts, by 1986 the company had developed an electronic document management system (EDMS), a process for transforming engineering drawings and similar documents into a computer database. Unisys Corp. manufactures a variety of computers. Unisys decided to market the Advent system in the United States. In June 1987, Unisys and Advent signed several agreements whereby Advent agreed to provide the software and hardware making up the document systems to be sold by Unisys in the United States. Advent was also obligated to provide sales and marketing material and staff as well as technical personnel to work with Unisys employees in building and installing the document systems. The agreement was to continue for two years, subject to automatic renewal or termination on notice.

During the summer of 1987, Unisys attempted to sell the document system to Arco, a large oil company, but was unsuccessful. Although the Unisys-Advent relationship was satisfactory initially, it soon came to an end. Unisys, which was in the throes of restructuring, decided it would be better served by developing its own document system. Accordingly, in December 1987, Unisys told Advent that their arrangement had ended. Advent filed a complaint against Unisys alleging, among other things, breach of contract and fraud. One of the issues in the lawsuit was whether the relationship between Advent and Unisys was one for the sale of goods—and hence subject to the statute of frauds provisions of the Uniform Commercial Code. The district court ruled that the UCC did not apply because although goods were to be sold, the services aspect of the contract predominated. Unisys appealed a judgment against it of $4,550,000 on the breach of contract claim.

Weis, Circuit Judge The district court ruled that as a matter of law the arrangement between the two parties was not within the Uniform Commercial Code and, consequently, the statute of frauds was not applicable. As the district court appraised the transaction, provisions for services outweighed those for products and, consequently, the arrangement was not predominately one for the sale of goods.

The Code "applies to transactions in goods." Sec. 2–102. Goods are defined as "all things (including specially manufactured goods) which are moveable at the time of identification for sale." Sec. 2–105. The Pennsylvania courts have recognized that "goods" has a very expansive meaning under the UCC.

Our court has addressed computer package sales in other cases, but has not been required to consider whether the UCC applied to software per se.

Computer programs are the product of an intellectual process, but once implanted in a medium are widely distributed to computer owners. An analogy can be drawn to a compact disc recording of an orchestral rendition. The music is produced by the artistry of musicians and in itself is not a "good," but when transferred to a laser-readable disc becomes a readily merchantable commodity. Similarly, when a professor delivers a lecture, it is not a good, but when transcribed as a book it becomes a good.

That a computer program may be copyrightable as intellectual property does not alter the fact that when in the form of a floppy disc or other medium, the program is tangible, moveable and available in the marketplace. The fact that some programs may be tailored for specific purposes need not alter their status as "goods" because the Code definition includes "specially manufactured goods."

Applying the UCC to computer software offers substantial benefits to litigants and the courts. The Code offers a uniform body of law on a wide range of questions likely to arise in computer software disputes: implied warranties, consequential damages, disclaimers of liability, the statute of limitations, to name a few.

The importance of software to the commercial world and the advantages to be gained by the uniformity in the UCC are strong policy arguments favoring inclusion. The contrary arguments are not persuasive, and we hold that software is a "good" within the definition in the Code.

The relationship at issue here is a typical mixed goods and services arrangement. The services are not substantially different from those generally accompanying package sales of hardware and software.

Although determining the applicability of the UCC to a contract by examining the predominance of goods or services has been criticized, we see no reason to depart from the practice here. As we pointed out in *De Flippo v. Ford Motor Co.,* segregating goods from non-goods and insisting that the Statute of Frauds apply only to a portion of the contract would be to make the contract divisible and impossible of performance within the intention of the parties.

We consider the purpose or essence of the contract. Comparing the relative costs of the materials supplied with the costs of the labor may be helpful in this analyis, but not dispositive. In this case the contract's main objective was to transfer "products." The specific provisions for training of Unisys personnel by Advent were but a small part of the parties' contemplated relationship.

The compensation structure of the agreement also focuses on "goods." The projected sales figures introduced during the trial demonstrate that in the contemplation of the parties the sale of goods clearly predominated.

We are persuaded that the transaction at issue here was within the scope of the Uniform Commercial Code.

Judgment in favor of Advent reversed.

Thus, the first question you should ask when faced with a contracts problem is: Is this a contract for the sale of goods? If it is not, then the principles of common law that were discussed in Part 3, Contracts, apply. If the contract is one for the sale of goods, then the Code applies. This analysis is illustrated in Figure 1.

LEASES

A lease of goods is a transfer of the right to possess and use goods belonging to another. Although the rights of one who leases goods (a lessee) do not constitute ownership of the goods, leasing is mentioned here because it is becoming an increasingly important way of acquiring the use of many kinds of goods, from automobiles to farm equipment. In some states, Article 2 and Article 9 of the UCC are applied to such leases by analogy. However, rules contained in these articles sometimes are inadequate to resolve special problems presented by leasing. For this reason, a new article of the UCC dealing exclusively with leases of goods, Article 2A, was written in 1987 and presented to state legislatures for possible adoption. Forty states have adopted Article 2A as of the time of this writing. Because of space limitations, this textbook does not cover Article 2A in detail.

MERCHANTS

Many of the Code's provisions apply only to **merchants** or to transactions between merchants.[1] In addition, the Code sets a higher standard of conduct for merchants because persons who regularly deal in goods are expected to be familiar with the practices of that trade and with commercial law. Ordinary consumers and nonmerchants frequently have little knowledge of or experience in these matters.

---

[1]Under the Code, a "merchant" is defined as a "person who deals in goods of the kind or otherwise by his occupation holds himself out as having knowledge or skill peculiar to the practices or goods involved in the transaction or to whom such knowledge or skill may be attributed by his employment of an agent or broker or other intermediary who by his occupation holds himself out as having such knowledge or skill" [2–104(1)].

FIGURE 1   Choice of Law

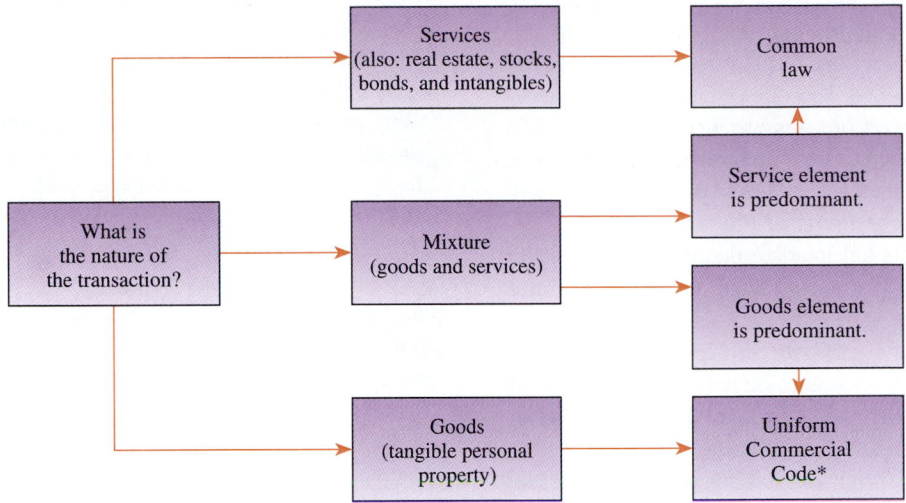

*If there is no specific Uniform Commercial Code provision governing the transaction, use the common law.

Code Requirements

The Code requires that parties to sales contracts act in good faith and in a commercially reasonable manner. Further, when a contract contains an unfair or unconscionable clause, or the contract as a whole is unconscionable, the courts have the right to refuse to enforce the unconscionable clause or contract [2–302].[2] The Code's treatment of unconscionability is discussed in detail in Chapter 15, Illegality.

A number of the Code provisions concerning the sale of goods were discussed in the chapters on Contracts. The following is a list of some of the important provisions discussed earlier, together with the section of the Code and the chapters in the text where the discussion can be found.

1. *Firm offers.* Under the Code, an offer in writing by a merchant that gives assurance that the offer will be held open is not revocable for lack of consideration during the time stated, or for a reasonable time if no time is stated, up to a period of three months [2–205]. (See Chapter 10, The Agreement: Offer.)

2. *Formation.* Under the Code, a contract for the sale of goods may be made in any manner that shows that the parties reached agreement, even though no particular moment can be pointed to as the time when the contract was made. Where the parties intended to make a contract but left one or more terms open, the contract is valid despite the lack of definiteness so long as the court has a basis for giving a remedy [2–204]. (See Chapter 10.)

3. *Additional terms in acceptances.* The Code states that an expression of acceptance or written confirmation sent within a reasonable time operates as an acceptance even if it states terms additional to or different from those offered, unless acceptance is expressly conditional on assent to the additional or different terms [2–207]. (See Chapter 11, The Agreement: Acceptance.)

4. *Statute of frauds.* The statute of frauds in the Code applies to the sale of goods at a price of $500 or more. The Code makes special exceptions for written confirmations between merchants, part payment or part delivery, admissions in legal proceedings, and specially manufactured goods [2–201]. (See Chapter 16, Writing.)

---

[2]The numbers in brackets refer to sections of the Uniform Commercial Code.

TERMS OF THE CONTRACT

General Terms

Within broad limits, the parties to a contract to sell goods may include any terms on which they agree. Many practices have become common in the everyday transactions of business, and under the Code, if a particular matter is not covered specifically in a contract or is unclear, common trade practices are used to fill out the terms of the contract.

The Code sets out in some detail the rights of the parties when they use certain terms, and those meanings apply unless the parties agree otherwise. For example, if a contract includes an open-price clause where the price is to be determined later, or if a contract is silent about price, the price is what would be considered *reasonable* at the time of delivery. If the price is to be fixed by either the buyer or the seller, that person must act in *good faith* in setting the price. However, if it is clear from their negotiations that the parties do not intend to be bound unless they agree on a price, and the price is not agreed on or fixed, no contract results [2–305].

Quantity Terms

In some cases, the parties may state the quantity of goods covered by their sales contract in an indefinite way. Contracts that obligate a buyer to purchase a seller's *output* of a certain item or all of the buyer's *requirements* of a certain item are commonly encountered. These contracts caused frequent problems under the common law because of the indefiniteness of the parties' obligations. If the seller decided to double its output, did the buyer have to accept the entire amount? If the market price of the item soared much higher than the contract price, could the buyer double or triple its demands?

Output and Needs Contracts

In an "output" contract, one party is bound to sell its entire output of particular goods and the other party is bound to buy that output. In a "needs" or "requirements" contract, the quantity of goods is based on the needs of the buyer. In determining the quantity of goods to be produced or taken pursuant to an output or needs contract, the rule of *good faith* applies. Thus, the buyer may not demand or take a quantity that is unreasonably disproportionate to any stated estimate in the contract or to "normal" prior output or requirements if no estimate is stated [2–306(2)]. Similarly, the seller may not insist that the buyer take more than the estimate or prior output or requirements.

For example, Farmer contracts to supply Sam's Grocery with all of the apples Sam's requires for sale to customers. If Sam's has sold between 500 and 700 bushels of apples a year over the past 10 years, Sam could not require Farmer to deliver 5,000 bushels of apples to Sam's one year because Sam had an unusual demand for them. Similarly, it would not be reasonable for Sam to say he would take only 10 bushels in one year.

Exclusive Dealing Contracts

The Code takes a similar approach to *exclusive dealing contracts.* Under the common law, these contracts were sources of difficulty due to the indefinite nature of the parties' duties. Did the dealer have to make any effort to sell the manufacturer's products, and did the manufacturer have any duty to supply the dealer? The Code provides that unless the parties make a different agreement, sellers have an obligation to use their best efforts to supply the goods to the buyer and buyers have obligations to use their best efforts to promote their sale [2–306(2)].

Time for Performance

If no time for performance is stated in the sales contract, the Code implies a *reasonable time* for performance. If a contract requires successive performances over an indefinite period of time, the contract is valid for a reasonable time; however, either party can terminate it at any time upon the giving of reasonable notice unless the parties have agreed otherwise as to termination [2–309]. For example, Farmer Jack agrees to sell his entire output of apples each fall to a cannery at the then-current market price. If the contract does not contain a provision spelling out how and when the parties may terminate the contract, Farmer Jack can terminate it if he gives the cannery a reasonable time to make arrangements to acquire apples from someone else.

Delivery Terms

Sales contracts customarily use standardized shipping terms that have specific commercial meanings. The terms **FOB (free on board)** and **FAS (free alongside ship)** are basic delivery terms. If the delivery term of the contract is FOB or FAS (and the contract also states the place at which the goods originate in connection with the FOB or FAS term), the seller must deliver to the carrier goods that (1) *conform to the contract* and (2) *are properly prepared for shipment* to the buyer. The seller also must make a *reasonable contract for transportation of the goods* on behalf of the buyer. Under such delivery terms, the goods are at the buyer's risk during transit and the buyer must pay the shipping charges. If the shipping term is *FOB destination,* the seller must deliver the goods to the designated destination and bears risk and expense during transit. These terms will be discussed in more detail later in this chapter.

TITLE

Passage of Title

Title to goods cannot pass from the seller to the buyer until the goods are identified to the contract [2–401(1)]. For example, if Seller agrees to sell Buyer 50 chairs and Seller has 500 chairs in his warehouse, title to 50 chairs will not pass from Seller to Buyer until Seller selects the 50 chairs that Buyer has purchased and identifies them as the chairs sold to Buyer.

The parties may agree between themselves when title to the goods will pass from the seller to the buyer. If there is no agreement, then the general rule is that the *title to the goods passes to the buyer when the seller completes his obligations as to delivery of the goods:*

1. If the contract requires the seller to "ship" the goods to the buyer, then title passes to the buyer when the seller delivers conforming goods to the carrier.

2. If the contract requires the seller to "deliver" the goods to the buyer, title does not pass to the buyer until the goods are delivered and tendered to the buyer.

3. If delivery is to be made without moving the goods, then title passes at the time and place of contracting. An exception is made if title to the goods is represented by a document of title such as a warehouse receipt; then, title passes when the document of title is delivered to the buyer.

4. If the buyer rejects goods tendered to him, title reverts to the seller [2–401(4)].

Importance of Title

Common law determined most of the problems relating to risks, insurable interests in goods, remedies, and similar rights and liabilities on the basis of who was the technical title owner at the particular moment the right or liability arose. The Code, however, determines the rights of the seller and buyer and of third persons irrespective of the technicality of who has the title, unless the provision of the Code expressly refers to title.

Determination of who has title to the goods is important in instances in which the rights of the seller's or the buyer's creditors in the goods are an issue. The *Russell v. Transamerica Insurance Co.* case, which follows, illustrates another instance in which determination of the title holder may be important—whether the seller's insurance policy covers a particular loss.

RUSSELL V. TRANSAMERICA INSURANCE CO.
322 N.W.2d 178 (Mich. Ct. App. 1982)

Russell, a full-service boat dealer and marine equipment service company, entered into an agreement to sell a 19-foot Kinsvater boat to Robert Clouser for $8,500. Pursuant to the agreement, Clouser made a down payment of $1,700, with the balance of the purchase price to be paid when he took possession of the boat. Under the agreement, Russell was to retain possession of the boat in order to transfer an engine and drive train from another boat. Upon the completion of these alterations, Clouser was to take delivery of the boat at Russell's marina.

While the boat was being tested by employees of Russell, prior to delivery to Clouser, it hit a seawall and was destroyed. Transamerica Insurance insured Russell under a policy that excluded watercraft hazards, except for damage to any watercraft under 26 feet in length not owned by Russell. Transamerica refused to honor a claim from Russell for the damage to Clouser's boat, contending that the policy excluded damage because Russell owned the boat at the time of the accident. Russell then brought suit against Transamerica Insurance. The trial court ruled in favor of Transamerica Insurance, and Russell appealed.

Lambros, Judge   The trial court, granting summary judgment in favor of Transamerica, stated: The facts reflect that the boat was in possession of Russell on August 4, 1977. Robert Clouser could not have taken delivery of the boat on the day in question. Under § 2–401(2), therefore, title had not passed to Clouser. . . . Effectively speaking, the risk of loss was, on August 4, 1977, on Russell's shoulders.

Under subsection (3)(b) of § 2–401, if delivery is to be made without moving the goods and no documents of title are involved, title passes at the time of contracting if the goods are already identified at the time of contracting. We note that goods need not be in a deliverable state to be identified to the contract.

In the instant case, because the 19-foot Kinsvater boat had been identified at the time the parties contracted for sale, because no documents of title were to be delivered by the sellers, there being no Michigan requirement for certificates of title for boats at that time, and because delivery of the boat was to be effected without its being moved, title passed to the buyer at the time of contracting under § 2–401(3)(b). The fact that the boat was not outfitted with all the equipment specified in the contract did not prevent its identification to the contract nor did it prevent title from passing at that time.

In addition, we find that the trial court erred in its decision in equating risk of loss with title. Under § 2–509, risk of loss passes to the buyer on his receipt of the goods or on tender of delivery by the seller. Risk of loss, then, does not necessarily follow title. In the instant case, because Russell retained possession of the boat after title passed, he bore the risk of loss. Title in the buyer, however, triggered the policy exception to the watercraft hazard exclusion regardless of where risk of loss lay.

We hold that the trial court erred in granting summary judgment in favor of Transamerica because title in the boat at the time of the accident was in one other than Russell and the boat was, thus, covered under Russell's policy.

Judgment reversed in favor of Russell.

TITLE AND THIRD PARTIES

Obtaining Good Title

A fundamental rule of property law is that a buyer cannot receive better title to goods than the seller had. If Thief steals a television set from Adler and sells it to Brown, Brown does not get good title to the set, because Thief had no title to it. Adler would have the right to recover the set from Brown. Similarly, if Brown sold the set to Carroll, Carroll could get no better title to it than Brown had. Adler would have the right to recover the set from Carroll.

The Code provides several exceptions to the general rule that a buyer cannot get better title to goods than his seller had. The most important exceptions include the following: (1) a person who has a voidable title to goods can pass good title to a bona fide purchaser for value; (2) a person who buys goods in the regular course of a retailer's business takes free of any interests in the goods that the retailer has given to others; and (3) a person who buys goods in the ordinary course of a dealer's business takes free of any claim of a person who entrusted those goods to the dealer (such as a person who left his watch with a jeweler for repair).

Transfers of Voidable Title

A seller who has a **voidable title** has the power to pass good title to a *good faith purchaser for value* [2–403(1)]. A seller has a voidable title to goods if he has obtained his title through fraudulent representations. For example, a person would have a voidable title if he obtained goods by impersonating another person or by paying for them with a bad check or if he obtained goods without paying the agreed purchase price when it was agreed that the transaction was to be a cash sale. Under the Code, **good faith** means "honesty in fact in the conduct or transaction concerned" [1–201(19)] and a buyer has given **value** if he has given any consideration sufficient to support a simple contract [1–201(44)].

For example, Jones goes to the ABC Appliance Store, convinces the clerk that he is really Clark, who is a good customer of ABC, and leaves with a stereo charged to Clark's account. If Jones sells the stereo to Davis, who gives Jones value for it and has no knowledge of the fraud that Jones perpetrated on ABC, Davis gets good title to the stereo. ABC cannot recover the stereo from Davis. Instead, ABC must look for Jones, the person who deceived it. In this situation, both ABC and Davis were innocent of wrongdoing, but the law considers Davis to be the more worthy of its protection for two reasons: (1) because ABC was in a better position to have prevented the wrongdoing by Jones and (2) because Davis bought the goods in good faith and for value. The Code would reach the same result if Jones had given ABC a check that later bounced and then sold the stereo to Davis, who was a good faith purchaser for value. Davis would have good title to the stereo, and ABC would have to pursue its right against Jones on the bounced check.

The *Charles Evans BMW, Inc. v. Williams* case, which follows, illustrates the importance of determining the identity and creditworthiness of a person to whom one sells goods. It also shows the importance of a subsequent buyer qualifying as a good faith purchaser for value so that it is able to get good title from a seller who had only a voidable title.

CHARLES EVANS BMW, INC. V. WILLIAMS

395 S.E.2d 650 (Ga. Ct. App. 1990)

Williams agreed to sell his car to an individual named Hodge and accepted a cashier's check from Hodge as payment. Without indicating on the certificate of title that Hodge was the purchaser, Williams signed the title in his capacity as seller and delivered the document and the car to Hodge. The next day, Hodge, representing himself to be Williams, offered to sell the car to Charles Evans BMW. When a price was agreed on, Hodge presented the certificate of title containing Williams's signature as seller and received a check that named Williams as payee. Hodge cashed the check after he produced as identification a Kentucky driver's license bearing the same number as that issued to Williams. After the car had been purchased by Evans BMW from Hodge, Williams learned that the cashier's check he had accepted from Hodge was a forgery. By the time that Evans BMW became aware of the fact that it had not actually purchased the car from Williams, but rather from Hodge representing himself to be Williams, it had already resold the car.

At the direction of the local police authorities, the car and the certificate of title were returned to Evans BMW and it refunded the purchase price. Subsequently, the police directed Evans BMW to return the car to Williams. However, Evans BMW retained the certificate of title and then brought a lawsuit against Williams to determine who was the owner of the automobile. The trial court found in favor of Williams and Evans BMW appealed.

Carley, Chief Judge Section 2–403(1) provides in relevant part, that "[a] purchaser of goods acquires all title which his transferor had or had power to transfer. . . . A person with voidable title has power to transfer a good title to a good faith purchaser for value. When goods have been *delivered* *under a transaction of purchase* the purchaser has such power even though: (a) The transferor was deceived as to the identity of the purchaser, or (b) The delivery was in exchange for a check which was later dishonored; or . . . (d) The delivery was procured through fraud punishable as larcenous under the criminal law." (Emphasis supplied.)

Williams was not deprived of his car by a physical taking of which he was unaware. The undisputed evidence shows that Williams *delivered his car under a transaction of purchase* procured by the perpetration of a criminal fraud whereby he was deceived as to the identity of the purchaser who gave him a check that was later dishonored. In these circumstances, Williams conveyed *voidable title* to Hodge and Hodge, having voidable rather than void title, had the power to transfer *good title* to a good faith purchaser for value. Section 2–403(1) empowers a purchaser with a voidable title to confer good title upon a good faith purchaser for value where the good[s] were procured through fraud punishable as larcenous under the criminal law. The distinction between *theft* and *fraud* in this context is found in the statutory definitions of "delivery" and "purchase." Delivery concerns a voluntary transfer of possession and purchase refers to a voluntary transaction creating an interest in property. In the present case, Williams voluntarily relinquished possession to Hodge. As one commentator has pointed out, "a thief who wrongfully takes goods is not a purchaser . . . but a swindler who fraudulently induces the victim to voluntarily deliver them is a purchaser."

It follows that if Evans BMW was a good faith purchaser for value, it acquired good title to the car from Hodge. " 'Good faith' means honesty in fact in the conduct or transaction concerned." Sec. 1–201(19). " 'Good faith' in the case of a merchant

means honesty in fact and the observance of reasonable commercial standards of fair dealing in the trade." Sec. 2–103(1)(b). There is ample evidence of Evans BMW's "good faith" in its transaction with Hodge. Evans BMW's agent who actually negotiated the purchase neither knew nor had reason to know that Hodge's representations were false. When the agent noticed an error on the registration form, Hodge was told that he would have to obtain a corrected registration from the county. When Hodge left and returned with the corrected form, this gave additional credence to his representations that he was Williams and the owner of the car. Hodge also presented a certificate of title which bore William's unforged signature as seller. The price that Evans BMW agreed to pay for the car was not nominal. Evans BMW gave Hodge a check made out to Williams and Hodge was successful in cashing that check by using a driver's license bearing the same number of the license that had actually been issued to Williams. Thus, Hodge's scheme to impersonate Williams not only duped Evans BMW, but was also successful against the county and the bank.

In opposition, there was no evidence to show that, in negotiating and consummating the purchase from Hodge, Evans had been less than honest or had failed to observe reasonable commercial standards of fair dealing. Therefore, on the undisputed evidence of record, Evans BMW was, as a matter of law, a good faith purchaser for value when it bought the car from Hodge. It retains that good title as against Williams who conveyed voidable title to Hodge.

Judgment reversed in favor of Charles Evans BMW.

Buyers in the Ordinary Course of Business

A person who buys goods in the ordinary course of business from a person dealing in goods of that type takes free of any security interest in the goods given by his seller to another person [9–307(1)]. A **buyer in ordinary course** is a person who in good faith, and without knowledge that the sale to him is in violation of the ownership rights of a third party, buys goods in the ordinary course of business of a

person selling goods of that kind, other than a pawnbroker [1–201(9)].

For example, Brown Buick may borrow money from Bank in order to finance its inventory of new Buicks; in turn, Bank may take a security interest in the inventory to secure repayment of the loan. If Carter buys a new Buick from Brown Buick, he gets good title to the Buick free and clear of the Bank's security interest if he is a buyer in the ordinary course of business. The basic purposes of this exception are (1) to protect those who innocently buy from merchants and (2) to promote confidence in such commercial transactions. The exception also reflects the fact that the bank is more interested in the proceeds from the sale than in the inventory. Security interests and the rights of buyers in the ordinary course of business are discussed in more detail in Chapter 28, Security Interests in Personal Property.

Entrusting of Goods

A third exception to the general rule is that if an owner *entrusts* goods to a merchant who deals in goods of that kind, the merchant has the power to transfer all rights of the entruster to a buyer in the ordinary course of business [2–403(2)]. For example, Gail takes her watch to Jeweler, a retail jeweler, to have it repaired, and Jeweler sells the watch to Mary. Mary would acquire good title to the watch, and Gail would have to proceed against Jeweler for conversion of her watch. The purpose behind this rule is to protect commerce by giving confidence to buyers that they will get good title to the goods they buy from merchants in the ordinary course of business. However, a merchant-seller cannot pass good title to stolen goods even if the buyer is a buyer in the ordinary course of business. This is because the original owner did nothing to facilitate the transfer.

CONCEPT REVIEW

TITLE AND THIRD PARTIES

General Rule	A seller cannot pass better title to goods than he has.
Exceptions to General Rule	1. A person who has voidable title to goods can pass good title to a bona fide purchaser for value.
	2. A buyer in the ordinary course of a retailer's business takes free of any interests in the goods that the retailer has given to others.
	3. A person who buys goods in the ordinary course of a dealer's business takes free of any claims of a person who entrusted those goods to the dealer.

RISK OF LOSS

The transportation of goods from sellers to buyers can be a risky business. The carrier of the goods may lose, damage, or destroy them; floods, tornadoes, and other natural catastrophes may take their toll; thieves may steal all or part of the goods. If neither party is at fault for the loss, who should bear the risk? If the buyer has the risk when the goods are damaged or lost, the buyer is liable for the contract price. If the seller has the risk, he is liable for damages unless he can tender substitute performance.

The common law placed the risk on the party who had technical title at the time of the loss. The Code rejects this approach and provides specific rules governing risk of loss that are designed to provide certainty and to place the risk on the party best able to protect against loss and most likely to be insured against it. Risk of loss under the Code depends on the terms of the parties' agreement, on the moment the loss occurs, and on whether one of the parties was in breach of contract when the loss occurred.

Terms of the Agreement

The contracting parties, subject to the rule of good faith, may specify who has the risk of loss in their agreement [2–509(4)]. This they may do directly or by using certain commonly accepted shipping terms in their contract. In addition, the Code has certain general rules on risk of loss that amplify specific shipping terms and control risk of loss in cases where specific terms are not used [2–509].

Shipment Contracts

If the contract requires the seller to ship the goods by carrier but does not require their delivery to a specific destination, the risk passes to the buyer when the seller delivers the goods to the carrier [2–509(1)(a)]. Shipment contracts are considered to be the normal contract in which the contract requires the seller to send goods to the buyer but does not require the seller to guarantee delivery at a particular location.

The following are common shipping terms that create shipment contracts:

1. *FOB (free on board) point of origin.* This term calls for the seller to deliver the goods free of expense and at the seller's risk at the place *designated.* For example, a contract between a seller located in Chicago and a buyer in New York calls for delivery "FOB Chicago." The seller at his expense and at his risk must deliver the goods to a carrier in the place designated in the contract, namely Chicago, and arrange for their carriage to New York. Because the shipment term in this example is "FOB Chicago," the seller is not responsible for delivering the goods to a specific destination; for example, the buyer's place of business. If the term is "FOB vessel, car, or other vehicle," the seller must load the goods on board at his own risk and expense [2–319(1)].

2. *FAS (free alongside ship).* This term is common in maritime contracts and the contract normally specifies the name of a specific vessel and port—for example, "FAS Calgary [the ship], Chicago Port Authority." The seller must deliver the goods alongside the vessel *Calgary* at the Chicago Port Authority at his own risk and expense [2–319(2)].

3. *CIF (cost, insurance, and freight).* This term means that the price of the goods includes the cost of shipping and insuring them. The seller bears this expense and the risk of loading the goods [2–320].

4. *C & F.* This term is the same as CIF except that the seller is not obligated to insure the goods [2–320].

The *Morauer v. Deak & Co., Inc.* case, which follows, provides an example of the risk borne by a buyer in a shipment contract.

Morauer v. Deak & Co., Inc.
26 UCC Rep. 1142 (D.C. Super. Ct. 1979)

On March 12, 1975, Raymond Morauer contracted with Deak & Co., a dealer in foreign currency, to purchase for investment purposes several bags of silver coins and a quantity of gold coins. He paid for his purchase with personal checks totaling $35,000. After his checks had cleared, he came to Deak's place of business to take delivery. Morauer had a discussion with Deak's assistant manager about the District of Columbia tax on the sale of gold. Both parties agreed that in order to avoid the tax, an admittedly legal endeavor, Deak would ship all of Morauer's gold coins to his residence in suburban Maryland. There was no District of Columbia tax on silver coins, so Morauer took possession of them.

Deak placed the gold coins in two packages and, as authorized by Morauer, sent the packages to his house by registered mail, return receipt requested. Deak did not insure the packages with the U.S. Postal Service but instead, in accordance with its custom, relied on its own insurance contract with its insurer to cover any risk of loss. Only one package was received by Morauer; however, he did not open it and thus did not realize at the time that he had received only a portion of his gold coins. More than two years later, while making an inventory of his collection, Morauer discovered the problem and notified Deak. By that time, the post office had destroyed its records of the shipment and Deak's insurance coverage for that shipment had expired. Morauer then brought a lawsuit asking the value at their time of purchase of the gold coins that he had not received.

Smith, Judge The court must determine whether the risk of loss of the gold coins in question passed from the defendant Deak to Morauer upon Deak's delivery of the coins to the Post Office for shipment to Morauer. If so, then Deak is not liable to Morauer for the value of the lost shipment. If the risk of loss did not pass, however, then Deak is liable for the full value of the coins at time of purchase.

The case is governed by § 2–509(1) of the UCC, and the court must determine whether paragraph (a) or paragraph (b) of subsection (1) controls. If the contract was a so-called "shipment" contract, then the risk of loss passed to

Morauer, the buyer, on Deak's delivery to the carrier, § 2–509(1) (a), provided, however, that Deak also satisfied the UCC's requirements for a valid "shipment" contract, § 2–504. If, on the other hand, the contract called for delivery at a particular destination, then the risk of loss never passed to Morauer, because the goods were never delivered, and Morauer must prevail, § 2–509(1) (b).

The fact that the parties had agreed that Deak would ship the coins to Morauer's residence in Maryland is not dispositive of this controversy. A "ship to" term in a sales contract has no significance in determining whether the agreement is a "shipment" or "destination" contract. Moreover, there is a preference in the UCC for "shipment" contracts. The drafters of the UCC state the preference and give the reasons for it in the following manner:

For the purposes of subsections (2) and (3) there is omitted from this Article the rule under prior uniform legislation that a term requiring the seller to pay the freight or cost of transportation to the buyer is equivalent to an agreement by the seller to deliver to the buyer or at an agreed destination. This omission is with the specific intention of negating the rule, for *under this Article the "shipment" contract is regarded as the normal one and the "destination" contract as the variant type. The seller is not obligated to deliver at a named destination and bear the concurrent risk of loss until arrival, unless he has specifically agreed so to deliver or the commercial understanding of the terms used by the parties contemplates such delivery.* Uniform Commercial Code Comment No. 5; § 2–503.

Here we have an order and payment by Morauer in person to Deak with receipts signed by Kirsch, Deak's agent, indicating Morauer's home address and, in one instance, including the further instruction, "c/o Mrs. Geraldine Morauer." Morauer and Kirsch discussed delivery of the coins, and Morauer decided that to avoid payment of the District of Columbia sales tax, he would have them shipped to his residence. Deak mailed the gold coins in two packages, both of which were properly addressed, stamped and deposited at the United States Post Office. Deak also included the cost of postage as part of Morauer's total bill. Therefore, we hold that Deak was authorized by the contract to ship the gold coins to Morauer by carrier, and that the risk of loss passed from Deak to Morauer on delivery of the packages of coins to the Post Office.

Although the court's finding that the parties were operating under a "shipment" contract puts the risk of loss on Morauer from the time of Deak's delivery to the authorized carrier, there remains the question whether defendant Deak met all the statutory requirements of "shipment" contracts under the applicable UCC section 2–504. That section states:

Where the seller is required or authorized to send the goods to the buyer and the contract does not require him to deliver them at a particular destination, then unless otherwise agreed he must

(a) put the goods in the possession of such a carrier and make such a contract for their transportation as may be reasonable having regard to the nature of the goods and other circumstances of the case; and

(b) obtain and promptly deliver or tender in due form any document necessary to enable the buyer to obtain possession of the goods or otherwise required by the agreement or by usage of trade; and

(c) promptly notify the buyer of the shipment.

Failure to notify the buyer under paragraph (c) or to make a proper contract under paragraph (a) is a ground for rejection only if material delay or loss ensues.

In the case now before this court Deak followed its regular practice of insuring the shipments with its own insurance company, properly addressed each package and sent both by first-class, registered mail, with a return receipt requested. Deak therefore made all arrangements with the carrier, the United States Postal Service, as were "reasonable having regard to the nature of the goods and other circumstances of the case." § 2–504(a). Deak had no obligation under paragraph (b) of § 2–504, insofar as there were no documents necessary to enable Morauer to obtain possession of the goods, and none "otherwise required by the agreement or by usage of trade." And finally, Deak was in compliance with § 2–504(c) in that Kirsch notified Morauer of the mailing of the gold coins when Morauer went to Deak's office to take delivery personally of the silver coins he had also purchased.

Judgment in favor of Deak.

Destination Contracts

If the contract requires the seller to deliver the goods to a specific destination, the seller bears the risk and expense of delivery to that destination [2–509(1)(b)]. The following are commonly used shipping terms that create destination contracts:

1. *FOB destination.* An FOB term coupled with the place of destination of the goods puts the expense and risk of delivering the goods to that destination on the seller [2–319(1)(b)]. For example, a contract between a seller in Chicago and a buyer in Phoenix might call for shipment FOB Phoenix. The seller must ship the goods to Phoenix at her own expense, and she also retains the risk of delivery of the goods to Phoenix.

2. *Ex-ship.* This term does not specify a particular ship, but it places the expense and risk on the seller until the goods are unloaded from whatever ship is used [2–322].

3. *No arrival, no sale.* This term places the expense and risk during shipment on the seller. If the goods fail to arrive through no fault of the seller, the seller has no further liability to the buyer [2–324]—that is, the buyer cannot sue for breach for nondelivery.

For example, a Chicago-based seller contracts to sell a quantity of shirts to a buyer FOB Phoenix, the buyer's place of business. The shirts are destroyed en route when the truck carrying the shirts is involved in an accident. The risk of the loss of the shirts is on the seller, and the buyer is not obligated to pay for them. The seller may have the right to recover from the trucking company, but between the seller and the buyer, the seller has the risk of loss. If the contract had called for delivery FOB the seller's manufacturing plant, then the risk of loss would have been on the buyer. The buyer would have had to pay for the shirts and then pursue any claims that he had against the trucking company.

Goods in the Possession of Third Parties

If the goods are in the possession of a bailee and are to be delivered without being moved, the risk of loss passes to the buyer upon delivery to him of a *negotiable document of title* for the goods; if no negotiable document of title has been used, the risk of loss passes when the bailee indicates to the buyer that the buyer has the *right to the possession of the goods* [2–509(2)]. For example, if Farmer sells Miller a quantity of grain currently stored at Grain Elevator, the risk of loss of the grain will shift from Farmer to Miller (1) when a negotiable warehouse receipt for the grain is delivered to Miller or (2) when Grain Elevator notifies Miller that it is holding the grain for Miller.

Risk Generally

If the transaction does not fall within the situations discussed above, the risk of loss passes to the buyer upon *receipt* of the goods if the seller is a merchant; if the seller is not a merchant, then the risk of loss passes to the buyer upon the *tender of delivery* of the goods to the buyer [2–509(3)]. If Jones bought a television set from ABC Appliance on Monday, intending to pick it up on Thursday, and the set was stolen on Wednesday, the risk of loss remained with ABC. However, if Jones had purchased the set from his next-door neighbor and could have taken delivery of the set on Monday (i.e., delivery was tendered then), the risk of loss was Jones's.

Effect of Breach on Risk of Loss

When a seller tenders goods that do not conform to the contract and the buyer has the right to reject the goods, the risk of loss remains with the seller until any defect is cured or until the buyer accepts the goods [2–510(1)]. Where the buyer rightfully revokes his acceptance of goods, the risk of loss is with the seller to the extent that any loss is not covered by the buyer's insurance [2–510(2)]. This rule gives the seller the benefit of any insurance carried by the buyer.

For example, if Adler bought a new Buick from Brown Buick that he later returned to Brown because of serious defects in it and if through no fault of Adler's the automobile was damaged while in his possession, then the risk of loss would be with Brown. However, if Adler had insurance on the automobile covering the damage to it and recovered from the insurance company, Adler would have to turn the insurance proceeds over to Brown or use them to fix the car before returning it to Brown.

When a buyer repudiates a contract for goods and those goods have already been set aside by the seller, the risk of loss stays with the buyer for a commercially reasonable time after the repudiation if the seller's insurance is not sufficient to cover any loss. [2–510(3)]. Suppose Cannery contracts to buy Farmer's entire crop of peaches. Farmer picks the peaches, crates them, tenders delivery to Cannery, and stores them in his barn. Cannery then tells Farmer that it does not intend to honor the contract. Shortly thereafter, but before Farmer has a chance to find another buyer, the peaches are spoiled by a fire. If Farmer's insurance covers only part of the loss, Cannery must bear the rest of the loss.

Insurable Interest

The Code recognizes the general commercial practice of insuring risks. A buyer may protect his interest in goods that are the subject matter of a sales contract before he actually obtains title. The buyer obtains an insurable interest in existing goods when they are identified as the goods covered by the contract even though they are in fact nonconforming. The seller retains an insurable interest in goods so long as he has either title or a security interest in them [2–501(2)]. The importance of the seller's retention of an insurable interest in goods he has sold is illustrated in the *Russell v. Transamerica Insurance Co.* case, which appeared earlier in this chapter.

CONCEPT REVIEW

Risk of Loss

The point at which the risk of loss or damage to goods identified to a contract passes to the buyer is as follows:

1. If there is an agreement between the parties, the risk of loss passes to the buyer at the time they have agreed to.
2. If the contract requires the seller to ship the goods by carrier but does not require that the seller guarantee their delivery to a specific destination (shipment contract), the risk of loss passes to the buyer when the seller has delivered the goods to the carrier and made an appropriate contract for their carriage.
3. If the contract requires the seller to guarantee delivery of the goods to a specific destination (destination contract), the risk of loss passes to the buyer when the seller delivers the goods to the designated destination.
4. If the goods are in the hands of a third person and the contract calls for delivery without moving the goods, the risk of loss passes to the buyer when the buyer has the power to take possession of the goods—for example, when he receives a document of title.
5. In any situation other than those noted above where the seller is a merchant, the risk of loss passes to the buyer on his receipt of the goods.
6. In any situation other than those noted above where the seller is not a merchant, the risk of loss passes to the buyer on the tender of delivery to the buyer by the seller.
7. When a seller tenders goods that the buyer lawfully could reject because they do not conform to the contract description, the risk of loss stays on the seller until the defect is cured or the buyer accepts them.
8. When a buyer rightfully revokes acceptance of goods, the risk of loss is on the seller from the beginning to the extent it is not covered by the buyer's insurance.
9. If a buyer repudiates a contract for identified, conforming goods before risk of loss has passed to the buyer, the buyer is liable for a commercially reasonable time for any loss or damage to the goods that is not covered by the seller's insurance.

SALES ON TRIAL

A common commercial practice is for a seller of goods to entrust possession of goods to a buyer to either give the buyer an opportunity to decide whether or not to buy them or to try to resell them to a third person. The entrusting may be known as a **sale on approval,** a **sale or return,** or a **consignment,** depending on the terms of the entrusting. Occasionally, the goods may be damaged, destroyed, or stolen, or the creditors of the buyer may try to claim them. On such occasions, the form of the entrusting will determine whether the buyer or the seller had the risk of loss and whether the buyer's creditors successfully can claim the goods.

Sale on Approval

In a sale on approval, the goods are delivered to the buyer with an understanding that he may use or test them for the purpose of determining whether he wishes to buy them [2–326(1)(a)]. In a sale on approval, neither the risk of loss nor title to the goods passes to the buyer until he accepts the goods. The buyer has the right to use the goods in any manner consistent with the purpose of the trial, but any unwarranted exercise of ownership over the goods is considered to be an acceptance of the goods. Similarly, if the buyer fails to notify the seller of his election to return the goods, he is considered to have accepted them [2–327]. For example, if Dealer agrees to let Hughes take a new automobile home to drive for a day to see whether she wants to buy it and Hughes takes the car on a two-week vacation trip, Hughes will be considered to have accepted the automobile because she used it in a manner beyond that contemplated by the trial and as if she were its owner. If Hughes had driven the automobile for a day, decided not to buy it, and parked it in her driveway for two weeks without telling Dealer of her intention to return it, Hughes would also be deemed to have accepted the automobile.

Once the buyer has notified the seller of his election to return the goods, the return of the goods is at the seller's expense and risk. Because the title and risk of loss of goods delivered on a sale on approval remain with the seller, goods held on approval are not subject to the claims of the buyer's creditors until the buyer accepts them [2–326].

Sale or Return

In a sale or return, the seller delivers goods to a buyer for resale with the understanding that the buyer has the right to return them [2–326(1)(b)]. Under a sale or return, the title and risk of loss are with the buyer. While the goods are in the buyer's possession, they are subject to the claims of his creditors [2–326 and 2–327]. For example, if Publisher delivers some paperbacks to Bookstore on the understanding that Bookstore may return any of the paperbacks that remain unsold at the end of six months, the transaction is a sale or return. If Bookstore is destroyed by a fire, the risk of loss of the paperbacks was Bookstore's and it is responsible to Publisher for the purchase price. Similarly, if Bookstore becomes insolvent and is declared a bankrupt, the paperbacks will be considered part of the bankruptcy estate. If the buyer elects to return goods held on a sale or return basis, the return is at the buyer's risk and expense.

Sale on Consignment

Sometimes, goods are delivered to a merchant on consignment. If the merchant to whom goods are consigned maintains a place of business dealing in goods of that kind under a name other than that of the person consigning the goods, then the consignor must take certain steps to protect his interest in the goods or they will be subject to the claims of the merchant's creditors. The consignor must (1) make sure that a sign indicating the consignor's interest is prominently posted at the place of business, or (2) make sure that the merchant's creditors know that he is generally in the business of selling goods owned by others, or (3) comply with the filing provisions of Article 9 of the Code—Secured Transactions.

For example, Jones operates a retail music store under the name of City Music Store. Baldwin Piano Company delivers some pianos to Jones on consignment. If no notices are posted indicating Baldwin's interest in the pianos, if Jones is not generally known to be selling from a consigned inventory, and if Baldwin does not file its interest with the recording office pursuant to Article 9 of the Code, then the goods are subject to the claims of Jones's creditors. This is crucial to Baldwin because it may have intended to retain title. However, the Code treats a consignment to a person doing business under a name other than that of the consignor as a "sale or return" [2–326(3)]. If Jones did business as the Baldwin Piano Company, Baldwin's interest would be protected from the claims of Jones's creditors without the need for Baldwin to post a sign or to file under Article 9.

The case that follows, *In Re Auclair*, illustrates the risks borne by a person who makes goods available on a sale or return or consignment basis.

In Re Auclair
McGregor v. Jackson
131 BR 185 (Bankr. M.D. Ala. 1991)

Edd and Diane Auclair maintained a place of business in Covington County, Alabama, where they operated a gun shop and convenience store named Heath Grocery and Final Chapter Firearms. In November 1989, Luke Jackson delivered about 70 firearms to the Auclairs to sell on consignment. The consignment agreement provided as follows:

I, Edd Auclair, have received a number of guns, of which a list will be attached and I will sign. As I sell a gun I will pay James E. "Luke" Jackson or Betty King, with them giving me a receipt for that particular gun. If something should happen to Luke Jackson the guns are to be returned to Betty King or at that time Betty King and Edd Auclair can enter into an agreement. If something should happen to Edd Auclair, Diane agrees to return all guns that have not been paid for to Luke Jackson or Betty King and pay for any that has [sic] been sold.

The agreement was signed by Jackson, King, and the Auclairs.

On June 28, 1990, the Auclairs filed a petition in bankruptcy under Chapter 11 of the Bankruptcy Act. Shortly thereafter, Jackson removed the firearms he had consigned from the Auclairs' store. The bankruptcy trustee (McGregor) representing the Auclairs' creditors claimed that the firearms were the property of the bankruptcy estate.

Gordon, Bankruptcy Judge   Both parties agree that Section 2–326(3) regarding consignments applies to the facts of this case. Under that subsection, goods delivered on consignment are "deemed to be on sale or return." Thus, by deeming the consignee a *purchaser* of the goods, the consignor is precluded from asserting an ownership claim to the goods vis-a-vis the consignee's creditors.

Applying that section to the instant case, Jackson is precluded from asserting his ownership of the firearms vis-a-vis the trustee. However, the subsection is not applicable to a consignor who—

(a) Complies with an applicable law providing for a consignor's interest or the like to be evidenced by a sign, or
(b) Establishes that the person conducting the business is generally known by his creditors to be substantially engaged in selling the goods of others, or
(c) Complies with the filing provisions of the article on secured transactions (Article 9). Section 2–326(3).

Jackson is not protected under (a) because Alabama does not have a sign law applicable to consignments. Jackson is not protected under (c) because he did not comply with the filing provisions of Article 9.

Jackson contends, but has failed to prove, that he is protected under (b). The evidence does not reflect that the debtors were "generally known by [their] creditors to be substantially engaged in selling the goods of others."

Jackson admitted that he did not notify any of the Auclairs' creditors that the firearms were placed with the Auclairs on consignment. The evidence reveals, *at best,* that only one of the Auclairs' eighteen creditors had knowledge of the consignment. The court concludes that the debtors were not "generally known by [their] creditors to be substantially engaged in selling" consigned firearms.

The court holds that the firearms in question are property of this bankruptcy estate which the trustee may sell. A separate order will be entered requiring Jackson to deliver the firearms to the trustee and to account for such property or its value. Jackson will have an unsecured claim for the value of the property returned to the trustee, for which he may file a proof of claim in this case.

Judgment in favor of bankruptcy estate and against Jackson.

BULK TRANSFERS

Bulk Transfer Legislation

There is one other situation where the creditors of a party to a sales contract may claim an interest (other than an Article 9 security interest) in the goods. This is in the case of a bulk transfer as covered by Article 6 of the Code. A **bulk transfer** occurs when a person whose main business is selling goods from stock (a retailer, a wholesaler, and in some cases a manufacturer) sells a major part of the materials, supplies, merchandise, or other inventory of the business in bulk and not in the ordinary course of business [6–102].

The danger in such cases is that financially troubled sellers may dispose of their assets secretly, pocket the proceeds, and disappear. In order to protect such a seller's creditors from being defrauded in this manner, Article 6 is designed to give them notice of the sale and enable them to file any claims they may have against the goods. The seller must give the buyer a sworn list of the seller's creditors and a schedule of the property to be transferred [6–104]. The buyer must keep this list available for inspection and copying by the seller's creditors for six months after the sale [6–104].

Notice to Creditors

The buyer must notify all known creditors of the sale at least 10 days before taking possession of the goods [6–105]. Failure to comply with the requirements means that the buyer holds the goods in trust for the seller's creditors. In some states, an optional provision of the Code has been enacted requiring that the proceeds of the bulk transfer be paid to the seller's creditors [6–106].

Statute of Limitations

Creditors have only six months from the time the transfer took place to enforce their rights under Article 6, unless the transfer was concealed from them. In such a case, they have six months after the transfer was discovered [6–111].

Current Developments

For some time, there has been general dissatisfaction with the current bulk sales law. The National Conference of Commissioners on Uniform State Laws has prepared a draft revision to UCC Article 6 (Bulk Sales) for consideration by the states; at the same time, the commissioners have voted to recommend to the states that they repeal Article 6 and do without a bulk sales law. Thus, the future for bulk sales laws is in doubt.

ETHICAL AND PUBLIC POLICY CONCERNS

1. Suppose you are the owner of a small jewelry store that sells new and antique jewelry. A customer leaves a family heirloom—an elaborate diamond ring—with you for cleaning and resetting. By mistake, a clerk in your store sells it to another customer. What would you do? If you were the buyer of the ring and had given it to your fiancé as a gift and then were informed of the circumstances, what would you do?

2. Under the pre-Code law, most issues relating to risks and insurable interests in goods were determined on the basis of who was technical title owner at the particular moment the problem of a right or liability arose. What policy considerations do you believe were involved in the decision by the drafters of the Code to provide for resolution of issues concerning risk of loss and insurable interest independent of who was the technical title owner?

3. In the *In Re Auclair* case, the owner that made the firearms available to the retailer for resale lost out to other creditors of the retailers when they filed for bankruptcy. Does this strike you as a reasonable result? What policy considerations underlie the Code provisions on which the court based its decision?

PROBLEMS AND PROBLEM CASES

1. Mr. and Mrs. Abelman engaged the Capitol Termite and Pest Control Company to treat their home for a termite infestation. The chemical used by Capitol was Gold Crest Termide manufactured by Velsicol Chemical Corporation. Velsicol sold the Gold Crest Termide to a distributor, which in turn sold it to Capitol in bulk—in 55-gallon drums. Capitol did not buy materials specifically for each termite job. One 55-gallon drum would service many homes. Employees of Capitol pumped the chemical from the 55-gallon drums into a 5-gallon pail at Capitol's premises. Employees then poured the solution from the 5-gallon pail into a 1-gallon pail, which they filled half full. Next, they poured the half-gallon of Gold Crest Termide into a fixed 50-gallon tank on the back of Capitol's trucks and then filled the tank to capacity with water. Capitol's employees then applied this solution to the Abelman's residence. The Abelmans abandoned their home the day after Capitol completed treatment. Three years later, they brought suit against Capitol and Velsicol, contending that the termiticide had caused personal injuries and property damages. Among other things, they claimed there was a breach of express and implied warranties provided by the Uniform Commercial Code (discussed in Chapter 20). Velsicol and Capitol sought to dismiss these claims on the ground that there had not been a sale of goods and thus no warranties had arisen. Was the contract to obtain treatment for termites a sale of goods under the Uniform Commercial Code?

2. Suchy Funeral Home brought suit against Waldenmaier to recover the contracted price for a funeral, including the provision of a casket. Waldenmaier claimed that the lawsuit was commenced more than four years after the funeral and thus was barred by the Code's four-year statute of limitations. Suchy contended that the Code's statute of limitations did not apply because no "sale of goods" was involved. Should the court apply the Code's provisions to this contract?

3. Clive Lapp purchased a 1978 Chrysler Cordoba from Prospector Chevrolet on July 24, 1980. Lapp paid cash for the car, secured a temporary license sticker, and drove the car away. Three months after the sale, Prospector sent the title documents for the car to the County Treasurer's Office. When Lapp tried to pick up the title, the Treasurer informed him that the title could not be transferred to him because the application for title was in the name of Olive Lapp instead of Clive Lapp. Lapp did not notify Prospector of the error or take any other action to cause a valid title to be issued to him. Instead, he took the license plates from another car and illegally used them on the Cordoba. On September 16, 1981, Lapp was driving the Cordoba when he struck and killed Merlin Benjamin. Benjamin's estate sued Prospector, alleg-

ing that Prospector still had title to the Cordoba. Safeco Insurance, Prospector's insurer, argued that title had passed to Lapp. Did title pass to Lapp despite the fact that a certificate of title was not issued in his name?

4. Club Pro Golf Products was a distributor of golf products. It employed salesmen who called on customers to take orders for merchandise. The merchandise was sent by Club Pro directly to the purchaser, and payment was made by the purchaser directly to Club Pro. A salesman for Club Pro, Carl Gude, transmitted orders for certain merchandise to Club Pro for delivery to several fictitious purchasers. Club Pro sent the merchandise to the fictitious purchasers at the fictitious addresses, where it was picked up by Gude. Gude then sold the merchandise, worth approximately $19,000, directly to Simpson, a golf pro at a golf club. Gude retained the proceeds of sale for himself. Club Pro discovered the fraud and brought suit against Simpson to recover the merchandise. Club Pro alleged that Gude "stole" the merchandise from it "with intent to defraud it" and as a result had no authority to transfer title to Simpson. Did Gude have a void or a voidable title to the merchandise when he obtained it from Club Pro?

5. Lane, a dealer in new and used boats, sold a new boat and trailer to Johnson. Johnson paid for the boat and trailer by a check that the bank later dishonored. Johnson then resold the boat and trailer to Honeycutt. Lane attempted to get the boat and trailer from Honeycutt. Can Lane recover them?

6. In June, Ramos entered into a contract to buy a motorcycle from Big Wheel Sports Center. He paid the purchase price of $893 and was given the papers necessary to register the cycle and get insurance on it. Ramos registered the cycle but had not attached the license plates to it. He left on vacation and told the salesperson for Big Wheel Sports Center that he would pick up the cycle on his return. While Ramos was on vacation, there was an electric power blackout in New York City and the cycle was stolen by looters. Ramos then sued Big Wheel Sports Center to get back his $893. Did Big Wheel Sports Center have the risk of loss of the motorcycle?

7. Debs, a dress manufacturer, sold Rose Stores 288 dresses. The order was on a Rose Stores printed

form that stated, "Ship via Stuarts Express." Stuarts Express picked up the dresses at Debs, then one week later wrote Debs a letter informing it that the entire shipment was lost. Since Stuarts's liability is extremely limited by the shipping contract, who, between Debs and Rose, must absorb the risk of loss?

8. Legendary Homes, a home builder, purchased various appliances from Ron Mead T.V. & Appliance, a retail merchant selling home appliances. They were intended to be installed in one of Legendary Homes's houses and were to be delivered on February 1, 1984. At 5 o'clock on that day, the appliances had not been delivered. Legendary Homes's employees closed the home and left. Sometime between 5 and 6:30, Ron Mead delivered the appliances. No one was at the home so the deliveryman put the appliances in the garage. During the night, someone stole the appliances. Legendary Homes denied it was responsible for the loss and refused to pay Ron Mead for the appliances. Ron Mead then brought suit for the purchase price. Did Legendary Homes have the risk of loss of the appliances?

9. Collier, a retail store operator, accepted a delivery of stereo tapes, cartridges, and equipment from B & B Sales. The invoice noted that the goods had been "sold to" Collier and stated: "Terms 30-60-90; this equipment will be picked up if not sold in 90 days." Shortly thereafter, Collier's store was burglarized and all the merchandise was stolen. B & B filed suit against Collier for the purchase price of the merchandise, claiming that the transaction was a sale and that Collier was liable to pay for the merchandise. Collier argued that the transaction was a consignment and that B & B had the risk of loss. Did Collier or B & B have the risk of loss of the merchandise?

10. Curtina International was a corporation engaged in the business of importing and distributing confectionery products, mainly varieties of wafers manufactured in Austria. From its inception in 1979, Curtina's business was not financially successful. By early 1981, Curtina was insolvent. Its largest unsecured creditor was one of its Austrian suppliers of wafers. In February 1981, Curtina's president approached Plymouth Enterprises, a corporation engaged in the business of buying and selling close-outs (excess, old, or out-of-season inventory) from manufacturers and wholesalers at a fraction of their normal selling prices. He offered to sell Plymouth Curtina's line of wafers. In March, Plymouth agreed to purchase substantially all of Curtina's inventory of wafers at approximately $12 per case, for a total of about $66,000; the wafers usually sold for about $50 a case to retail stores. Plymouth's representative was not aware that wafers constituted Curtina's entire inventory. At no time did Plymouth ask Curtina for a list of its creditors, and Plymouth did not furnish notice of the sale to Curtina's creditors. It took Plymouth approximately nine months to resell the wafers. Curtina was thrown into involuntary bankruptcy in April 1981. Murdock, the trustee in bankruptcy, sought to avoid the sale of the wafers to Plymouth, contending that it was made in violation of the state bulk sales law. Should the sale be voided for failing to comply with the bulk sales law?

11. [image] *Video Case.* See "Software Horror Story." Chuck Mason, a computer consultant, was hired to develop customized software for a client, Ms. Clark. His plan was to purchase off-the-shelf software and to modify it to meet the customer's need. After identifying several software packages that might meet his need, he contacted a software retailer, Bits and Bytes, by phone and explained that he needed to be able to modify the package at the source code level and to have the source code. He then asked Bits and Bytes to recommend a package that would meet these criteria and be easy to modify. After receiving the recommended software (D-Base Hit) from Bits and Bytes, Chuck modified the software but was unable to get it to work as envisioned. Bits and Bytes refused to take it back because Chuck's modifications prevented it from being resold or returned to the software publisher. Chuck refused to pay Bits and Bytes for the package. Chuck then purchased a different software package (Customized Amazing Base) and customized it for his client. However, the customized software never functioned satisfactorily for the client, and she refused to pay Chuck for it. Does the UCC apply to the sale of the software by the retailer? Does it apply to the sale of the customized software by the consultant to the customer?

12. [image] *Video Case.* See "TV Repair." Arnold took his old TV to an appliance store for repair. The appliance store developed financial problems and was unable to pay its debts to its creditors as they became due. Facing bankruptcy, the appliance store held a going-out-of-business sale and sold everything in the store, including Arnold's TV, to individual customers who had no knowledge of anyone else's interest in the goods. Does Arnold have the legal right to recover the TV from the person who bought it at the going-out-of-business sale?

13. 　　　 *Video Case.* See "Sour Grapes." Jelly Manufacturer, a food processor in Chicago, placed a phone order with Grape Grower, a grower in California, for a quantity of perishable produce. The shipping term was *CIF* with payment to be made on delivery (COD). Grower delivered the goods called for in the contract to a carrier and contracted for their shipment. However, it neglected to provide that the goods be shipped under refrigeration. The goods were loaded on a nonrefrigerated boxcar, and as a result, the produce was spoiled when it reached Chicago. Who had the risk of loss, Grape Grower or Jelly Manufacturer?

CHAPTER

20

PRODUCT LIABILITY

INTRODUCTION

Suppose you are the president of a firm making products for sale to the public. One of your concerns would be the company's exposure to civil liability for defects in those products. As president, therefore, you would worry about changes in the law that make such liability more likely or more expensive. In other contexts, however, the same changes might appeal to you. This is especially true if you *are harmed by defective products you purchase as a consumer. Such changes might also appeal to you if your firm wants to sue a supplier that has sold it defective products.*

Each of these situations involves the law of product liability. *Product liability law is the body of legal rules governing civil suits for losses resulting from defective goods.[1] After sketching product liability law's historical evolution, this chapter discusses the most important* theories of product liability recovery. *These theories are rules of law allowing plaintiffs to recover for losses resulting from defective goods once they prove certain facts. The second half of the chapter considers certain legal problems that are common to all the theories of recovery but that may be resolved differently from theory to theory.*

THE EVOLUTION OF PRODUCT LIABILITY LAW

The 19th Century

A century ago, the rules governing suits for defective goods were very much to sellers' and manufacturers' advantage. This was the era of *caveat emptor* (let the buyer beware). In contract suits, there was usually no liability unless the seller had made an express promise to the buyer and the goods did not conform to that promise. Some courts even required that the words *warrant* or *guarantee* accompany the promise before liability would exist. In negligence suits, the maxim of "no liability without fault" was widely accepted, and plaintiffs frequently had diffi-

---

[1]This chapter does not discuss the various federal consumer protection laws involving the payment and credit aspects of consumer transactions. Nor does it discuss product safety regulation. For these subjects, see Chapter 47.

culty proving negligence because the necessary evidence was under the defendant's control. In both contract and negligence cases, finally, the doctrine of "no liability outside privity of contract" often prevented plaintiffs from recovering against parties with whom they had not directly dealt.[2]

The social and economic conditions that prevailed for much of the 19th century help explain these prodefendant rules. At that time, laissez-faire values strongly influenced public policy and the law. One expression of those values was the belief that sellers and manufacturers should be contractually bound only when they deliberately assumed such liability by actually making a promise to someone with whom they dealt directly. Another factor limiting manufacturers' liability for defective products, some say, was the desire to promote industrialization by preventing potentially crippling damage recoveries against infant industries.

Certain features of the 19th-century economy, however, made that century's product liability rules less hard on plaintiffs than would otherwise have been the case. Chains of distribution tended to be short, so the no-liability-outside-privity defense was not always available. Because goods tended to be simple, buyers could sometimes inspect them for defects. Before the emergence of large corporations late in the 19th century, sellers and buyers were often of relatively equal size, sophistication, and bargaining power. This meant that they could deal on a relatively equal footing.

The 20th Century

Today, many 19th-century social and economic tendencies are conspicuous by their absence. Laissez-faire values do not exercise the influence they did a century ago. Instead, a more protective, interdependent climate has emerged. With the development of a viable industrial economy, there has been less perceived need to protect manufacturers from liability for defective goods. The emergence of long chains of distribution has meant that consumers often do not deal directly with the parties responsible for defects in the products they buy. Because

sizable corporations tend to dominate the economy, consumers are less able to bargain equally with such parties in any event. Finally, the growing complexity of goods has made buyer inspections more difficult.

Due to such developments, product liability law has moved from its earlier *caveat emptor* emphasis to a stance of *caveat venditor* (let the seller beware). To protect consumers, modern courts and legislatures intervene in private contracts for the sale of goods and impose liability regardless of fault. As a result, sellers and manufacturers face greater liability and higher damage recoveries for defects in their products. Underlying the shift toward *caveat venditor* is the belief that sellers, manufacturers, and their insurers are best able to bear the economic costs associated with product defects and that they can usually pass on these costs through higher prices. Thus, the economic risk associated with defective products has been effectively spread throughout society, or socialized.

The Current "Crisis" in Product Liability Law

Modern product liability law and its socialization-of-risk strategy have come under increasing attack over the past 15 to 20 years. Such attacks often focus on the difficulty sellers and manufacturers have encountered in obtaining product liability insurance and the increased costs of such insurance. Some observers blame the insurance industry for these problems, while others trace them to the increased liability and greater damage recoveries just discussed. Whatever their origin, the crisis in the liability insurance system has put sellers and manufacturers in a bind. Businesses unwilling or unable to buy expensive product liability insurance run the risk of being crippled by large damage awards unless they self-insure, which itself can be an expensive option today. Firms that purchase insurance, on the other hand, must pay a higher price for it. In either case, the resulting costs may be difficult to completely pass on. In addition, those costs may deter the development and marketing of innovative new products.

For these reasons and others, recent years have witnessed many efforts to scale back the proplaintiff thrust of modern product liability law. This is one aspect of the "tort reform" movement discussed in

---

[2]Privity of contract is the existence of a direct contractual relationship between two parties. Chapter 1 discusses the gradual demise of the no-liability-outside-privity rule in New York.

Chapter 7. However, despite the introduction of several federal reform bills, Congress has yet to make any major changes in product liability law. As we note later in this chapter, however, tort reform efforts have occasionally been successful in the states.

THEORIES OF PRODUCT LIABILITY RECOVERY

Technically, some theories of product liability recovery are contractual and some are tort-based. The contract theories involve a product **warranty**—a contractual promise about the nature of the product sold. In warranty cases, plaintiffs claim that the product failed to live up to the seller's promise. In tort cases, on the other hand, plaintiffs usually argue that the defendant was negligent or that strict liability should apply.[3]

Express Warranty

Creating an Express Warranty   UCC section 2–313(1) states that an **express warranty** is created in any of three ways.

   1. Any *affirmation of fact or promise* regarding the goods creates an express warranty that the goods will conform to that affirmation. For instance, a computer seller's statement that a particular computer has a certain amount of memory creates an express warranty to that effect.

   2. Any *description* of the goods creates an express warranty that the goods will conform to the description. This category includes: (1) statements that goods are of a certain brand, type, or model (e.g., an IBM dot-matrix computer printer); (2) descriptive adjectives characterizing the product (e.g., shatterproof glass); and (3) drawings, blueprints, and technical specifications.

   3. A *sample* or *model* of goods to be sold creates an express warranty that the rest of the goods will conform to the sample or model. A sample is an object drawn from an actual collection of goods to be sold, while a model is a replica offered for the

buyer's inspection when the goods themselves are unavailable.

   The first two kinds of express warranties probably overlap; also, each can be either written or oral. In addition, magic words like *warrant* or *guarantee* no longer are needed to create an express warranty.

Value, Opinion, and Sales Talk   Statements of *value* ("This chair would bring you $2,000 at an auction") or *opinion* ("I think that this chair is a genuine antique Louis XIV") do not create an express warranty. The same is true of statements that amount to *sales talk* or *puffery* ("This chair is a good buy"). Of course, no sharp line separates such statements from express warranties. In close cases, a statement is more likely to be an express warranty if it is specific rather than indefinite, if it is stated in the sales contract rather than elsewhere,[4] or if it is unequivocal rather than hedged or qualified. The relative knowledge possessed by the seller and the buyer can also be an important factor. A car salesperson's statement about a used car, for instance, stands a greater chance of being an express warranty where the buyer knows little about cars than where the buyer is another car dealer. The following *Hall Farms* case discusses some of the points made in this paragraph.

The Basis-of-the-Bargain Problem   Under pre-Code law, there was no recovery for breach of an express warranty unless the buyer *relied* on that warranty in making the purchase. The UCC, however, ambiguously requires that the warranty be *part of the basis of the bargain.* Some courts read the Code's basis-of-the-bargain test as saying that full reliance is necessary. Others only require that the seller's warranty have been a *contributing factor* in the buyer's decision to purchase.

Advertisements   Statements made in advertisements, catalogs, or brochures *may* be express warranties. Such sources, however, are often filled with sales talk. Also, basis-of-the-bargain problems may

---

[3]Negligence and strict liability are discussed in Chapter 7.

[4]Parol evidence rule problems can arise in express warranty cases. For example, a seller who used a written sale contract may argue that the rule excludes an alleged oral warranty. For the parol evidence rule, see Chapter 16.

arise if it is unclear whether or to what degree the statement really induced the buyer to make the purchase. For example, a buyer who reads an advertisement containing an express warranty one month before actually purchasing the product may or may not have been induced to purchase by the express warranty in the advertisement.

Multiple Express Warranties What happens when the seller gives two or more express warranties and those warranties arguably conflict? UCC section 2–317 says that such warranties should be read as consistent with each other and as cumulative if this is reasonable. If not, the parties' intention controls. In determining that intention: (1) exact or technical specifications defeat a sample, a model, or general descriptive language; and (2) a sample defeats general descriptive language.

MARTIN RISPENS & SON V. HALL FARMS, INC.
601 N.E.2d 429 (Ind. Ct. App. 1992)

Hall Farms, Inc. ordered 40 pounds of Prince Charles watermelon seed from Martin Rispens & Son, a seed dealer. Rispens had obtained the seed from Petoseed Company, Inc., a seed producer. The label on Petoseed's can stated that the seeds are "top quality seeds with high vitality, vigor and germination." Hall Farms germinated the seeds in a greenhouse before transplanting the small watermelon plants to its fields. Although the plants had a few abnormalities, they grew rapidly. By mid-July, however, purple blotches had spread over most of the crop, and by the end of July the crop was ruined. It was later determined that the crop had been destroyed by "watermelon fruit blotch." Hall Farms's lost profits on the crop came to $180,000.

Hall Farms sued Petoseed for, among other things, breach of express warranty. Petoseed moved for summary judgment, but the trial court denied the motion. Petoseed appealed.

Baker, Judge An express warranty is created by an affirmation of fact or promise made by the seller to the buyer which relates to the goods and becomes part of the basis of the bargain; it warrants that the goods shall conform to the affirmation or promise. It is not necessary that the seller use formal words such as "warrant" or "guarantee" or that he have a specific intention to make a warranty. On the other hand, an affirmation merely of the value of the goods or a statement purporting to be merely the seller's opinion or commendation of the goods does not create a warranty.

Whether a given representation is a warranty or merely an expression of the seller's opinion is determined in part by considering whether the seller asserts a fact of which the buyer is ignorant, or merely states an opinion or judgment on a matter of which the seller has no special knowledge and on which the buyer may be expected also to have an opinion and to exercise his judgment. Courts must also consider the degree of specificity expressed in the representation.

The label on Petoseed's can stated that the seeds are "top quality seeds with high vitality, vigor and germination." We consider the words "top quality seeds" as a classic example of puffery. The precise meaning of "top quality" is subject to considerably different interpretations.

Petoseed [also] claimed that its seeds possessed "high vitality, vigor and germination." Although reasonable people may differ as to the particular degree of vitality, vigor, and germination meant by the word "high," Petoseed did expressly warrant that its seeds would possess at least a modicum of vitality, vigor, and germination. If this affirmation became a basis of the bargain, an express warranty was created. We need not address this question, however, because even assuming Hall Farms relied on the affirmation, no breach occurred.

"Vitality" is the capacity to live, grow, or develop. "Vigor" is the capacity for natural growth and survival. "Germination" is the beginning of growth or sprouting. Here, there is no dispute that the watermelon seeds sprouted, grew, and developed a normal fruit set. Thus, the seeds conformed to the affirmation on Petoseed's labels; consequently, there was no breach. Partial summary judgment is appropriate when there is no conflict over facts dispositive of a portion of the litigation. Hall Farms may not recover from Petoseed based on an express warranty theory.

Trial court decision denying Petoseed's motion for summary judgment on Hall Farms' express warranty claim reversed.

Implied Warranty of Merchantability

An **implied warranty** is a warranty created by *operation of law* rather than the seller's voluntary express statements. UCC section 2–314(1) creates the Code's **implied warranty of merchantability** by stating that "a warranty that the goods shall be merchantable is implied in a contract for their sale if the seller is a merchant with respect to goods of that kind." This is a clear example of the 20th-century tendency for government to intervene in private contracts to protect allegedly weaker parties.

In an implied warranty of merchantability case, the plaintiff argues that the seller breached the warranty by selling nonmerchantable goods. Under section 2–314, such claims can succeed only where the seller is a *merchant with respect to goods of the kind sold.*[5] A housewife's sale of homemade preserves or a hardware store owner's sale of a used car, for example, do not trigger the implied warranty of merchantability.

UCC section 2–314(2) states that, to be merchantable, goods must at least: (1) pass without objection in the trade; (2) be fit for the ordinary purposes for which such goods are used; (3) be of even kind, quality, and quantity within each unit (case, package, or carton) and among all units; (4) be adequately contained, packaged, and labeled; (5) conform to any promises or statements of fact made on the container or label; and (6) in the case of fungible goods, be of fair average quality. The most important of these requirements is that the goods must be *fit for the ordinary purposes for which such goods are used.* The goods need not be perfect to be fit for their ordinary purposes. Rather, they need only meet the reasonable expectations of the average consumer.

Such broad, flexible tests of merchantability are almost inevitable given the wide range of products sold in the United States today and the varied defects they can present. Still, a few generalizations about merchantability determinations are possible. Goods that fail to function properly or that have harmful side effects generally are not merchantable. A computer that fails to work properly or that destroys the owner's programs, for example, is not fit for the ordinary purposes for which computers are used. In cases involving allergic reactions to drugs or other products, courts frequently find the defendant liable if it was reasonably foreseeable that an appreciable number of consumers would suffer the reaction. As the following *Marriott* case reveals, there is some disagreement about the standard for food products that are alleged to be unmerchantable because they contain harmful objects or substances. Under the *foreign-natural* test, the defendant is liable if the object or substance is "foreign" to the product, but not liable if it is "natural" to that product. Increasingly, however, courts ask whether the food product met the consumer's *reasonable expectations.*

---

[5]The term *merchant* is defined in Chapter 9.

YONG CHA HONG V. MARRIOTT CORPORATION
3 UCC Rep. Serv. 2d 83 (D. Md. 1987)

Yong Cha Hong bought some take-out fried chicken from a Roy Rogers Family Restaurant owned by the Marriott Corporation. While eating a chicken wing from her order, she bit into an object that she perceived to be a worm. Claiming permanent injuries and great physical and emotional upset from this incident, Hong sued Marriott for $500,000 in federal district court under the implied warranty of merchantability. After introducing an expert's report alleging that the object in the chicken wing was not a worm, Marriott moved for summary judgment. It claimed that the case involved no disputed issues of material fact, and that there was no breach of the implied warranty of merchantability as a matter of law.

Smalkin, District Judge   It appears that the item encountered by plaintiff was probably not a worm or other parasite, although plaintiff, in her deposition, steadfastly maintains that it was a worm. If it was not a worm (i.e., if the expert analysis is correct), it was either one of the chicken's major blood vessels (the aorta) or its trachea, both of which would appear worm-like (although not meaty like a worm, but hollow). For [present] purposes, the court will assume that the item was not a worm. Precisely how the aorta or trachea wound up in this hapless chicken's wing is a fascinating, but as yet unanswered (and presently immaterial), question.

Does Maryland law provide a breach of warranty remedy for personal injury flowing from an unexpected encounter with an inedible part of the chicken's anatomy in a piece of fast food fried chicken? Marriott contends that there can be no recovery unless the offending item was a foreign object, i.e., not part of the chicken itself.

In many cases that have denied [implied] warranty recovery as a matter of law, the injurious substance was, as in this case, a natural (though inedible) part of the edible item consumed. Thus, in *Shapiro v. Hotel Statler Corp.* (1955), recovery was denied for a fish bone in "Hot Barquette of Seafood Mornay." But in all these cases the natural item was reasonably to be expected in the dish by its very nature, under the prevailing expectation of any reasonable consumer. Indeed, precisely this "reasonable expectation" test has been adopted in a number of cases. The reasonable expectation test has largely displaced the foreign-natural test adverted to by Marriott. This court is confident that Maryland would apply the reasonable expectation rule.

The court cannot conclude that the presence of a trachea or an aorta in a fast food fried chicken wing is so reasonably to be expected as to render it merchantable, as a matter of law. This is not like the situation [in a previous case] involving a one centimeter bone in a piece of fried fish. Everyone but a fool knows that tiny bones may remain in even the best filets of fish. This case is more like [another decision], where the court held that the issue was for the trier of fact, on a claim arising from a cherry pit in cherry ice cream. Thus, a question is presented that precludes the grant of summary judgment. The jury must determine whether a piece of fast food fried chicken is merchantable if it contains an inedible item of the chicken's anatomy. Of course, the jury will be instructed that the consumer's reasonable expectations form a part of the merchantability concept.

Marriott's motion for summary judgment denied.

Implied Warranty of Fitness

UCC section 2–315's **implied warranty of fitness for a particular purpose** arises where: (1) the seller has reason to know a particular purpose for which the buyer requires the goods, (2) the seller has reason to know that the buyer is relying on the seller's skill or judgment to select suitable goods, and (3) the buyer actually relies on the seller's skill or judgment in purchasing the goods. If these tests are met, there is an implied warranty that the goods will be fit for the buyer's *particular* purpose.

In many fitness warranty cases, buyers effectively put themselves in the seller's hands by making their needs known and saying that they are relying on the seller to select goods that will satisfy those needs. This may happen, for example, where a seller sells a computer system specially manufactured or customized for a buyer's particular needs. But sellers can also be liable where the circumstances reasonably indicate that the buyer has a particular purpose and is relying on the seller to satisfy that purpose, even though the buyer fails to make either explicit. However, buyers may have trouble recovering where they are more expert than the seller, submit specifications for the goods they wish to buy, inspect the goods, actually select them, or insist on a particular brand.

As the following *Dempsey* case makes clear, the implied warranty of fitness clearly differs from the implied warranty of merchantability. The tests for the creation of each warranty are plainly not the same. Under section 2–315, moreover, sellers only warrant that the goods are fit for the buyer's *particular* purposes, not the *ordinary* purposes for which such goods are used. If a 400-pound man asks a department store for a hammock that will support his weight but is sold a hammock that only can support normally sized people, there is a breach of the implied warranty of fitness but no breach of the implied warranty of merchantability. If the hammock cannot support *anyone's* weight, however, both warranties are breached.

DEMPSEY V. ROSENTHAL
468 N.Y.S.2d 441 (N.Y. Civ. Ct. 1983)

Ruby Dempsey purchased a nine-week-old pedigreed male poodle from the American Kennels Pet Stores. She named the poodle Mr. Dunphy. Dempsey later testified that before making the purchase, she told the salesperson that she wanted a dog suitable for breeding purposes. Five days after the sale, she had Mr. Dunphy examined by a veterinarian, who discovered that the poodle had one undescended testicle. This condition did not seriously affect Mr. Dunphy's fertility, but it was a genetic defect that would probably be passed on to any offspring sired. Also, a dog with this condition could not be used as a show dog.

Dempsey demanded a refund from American Kennels, but her demand was denied. She then sued in small claims court, alleging that American Kennels had breached the implied warranty of fitness.

Saxe, Judge   UCC sections 2–314 and 2–315 make it clear that the warranty of fitness for a particular purpose is narrower, more specific, and more precise than the warranty of merchantability, which involves fitness for the *ordinary* purposes for which goods are used. The following are the conditions that are not required by the implied warranty of merchantability, but that must be present if a plaintiff is to recover on the basis of the implied warranty of fitness: (1) the seller must have reason to know the buyer's particular purpose, (2) the seller must have reason to know that the buyer is relying on the seller's skill or judgment to furnish appropriate goods, and (3) the buyer must, in fact, rely upon the seller's skill or judgment.

I find that the warranty of fitness for a particular purpose has been breached. Dempsey testified that she specified to the salesperson that she wanted a dog that was suitable for breeding purposes. Although this is disputed by the defendant, the credible testimony supports Dempsey's version of the event. Further, it is reasonable for the seller of a pedigreed dog to assume that the buyer intends to breed it. But it is undisputed by the experts here (for both sides) that Mr. Dunphy was as capable of siring a litter as a male dog with two viable and descended

testicles. This, the defendant contends, compels a finding in its favor. I disagree. While it is true that Mr. Dunphy's fertility level may be unaffected, his stud value, because of this hereditary condition (which is likely to be passed on to future generations), is severely diminished.

Judgment for Dempsey.

Negligence

Product liability suits based on the theory of **negligence** discussed in Chapter 7 usually allege that the seller or manufacturer breached a duty to the plaintiff by failing to eliminate a reasonably foreseeable risk of harm associated with the product.[6] Such suits typically claim one or more of the following: (1) improper *manufacture* of the goods (including improper materials and packaging), (2) improper *inspection,* (3) a failure to provide *adequate warnings* of hazards or defects, and (4) improper *design.*

Improper Manufacture   Negligence suits alleging the manufacturer's improper assembly, materials, or packaging often encounter problems because the evidence needed to prove a breach of duty is under the defendant's control.[7] However, liberal modern discovery rules and the doctrine of *res ipsa loquitur* can help plaintiffs establish a breach in such situations.[8]

Improper Inspection   Manufacturers have a duty to inspect their products for defects that create a reasonably foreseeable risk of harm, if such an

inspection would be practicable and effective. As before, *res ipsa loquitur* and modern discovery rules can help plaintiffs prove their case against the manufacturer.

Most courts have held that middlemen such as retailers and wholesalers have a duty to inspect the goods they sell only when they have actual knowledge or reason to know of a defect. In addition, such parties generally have no duty to inspect where this would be unduly difficult, burdensome, or time-consuming. Unless the product defect is obvious, for example, middlemen usually are not liable for failing to inspect goods sold in the manufacturer's original packages or containers.

On the other hand, sellers who prepare, install, or repair the goods they sell ordinarily have a duty to inspect those goods. Examples include restaurants, automobile dealers, and installers of household products. Usually, however, the scope of the inspection need only be consistent with the preparation, installation, or repair work performed. Thus, it is unlikely that such sellers must unearth hidden or latent defects.

If there is a duty to inspect and the inspection reveals a defect, further duties can arise. For example, a seller or manufacturer may be required not to sell the product in its defective state, or at least to give a suitable warning.

Failure to Warn   Sellers and manufacturers have a duty to give an appropriate warning when their products pose a reasonably foreseeable risk of harm. But in determining whether there was a duty to warn and whether the defendant's warning was adequate, courts often consider other factors besides

---

[6]Occasionally, such suits may proceed under the theory of *negligence per se* discussed in Chapter 7—for example, where the product violates a consumer product safety regulation or pure food law.

[7]Another problem concerns the negligence liability of computer designers and programmers. Some courts have held such parties to a higher standard of care when they develop custom application software, but others reject such claims.

[8]Chapter 2 discusses discovery, and Chapter 7 discusses *res ipsa loquitur.*

the reasonable foreseeability of the risk. These include the *magnitude or severity* of the likely harm, the *ease or difficulty of providing an appropriate warning*, and the likely *effectiveness of a warning*. As the following *Daniell* case makes clear, moreover, there is no duty to warn where the risk is *open and obvious*.

Design Defects

Manufacturers have a duty to design their products so as to avoid reasonably foreseeable risks of harm. Like failure-to-warn cases, however, design defect cases frequently involve other factors besides the reasonable foreseeability of harm. As before, one of these factors is the *magnitude or severity* of the foreseeable harm. Three others are *industry practices* at the time the product was manufactured, the *state of the art* (the

state of existing scientific and technical knowledge) at that time, and the product's compliance or noncompliance with *government safety regulations.*[9]

Sometimes courts employ *risk-benefit analysis* when weighing these factors. In such analyses, three other factors—the design's *social utility,* the *effectiveness of alternative designs,* and the *cost of safer designs*—may figure in the weighing process. Even where the balancing process indicates that the design was not defective, courts may still require a suitable warning.

---

[9]Some states have statutes stating that a product's compliance with state or federal product safety regulations creates a rebuttable presumption that it was not defective. Also, a few states have a statutory state-of-the-art defense.

DANIELL V. FORD MOTOR COMPANY
581 F. Supp. 728 (D.N.M. 1984)

Connie Daniell attempted to commit suicide by locking herself inside the trunk of her 1973 Ford LTD. Daniell remained in the trunk for nine days, but survived after finally being rescued. Later, Daniell sued Ford in negligence to recover for her resulting physical and psychological injuries. She contended that the LTD was defectively designed because its trunk did not have an internal release or opening mechanism. She also argued that Ford was liable for negligently failing to warn her that the trunk could not be unlocked from within. Ford moved for summary judgment.

Baldock, District Judge   As a general principle, a design defect is actionable only where the condition of the product is unreasonably dangerous to the user or consumer. Under negligence, a manufacturer has a duty to consider only those risks of injury which are foreseeable. A risk is not foreseeable where a product is used in a manner which could not reasonably be anticipated by the manufacturer and that use is the cause of the plaintiff's injury.

The purposes of an automobile trunk are to transport, stow, and secure the spare tire, luggage, and other goods and to protect those items from the weather. The design features of a trunk make it well near impossible that an adult intentionally would enter the trunk and close the lid. The dimensions of a trunk, the height of its sill and its load floor, and the efforts to first lower the lid and then to engage its latch, are among the design features which

encourage closing and latching the trunk lid while standing outside the vehicle. The court holds that the plaintiff's use of the trunk compartment as a means to attempt suicide was an unforeseeable use as a matter of law. Therefore, the manufacturer had no duty to design an internal release or opening mechanism that might have prevented this occurrence.

Nor did the manufacturer have a duty to warn the plaintiff of the danger of her conduct, given the plaintiff's unforeseeable use of the product. Another reason why the manufacturer had no duty to warn the plaintiff of the risk inherent in crawling into an automobile trunk and closing the lid is [that] such a risk is obvious. There is no duty to warn of known dangers. Moreover, the potential efficacy of any warning, given the plaintiff's use of the trunk for a deliberate suicide attempt, is questionable.

Having held that the plaintiff's conception of the manufacturer's duty is in error, the court need not reach the issues of comparative negligence or other defenses such as assumption of risk.

Ford's motion for summary judgment granted; Daniell loses.

Strict Liability

Strict products liability is a relatively recent development. Only in the 1960s did courts begin to impose such liability in significant numbers. The movement toward strict liability received a big boost when the American Law Institute promulgated section 402A of the *Restatement (Second) of Torts* in 1965. By now, the vast majority of the states have adopted some form of strict products liability. The most important reason is the socialization-of-risk strategy discussed earlier. Another common justification for strict products liability is that it stimulates manufacturers to design and build safer products. Strict liability also removes a problem that has long plagued plaintiffs in negligence suits—the need to prove a breach of duty.

Section 402A's Requirements   Because it is the most common version of strict products liability, we limit our discussion of the subject to section 402A. Section 402A provides that a "seller . . . engaged in the business of selling" a particular product is liable for physical harm or property damage suffered by the ultimate user or consumer of that product if the product was "in a defective condition unreasonably dangerous to the user or consumer or to his property." This rule applies even though "the seller has exercised all possible care in the preparation and sale of his product." Thus, section 402A states a rule of strict liability that eliminates the plaintiff's need to prove a breach of duty.

However, the liability imposed by section 402A is not absolute, for the section applies only if certain tests are met.

1. The seller must be *engaged in the business of selling the product that harmed the plaintiff.* Thus, section 402A only binds parties who resemble UCC merchants because they regularly sell the product at issue. For example, the section does not apply to a college professor's or a clothing store's sale of a used car.

2. The product must be in a *defective condition* when sold, and also must be *unreasonably dangerous* because of that condition. The usual test of a product's defective condition is whether the product meets the reasonable expectations of the average consumer. An unreasonably dangerous product is one that is dangerous to an extent beyond the reasonable contemplation of the average consumer. For example, good whiskey is not unreasonably dangerous even though it can cause harm, but whiskey contaminated with a poisonous substance qualifies. However, some courts balance the product's social utility against its danger when determining whether it is unreasonably dangerous.

Due to section 402A's unreasonably dangerous requirement, it covers a smaller range of product defects than the implied warranty of merchantability. A power mower that simply fails to operate, for instance, is not unreasonably dangerous, although it would violate the merchantability standard. Some courts, however, blur the defective condition and unreasonably dangerous requirements, and a few have done away with the latter test.

3. Finally, defendants can avoid section 402A liability where the product was *substantially modified* by the plaintiff or another party after the sale, and the modification contributed to the plaintiff's injury or other loss.

Applications of Section 402A   As the following *Toney* case makes clear, design defect and failure-to-warn suits can be brought under section 402A. Even though section 402A is a strict liability provision, the standards applied in such cases often resemble the negligence standards discussed in the previous section.

Because it applies to sellers, section 402A covers retailers and other middlemen who market goods containing defects that they did not create and may not have been able to discover. Even though such parties often escape negligence liability, some courts have found them liable under section 402A's strict liability rule. However, other states have given middlemen some protection against 402A liability, and/or have required the manufacturer or other responsible party to indemnify them.

What about products (such as some drugs) that have great social utility, but that pose serious risks which cannot be eliminated? Imposing strict liability on such "unavoidably unsafe" products might deter manufacturers from developing and marketing them. Where products of this kind cause harm and a lawsuit follows, many courts follow comment *k* to section 402A. Comment *k* says that unavoidably unsafe products are neither defective nor unreasonably dangerous if they are properly prepared and accompanied by proper directions and a proper warning. For this rule to apply, of course, the product must be genuinely incapable of being made safer.

Toney v. Kawasaki Heavy Industries, Ltd.
975 F.2d 162 (5th Cir. 1992)

Shortly after Billy Toney bought a used Kawasaki 750 motorcycle, he was struck from the side by a truck while riding the motorcycle on a highway. As a result, he suffered severe injuries to his left leg, leading to its eventual amputation. Toney sued Kawasaki in a Mississippi trial court, alleging that the motorcycle was improperly designed because it was not equipped with leg-protection devices, and that Kawasaki improperly failed to warn users about the dangers posed by the absence of such devices. After Kawasaki removed the case to federal district court, the district court granted Kawasaki's motion for summary judgment on Toney's section 402A claim. Toney appealed.

Jolly, Circuit Judge   To recover under Mississippi product strict liability law, the injured plaintiff must show that the product was "in a defective condition unreasonably dangerous." Mississippi has adopted the objective "consumer expectations" test to determine whether a product is unreasonably dangerous. The plaintiff must establish that the product was dangerous to an extent beyond that which would be contemplated by the ordinary consumer who purchases it, with the ordinary knowledge common to the community as to its characteristics. Furthermore, a product that has an open and obvious danger is not more dangerous than contemplated by the consumer, and hence cannot be unreasonably dangerous.

The ordinary consumer could see that [Toney's] motorcycle had no leg protection and, thus, could fully appreciate the motorcycle's design and its open and obvious dangers. An ordinary consumer would fully appreciate the danger that, if an automobile struck the side of the motorcycle, the rider's leg would be ruinously crushed. The danger of the product thus revealed and appreciated, it was not an unreasonably dangerous product for a manufacturer to market.

Toney next asserts that the district court erred in failing to consider his subjective state of mind in determining whether the danger presented by the design of his motorcycle was patent or latent. He testified that he did not appreciate the danger involved in riding a motorcycle without any leg protection features. Notwithstanding Toney's argument, the Mississippi Supreme Court has adopted an objective test of "consumer expectations" under section 402A. The test is the objective measure of the expectations of the generic consumer who has ordinary knowledge common to the community. The question in product strict liability cases is not whether the product is unreasonably dangerous to a given individual. Modern products are sold by the millions in markets comprising a cross section of the population and therefore are used by people with varying levels of education, experience, and ordinary common sense. The focus in product liability cases is on the product, not the individual purchaser.

District court decision granting Kawasaki's motion for summary judgment affirmed.

CONCEPT REVIEW

COMPARING THE MAJOR PRODUCT LIABILITY THEORIES—THE BASICS

Theory	Tort or Contract	Type of Defendant	Nature of Goods Sold	Remarks
Express Warranty	Contract	Seller of goods	Not as warranted by affirmation of fact or promise, description, sample, or model	Exemption for statements of value, opinion, or sales talk
Implied Warranty of Merchantability	Contract	Merchant for goods sold	Not merchantable; usually, not fit for ordinary purposes for which such goods used	Merchantability has other aspects
Implied Warranty of Fitness	Contract	Seller of goods	Not fit for buyer's particular purposes	Seller must have reason to know of buyer's needs and buyer's reliance, and buyer must actually rely
Negligence	Tort	Manufacturer or seller of goods	"Defective" due to improper manufacture, inspection, design, or failure to give suitable warning	Limited inspection duty for middlemen
Section 402A	Tort	Seller engaged in business of selling product sold	Defective and unreasonably dangerous	Strict liability; design defect and failure-to-warn suits possible

Other Theories of Recovery

Warranty of Title   Normally, a seller of goods impliedly warrants that: (1) the title he conveys is good and transfer of that title is rightful, and (2) the goods are free from any lien or security interest of which the buyer lacks knowledge. Thus, a buyer may recover damages against his seller where, for example, the seller has marketed stolen goods or goods that are subject to a third party's security interest. Also, a seller who is a merchant in goods of the kind sold normally warrants that the goods are free of any rightful patent or trademark infringement claim, or any similar claim, by a third party.

The Magnuson-Moss Act   The relevant civil-recovery provisions of the federal Magnuson-Moss Warranty Act apply to sales of *consumer products* costing more than *$10 per item.*[10] A consumer

product is tangible personal property normally used for personal, family, or household purposes. If a seller gives a *written warranty* for such a product to a *consumer,* the warranty must be designated full or limited. A seller who gives a full warranty promises to: (1) *remedy* any defects in the product and (2) *replace* the product or *refund* its purchase price if, after a reasonable number of attempts, it cannot be repaired.[11] A seller who gives a limited warranty is bound to whatever promises it actually makes. However, neither warranty applies if the seller simply declines to give a written warranty.

---

[10]Other portions of the Magnuson-Moss Act are discussed later in this chapter and in Chapter 47.

[11]Also, many states have enacted so-called lemon laws that may apply only to motor vehicles, or to various other consumer products as well. The versions applying to motor vehicles generally require the manufacturer to replace the vehicle or refund its purchase price once certain conditions are met. These conditions may include the following: a serious defect covered by warranty, a certain number of unsuccessful attempts at repair or a certain amount of downtime due to attempted repairs, and the manufacturer's failure to show that the defect is curable.

Misrepresentation   Section 402B of the *Restatement (Second) of Torts* lets *consumers* recover for *personal injury* resulting from certain *misrepresentations* about goods they have purchased. The misrepresentation must: (1) be made by a party engaged in the business of selling goods of the kind purchased; (2) be made to the public by advertising, labels, or similar means; (3) concern a fact *material* to the goods purchased; and (4) be *actually and justifiably* relied on by the consumer. Suppose the manufacturer of a laxative states in its advertising that the laxative has no adverse side effects if used as directed. Smith, who has been influenced by the advertisements and has no reason to doubt their accuracy, buys a bottle of the laxative. If, after using it according to directions, Smith suffers injury to his digestive system, he can recover from the manufacturer for that injury.

INDUSTRYWIDE LIABILITY

The development we call industrywide liability is a way for plaintiffs to bypass problems of causation that exist where several firms within an industry have manufactured a harmful standardized product, and it is impossible for the plaintiff to prove *which* firm produced the product that injured her. In such cases, each potential defendant can argue that the plaintiff should lose because she cannot show that *its* product caused the harm of which she complains. The usual reasons for the plaintiff's proof problems are the number of firms producing the product and the time lag between exposure to the product and the appearance of the injury. Many of the cases presenting this problem have involved DES (an antimiscarriage drug that has produced various ailments in daughters of the women to whom it was administered) or diseases resulting from long-term exposure to asbestos.

In such cases, some courts continue to deny recovery under traditional causation rules. However, using various theories whose many details are beyond the scope of this text, other courts have made it easier for plaintiffs to recover. Where recovery is allowed, some of these courts have *apportioned* damages among the firms that might have produced the harm-causing product. Typically, the apportionment is based on market share at some chosen time.

DAMAGES IN PRODUCT LIABILITY SUITS

At this point, we begin to consider several problems that are common to each major theory of product liability recovery but that may be resolved differently from theory to theory.[12] The first such problem, the damages obtainable under each theory, strongly influences a plaintiff's strategy in a product liability suit. Here, we describe the major kinds of damages recoverable in products liability cases, along with the theories under which each can be recovered. One lawsuit can involve claims for all these sorts of damages.

1. Basis-of-the-bargain damages. Buyers of defective goods have not received full value for their purchase price. The resulting loss, usually called basis-of-the-bargain damages or direct economic loss, is the value of the goods as promised under the contract, minus the value of the goods actually received.

Where Awarded: Basis-of-the-bargain damages are usually *not* recoverable in *negligence* and *strict liability* cases. In *express* and *implied warranty* suits under the UCC, however, basis-of-the-bargain damages are recoverable where there was *privity of contract* (a direct contractual relation) between the plaintiff and the defendant. As discussed in the next section, however, only occasionally will a warranty plaintiff who lacks privity with the defendant obtain basis-of-the-bargain damages. Basis-of-the-bargain recoveries most often occur where an express warranty was made to a remote plaintiff through advertising, brochures, or labels.

2. Consequential damages. Consequential damages include: **personal injury, property damage** (damage to the plaintiff's other property), and **indirect economic loss** (e.g., lost profits or lost business reputation) resulting from a product defect. Consequential damages also include **noneconomic loss**— for example, pain and suffering, physical impairment, mental distress, loss of enjoyment of life, loss of companionship or consortium, inconvenience, and disfigurement. Noneconomic loss is usually part of the plaintiff's personal injury claim. Recently,

---

[12]We do not consider how these problems are resolved under the warranty of title, the Magnuson-Moss Act, or section 402B.

several states have limited noneconomic loss recoveries, typically by imposing a dollar cap on them.

Where awarded: Plaintiffs in *negligence* and *strict liability* cases normally can recover for personal injury and property damage. Recoveries for foreseeable indirect economic loss are sometimes allowed.

In UCC *express* and *implied warranty* suits where *privity exists* between the plaintiff and the defendant, the plaintiff can recover for: (1) personal injury and property damage, if either proximately resulted from the breach of warranty; and (2) indirect economic loss, if the defendant had reason to know that this was likely. As discussed in the next section, a UCC plaintiff who *lacks privity* with the defendant has a fairly good chance of recovering for personal injury or property damage. But recovery for indirect economic loss is rare because remote sellers usually cannot foresee such losses.

3. Punitive damages. Punitive (or exemplary) damages are intended to punish defendants who have acted in an especially outrageous fashion, and to deter them and others from so acting in the future. Of the various standards for awarding punitive damages, perhaps the most common is the defendant's conscious or reckless disregard for the safety of those likely to be affected by the goods. Examples include concealment of known product hazards, knowing violation of government or industry product safety standards, failure to correct known dangerous defects, and grossly inadequate product testing or quality control procedures.

Due to their perceived frequency, size, and effect on business and the economy, punitive damages have been subjected to state tort reform regulation throughout the 1980s. The approaches taken by these statutes vary. Many set the standards for punitive damage recovery and the plaintiff's burden of proof; some articulate factors courts should consider when ruling on punitive damage awards; and some create special procedures for punitive damage determinations. Also, several states have limited the size of punitive damage recoveries, usually by restricting them to some multiple of the plaintiff's actual damages, or by putting a flat dollar cap on them.

Where awarded: Assuming that the standards just described have been met, punitive damages are recoverable in *negligence* and *strict liability* cases. Due to the traditional rule that punitive damages are not available in contract cases, they are usually not awarded in *express* and *implied warranty* suits.

Figure 1 summarizes the plaintiff's chances of recovering the most important kinds of damages in contract and tort cases.

THE NO-PRIVITY DEFENSE

Today, defective products often move through long chains of distribution before reaching the person they harm. This means that a product liability

---

FIGURE 1   When the Various Kinds of Damages Are Recoverable

Type of Damages	Express and Implied Warranty	Negligence and Section 402A
Basis of the Bargain	Within privity: Yes Outside privity: Occasionally	Rarely
Personal Injury and Property Damage	Within privity: If proximate result of breach Outside privity: Fairly good chance	Yes
Indirect Economic Loss	Within privity: If defendant has reason to know this likely Outside privity: Rarely	Sometimes
Punitive Damages	Rarely	Yes, in appropriate cases

plaintiff often has not dealt directly with the party ultimately responsible for his losses. Figure 2 depicts a hypothetical chain of distribution in which goods defectively produced by a manufacturer of component parts move vertically through the manufacturer of a product in which those parts are used, a wholesaler, and a retailer, ultimately reaching the buyer. The defect's consequences may move horizontally as well, affecting members of the buyer's family, guests in his home, and even bystanders. If the buyer or one of these parties suffers loss due to the defect in the component parts, can he successfully sue the component parts manufacturer or any other party in the vertical chain of distribution with whom he did not directly deal?

Because at that time there was no recovery for defective goods without privity of contract between the plaintiff and the defendant, such suits were unlikely to succeed under 19th-century law. In the preceding example the buyer would have been required to sue his dealer. If the buyer was successful, the retailer might have sued the wholesaler, and so on up the chain. For a variety of reasons (including a middleman's limited negligence liability for failure to inspect), the party ultimately responsible for the defect often escaped liability.

Negligence and Strict Liability Cases

By now, the old no-liability-outside-privity rule has been severely eroded in tort suits. It has little, if any, effect in *strict liability* cases, where even bystanders can recover against remote manufacturers. In *negligence* cases, a plaintiff generally recovers against a remote defendant if the plaintiff's loss was a reasonably foreseeable consequence of the defect. Depending on the circumstances, therefore, bystanders and other distant parties might recover against a manufacturer in negligence as well.

Warranty Cases

The no-privity defense still retains some vitality in UCC cases. Unfortunately, the "law" on this subject is complex and confusing. Under the Code, the privity question is formally governed by section 2–318, which comes in three alternative versions. Section 2–318's language, however, is a questionable guide to the courts' actual behavior in UCC privity cases.

FIGURE 2   **A Hypothetical Chain of Distribution**

UCC Section 2–318   Alternative A to section 2–318 says that a seller's express or implied warranty runs to natural persons in the family or household of *his* (the seller's) buyer and to guests in his buyer's home if they suffer personal injury and if it was reasonable to expect that they might use, consume, or be affected by the goods sold. On its face, Alternative A does little to undermine the traditional no-privity defense. In Figure 2, Alternative A would merely allow the buyer, his family, and guests in his home to sue the *retailer* for their personal injury.

Alternatives B and C go much further. Alternative B extends the seller's express or implied warranty to any natural person who has suffered personal injury, if it was reasonable to expect that this person would use, consume, or be affected by the goods. Alternative C is much the same, but it extends the warranty to any person (not just natural persons) and to those suffering injury in general (not just personal injury). If the reasonable-to-expect test is met, these two provisions should extend the warranty to many remote parties, including bystanders.

Departures from UCC Section 2–318   For various reasons, section 2–318's literal language is of questionable relevance in UCC privity cases. Some states have adopted privity statutes that differ from any version of section 2–318. Also, one of the comments to section 2–318 lets courts extend liability farther than the section expressly permits. Finally, versions B and C are fairly open ended as written. Thus, the plaintiff's ability to recover outside privity in warranty cases varies from state to state and situation to situation. The most important factors affecting resolution of this question include the following:

1. Whether it is *reasonably foreseeable* that a party such as the plaintiff would be harmed by the product defect in question.
2. The *status of the plaintiff*. On the average, consumers and other natural persons fare better outside privity than corporations and other business concerns.
3. The *type of damages* the plaintiff has suffered. In general, remote plaintiffs are: (a) most likely to recover for personal injury, (b) somewhat less likely to recover for property damage, (c) occasionally able to obtain basis-of-the-bargain damages, and (d) rarely able to recover for indirect economic loss. Recall from the previous section that a remote plaintiff is most likely to receive basis-of-the-bargain damages where an express warranty was made to him through advertising, brochures, or labels.

DISCLAIMERS AND REMEDY LIMITATIONS

Introduction

A product liability **disclaimer** is a clause in the sales contract whereby the seller tries to eliminate its *liability* under one or more theories of recovery. A **remedy limitation** is a clause attempting to block

recovery of certain kinds of *damages*. Disclaimers attack the plaintiff's theory of recovery; if the disclaimer is effective, no damages of any sort are recoverable under that theory. A successful remedy limitation prevents the plaintiff from recovering certain types of damages but does not attack the plaintiff's theory of recovery. Damages not excluded may still be recovered, because the theory is left intact.

The main justification for enforcing disclaimers and remedy limitations is freedom of contract. Also, because goods accompanied by an effective disclaimer or remedy limitation are apt to be cheaper than other goods, enforcing such clauses gives buyers the flexibility to get a lower price by accepting a greater risk of uncompensated defects. For purchases by ordinary consumers and other unsophisticated buyers, however, these arguments are sometimes illusory. Often, the seller presents the disclaimer or remedy limitation in a standardized, take-it-or-leave-it fashion. In addition, it is doubtful whether many consumers read disclaimers and remedy limitations at the time of purchase or would comprehend them if they were read. As a result, there usually is little or no genuine bargaining over disclaimers or remedy limitations in consumer situations. Instead, they are often effectively dictated by a seller with superior size and organization. These observations, however, are less valid where the buyer is a business entity with the capability to engage in genuine bargaining with sellers.

Because the realities surrounding the sale differ from situation to situation, and because some theories of recovery are more hospitable to contractual limitation than others, the law on product liability disclaimers and remedy limitations is complicated. We begin with a lengthy discussion of implied warranty disclaimers. Then we examine disclaimers of express warranty liability, negligence liability, and strict liability before considering remedy limitations separately.

Implied Warranty Disclaimers

To determine the enforceability of implied warranty disclaimers, we must consider several sets of legal rules.[13] Figure 3 structures the steps in this analysis.

---

[13]The same rules probably apply where a seller tries to modify an implied warranty or to limit its duration.

FIGURE 3   The Enforceability of Implied Warranty Disclaimers

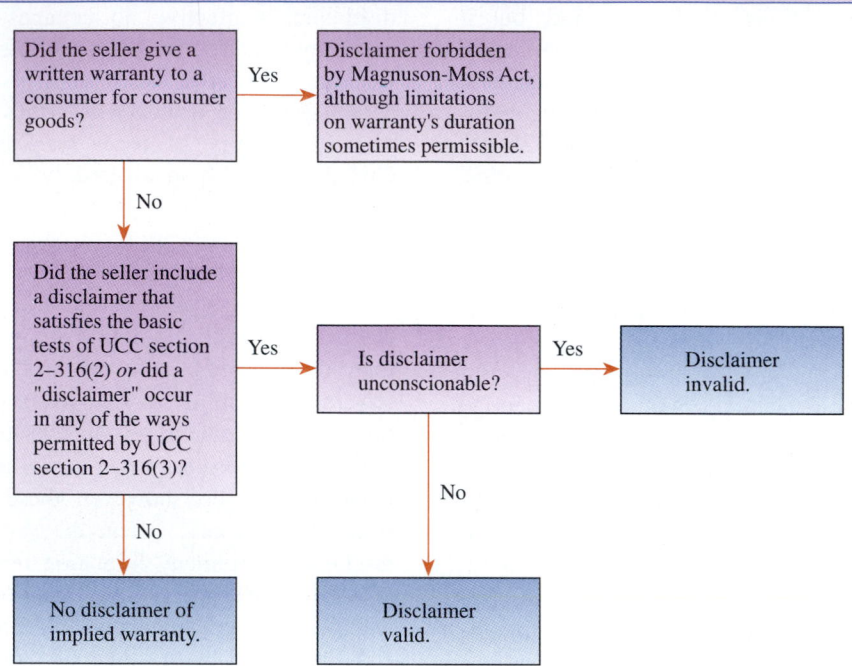

The Basic Tests of UCC Section 2–316(2)

UCC section 2–316(2) apparently makes it easy for sellers to disclaim the implied warranties of merchantability and fitness for a particular purpose. The section states that to exclude or modify the implied warranty of merchantability, a seller must: (1) use the word *merchantability,* and (2) make the disclaimer conspicuous if it is written. To exclude or modify the implied warranty of fitness, a seller must: (1) use a writing, and (2) make the disclaimer conspicuous. A disclaimer is conspicuous if it is written so that a reasonable person ought to have noticed it. Capital letters, larger type, contrasting type, and contrasting colors usually suffice.

Unlike the fitness warranty disclaimer, a disclaimer of the implied warranty of merchantability can be oral. Also, while disclaimers of the latter warranty must always use the word *merchantability,* no special language is needed to disclaim the implied warranty of fitness. For example, a conspicuous written statement that "THERE ARE NO WARRANTIES WHICH EXTEND BEYOND THE DESCRIPTION ON THE FACE HEREOF" disclaims the implied warranty of fitness but not the implied warranty of merchantability.

Other Ways to Disclaim Implied Warranties: UCC Section 2–316(3)

According to UCC section 2–316(3)(a), sellers can also disclaim either implied warranty by using such terms as "with all faults," "as is," and "as they stand." Some courts have held that these terms must be conspicuous to be effective as disclaimers.

UCC section 2–316(3)(b) describes two situations where the buyer's *inspection* of the goods or her *refusal to inspect* can act as a disclaimer. If a buyer examines the goods before the sale and fails to discover a defect that should have been reasonably apparent to her, there can be no implied warranty suit based on that defect. Also, if a seller requests that the buyer examine the goods and the buyer refuses, the buyer cannot base an implied warranty suit on a defect that would have been reasonably apparent had she made the inspection. The definition of a reasonably apparent defect varies with the buyer's expertise. Unless the defect is blatant, ordinary consumers may have little to fear from section 2–316(3)(b).

Finally, UCC section 2–316(3)(c) says that an implied warranty can be excluded or modified by *course of dealing* (the parties' previous conduct), *course of performance* (the parties' previous conduct under the same contract), or *usage of trade* (any practice regularly observed in the trade). For example, if it is accepted in the local cattle trade that buyers who inspect the seller's cattle and reject certain animals must accept all defects in the cattle actually purchased, such buyers cannot mount an implied warranty suit for those defects.

Unconscionable Disclaimers   From the previous discussion, it seems that any seller who retains a competent attorney can escape implied warranty liability at will. In fact, however, a seller's ability to disclaim implied warranties is restricted in various ways. One of these restrictions is the doctrine of **unconscionability** established by UCC section 2–302 and discussed in Chapter 15.

By now, almost all courts apply section 2–302's unconscionability standards to implied warranty disclaimers even though those disclaimers satisfy UCC section 2–316(2). Despite a growing willingness to protect smaller firms that deal with corporate giants, courts still tend to reject unconscionability claims where business parties have contracted in a commercial context. However, implied warranty disclaimers are often declared unconscionable in personal injury suits by ordinary consumers.

The Impact of Magnuson-Moss   The Magnuson-Moss Act creates other important limitations on a seller's ability to disclaim implied warranties. If a seller gives a consumer a full warranty on consumer goods, the seller may not disclaim, modify, or limit the duration of any implied warranty. If a limited warranty is given, the seller may not disclaim or modify any implied warranty but may limit its duration to the duration of the limited warranty if this is done conspicuously and if the limitation is not unconscionable. Presumably, however, a seller can still disclaim by refusing to give a written warranty while placing the disclaimer on some other writing.

Express Warranty Disclaimers

UCC section 2–316(1) says that an express warranty and a disclaimer should be read consistently if possible, but that the disclaimer must yield if such a reading is unreasonable. Because it is normally unreasonable for a seller to exclude with one hand

what he has freely and openly promised with the other, it is very difficult to disclaim an express warranty.

Negligence and Strict Liability Disclaimers

Disclaimers of negligence liability and strict liability are usually ineffective in cases involving ordinary consumers. However, some courts enforce such disclaimers where both parties are business entities that: (1) dealt in a commercial setting, (2) had relatively equal bargaining power, (3) bargained the product's specifications, and (4) negotiated the risk of loss from product defects (e.g., the disclaimer itself).

Limitation of Remedies

Due to the expense they can create for sellers, consequential damages are the usual target of remedy limitations. Where a limitation of consequential damages succeeds, buyers of the product may suffer. For example, suppose that Dillman buys a computer system for $20,000 under a contract that excludes consequential damages and limits the buyer's remedies to the repair or replacement of defective parts. Suppose also that the system never works properly, causing Dillman to suffer $10,000 in lost profits. If the remedy limitation is enforceable, Dillman could only have the system replaced or repaired by the seller, and could not recover his $10,000 in consequential damages.

In negligence and strict liability cases, the tests for the enforceability of remedy limitations resemble the previous tests for disclaimers. Under the UCC, however, the standards for remedy limitations differ from those for disclaimers.

UCC section 2–719(3) allows the limitation of consequential damages in express and implied warranty cases, but also states that such a limitation may be unconscionable. The section adds that a limitation of consequential damages is quite likely to be unconscionable where the sale is for *consumer goods* and the plaintiff has suffered *personal injury.* Where the loss is "commercial," however, the limitation may or may not be unconscionable. The meaning of commercial loss is unclear. But in cases where it exists, courts must consider the many factors relevant to unconscionability determinations on a case-by-case basis.

Time Limitations

Traditionally, the main time limits on product liability suits have been the applicable contract and tort statutes of limitations. The usual UCC statute of limitations for express and implied warranty claims is four years after the seller offers the defective goods to the buyer (usually, four years after the sale).[14] In negligence and strict liability cases, the applicable tort statute of limitations is generally shorter. But it only begins to run when the defect was or should have been discovered—often, the time of the injury.

Due in part to tort reform, some states now impose various other limitations on the time within which product liability suits must be brought. Often, these limitations apply only to claims for death, personal injury, and property damage, but they override the states' other time limitations where they do apply. Among these additional time limitations are: (1) special statutes of limitations for product liability cases involving death, personal injury, or property damage (e.g., from one to three years after the time the injury or death occurred or should have been discovered); (2) special time limits for "delayed manifestation" injuries such as those resulting from exposure to asbestos; (3) useful safe life defenses (which prevent plaintiffs from suing once the product's "useful safe life" has passed); and (4) statutes of repose (whose aim is similar). Statutes of repose usually run for a 10- to 12-year period that begins when the product is sold to the first buyer not purchasing for resale—usually an ordinary consumer. In a state with a 10-year statute of repose, for example, such parties cannot recover for injuries that occur more than 10 years after they purchased the product causing the injury. This is true even when the suit is begun quickly enough to satisfy the applicable statute of limitations.

Defenses

Many things—for example, the absence of privity or a valid disclaimer—can be considered defenses to a product liability suit. Here, however, our concern is with product liability defenses that involve the plaintiff's behavior.

The Traditional Defenses

Traditionally, the three main defenses in a product liability suit have been the overlapping trio of product misuse, assumption of risk, and contributory negligence.[15] **Product misuse** (or abnormal use) occurs when the plaintiff uses the product in some unusual, unforeseeable way, and this causes the loss for which she sues. Examples include ignoring the manufacturer's instructions, mishandling the product, and using the product for purposes for which it was not intended. But if the defendant had reason to foresee the misuse and failed to take reasonable precautions against it, there is no defense. Product misuse is usually available in warranty, negligence, and strict liability cases.

Assumption of risk is the plaintiff's voluntary consent to a known danger. It can occur any time the plaintiff willingly exposes herself to a known product hazard—for example, by consuming obviously adulterated food. Like product misuse, assumption of risk ordinarily is a defense in warranty, negligence, and strict liability cases.

Contributory negligence is the plaintiff's failure to act with reasonable, prudent, self-protectiveness. In the product liability context, perhaps the most common example is the simple failure to notice a hazardous product defect. Contributory negligence is clearly a defense in a negligence suit, but courts disagree about whether or when it should be a defense in warranty and strict liability cases.

Comparative Principles

Where they are allowed and proven, the three traditional product liability defenses completely absolve the defendant from liability. Dissatisfaction with this all-or-nothing situation has spurred the increasing use of *comparative* principles in product liability cases.[16] Rather than letting the traditional defenses completely absolve the defendant, courts

---

[14]Also, in express and implied warranty cases, the buyer must notify the seller of the breach within a reasonable time after the buyer discovers or should have discovered it. There is no notice requirement for negligence and strict liability suits.

[15]Chapter 7 discusses contributory negligence and assumption of risk.

[16]Comparative negligence is discussed in Chapter 7. Some of the newer state statutes, however, speak of comparative *fault*. Although courts and commentators often use the terms *comparative fault* and *comparative negligence* interchangeably, it is not always clear whether comparative negligence embraces forms of fault other than the plaintiff's negligence.

and legislatures now apportion damages on the basis of relative fault. They do so by requiring that the fact finder establish the plaintiff's and the defendant's percentage shares of the total fault for the injury, and then award the plaintiff his total provable damages times the defendant's percentage share of the fault.

Unsettled questions persist among the states that have adopted comparative principles. First, it is not always clear what kinds of fault will reduce the plaintiff's recovery. However, some state comparative negligence statutes have been read as embracing assumption of risk and product misuse, and state comparative fault statutes usually define fault broadly. Second, comparative principles may assume either the *pure* or the *mixed* forms described in Chapter 7. In states that use the mixed form, for example, the defendant has a complete defense where the plaintiff is more at fault than the defendant. Finally, there is some uncertainty about the theories of recovery and the types of damage claims to which comparative principles apply.

STATES V. R. D. WERNER COMPANY
799 P.2d 427 (Colo. Ct. App. 1990)

Lloyd States was injured after falling from a step ladder at a construction site. He had placed the ladder's front feet (which are on the same side of the ladder as its steps) on a sidewalk, with its rear feet on the surface of an unfinished parking lot that was 6 to 9 inches below the front feet. This was contrary to the manufacturer's instructions for the use of the ladder, which were affixed to it. Then States climbed the ladder, turned on the steps so that his back was to them, and leaned over toward a building. He did so in order to attach a sign to the building with a power wrench while the sign was being held in place by an overhead crane. States pressed against the sign with one hand while using his other hand to apply pressure on the power wrench. As he did so, the ladder moved away from him and he fell.

States sued R. D. Werner Co., the manufacturer of the ladder, in a Colorado trial court under section 402A of the *Restatement (Second) of Torts.* He alleged that a defect in the ladder caused his fall and his injuries. After trial, the jury found for R. D. Werner. States appealed, attacking the trial court's instruction to the jury. The jury had been instructed that: (1) if both a defective product and the plaintiff's conduct contributed to his injury, the plaintiff's recovery must be reduced in proportion to his percentage share of the fault causing the injury; and (2) if the plaintiff's misuse of a product was the sole cause of his injuries, and the alleged product defect played no role in producing them, the seller or manufacturer of that product cannot be liable.

Pierce, Judge   Misuse of a product by the injured person is a recognized defense to a section 402A action. Misuse concerns an issue of causation and provides a complete defense to liability, regardless of any defective condition, if an unforeseeable and unintended use of the product, and not the alleged defect, caused the plaintiff's injuries. Plaintiff argues that the concept of comparative [fault] is to be applied to all product liability actions. He asserts that the [second] instruction [stated above] erroneously converts the statutory concept of comparative fault into a recovery bar, rather than a damage diminution remedy.

Section 13–21–406 [of the Colorado Revised Statutes] provides in pertinent part:

Comparative fault as measure of damages.
(1) In any product liability action, the fault of the person suffering the harm, as well as the fault of all others who are parties to the action for causing the harm, shall be compared by the trier of fact in accordance with this section. The fault of the person suffering the harm shall not bar such person . . . from recovering damages, but the award of damages to such person . . . shall be diminished in proportion to the amount of causal fault attributed to the person suffering the harm.

* * * *

(4) The provisions of [Colorado's comparative negligence statute] do not apply to any product liability action.

We interpret section 13–21–406 to mean that once it has been established that the product is defective, if both the defective product and the injured person's conduct contributed to the injury underlying plaintiff's claim, then the plaintiff's recovery must be reduced by a percentage representing the amount of fault attributable to his own conduct. Here, the jury was properly so instructed. Depending on the facts of the case, the injured person's misuse of the product could constitute comparative fault which would reduce the plaintiff's recovery. However, if the misuse is the *sole* cause of damages, and thus the alleged defect was not a cause thereof, then the plaintiff cannot recover under [section 402A]. Here, the instruction given to the jury provided that if Lloyd's misuse of the ladder, *rather than a defect*, caused Lloyd's injuries, R. D. Werner could not be held legally responsible for those injuries. The trial court did not err in giving this instruction.

Trial court verdict for R. D. Werner affirmed.

ETHICAL AND PUBLIC POLICY CONCERNS

1. As suggested earlier in this chapter, one explanation for the prodefendant thrust of 19th-century product liability law is the courts' desire to protect infant industries by preventing them from suffering potentially crippling damage awards. If this explanation is accurate, it means that those injured by defective products and the survivors of those killed by such products were denied compensation so that the country might be industrialized. Is this right? Should people's rights be sacrificed in this way? In answering this question, assume for the sake of argument that these denials of recovery actually were necessary for industrialization to proceed.

2. Courts are much more likely to find disclaimers and remedy limitations enforceable when the plaintiff is a business firm than when the plaintiff is an ordinary consumer. What is the justification for this difference in treatment?

One possible way to get around the arguments against enforcing disclaimers and remedy limitations in consumer cases is to enforce them when the seller has used various kinds of "superdisclosure" to make buyers aware of the disclaimer. Possibilities include: positioning the disclaimer or limitation outside the product package, using signs to alert buyers to it, explaining it to buyers, and requiring the buyer to sign separately near a conspicuous disclaimer or limitation. Try to think of some problems with superdisclosure itself and with allowing disclaimers and remedy limitations to be enforced on this basis.

3. Most likely, consumers would pay a somewhat lower price for the products they purchase if the implied warranty of merchantability did not exist. Why is this so? Assuming that it is so, why shouldn't consumers have the choice whether to buy products with the "insurance policy" the warranty provides, or to get a lower price by forgoing this protection? Or would this choice be too difficult for individual sellers and manufacturers to provide? Nonetheless, shouldn't consumers at least know what deal sellers are offering so that they can pick the seller whose terms they prefer? In theory, how does current law make this possible? What would probably *really* be necessary for consumers to get the necessary information? *Hint:* look at the second paragraph of the previous question.

PROBLEMS AND PROBLEM CASES

1. *Video Case.* See "TV Repair." Allen, a salesperson for an electronics store, is talking to Arnold, a customer, while Arnold picks up a portable TV and puts it on the counter preparatory to buying it. Allen tells Arnold that he "won't have any problems" with the set because he's "buying the best." He also tells Arnold that "I'm sure you'll enjoy your new set." After purchasing the set, taking it home, and plugging it in, Arnold finds that the set does not work. Assuming that Allen has the authority to bind the store, has the store breached an express warranty to Arnold? Assuming that the store is a merchant and has not disclaimed the implied warranty of merchantability, is it liable on that basis?

2. Ewers, who owns a saltwater aquarium with tropical fish, bought several seashells, a piece of coral, and a driftwood branch from the Verona Rock Shop. Just before the purchase, the salesclerk told Ewers that these items were "suitable for saltwater aquariums, if they [are] rinsed." After making the purchase, Ewers took the items home, rinsed them for 20 minutes in a saltwater solution, and put them in his aquarium. Within a week, 17 of his tropical fish died. The "rinsing" required to prevent their deaths is a week-long cleansing process that involves soaking the shells and the coral in boiling water. Suppose that you are Ewers's attorney in his express warranty suit against the shop. Make an argument that the clerk's statement is an express warranty. Make an argument that this warranty was breached.

3. Steven Taterka purchased a 1972 Ford Mustang from a Ford dealer in January 1972. In October 1974, after Taterka had put 75,000 miles on the car and Ford's express warranty had expired, he discovered that the tail-light assembly gaskets on his Mustang had been installed in such a way that water was permitted to enter the tail-light assembly, causing rust to form. Even though the rusting problem was a recurrent one of which Ford was aware, Ford did nothing for Taterka. Is Ford liable to Taterka under the implied warranty of merchantability?

4. Cathy Adelman-Tremblay purchased a "Nailene Nail Kit" at a drugstore. The kit included artificial fingernails, a nail sander file, and a tube of cyanoacrylate liquid glue (also known as Super Glue). After attaching the artificial nails to her fingernails with the glue, Adelman-Tremblay experienced pain and eventually suffered the permanent loss of all of her natural fingernails. The cause of the loss was an allergic reaction called "allergic contact dermatitis."

The manufacturer of the Nailene kit had sold more than 1 million such kits, and Adelman-Tremblay's reaction was the only known adverse reaction to the glue. Also, the relevant medical literature indicated that allergic reactions to the glue were virtually impossible. Nonetheless, a few cases of allergic contact dermatitis from exposure to the glue occurred after Adelman-Tremblay suffered her reaction. Is the manufacturer liable in negligence for

failing to warn users of the possibility of such an allergic reaction? Can Adelman-Tremblay recover under the implied warranty of merchantability?

5. 🎞 *Video Case.* See "Software Horror Story." Chuck contacts the Bits and Bites Computer Superstore to get a software package suitable for some customized computer program work he is performing for a client. He tells the store's salesperson that he needs a database management system that he can customize at the source code level. However, there is little discussion of his other needs, including the work Chuck is doing for the client. The salesperson recommends a system called "D-Base Hit" for $649, and Chuck relies on the salesperson's judgment in buying that package. As it turns out, D-Base Hit *can* be modified at the source code level, but it is otherwise unsuitable for the job Chuck is doing. Assuming that Article 2 of the UCC applies, has Bits and Bites breached the implied warranty of fitness for a particular purpose?

6. Gari West used Ovulen-28, a birth control medication manufactured by Searle & Company. She claimed that the Ovulen-28 caused her to develop a hepatic adenoma (a benign liver tumor), which eventually ruptured, causing a life-threatening situation. Assuming that the Ovulen-28 actually caused West's problem, what argument can Searle make to avoid the imposition of strict liability under section 402A? *Hint*: Assume that the Ovulen-28 has considerable social utility and cannot feasibly be made safer than it now is.

7. Curtis Hagans lost the ring finger of his left hand while operating an industrial table saw manufactured by the Oliver Machinery Company. The saw was originally equipped with a detachable blade guard assembly that would have prevented Hagans's injury had it been attached to the saw while Hagans was working. This assembly was detachable rather than permanently affixed to the saw because many common woodworking functions could not be performed with the assembly in place. Also, the saw exceeded industry safety practices and national and associational safety standards in effect at the time of its manufacture. In addition, few competing manufacturers included blade guards as standard equipment, and none offered a table saw with a permanently affixed blade guard.

Hagans sued Oliver in negligence and under *Restatement (Second) of Torts* section 402A, alleging that the saw was defectively designed because it did not include a permanent blade guard assembly. Did Hagans win? You can assume that injuries of the kind Hagans suffered were foreseeable consequences of manufacturing the saw without a permanent guard, and that Hagans was not careless in his operation of the saw.

8. Floyd Roysden had long smoked Camel and Winston cigarettes, both of which are products of the R. J. Reynolds Tobacco Company. In 1983, Roysden's severe peripheral atherosclerotic vascular disease became so severe that his left leg was amputated below the knee. Some medical evidence links this disease to cigarette smoking. Assuming that they were not improperly manufactured and did not contain any dangerous impurities, were the cigarettes Roysden smoked "defective" under section 402A? Were they "unreasonably dangerous?" Does it matter that there is little public knowledge about the link between cigarette smoking and the specific disease from which Roysden suffered (as opposed to the general health risks cigarette smoking creates)?

9. Joe Kysar purchased a baler built by the Vermeer Manufacturing Company after a Vermeer sales representative told him that the baler in question would produce bales weighing 3,000 pounds. In fact, the baler never produced a 3,000-pound bale. Kysar eventually sued Vermeer in a Wyoming trial court. The court found Vermeer liable under the UCC, but did not specify the exact basis of its holding. As a remedy, it ordered Vermeer to return the purchase price to Kysar, after which Kysar was to return the baler to Vermeer. Assuming that Vermeer breached either an express warranty or the implied warranty of fitness, was this the proper measure of recovery for defective goods under the UCC? Assume for the sake of argument that Kysar suffered no consequential damages of any kind.

10. Arlyn and Rose Spindler were dairy farmers who leased a feed storage silo from Agristor Leasing. The silo was supposed to limit the oxygen reaching the feed and thus to hinder its spoilage. The Spindlers alleged that the silo was defective and that the dairy feed it contained was spoiled as a result. They further alleged that due to the spoilage of the feed, their dairy herd suffered medically and reproductively and their milk production dropped. The Spindlers sued Agristor in negligence and under section 402A for their resulting lost income. What *type* of damages are they claiming? Under the majority rule, can they recover for such damages in negligence or under section 402A? Would your answer be different if the Spindlers had sued for the damage to the *dairy feed* itself? Assume for purposes of argument that both section 402A and negligence suits are possible under this equipment lease.

11. ▣ *Video Case.* See "Car Deals." Jake, a car salesman, is discussing a particular car with Jones, a customer at Jake's dealership. Jake tells Jones "you won't find a car like this at any price. This car is a crown jewel." Later, Jake says that he bought the car at an auction in Kentucky. Influenced by these statements, Jones buys the car. The bill of sale conspicuously says that the car is being sold "AS IS," and that no warranties or representations concerning the car have been made or given, except as stated in the bill of sale. Later, Jones discovers that the car's brakes are so defective that the car is unsafe to drive.

Which, if any, of Jake's statements are express warranties? Which, if any, have been breached here? Does the language in the bill of sale disclaim any express warranties that might exist? Does the language in the bill of sale disclaim the implied warranty of merchantability? Assuming that the implied warranty of merchantability has not been disclaimed, is it breached here?

12. Duane Martin, a small farmer, placed an order for cabbage seed with the Joseph Harris Company, a large national producer and distributor of seed. Harris's order form included the following language:

NOTICE TO BUYER: Joseph Harris Company, Inc. warrants that seeds and plants it sells conform to the label descriptions as required by Federal and State seed laws. IT MAKES NO OTHER WARRANTIES, EXPRESS OR IMPLIED, OF MERCHANTABILITY, FITNESS FOR PURPOSE, OR OTHERWISE, AND IN ANY EVENT ITS LIABILITY FOR BREACH OF ANY WARRANTY OR CONTRACT WITH RESPECT TO SUCH SEEDS OR PLANTS IS LIMITED TO THE PURCHASE PRICE OF SUCH SEEDS OR PLANTS.

All of Harris's competitors used similar clauses in their contracts.

After Martin placed his order, and unknown to Martin, Harris stopped using a cabbage seed treatment that had been effective in preventing a certain cabbage fungus. Later, Martin planted the seed he had ordered from Harris, but a large portion of the resulting crop was destroyed by fungus because the seed did not contain the treatment Harris had previously used. Martin sued Harris for his losses under the implied warranty of merchantability.

Which portion of the notice quoted above is an attempted disclaimer of implied warranty liability, and which is an attempted limitation of remedies? Will the disclaimer language disclaim the implied warranty of merchantability under UCC section 2–316(2)? If Martin had sued under the implied warranty of fitness for a particular purpose, would the disclaimer language disclaim that implied warranty as well? Assuming that the disclaimer and the remedy limitation contained the correct legal boilerplate needed to make them effective, what argument could Martin still make to block their operation? What are his chances of success with this argument?

13. Moulton purchased a 1969 Ford LTD from Hull-Dobbs, a Ford dealer. His sales contracts with Ford and Hull-Dobbs contained valid disclaimers of the implied warranty of merchantability that satisfied UCC section 2–316(2). One year later, while Moulton was driving his car along an interstate highway, the Ford suddenly veered to the right, jumped the guardrail, and fell 26 feet to the street below. The accident was caused by a defect in the car's steering mechanism, and Moulton was seriously injured. Moulton sued Ford under the implied warranty of merchantability. Ford defended on the basis of its disclaimer. Moulton argued that the disclaimer was invalid in a personal injury case under UCC section 2–719(3), which makes the exclusion of consequential damages unconscionable in a case involving consumer goods and personal injury. Did Moulton's argument succeed?

PERFORMANCE OF

SALES CONTRACTS

INTRODUCTION

In the two previous chapters, we discussed the formation and terms of sales contracts, including those terms concerning express and implied warranties. In this chapter, the focus is on the legal rules that govern the performance of contracts. Among the topics covered are the basic obligations of the buyer and seller with respect to delivery and payment, the rights of the parties when the goods delivered do not conform to the contract, and the circumstances that may excuse the performance of a party's contractual obligations.

GENERAL RULES

The parties to a contract for the sale of goods are obligated to perform the contract according to its terms. The Uniform Commercial Code (UCC or Code) gives the parties great flexibility in deciding between themselves how they will perform a contract. The practices in the trade or business as well as any past dealings between the parties may supplement or explain the contract. The Code gives both the buyer and the seller certain rights, and it also sets out what is expected of them on points that they did not deal with in their contract. It should be kept in mind that the Code changes basic contract law in a number of respects.

Good Faith

The buyer and seller must act in **good faith** in the performance of a sales contract [1–203].[1] Good faith is defined to mean "honesty in fact" in performing the duties assumed in the contract or in carrying out the transaction [1–201(19)]. Thus, if the contract requires the seller to select an assortment of goods for the buyer, the selection must be made in good faith; the seller should pick out a reasonable assortment [2–311]. It would not, for example, be good faith to include only unusual sizes or colors.

---

[1]The numbers in brackets refer to sections of the Uniform Commercial Code.

Course of Dealing

The terms in the contract between the parties are the primary means for determining the obligations of the buyer and seller. The meaning of those terms may be explained by looking at any performance that has already taken place. For example, a contract may call for periodic deliveries of goods. If the seller has made a number of deliveries without objection by the buyer, the way the deliveries were made shows how the parties intended them to be made. Similarly, if there were any past contracts between the parties, the way the parties interpreted those contracts is relevant to the interpretation of the present contract. If there is a conflict between the express terms of the contract and the past course of dealing between the parties, the express terms of the contract prevail [1–205(4)].

Usage of Trade

In many kinds of businesses, there are customs and practices of the trade that are known by people in the business and that are usually assumed by parties to a contract for goods of that type. Under the Code, the parties and courts may use these trade customs and practices—known as usage of trade—in interpreting a contract [2—202; 1–205]. If there is a conflict between the express terms of the contract and trade usage, the express terms prevail [1–205(4)].

The *Weisz Graphics v. Peck Industries* case illustrates how a court may consider the terms of a contract, the course of dealing between the parties, and trade usage in determining the interpretation of a contract between merchants.

WEISZ GRAPHICS DIVISION OF THE FRED B. JOHNSON CO., INC. V. PECK INDUSTRIES, INC.

403 S.E.2d 146 (S.C. Ct. App. 1991)

Weisz Graphics is a custom manufacturer and seller of decals, markings, and other graphic materials and competes in a national market. Weisz manufactures its products to customer specifications based on blueprints, samples, art, or mechanical drawings. It manufactures only to order and does not maintain a general inventory. However, it regularly engages in what are known as "release programs" with its customer; such programs are common in the industry. Under a release program, Weisz manufactures a large quantity of goods to customer order, then warehouses the goods for the customer. As the customer needs the goods, Weisz releases them in specified lots and bills the buyer when it ships the goods. Release programs in the industry are generally limited to one year, due in part to the shelf life of the goods.

Peck Industries, a manufacturer of commercial signs for national and Memphis, Tennessee, accounts, uses pressure sensitive vinyl letters, numbers, and other products. Beginning in 1985, Peck began purchasing some of its requirements from Weisz; some contracts were for immediate manufacture and delivery while others were for extended delivery under a release program. A November 1985 order (P.O. 4426) provided: "BREAK UP INTO MULTIPLE SHIPMENTS." Weisz's acknowledgment contained the following shipment term: "On Releases Bill & Ship on release for 12 months." In April 1986, Peck sent a purchase order (P.O. 5885) for a quantity of goods that provided "TO BE BILLED AND SHIPPED AS RELEASED." Weisz sent back its standard acknowledgment form on which a clerk had typed "On Releases over 12 months." Other orders (P.O. 4037 and P.O. 4426)) were placed by Peck that stated on their face: "ORDER AS NEEDED FOR A PERIOD OF 1 YEAR." In each case, Weisz immediately manufactured the items ordered and over a period of a year released and billed shipments at Peck's request. At the end of the 12 months, Weisz refused to make further shipments until Peck paid in full the remaining balance on the shipment. Peck refused to pay, choosing instead to obtain its requirements from other manufacturers at higher prices. Weisz then brought suit for the balance due on the goods sold to Peck.

Bell, Judge   Section 1–205(3) states:

A course of dealing between parties and any usage of trade in the . . . trade in which they are engaged or should be aware [sic] give particular meaning to supplement or qualify terms of the agreement.

Similarly, section 2–208(1) provides that a course of performance between the parties which is accepted or acquiesced in without objection by a party with opportunity to object is relevant to determine the meaning of the agreement.

As to Purchase Order 4037, Peck itself specified that delivery was on release for one year. There is no evidence that Weisz's acknowledgment contained a similar notation. However, Weisz did not object and began delivering the goods on release.

Purchase Order 4426 specified multiple shipments, but no release period. Weisz's uncontradicted evidence showed that a time limitation is standard in the industry. It also showed that its prior course of dealing with Peck had been to ship on twelve-month release. None of its release contracts with Peck exceeded twelve months. Moreover, Peck accepted performance of Order 4426 without objection. Therefore, under sections 1–205(3) and 2–208(1), the twelve-month release period that supplemented the express provisions of the written form was part of the contract.

The same is true of Purchase Order 5885. Like Purchase Order 4426, it specified no release period. However, its express provisions were supplemented by trade usage and prior course of dealing which established the twelve month release period as a term of the contract.

In the alternative, the twelve-month release period became a term of the contract under section 2–207(2). In response to Purchase Order 4426 and 5885, Weisz's acknowledgment forms added a twelve-month release period. Neither of Peck's orders expressly limited Weisz's acceptance to the express terms of its standard form. Nor did Peck give Weisz a notification of objection to the acknowledgments. Instead, Peck began accepting performance of the contract without objection. Finally, the twelve-month limit was not a material alteration of the contract. Because it conformed to existing trade usage and prior course of dealing between the parties, it did not result in unreasonable surprise or hardship. Accordingly, both contracts incorporated a term for delivery on twelve-month release. Payment in full of the balance on the purchase price was due at the end of the twelfth month.

Judgment for Weisz.

Modification

Under the Code, consideration is not required to support a modification or rescission of a contract for the sale of goods. However, the parties may specify in their agreement that modification or rescission must be in writing, in which case a signed writing is necessary for enforcement of any modification to the contract or its rescission [2–209].

Waiver

In a contract that entails a number of instances of partial performance (such as deliveries or payments) by one party, the other party must be careful to object to any late deliveries or payments. If the other party does not object, it may waive its rights to cancel the contract if other deliveries or payments are late [2–208(3), 2–209(4)]. For example, a contract calls for a fish market to deliver fish to a supermarket every Thursday and for the supermarket to pay on delivery. If the fish market regularly delivers the fish on Friday and the supermarket does not object, the supermarket will be unable to cancel the contract for that reason. Similarly, if the supermarket does not pay cash but sends a check the following week, then unless the fish market objects, it will not be able to assert the late payments as grounds for later canceling the contract. A party that has waived rights to a portion of the contract not yet performed may retract the waiver by giving reasonable notice to the other party that strict performance will be required. The retraction of the waiver is effective unless it would be unjust because of a material change of position by the other party in reliance on the waiver [2–209(5)].

Assignment

Under the Code, the buyer and/or the seller may generally delegate their duties to someone else. If there is a strong reason for having the original party perform the duties, perhaps because the quality of the performance might differ otherwise, the parties may not delegate their duties. Also, they may not delegate their duties if the parties agree in the contract that there is to be no assignment of duties. However, they may assign rights to receive performance—for example, the right to receive goods or payment [2−210].

DELIVERY

Basic Obligation

The basic duty of the seller is to deliver the goods called for by the contract. The basic duty of the buyer is to accept and pay for the goods if they conform to the contract [2−301]. The buyer and seller may agree that the goods are to be delivered in several lots or installments. If there is no such agreement, then a single delivery of all the goods must be made. Where delivery is to be made in lots, the seller may demand the price of each lot upon delivery unless there has been an agreement for the extension of credit [2−307].

Place of Delivery

The buyer and seller may agree on the place where the goods will be delivered. If no such agreement is made, then the goods are to be delivered at the seller's place of business. If the seller does not have a place of business, then delivery is to be made at his home. If the goods are located elsewhere than the seller's place of business or home, the place of delivery is the place where the goods are located [2−308].

Seller's Duty of Delivery

The seller's basic obligation is to tender delivery of goods that conform to the contract with the buyer. Tender of delivery means that the seller must make the goods available to the buyer. This must be done during reasonable hours and for a reasonable period of time, so that the buyer can take possession of the goods [2−503]. The contract of sale may require the seller to merely ship the goods to the buyer but not to deliver the goods to the buyer's place of business. If this is the case, the seller must put the goods into the possession of a carrier, such as a trucking company or a railroad. The seller must also make a reasonable contract with the carrier to take the goods to the buyer. Then, the seller must notify the buyer that the goods have been shipped [2−504]. Shipment terms were discussed in Chapter 19, Formation and Terms of Sales Contracts.

If the seller does not make a reasonable contract for delivery or notify the buyer and a material delay or loss results, the buyer has the right to reject the shipment. Suppose the goods are perishable, such as fresh produce, and the seller does not ship them in a refrigerated truck or railroad car. If the produce deteriorates in transit, the buyer can reject the produce on the ground that the seller did not make a reasonable contract for shipping it.

In some situations, the goods sold may be in the possession of a bailee such as a warehouse. If the goods are covered by a negotiable warehouse receipt, the seller must indorse the receipt and give it to the buyer [2−503(4)(a)]. This enables the buyer to obtain the goods from the warehouse. Such a situation exists when grain being sold is stored at a grain elevator. The law of negotiable documents of title, including warehouse receipts, is discussed in Chapter 33, Checks and Documents of Title.

If the goods in the possession of a bailee are not covered by a negotiable warehouse receipt, then the seller must notify the bailee that it has sold the goods to the buyer and must obtain the bailee's consent to hold the goods for delivery to the buyer or release of the goods to the buyer. The risk of loss as to the goods remains with the seller until the bailee agrees to hold them for the buyer [2−503(4)(b)].

INSPECTION AND PAYMENT

Buyer's Right of Inspection

Normally, the buyer has the right to inspect the goods before he accepts or pays for them. The buyer and seller may agree on the time, place, and manner in which the buyer will inspect the goods. If no agreement is made, then the buyer may inspect the goods at any reasonable time and place and in any reasonable manner [2–513(1)].

If the shipping terms are cash on delivery (COD), then the buyer must pay for the goods before inspecting them unless they are marked "Inspection Allowed." However, if it is obvious even without inspection that the goods do not conform to the contract, the buyer may reject them without paying for them first [2–512(1)(a)]. For example, if a farmer contracted to buy a bull and the seller delivered a cow, the farmer would not have to pay for it. The fact that a buyer may have to pay for goods before inspecting them does not deprive the buyer of remedies against the seller if the goods do not conform to the contract [2–512(2)].

If the goods conform to the contract, the buyer must pay the expenses of inspection. However, if the goods are nonconforming, he may recover his inspection expenses from the seller [2–513(2)].

Payment

The buyer and seller may agree in their contract that the price of the goods is to be paid in money or in other goods, services, or real property. If all or part of the price of goods is payable in real property, then only the transfer of goods is covered by the law of sales of goods. The transfer of the real property is covered by the law of real property [2–304].

The contract may provide that the goods are sold on credit to the buyer and that the buyer has a period of time to pay for them. If there is no agreement for extending credit to the buyer, the buyer must pay for them upon delivery. The buyer usually can inspect goods before payment except where the goods are shipped COD, in which case the buyer must pay for them before inspecting them.

Unless the seller demands cash, the buyer may pay for the goods by personal check or by any other method used in the ordinary course of business. If the seller demands cash, the seller must give the buyer a reasonable amount of time to obtain it. If payment is made by check, the payment is conditional on the check being honored by the bank when it is presented for payment [2–511(3)]. If the bank refuses to pay the check, the buyer has not satisfied the duty to pay for the goods. In that case, the buyer does not have the right to retain the goods and must give them back to the seller.

ACCEPTANCE, REVOCATION, AND REJECTION

Acceptance

Acceptance of goods occurs when a buyer, after having a reasonable opportunity to inspect them, either indicates that he will take them or fails to reject them. To **reject** goods, the buyer must notify the seller of the rejection and specify the defect or nonconformity. If a buyer treats the goods as if he owns them, the buyer is considered to have accepted them [2–606].

For example, Ace Appliance delivers a new color television set to Baldwin. Baldwin has accepted the set if, after trying it and finding it to be in working order, she says nothing to Ace or tells Ace that she will keep it. Even if the set is defective, Baldwin is considered to have accepted it if she does not give Ace timely notice that she does not want to keep it because it is not in working order. If she takes the set on a vacation trip even though she knows that it does not work properly, this is also an acceptance. In the latter case, her use of the television set would be inconsistent with its rejection and the return of ownership to the seller.

If a buyer accepts any part of a **commercial unit** of goods, he is considered to have accepted the whole unit [2–606(2)]. A commercial unit is any unit of goods that is treated by commercial usage as a single whole. It can be a single article (such as a machine), a set or quantity of articles (such as a dozen, bale, gross, or carload), or any other unit treated as a single whole [2–105(6)]. Thus, if a bushel of apples is a commercial unit, then a buyer purchasing 10 bushels of apples who accepts 8½ bushels is considered to have accepted 9 bushels.

Effect of Acceptance

Once a buyer has accepted goods, he cannot later reject them unless at the time they were accepted, the buyer had reason to believe that the nonconformity would be cured. By accepting goods, the buyer does not forfeit or waive remedies against the seller for any nonconformities in the goods. However, if the buyer wishes to hold the seller responsible, he must give the seller *timely notice* that the goods are nonconforming.

The buyer is obligated to pay for goods that are accepted. If the buyer accepts all of the goods sold, she is, of course, responsible for the full purchase price. If the buyer accepts only part of the goods, she must pay for that part at the contract rate [2–607(1)].

Revocation of Acceptance

Under certain circumstances, a buyer may **revoke** or undo the acceptance. A buyer may revoke acceptance of nonconforming goods where: (1) the nonconformity *substantially impairs* the value of the goods and (2) the buyer accepted them without knowledge of the nonconformity because of the difficulty of discovering the nonconformity, or the buyer accepted the goods because of the seller's *assurances* that it would cure the defect [2–608(1)].

The buyer must exercise her right to revoke acceptance within a reasonable time after the buyer discovers or should have discovered the nonconformity. Revocation is not effective until the buyer notifies the seller of the intention to revoke acceptance. After a buyer revokes acceptance, her rights are the same as they would have been if the goods had been rejected when delivery was offered [2–608].

The right to revoke acceptance could arise, for example, where Arnold buys a new car from Dealer. While driving the car home, Arnold discovers that it has a seriously defective transmission. When she returns the car to Dealer, Dealer promises to repair it, so Arnold decides to keep the car. If the dealer does not fix the transmission after repeated efforts to fix it, Arnold could revoke her acceptance on the grounds that the nonconformity substantially impairs the value of the car, that she took delivery of the car without knowledge of the nonconformity, and that her acceptance was based on Dealer's assurances that he would fix the car. Similarly, revocation of acceptance might be involved where a serious problem with the car not discoverable by inspection shows up in the first month's use.

Revocation must occur prior to any *substantial change* in the goods, however, such as serious damage in an accident or wear and tear from using them for a period of time. What constitutes a "substantial impairment in value" and when there has been a "substantial change in the goods" are questions that courts frequently have to decide when an attempted revocation of acceptance results in a lawsuit. The case below of *North River Homes, Inc. v. Bosarge* illustrates a number of the issues that arise in situations where a buyer is seeking to revoke her acceptance.

North River Homes, Inc. v. Bosarge
17 UCC Rep.2d 121 (Miss. Sup. Ct. 1992)

On August 20, 1983, Elmer and Martha Bosarge purchased from J & J Mobile Home Sales a furnished mobile home manufactured by North River Homes. The mobile home, described by a J & J salesperson as the "Cadillac" of mobile homes, cost $23,900. Upon moving into their new home, the Bosarges immediately discovered defect after defect. The defects included a bad water leak that caused water to run all over the trailer and into the insulation, which in turn caused the trailer's underside to ballon downward, loose moldings, a warped dishwasher door, a warped bathroom door, holes in the walls, a defective heating and cooling system, cabinets with chips and holes in them, furniture that fell apart, rooms that remained moldy and mildewed, a closet that leaked rainwater, and spaces between the doors and windows and their frames that allowed the elements to come in. The Bosarges had not been able to spot the defects before taking delivery because they viewed the mobile home at night on J & J's lot and there was no light on in the mobile home.

The Bosarges immediately and repeatedly notified North River Homes of the defects, but it failed to repair the home satisfactorily. In November 1983, the Bosarges informed North River of their decision to revoke their acceptance of the defective home. On some occasions, repairmen came but did not attempt to make repairs, saying they would come back. Other times, the repairs were inadequate. For example, while looking for the water leak, a repairman cut open the bottom of the mobile home and then taped it back together with masking tape that failed to hold and resulted in the floor bowing out. Another repairman inadvertently punctured a septic line and did not properly repair the puncture, resulting in a permanent stench. Other repairmen simply left things off at the home, such as a new dishwasher door and a countertop, saying they did not have time to make the repairs.

In June 1984, the Bosarges provided North River with an extensive list of problems that had not been corrected. When they did not receive a satisfactory response, they sent a letter on October 4, 1984, saying they would make no further payments. North River made no further efforts to correct the problems. In March 1986, the Bosarges's attorney wrote to North River formally revoking acceptance of the mobile home because of its substantially impaired value, tendering the mobile home back to it, and advising North River that it could pick the home up at its earliest convenience. They then brought a lawsuit requesting return of the purchase price and seeking damages for breach of various warranties.

Prather, Justice   When a consumer has accepted goods and subsequently discovers defects or a breach of implied merchantability, the consumer may invoke statutory and case law which conditions revocation of acceptance on:

(1) a nonconformity [or defect] which substantially impairs the value of the "lot or commercial unit;"
(2) an acceptance
   (a) (with discovery of the defect) on the reasonable assumption that the nonconformity [or defect] would be cured or
   (b) (without discovery) reasonably induced by the difficulty of the discovery or by the seller's assurances;
(3) revocation within a reasonable time after the nonconformity [or defect] was discovered or should have been discovered; and
(4) revocation before a substantial change occurs in the condition of the goods not caused by their own defects.

Once the consumer has properly notified the seller of his or her intent to revoke acceptance, the seller has a right to attempt to cure the alleged defect. This right is not unlimited; that is Mississippi law does not permit a seller to postpone revocation in perpetuity by fixing everything that goes wrong with the good. "There is a time when enough is enough"—when a consumer no longer must tolerate or endure a seller's repeated (though good faith) attempts to cure the defect. As aptly stated by a Florida Court of Appeals:

The buyer . . . is not bound to permit the seller to tinker with the article indefinitely in the hope it may ultimately be made to comply with the warranty. At some point in time, if major problems continue . . ., it must become obvious to all people that a particular [article] simply cannot be repaired or parts replaced so that the same is made free of defect.

When the "time has come," the consumer may revoke once and for all.

North River contends that the Bosarges' failure to move out of their mobile home after "rejecting it" constituted an exercise of ownership (or dominion) and waiver of their right to revoke acceptance. The Bosarges did not move out of their home in November 1983 and in October 1984—the dates when they notified North River of their intention to revoke acceptance—because they were repeatedly assured that the defects would be repaired. Their mistaken belief that North River would fulfill its assurances to repair the defects is but one reason why the Bosarges did not move out of their home. Another reason is simple and understandable:

When you tie up all your savings into purchasing a home, you cannot take it and park it somewhere. You have to live in it until you can get the people to clear your lot so you can put another one on it. Its just not like a car you can drive on the lot and hand them the keys and say, its yours. (Testimony of Martha Bosarge).

North River's contention that the Bosarges should have moved out reflects ignorance of case law which requires a consumer, who expresses an intention to revoke acceptance, to provide a seller with a reasonable attempt to cure the defect. The evidence unequivocally shows that the Bosarges complied with this law; indeed, one could arguably contend that they complied to an unnecessary extent. But the Bosarges' great patience is not surprising in view of their financial inability to move elsewhere.

Any excessive or unreasonable use of the home by the Bosarges may be remedied through quantum meruit recovery—*not* through ineffectuation of revocation.

North River also contends that the Bosarges "failed to prove that the mobile home in question was substantially impaired." The Bosarges counter "that the evidence showed that their North River trailer was literally falling apart." The Bosarges

testimony revealed that each North River repairman who visited their home admitted to the Bosarges that their home was so defective that it "ought to be replaced." Notably, Ronnie Wilson, a HUD mobile home inspector provided testimony which is also supportive of the jury's finding; When asked if he would live in that kind of home (heating, cooling, leaking roof, mildew, ice), he answered "No, sir, my wife wouldn't let me, sir."

In sum the record is replete with evidence to support the jury's finding that the Bosarges' home was substantially impaired.

Judgment for Bosarges affirmed.

Buyer's Rights on Improper Delivery

If the goods delivered by the seller do not conform to the contract, the buyer has several options. The buyer can (1) reject all of the goods, (2) accept all of them, or (3) accept any commercial units and reject the rest [2–601]. The buyer, however, cannot accept only part of a commercial unit and reject the rest. The buyer must pay for the units accepted at the price per unit provided in the contract.

Where the contract calls for delivery of the goods in separate installments, the buyer's options are more limited. The buyer may reject an installment delivery only if the nonconformity *substantially affects the value* of that delivery and *cannot be corrected* by the seller in a timely fashion. If the nonconformity is relatively minor, the buyer must accept the installment. The seller may offer to replace the defective goods or give the buyer an allowance in the price to make up for the nonconformity [2–612].

Where the nonconformity or defect in one installment impairs the value of the whole contract, the buyer may treat it as a breach of the whole contract but must proceed carefully so as not to reinstate the remainder of the contract [2–612(3)].

Rejection

If a buyer has a basis for rejecting a delivery of goods, the buyer must act within a *reasonable time*

after delivery. The buyer must also give the seller *notice* of the rejection, preferably in writing [2–602]. The buyer should be careful to state all of the defects on which he is basing the rejection, including all of the defects that a reasonable inspection would disclose. This is particularly important if these are defects that the seller might cure (remedy) and the time for delivery has not expired. In that case, the seller may notify the buyer that he intends to redeliver conforming goods.

If the buyer fails to state in connection with his rejection a particular defect that is ascertainable by reasonable inspection, he cannot use the defect to justify his rejection if the seller could have cured the defect had he been given reasonable notice of it. In a transaction taking place between merchants, the seller has, after rejection, a right to a written statement of all the defects in the goods on which the buyer bases his right to reject, and the buyer may not later assert defects not listed in justification of his rejection [2–605].

In the case that follows, *Tai Wah Radio Manufactory Ltd. v. Ambassador Imports Ltd.,* the buyer kept a shipment of defective goods to use as leverage against the seller concerning a claim for damages on an earlier defective shipment. The court found that the buyer had accepted the shipment because it had not rejected it in a timely fashion.

Tai Wah Radio Manufactory Ltd. v. Ambassador Imports Ltd.
3 UCC Rep.2d 117 (S.D.N.Y. 1987)

Tai Wah Manufactory Ltd., a Hong Kong company, is a manufacturer of electronic goods. Ambassador Imports Ltd., a New York company, is an importer and wholesale distributor of various products, including electronic goods. The two companies had been doing business with each other for about five years when in February 1985 Ambassador placed an order with Tai Wah for 2,000 stereo cassette recorders, which were delivered to and accepted by Ambassador in Los Angeles on April 15. On April 4, Ambassador placed another order for cassette recorders with Tai Wah, this time for 2,040 units.

Ambassador claimed that in May it began to receive complaints from its customers about the recorders from the first shipment, and several hundred units were returned to Ambassador before June 24. On May 31 and June 7, Ambassador sent telexes to Tai Wah advising it of problems with the quality of the plastic in the dial and with breakage of the cassette door, and asking that the problem be corrected for all future orders. On June 1, Tai Wah indicated that it was trying to improve the quality of the plastic and that future orders would be corrected. It also advised Ambassador that the second shipment had been sent on May 24. Despite the complaints about the quality of the recorders, Ambassador picked up the second shipment of recorders in Los Angeles on June 24. It made no effort to inspect the goods. On June 29, it notified Tai Wah that it did not want the second shipment, that it had picked it up only to hold as collateral to ensure that it would be compensated for its damages on the first shipment, and that it would return the second shipment when such compensation was arranged.

Tai Wah then brought a lawsuit against Ambassador to recover the contract price of the second shipment of recorders.

Motley, District Judge   Tai Wah asserts that it is entitled to judgment as a matter of law because Ambassador did not timely reject the second shipment of recorders as required by the Uniform Commercial Code. Ambassador contends that the notice of defects in the first shipment constituted notice of defects in the second shipment.

It is undisputed that Ambassador accepted the second shipment for the sole purpose of negotiating a settlement with Tai Wah concerning money owing on the first shipment. Ambassador obviously did not intend to pay for the second shipment with the knowledge that it would reject the recorders. In addition, it knew that the recorders were allegedly defective at the time of acceptance.

Section 2–608 of the UCC provides:

(1) The buyer may revoke his acceptance of a lot or commercial unit whose non-conformity substantially impairs its value to him if he has accepted it
    (a) on the reasonable assumption that its non-conformity would be cured and it has not been seasonably cured; or
    (b) without discovery of such non-conformity if his acceptance was reasonably induced either by the difficulty of discovery before acceptance or by the seller's assurances.

Thus, a buyer with knowledge that goods are defective when he accepts them does not lose his right to revoke the acceptance if the acceptance was based on the reasonable assumption that the non-conformity would be seasonably cured but the cure was not effected. In addition, acceptance may be revoked if the buyer, without discovering the non-conformity, was reasonably induced to accept the goods either by the difficulty of discovery before acceptance or by the seller's assurances. Neither of these exceptions is applicable to this case. When Ambassador accepted the second shipment of cassette recorders, it had knowledge of the recorder's allegedly defective nature. Ambassador did not assume Tai Wah would cure the nonconformity. Thus, Ambassador did not have the right to revoke the contract for the second shipment.

Although Ambassador may not have intended to keep the products when it took possession of the second shipment, this does not change the result. From the undisputed facts in this case, it is obvious that Ambassador was attempting to engage in a form of commercial "kidnapping" to compel Tai Wah to resolve its differences with Ambassador. Ambassador, instead of taking possession of the second shipment of recorders, should have rejected the second shipment. Tai Wah, in telexes, had advised Ambassador, prior to Ambassador's receipt of the second shipment, that the recorders had been shipped prior to Tai Wah's receipt of Ambassador's first complaints about the first shipment and prior to Tai Wah having the opportunity to make the needed corrections. Thus, Ambassador, with knowledge of the allegedly defective nature of the goods, should have rejected them. Accordingly, Tai Wah is entitled to payment for the second shipment.

However, if it is established at trial that Ambassador complained in a timely manner about the defects in the goods, Ambassador is entitled to damages for breach of warranty—the difference between the contract price of the recorders and their actual value. This would be an offset against the money Ambassador owes Tai Wah.

Partial summary judgment awarded to Tai Wah.

ACCEPTANCE, REVOCATION, AND REJECTION

Acceptance	1. Occurs when buyer, having had a reasonable opportunity to inspect goods, either (a) indicates he will take them or (b) fails to reject them.
	2. If buyer accepts any part of a commercial unit, he is considered to have accepted the whole unit.
	3. If buyer accepts goods, he cannot later reject them *unless* at the time they were accepted buyer had reason to believe that the nonconformity would be cured.
	4. Buyer is obligated to pay for goods that are accepted.
Revocation	1. Buyer may revoke acceptance of nonconforming goods where (a) the nonconformity *substantially impairs the value* of the goods and, (b) buyer accepted the goods without knowledge of the nonconformity because of the difficulty of discovering the nonconformity *or* buyer accepted because of assurances by the seller.
	2. Right to revoke must be exercised within a *reasonable* time after buyer discovers *or* should have discovered the nonconformity.
	3. Revocation must be invoked before there is any *substantial* change in the goods.
	4. Revocation is not effective until buyer notifies seller of his intent to revoke acceptance.
Rejection	1. Where the goods delivered do not conform to the contract, buyer may (a) reject all of the goods, (b) accept all of the goods, or (c) accept any commercial unit and reject the rest. Buyer must pay for goods accepted.
	2. Where the goods are to be delivered in installments, an installment delivery may be rejected *only if* the nonconformity substantially affects the value of that delivery and cannot be corrected by the seller.
	3. Buyer must act within a reasonable time after delivery.

Right to Cure

If the seller has some reason to believe that the buyer would accept nonconforming goods, then the seller can take a reasonable time to reship conforming goods. The seller has this opportunity even if the original time for delivery has expired. For example,

Ace Manufacturing contracts to sell 200 red baseball hats to Sam's Sporting Goods, with delivery to be made by April 1. On March 1, Sam's receives a package from Ace containing 200 blue baseball hats and refuses to accept them. Ace can notify Sam's that it intends to cure the improper delivery by supplying 200 red hats, and it has until April 1 to deliver the red hats to Sam's. If Ace thought that Sam's would accept the blue hats because on past shipments Sam's did not object to the substitution of blue hats for red, then Ace has a reasonable time even after April 1 to deliver the red hats [2–508].

If the buyer wrongfully rejects goods, she is liable to the seller for breach of the sales contract [2–602(3)].

Buyer's Duties after Rejection

If the buyer is a merchant, then the buyer owes certain duties concerning the goods that he rejects. First, the buyer must follow any reasonable instructions that the seller gives concerning disposition of the goods. The seller, for example, might request that the rejected goods be shipped back to the seller. If the goods are perishable or may deteriorate rapidly, then the buyer must make a reasonable effort to sell the goods. The seller must reimburse the buyer for any expenses that the buyer incurs in carrying out the seller's instructions or in trying to resell perishable goods. In reselling goods, the buyer must act reasonably and in good faith [2–603(2) and (3)].

If the rejected goods are not perishable or if the seller does not give the buyer instructions, then the buyer has several options. First, the buyer can store the goods for the seller. Second, the buyer can reship them to the seller. Third, the buyer can resell them for the seller's benefit. If the buyer resells the goods, the buyer may keep his expenses and a reasonable commission on the sale. If the buyer stores the goods, the buyer should exercise care in handling them. The buyer also must give the seller a reasonable time to remove the goods [2–604].

If the buyer is not a merchant, then her obligation after rejection is to hold the goods with reasonable care for a sufficient time to give the seller an opportunity to remove them. The buyer is not obligated to ship the goods back to the seller [2–602]. The case that follows, *Lykins Oil Company v. Fekkos,* illustrates these principles.

LYKINS OIL COMPANY V. FEKKOS
507 N.E.2d 795 (Ohio Ct. Comm. Pl. 1986)

Haralambos Fekkos purchased from Lykins Sales & Service a Yammar Model 165D, 16-horsepower diesel tractor and various implements. On Saturday, April 27, Fekkos gave Lykins a check for the purchase price, less trade-in, of $6,596, and had the items delivered to his residence. The next day, while attempting to use the tractor for the first time, Fekkos discovered it was defective. The defects included a dead battery requiring jump starts, overheating while pulling either the mower or the tiller, missing safety shields over the muffler and the power takeoff, and a missing water pump.

On Monday, Fekkos contacted Lykins's sales representative, who believed his claims to be true and agreed to have the tractor picked up from Fekkos's residence; Fekkos also stopped payment on his check. Fekkos placed the tractor with the tiller attached in his front yard as near as possible to the front door without driving it onto the landscaped area closest to the house. Fekkos left the tractor on his lawn because his driveway was broken up for renovation and his garage was inaccessible, and because the tractor would have to be jump started by Lykins's employees when they picked it up. On Tuesday, Fekkos went back to Lykins's store to purchase an Allis-Chalmers tractor and reminded Lykins's employees that the Yammar tractor had not been picked up and remained on his lawn.

On Wednesday, May 1, at 6:00 A.M., Fekkos discovered that the tractor was missing although the tiller had been unhitched and remained in the yard. Later that day, Lykins picked up the remaining implements. The theft was reported to the police. On several occasions, Fekkos was assured that Lykins's insurance would cover the stolen tractor, that it was Lykins's fault for not picking it up, and that Fekkos had nothing to worry about. However, Lykins subsequently brought suit against Fekkos to recover the purchase price of the Yammar tractor. Both Lykins and Fekkos moved for summary judgment in their favor.

Watson, Judge   Lykins argues in support of its motion for summary judgment that section 2–602 applies to this matter. Subsections 2(a) and (b) provide that:

Subject to the provisions of the two following sections on rejected goods:
(a) after rejection any exercise of ownership by the buyer with respect to any commercial unit is wrongful as against the seller; and
(b) if the buyer has before rejection taken physical possession of goods in which he does not have a security interest under the provisions of this Article (subsection (3) of Section 2–711), he is under a duty after rejection to hold them with reasonable care at the seller's disposition for a sufficient time to permit the seller to remove them.

Lykins argues that because Fekkos was already in possession of the tractor at the time he rejected it, he had the duty to hold it for a sufficient length of time for Lykins to remove it from Fekkos's premises. Lykins asserts that Fekkos breached this duty and is liable to Lykins because the tractor was unavailable to be picked up by Lykins on May 1, the day after the purchase order was cancelled and two days after Fekkos rejected the tractor.

On the other hand, Fekkos, in support of his motion for summary judgment argues that section 2–510 controls the matter. Section 2–510(1) provides:

(1) Where a tender or delivery of goods so fails to conform to the contract so as to give a right of rejection the risk of their loss remains on the seller until cure or acceptance.

Fekkos argues that because the tractor was of no use to him as delivered, it failed to conform to the contract so as to give him the right to reject it. Thus, Fekkos asserts, under section 2–510 the risk of loss remained on the seller at the point of the tractor's theft on May 1, 1985, because no cure or acceptance had been made at that point.

Alternatively, Fekkos argues that if section 2–602 is applicable to the case, he still is entitled to summary judgment because subsequent to his rejection he held the tractor with reasonable care, forced because of the necessity of jump starting, the impassibility of his driveway and inaccessibility of his garage. Fekkos argues that it would be unreasonable to assume that he could have anticipated that someone would "go to the trouble of removing the tiller, and then push or winch a 1,200-plus pound tractor onto a truck or drag or whatever."

The court in its research of Ohio sales law discovered no Ohio case law on the precise issue presented in this case. Indeed, there is little case law nationwide on this issue. However, the court sees no reason that the two aforementioned statutes are not to be read in *pari materia* to provide the law to be applied.

As to the instant case, while it may be said that Lykins retained the risk of loss of the nonconforming tractor, the liability for loss would fall on Fekkos if the facts show that Fekkos breached his duty to hold the tractor with reasonable care for sufficient time for removal, after notification of rejection to seller.

On the facts, the court finds that the actions taken by Fekkos were reasonable under all the circumstances and that Fekkos did not breach his duty to use reasonable care to hold the tractor until Lykins would retrieve it. The court notes that there is no evidence whatsoever that any of Lykins's employees indicated their dissatisfaction with Fekkos's decision to park the tractor on his front lawn when told by Fekkos that that was where he would leave it until they came. The evidence shows to this court's satisfaction that Fekkos acted reasonably because of the inaccessibility of his garage on account of the demolition of his driveway.

Summary judgment for Fekkos.

ASSURANCE, REPUDIATION, AND EXCUSE

Assurance

The buyer or seller may become concerned that the other party may not be able to perform his contract obligations. If there is a reasonable basis for that concern, the buyer or seller can demand **assurance** from the other party that the contract will be performed. If such assurances are not given within a reasonable time not exceeding 30 days, the party is considered to have repudiated the contract [2–609].

For example, a farmer contracts to sell 1,000 bushels of apples to a canner, with delivery to be made in September. In March, the canner learns that a severe frost has damaged many of the apple blossoms in the farmer's area and that 50 percent of the crop has been lost. The canner has the right to demand assurances in writing from the farmer that he will be able to fulfill his obligations in light of the frost. The farmer must provide those assurances within 30 days. Thus, he might advise the canner that his crop sustained only relatively light damage or that he had made commitments to sell only a small percentage of his total crop and expects to be able to fulfill his obligations. If the farmer does not provide such assurances in a timely manner, he is considered to have repudiated the contract. The canner then has certain remedies against the farmer for breach of contract. These remedies are discussed in the next chapter.

The *LNS Investment Company, Inc. v. Phillips 66 Company* case, which follows, illustrates a situation where a buyer became concerned about the seller's ability to perform and demanded assurances from the seller.

LNS Investment Company, Inc. v. Phillips 66 Company
731 F.Supp. 1484 (D. Kansas 1990)

LNS Investment Company is the successor to the Compu-Blend Corporation (CBC), which blended, labeled, and packaged quart plastic bottles of motor oil for, among others, the Phillips 66 Company. On July 29, Peter Buhlinger, Phillips' manager of lubricants, wrote a letter to CBC that read as follows:

This will confirm our verbal agreement whereby Phillips will purchase additional quantities of plastic bottles from CBC during 1986.

CBC, in an effort to increase their packaging capacity, has committed to purchase several additional molds to blow the Phillips one-quart container. In order to amortize the cost of the additional equipment, Phillips has agreed to take delivery of a maximum of 4,000,000 bottles to be made available by December 31, 1986. This agreement includes the production available now and to be supplemented by the additional equipment. Should CBC be not able to produce the full 4,000,000 quarts by December 31, 1986, this agreement shall be considered satisfied.

Phillips' desire is to receive as many bottles packaged with Phillips motor oil in 1986 from CBC as possible. It is our intention to change to a different type of plastic one-quart container beginning in 1987 and therefore this agreement cannot extend past the December 31, 1986 deadline. All production would have to be of high resaleable [sic] plastic quarts filled with the appropriate Phillips products and labeled accordingly. The production would be required to be available on an even weekly basis in order to facilitate movement of the product to the warehouse and customers.

Although the agreement called for CBC to increase its production capacity, CBC experienced numerous problems in maintaining even its precontract capacity. Moreover, the quality of goods CBC was able to deliver was frequently unacceptable to Phillips. On September 18, a Phillips representative wrote to CBC complaining about the quality of goods Phillips was receiving, specifically mentioning neck finish and label application problems. The letter also noted that if Phillips had known how CBC would perform, it would not have committed to purchase CBC's hoped-for increase in production. CBC's chairman responded on September 29, acknowledging certain deficiencies, offering a number of reasons for the inability to perform, and stating that he was sure CBC would be showing "marked improvement in deliveries in the coming week and even more in another two or three weeks."

On October 15, the Phillips representative reiterated its continued dissatisfaction with CBC's products, indicating "we definitely do not want bottles on the shelf of the quality submitted." And, on December 16, he advised CBC that Phillips would not renew any commitments to purchase goods from CBC after March 31, 1987, because of CBC's poor performance under the July 29 agreement. In May 1987, CBC brought suit against Phillips, alleging that Phillips breached the July 29 agreement by failing to purchase CBC's full output of plastic bottles through December 31, 1986.

O'Connor, Chief Judge   CBC's failure to provide either the quantity or quality of goods contemplated by the July 29 agreement entitled Phillips to suspend its performance. Section 2−609 of the Code states as follows:

Right to adequate assurance of performance.

(1) A contract for sale imposes an obligation on each party that the other's expectations will not be impaired. When reasonable grounds for insecurity arise with respect to the performance of either party, the other may in writing demand adequate assurance of due performance and until he receives such assurance may if commercially reasonable suspend any performance for which he has not already received the agreed return.

(2) Between merchants the reasonableness of grounds for insecurity and the adequacy of any assurance offered shall be determined according to commercial standards.

(3) Acceptance of any improper delivery or payment does not prejudice the aggrieved party's right to demand adequate assurance of future performance.

(4) After receipt of a justified demand failure to provide within a reasonable time not exceeding thirty days such assurance of due performance as is adequate under the circumstances of the particular case is a repudiation of the contract.

To suspend its performance pursuant to this section, Phillips must (1) have had reasonable grounds for insecurity regarding CBC's performance under the contract, (2) have demanded in writing adequate assurance of CBC's future performance and (3) have not received from CBC such assurances.

Phillips had reasonable grounds for insecurity regarding CBC's performance. The evidence conclusively demonstrated that CBC suffered numerous setbacks in its attempt to increase its capacity to produce plastic bottles for Phillips. Specifically, both the quantity and quality of the bottles were chronically poor. Indeed, Phillips was arguably entitled to cancel the contract soon after CBC's unacceptable performance began. Sec. 2−607(3)(a); 2−711(1). Although Phillips lost its right to cancel the contract by failing to elect that remedy within a reasonable time, the above circumstances were sufficient to establish Phillip's right to adequate assurance of CBC's future performance under Section 2−609.

Phillips demanded, in writing, assurance from CBC regarding CBC's future performance. Phillips notified CBC of the inadequacies of CBC's goods and requested assurance that CBC would take steps to rectify the same. Thus it was incumbent on CBC to provide adequate assurance of its future performance to Phillips.

CBC failed to provide Phillips with adequate assurance of its future performance. CBC's continual excuses for failing to perform, unaccompanied by corresponding remedial action, cannot be deemed adequate assurance under the Code. Accordingly, Phillips was entitled to suspend its own performance of the contract by refusing to place orders with CBC and/or cancelling orders already placed, thirty days after either or both the September 18, 1986, and October 15, 1986, letters. In view of this conclusion, Phillips did not breach the contract by suspending performance in December, 1986.

Judgment for Phillips.

Anticipatory Repudiation

Sometimes, one of the parties to a contract *repudiates* the contract by advising the other party that he does not intend to perform his obligations. When one party repudiates the contract, the other party may suspend his performance. In addition, he may either await performance for a reasonable time or use the remedies for breach of contract that are discussed in the next chapter [2−610].

Suppose the party who repudiated the contract changes his mind. Repudiation can be withdrawn by clearly indicating that the person intends to perform his obligations. The repudiating party must do this before the other party has canceled the contract or has materially changed position by, for example, buying the goods elsewhere [2−611].

Excuse

Unforeseen events may make it difficult or impossible for a person to perform his contractual obligations. The Code rules for determining when a person is excused from performing are similar to the general contract rules. General contract law uses the test of **impossibility.** In most situations, however, the Code uses the test of **commercial impracticability.**

The Code attempts to differentiate events that are unforeseeable or uncontrollable from events that were part of the risk borne by a party. If the goods required for the performance of a contract are destroyed without fault of either party prior to the time that the risk of loss passed to the buyer, the contract is voided [2–613]. Suppose Jones agrees to sell and deliver an antique table to Brown. The table is damaged when Jones's antique store is struck by lightning and catches fire. The specific table covered by the contract was damaged without fault of either party prior to the time that the risk of loss was to pass to Brown. Under the Code, Brown has the option of either canceling the contract or accepting the table with an allowance in the purchase price to compensate for the damaged condition [2–613].

If unforeseen conditions cause a delay or the inability to make delivery of the goods and thus make performance impracticable, the seller is excused from making delivery. However, if a seller's capacity to deliver is only partially affected, the seller must allocate production in any fair and reasonable manner among his customers. The seller has the option of including any regular customer not then under contract in his allocation scheme. When the seller allocates production, he must notify the buyers [2–615]. When a buyer receives this notice, the buyer may either terminate the contract or agree to accept the allocation [2–616].

For example, United Nuclear contracts to sell certain quantities of fuel rods for nuclear power plants to a number of electric utilities. If the federal government limits the amount of uranium that United has access to, so that United is unable to fill all of its contracts, United is excused from full performance on the grounds of commercial impracticability. However, United may allocate its production of fuel rods among its customers by reducing each customer's share by a certain percentage and giving the customers notice of the allocation. Then, each utility can decide whether to cancel the contract or accept the partial allocation of fuel rods.

In the absence of compelling circumstances, courts do not readily excuse parties from their contractual obligations, particularly where it is clear that the parties anticipated a problem and sought to provide for it in the contract.

ETHICAL AND PUBLIC POLICY CONCERNS

1. Problem case 1 in this chapter illustrates a problem that can arise in situations where supplies of the goods that are the subject of a contract are either in significantly shorter, or more plentiful, supply than when the agreement was made and/or there has been a significant change in the market price. When, if ever, is a buyer or seller ethically justified in trying to find a way out of a contractual obligation because the supply or market price conditions have so changed that he can make a better deal elsewhere? Concomitantly, are there circumstances under which the other party, acting in an ethically responsible manner, should voluntarily release the disadvantaged party from her contractual commitment?

2. Suppose that you recently purchased a new automobile. The automobile has a number of problems that the dealer is unable to completely fix after you have left it with the dealer on two occasions. Although the dealer indicates a willingness to fix the remaining problems and confidence that they can be remedied quickly and completely, you have now concluded that you would prefer to have a car made by another manufacturer. Are there any ethical considerations involved in a decision on your part to attempt to revoke your acceptance of the automobile?

3. Where a contract calls for delivery in installments, the buyer can reject an installment delivery containing nonconforming goods only where the nonconformity substantially affects the value of the delivery and cannot be corrected; where the defects are relatively minor the buyer has to keep the installment if the seller, for example, offers an allowance to make up for the nonconformity. Suppose you are a seller with some goods you know have minor defects and that you would like to get rid of. Would it be ethical for you to send them to a customer with whom you have a contract for installment deliveries of the goods, knowing that they do not conform to the contract and that the customer will have to accept them as long as you give him a price allowance?

PROBLEMS AND PROBLEM CASES

1. Baker was a buyer and distributor of popcorn. Ratzlaff was a farmer who grew popcorn. In 1983, Baker and Ratzlaff entered into a written contract pursuant to which Ratzlaff agreed that in 1983 he would raise 380 acres of popcorn and sell the popcorn to Baker. Baker agreed to furnish the seed popcorn and to pay $4.75 per hundred pounds of popcorn. The popcorn was to be delivered to Baker as he ordered it, and Baker was to pay for the popcorn as it was delivered. At Baker's request, the first delivery was made on February 2 of the following year and the second on February 4. On neither occasion did Ratzlaff ask Baker to pay or Baker offer to pay. During that week, Ratzlaff and Baker had several phone conversations about further deliveries, but there was no discussion about payments. On February 11, Ratzlaff sent written notice to Baker that he was terminating the contract because Baker had not paid for the two loads of popcorn that had been delivered. In the meantime, Ratzlaff sold his remaining 1.6 million pounds of popcorn to another buyer at $8 per 100 pounds. Baker then sued Ratzlaff for breach of contract. Did Ratzlaff act in good faith in terminating the contract?

2. Ray Williams, a resident of Georgia, contracted to sell the "slaw cabbage" to be grown on 30 acres of farmland in Georgia to Thomas Curtin, a resident of New York, who intended to resell the cabbage to cole slaw manufacturers. The expected yield was 600 to 800 tons of cabbage, and the agreed price was $136 per ton. Large cabbages are generally preferable for making cole slaw, and Curtin orally advised Williams that he desired large cabbages (i.e., 12 heads or less per 50-pound bag); this request was not, however, incorporated into the written memorandum of agreement. Earlier agreements between Williams and Curtin had called for the sale of "large cabbage." The cabbage was planted in a way to provide the best assurance possible that the cabbage would be large cabbage as requested by Curtin. As a result of poor growing conditions, most of the cabbages grown on the acreage were small; moreover, prices for cabbage were generally higher than the price at which Williams had agreed to make the sale to Curtin. Curtin inspected the cabbage during the growing season and was aware of the small size of the cabbage. He advised Williams that he wanted all of the cabbage from the 30 acres, regardless of size. Williams, however, delivered only the large cabbages to Curtin (approximately 150 tons) and sold the smaller cabbages to other buyers at a price about three times higher than the price at which he had contracted to sell cabbage to Curtin. Williams claimed that in the trade in Georgia, "slaw cabbage" referred only to large cabbage with 12 cabbage heads or less per 50-pound bag. However, the other witnesses said that the term *slaw cabbage* was seldom used, that in their experience it had never been used to define a specific cabbage size, and that it meant simply cabbage suitable for processing into cole slaw. Did trade usage support Williams's contention that he was obligated to deliver only the large cabbages?

3. Harold Ledford agreed to purchase three used Mustang automobiles (a 1966 Mustang coupe, a 1965 fastback, and a 1966 convertible) from J. L. Cowan for $3,000. Ledford gave Cowan a cashier's check for $1,500 when he took possession of the coupe, with the understanding he would pay the remaining $1,500 on the delivery of the fastback and the convertible. Cowan arranged for Charles Canterberry to deliver the remaining vehicles to Ledford. Canterberry dropped the convertible off at a lot owned by Ledford and proceeded to Ledford's residence to deliver the fastback. He refused to unload it until Ledford paid him $1,500. Ledford refused to make the payment until he had an opportunity to inspect the convertible, which he suspected was not in the same condition that it had been in when he purchased it. Canterberry refused this request and returned both the fastback and the convertible to Cowan. Cowan then brought suit against Ledford to recover the balance of the purchase price. Was Ledford entitled to inspect the car before he paid the balance due on it?

4. Spada, an Oregon corporation, agreed to sell Belson, who operated a business in Chicago, two carloads of potatoes at "4.40 per sack, FOB Oregon shipping point." Spada had the potatoes put aboard railroad cars; however, it did not have floor racks

placed under the potatoes, as was customary during the winter months. As a result, there was no warm air circulating and the potatoes were frozen while in transit. Spada claims that its obligations ended with the delivery to the carrier and that the risk of loss was on Belson. What argument would you make for Belson?

5. In April, Reginald Bell contracted to sell potatoes to Red Ball Potato Company for fall delivery. The contract specified that the potatoes were to be "85 percent U.S. 1's." In Red Ball's dealings with Bell and other farmers, potatoes were delivered and paid for in truckload quantities. In the fall, Bell delivered several truckloads of potatoes. Samples of each load were taken for testing, and most of the loads were determined to be below 85 percent U.S. No 1. What options are open to Red Ball?

6. In February 1988, Jeannie Fannin agreed to manufacture and install custom-made draperies in Mary Ann George's home for a total purchase price of $4,000. George selected an appropriate fabric from Fannin's swatch book and paid $1,500 on execution of the contract. In May, Fannin told George that she could not obtain the fabric initially selected, but that she could provide a substitute that was slightly different in color. After inspecting the substitute material, George agreed to the substitution. The draperies were completed and installed in July. George concluded that the draperies failed to close, did not hang right, failed to to keep out sunlight, heat, and cold, and had other deficiencies. She told Fannin that the workmanship was "shoddy" and Fannin agreed to make adjustments. When Fannin failed to return to make the adjustments, George refused to pay the $500 she owed on the drapes. In October, Fannin filed suit in small claims court to recover the balance, and George counterclaimed to recover the $3,500 she had already paid. At the time of the trial in July 1989, the drapes were still in use at George's house. Had George made an effective rejection of the drapes?

7. On May 23, 1978, Deborah McCullough, a secretary, purchased a 1978 Chrysler LeBaron from Bill Swad Chrysler-Plymouth. The automobile was covered by both a limited warranty and a vehicle service contract (extended warranty). Following delivery, McCullough advised the salesperson that she had noted problems with the brakes, transmission, air conditioning, paint job, and seat panels, as well as the absence of rustproofing. The next day, the brakes failed and the car was returned to the dealer

for the necessary repairs. When the car was returned, McCullough discovered that the brakes had not been properly repaired and that none of the cosmetic work had been done. The car was returned several times to the dealer to correct these problems and others that developed subsequently. On June 26, the car was again returned to the dealer, who kept it for three weeks. Many of the defects were not corrected, however, and new problems with the horn and brakes arose. While McCullough was on a shopping trip, the engine abruptly shut off and the car had to be towed to the dealer. Then, while she was on her honeymoon, the brakes again failed. The car was taken back to the dealer with a list of 32 defects that needed correction. After repeated efforts to repair the car were unsuccessful, McCullough sent a letter to the dealer calling for rescission of the purchase, requesting return of the purchase price, and offering to return the car on receipt of shipping instructions. She received no answer and continued to drive it. McCullough then filed suit. In May 1979, the dealer refused to do any further work on the car, claiming that it was in satisfactory condition. By the time of the trial, in June 1980, it had been driven 35,000 miles, approximately 23,000 of which had been logged after McCullough mailed her notice of revocation. By continuing to operate the vehicle after notifying the seller of her intent to rescind the sale, did McCullough waive her right to revoke her original acceptance?

8. Walters, a grower of Christmas trees, contracted to supply Traynor with "top quality trees." When the shipment arrived and was inspected, Traynor discovered that some of the trees were not top quality. Within 24 hours, Traynor notified Walters that he was rejecting the trees that were not top quality. Walters did not have a place of business or an agent in the town where Traynor was. Christmas was only a short time away. The trees were perishable and would decline in value to zero by Christmas Eve. Walters did not give Traynor any instructions, so Traynor sold the trees for Walters's account. Traynor then tried to recover from Walters the expenses he incurred in caring for and selling the trees. Did Walters act properly in rejecting the trees and reselling them for the seller?

9. Creusot-Loire, a French manufacturing and engineering concern, was the project engineer to construct ammonia plants in Yugoslavia and Syria. The design process engineer for the two plants—as well as a plant being constructed in Sri Lanka—

specified burners manufactured by Coppus Engineering Corporation. After the burner specifications were provided to Coppus, it sent technical and service information to Creusot-Loire. Coppus expressly warranted that the burners were capable of continuous operation using heavy fuel oil with combustion air preheated to 260 degrees Celsius. The warranty extended for one year from the start-up of the plant but not exceeding three years from the date of shipment. In January 1979, Creusot-Loire ordered the burners for the Yugoslavia plant and paid for them; in November 1979, the burners were shipped to Yugoslavia. Due to construction delays, the plant was not to become operational until the end of 1983. In 1981, however, Creusot-Loire became aware that there had been operational difficulties with the Coppus burners at the Sri Lanka and Syria plants and that efforts to modify the burners had been futile. Creusot-Loire wrote to Coppus expressing concern that the burners purchased for the Yugoslavia plant, like those in the other plants, would prove unsatisfactory and asking for proof that the burners would meet contract specifications. When subsequent discussions failed to satisfy Creusot-Loire, it requested that Coppus take back the burners and refund the purchase price. Coppus refused. Finally, Creusot-Loire indicated that it would accept the burners only if Coppus extended its contractual guarantee to cover the delay in the start-up of the Yugoslavia plant and if Coppus posted an irrevocable letter of credit for the purchase price of the burners. When Coppus refused, Creusot-Loire brought an action for breach of contract, seeking a return of the purchase price. Coppus claimed that Creusot-Loire's request for assurance was unreasonable. How should the court rule?

10. In July 1980, Alimenta (U.S.A.), Inc., and Gibbs, Nathaniel (Canada), Ltd., each an international dealer in agricultural commodities, entered into three separate contracts in advance of the 1980 peanut harvest. Each contract called for the delivery in installments by Gibbs to Alimenta of "1980 crop U.S. runner split peanuts." When Gibbs failed to make delivery of the quantities specified in the contract, and made some deliveries later than the scheduled dates, Alimenta brought suit against Gibbs seeking damages for breach of contract. Gibbs claimed that it was excused from full performance by the occurrence of a drought in the peanut-growing areas.

The 1980 peanut crop had been planted in April and May. Rainfall was adequate in April, May, and June, and the crop came up in good condition. In the 25 years preceding 1980, the nation's peanut industry had experienced a steady growth in total production, with yield per acre increasing 250 percent over that period. In addition to Alimenta, Gibbs sold 1980 crop peanuts to 75 other customers and had contracted to purchase peanuts from 15 shellers in quantities 7 percent in excess of its sales. In early July, a hot and dry spell developed and became a full-fledged drought that did not break until late September. July and August were among the hottest and driest months on record in the last 100 years. In October, Gibbs received notices from 13 of its 15 shellers stating that because of the crop shortage, they were invoking Section 2–615 of the UCC and would be delivering only a portion of the peanuts they had contracted to deliver. Gibbs expected to receive only 52 percent of the peanuts it had contracted for, and in turn notified its customers, including, Alimenta, to expect reduced quantities. Alimenta ultimately received 87 percent of the contract quantity from Gibbs. Was Gibbs excused from full performance of its contract by the occurrence of the drought?

11. 🎞️ *Video Case.* See "Sour Grapes." Jelly Manufacturer, a food processor in Chicago, placed a phone order with Grape Grower, a grower in California, for a quantity of perishable produce. The shipping term was CIF with payment to be made on delivery (COD). Grower delivered the goods called for in the contract to a carrier and contracted for their shipment. However, it neglected to provide that the goods be shipped under refrigeration. The goods were loaded on a nonrefrigerated boxcar, and as a result, the produce was spoiled when it reached Chicago. Jelly Manufacturer, as required by the COD term, paid for the produce by check before discovering the spoilage. By paying for the produce, has Jelly Manufacturer "accepted" the goods so that it cannot subsequently "reject" them as nonconforming?

When Jelly Manufacturer called Grower to complain, Grower offered to rush a replacement shipment. Jelly Manufacturer declined the offer, stating that it would not arrive in time for the produce to be processed and delivered to Grocery Chain in time to meet Jelly Manufacturer's contract with Grocery Chain. Was Jelly Manufacturer required to accept Grower's promise to make a replacement shipment?

REMEDIES FOR BREACH OF SALES CONTRACTS

INTRODUCTION

Usually, both parties to a contract for the sale of goods perform the obligations that they assumed in the contract. Occasionally, however, one of the parties to a contract fails to perform her obligations. When this happens, the Uniform Commercial Code (UCC or Code) provides the injured party with a variety of remedies for breach of contract. This chapter will set forth and explain the remedies available to an injured party, as well as the Code's rules that govern buyer-seller agreements as to remedies, and the Code's statute of limitations. The objective of the Code remedies is to put the injured person in the same position that he would have been in if the contract had been performed. Under the Code, an injured party may not recover consequential or punitive damages unless such damages are specifically provided for in the Code or in another statute [1–106].[1]

AGREEMENTS AS TO REMEDIES

The buyer and seller may provide their own remedies in the contract, to be applied in the event that one of the parties fails to perform. They may also limit either the remedies that the law makes available or the damages that can be covered [2–719(1)]. If the parties agree on the amount of damages that will be paid to the injured party, this amount is known as **liquidated damages.** An agreement for liquidated damages is enforced if the amount is *reasonable* and if *actual* damages would be *difficult to prove* in the event of a breach of the contract. The amount is considered reasonable if it is not so large as to be a *penalty* or so small as to be *unconscionable* [2–718(1)].

   For example, Carl Carpenter contracts to build and sell a display booth for $5,000 to Hank Hawker for Hawker to use at the state fair. Delivery is to be made to Hawker by September 1. If the booth is not delivered on time, Hawker will not be able to sell his wares at the fair. Carpenter and Hawker might agree that if delivery is not made by September 1, Carpenter will pay Hawker $2,750 as liquidated damages. The actual sales that Hawker might lose without a booth would be very

---

[1]The numbers in brackets refer to sections of the Uniform Commercial Code.

hard to prove, so Hawker and Carpenter can provide some certainty through the liquidated damages agreement. Carpenter then knows what he will be liable for if he does not perform his obligation. Similarly, Hawker knows what he can recover if the booth is not delivered on time. The $2,750 amount is probably reasonable. If the amount were $500,000, it likely would be void as a penalty because it is way out of line with the damages that Hawker would reasonably be ex-

pected to sustain. And if the amount were too small, say $1, it might be considered unconscionable and therefore not enforceable.

If a liquidated damages clause is not enforceable because it is a penalty or unconscionable, the injured party can recover the actual damages that he suffered. The *Baker v. International Record Syndicate, Inc.* case, which follows, illustrates a situation where a court enforced a liquidated damages clause in a contract.

BAKER V. INTERNATIONAL RECORD SYNDICATE, INC.
812 S.W.2d 53 (Ct. App. Tex. 1991)

International Record Syndicate (IRS) hired Jeff Baker to take photographs of the musical group Timbuk-3. Baker mailed 37 "chromes" (negatives) to IRS via the business agent of Timbuk-3. When the chromes were returned to Baker, holes had been punched in 34 of them. Baker brought an action for breach of contract to recover for the damage done to the chromes.

A provision printed on Baker's invoice to IRS stated: "[r]eimbursement for loss or damage shall be determined by a photograph's reasonable value which shall be no less than $1,500 per transparency."

Enoch, Chief Judge   The Uniform Commercial Code provides:

Damages for breach by either party may be liquidated in the agreement but only at an amount which is reasonable in light of the anticipated harm caused by the breach, the difficulties of proof of loss, and the inconvenience or non-feasibility of otherwise obtaining an adequate remedy. A term fixing unreasonably large liquidated damages is void as a penalty.

Under Texas law a liquidated damages provision will be enforced when the court finds (1) the harm caused by the breach is incapable of estimation, and (2) the amount of liquidated damages is a reasonable forecast of just compensation. This might be termed the "anticipated harm" test. The party asserting that a liquidated damages clause is, in fact, a penalty provision has the burden of proof. Evidence related to the difficulty of estimation and the reasonable forecast must be viewed as of the time the contract was executed.

Baker testified that he had been paid as much as $14,000 for a photo session, which resulted in twenty-four photographs and that several of these photographs had also been resold. Baker further

testified that he had received as little as $125 for a single photograph. Baker also testified that he once sold a photograph for $500. Subsequently, he sold reproductions of the same photograph three additional times at various prices; the total income from this one photograph was $1,500. This particular photograph was taken in 1986 and was still producing income in 1990. Baker demonstrated, therefore, that an accurate demonstration of the damages from a single photograph is virtually impossible.

Timbuk-3's potential for fame was also an important factor in the valuation of the chromes. At the time of the photo session, Timbuk-3's potential was unknown. In view of the difficulty in determining the value of a piece of art, the broad range of values and long-term earning power of photographs, and the unknown potential for fame of the subject, $1,500 is not an unreasonable estimate of Baker's actual damages.

Additionally, liquidated damages must not be disproportionate to actual damages. If the liquidated damages are shown to be disproportionate to the actual damages, then the liquidated damages can be declared a penalty and recovery limited to actual damages proven. This might be called the "actual harm" test. The burden of proving this defense is upon the party seeking to invalidate the clause. The party asserting this defense is required to prove the amount of the other party's actual damages, if any, to show that the actual loss was not an approximation of the stipulated sum.

While evidence was presented that showed the value of several of Baker's other projects, this was not evidence of the photographs in question. The evidence clearly shows that photographs are unique items with many factors bearing on their actual value. Each of the thirty-four chromes may have had a different value. Proof of this loss is difficult; where damages are real but difficult to prove, injustice will be done the injured party if the court substitutes the requirements of judicial proof for the parties' own informed agreement as to what is a reasonable measure of damages. The evidence offered to prove Baker's actual damages lacks probative force. IRS failed to establish Baker's actual damages as to these particular photographs.

Judgment reversed in favor of Baker.

Liability for consequential damages resulting from a breach of contract (such as lost profits or damage to property) may also be limited or excluded by agreement. The limitation or exclusion is not enforced if it would be unconscionable. Any attempt to limit consequential damages for injury caused to a person by consumer goods is considered prima facie unconscionable [2–719(3)].

Suppose an automobile manufacturer makes a warranty as to the quality of an automobile that is purchased as a consumer good. It then tries to disclaim responsibility for any person injured if the car does not conform to the warranty and to limit its liability to replacing any defective parts. The disclaimer of consequential injuries in this case would be unconscionable and therefore would not be enforced. Exclusion of or limitation on consequential damages is permitted where the loss is commercial, as long as the exclusion or limitation is not unconscionable.

The *Hartzell v. Justus Co., Inc.* case, which follows, illustrates how the Code applies to a situation where circumstances cause a limited remedy agreed to by the parties to fail in its essential purpose. When this happens, the limited remedy is not enforced and the general Code remedies are available to the injured party.

HARTZELL V. JUSTUS CO., INC.
693 F.2d 770 (8th Cir. 1982)

Dr. Allan Hartzell purchased a log home construction kit manufactured by Justus Homes. Hartzell purchased the package for $38,622 from Del Carter, who was Justus Homes's dealer for the Sioux Falls area. He also hired Carter's construction company to build the house, which eventually cost about $150,000. Hartzell was dissatisfied with the house in many respects. His chief complaints were that knotholes in the walls and ceilings leaked rain profusely and that the home was not weathertight because flashings were not included in the roofing materials and because the timbers were not kiln-dried and therefore shrank. He also complained that an undersized support beam, which eventually cracked, was included in the package. This defect resulted in floor cracks and in inside doors that would not close. Hartzell claimed that the structural defects were only partially remediable and that the fair market value of the house was reduced even after all practicable repairs had been made.

Hartzell brought suit against Justus Homes, alleging negligence and breach of implied and express warranties and seeking damages for loss in value and the cost of repairs. A jury awarded Hartzell a verdict of $34,794.67. Justus Homes appealed.

Arnold, Circuit Judge Justus Homes contends the district court failed to adequately consider a limitation-of-remedies clause contained in its contract with Hartzell. Justus Homes relies on Clause 10c of the contract, which says that Justus will repair or replace defective materials, and Clause 10d, which states that this limited repair or replacement clause is the exclusive remedy available against Justus. These agreements, Justus asserts, are valid under the Uniform Commercial Code, § 2–719(1). Section 2–719(1) states:

(1) Subject to the provisions of subsections (2) and (3) of this section and of § 2–718 on liquidation and limitation of damages,

(a) The agreement may provide for remedies in addition to or in substitution for those provided in this article and may limit or alter the measure of damages recoverable under this article, as by limiting the buyer's remedies to return of the goods and repayment of the price or to repair and replacement of nonconforming goods or parts; and

(b) Resort to a remedy as provided is optional unless the remedy is expressly agreed to be exclusive, in which case it is the sole remedy.

Subsection (1) of § 2–719 is qualified by subsection (2): "Where circumstances cause an exclusive or limited remedy to fail of its essential purpose, remedy may be had as provided in this title." The jury's verdict for Hartzell in an amount almost exactly equal to Hartzell's evidence of cost of repairs plus diminution in market value means it must have found that the structural defects were not entirely remediable. Such a finding necessarily means that the limited warranty failed of its essential purpose.

Two of our recent cases support this conclusion. In *Soo Line R.R. v. Fruehauf Corp.*, the defendant claimed, relying on a limitation-of-remedies clause similar to the one involved here, that the plaintiff's damages should be limited to the reasonable cost of repairing the railroad cars that plaintiff had bought from defendant. The jury verdict included, among other things, an award for the difference between the value of the cars as actually manufactured and what they would have been worth if they had measured up to the defendant's representations. This court affirmed the verdict for the larger amount. We held, construing the Minnesota UCC, which is identical to 2–719 as adopted in South Dakota, that the limitation-of-

remedies clause was ineffective because the remedy as thus limited failed of its essential purpose. The defendant, though called upon to make the necessary repairs, had refused to do so, and the repairs as performed by the plaintiff itself "did not fully restore the cars to totally acceptable operating conditions."

Here, Justus Homes attempted to help with the necessary repairs, which is more than Fruehauf did in the *Soo Line* case, but after the repairs had been completed, the house was still, according to the jury verdict, not what Justus had promised it would be. The purpose of a remedy is to give to a buyer what the seller promised him—that is, a house that did not leak. If repairs alone do not achieve that end, then to limit the buyer's remedy to repair would cause that remedy to fail of its essential purpose.

An analogous case is *Select Port, Inc. v. Babcock Swine, Inc.*, applying 2–719 as adopted in Iowa. The defendant had promised to deliver to plaintiff certain extraordinary pigs known as Midwestern Gilts and Meatline Boars. Instead, only ordinary pigs were delivered. Plaintiff sued for breach of warranty, and defendant claimed that its damages, if any, should be limited to a return of the purchase price by an express clause to that effect in the contract. The district court held that the clause was unenforceable because it was unconscionable, see § 2–719(3), and because it failed of its essential purpose. We affirmed. "Having failed to deliver the highly-touted special pigs, defendants may not now assert a favorable clause to limit their liability."

So here, where the house sold was found by the jury to fall short of the seller's promises, and where repairs could not make it right, Justus Homes's liability cannot be limited to the cost of repairs. If the repairs had been adequate to restore the house to its promised condition, and if Dr. Hartzell had claimed additional consequential damages, for example, water damage to a rug from the leaky roof, the limitation-of-remedies clause would have been effective. But that is not this case.

The evidence in the record all demonstrates that the repair or replacement clause was a failure under the circumstances of this case. Some of the house's many problems simply could not be remedied by repair or replacement. The clause having failed of its essential purpose, that is, effective enjoyment of implied and express warranties, Dr. Hartzell was entitled, under UCC 2–719(2), to any of the buyer's remedies provided by the Code. Among these rem-

edies are consequential damages as provided in 2–714 and 2–715(2).

Judgment for Hartzell affirmed.

Statute of Limitations

The Code provides that a lawsuit for breach of a sales contract must be filed within four years after the breach occurs. The parties to a contract may shorten this period to one year, but they may not extend it for longer than four years [2–725]. Normally, a breach of warranty is considered to have occurred when the goods are delivered to the buyer. However, if the warranty covers future performance of goods (for example, a warranty on a tire for four years or 40,000

miles), then the breach occurs at the time the buyer should have discovered the defect in the product. If, for example, the buyer of the tire discovers the defect after driving 25,000 miles on the tire over a three-year period, he would have four years from that time to bring any lawsuit to remedy the breach.

In the *Wilson v. Hammer Holdings, Inc.* case, which follows, the court rejected the argument that a warranty given in connection with the sale of a painting extended to the future performance of the painting.

WILSON V. HAMMER HOLDINGS, INC.
6 UCC Rep.2d 321 (1st Cir. 1988)

In 1961, Dorothy and John Wilson purchased a painting entitled *Femme Debout* from the Hammer Galleries. They paid $11,000 for the work that was expressly guaranteed to be an original work of art by Edouard Vuillard. The purchase agreement stated that "the authenticity of this picture is guaranteed." In 1984, in preparation for selling it, the Wilsons had the picture examined by an expert. The expert determined that the painting was not done by the French artist Vuillard, and he refused to authenticate it.

The Wilsons returned the painting to the Hammer Galleries, and then brought a lawsuit seeking damages for breach of warranty. Hammer Galleries asserted that the claim was barred by the UCC's four-year statute of limitations. The district court held that the claim was barred by the statute of limitations, and Wilson appealed.

Coffin, Circuit Judge   The Massachusetts statute of limitations for breach of a sales contract is set out in section 2–725. That section provides that

(1) An action for breach of any contract for sale must be commenced within four years after the cause of action has accrued.

(2) A cause of action accrues when the breach occurs, regardless of the aggrieved party's lack of knowledge of the breach. A breach of warranty occurs when tender of delivery is made, except that where a warranty explicitly extends to future performance of the goods and discovery must await the time of such

performance, the cause of action accrues when the breach is or should have been discovered.

There is no question that the Wilsons' action was untimely under this statute if it accrued at the time they purchased the painting and received the warranty because those events occurred twenty-six years before suit was filed. The Wilsons therefore contend that this case falls within the exception to section 2–725(2), and they argue that their cause of action accrued upon their discovery in 1985 that the painting was not authentic.

The district court found the exception in section 2–725(2) to be inapplicable because Hammer's warranty made no explicit reference to future performance as required by the statute. The Wilsons do not argue that the district court erred in reading the warranty to lack an explicit promise of future performance. Rather, they argue that a warranty of authenticity necessarily relates to the future condition of the artwork, despite the absence of explicit language to that effect, and for that reason, they claim that the exception in section 2–725(2) should apply to them. Section 2–725(2) refers to a warranty of "future performance," and so the Wilsons' theory depends first on extending the concept of a "performance" to a painting. They concede that paintings, unlike consumer goods like automobiles and washing machines, generally are not purchased based on how they "perform" or "function." They suggest, however, that a painting "performs" "by being what it is represented to be." In this case, they say, "Femme Debout" could "perform" only by being an authentic Vuillard.

Accepting at least for the sake of argument that a painting does "perform" by being genuine, the question then becomes whether Hammer's express warranty of authenticity not only guaranteed the present "being" of the painting as an authentic Vuillard but also extended, as required by section 2–725(2), to the future existence of a painting as a Vuillard. On this point, the Wilsons argue that because the authenticity of a painting does not change over time, Hammer's warranty necessarily guaranteed the present and future existence of the painting as an authentic Vuillard. Therefore, they contend, explicit words warranting future performance would be superfluous in this context.

One difficulty with this argument, however, is that it asks us to ignore the literal language of the statute requiring an explicit promise of future performance. The Wilsons argue essentially that because the statutory exception's requirement of an explicit prospective warranty does not make sense in the context of the sale of paintings, we should dispense with that requirement. We are reluctant, however, to waive the specific eligibility requirements established by the legislature for what, it must be remembered, is an exception to the general limitations rule.

Even if we were to accept the Wilsons' argument that Hammer's warranty necessarily extended to future performance of the painting, and thus met the prospective warranty requirement of section 2–725(2), we nevertheless would conclude that their action is time-barred. The statute also requires that discovery of the breach "must await" the time of such future performance. That is not the case here. Because of the static nature of authenticity, the Wilsons were no less capable of discovering that "Femme Debout" was a fake at the time of purchase than they were at a later time.

Our reluctance to enlarge the scope of the exception in section 2–725(2) is strengthened by the recognition that the statute of limitations for art buyers could run indefinitely. Indeed, in this case suit was filed 26 years after the purchase. Although Massachusetts legislators may choose to provide perpetual protection for consumers of artistic products, it would be presumptuous for us to assume they would. Moreover, we think it is more likely that, if Massachusetts chooses to extend protection to art buyers in the way the Wilsons suggest, the legislature would fix some endpoint to the seller's possible liability—perhaps similar to the 20-year limitations period for an action seeking the recovery of land.

Judgment in favor of Hammer Galleries affirmed.

SELLER'S REMEDIES

Remedies Available to an Injured Seller

A buyer may breach a contract in a number of ways. The most common are: (1) by wrongfully refusing to accept goods, (2) by wrongfully returning goods, (3) by failing to pay for goods when payment is due, and (4) by indicating an unwillingness to go ahead with the contract.

When a buyer breaches a contract, the seller has a number of remedies under the Code, including the right to:

- Cancel the contract [2–703(f)].
- Withhold delivery of undelivered goods [2–703(a)].
- Resell the goods covered by the contract and recover damages from the buyer [2–706].
- Recover from the buyer the profit that the seller would have made on the sale or the damages that the seller sustained [2–708].
- Recover the purchase price of goods delivered to or accepted by the buyer [2–709].

In addition, a buyer may become insolvent and thus unable to pay the seller for goods already delivered or for goods that the seller is obligated to deliver. When a seller learns of a buyer's insolvency, the seller has a number of remedies, including the right to:

- Withhold delivery of undelivered goods [2–703(a)].
- Recover goods from a buyer upon the buyer's insolvency [2–702].
- Stop delivery of goods that are in the possession of a carrier or other bailee [2–705].

Cancellation and Withholding of Delivery

When a buyer breaches a contract, the seller has the right to cancel the contract and to hold up her own performance of the contract. The seller may then set aside any goods that were intended to fill her obligations under the contract [2–704].

If the seller is in the process of manufacturing the goods, she has two choices. She may complete manufacture of the goods, or she may stop manufacturing and sell the uncompleted goods for their scrap or salvage value. In choosing between these alternatives, the seller should select the alternative that will minimize the loss [2–704(2)]. Thus, a seller would be justified in completing the manufacture of goods that could be resold readily at the contract price. However, a seller would not be justified in completing specially manufactured goods that could not be sold to anyone other than the buyer who ordered them.

The purpose of this rule is to permit the seller to follow a reasonable course of action to mitigate (minimize) the damages. In *Madsen v. Murrey & Sons Co., Inc.,* which follows, the seller, who did not complete the manufacture of goods on the buyer's repudiation, but rather dismantled and largely scrapped the existing goods, was held not to have acted in a commercially reasonable manner.

MADSEN V. MURREY & SONS CO., INC.

743 P.2d 1212 (Utah Sup. Ct. 1987)

Murrey & Sons Co., Inc. (Murrey), was engaged in the business of manufacturing and selling pool tables. Erik Madsen was working on an idea to develop a pool table that would, through the use of electronic devices installed in the rails of the table, produce lighting and sound effects in a fashion similar to a pinball machine. Murrey and Madsen entered into a written contract whereby Murrey agreed to manufacture 100 of its M1 4-foot by 8-foot six-pocket coin operated pool tables with customized rails capable of incorporating the electronic lighting and sound effects desired by Madsen. Under the agreement, Madsen would design the rails and provide the drawings to Murrey, who would manufacture them to Madsen's specifications. Madsen was to design, manufacture, and install the electronic components for the tables. Madsen agreed to pay $550 per table or a total of $55,000 for the 100 tables and made a $42,500 deposit on the contract.

Murrey began the manufacture of the tables while Madsen continued to work on the design of the rails and electronics. Madsen encountered significant difficulties and notified Murrey that he would be unable to take delivery of the 100 tables. Madsen then brought suit to recover the $42,500 he had paid Murrey.

Following Madsen's repudiation of the contract, Murrey dismantled the pool tables and used salvageable materials to manufacture other pool tables. A good portion of the material was simply used as firewood. Murrey made no attempt to market the 100 pool tables at a discount or at any other price in order to mitigate the damages. It claimed the salvage value of the materials it reused as $7,448. The trial court ordered Murrey to return $21,250 to Madsen and Murrey appealed.

Howe, Justice   Murrey contends that the trial court erred in concluding that it had failed to mitigate or minimize its damages in a commercially reasonable manner by not attempting to sell the 100 pool tables on the open market. It is a well-settled rule of the law of damages that "no party suffering a loss as the result of a breach of contract is entitled to any damages which could have been avoided if the aggrieved party had acted in a reasonably diligent manner in attempting to lessen his losses as a consequence of that breach." We have held:

Where a contractual agreement has been breached by a party thereto, the aggrieved party is entitled to those damages that will put him in as good a position as he would have been had the other party performed pursuant to the agreement. A corollary to this rule is that the aggrieved party may not, either by action or inaction, aggravate the injury occasioned by the breach, but has a duty actively to mitigate his damages.

Murrey asserts that it sufficiently mitigated its damages by dismantling the pool tables and salvaging various components that could be used to manufacture other pool tables. The salvage value to Murrey was claimed to be $7,448. Murrey presented testimony that selling the tables as "seconds" would damage its reputation for quality and that the various holes, notches and routings placed in the tables to accommodate the electrical components to be installed by buyer weakened the structure of the tables so as to submit seller to potential liability if they were sold on the market.

On the other hand, Ronald Baker, who had been involved with the manufacturing and marketing of pool tables for 25 years testified on behalf of the buyer that the notches, holes and routings made in the frame to accommodate electrical wiring would not adversely affect the quality or marketability of the 100 pool tables. According to Baker, the tables could have been sold at full value or at a discounted price. In addition to this testimony, the trial court had the opportunity to view the experimental table developed by Madsen and his associates and observe the holes, notches, and routings necessary for the electrical components.

The trial court found that Murrey's action in dismantling the tables and using the materials for salvage and firewood, rather than attempting to sell or market the tables at full or discounted price, was not commercially reasonable. The court then concluded that seller had a duty to mitigate its damages and failed to do so. The finding is supported by competent evidence.

Applying the trial court's finding that the pool tables, if completed, could have been sold for at least $21,250, Murrey's damages are the difference between the market price ($21,250) and the contract price ($55,000) or $33,750. The trial court found that Murrey was not entitled to any incidental damages. Under section 2–718(2), (3), Madsen's right to restitution of advance payments on the contract ($42,500) is subject to offset to the extent that seller establishes damages ($33,750), for a total recovery of $8,750.

Judgment for Madsen affirmed, with the recovery set at $8,750.

Resale of Goods

If the seller sets aside goods intended for the contract or completes the manufacture of such goods, he is not obligated to try to resell the goods to someone else. However, he may resell them and recover damages. The seller must make any resale in good faith and in a commercially reasonable manner. If the seller does so, he is entitled to recover from the buyer as damages the difference between the resale price and the price the buyer agreed to pay in the contract [2–706].

If the seller resells, he may also recover incidental damages, but the seller must give the buyer credit for any expenses that the seller saved because of the buyer's breach of contract. Incidental damages include storage charges and sales commissions paid when the goods were resold [2–710]. Expenses saved might be the cost of packaging the goods and/or shipping them to the buyer.

If the buyer and seller have agreed as to the manner in which the resale is to be made, the courts will enforce the agreement unless it is found to be unconscionable [2–302]. If the parties have not entered into an agreement as to the resale of the goods, they may be resold at public or private sale, but in all events the resale must be made in good faith and in a commercially reasonable manner. The seller should make it clear that the goods he is selling are those related to the broken contract.

If the goods are resold at private sale, the seller must give the buyer reasonable notification of his intention to resell [2–706(3)]. If the resale is a public sale, such as an auction, the seller must give the buyer notice of the time and place of the sale unless the goods are perishable or threaten to decline in value rapidly. The sale must be made at a usual place or market for public sales if one is reasonably available; and if the goods are not within the view of those attending the sale, the notification of the sale must state the place where the goods are located and provide for reasonable inspection by prospective bidders. The seller may bid at a public sale [2–706(4)].

The purchaser at a public sale who buys in good faith takes free from any rights of the original buyer even though the seller has failed to conduct the sale in compliance with the rules set out in the Code [2–706(5)]. The seller is not accountable to the buyer for any profit that the seller makes on a resale [2–706(6)].

Recovery of the Purchase Price

In the normal performance of a contract, the seller delivers conforming goods (goods that meet the contract specifications) to the buyer. The buyer accepts the goods and pays for them. The seller is entitled to the purchase price of all goods accepted by the buyer. She also is entitled to the purchase price of all goods that conformed to the contract and were lost or damaged after the buyer assumed the risk for their loss [2–709].

For example, a contract calls for Frank, a farmer, to ship 1,000 dozen eggs to Sutton, a grocer, with shipment "FOB Frank's Farm." If the eggs are lost or damaged while on their way to Sutton, she is responsible for paying Frank for them. Risk of loss is discussed in Chapter 19, Formation and Terms of Sales Contracts.

In one other situation, the seller may recover the purchase or contract price from the buyer. This is where the seller has made an honest effort to resell the goods and was unsuccessful or where it is apparent that any such effort to resell would be unsuccessful. This might happen where the seller manufactured goods especially for the buyer and the goods are not usable by anyone else. Assume that Sarton's Supermarket sponsors a bowling team. Sarton's orders six green-and-red bowling shirts to be embroidered with "Sarton's Supermarket" on the back and the names of the team members on the pocket. After the shirts are completed, Sarton's wrongfully refuses to accept them. The manufacturer will be able to recover the agreed purchase price if it cannot sell the shirts to someone else.

If the seller sues the buyer for the contract price of the goods, she must hold the goods for the buyer. Then, the seller must turn the goods over to the buyer if the buyer pays for them. However, if resale becomes possible before the buyer pays for the goods, the seller may resell them. Then, the seller must give the buyer credit for the proceeds of the resale [2–709(2)].

Damages for Rejection or Repudiation

When the buyer refuses to accept goods that conform to the contract or repudiates the contract, the seller does not have to resell the goods. The seller has two other ways of determining the damages that the buyer is liable for because of the breach of contract: (1) the difference between the contract price and the market price at which the goods are currently selling and (2) the "profit" that the seller lost when the buyer did not go through with the contract [2–708].

The seller may recover as damages the difference between the contract price and the market price at the time and place the goods were to be delivered to the buyer. The seller may also recover any incidental damages, but must give the buyer credit for any expenses that the seller has saved [2–708(1)]. This measure of damages most commonly is sought by a seller when the market price of the goods dropped substantially between the time the contract was made and the time the buyer repudiated the contract.

For example, on January 1, Toy Maker, Inc., contracts with the Red Balloon Toy Shop to sell the shop 100,000 hula hoops at $3.50 each, with delivery to be made in Boston on June 1. By June 1, the hula hoop fad has passed and hula hoops are selling for $1 each in Boston. If Toy Shop repudiates the contract on June 1 and refuses to accept delivery of the 100,000 hula hoops, Toy Maker is entitled to the difference between the contract price of $350,000 and the June 1 market price in Boston of $100,000. Thus, Toy Maker could recover $250,000 in damages plus any incidental expenses, but less any expenses saved by it in not having to ship the hula hoops to Toy Shop (such as packaging and transportation costs).

If getting the difference between the contract price and the market price would not put the seller in as good a financial position as the seller would have been in if the contract had been performed, the seller may choose an alternative measure of damages based on the lost profit and overhead that the seller would have made if the sale had gone through. The seller can recover this lost profit and overhead plus any incidental expenses. However, the seller must give the buyer credit for any expenses saved as a result of the buyer's breach of contract [2–708(2)].

Using the hula hoop example, assume that the direct labor and material cost to Toy Maker of making the hoops was 75 cents each. Toy Maker could recover as damages from Toy Shop the profit Toy Maker lost when Toy Shop defaulted on the contract. Toy Maker would be entitled to the difference between the contract price of $350,000 and its direct cost of $75,000. Thus, Toy Maker could recover $275,000 plus any incidental expenses and less any expenses saved.

Seller's Remedies Where Buyer Is Insolvent

If the seller has not agreed to extend credit to the buyer for the purchase price of goods, the buyer must make payment on delivery of the goods. If the seller tenders delivery of the goods, he may withhold delivery unless the agreed payment is made. Where the seller has agreed to extend credit to the buyer for the purchase price of the goods, but discovers before delivery that the buyer is insolvent, the seller may refuse delivery unless the buyer pays cash for the goods together with the unpaid balance for all goods previously delivered under the contract [2–702(1)].

At common law, a seller had the right to rescind a sales contract induced by fraud and to recover the goods unless they had been resold to a bona fide purchaser for value. Based on this general legal principle, the Code provides that where the seller discovers that the buyer has received goods while insolvent, the seller may reclaim the goods upon demand made within 10 days after their receipt. This right granted to the seller is based on constructive deceit on the part of the buyer. Receiving goods while insolvent is equivalent to a false representation of solvency. To protect his rights, all the seller must do is to make a demand within the 10-day period; he need not actually repossess the goods.

If the buyer has misrepresented his solvency to this particular seller in writing within three months before the delivery of the goods, the 10-day limitation on the seller's right to reclaim the goods does not apply. However, the seller's right to reclaim the goods is subject to the prior rights of purchasers in the ordinary course of the buyer's business, good faith purchasers for value, creditors with a perfected lien on the buyer's inventory [2–702(2) and (3)], and a trustee in bankruptcy. The relative rights of creditors to their debtor's collateral are discussed in Chapter 28, Security Interests in Personal Property.

The case that follows, *Conoco, Inc. v. Braniff, Inc.,* illustrates some of issues that may arise when a creditor seeks to reclaim goods from an insolvent buyer.

CONOCO, INC. V. BRANIFF, INC.
11 UCC Rep.2d 519 (Bankr. M.D. Fla. 1990)

Braniff, an airline, had an agreement with Conoco whereby Conoco supplied Braniff with its needs for Jet A aviation fuel. The fuel was sent through an interstate common carrier pipeline used by numerous suppliers, including Conoco. The pipeline contained breakout points where fuel was directed out of the pipeline and into tank farm storage facilities operated by Ogden Allied Aviation Services, Braniff's designated fueling agent, at the Dallas–Fort Worth and Kansas City airports.

The agreement called for Braniff to make advance payments for its designated fuel needs for the following week, with settlement of overages or shortages on a monthly basis. Braniff made a payment of $320,000 on September 20, 1989, for its anticipated needs through September 27 and was scheduled to make a $420,000 payment on September 27, 1989. The payment was not made on September 27, and early the next morning Braniff filed a petition in bankruptcy under Chapter 11 of the Bankruptcy Code.

On September 29, 1989, Conoco sent Braniff a "Notice of Reclamation" seeking reclamation of unpaid fuel delivered into the tank farms at the Dallas–Fort Worth airports and Kansas City during the previous 10-day period. The reclamation notice identified the fuel it sought to reclaim by specifying 14 bills of lading representing unpaid shipments occurring from September 19 through September 27.

Corcoran, Bankruptcy Judge In order to establish entitlement to reclamation from a debtor under section 2–702 of the UCC and section 546 of the Bankruptcy Code, a reclaiming seller must satisfy the following four-part test:

1. The debtor was insolvent at the time the goods were delivered by the seller;
2. A written demand was made on the debtor within ten days after the goods were delivered to the debtor;
3. The goods were identifiable at the time the demand was made; and
4. The goods were in the possession and control of the debtor at the time the demand was made.

Braniff contends that the fuel at issue here was neither identifiable nor in its possession and control at the time the reclamation demand was made because of the commingling that occurred in the common carrier pipelines and at the airport tank farms. Braniff points out that the fuel was pumped through a common carrier pipeline from Conoco's refineries with petroleum products belonging to numerous other suppliers. Once the fuel was received at the Ogden Allied tank farms, it was then commingled in large tanks with fuel supplied by other suppliers and allocated to and for the use of numerous users. At Dallas–Fort Worth, the commingled fuel allocated to Braniff had been supplied solely by Conoco. At Kansas City, the fuel allocated to Braniff had been supplied by four suppliers, including Conoco.

In the case of fungible, bulk petroleum products, such as jet fuel, the "identification" and "possession and control" requirements of the Code and the UCC mandate that the reclaiming party:

trace the [fuel] from its possession into an identifiable mass and to show that the mass contains only [fuel] of like kind and grade. If the mass of [fuel into which the fuel is traced] is subject to [the debtor's] control, then it is both "identifiable" and "in the possession of the debtor."

In this case the jet fuel type A was shipped from Conoco's refineries through a common carrier pipeline where it was commingled with other jet fuel type A refined by other suppliers and sold to other users. The commingling further occurred in the airport tank farms, from which many airlines withdrew the fuel that was ultimately pumped into airplanes. Plainly, on these facts, Conoco has traced its fuel into an identifiable mass containing only fuel of like grade and quality.

Likewise Conoco has shown that the mass of fuel in the airport tank farms was subject to Braniff's control. The tank farms were owned and operated by Braniff's fueling agent. The fueling agent would then draw down from the fuel in the storage tanks the amount needed to fuel Braniff aircraft. On this record, it is clear that the fueling agent abided by Braniff's instructions.

The fact that the tanks contained fuel allocated to other airlines, by itself, is irrelevant to the "identification" and "possession and control" issue. The inquiry here deals solely with the fuel in the tanks allocated to Braniff.

The fact that the fueling agent also served as fueling agent for other airlines and that other airlines controlled their allocable portion of the fuel in the tank farm storage tanks does not diminish the control Braniff exercised over its allocable portion. The point, of course, is that Braniff had the ability and authority to control the disposition of its fuel at the time the reclamation notice was received.

Conoco desires to reclaim 284,107 gallons for which it is unpaid from the ending pool of 397,735. In effect, Conoco wants the court to assume that Braniff used during the ten-day reclamation period the fuel that it had on hand before the period began, the fuel that Conoco supplied during the reclamation period for which payment was made, and the fuel provided by three other suppliers during the reclamation period. In other words, Conoco says only Conoco fuel for which payment had not been made was left in the tank at the end of the reclamation period and that Conoco can now claim this "identified" fuel.

Braniff, of course, contends just the opposite. Braniff would have the court assume that Braniff used during the ten-day reclamation period the Conoco fuel for which payment was not made so that the fuel remaining in the tank at the end of the period represents only fuel that was there before the reclamation period began, fuel supplied by Conoco for which payment was made during the reclamation period, and fuel supplied by other suppliers.

The court concludes that it is required to reject both approaches. Where, as here, there are several suppliers delivering fungible, bulk goods into a common tank, the supplier must do more than merely trace its fungible, bulk goods into the pool. The supplier must go further and show what quantity of goods was in the pool at the beginning of the relevant reclamation period. The supplier must also show when, and how much of the goods, each of the suppliers contributed to the pool during that period. Finally, the supplier must show how much of the total remained in the pool at the end of the relevant period. With that information the court can then determine the amount of each bulk shipment that was consumed by the debtor during the period. The court also can determine to which supplier the amount remaining in the tank at the end of the period should be attributed or the proportional way in which the amount remaining should be allocated among the suppliers. Implicit in the rule the court states here is a "first in, first out" theory of bulk fuel use to be used in cases such as this where fungible, bulk goods are pooled or commingled.

On the evidence presented, Conoco established its right to reclaim only the 100,002 gallons of fuel it delivered to Dallas–Fort Worth on September 26.

Judgment for Conoco.

Seller's Right to Stop Delivery

If the seller discovers that the buyer is insolvent, he has the right to stop the delivery of any goods that he has shipped to the buyer, regardless of the size of the shipment. If a buyer repudiates a sales contract or fails to make a payment due before delivery, the seller has the right to stop delivery of any large shipment of goods, such as a carload, a truckload, or a planeload [2–705].

To stop delivery, the seller must notify the carrier or other bailee in time for the bailee to prevent delivery of the goods. After receiving notice to stop delivery, the carrier or other bailee owes a duty to hold the goods and deliver them as directed by the seller. The seller is liable to the carrier or other bailee for expenses incurred or damages resulting from compliance with his order to stop delivery. If a nonnegotiable document of title has been issued for the goods, the carrier or other bailee does not have a duty to obey a stop-delivery order issued by any person other than the person who consigned the goods to him [2–705(3)].

Liquidated Damages

If the seller has justifiably withheld delivery of the goods because of the buyer's breach, the buyer may recover any money or goods he has delivered to the seller over and above the agreed amount of liquidated damages. If there is no such agreement, the seller may not retain an amount in excess of $500 or 20 percent of the value of the total performance for which the buyer is obligated under the contract, whichever is smaller. This right of restitution is subject to the seller's right to recover damages under other provisions of the Code and to recover the amount of value of benefits received by the buyer directly or indirectly by reason of the contract [2–718].

CONCEPT REVIEW

SELLER'S REMEDIES (ON BREACH BY BUYER)

Problem	Seller's Remedy

Buyer Refuses to Go Ahead with Contract and Seller Has Goods	1. Seller may cancel contract, suspend performance, and set aside goods intended to fill the contract.
	  a. If seller is in the process of manufacturing, he may complete manufacture or stop and sell for scrap, picking alternative that in his judgment at the time will minimize the seller's loss.
	  b. Seller can resell goods covered by contract and recover difference between contract price and proceeds of resale.
	  c. Seller may recover purchase price where resale is not possible.
	  d. Seller may recover damages for breach based on difference between contract price and market price, or in some cases based on lost profits.

Goods Are in Buyer's Possession	1. Seller may recover purchase price. 2. Seller may reclaim goods in possession of insolvent buyer by making a demand within 10 days after their receipt. If the buyer represented solvency to the seller in writing within three months before delivery, the 10-day limitation does not apply.
Goods Are in Transit	1. Seller may stop any size shipment if buyer is insolvent. 2. Seller may stop carload, truckload, planeload, or other large shipment for reasons other than buyer's insolvency.

BUYER'S REMEDIES

Buyer's Remedies in General

A seller may breach a contract in a number of ways. The most common are: (1) failing to make an agreed delivery, (2) delivering goods that do not conform to the contract, and (3) indicating that he does not intend to fulfill the obligations under the contract.

A buyer whose seller breaks the contract is given a number of alternative remedies. These include:

· Buying other goods (covering) and recovering damages from the seller based on any additional expense that the buyer incurs in obtaining the goods [2–712].

· Recovering damages based on the difference between the contract price and the current market price of the goods [2–713].

· Recovering damages for any nonconforming goods accepted by the buyer based on the difference in value between what the buyer got and what he should have gotten [2–714].

Obtaining specific performance of the contract where the goods are unique and cannot be obtained elsewhere [2–716].

In addition, the buyer can in some cases recover consequential damages (such as lost profits) and incidental damages (such as expenses incurred in buying substitute goods).

Buyer's Right to Cover

If the seller fails or refuses to deliver the goods called for in the contract, the buyer can purchase substitute goods; this is known as **cover.** If the buyer does purchase substitute goods, the buyer can recover as damages from the seller the difference between the contract price and the cost of the substitute goods [2–712]. For example, Frank Farmer agrees to sell Ann's Cider Mill 1,000 bushels of apples at $10 a bushel. Farmer then refuses to deliver the apples. Cider Mill can purchase 1,000 bushels of similar apples, and if it has to pay $11 a bushel, it can recover the difference ($1 a bushel) between what it paid ($11) and the contract price ($10). Thus, Cider Mill could recover $1,000 from Farmer.

The buyer can also recover any incidental damages sustained, but must give the seller credit for any expenses saved. In addition, he may be able to obtain consequential damages. The buyer is not required to cover, however. If he does not cover, the other remedies under the Code are still available [2–712].

The case that follows, *Saboundjian v. Bank Audi (USA)*, illustrates that a court will not allow an aggrieved party to speculate on the market at the defaulting party's expense.

SABOUNDJIAN V. BANK AUDI (USA)
11 UCC Rep.2d 1165 (N.Y. Sup. Ct., App. Div. 1990)

Vrej Saboundjian, a customer of Bank Audi, was a sophisticated international businessman well acquainted with the foreign exchange market. In April 1986, he began to speculate in foreign currency through the bank. The foreign currency trading market, which is global, operates without a central exchange and with individual banks throughout the world setting their own rates. Thus, a foreign exchange speculator like Saboundjian, by sending orders to Far East, Middle East, and European markets, is able to participate in foreign exchange trading even after the close of business at domestic banks.

On January 7, 1987, Saboundjian was holding a short position in deutsche marks. That afternoon, he asked the foreign exchange trader at Bank Audi (USA) to liquidate his short position when "deutsche marks reached 1.9360 per dollar." As was customary for the bank when an order was placed in the late afternoon or evening and the customer's price was not available in the domestic mark, Bank Audi relayed the order to a foreign bank, in this case, Investbank in the United Arab Emirates, to be executed. The bank's commission covering profit and expenses for performing the trade was added to the price requested by Saboundjian. Thus, the order placed at 3:24 P.M., eastern standard time, called for the bank to sell $2 million against deutsche marks at the rate of 1.9380 deutsche marks per dollar.

At 8 A.M. the following morning, the Bank Audi trader noticed that confirmation of the requested trade had not been received and telephoned Investbank and was advised that it had been unable to execute the requested trade. He was advised by Bank Audi (Paris) that the market had been very hectic and that the requested price had been quoted in the market only very briefly and thereafter dropped quickly.

At about 9 A.M., Saboundjian was advised that Investbank had been unable to effect the order; he was also advised of the current market price and that his order could be executed at that price if he desired. He indicated that he did not want the bank to execute at that price and that he was "bullish." At the time, he could have made a profit of approximately $4,700, somewhat less than the approximately $8,000 he would have made if his requested trade had been executed. He subsequently testified that "I thought if I wait maybe a couple of hours or one day, that I could see my price again and if I don't see the price, I said, you have to take the loss as the bank."

During the day, Saboundjian's position deteriorated to a small loss by the end of the day. He did not ask the bank to close out his position until February 6, 1987, at which time the value of the dollar in terms of deutsche marks had fallen to 1.8695. His losses exceeded $420,000. He subsequently brought an action against Bank Audi for failure to execute the January 6 trade and sought consequential damages in excess of $400,000. The bank filed a motion for partial summary judgment, seeking to limit its liability to the difference between Saboundjian's profit had the transaction been carried out as requested and the smaller profit he would have made had he acted to cover on January 8 when he learned of the failure of the January 7 trade. The trial court denied the motion and the bank appealed.

Sullivan, Judge   Even assuming the bank is liable for failing to execute the January 7, 1987, trade, liability is limited to the difference between the price at which Saboundjian could have executed the trade at issue were it not for the failure to carry it out, and the price at which he could have executed the transaction within a reasonable time after he learned that it had not been effected earlier. Since Saboundjian had a duty to act reasonably and mitigate any damages he may have sustained, the bank cannot be liable for his entire speculation, including losses realized on unrelated transactions. Thus, when a broker rightfully fails to purchase or sell a security as directed, the customer's damages are limited to the cost of covering or replacing the security. If the customer fails to cover within a reasonable time, damages are limited to the potential cost to cover as measured from the time he learns of the broker's failure and for a reasonable time thereafter in which he must decide on his course of action. A customer may not refuse to cover a transaction previously requested and thereby speculate on the market entirely at the risk of the broker.

Article 2 of the Uniform Commercial Code is instructive on the issue of damages. Under section 2–712(1), in the event of a breach, "the buyer may 'cover' by making in good faith and without unreasonable delay any reasonable purchase or contract to purchase goods in substitution for those due from the seller." The buyer may only recover from the seller "as damages the difference between the cost of cover and the contract price together with any incidental or consequential damages." Consequential damages are restricted, however, to those "which could not reasonably be prevented by cover or otherwise." Section 2–715(2). Thus Saboundjian is not entitled to consequential damages since he was in a position to effect cover immediately after having been notified of the bank's failure to execute the January 7 order.

Saboundjian's damages are therefore limited to no more than the difference between the profit he would have earned had the subject trade been executed on January 7, 1987, or approximately $8,000 as alleged in the complaint, and the profit that Saboundjian would have earned had he directed the execution of the trade within a reasonable time after he learned that his original order had not been executed.

Judgment reversed in favor of Bank Audi.

Incidental Damages

Incidental damages include expenses that the buyer incurs in receiving, inspecting, transporting, and storing goods shipped by the seller that do not conform to those called for in the contract. Incidental damages also include any reasonable expenses or charges that the buyer has to pay in obtaining substitute goods [2–715(1)].

Consequential Damages

In certain situations, an injured buyer is able to recover consequential damages such as the buyer's lost profits caused by the seller's breach of contract. The buyer must be able to show that the seller knew or should have known at the time the contract was made that the buyer would suffer special damages if the seller did not perform his obligations. The buyer must also show that he could not have prevented the damage by obtaining substitute goods [2–715(2)].

Suppose Knitting Mill promises to deliver 15,000 yards of a special fabric to Dorsey by September 1. Knitting Mill knows that Dorsey wants to acquire the material to make garments suitable for the Christmas season. Knitting Mill also knows that in reliance on the contract with it, Dorsey will enter into contracts with department stores to deliver the finished garments by October 1. If Knitting Mill fails to deliver the fabric or delivers the fabric after September 1, it may be liable to Dorsey for any consequential damages that she sustains if she is unable to acquire the same material elsewhere in time to fulfill her October 1 contracts.

Consequential damages can also include an injury to a person or property caused by a breach of warranty. For example, an electric saw is defective. Hanson purchases the saw, and while he is using it, the blade comes off and severely cuts his arm. The injury to Hanson is consequential damage resulting from a nonconforming or defective product.

Damages for Nondelivery

If the seller fails or refuses to deliver the goods called for by the contract, the buyer has the option of recovering damages for the nondelivery. Thus, instead of covering, the buyer can get the difference between the contract price of the goods and their market price at the time he learns of the seller's breach. In addition, the buyer may recover any incidental damages and consequential damages, but must give the seller credit for any expenses saved [2–713].

Suppose Biddle agreed on June 1 to sell and deliver 1,500 bushels of wheat to a grain elevator on September 1 for $7 per bushel and then refused to deliver on September 1 because the market price was then $8 per bushel. The grain elevator could recover $1,500 damages from Biddle, plus incidental damages that could not have been prevented by cover.

The *Sun Maid Raisin Growers of California v. Victor Packing Co.* case, which follows, illustrates the application of the measure of damages for nondelivery. In this case, the market price of the goods at the time of delivery was significantly higher than the contract price, and the seller, who had gambled that the price would fall, had to pay substantial damages.

SUN MAID RAISIN GROWERS OF CALIFORNIA V. VICTOR PACKING CO.
194 Cal. Rptr. 612 (Cal. Ct. App. 1983)

In November 1975, Victor Packing Company agreed to sell Sun Maid Raisin Growers 1,900 tons of raisins. The first 100 tons were sold at 39 cents per pound and the remainder at 40 cents per pound. No specific delivery date was agreed on. Victor indicated to Sun Maid on August 10, 1976, that it would not complete performance, being unable to deliver the last 610 tons. Sun Maid was able to purchase 200 tons at 43 cents per pound. Because of heavy rains in September 1976, the new crop of raisins suffered extensive damage and the price of raisins increased dramatically.

Sun Maid brought suit against Victor to recover damages. The trial court awarded $307,339 in damages to Sun Maid. Victor appealed, claiming that the increase in the lost profits due to the disastrous rain damage was not foreseeable.

Franson, Acting Presiding Judge   The basic measure of damages for a seller's nondelivery or repudiation is the difference between the market price and the contract price.

In addition to the difference between the market price and the contract price, the buyer can recover incidental damages such as expenses of cover and consequential damages such as lost profits to the extent that they could not have been avoided by cover. The inability to cover after a prompt and reasonable effort to do so is a prerequisite to recovery of consequential damages. If the buyer is only able to cover in part, he is entitled to the net cost of cover (the difference between the cover price and the contract price plus expenses) together with any consequential damages but less expenses saved in consequence of the seller's breach.

Under 2–715(2)(a), consequential damages include "any loss resulting from general or particular requirements and needs of which the seller at the time of contracting had reason to know and which could not reasonably be prevented by cover or otherwise." The "reason to know" language concerning the buyer's particular requirements and needs arises from *Hadley v. Baxendale*. The Code, however, has imposed an objective rather than a subjective standard in determining whether the seller should have anticipated the buyer's needs. Thus, actual knowledge by the seller of the buyer's requirements is not required. The only requirement under 2–715(2)(a) is that the seller reasonably should have been expected to know of the buyer's exposure to loss.

Furthermore, comment 6 to § 2–715 provides that if the seller knows that the buyer is in the business of reselling the goods, the seller is charged with knowledge that the buyer will be selling the goods in anticipation of a profit. "Absent a contractual provision against consequential damages a seller in breach will therefore always be liable for the buyer's resulting loss of profit."

Finally, a buyer's failure to take any other steps by which the loss could reasonably have been prevented bars him from recovering consequential damages. This is merely a codification of the rule that the buyer must attempt to minimize damages. In the present case, the evidence fully supports the finding that after Victor's breach of the contract on August 10, 1976, Sun Maid acted in good faith in a commercially reasonable manner and was able to cover by purchase only some 200 tons of substitute raisins at a cost of 43 cents per pound. There were no other natural Thompson seedless free tonnage raisins available for purchase in the market at or within a reasonable time after Victor's breach. Although the evidence indicates that Sun Maid actually was able to purchase an additional 410 tons of raisins after the September rainfall in its efforts to effect cover, these were badly damaged raisins which had to be reconditioned at a substantial cost to bring them up to market condition. According to Sun Maid, if the trial court had used the total cost of cover of the full 610 tons as the measure of damages rather than lost profits on resale, its damages would have totaled $377,720.

Although the trial court did not specify why it determined damages by calculating lost profits instead of the cost of cover, the court probably found that damages should be limited to the amount that would have put Sun Maid in "as good a position as if the other party had fully performed." Thus, Sun Maid was awarded the lesser of the actual cost of cover (treating the reconditioning of the 410 tons as a cost) and the loss of prospective profits.

In contending that the foreseeability requirement applies to the amount of the lost profits and not just to the fact of lost profits, Victor apparently acknowledges that it knew at the time of contracting that Sun Maid would be reselling the raisins to its customers in the domestic market. Victor has no alternative to this concession since it was an experienced packer and knew that Sun Maid marketed raisins year round in the domestic market. Further-

more, Victor must be presumed to have known that if it did not deliver the full quota of raisins provided under the contracts (1,900 tons) by the end of the crop year or before such reasonable time as thereafter might be agreed to, Sun Maid would be forced to go into the market to attempt to cover its then existing orders for sale of raisins. This is exactly what occurred.

Victor nonetheless contends it should not be liable for damages based on the extraordinarily high price of raisins in the fall of 1976 which was caused by the "disastrous" rains in September. These rains reportedly caused a 50 percent loss of the new crop which with the lack of a substantial carryover of 1975 raisins drove the market price from approximately $860 per packed weight ton to over $1,600 per packed weight ton. Victor does not assert the doctrine of impossibility or impracticability of performance as a defense [§ 2–615]. This is understandable since the nondelivery of raisins was not caused by the failure of a presupposed condition (continuance of the $860 per ton market price) but solely by Victor's failure to deliver the 610 tons of raisins during the 1975 crop year.

This is where the trial court's findings of Victor's bad faith becomes pertinent. A reasonable inference may be drawn that from early spring Victor was gambling on the market price of raisins in deciding whether to perform its contracts with Sun Maid. If the price would fall below the contract price, Victor would buy raisins and deliver them to Sun Maid. If the market price went substantially above the contract price, Victor would sit tight. While we cannot read Victor's mind during the late spring and summer months, we can surmise that it speculated that the market price would remain below the contract price after the current crop year so that it could purchase new raisins for delivery to Sun Maid at the contract price. It threw the dice and lost. The possibility of "disastrous" rain damage to the 1976 raisin crop was clearly foreseeable to Victor. Such rains have occurred at sporadic intervals since raisins have been grown in the San Joaquin Valley. Raisin packers fully understand the great risk in contracting to sell raisins at a fixed price over a period of time extending into the next crop year. The market price may go up or down depending on consumer demand and the supply and quality of raisins. If the seller does not have sufficient inventory to fulfill his delivery obligations within the time initially required or as subsequently modified by the parties, he will have to go into the market to purchase raisins. The fact that he may be surprised by an extraordinary rise in the market price does not mean that the buyer's prospective profits on resale are unforeseeable as a matter of law.

Judgment for Sun Maid affirmed.

Damages for Defective Goods

If a buyer accepts defective goods and wants to hold the seller liable, the buyer must give the seller notice of the defect within a reasonable time after the buyer discovers the defect [2–607(3)]. Where goods are defective or not as warranted and the buyer gives the required notice, he can recover damages. The buyer is entitled to recover the difference between the value of the goods received and the value the goods would have had if they had been as warranted. He may also be entitled to incidental and consequential damages [2–714].

For example, Al's Auto Store sells Anders an automobile tire, warranting it to be four-ply construction. The tire goes flat when it is punctured by a nail, and Anders discovers that the tire is really only two-ply. If Anders gives the store prompt notice of the breach, she can keep the tire and recover from Al's the difference in value between a two-ply and a four-ply tire.

Buyer's Right to Specific Performance

Sometimes, the goods covered by a contract are unique and it is not possible for a buyer to obtain substitute goods. When this is the case, the buyer is entitled to specific performance of the contract.

Specific performance means that the buyer can require the seller to give the buyer the goods covered by the contract [2–716]. Thus, the buyer of an antique automobile such as a 1910 Ford might have a court order the seller to deliver the specified automobile to the buyer because it was one of a kind. On the other hand, the buyer of grain in a particular storage bin could not get specific performance if he could buy the same kind of grain elsewhere.

Buyer and Seller Agreements as to Remedies

As mentioned earlier in this chapter, the parties to a contract may provide remedies in addition to or as substitution for those expressly provided in the Code [2–719]. For example, the buyer's remedies may be limited by the contract to the return of the goods and the repayment of the price or to the replacement of nonconforming goods or parts. However, a court looks to see whether such a limitation was freely agreed to or whether it is unconscionable. In the latter case, the court does not enforce the limitation and the buyer has all the rights given to an injured buyer by the Code.

CONCEPT REVIEW

BUYER'S REMEDIES (ON BREACH BY SELLER)

Problems	Buyer's Remedy
Seller Fails to Deliver Goods or Delivers Nonconforming Goods that Buyer Rightfully Rejects or Justifiably Revokes Acceptance of	1. Buyer may cancel the contract and recover damages. 2. Buyer may "cover" by obtaining substitute goods and recover difference between contract price and cost of cover. 3. Buyer may recover damages for breach based on difference between contract price and market price.

Problems	Buyer's Remedy
Seller Delivers Nonconforming Goods that Are Accepted by Buyer	Buyer may recover damages based on difference between value of goods received and value of goods if they had been as warranted.
Seller Has the Goods but Refuses to Deliver Them and Buyer Wants Them	Buyer may seek specific performance if goods are unique and cannot be obtained elsewhere, or buyer may replevy goods identified to contract if buyer cannot obtain cover.

ETHICAL AND PUBLIC POLICY CONCERNS

1. In the *Wilson v. Hammer Holdings, Inc.,* case, the court held that the statute of limitations barred a claim of breach of warranty. Even if the gallery is not legally obligated to make good on its "guarantee" of authenticity, does it have any ethical responsibility to the purchaser for selling a painting that was not painted by the artist to whom it was attributed at the time of the sale?

2. Problem case 8 involves the sale of a yacht as new that previously had sunk in salt water. How would you assess the ethicality of the representations made by the salesperson to the purchaser in response to his question? In a case like this, should it be incumbent on a purchaser to ask the "right" questions in order to protect himself, or should there be an ethical obligation on the seller to disclose voluntarily material facts that may be relevant to the purchaser making an informed decision?

3. Suppose you own an automobile dealership. The manufacturer whose cars you sell produces a limited edition of a particular model, sets a sticker price of $60,000 on it, and makes only two of the cars available to you. You agree to sell one of the cars to a customer for $60,000. Before you deliver the car, another customer, who collects rare and classic cars, offers you a $30,000 per car premium over the sticker price if you will sell both cars to him. Would you accept his offer? What ethical considerations are involved in making your decision?

PROBLEMS AND PROBLEM CASES

1. Lobianco contracted with Property Protection, Inc., for the installation of a burglar alarm system. The contract provided in part:

Alarm system equipment installed by Property Protection, Inc., is guaranteed against improper function due to manufacturing defects of workmanship for a period of 12 months. The installation of the above equipment carries a 90-day warranty. The liability of Property Protection, Inc., is limited to repair or replacement of security alarm equipment and does not include loss or damage to possessions, persons, or property.

As installed, the alarm system included a standby battery source of power in the event that the regular source of power failed. During the 90-day warranty period, burglars broke into Lobianco's house and stole $35,815 worth of jewelry. First, they destroyed the electric meter so that there was no electric source to operate the system, and then they entered the house. The batteries in the standby system were dead, and thus the standby system failed to operate. Accordingly, no outside siren was activated and a telephone call that was supposed to be triggered was not made. Lobianco brought suit, claiming damage in the amount of her stolen jewelry because of the failure of the alarm system to work properly. Did the disclaimer effectively eliminate any liability on the alarm company's part for consequential damages?

2. On April 11, 1984, Neville Riley purchased a new Chevrolet Camaro from a Chevrolet dealer in Boston, Massachusetts. The car came equipped with a hydraulic jack that was designed, manufactured and sold by General Motors. The Camaro and jack subsequently changed hands several times and were sold to Jay Ronyak on July 24, 1989. While using the jack on August 29, 1989, to raise the Camaro, it malfunctioned, causing the car to fall on Ronyak. He died several days later as a result of the accident. The administrator of Ronyak's estate brought suit against General Motors for breach of warranty. General Motors asserted that the lawsuit was barred by the statute of limitations, but the administrator contended that the warranties in this instance extended to the future performance of the automobile and the jack. She reasoned that "a person who purchases a jack as part of an automobile purchase will have no need for the jack at the time of the purchase, and indeed may not have needed the jack for months or even years after the purchase." Was the lawsuit barred by the four-year statute of limitations in the UCC?

3. Bechtel ordered an alabaster-colored mink coat from Pollock Furs. The coat had been specially made because she required an unusually large size and requested a particular styling. The coat cost $5,500, of which Bechtel paid $250. Several months later, she decided that she did not want the coat and canceled the order, even though Pollack Furs had completed the coat. Pollack Furs then filed suit for the balance of the purchase price. What can Bechtel argue in defense?

4. Cohn advertised a 30-foot sailboat for sale in *The New York Times*. Fisher saw the ad, inspected the sailboat, and offered Cohn $4,650 for the boat. Cohn accepted the offer. Fisher gave Cohn a check for $2,535 as a deposit on the boat. He wrote on the check, "Deposit on aux sloop, D'arc Wind, full amount $4,650." Fisher later refused to go through with the purchase and stopped payment on the deposit check. Cohn readvertised the boat and sold it for the highest offer he received, which was $3,000. Cohn then sued Fisher for breach of contract. He asked for damages of $1,679.50. This represented the $1,650 difference between the contract price and the sale price plus $29.50 in incidental expenses in reselling the boat. Is Cohn entitled to this measure of damages?

5. Dubrow, a widower, was engaged to be married. In October, he placed a large order with a furniture store for delivery the following January. The order included rugs cut to special sizes for the prospective couple's new house and many pieces of furniture for various rooms in the house. One week later, Dubrow died. When the order was delivered, his only heir, his daughter, refused to take the furniture and carpeting. The furniture store then sued his estate to recover the full purchase price. It had not tried to resell the furniture and carpeting to anyone else. Under the circumstances, was the seller entitled to recover the purchase price of the goods?

6. McCain Foods sold on credit and delivered a quantity of frozen french fries to Flagstaff Food Service Company. Several days later, when the

potatoes had not yet been paid for, McCain discovered that Flagstaff was insolvent and had just filed a petition in bankruptcy. What would you advise McCain Foods to do?

7. Kneale bought two chairs from Modernage Furniture that were on sale for $97.50 apiece. The regular price of the chairs was $147.57 each, or $50.07 more than the sale price. Because the store had oversold that particular chair, it failed to deliver the items to Kneale, although she had paid the full purchase price in cash. She brought suit for breach of contract against Modernage Furniture. Modernage contended that its liability was limited to return of the purchase price. Was Modernage's liability for breach of contract limited to return of the purchase price?

8. Barr purchased from Crow's Nest Yacht Sales a 31-foot Tiara pleasure yacht manufactured by S-2 Yachts. He had gone to Crow's Nest knowing the style and type yacht he wanted. He was told that the retail price was $102,000 but that he could purchase the model they had for $80,000. When he asked about the reduction in price he was told that Crow's Nest had to move it because there was a change in the model and they had new ones coming in. He was assured that the yacht was new, that there was nothing wrong with it, and that it only had 20 hours on the engines. Barr installed a considerable amount of electronic equipment on the boat. When he began to use it, he experienced tremendous difficulties with equipment malfunctions. On examination by a marine expert it was determined that the yacht had earlier been sunk in salt water, resulting in significant rusting and deterioration in the engine, equipment, and fixtures. Other experts concluded that significant replacement and repair was required, that the engines would have only 25 percent of their normal expected life, and that following its sinking, the yacht would have only half of its original value. Barr then brought suit against Crow's Nest and S-2 Yachts for breach of warranty. To what measure of damages is Barr entitled to recover for breach of warranty?

9. Certina USA is a watch manufacturer that sells its watches through traveling salespeople paid by it. Migerobe, Inc., owns and operates jewelry counters in McRae's department stores, which are located throughout the Southeast. In the summer of 1987, Migerobe contacted Gerald Murff, a Certina salesperson from whom it had previously purchased watches. It notified him that Migerobe was interested in buying Certina watches if the company decided to sell a large portion of its inventory at reduced prices. Migerobe had some reason to believe that Certina had excess inventory, and Certina in fact decided to eliminate its inventory as a result of a corporate decision to withdraw its watches from the U.S. market. Migerobe was hoping to acquire the Certina watches so that they could be used as "doorbusters" for an after-Thanksgiving sale. Doorbusters or "loss leaders" are items offered at a low price, which are designed to increase the traffic flow through a store and, thereby, increase corollary sales (the sale of nonadvertised items). On October 29, the parties agreed on the sale of over 2,000 watches at a price of $45 per watch. On November 4, the national accounts manager for Certina called Migerobe to say that Certina would not ship the watches. Migerobe brought suit against Certina to recover damages for breach of contract, including consequential damages in the form of lost profits on corollary sales. Migerobe asserted that the Certina salesperson was aware of its plan to use the watches as a loss leader by featuring them in a "doorbuster" Thanksgiving advertisement at a 50 percent discount. It also had data that showed it previously had increased its corollary sales by 69 to 87 percent when it had used similar doorbuster promotions. Was Migerobe entitled to recover the lost profits on corollary sales as consequential damages caused by Certina's breach of contract?

10. In 1972, Schweber contracted to purchase a certain black 1973 Rolls-Royce Corniche automobile from Rallye Motors. He made a $3,500 deposit on the car. Rallye later returned his deposit to him and told him that the car was not available. However, Schweber learned that the automobile was available to the dealer and was being sold to another customer. The dealer then offered to sell Schweber a similar car but with a different interior design. Schweber brought a lawsuit against the dealer to prevent it from selling the Rolls-Royce Corniche to anyone else and to require that it be sold to him. Rallye Motors claimed that he could get only damages and not specific performance. Approximately 100 Rolls-Royce Corniches were being sold each year in the United States, but none of the others would have the specific features and detail of this one. Is the remedy of specific performance available to Schweber?

11. [▣] *Video Case.* See "Sour Grapes." Jelly Manufacturer, a food processor in Chicago, placed a phone order with Grape Grower, a grower in California for a quantity of perishable produce. The shipping term was CIF with payment to be made on delivery (COD). Grape Grower delivered the goods called for in the contract to a carrier and contracted for their shipment. However, it neglected to provide that the goods be shipped under refrigeration. The goods were loaded on a nonrefrigerated boxcar, and as a result, the produce was spoiled when it reached Chicago. Jelly Manufacturer, as required by the COD term, paid for the produce by check before discovering the spoilage. When Jelly Manufacturer called Grape Grower to complain, Grower offered to rush a replacement shipment. Jelly Manufacturer declined the offer, stating that it would not arrive in time for the produce to be processed and delivered to Grocery Chain in time to meet Jelly Manufacturer's contract with Grocery Chain. Jelly Manufacturer arranged for a rush replacement shipment from a nearby source, but had to pay 150 percent of the prevailing market price for the produce. Even so, Jelly Manufacturer was unable to deliver the finished products to Grocery Chain and was required to pay a penalty for late delivery as provided in its contract with Grocery Chain. Can Jelly Manufacturer recover damages from Grape Grower for breach of contract? If so, what elements can be recovered? Can Grocery Chain recover the penalty from Jelly Manufacturer?

PART — 5

PROPERTY

PERSONAL PROPERTY

AND BAILMENTS

INTRODUCTION

The concept of property is crucial to the organization of society. The essential nature of a particular society is often reflected in the way it views property, including the degree to which property ownership is concentrated in the state, the extent it permits individual ownership of property, and the rules that govern such ownership. History is replete with wars and revolutions that arose out of conflicting claims to, or views concerning, property. Significant documents in our own Anglo-American legal tradition, such as the Magna Carta and the Constitution, deal explicitly with property rights. This chapter will discuss the nature and classification of property. It will also examine the various ways that interests in personal property can be obtained and transferred, such as by production, purchase, or gift. The last half of the chapter explores the law of bailments. A bailment is involved, for example, when you check your coat in a coatroom at a restaurant or when you park your car in a public parking garage and leave your keys with the attendant.

NATURE OF PROPERTY

The word **property** is used in several distinct ways. The word is sometimes used to refer to a thing that is capable of being owned. It is also used to refer to a right or interest associated with a thing that gives the owner the ability to exercise dominion over that thing.

When we talk about ownership of property, we are talking about a bundle of rights that are recognized and enforced by the law. For example, ownership of a building includes the exclusive right to use, enjoy, sell, mortgage, or rent the building. If someone else tries to use the property without the owner's consent, the owner can use the courts and legal procedures to eject that person. Ownership of a patent includes the right to sell it, to license others to use it, or to produce the patented article personally.

In the United States, private ownership of property is protected by the Constitution, which provides that the government shall deprive no person of "life, liberty or property without due process of law." We recognize and encourage the rights of individuals to acquire, enjoy, and use property.

These rights, however, are not unlimited. For example, a person cannot use property in an unreasonable manner to the injury of others. Also, the state has **police power** through which it can impose reasonable regulations on the use of property, tax it, and take it for public use by paying the owner compensation for it.

Property can be divided into a number of categories based on its characteristics. The same piece of property may fall into more than one class. The following discussion explores the meaning of **personal property** and the numerous ways of classifying property.

CLASSIFICATIONS OF PROPERTY

Personal Property versus Real Property

Personal property is defined by process of exclusion. The term *personal property* is used in contrast to *real property*. Real property is the earth's crust and all things firmly attached to it.[1] For example, land, office buildings, and houses are all considered to be real property. All other objects and rights that can be owned are personal property. Clothing, books, bank accounts, and stock in a corporation are all examples of personal property.

Real property can be turned into personal property if it is detached from the earth. Similarly, personal property can be attached to the earth and become real property. For example, marble in the ground is real property. When the marble is quarried, it becomes personal property, but if it is used in constructing a building, it becomes real property again. Perennial vegetation that does not have to be seeded every year, such as trees, shrubs, and grass, is usually treated as part of the real property on which it is growing. When trees and shrubs are severed from the land, they become personal property. Crops that must be planted each year, such as corn, oats, and potatoes, are usually treated as personal property. However, if the real property on which they are growing is sold, the new owner of the real property also becomes the owner of the crops.

When personal property is attached to, or used in conjunction with, real property in such a way as to be treated as part of the real property, it is known as a **fixture.** The law concerning fixtures is discussed in the next chapter.

Tangible versus Intangible Personal Property

Personal property can be either tangible or intangible. Tangible property has a physical existence. Cars, animals, and computers are examples. Property that has no physical existence is called intangible property. For example, rights under a patent, copyright, or trademark would be intangible property.[2]

The distinction between tangible and intangible property is important primarily for tax and estate planning purposes. Generally, tangible property is subject to tax in the state in which it is located, whereas intangible property is usually taxable in the state where its owner lives.

Public and Private Property

Property is also classified as public or private based on the ownership of the property. If the property is owned by the government or a governmental unit, it is classified as public property. If it is owned by an individual, a group of individuals, a corporation, or some other business organization, it is private property.

ACQUIRING OWNERSHIP OF PERSONAL PROPERTY

Production or Purchase

The most common ways of obtaining ownership of property are by producing it or purchasing it. A person owns the property that she makes unless the person has agreed to do the work for someone else. In that case, the employer is the owner of the product of the work. For example, a person who creates a painting, knits a sweater, or develops a computer program is the owner unless she has been hired by someone to do the painting, knit the sweater, or develop the program. Another major way of acquiring property is by purchase. The law regarding the purchase of tangible personal property (that is, sale of goods) is discussed in Chapter 19.

---

[1]The law of real property is treated in Chapter 24.

[2]These important types of intangible property are discussed in Chapter 8.

Possession of Unowned Property

In very early times, the most common way of obtaining ownership of personal property was simply by taking possession of unowned property. For example, the first person to take possession of a wild animal became its owner. Today, one can still acquire ownership of personal property by possessing it if the property is unowned. The two major examples of unowned property that can be acquired by possession are wild animals and abandoned property. Abandoned property will be discussed in the next section, which focuses on the rights of finders.

The first person to take possession of a wild animal property normally becomes the owner.[3] To acquire ownership of a wild animal by taking possession, a person must obtain enough control over it to deprive it of its freedom. If a person fatally wounds a wild animal, the person becomes the owner. Wild animals caught in a trap or fish caught in a net are usually considered to be the property of the person who set the trap or net. If a captured wild animal escapes and is caught by another person, that person generally becomes the owner. However, if that person knows that the animal is an escaped animal and that the prior owner is chasing it to recapture it, then he does not become the owner.

Rights of Finders of Lost, Mislaid, and Abandoned Property

The old saying "finders keepers, losers weepers" is not a reliable way of predicting the legal rights of those who find personal property that originally belonged—or still belongs—to another. The rights of the finder will be determined by whether the property he finds is classified as abandoned, lost, or mislaid.

1. *Abandoned property.* Property is considered to be abandoned if the owner intentionally placed the property out of his possession with the intent to relinquish ownership of it. For example, Norris takes his TV set to the city dump and leaves it there. The finder of abandoned property who takes possession of abandoned property with intent to claim ownership becomes the owner of the property. This means he acquires better rights to the property than anyone else in the world, including the original owner. For example, if Fox finds the TV set, puts it in his car, and takes it home, Fox becomes the owner of the TV set.

2. *Lost property.* Property is considered to be lost when the owner did not intend to part with possession of the property. For example, if Barber's camera fell out of her handbag while she was walking down the street, it would be considered lost property. The person who finds lost property does not acquire ownership of it, but he acquires better rights to the lost property than anyone other than the true owner. For example, suppose Lawrence finds Barber's camera in the grass where it fell. Jones then steals the camera from Lawrence's house. Under these facts, Barber is still the owner of the camera. She has the right to have it returned to her if she discovers where it is—or if Lawrence knows that it belongs to Barber. As the finder of lost property, though, Lawrence has a better right to the camera than anyone else except Barber. This means that Lawrence has the right to require Jones to return it to him if he finds out that Jones has it.

If the finder does not know who the true owner is or cannot easily find out, the finder must still return the property if the real owner shows up and asks for the property. If the finder of lost property knows who the owner is and refuses to return it, the finder is guilty of conversion and must pay the owner the fair value of the property.[4]

A finder who sells the property that he has found can only pass to the purchaser those rights that he has; he cannot pass any better title to the property than he himself has. Thus, the true owner could recover the property from the purchaser.

3. *Mislaid property.* Property is considered to be mislaid if the owner intentionally placed the property somewhere and accidentally left it there, not intending to relinquish ownership of the property. For example, Fields places her backpack on a coatrack at Campus Bookstore while shopping for textbooks. Forgetting the backpack, Fields leaves the store and goes home. The backpack would be considered to be mislaid rather than lost because Fields intentionally and voluntarily placed it on the coatrack. The consequences of property being classified as mislaid are that the finder acquires no rights to

---

[3]As wildlife is increasingly protected by law, however, some wild animals cannot be owned because it is illegal to capture them (e.g., endangered species).

[4]The tort of conversion is discussed in Chapter 6.

the property. Rather, the person in possession of the real property on which the personal property was mislaid has the right to hold the property for the true owner and has better rights to the property than anyone other than the true owner. For example, if Stevens found Fields's backpack in Campus Bookstore, Campus Bookstore would have the right to hold the mislaid property for Fields. Stevens would acquire neither possession nor ownership of the backpack.

The rationale for this rule is that it increases the chances that the property will be returned to its real owner. A person who knowingly placed the property somewhere but forgot to pick it up might well remember later where she left the property and return for it.

Some states have a statute that allows finders of property to clear their title to the property. The statutes generally provide that the person must give public notice of the fact that the property has been found, perhaps by putting an ad in a local newspaper. All states have statutes of limitations that require the true owner of property to claim it or bring a legal action to recover possession of it within a certain number of years. A person who keeps possession of lost or unclaimed property for longer than that period of time will become its owner.

The following case, *Michael v. First Chicago Corporation,* presents an example of a conflict between a finder and an original owner over rights to personal property.

MICHAEL V. FIRST CHICAGO CORPORATION
487 N.E.2d 403 (Ill. Ct. App. 1986)

First National Bank of Chicago (First Chicago) sold a number of used file cabinets on an "as is" basis to Zibton, a new and secondhand office supply and furniture dealer. Zibton had bought used furniture from First Chicago before. On this and previous occasions, Zibton bought the used furniture as a group even if some pieces were damaged or locked.

In the summer of 1983, Zibton sold some of these cabinets to Charles Strayve. Strayve gave one of the cabinets, a locked one with no keys, to his friend, Richard Michael. About six weeks later, Michael was moving the file cabinet in his garage when it fell over and several of the locked drawers opened. Inside were more than 1,600 certificates of deposit (CDs), including seven that had not been canceled or stamped paid and that were worth a total of $6,687,948.85, with maturity dates ranging from October 1982 to January 1983. Six of the CDs were payable to "Bearer."

First Chicago had placed the CDs in the cabinet between March and May 1983, when the responsibility for storing paid CDs was changed to a different unit of the bank. The CDs were moved from a vault to file cabinets at that time. Each drawer had been labeled with a card stating "Paid Negotiable CDs" and indicating the numbers of the CDs contained in the drawer. The new unit responsible for storing CDs determined that they could not use the file cabinets, so the CDs were transferred to tote boxes. First Chicago employees randomly checked to determine if the contents were gone and then transferred the file cabinets to the warehouse for sale.

Michael called the FBI, which took possession of all of the CDs. Michael and his wife then filed this declaratory judgment to determine who owned the CDs. The trial court ruled in favor of First Chicago, and the Michaels appealed.

Reinhard, Justice   The Michaels' primary argument is that they were entitled to possession of the CDs because the certificates were the subject of a sale from First Chicago. They maintain that First Chicago's actions in the handling and sale of the CDs showed an objective intent to transfer the certificates along with the used file cabinets in which the documents were stored.

Here, First Chicago was selling only used furniture to Zibton. Neither First Chicago nor Zibton suspected that CDs or any other type of valuable had been left in the file cabinet. The evidence clearly shows that the intention of the parties was for First Chicago to sell used furniture only, and Zibton was not speculating that other valuable items might be contained in the used furniture.

Where both buyer and seller were ignorant of the existence or presence of the concealed valuable, and the contract was not broad enough to indicate an intent to convey all the contents, known or unknown, the courts have generally held that as between the owner and purchaser, title to the hidden article did not pass by the sale. The evidence here is that used office furniture was being sold, and the possibility that something valuable might be in any of the used furniture had nothing to do with the sale. The fact that the sale of the used furniture was "as is" indicates the furniture was sold in its present condition, damaged or otherwise, and does not show an intent to sell the contents of the used furniture. Accordingly, the evidence does not support the Michaels' contention that the CDs as contents of the used furniture were intended by either party to the sale to be sold along with the furniture.

The Michaels' alternative contention is that the CDs are abandoned property, rather than lost or mislaid property, which the finder is entitled to keep. Mislaid property is that which is intentionally put in a certain place and later forgotten; property is lost when it is unintentionally separated from the dominion of its owner; and property is abandoned when the owner, intending to relinquish all rights to the property, leaves it free to be appropriated by any other person. A finder of property acquires no rights in mislaid property, is entitled to possession of lost property against everyone except the true owner, and is entitled to keep abandoned property.

For the purposes of this appeal, we need only determine whether the CDs are abandoned property. If otherwise, the owner is entitled to possession. Abandonment is generally defined as an intentional relinquishment of a known right. As a general rule, abandonment is not presumed and the party seeking to declare an abandonment must prove the abandoning party intended to do so.

The Michaels basically argue that the CDs were abandoned as shown by evidence that they were intentionally placed in the cabinets, they were not forgotten, and the cabinets were sold with no reservations. We disagree. It is readily apparent from the evidence that the CDs were to be transferred to other storage and some simply were overlooked and left in the file cabinets. The relinquishment of possession, under the circumstances here, without a showing of an intention to permanently give up all right to the CDs is not enough to show abandonment.

Judgment for First Chicago affirmed.

CONCEPT REVIEW

RIGHTS OF FINDERS OF PERSONAL PROPERTY

Character of Property	Description	Rights of Finder	Rights of Original Owner
Lost	Owner unintentionally parted with possession	Rights superior to everyone except the owner	Retains ownership; has the right to the return of the property
Mislaid	Owner intentionally put property in a place but unintentionally left it there	None; person in possession of real property on which mislaid property was found holds it for the owner, and has rights superior to everyone except owner	Retains ownership; has the right to the return of the property
Abandoned	Owner intentionally placed property out of his possession with intent to relinquish ownership of it	Finder who takes possession with intent to claim ownership acquires ownership of property	None

Leasing

A lease of personal property is a transfer of the right to possess and use personal property belonging to another.[5] Although the rights of one who leases personal property (a lessee) do not constitute ownership of personal property, leasing is mentioned here because it is becoming an increasingly important way of acquiring the use of many kinds of personal property, from automobiles to farm equipment.

In most states, Article 2 and Article 9 of the UCC are applied to personal property leases by analogy. However, rules contained in these articles are sometimes inadequate to resolve special problems presented by leasing. For this reason, a new article of the UCC dealing exclusively with leases of goods, Article 2A, was written in 1987. Article 2A has been presented to state legislatures for possible adoption, but 40 states have adopted Article 2A as of the time of this writing.

Gifts

Title to personal property can be obtained by **gift.** A gift is a voluntary transfer of property to the **donee** (the person who receives a gift), for which the **donor** (the person who gives the gift) gets no consideration in return. To have a valid gift, all three of the following elements are necessary:

1. The donor must *intend* to make a gift.
2. The donor must make *delivery* of the gift.
3. The donee must *accept* the gift.

The most critical requirement is delivery. The person who makes the gift must actually give up possession and control of the property either to the donee or to a third person to hold it for the donee. Delivery is important because it makes clear to the donor that he is voluntarily giving up ownership without getting something in exchange. A promise to make a gift is usually not enforceable;[6] the person must actually part with the property. In some cases, the delivery may be symbolic or constructive. For example, handing over the key to a strongbox can be symbolic delivery of the property in the strongbox.

There are two kinds of gifts: gifts *inter vivos* and gifts *causa mortis.* A gift *inter vivos* is a gift between two living persons. For example, when Tweedle's parents give her a car for her 21st birthday, that is a gift inter vivos. A gift *causa mortis* is a gift made in contemplation of death. For example, Uncle John, who is about to undergo a serious heart operation, gives his watch to his nephew, Sam, and tells Sam that he wants him to have it if he does not survive the operation.

A gift *causa mortis* is a conditional gift and is effective unless any of the following occurs:

1. The donor recovers from the peril or sickness under fear of which the gift was made, or
2. The donor revokes or withdraws the gift before he dies, or
3. The donee dies before the donor.

If one of these events takes place, ownership of the property goes back to the donor.

Conditional Gifts

Sometimes a gift is made on condition that the donee comply with certain restrictions or perform certain actions. A conditional gift is not a completed gift, and it may be revoked by the donor before the donee complies with the conditions. Gifts in contemplation of marriage, such as engagement rings, are the primary example of a conditional gift. Such gifts are generally considered to have been made on an implied condition that marriage between the donor and donee take place. If the donee breaks the engagement without legal justification or if the engagement is broken by mutual consent, the donor will be able to recover the ring or other engagement gift. However, if the engagement is unjustifiably broken by the donor, he or she is generally not entitled to recover gifts made in contemplation of marriage. As is detailed in the case of *Fierro v. Hoel,* which follows, these rules are not uniformly applied in all states, however. Some states have enacted legislation prescribing the rules applicable to the return of engagement presents.

---

[5]A lease of personal property is a form of bailment, a "bailment for hire." Bailments are discussed later in this chapter.

[6]The idea is discussed in Chapter 12.

FIERRO V. HOEL

465 N.W.2d 669 (Ct. App. Iowa 1990)

John Fierro and Janan Hoel became engaged to be married shortly before Thanksgiving in 1987. At the time of the proposal, Fierro presented Hoel with a 1.37 carat diamond in a platinum setting valued at approximately $9,000. The news of their engagement was shared with family and friends, and they started making wedding plans. After they located a condominium to purchase in New York City, Hoel refused to sign mortgage documents recognizing that Fierro's parents had loaned them money to make the purchase. Shortly thereafter, in March 1988, Fierro broke off the engagement. He asked Hoel to return the ring but she refused.

Fierro then filed a lawsuit seeking to establish ownership of the ring. He asserted that the ring was symbolic of the parties' intent to marry and inherently conditioned on their subsequent marriage. He contended that when a couple terminates their engagement, the ring must be returned to the donor. Hoel, on the other hand, took the position that Fierro had not expressly stated the condition when he gave the ring to her and that it should be viewed as a completed gift. The trial entered judgment for Hoel and Fierro appealed.

Donielson, Judge   The question before us is whether an engagement ring is a conditional gift or a completed gift upon delivery. The district court concluded that because John Fierro had placed no express conditions on the ring at the time possession was transferred to Janan Hoel, the engagement ring was a completed gift upon delivery. We hold an engagement ring is an inherently conditional gift and therefore reverse.

An engagement ring given in contemplation of marriage is an impliedly conditional gift. The jurisdictions which have considered cases dealing with the gift of an engagement ring uniformly hold that marriage is an implied condition of the transfer of title and that the gift does not become absolute until the marriage occurs. One court explained:

Where a gift of personal property is made with the intent to take place irrevocably, and is fully executed by unconditional delivery, it is a valid gift *inter vivos.* Such a gift is absolute and, once made, cannot be revoked. A gift, however, may be conditioned on the performance of some act by the donee, and if the condition is not fulfilled the donor may recover the gift. We find the conditional gift theory particularly appropriate when the contested property is an engagement ring. The inherent symbolism of this gift forecloses the need to establish an express condition that marriage will ensue. Rather the condition may be implied in fact or imposed by law in order to prevent unjust enrichment.

Once we recognize an engagement ring is a conditional gift, the question still remains: who gets the gift when the condition is not fulfilled. The obvious answer is the gift must be returned to the donor. However, an older majority line of cases follows the general principle that the donor of an engagement ring can recover the gift only if the engagement is dissolved by agreement or if the engagement is unjustifiably broken by the donee. The critical inquiry in cases following this principle is who was at "fault" for the termination of the relationship. The party to an engagement who was unjustifiably jilted became the owner of the ring—a type of "consolation prize."

What fact justifies the breaking of an engagement? The absence of a sense of humor? Differing musical tastes? Differing political views? The painfully learned fact is that marriages are made on earth, not in heaven. They must be approached with intelligent care and should not happen without a decent assurance of success. When either party lacks that assurance, for whatever reason, the engagement should be broken. No justificaiion is needed. Either party may act. Fault, impossible to fix, does not count. This court believes fault, in an engagement setting, is irrelevant.

This court adopts the "no fault" approach followed in a minority of jurisdictions. Since the major purpose of the engagement period is to allow a couple time to test the permanency of their feelings, it would seem highly ironic to penalize the donor for taking steps to prevent a possibly unhappy marriage.

In summary, we hold an engagement ring given in contemplation of marriage is an impliedly conditional gift; it is a completed gift only upon marriage. If the wedding is called off, for whatever reason, the gift is not capable of becoming a completed gift and must be returned to the donor.

Reversed in favor of Fierro.

Hayden, Judge (dissenting)   The additional factual background in this case is John had given Janan a pin that belonged to his grandmother. He told Janan explicitly the pin was to be returned to him if they ever broke up. Later when John gave her the ring he placed no conditions on it when she received it. The trial court weighed and considered this evidence. The trial court ruled John had ended the engagement and had placed no conditions on the ring as he had done on the heirloom pin.

The question before us in this case is was the ring a gift conditioned on marriage or was the ring an unconditional gift. The Iowa Supreme Court has stated what the appropriate burden of proof should be when it is claimed there is a conditional gift: If an unqualified transfer to the donee is proved, one asserting the delivery was made on some condition or trust has the burden of establishing such condition or trust. Thus, if the gift elements are proven, John has the burden of proof to show the gift was conditioned on marriage.

The three essential elements for an *inter vivos* gift are donative intent, delivery and acceptance. There is no question there has been a delivery and an acceptance. The remaining question is what was John's intent at the time he gave Janan the ring.

In this case the intention of John was evident from the testimony presented. Janan was responsible for the purchase and payment of the insurance on the ring. Also the ring was referred to by the parties at all times as "her ring." Finally, a demand for the ring was not made until nearly 30 days after John called off the engagement. Thus, it is evident the requirements for a gift were completed unless a condition was proved otherwise.

If John had imposed a condition of marriage on the gift of the ring, such a requirement must have been explicit and known. Thus, if John had wanted such a condition on the gift, he should have made this known and clearly understood at the time he gave possession of the ring to Janan.

There is evidence John was aware of the need to clearly express such a condition when giving this type of gift. John had made a condition of marriage a requirement for the previous gift of heirloom jewelry he had given to Janan. If the engagement was broken, the piece of heirloom jewelry would be returned. After the engagement was broken, the piece of heirloom jewelry was promptly returned. If John wanted the ring returned, he could have expressed such a condition as he did with the heirloom jewelry. Absent any such evidence of condition, I determine the giving of the ring is a valid completed gift.

I acknowledge parties are free to return engagement gifts. However, proper social etiquette does not demand their return, and neither should the courts as a matter of law.

Uniform Transfers to Minors Act

The Uniform Transfers to Minors Act, which has been adopted in one form or another in every state, provides a fairly simple and flexible method for making gifts and other transfers of property to minors.[7] As defined in this act, a minor is anyone under the age of 21. Under the act, an adult may transfer money, securities, real property, insurance policies, and other property. The specific ways of doing this vary according to the type of property transferred. In general, however, the transferor (the person who gives or otherwise transfers the property) delivers, pays, or assigns the property to, or registers the property with, a custodian who acts for the benefit of the minor "under the Uniform Transfers

---

[7]This statute was formerly called, and is still called in some states, the Uniform Gift to Minors Act.

to Minors Act." The custodian is given fairly broad discretion to use the gift for the minor's benefit and may not use it for the custodian's personal benefit. The custodian may be the transferor himself, another adult, or a trust company, depending again on the type of property transferred. If the donor or other transferor fully complies with the Uniform Transfers to Minors Act, the transfer is considered to be irrevocable.

Will or Inheritance

Ownership of personal property can also be transferred upon the death of the former owner. The property may pass under the terms of a will if the will was validly executed. If there is no valid will, the property is transferred to the heirs of the owner according to state laws. Transfer of property at the death of the owner will be discussed in Chapter 26, Estates and Trusts.

Confusion

Title to personal property can be obtained by **confusion.** Confusion is the intermixing of goods that belong to different owners in such a way that they cannot later be separated. For example, suppose wheat belonging to several different people is mixed in a grain elevator. If the mixing was by agreement or if it resulted from an accident without negligence on anyone's part, each person owns his proportionate share of the entire quantity of wheat. However, a different result would be reached if the wheat was wrongfully or negligently mixed. Suppose a thief steals a truckload of Grade #1 wheat worth $8.50 a bushel from a farmer. The thief dumps the wheat into his storage bin, which contains a lower-grade wheat worth $4.50 a bushel, with the result that the mixture is worth only $4.50 a bushel. The farmer has first claim against the entire mixture to recover the value of his wheat that was mixed in. The thief, or any other person whose intentional or negligent act results in confusion of goods, must bear any loss caused by the confusion.

Accession

Ownership of personal property can also be acquired by **accession.** Accession means increasing the value of property by adding materials or labor, or both. As a general rule, the owner of the original property becomes the owner of the improvements. This is particularly likely to be true if the improvement was done with the permission of the owner. For example, Hudson takes his automobile to a shop that replaces the engine with a larger engine and puts in a new four-speed transmission. Hudson is still the owner of the automobile as well as the owner of the parts added by the auto shop.

Problems can arise if materials are added or work is performed on personal property without the consent of the owner. If property is stolen from one person and improved by the thief, the original owner can get it back and does not have to reimburse the thief for the work done or the materials used in improving it. For example, a thief steals Rourke's used car, puts a new engine in it, replaces the tires, and repairs the muffler. Rourke is entitled to get his car back from the thief and does not have to pay him for the engine, tires, or muffler.

The result is less easy to predict, however, if property is mistakenly improved in good faith by someone who believes that he is the owner of the property. In such a case, a court must weigh the respective interests of two innocent parties: the original owner and the improver.

For example, Johnson, a stonecarver, finds a block of limestone by the side of the road and, assuming that it has been abandoned, takes it home and carves it into a sculpture. In fact, the block was owned by Hayes and, having fallen off a flatbed truck during transportation, is merely lost property, which Hayes ordinarily could recover from the finder. In a case such as this, a court could decide the case in one of two ways. The first alternative would be to give the original owner (Hayes) ownership of the improved property, but to allow the person who has improved the property in good faith (Johnson) to recover the cost of the improvements. The second alternative would be to hold that the improver, Johnson, has acquired ownership of the sculpture, but that he is required to pay the original owner the value of the property as of the time he obtained it. The greater the extent to which the improvements have increased the value of the property, the more likely it is that the court will choose the second alternative and permit the improver to acquire ownership of the improved property.

BAILMENTS

Nature of Bailments

A **bailment** is the delivery of personal property by its owner or one who has the right to possess it (the **bailor**) to another person (the **bailee**) who accepts it and is under an express or implied agreement to return it to the bailor or to someone designated by the bailor. Only personal property can be the subject of bailments.

Although the legal terminology used to describe bailments might be unfamiliar to most people, everyone is familiar with transactions that consti- tute bailments. For example, Lincoln takes his car to a parking garage where the attendant gives Lincoln a claim check and then drives the car down the ramp to park it. Charles borrows his neighbor's lawn mower to cut his grass. Carne, who lives next door to Axe, agrees to take care of Axe's cat while Axe goes on a vacation. These are just a few of the everyday situations that involve bailments. The case of *York v. Jones,* which follows, involves a bailment that is much more unusual but nevertheless illustrates the essential characteristics of a bailment.

YORK v. JONES

717 F. Supp. 421 (E.D. Va. 1989)

Steven York and Risa Adler-York contacted the Jones Institute for Reproductive Medicine to determine if they were viable candidates for in vitro fertilization (IVF). This process involves removing one or more oocytes or eggs from the woman's body, fertilizing those eggs in vitro (outside of the womb) with the husband's sperm, and then depositing the developing masses into the woman's uterus. The Yorks were accepted into the Jones Institute's IVF program.

In May 1987, the Yorks signed a Cryopreservation Agreement outlining the procedure for cryopreservation or freezing of pre-zygotes and detailing the Yorks' rights in the frozen pre-zygote. The agreement explained that the cryopreservation procedure is available if more than five pre-zygotes are retrieved during the IVF treatment, so that the possibility for multiple births could be reduced while maintaining optimal chances for pregnancy. The agreement also provided in part:

We may withdraw our consent and discontinue participation at any time . . . and we understand our pre-zygotes will be stored only as long as we are active IVF patients at . . . Jones Institute. . . . We have the principal responsibility to decide the disposition of our pre-zygotes. Our frozen pre-zygotes will not be released from storage for the purpose of intrauterine transfer without the written consent of us both. In the event of divorce, we understand legal ownership of any stored pre-zygotes must be determined in a property settlement. . . . Should we for any reason no longer wish to attempt to initiate a pregnancy, we understand we may choose one of three fates for our pre-zygotes that remain in frozen storage. Our pre-zygotes may be: 1) donated to another infertile couple. . . . 2) donated for approved research investigation, and 3) thawed but not allowed to undergo further development.

The Yorks underwent IVF treatment on four occasions. Six eggs were removed from Mrs. York and fertilized with her husband's sperm, creating six embryos. Five of these embryos were transferred to Mrs. York's uterus, and the remaining embryo was cryogenically preserved in accordance with the procedures outlined in the Cryopreservation Agreement. None of the in vitro fertilization attempts resulted in pregnancy.

During the course of treatment, the Yorks moved to California. They sought to have the remaining frozen pre-zygote transferred from the Jones Institute in Norfolk, Virginia, to the Institute for Reproductive Research in Los Angeles, where the Yorks planned to attempt in vitro fertilization again. The Yorks arranged for proper transportation and handling of the pre-zygote, but the Jones Institute refused to allow such a transfer.

The Yorks brought suit against the Jones Institute and its physicians, claiming that its continued dominion and control over the pre-zygote was contrary to law and the parties' agreement. The Jones Institute filed a motion to dismiss, alleging that the Yorks' complaint did not state a claim on which relief could be granted. This is the trial court's ruling on that motion.

Clarke, Jr., District Judge The Yorks' complaint in this case raises an issue of first impression in the rapidly developing field of human reproductive technology. The Jones Institute argues that the Yorks' proprietary rights in the pre-zygote are limited to the "three fates" enumerated in the [Cryopreservation Agreement] because there is no established protocol for the inter-institutional transfer of pre-zygotes.

The court begins its analysis by noting that the Cryopreservation Agreement created a bailor-bailee relationship between the Yorks and Jones Institute. While the parties in this case expressed no intent to create a bailment, under Virginia law, no formal contract or actual meeting of the minds is necessary. Rather, all that is needed is the element of lawful possession however created, and duty to account for the thing as the property of another that creates the bailment. The essential nature of a bailment relationship imposes on the bailee, when the purpose of the bailment has terminated, an absolute obligation to return the subject matter of the bailment to the bailor. The obligation to return the property is implied from the fact of lawful possession of the personal property of another.

In the instant case, the requisite elements of a bailment relationship are present. The Jones Institute consistently refers to the pre-zygote as the "property" of the Yorks. Although the Cryopreservation Agreement constitutes a bailment contract, the Agreement is nevertheless governed by the same principles as apply to other contracts.

The Cryopreservation Agreement should be more strictly construed against the Jones Institute, the parties who drafted the Agreement. The Jones Institute has defined the extent of its possession interest as bailee of the pre-zygote by the following provision of the Agreement: "We may withdraw our consent and discontinue participation at any time . . . and . . . our pre-zygote will be stored only as long as we are active IVF patients at the [Jones Institute.]" The Jones Institute has further defined the limits of its possessory interest by recognizing the Yorks' proprietary rights in the pre-zygote. The Agreement repeatedly refers to "our pre-zygote" and further provides that the Yorks have the "principal responsibility to decide the disposition" of the pre-zygote.

The Jones Institute takes the position that the plain language of the Cryopreservation Agreement limits the Yorks' proprietary right to the pre-zygote to the "three fates" listed in the Agreement. The Court finds, however, that the applicability of the three fates is limited by the following language, "Should we for any reason no longer wish to initiate a pregnancy, we understand we may choose one of three fates for our pre-zygotes. . . ." The allegations of the Yorks' complaint and the entire thrust of this litigation suggest that the Yorks continue to desire to achieve pregnancy. The Agreement does not state that the attempt to initiate a pregnancy is restricted to procedures employed at the Jones Institute. The "three fates" are therefore inapplicable to the case at bar. For the reasons stated, the Court finds that the Yorks' complaint states a claim upon which relief can be granted.

Motion to dismiss denied in favor of the Yorks.

Elements of a Bailment

The essential elements of a bailment are:

1. The bailor must own or have the right to possess the property.

2. The bailor must deliver exclusive possession of and control over the property to the bailee.

3. The bailee must knowingly accept the property with the understanding that he owes a duty to return the property as directed by the bailor.

FIGURE 1   **Creation of a Bailment**

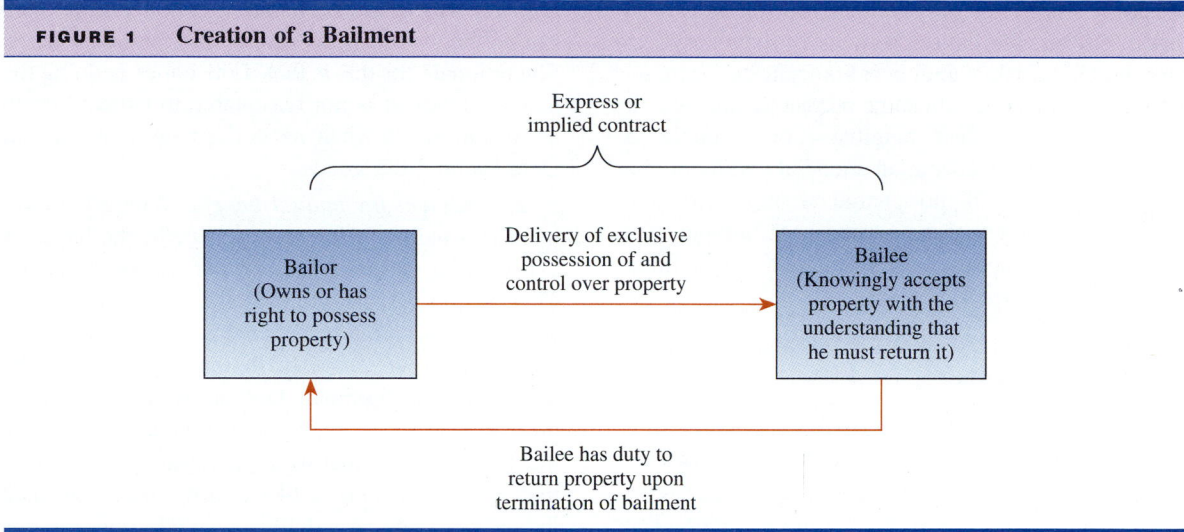

Creation of a Bailment

A bailment is created by an express or implied contract. Whether the elements of a bailment have been fulfilled is determined by examining all the facts and circumstances of the particular situation. For example, a patron goes into a restaurant and hangs her hat and coat on an unattended rack. It is unlikely that this created a bailment, because the restaurant owner never assumed exclusive control over the hat and coat. However, if there is a checkroom and the hat and coat are checked with the attendant, a bailment will arise.

If a customer parks his car in a parking lot, keeps the keys, and can drive the car out himself whenever he wishes, a bailment has not been created. The courts treat this situation as a lease of space. Suppose he takes his car to a parking garage where an attendant gives him a claim check and then the attendant parks the car. There is a bailment of the car because the parking garage has accepted delivery and possession of the car. However, a distinction is made between the car and some packages locked in the trunk. If the parking garage was not aware of the packages, it would probably not be a bailee of them as it did not knowingly accept possession of them. The creation of a bailment is illustrated in Figure 1.

Types of Bailments

Bailments are commonly divided into three different categories:

1. Bailments for the sole benefit of the bailor.
2. Bailments for the sole benefit of the bailee.
3. Bailments for mutual benefit.

The type of bailment involved in a case can be important in determining the liability of the bailee for loss of or damages to the property. As will be discussed later, however, some courts no longer rely on these distinctions for this purpose.

Bailments for Benefit of Bailor   A bailment for the sole benefit of the bailor is one in which the bailee renders some service but does not receive a benefit in return. For example, Brown allows his neighbor, Reston, to park her car in Brown's garage while she is on vacation and Brown does not ask for any compensation. Here, Reston, the bailor, has received a benefit from the bailee, Brown, but Brown has not received a benefit in return.

Bailments for Benefit of Bailee   A bailment for the sole benefit of the bailee is one in which the owner of the goods allows someone else to use them free of charge. For example, Anderson lends a lawn mower to her neighbor, Moss, so he can cut his grass.

Bailments for Mutual Benefit   If both the bailee and the bailor receive benefits from the bailment, it is a bailment for mutual benefit. For example, Sutton rents china for his daughter's wedding from E-Z Party Supplies for an agreed-on price. Sutton, the bailee, benefits by being able to use the china, while E-Z benefits from his payment of the rental charge. On some occasions, the benefit to the bailee is less tangible. For example, a customer checks a coat at an attended coatroom at a restaurant. Even if no charge is made for the service, it is likely to be treated as a bailment for mutual benefit because the restaurant is benefiting from the customer's patronage.

Special Bailments

Certain kinds of professional bailees, such as innkeepers and common carriers, are treated somewhat differently by the law and are held to a higher level of responsibility than is the ordinary bailee. The rules applicable to common carriers and innkeepers are detailed later in this chapter.

Duties of the Bailee

The bailee has two basic duties:

1. To take care of the property that has been entrusted to her.
2. To return the property at the termination of the bailment.

The following discussion examines the scope of these duties.

Duty of Bailee to Take Care of Property

The bailee is responsible for taking steps to protect the property during the time he has possession of it. If the bailee does not exercise proper care and the property is lost or damaged, the bailee is liable for negligence. The bailee would then be required to reimburse the bailor for the amount of loss or damage. If the property is lost or damaged without the fault or negligence of the bailee, however, the bailee is not liable to the bailor. The degree of care required of the bailee traditionally has depended in large part on the type of bailment involved—that is, which party or parties are benefiting from the bailment.

1. *Bailment for the benefit of the bailor.* If the bailment is solely for the benefit of the bailor, the bailee is expected to exercise only a minimal, or slight, degree of care for the protection of the bailed property. He would be liable, then, only if he were grossly negligent in his care of the bailed property. The rationale for this is that if the bailee is doing the bailor a favor, it is not reasonable to expect him to be as careful as when he is deriving some benefit from keeping the goods.

2. *Bailment for mutual benefit.* Where the bailment is a bailment for mutual benefit, the bailee is expected to exercise ordinary or reasonable care. This degree of care requires the bailee to use the same kind of care a reasonable person would use to protect his own property in that situation. If the bailee is a professional that holds itself out as a professional bailee, such as a warehouse, it must use the degree of care that would be used by a person in that profession. This is likely to be more care than the ordinary person would use. In addition, there is usually a duty on a professional bailee to explain any loss or damage to property—that is, to show it was not negligent. If it cannot do so, it will be liable to the bailor.

3. *Bailment for the benefit of the bailee.* If the bailment is solely for the benefit of the bailee, the bailee is expected to exercise a high degree of care. A person who lends a sailboat to a neighbor would probably expect the neighbor to be even more careful with the sailboat than the owner might be, for example. In such a case, the bailee would be liable for damage to the property if he committed a relatively small degree of negligence.

A number of courts today view the type of bailment involved in a case as just one factor to be considered in determining whether the bailee should be liable for loss or damage to bailed goods. The modern trend appears to be moving in the direction of imposing a duty of reasonable care on bailees, regardless of the type of bailment. This flexible standard of care permits courts to take into account a variety of factors such as the nature and value of the property, the provisions of the parties' agreement, the payment of consideration for the bailment, and the experience of the bailee. In addition, the bailee is required to use the property only as was agreed between the parties. For example, Jones borrows Morrow's lawn mower to mow his lawn. If Jones uses the mower to cut the weeds on a trash-filled vacant lot and the mower is damaged, he would be liable because he was exceeding the agreed purpose of the bailment—to cut his lawn.

Bailee's Duty to Return the Property

One of the essential elements of a bailment is the duty of the bailee to return the property at the termination of the bailment. If the bailed property is taken from the bailee by legal process, the bailee should notify the bailor and must take whatever action is necessary to protect the bailor's interest. In most instances, the bailee must return the identical property that was bailed. A person who lends a 1985 Volkswagen Rabbit to a friend expects to have that particular car returned. In some cases, the bailor does not expect the return of the identical goods. For example, a farmer who stores 1,500 bushels of Grade #1 wheat at a local grain elevator expects to get back 1,500 bushels of Grade #1 wheat when the bailment is terminated, but not the identical wheat he deposited.

The bailee must return the goods in an undamaged condition to the bailor or to someone designated by the bailor. If the goods have been damaged, destroyed, or lost, there is a rebuttable presumption of negligence on the part of the bailee. To overcome the presumption, the bailee must come forward with evidence showing that the accident, damage, or loss resulted from some cause consistent with the exercise of the relevant level of due care on his part. The operation of the rebuttable presumption can be seen in the *Magee v. Walbro* case, which follows. If the property is lost or damaged without the fault or negligence of the bailee, however, the bailee is not liable to the bailor.

Magee v. Walbro, Inc.
525 N.E.2d 975 (Ill. Ct. App. 1988)

Walbro, Inc., doing business as Mysel Furs, was in the business of storing furs. It had arranged for United Parcel Service (UPS) to pick up furs from its customers and deliver them to Mysel's. In May 1982, Mysel's solicited Crella Magee's business to store her furs for the summer, and Magee agreed. Pursuant to an arrangement with Mysel's to pick up three furs from Magee, UPS delivered three empty boxes labeled with unique call numbers to Magee on May 25. Magee inserted a fur in each of the boxes, and UPS then picked up the three boxes, giving Magee's husband three tickets bearing call numbers identical to those marked on the boxes. UPS delivered the boxes to Mysel's on May 26. A Mysel's employee signed for the boxes but did not check to be sure that none of the boxes was empty. In July, Mysel's issued a storage receipt to Magee that showed only two furs. This storage receipt also contained a term that limited Mysel's liability for lost property to $100. Magee called Mysel's immediately and received assurances that the three furs were in storage.

When Magee went to pick up her three furs in October 1982, however, one of them—a blue fox jacket worth $3,400—was missing. Mysel's did not compensate Magee, arguing that its liability for lost articles was limited to $100. Magee then brought suit against Walbro, Mysel's, and UPS for breach of bailment and conversion. The trial court ruled for the defendants, and Magee appealed. (Magee voluntarily dismissed her case against UPS, so its liability is not involved in this appeal.)

O'Connor, Justice   Establishing a prima facie case of bailment raises a presumption of negligence by the defendant, which the defendant must rebut with evidence sufficient to support a finding of the nonexistence of the presumed fact. The trial court ruled that the evidence established a bailment between Magee and Walbro and Mysel's, thus raising the presumption of negligence. Walbro and Mysel produced no evidence, however, to rebut the presumption of negligence.

Based on the evidence presented, the trial court ruled that the lost jacket was delivered to Mysel Furs. Walbro and Mysel's argued that, assuming delivery of the jacket, any presumption of negligence was defeated by the procedures used in storing furs. The furs were placed in a locked, alarmed vault to which several, identifiable Mysel's employees had access. Mysel's then prepared and issued a storage receipt to the customer. Walbro presented no evidence to show that these procedures were followed for Magee's furs, and the storage receipt was not issued until six weeks after the jacket was delivered. It is reasonable to assume that the defendants' procedures and security precautions customarily resulted in the return of the customer's fur. Magee's fur was not returned; therefore, without showing more than the mere existence of safety and security measures, the defendants failed to rebut the presumption of negligence. Magee was therefore entitled to recover her damages.

Finally, the defendants asserted the defense of limitation of liability. Walbro and Mysel's argue that they effectively limited their liability to $100, citing *Schoen v. Wallace,* which upheld an agreement between a fur owner and fur storage company to limit the storage company's liability to $100. *Schoen* and [other cases] indicate, however, that the customer was aware of the limitation of liability before the furs were placed in storage. The *Schoen* decision was based in part on the fact that the plaintiff had dealt with the defendant before, knew of its insurance practices, [and] could have chosen another furrier had she found the limitation objectionable.

In the instant case, Magee testified that she was not told of the limitation until after the fur was lost. Defendants rely on the receipt of July 1982, which stated that liability was limited to $100. Magee should have known of the limitation after she received the receipt in July, but by that time her furs had been at Mysel's for six weeks.

The limitation does not apply in the instant case because Magee had no knowledge of the limitation before agreeing to store her furs. In *Schoen,* the court stated that it would be "unjust to permit the plaintiff to repudiate [the agreement to limit liability] because the coat was lost." In the instant case, it would be unjust to permit Mysel and Walbro to assert a limitation that was not made clear at the time that the bailment contract was made because the coat was lost. We therefore hold that the $100 limitation of liability is inapplicable in this case.

For the foregoing reasons, judgment in favor of the defendants is reversed, and this case is remanded to the trial court to enter judgment against Walbro and Mysel's and in favor of Magee in the amount of $3,400.

Reversed and remanded in favor of Magee.

Bailee's Liability for Misdelivery

The bailee is also liable to the bailor if he misdelivers the bailed property at the termination of the bailment. The property must be returned to the bailor or to someone specified by the bailor.

If a third person claims to have rights in the bailed property that are superior to the rights of the bailor and demands possession of the bailed property, the bailee is in a dilemma. If the bailee refuses to deliver the bailed property to the third-person claimant and the third-person claimant is entitled to its possession, the bailee is liable to the claimant. If the bailee delivers the bailed property to the third-party claimant and the third-party claimant is not entitled to possession, the bailee is liable to the bailor. The circumstances may be such that the conflicting claims of the bailor and the third-person claimant can be determined only by judicial decision. In some cases, the bailee may protect himself by bringing the third-party claimant into a lawsuit along with the bailor so that all the competing claims can be adjudicated by the court before the bailee releases the property, but this remedy is not always available.

Limits on Liability

Bailees may try to limit or relieve themselves of liability for the bailed property. Some examples include the storage receipt purporting to limit liability to $100 in the *Magee v. Walbro, Inc.* case, signs near checkrooms, such as "Not responsible for loss of or damage to checked property," and disclaimers on claim checks, such as "Goods left at owner's risk." The standards used to determine whether such limitations and disclaimers are enforceable are discussed in detail in Chapter 15, Illegality.

Any attempt by the bailee to be relieved of liability for intentional wrongful acts is against public policy and will not be enforced. A bailee's ability to be relieved of liability for negligence is also limited. Courts look to see whether the disclaimer or limitation of liability was communicated to the bailor at the time of the bailment. Did the attendant point out the sign near the checkroom to the person when the coat was checked? Did the parking lot attendant call the person's attention to the disclaimer on the back of the claim check?

If not, as in the *Magee* case, the court may hold that the disclaimer was not communicated to the bailor and did not become part of the bailment contract. Even if the bailor was aware of the disclaimer, it still may not be enforced on the ground that it is contrary to public policy.

If the disclaimer was offered on a take-it-or-leave-it basis and was not the subject of arm's-length bargaining, it is less likely to be enforced than if it has been negotiated and voluntarily agreed on. A bailee may be able to limit liability to a certain amount or to relieve himself of liability for certain perils. Ideally, the bailee will give the bailor a chance to declare a higher value and to pay an additional charge to be protected up to the declared value of the goods. Common carriers, such as railroads and trucking companies, often take this approach. Courts do not look with favor on efforts by a person to be relieved of liability for negligence. For this reason, terms limiting the liability of a bailee stand a better chance of being enforced than do terms completely relieving the bailee of liability.

The bailor's knowledge of the bailee's facilities or of his method of doing business or the nature of prior dealings may give rise to an implied agreement as to the bailee's duties. The bailee may, if he wishes, assume all the risks incident to the bailment and contract to return the bailed property undamaged or to pay any damage to or loss of the property.

Right to Compensation

The express or implied contract creating the bailment controls whether the bailee has the right to receive compensation for keeping the property or must pay for having the right to use it. If the bailment is made as a favor, then the bailee is not entitled to compensation even though the bailment is for the sole benefit of the bailor. If the bailment is the rental of property, then the bailee must pay the agreed rental rate. If the bailment is for the storage or repair of property, then the bailee is entitled to the contract price for the storage or repair services. If no

specific price was agreed on, yet compensation was contemplated by the parties, then the bailee gets the reasonable value of the services provided.

In many instances, the bailee will have a lien (a charge against property to secure the payment of a debt) on the bailed property for the reasonable value of the services. For example, Silver takes a chair to Ace Upholstery to have it recovered. When the chair has been recovered, Ace has the right to keep it until the agreed price—or, if no price was set, the reasonable value of the work—is paid. This is an example of an **artisan's lien,** which is discussed in greater detail in Chapter 28, Security Interests in Personal Property.

Bailor's Liability for Defects in the Bailed Property

When personal property is rented or loaned, the bailor makes an implied warranty that the property has no hidden defects that make it unsafe for use. If the bailment is for the sole benefit of the bailee, then the bailor is liable for injuries that result from defects in the bailed property only if the bailor knew about the defects and did not tell the bailee. For example, Price lends his car, which he knows has bad brakes, to Sloan. If Price does not tell Sloan about the bad brakes and if Sloan is injured in an accident because the brakes fail, Price is liable for Sloan's injuries.

If the bailment is a bailment for mutual benefit, then the bailor has a larger obligation. The bailor must use reasonable care in inspecting the property and seeing that it is safe for the purpose for which it is intended. The bailor is liable for injuries suffered by the bailee because of defects that the bailor either knew about or should have discovered by reasonable inspection. For example, Friedman's Rent-All, which rents trailers, does not inspect the trailers after they are returned. A wheel has come loose on a trailer that Friedman's rents to Hirsch. If the wheel comes off while Hirsch is using the trailer and the goods Hirsch is carrying in it are damaged, Friedman's is liable to Hirsch.

In addition, product liability doctrines that apply a higher standard of legal responsibility have been applied to bailors who are commercial lessors of personal property.[8] Express or implied warranties of

---

[8]Product liability doctrines are discussed in Chapter 20.

quality under either Article 2 or Article 2A of the UCC may apply. Liability under these warranties does not depend on whether the bailor knew about or should have discovered the defect. The only question is whether the property's condition complied with the warranty. Some courts have also imposed strict liability on lessors-bailors of goods that cause personal injury or property damage to the lessee-bailee because they are defective and unreasonably dangerous. This liability is imposed regardless of whether the lessor was negligent.

CONCEPT REVIEW

DUTIES OF BAILEES AND BAILORS

Type of Bailment	Duties of Bailee	Duties of Bailor
Sole Benefit of Bailee	1. Must use great care; liable for even slight negligence. 2. Must return goods to bailor or dispose of them at his direction. 3. May have duty to compensate bailor.	1. Must notify the bailee of any known defects.
Mutual Benefit	1. Must use reasonable care; liable for ordinary negligence. 2. Must return goods to bailor or dispose of them at his direction. 3. May have duty to compensate bailor.	1. Must notify bailee of all known defects and any defects that could be discovered on reasonable inspection. 2. Commercial lessors may be subject to warranties of quality and/or strict liability in tort. 3. May have duty to compensate bailee.
Sole Benefit of Bailor	1. Must use at least slight care; liable for gross negligence. 2. Must return goods to bailor or dispose of them at his direction.	1. Must notify bailee of all known defects and any hidden defects that are known or could be discovered on reasonable inspection. 2. May have duty to compensate bailee.

SPECIAL BAILMENTS

Common Carriers

Bailees that are common carriers are held to a higher level of responsibility than that to which bailees that are private carriers are held. Common carriers are licensed by governmental agencies to carry the property of anyone who requests the service. Airlines licensed by the Department of Transportation and trucks and buses licensed by the Interstate Commerce Commission are examples of common carriers. Private contract carriers carry goods only for persons selected by the carrier.

Both common carriers and private contract carriers are bailees. However, the law makes the common carrier an absolute insurer of the goods it carries. The common carrier is responsible for any loss of or damage to goods entrusted to it. The common carrier can avoid responsibility only if it can show that the loss or damage was caused by one of the following:

1. An act of God.
2. An act of a public enemy.
3. An act or order of the government.
4. An act of the person who shipped the goods.
5. The nature of the goods themselves.

The common carrier is liable if goods entrusted to it are stolen by some unknown person but not if the goods are destroyed when a tornado hits the warehouse. If goods are damaged because the shipper improperly packages or crates them, then the carrier is not liable. Similarly, if perishable goods are not in suitable condition to be shipped and deteriorate in the course of shipment, the carrier is not liable so long as it used reasonable care in handling them.

Common carriers are usually permitted to limit their liability to a stated value unless the bailor declares a higher value for the property and pays an additional fee.

Hotelkeepers

Hotelkeepers are engaged in the business of offering food and/or lodging to transient persons. They hold themselves out to serve the public and are obligated to do so. Like the common carrier, the hotelkeeper is held to a higher standard of care than that of the ordinary bailee. The hotelkeeper is not a bailee in the strict sense of the word. The guest does not usually surrender the exclusive possession of his property to the hotelkeeper. However, the hotel-keeper is treated as the virtual insurer of the guest's property. The hotelkeeper is not liable for loss of or damage to property if she can show that it was caused by one of the following:

1. An act of God.
2. An act of a public enemy.
3. An act of a governmental authority.
4. The fault of a member of the guest's party.
5. The nature of the goods.

Most states have passed laws that limit the hotel-keeper's liability, however. Commonly, the law requires the hotel owner to post a notice advising guests that any valuables should be checked into the hotel vault. The hotelkeeper's liability is then limited, usually to a fixed amount, for valuables that are not so checked. The following case, *Gooden v. Day's Inn,* illustrates the application of such a state statute.

Gooden v. Day's Inn
385 S.E.2d 876 (Ct. App. Ga. 1990)

Marvin Gooden checked into a Day's Inn in Atlanta, Georgia, on March 3, 1988, paying in advance for two days' lodging. The next day he temporarily left his room, leaving a paper bag filled with approximately $9,000. Shortly thereafter, Mary Carter, a housekeeper, went into Gooden's room to clean it and found the bag of money. Seeing no other personal effects, she assumed that Gooden had checked out. Accordingly, she turned the bag over to her immediate supervisor, Vivian Clark, who in turn gave the bag of money to Dempsey Wilson who was responsible for general supervision and the maintenance of the grounds. Wilson had been employed by Day's Inn for approximately three years, and during that time he was occasionally given items of value to turn into the office. He always did so until this occasion when he decided to abscond with the bag of money.

A safe was located on the premises of Day's Inn for the use of guests. Day's Inn posted a notice concerning the availability of the safe on the door of the room that Gooden occupied. Pursuant to this notice, Day's Inn disclaimed liability for guests' valuables unless they were placed in the safe. At no point did Gooden seek the use of the safe.

Georgia law (OCGA Sec. 43-21-10) provides in pertinent part that: "The innkeeper may provide a safe or other place of deposit for valuable articles and, by posting a notice thereof, may require the guests of the innkeeper to place such valuable articles therein or the innkeeper shall be relieved from responsibility for such articles."

Gooden brought a tort action against, among others, Day's Inn seeking damages in the amount of $9,000. Day's Inn contended that it could not be held responsible for the loss of Gooden's money since it posted notice concerning the availability of the safe and Gooden failed to take advantage of it. Gooden, in turn, argued that the Georgia statute could not insulate an innkeeper from liability where the loss of a guest's valuables is occasioned by the negligent or tortious conduct of the innkeeper's employees. The trial court granted summary judgment in favor of Day's Inn, Carter, and Clark, and Gooden appealed.

McMurray, Presiding Judge   The Georgia statute carves out no exception for losses occasioned by the negligence of the innkeeper. Thus, if the innkeeper posts notice of the availability of a safe pursuant to the statute, it is not liable for articles stolen from a guest's room even if its negligence contributed to the loss. Likewise, the statute carves out no exception for losses occasioned by the negligence or intentional torts of the innkeeper's employees. Thus, if the innkeeper posts notice in accordance with the statute, it is not liable for articles stolen from a guest's room even if its own employees were negligent in preventing the theft or were actually parties to the theft.

Gooden contends that, notwithstanding the protection afforded to innkeepers under OCGA Sec. 43-21-10, Day's Inn, Carter and Clark are liable under an implied "bailment" theory since they actually took possession of Gooden's bag of money for safekeeping. Assuming arguendo, the validity of Gooden's contention, we must conclude, nonetheless, that the trial court properly denied Gooden's motion for summary judgment and properly granted the defendants' motion for summary judgment.

"All bailees are required to exercise care and diligence to protect the thing bailed and to keep it safe. Different degrees of diligence are required according to the nature of the bailments." OCGA Sec. 44-12-43. If the bailment is for the exclusive benefit of the bailor, only slight diligence is required; if the bailment is for the mutual benefit of the parties, ordinary diligence is required; and if the bailment is for the exclusive benefit of the bailee, extraordinary diligence is required.

A bailee is discharged from liability when he shows the exercise of that degree of diligence required by his class of bailment. We assume, without deciding, that any bailment in this case was for the mutual benefit of the parties and that the degree of diligence required of Day's Inn, Carter and Clark was ordinary diligence. Even so, we find them to be discharged of liability. Why? Because they demonstrated that they acted with ordinary care and diligence concerning the bag of money. After all, Ms. Carter simply turned the bag of money over to her immediate supervisor, Ms. Clark, who in turn, gave the bag of money to the "senior technician," Dempsey Wilson, a person with general supervisory powers. Mr. Wilson had been entrusted with guests' valuables in the past and he always acted responsibly with regard to those valuables. The defendants had no way of knowing that Mr. Wilson would abscond with Gooden's bag of money and thus cannot be said to have acted negligently in turning the money over to him.

Judgment affirmed.

Safe-Deposit Boxes

If a person rents a safe-deposit box at a local bank and places some property in the box, the box and the property are in the manual possession of the bank. However, it takes both the renter's key and the key held by the bank to open the box, and in most cases the bank does not know the nature, amount, or value of the goods in the box. Although a few courts have held the rental of a safe-deposit box not to be a bailment, most courts have found that the renter of the box is a bailor and the bank is a bailee. As such, the bank is not an insurer of the contents of the box. However, it is obligated to use due care and to come forward and explain loss of or damage to the property entrusted to it.

Involuntary Bailments

Suppose a person owns a cottage on a beach. After a violent storm, a sailboat washed up on his beach. As the finder of lost or misplaced property, he may be considered the **involuntary bailee** or **constructive bailee** of the sailboat. This relationship may arise when a person finds himself in possession of property that belongs to someone else without having agreed to accept possession.

The duties of the involuntary bailee are not well defined. The bailee does not have the right to destroy the property or to use it. If the true owner shows up, the property must be returned to him. Under some circumstances, the involuntary bailee may be under an obligation to assume control of the property or to take some minimal steps to ascertain who the owner is, or both.

ETHICAL AND PUBLIC POLICY CONCERNS

1. Does a finder of lost or mislaid property have an ethical duty to look for the owner of the property? How effective are the legal principles that you learned in encouraging a finder to do so?

2. What part does ethical conduct play in determining whether a person acquires ownership of personal property by confusion? By accession?

3. You learned that, in formulating the degree of care that a bailee must exercise over bailed property, courts traditionally have applied standards based on the amount of relative benefit the parties derive from the bailment. Where both parties benefit, reasonable care is required; where the bailee alone benefits, great care is required; and where the bailor alone benefits, only slight care is required. Modern courts seem to be moving in the direction of applying a standard of reasonable care to all bailments, however. Which approach is preferable, and why?

PROBLEMS AND PROBLEM CASES

1. In 1945, Lieber was serving in the U.S. Army. He was one of the first soldiers to occupy Munich, Germany. He and some other soldiers entered Adolf Hitler's apartment and removed various items of Hitler's personal belongings. Lieber brought his share to his home in Louisiana. It included Hitler's uniform jacket and cap and some of his decorations and personal jewelry. Lieber's possession of these items was well known. There were several feature articles about them, and they were occasionally displayed to the public. Many years later, Lieber's chauffeur stole the collection and sold it to a dealer of historical material in New York. The dealer sold it to Mohawk Arms, which had no knowledge that it had been stolen. Lieber learned that Mohawk Arms had the collection and demanded that the company return it. Mohawk Arms claimed that it did not have to return the collection to Lieber because the collection properly belonged to the occupational military authority or to the Bavarian government and not to Lieber. Was Lieber entitled to the return of the collection that had been stolen from him?

2. The Kahrs put their silver (worth about $3,800), jewelry, and a wallet containing their credit cards in bags and stored them in their attic while they were on vacation. After they returned, they retrieved the bags containing the valuables and placed them on their dining room table along with bags containing some used clothing that they had decided to donate to Goodwill. Mr. Kahr mistakenly picked up the bags containing the silver and wallet and delivered them to Goodwill along with the bags of used clothing. He told Goodwill at that time that he was donating used clothing. A Goodwill employee who was marking the items for resale found the Kahrs' wallet in a bag and, realizing it was a mistake, called the Kahrs' residence about the wallet. She did not mention the silver, though, because she had not yet found it. Even when she did find it, she did not realize that it was sterling silver. The Kahrs realized the mistake about two hours later. They called Goodwill only to find that the silver had been sold for $15 to Markland. Markland refused to return the silver, and the Kahrs brought suit against Goodwill and Markland. Can the Kahrs get their silver back?

3. Bernice Paset, a customer of the Old Orchard Bank, found $6,325 in currency on the seat of a chair in an examination booth in the bank's safety-deposit vault. The chair was partially under a table. Paset notified officers of the bank and turned the money over to them. She was told by the bank officials that the bank would try to locate the owner and that she could have the money if the owner was not located within one year. The bank wrote to everyone who had been in the safety-deposit vault area either on the day of, or on the day preceding, the discovery, stating that some property had been found and inviting the customers to describe any property they might have lost. No one reported the loss of any currency, and the money remained unclaimed a year after it had been found. The bank refused to deliver the money to Paset, contending it was mislaid, not lost, property and that it had a better right to it. Was the money found on the chair in the safe-deposit vault mislaid property?

4. In October 1973, Richard Welton, a businessman in his late 60s, met Florence Gallagher, a widow in her late 40s. Welton subsequently underwent several operations for cancer. After he was released from the hospital, Gallagher devoted much time and attention to him. In 1975, she helped him operate an ice cream business he had purchased. Shortly thereafter, he moved into her house and spent considerable money fixing it up. Welton subsequently moved out to live with Gallagher's niece, Sandra Kwock, a woman in her 20s, who agreed to take care of him for the rest of his life in return for his giving her $25,000 in bearer bonds. Kwock left town with the bonds, much to Welton's dismay. In April 1976, Welton moved back in with Gallagher, gave her $20,000 in bearer bonds, and told her to place them in her safe-deposit box. Gallagher said that he told her he wanted her to have them as a gift because she was much more deserving than her niece. Later in 1976, Welton and Gallagher ended their relationship and he moved out of her house. He also demanded that she return the bonds, but she refused. Had Welton made a completed *inter vivos* gift of the bonds to Gallagher?

5. Ochoa's Studebaker automobile was stolen. Eleven months later, the automobile somehow found its way into the hands of the U.S. government, which sold it to Rogers at a "junk" auction for $85. At the time it was purchased by Rogers, no part of the car was intact. It had no top except a part of the frame; it had no steering wheel, tires, rims, cushions, or battery; the motor, radiator, and gears were out of the car; one wheel was gone, as was one axle; the fenders were partly gone; and the frame was broken. It was no longer an automobile but a pile of broken and dismantled parts of what was once Ochoa's car. Having purchased these parts, Rogers used them in the construction of a delivery truck at an expense of approximately $800. When the truck was completed, he put it to use in his furniture business. Several months later, Ochoa was passing Rogers's place of business and recognized the vehicle from a mark on the hood and another on the radiator. He discovered that the serial and engine numbers matched those on the car he had owned. Ochoa demanded the vehicle from Rogers, who refused to surrender it. Ochoa brought suit to recover possession of the property. In the alternative, he asked for the value of the vehicle at the time of the suit, which he alleged to be $1,000, and for the value of the use of the car from the time Rogers purchased it from the government. Was Ochoa entitled to recover possession of his property, which Rogers had substantially improved?

6. R. B. Bewley and his family drove to Kansas City to attend a week-long church convention. When they arrived at the hotel where they had reservations, they were unable to park their car and unload their luggage because of a long line of cars. They then drove to a nearby parking lot where they took a ticket, causing the gate arm to open, and drove in 15 or 20 feet. A parking attendant told them that the lot was full, that they should leave the keys with him, and that he would park the car. They told the attendant that they had reservations at the nearby hotel and that after they checked in they would come back for their luggage. Subsequently, someone broke into the Bewleys' car and stole their personal property from the car and its trunk. Was the parking lot a bailee of the property?

7. Georgie Simon entrusted 14 gold and silver coins to her ex-husband, Hardie Maloney, to take to a coin show in Atlanta, Georgia. He was to try to sell the coins, for which he would receive a 7 percent commission. Maloney traveled to the coin show along with his girlfriend, Ann Williams, and a male friend, Herbert Pellegrini, with whom he had previously traveled to 40 or 50 coin shows. Just before they got ready to leave the Waverly Hotel, where the show had been held, Maloney and Williams went up to Pellegrini's room. Pellegrini would not permit Williams to use the bathroom because he wanted to check out before the deadline and avoid being charged for another day. Williams and Maloney helped Pellegrini carry his three pieces of luggage to the lobby. While Pellegrini checked out, Williams went to the ladies' room in the lobby of the hotel. While Williams was in the bathroom, Maloney went to get his car, on the suggestion and insistence of Pellegrini. He resisted the suggestion because he was carrying a briefcase containing Georgie Simon's coins, as well as the coins he had brought to, and purchased at, the show. Maloney wanted to wait until they could all walk over to the car together for protection. However, after being assured by Pellegrini that he would watch the briefcase, Maloney went to get the car. Maloney set the briefcase down beside Pellegrini's three bags in front of the hotel. When Maloney returned with the car, Pellegrini walked up to the vehicle carrying all three pieces of his luggage but left Maloney's briefcase in front of the hotel. When Maloney asked about the whereabouts of the briefcase, Pellegrini

replied that he did not know where it was. It was never found. Georgie Simon brought suit against Maloney for $19,000, the value of the coins she had entrusted to him, and Maloney, in turn, filed a claim against Pellegrini for the loss of those coins as well as for the $12,300 in coins that he had entrusted to Pellegrini. Was Pellegrini liable for the loss of the coins entrusted to him?

8. Pringle, the head of the drapery department at Wardrobe Cleaners, went to the Axelrods' home to inspect some dining room draperies for dry-cleaning purposes. He spent about 30 minutes looking at the drapes and inspected both the drapes and the lining. He pointed out some roach spots on the lining that could not be removed by cleaning, but this was not of concern to the Axelrods. He did not indicate to them that the fabric had deteriorated from sunburn, age, dust, or air conditioning so as to make it unsuitable for dry cleaning. He took the drapes and had them dry cleaned. When the drapes were returned, they were unfit for use. The fabric had been a gold floral design on an eggshell-white background. When returned, it was a blotchy gold. Wardrobe Cleaners stated that it was difficult to predict how imported fabrics would respond to the dry-cleaning process and that the company was not equipped to pretest the fabric to see whether it was colorfast. The Axelrods sued Wardrobe Cleaners for $1,000, the replacement value of the drapes. Was Wardrobe Cleaners liable for the damage caused to the drapes during the dry-cleaning process?

9. In April, Carter brought her fur coat to Reichlin Furriers for cleaning, glazing, and storage until the next winter season. She was given a printed form of receipt, upon the front of which an employee of Reichlin had written $100 as the valuation of the coat. There was no discussion of the value of the coat, and Carter did not realize that such a value had been written on the receipt, which she did not read at the time. A space for the customer's signature on the front of the receipt was left blank. Below this space in prominent type appeared a notice to "see reverse side for terms and conditions." The other side of the receipt stated that it was a storage contract and that by its acceptance the customer would be deemed to have agreed to its terms unless notice to the contrary were given within 10 days. Fifteen conditions were listed. One of the conditions was as follows: "Storage charges are based upon valuation herein declared by the depositor, and amount recoverable for loss or damage to the article shall not exceed its actual value or the cost of repair or replacement with materials of like kind and quality or the depositor's valuation appearing in this receipt, whichever is less." In the fall of the year, after Carter had paid the bill for storage and other services on the coat, Reichlin informed her that the coat was lost. At that time, the fair market value of the coat was $450. Carter sued Reichlin for loss of the coat and sought $450 damages. Reichlin claimed that its liability was limited to $100. Is this correct?

10. On May 16, Mathilda Durandy, a resident of Paris, France, registered at the Fairmont Roosevelt Hotel in New Orleans. She was assigned to room 436 and to safe-deposit box 8. Over the next few days she used the box on numerous occasions, taking jewelry from it when she left for social engagements and replacing the jewelry in it on her return. At 5:30 A.M. on May 22, Durandy returned from a dinner dance and went to the front desk of the hotel to deposit her jewelry. She waited about 15 or 20 minutes but no hotel employer was visible and she could not see any call bell or telephone. Finally, she returned to her room, where she locked her door and secured the chain. She removed her jewelry, including a 16-carat diamond ring and other pieces containing diamonds, rubies, and sapphires. Sometime thereafter, someone cut the chain, entered the room, cut the telephone cord, and stole Durandy's jewels. Under Louisiana law, an innkeeper is responsible for the effects of its guests and also must provide "an iron chest or other safe deposit for valuable articles." If the innkeeper provides safe-deposit procedures and appropriate notice to its guests, its liability is limited to $100. The Fairmont Roosevelt did have appropriate notices posted in its rooms. Was the hotel's liability for the stolen jewelry limited to $100?

CHAPTER 24

REAL PROPERTY

INTRODUCTION

Land's special importance in the law has long been recognized. In the agrarian society of previous eras, land served as the basic measure and source of wealth. In today's industrialized society, land functions not only as a source of food, clothing, and shelter but also as an instrument of commercial and industrial development. It is not surprising, then, that a complex body of law—the law of real property—*exists regarding the ownership, acquisition, and use of land.*

This chapter discusses the scope of real property and the various ownership interests in it. In addition, the chapter examines the ways in which real property is transferred and the controls society places on an owner's use of real property.

SCOPE OF REAL PROPERTY

Real property includes not only land but also things firmly attached to or embedded in land. Buildings and other permanent structures thus are considered real property. The owner of a tract of real property also owns the air above it, the minerals below its surface, and any trees or other vegetation growing on the property.[1]

Unlike readily movable personal property, real property is immovable or attached to something immovable. Distinguishing between real and personal property is important because rules of law governing real property transactions such as sale, taxation, and inheritance are frequently different from those applied to personal property transactions.

Fixtures

An item of personal property may, however, be attached to or used in conjunction with real property in such a way that it ceases being personal property and instead becomes part of the real property. This type of property is called a **fixture.**

Fixtures belong to the owner of the real property. One who provides or attaches fixtures to real property without a request to that effect from the owner of the real property is normally not entitled to

---

[1]Ownership of air above one's property is not an unlimited interest, however. Courts have held that the flight of aircraft above property does not violate the property owner's rights, so long as it does not unduly interfere with the owner's enjoyment of her land.

compensation from the owner. A conveyance (transfer of ownership) of real property also conveys the fixtures associated with that property, even if the fixtures are not specifically mentioned.

People commonly install items of personal property on the real property they own or rent. Disputes may arise regarding rights to such property. Suppose that Jacobsen buys an elaborate ceiling fan and installs it in his home. When he sells the house to Orr, may Jacobsen remove the ceiling fan, or is it part of the home Orr has bought? Suppose that Luther, a commercial tenant, installs showcases and tracklights in the store she leases from Nelson. May Luther remove the showcases and the lights when her lease expires, or do the items now belong to Nelson? If the parties' contracts are silent on these matters, courts will resolve the cases by applying the law of fixtures. As later discussion will reveal, Jacobsen probably cannot remove the ceiling fan because it is likely to be considered part of the real property purchased by Orr. Luther, on the other hand, may be entitled to remove the showcases and the lights under the special rules governing trade fixtures.

Factors Indicating Whether an Item Is a Fixture

There is no mechanical formula for determining whether an item has become a fixture. Courts tend, however, to consider these factors:

1. *Attachment.* One factor helping to indicate whether an item is a fixture is the degree to which the item is **attached** or **annexed** to the real property. If firmly attached to the real property so that it cannot be removed without damaging the property, the item is likely to be considered a fixture. An item of personal property that may be removed with little or no injury to the property is less likely to be considered a fixture.

Actual physical attachment to real property is not necessary, however. A close physical connection between the item of personal property and the real property may enable a court to conclude that the item is **constructively annexed**. For example, heavy machinery or remote control devices for automatic garage doors may be considered fixtures even though they are not physically attached to real property.

2. *Adaptation.* Another factor to be considered is **adaptation**—the degree to which the item's use is necessary or beneficial to the use of the real property. Adaptation is a particularly relevant factor when the item is not physically attached to the real property or is only slightly attached. When an item would be of little value except for use with certain real property, the item is likely to be considered a fixture even if it is unattached or could easily be removed. For example, keys and custom-sized window screens and storm windows have been held to be fixtures.

3. *Intent.* The third factor to be considered is the **intent** of the person who installed the item. Intent is judged not by what that person subjectively intended, but by what the circumstances indicate he intended. To a great extent, intent is indicated by the annexation and adaptation factors. An owner of real property who improves it by attaching items of personal property presumably intended those items to become part of the real estate. If the owner does not want an attached item to be considered a fixture, he must specifically reserve the right to keep the item. For instance, if a seller of a house wants to keep an antique chandelier that has been installed in the house, she should either replace the chandelier before the house is shown to prospective purchasers or specify in the contract of sale that the chandelier will be excluded from the sale.

Ford v. Venard presents a typical judicial analysis of whether an item of personal property has become a fixture.

FORD v. VENARD

340 N.W.2d 270 (Iowa Sup. Ct. 1983)

In 1973, Norman Van Sickle moved his double wide mobile home to a plot of land owned by Luelia Jedlicka. Van Sickle had the real estate landscaped, a foundation poured, concrete blocks set, and steel girders aligned on the blocks. After removing the hitches and wheels from the mobile home, he had the mobile home set on and hooked to the foundation. Thereafter, Van Sickle substantially modified his double-wide unit by welding it into a single unit, placing a roof over the entire building, and joining the exterior with siding. As a result, the structure could not be disassembled without tearing it apart and could not be moved as one unit except by a house mover.

Van Sickle had paid Jedlicka $500 as a down payment for the purchase of the land back in 1973, but had never made any further payments. He had never been asked to pay taxes and was told by Jedlicka that she paid them. Van Sickle had been told by the bank holding a security interest on the mobile home that the house would become part of Jedlicka's real estate after it was set on a foundation. Van Sickle did not consider himself the owner of the real estate; he believed the land belonged to Jedlicka.

In 1977, Henry Edsel Ford contracted with Jedlicka to buy the land. A clause in the Ford-Jedlicka contract specified that all "attached fixtures" were included as part of the real estate being sold. The question of ownership of the mobile home came to a head in 1982, when William Venard, a creditor of Van Sickle's, attempted to enforce a judgment against Van Sickle by attaching the mobile home and executing against it. Ford brought this action, claiming that he owned the mobile home and requesting an injunction to restrain Venard from executing against the mobile home. The trial court granted the injunction. Venard appealed.

Harris, Justice   The question is whether the mobile home was a fixture included under the terms of the land contract between Jedlicka and Ford. We think it plainly was. Under our common law rule, personal property becomes a fixture when:

(1) it is actually annexed to the realty, or to something appurtenant thereto;
(2) it is put to the same use as the realty with which it is connected; and
(3) the party making the annexation intends to make a permanent accession to the freehold.

The intention of the party annexing the improvement is the "paramount factor" in determining whether the improvement is a fixture. Physical attachment of the structure to the soil or to an appurtenance thereto is not essential to make the structure a part of the realty. On the other hand, a building which cannot be removed without destruction of a substantial part of its value becomes almost unavoidably an integral part of the real estate.

Venard argues that Van Sickle's home was not physically annexed to the realty and that Van Sickle never intended for his home to be permanently attached to the freehold. Ford, on the other hand, relies on these facts: the home's tongues and wheels have been removed; the home was set on a foundation and girders; it has been extensively remodeled into a single unit; and its removal would be expensive and damaging. He points out that the home was used as a homestead, which is the use for which the realty had been appropriated. He points to the bank's advice to Van Sickle that his home would become the property of Jedlicka when set on her land.

We have found buildings to be fixtures in a number of cases. We are convinced the home became attached to the land. It could not be removed from its present location except in the sense that any permanent home could be. We hold that it has become an integral part of the real estate. The trial court was correct in ordering the issuance of the permanent injunction.

Affirmed in favor of Ford.

Express Agreement   If the parties to an express agreement have clearly stated their intent about whether a particular item is to be considered a fixture, a court will generally enforce that agreement. For example, the buyer and seller of a house might agree to permit the seller to remove a fence or shrubbery that would otherwise be considered a fixture.

Trade Fixtures   An exception to the usual fixture rules is recognized when a *tenant* attaches personal property to leased premises for the purpose of carrying on her trade or business. Such fixtures, called **trade fixtures**, remain the personal property of the tenant and may normally be removed at the termination of the lease. This trade fixtures exception encourages commerce and industry. It recognizes that the commercial tenant who affixed the item of personal property did not intend a permanent improvement of the leased premises.

The tenant's right to remove trade fixtures is subject to two limitations. First, the tenant cannot remove the fixtures if doing so would cause substantial damage to the landlord's realty. Second, the tenant must remove the fixtures by the end of the lease if the lease is for a definite period; if the lease is for an indefinite period, the tenant usually has a reasonable time after the expiration of the lease to remove the fixtures. Trade fixtures not removed within the appropriate time become the landlord's property.

Leases may contain terms expressly addressing the parties' rights in any fixtures. A lease might give the tenant the right to attach items or make other improvements, and to remove them later. The reverse may also be true. The lease could state that any improvements made or fixtures attached will become the landlord's property at the termination of the lease. Courts generally enforce parties' agreements on fixture ownership.

Security Interests in Fixtures   Special rules apply to personal property subject to a lien or security interest at the time it is attached to real property. Assume, for example, that a person buys a dishwasher on a time-payment plan from an appliance store and has it installed in his kitchen. To protect itself, the appliance store takes a security interest in the dishwasher and perfects that interest by filing a financing statement in the appropriate real estate records office within the period of time specified by the Uniform Commercial Code. The appliance store then is able to remove the dishwasher if the buyer defaults in his payments. The store could be liable, however, to third parties such as prior real estate mortgagees for any damage removal of the dishwasher caused to the real estate. The rules governing security interests in personal property that will become fixtures are explained more fully in Chapter 28, Security Interests in Personal Property.

CONCEPT REVIEW

Fixtures

Concept	A *fixture* is an item of personal property attached to or used in conjunction with real property in such a way that it is treated as being part of the real property.
Significance	A conveyance of the real property will also convey the fixtures on that property.
Factors Considered in Determining Whether Property Is a Fixture	1. Attachment: Is the item physically attached or closely connected to the real property? 2. Adaptation: How necessary or beneficial is the item to the use of the real property? 3. Intent: Did the person who installed the item manifest intent for the property to become part of the real property?
Express Agreement	Express agreements clearly stating intent about whether property is a fixture are generally enforceable.
Trade Fixtures (Tenants' Fixtures)	Definition of *trade fixture:* personal property attached to leased real property by a tenant for the purpose of carrying on his trade or business. Trade fixtures can be removed and retained by the tenant at the termination of the lease except when one or more of the following apply: 1. Removal would cause substantial damage to the landlord's real property. 2. Tenant fails to remove the fixtures by the end of the lease (or within a reasonable time, if the lease is for an indefinite period of time). 3. An express agreement between the landlord and tenant provides otherwise.

Rights and Interests in Real Property

When we think of real property ownership, we normally envision one person owning all of the rights in a particular piece of land. Real property, however, involves a bundle of rights subject to ownership—sometimes by different people. This discussion examines the most common forms of present *possessory interests* (rights to exclusive possession of real property): **fee simple absolute** and **life estate**. It also explores the various ways in which two or more persons may share ownership of a possessory interest. Finally, it discusses the interests and rights one may have in another person's real property, such as the right to use the property or restrict the way the owner uses it.

Estates in Land

The term **estate** is used to describe the nature of a person's ownership interest in real property. Estates in land are classified as either **freehold estates** or **nonfreehold estates**. Nonfreehold (or leasehold) estates are those held by persons who lease real property. They will be discussed in the next chapter, which deals with landlord-tenant law. Freehold estates are ownership interests of uncertain duration. The most common types of freehold estates are fee simple absolute and life estates.

Fee Simple Absolute   The **fee simple absolute** is what we normally think of as "full ownership" of land. One who owns real property in fee simple absolute has the right to possess and use the property for an unlimited period of time, subject only to governmental regulations or private restrictions. She also has the unconditional power to dispose of the property during her lifetime or upon her death. A person who owns land in fee simple absolute may grant many rights to others without giving up fee simple ownership. For example, she may grant a mortgage on the property to a party who has loaned her money, lease the property to a tenant, or grant rights such as those to be discussed later in this section.

Life Estate   The property interest known as a **life estate** gives a person the right to possess and use property for a time measured by his or another person's lifetime. For example, if Haney has a life estate (measured by his life) in a tract of land known as Greenacre, he has the right to use Greenacre for the remainder of his life. At Haney's death, the property will revert to the person who conveyed the estate to him or will pass to some other designated person. Although a life tenant such as Haney has the right to use the property, he is obligated not to commit acts that would result in permanent injury to the property.

Co-Ownership of Real Property

Co-ownership of real property exists when two or more persons share the same ownership interest in the same property. The co-owners do not have separate rights to any portion of the real property; each has a share in the whole property. Seven types of co-ownership are recognized in the United States.

Tenancy in Common   Persons who own property under a **tenancy in common** have undivided interests in the property and equal rights to possess it. When property is transferred to two or more persons without specification of their co-ownership form, it is presumed that they acquire the property as tenants in common. The respective ownership interests of the tenants in common may be, but need not be, equal. One tenant, for example, could have a two-thirds ownership interest in the property, with the other tenant having a one-third interest.

Each tenant in common has the right to possess and use the property. Individual tenants, however, cannot exclude the other tenants in common from also possessing and using the property. If the property is rented or otherwise produces income, each tenant is entitled to share in the income in proportion to her ownership share. Similarly, each tenant must pay her proportionate share of property taxes and necessary repair costs. If a tenant in sole possession of the property receives no rents or profits from the property, she is not required to pay rent to her cotenant unless her possession is adverse to or inconsistent with her cotenant's property interests.

A tenant in common may dispose of his interest in the property during life and at death. Similarly, his interest is subject to his creditors' claims. When a tenant dies, his interest passes to his heirs or, if he has made a will, to the person or persons specified in the will. Suppose Peterson and Sievers own

Blackacre as tenants in common. Sievers dies, having executed a valid will in which he leaves his Blackacre interest to Johanns. In this situation, Peterson and Johanns become tenants in common.

Tenants in common may sever the cotenancy by agreeing to divide the property or, if they are unable to agree, by petitioning a court for *partition*. The court will physically divide the property if that is feasible, so that each tenant receives her proportionate share. If physical division is not feasible, the court will order that the property be sold and that the proceeds be appropriately divided.

Joint Tenancy

A **joint tenancy** is created when equal interests in real property are conveyed to two or more persons by means of a document specifying that they are to own the property as joint tenants. The rights of use, possession, contribution, and partition are the same for a joint tenancy as for a tenancy in common. The joint tenancy's distinguishing feature is that it gives the owners the **right of survivorship**, which means that upon the death of a joint tenant, the deceased tenant's interest automatically passes to the surviving joint tenant(s). The right of survivorship makes it easy for a person to transfer property at death without making a will. For example, Devaney and Osborne purchase Redacre and take title as joint tenants. At Devaney's death, his Redacre interest will pass to Osborne even if Devaney did not have a will setting forth such an intent. By the same token, even if Devaney had a will that purported to leave his Redacre interest to someone other than Osborne, the will's Redacre provision would be ineffective.

A joint tenant may mortgage, sell, or give away her interest in the property during her lifetime. Her interest in the property is subject to her creditors' claims. When a joint tenant transfers her interest, the joint tenancy is severed and a tenancy in common is created as to the share affected by the transaction. When a joint tenant sells her interest to a third person, the purchaser becomes a tenant in common with the remaining joint tenant(s).

Tenancy by the Entirety

Approximately half of the states permit married couples to own real property under a **tenancy by the entirety**. This tenancy is essentially a joint tenancy with the added requirement that the owners be married. As does the joint tenancy, the tenancy by the entirety features the right of survivorship. Neither spouse can transfer the property by will if the other is still living. Upon the death of the husband or wife, the property passes automatically to the surviving spouse.[2]

A tenancy by the entirety cannot be severed by the act of only one of the parties. Neither spouse can transfer the property unless the other one also signs the deed. Thus, a creditor of one tenant cannot claim an interest in that person's share of property held in tenancy by the entirety. Divorce, however, severs a tenancy by the entirety and transforms it into a tenancy in common. Figure 1 compares the features of tenancy in common, joint tenancy, and tenancy by the entirety.

Community Property

A number of western and southern states recognize the **community property** system of co-ownership of property by married couples. This type of co-ownership assumes that marriage is a partnership in which each spouse contributes to the family's property base. Property acquired during the marriage through a spouse's industry or efforts is classified as *community* property. Each spouse has an equal interest in such property regardless of who produced or earned the property. Because each spouse has an equal share in community property, neither can convey community property without the other's joining in the transaction. Various community property states permit the parties to dispose of their interests in community property at death. The details of each state's community property system vary, depending on the specific provisions of that state's statutes.

Not all property owned by a married person is community property, however. Property a spouse owned before marriage or acquired during marriage by gift or inheritance is *separate* property. Neither spouse owns a legal interest in the other's separate property. Property exchanged for separate property also remains separately owned.

Tenancy in Partnership

When a partnership takes title to property in the partnership's name, the co-ownership form is called **tenancy in partnership**. This form of co-ownership is discussed in

---

[2]In states that do not recognize the tenancy by the entirety, married couples often own real property in joint tenancy, but they are not required to elect that co-ownership form.

	Tenancy in Common	Joint Tenancy	Tenancy by the Entirety
FIGURE 1 Tenancy in Common, Joint Tenancy, and Tenancy by the Entirety			
Equal Possession and Use?	Yes	Yes	Yes
Share Income?	Yes	Yes	Presumably
Contribution Requirement?	Generally	Generally	Generally
Free Conveyance of Interest?	Yes; transferee becomes tenant in common	Yes, but joint tenancy is severed on conveyance and reverts to tenancy in common	Both must agree; divorce severs tenancy
Effect of Death?	Interest transferable at death by will or inheritance	Right of survivorship; surviving joint tenant takes decedent's share	Right of survivorship; surviving spouse takes decedent's share

Chapter 36, Introduction to Forms of Business and Formation of Partnerships.

Condominium Ownership   Condominiums have become very common in the United States in recent years, even in locations outside urban and resort areas. Under condominium ownership, a purchaser takes title to her individual unit and becomes a tenant in common with other unit owners in shared facilities such as hallways, elevators, swimming pools, and parking areas. The condominium owner pays property taxes on her individual unit and makes a monthly payment for the maintenance of the common areas. She may generally mortgage or sell her unit without the other unit owners' approval. For federal income tax purposes, the condominium owner is treated as if she owned a single-family home, and is thus allowed to deduct her property taxes and mortgage interest expenses.

Cooperative Ownership   In a cooperative, a building is owned by a corporation or group of persons. One who wants to buy an apartment in the building purchases stock in the corporation and holds his apartment under a long-term, renewable lease called a *proprietary lease*. Frequently, the cooperative owner must obtain the other owners' approval to sell or sublease his unit.

INTERESTS IN REAL PROPERTY OWNED BY OTHERS

In various situations, a person may hold a legally protected interest in real property owned by someone else. Such interests, to be discussed below, are not possessory because they do not give their holder the right to complete dominion over the land. Rather, they give him the right to use another person's property or to limit the way in which the owner uses the property.

Easements

An **easement** is the right to make certain uses of another person's property (*affirmative easement*) or the right to prevent another person from making certain uses of his own property (*negative easement*). The right to run a sewer line across someone else's property would be an affirmative easement. Suppose an easement prevents Rogers from erecting, on his land, a structure that would block his neighbor McFeely's solar collector. Such an easement would be negative in nature.

If an easement qualifies as an **easement appurtenant**, it will pass with the land. This means that if the owner of the land benefited by an easement appurtenant sells or otherwise conveys the property, the new owner also acquires the right contemplated by the easement. An easement appurtenant is primarily designed to benefit a certain tract of land, rather than merely giving an individual a personal right. For example, Agnew and Nixon are next-door neighbors. They share a common driveway that runs along the borderline of their respective properties. Each has an easement in the portion of the driveway that lies on the other's property. If Agnew sells his property to Ford, Ford also obtains the easement in the driveway portion on Nixon's land. Nixon, of course, still has an easement in the driveway portion on Ford's land.

Creation of Easements

Easements may be acquired in any of the following ways:

1. *By grant.* When an owner of property expressly provides an easement in his property to another while retaining ownership of the property, he is said to **grant** an easement. For example, Monroe may sell or give Madison, who owns adjoining property, the right to go across Monroe's land to reach an alley behind that land.

2. *By reservation.* When one transfers ownership of her land but retains the right to use it for some specified purpose, she is said to **reserve** an easement in the land. For example, Smythe sells land to Jones but reserves the mineral rights to the property as well as an easement to enter the land to remove the minerals.

3. *By prescription.* An easement by **prescription** is created when one person uses another's land openly, continuously, and in a manner adverse to the owner's rights for a period of time specified by state statute (the necessary period of time varying state to state). In such a situation, the property owner presumably is on notice that someone else is acting as if she possesses rights to use the property. If the property owner does not take action during the statutory period to stop the other person from making use of his property, he may lose his right to stop that use. Suppose, for instance, that State X allows easements by prescription to be obtained through 15 years of prescriptive use. Tara, who lives in State X, uses the driveway of her next-door neighbor, Kyle. Tara does this openly, on a daily basis, and without Kyle's permission. If this use by Tara continues for the 15-year period established by statute and Kyle takes no action to stop Tara within

that time span, Tara will obtain an easement by prescription. In that event, Tara will have the right to use the driveway not only while Kyle owns the property but also when Kyle sells the property to another party. Easements by prescription resemble *adverse possession*, a concept discussed later in this chapter.

4. *By implication.* Sometimes, easements are implied by the nature of the transaction rather than created by express agreement of the parties. Such easements, called **easements by implication**, take either of two forms: easements by prior use and easements by necessity.

An *easement by prior use* is created when land is subdivided and a path, road, or other apparent and beneficial use exists when part of the land is conveyed to another person. In this situation, the new owner of the conveyed portion of the land has an easement to continue using the path, road, or other prior use running across the nonconveyed portion of the land. Assume, for example, that a private road runs through Greenacre from north to south, linking the house located on Greenacre's northern portion to the public highway that lies south of Greenacre. Douglas, the owner of Greenacre, sells the northern portion to Kimball. On these facts, Kimball has an easement by implication to continue using the private road even where it runs across the portion of Greenacre retained by Douglas. To prevent such an easement from arising, Douglas and Kimball would need to have specified in their contract of sale that the easement would not exist.

An *easement by necessity* is created when real property once held in common ownership is subdivided in such a fashion that the only reasonable way a new owner can gain access to her land is through passage over another's land that was once part of the same tract. Such an easement is based on the necessity of obtaining access to property. Assume, for instance, that Tinker, the owner of Blackacre, sells Blackacre's northern 25 acres to Evers and its southern 25 acres to Chance. In order to have any reasonable access to her property, Chance must use a public road that runs alongside and just beyond the northern border of the land now owned by Evers; Chance must then go across Evers's property to reach hers. On these facts, Chance is entitled to an easement by necessity to cross Evers's land in order to go to and from her property.

Easements and the Statute of Frauds As interests in land, easements are potentially within the coverage of the statute of frauds. To be enforceable, an express agreement granting or reserving an easement must be evidenced by a suitable writing signed by the party to be charged.[3] An express grant of an easement normally must be executed with the same formalities observed in executing the grant of a fee simple interest. However, easements not granted expressly (such as easements by prior use, necessity, or prescription) are enforceable despite the lack of a writing.

Profits

A **profit** is a right to enter another person's land and remove some product or part of the land. Timber, gravel, minerals, and oil are among the products and parts frequently made the subject of profits. Generally governed by the same rules applicable to easements, profits are sometimes called *easements with a profit.*

Licenses

A **license** is a temporary right to enter another's land for a specific purpose. Ordinarily, licenses are more informal than easements. Licenses may be created orally or in any other manner indicating the landowner's permission for the licensee to enter the property. Because licenses are considered to be personal rights, they are not true interests in land. The licensor may revoke a license at his will unless the license is coupled with an interest (such as the licensee's ownership of personal property located on the licensor's land) or the licensee has paid money or provided something else of value either for the license or in reliance on its existence. For example, Branch pays Leif $900 for certain trees on Leif's land. Branch is to dig up the trees and haul them to her own property for transplanting. Branch has an irrevocable license to enter Leif's land to dig up and haul away the trees.

Restrictive Covenants

Within certain limitations, real estate owners may create enforceable agreements that restrict the use of real property. These private agreements are called

---

[3]Chapter 16 discusses the statute of frauds and compliance with the writing requirement it imposes when it is applicable.

restrictive covenants. For example, Grant owns two adjacent lots. She sells one to Lee subject to the parties' agreement that Lee will not operate any liquor-selling business on the property. This use restriction appears in the deed Grant furnishes Lee. As another illustration, a subdivision developer sells lots in the subdivision and places a provision in each lot's deed regarding the minimum size of house to be built on the property.

The validity and enforceability of such private restrictions on the use of real property depend on the purpose, nature, and scope of the restrictions. A restraint that violates a statute or other expression of public policy will not be enforced. For example, the federal Fair Housing Act (discussed later in this chapter) would make unlawful an attempt by a seller or lessor of residential property to refuse to sell or rent to certain persons because of an existing restrictive covenant that purports to disqualify those prospective buyers or renters on the basis of their race, color, religion, sex, handicap, familial status, or national origin.

Public policy generally favors the unlimited use and transfer of land. A restrictive covenant therefore is unenforceable if it effectively prevents the sale or transfer of the property. Similarly, ambiguous language in a restrictive covenant is construed in favor of the less restrictive interpretation. A restraint is enforceable, however, if it is clearly expressed and neither unduly restrictive of the use and transfer of the property nor otherwise violative of public policy. Restrictions usually held enforceable include those relating to minimum lot size, building design and size, and maintenance of an area as a residential community.

An important and frequently arising question is whether subsequent owners of property are bound by a restrictive covenant even though they were not parties to the original agreement that established the covenant. Under certain circumstances, restrictive covenants are said to "run with the land" and thus bind subsequent owners of the restricted property. For a covenant to run with the land, it must have been *binding* on the original parties to it, and those parties must have *intended that the covenant bind their successors.* The covenant must also *"touch and concern"* the restricted land. This means that the covenant must involve the use, value, or character of the land, rather than being merely a personal obligation of one of the original parties. In addition, a covenant will not bind a subsequent purchaser unless she had notice of the covenant's existence when she took her interest. This notice would commonly be provided by the recording of the deed (a subject discussed later in this chapter) or other document containing the covenant.

Restrictive covenants may be enforced by the parties to them, by persons meant to benefit from them, and—if the covenants run with the land—by successors of the original parties to them. If restric-

tive covenants amounting to a general building scheme are contained in a subdivision plat (recorded description of a subdivision), property owners in the subdivision may be able to enforce them against noncomplying property owners.

Mains Farm Homeowners Association v. Worthington illustrates the difficult interpretation, enforceability, and public policy questions sometimes presented by litigation over restrictive covenants that run with the land.

MAINS FARM HOMEOWNERS ASSOCIATION V. WORTHINGTON
854 P.2d 1072 (Wash. Sup. Ct. 1993)

A declaration of restrictive covenants for the platted Mains Farm subdivision was recorded in 1962. Worthington purchased a residential lot in Mains Farm in 1987. A house already existed on the property. Before purchasing, Worthington obtained and read a copy of the restrictive covenants, which stated, in pertinent part, that all lots in Mains Farm "shall be designated as 'Residence Lots' and shall be used for single family residential purposes only." Worthington later began occupying the residence along with four adults who paid her for 24-hour protective supervision and care. These four adults, who were not related to Worthington, were unable to do their own housekeeping, prepare their own meals, or attend to their personal hygiene. In providing this supervision and care on a for-profit basis, Worthington complied with the licensing and inspection requirements established by Washington law governing such enterprises.

The Mains Farm Homeowners Association (Association), which consisted of owners of property in the subdivision, filed suit against Worthington and asked the court to enjoin her from using her property as an adult family home business. Association asserted that Worthington's use violated the restrictive covenants quoted above. The trial court granted Association's motion for summary judgment and issued the requested injunction against Worthington's use. The Washington Court of Appeals affirmed. Worthington appealed to the Washington Supreme Court. Various organizations representing the interests of disabled adults submitted amicus curiae (friend of the court) briefs urging reversal.

Brachtenbach, Justice *Before* defendant Worthington bought the premises, she *read* the restrictive covenants. Written opposition by other property owners was made known to her immediately after her purchase. Despite that knowledge, Worthington applied for a building permit to add a fifth bedroom to the house. She was advised by the county that her intended facility did not comply with applicable zoning. Worthington later obtained the permit by stating that only her family would be living with her. In her words: "I told them what they wanted to hear." These equitable considerations must be kept in mind when we interpret the restrictive covenants at issue here. Our analysis

leads to the conclusion that Worthington's commercial use is prohibited.

To reach this conclusion, we consider the meaning of "single family." The cases interpreting "family" are legion. Any of the cases must be used with caution. Some involve a state statute which bears a different relationship to zoning powers than to vested property rights embodied in a restrictive covenant. No purpose will be served by examining and comparing in detail the numerous cases which define "family." Because of the widely differing documents being interpreted, the contexts in which the word is used, and the fact-specific circumstances, it is impossible to arrive at a single, all-purpose definition of "family." The possibilities range from the traditional notion of persons related by blood, marriage, or adoption to the broader concept of a group of people who live, sleep, cook, and eat upon the premises as a single housekeeping unit. Likewise, attempting to use one of the many dictionary classifications solves nothing. For similar reasons, the use of a phrase or two out of a dictionary to define "residential" for purposes of this covenant is not acceptable.

Some reflection leads us to attribute certain characteristics to a concept of "family," even in an extended sense. These include: (1) a sharing of responsibilities among the members and a mutual caring whether physical or emotional, (2) some commonality whether it be friendship, shared employment, mutual social or political interest, (3) some degree of existing or contemplated permanency to the relationship, and (4) a recognition of some common purpose—persons brought together by reasons other than a referral by a state agency. Here, we have four persons, all strangers before arriving at this residence. By law, they cannot be related to Worthington by birth, adoption, or marriage. By law, they cannot be below the age of 18. By regulatory definition, they must require 24-hour protective supervision and care. Worthington could not form this "family" without a license from the State, which must approve the site and is free to inspect it. Worthington meets these qualifications and provides around-the-clock care as a means of making a living.

These are not the characteristics of a single family residence. Our primary goal is to ascertain the intent of the restrictive covenants and to accord the words their ordinary and common usage. The reasonable expectations of the other lot owners who bought their family houses in reliance on the long recorded covenants would not include a State-licensed, 24-hour operating business. In this case, Worthington's main use of her property is not to provide a single family residence, but to provide 24-hour protective care and supervision in exchange for money. It must therefore be concluded that the other lot owners are entitled in equity to the injunction granted by the trial court.

As an alternative ground for reversing the trial court, Worthington argues that the restrictive covenant violates a legislative declaration of public policy and is therefore void. The public policy question should not be resolved in this case, for various reasons. First, the record made in the trial court is not adequate to identify the facts and bases upon which such a significant public policy should be considered. It is true that the Legislature has found "that adult family homes are an important part of the state's long-term care system" [citation to statute omitted]. Unfortunately, this record shows little more. We know that the Legislature has not implemented this finding beyond declaring that such homes are considered residential for *zoning* purposes. We know nothing of the number of persons qualified for adult family homes or of whether that need is being met. We know nothing of the situation along those lines in the community or county in which the Mains Farm subdivision is located. We do not know whether there exists an adequate supply of adult family homes in areas not subject to restrictive covenants. We are unaware whether efforts by individual or governmental units have been successful in locating such homes either without neighborhood opposition or by successful negotiation with concerned owners. We have not been made aware of what coordinated efforts, if any, are being made by state or local agencies to establish adult family homes. All of these considerations would be relevant to any possible court finding that a significant public policy overrides the existing restrictive covenants at issue in this case.

In addition, the statute relied upon by Worthington as the source of a legislative declaration of public policy favoring adult family homes was not effective until after the written opinion of the trial court, and was not cited to the trial court. Moreover, the statute, in stating that an adult family home should be permitted in an area zoned for single-family dwellings, is by its very terms limited to *zoning*. When the Legislature intends to affect a *private land use restriction* (i.e., a covenant) as compared to *zoning*, it normally does so explicitly.

The cases from other jurisdictions cited by Worthington either do not reach the policy conflict presented here or are based upon entirely different statutory direction or even constitutional dictates. The various amici curiae raise a claimed violation of the federal Fair Housing Act. We do not consider issues raised first and only by amicus.

We hold that under the equities of these particular facts, the discretionary grant of an injunction was proper. We caution that the interpretation of a particular restrictive covenant is largely dependent upon the facts of the case at hand. Our holding should not be construed as an encompassing declaration concerning covenants and uses under other circumstances. Likewise, our rejection of the claimed public policy is limited to the facts herein, especially due to the record's lack of any compre-

hensive presentation of governmental goals, efforts, needs, and successes existing in fact.

Injunction in favor of Association and against Worthington's use of property affirmed.

Termination of Restrictive Covenants   Restrictive covenants may be terminated in a variety of ways, including voluntary relinquishment or *waiver*. They may also be terminated *by their own terms* (such as when the covenant specifies that it is to exist for a certain length of time) or *by dramatically changed circumstances*. If Oldcodger's property is subject, for instance, to a restrictive covenant allowing only residential use, the fact that all of the surrounding property has come to be used for industrial purposes may operate to terminate the covenant. When a restrictive covenant has been terminated or held invalid, the deed containing the restriction remains a valid instrument of transfer but is treated as if the restriction had been removed from the document.

ACQUISITION OF REAL PROPERTY

Title to real property may be obtained in various ways, including purchase, gift, will or inheritance, tax sale, and adverse possession. Original title to land in the United States was acquired either from the federal government or from a country that held the land prior to its acquisition by the United States. The land in the 13 original colonies had been granted by the king of England either to the colonies or to certain individuals. The states ceded the land in the Northwest Territory to the federal government, which in turn issued grants or patents of land. Original ownership of much of the land in Florida and the southwest came by grants from Spain's rulers.

Acquisition by Purchase

Selling one's real property is a basic ownership right. Unreasonable restrictions on an owner's right to sell her property are considered unenforceable as against public policy. Most owners of real property acquired title by purchasing the property. Each state

sets the requirements for proper conveyances of real property located in that state. The various elements of selling and buying real property are discussed later in this chapter.

Acquisition by Gift

Real property ownership may be acquired by gift. For a gift of real property to be valid, the donor must deliver a properly executed deed to the property to the donee or to some third person who is to hold it for the donee. Neither the donee nor the third person needs to take actual possession of the property. The gift's essential element is delivery of the deed. Suppose that Fields executes a deed to the family farm and leaves it in his safe-deposit box for delivery to his daughter (the intended donee) when he dies. The attempted gift will not be valid, because Fields did not deliver the gift during his lifetime.

Acquisition by Will or Inheritance

The owner of real property generally has the right to dispose of the property by will. The requirements for a valid will are discussed in Chapter 26, Estates and Trusts. If the owner of real property dies without a valid will, the property passes to his heirs as determined under the laws of the state in which the property is located.

Acquisition by Tax Sale

If taxes assessed on real property are not paid when due, they become a *lien* on the property. This lien has priority over other claims to the land. If the taxes remain unpaid, the government may sell the land at a tax sale. Although the purchaser at the tax sale acquires title to the property, a number of states have statutes giving the original owner a limited time (such as a year) within which to buy the property from the tax sale purchaser for the price paid by the purchaser, plus interest.

Acquisition by Adverse Possession

Each state has a statute of limitations that gives an owner of land a specific number of years within which to bring suit to regain possession of her land from someone who is trespassing on it. This period varies from state to state, generally ranging from 5 to 20 years. If someone wrongfully possesses land and acts as if he were the owner, the actual owner must take steps to have the possessor ejected from the land. If the owner fails to do this within the statutory period, she loses her right to eject the possessor.

Assume, for example, that Titus owns a vacant lot next to Holdeman's house. Holdeman frequently uses the vacant lot for a variety of activities and appears to be the property's only user. In addition, Holdeman regularly mows and otherwise maintains the vacant lot. He has also placed a fence around it. By continuing such actions and thus staying in possession of Titus's property for the statutory period (and by meeting each other requirement about to be discussed), Holdeman may position himself to acquire title to the land by **adverse possession.**

To acquire title by adverse possession, one must possess land in a manner that puts the true owner on notice of the owner's cause of action against the possessor. The adverse possessor's acts of possession must be (1) *open,* (2) *actual,* (3) *continuous,* (4) *exclusive,* and (5) *hostile* (or adverse) *to the owner's rights.* The hostility element is not a matter of subjective intent. Rather, it means that the adverse possessor's acts of possession must be inconsistent with the owner's rights. If a person is in possession of another's property under a lease, as a cotenant, or with the permission of the owner, his possession is not hostile. In some states, the possessor of land must also pay the property taxes in order to gain title by adverse possession.

It is not necessary that the same person occupy the land for the statutory period. The periods of possession of several adverse possessors may be "tacked" together when calculating the period of possession if each possessor claimed rights from another possessor. The possession must, however, be continuous for the requisite time.

TRANSFER BY SALE

Steps in a Sale

The major steps normally involved in the sale of real property are:

1. Contracting with a real estate broker to locate a buyer.
2. Negotiating and signing a contract of sale.
3. Arranging for the financing of the purchase and satisfying other requirements, such as having a survey conducted or acquiring title insurance.
4. Closing the sale, which involves payment of the purchase price and transfer of the deed, as well as other matters.
5. Recording the deed.

Contracting with a Real Estate Broker

Although engaging a real estate broker is not a legal requirement for the sale of real property, it is common for one who wishes to sell his property to "list" the property with a broker. A listing contract empowers the broker to act as the seller's agent in procuring a ready, willing, and able buyer and in managing details of the property transfer. A number of states' statutes of frauds require listing contracts to be evidenced by a writing and signed by the party to be charged.

Real estate brokers are regulated by state and federal law. They owe *fiduciary duties* (duties of trust and confidence) to their clients. Chapter 34, The Agency Relationship, contains additional information regarding the duties imposed on such agents.

Types of Listing Contracts   Listing contracts specify such matters as the listing period's duration, the terms on which the seller will sell, and the amount and terms of the broker's commission. There are different types of listing contracts.

1. *Open listing.* Under an open listing contract, the broker receives a *nonexclusive* right to sell the property. This means that the seller and third parties (for example, other brokers) also are entitled to find a buyer for the property. The broker operating under an open listing is entitled to a commission only if he was the first to find a ready, willing, and able buyer.

2. *Exclusive agency listing.* Under an exclusive agency listing, the broker earns a commission if he *or any other agent* finds a ready, willing, and able buyer during the period of time specified in the contract. Thus, the broker operating under such a listing would have the right to a commission even if another broker actually procured the buyer. Under the exclusive agency listing, however, the seller has the right to sell the property himself without being obligated to pay the broker a commission.

3. *Exclusive right to sell.* An exclusive right to sell contract provides the broker the exclusive right to sell the property for a specified period of time and entitles her to a commission no matter who procured the buyer. Under this type of listing, a seller must pay the broker her commission even if it was the seller or some third party who found the buyer during the duration of the listing contract.

Contract of Sale

The contract formation, performance, assignment, and remedies principles about which you read in earlier chapters apply to real estate sales contracts. Such contracts identify the parties and subject property, and set forth the purchase price, the type of deed the purchaser will receive, the items of personal property (if any) included in the sale, and other important aspects of the parties' transaction. Real estate sales contracts often make the closing of the sale contingent on the buyer's obtaining financing at a specified rate of interest, on the seller's procurement of a survey and title insurance, and on the property's passing a termite inspection. Because they are within the statute of frauds, real estate sales contracts must be evidenced by a suitable writing signed by the party to be charged in order to be enforceable.

Fair Housing Act

The Fair Housing Act, enacted by Congress in 1968 and substantially revised in 1988, is designed to prevent discrimination in the housing market. Its provisions apply to real estate brokers, sellers (other than those selling their own single-family dwellings without the use of a broker), lenders, lessors, and appraisers. Originally, the act prohibited discrimination on the basis of race, color, religion, sex, and national origin. The 1988 amendments added handicap and "familial status" to this list. The familial status category was intended to prevent discrimination in the housing market against pregnant women and families with children.[4] "Adult" or "senior citizen" communities restricting residents' age do not violate the Fair Housing Act even though they exclude families with children, so long as the housing meets the requirements of the act's "housing for older persons" exemption.[5]

The act prohibits discrimination on the above-listed bases in a wide range of matters relating to the sale or rental of housing. These matters include refusals to sell or rent, representations that housing is not available for sale or rental when in fact it is, and discriminatory actions regarding terms, conditions, or privileges of sale or rental or regarding the provision of services and facilities involved in sale or rental.[6] The act also prohibits discrimination in connection with brokerage services, appraisals, and financing of dwellings.

Included within prohibited discrimination on the basis of handicap are refusals to permit a handicapped person to make (at his own expense) reasonable modifications to the property and refusals to make reasonable accommodations in property-related rules, policies, practices, or services when such modifications or accommodations are necessary to afford the handicapped person full enjoyment of the property. The act also outlaws the building of multifamily housing that is inaccessible to persons with handicaps.

A violation of the Fair Housing Act can result in a civil action brought by either the government or the aggrieved individual. If the aggrieved individual

---

[4]"Familial status" is defined as an individual or individuals under the age of 18 who is/are domiciled with a parent, some other person who has custody over him/her/them, or the designee of the parent or custodial individual. The familial status classification also applies to one who is pregnant or in the process of attempting to secure custody of a child or children under the age of 18.

[5]The Fair Housing Act defines "housing for older persons" as housing provided under any state or federal program found by the Secretary of HUD to be specifically designed and operated to assist elderly persons, housing intended for and solely occupied by persons 62 years old or older, or housing that meets the requirements of federal regulations and is intended and operated for occupancy by at least one person 55 years old or older.

[6]Chapter 25 discusses the Fair Housing Act's application to rentals of residential property.

brings suit and prevails, the court may issue injunctions, award actual and punitive damages, assess attorney's fees and costs, and grant other appropriate relief. Finally, the Fair Housing Act invalidates any state or municipal law requiring or permitting an action that would be a discriminatory housing practice under federal law.

Financing the Purchase   The various arrangements for financing the purchase of real property—such as mortgages, land contracts, and deeds of trust—are discussed in Chapter 27, Introduction to Credit and Secured Transactions.

Deeds

Each state's statutes set out the formalities necessary to accomplish a valid conveyance of land. As a general rule, a valid conveyance is brought about by the execution and delivery of a **deed**, a written instrument that transfers title from one person (the grantor) to another (the grantee). Three types of deeds are in general use in the United States: *quitclaim deeds*, *warranty deeds*, and *deeds of bargain and sale* (also called *grant deeds*). The precise rights contemplated by a deed depend on the type of deed the parties have used.

Quitclaim Deeds   A **quitclaim deed** conveys whatever title the grantor has at the time he executes the deed. It does not, however, contain warranties of title. The grantor who executes a quitclaim deed does not claim to have good title—or any title, for that matter. The grantee has no action against the grantor under a quitclaim deed if the grantee does not acquire good title. Quitclaim deeds are frequently used to cure technical defects in the chain of title to property.

Warranty Deeds   A **warranty deed**, unlike a quitclaim deed, contains covenants of warranty. Besides conveying title to the property, the grantor who executes a warranty deed guarantees the title she has conveyed. There are two types of warranty deeds.

1. *General warranty deed.* Under a general warranty deed, the grantor warrants against (and agrees to defend against) all title defects and encumbrances (such as liens and easements), including those that arose before the grantor received her title.

2. *Special warranty deed.* Under a special warranty deed, the grantor warrants against (and agrees to defend against) title defects and encumbrances that arose after she acquired the property. If the property conveyed is subject to an encumbrance such as a mortgage, a long-term lease, or an easement, the grantor frequently provides a special warranty deed that contains a provision excepting those specific encumbrances from the warranty.

Deed of Bargain and Sale   In a **deed of bargain and sale** (also known as a **grant deed**), the grantor makes no covenants. The grantor uses language such as "I grant" or "I bargain and sell" or "I convey" property. Such a deed does contain, however, the grantor's implicit representation that he owns the land and has not previously encumbered it or conveyed it to another party.

Form and Execution of Deed

Some states' statutes suggest a form for deeds. Although the requirements for execution of deeds are not uniform, they do follow a similar pattern. As a general rule, a deed states the *name of the grantee*, contains a *recitation of consideration and a description of the property conveyed,* and is *signed by the grantor*. Most states require that the deed be notarized (acknowledged by the grantor before a notary public or other authorized officer) in order to be eligible for recording in public records.

No technical words of conveyance are necessary for a valid deed. Any language is sufficient if it indicates with reasonable certainty the grantor's intent to transfer ownership of the property. The phrases "grant, bargain, and sell" and "convey and warrant" are commonly used. Deeds contain recitations of consideration primarily for historical reasons. The consideration recited is not necessarily the purchase price of the property. Deeds often state that the consideration for the conveyance is "one dollar and other valuable consideration."

The property conveyed must be described in such a manner that it can be identified. This usually means that the legal description of the property must be used. Several methods of legal description are used in the United States. In urban areas, descriptions are usually by lot, block, and plat. In rural areas where the land has been surveyed by the government, property is usually described by reference to

FIGURE 2	Three Basic Types of Priority Systems for Recording Deeds
Race Statutes	Under a race statute—so named because the person who wins the race to the courthouse wins the property ownership "competition"—the first grantee who records a deed to a tract of land has superior title. For example, if Grantor deeds Blackacre to Kerr on March 1 and to Templin on April 1, Templin will have superior title to Blackacre if she records her deed before Kerr's is recorded. Race statutes are relatively uncommon today.
Notice Statutes	Under a notice system of priority, a later grantee of property has superior title if he acquired his interest without notice of an earlier grantee's claim to the property under an unrecorded deed. For example, Grantor deeds Greenacre to Jonson on June 1, but Jonson does not record his deed. On July 1, Marlowe purchases Greenacre without knowledge of Jonson's competing claim. Grantor executes and delivers a deed to Marlowe. In this situation, Marlowe would have superior rights to Greenacre even if Jonson ultimately records his deed before Marlowe's is recorded.
Race-Notice Statutes	The race-notice priority system combines elements of the systems just discussed. Under race-notice statutes, the grantee having priority is the one who *both takes his interest without notice* of any prior unrecorded claim and *records first*. For example, Grantor deeds Redacre to Frazier on September 1. On October 1 (at which time Frazier has not yet recorded his deed), Grantor deeds Redacre to Dixon, who is then unaware of any claim by Frazier to Redacre. If Dixon records his deed before Frazier's is recorded, Dixon has superior rights to Redacre.

the government survey. It may also be described by a metes and bounds description that specifies the boundaries of the tract of land.

Recording Deeds

Delivery of a valid deed conveys title from a grantor to a grantee. Even so, the grantee should promptly **record** the deed in order to prevent his interest from being defeated by third parties who may claim interests in the property. The grantee must pay a fee to have the deed recorded, a process that involves depositing and indexing the deed in the files of a government office designated by state law. A recorded deed operates to provide the public at large with notice of the grantee's property interest.

Recording Statutes   Each state has a **recording statute** that establishes a system for the recording of all transactions affecting real property ownership. These statutes are not uniform in their provisions. In general, however, they provide for the recording of all deeds, mortgages, land contracts, and similar documents.

Types of Recording Statutes   State recording statutes also provide for priority among competing claimants to rights in real property, in case conflicting rights or interests in property should be deeded to (or otherwise claimed by) more than one person. (Obviously, a grantor has no right to issue two different grantees separate deeds to the same property, but if this should occur, recording statutes provide rules to decide which grantee has superior title.) These priority rules apply only to grantees who have given value for their deeds or other interest-creating documents (primarily purchasers and lenders), and not to donees. A given state's recording statute will set up one of three basic types of priority systems: race statues, notice statutes, and race-notice statues. Figure 2 explains these priority systems. Although each of the examples used in Figure 2 deal with recorded and unrecorded deeds, recording statutes apply to other documents that create interests in real estate. Chapter 27, Introduction to Credit and Secured Transactions, discusses the recording of mortgages, as well as the adverse security interest–related consequences a mortgagee may experience if its mortgage goes unrecorded.

Methods of Assuring Title

In purchasing real property, the buyer is really acquiring the seller's ownership interests. Because the buyer does not want to pay a large sum of money for something that proves to be of little or no value, it is important for her to obtain assurance that the seller has good title to the property. This is commonly done in one of three ways:

1. *Title opinion.* In some states, it is customary to have an attorney examine an **abstract of title**. An abstract of title is a history of what the public records show regarding the passage of title to (and other interests in) a parcel of real property. It is not a guarantee of good title. After examining the abstract, the attorney renders an opinion about whether the grantor has **marketable title** to the property. Marketable title is title free from defects or reasonable doubt about its validity. If the grantor's title is defective, the nature of the defects will be stated in the attorney's title opinion.

2. *Torrens system.* A method of title assurance available in a few states is the **Torrens system** of title registration. Under this system, one who owns land in fee simple obtains a certificate of title. When the property is sold, the grantor delivers a deed and a certificate of title to the grantee. All liens and encumbrances against the title are noted on the certificate, thus assuring the purchaser that the title is good except as to the liens and encumbrances noted on the certificate. However, some claims or encumbrances, such as those arising from adverse possession, do not appear on the records and must be discovered through an inspection of the property. In some Torrens states, encumbrances such as tax liens, short-term leases, and highway rights are valid against the purchaser even though they do not appear on the certificate.

3. *Title insurance.* Purchasing a policy of **title insurance** provides the preferred and most common means of protecting title to real property. Title insurance obligates the insurer to reimburse the insured grantee for loss if the title proves to be defective. In addition, title insurance covers litigation costs if the insured grantee must go to court in a title dispute. Lenders commonly require that a separate policy of title insurance be obtained for the lender's protection. Title insurance may be obtained in combination with the other previously discussed methods of assuring title.

SELLER'S RESPONSIBILITIES REGARDING THE QUALITY OF RESIDENTIAL PROPERTY

Buyers of real estate normally consider it important that any structures on the property be in good condition. This factor becomes especially significant if the buyer intends to use the property for residential purposes. The rule of *caveat emptor* (let the buyer beware) traditionally applied to the sale of real property unless the seller committed misrepresentation or fraud or made express warranties about the property's condition. In addition, sellers had no duty to disclose hidden defects in the property. In recent years, however, the legal environment for sellers—especially real estate professionals such as developers and builder-vendors of residential property—has changed substantially. This section examines two important sources of liability for sellers of real property.

Implied Warranty of Habitability

Historically, sellers of residential property were not regarded as making any **implied warranty** that the property was habitable or suitable for the buyer's use. The law's attitude toward the buyer-seller relationship in residential property sales began to shift, however, as product liability law underwent rapid change in the late 1960s. Courts began to see that the same policies favoring the creation of implied warranties in the sale of goods applied with equal force to the sale of residential real estate.[7] Both goods and housing are frequently mass-produced. The disparity of knowledge and bargaining power often existing between a buyer of goods and a professional seller is also likely to exist between a buyer of a house and a builder-vendor (one who builds and sells houses). Moreover, many defects in houses are not readily discoverable during a buyer's inspection. This creates the possibility of serious loss, because the purchase of a home is often the largest single investment a person ever makes.

For these reasons, courts in most states now hold that builders, builder-vendors, and developers make an implied warranty of habitability when they build or sell real property for residential purposes. An ordinary owner who sells her house—in other

---

[7]See Chapter 20 for a discussion of the development of similar doctrines in the law of product liability.

words, a seller who was neither the builder nor the developer of the residential property—does not make an implied warranty of habitability.

The implied warranty of habitability amounts to a guarantee that the house is free of latent (hidden) defects that would render it unsafe or unsuitable for human habitation. A breach of this warranty subjects the defendant to liability for damages, measured by either the cost of repairs or the loss in value of the house.[8]

A related issue that has led to considerable litigation is whether the implied warranty of habitability extends to subsequent purchasers of the house. For example, PDQ Development Co. builds a house and sells it to Johnson. If Johnson later sells the house to McClure, may McClure successfully sue PDQ for breach of warranty if a serious defect renders the house uninhabitable? Although some courts have rejected implied warranty actions brought by subsequent purchasers, many courts today hold that an implied warranty made by a builder-vendor or developer would extend to a subsequent purchaser.

May the implied warranty of habitability be *disclaimed* or *limited* in the contract of sale? It appears at least possible to disclaim or limit the warranty by a contract provision, subject to limitations imposed by the unconscionability doctrine, public policy concerns, and contract interpretation principles.[9] Courts construe attempted disclaimers

very strictly against the builder-vendor or developer, and often reject disclaimers that are not specific regarding rights supposedly waived by the purchaser.

Duty to Disclose Hidden Defects

Traditional contract law provided that a seller had no duty to disclose to the buyer defects in the property being sold, even if the seller knew about the defects and the buyer could not reasonably find out about them on his own. The seller's failure to volunteer information, therefore, could not constitute misrepresentation or fraud. This traditional rule of nondisclosure was another expression of the prevailing *caveat emptor* notion. Although the nondisclosure rule was subject to certain exceptions,[10] the exceptions seldom applied. Thus, there was no duty to disclose in most sales of real property.

Today, courts in many jurisdictions have substantially eroded the traditional nondisclosure rule and have placed a duty on the seller to disclose any known defect that materially affects the property's value and is not reasonably observable by the buyer. The seller's failure to disclose such defects effectively amounts to an assertion that the defects do not exist—an assertion on which a judicial finding of misrepresentation or fraud may be based.[11] *Johnson v. Davis* illustrates the trend toward expansion of the duty to disclose.

---

[8]Measures of damages are discussed in Chapter 18.

[9]The unconscionability doctrine and public policy concerns are discussed in Chapter 15. Chapter 16 addresses contract interpretation.

---

[10]These exceptions are discussed in Chapter 13.

[11]Misrepresentation and fraud are discussed in Chapter 13.

JOHNSON V. DAVIS
480 So. 2d 625 (Fla. Sup. Ct. 1985)

In May 1982, Morton and Edna Davis entered into a contract to buy a house from Clarence and Dana Johnson for $310,000. The house was three years old. The contract required a $5,000 initial deposit payment and an additional $26,000 deposit payment within five days. After the Davises had paid the initial $5,000 deposit but before they had paid the $26,000 deposit, Mrs. Davis noticed some buckling and peeling plaster around the corner of a window frame, as well as stains on ceilings in several rooms. When Mrs. Davis inquired about this, Mr. Johnson told her that the window had had a minor problem which was corrected long ago and that the stains were wallpaper glue. (The parties disagreed, at trial, about whether Mr. Johnson told Mrs. Davis at this time that there had never been any problems with the roof or ceilings.) The Davises then paid the remaining

$26,000 deposit, and the Johnsons moved out of the house. Several days later, following a heavy rain, Mrs. Davis entered the house and discovered water gushing in from around the window frame, the ceiling of the family room, the light fixtures, the glass doors, and the stove in the kitchen. The Davises hired roofers, who reported that the roof was inherently defective and that any repairs would be temporary because the roof was "slipping." Only a new roof, at a cost of $15,000, could be watertight. The Davises then filed this action alleging breach of contract, fraud, and misrepresentation. They sought rescission of the contract and return of their deposit payments. The trial court awarded the Davises $26,000 plus interest but permitted the Johnsons to keep the initial $5,000 deposit plus interest. Both parties appealed to the District Court of Appeals, which held that the entire deposit should have been returned to the Davises. The Johnsons appealed.

Adkins, Justice   We agree with the district court's conclusions under a theory of fraud and find that the Johnsons' statements to the Davises regarding the condition of the roof constituted a fraudulent misrepresentation entitling the Davises to the return of the $26,000 deposit payment. The record reflects that the statement made by the Johnsons was a false representation of material fact, made with knowledge of its falsity, upon which the Davises relied to their detriment as evidenced by the $26,000 paid to the Johnsons. The fact that the false statements as to the quality of the roof were made after the signing of the purchase agreement does not excuse the seller from liability where the misrepresentations were made prior to the conveyance of the property.

In determining whether a seller of a home has a duty to disclose latent material defects to a buyer, the established tort law distinction between misfeasance and nonfeasance, action and inaction, must carefully be analyzed. The highly individualistic philosophy of the earlier common law consistently imposed liability upon the commission of affirmative acts of harm, but shrank from converting the courts into an institution for forcing men to help one another. Liability for nonfeasance has therefore been slow to receive recognition in the evolution of tort law.

In theory, the difference between misfeasance and nonfeasance is quite simple and obvious; however, in practice it is not always easy to draw the line and determine whether conduct is active or passive. That is, where failure to disclose a material fact is calculated to induce a false belief, the distinction between concealment and affirmative representations is tenuous. Both proceed from the same motives and are attended with the same consequences; both are violative of the principles of fair dealing and good faith.

Still there exists in much of our case law the old tort notion that there can be no liability for nonfeasance. The courts in some jurisdictions hold that where the parties are dealing at arm's length and the facts lie equally open to both parties, with equal opportunity of examination, mere nondisclosure does not constitute a fraudulent concealment.

These unappetizing cases are not in tune with the times and do not conform with current notions of justice, equity, and fair dealing. One should not be able to stand behind the impervious shield of caveat emptor and take advantage of another's ignorance. Our courts have taken great strides since the days when the judicial emphasis was on rigid rules and ancient precedents. Modern concepts of justice and fair dealing have given our courts the opportunity and latitude to change legal precepts in order to conform to society's needs. Thus, the tendency of the more recent cases has been to restrict rather than extend the doctrine of caveat emptor. The law appears to be working toward the ultimate conclusion that full disclosure of all material facts must be made whenever elementary fair conduct demands it.

The harness placed on the doctrine of caveat emptor in a number of other jurisdictions has resulted in the seller of a home being liable for failing to disclose material defects of which he was aware. We are of the opinion that the same philosophy regarding the sale of homes should also be the law in the state of Florida. Accordingly we hold that where the seller of a home knows of facts materially affecting the value of the property which are not readily observable and are not known to the buyer, the seller is under a duty to disclose them to the buyer. This duty is equally applicable to all forms of real property, new and used.

In the case at bar, the evidence shows that the Johnsons knew of and failed to disclose that there had been problems with the roof of the house. Mr. Johnson admitted during his testimony that the Johnsons were aware of roof problems prior to entering into the contract of sale and receiving the $5,000 deposit payment. Thus, we find that the Johnsons' fraudulent concealment also entitles the Davises to the return of the $5,000 deposit payment plus interest.

Judgment for the Davises affirmed.

OTHER PROPERTY CONDITION–RELATED OBLIGATIONS OF REAL PROPERTY OWNERS AND POSSESSORS

In recent years, the law has increasingly required real property owners and possessors to take steps to further the safety of persons on the property and to make the property more accessible to disabled individuals. This section discusses two legal developments along these lines: the trend toward expansion of *premises liability* and the inclusion of property-related provisions in the *Americans with Disabilities Act.*

Expansion of Premises Liability

Premises liability is the name sometimes used for negligence cases in which property owners or possessors (such as business operators leasing commercial real estate) are held liable to persons injured while on the property. As explained in Chapter 7, Negligence and Strict Liability, property owners and possessors face liability when their *failures to exercise reasonable care* to keep their property reasonably safe result in injuries to persons lawfully on the property.[12] The traditional premises liability case was one in which a property owner's or possessor's negligence led to the existence of a potentially hazardous condition on the property (e.g., a dangerously slick floor or similar physical condition at a business premises), and a person justifiably on the premises (e.g., a

business customer) sustained personal injury upon encountering that unexpected condition (e.g., by slipping and falling).

Security Precautions against Foreseeable Criminal Acts   Recent years have witnessed a judicial inclination to expand premises liability to cover other situations in addition to the traditional scenario. A key component of this expansion has been many courts' willingness to reconsider the once-customary holding that a property owner or possessor had no legal obligation to implement security measures to protect persons on the property from the wrongful acts of third parties lacking any connection with the owner or possessor. Today, courts frequently hold that a property owner's or possessor's duty to exercise reasonable care includes the obligation to take *reasonable security precautions* designed to protect persons lawfully on the premises from *foreseeable* wrongful (including criminal) acts by third parties.

This expansion has caused hotel, apartment building, and convenience store owners and operators to be among the defendants held liable—sometimes in very large damage amounts—to guests, tenants, and customers on whom violent third-party attackers inflicted severe physical injuries. In such cases, the property owners' or possessors' negligent failures to take security precautions restricting such wrongdoers' access to the premises served as at least a *substantial factor* leading to the plaintiffs' injuries.[13] The security lapses amounting to a lack of reasonable care in a particular case may have been, for instance, failures to install deadbolt locks, provide adequate locking devices on sliding glass doors, maintain sufficient lighting, or employ security guards.

---

[12]Chapter 7 explains the law's traditional view that real property owners and possessors owe persons who come on the property certain duties that vary depending on those persons' invitee, licensee, or trespasser status. It also discusses courts' increasing tendency to merge the traditional invitee and licensee classifications and to hold that property owners and possessors owe invitees and licensees the duty to exercise reasonable care to keep the premises reasonably safe.

---

[13]See Chapter 7's discussion of the *causation* element of a negligence claim.

Determining Foreseeability   The security precautions component of the reasonable care duty is triggered only when criminal activity on the premises is foreseeable. It therefore becomes important to determine whether the foreseeability standard has been met. In making this determination, courts look at such factors as whether previous crimes had occurred on or near the subject property (and if so, the nature and frequency of those crimes), whether the property owner or possessor knew or should have known of those prior occurrences, and whether the property was located in a high-crime area. The fact-specific nature of the foreseeability and reasonable care determinations makes the outcome of a given premises liability case difficult to predict in advance. Nevertheless, there is no doubt that the current premises liability climate gives property owners and possessors more reason than ever before to be concerned about security measures.

Americans with Disabilities Act

In 1990, Congress enacted the broad-ranging Americans with Disabilities Act (ADA). This statute was designed to eliminate longstanding patterns of discrimination against disabled persons in matters such as employment, access to public services, and access to business establishments and similar facilities open to the public. The ADA's Title III focuses on places of *public accommodation*.[14] It imposes on certain property owners and possessors the obligation to take reasonable steps to make their property accessible to disabled persons (individuals with a physical or mental impairment that substantially limits one or more major life activities).

Places of Public Accommodation   Title III of the ADA classifies numerous businesses and nonbusiness enterprises as places of **public accommodation**. These include hotels, restaurants, bars, theaters, concert halls, auditoriums, stadiums, shopping centers, stores at which goods are sold or rented, service-oriented businesses (running the gamut from gas stations to law firm offices), museums, parks, schools, social services establishments (day-care centers, senior citizen centers, homeless shelters, and the like),

places of recreation, and various other enterprises, facilities, and establishments. Private clubs and religious organizations, however, are not treated as places of public accommodation for purposes of the statute.

Modifications of Property   Under the ADA, the owner or operator of a place of public accommodation cannot exclude disabled persons from the premises or otherwise discriminate against them in terms of their ability to enjoy the public accommodation. Avoiding such exclusion or other discrimination may require alteration of the business or nonbusiness enterprise's practices, policies, and procedures. Moreover, using language contemplating the possible need for physical modifications of property serving as a place of public accommodation, the ADA includes within prohibited discrimination the property owner's or possessor's "failure to take such steps as may be necessary to ensure that no individual with a disability is excluded" or otherwise discriminated against in terms of access to what nondisabled persons are provided. The failure to take these steps does not violate the ADA, however, if the property owner or possessor demonstrates that implementing such steps would "fundamentally alter the nature" of the enterprise or would "result in an undue burden."

Prohibited discrimination may also include the "failure to remove architectural barriers and communication barriers that are structural in nature," if removal is "readily achievable." When the removal of such a barrier is not readily achievable, the property owner or possessor nonetheless engages in prohibited discrimination if he, she, or it does not adopt "alternative methods" to ensure access to the premises and what it has to offer (assuming that the alternative methods are themselves readily achievable). The ADA defines *readily achievable* as "easily accomplishable and able to be carried out without much difficulty or expense." The determination of whether an action is readily achievable involves consideration of factors such as the action's nature and cost, the nature of the enterprise conducted on the property, the financial resources of the affected property owner or possessor, and the effect the action would have on expenses and resources of the property owner or possessor.

New Construction   Newly constructed buildings on property used as a place of public accommodation must contain physical features making the

---

[14]42 U.S.C. §§ 12181-12189 (1990). These sections examine only Title III of the ADA. Chapter 50 discusses the employment-related provisions set forth in Title I of the statute.

buildings *readily accessible* to disabled persons. The same is true of additions built on to previous structures. The ADA is supplemented by federal regulations setting forth property accessibility guidelines designed to lend substance and specificity to the broad legal standards stated in the statute. In addition, the federal government has issued technical assistance manuals and materials in an effort to educate public accommodation owners and operators regarding their obligations under the ADA.

Remedies   A person subjected to disability-based discrimination in any of the respects discussed above may bring a civil suit for injunctive relief. An injunction issued by a court must include "an order to alter facilities" to make the facilities "readily accessible to and usable by individuals with disabilities to the extent required" by the ADA. The court has discretion to award attorney's fees to the prevailing party. The U.S. Attorney General also has the legal authority to institute a civil action alleging a violation of Title III of the ADA. In such a case, the court may choose to grant injunctive and other appropriate equitable relief, award compensatory damages to aggrieved persons (when the Attorney General so requests), and assess civil penalties (up to $50,000 for a first violation and up to $100,000 for any subsequent violation) "to vindicate the public interest." When determining the amount of any such penalty, the court is to give consideration to any good faith effort by the property owner or possessor to comply with the law. The court must also consider whether the owner or possessor could reasonably have anticipated the need to accommodate disabled persons.

LAND USE CONTROL

Although a real property owner generally has the right to use his property as he desires, society has placed certain limitations on this right. This section examines the property use limitations imposed by nuisance law and by zoning and subdivision ordinances. It also discusses the ultimate land use restriction—the eminent domain power—which enables the government to deprive property owners of their land.

Nuisance Law

One's enjoyment of her own land depends to a great extent on the uses her neighbors make of their land. When the uses of neighboring landowners conflict, the aggrieved party frequently institutes litigation to resolve the conflict. A property use that unreasonably interferes with another person's ability to use or enjoy her own property may lead to an action for **nuisance** against the landowner or possessor engaging in the objectionable use.

The term *nuisance* has no set definition. It is often regarded, however, as encompassing any property-related use or activity that unreasonably interferes with the rights of others. Property uses potentially constituting nuisances include uses that are inappropriate to the neighborhood (such as using a vacant lot in a residential neighborhood as a garbage dump), bothersome to neighbors (such as keeping a pack of barking dogs in one's backyard), dangerous to others (such as storing large quantities of gasoline in 50-gallon drums in one's garage), or of questionable morality (such as operating a house of prostitution). To amount to a nuisance, a use need not be illegal. The fact that relevant zoning laws allow a given use does not mean that the use cannot be a nuisance. The use's having been in existence before complaining neighbors acquired their property does not mean that the use cannot be a nuisance, though it does lessen the likelihood that the use would be held a nuisance.

The test for determining the presence or absence of a nuisance is necessarily flexible and highly dependent on the individual case's facts. Courts balance a number of factors, such as the social importance of the parties' respective uses, the extent and duration of harm experienced by the aggrieved party, and the feasibility of abating (stopping) the nuisance.

Nuisances may be private or public. To bring a *private nuisance* action, the plaintiff must be a landowner or occupier whose enjoyment of her own land is substantially lessened by the alleged nuisance. The remedies for private nuisance include damages and injunctive relief designed to stop the offending use. A *public nuisance* occurs when a nuisance harms members of the public, who need not be injured in their use of property. For example, if a power plant creates noise and emissions posing a health hazard to pedestrians and workers in nearby buildings, a public nuisance may exist even though the nature of the harm has nothing to do with any loss of enjoyment of property. Public nuisances involve a broader class of affected parties than do private nuisances. The action to abate a public nuisance must usually be brought by the government. Remedies generally include injunctive relief and civil penalties that resemble fines. Private parties may sue for abatement of a public nuisance or for damages caused by one only when they suffered unique harm different from that experienced by the general public.

Wood v. Picillo illustrates the application of nuisance law to a property owner who maintained a hazardous waste dump.

WOOD V. PICILLO
443 A.2d 1244 (R.I. Sup. Ct. 1982)

The Picillos maintained a chemical dump site on a clearing on their land. The site was a huge trench about 200 feet long, 15 to 30 feet wide, and 15 to 20 feet deep. A thick layer of pungent, varicolored liquid covered the trench bottom. Along the periphery of the pit lay more than 100 55-gallon drums and 5-gallon pail containers. Some of these were upright and sealed, some were tipped, and some were partially buried. About 600 feet downhill from this site was a marshy wetland that drained into a river and several ponds. A witness testified that he saw the operator of a truck knock barrels marked "Combustible" off the truck's tailgate directly to the ground, where chemicals poured freely from the damaged barrels into the trench. Neighbors smelled "sickening," "heavy," and "terrible" odors that forced them to stay inside their homes. Several neighbors were made ill by the odors.

The attention of state officials was drawn to the site when an enormous explosion erupted into 50-foot flames in a trench on the Picillos' land, and the fire could not be extinguished. Investigators from the state environmental management department began an investigation of the site. The state fire marshal ordered the dumping to cease, but dumping operations continued. Edward Wood and other plaintiffs brought a nuisance action against the Picillos. The trial court found that the dumping operation was a nuisance. It issued an injunction against further chemical disposal operations on the Picillo property and ordered the Picillos to finance the cleanup and removal of the toxic wastes. The Picillos appealed.

Weisberger, Judge   The dump site proper might best be described in the succinct expression of the trial justice as "a chemical nightmare." At trial expert witnesses developed a scientific connection between the neighbors' experiences and the Picillos' operations. Laboratory analyses of samples taken from the trench, monitoring wells, and adjacent waters revealed the presence of five chemicals: toluene, xylene, chloroform, III trichloroethane, and trichloroethylene. According to the experts, the chemicals present on the Picillos' property and in the marsh, if left unchecked, would eventually threaten wildlife and humans well downstream from the dump site. Expert testimony further revealed that the chemicals had traveled and would continue to travel from the dump site into the marsh at the rate of about one foot per day. From the marsh, predicted the experts, the chemicals would flow into waters inhabited by fish and used by humans for recreational and agricultural purposes.

The Picillos contend that the evidence adduced at trial was insufficient to support a finding of public and private nuisance. We find this to be without merit. The essential element of an actionable nuisance is that persons have suffered harm or are threatened with injuries that they ought not to have to bear. Distinguished from negligence liability, liability in nuisance is predicated upon unreasonable injury rather than upon unreasonable conduct. Thus, plaintiffs may recover in nuisance despite the otherwise nontortious nature of the conduct which creates the injury.

The Picillos have accurately stated that the injury produced by an actionable nuisance "must be real and not fanciful or imaginary." The Picillos next suggest that the injuries in the case at bar are of the insubstantial, unactionable type. It is this statement, however, rather than the purported injuries, that is fanciful. The testimony to which reference is made in this opinion clearly establishes that the Picillos' dumping operations have already caused substantial injury to their neighbors and threaten to cause incalculable damage to the general public. The Picillos' neighbors have displayed physical symptoms of exposure to toxic chemicals and have been restricted in the reasonable use of their property.

Moreover, expert testimony showed that the chemical presence on the Picillos' property threatens both aquatic wildlife and human beings with possible death, cancer, and liver disease. Thus, there was ample evidence at trial to support the finding of substantial injury.

For the reasons stated, the Picillos' appeal is dismissed.

Judgment for Wood affirmed.

Eminent Domain

The Fifth Amendment to the Constitution provides that private property shall not be taken for public use without "just compensation." Implicit in this provision is the principle that the government has the power to take property for public use if it pays "just compensation" to the owner of the property. This power, called the power of **eminent domain**, makes it possible for the government to acquire private property for highways, water control projects, municipal and civic centers, public housing, urban renewal, and other public uses. Governmental units can delegate their eminent domain power to private corporations such as railroads and utility companies.

Although the eminent domain power is a useful tool of efficient government, there are problems inherent in its use. Determining when the power can be properly exercised presents an initial problem. When the governmental unit itself uses the property taken, as would be the case with property acquired for construction of a municipal building or a public highway, the exercise of the power is proper. The use of eminent domain is not so clearly justified, however, when the government acquires the property and resells it to a private developer. Although such acquisitions may be more vulnerable to challenge, recent cases have applied a very lenient standard in determining what constitutes a public use.[15]

Determining *just compensation* in a given case poses a second and frequently encountered eminent domain problem. The property owner is entitled to receive the "fair market value" of his property. Critics assert, however, that this measure of compensation falls short of adequately compensating the owner for her loss, because *fair market value* does not cover such matters as the lost goodwill of a business or one's emotional attachment to his home.

A third problem sometimes encountered is determining when there has been a "taking" that triggers the government's just compensation obligation. The answer is easy when the government institutes a formal legal action to exercise the eminent domain power (often called an action to *condemn* property). In some instances, however, the government causes or permits a serious physical invasion of a landowner's property without having instituted formal condemnation proceedings. For example, the government's dam-building project results in persistent flooding of a private party's land. Courts have recognized the right of property owners in such cases to institute litigation seeking compensation from the governmental unit whose actions effectively amounted to a physical taking of their land. In these so-called **inverse condemnation** cases, the property owner sends the message that "you have taken my land; now pay for it." *Yee v. City of Escondido*,[16] which appears later in this chapter's discussion of other takings issues, involved an unsuccessful attempt by landowners to stretch the *physical taking* concept further, however, than the Supreme Court was prepared to allow.

Zoning and Subdivision Laws

State legislatures commonly delegate to cities and other political subdivisions the power to impose reasonable regulations designed to promote the public health, safety, and welfare (often called the *police*

---

[15]This issue is discussed further in Chapter 3, as are other issues relating to eminent domain.

[16]112 S. Ct. 1522 (U.S. Sup. Ct. 1992).

power). Zoning ordinances, which regulate real property use, stem from the exercise of the police power. Normally, zoning ordinances divide a city or town into various districts and specify or limit the uses to which property in those districts may be put. They also contain requirements and restrictions regarding improvements built on the land.

Zoning ordinances frequently contain direct restrictions on land use, such as by limiting property use in a given area to single-family or high-density residential uses, or to commercial, light industry, or heavy industry uses. Other sorts of use-related provisions commonly found in zoning ordinances include restrictions on building height, limitations on the portion of a lot that can be covered by a building, and specifications of the distance buildings must be from lot lines (usually called *setback* requirements). Zoning ordinances also commonly restrict property use by establishing population density limitations. Such restrictions specify the maximum number of persons who can be housed on property in a given area and dictate the amount of living space that must be provided for each person occupying residential property. In addition, zoning ordinances often establish restrictions designed to maintain or create a certain aesthetic character in the community. Examples of this type of restriction include specifications of buildings' architectural style, limitations on billboard and sign use, and designations of special zones for historic buildings.

Many local governments also have ordinances dealing with proposed subdivisions. These ordinances often require the subdivision developer to meet certain requirements regarding lot size, street and sidewalk layout, and sanitary facilities. They also require that the city or town approve the proposed development. Such ordinances are designed to further general community interests and to protect prospective buyers of property in the subdivision by ensuring that the developer meets minimum standards of suitability.

Nonconforming Uses   A zoning ordinance has *prospective* effect. This means that the uses and buildings already existing when the ordinance is passed (**nonconforming uses**) are permitted to continue. The ordinance may provide, however, for the gradual phasing out of nonconforming uses and buildings that do not fit the general zoning plan.

Relief from Zoning Ordinances   A property owner who wishes to use his property in a manner

prohibited by a zoning ordinance has more than one potential avenue of relief from the ordinance. He may, for instance, seek to have the ordinance **amended**—in other words, attempt to get the law changed—on the ground that the proposed amendment is consistent with the essence of the overall zoning plan.

A different approach would be to seek permission from the city or political subdivision to deviate from the zoning law. This permission is called a **variance**. A person seeking a variance usually claims that the ordinance works an undue hardship on her by denying her the opportunity to make reasonable use of her land. Examples of typical variance requests include a property owner's seeking permission to make a commercial use of her property even though it is located in an area zoned for residential purposes, or permission to deviate from normal setback or building size requirements.

Attempts to obtain variances and zoning ordinance amendments frequently clash with the interests of other owners of property in the same area—owners who have a vested interest in maintaining the status quo. As a result, variance and amendment requests often produce heated battles before local zoning authorities.

Challenges to the Validity of the Zoning Ordinance   A disgruntled property owner might also attack the zoning ordinance's validity on constitutional grounds. Litigation challenging zoning ordinances has become frequent in recent years, as cities and towns have used their zoning power to achieve social control. For example, assume that a city creates special zoning requirements for adult bookstores or other uses considered moral threats to the community. Such uses of the zoning power have been challenged as unconstitutional restrictions on freedom of speech. In *City of Renton v. Playtime Theatres, Inc.*, however, the Supreme Court upheld a zoning ordinance that prohibited the operation of adult bookstores within 1,000 feet of specified uses such as residential areas and schools.[17]

---

[17]475 U.S. 41 (U.S. Sup. Ct. 1986). A later case, *FW/PBS, Inc. v. City of Dallas,* 493 U.S. 215 (U.S. Sup. Ct. 1990), presented a different sort of restriction on adult businesses and resulted in a different outcome. There, the Court held that a comprehensive ordinance requiring licensing of adult cabarets and other adult entertainment establishments violated the First Amendment because the ordinance did not have appropriate procedural safeguards against arbitrary denials of licenses. The ordinance's chief defect was its failure to establish a time limit within which city authorities were required to act on license applications.

The Court established that the First Amendment rights of operators of adult businesses would not be violated by such an ordinance so long as the city provided them a "reasonable opportunity to open and operate" their businesses within the city. The reasonable opportunity test was satisfied in *City of Renton* even though the ordinance at issue effectively restricted adult bookstores to a small area of the community in which no property was then available to buy or rent. As lower court cases reveal, however, the fact-specific nature of the inquiry contemplated by the reasonable opportunity test means that the government is not guaranteed of passing the test in every case.[18]

Other litigation has stemmed from ordinances by which municipalities have attempted to "zone out" residential facilities such as group homes for mentally retarded adults. In a leading case, the Supreme Court held that the Constitution's Equal Protection Clause was violated by a zoning ordinance that required a special use permit for a group home for the mentally retarded.[19] (For a case indicating that similar issues nonetheless may be treated differently in the *restrictive covenant*—as opposed to zoning—setting, see *Mains Farm Homeowners Association v. Worthington*, which appears earlier in this chapter.) The Fair Housing Act, which forbids discrimination on the basis of handicap and familial status, has also been used as a basis for challenging decisions that zone out group homes. Such a challenge has a chance of success when the plaintiff demonstrates that the zoning board's actions were a mere pretext for discrimination.[20]

Many cities and towns have attempted to restrict single-family residential zones to living units of traditional families related by blood or marriage. In enacting ordinances along those lines, municipalities have sought to prevent the presence of groups of unrelated students, commune members, or religious cult adherents by specifically defining the term *family* in a way that excludes these groups. In *Belle Terre v. Boraas*,[21] the Supreme Court upheld such an ordinance as applied to a group of unrelated students. The Court later held, however, that an ordinance defining *family* so as to prohibit a grandmother from living with her grandsons was an unconstitutional intrusion on personal freedom regarding family life.[22] Restrictive definitions of *family* have been held unconstitutional under state constitutions in some cases but narrowly construed by courts in other cases.

Land Use Regulation and Taking

Another type of litigation seen with increasing frequency in recent years centers around zoning laws and other land use regulations that make the use of property less profitable for development.[23] Affected property owners have challenged the application of such regulations as unconstitutional takings of property without just compensation, even though these cases do not involve the actual physical invasions present in the inverse condemnation cases discussed earlier in this chapter.

States normally have broad discretion to use their police power for the public benefit, even when that means interfering to some extent with an owner's right to develop her property as she desires. Some regulations, however, may interfere with an owner's use of his property to such an extent that they constitute a taking. For instance, in *Nollan v. California Coastal Commission*,[24] the owners of a beach-front lot (the Nollans) wished to tear down a small house on the lot and replace that structure with a larger house. The California Coastal Commission conditioned the grant of the necessary coastal development permit on the

---

[18]See, for example, *Topanga Press, Inc. v. City of Los Angeles*, 989 F.2d 1524 (9th Cir. 1993). In that case, the Ninth Circuit Court of Appeals upheld the trial court's issuance of a preliminary injunction against the city's *City of Renton*-like zoning ordinance regarding adult businesses. The reasonable opportunity test was not passed by the city, given that much of the real estate supposedly still "available" for relocation of the adult businesses was submerged beneath the Pacific Ocean or was used as a landfill, for petroleum storage, for airport runways, or for some other purpose inconsistent with the notion that the property could somehow become available for use by adult businesses.

[19]*City of Cleburne v. Cleburne Living Centers*, 473 U.S. 432 (U.S. Sup. Ct. 1985).

[20]See, for example, *Baxter v. City of Nashville*, 720 F. Supp. 720 (S.D. Ill. 1989), which involves a challenge by a hospice for AIDS patients to a city's denial of a special use permit.

[21]416 U.S. 1 (U.S. Sup. Ct. 1974).

[22]*Moore v. City of East Cleveland*, 431 U.S. 494 (U.S. Sup. Ct. 1977).

[23]This issue is also discussed in Chapter 3.

[24]483 U.S. 825 (U.S. Sup. Ct. 1987).

Nollans' agreeing to allow the public an easement across their property. This easement would have allowed the public to reach certain nearby public beaches more easily. The Nollans challenged the validity of the Coastal Commission's action. Ultimately, the Supreme Court concluded that the Coastal Commission's placing the easement condition on the issuance of the permit amounted to an impermissible regulatory taking of the Nollans' property. In reaching this conclusion, the Court held that the state could not avoid paying compensation to the Nollans by choosing to do by way of the regulatory route what it would have had to pay for if it had followed the formal eminent domain route.

Regulations Denying Economically Beneficial Uses

What about a land use regulation that allows the property owner no *economically beneficial use* of his property? *Lucas v. South Carolina Coastal Commission*[25] was brought by a property owner, Lucas, who had paid nearly $1 million for two residential beach-front lots before South Carolina enacted a coastal protection statute. This statute's effect was to bar Lucas from building any permanent habitable structures on the lots. The trial court held that the statute rendered Lucas's property "valueless" and that an unconstitutional taking had occurred, but the South Carolina Supreme Court reversed. The U.S. Supreme Court, however, held that when a land use regulation denies "all economically beneficial use" of property, there normally has been a taking for which just compensation must be paid. The exception to this rule, according to the Court, would be when the economically productive use being prohibited by the land use regulation was already disallowed anyway by nuisance law or other comparable property law principles. The Court therefore reversed and remanded the case for determination of whether there had been a taking under the rule crafted by the Court, or instead an instance in which the "nuisance" exception applied. On remand, the South Carolina Supreme

Court concluded that a taking calling for compensation had occurred (and, necessarily, that the nuisance exception did not apply to Lucas's intended residential use).[26]

The mere fact that a land use regulation deprives the owner of the *highest and most profitable use* of his property does not mean, however, that there has been a taking. If the regulation still allows a use that is economically beneficial in a meaningful sense—even though not the most profitable use—the *Lucas* analysis would seem to indicate that an unconstitutional taking probably did not occur. At the same time, *Lucas* offered hints that less-than-total takings (in terms of restrictions on economically beneficial uses) may sometimes trigger a right of compensation on the landowner's part. Thus, it appears that even as to land use regulations that restrict some but not all economically beneficial uses, property owners are likely to continue arguing (as they have in recent years) that the regulations go "too far" and amount to a taking.

There is no set formula for determining whether a regulation has gone too far. Courts look at the relevant facts and circumstances and weigh a variety of factors, such as the economic impact of the regulation, the degree to which the regulation interferes with the property owner's reasonable expectations, and the character of the government's invasion. The weighing of these factors occurs against the backdrop of a general presumption that state and local governments should have reasonably broad discretion to develop land use restrictions pursuant to the police power. As a result, the outcome of a case in which *regulatory taking* allegations are made is less certain than when a *physical taking* (a physical invasion of the sort addressed in the earlier discussion of inverse condemnation cases) appears to have occurred. *Yee v. City of Escondido*, which follows, illustrates an unsuccessful attempt by property owners to have an arguable case of regulatory taking (if any sort of taking at all) analyzed as if it were a physical taking.

---

[25]112 S. Ct. 2886 (U.S. Sup. Ct. 1992). The *Lucas* case appears in Chapter 3.

[26]424 S.E.2d 484 (S.C. Sup. Ct. 1992).

YEE V. CITY OF ESCONDIDO
112 S. Ct. 1522 (U.S. Sup. Ct. 1992)

Mobile home owners commonly place their mobile homes on small plots of land (often called *pads*) they have leased in a mobile home park. In 1978, California enacted the Mobilehome Residency Law. This statute prohibited mobile home park owners from evicting mobile home owners from leased pads unless the mobile home owner defaulted on rental payments or violated park rules, or the park owner decided to change the property from a mobile home park to a different land use. The statute also prohibited the park owner from requiring that a mobile home be removed from a pad when the mobile home was sold to a responsible purchaser who wished to lease the same pad from the park owner.

The City of Escondido later enacted a mobile home rent control ordinance. This ordinance rolled back rents charged by park owners to their 1986 levels and required park owners to obtain City Council approval before raising rents. John and Irene Yee owned two mobile home parks in Escondido. They and other park owners (referred to here collectively as "the Yees") sued the city. The Yees alleged that Escondido's rent control ordinance, when viewed against the backdrop of California's Mobilehome Residency Law, effected a *physical taking* of their property without just compensation. Specifically, the Yees asserted that the rent control ordinance "had the effect of depriving the plaintiffs of all use and occupancy of [their] real property and granting to the tenants of mobilehomes presently in [the plaintiffs' parks], as well as the successors in interest of such tenants, the right to physically permanently occupy and use the [plaintiffs'] real property." The Superior Court sustained the city's demurrer. The California Court of Appeal affirmed, concluding that the rent control ordinance could not constitute a *physical* taking. After the California Supreme Court denied review, the U.S. Supreme Court granted the Yees' petition for certiorari.

O'Connor, Justice   Most of our cases interpreting the Takings Clause of the Fifth Amendment fall within two distinct classes. Where the government authorizes a physical occupation of property (or actually takes title), the Takings Clause generally requires compensation. But where the government merely regulates the use of property, compensation is required only if considerations such as the purpose of the regulation or the extent to which it deprives the owner of the economic use of the property suggest that the regulation has unfairly singled out the property owner to bear a burden that should be borne by the public as a whole. The first category of cases requires courts to apply a clear rule; the second necessarily entails complex factual assessments of the purposes and economic effects of government actions.

The Yees' argument is predicated on the unusual economic relationship between park owners and mobile home owners. Park owners may no longer set rents or decide who their tenants will be. As a result, according to the Yees, any reduction in the rent for a mobile home pad causes a corresponding increase in the value of a mobile home, because the mobile home owner now owns, in addition to a mobile home, the right to occupy a pad at a rent below the value that would be set by the free market. Because (the argument goes) the California Mobilehome Residency Law makes it difficult to evict a mobile home owner or to require the mobile home's removal when it is sold to a purchaser who wishes to lease the same pad, the mobile home owner (or purchaser to whom he or she sells) is effectively a perpetual tenant of the park with a right to occupy a pad at below-market rent indefinitely. As a result, the Yees conclude, the rent control ordinance has transferred a discrete interest in land—the right to occupy the land indefinitely at a sub-market rent—from the park owner to the mobile home owner. The Yees contend that this transfer is no less than a right of physical occupation of the park owner's land.

This argument, while perhaps within the scope of our regulatory taking cases, cannot be squared easily with our cases on physical takings. The government effects a physical taking only where it *requires* the landowner to submit to the physical occupation of his land. Thus, whether the government floods a landowner's property or does no more than require the landowner to suffer the installation of a cable, the Takings Clause requires compensation if the government authorizes a compelled physical invasion of property.

But the Escondido rent control ordinance, even when considered in conjunction with the California Mobilehome Residency law, authorizes no such thing. The Yees voluntarily rented their land to mobile home owners. Neither the City nor the State compels park owners, once they have rented their property to tenants, to continue doing so forever. To the contrary, the Mobilehome Residency Law provides that the park owner who wishes to change the use of his land may evict his tenants, albeit with six or twelve months notice. Put bluntly, no government has required any physical invasion of the Yees' property. Their tenants were invited by them, not forced upon them by the government. While the right to exclude is doubtless one of the most essential sticks in the bundle of rights that are commonly characterized as property, we do not find that right to have been taken from the Yees on the mere face of the Escondido ordinance.

The state and local laws at issue here merely regulate *use* of land by regulating the relationship between landlord and tenant. This Court has consistently affirmed that States have broad power to regulate housing conditions in general and the landlord-tenant relationship in particular without paying compensation for all economic injuries that such regulation entails. When a landowner decides to rent his land to tenants, the government may place ceilings on the rents the landowner can charge, or require the landowner to accept tenants he does not like, without automatically having to pay compensation. Such forms of regulation are analyzed by engaging in the factual inquiries necessary to determine whether a regulation goes "too far" and thus constitutes a regulatory taking.

The Yees emphasize that the ordinance transfers wealth from park owners to incumbent mobile home owners. Other forms of land use regulation, however, can also be said to transfer wealth from the one who is regulated to another. The existence of the transfer in itself does not convert regulation into physical invasion. The ordinance does not have the effect of requiring park owners to submit to the physical occupation of their land.

The same may be said of the Yees' contention that the ordinance, when considered alongside the State's Mobilehome Residency Law, effectively amounts to compelled physical occupation because it deprives park owners of the ability to choose their incoming tenants [by removing park owners' ability to threaten disfavored would-be purchasers with higher pad rents]. Such an effect, however, does not convert regulation into the unwanted physical occupation of land. Because they voluntarily open their property to occupation by others, the Yees cannot assert a *per se* right to compensation based on this inability to exclude particular individuals.

We made this observation in *Loretto v. Teleprompter Manhattan CATV Corp.* (1982):

We affirm the traditional rule that a permanent physical occupation of property is a taking. In such a case, the property owner entertains a historically rooted expectation of compensation, and the character of the invasion is qualitatively more intrusive than perhaps any other category of property regulation. We do not, however, question the equally substantial authority upholding a State's broad power to impose appropriate restrictions upon an owner's *use* of his property.

We continue to observe this distinction today. Because the Escondido rent control ordinance does not compel a landowner to suffer the physical occupation of his property, it does not effect a *per se* taking.

Judgment for the City of Escondido affirmed.

In another portion of the opinion not set forth here, the Court declined to rule on the Yees' alternative claim of an impermissible *regulatory* taking. Because the Yees' petition for certiorari had referred only to the *physical* taking question, the Court concluded that it would be inappropriate to consider the regulatory taking issue.

ETHICAL AND PUBLIC POLICY CONCERNS

1. You read that a person may acquire title to another person's real property by adversely possessing that property for a certain period of time. What are some justifications for this doctrine?

2. As you read, restrictive covenants and zoning ordinances are sometimes relied upon by opponents of plans to place group homes for the retarded or disabled in certain residential neighborhoods. What are the major ethical considerations suggested by such uses of restrictive covenants and zoning ordinances? What are the major ethical considerations suggested by attempts to place group homes in certain locations despite arguably contrary language in restrictive covenants and zoning ordinances?

3. In recent years, the law has placed increasing duties on sellers of real property regarding the quality of their property, such as the implied warranty of habitability and a seller's duty to disclose hidden defects in property. Do these developments constitute steps in the right direction? Should the law go farther and impose the implied warranty of habitability on all sellers, not just on builder-vendors and developers? Should it require disclosure of all defects, not just hidden ones?

PROBLEMS AND PROBLEM CASES

1. In 1971, Swafford bought three metal buildings and installed them on his ranch. The buildings included (1) a horse barn with a dirt floor middle; (2) an office, a trophy room, and a tack room; and (3) an open-air hay shed with no siding. The buildings were prefabricated at a factory and were assembled at the ranch by Swafford's agent and bolted to concrete slabs. They were never moved after their assembly and installation. In 1973, Swafford mortgaged the property to Kerman. Swafford later defaulted on the debt, and Kerman instituted foreclosure proceedings. Kerman bought the ranch at the foreclosure sale. Swafford claims that the portable buildings belong to him and that he can remove them. Do they belong to Swafford?

2. In 1957 or 1958, the Hibbards cleared their land of overgrowth and set up a trailer park. There was no obvious boundary between their land and that of their neighbor to the east, so the Hibbards cleared the land up to a deep drainage ditch. They also built a road for use in entering and leaving the trailer park. In 1960, the Hibbards' neighbor, McMurray, discovered through a survey that the Hibbards had encroached on his land (the eastern parcel) by 20 feet. He so informed the Hibbards. The western parcel later changed hands several times until the Sanderses bought it in 1976. The use of the western parcel changed little over the years. The road remained in continuous use in connection with the trailer park. The area between the road and the drainage ditch was also used by trailer park residents for parking, storage, garbage removal, and picnicking. Trailer personnel and tenants mowed grass up to the drainage ditch and planted flowers. The Sanderses installed underground wiring and surface power poles in the area between the road and the drainage ditch. In 1978, the Chaplins bought the eastern parcel. Shortly thereafter, they had a survey conducted. This survey revealed the Sanderses' encroachments. The Chaplins then sued to quiet title to the road and its shoulder (Parcel A) and the area between the road and the drainage ditch (Parcel B). With 10 years being the relevant possession period under state law, the Sanderses asserted that they owned Parcels A and B by virtue of adverse possession. Were the Sanderses correct?

3. The Wakes owned a tract of land. They used one part of the tract as a farm and the other part as a cattle ranch. Each spring and fall, the Wakes drove cattle from the ranch over an access road on the farm to Butler Springs, which was also located on the farm. From Butler Springs, they ranged the cattle eastward to adjacent government land, where they held grazing rights. In December 1956, the Wakes sold the farm portion of the land on contract to the Hesses. The contract of sale expressly reserved an easement in the Wakes to use the Butler Springs water and the right-of-way from Butler Springs across the property to the federal land. The contract described the Butler Springs area but did not describe the access road leading to Butler Springs from the county road. In 1963, the Hesses sold the farm to the Johnsons. These parties' contract referred to the Wakes' easement. The Wakes continued to use the access road and Butler Springs until 1964, when they sold their ranch and granted the Butler Springs easement to the purchasers. The ranch later changed hands several times, but each owner continued to use the access road and Butler Springs. In 1978, shortly after the Nelsons bought the ranch, the Johnsons sent them a letter "revoking permission" to use the access road. The Johnsons later placed locks on the gates across the access road. The Nelsons alleged that they had easement rights in the Butler Springs area and the access road leading to it. Were they correct?

4. Major developed a subdivision in which he built a number of houses and offered them for sale. The Rozells bought one of the houses. Upon the first rain, water entered under the crawl space of the house. Water then accumulated to a depth of 17 inches in a room where the furnace and water heater were located. This frequently caused the water heater not to work. Major's attempts to keep the water out were unsuccessful. Water continued to accumulate in the room whenever there was a rainfall of any consequence. As a result, the house was damp and had a peculiar odor. Mildew also became a problem. Did the Rozells have a cause of action against Major? If so, what cause of action?

5. A restrictive covenant applicable to most lots in an industrial park was recorded in 1957. The restrictive covenant prohibited property improvements taller than 45 feet. It also forbade billboards and advertising signs except those identifying the name, business, and products of the person or firm occupying the property on which the billboards or signs appeared. In other words, billboards or signs promoting businesses located elsewhere (off-premises advertising) were prohibited. The City of Rolling Meadows acquired property in the industrial park in 1960. Shortly thereafter, approximately one tenth of the park's 201 acres were condemned so that a new public highway, Route 53, could run through the park. National Advertising Company and Universal Outdoor, Inc., leased industrial park property during the 1980s and began constructing billboards on their leased property. They intended these billboards to be between 49 and 56 feet tall and available for advertising use by other businesses (i.e., for off-premises advertising). The City of Rolling Meadows learned of the restrictive covenant shortly after construction of the billboards began. The city then filed suit against National and Universal in an effort to enforce the restrictive covenant and halt the billboard construction. National and Universal argued, among other things, that the character of the industrial park area had changed

substantially and that the restrictive covenant therefore should no longer be enforceable. As of the time of the litigation, Route 53 was a six-lane highway carrying approximately 100,000 to 150,000 cars per day through the industrial park. Was there a sufficient change in circumstances to justify a conclusion that the restrictive covenant was no longer enforceable?

6. The Parkers used part of their property for housing, breeding, raising, and selling German shepherd dogs. As many as 25 dogs were on the Parkers' property at one time. Many of the dogs were trained as guard, protection, or attack dogs. The dogs' barking and offensive odors annoyed adjacent property owners. The Parkers sometimes let some of the dogs wander around the neighborhood unsupervised. This caused neighbors to be concerned about the safety of their children. The Parkers' property was subject to a restriction prohibiting noxious or offensive activity and providing that no animal could be raised, bred, or kept for any purpose other than serving as household pets. Three owners of adjacent homes brought suit against the Parkers, seeking to have them enjoined from keeping a number of dogs. The Parkers argued that the subdivision restriction did not prohibit them from keeping the dogs. Were the neighbors entitled to obtain an injunction against the Parkers? If so, on what grounds?

7. Davis bought a 12-acre tract of land in 1967. The tract was landlocked, although it had some frontage on Beaver Lake, a navigable watercourse. At one time, a single owner, Clark, had owned all the land now owned by Davis, her neighbors the Attaways, and others in the area. At first, Davis reached her property by using an old trail across the Attaways' property and another tract. In 1975, however, the Attaways put in a gate to obstruct the trail. After that, Davis walked to her land. She later filed suit to acquire a right-of-way giving her access from a public road (Walnut Road) to her land. Was Davis entitled to such access?

8. Elliot and Davis owned property in Athens, Georgia, where the University of Georgia is located. Their property was in an area whose residential-purpose zoning allowed an unlimited number of related persons to occupy the same residence but no more than four unrelated persons to occupy the same residence. Elliott and Davis sought to sell their property to The Potter's House, an entity that planned to operate an alcohol and drug rehabilitation center on the property. This center would house 12 rehabilitation program participants (all unrelated persons) plus an employee of The Potter's House. The rehabilitation center therefore would not have complied with applicable zoning. The sale from Elliott and Davis to The Potter's House was conditional on the ability to obtain zoning changes to accommodate the rehabilitation center. After the City of Athens refused requests that the area's zoning be altered to accommodate the rehabilitation center, Elliott, Davis, and The Potter's House sued the city on the theory that the city's refusal to make a zoning accommodation violated the federal Fair Housing Act's provisions prohibiting discrimination on the basis of handicap. All parties to the case agreed that the rehabilitation center's inhabitants would be considered handicapped for purposes of the Fair Housing Act. The city argued, however, that it qualified for an exemption set forth in the Fair Housing Act for reasonable maximum occupancy restrictions imposed by local law. According to the city, its ordinance restricting the number of unrelated persons who could live together was designed to regulate the large university student population in Athens and to guard against extreme density-oriented problems in areas near the University of Georgia. Was the zoning ordinance a reasonable maximum occupancy restriction exempting the city from responsibility under the Fair Housing Act?

9. Glover and Santangelo owned adjacent parcels of property in Oregon. Both lots were on a hillside allowing views of Mt. Shasta, Lake Ewana, and the downtown area of Klamath Falls. Santangelo's lot (Lot 10), which was on the downhill side of Glover's lot (Lot 9), was encumbered by a restrictive covenant executed at a time when Glover's house was almost completed and Lot 10 was bare. The covenant prohibited any second story from ever being erected on any building in a specified area of Lot 10. The covenant expressly stated that it was intended to run with the land and that it was executed "so that the value of Lot 9 as a 'view lot' would not be impaired" by future construction on Lot 10. Santangelo began construction on his house, a substantial proportion of which lay in the portion of Lot 10 that was covered by the restrictive covenant. The house consisted of a main level and a "daylight basement." On the uphill side of the house, approximately one third of the basement was constructed above what would have been the original grade of the property. This basement had windows on the uphill side. The main floor was raised several feet off the ground. The house substantially impaired Glover's western view, but did not disturb Glover's view to the south, across another neighbor's land. As it became apparent to Glover that the house would impair his western view, he attempted to halt the construction. With full knowledge of Glover's complaint, Santangelo proceeded to complete the house. What legal rights did Glover have in this case?

10. Emma Yocum was married to James Yocum as of the time of her death in 1990. She and James had begun living together in March 1959. In July 1959, by way of a warranty deed that referred to them as "husband and wife," Emma and James took ownership of a home. She and James, however, were not yet married. Emma was still married to Joseph Perez, from whom she was divorced in April 1960. Emma and James were married in July 1960. When they acquired their home in 1959, James had provided the down payment. A mortgage executed by Emma and James at that time also referred to them as husband and wife even though they were not then married. After Emma's death in 1990, her children by her marriage to Joseph Perez filed suit in an effort to have the court determine present ownership of the home Emma and James had owned during her lifetime. Had Emma and James owned the home as *tenants in common* (meaning that Emma's interest in the property would pass to her estate, in which her children were entitled to share), or instead as either *tenants by the entirety* or *joint tenants* (meaning that James would then solely own the home by virtue of the right of survivorship)?

11. The Duchaines leased their property to Southern Massachusetts Broadcasters for a five-year period. While occupying the leased property, Southern installed a radio tower, which it used to transmit radio broadcasts. The tower was a 390-foot steel-frame structure that stood on three legs and was attached by iron bolts to five-foot-square cement foundations. Although it was possible to remove the tower from the property, Southern neither attempted to remove it nor claimed the right to do so until two and one-quarter years after vacating the Duchaines' property. Southern then filed suit, claiming ownership of the tower. Was Southern entitled to prevail?

CHAPTER

25

LANDLORD AND TENANT

INTRODUCTION

Landlord-tenant law has undergone dramatic change during the past two decades, due in large part to the changing nature of the relationship between landlords and tenants. In England and in early America, farms were the usual subjects of leases. The tenant's primary object was to lease land on which to grow crops or graze cattle. Accordingly, traditional landlord-tenant law viewed the lease as primarily a conveyance of land and paid relatively little attention to its contractual aspects.

In today's industrialized society, however, the landlord-tenant relationship is typified by the lease of property for residential or commercial purposes. The tenant occupies only a small portion of the total property. He bargains primarily for the use of structures on the land rather than for the land itself. He is likely to have signed a form lease provided by the landlord, the terms of which he may have had little opportunity to negotiate. In areas with a shortage of affordable housing, a residential tenant's ability to bargain for favorable lease provisions is further hampered. Because the typical landlord-tenant relationship can no longer fairly be characterized as one in which the parties have equal knowledge and bargaining power, it is not always realistic to presume that tenants are capable of negotiating to protect their own interests.

Although it was initially slow to recognize the changing nature of the landlord-tenant relationship, the law now tends to place greater emphasis than it once did on the contract components of the relationship. As a result, modern contract doctrines such as unconscionability, constructive conditions, the duty to mitigate damages, and implied warranties are applied to leases. Such doctrines may operate to compensate for tenants' lack of bargaining power. In addition, state legislatures and city councils have enacted statutes and ordinances that increasingly regulate leased property and the landlord-tenant relationship.

This chapter's discussion of landlord-tenant law will focus on the nature of leasehold interests, the traditional rights and duties of landlords and tenants, and recent statutory and judicial developments affecting those rights and duties.

LEASES AND TENANCIES

Nature of Leases

A **lease** is a contract under which an owner of property, the **landlord** (also called the *lessor*), conveys to the **tenant** (also called the *lessee*) the exclusive right to possess property for a period of time. The property interest conveyed to the tenant is called a **leasehold estate.**

Types of Tenancies

The duration of the tenant's possessory right depends upon the type of **tenancy** established by or resulting from the lease. There are four main types of tenancies.

1. *Tenancy for a term.* In a **tenancy for a term** (also called a *tenancy for years*), the landlord and tenant have agreed on a specific duration of the lease and have fixed the date on which the tenancy will terminate. For example, if Dudley, a college student, leases an apartment for the academic year ending May 30, 1995, a tenancy for a term will have been created. The tenant's right to possess the property ends on the date agreed upon without any further notice, unless the lease contains a provision permitting extension.

2. *Periodic tenancy.* A **periodic tenancy** is created when the parties agree that rent will be paid in regular successive intervals until notice to terminate is given, but do not agree on a specific lease duration. If the tenant pays rent monthly, the tenancy is from month to month; if the tenant pays yearly, as is sometimes done under agricultural leases, the tenancy is from year to year. (Periodic tenancies therefore are sometimes called *tenancies from month to month* or *tenancies from year to year*.) To terminate a periodic tenancy, either party must give advance notice to the other. The precise amount of notice required is often defined by state statutes. For example, to terminate a tenancy from month to month, most states require that the notice be given at least one month in advance.

3. *Tenancy at will.* A **tenancy at will** occurs when property is leased for an indefinite period of time and either party may choose to conclude the tenancy at any time. Generally, tenancies at will involve situations in which the tenant either does not pay rent or does not pay it at regular intervals. For example, Landon allows her friend Trumbull to live in the apartment over her garage. Although this tenancy's name indicates that it is terminable "at [the] will" of either party, most states require that the landlord give reasonable advance notice to the tenant before exercising the right to terminate the tenancy.

4. *Tenancy at sufferance.* A **tenancy at sufferance** occurs when a tenant remains in possession of the property (holds over) after a lease has expired. In this situation, the landlord has two options: (1) treating the holdover tenant as a trespasser and bringing an action to eject him; and (2) continuing to treat him as a tenant and collecting rent from him. Until the landlord makes her election, the tenant is a tenant at sufferance. Suppose that Templeton has leased an apartment for one year from Larson. At the end of the year, Templeton holds over and does not move out. Templeton is a tenant at sufferance. Larson may have him ejected or may continue treating him as a tenant. If Larson elects the latter alternative, a new tenancy is created. The new tenancy will be either a tenancy for a term or a periodic tenancy, depending on the facts of the case and any presumptions established by state law. Thus, a tenant who holds over for even a few days runs the risk of creating a new tenancy he might not want.

CONCEPT REVIEW

TYPES OF TENANCIES

Type of Lease	Characteristics	Termination
Tenancy for a Term	Landlord and tenant agree on a specific duration of the lease and fix the date on which the tenancy will end	Ends automatically on the date agreed upon; no additional notice necessary
Periodic Tenancy	Landlord and tenant agree that tenant will pay rent at regular, successive intervals (e.g., month to month)	Either party may terminate by giving the amount of advance notice required by state law

Type of Lease	Characteristics	Termination
Tenancy at Will	Landlord and tenant agree that tenant may possess property for an indefinite amount of time, with no agreement to pay rent at regular, successive intervals	May be terminated "at will" by either party, but state law requires advance notice
Tenancy at Sufferance	Tenant remains in possession after the termination of one of the leaseholds described above, until landlord has brought ejectment action against tenant or collected rent from him	Landlord has choice of: 1. Treating tenant as a trespasser and bringing ejectment action against him, or 2. Accepting rent from tenant, thus creating a new leasehold

Execution of a Lease

As transfers of interests in land, leases may be covered by the statute of frauds. In most states, a lease for a term of more than one year from the date it is made is unenforceable unless it is evidenced by a suitable writing signed by the party to be charged. A few states, however, require leases to be evidenced by a writing only when they are for a term of more than three years.

Good business practice demands that leases be carefully drafted to make clear the parties' respective rights and obligations. Care in drafting leases is especially important in cases of long-term and commercial leases. Lease provisions normally cover such essential matters as the term of the lease, the rent to be paid, the uses the tenant may make of the property, the circumstances under which the landlord may enter the property, the parties' respective obligations regarding the condition of the property, and the responsibility (as between landlord and tenant) for making repairs. In addition, leases often contain provisions allowing a possible extension of the term of the lease and purporting to limit the parties' rights to assign the lease or sublet the property. State or local law often regulates lease terms. For example, the Uniform Residential Landlord and Tenant Act (URLTA) has been enacted in a substantial minority of states. The URLTA prohibits the inclusion of certain lease provisions, such as a clause by which the tenant supposedly agrees to pay the landlord's attorney's fees in an action to enforce the lease. In states that have not enacted the URLTA, lease terms are likely to be regulated at least to a moderate degree by some combination of state statutes, common law principles, and local housing codes.

RIGHTS, DUTIES, AND LIABILITIES OF THE LANDLORD

Landlord's Rights

The landlord is entitled to receive the *agreed rent* for the term of the lease. Upon expiration of the lease, the landlord has the right to the *return of the property in as good a condition as it was when leased,* except for normal wear and tear and any destruction caused by an act of God.

Security Deposits Landlords commonly require tenants to make security deposits or advance payments of rent. Such deposits operate to protect the landlord's right to receive rent as well as her right to reversion of the property in good condition. In recent years, many cities and states have enacted statutes or ordinances designed to prevent landlord abuse of security deposits. These laws typically limit the amount a landlord may demand and require that the security deposit be refundable, except for portions withheld by the landlord due to the tenant's nonpayment of rent or tenant-caused property damage beyond ordinary wear and tear. Some statutes or ordinances also require the landlord to place the funds in interest-bearing accounts when the lease is for more than a minimal period of time. As a general rule, these laws require landlords to provide tenants a written accounting regarding their security deposits and any portions being withheld. Such an accounting normally must be provided within a specified period of time (30 days, for example) after the termination of the lease. The landlord's failure to comply with statutes and ordinances regarding security deposits may cause the landlord to experience adverse consequences that vary state by state.

Landlord's Duties

Fair Housing Act
As explained in Chapter 24, the Fair Housing Act prohibits housing discrimination on the basis of race, color, sex, religion, national origin, handicap, and familial status.[1] The Fair Housing Act prohibits discriminatory practices in various transactions affecting housing, including the rental of dwellings.[2] Included within the act's prohibited instances of discrimination against a protected person are refusals to rent property to such a person, discrimination against him or her in the terms, conditions, or privileges of rental, publication of any advertisement or statement indicating any preference, limitation, or discrimination operating to the disadvantage of a protected person, and representations that a dwelling is not available for rental to such a person when, in fact, it is available.

The act also makes it a discriminatory practice for a landlord to refuse to permit a tenant with a handicap to make—at his own expense—reasonable modifications to leased property. The landlord may, however, condition this permission on the tenant's agreement to restore the property to its previous condition upon termination of the lease, reasonable wear and tear excepted. In addition, landlords are prohibited from refusing to make reasonable accommodations in rules, policies, practices, or services if such accommodations are necessary to afford a handicapped tenant equal opportunity to use and enjoy the leased premises. When constructing certain types of multifamily housing for first occupancy, property owners and developers risk violating the act if they fail to make the housing accessible to persons with handicaps.

Due to a perceived increase in the frequency with which landlords would refuse to rent to families with children, the act prohibits landlords from excluding families with children. If, however, the dwelling falls within the act's "housing for older persons" exception, this prohibition does not apply.[3]

In *Walker v. Crigler,* which follows, the court demonstrates the importance of the public policy notions underlying the Fair Housing Act by holding that a property owner may be held liable for his agent's discriminatory actions even if the property owner has instructed the agent to comply with applicable anti-discrimination laws.

[1]Familial status is defined in Chapter 24.

[2]The act provides an exemption for certain persons who own and rent single-family houses. To qualify for this exemption, owners must not use a real estate broker or an illegal advertisement and cannot own more than three such houses at one time. It also exempts owners who rent rooms or units in dwellings in which they themselves reside, if those dwellings house no more than four families.

[3]The "housing for older persons" exception is described in Chapter 24.

WALKER V. CRIGLER
976 F.2d 900 (4th Cir. 1992)

Alleging that the following facts amounted to discrimination on the basis of sex in the rental of housing and that the Fair Housing Act was therefore violated, Darlene Walker filed suit against property owner Frank Whitesell and his property manager, Constance Crigler. Walker, a single mother of one son, worked in Falls Church, Virginia and wished to rent an apartment there for herself and her son. In July 1989, Walker sought the assistance of the Town and Country Properties (TCP) firm. TCP agents showed Walker the Multiple Listing Service (MLS) listings of available rental properties in Falls Church. After reviewing these listings, Walker became interested in an apartment located at 124 Falls Avenue. Whitesell owned this property. Crigler, a professional realtor, served as Whitesell's property manager for 124 Falls Avenue and other rental properties owned by Whitesell. Crigler's responsibilities included finding financially-qualified tenants for Whitesell's properties.

The MLS listing for 124 Falls Avenue specified $600 per month as the rent and described the property as a two-bedroom apartment that was "ideal for two men." Walker decided that she wanted to rent the apartment because it was close to a school for her son and was accessible to public transportation facilities. A TCP agent testified at trial that when he told Crigler he intended to submit the rental application of a financially-qualified single mother (Walker), Crigler stated that she would not rent to a female applicant under any circumstances. Another TCP agent contacted Crigler on Walker's behalf; Crigler reiterated her policy of not renting to women. Walker testified that when she personally telephoned Crigler regarding the apartment, Crigler stated essentially the same thing and added that in the past, boyfriends of single female tenants had caused problems. Roughly two months after these conversations took place, the 124 Falls Avenue apartment was rented to two men who paid a total monthly rent of $580—$20 per month less than what Walker had been willing to pay.

Crigler testified that she never told anyone she would not rent the apartment to a single woman. The evidence revealed that in January 1989 (approximately six months before Walker's unsuccessful attempt to rent the apartment), Whitesell's awareness of housing discrimination suits against landlords caused him to send Crigler a memorandum instructing her to comply with applicable antidiscrimination laws in screening possible tenants for his rental properties.

An instruction given by the trial judge to the jury stated that if the jury found Fair Housing Act violations on Crigler's part, Whitesell would also be liable if Crigler was Whitesell's agent and was acting within the scope of her employment at the time she engaged in discrimination. The jury returned a verdict in Walker's favor against Crigler for $5,000 in compensatory damages. The jury ruled in Whitesell's favor, however, on Walker's claim against him. The trial judge denied Walker's motions for judgment notwithstanding the verdict and for a new trial. Walker appealed.

––––––––––– ■ –––––––––––

Murnaghan, Circuit Judge   The jury ruled in Whitesell's favor, holding, apparently, that Crigler [despite clearly being Whitesell's agent] was not acting in the scope of her employment when she denied Walker's attempts to rent the 124 Falls Avenue premises because Walker was a woman. The sole evidence to support the jury's conclusion that Whitesell was not liable for damages for the discrimination was the evidence indicating that Crigler was instructed not to refuse to rent on discriminatory grounds. In denying the motion for judgment notwithstanding the verdict, the trial judge concluded that the evidence of Whitesell's instruction was sufficient to support the jury's verdict. We find, however, that the court's conclusion is based on an erroneous theory of law. Since there is no unsettled question of fact to be submitted for decision by the jury, it is appropriate to reverse the judgment that Whitesell was not liable for compensatory damages and to direct entry of judgment against Whitesell in Walker's favor in the amount of $5,000.

The evidence is sufficient to support the conclusion that Whitesell specifically intended that Crigler not discriminate. In many cases involving issues other than housing discrimination, such a finding would refute the assertion that Crigler acted within the scope of employment and would concurrently shield Whitesell from any liability as principal. However, the arguable conclusion that Crigler acted outside the scope of employment is irrelevant in the present case, for Whitesell could not insulate himself from liability for sex discrimination in regard to living premises owned by him and managed for his benefit merely by relinquishing the responsibility for preventing such discrimination to another party. We adopt the general rule applied by other federal courts that the duty of a property owner not to discriminate in the leasing or sale of that property is nondelegable.

We are not unmindful of the arguable incongruity of applying liability to Whitesell and . . . similarly situated [property owners] who are apparently non-culpable in a housing discrimination instance but must still bear the burden of liability. The central question to be decided in a case such as this, however, is which innocent party—the owner whose agent acted contrary to his instruction, or the potential renter who felt the direct harm of the agent's discriminatory failure to offer the residence for rental—will ultimately bear the burden of the harm caused. It is clear that the overriding societal priority of the provision of "fair housing throughout the United States" (clearly set out in the Fair Housing Act) indicates that the one innocent party with the power to control the acts of the agent—the owner of the property or other responsible superior—must act to compensate the injured party for the harm and to ensure that similar harm will not occur in the future.

It must not be overlooked that although the property owner's duty to prevent discrimination is nondelegable, the owner [usually] will not be subjected to liability for the full amount of all successful claims, [because] contribution from other liable parties may offset some or all of the payment for which the owner is responsible. [Although Crigler, in a separate legal proceeding, filed for bankruptcy and obtained a discharge of her judgment debt to Walker and any contribution-related obligation to Whitesell,] we may assume in the great majority of cases that real estate agents will not turn bankrupt or otherwise [become] judgment-proof. They will remain liable for damages flowing from flaunting a principal's intentions.

Just as we feel no qualms in holding a property owner responsible for paying property taxes, meeting health code safety requirements, or ensuring that other responsibilities to protect the public are met—

and we refuse to allow the owner to avoid these responsibilities with an assertion that he conferred the duty to another—we must hold those who benefit from the sale and rental of property to the public to the specific mandates of antidiscrimination law if the goal of equal housing opportunity is to be reached. Whitesell, despite forbidding discrimination on the part of Crigler, cannot, under the Fair Housing Act, dispose of his duty to prevent sexual discrimination in the rental of 124 Falls Avenue, a property which he owned and which was operated for his benefit.

Judgment in favor of Whitesell reversed; trial court ordered to enter judgment in favor of Walker and against Whitesell for $5,000 in compensatory damages.

Implied Warranty of Possession

Landlords have certain obligations that are imposed by law whenever property is leased. One of these obligations stems from the landlord's **implied warranty of possession**. This warranty guarantees the tenant's right to possess the property for the term of the lease. Suppose that Turner rents an apartment from Long for a term to begin on September 1, 1994, and to end on August 31, 1995. When Turner attempts to move in on September 1, 1994, she finds that Carlson, the previous tenant, is still in possession of the property. In this case, Long has breached the implied warranty of possession.

Implied Warranty of Quiet Enjoyment

By leasing property, the landlord also makes an **implied warranty of quiet enjoyment** (or *covenant of quiet enjoyment*). This covenant guarantees that the tenant's possession will not be interfered with as a result of the landlord's act or omission. In the absence of an emergency that threatens the property or a contrary provision in the lease, the landlord may not enter the leased property during the term of the lease. If he does, he will be liable for trespass. In some cases, courts have held that the covenant of quiet enjoyment was violated when the landlord failed to stop third parties, such as trespassers or other tenants who make excessive noise, from interfering with the tenant's enjoyment of the leased premises.

Constructive Eviction

The doctrine of **constructive eviction** may aid a tenant when property becomes unsuitable for the purposes for which it was leased because of the landlord's act or omission, such as the breach of a duty to repair or the covenant of quiet enjoyment. Under this doctrine, which applies both to residential and commercial property, the tenant may terminate the lease because he has effectively been evicted as a result of the poor condition or the objectionable circumstances there. Constructive eviction gives a tenant the right to vacate the property without further rent obligation if he does so *promptly* after giving the landlord reasonable notice and an opportunity to correct the problem. Because constructive eviction requires the tenant to vacate the leased premises, it is an unattractive option, however, for tenants who cannot afford to move or do not have a suitable alternative place to live.

Landlord's Responsibility for Condition of Leased Property

The common law historically held that landlords made no implied warranties regarding the *condition* or *quality* of leased premises. As an adjunct to the landlord's right to receive the leased property in good condition at the termination of the lease, the common law imposed on the *tenant* the duty to make repairs. Even when the lease contained a landlord's express warranty or express promise to make repairs, a tenant was not entitled to withhold rent if the landlord failed to carry out his obligations. This was because a fundamental contract performance principle—that a party is not obligated to perform if the other party fails to perform—was considered inapplicable to leases. In recent years, however, changing views of the landlord-tenant relationship have resulted in dramatically increased legal responsibility on the part of landlords for the condition of leased residential property.

Implied Warranty of Habitability   The legal principle that landlords made no implied warranty regarding the condition of leased property arose during an era when tenants used land primarily for agricultural purposes. Buildings existing on the property were frequently of secondary importance. They also tended to be simple structures, lacking modern conveniences such as plumbing and wiring. These buildings were fairly easily inspected and repaired by the tenant, who was generally more self-sufficient than today's typical tenant. In view of the relative simplicity of the structures, landlord and tenant were considered to have equal knowledge of the property's condition upon commencement of the lease. Thus, a rule requiring the tenant to make repairs seemed reasonable.

The position of modern residential tenants differs greatly from that of an earlier era's agricultural tenants. The modern residential tenant bargains not for the use of the ground itself, but for the use of a building (or portion thereof) as a dwelling. The structures on land today are complex, frequently involving systems (such as plumbing and electrical systems) to which the tenant does not have physical access. Besides decreasing the likelihood of perceiving defects during inspection, this complexity compounds the difficulty of making repairs—something at which today's tenant already tends to be less adept than his grandparents were. Moreover, placing a duty on tenants to negotiate for express warranties and duties to repair is no longer feasible. Residential leases are now routinely executed on standard forms provided by landlords.

For these reasons, statutes or judicial decisions in most states now impose an **implied warranty of habitability** on landlords leasing residential property. According to the vast majority of cases, this warranty is applicable only to *residential* property, and not to property leased for commercial uses. The implied warranty of habitability's content in lease settings is basically the same as in the sale of real estate—the property must be safe and suitable for human habitation. In lease settings, however, the landlord not only must deliver a habitable dwelling at the beginning of the lease but also must *maintain* the property in a habitable condition during the term of the lease. Various statutes and judicial decisions provide that the warranty includes an obligation that the leased property comply with any applicable housing codes. From a tenant's point of view, the implied warranty of habitability is superior to constructive eviction because a tenant does not have to vacate the leased premises in order to seek a remedy for breach of the warranty.

Remedies for Breach of Implied Warranty of Habitability   The particular remedies for breach of the implied warranty of habitability differ from state to state. Some of the remedies a tenant may pursue include:

1. *Action for damages.* The breach of the implied warranty of habitability violates the lease and renders the landlord liable for damages. The damages generally are measured by the diminished value of the leasehold. The landlord's breach of the implied warranty of habitability may also be asserted by the tenant as a counterclaim and defense in the landlord's action for eviction and/or nonpayment of rent.

2. *Termination of lease.* In extreme cases, the landlord's breach of the implied warranty of habitability may justify the tenant's termination of the lease. For this remedy to be appropriate, the landlord's breach must have been substantial enough to constitute a material breach.

3. *Rent abatement.* Some states permit rent abatement, a remedy under which the tenant withholds part of the rent for the period during which the landlord was in breach of the implied warranty of habitability. Where authorized by law, this approach allows the tenant to pay a reduced rent that reflects the *actual* value of the leasehold in its defective condition. There are different ways of computing this value. State law determines the amount by which the rent will be reduced.

4. *Repair-and-deduct.* A growing number of states have statutes permitting the tenant to have defects repaired and to deduct the repair costs from her rent. The repairs authorized in these statutes are usually limited to essential services such as electricity and plumbing. They also require that the tenant give the landlord notice of the defect and an adequate opportunity to make the repairs himself.

Housing Codes   Many cities and states have enacted housing codes that impose duties on property owners with respect to the condition of leased property. Typical of these provisions is Section 2304 of the District of Columbia Housing Code, which provides: "No person shall rent or offer to rent any habitation or the furnishing thereof unless such habitation and its furnishings are in a clean, safe and sanitary condition, in repair and free from rodents or vermin." Such codes commonly call for the provision and maintenance of necessary services such as heat, water, and electricity, as well as suitable bathroom and kitchen facilities. Housing codes also usually require that specified minimum space-per-tenant standards be met, that windows, doors, floors, and screens be kept in repair, that the property be painted and free of lead paint, that keys and locks meet certain specifications, and that the landlord issue written receipts for rent payments. A landlord's failure to comply with an applicable housing code may result in a fine or in liability for injuries resulting from the property's disrepair. The noncompliance may also result in the landlord's losing part or all of his claim to the agreed-upon rent. Some housing codes establish that tenants have the right to withhold rent until necessary repairs have been made and the right to move out in cases of particularly egregious violations of housing code requirements. As revealed by the following *Breezewood Management* case, the violation of an applicable housing code may also give rise to or strengthen a tenant's claim that the implied warranty of habitability was breached.

BREEZEWOOD MANAGEMENT COMPANY V. MALTBIE
411 N.E.2d 670 (Ind. Ct. App. 1980)

On August 2, 1978, Dan Maltbie and John Burke, students at Indiana University, entered into a one-year written lease with Breezewood Management Company for the rental of an apartment in an older house in Bloomington, Indiana. The agreed rent was $235 per month. When Burke and Maltbie moved in, they discovered numerous defects: rotting porch floorboards, broken and loose windows, an inoperable front door lock, leaks in the plumbing, a back door that would not close, a missing bathroom door, inadequate water pressure, falling plaster, exposed wiring over the bathtub, and a malfunctioning toilet. Later, they discovered more leaks in the plumbing, a leaking roof, the absence of heat and hot water, cockroach infestation, and pigeons in the attic.

The City of Bloomington had a housing code in effect at that time. Code enforcement officers inspected the apartment and found over 50 violations, 11 of which were "life-safety" violations (defined as conditions that might be severely "hazardous to health of the occupant"). These conditions remained largely uncorrected after notice by the code officers and further complaints by Burke and Maltbie.

On May 3, 1979, Maltbie vacated the apartment, notified Breezewood, and refused to pay any further rent. Breezewood agreed to let Burke remain and pay $112.50 per month. Breezewood then filed suit against Burke and Maltbie for $610.75, which was the balance due under the written rental contract plus certain charges. Burke and Maltbie each filed counterclaims against Breezewood, claiming damages and abatement of the rent for breach of the implied warranty of habitability. At trial, Burke and Maltbie presented evidence showing that the reasonable rental value of the apartment in its defective condition was only $50 per month during colder weather and $75 per month during warmer weather. The trial court entered judgment against Breezewood on its claim and awarded Burke and Maltbie a total of $1,030 in damages on their counterclaims. Breezewood appealed.

Robertson, Presiding Judge Over time, many exceptions have eroded the common law doctrine of *caveat lessee*. In most circumstances, the modern tenant lacks the skill and "know-how" to inspect and repair housing to determine whether it is fit for its particular purpose. In *Boston Housing Authority v. Hemingway*, the court treated the lease agreement as a contract in which the landlord promised to deliver premises suitable to the tenant's purpose in return for the tenant's promise to pay rent. In *Javins v. First National Realty Corporation*, the United States Court of Appeals for the District of Columbia found an implied warranty of habitability in the lease agreement, the minimum habitability standards being established by the Housing Regulations for the District of Columbia. The court stated that landlord-tenant law should be governed by the same implied warranty of fitness which covers a sale of goods under the Uniform Commercial Code. The court said:

In the case of the modern apartment dweller, the value of the lease is that it gives him a place to live. The city dweller who seeks to lease an apartment on the third floor of a tenement has little interest in the land 30 or 40 feet below, or even in the bare right to possession within the four walls of his apartment. When American city dwellers seek shelter today, they seek a well known package of goods and services—a package which includes not merely walls and ceilings, but also adequate heat, light, and ventilation, serviceable plumbing facilities, secure windows and doors, proper sanitation, and proper maintenance.

In the case at bar, the Bloomington Housing Code was in effect at the time of the lease agreement, and, by law, was incorporated into it. Burke and Maltbie had a reasonable expectation that their basic housing needs would be met: heating, plumbing, electricity, and structural integrity of the premises. For the reasons that a housing code was in effect and the premises violated many of its provisions, we hold that Breezewood breached an implied warranty of habitability.

Judgment for Burke and Maltbie affirmed.

Americans with Disabilities Act Landlords leasing property constituting a *place of public accommodation* (primarily commercial property as opposed to private residential property) must pay heed to Title III of the Americans with Disabilities Act. Under Title III, owners and possessors of real property that is a place of public accommodation may be expected to make reasonable accommodations, including physical modifications of the property, in order to allow disabled persons to have access to the property. Chapter 24 contains a detailed discussion of Title III's provisions.

Landlord's Tort Liability

Traditional No-Liability Rule There were two major effects of the traditional rule that a landlord had no legal responsibility for the condition. The first effect—that the uninhabitability of the premises traditionally did not give a tenant the right to withhold rent, assert a defense to nonpayment, or terminate a lease—has already been discussed. The second effect was that landlords normally could not be held liable in tort for injuries suffered by tenants on leased property. This state of affairs stemmed from the notion that the tenant had the ability and responsibility to inspect the property for defects before leasing it. By leasing the property, the tenant was presumed to take it as it was, with any existing defects. As to any defects that might arise during the term of the lease, the landlord's tort immunity was seen as justified by his lack of control over the leased property once he had surrendered it to the tenant.

Traditional Exceptions to No-Liability Rule Even before the current era's pro-tenant legal developments, however, courts created exceptions to the no-liability rule. In the following situations, landlords have traditionally owed the tenant (or an appropriate third party) a duty, the breach of which could constitute a tort:

1. *Duty to maintain common areas.* Landlords have a duty to use reasonable care to *maintain the common areas* (such as stairways, parking lots, and elevators) over which they retain control. If a tenant or a tenant's guest sustains injury as a result of the landlord's negligent maintenance of a common area, the landlord is liable.

2. *Duty to disclose hidden defects.* Landlords have the duty to disclose hidden defects about which they know, if the defects are not reasonably discoverable by the tenant. The landlord is liable if a tenant or appropriate third party suffers injury because of a hidden danger that was known to the landlord but undisclosed.

3. *Duty to use reasonable care in performing repairs.* If a landlord repairs leased property, he must *exercise reasonable care in making the repairs*. The landlord may be liable for the consequences stemming from negligently performed repairs, even if he was not obligated to perform them.

4. *Duty to maintain property leased for admission to the public.* The landlord has a duty to suitably maintain property that is leased for *admission to the public*. A theater would be an example.

5. *Duty to maintain furnished dwellings.* The landlord who rents a *fully furnished dwelling* for a short time impliedly warrants that the premises are safe and habitable.

Except for the above circumstances, the landlord traditionally was not liable for injuries suffered by the tenant on leased property. Note that none of these exceptions would apply to one of the most common injury scenarios—when the tenant was injured by a defect in her own apartment and the defect resulted from the landlord's failure to repair rather than from negligently performed repairs.

Current Trends in Landlord's Tort Liability
Today, there is a strong trend toward abolition of the traditional rule of landlord tort immunity. The proliferation of housing codes and the development of the implied warranty of habitability have persuaded a sizable number of courts to impose on landlords the duty to use *reasonable care* in their maintenance of the leased property. As discussed earlier, a landlord's duty to keep the property in repair may be based on an express clause in the lease, the implied warranty of habitability, or provisions of a housing code or statute.

The landlord now may be liable if injury results from her negligent failure to carry out her duty to make repairs. As a general rule, a landlord will not be liable unless she had *notice* of the defect and a reasonable opportunity to make repairs.

The duty of care landlords owe tenants has been held to include the duty to take reasonable steps to protect tenants from substantial risks of harm created by other tenants. Courts have held landlords liable for tenants' injuries resulting from dangerous conditions (such as vicious animals) maintained by other tenants when the landlord knew or had reason to know of the danger.

It is not unusual for landlords to attempt to insulate themselves from negligence liability to tenants by including an *exculpatory clause* in the standard form leases they expect tenants to sign. An exculpatory clause purports to relieve the landlord from legal responsibility that the landlord could otherwise face (on negligence or other grounds) in certain instances of premises-related injuries suffered by tenants. In recent years, a number of state legislatures and courts have frowned upon exculpatory clauses when they are included in leases of residential property. The *Crawford v. Buckner* case, which follows shortly, illustrates the increasing judicial tendency to limit the effect of exculpatory clauses or declare them unenforceable on public policy grounds when they are included in residential leases.

Another area of possible future expansion of landlords' liability could be the application of product liability principles to the residential lease setting. The California Supreme Court, for instance, has held a landlord strictly liable for a tenant's physical injuries that resulted from a hidden defect present when the tenant leased the property.[4]

---

[4]*Becker v. IRM Corp.,* 213 Cal. Rptr. 213 (Cal. Sup. Ct. 1985).

CRAWFORD V. BUCKNER
839 S.W.2d 754 (Tenn. Sup.Ct. 1992)

In order to rent an apartment in a building owned by Tobe McKenzie and McKenzie Development Corporation (MDC), Linda Crawford was required to sign a standard form lease provided by McKenzie and MDC. This lease contained an exculpatory clause stating that McKenzie and MDC "shall not be liable" to Crawford "for any injury to [Crawford's] person or loss of or damage to property for any cause." Two months after Crawford rented the apartment (which was located on the building's second floor), a fire broke out in the first-floor apartment of Debra and Larry Buckner. The fire spread to Crawford's apartment and blocked Crawford from escaping through the front (and only) door of her apartment. To escape the fire, Crawford jumped from a second-story window. When she landed, she sustained numerous injuries, partly due to debris on the ground behind the apartment building.

Crawford filed a negligence suit against the Buckners, McKenzie, and MDC. She alleged that McKenzie and MDC were negligent in failing to maintain the building's fire alarm system, in failing to maintain the ground area behind the apartment building, and in continuing to allow the Buckners to reside in the apartment complex despite numerous complaints to McKenzie and MDC about the Buckners' behavior. McKenzie and MDC asserted that the exculpatory clause in their lease with Crawford barred her negligence claim against them. The trial court agreed and granted those defendants' motion for summary judgment. When Tennessee's intermediate court of appeals affirmed, Crawford appealed to the Tennessee Supreme Court.

Anderson, Justice   The determinative issue raised in this appeal is whether an exculpatory clause in a residential lease bars recovery against the landlord for negligence which caused the tenant injury. An exculpatory clause in the context of a landlord-tenant relationship refers to a clause which deprives the tenant of the right to recover damages . . . by releasing the landlord from liability for future acts of negligence. [T]he argument for enforceability of such clauses has often been based upon the doctrine of freedom of contract. Some cases, especially older ones, have reasoned that the relationship of landlord and tenant is in no event a matter of public interest, but is purely a private affair, so that such clauses cannot be held void on public policy grounds. However, because of the burden-shifting effect of such clauses, which [purport to] grant immunity from [liability], it is not surprising that their validity has been challenged and that courts have reached different conclusions as to their enforceability.

McKenzie and MDC contend that freedom to contract in the residential lease setting is the majority rule in the United States, and that holding exculpatory provisions in residential leases invalid on public policy grounds would require this court to adopt the minority rule. We find, as the Washington Supreme Court found in *McCutcheon v. United Homes Corp.* (1971), that there is no majority rule, "only numerous conflicting decisions . . . and a disposition of the courts to emasculate such exculpatory clauses by means of strict construction."

Tennessee courts have long recognized that, subject to certain exceptions, parties may contract that one shall not be liable for his negligence to another. We held in *Olson v. Molzen* (1977), however, that if an exculpatory provision [adversely affects] the public interest, it is void as against public policy, despite the general rule that parties may contract that one shall not be liable for his negligence to another. In *Olson,* we said that a exculpatory clause signed by a patient as a condition of receiving medical treatment is invalid as contrary to public policy and may not be pleaded as a bar to the patient's suit for negligence.

Crawford contends in this case that the exculpatory provision in her lease falls squarely within criteria set forth in *Olson* [and that] the exculpatory provision [should therefore be held] void as against public policy. In order to determine whether an exculpatory provision [adversely] affects the public interest, we adopted the following criteria in *Olson:*

1. It concerns a business of a type generally thought suitable for public regulation.

2. The party seeking exculpation is engaged in performing a service of great importance to the public (often a matter of practical necessity for some members of the public).

3. The party [seeking exculpation] holds himself out as willing to perform this service for any member of the public who seeks it, or at least for any member coming within certain established standards.

4. As a result of the essential nature of the service, in the economic setting of the transaction, the party invoking exculpation possesses a decisive advantage of bargaining strength against any member of the public who seeks his services.

5. In exercising a superior bargaining power, that party confronts the public with a standardized adhesion contract of exculpation, and makes no provision whereby a purchaser [or lessee] may pay additional reasonable fees and obtain protection against negligence.

6. As a result of the transaction, the person or property of the purchaser [or lessee] is placed under the control of the seller [or lessor], subject to the risk of carelessness by the seller [or lessor] or his agents.

In adopting these factors, we stated that "it is not necessary that all be present . . . , but generally a transaction that has some of these characteristics would be offensive."

[W]e conclude that a residential lease concerns a business of a type generally thought suitable for public regulation. Our conclusion is bolstered by the fact that the legislature of this state has seen fit to regulate [some aspects of the residential landlord-tenant relationship]. [W]e no longer live in a society where land, not housing, was the important part of a rental agreement. Residential landlords offer shelter, a basic necessity of life, to more than a million inhabitants of this state. Accordingly, it is self-evident that a residential landlord is engaged in performing a service of great importance to the public [and that this service] is often a matter of practical necessity for some members of the public. In addition, a residential landlord holds itself out as willing to perform a service for any member of the public who seeks it.

As a result of the essential nature of the service and the economic setting of the transaction, a residential landlord has a decisive advantage in bargaining strength against any member of the public who seeks its services. A potential tenant is usually confronted with a "take it or leave it" form contract, which the tenant is powerless to alter. Moreover, due to its superior bargaining position, a residential landlord confronts the public with a standardized adhesion contract of exculpation, which contains no provision whereby a tenant can pay additional reasonable fees to obtain protection from the landlord's negligence. Finally, we conclude that by definition, a residential lease places the person and the property of the tenant under the control of the landlord, subject to the risk of carelessness by the landlord and his agents. The allegations of this case [provide] common examples of landlord negligence [allegedly] causing injury to either the person or property of the tenant.

Accordingly, we find that the residential landlord-tenant relationship here satisfies all six of the public interest criteria adopted in *Olson v. Molzen.* However, McKenzie and MDC insist that a residential lease between a landlord and a tenant is a purely private affair. We disagree. We find persuasive the reasoning of the Washington Supreme Court, which, in response to the very same argument, stated:

[W]e are not faced merely with the theoretical duty of construing a provision in an isolated contract specifically bargained for by *one landlord and one tenant* as a purely *private affair.* Considered realistically, we are asked to construe an exculpatory clause, the generalized use of which may have an impact upon thousands of potential tenants.

McCutcheon v. United Homes Corp. (1971) (emphasis in original).

Based on the foregoing, we conclude that the exculpatory clause in the residential lease in this case is contrary to public policy. In reaching this conclusion, we join a growing number of states, [which either by statute or judicial decision] have declared exculpatory clauses [in residential leases] void as against public policy.

Summary judgment for McKenzie and MDC reversed; case remanded to trial court for further proceedings.

Landlord's Liability for Injuries Resulting from Others' Criminal Conduct   Another aspect of the trend toward increasing landlords' legal accountability is that many courts have imposed on landlords the duty to take reasonable steps to protect tenants and others on their property from foreseeable criminal conduct.[5] Although landlords are not insurers of the safety of persons on their property, an increasing number of courts have found them liable for injuries sustained by individuals who were criminally attacked on the landlord's property, if the attack was facilitated by the landlord's failure to comply with housing codes or maintain reasonable security. This liability has been imposed on residential and commercial landlords (such as shopping mall owners). Some courts have held that the implied warranty of habitability includes the obligation to provide reasonable security, but in most

---

[5]Chapter 24 contains a more extensive discussion of courts' recent inclination to impose this duty on owners and possessors of property.

states that have imposed this type of liability, principles of negligence or negligence per se furnish the controlling rationale.[6]

_____

[6]The law of negligence is covered in detail in Chapter 7.

Muniz v. Lefran Realty Corp. builds on these principles in holding that a pedestrian injured by criminal conduct on the landlord's property stated a cause of action against the landlord, when the criminal conduct was made more likely by a tenant's known and unlawful use of the leased property.

MUNIZ V. LEFRAN REALTY CORP.
553 N.Y.S.2d 313 (Sup. Ct. of N.Y., App. Div. 1990)

Miguel Muniz, a nine-year-old boy, was permanently blinded when he was shot in the head while passing in front of a building owned by Lefran Realty. The bullet that struck Miguel was shot from inside Lefran Realty's building during a robbery of the allegedly known, illegal "drug supermarket" operated by the tenant of a store located in the building. The illegal use of the store was well known to many people prior to the day when Miguel was shot. Although it had been raided by police on five occasions, the store reopened with the sale of drugs and narcotics soon after each raid. The building superintendent stated that patrons of the store went there to buy drugs rather than clothing and that he had reported the misuse of the store to the landlord several times before the shooting. The executive director of the neighborhood association had received many complaints about the store from persons in the neighborhood.

Miguel and his mother brought suit against Lefran Realty. The trial court granted summary judgment in favor of Lefran Realty and dismissed the case. The Munizes appealed.

Rosenberger, Justice The [lower court] concluded that even if the landlord had knowledge of the drug operation, it "stretches foreseeability much too far" to conclude the landlord should have foreseen an attempted robbery of the drug operation. We disagree.

While the intervening criminal act of a third person will generally be deemed a superseding cause which severs the liability of the original tort-feasor, this is not the case "when the intentional or criminal intervention of a third party is reasonably foreseeable." Thus, a landlord may be held liable for the personal injury inflicted upon a tenant or guest by a criminal intruder in a common area of the building if the landlord should have anticipated a risk of harm from criminal activity to persons on the premises.

In this case, however, neither the injured infant nor his mother had any relationship with Lefran Realty; they were merely passersby. Consequently, Lefran Realty argues, the Munizes were not within the orbit of duty imposed on the owner of the building, and a landlord has no duty to the public at large, with no connection to the premises, who might be victimized by street predators.

The Munizes contend that the crime which led to the infant's injury was directly related to the illegal drug operation which was openly and notoriously conducted on Lefran Realty's premises. Lefran Realty's building was not merely a fortuitous site randomly chosen by a malefactor, but was itself the scene of an unlawful activity which is known to attract violent crime.

It is the duty of the owner of a building, abutting upon a public street, to maintain it in such a condition that it shall not become dangerous to the traveling public. We need not look to the terms of the lease to determine whether the landlord retained the power to remedy a dangerous condition arising from unlawful activity on his premises. Under Real Property Law section 231, an owner of real property who knowingly allows that property to be used or occupied for any unlawful trade, manufacture, or business is liable for any damage resulting from such unlawful use. This statute expresses the clear public policy of the state which requires that owners of real property be vigilant in preventing their property from being used for unlawful purposes. To this end, [the law] provides that whenever a lessee uses any part of a building for an unlawful trade or business, the lease shall thereupon become void, and the landlord of such lessee may enter upon the premises so let. It is to be noted that the owner of these premises was not reluctant to enlist the aid of the courts when the tenant of the premises was late in rent payments, having twice commenced summary proceedings for non-payment. The common law also imposes a duty upon landlords to control the conduct of persons on their premises when they are reasonably aware of the necessity to do so. This duty extends to the protection of persons lawfully present in public places adjacent to the landlords' premises.

These compelling reasons of public policy lead us to conclude that the intervening criminal act of another is not a superseding cause which will relieve a landlord, who knows or has reason to know of illegal activities on his premises, of liability for injuries to innocent persons not in privity with the landlord where the intervening criminal act is a reasonably foreseeable sequela of such illegal use. Public policy is furthered by requiring that property owners not permit illegal enterprises which attract violent confrontations to flourish on their premises.

The plaintiffs' allegations are legally sufficient to state a cause of action against Lefran Realty.

Summary judgment for Lefran Realty reversed.

RIGHTS, DUTIES, AND LIABILITIES OF THE TENANT

Rights of the Tenant

The tenant has the right to *exclusive possession* and *quiet enjoyment* of the property during the term of the lease. The landlord is not entitled to enter the leased property without the tenant's consent, unless an emergency threatens the property or the landlord is acting under an express lease provision giving her the right to enter. The tenant may use the leased premises for any lawful purpose that is reasonable and appropriate, unless the purpose for which it may be used is expressly limited in the lease. Furthermore, the tenant has both the right to receive leased residential property in a habitable condition at the beginning of the lease and the right to have the property maintained in a habitable condition for the duration of the lease.

Duty to Pay Rent

The tenant, of course, has the duty to pay rent in the agreed amount and at the agreed times. If two or more persons are cotenants, their liability under the lease is *joint and several*. This means that each cotenant has complete responsibility—not just partial responsibility—for performing the tenants' duties under the lease. For example, Alberts and Baker rent an apartment from Caldwell, with both Alberts and Baker signing a one-year lease. If Alberts moves out after three months, Caldwell may hold Baker responsible for the entire rent, not just half of it. (Naturally, Alberts remains liable on the lease—as well as to Baker under any rent-sharing agreement the two of them had—but Caldwell is free to proceed against Baker solely if Caldwell so chooses.)

Duty Not to Commit Waste

The tenant also has the duty not to commit **waste** on the property. This means that the tenant is responsible for the routine care and upkeep of the property and that he has the duty not to commit any act that would harm the property. In the past, fulfillment of this duty required that the tenant perform necessary repairs. Today, the duty to make repairs has generally been shifted to the landlord by court ruling, statute, or lease provision. The tenant now has no duty to make major repairs unless the relevant damage was caused by his own negligence. When damage exists through no fault of the tenant and the tenant therefore is not obligated to make the actual repairs, the tenant nonetheless has the duty to take reasonable interim steps to prevent further damage from the elements. This duty would include, but not necessarily be limited to, informing the landlord of the problem. The duty would be triggered, for instance, when a window breaks or the roof leaks.

Assignment and Subleasing

As with rights and duties under most other types of contracts, the rights and duties under a lease may generally be assigned and delegated to third parties. **Assignment** occurs when the landlord or the tenant transfers all of her remaining rights under the lease to another person. For example, a landlord may sell an apartment building and assign the relevant leases to the buyer, who will then become the new landlord. A tenant may assign the remainder of her lease to someone else, who then acquires whatever rights the original tenant had under the lease (including, of course, the right to exclusive possession of the leased premises).

Subleasing occurs when the tenant transfers to another person some, but not all, of his remaining right to possess the property. The relationship of tenant to sublessee then becomes one of landlord and tenant. For example, Dorfman, a college student whose 18-month lease on an apartment is to terminate on December 31, 1995, sublets his apartment to Wembley for the summer months of 1995. This is a sublease rather than an assignment, because Dorfman has not transferred all of his remaining rights under the lease.

The significance of the assignment-sublease distinction is that an assignee acquires rights and duties under the lease between the landlord and the original tenant, but a sublessee does not. An assignee steps into the shoes of the original tenant and acquires any rights she had under the lease.[7] For example, if the lease contained an option to renew, the assignee would have the right to exercise this option if he desired to do so. The assignee, of course, becomes personally liable to the landlord for the payment of rent.

Under both an assignment and a sublease, the original tenant remains liable to the landlord for the commitments made in the lease. If the assignee or sublessee fails to pay rent, for example, the tenant has the legal obligation to pay it. Figure 1 compares the characteristics of assignments and subleases.

Lease Provisions Limiting Assignment   Leases commonly contain limitations on assignment and subleasing. This is especially true of commercial leases. Such provisions typically require the landlord's consent to any assignment or sublease, or purport to prohibit such a transfer of the tenant's interests. Provisions requiring the landlord's consent are upheld by the courts, although some courts hold that the landlord cannot

---

[7]Assignment is discussed in detail in Chapter 17.

FIGURE 1 Comparison of Assignment and Sublease		
	Assignment	**Sublease**
Does the tenant transfer to the third party *all* his remaining rights under the lease?	Yes	No
Does the tenant remain liable on the lease?	Yes	Yes
Does the third party (assignee or sublessee) acquire rights and duties under the tenant's lease with the landlord?	Yes	No

withhold consent unreasonably. Total prohibitions against assignment may be enforced as well, but they are disfavored in the law. Courts usually construe them narrowly, resolving ambiguities against the landlord.

Tenant's Liability for Injuries to Third Persons

The tenant is normally liable to persons who suffer harm while on the portion of the property over which the tenant has control, *if the injuries resulted from the tenant's negligence.*

TERMINATION OF THE LEASEHOLD

A leasehold typically terminates because the lease term has expired. Sometimes, however, the lease is terminated early because of a party's material breach of the lease or because of mutual agreement.

Eviction

If a tenant breaches the lease (most commonly, by nonpayment of rent), the landlord may take action to **evict** the tenant. State statutes usually establish a relatively speedy eviction procedure. The landlord who desires to evict a tenant must be careful to comply with any applicable state or city regulations governing evictions. These regulations usually forbid self-help measures on the landlord's part, such as forcible entry to change locks. At common law, a landlord had a lien on the tenant's personal property. The landlord therefore could remove and hold such property as security for the rent obligation. This lien has been abolished in many states. Where the lien still exists, it is subject to constitutional limitations requiring that the tenant be given notice of the lien, as well as an opportunity to defend and protect his belongings before they can be sold to satisfy the rent obligation.

Agreement to Surrender

A lease may terminate prematurely by mutual agreement between landlord and tenant to **surrender** the lease (i.e., return the property to the landlord prior to the end of the lease). A valid surrender discharges the tenant from further liability under the lease.

Abandonment

Abandonment occurs when the tenant unjustifiably and permanently vacates the leased premises before the end of the lease term, and defaults in the payment of rent. If a tenant abandons the leased property, he is making an offer to surrender the leasehold. As shown in Figure 2, the landlord must

FIGURE 2   **Termination of a Leasehold by Abandonment**

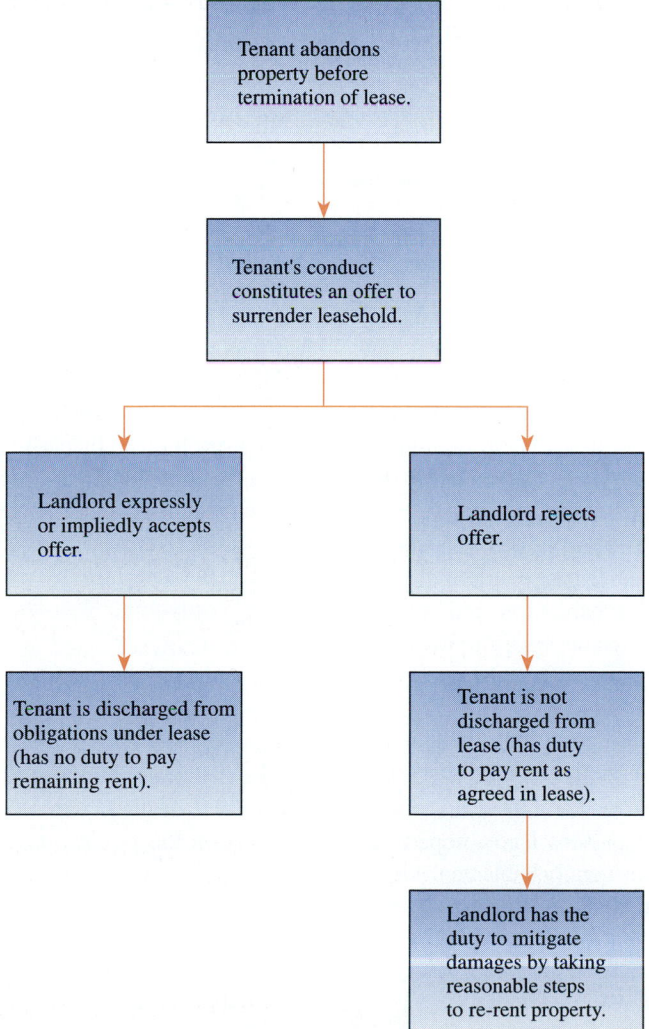

make a decision at this point. If the landlord's conduct shows acceptance of the tenant's offer of surrender, the tenant is relieved of the obligation to pay rent for the remaining period of the lease. If the landlord does not accept the surrender, she may sue the tenant for the rent due until such time as she (the landlord) rents the property to someone else, or, if she cannot find a new tenant, for the rent due for the remainder of the term.

At common law, the landlord had no obligation to mitigate (decrease) the damages caused by the abandonment by attempting to rent the leased property to a new tenant. In fact, taking possession of the property for the purpose of trying to rent it to someone else was a risky move for the landlord—her retaking of possession might be construed as acceptance of the surrender. Many states now place the duty on the landlord to attempt to mitigate damages by making a reasonable effort to rerent the property. These states also hold that the landlord's retaking of possession for the purpose of rerenting does not constitute a waiver of her right to pursue an action to collect unpaid rent.

ETHICAL AND PUBLIC POLICY CONCERNS

1. Suppose you own an older house and have rented it to a family with three young children. A state statute forbids painting new property with lead-based paint, but it does not forbid renting older property previously painted with lead-based paint. Should you disclose the lead-based paint to your tenants? Would current landlord-tenant law require you to do so?

2. As discussed earlier, the implied warranty of habitability guarantees that leased residential property will be fit for human habitation and that the landlord will take the actions necessary to keep it in this condition during the term of the lease. Should this warranty be applied to landlords who are not in the business of leasing property but make occasional rentals? Should it apply to obviously rundown housing leased at very low rents?

3. When two or more persons lease property together, they are jointly and severally liable on the lease. This means that any one of them could be held liable to the landlord for 100 percent of the rent or damages. Is it ethical for one tenant to abandon leased property and leave his fellow cotenants with this liability?

1. Dr. Kaminsky performed elective abortions in his medical practice. He leased office space from Fidelity in the Red Oak Atrium Building for a two-year term, beginning June 1983. The written lease included an express covenant of quiet enjoyment. In June 1984, anti-abortion demonstrators began picketing at the building on Saturdays, when Dr. Kaminsky scheduled abortions. Singing and chanting demonstrators picketed in the building's parking lot, inner lobby, and atrium area. They approached patients to discourage them from entering the building, accused Dr. Kaminsky of killing babies, and distributed literature. The demonstrators frequently occupied the stairs leading to Dr. Kaminsky's office and prevented patients from entering the office by blocking the doorway. Occasionally, they gained access to the office waiting area. Dr. Kaminsky asked Fidelity for help in keeping the demonstrators away, but became frustrated by Fidelity's failures to respond. No security personnel were present on Saturdays, even though the lease obligated Fidelity to provide security service on Saturdays. Fidelity's attorneys prepared a notice to inform the demonstrators that they risked prosecution by not leaving when asked to do so, but Fidelity's agent did not distribute the notice. The Sheriff's office refused to ask the demonstrators to leave without a directive from Fidelity, whose only response was to state that it was aware of Dr. Kaminsky's problems. In early December 1984, Dr. Kaminsky abandoned the property and ceased paying rent. Fidelity sued for the balance due under the lease. Dr. Kaminsky argued that Fidelity constructively evicted him by breaching the covenant of quiet enjoyment. Was Dr. Kaminsky correct?

2. Garwacki and Mastello shared a second-story apartment, which Garwacki rented from LaFraneire. Mastello invited Young to attend a dinner party at the apartment. Young went to the porch of the apartment to call down to Mastello, who was in the driveway below. As she placed her hands on the porch railing and leaned forward, the railing gave way. Young fell to the ground and was injured. The porch was accessible only from the living room of the apartment and was not a common area shared with other tenants. Should LaFraneire be liable for Young's injuries?

3. Skiver rented an apartment from Brighton for a 12-month period beginning May 1, 1990. His monthly rent was $430.83. Skiver paid Brighton a $350 security deposit. Skiver moved elsewhere in June 1990. He paid $100 toward the June rent, and nothing thereafter. A substitute tenant was not located until March 1991. Brighton retained Skiver's security deposit and sued him in small claims court for unpaid rent. State law allowed landlords to retain security deposits to satisfy all or part of a rent arrearage and to compensate for "actual damages to the rental unit." However, a state statute also provided that "[i]n the case of damage to the rental unit or other obligation against the security deposit, the landlord shall mail to the tenant, within 45 days after the termination of occupancy, an itemized list of damages claimed for which the security deposit may be used." Another statute stated that if the landlord failed to provide such a list within the 45-day period, the landlord was obligated to refund the full security deposit and was disqualified from recovering damages from the tenant. Brighton provided no itemized list to Skiver. The small claims court concluded that Skiver owed Brighton eight months' rent plus the unpaid portion of the June 1990 rent. It granted Brighton a judgment of $2,650 (the court's $3,000 jurisdictional limit minus the retained security deposit). The court determined that Brighton did not need to provide an itemized list because Brighton did not claim that Skiver had caused any physical damage to the premises. Skiver appealed. Was Brighton entitled to retain the security deposit? Was Brighton entitled to judgment against Skiver for the rent arrearage exceeding the security deposit amount?

4. Kridel entered into a lease with Sommer, owner of the Pierre Apartments, to lease apartment 6-L for two years. Kridel, who was to be married in June, planned to move into the apartment in May. His parents and future parents-in-law had agreed to assume responsibility for the rent, because Kridel was a full-time student who had no funds of his own. Shortly before Kridel was to have moved in, his engagement was broken. He wrote Sommer a letter explaining his situation and stating that he could not take the apartment. Sommer did not answer the letter. When another party inquired about renting apartment 6-L, the person in charge told her that the apartment was already rented to Kridel. Sommer did not enter the apartment or show it to anyone until he rented apartment 6-L to someone else when there were ap-

proximately eight months left on Kridel's lease. He sued Kridel for the full rent for the period of approximately 16 months before the new tenant's lease took effect. Kridel argued that Sommer should not be able to collect rent for the first 16 months of the lease because he did not take reasonable steps to rerent the apartment. Was Sommer entitled to collect the rent he sought?

5. Brock, the administrator of Jackson's estate, sued Levie and Watts Realty in a wrongful death action. Prior to her death, Jackson lived in a Birmingham, Alabama, apartment building owned by Levie. Watts Realty had leased the apartment to Jackson. In her complaint, Brock alleged that Jackson had twice asked the defendants to repair the locks on the back door of Jackson's apartment, but that the defendants had failed to respond. After Jackson made these requests, she notified the police that a prowler was at the "back part" of the apartment. When the police came to the apartment to investigate, they discovered that Jackson had been fatally stabbed. Brock's complaint alleged that Jackson's murderer acquired access to the apartment because of the broken locks on the back door, and that Levie and Watts Realty should be held liable because they violated two Birmingham ordinances in failing to maintain the locks. These ordinances required locks on exterior doors and specified that the locks must be kept "in sound working condition and good repair." Apparently concluding as a matter of law that Levie and Watts Realty could not be held liable for Jackson's death at the hand of a murderer, the trial judge granted summary judgment in favor of Levie and Watts Realty. Was the trial judge correct in doing so?

6. Kessler was employed as a part-time rental agent at White Oak Park Apartments. Her duties included showing and renting apartments, receiving rent money, arranging for repairs, and similar responsibilities. According to Kessler, her supervisor, Chase, instructed her to enter (while the tenants were not present) the apartments of tenants whose rent was overdue, to "snoop" around the apartments, and to look through private papers in order to obtain information regarding their places of employment, wage or salary information, and other information that might be helpful in collecting overdue rent. Kessler did so reluctantly a few times, but felt bad about having done so. She told Chase that she would not do this any more. Kessler was ultimately discharged. She alleged that she was discharged because of her refusal to carry out her supervisor's instructions regarding snooping into tenants' apartments. Is the type of entry that Kessler was allegedly instructed to conduct lawful?

7. From 1984 to 1986, Hardy occupied an apartment at 18 Arthur Street, which she leased from Griffin. Griffin had painted the apartment, but the previous coat of paint had not been scraped off. It was described as "thick, chipped, and peeling." Hardy saw her young son, Verron, eating paint chips in the apartment. This prompted her to have him tested for the presence of lead in his blood. She learned that Verron had abnormally high levels of lead in his blood and that this condition was due to his exposure to the lead-based paint present at 18 Arthur Street. Verron suffered severe brain damage as a result. Griffin admitted that in January 1987, he had received notice from the city about the presence of lead paint at 18 Arthur Street. On previous occasions, he had been put on notice that repairs to Hardy's unit were necessary. A state statute provided that "[t]he presence of paint which does not conform to federal standards as required in accordance with the Lead-Based Paint Poisoning Prevention Act . . . or of cracked, chipped, blistered, flaking, loose or peeling paint which constitutes a health hazard on accessible surfaces in any dwelling unit, tenement or any real property intended for human habitation shall be construed to render such dwelling unit . . . unfit for human habitation. . . ." A city ordinance imposed a duty on landlords to "make all repairs and do whatever is necessary to put and keep the premises in a fit and habitable condition." Hardy brought suit against Griffin for Verron's injuries. Should Griffin be liable?

8. In October 1981, Cook entered into an oral lease to rent a residence to Melson. Melson agreed to pay $400 per month, in advance, as rent. In November 1987, Cook sent Melson a letter advising that the rent would be increased to $525 per month, effective January 1, 1988, and asking whether Melson was going to pay. On December 10, 1987, Melson replied that he would not pay the increased rent. On January 2, 1988, Melson sent Cook a check for $400 as rent for January. Cook returned the check and stated that the rent was now $525. Melson did not vacate the premises until February 1, 1988. Cook brought a suit against Melson for

$525, allegedly the unpaid rent for the month of January. Was Melson liable for the $525?

9. Sippin owned property on Main Street in Monroe, Connecticut. He rented this property to Longo and Ellam pursuant to a written lease, which stipulated that the premises was to be used exclusively for Longo's and Ellam's real estate business. Longo and Ellam did not know that the deed by which Sippin had acquired the property contained a restrictive covenant barring any commercial use of the property. After Longo and Ellam had been in possession of the property for a few months, the local zoning enforcement agency ordered them to remove a commercial real estate sign and to cease operating their business on the property because it was located in a residential zone. Although the residential zoning of the property was in effect at the time they entered into their lease with Sippin, Longo and Ellam had not previously known of this zoning designation. Further zoning enforcement action caused Longo and Ellam to wind up their real estate business and to vacate the property (without paying further rent) prior to the expiration of the term contemplated by their lease with Sippin. Sippin sued Longo and Ellam in an effort to recover the unpaid rent (as called for by the lease) for the remainder of the lease term, or, in the alternative, to recover the fair rental value of the premises pursuant to a line of Connecticut cases allowing landlords to collect the fair rental value of property from any tenant at sufferance. When the trial court ruled in favor of Long and Ellam, Sippin appealed. Was Sippin entitled to a judgment for the unpaid rent contemplated by the lease? Alternatively, did the line of cases dealing with tenants at sufferance entitle Sippin to a judgment for the fair rental value of the premises?

10. Norman owned a three-bedroom duplex in Dane County, Wisconsin. He adopted a policy of renting to married persons (and their families) or to a divorced, widowed, separated, or single person. Norman would not, however, rent to any *group of unrelated* individuals. A Dane County ordinance prohibited landlords from discriminating against potential tenants on the basis of "marital status." When Norman refused to rent his duplex to a group of three single women and to a later group consisting of two women plus a child of one of the women, Dane County instituted legal proceedings against Norman. The county alleged that he violated the ordinance referred to above. Did Norman violate the ordinance?

ESTATES AND TRUSTS

INTRODUCTION

One of the basic features of the ownership of property is the right to dispose of the property during life and at death. You have already learned about the ways in which property is transferred during the owner's life. The owner's death is another major event for the transfer of property. Most people want to be able to choose who will get their property when they die. There are a variety of ways in which a person may control the ultimate disposition of his property. He may take title to the property in a form of joint ownership that gives his co-owner a right of survivorship. He may create a trust and transfer property to it to be used for the benefit of a spouse, child, elderly parent, or other beneficiary. He may execute a will in which he directs that his real and personal property be distributed to persons named in the will. If, however, a person makes no provision for the disposition of his property at his death, his property will be distributed to his heirs as defined by state law. This chapter focuses on the transfer of property at death and on the use of trusts for the transfer and management of property, both during life and at death.

THE LAW OF ESTATES AND TRUSTS

Each state has its own statutes and common law regulating the distribution of property upon death. Legal requirements and procedures may vary from state to state, but many general principles can be stated. The **Uniform Probate Code (UPC)** is a comprehensive, uniform law that has been enacted in 16 states. It is intended to update and unify state law concerning the disposition and administration of property at death. Several relevant UPC provisions will be discussed in this chapter.

Estate Planning

A person's **estate** is all of the property owned by that person. **Estate planning** is the popular name for the complicated process of planning for the transfer of a person's estate in later life and at death. Estate planning also concerns planning for the possibility of prolonged illness or disability. An attorney who is creating an estate plan will take an inventory of the client's assets, learn the client's objectives, and draft the instruments necessary to carry out the plan. This plan is normally guided by the desire to reduce the amount of tax liability and to provide for the orderly disposition of the estate.

WILLS

Right of Disposition by Will

The right to control the disposition of property at death has not always existed. In the English feudal system, the king owned all land. The lords and knights had only the right to use land for their lifetime. A landholder's rights in land terminated upon his death, and no rights descended to his heirs. In 1215, the king granted the nobility the right to pass their interest in the land they held to their heirs. Later, that right was extended to all property owners. In the United States, each state has enacted statutes that establish the requirements for a valid will, including the formalities that must be met to pass property by will.

Nature of a Will

A **will** is a document executed with specific legal formalities by a **testator** (person making a will) that contains his instructions about the way his property will be disposed of at his death. A will can dispose only of property belonging to the testator at the time of his death. Furthermore, wills do not control property that goes to others through other planning devices (such as life insurance policies) or by operation of law (such as by right of survivorship). For example, property held in joint tenancy or tenancy by the entirety is not controlled by a will, because the property passes automatically to the surviving co-tenant by right of survivorship. In addition, life insurance proceeds are controlled by the insured's designation of beneficiaries, not by any provision of a will. (Because joint tenancy and life insurance are ways of directing the disposition of property, they are sometimes referred to as "will substitutes.")

Common Will Terminology

Some legal terms commonly used in wills include the following:

1. *Bequest.* A **bequest** (also called **legacy**) is a gift of personal property or money. For example, a

will might provide for a bequest of a family heirloom to the testator's daughter. Since a will can direct only property that is owned by the testator at the time of his death, a specific bequest of property that the testator has disposed of before his death is ineffective. This is called **ademption.** For example, Samuel's will states that Warren is to receive Samuel's collection of antique guns. If the guns are destroyed before Warren's death, however, the bequest is ineffective because of ademption.

2. *Devise.* A **devise** is a gift of real property. For example, the testator might devise his family farm to his grandson.

3. *Residuary.* The **residuary** is the balance of the estate that is left after specific devises and bequests are made by the will. After providing for the disposition of specific personal and real property, a testator might provide that the residuary of his estate is to go to his spouse or be divided among his descendants.

4. *Issue.* A person's **issue** are his lineal descendants (children, grandchildren, great-grandchildren, and so forth). This category of persons includes adopted children.

5. *Per capita.* This term and the next one, *per stirpes*, are used to describe the way in which a group of persons are to share a gift. **Per capita** means that each of that group of persons will share equally. For example, Grandfather dies, leaving a will that provides that the residuary of his estate is to go to his issue or descendants *per capita*. Grandfather had two children, Mary and Bill. Mary has two children, John and James. Bill has one child, Margaret. Mary and Bill die before Grandfather (in legal terms, *predecease* him), but all three of Grandfather's grandchildren are living at the time of his death. In this case, John, James, and Margaret would each take one third of the residuary of Grandfather's estate.

6. *Per stirpes.* When a gift is given to the testator's issue or descendants **per stirpes** (also called **by right of representation**), each surviving descendant divides the share that his or her parent would have taken if the parent had survived. In the preceding example, if Grandfather's will had stated that the residuary of his estate was to go to his issue or descendants *per stirpes*, Margaret would take one half and John and James would take one quarter each (that is, they would divide the share that would have gone to their mother).

Testamentary Capacity

The capacity to make a valid will is called **testamentary capacity**. To have testamentary capacity, a person must be *of sound mind* and *of legal age*, which is 18 in most states. A person does not have to be in perfect mental health to have testamentary capacity. Because people often delay executing wills until they are weak and in ill health, the standard for mental capacity to make a will is fairly low. To be of "sound mind," a person need only be sufficiently rational to be capable of understanding the nature and character of his property, of realizing that he is making a will, and of knowing the persons who would normally be the beneficiaries of his affection. A person could move in and out of periods of lucidity and still have testamentary capacity if he executed his will during a lucid period.

Lack of testamentary capacity is a common ground upon which wills are challenged by persons who were excluded from a will. *Fraud* and *undue influence* are also common grounds for challenging the validity of a will.[1] Testamentary capacity and undue influence are discussed in the following case, *In the Matter of the Estate of Davidson.*

---

[1] Fraud and undue influence are discussed in detail in Chapter 13.

IN THE MATTER OF THE ESTATE OF DAVIDSON
839 S.W.2d 214 (Sup. Ct. Ark. 1992)

Charlye Vera Forrester Davidson died in a nursing home at the age of 90, leaving an estate in excess of $2 million. For a number of years before Davidson's death, Donald Goodner had served as her lawyer. Goodner and his wife also ran personal errands for Davidson. In 1984, Goodner prepared a will for Davidson in which he was appointed her executor and was given, after other bequests, the residue and remainder of her property. Later, in 1985, Goodner prepared another will for Davidson in which he was named coexecutor and from which he was dropped as residual beneficiary in favor of Davidson's nephews, John and William Forrester. Over the next three years, Davidson gave Goodner and his wife gifts totaling $60,000.

Following Davidson's death in 1989, her 1984 will was admitted to probate. William Forrester challenged the will on the ground of undue influence and Davidson's allegedly unsound mind. After the will contest was filed, Goodner found Davidson's 1985 will behind a dishwasher in her house. A petition to admit the 1985 will to probate was filed, and that will was contested by Forrester on the same grounds—undue influence and unsound mind. The probate court decided that the 1985 will revoked the 1984 will and it admitted the 1985 will to probate and appointed Goodner as executor. The court also found that Davidson was "in all respects competent, and was not acting under restraint or undue influence." Forrester appealed, seeking to invalidate both the 1984 and the 1985 wills on the ground of lack of testamentary capacity and to have the estate pass by intestacy.

Brown, Justice   Once the proponent of a will shows that the will is rational on its face and has been executed and witnessed in accordance with testamentary formalities, the party challenging the will's validity is required to prove by a preponderance of the evidence that the testator lacked mental capacity or was unduly influenced at the time the will was executed.

Davidson's physician, Dr. Lambiotte, testified that between 1960 and 1985, Mrs. Davidson began suffering from diseases associated with aging. He further testified that she always recognized him and knew where she was. A psychiatrist who saw Davidson in 1985 diagnosed her primary problem as deteriorating memory caused by either Alzheimer's dementia or multi-infarct dementia. Other witnesses described Mrs. Davidson as strongwilled, eccentric, and "nutty." Toward the end of her life, and in 1985, she was obsessed by the fact that someone was trying to enter her house and take her things. This caused her to lock her house and nail her doors shut.

Our generally expressed rule for testamentary capacity is that the testatrix must be able to know the natural objects of her bounty and the extent of her property; to understand to whom the property is being given; and to realize those who are being excluded from the will. In the present case, nothing before us suggests the elements of mental competency were not present when Davidson executed her 1985 will. Three witnesses attested to her signature on the will, and none espoused the view that there was any unusual behavior on Davidson's part or any problem concerning soundness of mind. Two witnesses in fact recall Mrs. Davidson's specifically declaring that she was there to sign her will. Moreover, there was testimony that at the time Davidson was aware of the property she owned by Lake Waldron and of her properties in Colorado and Texas.

Our probate law does not require that a testatrix mete out exact justice in the devise of her property. So long as she has the capacity to make a will, she may be unfair, eccentric, injudicious, or capricious in making distribution. Moreover, the fact that Davidson was suffering ideation relative to her house and incipient dementia does not, in itself, establish an impairment of testamentary capacity. As Dr. Lambiotte testified, this could represent only "a slot of abnormality."

Any assertion that Davidson was unfair to her nephews is difficult to fathom in light of the fact that they received almost ninety percent of the estate's assets as residuary beneficiaries under the 1985 will. But, more importantly, the proposition that she did not know her property or who her heirs were and was unable to interrelate those factors was simply not proven. Because there was insufficient proof that the testatrix lacked the requisite mental capacity to make a will in 1985, Forrester's contest must fail.

The additional assertion of undue influence really pertains more to the 1984 will where Goodner was a residuary beneficiary than to the 1985 will where he was not a recipient of the residuary estate. Forrester contends, however, that the circumstances surrounding the two wills taints the 1985 will. He further looks to Davidson's signature on the 1985 will which, he urges, indicates that she was assisted in her execution, the $60,000 in gifts to Goodner and his wife, and the line and different type for the residuary beneficiaries in the 1985 will as highly suspicious.

Undue influence sufficient to void a will must not spring from natural affection but must result from fear and coercion so as to deprive a testatrix of free will and direct the benefits of the will to particular parties. Undue influence is generally difficult of proof. Because of the allocation of the assets of her estate, it is difficult to discern a sinister or insidious effect from the 1985 will. It is true that Goodner had a confidential relationship with Davidson. Beyond that, we can only speculate about what her susceptibility to any testamentary suggestions by Goodner might have been. Our major problem with Forrester's argument is that neither Goodner nor any persons associated with him are distributees under the 1985 will. Without some assets flowing to particular parties sought to be benefitted by the supposed culprit, an undue influence claim is hard to sustain. Here, the proof was deficient and the claim of undue influence cannot prevail.

Probate of the will affirmed.

Execution of a Will

Unless a will is executed with the formalities required by state law, it is *void*. The courts are strict in interpreting statutes concerning the execution of wills. If a will is declared void, the property of the deceased person will be distributed according to the provisions of state laws that will be discussed later.

The formalities required for a valid will differ from state to state. For that reason, an individual should consult the laws of his state before making a will. If he should move to another state after having executed a will, he should consult a lawyer in his new state to determine whether a new will needs to be executed. All states require that a will be *in writing*. State law also requires that a formal will be *witnessed*, generally by two or three *disinterested* witnesses (persons who do not stand to inherit any property under the will), and that it be *signed* by the testator or by someone else at the testator's direction. Most states also require that the testator *publish* the will—that is, declare or indicate at the time of signing that the instrument is his will. Another formality required by most states is that the testator sign the will in the presence and the sight of the witnesses and that the witnesses sign in the presence and the sight of each other. As a general rule, an **attestation clause**, which states the formalities that have been followed in the execution of the will, is written following the testator's signature. These detailed formalities are designed to prevent fraud. Section 2–502 of the UPC requires that a will must be in writing, signed by the testator (or in the testator's name by some other individual in the testator's conscious presence and by the testator's direction), and signed by at least two individuals, each of whom signed within a reasonable time after he witnessed either the signing of the will or the testator's acknowledgment of that signature or will. Also, under the UPC, any individual who is generally competent to be a witness may witness a will, and the fact that the witness is an interested party does not invalidate the will [2–505]. When a testator has made a technical error in executing a will, however, the UPC permits the document to be treated as if it had been executed properly if it can be proven by clear and convincing evidence that the testator intended the document to constitute his will [2–503].

In some situations, a lawyer might arrange to have the execution of a will *videotaped* to provide evidence relating to the testator's capacity and the use of proper formalities. (Note that the will is executed in the normal way; the videotape merely records the execution of the will.) Some state probate codes specifically provide that videotapes of the executions of wills are admissible into evidence.

Incorporation by Reference

In some situations, a testator might want his will to refer to and incorporate an existing writing. For example, the testator may have created a list of specific gifts of personal property that he wants to incorporate in the will. A writing such as this is called an **extrinsic document**—that is, a writing apart from the will. In most states, the contents of extrinsic documents can be essentially incorporated into the will when the circumstances satisfy rules that have been designed to ensure that the document is genuine and that it was intended by the testator to be incorporated in the will. This is called **incorporation by reference**. For an extrinsic document to be incorporated by reference, it must have been *in existence at the time the will was executed*. In addition, the writing and the will must refer to each other so that the extrinsic document can be identified and so that it is clear that the testator intended the extrinsic document to be incorporated in the will. Under the UPC, incorporation by reference is allowed when the extrinsic document was in existence when the will was executed, the language of the will manifests the intent to incorporate the writing, and the will describes the writing sufficiently to identify it [2–510].

Informal Wills

Some states recognize certain types of wills that are not executed with these formalities. These are:

1. *Nuncupative wills.* A **nuncupative** will is an oral will. Such wills are recognized as valid in some states, but only under limited circumstances and to a limited extent. In a number of states, for example, nuncupative wills are valid only when made by soldiers in military service and sailors at sea, and even then they will be effective only to dispose of personal property that was in the actual possession of the person at the time the oral will was made. Other states place low dollar limits on the amount of property that can be passed by a nuncupative will.

2. *Holographic wills.* **Holographic wills** are wills that are written and signed in the testator's handwriting. The fact that holographic wills are not properly witnessed makes them suspect. They are recognized in about half of the states and by section 2–502(b) of the UPC, even though they are not executed with the formalities usually required of valid wills. For a holographic will to be valid in the states that recognize them, it must evidence testamentary intent and must actually be *handwritten* by the testator. A typed holographic will would be invalid. Some states require that the holographic will be *entirely* handwritten—although the UPC requires only that the signature and material portions of the will be handwritten by the testator [2–502(b)]—and some also require that the will be dated.

Joint and Mutual Wills

In some circumstances, two or more people—a married couple, for example—decide together on a plan for the disposition of their property at death. To carry out this plan, they may execute a **joint will** (a single instrument that constitutes the will of both or all of the testators and is executed by both or all) or they may execute **mutual wills** (joint or separate, individual wills that reflect the common plan of distribution).

Underlying a joint or mutual will is an agreement on a common plan. This common plan often includes an express or implied contract (a contract to make a will or not to revoke the will). One issue that sometimes arises is whether a testator who has made a joint or mutual will can later change his will. Whether joint and mutual wills are revocable depends on the language of the will, on state law, and on the timing of the revocation. For example, a testator who made a joint will with his spouse may be able to revoke his will during the life of his spouse, because the spouse still has a chance to change her own will, but he may be unable to revoke or change the will after the death of his spouse. The UPC provides that the mere fact that a joint or mutual will has been executed does *not* create the presumption of a contract not to revoke the will or wills [2–514].

Construction of Wills

Even in carefully drafted wills, questions sometimes arise as to the meaning or legal effect of a term or provision. Disputes about the meaning of the will are even more likely to occur in wills drafted by the testator himself, such as holographic wills. To interpret a will, a court will examine the entire instrument in an attempt to determine the testator's intent. The following case, *Haag v. Stickley*, provides a good example of the methods and principles courts use to interpret wills.

Haag v. Stickley
389 S.E.2d 691 (Va. Sup. Ct. 1990)

Kenneth Haag owned Front Royal Supply Company. Charles Smoot had worked for Haag as the manager of the Front Royal store for a number of years. John Stickley was the manager of the company's Winchester store, but had not worked for Haag as long as Smoot had. Wayne Blye was assistant manager of the Winchester store, and had worked for the company for a lesser amount of time than had Stickley. Melvin Printz was also an employee of Haag's, but was fired in 1984–85.

On January 20, 1983, Haag executed a holographic will. The will contained a specific bequest of stock to his employees who were still with Front Royal at the time of his death. It stated as follows:

In October 1985, Haag executed a holographic codicil. This codicil provided that "In case Chs. Smoot is deceased or any other receipitent [sic] their stare [sic] will go back in the estate." Haag died in 1986. His will was admitted to probate, and his former wife, Helen, was named executor. At the time of Haag's death, he owned 689 shares of Front Royal stock, the value of which was at least $254,000. A dispute arose between Mrs. Haag, as executor, and Stickley and Blye about whether they were entitled to any shares. Mrs. Haag maintained that the will should be interpreted to give 500 shares of stock to Smoot, and none to Stickley and Blye, with the remaining 189 shares going into the residuary of the estate. Stickley and Blye filed this action asking the court to construe and interpret the will in order to determine their rights to the shares of stock. The court determined that Smoot should get the first 500 shares, and the remaining 189 shares should be divided equally between Stickley and Blye, with the odd share going to the person with longer service. Mrs. Haag appealed.

Compton, Justice   In construing a will, the testator's intention controls, unless contrary to an established rule of law. The whole will must be examined to determine the testator's intention and effect should be given to all parts of the document, as far as possible. Even though the language of the will may be obscure or uncertain, the testator's intention will prevail, if it can be ascertained.

Moreover, when the words of the will are capable of two different constructions, that should be adopted which is most consistent with the intention of the testator as ascertained by other provisions in the will; and when the intention of the testator is incorrectly expressed, the court will effectuate it by supplying the proper words.

It is true that in ascertaining the testator's intent we examine the words used in light of the circumstances surrounding the testator at the time of the will's execution. However, we cannot ignore subsequent changes to the will as we consider that intent. A will is an ambulatory instrument, not intended or allowed to take effect until the death of the maker. It may be changed during life as often as the mind and purposes of the testator change.

Against the background of the foregoing principles, we cannot say that the chancellor misinterpreted or misconstrued the testamentary documents. Insofar as the bequest of company stock is concerned, the testator's plan clearly appears from the will and from the circumstances prevailing at the time the will was drawn. The testator wished to reward company employees for their past and continued service by leaving all his stock in the company to such of those employees who were living and still working for the company at the time of his death.

Thus, he bequeathed "my shares of the stock" in the company, intending to give all the shares he owned. The quantity "500 shares" follows Smoot's name. No quantity is shown after Stickley's or Blye's names. Mrs. Haag contends the bequest is incomplete because it contains what she has labeled "blanks" or omissions. We perceive no blanks or omissions. Rather, we view the terms to state individual bequests.

Where a bequest is to several individuals, whatever may be their relationship to each other, equality is the rule, unless the testator has established a different one. Therefore, we conclude from the language and arrangement of the words that the testator intended to make a gift of all of his shares to three persons with one receiving 500 shares and the other two receiving the balance, which they divide equally, the longer in service to the company receiving the odd share.

The testator's intent is further indicated by the manner in which he made corrections on the holograph. He struck through the name of Melvin Printz, probably after Printz had been fired in 1984–85. He initialled the deletion writing "no" before "shares." This demonstrates the testator's method of deleting a beneficiary and canceling a bequest. He made other deletions in other portions of the will and codicil and initialled them also. In contrast, the names of Stickley and Blye remained in the will without being initialled but separately joined to the words "shares" by dashes or connecting lines, not blanks. The lines are undulating and not straight as a blank line usually appears. It cannot be successfully argued that these lines serve to negate the bequest to Stickley or Blye. There are at least two plausible reasons why the testator did not specify the number of shares allocated to Stickley or Blye. First, the testator was probably uncertain whether both would remain company employees until his death. Second, the testator was uncertain about the number of shares of company stock he would own when he died. For these reasons, the testator probably concluded that the exact number of shares passing to these two employees could be more accurately determined after his death.

For these reasons, we find no error in the decision of the trial court.

Judgment for Stickley and Blye affirmed.

Limitations on Disposition by Will

A person who takes property by will takes it subject to all outstanding claims against the property. For example, if real property is subject to a mortgage or other lien, the beneficiary who takes the property gets it subject to the mortgage or lien. In addition, the rights of the testator's creditors are superior to the rights of beneficiaries under his will. Thus, if the testator was insolvent (his debts exceeded his assets), persons named as beneficiaries do not receive any property by virtue of the will.

Under the laws of most states, the surviving spouse of the testator has statutory rights in property owned solely by the testator that cannot be defeated by a contrary will provision. This means that a husband cannot effectively disinherit his wife, and vice versa. Even if the will provides for the surviving spouse, he or she can elect to take the share of the decedent's estate that would be provided by state law rather than the amount specified in the will. In some states, personal property, such as furniture, passes automatically to the surviving spouse.

At common law, a widow had the right to a life estate in one third of the lands owned by her husband during their marriage. This was known as a widow's **dower right**. A similar right for a widower was known as **curtesy**. A number of states have changed the right by statute to give a surviving spouse a one-third interest in fee simple in the real and personal property owned by the deceased spouse at the time of his or her death. (Naturally, a testator can leave his spouse more than this if he desires.) Under UPC 2–201, the surviving spouse's elective share varies depending on the length of the surviving spouse's marriage to the testator—the elective share increases with the length of marriage.

As a general rule, a surviving spouse is given the right to use the family home for a stated period as well as a portion of the deceased spouse's estate. In community property states, each spouse has a one-half interest in community property that cannot be defeated by a contrary will provision. (Note that the surviving spouse will obtain *full* ownership of any property owned by the testator and the surviving spouse as joint tenants or tenants by the entirety.)

Children of the testator who were born or adopted after the will was executed are called **preterminated** children. There is a presumption that the testator intended to provide for such a child, unless there is evidence to the contrary. State law gives preterminated children the right to a share of the testator's estate. For example, under section 2–302 of the Uniform Probate Code, a preterminated child has the right to receive the share he would have received under the state intestacy statute unless it appears that the omission of this child was intentional, the testator gave substantially all of his estate to the child's other parent, or the testator provided for the child outside of the will.

Revocation of Wills

One important feature of a will is that it is *revocable* until the moment of the testator's death. For this reason, a will confers *no present interest* in the testator's property. A person is free to revoke a prior will and, if she wishes, to make a new will. Wills can be revoked in a variety of ways. Physical destruction and mutilation done with intent to revoke a will constitute revocation, as do other acts such as crossing out the will or creating a writing that expressly cancels the will.

In addition, a will is revoked if the testator later executes a valid will that expressly revokes the earlier will. A later will that does not *expressly* revoke an earlier will operates to revoke only those portions of the earlier will that are inconsistent with the later will. Under the UPC, a later will that does not expressly revoke a prior will operates to revoke it by inconsistency if the testator intended the subsequent will to *replace* rather than *supplement* the prior will [2–507(b)]. Furthermore, the UPC presumes that the testator intended the subsequent will to replace rather than supplement the prior will if the subsequent one makes a complete disposition of her estate, but it presumes that the testator intended merely to supplement and not replace the prior will if the subsequent will disposes of only part of her estate [2–507(c), 2–507(d)]. In some states, a will is presumed to have been revoked if it cannot be located after the testator's death, although this presumption can be rebutted with contrary evidence.

Wills can also be revoked by operation of law without any act on the part of the testator signifying revocation. State statutes provide that certain changes in relationships operate as revocations of a will. In some states, marriage will operate to revoke a will that was made when the testator was single. Similarly, a divorce may revoke provisions in a will made during marriage that leave property to the divorced spouse. Under the laws of some states, the birth of a child after the execution of a will may operate as a partial revocation of the will.

Codicils

A **codicil** is an amendment of a will. If a person wants to change a provision of a will without making an entirely new will, she may amend the will by executing a codicil. One may *not* amend a will by merely striking out objectionable provisions and inserting new provisions. The same formalities are required for the creation of a valid codicil as for the creation of a valid will.

ADVANCE DIRECTIVES: PLANNING FOR DISABILITY

Advances in medical technology now permit a person to be kept alive by artificial means, even in many cases in which there is no hope of the person being able to function without life support. Many people are opposed to their lives being prolonged with no chance of recovery. In response to these concerns, almost all states have enacted statutes permitting individuals to state their choices about the medical procedures that should be administered or withheld if they should become incapacitated in the future and cannot recover. Collectively, these devices are called **advance directives**. An advance directive is a written document (such as a living will or durable power of attorney) that directs others how future health care decisions should be made in the event that the individual becomes incapacitated.

Living Wills

Living wills are documents in which a person states in advance his intention to forgo or obtain certain life prolonging medical procedures. Almost all states have enacted statutes recognizing living wills. These statutes also establish the elements and formalities required to create a valid living will and describe the legal effect of living wills. Currently, the law concerning living wills is primarily a matter of state law and differs from state to state. Living wills are typically included with a patient's medical records. Many states require physicians and other health care providers to follow the provisions of a valid living will. Because living wills are created by statute, it is important that all terms and conditions of the statute be followed. Figure 1 shows a living will form that is contained in Indiana's current living will statute.[2]

The importance of living wills and durable powers of attorney (which are discussed in the next section) was underscored in a 1990 U.S. Supreme Court case, *Cruzan v. Director, Missouri Department of Health. Cruzan*, which follows, held that it was constitutionally permissible for a state to refuse to permit the guardians of an incompetent person to terminate life support without clear and convincing evidence that the incompetent person would consent to such termination.

---

[2]Indiana Code 16-36-4-10 (1993).

FIGURE 1   Living Will

LIVING WILL DECLARATION

Declaration made this _____ day of _____ , _____ . I, _____ , being at least eighteen (18) years of age and of sound mind, willfully and voluntarily make known my desires that my dying shall not be artificially prolonged under the circumstances set forth below, and I declare:

If at any time I have an incurable injury, disease, or illness certified in writing to be a terminal condition by my attending physician, and my attending physician has determined that my death will occur within a short time, and the use of life prolonging procedures would serve only to artificially prolong the dying process, I direct that such procedures be withheld or withdrawn and that I be permitted to die naturally with only the provision of appropriate nutrition and hydration and the administration of medication and the performance of any medical procedure necessary to provide me with comfort, care, or to alleviate pain.

In the absence of my ability to give directions regarding the use of life prolonging procedures, it is my intention that his declaration be honored by my family and physicians as the final expression of my legal right to refuse medical or surgical treatment and accept the consequences of the refusal.

I understand the full import of this declaration,

Signed: _____

City, County, and State of Residence

The declarant has been personally known to me, and I believe (him/her) to be of sound mind. I did not sign the declarant's signature above for or at the direction of the declarant. I am not a parent, spouse, or child of the declarant. I am not entitled to any part of the declarant's estate or directly financially responsible for the declarant's medical care. I am competent and at least eighteen (18) years of age.

Witness _____ Date _____
Witness _____ Date _____

CRUZAN V. DIRECTOR, MISSOURI DEPARTMENT OF HEALTH
110 S. Ct. 2841 (U.S. S. Ct. 1990)

On the night of January 11, 1983, 25-year-old Nancy Cruzan lost control of her car while driving down Elm Road in Jasper County, Missouri. The vehicle overturned and Cruzan was discovered lying face down in a ditch without detectable respiratory or cardiac function. Paramedics were able to restore her breathing and heartbeat at the accident site and she was transported to a hospital. There she was diagnosed as having sustained probable cerebral contusions compounded by significant anoxia (lack of oxygen). She remained in a coma for three weeks and then progressed to an unconscious state in which she was able to orally ingest some nutrition. To ease feeding and further her recovery, surgeons implanted a gastrostomy feeding and hydration tube. She then remained in a Missouri state hospital in what is commonly referred to as a persistent vegetative state.

After it became apparent that Cruzan had virtually no chance of regaining her mental faculties, her parents (also her legal guardians) asked hospital employees to terminate the artificial nutrition and hydration procedures, which would cause her death. The employees refused to do so without court approval. The parents then sought authorization from the state trial court for termination. Cruzan had not executed a living will, but a former roommate of Cruzan's testified that Cruzan had told her that if she were sick or injured she would not wish to continue her life unless she could live at least halfway normally. The trial court granted authorization to terminate nutrition and hydration, holding that a person in Cruzan's position had a fundamental constitutional right to refuse or direct the withdrawal of "death prolonging procedures." It also found that Cruzan's conversation with her roommate indicated that she would not want to continue with life support. The Supreme Court of Missouri reversed on the ground that no one can assume the choice regarding termination of medical treatment for an incompetent person in the absence of the formalities required under the Living Will Statute or clear and convincing evidence, which evidence it found to be lacking in this case. The U.S. Supreme Court then granted certiorari to consider whether the U.S. Constitution would require the hospital to withdraw life-sustaining treatment from Cruzan under these circumstances.

Rehnquist, Chief Justice   Petitioners insist that the forced administration of life-sustaining medical treatment, and even of artificially-delivered food and water essential to life, would implicate a competent person's liberty interest. For purposes of this case, we assume that the United States Constitution would grant a competent person a constitutionally protected right to refuse lifesaving hydration and nutrition.

Petitioners go on to assert that an incompetent person should possess the same right in this respect as is possessed by a competent person. The difficulty with petitioner's claim is that an incompetent person is not able to make an informed and voluntary choice to exercise a hypothetical right to refuse treatment or any other right. Such a "right" must be exercised for her, if at all, by some sort of surrogate. Here, Missouri has in effect recognized that under certain circumstances a surrogate may act for the patient in electing to have hydration and nutrition withdrawn in such a way as to cause death, but it has established a procedural safeguard to assure that the action of the surrogate conforms as best it may to the wishes expressed by the patient while competent. Missouri requires that evidence of the incompetent's wishes as to the withdrawal of treatment be proved by clear and convincing evidence. The question, then, is whether the United States Constitution forbids the establishment of this procedural requirement by the State. We hold that it does not.

The choice between life and death is a deeply personal decision of obvious and overwhelming finality. We believe Missouri may legitimately seek to safeguard the personal element of this choice through the imposition of heightened evidentiary requirements. It cannot be disputed that the Due Process Clause protects an interest in life as well as an interest in refusing life-sustaining medical treatment.

Not all incompetent patients will have loved ones available to serve as surrogate decisionmakers. And even where family members are present, there will, of course, be some unfortunate situations in which family members will not act to protect a patient. A State is entitled to guard against potential abuses in such situations. Similarly, a State is entitled to consider that a judicial proceeding to make a determination regarding an incompetent's wishes may very well not be an adversarial one, with the added guarantee of accurate factfinding that the adversary process brings with it. Finally, we think a State may properly decline to make judgments about the "quality" of life that a particular individual may enjoy, and simply assert an unqualified interest in the preservation of human life to be weighed against the constitutionally protected interests of the individual.

It is also worth noting that most, if not all, States simply forbid oral testimony entirely in determining the wishes of parties in transactions which, while important, simply do not have the consequences that a decision to terminate a person's life does. In most states, the parol evidence rule prevents the variations of the terms of a written contract by oral testimony. The statute of frauds makes unenforceable oral contracts to leave property by will, and statutes regulating the making of wills universally require that those instruments be in writing. There is no doubt that [these statutes] on occasion frustrate effectuation of the intent of a particular decedent just as Missouri's requirement of proof in this case may have frustrated the effectuation of the not-fully-expressed desires of Nancy Cruzan. But the Constitution does not require general rules to work faultlessly; no general rule can.

In sum, we conclude that a State may apply a clear and convincing evidence standard in proceedings where a guardian seeks to discontinue nutrition and hydration of a person diagnosed to be in a persistent vegetative state. The Supreme Court of Missouri held that the testimony adduced at trial did not amount to clear and convincing proof of the patient's desire to have hydration and nutrition withdrawn. We cannot say that the Supreme Court of Missouri committed constitutional error in reaching the conclusion that it did.

Judgment for the Missouri Department of Health affirmed.

Durable Power of Attorney

Another technique of planning for the eventuality that one may be unable to make decisions for oneself is to execute a document that gives another person the legal authority to act on one's behalf in the case of mental or physical incapacity. This document is called a **durable power of attorney**.

A *power of attorney* is an express statement in which one person (the **principal**) gives another person (the **attorney in fact**) the authority to do an act or series of acts on his behalf. For example, Andrews enters into a contract to sell his house to Willis, but he must be out of state on the date of the real estate closing. He gives Paulsen a power of attorney to attend the closing and execute the deed on his behalf. Ordinary powers of attorney terminate upon the principal's incapacity. By contrast, the *durable power of attorney* is not affected if the principal becomes incompetent.

A durable power of attorney permits a person to give someone else extremely broad powers to make decisions and enter transactions such as those involving real and personal property, bank accounts, and health care, and to specify that those powers will not terminate upon incapacity. The durable power of attorney is an extremely important planning device. For example, a durable power of attorney executed by an elderly parent to an adult child at a time in which the parent is competent would permit the child to take care of matters such as investments, property, bank accounts, and hospital admission. Without the durable power of attorney, the child would be forced to apply to a court for a guardianship, which is a more expensive, and often a less efficient manner in which to handle personal and business affairs.

Durable Power of Attorney for Health Care

The majority of states have enacted statutes specifically providing for **durable powers of attorney for health care** (sometimes called **health care representatives**). This is a type of durable power of attorney in which the principal specifically gives the attorney in fact the authority to make certain health care decisions for him if the principal should become incompetent. Depending on state law and the instructions given by the principal to the attorney in fact, this could include decisions such as consenting or withholding consent to surgery, admitting the principal to a nursing home, and possibly withdrawing or prolonging life support. Note that the durable power of attorney becomes relevant only in the event that the principal becomes incompetent. So long as the principal is competent, he retains the ability to make his own health care decisions. This power of attorney is also revocable at the will of the principal. The precise requirements for creation of the durable power of attorney differ from state to state, but all states require a written and signed document executed with specified formalities, such as witnessing by disinterested witnesses.

Federal Law and Advance Directives

A new federal statute, The Patient Self-Determination Act,[3] requires health care providers to take active steps to educate people about the opportunity to make advance decisions about medical care and the prolonging of life and to record the choices that they make. This statute, which became effective in 1992, requires health care providers such as hospitals, nursing homes, hospices, and home health agencies, to provide written information to adults receiving medical care about their rights concerning the ability to accept or refuse medical or surgical treatment, the health care provider's policies concerning those rights, and their right to formulate advance directives. The act also requires the provider to document in the

---

[3]42 U.S.C. section 1395cc (1993).

FIGURE 2	Example of a Distribution Scheme under an Intestacy Statute

Person Dying Intestate Is Survived by	Result
1. Spouse* and child or issue of a deceased child	Spouse ½, Child ½
2. Spouse and parent(s) but no issue	Spouse ¾, Parent ¼
3. Spouse but no parent or issue	All of the estate to spouse
4. Issue but no spouse	Estate is divided among issue
5. Parent(s), brothers, sisters, and/or issue of deceased brothers and sisters but no spouse or issue	Estate is divided among parent(s), brothers, sisters, and issue of deceased brothers and sisters
6. Issue of brothers and sisters but no spouse, issue, parents, brothers, and sisters	Estate is divided among issue of deceased brothers and sisters
7. Grandparents, but no spouse, issue, parents, brothers, sisters, or issue of deceased brothers and sisters	All of the estate goes to grandparents
8. None of the above	Estate goes to the state

*Note, however, second and subsequent spouses who had no children by the decedent may be assigned a smaller share.

patient's medical record whether the patient has executed an advance directive, and it forbids discrimination against the patient based on the individual's choice regarding an advance directive. In addition, the provider is required to ensure compliance with the requirements of state law concerning advance directives and to educate its staff and the community on issues concerning advance directives.

INTESTACY

If a person dies without making a will, or if he makes a will that is declared invalid, he is said to have died **intestate**. When that occurs, his property will be distributed to the persons designated as the intestate's heirs under the appropriate state's **intestacy** or **intestate succession** statute. The intestate's real property will be distributed according to the intestacy statute of the state in which the property is located. His personal property will be distributed according to the intestacy statute of the state in which he was **domiciled** at the time of his death. A domicile is a person's permanent home. A person can have only one domicile at a time. Determinations of a person's domicile turn on facts that tend to show that person's intent to make a specific state his permanent home.

Characteristics of Intestacy Statutes

The provisions of intestacy statutes are not uniform. Their purpose, however, is to distribute property in a way that reflects the *presumed intent* of the deceased—that is, to distribute it to the persons most closely related to him. In general, such statutes first provide for the distribution of most or all of a person's estate to his surviving spouse, children, or grandchildren. If no such survivors exist, the statutes typically provide for the distribution of the estate to parents, siblings, or nieces and nephews. If no relatives at this level are living, the property may be distributed to surviving grandparents, uncles, aunts, or cousins. Generally, persons with the same degree of relationship to the deceased person take equal shares. If the deceased had no surviving relatives, the property **escheats** (goes) to the state.

Figure 2 shows an example of a distribution scheme under an intestacy statute.

Special Rules

Under intestacy statutes, a person must have a relationship to the deceased person through blood or marriage in order to inherit any part of his property. State law includes adopted children within the definition of "children," and treats adopted children in the same way as it treats biological children. (An adopted child would inherit from his adoptive parents, not from his biological parents.) Half brothers and half sisters are usually treated in the same way as brothers and sisters related by whole blood. An illegitimate child may inherit from his mother, but as a general rule, illegitimate children do not inherit from their fathers unless paternity has been either acknowledged or established in a legal proceeding.

A person must be alive at the time the decedent dies to claim a share of the decedent's estate. An exception may be made for pretermitted children or other descendants who are born *after* the decedent's death. If a person who is entitled to a share of the decedent's estate survives the decedent but dies before receiving his share, his share in the decedent's estate becomes part of his own estate.

Simultaneous Death

A statute known as the Uniform Simultaneous Death Act provides that where two persons who would inherit from each other (such as husband and wife) die under circumstances that make it difficult or impossible to determine who died first, each person's property is to be distributed as though he or she survived. This means, for example, that the husband's property will go to his relatives and the wife's property to her relatives.

ADMINISTRATION OF ESTATES

When a person dies, an orderly procedure is needed to collect his property, settle his debts, and distribute any remaining property to those who will inherit it under his will or by intestate succession. This process occurs under the supervision of a probate court and is known as the **administration process** or the **probate process**. Summary (simple) procedures are sometimes available when an estate is relatively small—for example, when it has assets of less than $7,500.

The Probate Estate

The probate process operates only on the decedent's property that is considered to be part of his **probate estate**. The probate estate is that property belonging to the decedent at the time of his death other than property held in joint ownership with right of survivorship, proceeds of insurance policies payable to a trust or a third party, property held in a revocable trust during the decedent's lifetime in which a third party is the beneficiary, or retirement benefits, such as pensions, payable to a third party. Assets that pass by operation of law and assets that are transferred by other devices such as trusts or life insurance policies do not pass through probate.

Note that the decedent's probate estate and his *taxable estate* for purposes of federal estate tax are two different concepts. The taxable estate includes all property owned or controlled by the decedent at the time of his death. For example, if a person purchased a $1 million life insurance policy made payable to his spouse or children, the policy would be included in his taxable estate, but not in his probate estate.

Determining the Existence of a Will

The first step in the probate process is to determine whether the deceased left a will. This may require a search of the deceased person's personal papers and safe-deposit box. If a will is found, it must be *proved* to be admitted to probate. This involves the testimony of the persons who witnessed the will, if they are still alive. If the witnesses are no longer alive, the signatures of the witnesses and the testator will have to be established in some other way. In many states and under UPC section 2–504, a will may be proved by an affidavit (declaration under oath) sworn to and signed by the testator and the witnesses at the time the will was executed. This is called a **self-proving affidavit**. If a will is located and proved, it will be admitted to probate and govern many of the decisions that must be made in the administration of the estate.

Selecting a Personal Representative

Another early step in the administration of an estate is the selection of a personal representative to administer the estate. If the deceased left a will, it is likely that he designated his personal representative in the will. The personal representative under a will is also known as the **executor**. Almost anyone could serve as an executor. The testator may have chosen, for example, his spouse, a grown child, a close friend, an attorney, or the trust department of a bank.

If the decedent died intestate, or if the personal representative named in a will is unable to serve, the probate court will name a personal representative to administer the estate. In the case of an intestate estate, the personal representative is called an **administrator**. A preference is usually accorded to a surviving spouse, child, or other close relative. If no relative is available and qualified to serve, a creditor, bank, or other person may be appointed by the court.

Most states require that the personal representative *post a bond* in an amount in excess of the estimated value of the estate to ensure that her duties will be properly and faithfully performed. A person making a will often directs that his executor may serve without posting a bond, and this exemption may be accepted by the court.

Responsibilities of the Personal Representative

The personal representative has a number of important tasks in the administration of the estate. She must see that an inventory is taken of the estate's assets and that the assets are appraised. Notice must then be given to creditors or potential claimants against the estate so that they can file and prove their claims within a specified time, normally five months. As a general rule, the surviving spouse of the deceased person is entitled to be paid an allowance during the time the estate is being settled. This allowance has priority over other debts of the estate. The personal representative must see that any properly payable funeral or burial expenses are paid and that the creditors' claims are satisfied.

Both federal and state governments impose estate or inheritance taxes on estates of a certain size. The personal representative is responsible for filing estate tax returns. The federal tax is a tax on the deceased's estate, with provisions for deducting items such as debts, expenses of administration, and charitable gifts. In addition, an amount equal to the amount left to the surviving spouse may be deducted from the gross estate before the tax is computed. State inheritance taxes are imposed on the person who receives a gift or statutory share from an estate. It is common, however, for wills to provide that the estate will pay all taxes, including inheritance taxes, so that the beneficiaries will not have to do so. The personal representative must also make provisions for filing an income tax return and for paying any income tax due for the partial year prior to the decedent's death.

When the debts, expenses, and taxes have been taken care of, the remaining assets of the estate are distributed to the decedent's heirs (if there was no will) or to the beneficiaries of the decedent's will. Special rules apply when the estate is too small to satisfy all of the bequests made in a will or when some or all of the designated beneficiaries are no longer living.

When the personal representative has completed all of these duties, the probate court will close the estate and discharge the personal representative.

TRUSTS

Nature of a Trust

A **trust** is a legal relationship in which a person who has legal title to property has the duty to hold it for the use or benefit of another person. The person benefited by a trust is considered to have **equitable title** to the property, because it is being maintained for his benefit. This means that he is the real owner even though the trustee has the legal title in his or her name. A trust can be created in a number of ways. An owner of property may *declare* that he is holding certain property in trust. For example, a mother might state that she is holding 100 shares of General Motors stock in trust for her daughter. A trust may also arise *by operation of law*. For example, when a lawyer representing a client injured in an automobile accident receives a settlement payment from an insurance company, the lawyer holds the settlement payment as trustee for the client. Most commonly, however, trusts are created through *express instruments* whereby an owner of property transfers title to the property to a trustee who is to hold, manage, and invest the property for the benefit of either the original owner or a third person. For example, Long transfers certain stock to First Trust Bank with instructions to pay the income to his daughter during her lifetime and to distribute the stock to her children after her death.

Trust Terminology

A person who creates a trust is known as a **settlor** or **trustor**. The person who holds the property for the benefit of another person is called the **trustee**. The person for whose benefit the property is held in trust is the **beneficiary**. Figure 3 illustrates the relationship between these parties. A single person may occupy more than one of these positions; however,

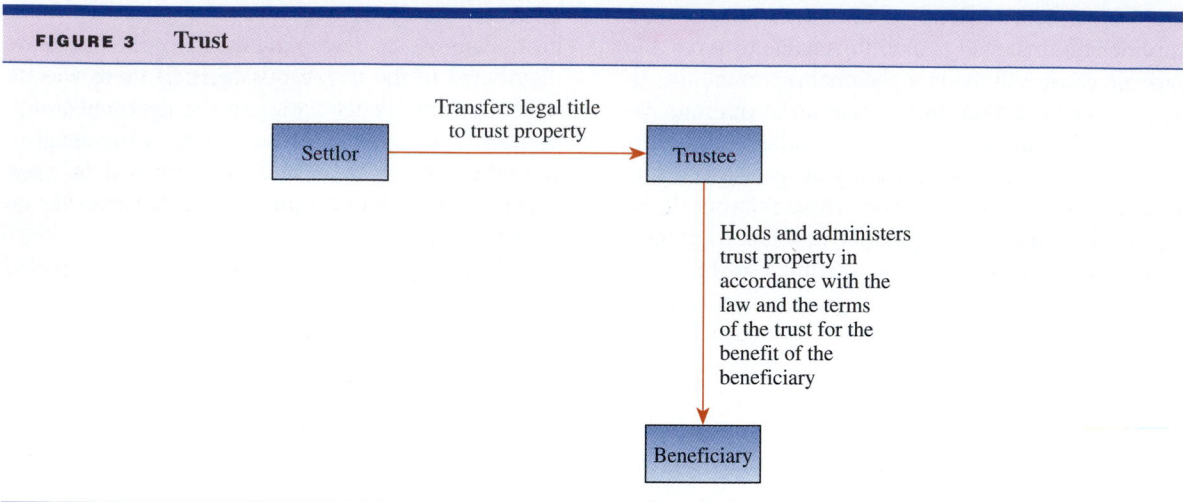

FIGURE 3   Trust

Transfers legal title to trust property

Settlor → Trustee

Holds and administers trust property in accordance with the law and the terms of the trust for the benefit of the beneficiary

Beneficiary

if there is only one beneficiary, he cannot be the sole trustee. The property held in trust is called the **corpus** or **res**. A distinction is made between the property in trust, which is the principal, and the income that is produced by the principal.

A trust that is established and effective during the settlor's lifetime is known as an **inter vivos trust**. A trust can also be established in a person's will. Such trusts take effect only at the death of the settlor. They are called **testamentary trusts**.

Why People Create Trusts

Bennett owns a portfolio of valuable stock. Her husband has predeceased her. She has two children and an elderly father for whom she would like to provide. Why might it be advantageous to Bennett to transfer the stock to a trust for the benefit of the members of her family?

First, there may be income tax or estate tax advantages in doing so, depending on the type of trust she establishes and the provisions of that trust. For example, she can establish an irrevocable trust for her children and remove the property transferred to her trust from her estate so that it is not taxable at her death. In addition, the trust property can be used for the benefit of others and may even pass to others after the settlor's death without the necessity of having a will. Many people prefer to pass their property by trust rather than by will because trusts afford more privacy: unlike a probated will, they do not become an item of public record. Trusts also afford greater opportunity

for postgift management than do outright gifts and bequests. If Bennett wants her children to enjoy the income of the trust property during their young adulthood without distributing unfettered ownership of the property to them before she considers them able to manage it properly, she can accomplish this through a trust provision. A trust can prevent the property from being squandered or spent too quickly. Trusts can be set up so that a beneficiary's interest cannot be reached by his creditors in many situations. Such trusts, called **spendthrift trusts**, will be discussed later.

Placing property in trust can operate to increase the amount of property held for the beneficiaries if the trustee makes good investment decisions. Another important consideration is that a trust can be used to provide for the needs of disabled beneficiaries who are not capable of managing funds.

Creation of Express Trusts

There are five basic requirements for the creation of a valid express trust, although special and somewhat less restrictive rules govern the establishment of charitable trusts. The requirements for forming an express trust are:

1. *Capacity.* The settlor must have had the **legal capacity** to convey the property to the trust. This means that the settlor must have had the capacity needed to make a valid contract if the trust is an *inter vivos* trust or the capacity to make a will if the trust is a testamentary trust. For example, a trust would fail under this requirement if at the time the trust was created, the settlor had not attained the age required by state law for the creation of valid wills and contracts (age 18 in most states).

2. *Intent and formalities.* The settlor must *intend* to create a trust at the present time. To impose enforceable duties on the trustee, the settlor must meet certain formalities. Under the laws of most states, for example, the trustee must accept the trust by signing the trust instrument. In the case of a trust of land, the trust must be in writing so as to meet the statute of frauds. If the trust is a testamentary trust, it must satisfy the formal requirements for wills.

3. *Conveyance of specific property.* The settlor must convey *specific property* to the trust. The property conveyed must be property that the settlor has the *right to convey*.

4. *Proper purpose.* The trust must be created for a *proper purpose*. It cannot be created for a reason that is contrary to public policy, such as the commission of a crime.

5. *Identity of the beneficiaries.* The *beneficiaries* of the trust must be described clearly enough so that their identities can be ascertained. Sometimes, beneficiaries may be members of a specific class, such as "my children."

Charitable Trusts

A distinction is made between private trusts and trusts created for charitable purposes. In a private trust, property is devoted to the benefit of specific persons, whereas in a charitable trust, property is devoted to a charitable organization or to some other purposes beneficial to society. While some of the rules governing private and charitable trusts are the same, a number of these rules are different. For example, when a private trust is created, the beneficiary must be known at the time or ascertainable within a certain time (established by a legal rule known as the **rule against perpetuities**). However, a charitable trust is valid even though no definitely ascertainable beneficiary is named and even though it is to continue for an indefinite or unlimited period.

Doctrine of Cy Pres

A doctrine known as **cy pres** is applicable to charitable trusts when property is given in trust to be applied to a particular charitable purpose that becomes impossible, impractical, or illegal to carry out. Under the doctrine of *cy pres*, the trust will not fail if the settlor indicated a general intention to devote the property to charitable purposes. If the settlor has not specifically provided for a substitute beneficiary, the court will direct the application of the property to some charitable purpose that falls within the settlor's general charitable intention.

Totten Trusts

A **Totten trust** is a deposit of money in a bank or other financial institution in the name of the depositor *as trustee* for a named beneficiary. For example, Bliss deposits money in First Bank in trust for his daughter, Bessie. The Totten trust creates a revocable living trust. At Bliss's death, if he has not revoked this trust, the money in the account will belong to Bessie.

Powers and Duties of the Trustee

In most express trusts, the settlor names a specific person to act as trustee. If the settlor does not name a trustee, the court will appoint one. Similarly, a court will replace a trustee who resigns, is incompetent, or refuses to act.

The trust codes of most states contain provisions giving trustees broad management powers over trust property. These provisions can be limited or expanded by express provisions in the trust instrument. The trustee must use a *reasonable degree of skill, judgment, and care* in the exercise of his duties unless he holds himself out as having a greater degree of skill, in which case he will be held to a higher standard. Section 7–302 of the UPC provides that the trustee is held to the standard of a prudent person dealing with the property of another, and if he has special skills or is named trustee based on a representation of special skills, he is required to use those special skills. He *may not commingle* the property he holds in trust with his own property or with that of another trust.

A trustee owes a *duty of loyalty* (fiduciary duty) to the beneficiaries. This means that he must administer the trust for the benefit of the beneficiaries and avoid any conflict between his personal interests and the interest of the trust. For example, a trustee cannot do business with a trust that he administers without express permission in the trust agreement. He must not prefer one beneficiary's interest to another's, and he must account to the beneficiaries for all transactions. Unless the trust agreement provides otherwise, the trustee must make the trust productive. He may not delegate the performance of discretionary duties (such as the duty to select investments) to another, but he may delegate the performance of ministerial duties (such as the preparation of statements of account).

A trust may give the trustee discretion as to the amount of principal or income paid to a beneficiary. In such a case, the beneficiary cannot require the trustee to exercise his discretion in the manner desired by the beneficiary.

Allocating between Principal and Income

One of the duties of the trustee is to distribute the principal and income of the trust in accordance with the terms of the trust instrument. Suppose Wheeler's will created a testamentary trust providing that his wife was to receive the income from the trust for life, and at her death, the trust property was to be distributed to his children. During the duration of the trust, the trust earns profits, such as interest or rents, and has expenses, such as taxes or repairs. How should the trustee allocate these items as between Wheeler's surviving spouse, who is an **income beneficiary**, and his children, who are **remaindermen**?

The terms of the trust and state law bind the trustee in making this determination. As a general rule, ordinary profits received from the investment of trust property are allocated to income. For example, interest on trust property or rents earned from leasing real property held in trust would be allocated to income. Ordinary expenses such as insurance premiums, the cost of ordinary maintenance and repairs of trust property, and property taxes, would be chargeable to income. The principal of the trust includes the trust property itself and any extraordinary receipts, such as proceeds or gains derived from the sale of trust property. Extraordinary expenses—for example, the cost of long-term permanent improvements to real property or expenses relating to the sale of property—would ordinarily be charged against principal.

Liability of Trustee

A trustee who breaches any of the duties of a trustee or whose conduct falls below the standard of care applicable to trustees may incur personal liability. For example, if the trustee invests unwisely and imprudently, the trustee may be personally liable to reimburse the trust estate for the shortfall. The language of the trust affects the trustee's liability and the level of care owed by the trustee. A settlor might, for example, include language lowering the trustee's duty of care or relieving the trustee of some liability that he might otherwise incur. The following *Neuhaus v. Richards* case discusses both trustee liability and the extent to which a trust instrument can limit the trustee's liability.

The trustee can also have liability to third persons who are injured by the operation of the trust. Because a trust is not in itself a legal entity that can be sued, a third party who has a claim (such as a tort claim or a claim for breach of contract) must file his claim against the trustee of the trust. The trustee's actual personal liability to a third party depends on the language of the trust and of any contracts he might enter on behalf of the trust as well as the extent to which the injury complained of by the third party was a result of the personal fault or omission of the trustee.

Neuhaus v. Richards

846 S.W.2d 70 (Tex. Ct. App. 1992)

In 1976, V. F. and Gertrude Neuhaus executed a Trust Indenture Creating the Neuhaus Family Trusts, which established a number of separate individual trusts for the benefit of their children and grandchildren, Vernon and Lacey Neuhaus. The trusts were both managed by the same cotrustees, Grace Neuhaus Richards and Robert Schwarz. The initial corpus of both trusts consisted of stock in McAllen State Bank. However, in 1982, First City Bancorporation of Texas acquired all the stock of McAllen State Bank, and First City substituted its own stock for the McAllen State Bank Stock in the trusts. From 1985 through 1987, the First City stock declined in value, but the trustees refused to sell until the stock in Lacey Neuhaus's trust became virtually worthless, and they delayed selling the stock in Vernon Neuhaus's trust until significant losses had been sustained. The Neuhauses sued both trustees alleging a breach of fiduciary duties, including a failure to exercise judgment and care, willful misconduct, and conscious disregard for the rights and welfare of the beneficiaries, among other claims. The trial court granted a summary judgment against the Neuhauses, and the Neuhauses appealed.

———————————————■———————————————

Hinojosa, Justice   The fundamental duties of a trustee include the use of the skill and prudence that an ordinary, capable, and careful person would use in the conduct of his own affairs and loyalty to the beneficiaries of the trust. In particular, one of the basic duties of a trustee is to make the assets of the trust productive while at the same time preserving the assets. Under these principles, it would appear in the present case that the trustees could be held liable for failing to sell the First City stock if their decision not to sell was imprudent. However, the settlor may within the trust instrument relieve the trustee of certain duties, restrictions, responsibilities, and liabilities imposed by statute. However, exculpatory clauses are strictly construed, and the trustee is relieved of liability only to the extent that the trust instrument clearly provides that he shall be excused.

In the present case, the trustees point to two supposedly exculpatory provisions in the present trust indenture: section V(k) and section V(v). Section V(k) provides that:

All property transferred by gift to any trust and any property acquired by the Trustees . . . shall be deemed a proper investment, and the Trustees shall be under no obligation to dispose of or convert any such property.

The trustees suggest that section V(k) completely relieves them of any duty to sell the First City stock. However, we hold that this provision is ambiguous. Section V(k) leaves uncertain whether the trustees are still under a duty to prudently manage and, if need be, sell an investment that is otherwise deemed proper, and whether the obligation to dispose of assets includes the generalized duty to manage the trust prudently or merely relieves the trustees of any specific obligation to sell a particular kind or class of investments. Even if we were to accept the trustees' interpretation that this section generally relieved them of a duty to sell or of liability for failing to sell the First City stock, nevertheless, it could not have validly relieved them of all liability for failing to sell the stock. Under Texas law, an exculpatory provision in the trust instrument is not effective to relieve the trustee of liability for action taken in bad faith or for acting intentionally adverse or with reckless indifference to the interests of the beneficiary. Courts have held that the trust instrument may relieve the trustee of the duty to act as a prudent man in determining to retain unproductive property, but not of the duty to do so honestly, in good faith, and without willful misconduct or reckless indifference to the interests of the beneficiaries. In other words, the trustee's determination to retain unproductive investments is generally protected as long as that determination was not made dishonestly, in bad faith, recklessly, or with the intent to harm the trust.

Turning to the second exculpatory provision relied upon by the trustees, section V(v) provides that "no Trustee shall be liable for negligence or error of judgment but shall be liable only for his willful misconduct or personal dishonesty." Thus, under this general exculpatory provision, the trustees are not held to the prudent person standard but may be liable only for willful misconduct or personal dishonesty. As we stated earlier, the Neuhauses alleged that in failing to sell the First City stock the trustees not only failed to act prudently but also that they acted out of willful misconduct. Because the trustees made no attempt by summary judgment evidence to negate these allegations of willful misconduct, summary judgment should not have been granted in their favor on the basis of exculpatory provisions of the trust indenture.

Reversed in favor of the Neuhauses and remanded for trial.

Spendthrift Trusts

Generally, the beneficiary of a trust may voluntarily assign his rights to the principal or income of the trust to another person. In addition, any distributions to the beneficiary are subject to the claims of his creditors. Sometimes, however, trusts contain provisions known as **spendthrift clauses**, which restrict the voluntary or involuntary transfer of a beneficiary's interest. Such clauses are generally enforced, and they preclude assignees or creditors from compelling a trustee to recognize their claims to the trust. The enforceability of such clauses is subject to four exceptions, however:

1. A person cannot put his own property beyond the claims of his own creditors. Thus, a spendthrift clause is not effective in a trust when the settlor makes himself a beneficiary.
2. Divorced spouses and minor children of the beneficiary can compel payment for alimony and child support.
3. Creditors of the beneficiary who have furnished necessaries can compel payment.
4. Once the trustee distributes property to a beneficiary, it can be subject to valid claims of others.

Termination and Modification of a Trust

Normally, a settlor cannot revoke or modify a trust unless he reserves the power to do so at the time he establishes the trust. However, a trust may be modified or terminated with the consent of the settlor and all of the beneficiaries. When the settlor is dead or otherwise unable to consent, a trust can be modified or terminated by consent of all the persons with a beneficial interest, but only when this would not frustrate a material purpose of the trust. Because trusts are under the supervisory jurisdiction of a court, the court can permit a deviation from the terms of a trust when unanticipated changes in circumstances threaten accomplishment of the settlor's purpose.

Implied and Constructive Trusts

Under exceptional circumstances in which the creation of a trust is necessary to effectuate a settlor's intent or avoid unjust enrichment, the law *implies* or imposes a trust even though no express trust exists or an express trust exists but has failed. One trust of this type is a **resulting trust**, which arises when there has been an incomplete disposition of trust property. For example, if Hess transferred property to Wickes as trustee to provide for the needs of Hess's grandfather and the grandfather died before the trust funds were exhausted, Wickes will be deemed to hold the property in a resulting trust for Hess or Hess's heirs. Similarly, if Hess had transferred the property to Wickes as trustee and the trust had failed because Hess did not meet one of the requirements of a valid trust, Wickes would not be permitted to keep the trust property as his own. A resulting trust would be implied.

A **constructive trust** is a trust created by operation of law to avoid fraud, injustice, or unjust enrichment. This type of trust imposes on the constructive trustee a duty to convey property he holds to another person on the ground that the constructive trustee would be unjustly enriched if he were allowed to retain it. For example, when a person procures the transfer of property by means of fraud or duress, he becomes a constructive trustee and is under an obligation to return the property to its original owner.

ETHICAL AND PUBLIC POLICY CONCERNS

1. What are some of the ethical implications a state legislature should take into account before adopting a living will statute or a durable power of attorney for health care statute?

2. Why should the law require so much formality to create a valid will? Would it be preferable for the law to lift some of the formalities surrounding wills and allow people to make valid wills orally, by informal letters, or by videotapes or audio recordings?

3. What is the ethical basis of a constructive trust?

PROBLEMS AND PROBLEM CASES

1. Cunningham died in 1983, leaving a writing that purported to be his will. The writing was on a preprinted will form in which the first and last part of the will were printed and the rest of the will was

handwritten by Cunningham. The first paragraph reads: "In the name of God, Amen. I," which is printed, followed by the handwriting: "Thomas John Cunningham—Social Security number 55–24–3083," which in turn is followed by printing: "being of sound mind, memory and understanding, do make and publish this my Last Will and Testament, in the manner following, that is to say: . . ." This is followed by the body of the will in Cunningham's handwriting, which gives instructions concerning the donation of bodily remains, specific bequests, and the distribution of the remainder of his estate. A printed clause appears after the body of the will, and immediately below this clause is a printed line upon which a testator normally signs his name, at the end of which is printed "Seal." Cunningham did not sign his name on this line; instead, the line contains the signature of a Notary Public of New Jersey, together with his notarial seal impressed over the printed word "Seal." Two people, a realtor (who was also the notary) and the realtor's secretary, witnessed the writing. Cunningham came to the realtor's office with the proposed will fully completed except for the witnesses' signatures. The writing was offered for probate as a will. Is the will valid?

2. Prigge died in 1982, survived by two sisters, Marian and Jean; one brother, Louis; and some nephews and nieces. John had never married and had been a farmer all his life. In 1980, he sold his farm and moved in with his sister Marian. While John was living with her, Marian, at John's request, prepared a handwritten document expressing his testamentary intent. John took the document to a lawyer, who prepared a will based on the contents of the document. John executed the will in 1981. In the will, John devised his entire estate to Marian and her six children in equal shares and specifically excluded Louis and Jean. John died in 1982. Louis and Jean contested the will on grounds of lack of testamentary capacity and undue influence. Was the will valid?

3. Roy and Icie Johnson established two revocable *inter vivos* trusts in 1966. The trusts provided that upon Roy and Icie's deaths, income from the trusts was to be paid in equal shares to their two sons, James and Robert, for life. Upon the death of the survivor of the sons, the trust was to be *divided equally between all of my grandchildren, per stirpes.* James had two daughters, Barbara and Elizabeth. Robert had four children, David, Rosalyn, Catherine, and Elizabeth. James and Robert disclaimed their interest in the trust in 1979, and a dispute arose about how the trust should be distributed to the grandchildren. The trustee filed an action seeking instructions on how the trusts should be distributed. What should the court hold?

4. Bruce Tidrow, a mentally retarded adult, was cared for at home until his mother became critically ill. When his mother died, his father applied for future residential services for him, which at that time cost $1,234 per month. Mr. Tidrow was aware that funds were generally available for financial assistance of residential-type programs and that his son would have to be institutionalized as long as he lived. A week after making this application, Mr. Tidrow executed a will, leaving the bulk of his estate in a discretionary, spendthrift trust for the benefit of Bruce, and secondarily for the benefit of his other son, Kim, with the remainder to go to Kim outright upon Bruce's death. The assets of the trust, valued at approximately $175,000, consisted mainly of a residence and proceeds of life insurance policies. Mr. Tidrow died in July 1981, and Bruce was placed in a residential program. Medical assistance to pay the cost of this residential care was applied for. State law prohibits assistance payments to anyone who is the owner or beneficial owner of cash or securities in the amount of $1,000 or more or any kind of property of a value in excess of $20,500. The Division of Family Services imputed the $175,000 trust assets to Bruce and denied his application on the ground that he had "resources in excess of the maximum allowed," and was thus financially unqualified for public assistance. Was it correct to conclude that Bruce was the beneficial owner of the trust assets?

5. Crawshaw bequeathed the bulk of his estate to two residuary beneficiaries, the Salvation Army and Marymount College. Crawshaw's will provided for 15 percent of the residue to go to the Salvation Army outright and 85 percent to Marymount College in trust. The stated purpose of this trust was to provide loans to nursing and other students at Marymount. Marymount ceased operation on June 30, 1989. It sought to have the trust funds directed to Marymount Memorial Educational Trust Fund. The Salvation Army challenged this, arguing that Crawshaw did not intend to benefit students attending colleges other than Marymount. It asked that the court distribute the trust funds to the Salvation Army as the remaining beneficiary of Crawshaw's residuary estate. What should the court do?

6. Hotarek's parents were divorced when he was two. For about 13 years after that, Hotarek's mother, Benson, had no contact with him, did not provide financial support to him, and did not display interest in her son. In 1986, at the age of 15, Hotarek was killed in an automobile accident. After his death, his estate settled a claim against the other driver for $20,000 and was awarded uninsured motorist's benefits in the amount of $525,000. These proceeds made up Hotarek's estate. Following Hotarek's death, Benson could not be located. Once she was located, the probate court ordered half of Hotarek's estate distributed to her in accordance with Connecticut's intestacy statute. It provides that if a person dies intestate leaving no spouse or children, the residue of the state shall be distributed equally to the decedent's parent or parents. Hotarek's father objected to the distribution to Benson on the ground that she had abandoned her minor child during his life and should not be entitled to share in his estate after his death. Is Benson entitled to share in her intestate son's estate?

7. Fickes, a resident of Washington, died in December 1943, leaving a will dated November 19, 1940. The will provided for the creation of a trust upon his death. The will also provided that upon the death of Fickes's last surviving child, one half of the trust property was to be distributed to Renssalaer Polytechnic Institute and the other half of the trust property distributed "in equal portions" between Fickes's "grandchildren then living." At the time of death of Fickes's last surviving child, there were four biological grandchildren living. In addition, there were four adopted grandchildren living. Two of them, grandsons, had been adopted by Fickes's son while Fickes was still living. The other two, granddaughters, were adopted by Fickes's son in 1962 and 1965, long after Fickes's death. Were the granddaughters entitled to share in the trust distribution?

CREDIT

INTRODUCTION TO CREDIT AND SECURED TRANSACTIONS

In the United States, a substantial portion of business transactions involves the extension of credit. The term credit *has many meanings. In this chapter, it will be used to mean transactions in which goods are sold, services are rendered, or money is loaned in exchange for a promise to pay for them at some future date.*

In some of these transactions, a creditor is willing to rely on the debtor's promise to pay at a later time; in others, the creditor wants some further assurance or security that the debtor will make good on his promise to pay. This chapter will discuss the differences between secured and unsecured credit and will detail various mechanisms that are available to the creditor who wants to obtain security. These mechanisms include obtaining liens or security interests in personal or real property, sureties, and guarantors. Security interests in real property, sureties and guarantors, and common law liens on personal property will be covered in this chapter, and the Uniform Commercial Code (UCC or Code) rules concerning security interests in personal property will be covered in Chapter 28, Security Interests in Personal Property. The last chapter in this part deals with bankruptcy law, which may come into play when a debtor is unable to fulfill his obligation to pay his debts when they are due.

CREDIT

Unsecured Credit

Many common transactions are based on unsecured credit. For example, a person may have a charge account at a department store or a MasterCard account. If the person buys a sweater and charges it to his charge account or MasterCard account, unsecured credit has been extended to him. He has received goods in return for his promise to pay for them later. Similarly, if a person goes to a dentist to have a tooth filled and the dentist sends her a bill payable by the end of the month, services have been rendered on the basis of unsecured credit. Consumers are not the only people who use unsecured credit. Many transactions between businesspeople utilize it. For example, a retailer buys merchandise or a manufacturer buys raw materials, promising to pay for the merchandise or materials within 30 days after receipt.

The unsecured credit transaction involves a maximum of risk to the creditor—the person who extends the credit. When goods are delivered, services are rendered, or money is loaned on unsecured credit, the creditor gives up all rights in the goods, services, or money. In return, the creditor gets a promise by the debtor to pay or to perform the promised act. If the debtor does not pay or keep the promise, the creditor's options are more limited than if he had obtained security to ensure the debtor's performance. One course of action is to bring a lawsuit against the debtor and obtain a judgment. The creditor might then have the sheriff execute the judgment on any property owned by the debtor that is subject to execution. The creditor might also try to **garnish** the wages or other moneys to which the debtor is entitled. However, the debtor might be **judgment-proof;** that is, the debtor may not have any property subject to execution or may not have a steady job. Under these circumstances, execution or garnishment would be of little aid to the creditor in collecting the judgment.

A businessperson may obtain credit insurance to stabilize the credit risk of doing business on an unsecured credit basis. However, he passes the costs of the insurance to the business, or of the unsecured credit losses that the business sustains, on to the consumer. The consumer pays a higher price for goods or services purchased, or a higher interest rate on any money borrowed, from a business that has high credit losses.

Secured Credit

To minimize his credit risk, a creditor may contract for security. The creditor may require the debtor to convey to the creditor a security interest or lien on the debtor's property. Suppose a person borrows $3,000 from a credit union. The credit union might require her to put up her car as security for the loan or might ask that some other person agree to be liable if she defaults. For example, if a student who does not have a regular job goes to a bank to borrow money, the bank might ask that the student's father or mother cosign the note for the loan.

When the creditor has security for the credit he extends and the debtor defaults, the creditor can go against the security to collect the obligation. Assume that a person borrows $18,000 from a bank to buy a new car and that the bank takes a security interest (lien) on the car. If the person fails to make his monthly payments, the bank has the right to repossess the car and have it sold so that it can recover its money. Similarly, if the borrower's father cosigned for the car loan and the borrower defaults, the bank can sue the father to collect the balance due on the loan.

Development of Security

Various types of security devices have been developed as social and economic need for them arose. The rights and liabilities of the parties to a secured transaction depend on the nature of the security—that is, on whether (1) the security pledged is the promise of another person to pay if the debtor does not, or (2) a security interest in goods, intangibles, or real estate is conveyed as security for the payment of a debt or obligation.

If personal credit is pledged, the other person may guarantee the payment of the debt—that is, become a guarantor—or the other person may join the debtor in the debtor's promise to pay, in which case the other person would become surety for the debt.

The oldest and simplest security device was the pledge. To have a pledge valid against third persons with an interest in the goods, such as subsequent purchasers or creditors, it was necessary that the property used as security be delivered to the pledgee or a pledge holder. Upon default by the pledger, the pledgee had the right to sell the property and apply the proceeds to the payment of the debt.

Situations arose in which it was desirable to leave the property used as security in the possession of the debtor. To accomplish this objective, the debtor would give the creditor a bill of sale to the property, thus passing title to the creditor. The bill of sale would provide that if the debtor performed his promise, the bill of sale would become null and void, thus revesting title to the property in the debtor. A secret lien on the goods was created by this device, and the early courts held that such a transaction was a fraud on third-party claimants and void as to them. An undisclosed or secret lien is unfair to creditors who might extend credit to the debtor on the strength of property that they see in the debtor's possession but that in fact is subject to the prior claim of another creditor. Statutes were enacted providing for the recording or filing of the bill of sale, which was later designated as a chattel mortgage. These statutes were not uniform in their provisions. Most of them set up formal requirements for the execution of the chattel mortgage and also stated the effect of recording or filing on the rights of third-party claimants.

To avoid the requirements for the execution and filing of the chattel mortgage, sellers of goods would sell the goods on a "conditional sales contract" under which the seller retained title to the goods until their purchase price had been paid in full. Upon default by the buyer, the seller could (a) repossess the goods or (b) pass title and recover a judgment for the unpaid balance of the purchase price. Abuses of this security device gave rise to some regulatory statutes. About half of the states enacted statutes providing that the conditional sales contract was void as to third parties unless it was filed or recorded.

No satisfactory device was developed whereby inventory could be used as security. The inherent difficulty is that inventory is intended to be sold and turned into cash and the creditor is interested in protecting his interest in the cash rather than in maintaining a lien on the sold goods. Field warehousing was used under the pledge, and an after-acquired property clause in a chattel mortgage on a stock of goods held for resale partially fulfilled this need. One of the devices used was the trust receipt. This short-term marketing security arrangement had its origin in the export-import trade. It was later used extensively as a means of financing retailers of consumer goods having a high unit value.

Security Interests in Personal Property

Chapter 28 will discuss how a creditor can obtain a security interest in the personal property or fixtures of a debtor. It will also explain the rights to the debtor's property of the creditor, the debtor, and other creditors of the debtor. These security interests are covered by Article 9 of the Uniform Commercial Code, which sets out a comprehensive scheme for regulating security interests in personal property and fixtures. The Code abolishes the old formal distinctions between different types of security devices used to create security interests in personal property.

Security Interests in Real Property

Three types of contractual security devices have been developed by which real estate may be used as security: (1) the real estate mortgage, (2) the trust deed, and (3) the land contract. In addition to these contract security devices, all of the states have enacted statutes granting the right to mechanic's liens on real estate. Security interests in real property are covered later in this chapter.

SURETYSHIP AND GUARANTY

Sureties and Guarantors

As a condition of making a loan, granting credit, or employing someone (particularly as a fiduciary), a creditor may demand that the debtor, contractor, or employee provide as security for his performance the liability of a third person as surety or guarantor. The purpose of the contract of suretyship or guaranty is to provide the creditor with additional protection against loss in the event of default by the debtor, contractor, or employee.

A **surety** is a person who is *liable for the payment of another person's debt or for the performance of another person's duty.* The surety joins with the person primarily liable in promising to make the payment or to perform the duty. For example, Kathleen Kelly, who is 17 years old, buys a used car on credit from Harry's Used Cars. She signs a promissory note, agreeing to pay $75 a month on the note until the note is paid in full. Harry's has Kathleen's father cosign the note; thus, her father is a surety. Similarly, the city of Chicago hires the B&B Construction Company to build a new sewage treatment plant. The city will probably require B&B to have a surety agree to be liable for B&B's performance of its contract. There are insurance companies that, for a fee, will agree to be a surety on the contract of a company such as B&B.

If the person who is primarily liable (the principal) defaults, the surety is liable to pay or perform. Upon default, the creditor may ask the surety to pay even if he has not asked the principal debtor to pay. If the surety makes good on his contract of suretyship, he is entitled to be reimbursed by the principal. While a contract of surety does not have to be in writing to be enforceable, it normally is.

A guaranty contract is similar to a suretyship contract in that the promisor agrees to answer for the obligation of another. However, a guarantor does not join the principal in making a promise; rather, a guarantor makes a separate promise and agrees to be liable upon the happening of a certain event. For example, a father tells a merchant, "I will guarantee payment of my daughter Rachel's debt to you if she does not pay it," or "If Rachel becomes bankrupt, I will guarantee payment of her debt to you." While a surety is *primarily liable,* a guarantor is *secondarily* liable and can be held to his guarantee only after the principal defaults and cannot be held to his promise or payment. Generally, a guarantor's promise must be made in writing to be enforceable under the statute of frauds.

The rights and liabilities of the surety and the guarantor are substantially the same. No distinction will be made between them in this chapter except where the distinction is of basic importance. Moreover, most commercial contracts and promissory notes today that are to be signed by multiple parties provide for the parties to be "jointly and severally" liable, thus making the surety relationship the predominate one.

Creation of Principal and Surety Relation

The relationship of principal and surety, or that of principal and guarantor, is created by contract. The basic rules of contract law apply in determining the existence and nature of the relationship as well as the rights and duties of the parties.

Defenses of a Surety

Suppose Jeffrey's mother agrees to be a surety for Jeffrey on his purchase of a motorcycle. If the motorcycle was defectively made and Jeffrey refuses to make further payments on it, the dealer might try to collect the balance due from Jeffrey's mother. As a surety, Jeffrey's mother can use any defenses against the dealer that Jeffrey has if they go to the merits of the primary contract. Thus, if Jeffrey has a valid defense of breach of warranty against the dealer, his mother can use it as a basis for not paying the dealer.

Other defenses that go to the merits include (1) lack or failure of consideration, (2) inducement of the contract by fraud or duress, and (3) breach of contract by the other party. Certain defenses of the principal cannot be used by the surety. These defenses include lack of capacity, such as minority or insanity, and bankruptcy. Thus, if Jeffrey is only 17 years old, the fact that he is a minor cannot be used by Jeffrey's mother to defend against the dealer. This defense of Jeffrey's lack of capacity to contract does not go to the merits of the contract between Jeffrey and the dealer and cannot be used by Jeffrey's mother.

A surety contracts to be responsible for the performance of the principal's obligation. If the principal and the creditor change that obligation by agreement, the surety is relieved of responsibility unless the surety agrees to the change. This is because the surety's obligation cannot be changed without his consent.

For example, Fredericks cosigns a note for his friend Kato, which she has given to Credit Union to secure a loan. Suppose the note was originally for $2,500 and payable in 12 months with interest at 11 percent a year. Credit Union and Kato later agree that Kato will have 24 months to repay the note but that the interest will be 13 percent per year. Unless Fredericks consents to this change, he is discharged from his responsibility as surety. The obligation he agreed to assume was altered by the changes in the repayment period and the interest rate.

The most common kind of change affecting a surety is an extension of time to perform the contract. If the creditor merely allows the principal more time without the surety's consent, this does not relieve the surety of responsibility. The surety's consent is required only where there is an actual binding agreement between the creditor and the principal as to the extension of time.

In addition, the courts usually make a distinction between **accommodation sureties** and **compensated sureties.** An accommodation surety is a person who acts as a surety without compensation, such as a friend who cosigns a note as a favor. A compensated surety is a person, usually a professional such as a bonding company, who is paid for serving as a surety.

The courts are more protective of accommodation sureties than of compensated sureties. Accommodation sureties are relieved of liability unless they consent to an extension of time. Compensated sureties, on the other hand, must show that they will be harmed by an extension of time before they are relieved of responsibility because of a binding extension without their consent. A compensated surety must show that a change in the contract was both material and prejudicial to him if he is to be relieved of his obligation as surety. This principle is illustrated in the *United States v. Reliance Insurance Co.* case, which follows.

If the debtor's obligation to the creditor is paid or satisfied, the surety is discharged from her obligation.

UNITED STATES v. RELIANCE INSURANCE CO.
799 F.2d 1382 (9th Cir. 1986)

On February 18, 1983, the Army-Navy Foundation, a nonprofit organization formed to facilitate preparations for the 1983 Army-Navy game, and the U.S. Military and Naval Academies entered into a contract to play the game at the Rose Bowl in Pasadena. Traditionally, the game was played in Philadelphia. The parties drew the contract to ensure that the Academies would receive approximately the same revenue from the 1983 game as they had received from the 1982 game and would not incur additional expenses as a result of the change in location.

The Foundation was entitled to "revenue generated from ticket sales and broadcast rights." The Foundation was required to pay each Academy $875,000—$550,000 from television revenues and $325,000 from ticket sales and concession proceeds. The Foundation agreed also to compensate each Academy up to $100,000 for additional costs that were "in excess of those expenses actually incurred by the Army and Navy in conjunction with the 1982 Army-Navy game." Finally, the Foundation agreed to provide funds to transport cadets, midshipmen, and support personnel to Pasadena and to provide housing and meals for them while there.

The contract required the Foundation to obtain two bonds. One bond guaranteed the Foundation's obligation of $650,000 for ticket sales and concession proceeds. The Academies released this bond when they collected the money. The second bond guaranteed the Foundation's obligation to pay up to $200,000 to cover additional expenses incurred by the Academies.

An insurance broker put the Foundation in touch with Reliance Insurance Company to obtain the bonds. Because the Foundation had no assets, Reliance required 100 percent collateral. The Foundation assured Reliance that it was entitled to the television proceeds from the game and by letter dated February 18 assured Reliance that it would assign the television proceeds to it up to the face amount of the bonds. Although initially estimated to be $1,100,000, after negotiation with ABC, the television contract amounted to $1,450,000. The Foundation never made the assignment and on their face the bonds did not mention an assignment of the television proceeds.

Subsequent to the issuance of the bonds, the Academies and the Foundation executed three modifications to the contract. The first modification changed the date of the game from December 3 to November 25; this change was required by ABC. The second modification was required by the National Collegiate Athletic Association and changed the contract to direct payment of the television proceeds to the Army as the host school, rather than to the Foundation. As a result of this modification, the Foundation was entitled to only $350,000 of the television proceeds; however, it was relieved of its $1,100,000 obligation to the Academies.

Finally, less than a week before the game, a third modification to the contract was executed. Because the air carriers hired to transport the cadets, midshipmen, and support personnel to Pasadena unexpectedly required payment prior to takeoff and the Foundation was unable to meet its contractual responsibility to make such payments because it had not yet received any ticket or television revenue, the Academies made the payments. In turn, the Foundation waived its rights to ticket revenue already retained by the Academies, which was payable to the Foundation, and to television revenues in excess of $1,100,000 (i.e., $350,000).

The only persons who had knowledge of both the Foundation's assurance that Reliance would receive an assignment of the television proceeds and the three subsequent modifications to the contract were the officers of the Foundation. Reliance knew nothing of the modifications to the contract and the Academies knew nothing of the agreement to assign the television proceeds to Reliance. When the Foundation failed to pay for the Academies' additional expenses, the Academies brought suit to recover on the bond provided by Reliance. The trial court held for Reliance and the Foundation (which was involved in the case as a third-party defendant) appealed.

Jameson, District Judge   The primary issue is whether modifications of the bonded contract exonerate Reliance. As a general rule a surety will be discharged where a bonded contract is materially altered or changed without the surety's knowledge or consent. In addition, where, as here, a compensated surety seeks exoneration, it must show that the alteration caused prejudice or damage. Thus Reliance must demonstrate that the modifications were material and that some prejudices resulted.

The second modification had no net effect. The Foundation lost the rights to $1,100,000 in television revenues, but it was also relieved of its obligation to guarantee that amount. The third modification did not relieve the Foundation of its obligation to pay the airlines. The language of the third modification clearly indicates that the Foundation remained liable for the costs of transportation. The third modification merely shifted from the Foundation to the Academies the immediate burden of providing funds for transportation. In exchange, the Foundation relinquished its sole remaining right of any significance under the contract—the right to receive the excess television revenues.

The Academies argue that this court should view the modifications of the contract only to the extent they modify the Foundation's obligation which was the subject of the bond in question—the obligation to cover the Academies' additional expenses for the football team. Because the modifications did not affect this obligation, the Academies argue that there was no material alteration of the bonded contract. This view is much too narrow.

First, courts construe a bond and its underlying contract together. Second, the bond specifically incorporated the contract. Reliance guaranteed the Foundation's obligation on the basis of the entire contract, not just a single provision. When the bond and its underlying contract are viewed together, it is clear that the modifications were both material and prejudicial.

The contract funded the otherwise assetless Foundation with ticket, concession, and television proceeds. These funds provided the Foundation with a means to satisfy its obligations. As evidenced by the Foundation's February 18 letter promising to assign television proceeds, Reliance relied on the Foundation's funding as provided in the original contract. As the District Court concluded, "The impact of the third modification on the Foundation was that it was deprived of the excess television revenues on which it depended to meet its contractual obligations, including those secured by the bond in question." Absent the provision that the Foundation would receive the television proceeds, Reliance would likely have determined the risk was too great and declined to issue the bonds. Had there been no third modification, the Foundation may have had funds available to cover its obligations. The prejudice suffered by Reliance is the increased risk resulting from the modifications. As the Court of Appeals for the District of Columbia has stated:

A surety company is not a public utility. It may, for any or no reason conclude not to furnish its bond with respect to a particular contract. When it has committed itself with respect to one contract, amendments which convert that agreement into a significantly different one should be brought to the attention of the surety so that it may exercise its own business judgment as to whether it wishes to continue its commitment. It is not for the parties to the contract to decide among themselves that their amendments are of no interest to the surety, at least when, as here, those amendments go beyond mere matters of form.

The modifications of the contract between the Academies and the Foundation were material, at least one of which, the third, was prejudicial to the rights of Reliance as surety. Reliance had no knowledge of the modifications and did not consent to them.

Judgment for Reliance affirmed.

Creditor's Duties to Surety

The creditor is required to disclose any material facts about the risk involved to the surety. If he does not do so, the surety is relieved of liability. For example, a bank (creditor) knows that an employee, Arthur, has been guilty of criminal conduct in the past. If the bank applies to a bonding company to obtain a bond on Arthur, the bank must disclose this information about Arthur. Similarly, suppose the bank has an employee, Alison, covered by a bond and discovers that Alison is embezzling money. If the bank agrees to give Alison another chance but does not report her actions to the bonding company, the bonding company is relieved of responsibility for further wrongful acts by Alison.

If the debtor posts security for the performance of an obligation, the creditor must not surrender the security without the consent of the surety. If the creditor does so, the surety is relieved of liability to the extent of the value surrendered.

Subrogation, Reimbursement, and Contribution

If the surety has to perform or pay the principal's obligation, then the surety acquires all of the rights that the creditor had against the principal. This is known as the surety's **right of subrogation.** The rights acquired could include the right to any collateral in the possession of the creditor, any judgment right the creditor had against the principal on the obligation, and the rights of a creditor in bankruptcy proceedings.

If the surety performs or pays the principal's obligation, she is entitled to recover her costs from the principal; this is known as the surety's **right to reimbursement.** For example, Amado cosigns a promissory note for $250 at the credit union for her friend Anders. Anders defaults on the note, and the credit union collects $250 from Amado on her suretyship obligation. Amado then not only gets the credit union's rights against Anders, but also the right to collect $250 from Anders.

Suppose several persons (Tom, Dick, and Harry) are cosureties of their friend Sam. When Sam defaults, Tom pays the whole obligation. Tom is entitled to collect one third from both Dick and Harry since he paid more than his prorated share. This is known as the cosurety's **right to contribution.** The relative shares of cosureties, as well as any limitations on their liability, are normally set out in the contract of suretyship.

LIENS ON PERSONAL PROPERTY

Common Law Liens

Under the common—or judge-made—law, artisans, innkeepers, and common carriers (such as airlines and trucking companies) were entitled to liens to secure the reasonable value of the services they performed. An artisan such as a furniture upholsterer or an auto mechanic uses his labor or materials to improve personal property that belongs to someone else. The improvement becomes part of the property and belongs to the owner of the property. Therefore, the artisan who made the improvement is given a **lien** on the property until she is paid.

For example, the upholsterer who recovers a sofa for a customer is entitled to a lien on the sofa. The innkeeper and common carrier are in business to serve the public and are required by law to do so. Under the common law, the innkeeper, to secure payment for his reasonable charges for food and lodging, was allowed to claim a lien on the property that the guest brought to the hotel or inn. Similarly, the common carrier, such as a trucking company, was allowed to claim a lien on the goods carried for the reasonable charges for the service. The justification for such liens was that the innkeeper and common carrier were entitled to the protection of a lien because they were required by law to provide the service to anyone seeking it.

Statutory Liens

While common law liens are still generally recognized today, many states have incorporated this concept into statutes. Some of the state statutes have created additional liens, while others have modified the common law liens to some extent. The statutes commonly provide a procedure for foreclosing the lien. **Foreclosure** is the method by which the rights of the property owner are cut off so that the lienholder can realize her security interest. Typically, the statutes provide for a court to authorize the sale of the personal property subject to the lien so that the creditor can obtain the money to which she is entitled.

Carriers' liens and warehousemen's liens are provided for in Article 7, Documents of Title, of the Uniform Commercial Code. They are covered in Chapter 33, Checks and Documents of Title.

Characteristics of Liens

The common law lien and most of the statutory liens are known as **possessory liens.** They give the artisan or other lienholder the right to keep possession of the debtor's property until the reasonable charges for services have been paid. For the lien to come into play, possession of the goods must have been entrusted to the artisan. Suppose a person takes a chair to an upholsterer to have it repaired. The upholsterer can keep possession of the chair until the person pays the reasonable value of the repair work. However, if the upholsterer comes to the person's home to make the repair, the upholsterer would not have a lien on the chair as the person did not give up possession of it.

The two essential elements of the lien are: (1) possession by the improver or the provider of services and (2) a debt created by the improvement or the provision of services concerning the goods. If the artisan or other lienholder gives up the goods voluntarily, he loses the lien. For example, if a person has a new engine put in his car and the mechanic gives the car back to him before he pays for the engine, the mechanic loses the lien on the car to secure the person's payment for the work and materials. However, if the person uses a spare set of keys to regain possession, or does so by fraud or another illegal act, the lien is not lost. Once the debt has been paid, the lien is terminated and the artisan or other lienholder no longer has the right to retain the goods. If the artisan keeps the goods after the debt has been paid, or keeps the goods without the right to a lien, he is liable for conversion or unlawful detention of goods.

Another important aspect of common law liens is that the work or service must have been performed at the request of the owner of the property. If the work or service is performed without the consent of the owner, no lien is created. This is one of the issues raised in the *Navistar Financial Corporation v. Allen's Corner Garage and Towing Service, Inc.* case, which follows.

NAVISTAR FINANCIAL CORPORATION V. ALLEN'S CORNER GARAGE AND TOWING SERVICE, INC.

505 N.E.2d 1321 (Ill. App. Ct. 1987)

Wieslaw Wik was the owner of a truck tractor on which Navistar Financial Corporation held a lien to secure a purchase loan agreement. On February 21, 1986, Wik was driving his truck tractor and pulling a trailer owned by the V. Seng Teaming Company. The tractor/trailer unit overturned in a ditch. Allen's Corner Garage and Towing Service was called by the Illinois State Police. Its crew removed the cargo from the trailer and hoisted the tractor and trailer out of the ditch and onto the highway. They then took the truck, trailer, and cargo to Allen's garage for storage. The uprighting and towing of semitrailer trucks is an intricate process and involves a good deal of specialized equipment. Allen's was licensed by the Interstate Commerce Commission and the Illinois Commerce Commission as a common carrier and owned over 50 specialized trucks and trailers for such operations.

Wik defaulted on his loan agreement with Navistar, and the right to possession passed to Navistar. One of its employees contacted Allen's and offered to pay the towing plus storage charges on the truck in exchange for possession of it. Allen's refused, saying it would not release the truck unless the charges for the truck, trailer, and cargo were all paid. Navistar then brought suit against Allen's to recover possession of the truck. Subsequently, V. Seng Teaming Company paid $13,000 in towing and storage charges on the trailer and cargo and took possession of them. Navistar then reiterated its willingness to pay the towing charges but refused to pay any storage charges accruing after its initial offer.

The trial court held that Allen's had a common law artisan's lien against the tractor for towing charges but not for storage fees. It held that Navistar was entitled to possession of the tractor, subject to payment of $1,162 for towing. Allen's appealed and Navistar cross-appealed the portion of the order granting Allen's a common law lien for towing.

------------◼------------

Unverzagt, Judge   Illinois recognizes the common law possessory lien. Such liens are fundamentally consentual in nature and can be created only by agreement, by some fixed rule of law, or by usage of trade or commerce. The common law lien has no provision for forfeiture and sale, but is limited to the right to possession of the chattel until all charges are paid. The lien applies to categories of persons: (1) those who impart added value to the property and (2) common carriers who are bound by law to accept and carry the goods. In Illinois, a common carrier has a lien on goods delivered to it for carriage; the carrier is not bound to part with the goods until the charges are paid.

Allen's argues that its services fall within both categories of common law liens. It claims that its towing and cargo salvaging operations are so specialized as to qualify it as an artisan, or alternatively, that it is a common carrier. Navistar responds that Allen's is not an artisan, citing a number of cases from Illinois and from foreign jurisdictions for the principle that mere towing of a vehicle, no matter how difficult or specialized, does not give rise to a common law lien. Most of these cases are distinguishable as they involve towing of a vehicle without the owner's consent. Nonetheless, we agree with Navistar that mere towing of a vehicle from one place to another does not add anything of value to the "intrinsic value" of the vehicle towed.

We agree with Allen's, however, that it is entitled to a lien as a common carrier. As a common carrier, it is entitled to a lien for carriage charges. Navistar does not directly challenge this conclusion, but argues that Allen's towed the tractor without its consent. As an agreement is a necessary element of a common law lien, Navistar's lack of consent would defeat Allen's lien. Although police have the power to remove disabled vehicles from highways, they may not create a lien upon a vehicle without the owner's consent. John Allen testified that a representative from Seng was at the scene when he arrived and that the entire unit was under Seng's control. Allen also testified that the driver came to Allen's place of business the following day. Testifying later, Allen stated unequivocally that Allen's Corner Garage was authorized to make the tow. The court could have concluded that the representative of Seng was authorized to and did give his consent to the towing, or that the driver subsequently ratified these actions.

Having decided that Allen's was entitled to a common law lien as a common carrier, we now turn to the question of whether it may also claim a lien for storage charges. The rule has been stated that when a common carrier hauls freight and then stores it at the destination until claimed by the receiver, the carrier becomes a warehouseman and obtains a lien for storage charges. [Citations omitted.] In those cases, the commodities involved, coal and grain, required special handling and storage. The carrier in each case sustained some inconvenience or expense by storing the property until the receiver was ready to remove it.

In the present case, Allen's did not keep the truck on the lot for the benefit of Navistar, but did so only to preserve its lien right. A garage owner is not entitled to a lien for storage in a garage. Since Allen's retained and stored the truck for no reason other than to be able to insist on its lien rights, the trial court was correct in denying it a lien for storage charges.

Judgment affirmed.

Foreclosure of Lien

The right of a lienholder to possess goods does not automatically give the lienholder the right to sell the goods or to claim ownership if his charges are not paid. Commonly, there is a procedure provided by statute for selling property once it has been held for a certain period of time. The lienholder is required to give notice to the debtor and to advertise the proposed sale by posting or publishing notices. If there is no statutory procedure, the lienholder must first bring a lawsuit against the debtor. After obtaining a judgment for his charges, the lienholder can have the sheriff seize the property and have it sold at a judicial sale.

SECURITY INTERESTS IN REAL PROPERTY

There are three basic contract devices for using real estate as security for an obligation: (1) the real estate mortgage, (2) the deed of trust, and (3) the land contract. In addition, the states have enacted statutes giving mechanics such as carpenters and plumbers, and materialmen such as lumberyards, a right to a lien on real property into which their labor or materials have been incorporated.

Historical Developments of Mortgages

A **mortgage** is a security interest in real property or a deed to real property that is given by the owner (the **mortgagor**) as security for a debt owed to the creditor (the **mortgagee**). The real estate mortgage was used as a form of security in England as early as the middle of the 12th century, but our present-day mortgage law developed from the common law mortgage of the 15th century. The common law mortgage was a deed that conveyed the land to the mortgagee, with the title to the land to return to the mortgagor upon payment of the debt secured by the mortgage. The mortgagee was given possession of the land during the term of the mortgage. If the mortgagor defaulted on the debt, the mortgagee's title to the land became absolute. The land was forfeited as a penalty, but the forfeiture did not discharge the debt. In addition to keeping the land, the mortgagee could sue on the debt, recover a judgment, and seek to collect the debt.

The early equity courts did not favor the imposition of penalties and would relieve mortgagors from such forfeitures, provided that the mortgagor's default was minor and was due to causes beyond his

control. Gradually, the courts became more lenient in permitting redemptions and allowed the mortgagor to **redeem** (reclaim his property) if he tendered performance without unreasonable delay. Finally, the courts of equity recognized the mortgagor's right to redeem as an absolute right that would continue until the mortgagee asked the court of equity to decree that the mortgagor's right to redeem be foreclosed and cut off. Our present law regarding the foreclosure of mortgages developed from this practice.

Today, the mortgage is generally viewed as a lien on land rather than a conveyance of title to the land. There are still some states where the mortgagor goes through the process of giving the mortgagee some sort of legal title to the property. Even in these states, however, the mortgagee's title is minimal and the real ownership of the property remains in the mortgagor.

Form, Execution, and Recording

Because the real estate mortgage conveys an interest in real property, it must be executed with the same formality as a deed. Unless it is executed with the required formalities, it will not be eligible for recording in the local land records. Recordation of the mortgage does not affect its validity as between the mortgagor and the mortgagee. However, if it is not recorded, it will not be effective against subsequent purchasers of the property or creditors, including other mortgagees, who have no notice of the earlier mortgage. It is important to the mortgagee that the mortgage be recorded so that the world will be on notice of the mortgagee's interest in the property. See Figure 1 for an example of a mortgage.

Rights and Liabilities

The owner (mortgagor) of property subject to a mortgage can sell the interest in the property without the consent of the mortgagee. However, the sale does not affect the mortgagee's interest in the property or the mortgagee's claim against the mortgagor. In some cases, the mortgage may provide that if the property is sold, then any remaining balance becomes immediately due and payable. This is known as a "due on sale" clause.

Suppose Erica Smith owns a lot on a lake. She wants to build a cottage on the land, so she borrows $55,000 from First National Bank. She signs a note

FIGURE 1 **A Mortgage**

MORTGAGE

THIS INDENTURE, made this 18th day of October, A.D. 1995, BETWEEN Raymond A. Dole and Deborah H. Dole, hereinafter called the Mortgagor, and First Federal Savings and Loan Association, hereinafter called the Mortgagee,

WITNESSETH, That the said Mortgagor, for and in consideration of the sum of One Dollar, to us in hand paid by the said Mortgagee, the receipt whereof is hereby acknowledged, have granted, bargained, and sold to the said Mortgagee, its heirs and assigns forever, the following described land situate, lying and being in the County of Genesee, State of Michigan, to wit:

All that certain plot, piece, or parcel of land located in the County of Genesee, State of Michigan and known and described as Lot number Thirty-nine (39) in William D. Green's subdivision of part of Lot numbered Twenty-two (22) in Square numbered Twelve Hundred Nineteen (1219), as per plot recorded in the Office of the Surveyor for the County of Genesee in Liber 30 at folio 32, together with the buildings and improvements thereon, and the said Mortgagor do hereby fully warrant the title to said land, and will defend the same against the lawful claims of all persons whomsoever.

PROVIDED ALWAYS, That if said Mortgagor, their heirs, legal representatives, or assigns shall pay unto the said Mortgagee, its legal representatives or assigns, a certain promissory note dated the 18th day of October, A.D. 1995, for the sum of Thirty-eight Thousand Dollars ($38,000.00), payable in monthly installments of Three Hundred Fifteen Dollars ($315.00) with interest at ten percent (10%) beginning on November 18, 1995, and signed by Raymond A. Dole and Deborah H. Dole and shall perform, comply with, and abide by this mortgage, and shall pay all taxes which may accrue on said land and all costs and expenses said Mortgagee may be put to in collecting said promissory note by foreclosure of this mortgage or otherwise, including a reasonable attorney's fee, then this mortgage and the estate hereby created shall cease and be null and void.

IN WITNESS WHEREOF, the said Mortgagor hereunto set their hands and seals the day and year first above written. Signed, sealed, and delivered in presence of us:

John R. Bacon)
)
James A. Brown)
)

Raymond A. Dole

Deborah H. Dole

ACKNOWLEDGMENT OF MORTGAGE
State of Michigan)
County of Genesee) ss

I, an officer authorized to take acknowledgments according to the laws of the State of Michigan, duly qualified and acting, HEREBY CERTIFY that Raymond A. Dole and Deborah H. Dole to me personally known, this day personally appeared and acknowledged before me that they executed the foregoing Mortgage, and I further certify that I know the said persons making said acknowledgment to be the individuals described in and who executed the said Mortgage.
Susan B. Clark
Notary Public

Susan B. Clark

Susan B. Clark
Notary Public

for $55,000 and gives the bank a $55,000 mortgage on the land and cottage as security for her repayment of the loan. Several years later, Smith sells her land and cottage to Melinda Mason. The mortgage she gave First National might make the unpaid balance due on the mortgage payable on sale. If it does not, Smith can sell the property with the mortgage on it. If Mason defaults on making the mortgage payments, the bank can foreclose on the mortgage. If at the foreclosure sale the property does not bring enough money to cover the costs, interest, and balance due on the mortgage, First National is entitled to a deficiency judgment against Smith. However, some courts are reluctant to give deficiency judgments where real property is used as security for a debt. If on foreclosure the property sells for more than the debt, Mason is entitled to the surplus.

A purchaser of mortgaged property may buy it **subject to** the mortgage or may **assume** the mortgage. If she buys subject to the mortgage and there is a default and foreclosure, the purchaser is not personally liable for any deficiency. The property is liable for the mortgage debt and can be sold to satisfy it in case of default; in addition, the original mortgagor remains liable for its payment. If the buyer assumes the mortgage, then she becomes personally liable for the debt and for any deficiency on default and foreclosure.

The creditor (mortgagee) may assign his interest in the mortgaged property. To do this, the mortgagee must assign the mortgage as well as the debt for which the mortgage is security. In most jurisdictions, the negotiation of the note carries with it the right to the security and the holder of the note is entitled to the benefits of the mortgage.

Foreclosure

Foreclosure is the process by which any rights of the mortgagor or the current property owner are cut off. Foreclosure proceedings are regulated by statute in the state in which the property is located. In many states, two or more alternative methods of foreclosure are available to the mortgagee or his assignee. The methods in common use today are (1) strict foreclosure, (2) action and sale, and (3) power of sale.

A small number of states permit what is called **strict foreclosure.** The creditor keeps the property in satisfaction of the debt, and the owner's rights are cut off. This means that the creditor has no right to a deficiency and the debtor has no right to any surplus. Strict foreclosure is normally limited to situations where the amount of the debt exceeds the value of the property.

Foreclosure by **action and sale** is permitted in all states, and it is the only method of foreclosure permitted in some states. Although the state statutes are not uniform, they are alike in their basic requirements. In a foreclosure by action and

sale, suit is brought in a court having jurisdiction. Any party having a property interest that would be cut off by the foreclosure must be made a defendant, and if any such party has a defense, he must enter his appearance and set up his defense. After the case is tried, a judgment is entered and a sale of the property ordered. The proceeds of the sale are applied to the payment of the mortgage debt, and any surplus is paid over to the mortgagor. If there is a deficiency, a deficiency judgment is, as a general rule, entered against the mortgagor and such other persons as are liable on the debt. Deficiency judgments are generally not permitted where the property sold is the residence of the debtor.

The right to foreclose under a **power of sale** must be expressly conferred on the mortgagee by the terms of the mortgage. If the procedure for the exercise of the power is set out in the mortgage, that procedure must be followed. Several states have enacted statutes that set out the procedure to be followed in the exercise of a power of sale. No court action is required. As a general rule, notice of the default and sale must be given to the mortgagor. After the statutory period, the sale may be held. The sale must be advertised, and it must be at auction. The sale must be conducted fairly, and an effort must be made to sell the property at the highest price obtainable. The proceeds of the sale are applied to the payment of costs, interest, and the principal of the debt. Any surplus must be paid to the mortgagor. If there is a deficiency and the mortgagee wishes to recover a judgment for the deficiency, she must bring suit on the debt.

Right of Redemption

At common law and under existing statutes, the mortgagor or an assignee of the mortgagor has what is called an **equity of redemption** in the mortgaged real estate. This means that he has the absolute right to discharge the mortgage when due and to have title to the mortgaged property restored free and clear of the mortgage debt. Under the statutes of all states, the mortgagor or any party having an interest in the mortgaged property that will be cut off by the foreclosure may redeem the property after default and before the mortgagee forecloses the mortgage. In several states, the mortgagor or any other party in interest is given by statute what is known as a redemption period (usually six months or one year, beginning either after the foreclosure proceedings are started or after a foreclosure sale of the mortgaged property has been made) in which to pay the mortgaged debt, costs, and interest and to redeem the property.

As a general rule, if a party in interest wishes to redeem, he must, if the redemption period runs after the foreclosure sale, pay to the purchaser at the foreclosure sale the amount that the purchaser has paid plus interest up to the time of redemption. If the redemption period runs before the sale, the party in interest must pay the amount of the debt plus the costs and interest. The person who wishes to redeem from a mortgage foreclosure sale must redeem the entire mortgage interest; he cannot redeem a partial interest by paying a proportionate amount of the debt or by paying a proportionate amount of the price bid at the foreclosure sale.

Deed of Trust

States typically use either the mortgage or the **deed of trust** as the primary mechanism for holding a security interest in real property. There are three parties to a deed of trust: (1) the owner of the property who borrows the money (the debtor), (2) the trustee who holds legal title to the property put up as security, and (3) the lender who is the beneficiary of the trust. The trustee serves as a fiduciary for both the creditor and the debtor. The purpose of the deed of trust is to make it easy for the security to be liquidated. However, most states treat the deed of trust like a mortgage in giving the borrower a relatively long period of time to redeem the property, thereby defeating this rationale for the arrangement.

In a deed of trust transaction, the borrower deeds to the trustee the property that is to be put up as security. See Figure 2 for an example of a deed of trust. The trust agreement usually gives the trustee the right to foreclose or sell the property if the debtor fails to make a required payment on the debt. Normally, the trustee does not sell the property until the lender notifies him that the borrower is in default and demands that the property be sold. The trustee must notify the debtor that he is in default and that the land will be sold. The trustee advertises

the property for sale. After the statutory period, the trustee will sell the property at a public or private sale. The proceeds are applied to the costs of the foreclosure, interest, and debt. If there is a surplus, it is paid to the borrower. If there is a deficiency, the lender has to sue the borrower on the debt and recover a judgment.

Land Contracts

The **land contract** is a device for securing the balance due the seller on the purchase price of real estate. Essentially, it is an installment contract for the purchase of land. The buyer agrees to pay the purchase price over a period of time. The seller agrees to convey title to the property to the buyer when the full price is paid. Usually, the buyer takes possession of the property, pays the taxes, insures the property, and assumes the other obligations of an owner. However, the seller keeps legal title and does not turn over the deed until the purchase price is paid.

If the buyer defaults, the seller usually has the right to declare a forfeiture and take over possession of the property. The buyer's rights to the property are cut off at that point. Most states give the buyer on a land contract a limited period of time to redeem his interest. Moreover, some states require the seller to go through a foreclosure proceeding. Generally, the procedure for declaring a forfeiture and recovering property sold on a land contract is simpler and less time-consuming than foreclosure of a mortgage. In most states, the procedure in case of default is set out by statute. If the buyer, after default, voluntarily surrenders possession to the seller, no court procedure is necessary; the seller's title will become absolute, and the buyer's equity will be cut off.

Purchases of farm property are commonly financed through the use of land contracts. See Figure 3 for an example of a land contract. As an interest in real estate, a land contract should be in writing and recorded in the local land records so as to protect the interests of both parties.

As can be seen in the following case, *Looney v. Farmers Home Administration*, some courts have invoked the equitable doctrine against forfeitures and have required that the seller on a land contract must foreclose on the property in order to avoid injustice to a defaulting buyer.

FIGURE 2   A Deed of Trust

DEED OF TRUST

THIS DEED made this 14th day of August, 1995, by and between Harold R. Holmes, grantor, party of the first part, and Frederick B. Cannon, trustee, party of the second part, and Sarah A Miles, party of the third part,

WITNESSETH:

The party of the first part does hereby grant unto the party of the second part, the following described property located in the District of Columbia and known as Lot number One Hundred Fourteen (114) in James B. Nicholson's subdivision in Square numbered Twelve Hundred Forty-seven (1247), formerly Square numbered Seventy-seven (77), "Georgetown," as per plat recorded in the Office of the Surveyor for the District of Columbia in Liber Georgetown 2 at folio 34, in trust, however, to secure the balance only of the purchase price of the above described premises, evidenced by the following described obligation:

Promissory note executed by the party of the first part, payable to the party of the third part and dated August 14, 1995, in the principal sum of Sixty-four Thousand Dollars ($64,000.00) bearing interest at the rate of ten percent (10%) per annum until paid. Said principal and interest are payable in monthly installments of Seven Hundred Thirty-five Dollars ($735.00) on the 14th day of each and every month beginning September 14, 1995, and continuing every month thereafter, with the unpaid balance of said principal and interest due and payable in full on August 14, 2005.

IN WITNESS WHEREOF, the party of the first part has set his hand and seal this the day and year first above written.

Harold R. Holmes

(SEAL)

Acknowledgment

This Deed of Trust accepted this 14th day of August, 1995.

Frederick B. Cannon

Trustee

LOONEY V. FARMERS HOME ADMINISTRATION

794 F.2d 310 (7th Cir. 1986)

On October 7, 1976, Lowry and Helen McCord entered into a land contract to purchase a 260-acre farm from John and Esther Looney for $250,000. The contract specified that this was to be amortized over a 20-year period at an annual interest rate of 7 percent. The McCords were to make annual payments of $23,280 on November 15 of each year until the purchase price and all accrued interest was paid. They also agreed to pay real estate taxes, insurance, and maintenance costs for the property.

Four years later, the McCords received an economic emergency loan of $183,000 from the Farmers Home Administration (FmHA). They signed a promissory note for the amount of the loan with interest at 11 percent and, as security, also granted the FmHA a second mortgage on the land subject to the land sales contract.

The McCords subsequently defaulted on their obligations to the Looneys. At the time of the default, the McCords had paid $123,280 to the Looneys but still owed $249,360.12 on the contract price. At the time, the property was worth $455,000. The Looneys brought suit against the McCords and the FmHA seeking to eject the McCords from the property and forfeiture of the contract. The FmHA objected to the proposed forfeiture and argued that the court should order foreclosure proceedings.

The district court denied the FmHA's motion for foreclosure. It held that the traditional presumption under Indiana law did not apply because the McCords had made only minimal payments on the contract and had not paid their fall taxes or insurance installments. Because $249,360.12 was still owed on an initial base price of $250,000, the court found the McCords's equity to be $639.88, only .26 percent of the principal. The court therefore found forfeiture appropriate, awarded the FmHA $639.88, and extinguished the FmHA's mortgage. The FmHA appealed.

Cudahy, Circuit Judge Under Indiana law a conditional land sales contract is considered in the nature of a secured transaction, "the provisions of which are subject to all proper and just remedies at law and in equity." *Skendzel v. Marshall.* Recognizing the common law maxim that "equity abhors forfeitures," the *Skendzel* court concluded that "judicial foreclosure of a land sales contract is in consonance with the notions of equity developed in American jurisprudence." Foreclosure generally protects the rights of all parties to a contract. Upon judicial sale the proceeds are first applied to the balance of the contract principal and interest owed the seller. Then, any junior lien-holders take their share. Any surplus goes to the buyer.

Skendzel recognized, however, two instances where forfeiture was the appropriate remedy:

In the case of an abandoning, absconding vendee, forfeiture is a logical and equitable remedy. Forfeiture would also be appropriate where the vendee has paid a minimal amount on the contract at the time of default and seeks to retain possession while the vendor is paying taxes, insurance, and other upkeep in order to preserve the premises.

The district court did not rely on the first *Skendzel* exception in finding forfeiture appropriate. No evidence in the record supports such a finding. If forfeiture is justified, then, it is only because the second *Skendzel* exception is met. This requires that the vendee have paid only a minimum amount on the contract at the time of default. In this case, the district court concluded that "this is patently a situation contemplated by the court in *Skendzel* in which forfeiture is the logical and equitable remedy."

However, the buyers in *Skendzel* had in fact paid more than a minimum amount on the contract and the court cited no examples of what would "patently" constitute a "minimum amount." Rather, later Indiana cases have interpreted *Skendzel* as requiring a case by case analysis that examines the totality of circumstances surrounding the contract and its performance. Here, while $123,280 was paid to the Looneys, the court considered all but $639.88 to be interest rather than a part of the contract price. The court equated contract price with what was paid to reduce principal. But nothing in Indiana law compels the district court's construction of payments on the contract. On the contrary, several Indiana courts have considered and given weight to both payments to reduce principal and those to reduce interest in determining whether a buyer falls within the second *Skendzel* exception.

Even where no principal is paid, a buyer's stake in the property may be sufficient to justify foreclosure. Here, two uncontested affidavits indicate the property to be worth over $200,000 more than the McCords owe the Looneys. With the evidence of appreciation, the court was incorrect to conclusively value the McCords' equity at only $639.88.

When the second *Skendzel* exception has been invoked it frequently has been because the vendee is contributing to a decline in the value of the security. There is no allegation or evidence of waste in this case. Even the Looneys admit that the buyers "had paid substantial monies pursuant to the terms of the contracts." The Looneys received $123,280 and the McCords paid the necessary real estate taxes, insurance premiums and upkeep expenses for over six years. The Looneys make no showing that foreclosure would not satisfy their interest and the court below made no such determination. While foreclosure would appear to satisfy all parties' needs, forfeiture leaves the FmHA with a $639.88 recovery on a $183,800 loan. In view of the "totality of circumstances" this result seems inequitable.

Judgment reversed in favor of Farmers Home Administration.

FIGURE 3   **A Land Contract**

LAND CONTRACT

THIS AGREEMENT, made this 15th day of September, A.D. 1995, between Sarah A. Collins, a single woman, hereinafter designated "Vendor," and Robert H. Bowen, a single man, hereinafter designated "Vendee," in the manner following: The Vendor hereby agrees to sell and the Vendee agrees to buy all that certain piece or parcel of land being in the Township of Fenton, County of Genesee and State of Michigan, and more particularly described as follows:

Part of the Northeast $\frac{1}{4}$ of the Northwest $\frac{1}{4}$ of Section 20, Township 5 North, Range 5 East, described as follows: Beginning at a point on the North line of said Section 20, which is West along said North line, 797.72 feet from the North $\frac{1}{4}$ corner of said Section 20; thence continuing West along said North line, 522.72 feet; thence South 0 degrees, 18 minutes, 12 seconds East along the West $\frac{1}{8}$ line of said Section, 1000.0 feet; thence East parallel to the North line of said Section, 522.72 feet; thence North 0 degrees, 18 minutes, 12 seconds West parallel to said West $\frac{1}{8}$ line 1000.0 feet to the point of beginning, containing 12.0 acres of land, more or less, and known as 1135 Long Lake Road.

Subject to all easements, laws, ordinances, reservations, applying to this property.

For the sum of Sixty-four Thousand Nine Hundred Dollars ($64,900.00), payable as follows: Ten Thousand Dollars ($10,000.00), cash in hand, receipt of which is hereby acknowledged before the signing of this contract and the balance payable as follows: Three Hundred Dollars ($300.00) or more payable on the 1st day of November, 1995, and a like amount on the 1st day of each and every month thereafter until the full sum of both interest and principal has been paid in full. Interest at the rate of ten percent (10%) per annum, starting October 1, 1995, shall be deducted from each and every monthly payment and the balance applied on the principal. The entire balance, both principal and interest, to be paid in full on or before 5 years from date of closing. It is understood and agreed that the above monthly payment includes taxes and insurance that may become due and payable subsequent to the date of this contract; said amounts to be paid by Vendor and added to the principal balance.

Vendee also agrees to pay all taxes and assessments extraordinary as well as ordinary that may be levied thereon, including taxes for the year 1995, and also deferred payments on special assessments that shall become due and payable after the date thereof to be prorated to date.

The Vendee agrees to keep the buildings upon or to be placed upon the premises insured against damage by fire and wind, in such company and amount as is approved by the Vendor, for the benefit of all parties in interest; such policies shall be delivered to and held by the Vendor.

And Vendee agrees to keep the buildings and other improvements on the premises in good repair. In case the Vendee shall fail to pay taxes, effect insurance, or make necessary repairs, the Vendor may do any or all of these things and the amount paid therefore by the Vendor shall be deemed a part of the principal sum under this contract and become payable immediately with interest at the rate of ten percent (10%) per annum until paid.

The Vendor on receiving payment in full of the principal and interest, and of all other sums chargeable under the contract, agrees, at his own proper cost and expense, to execute and deliver to the Vendee, or to his assigns, upon surrender of this contract, a good and sufficient conveyance in fee simple of the above described premises, free and clear of all liens and encumbrances, except such as may have accrued thereon subsequent to the date of this contract by or through the acts or negligences of others than the Vendor, and at the option of the Vendor furnish the Vendee an abstract of title or a policy of title insurance in an amount equal to the purchase price under this contract. The Vendor hereby reserves the right to mortgage said premises at any time in an amount not in excess of the amount then due on this contract, and the Vendee agrees that the said mortgage shall be a first lien on the premises.

It is mutually agreed that the Vendee shall have possession of said premises from and after October 1, 1995.

If the Vendee shall fail to comply with the terms of this contract, the Vendor may take possession of the property and all the improvements on it and treat the Vendee as a tenant holding over without permission and remove him therefrom and retain any money paid hereon as stipulated damages for nonperformance of this contract. It is hereby expressly understood and declared that time is and shall be taken as of the very essence of this contract. Notice of said forfeiture may be given by depositing the notice in post office, addressed to Vendee at his last known address.

It is agreed that the stipulations contained in this contract are to apply to and bind the heirs, executors, administrators, and assigns of the respective parties to this contract.

In witness whereof, the said parties have set their hands and seals the day and year first above written.

Signed, sealed and delivered in presence of:

Harriet Greene)   *Sarah A. Collins*
                                        Sarah A. Collins

Samuel A. Giggs)   *Robert H. Bowen*
                                        Robert H. Bowen

CONCEPT REVIEW
SECURITY INTERESTS IN REAL PROPERTY

Type of Security Instrument	Parties	Features
Mortgage	1. Mortgagor (property owner/debtor) 2. Mortgagee (creditor)	1. Mortgagee holds a security interest (and in some states, title) in real property as security for a debt. 2. If mortgagor defaults on her obligation, mortgagee must *foreclose* on property to realize on his security interest. 3. Mortgagor has a limited time after foreclosure to *redeem* her interest.
Deed of Trust	1. Owner/debtor 2. Lender/creditor 3. Trustee	1. Trustee holds legal title to the real property put up as security. 2. If debt is satisfied, the trustee conveys property back to owner/debtor. 3. If debt is not paid as agreed, creditor notifies trustee to sell the property. 4. While intended to make foreclosure easier, most states treat it like a mortgage for purposes of foreclosure.
Land Contract	1. Buyer 2. Seller	1. Seller agrees to convey title when full price is paid. 2. Buyer usually takes possession, pays property taxes and insurance, and maintains the property. 3. If buyer defaults, seller may declare a forfeiture and retake possession (most states) after buyer has limited time to redeem; some states require foreclosure.

MECHANIC'S AND MATERIALMAN'S LIENS

Each state has a statute that permits persons who contract to furnish labor or materials to improve real estate to claim a lien on the property until they are paid. There are many differences among states as to exactly who can claim such a lien and the requirements that must be met to do so.

Rights of Subcontractors and Materialmen

A general contractor is a person who has contracted with the owner to build, remodel, or improve real property. A subcontractor is a person who has contracted with the general contractor to perform a stipulated portion of the general contract. A materialman is a person who has contracted to furnish certain materials needed to perform a designated general contract.

Two distinct systems—the New York system and the Pennsylvania system—are followed by the states in allowing mechanic's liens on real estate to subcontractors and materialmen. The New York system is based on the theory of subrogation, and the subcontractors or materialmen cannot recover more than is owed to the contractor at the time they file a lien or give notice of a lien to the owner. Under the Pennsylvania system, the subcontractors or materialmen have direct liens and are entitled to liens for the value of labor and materials furnished, irrespective of the amount due from the owner to the contractor. Under the New York system, the general contractor's failure to perform his contract or his abandonment of the work has a direct effect on the lien rights of subcontractors and materialmen, whereas under the Pennsylvania system, such breach or abandonment by the general contractor does not directly affect the lien rights of subcontractors and materialmen.

Basis for Mechanic's or Materialman's Lien

Some state statutes provide that no lien shall be claimed unless the contract for the improvement is in writing and embodies a statement of the materials to be furnished and a description of the land on which the improvement is to take place and of the work to be done. Other states permit the contract to be oral, but in no state is a licensee or volunteer entitled to a lien. No lien can be claimed unless the work is done or the materials are furnished in the performance of a contract to improve specific real property. A sale of materials without reference to the improvement of specific real property does not entitle the person furnishing the materials to a lien on real property that is, in fact, improved by the use of the materials at some time after the sale.

Unless the state statute specifically includes submaterialmen, they are not entitled to a lien. For example, if a lumber dealer contracts to furnish the lumber for the erection of a specific building and orders from a sawmill a carload of lumber that is needed to fulfill the contract, the sawmill will not be entitled to a lien on the building in which the lumber is used unless the state statute expressly provides that submaterialmen are entitled to a lien.

At times, the question has arisen as to whether materials have been furnished. Some courts have held that the materialman must prove that the material furnished was actually incorporated into the structure. Under this ruling, if material delivered on the job is diverted by the general contractor or others and not incorporated into the structure, the materialman will not be entitled to a lien. Other courts have held that the materialman is entitled to a lien if he can provide proof that the material was delivered on the job under a contract to furnish the material.

Requirements for Obtaining Lien

The requirements for obtaining a mechanic's or materialman's lien must be complied with strictly. Although there is no uniformity in the statutes as to the requirements for obtaining a lien, the statutes generally require the filing of a notice of lien with a county official such as the register of deeds or the county clerk, which notice sets forth the amount claimed, the name of the owner, the names of the contractor and the claimant, and a description of the property. Frequently, the notice of lien must be verified by an affidavit of the claimant. In some states, a copy of the notice must be served on the owner or be posted on the property.

The notice of lien must be filed within a stipulated time. The time varies from 30 to 90 days, but the favored time is 60 days after the last work performed or after the last materials furnished. Some statutes distinguish between labor claims, materialmen's claims, and claims of general contractors as to time of filing. The lien, when filed, must be foreclosed within a specified time, which generally varies from six months to two years.

Priorities and Foreclosure

The provisions for priorities vary widely, but most of the statutes provide that a mechanic's lien has priority over all liens attaching after the first work is performed or after the first materials are furnished. This statutory provision creates a hidden lien on the property, in that a mechanic's lien, filed within the allotted period of time after completion of the work, attaches as of the time the first work is done or the first material is furnished, but no notice of lien need be filed during this period. And if no notice of lien is filed during this period, third persons would have no means of knowing of the existence of a lien. There are no priorities among lien claimants under the majority of the statutes.

The following case, *In Re Skyline Properties,* illustrates a number of issues that can arise when a mechanic's claim that he has a lien on certain property because of work he did concerning it is challenged by another party claiming a competing interest in the property.

In Re Skyline Properties, Inc.
Century National Bank and Trust Co. v. Skyline Properties, Inc.
134 B.R. 830 (Bankr. W.D.Pa. 1992)

In 1987, Skyline Properties commenced development of an integrated, multifaceted resort encompassing approximately 1,000 acres to be known as Hunter's Station. David Mealy was engaged to perform excavating and grading work on the project and commenced visible work on April 20, 1987. Mealy's work included bulldozing new roads, constructing parking areas, digging footers and drainage ditches, grading a basement for a new building used as a tack shop, excavation of crawl spaces for new additions to an existing building subsequently used as a sales office, grading an area for a new horse barn, and the installation of drains and fencing on the property. The sales office was substantially complete and opened for business on June 4, 1987, while work continued on construction of the tack shop.

On June 5, 1987, Century National Bank extended $150,000 credit to Skyline, took as collateral a mortgage on several of the parcels in the development, and recorded the mortgage on June 5, 1987. Mealy completed his work on August 3, 1987, and filed a notice of a mechanic's lien claim on September 23, 1987. Pennsylvania law requires that claims for such liens be filed within four months after the completion of the work.

In October 1988, the bank filed a mortgage foreclosure action against Skyline's property that it held as security for the loan. In September 1989, Mealy obtained a judgment on his claim and scheduled a sheriff's sale of the Skyline property. The sale was halted by the filing of an involuntary petition in bankruptcy. One of the issues in the bankruptcy proceeding was the relative priority of the claims of the bank and Mealy to the Skyline property.

Bemtz, Bankruptcy Judge   A mechanic's lien for services which constitute alterations and repairs takes effect and has priority as of the date the mechanic's lien claim is filed. 49 Pa.Stat.Ann. Sec. 1508(b). In the case of services constituting erection and construction, the lien of a claim takes effect and has priority "as of the date of the visible commencement upon the ground of the work of erecting or constructing the improvement." 49 Pa.Stat. Ann. Sec. 1508(a).

This matter involves the following relevant dates:

Visible commencement of construction:	April 20, 1987
Bank's mortgage:	June 5, 1987
Mealy Claim filed:	September 23, 1987

Thus, if Mealy's work is erection and construction, Mealy's Claim has priority over the Bank; if the work is alteration or repair, the Bank's mortgage takes priority.

Section 1201(10) of the Mechanic's Lien Law defines "erection and construction" as follows:

"Erection and construction" means the erection and construction of a new improvement or of a substantial addition to an existing improvement or any adaption of an existing improvement rendering the same fit for a new or distinct use and effecting a material change in the interior or exterior thereof.

The Bank asserts that no buildings were erected or constructed in conjunction with Mealy's work and Mealy's lien is for alterations and repairs. Thus the Bank asserts that Mealy's lien takes priority as of the date of filing of the Claim and not the date of visible commencement of the work.

The concern in determining whether the work is "erection and construction" or "alterations or repairs" is whether a substantial change to the existing structure has occurred such that any third party, such as the Bank, would be on notice that potential liens could exist. A change in the appearance or use of a building is sufficient to give such notice.

In the present case, the evidence reveals that a farmhouse on the property, formerly used as a residential dwelling, was converted into a sales office used to sell ownership interests in the development. Skyline converted an existing farmhouse into a sales office by essentially "gutting" the structure and constructing additions to the original dwelling. The appearance of the house was transformed into a commercial building and the use was altogether different. The addition to the building made it substantially larger than it had been as a private residence. The additions are substantial enough to be considered new construction. The work was substantially completed and the sales office open for business on June 4, 1987, one day *before* the Bank recorded its mortgage. Had the Bank, which was aware of the scope of the planned construction, viewed the property at the time it recorded its mortgage, it certainly would have known that potential liens could exist.

The tack shop was built on existing concrete blocks which had served as the foundation for a building that [had] previously fallen down or been removed. The tack shop has both a "new use" and a "new appearance" and constitutes erection and construction.

Grading and excavation is the type of work which is properly lienable as incident to the erection or construction of an improvement. Another way of stating the test utilized by the Pennsylvania courts in determining whether a certain type of work is lienable is whether the work is incident to the construction of an improvement. Mealy graded the area for four structures—the sales office, the tack shop, the horse barn and arena, and the guardhouse. Mealy dug footers and drainage ditches for the sales office and the guardhouse and installed drains for the tack shop. The work Mealy performed was incident to the construction of these improvements and also designed to enhance their value by building a resort around them.

Mealy's lienable work, incident to the erection and construction of four structures, as opposed to merely alteration and repair, entitles Mealy to a claim which relates back in time to the date upon which work was commenced and therefore, is prior to the Bank's mortgage interest.

Order upholding Mealy's lien claim.

The procedure followed in the foreclosure of a mechanic's lien on real estate follows closely the procedure followed in a court foreclosure of a real estate mortgage. The rights acquired by the filing of a lien and the extent of the property covered by the lien are set out in some of the mechanic's lien statutes. In general, the lien attaches only to the interest that the person has in the property that has been improved at the time the notice is filed. Some statutes provide that the lien attaches to the building and to the city lot on which the building stands, or if the improvement is to farm property, the lien attaches to a specified amount of land.

Waiver of Lien

The question often arises as to the effect of an express provision in a contract for the improvement of real estate that no lien shall attach to the property for the cost of the improvement. In some states, there is a statute requiring the recording or filing of the contract and making such a provision ineffective if the statute is not complied with. In some states, courts have held that such a provision is effective against everyone; in other states, courts have held that the provision is ineffective against everyone except the contractor; and in still other states, courts have held that such a provision is ineffective as to subcontractors, materialmen, and laborers. Whether the parties to the contract have notice of the waiver of lien provision plays an important part in several states in determining their right to a lien.

It is common practice that before a person who is having improvements made to his property makes final payment, he requires the contractor to sign an affidavit that all materialmen and subcontractors have been paid and to supply him with a release of lien signed by the subcontractors and materialmen.

ETHICAL AND PUBLIC POLICY CONCERNS

1. Suppose you operate an appliance store in an inner city neighborhood. Many of your potential customers do not have sufficient income to pay cash for goods such as television sets, VCRs, and stereo sets, and they also have difficulty qualifying for credit cards or store charge accounts. You develop a "lease to buy" sales program whereby you offer those prospective customers the opportunity to lease a TV, VCR, or stereo on a weekly rental basis, and after they have leased it for two years, they will be the owner of it. The total amount they would pay as rent for the item over the two years is about three times the retail cash price for the item. This element is not disclosed in your ads; rather, the focus is on the "opportunity to own" and the "low weekly payment." What ethical considerations are involved in your proposed sales program?

2. Suppose you own and operate a small loan business. A young man applies for a $1,000 loan. When you run a credit check on him, you find that he has had difficulty holding a job and has a terrible credit record. You conclude that he is a poor credit risk and inform him that you are willing to make the requested loan only if he can find someone who has a good credit rating to cosign a promissory note with him. The next day he comes by the office with a young woman who meets your criteria for a good credit rating and who indicates she is willing to cosign the note. Do you have any ethical obligation to share with the young woman the information you have about the young man's employment and credit history?

3. Suppose you have sold a farm to a young couple on a land contract that calls for them to pay off the purchase price over a 10-year period. After the couple has paid about a third of the purchase price, a serious drought damages their crop and they miss several payments, triggering your right to declare a default and reclaim possession of the property. Are there any ethical considerations involved in your taking such an action that you are otherwise legally entitled to take? If you proceed with a forfeiture action in court, what policy considerations should the court take into account in deciding whether to grant your request?

1. Bayer was the general contractor on a Massachusetts state highway contract. He hired Deschenes as a subcontractor to do certain excavation work. Deschenes was to start the job by November 24, 1988, and to complete it on or before March 1, 1989. Deschenes was required to furnish a bond of $91,000 to ensure his faithful performance of the subcontract, and he purchased such a bond from Aetna Insurance Company. Deschenes began the work on December 1, 1988, and quit on June 22, 1989, after completing only about half of the work. Bayer had made numerous efforts to get Deschenes to do the work and then completed the job himself when Deschenes walked off the job. Bayer brought a lawsuit against Aetna on the bond, and Aetna claimed that it was discharged by the extension of time given to Deschenes. Should Bayer recover on the bond?

2. Rusty Jones, a used car dealer, applied to First Financial Federal Savings and Loan Association for a $50,000 line of credit to purchase an inventory of used cars. First Financial refused to make the loan to Jones alone but agreed to do so if Worth Camp, an attorney and friend of Jones, would cosign the note. Camp agreed to cosign as an accommodation maker or surety. The expectation of the parties was that the loans cosigned by Camp would be repaid from the proceeds of the car inventory. The original note for $25,000 was signed on August 2, 1984, and renewals were executed on January 25, 1985, September 11, 1985, and March 15, 1986, and the amount was eventually increased to $50,000. In August 1985, as Camp was considering whether to sign the September renewal note, he was advised by First Financial's loan officer that the interest on the loan had not been paid. In fact, interest payments were four months delinquent. In addition, unknown to Camp, as the $50,000 credit limit was approached, First Financial began making side, or personal, loans to Jones totaling about $25,000, which were also payable out of the used car inventory. Camp knew nothing of these loans and thought that Jones's used car business was making payments only on the loans he had cosigned. Jones defaulted on the $50,000 note cosigned by Camp and First Financial brought suit against Camp on his obligation as surety on the note. Was Camp relieved of his obligation as surety by First Financial's failure to disclose material facts to him?

3. Maxwell owned the timber on a certain tract of land. He hired Fitzgerald to cut the timber into logs and to put the logs in Maxwell's mill pond. Fitzgerald did the work but was not paid for it as promised. He claims a common law lien on the logs for his work in cutting and hauling them. Is Fitzgerald entitled to a common law lien on the logs?

4. During May and June, John Shumate regularly parked his automobile on a vacant lot in downtown Philadelphia. At that time, no signs were posted prohibiting parking on the lot or indicating that vehicles parked there without authorization would be towed. On July 7, Shumate again left his car on the lot. When he returned two days later, the car was gone and the lot was posted with signs warning that parking was prohibited. Shumate learned that his car had been towed away by Ruffie's Towing Service and that the car was being held by Ruffie's at its place of business. Ruffie's refused to release the car until Shumate paid a towing fee of $44.50 plus storage charges of $4 per day. Shumate refused to pay the fee, and Ruffie's kept possession of the car. Did Ruffie's have a common law possessory lien on the car?

5. Betty Nelson signed a promissory note payable to Family Bank in return for a loan the bank had made to her. The note was secured by a deed of trust on a duplex owned by Nelson. When the note was signed, the duplex was rented to third parties. Nelson defaulted on the note and Family Bank filed a complaint to foreclose the trust deed. Nelson advised the bank that she and her son were occupying the duplex as their residence. Under Oregon law, a lender can obtain a deficiency judgment in connection with the foreclosure of a commercial deed of trust; however, a deficiency judgment is not available in connection with the foreclosure of a noncommercial (residential) deed of trust. If Family Bank went forward with foreclosure of the deed of trust, could it obtain a deficiency judgment against Nelson if the sale of the property produced less than the amount of the debt?

6. Philip and Edith Beh purchased some property from Alfred M. Gromer and his wife. Sometime earlier, the Gromers had borrowed money from City Mortgage. They had signed a note and had given City Mortgage a second deed of trust on the property. There was also a first deed of trust on the property at the time the Behs purchased it. In the contract of sale between the Behs and the Gromers, the Behs promised to "assume" the second deed of trust of approximately $5,000 at 6 percent interest. The Behs later defaulted on the first deed of trust. Foreclosure was held on the first deed of trust, but the proceeds of the sale left nothing for City Mortgage on its second deed of trust. City Mortgage then brought a lawsuit against the Behs to collect the balance due on the second deed of trust. When the Behs "assumed" the second deed of trust, did they become personally liable for it?

7. Pope agreed to sell certain land to Pelz and retained a mortgage on the property to secure payment of the purchase price. The mortgage contained a clause providing that if Pelz defaulted, Pope had the "right to enter upon the above-described premises and sell the same at public sale" to pay the balance of the purchase price, accounting to Pelz for any surplus realized on the sale. What type of foreclosure does this provision contemplate: (1) strict foreclosure, (2) action and sale, or (3) private power of sale?

8. In October 1972, Verda Miller sold her 107-acre farm for $30,000 to Donald Kimball, who was acting on behalf of his own closely held corporation, American Wonderlands. Under the agreement, Miller retained title and Kimball was given possession pending full payment of all installments of the purchase price. The contract provided that Kimball was to pay all real estate taxes. If he did not pay them, Miller could discharge them and either add the amounts to the unpaid principal or demand immediate payment of the delinquencies plus interest. Miller also had the right to declare a forfeiture of the contract and regain possession if the terms of the agreement were not met. In 1975, Miller had to pay the real estate taxes on the property in the amount of $672.78. She demanded payment of this amount plus interest from Kimball. She also served a notice of forfeiture on him that he had 30 days to pay. Kimball paid the taxes but refused to pay interest of $10.48. Miller made continued demands on Kimball for two months, then filed notice of forfeiture with the county recorder in August 1975. She also advised Kimball of this. Was Miller justified in declaring a forfeiture and taking back possession of the land?

9. Edwin Bull was the owner of an 80-foot fishing trawler named the *Bull Head* that had been leased for use in dismantling a bridge over the Illinois River at Pekin, Illinois. At the termination of the lease, the *Bull Head* was towed upriver to Morris, Illinois, not operating on its own power. At Morris, a tugboat owned by Iowa Marine Repair Corporation was used to remove the *Bull Head* from the tow and to move it to the south bank of the river where it was tied up. Several months later, the *Bull Head* was moved across the river by Iowa Marine and moored at a place on the north bank where it maintained its fleeting operations. The *Bull Head* remained there for several years and greatly deteriorated. Iowa Marine sent Bull a bill for switching, fleeting, and other services. Bull refused to pay and brought suit against Iowa Marine to recover possession of the boat. In turn, Iowa Marine claimed that it had a mechanic's lien on the *Bull Head* and that the boat should be sold to satisfy the lien. Illinois law provides that:

any architect, contractor, subcontractor, materialman, or other person furnishing services, labor, or material for the purpose of, or in constructing, building, altering, repairing or ornamenting a boat, barge, or watercraft shall have a lien on such boat for the value of such services, labor, or material in the same manner as in this act provided for the purpose of building, altering, repairing, or ornamenting a house or other building.

Does Iowa Marine have a valid mechanic's lien on the boat for its switching, fleeting, and storage services?

10. Albert Sharkey was the owner of a commercial building that was leased to Consolidated Freightways for more than 10 years before the lease was terminated by Consolidated on October 25, 1982. Consolidated's lease with Sharkey provided that Consolidated would leave the property in as good condition as received. Consolidated was responsible for damaging 10 overhead doors and contacted Dewco Building Systems to repair the damage. Dewco ordered new doors from Overhead. Overhead specially ordered the doors and paid for them on delivery from the manufacturer. On March 18, 1983, Overhead submitted its bill to Dewco. Overhead was unable to collect since Dewco had gone out of business and filed for bankruptcy. Dewco had already collected $10,397 from Consolidated and owed $6,685 to Overhead. On May 10, 1983, Overhead filed a mechanic's lien against Sharkey's property and brought a lawsuit to enforce the lien. Iowa Code Section 572.2 provides that:

Every person who shall furnish any material or labor for, or perform any labor, upon any building or land for improvement, alteration or repair thereof, including those engaged in the construction or repair of any work of internal or external improvement . . . by virtue of any contract with the owner, his agent, trustee, contractor, or subcontractor shall have a lien upon such building or improvement, and land belonging to the owner on which the same is situated . . . , to secure payment for material or labor furnished or labor performed.

Does Overhead have a valid claim for a mechanic's lien on Sharkey's property?

SECURITY INTERESTS

IN

PERSONAL PROPERTY

INTRODUCTION

In many credit transactions the creditor, in order to protect his investment, takes a security interest, or lien, in personal property belonging to the debtor. The law covering security interests in personal property is set forth in Article 9 of the Uniform Commercial Code. Article 9, entitled Secured Transactions, applies to situations that consumers and businesspeople commonly face; for example, the financing of an automobile, the purchase of a refrigerator on a time-payment plan, or the financing of business inventory.

ARTICLE 9

If a creditor wants to obtain a security interest in the personal property of the debtor, he also wants to be sure that his interest is superior to the claims of other creditors. To do so, the creditor must carefully comply with Article 9. In Part IV, Sales, we pointed out that businesspersons sometimes leave out important terms in a contract or insert vague terms to be worked out later. Such looseness is a luxury that is not permitted in secured transactions. If a debtor gets into financial difficulties and cannot meet her obligations, even a minor noncompliance with Article 9 may cause the creditor to lose his preferred claim to the personal property of the debtor. A creditor who loses his secured interest is only a general creditor if the debtor is declared bankrupt. As a general creditor in bankruptcy proceedings, he may have little chance of recovering the money owed by the debtor because of the relatively low priority of such claims. Chapter 29, Bankruptcy, covers this in detail.

Article 9 has not been adopted in exactly the same form in every state. The law of each state must be examined carefully to determine the procedure for obtaining a secured interest and the rights of creditors and debtors in that state. The general concepts are the same in every state, however, and these concepts are the basis of our discussion in this chapter.

SECURITY INTERESTS UNDER THE CODE

Security Interests

Basic to a discussion of secured consumer and commercial transactions is the term **security interest**. A security interest is an interest in personal property or fixtures obtained by a creditor to secure payment or performance of an obligation [1–201(37)].[1] For example, when a person borrows money from a bank to buy a new car, the bank takes a security interest, or puts a lien, on the car until the loan is repaid. If the person defaults on the loan, the bank can repossess the car and have it sold to cover the unpaid balance. A security interest is a property interest in the collateral.

While one usually thinks of goods as being put up as collateral, the Code actually covers secured interests in a much broader grouping of personal property. The Code breaks down personal property into a number of different classifications that are important in determining how a creditor acquires an enforceable security interest in a particular collateral. The Code classifications are:

1. *Instruments.* This category includes checks, notes, drafts, stocks, bonds, and other investment securities [9–105(i)].

2. *Documents of title.* This category includes bills of lading, dock warrants, dock receipts, and warehouse receipts.

3. *Accounts.* This category includes rights to payment for goods sold or leased or for services rendered that are not evidenced by instruments or chattel paper but are carried on open account. The category includes such rights to payment whether or not they have been earned by performance [9–106].

4. *Chattel paper.* This category includes written documents that evidence both an obligation to pay money and a security interest in specific goods [9–105]. A typical example of chattel paper is what is commonly known as a conditional sales contract. This is the type of contract that a consumer might sign when she buys a large appliance, such as a refrigerator, on a time-payment plan.

5. *General intangibles.* Among the items in this catchall category are patents, copyrights, literary royalty rights, franchises, and money [9–106].

6. *Goods.* Goods are divided into several classes; the same item of collateral may fall into different classes at different times, depending on its use.

   a. Consumer goods. These goods are used or bought for use primarily for personal, family, or household purposes. They include automobiles, furniture, and appliances.

   b. Equipment. This includes goods used or bought for use primarily in business, including farming and professions.

   c. Farm products. These are crops, livestock, or supplies used or produced in farming operations as long as they are still in the possession of a debtor engaged in farming.

   d. Inventory. This includes goods held for sale or lease or for use under contracts of service as well as raw materials, work in process, and materials used or consumed in a business.

   e. Fixtures. These are goods so affixed to real property as to be considered a part of it [9–109].

In different situations, an item such as a stove could be classified as inventory, equipment, or consumer goods. In the hands of the manufacturer or an appliance store, the stove is "inventory" goods. If it is used in a restaurant, it is "equipment." If it was purchased by a consumer for use in her home, it is "consumer goods."

Obtaining a Security Interest

The goal of a creditor is to obtain a security interest in certain personal property that will be good against: (1) the debtor, (2) other creditors of the debtor, and (3) a person who might purchase the property from the debtor. In case the debtor defaults on the debt, the creditor wants to have a better right to claim the property than anyone else. Obtaining an enforceable security interest is a two-step process—attachment and perfection.

ATTACHMENT OF THE SECURITY INTEREST

Attachment

A security interest is not legally enforceable against a debtor until it is attached to one or more particular items of the debtor's property. The **attachment** of the security interest takes place in a legal sense rather than in a physical sense. There are three basic requirements for a security interest to be attached to the goods of a debtor [9–203]: First is an *agreement* in which the debtor grants the creditor a security interest in particular property (collateral) in which the

---

[1]The numbers in brackets refer to sections of the Uniform Commercial Code.

debtor has an interest. Second, the debtor must have *rights in the collateral.* Third, the creditor must give value to the debtor. The creditor must, for example, lend money or advance goods on credit to the debtor. Unless the debtor owes a debt to the creditor, there can be no security interest. The purpose of obtaining a security interest is to secure a debt.

The Security Agreement

The agreement in which a debtor grants a creditor a security interest in the debtor's property must generally be in writing and signed by the debtor. A written agreement is required in all cases except where the creditor has possession of the collateral [9–203]. Suppose Cole borrows $50 from Fox and gives Fox her wristwatch as a security for the loan. The agreement whereby Cole put up her watch as collateral does not have to be in writing to be enforceable. Because the creditor (Fox) is in possession of the collateral, an oral agreement is sufficient.

The security agreement must reasonably describe the collateral so that it can readily be identified. For example, it should list the year, make, and serial number of an automobile. The security agreement usually spells out the terms of the arrangement between the creditor and the debtor. Also, it normally contains a promise by the debtor to pay certain amounts of money in a certain way. The agreement specifies which events, such as nonpayment by the buyer, constitute a default. In addition, it may contain provisions that the creditor feels are necessary to protect his security interest. For example, the debtor may be required to keep the collateral insured, not to move it without the creditor's consent, or to periodically report sales of secured inventory goods. See Figure 1 for an example of a security agreement.

In the case that follows, *In Re Hardage,* Sears was deemed to have obtained a valid security agreement from its debtor even though the document constituting it was missing certain critical terms.

In Re Hardage

99 BR 738 (Bankr. N.D. Tex. 1989)

On June 14, 1986, Jimmy Hardage purchased a videocassette recorder for $315.36 from Sears Roebuck & Co. (Sears), and on November 8, 1987, he purchased a guitar board from Sears for $181.89. In each case he used his Sears charge card to make the purchase and signed the sales slips at the time of purchase. The sales slips contained, among other things, this information:

1. Hardage's credit account number.
2. Hardage's name.
3. The date of purchase.
4. The amount of the purchase.
5. A brief description of the goods sold.
6. An invoice number.
7. Hardage's address.
8. Hardage's signatures immediately below the following legend:

This purchase is subject to the approval of the Sears Credit Sales Department and is made under my SearsCharge Account Security Agreement for my SearsCharge Modernizing Credit Plan Security Agreement which is incorporated herein by reference. I agree that Sears retains a security interest under the Uniform Commercial Code in the merchandise purchased until fully paid.

On December 17, 1987, Hardage and his wife, Danelle, filed for relief under Chapter 7 of the Bankruptcy Code. They listed Sears as an unsecured creditor to whom they owed $1,453.07. Sears claimed that it had a security interest in the videocassette recorder and the guitar board for the amount of $402.64 (the balance remaining unpaid on the two items).

Akard, Bankruptcy Judge   The issue before the court is: Do the sales slips denominated "credit billing copy," of Sears, Roebuck & Co. (Sears), constitute valid security agreements such that pursuant to Uniform Commercial Code (UCC) Article 9 Sears has perfected security interests in the consumer goods sold?

The Texas version of the UCC sets forth the formal requisite a party must follow to create an Article 9 security interest enforceable against the buyer or third parties with respect to the collateral. In pertinent part, these steps are: (1) the debtor signs a security agreement which contains a description of the collateral; (2) value has been given; and (3) the debtor has rights in the collateral. Section 9–203(a). A financing statement is not necessary to perfect a purchase money security interest in consumer goods.

The writing requirement may be simply expressed as follows; it must: (1) contain sufficient language to embody a "security agreement"; (2) include an adequate description of the collateral; and (3) be signed by the debtor. Since items 2 and 3 are not in dispute, we turn to item one, the sufficiency of the language to embody a security agreement.

Section 9–105(a)(12) states a security agreement means "an agreement which creates or provides for a security interest." Where the parties are in dispute on the issue, the court may have to resolve first, as a question of law, whether the language in the agreement objectively indicates the parties may have intended to create or provide for a security interest.

Although some courts read "may have intended" to require more, other courts rely on Comment 5 to section 9–203, which states that the writing requirement is more in the nature of satisfaction of the statute of frauds.

The UCC does not require special words or any special form to show a possible security interest. Further, the courts have recognized unorthodox documents containing certain words as adequate security agreements. Even when conventional words do not appear, some courts find security agreements. Or, where one document is not sufficient to create a valid security interest, creditors may show such creation by introducing multiple executed documents. Therefore, once the agreement meets the section 9–203 writing requirement, the court may or may not ask for other evidence of whether the parties actually intended to create a security interest, a question of fact.

The court concludes that as a matter of law the sales slips retained a security interest in the items purchased. Clearly Sears intended for the sales slips to be a security agreement and the intention of Mr. Hardage for the sales slips to be a security agreement must be found from the fact that he signed the sales slips immediately below the language creating the security interest.

Judgment for Sears.

Future Advances

A security agreement may stipulate that it covers advances of credit to be made at some time in the future [9–204(3)]. Such later extensions of credit are known as **future advances.** Future advances would be involved where, for example, a bank grants a business a line of credit for $100,000 but initially advances only $20,000. When the business draws further against its line of credit, it has received a future advance and the bank is considered to have given additional "value" at that time. The security interest that the creditor obtained earlier also covers these later advances of money.

After-Acquired Property

A security agreement may be drafted to grant a creditor a security interest in the **after-acquired property** of the debtor. After-acquired property is property that the debtor does not currently own or have rights in but that he may acquire in the future. However, the security interest does not attach until the debtor actually obtains some rights to the new property [9–204].[2] For

---

[2]The Code imposes an additional requirement as to security interests in after-acquired consumer goods. Security interests do not attach to consumer goods other than accessions unless the consumer acquires them within 10 days after the secured party gave value [9–204(2)].

FIGURE 1   **A Security Agreement**

BUYER ~~Mr. and Mrs.~~ ~~Mrs.~~ Miss *Cheryl Cole*

ADDRESS *542 Oakdale*

CITY *Chicago, Il.*   TEL. NO. *828-0290*

DELIVER TO: *542 Oakdale*

Account No.

C-1005

Date

SECURITY AGREEMENT
ACE APPLIANCE

THIS AGREEMENT, executed between Ace Appliance, as Secured Party ("Seller"), and Buyer named above, as Debtor ("Buyer"): Seller agrees to sell and Buyer agrees to purchase, subject to the terms, conditions, and agreements stated in this agreement, the goods described below (the "Collateral"), Seller reserving and Buyer granting a purchase money security interest in the Collateral to secure the payment of the balance owed (Item 7) and all other present and future obligations of Buyer to Seller.

DESCRIPTION OF COLLATERAL

Quan.	Article	Unit Price	Total		TERMS	
1	Refrig	545	—	545	(1) Cash Price	104 00
1	Stove	495	—	495	(2) Down Payment	100 00
					Trade-in	
					Unpaid Principal	
					(3) Balance Owed	94 00
					(4) Finance Charge	100 00
					Time Balance	
					(5) Owed	1040 00
					(6) Sales tax	40 00
					(7) Balance Owed	1080 00

Buyer agrees to pay Seller, without relief from valuation and appraisement laws, the balance owed (Item 7) of $ *1080 00*

in *11* successive ~~weekly~~ monthly installments of $ *90 00* each and a final installment of $ *90 00* , commencing on

Jan. 1 , 19 *95* and continuing thereafter on the same day of each ~~week~~ month until paid, together with all deliquent charges, costs of repossession, collection, disposition, maintenance, and other like charges, allowed by law, and reasonable attorney's fees.

   This sale is made subject to the terms, conditions, and agreements stated above on the reverse side. Buyer represents that the correct name and address of Buyer is as stated above, and that all statements made by buyer as to financial condition and credit information are true.

   Buyer acknowledges delivery by Seller to Buyer of a copy of this agreement.

   Buyer warrants and represents that the Collateral will be kept at Buyer's address unless otherwise specified as follows: _____

and will be used or is purchased for use primarily for: (check one) family or household purposes ☒; business use ☐; farming operations ☐. The Collateral will not be affixed to real estate unless checked here ☐. If the Collateral is to be affixed to real estate, a description of the real estate is as follows: _____

and the name of the record owner is _____

FIGURE 1 *(concluded)*

IN WITNESS WHEREOF, the parties have executed this agreement on this *1st* day of *Dec*,19 *94*.
BUYER'S SIGNATURE (Ace Appliance) Seller (as Secured party) *Cheryl Cole* By *Frank Singer*
(as debtor)

TERMS, CONDITIONS, AND AGREEMENTS

1. The security interest of Seller shall extend to all replacements, proceeds (including tort claims and insurance), and accessories, and shall continue until full performance by Buyer of all conditions and obligations under this agreement.

2. Buyer shall maintain the Collateral in good repair, pay all taxes and other charges levied upon the Collateral when due, and shall defend the Collateral against any claims. Buyer shall not permit the Collateral to be removed from the place where kept without the prior written consent of Seller. Buyer shall give prompt witten notice to Seller of any transfer, pledge, assignment, or any other process or action taken or pending, voluntary or involuntary, whereby a third party is to obtain or is attempting to obtain possession of or any interest in the Collateral. Seller shall have the right to inspect the Collateral at all reasonable times. At its option, but without obligation to Buyer and without relieving Buyer from any default, Seller may discharge any taxes, liens, or other encumbrances levied or placed upon the Collateral for which Buyer agrees to reimburse Seller upon demand.

3. If the Collateral is damaged or destroyed in any manner, the entire balance remaining unpaid under this agreement (the "Agreement Balance") shall immediately become due and payable and Buyer shall first apply any insurance or other receipts compensating for such loss to the Agreement Balance. Buyer shall fully insure the Collateral, for the benefit of both Seller and Buyer, against loss of fire, theft, and other casualties by comprehensive extended coverage insurance in an amount equal to the balance owed under this agreement.

4. Buyer shall pay all amounts payable when due at the store of Seller from which this sale is made or at Seller's principal office in *Gary* , Indiana, and upon default shall pay the maximum delinquent charges permitted by law. Upon prepayment of the Agreement Balance, Seller shall allow the minimum discount permitted by law.

5. Time is of the essence of this agreement. Buyer agrees that the following shall constitute an event of default under this Security Agreement: (*a*) the failure of Buyer to perform any condition or obligation contained in this agreement; (*b*) when any statement, representation, or warranty made by Buyer shall be found to have been untrue in any material respect when made; or (*c*) if Seller in good faith believes that the prospect of payment or performance is impaired. Upon a default, Seller, at its option and without notice or demand to Buyer, shall be entitled to declare the Agreement Balance immediately due and payable, take immediate possession of the Collateral and enter the premises at which the Collateral is located for such purpose or to render the Collateral unusable. Upon request, Buyer shall assemble and make the Collateral available to Seller at a place to be designated by Seller which is reasonably convenient to both parties. Upon repossession, Seller may retain or dispose of any or all of the collateral in the manner prescribed by the Indiana Uniform Commercial Code and the proceeds of any such disposition shall be first applied in the following order: (*a*) to the reasonable expenses of retaking, holding, preparing for sale, selling, and the like; (*b*) to the reasonable attorney's fees and legal expenses incurred by Seller; and (*c*) to the satisfaction of the indebtedness secured by this security interest. Buyer convenants to release and hold harmless Seller from any and all claims arising out of the repossession of the Collateral. No waiver of any default or any failure or delay to exercise any right or remedy by Seller shall operate as a waiver of any other default, or of the same default in the future or as a waiver of any right or remedy with respect to the same or any other occurrence.

6. All rights and remedies of seller specified in this agreement are cumulative and are in addition to, and shall not exclude, any rights and remedies Seller may have by law.

7. Seller shall not be liable for any damages, including special or consequential damages, for failure to deliver the Collateral or for any delay in delivery of the Collateral to Buyer.

8. Buyer agrees that Seller may carry this agreement, together with any other agreements and accounts, with Buyer in one account upon its records and unless otherwise instructed in writing by Buyer, any payment of less than all amounts then due on all agreements and accounts shall be applied to any accrued delinquent charges, costs of collection and maintenance, and to the balances owing under all agreements or accounts in such oder as Seller in its discretion shall determine.

9. Buyer authorizes Seller to execute and file financing statements signed only by Seller covering the Collateral described.

10. Any notice required by this agreement shall be deemed sufficient when mailed to Seller (state Seller's address), or to Buyer at the address at which the Collateral is kept.

11. Buyer shall have the benefit of manufacturers' warranties, if any; however, Seller makes no express warranties (except a warranty of title) and no implied warranties, including any warranty of MERCHANTABILITY or FITNESS. Buyer agrees that there are no promises or agreements between the parties not contained in this agreement. Any modification or rescission of this agreement shall be ineffective unless in writing and signed by both Seller and Buyer.

12. ANY HOLDER OF THIS CONSUMER CREDIT CONTRACT IS SUBJECT TO ALL CLAIMS AND DEFENSES WHICH THE DEBTOR COULD ASSERT AGAINST THE SELLER OF GOODS OR SERVICES OBTAINED WITH THE PROCEEDS HEREOF. RECOVERY HEREUNDER BY THE DEBTOR SHALL NOT EXCEED AMOUNTS PAID BY THE DEBTOR HEREUNDER.

example, Dan's Diner borrows $25,000 from the bank and gives it a security interest in all of its present restaurant equipment as well as all of the restaurant equipment that it may "hereafter acquire." If Dan's owns only a stove at the time, then the bank has a security interest only in the stove. However, if a month later Dan's buys a refrigerator, the bank's security interest would "attach" to the refrigerator when Dan's acquires some rights to it.

A security interest in after-acquired property may not have priority over certain other creditors if the debtor acquires his new property subject to what is known as a **purchase money security interest.** When the seller of goods retains a security interest in goods until they are paid for, or when money is loaned for the purpose of acquiring certain goods and the lender takes a security interest in those goods, the security interest is a purchase money security interest. Later in this chapter, the section entitled Priority Rules discusses the rights of the holder of a purchase money security interest versus the rights of another creditor who filed earlier on after-acquired property of the debtor.

Proceeds

The creditor is commonly interested in having his security interest cover not only the collateral described in the agreement but also the **proceeds** on the disposal of the collateral by the debtor. For example, if a bank lends money to Dealer to enable Dealer to finance its inventory of new automobiles and the bank takes a security interest in the inventory, the bank wants its interest to continue in any cash proceeds obtained by Dealer when the automobiles are sold to customers. Under the 1972 amendments to Article 9, these proceeds are automatically covered unless the security agreement specifically excludes them [9–203(3)].

Assignment

In the past, installment sales contracts and security agreements commonly included a provision that the buyer would not assert against the assignee of a sales contract any claims or defenses that the buyer had against the seller. Such clauses made it easier for a retailer to assign its installment sales contracts, or security agreements, to a financial institution

such as a bank. The bank knew that it could collect from the buyer without having to worry about any claims that the buyer had against the retailer, such as for breach of warranty. The waiver clauses were usually presented to the buyer on a take-it-or-leave-it basis.

Such clauses can operate to the disadvantage of the buyer. For example, Ellen Horn agrees to buy some storm windows from Ace Home Improvement Company. She signs an installment sales contract, or security agreement, promising to pay $50 a month for 24 months and giving the company a security interest in the windows. The contract contains a waiver of defenses clause. Ace assigns the contract to First Bank and goes out of business. If the storm windows were of a poorer quality than was called for by the contract, Horn would have a claim of breach of warranty against Ace. She would not have to pay Ace the full amount if it tried to collect from her. Under these circumstances, however, Horn has to pay the full amount to the bank; then she can try to collect from Ace for breach of warranty. Here, Horn might be out of luck.

Under the Uniform Commercial Code, an express or implied waiver of defenses is generally valid and enforceable by an assignee who takes his assignment for value, in good faith, and without notice of a claim or defense [9–206(1)]. The two exceptions to this rule are (1) the waiver is not effective as to any type of defense that could be asserted against a holder in due course of a negotiable instrument; (2) the waiver is not effective if a statute or court decision establishes a different rule for buyers of consumer goods [9–206(1)].

Some states have enacted comprehensive legislation to abolish waiver of defenses clauses in consumer contracts, and other states have limited their use. The Uniform Consumer Credit Code (UCCC), which has been adopted by a number of states, gives the adopting states two alternatives regarding waiver of defenses clauses: Alternative A provides that an assignee of a consumer sales contract takes subject to all of the defenses that the buyer has against the seller arising out of the sale, regardless of whether the contract contains a waiver of defenses clause. Alternative B permits the enforcement of such clauses only by an assignee who is not related to the seller and who acquires the assignment of the contract in good faith and for value, gives the buyer notice of the assignment, and is not advised by the buyer in writing within three months that the buyer has any claims or defenses against the seller.

In addition, the Federal Trade Commission has promulgated a regulation that applies to situations in which a buyer signs a waiver of defenses clause as part of an installment sales contract. For a detailed discussion of this regulation, see Chapter 31, Negotiation and Holder in Due Course. The FTC regulation requires that a seller or financing agency insert in all consumer contracts and direct loan agreements a clause putting any holder of the contract on notice that the holder is subject to all of the claims and defenses that the buyer-debtor could assert against the seller of the goods or services covered by the contract.

PERFECTING THE SECURITY INTEREST

Perfection

While attachment of a security interest to collateral owned by the debtor gives the creditor rights vis-à-vis the debtor, a creditor is also concerned about making sure that she has a better right to the collateral than any other creditor if the debtor defaults. In addition, a creditor may be concerned about protecting her interest in the collateral if the debtor sells it to someone else. The creditor gets protection against other creditors or purchasers of the collateral by perfecting her security interest. Perfection is not effective without an attachment of the security interest [9–303].

Under the Code, there are three main ways of perfecting a security interest:

1. By filing a public notice of the security interest.
2. By the creditor taking possession of the collateral.
3. In certain transactions, by mere attachment of the security interest; this is known as automatic perfection.

Perfection by Public Filing

The most common way of perfecting a security interest is to file a **financing statement** in the appropriate public office. The financing statement serves as constructive notice to the world that the creditor claims an interest in collateral that belongs to a certain named debtor. The financing statement usually consists of a multicopy form that is available from the office of the secretary of state. (See Figure 2.) However, the security agreement can be filed as the financing statement if it contains the required information and has been signed by the debtor.

To be sufficient, the financing statement must (1) contain the names of the debtor and of the secured party, or creditor; (2) be signed by the debtor; (3) give an address of the secured party from which additional information about the security interest can be obtained; (4) give a mailing address for the debtor; and (5) contain a statement listing the collateral or a description of the collateral. If the financing statement covers goods that are to become fixtures, a description of the real estate must be included.

Each state specifies by statute where the financing statement has to be filed. In all states, a financing statement that covers fixtures must be filed in the office where a mortgage on real estate would be filed [9–401]. To obtain maximum security, the secured party acquiring a security interest in property that is a fixture or is to become a fixture should double file—that is, file the security interest as a fixture and as a nonfixture.

In regard to collateral other than fixtures, the state may require only central filing, usually in the office of the secretary of state. However, most states require the local filing of local transactions, such as transactions in which the collateral is equipment used in farming operations; farm products; accounts, contract rights, or general intangibles arising from or relating to the sale of farm products by a farmer; or consumer goods.

A financing statement is effective for a period of five years from the date of filing, and it lapses then unless a continuation statement has been filed before that time. An exception is made for real estate mortgages that are effective as fixture filings—they are effective until the mortgage is released or terminates [9–403].

A **continuation statement** may be filed within six months before the five-year expiration date. The continuation statement must be signed by the secured party, identify the original statement by file number, and state that the original statement is still effective. Successive continuation statements may be filed [9–403(3)].

FIGURE 2   **A Financing Statement**

UNIFORM COMMERCIAL CODE   STATE OF INDIANA   FORM UCC-1
                                          FINANCING STATEMENT

INSTRUCTIONS

1. Please type this form. Fold only along perforation for mailing.
2. Remove Secured Party and Debtor copies and send other three copies with interleaved carbon paper to the filing officer. Enclose filing fee of $1.00.
   (plus $ .50 if collateral is or to become a fixture).
3. When filing is to be with more than one office, Form UCC-2 may be placed over this set to avoid double typing.
4. If the space provided for any item(s) is inadequate, the item(s) may be continued on additional sheets, preferably 5"x 8" or sizes convenient to
   secured party in case of long schedules, indentures, etc. Only one sheet is required. Extra names of debtors may be continued below box "1" in
   space for description of property.
5. If the collateral is crops or goods which are or are to become fixtures, describe the goods and also the real estate with the name of the record owner
   if he is other than the debtor.
6. Persons filing a security agreement (as distinguished from a financing statement) are urged to complete this form with or without signature and send
   with security agreement.
7. If collateral is goods which are or are to become fixtures, use Form UCC-1a over this Form to avoid double typing, and enclose regular fee plus $ .50
8. The filing officer will return the third page of this Form as an acknowledgement. Secured party at a later time may use third page as a Termination
   Statement by dating and signing the termination legend on that page.

This Financing Statement is presented to Filing Officer for filing pursuant to the UCC: 3. Maturity Date (if any):

1. Debtor(s) (Last Name First) and Address(es)	2. Secured Party(ies) and Address(es)	For Filing Officer (Date, Time, Number, and Filing Office)

4. This financing statement covers the following types (or items) of property (also describe realty
   where collateral is crops or fixtures):

Assignee of Secured Party

This statement is filed without the debtor's signature to perfect a security interest in collateral
(check ☐ if so)

☐ under a security agreement signed by debtor authorizing secured party to file this statement, or
☐ already subject to a security interest in another jurisdiction when it was brought into this state, or
☐ which is proceeds of the following described original collateral which was perfected:

Check ☐ if covered: ☐ Proceeds of Collateral are also covered.   ☐ Products of Collateral are also covered.   No. of additional Sheets presented:

Filed with: ☐ Secretary of State   ☐ Recorder of _____ County

By: _____   By: _____
    Signature(s) of Debtor(s)   Signature(s) of Secured Party(ies)

(1) Filing Officer Copy—Alphabetical   Approved by:
    FORM UCC-1—INDIANA UNIFORM COMMERCIAL CODE
                                                                            Secretary of State

---

When a consumer debtor completely fulfills all debts and obligations secured by a financing statement, she is entitled to a **termination statement** signed by the secured party or an assignee of record. Failure of the affected secured party to furnish a termination statement after proper demand subjects him to a fine of $100 plus damages for any loss caused to the debtor by such failure [9–404].

Possession by Secured Party as Public Notice

Public filing of a security interest is intended to put any interested members of the public on notice of the security interest. A potential creditor of the debtor, or a potential buyer of the collateral, can check the records to see whether anyone else claims an interest in the debtor's collateral. The same objective can be reached if the debtor gives up possession of the collateral to the creditor or to a third person who holds the collateral for the creditor. If a debtor does not have possession of collateral that he claims to own, then a potential creditor or debtor is on notice that someone else may claim an interest in it. Thus, a security interest is perfected by change of possession of collateral from the debtor to the creditor/secured party or his agent [9–302(1)(a)]. For example, Simpson borrows $50 from a pawnbroker and leaves his guitar as collateral for the loan. The pawnbroker's security interest in the guitar is perfected by virtue of her possession of the guitar.

Generally, possession by the secured party is the means for perfecting a security interest in instruments such as checks or notes and in money.[3] Possession of the collateral by the secured party is an alternative means, and often the most satisfactory means, of perfecting a security interest in chattel paper and negotiable documents of title. Possession is also a possible means for perfecting a security interest in inventory. This is sometimes done through the **field warehousing** arrangement, whereby part of the debtor's inventory is fenced off and withdrawals from it are permitted only on the approval of the secured party or his on-the-scene representative.

Possession by the secured party is usually not a practical means for perfecting a security interest in equipment or consumer goods because the debtor normally wants to retain possession to make use of the equipment or goods. Of course, possession by the secured party is not possible at all with accounts or general intangibles. The person to whom the collateral is delivered holds it as bailee, and he owes the duties of a bailee to the parties in interest [9–207].

Perfection by Attachment

Perfection by mere attachment of the security interest, sometimes known as automatic perfection, is

the only form of perfection that occurs without the giving of public notice. It occurs automatically when all the requirements of attachment are complete. This form of perfection is limited to certain classes of collateral; in addition, it may be only a temporary perfection in some situations.[4]

A creditor who sells goods to a consumer on credit, or who lends money to enable a consumer to buy goods, can obtain limited perfection of a security interest merely by attaching the security interest to the goods. A creditor under these circumstances has what is called a **purchase money security interest in consumer goods.** For example, an appliance store sells a television set to Margaret Morse on a conditional sales contract, or time-payment plan. The store does not have to file its purchase money security interest in the set. The security interest is considered perfected just by virtue of its attachment to the set in the hands of the consumer.

In the case that follows, *In Re Phillips,* the court rejected a creditor's claims that its security interest was perfected by attachment, holding that the goods were equipment and not consumer goods.

---

[3]Sections 9–304(4) and (5) permit a 21-day temporary perfection.

[4] Temporary perfection without filing or possession is automatically obtained for 21 days after attachment of the security interest in instruments and negotiable documents [9–304]. To get protection beyond the 21-day period, the secured party must perfect by filing or possession. During the 21-day period of temporary perfection, however, any holder in due course of commercial paper or any bona fide purchaser of a security or a negotiated document will prevail over the secured party relying on temporary perfection [9–309].

In Re Phillips
Creditway of America v. Phillips
42 UCC Rep. 679 (Bankr. W.D. Va. 1985)

Jacob Phillips and his wife, Charlene, jointly owned the Village Variety 5&10 Store in Bluefield, Virginia. In addition, Mrs. Phillips was a computer science teacher at the Wytheville Community College. On December 1, 1984, Mrs. Phillips entered into a retail installment sales contract with Holdren's, Inc., for the purchase of a Leading Edge color computer and a Panasonic printer. The contract, which was also a security agreement, provided for a total payment of $3,175.68, with monthly payments of $132.32 to begin on March 5, 1985. On December 1, 1984, Holdren's assigned the contract to Creditway of America.

At the time of purchase, Mrs. Phillips advised Holdren's that she was purchasing the computer for professional use in her teaching assignments as well as for use in the variety store. One of the software programs purchased was a practical accounting program for business transactions. Mrs. Phillips also received a special discount price given by Holdren's to state instructors buying for their teaching use. She used the computer in the Village Variety 5&10 Store until it closed in April 1985. In June, the Phillips filed a petition under Chapter 7 of the Bankruptcy Act. At the time, they owed $2,597.79 on the computer. No financing statement was ever filed.

Creditway filed a motion in the bankruptcy proceeding, claiming that it had a valid lien on the computer and seeking to be permitted to repossess it.

Pearson, Bankruptcy Judge   The key factor in determining whether to grant Creditway's motion for relief is the classification of the collateral. Virginia Code Section 9–302(1)(d) provides that "a financing statement shall be filed to perfect all security interests except a purchase money security interest in consumer goods." If the computer goods are classified as consumer goods, then Creditway, as assignee of Holdren's, would not need to file a financing statement to have a perfected security interest in the collateral. However, if the computer items are classified as equipment, then, pursuant to Section 9–401(1)(c), it would be necessary for Creditway to have a dual filing to perfect its security interest.

Virginia Code Section 9–109 outlines the classification of collateral. In pertinent part it provides that

Goods are
   (1) "consumer goods" if they are used or bought for use primarily for personal, family, or household purposes;
   (2) "equipment" if they are used or bought for use primarily in business (including farming or a profession).

The test for the classification of goods is the owner's use of the goods. The two classes of goods are mutually exclusive. The same property cannot be in two classes at the same time and as to the same person. Thus, an item cannot, for example, be classified as both consumer goods and equipment.

The evidence before this court indicates that the computer items were purchased for use primarily in business rather than for personal, family, or household purposes. Mrs. Phillips' uncontradicted testimony is that at the time of purchase she informed the salesperson at Holdren's that the computer would be used for her teaching assignments as well as in the variety store. She received a special discount as a state instructor for purchase of the items for use in teaching. Mrs. Phillips also indicated that she purchased this computer with its memory capability to handle business transactions, and that she purchased a software package on Practical Accounting for business billing. These facts and circumstances should have provided sufficient notice of the use of the items for classification purposes such that financing statements could have been filed properly to perfect the security interest.

Courts have held without exception that the Uniform Commercial Code filing requirements are mandatory and that the filing of a financing statement in an improper place or not in all the places required is ineffective to perfect a security interest. Although the application of rules in a given case may be harsh, any other result would invite inconsistency which the Uniform Commercial Code was enacted to avoid. On the evidence presented the collateral should be found to be classified as equipment and, having not filed in all places required, Creditway holds an unperfected security interest against the debtor.

Motion of Creditway to repossess the collateral denied.

Perfection by attachment is not effective if the consumer goods are motor vehicles for which the state issues certificates of title and has only limited effectiveness if the goods are fixtures [9–302]. A later section of this chapter discusses the special rules covering these kinds of collateral.

There are also major limitations to the perfection by attachment principle. As discussed in the Priority section of this chapter, relying on attachment for perfection does not, in some instances, provide as much protection to the creditor as does public filing.

One potential concern for a creditor is that the use of the collateral will change from that anticipated when the security interest was obtained. For example, in the *Phillips* case, assume that the computer was originally purchased to be used in the home and later converted to use in the business. It is important that the creditor properly perfect the security interest initially so that it will not be adversely affected by a subsequent change in use and will continue to have the benefit of its initial perfection.

Motor Vehicles

If state law requires a certificate of title for motor vehicles, then a creditor who takes a security interest in a motor vehicle (other than a creditor holding a security interest in inventory held for sale by a person in the business of selling goods of that kind) must have the security interest noted on the title [9–302]. Suppose a credit union lends Carlson money to buy a new car in a state that requires certificates of title for cars. The credit union cannot rely on filing or on attachment of its security interest in the car to perfect that interest; rather, it must have its security interest noted on the certificate of title.

This requirement protects the would-be buyer of the car or another creditor who might extend credit based on Carlson's ownership of the car. By checking the certificate of title to Carlson's car, a potential buyer or creditor would learn about the credit union's security interest in the car. If no security interest is noted on the certificate of title, the buyer can buy—or the creditor can extend credit—with confidence that there are no undisclosed security interests that would be effective against him.

Fixtures

The Code also provides special rules for perfecting security interests in consumer goods that become fixtures by virtue of their attachment to or use with real property. A creditor with a security interest in consumer goods (including consumer goods that will become fixtures) obtains perfection merely by attachment of her security interest to a consumer good. However, as discussed in the Priority section of this chapter, a creditor who relies on attachment for perfection will not, in some instances, prevail against other creditors who hold an interest in the real estate to which the consumer good is attached unless a financing statement is filed with the real estate records to perfect the security interest [9–401(1)(a)].

Removal of Collateral

Even where a creditor has a perfected security interest in the collateral of her debtor, she needs to be concerned about the possibility that the debtor can take the collateral from the state where the creditor has filed on it to another state where the creditor does not have her claim filed on the public record. Commonly, the security agreement between the creditor and the debtor provides where the collateral is to be kept and stipulates that it is not to be moved unless the debtor gives notice to and/or obtains the permission of the creditor. There is, however, no absolute assurance that the debtor will be faithful to such an agreement.

Under the Code, a secured creditor who has perfected his security interest generally has four months after the collateral is brought into the new state to perfect his security interest in that state. If the creditor does not reperfect within the four months, his security interest becomes unperfected and he could lose the collateral to a person who purchases it, or takes an interest in it, after it has been removed [9–103(1)]. If the creditor has not perfected his security interest by the time the collateral is removed, or within the time period that the creditor has to perfect his security interest in the former location of the collateral, then his interest is unperfected and he does not obtain the advantage of the four-month grace period.

The Code rules that govern the removal of collateral covered by a state certificate of title—such as an automobile—are more complicated. If an automobile covered by a certificate of title on which a security interest is noted is moved to another state, the perfected security interest is perfected for four months in the new state, or until the automobile is registered in the new state. If the original state did not require that security interests be noted on the title, and if a new title is used in the second state without notation of the security interest, then under certain circumstances a buyer of the automobile can take free of the original security interest. To qualify, the buyer must not be in the business of buying and selling automobiles and must (1) give value, (2) take delivery after issuance of the new title, and (3) buy without notice of the security interest [9–103(2)].[5]

[5]Other rules are set out in the Code for accounts, general intangibles, chattel paper, and mobile goods removed to other states [9–103(3) and (4)].

OBTAINING AN ENFORCEABLE SECURITY INTEREST

Step	Purpose	Necessary Action
Attachment of Security Interest	To secure a debt. The debtor gives the creditor rights in the debtor's property to secure the debt owed by the creditor to the debtor.	1. Agreement by the debtor giving the creditor a security interest in specific property (collateral) in which the debtor has a legal interest. This can include after-acquired property and proceeds of the collateral. 2. The debtor must have a legal interest in the collateral. 3. The creditor must give value to the debtor (e.g., money or goods). Future advances are value when actually given to the debtor.
Perfection	To obtain protection against other creditors of the debtor and against purchasers of the collateral from the debtor.	1. *Public filing.* Filing a financing statement with the appropriate state or local office to put the world on notice that the creditor claims an interest in specific collateral belonging to the debtor; or in the case of a motor vehicle, noting the security interest on the certificate of title; or 2. *Possession by creditor.* The creditor may take possession of the collateral, thus putting other creditors and potential purchasers on notice that the creditor has an interest in the collateral (this is not practical for all kinds of collateral); or 3. *Perfection by attachment.* Limited perfection merely by attachment of the security interest is obtained where (a) a creditor sells consumer goods to a consumer on credit or (b) a creditor loans money to a consumer to enable him to buy consumer goods.

PRIORITY RULES

Importance of Determining Priority

Because several creditors may claim a security interest in the same collateral of a debtor, the Code establishes a set of rules for determining which of the conflicting security interests has priority. Determining which creditor has priority, or the best claim, takes on particular importance in bankruptcy situations, where unless a creditor has a preferred secured interest in collateral that fully protects the obligation owed to him, the creditor may realize nothing or only a few cents on every dollar owed to him.

General Priority Rules

The basic rule established by the Code is that when more than one security interest in the same collateral has been filed or otherwise perfected, the first security interest to be filed or perfected has priority over any that are filed or perfected later. If only one security interest has been perfected—for example, by filing—then that security interest has priority. However, if none of the conflicting security interests has been perfected, then the first security interest to be attached to the collateral has priority [9–312(5)].

Thus, if Bank A filed a financing statement covering a retailer's inventory on February 1, 1995, and Bank B filed a financing statement covering that same inventory on March 1, 1995, Bank A would have priority over Bank B even though Bank B might have made its loan and attached its security interest to the inventory before Bank A did so. However, if Bank A neglected to perfect its security interest by filing and Bank B did perfect, then Bank B, as the holder of the only perfected security interest in the inventory, would prevail.

If both of the creditors neglected to perfect their security interest, then the first security interest that attached would have priority. For example, if Bank Y has a security agreement covering a dealer's equipment on June 1, 1995, and advances money to the dealer on that date, whereas Bank Z does not obtain a security agreement covering that equipment or advance money to the dealer until July 1, 1995, then Bank Y would have priority over Bank Z. In connection with the last situation, unperfected secured creditors do not enjoy a preferred position in bankruptcy proceedings, thus giving additional impetus to the desirability of filing or otherwise perfecting a security interest.

Purchase Money Security Interests in Inventory

There are several very important exceptions to the general priority rules. First, a *perfected purchase money security interest in inventory* has priority over a conflicting security interest in the same inventory *if the purchase money security interest is perfected at the time the debtor receives possession of the inventory* and if the purchase money secured party gives *notification in writing* to the prior secured creditor *before* the debtor receives the inventory [9–312(3)].

Assume that Bank A takes and perfects a security interest in all the present and after-acquired inventory of a debtor. Then, the debtor acquires some additional inventory from a wholesaler, who retains a security interest in the inventory until the debtor pays for it and perfects this security interest. The wholesaler has a purchase money security interest in inventory goods and has priority over the prior secured creditor (Bank A) if the wholesaler has perfected the security interest by the time the collateral reaches the debtor and if the wholesaler sends notice of her purchase money security interest to Bank A before shipping the goods. Thus, to protect itself, the wholesaler must check the public records to see whether any of the debtor's creditors are claiming an interest in the debtor's inventory. When the wholesaler discovers that some are claiming an interest, it should file its own security interest and give notice to the existing creditors.

As the following *Borg-Warner Acceptance Corp.* case illustrates, the subsequent seller of inventory can obtain a priority position if it files a financing statement and notifies the prior secured party in a timely fashion.

Borg-Warner Acceptance Corp. v. Tascosa National Bank
784 S.W.2d 129 (Tex. Ct. App. 1990)

On March 1, 1982, the Tascosa National Bank of Amarillo (Bank) extended a loan to T & L Ventures, Inc., doing business as (d/b/a) The Video Connection (T & L) in the amount of $30,006. A financing statement was obtained and filed with the secretary of state on March 4, 1982. The Bank's financing statement described the collateral as:

Video software and hardware, computer games hardware and software, all inventory, furniture, fixtures of above located at Amarillo, Potter County, Texas.

From time to time, the indebtedness was renewed and extended and additional funds were provided T & L, with the last note dated April 18, 1986, in the principal amount of $153,613.84. All indebtedness was evidenced by notes and secured by the same collateral.

On March 7, 1982, Borg-Warner Acceptance Corporation (Borg-Warner) entered into an Inventory Security Agreement pursuant to which T & L granted to Borg-Warner a security interest in its inventory purchased with the proceeds of loans made by Borg-Warner. Borg-Warner perfected its security interest as a purchase money security interest (PMSI) under section 9–312(3) by: (1) filing on March 11, 1982, a financing statement describing the collateral with the secretary of state's office; and (2) notifying the Bank of Borg-Warner's interest in T & L's inventory.

Following the perfection of Borg-Warner's PMSI, Borg-Warner commenced financing the acquisition of inventory by T & L and continued such financing through May 22, 1986. Pursuant to a "floor-planning arrangement," Borg-Warner purchased from vendors and paid directly to vendors the invoice purchase price of inventory acquired by T & L for resale. Indebtedness to Borg-Warner was not incurred for any purpose other than the purchase of inventory.

T & L defaulted on its indebtedness. On May 11, 1986, the Bank repossessed T & L's inventory, removed it from T & L's premises, and placed it in a warehouse. Borg-Warner demanded that the Bank deliver the inventory to it on the grounds it had a superior claim to it. The Bank refused and Borg-Warner brought suit against the Bank. The trial court granted summary judgment in favor of the Bank, and Borg-Warner appealed.

Dodson, Judge   The determinative issue on Borg-Warner's appeal is the priority of liens question. If Borg-Warner's security interest qualifies as a PMSI under section 9–312(3), Borg-Warner prevails. However, if Borg-Warner's security interest does not so qualify, then the Bank prevails under the "first to file rule." Section 9–312(5)(1).

The Uniform Commercial Code defines two types of PMSIs, those claimed by sellers and those claimed by financing agencies:

A security interest is a "purchase money security interest" to the extent that it is

(1) taken or retained by the seller of the collateral to secure all or part of its price; or

(2) taken by a person who by making advances or incurring an obligation gives value to enable the debtor to acquire rights in or the use of collateral if such value is so used. Section 9–107.

We reiterate, the general rule of priority among conflicting security interests in the same collateral where both interests are perfected by filing, is that the secured party who first files a financing statement prevails. Section 9–312(5)(1). However, section 9–312(3) states a special rule for a PMSI in inventory. That subsection reads in full as follows:

(3) A perfected purchase money security interest in inventory has priority over a conflicting security interest in the same inventory and also has priority in identifiable cash proceeds received on or before the delivery of the inventory to a buyer if

(1) the purchase money security interest is perfected at the time the debtor receives possession of the inventory; and

(2) except where excused by section 9–319 (oil and gas production), the purchase money secured party gives notification in writing to the holder of the conflicting security interest if the holder had filed a financing statement covering the same types of inventory (i) before the date of the filing made by the purchase money secured party, or (ii) before the beginning of the 21-day period where the purchase money security interest is temporarily perfected without filing or possession (Subsection (e) of Section 9–304); and

(3) the holder of the conflicting security interest receives any required notification within five years before the debtor receives possession of the inventory; and

(4) the notification states that the person giving the notice has or expects to acquire a purchase money security interest in inventory of the debtor, describing such inventory by item or type. [Emphasis added.] Section 9–312(3).

Under the above provisions, Borg-Warner's security interest is a PMSI to the extent that it is taken by Borg-Warner who by incurring an obligation gave value to enable T & L to acquire rights in or the use of collateral if such value was in fact used.

In determining the priority between Borg-Warner and the Bank, we note that the legislature has provided that a PMSI in inventory such as Borg-Warner's has priority over a conflicting security interest in the same inventory if: (1) the PMSI was perfected at the time T & L received possession of the inventory; (2) Borg-Warner gave notice in writing to the Bank who had filed a financing statement covering the same type of inventory before the date of the filing by Borg-Warner; (3) the Bank received any required notification within five years before T & L received possession of the inventory; and (4) the notification stated that Borg-Warner expected to ac-

quire a PMSI in the inventory of T & L, describing such inventory by item or type. Section 9–312(3).

Our earlier explication of the undisputed facts reveals that Borg-Warner complied with the statutory code requirements.

Judgment reversed in favor of Borg-Warner.

Purchase Money Security Interests in Noninventory Collateral

The second exception to the general priority rule is that a *purchase money security interest in collateral other than inventory* has priority over a conflicting security interest in the same collateral *if the purchase money security interest is perfected at the time the debtor receives the collateral* or *within 10 days afterward* [9–312(4)].

Assume that Bank B takes and perfects a security interest in all the present and after-acquired equipment belonging to a debtor. Then, a supplier sells some equipment to the debtor, reserving a security interest in the equipment until it is paid for. If the supplier perfects the purchase money security interest by filing at the time the debtor obtains the collateral or within 10 days thereafter, it has priority over Bank B. This is because its purchase money security interest in noninventory collateral prevails over a prior perfected security interest if the purchase money security interest is perfected at the time the debtor takes possession or within 10 days afterward.

Rationale for Protecting Purchase Money Security Interests

The preference given to purchase money security interests, provided that their holders comply with the statutory procedure in a timely manner, serves several ends. First, it prevents a single creditor from closing off all other sources of credit to a particular debtor and thus possibly preventing the debtor from obtaining additional inventory or equipment needed to maintain his business. Second, the preference makes it possible for a supplier to have first claim on inventory or equipment until it is paid for, at which time it may become subject to the after-acquired property clause of another creditor's secu-

rity agreement. By requiring that the first perfected creditor be given notice of a purchase money security interest at the time the new inventory comes into the debtor's inventory, the Code serves to alert the first creditor to the fact that some of the inventory on which it may be relying for security is subject to a prior secured interest until it is paid for.

Buyers in the Ordinary Course of Business

A third exception to the general priority rule is that a **buyer in the ordinary course of business** (other than a person buying farm products from a person engaged in farming operations) takes free from a security interest created by his seller even though the security interest is perfected and even though the buyer knows of its existence [9–307(1)]. For example, a bank loans money to a dealership to finance that dealership's inventory of new automobiles and takes a security interest in the inventory, which it perfects by filing. Then, the dealership sells an automobile out of inventory to a customer. The customer takes the automobile free of the bank's security interest even though the dealership may be in default on its loan agreement and even if the customer knows about the bank's interest. As long as the customer is a buyer in the ordinary course of business, she is protected. The reasons for this rule are that a bank really expects to be paid from the proceeds of the dealership's automobile sales and that the rule is necessary to the smooth conduct of commerce. Customers would be very reluctant to buy goods if they could not be sure they were getting clear title to them from the merchants from whom they buy.

In the following case, *DBC Capital Fund, Inc. v. Snodgrass,* a buyer of an automobile from a dealer obtained title free of a security interest previously given by the dealer to his creditor.

DBC Capital Fund, Inc. v. Snodgrass

551 N.E.2d 475 (Ind. Ct. App. 1990)

On February 19, 1988, DBC Capital Fund, Inc. (DBC), entered into an agreement with the owner of Devers Auto Sales whereby DBC obtained a security interest in the automobile inventory maintained by Devers. This security interest was perfected by filing with the secretary of state on February 25, 1988.

On March 24, 1989, Cheryl Snodgrass purchased a 1984 Oldsmobile from Devers for $5,000 in cash. This automobile was taken from the inventory covered by DBC's security interest, although Snodgrass was not made aware of the financing agreement between Devers and DBC. When Snodgrass took possession of the Oldsmobile, Devers told her that the automobile's certificate of title would be mailed to her. In the meantime, she was issued a temporary registration.

On April 28, 1989, Snodgrass was informed by letter that DBC had physical possession of the certificate of title for the Oldsmobile and that DBC considered itself to have a valid lien on the automobile. In a later telephone conversation, DBC's attorney informed Snodgrass that DBC would not release the certificate of title to the 1984 Oldsmobile until Snodgrass paid DBC $4,200.

On April 25, 1989, the temporary registration issued to Snodgrass by Devers expired. Because Snodgrass was not in possession of the certificate of title for the Oldsmobile, she was unable to obtain proper licensing for the vehicle and, therefore, could not use the automobile. In an effort to obtain the certificate of title, Snodgrass then filed suit against DBC. The trial court entered judgment in her favor on June 28, 1989, awarding her $1,920 in triple damages and $1,748.45 in attorney's fees. DBC appealed.

Ratliff, Judge   DBC first contends that the trial court erred in determining that Snodgrass was a buyer in the ordinary course of business, and that, therefore, the trial court failed to recognize that, as a holder of a valid secured interest, DBC was entitled to possession of the certificate of title to the 1984 Oldsmobile. We disagree.

At the hearing the parties stipulated to the fact that DBC had a valid security interest in the 1984 Oldsmobile. The main issue litigated at trial was whether Snodgrass was in a legal position which would make her claim to the automobile superior to that of DBC. Under the relevant provision of the Uniform Commercial Code (UCC) the interest of a "buyer in the ordinary course of business" is superior to that of a holder of valid secured interest. Section 9–307(1).

DBC claims that Snodgrass cannot be considered a buyer in the ordinary course of business "because she failed to require delivery of the title at the time of purchase." According to DBC Snodgrass was charged with knowledge of Indiana Code sections 9-1-2-2(a) and 9-1-2-3(b) which made it unlawful for Devers to fail to deliver a certificate of title at the time of purchase. Because Devers failed to deliver the certificate of title at the time of sale, Snodgrass knew or should have known that the sale of the 1984 Oldsmobile was in violation of the ownership rights of a third party. DBC concludes that because Snodgrass was not a buyer in the ordinary course of business, Snodgrass cannot defeat DBC's valid security interest.

It is true that if there are grounds for suspecting that a security interest is being imperiled by a mode of dealing, a transaction cannot be considered in the ordinary course of business. However, we conclude that DBC has failed to prove that the mode of dealing in the present case was grounds for such a suspicion. DBC's analysis is flawed in that it rests on the supposition that sections 9-1-2-2(a) and 9-1-2-3(b) were enacted to protect the interests of secured creditors. Such simply is not the case. The plain purpose for enacting these statutes was to impede the trade in stolen vehicles. As stated by Judge Posner of the United States Court of Appeals, "as the statute is intended to protect purchasers . . . rather than lenders, there would be a considerable paradox in interpreting the statute to defeat the purchaser's interest." Therefore, we reject DBC's contention that these statutes create a duty on behalf of a purchaser to demand delivery of the certificate of title to an automobile at the time of sale.

Absent such a duty, nothing in the evidence suggests that Snodgrass' purchase of the 1984 Oldsmobile was outside the ordinary course of business. Therefore, under the provisions of section 9–307(1), as a buyer in the ordinary course of business, Snodgrass took free of the security interest held by DBC.

Judgment in favor of Snodgrass.

Artisan's and Mechanic's Liens

The Code also provides that certain liens arising by operation of law (such as an artisan's lien) have priority over a perfected security interest in the collateral [9–310]. For example, Marshall takes her automobile, on which a credit union has a perfected security interest, to Frank's Garage to have it repaired. Under common or statutory law, Frank's may have a lien on the car to secure payment for the repair work; such a lien permits Frank's to keep the car until it receives payment. If Marshall defaults on her loan to the credit union, refuses to pay Frank's for the repair work, and the car is sold to satisfy the liens, Frank's is entitled to its share of the proceeds before the credit union gets anything.

Liens on Consumer Goods Perfected by Attachment

A retailer of consumer goods who relies on attachment of a security interest to perfect it prevails over other creditors of the debtor-buyer. However, the retailer does not prevail over someone who buys the collateral from the debtor if the buyer (1) has no knowledge of the security interest; (2) gives value for the goods; and (3) buys the goods for his personal, family, or household use [9–307(2)]. The retailer does not have priority over such a **bona fide purchaser** unless it filed its security interest.

For example, an appliance store sells a television set to Arthur for $750 on a conditional sales contract, reserving a security interest in the set until Arthur has paid for it. The store does not file a financing statement but relies on attachment for perfection. Arthur later borrows money from a credit union and gives it a security interest in the television set. When Arthur defaults on his loans and the credit union tries to claim the set, the appliance store has a better claim to the set than does the credit union. The credit union then has the rights of an unsecured creditor against Arthur.

Now, suppose Arthur sells the television set for $500 to his neighbor Andrews. Andrews is not aware that Arthur still owes money on the set to the appliance store. Andrews buys it to use in her home. If Arthur defaults on his obligation to the store, it cannot recover the television set from Andrews. To be protected against such a purchaser from its debtor, the appliance store must file a financing statement rather than relying on attachment for perfection.

Fixtures

A separate set of problems arise when the collateral is goods that become fixtures by being so related to particular real estate that an interest in them arises under real estate law. Determining the priorities among a secured party with an interest in the fixtures, subsequent purchasers of the real estate, and those persons who have a secured interest—such as a mortgage—on the real property can involve both real estate law and the Code. However, the Code does set out rules for determining when the holder of a perfected security interest in fixtures has priority over an encumbrancer or owner of the real estate. Some of the Code priority rules are as follows:

First, the holder of the secured interest in a fixture has priority if: (1) her interest is a purchase money security interest obtained prior to the time the goods become fixtures; (2) the security interest is perfected by "fixture filing"—that is, by filing in the recording office where a mortgage on the real estate would be filed prior to, or within 10 days of, the time when the goods become fixtures; and (3) the debtor has a recorded interest in the real estate or is in possession of it [9–313(4)(a)].

For example, Restaurant Supply sells Arnold Schwab, the operator of Arnie's Diner, a new gas stove on a conditional sales contract, reserving a security interest until the purchase price of the stove is paid. The stove, a replacement for an existing stove, is to be installed in a building owned by Arnold Schwab on which First National Bank holds a real estate mortgage. Restaurant Supply can ensure that its security interest in the stove has priority over any claims to it by First National Bank. To do this, Restaurant Supply must (1) enter into a security agreement with Schwab before the stove is delivered to him; and (2) perfect its security interest by fixture filing before the stove is hooked up by a plumber or within 10 days of that time.

Second, the secured party whose interest in fixtures is perfected has priority where: (1) the fixtures are removable factory or office machines or readily removable replacements of domestic appliances that are consumer goods; and (2) the security interest was perfected before the goods became fixtures [9–313(4)(c)]. For example, Harriet Hurd's dishwasher breaks down and she contracts with The Appliance Store to buy a new one on a time-payment plan. The mortgage on Hurd's house provides that it covers the real property along with all kitchen appliances or their replacements. The Appliance Store's security interest in the dishwasher has priority over the interest of the holder of the mortgage if The Appliance Store perfects its security interest before the new dishwasher is installed in Hurd's home. Perfection in consumer goods can, of course, be obtained merely by attaching the security interest through the signing of a valid security agreement.

Note that a creditor holding a security interest in consumer goods that become fixtures who relies on attachment for perfection prevails over other creditors with an interest in the real property *only* where the consumer goods are "readily removable replacements for domestic appliances."

Suppose a hardware store takes a security interest in some storm windows. Because the storm windows are likely to become fixtures through their use with the homeowner's home, the hardware store cannot rely merely on attachment to protect its security interest. It should file a financing statement to protect that security interest against other creditors of the homeowner with an interest in his home. This rule helps protect a person interested in buying the real property or a person considering lending money based on the real property. By checking the real estate records, the potential buyer or creditor would learn of the hardware store's security interest in the storm windows.

Once a secured party has filed his security interest as a fixture filing, he has priority over purchasers or encumbrancers whose interests are filed after that of the secured party [9–313(4)(b) and (d)].

Where the secured party has priority over all owners and encumbrancers of the real estate, he generally has the right on default to remove the collateral from the real estate. However, he must make reimbursement for the cost of any physical injury caused to the property by the removal [9–313(8)].

CONCEPT REVIEW

PRIORITY RULES

Parties	Rule
Buyer of Collateral from Debtor versus Creditor with a Security Interest in the Collateral	1. A *buyer in ordinary course of business* (other than a person buying farm products from a person engaged in farming operations) takes *free* of a security interest created by his seller even though the security interest is *perfected* and even though the buyer knows of its existence. 2. A *bona fide purchaser* of collateral that is *consumer goods* from a debtor has priority over a creditor who holds a purchase money security interest in the collateral but did not file its security interest if the buyer (a) has no knowledge of the security interest, (b) gives value for the goods, and (c) buys them for her own personal, family, or household use. 3. Otherwise, buyers take subject to perfected or known security interests but free of unperfected and unknown security interests.

Parties	Rule

Secured Creditor versus Other Creditors	1. As to collateral *other than fixtures,* the general rule is that when more than one security interest in the same collateral has been filed (or otherwise perfected), the first security interest to be filed or perfected has priority over other security interests.
	2. Exceptions to this general rule are:
	  a. Inventory. A perfected purchase money security interest in inventory has priority over a conflicting security interest in the same inventory *if* the purchase money security interest is perfected at the time the debtor receives possession of the inventory *and* if the purchase money secured party gives notification in writing to the prior secured creditor *before* the debtor receives the inventory.
	  b. Noninventory. A purchase money security interest in noninventory collateral prevails over a prior perfected security interest *if* the purchase money security interest is perfected at the time the debtor takes possession or within 10 days afterward.
	  c. Liens by operation of law. Liens that arise by operation of law—such as artisan's liens—have priority over even perfected security interests in collateral.
	3. If none of the conflicting security interests has been perfected, then the *first* security interest to be *attached* to the collateral has priority.

Secured Creditor versus Other Persons with an Interest in Real Property on which Fixture Is Located	1. As to collateral that will become a *fixture:*
	  a. A creditor with a secured interest in a fixture has priority if (1) the interest is a purchase money security interest that was obtained prior to the time the goods became fixtures; (2) the security interest was perfected by fixture filing prior to, or within 10 days of, the time when the goods became fixtures; and (3) the debtor has a recorded interest in the real estate or is in possession of it.
	  b. A creditor with a perfected secured interest in fixtures will have priority where: (1) the fixtures are removable factory or office machines or readily removable replacements of domestic appliances that are consumer goods; and (2) the security interest is perfected *prior* to the time the goods become fixtures.

DEFAULT AND FORECLOSURE

Default

Usually, the creditor and debtor state in their agreement which events constitute a default by the buyer. The Code does not define what constitutes default. Defining default is left to the parties' agreement, subject to the Code requirement that the parties act in good faith in doing so. If the debtor defaults, the secured creditor has several options:

1. Forget the collateral, and sue the debtor on his note or promise to pay.

2. Repossess the collateral, and use strict foreclosure—in some cases—to keep the collateral in satisfaction of the remaining debt.

3. Repossess and foreclose on the collateral, and then, depending on the circumstances, either sue for any deficiency or return the surplus to the debtor.

Right to Possession

The agreement between the creditor and the debtor may authorize the creditor to repossess the collateral in case of default. If the debtor does default, the creditor is entitled under the Code to possession of the collateral. If through self-help the creditor can obtain possession peaceably, he may do so. However, if the collateral is in the possession of the debtor and cannot be obtained without disturbing the peace, then the creditor must take court action to repossess the collateral [9–503]. See the *Ivy v. General Motors Acceptance Corp.* case, which follows shortly, for a discussion of what constitutes repossession without breach of the peace.

If the collateral is intangible, such as accounts, chattel paper, instruments, or documents, and performance has been rendered to the debtor, the secured party may give notice and have payments made or performance rendered to her [9–502].

Sale of the Collateral

The secured party may dispose of the collateral by sale or lease or in any manner calculated to produce the greatest benefit to all parties concerned. However, the method of disposal must be commercially reasonable [9–504]. Notice of the time and place of a public sale must be given to the debtor, as must notice of a private sale. If the creditor decides to sell the collateral at a public sale such as an auction, then the creditor must give the debtor notice of the time and place of the public sale. Similarly, if the creditor proposes to make a private sale of the collateral, notice must be given to the debtor. This gives the debtor a chance to object to the proposed private sale if she considers it not to be commercially reasonable or to otherwise protect her interests [9–504].

Until the collateral is actually disposed of by the creditor, the buyer has the right to **redeem** it. This means that if the buyer tenders fulfillment of all obligations secured by the collateral as well as of the expenses incurred by the secured party in retaking, holding, and preparing the collateral for disposition, she can recover the collateral from the creditor [9–506].

Consumer Goods

If the creditor has a security interest in consumer goods and the debtor has paid 60 percent or more of the purchase price or debt (and has not agreed in writing to a strict foreclosure), the creditor must sell the repossessed collateral. If less than 60 percent of

the purchase price or debt related to consumer goods has been paid, and as to any other security interest, the creditor may propose to the debtor that the seller keep the collateral in satisfaction of the debt. The consumer-debtor has 21 days to object in writing. If the consumer objects, the creditor must sell the collateral. Otherwise, the creditor may keep the collateral in satisfaction of the debt [9–505].

Distribution of Proceeds

The Code sets out the order in which any proceeds are to be distributed after the sale of collateral by the creditor. First, any expenses of repossessing, storing, and selling the collateral, including reasonable attorney's fees, are paid. Second, the proceeds are used to satisfy the debt. Third, any junior liens are paid. Finally, if any proceeds remain, the debtor is entitled to them. If the proceeds are not sufficient to satisfy the debt, then the creditor is usually entitled to a **deficiency judgment.** This means that the debtor remains personally liable for any debt remaining after the sale of the collateral [9–504].

For example, suppose a loan company lends Christy $5,000 to purchase a car and takes a security interest. After making several payments and reducing the debt to $4,800, Christy defaults. The loan company pays $50 to have the car repossessed and then has it sold at an auction, where it brings $4,500, thus incurring a sales commission of 10 percent ($450) and attorney's fees of $150. The repossession charges, sales commission, and attorney's fees, totaling $650, are paid first from the $4,500 proceeds. The remaining $3,850 is applied to the $4,800 debt, leaving a balance due of $950. Christy remains liable to the loan company for the $950.

Liability of Creditor

A creditor who holds a security interest in collateral must be careful to comply with the provisions of Article 9 of the Code. A creditor acting improperly in repossessing collateral or in its foreclosure and sale is liable to the parties injured. Thus, a creditor can be liable to a debtor if she acts improperly in repossessing or selling collateral [9–507]. This potential liability is illustrated in the case of *Ivy v. General Motors Acceptance Corp.*

IVY V. GENERAL MOTORS ACCEPTANCE CORP.
612 So.2d 1108 (Sup. Ct. Miss. 1992)

Lester Ivy borrowed money from General Motors Acceptance Corp. (GMAC) to purchase a van, and GMAC acquired a security interest in the van. The security agreement contained a so-called insecurity clause that provided GMAC with the right to immediately repossess the van upon default; notice was not a prerequisite to repossession. Ivy defaulted on his obligation on the loan, and GMAC hired American Lenders Service of Jackson to repossess Ivy's van. About 6:30 A.M., Dax Freeman and Jonathan Baker of American Lenders Service drove to Ivy's home. They drove on Ivy's gravel driveway, which is about a quarter-mile long, past a chicken house and the van parked near Ivy's mobile home. They quietly attempted to start the van, but their attempt failed. They then hitched the van to their tow truck and towed it away.

When Freeman and Baker reached the end of Ivy's driveway, Freeman stopped the tow truck and checked the van. At that point, he saw someone running from the chicken house toward the mobile home. Ivy testified that prior to running toward the mobile home, he ran toward the tow truck "hollering and flagging for them to stop" but Freeman and Baker apparently did not see or hear Ivy at the time. Freeman jumped back into the tow truck, drove off Ivy's property, and onto an adjacent road. Ivy decided to chase after Freeman and Baker because he thought they were stealing his van. He jumped into a pickup truck, passed Freeman and Baker, and—according to them—pulled in front of the tow truck and slammed on his brakes. Freeman claimed he was forced to slam on his brakes but was unable to avoid a slight collision with the rear bumper of Ivy's truck. Ivy claimed that he stopped well ahead of the tow truck, affording Freeman plenty of time to stop, but that he reved the engine and "rammed him." Ivy claimed that his head hit the rear window of the truck as a result of the collision and that he sustained a "severe vertical sprain." However, Ivy's medical bill totaled only $20 and he did not miss any work.

When Ivy exited his truck, Freeman showed him some "official looking documents," advised him that he worked for American Lenders, and stated that they were repossessing his truck at GMAC's request. There was a dispute as to whether Ivy sought to have the sheriff called concerning the accident. Freeman allowed Ivy to retrieve some personal belongings from the van and gave Ivy a telephone number to call to get his van back; at that point, they all departed the scene.

Seven months later, on October 20, Ivy filed a complaint against GMAC and American Lenders contending that the repossession of his van was invalid because there was a breach of the peace and he had been caused "personal injuries." Ivy sought actual and punitive damages. At the conclusion of a jury trial, the jury awarded Ivy $5,000 in actual damages and $100,000 in punitive damages. The trial court judge set aside the punitive damage award and both parties appealed.

———————————————■———————————————

Prather, Judge   GMAC contends that its agents did not breach the peace and, therefore, it should not have been liable for actual damages. Ivy, of course, disagrees.

Mississippi law authorizes a creditor or secured party to repossess collateral without judicial process if he or she can do so without breaching the peace. Sec. 9–503. The legislature did not define "breach of peace," but this Court has provided some indication. For example, this court has held that entering a private driveway to repossess collateral without use of force does not constitute a breach of peace. This Court has also held that a creditor, who repossesses collateral despite the fact that the debtor has withheld his or her consent or has strongly objected, did not breach the peace. And, courts in other jurisdictions have generally held that the use of trickery or deceit to peaceably repossess collateral does not constitute a breach of peace.

On the other hand, a Florida Court of Appeal opined that a debtor's "physical objection"—"even from a public street"—bars repossession. A Georgia Court of Appeal found a breach of peace in a case in which: (1) the creditor repossessed the debtor's automobile by blocking it with another automobile; (2) the creditor informed the debtor that he could just "walk his a-- home"; and (3) the debtor "unequivocally protested" the manner of repossession. The Ohio Supreme Court opined that the use of intimidation or acts "fraught with the likelihood of violence" constitutes a breach of peace.

In sum, much of the litigation involving self-help repossession statutes involves the issue of whether a breach of peace has occurred. Disposition of this issue is not a simple task: Since physical violence will ordinarily result in a breach of peace, the secured party's right to repossession will end if repossession evokes physical violence, either on the part of the debtor or the secured party. At the other end from physical violence, a secured party may peaceably persuade the debtor to give up the collateral so that no breach of peace occurs. Between those two ex-treme situations—one in which violence occurs and the other in which the debtor peaceably gives up the collateral—lies the line which divides those cases in which the secured party may exercise self-help repossession and those in which he must resort to the courts. As with most dividing lines, the line between the two extremes is sometimes hard to locate, and even if it is located, it sometimes moves.

Application of the foregoing principles to the evidence viewed in the light most favorable to the verdict leads this Court to conclude that a breach of peace did occur. This Court, therefore, affirms on this issue.

Judgment affirmed awarding actual damages and denying punitive damages.

McRae, Justice (concurring in part and dissenting in part)   The majority complains that Mississippi case law provides little guidance on determining whether a creditor or agent's conduct is so malicious, oppressive or fraudulent that an award of punitive damages is warranted. While it is true that this Court has not often confronted this issue, the principle is well settled throughout the jurisdictions that punitive damages are proper where creditors seize property in a manner that reflects malice, fraud, oppression, gross negligence, or reckless disregard of the rights of the chattel holder.

In *Kirkwood v. Hickman,* perhaps the only Mississippi case to directly address this question, the Court found that when a creditor commits a trespass to retrieve secured property in an "intentional and highhanded manner," punitive damages are in order even if the trespass involved no violence. What could possibly be more "highhanded" than going onto a debtor's property without permission, hooking the debtor's van to a tow truck, and hauling it away in plain view of the debtor with no explana-tion whatsoever? In such circumstances the debtor would naturally think his property was being stolen and would set about to recapture the property. If the conduct of GMAC and American Lenders does not qualify as "reckless disregard for the rights of the chattel holder," then I am at a loss to imagine what might fit the description.

Clearly, given Ivy's version of the events the jury was justified in concluding that the conduct of GMAC and American Lenders was oppressive, high-handed and recklessly unmindful of Ivy's rights.

This entire misadventure might have been avoided if the creditor had simply followed the replevin procedures set out in the Mississippi Code. While Mississippi still permits creditors to employ the remedy of self-help when retrieving their property from chattel holders, creditors follow that path at their peril. GMAC and American Lenders in this case took the law into their own hand, and so could be held fully responsible for the consequences. I would reverse the judgment not withstanding the verdict and reinstate the jury's award of punitive damages.

Constitutional Requirements in Regard to Repossession

In 1972, in *Fuentes v. Shevin,* the U.S. Supreme Court held that state repossession statutes that authorize summary seizure of goods and chattels by state agents such as a sheriff, on an application by some private person who claims he is lawfully entitled to the property and posts a bond, are unconstitutional.[6] This is

---

[6] 407 U.S. 67 (1972).

because these statutes deny the current possessor of the property an opportunity to be heard in court before the property is taken from him. The Court did not accept the argument that because the possessors of the property in question had signed conditional sales contracts authorizing the sellers to take back or repossess the property on default, they had waived their rights to a hearing. This decision raised some speculation that the provisions of the Code permitting secured parties to repossess collateral, in some cases without even judicial process, might be constitutionally defective.

Then, in 1974, in *Mitchell v. W. T. Grant,* the Supreme Court limited the *Fuentes* holding to a requirement that where only property rights are involved, there must be some opportunity for a judicial hearing prior to any final determination of the rights of the parties claiming an interest in the property in question.[7] This decision permits property to be seized by state officials, following the filing of an application and the posting of a bond, so long as the person from whom the property is seized has a later opportunity in court to assert his rights to the property.

The repossession provisions of the Code have been attacked in court as lacking in due process. However, the courts to date have upheld the Code repossession provisions as they relate to private repossession without judicial process.[8] Where judicial process is used, the procedures must conform to the standards laid down in *Fuentes* and *Mitchell.*

ETHICAL AND PUBLIC POLICY CONCERNS

1. In the *Ivy v. GMAC* case, presented earlier in this chapter, a car was repossessed by towing it away from the debtor's residence early in the morning. In Problem case 10 of this chapter, the car was repossessed by driving it away from the owner's residence at 2:00 A.M. In another recent case, an automobile was repossessed by forcing it off the road and then forcing the driver to drive it to the dealer/creditor. Are the repossession techniques used in these cases ethical?

2. Should creditors be able to obtain deficiency judgments against consumers who default on their obligations in connection with the time-purchase of consumer goods and where the proceeds on resale are not sufficient to satisfy the balance due? Or should the creditor have to look solely to the collateral for his security?

3. Suppose that you own an appliance business in a working-class neighborhood that makes most of its sales on credit. What considerations would you take into account in determining whether and when to foreclose or repossess items on which customers have fallen behind in making their payments? Should you be swayed by the personal circumstances of your debtor or look only to protecting your financial interests? For example, would you consider the value of the item to the debtor—such as whether it is a necessity for her life, such as a refrigerator, or a luxury? Would you consider the reason the person had fallen behind—that is, whether she had been ill or had recently lost her job?

PROBLEMS AND PROBLEM CASES

1. Symons, a full-time insurance salesperson, bought a set of drums and cymbals from Grinnel Brothers. A security agreement was executed between them but was never filed. Symons purchased the drums to supplement his income by playing with a band. He had done this before, and his income from his two jobs was about equal. He also played several other instruments. Symons became bankrupt, and the trustee tried to acquire the drums and cymbals as part of his bankruptcy estate. Grinnel's claimed that the drums and cymbals were consumer goods and thus it had a perfected security interest merely by attachment of the security interest. Were the drums and cymbals consumer goods?

2. Robert and Billie Brown operated a paint and gift store. They borrowed $36,628.31 from the First National Bank of Dewey and gave the bank a security interest in "all goods, wares, merchandise, gifts, inventory, fixtures, and accounts receivable owned or thereafter acquired and used in the business." The security agreement also covered "all additions, accessions, and substitutions" to or for collateral and required the Browns to insure the collateral for the benefit of the bank. The bank perfected its security interest. The Browns obtained

---

[7]407 U.S. 600 (1974).

[8]See, for example, *Gibbs v. Titleman,* 502 F.2d 1107 (3rd Cir. 1974) and cases cited therein.

fire insurance but did not name the bank as a loss payee. The Browns' business was destroyed by fire, and the Browns received a $25,000 check from the insurance company for the loss of inventory. The bank then filed suit to obtain the check. Shortly thereafter, the Browns were adjudicated bankrupt. Does the bank have a perfected security interest in the insurance check?

3. Ronald Allegretti purchased a bedroom set valued at $900 and a television set valued at $350 from Goldblatt Brothers, a furniture and appliance store, on a revolving credit account. Under the terms of the revolving credit agreement and the credit slip that was signed at the time of each purchase, Goldblatt's reserved a security interest in all goods sold on credit to Allegretti. Goldblatt's then assigned its interest in the extended credit agreement to General Electric Credit Corporation. Neither filed a financing statement. Allegretti subsequently filed a voluntary petition in bankruptcy, and one of the questions in the bankruptcy action was whether Goldblatt's, and in turn General Electric Credit Corporation, held a perfected security interest in the bedroom set and the television. Did the creditors hold a perfected secured interest in the bedroom set and the television set even though they had not filed financing statements?

4. On October 28, 1983, Steve Gresham, doing business as Midway Cycle Sales, entered into a Wholesale Financing Agreement with ITT Commercial Finance Corporation. The agreement was to finance the purchase of new motorcycles from Suzuki Motor Corporation. ITT filed a financing statement with the Indiana secretary of state on December 16, 1983. The description of the collateral in which ITT asserted a security interest included "all inventory . . . replacements and proceeds." On January 9, 1984, Union Bank filed a financing statement with the Indiana secretary of state claiming it was engaged in "floor planning of new motorcycles" for Midway Cycle Sales. In August 1984, ITT began paying Suzuki invoices for Gresham. In July 1985, ITT sent a letter to Union Bank notifying it that it expected to acquire purchase money security interests in the inventory of Stephan Gresham d/b/a Midway Cycle Sales. In early 1986, Union Bank began loaning money to Gresham under its floor planning agreement with him. Actually, Gresham was "double floor planning"—that is, he was taking invoices for motorcycles that had been paid for by

ITT to the Union Bank and claiming that he had paid for the motorcycles but had decided to floor plan them. When Union Bank advanced money to him, he used the money to make payments on the loans to ITT. He made no payments to Union Bank and did not pay off all of his loan to ITT. Midway Cycle Sales went bankrupt when Union Bank repossessed 22 new Suzuki motorcycles. ITT brought suit against Union Bank, claiming it had paid for the motorcycles and had a perfected security interest in the motorcycles that had priority over Union Bank's security interest in them. Did ITT's security interest have priority over Union Bank's security interest?

5. On November 18, Firestone & Company made a loan to Edmund Carroll, doing business as Kozy Kitchen. To secure the loan, a security agreement was executed, which listed the items of property included, and concluded as follows: "together with all property and articles now, and which may hereafter be, used or mixed with, added or attached to, and/or substituted for any of the described property." A financing statement that included all the items listed in the security agreement was filed with the town clerk on November 18, and with the secretary of state on November 22. On November 25, National Cash Register Company delivered a cash register to Carroll on a conditional sales contract. National Cash Register filed a financing statement on the cash register with the town clerk on December 20, and with the secretary of state on December 21. Carroll defaulted in his payments to both Firestone and National Cash Register. Firestone repossessed all of Carroll's fixtures and equipment covered by its security agreement, including the cash register, and then sold the cash register. National Cash Register claimed that it was the title owner of the cash register and brought suit against Firestone for conversion. Did Firestone or National Cash Register have the better right to the cash register?

6. Glatfelter purchased a stereo set under a purchase money security agreement from Mahaley's Store. This agreement was not perfected by filing. She sold the set to Colonial Trading Company, which in turn resold it. When Glatfelter did not meet her obligations, Mahaley's sued Colonial Trading for conversion of the stereo set in which it claimed a security interest. Is Colonial Trading liable for selling the stereo set in which Mahaley has a security interest?

7. Grimes purchased a new Dodge car from Hornish, a franchised Dodge dealer. The sale was made in the ordinary course of Hornish's business. Grimes paid Hornish the purchase price of the car at the time of the sale. Hornish had borrowed money from Sterling Acceptance and had given it a perfected security interest in its inventory, including the car Grimes bought. Hornish defaulted on its loan to Sterling and Sterling then tried to recover the Dodge from Grimes. Was the car Grimes bought from Hornish still subject to Sterling Acceptance's security interest?

8. On April 10, Benson purchased a new Ford Thunderbird automobile. She traded in her old automobile and financed the balance of $4,325 through the Magnavox Employees Credit Union, which took a security interest in the Thunderbird. In July, the Thunderbird sustained major damage in two accidents. It was taken to ACM Garage for repairs that took seven months to make and resulted in charges of $2,139.54. Benson was unable to pay the charges, and ACM claimed a garageman's lien. Does Magnavox Credit Union's lien or ACM's lien have priority?

9. Kahn applied for a home improvement loan to construct an in-ground swimming pool. Union National Bank approved the loan, and construction began on Kahn's land. State Bank held a valid mortgage on this land. After the pool was completed, Union National gave Kahn the money with which he paid the contractor. Union National then perfected its interest by filing. State Bank later attempted to foreclose on its mortgage. Union National claimed the value of the pool. Is Union National entitled to recover the value of the pool?

10. In August 1979, Norma Wade purchased a Ford Thunderbird automobile and gave Ford Motor Credit a security interest in it to secure her payment of the $7,000 balance of the purchase price. When Wade fell behind on her monthly payments, Ford engaged the Kansas Recovery Bureau to repossess the car. On February 10, 1980, an employee of the Recovery Bureau located the car in Wade's driveway, unlocked the door, got in, and started it. He then noticed a discrepancy between the serial number of the car and the number listed in his papers. He shut off the engine, got out, and locked the car. When Wade appeared at the door to her house, he advised her that he had been sent by Ford to repossess the car but would not do so until he had

straightened out the serial number. She said that she had been making payments, that he was not going to take the car, and that she had a gun, which she would use. He suggested that Wade contact Ford to straighten out the problem. She called Ford and advised its representative that if she caught anybody on her property again trying to take her car, she would use her gun to "leave him laying right where I saw him." Wade made several more payments, but Ford again contracted to have the car repossessed. At 2:00 A.M. on March 5, 1980, the employee of the Kansas Recovery Bureau successfully took the car from Wade's driveway. She said that she heard a car burning rubber, looked out of her window, and saw that her car was missing. There was no confrontation between Wade and the employee since he had safely left the area before she discovered that the car had been taken. Wade then brought a lawsuit against Ford claiming that the car had been wrongfully repossessed. She sought actual and punitive damages, plus attorney's fees. Should Ford be held liable for wrongful repossession?

11. Gibson, a collector of rare old Indian jewelry, took two of his pieces to Hagberg, a pawnbroker. The two pieces, a silver belt and a silver necklace, were worth $500 each. Hagberg loaned only $45 on the belt and $50 on the necklace. Gibson defaulted on both loans, and immediately and without notice, the necklace was sold for $240. A short time later, the belt was sold for $80. At the time of their sale, Gibson owed interest on the loans of $22. Gibson sued Hagberg to recover damages for improperly disposing of the collateral. Is Gibson entitled to damages because of Hagberg's actions in disposing of the collateral?

12. 🎞 *Video Case.* See "A Good Night's Sleep." Appliance Dealer needed additional working capital, so it obtained a loan from bank, which took—and perfected by filing—a security interest in all present and after-acquired inventory and equipment of Appliance Dealer. Subsequently, the Appliance Dealer obtained inventory on credit from a Wholesaler, who retained and perfected a security interest in the inventory until Appliance Dealer paid for it. Appliance Dealer also purchased from Computer Retailer a computer for use in the store; Computer Retailer took and perfected a security interest in the computer before it was delivered. Can the bank obtain a security interest in the inventory and computer even though Appliance Dealer did not own them at the time it borrowed the money from Bank and gave it a security interest?

Cook, a Customer, buys a microwave oven and built-in range/oven on credit from Appliance Dealer. Both items were among the inventory that Appliance Dealer had purchased from Wholesaler, but it has not yet paid Wholesaler for either item. Appliance Dealer retained a security interest in the items it sold to Cook but it did not file a financing statement. Cook sold the microwave to her neighbor for about 60 percent of the price she agreed to pay Appliance Dealer. If Cook subsequently defaulted on her obligation to Appliance Dealer, could it recover the stove from Cook? Would your answer be different if the oven had been installed in a building on which Mortgage Company held a mortgage? Who would have the better right to the oven, Appliance Dealer or Mortgage Company? Does Appliance Dealer have the right to recover the microwave from Cook's neighbor?

If Appliance Dealer subsequently defaulted on its obligations to Bank, to Wholesaler, and to Computer Retailer, who would have the priority security interest in the appliances that remain in Appliance Dealer's inventory, the bank or Wholesaler? Would either have the legal right to recover the microwave or the stove that were sold to Cook? Who would have the priority security interest in the computer, Bank or Computer Retailer?

13. ▣ *Video Case.* See "TV Repair." Appliance Store acquired inventory on credit from TV Manufacturer, which retained and perfected a security interest in the TV sets until they were paid for. Appliance Store subsequently experienced financial difficulties and held a going-out-of-business sale. If TV Manufacturer had not been paid for the TV sets, would it have the legal right to recover them from individual customers who purchased them at the going-out-of-business sale?

BANKRUPTCY

INTRODUCTION

When an individual, a partnership, or a corporation is unable to pay its debts to creditors, problems can arise. Some creditors may demand security for past debts or start court actions on their claims in an effort to protect themselves. Such actions may adversely affect other creditors by depriving them of their fair share of the debtor's assets. Also, quick depletion of the debtor's assets may effectively prevent the debtor who needs additional time to pay off his debts from having an opportunity to do so.

At the same time, creditors need to be protected against the actions a debtor in financial difficulty might be tempted to take to their detriment. For example, the debtor might run off with his remaining assets or might use them to pay certain favored creditors, leaving nothing for the other creditors. Finally, a means is needed by which a debtor can get a fresh start financially and not continue to be saddled with debts beyond his ability to pay. This chapter focuses on the body of law and procedure that has developed to deal with the competing interests when a debtor is unable to pay his debts in a timely manner.

THE BANKRUPTCY ACT

The Bankruptcy Act is a federal law that provides an organized procedure under the supervision of a federal court for dealing with insolvent debtors. Debtors are considered insolvent if they are unable or fail to pay their debts as they become due. The power of Congress to enact bankruptcy legislation is provided in the Constitution. Through the years, there have been many amendments to the Bankruptcy Act. Congress completely revised the act in 1978 and then passed significant amendments to it in 1984. In 1986, Congress added provisions dealing with family farms.

The Bankruptcy Act has several major purposes. One is to ensure that the debtor's property is fairly distributed to the creditors and that some creditors do not obtain unfair advantage over the others. At the same time, the act protects all of the creditors against actions by the debtor that would unreasonably diminish the debtor's assets to which they are entitled. The act also provides the honest debtor with a measure of protection against the demands for payment by his creditors. Under some circumstances, the debtor is given additional time to pay the creditors, freeing him of those pressures creditors might otherwise exert. If the debtor makes a full and honest accounting of his assets and liabilities and deals fairly with his creditors, the debtor may have most—if not all—of the debts discharged so as to have a fresh start.

At one time, **bankruptcy** carried a strong stigma for the debtors who became involved in it. Today, this is less true. It is still desirable that a person conduct her financial affairs in a responsible manner. However, there is a greater understanding that such events as accidents, natural disasters, illness, divorce, and severe economic dislocations are often beyond the ability of individuals to control and may lead to financial difficulty and bankruptcy.

Bankruptcy Proceedings

The Bankruptcy Act covers a number of bankruptcy proceedings. In this chapter, our focus will be on:

1. Straight bankruptcy (liquidations).
2. Reorganizations.
3. Family farms.
4. Consumer debt adjustments.

The Bankruptcy Act also contains provisions regarding municipal bankruptcies, which are not covered in this chapter.

Liquidations

A liquidation proceeding, traditionally called **straight bankruptcy,** is brought under Chapter 7 of the Bankruptcy Act. The debtor must disclose all of the property she owns and surrender this bankruptcy estate to the **bankruptcy trustee.** The trustee separates out certain property that the debtor is permitted to keep and then administers, liquidates, and distributes the remainder of the bankrupt debtor's estate. There is a mechanism for determining the relative rights of the creditors, for recovering any preferential payments made to creditors, and for disallowing any preferential liens obtained by creditors. If the bankrupt person has been honest in his business transactions and in the bankruptcy proceedings, she is usually given a **discharge** (relieved) of her debts.

Reorganizations

Chapter 11 of the Bankruptcy Act provides a proceeding whereby a debtor can work out a plan to solve its financial problems under the supervision of a federal court. A reorganization plan is essentially a contract between a debtor and its creditors. The proceeding is intended for debtors, particularly businesses, whose financial problems may be solvable if they are given some time and guidance and if they are relieved of some pressure from creditors.

Family Farms

Historically, farmers have been accorded special attention in the Bankruptcy Code. Chapter 12 of the Bankruptcy Act provides a special proceeding whereby a debtor involved in a family farming operation can develop a plan to work out his financial difficulties. Generally, the debtor remains in possession of the farm and continues to operate it while the plan is developed and implemented.

Consumer Debt Adjustments

Under Chapter 13 of the Bankruptcy Act, individuals with regular incomes who are in financial difficulty can develop plans under court supervision to satisfy their creditors. Chapter 13 permits compositions (reductions) of debts and/or extensions of time to pay debts out of the debtor's future earnings.

The Bankruptcy Courts

Bankruptcy cases and proceedings are filed in federal district courts. The district courts have the authority to refer the cases and proceedings to bankruptcy judges, who are considered to be units of the district court. If a dispute falls within what is known as a **core proceeding,** the bankruptcy judge can hear and determine the controversy. Core proceedings include a broad list of matters related to the administration of a bankruptcy estate. However, if a dispute is not a core proceeding but rather involves a state law claim, then the bankruptcy judge can only hear the case and prepare draft findings and conclusions for review by the district court judge.

Certain proceedings affecting interstate commerce have to be heard by the district court judge if any party requests that this be done. Moreover, even the district courts are precluded from deciding certain state law claims that could not normally be brought in federal court, even if those claims are related to the bankruptcy matter. Bankruptcy judges are appointed by the president for terms of 14 years.

CHAPTER 7: LIQUIDATION PROCEEDINGS

Petitions

All bankruptcy proceedings, including liquidation proceedings, are begun by the filing of a petition. The petition may be either a **voluntary petition** filed by the debtor or an **involuntary petition** filed by a creditor or creditors of the debtor. A voluntary petition in bankruptcy may be filed by an individual, a partnership, or a corporation. However, municipal, railroad, insurance, and banking corporations and savings or building and loan associations are not permitted to file for straight bankruptcy proceedings. A person filing a voluntary petition need not be insolvent—that is, her debts need not be greater than her assets. However, the person must be able to allege that she has debts. The primary purpose for filing a voluntary petition is to obtain a discharge from some or all of the debts.

Involuntary Petitions

An involuntary petition is a petition filed by creditors of a debtor. By filing it, they seek to have the debtor declared bankrupt and his assets distributed to the creditors. Involuntary petitions may be filed against many debtors. However, involuntary petitions in straight bankruptcy cannot be filed against (1) farmers; (2) ranchers; (3) nonprofit organizations; (4) municipal, railroad, insurance, and banking corporations; (5) credit unions; and (6) savings or building and loan associations. If a debtor has 12 or more creditors, an involuntary petition to declare him bankrupt must be signed by at least 3 creditors. If there are fewer than 12 creditors, then an involuntary

petition can be filed by a single creditor. The creditor or creditors must have valid claims against the debtor exceeding the value of any security they hold by $5,000 or more. To be forced into involuntary bankruptcy, the debtor must be unable to pay his debts as they become due—or have had a custodian for his property appointed within the previous 120 days.

If an involuntary petition is filed against a debtor engaged in business, the debtor may be permitted to continue to operate the business. However, the court may appoint an **interim trustee** if this is necessary to preserve the bankruptcy estate or to prevent loss of the estate. A creditor who suspects that a debtor may dismantle her business or dispose of its assets at less than fair value may apply to the court for protection.

Automatic Stay Provisions

The filing of a bankruptcy petition operates as an automatic stay, holding in abeyance various forms of creditor action against a debtor or her property. These actions include: (1) beginning or continuing judicial proceedings against the debtor; (2) actions to obtain possession of the debtor's property; (3) actions to create, perfect, or enforce a lien against the debtor's property; and (4) setoff of indebtedness owed to the debtor before commencement of the bankruptcy proceeding. A court may give a creditor relief from the stay if the creditor can show that the stay does not give her "adequate protection" and jeopardizes her interest in certain property. The relief to the creditor might take the form of periodic cash payments or the granting of a replacement lien or an additional lien on property.

The case that follows, *In Re Ionosphere Clubs, Inc.,* is an example of creditors trying to proceed independent of a bankruptcy court and having their efforts blocked.[1]

---

[1]While this case involved a petition for relief under Chapter 11 (Reorganization), the automatic stay provisions of the bankruptcy title of the U.S. Code are applicable to both Chapter 7 and Chapter 11 proceedings.

In Re Ionosphere Clubs, Inc.
111 B.R. 423 (Bankr. S.D. N.Y. 1990)

On March 4, 1989, the International Association of Machinists and Aerospace Workers, AFL-CIO (IAM), initiated a strike against Eastern Air Lines, Inc. Thereafter, both the Airline Pilots Association (ALPA) and the Transport Workers Union of America (TWU) initiated a sympathy strike. As a result, on March 9, 1989, Eastern and its affiliate, Ionosphere Clubs, Inc., each filed a voluntary petition for relief under Chapter 11. After the bankruptcy filing, Eastern and Ionosphere continued to operate their businesses as debtors in possession.

During the strike, Eastern hired new pilots as permanent replacements for the striking pilots. On November 22, 1989, the ALPA notified Eastern that the sympathy strike had been concluded and that the approximately 2,000 striking pilots were willing to return to work. Eastern was not willing to displace the replacement pilots to make room for the returning strikers.

In February 1990, Morteson Rolleston and 17 formerly striking pilots filed a class action lawsuit in federal district court in Atlanta, claiming, among other things, that Eastern had failed to fund its pilot pension plan and to pay interest on certain pension benefits that had already been paid. The lawsuit sought to freeze the assets of Eastern until amounts allegedly due to certain benefit plans were paid. Eastern sought an injunction from the bankruptcy court enjoining the Rolleston lawsuit as a violation of the automatic stay provisions of the Bankruptcy Act.

Lifland, Chief Judge   Section 362(a)(3) of the [Bankruptcy] Code provides in pertinent part as follows:

(a) . . . a petition filed under . . . this title . . . operates as a stay, applicable to all entities, of—

(1) the commencement or continuation . . . of a judicial, administrative or other proceeding against the debtor that was or could have been commenced before the commencement of the case under this title, or to recover a claim against the debtor that arose before the commencement of the case under this title;

* * * * *

(3) an act to obtain possession of the property of the estate or of property from the estate or to exercise control over property of the estate;

* * * * *

(6) any act to collect, assess or recover a claim against the debtor that arose before the commencement of the case under this title.

It is beyond dispute that the Rolleston Plaintiffs seek to exercise control of at least $281 million of the cash assets of Eastern's estate by seeking to secure a court order "freezing" Eastern's assets and directing Eastern to pay this amount to the pilot pension plans. Additionally, the Rolleston Plaintiffs appear to request a temporary restraining order that would prohibit distributions under a reorganization plan, because "if the assets are distributed to creditors, it will be impossible for Plaintiffs to recover those assets." This direct attempt to secure preferred status for a discrete group of creditors runs directly counter to the distribution and oversight scheme established by the Code.

The Rolleston Plaintiffs also allege that the funds they seek to recover from Eastern on behalf of the pension plans "are not Eastern's assets but . . . are assets of the [Rolleston] Plaintiffs." It would appear that the Rolleston Plaintiffs are merely asserting unliquidated, contingent pre-petition claims against the Eastern estate and have no specific interest (other than the interest that all of Eastern's creditors have in property of the estate) in the property which they are attempting to gain control over.

Any attempt to "freeze" Eastern's assets and obtain an order requiring Eastern to transfer cash from its estate to the pilot pension plans is a direct and blatant attempt to assert control over the assets of the estate for the benefit of the Rolleston Plaintiffs. Such a distribution will reduce the amount to be paid to creditors and have an adverse effect on the feasibility of any plan of reorganization.

Additionally, the Rolleston lawsuit interferes with this court's jurisdiction over essential core matters in the Eastern case, including claims issues and confirmation of a plan of reorganization.

Judgment in favor of Eastern enjoining the Rolleston lawsuit.

Order of Relief

Once a bankruptcy petition has been filed, the first step is a court determination that relief should be ordered. If a voluntary petition is filed by the debtor, or if the debtor does not contest an involuntary petition, this step is automatic. If the debtor contests an involuntary petition, then a trial is held on the question of whether the court should order relief. The court orders relief only (1) if the debtor is generally not paying his debts as they become due, or (2) if within four months of the filing of the petition a custodian was appointed or took possession of the debtor's property. The court also appoints an interim trustee pending election of a trustee by the creditors.

Meeting of Creditors and Election of Trustee

The bankrupt person is required to file a list of her assets, liabilities, and creditors and a statement of her financial affairs. Then, the court calls a meeting of the creditors. The creditors may elect a creditors' committee and a trustee who, if approved by the judge, takes over administration of the bankrupt's estate. The trustee represents the creditors in handling the estate. At the meeting, the creditors have a chance to ask the debtor questions about her assets, liabilities, and financial difficulties. These questions commonly focus on whether the debtor has concealed or improperly disposed of assets. See Figure 1.

Duties of the Trustee

The trustee takes possession of the debtor's property and has it appraised. The debtor must also turn over her records to the trustee. For a time, the trustee may operate the debtor's business. The trustee sets aside the items of property that a debtor is permitted to keep under state exemption statutes or federal law.

The trustee examines the claims filed by various creditors and objects to those that are improper in any way. The trustee separates the unsecured property from the secured and otherwise exempt property. He also sells the bankrupt's nonexempt property as soon as possible, consistent with the best interest of the creditors.

The trustee is required to keep an accurate account of all the property and money he receives and to promptly deposit moneys into the estate's accounts. At the final meeting of the creditors, the trustee presents a detailed statement of the administration of the bankruptcy estate.

Exemptions

Even in a liquidation proceeding, the bankrupt is generally not required to give up all of his property; he is permitted to **exempt** certain items of property. Under the new Bankruptcy Act, the debtor may choose to keep certain items or property either exempted by state law, or exempt under federal law—unless state law specifically forbids use of the federal exemptions. However, any such property concealed or fraudulently transferred by the debtor may not be retained.

The debtor must elect to use *either* the set of exemptions provided by the state or the set provided by the federal bankruptcy law; she may not pick and choose between them. A husband and wife involved in bankruptcy proceedings must both elect either the federal or the state exemptions; where they cannot agree, the federal exemptions are deemed elected.

The exemptions permit the bankrupt person to retain a minimum amount of the assets considered necessary to life and to his ability to continue to earn a living. They are part of the fresh start philosophy that is one of the purposes of the Bankruptcy Act. The general effect of the federal exemptions is to make a minimum exemption

FIGURE 1   **Order and Notice of Chapter 7 Bankruptcy Filing**

B16A	United States Bankruptcy Court for the District of Maryland	ORDER AND NOTICE OF CHAPTER 7 BANKRUPTCY FILING, MEETING OF CREDITORS, AND FIXING OF DATES (Individual or Joint Debtor No Asset Case)

A. GENERAL INFORMATION

Name of Debtor
  John B. Jones
  D/B/A THE BATH SHOP
	Address of Debtor
	  195 MAIN STREET
	  ANNAPOLIS MD. 21401		

		Date Filed 01/24/95	Case Number 9060300-SD	Soc. Sec. Nos./Tax ID Nos. 050-30-4701

Addressee:
  WICKER PRODUCTS, INC.
  2000 SMITH PIKE
  ALMA, MI 48030
	Address of the Clerk of the Bankruptcy Court
	  United States Bankruptcy Court
	  101 W. Lombard Street
	  Baltimore, MD 21201

Name and Address of Attorney for Debtor
  MARC A. BURNS
  215 WATER STREET,
  BALTIMORE MD 21202
	Name and Address of Trustee
	  BRUCE A. SMITH
	  136 S. CHARLES STREET,
	  BALTIMORE MD 21201

B. DATE, TIME AND LOCATION OF MEETING OF CREDITORS
February 28, 1995, 09:15 A.M., U.S. Trustee, Fallon Federal Bldg., Rm. G-13, 31 Hopkins Plaza, Baltimore, MD 21201

C. DISCHARGE OF DEBTS
Deadline to File a Complaint Objecting to the Discharge of the Debtor or Dischargeability of a Debt: April 30, 1995

D. BANKRUPTCY INFORMATION

THERE APPEAR TO BE NO ASSETS AT THIS TIME FROM WHICH PAYMENT MAY BE MADE TO CREDITORS. DO NOT FILE A PROOF OF CLAIM UNTIL YOU RECEIVE NOTICE TO DO SO.

FILING OF A BANKRUPTCY CASE. A bankruptcy petition has been filed in this court for the person or persons named above as the debtor, and an order for relief has been entered. You will not receive notice of all documents filed in this case. All documents which are filed with the court, including lists of the debtor's property and debts, are available for inspection at the office of the clerk of the bankruptcy court.

CREDITORS MAY NOT TAKE CERTAIN ACTIONS. Anyone to whom the debtor owes money or property is a creditor. Under the bankruptcy law, the debtor is granted certain protection against creditors. Common examples of prohibited actions are contacting the debtor to demand repayment, taking action against the debtor to collect money owed to creditors or to take property of the debtor, except as specifically permitted by the bankruptcy law, and starting or continuing foreclosure actions, repossessions, or wage deductions. If unauthorized actions are taken by a creditor against a debtor, the court may punish that creditor. A creditor who is considering taking action against the debtor or the property of the debtor should review 11 U.S.C. § 362 and may wish to seek legal advice. The staff of the clerk's office is not permitted to give legal advice to anyone.

MEETING OF CREDITORS. The debtor (both husband and wife in a joint case) shall appear at the meeting of creditors at the date and place set forth above in box 'B' for the purpose of being examined under oath. ATTENDANCE BY CREDITORS AT THE MEETING IS WELCOMED, BUT NOT REQUIRED. At the meeting the creditors may elect a trustee as permitted by law, elect a committee of creditors, examine the debtor, and transact such other business as may properly come before the meeting. The meeting may be continued or adjourned from time to time without further written notice to the creditors.

LIQUIDATION OF THE DEBTOR'S PROPERTY. A trustee has been appointed in this case to collect the debtor's property, if any, and turn it into money. At this time, however, it appears from the schedules of the debtor that there are no assets from which any dividend can be paid to creditors. If at a later date it appears that there are assets from which a dividend may be paid, creditors will be notified and given an opportunity to file claims.

EXEMPT PROPERTY. Under state and federal law, the debtor is permitted to keep certain money or property as exempt. If a creditor believes that an exemption of money or property is not authorized by law, the creditor may file an objection. Any objection must be filed no later than 30 days after the conclusion of the meeting of creditors.

DISCHARGE OF DEBTS. The debtor is seeking a discharge of debts. A discharge means that certain debts are made unenforceable. Creditors whose claims against the debtor are discharged may never take action to collect the discharged debts. If a creditor believes the debtor should not receive a discharge under 11 U.S.C. § 727 or a specific debt should not be discharged under 11 U.S.C. § 523(c) for some valid reason specified in the bankruptcy law, the creditor must take action to challenge the discharge. The deadline for challenging a discharge is set forth above in box 'C.' Creditors considering taking such action may wish to seek legal advice.

DO NOT FILE A PROOF OF CLAIM UNLESS YOU RECEIVE A COURT NOTICE TO DO SO

For the Court: January 31, 1995 ——————————————— Date	 Michael Kostishak ——————————————— Clerk of the Bankruptcy Court

available to debtors in all states. States that wish to be more generous to debtors can provide more liberal exemptions.

The specific items that are exempt under state statutes vary from state to state. Some states provide fairly liberal exemptions and are considered "debtors havens." For example, in Florida none of the equity in the debtor's homestead can be used to pay off unsecured creditors, thus allowing even relatively well-off individuals to shield significant assets from creditors. Items that are commonly made exempt from sale to pay debts owed creditors include the family Bible, tools or books of the trade; life insurance policies; health aids such as wheelchairs and hearing aids; personal and household goods, and jewelry, furniture, and motor vehicles worth up to a certain amount.

The case that follows, *In re Griffin,* illustrates a claim by a debtor for an exemption under a state statute.

In Re Griffin
139 B.R. 415 (Bankr. W.D. Tex. 1992)

Troy Griffin was a debtor in a Chapter 7 bankruptcy proceeding. He claimed that his 1985 Hobie Magnum sailboat was exempt from his creditors under a Texas statute that provided an exemption for "athletic and sporting" equipment. A creditor objected to the claim of exemption.

King, Bankruptcy Judge   The question in this case is whether a sailboat may be claimed as exempt under the "athletic and sporting equipment" category of section 42,002(a)(8) of the Texas Property Code. This Court holds that a sailboat is not included within the Texas exemption for athletic and sporting equipment, and, therefore, the objection to the claim of exemption is sustained and the exemption is denied.

The exemption statutes in Texas were amended in May, 1991. Prior to the amendments, certain items of personal property were not exempt unless the property was reasonably necessary for the family or single adult. After the amendments, however, athletic and sporting equipment were no longer required to be reasonably necessary for the family to qualify as exempt property.

The most extensive discussion of the athletic and sporting equipment exemption is found in an unreported opinion by Judge Clark, *In re Schwarzbach,* in which he determined that a sixteen foot bass boat was not exempt as athletic or sporting equipment. *Schwarzbach* agreed with the analysis of an earlier case that "athletic and sporting equipment" is limited to small items for personal use. *Schwarzbach* also compared the language of two different exemptions and concluded that the Legislature contemplated an exemption for a boat only if the boat is used in a trade or profession. At the time *Schwarzbach* was decided, section 42.002(3)(B) allowed an exemption for "tools, equipment, books, and apparatus, including a boat, used in a trade or profession." Today, that section includes "boats and motor vehicles." In contrast, the current 42.002(a)(8) exemption for athletic and sporting equipment expressly includes bicycles, but not boats.

The purpose of exemption laws is to work a balance between protecting the debtor from destitution and allowing creditors to obtain payment on legitimate debts from the debtor's assets. This court agrees with *Schwarzbach* in holding that "athletic and sporting equipment" under the Texas exemption statute should be limited to small items for individual use. Allowing exemption of a sailboat or ski boat as "athletic and sporting equipment" would permit debtors to take undue advantage of the exemption laws and shield assets which are not necessary to a fresh start from the just claims of creditors. As so apply stated by *In re Henricksen,* "Bankruptcy is intended to provide debtors with a fresh start, not with a fine finish."

Claim of exemption denied.

Eleven categories of property are exempt under the federal exemptions, which the debtor may elect in lieu of the state exemptions. The federal exemptions include:

1. The debtor's interest (not to exceed $7,500 in value) in real or personal property that the debtor or a dependent of the debtor uses as a residence.

2. The debtor's interest (not to exceed $1,200 in value) in one motor vehicle.

3. The debtor's interest (not to exceed $200 in value for any particular item) up to a total of $4,000 in household furnishings, household goods, wearing apparel, appliances, books, animals, crops, or musical instruments that are held primarily for the personal, family, or household use of the debtor or a dependent of the debtor.

4. The debtor's aggregate interest (not to exceed $500 in value) in jewelry held primarily for the personal, family, or household use of the debtor or a dependent of the debtor.

5. $400 in value of any other property of the debtor's choosing, plus up to $3,750 of any unused homestead exemption.

6. The debtor's aggregate interest (not to exceed $750 in value) in any implements, professional books, or tools of the trade.

7. Life insurance contracts.

8. Interest up to $4,000 in specified kinds of dividends or interest in certain kinds of life insurance policies.

9. Professionally prescribed health aids.

10. Social security, disability, alimony, and other benefits reasonably necessary for the support of the debtor or his dependents.

11. The debtor's right to receive certain insurance and liability payments.

The term *value* means "fair market value as of the date of the filing of the petition." In determining the debtor's interest in property, the amount of any liens against the property must be deducted. Note, also, that the amount of the exemptions is doubled where a husband and wife are jointly involved in a single bankruptcy proceeding.

Avoidance of Liens

The debtor is also permitted to **void** certain liens against exempt properties that impair her exemptions. Liens that can be voided on this basis are judicial liens or nonpossessory, nonpurchase money security interests in: (1) household furnishings, household goods, wearing apparel, appliances, books, animals, crops, musical instruments, or jewelry that are held primarily for the personal, family, or household use of the debtor or a dependent of the debtor; (2) implements, professional books, or tools of the trade of the debtor or a dependent of the debtor; and (3) professionally prescribed health aids for the debtor or a dependent of the debtor. Debtors are also permitted to **redeem** exempt personal property from secured creditors by paying them the value of the collateral. Then, the creditor is an unsecured creditor as to any remaining debt owed by the debtor.

Preferential Payments

A major purpose of the Bankruptcy Act is to ensure equal treatment for the creditors of an insolvent debtor. The act also seeks to prevent an insolvent debtor from distributing her assets to a few favored creditors to the detriment of the other creditors. Thus, the trustee has the right to recover for the benefit of the bankruptcy estate all **preferential payments** in excess of $600 made by the bankrupt person.[2] A preferential payment is a payment made by an insolvent debtor within 90 days of the filing of the bankruptcy petition that enables a creditor to obtain a greater percentage of a preexisting debt than other similar creditors of the debtor. It is irrelevant whether the creditor knew that the debtor was insolvent. A debtor is presumed to have been insolvent on and during the 90 days immediately preceding the filing of a petition.

For example, Fredericks has $1,000 in cash and no other assets. He owes $650 to his friend Roberts, $1,500 to a credit union, and $2,000 to a finance company. If Fredericks pays $650 to Roberts and

---

[2]In the case of an individual debtor whose debts are primarily consumer debts, the trustee is not entitled to avoid preferences unless the aggregate value of the property is $600 or more.

then files for bankruptcy, he has made a preferential payment to Roberts. Roberts has had his debt paid in full, whereas only $350 is left to satisfy the $3,500 owed to the credit union and finance company. They stand to recover only 10 cents on each dollar that Fredericks owes them. The trustee has the right to get the $650 back from Roberts.

If the favored creditor is an insider—a relative of an individual debtor or an officer, director, or related party of a company—who had reasonable cause to believe the debtor was insolvent at the time the transfer was made, then a preferential payment made to that creditor between 90 days and one year prior to the filing of the petition can be recovered by the trustee.

Preferential Liens

Preferential liens are treated in a similar manner. A creditor might try to obtain an advantage over other creditors by obtaining a lien on the debtor's property to secure an existing debt. The creditor might seek to get the debtor's consent to a lien or to obtain a lien by legal process. Such liens are considered *preferential* and are invalid if they are obtained on property of an insolvent debtor within 90 days of the filing of a bankruptcy petition and if their purpose is to secure a preexisting debt. In addition, a preferential lien obtained by an insider (who had reasonable cause to believe the debtor was insolvent at the time the lien was obtained) between 90 days and one year prior to the filing of the bankruptcy petition can be avoided.

Transactions in the Ordinary Course of Business

The Bankruptcy Act provides several exceptions to the trustee's avoiding power that are designed to allow a debtor and his creditors to engage in ordinary business transactions. The exceptions include (1) transfers that are intended by the debtor and creditor to be a contemporaneous exchange for new value or (2) the creation of a security interest in new property where new value was given by the secured party to enable the debtor to obtain the property and where the new value was in fact used by the debtor to obtain the property.

For example, George Grocer is insolvent. He is permitted to purchase and pay cash for new inventory, such as produce or meat, without the payment being considered preferential. His assets have not been reduced. He has simply traded money for goods to be sold in his business. Similarly, he could buy a new display counter and give the seller a security interest in the counter until he has paid for it. This would not be considered a preferential lien. The seller of the counter has not gained an unfair advantage over other creditors, and Grocer's assets have not been reduced by the transaction. The unfair advantage comes where an existing creditor tries to take a lien or obtain a payment of more than his share of the debtor's assets. Then, the creditor has obtained a preference over other creditors, which is what the trustee is allowed to avoid.

The Bankruptcy Act also excepts transfers made in payment of a debt incurred in the ordinary course of the business or financial affairs of the debtor and the transferee and made according to ordinary business terms. The payment (transfer by the debtor) must be made not later than 45 days after the debt was incurred in the ordinary course of business. Thus, for example, a consumer could pay her monthly utility bills in a timely fashion without the creditor/utility being vulnerable to having the transfer of funds avoided by a trustee. The purpose of this exception is to leave undisturbed normal financial relations, and it is consistent with the general policy of the preference section of the Act to discourage *unusual* action by either a debtor or her creditors when the debtor is moving toward bankruptcy.

Exceptions to the trustee's avoidance power are also made for certain statutory liens, certain other perfected security interests, and cases filed by individual debtors whose debts are primarily consumer debts and the aggregate value of all property affected by the transfer is less than $600.

Fraudulent Transfers

If a debtor transfers property or incurs an obligation with *intent to hinder, delay, or defraud creditors,* the transfer is *voidable* by the trustee. Transfers of property for less than reasonable value are similarly voidable. Suppose Kasper is in financial difficulty.

She "sells" her $15,000 car to her mother for $100 so that her creditors cannot claim it. Kasper did not receive fair consideration for this transfer. The transfer could be declared void by a trustee if it was made within a year before the filing of a bankruptcy petition against Kasper. The provisions of law concerning **fraudulent transfers** are designed to prevent a debtor from concealing or disposing of his property in fraud of creditors. Such transfers may also subject the debtor to criminal penalties and prevent discharge of the debtor's unpaid liabilities.[3]

The *In Re Beckman* case, which follows, illustrates the attempt of some debtors in anticipation of bankruptcy to put some of their assets beyond the reach of their creditors and the response of the trustee who was able to avoid the transfers as fraudulent.

[3]Bulk sales of a debtor's materials, supplies, merchandise, or other inventory of the business in bulk and not in the ordinary course of business have the potential to defraud creditors. See Chapter 19, page 376, for a discussion of Article 6: Bulk transfers and the rights it provides to creditors.

In Re Beckman
104 B.R. 866 (Bankr. S.D. Ohio 1989)

In September 1985, Richard and Nancy Beckman believed they collectively owned assets in excess of $3 million and had a joint net worth in excess of $1.5 million. However, after consulting an attorney and having their assets appraised, it became apparent during October 1985 that they had a negative net worth, that they were insolvent, and that bankruptcy was inevitable.

In December, the Beckmans each signed applications to Bankers National Life Insurance Company to purchase $100,000 worth of additional life insurance. At the time, Richard Beckman already had $300,000 in term life insurance, $100,000 in accidental life insurance, $10,000 in whole life, and $14,000 in credit life insurance. On January 11, 1986, Richard Beckman delivered $15,000 in cash to Bankers Life as the initial premium on the two policies ($10,000 on his policy and $5,000 on her policy). The source of the funds was fees earned in his dentistry practice during the preceding October through December. The beneficiaries on all of the insurance policies (except the credit life policy) were either the Beckmans or their children.

On January 9, 1986, the Beckmans signed a Chapter 7 bankruptcy petition, and it was filed on January 14, 1986. The trustee sought to avoid the purchase of insurance from Bankers Life as a fraud on creditors.

Cole, Bankruptcy Judge   The Beckmans argue that it was perfectly proper and, hence, not fraudulent, to convert nonexempt cash to exempt property—the life insurance policies—on the eve of bankruptcy. Further, according to the Beckmans, the insurance purchase was made merely to "provide for each other and their children in the event that one or both of them died." For these reasons, the Beckmans submit that because the insurance purchase was not fraudulent under either federal or state law, the transfer of $15,000 is not avoidable.

The Trustee maintains the insurance purchase was undertaken with actual intent to hinder, delay and defraud the creditors of the estate, thereby rendering the transaction avoidable pursuant to Bankruptcy Code section 548(a)(1). This section states:

(a) The trustee may avoid any transfer of an interest of the debtor in property or any obligation incurred by the debtor that was made or incurred on or within one year before the date of the filing of the petition, if the debtor voluntarily or involuntarily

(1) made such transfer or incurred such obligation with actual intent to hinder, delay or defraud any entity to which the debtor was or became, on or after the date that such transfer was made or such obligation was incurred, indebted;

The issue for decision is whether the Beckmans' eve-of-bankruptcy conversion of non-exempt cash into exempt life insurance policies constitutes fraudulent conduct or merely prudent pre-bankruptcy planning.

Considerable debate in the case law has been engendered by pre-bankruptcy engineering—i.e., the practice of converting non-exempt property into exempt property in contemplation of filing a bankruptcy case. The general rule which has emerged from the decisional law is that mere conversion of property from non-exempt to exempt status on the eve of bankruptcy does not establish fraud. However, if extrinsic evidence of intent to defraud creditors is adduced, courts have: (1) disallowed the debtor's exemption claim and (2) held that the pre-bankruptcy transactions constitute avoidable fraudulent transfers.

Hence, the Court must determine here whether the Trustee has shown the existence of extrinsic evidence of fraud. Among the circumstances which courts focus upon in determining a debtor's intent in purchasing exempt life insurance on the eve of bankruptcy are the following:

1. Whether there was fair consideration paid for the life insurance policy;
2. Whether the debtor was solvent or insolvent as a result of the transfer or whether he was insolvent at the time of the transfer;
3. The amount of the policy;
4. Whether the debtor intended, in good faith, to provide by moderate premiums some protection to those to whom he had a duty to support;
5. The length of time between the purchase of a life insurance policy and the filing of the bankruptcy;
6. The amount of non-exempt property which the debtor had after purchasing the life insurance policy; and
7. The debtor's failure to produce available evidence and to testify with significant preciseness as to the pertinent details of his activities shortly before filing the bankruptcy petition.

Utilizing the foregoing factors as a guide, the Court concludes that in carrying out the insurance purchase the Beckmans intended to defraud their creditors. The factors delineated in paragraphs (2), (5) and (6) of the above list are clearly present. Debtors converted all of their remaining non-exempt property (p6) two days before their bankruptcy petition was filed (p5) and while they were admittedly insolvent (p2).

The amount of insurance purchased by the Beckmans (p3) likewise evinces a fraudulent purpose on their part. Notwithstanding the substantial amount of life insurance they had, the Beckmans consummated the purchase of additional insurance a mere three days prior to their bankruptcy filing. The Beckmans maintain the additional coverage was necessary for the protection of their family. But, having considered the record as a whole, the Court concludes that this testimony is not credible. To purchase an additional $200,000 in life insurance on the eve of bankruptcy and pre-pay the premiums thereon so that the cash surrender value of the policies would be obtainable by the Beckmans upon the termination of their bankruptcy proceeding goes far beyond "providing in good faith by moderate premiums some protection to those to whom they had a duty to support."

Perhaps the most telling indicator of the Beckmans fraudulent intent is their attempted concealment or, at best, obfuscation of the insurance purchase in their bankruptcy schedule and the accompanying schedules.

Judgment in favor of Trustee avoiding the insurance purchase as made in fraud of creditors.

Claims

If creditors wish to participate in the estate of a bankrupt debtor, they must file a **proof of claim** in the estate within a certain time—usually six months—after the first meeting of creditors. Only unsecured creditors are required to file proofs of claims. However, a secured creditor whose secured claim exceeds the value of the collateral is an unsecured creditor to the extent of the deficiency. That creditor must file a proof of claim to support the recovery of the deficiency.

Allowable Claims

The fact that a proof of claim is filed does not ensure that a creditor can participate in the distribution of the assets of the bankruptcy estate. The claim must also be allowed. If the trustee has a valid defense to the claim, he can use the defense to disallow or reduce it. For example, if the claim is based on goods sold to the debtor and the seller breached a warranty, the trustee can assert the breach as a defense. All of the defenses available to the bankrupt person are available to the trustee.

Secured Claims

The trustee must also determine whether a creditor has a lien or secured interest to secure an allowable claim. If the debtor's property is subject to a secured claim of a creditor, that creditor has first claim to it. The property is available to satisfy claims of other creditors only to the extent that its value exceeds the amount of the debt secured.

Priority Claims

The Bankruptcy Act declares certain claims to have **priority** over other claims. The six classes of priority claims are:

1. Expenses and fees incurred in administering the bankruptcy estate.
2. Unsecured claims in involuntary cases that arise in the ordinary course of the debtor's business after the filing of the petition but before the appointment of a trustee or the order of relief.
3. Unsecured claims of up to $2,000 per individual for employees' wages earned within 90 days before the petition was filed.
4. Contributions to employee benefit plans up to $2,000 per person (moreover, the claim for wages plus pension contribution is limited to $2,000 per person).
5. Claims of up to $900 each by individuals for deposits made on goods or services for personal use that were not delivered or provided.
6. Certain taxes owed to governmental units.

Distribution of the Debtor's Estate

The priority claims are paid *after* secured creditors realize on their collateral but *before* other unsecured creditors are paid. Payments are made to the six priority classes, in order, to the extent there are funds available. Each class must be paid in full before the next class is entitled to receive anything. To the extent there are insufficient funds to satisfy all the creditors within a class, each class member receives a pro rata share of his claim.

Unsecured creditors include: (1) those creditors who had not taken any collateral to secure the debt owed to them; (2) secured creditors to the extent their debt was not satisfied by the collateral they held; and (3) priority claimholders to the extent their claims exceed the limits set for priority claims.

Unsecured creditors, to the extent any funds are available for them, share in proportion to their claims. Unsecured creditors frequently receive little or nothing on their claims. Secured claims, trustee's fees, and other priority claims often consume a large part of the bankruptcy estate.

Special rules are set out in the Bankruptcy Act for distribution of the property of a bankrupt stockbroker or commodities broker.

DISTRIBUTION OF A DEBTOR'S ESTATE (CHAPTER 7)

Secured creditors proceed directly against the collateral. If debt if fully satisfied, they have no further interest; if debt is only partially satisfied, they are treated as general creditors for the balance.

↓

Debtor's Estate Is Liquidated and Distributed

↓

Priority Creditors (six classes)

1. Costs and expenses of administration.
2. If involuntary proceeding, expenses incurred in the ordinary course of business after petition filed but before appointment of trustee.
3. Claims for wages, salaries, and commissions earned within 90 days of petition; limited to $2,000 per person.
4. Contributions to employee benefit plans arising out of services performed within 180 days of petition; limit of $2,000 (including claims for wages, salaries, and commissions) per person.
5. Claims of individuals, up to $900 per person, for deposits made on consumer goods or services that were not received.
6. Government claims for certain taxes.

---

a. Distribution is made to the six classes of priority claims in order.
b. Each class must be fully paid before the next class receives anything.
c. If funds available are not sufficient to satisfy everyone in a class, then each member of the class receives the same proportion of claim.

↓

General Creditors

1. General unsecured creditors.
2. Secured creditors for the portion of their debt that was not satisfied by collateral.
3. Priority creditors for amounts beyond priority limits.

If funds remaining are not sufficient to satisfy all general creditors, then they each receive the same proportion of their claims.

↓

Debtor

Debtor receives any remaining funds.

DISCHARGE IN BANKRUPTCY

Discharge

A bankrupt person who has not been guilty of certain dishonest acts and has fulfilled his duties as a bankrupt is entitled to a **discharge** in bankruptcy. A discharge relieves the bankrupt person of further responsibility for dischargeable debts and gives him a fresh start. A corporation or a partnership is not eligible for a discharge in bankruptcy. A bankrupt person may file a written waiver of his right to a discharge. An individual may not be granted a discharge if she obtained one within the previous six years.

Objections to Discharge

After the bankrupt has paid all of the required fees, the court gives creditors and others a chance to file objections to the discharge of the bankrupt. Objections may be filed by the trustee, a creditor, or the U.S. attorney. If objections are filed, the court holds a hearing to listen to them. At the hearing, the court must determine whether the bankrupt person has committed any act that is a bar to discharge. If the bankrupt has not committed such an act, the court grants the discharge. If the bankrupt has committed an act that is a bar to discharge, the discharge is denied. The discharge is also denied if the bankrupt fails to appear at the hearing on objections or if he refused earlier to submit to the questioning of the creditors.

Acts that Bar Discharge

Discharges in bankruptcy are intended for honest debtors. Therefore, the following acts bar a debtor from being discharged: (1) the unjustified falsifying, concealing, or destroying of records; (2) making false statements, presenting false claims, or withholding recorded information relating to the debtor's property or financial affairs; (3) transferring, removing, or concealing property in order to hinder, delay, or defraud creditors; (4) failing to account satisfactorily for any loss or deficiency of assets; and (5) failing to obey court orders or to answer questions approved by the court.

Nondischargeable Debts

Certain debts are not affected by the discharge of a bankrupt debtor. The Bankruptcy Act provides that a discharge in bankruptcy releases a debtor from all provable debts except those that:

1. Are due as a tax or fine to the United States or any state or local unit of government.
2. Result from liabilities for obtaining money by false pretenses or false representations.
3. Are due for willful or malicious injury to a person or his property.
4. Are due for alimony or child support.
5. Were created by the debtor's larceny or embezzlement or by the debtor's fraud while acting in a fiduciary capacity.
6. Are certain kinds of educational loans that became due within five years prior to the filing of the petition.
7. Were not scheduled in time for proof and allowance because the creditor holding the debt did not have notification of the proceeding even though the debtor was aware that he owed money to that creditor.

The case that follows, *In Re Hott*, involves a denial of discharge of a debt on the grounds that the debtor obtained a loan using a materially false financial statement.

In Re Hott

99 B.R. 664 (Bankr. W.D. Pa. 1989)

David Hott was a college graduate with a degree in business administration who was employed as an insurance agent. He and his wife graduated from college in 1986. At the time he graduated, Hott had outstanding student loans of $14,500 for which he was given a grace period before he had to repay them.

Hott became unemployed. Bills began to accumulate and a number of outstanding bills were near the credit limits on his accounts. About that time, he received a promotional brochure by mail from Signal Consumer

Discount Company, offering the opportunity to borrow several thousand dollars. The Hotts decided that it appeared to be an attractive vehicle for them to use to consolidate their debts. Hott went to the Signal office and filled out a credit application. He did not list the student loan as a current debt. He later claimed that someone in the office told him he didn't have to list it if he owned an automobile, but there was significant doubt about this claim. Had he listed it, he would not have met the debt/income ratio required by Signal and it would not have made the loan. As it was, Signal agreed to make the loan on the condition that Hott pay off a car debt in order to reduce his debt/income ratio and Hott agreed to do so. On March 30, 1987, Signal loaned the Hotts $3,458.01.

On June 24, 1988, the Hotts filed for bankruptcy. Signal objected to the discharge of the balance remaining on its loan on the grounds that it had been obtained through the use of a materially false financial statement.

Markovitz, Bankruptcy Judge Section 523(a)(2)(B) provides that a discharge under section 72 . . . does not discharge an individual debtor from any debt—

(2) for money . . . to the extent obtained by—
(B) use of a statement in writing—
(i) that is materially false;
(ii) respecting the debtor's financial condition;
(iii) on which the creditor to whom the debtor is liable for such money . . . reasonably relied; and
(iv) that the debtor caused to be made with intent to deceive.

The parties agree that Hott did in fact obtain money as a result of his submission to Signal of a written statement of his financial condition. It appears that Hott does not contest Signal's reliance on the statement and it is clear that Signal's loss was proximately caused by Hott's financial statement. It is not clear if Hott concedes that the omission of the student loan caused the statement to be materially false. The major contested issue is whether Hott intentionally deceived Signal as to his true financial status in order to obtain the funds.

Material falsity has been defined as "an important or substantial untruth." It includes any omission, concealment or understatement of the Hotts' material liabilities. By omitting his single largest debt, a debt which by itself is as great as the remainder of his debt in combination, Hott created a material falsity in his financial statement.

Hott asserts that he fully intended to list his student loan debt on the application. He claims that said debt was in fact listed on the payment schedule his wife had prepared for him to take to Signal's office. That paper has admittedly long since been destroyed. Hott claims to have discussed the placement of the student loan with one of Signal's employees. Hott provided a physical description of the alleged employee. Signal's manager advised that the office had only three employees including himself. None of the three people even vaguely matched Hott's description.

Hott claims that the employee told him not to worry about the debt, so he did not. Given the size of the student loan in relation to the remainder of his debt, Hott's attitude certainly qualified as indifference and/or reckless disregard for accuracy.

We additionally reiterate Hott's education and qualifications in relation to his claim of innocence. Hott has a Bachelor's Degree in Business. He admits to having a knowledge of the concept called debt/income ratio and its purpose. Hott would easily have been able to determine that inclusion of his student loan on his application would cause his debt/income ratio to skyrocket. Hott asserts that he never stopped to perform any of the calculations. Hott may not assume the position of an ostrich with his head in the sand and ignore facts which were readily available.

This court finds that Hott's position lacks credibility and that Signal's witness was fully credible. We find at the very least Hott recklessly omitted the existence of his student loan when completing the credit application submitted for Signal's approval. Therefore, the debt must be found to be nondischargeable.

Judgment in favor of Signal.

The 1984 amendments established several additional grounds for nondischargeability relating to debts incurred in contemplation of bankruptcy. Congress was concerned about debtors who ran up large expenditures on credit cards shortly before filing for bankruptcy relief. Cash advances in excess of $1,000 obtained by use of a credit card and a revolving line of credit at a credit union obtained within 20 days of filing a bankruptcy petition are presumed to be nondischargeable. Similarly, a debtor's purchase of more than $500 in *luxury goods or services* on credit from a single creditor within 40 days of filing a petition is presumed to be nondischargeable.

There is also an exception from dischargeability for debts reflected in a judgment arising out of a debtor's operation of a motor vehicle while legally intoxicated.

All of these nondischargeable debts are provable debts. The creditor who owns these claims can participate in the distribution of the bankrupt's estate. However, the creditor has an additional advantage: His right to recover the unpaid balance is not cut off by the bankrupt's discharge. All other provable debts are dischargeable; that is, the right to recover them is cut off by the bankrupt's discharge.

Reaffirmation Agreements

Sometimes, creditors put pressure on debtors to reaffirm, or to agree to pay, debts that have been discharged in bankruptcy. When the 1978 amendments to the Bankruptcy Act were under consideration, some individuals urged Congress to prohibit such agreements. They argued that reaffirmation agreements were inconsistent with the fresh start philosophy of the Bankruptcy Act. Congress did not agree to a total prohibition; instead, it set up a rather elaborate procedure for a creditor to go through to get a debt reaffirmed. Essentially, the creditor must do so before the discharge is granted, and the court must approve the reaffirmation. The debtor has 60 days after he agrees to a reaffirmation to rescind it. Court approval is not required for the reaffirmation of loans secured by real estate.

A debtor may voluntarily pay any dischargeable obligation without entering into a reaffirmation agreement.

Dismissal for Substantial Abuse

As it considered the 1984 amendments to the Bankruptcy Act, Congress was concerned that too many individuals with an ability to pay their debts over time pursuant to a Chapter 13 plan (discussed later in this chapter) were filing petitions to obtain Chapter 7 discharges of liability. The consumer finance industry urged Congress to preclude Chapter 7 petitions where a debtor had the prospect of future disposable income to satisfy more than 50 percent of his prepetition unsecured debts. Although Congress rejected this approach, it did authorize Bankruptcy Courts to dismiss cases that they determined were a **substantial abuse** of the bankruptcy process. This provision appears to cover situations where a debtor has acted in bad faith or where she has the present or future ability to pay a significant portion of her current debts.

The case that follows, *In Re Newsom*, illustrates a situation where the court found the filing of a Chapter 7 petition by debtors with the ability to eventually pay off much of the unsecured debt they had accumulated to be a "substantial abuse" of the bankruptcy process.

IN RE NEWSOM
69 B.R. 801 (Bankr. D. N.D. 1987)

John and Christine Newsom were noncommissioned officers in the U.S. Air Force who each earned $1,408 net a month. In October 1986, they filed a voluntary petition in bankruptcy under Chapter 7. At the time, they had three secured debts totaling $21,956, $21,820 of which stemmed from the purchase of a 1986 Ford Bronco and a 1985 Pontiac Trans Am. They proposed to surrender the Bronco and a secured television set to the trustee, leaving $10,000 owing on the Pontiac as the only secured debt. Their unsecured debts totaled $20,911: $6,611 from bank card use, $12,764 from retail credit, and $1,350 from credit union loans. Of the unsecured debt, $11,563 was incurred in 1986.

The Newsoms filed an income and expense schedule showing that their monthly expenses totaled $2,232, including $100 per month for recreation and $150 for cigarettes and "walk around money." This left a surplus of $276 per month. The Bankruptcy Court, on its own motion, issued an order to the Newsoms to show why their petition should not be dismissed pursuant to the substantial abuse provision of the Bankruptcy Code.

Hill, Bankruptcy Judge   Section 707(b) of the Bankruptcy Code, providing for the dismissal of Chapter 7 cases, provides as follows:

(b) After notice and a hearing, the court on its own motion or on a motion by the United States Trustee but not at the request or suggestion of any party in interest, may dismiss a case filed by an individual debtor under this chapter whose debts are primarily consumer debts if it finds that the granting of relief would be a substantial abuse of the provisions of this chapter. There shall be a presumption in favor of granting the relief requested by the debtor.

This section was enacted as part of the consumer credit amendments to the Bankruptcy Act in 1984 as a means of combating what Congress viewed as an abuse of Chapter 7 by consumer debtors who had the ability to pay.

From the developing case law, this court has adopted the following as criteria against which the facts of a particular case ought to be judged in determining whether substantial abuse exists sufficient to mandate dismissal under section 707(b):

1. Whether the debtors have a likelihood of sufficient future income to fund a Chapter 13 plan which would pay a substantial portion of the secured claims;

2. Whether the debtors' petition was filed as a consequence of illness, disability, unemployment or some other calamity;

3. Whether the schedules suggest the debtors incurred cash advances and consumer purchases in an excess of their ability to repay them;

4. Whether the debtors' proposed family budget is excessive or extravagant;

5. Whether the debtors' statement of income and expenses is misrepresentative of their true financial condition.

The Newsoms' unsecured obligations are comprised exclusively of consumer debt. Their schedule of unsecured debt is highly suggestive of individuals who, already aware of their financial limitations and already faced with financial difficulties, went ahead and rang up at least $11,500 of consumer debt in 1986—an amount equal to thirty percent of their combined annual net income and which was incurred when they already had unsecured obligations of over $9,000. Even worse, they apparently purchased a second vehicle during this time period. Such action can only be regarded by the court as a completely irresponsible use of credit for non-essential items.

The Newsoms' proposed family budget seems extravagant insofar as they profess to need $250 for entertainment and recreation, including $150 for cigarettes and "walk around money." The court finds this aspect of the budget as unacceptable. It appears that the Newsoms are making no effort to tighten their belts or maintain a conservative life style. With a combined annual net income of nearly $34,000 and no dependents, the Newsoms are far better off than many and ought to be able to live quite comfortably while at the same time making an effort to pay back at least a portion of their unsecured creditors.

The ability to pay back a substantial portion of unsecured debt does not require an ability to pay back one hundred percent. All that is required is that the payback be significant and that there be a likelihood of sufficient future income to maintain such a payback. In the present case, assuming future income and expenses remain stable, the Newsoms would at a minimum, be able to contribute $276 per month or $3,312 per year toward a repayment plan. Over a three-year period, they would have contributed $9,936 resulting in a repayment of forty-seven percent of their unsecured claims. Contributions over a five-year period would result in an eighty-percent payback. None of these figures can be regarded as insignificant as far as creditors are concerned and strongly suggest that a meaningful payback could be accomplished. An even greater payback could be accomplished by honing the Newsoms' entertainment budget to a more realistic level. At any rate, this court believes that the Newsoms have the financial means at hand and will continue to have the means to fund a Chapter 13 plan which would retire a substantial portion of the unsecured claims.

Newsoms' petition for Chapter 7 relief dismissed.

CHAPTER 11: REORGANIZATIONS

Reorganization Proceeding

Sometimes, creditors benefit more from the continuation of a bankrupt debtor's business than from the liquidation of the debtor's property. Chapter 11 of the Bankruptcy Act provides a proceeding whereby, under the supervision of the Bankruptcy Court, the debtor's financial affairs can be reorganized rather than liquidated. Chapter 11 proceedings are available to individuals and to virtually all business enterprises, including individual proprietorships, partnerships, and corporations (except banks, savings and loan associations, insurance companies, commodities brokers, and stockbrokers).

Petitions for reorganization proceedings can be filed voluntarily by the debtor or involuntarily by its creditors. Once a petition for a reorganization proceeding is filed and relief is ordered, the court usually appoints (1) a committee of creditors holding unsecured claims, (2) a committee of equity security holders (shareholders), and (3) a trustee. The trustee may be given the responsibility for running the debtor's business. He is also usually responsible for developing a plan for handling the various claims of creditors and the various interests of persons such as shareholders.

The reorganization plan is essentially a contract between a debtor and its creditors. This contract may involve recapitalizing a debtor corporation and/or giving creditors some equity, or shares, in the corporation in exchange for part or all of the debt owed to them. The plan must (1) divide the creditors into classes; (2) set forth how each creditor will be satisfied; (3) state which claims, or classes of claims, are impaired or adversely affected by the plan; and (4) provide the same treatment to each creditor in a particular class, unless the creditors in that class consent to different treatment.

The plan is then submitted to the creditors for approval. Approval generally requires that creditors holding two thirds in amount and one half in number of each class of claims impaired by the plan must accept it. Once approved, the plan goes before the court for confirmation. If the plan is confirmed, the debtor is responsible for carrying it out.

The case that follows, *Official Committee of Equity Security Holders v. Mabey,* shows that until a plan is confirmed, the bankruptcy court has no authority to distribute a portion of the bankruptcy assets to a portion of the unsecured creditors.

OFFICIAL COMMITTEE OF EQUITY SECURITY HOLDERS v. MABEY
832 F.2d 299 (4th Cir. 1987)

The A. H. Robins Company is a publicly held company that filed a voluntary petition for relief under Chapter 11 of the Bankruptcy Code. Robins sought refuge in Chapter 11 because of a multitude of civil actions filed against it by women who alleged they were injured by use of the Dalkon Shield intrauterine device that it manufactured and sold as a birth control device. Approximately 325,000 notices of claim against Robins were received by the Bankruptcy Court.

In 1985, the court appointed the Official Committee of Equity Security Holders to represent the interest of Robins's public shareholders. In April 1987, Robins filed a proposed plan of reorganization, but no action was taken on the proposed plan because of a merger proposal submitted by Rorer Group, Inc. Under this plan, Dalkon Shield claimants would be compensated out of a $1.75 billion fund, all other creditors would be paid in full, and Robins's stockholders would receive stock of the merged corporation. However, at the time of other critical activity in the bankruptcy proceeding, no revised plan incorporating the merger proposal had been filed or approved.

Earlier, in August 1986, the court had appointed Ralph Mabey as an examiner to evaluate and suggest proposed elements of a plan of reorganization. On Mabey's suggestion, a proposed order was put before the district court supervising the proceeding that would require Robins to establish a $15 million emergency treatment fund "for the purpose of assisting in providing tubal reconstructive surgery or in-vitro fertilization to eligible Dalkon Shield claimants." The purpose of the emergency fund was to assist those claimants who asserted that they had become infertile as a consequence of their use of the product. A program was proposed for administering the fund and for making the medical decisions required.

On May 21, 1987, the district court ordered that the emergency treatment fund be created, and the action was challenged by the committee representing the equity security holders.

Chapman, Circuit Judge   The May 21, 1987, order of the district court approving the Emergency Treatment Fund makes no mention of its authority to establish such a fund prior to the allowance of the claims of the women who would benefit from the fund, and prior to the confirmation of a plan of reorganization of Robins. In its order denying the Equity Committee's Motion for a Stay Pending Appeal of the May 21 order, the district court relied on the "expansive equity power" of the court to justify its action.

While one may understand and sympathize with the district court's concern for the Dalkon Shield claimants who may desire reconstructive surgery or in-vitro fertilization, the creation of the Emergency Treatment Fund at this stage of the Chapter 11 bankruptcy proceedings violates the clear language and intent of the Bankruptcy Code, and such action may not be justified as an exercise of the court's equitable powers.

The Bankruptcy Code does not permit a distribution to unsecured creditors in a Chapter 11 proceeding except under and pursuant to a plan of reorga-

nization that has been properly presented and approved. Sections 1122–1129 of the Bankruptcy Code set forth the required contents of the reorganization plan, the classification of claims, the requirements of disclosure of the contents of the plan, the method for accepting the plan, the hearing required on confirmation of the plan, and the requirements for confirmation. The clear language of these statutes does not authorize the payment in part or full, or the advance of monies to or for the benefit of unsecured claimants prior to the approval of the plan of reorganization. The creation of the Emergency Treatment Fund has no authority to support it in the Bankruptcy Code and violates the clear policy of Chapter 11 reorganizations by allowing piecemeal pre-confirmation payments to certain unsecured creditors. Such action also violates Bankruptcy Rule 3021 which allows distribution to creditors only after the allowance of claims and the confirmation of a plan.

Judgment reversed in favor of Official Committee of Equity Security Holders.

Use of Chapter 11

During the 1980s, attempts by a number of corporations to seek refuge in Chapter 11 as a means of escaping problems they were facing received consid-

erable public attention. Some of the most visible cases involved efforts to obtain some protection against massive product liability claims and judgments for damages for breach of contract and to escape from collective bargaining agreements. Thus, for example, Johns-Manville Corporation filed under Chapter 11 because of the claims against it arising out of its production and sale of asbestos years earlier, while A. H. Robins Company, as illustrated in the preceding case, was concerned about a surfeit of claims arising out of its sale of the Dalkon Shield, an intrauterine birth control device. And, in 1987, Texaco, Inc., faced with a $10.3 billion judgment in favor of Pennzoil in a breach of contract action, filed a petition for reorganizational relief under Chapter 11. Companies such as LTV and Allegheny Industries sought changes in retirement and pension plans, and other companies such as Eastern Airlines sought refuge in Chapter 11 while embroiled in labor disputes.

As the 1990s began, a number of companies that were the subject of highly leveraged buyouts (LBOs) financed with so-called junk bonds, including a number of retailers, resorted to Chapter 11 to seek restructuring and relief from their creditors. Similarly, companies such as Pan Am and TWA that were hurt by the economic slowdown and the increase in fuel prices filed Chapter 11 petitions.

In recent years, Chapter 11 has been the subject of significant criticism and calls for its revision. Critics point out that many of the Chapter 11 cases are permitted to drag on for years, thus depleting the assets of the debtor through payments to trustees and lawyers involved in administration and diminishing the assets available to creditors.

Collective Bargaining Agreements

Collective bargaining contracts pose special problems. Prior to the 1984 amendments, there was concern that some companies would use Chapter 11 reorganizations as a vehicle to avoid executed collective bargaining agreements. The concern was heightened by the Supreme Court's 1984 decision in *NLRB v. Bildisco and Bildisco.* In that case, the Supreme Court held that a reorganizing debtor did not have to engage in collective bargaining before modifying or rejecting portions of a collective bargaining agreement and that such unilateral alterations by a debtor did not violate the National Labor Relations Act.

Congress then acted to try to prevent the misuse of bankruptcy proceedings for collective bargaining purposes. The act's 1984 amendments adopt a rigorous multistep process that must be complied with in determining whether a labor contract can be rejected or modified as part of a reorganization. Among other things that must be done before a debtor or trustee can seek to avoid a collective bargaining agreement are the submission of a proposal to the employees' representative that details the "necessary" modifications to the collective bargaining agreement and ensures that "all creditors, the debtor and all affected parties are fairly treated." Then, before the bankruptcy court can authorize a rejection of the original collective bargaining agreement, it must review the proposal and find that (1) the employees' representative refused to accept it without good cause, and (2) the balance of equities clearly favors the rejection of the original collective bargaining agreement.

The following case, *In Re Royal Composing Room, Inc.,* shows the scrutiny that the court gives the action of a debtor seeking to avoid a collective bargaining agreement.

In Re Royal Composing Room, Inc.

78 B.R. 671 (S.D. N.Y. 1987)

Royal Composing Room, Inc., is an advertising typography company, one of the last unionized shops in an industry that was subjected to considerable stress as computer technology replaced the linotype machine. Royal was a party to a collective bargaining agreement with Typographical Union No. 6. Royal was a profitable company until 1982, when its gross revenues declined by $2 million; over the next four years, it sustained operating losses. Confronted with these difficulties, in 1983 Royal began to cut expenses by sharply cutting the compensation of its principal executives, freezing the salaries of salespeople and middle management foremen, eliminating company automobiles, and moving to a smaller location to save rent. At the start of 1986, Royal lost its largest customer, Doyle Dane Bernbach, Inc., and sought to convince the union, which theretofore had not made any sacrifices or concessions, to forgo a 3 percent wage increase agreed to earlier. When the union refused, Royal filed a petition for reorganization under Chapter 11 and sought to reject its collective bargaining agreement.

Under section 1113(b) of the Bankruptcy Code, before it could reject the collective bargaining agreement, Royal was required to make a proposal to the union "which provides for those necessary modifications in the employees' benefits and protections that are necessary to permit the reorganization of the debtor and assures that all creditors, the debtor and all of the affected parties are treated fairly and equally." Royal held a meeting with officals of the union and offered a proposal that included a reduction of benefits, changes in work rules, the elimination of the scheduled wage increase, and the elimination of the union's right to arbitration as the way to change the contract. The union rejected the proposal and did not negotiate.

After a trial before the bankruptcy judge, Royal's motion to reject the existing collective bargaining contract was granted. The union then appealed to the District Court.

Keenan, District Judge   Local 6 raises two arguments on appeal: (1) the Bankruptcy Court did not apply the proper definition of "necessary" under section 1113, and (2) Royal's proposal did not treat all affected parties fairly and equitably. Both positions are unavailing.

The Second Circuit has indicated that the term "necessary" contained in section 1113 does not mean "essential" or "bare minimum." It has ruled that "the necessary requirement places on the debtor the burden of proving that its proposal is made in good faith, and that it contains necessary, but not absolutely minimal, changes that will enable the debtor to complete the reorganization process successfully."

Applying the standard of necessity endorsed by the Second Circuit, Bankruptcy Judge Abram found that Royal had, "established that it had in good faith attempted to negotiate for necessary changes but had been unsuccessful because of the union's unwillingness to engage in serious discussions." The record supports this finding. Local 6 was unresponsive and dilatory in the face of management's financial condition and resulting proposal. Likewise, Judge Abram was correct in her analysis of Royal's proposal. She found that Royal had cut nonunion management and executive salaries, eliminated trade association memberships, and even reused old doorknobs. During this time, union labor costs were the only expenses not cut.

The correctness of Judge Abram's legal conclusion is bolstered by the Second Circuit's statement in *Carey Transportation* that courts "must consider whether rejection of a collective bargaining agreement would increase the likelihood of successful reorganization." This court cannot envision Royal being able to successfully reorganize absent at least enforcement of its proposal under section 1113. Rejection clearly increases the likelihood of successful reorganization.

Local 6 further asserts that Royal did not satisfy the statutory requirement that under the proposal "all creditors, the debtor and all affected parties are treated fairly and equitably." Judge Abram correctly found that Royal "had spread the burden of financial sacrifice." As noted earlier, Royal cut costs in many ways, including a decrease in executive compensation, the rescinding of raises and freezing of salaries of salesmen and middle level management, the elimination of company cars, and the moving of its premises to smaller quarters. The union's wages were neither frozen nor cut. The Second Circuit observed that a debtor need not show that managers and nonunion employees have their benefits cut to the degree union benefits are cut. In this case, the union's benefits were the last to be cut, and it certainly was not the only constituency in Royal to feel the financial pinch. Royal's proposal satisfied the statute's requirement of fairness and equity.

Judgment of the Bankruptcy Court rejecting the collective bargaining agreement affirmed.

Chapter 12: Family Farms

Relief for Family Farmers

Historically, farmers have been accorded special treatment in the Bankruptcy Code. In the 1978 act, as in earlier versions, small farmers were exempted from involuntary proceedings. Thus, a small farmer who filed a voluntary Chapter 11 or 13 petition could not have the proceeding converted into a Chapter 7 liquidation over his objection so long as he complied with the act's requirements in a timely fashion. Additional protection was also accorded through the provision allowing states to opt out of the federal exemption scheme and to provide their own exemptions. A number of states used this flexibility to provide generous exemptions for farmers so they would be able to keep their tools and implements.

Despite these provisions, the serious stress on the agricultural sector in the mid-1980s led Congress in 1986 to further amend the Bankruptcy Act by adding a new Chapter 12 targeted to the financial problems of the family farm. During the 1970s and 1980s, farmland prices appreciated and many farmers borrowed heavily to expand their productive capacity, creating a large debt load in the agricultural sector. When land values subsequently dropped and excess production in the world kept farm product prices low, many farmers faced extreme financial difficulty.

Chapter 12 is modeled after Chapter 13, which is discussed next. It is available only for family farmers with regular income. To qualify, a farmer and spouse must have not less than 80 percent of their total noncontingent, liquidated debts arising out of their farming operations. The aggregate debt must be less than $1.5 million, and at least 50 percent of an individual's or couple's income during the year preceding the filing of the petition must have come from the farming operation. A corporation or partnership can also qualify, provided that more than 50 percent of the stock or equity is held by one family or its relatives and they conduct the farming operation. Again, 80 percent of the debt must arise from the farming operation; the aggregate debt ceiling is $1.5 million.

The debtor is usually permitted to remain in possession to operate the farm. Although the debtor in possession has many of the rights of a Chapter 11 trustee, a trustee is appointed under Chapter 12 and the debtor is subject to his supervision. The trustee is permitted to sell unnecessary assets, including farmland and equipment, without the consent of secured creditors and before a plan is approved. However, the secured creditor's interest attaches to the proceeds of the sale.

The debtor is required to file a plan within 90 days of the filing of the Chapter 12 petition—although the bankruptcy court has the discretion to extend the time. A hearing is held on the proposed plan, and it can be confirmed over the objection of creditors. The debtor may release to any secured party the collateral that secures the claim to obtain confirmation without the acceptance by that creditor.

Unsecured creditors are required to receive at least liquidation value under the Chapter 12 plan. If an unsecured creditor or the trustee objects to the plan, the court may still confirm the plan despite the objection so long as it calls for full payment of the unsecured creditor's claim or it provides that the debtor's disposable income for the duration of the plan is applied to making payments on it. A debtor who fulfills his plan, or is excused from full performance because of subsequent hardship, is entitled to a discharge.

Chapter 13: Consumer Debt Adjustments

Relief for Individuals

Chapter 13 of the Bankruptcy Act, entitled Adjustments of Debts for Individuals, gives individuals who do not want to be declared bankrupt an opportunity to pay their debts in installments under the protection of a federal court. Under Chapter 13, the debtor has this opportunity free of such problems as garnishments and attachments of her property by creditors. Only individuals with regular incomes (including sole proprietors of businesses) who owe individually (or with their spouse) liquidated, unsecured debts of less than $100,000 and secured debts of less than $350,000 are eligible to file under Chapter 13. Under the pre-1978 Bankruptcy Act, Chapter 13 proceedings were known as "wage earner plans." The 1978 amendments expanded the coverage of these proceedings.

Procedure

Chapter 13 proceedings are initiated only by the voluntary petition of a debtor filed in the Bankruptcy Court. Creditors of the debtor may not file an involuntary petition for a Chapter 13 proceeding. The debtor in the petition states that he is insolvent or unable to pay his debts as they mature and that he desires to effect a composition or an extension, or both, out of future earnings or income. A **composition of debts** is an arrangement whereby the amount the person owes is reduced, whereas an **extension** provides the person a longer period of time in which to pay his debts. Commonly, the debtor files at the same time a list of his creditors as well as a list of his assets, liabilities, and executory contracts.

Following the filing of the petition, the court calls a meeting of creditors, at which time proofs of claims are received and allowed or disallowed. The debtor is examined, and she submits a plan of payment. The plan is submitted to the secured creditors for acceptance. If they accept the plan and if the court is satisfied that the plan is proposed in good faith, meets the legal requirements, and is in the interest of the creditors, the court approves the plan. The court then appoints a trustee to carry out the plan. The plan must provide for payments over three years or less, unless the court approves a longer period of up to five years.

No plan may be approved if the trustee or an unsecured creditor objects, unless the plan provides for the objecting creditor to be paid the present value of what he is owed or provides for the debtor to commit all of his projected disposable income for a three-year period to pay his creditors.

The case that follows, *In Re Tucker,* deals with the issue of whether a proposed plan that provided for the commitment of all disposable income for a four-year period should be rejected because it unfairly discriminated against a class of unsecured creditors.

IN RE TUCKER
159 B.R. 325 (Bankr. D.Mont. 1993)

Daniel and Betty Tucker filed a voluntary Chapter 13 petition on March 10, 1993, listing personal property totaling $3,015. They claimed virtually all of the personal property as exempt, except for $180 worth of an automobile that exceeded the allowed exemption. Their real property was either encumbered or exempt, leaving little available for distribution to unsecured creditors in the event of liquidation. They also listed unsecured claims in the amount of $14,208, of which $4,183 were claims for student loans. The remainder of claims were for services and purchases, all of which would be dischargeable.

In August 1993, the Tuckers filed a Chapter 13 plan that provided for monthly payments in the amount of $115, which corresponded to the difference between their current income and expenditures as shown on the schedules they filed with their petition. The plan provided for payment in full of the student loan debts over a 48-month period and 29 percent of the claims to the other unsecured creditors. The Trustee, relying on objections from unsecured creditors, filed an objection to the plan on the grounds that it discriminated unfairly against a class of unsecured claims.

Peterson, Bankruptcy Judge   At issue is whether the Plan unfairly discriminates against the unsecured creditors in violation of Bankruptcy Code section 1322(b)(1) by paying nondischargeable student loan debts in full while only paying a 29% dividend on the other secured claims. The Tuckers argue that the discrimination in the Plan is fair because it allows them to pay the student loans in full, which fulfills the intent of Congress in making student loans nondischargeable; the Plan pays 29% to the unsecured creditors where they would receive virtually nothing if the case were in Chapter 7; and finally it gives the Tuckers a "fresh start."

In determining whether a Plan discriminates unfairly against a class of unsecured claims, courts have developed a four-part test: (1) whether the discrimination has a reasonable basis; (2) whether the Debtor can carry out a Plan without discrimination; (3) whether the discrimination is proposed in good faith; and (4) whether the degree of discrimination is directly related to the basis or rationale for the discrimination.

The court in *In re Smallberger* (Bankr. D.Or. 1993) found discrimination in favor of student loans unfair and refused to allow separate classification simply on the basis that they were nondischargeable or in the interests of the debtor's "fresh start." The court in *In re Tucker* (Bankr. N.D.Ohio 1992) likewise found unfair discrimination in a plan which proposed paying 100% of student loans over 48 months while paying the unsecured claims five percent. The court deemed repayment of nondischargeable student loans to be the debtor's problem "which he cannot foist off on his other unsecured creditors."

Even the court in *Smallberger* notes that a "debtor might accomplish the result sought here by filing a chapter 7 case and then a chapter 13 case to deal with the nondischargeable obligations." This focuses the inquiry on whether the discrimination is indeed "unfair." Debtors in Chapter 13 have the unwaivable right to convert to Chapter 7 at any time. The parties agree that if the Debtors converted this case to Chapter 7 all of the unsecured claims would get virtually nothing after administrative expenses and their claims would be discharged with the exception of the student loan debts. The student loan debts, while not discharged, would be paid voluntarily by the Debtors from post-petition income in Chapter 7 as they would be under the proposed Chapter 13 Plan. By preventing the discrimination in favor of nondischargeable student loans, the courts in *Smallberger* and *Tucker* encourage debtors to utilize Chapter 7 instead of Chapter 13, despite Congressional intent favoring Chapter 13.

This court, looking at the facts on a case-by-case basis, deems a liquidation analysis highly significant. If this case is converted to a Chapter 7 case, the unsecured creditors will receive nothing and have their claims discharged. If the Plan is confirmed, they will receive 29% of their claims. The fairer treatment for the creditors is clearly the 29% dividend in Chapter 13 which Congress encourages Debtors to use in lieu of Chapter 7. The creditors who filed the rejections of the proposed Plan cannot hope to thereby force a larger dividend upon these Debtors (the Tuckers), who have nothing to lose by converting to Chapter 7, except all the unsecured claims which are not student loan debts.

Turning to the four-part test, I first find that the discrimination has a reasonable basis, i.e. that it provides for the payment in full of nondischargeable student loans. Second, I find that the Debtor cannot carry out a Plan without the discrimination. The Debtors already have extended the Plan period to four years, longer than the three year period of Bankruptcy Code section 1322(c). If the discrimination is not allowed the Plan payments would be completed without the student loans paid in full, thereby leaving the Debtors saddled with debt after four years under a Plan and defeating their "fresh start."

Third, I find that the discrimination is proposed in good faith. There is nothing to suggest that these Debtors proposed the discrimination in bad faith. Fourth, I find the degree of discrimination is directly related to the basis or rationale for the discrimination. They commit their disposable income for four years to the Plan, thereby providing a 29% dividend for creditors who would otherwise be left out in the cold in Chapter 7. The Plan pays in full a nondischargeable student loan and provides the Debtors with a "fresh start" at the end of 48 months free from all debts.

Objections to confirmation overruled.

Under the 1984 amendments, a Chapter 13 debtor must begin making the installment payments proposed in her plan within 30 days after the plan is filed. The interim payments must continue to be made until the plan is confirmed or denied. If the plan is denied, the money, less any administrative expenses, is returned to the debtor by the trustee. The interim payments give the trustee an opportunity to observe the debtor's performance and thus to be in a better position to make a recommendation about whether the plan should be approved.

Once approved, a plan may be subsequently modified on petition of a debtor or a creditor where there is a material change in the debtor's circumstances.

Suppose Curtis Brown has a monthly take-home pay of $1,000 and a few assets. He owes $1,500 to the credit union, borrowed for the purchase of furniture; he is supposed to repay the credit union $75 per month. He owes $1,800 to the finance company on the purchase of a used car; he is supposed to repay the company $90 a month. He has also run up charges of $1,200 on a MasterCard account, primarily for emergency repairs to his car; he must pay $60 per month to MasterCard. His rent is $350 per month, and food and other living expenses run him another $425 per month. Curtis was laid off from his job for a month and fell behind on his payments to his creditors. He then filed a Chapter 13 petition. In his plan, he might, for example, offer to repay the credit union $50 a month, the finance company $60 a month, and MasterCard $40 a month—with the payments spread over three years rather than the shorter time for which they are currently scheduled.

Discharge

When the debtor has completed her performance of the plan, the court issues an order that discharges her from the debts covered by the plan. The debtor may also be discharged even though she did not complete her payments within the three years if the court is satisfied that the failure is due to circumstances for which the debtor cannot justly be held accountable. An active Chapter 13 proceeding stays, or holds in abeyance, any straight bankruptcy proceedings and any actions by creditors to collect consumer debts. However, if the Chapter 13 proceeding is dismissed (for example, because the debtor fails to file an acceptable plan or defaults on an accepted plan), straight bankruptcy proceedings may begin.

Advantages of Chapter 13

A debtor may choose to file under Chapter 13 to avoid the stigma of bankruptcy or to retain more of his property than is exempt from bankruptcy under state law. Chapter 13 can provide some financial discipline to a debtor as well as an opportunity to get his financial affairs back in good shape. It also gives him relief from the pressures of individual creditors so long as he makes the payments called for by the plan. The debtor's creditors may benefit by recovering a greater percentage of the debt owed to them than would be obtainable in straight bankruptcy.

CONCEPT REVIEW

COMPARISON OF MAJOR FORMS OF BANKRUPTCY PROCEEDINGS

Purpose	Chapter 7 Liquidation	Chapter 11 Reorganization	Chapter 12 Adjustments of Debts	Chapter 13 Adjustments of Debts
Eligible Debtors	Individuals, partnerships, and corporations *except* municipal corporations, railroads, insurance companies, banks, and savings and loan associations. Farmers and ranchers are eligible only if they petition voluntarily.	Generally same as Chapter 7 except a railroad may be a debtor, and a stockbroker and commodity broker may not be a debtor under Chapter 11.	Family farmer with regular income, at least 50 percent of which comes from farming, and less than $1.5 million in debts, at least 80 percent of which is farm related.	Individual with regular income with liquidated unsecured debts less than $100,000 and secured debts of less than $350,000.

Purpose	Chapter 7 Liquidation	Chapter 11 Reorganization	Chapter 12 Adjustments of Debts	Chapter 13 Adjustments of Debts
Initiation of Proceeding	Petition by debtor (voluntary). Petition by creditors (involuntary).	Petition by debtor (voluntary). Petition by creditors (involuntary).	Petition by debtor.	Petition by debtor.
Basic Procedure	1. Appointment of trustee. 2. Debtor retains exempt property. 3. Nonexempt property is sold and proceeds distributed based on priority of claims. 4. Dischargeable debts are terminated.	1. Appointment of trustee and committees of creditors and equity security holders. 2. Debtor submits reorganization plan. 3. If plan is approved and implemented, debts are discharged.	1. Trustee is appointed but debtor usually remains in possession of farm. 2. Debtor submits a plan in which unsecured creditors must receive at least liquidation value. 3. If plan is approved and fulfilled, debtor is entitled to a discharge.	1. Debtor indicates in petition that he is seeking a composition of debts or an extension. 2. If plan is approved after submitted to creditors, then trustee is appointed. 3. If plan is approved and fulfilled, debts covered by plan are discharged.
Advantages	After liquidation and distribution of assets, most or all of debts may be discharged and debtor gets a fresh start.	Debtor remains in business and debts are liquidated through implementation of approved reorganization plan.	Debtor generally remains in possession and has opportunity to work out of financial difficulty over period of time (usually three years) through implementation of approved plan.	Debtor has opportunity to work out of financial difficulty over period of time (usually three years) through implementation of approved plan.

ETHICAL AND PUBLIC POLICY CONCERNS

1. If a person receives a discharge of debts in bankruptcy, should the person feel an ethical obligation to reaffirm or to repay the debts that were discharged?

2. Is it ethical for a person facing the prospect of seeking relief under the bankruptcy laws to try to convert nonexempt property into exempt property on the eve of the filing of his petition? Does the relative economic condition of the debtor have any bearing on your response to this question?

3. As you have learned in this chapter, during the past decade corporations have filed petitions under Chapter 11 in order to deal with a variety of problems, including the threat of massive product liability claims and the desire of the company to get out of labor contracts. Is it ethical for a company to use Chapter 11 to try to get out of, or to modify, labor contracts or pension agreements that it now deems unfavorable to its interests? Is it ethical for a company to seek the shelter of Chapter 11 when faced with claims for product liability? Is the decision of the appeals court in *Official Committee of Equity Security Holders v. Mabey* to disallow the proposed emergency treatment fund good public policy?

4. As was discussed in this chapter, the federal bankruptcy law makes special provision for small farmers, and some states are particularly generous in the exemptions they make available to farmers. Is this special treatment of farmers justifiable as sound and fair public policy?

PROBLEMS AND PROBLEM CASES

◆

1. Gilbert and Kimberly Barnes filed a voluntary Chapter 7 petition in the U.S. Bankruptcy Court for the District of Maryland. Subsequently, they moved to avoid a nonpurchase money lien held by ITT Financial Services on their exempt "household goods." Among the goods that the Barneses were claiming as "household goods" were a videocassette recorder (VCR), a 12-gauge pump shotgun, a 20-gauge shotgun, a 30–06 rifle, and a .22 pistol. ITT contended that the VCR and the firearms were not household goods that they could exempt. Under Maryland law, household goods are items of personal property reasonably necessary for the day-to-day existence of people in the context of their homes. Should the court consider the VCR and firearms to be "household goods"?

2. On June 29, 1979, Gary Johnson filed a Chapter 13 bankruptcy petition. Acting on the advice of his lawyer shortly before filing the petition, Johnson sold an interest in real estate and used the proceeds to buy a life insurance policy with a face value of $31,460 and a cash value of $12,118. His wife was named as the beneficiary. Johnson claimed that the policy was exempt under South Dakota law, which provides for an exemption of up to $20,000 for the proceeds of a life insurance policy payable directly to the insured, his surviving spouse, or his family. A creditor objected to the exemption but made no showing of fraudulent intent on Johnson's part. Should the exemption be allowed?

3. On October 19, 1976, Wallace Tuttle, an attorney, and Peninsula Roofing entered into a retainer agreement for the performance of legal services at a stipulated hourly rate. In 1978 and 1979, Peninsula became delinquent in its payments for attorney's fees. The delinquencies reflected overall corporate financial problems that resulted in the permanent closing of Peninsula on July 25, 1979. On August 6, 1979, Peninsula received a check for $3,250 representing an account receivable due it. Peninsula turned the check over to Tuttle, who deposited it to his trust account, credited $1,946.96 against the past-due account, and created a trust fund from which payments for current services and disbursements would be made. On October 18, 1979, an involuntary petition was filed against Peninsula. The bankruptcy trustee sought to require Tuttle to return the $3,250 to him as a preferential payment. Should Tuttle be required to return the money he received?

4. William Kranich, Jr., was the sole shareholder in the DuVal Financial Corporation (DFC). On November 10, 1981, Kranich filed a voluntary petition for relief under Chapter 7; on January 6, 1982, DFC also filed a voluntary petition under Chapter 7. Prior to the commencement of the Chapter 7 proceedings, Kranich conveyed his personal residence in Clearwater, Florida, to DFC. The transfer was wholly without consideration. Shortly thereafter, DFC transferred the property to William Kranich III and June Elizabeth Kranich, Kranich's son and daughter, as tenants in common. This transfer was also without consideration. The bankruptcy trustee brought suit to recover the property from the son and daughter on the grounds that the transfer was fraudulent. Could the trustee recover the property on the grounds that its transfer, without consideration, was fraudulent?

5. Barnhart had borrowed money from Credit Plan and was behind in her payments. She applied for a new loan with which she intended to pay the existing loan and the interest on it. At the time the new loan was granted, the agent of Credit Plan prepared a financial statement showing that Barnhart owed $837.50. In fact, she owed approximately $1,800. The agent was a schoolmate of Barnhart's and was familiar with her financial affairs. At the time the statement was prepared, Barnhart talked to the agent about her other debts. She signed the statement without reading it. Credit Plan filed objections to Barnhart's discharge on the ground that she had obtained credit on a materially false credit statement in writing. Should Barnhart be denied a discharge on this ground?

6. While attending college, Barbara Barrington obtained a student loan from the New York State Higher Education Services Corporation. Barrington had had depressive illnesses all her life, as had previous generations in her family: Her grandmother was institutionalized for depression, and her mother had been on medication to treat depression for a long time. Barrington was discharged by Eastman Kodak Company because she could not face the problems and stress of her job. Since that time, she had stayed at home, slept a lot, and played with her dog. She made little or no effort to find other employment because of her depressed condition. She also filed for bankruptcy. In the bankruptcy proceeding, one of the questions was whether payment of her student loan would impose an undue hardship on Barrington, and thus whether the loan was dischargeable. Should the student loan be discharged?

7. On December 19, 1986, Brian Scholz was involved in an automobile collision with a person insured by The Travelers Insurance Company. At the time, Scholz was cited for, and plead no contest to, a criminal charge of driving under the influence of alcohol arising out of the accident. The Travelers paid its insured $4,303.68 and was subrogated to the rights of its insured against Scholz. Subsequently, The Travelers filed a civil action against Scholz to recover the amount it had paid, and a default judgment was entered against Scholz. Eleven months later, Scholz sought relief from the bankruptcy court by filing a voluntary petition under Chapter 7. One of the questions in the bankruptcy proceeding was whether the debt owing to The Travelers was nondischargeable. Is the debt dischargeable?

8. Bryant filed a Chapter 7 petition on January 7, 1984. On March 8, she filed an application to reaffirm an indebtedness owed to General Motors Acceptance Corporation (GMAC) on her 1980 Cadillac automobile. Bryant was not married, and she supported two teenage daughters. She was not currently employed, and she collected $771 a month in unemployment benefits and $150 a month in rental income from her mother. Her monthly house payments were $259. The present value of the Cadillac was $9,175; she owed $7,956.37 on it, and her monthly payments were $345.93. Bryant indicated that she wanted to keep the vehicle because it was reliable. GMAC admitted that Bryant had been, and continued to be, current in her payments. GMAC said that the car was in no danger of being repossessed but that, absent reaffirmation, it might decide to repossess it. Should the court grant Bryant's application to reaffirm her indebtedness to GMAC?

9. Winifred Doersam was the borrower on three student loans made to her by First Federal Savings and Loan and guaranteed by the state of Ohio Student Loan Commission (OSLC) totaling $10,000 to finance her graduate education at the University of Dayton. Doersam also signed as the cosigner for a $5,000 student loan for her daughter, also made by First Federal and guaranteed by OSLC. With the use of the loans, she was able to obtain a position as a systems analyst with NCR Corporation, which required her to obtain a master's degree in order to retain her position at an annual salary of $24,000. Approximately six weeks before her graduation, and before the first payment on her student loans was due, Doersam filed a petition and plan under Chapter 13. In her plan, she proposed to pay $375 a month to her unsecured creditors over a 36-month period. Doersam's total unsecured debt was $18,418, 81 percent of which was comprised of the outstanding student loans. Her schedules provided for payment of rent of $300 per month and food of $400 per month. Her listed dependents included her 23-year-old daughter and her 1-year-old grandaughter. At the time, her daughter was employed in the Ohio Work Program, a program designed to help welfare recipients, for which she was paid a small salary. The OLSC objected to the plan proposed by Doersam on the grounds that it was filed in bad faith. Should the bankruptcy court refuse to confirm the plan on the grounds it was not filed in good faith?

10. On December 8, 1981, Thomas Thompson filed a petition under Chapter 13 to pay his debts through a wage earner plan. After the notice to creditors, Ford Motor Credit Company, a secured creditor to which Thompson was indebted for payments on a 1980 Ford, filed a proof of claim and rejected the plan. The plan was confirmed over Ford's objections. It provided for payments to Ford of $22.90 a week, equivalent to the same rate and adding up to the same total as in the original sales contract, and enjoined Ford from foreclosing on the automobile. In 1982, Thompson was injured at work and able to work only part time. He then fell behind in his payments to Ford, even though he was regularly submitting his disability checks to the trustee. Ford then filed a petition to reclaim the car, alleging that Thompson had failed to make the payments due on the car. Should Ford be permitted to have the plan disregarded so that it can foreclose its security interest on the car?

COMMERCIAL PAPER

NEGOTIABLE

INSTRUMENTS

As commerce and trade developed, people moved beyond exclusive reliance on barter to the use of money and then to the use of substitutes for money. The term commercial paper *encompasses such substitutes in common usage today as checks, promissory notes, and certificates of deposit.*

History discloses that every civilization that engaged to an appreciable extent in commerce used some form of commercial paper. Probably the oldest commercial paper used in the carrying on of trade is the promissory note. Archaeologists found a promissory note made payable to bearer that dated from about 2100 B.C. The merchants of Europe used commercial paper—which, under the law merchant, was negotiable—in the 13th and 14th centuries. Commercial paper does not appear to have been used in England until about A.D. 1600.

This chapter and the three following chapters outline and discuss the body of law that governs commercial paper. Of particular interest are those kinds of commercial paper having the attribute of negotiability—that is, they can generally be transferred from party to party and accepted as a substitute for money. This chapter discusses the nature and benefits of negotiable instruments and then outlines the requirements an instrument must meet to qualify as a negotiable instrument. Subsequent chapters discuss transfer and negotiation of instruments, the rights and liabilities of parties to negotiable instruments, and the special rules applicable to checks.

NATURE OF NEGOTIABLE INSTRUMENTS

When a person buys a television set and gives the merchant a check drawn on his checking account, that person uses a form of negotiable commercial paper. Similarly, a person who goes to a bank or a credit union to borrow money might sign a promissory note agreeing to pay the money back in 90 days. Again, the bank and borrower use a form of negotiable commercial paper.

Commercial paper is basically a *contract for the payment of money*. It may serve as a substitute for money payable immediately, such as a check. Or, it can be used as a means of extending credit.

When a television set is bought by giving the merchant a check, the check is a substitute for money. If a credit union loans a borrower money now in exchange for the borrower's promise to repay it later, the promissory note signed by the borrower is a means of extending credit.

Uniform Commercial Code

The law of commercial paper is covered in Article 3 (Negotiable Instruments) and Article 4 (Bank Deposits and Collections) of the Uniform Commercial Code. Other negotiable documents, such as investment securities and documents of title, are treated in other articles of the Code. The original Code Articles 3 and 4, adopted initially in the 1960s, generally followed the basic, centuries-old rules governing the use of commercial paper; but at the same time they adopted modern terminology and coordinated, clarified, and simplified the law. However, business practices continued to evolve and new technological developments have changed the way that banks process checks. Accordingly, in 1990, a joint effort by the American Law Institute and the National Conference of Commissioners on Uniform State Laws produced a Revised Article 3 and related amendments to Articles 1 and 4. The purpose was to clarify Articles 3 and 4, to bring them into better harmony with current business practice, and to acknowledge recent technological developments.

Because a majority of the states have now adopted the 1990 revision to Article 3 and the related amendments, we use them as the basis for this edition of the textbook. The reader should ascertain whether the state in which she lives has adopted the revised article/amendments and also should keep in mind that instruments may be interpreted under the version of the Code that was in effect when the instruments were issued. Moreover, for the period between the first adoption of the revised article/amendments by a state (Arkansas) and the adoption by the last state or the District of Columbia, the "uniform law" concerning negotiable instruments will be anything but uniform.

For the student of negotiable instruments law, this is an interesting—but also a particularly difficult—time to study this area of the law. Revised Article 3 and the related amendments introduce new concepts, change definitions and the wording of key elements, and delete numerous provisions from the original version of Article 3. As a result, in drafting this chapter and the three chapters that follow, the authors have relied heavily on tracking the language of the revised article and on statements by the drafters as to their intent. Further complicating the picture is the fact that, in a number of respects, the revision is more complex than the original version. Moreover, while more than 30 years of case law had helped flesh out the meaning of the original Article 3, the revision has diminished much of the value of that case law. Virtually all of the cases to date arose under the original version of Article 3 and are of mixed—and sometimes very limited—value in trying to assess how courts will decide issues under the revision.

Just as these factors posed a challenge to the authors of this edition of the textbook, they will pose a challenge to you and your instructor as you work your way through the material on negotiable instruments. More questions are likely to be left up in the air than is true in other, more settled areas of the law. It will take a number of years, considerable experience, and new case law to flesh out the updated law of negotiable instruments.

Negotiable Instruments

The two basic types of negotiable instruments are *promises to pay money* and *orders to pay money*. Promissory notes and certificates of deposit issued by banks are promises to pay someone money. Checks and drafts are orders to another person to pay money to a third person. A check, which is a type of draft, is an order directed to a certain kind of person, namely a bank, to pay money from a person's account to a third person.

Negotiability

Negotiable instruments are a special kind of commercial paper that can pass readily through our financial system and is accepted in place of money. This gives negotiable instruments many advantages.

For example, Searle, the owner of a clothing store in New York, contracts with Amado, a swimsuit manufacturer in Los Angeles, for $10,000 worth of swimsuits. If negotiable instruments did not exist, Searle would have to send or carry $10,000 across the country, which would be both inconvenient and risky. If someone stole the money along the way, Searle would lose the $10,000 unless he could

FIGURE 1   Promissory Note

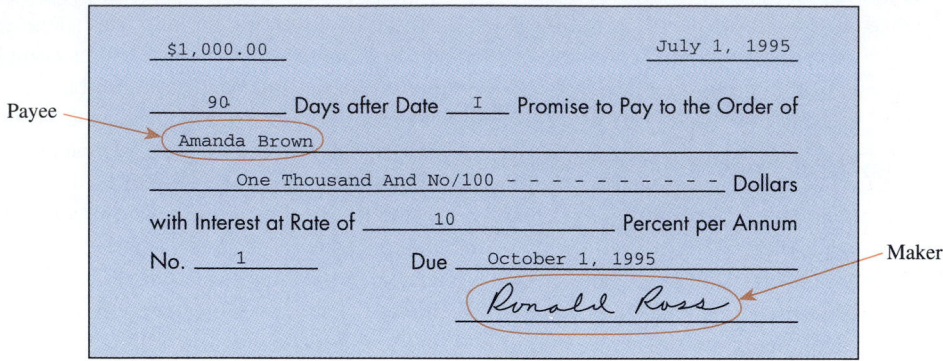

locate the thief. By using a check in which Searle orders his bank to pay $10,000 from his account to Amado, or to someone designated by Amado, Searle makes the payment in a far more convenient manner. He sends only a single piece of paper to Amado. If the check is properly prepared and sent, sending the check is less risky than sending money. Even if someone steals the check along the way, Searle's bank may not pay it to anyone but Amado or someone authorized by Amado. And, because the check gives Amado the right either to collect the $10,000 or to transfer the right to collect it to someone else, the check is a practical substitute for cash to Amado as well as Searle.

In this chapter and in the three following chapters, we discuss the requirements necessary for a contract for the payment of money to qualify as a negotiable instrument. We also explain the features that not only distinguish a negotiable instrument from a simple contract but also led to the widespread use of negotiable instruments as a substitute for money.

KINDS OF NEGOTIABLE INSTRUMENTS

Promissory Notes

The promissory note is the simplest form of commercial paper; it is simply a promise to pay money. A **promissory note** is a two-party instrument in which one person (known as the **maker**) makes an unconditional promise in writing to pay another person (the **payee**), a person specified by that person, or the bearer of the instrument, a fixed amount of money, with or without interest, either on demand or at a specified, future time [3–104].[1]

The promissory note, shown in Figures 1 and 2, is a credit instrument; it is used in a wide variety of transactions in which credit is extended. For example, if a person purchases an automobile using money borrowed from a bank, the bank has the person sign a promissory note for the unpaid balance of the purchase price. Similarly, if a person borrows money to purchase a house, the lender who makes the loan and takes a mortgage on the house has the person sign a promissory note for the amount due on the loan. The note probably states that it is secured by a mortgage. The terms of payment on the note should correspond with the terms of the sales contract for the purchase of the house.

Certificates of Deposit

The certificate of deposit given by a bank or a savings and loan association when a deposit of money is made is a type of note—namely, a note of a bank. A **certificate of deposit** is an instrument containing (1) an acknowledgment by a bank that it has received a deposit of money and (2) a promise by the bank to repay the sum of money

---

[1]The numbers in brackets refer to the sections of the 1990 Revised Article 3 (and the conforming amendments to Articles 1 and 4) of the Uniform Commercial Code.

FIGURE 2   Promissory Note (Consumer Loan Note)

The National
**BANK OF
WASHINGTON**
CONSUMER LOAN NOTE
Date _November 21,_ , 19 _95_

The words I and me mean all borrowers who signed this note. The word bank means The National Bank of Washington.

Promise to Pay
30___ months from today, I promise to pay to the order of The National Bank of Washington   ← **Payee**
Seventy-Eight Hundred Seventy Five and no/100 - - - - - - - - - - - dollars ($ 7,875.00).

Responsibility
Although this note may be signed below by more than one person, I understand that we are each as individuals responsible for paying back the full amount.

Breakdown of Loan
This is what I will pay:

Amount of loan	1.$	6,800.00
Credit Life Insurance (optional)	2.$	100.00
Other (describe) _____	3.$	-0-
Amount Financed (Add 1 and 2 and 3)	4.$	6,900
FINANCE CHARGE	5.$	975.00
Total of Payments (Add 4 and 5)	$	7,875.00
ANNUAL PERCENTAGE RATE		10.5 %

Repayment
This is how I will repay:
I will repay the amount of this note in ___30___ equal uninterrupted monthly installments of $ 262.50 each on the _1st_ day of each month starting on the _1st_ day of _December_ , 19 _95_ and ending on _May 1_ , _____ , 19 _98_ .

Prepayment
I have the right to prepay the whole outstanding amount of this note at any time. If I do, or if this loan is refinanced—that is, replaced by a new note—you will refund the unearned finance charge, figured by the rule of 78—a commonly used formula for figuring rebates on installment loans.

Late Charge
Any installment not paid within ten days of its due date shall be subject to a late charge of 5% of the payment, not to exceed $5.00 for any such late installment.

Security
To protect the National Bank of Washington, I give what is known as a security interest in my auto and/or other: (Describe) _Ford Thunderbird_
_____ # Serial #115117-12-
See the security agreement.

Credit Life Insurance
Credit life insurance is not required to obtain this loan. The bank need not provide it and I do not need to buy it unless I sign immediately below. The cost of credit life insurance is $ 100.00 for the term of the loan.

Signed: _A. J. Smith_
Date: _November 21, 1995_

Default
If for any reason I fail to make any payment on time, I shall be in default. The bank can then demand immediate payment of the entire remaining unpaid balance of this loan, without giving anyone further notice. If I have not paid the full amount of the loan when the final payment is due, the bank will charge me interest on the unpaid balance at six percent (6%) per year.

Right of Offset
If this loan becomes past due, the bank will have the right to pay this loan from any deposit or security I have at this bank without telling me ahead of time. Even if the bank gives me an extension of time to pay this loan, I still must repay the entire loan.

Collection Fees
If this note is placed with an attorney for collection, then I agree to pay an attorney's fee of fifteen percent (15%) of the unpaid balance. This fee will be added to the unpaid balance of the loan.

Co-borrowers
If I am signing this note as a co-borrower, I agree to be equally responsible with the borrower for this loan. The bank does not have to notify me that this note has not been paid. The bank can change the terms of payment and release any security without notifying or releasing me from responsibility for this loan.

Copy Received
I received a completely filled in copy of this note. If I have signed for Credit Life Insurance, I received a copy of the Credit Life Insurance certificate.

Borrower: _A. J. Smith_   ← **Maker**
A. J. Smith
3412 Brookdale, S. W. Washington D.C.
Address
Co-borrower: _Andrea H Smith_   ← **Comaker**
Andrea H. Smith
3412 Brookdale, S. W. Washington D.C.
Address
Co-borrower: _____
Address

CONSUMER CREDIT HOTLINE: If you have any questions, please call us immediately at (202) 624-3450.
NBW 437 (Rev. 11-78)   1-Bank's copy 2-File copy 3-Customer's copy

[3–104(j)]. Figure 3 is an example of a certificate of deposit.

Many banks no longer issue certificates of deposit (CD) in paper form. Rather, the bank maintains an electronic deposit and provides the customer with a statement indicating the amount of principal held on a CD basis and the terms of the CD, such as the maturity and interest rate. In these instances, the certificate of deposit is not in negotiable instrument form.

FIGURE 3   Certificate of Deposit

Maker —→

Payee —→

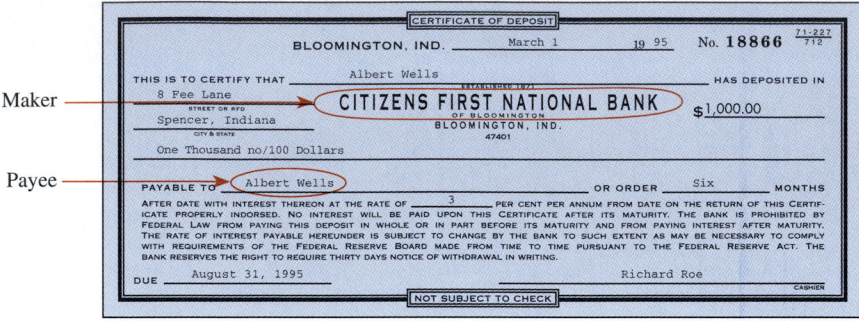

Drafts

A **draft** is a form of commercial paper that involves an *order* to pay money rather than a promise to pay money [3–104(e)]. The most common example of a draft is a check. A draft has three parties to it: one person (known as the **drawer**) orders a second person (the **drawee**) to pay a certain sum of money to a third person (the **payee**), to a person specified by that person, or to bearer.

Drafts other than checks are used in a variety of commercial transactions. If Brown owes Ames money, Ames may draw a draft for the amount of the debt, naming Brown as drawee and herself or her bank as payee, and send the draft to Brown's bank for payment. Alternatively, Ames might send a draft providing for payment on a certain day in the future to Brown for "acceptance." Brown could "accept" the draft by signing his name to it, thereby obligating himself to pay the amount specified in the draft on that day in the future to Ames or to someone specified by Ames.

In freight shipments in which the terms are "cash on delivery," the seller commonly ships the goods to the buyer on an "order bill of lading" consigned to himself at the place of delivery. The seller then indorses the bill of lading and attaches a draft naming the buyer as drawee. He then sends the bill of lading and the draft through banking channels to the buyer's bank. A bank in the buyer's locale presents the draft to the buyer's bank for payment, and when the former bank receives payment, delivers the bill of lading to the buyer. Through this commercial transaction, the buyer gets the goods and the seller gets his money.

When credit is extended, the same procedure is followed, but the seller uses a time draft—a draft payable at some future time. See Figure 4. In such a transaction, the buyer "accepts" the draft (instead of paying it) and obligates herself to pay the amount of the draft when due. In these cases, the *drawee* (now called the **acceptor**) should date her signature so that the date at which payment is due is clear to all [3–409(c)].

Checks

A **check** is a *draft payable on demand* and drawn on a bank (i.e., a bank is the drawee or person to whom the order to pay is addressed). Checks are the most widely used form of commercial paper. The issuer of a check orders the bank at which she maintains an account to pay a specified person, or someone designated by that person, a fixed amount of money from the account. For example, Elizabeth Brown has a checking account at the National Bank of Washington. She goes to Sears Roebuck & Co. and agrees to buy a washing machine priced at $459.95. If she writes a check to pay for it, she is the drawer of the check, the National Bank of Washington is the drawee, and Sears is the payee. By writing the check, Elizabeth is ordering her bank to pay $459.95 from her account to Sears or to Sears's order—that is, to whomever Sears asks the bank to pay the money. See Figure 5.

An instrument may qualify as a "check" and be governed by Article 3 even though it is described on its face by another term such as "money order." The Code definition of a "check" includes a "cashier's check" and a "teller's check." A **cashier's check** is a draft on which the drawer and drawee are the same

FIGURE 4   **Draft**

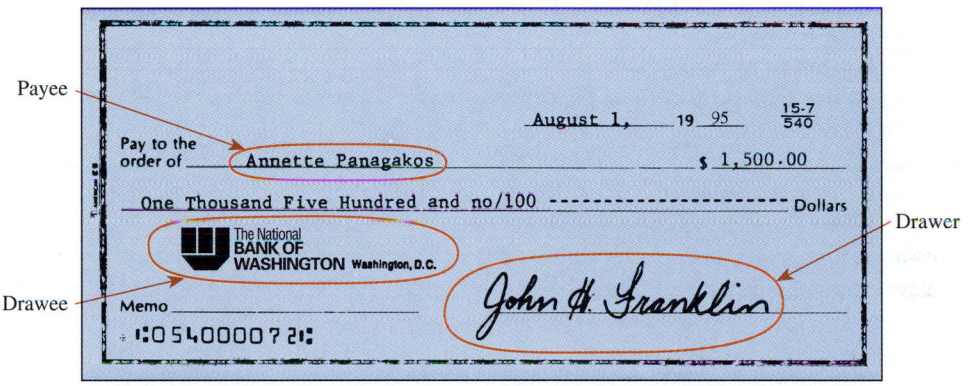

FIGURE 5   **Check**

bank (or branches of the same bank); a **teller's check** is a draft drawn by a bank (as drawer) on another bank or payable at or through a bank [3–104(g) and (h)]. For example, a check drawn by a credit union on its account at a federally insured bank would be a teller's check.

BENEFITS OF NEGOTIABLE INSTRUMENTS

Rights of an Assignee of a Contract

As we noted in Chapter 17, Rights of Third Parties, the assignee of a contract can obtain no greater rights than the assignor had at the time of the assignment. For example, Frank Farmer and Neam's Market enter into a contract providing that Farmer will sell Neam's a dozen crates of fresh eggs a week for a year and that Neam's will pay Farmer $4,000 at the end of the year. If at the end of the year Farmer assigns to Bill Sanders his rights under the contract—including the right to collect the money from Neam's—then Sanders has whatever rights Farmer had at that time. If Farmer has delivered all the eggs to Neam's as he promised, then Farmer would be entitled to $4,000 and Sanders would obtain that right from him. However, if Farmer has not delivered all the eggs that he had promised to deliver, or if the eggs he delivered were not fresh, then Neam's might have a valid defense or reason to refuse to pay the full $4,000. In that case, Sanders would have only what rights Farmer had and also would be subject to the defense Neam's has against full payment.

Taking an assignment of a contract involves assuming certain risks. The assignee (Sanders) may not be aware of the nature and extent of any defenses that the party liable on the contract (Neam's) might have against the assignor (Farmer). An assignee who does not know what rights he is getting, or which risks he is assuming, may be reluctant to take an assignment of the contract.

Rights of a Holder of a Negotiable Instrument

The object of a negotiable instrument is to have it accepted readily as a substitute for money. In order to accept it readily, a person must be able to take it free of many of the risks assumed by the assignee of a regular contract. Under the law of negotiable instruments, this is possible if two conditions are met: (1) the contract for the payment of money must meet the formal requirements to qualify as a negotiable instrument; and (2) the person who acquires the instrument must qualify as a holder in due course. Basically, a *holder in due course* is a person who has good title to the instrument, paid value for it, acquired it in good faith, and had no notice of certain claims or defenses against payment. In addition, the instrument cannot bear facial irregularities (evidence of forgery or alteration or questions concerning its authenticity).

The next section of this chapter discusses the formal requirements for a negotiable instrument. Chapter 31, Negotiation and Holder in Due Course, outlines the requirements that a person must meet to qualify as a holder in due course.

A holder in due course of a negotiable instrument takes the instrument free of all defenses and claims to the instrument except those that concern its validity. For example, a holder in due course of a note given in payment for goods may enforce the obligation in spite of the buyer's claim that the seller breached a warranty. However, if the maker of a note wrote it under duress, such as a threat of force, or was a minor, then even a holder in due course is subject to the defenses of duress or infancy to the extent other law (1) would nullify the obliga-

tion for duress or (2) would permit infancy as a defense to a simple contract. In those instances, the person who holds the note could not obtain the payment from the maker but would have to recover from the person from whom he got the note.

The Federal Trade Commission (FTC) has adopted a regulation that alters the rights of a holder in due course in consumer purchase transactions. This regulation allows a consumer who gives a negotiable instrument to use additional defenses (such as breach of warranty or fraudulent inducement) against payment of the instrument against even a holder in due course. Similarly, some states have enacted the Uniform Consumer Credit Code (UCCC), which produces a similar result. Chapter 31 discusses the rights of a holder in due course, as well as the FTC rule.

FORMAL REQUIREMENTS FOR NEGOTIABILITY

Basic Requirements

An instrument such as a check or a note must meet certain formal requirements to be a negotiable instrument. If the instrument does not meet these requirements, it is non-negotiable; that is, it is treated as a simple contract and not as a negotiable instrument. A primary purpose for these formal requirements is to ensure the willingness of prospective purchasers of the instrument, particularly financial institutions such as banks, to accept it as a substitute for money.

For an instrument to be negotiable, it must:

1. Be in writing.
2. Be signed by the issuer (the *maker* in the case of a person undertaking to pay or the *drawer* in the case of a person giving an order or instruction to pay).
3. Contain an unconditional promise or order to pay a fixed amount of money, with or without interest or other charges described in the promise or order.
4. Be payable to order or to bearer at the time it is issued or first comes into possession of a holder.
5. Be payable on demand or at a definite time.
6. Not state any other undertaking or instruction by the person promising or ordering to do any

act in addition to the payment of money (but it may contain (*a*) an undertaking or promise relative to collateral to secure payment, (*b*) an authorization for confession of judgment, or (*c*) a waiver of benefit of any law intended for the advantage or protection of an obligor). [3–103; 3–104].

In addition, an instrument that otherwise qualifies as a check can be a negotiable even if it is not explicitly payable to order or to bearer [3–104(c)]. As explained later, this means that a check reading "pay John Doe" could be negotiable even though the normal form for a check is "pay to the order of _____ ."

A promise or order other than a check is not a negotiable instrument if at the time it is issued or first comes into the possession of a holder it contains a conspicious statement that the promise or order is not negotiable or is not an instrument governed by Article 3 [3–104(d)]. For example, if a promissory note contained the legend "NON–NEGOTIABLE," it would not qualify as a negotiable instrument even if it otherwise met the formal requirements for one.

Importance of Form

Whether or not an instrument satisfies these formal requirements is important only for the purpose of determining whether an instrument is negotiable or nonnegotiable. Negotiability should not be confused with validity or collectibility. If an instrument is negotiable, the law of negotiable instruments in the Code controls in determining the rights and liabilities of the parties to the instrument. If an instrument is non-negotiable, the general rules of contract law control. The purpose of determining negotiability is to ascertain whether a possessor of the instrument can become a holder in due course.

An instrument that meets all of the formal requirements is a negotiable instrument even though it is void, voidable, unenforceable, or uncollectible for other reasons. Negotiability is a matter of form and nothing else. Suppose a person gives an instrument in payment of a gambling debt in a state that has a statute declaring that any instrument or promise given in payment of a gambling debt is void. The instrument is a negotiable instrument if it is negotiable in form even though it is absolutely void. Also, an instrument that is negotiable in form is a

negotiable instrument even though it is issued by a minor. The instrument is voidable at the option of the minor if state law makes infancy a defense to a simple contract, but it is negotiable.

In Writing

To be negotiable, an instrument must be in writing. An instrument that is handwritten, typed, or printed is considered to be in writing [1–201(46)]. The writing does not have to be on any particular material; all that is required is that the instrument be in writing. A person could create a negotiable instrument in pencil on a piece of wrapping paper. It would be poor business practice to do so, but the instrument would meet the statutory requirement that it be in writing.

Signed

To qualify as a negotiable instrument, an instrument in the form of a note must be signed by the person undertaking to pay (the maker) and an instrument in the form of a draft must be signed by the person giving the instruction to pay (the drawer) [3–103]. An instrument has been signed if the maker or drawer has put a name or other symbol on it with the intention of validating it [3–401(b)]. Normally, the maker or drawer signs an instrument by writing his name on it; however, this is not required. A person or company may authorize an agent to sign instruments for it. A typed or rubber-stamped signature is sufficient if it was put on the instrument to validate it. A person who cannot write her name might make an X and have it witnessed by someone else.

Unconditional Promise or Order

Requirement of a Promise or Order

If an instrument is promissory in nature, such as a note or a certificate of deposit, it must contain an unconditional promise to pay or it cannot be negotiable. Merely acknowledging a debt is not sufficient [3–103(9)]. For example, the statement "I owe you $100," does not constitute a promise to pay. An IOU in this form is not a negotiable instrument.

If an instrument is an order to pay, such as a check or a draft, it must contain an unconditional order. A simple request to pay as a favor is not sufficient; however, a politely phrased demand, such as "please pay," can meet the requirement. Checks commonly use the language "Pay to the order of." This satisfies the requirement that the check contain an order to pay. The order is the word "pay," not the word "order." The word "order" has another function—that of making the instrument payable "to order or to bearer."

Promise or Order Must Be Unconditional

An instrument is not negotiable unless the promise or order is unconditional. For example, a note that provides, "I promise to pay to the order of Karl Adams $1,000 if he replaces the roof on my garage," is not negotiable because it is payable on a condition.

To be negotiable, an instrument must be written so that a person can tell from reading the instrument alone what the obligations of the parties are. If a note contains the statement, "Payment is subject to the terms of a mortgage dated November 20, 1995," it is not negotiable. To determine the rights of the parties on the note, one would have to examine another document—the mortgage.

However, a reference to another document for a statement of rights with respect to collateral, prepayment, or acceleration does not destroy the negotiability of a note [3–106(b)]. For example, a note could contain this statement: "This note is secured by a mortgage dated August 30, 1995" without affecting its negotiability. In this case, the mortgage does not affect rights and duties of the parties to the note. It would not be necessary to examine the mortgage document to determine the rights of the parties to the note; the parties only need examine the note.

The negotiability of an instrument is not affected by a statement of the consideration for which the instrument was given or by a statement of the transaction that gave rise to the instrument. For example, a negotiable instrument may state that it was given in payment of last month's rent or that it was given in payment of the purchase price of goods. The statement does not affect the negotiability of the instrument. The effect of a notation in the lower left corner of a check following the printed word *memo* is discussed in the *Western Bank v. RaDEC Construction Co., Inc.* case, which follows.

WESTERN BANK v. RaDEC CONSTRUCTION CO., INC.
42 UCC Rep. 1340 (S.D. Sup. Ct. 1986)

RaDEC Construction Company was the general contractor in the construction of a medical center in Huron, South Dakota. One of RaDEC's subcontractors on this job was Carpet Center. RaDEC became aware that Carpet Center's financial problems were making it difficult for Carpet Center to furnish the necessary materials and labor for the medical center job. RaDEC's president, Clarence Hoesing, had a conversation with Carpet Center on December 13, 1982, in which he agreed to send a check for $8,743.52 to Carpet Center, provided that Carpet Center (1) furnish certain paid invoices for material delivered, (2) provide certain additional material, and (3) ensure the installation of the material on December 14. Hoesing then made out a handwritten check to Carpet Center. In the lower left corner of the check following the printed word *memo* Hoesing typed the phrase, "Payee must prove clear title to material." Hoesing considered the check to be conditioned on Carpet Center's performance of the three conditions. After the check was delivered on December 14, Carpet Center deposited the check in the Western Bank, which allowed it to make an immediate withdrawal of the money. Later that day, RaDEC learned that Carpet Center had not performed the three requirements and filed a stop payment order on the check.

Unable to recover the money from Carpet Center, which was insolvent, the bank brought suit against RaDEC, claiming to be a holder in due course of the check. The trial court held in favor of the bank and RaDEC appealed.

Hertzel, Justice   The trial court held as a matter of law that the phrase typed in at the lower left hand corner of the check, "Payee must prove clear title to material," did not have the effect of making the check conditional and that the bank was a bona fide holder in due course.

Section 3–104(1) sets forth four elements necessary to constitute a negotiable instrument: (a) It must be signed by the maker; (b) contain an unconditional promise or order to pay a sum certain in money and no other promise, order, obligation or power given by the maker or drawer except as authorized by this chapter; (c) be payable on demand or at a definite time; and (d) be payable to order or to bearer.

In this case there is no dispute that elements (a), (c) and (d) have been fulfilled. RaDEC claims, however, that element (b) has not been met because the check was a "conditional instrument" and therefore subject to its defenses.

RaDEC relies heavily on our decision in *Bank of America v. Butterfield*. In that case, the draft in question stated: "Subject to approval of title, pay to the order of Vernon H. Butterfield and Laura E. Butterfield." It is important to note that the phrase "subject to approval of title," immediately precedes the standard phrase, "Pay to the order of." In affirming the trial court we said: "The promise to pay money contained in the draft in question is clearly not unconditional. The payment ordered is subject to approval of title. Consequently, it is not a negotiable instrument."

Negotiability is determined from the face of the instrument without reference to extrinsic facts. The conditional or unconditional character is to be determined by what is expressed in the instrument itself.

RaDEC claims that the check was not a negotiable instrument because of the condition written on its face. Moreover, RaDEC argues that the location of the conditional language in the place usually reserved for "memo" is of little consequence, since the language itself was sufficient to give the bank notice that RaDEC's obligation to pay was conditioned upon Carpet Center's having proved clear title to the material. The bank, on the other hand, argues that the instant factual situation can be distinguished from that of *Bank of America* because in that case the conditional language, i.e., "subject to approval of title," preceded the words "Pay to the order of."

We conclude that the phrase "payee must prove clear title to material" written where it was, did not make the check conditional thereby depriving the bank of its status as a holder in due course. It appears that the notation in the "memo" area of the check is nothing more than a self-serving declaration by RaDEC for its own benefit and recordkeeping and for informational purposes only. An otherwise unconditional instrument cannot be rendered conditional by such a device.

Judgment for Western Bank affirmed.

Note: Although this decision predates Revised Article 3, which modified the requirements for a negotiable instrument set out in original § 3–104, the result in this case would be the same under Revised Article 3.

A check may reference the account to be debited without making the check non-negotiable. For example, a check could contain the notation, "payroll account" or "petty cash." Similarly, the account number that appears on personal checks does not make the instrument payable only out of a specific fund. Under original Article 3, a check (other than a governmental check) that stated that it was payable only out of a specific fund or account was treated as a conditional order and thus was not negotiable. Revised Article 3 changed this rule so that limiting payment to a particular fund or source does not make the promise or order conditional [3–106(b)].

Revised Article 3 also addresses the negotiability of traveler's checks that commonly require, as a condition to payment, a countersignature of a person whose specimen signature appears on the draft. Under the revision, the condition does not prevent the instrument from meeting the "unconditional promise or order" requirement [3–106(c)]. However, if the person whose specimen signature appears on the instrument fails to countersign it, the failure to sign becomes a defense to the obligation of the issuer to pay. This concept will be discussed in the following chapter.

A conditional indorsement does not destroy the negotiability of an otherwise negotiable instrument and it is not affected by subsequent indorsement.

The Code determines negotiability at issuance, so that later indorsements do not affect the underlying negotiability of the instrument. We discuss conditional indorsements in Chapter 31, Negotiation and Holder in Due Course.

FIXED AMOUNT OF MONEY

Fixed Amount

The promise or order in an instrument must be to pay a fixed amount of money, with or without interest or other charges described in the promise or order. The requirement of a "fixed amount" applies only to principal, and the amount of any interest payable is that described in the instrument. If a variable rate of interest is prescribed, the amount of interest is calculated by reference to the formula or index referenced in the instrument. If the description of interest in the instrument does not allow the amount of interest to be ascertained, then interest is payable at the judgment rate in effect at the place of payment at the time interest first accrues [3–112].

The judgment rate is the rate of interest courts impose on losing parties until they pay the winning parties.

Under the original version of Article 3, a promise or order had to be to pay a "sum certain." Generally, to meet this requirement, a person had to be able to compute from the information in the instrument the amount required to discharge—or pay off—the instrument at any given time. Among other things, this caused problems when applied to variable rate instruments that came into common commercial usage in the United States after the original Article 3 was drafted. Some state courts held that instruments providing for variable interest rates ascertainable through reference to indexes outside the instrument were not negotiable; other courts sought to interpret the Code to accommodate this new commercial practice.

The case that follows, *Carnegie Bank v. Shalleck*, illustrates the challenge faced by a court presented with a variable rate note—drafted when the original Article 3 requirement for a sum certain was in effect—in a state that has now adopted Revised Article 3.

CARNEGIE BANK V. SHALLECK
17 UCC Rep.2d 799 (Sup. Ct. N.J. 1992)

On July 11, 1988, Ann Anderson borrowed $150,000 from the Carnegie Bank and executed a note payable to the order of "Carnegie Bank." Her loan was secured by a mortgage and note also dated July 11, 1988 in favor of Anderson and signed by Alan B. Shalleck in his individual capacity and as president of two corporations. The note provided for interest at "two (2%) percent in excess of the Floating Base Rate at Carnegie Bank, as adjusted from time to time, provided, however, that at no time shall the rate be less than fifteen (15%) per annum." Anderson assigned the Shalleck mortgage and note to Carnegie Bank as security for her loan.

Shalleck defaulted on his note to Anderson and she, in turn, defaulted on her loan to Carnegie Bank. The Bank sued Shalleck to recover on the note that Anderson had assigned to it. One of the questions in the litigation was whether the note was a negotiable instrument. The trial court held that it was not negotiable.

Coleman, Presiding Judge We consider whether the Shalleck note was rendered non-negotiable because it provided for repayment at a variable interest rate rather than a rate fixed by the four corners of the note. If the note was not negotiable, Carnegie Bank could not become a holder in due course. The trial court found that the

"sum certain" requirement of section 104(1)(b) was not satisfied by the note.

The Code does not define "sum certain"; it only enumerates factors which do not destroy the "sum certain" requirement for negotiability. Sec. 106 (1). Official Comment 1 to sec. 3–106 of the Code states that the interest computation must be one which can be made from the instrument itself without reference to any outside source, and this section does not make negotiable a note payable with interest "at the current rate." The comment does not, however, cover a situation where the rate can be determined by reference to a generally accepted published index.

Whether a variable interest rate renders the instrument non-negotiable raises a question of first impression in this state. Some states have held generally that variable rate notes are not negotiable. Yet, some courts have held that certain variable rate provisions in notes do not affect negotiability.

Prior to the trial in this case, the National Conference of Commissioners on Uniform State Laws proposed an amendment to section 3–112 of the Uniform Commercial Code to permit the use of variable interest rates without affecting negotiability. The proposal was approved by the American Law Institute in 1990. The new revision with Comment is [in pertinent part] as follows:

Sec. 3–112. Interest

  (a)   *   *   *   *

(b) Interest may be stated in an instrument as a fixed or variable amount of money or it may be expressed as a fixed or variable rate or rates. The amount of interest may be stated or described in the instrument in any manner and may require reference to information not contained in the instrument. If an instrument provides for interest, but the amount of interest payable cannot be ascertained from the description, interest is payable at the judgment rate in effect at the place of payment of the instrument and at the time interest first accrues.

OFFICIAL COMMENT

1. Under Section 3–104(a) the requirement of a "fixed amount" applies only to principal. The amount of interest payable is that described in the instrument. If the description of interest in the instrument does not allow for the amount of interest to be ascertained, interest is payable at the judgment rate. Hence, if an instrument calls for interest, the amount of interest will always be determinable. If a variable rate of interest is prescribed, the amount of interest is ascertainable by reference to the formula or index described or referred to in the instrument.

Two months before The American Law Institute was scheduled to discuss the proposed amendment in May 1990 and before the trial in this case, Senate

Bill No. 2431 was introduced in the New Jersey Senate essentially to adopt the proposal submitted to The American Law Institute. Senate Bill 2431 was enacted into law on January 9, 1992, effective immediately, and [among other things] adds Section 3–106(3) which reads:

A rate of interest that cannot be calculated by looking only to the instrument is a "stated rate of interest" in subsection (1) of this section if the rate is readily ascertainable by reference in the instrument to a published statute, regulation, rule of court, generally accepted commercial or financial index, compendium of interest rates, or announced or established rate of a named financial institution.

We recognize that as a general rule, New Jersey courts favor prospective application of new statutory amendments. The reason for this general rule is that retroactive application of new statutes carries a high risk of unfairness. However, there are three recognized exceptions to the general rule: (1) where the Legislature expressly or impliedly intends retroactive application; (2) where a statute is ameliorative or curative, and (3) where the expectations of the parties will be enhanced.

A statement attached to the legislation is a useful aid in ascertaining legislative intent. The sponsor's statement as well as the Senate Committee's statement to the legislation provide that:

This bill amends one of the provisions in the Uniform Commerical Code which establish the criteria for a negotiable instrument by providing that a variable rate of interest which requires reference to a source outside the instrument in order to ascertain the amount due would not make the instrument non-negotiable. Some courts in other states have ruled that instruments with variable insterest rates tied to a market or other index are non-negotiable.

The clear implication is that, while no New Jersey decision has found that Section 106 rendered instruments with variable interest rates non-negotiable, other courts have and the Legislature wanted to clarify New Jersey's position on the issue before any decisions were rendered.

We believe the 1992 amendment is curative and it also enhances the expectations of the parties.

Held that the sum certain requirement was satisfied by the variable rate note.

Payable in Money

The amount specified in the instrument must be payable in money, which is a medium of exchange authorized or adopted by a domestic or foreign government and includes a monetary unit of account established by an intergovernmental organization or by agreement between two or more nations [1–201(24)]. Unless the instrument otherwise provides, an instrument that states the amount payable in foreign money may be paid in the foreign money or in an equivalent dollar amount [3–107]. If the person obligated to pay off an instrument can do something other than pay money, the instrument is not negotiable. For example, if a note reads, "I promise to pay to the order of Sarah Smith, at my option, $40 or five bushels of apples, John Jones," the note is not negotiable.

PAYABLE ON DEMAND OR AT A DEFINITE TIME

To be negotiable, the promise or order must be payable either on demand or at a specified time in the future. This is so that the time when the instrument is payable can be determined with some certainty. An instrument that is payable on the happening of some uncertain event is not negotiable. Thus, a note payable "when my son graduates from college" is not negotiable, even though the son does graduate subsequently.

Payable on Demand

A promise or order is "payable on demand" if (1) it states that it is payable on "demand" or "sight" (or otherwise at the will of the holder of the instrument) or (2) does not state any time for payment [3–108(a)]. For example, if the maker forgets to state when a note is payable, it is payable immediately at the request of the holder of the note.

An instrument may be antedated or postdated, and normally an instrument payable on demand is not payable before the date of the instrument. [3–113(a)] Revised Article 3 makes an important exception for checks; a payor bank (a bank that is the drawee of a draft) may pay a postdated check before the stated date *unless* the drawer has notified the bank of postdating pursuant to a procedure set out in the Code [3–113(a); 4–401(c)].

Payable at a Definite Time

A promise or order is "payable at a definite time" if it is payable at a fixed date or dates or at a time or times readily ascertainable at the time the promise or order is issued [3–108(b)]. Thus, a note dated March 25, 1995, might be made payable at a fixed time after a stated date, such as "30 days after date."

Under the Code, an instrument that names a fixed date or time for payment—without losing its negotiable character—may also contain a clause permitting the time for payment to be accelerated at the option of the maker. Similarly, an instrument may allow an extension of time at the option of the holder or allow a maker or acceptor to extend payment to a further definite time. Or, the due date of a note might be triggered by the happening of an event, such as the filing of a petition in bankruptcy against the maker. The Code permits these clauses so long as one can determine the time for payment with certainty [3–108].

A promise or order is also "payable at a definite time" if it is payable on elapse of a definite period of time after "sight" or "acceptance." A draft payable at a specified time—such as "15 days after sight"—is, in effect, payable at a fixed time after the draft is presented to the drawee for acceptance.

If an instrument is undated, its "date" is the date it is issued by the maker or drawer [3–113(b)].

PAYABLE TO ORDER OR BEARER

Except for checks, to be negotiable an instrument must be "payable to order or to bearer." A note that provides, "I promise to pay to the order of Sarah Smith" or "I promise to pay to Sarah Smith or bearer" is negotiable. However, one that provides "I promise to pay to Sarah Smith" is not. The words "to the order of" or "to bearer" show that the drawer of a draft, or the maker of a note, intends to issue a negotiable instrument. The drawer or maker is not restricting payment of the instrument to just Sarah Smith but is willing to pay someone else designated by Sarah Smith. This is the essence of negotiability.

In the original version of Article 3, an order in the form of a check also had to be "payable to order or bearer" to qualify as a negotiable instrument. However, the drafters of Revised Article 3 created an exception for instruments that otherwise meet the requirements for a negotiable instrument as well as the definition of a check [3–104(c)]. Under the revised article, a check that reads "Pay John Doe" could qualify as a negotiable instrument. As a result, the Code treats checks, which are payment instruments, as negotiable instruments whether or not they contain the words "to the order of." The drafters explained that most checks are preprinted with these words but that occasionally the drawer may strike out the words before issuing the check and that a few check forms have been in use that do not contain these words. In these instances, the drafters preferred not to limit the rights of holders of such checks who may pay money or give credit for a check without being aware that it is not in the conventional form for a negotiable instrument.

The most common forms of a promise or order being payable to bearer use the words "payable to bearer," "payable to the order of bearer," "payable to cash," or "payable to the order of cash" [3–109(a)]. A promise or order is considered to be payable "to order" if it is payable (1) to the order of an identified person or (2) to an identified person or that person's order [3–109(b)]. Examples would include: "Pay to the order of Sandy Smith" and "Pay to Sandy Smith or order." A check sent with the payee line blank is payable to bearer. However, it is also considered an incomplete instrument, the rules concerning which will be discussed in the following two chapters.

The original payee of a check or a note can transfer the right to receive payment to someone else. By making the instrument payable "to the order of" or "to bearer," the drawer or maker is giving the payee the chance to negotiate the instrument to another person and to cut off certain defenses that the drawer or maker may have against payment of the instrument.

A check that is payable to the order of a specific person is known as "order paper." Order paper can be negotiated or transferred only by indorsement. A check payable "to bearer" or "to cash" is known as "bearer paper"; it can be negotiated or transferred without indorsement [3–201(b)]. The rules governing negotiation of instruments will be detailed in the next chapter.

An instrument can be made payable to two or more payees. For example, a check could be drawn payable "to the order of John Jones and Henry Smith." Then, both Jones and Smith have to be involved in negotiating it or enforcing its payment. An instrument also can be made payable to alternative persons—for example, "to the order of Susan Clark or Betsy Brown." In this case, either Clark or Brown could negotiate it or enforce its payment [3–110(d)].

SPECIAL TERMS

Additional Terms

Generally, if an instrument is to qualify as a negotiable instrument, the person promising or ordering payment may not state undertakings or instructions in additon to the payment of money [3–104(a)(3). However, the instrument may include clauses concerning (1) giving, maintaining, or protecting collateral to secure payment, (2) an authorization to confess judgment or to realize on or dispose of collateral, and (3) waiving the benefit of any law intended for the protection or benefit of any person obligated on the instrument.

Thus, a term authorizing the confession of judgment on an instrument when it is due does not affect the negotiability of the instrument. A confession of judgment clause authorizes the creditor to go into court if the debtor defaults and, with the debtor's acquiescence, to have a judgment entered against the debtor. However, some states prohibit confessions of judgment.

Banks and other businesses often use forms of commercial paper that meet their particular needs. These forms may include certain other terms that do not affect the negotiability of an instrument. For example, a note may designate a place of payment without affecting the instrument's negotiability. Where the instrument does not specify a place of payment, the Code sets out rules for ascertaining where payment is to be made [3–111].

CONCEPT REVIEW

REQUIREMENTS FOR NEGOTIABILITY

Requirement	Basic Rules
Must Be in Writing	1. The instrument may be handwritten, typed, or printed.
Must Be Signed by the Maker or Drawer	1. Person issuing the instrument must sign with intent of validating his or her obligation. 2. Person issuing may affix the signature in a variety of ways—for example, by word, mark, or rubber stamp. 3. Agent or authorized representative may supply the "signature."
Must Contain a Promise or Order to Pay	1. Promise must be more than acknowledgment of a debt. 2. Order requirement is met if the drawer issues an instruction to "pay".
Promise or Order Must Be Unconditional	1. Entire obligation must be found in the instrument itself and not in another document or documents. 2. Payment cannot be conditioned on the occurrence of an event.
Must Call for Payment of a Fixed Amount of Money	1. Must be able to ascertain the principal from the face of the instrument. 2. May contain a clause providing for payment of interest or other charges such as collection or attorney's fees.
Must Be Payable in Money	1. Obligation must be payable in a medium of exchange authorized or adopted by a government or by an international organization or agreement between two or more nations. 2. Maker or drawer cannot have the option to pay in something other than money.
Must Be Payable on Demand or at a Definite Time	1. Requirement is met if instrument says it is payable on demand or if no time for payment is stated (then it is payable on demand). 2. Requirement is met if it is payable on a stated date, at a fixed time after a stated date, or a fixed time "after sight." 3. Instrument may contain an acceleration clause or a clause allowing maker or holder to extend the payment date.
Generally Must Be Payable to Bearer or to Order	1. Bearer requirement is met if instrument is payable "to bearer" or "to cash." 2. Order requirement is met if instrument is payable "to the order of" a specified person or persons. 3. Exception from requirement is made for instruments meeting both the definition of a check and all the other requirements for a negotiable instrument.
May Not State Any Other Undertaking or Instruction by the Person Promising or Ordering Payment to Do Any Act in Addition to the Payment of Money	1. However, it may contain (*a*) an undertaking or power to give, maintain, or protect collateral to secure payment, (*b*) an authorization or power to the holder to confess judgment or realize on or dispose of collateral, or (*c*) a waiver of the benefit of any law intended for the advantage or protection of an obligor on the instrument.

Ambiguous Terms

Occasionally, a person may write or receive a check on which the amount written in figures differs from the amount written in words. Or a note may have conflicting terms or an ambiguous term. Where a conflict or an ambiguous term exists, there are general rules of interpretation that are applied to resolve the conflict or ambiguity: Typewritten terms prevail over printed terms, handwritten terms prevail over printed and typewritten terms, and where words and numbers conflict, the words control the numbers [3–114].

The following *Galatia Community State Bank v. Kindy* case involves a check on which there was a difference between the numbers on a check placed there by a check-writing machine and those written by hand.

GALATIA COMMUNITY STATE BANK V. KINDY
307 Ark. 467 (Ark. Sup. Ct. 1991)

Galatia Community State Bank honored a check it took for collection for $5,500, which was the amount imprinted by a check-writing machine in the center underline section of the check commonly used for stating the amount in words. The imprint looked like this:

RegistereD
No. 497345   **5550 DOL'S 00 CTS

The impression made by the check-writing machine could be felt on the front and back of the check, and "**5550 DOL'S 00 CTS" was imprinted in red ink. In the box on the right-hand side of the check commonly used for numbers, "6,550.00" appeared in handwriting. The check was in partial payment of the purchase price of two engines that Eugene Kindy was buying from the payee on the check, Tony Hicks. Kindy postdated the check by a month and deliberately placed two different amounts on the check because he thought the bank would check with him before paying it. Kindy wanted to be sure that the engines had been delivered to Canada before he paid the $6,550 balance of the purchase price.

After the check was deposited in the Galacia Bank and Hicks was given $5,550, an employee of the bank altered the "6" by hand to read "5." Because Kindy had stopped payment on the check, the drawee bank refused to pay it to Galatia Bank. Galatia Bank then brought suit against Kindy as the drawer of the check. One of the issues in the lawsuit was how the check should be constructed. The trial court found that the rules on construction provided in the Code were not helpful because they were contradictory.

Newbern, Justice   The trial court reviewed Code section 3–118(b) and (c) (1987) which has since been superceded by section 3–114 (1991) but which was in effect at the time in question in this case. The statute provided in relevant part:

3–118. Ambiguous terms and rules of construction.
The following rules apply to every instrument:

* * * *

(b) Handwritten terms control typewritten and printed terms, and typewritten control printed.
(c) Words control figures except that if the words are ambiguous figures control.

The frustration expressed by the trial court with respect to section 3–118 which stated the applicable rules of construction for negotiable instruments is understandable.

The 5550.00 amount imprinted by the checkwriting machine upon the line customarily used for words is expressed in figures and not in words. One question is whether imprinted numbers located where words are customarily placed on a check control figures placed where figures are customarily placed. Another question is whether handwritten figures control printing.

We find both questions satisfactorily answered in *St. Paul Fire & Marine Ins. Co. v. Bank of Salem*

[Ind. App. 1980]. In that case, there was a conflict between an amount imprinted by a check imprinting machine and numbers expressed in typewritten figures. The court recognized the imprinted amount was not expressed in words but held "the purposes of the UCC are best served by considering an amount imprinted by a checkwriting machine as 'words' for the purpose of resolving an ambiguity between an amount and an amount entered upon the line usually used to express the amount in figures." The court quoted from a pre-UCC case, *United States Fidelity and Guaranty Co. v. First National Bank of South Carolina* (1964), as follows:

A prime purpose, as we see it, of making a sum payable when expressed in words controlling over the sum payable expressed in figures is the very fact that words are much more difficult to alter. The perforated imprinting by a check-writing machine, while fully expressing the sum payable in figures, is even more difficult to successfully alter than a sum payable in written words.

Because a check imprinting machine's purpose is to protect against alterations, the amount shown on the imprint should control whether the number is in words or figures.

Turning to the question of whether typewriting controls printing, the Indiana court [in *St. Paul Fire & Marine Ins. Co. v. State Bank of Salem*] stated:

As the section makes clear, in the event of an ambiguity between printed terms and typewritten terms, the latter would control. We do not consider the impression made by the check imprinter to be 'printed terms' under this section.

A conflict between the two amounts on a check would be resolved by section 3–118(c) which states that words control figures. Arguably, the amount imprinted by the checkwriting machine upon the line customarily expressing the amount in words, is expressed in figures. . . . We think, however, that the purposes of the UCC are best served by considering an amount imprinted by a checkwriting machine as "words" for the purpose of resolving an ambiguity between that amount and an amount entered upon the line usually used to express the amount in figures.

Although the court did not say specifically that it regarded the portion written by the checkwriting machine was the equivalent of handwriting, that is the clear effect of the decision.

Judgment for Kindy reversed on other grounds.

Note: The court here concluded that a conflict between the words and figures did not serve as "notice of a claim or defense" and thus did not prevent Galatia Bank from becoming a holder in due course who could recover from Kindy. The court's rationale was that section 118 treats the situation as a "mistake" which can be resolved through the rules of construction. Although, as the court notes, this case was decided under the original version of Article 3, the dilemma posed, and the statements made by the court concerning the construction of the check, would likely be the same if the dilemma came up under Revised Article 3.

ETHICAL AND PUBLIC POLICY CONCERNS

1. The Uniform Commercial Code currently provides that in the case of ambiguity or conflict between the words and numbers on a negotiable instrument, the words control the numbers. A group of banks argue that in an era of computers, they encode checks based on the amount stated in figures and that the Code should be changed to provide for the dominance of figures over words. What policy considerations are involved in deciding whether or not the bank's position should be adopted in the Code?

1. Is the following instrument a note, a check, or a draft? Why? If it is not a check, how would you have to change it to make it a check?

To: Arthur Adams January 1, 1995
TEN DAYS AFTER DATE PAY TO THE ORDER OF:
Bernie Brown
THE SUM OF: Ten and no/100 DOLLARS
SIGNED: Carl Clark

2. Wiley, Tate & Irby, buyers and sellers of used cars, sold several autos to Houston Auto Sales. Houston wrote out the order for payment on the outside of several envelopes. He signed them and they were drawn on his bank, Peoples Bank & Trust Co., to be paid on the demand of Wiley, Tate & Irby. Can the envelopes qualify as negotiable instruments?

3. Is the following a negotiable instrument?

IOU, A. Gay, the sum of seventeen and 5/100 dollars for value received.
John R. Rooke

4. Is the following a negotiable instrument?

Subject to Approval of Title
Pay to the Order of Vernon Butterfield
$1,997,90.

The Culver Company
By A. M. Culver

5. A promissory note provides as follows:

FOR VALUE RECEIVED, the undersigned promises to pay to the order of J. MONTE WILLIAMSON . . . the principal sum of Four Thousand Dollars ($4,000) payable as set forth in that certain agreement dated March 15, 1976, an executed copy of which is attached hereto and made a part thereof by this reference.

Is the note negotiable?

6. Strickland ordered a swimming pool from Kafko Manufacturing and gave it a check for the purchase price that included the following words in the space following the word memo: "for pool kit to be delivered." Is the check negotiable?

7. Olde Town Investment Corporation borrowed $18,000 from VMC Mortgage Company and signed a promissory note secured by a deed of trust on land it owned. The note provided for interest at "three percent (3.00%) over Chase Manhattan Prime to be adjusted monthly." Is a note providing for a variable amount of interest, not ascertainable from the face of the note, a negotiable instrument?

8. Nation-Wide Check Corporation sold money orders to drugstores. The money orders contained the words, "Payable to," followed by a blank. Can the money order qualify as a negotiable instrument?

9. Holliday made out a promissory note to Anderson, leaving the date of payment of the note blank. Anderson filled in the words "on demand" in the blank without Holliday's knowledge. Does this alter the rights or obligations of the parties?

10. Emmett McDonald, acting as the personal representative of the estate of Marion Cahill, wrote a check payable to himself, individually, on the estate checking account in the Commercial Bank & Trust Company. The instrument contained an obvious variance between the numbers and the written words that indicated the amount of the check. It said: "Pay to the order of Emmett E. McDonald $10075.00 Ten hundred seventy five . . . Dollars." The bank paid the $10,075 sum stated by the numerals to McDonald, who absconded with the funds. Yates, the successor representative, sued the bank on behalf of the estate to recover the $9,000 difference between that amount and the $1,075 that was written out. Did the bank pay the correct amount on the check?

NEGOTIATION AND HOLDER IN DUE COURSE

INTRODUCTION

The preceding chapter discussed the nature and benefits of negotiable instruments. It also outlined the requirements an instrument must meet to qualify as a negotiable instrument and thus possess the qualities that allow it to be accepted as a substitute for money.

This chapter focuses on negotiation—the process by which rights to a negotiable instrument pass from one person to another. Commonly, this involves an indorsement and transfer of the instrument. This chapter also develops the requirements that a transferee of a negotiable instrument must meet to qualify as a holder in due course and to thus attain special rights under negotiable instruments law. These rights, which put a holder in due course in an enhanced position compared to an assignee of a contract, are discussed in some detail.

NEGOTIATION

Nature of Negotiation

Under Revised Article 3, **negotiation** is the transfer of possession (whether voluntary or involuntary) of a negotiable instrument by a person (other than the issuer) to another person who becomes its *holder* [3–201]. A person is a **holder** if she is in possession of an instrument (1) that is payable to bearer or (2) made payable to an identified person and she is that identified person [1–201(20)].[1]

For example, when an employer gives an employee, Susan Adams, a paycheck payable "to the order of Susan Adams," she is the holder of the check because she is in possession of an instrument payable to an identified person (Susan Adams) and she is that person. When she indorses (writes her name) on the back of the check and exchanges it for cash and merchandise at Ace Grocery, she has negotiated the check to the grocery store and the store is now the holder because it is in possession by transfer of a check that now is payable to bearer. Similarly, if Susan Adams indorsed the check "Pay to the Order of Ace Grocery, Susan Adams" and transferred it to the grocery store, it would be a

---

[1] The numbers in parentheses refer to sections of the Uniform Commercial Code (UCC), which is reproduced in the appendix.

holder through the negotiation of the check to it. The grocery store would be in possession of an instrument payable to an identified person (Ace Grocery) and is the person identified in the check.

In certain circumstances, Revised Article 3 allows a person to become a holder by negotiation even though the transfer of possession is involuntary. For example, if a negotiable instrument is payable to bearer and is stolen by Tom Thief or found by Fred Finder, Thief or Finder becomes the holder when he obtains possession. The involuntary transfer of possession of a bearer instrument results in a negotiation to Thief or Finder.

Formal Requirements for Negotiation

The formal requirements for negotiation are very simple. If an instrument is payable to the order of a specific payee, it is called **order paper** and it can be negotiated by transfer of possession of the instrument after indorsement by the person specified [3–201(b)].

For example, if Rachel's father gives her a check payable "to the order of Rachel Stern," then Rachel can negotiate the check by indorsing her name on the back of the check and giving it to the person to whom she wants to transfer it. Note that the check is order paper, not because the word *order* appears on the check but rather because it named a specific payee, Rachel Stern.

If an instrument is payable to bearer or to cash, it is called **bearer paper** and negotiating it is even simpler. An instrument payable to bearer may be negotiated by transfer of possession alone [3–201(b)]. Thus, if someone gives you a check that is made payable "to the order of cash," you can negotiate it simply by giving it to the person to whom you wish to transfer it. No indorsement is necessary to negotiate an instrument payable to bearer. However, the person who takes the instrument may ask for an indorsement for her protection. By indorsing the check, you agree to be liable for its payment to that person if it is not paid by the drawee bank when it is presented for payment. This liability will be discussed in Chapter 32, Liability of Parties.

Nature of Indorsement

An indorsement is made by adding the signature of the holder of the instrument to the instrument, usually on the back of it, either alone or with other words. **Indorsement** is defined to mean "a signa-ture (other than that of a maker, drawer or acceptor) that alone or accompanied by other words, is made on an instrument for purpose of (i) negotiating the instrument, (ii) restricting payment of the instrument, or (iii) incurring indorser's liability on the instrument" [3–204(a)]. The negotiation and restriction of payment aspects of indorsements will be discussed below; indorser's liability will be covered in the next chapter.

The signature constituting an indorsement can be put there either by the holder or by someone who is authorized to sign on behalf of the holder. For example, a check payable to "H&H Meat Market" might be indorsed "H&H Meat Market by Jane Frank, President," if Jane is authorized to do this on behalf of the market.

Wrong or Misspelled Name

When indorsing an instrument, the holder should spell his name in the same way as it appears on the instrument. If the holder's name is misspelled or wrong, then legally the indorsement can be made either in his name or in the name that is on the instrument. However, any person who pays the instrument or otherwise gives value for it may require the indorser to sign both names [3–204(d)].

Suppose Joan Ash is issued a check payable to the order of "Joanne Ashe." She may indorse the check as either "Joan Ash" or "Joanne Ashe." However, if she takes the check to a bank to cash, the bank may require her to sign both "Joanne Ashe" and "Joan Ash."

Checks Deposited without Indorsement

Occasionally, when a customer deposits a check to her account with a bank, she may forget to indorse the check; it is common practice for depositary banks to receive unindorsed checks under what are known as "lock-box" arrangements with customers who receive a high volume of checks. Normally, a check payable to the order of an identified person would require the indorsement of that person in order for a negotiation to the depositary bank to take place and for it to become a holder. Under the original Article 3, the depositary bank, in most cases, had the right to supply the customer's indorsement. Instead of actually signing the customer's name to the check as the indorsement, the bank might just stamp on it that it was deposited by the customer or credited to her account. Banks did not have the right to put the customer's indorsement on a check that the customer has deposited if the check specifically required the payee's signature. Insurance and government checks commonly require the payee's signature.

The revision to Article 3 and the conforming amendments to Articles 1 and 4 address the situation where a check is deposited in a depositary bank without indorsement differently. The depositary bank becomes a holder of a item delivered to it for collection, whether or not it is indorsed by the customer, if the customer at the time of delivery qualified as a holder [4–205]. Concomitantly, the depositary bank warrants to other collecting banks, the payor bank (drawee), and the drawer that it paid the amount of the item to the customer or deposited the amount to the customer's account.

Transfer of Order Instrument

Except for the special provisions concerning depositary banks, if an order instrument is transferred without indorsement, the instrument has not been negotiated and the transferee cannot qualify as a holder. For example, Sue Brown gives a check payable "to the order of Susan Brown" to a drugstore in payment for some cosmetics. Until Sue indorses the check, she has not negotiated it and the druggist could not qualify as a holder of the check.

Transfer of an instrument, whether or not the transfer is a negotiation, vests in the transferee any right of the transferor to enforce the instrument. However, the transferee cannot obtain the rights of a holder in due course (discussed later in this chapter) if he is engaged in any fraud or illegality affecting the instrument. Unless otherwise agreed, if an instrument is transferred for value but without a required indorsement, the transferee has the right to the unqualified indorsement of the transferor; however, the negotiation only takes place when the transferor applies her indorsement [3–203(c)].

INDORSEMENTS

Effects of an Indorsement

There are three functions to an indorsement. First, an indorsement is necessary in order for the negotiation of an instrument that is payable to the order of a specified person. Thus, if a check is payable "to the order of James Lee," James must indorse the check before it can be negotiated. Second, the form of the indorsement that the indorser uses also affects future attempts to negotiate the instrument. For example, if James indorses it "Pay to the order of Sarah Hill," Sarah must indorse it before it can be negotiated further.

Third, an indorsement generally makes a person liable on the instrument. By indorsing an instrument, a person incurs an obligation to pay the instrument if the person primarily liable on it (for example, the maker of a note) does not pay it. We discuss the contractual liability of indorsers in Chapter 32. In this chapter, we discuss the effect of an indorsement on further negotiation of an instrument.

Kinds of Indorsements

There are three basic kinds of indorsements: (1) special, (2) blank, and (3) restrictive. In addition, an indorsement may be "qualified."

Special Indorsement   A **special indorsement** contains the signature of the indorser along with words indicating to whom, or to whose order, the instrument is payable. For example, if a check is drawn "Pay to the Order of Marcia Morse" and Marcia indorses it "Pay to the Order of Sam Smith, Marcia Morse" or "Pay to Sam Smith, Marcia Morse," it has been indorsed with a special indorsement. An instrument that is indorsed with a special indorsement remains order paper. It can be negotiated only with the indorsement of the person specified [3–205(a)]. In this example, Sam Smith must indorse the check before he can negotiate it to someone else.

Blank Indorsement   If an indorser merely signs his name and does not specify to whom the instrument is payable, he has indorsed the instrument **in blank**. For example, if a check drawn "Pay to the Order of Natalie Owens" is indorsed "Natalie Owens" by Natalie, Natalie has indorsed it in blank. An instrument indorsed in blank is payable to the bearer (person in possession of it) and from that act is "bearer paper." As such, the bearer negotiates it by transfer alone and no further indorsement is necessary for negotiation [3–205(b)].

If Natalie indorsed the check in blank and gave it to Kevin Foley, Kevin would have the right to convert the blank indorsement into a special indorsement [3–205(c)]. He could do this by writing the words "Pay to the Order of Kevin Foley" above Natalie's indorsement. Then the check would have to be indorsed by Kevin before it could be negotiated further.

If Kevin took the check indorsed in blank to a bank and presented it for payment or for collection, the bank would normally ask him to indorse the check. It does this not because it needs his indorsement for the check to be negotiated to it; the check indorsed in blank can be negotiated merely by delivering it to the bank cashier. Rather, the bank asks for his indorsement because it wants to make him liable on the check if it is not paid when the bank sends it to the drawee bank for payment. Chapter 32 discusses the liability of indorsers.

Restrictive Indorsement   A **restrictive indorsement** is one that specifies the purpose of the indorsement or specifies the use to be made of the instrument. Among the more common restrictive indorsements are:

1. Indorsements for deposit. For example, "For Deposit Only" or "For Deposit to My Account at First National Bank."

2. Indorsements for collection, which are commonly put on by banks involved in the collection process. For example, "Pay any bank, banker, or trust company" or "For collection only."

3. Indorsements indicating that the indorsement is for the benefit of someone other than the person to whom it is payable. For example, "Pay to Arthur Attorney in Trust for Mark Minor."

Generally, the person who takes an instrument with a restrictive indorsement must pay or apply any money or other value he gives for the instrument consistently with the indorsement. In the case of a check indorsed "for deposit" or "for collection," any person other than a bank who purchases the check is considered to have **converted** the check unless (1) the indorser received the amount paid for it or (2) the bank applied the amount of the check consistently with the indorsement (e.g., deposited it to the indorser's account). Similarly, a depositary bank (a bank that takes an item for collection) or payor bank (the drawee bank) that takes an instrument for deposit or for immediate payment over the counter that has been indorsed "for deposit" or "for collection" will be liable for conversion unless the indorser received the amount paid for the instrument or the proceeds or the bank applied the amount consistently with the indorsement [3–206(c)].[2]

By way of illustration, assume that Robert Franks has indorsed his paycheck "For Deposit to My Account No. 4068933 at Bank One." While on his way to the bank he loses the check, and Fred Finder finds it. If Finder tries to cash the check at a check-cashing service, the service must ensure that any value it gives for the check either is deposited to Franks' account at Bank One or is received by Franks. If it gives the money to Finder, it will be liable to Franks for converting his check. This principle is illustrated in the following case, *Lehigh Presbytery v. Merchants Bancorp, Inc.*, which involves a bank that failed to apply value given for checks consistently with restrictive indorsements on the checks.

---

[2] Otherwise, a payor bank as well as an intermediary bank may disregard the indorsement and is not liable if the proceeds of the instrument are not received by the indorser or applied consistently with the indorsement [3–206(c)(4)].

LEHIGH PRESBYTERY V. MERCHANTS BANCORP, INC.
17 UCC Rep.2d 163 (Pa. Super. Ct. 1991)

Mary Ann Hunsberger was hired by the Lehigh Presbytery as a secretary/bookkeeper. In this capacity, she was responsible for opening the Presbytery's mail, affixing a rubber stamp indorsement to checks received by the Presbytery, and depositing the checks into the Presbytery's account at Merchants Bancorp, Inc. Over a period of more than five years, Hunsberger deposited into her own account 153 of these checks. Each check was indorsed: "For Deposit Only To The Credit of Presbytery of Lehigh, Ernest Hutcheson, Treas." The bank credited the checks to Hunsberger's account, despite the rubber stamp restrictive indorsement, because it relied solely on the account number handwritten on the deposit slips submitted by Hunsberger with the checks at the time of deposit. Hunsberger obtained the deposit slips in the lobby of the bank, wrote the proper account title, "Lehigh Presbytery," but inserted her own account number rather than the account number of her employer.

When Lehigh Presbytery discovered the diversionary scheme, it sued the bank to recover the funds credited to Hunsberger's account. The primary issue in the case was whether the bank was bound to follow the restrictive indorsements on the 153 checks that it instead had deposited to the personal account of Hunsberger. The trial court ruled in favor of the bank and Lehigh Presbytery appealed.

McEwen, Judge   UCC Section 3–205 provides:

An indorsement is restrictive which either:

* * * *

(3) includes the words "for collection," "for deposit," "pay any bank," or like terms signifying a purpose of deposit or collection; or

* * * *

It is undisputed that the indorsement stamped on each check by Ms. Hunsberger is a restrictive indorsement within the meaning of section 3–205.

Section 3–206 of the UCC addresses the effect of such an indorsement and provides, in pertinent part:

(c) Conditional or specified purpose indorsement.— Except for an intermediary bank, any transferee under an indorsement which is conditional or includes the words "for collection," "for deposit," "Pay any bank," or like terms (section 3–205(1) and (3) (relating to restrictive indorsements) must pay or apply any value given by him for or on the security of the instrument consistently with

the indorsement and to the extent he does he becomes a holder for value.

Thus, the UCC mandates application of the value of the checks consistently with the indorsement, i.e., for deposit to Lehigh Presbytery's account.

Courts considering the significance of a restrictive indorsement have consistently concluded that the UCC imposes an unwaivable obligation upon the bank to follow the indorsement. New York State's highest court has held that "[t]he presence of a restriction imposes upon the depositary bank an obligation not to accept that item other than in accord with the restriction. By disregarding the restriction, it not only subjects itself to liability for any losses resulting from its actions, but it also passes up what may be the best opportunity to prevent the fraud."

Judgment reversed in favor of Lehigh Presbytery.

Note: Although this case was decided under the original version of Article 3, the same result would be expected under Revised Article 3.

Some indorsements indicate payment to the indorsee as an agent, trustee, or fiduciary. A person who takes an instrument containing such an indorsement from the indorsee may pay the proceeds to the indorsee without regard to whether the indorsee violates a fiduciary duty to the indorser *unless* he is on *notice* of any breach of fiduciary duty that the indorser may be committing [3–206(d)]. A person would have such notice if he took the instrument in any transaction that benefited the indorsee personally [3–307]. Suppose a person takes a check indorsed to "Arthur Attorney in Trust for Mark Minor." The money given for the

check should be put in Mark Minor's trust account. A person would not be justified in taking the check in exchange for a television set that he knew Attorney was acquiring for his own—rather than Minor's—use.

There are two other kinds of indorsements that original Article 3 treated as restrictive indorsements but that Revised Article 3 no longer considers as restrictive indorsements. They are:

1. Indorsements purporting to prohibit further negotiation. For example, "Pay to Carl Clark Only."

2. Conditional indorsements, which indicate that they are effective only if the payee satisfies a certain condition For example, "Pay to Bernard Builder Only if He Completes Construction on My House by November 1, 1995."

Under Revised Article 3, any indorsement that purports to limit payment to a particular person, or to prohibit further transfer or negotiation of the instrument, is not effective to prevent further transfer or negotiation [3–206(a)]. Thus, if a note is indorsed "Pay to Carl Clark Only" and given to Clark, he may negotiate the note to subsequent holders who may ignore the restriction on the indorsement.

Indorsements that state a condition to the right of the indorsee to receive payment do not affect the right of the indorsee to enforce the instrument. Any person who pays the instrument or takes it for value or for collection may disregard the condition. Moreover, the rights and liabilities of the person are not affected by whether the condition has been fulfilled [3–206(b)].

Qualified Indorsement A **qualified indorsement** is one where the indorser disclaims her liability to make the instrument good if the maker or drawer defaults on it. Words such as "Without Recourse" are used to qualify an indorsement. They can be used with either a blank indorsement or a special indorsement and thus make it a qualified blank indorsement or a qualified special indorsement. The use of a qualified indorsement does not change the negotiable nature of the instrument. Its effect is to eliminate the contractual liability of the indorser. Chapter 32 will discuss this liability in detail.

CONCEPT REVIEW

INDORSEMENTS

(Assume a check is payable "To The Order of Mark Smith.")

Type	Example	Consequences
Blank	Mark Smith	1. Satisfies the indorsement requirement for the negotiation of order paper. 2. The instrument becomes bearer paper and can be negotiated by delivery alone. 3. The indorser becomes obligated on the instrument. (See Chapter 32, Liability of Parties.)
Special	Pay to the Order of Joan Brown, Mark Smith	1. Satisfies the indorsement requirement for the negotiation of order paper. 2. The instrument remains order paper and Joan Brown's indorsement is required for further negotiation. 3. The indorser becomes obligated on the instrument. (See Chapter 32.)
Restrictive	For deposit only to my account in First American Bank Mark Smith	1. Satisfies the indorsement requirement for the negotiation of order paper. 2. The person who pays value for the instrument is obligated to pay it consistent with the indorsement (i.e., to pay it into Mark Smith's account at First American Bank). 3. The indorser becomes obligated on the instrument. (See Chapter 32.)
Qualified	Mark Smith (without recourse)	1. Satisfies the indorsement requirement for negotiation of order paper. 2. Eliminates the indorser's obligation. (See Chapter 32.)

Rescission of Indorsement

Negotiation is effective to transfer an instrument even if the negotiation is (1) made by a minor, a corporation exceeding its powers, or any other person without contractual capacity; (2) obtained by fraud, duress, or mistake of any kind; (3) made in breach of duty; or (4) part of an illegal transaction. A negotiation made under the preceding circumstances is subject to **rescission** before the instrument has been negotiated to a transferee who can qualify as a holder in due course [3–202]. The situation in such instances is analogous to a sale of goods where the sale has been induced by fraud or misrepresentation. In such a case, the seller may rescind the sale and recover the goods, provided that the seller acts before the goods are resold to a bona fide purchaser for value.

HOLDER IN DUE COURSE

A person who qualifies as a holder in due course of a negotiable instrument gets special rights. Normally, the transferee of an instrument—like the assignee of a contract—gets only those rights in the instrument that are held by the person from whom he got the instrument. But a holder in due course can get better rights. A holder in due course takes a negotiable instrument free of all **personal defenses, claims to the instrument**, and **claims in recoupment** either of the obligor or of a third party. A holder in due course does not take free of the **real defenses**, which go to the validity of the instrument or of claims that develop after he becomes a holder. We develop the differences between personal and real defenses in more detail later in this chapter and also explain claims to the instrument and claims in recoupment. The following example illustrates the advantage that a holder in due course of a negotiable instrument may have.

Assume that Carl Carpenter contracts with Helen Homeowner to build her a garage for $9,500, payable on October 1 when he expects to complete the garage. Assume further that Carpenter assigns his right to the $9,500 to First National Bank in order to obtain money for materials. If the bank tries to collect the money from Homeowner on October 1 but Carpenter has not finished building the garage, then Homeowner may assert the fact that the garage is not complete as a defense to paying the bank. As assignee of a simple contract, the bank has only those rights that its assignor, Carpenter, has and is subject to all claims and defenses that Homeowner has against Carpenter.

Now assume that instead of simply signing a contract with Homeowner, Carpenter had Homeowner give him a negotiable promissory note in the amount of $9,500 payable to the order of Carpenter on October 1 and that Carpenter then negotiated the note to the bank. If the bank is able to qualify as a holder in due course, it may collect the $9,500 from Homeowner on October 1 even though she might have a personal defense against payment of the note because Carpenter had not completed the work on the garage. Homeowner cannot assert that personal defense against a holder in due course. She would have to pay the note to the bank and then independently seek to recover from Carpenter for breach of their agreement. The bank's improved position is due to its status as a holder in due course of a negotiable instrument. If the instrument in question was not negotiable, or if the bank could not qualify as a holder in due course, then it would be in the same position as the assignee of a simple contract and would be subject to Homeowner's personal defense.

We turn now to a discussion of the requirements that must be met for the possessor of a negotiable instrument to qualify as a holder in due course.

General Requirements

In order to become a **holder in due course**, a person who takes a negotiable instrument must be a *holder*, and take the instrument for *value*, in *good faith*, *without notice* that it is *overdue* or has been *dishonored* or that there is any uncured default with respect to payment of another instrument issued as part of the same series, *without notice that the instrument contains an unauthorized signature or has been altered, without notice of any claim of a property or possessory interest in it*, and *without notice* that any party has any *defense against it* or *claim in recoupment to it* [3–302(a)(2)].

In addition, the revision to Article 3 requires "that the instrument when issued or negotiated to the holder does not bear such *apparent evidence of forgery or alteration* or is not otherwise so *irregular or incomplete* as to call into question its authenticity" [3–302(a)(1)].

If a person who takes a negotiable instrument does not meet these requirements, he is not a holder in due course. Then the person is in the same position as an assignee of a contract.

Holder

As noted earlier in this chapter, to be a **holder** of a negotiable instrument, a person must have possession of an instrument that is either payable to bearer or that is payable to him. For example, if Teresa Gonzales is given a check by her grandmother that is made payable "to the order of Teresa Gonzales," Teresa is a holder of the check because it is made out to her. If Teresa indorses the check "Pay to the order of Ames Hardware, Teresa Gonzales" and gives it to Ames Hardware in payment for some merchandise, then Ames Hardware is the holder of the check. Ames Hardware is a holder because it is in possession of a check that is indorsed to its order. If Ames Hardware indorses the check "Ames Hardware" and deposits it in its account at First National Bank, the bank becomes the holder. The bank is in possession of an instrument that is indorsed in blank and thus is payable to bearer.

It is important that all indorsements on the instrument at the time it is payable to the order of someone are *authorized indorsements*. With limited exceptions (discussed later), a forged indorsement is not an effective indorsement and prevents a person from becoming a holder.

To be a holder, a person must have a complete chain of authorized indorsements. Suppose the Internal Revenue Service mails to Robert Washington an income tax refund check payable to him. Tom Turner steals the check from Washington's mailbox, signs (indorses) "Robert Washington" on the back of the check, and cashes it at a shoe store. The shoe store is not a holder of the check because its transferor, Turner, was not a holder and because it needs Washington's signature to have a good chain of authorized indorsements. Robert Washington has to indorse the check in order for there to be a valid chain of indorsements. Turner's signature is not effective for this purpose because Washington did not authorize him to sign Washington's name to the check [1–201(20); 3–403(a); 3–416(a)(2)].

The case that follows, *LaJunta State Bank v. Travis*, illustrates that a party in possession of a check indorsed in blank is a holder of the instrument.

LA JUNTA STATE BANK v. TRAVIS
727 P.2d 48 (Sup. Ct. Colo. 1986)

On November 15, 1979, Katherine Warnock purchased a cashier's check in the amount of $53,541.93 payable to her order and drawn on the Pueblo Bank and Trust Company. At some time between November 15 and November 30, Warnock indorsed "Katherine Warnock" on the reverse side of the check, and Warnock's attorney, Jerry Quick, wrote the words "deposit only" under Warnock's indorsement. On November 30, Quick deposited the check into a trust account he maintained at the La Junta State Bank. Warnock did not maintain any type of account with La Junta State Bank. La Junta collected the amount of the check from Pueblo Bank.

Warnock died on November 10, 1981. Robert Travis, Warnock's personal representative, was unable to find a receipt in her personal papers for the sum of $53,541.93. On June 24, Travis demanded that the La Junta Bank repay that sum to Warnock's estate. At the time, no funds remained in Quick's trust account at the bank. When the La Junta Bank refused the representative's demand, he brought suit against the bank claiming it had improperly paid the check by allowing it into any account other than one in Warnock's name. The trial court determined that Warnock had indorsed the check in blank and delivered it to Quick, that the check therefore became bearer paper upon Warnock's indorsement, and that the check was negotiable on delivery alone; it granted judgment to the bank. A divided court of appeals reversed in favor of the representative, holding that Quick's addition of the words "deposit only" below Warnock's signature created a restrictive indorsement and that because the bank failed to treat it as such, it was liable to the representative for the full amount of the check. The bank appealed.

Kirshbaum, Justice   It is undisputed that when Warnock indorsed the check in blank and delivered it to Quick, it was converted from order paper to bearer paper, negotiable by delivery alone until specially indorsed [3–204(2)]. The trial court also concluded that Quick's addition of "deposit only" below Warnock's signature did not convert Warnock's blank indorsement into a special indorsement.

Implicit in the trial court's conclusions is the assumption that Quick added the words "deposit only" to the check some time after Warnock's indorsement thereof. This implicit finding is supported by the stipulation of facts and the evidence disclosed by the record. Therefore, we also conclude that when Warnock indorsed the check in blank and delivered it to Quick, Quick became a holder of the instrument in bearer form with the right to transfer or negotiate it by delivery alone.

Warnock's representative argues that, assuming Quick was initially a holder of a check in bearer form, his act of affixing the words "deposit only" to the check deprived him of that status, destroyed the negotiability of the check, and converted Warnock's blank indorsement into a restrictive indorsement. This argument is untenable.

Quick, as holder of an instrument, was not authorized by any Code provision to convert this transferor's blank indorsement into a restrictive one (see section 3–204(3): "The holder may convert a blank indorsement by writing over the signature of the indorser in blank any contract consistent with the character of the indorsement."). Furthermore, the representative incorrectly assumes that a blank indorsement and a restrictive indorsement create mutually exclusive methods for negotiation. As UCC section 3–206 official comment 5 (1978) indicates, "indorsements 'for collection' or 'for deposit' may be either special or blank." A single indorsement, therefore, may be both in blank and restrictive. The nonrestrictive character of Warnock's indorsement was determined when she affixed her signature to the check.

The fact that Quick was a holder of bearer paper does not end the inquiry into the propriety of the bank's conduct. Section 3–206(3) of the Code requires a depository bank, upon being presented with a negotiable instrument containing an indorsement which includes the words "for deposit" or like terms, to "pay or apply any value given by him for or on the security of the instrument consistently with the indorsement. . . ." This obligation affords protection to payees or indorsers who indorse items "for deposit" in the belief that such indorsement will guard against further negotiation of the instrument to a holder in due course by a finder or a thief.

In this case the bank, as a depository bank, received a check containing what appeared to be a restrictive indorsement by Katherine Warnock. The record does not reveal who actually delivered the check and deposit slip to the bank. Thus, at the moment it received the restrictively indorsed check, the bank appeared to owe a duty to Warnock to either comply with the directions of the indorsement or to inquire further concerning the transaction because of the simultaneous receipt of a deposit slip into an account other than Warnock's. However, because the check was bearer paper when Quick received it, he was free to direct its deposit in any manner he elected. Any inquiry by the bank would have revealed that, although the language inscribed on the instrument appeared to constitute a restrictive indorsement by Katherine Warnock, the words "deposit only" had been added by Quick on his own behalf; and the bank owed a duty to Quick on November 30, 1979, to honor his restrictive indorsement. Under the circumstances of the case, the bank owed no duty to Warnock and Warnock's representative is entitled to no damages.

Judgment for La Junta State Bank.

Note: Although this case was decided under the original version of Article 3, the same result would be anticipated under Revised Article 3.

Value

To qualify as a holder in due course of a negotiable instrument, a person must give **value** for it. Value is not identical to simple consideration. Under the provisions of the Revised Article 3, a holder takes for value if: (1) the agreed-on promise of performance has been performed—for example, if the instrument was given in exchange for a promise to deliver a refrigerator and the refrigerator has been delivered; (2) he acquires a security interest in, or a lien on, the instrument; (3) he takes the instrument in payment of, or as security for, an antecedent claim; (4) he gives a negotiable instrument for it; or (5) he makes an irrevocable commitment to a third person [3–303]. Thus, a person who gets a check as a gift or merely makes an executory promise in return for a check has not given value for it and cannot qualify as a holder in due course.

A bank or any person who discounts an instrument in the *regular course of trade* has given value for it. In this context, the discount is essentially a means for increasing the return or the rate of interest on the instrument. Likewise, if a loan is made and an instrument is pledged as security for the repayment of the loan, the secured party has given value for the instrument to the amount of the loan. If Axe, who owes Bell a past-due debt, indorses and delivers to Bell, in payment of the debt or as security for its repayment, an instrument issued to Axe, Bell has given value for the instrument. If a bank allows a customer to draw against a check deposited for collection, it has given value to the extent of the credit drawn against.

If the promise of performance that is the consideration for an instrument has been partially performed, the holder may assert rights as a holder in due course of the instrument only to the fraction of the amount payable under the instrument equal to the partial performance divided by the value of the promised performance [3–302(d)]. For example, Arthur Wells agrees to purchase a note payable to the order of Helda Parks. The note is for the sum of $5,000. Wells pays Parks $1,000 on the negotiation of the note to him and agrees to pay the balance of $4,000 in 10 days. Initially, Wells is a holder in due course for one fifth of the amount of the note. If he later pays the $4,000 due he may become a holder in due course for the full amount.

Good Faith

To qualify as a holder in due course of a negotiable instrument, a person must take it in **good faith**, which means that the person obtained it honestly and in the observance of reasonable commercial standards of fair dealing [3–103(a)(4)]. If a person obtains a check by trickery or with knowledge that it has been stolen, the person has not obtained the check in good faith and cannot be a holder in due course. A person who pays too little for an instrument, perhaps because she suspects that something

may be wrong with the way it was obtained, may have trouble meeting the good faith test. Suppose a finance company works closely with a door-to-door sales company that engages in shoddy practices. If the finance company buys the consumers' notes from the sales company, it will not be able to meet the good faith test and qualify as a holder in due course of the notes.

Overdue or Dishonored

In order to qualify as a holder in due course, a person must take a negotiable instrument before he has notice that it either is **overdue** or has been **dishonored**. The reason for this is that one should perform obligations when they are due. If a negotiable instrument is not paid when it is due, the Code considers the person taking it to be on notice that there may be defenses to the payment of it.

Overdue Instruments If a negotiable instrument is payable on demand, it is overdue: (1) the day after demand for payment has been made in a proper manner and form; (2) 90 days after its date if it is a check; and (3) if it is an instrument other than a check, when it has been outstanding for an unreasonably long period of time in light of the nature of the instrument and trade practice [3–304(a)]. Thus, a check becomes stale after 90 days and, for other kinds of instruments, one must consider trade practices and the facts of the particular case. In a farming community, the normal period for loans to farmers may be six months. A demand note might be outstanding for six or seven months before it is considered overdue. On the other hand, a demand note issued in an industrial city where the normal period of such loans is 30 to 60 days would be considered overdue in a much shorter period of time.

If a negotiable instrument due on a certain date is not paid by that date, then normally it is overdue at the beginning of the next day after the due date. For example, if a promissory note dated January 1 is payable "30 days after date," it is due on January 31. If it is not paid by January 31, it is overdue beginning on February 1.

As to instruments payable at a definite time, Revised Article 3 sets out four rules: (1) if the principal is not payable in installments and the due date has not been accelerated, the instrument is overdue on the day after the due date; (2) if the principal is due in installments and a due date has not been accelerated, the instrument is overdue upon default for nonpayment of an installment and remains overdue until the default is cured; (3) if a due date for the principal has been accelerated, the instrument is overdue on the day after the accelerated due date; and (4) unless the due date of the principal has been accelerated, an instrument does not become overdue if there is a default in payment of interest but no default in payment of principal [3–304(b)].

Dishonored Instruments   To be a holder in due course, a person not only must take a negotiable instrument before he has notice that it is overdue but also must take it before it has been dishonored. A negotiable instrument has been *dishonored* when the holder has presented it for payment (or acceptance) and payment (or acceptance) has been refused.

For example, Susan writes a check on her account at First National Bank that is payable "to the order of Sven Sorensen." Sven takes the check to First National Bank to cash it but the bank refuses to pay it because Susan has insufficient funds in her account to cover it. The check has been dishonored. If Sven then takes Susan's check to Harry's Hardware and uses it to pay for some paint, Harry's cannot be a holder in due course of the check if it is on notice that the check has been dishonored. Harry's would have such notice if First National had stamped the check "Payment Refused NSF" (not sufficient funds).

Similarly, suppose Carol Carson signs a 30-day note payable to Ace Appliance for $500 and gives it to Ace as payment for a stereo set. When Ace asks Carol for payment, she refuses to pay because the stereo does not work properly. If Ace negotiates the note to First National Bank, First National cannot be a holder in due course if it knows about Carol's refusal to pay.

Notice of Unauthorized Signature or Alteration

A holder who has notice that an instrument contains an unauthorized signature or has been altered cannot qualify as a holder in due course of the instrument. For example, Frank makes out a check in the amount of $5.00 payable to George Grocer and gives it to his daughter, Jane, to take to the grocery store to purchase some groceries. The groceries

Frank wants cost $20.00 and Jane changes the check to read $25.00, giving it to Grocer in exchange for the groceries and $5.00 in cash. Grocer cannot qualify as a holder in due course if he sees Jane make the alteration to the check or otherwise is on notice of it.

Notice of Claims

If a person taking a negotiable instrument is *on notice of an adverse claim* to the instrument by someone else (for example, that she is the rightful owner of the instrument) or that someone is seeking to rescind a prior negotiation of the instrument, the current holder cannot qualify as a holder in due course. For example, a U.S. Treasury check is payable to Susan Samuels. Samuels loses the check and it is found by Robert Burns. Burns takes the check to a hardware store, signs "Susan Samuels" on the back of the check in the view of a clerk, and seeks to use it in payment of merchandise. The hardware store cannot be a holder in due course because it is on notice of a potential claim to the instrument by Susan Samuels.

Notice of Breach of Fiduciary Duty   One situation in which the Code considers a person to be on notice of a claim is if she is taking a negotiable instrument from a fiduciary, such as a trustee. If a negotiable instrument is payable to a person as a trustee or an attorney for someone, then any attempt by that person to negotiate it for his own behalf or for his use (or benefit) or to deposit it in an account other than that of the fiduciary puts the person on notice that the beneficiary of the trust may have a claim [3–307].

For example, a check is drawn "Pay to the order of Arthur Adams, Trustee for Mary Minor." Adams takes the check to Credit Union, indorses his name to it, and uses it to pay off the balance on a loan Adams had from Credit Union. Credit Union cannot be a holder in due course because it should know that the negotiation of the check is in violation of the fiduciary duty Adams owes to Mary Minor. Credit Union should know this because Adams is negotiating the check for his own benefit, not Mary's. The case that follows, *Smith v. Olympic Bank*, illustrates the consequences to a bank of not being careful in taking an instrument from a fiduciary.

SMITH V. OLYMPIC BANK
693 P.2d 92 (Sup. Ct. Wash. 1985)

Charles Alcombrack was appointed guardian for his son, Chad Alcombrack, who was seven years old and the beneficiary of his grandfather's life insurance policy. The insurance company issued a check for $30,588.39 made payable to "Charles Alcombrack, Guardian of the Estate of Chad Stephen Alcombrack, a Minor." The attorney for the son's estate directed the father to take the check, along with the letters of guardianship issued to the father, to the bank and open a guardianship savings and checking account. Instead, the father took the check, without the letters of guardianship, to the Olympic Bank and opened a personal checking and a personal savings account.

Despite the fact that the check was payable to the father in his guardianship capacity, the bank allowed the father to place the entire amount in his newly opened personal accounts. The father used all but $320.60 of the trust money for his own benefit. A new guardian, J. David Smith, was appointed for Chad. Smith brought suit against the Olympic Bank, on Chad's behalf, to recover the amount of the check. The trial court granted judgment in favor of the bank and Smith appealed.

Dore, Justice   Olympic Bank claims that it is a holder in due course (HIDC) and, as such, is not subject to the claims of Smith. In order to qualify as a HIDC, the bank must meet five requirements. It must be (1) a holder (2) of a negotiable instrument, (3) that took the instrument for value (4) in good faith and (5) without notice that it was overdue, dishonored, or of any defense or claim to it on the part of any person. We need not decide whether the bank met the first four conditions as we hold that the bank took the check with notice of an adverse claim to the instrument and, therefore, is not a holder in due course. Consequently, the bank is liable to the son's estate.

A purchaser has notice of an adverse claim when "he has knowledge that a fiduciary has negotiated the instrument in payment of or as security for his own debt or in any transaction for his own benefit or otherwise in breach of duty." Section 3–304(2). Thus the issue raised by this case is whether the bank had knowledge that the guardian was breaching his fiduciary duty when it allowed him to deposit a check, made payable to him in his guardianship capacity, into his personal accounts.

The bank knew it was dealing with guardianship funds. The check was payable to the father as guardian and not to him personally. The father indorsed it in his guardianship capacity. The bank received a call from the guardian's attorney inquiring about the fee charged for guardianship accounts,

and a trust officer for the bank replied in a letter referring to the "Estate of Chad Alcombrack."

Reasonable commercial practices dictate that when the bank knew that the funds were deposited in a personal account instead of a guardianship account, it knew that the father was breaching his fiduciary duty. The funds lost the protection they would have received in a guardianship account. If the funds had been placed in a guardianship account, the bank would not have been permitted to accept a check drawn on the guardianship account, from the father in satisfaction of the father's unsecured personal loan in the amount of approximately $3,000. Nor could the father, or bank, have authorized his new wife to write checks against the guardianship account without court approval. A fiduciary has a duty to ensure that trust funds are protected. Here, the father breached his duty.

The policy reasons for holding a bank liable are compelling—especially in the situation presented in this case. The ward has no control of his own estate. He must rely on his guardian and on the bank for the safekeeping of his money. In order to protect the ward, the guardian and bank must be held to a high standard of care. For the guardian, this means that he must deposit guardian funds in a guardianship account. For the bank, it means that when it receives a check made payable to an individual as a guardian, it must make sure that the check is placed in a guardianship account. This will not place an undue burden on either banks or guardians and will have the beneficial effect of protecting the ward.

Judgment reversed in favor of son's guardian.

Note: Although this case was decided under the original version of Article 3 and the applicable language has been changed, the decision is consistent with Revised Article 3's treatment of negotiations involving fiduciaries. See section 3–307.

Notice of Defenses and Claims in Recoupment

To qualify as a holder in due course, a person must also acquire a negotiable instrument without notice that any party to it has any **defenses** or **claims in recoupment**. Potential defenses include infancy, duress, fraud, and failure of consideration. Thus, if a person knows that a signature on the instrument was obtained by fraud, misrepresentation, or duress, the person cannot be a holder in due course.

A *claim in recoupment* is a claim of the obligor against the original payee of the instrument. The claim must arise from the transaction that gave rise to the instrument. An example of a claim in recoupment would be as follows: Buyer purchases a used automobile from Dealer for $8,000, giving the dealer a note for $8,000 payable in one year. Because the automobile is not as warranted, Buyer has a breach of warranty claim that could be asserted against Dealer as counterclaim or "claim in recoupment" to offset the amount owing on the note.

The following case, *Parkhill v. Nusor*, illustrates the factors a court may consider in determining whether a person should be on notice of possible defenses or adverse claims by a party to a negotiable instrument and thus not able to claim the status of a holder in due course.

IN RE NUSOR
PARKHILL V. NUSOR
13 UCC Rep.2d 773 (Bankr. App., 9th Cir. 1991)

In the fall of 1987, Irene Nusor was behind in her mortgage payments. She received advertisements from Best Financial Consultants offering attractive refinancing opportunities. On October 14, 1987, she attended a meeting with Best representatives at a McDonald's restaurant who told her that Best would arrange for a complete refinancing of her home in the amount of $98,000, pay off the two existing lienholders, and provide Nusor with an additional $5,000 in spending money. In consideration for these services, Nusor was told that she would owe Best only $4,000.

Nusor agreed to the arrangement and proceeded to sign a fee agreement and a promissory note entitled "Installment Note" that was blank at the time and Best representatives later completed. As completed, it provided that Best would loan her a total sum of $14,986.61 payable in full in 60 days (on December 23, 1987) with an annual interest rate of 18 percent. Where the note provided for the name of the promissor to be filled in, the following words had been typed in: "I, the undersigned, Irene Vazquez Nusor, a married woman, as her sole and separate property." The note was payable to "Best Financial Consultants, a California Sole Proprietorship, or order." The note also contained the following statement: "This note is a [sic] junior to a first deed of trust of record." On November 13, 1987, Nusor went to a second meeting with Best representatives and signed a "short form deed of trust and assignment of rents." The deed indicated that it was secured by a promissory note in the amount of $14,986.61.

On December 2, 1987, Best assigned the note to Robin Parkhill for the discounted price of $13,812.19. Over the term of the note, Parkhill's total anticipated return was $1,624.02, representing the equivalent of an annual interest rate of over 203 percent. Parkhill, who responded to a newspaper ad placed by Best, bought the note without actual notice of the misrepresentations made to Nusor by Best. Nusor received only a single payment of $5,997.25 from Best to one of her lienholders; Best never refinanced Nusor's home or fulfilled its other promises. In June 1988, Nusor filed a Chapter 13 bankruptcy petition. One of the questions in the bankruptcy proceeding was the status of the promissory note that Parkhill claimed Nusor owed to her. A key issue was whether Parkhill was a holder in due course of a negotiable promissory note and thus not subject to the defenses of fraud in the inducement and failure of consideration that Nusor had against Best. The trial court held in favor of Nusor and Parkhill appealed.

Volinn, Bankruptcy Judge   Whether Parkhill is a holder in due course turns on Parkhill satisfying the requirements of Code Section 3–302. Nusor argues that Parkhill fails to meet this standard because of the note's clumsy draftsmanship and its exceptional rate of return (i.e., the maturation of the discounted note 21 days from the date of the assignment) gave Parkhill at least constructive notice of Nusor's defenses. Nusor states that these "irregularities ... would certainly cause a reasonably prudent person to question the note's validity and thereby be placed on notice." We agree and hold that Parkhill was not a holder in due course.

Code section 3–304(1) sets forth the conditions under which "irregularities" in the instrument puts the holder on notice:

(1) The purchaser has *notice of a claim or defense* if (a) the instrument is so incomplete, bears such visible evidence of forgery or alteration, or *is otherwise so irregular as to call into question its validity, terms or ownership* or to create an ambiguity as to the party to pay; [Emphasis added.]

The term "notice" is further defined in section 1–201(25)(c), which provides that one has notice of a fact when "[f]rom all the facts and circumstances known to him at the time in question he or she has *reason to know* that it exists." [Emphasis added.]

In this case, Parkhill did not seek interest income in the usual manner. She answered a newspaper advertisement. Presumably, after communicating with Best, she calcualted the rate of return. The content of the Installment Note, particularly its extraordinarily favorable terms, clearly indicated that this was an unusual type of commercial trans-

action. For the discounted price of $13,812.19, Parkhill was assigned a note designed to provide her in 21 days (on December 23, 1987) the face value of the Installment Note ($14,986.61) plus 18% per annum interest that would accrue over the term of the note. Thus, Parkhill's total anticipated return was $1,624.02. This amount represents the equivalent of an annual rate of return of over 203%, a return far in excess of the reasonable expectations of any investor who in good faith seeks a favorable rate of return. In addition, we find it significant that Parkhill made no inquiry about the note's origins notwithstanding its manifestly unusual terms. See *Stewart v. Thornton* (holder in due course protection cannot be used to shield one who simply refuses to investigate when the facts known to him suggest an irregularity concerning the commercial paper he purchases).

The imprecise form of the Installment Note, combined with its exorbitant rate of return, were sufficient to divest Parkhill of holder in due course status and to subject her to Nusor's defenses against the note's enforceability. Accordingly, we hold that Parkhill is not a holder in due course and is therefore subject to Nusor's defenses of fraud in the inducement and failure of consideration.

Judgment in favor of Nusor affirmed.

Note: Although this case was decided under the original Article 3, the same result would be anticipated under Revised Article 3. And, as noted below, Revised Article 3 explicitly provides that a person cannot become a holder in due course of an instrument that is so irregular as to call into question its authenticity [3–302(a)(1)].

Irregular and Incomplete Instruments

A person cannot be a holder in due course of a negotiable instrument if, when she takes it, it is irregular or some important or **material term** is blank.

If the negotiable instrument contains a facial irregularity, such as an obvious alteration in the amount, then it is considered to be **irregular paper**. If you take an irregular instrument, you are considered to be on notice of any possible defenses to it. For example, Kevin writes a check for "one dollar" payable to Karen. Karen inserts the word "hundred" in the amount, changes the figure "$1" to "$100," and gives the check to a druggist in exchange for a purchase of goods. If the alterations in the amount should be obvious to the druggist, perhaps because there are erasures, different handwritings, or different inks, then the druggist cannot be a holder in due course. She would have taken irregular paper and would be on notice that there might be defenses to it. These defenses include Kevin's defense that he is liable for only $1 because that is the amount for which he made the check.

Similarly, if someone receives a check that has been signed but the space where the amount of the check is to be written is blank, then the person cannot be a holder in due course of that check. The fact that a material term is blank means that the instrument is **incomplete** and should put the person on notice that the drawer may have a defense to payment of it. To be material, the omitted term must be one that affects the legal obligation of the parties to the negotiable instrument. Material terms include the amount of the instrument and the name of the payee. If a negotiable instrument is completed after the obligor signed it but before a person acquires it, the person can qualify as a holder in due course if she had no knowledge about the completion.

Payee as Holder in Due Course

The original Article 3 provided explicitly that a *payee* could be a holder in due course if he complied with all the requirements for a holder in due course. Revised Article 3 drops the explicit statement; the drafters stated they intended no change in the law but that they were concerned that the explicit provision suggested that use of holder in due course status by payees was the normal situation. It is not the normal situation because a payee usually will have notice or knowledge of any defenses to the instrument and will know whether it is overdue or has been dishonored; consequently, the payee is unlikely to qualify as a holder in due course. For example, Drew draws a check on First Bank as drawee, payable to the order of Parks but leaves the amount blank. Drew delivers the check to Axe, his agent, and instructs Axe to fill in $300 as the amount. Axe, however, fills in $500 as the amount, and Parks gives Axe $500 for the check.

Axe then gives Drew $300 and absconds with the extra $200. In such a case, Parks, as payee, is a holder in due course of the check because he has taken it for value, in good faith, and without notice of defenses.

Similarly, assume that Jarvis owes Fields $200. Jarvis agrees to sell Kirk a used television set for $200; Jarvis assures Kirk that it is in working condition. In fact, the set is broken. Jarvis asks Kirk to make her check for $200 payable to Fields and then delivers the check to Fields in payment of the debt. Fields, as the payee, can be a holder in due course of the check if he is not aware of the misrepresentation that Jarvis made to Kirk in order to obtain the check.

Shelter Rule

The transferee of an instrument—whether or not the transfer is a negotiation—obtains those rights that the transferor had, including (1) the transferor's right to enforce the instrument and (2) any right as a holder in due course [3–203(b)]. This means that any person who can trace his title to an instrument back to a holder in due course receives rights similar of a holder in due course even if he cannot meet the requirements himself. This is known as the **shelter rule** in Article 3. For example, Archer makes a note payable to Bryant. Bryant negotiates the note to Carlyle, who qualifies as a holder in due course. Carlyle then negotiates the note to Darby, who cannot qualify as a holder in due course because she knows the note is overdue. Because Darby can trace her title back to a holder in due course (Carlyle), Darby has rights like a holder in due course when she seeks payment of the note from Archer.

There is, however, a limitation on the shelter rule. A transferee who has himself been a party to any fraud or illegality affecting the instrument cannot improve his position by taking, directly or indirectly, from a later holder in due course [3–203(b)]. For example, Archer, through fraudulent representations, induced Bryant to execute a negotiable note payable to Archer and then negotiated the instrument to Carlyle, who took as a holder in due course. If Archer thereafter took the note for value from Carlyle, Archer could not acquire Carlyle's rights as a holder in due course. Archer was a party to the fraud that induced the note, and, accordingly, cannot improve his position by negotiating the instrument and then reacquiring it.

REQUIREMENTS FOR A HOLDER IN DUE COURSE

Requirement	Rule
1. Must be a *holder*	A holder is a person in possession of an instrument payable to bearer or payable to an identified person and he is that person.
2. Must take *for value*	A holder has given value: *a.* To the extent the agreed-on consideration has been paid or performed. *b.* To the extent a security interest or lien has been obtained in the negotiable instrument. *c.* By taking the negotiable instrument in payment of—or as security for—an antecedent claim. *d.* By giving a negotiable instrument for it. *e.* By making an irrevocable commitment to a third person.
3. Must take in *good faith*	Good faith means honesty in fact and the observance of reasonable commercial standards of fair dealing.
4. Must take *without notice* that the instrument is *overdue*	An instrument payable on demand is overdue the day after demand for payment has been duly made. A check is overdue 90 days after its date. If it is an instrument other than a check and payable on demand, when it has been outstanding for an unreasonably long period of time in light of nature of the instrument and trade practice. If it is an instrument due on a certain date, then it is overdue at the beginning of the next day after the due date.
5. Must take *without notice that the instrument has been dishonored.*	An instrument has been dishonored when the holder has presented it for payment (or acceptance) and payment (or acceptance) has been refused.
6. Must take *without notice* of any *uncured default* with respect to payment of another instrument issued as part of the same series.	If there is a series of notes, holder must take without notice that there is an uncured default as to any other notes in the series.
7. Must take *without notice* that the instrument contains an *unauthorized signature* or has been *altered.*	Notice of unauthorized signature or alteration—i.e., a change in a material term—prevents holder from obtaining HDC status.
8. Must take *without notice* of any *claim of a property or possessory interest* in it.	Claims of property or possessory interest include: *a.* Claim by someone that she is the rightful owner of the instrument. *b.* Person seeking to rescind a prior negotiation of the instrument. *c.* Claim by a beneficiary that a fiduciary negotiated the instrument for his own benefit.
9. Must take *without notice* that any party has a *defense* against it.	Defenses include real defenses that go to the validity of the instrument and personal defenses that commonly are defenses to a simple contract.
10. Must take *without notice* of a *claim in recoupment* to it.	A claim in recoupment is a claim of the obligor on the instrument against the original payee that arises from the transaction that gave rise to the instrument.
11. The instrument must not bear *apparent evidence of forgery or alteration* or be *irregular* or *incomplete.*	The instrument must not contain obvious reasons to question its authenticity.

RIGHTS OF A HOLDER IN DUE COURSE

Claims and Defenses Generally

Revised Article 3 establishes four categories of claims and defenses. They are:

1. Real defenses—which go to the validity of the instrument.
2. Personal defenses—which generally arise out of the transaction that gave rise to the instrument.
3. Claims to an instrument—which generally concern property or possessory rights in an instrument or its proceeds.
4. Claims in recoupment—which also arise out of the transaction that gave rise to the instrument.

These defenses and claims are discussed in some detail below.

Importance of Being a Holder in Due Course

In the preceding chapter, we discussed that one advantage of negotiable instruments over other kinds of contracts is that they are accepted as substitutes for money. People are willing to accept them as substitutes for money because, generally, they can take them free of claims or defenses to payment between the original parties to the instrument. On the other hand, a person who takes an assignment of a simple contract gets only the same rights as the person had who assigned the contract.

There are two qualifications to the ability of a person who acquires a negotiable instrument to be free of claims or defenses between the original parties. First, the person in possession of a negotiable instrument must be a *person entitled to enforce the instrument* as well as a *holder in due course* (or must be a holder who has the rights of a holder in due course through the shelter rule). If the person is neither, then she is subject to all claims or defenses to payment that any party to it has. Second, the only claims or defenses that the holder in due course has to worry about are so-called real defenses—those that affect the validity of the instrument—or claims that arose after she became a holder. For example, if the maker or drawer did not have legal capacity because she was a minor, the maker or drawer has a real defense. The holder in

due course does not have to worry about other defenses and claims that do not go to the validity of the instrument—the so-called personal defenses.

Real Defenses

There are some claims and defenses to payment of an instrument that go to the validity of the instrument. These claims and defenses are known as **real defenses**. They can be used as reasons against payment of a negotiable instrument to any holder, including a holder in due course (or a person who has the rights of a holder in due course). Real defenses include:

1. Minority or infancy that under state law makes the instrument void or voidable; for example, if Mark Miller, age 17, signs a promissory note as maker, he can use his lack of capacity to contract as a defense against paying it even to a holder in due course.

2. Incapacity that under state law makes the instrument void; for example, if a person has been declared mentally incompetent by a court, then the person has a real defense if state law declares all contracts entered into by the person after the adjudication of incompetency to be void.

3. Duress that voids or nullifies the obligation of a party liable to pay the instrument; for example, if Harold points a gun at his grandmother and forces her to execute a promissory note, the grandmother can use duress as a defense against paying it even to a holder in due course.

4. Illegality that under state law renders the obligation void; for example, in some states, checks and notes given in payment of gambling debts are void.

5. Fraud in the execution (or fraud in the factum). This occurs where a person signs a negotiable instrument without knowing or having a reasonable opportunity to know that it is a negotiable instrument or of its essential terms. For example, Amy Jones is an illiterate person who lives alone. She signs a document that is actually a promissory note but she is told that it is a grant of permission for a television set to be left in her house on a trial basis. Amy has a real defense against payment of the note even to a holder in due course. Fraud in the execution is distinguished from fraud in the inducement, which is only a personal defense.

6. Discharge in bankruptcy; for example, if the maker of a promissory note has had the debt discharged in a bankruptcy proceeding, she no longer is liable on it and has a real defense against payment [3–305(a)(1)].

Real defenses can be asserted even against a holder in due course of a negotiable instrument because it is more desirable to protect people who have signed negotiable instruments in these situations than it is to protect persons who have taken negotiable instruments in the ordinary course of business.

In addition to the real defenses discussed above, there are several other reasons why a person otherwise liable to pay an instrument would have a defense against payment that would be effective, even against a holder in due course. They include:

1. Forgery; for example, if a maker's signature has been put on the instrument without his authorization and without his negligence, the maker has a defense against payment of the note.

2. Alteration of a completed instrument. This is a partial defense against a holder in due course (or a person having the rights of a holder in due course), and a complete defense against a nonholder in due course. A holder in due course can enforce an altered instrument against the maker or drawer according to its original tenor.

3. Discharge. If a person takes an instrument with knowledge that the obligation of any party obligated on the instrument has been discharged, the person takes subject to the discharge even if the person is a holder in due course.

Personal Defenses

Personal defenses are legal reasons for avoiding or reducing liability of a person who is liable on a negotiable instrument. Generally, personal defenses arise out of the transaction in which the negotiable instrument was issued and are based on negotiable instruments law or contract law. A holder in due course of a negotiable instrument (or one who can claim the rights of one) is not subject to any personal defenses or claims that may exist between the original parties to the instrument. Personal defenses include:

1. Lack or failure of consideration; for example, a promissory note for $100 was given to someone without intent to make a gift and without receiving anything in return [3–303(b)].

2. Breach of contract, including breach of warranty; for example, a check was given in payment for repairs to an automobile but the repair work was defective.

3. Fraud in the inducement of any underlying contract; for example, an art dealer sells a lithograph to Cheryl, telling her that it is a Picasso, and takes Cheryl's check for $500 in payment. The art dealer knows that the lithograph is not a genuine Picasso but a forgery. Cheryl has been induced to make the purchase and to give her check by the art dealer's fraudulent representation. Because of this fraud, Cheryl has a personal defense against having to honor her check to the art dealer.

4. Incapacity to the extent that state law makes the obligation voidable, as opposed to void; for example, where state law makes the contract of a person of limited mental capacity but who has not been adjudicated incompetent voidable, the person has a personal defense to payment.

5. Illegality that makes a contract voidable, as opposed to void; for example, where the payee of a check given for certain professional services was required to have a license from the state but did not have one.

6. Duress, to the extent it is not so severe as to make the obligation void but rather only voidable; for example, if the instrument was signed under a threat to prosecute the maker's son if it was not signed, the maker might have a personal defense.

7. Unauthorized completion or material alteration of the instrument; for example, the instrument was completed in an unauthorized manner, or a material alteration was made to it, after it left the maker's or drawer's possession.

8. Nonissuance of the instrument, conditional issuance, and issuance for a special purpose; for example, the person in possession of the instrument obtained it by theft or by finding it, rather than through an intentional delivery of the instrument to him [3–105(b)].

9. Failure to countersign a traveler's check [3–106(c)].

10. Modification of the obligation by a separate agreement [3–117].

11. Payment that violates a restrictive indorsement [3–206(f)].

12. Breach of warranty when a draft is accepted (discussed in following chapter) [3–417(b)].

The following example illustrates the limited extent to which a maker or drawer can use personal defenses as a reason for not paying a negotiable instrument he signed. Suppose Trent Tucker bought a used truck from Honest Harry's and gave Harry a 60-day promissory note for $2,750 in payment for the truck. Honest Harry's "guaranteed" the truck to be in "good working condition," but in fact the truck had a cracked engine block. If Harry tries to collect the $2,750 from Trent, Trent could claim breach of warranty as a reason for not paying Harry the full $2,750 because Harry is not a holder in due course. However, if Harry negotiated the note to First National Bank and the bank was a holder in due course, the situation would be changed. If the bank tried to collect the $2,750 from Trent, Trent would have to pay the bank.

Trent cannot use his defense or claim of breach of warranty as a reason for not paying the bank, which qualified as a holder in due course. It is a personal defense. Trent must pay the bank the $2,750 and then pursue his breach of warranty claim against Harry.

The case below, *Standard Finance Co., Ltd. v. Ellis*, illustrates the distinction between fraud in the essence (a real defense) and fraud in the inducement (a personal defense) and discusses the real defense of duress and the personal defense of failure of consideration. In this case the court followed the Restatement (Second) of Contracts narrow interpretation of duress as excluding one spouse's alleged abuses of the other because the spouse claiming abuse did not prove that actual physical abuse compelled her to sign the instrument in question.

STANDARD FINANCE CO., LTD. v. ELLIS
657 P.2d 1056 (Hawaii Ct. App. 1983)

On September 30, 1976, Betty Ellis and her then husband, W. G. Ellis, executed and delivered a promissory note for $2,800 payable to Standard Finance Company. They paid nothing on the note, and on May 15, 1980, Standard Finance brought a collection action against Betty Ellis, who was divorced from W. G. The trial court awarded a judgment of $5,413.35 against Ellis. She appealed, claiming that she had defenses against payment of misrepresentation, duress, and failure of consideration.

Tanaka, Justice Betty Ellis indicates that "shortly before" W. G. Ellis executed the note, he gave her "constant assurance" that her "signature was a formality and that he alone was liable and that the debt would be repaid without any participation by her." Thereafter, Betty Ellis accompanied W. G. Ellis to Standard Finance's office and executed the note. Betty Ellis argues that W. G. Ellis's misrepresentation induced her to sign the note and since such misrepresentation dealt with its essential terms, her execution of the note was not a manifestation of her assent. Consequently, the note was *void ab initio* and unenforceable as to her.

The principles of law as to when misrepresentation prevents the formation of a contract and when it makes a contract voidable are set forth in Restatement (Second) of Contracts. Section 163 states:

Section 163. When a Misrepresentation Prevents Formation of a Contract.

If a misrepresentation as to the character or essential terms of a proposed contract induces conduct that appears to be a manifestation of assent by one who neither knows nor has reasonable opportunity to know of the character or essential terms of the proposed contract, his conduct is not effective as a manifestation of assent.

Comment a to Section 163 provides in part as follows:

This Section involves an application of that principle where a misrepresentation goes to what is sometimes called the "factum" or the "execution" rather than merely the "inducement." If, because of a misrepresentation as to the character or essential terms of a proposed contract, a party does not know or have reasonable opportunity to know of its character or essential terms, then he neither knows nor has reason to know that the other party may infer from his conduct that he assents to that contract. In such a case there is no effective manifestation of assent and no contract at all.

Based on the facts in the record, we hold as a matter of law that the misrepresentation by W. G. Ellis was not a "fraud in the factum" or a "fraud in the execution" to render the note void at its inception.

A common illustration of "fraud in the factum" is that of the "maker who is tricked into signing a note in the belief that it is merely a receipt or some other document."

In the instant case, no representation was made to Betty Ellis that the note was anything other than a note. In fact, as indicated above, it is uncontradicted that Standard Finance's representative explained the "terms and conditions of the note" to Betty and W. G. Ellis prior to their execution of the note. Comment 7 to Section 3–305 further states that the defense of "fraud in the factum" is that of "excusable ignorance of the contents of the writing signed" and the party claiming such fraud "must also have had no reasonable opportunity to obtain knowledge." *Page v. Krekey* and *First National Bank of Odessa v. Fazzari*, both cited by Betty Ellis, are examples in this category of "fraud in the factum." In *Page,* an intoxicated, illiterate defendant, who could not read or write, was induced to sign a guaranty on a false representation that it was an application for a license. In *Fazzari,* a defendant who was unable to read or write English was induced to sign a note upon the misrepresentation that it was a statement of wages earned.

The record in this case fails to show any fact constituting "excusable ignorance" of the contents of the paper signed or "no reasonable opportunity to obtain knowledge" on the part of Betty Ellis.

In her answers to interrogatories, Betty Ellis states that she was "forced" to sign the note under duress. "Physical beatings" and "psychological pressure" on her by Ellis for at least three years prior to signing the note constituted the duress. She argues that her execution of the note which was compelled by duress was not a manifestation of her assent. Thus, the note is void and unenforceable.

The law concerning duress resulting in void or voidable contracts is discussed in Restatement (Second) of Contracts.

Section 174 reads:

Section 174. When Duress by Physical Compulsion Prevents Formation of a Contract.

If conduct that appears to be a manifestation of assent by a party who does not intend to engage in that conduct is physically compelled by duress, the conduct is not effective as a manifestation of assent.

Comment a to Section 174 provides in part:

This Section involves an application of that principle to those relatively rare situations in which actual physical force has been used to compel a party to appear to assent to a contract. . . . The essence of this type of duress is that a party is compelled by physical force to do an act that he has no intention of doing.

We hold that as a matter of law the facts in the record do not constitute the type of duress which renders the note void under § 174. Such duress involves the use of actual physical force to compel a person to sign a document. It may include the example given in Comment 6 to Section 3–305 of an "instrument signed at the point of a gun" being void.

Here, the only evidence of duress is "physical beatings" and "psychological pressure" by W. G. Ellis on Betty Ellis over a course of three years prior to her signing of the note. Without more, such evidence does not constitute duress resulting in the voiding of the note. From such evidence it cannot reasonably be inferred that the physical beatings by W. G. Ellis directly resulted in Betty Ellis signing the note in question.

Finally, Betty Ellis claims that the entire amount of the loan of $2,800 went to Ellis and she received no part of it. Thus, there was lack or failure of consideration and summary judgment was improper. We cannot agree.

Standard Finance's check for $2,800 was made payable to "W. G. Ellis and Betty Ellis." The reverse side of the check bears the indorsement of "Betty Ellis." This was sufficient evidence of consideration for the transaction involved.

However, Betty Ellis states that she "never got the money or the use of it" and "it all went to my ex-husband and this was understood by Standard Finance." This fact does not constitute lack or failure of consideration. It is fundamental that consideration received by a co-maker on a note from the payee is sufficient consideration to bind the other co-maker.

Judgment for Standard Finance affirmed.

Note: Although this case was decided under the original version of Article 3, the same result would be anticipated under Revised Article 3.

The rule that a holder in due course takes a negotiable instrument free of any personal defenses or claims to it has been modified to some extent, particularly in relation to instruments given by consumers. These modifications will be discussed in the next section of this chapter.

Claims to the Instrument

For purposes of Revised Article 3, the term *claims* to an instrument can include:

1. A claim to ownership of the instrument by one who asserts that he is the owner and was wrongfully deprived of possession.
2. A claim of a lien on the instrument.
3. A claim for rescission of an indorsement.

A holder in due course takes free of claims that arose before she became a holder, but is subject to those arising when or after she becomes a holder in due course. For example, if a holder impairs the collateral given for an obligation, he may be creating a defense for an obligor.

Claims in Recoupment

A *claim in recoupment* is not actually a defense to an instrument but rather an *offset to liability*. For example, Ann Adams purchases a new automobile from Dealership, giving it a note for the balance of the purchase price beyond her down payment. After accepting delivery, she discovers a breach of warranty that the dealer fails to remedy. If Dealer has sold the note to a bank that subsequently seeks payment on the note from Adams, she has a claim in recoupment for breach of warranty. If the bank is a holder in due course, the claim in recoupment cannot be asserted against it. However, if the bank is a not a holder in due course, then Adams can assert the claim in recoupment to reduce the amount owing on the instrument at the time the action is brought against her on the note. Her claim could serve only to reduce the amount owing and not as a basis for a net recovery from the bank. However, if Dealer was the person bringing an action to collect the note Adams could assert the breach of warranty claim as a counterclaim and potentially might recover from Dealer any difference between the claim and the damages due for breach of warranty.

The obligor may assert a claim up to the amount of the instrument if the holder is the original payee, but cannot assert claims in recoupment against a holder in due course. In addition, the obligor may assert a claim against a transferee who does not qualify as a holder in due course, but only up to the amount owing on the instrument at the time it brought the claim in recoupment.

CLAIMS AND DEFENSES AGAINST PAYMENT OF NEGOTIABLE INSTRUMENTS

Claim or Defense	Examples
Real Defense Valid against all holders, including holders in due course and holders who have the rights of holders in due course.	1. Minority that under state law makes the contract void or voidable. 2. Other lack of capacity that makes the contract void. 3. Duress that makes the contract void. 4. Illegality that makes the contract void. 5. Fraud in the essence (fraud in the factum). 6. Discharge in bankruptcy.
Personal Defense Valid against plain holders of instruments—but not against holders in due course or holders who have the rights of in due course holders through the shelter rule.	1. Lack or failure of consideration. 2. Breach of contract (including breach of warranty). 3. Fraud in the inducement. 4. Lack of capacity that makes the contract voidable (except minority). 5. Illegality that makes the contract voidable. 6. Duress that makes the contract voidable

Claim or Defense	Examples
	7. Unauthorized completion of an incomplete instrument, or material alteration of the instrument.
	8. Nonissuance of the instrument.
	9. Failure to countersign a traveler's check.
	10. Modification of the obligation by a separate agreement.
	11. Payment that violates a restrictive indorsement.
	12. Breach of warranty when a draft is accepted.
Claim to an Instrument	1. Claim of ownership by someone who claims to be the owner and that he was wrongfully deprived of possession.
	2. Claim of a lien on the instrument.
	3. Claim for rescission of an indorsement.
Claims in Recoupment	1. Breach of warranty in the sale of goods for which the instrument was issued.

CHANGES IN THE HOLDER IN DUE COURSE RULE

Consumer Disadvantages

The rule that a holder in due course of a negotiable instrument is not subject to personal defenses between the original parties to it makes negotiable instruments a readily accepted substitute for money. This rule also can result in serious disadvantages to consumers. Consumers sometimes buy goods or services on credit and give the seller a negotiable instrument such as a promissory note. They often do this without knowing the consequences of their signing a negotiable instrument. If the goods or services are defective or not delivered, the consumer would like to withhold payment of the note until the seller corrects the problem or makes the delivery. Where the note is still held by the seller, the consumer can do this because any defenses of breach of warranty or nonperformance are good against the seller.

However, the seller may have negotiated the note at a discount to a third party such as a bank. If the bank qualifies as a holder in due course, the consumer must pay the note in full to the bank. The consumer's personal defenses are not valid against a holder in due course. The consumer must pay the holder in due course and then try to get her money back from the seller. This may be difficult if the seller cannot be found or will not accept responsibility. The consumer would be in a much stronger position if she could just withhold payment, even against the bank, until the goods or services are delivered or the performance is corrected.

State Legislation

Some state legislatures and courts have limited the holder in due course doctrine, particularly as it affects consumers. State legislation limiting the doctrine typically ammended state laws dealing with consumer credit transactions. For example, some state laws prohibit a seller from taking a negotiable instrument other than a check from a consumer in payment for consumer goods and services. Other state laws require promissory notes given by consumers in payment for goods and services to carry the words *consumer paper*; these state laws treat instruments with this legend as non-negotiable.[3] Thus, the rights of a consumer who has signed a negotiable instrument vary from state to state.

Federal Trade Commission Rules

The Federal Trade Commission (FTC) has promulgated a regulation designed to protect consumers against operation of the holder in due course rule. The FTC rule applies to persons who sell to consumers on credit and have the consumer sign a note

---

[3] Revised Article 3 expressly deals with these state variations in Section 3-106(d) and Official Comments 3 to 3-106 and Comments 3 to 3-305. Section 3-106(d) permits instruments containing legends or statements required by statutory or administrative law that preserve the obligor's rights to assert claims or defenses against subsequent holders as within Article 3 except that no holder can be a holder in due course.

or an installment sale contract or arrange third-party financing of the purchase. The seller must ensure that the note or the contract contains the following clause:

NOTICE: ANY HOLDER OF THIS CONSUMER CREDIT CONTRACT IS SUBJECT TO ALL CLAIMS AND DEFENSES WHICH THE DEBTOR COULD ASSERT AGAINST THE SELLER OF THE GOODS OR SERVICES OBTAINED PURSUANT HERETO OR WITH THE PROCEEDS HEREOF. RECOVERY HEREUNDER BY THE DEBTOR SHALL NOT EXCEED AMOUNTS PAID BY THE DEBTOR HERE-UNDER.

The effect of the notice is to make a potential holder of the note or contract subject to all claims and defenses of the consumer. This is illustrated in the *Ford Motor Credit Co. v. Morgan* case, which follows. If the note or contract does not include the clause required by the FTC rule, the consumer does not gain any rights that he would not otherwise have under state law, and a subsequent holder may qualify as a holder in due course. However, the FTC does have the right to seek a fine of as much as $10,000 against the seller who failed to include the notice.

FORD MOTOR CREDIT CO. v. MORGAN
536 N.E.2d 587 (Sup. Jud. Ct. Mass. 1989)

Rose and William Morgan purchased a new Mercury automobile from Neponset Lincoln Mercury, Inc. In order to finance their purchase through Ford Motor Credit Company, they signed a Note/Massachusetts Retail Installment Contract, a standard printed form contract prepared by Ford Credit. Printed in capital letters at the bottom of the first page of the form was the following statement:

NOTICE: ANY HOLDER OF THIS CONSUMER CREDIT CONTRACT IS SUBJECT TO ALL CLAIMS AND DEFENSES WHICH THE DEBTOR COULD ASSERT AGAINST THE SELLER OF GOODS OR SERVICES OBTAINED PURSUANT HERETO OR WITH THE PROCEEDS HEREOF. RECOVERY HEREUNDER BY THE DEBTOR SHALL NOT EXCEED AMOUNTS PAID BY THE DEBTOR HEREUNDER.

Ford Credit financed the car for $3,833, with payment to be made in 36 consecutive monthly installments of $137.13. During the first 18 months they owned the car, the Morgans experienced problems with it. These included water leaking into the trunk, a faulty head gasket, rust, hood misalignment, lack of shine, and, when left unattended, the car would shift from "park" to "reverse" and would have to be shifted back to "park" before it could be started. After making 15 payments totaling $2,056.95, the Morgans defaulted on their remaining obligation to Ford Credit. Before the car could be resold by Ford Credit, it was extensively vandalized; the Morgans had not maintained insurance coverage on it and it was a total loss.

Ford Credit sued the Morgans on the note, seeking recovery of $2,628.87 plus attorney's fees. The Morgans counterclaimed, seeking recovery against Ford Credit of claims for fraud and deceit, unfair and deceptive practices, and breach of express and implied warranties. In a special verdict, a jury found that the dealer knowingly made false representations to the Morgans, on which the Morgans relied. In turn, the trial court judge determined that this gave the Morgans a valid defense that extinguished the claim of Ford Motor Credit for the balance due on the credit contract. He also denied the Morgan's claim for an affirmative recovery against Ford Motor Credit on their counterclaim. The Morgans appealed to the Appeals Court, which transferred the case to the Supreme Judicial Court.

O'Connor, Justice The Morgans' first contention is that the explicit language of the notice provision contained in the contract, which subjects holder to all "claims and defenses which the debtor could assert against the seller" permits them to recover from Ford Credit for the dealer's wrongdoing. As the Morgans acknowledge, that notice provision is mandated by a Federal Trade Commission (FTC) rule that provides that it is an unfair or deceptive act or practice to take or receive a consumer credit contract which fails to include that provision. Therefore, we look to the FTC's purpose in enacting the rule as a guide to our interpretation of the contract provision.

The rule was designed to preserve the consumer's claims and defenses by cutting off the creditor's rights as a holder in due course. Under the holder in due course principle, which would apply were it not for the contract provision mandated by the FTC rule, the creditor could "assert his right to be paid by the consumer despite misrepresentation, breach of warranty or contract, or even fraud on the part of the seller, and despite the fact that the consumer's debt was generated by the sale. Thus, "being prevented from asserting the seller's breach of warranty or failure to perform against the assignee of the consumer's instrument, the consumer would be deprived of his most effective weapon—nonpayment." Eliminating holder in due course status prevents the assignee from demanding further payment when there has been assignor wrongdoing, and rearms the consumer with the "weapon" of nonpayment.

The FTC anticipated that in addition to nonpayment, affirmative recovery, a judgment for damages against the assignee-creditor, would be available in limited circumstances. Thus, in its statement of policy and purpose, the FTC spelled out the avenues of relief under the rule as follows: "A consumer can (1) defend a creditor suit for payment of an obligation by raising a valid claim against a seller as a setoff, and (2) maintain an affirmative action against a creditor who has received for a return of moneys paid on account."

However, the FTC made clear that "The latter alternative will only be available where a seller's breach is so substantial that a court is persuaded that rescission and restitution are justified. The most typical example of such a case would involve non-delivery, where delivery was scheduled after the date payments to a creditor commenced."

The FTC re-emphasized this point in stating, "consumers will not be in a position to obtain an affirmative recovery, unless they have actually commenced payments and received little or nothing of value from the seller. In the case of non-delivery, we believe the consumer is entitled to a refund of monies paid on account." Finally, the FTC anticipated that the rule would allow the courts to weigh the equities in the underlying sale, and "remain the final arbiters of equities between a seller and a consumer." Thus, the function of the rule is to allow consumers to stop payments, and, in limited circumstances not present here, where equity requires, to provide for a return of monies paid. The FTC did not intend that the rule would, as a matter of course, entitle a consumer to a full refund of monies paid on account. It follows, of course, that there is no merit to the Morgans' assertions that the contractual language allows them affirmative recovery even beyond the amount they paid in. To expose a creditor to further affirmative recovery would not only contravene the intention of the FTC, but "would place the creditor in the position of an absolute insurer or guarantor of the seller's performance." This we decline to do.

Judgment affirmed.

ETHICAL AND PUBLIC POLICY CONCERNS

1. If you are in the business of buying commercial paper—such as consumer notes—from businesses such as home improvement companies, how much of an ethical obligation, if any, do you have to look into the sales practices and performance records of the companies to whom the consumers have made the notes payable?

2. Suppose you have given a check in payment of a gambling debt in a state that makes such obligations void. Are there any ethical considerations involved as to whether you should assert the real defense of illegality against payment of the check to a holder in due course?

PROBLEMS AND PROBLEM CASES

1. Stone & Webster drew three checks in the total amount of $64,755.44 payable to the order of Westinghouse Electric Corporation. An employee of Stone & Webster obtained possession of the checks, forged Westinghouse's indorsement to them, and cashed them at the First National Bank & Trust Company and put the proceeds to his own use. The first two checks were indorsed in typewriting, "For Deposit Only: Westinghouse Electric Corporation By: Mr. O. D. Costine, Treasury Representative," followed by the ink signature "O. D. Costine." The third check was indorsed in typewriting, "Westinghouse Electric Corporation by: [Sgd.] O. D. Costine, Treasury Representative." Were the checks negotiated to the bank?

2. Louis Agaliotis took out a policy of insurance on his son, Robert. Louis paid all of the premiums on the policy, and under the terms of the policy he was entitled to any refunds on the premiums. The insurance company sent a refund check for $1,852 to Louis. By mistake, the check was made payable to "Robert L. Agaliotis." Louis indorsed the check "Robert L. Agaliotis"and cashed it. Robert then sued Louis to get the $1,852. Was Louis entitled to sign his son's name to the check and to keep the money when he cashed it?

3. Reliable Janitorial Service, Inc., maintained a bank account with AmSouth Bank. Rosa Pennington was employed by Reliable as a bookkeeper/office manager. She deposited checks made payable to Reliable but did not have authority to write checks on Reliable's account. Beginning in January 1985, Pennington obtained counter deposit slips from AmSouth. She wrote on the deposit slips that the depositor was "Reliable Janitorial Services, Inc.," but in the space for the account number, Pennington wrote the account number for her own personal account with AmSouth. She stamped the checks that were made payable to "Reliable Janitorial Service, Inc." with the indorsement "For Deposit Only, Reliable Carpet Cleaning, Inc." Over an 11-month period, Pennington was able to deposit 169 checks so indorsed. AmSouth credited the deposits to Pennington, not Reliable. Pennington spent all the funds that she diverted to her account. When Reliable discovered the fraud, it brought suit against AmSouth for conversion and sought to have its account credited with the improperly paid checks. Was AmSouth Bank liable to Reliable for the value of the restrictively indorsed checks that it paid inconsistently with the indorsement?

4. Reggie Bluiett worked at the Silver Slipper Gambling Hall and Saloon. She received her weekly paycheck made out to her from the Silver Slipper. She indorsed the check in blank and left it on her dresser at home. Fred Watkins broke into Bluiett's house and stole the check. Watkins took the check to the local auto store, where he bought two tires at a cost of $71.21. He obtained the balance of the check in cash. Could the auto store qualify as a holder in due course?

5. Horton wrote a check for $20,000 to Axe, who in turn indorsed it to Halbert. In return, Halbert advanced $8,000 in cash to Axe and promised to cancel a $12,000 debt owed him by Axe. The check, when presented by Halbert to the bank, was not paid due to insufficient funds. Halbert thus never regarded the debt as canceled. To what extent can Halbert be a holder in due course of the check?

6. In 1981, Anthony Maggio purchased a limited partnership interest in a new venture created by a former astronaut to develop an optoelectronic scanner designed to provide perimeter security for sprawling properties such as airfields, oil fields, and pipelines. As consideration for his partnership interest, Maggio gave the partnership a noninterest-bearing note for $55,000 maturing October 31, 1990. The partnership negotiated the note to a venture-capital company that in turn negotiated it to Goldman Sachs, which in turn negotiated it in 1988 to Northwestern National Insurance Company. Maggio's note was negotiated, along with a number of notes from other limited partners, at a 50 percent discount. On the due date, Northwestern demanded payment in full and Maggio refused, claiming that he was induced to enter the limited partnership by fraud. Could Northwestern be a holder in due course—and thus not subject to defense of fraud in the inducement—if it took the note at a 50 percent discount?

7. Eric Strober, the chairman of the board of Strober Bros., Inc., was approached by a business acquaintance, Sidney Pal, to make a short-term loan of $150,000 to a business venture operated by Pal. Pal indicated the loan would be collateralized by a negotiable certificate of deposit. Strober agreed to make the loan and made out a check for $150,000 drawn on the Strober Bros. account and made payable to the Tamara Trust, Pal's business venture. Pal urged the immediate delivery of the check to him and promised to deliver the negotiable certificate of deposit the next day. Strober agreed to deliver the check only on the condition that it be made non-negotiable, that a stop-payment order would be placed on it, and that a trust agreement and the certificate of deposit be delivered by 4 o'clock the following day, at which point the stop-payment order would be removed. Strober struck out the words "the order of" on the check so that it read "pay to Tamara Trust" and placed a stop-payment order on the check. Pal deposited the check in an account at the Key Bank and was allowed to draw out the funds in the account. When the check was sent to Strober's bank, payment was refused and it was returned marked "Payment Stopped." Pal never delivered a negotiable certificate of deposit. Key Bank brought suit against Strober Bros. on the check seeking to hold Strober Bros. liable on the basis of its drawer's liability on the check. Key Bank claimed to be a holder in due course of the check who held it free of any defenses Strober Bros. might have against Pal and the Tamara Trust. Was Key Bank a holder in due course of the check?

8. Two smooth-talking salesmen for Rich Plan of New Orleans called on Leona and George Henne at their home. They sold the Hennes a home food plan. One of the salesmen suggested that the Hennes sign a blank promissory note. The Hennes refused. The salesman then wrote in ink "$100" as the amount and "4" as the number of installments in which the note was to be paid, and the Hennes signed the note. Several days later, the Hennes received a payment book from Nationwide Acceptance. The payment book showed that a total of $843.38 was due, payable in 36 monthly installments. Rich Plan had erased the "$100" and "4" on the note and typed in the figures "$843.38" and "36." The erasures were cleverly done but were visible to the naked eye. Rich Plan then negotiated the Hennes' note to Nationwide Acceptance. The Hennes refused to pay the note. Nationwide claimed that it was a holder in due course and was entitled to receive payment. Was Nationwide Acceptance a holder in due course?

9. Culver, a farmer, entered into a business arrangement with Nasib Kalliel whereby Kalliel was to assume control over the financial aspects of Culver's farm while Culver was to manage the farming operation. Subsequently, Culver notified Kalliel that he urgently needed money to stave off foreclosure. One week later, $30,000 was wire-transferred from the Rexford State Bank in Rexford, Kansas, to Culver's bank account in King City, Missouri. Culver knew that the money had come from the Rexford State Bank but thought that Kalliel would be responsible for its repayment. A week later, Culver was approached by one of Kalliel's employees, Jerry Gilbert, who told him that "Rexford State Bank wanted to know where the $30,000 went . . . for their records." Gilbert presented Culver with a document and asked him to sign it. Gilbert led Culver to believe he was merely signing a receipt for the $30,000 he had received. In fact, Culver had signed a preprinted promissory note form that contained a number of blanks. The name of the payee, "The Rexford State Bank," was printed on the note along with a provision that principal and accrued interest were to be paid to the payee at its offices. While Culver assumed that the figure $30,000 would eventually be written on the document, someone completed the note showing the principal amount as $50,000, the execution date as August 2, 1984, the maturity date as February 2, 1985, and that interest would be 14½ percent per annum until maturity and 18½ percent after that. Although Culver received only $30,000, Rexford State Bank deposited the full $50,000 in an account controlled by Kalliel. The Rexford Bank became insolvent and the Federal Deposit Insurance Corporation took over as its receiver and purchased a number of the bank's assets, including the note signed by Culver. At the time, the FDIC had no knowledge of the circumstances surrounding the signing and completion of the note. The FDIC brought suit against Culver to collect on the note. Culver sought to defend on the grounds he had been tricked into signing the note thinking it was only a receipt. He claimed he had a defense of "fraud in the factum" that was good even against a holder in due course (the FDIC). Did Culver have a real defense of fraud in the factum that could be asserted as a defense against payment of the promissory note to a holder in due course?

10. Ralph Herrmann wrote a check for $10,000 payable to Ormsby House, a hotel-casino in Carson City, Nevada, and exchanged it for three counter checks he had written earlier that evening to acquire gaming chips. Ormsby House was unable to collect the proceeds from the check because Herrmann had insufficient funds in his account. The debt evidenced by the check was assigned to Sea Air Support, Inc., d/b/a Automated Accounts Associates, for collection. Sea Air was also unsuccessful in its attempts to collect and filed a lawsuit against Herrmann to recover on the dishonored check. Nevada law then provided that all instruments drawn for the purpose of reimbursing or repaying any money knowingly lent or advanced for gaming are "utterly void, frustrate, and of none effect." Is Herrmann still liable to Sea Air?

11. Pedro and Paula de la Fuente were visited by a representative of Aluminum Industries, Inc., who was seeking to sell them aluminum siding for their home. They agreed to purchase the siding and signed a number of documents, including a retail installment contract and a promissory note for $9,138.24. The contract granted Aluminum Industries, Inc., a first lien on the de la Fuentes' residence; this was in violation of the Texas Civil Code, which prohibited such provisions. The promissory note contained a notice in bold type as required by the Federal Trade Commission. It read in part:

NOTICE: ANY HOLDER OF THIS CONSUMER CREDIT CONTRACT IS SUBJECT TO ALL CLAIMS AND DEFENSES WHICH THE DEBTOR COULD ASSERT AGAINST THE SELLER OF GOODS OR SERVICES OBTAINED PURSUANT HERETO WITH THE PROCEEDS THEREOF.

Aluminum Industries assigned the promissory note and first lien to Home Savings Association. Aluminum Industries subsequently went out of business.

Home Savings brought suit against the de la Fuentes to collect the balance due on the note. Home Savings contended that it was a holder in due course and that the de la Fuentes could not assert any defenses against it that they had against Aluminum Industries. Can an assignee of a consumer promissory note that includes the notice required by the FTC qualify as a holder in due course?

12. *Video Case.* See "TV Repair." Arnold takes his old TV set to an appliance store for repair and purchases a new TV from the store. He signs a promissory note, which provides for installment payments, for the balance due on the new set. The note contains the notice that the FTC requires be included in consumer credit instruments. Arnold discovers that the TV is defective after making the first payment on the note to the appliance store. The appliance store assigns the promissory note to Acme Finance Company, which notifies Arnold of its interest in the note and that he should make his payments on the note to it. Arnold advises Acme Finance that he will not make any further payments on the promissory note until the TV is repaired. If Arnold has a valid claim for breach of warranty of merchantability of the TV set, can he assert this as a defense against paying the note to the appliance store and/or to Acme Finance?

CHAPTER
3 2

LIABILITY OF

PARTIES

INTRODUCTION

Thus far in Part 7, Commercial Paper, the focus has been on the nature of and requirements for negotiable instruments, as well as the rights that an owner of an instrument can obtain and how to obtain them. Another important aspect to negotiable instruments concerns how a person becomes liable on a negotiable instrument and the nature of the liability incurred.

When a person signs a promissory note, he expects to be liable for paying the note on the day it is due. Similarly, when a person signs a check and mails it off to pay a bill, she expects that the drawee bank will pay it from funds in her checking account and that if her account contains insufficient funds to cover it, she will have to make it good out of other funds she has. These liabilities concerning instruments are commonly understood.

However, there are a number of other ways in which a person can become liable on a negotiable instrument. For example, a person who indorses a paycheck assumes liability on it; and a bank that cashes a check with a forged indorsement on it is liable for conversion of the check. This chapter and the following chapter discuss the liabilities of the various parties to a negotiable instrument. These two chapters also explain what happens when an instrument is not paid when it is supposed to be paid. For example, a check usually should not be paid if the drawer's account contains insufficient funds or if the check has been forged. In addition, this chapter discusses the ways in which liability on an instrument can be discharged.

LIABILITY IN GENERAL

Liability on negotiable instruments flows from signatures on the instruments as well as actions taken concerning them. It can arise from the fact that a person has signed a negotiable instrument or has authorized someone else to sign it. The liability depends on the capacity in which the person signs the instrument. Liability also arises from (1) transfer or presentment of an instrument, (2) negligence relating to the issuance, alteration, or indorsement of the instrument, (3) improper payment, or (4) conversion.

CONTRACTUAL LIABILITY

When a person signs a negotiable instrument, whether as maker, drawer, or indorser, or in some other capacity, she generally becomes contractually liable on the instrument. As mentioned above, this contractual liability depends on the capacity in which the person signed the instrument. The terms of the contract of the parties to a negotiable instrument are not set out in the text of the instrument. Rather, Article 3 of the Uniform Commercial Code supplies the terms, which are as much a part of the instrument as if they were part of its text.

Primary and Secondary Liability

A party to a negotiable instrument may be either *primarily liable* or *secondarily liable* for payment of it. A person who is primarily liable has agreed to pay the negotiable instrument. For example, the maker of a promissory note is the person who is primarily liable on the note. A person who is secondarily liable is like a guarantor on a contract; Article 3 requires a secondary party to pay the negotiable instrument only if a person who is primarily liable defaults on that obligation. Chapter 27, Introduction to Credit and Secured Transactions, discusses guarantors.

Obligation of a Maker

The **maker** of a promissory note is primarily liable for payment of it. The maker makes an unconditional promise to pay a fixed amount of money and is responsible for making good on that promise. The obligation of the maker is to pay the negotiable instrument according to its terms at the time he issues it or, if it is not issued, then according to its terms at the time it first came into possession of a holder [3–412].[1] If the material terms of the note are not complete when the maker signs it, then the maker's obligation is to pay the note as it is completed, provided that the terms filled in are as authorized. If the instrument is incomplete when the maker signs it and it is completed in an unauthorized manner, then the maker's liability will depend on whether the person seeking to enforce the instrument can qualify as a holder in due course.

The obligation of the maker is owed to (1) a *person entitled to enforce the instrument* or (2) any indorser who paid the instrument pursuant to her indorser's liability (discussed below). A person entitled to enforce an instrument includes: (1) the holder of the instrument, (2) a nonholder in possession of the instrument who has the rights of a holder, and (3) a person not in possession of the instrument who has the right to enforce the instrument under section 3–309 that deals with lost, destroyed, or stolen instruments.

Revised Article 3 provides that the *drawer of a cashier's check* has the same obligation as the maker or issuer of a note. Thus, it treats a draft drawn on a bank drawer the same as a note for purposes of the issuer's liability rather than treating the issuer as a drawer of a draft [3–412].

Obligation of a Drawee or an Acceptor

The **acceptor** of a draft is obligated to pay the draft according to the terms at the time of its acceptance. As was discussed in Chapter 30, acceptance is the drawee's signed engagement to honor the draft as presented—and is commonly indicated by the signature of the acceptor on the instrument itself. The acceptor's obligation extends to (1) a person entitled to enforce the draft, (2) the drawer, and (3) an indorser who paid the instrument pursuant to her indorser's liability [3–413].

If the certification of a check or other acceptance of a draft states the amount certified or accepted, the obligation of the acceptor is that amount. If the certification or acceptance does not state an amount, or if the amount of the instrument is subsequently raised, and then the instrument is negotiated to a holder in due course, the obligation of the acceptor is the amount of the instrument at the time a holder in due course takes it [3–413(b)].

At the time a check or other draft issues, no party is primarily liable on it. Usually, the drawee bank pays a check when it is presented for payment and no person becomes primarily liable. However, the drawer or a holder of the check may ask the drawee bank to accept or certify the check. The drawee bank certifies the check by signing its name to the check and, with that act, accepts liability as acceptor. The drawee bank debits, or takes the money out of, the drawer's account and holds the money to pay the check. If the drawee bank certifies the check, it becomes primarily, or absolutely, liable for paying

---

[1]The numbers in brackets refer to sections of the Uniform Commercial Code (UCC), which is reproduced in the appendix.

the check as it reads at the time of its acceptance, [3–413]. Similarly, when a trade draft is presented for acceptance or payment, no party is liable on it. If the named drawee accepts it, perhaps by writing his name on the face of it, then he accepts the obligations set forth in the instrument.

A drawee has no liability on a check or other draft unless it certifies or accepts the check or draft—that is, agrees to be liable on it. However, a drawee bank that refuses to pay a check when it is presented for payment may be liable to the drawer for wrongfully refusing payment, assuming the drawer had sufficient funds in his checking account to cover it. The next chapter discusses this liability of a drawee bank.

Obligation of a Drawer

The **drawer**'s obligation is that if the drawee dishonors an unaccepted check (or draft), the drawer will pay the check (or draft) according to its terms at the time he issued it or, if it was not issued, according to its terms at the time it first came into possession of a holder. If the draft was not complete when issued but was completed as authorized, then the obligation is to pay it as completed. If any completion is not authorized, then the obligation will depend on whether the person seeking to enforce the instrument can qualify as a holder in due course. A person entitled to enforce the draft or an indorser who paid the draft pursuant to his indorser's liability may enforce the drawer's obligation [3–414(b)].

For example, Janis draws a check on her account at First National Bank payable to the order of Collbert. If First National does not pay the check when Collbert presents it for payment, then Janis is liable to Collbert on the basis of her drawer's obligation.

If a draft is accepted by a bank—for example, if the drawee bank certifies a check—the drawer is discharged of her drawer's obligation. If someone other than a bank accepts a draft, then the obligation of the drawer to pay the draft, if the draft is dishonored, is the same as an indorser (discussed next) [3–414(c) and (d)].

The case that follows, *First American Bank of Virginia v. Litchfield Company of South Carolina, Inc.*, illustrates circumstances under which a drawer might be liable on its drawer's contractual obligation.

FIRST AMERICAN BANK OF VIRGINIA v. LITCHFIELD COMPANY OF SOUTH CAROLINA, INC.
353 S.E.2d 143 (S.C. Ct. App. 1987)

On February 9, 1983, Litchfield Company drew a check payable to Jensen Farley Pictures, Inc., in the amount of $13,711.11, on its account with Bankers Trust of South Carolina. Litchfield sent the check to Jensen Farley, which negotiated the check on September 16 to First American Bank of Virginia with whom it had a checking account. First American gave Jensen Farley immediate credit on the check and forwarded it to Bankers Trust for payment. Unknown to First American, Litchfield had given Bankers Trust an oral stop-payment order on the check. On September 19, Jensen Farley withdrew most of the balance in its First American account; it subsequently filed for bankruptcy. On September 21, Bankers Trust returned the Litchfield check to First American marked "payment stopped."

First American then sued Litchfield, claiming that as drawer of the check, it was liable to First American, a holder in due course of the check. The trial court awarded First American Bank judgment for $9,369.37 (representing the amount it had been unable to recover from Jensen Farley), and Litchfield appealed.

Bell, Judge   The drawer of a check engages that upon dishonor he will pay the amount of the draft to a holder in due course. Section 3–413(2). The drawer has the right to stop payment, but remains liable on the instrument to a holder in due course. Section 4–403 and comment 8; section 3–413(2). Since Litchfield has conceded First American was a holder in due course, Litchfield remains liable on the instrument unless it can establish a valid defense or set off.

Litchfield argues that its liability was discharged by First American's failure to give timely notice the check had been dishonored. This defense is unavailing for two reasons.

First, failure to give notice of dishonor discharges a drawer only to the extent he is deprived of funds maintained with the drawee bank to cover the check because the drawee bank became insolvent during the delay. Sections 3–501(2)(b) and 3–502(1)(b). A drawer is not otherwise discharged. In this case, Litchfield was not deprived of any funds in its account with Bankers Trust nor did Bankers Trust become insolvent during the delay.

Second, notice of dishonor is excused when the party to be charged has himself countermanded payment. Section 3–511(2)(b). Since Litchfield ordered payment stopped, it was not entitled to notice of dishonor.

Litchfield argues strenuously that it is unfair to apply section 3–511(2)(b) to the drawer of a check who has no means of knowing whether the check has been negotiated to a holder. This reasoning misses the mark. The maker of an outstanding negotiable instrument is presumed to know the instrument is subject to transfer to a holder in due course. The drawer is often without actual knowledge that his check has been negotiated, but that ignorance in no way diminishes the rights of a holder in due course. To hold otherwise would, as a practical matter, destroy the negotiability of a check.

Judgment for First American affirmed.

Note: Although this case was decided under the original Article 3 and Revised Article 3 restates the obligation of a drawer, the same result would be anticipated under Revised Article 3.

Obligation of an Indorser

A person who indorses a negotiable instrument usually is secondarily liable. Unless the indorser qualifies or otherwise disclaims liability, the **indorser**'s obligation on dishonor of the instrument is to pay the amount due on the instrument according to its terms at the time he indorsed it or if he indorsed it when incomplete, then according to its terms when completed, provided that it is completed as authorized. The indorser owes the obligation to a person entitled to enforce the instrument or to any subsequent indorser who had to pay it [3–415].

The indorser can avoid this liability only by qualifying its indorsement, such as ''without recourse,'' on the instrument when he indorses it [3–415(b)].

Indorsers are liable to each other in the chronological order in which they indorse, from the last indorser back to the first. For example, Mark Maker gives a promissory note to Paul Payee. Payee indorses it and negotiates it to Fred First, who indorses it and negotiates it to Shirley Second. If Maker does not pay the note when Second takes it to him for payment, then Second can require First to pay it to her. First is secondarily liable on the basis of his indorsement. First, in turn, can require Payee to pay him because Payee also became secondarily

liable when he indorsed it. Then, Payee is left to try to collect the note from Maker. Second also could have skipped over First and proceeded directly against Payee on his indorsement. First has no liability to Payee, however, because First indorsed after Payee indorsed the note.

If a bank accepted a draft (for example, by certifying a check) after an indorsement is made, the acceptance discharges the liability of the indorser [3–415(d)]. If notice of dishonor is required and proper notice is not given to the indorser, she is discharged of liability [3–415(c)]. And, where no one presents a check or gives it to a depositary bank for collection within 30 days after the date of an indorsement, the indorser's liability is discharged [3–415(e)].

Obligation of an Accommodation Party

An **accommodation party** is a person who signs a negotiable instrument for the purpose of lending her credit to another party to the instrument but is not a direct beneficiary of the value given for the instrument. For example, a bank might be reluctant to lend money to—and take a note from—Payee because of his shaky financial condition. However, the bank may be willing to lend money to Payee if he signs the note and has a relative or a friend also sign the note as an accommodation maker.

The obligation of an accommodation party depends on the capacity in which the party signs the instrument [3–419]. If Payee has his brother Sam sign a note as an accommodation maker, then Sam has the same contractual liability as a maker. Sam is primarily liable on the note. The bank may ask Sam to pay the note before asking Payee to pay. However, if Sam pays the note to the bank, he has the right to recover his payment from Payee, the person on whose behalf he signed.

Similarly, if a person signs a check as an accommodation indorser, his contractual liability is that of an indorser. If the accommodation indorser has to make good on that liability, he can collect in turn from the person on whose behalf he signed.

Signing an Instrument

No person is contractually liable on a negotiable instrument unless she or her authorized agent has signed it and the signature is binding on the represented person. A signature can be any name, word, or mark used in place of a written signature [3–401]. As discussed earlier, the capacity in which a person signs an instrument determines his liability on the instrument.

Signature by an Authorized Agent

An authorized agent can sign a negotiable instrument. If Sandra Smith authorized her attorney to sign checks as her agent, then she is liable on any checks properly signed by the attorney as her agent. All negotiable instruments signed by corporations have to be signed by an agent of the corporation who is authorized to sign negotiable instruments.

If a person purporting to act as a representative signs an instrument by signing either the name of the represented person or the name of the signer, that signature binds the represented person to the same extent she would be bound if the signature were on a simple contract. If the represented person has authorized the signature of the representative, it is the "authorized signature of the represented person" and the represented person is liable on the instrument, whether or not identified in the instrument. This brings the Code in line with the general principle of agency law that binds an undisclosed

principal on a simple contract. For example, if Principal authorizes Agent to borrow money on Principal's behalf and Agent signs her name to a note without disclosing that the signature was on behalf of Principal, Agent is liable on the note. In addition, if the person entitled to enforce the note can show that Principal authorized Agent to sign on his behalf, then Principal is liable on the note as well.

When a representative signs an authorized signature to an instrument, then the representative is not bound provided the signature shows "unambiguously" that the signature was made on behalf of the represented person who is named in the instrument [3–402(b)(1)]. For example, if a note is signed "XYZ, Inc., by Flanigan, Treasurer," Flanigan is not liable on the instrument in his own right, but XYZ, Inc., is liable.

If an authorized representative signs his name as the representative of a drawer of a check without noting his representative status but the check is payable from an account of the represented person who is identified on the check, the signer is not liable on the check as long as his signature was authorized [3–402(c)]. The rationale for this provision is that because most checks today identify the person on whose account the check is drawn, no one is deceived into thinking that the person signing the check is meant to be liable.

Except for the check situation noted above, a representative is personally liable to a holder in due course that took the instrument without notice that the representative was not intended to be liable if (1) the form of the signature does not show unambiguously that the signature was made in a representative capacity or (2) the instrument does not identify the represented person. As to persons other than a holder in due course without notice of the representative nature of the signature, the representative is liable *unless* she can prove that the original parties did not intend her to be liable on the instrument [3–402(b)(2)].

Thus, if an agent or a representative signs a negotiable instrument on behalf of someone else, the agent should indicate clearly that he is signing as the representative of someone else. For example, Kim Darby, the president of Swimwear, Inc., is authorized to sign negotiable instruments for the company. If Swimwear borrows money from the bank and the bank asks her to sign a 90-day promissory note, Darby should sign it either "Swimwear, Inc. by Kim Darby, President" or

"Kim Darby, President, for Swimwear, Inc." If Kim Darby signed the promissory note merely "Kim Darby," she could be personally liable on the note. Similarly, if Clara Carson authorizes Arthur Anderson, an attorney, to sign checks for her, Anderson should make sure either that the checks identify Clara Carson as the account involved or should sign them "Clara Carson by Arthur Anderson, Agent." Otherwise, he risks being personally liable on them.

The liability of an authorized representative is discussed in the case that follows, *Mestco Distributors, Inc., v. Stamps.*

MESTCO DISTRIBUTORS, INC. v. STAMPS
17 UCC Rep.2d 174 (Tex. Ct. App. 1992)

On seven separate occasions between May 1985 and December 1986, Mestco Distributors, Inc., loaned funds for business operations to Innovative Timber Specialties, Inc. (ITS), in which Mestco was a shareholder. The seven notes were signed as follows:

Promissory note 1, May 17, 1985, signed:

I.T.S. Inc.
by Ralph W. Stamps
Secty. Treas

Promissory note 2, June 25, 1985, signed:

Ralph W. Stamps

Promissory note 3, December 23, 1985, signed:

Innovative Timber Specialties
Inc.
by Secty-treas
Ralph W. Stamps

Promissory note 4, July 16, 1985, signed:

Ralph W. Stamps
Secty-Treas. I.T.S. Inc.

Promissory note 5, December 9, 1985, signed:

Ralph W. Stamps

Promissory note 6, August 6, 1986, signed:

Innovative Timber Specialties
Inc.
by Ralph W. Stamps

Promissory note 7, December 31, 1986, signed:

Ralph W. Stamps
Innovative Timber Specialties
Inc.
by: Secretary

The notes were not paid and Mestco sued Stamps, seeking to hold him personally liable for paying the seven notes. The trial court held in favor of Stamps, and Mestco appealed.

Ellis, Judge   Mestco argues that none of the promissory notes meet the requirements of Section 3–403, and, therefore, Stamps was required to present evidence to overcome the presumption of individual liability as to all seven notes. We disagree.

Section 3–403(c) provides that a signature is established as being in a representative capacity *if it has the name of an organization preceded or followed by an authorized individual's name and office.* Four of the promissory notes meet these requirements (May 17, 1985; December 23, 1985; July 16, 1986; December 31, 1986). Clearly, these notes listed the names of the organization followed or preceded by Ralph Stamps' name and his office, designated as Secretary or Scty-Treas. Accordingly, there was evidence to support the trial court's finding that these four notes were executed in a representative capacity.

Three of the promissory notes clearly did not meet the requirements of Section 3–403. Two notes were signed solely with Ralph Stamps' name and one note was signed "Innovative Timber Specialties, Inc. by Ralph W. Stamps." As Mestco correctly points out, if a signature is not shown to be in a representative capacity pursuant to Section 3–403(c), the signer/maker, in a dispute between the immediate parties, has the burden to offer proof that he signed only in a representative capacity.

Although there is no evidence in the present case that Stamps actually told Mestco that he was signing the notes in a representative capacity, there was evidence of prior dealings between the parties as well as circumstances that communicated to Mestco that Stamps was executing the notes in a representative capacity.

The evidence before the court was as follows. Henry Mest was president and owner of Mestco Distributors, Inc. He was in business for 30 years in La Marque, Texas. Stamps and Mest knew each other for more than 30 years. Stamps approached Mest regarding investing in ITS after its original formation in 1982. They each became shareholders in ITS, neither being majority shareholders. Both became officers and Mest became a director. The chief operating officer and president resigned in 1985 and Mest took over. In 1985 Mest went to ITS's job site once or twice a week and was fully aware of what was going on with the business.

Stamps managed ITS from 1985 to 1986 per an agreement with Mest. Stamps would also let Mestco know of ITS's financial need. Mestco and Stamps both from time to time loaned money to ITS as needed. In 1986, both Mestco and Stamps repaid in equal amounts a loan made to ITS in the amount of $150,000. Mestco received at least seven notes in addition to the notes the subject of this suit. These notes were later written off by Mestco as bad debts. The seven promissory notes involved in the present suit were prepared at Mest's direction. The payment of each of the notes was a promise of ITS's named in the subject notes and there was no understanding that the loans represented loans to Stamps individually. The funding of the notes was to ITS directly and were often deposited to ITS's bank account by Mestco's accountant. Also the notes were carried on Mestco's books as notes receivable from ITS and not as notes receivable from Stamps. Further, the notes were charged-off by Mestco in 1986 and 1987.

Accordingly, there was sufficient evidence showing that Mestco knew the notes were executed in a representative capacity and not Stamps individually, and past dealings supported that Stamps executed in a representative capacity.

Judgment for Stamps affirmed.

Note: Although this case was decided under the original version of Article 3, the same result would likely be reached under Revised Article 3.

Unauthorized Signature

If someone signs a person's name to a negotiable instrument without that person's authorization or approval, the signature does not bind the person whose name appears. However, the signature is effective as the signature of the unauthorized signer in favor of any person who in good faith pays the instrument or takes it for value [3–403(a)]. For example, if Tom Thorne steals Ben Brown's checkbook and signs Brown's name to a check, Brown is not liable on the check because Brown had not authorized Thorne to sign Brown's name. However,

Thorne can be liable on the check because he did sign it, even though he did not sign it in his own name. Thorne's forgery of Brown's signature operates as Thorne's signature. Thus, if Thorne cashed the check at the bank, Thorne would be liable to it; or if he negotiated it to a store for value, he would be liable to the store to make it good.

Even though a signature is not "authorized" when it is put on an instrument initially, it can be ratified later by the person represented [3–403(a)]. It should also be noted that if more than one person must sign to constitute the authorized signature of an organization, the signature of the organization is unauthorized if one of the required signatures is lacking [3–403(b)]. Corporate and other accounts sometimes require multiple signatures as a matter of maintaining sound financial control.

CONTRACTUAL LIABILITY IN OPERATION

To bring the contractual liability of the various parties to a negotiable instrument into play, it is generally necessary that the instrument be *presented for payment*. In addition, to hold the parties that are secondarily liable on the instrument to their contractual liability, it is generally necessary that the instrument be *presented for payment* and *dishonored*.

Presentment of a Note

The maker of a note is primarily liable to pay it when it is due. Normally, the holder takes the note to the maker at the time it is due and asks the maker to pay it. Sometimes, the note may provide for payment to be made at a bank, or the maker sends the payment to the holder at the due date. The party to whom the holder presents the instrument, without dishonoring the instrument, may (1) require the exhibition of the instrument, (2) ask for reasonable identification of the person making presentment, (3) ask for evidence of his authority to make it if he is making it for another person, or (4) return the instrument for lack of any necessary indorsement, (5) ask that a receipt be signed for any payment made, and (6) ask for surrender of the instrument if full payment is made [3–501].

Dishonor of a note occurs if the maker does not pay the amount due when: (1) it is presented in the case of (*a*) a demand note or (*b*) a note payable at or through a bank on a definite date that is presented

on or after that date, or (2) if it is not paid on the date payable in the case of a note payable on a definite date but not payable at or through a bank [3–502]. If the maker or payor dishonors the note, the holder can seek payment from any persons who indorsed the note before the holder took it. The basis for going after the indorsers is that they are secondarily liable. To hold the indorsers to their contractual obligation, the holder must give them notice of the dishonor. The notice can be either written or oral [3–503].

For example, Susan Strong borrows $1,000 from Jack Jones and gives him a promissory note for $1,000 at 9 percent annual interest payable in 90 days. Jones indorses the note "Pay to the order of Ralph Smith" and negotiates the note to Ralph Smith. At the end of the 90 days, Smith takes the note to Strong and presents it for payment. If Strong pays Smith the $1,000 and accrued interest, she can have Smith mark it "paid" and give it back to her. If Strong does not pay the note to Smith when he presents it for payment, then she has dishonored the note. Smith should give notice of the dishonor to Jones and advise him that he intends to hold Jones secondarily liable on his indorsement. Smith may collect payment of the note from Jones. Jones, after making the note good to Smith, can try to collect the note from Strong on the ground that she defaulted on the contract she made as maker of the note. Of course, Smith could also sue Strong on the basis of her maker's obligation.

Presentment of a Check or a Draft

The holder should present a check or draft to the drawee. The presentment can be either for payment or for acceptance (certification) of the check or draft. Under Revised Article 3, the presentment may be made by any commercially reasonable means, including a written, oral, or electronic communication [3–501]. No one is primarily obligated on a check or draft, and the drawee is not obligated on a check or draft unless it accepts (certifies) it [3–408]. An acceptance of a draft is the drawee's signed commitment to honor the draft as presented. The acceptance must be written on the draft, and it may consist of the drawee's signature alone [3–409].

A drawer who writes a check issues an order to the drawee to pay a certain amount out of the drawer's account to the payee (or to someone authorized by the payee). This order is not an assignment of the funds in the drawer's account [3–408]. The drawee bank does not have an obligation to the payee to pay the check unless it certifies the check. However, the drawee bank usually does have a separate contractual obligation (apart from Article 3) to the drawer to pay any properly payable checks for which funds are available in the drawer's account.

For example, Janet Payne has $100 in a checking account at First National Bank and writes a check for $10 drawn on First National and payable to Ralph Smith. The writing of the check is the issuance of an order by Payne to First National to pay $10 from her account to Smith or to whomever Smith requests it to be paid. First National owes no obligation to Smith to pay the $10 unless it has certified the check. However, if Smith presents the check for payment and First National refuses to pay it even though there are sufficient funds in Payne's account, then First National is liable to Payne for breaching its contractual obligation to her to pay items properly payable from existing funds in her account. Chapter 33, Checks and Documents of Title, discusses the liability of a bank for wrongful dishonor of checks in more detail.

If the drawee bank does not pay or certify a check when it is properly presented for payment or acceptance (certification), the drawee bank has dishonored the check [3–502]. Similarly, if a draft is not paid on the date it is due (or accepted by the drawee on the due date for acceptance), it has been dishonored. The holder of the draft or check then can proceed against either the drawer or any indorsers on their secondary liability. To do so, the holder must give them notice of the dishonor [3–503]. Notice of dishonor, like presentment, can be by any commercially reasonable means, including oral, written, or electronic communication. Under certain circumstances, set out in section 3–504, presentment or notice of dishonor may be excused.

Suppose Matthews draws a check for $100 on her account at a bank payable to the order of Williams. Williams indorses the check "Pay to the order of Clark, Williams" and negotiates it to Clark. When Clark takes the check to the bank, it refuses to pay the check because there are insufficient funds in Matthews's account to cover the check. The check has been presented and dishonored. Clark has two options: He can proceed against Williams on Williams's secondary liability as an indorser (be-

cause by putting an unqualified indorsement on the check, Williams is obligated to make the check good if it was not honored by the drawee). Or, he can proceed against Matthews on Matthews's obligation as drawer because in drawing the check, Matthews must pay any person entitled to enforce the check if it is dishonored and he is given notice. Because Clark dealt with Williams, Clark is probably more likely to return the check to Williams for payment. Williams then has to go against Matthews on Matthews's liability as drawer.

Time of Presentment

If an instrument is payable at a definite time, the holder should present it for payment on the due date. In the case of a demand instrument, the nature of the instrument, trade or bank usage, and the facts of the particular case determine a reasonable time for presentment for acceptance or payment. In a farming community, for example, a reasonable time to present a promissory note that is payable on demand may be six months or within a short time after the crops are ready for sale, because the holder commonly expects payment from the proceeds of the crops.

WARRANTY LIABILITY

Whether or not a person signs a negotiable instrument, a person who transfers such an instrument or presents it for payment or acceptance may incur liability on the basis of certain implied warranties. These warranties are (1) **transfer warranties**, which persons who transfer negotiable instruments make to their transferees; and (2) **presentment warranties**, which persons who present negotiable instruments for payment or acceptance (certification) make to payors and drawees.

Transfer Warranties

A person who transfers a negotiable instrument to someone else and for consideration makes five warranties to his immediate transferee. If the transfer is by indorsement, the transferor makes these warranties to all subsequent transferees. The five transfer warranties are:

1. The warrantor is a person entitled to enforce the instrument. In essence the transferor warrants that there are no unauthorized or missing indorsements that prevent the transferor from making the transferee a person entitled to enforce the instrument.

2. All signatures on the instrument are authentic or authorized.

3. The instrument has not been altered.

4. The instrument is not subject to a defense or a claim in recoupment that any party can assert against the warrantor.

5. The warrantor has no knowledge of any insolvency proceedings commenced with respect to the maker or acceptor or, in the case of an unaccepted draft, the drawer [3–416(a)]. Note that this is not a warranty against difficulty in collection or insolvency—the warranty stops with the warrantor's knowledge.

Revised Article 3 provides that in the event of a breach of a transfer warranty, a beneficiary of the transfer warranties who took the instrument in good faith may recover from the warrantor an amount equal to the loss suffered as a result of the breach. However, the damages recoverable may not be more than the amount of the instrument plus expenses and loss of interest incurred as a result of the breach [3–416(b)].

Transferors of instruments other than checks may disclaim the transfer warranties. Unless the warrantor receives notice of a claim for breach of warranty within 30 days after the claimant has reason to know of the breach and the identity of the warrantor, the delay in giving notice of the claim may discharge the warrantor's liability to the extent of any loss the warrantor suffers from the delay, such as the opportunity to proceed against the transferor [3–416(c)].

Although contractual liability often furnishes a sufficient basis for suing a transferor when the party primarily obligated does not pay, warranties are still important. First, they apply even when the transferor did not indorse. Second, unlike contractual liability, they do not depend on presentment, dishonor, and notice, but may be utilized before presentment has been made or after the time for giving notice has expired. Third, a holder may find it easier to return the instrument to a transferor on the ground of breach of warranty than to prove her status as a holder in due course against a maker or drawer.

CONCEPT REVIEW

TRANSFER WARRANTIES

The five transfer warranties made by a person who transfers a negotiable instrument to someone else for consideration are:

1. The warrantor is entitled to enforce the instrument.
2. All signatures on the instrument are authentic or authorized.
3. The instrument has not been altered.
4. The instrument is not subject to a defense or a claim in recoupment that any party can assert against the warrantor.
5. The warrantor has no knowledge of any insolvency proceedings commenced with respect to the maker or acceptor or, in the case of an unaccepted draft, the drawer.

Who	What Warranties	To Whom
Nonindorsing Transferor	Makes all five transfer warranties	To his immediate transferor only
Indorsing Transferor	Makes all five transfer warranties	To all subsequent transferors

---

Presentment Warranties

Persons who present negotiable instruments for payment or drafts for acceptance also make warranties, but their warranties differ from those transferors make. If an unaccepted draft (such as a check) is presented to the drawee for payment or acceptance and the drawee pays or accepts the draft, then the person obtaining payment or acceptance warrants to the drawee making payment or accepting the draft in good faith that:

1. The warrantor is, or was, at the time the warrantor transferred the draft, a person entitled to enforce the draft or authorized to obtain payment or acceptance of the draft on behalf of a person entitled to enforce the draft.

2. The draft has not been altered.

3. The warrantor has no knowledge that the signature of the drawer of the draft has not been authorized [3–417(a)].

These warranties are also made by any prior transferor of the instrument at the time the person transfers the instrument; the warranties run to the drawee who makes payment or accepts the draft in good faith. Such a drawee would include a drawee bank paying a check presented to it for payment directly or through the bank collection process.

The effect of the third presentment warranty is to leave with the drawee the risk that the drawer's signature is unauthorized, unless the person presenting the draft for payment, or a prior transferor, had knowledge of any lack of authorization.

A drawee who makes payment may recover as damages for any breach of a presentment warranty an amount equal to the amount paid by the drawee less the amount the drawee received or is entitled to receive from the drawer because of the payment. In addition, the drawee is entitled to compensation for expenses and loss of interest resulting from the breach [3–417(b)]. The drawee's right to recover damages for breach of warranty is not affected by any failure on the part of the drawee to exercise ordinary care in making payment.

If a drawee asserts a claim for breach of a presentment warranty based on an unauthorized indorsement of the draft or an alteration of the draft, the warrantor may defend by showing that the indorsement is effective under the *impostor* or *fictitious payee* rules (discussed later in this chapter) or that the drawer's negligence precludes him from asserting against the drawee the unauthorized indorsement or alteration (also discussed below) [3–417(c)].

If (1) a *dishonored draft* is presented for payment to the drawer or an indorser or (2) any other instrument (such as a note) is presented for payment to a party obligated to pay the instrument and the presenter receives payment, the presenter makes the following presentment warranty:

The person obtaining payment is a person entitled to enforce the instrument or authorized to obtain payment on behalf of a person entitled to enforce the instrument [3–417(d)].

On breach of this warranty, the person making the payment may recover from the warrantor an amount equal to the amount paid plus expenses and loss of interest resulting from the breach.

With respect to checks, the party presenting the check for payment cannot disclaim the presentment warranties [3-417(e)]. Unless the payor or drawee provides notice of a claim for breach of a presentment warranty to the warrantor within 30 days after the claimant has reason to know of the breach and the identity of the warrantor, the warrantor is discharged to the extent of any loss caused by the delay in giving notice of the claim of breach.

Payment or Acceptance by Mistake

A longstanding general rule of negotiable instruments law is that payment or acceptance is final in favor of a holder in due course or payee who changes his position in reliance on the payment or acceptance. Revised Article 3 retains this concept by making payment final in favor of a person who took the instrument in good faith and for value. However, payment is not final—and may be recovered from—a person who does not meet these criteria where the drawee acted on the mistaken belief that (1) payment of a draft or check has not been stopped, (2) the signature of the purported drawer of the draft was authorized, and (3) the balance in the drawer's account with the drawee represented available funds [3–418(a)].

As a result, this means that if the drawee bank mistakenly paid a check over a stop-payment order, paid a check with a forged or unauthorized drawer's signature on it, or paid despite the lack of sufficient funds in the drawer's account to cover the check, the bank cannot recover if it paid the check to a presenter who had taken the instrument in good faith and for value. In that case, the drawee bank would have to pursue someone else, such as the forger or unauthorized signer, or the drawer in the case of insufficient funds. On the other hand, if the presenter had not taken in good faith or for value, the bank could, in these enumerated instances, recover from the presenter the payment it made by mistake.

The *Garnac Grain Co. Inc. v. Boatmen's Bank & Trust Co. of Kansas City* case, which follows, illustrates the operation of presentment and transfer warranties.

GARNAC GRAIN CO., INC. V. BOATMEN'S BANK & TRUST CO. OF KANSAS CITY

694 F. Supp 1389 (W.D. Mo. 1988)

Katherine Millison was employed by the Garnac Grain Company as a bookkeeper. She developed a scheme to embezzle money from Garnac whereby she would take home fully executed and valid checks payable to freight vendors and type "or L. R. Millison" (her husband's name) under the named payee with her manual typewriter. She would then indorse the check "L. R. Millison" on the back and deposit the check in a joint account she and her husband maintained at the State Bank of Oskaloosa. The bank forwarded the altered checks through the Federal Reserve System (through First National Bank of Kansas City), which presented them for payment to the drawee bank, Boatmen's Bank & Trust Company of Kansas City. Boatmen's paid the checks. Millison then would intercept the monthly bank statements from Boatmen's Bank & Trust, remove the altered checks, and obliterate the "or L. R. Millison" on the face of the checks and the indorsement on the back.

The scheme was discovered and Millison was convicted of embezzlement. Garnac brought suit against Boatmen's Bank & Trust, alleging that it wrongfully paid the altered checks. It settled with Garnac and then sued the State Bank of Oskaloosa, contending that it breached the UCC transfer warranties when it forwarded the altered checks for payment.

Hunter, Senior District Judge   Boatmen's and First National contend that Oskaloosa is liable for the amount of their settlement with Garnac because it breached the UCC transfer warranties it made to them when it sent the checks altered by Millison to First National for payment by Boatmen's. Specifically it alleges that Oskaloosa breached the good title, material alterations, and genuine signature warranties.

Section 4–207 provides in pertinent part:

(1) Each customer or collecting bank who obtains payment or acceptance of an item and each prior customer and collecting bank warrants to the payor bank or other payor who in good faith pays or accepts the item that

(a) he has good title to the item or is authorized to obtain payment or acceptance on behalf of one who has a good title; and

(b) he has no knowledge that the signature of the maker or drawer is unauthorized . . .; and

(c) the item has not been materially altered . . .

(2) Each customer and collecting bank who transfers an item and receives a settlement or other consideration for it warrants to his transferee and to any subsequent collecting bank who takes the item in good faith that

(a) he has a good title to the item or is authorized to obtain payment or acceptance on behalf of one who has a good title and the transfer is otherwise rightful; and

(b) all signatures are genuine and authorized; and

(c) the item has not been materially altered;

Under this system, a payor bank in possession of a check containing, for example, a material alteration has the choice of bringing a warranty claim against the bank that transferred the check to it, or any other intermediate collecting bank or the depositary bank. If the payor bank brings the action against a bank other than the depositary bank, that bank can bring a claim against its transferor bank or any other previous collecting bank. As between the banks involved in the collection process, the liability for a materially altered check falls on the depositary bank. This is in accord with the loss allocation framework of Articles 3 and 4 of the UCC which generally places the loss of a forged or altered item on the person or bank who dealt with the wrongdoer if the wrongdoer cannot be found or is judgment proof. Since there is no knowledge or notice requirement with respect to the material alteration warranties, the question of whether or not a party breached these warranties is simply a question of whether or not the checks were materially altered.

There seems to be no serious dispute among the parties but that the alterations made by Millison were material. Each check was drawn on Garnac's account at Boatmen's, was properly made out to barge freight vendors, and was properly signed by authorized representatives of Garnac. Millison altered the checks by typing "or L. R. Millison" underneath the payee's name. The court finds that, as a matter of law, an alteration which adds an alternative payee is a material alteration as that term is used in the UCC. See section 3–407. Thus, both Oskaloosa and First National breached their 3–207(1) warranties of no material alteration to Boatmen's; Oskaloosa breached its 4–207(2) warranty of no material alterations.

There is also no question that Oskaloosa breached its warranty of good title. Without the indorsement of the intended payees on the checks (i.e., the barge freight vendors) Oskaloosa could not obtain good title to the checks. The only indorsement on the back of the checks was "L. R. Millison." Neither Millison nor her husband was authorized to indorse the checks on behalf of the barge freight vendors shown as payees on the altered checks. Since Oskaloosa did not have good title when it transferred the checks to First National, it breached its section 4–207(1)(a) warranty to Boatmen's and its 4–207(2)(a) warranty to First National.

Summary judgment in favor of Boatmen's on its claims that the State Bank of Oskaloosa breached its warranties of good title and no material alterations.

Note: The court found that there were issues of material fact as to whether Garnac had exercised reasonable care and promptness in examining its bank statement to discover unauthorized signatures and alterations and whether Boatmen's had exercised ordinary care in paying the checks in question. It should also be noted that this case was decided under the original version of Articles 3 and 4. Revised Article 3 and the conforming amendments to Articles 1 and 4 change the wording of the transfer and presentment warranties and the warranties appear under different section numbers. However, the result reached in this case would be the same under the revisions to the Code.

CONCEPT REVIEW

PRESENTMENT WARRANTIES

If an unaccepted draft (such as a check) is presented for payment or acceptance and the drawee pays or accepts the draft, then the person obtaining payment or acceptance warrants to the drawee:

1. The warrantor is a person entitled to enforce payment or authorized to obtain payment or acceptance on behalf of a person entitled to enforce the draft.
2. The draft has not been altered.
3. The warrantor has no knowledge that the signature of the drawer of the draft has not been authorized.

If (*a*) a dishonored draft is presented for payment to the drawer or indorser or (*b*) any other instrument (such as a note) is presented for payment to a party obligated to pay the instrument and the presenter receives payment, the presenter (as well as a prior transferor of the instrument) makes the following warranty to the person making payment in good faith:

The person obtaining payment is a person entitled to enforce the instrument or authorized to obtain payment on behalf of a person entitled to enforce the instrument.

Operation of Warranties

The following are three scenarios that show how the transfer and presentment warranties shift the liability back to a wrongdoer or to the person who dealt immediately with a wrongdoer and thus was in the best position to avert the wrongdoing.

Scenario 1   Arthur makes a promissory note for $200 payable to the order of Betts. Carlson steals the note from Betts, indorses her name on the back, and gives it to Davidson in exchange for a television set. Davidson negotiates the note for value to Earle, who presents the note to Arthur for payment. Assume that Arthur refuses to pay the note because Betts has advised him that it has been stolen and that he is the person entitled to enforce the instrument. Earle then can proceed to recover the face amount of the note from Davidson on the grounds that as a transferor Davidson has warranted that he is a person entitled to enforce the note and that all signatures were authentic. Davidson, in turn, can proceed against Carlson on the same basis — if he can find Carlson. If he cannot, then Davidson must bear the loss caused by Carlson's wrongdoing. Davidson was in the best position to ascertain whether Carlson was the owner of the note and whether the indorsement of Betts was genuine. Of course, even though Arthur does not have to pay the note to Earle, Arthur remains liable for his underlying obligation to Betts.

Scenario 2   Anderson draws a check for $10 on her checking account at First Bank payable to the order of Brown. Brown cleverly raises the check to $110, indorses it, and negotiates it to Carroll. Carroll then presents the check for payment to First Bank, which pays her $110 and charges Anderson's account for $110. Anderson then asks the bank to recredit her account for the altered check, and it does so. The bank can proceed against Carroll for breach of the presentment warranty that the instrument had not been altered, which she made to the bank when she presented the check for payment. Carroll in turn can proceed against Brown for breach of her transfer warranty that the check had not been altered — if she can find her. Unless she was negligent in drawing the check, Article 3 limits Anderson's liability to $10 because her obligation is to pay the amount in the instrument at the time she issued it.

Scenario 3   Bates steals Albers's checkbook and forges Albers's signature to a check for $100 payable to "cash," which he uses to buy $100 worth of groceries from a grocer. The grocer presents the check to Albers's bank. The bank pays the amount of the check to the grocer and charges Albers's account. Albers then demands that the bank recredit his account. The bank can recover against the grocer only if the grocer knew that Albers's signature had been forged. Otherwise, the bank must look for Bates. The bank had the responsibility to recognize the true signature of its drawer, Albers, and not to pay the check that contained an unauthorized signature. The bank may be able to resist recrediting Albers's account if it can show he was negligent. The next section of this chapter discusses negligence.

OTHER LIABILITY RULES

Normally, a bank may not charge against (debit from) the drawer's account a check that has a forged payee's indorsement. Similarly, a maker does not have to pay a note to the person who currently possesses the note if the payee's signature has been forged. If a check or note has been altered — for example, by raising the amount — the drawer or maker is usually liable only for the instrument in the amount for which he originally issued it. However, there are a number of exceptions to these usual rules. These exceptions, as well as liability based on conversion of an instrument, are discussed below.

Negligence

A person can be so negligent in writing or signing a negotiable instrument that she in effect invites an alteration or an unauthorized signature on it. If a person has been negligent, Article 3 precludes her from using the alteration or lack of authorization as a reason for not paying a person that in good faith pays the instrument or takes it for value [3–406]. For example, Mary Maker makes out a note for $10 in such a way that someone could alter it to read $10,000. Someone alters the note and negotiates it to Katherine Smith, who can qualify as a holder in due course. Smith can collect $10,000 from Maker. Maker's negligence precludes her from claiming alteration as a defense to paying it. Maker then has to find the person who "raised" her note and try to collect the $9,990 from him.

Where the person asserting the preclusion failed to exercise ordinary care in taking or paying the instrument and that failure substantially contributed to the loss, Article 3 allocates the loss between the two parties based on their comparative negligence [3–406(b)]. Thus, if a drawer was so negligent in drafting a check that he made it possible for the check to be altered and the bank that paid the check, in the exercise of ordinary care, should have noticed the alteration, then any loss occasioned by the fact that the person who made the alteration could not be found would be split by the drawer and the bank based on their comparative fault.

Impostor Rule

Article 3 establishes special rules for negotiable instruments made payable to impostors and fictitious persons. An **impostor** is a person who poses as someone else and convinces a drawer to make a check payable to the person being impersonated—or to an organization the person purports to be authorized to represent. When this happens, the Code makes any indorsement "substantially similar" to that of the named payee effective [3–404(a)]. Where the impostor has impersonated a person authorized to act for a payee, such as claiming to be Jack Jones, the president of Jones Enterprises, the impostor has the power to negotiate a check to Jones Enterprises.

An example of a situation involving the impostor rule would be the following: Arthur steals Paulsen's automobile and finds the certificate of title in the automobile. Then, representing himself as Paulsen, he sells the automobile to Berger Used Car Company. The car dealership draws its check payable to Paulsen for the agreed purchase price of the automobile and delivers the check to Arthur. Any person can negotiate the check by indorsing it in the name of Paulsen.

The rationale for the impostor rule is to put the responsibility for determining the true identity of the payee on the drawer or maker of a negotiable instrument. The drawer is in a better position to do this than some later holder of the check who may be entirely innocent. The impostor rule allows that later holder to have good title to the check by making the payee's signature valid although it is not the signature of the person with whom the drawer or maker thought he was dealing. It forces the drawer or maker to find the wrongdoer who tricked him into signing the negotiable instrument or to bear the loss himself.

Fictitious Payee Rule

A **fictitious payee** commonly arises in the following situation: A dishonest employee draws a check payable to someone who does not exist—or to a real person who does business with the employer but to whom the dishonest employee does not intend to send the check. If the employee has the authority to do so, he may sign the check himself. If he does not have such authority, he gives the check to his employer for signature and represents that the employer owes money to the person named as the payee of the check. The dishonest employee then takes the check, indorses it in the name of the payee, presents it for payment, and pockets the money. The employee may be in a position to cover up the wrongdoing by intercepting the canceled checks or juggling the company's books.

The Code allows any indorsement in the name of the fictitious payee to be effective as the payee's indorsement in favor of any person that pays the instrument in good faith or takes it for value or for collection [3–404(b) and (c)]. For example, Anderson, an accountant in charge of accounts payable at Moore Corporation, prepares a false invoice naming Parks, Inc., a supplier of Moore Corporation, as having supplied Moore Corporation with goods, and draws a check payable to Parks, Inc., for the amount of the invoice. Anderson then presents the check to Temple, Treasurer of Moore Corporation, together with other checks with invoices attached. Temple signs all of these checks and returns them to Anderson for mailing. Anderson then withdraws the check payable to Parks, Inc. Anyone, including Anderson, can negotiate the check by indorsing it in the name of Parks, Inc.

The rationale for the fictitious payee rule is similar to that for the impostor rule. If someone has a dishonest employee or agent who is responsible for the forgery of some checks, the employer of the wrongdoer should bear the immediate loss of those checks rather than some other innocent party. In turn, the employer must locate the unfaithful employee or agent and try to recover from him.

The *City of Phoenix v. Great Western Bank & Trust* case, which follows, illustrates the operation of the fictitious payee rule. As you read the case, determine what the City should have done to prevent the loss it suffered.

CITY OF PHOENIX V. GREAT WESTERN BANK & TRUST

42 UCC Rep. 1364 (Ariz. Ct. App. 1985)

Gary Hann opened a checking account at the Tucson branch of Great Western Bank & Trust in the name of Duncan Industries with a cash deposit of $200. He told the bank that Duncan Industries was a sole proprietorship involved in investments. Hann listed the mailing address of the business as a post office box and designated himself as the authorized signature on the account. Hann's confederate, Jay Maisel, worked for the City of Phoenix in a government-funded program to assist ex-convicts. Maisel had served nine years in prison for theft. City officials were aware of his background and initially placed him in a nonsensitive position. However, the City promoted Maisel to a position in which he was responsible for preparing the documentation to pay the City's vendors. Six months after his promotion, Maisel prepared two claims packages for one vendor, Duncan Industries, causing the City to issue duplicate checks to the order of Duncan Industries, each in the amount of $514,320.40. The legitimate check was mailed to the vendor in Chicago; the fraudulent check was mailed to Hann in Tucson.

Hann deposited the check in the Duncan Industries account he had established, where it was subjected to a four-day hold. Once the hold expired, Hann withdrew over $441,000 from the account, much of it in cashier's checks made payable to coin, stamp, diamond, or bullion dealers. The City, on its own behalf and as assignee of the rights of the drawee bank, brought suit against the Great Western Bank to recover the amount of the check taken for deposit by it, contending, among other things, that the check contained a forged payee's indorsement. The trial court ruled in favor of the bank and the City appealed.

Corcoran, Judge Section 3–405 provides an exception to the general rule that forged indorsements are ineffective to pass title or to authorize a drawee to pay. Under section 4–401, a drawer can usually require the drawee bank to recredit the drawer account when the drawee pays a check on which a necessary indorsement is forged. The drawee bank can then shift the loss to previous indorsers on the ground of breach of warranty. The loss under the general rule will ultimately rest with the person who forged the instrument or the bank which took the instrument from the forger.

Section 3–405(1)(c), often referred to as the "fictitious payee rule," provides in pertinent part:

A. An indorsement by any person in the name of a named payee is effective if: . . . 3. An agent or employee of the maker or drawer has supplied him with the name of the payee intending the latter to have no such interest.

The exception places the loss from the activities of a faithless employee upon the employer rather than on the drawee bank. The loss is shifted by making the indorsement "effective" although it is unauthorized. Since the indorsement is "effective," the instrument passes as though there had been no forgery and as between a collecting bank and the drawer of the check, the loss must fall on the drawer employer. The rule, as applied, also eliminates any liability of a collecting bank for breach of warranty of the genuineness of the signatures because a signature that is "effective" is to be regarded as "genuine" for the purpose of warranty liability. Thus, in this case, the City, as assignee of its drawee bank, has no recourse against Great Western Bank based on the warranties contained in sections 3–417 and 4–207 owed by Great Western Bank to the drawee.

The basis of the fictitious payee rule is explained in section 3–405, Official Comment 4: The principle followed is that the loss should fall upon the employer as a risk of his business enterprise rather than upon the subsequent holder or drawee. The reasons are that the employer is normally in a better position to prevent such forgeries by reasonable care in the selection or supervision of his employees, or, if he is not, is at least in a better position to cover the loss by fidelity insurance: and that the cost of such insurance is properly an expense of his business rather than of the business of the holder or drawee.

The factual circumstances for application of the fictitious payee rule are met in this case. Maisel, an "employee" of the drawer, the City of Phoenix, supplied the City, as to the duplicate check, with the name of a "payee," Duncan Industries, with the intent of creating no interest in Duncan Industries.

Judgment for Great Western Bank affirmed.

Note: This case was decided under the original version of Article 3. Although Revised Article 3 changes the wording of the "fictitious payee rule" and sets it out in section 3–404 of Revised Article 3, the result would be the same under the revision.

Comparative Negligence Rule Concerning Impostors and Fictitious Payees

Revised Article 3 also establishes a comparative negligence rule if (1) the person, in a situation covered by the impostor or fictitious payee rule, pays the instrument or takes it for value or collection without exercising ordinary care in paying or taking the instrument, and (2) that failure substantially contributes to the loss resulting from payment of the instrument. In these instances, the person bearing the loss may recover an allocable share of the loss from the person who did not exercise ordinary care [3–404(d)].

Fraudulent Indorsements by Employees

Revised Article 3 specifically addresses employer responsibility for fraudulent indorsements by employees and adopts the principle that the risk of loss for such indorsements by employees who are entrusted with responsibilities for instruments (primarily checks) should fall on the employer rather than on the bank that takes the check or pays it [3–405]. As to any person who in good faith pays an instrument or takes it for value, a fraudulent indorsement by a responsible employee is effective as the indorsement of the payee if it is made in the name of the payee or in a substantially similar name [3–405(b)]. If the person taking or paying the instrument failed to exercise ordinary care and that failure substantially contributed to loss resulting from the fraud, the comparative negligence doctrine guides the allocation of the loss.

A fraudulent indorsement includes a forged indorsement purporting to be that of the employer on an instrument payable to the employer; it also includes a forged indorsement purporting to be that of the payee of an instrument on which the employer is drawer or maker [3–405(a)(2)]. "Responsibility" with respect to instruments means the authority (1) to sign or indorse instruments on behalf of the employer, (2) to process instruments received by the employer, (3) to prepare or process instruments for issue in the name of the employer, (4) to control the disposition of instruments to be issued in the name of the employer, or (5) to otherwise act with respect to instruments in a responsible capacity. "Responsibility" does not cover those who simply have access to instruments as they are stored, transported, or that are in incoming or outgoing mail [3–405(a)(3)].

Conversion

Conversion of an instrument is an unauthorized assumption and exercise of ownership over it. A negotiable instrument can be converted in a number of ways. For example, it might be presented for payment or acceptance, and the person to whom it is presented might refuse to pay or accept and refuse to return it. An instrument is also converted if a person pays an instrument to a person not entitled to payment—for example, if it contains a forged indorsement.

Revised Article 3 modifies and expands the previous treatment of conversion and provides that the law applicable to conversion of personal property applies to instruments. It also specifically provides that conversion occurs if (1) an instrument lacks an indorsement necessary for negotiation and (2) it is (*a*) purchased, (*b*) taken for collection, or (*c*) paid by a drawee to a person not entitled to payment. An action for conversion may not be brought by (1) the maker, drawer, or acceptor of the instrument or (2) a payee or an indorsee who did not receive delivery of the instrument either directly or through delivery to an agent or copayee [3–420].

Thus, if a bank pays a check that contains a forged indorsement, the bank has converted the check by wrongfully paying it. The bank then becomes liable for the face amount of the check to the person whose indorsement was forged [3–420]. For example, Arthur Able draws a check for $50 on his account at First Bank, payable to the order of Bernard Barker. Carol Collins steals the check from Barker, forges Barker's indorsement on it, and cashes it at First Bank. First Bank has converted Barker's property, because it had no right to pay the check without Barker's valid indorsement. First Bank must pay Barker $50, and then it can try to locate Collins to get the $50 back from her.

As is true under the original version of Article 3, if a check contains a restrictive indorsement (such as "for deposit" or "for collection") that shows a purpose of having the check collected for the benefit of a particular account, then any person who purchases the check or any depositary bank or payor bank that takes it for immediate payment converts the check unless the indorser receives the proceeds or the bank applies them consistent with the indorsement [3–206]. This principle is illustrated in the case that follows, *Kelly v. Central Bank & Trust Co. of Denver*.

Kelly v. Central Bank & Trust Co. of Denver
794 P.2d 1037 (Colo. Ct. App. 1990)

A number of investors, including Kelly, invested in a Cayman Islands entity, Tradecom, Ltd., a business involved in precious metals arbitrage. Their investments, in the form of cashier's checks, were payable to Tradecom and delivered to Arvey Down, Tradecom's agent. Down indorsed the checks and deposited them at the Central Bank & Trust Company of Denver into a checking account.

Most of the 934 checks, which were worth $11,227,473, were indorsed:

Tradecom Limited For deposit only 072 575

Other checks, totaling $576,850, were indorsed:

For deposit only 072 575

This included one check for $57,000, which apparently was deposited without indorsement and was indorsed by Central Bank's officer:

For deposit only 072 575 Tradecom by Mark E. Thompson Commercial Loan officer

The referenced account, No. 072 575, was not that of Tradecom (which had no accounts at Central Bank) but rather was that of Equity Trading Corporation, a company owned and managed by Down, also purportedly an agent of Tradecom.

The investors subsequently lost most of their investments in Tradecom, and they sued Central Bank for, among other things, conversion. They alleged that: (1) neither Down nor Equity Trading was an agent of Tradecom and that the check indorsements were unauthorized and ineffective; (2) over the course of 13 months, the bank negligently or recklessly permitted Down to divert the checks payable to Tradecom into Equity Trading's checking account; and (3) Central Bank did not follow reasonable commercial standards. Central Bank moved for summary judgment and in support of its motion submitted an executed power of attorney that indicated Down had the authority to indorse checks on behalf of Tradecom. The trial court awarded summary judgment to the Central Bank and the investors appealed.

Tursi, Judge   Because there was no triable issue of fact concerning Down's agency and authority to indorse and deposit the cashier's checks, and because proof of a forged or unauthorized indorsement is a necessary predicate to Central Bank's liability, the investors could not prevail as to the 11 million dollars of checks that contained an indorsement which included the "Tradecom Limited" name. Consequently, with respect to the checks indorsed with Tradecom's name, we conclude that the trial court properly granted summary judgment for Central Bank.

The trial court erred, however, in granting Central Bank summary judgment on the $57,000 check indorsed by Central Bank's commercial loan officer. In order for Central Bank to have become a holder under this indorsement, and thus have obtained title, Central Bank would have had to have been authorized to provide Tradecom's indorsement under section 4–205(1). This, however, was impossible since Tradecom was not Central Bank's "customer." Consequently, this indorsement is unauthorized as a matter of law, and summary judgment should not have been ordered for Central Bank on this check.

The investors also contend that the trial court erred in granting summary judgment for Central Bank on the remaining $519,850 of cashier's checks lacking any signature and merely indorsed "For deposit only 072 575." We agree.

Under section 3–419(1)(c), a check is converted when it is paid on a forged indorsement. In this context, a collecting or paying bank "pays" a check when it credits its customer's account with the proceeds of a check collected from the drawee bank. If such a payment occurs on a check with no indorsement or a missing indorsement, it is the legal equivalent of payment on a forged indorsement.

The term "indorsement" is generally understood to mean the indorser's writing of his or her signature on the instrument or the affixing of the indorser's name or some designation identifying the indorser on the instrument. A check simply inscribed "For deposit only" to an account other than payee's account and without the payee's signature is not an effective "indorsement." If the instrument is order paper and the depository bank does not, or cannot, supply the missing indorsement of its customer, the absence of the indorsement can be fatal to negotiation and transfer of title. One such situation is when the depository bank's customer and the payee are not the same person. In this case, the depository bank is unauthorized to, and cannot, supply the missing indorsement of the payee since the payee is not the bank's "customer" under section 4–205. In this situation, the depository bank does not become a holder of the checks and does not obtain good title to them. Payment of such proceeds to its depositor subjects the depository bank to liability for conversion.

In this case it was undisputed that Down, or someone in his employ, deposited $519,850 worth of cashier's checks at Central Bank bearing the simple inscription "For Deposit only 072 575." These checks, which bore no signature indorsement of the payee, Tradecom, or anyone else, were paid and credited to account 072 575. This was not an account of Tradecom, which was not a customer of Central Bank. Under these circumstances, Central Bank was not a holder of these checks by negotiation. It obtained no title to these checks. It is, consequently, subject to conversion liability under section 3–419(1)(c) for making payment on the equivalent of a forged indorsement.

Judgment for Central Bank reversed in part.

Note: Although this case was decided under original Article 3, the same result would be expected under Revised Article 3.

DISCHARGE OF NEGOTIABLE INSTRUMENTS

Discharge of Liability

The obligation of a party to pay an instrument is discharged (1) if he meets the requirements set out in Revised Article 3 or (2) by any act or agreement that would discharge an obligation to pay money on a simple contract. Discharge of an obligation is not effective against a person who has the rights of a holder in due course of the instrument and took the instrument without notice of the discharge [3–601].

The most common ways that an obligor on an instrument is discharged from her liability are:

1. Payment of the instrument.
2. Cancellation of the instrument.
3. Alteration of the instrument.
4. Modification of the principal's obligation that causes loss to a surety or impairs the collateral.
5. Unexcused delay in presentment or notice of dishonor with respect to a check (discussed earlier in this chapter).
6. Acceptance of a draft but varying the terms from the draft as presented (this entitles the holder to treat the draft as dishonored and the drawee, in turn, to cancel the acceptance). [3–410]

In addition, as noted earlier in the chapter, a drawer is discharged of liability of a draft that is accepted by a bank (e.g., if a check is certified by a bank) because at that point, the holder is looking to the bank to make the instrument good.

Discharge by Payment

Generally, payment in full discharges liability on an instrument to the extent payment is (1) by or on behalf of a party obligated to pay the instrument and (2) to a person entitled to enforce the instrument. To the extent of payment, the obligation of a party to pay the instrument is discharged even though payment is made with knowledge of a claim to the instrument by some other person. However, the obligation is not discharged if: (1) there is a claim enforceable against the person making payment and payment is made with knowledge of the fact that payment is prohibited by an injunction or similar legal process, or (2) in the case of an instrument other than a cashier's, certified, or teller's check, the person making the payment had accepted from the person making the claim indemnity against loss for refusing to make payment to the person entitled to enforce payment. It is also not discharged if he knows the instrument is a stolen instrument and pays someone he knows is in wrongful possession of the instrument [3–602].

Also, if the holder has indorsed a negotiable instrument restrictively, the person who pays must comply with the restrictive indorsement to be discharged [3–603(1)(b)]. For example, Arthur makes a note of $100 payable to the order of Bryan. Bryan indorses the note "Pay to the order of my account no. 16154 at First Bank, Bryan." Bryan then gives the note to his employee, Clark, to take to the bank. Clark takes the note to Arthur, who pays Clark the $100. Clark then runs off with the money. Arthur is not discharged of his primary liability on the note because he did not make his payment consistent with the restrictive indorsement. To be discharged, Arthur has to pay the $100 into Bryan's account at First Bank.

Discharge by Cancellation

A person entitled to enforce a negotiable instrument may discharge the liability of the parties to the instrument by canceling or renouncing it. If the holder mutilates or destroys a negotiable instrument with the intent that it no longer evidences an obligation to pay money, the holder has canceled that obligation [3–604]. For example, a grandfather lends $1,000 to his grandson for college expenses. The grandson gives his grandfather a promissory note for $1,000. If the grandfather later tears up the note with the intent that the grandson no longer owes him $1,000, the grandfather has canceled the note.

An accidental destruction or mutilation of a negotiable instrument is not a cancellation and does not discharge the parties to it. If an instrument is lost, mutilated accidentally, or destroyed, the person entitled to enforce it can still enforce the instrument. In such a case, the person must prove that the instrument existed and that she was its holder when it was lost, mutilated, or destroyed.

Altered Instruments; Discharge by Alteration

A person paying a fraudulently altered instrument, or taking it for value, in good faith, and without notice of the alteration, may enforce the instrument (1) according to its original terms or (2) in the case of an incomplete instrument later completed in an unauthorized manner, according to its terms as completed [3–407(c)]. An alteration occurs if there is (1) an unauthorized change that modifies the obligation of a party to the instrument or (2) an unauthorized addition of words or numbers or other change to an incomplete instrument that changes the obligation of any party [3–407(a)]. A change that does not affect the obligation of one of the parties, such as dotting an *i* or correcting the grammar, is not considered to be an alteration.

Two examples illustrate the situations where Revised Article 3 allows fraudulently altered instruments to be enforced. First, assume the amount due on a note is fraudulently raised from $100 to $10,000 without any negligence on the maker's part. The contract of the maker has been changed: The maker promised to pay $100, but after the change has been made, he would be promising to pay much more. If the note is negotiated to a person who can qualify as a holder in due course who was without notice of the alteration, that person can enforce the note against the maker for its original terms, i.e., $100.

Second, assume Swanson draws a check payable to Frank's Nursery, leaving the amount blank. He gives it to his gardener with instructions to purchase some fertilizer at Frank's and to fill in the purchase price of the fertilizer when it is known. The gardener fills in the check for $100 and gives it to Frank's in exchange for the fertilizer ($7.25) and the difference in cash ($92.75). The gardener then leaves town with the cash. If Frank's had no knowledge of the unauthorized completion, it could enforce the check for $100 against Swanson. A similar situation is illustrated in the case that follows, *American Federal Bank, FSB v. Parker*.

AMERICAN FEDERAL BANK, FSB V. PARKER
392 SE2d 798 (Ct. App. S.C. 1990)

Thomas Kirkman was involved in the horse business and was a friend of John Roundtree, a loan officer for American Federal Bank. Kirkman and Roundtree conceived a business arrangement in which Kirkman would locate buyers for horses and the buyers could seek financing from American Federal. Roundtree gave Kirkman blank promissory notes and security agreements from American Federal. Kirkman was to locate the potential purchaser, take care of the paperwork, and bring the documents to the bank for approval of the purchaser's loan.

Kirkman entered into a purchase agreement with Gene Parker, a horse dealer, to copurchase for $35,000 a horse named Wills Hightime that Kirkman represented he owned. Parker signed the American Federal promissory note in blank and also executed in blank a security agreement that authorized the bank to disburse the funds to the seller of the collateral. Kirkman told Parker he would cosign the note and fill in the details of the transaction with the bank. While Kirkman did not cosign the note, he did complete it for $85,000 as opposed to $35,000. Kirkman took the note with Parker's signature to Roundtree at American Federal and received two checks from the bank payable to him in the amounts of $35,000 and $50,000. Kirkman took the $35,000 and gave it to the real owner of the horse. Parker then received the horse.

Parker began making payments to the bank and called on Kirkman to assist in making the payments pursuant to their agreement. However, Kirkman skipped town, taking the additional $50,000 with him. Parker repaid the $35,000 but refused to pay any more. He argued that he only agreed to borrow $35,000 and the other $50,000 was unauthorized by him. American Federal Bank filed suit to recover the balance due on the note. The trial court held in favor of the bank, and Parker appealed.

Cureton, Judge   Parker executed a promissory note in blank. Under the Uniform Commercial Code, the maker of a note agrees to pay the instrument according to its tenor at the time of engagement "or as completed pursuant to Section 3–115 on incomplete instruments." Under Section 3–115(2) if the completion of an instrument is unauthorized the rules as to material alteration apply. Under Section 3–407(1)(b) the completion of an incomplete instrument otherwise than as authorized is considered an alteration. However, under Section 3–407(3) a subsequent holder in due course may enforce an incomplete instrument as completed. Official Comment 4 indicates that where blanks are filled or an incomplete instrument is otherwise completed, the loss is placed upon the party who left the instrument incomplete and the holder is permitted to enforce it according to its completed form.

We agree with the trial court that the bank was entitled to the directed verdicts. The responsibility for the situation rests with Parker. He and Kirkman negotiated their deal. Parker signed a blank promissory note. He relied upon Kirkman to cosign the note and fill it in for $35,000. Parker's negligence substantially contributed to the material alteration as a matter of law.

Parker argues that its was not reasonable commercial practice for American Federal to give Kirkman possession of blank promissory notes. After the fact, Parker argues the bank should have contacted him or checked to be sure everything was correct before disbursing the proceeds of the loan to Kirkman. There is no evidence in the record to establish the bank had any reason to inquire into the facial validity of the note. The note was complete when presented to the bank and there were no obvious alterations on it.

The record establishes American Federal took the note in good faith and without notice of any defense to it by Parker. American Federal gave value for the note when it disbursed the funds to Kirkman. As a holder in due course, American Federal may enforce the note against Parker as completed. Sections 3–302; 3–407(3).

Judgment for American Federal affirmed.

Note: Although this case was decided under the original version of Article 3, the same result would be reached under Revised Article 3 so long as the court found Kirkman's completion (alteration) to be fraudulent.

In any other case, a fraudulent alteration **discharges** any party whose obligation is affected by the alteration *unless* (1) the party assents or (2) is precluded from asserting the alteration (e.g., because of the party's contributory negligence). Assume that Anderson signs a promissory note for $100 payable to Bond. Bond indorses the note "Pay to the order of Connolly, Bond" and negotiates it to Connolly. Connolly changes the $100 to read $100,000. Connolly's change is unauthorized and fraudulent. As a result, Anderson is discharged from her primary liability as maker of the note and Bond is discharged from her secondary liability as indorser. Neither of them has to pay Connolly. The obligations of both Anderson and Bond were changed because the amount for which they are liable was altered.

No other alteration—that is, one that is not fraudulent—discharges any party, and a holder may enforce the instrument according to its *original* terms [3–407(b)]. Thus, there would no discharge if a blank is filled in the honest belief that it is authorized or if a change is made, without any fraudulent intent, to give the maker on a note the benefit of a lower interest rate.

Discharge of Indorsers and Accommodation Parties

If a person entitled to enforce an instrument agrees, with or without consideration, to a material modification of the obligation of a party to the instrument, including an extension of the due date, then any accommodation party or indorser who has a right of recourse against the person whose obligation is modified is discharged *to the extent the modification causes a loss to the indorser or accommodation party*. Similarly, if collateral secures the obligation of a party to an instrument and a person entitled to enforce the instrument impairs the value of the collateral, the obligation of the indorser or accommodation party having the right of recourse against the obligor is discharged to the extent of the impairment. These discharges are not effective unless the person agreeing to the modification or causing the impairment knows of the accommodation or has notice of it. Also, no discharge occurs if the obligor assented to the event or conduct, or if the obligor has waived the discharge [3–605].

For example, Frank goes to Credit Union to borrow $4,000 to purchase a used automobile. The credit union has Frank sign a promissory note and takes a security interest in the automobile (i.e., takes it as collateral for the loan). It also asks Frank's brother Bob to sign the note as an accommodation maker. Subsequently, Frank tells the credit union he wants to sell the automobile and it releases its security interest. Because release of the collateral adversely affects Bob's obligation as accommodation maker, he is discharged from his obligation as accommodation maker in the amount of the value of the automobile.

ETHICAL AND PUBLIC POLICY CONCERNS

1. Suppose you have taken a promissory note for $1,000 as payment for some carpentry work you did for a friend. You have some reason to believe that the maker is having some financial difficulty and may not be able to pay the note when it is due. You discuss the possible sale of the note to an elderly neighbor as an investment and she agrees to buy it. Would it be ethical for you to indorse the note with a qualified indorsement ("without re-course")?

2. In problem case 10, a creditor made a mistake and returned a note marked "canceled" to the maker without collecting all of the interest due on it. Suppose, instead, that the maker/borrower realized that Crown Financial had made an error in not including in the subsequent note the interest due on the original note. Should the maker/borrower feel compelled by ethical considerations to pay the interest, even if not legally required to do so?

PROBLEMS AND PROBLEM CASES

1. American Music Industries, Inc., and Disneyland Vista Records had ongoing business dealings during 1975 and 1976. As of May 21, 1976, American owed Disneyland over $93,000. As evidence of that indebtedness, American issued 10 promissory notes, payable to Disneyland and signed by Irv Schwartz, the president of American Music. The notes contained no reference to American Music Industries, Inc., nor was there any indication that Schwartz signed in a representative capacity. American paid four of the notes, then defaulted on the rest. Disneyland brought suit against Schwartz to recover on the remaining six promissory notes. Schwartz claimed that the notes had been prepared by Disneyland; that they did not reflect correctly the intent of the parties, because they did not name American as the maker; and that he signed the notes individually by mistake. Is Schwartz individually liable on the notes?

2. Frederick Dowie was the president and sole stockholder of Fred Dowie Enterprises, Inc., a catering company. He obtained the opportunity to operate the concession stands at the Living History Farms during the pope's visit to Des Moines, Iowa. With high expectations, Dowie ordered 325,000 hot dog buns from Colonial Baking Company. Before the buns were delivered, he presented to Colonial Baking a postdated check in the amount of $28,640. The check showed the name of the corporation and its address in the upper left-hand corner. The signature on the check read "Frederick J. Dowie," and there were no other words of explanation. Unfortunately, only 300 buns were sold. Following a dispute over the ownership and responsibility for the remaining buns, Dowie stopped payment on the check. Colonial Baking then sued Dowie in his personal capacity as signer of the check. Is Dowie personally liable for the check?

3. Clay Haynes was the bookkeeper for Johnstown Manufacturing, Inc. He had express check-signing authority, and his signature was on the signature card for the account that Johnstown maintained at BancOhio National Bank. Haynes was also the bookkeeper of another corporation, Lynn Polymers, Inc., which was operated by the same individuals that operated Johnstown. Over a period of a year, Haynes engaged in a check-cashing scheme from which he pocketed approximately $70,000. Haynes wrote 35 corporate checks to the order of BancOhio National Bank, and the bank, in return, gave the cash to Haynes. Johnstown brought suit against BancOhio to recover $300 for the one check written on the Johnstown account that the bank paid to Haynes. (The other checks were written on the Polymers's account.) Johnstown claimed that the check was written without the express authority of the corporation, and thus it contained an "unauthorized" signature. Was Haynes's signature on the check unauthorized as that term is used in the Uniform Commercial Code?

4. Gish operated a retail business under the name of Gish's General Store. He agreed to sell his business to Kenneth Smith and Barry Gill in exchange for two houses to be built for Gish by Smith and Gill. The transaction was to be consummated on completion of the houses. In the interim, Smith and Gill were to familiarize themselves with the business by assisting in its operation. However, without Gish's knowledge, Smith and Gill opened a checking account at Springhill Bank in the name of Gish's General Store. They then stole a number of checks from Gish's cash register, indorsed them with Gish's signature stamped "For deposit only, Gish's General Store," and deposited them to the account at Springfield Bank. Subsequently, Smith and Gill withdrew the money from the account and disappeared. Several of the checks were returned to Springfield Bank because the drawers had stopped payment on them. Springfield Bank then brought suit against Gish to recover the amount of the dishonored checks, claiming that he was liable as indorser of the checks because of the stamped indorsement. Was Gish liable as indorser of the dishonored checks?

5. Willard Cobb operated an insurance agency in Brattleboro, Vermont. Cobb received a check in the amount of $13,750 issued by the Hartford Insurance Company and payable to R. A. McQuaide Milk Transport. The check was issued in payment of a property loss incurred by McQuaide under a policy issued by Hartford Insurance through Cobb's agency. Willard Cobb, without authorization from McQuaide, fraudulently indorsed McQuaide's name to the check. He then added his own indorsement: "For Deposit Only—Franklin County Trust Co., Willard D. Cobb." He gave the check to his brother Leon to deposit at Franklin County Trust in a new partnership account they had opened in the name of "Econo Car Rental Center." The bank credited the partnership account with the money. Willard took the money from the account and left town. The bank had to pay back Hartford Insurance for the check it had wrongfully paid to Willard and Leon rather than to McQuaide. Then it sued Willard and Leon Cobb to recover the money from them. Were Leon and Willard liable to the bank on the ground that they breached transfer warranties?

6. Mrs. Gordon Neely hired Louise Bradshaw as the bookkeeper for a Midas Muffler shop she and her husband owned and operated as a corporation, J. Gordon Neely Enterprises, Inc. (Neely). Bradshaw's duties included preparing company checks for Mrs. Neely's signature and reconciling the checking account when the company received bank statement and canceled checks each month. Bradshaw prepared several checks payable to herself and containing a large space to the left of the amount written on the designated line. When Mrs. Neely signed the checks, she was aware of the large gaps. Subsequently, Bradshaw altered the checks by adding a digit or two to the left of the original amount and then cashed them at American National Bank, the drawee bank. Several months later, the Neelys hired a new accountant, who discovered the altered checks. Neely brought suit against American National Bank to have its account recredited for the altered checks, claiming that American was liable for paying out on altered instruments. The bank contended that Neely's negligence substantially contributed to a material alteration of the instrument and thus Neely was precluded from asserting the alteration against the bank. Between Neely and American National Bank, who should bear the loss caused by Bradshaw's fraud?

7. Mrs. Johnson mailed a loan application to First National Bank in her husband's name and without his knowledge. Having dealt with her husband before, the bank approved the application and mailed a check in the amount requested to Mr. Johnson. Mrs. Johnson then indorsed the check in her husband's name and cashed it at Merchant's Bank. Merchant's Bank indorsed the check and presented it for payment. First National, having discovered the deception, refused to pay. Is First National liable on the check?

8. Clarice Rich was employed by the New York City Board of Education as a clerk. It was her duty to prepare requisitions for checks to be issued by the board, to prepare the checks, to have them signed by the authorized personnel, and to send the checks to the recipients. In some instances, however, she retained them. Also, on a number of occasions, she prepared duplicate requisitions and checks that, when signed, she likewise retained. She then forged the indorsement of the named payees on the checks she had retained and cashed the checks at Chemical Bank, where the Board of Education maintained its account. After the board discovered the forgeries, it demanded that Chemical Bank credit its account for the amount of the forged checks. Is Chemical Bank required to credit the board's account as requested?

9. Wilson was presented with a check payable to Jones and Brown and drawn on Merchant's Bank. The check was indorsed by Brown alone. Wilson accepted the check, indorsed it, and submitted it to Merchant's Bank for payment. Merchant's Bank paid Wilson. Does Merchant's Bank have any liability to Jones?

10. Charles Peterson, a farmer and rancher, was indebted to Crown Financial Corporation on a $4,450,000 promissory note that was due on December 29, 1972. Shortly before the note was due, Crown sent Peterson a statement of interest due on the note ($499,658.85). Peterson paid the interest and executed a new note in the amount of $4,450,000 that was to mature in December 1975. The old note was then marked "canceled" and returned to Peterson. In 1975, Crown billed Peterson for $363,800 in interest that had been due on the first note but apparently not included in the statement. Peterson claimed that the interest had been forgiven and that he was not obligated to pay it. Was Peterson still obligated to pay interest on the note that had been returned to him marked "canceled"?

11. 〔■■〕 *Video Case.* See "Cafeteria Conversion." Steve, an individual with a gambling and substance abuse problem, works in the accounts payable department of a company. He issues checks drawn on his employer's account that are made payable to suppliers who do business with his employer but who are not currently owed money. Then he forges the signature of the named payees, obtains payment of the checks from the drawee bank, and uses the funds to support his habits. Because Steve's responsibilities include reconciling the bank statements, his forgery scheme is not discovered for a considerable period of time. When it is discovered, is the drawee bank required to recredit the employer's account for the forged checks that were paid from it?

CHECKS AND DOCUMENTS OF TITLE

INTRODUCTION

For most people, a checking account provides the majority of their contact with negotiable instruments. This chapter focuses on the relationship between the drawer with a checking account and the drawer's bank, known as the drawee bank. It addresses such common questions as: What happens when a bank refuses to pay a check even though the depositor has sufficient funds in her account? Does the bank have the right to create an overdraft in a depositor's account by paying an otherwise properly payable check? What are the depositor's rights and the bank's obligation when the depositor stops payment on a check? What is the difference between a certified check and a cashier's check? What are the depositor's responsibilities when she receives her monthly statement and canceled checks? The second half of the chapter discusses the Code rules that apply to negotiable documents of title such as warehouse receipts and bills of lading.

THE DRAWER-DRAWEE RELATIONSHIP

There are two sources that govern the relationship between the depositor and the drawee bank: the deposit agreement and Articles 3 and 4 of the Code. Article 4, which governs Bank Deposits and Collections, allows the depositor and drawee bank (which Article 4 calls the "payor bank") to vary Article 4's provisions with a few important exceptions. The deposit agreement cannot disclaim the bank's responsibility for its own lack of good faith or failure to exercise ordinary care or limit the measure of damages for the lack or failure; however, the parties may determine by agreement the standards by which to measure the bank's responsibility so long as the standards are not manifestly unreasonable [4–103].

The deposit agreement establishes many important relationships between the depositor and drawee/payor bank. The first of these is their relationship as creditor and debtor, respectively, so that when a person deposits money in an account at the bank, the law no longer considers him the owner of the money. Instead, he is a creditor of the bank to the extent of his deposits and the bank becomes his debtor. Also, when the depositor deposits a check to a checking account, the bank also becomes his agent for collection of the check. The bank as the person's agent owes a duty to him to follow his reasonable instructions concerning payment of checks and other items from his account and a duty of ordinary care in collecting checks and other items deposited to the account.

Bank's Duty to Pay

When a bank receives a properly drawn and payable check on a person's account and there are sufficient funds to cover the check, the bank is under a duty to pay it. If the person has sufficient funds in the account and the bank refuses to pay, or dishonors, the check, the bank is liable for the actual damages proximately caused by its wrongful dishonor as well as consequential damages [4–402]. Actual damages may include charges imposed by retailers for returned checks as well as damages for arrest or prosecution of the customer. Consequential damages include injury to the depositor's credit rating that results from the dishonor.

For example, Donald Dodson writes a check for $1,500 to Ames Auto Sales in payment for a used car. At the time that Ames Auto presents the check for payment at Dodson's bank, First National Bank, Dodson has $1,800 in his account. However, a teller mistakenly refuses to pay the check and stamps it NSF (not sufficient funds). Ames Auto then goes to the local prosecutor and signs a complaint against Dodson for writing a bad check. As a result, Dodson is arrested. Dodson can recover from First National the damages that he sustained because the bank wrongfully dishonored his check, including the damages involved in his arrest, such as his attorney's fees.

In the case that follows, *Buckley v. Trenton Savings Fund Society,* the bank is potentially liable for consequential damages sustained by the drawer because it wrongfully dishonored a customer's check. In reading the case, you should keep in mind that Revised Article 3 deletes any reference to "mistake" by the bank; thus, the proof and measure of damages no longer turns on whether the bank can establish that it dishonored a check by mistake.

Buckley v. Trenton Savings Fund Society

524 A.2d 886 (N.J. Super. Ct. 1987)

Buckley maintained a checking account at the Trenton Savings Fund Society. In 1981, he separated from his wife, Linda, and entered into a consent agreement with her in which he agreed to pay her $150 per week for food and support for herself and their children. On January 13, 1984, Buckley wrote a check for $150 and gave it to his wife. The next Saturday, she presented it for payment at one of Trenton Savings' branches but payment was refused even though Buckley had $900 in the account at the time. The following Monday, she took it to another branch where payment was refused again. The bank told Linda that it would not cash the check for her because Linda did not have an account at the bank. Subsequently, the bank agreed to cash checks for Linda, but on March 4, 1984, the bank again refused to pay one of Buckley's checks that she presented for payment. Linda was known to the bank because it held a mortgage on the home that she and Buckley jointly owned.

Shortly after Trenton Bank's failure to cash the two checks, Buckley received an irate call from Linda. He also received calls from his parents, his sister, and his best friend inquiring as to why he was not making the support payments. In addition, his children inquired "why daddy wouldn't give them food money." Buckley incurred severe emotional distress over the matter. He brought suit against Trenton Savings for wrongful dishonor and sought compensatory damages, as well as punitive damages, for the mental anguish he sustained. The trial court entered judgment for Buckley based on a jury verdict for $25,000, and the bank appealed.

Stern, Judge   The bank contends that the jury should not have been permitted to award damages for emotional distress under the facts of this case. A bank's liability for wrongful dishonor of a customer's check is defined in section 4–402 of the Uniform Commercial Code:

A payor bank is liable to its customer for damages proximately caused by the wrongful dishonor of an item. When the dishonor occurs through mistake, liability is limited to actual damages proved. If so proximately caused and proved, damages may include damages for an arrest or prosecution of the customer or other consequential damages. Whether any consequential damages are proximately caused by the wrongful dishonor is a question of fact to be determined in each case.

The UCC does not indicate the theory or basis for a bank's liability for wrongful dishonor. As explained in the UCC official comment to section 4–402, "The liability of the drawee for dishonor has sometimes been stated as one for breach of contract, sometimes as for negligence or other breach of a tort duty, and sometimes as for defamation." The drafters of the UCC did not intend to exclude the possibility of mental distress damages upon a wrongful dishonor by a bank. Since section 4–402 is silent on any restriction of damages when the dishonor is grounded on an action other than mistake, it implies that these damages are not precluded by the Code. Thus, out-of-state courts interpreting section 4–402 have concluded that mental suffering is compensable under this section.

The Legislature adopted section 4–402 as promulgated in the Uniform Commercial Code without substantive change. The section expressly limits recovery for "actual damages" when the dishonor results from "mistake" but otherwise expressly permits recovery of "consequential damages" proximately caused. As White and Summer explains:

When wrongful dishonors occur not "through mistake" but willfully, the court may impose damages greater than "actual damages."

* * * *

Might one argue that "actual damages" excludes recovery for mental distress? We think not. In the first place, the drafters went to great efforts to assure that customers can recover for arrest and prosecution. It is inconsistent to allow recovery for embarrassment and mental distress deriving from arrest and prosecution and to deny similar recovery in other cases. Moreover, cases under the predecessor to 4–402, the American Association Statute, held that "actual damages" includes damages for mental distress. Thus we believe . . . that the Code drafters intended to allow recovery for mental distress and other intangible injury.

In this case the judge's instructions failed to delineate the distinction between mistake and intentional mistake and an intentional breach or wilful, wanton or reckless conduct. As a result, the matter must be remanded for a new trial and for a determination of damages based on appropriate instructions.

We preclude an award of punitive damages. Punitive damages are not generally recoverable for breach of contract, at least when the breach of contract does not also constitute a tort for which punitive damages are recoverable.

Reversed and remanded for new trial.

Note: This case was decided under the original version of Article 3 under which courts found that the Code appeared to allow a different measure of damages if the dishonor was other than by mistake. Revised Article 3 eliminates any distinction turning on mistake and provides that the depositor may recover actual damages, including consequential damages, proximately caused by a dishonor.

Bank's Right to Charge to Customer's Account

The drawee bank has the right to charge any properly payable check to the account of the customer or drawer. The bank has this right even though payment of the check creates an overdraft in the account [4–401]. If an account is overdrawn, the customer owes the bank the amount of the overdraft and the bank may take that amount out of the next deposit that the customer makes or from another account that the depositor maintains with the bank. Alternatively, the bank might seek to collect the amount directly from the customer. If there is more than one customer who can draw from an account, only that customer—or those customers—who sign the items or who benefit from the proceeds of an overdraft are liable for the overdraft.

Stale Checks   The bank does not owe a duty to its customer to pay any checks out of the account that are more than six months old. Such checks are called **stale checks.** However, the bank acting in good faith may pay a check that is more than six months old and charge it to the drawer-depositor's account [4–404].

Altered and Incomplete Items   If the bank in good faith pays a check drawn by the drawer-depositor but subsequently altered, it may charge the customer's account with the amount of the check as originally drawn. Also, if an incomplete check of a customer gets into circulation, is completed, and is presented to the drawee bank for payment, and the bank pays the check, the bank can charge the amount as completed to the customer's account even though it knows that the check has been completed, unless it has notice that the completion was improper [4–401(d)]. The respective rights, obligations, and liabilities of drawee banks and their drawer-customers concerning forged and altered checks are discussed in more detail later in this chapter.

Limitations on Bank's Right or Duty   Article 4 recognizes that the bank's right or duty to pay a check or to charge the depositor's account for the check (including exercising its right to set off an amount due to it by the depositor) may be terminated, suspended, or modified by the depositor's order to stop payment (which is discussed in the next section of this chapter). In addition, it may be stopped by events external to the relationship between the depositor and the bank. These external events include the filing of a bankruptcy petition by the depositor or by the depositor's creditors, and the garnishment of the account by a creditor of the depositor. The bank must receive the stop-payment order from its depositor or the notice of the bankruptcy filing or garnishment before the bank has certified the check, paid it in cash, settled with another bank for the amount of the item without a right to revoke the settlement, completed the process necessary to its decision to pay the check, or otherwise become accountable for the amount of the check under Article 4 [4–303]. These restrictions on the bank's right or duty to pay are discussed in later sections of this chapter.

Postdated Checks   Under original Articles 3 and 4, a postdated check was not properly payable by the drawee bank until the date on the check. The recent amendments to Article 4 change this. Under the revision, an otherwise properly payable postdated check that is presented for payment before the date on the check may be paid and charged to the customer's account *unless* the customer has given notice of it to the bank. The customer must give notice of the postdating in a way that describes the check with reasonable certainty. It is effective for the same time periods as Article 4 provides for stop-payment orders (discussed below). The customer must give notice to the bank at such time and in such manner as to give the bank an opportunity to act on it before the bank takes any action with respect to paying the check. If the bank charges the customer's account for a postdated check before the date stated in the notice given to the bank, the bank is liable for damages for any loss that results. Such damages might include that associated with the bank's dishonor of subsequent items [3–113(a); 4–401(c)].

There are a variety of reasons why a person might want to postdate a check. For example, a person might have a mortgage payment due on the first of the month at a bank located in another state. To make sure that the check arrives on time, the customer may send the payment by mail several days before the due date. However, if the person is depending on a deposit of her next monthly paycheck on the first of the month to cover the mortgage payment, she might postdate the check to the first of the following month. Under the original version of Articles 3 and 4, the bank could not properly pay the check until the first of the month. However, under the revisions it could be properly paid by the bank before that date if presented earlier. To avoid the risk that the bank would dishonor the check for insufficient funds if presented before the first, the customer should notify the drawee bank in a manner similar to that required for stop payment of checks.

Stop-Payment Order

A **stop-payment order** is a request made by a customer of a drawee bank instructing it not to pay or certify a specified check. As the drawer's agent in the payment of checks, the drawee bank must

---

---

follow the reasonable orders of the customer/ drawer about payments made on the drawer's behalf. Any person authorized to draw a check may stop payment of it. Thus, any person authorized to sign a check on the account may stop payment even if she did not sign the check in question [4–403(a)].

To be effective, the payor bank must receive the stop-payment order in time to give the bank a reasonable opportunity to act on the order. This means that the bank must receive the stop-payment order before it has paid or certified the check. In addition, the stop-payment order must come soon enough to give the bank time to instruct its tellers and other employees that they should not pay or certify the check [4–403(a)]. The stop-payment order must also describe the check with "reasonable certainty" so as to provide the bank's employees the ability to recognize it as the check corresponding to the stop-payment order.

The customer may give an oral stop-payment order to the bank, but it is valid for only 14 days unless the customer confirms it in writing during that time. A written stop-payment order is valid for six months and the customer can extend it for an additional six months by giving the bank instructions in writing to continue the order [4–403(b)]. See Figure 1.

Sometimes the information given the bank by the customer concerning the check on which payment is to be stopped is incorrect. For example, there may be an error in the payee's name, the amount of the check, or the number of the check. The question then arises whether the customer has accorded the bank a reasonable opportunity to act on his request. A common issue is whether the stop-payment order must have the dollar amount correct to the penny. Banks usually take the position that the stop-payment order must be correct to the penny because they program and rely on computers to focus on the customer's account number and the amount of the check in question to avoid paying an item subject to a stop-payment order.

The amendments to Article 4 do not resolve this question. In the Official Comments, the drafters indicate that "in describing an item, the customer, in the absence of a contrary agreement, must meet the standard of what information allows the bank under the technology then existing to identify the check with reasonable certainty." The following *FJS Electronics v. Fidelity Bank* case involves a situation in which the amount set out in a stop-payment order differed by $.50 from the amount actually on the check.

FJS ELECTRONICS, INC. v. FIDELITY BANK
28 UCC Rep. 1462 (Pa. Ct. C.P. 1980)

On February 27, 1976, Multi-Tek issued check number 896 in the face amount of $1,844.98, drawn on Multi-Tek's account at Fidelity and made payable to Multilayer Computer Circuits. However, on March 9, 1976, Frank J. Suttill, Multi-Tek's president, telephoned Fidelity and placed a stop-payment order on the check. Rosana M. Sanders, Fidelity's employee, received and simultaneously recorded the order. This recordation contained the following information: the name of the account, the account number, the check number, the date of the check, the date and hour the stop-payment order was received, and the amount of the check as $1,844.48. This recordation was correct in most respects, except for a 50-cent difference between the face amount ($1,844.98) and the amount listed in the stop-payment order ($1,844.48).

Subsequently, Fidelity mailed a confirmation notice bearing the date "03/ 76" to Multi-Tek. It contained, among other things, the following information:

PAYEE: MULTILAYER COMPUTER CIRCUITS AMOUNT: $1,844.48
CK: NO.: 896
DATE: 02/ 27/76

The instructions in this confirmation notice concluded with: PLEASE ENSURE AMOUNT IS CORRECT. Suttill signed this confirmation notice and returned it to Fidelity.

Fidelity programmed its computer to pull checks only if all of the digits on the stop-payment order agreed with those on the check. As a result, Fidelity honored check number 896 and charged it to Multi-Tek's account. Multi-Tek then brought suit against Fidelity to recover $1,844.98 because the check was paid over the stop-payment order.

———————————————— ■ ————————————————

Marutani, Judge   The Uniform Commercial Code, Section 4–403(1), provides in pertinent part that: "A customer may by order to his bank stop payment of any item payable for his account but the order must be received at such time and in such manner as to afford the bank a reasonable opportunity to act on it prior to any action by the bank with respect to the item." In this case, there is no question that the transmittal of the stop-payment order was made timely; this leaves for resolution only whether such order was given "in such *manner* as to afford the bank a reasonable opportunity to act on it": UCC Section 4–403(1); emphasis added. While the parties "may by agreement determine the standards by which [the bank's] responsibility is to be measured if such standards are not manifestly unreasonable," at the same time "no agreement can disclaim a bank's responsibility for its failure to exercise ordinary care": UCC Section 4–103(1).

The decisional law construing Section 4–403(1) appears to vary. Thus, in a recent decision of a trial court wherein the customer identified the check correctly as to the payee, the check number, and the

date of issuance, but erred by 10 cents as to the amount of the check—$1,804.00 instead of the correct amount of $1,804.10—it was held that "the check was described with sufficient particularity and accuracy so that the bank should have known to give effect to the stop-payment order." However, where the customer provided the correct amount of the check but erred as to the date and name of the payee—one-day error in date, "Walter Morris Buick" instead of the correct name "Frank Morris Buick" —the Alabama Supreme Court held such to be insufficient notice.

In this case, as the parties by the stipulation agreed, "the Bank did not tell Mr. Suttill, nor did he request, information as to the procedure whereby the computer pulls checks on which stop payments have been issued." Under such circumstances, where the customer (Mr. Suttill) was called upon by the bank (Fidelity) to provide numerous data relating to the check in question, but the bank failed to emphasize to him that all such information may well be ineffective unless the amount of the check were absolutely accurate, we are constrained to be guided by the official comment to Section 4–403 under "Purposes," which reads:

2. The position taken by this section is that stopping payment is a service which depositors expect and are entitled to receive from banks notwithstanding its difficulty, inconvenience and expense. The inevitable occasional losses through failure to stop should be borne by the banks as a cost of the business of banking.

Judgment for Multi-Tek.

Note: As noted above, the recent revisions of Articles 3 and 4 require the item to be described "with reasonable certainty" and do not explicitly address the question of whether the amount of the item has to be correct to the penny. It is not clear whether another court now faced with this same set of facts would find that the description of the item here would "meet the standard of what information allows the bank under the technology then existing to identify the item with reasonable certainty," as the drafters amplify the test in the Official Comments.

Bank's Liability for Payment after Stop-Payment Order

While a stop-payment order is in effect, the drawee bank is liable to the drawer of a check that it pays for any loss that the drawer suffers by reason of such payment. However, the drawer-customer has the burden of establishing the fact and amount of the loss. To show a loss, the drawer must establish that the drawee bank paid a person against whom the drawer had a valid defense to payment. To the extent that the drawer has such a defense, he has suffered a loss due to the drawee's failure to honor the stop-payment order.

For example, Brown buys what is represented to be a new car from Foster Ford and gives Foster Ford his check for $12,280 drawn on First Bank. Brown then discovers that the car is in fact a used demonstrator model and calls First Bank, ordering it to stop payment on the check. If Foster Ford presents the check for payment the following day and First Bank pays the check despite the stop-payment order, Brown can require the bank to recredit his account. (The depositor-drawee bases her claim to recredit on the fact that the bank did not follow her final instruction—the instruction not to pay the check.) Brown had a valid defense of misrepresentation that she could have asserted against Foster Ford if it had sued her on the check. Foster Ford would have been required to sue on the check or on Brown's contractual obligation to pay for the car.

Assume, instead, that Foster Ford negotiated the check to Smith and that Smith qualified as a holder in due course. Then, if the bank paid the check to Smith over the stop-payment order, Brown would not be able to have his account recredited, because Brown would not be able to show that he sustained any loss. If the bank had refused to pay the check, so that Smith came against Brown on his drawer's liability, Brown cannot use his personal defense of misrepresentation of the proper use of the car as a reason for not paying Smith. Brown's only recourse would be to pursue Foster Ford on his misrepresentation claim.

The bank may ask the customer to sign a form in which the bank tries to disclaim or limit its liability for the stop-payment order. As explained at the beginning of this chapter, the bank cannot disclaim its responsibility for its failure to act in good faith or to exercise ordinary care in paying a check over a stop-payment order [4–103].

If a bank pays a check after it has received a stop-payment order and has to reimburse its customer for the improperly paid check, it acquires all the rights of its customer against the person to whom it originally made payment, including rights arising from the transaction on which the check was based [4–407]. In the previous example involving Brown and Foster Ford, assume that Brown was able to have his account recredited because First Bank had paid the check to Foster Ford over his stop-payment order. Then, the bank would have any rights that Brown had against Foster Ford for the misrepresentation.

If a person stops payment on a check and the bank honors the stop-payment order, the person may still be liable to the holder of the check. Suppose Peters writes a check for $450 to Ace Auto Repair in payment for repairs to her automobile. While driving the car home, she concludes that the car was not repaired properly. She calls her bank and stops payment on the check. Ace Auto negotiated the check to Sam's Auto Parts, which took the check as

FIGURE 2   **Certified Check**

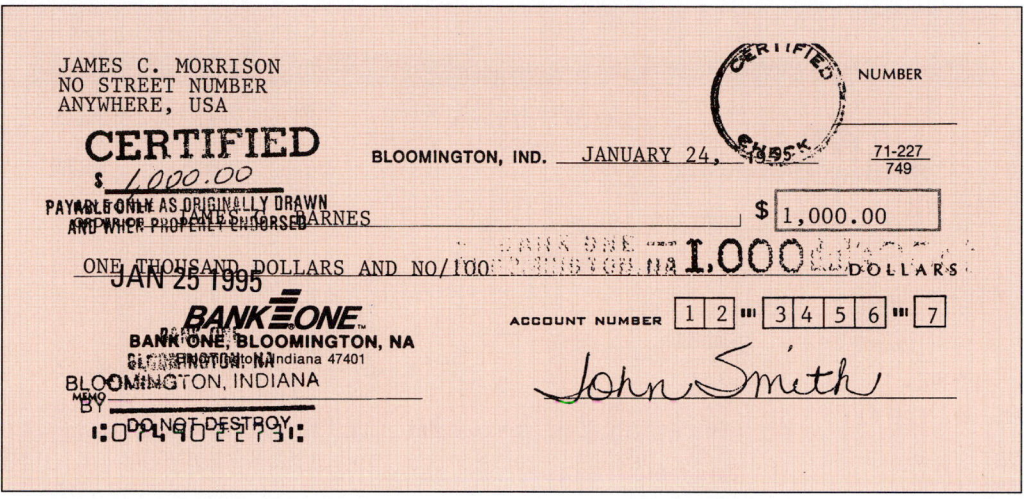

a holder in due course. When Sam's takes the check to Peters's bank, the bank refuses to pay because of the stop-payment order. Sam's then comes after Peters on her drawer's liability. All Peters has is a personal defense against payment, which is not good against a holder in due course. So, Peters must pay Sam's the $450 and pursue her claim separately against Ace. If Ace were still the holder of the check, however, the situation would be different. Peters could use her personal defense concerning the faulty work against Ace to reduce or possibly to cancel her obligation to pay the check.

Certified Check

Normally, a drawee bank is not obligated to certify a check. When a drawee bank does certify a check, it substitutes its undertaking (promise) to pay the check for the drawer's undertaking and becomes obligated to pay the check. At the time the bank certifies a check, the bank usually debits the customer's account for the amount of the certified check and shifts the money to a special account at the bank. It also adds its signature to the check to show that it has accepted primary liability for paying it. The bank's signature is an essential part of the certification—the bank's signature must appear on the check [3–409]. If the holder of a check chooses to have it certified, rather than seeking to

have it paid at that time, the holder has made a conscious decision to look to the certifying bank for payment and no longer may rely on the drawer or the endorsers to pay it. See Figure 2 for an example of a certified check.

If the drawee bank certifies a check, then the drawer and any persons who previously endorsed the check are discharged of their liability on the check [3–414(c); 3–415(d)].

Cashier's Check

A cashier's check differs from a certified check. A check on which a bank is both the drawer and the drawee is a cashier's check. The bank is primarily liable on the cashier's check. See Figure 3 for an example of a cashier's check. A teller's check is similar to a cashier's check in that it is a check on which one bank is the drawer and another bank is the drawee. An example of a teller's check is a check drawn by a credit union on its account at a bank.

Death or Incompetence of Customer

Under the general principles of agency law, the death or incompetence of the principal terminates the agent's authority to act for the principal. However, slightly different rules apply to the authority of

FIGURE 3   **Cashier's Check**

a bank to pay checks out of the account of a deceased or incompetent person. The bank has the right to pay the checks of an incompetent person until it has notice that a court has determined that the person is incompetent. Once the bank learns of this fact, it loses its authority to pay that person's checks—because the depositor is not competent to issue instructions to pay.

Similarly, a bank has the right to pay the checks of a deceased customer until it has notice of the customer's death. Even if a bank knows of a customer's death, for a period of 10 days after the customer's death, it can pay checks written by the customer prior to his death. However, the deceased person's heirs or other persons claiming an interest in the account can order the bank to stop payment [4–405].

FORGED AND ALTERED CHECKS

Bank's Right to Charge Account

A check that bears a forged signature of the drawer or payee is generally not properly payable from the customer's account because the bank is not following the instructions of the depositor precisely as he gave them. The bank is expected to be familiar with the authorized signature of its depositor. If it pays such a check, Article 4 will treat the transaction as

one in which the bank paid out its own funds, rather than the depositor's funds.

Similarly, a check that was altered after the drawer made it out—for example, by increasing the amount of the check—is generally not properly payable from the customer's account. However, as noted earlier, if the drawer is negligent and contributes to the forgery or alteration, he may be barred from claiming it as the reason that a particular check should not be charged to his account.

For example, Barton makes a check for $1 in a way that makes it possible for someone to easily alter it to read $101, and it is so altered. If the drawee bank pays the check to a holder in good faith, it can charge the $101 to Barton's account if Barton's negligence contributed to the alteration. Similarly, if a company uses a mechanical check-writer to write checks, it must use reasonable care to see that unauthorized persons do not have access to blank checks and to the checkwriter.

If the alteration is obvious, the bank should note that fact and refuse to pay the check when it is presented for payment. Occasionally, the alteration is so skillful that the bank cannot detect it. In that case, the bank is allowed to charge to the account the amount for which the check originally was written.

The bank has a duty to exercise "ordinary care" in the processing of negotiable instruments; it must observe the reasonable commercial standards prevailing among other banks in the area in which it does business. In the case of banks that take checks for collection or payment using automated means, it is important to note that reasonable commercial standards do not require the bank to examine every item *if* the failure to examine does not violate the bank's prescribed procedures and those procedures do not vary unreasonably from general banking practice or are not disapproved by the Code [3–103(a)(7); 4–103(c)]. For example, the bank's practice may be to examine those checks for more than $1,000 and a sample of smaller checks. Thus, if it did not examine a particular check in the amount of $250 for evidence of alteration or forgery, its actions would be commercially reasonable so long as (1) it followed its own protocol, (2) that protocol was not a great variance from general banking usage, and (3) the procedure followed was not specifically disallowed in the Code.

In a case where both a bank and its customer fail to use ordinary care, a comparative negligence standard is used [4–406(e)].

Customer's Duty to Report Forgeries and Alterations

A bank must send a monthly (or quarterly) statement listing the transactions in an account and commonly returns the cancelled checks to the customer. Revised Article 3 recognizes the modern bank practice of truncating (or retaining) checks and permits the bank to supply only a statement showing the item number, amount, and date of payment [4–406(a)]. When the bank does not return the paid items to the customer, the bank must either retain the items or maintain the capacity to furnish legible copies of the items for seven years after their receipt. The customer may request an item and the bank has a reasonable time to provide either the item or a legible copy of it [4–406(b)].

If the bank sends or makes available a statement of account or items, the customer must exercise reasonable promptness to examine the statement or items to determine whether payment was not authorized because of an alteration of any item or because a signature of the customer was not authorized. If, based on the statement or items provided, the customer should discover the unauthorized payment, the customer must notify the bank of the relevant facts promptly [4–406(c)].

Multiple Forgeries or Alterations

Revised Article 3 provides a special rule to govern the situation in which the same wrongdoer makes a series of unauthorized drawer's signatures or alterations. The customer generally cannot hold the bank responsible for paying, in good faith, any such checks after the statement of account or item that contained the first unauthorized customer's signature or an alteration was available to the customer for a reasonable period, not exceeding 30 calendar days. This rule holds (1) if the customer did not notify the bank of the unauthorized signature or alteration and (2) the bank proves it suffered a loss because of the customer's failure to examine his statement and notify the bank [4–406(d)]. Unless the customer has notified the bank about the forgeries or alterations that he should have discovered by reviewing the statement or item, the customer generally bears responsibility for any subsequent forgeries or alterations by the same wrongdoer.

Suppose that Allen employs Farnum as an accountant and that over a period of three months, Farnum forges Allen's signature to 10 checks and cashes them. One of the forged checks is included in the checks returned to Allen at the end of the first month. Within 30 calendar days after the return of these checks, Farnum forges two more checks and cashes them. Allen does not examine the returned checks until three months after the checks that included the first forged check were returned to her. The bank would be responsible for the first forged check and for the two checks forged and cashed within the 30-day period after it sent the first statement and the canceled checks (unless the bank proves that it suffered a loss because of the customer's failure to examine the checks and notify it more promptly). It would not be liable for the seven forged checks cashed after the expiration of the 30-day period.

The case that follows, *Rhode Island Hospital Trust National Bank v. Zapata,* illustrates how the UCC applies to a series of forgeries. It was decided under the original version of Article 3, which provided a 14-day period for a customer to review a statement and notify the bank of any alterations or unauthorized signatures of the customer.

RHODE ISLAND HOSPITAL TRUST NATIONAL BANK v. ZAPATA CORP.
6 UCC Rep.2d 1 (1st Cir. 1988)

In early 1985, an employee of the Zapata Corporation stole some blank checks from the company. She wrote a large number of forged checks, almost all in amounts of $150 to $800 each, on Zapata's account at Rhode Island Hospital Trust National Bank. The bank, from March through July 1985, received and paid them. Bank statements that the bank regularly sent Zapata first began to reflect the forged checks in early 1985. Zapata failed to examine its statements closely until July 1985, when it found the forgeries. It immediately notified the bank, which then stopped clearing the checks. The bank already had processed and paid checks containing forged drawer's signatures totaling $109,247.16. Zapata then brought suit against the bank to have its account recredited for the checks.

The district court held that the bank was liable to reimburse Zapata for the checks that it paid before April 25, 1985 (two weeks after Zapata received the first statement containing the forged checks), but held in favor of the bank as to the remaining checks. Zapata appealed.

Breyer, Circuit Judge   The issue that this appeal presents is whether Zapata Corporation has shown that the system used by Rhode Island Hospital Trust National Bank for detecting forged checks—a system used by a majority of American banks—lacks the "ordinary care" that a bank must exercise under the Uniform Commercial Code section 4–406(3). The question arises out of the following district court determinations, all of which are adequately supported by the record and by Rhode Island law.

The Bank will (and legally must) reimburse Zapata in respect to all checks it cleared before April 25 (or for at least two weeks after Zapata received the statement that reflected the forgeries). See sections 3–401(1), 4–406(2). In respect to checks cleared on and after April 25, the Bank need not reimburse Zapata because Zapata failed to "exercise reasonable care and promptness to examine the [bank] statements." Section 4–406(1).

The question before us is whether this last-mentioned conclusion is correct or whether Zapata can recover for the post–April 24 checks on the theory that, even if it was negligent, so was the Bank.

To understand this question, one must examine UCC section 4–406. Ordinarily a bank must reimburse an innocent customer for forgeries that it honors, section 3–401(1), but section 4–406 makes an important exception to the liability rule. The exception operates in respect to a series of forged checks, and it applies once a customer has had a chance to catch the forgeries by examining his bank statements and notifying the bank but has failed to do so.

The statute, in relevant part, reads as follows:

(1) When a bank sends to its customer a statement of account accompanied by items paid in good faith in support of the debit entries or holds the statement and items pursuant to a request or instructions of its customer or otherwise in a reasonable manner makes the statement and items available to the customer, the customer must exercise reasonable care and promptness to examine the statement and items to discover his unauthorized signature or any alteration on an item and must notify the bank promptly after discovery thereof.

(2) If the bank establishes that the customer failed with respect to an item to comply with the duties imposed on the customer by subsection (1) the customer is precluded from asserting against the bank (a) His unauthorized signature or any alteration on the item if the bank also establishes that it suffered a loss by reason of such failure; and (b) An unauthorized signature or alteration by the same wrongdoer on any other item paid in good faith by the bank after the first item and statement was available to the customer for a reasonable period not exceeding fourteen (14) calendar days and before the bank receives notification from the customer of any such unauthorized signature or alteration. Section 4–406(1) and (2). (Emphasis added.)

The statute goes on to specify an important exception. It says:

(3) The preclusion under subsection (2) does not apply if the customer establishes lack of ordinary care on the part of the bank in paying the item(s). Section 4–406(3).

Zapata's specific claim on this appeal is that it falls within this "exception to the exception"—that the bank's treatment of the post–April 24 checks lacked "ordinary care." The statute places the burden of proof on Zapata. It says that strict bank liability terminates fourteen days after the customer receives the bank's statement unless "the customer establishes lack of ordinary care." The record convinces us that Zapata failed to carry its burden of establishing "lack of ordinary care" on the part of the Bank.

First the Bank described its ordinary practices as follows: The Bank examines all signatures on checks for more than $1,000. It examines signatures on checks between $100 and $1,000 (those at issue here) if it has reason to suspect a problem, e.g., if a customer has warned it of a possible forgery or if the check was drawn on an account with insufficient funds. It examines the signatures of a randomly chosen one percent of all other checks between $100 and $1,000. But it does not examine the signatures on other checks between $100 and $1,000. Through expert testimony, the Bank also established that most other banks in the nation follow this practice and that banking industry experts recommend it. Indeed, the Bank's practices are conservative in this regard, as most banks set $2,500 or more, not $1,000, as the limit beneath which they will not examine each signature. This testimony made out a prima facie case of "ordinary care."

Second, both bank and industry experts pointed out that this industry practice, in general and in the particular case of the Bank, saved considerable expense, compared with the Bank's pre-1981 practice of examining each check by hand. To be specific, the change saved the bank about $125,000 annually.

Third, both a Bank official and an industry expert testified that changing from an "individual signature examination" system to the new "bulk-filing" system led to no significant increase in the number of forgeries that were detected. Under the Bank's prior "individual signature examination" some forgeries still slipped through.

Fourth, even if one assumes, contrary to this uncontradicted evidence, that the new system meant some increase in the number of undetected forged checks, Zapata still could not prevail, for it presented no evidence tending to show any such increased loss unreasonable in light of the costs that the new practice would save.

Judgment for Rhode Island Hospital Trust National Bank affirmed.

Regardless of which party may have been negligent, a customer must discover and report to the bank any unauthorized customer's signature or any alteration within one year from the time after the statement or items are made available to him. If the customer does not do so, he cannot require the bank to recredit his account for such items. Similarly, a customer has three years from the time his statement or item is made available to discover and report any unauthorized indorsement on the item. The customer's failure to discover and report these irregularities within the one- or three-year periods specified ends his right to have his account recredited for the amount of the checks [4–406(f)].

CONCEPT REVIEW

Liability for Multiple Forgeries or Alterations by the Same Person

Date First Statement Disclosing an Altered or Forged Check Is Available to Customer	Date 30 Days Later	Date Customer Gives Notice of Alteration or Forgery
Customer is not liable for forged/altered checks paid during this period unless bank suffers a loss from customer's unreasonable delay in notifying bank of forgery or alteration.	Customer is liable for forged or altered checks paid during this period unless customer gives bank notice of forgery or alteration within a reasonable time after date the first statement containing a forged or altered check was available to customer.	Customer is not liable for forged or altered checks paid during this period.

CHECK COLLECTION AND FUNDS AVAILABILITY

Check Collection

As Chapter 30, Negotiable Instruments, describes, checks and other drafts collected through the banking system usually have at least three parties—the drawer, the drawee bank, and the payee. If the payee deposits the check at the same bank as the drawee bank, the latter will take a series of steps necessary to reflect the deposit as a credit to the payee's account and to decide whether to pay the check from the drawer's account. In connection with its handling of the deposit for the payee's benefit, it will make one ledger entry showing the deposit as a credit to the payee's account. In connection with its decision to pay, the bank's employees and computers will perform several steps commonly referred to as the process of posting.

Original Article 4 contained special rules describing the process of posting and the legal effect. The amendments to Article 4 deleted these special rules because automated check processing limited the legal significance of particular acts in posting [4–109 and 4–213(a)]. These steps need not be taken in any particular order, but they customarily include determining whether there are sufficient funds to pay, debiting the drawer's account for the amount of the check, and placing the check into a folder for later return to the drawer (to satisfy its obligations under the "bank statement" rule [4–406]. Banks in those states that have not enacted the amendments to Article 4 also will compare the drawer's signature on the check with that on the deposit agreement as part of this process.

If the payee deposits the check at a bank other than the drawee bank, the depositary bank, acting as the agent of the payee, will make the ledger entry showing the deposit as a credit to the payee's account. The next step of the collection process depends on where the depositary bank is located. If the drawee and depositary banks are in the same town or county, the depositary bank will indorse the check and deliver (present) it to the drawee bank for payment. It may deliver it by courier or through a local association of banks known as a *"clearinghouse"* [4–104(1)(d)]. The drawee-payor bank must settle for the check before midnight of the banking day of its receipt of the check, which means that it must give the depositary bank funds or a credit

equal to the amount of the check. Once it settles for the check, the drawee-payor bank has until midnight of the banking day after the banking day of receipt to pay the check or to return the check or send notice of dishonor. This deadline for the drawee-payor bank's action on the check is known as the bank's "midnight deadline" [4–104(1)(h)]. The drawee-payor bank's failure to settle by midnight of the banking day of receipt, or its failure to pay or return the check, or send notice of dishonor, results in the drawee-payor bank becoming "accountable" for the amount of the check, which means it must pay the amount of the check [4–302(a)].

If the drawee and depositary banks are located in different counties, or in different states, the depositary bank will use an additional commercial bank, and one or more of the regional Federal Reserve Banks, in the collection of the check. In these cases, the depositary bank will send the check on to the drawee-payor bank through these "collecting banks." Each bank in the sequence must use ordinary care in presenting the check or sending it for presentment, and in sending notice of dishonor or returning the check after learning that the check has not been paid [4–202(a)]. The depositary and collecting banks have until their respective midnight deadlines—or, in some cases, a further reasonable time—to take the action required of them in the sequence of collection steps.

If the drawee-payor bank dishonors the check prior to its midnight deadline or shortly after the midnight deadline under circumstances specified in "Regulation CC" of the Federal Reserve Board (described in the next section of this chapter), it will send the check back to the depositary bank. Until September 1, 1988, the drawee-payor bank customarily sent the dishonored check back to the collecting bank from which it received the check, and the collecting bank sent it back to the bank from which it had received it, and through any other bank that handled the check in the "forward collection" process until the check again reached the depositary bank. The provisions of Article 4 still describe this sequence as the "return collection" process, although Regulation CC imposes new responsibilities on the payor bank and on any other returning bank. Each bank in the return sequence adjusts its accounts to reflect the return and has until its midnight deadline to send the check back to the bank from which it originally had received the check. After

September 1, 1988 (or in states that previously had adopted "direct return" [4–212(b), the drawee-payor bank may return the check directly to the depositary bank—skipping all of the collecting banks and the delay represented by the midnight deadlines that each bank otherwise would have had.

Direct return also increases the likelihood that the depositary bank will know whether the check has been dishonored by the day on which Regulation CC requires the depositary bank to allow the payee to write checks or otherwise make withdrawals against the deposit. The next section of this chapter discusses this aspect of Regulation CC in more detail.

On receipt of the dishonored check, the depositary bank will return the check or otherwise notify its depositor (the payee) of the dishonor and will debit or charge back her account for the check it did not collect. The depositary bank may charge back the deposit even if it previously had allowed the payee-depositor to withdraw against the credit given for the deposit.

When the depositor receives the notice of dishonor and returned check, it will take one of several steps, depending on whether it received the check directly from the drawer or took it by indorsement from another person. If the depositor was not the original payee of the check, it usually will prefer to return the check—giving notice of dishonor unless already given by the drawee bank or another collecting bank—to the person who negotiated the check to her, the prior indorser. Recall that an indorser is obligated to pay the check following dishonor and notice of dishonor [3–415].

If the depositor received the check directly from the drawer, for example as payee, the depositor will normally demand payment from the drawer. Recall that the drawer is obligated to pay the check upon dishonor and notice of dishonor [3–414]; alternatively, the payee may seek to enforce the underlying obligation for which the drawer originally issued the check, such as the purchase of groceries or an automobile.

Funds Availability

When a bank taxes a check for deposit to a customer's account, it typically places a hold on the funds represented by the deposited check because it runs a number of risks in allowing a customer to withdraw deposits that it has not collected from the drawee bank. The risks that the check may be returned include: (1) there may be insufficient funds in the drawer's account or the account may have been closed; (2) the check may contain a forged drawer's or indorser's signature, or there may have been a material alteration of the check; (3) the possibility that the drawer is kiting checks or playing two accounts against each other; or (4) a stop-payment order may have been placed against the check. These are real concerns to a depositary bank, and it has a significant interest in protecting itself against these possibilities.

Until recently, the risks run by a depositary bank were complicated by a very slow process used by drawee-payor banks in returning a dishonored check or notifying the bank of the dishonor. Moreover, depositary banks do not get direct notice from drawee-payor banks when they pay checks. Accordingly, banks often restricted the depositor's use of the deposit by placing relatively long holds on checks deposited with them for collection; these sometimes ran 15 to 20 days for items drawn on other than local banks.

The extensive use of holds, and a growing public sentiment that they were excessive and often unfair, led to the passage by Congress in 1987 of the Expedited Funds Availability Act. In the act, Congress set out mandatory schedules limiting check holds and specifying when funds are to be made available to customers by depositary institutions. The act also delegated to the Federal Reserve Board the authority to speed up the check-processing system. The regulations adopted by the Board to speed up check processing supersede the provisions of Article 4 of the UCC (Bank Deposits and Collections) in a number of respects but will not be covered in this text.

The key elements of the mandatory funds availability schedules, which are set out in Federal Reserve Board Regulation CC, are:

1. Local checks (those drawn on banks in the same Federal Reserve check-processing region as the depositary bank) must be made available for the depositor to draw against by the second business day following deposit.

2. Nonlocal checks (those drawn on banks located in the United States but outside the Federal Reserve check-processing region in which the depositary bank is located) must be made available by the fifth business day following deposit.

3. Certain items must be made available by the next day after the day of deposit. These include:

   a. Cash deposits where the deposit is banked in person to an employee of the depositary bank (i.e., not at an ATM).

   b. Electronic payments.

   c. Checks drawn on the U.S. Treasury.

   d. U.S. Postal Service money orders.

   e. Checks drawn on a Federal Reserve Bank or Federal Home Loan Bank.

   f. Checks drawn by a state or a unit of local government (under certain conditions).

   g. Cashier's, certified, or teller's checks.

   h. Checks drawn on the depositary bank.

   i. The lesser of $100 or the aggregate deposit on any one banking day.

4. If the next-day items are not deposited in person with an employee of the depositary institution but rather are deposited in an ATM machine or by mail, then the deposit does not have to be made available for withdrawal until the second business day after deposit.

5. Generally, the depository bank must begin accruing interest to a depositor's interest-bearing account from the day it receives credit for cash and check deposits to an interest-bearing account.

There are six major exceptions to the mandatory availability schedules set out above that are designed to safeguard depositary banks against higher risk situations. The exceptions are:

1. *New account exception.* The depositary bank may suspend the availability rules for new accounts and can limit the next-day and second-day availability to the first $5,000 deposited.

2. *Large deposit exception.* The hold periods can be extended to the extent the aggregate deposit on any banking day exceeds $5,000.

3. *Redeposited check exception.* The hold period can be extended where a check has been returned one or more times.

4. *Repeated overdraft exception.* A longer hold period may be required for deposits to accounts that have been overdrawn repeatedly.

5. *Reasonable cause exception.* The scheduled availability may be extended where the bank has reasonable cause to believe the check is uncollectible.

6. *Emergency conditions exception.* The scheduled availability may be extended under certain emergency conditions such as a communications interruption or a computer failure.

Banks are required to disclose their funds availability policy to all of their customers; they may provide different policies to different classes or categories of customers.

ELECTRONIC BANKING

With the development of computer technology, many banks encourage their customers to transfer funds electronically by using computers rather than paper drafts and checks. A bank customer may use a specially coded card at terminals provided by the bank to make deposits to an account, to transfer money from one checking or savings account to another, to pay bills, or to withdraw cash from an account. These new forms of transferring money have raised questions about the legal rules that apply to them, and the questions are only beginning to be resolved.

Electronic Funds Transfer Act

The consumer who used electronic funds transfer systems (EFTs), the so-called cash machines or electronic tellers, in the early years often experienced problems in identifying and resolving mechanical errors resulting from malfunctioning EFTs. In response to these problems, Congress passed the Electronic Funds Transfer Act in 1978 to provide "a basic framework, establishing the rights, liabilities, and responsibilities of participants in electronic funds transfer systems" and especially to provide "individual consumer rights."

The four basic EFT systems are automated teller machines; point-of-sale terminals, which allow consumers to use their EFT cards like checks at retail establishments; preauthorized payments, such as automatic paycheck deposits or mortgage or utility payments; and telephone transfers between accounts or to pay specific bills by phone.

Similar to the Truth in Lending Act and the Fair Credit Billing Act (FCBA) discussed in Chapter 47, The Federal Trade Commission Act and Consumer Protection Laws, the EFT Act requires disclosure of the terms and conditions of electronic fund transfers at the time the consumer contracts for the EFT service. Among the nine disclosures required are the following: the consumer's liability for unauthorized electronic fund transfers (those resulting from loss or theft), the nature of the EFT services under the consumer's account, any pertinent dollar or frequency limitations, any charges for the right to make EFTs, the consumer's right to stop payment of a preauthorized transfer, the financial institution's liability to the consumer for failure to make or stop payments, and the consumer's right to receive documentation of transfers both at the point or time of transfer and periodically. The act also requires 21 days' notice prior to the effective date of any change in the terms or conditions of the consumer's account that pertains to the required disclosures.

The EFT Act does differ from the Fair Credit Billing Act in a number of important respects. For example, under the EFT Act, the operators of EFT systems are given a maximum of 10 working days to investigate errors or provisionally recredit the consumer's account, whereas issuers of credit cards are given a maximum of 60 days under the FCBA. The liability of the consumer is also different if an EFT card is lost or stolen than it is if a credit card is lost or stolen.

The case that follows, *Kruser v. Bank of America NT & SA,* illustrates the application of the EFT Act's provisions that require a customer to provide timely notification of any unauthorized use of his card in order to limit his liability for the unauthorized use of the card.

KRUSER v. BANK OF AMERICA NT & SA
281 Cal.Rptr. 463 (Cal. Ct. App. 1991)

Lawrence and Georgene Kruser maintained a joint checking account with the Bank of America, and the bank issued each of them a "Versatel" card and separate personal identification numbers that would allow access to funds in their account from automatic teller machines. The Krusers also received with their cards a "Disclosure Booklet" that provided to the Krusers a summary of consumer liability, the bank's business hours, and the address and telephone number by which they could notify the bank in the event they believed an unauthorized transfer had been made.

The Krusers believed Mr. Kruser's card had been destroyed in September 1986. The December 1986 account statement mailed to the Krusers by the bank reflected a $20 unauthorized withdrawal of funds by someone using Mr. Kruser's card at an automatic teller machine. The Krusers reported this unauthorized transaction to the bank when they discovered it in August or September 1987.

Mrs. Kruser underwent surgery in late 1986 or early 1987 and remained hospitalized for 11 days. She then spent a period of six or seven months recuperating at home. During this time, she reviewed the statements the Krusers received from the bank.

In September 1987, the Krusers received bank statements for July and August 1987 that reflected 47 unauthorized withdrawals totaling $9,020 made from an automatic teller machine, again by someone using Mr. Kruser's card. They notified the bank of these withdrawals within a few days of receiving the statements. The bank refused to credit the Kruser's account with the amount of the unauthorized withdrawals. The Krusers sued the bank, claiming damages for the unauthorized withdrawals from their account. The trial court ruled in favor of the bank on the grounds that the Krusers had failed to comply with the note and reporting requirements of the Electronic Funds Transfer Act (EFTA). The Krusers appealed.

Stone, Associate Justice   The ultimate issue we address is whether, as a matter of law, the unauthorized $20 withdrawal which appeared on the December 1986 statement barred the Krusers from recovery for the losses incurred in July and August 1987. Resolution of the issue requires the interpretation of the EFTA and section 205.6 of Regulation E, one of the regulations prescribed by the Board of Governors of the Federal Reserve System in order to carry out the EFTA.

Section 205.6 of Regulation E mirrors [the EFTA] and in particular provides:

(b) Limitations on amount of liability. The amount of a consumer's liability for an unauthorized electronic fund transfer or a series of related unauthorized transfers shall not exceed $50 or the amount of unauthorized transfers that occur before notice to the financial institution . . ., whichever is less, unless one of the following exceptions apply:

* * * * *

(2) If the consumer fails to report within 60 days of transmittal of the periodic statement any unauthorized electronic fund transfer that appears on the statement, the consumer's liability shall not exceed the sum of (i) The lesser of $50 or the amount of unauthorized electronic fund transfers that appear on the periodic statement during the 60-day period and (ii) The amount of unauthorized electronic fund transfers that occur after the close of the 60 days and before notice to the financial institution and that the financial institution establishes would not have occurred but for the failure of the consumer to notify the financial institution within that time.

* * * * *

(4) If a delay in notifying the financial statements was due to extenuating circumstances, such as extended travel or hospitalization, the time periods specified above shall be extended to a reasonable time.

The trial court concluded the Bank was entitled to judgment as a matter of law because the unauthorized withdrawals of July and August 1987 occurred more than 60 days after the Krusers received a statement which reflected an unauthorized transfer in December 1986. The court relied upon section 205.6(b)(2) of Regulation E.

The Krusers contend the December withdrawal of $20 was so isolated in time and minimal in amount that it cannot be considered in connection with the July and August withdrawals. They assert the court's interpretation of section 205.6(b)(2) of Regulation E would have absurd results which would be inconsistent with the primary objective of the EFTA—to protect the consumer. They argue that if a consumer receives a bank statement which reflects an unauthorized minimal electronic transfer and fails to report the transaction to the bank within 60 days of transmission of the bank statement, unauthorized transfers many years later, perhaps totalling thousands of dollars, would remain the responsibility of the consumer.

The result the Krusers fear is avoided by the requirement that the bank establish the subsequent unauthorized transfers could have been prevented had the consumer notified the bank of the first unauthorized transfer. Here, although the unauthorized transfer of $20 occurred approximately seven months before the unauthorized transfers totalling $9,020, it is undisputed that all transfers were made by using Mr. Kruser's card which the Krusers believed had been destroyed prior to December 1986. According to the declaration of Yvonne Maloon, the Bank's Versatel risk manager, the Bank could have and would have cancelled Mr. Kruser's card had it been timely notified of the December unauthorized transfer. In that event Mr. Kruser's card could not have been used to accomplish the unauthorized transactions in July and August 1987.

In the alternative, the Krusers contend the facts establish that Mrs. Kruser, who was solely responsible for reconciling the bank statements, was severely ill and was also caring for a terminally ill relative when the December withdrawal occurred. Therefore they claim they were entitled to an extension of time within which to notify the bank.

The evidence the Krusers rely upon indicates in late 1986 or early 1987 Mrs. Kruser underwent surgery and remained in the hospital for 11 days. She left her house infrequently during the first six or seven months of 1987 during which she was recuperating. Mrs. Kruser admits, however, she received and reviewed bank statements during her recuperation. Therefore, we need not consider whether Mrs. Kruser's illness created circumstances which might have excused her failure to notice the unauthorized withdrawal pursuant to the applicable sections. She in fact did review the statements in question.

Judgment for Bank of America affirmed.

DOCUMENTS OF TITLE

Introduction

Storing or shipping goods, giving a warehouse receipt or bill of lading representing the goods, and transferring such a receipt or bill of lading as representing the goods are practices of ancient origin. The warehouseman or the common carrier is a bailee of the goods who contracts to store or transport the goods and to deliver them to the owner or to act otherwise in accordance with the lawful directions of the owner. The **warehouse receipt** or the **bill of lading** may be either negotiable or non-negotiable. To be negotiable, a warehouse receipt, bill of lading, or other document of title must provide that the goods are to be delivered to the bearer or to the order of a named person [7–104(1)]. The primary differences between the law of negotiable instruments and the law of negotiable documents of title are based on the differences between the obligation to pay money and the obligation to deliver specific goods.

Warehouse Receipts

A warehouse receipt, to be valid, need not be in any particular form, but if it does not embody within its written or printed form each of the following, the warehouseman is liable for damages caused by the omission to a person injured as a result of it: (1) the location of the warehouse where the goods are stored; (2) the date of issue; (3) the consecutive number of the receipt; (4) whether the goods are to be delivered to the bearer or to the order of a named person; (5) the rate of storage and handling charges; (6) a description of the goods or of the packages containing them; (7) the signature of the warehouseman or his agent; (8) whether the warehouseman is the owner of the goods, solely, jointly, or in common with others; and (9) a statement of the amount of the advances made and of the liabilities incurred for which the warehouseman claims a lien or security interest. Other terms may be inserted [7–202].

A warehouseman is liable to a purchaser for value in good faith of a warehouse receipt for nonreceipt or misdescription of goods. The receipt may conspicuously qualify the description by a statement such as "contents, condition, and quantity unknown" [7–203].

Because a warehouseman is a bailee of the goods, he owes to the holder of the warehouse receipt the duties of a mutual benefit bailee and must exercise reasonable care [7–204]. Chapter 23, Personal Property and Bailments, discusses the duties of a bailee in detail. The warehouseman may terminate the relation by notification where, for example, the goods are about to deteriorate or where they constitute a threat to other goods in the warehouse [7–206]. Unless the warehouse receipt provides otherwise, the warehouseman must keep separate the goods covered by each receipt; however, different lots of fungible goods such as grain may be mingled [7–207].

A warehouseman has a lien against the bailor on the goods covered by his receipt for his storage and other charges incurred in handling the goods [7–209]. The Code sets out a detailed procedure for enforcing this lien [7–210].

Bills of Lading

In many respects, the rights and liabilities of the parties to a negotiable bill of lading are the same as the rights and liabilities of the parties to a negotiable warehouse receipt. The contract of the issuer of a bill of lading is to transport goods, whereas the contract of the issuer of a warehouse receipt is to store goods. Like the issuer of a warehouse receipt, the issuer of a bill of lading is liable for nonreceipt or misdescription of the goods, but he may protect himself from liability where he does not know the contents of packages by marking the bill of lading "contents or condition of packages unknown" or similar language. Such terms are ineffective when the goods are loaded by an issuer who is a common carrier unless the goods are concealed by packages [7–301].

Duty of Care

A carrier who issues a bill of lading, or a warehouse operator who issues a warehouse receipt, must exercise the same degree of care in relation to the goods as a reasonably careful person would exercise under similar circumstances. Liability for damages not caused by the negligence of the carrier may be imposed on him by a special law or rule of law. Under tariff rules, a common carrier may limit her liability to a shipper's declaration of value, provided that the rates are dependent on value [7–309]. In the case that follows, *Calvin Klein Ltd. v. Trylon Trucking Corp.,* a court enforced a $50 per shipment limitation that had been part of a long series of shipping contracts where the customer had the opportunity to declare a higher value and failed to do so.

Calvin Klein Ltd. v. Trylon Trucking Corp.
892 F.2d 191 (2d Cir. 1989)

Trylon Trucking Corporation is a New Jersey trucking firm that engaged in the business of transporting goods from New York City's airports for delivery to its customers' facilities. For three years prior to 1986, Calvin Klein, a New York clothing company, used the services of Trylon involving hundreds of shipments. Calvin Klein, through its customs broker, would contact Trylon to pick up the shipment from the airport for delivery to Calvin Klein's facility. After completing the delivery carriage, Trylon would forward to Calvin Klein an invoice, which contained a limitation of liability provision as follows:

In consideration of the rate charged, the shipper agrees that the carrier shall not be liable for more than $50.00 on any shipment accepted for delivery to one consignee unless a greater value is declared, in writing, upon receipt at time of shipment and charge for such greater value paid, or agreed to be paid, by the shipper.

A shipment of 2,833 blouses from Hong Kong arrived at John F. Kennedy International Airport for Calvin Klein on March 27, 1986. Calvin Klein arranged for Trylon to pick up the shipment and deliver it to Calvin Klein's New Jersey warehouse. On April 2, Trylon dispatched its driver, J. Jefferson, to pick up this shipment. Jefferson signed a receipt for the shipment from Calvin Klein's broker. Later, on April 2, the parties discovered that Jefferson had stolen Trylon's truck and its shipment. The shipment was never recovered.

Calvin Klein sent a claim letter to Trylon for the full value of the lost blouses. When it did not receive a response from Trylon, Calvin Klein filed suit against Trylon, seeking to recover $150,000, the alleged value of the blouses. In the pleadings before the court, the parties agreed that Trylon was liable to Calvin Klein for the loss of the shipment and that it had been grossly negligent in the hiring and supervision of Jefferson. They also agreed that "the terms and conditions of Trylon's carriage were that liability for loss or damage to cargo is limited to $50 in accordance with the provision in Trylon's invoice forms." Calvin Klein conceded that it was aware of the limitation of liability and that it did not declare a value on the blouses at the time of shipment.

Trylon contended that its liability was limited to $50 in accordance with the provision in its invoice forms. Calvin Klein argued that the limitation clause was not enforceable for two reasons: (1) no agreement existed between it and Trylon as to the limitation of liability; and (2) even if an agreement existed, public policy would prevent its enforcement because of Trylon's gross negligence. The district court held that Calvin Klein had not assented to the limitation clause for this shipment and awarded damages to Calvin Klein of $101,542.62. Trylon appealed.

Miner, Circuit Judge A common carrier is strictly liable for the loss of goods in its custody. Where the loss is not due to excepted causes [that is, act of God or public enemy, inherent nature of goods, or shipper's fault], it is immaterial whether the carrier was negligent or not. Even in the case of loss from theft by third parties, liability may be imposed upon a negligent common carrier.

A shipper and a common carrier may contract to limit the carrier's liability in cases of loss to an amount agreed to by the parties, so long as the language of the limitation is clear, the shipper is aware of the terms of the limitation, and the shipper can change the terms by indicating the true value of the goods being shipped. Section 7–309(2). Such a limitation agreement is generally valid and enforceable despite carrier negligence. The limitation of liability provision involved here clearly provides that, at the time of delivery, the shipper may increase the limitation by written notice of the value of the goods to be delivered and by payment of a commensurately higher fee.

The parties stipulated to this fact that the $50 limitation of liability was a term and condition of carriage and that Calvin Klein was aware of that limitation. This stipulated fact removes the first issue, namely whether an agreement existed as to a liability limitation between the parties. Calvin Klein's argument that it never previously acknowledged this limitation by accepting only $50 in settlement of a larger loss does not alter this explicit stipulation. The district court erred in not accepting the limitation of liability as stipulated.

The remaining issue concerns the enforceability of the limitation clause in the light of Trylon's conceded gross negligence.

Since carriers are strictly liable for loss of shipments in their custody and are insurers of those goods, the degree of carrier negligence is immaterial. The common carrier must exercise reasonable care in relation to the shipment in its custody. Section 7–309(2). Carriers can contract with their shipping customers on the amount of liability each party will bear for the loss of a shipment, regardless of the amount of carrier negligence. Unlike a merchant acquiring a burglar alarm, the shipper can calculate the specific amount of its potential damages in advance, declare the value of the shipment based on that calculation, can pay a commensurately higher rate to carry the goods, in effect buying additional insurance from the common carrier.

In this case Calvin Klein and Trylon were business entities with an ongoing commercial relationship involving numerous carriages of Calvin Klein goods by Trylon. Where such entities deal with each other in a commercial setting, and no special relationship exists between the parties, clear limitations between them will be enforced. Here, each carriage was under the same terms and conditions as the last, including a limitation of Trylon's liability. This is not a case in which the shipper was dealing with the common carrier for the first time or contracting under new or changed conditions. Calvin Klein was aware of the terms and was free to adjust the limitation upon a written declaration of the value of a given shipment, but failed to do so with the shipment at issue here. Since Calvin Klein failed to adjust the limitation, the limitation applies here, and no public policy that dictates otherwise can be identified.

Calvin Klein also argues that the limitation is so low as to be void. The amount is immaterial because Calvin Klein had the opportunity to negotiate the amount of coverage by declaring the value of the shipment. Commercial entities can easily negotiate the degree of risk each party will bear and which party will bear the cost of insurance. Calvin Klein had the opportunity to declare a higher value and we find all of its arguments relating to the unreasonableness of the limitation to be without merit.

District court judgment reversed with instructions to enter judgment for Calvin Klein for $50.

Negotiation of Document of Title

A negotiable document of title and a negotiable instrument are negotiated in substantially the same manner. If the document of title provides for the delivery of the goods to bearer, it may be negotiated by delivery. If it provides for delivery of the goods to the order of a named person, it must be indorsed by that person and delivered. If an order document of title is indorsed in blank, it may be negotiated by delivery unless it bears a special indorsement following the blank indorsement, in which event it must be indorsed by the special indorsee and delivered [7–501].

A person taking a negotiable document of title takes as a bona fide holder if she takes in good faith and in the regular course of business. The bona fide holder of a negotiable document of title has substantially the same advantages over a holder who is not a bona fide holder or over a holder of a non-negotiable document of title as does a holder in due course of a negotiable instrument over a holder who is not a holder in due course or over a holder of a non-negotiable instrument.

Rights Acquired by Negotiation

A person who acquires a negotiable document of title by due negotiation acquires (1) title to the document, (2) title to the goods, (3) the right to the goods delivered to the bailee after the issuance of the document, and (4) the direct obligation of the issuer to hold or deliver the goods according to the terms of the document [7–502(1)].

Under the broad general principle that a person cannot transfer title to goods he does not own, a thief—or the owner of goods subject to a perfected security interest—cannot, by warehousing or shipping the goods on a negotiable document of title and then negotiating the document of title, transfer to the purchaser of the document of title a better title than he has [7–503].

Warranties of ᵗsferor of Document of Title

The transferor of a negotiable document of title warrants to his immediate transferee, in addition to any warranty of goods, only that the document is genuine, that he has no knowledge of any facts that would impair its validity or worth, and that his negotiation or transfer is rightful and fully effective with respect to the title to the document and the goods it represents [7–507].

ETHICAL AND PUBLIC POLICY CONCERNS

1. Suppose you take your car to a garage to have it repainted. When you go to pick it up, you are not happy with the quality of the work, but the garage owner refuses to release the car to you unless you pay him in full for the work. You give him a check in the amount requested, and on the way home stop at your bank and request that the bank stop payment on the check you have just written, an action you decided to take when you were writing out the check. Have you acted ethically?

2. Some banks take the position that because they process checks with the use of computers, a customer seeking to stop payment on a check must provide them with the amount of the check with every digit correct in order for the bank to be able to stop payment. What policy considerations are involved in deciding whether the bank's position should establish the minimum information required for a bank to have a "reasonable opportunity" to respond to the customer's request?

3. Suppose that you own and operate a warehouse. A local liquor store owner occasionally uses your facilities to store shipments of wine from France until he has room for the wine in his store. You are aware that from time to time your warehouse employees "borrow" a bottle from the crates of wine being stored in your warehouse. After a number of crates with a total of four bottles missing are delivered to the liquor store, the store owner queries you about the missing bottles and you tell him that they must have been broken in transit to your warehouse. Have you acted ethically?

PROBLEMS AND PROBLEM CASES

1. J. E. B. Stewart received a check in the amount of $185.48 in payment of a fee from a client. Stewart presented the check, properly indorsed, to the Citizen's & Southern Bank. The bank refused to cash the check even though there were sufficient funds in the drawer's account. Stewart then sued the bank for actual damages of $185.48 and for punitive damages of $50,000 for its failure to cash a valid check drawn against a solvent account in the bank. Does Stewart have a good cause of action against the bank?

2. Louise Kalbe signed a check drawn on her account at the Pulaski State Bank; later, that check was lost or stolen. The check was drafted for $7,260 payable to cash. The bank paid the check, which created an overdraft of $6,542.12 in Kalbe's account. The bank brought a lawsuit against Kalbe to recover the overdraft. Kalbe asserted that the check was not properly payable from her account. Was the bank legally entitled to pay a check that exceeded the balance in her account and to recover the overdraft from her?

3. On November 15, Midgen, the drawer of a check, issued a written stop-payment order to Chase

Manhattan Bank, the drawee on the check. Midgen provided the correct payee, check date, and account and check number. However, he incorrectly stated the amount of the check to be $759.92. In fact, the amount was $754.92. Chase Manhattan paid the check on December 7. Should the $5 difference in the amount relieve Chase Manhattan of liability for paying the check over the stop-payment order?

4. In November 1981, Marc Gardner, the president of M. G. Sales, Inc., made out two checks on the account of M. G. Sales at Chemical Bank. The checks were both in the amount of $6,000 and were payable to, signed, and indorsed by Gardner. Apparently, he lost both checks. Consequently, on November 16, 1981, he went to Chemical Bank and obtained two stop-payment orders that, by their terms, were valid for six months. In January and February 1983, the checks were deposited into an account at another branch of Chemical Bank and the proceeds were credited to that account. M. G. Sales then brought an action against Chemical Bank for paying the checks despite the earlier stop-payment order and the fact the check was more than six months old and thus "stale." Is M. G. Sales entitled to have its account recredited?

5. In December, Whalley Company hired Nancy Cherauka as its bookkeeper. Her duties included preparing checks, taking deposits to the bank, and reconciling the monthly checking account statements. She was not authorized to sign or cash checks. Between the following January 24 and May 31, Cherauka forged 49 checks on the Whalley account at National City Bank. Each month, National City Bank sent Whalley a statement and the canceled checks (including the forgeries) it had paid the previous month. The president of Whalley looked at the statement to see the balance in the account but he did not look at the individual checks. Then he gave the statement and checks to the bookkeeper. The January 24 forged check was sent to Whalley on February 3. In June, Whalley discovered that Cherauka was forging checks and fired her. It then brought a lawsuit against National City Bank to force it to recredit Whalley's account with the total amount of the 49 checks. Whalley claimed that the checks were not properly payable from the account. Is National City required to recredit Whalley's account?

6. Two couples, Edna and Larry Brown and Mary and James Knight, formed a cable television construction business known as Knight Communications, Inc., with the four principals as directors. The Browns provided about $50,000 in capital and the Knights operated the company. According to the deposit/account agreement for the corporate checking account opened in January 1986 at the Boatmen's National Bank of St. Louis and the understanding of the parties, each check required the signature of one of the Knights and one of the Browns. Beginning February 21, 1986, the bank began honoring checks with the signature of only one or both Knights. Between February and May 1986, 105 checks lacking a Brown signature (out of over 500 checks issued by the corporation during this time) were paid by the bank. The total of the improperly payable checks payable to the Knights was $7,696.94. One of the bank officers asserted that he had oral permission of Mr. Brown to pay the checks but Mr. Brown later denied that he ever gave oral or written permission to the bank to honor checks without a Brown signature. The bank regularly returned the cancelled checks to the corporation along with a periodic statement of account, but the corporation made no contemporaneous objection to the lack of signatures by a Brown. The Brown-Knight joint enterprise effectively ended in August 1986. At that time, Mr. Brown delivered some of the improperly paid checks to his attorney and other cancelled checks were delivered to that attorney by the Knights. In September 1988, a lawsuit was filed in the name of Knight Communications against the bank for breach of contract for unauthorized payment of the checks without the required Brown signature. This was the first time that the lack of authorization issue was raised with the bank. Is the drawee bank liable to the drawer for the amount of checks it paid containing unauthorized drawer's signatures when it is notified of that fact two years after the checks were made available to the drawer?

7. On August 16, 1981, Frederick Ognibene went to the ATM area at a Citibank branch and activated one of the machines with his Citibank card, pressed in his personal identification code, and withdrew $20. When he approached the machine a person was using the customer service telephone located between two ATM machines and appeared to be telling customer service that one of the machines was malfunctioning. As Ognibene was making his withdrawal, the person said into the telephone, "I'll see if his card works in my machine." He then asked Ognibene if he could use his card to see if the other machine was working. Ognibene handed his card to him and saw him insert it into the adjoining machine at least two times while saying into the telephone, "Yes, it seems to be working." When Ognibene received his Citibank statement, it showed that two withdrawals of $200 each from his account were made at 5:42 P.M. and 5:43 P.M., respectively, on August 16. His own $20 withdrawal was made at 5:41 P.M.. At that time, Ognibene was unaware that any withdrawals from his account were being made from the adjoining machine. Ognibene sought to have his account recredited for $400, claiming that the withdrawals had been unauthorized. Citibank had been aware for some time of a scam being perpetrated against its customers by persons who observed the customer inserting his personal identification number into an ATM and then obtained access to the customer's ATM card in the same manner as Ognibene's card was obtained. After learning about the scam, Citibank posted signs in ATM areas containing a red circle approximately 2 ½ inches in diameter in which was written "Do Not Let Your Citicard Be Used For Any Transaction But Your Own." Was Citibank required under the Electronic Fund Transfer Act to recredit Ognibene's account on the grounds that the withdrawal of the $400 was unauthorized?

8. Griswold and Bateman Warehouse Company stored 337 cases of Chivas Regal Scotch Whiskey for Joseph H. Reinfeld, Inc., in its bonded warehouse. The warehouse receipt issued to Reinfeld limited Griswold and Bateman's liability for negligence to 250 times the monthly storage rate, a total of $1,925. When Reinfeld sent its truck to pick up the whiskey, 40 cases were missing. Reinfeld then brought suit seeking the wholesale market value of the whiskey, $6,417.60. Reinfeld presented evidence of the delivery of the whiskey, the demand for its return, and the failure of Griswold and Bateman to return it. Reinfeld claimed that the burden was on Griswold and Bateman to explain the disappearance of the whiskey. Griswold and Bateman admitted that it had been negligent, but sought to limit its liability to $1,925. Is Griswold and Bateman's liability limited to $1,925?

9. Everlens Mitchell entered into a written contract with All American Van & Storage to transport and store her household goods. She was to pay the storage charges on a monthly basis. As security, she granted All American a warehouseman's lien. All American had the right to sell the property if the charges remained unpaid for three months and if, in the opinion of the company, such action was necessary to protect the accrued charges. Mitchell fell eight months behind on her payments. On October 20, 1985, she received notice that if the unpaid charges, totaling $804.30, were not paid by October 31, her goods would be sold on November 7. Mitchell advised All American that she had a claim pending with the Social Security Administration and would soon receive a large sum of money. This was confirmed to All American by several government officials. However, All American sold Mitchell's property on November 7 for $925.50. At the end of the month, Mitchell received a $5,500 disability payment. She sued All American for improperly selling her goods. The trial court awarded judgment to All American. Should the decision be reversed on appeal?

10. On October 15, Young delivered 207 bags of rice to Atteberry's warehouse and received a non-negotiable receipt. Young then transferred the receipt to Brock for a valuable consideration, and Brock notified Atteberry of the transfer on November 3. Prior to November 3, however, Young had procured a negotiable receipt for the rice along with some other rice he had deposited with Atteberry. Brock presented his non-negotiable receipt to Atteberry and demanded delivery of the rice. Atteberry contended that no rice was being held at the warehouse on Brock's account. Who is correct?

11. 📼   *Video Case* See "Sour Grapes." Jelly Manufacturer orders some grapes by phone from Grape Grower in California on a COD basis. When the grapes arrive, Jelly Manufacturer pays for them by check before discovering that they had spoiled enroute because they had been shipped in a nonrefrigerated truck. After calling Grape Grower to complain, Jelly Manufacturer calls its bank and places a stop-payment order on the check. The bank's computer fails to catch the check and the check is paid to Grape Grower. Does Jelly Manufacturer have any recourse against the bank for paying the check over the stop-payment order?

AGENCY

LAW

CHAPTER

3 4

THE AGENCY RELATIONSHIP

INTRODUCTION

Frequently, businesses are legally bound by the actions of their employees or other representatives. For example, corporations frequently are liable on contracts their employees make or for torts those employees commit. We take such liability for granted, but it is not immediately obvious why we should. A corporation is an artificial legal person distinct from the officers, employees, and other representatives who contract on its behalf and who may commit torts while performing their duties. Similarly, a sole proprietor is distinct from the people he may employ. How can these and other business actors be bound on contracts they did not make or for torts they did not commit? The reason is the law of agency.

DEFINITION OF AGENCY

Agency is a two-party relationship in which one party (the **agent**) is authorized to act on behalf of, and under the control of, the other party (the **principal**). Simple examples include hiring a salesperson to sell goods, retaining an attorney, and engaging a real estate broker to sell a house. Agency law's most important social function is to stimulate business and commercial activity. It does so by enabling businesses to increase the number of transactions they can complete within a given time. Without agency, for instance, a sole proprietor's ability to engage in trade would be limited by the need to make each of her purchase or sale contracts in person. As artificial persons, moreover, corporations can only act through their agents.

Agency law divides into two rough categories. The first involves legal relations *between the principal and the agent.* These include the rules governing formation of an agency, the duties the principal and the agent owe each other, and the ways an agency can be terminated. These topics are the main concern of this chapter. Chapter 35 discusses the principal's and the agent's relations with *third parties.* Here, our main concerns are the principal's and the agent's liability on contracts the agent makes and for torts the agent commits.

CREATION OF AN AGENCY AND RELATED MATTERS

Formation

An agency is created by the manifested agreement of two parties that one party (the agent) will act for the benefit of the other (the principal) under the principal's direction.[1] As the term *manifested* suggests, the test for an agency's existence is *objective*. If the parties' behavior and the surrounding facts and circumstances indicate an agreement that one person is to act for the benefit and under the control of another, courts hold that the relationship exists. If the facts establish an agency, it is immaterial whether either party knows about the agency's existence or subjectively desires that it exist. In fact, an agency may be present even where the parties expressly state that they do not intend to create it or intend to create some other legal relationship instead.

Often, parties create an agency by a written contract. But an agency contract may be oral unless state law provides otherwise.[2] Some states, for example, require written evidence of contracts to pay an agent

a commission for the sale of real estate. More importantly, the agency relation need not be contractual at all. Thus, consideration is not necessary to form an agency. As the *Warren* case (which follows shortly) illustrates, courts sometimes imply an agency from the parties' behavior and the surrounding circumstances without discussing the need for a contract or for consideration.

Capacity

A principal or agent who lacks the necessary mental capacity when the agency is formed ordinarily can release himself from the agency at his option. Examples include those who are minors or are mentally incapacitated when the agency is created. Of course, incapacity may occur at other times as well; we discuss such situations at various points in this chapter and Chapter 35.

As you have seen, corporations can and must appoint agents. In a partnership, each partner normally acts as the agent of the partnership in transacting partnership business,[3] and partnerships can appoint nonpartner agents as well. In addition, corporations, partnerships, and other business organizations themselves can act as agents.

Nondelegable Obligations

Certain duties or acts must be performed personally and cannot be delegated to an agent. Examples include making statements under oath, voting in public elections, and signing a will. The same is true for service contracts in which the principal's personal performance is crucial—for example, certain contracts by lawyers, doctors, artists, and entertainers.

---

[1]Sometimes it is said that an agency may also be created by *ratification, estoppel,* or *operation of law.* Usually, however, ratification and estoppel are regarded as ways of binding the principal to an agent's actions, not as ways of forming an agency in the first place. Ratification is discussed in Chapter 35, and estoppel resembles the concept of apparent authority discussed later in this chapter and in Chapter 35. It is unusual for an agency to be created by operation of law. An example might be a statute designating a state's secretary of state as an out-of-state motorist's "agent" for purposes of receiving a summons and a complaint in a lawsuit against the motorist.

[2]Usually, the state law in question is the statute of frauds, which is discussed in Chapter 16. Also, it sometimes is said that if the contract the agent is to form must be in writing, the agency agreement likewise must be written. However, it is doubtful whether this "equal dignity rule" enjoys widespread acceptance.

[3]Chapter 37 discusses how agency law operates in the partnership context.

WARREN v. UNITED STATES
613 F.2d 591 (5th Cir. 1980)

For two years, Bobby and Modell Warren took their cotton crops to certain cotton gins that ginned and baled the cotton. After being so instructed by the Warrens, the gins obtained bids for the cotton from prospective buyers and the Warrens told the gins which bids to accept. Then the gins sold the cotton to the designated buyers, collecting the proceeds. At the Warrens' instruction, the gins deferred payment of the proceeds to the Warrens until the year after the one in which each sale was made.

The Warrens did not report the proceeds as taxable income for the year when the gins received the proceeds, instead including the proceeds in their return for the following year. After an IRS audit, the Warrens were compelled to treat the proceeds as taxable income for the year when the proceeds were received, and to pay accordingly. The Warrens eventually won a refund action in federal district court. The government appealed, arguing that the gins were agents of the Warrens. Because receipt of proceeds by an agent is receipt by the principal, this would mean that the proceeds were taxable income for the year when they were received by the gins.

Johnson, Circuit Judge   The relationship between the Warrens and the gins for the purpose of selling the cotton was indisputably that of principal and agent. The Warrens instructed the gins to solicit bids, the Warrens decided whether to accept the highest price offered, and the Warrens determined whether or not to instruct the gins to hold the proceeds from the sale until the following year. The gins' role in the sale of the cotton was to adhere to the Warrens' instructions. The Warrens were the owners of the cotton held for sale; the Warrens were in complete control of its disposition.

This case is distinguishable from those cases where it was recognized that proceeds from the sale of a crop by a farmer, pursuant to a bona fide arm's-length contract between the buyer and seller calling for payment in the taxable year following delivery, are includable in gross income for the taxable year in which payment is received. In the case at bar the bona fide arm's-length agreement was not between the buyer and seller but rather between the seller and his agent. The income was received by the Warrens' agents in the year of the sale. The fact that the Warrens restricted their access to the sales proceeds does not change the tax status of the money received.

Judgment reversed in favor of the government.

AGENCY CONCEPTS, DEFINITIONS, AND TYPES

Agency law includes various concepts, definitions, and distinctions. These matters often determine the rights, duties, and liabilities of the principal, the agent, and third parties. In addition, they sometimes are important outside agency law. Because these basic topics are so crucial in so many different contexts, we outline them together here.

Authority

Although agency law lets people multiply their dealings by employing agents, a principal should not be liable for *any* deal his agent concludes. Thus, agency law normally lets an agent bind his principal only when the agent has **authority** to do so. Authority is an agent's ability to affect his principal's legal relations. Authority comes in two main forms: **actual authority** and **apparent authority.** Each is based on the principal's manifested consent that the agent may act for and bind the principal. For actual authority, this consent is communicated to the *agent;* for apparent authority, it is communicated to the *third party.*

Actual authority comes in two forms: **express authority** and **implied authority.** Express authority is created by the principal's actual words (whether written or oral). Thus, an agent has express authority to bind her principal in a certain fashion only when the principal has made a fairly precise statement to that effect. Often, however, it is impractical for a principal to specify the agent's authority fully and exactly. Thus, to avoid unnecessarily restricting an agent's ability to represent her principal, agency law also gives agents *implied authority* to bind their principals. An agent generally has implied authority to do whatever it is reasonable to assume that the principal wanted him to do, given the principal's express statements and the surrounding circumstances. Relevant factors include the principal's express statements, the nature of the agency, the acts reasonably necessary to carry on the agency business, and the acts customarily done when conducting that business.

Sometimes, an agent who lacks actual authority may still *appear* to have such authority, and third parties may reasonably rely on this appearance of authority. To protect third parties in such situations, agency law lets agents bind the principal on the basis of their *apparent authority*. Apparent authority arises when the principal's behavior causes a third party to form a reasonable belief that the agent is authorized to act in a certain way. Apparent authority depends on what the principal communicates to the third party—either directly or through the agent. A principal might clothe an agent with apparent authority by making direct statements to the third party, telling an agent to do so, or allowing an agent to behave in a way that creates an appearance of authority. Communica-tions to the agent are irrelevant unless they become known to the third party or affect the agent's behavior. Also, agents cannot give them-selves apparent authority, and apparent authority does not exist where the agent creates an appearance of authority without the principal's consent. Finally, the third party must *reasonably* believe in the agent's authority. Trade customs and business practices can help courts determine whether such a belief was reasonable.

Authority is important in a number of agency contexts. Chapter 35 examines its most important application—determining a principal's liability on contracts made by his agent. As the following *Towers* case illustrates, moreover, authority finds application outside agency law as well.

TOWERS WORLD AIRWAYS v. PHH AVIATION SYSTEMS
933 F.2d 174 (2d Cir. 1991)

PHH Aviation Systems leased a corporate jet to Towers World Airways. PHH also issued a credit card to Towers to buy fuel for the jet from sellers of airplane fuel. The contract between PHH and Towers made Towers liable to PHH for fuel purchases Towers made with the card. A Towers officer allowed Fred Jay Schley, the jet's chief pilot, to use the card to make fuel purchases for *noncharter* flights. However, there was conflicting testimony regarding Schley's authorization to use the card for *chartered* flights. Nonetheless, Schley charged over $89,000 to Towers in connection with fuel purchases for chartered flights.

Claiming that it was not liable to PHH for the $89,000 because the Truth-in-Lending Act limited its liability to $50, Towers sued for a declaratory judgment to that effect. PHH counterclaimed for the $89,000 and then successfully moved for summary judgment. Towers appealed.

Newman, Circuit Judge   Congress enacted the 1970 amendments to the Truth-in-Lending Act to protect credit cardholders from unauthorized use by those able to obtain possession of a card from its original owner. The amendments enacted a scheme for limiting the liability of cardholders for all charges by third parties made without "actual [ex-press], implied, or apparent authority." Where an unauthorized use has occurred, the cardholder can be held liable only up to a limit of $50, if certain conditions are satisfied.

Congress apparently contemplated reliance on background principles of agency law in determining the liability of cardholders for charges incurred by third-party card bearers. A cardholder, as principal, can create express and implied authority only through manifestations to the user of consent to the particular transactions into which the user has en-tered. There remains an unresolved issue of fact as to whether the Towers officer who dealt with Schley expressly or impliedly authorized Schley to pur-chase fuel on chartered flights. Accordingly, we cannot affirm the grant of summary judgment on the theory that Schley possessed express or implied authority.

Unlike express or implied authority, apparent authority exists apart from the principal's manifes-tations of consent to the agent. Rather, the card-holder, as principal, creates apparent authority through words or conduct that, reasonably inter-preted by a third party from whom the card bearer makes purchases, indicate that the card user acts with the cardholder's consent. Though a cardholder's relinquishment of possession may create in another the appearance of authority to use the card, the statute clearly precludes a finding of apparent authority where the transfer of the card was without the cardholder's consent, as in cases involving theft, loss, or fraud. Because the statute provides no guidance as to uses arising from the *voluntary* transfer of credit cards, the general principles of agency law govern disputes over whether a resulting use was unauthorized. These disputes frequently involve, as in this case, a cardholder's claim that the card bearer was given permission to use a card for only a limited purpose and that subsequent charges exceeded the consent originally given by the cardholder. Several state courts have declined to apply the Truth-in-Lending Act to limit the cardholder's liability [in such situations], reasoning that the cardholder's voluntary relinquishment of the card for one purpose gives the bearer apparent authority to make additional charges.

We need not decide whether voluntary relinquishment for one purpose creates in every case apparent authority to incur other charges. The appearance of authority for Schley to purchase fuel on chartered flights was established not only by Towers's consent to Schley's unrestricted access to the PHH card but by other conduct and circumstances as well. Nothing about the PHH card or the circumstances surrounding the purchases gave fuel sellers reason to distinguish the clearly authorized fuel purchases made in connection with non-charter flights from the purchases for chartered flights. It was the industry custom to entrust credit cards used to make airplane-related purchases to the pilot of the plane. By designating Schley as the pilot and subsequently giving him the card, Towers thereby imbued him with more apparent authority than might arise from voluntary relinquishment of a credit card in other contexts. In addition, with Towers's blessing Schley had used the card to purchase fuel on non-charter flights for the same plane. The only difference between those uses expressly authorized and those now claimed to be unauthorized—the identity of the passengers—was insufficient to provide notice to those who sold the fuel that Schley lacked authority for the charter flight purchases.

Summary judgment for PHH affirmed.

General and Special Agents

Although it may be falling out of favor with courts, the blurred distinction between general agents and special agents still has some importance. A **general agent** is *continuously* employed to conduct a series of transactions, while a **special agent** is employed to conduct a single transaction or a small, simple group of transactions. Thus, a continuously employed general manager, construction project supervisor, or purchasing agent is normally a general agent; and a person employed to buy or sell a few objects on a one-shot basis is usually a special agent. In addition to being employed on a continuous basis, general agents often serve for longer periods, perform more acts, and deal with more parties than do special agents.

Gratuitous Agents

An agent who receives no compensation for his services is called a **gratuitous agent.** Gratuitous agents have the same power to bind their principals as do paid agents with the same authority. As you will see, however, the fact that an agent is gratuitous sometimes lowers the duties principal and agent owe each other and may also increase the parties' ability to terminate the agency without incurring liability.

Subagents

A **subagent** is basically an agent of an agent. More precisely, a subagent is a person appointed by an agent to perform functions that the agent has undertaken to perform for his principal. For example, if you retain an accounting firm as your agent, the accountant actually handling your affairs is the firm's agent and your subagent. For a subagency to exist, the agent must have the authority to make the subagent *his agent* for conducting the principal's business. Sometimes, however, a party appointed by an agent is not a subagent because the appointing agent only had authority to appoint agents *for the*

FIGURE 1   **Agents, Employees, and Independent Contractors as the *Restatement (Second) of Agency* Sees Them**

principal. For instance, sales agents appointed by a corporation's sales manager probably are agents of the corporation, not agents of the sales manager.

When an agent appoints a true subagent, the agent becomes a principal with respect to the subagent, his agent. Thus, the legal relations between agent and subagent closely parallel the legal relations between principal and agent. But a subagent is also the *original principal's* agent. Here, though, the normal rules governing principals and agents do not always apply. We occasionally refer to such situations in the pages ahead.

Employees and Independent Contractors

Many important legal questions hinge on a distinction between two relationships that overlap with the principal-agent relationship. These are an employer's (or master's) relationship with his **employee** (or servant), and a principal's relationship with an **independent contractor.** No sharp line separates these two relationships; the following *VIP Tours* case lists some factors considered in making such determinations. The most important of these factors is the principal's *right to control the physical details of the work.* Employees are typically subject to such control. Independent contractors, on the other hand, generally contract with the principal to produce some result, and determine for themselves how that result will be accomplished.

Although many employees perform physical labor or are paid on an hourly basis, corporate officers are usually employees as well. Profession-als such as brokers, accountants, and attorneys are often independent contractors, although they are sometimes employees. Consider the difference between a corporation represented by an attorney engaged in her own practice and a corporation that maintains a staff of salaried in-house counsel. Finally, franchisees are usually independent contractors.

When are employees and independent contractors agents? Although there is little consensus on this question, this text follows the *Restatement* position. According to the *Restatement*, employees are *always* agents, while independent contractors *may or may not* be agents.[4] An independent contractor is an agent when the tests for the existence of an agency—most importantly, sufficient control by the principal—are met. Figure 1 sketches the *Restatement* position on the relationships among agents, employees, and independent contractors.

As Chapter 35 makes clear, the employee–independent contractor distinction is often crucial in determining the principal's liability for an agent's torts. The distinction also helps define the coverage of some employment regulations discussed in Chapter 50. Unemployment compensation (the subject of *VIP Tours*) and workers' compensation are two clear examples.

---

[4]*Restatement (Second) of Agency* §§ 2, 14N, 25, and the Introductory Note following § 218 (1959).

VIP TOURS, INC. V. FLORIDA
449 So. 2d 1307 (Fla. Ct. App. 1984)

VIP Tours, Inc. arranged tours of central Florida's attractions. Cynthia Hoogland conducted 29 such tours for VIP between July 1980 and March 1981. Both Hoogland and VIP considered Hoogland an independent contractor. She worked for VIP only when it needed her services and she could reject particular assignments. She was also free to work for other tour services, and she did so.

Once Hoogland accepted a job from VIP, she was told where to report and was given instructions about the job. She also had to use a VIP-furnished vehicle and wear a uniform with the VIP logo when conducting tours. Aside from ensuring that she departed on time, however, VIP did not tell her how long to stay or what kind of tour to conduct at each tourist attraction. Finally, Hoogland was paid on a per tour basis.

Hoogland later filed a claim for unemployment compensation benefits with the Florida Division of Labor and Employment Security. The Division concluded that she was entitled to these benefits because she was VIP Tours' employee. VIP appealed the Division's order to an intermediate appellate court.

Upchurch, Judge   The [Florida] Supreme Court has approved the test set out in *Restatement (Second) of Agency* section 220 for determining whether one is an employee or an independent contractor:

In determining whether one acting for another is a servant or an independent contractor, the following matters of fact, among others, are considered:

(a) the extent of control which, by the agreement, the master may exercise over the details of the work;

(b) whether or not the one employed is engaged in a distinct occupation or business;

(c) the kind of occupation, with reference to whether, in the locality, the work is usually done under the direction of the employer or by a specialist without supervision;

(d) the skill required in the particular occupation;

(e) whether the employer or the workman supplies the instrumentalities, tools, and the place of work for the person doing the work;

(f) the length of time for which the person is employed;

(g) the method of payment, whether by the time or by the job;

(h) whether or not the work is part of the regular business of the employer;

(i) whether or not the parties believe that they are creating the relationship of master and servant; and

(j) whether the principal is or is not in business.

It has been said repeatedly that of all the factors, the right of control as to the mode of doing the work is the principal consideration.

VIP had no right of control over the tour guides other than to require them to show up at a particular place at a particular time wearing the VIP uniform and to travel in VIP transportation. VIP had little interest in the details of the guides' work, as is illustrated by the fact that the guides controlled the number of hours spent at a particular attraction and the nature of the tour at each exhibit. In addition, the guides were free to contract with other tour companies, as Hoogland did, and could accept or reject any assignment, factors further indicating a lack of control by VIP.

Other factors in the *Restatement* also point toward independent contractor status. The tour guides were engaged in a distinct occupation. They worked and were paid on a per-job basis. Both VIP and Hoogland considered the guides to be independent contractors.

Division order reversed.

DUTIES OF AGENT TO PRINCIPAL

If an agency is created by contract, the agent must perform according to its terms. Regardless of whether the relationship is contractual, agency law also establishes certain *fiduciary duties* that the agent owes the principal. These duties supplement the duties created by an agency contract. They exist because agency is a relationship of trust and confidence. Often, however, the parties may eliminate or modify fiduciary duties by agreement.

Despite certain exceptions noted later, a *gratuitous agent* usually has the same fiduciary duties as a paid agent. But this is true only so long as a gratuitous agent continues to act as an agent. In other words, a gratuitous agent need not perform as promised, he normally can terminate the agency without incurring liability, and his fiduciary duties cease once the agency ends. However, a gratuitous agent *is* liable for failing to perform as promised when his promise causes the principal to rely on him to undertake certain acts, and the principal suffers losses because she refrained from performing those acts herself. For example, suppose the principal refrains from bidding at an auction because her agent has gratuitously promised to bid for her, the agent attends the auction but fails to make the bid, and the bid would have succeeded had it been made.

A *subagent* owes the agent (his principal) all the duties agents owe their principals. A subagent who knows of the original principal's existence also owes that principal all the duties agents owe their principals, except for duties arising solely from the original principal's contract with the agent. Finally, the agent who appointed the subagent is generally liable to the original principal when the principal is harmed by the subagent's conduct.

Agent's Duty of Loyalty

Because agency is a relationship of trust and confidence, an agent has a **duty of loyalty** to his principal. Thus, an agent must subordinate personal concerns by: (1) avoiding conflicts of interest with the principal, and (2) not disclosing confidential information received from the principal.

Conflicts of Interest   An agent whose interests conflict with the principal's interests may be unable to represent his principal effectively. When conducting the principal's business, therefore, an agent is forbidden to *deal with himself.* For example, an agent authorized to sell property cannot sell that property to himself. This rule often includes an agent's transactions with his relatives or business associates, or with business organizations in which he has an interest. However, an agent may engage in self-dealing transactions if the principal consents. For this consent to be effective, the agent must disclose all relevant facts to the principal before dealing with the principal on his own behalf.

Unless the principal agrees otherwise, an agent is also forbidden to *compete with the principal* regarding the agency business so long as he remains an agent. Thus, an agent employed to purchase specific property may not buy it himself if the principal still desires it. As the following *Chernow* case states, moreover, an agent ordinarily may not solicit customers for a planned competing business while still employed by the principal.

Finally, an agent who is authorized to make a certain transaction cannot *act on behalf of the other party* to the transaction unless the principal knowingly consents. Thus, one ordinarily cannot act as agent for both parties to a transaction without first disclosing the double role to, and obtaining the consent of, both principals. Here, the agent must disclose to each principal all the factors reasonably affecting each principal's decision. Occasionally, though, an agent who acts as a middleman may serve both parties to a transaction without notifying either. For instance, an agent may simultaneously be employed as a "finder" by a firm seeking suitable businesses to acquire and a firm looking for prospective buyers, so long as neither principal expects the agent to advise it or negotiate for it.

CHERNOW V. REYES
570 A.2d 1282 (N.J. Ct. App. 1990)

Ronald Chernow is in the business of auditing telephone bills for customers. Typically, he determines whether the customers' phone equipment is in place, properly billed, and in working order; checks for overcharges; and receives half of any overcharge refund the customer receives from the telephone company. In October 1982, Chernow hired Angelo Reyes as an auditor. The employment lasted until July 1983, when Reyes either quit or was fired.

Prior to leaving Chernow's employ and without his knowledge, Reyes took various steps to form and operate a business that competed with Chernow's business. Most importantly, he obtained three auditing contracts and performed work under those contracts during that period. He also solicited a fourth account, but did no work for that firm until after ceasing to work for Chernow. None of these businesses was an existing customer of Chernow. Reyes's soliciting and auditing activities did not take place during his regular working hours, which he devoted to Chernow's business.

Chernow sued Reyes for breach of his agent's duty of loyalty. The trial court held for Reyes. Its main reason was that Reyes's customers were neither clients of Chernow nor within the pool of businesses Chernow was soliciting. Chernow appealed.

Stein, Judge   An employee owes a duty of loyalty to the employer and must not, while employed, act contrary to the employer's interest. "Unless otherwise agreed, an agent is subject to a duty not to compete with the principal concerning the subject matter of his agency." *Restatement (Second) of Agency* section 393. Comment e to section 393 states:

... [B]efore the end of his employment, [the agent] can properly purchase a rival business and upon termination of employment immediately compete. *He is not, however, entitled to solicit customers for such rival business before the end of his employment nor can he properly do other similar acts in direct competition with the employer's business* [emphasis added].

By engaging in a competitive enterprise, Reyes crossed the line between permissible preparation to change jobs and actionable conduct. Chernow was entitled to expect that a person on his payroll would not undertake to pursue competitive commercial opportunities. The protection accorded is not limited to the diversion of an employer's customers. It extends to pursuing and transacting business within the larger pool of potential customers who might have been solicited by the employer.

Judgment reversed in favor of Chernow.

Confidentiality   Unless otherwise agreed, an agent may not *use or disclose confidential information* acquired through the agency. Confidential information means facts that are valuable to the principal because they are not widely known, or that would harm the principal's business if they became widely known. Examples include the principal's business plans, financial condition, contract bids, technological discoveries, manufacturing methods, customer files, and other trade secrets.[5] In the absence of an agreement to the contrary,[6] an agent may compete with her principal after termination of the agency. But as the following *ABKCO* case

---

[5]Liability for misappropriation of trade secrets is discussed in Chapter 8.

[6]Agreements not to compete are discussed in Chapter 15.

illustrates, the duty not to use or disclose confidential information continues.[7] The former agent may, however, utilize general knowledge and skills acquired during the agency.

[7]On the patent and trade secrets problems that arise when an employee or a former employee tries to utilize ideas, discoveries, or inventions found or created during the course of her employment, see Chapter 8.

ABKCO MUSIC, INC. v. HARRISONGS MUSIC, LTD.
722 F.2d 988 (2d Cir. 1983)

In 1963, a song called "He's So Fine" was a huge hit in the United States and Great Britain. In February 1971, Bright Tunes Music Corporation, the copyright holder of "He's So Fine," sued ex-Beatle George Harrison and Harrisongs, Music, Ltd. in federal district court. Bright Tunes claimed that the Harrison composition "My Sweet Lord" infringed its copyright to "He's So Fine." At this time, Harrison's business affairs were handled by ABKCO Music, Inc. and Allen B. Klein, its president. Shortly after the suit began, Klein unsuccessfully tried to settle it by having ABKCO purchase Bright Tunes.

Shortly thereafter, Bright Tunes went into receivership, and it did not resume the suit until 1973. At this time, coincidentally, ABKCO's management contract with Harrison expired. In late 1975 and early 1976, however, Klein continued his efforts to have ABKCO purchase Bright Tunes. As part of these efforts, he gave Bright Tunes three schedules summarizing Harrison's royalty income from "My Sweet Lord," information he possessed because of his previous service to Harrison. Throughout the 1973–76 period, Harrison's attorneys had been trying to settle the copyright infringement suit with Bright Tunes. Because Klein's activities not only gave Bright Tunes information about the economic potential of its suit but also gave it an economic alternative to settling with Harrison, Klein may have impeded Harrison's efforts to settle.

When the copyright infringement suit finally came to trial in 1976, the court found that Harrison had infringed Bright Tunes' copyright. The issue of damages was scheduled for trial at a later date, and this trial was delayed for some time. In 1978, ABKCO purchased the "He's So Fine" copyright and all rights to the infringement suit from Bright Tunes. This made ABKCO the plaintiff in the 1979 trial for damages on the infringement suit. At trial, Harrison counterclaimed for damages resulting from Klein's and ABKCO's alleged breaches of the duty of loyalty. Finding a breach of duty, the district judge issued a complex order reducing ABKCO's recovery. ABKCO appealed.

Pierce, Circuit Judge   The relationship between Harrison and ABKCO prior to termination of the management agreement in 1973 was that of principal and agent. An agent has a duty not to use confidential knowledge acquired in his employment in competition with his principal. This duty exists as well after the employment as during its continuance. On the other hand, use of information based on general business knowledge is not covered by the rule, and the former agent is permitted to compete with his former principal in reliance on such publicly available information. The principal issue before us, then, is whether Klein (hence, ABKCO) improperly used confidential information, gained as Harrison's former agent, in negotiating for the purchase of Bright Tunes' stock in 1975–76.

One aspect of this inquiry concerns the nature of the schedules of "My Sweet Lord" earnings which Klein furnished to Bright Tunes in connection with the 1975–76 negotiations. It appears that at least some of [this] information was confidential. The evidence is not at all convincing that the information was publicly available.

Another aspect of the breach of duty issue concerns the timing and nature of Klein's entry into the negotiation picture and the manner in which he became a plaintiff in this action. We find this case analogous to those where an employee, with the use of information acquired through his former employment, completes for his own benefit a transaction originally undertaken on the former employer's behalf. Klein had commenced a purchase transaction with Bright Tunes in 1971 on behalf of Harrison, which he pursued on his own account after termination of his fiduciary relationship with Harrison. Klein pursued the later discussions armed with the intimate knowledge not only of Harrison's business affairs, but of the value of this lawsuit. Taking all of these circumstances together, we agree that Klein's conduct during the period 1975–78 did not meet the standard required of him as a former fiduciary.

District court decision in Harrison's favor on the breach of duty issue affirmed.

Agent's Duty to Obey Instructions

Because an agent acts under the principal's control and for the principal's benefit, she has a duty to *obey the principal's reasonable instructions* for carrying out the agency business. However, a gratuitous agent need not obey his principal's order to continue to act as an agent. Also, agents generally have no duty to obey orders to behave illegally or unethically. Thus, a sales agent need not follow directions to misrepresent the quality of the principal's goods, and professionals such as attorneys and accountants are not obligated to obey directions that conflict with the ethical rules of their professions.

Agent's Duty to Act with Care and Skill

A paid agent must *possess and exercise the degree of care and skill* that is standard in the locality for the kind of work the agent performs. A gratuitous agent need only exercise the care and skill required of nonagents who perform similar gratuitous undertakings. Paid agents who represent that they possess a higher than customary level of skill may be held to a correspondingly higher standard of performance.

Similarly, an agent's duty may change if the principal and the agent agree that the agent must possess and exercise greater or lesser than customary care and skill.

Agent's Duty to Notify the Principal

An agent must promptly communicate to the principal matters within his knowledge that are reasonably relevant to the agency business and that he knows or should know are of concern to the principal. As the following *Levin* case suggests, this *duty to notify* is sometimes treated as one facet of the duty to act with care and skill. The basis for the duty to notify is the principal's interest in being informed of matters that are important to the agency business.

However, there is no duty to notify where the agent receives privileged or confidential information. For example, an attorney may acquire confidential information from a client and thus be obligated not to disclose it to a second client. If the attorney cannot properly represent the second client without revealing this information, he should refuse to represent that client.

LEVIN V. KASMIR WORLD TRAVEL
540 N.Y.S.2d 639 (N.Y. Civ. Ct. 1989)

In July 1987, Marsha Levin bought her daughter a round-trip plane ticket from New York City to Paris from Kasmir World Travel, Inc. Upon arriving in Paris, Mrs. Levin's daughter was denied entry and was placed on the next return flight to the United States because she did not have a visa. The apparent reason for the visa requirement was the French government's effort to deal with terrorist activities directed at Americans abroad.

Neither Mrs. Levin nor her daughter was aware of the requirement; indeed, a few years earlier Mrs. Levin had traveled to France without being required to present a visa.

Levin sued Kasmir for failing to notify her about the visa requirement. Kasmir moved to dismiss her complaint.

Saxe, Judge   The duty of a travel agent includes such responsibilities as verifying or confirming reservations. Travel agents are required to have the degree of skill and knowledge requisite to the calling; to exercise good faith and reasonable skill, care, and diligence; and to possess reasonable knowledge of the types of carriers, lines, and accommodations that they select for their principals, and all significant attendant matters. Beyond the duty to confirm travel reservations, travel agents should provide information which is necessary and of importance to the traveler.

Kasmir had a duty to notify the traveler about the need for a visa before entering France. This is in accord with the expanding role of the travel agent to provide all relevant and necessary information to the consumer who reasonably relies on the agent's expertise. Here, it was reasonable to expect Kasmir to alert its [principal] to important changes in the visa requirements of foreign nations. It was also reasonable for Mrs. Levin to rely on Kasmir to supply this information. The travel agency was clearly in a position to assemble and disseminate this basic and significant type of travel information.

I am aware of Kasmir's contention that its relationship to the claimant was merely that of a ticketing agent, and that consequently duties beyond the actual sale of the ticket could not implicate such an agent. [But] information concerning entry or visa requirements into foreign lands is so basic to the purchase or sale of the ticket that the seller must be obliged to furnish it to all affected consumers.

Kasmir's motion to dismiss denied.

Agent's Duties to Account

An agent's duties of loyalty and care require that she give the principal any money or property received in the course of the agency business. This includes profits resulting from the agent's breach of the duty of loyalty, or other duties. It also includes incidental benefits received through the agency business. Examples include bribes, kickbacks, and gifts from parties with whom the agent deals on the principal's behalf. However, the principal and the agent may agree that the agent can retain certain benefits received during the agency. Courts may imply such an agreement when it is customary for agents to retain tips or accept entertainment while doing the principal's business.

Another type of *duty to account* concerns agents whose business involves collections, receipts, or expenditures. Such agents must keep accurate records and accounts of all transactions, and disclose these to the principal once the principal makes a reasonable demand for them. Also, an agent who obtains or holds property for the principal usually may not commingle that property with her own property. For example, an agent ordinarily cannot deposit the principal's funds in her own name or in her own bank account.

Remedies of the Principal

Many claims and remedies are possible when an agent breaches a duty to her principal. If the agency was created by contract, for example, the agent's wrongdoing may breach that contract and may enable the principal to obtain the various kinds of contract damages. Also, a principal may obtain injunctive relief where, for instance, an agent discloses or threatens to disclose confidential information, or misappropriates or threatens to misappropriate the principal's property. In addition, a principal may rescind contracts made by an agent who has represented two principals without the knowledge of one or both, has dealt with himself, or has failed to disclose relevant facts. Finally, agents who retain money or property due the principal (including bribes or gifts), or who profit from the breach of duty, may be liable for the amount of their unjust enrichment.

Tort claims are possible when the agent has misbehaved. A principal may recover for losses caused by his agent's negligent failure to follow instructions, to notify, or to perform with appropriate skill and care. The tort of conversion is available where an agent has unjustifiably retained, stolen, transferred, destroyed, failed to separate, or otherwise misappropriated the principal's property.

DUTIES OF PRINCIPAL TO AGENT

If an agency is formed by contract, the contract normally states the duties the principal owes the agent. In addition, the law implies certain duties from the existence of an agency relationship, however formed. The most important of these duties are the principal's obligations to **compensate** the agent, to **reimburse** the agent for money spent in the principal's service, and to **indemnify** the agent for losses suffered in conducting the principal's business.[8] These duties can generally be eliminated or modified by agreement between the parties. Although there is no duty to compensate a gratuitous agent, the principal still owes such an agent the other two duties unless there is an agreement to the contrary.

An agent's duties to a subagent are the same as a principal's duties to an agent. If there is no agreement to the contrary, however, the original principal has no contractual liability to a subagent. For example, such a principal is normally not obligated to compensate a subagent. But a principal must reimburse and indemnify subagents as he would agents.

Duty to Compensate Agent

Where an agency contract states the agent's compensation, the contract generally controls questions on that issue. In other cases, the relationship of the parties and the surrounding circumstances deter-

mine whether and in what amount the agent is to be compensated. If there is no contract provision on compensation, for example, a principal generally is not required to pay for undertakings that she did not request, services to which she did not consent, and tasks that typically are undertaken without pay. Also, a principal usually need not compensate an agent who has materially breached the agency contract or has committed a serious breach of a fiduciary duty. Where compensation is due but its amount is not expressly stated, the amount is the market price or the customary price for the agent's services, or, if neither is available, their reasonable value.

Sometimes an agent's compensation depends on the accomplishment of a specific result. For instance, a plaintiff's attorney may be retained on a contingent fee basis (being paid a certain percentage of the recovery if the suit succeeds or is settled), or a real estate broker may be entitled to a fee only if a suitable buyer is found. In such cases, the agent is not entitled to compensation unless he achieves the result within the time stated or, if no time is stated, within a reasonable time. This is true no matter how much effort or money the agent expends. However, the principal must cooperate with the agent in achieving the result and must not do anything to frustrate the agent's efforts. Otherwise, the agent is entitled to compensation despite the failure to perform as specified.

Duties of Reimbursement and Indemnity

If, while acting on the principal's behalf, an agent makes expressly or impliedly authorized expenditures, the agent is entitled to **reimbursement** for those expenditures if there is no agreement to the contrary. Unless otherwise agreed, for example, an agent requested to make overnight trips as part of his agency duties can recover reasonable transportation and hotel expenses.

A principal's duty of reimbursement overlaps with her duty of **indemnity.** Agency law implies a promise by the principal to indemnify an agent for losses that result from the agent's authorized activities. These include authorized payments made on the principal's behalf and payments on contracts on which the agent was authorized to become liable. A principal may also have to indemnify an agent if the agent's authorized acts constitute a breach of contract or a tort for which the agent is required to pay damages to a third party.

---

[8]A principal may also have other duties, including the duties to: provide the agent with an opportunity for service, not interfere with the agent's work, keep accounts, act in a manner not harmful to the agent's reputation or self-esteem, and (in the case of employees) maintain a safe workplace. The last duty has been greatly affected, if not superseded, by workers' compensation systems and the Occupational Safety and Health Act, which are discussed in Chapter 50.

So long as the principal did not benefit from such behavior, however, he is *not* required to indemnify an agent for losses resulting: (1) from unauthorized acts, or (2) solely from the agent's negligence or other fault. Even where the principal directed the agent to commit a tortious act, moreover, there is no duty to indemnify if the agent knew the act was tortious. But the principal must indemnify the agent for tort damages resulting from authorized conduct that the agent did not believe was tortious. For example, if a principal directs his agent to repossess goods located on another's property and the agent, believing her acts legal, becomes liable for conversion or trespass, the principal must indemnify the agent for the damages the agent pays.

Remedies of the Agent

An agent's claim for breach of the duties just discussed is often contractual, and normal contract remedies—except specific performance—are available. In some cases, a principal's failure to pay, indemnify, or reimburse an agent enables the agent to acquire a lien on property or funds of the principal that are in the agent's possession. This usually allows the agent to hold the property or funds until the principal pays his obligation. Also, an agent whose principal violates the duties to pay, indemnify, or reimburse can refuse to render further services to the principal.

Of course, an agent's *own* breach of duty—especially the duties of loyalty and obedience—may defeat his claim against the principal. Where the breach is not serious enough to give the principal a complete defense, the principal may still set off losses caused by the breach against the agent's recovery.

TERMINATION OF THE AGENCY RELATIONSHIP

An agency can terminate in many ways.[9] Such terminations fall under two general headings: (1) termination by act of the parties, and (2) termination by operation of law.

---

[9]The rules stated below generally apply to the termination of a subagent's authority as well. In general, a subagency terminates when relations between either the principal and the agent or the agent and the subagent are terminated in any of the ways to be described.

Termination by Act of the Parties

Termination by act of the parties occurs:

1. *At a time or upon the happening of an event stated in the agreement.* If no such time or event is stated, the agency terminates after a reasonable time.

2. *When a specified result has been accomplished, if the agency was created to accomplish a specified result.* For example, if an agency's only objective is to sell certain property, the agency terminates when the property is sold.

3. *By mutual agreement of the parties,* at any time.

4. *At the option of either party.* This is called **revocation** when done by the principal and **renunciation** when done by the agent. Revocation or renunciation occurs when either party manifests to the other that he does not wish the agency to continue. This includes conduct inconsistent with the agency's continuance. For example, an agent may learn that his principal has hired another agent to perform the same job.

A party can revoke or renounce even if this violates the agency agreement. However, although either party has the *power* to terminate in such cases, there is no *right* to do so. This means that where one party terminates in violation of the agreement, she need not perform any further, but she may be liable for damages to the other party. However, a gratuitous agency is normally terminable by either party without liability. Also, the terminating party is not liable where the revocation or renunciation is justified by the other party's serious breach of a fiduciary duty.

Termination by Operation of Law

Termination by operation of law normally involves situations where it is reasonable to believe that the principal would not wish the agent to act further, or where accomplishment of the agency objectives has become impossible or illegal. Although courts may recognize exceptions in certain cases, an agency relationship is usually terminated by:

1. *The death of the principal.* This normally is true even where the agent has no notice of the principal's death.

2. *The death of the agent.*

3. *The principal's permanent loss of capacity.* This is a *permanent* loss of capacity occurring *after* creation of the agency—most likely due to the principal's insanity. The principal's permanent incapacity ends the agency even without notice to the agent. But a brief period of insanity may only temporarily suspend the agency for the time the principal is insane.

4. *The agent's loss of capacity to perform the agency business.* The scope of this basis for termination is unclear. As Chapter 35 relates, an agent who becomes insane or otherwise incapacitated after the agency is formed still can bind his principal to contracts with third parties. Thus, it probably makes little sense to treat the agency relationship as terminated in such cases. As a result, termination under this heading may be limited to such situations as the loss of a license needed to perform agency duties.

5. *Changes in the value of the agency property or subject matter* (e.g., a significant decline in the value of land to be sold by an agent).

6. *Changes in business conditions* (e.g., a much lower supply and a much increased price for goods to be purchased by an agent).

7. *The loss or destruction of the agency property or subject matter or the termination of the principal's interest therein* (e.g., where a house to be sold by a real estate broker burns down or is taken by a mortgage holder to satisfy a debt owed by the principal).

8. *Changes in the law that make the agency business illegal* (e.g., where drugs to be sold by an agent are banned by the government).

9. *The principal's bankruptcy*—as to transactions the agent should realize the principal no longer desires. For example, consider the likely effect of the principal's bankruptcy on an agency to purchase antiques for the principal's home versus its likely effect on an agency to purchase necessities of life for the principal.

10. *The agent's bankruptcy*—where the agent's financial condition affects his ability to serve the principal. This could occur where an agent is employed to purchase goods on his own credit for the principal.

11. *Impossibility of performance by the agent.* This covers various events, some of which fall within the categories just stated. The *Restatement*'s definition of impossibility, for example, includes: (*a*) destruction of the agency subject matter, (*b*)

termination of the principal's interest in the agency subject matter (as, for example, by the principal's bankruptcy), and (*c*) changes in the law or in other circumstances that make it impossible for the agent to accomplish the agency's aims.

12. *A serious breach of the agent's duty of loyalty.*

13. *The outbreak of war*—where this leads the agent to the reasonable belief that his services are no longer desired. An example might be the outbreak of war between the principal's country and the agent's country.

Termination of Agency Powers Given as Security

An agency power given as security for a duty owed by the principal, sometimes called an *agency coupled with an interest,* is an exception to some of the termination rules just discussed. Here, the agent has an interest in the subject matter of the agency that is distinct from the principal's interest and that is not exercised for the principal's benefit. This interest exists to benefit the agent or a third person by securing performance of an obligation owed by the principal. A common example is a secured loan agreement authorizing a lender (the agent) to sell property used as security if the debtor (the principal) defaults. For instance, suppose that Allen lends Peters $100,000 and Peters gives Allen a lien or security interest on Peters's land to secure the loan. The agreement might authorize Allen to act as Peters's "agent" to sell the land if Peters fails to repay the loan.

Because the power given the "agent" in such cases is not for the principal's benefit, it is sometimes said that an agency coupled with an interest is not truly an agency. In any event, courts distinguish it from genuine agency relations in which the agent is compensated from the profits or proceeds of property held for the principal's benefit. For example, if an agent is promised a commission for selling the principal's property, the relationship is not an agency coupled with an interest. Here, the power exercised by the agent (selling the principal's property) benefits the principal. The following *Smith* case provides another example.

Why is the agency coupled with an interest important? The main reason is that it is *not terminated* by: (1) the principal's revocation, (2) the

---

FIGURE 2   **Termination of an Agent's Authority after Termination of the Agency**

Type of Termination	Actual Authority	Apparent Authority
By Acts of the Parties	Ceases	Persists unless appropriate notice or notification to third party
By Operation of Law	Ceases	Ceases if termination by principal's death or loss of capacity, or by impossibility; persists in other cases unless appropriate notice or notification to third party

---

principal's or the agent's loss of capacity, (3) the agent's death, and (4) (usually) the principal's death. However, unless an agency coupled with an interest is held for the benefit of a third party, the agent can voluntarily surrender it. Of course, an agency coupled with an interest terminates when the principal performs her obligation.

Effect of Termination on Agent's Authority

Sometimes, former agents continue to act on their ex-principals' behalf even though the agency has ended. Do such "agents" still have authority to bind their former principals? As Figure 2 states, once an agency terminates by any of the means just described, the agent's *express* and *implied* authority end as well.

Third parties who are unaware of the termination, however, may reasonably believe that an ex-agent still has authority. To protect third parties who rely on such a reasonable appearance of authority, an agent's *apparent authority* often persists after termination. Thus, a former agent may be able to bind the principal under his apparent authority even though the agency has ended. But as Figure 2 also states, apparent authority ends where the termination was caused by: (1) the *principal's death*, (2) the *principal's loss of capacity*, or (3) *impossibility*.[10] Note from the previous discussion that certain other

bases for termination may also end the agent's apparent authority because they fit within the broad category of impossibility.

Notice to Third Parties   Apparent authority ends when the third party receives appropriate *notice* of the termination. In general, any facts known to the third party that reasonably indicate the agency's termination constitute suitable notice. Some bases for termination by operation of law (e.g., changed business conditions) may provide such notice.

To protect themselves against unwanted liability, however, prudent principals may want to notify third parties themselves. The required type of notification varies with the third party in question.

1. *For third parties who have previously dealt with the agent or who have begun to deal with the agent,* **actual notification** *is necessary.* This can be accomplished by: (*a*) a direct personal statement to the third party; or (*b*) a writing delivered to the third party personally, to his place of business, or to some other place reasonably believed to be appropriate.

2. *For all other parties,* **constructive notification** *suffices.* Usually, these other parties are aware of the agency but did no business with the agent. Constructive notification can normally be accomplished by advertising the agency's termination in a newspaper of general circulation in the place where the agency business is regularly carried on. If no suitable publication exists, notification by other means reasonably likely to inform third parties—for example, posting a notice in public places—may suffice.

---

[10]*Restatement (Second) of Agency* § 124A, comment *a*; and § 133 (1959). Subject to certain exceptions; moreover, § 132 of the *Restatement (Second)* says that the apparent authority of a *special agent* terminates along with termination of the agency.

Smith v. Cynfax Corporation
618 A.2d 937 (N.J. Super. Ct. 1992)

Brenda Smith was injured by a falling ceiling in a building owned by the Cynfax Corporation. She retained Floyd Goldsman as her attorney, and Goldsman sued Cynfax on her behalf. On February 4, 1992, Cynfax's insurer, the Cumberland Mutual Fire Insurance Company, made Smith a $7,000 settlement offer through Goldsman. Goldsman immediately tried to inform Smith of the offer, but learned that she had died on February 2.

Goldsman later accepted Cumberland's offer to Smith. Still later, Cumberland refused to pay Smith's estate the $7,000. Smith's estate then moved to enforce the alleged settlement agreement. One issue before the court was whether Goldsman had authority to accept Cumberland's offer on Smith's behalf.

Yanoff, Judge   As Mrs. Smith's attorney, Goldsman was an agent of his client. For Goldsman to have accepted the settlement offer, his agency must have survived the death of his client. Goldsman's agency immediately ceased when his client died. It makes no difference that the settlement negotiations were undertaken in good faith and in ignorance of Smith's death. A general principle of agency is that the death of the principal terminates the authority of the agent. Knowledge of the principal's death only becomes an issue where the agency is derived from a written power of attorney [citing a New Jersey statute].

An agency coupled with an interest survives the principal, even after notice of his death. This requires that the agent have some interest, such as a security interest, in the subject-matter of the agency independent of the power conferred upon him by the principal. An interest merely in the proceeds which will arise from the exercise of the power of the agency is not sufficient for this purpose. Goldsman's agency was controlled by an agreement which provided that "the law firm will protect your legal rights and do all necessary legal work to represent you in this matter" in exchange for a percentage contingency fee. This created an interest in the proceeds of a successful exercise of the powers of the agency, not in its subject-matter. An attorney's contingent fee contract creates an agency which is not coupled with an interest and which terminates upon the death of the principal.

Motion of Smith's estate denied; Cumberland wins.

Ethical and Public Policy Concerns

1. Under one of the agent's duties to account, an agent might be required to return to the principal gifts from third parties with whom the agent deals on the principal's behalf. Where the gift is a genuine token of appreciation, the principal may be getting a windfall. What can justify this result?

2. A well-known ethical theory called utilitarianism generally asserts that the moral worth of actions should be judged by their tendency to promote net aggregate satisfaction. Some people regard the maximization of social wealth as a reasonable measuring rod for net aggregate satisfaction. Under a wealth-maximization criterion, does the rule forbidding ex-agents from using or disclosing confidential information make sense? How might the rule promote wealth-maximization? How might it hinder wealth-maximization? In attempting to answer this question, you might consult the introduction to the section on trade secrets in Chapter 8.

What other ethical considerations might justify the rule against the disclosure of confidential information by an ex-agent? Are they utilitarian in the sense defined above?

PROBLEMS AND PROBLEM CASES

1. Joan Marie Ottensmeyer was a contestant for the title of Miss Hawaii-USA 1974. The pageant was run by Richard You as a franchisee of Miss Universe, Inc. After finishing as first runner-up, Ottensmeyer sued Miss Universe, arguing that as its agent You had prevented her from winning a title to which she was rightfully entitled and from obtaining the benefits thereof. The franchise agreement between Miss Universe and You explicitly stated that You was not Miss Universe's agent. By itself, is this statement sufficient to prevent the formation of an agency relationship between Miss Universe and You?

2. Norman Finnegan purchased a 1986 Lincoln town car from Tri-County Auto Group, Inc., for $8,093. The purchase agreement provided "30-day interest-free finance." At the time of the sale, Finnegan also completed an installment payment finance agreement with General Motors Acceptance Corporation (GMAC). Later, within the 30-day period, Finnegan paid Tri-County the entire balance due on the car. Previously, GMAC had allowed customers to pay off its installment contracts through dealerships in this fashion. Generally, the dealership would then send a check to GMAC to complete the payment.

Rather than forwarding Finnegan's lump-sum payment to GMAC, however, Tri-County began to pay GMAC Finnegan's monthly installments under the contract. After making four such payments, Tri-County became insolvent. GMAC then sued Finnegan for the balance due on the contract. Finnegan argued that Tri-County was GMAC's agent for the purpose of collecting payment, that Tri-County had authority to collect his payment, and that payment to Tri-County therefore was payment to GMAC. Did Tri-County have apparent authority to receive Finnegan's payment for GMAC? Assume that at the time he paid Tri-County, Finnegan was aware of GMAC's practice of letting installment contract customers pay the balance through the dealership.

3. 📼 *Video Case* See "In the Cards." Jack runs a video card shop. Linda, who knows little or nothing about baseball or baseball cards, agreed to run the shop for Jack while he went out for dinner. Jack told Linda that she could sell any card for the price marked on the card. Then, he pointed to a case containing the more expensive cards, and said that he might negotiate the price on those cards if customers would wait until he returned. Shortly after Jack left, Linda sold a small boy an Ernie Banks rookie card for $12. The card bore a price sticker that stated: "1200." The boy apparently was unaware of the card's true value and did not try to negotiate its price. Did Linda have express, implied, or apparent authority to sell the card for $12? In any event, on what bases might Jack sue her for his losses?

4. 📼 *Video Case* "See Martin Manufacturing." Mr. Martin, the president of Martin Manufacturing, fires a purchasing agent named Mitch. The reason is that Mitch has been taking kickbacks from suppliers. Martin also withholds Mitch's last paycheck until Martin can determine how much Mitch's misbehavior has cost him.

Has Mitch breached any fiduciary duty or duties to Martin? If so, which ones? Will Mitch be required to give Martin the amount of any kickbacks he has received? Can Martin fire Mitch without incurring liability under these circumstances? Finally, is Martin justified in withholding Mitch's paycheck?

5. Mark and Roberta Murray purchased a single-family home. Some time after they moved in, cracks appeared at various places in the house, and the Murrays eventually discovered that its foundation was defective. They sued the real estate broker who had represented them in the purchase, arguing that he breached his duty of care and skill by failing to conduct a reasonable investigation of the house. Did their broker owe the Murrays such a duty? Assume that the *seller's* broker had a duty to make such an inspection and to disclose to the purchaser all facts materially affecting the value or desirability of the house.

6. Ted and Sharon Markland arranged for a trip to the Virgin Islands with Travel Travel Southland, Inc. Travel Travel made the necessary arrangements with Eastern Airlines, which was having financial problems. The Marklands then paid Travel Travel $6,548 for the trip. There was conflicting testimony as to whether Travel Travel warned the Marklands about Eastern's difficulties, and for purposes of this question assume that it did not. It is also unclear how much the Marklands knew about Eastern's troubles, but assume that they had at least a general knowledge of them.

Ten days after the Marklands reached the Virgin Islands, their hotel informed them that their reservations were no longer valid because Eastern had not paid for them and (due to its declaring bankruptcy) most likely would not. The Marklands wound up having to pay the hotel an additional $4,900, and also had to expend another $1,756 for a return flight to the United States. Afterwards, they sued Travel Travel for failing to advise them about Eastern's precarious position. Did Travel Travel breach either its duty of care and skill or its duty to notify?

7. In February 1989, Thomas Fix arranged for a Florida vacation package for himself and his sister with Travel Help, a travel agency. The travel agent selected an Eastern Airlines package that included Eastern vouchers for a rental car, Howard Johnson's Fountain Park, and Sea World. Aware of the labor and other problems Eastern was experiencing at that time, Fix's sister contacted the agent several times requesting that all the arrangements be made with another airline. The agent assured her that the flights could be changed and that the vouchers would be honored. After Eastern went into bankruptcy on March 9, 1989, the agent arranged for Fix and his sister to be transported to Florida on a different airline. After they arrived, however, the providers of the voucher bookings refused to honor Eastern's vouchers. Did the agent breach a duty to Fix (and his sister)? If so, which one? You can assume that the travel agent was acting for both Fix and his sister, and that the communications to the agent by Fix's sister were communications to an agent by his principal.

8. Southeastern Agri-Systems, Inc., was an agent for Otto Niederer. James Stanford was Agri-Systems' president and sole employee. Niederer instructed Stanford to accept payment for the sale of some equipment owned by Niederer, to deduct his commission from the payment, and to wire the remainder to Niederer. Instead, Stanford diverted the funds to his own purposes and refused to pay Niederer the amount due. When sued individually for breach of the agent's duty to obey, Stanford argued that Niederer had employed Agri-Systems as its agent, that he was merely an employee of Agri-Systems, and that he thus owed no duty to Niederer. Is Stanford correct?

9. Stanley Mazur owned an Oldsmobile Cutlass and a small Subaru pickup truck. He asked his insurance agent, Ken Curtis, to arrange "full coverage" on the truck similar to the coverage on his Cutlass. Although the policy on the Cutlass included personal injury protection, Curtis negligently failed to include such protection in the policy he obtained for the Subaru. Later, Mazur suffered personal injury from an accident in which he was involved while driving the Subaru. Because the policy did not cover such injury, he was unable to recover for it from the insurer, the Selected Risks Insurance Company.

Mazur recovered against Curtis for Curtis's failure to procure the requested coverage. Curtis then sued to have Selected indemnify him for this loss. Is Selected required to indemnify Curtis? Why or why not? Assume that Curtis was acting as an agent for Selected as well as for Mazur.

10. 📼   *Video Case*   See "Martin Manufacturing." Immediately after being fired by Martin Manufacturing in Problem Case 4 above, Mitch decides to squeeze one last bit of profit from his relationship with Martin. Thus, he calls a customer with whom he has dealt on many occasions, and orders several cases of fasteners on Martin's behalf. Later, he resells the fasteners himself, pocketing the money. Is Martin liable to the supplier for the fasteners? In any event, what should Martin do to protect itself in cases like this one?

CHAPTER

35

THIRD-PARTY RELATIONS OF THE PRINCIPAL AND THE AGENT

INTRODUCTION

By letting principals contract through their agents and thereby multiply their dealings, agency law stimulates business activity. For this process to succeed, there must be rules for determining when the principal and the agent are liable on the agent's contracts. Principals need to predict and control their liability on agreements their agents make. Also, third parties need assurance that such agreements really bind the principal. Furthermore, both agents and third parties have an interest in knowing when an agent is bound on these contracts. The first half of this chapter discusses the principal's and the agent's contract liability.

While acting on the principal's behalf, agents sometimes harm third parties in various ways. Normally, this makes the agent liable to the injured party in tort. Sometimes, moreover, a principal is liable for his agent's torts. Because tort judgments can be expensive, the rules for determining the principal's and the agent's tort liability are of great concern to principals, their agents, and third parties. Thus, we examine these subjects in this chapter's second half.

CONTRACT LIABILITY OF THE PRINCIPAL

A principal is normally liable on a contract made by his agent if the agent had **express, implied, or apparent authority** to make the contract. Occasionally, however, a principal's contract liability may be affected by other factors. Even where the agent lacked authority to contract, moreover, a principal may bind herself by later **ratifying** the agent's contract.

Express Authority

As discussed in Chapter 34, **express authority** is created by a principal's *words* to his agent, whether written or oral. Thus, an agent has express authority to bind her principal to a particular contract if the principal clearly told the agent that she could make that contract on the principal's behalf. For example, suppose that Payne instructs his agent Andrews to contract to sell a specific antique chair for $400 or more. If Andrews contracts to sell the chair to

Tucker for $425, Payne is liable to Tucker on the basis of Andrews's express authority. However, Andrews would not have express authority to sell the chair for $375, or to sell a different chair.

Implied Authority

Often, it is difficult or impossible for a principal to specify his agent's authority completely and precisely. Thus, agents also can bind their principals on the basis of the agent's **implied authority.** As Chapter 34 states, an agent generally has implied authority to do whatever it is reasonable to assume that his principal wanted him to do, in light of the principal's express statements and the surrounding circumstances. Relevant factors include the principal's express statements, the nature of the agency, the acts reasonably necessary to carry on the agency business, the acts customarily done when conducting that business, and the relations between principal and agent.

Implied authority often derives from a grant of express authority or some other express statement by the principal. Ordinarily, an agent has implied authority to make those contracts that are reasonably necessary for conducting the business he has been expressly authorized to perform, or that are customarily made in conducting that business. Implied authority, however, cannot conflict with the principal's express statements. Thus, there is no implied authority to contract where a principal has limited her agent's authority by express statement or clear implication and the contract would conflict with that limitation.

On occasion, implied authority may exist even though there is no relevant grant of express authority. Here, courts generally derive implied authority from the nature of the agency business, the relations between principal and agent, customs in the trade, and other facts and circumstances. For example, there may be implied authority to make a certain contract if the agent has made similar past contracts with the principal's knowledge and without his objection.

Examples of Implied Authority   Courts have created general rules or presumptions for determining the implied authority of certain agents in certain situations. For example:

1. An agent hired to *manage a business* normally has implied authority to make those contracts that are reasonably necessary for conducting the business or

that are customary in the business. These include contracts for obtaining equipment and supplies, making repairs, employing employees, and selling goods or services. However, a manager has no power to borrow money or issue negotiable instruments in the principal's name unless the principal is a banking or financial concern regularly performing such activities.

2. An agent given *full control over real property* has implied authority to contract for repairs and insurance, and may rent the property if this is customary. But such an agent may not sell the property or allow any third-party liens or other interests to be taken on it.

3. Agents appointed to *sell the principal's goods* may have implied authority to make customary warranties on those goods. In states that still recognize the distinction, the *general agent* described in Chapter 34 is more likely to have such authority than a *special agent.*

Apparent Authority

As discussed in Chapter 34, **apparent authority** arises when the *principal's behavior* causes a third party to form a *reasonable belief* that the agent is authorized to act in a certain way. Principals can give their agents apparent authority through the statements they make, or tell their agents to make, to third parties, and through the actions they knowingly allow their agents to take. Background factors such as trade customs and established business practices often determine whether it is reasonable for the third party to believe such manifestations of authority. For instance, if a principal appoints his agent to a position such as general manager that customarily involves the power to make certain contracts, the agent normally has apparent authority to make those contracts. Here, the principal's behavior in appointing the agent to the position, as reasonably interpreted in light of business customs, creates apparent authority in the agent. This is true even if the principal expressly told the agent not to make such contracts, so long as this limitation remains unknown to the third party. Because agents cannot give themselves apparent authority, however, there would be no such authority if an agent falsely told third parties that he had been promoted to general manager without the principal's knowledge or permission.

Established business customs can help create apparent authority in other ways as well. For example, an agent can often bind his principal to forbidden promises that customarily accompany contracts the agent actually is authorized to complete, if the third party is unaware that the promises were forbidden. In states that still recognize the distinction, general agents are more likely to have this kind of apparent authority than are special agents. Suppose that Perry employs Arthur as general sales agent for his manufacturing business. Certain warranties customarily accompany the products Perry sells, and agents like Arthur are ordinarily empowered to give these warranties. But Perry tells Arthur not to make any such warranties to buyers, thus cutting off Arthur's express and implied authority. Despite Perry's orders, however, Arthur makes the usual warranties in a sale to Thomas, who is familiar with customs in the trade. If Thomas did not know about the limitation on Arthur's authority, Perry is bound by Arthur's warranties.

Finally, apparent authority may exist where a principal has, to the knowledge of a third person, permitted his agent to make contracts that the agent was expressly forbidden to make. Suppose Potter has told Abram, the manager of his business, to hire loaders for his trucks for no more than one day at a time. No one else knows about this limitation on Abram's actual authority. With Potter's knowledge and without his objection, however, Abram frequently has employed loaders by the week. Then Abram agrees to employ Trapp as a loader for a week. If Trapp knew about the earlier employment by the week, Potter would be bound to the one-week employment contract on the basis of Abram's apparent authority.

Other Factors Affecting a Principal's Contract Liability

Agent's Notification and Knowledge
Sometimes the general agency rules regarding *notification* and *knowledge* affect a principal's contract liability. If a third party gives proper notification to an agent with actual or apparent authority to receive it, the principal is bound as if the notification had been given directly to him. For example, where a contract between Phillips and Thomas made by Phillips's agent Anderson contains a clause allowing Thomas to cancel if she notifies Phillips, she can cancel by notifying Anderson if Anderson has actual or apparent authority to receive the notification. Similarly, notification *to* a third party *by* an agent with the necessary authority is considered notification by the principal.

In certain circumstances, an agent's knowledge of certain facts is imputed to the principal. This means

that the principal's rights and liabilities are what they would have been if the principal had known what the agent knew. Generally, an agent's knowledge is imputed to a principal when it is relevant to activities that the agent is authorized to undertake, or when the agent is under a duty to disclose the knowledge to the principal. Suppose that Ames contracts with Timmons on Pike's behalf, knowing that Timmons is completely mistaken about a matter material to the contract. Even though Pike knew nothing about Timmons's unilateral mistake, Timmons probably can avoid his contract with Pike.[1]

Incapacity of Principal or Agent
As discussed in Chapter 34, a principal who lacks capacity at the time an agency is formed may usually avoid the agency, and a principal's permanent loss of capacity after the agency's formation terminates the agency. Where the agency continues to exist, is a minor or a person of limited mental capacity bound on contracts made by his agent? Subject to the exceptions discussed in Chapter 14, such contracts are voidable at the principal's option. These contracts would normally be voidable if made by the principal himself, and it is difficult to see why acting through an agent should increase the principal's capacity.

Like the principal, an agent can avoid the agency agreement if she lacks capacity at the time it is formed. Where the agency survives, however, the agent's incapacity usually does *not* affect the contract liability of a principal who has capacity. Just as an agent cannot increase the principal's capacity, neither can she diminish it. However, the principal may sometimes escape liability where an agent's incapacity is so extreme that the agent cannot receive or convey ideas, or cannot follow the principal's instructions.

Ratification

Ratification is a process whereby a principal binds himself to an unauthorized act done by an agent or by a person purporting to act as an agent. Ratification relates back to the time when the act was performed. For contracts, its effect is to bind the principal as if the agent had possessed authority at the time the contract was made.

Conduct Amounting to Ratification
Ratification can be express or implied. An *express ratification*

---

[1] Unilateral mistake is discussed in Chapter 13.

occurs when the principal communicates an intent to ratify by written or oral words to that effect. *Implied ratification* arises when the principal's behavior evidences an intent to ratify. Part performance of the agent's contract by a principal or a principal's acceptance of benefits under the contract may work an implied ratification. Sometimes even a principal's silence, acquiescence, or failure to repudiate the transaction may constitute ratification. This can occur where the principal would be expected to object if he did not consent to the contract, the principal's silence leads the third party to believe that he does consent, and the principal is aware of all relevant facts.

Additional Requirements   Even if a principal's words or behavior indicate an intent to ratify, other requirements must be met before ratification occurs. These requirements have been variously stated; the following list is typical.

1. The act ratified must be one that was *valid* at the time it was performed. For example, an agent's illegal contract cannot be made binding by the principal's subsequent ratification. However, a contract that was voidable when made due to the principal's incapacity may be ratified by a principal who has later attained or regained capacity.

2. The principal must have been *in existence* at the time the agent acted. However, as discussed in Chapter 41, corporations may bind themselves to their promoters' preincorporation contracts by adopting such contracts.

3. When the act to be ratified occurred, the agent must have indicated to the third party that she was acting for *a* principal and not for herself. But the agent need not have disclosed the principal's identity.

4. The principal must be *legally competent* at the time of ratification. For instance, an insane principal cannot ratify.

5. The principal must have *knowledge* of all material facts regarding the prior act or contract at the time it is ratified. Here, an agent's knowledge is not imputed to the principal. In the following *Adams* case, the principal did not ratify because it lacked sufficient knowledge.

6. The principal must ratify the *entire* act or contract. He cannot ratify the beneficial parts of a contract and reject those that are detrimental.

7. In ratifying, the principal must use the *same formalities* required to give the agent authority to execute the transaction. As Chapter 34 related, few formalities are normally needed to give an agent authority. But where the original agency contract requires a writing, ratification likewise must be written.

Intervening Events   Certain events occurring after an agent's contract but before the principal's ratification may cut off the principal's power to ratify. These include: (1) the third party's *withdrawal* from the contract; (2) the third party's *death* or *loss of capacity*; (3) the principal's *failure to ratify within a reasonable time* (assuming that the principal's silence did not already work a ratification); and (4) *changed circumstances* (especially where the change places a greater burden on the third party than he assumed when the contract was made).

ADAMS V. LOUISIANA COCA-COLA BOTTLING CO.
531 So. 2d 501 (La. Ct. App. 1988).

Rosia Adams, an employee at a Jefferson Parish School Board warehouse, was injured when she slipped on a wet floor at the warehouse. The floor was wet because it had been mopped to clean a spill from a malfunctioning Coca-Cola vending machine leased to the school board by the Louisiana Coca-Cola Bottling Company (Coca-Cola). A warehouse inventory clerk signed the lease on behalf of the school board.

Adams sued Coca-Cola for her injuries. Coca-Cola then filed a third-party action against the school board, alleging that under the terms of the lease the school board was required to indemnify and insure Coca-Cola against injuries to employees like Adams. After trial, Adams obtained a jury verdict against Coca-Cola, and the trial judge dismissed Coca-Cola's claim against the school board. Coca-Cola then appealed the trial judge's decision dismissing its claim against the school board.

Ciaccio, Judge   The question is whether the school board is obligated under the lease. The clerk who signed the lease did not have express authority to do so. Whether he had implied authority, the other component of actual authority, is determined by inference from the circumstances, purposes, and nature of the agency. An agent is invested with the implied authority to do all those things necessary or incidental to the accomplishment of the purpose of the agency. Coca-Cola argues that the clerk was empowered with general authority to operate the warehouse. Such a mandate confers only a power of administration. The proof does not establish any particular circumstances, purposes, or nature of the agency beyond receiving and inventorying goods delivered to the warehouse. We do not find therein any implied authority to agree to indemnify and insure the lessor of a vending machine placed on the premises.

For apparent authority to apply, the principal must first act to manifest the agent's authority to [a] third party. Second, the third party must rely reasonably on the manifested authority of the agent. In support of its argument for the clerk's apparent authority to execute this lease on behalf of the board, Coca-Cola relies on the following facts. The clerk has worked for the school board for twenty years. During this time he has always handled soft drink vending machines on the premises. Either he or another school board employee initially contacted Coca-Cola to have a machine installed at the warehouse. The school board's representative admitted that employees all over the school board system were signing similar leases. He also admitted that some of the seven thousand school board employees have previously bound the school board without formal authorization.

There is no indication that the school board acted to manifest authority for the clerk to execute this lease. There is no evidence that the school board knew of the lease, much less its provisions. The board's role was passive; it apparently paid no attention to the vending machines on its premises. We do not find that this passiveness manifested authority in its employees to agree to indemnify and insure the lessor of these machines.

Further, we find unreasonable any reliance by Coca-Cola upon any perception of authority in the clerk. Coca-Cola did not inquire into the nature and extent of the clerk's authority. Agreeing to indemnify and insure Coca-Cola as lessor requires greater authority than one would reasonably perceive to be vested in an inventory clerk.

Coca-Cola finally argues that the school board ratified the lease by permitting the machine to remain at the warehouse, permitting another machine to be placed there, and [later] permitting over one hundred other machines to be placed at various other school board locations under similar lease conditions. There is no indication that the school board was aware that the machines were being leased, that the leases were being executed in its name, or that the leases contained onerous provisions that the board indemnify and insure Coca-Cola as lessor. We do not find the board's permitting the presence of the machines to be a ratification of the lease provisions confected by Coca-Cola.

Judgment in favor of the school board on Coca-Cola's third-party claim affirmed.

Contracts Made by Subagents

The rules governing a principal's liability for her agent's contracts generally apply to contracts made by her subagents. If an agent has authorized his subagent to make a certain contract and this authorization is within the authority granted the agent by his principal, the principal is bound to the subagent's contract. Suppose that Peters employs the Ajax Company to sell certain personal property while she is out of the country, with the understanding that one of Ajax's agents will handle the sale from start to finish. If Ajax authorizes its agent Sampson (Peters's subagent) to contract to sell the property and Sampson does so, Peters is bound to the contract.

Because the relationship between agent and subagent closely resembles the relationship between principal and agent, a subagent acting within the authority conferred by her principal (the agent) can bind the *agent* in contract. Finally, although the authorities do not clearly address the subject, both the principal and the agent can probably ratify the contracts of subagents.

Contract Liability of the Agent

An *agent's* liability on contracts he makes for the principal usually depends on a different set of factors than the factors determining the principal's liability.[2] The most important of these variables is the *nature of the principal*. Thus, this section first examines the liability of agents who contract for several distinct kinds of principals. Then it discusses two ways that an agent can be bound after contracting for almost any type of principal—by agreeing to be liable, or by contracting without the necessary authority.

The Nature of the Principal

Disclosed Principal A principal is **disclosed** if a third party knows or has reason to know: (1) that the agent is acting for a principal, and (2) the principal's identity. Unless he agrees otherwise, an agent who represents a disclosed principal is *not liable* on authorized contracts made for such a principal. Suppose that Adkins, a sales agent for Parker, calls on Thompson and presents a business card clearly identifying her as Parker's agent. If Adkins contracts to sell Parker's goods to Thompson with authority to do so, Adkins is not bound because Parker is a disclosed principal. This rule is usually consistent with the third party's intentions; for example, Thompson probably intended to contract only with Parker. In the following *Cahn* case, the agents were bound even though they

---

[2]The rules stated here should generally govern the contract liability of subagents as well as agents. See *Restatement (Second) of Agency* § 361 (1959).

contracted for a disclosed principal, because they had impliedly agreed to be bound.

Partially Disclosed Principal A principal is **partially disclosed** if the third party: (1) knows or has reason to know that the agent is acting for *a* principal, but (2) lacks knowledge or reason to know the principal's *identity*. This can occur where an agent simply neglects to disclose his principal's identity. Also, a principal may tell her agent to keep her (the principal's) identity secret to preserve her bargaining position.

Among the factors affecting anyone's decision to contract are the integrity, reliability, and creditworthiness of the other party to the contract. Where the principal is partially disclosed, the third party ordinarily cannot judge these matters. As a result, he usually depends on the agent's reliability to some degree. For this reason, and to give the third party additional protection, an agent is liable on contracts made for a partially disclosed principal unless the parties agree otherwise.

Undisclosed Principal A principal is **undisclosed** where the third party lacks knowledge or reason to know *both* the principal's existence and the principal's identity. This can occur where a principal judges that he will get a better deal if his existence and identity remain secret, or where the agent simply neglects to make adequate disclosure.

A third party who deals with an agent for an undisclosed principal obviously cannot assess the principal's reliability, integrity, and creditworthiness. Indeed, here the third party reasonably believes that the *agent* is the other party to the contract. Thus, an agent is liable on contracts made for an undisclosed principal.

Cahn v. Fisher
805 P.2d 1040 (Ariz. Ct. App. 1991)

H. Richmond Fisher and Francis Smith, two attorneys, ordered three deposition transcripts from Harry Cahn and Conrad Blain, two court reporters. The attorneys did so as part of some litigation work they were performing for two clients. Fisher and Smith did not tell Cahn and Blain that they were acting on their clients' behalf when ordering the transcripts; nor did they specifically identify their clients to the court reporters. Presumably, however, the depositions contained a caption identifying those clients and suggesting that Fisher and Smith were acting in a representative capacity.

After the lawyers placed their order with Cahn and Blain, their clients went bankrupt. Thus, they did not pay the reporters' $579.95 bill for the transcripts. Cahn and Blain then sued Fisher and Smith for this amount.

Later, they moved for summary judgment. Included in their summary judgment motion was another court reporter's affidavit stating that it was the "custom and usage" of local court reporters to bill and extend credit to lawyers rather than their clients. The trial court granted the reporters' summary judgment motion, and the lawyers appealed.

Lankford, Judge   The lawyers argue that agency law protects an agent from liability on a contract entered into on behalf of a disclosed principal. Unless otherwise agreed, a person making or purporting to make a contract with another as agent for a disclosed principal does not become a party to the contract. Disclosure of the principal requires that the agent give the other party both notice that the agent is acting for a principal and the principal's identity. Reasonable inferences can be drawn that the court reporters were aware that the lawyers were ordering the transcripts not for themselves but on behalf of their clients, and that the reporters were aware of the clients' identities. Under these circumstances, agency law precludes a judgment resting on the theory that lawyers are generally liable on a contract with court reporters.

While the lawyers ordinarily would not be bound under agency law to a contract entered into on behalf of their disclosed principals, the parties were certainly free to agree otherwise. In this case, the court reporters attempted to show that "custom and usage" between court reporters and lawyers is that the lawyers are directly liable for the reporters' fees. Court reporters might also be able to establish such liability by proof of a course of dealing between the parties. The lawyers argued below that the affidavit offered by the reporters was insufficient to show custom and usage. However, they abandoned that argument on appeal and we therefore decline to consider the sufficiency of the affidavit. [This] evidence of custom and usage was uncontroverted. It showed that the parties' understanding was that the lawyers would be responsible for paying the reporters. This evidence fully sustains the [trial] court's entry of summary judgment against the lawyers.

Judgment for Cahn and Blain affirmed.

Nonexistent Principal   In the absence of an agreement to the contrary, an agent who purports to act for a **legally nonexistent** principal such as an unincorporated association is personally liable. This is true even where the third party knows that the principal is nonexistent.[3]

Principal Lacking Capacity   As stated earlier, a principal who lacks contractual capacity due to insanity or infancy can avoid contracts made by his agent. In this case, the *agent* also escapes liability unless: (1) she misrepresents the capacity of her principal, or (2) she has reason to believe that the third party is unaware of the principal's incapacity and she fails to disclose this. Also, unless the parties agree otherwise, an agent is liable on contracts made for a *wholly incompetent* principal such as a person who has been adjudicated insane.

Liability of Agent by Agreement

An agent may bind herself on contracts she makes for a principal by *expressly or impliedly agreeing* to be liable. This is true regardless of the principal's nature. An agent may expressly bind herself by: (1) making the contract in her own name rather than in the principal's name, (2) joining the principal as an obligor on the contract, or (3) acting as surety or guarantor for the principal.

Problems of contract interpretation can arise when it is claimed that an agent has expressly promised to be bound. The two most important factors affecting the agent's liability are the wording of the contract and the way the agent has signed it. An agent who wishes to avoid liability should make

---

[3]For a closely analogous situation, see Chapter 41's discussion of a promoter's liability on contracts made for a corporation before it comes into existence.

no express promises in her own name and should try to ensure that the agreement only obligates the principal. In addition, the agent should use a signature form that clearly identifies the principal and indicates the agent's representative capacity—for example, "Parker, by Adkins," or "Adkins, for Parker." Simply adding the word "agent" when signing her name (Adkins, Agent) or signing without any indication of her status (Adkins) could subject the agent to liability. Sometimes, as in the following *Wired Music* case, the body of the agreement suggests one result and the signature form another. Here, and generally, oral evidence or other extrinsic evidence of the parties' understanding may help resolve the uncertainty.[4]

---

[4]However, the introduction of such evidence may be blocked by the parol evidence rule. See Chapter 16.

Wired Music, Inc. v. Great River Steamboat Co.
554 S.W.2d 466 (Mo. Ct. App. 1977)

A sales representative of Wired Music, Inc., sold Frank Pierson, president of the Great River Steamboat Company, a five-year Muzak Program Service for a riverboat and restaurant owned by Great River. Pierson signed a form contract drafted by Wired Music in the following manner:

By /s/ Frank C. Pierson, Pres.

       Title

The Great River Steamboat Co.

~~Port of St. Louis Investments, Inc.~~

For the Corporation

In signing, Pierson crossed out "Port of St. Louis Investments, Inc.," which had been incorrectly listed as the name of the corporation, and inserted the proper name. The contract included the following clause arguably making Pierson a surety or guarantor for Great River: "The individual signing this agreement for the subscriber guarantees that all of the above provisions shall be complied with."

Great River made approximately four payments under the contract and then ceased to pay. Wired Music brought an action for contract damages against Pierson personally. The trial court ruled in Pierson's favor, and Wired Music appealed.

Gunn, Judge   The general rule regarding liability incurred by an individual who signs an instrument on behalf of another party is: where the principal is disclosed and the capacity in which the individual signs is evident, e.g., president, secretary, agent, the liability is the principal's and not that of the individual signing for the principal. Of course, where the circumstances surrounding the transaction disclose a mutual intention to impose personal responsibility on the individual executing the agreement, the individual may be personally liable even though the form of the signature is that of the agent.

The determinative issue here is whether, in view of the form of the signature to the agreement, the language of the so-called guaranty clause is sufficient to manifest a clear and explicit intent by Pierson to assume a personal guaranty contract. We hold that standing alone it does not. The contract language imposing a personal obligation is inconsistent with the form of execution, which positively limited Pierson's participation to his official corporate capacity and not as an individual. Such inconsistency creates at least a latent ambiguity which permits the admission of parol evidence to explain the true intent of the parties.

Pierson has stressed that he neglected to read the contract prior to its signing. One who signs a contract is presumed to have known its contents and accepted its terms. Thus, Pierson's failure to examine the terms of the instrument would afford no defense to the corporation regarding its obligations under the contract, as his signature was sufficient to bind the corporation. Such neglect *is* a relevant circumstance, however, in ascertaining Pierson's intent to assume personal liability, as his personal signature appeared nowhere on the instrument. Without knowledge of the guaranty clause he could not have possessed the requisite intent to assume obligations under it. The record is destitute of any indication that Pierson was ever made aware of potential personal liability under the guaranty clause, and he steadfastly denied any such knowledge. Wired Music drafted the contract, and its agents procured Pierson's corporate signature without explanation of or bargaining over its terms. Under these circumstances we find that there was an absence of the meeting of the minds as to the nature and the extent of the personal obligations imposed, essential to the formation of a binding guaranty.

Judgment for Pierson affirmed.

Agent's Liability on Unauthorized Contracts

An agent may also become liable to a third party if he contracts for the principal while *lacking authority* to do so. Here, the principal is not bound, and it is arguably unfair to leave the third party without any recovery. Thus, an agent is normally bound on the theory that he made an implied warranty of his authority to contract.[5] This liability exists regardless of whether the agent is otherwise bound to the third party.

To illustrate, suppose that Allen is a salesperson for Prine, a seller of furs. Allen has actual authority to receive offers for the sale of Prine's furs, but not to make contracts of sale, which must be approved by Prine himself. Prine has long followed this practice, and it is customary in the markets where his agents work. Representing himself as Prine's agent but saying nothing about his authority, Allen contracts to sell Prine's furs to Thatcher on Prine's behalf. Thatcher, who should have known better, honestly believes that Allen has authority to contract to sell Prine's furs. Prine is not liable on Allen's contract because Allen lacked actual or apparent authority to bind him. But Allen is liable to Thatcher for breaching his implied warranty of authority.

However, an agent is *not* liable for making an unauthorized contract if:

1. The third party *actually knows* that the agent lacks authority. However, note from the Allen-Prine example that the agent is still liable where the third party only had *reason to know* that authority was lacking.

2. The principal subsequently *ratifies* the contract. Here, the principal is bound and the agent is discharged. Because ratification relates back to the time the contract was made, the relation of the parties is the same as if the agent had possessed authority in the first place.

3. The agent adequately *notifies* the third party that he does not warrant his authority to contract.

CONTRACT SUITS AGAINST PRINCIPAL AND AGENT

Figure 1 sketches the most important situations where the principal, the agent, or both are liable due to the agent's contracts. As it suggests, a third party usually has *someone* to sue if neither the principal nor the agent performs.

Without ratification, a principal is not liable on contracts made by an agent who lacks authority. Here, though, the agent is usually bound under an implied warranty of authority. In addition, the agent is bound on the contract where the principal was partially disclosed, undisclosed, or legally nonexis-

---

[5]An agent who intentionally misrepresents his authority also may be liable to the third party in tort. In addition, some states may allow tort liability for negligent misrepresentations. Where the third party has a tort suit, he may often elect to recover damages or to rescind the contract.

FIGURE 1	Contract Liability of Principal and Agent: The Major Possibilities

Principal	Agent's Authority		
	Actual	**Apparent**	**None**
Disclosed	P liable; A not liable unless agreement	P liable; A not liable unless agreement	P not liable; A usually liable
Partially Disclosed	P liable; A liable	P liable; A liable	P not liable; A liable
Undisclosed	P liable; A liable	Impossible	P not liable; A liable

tent.[6] Authorized contracts for a disclosed principal do not bind an agent unless he has agreed to be bound. But here the agent's actual or apparent authority binds the principal.

As Figure 1 further illustrates, in certain situations both the principal and the agent are liable on a contract made by the agent. This can occur where an agent with appropriate authority contracts on behalf of a partially disclosed or undisclosed principal. Also, an agent can bind himself by express or implied agreement in situations where the principal is also bound. In such cases, which party is ultimately responsible to the third person? The complicated rules governing this question vary from situation to situation. Due to their complexity and variety, they are beyond the scope of this text.

TORT LIABILITY OF THE PRINCIPAL

A principal's liability for her agent's torts involves four distinct subjects, which we consider in turn.[7]

Respondeat Superior Liability

Under the doctrine of *respondeat superior* (let the master answer), a principal who is an **employer** is liable for torts committed by agents who are **employees** and who commit the tort while acting within the **scope of their employment.** This doctrine applies to an employee's negligence, recklessness, or intentional torts. Chapter 34 outlined the main factors courts consider when determining whether an agent is an employee.[8] The most important of these factors is a principal's right to control the physical details of an agent's work.

Respondeat superior is a rule of *imputed* or *vicarious* liability because it bases an employer's liability on his relationship with the employee rather than on his own fault. This imputation of liability reflects the following beliefs: (1) that the economic burdens of employee torts can best be borne by employers; (2) that employers can often protect themselves against such burdens by self-insuring or purchasing insurance; and (3) that the resulting costs can frequently be passed on to consumers, thus "socializing" the economic risk posed by employee torts. *Respondeat superior* also motivates employers to ensure that their employees avoid tortious behavior. Because they typically control the physical details of the work, employers are fairly well positioned to do so.

---

[6]Note, however, that it is impossible for an agent for an undisclosed principal to have apparent authority. Apparent authority exists when the principal's communications to the third party cause that party to reasonably believe that the agent has authority to contract for another. How can this occur when the principal is undisclosed?

[7]In addition to the various forms of tort liability discussed in this section, a principal can also *ratify* an agent's torts. Furthermore, the *Restatement* says that the rules governing a principal's liability for an agent's torts generally control a principal's liability for the torts of *subagents*. *Restatement (Second) of Agency* § 255 (1959).

[8]Recall from Chapter 34 that this text follows the *Restatement (Second) of Agency* by treating all employees as agents. Independent contractors, on the other hand, may or may not be agents.

Scope of Employment

Respondeat superior's scope-of-employment requirement has been stated in many ways and is notoriously ambiguous. In the past, for example, some courts considering this question asked whether the employee was on a "frolic" of his own, or merely made a "detour" from his assigned activity. According to the *Restatement,*[9] an employee's conduct is within the scope of his employment if it meets *each* of the following four tests:

1. It was of the *kind* that the employee was employed to perform. To meet this test, an employee's conduct need only be of the same general nature as work expressly authorized, or be incidental to its performance. For instance, the following *Gatzke* case treats on-the-job smoking as an act incidental to an employee's authorized work. But an employee hired only to care for his employer's horses is probably not within the scope of employment if he paints the employer's house without the employer's authorization.

Even criminal conduct may occasionally be within the scope of employment. Here, the test seems to be whether the employer could reasonably anticipate the criminal behavior in question. Thus, a delivery driver who exceeds the speed limit while on a rush job is probably covered, but a driver who shoots another driver after a traffic altercation almost certainly is not.

2. It occurred substantially within the authorized *time* period. This is simply the employee's assigned time of work. Beyond this, there is an extra period of time during which the employment may con- tinue. For instance, a security guard whose regular quitting time is 5:00 probably meets the time test if he unjustifiably injures an intruder at 5:15. Doing the same thing three hours later, however, would put the guard outside the scope of employment.

3. It occurred substantially within the *location* authorized by the employer. This includes locations not unreasonably distant from the authorized location. For example, a salesperson told to limit her activities to New York City probably would satisfy the location requirement while pursuing the employer's business in suburbs just outside the city limits but not while pursuing the same business in Philadelphia. Generally, the smaller the authorized area of activity, the smaller the departure from that area needed to put the employee outside the scope of employment. For example, consider the different physical distance limitations that should apply to a factory worker and a traveling salesperson.

4. It was motivated *at least in part* by the *purpose* of serving the employer. This test is met where the employee's conduct was motivated *to any appreciable extent* by the desire to serve the employer. Thus, an employee's tort may be within the scope of employment even if the motives for committing it were partly personal. For example, suppose that a delivery employee is behind schedule and for that reason has an accident while speeding to make a delivery in his employer's truck. The employee would be within the scope of employment even if another reason for his speeding was to impress a friend who was riding with him.

In the following *Gatzke* case, all four *Restatement* tests were met and the employer was liable. In applying those tests, was the court influenced by a desire to see the plaintiff recover?

---

[9]*Restatement (Second) of Agency* § 228(1) (1959). This section adds that if an employee intentionally uses force on another, this must have been "not unexpectable" by the employer to be within the scope of employment.

EDGEWATER MOTELS, INC. v. GATZKE
277 N.W.2d 11 (Minn. Sup. Ct. 1979)

A. J. Gatzke, a district manager for the Walgreen Company, spent several weeks in Duluth, Minnesota, supervising the opening of a new Walgreen restaurant there. He remained at the restaurant approximately 17 hours a day, and he was on call 24 hours a day to handle problems arising in other Walgreen restaurants in the district. While in Duluth, he lived at the Edgewater Motel at Walgreen's expense. After some heavy drinking late one night, Gatzke returned to his motel room and spent some time at a desk filling out an expense account required by his employer. Gatzke was a heavy smoker, and he testified that he probably smoked a cigarette while completing the expense account. Shortly after Gatzke went to bed, a fire broke out in his motel room. Gatzke escaped, but fire damage to the motel totaled over $330,000. An expert witness testified that the fire was caused by a burning cigarette or a match and that it started in or near a wastebasket located beside the desk at which Gatzke worked.

Edgewater sued Walgreen for Gatzke's negligence. The jury found for Edgewater, in the process concluding that Gatzke acted within the scope of his employment when he filled out the form and disposed of the cigarette. The trial court, however, granted Walgreen's motion for judgment notwithstanding the verdict. Edgewater appealed. The question for the appellate court was whether Gatzke's negligent conduct occurred within the scope of his employment.

Scott, Justice Gatzke's negligent smoking of a cigarette was a direct cause of the damages sustained by Edgewater. The question is whether the facts reasonably support the imposition of vicarious liability on Walgreen's for the conceded negligent act of its employee.

For an employer to be held vicariously liable for an employee's negligent conduct, the employee's wrongful act must be committed within the scope of his employment. To support [such] a finding, it must be shown that his conduct was, to some degree, in furtherance of the interests of his employer. This principle is recognized by *Restatement (Second) of Agency* section 235, which states: "An act of a servant is not within the scope of employment if it is done with no intention to perform it as a part of or incident to a service on account of which he is employed." Other factors to be considered in the scope-of-employment determination are whether the conduct is of the kind that the employee is authorized to perform and whether the act occurs substantially within authorized time and space restrictions.

The question is whether an employee's smoking of a cigarette can constitute conduct within his scope of employment. The courts which have considered the question have not agreed on its resolution. A number of courts have ruled that the act of smoking, even when done simultaneously with work-related activity, is not within the employee's scope of employment because it is a matter personal to the employee which is not done in furtherance of the employer's interest. Other courts have reasoned that the smoking of a cigarette, if done while engaged in the business of the employer, is within an employee's scope of employment because it is a minor deviation from the employee's work-related activities, and thus merely in-

cidental to employment. We agree with this analysis and hold that an employer can be vicariously liable for an employee's negligent smoking of a cigarette if he was otherwise acting in the scope of his employment at the time of the negligent act.

Thus, we must next determine whether Gatzke was otherwise in the scope of his employment at the time of his negligent act. Even assuming that Gatzke was outside the scope of his employment while he was at the bar, Gatzke resumed his employment activities after he returned to his motel room and filled out his expense account. The expense account was completed so that Gatzke could be reimbursed by Walgreen's for his work-related expenses. In this sense, Gatzke is performing an act for his own personal benefit. However, the completion of the expense account also furthers the employer's business in that it provides detailed documentation of business expenses so that they are properly deductible for tax purposes. In this light, the filling out of the expense form can be viewed as serving a dual purpose: that of furthering Gatzke's personal interests and promoting his employer's business purposes. Accordingly, the completion of the expense account is an act done in furtherance of the employer's business purposes.

Additionally, the record indicates that Gatzke was an executive type of employee who had no set working hours. He considered himself a 24-hour-a-day man; his room at the Edgewater Motel was his "office away from home." It [is] therefore reasonable to determine that the filling out of his expense account was done within authorized time and space limits of his employment.

Judgment reversed in favor of Edgewater.

Direct Liability

As the following *Victory Tabernacle* case makes clear, a principal's **direct liability** for an agent's torts differs considerably from *respondeat superior* liability. Here, the principal *himself* is at fault, and there is no need to impute liability to him. Also, no scope-of-employment requirement exists in direct liability cases, and the agent need not be an employee. Of course, a principal might incur both direct liability and *respondeat superior* liability in cases where due to the principal's fault, an employee commits a tort within the scope of her employment.

A principal is directly liable for an agent's tortious conduct if the principal *directs* that conduct and *intends* that it occur. In such cases, the *agent's* behavior might be intentional, reckless, or negli-gent. For instance, if Petty tells his agent Able to beat up Tabler and Able does so, Petty is directly liable to Tabler. Petty also would be liable for harm to third parties that results from his telling Able to do construction work in a negligent, substandard fashion.

The typical direct liability case, however, involves harm caused by the principal's *negligence* regarding the agent. Examples of direct liability for negligence include: (1) giving the agent improper or unclear instructions; (2) failing to make and enforce appropriate regulations to govern the agent's conduct; (3) hiring an unsuitable agent; (4) failing to discharge an unsuitable agent; (5) furnishing an agent with improper tools, instruments, or materials; and (6) carelessly supervising an agent.

J. v. VICTORY TABERNACLE BAPTIST CHURCH
372 S.E.2d 391 (Va. Sup. Ct. 1988)

A woman sued the Victory Tabernacle Baptist Church, alleging that due to its negligence her 10-year-old daughter had been repeatedly raped and sexually assaulted by a church employee. The plaintiff's complaint claimed that when the church hired the employee, it knew or should have known that he had recently been convicted of aggravated sexual assault on a young girl, that he was on probation for this offense, and that a condition of his probation was that he not be involved with children. Despite all this, the complaint continued, the employee's duties allowed him to freely come into contact with children, including the plaintiff's daughter, and he was given keys enabling him to lock and unlock all the church's doors.

The complaint alleged (among other things) negligent hiring on the church's part. The church filed a demurrer to the complaint, and the trial court sustained the demurrer. The plaintiff appealed this decision, and the case reached the Virginia Supreme Court.

Thomas, Justice   We decide only whether the allegations of negligent hiring state a cause of action in Virginia. Victory Baptist argues that the trial court properly sustained the demurrer on [this] question because plaintiff failed to allege that the harm to the victim was caused by negligence on the part of the employee. According to this argument, the negligent hiring cause of action requires that the negligently hired individual negligently injured the plaintiff. We disagree. The very thing that allegedly should have been foreseen in this case is that the employee would commit a violent act upon a child. To say that a negligently hired employee who acts willfully or criminally thus relieves his employer of liability for negligent hiring when willful or criminal conduct is precisely what the employer should have foreseen would rob the tort of vitality.

Victory Baptist also argues that the [plaintiff's] allegations do not establish a sufficient nexus among the employer's breach of duty, the employee's conduct, and the employee's employment. In oral argument, counsel explained that there were no allegations that the employee was engaged in the church's business when the child was injured—no allegation, for example, that the employee was on duty for the church at the time the girl was raped.

Counsel then made clear that what he was complaining about was that there were no allegations to bring the employee's conduct within the scope of his employment.

This argument demonstrates that Victory Baptist is confusing the doctrine of *respondeat superior* with the tort of negligent hiring. This distinction was succinctly stated in a recent law review article:

Under *respondeat superior,* an employer is vicariously liable for an employee's tortious acts committed within the scope of employment. In contrast, negligent hiring is a doctrine of primary liability; the employer is principally liable for negligently placing an unfit person in an employment situation involving an unreasonable risk of harm to others. Negligent hiring, therefore, enables plaintiffs to recover in situations where *respondeat superior's* scope of employment limitation previously protected employers from liability.

Thus, Victory Baptist's contention is misplaced.

In our opinion, the [complaint] was fully sufficient to state a claim of negligent hiring, and thus it was error for the trial court to sustain the demurrer on that issue.

Judgment for the church on the negligent hiring claim reversed. Case remanded for trial consistent with the Supreme Court's opinion.

Liability for Torts of Independent Contractors

A principal ordinarily is *not* liable for torts committed by **independent contractors.** As compared with employees, independent contractors are more likely to have the size and resources to insure against tort liability and to pass on the resulting costs themselves. Sometimes, therefore, the risk can still be socialized if only the independent contractor is held responsible. Because the principal does not control the manner in which an independent contractor's work is performed, moreover, he has less ability to prevent a contractor's torts than an employer has to prevent an employee's torts. Thus, imposing liability on principals for the torts of independent contractors may do little to eliminate the contractor's torts.

However, the rule that principals are not liable for torts committed by independent contractors has exceptions. For example:

1. A principal can be *directly* liable for tortious behavior connected with the retention of an independent contractor. One example is the hiring of a dangerously incompetent independent contractor.

2. A principal is liable for harm resulting from the independent contractor's failure to perform a *nondelegable duty.* A nondelegable duty is a duty whose proper performance is so important that a principal cannot avoid liability by contracting it away. Examples include a carrier's duty to transport its passengers safely, a municipality's duty to keep its streets in repair, a railroad's duty to maintain safe crossings, and a landlord's duties to make repairs and to use care in doing so. Thus, a landlord who retains an independent contractor to repair the stairs in an apartment building is liable for injuries caused by the contractor's failure to repair the stairs properly.

3. A principal is liable for an independent contractor's negligent failure to take the special precautions needed to conduct certain *highly dangerous* or *inherently dangerous* activities.[10] Examples of such activities include excavations in publicly traveled areas, the clearing of land by fire, the construction of a dam, and the demolition of a building. For example, a contractor engaged in demolishing a building presumably has duties to warn pedestrians and to keep them at a safe distance. If injury results from the independent contractor's failure to meet these duties, the principal is liable.

Liability for Agent's Misrepresentations

A principal's liability for misrepresentations made by agents to third parties involves both contract and tort principles.[11] A principal is *directly* liable for

---

[10]The range of activities considered "highly dangerous" or "inherently dangerous" is probably greater than the range of activities considered "ultrahazardous" or "abnormally dangerous" for strict liability purposes. On the latter activities, see Chapter 7.

[11]On fraud and misrepresentation in the tort and contract contexts, see Chapters 6 and 13.

misrepresentations made by her agent during authorized transactions if she *intended* that the agent make the misrepresentations. In some states, a principal may also be directly liable if she *negligently* allows the agent to make misrepresentations.

Even where a principal is not directly at fault, she may be liable for an agent's misrepresentations if the agent had *actual or apparent authority to make true statements on the subject.* Suppose that an agent to sell farmland falsely states that a stream on the land has never flooded the property when in fact it does so almost every year, and that this statement induces a third party to buy the land. The principal is directly liable if she intended that the agent make this false statement. Even if the principal is personally blameless, she is liable if the agent had actual or apparent authority to make true statements about the spring.

If the agent intended to make the misrepresentation, or if the principal intended that the agent make it, the third party can recover in tort for the losses that result. In some states, a third party may also recover in tort for misrepresentations resulting from the principal's or the agent's negligence. In either case, the third party can elect to rescind the transaction instead of pursuing a tort suit.

Exculpatory Clauses   Both honest and dishonest principals may try to escape liability for an agent's misrepresentations by including an exculpatory clause in contracts the agent makes with third parties. Such clauses typically state that the agent only has authority to make the representations contained in the contract and that only those representations bind the principal. Exculpatory clauses do not protect a principal who intends or expects that an agent will make false statements. Otherwise, though, they insulate the principal from *tort* liability if the agent misrepresents. But the third party still may *rescind* the transaction, because it would be unjust to let the principal benefit from the transaction while disclaiming responsibility for it.

CONCEPT REVIEW

An Outline of the Principal's Tort Liability

Respondeat Superior	1. Agent must be an employee, *and* 2. Employee must act within scope of employment while committing tort
Direct Liability	1. Principal intends and directs agent's intentional tort, recklessness, or negligence, *or* 2. Principal is negligent regarding agent
Torts of Independent Contractors	1. Principal generally is *not* liable 2. Exceptions for direct liability, highly dangerous activities, and nondelegable duties
Misrepresentation	1. Direct liability 2. Vicarious liability where agent had authority to make true statements on the subject of the misrepresentation 3. An exculpatory clause may eliminate the principal's tort liability, but the third party still can rescind
Torts of Subagents	The preceding rules govern the principal's liability, but their application varies

---

Tort Liability of the Agent

Agents are usually liable for their own torts.[12] Normally, they are not absolved from liability just because they acted at the principal's command. However, there are exceptions to this generalization.

1. An agent can escape liability if she is *exercising a privilege of the principal.* Suppose that Tingle grants Parkham a right-of-way to transport his farm products over a private road crossing Tingle's land. Parkham's agent Adams would not be liable in

---

[12]The rules stated in the previous section generally govern an agent's liability for torts committed by his subagents. *Restatement (Second) of Agency* § 362 (1959).

trespass for driving across Tingle's land to transport farm products if she did so at Parkam's command. However, an agent must not exceed the scope of the privilege and must act for the purpose for which the privilege was given. Thus, Adams would not be protected if she took her Jeep on a midnight joyride across Tingle's land. Also, the privilege given the agent must be delegable in the first place. If Tingle had given the easement to Parkham exclusively, Adams would not be privileged to drive across Tingle's land.

2. A principal who is *privileged to take certain actions in defense of his person or property* may often authorize an agent to do the same. In such cases, the agent escapes liability if the principal could have done so. For example, a properly authorized agent may use force to protect the life or property of his principal if the principal could have done the same.

3. An agent who makes *misrepresentations* while conducting the principal's business is not liable in tort unless he either *knew or had reason to know* their falsity. Suppose Parker authorizes Arnold to sell his house, falsely telling Arnold that the house is fully insulated. Arnold does not know that the statement is false, and could not discover its falsity through a reasonable inspection. If Arnold tells Thomas that the house is fully insulated and Thomas relies on this statement in purchasing the house, Parker is directly liable to Thomas, but Arnold is not liable.

4. An agent is not liable for injuries to third persons caused by *defective tools or instrumentalities* furnished by the principal unless the agent had actual knowledge or reason to know of the defect.

Tort Suits against Principal and Agent

Both principal and agent are sometimes liable for an agent's torts. Here, the parties are *jointly and severally* liable. This means that a third party may join the principal and the agent in one suit and get a judgment against each, or may sue either or both individually and get a judgment against either or both. However, once a third party actually collects in full from either the principal or the agent, no further recovery is possible.

In some cases, therefore, either the principal or the agent has to satisfy the judgment alone despite the other party's liability. Here, the other party is sometimes required to *indemnify* the party who has satisfied the judgment. As discussed in Chapter 34, for example, sometimes a principal is required to indemnify an agent for tort liability the agent incurs. On the other hand, some torts committed by agents may involve a breach of duty to their principal, and the principal may be able to recover from an agent on this basis.

ETHICAL AND PUBLIC POLICY CONCERNS

1. One of the justifications for *respondeat superior* is that employers are in a relatively good position to absorb the liability of employee torts, to insure against such liability, and to pass on the resulting costs. What are the advantages and disadvantages of applying this reasoning to make principals liable for all torts committed by *independent contractors* within the scope of their employment?

2. If the purposes underlying *respondeat superior* are sound ones, why limit the doctrine to employee torts committed within the scope of employment? In other words, why not make employers liable for *all* torts committed by their employees?

3. Agents who make unauthorized contracts are not liable if the principal later ratifies the contract. The official justification for this rule is that, because ratification relates back to the time the unauthorized contract was made, the relations of the parties are the same as if the agent had originally had authority. However, there is another, much more down-to-earth, justification for this rule. What is it?

PROBLEMS AND PROBLEM CASES

1. The Capital Dredge and Dock Corporation sued the city of Detroit for damages associated with certain construction work it had been performing for the city. One of the city's defenses was that Capital had released the city from liability on some of Capital's present claims during earlier, related litigation between Capital and the city. The releases were part of a settlement document signed by Capital Dredge's attorney, Alteri. Capital Dredge had held Alteri out as having authority to represent it in the relevant litigation, and this included authority to negotiate a settlement. However, unknown to the city, Capital Dredge had also specifically told Alteri not to compromise some of the claims he later settled. Under these circumstances, could Alteri have had implied authority to settle the claims in question? Could he have had apparent authority to do so?

2. Jeff Hartman, a hauler of hay, contracted to purchase Larry Draper's entire 1988 alfalfa hay crop. According to that contract, Hartman had to pay in advance for any hay taken from Draper's farm. Later, Hartman approached Cecil Hilt about buying some of the hay crop Hartman had purchased. Hartman told Hilt that the hay was from Draper's farm, but he did not say that he was acting as Draper's agent. Nonetheless, Hilt believed that Hartman was acting on Draper's behalf. On July 5, 1988, Hilt agreed to buy 400 tons of hay at $60 per ton. As part of the deal, he wrote a $3,000 check payable to Draper as a deposit. Hartman then gave the check to Draper, who indorsed and cashed it.

Much later, Hartman found himself unable to produce the money needed to get Hilt's hay from Draper. Draper eventually sold the hay to another party, and Hilt sued Draper for breach of contract. Assuming for the sake of argument that Hartman was Draper's agent, did Hartman have apparent authority to bind Draper to the deal with Hilt?

3. Roma Funk, who co-owned a piece of land along with her seven brothers and sisters, contracted to sell the land to her neighbors. It was unclear whether Funk had authority to sell the land on behalf of her siblings. For certain, there was no writing giving her such authority. Funk's siblings eventually backed out of the deal, and the buyers sued for specific performance. They argued that Funk's siblings had ratified her contract by failing to come forward and repudiate it. Can a contract ever be ratified in this way? Regardless of your answer to this question, there is another reason why Funk's siblings could not have ratified this particular contract. What is it? Assume that in this state an agent who executes an agreement conveying an interest in land on behalf of his principal must be authorized in writing.

4. Seascape Restaurants, Inc., operated a restaurant called The Magic Moment. Jeff Rosenberg was one-third owner and president of Seascape. Van D. Costas, the president of Van D. Costas, Inc., contracted to construct a "magical entrance" to the Magic Moment. Jeff Rosenberg signed the contract on a line under which appeared the words "Jeff Rosenberg, the Magic Moment." The contract did not refer to Seascape, and Costas knew nothing of Seascape's existence. After a dispute over performance of the contract, Costas sued Rosenberg for breach of contract. Is Rosenberg personally liable to Costas?

5. Dale F. Everett did business as the Dale F. Everett Company, Inc. (the Company). He also formed a retail business known as The Clubhouse, which had no legal status aside from its registration as a trade name for the Company. Everett contracted with James Smith for $8,424 of advertising time. Everett signed his contract with Smith as follows: "THE CLUBHOUSE, Client, By Dale F. Everett." Smith later sent billing statements for the ads to "The Clubhouse, Inc." Everett never paid Smith the $8,424, and Smith sued Everett personally. Is Everett personally liable on the contract with Smith?

6. ▣ *Video Case.*   See "Martin Manufacturing." Mr. Martin, the president of Martin Manufacturing, was talking with Arnold, a new traveling salesman, about Arnold's first week on the road. Arnold told Martin that he hit one of Martin's customers in the customer's store, causing the customer some physical harm. The blow came after Arnold and the customer got into an argument, during which the customer ordered Arnold out of his store. In striking the customer, Arnold was motivated at least in part by a feeling that no Martin employee should have to endure such disrespect.

Shortly after this, Martin also learned from Arnold that Arnold had gotten into an accident while driving a company van. The accident came after Arnold negligently ran a stop sign while thinking about the fight. The driver of the other car was seriously injured in the accident.

Assuming that Arnold is an employee, is Martin liable to the customer for any battery Arnold committed, and to the driver of the car for Arnold's negligence?

7. Redford had been a backhoe operator for five years. Although he had worked for other sign companies, he had spent 90 percent of his time during the past three years working for Tube Art Display, Inc. Redford generally dug holes exactly as directed by the sign company employing him. He did, however, pay his own business taxes, and he did not participate in any of the fringe benefits available to Tube Art employees.

Tube Art obtained a permit to install a sign in the parking lot of a combination commercial and apartment building. Telling Redford how to proceed, Tube Art's service manager laid out the exact location of a 4 × 4-foot square on the asphalt surface with yellow paint and directed that the hole be 6 feet deep. After Redford began the job, he struck a small natural gas pipeline with the backhoe. He examined the pipe, and, finding no indication of a leak or break, concluded that the line was not in use and left the worksite. Later, an explosion and fire occurred in the building serviced by the line. As a result, a business owned by Massey was destroyed. Massey sued Tube Art for Redford's negligence under the doctrine of *respondeat superior*. Will Massey recover? Assume that Redford was negligent.

8. John Hondzinski delivered newspapers in his own car for a newspaper called the *News Herald*. Under the contract between Hondzinski and the *News Herald*, Hondzinski was obligated to pick up and promptly deliver newspapers provided by the *News Herald*, but the means and the routes for doing so were within Hondzinski's control. While making deliveries for the *News Herald* one day, Hondzinski negligently allowed his car to collide with a car driven by Peter Janice. Janice sued the *News Herald* for Hondzinski's negligence. Can Janice recover against the *News Herald* under the doctrine of *respondeat superior*? Why or why not?

9. William Smith was employed by P&M Heating and Air Conditioning, Inc., as a service technician. Smith normally worked a 40-hour week. P&M provided Smith with a service van containing the tools he used in his work. P&M allowed Smith to drive his van home after work, keep it there overnight, call in to P&M to receive his first job assignment each morning, and travel to that assignment in the van.

On July 23, 1986, Smith worked a normal eight-hour day, finishing at 4:00 P.M. After Smith drove the van home and had dinner, his stepdaughter called to tell him that she was having problems with her home air-conditioning unit. As a favor to his stepdaughter, Smith, accompanied by his wife, drove the van to the stepdaughter's home to check out the unit. He did not tell P&M about this work, he did not fill out a customer receipt or any other paperwork for it, and P&M apparently never billed his stepdaughter for it. Smith finished working on his stepdaughter's unit about 10:45 P.M. After that, he took a swim in her pool. About midnight, Smith and his wife left for home. At about 1:00 A.M., the P&M van driven by Smith collided with a vehicle driven by Anthony S. Giannoble, killing Giannoble.

Assuming that the collision was due to Smith's negligence, is P&M liable to Giannoble's estate for that negligence? Assume that Smith was an employee of P&M.

10. Susie Mae Woodson's husband was killed due to a cave-in at a construction site where he was laying sewer pipe in a trench dug by an independent contractor of Davidson & Jones, Inc. (D&J). The trench in which Mr. Woodson was working had not been braced or shored to prevent a cave-in, and this was a violation of federal occupational safety regulations. Mrs. Woodson sued D&J for the independent contractor's negligence. Will she recover? Assume that D&J was not in any way *directly* liable regarding the independent contractor.

11. Edward J. Opatz maintained an investment account with John G. Kinnard and Company. Byron Jensen, a Kinnard broker, handled Opatz's account. In January 1985, Jensen told Opatz that he would buy three fourths of a $24,000 investment unit if Opatz would buy the remaining fourth. Relying on this statement and believing that the transaction was within Jensen's authority, Opatz gave Jensen a $6,000 check payable to Jensen. One week later, Jensen admitted to Opatz that he had never purchased the unit, and gave Opatz a personal check for $6,000. Still later, the check bounced and Jensen disappeared. Is Kinnard liable to Opatz for the $6,000? Assume that: (1) Jensen's statement that he would invest the $6,000 was actionable fraud, (2) Kinnard was not directly liable for Jensen's behavior, and (3) Kinnard did not expressly or impliedly authorize Jensen's statements to Opatz.

PARTNERSHIP

LAW

INTRODUCTION TO FORMS OF BUSINESS AND FORMATION OF PARTNERSHIPS

INTRODUCTION

In this chapter, you begin your study of business organizations. Early in this chapter, you will preview the basic characteristics of the most important forms of business and learn how to select an appropriate form for a business venture. Following that introduction, you will begin your in-depth study of partnerships, learning their characteristics and the formalities for their creation.

CHOOSING A FORM OF BUSINESS

One of the most important decisions made by a person beginning a business is choosing a **form of business**. This decision is important because the business owner's liability and control of the business vary greatly among the many forms of business. In addition, some business forms offer significant tax advantages to their owners.

Although other forms of business exist, usually a person starting a business will wish to organize the business as a sole proprietorship, partnership, limited liability partnership, limited partnership, corporation, or limited liability company.

Sole Proprietorship

A **sole proprietorship** has only one owner. The sole proprietorship is merely an extension of its only owner, the **sole proprietor**.

As the only owner, the sole proprietor has the right to make all the management decisions of the business. In addition, all the profits of the business are his. A sole proprietor assumes great liability: He is personally liable for all the obligations of the business. All the debts of the business, including debts on contracts signed only in the name of the business, are his debts. If the assets of the business are insufficient to pay the claims of its creditors, the creditors may require the sole proprietor to pay the claims using his individual, nonbusiness assets such as money from his bank account and the proceeds from the sale of his house. A sole proprietor may lose everything if his business becomes insolvent. Hence, the sole proprietorship is a risky form of business for its owner.

Despite this risk, there are two reasons why a person may organize a business as a sole proprietorship. First, the sole proprietorship is formed very easily and inexpensively. No formalities are necessary. Second, few people consider the business form decision. They merely begin their businesses. Thus, by default, a person going into business by herself automatically creates a sole proprietorship when she fails to choose another business form. These two reasons explain why the sole proprietorship is the most common form of business in the United States.

Because the sole proprietorship is merely an extension of its owner, it has no life apart from its owner. Therefore, while the business of a sole proprietorship may be freely sold to someone else, legally the sole proprietorship as a form of business cannot be transferred to another person. The buyer of the business must create his own form of business to continue the business.

A sole proprietorship is not a legal entity. It cannot sue or be sued. Instead, creditors must sue the owner. The sole proprietor—in his own name—must sue those who harm the business.

A sole proprietor may hire employees for the business, but they are employees of the sole proprietor. Under the law of agency, the sole proprietor is responsible for her employees' authorized contracts and for the torts they commit in the course of their employment. Also, a sole proprietorship is not a tax-paying entity for federal income tax purposes. All of the income of a sole proprietorship is income to its owner and must be reported on the sole proprietor's individual federal income tax return. Likewise, any business losses are deductible without limit on the sole proprietor's individual tax return. This loss-deduction advantage explains why some wealthier taxpayers use the sole proprietorship for selected business investments—when losses are expected in the early years of the business, yet the risk of liability is low. Such an investor may form a sole proprietorship and hire a professional manager to operate the business.

Many sole proprietorships have trade names. For example, Caryl Stanley may operate her bagel shop under the name Caryl's Bagel Shop. Caryl would be required to file the trade name under a state statute requiring the registration of fictitious business names. If she were sued by a creditor, the creditor would address his complaint to "Caryl Stanley, doing business as Caryl's Bagel Shop."

Partnership

A **partnership** has two or more owners, called **partners.** The partners have the right to make all the management decisions for the business. In addition, all the profits of the business are shared by the partners.

The partners assume personal liability for all the obligations of the business. All the debts of the business are the debts of all the partners. Likewise, partners are liable for the torts committed in the course of business by their partners or by partnership employees. If the assets of the business are insufficient to pay the claims of its creditors, the creditors may require one or more of the partners to pay the claims using their individual, nonbusiness assets. Thus, a partner may have to pay more than his share of partnership liabilities.

Like the sole proprietorship, the partnership is not a tax-paying entity for federal income tax purposes. All of the income of the partnership is income to its partners and must be reported on the individual partner's federal income tax return. Likewise, any business losses are deductible without limit on the partner's individual tax return.

The partnership has no life apart from its owners. When a partner dies or otherwise leaves the business, the partnership is dissolved. A partner's ownership interest in a partnership is not freely transferable: A purchaser of the partner's interest is not a partner of the partnership, unless the other partners agree to admit the purchaser as a partner.

Why would persons organize a business as a partnership? Formation of a partnership requires no formalities and may be formed by default. A partnership is created automatically when two or more persons own a business together without selecting another form. Also, each partner's right to manage the business and the deductibility of partnership losses on individual tax returns are attractive features.

Limited Liability Partnership

Reacting to the large personal liability sometimes imposed on lawyers and accountants for the professional malpractice of their partners, Texas enacted in 1991 the first statute permitting the formation of **limited liability partnerships (LLP).** An LLP is similar to a partnership, except that a partner's liability for his partners' professional malpractice is limited to the partnership's assets; a partner retains unlimited liability for his *own* malpractice and for all *non*professional obligations of the partnership.

An LLP is managed by its partners, who have equal say in the business of the partnership, unless they agree otherwise. An LLP has no life apart from its partners, and a partner's ownership interest in an LLP is not freely transferable: The purchaser will not be a partner of the partnership, unless the other partners agree that the purchaser may join the LLP.

The Internal Revenue Service has privately indicated that LLPs will be taxed like partnerships: the partnership pays no federal income tax; instead each partner reports his share of the LLP's profits and losses on his individual federal income tax return.

The formation of an LLP requires filing a form with the secretary of state and maintaining adequate professional liability insurance for the firm.

The LLP is an especially good form of business for professionals such as accountants, allowing them flexibility of management, while insulating them in part from personal liability. As more states adopt LLP statutes, the LLP will become the preferred form of business for professionals who do not incorporate. As of October 1994, seventeen states and the District of Columbia had passed LLP statutes.

Limited Partnership

A **limited partnership** has one or more general partners and one or more limited partners. General partners have rights and liabilities similar to partners in a partnership. They manage the business of the limited partnership and have unlimited liability for the obligations of the limited partnership. Typically, however, the only general partner is a corporation, thereby protecting the human managers from unlimited liability.

Because the limited partnership is not a taxpaying entity for federal income tax purposes, general partners report their shares of the limited partnership's income and losses on their individual federal income tax returns. For general partners, losses of the business are deductible without limit.

Limited partners usually have no liability for the obligations of the limited partnership once they have paid their capital contributions to the limited partnership. Limited partners have no right to manage the business and may lose their limited liability for the business's obligations if they do manage the business.

A limited partner must pay federal income tax on his share of the profits of the business, but he may deduct his share of losses only to the extent of his investment in the business. As a passive investor, a limited partner may use the losses only to offset income from other passive investments.

A limited partnership may have a life apart from its owners. When a limited partner dies or otherwise leaves the business, the limited partnership is not dissolved. When a general partner dies or withdraws, however, the limited partnership is dissolved in the absence of a contrary agreement. A general or limited partner's rights may not be wholly transferred to another person unless the other partners agree to admit the new person as a partner.

Unlike a sole proprietorship or partnership, a limited partnership may be created only by complying with a state statute permitting limited partnerships. Thus, no limited partnership may be created by default.

There are three main reasons why persons organize a business as a limited partnership. First, by using a corporate general partner, no human will have unlimited liability for the debts of the business. Second, losses of the business are deductible on the owners' federal income tax returns. Third, investors may contribute capital to the business yet avoid unlimited liability and the obligation to manage the business. Thus, the limited partnership has the ability to attract large amounts of capital, much more than the sole proprietorship, which has only one owner, or the partnership, whose partners' fear of unlimited liability restricts the size of the business. Hence, for a business needing millions of dollars of capital and expecting to lose money in its early years, the limited partnership is a particularly good form of business.

Corporation

A **corporation** is owned by shareholders who elect a board of directors to manage the business. The board of directors often selects officers to run the day-to-day affairs of the business. Consequently, ownership and management of a corporation may be completely separate: No shareholder has the right to manage, and no officer or director needs to be a shareholder.

Shareholders have limited liability for the obligations of the corporation, even if a shareholder is elected as a director or selected as an officer. Directors and officers have no liability for the contracts they or the corporation's employees negotiate in the name of the corporation. While managers have liability for their own misconduct, they have no liability for corporate torts committed by other corporate managers or employees. Therefore, shareholders, officers, and directors have limited liability for the obligations of the business.

The usual corporation is a tax-paying entity for federal income tax purposes. The corporation pays taxes on its profits. Shareholders do not report their shares of corporation profits on their individual federal income tax returns. Instead, only when the corporation distributes its profits to the shareholders in the form of dividends or the shareholders sell their investments at a profit do the shareholders report income on their individual returns. This creates a double-tax possibility, as profits are taxed once at the corporation level and again at the shareholder level when dividends are paid.

Also, shareholders do not deduct corporate losses on their individual returns. They may, however, deduct their investment losses after they have sold their shares of the corporation.

There is one important exception to these corporate tax rules. The shareholders may elect to have the corporation and its shareholders taxed under Subchapter S of the Internal Revenue Code. By electing **S Corporation** status, the corporation and its shareholders are taxed nearly entirely like a partnership: Income and losses of the business are reported on the shareholders' individual federal income tax returns. A corporation electing S Corporation status may have no more than 35 shareholders.

A corporation has a life separate from its owners and its managers. When a shareholder or manager dies or otherwise leaves the business, the corporation is not dissolved. A shareholder may sell his shares of the corporation to other persons without limitation unless there is a contrary agreement. The purchaser becomes a shareholder with all the rights of the selling shareholder.

There are several reasons why persons organize a business as a corporation. First, no human has unlimited liability for the debts of the business. As a result, businesses in the riskiest industries—such as manufacturing—incorporate. Second, because investors may contribute capital to the business, avoid unlimited liability, escape the obligation to manage the business, and easily liquidate their investments by selling their shares, the corporation has the ability to attract large amounts of capital, even more than the limited partnership, whose partnership interests are not as freely transferable. Thus, the corporation has the capacity to raise the largest amount of capital.

The S Corporation has an additional advantage: Losses of the business are deductible on individual federal income tax returns. However, because the S Corporation is limited to 35 shareholders—who must be individuals or estates of individuals—its ability to raise capital is severely limited. Also, while legally permitted to sell their shares, S corporation shareholders may be unable to find investors willing to buy their shares or may be restricted from selling their shares pursuant to an agreement between the shareholders.

Limited Liability Company

A **limited liability company (LLC)** is a new business form intended to combine the nontax advantages of corporations with the favorable tax treatment of partnerships. An LLC is owned by members, who may manage the LLC themselves or elect the manager or managers who will operate the business. Members have limited liability for the obligations of the LLC.

The LLC has the purported federal taxation advantage of the partnership—no federal income taxation at the firm level. Instead, LLC owners pay taxes on their shares of the firm's profits. However, partnership treatment appears to require a lack of free transferability of the members' ownership interests: Transfer of membership interests is prohibited without the consent of all the members. In addition, the death, retirement, or bankruptcy of any member dissolves and forces the liquidation of the LLC, unless all the remaining members vote to continue the business.

What are the advantages of the LLC? The LLC has the limited liability advantage and the management advantage of the corporation. The LLC and its members receive the same federal tax treatment as the S Corporation and its shareholders, yet the LLC has no limit on the number or type of owners, as does an S Corporation. The major disadvantage of the LLC, however, is that the death of a member requires a vote by the remaining members to continue the business. This requirement practically limits the number of members of an LLC.

See Figure 1 for a summary of the general characteristics of business forms.

Franchising

Franchising is an agreement by which a **franchisee** has the right to sell goods or services under a marketing plan prescribed in substantial part by a **franchisor**. Thus, when a franchisee purchases a franchise, the franchisee buys a *business opportunity*, which the franchisee may choose to operate as any form of business. For example, if you obtain a McDonald's restaurant franchise for the south side of Santa Fe, you will probably choose to operate the business as a corporation.

Franchising has advantages for both the franchisee and the franchisor. The franchisee receives the franchisor's assistance in setting up the business and training employees. In addition, the franchisee may benefit from the franchisor's national advertising and strong trademark and goodwill. For example, a McDonald's franchisee obtains instant visibility and credibility from displaying the McDonald's golden arches. In return for this assistance, the franchisee usually pays a substantial purchase price plus a fee based on income, sales, or the purchase price of specified supplies. For example, an ice-cream restaurant franchise may pay its franchisor 15 percent of the price it pays for its ice-cream mix. The fee is collected for the franchisor by an authorized supplier of the mix.

The franchisor also benefits. Instead of making a high investment in several business locations, the franchisor shifts most of the investment risk to the franchisees. Yet the franchisor receives income from the franchisees' operation of their businesses. And while the franchisor's profits are tied to the franchisees' success, the franchisees typically have a sizable investment in the franchises and have a strong incentive to succeed. Also, the franchisor can adopt standards to ensure it selects high-quality franchisees with superior financial strength. Using franchising allows a franchisor to exploit its trademark and goodwill yet also protect itself by requiring franchisees to adopt uniform image and marketing practices.

Nature of Franchisor/Franchisee Relationship
Because a franchisor may exercise some control over parts of a franchisee's business, there is a risk that the franchisor may be liable for the torts and contracts of the franchisee. Most franchising agreements provide that the franchisee is not an agent or partner of the franchisor. Some courts refuse to accept this characterization of the relationship, especially when the degree and type of control by the franchisor suggest an agency relationship. For example, when a franchisor has the right to control a franchisee's prices, the franchisor may be responsible for any resulting antitrust violation resulting from the franchisee's pricing decisions.

Franchisee Protection   In response to abuses by franchisors, the courts, the Federal Trade Commission, and the state legislatures have created rules that protect franchisees. The typical franchising agreement gives a franchisor wide latitude to terminate a franchisee. Some courts have invalidated such termination power or required that terminations be made in good faith. The Federal Trade Commission has issued a franchise disclosure rule and guidelines requiring franchisors to disclose their financial fees and charges, the franchisees' obligations to purchase supplies, and territorial restrictions on the franchisees. In addition, most of the states require disclosure and termination protection for franchisees.

PARTNERSHIPS

The basic concept of partnership is as ancient as the history of collective human activity. Partnerships were known in ancient Babylonia, ancient Greece, and the Roman Empire. Hammurabi's Code of 2300 B.C. regulated partnerships. The definition of a partnership in the 6th-century Justinian Code of the Roman Empire does not differ materially from that in our laws today. The partnership was likewise known in Asian countries, including China. During the Middle Ages, much trade between nations was carried on by partnerships.

By the close of the 17th century, the partnership was recognized in the English common law. When the United States became an independent nation and adopted the English common law in 1776, the English law of partnerships became a part of American

FIGURE 1 **General Characteristics of Forms of Business**

	Sole Proprietorship	Partnership	Limited Liability Partnership	Limited Partnership	Corporation	S Corporation	Limited Liability Company
Formation	When one person conducts business without forming a corporation	By agreement of owners *or* by default when two or more owners conduct business together without forming a limited partnership or a corporation	By agreement of owners; must comply with limited liability partnership statute	By agreement of owners; must comply with limited partnership statute	By agreement of owners; must comply with corporation statute	By agreement of owners; must comply with corporation statute; must elect S Corporation status under Subchapter S of Internal Revenue Code	By agreement of owners; must comply with limited liability company statute
Duration	Terminates on death or withdrawal of sole proprietor	Dissolves on death or withdrawal of partner	Dissolves on death or withdrawal of partner	Dissolves on death or withdrawal of general partner	Unaffected by death or withdrawal of shareholder	Unaffected by death or withdrawal of shareholder	Dissolves on death or withdrawal of member
Management	By sole proprietor	By partners	By partners	By general partners	By board of directors	By board of directors	By managers or members
Owner Liability	Unlimited	Unlimited	Unlimited for general obligations of partnership; limited to capital contribution for professional malpractice of a fellow partner	Unlimited for general partners; limited to capital contribution for limited partners	Limited to capital contribution	Limited to capital contribution	Limited to capital contribution
Transferability of Owners' Interest	None	None	None	None	Freely transferable	Freely transferable unless shareholders agree otherwise	None
Federal Income Taxation	Only sole proprietor taxed	Only partners taxed	Only partners taxed	Only partners taxed	Corporation taxed; shareholders taxed on dividends (double tax)	Only shareholders taxed	Only members taxed

---

FIGURE 2   Principal Characteristics of Partnerships under the UPA

1. A partnership may be created with no formalities. Two or more people merely need to agree to own and conduct a business together in order to create a partnership (aggregate theory).
2. Partners have unlimited liability for the obligations of the business (aggregate theory). However, a partner's personal creditors have first priority to that partner's assets, while partnership creditors have first priority to partnership assets (entity theory).
3. Each partner, merely by being an owner of the business, has a right to manage the business of the partnership (aggregate theory). He is an agent of the partnership and may make the partnership liable for contracts, torts, and crimes (entity theory). Because partners are liable for all obligations of the partnership, in effect each partner is an agent of the other partners. Each partner may hire agents, and every partner is liable for the agents' authorized contracts and for torts that the agents commit in the course of their employments (aggregate theory).
4. A partnership is not an employer of the partners, for most purposes. As a result, for example, a partner who leaves a partnership is not entitled to unemployment benefits (aggregate theory).
5. Partners are fiduciaries of the partnership. They must act in the best interests of the partnership, not in their individual best interests (entity theory).
6. The profits or losses of the business are shared by the partners, who report their shares of the profits or losses on their individual federal income tax returns, because the partnership does not pay federal income taxes (aggregate theory). Nonetheless, a partnership does keep its own financial records and must file an information return with the Internal Revenue Service (entity theory).*
7. A partnership may own property in its own name (entity theory).
8. A partnership may not sue or be sued in its own name. The partners must sue or be sued (aggregate theory).
9. A partner may not sue her partners. Her sole remedy is to seek an accounting between the partners (aggregate theory).
10. A partner's ownership interest in a partnership is not freely transferable. A purchaser of a partner's interest does not become a partner, but is entitled to receive only the partner's share of the partnership's profits (aggregate theory).
11. Generally, a partnership has no life apart from its owners. If a partner dies, the partnership dissolves and may be terminated (aggregate theory). Under certain circumstances, however, the partnership may continue after the death of a partner (entity theory).

---

*The federal income tax return filed by a partnership is merely an information return in which the partnership indicates its gross income and deductions and the names and addresses of its partners (IRC Sec. 6031). The information return allows the Internal Revenue Service to determine whether the partners accurately report partnership income on their individual returns.

law. In the early part of the 19th century, the partnership became the most important form of association in the United States.

Today, the American common law of partnership has been largely replaced by statutory law. Every state has a statute on partnership law. The Uniform Partnership Act (UPA) of 1914 has been adopted in 49 states (Louisiana is the exception) and the District of Columbia. The UPA is a model partnership statute that is the product of the National Conference of Commissioners on Uniform State Laws, a group of practicing lawyers, judges, and law professors. The aims of the UPA are to codify partnership law in one document, to make that law more nearly consistent with itself, and to attain uniformity throughout the country.

A Revised Uniform Partnership Act (RUPA) was proposed in 1992. As of February 1994, only Wyoming and Montana had adopted the RUPA. The

RUPA has been heavily criticized for changing partnership rules protecting creditors of partnerships and, therefore, is not likely to become law in a majority of states without some major changes. Because the UPA of 1914 has been adopted by nearly every state in the United States, the UPA is the framework of your study of partnerships.

Entity and Aggregate Theories

Studying the list of partnership characteristics in Figure 2, you may perceive that in some respects the partnership is treated as an **entity**—that is, as a person separate and distinct from its partners. In other respects, the partnership is viewed as an **aggregate** of the partners, with no life or powers apart from them. The UPA recognizes the partnership primarily as an aggregate of the partners. In a few situations, however, the UPA confers entity status on a partnership.

CREATION OF PARTNERSHIP

No formalities are necessary to create a partnership. Two or more persons may become partners in accordance with a written partnership contract (articles of partnership), they may agree orally to be partners, or they may become partners merely by arranging their affairs as if they were partners. If partners conduct business under a trade name, they must file the name with the secretary of state in compliance with state statutes requiring the registration of fictitious business names.

When people decide to become partners, they should employ a lawyer to prepare a written partnership agreement. Although such **articles of partnership** are not required to form a partnership, they are highly desirable for the same reasons that written contracts are generally preferred. In addition, the statute of frauds requires a writing for a partnership having a term exceeding one year.

When there is no written partnership agreement, a dispute may arise over whether persons who are associated in some enterprise are partners. For example, someone may assert that she is a partner and, therefore, claim a share of the value of a successful enterprise. More frequently, an unpaid creditor may seek to hold a person liable for a debt incurred by another person in the same enterprise. To determine whether there is a partnership in the absence of an express agreement, the courts use the definition of partnership in the UPA.

UPA Definition of Partnership

The UPA defines a partnership as an "association of two or more persons to carry on as co-owners a business for profit." If the definition is satisfied, then the courts will treat those involved as partners. A relationship may meet the UPA definition of partnership even when a person does not believe he is a partner, and occasionally, even if the parties agree that they are not partners.

Association of Two or More Persons   As an association, a partnership is a *voluntary and consensual relationship*. It cannot be imposed on a person; a person must agree expressly or impliedly to have a person associate with her. For example, a partner cannot force her partners to accept her daughter into the partnership.

No person can be a partner with herself—a partnership must have *at least two partners*. A person may be a partner with her spouse.

Not everyone or everything may be a partner. An individual, partnership, limited partnership, corporation, or other association may be a partner. Most states do not permit a trust to be a partner, but they allow the trustee of the trust to be a partner for the benefit of the trust.

Carrying On a Business   Any trade, occupation, or profession may qualify as a business. Carrying on a business usually requires a series of transactions conducted over a period of time. For example, a group of farmers that buys supplies in quantity to get lower prices is not carrying on a business but only part of one. If the group buys harvesting equipment with which it intends to harvest crops for others for a fee for many years, it is carrying on a business.

Co-Ownership   Partners must *co-own the business* in which they associate. There is no requirement that the capital contributions or the assets of the business be co-owned.

Also, by itself, co-ownership of assets does not establish a partnership. For example, two persons who own a building as joint tenants are not necessarily partners. To be partners, they must co-own a business.

The two most important factors in establishing co-ownership of the business are the sharing of profits and the sharing of management of the business. The UPA declares that a person's **sharing the profits** of a business is *prima facie* evidence that she is a partner in the business. This means that persons sharing profits are partners, unless other evidence exists to disprove they are partners. The rationale for this rule is that a person ordinarily would not be sharing the profits of a business unless she were a co-owner. This rule brings under partnership law many persons who fail to realize that they are partners. For example, two college students who purchase college basketball tickets, resell them, and split the profits are partners.

Sharing the gross revenues of a business does not create a presumption of partnership. The profits, not the gross receipts, must be shared. For example, a broker who receives a commission on a sale of land is not a partner of the seller of that land.

Although sharing profits usually is prima facie proof of partnership, the UPA provides that **no** presumption of partnership may be made when a share of profits is received:

1. By a creditor as payment on a debt.
2. By a creditor as interest on a loan.
3. By an employee as wages.
4. By a landlord as rent.
5. By a widow, widower, or representative of a deceased partner for the value of that partner's share of the partnership.
6. As consideration to the transferor of a business or other property for his sale of the goodwill of the business or other property.

These exceptions reflect the normal expectations of the parties that no partnership exists in such situations.

Sharing management of a business is additional evidence tending to prove the existence of a partnership. However, by itself, participation in management is not conclusive proof of the existence of a partnership. For example, a creditor may be granted considerable control in a business, such as a veto power over partnership decisions and the right of consultation, without becoming a partner. Also, a sole proprietor may hire someone to manage his business, yet the manager will not be a partner of the sole proprietor.

However, when the parties claim that they share profits for one of the six reasons above, the sharing of management may overcome the presumption that they are not partners. When the parties arrange their affairs in a manner that otherwise establishes an objective intent to create a partnership, the courts find that a partnership exists. For example, when a nonmanagerial employee initially shares profits as a form of employment compensation, the employee is not a partner of his employer. But when the employer and employee modify their relationship by having the employee exercise the managerial control of a partner and fail to reaffirm that the manager is merely an employee, a partnership may exist.

Creditors occupy a privileged position. Many cases have permitted creditors to share profits and to exercise considerable control over a business without becoming partners. Creditor control is often justified on the grounds that it is merely reasonable protection for the creditor's risk.

FIGURE 3   Important Consequences of Being a Partner

1. You share ownership of the business. For example, you want to bring an employee into your business, which is worth $250,000. If you and the employee conduct your affairs like partners, your employee will own half of your business.
2. You share the profits of the business.
3. You share management of the business. Your partner must be allowed to participate in management decisions.
4. Your partner is your agent. You are liable for your partner's torts and contracts made in the ordinary course of business.
5. You owe fiduciary duties to your partnership and your partner, such as the duties to devote full time to the business, not to compete with the business, not to self-deal, and not to disclose confidential matters.
6. Your have unlimited personal liability for all the obligations of the partnership.

For Profit   The owners of an enterprise must *intend to make a profit* to create a partnership. If the enterprise suffers losses, yet the owners intend to make a profit, a partnership may result. When an endeavor is carried on by several people for charitable or other nonprofit objectives, it is not a partnership. For example, Alex and Geri operate a restaurant booth at a county fair each year to raise money for a Boy Scout troop. Their relationship is not a partnership, but merely an association. (Nonetheless, like partners, they may be individually liable for the debts of the enterprise.)

Intent   Frequently, courts say that there must be intent to form a partnership. This rule is more correctly stated as follows: The *parties must intend to create a relationship that the law recognizes as a partnership*. A partnership may exist even if the parties entered it inadvertently, without considering whether they had created a partnership. A written agreement to the effect that the parties do not intend to form a partnership is not conclusive if their actions provide evidence of their intent to form a relationship that meets the UPA partnership test.

There are several important consequences of being a partner. See Figure 3 for a summary of the most important consequences.

Creation of Joint Ventures

Courts frequently distinguish **joint ventures** from partnerships. A joint venture may be found when a court is reluctant to call an arrangement a partnership because the purpose of the arrangement is not to establish an ongoing business involving many transactions; instead, it is limited to a single project. For example, an agreement to buy, develop, and resell for profit a particular piece of real estate is likely to be viewed as a joint venture rather than a partnership. In all other respects, joint ventures are created just as partnerships are created. The joint venturers may have a formal written agreement. In its absence, a court applies the UPA definition of partnership—modified so as not to require the carrying on of a business—to determine whether a joint venture has been created.

The legal implications of the distinction between a partnership and a joint venture are not entirely clear. Generally, partnership law applies to joint ventures. For example, all of the participants in a joint venture are personally liable for its debts, and joint venturers owe each other the fiduciary duties imposed on partners. Joint ventures are treated as partnerships for federal income tax purposes. The most significant difference between joint venturers and partners is that joint venturers are usually held to have *less implied and apparent authority* than partners, due to the limited scope of the enterprise.

The following case applies partnership law to the question of whether a joint venture has been created by players of the Illinois state lottery.

FITCHIE V. YURKO

570 N.E.2d 892 (Ill. App. Ct. 1991)

Phyllis Huisel operated a coffee shop called the Hitching-A-Ride, from which she sold tickets for the Illinois state lottery. A regular customer, Rick Yurko, frequently purchased lottery tickets from Phyllis. In mid-February 1990, Yurko purchased $100 dollars worth of $1 Fortune Hunt lottery tickets. The lottery tickets were the scratch-off variety, which revealed instant winners when the lottery player scratched off a film covering the tickets. Yurko asked Phyllis to help him scratch off the tickets, but she suggested that Judy Fitchie, one of her employees, should scratch off the tickets because Judy was luckier than Phyllis. Yurko placed several tickets in front of Judy and Frances Vincent, another customer at the coffee shop, and invited them to help him scratch them off. Yurko stated that if they would help him scratch off the lottery tickets, they would be his partners and would share in any winnings.

After playing for some time, Judy uncovered three television sets and announced that she had a winner. The ticket scratched by Judy gave the owner a chance to compete for a $100,000 prize. The owner of the ticket was required to complete the back of ticket, indicating the name, address, and phone number of the owner. Completed tickets were to be mailed to the Illinois Department of the Lottery; six tickets would be drawn and their owners would appear on the lottery television show.

Judy placed the ticket near Phyllis, and Yurko urged Phyllis to fill it out. Phyllis did not want to appear on television. Yurko indicated he would appear on television, and after discussion, Phyllis, Judy, Frances, and Yurko agreed that Yurko would be their representative and go on television. Yurko then printed on the back of the ticket "F.J.P. Rick Yurko." F.J.P. represented the first initials of Frances, Judy, and Phyllis. When Yurko started filling out the ticket, he told Phyllis that he was going to put all their initials and his name on the ticket and that they would be partners no matter what they might win.

The ticket was mailed to the Lottery and was one of six drawn for the lottery television show. Yurko appeared on the show and won the $100,000 prize. Thereafter, Yurko claimed all the $100,000 for himself. Phyllis, Judy, and Frances sued Yurko to recover shares of the winnings. The trial court held that they were partners or joint venturers entitled to an equal share of the winnings. Yurko appealed to the Appellate Court of Illinois.

Bowman, Justice The evidence indicates that the arrangement between Yurko, Phyllis, Judy, and Frances constituted a joint venture. A joint venture is essentially a partnership carried on for a single enterprise.

A joint venture is an association of two or more persons to carry out a single enterprise for profit. Whether a joint venture exists is a question of the intent of the parties. The elements to be considered in determining the parties' intent are: an agreement to carry on an enterprise; a demonstration of intent by the parties to be joint venturers; a joint interest, as reflected in the contribution of property, finances, effort, skill, or knowledge by each party; a measure of proprietorship or joint control over the enterprise; and a provision for sharing of profits and losses. A formal agreement is not essential to establish a joint venture. Rather, the existence of a joint venture may be inferred from facts and circumstances demonstrating that the parties, in fact, undertook a joint enterprise.

The parties entered into an agreement and showed their intent to be joint venturers when they started playing the lottery together. Yurko invited the women, both verbally and by placing tickets in front of them, to play the lottery with him. Yurko told them that if they would help him scratch tickets they would be his partners and would share in any prize winnings. They expressed agreement with Yurko's proposal when they began scratching off the tickets.

Both Judy and Frances uncovered tickets that were good for small cash prizes or more tickets. None of the players tried to claim any of those prizes as their own. Rather, the tickets were turned in for more tickets, and the players kept on scratching. After the winning ticket was revealed, there was discussion amongst all the parties as to who would appear on the television show. Together, not individually, they decided that Yurko would be the one to go. Yurko impliedly acknowledged a joint effort when he printed the women's initials right alongside his own name on the back of the winning ticket, again amidst talk that he and the women were partners.

A joint interest in the effort to win the lottery is also found in the evidence. It is undisputed that Yurko paid for the tickets. Frances and Judy expended their time and energy and put forth effort to scratch the tickets. While Phyllis's part in this is not altogether clear, Phyllis scratched off a couple of tickets, and it is evident the other parties considered her part of the enterprise.

Finally, with regard to provision for sharing of profits, Yurko told the women they would share in anything that was won if they helped scratch the tickets. Yurko also wrote the women's initials next to his own on the line provided on the lottery ticket for the ticket holder's name. This evidence proves that the joint venturers planned to share equally in any lottery prize ultimately won.

We acknowledge the informality of the arrangement between Yurko and the women. Nonetheless, the parties should be bound by the terms of their agreement to jointly carry out an enterprise for profit.

Judgment for Fitchie, Huisel, and Vincent affirmed.

Creation of Mining Partnerships

Although similar to an ordinary partnership or a joint venture, a mining partnership is recognized as a distinct relationship in a number of states. Persons who cooperate in the working of either a mine or an oil or gas well are treated as mining partners if there is (1) joint ownership of a mineral interest, (2) joint operation of the property, and (3) sharing of profits and losses. Joint operation requires more than merely financing the development of a mineral interest, but it does not require active physical participation in operations; it may be proved by furnishing labor, supplies, services, or advice. The delegation of sole operating responsibility to one of the participants does not bar treatment as a mining partnership.

Creation of Limited Liability Partnerships

Unlike an ordinary partnership, a limited liability partnership (LLP) may not be created merely by partners conducting a business together. The partners must expressly agree to create an LLP by complying with a limited liability partnership statute. In Texas—the first state to permit the formation of an LLP—the formation of an LLP requires filing a form with the secretary of state, paying an annual fee ($200 per partner), adding the words "Registered Limited Liability Partnership" or the acronym "LLP" to the partnership's name, and maintaining at least $100,000 of professional liability insurance for the firm.

Partnership by Estoppel

Two persons may not be partners, yet in the eyes of a third person they may **appear** to be partners. If the third person deals with one of the apparent partners, he may be harmed and seek to recover damages from both of the apparent partners. The question, then, is whether the third person may collect damages from both of the apparent partners.

For example, Thomas thinks that Wilson, a wealthy person, is a partner of Porter, a poor person. Thomas decides to do business with Porter on the grounds that if Porter does not perform as agreed, he can recover damages from Wilson. If Thomas is wrong and Wilson is not Porter's partner, Thomas ordinarily has no recourse against Wilson. UPA Section 7(1) states that "persons who are not partners as to each other are not partners as to third persons." However, if Thomas can prove that Wilson misled him to believe that Wilson and Porter were partners, he may sue Wilson for damages suffered when Porter failed to perform as agreed. This is an application of the doctrine of **partnership by estoppel**.

Partnership by estoppel is based on substantial, detrimental reliance on the appearance of partnership. Partnership by estoppel has three elements:

1. A person holds herself out or consents to being held out as a partner of another person.
2. A third party justifiably relies on the holding out.
3. The third person is injured as a result of the reliance.

The third party who is damaged may recover his loss from the person who held herself out or consented to being held out as the partner of the other person.

Holding Out

A person might hold himself out as a partner by referring to himself as another person's partner. Or he might appear frequently in the office of a purported partner and confer with him. Perhaps he and another person share office space, have one door to an office with both of their names on it, have one telephone number, and share a secretary who answers the phone giving the names of both persons.

More difficult is determining when a person *consents* to being held out as another's partner. Mere knowledge that one is being held out as a partner is not consent. But a person's silence in response to a statement that the person is another's partner is consent. For example, suppose Chavez tells Eaton that Gold is a partner in Birt's new retail shoe business. In fact, Gold is not Birt's partner. Later, Gold learns of the conversation between Chavez and Eaton. Gold does not have to seek out Chavez and Eaton to tell them that he is not Birt's partner in order to avoid being held liable as a partner for Birt's business debts. Had Chavez made the statement to Eaton in Gold's presence, however, Gold must deny the partnership relation or he will be held liable for Eaton's subsequent reliance on Gold's silence.

Reasonable Reliance and Injury

A partner by estoppel is liable only to those persons who reasonably rely on the holding out and suffer injury thereby. This means that partnership by estoppel is determined on a case-by-case basis.

A third person's reliance on the appearance of a partnership must be reasonable. When a person has information that would prevent a reasonable person from relying on the holding out, no partnership by estoppel may result. For example, Litz knows that Frank and Stump are employer and employee. Frank calls Stump "my partner" in the presence of Stump and Litz. Frank and Stump are not partners by estoppel. Because Litz knows that Frank and Stump are employer and employee, she may not reasonably rely on Frank's calling Stump "my partner."

The injury suffered by the third person must be the result of her reliance. If the third person would have done business with another person whether or not that person was a partner of someone held out as a partner, there is no injury as a result of reliance. Hence, there is no partnership by estoppel.

Effect of Partnership by Estoppel

Once partnership by estoppel has been proved, the person who held himself out or who consented to being held out is liable as though he were a partner. He is liable on contracts entered into by third persons on their belief that he was a partner. He is liable for torts committed during the course of relationships entered by third persons who believed he was a partner.

Although two parties are partners by estoppel to a person who knows of the holding out and who justifiably relies on it to his injury, the partners by estoppel are *not partners in fact* and do not share the profits, management, or value of the business of the purported partnership. Partnership by estoppel is merely a device to allow creditors to sue parties who mislead them into believing that a partnership exists.

In the following case, the appearance of partnership led the court to a finding of partnership by estoppel.

VOLKMAN V. DP ASSOCIATES
268 S.E.2d 265 (N.C. Ct. App. 1980)

Alvin and Carol Volkman decided to build a house. They contacted David McNamee for construction advice. McNamee informed the Volkmans that he was doing business with Phillip Carroll. Subsequently, the Volkmans received a letter from McNamee on DP Associates stationery. They assumed that the DP was derived from the first names of McNamee and Carroll: David and Phillip. Prior to the signing of the contract, McNamee introduced Carroll to Mr. Volkman at the DP Associates office, where Carroll said, "I hope we'll be working together." Carroll stated that McNamee would be the person at DP Associates primarily doing business with the Volkmans, but indicated that he also would be available for consultation.

The Volkmans reviewed the written contract in the DP Associates office with McNamee. McNamee suggested that they use a form to identify DP Associates as acting as a general contractor. He then left the room saying, "I will ask Phil." When he returned, he said that they would use the form.

After the contract was signed but before construction of the house began, Mr. Volkman visited the office of DP Associates. He again saw and spoke with Carroll, who said to him, "I am happy that we will be working with you." During construction, Mr. Volkman visited the office of DP Associates several times and saw Carroll there. During one visit, he expressed to Carroll his concern about construction delays, but Carroll told him not to worry because McNamee would take care of it.

When DP Associates failed to perform the contract, the Volkmans sued DP Associates, McNamee, and Carroll. Carroll argued that he could not be liable to the Volkmans because he and McNamee were not partners. The trial court agreed and refused to let the jury decide the case. The Volkmans appealed to the North Carolina Court of Appeals.

Vaughn, Judge   If the Volkmans are unable to prove a partnership in fact, they may be able to show that Carroll should be held as a partner by estoppel.

Liability by estoppel may result either from Carroll's representation of himself as a partner "by words spoken or written" or "by conduct" or Carroll's "consent" to such a representation by another. The Volkmans indicated they may be able to show that Carroll by his oral statements to them and conduct in their presence and by his consent to the representations of McNamee to the Volkmans, some of which were in the presence of Carroll, represented himself as a partner and should be estopped to deny such association. They may be able to show further they relied upon these representations not knowing them to be false and that based upon the representations of Carroll and McNamee, the Volkmans changed their position and were thereby damaged.

The liability of the person seeking to deny partner status is based on the objective theory of contract law, i.e., a person should be bound by his words and conduct. Thus, when Carroll told Mr. Volkman, "I am happy that we will be working with you," and conducted himself as he did in the DP

Associates office in the presence of Mr. Volkman, the jury may find that Carroll was indicating a willingness to be bound by the statements and acts of McNamee, that Carroll held himself out as a partner of McNamee in DP Associates, that Mc-Namee had apparent authority to act for Carroll, and that the Volkmans reasonably relied upon this holding out. If so, Carroll is bound as if he directly dealt with the Volkmans.

Judgment reversed in favor of the Volkmans. Remanded to the trial court for jury trial.

PARTNERSHIP CAPITAL

When a partnership or limited liability partnership is formed, partners contribute cash or other property to the partnership. The partners' contribution is called **partnership capital.** To supplement beginning capital, other property may be contributed to the partnership as needed, such as by the partners permitting the partnership to retain some of its profits. Partnership capital is the equity of the business.

Loans made by partners to a partnership are not partnership capital but instead are liabilities of the business. Partners who make loans to a partnership are both owners and creditors.

PARTNERSHIP PROPERTY

A partnership or limited liability partnership may own all or only a part of the property it uses. For example, it may own the business and perhaps a small amount of working capital in the form of cash or a checking account, yet own no other assets. All other tangible and intangible property used by the partnership may be individually or jointly owned by one or more of the partners or rented by the partnership from third parties. A determination of what is partnership property becomes essential when the partnership is dissolved and the assets are being distributed and when creditors of either the partnership or one of the partners is seeking assets to satisfy a debt.

The UPA provides that (1) all property originally brought into the partnership or subsequently acquired by purchase or otherwise, on account of the partnership, is partnership property, and (2) unless the contrary intention appears, property acquired with partnership funds is partnership property.

The intent of the partners controls whether the partnership or an individual partner owns the property. It is best to have a written record of the partners' intent as to ownership of all property used by the partnership, such as in the articles of partnership. Other writings—such as accounting records—show the partnership assets; assets appearing in the partnership's books are presumed to belong to the partnership. Also, the partnership's paying rent on property provides strong evidence that the property belongs to the partner receiving the rent.

The presumption is very strong that property purchased with partnership funds and used in the partnership is partnership property. No such presumption is accorded to a partner who purchases property with her own funds and then allows the partnership to use the property; other factors besides the partner's funding the purchase determine who owns the property.

If title is taken in the partnership name, it is presumed that the property is partnership property. However, the presumption is not as strong that real property held in the name of a partner is individual property. Other indicia may prove that property held in a partner's name belongs to the partnership. For example, the partnership's payment of property taxes or insurance premiums, the maintainance, repair, and improvement of property by the partnership, and the deduction of these expenses on the partnership income tax return are indications of the intent of the partners that property belongs to the partnership, despite title being held in the name of a partner.

Examples

A tax accountant discovers that a partnership is using a building to which a partner, Jacob Smith, holds title. The partnership pays rent monthly to Smith, but the partnership pays for all maintenance and repairs on the building. The accountant wants to know whether the partnership or Smith should be paying real property taxes on the building. Smith is the owner and should be paying taxes on it because his partners' intent to allow Smith to retain ownership is evidenced by the partnership paying rent to Smith.

Changing the facts, suppose the partnership pays no rent to Smith, the partnership maintains and repairs the building, and the partnership pays real property taxes on the building, but the title is in Smith's name. Who owns the building? The property belongs to the partnership, because all the objective criteria of ownership point toward partnership ownership, especially the payment of taxes. Therefore, when the partnership is liquidated, the building will be sold along with other partnership assets, and the proceeds of its sale will be distributed to partnership creditors and to all of the partners.

In the following case, the court held that a truck trailer held in the partnership's name was partnership property.

In Re Fulton
43 B.R. 273 (M.D. Tenn. 1984)

Padgett Carroll and Walter Fulton operated as a partnership a trucking business under the name of C & F Trucking. Carroll contributed a semi truck, which Fulton drove for the business. Carroll used $4,600 of his personal funds to purchase a used 42-foot trailer for C & F Trucking. The seller's invoice listed C & F Trucking as the purchaser of the trailer. The trailer's certificate of title listed C & F Trucking as the owner.

Fulton's personal financial problems forced him to file for bankruptcy. Fulton claimed ownership of the trailer among his assets. Carroll claimed that the trailer was his individual asset.

Paine, Bankruptcy Judge In determining whether property is partnership property or property owned by an individual, the court must focus primarily on the intentions of the partners at the time the property was acquired. Such intention of the partners must be determined from their apparent intention at the time the property was acquired and the conduct of the partners toward the property after the purchase.

Viewing evidence surrounding the purpose and use of the property, Tennessee courts have held that when property is titled in the name of the partnership, the party asserting that the property is not partnership property has the burden of proof.

The evidence establishes that the trailer is partnership property. Both a sales invoice and a certificate of title list the owner of the trailer as C & F Trucking. The trailer was purchased by Carroll for use in the C & F Trucking business and Fulton actually used the trailer in the business.

The claims of individual ownership asserted by both Fulton and Carroll lack substance. The property was indeed partnership property.

Judgment for Carroll.

PARTNERS' PROPERTY RIGHTS

In a partnership or limited liability partnership, a partner has three property rights:

1. Her rights in specific partnership property.
2. Her partnership interest.
3. Her right to participate in the management of the business.

The first two rights are discussed here. The management right is discussed in Chapter 37, Operation of Partnership and Related Forms.

Rights in Partnership Property

Partnership property is owned by partners as **tenants in partnership.** This means that the partners as a group own partnership property as a whole; the partners as individuals do not own proportionate interests in separate items of partnership property.

As a tenant in partnership, each partner has the right to possess partnership property for partnership purposes. A partner has no individual right to use or possess partnership property for her own purposes, such as paying a personal debt, unless she has the consent of the other partners. Likewise, a partner's personal creditor may not make a claim against partnership assets.

On the death or other withdrawal of a partner, his rights in partnership property pass to the surviving partners. This is called the **right of survivorship.**

Partnership Interest

As a co-owner of a partnership, a partner has an ownership interest in the partnership. A partner's ownership interest is called a **partnership interest** and is part of his personal property. Although a partner may not give his personal creditors any interest in separate items of partnership property, a partner may sell or **assign his partnership interest** to a creditor. And although a partner's personal creditor has no right to seize separate items of partnership property, a creditor may obtain rights in a partner's partnership interest by obtaining a **charging order** against that interest.

Assignment   The sale or **assignment of a partnership interest** is a voluntary act of a partner. It entitles the buyer or assignee to receive the assigning partner's share of the partnership's profits, but it does not make the assignee a partner of the partnership: The assignee has no right to inspect the partnership's books and records or to manage the partnership. The assignee's only other right beyond receiving a share of the profits is to ask a court to dissolve the partnership, but only if the partnership is at will. (A partnership at will has no term and may rightfully be dissolved by a partner at any time.) An assignee who obtains a judicial dissolution may obtain liquidation of the partnership's assets and obtain payment from the proceeds of the sale of the partnership's assets.

By itself a partner's assignment of his partnership interest does not dissolve the partnership; the assigning partner remains a partner and can continue to manage the partnership.

The nonassigning partners may not exclude the assigning partner from the partnership. They may, however, rightfully dissolve the partnership by their *unanimous* agreement, even if the term or objective of the partnership has not been met.

The following case illustrates that an assignee of a partnership interest has the right to receive profits but has no liability to partnership creditors due to the assignment.

CONNORS v. MIDDLE FORK CORP.
790 F.Supp. 6 (D.D.C. 1992)

In 1983, Odell Rogers, John Lockhart, and Caleb Cooley formed MFC Partnership, a partnership formed under the laws of Kentucky. In 1984, Odell Rogers made a gift of his 41 percent interest in MFC to his three sons: 4-year-old Shannon Rogers, 19-year-old James Rogers, and 20-year-old Arthur Rogers. Odell made the gift for the purpose of providing income to his sons to pay their college expenses. The Rogers sons received income from MFC, which was reported on both the partnership's and the sons' individual federal income tax returns. The sons were identified as partners on MFC's unaudited balance sheet of December 31, 1985. In addition, MFC's 1986 income statement listed the sons as partners.

In 1987, MFC incurred liability to an employee pension fund under the federal Employee Retirement Income Security Act (ERISA). Joseph Connors, a trustee for the fund, contended that the Rogers sons were partners of MFC and therefore were personally liable to the fund on MFC's ERISA liability. The Rogers sons asked the trial court to grant a summary judgment for the sons on the grounds that they were merely assignees of their father's partnership interest and had no liability for MFC's obligations.

Revercomb, District Judge   Under the Uniform Partnership Act, the receipt of profits from a business is *prima facie* evidence that one is a partner in the business. One may rebut this presumption by showing that one falls within a statutorily protected relationship. The Rogers sons argue that the 1984 transfer to them was no more than an assignment of Odell Rogers's partnership interest. An assignment of a partnership interest merely entitles the assignee to receive the assignor's profits from the firm, but does not entitle the assignee to interfere otherwise in the management of the firm. Assignees are not partners, and cannot be held personally liable for the firm's obligations.

Although the sharing of profits and losses is prima facie evidence of a partnership, the issue of control is the more important criterion in determining the existence of a partnership. Both Arthur and James Rogers did none of the acts which usually denote management or control of a partnership: request information about the firm's finances, attend its meetings or vote, attempt to withdraw its money, represent the firm to third parties, or even speak with the other partners about the firm. Neither James nor Arthur knew where the offices of MFC Partnership were located. Neither Arthur nor James was employed by MFC.

Connors notes that the Rogers sons on one occasion received "management fees" totalling $3,000, without any further showing of what these "fees" were paid for. The Court regards such evidence as no more than a mere scintilla upon which a jury could not reasonably find for Connors.

Thus, there can be *no* doubt that the transfer conveyed *less* than full partnership status. Connors has failed to carry his burden of proof of showing sufficient indicia of partnership. It follows that the Rogers sons are not jointly or severally liable to the pension fund as partners.

Motion for summary judgment granted in favor of the Rogers sons.

Charging Order   A partner's personal creditor with a judgment against the partner may ask a court to issue a **charging order**—that is, an order charging the partner's partnership interest with payment of the unsatisfied amount of the judgment. Unlike assignment, a charging order is obtained without the partner's consent. As with assignment, however, the partner remains a partner and may manage the partnership, and the creditor is entitled to receive only the partner's share of the profits. If the profits are insufficient to pay the debt, the creditor may ask the court to order foreclosure and to sell the partner's interest to satisfy the charging order.

Neither the issuance of a charging order nor the purchase of a partnership interest at a foreclosure sale causes a dissolution. But the purchaser of a partnership interest at the foreclosure sale may ask a court to dissolve a partnership at will. The other partners may eliminate this potential threat to the continuation of the partnership by **redeeming the charging order.** To redeem a charging order, the other partners must pay the creditor the amount due on the judgment against the partner. If the other partners so choose, however, they may dissolve the partnership by their unanimous agreement, even if the term or objective of the partnership has not been met.

Joint Venturers and Mining Partners   Transfers of interests in joint ventures are treated in the same way as transfers of partnership interests. However, a mining partner's interest is *freely transferable*. The transferee becomes a partner with all the rights of ownership and management, and the transferor loses all of his partnership rights. The other mining partners cannot object to the transfer, and their consent to a transfer is not required.

ETHICAL AND PUBLIC POLICY CONCERNS

1. A person who carefully considers which business form to use for his one-person business can achieve nearly any combination of results desirable to him. For example, by incorporating and electing S Corporation status, a person can limit his personal liability, deduct business losses on his individual federal income tax return, yet control the business by electing himself to the board of directors. Why should a careful planner obtain such advantages, while a person who merely begins his business has unlimited liability as a sole proprietor? Is the business of the careful planner more valuable to our society than the business of the person who does not choose a business form?

2. Why should all the partners in a partnership be individually liable for all the obligations of the partnership, while shareholders and managers of a corporation have no liability beyond their capital contributions? Is the corporate form of business or the business conducted by corporations more important to society than the partnership form or the business conducted by partnerships? Would benefits that businesses provide to society be reduced if limited liability were not extended to shareholders and managers of corporations?

3. What are the ethical underpinnings of partnership by estoppel? Why should a person be held liable for the business debts of another person when he does not benefit from the business? Could the person who relied on the appearance of partnership have protected himself by making inquiries? Should he be required to make such inquiries?

PROBLEMS AND PROBLEM CASES

1. *Video Case.* See "The Reunion." When friends reunite at a wedding, they reveal their plans for future business ventures. Al and Amy, an unmarried couple, propose opening a Thai restaurant. Al is a dentist, and Amy is director of public relations for a publishing company. Amy will quit her job eventually to manage the restaurant. They will hire a chef whose restaurant is about to close.

Carl is a successful real estate agent who wants to open his own real estate firm.

Bob has tried several business ventures, but all have failed, including a venture to manufacture ski racks for motorcycles.

Dave and Donna, the newly married couple, plan to quit their jobs, move to Wyoming, and open a software development business. They want the business to have few investors. They have lined up potential clients who will finance their initial efforts in return for software customization.

What business forms should they use for their business ventures? What additional questions do you want to ask to help you determine the best business forms for their ventures?

2. Daon Corporation developed a housing subdivision, improving the building lots for resale. To promote the sales of lots, Daon created a marketing scheme, named Showcase of Homes, that involved area builders. The builders, including Raymond Driesel, purchased lots from Daon and built custom homes on the homesites. Daon advertised the Showcase of Homes, decorated and furnished model homes, and provided a landscaping plan to the builders. Both Driesel and Daon benefited from the Showcase program. Driesel benefited from Daon's advertising and the chance to show his home, leading to future home-building jobs. Daon benefited from having homes constructed in the subdivision, proving to prospective lot buyers the feasibility and desirability of buying a lot from Daon, leading to further lot sales. Theo Dority purchased the home built by Driesel. All negotiations and documents for the sale were between Dority and Driesel. The home was defective. Driesel promised to correct the defects, but he failed to do so. Dority corrected the defects at a cost of $20,000. Will Dority successfully sue Daon for $20,000 on the grounds that Daon and Driesel were partners?

3. OWLP, a Hawaii limited partnership, owned the Outrigger West Hotel. OWLP and Hawaii Hotels Operating Company (HHOC) agreed that OWLP and HHOC would jointly operate the hotel and share its revenues, allocating 73 percent to OWLP and 27 percent to HHOC. The agreement provided that revenues would be collected from the hotel and allocated daily according to the percentages above.

However, the allocation percentages were changed six times during a four-year period to permit each party to recover out-of-pocket expenses and to provide a return of 98 percent of the net income to OWLP and of 2 percent of the net income to HHOC. Thus, any amount recovered by each party according to the predetermined percentage in excess of its expenses would be its profit. Losses were shared pro rata like the profits. Are OWLP and HHOC partners?

4. Vearle Edwards owned and operated Edwards IGA grocery. Vearle advertised his grocery in the South Sioux City *Star* but failed to pay for the advertising. When Vearle filed for bankruptcy, the *Star* sued Vearle's wife, Ila. The *Star*'s managing editor believed that the grocery was a family-owned business, but he said that he spoke very few times with Ila about advertising since "she was not around." At one time, Ila had done some bookkeeping at the store, but for the last seven years she had no dealings with the grocery. She at no time dealt directly with any suppliers, made any management decisions, ordered any food or supplies, supervised any employees, or placed any advertisements. She contributed no resources to the store. She did not share in the profits or losses of the store, except as the wife of Vearle. Is Ila obligated to pay for the advertising in the *Star?*

5. ▣ *Video Case.* See "The Partnership." Art, Ben, and Diedre are partners of Alphabet Builders, a partnership in the construction business. They meet at a restaurant with a prospective new partner, Don, who says he will decide whether to enter the partnership after discussing the matter with his wife. During the meeting, they are approached by John, with whom the partnership has been attempting to do business. Art introduces Don to John, stating, "We're celebrating Don's joining Alphabet Builders." Don and John shake hands, and John says, "Congratulations! Alphabet Builders has a very good reputation. In fact, I'm about to become one of your new clients. I signed the contract this morning." Don says nothing in response to John's statement. Subsequently, however, Don decides not to join Alphabet Builders. Nonetheless, when Alphabet Builders breaches its contract with John, John sues Don on the contract. Is Don liable to John?

6. Coy Stephens did business as Audio Works. When he needed a bank loan for the business, Coy and his father, Vastine Stephens, executed a document stating that they were partners in the business and that Coy had the authority to sign for the business in all respects. In fact, Coy and Vastine were not partners, but they executed the document solely to induce a bank to loan the necessary funds to Coy. Relying on the document, Angelina National Bank loaned $33,000 to Audio Works. Angelina would not have loaned the money to Audio Works had it not believed that Vastine was Coy's partner. When Coy failed to repay the loan, Angelina sued Vastine. Was Vastine liable to Angelina?

7. Barry Wilen owned a one-third interest in Bay Country Investments, a partnership. During the term of Barry's marriage to Loveta Wilen, Bay Country sold real property for $126,500. The partnership reinvested the proceeds in other real property. Subsequently, Loveta and Barry had marital problems. During a divorce proceeding, Loveta claimed that she was entitled to receive half of Barry's one-third share of the $126,500 proceeds. Was she correct?

8. Richard DeLong and Ken Birch formed a partnership to build houses. They agreed that all sales proceeds would be deposited in a partnership bank checking account and that both of them must sign all checks. For two years, Birch and DeLong signed all checks, but then DeLong agreed that Birch could sign partnership checks by himself. Six years later, DeLong discovered that Birch paid some of his personal expenses with partnership checks. DeLong reported his discovery to the Washington state prosecuting attorney, who prosecuted Birch for the crime of embezzlement. Embezzlement was defined in the Washington statute as exerting unauthorized control over the property of another. Has Birch committed embezzlement?

9. Claude Gauldin and Joe Corn formed a partnership to raise cattle and hogs on land owned by Corn. Partnership funds were used to build two buildings on the land for use by the partnership. Gauldin and Corn did not discuss who owned the buildings. Gauldin knew when the buildings were constructed that they would be permanent improvements to the land and would become part of it. The partnership paid no rent for the land, and there was no agreement to consider the use of the land as a contribution by Corn. The taxes on the land were paid by Corn, as was the cost of upkeep. When Corn left the partnership, Gauldin claimed that the buildings were partnership assets and that he was entitled to half of their fair market value. Was Gauldin correct?

OPERATION OF PARTNERSHIP AND RELATED FORMS

INTRODUCTION

*Two relationships are important during the opera-
tion of a partnership business: (1) the relation of
the partners to each other and the partnership;
and (2) the relation of the partners to third parties
who are affected by the business of the partnership.*

DUTIES OF PARTNERS TO THE PARTNERSHIP AND EACH OTHER

The relation between partners and the partnership
is a fiduciary relation of the highest order. It is one
of mutual trust, confidence, and honesty. Therefore, partners owe to the partnership and each
other the highest degree of *loyalty and good faith*
in all partnership matters. The duties partners owe
each other are the same in ordinary partnerships
and in limited liability partnerships.

Profiting Secretly

Unless there is a contrary agreement, a partner's
sole compensation from partnership affairs is a
share of partnership profits. Therefore, a partner
may not make a secret profit out of the transaction
of partnership business. For example, a partner
may not profit personally by receiving an undisclosed kickback from a partnership supplier. In
addition, a partner may not profit secretly when
she makes a contract with her partnership, such as
selling a building she owns to her partnership
without disclosing her ownership or her profit to
her partners.

   When a partner receives a secret profit, she has a
conflict of interests, and there is a risk that she may
prefer her own interests over those of the partnership. Therefore, the law permits a partner to profit
personally from partnership transactions only if she
deals in good faith, makes a full disclosure of all
material facts affecting the transaction, and obtains
approval from her partners. The remedy for a breach

of this duty not to make a secret profit is a return of the profit that she made in the transaction with the partnership.

The following case imposed liability on a partner who profited secretly from the sale of a jet plane to the partnership.

LEVY V. DISHAROON
749 P.2d 84 (N. Mex. Sup. Ct. 1988)

Walter Levy and Henry Disharoon formed a partnership to purchase a jet airplane and to operate a charter airline business. Disharoon located a jet and informed Levy that the price was $963,000. After Levy approved the purchase, Disharoon contracted to buy the jet for $860,000. The partnership borrowed $975,000 to pay for the jet. Disharoon paid the seller $860,000 and deposited in Disharoon's personal bank account the $103,000 difference between the actual purchase price and the purchase price represented to Levy.

Levy asked a trial court for a formal accounting of the partnership affairs. The trial court found that Disharoon misrepresented the purchase price of the jet with the intention of deceiving Levy. The trial court awarded Levy actual damages of $70,000 and punitive damages of $100,000. Disharoon appealed to the Supreme Court of New Mexico.

Sosa, Senior Justice   Each partner has the right to have his co-partner exercise good faith in partnership matters. A partner is not allowed to gain any advantage over a co-partner by fraud, misrepresentation, or concealment. For any advantage so obtained he must account to the co-partner. The jet was actually purchased for $860,000, but Disharoon told Levy the sale price was $963,000. The difference was wired to Disharoon's personal banking account in Chicago. Thus, Disharoon defrauded the partnership in the amount of $103,000.

We conclude the trial court was correct in holding Disharoon accountable, but erred in awarding Levy $70,000 in actual damages. Levy's compensatory damages were one-half of the misappropriated funds or $51,500.

The trial court also awarded Levy $100,000 in punitive damages. The amount of punitive damages is left to the discretion of the fact finder and will not be disturbed on appeal unless it is so unrelated to the injury and actual damages proven as to plainly manifest passion and prejudice rather than reason and justice. The $100,000 punitive damage award is not so unrelated to the actual damages to be clearly erroneous. Disharoon's conduct in misrepresenting the jet's actual sale price and misappropriating the partnership's funds deserves punishment.

Judgment for Levy affirmed as modified.

Competing against the Partnership

A partner may not compete against his partnership unless he obtains consent from the other partners. For example, a partner of a retail clothing store may not open a clothing store nearby. However, he may open a grocery store and not breach his fiduciary duty. The partnership has the remedy of recovering the profits of the partner's competing venture.

In the following case, a partner in an accounting partnership breached the duty not to compete by providing his own clients with the same types of accounting services that his accounting partnership could have provided.

VEALE V. ROSE

657 S.W.2d 834 (Tex. Ct. App. 1983)

Larry Rose, Paul G. Veale, Sr., Paul G. Veale, Jr., Gary Gibson, and James Parker offered professional accounting services as partners under the firm name Paul G. Veale and Co. Their written partnership agreement expressed the general duties of the partners, but it recognized that Veale, Sr., and Rose had outside investments and a number of other business commitments. All of the partners were allowed to pursue other business activities so long as the activities did not conflict with the partnership practice of public accounting or materially interfere with the partners' duties to the partnership.

While a partner of Paul G. Veale and Co., Larry Rose performed accounting services for Right Away Foods and Ed Payne. He was paid personally by those clients. Rose was an officer and shareholder of Right Away. When the other partners discovered these actions, they claimed Rose owed them a share of his profits from the actions, which competed with the partnership. The jury found that Rose had not competed with the partnership. Rose's partners appealed.

Nye, Chief Justice   Partners may be said to occupy a fiduciary relationship toward one another which requires of them the utmost degree of good faith and honesty in dealing with one another. Breaches of a partner's duty not to compete with the partnership are compensable at law by awarding to the injured partners their proportionate shares of the profits wrongfully acquired by the offending partner.

While a partner of Veale and Co., Rose rendered accounting services for Right Away Foods for which he billed and received payment personally. Rose admitted that he billed Right Away Foods for the services of a CPA. He also admitted that there was no reason why he could not have rendered the same services to Right Away Foods as a partner in the accounting firm. The preponderance of all of the evidence clearly establishes that Rose performed accounting services for Right Away Foods while a partner of Paul G. Veale and Co., in competition with the partnership.

Rose also admitted that he performed accounting services for various enterprises owned by Payne during his tenure as a partner at Veale, for which he billed and received payment personally. His later testimony that he performed these services, in effect, after hours, or in addition to his duties to the partnership, is of no value in light of the obligations imposed by the partnership agreement and by the common understanding of the term "competition."

Judgment reversed in favor of Rose's partners. Remanded for a new trial.

Duty to Serve

The duty to serve requires a partner to undertake his share of responsibility for running the day-to-day operations of the partnership business. The basis of this duty is the expectation that all partners will work. Sometimes, this duty is termed the duty to devote full time to the partnership.

Partners may agree to relieve a partner of the duty to serve. So-called *silent partners* merely contribute capital to the partnership. Silent partners do not have the duty to serve, but they have the same liability for partnership debts as any other partner.

The remedies for breach of the duty to serve include assessing the partner for the cost of hiring a person to do his work and paying the other partners additional compensation.

Duty of Care

In transacting partnership business, each partner owes a duty to use **reasonable skill and care.** A partner is not liable to her partnership for losses resulting from honest errors in judgment, but a partner is liable for losses resulting from her negligence or lack of skill and care. She must make a **reasonable investigation** before making a decision, so that she has an adequate basis for making the decision. The decision she makes must be that of an **ordinarily prudent business manager** in her position.

For example, a grocery store has stocked avocados for three years and has always sold them. If one of the partners buys the same amount of avocados as usual but they do not sell, the partner is not liable for the loss to the partnership. Her decision appears reasonable as of the time she made it. If prior to the time she made the decision, however, sales of avocados have fallen and trade magazines that she should have read published customer surveys showing lower expected sales of avocados, she would be liable.

Duty to Act within Actual Authority

A partner has the duty not to exceed the authority granted him by the partnership agreement or, if there is no agreement, the authority normally held by partners in his position. He is responsible to the partnership for losses resulting from unauthorized transactions negotiated in the name of the partnership. For example, suppose partners agree that no partner shall purchase supplies from Jasper Supply Company, which is unaware of the limitation on the partners' authority. When one partner purchases supplies from Jasper and the partnership suffers a loss because the supplies are of low quality, the wrongdoing partner must bear the loss due to her breach of the partnership agreement.

Duty to Account

Partners have a duty to account for their use or disposal of partnership funds and partnership property, as well as their receipt of any benefit or profit without the consent of the other partners. Partnership property should be used for partnership purposes, not for a partner's personal use.

For example, when a partner of a firm that leases residential property to college students allows his daughter to live in a partnership-owned apartment, the partner must collect rent for the partnership from his daughter or risk breaching the duty to account.

Each partner owes a duty to keep a reasonable record of all business transacted by him for the partnership and to make such records available to the person keeping the partnership books. The books must be kept at the partnership's principal place of business. Every partner must at all times have access to them and may inspect and copy them.

In addition to a right to inspect the books of the partnership, a partner has a right to a formal **accounting** of the partnership affairs. It is generally by an accounting that a partner can recover from his partners for their breaches of their fiduciary duties.

An accounting is not merely a presentation of financial statements. It is a judicial review of all partnership and partners' transactions to determine whether partners have properly used partnership assets and to award each partner his rightful share of partnership assets. The court takes into consideration breaches of fiduciary duties and adjusts appropriately the amounts payable to the partners.

An accounting is an extreme action and is ordinarily taken only after dissolution of a partnership. The Uniform Partnership Act (UPA), however, specifically permits an accounting prior to dissolution.

Closely related to the duty to account is the right of a partner to be **indemnified** for expenditures made from personal funds and for personal liabilities incurred during the ordinary conduct of the business. For example, a partner uses her own truck to pick up some partnership supplies, which she pays for with her personal check. The partner is entitled to be reimbursed for the cost of the supplies and for her cost of picking up the supplies, including fuel.

Other Duties

A partner must maintain the **confidentiality** of partnership information such as a trade secret or a customer list. This means a partner should not disclose to third parties confidential information of the partnership unless disclosure benefits the partnership.

On the other hand, each partner owes a duty to disclose to the other partners all information that is material to the partnership business. She also owes a duty to inform the partners of notices she has received that affect the rights of the partnership. For example, Gordon Gekko, a partner of a stock brokerage firm, learns that National Motors Corporation is projecting a loss for the current year. The projection reduces the value of National stock, which the firm has been recommending that its customers buy. Gekko has a duty to disclose the projection to his partners to allow them to advise customers of the brokerage.

CONCEPT REVIEW

Partner's Duties

1.   Duty not to make a secret profit while transacting for the partnership.

2.   Duty not to compete with the partnership.

3.   Duty to serve the partnership.

4.   Duty to exercise the skill and care of the ordinarily prudent business manager.

5.   Duty to act within the actual authority possessed by the partner.

6.   Duty to account for the use and disposal of partnership funds and property.

7.   Duty to indemnify other partners for expenditures they made from their personal funds and for liabilities they incurred on behalf of the partnership.

8.   Duty to maintain the confidentiality of partnership information.

9.   Duty to disclose to the other partners information material to the partnership business.

10.   Duty to inform partners of notices he has received.

Joint Ventures and Mining Partnerships

The fiduciary duties of partners also exist in joint ventures and mining partnerships, although there are a few special rules regarding their enforcement. For example, a joint venturer may seek an accounting to settle claims between the joint venturers, or he may sue his joint venturers to recover joint property or to be indemnified for expenditures that he has made on behalf of the joint venture. A mining partner's remedy against his partners is an accounting; however, a mining partner has a lien against his partners' shares in the mining partnership for his expenditures on behalf of the mining partnership. The lien can be enforced against purchasers of his partners' shares.

COMPENSATION OF PARTNERS

A partner's compensation for working for a partnership or limited liability partnership is a share of the profits of the business. Ordinarily, a partner is not entitled to a salary or wages, even if he spends a disproportionate amount of time conducting the business of the partnership.

Profits and Losses

Unless there is an agreement to the contrary, partners share partnership profits equally, according to the number of partners, and not according to their capital contributions or the amount of time that each devotes to the partnership. For example, a partnership has two partners, Juarez, who contributes $85,000 of capital to the partnership and does 35 percent of the work, and Easton, who contributes $15,000 and does 65 percent of the work. If they have made no agreement how to share profits, when the partnership makes a $50,000 profit in the first year, each partner receives $25,000, half of the profits.

Losses   When the partnership agreement is silent on how to share losses, losses are shared in the same proportion that profits are shared. The basis of this rule is the presumption that partners want to share benefits and detriments in the same proportions. Nonetheless, the presumption does not work in reverse. If a partnership agreement specifies how losses are shared but does not specify how profits are shared, profits are shared equally by the partners, not as losses are shared.

Examples   For example, when there is no agreement regarding how profits or losses are shared, profits are shared equally, and because losses are shared like profits, losses are shared equally as well. When two partners agree to share profits 70–30 and make no agreement on losses, both profits and losses are shared 70–30.

However, when two partners make no agreement how to share profits but agree to share losses 60–40, losses are shared in that proportion but profits are shared equally.

Partners may agree to split profits on one basis and losses on another basis for many reasons, including their making different capital and personal service contributions or a partner's having higher outside income than the other partners, which better enables him to use a partnership loss as a tax deduction.

Effect of Agreement on Creditors' Rights   Each partner has unlimited personal liability to partnership creditors. Loss-sharing agreements between partners do not bind partnership creditors unless the creditors agree to be bound. For example, two partners agree to share losses 60–40, the same proportion in which they contributed capital to the partnership. After the partnership assets have been distributed to the creditors, $50,000 is still owed to them. The creditors may collect the entire $50,000 from the partner who agreed to assume only 60 percent of the losses. That partner may, however, collect $20,000—40 percent of the amount from the other partner.

In the following case, the court held that the partners' oral agreement regarding partners' compensation bound the partners.

WARREN V. WARREN
784 S.W.2d 247 (Mo. App. 1989)

In 1969, brothers Harold and Ray Warren formed a partnership to operate a funeral home in Columbia, Missouri. In 1970, they created a second partnership, The Warren Yard and Tree Service. The brothers based their partnerships solely on oral agreements, never putting them in writing. They adopted a system under which each partner drew from the partnerships' funds a reasonable compensation for his actual services rendered to the two businesses.

After a few years, Harold—a licensed embalmer and funeral director—spent an increasing amount of his time in the funeral home, performing all the lab work and specialized mortuary services. By 1978, Harold spent nearly all his time at the funeral home. Ray—licensed only as a funeral director—devoted most of his time to the tree service partnership, spending only a few hours each week assisting with funerals. Consequently, during the term of their partnership, Harold drew large sums of compensation from the funeral home partnership and only about $400 from the tree service partnership. Ray drew his primary compensation from the tree service partnership and a smaller compensation from the funeral home partnership. Because the funeral home was the more profitable business, Harold's total compensation exceeded Ray's by a considerable amount.

In 1983, Ray sued Harold, claiming that he was entitled to receive compensation equal to Harold for the entire 14-year term of the funeral home partnership. Ray asked the trial court to order Harold to pay Ray an amount that would equalize their 14-year compensation. The trial court held that Ray was not entitled to additional compensation, and Ray appealed.

Nugent, Chief Judge   Ray Warren first asserts that the trial court erred in finding that an oral agreement bound each partner to draw compensa-tion commensurate with his services. The Warren brothers adopted a compensation system abstruse as to a method of payment but clear as to intent and business customs. There was an agreement between Ray and Harold under which Ray would run the tree service, Harold the funeral home, and each would draw compensation commensurate with his input of services. For nearly fifteen years, Ray knew of and did not protest the perquisites afforded his brother by the funeral home partnership, such as use of an apartment above the funeral home and of a car.

Section 18 of the Uniform Partnership Act enunciates the rules determining the rights and duties of a partner: "The rights and duties of the partners in relation to the partnership shall be determined, subject to any agreement between them, by the following rules: . . . (f) No partner is entitled to remuneration for acting in the partnership business." The oral agreement between the brothers negates the statute's proscription of compensation to partners. Missouri law recognizes the validity of oral and implied agreements between partners. Indeed, for more than a century, Missouri has recognized that, in the presence of an agreement linking compensation to a partner's efforts, partners providing services vital to the enterprise, or those devoting much of their time to the partnership's commonweal, deserve compensation often far in excess of that owed partners providing less important services or those giving only a little time to the business.

Harold provided the expert services vital to the partnership. His skills in the mortuary business far exceeded Ray's. The brothers agreed that Harold would run the funeral home and Ray, the tree service. Thus, implicitly if not expressly, they acknowledged each other's expertise, and, accordingly, each concentrated his efforts in the area of his own ability.

Moreover, Ray derived substantial financial benefit from the funeral home, to which he contributed but minimal efforts. Concomitantly, Harold succeeded in continuing to operate the business despite the effective withdrawal of Ray. Thus, Harold became entitled to suitable compensation for his efforts.

Judgment for Harold Warren affirmed.

CONCEPT REVIEW

PARTNERS' SHARE OF PROFITS AND LOSSES

Profits	Partners share profits equally, unless the partners agree otherwise.
Losses	Partners share losses in the same way they share profits, unless the partners agree to share losses in a different manner.
Tax Effect	A partner's share of partnership profits is income to the partner, on which the partner pays federal income tax. A partner's share of partnership losses may be deducted on the partner's individual federal income tax return.
Right of Contribution	A partner who pays more than his share of a partnership loss may collect the excess paid from those partners whose shares he paid.

MANAGEMENT POWERS OF PARTNERS

Individual Authority of Partners

In a partnership or limited liability partnership, every partner is a general manager of the business. This power is expressed in the UPA, which states that a partnership is bound by the act of every partner for apparently carrying on in the usual way the business of the partnership. Such authority is implied from the nature of the business. It permits a partner to bind the partnership and his partners for acts within the ordinary affairs of the business. The scope of this **implied authority** is determined with reference to what is usual business for partnerships of the same general type in the locality.

Implied authority of a partner may not contradict a partner's **express authority**, which is created by agreement of the partners. An agreement among the partners can expand, restrict, or even completely eliminate the implied authority of a partner. For example, the partners in a newspaper publishing business may agree that one partner shall have the authority to purchase a magazine business for the partnership and that another partner shall not have the authority to sell advertising space in the newspaper. The partners may agree also that all partners must consent to borrow money for the partnership. The partners' implied authority to be general managers is modified in accordance with these express agreements.

Express authority may be stated orally or in writing, or it may be obtained by acquiescence. Regardless of the method of agreement, all of the partners must agree to the modification of implied authority. Together, a partner's express and implied authority constitute her **actual authority.**

Apparent Authority   When implied authority is restricted or eliminated, the partnership risks the possibility that **apparent authority** to do a denied act will remain. Apparent authority exists because it reasonably appears a partner has authority to do an act. To prevent apparent authority from continuing when there is a limitation of a partner's actual authority, third persons with whom the partner deals must have knowledge of the limitation of his actual authority. Just as a principal must notify third persons of limitations of an agent's authority, so must a partnership notify its customers, suppliers, and others of express limitations of the actual authority of partners.

Suppose that Carroll, Melton, and Ramirez are partners and that they agree that Carroll will be the only purchasing agent for the partnership. This agreement must be communicated to third parties selling goods to the partnership, or Melton and Ramirez will have apparent authority to bind the partnership on purchase contracts. Melton and Ramirez do not have express authority to purchase goods, because they have agreed to such a restriction on their authority. They do not have implied authority to purchase, because implied authority may not contradict express authority.

Ratification   A partnership may ratify the unauthorized acts of partners. Essentially, **ratification** occurs when the partners accept an act of a partner who had no actual or apparent authority to do the act when it was done.

For example, suppose Cabrillo and Boeglin are partners in an accounting firm. They agree that only Cabrillo has authority to make contracts to perform audits of clients, an agreement known by Mantron Company. Nonetheless, Boeglin and Mantron contract for the partnership to audit Mantron's financial statements. At this point, the partnership is not liable on the contract, because Boeglin has no express, implied, or apparent authority to make the contract. But suppose Boeglin takes the contract to Cabrillo, who reads it and says, "OK, we'll do this audit." Cabrillo, as the partner with express authority to make audit contracts, has ratified the contract and thereby bound the partnership to the contract.

Special Transactions

The validity of some partner's actions is affected by special partnership rules that reflect a concern for protecting important property and the credit standing of partners. This concern is especially evident in the rules for conveying the partnership's real property and for borrowing money in the name of the partnership.

Power to Convey Partnership Real Property

To bind the partnership, an individual partner's conveyance of a partnership's real property must be expressly, impliedly, or apparently authorized or be ratified by the partnership. For example, the partners may expressly agree that a partner may sell the partnership's real property.

The more difficult determination is whether a partner has *implied* and *apparent* authority to convey real property. A partner has implied and apparent authority to sell real property if a partnership sells real property in the usual course of the partnership business. Such would be the case with the partner of a real estate investment partnership that buys and sells land as its regular business. By contrast, a partner has no implied or apparent authority to sell the building in which the partnership's retail business is conducted. Here, unanimous agreement of the partners is required, since the sale of the building may affect the ability of the firm to continue. In addition, a partner has no implied or apparent authority to sell land held for investment not in the usual course of business. A sale of such land would be authorized only if the partners concurred.

When title to partnership real property is recorded in the name of the partners and not the partnership, those partners in whose name title is recorded have apparent authority to convey title to a bona fide purchaser unaware of the partnership's interest in the real property.

Borrowing Money   Partnership law restricts the ability of a partner to borrow money in the name of a partnership. Essentially, a partner must possess express, implied, or apparent authority to borrow. Express authority presents few problems. Finding implied and apparent authority to borrow is more difficult.

Although the UPA does not explicitly recognize the distinction, a number of courts have distinguished between trading and nontrading partnerships for purposes of determining whether a partner has implied or apparent authority to borrow money on behalf of the partnership. A **trading partnership** has an inventory; that is, its regular business is buying and selling merchandise, such as retailing, wholesaling, importing, or exporting. For example, a toy store and a clothing store are trading partnerships. Since there is a time lag between the date they pay for their inventory and the date they sell inventory to their customers, these firms ordinarily need to borrow to avoid cash flow problems. Therefore, a partner of a trading partnership has implied and apparent authority to borrow money for the partnership.

A **nontrading partnership** has no substantial inventory and is usually engaged in providing services—for example, accounting services or real estate brokerage. Such partnerships have no normal borrowing needs. Therefore, a partner of a nontrading partnership has no implied or apparent authority to borrow money for the partnership.

The distinction between trading and nontrading partnerships is not always clear. Businesses such as general contracting, manufacturing, and dairy farming, although not exclusively devoted to buying and selling inventory, have been held to be trading partnerships. The rationale for their inclusion in this category is that borrowing is necessary in the ordinary course of business to augment their working capital.

This suggests why the distinction between trading partnerships and nontrading partnerships is useless or misleading. There is no necessary connection between borrowing money and buying and selling. The more important inquiry should be whether a partner's borrowing is in the ordinary course of business. When borrowing is in the ordinary course of business, a partner has implied and apparent authority to borrow money. If borrowing is not in the ordinary course of business, then no individual partner has implied or apparent authority to borrow money.

If a court finds that a partner has authority to borrow money, the partnership is liable for his borrowings on behalf of the partnership. There is a limit, however, to a partner's capacity to borrow. A partner may have authority to borrow, yet borrow beyond the ordinary needs of the business. A partnership will not be liable for any loan whose amount exceeds the ordinary needs of the business, unless otherwise agreed by the partners.

The power to borrow money on the firm's credit will ordinarily carry with it the power to grant the lender a lien or security interest in firm assets to secure the repayment of the borrowed money. Security interests are a normal part of business loan transactions.

Issuing Negotiable Instruments   A partner who has the authority to borrow money also has authority to issue negotiable instruments such as promissory notes for that purpose. When a partnership has a checking account and a partner's name appears on the signature card filed with the bank, the partner has express authority to draw checks. A partner whose name is not on the signature card filed with the bank has apparent authority to issue checks, but only in respect to a third person who has no knowledge of the limitation on the partner's authority.

Negotiating Instruments   A partnership receives many negotiable instruments during the course of its business. For example, an accounting firm's clients often pay fees by check. Even though borrowing money and issuing negotiable instruments may be beyond a partner's implied and apparent authority, a partner usually has implied and apparent authority to transfer or negotiate instruments on behalf of the partnership.

For example, when a partnership has a bank account, a partner has implied and apparent authority to indorse and deposit in the account checks drawn payable to the partnership. As a general rule, a partner also has implied and apparent authority to indorse and cash checks drawn payable to the order of the partnership.

Likewise, partners have implied authority to indorse drafts and notes payable to the order of the partnership and to sell them at a discount.

In the following case, the court found that a partner had implied authority to indorse and deposit checks payable to the partnership.

GROSBERG V. MICHIGAN NATIONAL BANK
62 N.W.2d 715 (Mich. Sup. Ct. 1984)

Mervin Grosberg and Sheldon Goldman, as partners, constructed and operated the Chatham Fox Hills Shopping Center. Grosberg and Goldman had agreed that Goldman would receive rental checks from the shopping center's tenants and deposit them in an account in Grosberg's name at Manufacturers National Bank.

Without Grosberg's knowledge or permission, Goldman opened an account in both their names at Michigan National Bank. Goldman deposited in that account checks relating to the partnership business that were payable to the partnership or its partners. Goldman indorsed each check by signing the name of the partnership or the partners. Later, Goldman embezzled $112,000 of the deposited funds. At no time was Michigan National Bank aware that Grosberg and Goldman were partners.

When Grosberg discovered Goldman's embezzlement, Grosberg sued Michigan National Bank for conversion for accepting checks on which Grosberg's or the partnership's indorsement was forged. The trial court found that Goldman had authority to indorse and to deposit partnership checks in the account. The court of appeals affirmed the trial court's decision, and Grosberg appealed.

Boyle, Justice Goldman had *express* authority to indorse and deposit checks only in the account maintained by Grosberg at Manufacturers National Bank. We find, however, that Goldman's partner status invested him with *implied* authority to indorse and deposit each of the incoming checks in the account at Michigan National Bank.

Section 9 of the Uniform Partnership Act states:

The act of every partner, including the execution in the partnership name of any instrument, for apparently carrying on in the usual way the business of the partnership of which he is a member binds the partnership, unless the partner so acting has in fact no authority to act for the partnership in the particular matter, and the person with whom he is dealing has knowledge of the fact that he has no such authority.

The UPA phrase "for apparently carrying on in the usual way the business of the partnership," although it contains the word "apparent," need not be read to exclude the implied-authority notion of powers *that naturally flow from the partnership relationship*. Accordingly, we find that section 9 of the UPA applies regardless of the bank's lack of knowledge of the partnership relationship.

Grosberg entrusted Goldman with responsibility to receive and deposit incoming partnership checks. In light of the partnership relationship, we easily conclude that Goldman had *implied* authority to indorse all incoming checks on behalf of the partnership and the partners. The possibility that Goldman may have secretly intended at the time of indorsement to embezzle the funds cannot detract from his authority to affix indorsements, since at that time he was "apparently carrying on in the usual way the business of the partnership."

The question remains whether Goldman's subsequent conduct in depositing the checks in the account at Michigan National Bank invalidates that authority. This case involves a partner with general authority to indorse, a diversion to a joint account in which Grosberg had an equal ownership interest, and diverted checks in which Goldman had a partial ownership interest. The present circumstances are not so inconsistent with "carrying on in the usual way the business of the partnership" that Goldman's authority to make the deposits at issue cannot be implied.

Goldman's inherent authority as a partner extended by implication to the deposit of partnership checks in an account ostensibly maintained in both partners' names.

Because of Goldman's implied authority both to indorse incoming checks and to deposit them in an account created in a manner consistent with "apparent partnership purposes," we conclude that no forgery occurred. Therefore, Michigan National Bank is free from liability in conversion.

Judgment for Michigan National Bank affirmed.

Admissions and Notice   A partnership is bound by admissions or representations made by a partner concerning partnership affairs that are within her express, implied, or apparent authority. Likewise, notice to a partner is considered to be received by the partnership. Also, a partner's knowledge of material information relating to partnership affairs is **imputed** to the partnership. These rules reflect the reality that a partnership speaks, sees, and hears through its partners.

Disagreement among Partners

Usually, partners will discuss management decisions among themselves before taking action, even when doing so is not required by a partnership agreement and even when a partner has the implied authority to take the action by herself. When partners discuss a prospective action, they will usually vote on what action to take. Each partner has one vote, regardless of the relative sizes of their partnership interests or their shares of the profits. The vote of a majority of the partners controls ordinary business decisions and, thereby, limits the actual authority of the partners. Nonetheless, the apparent authority of the partners to bind the partnership on contracts in the ordinary course of business is unaffected by the majority vote of partners, unless the limitation on the partners' actual authority is communicated to third parties.

Effect of Partnership Agreement

The partners may modify the rules of management by their unanimous agreement. They may agree that a partner will relinquish his management right, thus removing the partner's express and implied author-

ity to manage the partnership. They may grant sole authority to manage the business to one or more partners. Such removals or delegations of management powers will not, however, eliminate a partner's apparent authority to bind the partnership for his acts within the usual course of business.

A partnership agreement may create classes of partners, some of which will have the power to veto certain actions. Some classes of partners may be given greater voting rights. Unequal voting rights are often found in very large partnerships, such as an accounting firm with several hundred partners.

Unanimous Partners' Agreement Required

Some partnership actions are so important that one partner should not be able to do them by himself. To make clear that no single partner has implied or apparent authority to do certain acts, in the absence of a contrary agreement, the UPA requires unanimity for several actions. These actions are:

1. Assignment of partnership property for the benefit of creditors.
2. Disposal of the goodwill of the business (such as selling the right to do business with a firm's customers to another business).
3. Action making it impossible to carry on the ordinary business of the partnership (such as the distress sale of the entire inventory of a retailing partnership).
4. Confession of judgment against the partnership.
5. Submission of a partnership claim or liability to arbitration.
6. An agreement for the partnership to pay or assume an individual debt of a partner.

7. An agreement for the partnership to serve as a surety or guarantor of the debt of another (unless the partnership's ordinary business is suretyship and guaranty).

8. Any act not apparently for the carrying on of business of the partnership in the usual way.

Essentially, this list contains acts that are not in the usual course of business of the partnership. Such actions must be approved by all partners, unless there is a contrary agreement. For example, a decision to merge one accounting partnership with another partnership must be approved by all partners. Similarly, the decision of a grocery store partnership to move the business to another city requires unanimous partner approval.

In the following case, the court required unanimous partners' agreement for the sale of a motel building that housed the partnership's only business.

PATEL V. PATEL

260 Cal;. Rptr. 255 (Cal. Ct. App. 1989)

L. G. and S. L. Patel, husband and wife, owned the City Center Motel in Eureka, California. On April 16, 1986, the Patels formed a partnership with their son, Raj. The purpose of the partnership was to own and operate the motel. The partnership agreement required Raj's approval of any sale of the motel building. Real estate records were not changed, however, and the motel remained recorded only in the names of L. G. and S. L. Patel.

On May 2, 1986, L. G. and S. L. contracted to sell the motel to P. V. and Kirit Patel, who were unaware of Raj's interest as a partner in the motel. When Raj was informed of the contract to sell the motel, he refused to give his approval. Three weeks later, P. V. and Kirit sued L. G., S. L., and Raj for specific performance to compel them to sell the motel. The trial court held the contract unenforceable; P. V. and Kirit appealed.

Channel, Associate Justice Generally, every partner is an agent of the partnership for the purpose of its business, and the act of every partner to carry on the business of the partnership binds the partnership. UPA Section 9(1). However, partners acting without the approval of the remaining partners may not do any act that would make it impossible to carry on the ordinary business of the partnership. UPA Section 9(3)(c).

Historically, partnerships were divided into two types: commercial or trading partnerships and noncommercial or nontrading partnerships. Although this distinction has been rejected in California, it remains a valuable tool in considering whether L. G. and S. L. exceeded their statutory authority by entering into the real estate contract, thus making it impossible to carry on the ordinary business of the partnership. In the case of a commercial or trading partnership in which the usual partnership business is to hold and sell real property, a contract such as that involved in this case—to sell the sole partnership asset—would be enforceable. By contrast, when—as in the present case—the usual partnership business is to run a business, rather than to hold it in anticipation of its eventual sale, the partnership is not bound by a contract selling that business without the approval of all the partners. Under these circumstances, the trial court properly denied specific performance of the unauthorized contract in order to prevent destruction of the partnership.

Nevertheless, P. V. and Kirit contend that the trial court should have applied UPA Section 10(3). It states:

Where title to real property is in the name of one or more of the partners, whether or not the record discloses the right of the partnership, the partners in whose name the title stands may convey title to such property, but the partnership may recover such property unless the property has been conveyed to a bona fide purchaser for value without knowledge that the partner executing the conveyance has exceeded his authority.

P. V. and Kirit contend that they are bona fide purchasers for value because they had no knowledge of Raj's unrecorded interest in the motel.

To enforce the contract of sale without Raj's approval would frustrate the purpose of UPA Section 9(3)(c) by making it impossible for the partnership to continue. As the purpose of the partnership is to operate a motel, rather than to hold it for eventual sale, we believe that the better result would be to preserve the partnership and hold the contract unenforceable.

Judgment for L. G., S. L., and Raj Patel affirmed.

Joint Ventures and Mining Partnerships

Most of the authority rules of partnerships apply to joint ventures and mining partnerships. These business organizations are in essence partnerships with limited purposes. Therefore, their members have less implied and apparent authority than do partners. Joint venturers have considerable apparent authority if third persons are unaware of the limited scope of the joint venture. A mining partner has no implied authority to borrow money or issue negotiable instruments. As with partners, joint venturers and mining partners may by agreement expand or restrict each other's agency powers.

LIABILITY FOR TORTS AND CRIMES

Torts

The standards and principles of agency law's respondeat superior are applied in determining the liability of the partnership and of the other partners for the torts of a partner and other partnership employees. In addition, the partnership and the other partners are liable for the torts of a partner committed within the ordinary course of partnership business or within the ordinary authority of that partner. Finally, when a partner commits a breach of trust, the partnership and all of the partners are liable. For example, all of the partners in a stock brokerage firm are liable for a partner's embezzlement of a customer's securities and funds.

Intentional Torts While the doctrine of respondeat superior usually imposes liability on a partnership and its partners for a partner's negligence, the doctrine does not usually impose liability for a partner's intentional torts. The reason for this rule is that intentional torts are not usually within the ordinary scope of business or within the ordinary authority of a partner.

A few intentional torts impose liability on a partnership and its partners. For example, a partner who repossesses consumer goods from debtors of the partnership may trespass on consumer property or batter a consumer. Such activities have been held to be in the ordinary course of business. Also, a partner who authorizes a partner to commit an intentional tort is liable for such torts.

In the following case, a partner was not held liable for the intentional tort of her partner.

VRABEL V. ACRI
103 N.E.2d 564 (Ohio Sup. Ct. 1952)

On February 17, 1947, Stephen Vrabel and a companion went into the Acri Cafe in Youngstown, Ohio, to drink a few beers. While Vrabel and his companion were sitting at the bar drinking, a partner of the bar, Michael Acri, without provocation drew a .38-caliber handgun, shot and killed Vrabel's companion, and shot and seriously injured Vrabel. Michael Acri was convicted of murder and sentenced to a life term in the state prison.

Since 1933, Florence and Michael Acri, as partners, had owned and operated the Acri Cafe. From the time of his marriage to Florence in 1931 until 1946, Michael had been in and out of hospitals, clinics, and sanitaria for the treatment of mental disorders and nervousness. Although Michael beat Florence when they had marital difficulties, he had not attacked, abused, or mistreated anyone else. Florence and Michael separated in September 1946, and Florence sued Michael for divorce soon afterward. Before their separation, Florence had operated and managed the cafe primarily only when Michael was ill. Following the marital separation and up until the time he shot Vrabel, Michael was in exclusive control of the management of the cafe.

Vrabel brought suit against Florence to recover damages for his injuries on the ground that, as Michael's partner, she was liable for Michael's tort of battery of Vrabel. The trial court ordered Florence to pay Vrabel damages of $7,500. Florence appealed.

Zimmerman, Judge   When a partnership is shown to exist, each member of the partnership project acts both as principal and agent of the others as to those things done within the apparent scope of the business of the project and for its benefit.

However, it is equally true that where one member of a partnership commits a wrongful and malicious tort not within the actual or apparent scope of the agency or the common business of the particular venture, to which the other members have not assented and which has not been concurred in or ratified by them, they are not liable for the harm thereby caused.

Because at the time of Vrabel's injuries and for a long time prior thereto Florence had been excluded from the Acri Cafe and had no voice or control in its management, and because Florence did not know or have good reason to know that Michael was a dangerous individual prone to assault cafe patrons, the theory of negligence urged by Vrabel is hardly tenable. The willful and malicious attack by Michael Acri upon Vrabel in the Acri Cafe cannot reasonably be said to have come within the scope of the business of operating the cafe, so as to have rendered the absent Florence accountable.

Since the liability of a partner for the acts of his associates is founded upon the principles of agency, the statement is in point that an intentional and willful attack committed by an agent or employee, to vent his own spleen or malevolence against the injured person, is a clear departure from his employment, and his principal or employer is not responsible therefor.

Judgment reversed in favor of Florence Acri.

Partners' Remedies   When a partnership and the other partners are held liable for a partner's tort, they may, during an accounting, recover the amount of their vicarious liability from the wrongdoing partner. This rule places ultimate liability on the wrongdoing partner without affecting the ability of tort victims to obtain recovery from the partnership or the other partners.

Tort Liability and Limited Liability Partnerships

State legislatures created the limited liability partnership (LLP) as a means of reducing the personal liability of professional partners, such as accountants. Consequently, an innocent partner of an LLP has no liability for the professional malpractice of his partners. Arguably, LLP statutes grant partners broad protection, eliminating an innocent partner's liability for errors, omissions, negligence, incompetence, or malfeasance of his partners or employees.

That is the limit of protection, however. The LLP itself is liable for the tort of a wrongdoing partner or employee under the doctrine of respondeat superior. In addition, a wrongdoing partner is liable for his own malpractice or negligence. Also, the partner supervising the work of the wrongdoing partner has unlimited liability for the wrongdoing partner's tort. Thus, the LLP's assets, the wrongdoing partner's personal assets, and the supervising partners' personal assets are at risk. Finally, the LLP and its partners have unlimited liability for other debts of the business, such as a supplier's bill, lease obligations, and bank loans.

Crimes

When a partner commits a crime in the course and scope of transacting partnership business, rarely are his partners criminally liable. But when the partners have participated in the criminal act or authorized its commission, they are liable. They may also be liable when they know of a partner's criminal tendencies yet place him in a position in which he may commit a crime.

Until recent times, a partnership could not be held liable for a crime in most states because it was not viewed as a legal entity. However, modern criminal codes usually define a partnership as a "person" that may commit a crime when a partner, acting within the scope of his authority, engages in a criminal act.

LAWSUITS BY AND AGAINST PARTNERSHIPS AND PARTNERS

Under the UPA, a partnership may not sue in its own name; instead, all of the partners must join in the suit. This means that if the partnership wants to sue someone for breaching a contract or defaming the partnership business, all of the partners must agree to bring the suit. Especially for large partnerships, this requirement is cumbersome. Today, many state statutes differ from the UPA by permitting a partnership to sue in its own name.

Because the UPA imposes on partners a different type of liability for torts than it does for contracts, different rules apply to tort actions than apply to contract actions against the partnership and its partners. Partners are **jointly and severally** liable for partnership **torts.** This means that a tort victim may sue all of the partners (jointly) or sue fewer than all of the partners (severally). If a tort victim sues all of the partners jointly, the judgment may be satisfied against assets of the partnership and assets of the individual partners. If fewer than all of the partners are sued severally, the judgment may generally be satisfied from only the individual assets of the partners sued.

If fewer than all of the partners are sued and made to pay the entire amount of the tort victim's damages, those partners may seek **indemnification** or **contribution** from the other partners for their shares of the liability.

Partners are **jointly liable** for **contractual** obligations of the partnership. This means that all of the partners must be sued if the partnership has breached a contract. Otherwise, no individual partner may be required to pay a judgment and the assets of the partnership cannot be used to satisfy the contract creditor's judgment.

Courts and legislatures have fashioned many modifications to this requirement of joining all the partners in contract actions. Some states make partners jointly and severally liable for contracts. Others have joint debtor statutes that permit creditors—both contract and tort claimants—to sue fewer than all of the partners and yet collect from partnership property. Some courts refuse to permit partners to be sued on contract actions until partnership assets have been exhausted.

The UPA does not permit a partnership to be sued in its own name. This prohibition is especially cumbersome for a party suing for breach of contract because the UPA imposes joint liability on partners for partnership contracts. Thus, it is necessary to sue each of the partners, which is especially difficult when the partners live in a number of states.

Many states have responded to this difficulty by enacting statutes that make all joint obligations joint and several. In addition, *common-name statutes* permit suits against the partnership even if fewer than all of the partners are notified of the suit. Pursuant to such statutes, a judgment against the partnership is enforceable against the assets of the partnership and against the individual assets of those partners who have been served with process.

ETHICAL AND PUBLIC POLICY CONCERNS

1. Should the law require partners to owe each other fiduciary duties? Does a partner's breach of his fiduciary duty harm only the partners, or is society at large also harmed? Should partners be allowed to agree that they do not owe fiduciary duties to each other?

2. Why should a partner have greater implied authority than an agent who is a general manager? Is there a greater risk that an agent will do something imprudent with a business that belongs entirely to someone else than that a partner will do something imprudent with a business that belongs in part to that partner?

3. Is it fair that a partner is liable for the contracts of his partners? Is it fair that a partner is liable for the torts of his partners? Should a partnership be entirely a beneficial relationship for the partners, by which the partners reap the benefits of their relationship with each other but suffer none of the detriments?

PROBLEMS AND PROBLEM CASES

1. Saul Birnbaum, Jay Birnbaum, and Ilene Flaum owned a partnership that developed and operated a shopping center. Due to a conflict between the partners, Saul was the sole manager of the partnership. Rather than develop the shopping center himself, Saul hired Victoria Tree, who later became his wife, to develop the shopping center for the partnership. Saul paid Victoria from partnership funds. Saul did not disclose his hiring of Victoria to Jay and Ilene. Did Saul violate a fiduciary duty?

2. Larry Rose, a partner of an accounting firm, used the firm's employees and computers to render services to his personal clients. The partnership received no compensation from Rose for the use of its employees and computers. Has Rose breached a fiduciary duty?

3. Holiday Inns, Inc., and L & M Enterprises, Inc. (L & M), were 50–50 partners of Marina Associates, a partnership formed to develop a gambling casino in Atlantic City. Holiday Inns conducted the day-to-day operation of Marina. The partnership was unprofitable during its early years, and rather than contribute more capital to the partnership, L & M agreed to sell most of its 50 percent interest to Holiday Inns. Subsequently, the casino became profitable, a fact that was a matter of public record. Also, L & M was aware that Marina had become highly profitable. Nonetheless, L & M sold its remaining 1 percent interest to Holiday Inns. After a newspaper article suggested that Holiday Inns had taken advantage of L & M, L & M sued Holiday Inns. L & M argued that Holiday Inns breached a fiduciary duty by failing to provide to L & M a 35-year financial forecast prepared by Holiday Inns, which projected large cash flows and high profits for the casino. Was Holiday Inns held liable to L & M?

4. Russel Daub, Daniel Smith, and Frederick Stehlik formed a partnership. No formal partnership agreement was executed. During 1980, profits were distributed monthly, with Daub receiving $3,000 per month, Smith $1,500, and Stehlik $1,500. In the latter months of 1980, Stehlik received $1,700 per month, but the 1980 partnership tax return indicated that profits were divided 50 percent to Daub and 25 percent each to Smith and Stehlik. During 1981, profits were distributed 50 percent to Daub and 25 percent each to Smith and Stehlik. The 1981 partnership tax return showed the 50–25–25 profit ratio at the beginning of the year, but it showed a year-end ratio of one third to each partner. In 1982, profits were distributed 50–25–25. When the partnership was dissolved and liquidated, Smith and Stehlik argued that each was entitled to one third of the profits and one third of the value of the partnership. Are they correct?

5. Two brothers, Sydney and Ashley Altman, operated several partnerships in Pennsylvania. They shared equally in the management of the partnerships. They agreed that each would receive identical salaries and that each was permitted to charge an equal amount of personal expenses to the partnerships. After Sydney moved to Florida, Sydney commuted to Pennsylvania every week to work for two to three days. After a year passed, Sydney told Ashley that he was considering retiring and remaining in Florida permanently. They tried to reach an agreement on Ashley's purchase of Sydney's partnership interests but were unable to do so. Ashley continued to manage the businesses by himself for nearly four years. During that time, Ashley paid himself salaries in excess of what the brothers had agreed. Has Ashley received excessive compensation as a partner?

6. Roy Moyle and Kenneth McCue were the general partners of McCue-Moyle Development Company, a real estate investment partnership that bought, developed, and sold real estate. Robert Baker offered $1.1 million for one piece of partnership property. On behalf of the partnership, Moyle signed the offer. Subsequently, McCue objected to the sale price and argued that the contract was not binding on the partnership because McCue had not signed it. Was the partnership bound on the contract?

7. 📼   *Video Case.* See "The Partnership." Art is a partner of Alphabet Builders, a partnership in the construction business. The three partners of Alphabet Builders have agreed that the partnership may not borrow money unless all the partners approve the borrowing. In the name of the partnership but without the consent of his partners, Art borrows money from a bank. Art tells the bank that the partnership will use the money for general purposes. Art indorses the loan check in the name of the partnership but deposits the money in his personal account. Art uses the money to purchase commodities futures. Art loses money on the futures and is unable to repay the loan. The bank sues Alphabet Builders and its partners. Are Alphabet Builders and its partners liable to the bank on the loan? Does Art have any liability to his partners?

8. Harold Schwartz, Gerald Dowell, and Lester Dowell formed a partnership to develop residential real estate. The Dowells gave Schwartz complete responsibility to sell the land. Although Schwartz and the Dowells knew that the land had not been surveyed, they conducted no survey because of the high cost of surveying. Instead, Schwartz relied on boundary information from a survey map, from land to the east that had been surveyed, and from boundary stakes placed by previous owners. In preparation for sale, Schwartz marked the boundaries with stakes and surveyor's ribbons. A prospective purchaser, Charles Nuttall, saw the stakes and flags placed by Schwartz and was told that they were "accurate within a couple of feet at the most." Nuttall bought land from the partnership relying on the representations made by Schwartz. Subsequent survey proved the boundaries to be off by 130 feet,

resulting in damages of $1,900 to Nuttall. Nuttall sued the Dowells. Are they liable for Schwartz's misrepresentations?

9. Ramada Inn West was a partnership operating a motel in Asheville, North Carolina. The partners were James Brandis, Ann Brandis, and Wallace Hyde. One evening, a Ramada Inn West waitress served four double shots of Tequila and four bottles of beer to Wayne Jordan, an underage drinker. Driving a car on his way home, Jordan died in a one-car automobile accident allegedly caused by his intoxication. When Jordan's estate sued the partnership for causing his death by serving him alcoholic beverages when he was too young, to whom did it address the complaint?

10. Alvin Meyer was a resident of 100 Central Park South, an apartment building in Manhattan, New York, owned by a partnership, Park South Associates. Meyer sued the partnership and one of its partners, Donald Trump, on three grounds: for violation of the lease between Meyer and the partnership, for breach of the warranty of habitability, and for the tort of intentional infliction of emotional distress due to the partnership's harassment of Meyer. Meyer did not allege in his complaint that Park South Associates was insolvent or otherwise unable to pay its obligations. Trump asked the trial court to dismiss the suit against him on the grounds that he personally could not be sued on partnership obligations unless it was insolvent or otherwise unable to pay its obligations. Did the court agree with Trump?

CHAPTER

38

Dissolution, Winding Up, and Termination of Partnerships

INTRODUCTION

This chapter is about the death of partnerships. Three terms are important in this connection: dissolution, winding up, and termination. Dissolution is a change in the relation of the partners, as when a partner dies. Winding up, which may follow dissolution, is the orderly liquidation of the partnership assets and the distribution of the proceeds to those having claims against the partnership. Termination, the end of the partnership's existence, automatically follows winding up. A limited liability partnership is dissolved, wound up, and terminated in the same manner as an ordinary partnership.

DISSOLUTION

Dissolution is defined in the Uniform Partnership Act (UPA) as "the change in the relation of the partners caused by any partner ceasing to be associated in the carrying on as distinguished from the winding up of the business." A dissolution may be caused by a partner's retirement, death, or bankruptcy, among other things. Whatever the cause of dissolution, however, it is characterized by a partner's *ceasing to take part in the carrying on of the partnership's business.*

Dissolution is the starting place for the winding up (liquidation) and termination of a partnership. Although winding up does not always follow dissolution, it often does. Winding up usually has a severe effect on a business: It usually ends the business, because the assets of the business are sold and the proceeds of the sale are distributed to creditors and partners.

A partner has the *power* to dissolve the partnership *at any time*, such as by withdrawing from the partnership. A partner does not, however, always have the *right* to dissolve a partnership. A partner has the right to dissolve a partnership only when a dissolution does not violate the partnership agreement. For example, a partner has the power to withdraw from a partnership with a 20-year term before the term expires, but has no right to do so.

When a partner's dissolution does not violate the partnership agreement, the partner has the right to dissolve the partnership: Such a dissolution is **nonwrongful.** When a partner's dissolution violates the partnership agreement, the partner has the power—

but not the right—to dissolve the partnership: Such a dissolution is **wrongful.** The consequences that follow a nonwrongful dissolution may differ from those that follow a wrongful dissolution.

Nonwrongful Dissolution

A dissolution is nonwrongful when the dissolution does not violate the partnership agreement. The following actions are nonwrongful dissolutions:

1. Automatic dissolution at the end of the term stated in the partnership agreement. For example, a partnership with a 20-year term is automatically dissolved at the expiration of that term.

2. Automatic dissolution on the partnership's accomplishment of its objective. For example, a partnership organized to build 15 condominiums dissolves when it completes their construction.

3. Withdrawal of a partner at any time from a partnership at will. A partnership at will is a partnership whose partnership agreement does not specify any specific term or objective.

4. Unanimous agreement of the partners who have not assigned their partnership interests or suffered charging orders against their partnership interests.

5. Expulsion of a partner in accordance with the partnership agreement. For example, the removal of a partner who has stolen partnership property dissolves the partnership if the partnership agreement allows removal on such grounds.

6. The illegality of the partnership business.

7. The death of a partner.

8. The bankruptcy of a partner. The partner must be adjudicated a bankrupt. Mere insolvency does not effect a dissolution.

In addition, a partner or other may go to court to request that a judge order a judicial dissolution in several situations. The following grounds for **judicial dissolution** are nonwrongful:

9. The adjudicated insanity of a partner.

10. The inability of a partner to perform the partnership contract. For example, a two-person partnership that remodels kitchens may be dissolved by a court when one of the partners becomes paralyzed in an automobile accident.

11. The inability of the partnership to conduct business except at a loss. Often, a partnership is not making a profit because of irreconcilable differences among the partners that prevent the business from being conducted beneficially.

12. At the request of a purchaser of a partnership interest in a partnership at will. This allows the creditor to whom a partner has assigned his partnership interest to obtain a dissolution and then to seek a winding up. During winding up, the creditor is paid from the debtor/partner's share of the proceeds of the sale of partnership assets.

Consequences of Nonwrongful Dissolution

When a dissolution is nonwrongful, each partner, including the dissolving partner, may demand that the business of the partnership be wound up; also, each partner—unless deceased or bankrupt—may participate in the winding-up process. In addition, by their unanimous agreement, the partners—including the nonwrongfully dissolving partner—may decide to allow one or more of the partners to continue the business using the partnership's name. If unanimity to continue the business cannot be obtained, any partner may force the business to wind up.

Wrongful Dissolution

A partner wrongfully dissolves a partnership when she dissolves her partnership in violation of the partnership agreement. For example, a partner wrongfully dissolves a partnership by retiring before the partnership accomplishes its stated objective of building vacation homes in Aspen, Colorado.

In addition, some judicial dissolutions on the following grounds are wrongful dissolutions for the wrongdoing partner: (1) when a partner's conduct prejudicially affects the business, or (2) when a partner willfully and persistently breaches the partnership agreement or her fiduciary duties. For example, a partner may continually insult customers, causing a loss of business; or a partner may persistently and substantially use partnership property for his own benefit; or three partners may refuse to allow a fourth partner to manage the partnership's business. In all of these situations, the harmed partners may seek judicial dissolution. As to the harmed partners, the dissolution would be nonwrongful. As to the wrongdoing partners, the dissolution would be wrongful.

Consequences of Wrongful Dissolution   A partner who wrongfully dissolves a partnership (1) has no right to demand that the business be wound

up; (2) has no right to participate in the winding up if the business is wound up; (3) has no right to have the goodwill of the business taken into account in valuing his partnership interest; (4) may not use the firm's name in connection with any business he conducts after dissolution; and (5) is liable for damages for breach of the partnership agreement, such as loss of profits. Nonetheless, a wrongfully dissolving partner is entitled to his share of the value of the partnership, minus his share of the partnership goodwill and the damages he caused the partnership.

Right to Continue In the event of a wrongful dissolution, the innocent partners may continue the business themselves or with new partners. They may continue to use the partnership's name. This right to continue the business prevents a wrongfully dissolving partner from forcing a liquidation of the partnership. In addition, each of the innocent partners has all of the rights that are possessed by partners when there is a nonwrongful dissolution. This means that if there is a wrongful dissolution, any innocent partner may force a winding up. Usually, innocent partners choose to continue the business.

Acts Not Causing Dissolution

A partner's assignment of his partnership interest does not dissolve a partnership, and neither does a creditor's obtaining a charging order. Also, the addition of a partner to a partnership does not dissolve the partnership, because no one disassociates from the partnership.

Mere disagreements, even irreconcilable differences, between the partners are expectable, but they are not grounds for dissolution. If the disagreements threaten partnership assets or profitability, then a court may order dissolution.

The partnership agreement may state that death or withdrawal shall not cause a dissolution. Although death or withdrawal clearly disassociates a partner from the carrying on of the business, several states permit the partners to vary the definition of dissolution by their agreement. Other states permit the partners to eliminate the right to demand a winding up after the death or withdrawal of a partner.

Joint Ventures and Mining Partnerships

Essentially, the partnership rules of dissolution apply to joint ventures. It is more likely in a joint venture than in a partnership that a member's death will not dissolve the joint venture or not permit a demand to wind up; courts often find that joint venturers made an implied agreement that the limited objective of the joint venture be completed, as in *Rhue v. Dawson*, which follows.

Mining partnerships are more difficult to dissolve than general partnerships due to the free transferability of mining partnership interests. The death or bankruptcy of a mining partner does not effect a dissolution. In addition, a mining partner may sell his interest to another person and disassociate himself from the carrying on of the mining partnership's business without causing a dissolution. The other rules of partnership dissolution apply to mining partnerships.

RHUE V. DAWSON
841 P.2d 215 (Ariz. App. Div. 1992)

James Rhue and John Dawson formed a partnership or joint venture to acquire and develop a shopping center. They named the enterprise Shopping Center Enterprises of Arizona (SCEA). Rhue had shopping center expertise and handled day-to-day details. Dawson contributed most of the capital and promised to seek bank financing for the project. They agreed to share profits and equity equally. They did not immediately put their agreement in writing, although drafts of an agreement were circulated.

Rhue located two adjacent shopping centers that the partnership purchased for $7.2 million. The estimated cost of renovating the combined shopping centers was $4.6 million. To obtain bank financing of the purchase and development of the combined shopping centers, Dawson obtained an appraisal of the projected value of the combined shopping center assuming redevelopment according to the plans prepared by SCEA. The appraisal projected the value at $15.6 million, indicating a projected profit of $3.8 for the venture. Rhue's one-half share of the projected profits would have been $1.9 million.

Seven days after receiving the appraisal, Dawson asked Rhue to sign a form entitled "Joint Venture Agreement." Dawson pressured Rhue to sign the agreement before Rhue could read it. Rhue specifically asked whether certain changes that they had discussed and agreed on were in the written agreement. Dawson replied that they were included; however, Dawson failed to tell Rhue that the agreement contained an "Option to Purchase" clause. Previous drafts lacked this clause. The clause allowed Dawson to buy Rhue's interest in the partnership merely by returning Rhue's capital contribution. Because Rhue contributed mostly expertise, not capital, this clause was highly favorable to Dawson. Rhue signed the agreement without reading it.

Two months later, Rhue learned about the "Option to Purchase" clause and indicated to Dawson that he did not intend to be bound by it. Dawson answered by notifying Rhue of his intent to exercise the buyout provision. Dawson then locked Rhue out of the partnership's offices. Rhue sued Dawson, claiming wrongful dissolution by Dawson and asking for lost profits. The trial judge held that Dawson had wrongfully dissolved the partnership and ordered Dawson to pay Rhue $8.4 million, which included Rhue's attorney's fees, punitive damages of $2 million, and the profits Rhue would have made on the venture, which were tripled under Arizona's racketeering statute. Dawson appealed.

Lankford, Judge   Arizona law recognizes three types of partnerships differentiated by term: a partnership at will, a partnership for a particular undertaking, and a partnership for a definite term. A partnership for a definite term or for a particular undertaking may be dissolved without violating the partnership agreement only at the end of the term or on completion of the undertaking. Only a partnership having no specified definite term or particular undertaking is a partnership at will. Such a partnership is subject to dissolution by express will of a partner without violating the partnership agreement.

Evidence supports a finding of a partnership other than one at will. Rhue and Dawson contemplated purchase of a single shopping center. They anticipated no other undertakings. This suggests a partnership for a particular undertaking.

Dawson could dissolve the partnership only in accordance with the terms of the agreement. Dawson delivered a letter notifying Rhue of the buyout and dissolving the partnership. Dawson locked Rhue out of the partnership offices. These actions effectively ousted Rhue as a partner. Dawson's conduct wrongfully dissolved the partnership in contravention of the parties' agreement.

A partner who has been wrongfully excluded from the partnership has the right, as against the partner who wrongfully excluded him, to damages for breach of the agreement, including loss of probable profits. To prove lost profits, Rhue must establish a reasonably certain factual basis for computation of lost profits. Dawson objects to the lost profits as too uncertain because SCEA was a new business.

While SCEA was a new business association, the two pieces of property held by SCEA had been operated in the commercial real estate market for many years. The appraiser estimated the value of the property based on the assumption that the property was to be developed in accordance with SCEA's plans and specifications. Dawson himself had utilized the same appraisal after the dissolution in various financial statements to a lending institution. Valuation methods utilized by the appraiser included comparable sales, net income, discounted cash flows, and replacement costs. The evidence was sufficient to support an award of lost profits.

Dawson next argues that his conduct was not sufficiently outrageous to justify an award of punitive damages. Rhue's claim for punitive damages is proper. Both fraud and deliberate, overt, dishonest dealings will suffice to sustain punitive damages. Dawson deliberately misled Rhue and intended to injure Rhue. Moreover, the relationship between the parties affects whether punitive damages can be awarded. Rhue and Dawson were partners. Dawson failed to discharge his fiduciary duty and his duty to exercise the utmost good faith and to discharge the obligation of loyalty, fairness, and honesty in his dealings with Rhue.

Dawson acted with an evil mind. Dawson deliberately failed to disclose to Rhue that the agreement signed by the parties contained a buyout provision. Dawson locked Rhue out of the partnership offices. Dawson's actions were consciously malicious.

Dawson also questions whether punitive damages may be imposed in addition to civil racketeering treble damages. Appellate courts will not interfere with the trial court's verdict on damages unless the verdict is not supported by the evidence or unless it is so outrageously excessive as to suggest passion or prejudice. We remand for the trial court to review the amount of punitive damages in light of the trebled compensatory damages to ensure that the former are not excessive.

Judgment for Rhue affirmed; remanded to trial court for review of the punitive damage award.

CONCEPT REVIEW

CAUSES OF DISSOLUTION AND ACTS NOT CAUSING DISSOLUTION

Causes of Dissolution	**Wrongful Dissolutions**
	1. Any dissolution that violates the partnership agreement.
	2. Judicial dissolution due to a partner's conduct prejudicially affecting the business.
	3. Judicial dissolution due to a partner's willful and persistent breach of the partnership agreement or her fiduciary duties.
	Nonwrongful Dissolutions
	1. End of the term stated in the partnership agreement.
	2. The partnership's accomplishment of its objective.
	3. Withdrawal of a partner at any time from a partnership at will.
	4. Withdrawal of a partner in accordance with the partnership agreement.
	5. Expulsion of a partner in accordance with the partnership agreement.
	6. Unanimous agreement of the partners who have not assigned their partnership interests or suffered charging orders against their partnership interests.
	7. Illegality of the partnership business.
	8. Death of a partner.
	9. Bankruptcy of a partner.
	10. Judicial dissolution due to the adjudicated insanity of a partner.
	11. Judicial dissolution due to the inability of a partner to perform the partnership contract.
	12. Judicial dissolution due to the inability of the partnership to conduct business except at a loss.
	13. Judicial dissolution at the request of a purchaser of a partnership interest in a partnership at will.
Acts Not Causing Dissolution	1. A partner's assignment of a partnership interest.
	2. A creditor's obtaining a charging order against a partnership interest.
	3. Addition of a partner to a partnership.
	4. Disagreement among the partners that does not threaten partnership assets or profitability.
	5. Death or withdrawal of a partner, when the partnership agreement states that death or withdrawal shall not cause a dissolution.

WINDING UP THE PARTNERSHIP BUSINESS

When a partnership is to be terminated, the next step after dissolution is **winding up** the partnership's affairs. This involves the orderly liquidation—or sale—of the assets of the business. Liquidation may be accomplished asset by asset; that is, each asset may be sold separately. It may also be accomplished by a sale of the business as a whole. Or it may be accomplished by a means somewhere between these two extremes.

Winding up does not always require the sale of the assets or the business. When a partnership has valuable assets, the partners may wish to receive the assets rather than the proceeds from their sale. Such *distributions-in-kind* are rarely permitted. They are allowed when there are no creditors' claims against the partnership, the value of the assets can be ascertained, and the assets can be distributed in a manner that is fair to each partner.

During winding up, the partners continue as fiduciaries to each other, especially in negotiating sales or making distributions of partnership assets to members of the partnership. Nonetheless, there is a termination of the fiduciary duties unrelated to winding up. For example, a partner who is not winding up the business may compete with his partnership during winding up.

Demanding and Performing Winding Up

A partner who has not wrongfully dissolved the partnership may demand winding up. Thus, when a partnership has been dissolved nonwrongfully, any partner, even the dissolving partner, may demand winding up. If the partnership has been wrongfully dissolved, only the innocent partners may demand winding up.

Any surviving, nonbankrupt partner who has not wrongfully dissolved the partnership may perform the winding up. A partner who has wrongfully dissolved the partnership has no right to wind up the business. When a dissolution is caused by the death or bankruptcy of a partner, the surviving partners and the nonbankrupt partners have the right to wind up the business.

If the dissolution is by court decree, usually no partner winds up. Instead, a *receiver* is appointed by the court to wind up the business.

The compensation to a winding up partner is only his share of the profits, unless the partners agree to give special compensation to the winding up partner. In addition, when the winding up partner provides extraordinary services or is the sole surviving partner after dissolution by death, he is entitled to the reasonable value of his winding up services.

Partner's Authority during Winding Up

Express and Implied Authority
During winding up, a partner has the express authority to act as the partners have agreed. The implied authority of a winding up partner is the power to do those acts *reasonably necessary to the winding up* of the partnership affairs. That is, he has the power to bind the partnership in any transaction necessary to the liquidation of the assets. He may collect money due, sue to enforce partnership rights, prepare assets for sale, sell partnership assets, pay partnership creditors, and do whatever else is appropriate to wind up the business. He may maintain and preserve assets or enhance them for sale, for example, by painting a building or by paying a debt to prevent foreclosure on partnership land. A winding up partner may temporarily continue the business when the effect is to preserve the value of the partnership.

Performing Executory Contracts
The implied authority of a winding up partner includes the power to perform contracts made before dissolution. A partner may not enter into *new* contracts unless the contracts aid the liquidation of the partnership's assets. For example, a partner may fulfill a contract to deliver coal if the contract was made before dissolution. She may not make a new contract to deliver coal unless doing so disposes of coal that the partnership owns or has contracted to purchase.

Borrowing Money
Usually, the implied authority of a winding up partner includes no power to borrow money in the name of the partnership. Nonetheless, when a partner can preserve the assets of the partnership or enhance them for sale by borrowing money, he has implied authority to engage in new borrowing. For example, a partnership may have a valuable machine repossessed and sold far below its value at a foreclosure sale unless it can refinance a loan. A partner may borrow the money needed to refinance the loan, thereby preserving the asset. A partner may also borrow money to perform executory contracts.

Apparent Authority
Winding up partners have apparent authority to conduct business as they did before dissolution, when notice of dissolution is not given to those persons who knew of the partnership prior to its dissolution. For example, a construction partnership dissolves and begins winding up but does not notify anyone of its dissolution. After dissolution, a partner makes a contract with a customer to remodel the customer's building. The partner would have no implied authority to make the contract, because the contract is new business and does not help liquidate assets. Nonetheless, the

contract may be within the partner's apparent authority, because to persons unaware of the dissolution, it appears that a partner may continue to make contracts that have been in the usual course of business.

To eliminate this apparent authority to conduct business in the normal way, the partnership must do both of the following:

1. Give **actual**—or personal—**notice** of the dissolution to persons who extended credit to the partnership prior to dissolution, and

2. Give either actual notice or **constructive notice** of the dissolution to persons who were not creditors but had merely done business with the partnership without extending credit or had merely been aware of the existence of the partnership.

Actual notice may be given by telephone or by a letter mailed or faxed to the creditor's place of business. Creditors may also receive actual notice by hearing of the dissolution by word of mouth or reading of it in a newspaper.

Constructive notice is notice published in a newspaper of general circulation in the places where the partnership did business. Constructive notice eliminates apparent authority of the partners as to noncreditors even if the notice is not read by the noncreditors.

For persons who were previously unaware of the partnership's existence, no notice of any type need be given to eliminate apparent authority.

Disputes among Winding Up Partners   When more than one partner has the right to wind up the partnership, the partners may disagree concerning which steps should be taken during winding up. For decisions in the ordinary course of winding up, the decision of a majority of the partners controls. When the decision is an extraordinary one, such as continuing the business for an extended period of time, unanimous partner approval is required.

In the following case, the court found that the business of the partnership to train and race a horse should continue during winding up.

PACIARONI v. CRANE
408 A.2d 946 (Del. Ct. Ch. 1979)

Black Ace, a harness racehorse of exceptional speed, was the fourth best pacer in the United States in 1979. He was owned by a partnership: Richard Paciaroni owned 50 percent; James Cassidy, 25 percent; and James Crane, 25 percent. Crane, a professional trainer, was in charge of the daily supervision of Black Ace, including training. It was understood that all of the partners would be consulted on the races in which Black Ace would be entered, the selection of drivers, and other major decisions; however, the recommendations of Crane were always followed by the other partners because of his superior knowledge of harness racing.

In 1979, Black Ace won $96,969 through mid-August. Seven other races remained in 1979, including the prestigious Little Brown Jug and the Messenger at Roosevelt Raceway. The purse for these races was $600,000.

A disagreement among the partners arose when Black Ace developed a ringbone condition and Crane followed the advice of a veterinarian not selected by Paciaroni and Cassidy. The ringbone condition disappeared, but later Black Ace became uncontrollable by his driver, and in a subsequent race he fell and failed to finish the race. Soon thereafter, Paciaroni and Cassidy sent a telegram to Crane rightfully dissolving the partnership and directing him to deliver Black Ace to another trainer they had selected. Crane refused to relinquish control of Black Ace, so Paciaroni and Cassidy sued him in August 1979, asking the court to appoint a receiver who would race Black Ace in the remaining 1979 stakes races and then sell the horse. Crane objected to allowing anyone other than himself to enter the horse in races. Before the trial court issued the following decision, Black Ace had entered three additional races and won $40,000.

Brown, Vice Chancellor   It is generally accepted that once dissolution occurs, the partnership continues only to the extent necessary to close out affairs and complete transactions begun but not then finished. It is not generally contemplated that new business will be generated or that new contractual commitments will be made. This, in principle, would work against permitting Black Ace to participate in the remaining few races for which he is eligible.

However, in Delaware, there have been exceptions to this. Where, because of the nature of the partnership business, a better price upon final liquidation is likely to be obtained by the temporary continuation of the business, it is permissible, during the winding up process, to have the business continue to the degree necessary to preserve or enhance its value upon liquidation, provided that such continuation is done in good faith with the intent to bring affairs to a conclusion as soon as reasonably possible. And one way to accomplish this is through an application to the Court for a winding up under UPA Section 37, which carries with it the power of the Court to appoint a receiver for that purpose.

The business purpose of the partnership was to own and race Black Ace for profit. The horse was bred to race. He has the ability to be competitive with the top pacers in the country. He is currently "racing fit" according to the evidence. He has at best only seven more races to go over a period of the next six weeks, after which time there are established horse sales at which he can be disposed of to the highest bidder. The purse for these remaining stake races is substantial. The fact that he could possibly sustain a disabling injury during this six-week period appears to be no greater than it was when the season commenced. Admittedly, an injury could occur at any time. But this is a fact of racing life which all owners and trainers are forced to accept. And the remaining stake races are races in which all three partners originally intended that he would compete, if able.

Under these circumstances, I conclude that the winding up of the partnership affairs should include the right to race Black Ace in some or all of the remaining 1979 stakes races for which he is now eligible. The final question, then, is who shall be in charge of racing him.

On this point, I rule in favor of Paciaroni and Cassidy. They may, on behalf of the partnership, continue to race the horse through their new trainer, subject, however, to the conditions hereafter set forth. Crane does have a monetary interest in the partnership assets that must be protected if Paciaroni and Cassidy are to be permitted to test the whims of providence in the name of the partnership during the next six weeks. Accordingly, I make the following ruling:

1. Paciaroni and Cassidy shall first post security in the sum of $100,000 so as to secure to Crane his share of the value of Black Ace.

2. If Paciaroni and Cassidy are unable or unwilling to meet this condition, then they shall forgo the right to act as liquidating partners. In that event, each party, within seven days, shall submit to the Court the names of two persons who they believe to be qualified, and who they know to be willing, to act as receiver for the winding up of partnership affairs.

3. In the event that no suitable person can be found to act as receiver, or in the event that the Court should deem it unwise to appoint any person from the names so submitted, then the Court reserves the power to terminate any further racing by Black Ace and to require that he simply be maintained and cared for until such time as he can be sold as a part of the final liquidation of the partnership.

Judgment for Paciaroni and Cassidy.

CONCEPT REVIEW

Partner's Authority during Winding Up

Express Authority	· To do anything the partners agree a partner may perform.

Implied Authority	· To do those acts reasonably necessary to winding up.
	  · Preserve and enhance assets
	  · Sell assets
	  · Complete executory contracts

Apparent Authority	• To conduct business in the usual way, unless proper notice of dissolution has been given.
	• Actual notice—must be given to prior creditors of the partnership.
	• Constructive notice (or actual notice)—must be given to noncreditors who conducted business with the partnership.
	• Constructive notice (or actual notice)—must be given to persons who did not conduct business with the partnership but knew of its existence.
	• No notice—to persons who previously were unaware of the partnership's existence.

WHEN THE BUSINESS IS CONTINUED

Cessation of business need not follow dissolution of a partnership. The remaining partners could purchase the business during winding up, someone else could purchase the business, or the partnership agreement could provide that there will be no winding up and that the business may be carried on by the remaining partners.

When there is no winding up and the business is continued, the claims of creditors against the partnership and the partners may be affected, because old partners are no longer with the business and new partners may enter the business.

Successor's Liability for Predecessor's Obligations

When the business of a partnership is continued after dissolution, creditors of the old partnership are creditors of the person or partnership continuing the business. In addition, the original partners remain liable for obligations incurred prior to dissolution unless there is agreement with the creditors to the contrary. Thus, partners may not usually escape liability by forming a new partnership or a corporation to carry on the old business of the partnership.

Outgoing Partner's Liability for Obligations Incurred While a Partner

Outgoing partners remain liable to partnership creditors for partnership liabilities incurred while they were partners; however, an outgoing partner's liability may be eliminated by the process of **novation.** Novation occurs when the following two conditions are met:

1. The continuing partners release an outgoing partner from liability on a partnership debt, and
2. A partnership creditor releases the outgoing partner from liability on the same obligation.

Partners usually expressly release an outgoing partner from liability, but the release may be implied as well. To complete the requirements for novation, an outgoing partner must also secure his release by the partnership's creditors. A creditor's agreement to release an outgoing partner from liability may be express, but usually it is implied. *Implied* novation may be proved by a creditor's knowledge of a partner's withdrawal and his continued extension of credit to the partnership. In addition, a *material modification* of an obligation operates as a novation for an outgoing partner, when the creditor has knowledge that the continuing partners have released the outgoing partner from liability.

When former partners release an outgoing partner from liability but creditors do not, there is not a novation. As a result, creditors may enforce a partnership liability against an outgoing partner. However, the outgoing partner may recover from his former partners who have agreed to release him from liability.

Nonetheless, an outgoing partner may not enforce a release-of-liability agreement when he obtains the release by failing to disclose material facts to the partners or creditors. For example, an outgoing partner who obtains release from the partners without disclosing that he has bound the partnership on a contract retains his liability to the other partners.

In the following case, the court found both an implied novation and a material alteration operating as a novation. Consequently, the court relieved an outgoing partner from liability to a landlord.

Wester & Co. v. Nestle
669 P.2d 1046 (Colo. Ct. App. 1983)

Junior Nestle and Eric Ellis were the owners of Red Rocks Meat and Deli, a partnership. They had no partnership agreement and no specified term for the partnership. They operated the partnership in a building that they leased from Wester & Company. In October 1978, Nestle left the business. John Herline purchased Nestle's partnership interest, including Nestle's entire interest in partnership equipment, leases, and other assets. In return, a new partnership of Ellis and Herline agreed to assume all the liabilities of the former partnership and to release Nestle from liability. A copy of the purchase and release agreement was mailed to Wester & Co., giving notice to Wester & Co. that Nestle was no longer a partner. Ellis introduced Herline to Wester & Co. as his new partner. Wester & Co. did not object to a change in partners or request that Nestle remain liable.

Soon after, Herline left the partnership, and Ellis operated the business as a sole proprietorship. In January 1980, Wester & Co. and Ellis modified the original lease to include adjacent space and to increase the rent. When the lease was modified, it was clear to Wester & Co. that Ellis was then operating the business as a sole proprietor. The president of Wester & Co. was told when the lease was modified that Nestle was no longer a partner.

In May 1980, when Ellis failed to pay the rent, Wester & Co. sued Nestle for the rent. The court found that due to Wester & Company's knowledge of the situation and the parties' course of dealings, it had consented to Nestle's release from liability. The court also concluded that the modified lease materially altered Nestle's liability on the underlying lease, thereby discharging Nestle from liability. Wester & Co. appealed.

Steinberg, Judge   The dissolution of a partnership does not of itself discharge the existing liability of any partner. A partner is discharged from existing liability by an agreement to that effect between the withdrawing partner, the remaining partners, and the partnership creditor, and "such agreement may be inferred from the course of dealing between the creditor and the person or partnership continuing the business." A material alteration in an existing liabil-ity will discharge from liability a partner whose obligations have been assumed.

The trial court found that the conditions for discharge from liability under both of these subsections existed, and such factual findings, supported by the evidence, may not be disturbed upon appeal.

Judgment for Nestle affirmed.

Outgoing Partner's Liability for Obligations Incurred after Leaving the Partnership

Ordinarily, an outgoing partner has no liability on partnership obligations incurred after he leaves the partnership because he no longer controls the partnership or shares as a co-owner in its profits. Nonetheless, outgoing partners may be liable for obligations incurred by a person or partnership continuing the business after their departure, under the theory of *partnership by estoppel*. There is no such liability to creditors who are aware of the change in partners. Also, the risk of estoppel liability can be eliminated by giving the appropriate notice that the partner has left the partnership.

Actual—or personal—notice must be given to those persons who extended credit to the partnership prior to dissolution. Such notice may be either oral or written and must be actually delivered or received. Constructive notice—notice published several times in a newspaper of general circulation—is sufficient for those who knew of the partnership but were not prior creditors. No notice need be given to persons who were not previously aware of the partnership's existence or who knew of the dissolution.

Liability of Incoming Partners

A person joining an existing partnership has unlimited liability for all partnership obligations incurred *after* she becomes a partner. For partnership obligations incurred *before* she became a partner, she is liable as if she had been a partner when the obligations were incurred; however, her liability is limited to the partnership's assets. Once partnership assets are exhausted, she has no further liability for partnership obligations that were incurred prior to her affiliation with the partnership. Nonetheless, if she has expressly or impliedly agreed to undertake unlimited liability for prior obligations, her liability will be unlimited. For example, she may agree with an outgoing partner to assume the outgoing partner's partnership obligations.

In the following case, incoming partners had no liability beyond the assets of the partnership on a debt that arose prior to their joining the partnership.

KALICHMAN V. BEVERLY HOLDING CO.

520 N.Y.S.2d 255 (N.Y. App. Div. 1987)

Joseph Kalichman and Joseph Klein formed a partnership that owned and managed an apartment building in the Bronx, New York. The partnership borrowed $189,000 from National Savings Bank of Albany. Before the loan was repaid, Joseph Klein died, and his interest in the partnership passed to his sons, Jack and Frank, who received Joseph Klein's share of the partnership income. Jack and Frank did not, however, engage in management of the partnership business. When the partnership defaulted on the loans, National Savings Bank sued Kalichman. Kalichman settled the lawsuit by paying $100,000 to National Savings Bank and then sued Jack and Frank Klein to require them to pay their share of the liability. The trial court found Jack and Frank liable to Kalichman; Jack and Frank appealed.

Casey, Justice   Jack and Frank assert that the existence of a partnership arrangement does not demonstrate or indicate their assumption of a preexisting obligation on the bonds, rendering them personally liable for such debt. We agree. UPA section 41(7) provides:

The liability of a third person becoming a partner in the partnership continuing the business under this section to the creditors of the dissolved partnership shall be satisfied out of partnership property only.

Although the primary purpose of UPA section 41 is the protection of creditors, it also limits incoming partners' liability to the partnership property unless personal liability is expressly assumed through the partnership agreement or otherwise. Here, Joseph Klein's death dissolved his partnership with Kalichman. Kalichman then had the right to possess the property for a partnership purpose, as well as the duty to wind up the affairs of the partnership and to pay to Joseph Klein's legal representative Klein's proportionate share in partnership surplus. These events did not occur here, however, since Kalichman continued the partnership business with Jack and Frank's consent. Having continued to carry on the partnership business after Joseph Klein's death, Kalichman must bear all of the losses, while UPA section 41(7) limits Jack and Frank's liability to their interest in the Bronx property. Jack and Frank's only association with the partnership was to receive income from the same. While this fact might evidence the formation of a partnership between Jack, Frank, and Kalichman, it does not evidence that Jack and Frank ever assumed personal liability for preexisting loans incurred by Joseph Klein.

Judgment reversed in favor of Jack and Frank Klein.

Rights of Outgoing Partners

An outgoing partner is entitled to receive the value of his partnership interest. He becomes a creditor of the new partnership for the value of his partnership interest, but his claim is subordinate to the claims of other creditors of the partnership.

Valuation of the Outgoing Partner's Interest

The value of an outgoing partner's interest in the partnership is determined at the time of the dissolution. Often, the partnership agreement includes a method for calculating the value of a partnership interest.

The value of a partnership includes its goodwill. **Goodwill** is the well-founded expectation of continued public patronage of a business. It represents the difference between the going-concern value of a business and the liquidation value of its assets.

When a partnership business is continued after dissolution, it is frequently difficult to determine the value of the goodwill that is transferred to the continuing partners. In service partnerships, the goodwill may be so closely tied to the individual partners that no goodwill remains with the business when valuable partners withdraw from the partnership. These difficulties and uncertainties also make it advisable to have a partnership agreement on valuing the partnership, including the value of its goodwill.

Payment Options   In the absence of a contrary agreement, when dissolution results from death or retirement, the outgoing partner may choose one of the following payment options:

1. Taking the value of his partnership interest at the time of dissolution plus interest, or
2. Taking the value of his partnership interest at the time of dissolution plus a pro rata share of subsequent profits.

These options provide incentive for the continuing partners to settle promptly with an outgoing partner.

When there is no agreement and dissolution results from a cause other than death or retirement—as with dissolutions caused by bankruptcy or by willful, persistent breaches of the partnership agreement—the partner is entitled to receive the value of her interest at the time of dissolution. The outgoing partner may insist on immediate payment and receive interest for late payment.

Valuation of Interest of Wrongfully Dissolving Partner   A wrongfully dissolving partner must be paid the value of his partnership interest in cash by the continuing partners, or the partners must post a bond to have the privilege of continuing the business. In addition, they must agree to release him from all present and future partnership liabilities. However, goodwill is excluded from the valuation of the partnership interest of a partner who has wrongfully caused dissolution, and the valuation of that interest is further reduced by the damages that he has caused his partners due to his dissolution.

DISTRIBUTION OF ASSETS

After the partnership's assets have been sold during winding up, the proceeds are distributed to those persons who have claims against the partnership. Not only creditors but also partners have claims against the proceeds. As you might expect, the claims of creditors must be satisfied before the claims of partners may be paid. The UPA states the order of distribution of the partnership assets:

1. Those owing to creditors other than partners.
2. Those owing to partners other than for capital and profits.
3. Those owing to partners in respect of capital.
4. Those owing to partners in respect of profits.

Note that item 2 places partners who are also creditors of the partnership subordinate to other creditors. This is done to prevent partners from underfunding a partnership to the detriment of creditors. The subordination of partner-creditors also emphasizes that the partners are liable for all the partnership's liabilities.

A partner who is also a creditor of the partnership, however, is paid his claim as a creditor before any partner receives any return of his capital contribution. Thus, for example, a partner's loan to the partnership is repaid before any partner has his capital returned.

If a partnership has not suffered losses that impair its capital, few problems are presented in the distribution of its assets. Everyone having an interest in the partnership is paid in full. If there is a disagreement about the amount due to a claimant, the dispute is usually resolved by an accounting ordered by the court. In the following case, the court calculated each partner's share of the assets of a solvent partnership.

LANGNESS V. O STREET CARPET SHOP
353 N.W.2d 709 (Neb. Sup. Ct. 1984)

NFL Associates was a partnership of three partners: Herbert Friedman, Strelsa Lee Langness, and The O Street Carpet Shop, Inc. At the partnership's creation in 1973, O Street Carpet contributed a contract worth $9,000, Langness contributed $14,000 in cash, and Friedman contributed his legal services, which were not valued. The partners used part of Langness's contribution to make an $8,000 payment to O Street Carpet. They used the remaining $6,000 to purchase investment property and for working capital. Later, O Street Carpet contributed an additional $4,005 in capital. The partners agreed that Friedman would receive 10 percent of the profits and that each of the other two partners would receive 45 percent of the profits. The partners also agreed that Langness would receive payments of $116.66 each month.

During the five-year term of the partnership, Langness received checks totaling $6,300.30. Langness did not pay income tax on these monthly payments. The partnership did not take expense deductions for those payments on its information return filed with the Internal Revenue Service. In 1978, the partnership dissolved and wound up its business, selling its investment property for $52,001.20. After paying partnership liabilities of $3,176.79, Friedman distributed the remaining $48,824.41 to the partners. Langness received $16,792.01, O Street Carpet received $26,808.58, and Friedman received $5,223.82. Langness was unhappy with the distribution and sued Friedman and O Street Carpet for a larger share. The trial court held that Langness was entitled to receive $24,082.43. The court imposed liability on Friedman and O Street Carpet for $7,290.42, the additional amount Langness should have received. Friedman appealed.

Per Curiam   Friedman's appeal is best analyzed by reviewing the capital contributions made by the partners, the nature of the payments made to Langness, and the distributions made to each of the three partners upon the winding up of the partnership. O Street Carpet made a contribution of property worth $9,000. However, $8,000 of the $14,000 contributed by Langness went to O Street Carpet, thereby reducing its capital contribution at that time to $1,000. O Street Carpet contributed an additional $4,005 in capital. Thus, O Street Carpet's total capital contribution is $5,005.

Friedman contributed no money or property. It is the general rule that a partner who contributes only services to a partnership is not deemed to have made a capital contribution to the partnership, unless the partners have agreed to the contrary. Friedman argues that since, by agreement, he was given 10 percent of the partnership, he was entitled to be credited with a like amount of the partnership capital upon dissolution. While the agreement specifically states that Friedman is entitled to 10 percent of the partnership profits, it mentions nothing concerning his rights to partnership capital upon dissolution. Therefore, Friedman made no capital contribution to the venture.

We next address the nature of the payments made to Langness. The partnership agreement called for the partnership to pay to Langness $116.66 per month for the life of the partnership. While this provision of the articles is found under a section labeled "Distribution of Profits and Losses," the agreement does not state whether it is to be treated as an advance on profits or a capital withdrawal. Both accountants who testified at the trial stated that the payments were treated as capital withdrawals. Langness treated the payments as such when preparing her tax returns. The tax returns of the partnership did not treat them as expenses. We calculate her total capital withdrawals as $6,300.30, which reduced her capital in the partnership to $7,699.70.

We now reach the question of the appropriate amounts of the distribution to each of the partners. The partnership agreement provides: "Upon the dissolution of the partnership after settlement of all of its liabilities, the partners are entitled to all remaining assets of the partnership in equal proportions in liquidation of all of their respective interests in the partnership." Amounts owing to partners to reimburse them for capital contributions take priority over amounts owing to partners in respect to profits.

Of the $48,824.41 in assets remaining after payment of the partnership's debts, $7,699.70 is to be paid to Langness for her capital contribution and $5,005 to O Street Carpet for its capital contribution. The remaining $36,119.71 is to be divided according to the partners' share in the profits, which is on a 45–45–10 basis. This action requires $16,253.87 to be paid to Langness for profit, the same amount to O Street Carpet, and $3,611.97 to Friedman.

Therefore, Langness was entitled to a total distribution of $23,953.57. Since Langness was paid only $16,792.01, she is entitled to an additional $7,161.56.

Judgment for Langness affirmed as modified.

Distribution of Assets of Insolvent Partnership

When a partnership has suffered losses, distribution of the assets may be troublesome. For example, partnership creditors may compete with the creditors of individual partners to obtain payment from partnership assets and the assets of individual partners. Also, the partnership losses must be allocated among partners. In adjusting the rights of partnership creditors and the creditors of individual partners, the rule is usually that partnership creditors have first claim on partnership assets and that individual creditors have first claim on individual assets. This is called **marshaling of assets**.

Example   The distribution of assets and allocation of losses of an insolvent partnership can best be explained with an example. Suppose that Alden, Bass, and Casey form a partnership and that Alden contributes $25,000, Bass contributes $15,000, and Casey contributes $10,000. After operating for several years, the firm suffers losses and becomes insolvent. When the partnership is liquidated, its assets total $30,000 in cash. It owes $40,000 to partnership creditors. Therefore, the capital balance (net worth) of the partnership is a negative $10,000. This means that partnership losses totaled $60,000 ($50,000 of capital already contributed and lost plus the $10,000 negative net worth). The situation could be represented by the following equation:

$$\text{Profit} = \text{Ending owner's capital} - \text{Beginning owner's capital}$$
$$-\$60,000 = \quad -\$10,000 \quad - \quad \$50,000$$

Because the profit is negative, this is a loss of $60,000.

In the absence of a provision in the partnership agreement concerning the partners' shares of profits and losses, they are shared equally. Therefore, each partner's **share of the loss** is one third of the loss, $20,000. Their shares of the loss reduce the partners' capital claims against partnership assets, as shown in the following table.

	Capital at Beginning		Share of Loss		Capital at Liquidation
Alden	$25,000	–	$20,000	=	$ 5,000
Bass	15,000	–	20,000	=	(5,000)
Casey	10,000	–	20,000	=	(10,000)
Totals	$50,000	–	$60,000	=	$(10,000)

The table shows that while each partner should have assumed $20,000 of the loss, Alden has taken $25,000 of the loss due to her $25,000 capital contribution. Therefore, unless she has $5,000 of her capital returned, she has assumed $5,000 of the loss she should not have assumed. Bass and Casey, on the other hand, have assumed too little of the loss, because their capital contributions were less than $20,000. Bass should undertake $5,000 more of the loss, and Casey should assume $10,000 more, amounts reflected in the last column of the table.

Now we shall distribute partnership assets and pay the claims against the partnership. Following the order of distribution in the UPA, the $30,000 in cash from the liquidation is distributed pro rata to pay the nonpartner creditors of the partnership. Because the creditors are owed $40,000, the $30,000 payment leaves $10,000 of partnership debts to outsiders unpaid. The partners are liable for the remaining $10,000. Because the partnership assets are gone, the partners must pay the debt from their individual assets.

To undertake their **shares of the partnership liabilities**, Bass is legally liable to contribute $5,000 and Casey $10,000 to the partnership, the negative amounts in the Capital at Liquidation column in the table. This permits completion of the payment of the partnership creditors ($10,000) and the return of Alden's capital to the extent that it exceeded her share of the partnership loss—the $5,000 figure in the Capital at Liquidation column.

Unpaid partnership creditors have a right to collect from any solvent partner. Had they chosen to collect the entire amount from Alden, she would then have had to proceed against Bass and Casey for the amount she paid that Bass and Casey should have paid.

Termination

After the assets of a partnership have been distributed, **termination** of the partnership occurs automatically.

ETHICAL AND PUBLIC POLICY CONCERNS

1. Why should a partner have the power to dissolve a partnership at any time, while in general a shareholder of a corporation has no such power? Is it important to your answer that a partner has liability for his partners' contracts and torts, while a shareholder generally has no liability for the contracts or the torts of the corporation? Why should a partner not have the right to dissolve a partnership at any time? Who should determine when a partner has the right to dissolve a partnership? Should only the partners determine the scope of this right, or does society have the right to limit a partner's right to dissolve?

2. Why should a partnership give notice of the dissolution of a partnership? Why is the partnership liable to creditors who do not receive proper notice of the dissolution? Is fairness promoted by such a rule? Is economic efficiency promoted by such a rule?

3. Is it fair that a wrongfully dissolving partner is not entitled to receive a share of the value of the partnership's goodwill? What is goodwill? How much goodwill does the business lose when a dissolving partner leaves the partnership? Is more goodwill lost when a partner dissolves wrongfully than when he dissolves nonwrongfully? Do partners expect wrongful dissolutions? Do the expectations of the partners provide a rationale to deny goodwill to a wrongfully dissolving partner?

PROBLEMS AND PROBLEM CASES

1. Jackson Wanlass and D. W. Ogden operated a title search business as partners at will. After Ogden and Wanlass died, the Ogden children excluded Mrs. Wanlass from the business and converted partnership funds. Mrs. Wanlass claimed that these actions amounted to a wrongful dissolution by the Ogden children. Was she correct?

2. Hilolani Acres Joint Venture was a partnership of 42 partners, including Benjamin Aiu. Four of the partners were designated managing partners. The partnership agreement stated that the purpose of the partnership was "dealing with" the Hilolani Acres, a housing development in Hawaii. The partnership agreement also provided for continuation of the business of the partnership in the event of a withdrawal of partners from the partnership. In 1971, three of the managing partners withdrew from the partnership; in addition, title to Hilolani Acres was transferred to Great Hawaiian Mortgage Corporation, which would manage the development of Hilolani Acres for the partnership; Great Hawaiian received 35 percent of the profits from Hilolani Acres, the remainder going to the partnership. The nonmanaging partners claimed that these acts dissolved the partnership, and they sought to wind it up. Were they right?

3. Robert Cowan was a partner in a six-person law firm. The partnership agreement provided that the firm would not dissolve upon the withdrawal of a partner. Cowan initially indicated that he would withdraw from the partnership but later changed his mind. By that time, however, the other partners had resolved to force Cowan from the partnership. The other partners transferred all partnership funds to accounts in their names only. However, a few days later, they set up an escrow account to protect the value of Cowan's partnership interest. Did the other partners' actions entitle Cowan to obtain a judicial dissolution of the partnership?

4. Kenneth Flynn and Rick Haddad were partners owning a beachfront lot with a small inn on it.

Title to the lot was in both partners' names. Flynn gave Haddad a deed to Flynn's interest in the property, which was effective only upon Flynn's nonpayment of a loan. When the inn was destroyed by fire, the partners began construction of a new inn, but construction was stopped because it violated local zoning laws. The effect of halting construction was also to eliminate the market of potential buyers of the property. Haddad decided to sever his relationship with Flynn and, consequently, filed the deed to the property that had earlier been executed by Flynn, although Flynn had already repaid the loan. Has the partnership been dissolved? Should the property be sold during winding up, or should Haddad receive title to it and be required to pay Flynn his share of the value of the property?

5. Roger Steeby and Charles Fial were the only partners of an auditing firm. They contracted to provide audit services for their clients, but instead of performing the audits themselves, they hired independent contractors to do the audits. Because Fial generated about 80 percent of the business of the firm, he became unhappy with their profit-sharing agreement and dissolved the partnership. Fial terminated the contracts with the firm's clients and signed the clients to contracts with Fial's corporation, Audit Consultants of Colorado, Inc. Fial's corporation used the same independent contractors to perform audits for the clients. Has Fial acted properly?

6. Brothers Eugene and Marlowe Mehl operated a family farm as a partnership. Each partner was active in the partnership until Marlowe suffered a stroke. Eleven years later, the partnership was dissolved, and Eugene by himself wound up the partnership's affairs. Was Eugene entitled to wages as compensation for winding up the partnership?

7. Ralph Neitzert and his brother were the only partners of Jolly Jug Liquors, a retail liquor store. The partners signed a contract to lease refrigeration equipment from Colo-Tex Leasing, Inc. A month later, Ralph sold his interest in the partnership to his sister. Ralph did not notify Colo-Tex that he sold his interest to his sister. A year later, when the partnership breached the lease, Colo-Tex sued Ralph, his brother, and his sister. Is Ralph liable to Colo-Tex?

8. Weintraub, Gold & Alper, a law firm partnership, was dissolved. The firm's partners continued to occupy the same office space and to use the

firm's name and letterhead as an aid in the partners' transition to individual law practices. Roger Allen sought a $60,000 loan from Royal Bank. Allen told Royal Bank that the $60,000 would be kept in an escrow account of his lawyers, the firm of Weintraub, Gold & Alper. Allen gave Royal Bank a letter on the law firm's stationery addressed to Allen and signed by Weintraub acknowledging that the money would be placed in a firm escrow account. Royal Bank discovered that Weintraub, Gold, and Alper were listed separately in a lawyer directory as practicing law at the address given on the firm stationery. Royal Bank also found the firm listing in the current New York phone book at the address and phone number on the letterhead. When Royal Bank dialed the number, the receptionist answered, "Weintraub, Gold and Alper." Royal Bank spoke with Weintraub, who confirmed the escrow arrangement. That same day, Royal Bank made the loan to Allen, giving him a check payable to the law firm. The check was deposited in the escrow account. When the loan was due, the escrowed check was not returned and the loan was not repaid. Royal Bank sued Gold and Alper to recover the $60,000. Were Gold and Alper liable to Royal Bank?

9. In 1980, Southern Distilleries, a partnership, executed two promissory notes totaling $140,000 payable to Commercial State Bank. In 1981, the partnership admitted Julius Moselely as a partner. He contributed $100,000 to the partnership. Two months later, Southern Distilleries executed a new promissory note to replace the old notes. The old notes were marked paid. The new note was in the amount of $140,000 payable to Commercial State Bank. The note was not paid when it was due, and the bank sued Southern Distilleries and its partners. What is the amount of Moselely's liability to the bank on the $140,000 note?

10. 📼 *Video Case.* See "The Partnership." Art retires from Alphabet Builders, a partnership with Ben and Diedre. Zack agrees to replace Art in the partnership. Zack signs an agreement with Art assuming Art's liability for all partnership obligations. After Art leaves the partnership, Alphabet Builders falls behind in payments to its creditors, including the following:

a. The bank from which Art obtained a loan in the name of the partnership prior to his leaving the partnership. Art pocketed the bank loan and used it for his personal investment in commodities futures. Art did not disclose the loan to his partners or to Zack.

b. The creditor who leases office equipment to Alphabet Builders. The lease agreement predates the time Art left the partnership.

c. Subcontractors owed money on contracts entered into after Art left and Zack entered the partnership.

What is Art's liability on these obligations? What is Zack's liability on these obligations? What other facts do you need to help you answer these questions?

11. Thomas Bernabei, James Serra, and Howard Wenger formed a partnership, Fairway Development I. In 1981, Bernabei and Serra ceased their involvement with Fairway Development I and transferred all their rights in the partnership to Wenger and James Valentine. Wenger and Valentine continued the business as partners, using the name Fairway Development II. Subsequently, Fairway II sought to enforce Fairway I's contract with Title Insurance Company of Minnesota (TICOM). TICOM argued that it was liable to Fairway I only and that Fairway I had been dissolved and terminated. Therefore, TICOM argued that Fairway II was a new partnership, was not a party to the contract, and could not sue TICOM. Was TICOM correct?

LIMITED PARTNERSHIPS AND LIMITED LIABILITY COMPANIES

While the taxation advantages of the partnership form of business may attract investors to a partnership, the partners' unlimited liability for partnership debts scares away some investors. State legislatures and the Internal Revenue Service have cooperated to permit the creation of two business forms that offer taxation advantages similar to the partnership, yet extend limited liability to the owners of the business. These forms are the limited partnership and the limited liability company.

LIMITED PARTNERSHIPS

The partnership form—with managerial control and unlimited liability for all partners—is not acceptable for all business arrangements. Often, business managers want an infusion of capital into a business yet are reluctant to surrender managerial control to those contributing capital. Investors wish to contribute capital to a business and share in its profits yet limit their liability to the amount of their investment and be relieved of the obligation to manage the business.

The **limited partnership** serves these needs. The limited partnership has two classes of owners: **general partners**, who contribute capital to the business, manage it, share in its profits, and possess unlimited liability for its obligations; and **limited partners**, who contribute capital and share profits, but possess no management powers and have liability limited to their investments in the business.

In 1822, New York and Connecticut were the first states to recognize the limited partnership. Today, every state has a statute permitting the creation of limited partnerships, although Louisiana calls them partnerships *in commendam.*

The Uniform Limited Partnership Acts

The National Conference of Commissioners on Uniform State Laws—a body of lawyers, judges, and legal scholars—drafted the Uniform Limited Partnership Act (ULPA) in 1916. In 1976, the commissioners drafted the Revised Uniform Limited Partnership Act (RULPA), which more clearly and

---

FIGURE 1 **Principal Characteristics of Limited Partnerships**

1. A limited partnership may be *created only in accordance with a statute.*
2. A limited partnership has two types of partners: *general partners* and *limited partners.* It must have one or more of each type.
3. All partners, limited and general, *share the profits* of the business.
4. Each general partner has *unlimited liability* for the obligations of the business. Each limited partner has liability *limited to his capital contribution* to the business.
5. Each general partner has a *right to manage* the business, and she is an agent of the limited partnership. A limited partner has *no right to manage* the business or to act as its agent, but he does have the right to vote on fundamental matters. If a limited partner does manage the business, he may incur unlimited liability for partnership obligations.
6. General partners, as agents, are *fiduciaries* of the business. Limited partners are not fiduciaries.
7. A partner's interest in a limited partnership *is not freely transferable.* An assignee of a general or limited partnership interest is not a partner, but is entitled only to the assigning partner's share of capital and profits, absent a contrary agreement.
8. Withdrawal of a general partner *dissolves* a limited partnership absent a contrary agreement of the partners. The withdrawal of a limited partner does not automatically dissolve a limited partnership.
9. A limited partnership *pays no federal income taxes.* Its partners report their shares of the profits and losses on their individual federal income tax returns. A limited partnership files an *information return* with the Internal Revenue Service, notifying the IRS of each partner's share of the year's profit or loss.

---

comprehensively states the law of limited partnership. The RULPA was amended in several significant ways in 1985. Forty-eight states have adopted the RULPA, Vermont follows the ULPA, and Louisiana follows neither. The RULPA as amended in 1985 forms the foundation of the discussion in this chapter. References are made to the Uniform Partnership Act (UPA), which applies to limited partnerships in the absence of an applicable provision in the RULPA. As shown in Figure 1, many characteristics of a limited partnership under the RULPA are similar to those of a partnership under the UPA.

Use of Limited Partnerships

The limited partnership form is used primarily in tax shelter ventures and activities such as real estate investment, oil and gas drilling, and professional sports. Limited partnerships operate as tax shelters by allowing partners to reduce their personal federal income tax liability by deducting limited partnership losses on their individual income tax returns. General partners, however, receive a greater tax shelter advantage than do limited partners. Losses of the business allocated to a general partner offset his income from any other sources. Losses of the business allocated to

limited partners may be used to offset only income from other *passive* investments. If a limited partner has sold her limited partnership interest or the limited partnership has terminated, her loss offsets any income.

CREATION OF LIMITED PARTNERSHIPS

A limited partnership may be created only by complying with the applicable state statute. Yet the statutory requirements of the RULPA are minimal. A **certificate of limited partnership** must be executed and filed with the secretary of state. The certificate must be signed by all general partners. A limited partnership begins its existence at the time the certificate is filed with the office of the secretary of state or at any later time specified in the certificate. Figure 2 (on page 807) lists the contents of the certificate of limited partnership.

The certificate is not required to state the names of the limited partners, the partners' capital contributions, the partners' shares of profits and other distributions, or the acts that cause a dissolution of the limited partnership. Nonetheless, the partners will usually include those and other matters in the certificate or in a separate **limited partnership agreement.**

FIGURE 2   Contents of Certificate of Limited Partnership

The following must be in the certificate:

1. The name of the limited partnership, which must contain the words *limited partnership*. The name may not include the surname of a limited partner, unless it is the same as the surname of a general partner or unless the business of the limited partnership has been carried on under that name prior to the admission of the limited partner.
2. The name and address of each general partner. Each general partner must sign the certificate.
3. The latest date the limited partnership will dissolve.
4. The name and address of an agent for service of process. Designating an agent for service of process in the certificate eases a creditor's obligation to notify a limited partnership that it is being sued by the creditor.

Any *person* may be a general or limited partner. Persons include a natural person, partnership, limited partnership, trust, estate, association, or corporation. Hence, as commonly occurs, a corporation may be the sole general partner of a limited partnership.

The RULPA permits partners to make capital contributions of cash, property, services rendered, a promissory note, or a binding promise to contribute cash, property, or services.

Defective Compliance with Limited Partnership Statute

The RULPA requires at least *substantial compliance* with the previously listed requirements to create a limited partnership. If the persons attempting to create a limited partnership do not substantially comply with the RULPA, a limited partnership does not exist; therefore, a limited partner may lose her limited liability and become liable as a general partner. A lack of substantial compliance might result from failing to file a certificate of limited partnership or from filing a defective certificate. A defective certificate might, for example, misstate the name of the limited partnership.

Infrequently, a person will believe that she is a limited partner but discover later that she has been designated a general partner or that the general partners have not filed a certificate of limited partnership. In such circumstances and others, she will be liable as a general partner unless she in good faith believes she is a limited partner and upon discovering she is not a limited partner she either:

1. Causes a proper certificate of limited partnership (or an amendment thereto) to be filed with the secretary of state, or
2. Withdraws from future equity participation in the firm by filing a certificate declaring such withdrawal with the secretary of state.

However, such a person remains liable as a general partner to third parties who previously believed in good faith that the person was a general partner.

A limited partnership must keep its filed certificate current. Current filings allow creditors to discover current facts, not merely those facts that existed when the original certificate was filed. For example, a certificate amendment must be filed when a new general partner is admitted or withdraws.

In the following case, the court considered the liability of new investors who believed they were limited partners although a limited partnership certificate had not been filed.

Briargate Condominium Assoc. v. Carpenter
976 F.2d 868 (4th Cir. 1992)

In 1984, Judith Carpenter invested in Briargate Homes, a business that purchased several condominium units in the Briargate Condominium complex. Although Carpenter believed that Briargate was a limited partnership and that she was a limited partner, in fact Briargate Homes was a partnership and she was a general partner. No attempt had been made to achieve actual or substantial compliance with the North Carolina limited partnership statute.

Carpenter never signed the partnership agreement or saw copies of the partnership's K-1 tax returns, which clearly identified her as a general partner. However, deductions for partnership losses that Carpenter claimed on her individual income tax returns were allowable only if she was a general partner. In early 1987, Carpenter or her attorneys had possession of documents explicitly stating that Briargate Homes was a general partnership and that her interest was one of a general partner. In June and December 1987, Carpenter received additional documents identifying Briargate Homes as a general partnership. Carpenter was an experienced business-woman, served on the board of directors of a bank, and had ready access to legal and other professional advice.

As an owner of condominiums, the partnership was liable to the Briargate Condominium Association for assessments for maintenance, repair, and replacement of common areas in the complex. In late 1987 and early 1988, the partnership failed to pay the Association assessed fees of $85,106. The Association sued the partnership and its partners.

On February 5, 1988, Carpenter notified the other partners and the Association that she was withdrawing from any equity participation and renouncing any interest in the profits of the partnership.

At the trial, Carpenter contended that because she believed she was a limited partner, she should not be liable to the Association for the fees. The district court found that because Carpenter had not promptly withdrawn from the partnership upon discovering she was a general partner, she was liable for the full amount of the debt. Carpenter appealed.

Hamilton, Circuit Judge Carpenter's defense is grounded in the Revised Uniform Partnership Act sec. 304, which provides:

(a) Except as provided in subsection (b), a person who makes a contribution to a business enterprise and errone-ously but in good faith believes that he has become a limited partner in the enterprise is not a general partner in the enterprise and is not bound by its obligations, . . . if, on ascertaining the mistake, he:

> **(1)** Causes an appropriate certificate of limited part-nership to be executed and filed; or
>
> **(2)** Withdraws from future equity participation in the enterprise.

(b) A person who makes a contribution of the kind described in subsection (a) is liable as a general partner to any third party who transacts business with the enterprise (i) before the person withdraws from the enterprise, or (ii) before the person gives notice to the partnership of his withdrawal from future equity participation, but only if the third party actually believed in good faith that the person was a general partner at the time of the transaction.

First, the person must have a good faith belief that he has become a limited partner. Second, the person must on ascertaining the mistake take one of two courses of action. He may file an appropriate certificate of limited partnership. Under this option, the person may continue in the business with limited liability. In the alternative, the person may give notice and withdraw completely from future equity participation in the business. If the two elements are met, then the person is liable *only* as a limited partner, effectively cutting off all personal liability of a general partner, unless subsection (b) applies.

Subsection (b) sets forth the *only* circumstances under which a person who meets the requirements of subsection (a) may incur liability like a general partner. Personal liability to third parties arises when the third party transacts business with the enterprise before the person files a proper certificate or withdraws. Imposition of liability is limited, however, by the requirement that at the time he transacts business, the third party actually believed in good faith that the person was a general partner at the time of the transaction. Reliance of the third party in the resources of the general partner is absolutely essential before liability may be imposed for transactions occurring before withdrawal.

Unlike its predecessor statute, RULPA sec. 304 does not specify how quickly a proper certificate or notice of withdrawal must be filed after a person ascertains he is not a limited partner. The current statute deletes the word "promptly" contained in the prior statute. The present statute also added the language in subsection (b) regarding reliance. This difference between the old and new statutes reflects a shift in emphasis away from the speed with which withdrawal is effected to an emphasis on protection of reliance by third parties. The key to liability is reliance by the third party on a person's apparent status as a general partner.

Given this interpretation of the statute, we believe the judgment of the district must be vacated, and the case remanded to the district court for additional findings. First, the district court must determine whether or not Carpenter held a good faith belief that she was a limited partner at the time she initially joined and contributed to the partnership. The district court did conclude that by at least mid-1986, Carpenter could not have held a good faith belief she was a limited partner, but the key date is the date of the contribution to the enterprise. Should the district court conclude that Carpenter did not have a good faith belief that she was a limited partner at the time of the initial contribution, then the statute affords her no relief.

Second, assuming Carpenter demonstates a good faith belief at the time she invested, then her notice of withdrawal effectively cut off liability for any fees accrued after such notice. To hold Carpenter liable for fees accrued prior to the notice, the district court must determine if and when the Association actually believed in good faith that Carpenter was a general partner. Carpenter may be held liable only for those assessments made in reliance on the belief that the Association could look to assets of Carpenter as a general partner to satisfy the debt.

Carpenter points to statements indicating that agents of the Association apparently believed they were dealing with a limited partnership and were totally unaware of Carpenter's interest in the partnership until the time of her notice withdrawing from any equity participation and renouncing any interest in the profits of the partnership. We decline, however, to rule on the issue. It does not appear that this issue received much attention at trial. The district court should, on remand, review the record and may take additional evidence if necessary to aid its fact-finding on this issue.

Judgment for the Association vacated; remanded to the district court.

Foreign Limited Partnerships

A limited partnership is **domestic** in the state in which it is organized; it is **foreign** in every other state. The RULPA makes it clear that the laws of the domestic state apply to the internal affairs of the limited partnership, allowing a limited partner protection regardless of where business is conducted.

Nonetheless, to be privileged to do business in a foreign state, a limited partnership must *register* to do business in that state. To register, a limited partnership must file an **application for registration** with the secretary of state of the foreign state. The application must include the name and address of the limited partnership, the names and addresses of the general partners, the name and address of an agent for service of process, and the address of the office where the names, addresses, and capital contributions of the limited partners are kept. The application must be accompanied by the payment of a fee. The secretary of state reviews the application and, if all requirements are met, issues a **certificate of registration.**

There are few penalties for failing to register as a foreign limited partnership. Although the RULPA does not impose fines for a failure to register, a few states have amended it to do so. In addition, an unregistered foreign limited partnership may not use the foreign state's courts to sue to enforce any right or contract. Once it registers, a limited partnership may use the state's courts, even when it sues to enforce a contract that was made before it registered.

Failure to register does not invalidate any contracts made in the foreign state or prevent a limited partnership from defending itself in a suit brought in the state's courts. The failure to register, by itself, does not make a limited partner liable as a general partner.

Rights and Liabilities of Partners in Limited Partnerships

The partners of a limited partnership have many rights and liabilities. Some are identical to those of partners in an ordinary partnership, but others are special to limited partnerships. Some are common to both general and limited partners, while others are not shared.

Rights and Liabilities Shared by General and Limited Partners

Capital Contributions   A partner is obligated to contribute as capital the cash, property, or other services that he promised to contribute. This obligation may be enforced by the limited partnership or by any of its creditors.

Share of Profits and Losses   Under the RULPA, profits and losses are shared on the basis of the value of each partner's capital contribution unless there is a written agreement to the contrary. For example, if 2 general partners contribute $1,000 each and 20 limited partners contribute $20,000 each, and the profit is $40,200, each general partner's share of the profits is $100 and each limited partner's share is $2,000.

Because most limited partnerships are tax shelters, partnership agreements often provide for limited partners to take all the losses of the business, up to the limit of their capital contributions.

Voting Rights   The partnership agreement may require that certain transactions be approved by general partners, by limited partners, or by all the partners. The agreement may give each general partner more votes than it grants limited partners, or vice versa. The RULPA makes it clear that limited partners have no inherent right to vote on any matter as a class. They may receive such a right only by agreement of the partners.

Admission of New Partners   No new partner may be admitted unless each partner has consented to the admission. New partners may be admitted by unanimous written consent of the partners or in accordance with the limited partnership agreement.

Partnership Interest   Each partner in a limited partnership owns a partnership interest. It is his personal property. He may sell or assign it to others, such as his personal creditors. Or his personal creditor may obtain a charging order against it. Generally, a buyer or assignee—or a creditor with a charging order—is entitled to receive only the partner's share of distributions.

Nonetheless, when the limited partnership agreement so provides or all the partners consent, a buyer or assignee of a limited or a general partnership interest may become a limited partner. The new limited partner then assumes all the rights and liabilities of a limited partner, except for liabilities unknown to her at the time she became a partner.

A partner's assignment of his partnership interest terminates his status as a partner. The assignment does not, however, relieve him of liability for illegal distributions or for false filings with the secretary of state. When a court grants a charging order to a creditor, however, the partner remains a partner.

Right to Withdraw   Partners in a limited partnership have the power to withdraw from the partnership and receive the fair value of their partnership interests. Fair value includes the going concern value of the partnership business, that is, its goodwill.

A general partner may withdraw from a limited partnership at any time; if a general partner's withdrawal breaches the limited partnership agreement, the value of her interest is reduced by the damages suffered by the limited partnership. A limited partner may withdraw after giving six months' prior notice to each general partner.

When a partner withdraws from a limited partnership, the partner may receive a return of his capital contribution. However, the return of capital may not impair the limited partnership's ability to pay its creditors. After the withdrawal of capital, the fair value of partnership assets must at least equal the limited partnership's liabilities to creditors.

Other Rights of General Partners

A general partner has the same right to manage and the same agency powers as a partner in an ordinary partnership. He has the express authority to act as the partners have agreed he should and the implied authority to do what is in the usual course of business. In addition, he may have apparent authority to bind the partnership to contracts when his implied authority is limited yet no notice of the limitation has been given to third parties.

A general partner has no right to compensation beyond his share of the profits, absent an agreement to the contrary. Since most limited partnerships are tax shelters that are designed to lose money during their early years of operation, most limited partnership agreements provide for the payment of salaries to general partners.

Other Liabilities of General Partners

A general partner has unlimited liability to creditors of his limited partnership. In addition, a general partner is in a position of trust when he manages the business, and therefore owes fiduciary duties to the limited partnership and the limited partners (e.g., he may not profit secretly from limited partnership transactions or compete with the limited partnership). The following case imposed fiduciary liability on a general partner for misusing partnership property.

In re The Monetary Group
2 F.3d 1098 (11th Cir. 1993)

The Securities Group (TSG), The Monetary Group (TMG), and The Securities Group 1980 (TSG80) were New York limited partnerships. The Securities Groups (Groups) was a New York *general* partnership whose general partners included TSG, TMG, and TSG80. Charles Barnett and Randall Atkins were general partners of TSG; they were limited partners of TMG. Barnett was also a limited partner of TSG80.

In need of office space, TSG entered negotiations to purchase the Hotel Nassau and the adjacent Olivetti Building at 500 Park Avenue in New York City from Olivetti Properties. Eventually, it was decided that a Kentucky limited partnership—500 Park Avenue Associates (Associates)—would purchase the buildings for $22 million and lease three floors of the Olivetti Building to Groups. Atkins was a limited partner in Associates, which Atkins helped form for the express purpose of buying the buildings.

Under the lease agreement, Associates received a $1 million cash rent security deposit and a $4 million damage deposit from Groups. The $4 million damage deposit comprised marketable securities. Associates immediately gave the $1 million cash to Olivetti as a down payment on the buildings. Associates financed the remainder of the purchase price with a mortgage loan from Manufacturers Hanover Trust Company. Security for the loan was the buildings and the $4 million in marketable securities that Associates received from Groups. When Manufacturers Hanover required an additional $2.8 million collateral, Groups gave Associates another $2.8 million in marketable securities, which Associates transferred to Manufacturers Hanover.

Immediately after completing its purchase of the buildings, Associates placed the buildings on the market. A year and a half later, Associates sold the buildings to Equitable Life Assurance Company for $54.5 million plus a share of Equitable's future profits from developments on the Hotel Nassau site. As part of the sale, Associates assigned its lease with Groups to Equitable.

After six years, TMS, TMG, TMS80, and Groups sought Chapter 11 bankruptcy protection. The court-appointed administrator for the partnerships sued Barnett and Atkins on behalf of the partnership, alleging that they had breached their fiduciary duty to the partnership. The bankruptcy court found Barnett and Atkins liable for all gains received by them from the sale of the property, almost $32 million. Barnett and Atkins appealed to the district court, which affirmed the bankruptcy court's decision. Barnett and Atkins then appealed to the court of appeals.

Per Curiam   A general partner in a limited partnership stands in a fiduciary relationship with the limited partners of that limited partnership. Atkins was general partner of TSG. Thus, Atkins owed a fiduciary duty to TSG's limited partners. Additionally, TSG was a general partner of Groups. Therefore, Atkins' fiduciary duty extended to Groups.

A limited partner is liable to the other limited partners of a partnership where that limited partner acts in concert with a general partner of that partnership in derogation of that general partner's fiduciary duty. Atkins was a limited partner of TMG. TSG and TMG were partners operating as Groups. Thus, if Atkins violated his duty to TSG as general partner by participating in diverting partnership assets, then Atkins can be said to have joined in the wrong against TMG thereby necessitating the finding that Atkins is liable to the other limited partners of TMG.

A partner breaches his fiduciary where that partner diverts for non-partnership purposes monies belonging to the partnership. Partners are liable to each other for such wrongfully appropriated partnership property.

Funds and other assets of TSG, TMG, TSG80, and Groups were misused, thus enabling Associates to purchase the buildings. Negotiations were initiated on TSG's behalf. Even after Associates assumed the role of purchaser, the deal depended on the use of Groups' assets. The security deposits were obviously tailored to meet Associates' needs.

Atkins contends that such a transaction constitutes a valid lease agreement and should not be characterized as a misappropriation of partnership property. This court, however, need not determine whether the dubious lease agreement is an indirect misappropriation of partnership property, because there is ample evidence of a direct misappropriation of partnership property. When Associates' lender required an additional $2.8 million in security, the malefactors simply transferred an additional $2.8 million from Groups to Associates as an additional security. The additional $2.8 million was not transferred pursuant to an agreement. Groups was under no contractual obligation to pay Associates an additional security. The transfer of an extra $2.8 million represented nothing more than a naked misuse of the partnerships' property for Associates' benefit. Thus, Associates directly misappropriated at least $2.8 million worth of the partnerships' securities.

We must next consider whether Atkins was guilty of any wrongdoing. Atkins actively participated in the purchase of the property and facilitated the transfer of the security deposit from Groups to Associates. Moreover, Atkins enjoyed a personal windfall from the transactions through his limited partnership interest in Associates. Atkins' conduct directly violated his fiduciary duty as a partner of TSG and TMG to refrain from personally profiting from the misuse of partnership assets.

The bankruptcy court found that Barnett was liable by virtue of his position as a general partner of TSG. An innocent general partner may be held liable to third parties for the wrongful conduct of a fellow partner even though that partner had no knowledge of the offending partners' action. No cases have applied this principle of partnership liability in other than the third-party context. At least one state court has held that an innocent general partner does not bear agency liability to limited partners for another general partner's misuse of partnership funds. We decline to extend this principle of agency liability to the interpartnership suit context. Potentially, such an extension would make all innocent general partners in a partnership liable to each other for the secret misappropriation of partnership funds by one general partner. The bankruptcy court erred by imposing such liability on Barnett.

Judgment affirmed in favor of TMG against Atkins; judgment reversed in favor of Barnett.

Other Rights of Limited Partners

Limited partners have the right to be informed about partnership affairs. The RULPA obligates the general partners to provide financial information and tax returns to the limited partners on demand. In addition, a limited partner may inspect and copy a list of the partners, information concerning contributions by partners, the certificate of limited partnership, tax returns, and partnership agreements.

A limited partner may sue to enforce a limited partnership right of action against a person who has harmed the limited partnership. This right of action is called a **derivative suit** or a derivative action because it derives from the limited partnership. Any recovery obtained by the limited partner goes to the limited partnership, since it is the entity that was harmed. In addition, when a limited partnership is sued and the general partners fail to assert a defense, a limited partner may appear on behalf of the limited partnership and assert the defense.

Other Liabilities of Limited Partners

Once a limited partner has contributed all of his promised capital contribution, generally he has no further liability for partnership losses or obligations. In return for limited liability, however, a limited partner gives up the right to participate in the management of a limited partnership. When a limited partner engages in management activities, he may lose his limited liability.

Limited Partner Engaged in Management

A limited partner who participates in the control of the business may be liable to creditors of the limited partnership. Under the RULPA, a limited partner who participates in control is liable only to those persons who transact with the limited partnership reasonably believing, based on the limited partner's conduct, that the limited partner is a general partner. Thus, three elements must be met in order for a limited partner to be liable as a general partner due to his participation in management:

1. The limited partner must participate in the control of the limited partnership.
2. That participation must lead a person to believe reasonably that the limited partner is a general partner.
3. That person must transact with the limited partnership while holding that belief.

For example, Larry Link is a limited partner whom the general partners have allowed to make management decisions. A creditor of the partnership observes Link's management of the partnership, with the result that the creditor extends $10,000 credit to the limited partnership believing that Link is a general partner. Link is liable on the $10,000 debt to the creditor.

It is sometimes difficult to determine whether a limited partner's acts amount to control of the limited partnership. Control is best defined as participation in the firm's day-to-day management decisions as contrasted with isolated involvement with major decisions. For example, a limited

1. Being *an agent, an employee,* or *a contractor* for the limited partnership or a general partner; or being an officer, director, or shareholder of a general partner that is a corporation.
2. Being a *consultant* or *adviser* to a general partner.
3. Acting as a *surety* for the limited partnership or guaranteeing or assuming specific obligations of the limited partnership. However, a limited partner who specifically assumes liability on a partnership obligation is liable on that obligation.
4. Pursuing a derivative suit on behalf of the limited partnership.
5. Requesting or attending a meeting of partners.
6. Proposing or voting on such partnership matters as dissolution, sale of substantially all the assets, changes in the nature of the business, admissions and removals of general or limited partners, and amendments to the partnership agreement.
7. Winding up the limited partnership as permitted by the RULPA.

partner of a real estate investment partnership participates in control if she regularly decides which real estate the limited partnership should purchase. A limited partner who only once vetoed a loan agreement with a bank is not participating in control.

The RULPA lists the kinds of management activities that limited partners may perform without becoming personally liable for partnership debts. Therefore, a limited partner may perform these acts and still retain his limited liability. The list of such activities appears in Figure 3.

For most well-planned limited partnerships, the general partner is a corporation. Usually, the only shareholders, directors, and officers of the corporate general partner are the individuals who manage the limited partnership. Sometimes, these individuals are limited partners as well. These individuals will not have the liability of a general partner, because the RULPA permits limited partners to be officers, directors, or shareholders of a general partner (see item 1 of Figure 3).

In the following case, the court held that a limited partner had not exercised sufficient control over the limited partnership to render the limited partner liable as a general partner.

ALZADO V. BLINDER, ROBINSON & CO.
752 P.2d 544 (Colo. Sup. Ct. 1988)

In 1979, Blinder, Robinson & Co. as limited partner and Combat Promotions, Inc., as general partner created Combat Associates to promote an eight-round exhibition boxing match between Muhammad Ali and Lyle Alzado, the pro football player. Combat Promotions was owned entirely by Alzado, his accountant, and his professional agent. Alzado was also vice president of Combat Promotions. Combat Associates agreed to pay Alzado $100,000 for his participation in the match.

Few tickets were sold, and the match proved to be a financial debacle. Alzado received no payments for participating in the boxing match. Alzado sued Blinder, Robinson, claiming that because of its conduct, Blinder, Robinson must be deemed a general partner of Combat Associates and, therefore, liable to Alzado under the agreement between Alzado and the limited partnership for Alzado's participation in the match. The trial court agreed with Alzado, but Blinder, Robinson appealed to the court of appeals, which held that Blinder, Robinson had no liability to Alzado. Alzado appealed to the Supreme Court of Colorado.

Kirshbaum, Justice   A limited partner may become liable to partnership creditors as a general partner if the limited partner assumes control of partnership business. RULPA Section 303 provides that a limited partner does not participate in the control of partnership business solely by doing one or more of the following:

(a) Being a contractor for or an agent or employee of the limited partnership or of a general partner;

(b) Being an officer, director, or shareholder of a corporate general partner;

(c) Consulting with and advising a general partner with respect to the business of the limited partnership . . . .

Any determination of whether a limited partner's conduct amounts to control over the business affairs of the partnership must be determined by consideration of several factors, including the purpose of the partnership, the administrative activities undertaken, the manner in which the entity actually functioned, and the nature and frequency of the limited partner's purported activities.

The record here reflects that Blinder, Robinson used its Denver office as a ticket outlet, gave two parties to promote the exhibition match, and pro-

vided a meeting room for many of Combat Associates' meetings. Meyer Blinder, president of Blinder, Robinson, personally appeared on a television talk show and gave television interviews to promote the match. Blinder, Robinson made no investment, accounting or other financial decisions for the partnership; all such fiscal decisions were made by officers or employees of Combat Promotions, the general partner. The evidence established at most that Blinder, Robinson engaged in a few promotional activities. It does not establish that it took part in the management or control of the business affairs of the partnership.

Alzado finally asserts that Blinder, Robinson fostered the appearance of being in control of Combat Associates, that such actions rendered Blinder, Robinson liable as a general partner and that this conduct allowed third parties to believe that Blinder, Robinson was in fact a general partner. The evidence does not support this argument. Certainly, as Vice President of Combat Promotions, Alzado had no misconception concerning the function and role of Blinder, Robinson as a limited partner only.

Judgment for Blinder, Robinson affirmed.

Limited Partner's Name in Firm Name   Including a limited partner's *surname* in the name of a limited partnership may mislead a creditor to be-

lieve that a limited partner is a general partner. Under the RULPA, a limited partner who *knowingly* permits her name to be included in the firm name is liable to creditors who have *no actual knowledge* that she is a limited partner, unless a general partner has the same surname as that of the limited partner or the business of the limited partnership was conducted under that name prior to the limited partner's admission to the limited partnership.

DISSOLUTION AND WINDING UP OF A LIMITED PARTNERSHIP

Dissolution

A limited partnership may be dissolved and its affairs wound up. There are five causes of dissolution:

1. Expiration of the term specified in the certificate of limited partnership. For example, the certificate may provide that a limited partnership has a 20-year term.

2. Upon the happening of events specified in writing in the partnership agreement. For example, a written partnership agreement may provide for dissolution of a limited partnership after it has accomplished its objective of building a shopping mall.

3. By the written consent of all the partners.

4. Upon the withdrawal of a *general* partner, with few exceptions. Such a withdrawal includes retirement, death, bankruptcy, assignment of a general partnership interest, removal by the other partners, and adjudicated insanity. For a general partner that is not a natural person, such as a partnership or a corporation, its own dissolution is a withdrawal causing a dissolution of the limited partnership. The RULPA specifically permits a limited partnership to avoid dissolution after the withdrawal of a general partner if a written partnership agreement permits the business to be conducted by the remaining general partners or if all of the partners agree in writing to continue the business.

5. By court order, when it is *not reasonably practicable* to carry on the business in conformity with the limited partnership agreement. Judicial dissolution has frequently been granted when general partners continually violate their fiduciary duties, such as by secretly profiting from self-dealing with the limited partnership.

The RULPA requires a limited partnership to file a **certificate of cancellation** upon its dissolution and the commencement of winding up. The certificate of cancellation cancels the certificate of limited partnership. However, the failure to file a certificate of cancellation does not prevent a dissolution.

Winding Up

Winding up is the orderly liquidation of the limited partnership's assets and payment of the proceeds to creditors and other claimants. Dissolution requires the winding up of a limited partnership's affairs. The only way to prevent winding up is to prevent dissolution, such as by an agreement of the partners that an event shall not cause a dissolution.

General partners who have *not wrongfully dissolved* a limited partnership may perform the winding up. Wrongful dissolution includes a dissolution in violation of the limited partnership agreement or wrongful conduct that leads to a judicial dissolution, such as a general partner's breach of his fiduciary duties. Limited partners may wind up if there are no surviving general partners. In addition, any partner may *ask a court* to perform a winding up.

The winding up partner has express authority to act as the partners have agreed he should act. More importantly, he has the implied authority to do those acts that are reasonably necessary to liquidate the assets. He possesses the apparent authority to do all of the acts that he was able to do before dissolution, unless appropriate notice is given to persons who dealt with the partnership or knew of its existence.

Distribution of Assets   After the assets have been sold during winding up, the proceeds of the sale of assets are distributed to those persons having claims against the limited partnership. Figure 4 (see page 816) states the RULPA rule for distribution of limited partnership assets.

Continuation of the Business   Usually, the assets of a limited partnership are sold individually during winding up. However, all the assets of the business of the limited partnership could be sold to someone who desires to continue the business. For example, some of the partners may wish to continue the business despite dissolution. The continuing partners are required to pay the outgoing partners the fair value of their partnership interests, including goodwill.

Events Not Causing Dissolution   The death, bankruptcy, insanity, or withdrawal of a *limited* partner does not result in dissolution unless the certificate of limited partnership compels dissolution. Also, the *addition* of a partner—general or limited—does not cause a dissolution.

1. To firm *creditors,* including partners who are creditors, except for unpaid distributions to partners.
2. To partners for *unpaid distributions,* including the return of capital to previously withdrawn partners.
3. To partners to the extent of their *capital contributions.*
4. To partners in the proportion in which they share distributions. Hence, the partners share the proceeds that remain after all other claimants have been paid.

Between partners, the order of distribution may be changed by a partnership agreement. For example, a limited partnership agreement may combine priorities (2) and (3) to provide that unpaid distributions to partners shall be paid at the same time capital contributions are returned. However, the priority of creditors may not be harmed by a partner's agreement, such as an agreement to pay creditors *after* partners have received the return of their capital.

LIMITED LIABILITY COMPANIES

The limited liability company (LLC) is the product of attempts by state legislators to create a new business organization that combines the nontax advantages of the corporation and the favorable tax status of the partnership. Wyoming, in 1977, passed the first LLC statute. Florida followed in 1982. In 1988, the Internal Revenue Service ruled that a Wyoming LLC would be recognized as a partnership for federal income tax purposes. As a result, the LLC pays no federal income tax. Instead, all income and losses of the LLC are reported by the LLC's owners on their individual income tax returns. Typically, the LLC is a tax shelter for wealthy investors, allowing such investors to reduce their taxable income by deducting LLC losses on their federal income tax returns. Thirty-six states have adopted LLC laws, and it is expected that by 1995 nearly every state will have such a law.

Formation of LLCs

To create an LLC, two or more persons must file **articles of organization** with the secretary of state. The articles must include the name of the LLC, its duration, and the name and address of its registered agent. The name of the LLC must include the words "limited liability company" or some other words indicating that the liability of its owners is limited.

Although not required, an LLC will typically have an **operating agreement**, which is an agreement of the owners as to how the LLC will be operated.

Many states also require an LLC to file an annual report with the secretary of state. The annual report may include financial information such as the capital accounts of the owners and the LLC's balance sheet.

Owners of LLCs

Owners of LLCs are called **members.** Most statutes require an LLC to have at least two members at all times, although there is no maximum limit on members. An individual, partnership, corporation, and even another LLC may be a member of an LLC.

A member has no personal liability for LLC obligations. A member must, however, make capital contributions to the LLC as she has agreed.

LLC statutes restrict the members' ability to sell their interests in the LLC. An LLC interest is the personal property of the member and may be transferred as stated in the operating agreement; however, the transferee has no right to become a member or participate in management unless the other members consent to the transfer. The transferee who does not become a member is entitled only to the transferring member's share of profits.

A member is entitled to withdraw from the LLC and receive either the value of his interest or a return of his capital contribution. Such a distribution of assets to a member may be executed only if the LLC's assets exceed its liabilities after the distribution.

LLC as an Entity

The LLC is technically a corporation. Like any corporation, it is an entity separate from its owners. It may sue and be sued in its own name. It can buy, hold, and sell property. It can make contracts and incur liabilities.

Because the LLC is an entity liable for its own obligations, the members have no individual liability on LLC obligations. However, a court will pierce the veil between the LLC and its members and impose personal liability on the members when the LLC is used to defraud creditors. For example, suppose the members provide very little capital to an LLC that is engaging in a highly risky business. As a result, the business is unsuccessful and unable to pay its creditors. A court will likely require the members to pay the obligations of the business.

Management of LLCs

Members of an LLC share management power in proportion to their capital contributions to the LLC. If there is no member vote restricting the actual authority of a member, however, members have considerable implied and apparent authority to bind the LLC on transactions in the ordinary course of business.

The members may agree to entrust management to managers selected by the members. Managers of an LLC are comparable to directors of a corporation.

The members or managers who manage the LLC are fiduciaries of the LLC. They must manage the LLC in the best interest of the LLC and not prefer their individual interests over the interests of the LLC.

Dissolution of LLCs

An LLC must be easily dissolved to obtain partnership tax treatment under the Internal Revenue Code. Dissolution is caused by the death, retirement, bankruptcy, or dissolution of any member. However, the remaining members may avoid liquidation by *unanimously* agreeing to continue the business. Under most statutes, an LLC's term cannot exceed 30 years.

ETHICAL AND PUBLIC POLICY CONCERNS

1. Is it fair that a limited partner has limited liability for the obligations of a limited partnership? Is it fair that a general partner has unlimited liability while a limited partner has limited liability?

2. Limited partners have a limited right to deduct limited partnership losses on their individual federal income tax returns, while general partners are not restricted. Is this fair? Are the general partners' investments or activities more socially desirable than the limited partners' investments or activities?

3. By having a corporation as the sole general partner of a limited partnership, no human will have unlimited liability for the obligations of the limited partnership. Is this fair? Does this produce a socially desirable result?

4. Do you think limited partners should be allowed to participate in the control of a limited partnership and retain their limited liability?

PROBLEMS AND PROBLEM CASES

1. In 1979, Jeffrey Shaughnessy organized a limited partnership, Capital City Investments. The partnership agreement listed Shaughnessy as the sole general partner. Shaughnessy signed the agreement. The limited partners were listed in the agreement but none signed it. No certificate of limited partnership was filed in the county recorder's office, where recording was required. Has a limited partnership been created?

2. Brookwood Fund was a limited partnership formed to trade investment securities. The original certificate of limited partnership filed in April 1987 listed Kenneth Stein as the "General Partner" and Barbara Stein as the "Original Limited Partner." Between May and August 1987, additional limited partners were added to Brookwood. The new limited partners did not participate in the management of Brookwood. However, an amended certificate of limited partnership reflecting the new limited partners was not filed. What should the new limited partners do to protect themselves from having the liability of general partners?

3. Virginia Partners, Ltd., a limited partnership organized in Florida, was in the business of drilling oil wells. When Virginia Partners injected acid into an oil well in Kentucky, a bystander, Robert Day, was injured by acid that sprayed on him from a ruptured hose. Virginia Partners had failed to register as a foreign limited partnership in Kentucky. Are the limited partners of Virginia Partners liable to Day for his injuries?

4. Palmetto Federal Savings & Loan Association made real estate loans to Beacon Reef Limited Partnership. When Beacon Reef defaulted on the loans, Palmetto Federal sued Beacon Reef. Beacon Reef's general partners decided not to raise the defense that Palmetto Federal charged a usurious rate on the loan. May Howard Wulsin, the only limited partner, on behalf of Beacon Reef, assert the defense of usury against Palmetto Federal?

5. Cornel Peleo was a general partner of Livonia Associates, a limited partnership. On December 3, 1971, Peleo and his wife purchased land for $9,000. On April 15, 1972, they sold the land to Livonia Associates for $18,000. Peleo told one limited partner that he had an interest in the property, but he did not tell him the amount. Has Peleo breached a fiduciary duty?

6. Paul Linnane was the sole general partner and Richard Stover was the sole limited partner of Linnane Magnavox Home Entertainment Center, a limited partnership. Stover possessed no power to manage daily partnership affairs and took no part in any partnership business. Linnane negotiated with General Electric Credit Corporation (GE Credit) to obtain financing for Linnane Magnavox. Two written contracts were executed and signed by GE Credit, Linnane, and Stover. Stover signed one contract, "by Richard Stover (Officer, Partner, Owner)." He signed the other contract, "by Richard Stover (V. Pres., Secy., Treas., Partner)." GE Credit would not have extended financing to Linnane Magnavox had Stover not signed the contracts. GE Credit was not aware of the limited partnership agreement between Linnane and Stover, although it was aware that Stover was a silent partner of Linnane. Stover signed the contracts at the request of Linnane, intended the signatures to be only in the capacity of limited partner, but did not communicate that intention to GE Credit. Is Stover liable on the contracts with GE Credit?

7. The Securities Group 1980, a limited partnership, was created to provide tax deferral advantages for its limited partners. To offset a potential adverse tax consequence when the tax laws changed, the general partners arranged a sale of the limited partnership interests to a new partnership owned by the Securities Group's general partners. The limited partners received cash and promissory notes worth 105 percent of the net asset value of Securities Group. At that time, Securities Group was indebted to various creditors. The new partnership subsequently became insolvent, with the result that the Securities Group creditors were unpaid. Are the Securities Group creditors able to collect from the former limited partners of Securities Group?

8. OKC Corporation adopted a plan to become a limited partnership. Under the plan, the shareholders became limited partners in OKC Limited Partnership. They did not receive actual possession of their limited partnership interests. Instead, the limited partnership interests were deposited in MBank of Dallas, which then issued depositary receipts to the limited partners. The depositary receipts were traded on the Pacific Stock Exchange. Some of the limited partners sold their depositary receipts to other investors. In 1987, a committee of receipt holders attempted to replace the general partners, an action within the powers of the limited partners under the limited partnership agreement. The general partners opposed the action and claimed that only the original limited partners who were still receipt holders could vote to replace the general partners. Were the general partners correct?

9. Excel Associates was a New York limited partnership. Lipkin was Excel's only individual general partner. Tribute Music Inc. was the only other general partner. Chalpin, the only limited partner, was also the president and sole shareholder and director of Tribute Music. Chalpin hired Bernabe Gonzales to be the superintendent of Excel's apartment building in Long Beach, Long Island, New York. Later, Chalpin hired Gonzales to renovate the building. Chalpin signed all Excel's checks paying Gonzalez. Chalpin did not name Tribute Music on the checks or indicate that he was signing in a representative capacity. Chalpin terminated Gonzales's employment with Excel. Gonzales sued Excel for breach of an employment contract. Gonzales also claimed that Chalpin was liable on the breached contract. On what grounds did Gonzales base his argument for Chalpin's liability?

10. Canal East Company was a limited partnership formed to operate a commercial real estate project known as Packett's Landing. John Flowers was the sole general partner. Scott Arrington, William May, and Robert Klimasewski were the only limited partners. Fishers Development Company was another partnership in which Arrington, May, and Klimasewski were the only limited partners. Fishers Development bought restaurant equipment and leased it to a restaurant-tenant at Packett's Landing. Flowers and Arrington were guarantors of the lease obligation to Fishers Development. When the restaurant-tenant became bankrupt, Flowers and Arrington obtained possession of the equipment pursuant to an assignment from the restaurant-tenant. They assigned the equipment lease to Canal East, which agreed to assume Flowers and Arrington's guaranty of the lease and to indemnify them from their liabilities under the lease or guaranty. Flowers and Arrington signed the agreement as assignors. In addition, Flowers signed the agreement as the general partner of Canal East, the assignee. May and Klimasewski sought judicial dissolution of the limited partnership, claiming that Flowers and Arrington breached fiduciary duties. Will the court order dissolution?

CORPORATIONS

History

and Nature

of Corporations

INTRODUCTION

The modern corporation has facilitated the rapid economic development of the last 150 years by permitting businesses to attain economies of scale. Businesses organized as corporations can attain such economies because they have a greater capacity to raise capital than do other business forms. This capital-raising advantage is ensured by corporation law, which allows persons to invest their money in a corporation and become owners without imposing unlimited liability or management responsibilities on themselves. Many people are willing to invest their savings in a large, risky business if they have limited liability and no management responsibilities. Far fewer are willing to invest in a partnership or other business form in which owners have unlimited liability and management duties.

History of Corporations

Although modern corporation law emerged only in the last 150 years, ancestors of the modern corporation existed in the times of Hammurabi, ancient Greece, and the Roman Empire. As early as 1248 in France, privileges of incorporation were given to mercantile ventures to encourage investment for the benefit of society. In England, the corporate form was used extensively before the 16th century.

The famous British trading companies—such as the Massachusetts Bay Company—were the forerunners of the modern corporation. The British government gave these companies monopolies in trade and granted them powers to govern in the areas they colonized. They were permitted to operate as corporations due to the benefits they would confer on the British empire, such as the development of natural resources. Although these trading companies were among the few corporations of the time whose owners were granted limited liability, they sought corporate status primarily because the government granted them monopolies and governmental powers.

American Corporation Law

Beginning in 1776, corporation law in the United States evolved independently of English corporation law. Early American corporations received **special charters** from state legislatures. These charters

FIGURE 1 **Principal Characteristics of Corporations**

1. **Creation.** A corporation may be created only by **permission of a government.**

2. **Legal status.** A corporation is a legal person and a legal entity independent of its owners (**shareholders**) and its managers (officers and the **board of directors**). Its life is unaffected by the retirement or death of its shareholders, officers, and directors. A corporation is a person under the Constitution of the United States.

3. **Powers.** A corporation may **acquire, hold, and convey property** in its own name. A corporation may **sue and be sued** in its own name. Harm to a corporation is not harm to the shareholders; therefore, with few exceptions, a shareholder may not sue to enforce a claim of the corporation.

4. **Management.** Shareholders elect a board of directors, which manages the corporation. The board of directors may delegate management duties to officers. A shareholder has **no right or duty to manage** the business of a corporation, unless he is elected to the board of directors or is appointed an officer. The directors and officers need not be shareholders.

5. **Owners' liability.** The shareholders have **limited liability.** With few exceptions, they are not liable for the debts of a corporation after they have paid their promised capital contributions to the corporation.

6. **Transferability of owner's interest.** Generally, the ownership interest in a corporation is **freely transferable.** A shareholder may sell her shares to whomever she wants whenever she wants. The purchaser becomes a shareholder with the same rights that the seller had.

7. **Taxation.** A corporation pays **federal income taxes** on its income. Shareholders have personal income from the corporation only when the corporation makes a distribution of its income to them. For example, a shareholder would have personal income from the corporation when the corporation pays him a dividend. This creates a **double-taxation** possibility: The corporation pays income tax on its profits, and when the corporation distributes the after-tax profits as dividends, the shareholders pay tax on the dividends.

were granted one at a time by special action of the legislatures; few special charters were granted.

In the late 18th century, general incorporation statutes emerged in the United States. Initially, these statutes permitted incorporation only for limited purposes beneficial to the public, such as operating toll bridges and water systems. Incorporation was still viewed as a privilege, and many restrictions were placed on corporations: incorporation was permitted for only short periods of time; maximum limits on capitalization were low; ownership of real and personal property was often restricted.

During the last 150 years, such restrictive provisions have disappeared in most states. Today, modern incorporation statutes are mostly enabling, granting the persons who control a corporation great flexibility in establishing, financing, and operating it.

See Figure 1 for a statement of the characteristics of corporations.

Classifications of Corporations

Corporations may be divided into three classes: (1) corporations **for profit,** (2) corporations **not for** **profit,** and (3) **government-owned** corporations. State corporation statutes establish procedures for the incorporation of each of these classes and for their operation. In addition, a large body of common law applies to all corporations.

Most business corporations are **for-profit corporations.** For-profit corporations issue stock to their shareholders, who invest in the corporation with the expectation that they will earn a profit on their investment. That profit may take the form of dividends paid by the corporation or increased market value of their shares.

Nearly all for-profit corporations are incorporated under the **general incorporation law** of a state. All of the states require professionals who wish to incorporate, such as physicians, dentists, lawyers, and accountants, to incorporate under **professional corporation acts.** In addition, for-profit corporations that especially affect the public interest, such as banks, insurance companies, and savings and loan associations, are usually required to incorporate under special statutes.

For-profit corporations range from huge international organizations such as General Motors

Corporation to small, one-owner businesses. GM is an example of a **publicly held corporation** because its shares are generally available to public investors. The publicly held corporation tends to be managed by professional managers who own small percentages of the corporation. Nearly all the shareholders of the typical publicly held corporation are merely investors who are not concerned in the management of the corporation.

Corporations with very few shareholders whose shares are not available to the general public are called **close corporations.** In the typical close corporation, the controlling shareholders are the only managers of the business.

Usually, close corporations and publicly held corporations are subject to the same rules under state corporation law. Many states, however, allow close corporations greater latitude in the operation of their internal affairs than is granted to public corporations. For example, the shareholders of a close corporation may be permitted to dispense with the board of directors and manage the close corporation as if it were a partnership.

A Subchapter S corporation, or **S Corporation,** is a special type of close corporation. It is treated nearly like a partnership for federal tax purposes. Its shareholders report the earnings or losses of the business on their individual federal income tax returns. This means that an S Corporation's profits are taxed only once—at the shareholder level. Thus, electing S Corporation status eliminates the double-taxation penalty of incorporation. An S Corporation election is made by complying with Internal Revenue Code requirements, including the requirement that it have no more than 35 shareholders.

Not-for-profit corporations do not issue stock and do not expect to make a profit. Instead, they provide services to their members under a plan that eliminates any profit motive. These corporations have **members** rather than shareholders, and none of the surplus revenue from their operations may be distributed to their members. Since they generally pay no income tax, nonprofit corporations can reinvest a larger share of their incomes in the business than can for-profit corporations. Examples of nonprofit corporations are charities, churches, fraternal organizations, community arts councils, cooperative grocery stores, and cooperative farmers' feed and supplies stores.

Some corporations are owned by governments and perform governmental and business functions. A municipality (city) is one type of **government-owned corporation.** Other types are created to furnish more specific services—for example, school corporations and water companies. Others—such as the Tennessee Valley Authority and the Federal Deposit Insurance Corporation—operate much like for-profit corporations except that at least some of their directors are appointed by governmental officials, and some or all of their financing frequently comes from government. The TVA and the FDIC are chartered by Congress, but government-owned corporations may also be authorized by states. Government-operated businesses seek corporate status to free themselves from governmental operating procedures, which are more cumbersome than business operating procedures.

REGULATION OF FOR–PROFIT CORPORATIONS

To become a corporation, a business must **incorporate** by complying with an incorporation statute. Incorporation is a fairly simple process usually requiring little more than paying a fee and filing a document with a designated government official—usually the secretary of state of the state of incorporation. Incorporation of for-profit businesses has been entrusted primarily to the governments of the 50 states.

State Incorporation Statutes

State incorporation statutes set out the basic rules regarding the relationship between the corporation, its shareholders, and its managers. For example, an incorporation statute sets the requirements for a business to incorporate, the procedures for shareholders' election of directors, and the duties directors and officers owe to the corporation. Although a corporation may do business in several states, usually the relationship between the corporation, its shareholders, and its managers is regulated only by the state of incorporation.

The American Bar Association's Committee on Corporate Laws has prepared a *model* statute for adoption by state legislatures. The purpose of the model statute is to improve the rationality of corporation law. It is called the **Model Business Corporation Act (MBCA).** The MBCA has been amended many times, and it was completely revised in 1984.

The revised MBCA is the basis of corporation law in most states. Your study of statutory corporation law in this book concentrates on the revised MBCA. Delaware and several other major commercial and industrial states such as New York and California do not follow the MBCA. Therefore, selected provisions of the Delaware and other acts will be addressed.

Several states have special provisions or statutes that are applicable only to close corporations. The ABA's Committee on Corporate Laws has adopted the *Statutory Close Corporation Supplement to the Model Business Corporation Act.* The Supplement is designed to provide a rational, statutory solution to the special problems facing close corporations.

State Common Law of Corporations

Although nearly all of corporation law is statutory law, including the courts' interpretation of the statutes, there is a substantial body of common law of corporations (judge-made law). Most of this common law deals with creditor and shareholder rights. For example, the law of piercing the corporate veil, which you will study later in this chapter, is common law protecting creditors of corporations.

REGULATION OF FOREIGN CORPORATIONS

A corporation may be incorporated in one state yet do business in many other states in which it is not incorporated. The corporation's contacts with other persons in those states may permit the states to regulate the corporation's transactions with their citizens, to subject the corporation to suits in their courts, or to tax the corporation. The circumstances under which states may impose their laws on a business incorporated in another state is determined by the law of foreign corporations.

A corporation is a **domestic corporation** in the state that has granted its charter; it is a **foreign corporation** in all the other states in which it does business. For example, a corporation organized in Delaware and doing business in Florida is domestic in Delaware and foreign in Florida. Note that a corporation domiciled in one country is an **alien corporation** in other countries in which it does business. Many of the rules that apply to foreign corporations apply as well to alien corporations.

Generally, a state may impose its laws on a foreign corporation if such imposition does not violate the Constitution of the United States, notably the Due Process Clause of the Fourteenth Amendment and the Commerce Clause.

Due Process Clause

The Due Process Clause requires that a foreign corporation have sufficient contacts with a state before a state may exercise jurisdiction over the corporation. The leading case in this area is the *International Shoe* case.[1] In that case, the Supreme Court ruled that a foreign corporation must have "certain minimum contacts" with the state such that asserting jurisdiction over the corporation does not offend "traditional notions of fair play and substantial justice." The Supreme Court justified its holding with a **benefit theory**: When a foreign corporation avails itself of the protection of a state's laws, it should suffer any reasonable burden that the state imposes as a consequence of such benefit. In other words, a foreign corporation should be required to pay for the benefits that it receives from the state.

Commerce Clause

Under the Commerce Clause, the power to regulate interstate commerce is given to the federal government. The states have no power to exclude or to discriminate against foreign corporations that are engaged solely in *interstate* commerce. Nevertheless, a state may require a foreign corporation doing interstate business in the state to comply with its laws if the application of these laws does not unduly burden interstate commerce. When a foreign corporation enters interstate commerce to do *intrastate* business in a state, the state may regulate the corporation's activities, provided again that the regulation does not unduly burden interstate commerce.

---

[1]*International Shoe Co. v. State of Washington*, 326 U.S. 310 (1945).

A state statute does not unduly burden interstate commerce if (1) the statute serves a legitimate state interest, (2) the state has chosen the least burdensome means of promoting that interest, and (3) that legitimate state interest outweighs the statute's burden on interstate commerce. Because conducting intrastate business increases a corporation's contact with a state, it is easier to prove that the state has a legitimate interest and that there is no undue burden on interstate commerce when the corporation is conducting intrastate business.

Doing Business   To aid their determination of whether a state may constitutionally impose its laws on a foreign corporation, courts have traditionally used the concept of **doing business.** Courts have generally held that a foreign corporation is subject to the laws of a state when it is doing business in the state. The activities that constitute doing business differ, however, depending on the purpose of the determination. There are four such purposes: (1) to determine whether a corporation is subject to a lawsuit in a state's courts, (2) to determine whether the corporation's activities are subject to taxation, (3) to determine whether the corporation must qualify to carry on its activities in the state, and (4) to determine whether the state may regulate the internal affairs of the corporation.

Subjecting Foreign Corporations to Suit

The Supreme Court of the United States has held that a foreign corporation may be brought into a state's court in connection with its activities within the state, provided that the state does not violate the corporation's due process rights under the Fourteenth Amendment of the Constitution and its rights under the Commerce Clause.

The *International Shoe* minimum contacts test must be met. Subjecting the corporation to suit cannot offend "traditional notions of fair play and substantial justice." A court must weigh the corporation's contacts within the state against the inconvenience to the corporation of requiring it to defend a suit within the state. The burden on the corporation must be reasonable in relation to the benefit that it receives from conducting activities in the state.

Under the minimum contacts test, even an isolated event may be sufficient to confer jurisdiction on a state's courts. For example, driving a truck from Arizona through New Mexico toward a final destination in Florida provides sufficient contacts with New Mexico to permit a suit in New Mexico's courts against the foreign corporation for its driver's negligently causing an accident within New Mexico.

Most of the states have passed **long-arm statutes** to permit their courts to exercise jurisdiction under the decision of the *International Shoe* case. These statutes frequently specify several kinds of corporate activities that make foreign corporations subject to suit within the state, such as the commission of a tort, the making of a contract, or the ownership of property. Most of the long-arm statutes grant jurisdiction over causes of action growing out of any transaction within the state.

In the following case, the court applied the Louisiana long-arm statute.

HERVISH V. GROWABLES, INC.
449 So.2d 684 (La. Ct. App. 1984)

Growables, Inc., a manufacturer of furniture, was incorporated in St. Petersburg, Florida. In July 1982, Debra Hervish, a resident of Florida, obtained a brochure about Growables' line of children's furniture. She went to Growables' offices in Florida to place an order for 14 pieces of furniture. While at Growables' office, she deposited $2,000 toward the total purchase price of $2,662. She told Growables that she would soon be moving to Louisiana, and she asked that the furniture be shipped there. Growables agreed to do so.

In early August 1982, Mrs. Hervish moved to Kenner, Louisiana, and informed Growables of her new address. Thereafter, she contacted Growables three or four times to find out why shipment of the furniture had been delayed beyond the eight weeks estimated by Growables.

On November 2, 1982, the furniture was delivered to Mrs. Hervish by Ryder Truck Lines. At the time of delivery, she paid the Ryder driver the balance of the purchase price plus the shipping charges, a total of $877. Upon opening the cardboard cartons in which the furniture had been shipped, Mrs. Hervish discovered that every piece of furniture was damaged. After making futile demands for recovery from Ryder and Growables, she sued Growables in a Louisiana trial court.

Growables asked the trial court to dismiss the suit on the grounds that the Louisiana courts could not take long-arm jurisdiction over Growables. The trial court agreed with Growables and dismissed Hervish's suit. Hervish appealed.

Chehardy, Judge   The Louisiana long-arm statute provides, in pertinent part,

A court may exercise personal jurisdiction over a nonresident, who acts directly or by an agent, as to a cause of action arising from the nonresident's:

(a) transacting any business in this state;
(b) contracting to supply services or things in this state;
(c) causing injury or damage by an offense or quasi-offense committed through an act or omission in this state;
(d) causing injury or damage in this state by an offense or quasi-offense committed through an act or omission outside of this state, if he regularly does or solicits business, or engages in any other persistent course of conduct, or derives substantial revenue from goods used or consumed or services rendered, in this state.

This statute was intended by the Legislature to extend the personal jurisdiction of Louisiana courts over nonresidents to the full limits of due process under the Fourteenth Amendment.

In order for the proper exercise of jurisdiction over a nonresident, there must be sufficient minimum contacts between the nonresident defendant and the forum state to satisfy due process and traditional notions of fair play and substantial justice. Whether or not a particular defendant has sufficient minimum contracts with a state is to be determined from the facts and circumstances peculiar to each case.

It is essential in each case that there be some act by which the defendant purposefully avails itself of the privilege of conducting activities within the state, thus invoking the benefits and protections of its law.

It appears that knowledge alone or foreseeability that property will come to rest in a particular state is insufficient to subject a defendant to jurisdiction, unless the facts and circumstances lead to a conclusion that the defendant purposefully availed itself of the privilege of conducting activities within the forum state in such a manner that the defendant has clear notice that it would be subject to suit there.

Applying these standards to the case before us, we must examine the contacts between Growables, Inc., and Louisiana to determine whether the relationship is sufficient to satisfy due process requirements. At the time Mrs. Hervish ordered the furniture, she was a Florida resident. She obtained the brochure advertising the furniture in Florida; she went personally to the Growables office in Florida to place the order. The only incidents that took place in Louisiana are Mrs. Hervish's calls to Growables to question the delay in shipment, the delivery—through a third-party truck—of the furniture into this state, and Mrs. Hervish's payment of the balance of the purchase price to the truck driver upon delivery.

There is no evidence that Growables transacts any business in Louisiana, that its representatives or agents travel to Louisiana for business purposes, or that it advertises or otherwise solicits business in Louisiana or from Louisiana residents, either directly or by mail. There is no evidence that Growables derives any substantial revenue from business in Louisiana, or "engages in any persistent course of conduct" in this state.

In fact, the only classification of the long-arm statute Growables will fit into is subparagraph (b), "contracting to supply services or things in this state." We can, however, find no other case in which a Louisiana court has found an isolated incident of delivery, without other affiliating circumstances, sufficient to apply long-arm jurisdiction to a foreign corporation. This single transaction would not justify our concluding that Growables purposefully availed itself of the privilege of conducting activities within Louisiana in such a manner that it had clear notice it would be subject to suit here.

Accordingly, we conclude the district court properly found a lack of personal jurisdiction over Growables.

Judgment for Growables affirmed.

Taxation

A state may tax a foreign corporation if such taxation does not violate the Due Process Clause or the Commerce Clause. Generally, a state's imposition of a tax must serve a legitimate state interest and be reasonable in relation to a foreign corporation's contacts with the state. For example, a North Carolina corporation's property located in Pennsylvania is subject to property tax in Pennsylvania. The corporation enjoys Pennsylvania's protection of private property. It may be required to pay its share of the cost of such protection.

Greater contacts are needed to subject a corporation to state income and sales taxation in a state than are needed to subject it to property taxation. A state tax does not violate the Commerce Clause when the tax (1) is applied to an activity with a substantial connection with the taxing state, (2) is fairly apportioned, (3) does not discriminate against interstate commerce, and (4) is fairly related to the services provided by the state.

For example, New Jersey has been permitted to tax a portion of the entire net income of a corporation for the privilege of doing business, employing or owning capital or property, or maintaining an office in New Jersey when the portion of entire net income taxed is determined by an average of three ratios: in-state property to total property, in-state to total receipts, and in-state to total wages, salaries, and other employee compensation.[2] However, Pennsylvania could not assess a flat tax on the operation of all trucks on Pennsylvania highways. The flat tax imposed a disproportionate burden on interstate trucks as compared with intrastate trucks because interstate trucks traveled fewer miles per year on Pennsylvania highways.[3]

Qualifying to Do Business

A state may require that foreign corporations **qualify** to conduct **intrastate** business in the state. The level of doing business that constitutes intrastate business for qualification purposes has been difficult to define. To help clarify the confusion in this area, the MBCA lists several activities that do *not* require qualification. For example, soliciting—by mail or through employees—orders that require acceptance outside the state is not doing intrastate business requiring qualification. Selling through independent contractors or owning real or personal property does not require qualification.

Also classified as not doing business for qualification purposes is conducting an **isolated transaction** that is completed within 30 days and is not one in the course of repeated transactions of a like nature. This isolated transaction safe harbor allows a tree grower to bring Christmas trees into a state in order to sell them to one retailer. However, a Christmas tree retailer who comes into a state for 29 days before Christmas and sells to consumers from a street corner is required to qualify. Although both merchants have consummated their transactions within 30 days, the grower has engaged in only one transaction, but the retailer has engaged in a series of transactions.

Maintaining an office to conduct intrastate business, selling personal property not in interstate

---

[2]*Amerada Hess Corp. v. Director of Taxation,* 490 U.S. 66 (1989).

[3]*American Trucking Assns., Inc. v. Scheiner,* 483 U.S. 266 (1987).

commerce, entering into contracts relating to local business or sales, or owning or using real estate for general corporate purposes does constitute doing intrastate business. Passive ownership of real estate for investment, however, is not doing intrastate business.

Maintaining a stock of goods within a state from which to fill orders, even if the orders are taken or accepted outside the state, is doing intrastate business requiring qualification. Performing service activities such as machinery repair and construction work may be doing intrastate business.

In the next case, the court applied the isolated transaction safe harbor and held that providing services for four days annually to an independent in-state business was not doing intrastate business requiring qualification.

COMMONWEALTH OF KENTUCKY V. NATIONAL STEEPLECHASE AND HUNT ASS'N.

612 S.W.2d 347 (Ky. Ct. App. 1981)

The National Steeplechase and Hunt Association (NSHA) is a New York corporation that sanctions, regulates, and supervises steeplechase races. Its first sanctioned race was the Oxmoor Steeplechase, near Louisville, Kentucky, in 1948. It has supervised the High Hope Steeplechase in Fayette County, Kentucky, since 1967 and the Hard Scuffle Steeplechase in Oldham County, near Louisville, since 1975. Each of the sanctioned events lasts no more than three to four days every year.

The NSHA has never obtained from the Kentucky secretary of state a certificate to do business in Kentucky as a foreign corporation. No annual reports have been filed, and no registration fees have been paid. The NSHA does not maintain a registered office or a registered agent in the state.

In 1975, the Commonwealth of Kentucky sued the NSHA to collect all of the fees and penalties due to the Commonwealth as a result of the failure of the NSHA to qualify to do business in Kentucky. The trial court held that the NSHA was not doing business in Kentucky and therefore did not need to qualify. The Commonwealth appealed.

Wintersheimer, Judge   The sanctioning of steeplechase meetings does not constitute the transaction of business in Kentucky. The NSHA promulgates rules; approves the racecourses, race officials, and the financial responsibility of the sponsoring organization; receives entries for each meeting by telephone or mail; assembles the information on the meetings; and prepares a booklet and identification badges for each meet. All of these functions are performed in the New York office. The NSHA maintains no offices or employees in Kentucky. All communications are conducted by mail or telephone. The NSHA provides a service and information to the local sponsoring organization. The attendance by NSHA employees at the meetings does not constitute the transaction of business in Kentucky.

The leasing of fences and jumps by the NSHA to the local organizations in Kentucky is within the exception provided for interstate commerce in the Kentucky statute. The NSHA driver transporting the jumps to Kentucky does not assist the local organization in setting up the equipment. The NSHA employee does not deal with the equipment after it is delivered.

The isolated transaction section applies to the activities of the NSHA employees in Kentucky. The statute makes an exception for isolated transactions completed within 30 days and not in the course of a number of repeated transactions of a like nature. Here, the meetings generally last no more than three to four days. Three different locations are now used annually. The presence of the NSHA's employees at these meetings and the occasional utilization of them as stewards falls within the isolated transaction section.

Judgment for the NSHA affirmed.

Qualification Requirements   To qualify to do intrastate business in a state, a foreign corporation must apply for a **certificate of authority** from the secretary of state, pay an application fee, maintain a registered office and a registered agent in the state, file an annual report with the secretary of state, and pay an annual fee.

Doing intrastate business without qualifying usually subjects a foreign corporation to a fine, in some states as much as $10,000. The MBCA disables the corporation to use the state's courts to bring a lawsuit until it obtains a certificate of authority. The corporation may defend itself in the state's courts, however, even if it has no certificate of authority.

Regulation of a Corporation's Internal Affairs

Regulation of the internal affairs of a corporation—that is, the relation between the corporation and its directors, officers, and shareholders—is usually only exercised by the state of incorporation. Nonetheless, a foreign corporation may conduct most of its business in a state other than the one in which it is incorporated. Such a corporation is called a **pseudo-foreign corporation** in the state in which it conducts most of its business.

A few states subject pseudo-foreign corporations to extensive regulation of their internal affairs, regulation similar to that imposed on their domestic corporations. California's statute requires corporations that have more than 50 percent of their business and ownership in California to elect directors by cumulative voting, to hold annual directors' elections, and to comply with California's dividend payment restrictions. Foreign corporations raise many constitutional objections to the California statute, including violations of the Commerce Clause and the Due Process Clause.

Piercing the Corporate Veil

A corporation is a legal entity separate from its shareholders. Corporation law erects an imaginary wall between a corporation and its shareholders that protects shareholders from liability for a corporation's actions. Once shareholders have made their promised capital contributions to the corporation, they have no further financial liability. This means that contracts of a corporation are not contracts of its shareholders, and debts of a corporation are not debts of its shareholders.

Nonetheless, in order *to promote justice and to prevent inequity*, courts will sometimes ignore the separateness of a corporation and its shareholders by **piercing the corporate veil.** The primary consequence of piercing the corporate veil is that a corporation's shareholders may lose their limited liability.

Two requirements must exist for a court to pierce the corporate veil: (1) **domination** of a corporation by its shareholders; and (2) use of that domination for an **improper purpose.**

As an entity separate from its shareholders, a corporation should act for itself, not for its shareholders. If the shareholders cause the corporation to act to its detriment and to the personal benefit of shareholders, *domination*—the first requirement for piercing the corporate veil—is proved. For example, shareholders' directing a corporation to pay a shareholder's personal expenses is domination. Domination is also proved if the shareholders cause the corporation to fail to observe corporate formalities (such as failing to hold shareholder and director meetings or to maintain separate accounting records). Some courts say that shareholder domination makes the corporation the *alter ego* (other self) of the shareholders. Other courts say that domination makes the corporation an *instrumentality* of the shareholders.

To prove domination, it is not sufficient, or even necessary, to show that there is only one shareholder. Many one-shareholder corporations will never have their veils pierced. However, nearly all corporations whose veils are pierced are close corporations, since domination is more easily accomplished in a close corporation than in a publicly held one.

In addition to domination, there must be an *improper use* of the corporation. The improper use may be any of three types: defrauding creditors, circumventing a statute, or evading an existing obligation.

Shareholders must organize a corporation with sufficient capital to meet the initial capital needs of the business. Inadequate capitalization, called **thin capitalization**, is proved when capitalization is very small in relation to the nature of the business of the corporation and the risks the business necessarily entails.

Thin capitalization defrauds creditors of a corporation. An example of thin capitalization is forming a business with a high debt-to-equity ratio, such as a $10-million-asset business with only $1,000 of equity capital, with the shareholders sometimes contributing the remainder of the needed capital as secured creditors. By doing so, the shareholders elevate a portion of their bankruptcy repayment priority to a level above that of general creditors, thereby reducing the shareholders' risk. The high debt-to-equity ratio harms nonshareholder-creditors by failing to provide an equity cushion sufficient to protect their claims. In such a situation, either the shareholders will be liable for the corporation's debts or the shareholders' loans to the corporation will be subordinated to the claims of other creditors. As a result, the nonshareholder-creditors are repaid all of their claims prior to the shareholder-creditors receiving payment from the corporation.

In the next case, the court held that $3,000 was inadequate initial capital for a business with assets of $430,000.

J. L. BROCK BUILDERS, INC. v. DAHLBECK

391 N.W.2d 110 (Neb. Sup. Ct. 1986)

In 1971, Eric Dahlbeck incorporated Viking Construction, Inc. Its initial capital was $3,000. In addition, Dahlbeck made a $7,000 loan to Viking. It had as assets 65 lots of land for development, which cost $430,000. For its entire existence, Viking's liabilities exceeded the book value of its assets. From 1972 through 1974, Dahlbeck and another officer received salaries totaling $53,750. Beginning in 1975, Viking's business steadily declined and creditors' claims became overdue. No salaries were paid thereafter. In 1978, Viking began liquidation and transferred assets to Dahlbeck to repay loans that Dahlbeck had made to Viking. Viking dissolved in 1980, having not paid several creditors, including J. L. Brock Builders, which was owed about $16,000. Brock sued Dahlbeck personally, claiming that Viking's corporate veil should be pierced. The trial court refused to pierce Viking's veil. Brock appealed to the Supreme Court of Nebraska.

Shanahan, Justice   A creditor seeking to pierce the corporate veil and impose on a shareholder liability for a corporate debt has the burden to show that the corporate entity must be disregarded to prevent fraud or injustice to the creditor. One of the factors that is relevant in determining whether to disregard the corporate entity on the basis of fraud is grossly inadequate capitalization.

Viking was grossly inadequately capitalized at the time of its formation. Viking's capital was $3,000 at formation and it had as an asset 65 lots, 25 at $10,000 each and the remaining at $4,500 an acre. The scale of operations anticipated by both the number of lots and their value cannot be adequately capitalized by $3,000. The risk to creditors must be balanced by the availability of more capital should the corporation fail. In reaching our conclusion that Viking was inadequately capitalized, we note Dahlberg could have provided more capital to Viking at its formation, but chose instead to loan Viking $7,000.

Shareholders of an insolvent corporation cannot participate in the distribution of its assets until claims of creditors are paid. If the shareholders are allowed to withdraw assets leaving creditors unpaid, they may be compelled to repay what they have received.

Although he was aware of $78,000 in debts to Viking creditors, Dahlbeck, as Viking's sole shareholder, transferred all Viking's assets to himself.

Dahlbeck's action constitutes an improper use of corporate funds, an injustice perpetrated by a shareholder.

Viking's corporate existence was used to commit a fraud upon Brock. Viking's corporate entity should be disregarded and liability imposed on Dahlbeck for the debt incurred by Viking.

Judgment reversed in favor of Brock.

Transfers of corporate assets to shareholders for less than fair market value (called **looting**) also defraud creditors. For example, shareholder-managers loot a corporation by paying themselves excessively high salaries or by having the corporation pay their personal credit card bills. When such payments leave insufficient assets in the corporation to pay creditors' claims, a court will hold the shareholders liable to the creditors.

Frequently, the same shareholders may own two corporations that transact with each other. The shareholders may cause one corporation to loot the other. When such looting occurs between corporations of common ownership, courts pierce the veils of these corporations. This makes each corporation liable to the creditors of the other corporation. For example, a shareholder-manager operates two corporations from the same office. Corporation 1 transfers inventory to Corporation 2, but it receives less than fair market value for the inventory. Also, both corporations employ the same workers, but all of the wages are paid by Corporation 1. In such a situation, the veils of the corporations will be pierced, allowing the creditors of Corporation 1 to satisfy their claims against the assets of Corporation 2.

In the next case, the shareholders' looting of a corporation was grounds to pierce the corporate veil.

CASTLEBERRY V. BRANSCUM
721 S.W.2d 270 (Tex. Sup. Ct. 1986)

In September 1980, Joe Castleberry, Byron Branscum, and Michael Byboth incorporated their furniture-moving business as Texan Transfer, Inc. Each owned one third of the shares of Texan Transfer. Byboth was president, Castleberry was vice president, and Branscum was secretary-treasurer. Soon thereafter, Branscum formed Elite Moving Company, a business that competed with Texan Transfer. Castleberry discovered the existence of Elite Moving and sued to claim that Texan Transfer owned the assets and revenues of Elite Moving. As a result, Branscum became very upset and threatened that Castleberry would not receive any return on his investment in Texan Transfer unless Castleberry abandoned his attempts to claim ownership of Elite Moving.

In July 1981, Castleberry sold his Texan Transfer shares back to Texan Transfer in exchange for a $42,000 promissory note payable by Texan Transfer. After the sale, Elite Moving took over more and more of Texan Transfer's business. Controlled by Branscum and Byboth, Texan Transfer allowed Elite Moving to use its employees and trucks. Elite Moving advertised for furniture moving, but Texan Transfer did not. While Texan Transfer's business declined, Elite Moving's prospered. For the 18 months prior to Castleberry's sale of his shares, Texan Transfer had a net income of $65,479. After the sale, its net income fell to $2,814 for the second half of 1981. In 1982, it lost more than $16,000. By contrast, Elite Moving had income in 1982 of $195,765.

In 1982, Branscum told his wife that Castleberry "would never get a dime, that he would file bankruptcy before Castleberry got any money out of the company and that he would open the company in another name so that Joe wouldn't get paid." In September 1982, Byboth and Branscum started Custom Carriers, Inc. At that time, Byboth and Branscum terminated Texan Transfer's contract with Freed Furniture, which contract comprised the majority of Texan Transfer's business. Byboth and Branscum obtained for Custom Carriers an identical contract with Freed Furniture, doing the same deliveries at the same rate. Byboth and Branscum then sold Texan Transfer's trucks to drivers hired to make deliveries for Custom Carriers. With the proceeds of the sales, Byboth and Branscum paid themselves back salaries.

Castleberry was paid only $1,000 of the $42,000 promissory note. He sued Branscum and Byboth, claiming that the corporate veil of Texan Transfer should be pierced to make them personally liable on the promissory note. The trial court found Branscum and Byboth liable to Castleberry. Branscum and Byboth appealed. The court of appeals reversed and held for Branscum and Byboth. Castleberry appealed to the Supreme Court of Texas.

Spears, Justice   The corporate form normally insulates shareholders, officers, and directors from liability for corporate obligations; but when these individuals abuse the corporate privilege, courts will disregard the corporate fiction and hold them individually liable.

We disregard the corporate fiction when the corporate form has been used as part of a basically unfair device to achieve an inequitable result. Specifically, we disregard the corporate fiction:

1. When the fiction is used as a means of perpetrating fraud;

2. When the corporate fiction is resorted to as a means of evading an existing legal obligation;

3. When the corporate fiction is used to circumvent a statute.

We hold that there is some evidence of a sham to perpetrate a fraud. A jury could find that both Byboth and Branscum manipulated a closely held corporation—Texan Transfer—and formed competing businesses to ensure that Castleberry did not get paid.

The variety of shams is infinite, but many fit this case's pattern: a closely held corporation owes unwanted obligations; it siphons off corporate revenues, sells off much of the corporate assets, or does other acts to hinder the on-going business and its ability to pay off its debts; a new business then starts up that is basically a continuation of the old business with many of the same shareholders, officers, and directors.

Judgment reversed in favor of Castleberry.

Looting may occur also when one corporation (called the **parent corporation**) owns at least a majority of the shares of another corporation (called the **subsidiary corporation**). Ordinarily, the parent is liable for its own obligations and the subsidiary is liable for its own obligations, but the parent is not liable for its subsidiary's debts and the subsidiary is not liable for the parent's debts. Nonetheless, because a parent corporation is able to elect the directors of its subsidiary and therefore can control the management of the subsidiary, the parent may cause its subsidiary to transact with the parent in a manner that benefits the parent but harms the subsidiary.

For example, a parent corporation may direct its subsidiary to sell its assets to the parent for less than fair market value. Because the subsidiary has given more assets to the parent than it has received from the parent, creditors of the subsidiary have been defrauded. Consequently, a court will pierce the veil between the parent and its subsidiary and hold the parent liable to the creditors of the subsidiary.

A corporation should not engage in a course of conduct that is prohibited by a statute. For example, a city ordinance prohibits retail businesses from being open on consecutive Sundays. To avoid the statute, a retail corporation forms a subsidiary owned entirely by the retail corporation; on alternate weeks, it leases its building and inventory to the subsidiary. A court will pierce the veil because the purpose of creating the subsidiary corporation is to circumvent the statutory prohibition. Consequently, both the parent and the subsidiary will be liable for violating the statute.

Sometimes, a corporation will attempt to escape liability on a contract by reincorporating or by forming a subsidiary corporation. The new corporation will claim that it is not bound by the contract, even though it is doing the same business as was done by the old corporation. In such a situation, courts pierce the corporate veil and hold the new corporation liable on the contract.

For example, to avoid an onerous labor union contract, a corporation creates a wholly owned subsidiary

| | Proof of | Proof of | |
Event	Domination	Improper Purpose	Result
Sole shareholder/director causes corporation to pay shareholder's personal debt.	Sole shareholder/director controls corporation's use of assets.	Creditors defrauded when corporate assets used to pay shareholder's debt, not corporation's debt.	Shareholder liable to creditors of corporation.
Shareholders/directors fail to hold annual shareholders' and directors' meetings.	Shareholders and directors control corporation's decision to hold meetings.	Circumvention of incorporation statute requiring annual meetings.	Shareholders liable to creditors of corporation.
To avoid union contract, shareholders vote to transfer business of corporation to new corporation owned by the same shareholders.	Shareholders' vote controlled corporation's decision to transfer business to new corporation.	Obligation to employees evaded by the business.	New corporation liable to employees under union contract.
Parent of wholly owned subsidiary causes subsidiary to buy asset from parent at price higher than fair market value.	Parent owns 100% of subsidiary, elects its directors, and therby controls subsidiary.	Creditors of subsidiary defrauded when parent gives fewer assets to subsidiary than subsidiary gives to parent.	Parent liable to creditors of subsidiary.
Shareholders organize corporation by contributing $1,000 of capital and by loaning $99,000 to corporation. The loan is secured by all the corporation's assets.	Shareholders control organization of corporation.	Nonshareholder creditors defrauded by thin capitalization.	Part or all of loans treated as capital, thereby subordinating shareholder's loans to claims of nonshareholders.

FIGURE 2 Examples of Piercing the Corporate Veil

and sells its entire business to the subsidiary. The subsidiary will claim that it is not a party to the labor contract and may hire nonunion labor. A court will pierce the veil between the two corporations because the subsidiary was created only to avoid the union contract.

For a summary of the law of piercing the corporate veil, see Figure 2.

ETHICAL AND PUBLIC POLICY CONCERNS

1. Do you think it is right that shareholders of corporations have no liability for the obligations of their corporation once they have paid their promised capital contribution? What benefits does society receive from extending such a privilege to shareholders? What detriments does society suffer? Can those detriments be eliminated without changing corporation law, such as by prospective corporate creditors contracting for the unlimited liability of some or all shareholders of the corporations with whom they plan to transact? Why should shareholders have limited liability when sole proprietors and partners do not? Are the sole proprietorship and the partnership less socially desirable business forms than the corporation?

2. Should businesses be permitted to incorporate in a state that has a business incorporation law that extends the greatest freedom to managers of the business? Who benefits from businesses incorporating in such states? Who is harmed? Can the persons who are harmed protect themselves?

3. When a corporation engages in interstate business, should its managers attempt to reduce the risk that foreign states' courts will have jurisdiction over the corporation? Should the managers attempt to avoid taxation by foreign states? Should they try to avoid qualification requirements? Is it enough that the corporation complies exactly with the laws of the foreign states, or should the corporation attempt to return to the state—such as through taxes and qualification fees—an amount appropriate to the benefits it receives from customers in the foreign state? Is the corporation the only person benefiting from its doing business in a foreign state? What risk may arise if a state aggressively regulates foreign corporations?

4. Why should courts and corporation statutes require corporations to be adequately capitalized? Who is harmed by thin capitalization? Is it possible for creditors harmed by thin capitalization to protect themselves by examining the financial position of the corporation prior to extending credit to the corporation? Why should a court protect creditors who knowingly or carelessly extend credit to thinly capitalized corporations? Should a court treat a corporation's *contract* creditors differently from its *tort* creditors? Are a thinly capitalized corporation's *contract* creditors better able to protect themselves than are the corporation's *tort* victims?

PROBLEMS AND PROBLEM CASES

1. Nippon Electric Co., Ltd., a Japanese corporation with its principal place of business in Tokyo, manufactured telephone and computer equipment in Japan, which it sold to its wholly owned subsidiary, NEC America, a New York corporation authorized to do business in New Jersey. NEC America distributed Nippon equipment to its wholly owned subsidiary, NEC Telephone. NEC Telephone sold Nippon telephone equipment to Telecom Equipment Corporation, a New Jersey corporation. Telecom sold a portion of the equipment to Charles Gendler & Co. for installation at Gendler's place of business in New Jersey. The equipment failed to perform as promised, and Gendler sued Nippon in a New Jersey court. Nippon claimed that it could not be sued in a New Jersey court because it had not conducted any business in New Jersey, had no agents located there, had not advertised for or solicited business in New Jersey, did not have a telephone listing in the state, had not contracted with Gendler for the sale of the equipment, and had not received any direct income from Gendler or any other New Jersey resident. Nonetheless, Nippon acknowledged that the sale to Gendler was not an isolated transaction and that other Nippon equipment may have been sold in New Jersey. May Gendler sue Nippon in a New Jersey court?

2. A Hawaiian statute imposed a 20 percent wholesale excise tax on liquor sold in Hawaii. To encourage the development of Hawaiian liquor, the statute exempted from taxation Okolehao, a brandy distilled from the root of the ti plant, a native Hawaiian shrub. Bacchus Imports, a liquor wholesaler, claimed that the excise tax violated the Commerce Clause. Was Bacchus correct?

3. Campaign Works, Ltd., a business incorporated in Florida, was a consultant to candidates for political office. Campaign Works had offices in Florida and Washington, D.C. It had no office and no employees in Missouri and had not qualified to do business in Missouri. Campaign Works contracted to provide political consulting services to Doug Hughes, a candidate to the U.S. Congress for

Missouri. The contract was negotiated by telephone and concluded by mail between Campaign Works in Florida or Washington and Hughes in Missouri. The contract called for consultations with Hughes in Missouri and political research appropriate to his election campaign. Campaign Works actually performed election research for Hughes from its offices in Florida and Washington, and its president traveled to Missouri twice to consult with Hughes and his staff. The parties terminated the contract, with Hughes owing Campaign Works nearly $9,000. Hughes failed to pay this amount, and Campaign Works sued Hughes in a Missouri trial court. Does Campaign Works's failure to qualify to do business in Missouri prevent it from suing Hughes in a Missouri court?

4. Section 2115 of the California General Corporation Law requires that a foreign corporation doing a majority of its business in California (on the basis of its property, payroll, and sales) and having a majority of its outstanding voting securities owned by persons with addresses in California comply with certain internal governance provisions of the California corporation law, including section 708, which provides for the cumulative voting of shares for the election of directors. Louisiana-Pacific Resources, Inc., was a Utah corporation. The average of its property, payroll, and sales in California exceeded 50 percent, and more than 50 percent of its shareholders entitled to vote resided in California. Except for being domiciled in Utah and having a transfer agent there, Louisiana-Pacific had virtually no business connections with Utah. Its principal place of business was in California; its meetings of shareholders and directors were held in California; and all of its employees and bank accounts were in California. Louisiana-Pacific argued that application of section 2115 to Louisiana-Pacific violated the Constitution of the United States. Is it correct?

5. Pacific Development, Inc., was incorporated in the District of Columbia in 1968 to engage in the business of international brokerage and consulting. Tongsun Park was Pacific's founder, president, and sole shareholder. It was doubtful whether Pacific had a board of directors prior to December 1974. The directors met infrequently after 1974. When they did meet, they approved without discussion or question corporate decisions made by Park. Park wrote checks on Pacific's bank accounts to cover his unrelated personal and business expenses. Pacific

employees served as Park's household servants. Park made loans with Pacific funds to politically influential people and then forgave the loans. Pacific personnel provided administrative and managerial services for Park's other business ventures, and Pacific's profits were assigned to Park or to his other companies. In 1977, the Internal Revenue Service assessed $4.5 million in back income taxes against Park. To collect the taxes, the IRS seized some of Pacific's assets, claiming that the company was a mere alter ego of Park. Was the IRS correct?

6. Sea Pines Company owned 90 percent of the shares of Point South, Inc. The directors and officers of Point South were under the control of Sea Pines. Point South was organized with initial capital of $1,000. In February 1973, Point South had assets of $2.5 million and total net worth of $65,000, of which only $1,000 was capital contributions. By February 1974, Point South had become so unprofitable that it had a negative net worth of $177,000. During the period of unprofitability, Sea Pines paid the salary and expenses of Point South with the expectation that it would be reimbursed. In February 1974, when Point South was insolvent, its directors mortgaged a piece of property (worth $350,000) to secure a debt of Sea Pines. In exchange for the mortgage, Sea Pines reduced by $8,000 the amount it was owed by Point South. When Point South failed to repay a construction loan to American Bank & Trust Company, American sued Sea Pines. Was Sea Pines liable to American?

7. Vassilis Morfopolous was the sole shareholder of American Standards Testing Bureau (ASTB). ASTB was the sole shareholder of Architectural Research Corporation (ARC) and Ar-Lite Panelcraft, Inc. (API). ASTB, ARC, and API had the same officers, and Morfopolous ran all three businesses. ASTB made periodic loans to ARC that were secured by all of ARC's assets. When ARC defaulted on an obligation to Bodenhamer Building Corporation, Bodenhamer sued ARC and obtained a judgment for $50,000. To prevent Bodenhamer from collecting his judgment, ASTB foreclosed on its loan to ARC and obtained the auction sale of ARC's assets. At the auction, ASTB submitted the only bid, $115,000, which was considerably less than previous purchase offers ranging from $1 million to $2.2 million and earlier estimates that ARC's assets were worth from $345,000 to $600,000. ASTB took possession of the assets, leaving Bodenhamer and other ARC creditors unpaid. ARC ceased operations, and ASTB leased the purchased assets to API, which had been incorporated solely to continue ARC's business had Bodenhamer been successful in obtaining a judgment against ARC. Bodenhamer sued ASTB and API to obtain payment of the judgment. Are they liable to Bodenhamer?

8. New York law required that every taxicab company carry $10,000 of accident liability insurance for each cab in its fleet. The purpose of the law was to ensure that passengers and pedestrians injured by cabs operated by these companies would be adequately compensated for their injuries. Carlton organized 10 corporations, each owning and operating two taxicabs in New York City. Each of these corporations carried $20,000 of liability insurance. Carlton was the principal shareholder of each corporation. The vehicles, the only freely transferable assets of these corporations, were collateral for claims of secured creditors. The 10 corporations were operated more or less as a unit with respect to supplies, repairs, and employees. Walkovszky was severely injured when he was run down by one of the taxicabs. He sued Carlton personally, alleging that the multiple corporate structure amounted to fraud upon those who might be injured by the taxicabs. Should the court pierce the corporate veil to reach Carlton individually?

9. Denzil and Stephanie Cooper obtained a court judgment for $31,800 against Seaside Pools, Inc. (SPI), a wholly owned subsidiary of Seaside Industries, Inc. (SI). SPI had sufficient funds to pay the judgment. Two weeks later, Bernard Leff, the sole owner of SI, incorporated Seaside Pools of Texas, Inc. (SPOT), and Seaside Enterprises, Inc. (SE). Leff transferred all his SI shares to SE, which as a result owned all the shares of SI, which still owned SPI. In addition, SE was the only shareholder of SPOT. Leff was president of all the corporations. Two months later, SPI ceased business, but SPOT began business using the same location, personnel, telephone, trade name, and advertising as SPI. When SPI failed to pay the Coopers, they sued Leff, SPOT, SE, and SI. Did the Coopers succeed?

10. Maintenance Contractors, Inc., owed $13,600 to Westinghouse Electric Supply Co. Robert Pilkerton, the majority shareholder of Maintenance Contractors, caused Maintenance Contractors to cease operations. Twelve days later, Robert Pilkerton incorporated R.E. Pilkerton, Inc, which carried on the same business as Maintenance Contractors. Are Pilkerton and R.E. Pilkerton, Inc., liable to Westinghouse on the $13,600 debt?

ORGANIZATION AND FINANCIAL STRUCTURE OF CORPORATIONS

INTRODUCTION

A person desiring to incorporate a business must comply with the applicable corporation law. Failing to comply can create various problems. For example, a person may make a contract on behalf of the corporation before it is incorporated. Is the corporation liable on this contract? Is the person who made the contract on behalf of the prospective corporation liable on the contract? Do the people who thought that they were shareholders of a corporation have limited liability, or do they have unlimited liability as partners of a partnership?

PROMOTERS AND PREINCORPORATION TRANSACTIONS

A **promoter** of a corporation incorporates a business, organizes its initial management, and raises its initial capital. Typically, a promoter discovers a business or an idea to be developed, finds people who are willing to invest in the business, negotiates the contracts necessary for the initial operation of the proposed venture, incorporates the business, and helps management start the operation of the business. Consequently, a promoter may engage in many acts prior to the incorporation of the business. As a result, the promoter may have liability on the contracts he negotiates on behalf of the prospective corporation. In addition, the corporation may *not* be liable on the contracts the promoter makes on its behalf.

Corporation's Liability on Preincorporation Contracts

A nonexistent corporation has no liability on contracts made by a promoter prior to its incorporation. This is because the corporation does not exist.

Even when the corporation comes into existence, it does not automatically become liable on a preincorporation contract made by a promoter on its behalf. It cannot be held liable as a principal whose agent made the contracts because the promoter was not its agent and the corporation was not in existence when the contracts were made.

The only way a corporation may become bound on a promoter's preincorporation contracts is by the corporation's **adoption** of the promoter's contracts. For a corporation to adopt a promoter's contract, the corporation must accept the contract with knowledge of all its material facts.

Acceptance may be express or implied. The corporation's knowing receipt of the benefits of the contract is sufficient for acceptance. For example, a promoter makes a preincorporation contract with a genetic engineer, requiring the engineer to work for a prospective corporation for 10 years. After incorporation, the promoter presents the contract to the board of directors. Although the board takes no formal action to accept the contract, the board allows the engineer to work for the corporation for one year as the contract provides and pays him the salary required by the contract. The board's actions constitute an acceptance of the contract, binding the corporation to the contract for its 10-year term.

Promoter's Liability on Preincorporation Contracts

A promoter and her copromoters are jointly and severally liable on preincorporation contracts the promoter negotiates in the name of the nonexistent corporation. This liability exists even when the promoters' names do not appear on the contract. Promoters are also jointly and severally liable for torts committed by their copromoters prior to incorporation.

A promoter retains liability on a preincorporation contract until **novation** occurs. For novation to occur, the corporation and the third party must agree to release the promoter from liability and to substitute the corporation for the promoter as the party liable on the contract. Usually, novation will occur by express or implied agreement of all the parties.

If the corporation is not formed, a promoter remains liable on a preincorporation contract unless the third party releases the promoter from liability. In addition, the mere formation of the corporation does not release a promoter from liability. A promoter remains liable on a preincorporation contract even after the corporation's adoption of the contract, since adoption does not automatically release the promoter. The corporation cannot by itself relieve the promoter of liability to the third party; the third party must also agree, expressly or impliedly, to release the promoter from liability.

A few courts have held that a promoter is not liable on preincorporation contracts if the third party *knew of the nonexistence* of the corporation yet insisted that the promoter sign the contract on behalf of the nonexistent corporation. Other courts have found that the promoter is not liable if the third party clearly stated that he would *look only to the prospective corporation* for performance.

In the next case, the court held that a promoter failed to prove that the third party agreed to look only to the corporation for performance.

COOPERS & LYBRAND V. FOX
758 P.2d 683 (Colo. Ct. App. 1988)

On November 3, 1981, Garry Fox met with Coopers & Lybrand, a national accounting firm, to request a tax opinion and other accounting services. Fox told Coopers that he was acting on behalf of a corporation that he was in the process of forming, to be named G. Fox and Partners, Inc. Coopers accepted its engagement to provide services with the knowledge that the corporation was not yet in existence. Fox and Coopers had no agreement regarding Fox's personal liability for payment of the fee for the services.

G. Fox and Partners, Inc., was incorporated on December 4, 1981. Coopers completed its work on the contract by mid-December and billed "Mr. Garry Fox, Fox and Partners, Inc." in the amount of $10,827. When neither Fox nor the corporation paid the bill, Coopers sued Garry Fox individually based on the theory of promoter liability. The trial court held that Fox had no personal liability to Coopers. Coopers appealed to the Colorado Court of Appeals.

Kelly, Chief Judge   As a preliminary matter, we reject Fox's argument that he was acting only as an agent for the future corporation. One cannot act as the agent of a nonexistent principal.

On the contrary, the uncontroverted facts place Fox squarely within the definition of a promoter. A promoter is one who, alone or with others, undertakes to form a corporation and to procure for it the rights, instrumentalities, and capital to enable it to conduct business.

As a general rule, promoters are personally liable for the contracts they make, though made on behalf of a corporation to be formed. A well-recognized exception to the general rule of promoter liability is that if the contracting party knows the corporation is not in existence but nevertheless agrees to look solely to the corporation and not to the promoter for payment, then the promoter incurs no personal liability. In the absence of an express agreement, the existence of an agreement to release the promoter from liability may be shown by circumstances making it reasonably certain that the parties intended to and did enter into the agreement. Release of the promoter depends on the intent of the parties. The promoter has the burden of proving an alleged agreement to release the promoter from liability.

Fox seeks to bring himself within the exception to the general rule of promoter liability. However, as the proponent of the exception, he must bear the burden of proving the existence of the alleged agreement releasing him from liability. There was no agreement regarding Fox's liability. Thus, Fox failed to sustain his burden of proof, and the trial court erred in granting judgment in his favor.

Judgment reversed in favor of Coopers.

Obtaining a Binding Preincorporation Contract

While it may be desirable for the promoter to escape liability on a preincorporation contract, there is one disadvantage: Only when the promoter is liable on the preincorporation contract is the other party liable on the contract. This means that when the promoter is not liable on the contract, the other party to the contract may rescind the contract at any time prior to adoption by the corporation. Once the corporation has adopted the contract, the corporation and the third party are liable on it, and the contract cannot be rescinded without the consent of both parties.

To maintain the enforceability of a preincorporation contract prior to adoption, a promoter may want to be liable on a preincorporation contract at least until the corporation comes into existence and adopts the contract. To limit his liability, however, the promoter may wish to have his liability cease automatically upon adoption. The promoter should ensure that the contract has an **automatic novation clause**. For example, a preincorporation contract may read that "the promoter's liability on this contract shall terminate upon the corporation's adoption of this contract."

Instead of using automatic novation clauses, today most well-advised promoters incorporate the business prior to making any contracts for the corporation. By doing so, only the corporation and the third party—and not the promoter—have liability on the contract.

Preincorporation Share Subscriptions

Promoters sometimes use **preincorporation share subscriptions** to ensure that the corporation will have adequate capital when it begins its business. Under the terms of a share subscription, a prospective shareholder offers to buy a specific number of the corporation's shares at a stated price. Under the Model Business Corporation Act (MBCA), a prospective shareholder may not revoke a preincorporation subscription for a six-month period, in the absence of a contrary provision in the subscription. Generally, corporate acceptance of preincorporation subscriptions occurs by action of the board of directors after incorporation.

Promoters have no liability on preincorporation share subscriptions. They have a duty, however, to make a good faith effort to bring the corporation into existence. When a corporation fails to accept a preincorporation subscription or becomes insolvent, the promoter is not liable to the disappointed subscriber, in the absence of fraud or other wrongdoing by the promoter.

Today, most promoters incorporate the business and obtain promises to buy shares from prospective shareholders. These promises, which may take the form of postincorporation subscriptions, are discussed later in this chapter.

Relation of Promoter and Prospective Corporation

A promoter of a nonexistent corporation is not an agent of the prospective corporation but nonetheless owes fiduciary duties to it. A promoter is not an agent of prospective investors in the business because they did not appoint him and they have no power to control him.

Although not an agent of the proposed corporation or its investors, a promoter owes a **fiduciary duty** to the corporation and to its prospective investors. A promoter owes such parties a duty of full disclosure and honesty. For example, a promoter breaches this duty when she diverts money received from prospective shareholders to pay her expenses, unless the shareholders agree to such payment. The fiduciary duty also prevents a promoter from diverting a business opportunity from the corporation and giving it to himself instead. In addition, the promoter may not purchase shares of the corporation at a price lower than that paid by the public shareholders.

A promoter may not profit personally by transacting secretly with the corporation in his personal capacity. The promoter's failure to disclose her interest in the transaction and the material facts permits the corporation to rescind the transaction or to recover the promoter's secret profit. On the other hand, the promoter's full disclosure of her interest and the material facts of the transaction to an independent board of directors that approves the transaction prevents the corporation from recovering the promoter's profit. Note, however, that when a promoter is a director, approval of the transaction by the board of directors is not sufficient; the transaction must be intrinsically fair to the corporation.

In the following case, the court held that promoters are fiduciaries of the corporation they organize.

Smith v. Bitter
319 N.W.2d 196 (Iowa Sup. Ct. 1982)

Joseph J. Smith, Steve J. Smith, and Joseph Bitter planned to open a tavern in the college town of Dubuque, Iowa. In the name of Gomer's, Inc., a corporation not yet formed, all three signed an offer to purchase a building in which to operate the tavern. After Gomer's, Inc., had been incorporated, the Smiths as corporate officers signed a contract to purchase the building in the name of the corporation. Soon after business began, differences arose between the Smiths and Bitter. Despite Bitter's protests, the Smiths assumed control of the corporation, including the building. Bitter sued the Smiths, asking the court to declare that Bitter and the Smiths as individuals owned the building and that Gomer's, Inc., had no interest in the building. The trial court held that Gomer's, Inc., owned the building. Bitter appealed to the Supreme Court of Iowa.

LeGrand, Justice   This litigation culminates what started as a business venture among friends and terminated in acrimony and distrust.

In negotiating for the purchase of the real estate, Bitter and the Smiths were promoters acting for the corporation they were then in the process of organizing. A promoter stands in a fiduciary position toward both the corporation and its stockholders and is prohibited from acquiring a secret personal advantage from any action taken on behalf of the corporation.

The Smiths and Bitter owed a fiduciary duty to the corporation for which they were acting and to its shareholders. The fact that the promoters themselves were the stockholders does not alter that obligation. The record is clear that all negotiations for purchase of the real estate were made on behalf of Gomer's, Inc., which the Smiths and Bitter were then organizing. Bitter cannot profit personally from this transaction nor can he assert

personal ownership of the real estate against those toward whom he was bound to exercise the utmost good faith.

Judgment for the Smiths affirmed.

Liability of Corporation to Promoter

Valuable as the services of a promoter may be to a prospective corporation and to society, a corporation is generally not required to compensate a promoter for her promotional services, or even her expenses, unless the corporation has agreed expressly to compensate the promoter. The justification for this rule is that the promoter is self-appointed and acts for a corporation that is not in existence.

Nonetheless, a corporation may choose to reimburse the promoter for her reasonable expenses and to pay her the value of her services to the corpora-

tion. Corporations often compensate their promoters with shares. The MBCA permits the issuance of shares for a promoter's preincorporation services.

To ensure that she is compensated for her services, a promoter may tie herself to a person or property that the corporation needs to succeed. For example, a promoter may purchase the invention that the corporation was formed to exploit. Another way to ensure compensation is by the promoter dominating the board of directors during the early months of its life. By doing so, the promoter may direct the corporation to compensate her.

CONCEPT REVIEW

PREINCORPORATION CONTRACTS

Promoter Liability	A promoter is liable on a preincorporation contract unless either:
	 1. The third party knows of the nonexistence of the corporation and insists that the promoter sign in the name of the corporation, or
	 2. The third party knows of the nonexistence of corporation and agrees only to look to prospective corporation for performance, or
	 3. Novation occurs either:
	   a. By agreement of the corporation and the third party, or
	   b. By use of an automatic novation clause.

Corporation Liability	A corporation is *not* liable on a preincorporation contract until the board of directors adopts the contract.
Third-Party Liability	A third party is liable on a preincorporation contract if either the promoter or the corporation is liable on the contract

---

INCORPORATION

Anyone seeking to incorporate a business must decide where to do so. If the business of a proposed corporation is to be primarily *intrastate*, it is usually cheaper

to incorporate in the state where the corporation's business is to be conducted. For the business that is primarily *interstate*, however, the business may benefit by incorporating in a state different from the state in which it has its principal place of business.

Incorporation fees and taxes, annual fees, and other fees such as those on the transfer of shares or the dissolution of the corporation vary considerably from state to state. Delaware has been a popular state in which to incorporate because its fees tend to be low.

Promoters frequently choose to incorporate in a state whose corporation statute and court decisions grant managers broad management discretion. For example, it is easier to pay a large dividend and to effect a merger in Delaware than in many other states.

Steps in Incorporation

There are only a few requirements for incorporation. It is a fairly simple process and can be accomplished inexpensively in most cases. The steps prescribed by the incorporation statutes of the different states vary, but they generally include the following, which appear in the MBCA:

1. Preparation of articles of incorporation.
2. Signing and authenticating the articles by one or more incorporators.
3. Filing the articles with the secretary of state, accompanied by the payment of specified fees.
4. Receipt of a copy of the articles of incorporation stamped "Filed" by the secretary of state, accompanied by a fee receipt. (Some states retain the old MBCA rule requiring receipt of a certificate of incorporation issued by the secretary of state.)
5. Holding an organization meeting for the purpose of adopting bylaws, electing officers, and transacting other business.

Articles of Incorporation   The basic governing document of the corporation is the **articles of incorporation** (sometimes called the charter). The articles are similar to a constitution. They state many of the rights and responsibilities of the corporation, its management, and its shareholders. Figure 1 lists the contents of the articles.

The corporation must have a name that is distinguishable from the name of any other corporation incorporated or qualified to do business in the state. The name must include the word *corporation, incorporated, company,* or *limited,* or the abbreviation *corp., inc., co.,* or *ltd.*

The MBCA does not require the inclusion of a statement of purpose in the articles. When a purpose

---

FIGURE 1   Contents of Articles of Incorporation (pursuant to MBCA)

The following *must* be in the articles:

1. The name of the corporation.
2. The number of shares that the corporation has authority to issue.
3. The address of the initial registered office of the corporation and the name of its registered agent.
4. The name and address of each incorporator.

The following *may* be included in the articles:

1. The names and addresses of the individuals who are to serve as the initial directors.
2. The purpose of the corporation.
3. The duration of the corporation.
4. The par value of shares of the corporation.
5. Additional provisions not inconsistent with law for managing the corporation, regulating the internal affairs of the corporation, and establishing the powers of the corporation and its directors and shareholders.

---

is stated, it is sufficient to state, alone or together with specific purposes, that the corporation may engage in "any lawful activity."

The MBCA permits a corporation to have perpetual existence. If desired, the articles of incorporation may provide for a shorter duration.

Most of the state corporation statutes require the articles to recite the initial capitalization of the business. Usually, the statutes require that there be a minimum amount of initial capital, such as $1,000. Since such a small amount of capital is rarely enough to protect creditors adequately, the MBCA dispenses with the need to recite a minimum amount of capital.

The articles may contain additional provisions not inconsistent with law for managing the corporation, regulating the internal affairs of the corporation, and establishing the powers of the corporation and its directors and shareholders. For example, these additional provisions may contain the procedures for electing directors, the quorum requirements for shareholders' and directors' meetings, and the dividend rights of shareholders.

The MBCA specifies that one or more persons, including corporations, partnerships, and unincorporated associations, may serve as the **incorporators**.

Incorporators have no function beyond lending their names and signatures to the process of bringing the corporation into existence. No special liability attaches to a person merely because she serves as an incorporator.

Filing Articles of Incorporation

The articles of incorporation must be delivered to the office of the secretary of state, and a filing fee must be paid. The office of the secretary of state reviews the articles of incorporation that are delivered to it. If the articles contain everything that is required, the secretary of state stamps the articles "Filed" and returns a copy of the stamped articles to the corporation along with a receipt for payment of incorporation fees. Some states require a duplicate filing of the articles with an office—usually the county recorder's office—in the county in which the corporation has its principal place of business.

The existence of the corporation begins when the articles are filed by the secretary of state. Filing of the articles is conclusive proof of the existence of the corporation.

Because the articles of incorporation embody the basic contract between a corporation and its shareholders, shareholders must approve most changes in the articles. For example, when the articles are amended to increase the number of authorized shares, shareholder approval is required.

The Organization Meeting

After the articles of incorporation have been filed by the secretary of state, an organization meeting is held. Usually, it is the first formal meeting of the directors. Frequently, only bylaws are adopted and officers elected. The function of the bylaws is to supplement the articles of incorporation by defining more precisely the powers, rights, and responsibilities of the corporation, its managers, and its shareholders and by stating other rules under which the corporation and its activities will be governed. Its common contents are listed in Figure 2.

The MBCA gives the incorporators or the initial directors the power to adopt the initial bylaws. The board of directors holds the power to repeal and to amend the bylaws, unless the articles reserve this power to the shareholders. Under the MBCA, the shareholders, as the ultimate owners of the corporation, always retain the power to amend the bylaws,

---

FIGURE 2	**Contents of the Bylaws**

1. The authority of the officers and the directors, specifying what they may or may not do.
2. The time and place at which the annual shareholders' meetings will be held.
3. The procedure for calling special meetings of shareholders.
4. The procedures for shareholders' and directors' meetings, including whether more than a majority is required for approval of specified actions.
5. Provisions for special committees of the board, defining their membership and the scope of their activities.
6. The procedures for the maintenance of share records.
7. The machinery for the transfer of shares.
8. The procedures and standards for the declaration and payment of dividends.

---

even if the directors also have such power. To be valid, bylaws must be consistent with the law and with the articles of incorporation.

If the organization meeting is the first meeting of the board of directors, the board may adopt a corporate seal for use on corporate documents, approve the form of share certificates, accept share subscriptions, authorize the issuance of shares, adopt preincorporation contracts, authorize reimbursement for promoters' expenses, and fix the salaries of officers.

Filing Annual Report

To retain its status as a corporation in good standing, a corporation must file an annual report with the secretary of state of the state of incorporation and pay an annual franchise fee or tax. The amount of annual franchise tax varies greatly from state to state. While the annual report includes very little information and repeats information already filed in the articles of incorporation, failure to file an annual report or pay the annual fee or tax may result in a dissolution of the corporation and an imposition of monetary penalties.

Close Corporation Elections

Close corporations face problems that normally do not affect publicly held corporations. In recognition of these problems, nearly half of the states have statutes that attend to the special needs of close corporations. For example, some corporation statutes allow a close corporation to be managed by its shareholders.

To take advantage of these close corporation statutes, most statutes require that a corporation make an *election* to be treated as a close corporation. The Statutory Close Corporation Supplement to the MBCA permits a corporation with *fewer than 50 shareholders* to elect to become a close corporation. The Close Corporation Supplement requires the articles of incorporation to state that the corporation is a statutory close corporation.

There is no penalty for a corporation's failure to make a close corporation election. The only consequence of a failure to meet the requirements is that the close corporation statutory provisions are inapplicable. Instead, statutory corporation law will treat the corporation as it treats any other general corporation.

Note, however, that even when a corporation fails to meet the statutory requirements for treatment as a close corporation, a court may decide to apply special *common law* rules applicable only to close corporations.

DEFECTIVE ATTEMPTS TO INCORPORATE

When business managers attempt to incorporate a business, sometimes they fail to comply with all the conditions for incorporation. For example, the incorporators may not have filed articles of incorporation or the directors may not have held an organization meeting. These are examples of **defective attempts to incorporate,** which may result in the business managers and investors having personal liability for the obligations of the defectively formed corporation.

One possible consequence of defective incorporation is to make the managers and the purported shareholders *personally liable* for the obligations of the defectively formed corporation. For example, an employee of an insolvent corporation drives the corporation's truck over a pedestrian. If the pedestrian proves that the corporation was defectively formed, he may be able to recover damages for his injuries from the managers and the shareholders.

A second possible consequence of defective incorporation is that a party to a contract involving the purported corporation may claim nonexistence of the corporation in order to avoid a contract made in the name of the corporation. For example, a person makes an ill-advised contract with a corporation. If the person proves that the corporation was defectively formed, he may escape liability on the contract because he made a contract with a nonexistent person, the defectively formed corporation. As an alternative, the defectively formed corporation may escape liability on the contract on the grounds that its nonexistence makes it impossible for it to have liability.

The courts have tried to determine when these two consequences should arise by making a distinction between de jure corporations, de facto corporations, corporations by estoppel, and corporations so defectively formed that they are treated as being nonexistent.

De Jure Corporation

A de jure corporation is formed when the promoters substantially comply with each of the **mandatory conditions precedent** to the incorporation of the business. Mandatory provisions are distinguished from directory provisions by statutory language and the purpose of the provision. Mandatory provisions are those that the corporation statute states "shall" or "must" be done or those that are necessary to protect the public interest. Directory provisions are those that "may" be done and that are unnecessary to protect the public interest.

For example, statutes provide that the incorporators shall file the articles of incorporation with the secretary of state. This is a mandatory provision, due not only to the use of the word *shall* but also to the importance of the filing in protecting the public interest. Other mandatory provisions include conducting an organization meeting. Directory provisions include minor matters such as the inclusion of the incorporators' addresses in the articles of incorporation.

If a corporation has complied with each mandatory provision, it is a de jure corporation and is treated as a corporation for all purposes. The validity of a de jure corporation cannot be attacked, except in a few states in which the state, in a *quo warranto* proceeding, may attack the corporation for noncompliance with a condition subsequent to incorporation, such as a failure to file an annual report with the secretary of state.

De Facto Corporation

A de facto corporation exists when the incorporators fail in some material respect to comply with all of the mandatory provisions of the incorporation statute yet comply with most mandatory provisions. There are three requirements for a de facto corporation:

1. There is a valid statute under which the corporation could be organized.
2. The promoters or managers make an honest attempt to organize under the statute. This requires substantial compliance with the mandatory provisions taken as a whole.
3. The promoters or managers exercise corporate powers. That is, they act as if they were acting for a corporation.

Generally, failing to file the articles of incorporation with the secretary of state will prevent the creation of a de facto corporation. However, a de facto corporation will exist despite the lack of an organization meeting or the failure to make a duplicate filing of the articles with a county recorder.

A de facto corporation is treated as a corporation against either an attack by a third party or an attempt of the business itself to deny that it is a corporation. The state, however, may attack the claimed corporate status of the business in a *quo warranto* action.

Corporation by Estoppel

When people hold themselves out as representing a corporation or believe themselves to be dealing with a corporation, a court will estop those people from denying the existence of a corporation. This is called **corporation by estoppel**. For example, a manager states that a business has been incorporated and induces a third person to contract with the purported corporation. The manager will not be permitted to use a failure to incorporate as a defense to the contract because he has misled others to believe reasonably that a corporation exists.

Under the doctrine of estoppel, each contract must be considered individually to determine whether either party to the contract is estopped from denying the corporation's existence.

Liability for Defective Incorporation

If people attempt to organize a corporation but their efforts are so defective that not even a corporation by estoppel is found to exist, the courts have generally held such persons to be partners with unlimited liability for the contracts and torts of the business. However, most courts impose the unlimited *contractual* liability of a partner only on those who are *actively engaged in the management* of the business or who are responsible for the defects in its organization. *Tort* liability, however, is generally imposed on everyone—the managers and the purported shareholders of the defectively formed corporation.

Modern Approaches to the Defective Incorporation Problem

As you can see, the law of defective incorporation is confusing. It becomes even more confusing when you consider that many of the defective incorporation cases look like promoter liability cases, and vice versa. A court may have difficulty deciding whether to apply the law of promoter liability or the law of defective incorporation to preincorporation contracts. It is not surprising, therefore, that modern corporation statutes have attempted to eliminate this confusion by adopting simple rules for determining the existence of a corporation and the liability of its promoters, managers, and shareholders.

The MBCA states that incorporation occurs when the articles are filed by the secretary of state. The **filing** of the articles is **conclusive proof** of the existence of the corporation, except in a proceeding brought by the state. Consequently, the incorporators may omit even a mandatory provision, yet create a corporation, provided that the secretary of state has filed the articles of incorporation. Conversely, courts have held that a failure to obtain a filing of the articles is conclusive proof of the nonexistence of the corporation, on the grounds that the MBCA eliminates the concepts of de facto corporation and corporation by estoppel.

Figure 3 summarizes the preceding discussion.

Liability for Defective Incorporation under the MBCA   The MBCA imposes joint and several liability on those persons who purport to act on behalf of a corporation and know that there has been

FIGURE 3   **Defective Attempts to Incorporate**

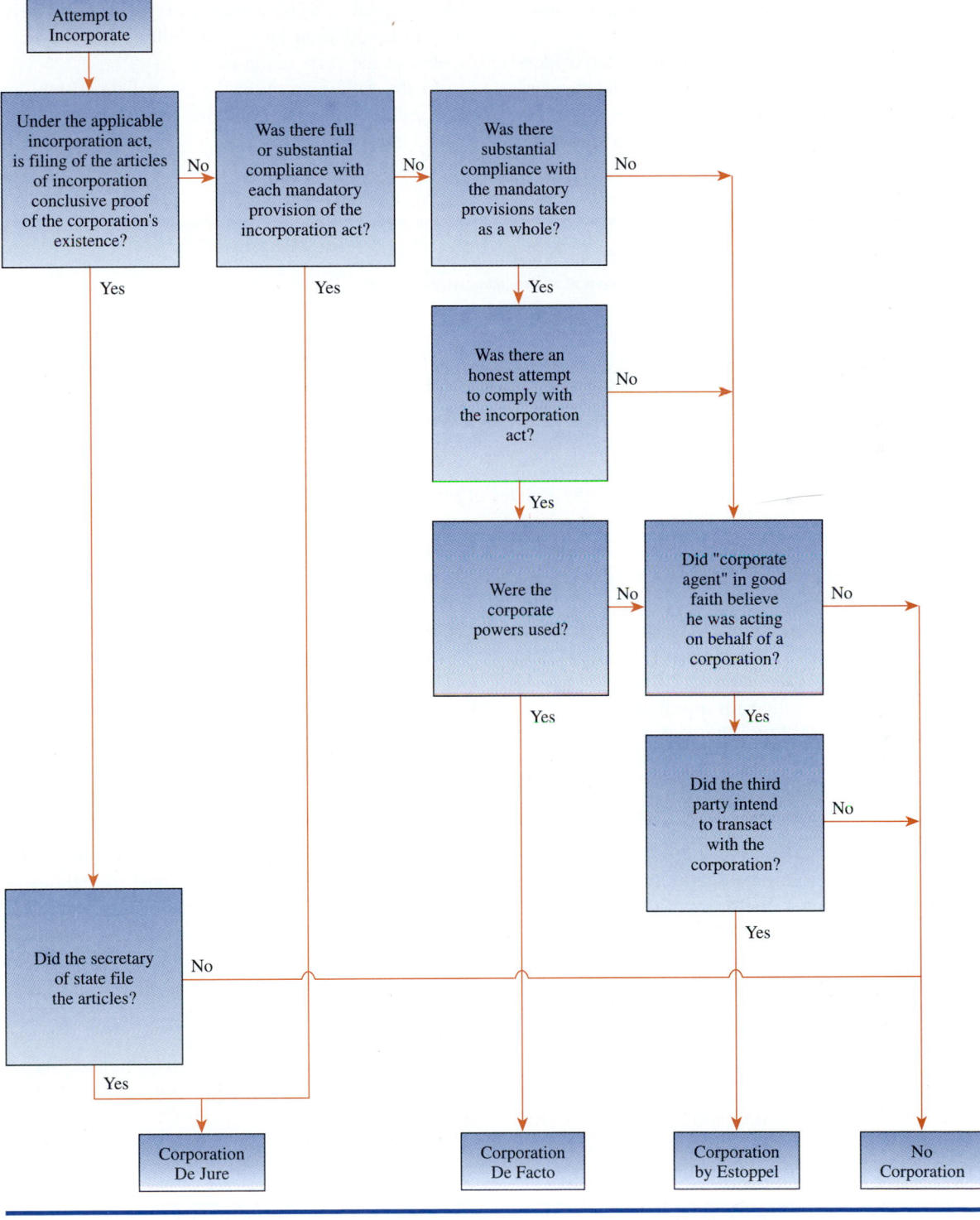

no incorporation. Managers and shareholders who both (1) *participate* in the operational decisions of the business and (2) *know* that the corporation does not exist are liable for the purported corporation's contracts and torts.

The MBCA releases from liability shareholders and others who either (1) take no part in the management of the defectively formed corporation *or* (2) mistakenly believe that the corporation is in existence.

Consequently, *passive* shareholders have no liability for the obligations of a defectively formed corporation even when they know that the corporation has not been formed. Likewise, managers of a defectively formed corporation have no liability when they believe that the corporation exists.

In the following case, the court held that filing the articles of incorporation conclusively established the existence of a closely held corporation.

WARTHAN V. MIDWEST CONSOLIDATED INSURANCE AGENCIES, INC.
450 N.W.2d 145 (Minn. Ct. App. 1990)

David Warthan and Mary Knettel owned an insurance agency in St. Cloud, Minnesota. Clifford Koltes, James McMahill, and Thomas Kellin owned an insurance agency in Minnetonka, Minnesota. The two groups agreed to combine their insurance agencies into one agency. They agreed that each group would own 50 percent of the new agency. They agreed to transfer their existing insurance policy business to a new corporation, to be named Midwest Consolidated Insurance Agencies, Inc. (MCIA), to renew insurance policies in the name of MCIA, and to seek new insurance business for MCIA. Articles of incorporation for MCIA were filed by the secretary of state of Minnesota.

Several contracts were made in the name of MCIA to purchase the businesses of three additional insurance agencies. However, the two groups had difficulty combining their operations. No shares of stock were issued. No formal shareholder or directors meetings were held. Although bylaws were drafted, they were never approved. Eventually, the groups agreed to separate their operations as they had existed prior to their combination. However, the Minnetonka group continued to operate the three agencies purchased in the name of MCIA, eventually transferring the agencies to MCI, Inc., a corporation owned by the Minnetonka group. The St. Cloud group filed for a judicial dissolution of MCIA on the grounds that the Minnetonka group had breached a fiduciary duty. The trial court held that MCIA never came into existence and that, therefore, no fiduciary duties existed and MCIA could not be dissolved. The St. Cloud group appealed.

Parker, Judge The trial court concluded that MCIA was not a closely held corporation in law or fact because it did not conform with the Minnesota Business Corporation Act (MBCA).

The corporate existence begins when the articles of incorporation are filed with the secretary of state accompanied by a payment of the incorporation and filing fees. The filing creates an irrefutable presumption that the corporation is and has been incorporated in this state.

Articles of incorporation were filed and the required fee paid on behalf of MCIA; as a matter of law, MCIA is a corporation and the trial court erred in concluding otherwise.

The trial court determined that because MCIA failed to follow certain organizational formalities in the Minnesota Business Corporation Act (MBCA), it was a defectively formed corporation. The MBCA provides that a closely held corporation may, but need not, have bylaws. Annual or otherwise regular meetings of the shareholders need only be held if required by the articles or bylaws or by demand. Unless provided for in the articles or bylaws, meetings of the board are not required unless called by a board member.

MCIA's articles do not require regular meetings. There is no evidence that any shareholder or director demanded or called a meeting. Therefore, the trial court erred in finding a deficiency in MCIA's failure to follow these particular organization guidelines. Further, the facts demonstrate that MCIA was more than a corporation in name only. Among other things, it entered into contracts to purchase the business of three insurance agencies, paid salaries, and maintained an office in Minnetonka.

The trial court's second conclusion of law is expressly based on its determination that MCIA is not a corporation; because erroneous, it must fail. This second conclusion concerns the fiduciary duties owed by the Minnetonka group to the St. Cloud group. As these parties were partners in a closely held corporation, they had a fiduciary duty to deal openly, honestly, and fairly with each other.

In determining whether to order dissolution involving a closely held corporation, the court shall take into consideration the duty which all shareholders in a closely held corporation owe one another to act in an honest, fair, and reasonable manner. The Minnetonka group controlled the operation of the newly acquired insurance agencies, eventually transferring them from MCIA to another corporation without consent of the St. Cloud group. The Minnetonka group therefore acted illegally and prejudicially toward the St. Cloud group.

Judgment reversed in favor of Warthan and Knettel; remanded to the trial court.

FINANCING THE CORPORATION

Any business needs money to operate and to grow. One advantage of incorporation is the large number of sources of funds that are available to businesses that incorporate. One such source is the sale of corporate **securities**, including shares, debentures, bonds, and long-term notes payable.

In addition to obtaining funds from the sale of securities, a corporation may be financed by other sources. A bank may lend money to the corporation in exchange for the corporation's short-term promissory notes, called commercial paper. Earnings provide a source of funds once the corporation is operating profitably. In addition, the corporation may use normal short-term financing, such as accounts receivable financing and inventory financing.

In this section, you will study only one source of corporate funds—a corporation's sale of securities. A corporate security may be either (1) a share in the corporation or (2) an obligation of the corporation. These two kinds of securities are called equity securities and debt securities.

Equity Securities

Every business corporation issues equity securities, which are commonly called stock or **shares.** The issuance of shares creates an ownership relationship: the holders of the shares—called stockholders or **shareholders**—are the owners of the corporation.

Modern statutes permit corporations to issue several classes of shares and to determine the rights of the various classes. Subject to minimum guarantees contained in the state business corporation law, the shareholders' rights are a matter of contract and appear in the articles of incorporation, in the bylaws, in a shareholder agreement, and on the share certificates.

Common Shares   Common shares (or common stock) are a type of equity security. Ordinarily, the owners of common shares—called **common shareholders**—have the exclusive right to elect the directors, who manage the corporation.

The common shareholders often occupy a position inferior to that of other investors, notably creditors and preferred shareholders. The claims of common shareholders are subordinate to the claims of creditors and other classes of shareholders when liabilities and dividends are paid and when assets are distributed upon liquidation.

In return for this subordination, however, the common shareholders have an exclusive claim to the corporate earnings and assets that exceed the claims of creditors and other shareholders. Therefore, the common shareholders bear the major risks of the corporate venture, yet stand to profit the most if it is successful.

Preferred Shares   Shares that have preferences with regard to assets or dividends over other classes of shares are called preferred shares (or preferred stock). **Preferred shareholders** are customarily given liquidation and dividend preferences over common shareholders. A corporation may have several classes of preferred shares. In such a situation, one class of preferred shares may be given preferences over another class of preferred shares. Under the MBCA, the preferences of preferred shareholders must be set out in the articles of incorporation.

The **liquidation preference** of preferred shares is usually a stated dollar amount. During a liquidation, this amount must be paid to each preferred shareholder before any common shareholder or other shareholder subordinated to the preferred class may receive his share of the corporation's assets.

Dividend preferences may vary greatly. For example, the dividends may be cumulative or noncumulative. Dividends on **cumulative** preferred shares, if not paid in any year, accumulate until paid. The entire accumulation must be paid before any dividends may be paid to common shareholders. Dividends on **noncumulative** preferred shares do not accumulate if unpaid. For such shares, only the current year's dividends must be paid to preferred shareholders prior to the payment of dividends to common shareholders.

Participating preferred shares have priority up to a stated amount or percentage of the dividends to be paid by the corporation. Then, the preferred shareholders participate with the common shareholders in additional dividends paid.

Some close corporations attempt to create preferred shares with a **mandatory dividend** right. These mandatory dividend provisions have generally been held illegal as unduly restricting the powers of the board of directors. Today, a few courts and some special close corporation statutes permit mandatory dividends.

A **redemption** provision in the articles allows a corporation at its option to repurchase preferred shareholders' shares at a price stated in the articles, despite the shareholders' unwillingness to sell. Some statutes permit the articles to give the shareholders the right to force the corporation to redeem preferred shares.

Preferred shares may be **convertible** into another class of shares, usually common shares. A **conversion** right allows a preferred shareholder to ex-

change her preferred shares for another class of shares, usually common shares. The conversion rate or price is stated in the articles.

Preferred shares have **voting rights** unless the articles provide otherwise. Usually, most voting rights are taken from preferred shares, except for important matters such as voting for a merger or a change in preferred shareholders' dividend rights. Rarely are preferred shareholders given the right to vote for directors, except in the event of a corporation's default in the payment of dividends.

Authorized, Issued, and Outstanding Shares

Authorized shares are shares that a corporation is permitted to issue by its articles of incorporation. A corporation may not issue more shares than are authorized. **Issued** shares are shares that have been sold to shareholders. **Outstanding** shares are shares that are currently held by shareholders. The distinctions between these terms are important. For example, a corporation pays cash, property, and share dividends only on outstanding shares. Only outstanding shares may be voted at a shareholders' meeting.

Canceled Shares   Sometimes, a corporation will purchase its own shares. A corporation may cancel repurchased shares. Canceled shares do not exist: they are neither authorized, issued, nor outstanding. Since canceled shares do not exist, they cannot be reissued.

Shares Restored to Unissued Status   Repurchased shares may be restored to unissued status instead of being canceled. If this is done, the shares are merely authorized and they may be reissued at a later time.

Treasury Shares   If repurchased shares are neither canceled nor restored to unissued status, they are called **treasury shares**. Such shares are authorized and issued, but not outstanding. They may be sold by the corporation at a later time. The corporation may not vote them at shareholders' meetings, and it may not pay a cash or property dividend on them.

The MBCA abolishes the concept of treasury shares. It provides that repurchased shares are restored to unissued status and may be reissued, unless the articles of incorporation require cancellation.

Options, Warrants, and Rights

Equity securities include options to purchase common shares and preferred shares. The MBCA expressly permits the board of directors to issue **options** for the purchase of the corporation's shares. Share options are often issued to top-level managers as an incentive to increase the profitability of the corporation. An increase in profitability should increase the market value of the corporation's shares, resulting in increased compensation to the employees who own and exercise share options.

Warrants are options evidenced by certificates. They are sometimes part of a package of securities sold as a unit. For example, they may be sold along with notes, bonds, or even shares. Underwriters may receive warrants as part of their compensation for aiding a corporation in selling its shares to the public.

Rights are short-term certificated options that are usually transferable. Rights are used to give present security holders an option to subscribe to a proportional quantity of the same or a different security of the corporation. They are most often issued in connection with a **preemptive right** requirement, which obligates a corporation to offer each existing shareholder the opportunity to buy the corporation's newly issued shares in the same proportion as the shareholder's current ownership of the corporation's shares.

Debt Securities

Corporations have inherent power to borrow money necessary for their operations by issuing debt securities. Debt securities create a debtor-creditor relationship between the corporation and the security holder. With the typical debt security, the corporation is obligated to pay interest periodically and to pay the amount of the debt (the principal) on the maturity date. Debt securities include debentures, bonds, and notes payable.

Debentures are long-term, unsecured debt securities. Typically, a debenture has a term of 10 to 30 years. Debentures usually have indentures. An indenture is a contract that states the rights of the debenture holders. For example, an indenture defines what acts constitute default by the corporation and what rights the debenture holders have upon default. It may place restrictions on the corporation's right to issue other debt securities.

Bonds are long-term, secured debt securities that usually have indentures. They are identical to debentures except that bonds are secured by collateral. The collateral for bonds may be real property such as a building, or personal property such as a commercial airplane. If the debt is not paid, the bondholders may force the sale of the collateral and take the proceeds of the sale.

Generally, **notes** have a shorter duration than debentures or bonds. They seldom have terms exceeding five years. Notes may be secured or unsecured.

It is not uncommon for notes or debentures to be **convertible** into other securities, usually preferred or common shares. The right to convert belongs to the holder of the convertible note or debenture. This conversion right permits an investor to receive interest as a debt holder and, after conversion, to share in the increased value of the corporation as a shareholder.

CONSIDERATION FOR SHARES

The board of directors has the power to issue shares on behalf of the corporation. The board must decide at what *price* and for what *type of consideration* it will issue the shares. Corporation statutes restrict the discretion of the board in accepting specified kinds of consideration and in determining the value of the shares it issues.

Quality of Consideration for Shares

Not all kinds of consideration in contract law are acceptable as legal consideration for shares in corporation law. To protect creditors and other shareholders, the statutes require legal consideration to have *real value*. Modern statutes, however, place few limits on the type of consideration that may be received for shares. The MBCA permits shares to be issued in return for any tangible or intangible *property* or *benefit to the corporation,* including cash, promissory notes, services performed for the corporation, contracts for services *to be performed* for the corporation, and securities of the corporation or another corporation. The rationale for the MBCA rule is a recognition that future services and promises of future services have value that is as real as that of tangible property. Consequently, for example, a corporation may issue common shares to its president in exchange for the president's commitment to work for the corporation for three years or in exchange for bonds of the corporation or debentures issued by another corporation. In addition, the MBCA permits corporations to issue shares to their promoters in consideration for their promoters' preincorporation services. This rule acknowledges that a corporation benefits from a promoter's preincorporation services.

Several states' constitutions place stricter limits on permissible consideration for shares. They provide that shares may be issued only for money paid to the corporation, labor done for the corporation, or property actually received by the corporation. Such a rule prohibits a corporation from issuing its shares for a promise to pay money or a promise to provide services to the corporation in the future.

Quantity of Consideration for Shares

The board is required to issue shares for an adequate dollar amount of consideration. Whether shares have been issued for an adequate amount of consideration depends in part on the *par value* of the shares. The more important concern, however, is whether the shares have been issued for *fair value*.

Par Value   Par value is an arbitrary dollar amount that may be assigned to the shares by the articles of incorporation. Par value does not reflect the fair market value of the shares, but par value is the minimum amount of consideration for which the shares may be issued.

Shares issued for less than par value are called **discount shares**. The board of directors is liable to the corporation for issuing shares for less than par

value. A shareholder who purchases shares from the corporation for less than par value is liable to the corporation for the difference between the par value and the amount she paid.

Fair Value   It is not always enough, however, for the board to issue shares for their par value. Many times, shares are worth more than their par value. In addition, many shares today do not have a par value. In fact, the MBCA purports to eliminate the concept of par value as it affects the issuance of shares. In such cases, the board must exercise care to ensure that the corporation receives the *fair value* of the shares it issues. If there are no par value problems, the board's judgment as to the amount of consideration that is received for the shares is *conclusive* when the board acts in good faith, exercises the care of ordinarily prudent directors, and acts in the best interests of the corporation.

Disputes may arise concerning the *value* of property that the corporation receives for its shares. The board's valuation of the consideration is conclusive if it acts in good faith with the care of prudent directors and in a manner it reasonably believes to be in the best interests of the corporation. When the board impermissibly overvalues the consideration for shares, the shareholder receives **watered shares**. Both the board and the shareholder are liable to the corporation when there is a watered shares problem.

When a shareholder pays less than the amount of consideration determined by the board of directors, the corporation or its creditors may sue the shareholder to recover the deficit. When a shareholder has paid the proper amount of consideration, the shares are said to be *fully paid and nonassessable*.

In the following case, the court considered whether a promissory note was legal and valuable consideration to be received for shares.

KIRK v. KIRK'S AUTO ELECTRIC, INC.
728 S.W.2d 529 (Ky. Sup. Ct. 1987)

Kirk's Auto Electric, Inc., issued 11 shares of common stock to Billy H. Bone, 10 shares to Andre Bone, and 5 shares to Joe T. Bone. In exchange for each issuance of shares, the Bones gave the corporation unsecured interest-bearing promissory notes payable on demand. The Bones were issued share certificates, which were signed on behalf of the corporation by Billy H. Bone, who was a director and president of the corporation, and by Clarence Kirk, who was a director and secretary of the corporation. No payments were made on the notes.

Later, Kirk contested the issuance on the grounds that the Bones had not paid proper or sufficient consideration for the shares. The trial court and the court of appeals held that Kirk could not contest the issuance of the shares because he had participated in the issuance. Kirk appealed to the Kentucky Supreme Court.

Lambert, Justice   Section 193 of the Constitution of Kentucky states:

No corporation shall issue stock, except for an equivalent in money paid or labor done, or property actually received and applied to the purposes for which such corporation was created, and neither labor nor property shall be received in payment of stock at a greater value than the market price at the time such labor was done or property delivered.

The constitutional provisions quoted herein evince a strong policy in this Commonwealth toward protecting corporations, shareholders, and corporate creditors from the dissipation of corporate assets. The issuance of shares must be attended by good faith and the corporation must receive value not disproportionate to the value of the shares issued.

The promissory notes received by Kirk's Auto Electric were unsecured and were payable only upon demand. The only persons eligible to demand payment from the makers of the notes were the members of the board of directors, Kirk and Billy

H. Bone, the same persons who authorized issuance of the shares and acceptance of the unsecured notes. Billy H. Bone was himself maker of one of the notes. Therefore, appropriate vigilance would be less than assured. This transaction well illustrates the need for strict enforcement of the constitutional requirements.

Our holding in this case may appear to be too restrictive and represent an interference with the power of a corporation to conduct its business affairs. In ordinary commercial transactions, unsecured promissory notes are essential and undoubtedly constitute valuable consideration. Nevertheless, the constitutional provisions are impressed with a public interest and their primary purpose is to prevent fraud and to protect creditors or purchasers of stock of corporations. If the public interest is to be protected, strict adherence to the law must be required.

Judgment reversed in favor of Kirk; remanded to the trial court.

Accounting for Consideration Received   The consideration received by a corporation for its equity securities appears in the equity or capital accounts in the shareholders' equity section of the corporation's balance sheet. The **stated capital** account records the product of the number of shares outstanding multiplied by the par value of each share. When the shares are sold for more than par value, the excess or surplus consideration received by the corporation is **capital surplus**.

Under the MBCA, the terms *stated capital* and *capital surplus* have been eliminated. All consideration received for shares is lumped under one accounting entry for that class of shares, such as common equity.

Resales of Shares   The par value of shares is important *only when the shares are issued* by the corporation. Since treasury shares are issued but not outstanding, the corporation does not issue treasury

shares when it resells them. Therefore, the board may sell treasury shares for less than par, provided that it sells the shares for an amount equal to their fair value.

Because par value and fair value are designed to ensure only that the corporation receives adequate consideration for its shares, a shareholder may buy shares from another shareholder for less than par value or fair value and incur no liability. However, if the purchasing shareholder *knows* that the selling shareholder bought the shares from the corporation for less than par value, the purchasing shareholder is liable to the corporation for the difference between the par value and the amount paid by the selling shareholder.

SHARE SUBSCRIPTIONS

Under the terms of a **share subscription**, a prospective shareholder promises to buy a specific number of shares of a corporation at a stated price. If the subscription is accepted by the corporation and the subscriber has paid for the shares, the subscriber is a shareholder of the corporation, even if the shares have not been issued. Under the MBCA, subscriptions need not be in writing to be enforceable. Usually, however, subscriptions are written.

Promoters use written share subscriptions in the course of selling shares of a proposed corporation to ensure that equity capital will be provided once the corporation comes into existence. These are called **preincorporation subscriptions**, which were covered in this chapter's discussion of promoters. Preincorporation subscriptions are not contracts binding on the corporation and the shareholders until the corporation comes into existence and its board of directors accepts the share subscriptions.

Close corporations may use share subscriptions when they seek to sell additional shares after incorporation. These are examples of **postincorporation subscriptions**, subscription agreements made *after* incorporation. A postincorporation subscription is a contract between the corporation and the subscriber at the time the subscription agreement is made.

A subscription may provide for payment of the price of the shares on a specified day, in installments, or upon the demand of the board of directors. The board may not discriminate when it demands payment: It must demand payment from all the subscribers of a class of shares or from none of them.

A share certificate may not be issued to a share subscriber until the price of the shares has been fully paid. If the subscriber fails to pay as agreed, the corporation may sue the subscriber for the amount owed.

ISSUANCE OF SHARES

Uniform Commercial Code (UCC) Article 8 regulates the issuance of securities. Under Article 8, a corporation has a duty to issue only the number of shares authorized by its articles. Overissued shares are void.

Even when a person is entitled to overissued shares, the corporation may not issue the shares. However, the person has two remedies. The corporation must obtain identical shares—if such shares are reasonably available—and deliver them to the person entitled to issuance. If identical shares are unavailable, the corporation must reimburse the person for the value paid for the shares plus interest.

The directors may incur liability, including criminal liability, for an overissuance of shares. To prevent overissuance through error in the issuance or transfer of their shares, corporations often employ a bank or a trust company as a registrar.

A share certificate is evidence that a person has been issued shares, owns the shares, and is a shareholder. The certificate states the corporation's name, the shareholder's name, and the number and class of shares. The certificate, however, is not the shares, which are intangible and cannot be possessed physically. A person can be a shareholder without receiving a share certificate, such as a holder of a share subscription. Under the MBCA, a corporation is not required to issue share certificates.

TRANSFER OF SHARES

Because share certificates are evidence of the ownership of shares, their transfer is evidence of the transfer of the ownership of shares. UCC Article 8 covers the registration and transfer of shares, as represented by certificates.

Share certificates are issued in *registered* form; that is, they are registered with the corporation in the name of a specific person. The indorsement of a share certificate on its back by its registered owner and the delivery of the certificate to another person transfers ownership of the shares to the other person. The transfer of a share certificate without naming a transferee creates a *street certificate*. A street certificate is similar to a bearer negotiable instrument. The transfer of a street certificate may be made by delivery without indorsement. Any holder of a street certificate is presumed to be the owner of the shares it represents. Therefore, a transferee should ask the corporation to reregister the shares in his name.

Under the UCC, a corporation owes a duty to register the transfer of any registered shares presented to it for registration, provided that the shares have been properly indorsed. If the corporation refuses to make the transfer, it is liable to the transferee for either conversion or specific performance.

When an owner of shares claims that his shares have been lost, destroyed, or stolen, the corporation must issue new shares to the owner unless the corporation has notice that the shares have been acquired by a bona fide purchaser. A **bona fide purchaser** is a purchaser of the shares for value in good faith with no notice of any adverse claim against the shares. If, after the issuance of the new shares, a bona fide purchaser of the original shares presents them for registration, the corporation must register the transfer, unless overissuance would result.

Restrictions on Transferability of Shares

Historically, a shareholder has been free to sell her shares to whomever she wants whenever she wants. The courts have been reluctant to allow restrictions on the free transferability of shares, even if the shareholder agreed to a restriction on the transfer of her shares. Gradually, the courts and the legislatures have recognized that there are good reasons to permit the use of some restrictions on the transfer of shares. Today, modern corporation statutes allow most transfer restrictions, especially for close corporations.

Types of Restrictions on Transfer   There are four categories of transfer restrictions that may be used to accomplish the objectives addressed above: (1) rights of first refusal and option agreements, (2) buy-and-sell agreements, (3) consent restraints, and (4) provisions disqualifying purchasers.

A **right of first refusal** grants to the corporation or the other shareholders the right to match the offer that a selling shareholder receives for her shares. An **option agreement** grants the corporation or the other shareholders an option to buy the selling shareholder's shares at a price determined by the agreement. An option agreement will usually state a formula used to calculate the price of the shares.

A **buy-and-sell agreement** compels a shareholder to sell his shares to the corporation or to the other shareholders at the price stated in the agreement. It also obligates the corporation or the other shareholders to buy the selling shareholder's shares at that price. The agreement is called a cross-purchase agreement when the shareholders are obligated to buy and sell. It is called a redemption agreement when the corporation is the person that is obligated to buy. The price of the shares is usually determined by a stated formula.

A **consent restraint** requires a selling shareholder to obtain the consent of the corporation or the other shareholders before she may sell her shares. A **provision disqualifying purchasers** may be used in rare situations to exclude unwanted persons from the corporation. For example, a transfer restriction may prohibit the shareholders from selling to a competitor of the business.

Uses of Transfer Restrictions   A corporation and its shareholders may use transfer restrictions to maintain the balance of shareholder power in the corporation. For example, four persons may own 25 shares each in a corporation. No single person can control such a corporation. If one of the four can buy 26 additional shares from the other shareholders, he will acquire control. The shareholders may therefore agree that each shareholder is entitled or required to buy an equal amount of any shares sold by any selling shareholder. The right of first refusal, option agreement, or buy-and-sell agreement may serve this purpose.

A buy-and-sell agreement may be used to guarantee a shareholder a market for his shares. For example, in a close corporation, there may be no ready market for the shares of the corporation. To ensure that a shareholder can obtain the value of her investment upon her retirement or death, the shareholders or the corporation may be required to buy a shareholder's shares upon the occurrence of a specific event such as death or retirement.

A buy-and-sell agreement may also be used to determine who should be required to sell and who should be required to buy shares when there is a severe disagreement between shareholders that threatens the profitability of the corporation.

In a close corporation, the shareholders may want only themselves or other approved persons as shareholders. A buy-and-sell agreement or right of first refusal may be used to prevent unwanted persons from becoming shareholders.

A provision disqualifying purchasers may be used in limited situations, such as when the purchaser is a competitor of the business or has a criminal background.

A consent restraint is used to preserve a close corporation or Subchapter S taxation election. Close corporation statutes and Subchapter S of the Internal Revenue Code limit the number of shareholders that a close corporation or S Corporation may have. A transfer restriction may prohibit the shareholders from selling shares if, as a result of the sale, there would be too many shareholders to preserve a close corporation or S Corporation election. A consent restraint is also used to preserve an exemption from registration of a securities offering. Under the Securities Act of 1933 and the state securities acts, an offering of securities is exempt from registration if the offering is to a limited number of investors, usually 35. A transfer restriction may require a selling shareholder to obtain permission from the corporation's legal counsel, which permission will be granted upon proof that the shareholder's sale of the shares does not cause the corporation to lose its registration exemption.

Legality of Transfer Restrictions   Corporation statutes permit the use of option agreements, rights of first refusal, and buy-and-sell agreements with virtually no restrictions. The MBCA authorizes transfer restrictions for any reasonable purpose. The reasonableness of a restraint is judged in light of the character and needs of the corporation.

Consent restraints and provisions disqualifying purchasers may be used if they are not *manifestly unreasonable*. The MBCA makes per se reasonable any consent restraint that maintains a corporation's status when that status is dependent on the number or identity of shareholders, as with close corporation

or S Corporation status. The MBCA also makes per se reasonable any restriction that preserves registration exemptions under the Securities Act of 1933 and state securities laws.

Enforceability   To be enforceable against a shareholder, a transfer restriction must be contained in the articles of incorporation, the bylaws, an agreement among the shareholders, or an agreement between the corporation and the shareholders. In addition, the shareholder must either agree to the restriction or purchase the shares with notice of the restriction. Under the MBCA, a purchaser of the shares has notice of a restriction if it is noted conspicuously on the face or the back of a share certificate or if it is a restriction of which he has knowledge.

The next case addresses the issue of whether a restriction is reasonable and whether it is conspicuously noted on the certificate.

LING AND CO. V. TRINITY SAVINGS AND LOAN ASS'N.
482 S.W.2d 841 (Tex. Sup. Ct. 1972)

When Bruce Bowman borrowed some money from Trinity Savings and Loan Association, he pledged 1,500 shares of Ling and Company Class A common stock as collateral for the loan. Bowman failed to repay Trinity. Trinity sued Bowman on the loan and asked the court to order the sale of the shares pledged as collateral. Ling and Company objected to the sale of the shares on the grounds that Ling's articles of incorporation restricted transfer of its shares. Trinity asked the court to invalidate the transfer restrictions. The restrictions appeared in Article 4 of Ling's articles of incorporation. One restriction was an option agreement that granted to the corporation and the other shareholders a 10-day option to buy the shares before the shares could be sold to any other person.

On the front side of the share certificate, in small print, it was stated that the shares were subject to the provisions of the articles of incorporation, that a copy of the articles could be obtained from the secretary of the corporation or the secretary of state, and that specific references to provisions setting forth restrictions were on the back of the certificate. On the back side, also in small type, the reference to the articles was repeated and specific mention was made of Article 4. Here, the option agreement was referred to but not stated fully.

The trial court held that the restrictions were invalid and ordered the sale of the shares. After the court of appeals affirmed the trial court's decision, Ling appealed to the Supreme Court of Texas.

Reavley, Justice   The court of civil appeals struck down the restrictions for the lack of conspicuous notice on the share certificate and the unreasonableness of the restrictions.

The Texas Business Corporation Act provides that a corporation may impose restrictions on the transfer of its shares, if they are "expressly set forth in the articles of incorporation and copied at length

or in summary form on the face or so copied on the back and referred to on the face of each certificate." The Legislature, at the same time, permitted an incorporation by reference on the face or back of a certificate of a provision in the articles of incorporation that restricts the transfer of the shares. In the present case, reference is made on the face of the certificate to the restrictions described on the reverse side; the notice on the reverse side refers to the particular article of the articles of incorporation as restricting the transfer or encumbrance of the shares and requiring "the holder thereof to grant options to purchase the shares represented hereby first to the Corporation and then pro rata to the other holders of the Class A Common Stock." We hold that the content of the certificate complies with the requirements of the Texas Business Corporation Act.

There remains the requirement that the restriction or reference on transferability be "noted conspicuously on the security." The UCC provides that a conspicuous term is so written as to be noticed by a reasonable person. Examples of conspicuous matter are given there as a "printed heading in capitals or larger or other contrasting type or color." This means that something must appear on the face of the certificate to attract the attention of a reasonable person when he looks at it. The line of print on the face of the Ling certificate does not stand out and cannot be considered conspicuous.

Our holding that the restriction is not noted conspicuously on the certificate does not entitle Trinity to a judgment under this record. The restriction is effective against a person with actual knowl-edge of it. The record does not establish conclusively that Trinity lacked knowledge of the restriction when Bowman executed an assignment of these shares to Trinity Savings and Loan.

A corporation may impose restrictions on the disposition of its shares, if the restrictions "do not unreasonably restrain or prohibit transferability." The court of appeals held that it is unreasonable to require a shareholder to notify all other record holders of Class A Common Stock of his intent to sell and give the other holders a 10-day option to buy. The record does not reveal the number of holders of this class of shares; we know only that there are more than 20. We find nothing unusual or oppressive in these first option provisions. Conceivably the number of shareholders might be so great as to make the burden too heavy upon the shareholder who wishes to sell and, at the same time, dispel any justification for contending that there exists a reasonable corporate purpose in restricting the ownership. There is, however, no proof of that.

Judgment reversed in favor of Ling. Case remanded to the trial court.

Although transfer restrictions are important to close corporations, many close corporation shareholders fail to address the share transferability problem. Therefore, a few states provide statutory resolution of the close corporation transferability problem. In these states, statutes offer solutions to the transferability problem that are similar to the solutions that the shareholders would have provided had they thought about the problem. Not all transferability problems are settled by the Close Corporation Supplement, however. For example, there is no statutory buy-and-sell provision.

ETHICAL AND PUBLIC POLICY CONCERNS

1. Suppose that a promoter of a prospective business, Promoter 1, chooses to incorporate the business prior to making any contracts for the prospective business. Because incorporation is a fairly simple process, Promoter 1 has done little more than Promoter 2, who makes preincorporation contracts. Yet Promoter 1 will not ordinarily have liability on contracts signed in the name of the corporation, while Promoter 2 will have liability. Does this distinction seem fair to the promoters? Is it fair to the other parties to the contract? Would your answers change if Promoter 1 incorporated the business with the minimum amount of capital required by the incorporation statute and then negotiated contracts obligating the business in amounts exceeding $100,000?

2. Under the Model Business Corporation Act, investors who believe that they have contributed capital to a corporation have no personal liability for the debts of the corporation even if it has been defectively formed. Why should such investors not be held liable as partners? Is it fair that the defectively formed corporation's creditors cannot sue the investors? Should it matter whether the investors are involved in the operation of the defectively formed corporation? Should it matter whether the creditors believed there was no corporation and thought the investors were partners? Should it matter whether the creditors are contract creditors (who could have checked into the status of the corporation and its investors prior to contracting with the business) or tort creditors (who have no ability to investigate the corporation and its investors prior to being injured by the person acting on behalf of the defectively formed corporation)?

3. Why should the law impose limits on the use of share transfer restrictions? Who may be harmed if there are no legal limits? Is it possible for those who would be harmed to be protected in ways other than by limiting the use of share transfer restrictions?

PROBLEMS AND PROBLEM CASES

1. RKO-Stanley Warner Theatres, Inc., contracted to sell a theater to Jack Jenofsky and Ralph Graziano, who were in the process of forming a corporation to be known as Kent Enterprises, Inc. The contract included the following, added by Jenofsky and Graziano's lawyer:

It is understood by the parties hereto that it is the intention of the Purchaser to incorporate. Upon condition that such incorporation be completed by the closing date, all agreements contained herein shall be construed to have been made between Seller and the resultant corporation.

Subsequently, Kent Enterprises, Inc., was incorporated. A final closing date was set, but the sale was never completed. RKO sued Jenofsky and Graziano on the contract. Jenofsky claimed that the quoted provision in the contract released him from any personal liability. Was he correct?

2. Max and Edward Gurwicz developed the Regency Towers Condominium (Towers), which sold condominium units to residents. The Gurwiczes also formed the Regency Towers Condominium Association (Association), which was to serve as an association of the condominium owners. Prior to the drafting of the Association's articles of incorporation, the Gurwiczes signed a lease in the name of the Association obligating the Association to make rental payment to Towers. Three weeks later, the articles were filed by the secretary of state. After the filing, the Association's board of directors took no action in respect to the lease

and made no rental payments to Towers. The condominium owners, who indirectly would be liable on the lease if the Association was bound by it, believed that the lease unreasonably burdened the Association. The condominium owners asked a court to rule that the Association was not liable on the lease. What did the court hold?

3. Stuart Lakes Club, Inc., a New York corporation, was a private game club owning 75 acres of land, two lakes, and a clubhouse. The board of directors adopted a bylaw provision that stated, "When any member ceases to be a member of the Club, either by death, resignation, or otherwise, his share shall be considered void and the certificate returned to the Treasurer for cancellation." The purpose of the bylaw provision was to make the last surviving member of the club its sole owner and therefore the beneficial owner of the club's valuable land and clubhouse. Has the board of directors adopted an enforceable bylaw?

4. On April 9, 1980, Bowers Building Co. and Division 8, Inc., entered a contract for Division 8 to provide labor and materials to Bowers for a construction project. Division 8 was unable to complete the contract, which it assigned to Altura Glass Co., Inc., on January 9, 1981. On that date, Altura's president, Jack Crownover, wrote Bowers a letter requesting that Bowers issue future checks to "Altura Glass Co." Crownover signed the letter "Pres. Jack Crownover." On that same date, Crownover delivered to Altura's lawyer its articles of incorporation, which the lawyer mailed to the secretary of state of Colorado. The secretary of state issued a certificate of incorporation to Altura on January 12, 1981. The next day, Bowers issued a check payable to Altura Glass Company, which Altura accepted. When Altura breached the contract, Bowers sued Altura and its president, Crownover. Are Altura and Crownover liable to Bowers?

5. Eugene Levy agreed to buy a retail record business from Martin Robertson. Levy submitted for filing the articles of incorporation for Record Shack, Inc., but they were rejected by the secretary of state. Six days later, Robertson sold the assets of the business to the Record Shack and received a promissory note for the purchase price signed "Penn Ave. Record Shack, Inc., by Eugene M. Levy, President." Subsequently, Levy resubmitted the articles, and a certificate of incorporation of

Penn Ave. Record Shack, Inc., was issued. Robertson accepted one payment on the promissory note from the corporation, but within six months, Record Shack ceased doing business; no assets remained. Robertson sued Levy for the balance of the promissory note. Was Levy liable on the promissory note?

6. Arthur Kaiser and Jerry Kaiser incorporated Jerry Kaiser & Associates, Inc., a real estate development company. Arthur told Jerry about the availability of some unimproved land. The land was subsequently acquired by Jerry Kaiser & Associates and developed as Sherwood Manor Apartments. At a meeting of the directors, Jerry, as the chairman of the board, announced that Arthur had rendered services to the corporation. The board then approved the issuance to Arthur of 25 shares of $10 par value Class A common stock. The corporation issued to Arthur share certificate number 1 for 25 shares "of the $10 par value Class A nonvoting stock of Jerry Kaiser & Associates, Inc., fully paid and non-assessable." Has Arthur paid for the stock with a proper type of consideration?

7. Dale Frey intended to develop a 33-acre apartment complex, to be operated by Mt. Carmel Apartments, Inc., a corporation not yet formed. To promote and develop the complex, Frey contracted with Jess Burge. Their agreement provided that Burge would receive $70,000 payable in 12.5 percent of the shares of the corporation. Subsequently, Burge consulted with architects, calculated construction costs, executed a loan application, and consulted with prospective contractors on behalf of the complex. After incorporation of Mt. Carmel Apartments, Inc., the board of directors accepted the agreement between Frey and Burge, placed a $70,000 value on his services performed prior to incorporation, and issued 12.5 percent of the corporation's shares to Burge. After a dispute arose between Burge and the corporation, Frey claimed that the corporation acted wrongly by issuing the shares to Burge. Was Frey correct?

8. John Gazda, Anthony Kolinski, and John Giamartino formed a corporation to operate Big Boy restaurants, with each owning one third of the shares. After a dispute resulted in the removal of Gazda as an officer, Kolinski and Giamartino as controlling directors voted to issue shares of the corporation for $100 per share. At the time, the book value of the corporation was $266 per share

and the fair market value was between $497 and $572 per share. Gazda opposed the issuance of the shares. Was he successful with stopping the issuance?

9. The shareholders of KBM, Inc., a close corporation, executed a shareholders' agreement that required a shareholder who resigned his employment with the corporation to first offer to sell all his shares to the corporation at book value. If the corporation did not buy all the shares, the shareholder was required to offer the unpurchased shares to the other shareholders. If there were any remaining unsold shares, the shareholder and the corporation were required to attempt to negotiate a "sale mutually satisfactory to all parties." If no mutually satisfactory agreement could be reached, the corporation was to be dissolved and liquidated, and its assets distributed to shareholders. Is this agreement legal?

10. Video Case. See "The Stock Option." An employee of FAMCO purchases common shares of FAMCO through its fringe benefit plan. Transfer of the shares purchased under the plan is restricted in two ways. First, when employment terminates for any reason, FAMCO has an option to purchase the shares at book value. Second, if an employee attempts to sell the shares while employed, FAMCO has a right of first refusal to purchase the shares at the sale price. FAMCO informs an employee that for the good of the company, she must sell her shares to FAMCO. She believes that she will be terminated unless she sells the shares to FAMCO, but nonetheless she sells the shares on the open market at a price much greater than book value. Can FAMCO invalidate the employee's sale of the shares?

11. Alice Marr owned 800 of the 11,340 shares outstanding of Gloucester Ice & Storage Co., a closely held corporation with no ready market for its shares. When Marr died, Thomas Goode, the administrator of her will, demanded that Gloucester or its majority shareholder purchase Marr's shares. No provision restricting the transfer of shares or requiring the corporation or remaining shareholders to purchase shares on the death of a shareholder appeared in the corporation's articles of incorporation, bylaws, or agreement among shareholders. Is Gloucester or its majority shareholder required to purchase Marr's shares at fair market value?

MANAGEMENT OF

CORPORATIONS

INTRODUCTION

Although shareholders own a corporation, they traditionally have possessed no right to manage the business of the corporation. Instead, shareholders elect individuals to a **board of directors***, to which management is entrusted. Often, the board delegates much of its management responsibilities to* **officers.**

This chapter explains the legal aspects of the board's and officers' management of the corporation. Their management of the corporation must be consistent with the objectives and powers of the corporation, and they owe duties to the corporation to manage it prudently and in the best interests of the corporation and the shareholders as a whole.

CORPORATE OBJECTIVES

The traditional objective of the business corporation has been to *enhance corporate profits and shareholder gain.* According to this objective, the managers of a corporation must seek the accomplishment of the profit objective to the exclusion of all inconsistent goals. Interests other than profit maximization may be considered, provided that they do not hinder the ultimate profit objective.

Nonetheless, some courts have permitted corporations to take *socially responsible actions* that are *beyond the profit maximization requirement.* In addition, every state recognizes corporate powers that are not economically inspired. For example, corporations may make contributions to colleges, political campaigns, child abuse prevention centers, literary associations, and employee benefit plans, regardless of economic benefit to the corporations. Also, every state expressly recognizes the right of shareholders to choose freely the extent to which profit maximization captures all of their interests and all of their sense of responsibility.

In the following case, the court held that the board of directors acted improperly by failing to maximize shareholder profit.

REVLON, INC. v. MACANDREWS & FORBES HOLDINGS, INC.
506 A.2d 173 (Del. Sup. Ct. 1986)

In 1985, Pantry Pride, Inc., informed Revlon, Inc., of its intent to acquire Revlon. Pantry Pride planned to "bust up" Revlon after the acquisition by selling its various lines of businesses individually. Revlon's board of directors rejected Pantry Pride's plan. Nonetheless, Pantry Pride made a hostile takeover bid for Revlon's shares at $47.50 per share.

In response to Pantry Pride's bid, Revlon's board sought to reduce the number of shares Pantry Pride could acquire by repurchasing some of it shares in exchange for new Senior Notes. The contract with the new Senior Noteholders protected the noteholders with covenants limiting Revlon's ability to incur more debt, sell assets, or pay dividends. The covenants, however, could be waived by the board's independent directors.

When this defense failed to deter Pantry Pride, the board recognized that a takeover was inevitable. Consequently, the board agreed to a friendly acquisition by Forstmann Little & Co. for $56 per share. Realizing the inevitability of a bust-up, Revlon's board agreed to break up its assets by selling its cosmetic division; Forstmann planned to sell two other divisions after the purchase.

In addition, Revlon's independent directors agreed to waive the Senior Note covenants. As a result, the value of the Senior Notes dropped 12 percent. Angry Senior Noteholders threatened to sue Revlon's directors. Concerned about their personal liability to the Senior Noteholders, the Revlon directors amended their agreement with Forstmann. Forstmann increased its offer to $57.25 per share and agreed to support the value of the Senior Notes. In return, Revlon gave Forstmann a lock-up option, promising to sell two valuable divisions to Forstmann at nearly $200 million below their market value if Pantry Pride was successful in taking over Revlon.

Pantry Pride sued Revlon to invalidate the lock-up option as beyond the objectives of the corporation. The trial court enjoined Revlon's directors from making concessions to Forstmann. Revlon appealed to the Supreme Court of Delaware.

———————————————— ■ ————————————————

Moore, Justice   The lock-up with Forstmann had as its emphasis shoring up the market value of the Senior Notes. The directors made support of the Senior Notes an integral part of the company's dealings with Forstmann, even though their primary responsibility at this stage was to the shareholders.

The original threat posed by Pantry Pride—the break-up of the company—had become a reality that even the directors embraced. Selective dealing to fend off a hostile bidder was no longer a proper objective. Instead, obtaining the highest price for the benefit of the shareholders should have been the central theme guiding director action.

The Revlon board argued that it acted in good faith in protecting the Senior Noteholders because Delaware law permits consideration of other corporate constituencies. Although such considerations may be permissible, there are fundamental limitations upon that prerogative. A board may have regard for various constituencies, provided there are rationally related benefits accruing to the shareholders. However, such concern for non-shareholder interests is inappropriate when an auction among active bidders is in progress, and the object no longer is to protect or maintain the corporate enterprise but to sell it to the highest bidder.

Revlon also contended that it had contractual obligations to the Senior Noteholders. However, any such duties are limited to the principle that one may not interfere with contractual relationships by improper actions. Here the rights of the Senior Noteholders were fixed by agreement, and there is nothing to suggest that any of those terms were violated. The Senior Notes covenants specifically contemplated a waiver.

In granting an asset option lock-up to Forstmann, the directors allowed considerations other than the maximization of shareholder profit to affect their judgment to the ultimate detriment of shareholders. No such defensive measure can be sustained.

Judgment for Pantry Pride affirmed.

(d) A director may, in considering the best interests of a corporation, consider the effects of any action on shareholders, employees, suppliers, and customers of the corporation, and the communities in which the offices or other facilities of the corporation are located, and any other factors the director considers pertinent

(f) [D]irectors are not required to consider the effects of a proposed corporate action of any particular corporate constituent group or interest as a dominant or controlling factor.

The decision in *Revlon* prodded most of the states to enact **corporate constituency statutes,** which broaden the legal objectives of corporations. Such statutes permit or require directors to take into account the interests of constituencies other than shareholders. These statutes direct the board to act in the best interests of the corporation, not just the interests of the shareholders, and to maximize corporate profits *over the long term.* The new laws recognize that a corporation is a collection of interests working together for the purpose of producing goods and services at a profit, and that the goal of corporate profit maximization over the long term is not necessarily the same as the goal of stock price maximization over the short term. For an example of the new statutes, see the excerpt from the Indiana statute in Figure 1.

CORPORATE POWERS

The actions of management are limited not only by the objectives of business corporations but also by the *powers* granted to business corporations. Such limitations may appear in the state statute, the articles of incorporation, and the bylaws.

The primary source of a corporation's powers is the corporation statute of the state in which it is incorporated. Some state corporation statutes expressly specify the powers of corporations. These powers include making gifts for charitable and educational purposes, lending money to corporate officers and directors, and purchasing and disposing of the corporation's shares. Other state corporation statutes limit the powers of corporations, such as prohibiting the acquisition of agricultural land by corporations.

Modern statutes attempt to authorize corporations to engage in any activity. The Model Business Corporation Act (MBCA) states that a corporation has the power to do *anything that an individual may do.*

Purpose Clauses in Articles of Incorporation

Most corporations state their purposes in the articles of incorporation. The purpose is usually phrased in broad terms, even if the corporation has been formed with only one type of business in mind. Most corporations have purpose clauses stating that they may engage in any lawful business.

Under the MBCA, the inclusion of a purpose clause in the articles is optional. Any corporation incorporated under the MBCA has the purpose of engaging in any lawful business, unless the articles state a narrower purpose.

The Ultra Vires Doctrine Historically, an act of a corporation beyond its powers was a nullity, as it was *ultra vires,* which is Latin for "beyond the powers." Therefore, any act not permitted by the corporation statute or by the corporation's articles of incorporation was void due to lack of capacity.

This lack of capacity or power of the corporation was a defense to a contract assertable either by the corporation or by the other party that dealt with the corporation. Often, *ultra vires* was merely a convenient justification for reneging on an agreement that was no longer considered desirable. This misuse of the doctrine has led to its near abandonment.

Today, the *ultra vires* doctrine is of small importance for two reasons. First, nearly all corporations have broad purpose clauses, thereby preventing any *ultra vires* problem. Second, the MBCA and most other statutes do not permit a corporation or the other party to an agreement to avoid an obligation on the ground that the corporate action is *ultra vires.*

Under the MBCA, *ultra vires* may be asserted by only three types of persons: (1) by a shareholder seeking to enjoin a corporation from executing a proposed action that is *ultra vires,* (2) by the corporation suing its management for damages caused by exceeding the corporation's powers, and

FIGURE 2	Primary Responsibilities of Directors

	Percent*
1. Ensure integrity of corporation's operations	60%
2. Counsel top management	58
3. Ensure strategic plan for the future	55
4. Monitor performance of the CEO	47
5. Ensure management succession	43
6. Serve the public interest	15
7. Monitor financial reporting	9

*Percent of directors surveyed citing each responsibility.
Source: Survey of directors, published by Arthur Young Executive Resource Consultants in *The New Director: Changing Views of the Board's Role* (1989).

(3) by the state's attorney general, who may have the power to enjoin an *ultra vires* act or to dissolve a corporation that exceeds its powers.

THE BOARD OF DIRECTORS

Traditionally, the **board of directors** has had the authority and the duty to manage the corporation. Yet in a large publicly held corporation, it is impossible for the board to manage the corporation on a day-to-day basis, because many of the directors are high-level executives in other corporations and devote most of their time to their other business interests. Therefore, the MBCA permits a corporation to be managed *under the direction of* the board of directors. Consequently, the board of directors delegates major responsibility for management to committees of the board such as an executive committee, to individual board members such as the chairman of the board, and to the officers of the corporation, especially the chief executive officer (CEO). In theory, the board supervises the actions of its committees, the chairman, and the officers to ensure that the board's policies are being carried out and that the delegatees are managing the corporation prudently. Figure 2 lists the results of a survey of directors concerning their primary responsibilities.

Board Authority under Corporation Statutes

A corporation's board of directors has the authority to do almost everything within the powers of the corporation. The board's authority includes not only the general power to manage or direct the corporation in the ordinary course of its business but also the power to issue shares of stock and to set the price of shares. Among its other powers, the board may repurchase shares, declare dividends, adopt and amend bylaws, elect and remove officers, and fill vacancies on the board.

Some corporate actions require *board initiative* and shareholder approval. That is, board approval is necessary to *propose such actions to the shareholders,* who then must approve the action. Board initiative is required for important changes in the corporation, such as amendment of the articles of incorporation, merger of the corporation, the sale of all or substantially all of the corporation's assets, and voluntary dissolution.

Committees of the Board

Most publicly held corporations have committees of the board of directors. These committees, which have fewer members than the board has, can more efficiently handle management decisions and exercise board powers than can a large board. Only directors may serve on board committees.

Although many board powers may be delegated to committees of the board, some decisions are so important that corporation statutes require their *approval by the board as a whole.* Under the MBCA, the powers that may not be delegated concern important corporate actions such as declaring dividends, filling vacancies on the board or its committees, adopting and amending bylaws, approving issuances of shares, and approving repurchases of the corporation's shares.

The most common board committee is the **executive committee.** It is usually given authority to act for the board on most matters when the board is not in session. Generally, it consists of the inside directors and perhaps one or two outside directors who can attend a meeting on short notice. An inside director is an officer of the corporation who devotes substantially full time to the corporation. Outside directors have no such affiliation with the corporation.

Audit committees recommend independent public accountants and supervise the public accountants' audit of the corporate financial records. Nearly all publicly held firms have audit committees comprising independent directors.

Nominating committees choose management's slate of directors that is to be submitted to shareholders at the annual election of directors. Nominating committees also often plan generally for management succession. Nominating committees wholly or largely comprise outside directors.

Compensation committees review and approve the salaries, bonuses, stock options, and other benefits of high-level corporate executives. Although compensation committees usually comprise directors who have no affiliation with the executives or directors whose compensation is being approved, compensation committees may also set the compensation of their members. Directors of a typical corporation receive annual compensation between $30,000 to $60,000.

A **shareholder litigation committee** is given the task of determining whether a corporation should sue someone who has allegedly harmed the corporation. Usually, the committee of disinterested directors is formed when a shareholder asks the board of directors to cause the corporation to sue some or all of the directors for mismanaging the corporation.

Powers, Rights, and Liabilities of Directors as Individuals

A director is not an agent of the corporation *merely* by being a director. The directors may manage the corporation only when they act as a board, unless the board of directors grants agency powers to the directors individually.

A director has the *right to inspect* corporate books and records that contain corporate information essential to the director's performance of her duties. The director's right of inspection is denied when the director has an interest adverse to the corporation, as in the case of a director who plans to sell a corporation's trade secrets to a competitor.

Normally, a director does not have any personal liability for the contracts and torts of the corporation.

Election of Directors

Generally, any individual may serve as a director of a corporation. A director need not even be a shareholder. Nonetheless, a corporation is permitted to specify qualifications for directors in the articles of incorporation.

A board of directors may not act unless it has the number of directors required by the state corporation law. The MBCA and several state corporation statutes require a minimum of one director, recognizing that in close corporations with a single shareholder-manager, additional board members are superfluous. Several statutes, including the New York statute, require at least three directors, unless there are fewer than three shareholders, in which case the corporation may have no fewer directors than it has shareholders.

A corporation may have more than the minimum number of directors required by the corporation statute. The articles of incorporation or bylaws will state the number of directors of the corporation. Most large publicly held corporations have boards with more than 10 members.

Directors are elected by the shareholders at the annual shareholder meeting. Usually, each shareholder is permitted to vote for as many nominees as there are directors to be elected. The shareholder may cast as many votes for each nominee as he has shares. The top votegetters among the nominees are elected as directors. This voting process, called **straight voting,** permits a holder of more than 50 percent of the shares of a corporation to dominate the corporation by electing a board of directors that will manage the corporation as he wants it to be managed.

To avoid domination by a large shareholder, some corporations allow class voting or cumulative voting. **Class voting** may give certain classes of shareholders the right to elect a specified number of directors. **Cumulative voting** permits shareholders to multiply the number of their shares by the number of directors to be elected and to cast the resulting total of votes for one or more directors. As a result, cumulative voting may permit minority shareholders to obtain representation on the board of directors.

Directors usually hold office for only one year, but they may have longer terms. The MBCA permits *staggered terms* for directors. A corporation having a board of nine or more members may establish either two or three approximately equal classes of directors, with only one class of directors coming up for election at each annual shareholders' meeting. If there are two classes of directors, the directors serve two-year terms; if there are three classes, they serve three-year terms.

The original purpose of staggered terms was to permit continuity of management. Staggered terms also frustrate the ability of minority shareholders to use cumulative voting to elect their representatives to the board of directors.

The Proxy Solicitation Process

Most individual investors purchase corporate shares in the public market to increase their wealth, not to elect or to influence the directors of corporations. Nearly all institutional investors—such as pension funds, mutual funds, and bank trust departments—have the same profit motive. Generally, they are passive investors with little interest in exercising their shareholder right to elect directors by attending shareholder meetings.

Once public ownership of the corporation's shares exceeds 50 percent, the corporation cannot conduct any business at its shareholder meetings unless some of the shares of these passive investors are voted. This is because the corporation will have a shareholder quorum requirement, which usually requires that 50 percent or more of the shares be voted for a shareholder vote to be valid. Since passive investors rarely attend shareholder meetings, the management of the corporation must solicit **proxies** if it wishes to have a valid shareholder vote. Shareholders who will not attend a shareholder meeting must be asked to appoint someone else to vote their shares for them. This is done by furnishing each such shareholder with a proxy form to sign. The proxy designates a person who may vote the shares for the shareholder.

Management Solicitation of Proxies

To ensure its perpetuation in office and the approval of other matters submitted for a shareholder vote, the corporation's management solicits proxies from shareholders for directors' elections and other important matters on which shareholders vote, such as mergers. The management designates an officer, a director, or some other person to vote the proxies received. The person who is designated to vote for the shareholder is also called a proxy. Typically, the chief executive officer (CEO) of the corporation, the president, or the chairman of the board of directors names the person who serves as the proxy.

Usually, the proxies are merely signed and returned by the public shareholders, including the institutional shareholders. Passive investors follow the **Wall Street rule:** Either support management or

sell the shares. As a result, management almost always receives enough votes from its proxy solicitation to ensure the reelection of directors and the approval of other matters submitted to the shareholders, even when other parties solicit proxies in opposition to management.

Management's solicitation of proxies produces a result that is quite different from the theory of corporate management that directors serve as representatives of the shareholders. The CEO usually nominates directors of his choice, and they are almost always elected. The directors appoint officers chosen by the CEO. The CEO's nominees for director are not unduly critical of his programs or of his methods for carrying them out. This is particularly true if a large proportion of the directors are officers of the company and thus are more likely to be dominated by the CEO. In such situations, the board of directors does not even function effectively as a representative of the shareholders in supervising and evaluating the CEO and the other officers of the corporation. The board members and the other officers are subordinates of the CEO, even though the CEO is not a major shareholder of the corporation.

Proposals for improving corporate governance in public-issue corporations seek to develop a board that is capable of functioning independently of the CEO by changing the composition or operation of the board of directors. Some corporate governance critics propose that a federal agency such as the Securities and Exchange Commission (SEC) appoint one or more directors to serve as watchdogs of the public interest. Other critics would require that shareholders elect at least a majority of directors without prior ties to the corporation, thus excluding shareholders, suppliers, and customers from the board. The New York Stock Exchange requires a minimum of two directors independent of management for its listed companies.

Other proposals recommend changing the method by which directors are nominated for election. One proposal would encourage shareholders to make nominations for directors. Supporters of this proposal argue that in addition to reducing the influence of the CEO, it would also broaden the range of backgrounds represented on the board. The SEC recommends that publicly held corporations establish a nominating committee composed of outside directors. Many publicly held corporations have nomination committees.

FIGURE 3	Influence of Board on Key Management Decisions		
	Strong	**Moderate**	**None or Unknown**
Compensation of top management	71%	27%	2%
Mergers and acquisitions	62	33	5
Capital expenditures	32	60	8
Selection of senior executives	22	64	14
Long-range planning	21	70	9

Note: Figures are percentages of directors surveyed citing the board's influence as strong, moderate, none, or unknown.
Source: Survey of directors, published by Arthur Young Executive Resource Consultants in *The New Director: Changing Views of the Board's Role* (1989).

Mostly due to SEC and public pressures for changes in corporate governance, current boards of directors operate significantly differently from the boards of the 1960s and the early 1970s. Boards supervise officers more closely. More directors are outside rather than inside directors. Boards meet more frequently, and more important, they have working committees that assume specific responsibilities. In addition, today's directors *perceive* themselves as being more nearly independent of the CEO. As a consequence, they *are* more nearly independent of the CEO. See Figure 3.

Vacancies on the Board

The MBCA permits the directors to fill vacancies on the board. A majority vote of the remaining directors is sufficient to select persons to serve out unexpired terms, even though the remaining directors are less than a quorum.

Removal of Directors

Modern corporation statutes permit shareholders to remove directors *with or without cause.* The rationale for the modern rule is that the shareholders should have the power to judge the fitness of directors at any time.

However, most corporations have provisions in their articles authorizing the shareholders to remove directors *only for cause.* Cause for removal would include mismanagement or conflicts of interest. Before removal for cause, the director must be given notice and an opportunity for a hearing.

A director elected by a class of shareholders may be removed only by that class of shareholders, thereby protecting the voting rights of the class. A director elected by cumulative voting may not be removed if the votes cast against her removal would have been sufficient to elect her to the board, thereby protecting the voting rights of minority shareholders.

In the following case, a director—a minority shareholder—would not have been removed as a director had there been cumulative voting of shares.

LEHMAN V. PIONTKOWSKI
460 N.Y.S.2d 817 (N.Y. App. Div. 1983)

Jacob Lehman and Shlomo Piontkowski were surgeons who practiced together in a professional corporation. They were the directors and only shareholders, Lehman owning six shares and Piontkowski owning four shares. Each was an employee of the corporation. Piontkowski's employment contract granted to the board of directors of the corporation the power to terminate his employment for "personal misconduct of such a material nature as to be professionally detrimental to the corporation."

From 1977 to 1979, Lehman and Piontkowski disagreed on the distribution of the corporation's income. Dissatisfied with his share of the income, Piontkowski canceled surgery, informed his patients that he was on vacation, and planned to open his own office nearby.

Acting as president of the corporation, Lehman sent Piontkowski a letter stating that Piontkowski's actions violated his employment contract. As president, Lehman stated that he deemed these actions to be personal misconduct so material as to be professionally detrimental to the corporation.

At a special shareholder meeting, Lehman proposed that Piontkowski be removed as a director and voted his six shares to oust Piontkowski. Piontkowski did not vote his four shares. Lehman then nominated himself as sole director, voted his shares to elect himself sole director, and adjourned the shareholder meeting. Lehman then called the special directors' meeting to order and, as the sole director, dismissed Piontkowski as an employee.

Afterward, Lehman and the corporation sued Piontkowski, seeking to recover damages of $500,000 for Piontkowski's breach of contract by opening a competing medical practice. Piontkowski argued that his expulsion from the corporation was illegal and that therefore the corporation was not entitled to enforce the contract. The trial court denied Piontkowski's motion for summary judgment, and Piontkowski appealed.

Memorandum by the Court   Piontkowski's expulsion as director and the termination of his employment were improper.

By letter, Piontkowski was informed that Lehman, as president, deemed Piontkowski's actions to be personal misconduct that was so material as to be professionally detrimental to the corporation. This opinion was not that of the board of directors, as was required by the employment contract, but rather was that of Lehman individually and as president of the corporation. The board had not formally met to make a determination that Piontkowski had committed detrimental misconduct as a material breach of the contract. Therefore, the letter was of no legal effect.

At the special shareholder meeting, Lehman's first order of business was to vote his majority of the shares to dismiss Piontkowski as a director. Such an act was of no effect in the present matter. The New York Business Corporation Law provides that "the number of directors . . . shall not be less than three, except that where all the shares of a corporation are owned . . . by less than three shareholders, the number of directors may be less than three but not less than the number of shareholders."

Here there were two shareholders at the commencement of the special shareholder meeting. Piontkowski's expulsion as a director and the election of Lehman as the sole director were therefore improper. The removal of Piontkowski as a director left the corporation with only one director and without a validly constituted board of directors. The New York statute prohibits such an occurrence. The subsequent act of an illegally constituted one-man board of directors in terminating Piontkowski's employment was invalid.

As Piontkowski's unilateral expulsion from the corporation was illegal, the corporation is not entitled to enforce Piontkowski's employment contract.

Judgment reversed in favor of Piontkowski.

DIRECTORS' MEETINGS

Traditionally, directors could act only when they were properly convened as a board. They could not vote by proxy or informally, as by telephone. This rule was based on a belief in the value of consultation and collective judgment.

Today, the corporation laws of a majority of the states and the MBCA specifically permit action by the directors without a meeting if all of the directors consent in writing to the action taken. Such authorization is useful for dealing with routine matters or for formally approving an action based on an earlier policy decision made after full discussion.

The MBCA also permits a board to meet by telephone or television hookup. This section permits a meeting of directors who may otherwise be unable to convene. The only requirement is that the directors be able to hear one another simultaneously.

Directors are entitled to reasonable notice of all *special meetings,* but not of regularly scheduled meetings. The MBCA does not require the notice for a special meeting to state the purpose of the meeting. A director's attendance at a meeting waives any required notice, unless at the beginning of the meeting the director objects to the lack of notice.

For the directors to act, a *quorum* of the directors must be present. The quorum requirement ensures that the decision of the board will represent the views of a substantial portion of the directors. A quorum is usually a *majority* of the number of directors.

Each director has *one vote.* If a quorum is present, a vote of a majority of the directors present is an act of the board, unless the articles or the bylaws require the vote of a greater number of directors. Such *supermajority voting provisions* are common in close corporations but not in publicly held corporations. The use of supermajority voting provisions by close corporations is covered later in this chapter.

OFFICERS OF THE CORPORATION

The board of directors has the authority to appoint the officers of the corporation. Many corporation statutes provide that the officers of a corporation shall be the *president,* one or more *vice presidents,* a *secretary,* and a *treasurer.* Usually, any two or more offices may be held by the same person, except for the offices of president and secretary.

The MBCA requires only that there be an officer performing the duties normally granted to a corporate secretary. Under the MBCA, one person may hold several offices, including the offices of president and secretary.

The officers are agents of the corporation. As agents, officers have *express authority* conferred on them by the bylaws or the board of directors. In addition, officers have *implied authority* to do the things that are reasonably necessary to accomplish their express duties. Also, officers have *apparent authority* when the corporation leads third parties to believe reasonably that the officers have authority to act for the corporation. Like any principal, the corporation may *ratify* the unauthorized acts of its officers. This may be done expressly by a resolution of the board of directors or impliedly by the board's acceptance of the benefits of the officer's acts.

The most perplexing issue with regard to the authority of officers is whether an officer has *inherent authority* merely by virtue of the title of his office. Courts have held that certain official titles confer authority on officers, but such powers are much more restricted than you might expect.

Traditionally, a *president* possesses no power to bind the corporation by virtue of the office. Instead, she serves merely as the presiding officer at shareholder meetings and directors' meetings. A president with an additional title such as *general manager* or *chief executive officer* has broad implied authority to make contracts and to do other acts in the ordinary business of the corporation.

A *vice president* has no authority by virtue of that office. An executive who is vice president of a specified department, however, such as a vice president of marketing, will have the authority to transact the normal corporate business falling within the function of the department.

The *secretary* usually keeps the minutes of directors' and shareholder meetings, maintains other corporate records, retains custody of the corporate seal, and certifies corporate records as being authentic. Although the secretary has no authority to make contracts for the corporation by virtue of that office, the corporation is bound by documents certified by the secretary.

The *treasurer* has custody of the corporation's funds. He is the proper officer to receive payments to the corporation and to disburse corporate funds for authorized purposes. The treasurer binds the corporation by his receipts, checks, and indorsements, but he does not by virtue of that office alone have authority to borrow money, to issue negotiable instruments, or to make other contracts on behalf of the corporation.

Like any agent, a corporate officer ordinarily has *no liability on contracts* that he makes on behalf of his principal, the corporation, if he signs for the corporation and not in his personal capacity.

Officers serve the corporation at the pleasure of the board of directors, which may remove an officer at any time with or without cause. An officer who has been removed without cause has no recourse against the corporation, unless the removal violates an employment contract between the officer and the corporation.

MANAGING CLOSE CORPORATIONS

Many of the management formalities that you have studied in this chapter are appropriate for publicly held corporations yet inappropriate for close corporations. Close corporations tend to be more loosely managed than public corporations. For example, they may have few board meetings. Each shareholder may want to be *involved in management* of the close corporation. If a shareholder is not involved in management, he may want to protect his interest by placing *restrictions on the managerial discretion* of those who do manage the corporation.

Modern close corporation statutes permit close corporations to dispense with most, if not all, management formalities. The Statutory Close Corporation Supplement to the MBCA permits a close corporation to *dispense with a board of directors* and to be *managed by the shareholders*. The California General Corporation Law permits the close corporation to be managed *as if it were a partnership.*

Because a minority shareholder of a close corporation may be dominated by the shareholders who control the board of directors, close corporation shareholders have resorted to two devices: **supermajority voting** requirements for board actions and **restrictions on the managerial discretion** of the board of directors.

Any corporation may require that board action be possible only with the approval of more than a majority of the directors, such as three fourths or unanimous approval. A supermajority vote is often required to terminate the employment contract of an employee-shareholder, to reduce the level of dividends, and to change the corporation's line of business. Supermajority votes are rarely required for ordinary business matters, such as deciding with which suppliers the corporation should deal.

Traditionally, shareholders could not restrict the managerial discretion of directors. This rule recognized the traditional roles of the board as manager and of the shareholders as passive owners. Modern close corporation statutes permit shareholders to intrude into the sanctity of the boardroom. The Statutory Close Corporation Supplement grants the shareholders *unlimited* power to restrict the discretion of the board of directors. For example, the shareholders may agree that the directors may not terminate or reduce the salaries of employee-shareholders and may not lower or eliminate dividends. And, as was stated above, close corporation statutes even permit the shareholders to dispense with a board of directors altogether and to manage the close corporation as if it were a partnership.

DIRECTORS' AND OFFICERS' DUTIES TO THE CORPORATION

Directors and officers are in positions of trust; they are entrusted with property belonging to the corporation and with power to act for the corporation. Therefore, directors and officers owe **fiduciary duties** to the corporation. They are the duties to act within the authority of the position and within the objectives and powers of the corporation, to act with due care in conducting the affairs of the corporation, and to act with loyalty to the corporation.

Acting within Authority

An officer or director has a duty to **act within the authority** conferred on her by the articles of incorporation, the bylaws, and the board of directors. The directors and officers must act within the scope of the powers of the corporation. An officer or a director may be liable to the corporation if it is damaged by an act exceeding that person's or the corporation's authority.

Duty of Care

Directors and officers are liable for losses to the corporation resulting from their lack of *care or diligence*. The MBCA expressly states the standard of care that must be exercised by directors and officers. MBCA Section 8.30 states:

(a) A director shall discharge his duties as a director, including his duties as a member of a committee:

 (1) in good faith;

 (2) with the care an ordinarily prudent person in a like position would exercise under similar circumstances; and

(3) in a manner he reasonably believes to be in the best interests of the corporation.

Managers need merely meet the standard of the **ordinarily prudent person in the same circumstances,** a standard focusing on the basic manager attributes of common sense, practical wisdom, and informed judgment. The duty of care does not hold directors and officers to the standard of a prudent businessperson, a person of some undefined level of business skill. A director or officer's performance is evaluated at the time of the decision, thereby preventing the application of hindsight in judging her performance.

The MBCA duty of care test requires that a director or officer make a **reasonable investigation** and **honestly believe** that her decision is in the **best interests of the corporation.** For example, the board of directors decides to purchase an existing manufacturing business for $15 million without inquiring into the value of the business or examining its past financial performance. Although the directors may believe that they made a prudent decision, they have no reasonable basis for that belief. Therefore, if the plant is worth only $5 million, the directors will be liable to the corporation for its damages—$10 million—for breaching the duty of care.

The Business Judgment Rule   The directors' and officers' duty of care is sometimes expressed as the **business judgment rule:** absent bad faith, fraud, or breach of fiduciary duty, the judgment of the board of directors is conclusive. When directors and officers have complied with the business judgment rule, they are protected from liability to the corporation for their unwise decisions. The business judgment rule precludes the courts from substituting their business judgment for that of the corporation's managers. The business judgment rule recognizes that the directors and officers—not the shareholders and the courts—are best able to make business judgments and should not ordinarily be vulnerable to second-guessing. Shareholders and the courts are ill-equipped to make better business decisions than those made by the officers and directors of a corporation, who have more business experience and are more familiar with the needs, strengths, and limitations of the corporation.

Three requirements must be met for the business judgment rule to protect managers from liability:

1. The managers must make an **informed decision.** They must take the steps necessary to become informed about the relevant facts before making a decision. These steps may include merely listening to a proposal, reviewing written materials, or making inquiries. Managers may rely on information collected and presented by other persons. In essence, the informed-decision component means that managers should do their homework if they want the protection of the business judgment rule.

2. The managers may have **no conflicts of interest.** The managers may not benefit personally—other than as shareholders—when they transact on behalf of the corporation.

3. The managers must have a **rational basis** for believing that the decision is in the best interests of the corporation. The rational basis element requires only that the managers' decision have a *logical connection to the facts* revealed by a reasonable investigation or that the decision *not be manifestly unreasonable.* Some courts have held that the managers' wrongdoing must amount to *gross negligence* for the directors to lose the protection of the business judgment rule.

If the business judgment rule does not apply because one or more of its elements are missing, a court may *substitute its judgment* for that of the managers.

Nonetheless, courts rarely refuse to apply the business judgment rule. As a result, the rule has been criticized frequently as providing too much protection for the managers of corporations. In one famous case, the court applied the business judgment rule to protect a 1965 decision made by the board of directors of the Chicago Cubs not to install lights and not to hold night baseball games at Wrigley Field.[1] Yet the business judgment rule is so flexible that it protected the decision of the Cubs' board of directors to install lights in 1988.

The *Trans Union* case[2] is one of the few cases that have held directors liable for failing to comply with the business judgment rule. The Supreme Court of Delaware found that the business judgment rule was not satisfied by the board's approval of an acquisition of the corporation for $55 per share. The board approved the acquisition after only two hours' consideration. The board received no documentation

---

[1] *Shlensky v. Wrigley,* 237 N.E.2d 776 (Ill. Ct. App. 1968).
[2] *Smith v. Van Gorkom,* 488 A.2d 858 (Del. Sup. Ct. 1985).

to support the adequacy of the $55 price. Instead, it relied entirely on a 20-minute *oral* report of the chairman of the board. No written summary of the acquisition was presented to the board. The directors failed to obtain an investment banker's report, prepared after careful consideration, that the acquisition price was fair.

In addition, the court held that the mere fact that the acquisition price exceeded the market price by $17 per share did not legitimize the board's deci-sion. The board had frequently made statements prior to the acquisition that the market had under-valued the shares, yet the board took no steps to determine the intrinsic value of the shares. Conse-quently, the court found that at a minimum, the directors had been grossly negligent.

In the following case, the court considered whether a bank loan officer complied with the business judgment rule.

OMNIBANK OF MANTEE V. UNITED SOUTHERN BANK
607 So.2d 76 (Miss. Sup. Ct. 1992)

James R. Gray was president and managing officer of the Peoples Bank and Trust Company in Olive Branch, Mississippi, a branch bank owned by United Southern Bank (USB). Gray had complete charge of the day-to-day banking business of Peoples Bank. He had discretionary loan authority, subject to USB's limits for all senior loan officers: $75,000 for unsecured loans and $150,000 for secured loans.

Frank Piecara was an established customer of Peoples Bank. Piecara was president of Mirage Construction, Inc., which was obligated on a subcontract to provide earthwork and roadwork for Rogers Construction Company at the Pacacho Pumping Plant in Arizona. Gray directed Peoples Bank to make loans in the amount of $536,000 to a trust managed by Piecara. The loan proceeds were used to provide working capital for Mirage. In addition, Gray directed Peoples Bank to issue a $300,000 irrevocable letter of credit to Rogers Construction for the purpose of securing Mirage's performance as Rogers's subcontractor. Gray called USB's senior vice president, Edward P. Peacock III, to request authorization of the letter of credit. Gray and Peacock each had $150,000 authority to make secured loans, which they combined to issue the letter of credit. As security for the loans and letter of credit, Gray obtained a security interest in Mirage's accounts receivable and contract rights, in particular the payments Rogers might make to Mirage under the subcontract. Gray did not perfect the security interest in the subcontract. Gray did not notify Rogers or the owner of the Pacacho Pumping Plant of the security interest or require Rogers or the owner to remit subcontract payments directly to Peoples Bank.

Piecara and Mirage defaulted on the loans and letter of credit, with USB suffering a loss of almost $600,000. USB sued Gray alleging his breach of a fiduciary duty. The trial court found Gray liable to USB. Gray appealed to the Mississippi Supreme Court.

Robertson, Justice The law devolves upon those in the upper echelons of a corporate entity certain duties owing to the entity, over and above those of an ordinary agent or employee. The question is whether Gray is one of those so burdened. We doubt a definitional line may be drawn with precision or permanence. For the moment, we are prepared to accept that

"Officer" means (a) the chief executive, operating, finan-cial, legal and accounting officers of a corporation; (b) to the extent not encompassed by the foregoing, the chair-man of the board of directors . . ., president, treasurer, and secretary, and a *vice-president or vice-chairman who is in charge of a principal business unit, division,* or function . . . and (c) any other individual designated by the corpo-ration as an officer.
American Law Institute, *Principles of Corporate Gover-nance: Analysis and Recommendations,* section 1.27.

His title aside, Gray served USB as the chief operating official at Peoples Bank where he had substantial discretionary authority. We think a bank-ing office such as the Peoples Bank branch as one of

USB's principal business units. Gray was the man in charge. He presided over a branch worth over twenty million dollars, had substantial loan authority, and had considerable autonomy in directing the day-to-day operations of the branch. The trial court was correct in treating Gray as an officer of USB.

By law, officer Gray owed USB two principal duties: a duty of care and a duty of loyalty and fair dealing. These duties differ in nature and content, though they doubtless intersect and overlap. There is a bit of lore born no doubt of thought of failed banks and helpless widows that we ought demand more of bank officers than one who runs a foundry or a pest control company.

We begin with the duty of care. A director or officer has a duty to the corporation to perform the director's or officer's functions in good faith, in a manner he or she reasonably believes to be in the best interests of the corporation, and with the care that an ordinarily prudent person would reasonably be expected to exercise in a like position and under similar circumstances. The duty includes the obligation to make, or cause to make, an inquiry when, but only when, the circumstances would alert a reasonable director or officer to the need therefor. The extent of such inquiry shall be such as the director or officer reasonably believes to be necessary.

We long ago recognized this duty in a banking setting and said an officer who "very negligently" makes unreasonably risky loans may on his borrowers' default be held personally to make good the bank's loss.

The duty of care is subject to a well-settled common law, known as the business judgment rule. That rule has recently been stated with care:

A director or officer who makes a business judgment in good faith fulfills the duty . . . [of care] if the director or officer:

(1) is not interested . . . in the subject of the business judgment;

(2) is informed with respect to the subject of the business judgment to the extent the director or officer reasonably believes to be appropriate under the circumstances; and

(3) rationally believes that the business judgment is in the best interests of the corporation.

Principles of Corporate Governance, section 4.01. *See* MBCA section 8.42.

Gray's defaults in the Piecara loans are apparent. To be sure, there is nothing improper about a banker securing a credit by taking a security interest in contract rights or assignment of accounts. On the other hand, there are risks associated with the receivables form of collateral not associated with more tangible security, and a prudent loan officer must reasonably assess and control these risks. These risks are exacerbated where, as here, the subcontract is to be performed some 1500 miles away.

Gray made no inquiry of the financial responsibility of Rogers or the owner of the Picacho Pumping Plant. A prudent loan officer taking such collateral will give notice of his bank's interest to the prime contractor and the owner and demand that all payments due under the subcontract be routed through the bank. Gray did none of this, nor did he monitor performance of the subcontract and have Piecara remit as his company was paid. Gray failed to perfect the security interest. Moreover, it appears clear the value of the collateral was far below what prudently should have been required for credit of this size. We accept the trial court's holding that Gray breached his duty of care to USB in handling the Piecara loans.

Gray's argument in reply is laced with implied references to the business judgment rule. He insists he acted in subjective good faith at all times, and of this there is little doubt. The trial court found Gray had no "interest" in any of the credits at issue. Gray insists he reasonably believed the debtors would respond to their obligations in a reasonably timely fashion. Gray insists he thought the risks reasonable and, where unsecured, backed by adequate financial statements. Reports of these loans, their terms, and periodic status were routinely available to USB, which offered nothing but praise until a state bank examiner's probe in January, 1985.

These are not irrelevancies. They are evidence that Gray may have acted with reasonable business judgment. Most assuredly, the duty of care holds no truck with Monday morning quarterbacking, and the business judgment rule stands to prevent this. A loan officer is no guarantor of the success of each credit extension. The prudence of the practice is judged objectively in the circumstances then existing and reasonably knowable by the officer.

The defense ultimately founders. The trial court impliedly found unreasonable Gray's belief regarding the extent to which he should have informed himself at the time regarding these debtors. Further, the court impliedly found there was no rational basis for a belief that his handling of these matters was in USB's best interest.

Judgment for United Southern Bank affirmed.

Recent Changes in the Duty of Care

In response to the *Trans Union* case and insurance companies' increasing unwillingness to insure directors and officers for breaches of their duty of care (and the resulting exodus of outside directors from corporate boards of directors), many state legislatures changed the wording of the duty of care, typically imposing liability only for willful or wanton misconduct or for gross negligence.

For example, Ohio protects directors from monetary liability except when clear and convincing evidence demonstrates the directors' deliberate intent to injure the corporation or the directors' reckless disregard for its welfare. Delaware corporation law and the MBCA allow corporations to amend their articles to reduce or eliminate directors' liability for monetary damages for breaches of the duty of care. Figure 4 contains the MBCA provision.

FIGURE 4   MBCA Section 2.02

(b) The articles of incorporation may set forth:

(4) a provision eliminating or limiting the liability of a director to the corporation or its shareholders for money damages for any action taken or any failure to take any action, as a director, except liability for

(A) the amount of financial benefit received by a director to which he is not entitled;

(B) an intentional infliction of harm on the corporation or the shareholders;

(C) a violation of Section 8.33 [illegal payment of dividends]; or

(D) an intentional violation of criminal law.

Board Opposition to Acquisition of Control of a Corporation

In the last 30 years, many outsiders have attempted to acquire control of publicly held corporations. Typically, these outsiders (called **raiders**) will make a **tender offer** for the shares of a corporation (called the **target**). A tender offer is an offer to the shareholders to buy their shares at a price above the current market price. The raider hopes to acquire a majority of the shares, which will give it control of the target corporation.

Most tender offers are opposed by the target corporation's management. The defenses to tender offers are many and varied, and they carry interesting names, such as the Pac-Man defense, the white knight, greenmail, the poison pill, and the lock-up option. See Figure 5 for definitions of these defenses.

When takeover defenses are successful, shareholders of the target may lose the opportunity to sell their shares at a price up to twice the market price of the shares prior to the announcement of the hostile bid. Frequently, the loss of this opportunity upsets shareholders, who then decide to sue the directors who have opposed the tender offer. Shareholders contend that the directors have opposed the tender offer only to preserve their corporate jobs. Shareholders also argue that the target corporation's interests would have been better served if the tender offer had succeeded.

Generally, courts have refused to find directors liable for opposing a tender offer because the business judgment rule applies to a board's decision to oppose a tender offer.

Nonetheless, the business judgment rule will not apply when the directors make a decision to oppose the tender offer before they have carefully studied it. In addition, if the directors' actions indicate that they opposed the tender offer in order to preserve their jobs, they will be liable to the corporation.

FIGURE 5   Tender Offer Defenses

Pac-Man

The target corporation turns the tables on the tender offeror or raider (which is often another publicly held corporation) by making a tender offer for the raider's shares. As a result, two tender offerors are trying to buy each other's shares. This is similar to the Pac-Man video game, in which Pac-Man and his enemies chase each other.

Greenmail

The target's repurchase of its shares from the raider at a substantial profit to the raider, upon the condition that the raider sign a standstill agreement in which it promises not to buy additional shares of the target for a stated period of time.

White Knight

A friendly tender offeror whom management prefers over the original tender offeror–called a black knight. The white knight rescues the corporation from the black knight (the raider) by offering more money for the corporation's shares. In the *Revlon* case that appeared earlier in the chapter, Forstmann was a white knight for Revlon.

Lock-Up Option

Used in conjunction with a white knight to ensure the success of the white knight's bid. The target and the white knight agree that the white knight will buy a highly valuable asset of the target at a very attractive price for the white knight (usually a below-market price) if the raider succeeds in taking over the target. For example, in the *Revlon* case, Revlon gave a lock-up option to Forstmann to reduce the amount of profit that Pantry Pride would make had it completed its takeover of Revlon.

Poison Pill

Also called a shareholders' rights plan. There are many types, but the typical poison pill involves the target's issuance of a new class of preferred shares to its common shareholders. The preferred shares have rights (share options) attached to them. These rights allow the target's shareholders to purchase shares of the raider or shares of the target at less than fair market value. The poison pill deters hostile takeover attempts by threatening the raider and its shareholders with severe dilutions in the value of the shares they hold.

Court decisions have seemingly modified the business judgment rule as it is applied in the tender offer context. For example, in *Unocal Corp. v. Mesa Petroleum Co.,*[3] the Supreme Court of Delaware upheld the application of the business judgment rule to a board's decision to block a hostile tender offer by making a tender offer for its own shares that excluded the raider.[4] But in so ruling, the court held that the board may use only those defense tactics that are *reasonable* compared to the takeover threat. The board may consider a variety of concerns, including the inadequacy of the price offered, nature and timing of the offer, questions of illegality, the impact on constituencies other than shareholders (i.e., creditors, customers, employees, and perhaps even the community generally), the risk of nonconsummation, and the quality of securities being offered in the exchange.

In *Unocal,* the threat was a two-tier, highly coercive tender offer. In the typical two-tier offer, the raider first offers cash for a majority of the shares. After acquiring a majority of the shares, the offeror initiates the second tier, in which the remaining shareholders are forced to sell their shares for a package of securities less attractive than the first tier. Because shareholders fear that they will be forced to take the less attractive second-tier securities if they fail to tender during the first tier, shareholders—including those who oppose the offer—are coerced into tendering during the first tier. *Unocal* and later cases specifically authorize the use of defenses to defeat a coercive two-tier tender offer.

Since its decision in *Unocal,* the Supreme Court of Delaware has applied this modified business judgment rule to validate a poison pill tender offer defense tactic in *Moran v. Household Int'l, Inc.*[5] and to invalidate a lock-up option tender offer defense in

---

[3]493 A.2d 946 (Del. Sup. Ct. 1985).

[4]Discriminatory tender offers are now illegal pursuant to Securities Act Rule 13e-4.

[5]500 A.2d 346 (Del. Sup. Ct. 1985).

the *Revlon* case, which appears earlier in this chapter. These cases confirmed the *Unocal* holding that the board of directors must show that:

1. It had reasonable grounds to believe that a danger to corporate policy and effectiveness was posed by the takeover attempt.
2. It acted primarily to protect the corporation and its shareholders from that danger.
3. The defense tactic was reasonable in relation to the threat posed to the corporation.

Such a standard appeared to impose a higher standard on directors than the rational basis requirement of the business judgment rule, which historically has been interpreted to require only that a decision of a board not be manifestly unreasonable. In addition, the *Revlon* case required the board to establish an auction market for the company and to sell it to the highest bidder when the directors have abandoned the long-term business objectives of the company by embracing a bust-up of the company.

In the following case, the Supreme Court of Delaware expanded board discretion in fighting hostile takeovers, holding that a board may oppose a hostile takeover provided the board had a *preexisting, deliberately conceived corporate plan* justifying its opposition. The existence of such a plan enabled Time's board to meet the reasonable-tactic element of the *Unocal* test.

PARAMOUNT COMMUNICATIONS, INC. v. TIME, INC.
571 A.2d 1140 (Del. Sup. Ct. 1989)

Since 1983, Time, Inc., had considered expanding its business beyond publishing magazines and books, owning Home Box Office and Cinemax, and operating television stations. In 1988, Time's board approved in principle a strategic plan for Time's acquisition of an entertainment company. The board gave management permission to negotiate a merger with Warner Communications, Inc. The board's consensus was that a merger of Time and Warner was feasible, but only if Time controlled the resulting corporation, preserving the editorial integrity of Time's magazines. The board concluded that Warner was the superior candidate because Warner could make movies and TV shows for HBO, Warner had an international distribution system, Warner was a giant in the music business, Time and Warner would control half of New York City's cable TV system, and the Time network could promote Warner's movies.

Negotiations with Warner broke down when Warner refused to agree to Time dominating the combined companies. Time continued to seek expansion, but informal discussions with other companies terminated when it was suggested the other companies purchase Time or control the resulting board. In January 1989, Warner and Time resumed negotiations, and on March 4, 1989, they agreed to a combination by which Warner shareholders would own 62 percent of the resulting corporation, to be named Time-Warner. To retain the editorial integrity of Time, the merger agreement provided for a board committee dominated by Time representatives.

On June 7, 1989, Paramount Communications, Inc., announced a cash tender offer for all of Time's shares at $175 per share. (The day before, Time shares traded at $126 per share.) Time's financial advisers informed the outside directors that Time's auction value was materially higher than $175 per share. The board concluded that Paramount's $175 offer was inadequate. Also, the board viewed the Paramount offer as a threat to Time's control of its own destiny and retention of the Time editorial policy; the board found that a combination with Warner offered greater potential for Time.

In addition, concerned that shareholders would not comprehend the long-term benefits of the merger with Warner, on June 16, 1989, Time's board recast its acquisition with Warner into a two-tier acquisition, in which it would make a tender offer to buy 51 percent of Warner's shares for cash immediately and later buy the remaining 49 percent for cash and securities. The tender offer would eliminate the need for Time to obtain shareholder approval of the transaction.

On June 23, 1989, Paramount raised its offer to $200 per Time share. Three days later, Time's board rejected the offer as a threat to Time's survival and its editorial integrity; the board viewed the Warner acquisition as offering greater long-term value for the shareholders. Time shareholders and Paramount then sued Time and its board to enjoin Time's acquisition of Warner. The trial court held for Time. Paramount and Time shareholders appealed to the Supreme Court of Delaware.

Horsey, Justice   Our decision does not require us to pass on the wisdom of the board's decision. That is not a court's task. Our task is simply to determine whether there is sufficient evidence to support the initial Time-Warner agreement as the product of a proper exercise of business judgment.

We have purposely detailed the evidence of the Time board's deliberative approach, beginning in 1983–84, to expand itself. Time's decision in 1988 to combine with Warner was made only after what could be fairly characterized as an exhaustive appraisal of Time's future as a corporation. Time's board was convinced that Warner would provide the best fit for Time to achieve its strategic objectives. The record attests to the zealousness of Time's executives, fully supported by their directors, in seeing to the preservation of Time's perceived editorial integrity in journalism. The Time board's decision to expand the business of the company through its March 4 merger with Warner was entitled to the protection of the business judgment rule.

The revised June 16 agreement was defense-motivated and designed to avoid the potentially disruptive effect that Paramount's offer would have had on consummation of the proposed merger were it put to a shareholder vote. Thus, we decline to apply the traditional business judgment rule to the revised transaction and instead analyze the Time board's June 16 decision under *Unocal.*

In *Unocal,* we held that before the business judgment rule is applied to a board's adoption of a defensive measure, the burden will lie with the board to prove (a) reasonable grounds for believing that a danger to corporate policy and effectiveness existed; and (b) that the defensive measure adopted was reasonable in relation to the threat posed.

Paramount argues a hostile tender offer can pose only two types of threats: the threat of coercion that results from a two-tier offer promising unequal treatment for nontendering shareholders; and the threat of inadequate value from an all-shares, all-cash offer at a price below what a target board in good faith deems to be the present value of its shares.

Paramount would have us hold that only if the value of Paramount's offer were determined to be clearly inferior to the value created by management's plan to merge with Warner could the offer be viewed—objectively—as a threat.

Paramount's position represents a fundamental misconception of our standard of review under *Unocal* principally because it would involve the court in substituting its judgment as to what is a "better" deal for that of a corporation's board of directors. The usefulness of *Unocal* as an analytical tool is precisely its flexibility in the face of a variety of fact scenarios. Thus, directors may consider, when evaluating the threat posed by a takeover bid, the inadequacy of the price offered, nature and timing of the offer, questions of illegality, the impact on constituencies other than shareholders, the risk of nonconsummation, and the quality of securities being offered in the exchange.

The Time board reasonably determined that inadequate value was not the only threat that Paramount's all-cash, all-shares offer could present. Time's board concluded that Paramount's offer posed other threats. One concern was that Time shareholders might elect to tender into Paramount's cash offer in ignorance or a mistaken belief of the strategic benefit which a business combination with Warner might produce.

Paramount also contends that Time's board had not duly investigated Paramount's offer. We find that Time explored the available entertainment companies, including Paramount, before determining that Warner provided the best strategic "fit." In addition, Time's board rejected Paramount's offer because Paramount did not serve Time's objectives or meet Time's needs. Time's board was adequately informed of the potential benefits of a transaction with Paramount. Time's failure to negotiate cannot be fairly found to have been uninformed. The evidence supporting this finding is materially enhanced by the fact that twelve of Time's sixteen board members were outside independent directors.

We turn to the second part of the *Unocal* analysis. The obvious requisite to determining the reasonableness of a defensive action is a clear identification of the nature of the threat. This requires an evaluation of the importance of the corporate objective threatened; alternative methods of protecting that objective; impacts of the defensive action, and other relevant factors.

The fiduciary duty to manage a corporate enterprise includes the selection of a time frame for achievement of corporate goals. Directors are not obliged to abandon a deliberately conceived corporate plan for a short-term shareholder profit unless there is clearly no basis to sustain the corporate strategy. Time's responsive action to Paramount's tender offer was not aimed at "cramming down" on its shareholders a management-sponsored alternative, but rather had as its goal the carrying forward of a pre-existing transaction in an altered form. Thus, the response was reasonably related to the threat. The revised agreement did not preclude Paramount from making an offer for the combined Time-Warner company or from changing the conditions of its offer so as not to make the offer dependent upon the nullification of the Time-Warner agreement. Thus, the response was proportionate.

Judgment for Time affirmed.

The *QVC* Decision   In February 1994, the Delaware Supreme Court confirmed its holdings in *Unocal* and *Revlon*. Some commentators have expressed that the decision also casts doubt on the future of the *Time* decision. In *Paramount Communications Inc. v. QVC Network Inc.,*[6] the Delaware Supreme Court enjoined defensive measures taken by Paramount's board of directors. The defensive tactics were designed to facilitate a friendly takeover of Paramount by Viacom Inc. (at $85 per share) and to thwart a more valuable unsolicited takeover bid by QVC (at $90 per share). The Paramount-Viacom agreement provided that Paramount's board would make Paramount's poison pill rights agreement inapplicable to Viacom's bid and grant Viacom a lock-up option to purchase almost 20 percent of Paramount's shares at a bargain price. In addition, Paramount promised to pay Viacom a termination fee of $100 million if Paramount's directors terminated the merger because of a competing transaction, if the directors recommended a competing merger, or if the shareholders failed to approve the merger. When Paramount's board rejected QVC's $90 offer, QVC sued Paramount to enjoin enforcement of the defense tactics preferring Viacom.

The Delaware Supreme Court pointed out that the Paramount-Viacom merger would result in a transfer of control of Paramount from public shareholders to a single shareholder, with the public shareholders receiving a minority voting position in the surviving company. Once control shifted, the public shareholders would have no leverage to demand another premium for transferring control to the majority shareholder. As a result, the Delaware court held that the public shareholders of Paramount were entitled to receive "a control premium and/or protective devices of significant value." The court held that when a corporation undertakes a transaction that will cause a change in corporate control, the directors have an obligation "to seek the best value reasonably available to the shareholders." Having decided to sell control of Paramount, the directors were obligated "to evaluate critically whether or not all material aspects of the Paramount-Viacom merger (separately and in the aggregate) were reasonable and in the best interests of the public stockholders."

Applying the standard above, the Delaware Supreme Court found that the Paramount directors' process was not reasonable and the result achieved for the shareholders was not reasonable. The court ruled that the Paramount directors had the opportunity to improve the economic terms of the Paramount-Viacom transaction, but failed to do so, ultimately squandering their "final opportunity to negotiate on the stockholders' behalf and to fulfill their obligation to seek the best value reasonably available." Rather than taking advantage of the

---

[6] 637 A.2d 34 (Del. Sup. Ct. 1994).

opportunity, the Paramount directors "chose to wall themselves off from material information that was reasonably available and to hide behind defensive measures as a rationalization for refusing to negotiate with QVC or seeking other alternatives." Consequently, the Delaware Supreme Court affirmed the lower court's grant of a preliminary injunction.

It is difficult at this time to assess the importance of the *QVC* decision. The ruling may signal a retreat from the Delaware court's decision in *Time,* which emphasized the need to defer to directors' judgments regarding long-term strategy and granted boards wide latitude to ignore unsolicited bids after a friendly merger was announced. The *QVC* decision may indicate that when there are two bids for a company, the board should not stand in the way of only one of them.

Duties of Loyalty

Directors and officers owe a duty of **utmost loyalty and fidelity** to the corporation. Judge Benjamin Cardozo stated this duty of trust. He declared that a director:

owes loyalty and allegiance to the corporation—a loyalty that is undivided and an allegiance that is influenced by no consideration other than the welfare of the corporation. Any adverse interest of a director will be subjected to a scrutiny rigid and uncompromising. He may not profit at the expense of his corporation and in conflict with its rights; he may not for personal gain divert unto himself the opportunities which in equity and fairness belong to his corporation.[7]

Directors and officers owe the corporation the same duties of loyalty that agents owe their principals, though many of these duties have special names in corporation law. The most important of these duties of loyalty are the duties not to *self-deal,* not to *usurp a corporate opportunity,* not to *oppress minority shareholders,* and not to *trade on inside information.*

Self-Dealing with the Corporation

When a director or officer *self-deals* with his corporation, the director or officer has a **conflict of interest** and may prefer his own interests over those of the corporation. The director's or officer's inter-

est may be *direct,* such as his interest in selling his land to the corporation, or it may be *indirect,* such as his interest in having another business of which he is an owner, director, or officer supply goods to the corporation. When a director has a conflict of interest, the director's transaction with the corporation may be voided or rescinded.

Under the MBCA, a self-dealing transaction will not be voided merely on the grounds of a director's conflict of interest when *any one* of the following is true:

1. The transaction has been approved by a majority of informed, disinterested directors,
2. The transaction has been approved by a majority of the shares held by informed, disinterested shareholders, or
3. The transaction is fair to the corporation.

Nonetheless, even when disinterested directors' or shareholders' approval has been obtained, courts will void a conflict-of-interest transaction that is unfair to the corporation. Therefore, every corporate transaction in which a director has a conflict of interest must be fair to the corporation. If the transaction is fair, the self-dealing (interested) director is excused from liability to the corporation. A transaction is fair if reasonable persons in an *arm's-length bargain* would have bound the corporation to it. This standard is often called the **intrinsic fairness standard.**

The function of disinterested director or disinterested shareholder approval of a conflict-of-interest transaction is merely to shift the burden of proving unfairness. Under the MBCA, the burden of proving fairness lies initially on the interested director. The burden of proof shifts to the corporation that is suing the officer or director for self-dealing if the transaction was approved by the board of directors or the shareholders. Nonetheless, when disinterested directors approve a self-dealing transaction, substantial deference is given to the decision in accordance with the business judgment rule, especially when the disinterested directors compose a majority of the board.

Generally, *unanimous* approval of a self-dealing transaction by informed shareholders *conclusively* releases an interested director or officer from liability for self-dealing even if the transaction is unfair to the corporation. The rationale for this rule is that fully informed shareholders should know what is best for themselves and their corporation.

---

[7]*Meinhard v. Salmon,* 164 N.E.2d 545, 546 (N.Y. Ct. App. 1928).

Loans to Directors

Under early corporation law, *loans* by the corporation *to directors* or *officers* were illegal, on the grounds that such loans might result in the looting of corporate assets. The MBCA allows loans to directors only after certain procedures have been followed. Either the shareholders must approve the loan, or the directors, after finding that the loan benefits the corporation, must approve it.

Parent-Subsidiary Transactions

Self-dealing is a concern when a parent corporation *dominates* a subsidiary corporation. Often, the subsidiary's directors will be directors or officers of the parent also. When persons with dual directorships approve transactions between the parent and the subsidiary, the opportunity for *overreaching* arises. There may be *no arm's-length bargaining* between the two corporations. Hence, such transactions must meet the *intrinsic fairness* test.

Usurpation of a Corporate Opportunity

Directors and officers may steal not only assets of their corporations (such as computer hardware and software) but also *opportunities* that their corporations could have exploited. Both types of theft are equally wrongful. As fiduciaries, directors and officers are liable to their corporation for **usurping corporate opportunities.**

The opportunity must come to the director or officer *in her corporate capacity*. Clearly, opportunities received at the corporate offices are received by the manager in her corporate capacity. In addition, courts hold that CEOs and other high-level officers are nearly always acting in their corporate capacities, even when they are away from their corporate offices.

The opportunity must have a *relation or connection* to an *existing or prospective* corporate activity. Some courts apply the *line of business test*, considering how closely related the opportunity is to the lines of business in which the corporation is engaged. Other courts use the *interest or expectancy test*, requiring the opportunity to relate to property in which the corporation has an existing interest or in which it has an expectancy growing out of an existing right.

The corporation must be *able financially* to take advantage of the opportunity. Managers are required to make a good faith effort to obtain external financing for the corporation, but they are not required to use their personal funds to enable the corporation to take advantage of the opportunity.

A director or officer is free to exploit an opportunity that has been rejected by the corporation.

In the following case, the court found that an opportunity to become the manufacturer of Pepsi-Cola syrup was usurped by the president of a corporation that manufactured beverage syrups and operated soda fountains.

GUTH V. LOFT, INC.

5 A.2d 503 (Del. Sup. Ct. 1939)

Loft, Inc., manufactured and sold candies, syrups, and beverages and operated 115 retail candy and soda fountain stores. Loft sold Coca-Cola at all of its stores, but it did not manufacture Coca-Cola syrup. Instead, it purchased its 30,000-gallon annual requirement of syrup and mixed it with carbonated water at its various soda fountains.

In May 1931, Charles Guth, the president and general manager of Loft, became dissatisfied with the price of Coca-Cola syrup and suggested to Loft's vice president that Loft buy Pepsi-Cola syrup from National Pepsi-Cola Company, the owner of the secret formula and trademark for Pepsi-Cola. The vice president said he was investigating the purchase of Pepsi syrup.

Before being employed by Loft, Guth had been asked by the controlling shareholder of National Pepsi, Megargel, to acquire the assets of National Pepsi. Guth refused at that time. However, a few months after Guth had suggested that Loft purchase Pepsi syrup, Megargel again contacted Guth about buying National Pepsi's secret formula and trademark for only $10,000. This time, Guth agreed to the purchase, and Guth and

Megargel organized a new corporation, Pepsi-Cola Company, to acquire the Pepsi-Cola secret formula and trademark from National Pepsi. Eventually, Guth and his family's corporation owned a majority of the shares of Pepsi-Cola Company.

Very little of Megargel's or Guth's funds were used to develop the business of Pepsi-Cola. Instead, without the knowledge or consent of Loft's board of directors, Guth used Loft's working capital, its credit, its plant and equipment, and its executives and employees to produce Pepsi-Cola syrup. In addition, Guth's domination of Loft's board of directors ensured that Loft would become Pepsi-Cola's chief customer.

By 1935, the value of Pepsi-Cola's business was several million dollars. Loft sued Guth, asking the court to order Guth to transfer to Loft his shares of Pepsi-Cola Company and to pay Loft the dividends he had received from Pepsi-Cola Company. The trial court found that Guth had usurped a corporate opportunity and ordered Guth to transfer the shares and to pay Loft the dividends. Guth appealed.

Layton, Chief Justice Public policy demands of a corporate officer or director the most scrupulous observance of his duty to refrain from doing anything that would deprive the corporation of profit or advantage. The rule that requires an undivided and unselfish loyalty to the corporation demands that there shall be no conflict between duty and self-interest.

The real issue is whether the opportunity to secure a very substantial stock interest in a corporation to be formed for the purpose of exploiting a cola beverage on a wholesale scale was so closely associated with the existing business activities of Loft, and so essential thereto, as to bring the transaction within that class of cases where the acquisition of the property would throw the corporate officer purchasing it into competition with his company.

Guth suggests a doubt whether Loft would have been able to finance the project. The answer to this suggestion is two-fold. Loft's net asset position was amply sufficient to finance the enterprise, and its plant, equipment, executives, personnel and facilities were adequate. The second answer is that Loft's resources were found to be sufficient, for Guth made use of no other resources to any important extent.

Guth asserts that Loft's primary business was the manufacturing and selling of candy in its own chain of retail stores, and that it never had the idea of turning a subsidiary product into a highly advertised, nation-wide specialty. It is contended that the Pepsi-Cola opportunity was not in the line of Loft's activities, which essentially were of a retail nature.

Loft, however, had many wholesale activities. Its wholesale business in 1931 amounted to over $800,000. It was a large company by any standard, with assets exceeding $9 million, excluding goodwill. It had an enormous plant. It paid enormous rentals. Guth, himself, said that Loft's success depended upon the fullest utilization of its large plant facilities. Moreover, it was a manufacturer of syrups and, with the exception of cola syrup, it supplied its own extensive needs. Guth, president of Loft, was an able and experienced man in that field. Loft, then, through its own personnel, possessed the technical knowledge, the practical business experience, and the resources necessary for the development of the Pepsi-Cola enterprise. Conceding that the essential of an opportunity is reasonably within the scope of a corporation's activities, latitude should be allowed for development and expansion. To deny this would be to deny the history of industrial development.

We cannot agree that Loft had no concern or expectancy in the opportunity. Loft had a practical and essential concern with respect to some cola syrup with an established formula and trademark. A cola beverage has come to be a business necessity for soft drink establishments; and it was essential to the success of Loft to serve at its soda fountains an acceptable five-cent cola drink in order to attract into its stores the great multitude of people who have formed the habit of drinking cola beverages.

When Guth determined to discontinue the sale of Coca-Cola in the Loft stores, it became, by his own act, a matter of urgent necessity for Loft to acquire a constant supply of some satisfactory cola syrup, secure against probable attack, as a replacement; and when the Pepsi-Cola opportunity presented itself, Guth having already considered the availability of the syrup, it became impressed with a Loft interest and expectancy arising out of the circumstances and the urgent and practical need created by him as the directing head of Loft.

The fiduciary relation demands something more than the morals of the marketplace. Guth did not offer the Pepsi-Cola opportunity to Loft, but captured it for himself. He invested little or no money of his own in the venture, but commandeered for his own benefit and advantage the money, resources, and facilities of his corporation and the services of his officials. He thrust upon Loft the hazard, while he reaped the benefit. In such a manner he acquired for himself 91 percent of the capital stock of Pepsi-Cola, now worth many millions. A genius in his line he may be, but the law makes no distinction between the wrongdoing genius and the one less endowed.

Judgment for Loft affirmed.

Oppression of Minority Shareholders

Directors and officers owe a duty to manage a corporation in the best interests of the corporation and the shareholders as a whole. When, however, a group of shareholders has been isolated for beneficial treatment to the detriment of another isolated group of shareholders, the disadvantaged group may complain of **oppression.**

For example, oppression may occur when directors of a close corporation who are also the majority shareholders pay themselves high salaries yet refuse to pay dividends or to hire minority shareholders as employees of the corporation. Since there is no market for the shares of a close corporation (apart from selling to the other shareholders), these oppressed minority shareholders have investments that provide them no return. They receive no dividends or salaries, and they can sell their shares only to the other shareholders, who are usually unwilling to pay the true value of the shares.

Generally, courts treat oppression of minority shareholders the same way courts treat director self-dealing: The transaction must be intrinsically fair to the corporation and the minority shareholders.

A special form of oppression is the **freeze-out.** A freeze-out is usually accomplished by merging a corporation with a newly formed corporation under terms by which the minority shareholders do not receive shares of the new corporation but instead receive only cash or other securities. The minority shareholders are thereby *frozen out as shareholders.*

Going private is a special term for a freeze-out of shareholders of *publicly owned corporations.*

Some public corporations discover that the burdens of public ownership—such as the periodic disclosure requirements of the SEC—exceed the benefits of being public. Many of these publicly owned companies choose to freeze out their minority shareholders to avoid such burdens. Often, going private transactions appear abusive because the corporation goes public at a high price and goes private at a much lower price.

Some courts have adopted a fairness test and a business purpose test for freeze-outs. Most states apply the **total fairness test** to freeze-outs. In the freeze-out context, total fairness has two basic aspects: *fair dealing* and *fair price.* Fair dealing requires disclosing material information to directors and shareholders and providing an opportunity for negotiation. A determination of fair value requires the consideration of all the factors relevant to the value of the shares, except speculative projections.

Some states apply the **business purpose test** to freeze-outs. This test requires that the freeze-out accomplish some legitimate business purpose and not serve the special interests of the majority shareholders or the managers.

Other states place no restrictions on freeze-outs provided a shareholder has a **right of appraisal,** which permits a shareholder to require the corporation to purchase his shares at a fair price.

In addition, the SEC requires a *publicly held* company to make a statement on the fairness of its proposed going private transaction and to discuss in detail the material facts on which the statement is based.

In the next case, the court required that a freeze-out of minority shareholders of the New England Patriots football team meet both the business purpose and intrinsic fairness tests. The court held that freezing out the minority shareholders merely to allow the corporation to repay the majority shareholder's personal debts was not a proper business purpose.

COGGINS V. NEW ENGLAND PATRIOTS FOOTBALL CLUB, INC.

492 N.E.2d 1112 (Mass. Sup. Jud. Ct. 1986)

In 1959, the New England Patriots Football Club, Inc. (Old Patriots), was formed with one class of voting shares and one class of nonvoting shares. Each of the original 10 voting shareholders, including William H. Sullivan, purchased 10,000 voting shares for $2.50 per share. The 120,000 nonvoting shares were sold for $5 per share to the general public in order to generate loyalty to the Patriots football team. In 1974, Sullivan was ousted as president of Old Patriots. In November 1975, Sullivan succeeded in regaining control of Old Patriots by purchasing all 100,000 voting shares for $102 per share. He again became a director and president of Old Patriots.

To finance his purchase of the voting shares, Sullivan borrowed $5,350,000 from two banks. The banks insisted that Sullivan reorganize Old Patriots so that its income could be used to repay the loans made to Sullivan and its assets used to secure the loans. To make the use of Old Patriots' income and assets legal, it was necessary to freeze out the nonvoting shareholders. In November 1976, Sullivan organized a new corporation called the New Patriots Football Club, Inc. (New Patriots). Sullivan was the sole shareholder of New Patriots. In December 1976, the shareholders of Old Patriots approved a merger of Old Patriots and New Patriots. Under the terms of the merger, Old Patriots went out of business, New Patriots assumed the business of Old Patriots, Sullivan became the only owner of New Patriots, and the nonvoting shareholders of Old Patriots received $15 for each share they owned.

David A. Coggins, a Patriots fan from the time of its formation and owner of 10 Old Patriots nonvoting shares, objected to the merger and refused to accept the $15 per share payment for his shares. Coggins sued Sullivan and Old Patriots to obtain rescission of the merger. The trial judge found the merger to be illegal and ordered the payment of damages to Coggins and all other Old Patriots shareholders who voted against the merger and had not accepted the $15 per share merger payment. Sullivan and Old Patriots appealed to the Massachusetts Supreme Judicial Court.

Liacos, Justice   When the director's duty of loyalty to the corporation is in conflict with his self-interest, the court will vigorously scrutinize the situation. The dangers of self-dealing and abuse of fiduciary duty are greatest in freeze-out situations like the Patriots merger, when a controlling shareholder and corporate director chooses to eliminate public ownership. Because the danger of abuse of fiduciary duty is especially great in a freeze-out merger, the court must be satisfied that the freeze-out was for the advancement of a legitimate corporate purpose. If satisfied that elimination of public ownership is in furtherance of a business purpose, the court should then proceed to determine if the transaction was fair by examining the totality of the circumstances. Consequently, Sullivan and Old Patriots bear the burden of proving, first, that the merger was for a legitimate business purpose, and second, that, considering the totality of circumstances, it was fair to the minority.

Sullivan and Old Patriots have failed to demonstrate that the merger served any valid corporate objective unrelated to the personal interests of Sullivan, the majority shareholder. The sole reason for the merger was to effectuate a restructuring of Old Patriots that would enable the repayment of the personal indebtedness incurred by Sullivan. Under the approach we set forth above, there is no need to consider further the elements of fairness of a transaction that is not related to a valid corporate purpose.

Judgment for Coggins affirmed as modified.

Trading on Inside Information

Officers and directors have *confidential access* to nonpublic information about the corporation. Sometimes, directors and officers purchase their corporation's securities with knowledge of confidential information. Often, disclosure of previously nonpublic, **inside information** affects the value of the corporation's securities. Therefore, directors and officers may make a profit when the prices of the securities increase after the inside information has been disclosed publicly. Shareholders of the corporation claim that they have been harmed by such activity, either because the directors and officers misused confidential information that should have been used only for corporate purposes or because the directors and officers had an unfair informational advantage over the shareholders.

In this century, there has been a judicial trend toward finding a duty of directors and officers to disclose information that they have received confidentially from the corporation before they buy or sell the corporation's securities. As will be discussed fully in Chapter 44, Securities Regulation, the illegality of insider trading is already federal law under the Securities Exchange Act; however, it remains only a minority rule under state corporation law.

Director's Right to Dissent

A director who assents to an action of the board of directors may be held liable for the board's exceeding its authority or its failing to meet its duty of due care or loyalty. A director who attends a board meeting is deemed to have assented to any action taken at the meeting, unless he dissents.

Under the MBCA, to register his **dissent** to a board action, and thereby to protect himself from liability, the director must **not vote in favor** of the action and **must make his position clear** to the other board members. His position is made clear either by requesting that his dissent appear in the minutes or by giving written notice of his dissent to the chairman of the board at the meeting or to the secretary immediately after the meeting. These procedures ensure that the dissenting director will attempt to dissuade the board from approving an imprudent action.

Generally, directors are not liable for failing to attend meetings. However, a director is liable for *continually failing* to attend meetings, with the result that the director is unable to prevent the board from harming the corporation by its self-dealing.

CORPORATE AND MANAGEMENT LIABILITY FOR TORTS AND CRIMES

When directors, officers, and other employees of the corporation commit torts and crimes while conducting corporate affairs, the issue arises concerning who has liability. Should the individuals committing the torts and crimes be held liable, the corporation, or both?

Liability of the Corporation

For torts, the vicarious liability rule of *respondeat superior* applies to corporations. The only issue is whether an employee acted within the scope of her employment, which encompasses not only acts the employee is authorized to commit but may also include acts that the employee is expressly instructed to avoid.

The traditional view was that a corporation could not be guilty of a crime because criminal guilt required intent. A corporation, not having a mind, could form no intent. Other courts held that a corporation was not a person for purposes of criminal liability.

Today, few courts have difficulty holding corporations liable for crimes. Modern criminal statutes either expressly provide that corporations may commit crimes or define the term *person* to include corporations. In addition, some criminal statutes designed to protect the public welfare do not require intent as an element of some crimes, thereby removing the grounds used by early courts to justify relieving corporations of criminal liability.

Courts are especially likely to impose criminal liability on a corporation when the criminal act is requested, authorized, or performed by:

1. The board of directors.
2. An officer.
3. Another person having responsibility for formulating company policy.
4. A high-level administrator having supervisory responsibility over the subject matter of the offense and acting within the scope of his employment.

In addition, courts hold a corporation liable for crimes of its agent or employee committed within the scope of his authority, even if a higher corporate official has no knowledge of the act and has not ratified it.

DIRECTORS' AND OFFICERS' LIABILITY FOR TORTS AND CRIMES

A person is always *liable for his own torts and crimes,* even when committed on behalf of his principal. Every person in our society is expected to exercise independent judgment and not merely to follow orders. Therefore, directors and officers are personally liable when they commit torts or crimes during the performance of their corporate duties.

A director or officer is usually not liable for the torts of employees of the corporation, since the corporation, not the director or the officer, is the principal. He will have **tort** liability, however, if he *authorizes* the tort or *participates* in its commission. A director or officer has **criminal** liability if she *requests, authorizes, conspires,* or *aids and abets* the commission of a crime by an employee.

In the next case, the court considered the criminal liability of a corporation and its officers.

UNITED STATES V. CATTLE KING PACKING CO., INC.
793 F.2d 232 (10th Cir. 1986)

On June 1, 1981, Butch Stanko started a meatpacking plant in Adams County, Colorado, under the name of Cattle King Packing Company, Inc. Stanko was an officer and shareholder of Cattle King. Gary Waderich was a general sales manager primarily responsible for commercial sales of meat food products and for the daily operation of Cattle King. Stanko set company policies and practices to circumvent the Federal Meat Inspection Act (FMIA), which policies and practices he instructed Waderich and other employees to follow. When Stanko returned to his home in Scottsbluff, Nebraska, he monitored operations by phone and visits to the plant to make certain that the policies and practices that he had established were being followed.

Among the violations of the Federal Meat Inspection Act were the following:

1. Stanko gave a Cattle King employee directions on how, when the government inspector was not around, to mix inedible scrap with edible meat and thereby increase the poundage of the meat.
2. When a shipment of meat was rejected by a grocer and returned to Cattle King, Waderich instructed an employee to rebox the meat and resell it, without government inspection. (The FMIA required all returned meat to be government inspected.) When a government veterinarian came on the reboxing scene and demanded to know what was going on, Waderich denied he knew of the reboxing. Later, Waderich told another employee, "Well, we tried, but we got caught."
3. Cattle King employees dated meat the date it was shipped rather than the date it was produced, as required by the FMIA.
4. Spoiled meat rejected by a buyer and returned to Cattle King was in bags that were puffy with gas caused by the spoilage. On instructions by Waderich, an employee reworked the meat by poking the bags to release the gas, and the meat was reshipped to the same buyer.

The U.S. Attorney General prosecuted Waderich, Stanko, and Cattle King for criminal violations of the FMIA. The jury convicted them, and all three defendants appealed.

McWilliams, Circuit Judge   There is little doubt that Cattle King's operation violated federal meat inspection law at about every turn. Cattle King employees adulterated the meat, misdated the meat, and evaded federal inspection when rejected meat was returned to the plant. Cattle King employees also reworked the returned meat and resold it. Because this activity directly involved Gary Waderich, his challenge of the sufficiency of the evidence must clearly fail.

Stanko would make much of the fact that he returned to Scottsbluff, Nebraska in February 1982, and points out that all of the crimes occurred after that date. He would have us believe that he was somehow insulated from transactions occurring in Colorado when he was in Nebraska. This is an overly simplistic view of the matter. The fact that Stanko was in Scottsbluff does not absolve him of the criminal acts, for example of Waderich, which were committed pursuant to instructions from Stanko himself.

As a variation on his "I-was-in-Scottsbluff" defense, Stanko charges that the trial court's reliance on *United States v. Park* (1975) was error. The rationale of the Supreme Court's decision in *Park* is based upon this premise: Companies that engage in the food business, and the people who manage them, have an affirmative duty to insure that the food they sell to the public is safe. Accordingly, a corporate officer, who is in a "responsible relationship" to some activity within a company that violates federal food laws, can be held criminally responsible even though that officer did not personally engage in that activity. The trial court gave the jury the opportunity to decide whether Butch Stanko was responsible for Cattle King's violations of federal meat inspection laws. The jury found that he was.

In any event, this is not an instance where Stanko was in Scottsbluff, Nebraska, *not* knowing what his employees were doing in Colorado. Rather, Stanko set in motion the very acts which were carried out, pursuant to his direction, by his employees. Scottsbluff is not a shield for Stanko.

The trial court instructed the jury that Cattle King could be found guilty only if one of its agents committed the crimes, and the other three elements were met:

1. The agent was acting within the scope of his or her employment.
2. The agent was authorized to do the act.
3. The agent was motivated, at least in part, to benefit the corporation.

Gary Waderich, an officer of Cattle King, was personally responsible for the commission of all the crimes. Given Waderich's position within Cattle King, there is no doubt that elements 1 and 2 are met. As for element 3, there is also no doubt that Cattle King benefited by the commission of these crimes. The principal effect of all the crimes committed was that Cattle King reaped great economic rewards. Selling meat which should be condemned, misdating boxes so that meat could be stockpiled and thus produced more cheaply, all directly benefited Cattle King economically. There is, therefore, sufficient evidence that Cattle King, as a company, is also guilty of all the crimes.

Judgment convicting Waderich, Stanko, and Cattle King affirmed.

Insurance and Indemnification

The extensive potential liability of directors deters many persons from becoming directors. They fear that their liability for their actions as directors may far exceed their fees as directors. To encourage persons to become directors, corporations **indemnify** them for their outlays associated with defending lawsuits brought against them and paying judgments and settlement amounts. In addition, or as an alternative, corporations purchase **insurance** that will make such payments for the directors.

Indemnification and insurance are provided for officers, also.

Mandatory Indemnification of Directors

Under the MBCA, a director is entitled to *mandatory indemnification* of her reasonable litigation expenses when she is sued and *wins completely* (is *wholly successful*). The greatest part of such expenses is attorney's fees. Because indemnification is mandatory in this context, when the corporation refuses to indemnify a director who has won completely, she may ask a court to order the corporation to indemnify her.

Permissible Indemnification of Directors

Under the MBCA, a director who loses a lawsuit *may* be indemnified by the corporation. This is called *permissible indemnification,* because the corporation is permitted to indemnify the director but is not required to do so.

The corporation must establish that the director acted in *good faith* and reasonably believed that she acted in the *best interests* of the corporation. When a director seeks indemnification for a *criminal* fine, the corporation must establish a third requirement—that the director had no reasonable cause to believe that her conduct was unlawful. Finally, any permissible indemnification must be approved by someone independent of the director receiving indemnification—a disinterested board of directors, disinterested shareholders, or independent legal counsel. Permissible indemnification may cover not only the director's reasonable expenses but also fines and damages that the director has been ordered to pay.

A corporation may not elect to indemnify a director who was found to have received a *financial benefit* to which he was not entitled. Such a rule tends to prevent indemnification of directors who acted from self-interest.

If a director received no financial benefit but was held liable to his corporation or paid an amount to the corporation as part of a *settlement,* the director may be indemnified only for his reasonable expenses, not for the amount that he paid to the corporation. The purpose of these rules is to avoid the circularity of having the director pay damages to the corporation and then having the corporation indemnify the director for the same amount of money.

Advances A director may not be able to afford to make payments to her lawyer prior to the end of a lawsuit. More important, a lawyer may refuse to defend a director who cannot pay legal fees. Therefore, the MBCA permits a corporation to make advances to a director to allow the director to afford a lawyer, if the director affirms that she meets the requirements for permissible indemnification and she promises to repay the advances if she is found not entitled to indemnification.

Court-Ordered Indemnification A court may order a corporation to indemnify a director if it determines that the director meets the standard for *mandatory* indemnification or if the director is *fairly and reasonably* entitled to indemnification in view of all the relevant circumstances.

Indemnification of Nondirectors Under the MBCA, officers and employees who are not directors are entitled to the same mandatory indemnification rights as directors.

Insurance

The MBCA does not limit the ability of a corporation to purchase insurance on behalf of its directors, officers, and employees. Insurance companies, however, are unwilling to insure all risks. In addition, some risks are *legally uninsurable as against public policy.* Therefore, liability for misconduct such as self-dealing, usurpation, and securities fraud is uninsurable.

ETHICAL AND PUBLIC POLICY CONCERNS

1. Do you agree that the primary objective of a corporation should be to maximize profits for its shareholders? What other objectives should a corporation have in addition to or instead of maximizing profits? Should the board of directors engage in an activity that maximizes profits but harms the community in which the corporation is located? Is it possible for a board to maximize profits and to be socially responsible to the community in which the corporation is located?

2. Should corporation law absolutely prevent CEO domination of a corporation or merely allow shareholders to restrict CEO power if shareholders choose? Why do shareholders invest in a corporation in which the CEO dominates the corporation? Why don't shareholders elect directors who control the CEO?

3. Should corporation law allow a board of directors great discretion in fighting hostile takeovers of a corporation? Is your answer affected by whether the raider is able to manage the corporation better than current management? Is your answer affected by whether the raider intends to move the operations of the target to another community? What other factors might affect your view of the law we have concerning takeover defenses? Suppose the raider plans to break up the corporation and to sell the divisible parts of the corporation's business to other corporations. Is board opposition to such a hostile bid more justifiable? Does society benefit from such a bust-up takeover?

PROBLEMS AND PROBLEM CASES

1. A ballot in the San Francisco city election included Proposition T, which would prohibit the construction of any building more than 72 feet high unless plans for the proposed building were approved in advance by the voters. Pacific Gas & Electric Company's (PG&E) management concluded that the proposition would raise its property taxes by an estimated $380,000 in the first year and by as much as $1,135,000 per year in 10 years and that the proposition would also require redesigning and obtaining additional land for an already planned electric power substation. Consequently, the executive committee approved a $10,000 political contribution to a group opposing Proposition T. Neither PG&E's articles of incorporation nor the laws of California expressly permitted PG&E to make political donations. Is the contribution *ultra vires*?

2. Pilot House Motor Inns, Inc., issued demand promissory notes for $540,000 to Marvin Herkowitz. No meeting of the directors was held to approve the issuance of the notes, but minutes of a supposed meeting at which the corporation resolved to issue the notes was signed by all the directors. The minutes stated, "We, the undersigned directors, hereby ratify and confirm the actions reflected in the foregoing minutes." Has the board officially acted to authorize the issuance of the notes?

3. Lillian Pritchard was a director of Pritchard & Baird Corporation, a business founded by her husband. After the death of her husband, her sons took control of the corporation. For two years, they looted the assets of the corporation through theft and improper payments. The corporation's financial statements revealed the improper payments to the sons, but Mrs. Pritchard did not read the financial statements. She did not know what her sons were doing to the corporation or that what they were

doing was unlawful. When Mrs. Pritchard was sued for failing to protect the assets of the corporation, she argued that she was a figurehead director, a simple housewife who served as a director as an accommodation to her husband and sons. Was Mrs. Pritchard held liable?

4. The Chicago National League Ball Club, Inc. (Chicago Cubs), operated Wrigley Field, the Cubs' home park. Through the 1965 baseball season, the Cubs were the only major league baseball team that played no home games at night because Wrigley Field had no lights for nighttime baseball. Philip K. Wrigley, director and president of the corporation, refused to install lights because of his personal opinion that baseball was a daytime sport and that installing lights and scheduling night baseball games would result in the deterioration of the surrounding neighborhood. The other directors assented to this policy. From 1961 to 1965, the Cubs suffered losses from their baseball operations. The Chicago White Sox, whose weekday games were generally played at night, drew many more fans than did the Cubs. A shareholder sued the board of directors to force them to install lights at Wrigley Field and to schedule night games. What did the court rule?

5. Paul Brane, Kenneth Richison, Ralph Dawes, and John Thompson were directors of LaFontaine Grain Co-op, a grain elevator cooperative. Co-op hired Eldon Richison as its manager with authority to buy and sell grain, which accounted for 90 percent of its business. After Co-op suffered a substantial loss in 1979, its independent accountant recommended to the directors that Co-op hedge its grain positions to protect itself from future losses. The directors authorized Eldon Richison to hedge for Co-op, but he was inexperienced in hedging. Moreover, the board failed to attain knowledge of the basic fundamentals of hedging to be able to direct hedging activities and supervise Eldon Richison. He hedged only $20,050 in 1980, whereas Co-op had $7,300,000 in grain sales. Co-op lost over $400,000 in 1980, due primarily to the failure to hedge. Did the directors have liability to Co-op?

6. The management of MacMillan Corporation recognized that it would not be able to prevent a takeover of the corporation. Therefore, management convinced the directors to authorize an auction of the company. Only two bidders emerged: Kohlberg Kravis Roberts & Co. (KKR) and Robert Maxwell. Management preferred KKR and took steps to ensure that KKR would win the auction. Only hours before the deadline for bids, MacMillan's chairman and CEO tipped KKR that Maxwell's bid was lower than KKR's. MacMillan's auctioneer understood that Maxwell would top any KKR bid yet allowed Maxwell to believe that he had made the higher bid. The board granted KKR a lock-up option of MacMillan's crown jewels—its most valuable assets. Has MacMillan's board acted properly?

7. CSX Corp. owned 100 percent of the stock of Chesapeake & Ohio Railway (C&O). C&O owned 98 percent of the stock of Baltimore & Ohio Railroad (B&O). B&O owed 66 percent of the stock of Western Maryland Railway Company; C&O owned 20 percent of Western Maryland. C&O also owned 100 percent of the stock of Peakbay Corporation. The directors of B&O were also the directors of C&O and Western Maryland. First Boston, an investment banking firm, prepared a study for CSX in which financial data for Western Maryland was compared with that of other railroad companies. Paul Goodwin, the senior vice president for finance for B&O and C&O, and his staff formulated a value of $55 per share for Western Maryland's stock. CSX proposed a merger of Western Maryland and Peakbay, by which each share of Western Maryland would be converted into the right to receive $55 cash or CSX common shares of equivalent value. The book value of Western Maryland shares was $63.43 per share; the market price of the shares, which were traded over-the-counter, was $31.50. The merger was approved by the appropriate boards of directors and shareholders. B&O elected to receive cash of $64 million for its Western Maryland shares. A minority B&O shareholder sued the B&O directors, alleging that the sale price was less than B&O would have received had it solicited bids from outside parties for the controlling interest in Western Maryland. What standard did the court apply in determining whether the B&O directors acted properly? Did the directors sell the shares for insufficient consideration?

8. Lindenhurst Drugs, Inc., was owned equally by Allen Becker, Burton Steinberg, and Marvin Steinberg. Each was also an officer and director. The corporation operated a drugstore in leased space in the Linden Plaza Shopping Center. Burton was the manager of the drugstore. In 1979, wanting more retail space to expand their product lines,

Becker and the Steinbergs offered to purchase the Ben Franklin store franchise in the Linden Plaza Shopping Center. Their offer was rejected, but the corporation still had an interest in buying the Ben Franklin store. In 1981, the Linden Plaza Shopping Center notified the corporation that its lease would not be renewed at the end of the year. Becker did not immediately inform the Steinbergs of the termination notice. He did nothing to find a new space for the store. Instead, Becker purchased the Ben Franklin store in the name of his own corporation and leased space for the Ben Franklin store from Linden Plaza Shopping Center. Has Becker done anything wrong?

9. Brothers Theodore and Lawrence Lerner were the only shareholders of Lerner Corporation, a real estate development and management company in Washington, D.C. Theodore owned 70 shares and Lawrence 25 shares of the corporation. Each was an officer and director. In April 1983, Lawrence discovered that Theodore was excluding Lawrence from the benefit of investment opportunities that had been developed through Lawrence's efforts and the use of the corporation's resources. Lawrence sued for judicial dissolution of the corporation. The suit was publicized in a Washington newspaper. Theodore believed that Lawrence would challenge future salary decisions and otherwise engage in behavior that would adversely affect the morale and productivity of key employees. He also believed that word of mouth and the newspaper notoriety about dissension in the corporation would cause prospective customers to prefer other real estate management companies. Theodore removed Lawrence as an officer and director and removed him from the payroll. Theodore also proposed to amend the articles to effect a 1-for-35 reverse stock split, by which Theodore's 70 shares would become 2 shares and Lawrence's 25 shares would become a fractional share. Corporation law allowed the corporation to purchase Lawrence's fractional share, which would result in Lawrence being forced to sell his interest in the corporation for $241,000. The articles amendment was approved by a majority of the outstanding shares. Lawrence sued to enjoin the reverse stock split. Should he be successful?

10. A school bus was returning children to their homes in Livingston County, Kentucky. Phillip Kirkham, age 10, and his sister, Windy Kirkham,

age 6, left the bus and attempted to cross the highway when a truck came on the scene. The truck was owned by Fortner LP Gas Company, Inc. The driver of the truck saw the bus, geared down, applied the brakes, but failed to stop the truck. The truck struck both children, injuring Phillip and killing Windy instantly. A subsequent inspection of the truck revealed grossly defective brakes. The Commonwealth of Kentucky prosecuted the corporation for manslaughter in the second degree for causing Windy's death. The corporation claimed that it could not commit the crime of manslaughter. Was it correct?

11. Shareholders collectively owning 80 percent of the shares of the Bank of New Mexico Holding Company made a shareholder's buy-sell agreement. Those shareholders included directors of the corporation. One of the agreeing shareholders sued the other shareholders, including the directors, to obtain a determination of the price of the shares under the agreement. The corporation reimbursed the legal expenses of the directors who, as shareholders, were defendants in the litigation. Did the corporation act properly in indemnifying the directors?

SHAREHOLDERS' RIGHTS AND LIABILITIES

INTRODUCTION

*The **shareholders** are the ultimate owners of a corporation, but a shareholder has **no right to manage** the corporation. Instead, a corporation is managed by its board of directors and its officers for the benefit of its shareholders.*

The shareholders' role in a corporation is limited to electing and removing directors, approving certain important matters, and ensuring that the actions of the corporation's managers are consistent with the applicable state corporation statute, the articles of incorporation, and the bylaws.

Shareholders also assume a few responsibilities. For example, all shareholders are required to pay the promised consideration for shares. Shareholders are liable for receiving dividends beyond the lawful amount. In addition, controlling shareholders may owe special duties to minority shareholders.

Close corporation shareholders enjoy rights and owe duties beyond the rights and duties of shareholders of publicly owned corporations. In addition, some courts have found close corporation shareholders to be fiduciaries of each other.

This chapter's study of the rights and responsibilities of shareholders begins with an examination of shareholders' meetings and voting rights.

SHAREHOLDERS' MEETINGS

The general corporation statutes of most states and the Model Business Corporation Act (MBCA) provide that an **annual meeting of shareholders** shall be held. The purpose of an annual shareholders' meeting is to elect new directors and to conduct other necessary business. Often, the shareholders are asked to approve the corporation's independent auditors and to vote on shareholders' proposals.

Special meetings of shareholders may be held whenever a corporate matter arises that requires immediate shareholders' action, such as the approval of a merger that cannot wait until the next annual shareholders' meeting. Under the MBCA, a special shareholders' meeting may be called by the board of directors or by a person authorized to do so by the bylaws, usually the president or the chairman of the board. In addition, the holders of at least 10 percent of the shares entitled to vote at the meeting may call a special meeting.

Notice of Meetings

To permit shareholders to arrange their schedules for attendance at shareholders' meetings, the MBCA requires the corporation to give shareholders **notice** of annual and special meetings of shareholders. Notice of a *special meeting* must list the purpose of the meeting. Under the MBCA, notice of an *annual meeting* need not include the purpose of the meeting unless shareholders will be asked to approve extraordinary corporate changes—for example, amendments to the articles of incorporation and mergers.

Notice need be given only to shareholders entitled to vote who are **shareholders of record** on a date fixed by the board of directors. Shareholders of record are those whose names appear on the share-transfer book of the corporation. Usually, only shareholders of record are entitled to vote at shareholders' meetings.

Conduct of Meetings

To conduct business at a shareholders' meeting, a **quorum** of the outstanding shares must be represented at the meeting. If the approval of more than one class of shares is required, a quorum of each class of shares must be present. A quorum is a majority of shares outstanding, unless a greater percentage is established in the articles. The president or the chairman of the board usually presides at shareholders' meetings. Minutes of shareholders' meetings are usually kept by the secretary.

A majority of the votes cast at the shareholders' meeting will decide issues that are put to a vote. If the approval of more than one class of shares is required, a majority of the votes cast by each class must favor the issue. The articles may require a greater than majority vote. Ordinarily, a shareholder is entitled to cast as many votes as he has shares.

Shareholders have a right of *full participation* in shareholders' meetings. This includes the right to offer resolutions, to speak for and against proposed resolutions, and to ask questions of the officers of the corporation.

Typical shareholder resolutions are aimed at protecting or enhancing the interests of minority shareholders and promoting current social issues. Proposals have included limiting corporate charitable contributions, restricting the production of nuclear power, banning the manufacture of weapons, and requiring the protection of the environment.

Shareholder Action without a Meeting

Generally, shareholders can act only at a properly called meeting. However, the MBCA permits shareholders to act without a meeting if *all of the shareholders entitled to vote consent in writing* to the action.

SHAREHOLDERS' ELECTION OF DIRECTORS

The most important shareholder voting right exercised at a shareholder meeting is the right to elect the directors. Normally, directors are elected by a single class of shareholders in **straight voting**, in which each share has one vote for each new director to be elected. With straight voting, a shareholder may vote for as many nominees as there are directors to be elected; a shareholder may cast for each such nominee as many votes as she has shares. For example, in a director election in which 15 people have been nominated for 5 director positions, a shareholder with 100 shares can vote for up to 5 nominees and can cast up to 100 votes for each of those 5 nominees.

Under straight voting, the nominees with the most votes are elected. Consequently, straight voting allows a majority shareholder to elect the entire board of directors. Thus, minority shareholders are unable to elect any representatives to the board without the cooperation of the majority shareholder.

Straight voting is also a problem in close corporations in which a few shareholders own equal numbers of shares. In such corporations, no shareholder individually controls the corporation, yet if the holders of a majority of the shares act together, those holders will elect all of the directors and control the corporation. Such control may be exercised to the detriment of the other shareholders.

Two alternatives to straight voting aid minority shareholders' attempts to gain representation on the board and prevent harmful coalitions in close corporations: cumulative voting and class voting.

Cumulative Voting   With cumulative voting, a corporation allows a shareholder to cumulate her votes by multiplying the number of directors to be elected by the shareholder's number of shares. A shareholder may then allocate her votes among the nominees as she chooses. She may vote only for as many nominees as there are directors to be elected,

---

FIGURE 1 **Cumulative Voting Formula**

The formula for determining the minimum number of shares required to elect a desired number of directors under cumulative voting is:

$$X = \frac{S \times R}{D + 1} + 1$$

X = Number of shares needed to elect the desired number of directors

S = Total number of shares voting at the shareholders' meeting

R = Number of director representatives desired

D = Total number of directors to be elected at the meeting

Example: Sarah Smiles wants to elect two of the five directors of Oates Corporation. One thousand shares will be voted. In this case:

$$S = 1,000$$

$$R = 2$$

$$D = 5$$

Therefore:

$$X = 334.33$$

Fractions are ignored; thus, Sarah will need to hold at least 334 shares to be able to elect two directors.

---

but she may vote for fewer nominees. For example, she may choose to cast all of her votes for only one nominee.

See Figure 1 for a further explanation of the mechanics of cumulative voting.

Classes of Shares

Classes of Shares A corporation may have several classes of shares. The two most common classes are *common shares* and *preferred shares*, but a corporation may have several classes of common shares and several classes of preferred shares. Many close corporations have two or more classes of common shares with different voting rights. Each class may be entitled to elect one or more directors, in order to balance power in a corporation.

For example, suppose a corporation has four directors and 100 shares held by four shareholders—each of whom owns 25 shares. With straight voting and no classes of shares, no shareholder owns enough shares to elect himself as a director, because 51 shares are necessary to elect a director. Suppose, however, that the corporation has four classes of shares, each with the right to elect one of the directors. Each class of shares is issued to only one shareholder. Now, as the sole owner of a class of shares entitling the class to elect one director, each shareholder can elect himself to the board.

Shareholder Control Devices

While cumulative voting and class voting are two useful methods by which shareholders can allocate or acquire voting control of a corporation, there are other devices that may also be used for these purposes: voting trusts; shareholder voting agreements; and proxies, especially irrevocable proxies.

Voting Trusts With a **voting trust**, shareholders transfer their shares to one or more voting trustees and receive voting trust certificates in exchange. The shareholders retain many of their rights, including the right to receive dividends, but the voting trustees vote for directors and other matters submitted to shareholders.

The purpose of a voting trust is to control the corporation through the concentration of shareholder voting power in the voting trustees, who often are participating shareholders. If several minority shareholders collectively own a majority of the shares of a corporation, they may create a voting trust and thereby control the corporation. You may ask why shareholders need a voting trust when they are in apparent agreement on how to vote their shares. The reason is that they may have disputes in the future that could prevent the shareholders from agreeing on how to vote. The voting trust ensures that the shareholder group will control the corporation despite the emergence of differences.

The MBCA limits the duration of voting trusts to 10 years, though the participating shareholders may agree to extend the term for another 10 years. Also, a voting trust must be made public, with copies of the voting trust document available for inspection at the corporation's offices.

Shareholder Voting Agreements   As an alternative to a voting trust, shareholders may merely agree how they will vote their shares. For example, shareholders collectively owning a majority of the shares may agree to vote for each other as directors, resulting in each being elected to the board of directors.

A shareholder voting agreement must be written; only shareholders signing the agreement are bound by it. When a shareholder refuses to vote as agreed, courts specifically enforce the agreement.

Shareholder voting agreements have two advantages over voting trusts. First, their duration may be *perpetual*. Second, they may be kept secret from the other shareholders; they usually do not have to be filed in the corporation's offices.

Proxies   A shareholder may appoint a **proxy** to vote his shares. If several minority shareholders collectively own a majority of the shares of a corporation, they may appoint a proxy to vote their shares and thereby control the corporation. The ordinary proxy has only a limited duration—11 months under the MBCA—unless a longer term is specified. Also, the ordinary proxy is *revocable* at any time. As a result, there is no guarantee that control agreements accomplished through the use of revocable proxies will survive future shareholder disputes.

However, a proxy is *irrevocable* if it is coupled with an interest. A proxy is coupled with an interest when, among other things, the person holding the proxy is a party to a shareholder voting agreement or a buy-and-sell agreement. The principal use of irrevocable proxies is in conjunction with shareholder voting agreements.

In the next case, the court considered the legality of a shareholder voting agreement.

Schreiber v. Carney

447 A.2d 17 (Del. Ch. Ct. 1982)

Texas International Airlines, Inc. (TIA), proposed a new corporate structure in order to strengthen its financial position. To effect the restructuring, TIA would merge with Texas Air Company. The merger required approval of each of the four classes of TIA shareholders. Jet Capital Corporation owned all of the shares of Class C stock. Although Jet Capital believed that the merger would benefit TIA and the other shareholders, Jet Capital would suffer adverse tax consequences if the merger was effected. Thus, Jet Capital decided to vote against the merger. Jet Capital's adverse tax burden was due to its ownership of warrants to purchase TIA shares. Jet Capital could eliminate the merger's adverse tax impact by exercising the warrants prior to the merger, an alternative that Jet Capital was unwilling to choose since it would require a cash payment of over $3 million. Beyond its shares of TIA, Jet Capital had assets of only $200,000. To borrow the $3 million at market interest rates was too expensive.

Therefore, TIA and Jet Capital agreed that TIA would loan Jet Capital $3 million at a below-market interest rate. Since Jet Capital would give the cash from the loan immediately back to TIA when it exercised the warrants, the loan had virtually no impact on TIA's cash position. As a condition of the loan, Jet Capital agreed to vote in favor of the merger. The loan agreement was approved by a majority of the shares held by shareholders other than Jet Capital. Subsequently, the merger was approved by the TIA shareholders.

Leonard Schreiber, a TIA shareholder, brought a derivative suit on behalf of TIA against TIA's directors, including Robert Carney. Schreiber argued that the loan transaction constituted vote-buying and, therefore, was an illegal voting agreement.

Hartnett, Vice Chancellor   There are essentially two principles regarding vote-buying that appear in the Delaware caselaw. The first is that vote-buying is illegal *per se* if its object or purpose is to defraud or disenfranchise the other shareholders.

The second principle is that vote-buying is illegal *per se* as a matter of public policy, the reason being that each shareholder should be entitled to rely upon the independent judgment of his fellow shareholders.

The agreement in question was entered into primarily to further the interests of TIA's other shareholders. Indeed, the shareholders voted overwhelmingly in favor of the loan agreement. Thus, the underlying rationale for the argument that vote-buying is illegal *per se*, as a matter of public policy, ceases to exist when measured against the undisputed reason for the transaction.

Moreover, the rationale that vote-buying is, as a matter of public policy, illegal *per se* is founded upon considerations of policy that are now outmoded as a necessary result of an evolving corporate environment. According to 5 Fletcher *Cyclopedia Corporation* (Perm.Ed.) section 2066:

The theory that each shareholder is entitled to the personal judgment of each other shareholder expressed in his vote, and that any agreement among shareholders frustrating it was invalid, is obsolete because it is both impracticable and impossible of application to modern corporations with many widely scattered shareholders.

In *Ringling Bros.-Barnum & Bailey Combined Shows v. Ringling* (1947), the Delaware Supreme Court adopted a liberal approach to voting agreements. The court stated:

Generally speaking, a shareholder may exercise wide liberality of judgment in the matter of voting, and it is not objectionable that his motives may be for personal profit, or determined by whims or caprice, so long as he violates no duty owed his fellow shareholders.

It is clear that Delaware has discarded the presumption against voting agreements. Thus, an agreement involving the transfer of share voting rights without the transfer of ownership is not necessarily illegal and each arrangement must be examined in light of its object or purpose. To hold otherwise would be to exalt form over substance. Voting agreements in whatever form, therefore, should not be considered to be illegal *per se* unless the object or purpose is to defraud or in some way disenfranchise the other shareholders. This is not to say, however, that vote-buying accomplished for some laudable purpose is automatically free from challenge. Because vote-buying is so easily susceptible of abuse, it must be viewed as a voidable transaction subject to a test for intrinsic fairness.

Schreiber's motion for summary judgment is denied.

FUNDAMENTAL CORPORATE CHANGES

Other matters besides the election of directors require shareholder action, some because they make fundamental changes in the structure or business of the corporation.

Because the articles of incorporation embody the basic contract between a corporation and its shareholders, shareholders must approve most **amendments of the articles of incorporation**. For example, when the articles are amended to increase the number of authorized shares or reduce the dividend rights of preferred shareholders, shareholder approval is needed.

A **merger** is a transaction in which one corporation merges into a second corporation. Usually, the first corporation dissolves; the second corporation takes all the business and assets of both corporations and becomes liable for the debts of both corporations. Usually, the shareholders of the dissolved corporation become shareholders of the surviving corporation. Ordinarily, both corporations' shareholders must approve a merger.

A **consolidation** is similar to a merger except that both old corporations go out of existence and a new corporation takes the business, assets, and liabilities of the old corporations. Both corporations' shareholders must approve the consolidation. Modern corporate practice makes consolidations obsolete, since it is usually desirable to have one of the old corporations survive. The MBCA does not recognize consolidations. However, the effect of a consolidation can be achieved by creating a new corporation and merging the two old corporations into it.

A **share exchange** is a transaction by which one corporation becomes the owner of all of the outstanding shares of a second corporation through a *compulsory* exchange of shares: The shareholders of the second corporation are compelled to exchange their shares for shares of the first corporation. The second corporation remains in existence and becomes a wholly owned subsidiary of the first corporation. Only the selling shareholders must approve the share exchange.

A **sale of all or substantially all of the assets** of the business other than in the regular course of business must be approved by the shareholders of the selling corporation, since it drastically changes the shareholders' investment. Thus, a corporation's sale of all its real property and equipment is a sale of substantially all its assets, even though the corporation continues its business by leasing the assets back from the purchaser. However, a corporation that sells its building, but retains its machinery with the intent of continuing operations at another location, has not sold all or substantially all of its assets.

A **dissolution** is the first step in the termination of the corporation's business. The typical dissolution requires shareholder approval. Dissolution of corporations is covered more fully at the end of this chapter.

The articles of incorporation and the bylaws may require or permit other matters to be submitted for shareholder approval. For example, loans to officers, self-dealing transactions, and indemnifications of managers for litigation expenses may be approved by shareholders. Also, many of the states require shareholder approval of share option plans for high-level executive officers, but the MBCA does not.

Procedures Required

Similar procedures must be met to effect each of the above fundamental changes. The procedures include approval of the board of directors, notice to all of the shareholders whether or not they are entitled to vote, and majority approval of the votes held by shareholders entitled to vote under the statute, articles, or bylaws. Majority approval will be insufficient if a corporation has a supermajority shareholder voting requirement, such as one requiring two-thirds approval.

If there are two or more classes of shares, the articles may provide that matters voted on by shareholders must be approved by each class substantially affected by the proposed transaction. For example, a merger may have to be approved by a majority of the preferred shareholders and a majority of the common shareholders. As an alternative, the articles may require only the approval of the shareholders as a whole.

Under the MBCA, voting by classes is required for mergers, share exchanges, and amendments of the articles if these would substantially affect the rights of the classes. For example, the approval of preferred shareholders is required if a merger would change the dividend rights of preferred shareholders.

In many states, no approval of shareholders of the *surviving corporation* is required for a merger *if* the merger does not fundamentally alter the character of the business or substantially reduce the shareholders' voting or dividend rights.

Also, many statutes, including the MBCA, permit a merger between a parent corporation and its subsidiary without the approval of the shareholders of either corporation. Instead, the board of directors of the parent approves the merger and sends a copy of the merger plan to the subsidiary's shareholders. This simplified merger is called a **short-form merger**. It is available only if the parent owns a high percentage of the subsidiary's shares—90 percent under the MBCA and the Delaware statute.

DISSENTERS' RIGHTS

Many times, shareholders approve a corporate action by less than a unanimous vote, indicating that some shareholders oppose the action. For the most part, the dissenting shareholders have little recourse. Their choice is to remain shareholders or to sell their shares. For close corporation shareholders, there is no choice—the dissenting close corporation shareholder has no ready market for her shares, so she will remain a shareholder.

Some corporate transactions, however, so materially change a shareholder's investment in the corporation or have such an adverse effect on the value of a shareholder's shares that it has been deemed unfair to require the dissenting shareholder either to remain a shareholder (because there is no fair market for the shares) or to suffer a loss in value when he sells his shares on a market that has been adversely affected by the news of the corporate action. Corporate law has therefore responded by creating **dissenters' rights** (a right of appraisal) for shareholders who disagree with specified fundamental corporate transactions. Dissenters' rights require the corporation to pay dissenting shareholders the *fair value* of their shares.

Under the MBCA, the dissenters' rights cover mergers, short-form mergers, share exchanges, significant amendments of the articles of incorporation, and sales of all or substantially all the assets other than in the ordinary course of business. Some statutes cover consolidations also.

A dissenting shareholder seeking payment of the fair value of his shares must have the *right to vote* on the action to which he objects; however, a shareholder of a subsidiary in a short-form merger has dissenters' rights despite his lack of voting power. In addition, the shareholder must *not vote in favor* of the transaction. The shareholder may either vote against the action or abstain from voting.

Most states' statutes exclude from dissenters' rights shares that are traded on a recognized securities exchange such as the New York Stock Exchange. Instead, these statutes expect a shareholder to sell his shares on the stock exchange if he dissents to the corporate action. The MBCA has no such exclusion, on the grounds that the market price may be adversely affected by the news of the proposed or consummated corporate action to which the shareholder objects.

Generally, a shareholder must notify the corporation of his intent to seek payment before the shareholders have voted on the action. Next, the corporation informs a dissenting shareholder how to demand payment. After the dissenting shareholder demands payment, the corporation and the shareholder negotiate a mutually acceptable price. If they cannot agree, a court will determine the fair value of the shares and order the corporation to pay that amount.

To determine fair value, most judges use the **Delaware Block Method**, a weighted average of several valuation techniques—such as market value, comparisons with other similar companies, capitalization of earnings, and book value.

In the following case, the court granted dissenters' rights to a shareholder of a corporation that sold substantially all its assets.

WATERS V. DOUBLE L, INC.
755 P.2d 1294 (Idaho Ct. App. 1987)

Dale Waters was a minority shareholder of Double L, Inc., a business engaged in manufacturing agricultural machinery and related products. When Double L became financially distressed, the directors agreed to sell to Pioneer Astro all of Double L's real property and equipment and to issue sufficient shares to make Pioneer Astro an 80 percent shareholder of Double L. To improve Double L's financial position, Pioneer Astro agreed to pay cash for the assets and shares and to loan money to Double L. To allow Double L to continue its business, Pioneer Astro agreed to lease the purchased assets back to Double L.

At a shareholder meeting, shareholders approved the transaction with Pioneer Astro. Waters, however, abstained from voting and demanded that Double L pay him the fair value of his shares pursuant to dissenters' rights under Idaho law. When Double L refused to buy Waters's shares, Waters sued. The trial court ordered Double L to buy Waters's shares. Double L appealed.

Burnett, Judge   Idaho Code section 30-1-80 lists the categories of corporate actions that trigger the right to dissent:

(a) Any shareholder of a corporation shall have the right to dissent from, and to obtain payment for his shares in the event of any of the following corporate actions:

* * * * *

(2) Any sale, lease, exchange, or other disposition of all or substantially all of the property and assets of the corporation not made in the usual or regular course of its business.

Double L points to the fact that it retained certain assets in the form of inventory, accounts receivable, and goodwill. However, in the deposition of Lynn

Johnson, Double L's president, Johnson testified as follows:

Q: You made an agreement whereby Pioneer Astro invested heavily in Double L; is that right?
A: Yes.
Q: Pioneer Astro bought your land, your machinery, and the buildings owned by Double L?
A: Yes.
Q: Was that substantially all of your assets?
A: Yes.

Moreover, the corporation's own conduct—seeking and obtaining shareholder approval of the Pioneer Astro transaction—implicitly indicated that the transaction comprised a sale of substantially all of the corporation's assets. Had the transaction not embraced substantially all of the assets, or the transaction been in the ordinary course of business, it would not have required shareholder approval.

The corporation would have us hold that because its business continued to operate after the transaction was consummated, the transaction could not be regarded as a sale of all or substantially all of the corporation's assets. However, the mere fact that the corporation remained in business under the same name is not the critical criterion. The nature of the transaction takes precedence over its form. Our focus is upon the relationship between the assets transferred and those remaining. Here, the corporation sold all of its hard assets, retaining intangible assets of admittedly dubious value. Only by renting the hard assets back from Pioneer Astro was the corporation able to continue its operations. This is a classic "sale of assets" transaction. The corporation after the Pioneer Astro transaction was not, in any real sense, the same entity that existed before the transaction.

Judgment for Waters affirmed.

SHAREHOLDERS' INSPECTION AND INFORMATION RIGHTS

Inspecting a corporation's books and records is sometimes essential to the exercise of a shareholder's rights. For example, a shareholder may be able to decide how to vote in a director election only after examining corporate financial records that reveal whether the present directors are managing the corporation profitably. Also, a close corporation shareholder may need to look at the books to determine the value of his shares.

Many corporate managers are resistant to shareholders inspecting the corporation's books and records, charging that shareholders are nuisances or that shareholders often have improper purposes for making such an inspection. Sometimes, management objects solely on the ground that it desires secrecy.

Most of the state corporation statutes specifically grant shareholders inspection rights. The purpose of these statutes is to facilitate the shareholder's inspection of the books and records of corporations whose managements resist or delay proper requests by shareholders. A shareholder's lawyer or accountant may assist the shareholder's exercise of his inspection rights.

The MBCA grants shareholders an **absolute right of inspection** of an alphabetical listing of the shareholders entitled to notice of a meeting, including the number of shares owned. Access to a shareholder list allows a shareholder to contact other shareholders about important matters such as shareholder proposals.

The MBCA also grants an absolute right of inspection of, among other things, the articles, bylaws, and minutes of shareholder meetings within the past three years.

Shareholders have a **qualified right to inspect** other records, however. To inspect accounting records, board and committee minutes, and shareholder minutes more than three years old, a shareholder must make the demand in *good faith* and have a *proper purpose*. Proper purposes include inspecting the books of account to determine the value of shares or the propriety of dividends. On the other hand, learning business secrets and aiding a competitor are clearly improper purposes.

In the next case, the court found that valuing shares and checking on allegations of corporate mismanagement were proper purposes.

CARTER V. WILSON CONSTRUCTION CO.
348 S.E.2d 830 (N.C. Ct. App. 1986)

William Carter owned 317 shares of Wilson Construction Company. He also owned 20 percent of the shares of Wilson Equipment Leasing, Inc., a company that leased equipment to and engaged in other transactions with Wilson Construction. Carter worked for Wilson Construction until he resigned his position in November 1983. Immediately, he organized and became a part owner and employee of C & L Contracting, Inc., a competitor of Wilson Construction. Carter offered to sell his shares to Wilson Construction, but his offer was rejected. In 1984, Carter demanded that Wilson Construction make available to him its books, records of account, minutes, and record of shareholders, on the grounds that he had been told and believed that the financial condition of Wilson Construction had deteriorated due to improper management. In addition, he requested the information to determine the value of his shares, the financial condition of the corporation, and whether it was efficiently managed in the best interests of the corporation. Wilson Construction refused the request. Carter sued Wilson Construction and its president, Ray Wilson. The trial court ordered the corporation to make the records available to Carter and allowed Carter to recover $500 in penalties from Wilson Construction and $500 in penalties from Ray Wilson. Wilson Construction and Ray Wilson appealed.

Johnson, Judge   North Carolina law does not give a shareholder an absolute right of inspection and examination for a mere fishing expedition, or for a purpose not germane to the protection of his economic interest as a shareholder of the corporation. For a shareholder to have the right to visit a corporation's office and possibly disrupt its normal operation in order to inspect corporate books and records of account, his motives must be "proper." Purposes that previously have been deemed proper are the shareholder's good faith desire to (1) determine the value of his shares; (2) investigate the conduct of management; and (3) determine the financial condition of the corporation. The burden of proof rests upon Wilson Construction, if it wishes to defeat Carter's demand, to show that Carter is motivated by some improper purpose.

Here, Carter stated a proper purpose. Carter tried to sell his shares in Wilson Construction back to Wilson Construction, which declined his offer to sell. Carter had personally guaranteed the debts of Wilson Equipment Leasing, a corporation that conducted related transactions with Wilson Construction, including indemnifying its debts and extending loans. Carter had reason to believe, based upon information from Wilson Construction's management consultant, that certain purchases had not been put on the corporate books and that funds were shuffled between Wilson Equipment Leasing and Wilson Construction, and that the net worth of Wilson Construction decreased from August 1983 to August 1984. This evidence supports Carter's allegation of a proper purpose.

The evidence produced by Wilson Construction showed that Carter is currently part owner and employee of C & L Contracting. According to Ray Wilson, "We are in direct competition on all work in the Piedmont, North Carolina, that is bridge work" and to allow Carter access to the books and records of Wilson Construction "would put us at a disadvantage."

This evidence is insufficient to override the presumption that Carter is acting in good faith. The mere possibility that a shareholder may abuse his right to gain access to corporate information will not be held to justify a denial of a legal right, if such right exists in the shareholder.

Judgment for Carter affirmed.

Shareholders also have the right to receive from the corporation **information** that is important to their voting and investing decisions. The MBCA requires a corporation to furnish its shareholders *financial statements*, including a balance sheet, an income statement, and a statement of changes in shareholders' equity. The Securities Exchange Act of 1934 also requires publicly held companies to furnish such statements, as well as other information that is important to a shareholders' voting and investing decisions.

PREEMPTIVE RIGHT

The market price of a shareholder's shares will be reduced if a corporation issues additional shares at a price less than the market price. In addition, a shareholder's proportionate voting, dividend, and liquidation rights may be adversely affected by the issuance of additional shares. For example, if a corporation's only four shareholders each own 100 shares worth $10 per share, then each shareholder has shares worth $1,000, a 25 percent interest in any dividends declared, 25 percent of the voting power, and a claim against 25 percent of the corporation's assets after creditors' claims have been satisfied. If the corporation subsequently issues 100 shares to another person for only $5 per share, the value of each shareholder's shares falls to $900 and his dividend, voting, and liquidation rights are reduced to 20 percent. In a worse scenario, the corporation issues 201 shares to one of the existing shareholders, giving that shareholder majority control of the corporation and reducing the other shareholders' interests to less than 17 percent each. As a result, the minority shareholders will be dominated by the majority shareholder and will receive a greatly reduced share of the corporation's dividends.

Such harmful effects of an issuance could have been prevented if the corporation had been required to offer each existing shareholder a percentage of the new shares equal to her current proportionate ownership. If, for example, in the situation described above, the corporation had offered 50 shares to each shareholder, each shareholder could have remained a 25 percent owner of the corporation; her interests in the corporation would not have been reduced, and her total wealth would not have been decreased.

Corporation law recognizes the importance of giving a shareholder the option of maintaining the value of his shares and retaining his proportionate interest in the corporation. This is the shareholder's **preemptive right**, an option to subscribe to a new issuance of shares in proportion to the shareholder's current interest in the corporation.

The MBCA adopts a comprehensive scheme for determining preemptive rights. It provides that the preemptive right does not exist except to the extent provided by the articles. The MBCA permits the corporation to state expressly when the preemptive right arises.

When the preemptive right exists, the corporation must notify a shareholder of her option to buy shares, the number of shares that she is entitled to buy, the price of the shares, and when the option must be exercised. Usually, the shareholder is issued a **right**, a written option that she may exercise herself or sell to a person who wishes to buy the shares.

DISTRIBUTIONS TO SHAREHOLDERS

During the life of a corporation, shareholders may receive distributions of the corporation's assets. Most people are familiar with one type of distribution—dividends—but there are other important types of distributions to shareholders, including payments to shareholders upon the corporation's repurchase of its shares.

There is one crucial similarity among all the types of distributions to shareholders: Corporate assets are transferred to shareholders. Consequently, an asset transfer to shareholders may harm the corporation's creditors and others with claims against the corporation's assets. For example, a distribution of assets may impair a corporation's ability to pay its creditors. In addition, a distribution to one class of shareholders may harm another class of shareholders that has a liquidation priority over the class of shareholders receiving the distribution. The existence of these potential harms compels corporation law to restrict the ability of corporations to make distributions to shareholders.

Dividends

One important objective of a business corporation is to make a profit. Shareholders invest in a corporation primarily to share in the expected profit either through appreciation of the value of their shares or through dividends. There are two types of dividends: *cash or property dividends* and *share dividends*. Only cash or property dividends are distributions of the corporation's assets. Share dividends are *not* distributions.

Cash or Property Dividends   Dividends are usually paid in cash. However, other assets of the corporation—such as airline discount coupons or shares of another corporation—may also be distributed as dividends. Cash or property dividends are declared by the board of directors and paid by the corporation on the date stated by the directors. Once declared, dividends are *debts* of the corporation and shareholders may sue to force payment of the dividends. The board's dividend declaration, including the amount of dividend and whether to declare a dividend, is protected by the business judgment rule.

Preferred shares nearly always have a set dividend rate stated in the articles of incorporation. Even so, unless the preferred dividend is mandatory, the board has discretion to determine whether to pay a preferred dividend and what amount to pay. Most preferred shares are *cumulative preferred shares*, on which unpaid dividends cumulate. The entire accumulation must be paid before common shareholders may receive any dividend. Even when preferred shares are noncumulative, the current dividend must be paid to preferred shareholders before any dividend may be paid to common shareholders.

The following, is one of the few cases in which a court ordered the payment of a dividend to common shareholders. The court found that Henry Ford had the wrong motives for causing Ford Motor Company to refuse to pay a dividend.

DODGE v. FORD MOTOR CO.
170 N.W. 668 (Mich. Sup. Ct. 1919)

In 1916, brothers John and Horace Dodge owned 10 percent of the common shares of the Ford Motor Company. Henry Ford owned 58 percent of the outstanding common shares and controlled the corporation and its board of directors. Starting in 1911, the corporation paid a regular annual dividend of $1.2 million, which was 60 percent of its capital stock of $2 million but only about 1 percent of its total equity of $114 million. In addition, from 1911 to 1915, the corporation paid special dividends totaling $41 million.

The policy of the corporation was to reduce the selling price of its cars each year. In June 1915, the board and officers agreed to increase production by constructing new plants for $10 million, acquiring land for $3 million, and erecting an $11 million smelter. To finance the planned expansion, the board decided not to reduce the selling price of cars beginning in August 1915 and to accumulate a large surplus.

A year later, the board reduced the selling price of cars by $80 per car. The corporation was able to produce 600,000 cars annually, all of which, and more, could have been sold for $440 instead of the new $360 price, a forgone revenue of $48 million. At the same time, the corporation announced a new dividend policy of paying no special dividend. Instead, it would reinvest all earnings except the regular dividend of $1.2 million.

Henry Ford announced his justification for the new dividend policy in a press release: "My ambition is to employ still more men, to spread the benefits of this industrial system to the greatest possible number, to help them build up their lives and their homes." The corporation had a $112 million surplus, expected profits of $60 million, total liabilities of $18 million, $52.5 million in cash on hand, and municipal bonds worth $1.3 million.

The Dodge brothers sued the corporation and the directors to force them to declare a special dividend. The trial court ordered the board to declare a dividend of $19.3 million. Ford Motor Company appealed.

Ostrander, Chief Justice   It is a well-recognized principle of law that the directors of a corporation, and they alone, have the power to declare a dividend of the earnings of the corporation, and to determine its amount. Courts will not interfere in the management of the directors unless it is clearly made to appear that they are guilty of fraud or misappropriation of the corporate funds, or they refuse to declare a dividend when the corporation has a surplus of net profits which it can, without detriment to the business, divide among its stockholders, and when a refusal to do so would amount to such an abuse of discretion as would constitute a fraud, or breach of that good faith that they are bound to exercise towards the shareholders.

The testimony of Mr. Ford convinces this court that he has to some extent the attitude towards shareholders of one who has dispensed and distributed to them large gains and that they should be content to take what he chooses to give. His testimony creates the impression that he thinks the Ford Motor Company has made too much money, has had too large profits, and that, although large profits might be still earned, a sharing of them with the public, by reducing the price of the output of the company, ought to be undertaken. We have no doubt that certain sentiments, philanthropic and altruistic, creditable to Mr. Ford, had large influence in determining the policy to be pursued by the Ford Motor Company.

There should be no confusion of the duties that Mr. Ford conceives that he and the shareholders owe to the general public and the duties that in law he and his co-directors owe to protesting, minority shareholders. A business corporation is organized and carried on primarily for the profit of the shareholders. The powers of the directors are to be employed for that end.

We are not, however, persuaded that we should interfere with the proposed expansion of the Ford Motor Company. In view of the fact that the selling price of products may be increased at any time, the ultimate results of the larger business cannot be certainly estimated. The judges are not business experts. It is recognized that plans must often be made for a long future, for expected competition, for a continuing as well as an immediately profitable venture. We are not satisfied that the alleged motives of the directors, in so far as they are reflected in the conduct of the business, menace the interests of shareholders.

Assuming the general plan and policy of expansion were for the best ultimate interest of the company and therefore of its shareholders, what does it amount to in justification of a refusal to declare and pay a special dividend? The Ford Motor Company was able to estimate with nicety its income and profit. It could sell more cars than it could make. The profit upon each car depended upon the selling price. That being fixed, the yearly income and profit was determinable, and, within slight variations, was certain.

There was appropriated for the smelter $11 million. Assuming that the plans required an expenditure sooner or later of $10 million for duplication of the plant, and for land $3 million, the total is $24 million. The company was a cash business. If the total cost of proposed expenditures had been withdrawn in cash from the cash surplus on hand August 1, 1916, there would have remained $30 million.

The directors of Ford Motor Company say, and it is true, that a considerable cash balance must be at all times carried by such a concern. But there was a large daily, weekly, monthly receipt of cash. The output was practically continuous and was continuously, and within a few days, turned into cash. Moreover, the contemplated expenditures were not to be immediately made. The large sum appropriated for the smelter plant was payable over a considerable period of time. So that, without going further, it would appear that, accepting and approving the plan of the directors, it was their duty to distribute on and near the 1st of August 1916, a very large sum of money to stockholders.

Judgment for the Dodge brothers affirmed.

To protect the claims of the corporation's creditors, all of the corporation statutes limit the extent to which dividends may be paid. The MBCA imposes two limits: (1) the *solvency test* and (2) the *balance sheet test*.

Solvency Test   A dividend may not make a corporation insolvent,—that is, unable to pay its debts as they come due in the usual course of business. This means that a corporation may pay a dividend to the extent it has *excess solvency*—that is, liquidity that it does not need to pay its currently maturing obligations. This requirement protects creditors, who are concerned primarily with the corporation's ability to pay debts as they mature.

Balance Sheet Test

After the dividend has been paid, the corporation's assets must be sufficient to cover its liabilities and the liquidation preference of shareholders having a priority in liquidation over the shareholders receiving the dividend. This means that a corporation may pay a dividend to the extent it has *excess assets*—that is, assets it does not need to cover its liabilities and the liquidation preferences of shareholders having a priority in liquidation over the shareholders receiving the dividends. This requirement protects not only creditors but also preferred shareholders. It prevents a corporation from paying to common shareholders a dividend that will impair the liquidation rights of preferred shareholders.

Example

Batt Company has $27,000 in excess liquidity that it does not need to pay its currently maturing obligations. It has assets of $200,000 and liabilities of $160,000. It has one class of common shareholders. Its one class of preferred shareholders has a liquidation preference of $15,000. Examining these facts, we find that Batt's excess solvency is $27,000, but its excess assets are only $25,000 ($200,000 − 160,000 − 15,000). Therefore, Batt's shareholders may receive a maximum cash or property dividend of $25,000, which will eliminate all of Batt's excess assets and leave Batt with $2,000 of excess solvency.

Share Dividends and Share Splits

Corporations sometimes distribute additional shares of the corporation to their shareholders. Often, this is done in order to give shareholders something instead of a cash dividend so that the cash can be retained and reinvested in the business. Such an action may be called either a **share dividend** or a **share split**.

A **share dividend** of a *specified percentage of outstanding shares* is declared by the board of directors. For example, the board may declare a 10 percent share dividend. As a result, each shareholder will receive 10 percent more shares than she currently owns. A share dividend is paid on outstanding shares only. Unlike a cash or property dividend, a share dividend may be revoked by the board after it has been declared.

A **share split** results in shareholders receiving a specified number of shares in exchange for each share that they currently own. For example, shares may be split two for one. Each shareholder will now have two shares for each share that he previously owned. A holder of 50 shares will now have 100 shares instead of 50.

The MBCA recognizes that a share split or a share dividend in the same class of shares does not affect the value of the corporation or the shareholders' wealth, because no assets have been transferred from the corporation to the shareholders. The effect is like that produced by taking a pie with four pieces and dividing each piece in half. Each person may receive twice as many pieces of the pie, but each piece is worth only half as much. The total amount received by each person is unchanged.

Therefore, the MBCA permits share splits and share dividends of the same class of shares to be made merely by action of the directors. The directors merely have the corporation issue to the shareholders the number of shares needed to effect the share dividend or split. The corporation must have a sufficient number of authorized, unissued shares to effect the share split or dividend; when it does not, its articles must be amended to create the required number of additional authorized shares.

Reverse Share Split

A *reverse share split* is a decrease in the number of shares of a class such that, for example, two shares become one share. Most of the state corporation statutes require shareholder action to amend the articles to effect a reverse share split because the number of authorized shares is reduced. The purpose of a reverse share split is usually to increase the market price of the shares.

Share Repurchases

Declaring a cash or property dividend is only one of the ways in which a corporation may distribute its assets. A corporation may also distribute its assets by repurchasing its shares from its shareholders. Such a repurchase may be either a *redemption* or an *open-market repurchase*.

The right of **redemption** (or a call) is usually a right of the corporation to force an *involuntary* sale by a shareholder at a fixed price. The shareholder must sell the shares to the corporation at the corporation's request; in most states, the shareholder cannot force the corporation to redeem the shares.

Under the MBCA, the right of redemption must appear in the articles of incorporation. It is common for a corporation to issue preferred shares subject to redemption at the corporation's option. Usually, common shares are not redeemable.

In addition, a corporation may repurchase its shares **on the open market**. A corporation is empowered to purchase its shares from any shareholder who is willing to sell them. Such repurchases are *voluntary* on the shareholder's part, requiring the corporation to pay a current market price to entice the shareholder to sell.

A corporation's repurchase of its shares may harm creditors and other shareholders. The MBCA requires a corporation repurchasing shares to meet tests that are the same as its cash and property dividend rules, recognizing that financially, a repurchase of shares is no different from a dividend or any other distribution of assets to shareholders.

1. **Solvency Test:** The repurchase may not make the corporation insolvent, that is, unable to pay its debts as they come due in the usual course of business. This means that a corporation may repurchase shares to the extent it has *excess solvency*.

2. **Balance Sheet Test:** After the repurchase of shares, the corporation's assets must be sufficient to cover its liabilities and the liquidation preference of shareholders having a priority in liquidation over the shareholders whose shares were repurchased. This means that a corporation may repurchase shares to the extent that it has *excess assets*.

SHAREHOLDERS' LAWSUITS

Shareholders' Individual Lawsuits

A shareholder has the right to sue in his own name to prevent or redress a breach of the shareholder's contract. For example, a shareholder may sue to recover dividends declared but not paid or dividends that should have been declared, to enjoin the corporation from committing an *ultra vires* act, to enforce the shareholder's right of inspection, and to enforce preemptive rights.

Shareholder Class Action Suits

When several people have been injured similarly by the same persons in similar situations, one of the injured people may sue for the benefit of all the people injured. Likewise, if several shareholders have been similarly affected by a wrongful act of another, one of these shareholders may bring a **class action** on behalf of all the affected shareholders.

An appropriate class action under state corporation law would be an action seeking a dividend payment that has been brought by a preferred shareholder for all of the preferred shareholders. Any recovery is prorated to all members of the class.

A shareholder who successfully brings a class action is entitled to be reimbursed from the award amount for his *reasonable expenses*, including attorney's fees. If the class action suit is unsuccessful and has no reasonable foundation, the court may order the suing shareholder to pay the defendants' reasonable litigation expenses, including attorney's fees.

Shareholders' Derivative Actions

When a corporation has been harmed by the actions of another person, the right to sue belongs to the corporation and any damages awarded by a court belong to the corporation. Hence, as a general rule, a shareholder has no right to sue in his own name when someone has harmed the corporation, and he may not recover for himself damages from that person. This is the rule even when the value of the shareholder's investment in the corporation has been impaired.

Nonetheless, one or more shareholders are permitted under certain circumstances to bring an action for the benefit of the corporation when the directors have failed to pursue a corporate cause of action. For example, if the corporation has a claim against its chief executive for wrongfully diverting corporate assets to her personal use, the corporation is unlikely to sue the chief executive because she controls the board of directors. Clearly, the CEO should not go unpunished. Consequently, corporation law authorizes a shareholder to bring a **derivative action** (or derivative suit) against the CEO on behalf of the corporation and for its benefit. Such a suit may also be used to bring a corporate claim against an outsider.

If the derivative action succeeds and damages are awarded, the damages ordinarily go to the corporate treasury for the benefit of the corporation. The suing shareholder is entitled only to reimbursement of his reasonable attorney's fees that he incurred in bringing the action.

Eligible Shareholders

Although allowing shareholders to bring derivative suits creates a viable procedure for suing wrongdoing officers and directors, this procedure is also susceptible to abuse. **Strike suits** (lawsuits brought to gain out-of-court settlements for the complaining shareholders personally or to earn large attorney's fees, rather than to obtain a recovery for the corporation) have not been uncommon. To discourage strike suits, the person bringing the action must be a current shareholder who also held his shares at the time the alleged wrong occurred. In addition, the shareholder must fairly and adequately represent the interests of shareholders similarly situated in enforcing the right of the corporation.

One exception to these rules is the **double derivative suit**, a suit brought by a shareholder of a parent corporation on behalf of a subsidiary corporation owned by the parent. Courts regularly permit double derivative suits.

Demand on Directors

Since a decision to sue someone is ordinarily made by corporate managers, a shareholder must first **demand** that the board of directors bring the suit. A demand informs the board that the corporation may have a right of action against a person that the board, in its business judgment, may decide to pursue. Therefore, if a demand is made and the board decides to bring the suit, the shareholder may not institute a derivative suit.

Ordinarily, a shareholder's failure to make a demand on the board prevents her from bringing a derivative suit. Nonetheless, the shareholder may initiate the suit if she proves that a demand on the board would have been useless or **futile**. Demand is futile, and therefore **excused**, if the board is unable to make a disinterested decision regarding whether to sue. Futility may be proved when all or a majority of the directors are interested in the challenged transaction, such as in a suit alleging that the directors issued shares to themselves at below-market prices.

If a shareholder makes a demand on the board and it **refuses** the shareholder's demand to bring a suit, ordinarily the shareholder is not permitted to continue the derivative action. The decision to bring a lawsuit is an ordinary business decision appropriate for a board of directors to make. The business judgment rule, therefore, is available to insulate from court review a board's decision not to bring a suit.

Of course, if a shareholder derivative suit accuses the board of harming the corporation, such as by misappropriating the corporation's assets, the board's refusal will not be protected by the business judgment rule because the board has a conflict of interest in its decision to sue. In such a situation, the shareholder may sue the directors despite the board's refusal.

Shareholder Litigation Committees

In an attempt to ensure the application of the business judgment rule in demand refusal and demand futility situations, interested directors have tried to isolate themselves from the decision whether to sue by creating a special committee of the board, called a *shareholder litigation committee* (SLC) (or independent investigation committee) whose purpose is to decide whether to sue. The SLC should consist of directors who are not defendants in the derivative suit, who are not interested in the challenged action, are independent of the defendant directors, and if possible, were not directors at the time the wrong occurred. Usually, the SLC has independent legal counsel that assists its determination whether to sue. Because the SLC is a committee of the board, its decision may be protected by the business judgment rule. Therefore, an SLC's decision not to sue may prevent a shareholder from suing.

Shareholders have challenged the application of the business judgment rule to an SLC's decision to dismiss a shareholder derivative suit against some of the directors. The suing shareholders argue that it is improper for an SLC to dismiss a shareholder derivative suit because there is a *structural bias*. That is, the SLC members are motivated by a desire to avoid hurting their fellow directors and adversely affecting future working relationships within the board.

When demand is **not futile**, most of the courts that have been faced with this question have upheld the decisions of special litigation committees that comply with the business judgment rule. The courts require that the SLC members be *independent* of the defendant directors, be *disinterested* with regard to the subject matter of the suit, make a *reasonable investigation* into whether to dismiss the suit, and act in *good faith*.

When demand is **futile or excused**, most courts faced with the decision of an SLC have applied the rule of the *Zapata* case, which follows.

ZAPATA CORP. v. MALDONADO
430 A.2d 779 (Del. Sup. Ct. 1981)

Zapata Corporation had a share option plan that permitted its executives to purchase Zapata shares at a below-market price. Most of the directors participated in the share option plan. In 1974, the directors voted to advance the share option exercise date in order to reduce the federal income tax liability of the executives who exercised the share options, including the directors. An additional effect, however, was to increase the corporation's federal tax liability.

William Maldonado, a Zapata shareholder, believed that the board action was a breach of a fiduciary duty and that it harmed the corporation. In 1975, he instituted a derivative suit in a Delaware court on behalf of Zapata against all of the directors. He failed to make a demand on the directors to sue themselves, alleging that this would be futile since they were all defendants.

The derivative suit was still pending in 1979, when four of the defendants were no longer directors. The remaining directors then appointed two new outside directors to the board and created an Independent Investigation Committee consisting solely of the two new directors. The board authorized the committee to make a final and binding decision regarding whether the derivative suit should be brought on behalf of the corporation. Following a three-month investigation, the committee concluded that Maldonado's derivative suit should be dismissed as against Zapata's best interests.

Zapata asked the Delaware court to dismiss the derivative suit. The court refused, holding that Maldonado possessed an individual right to maintain the derivative action and that the business judgment rule did not apply. Zapata appealed to the Supreme Court of Delaware.

Quillen, Justice   We find that the trial court's determination that a shareholder, once demand is made and refused, possesses an independent, individual right to continue a derivative suit for breaches of fiduciary duty over objection by the corporation, as an absolute rule, is erroneous.

Derivative suits enforce corporate rights, and any recovery obtained goes to the corporation. We see no inherent reason why a derivative suit should automatically place in the hands of the litigating shareholder sole control of the corporate right throughout the litigation. Such an inflexible rule would recognize the interest of one person or group to the exclusion of all others within the corporate entity.

When, if at all, should an authorized board committee be permitted to cause litigation, properly initiated by a derivative stockholder in his own right, to be dismissed? The problem is relatively simple. If, on the one hand, corporations can consistently wrest bona fide derivative actions away from well-meaning derivative plaintiffs through the use of the committee mechanism, the derivative suit will lose much, if not all, of its effectiveness as an intracorporate means of policing boards of directors. If, on the other hand, corporations are unable to rid themselves of meritless or harmful litigation and strike suits, the derivative action, created to benefit the corporation, will produce the opposite, unintended result. It thus appears desirable to us to find a balancing point where bona fide shareholder power to bring corporate causes of action cannot be unfairly trampled on by the board of directors, but the corporation can rid itself of detrimental litigation.

We are not satisfied that acceptance of the business judgment rationale at this stage of derivative litigation is a proper balancing point. We must be mindful that directors are passing judgment on fellow directors in the same corporation and fellow directors, in this instance, who designated them to serve both as directors and committee members. The question naturally arises whether a "there but for the grace of God go I" empathy might not play a role. And the further question arises whether inquiry as to independence, good faith and reasonable investigation is sufficient safeguard against abuse, perhaps subconscious abuse.

We thus steer a middle course between those cases that yield to the independent business judgment of a board committee and this case as determined below, which would yield to unbridled shareholder control.

We recognize that the final substantive judgment whether a particular lawsuit should be maintained requires a balance of many factors—ethical, commercial, promotional, public relations, employee relations, fiscal, as well as legal. We recognize the danger of judicial overreaching but the alternatives seem to us to be outweighed by the fresh view of a judicial outsider.

After an objective and thorough investigation of a derivative suit, an independent committee may cause its corporation to file a motion to dismiss the derivative suit. The Court should apply a two-step test to the motion. First, the Court should inquire into the independence and good faith of the committee and the bases supporting its conclusions. The corporation should have the burden of proving independence, good faith, and reasonable investigation, rather than presuming independence, good faith, and reasonableness. If the Court determines either that the committee is not independent or has not shown reasonable bases for its conclusions, or if the Court is not satisfied for other reasons relating to the process, including but not limited to the good faith of the committee, the Court shall deny the corporation's motion to dismiss the derivative suit.

The second step provides the essential key in striking the balance between legitimate corporate claims as expressed in a derivative stockholder suit and a corporation's best interests as expressed by an independent investigating committee. The Court should determine, applying its own independent business judgment, whether the motion should be granted. The second step is intended to thwart instances where corporate actions meet the criteria of step one, but the result does not appear to satisfy its spirit, or where corporate actions would simply prematurely terminate a stockholder grievance deserving of further consideration in the corporation's interest. The Court of course must carefully consider and weigh how compelling the corporate interest in dismissal is when faced with a non-frivolous lawsuit. The Court should, when appropriate, give special consideration to matters of law and public policy in addition to the corporation's best interests.

The second step shares some of the same spirit and philosophy of the statement of the trial court: "Under our system of law, courts and not litigants should decide the merits of litigation."

Judgment reversed in favor of Zapata. Case remanded to the trial court.

Litigation Expenses   If a shareholder is successful in a derivative suit, she is entitled to a reimbursement of her reasonable litigation expenses out of the corporation's damage award. On the other hand, if the suit is unsuccessful and has been brought without reasonable cause, the shareholder must pay the defendants' expenses, including attorney's fees. The purpose of this rule is to deter strike suits by punishing shareholders who litigate in bad faith.

Defense of Corporation by Shareholder

Occasionally, the officers or managers will refuse to defend a suit brought against a corporation. If a shareholder shows that the corporation has a valid defense to the suit and that the refusal or failure of the directors to defend is a breach of their fiduciary duty to the corporation, the courts will permit the shareholder to defend for the benefit of the corporation, its shareholders, and its creditors.

Shareholder Liability

Shareholders have many responsibilities and liabilities in addition to their many rights. You have already studied shareholder liability when a shareholder pays too little consideration for shares, when a corporation is defectively formed, and when a corporation's veil is pierced. In this section, four other grounds for shareholder liability are discussed.

Shareholder Liability for Illegal Distributions

Dividends and other distributions of a corporation's assets received by a shareholder with *knowledge of their illegality* may be recovered on behalf of the corporation. Under the MBCA, primary liability is placed on the directors who, failing to comply with the business judgment rule, authorized the unlawful distribution. However, the directors are entitled to contribution from shareholders who received an asset distribution knowing that it was illegally made. These liability rules enforce the limits on asset distributions that were discussed earlier in this chapter.

Shareholder Liability for Corporate Debts

One of the chief attributes of a shareholder is his *limited liability*: Ordinarily, he has no liability for corporate obligations beyond his capital contribution. Defective attempts to incorporate and piercing the corporate veil are grounds on which a shareholder may be held liable for corporate debts beyond his capital contribution. In addition, a few states impose personal liability on shareholders for *wages owed to corporate employees*, even if the shareholders have fully paid for their shares.

Sale of a Control Block of Shares

The per share value of the shares of a majority shareholder of a corporation is greater than the per share value of the shares of a minority shareholder. This difference in value is due to the majority shareholder's ability to control the corporation and to cause it to hire her as an employee at a high salary. Therefore, a majority shareholder can sell her shares for a *premium* over the fair market value of minority shares.

Majority ownership is not always required for control of a corporation. In a close corporation it is required, but in a publicly held corporation with a widely dispersed, hard-to-mobilize shareholder group, minority ownership of from 5 to 30 percent may be enough to obtain control. Therefore, a holder of minority control in such a corporation will also be able to receive a premium.

Current corporation law imposes no liability on any shareholder, whether or not the shareholder is a controlling shareholder, *merely* because she is able to sell her shares for a premium. Nonetheless, if the premium is accompanied by wrongdoing, controlling shareholders have been held liable either for the amount of the premium or for the damages suffered by the corporation.

For example, a seller of control shares is liable for selling to a purchaser who harms the corporation if the seller had or should have had a *reasonable suspicion* that the purchaser would mismanage or loot the corporation. A seller may be placed on notice of a purchaser's bad motives by facts indicating the purchasers' history of *mismanagement and personal use of corporate assets*, by the purchaser's *lack of interest in the physical facilities* of the corporation, or the purchaser's great *interest in the liquid assets* of the corporation. These factors tend to indicate that the purchaser has a short-term interest in the corporation.

The mere payment of a premium is not enough to put the seller on notice. If the *premium is unduly high*, however, such as a $50 offer for shares traded for $10, a seller must doubt whether the purchaser will be able to recoup his investment without looting the corporation.

When a seller has, or should have, a reasonable suspicion that a purchaser will mismanage or loot the corporation, he must not sell to the purchaser unless a *reasonable investigation* shows there is no reasonable risk of wrongdoing.

A few courts find liability when a selling shareholder takes or sells a *corporate asset*. For example, if a purchaser wants to buy the corporation's assets and the controlling shareholder proposes that the purchaser buy her shares instead, the controlling shareholder is liable for usurping a corporate opportunity.

A more unusual situation existed in *Perlman v. Feldman*.[1] In that case, Newport Steel Corporation had excess demand for its steel production, due to the Korean War. Another corporation, in order to guarantee a steady supply of steel, bought at a premium a minority yet controlling block of shares of Newport from Feldman, its chairman and president. The court ruled that Feldman was required to share the premium with the other shareholders because he had sold a corporate asset—the ability to exploit an excess demand for steel. The court reasoned that Newport could have exploited that asset to its advantage.

---

[1]219 F.2d 173 (2d Cir. 1955).

Oppression of Minority Shareholders

A few courts have recognized a fiduciary duty of controlling shareholders to use their ability to control the corporation in a fair, just, and equitable manner that benefits all of the shareholders proportionately. This is in part a duty to be impartial—that is, not to prefer themselves over the minority shareholders. For example, controlling shareholders have a fiduciary duty not to cause the corporation to repurchase their own shares or to pay themselves a dividend unless the same offer is made to the minority shareholder.

One of the most common examples of oppression is the **freeze-out** of minority shareholders. It occurs in close corporations when controlling shareholders pay themselves high salaries while not employing or paying dividends to noncontrolling shareholders. Since there is usually no liquid market for the shares of the noncontrolling shareholders, they have an investment that provides them no return, while the controlling shareholders reap large gains. Such actions by the majority are especially wrongful when the controlling shareholders follow with an offer to buy the minority's shares at an unreasonably low price.

In the following case, the court held that a majority shareholder violated a duty not to freeze out minority shareholders.

SUGARMAN V. SUGARMAN
797 F.2d 3 (1st Cir. 1986)

Three brothers—Joseph, Myer, and Samuel Sugarman—owned equal amounts of the shares of Statler Tissue Corporation. Although ownership was initially balanced, a series of stock transactions resulted in Myer's son Leonard becoming the majority shareholder of the corporation. Samuel gave some of his shares to his son Hyman and to Hyman's children, James, Marjorie, and Jon Sugarman. Hyman sold his shares to Leonard. Joseph Sugarman's shares were repurchased by the corporation. By 1974, Leonard owned 61 percent of the shares and was president and chairman of the board. James, Marjorie, and Jon Sugarman owned 22 percent of the shares.

Marjorie had sought employment with the corporation but was not hired. Jon was employed from 1974 until his discharge in 1978. James never sought employment with the company. After 1975, Myer's value to the corporation was near zero because he had Alzheimer's disease; nonetheless, Myer was employed by the corporation and received a salary equal to Hyman's salary. In 1980, Leonard caused the company to double Myer's salary to $85,000 for 1980 and 1981, when Myer was 87 and 88 years of age. Hyman received no such increase. When Myer retired in 1982, Leonard caused the corporation to pay Myer a yearly pension of $75,000. When Hyman retired in 1980, he received no pension.

The corporation paid no dividends. In 1980, Leonard offered to buy Jon's and Marjorie's shares for $3.33 per share. At that time, Price Waterhouse had advised Leonard that the book value of the corporation's shares was $16.30 per share. Jon and Marjorie refused to sell their shares and instead sued Leonard, alleging he had frozen them out of the corporation by depriving them of employment, paying himself and Myer excessive salaries, and refusing to pay dividends. The district court found Leonard liable to Jon and Marjorie for $538,000. Leonard appealed.

Coffin, Circuit Judge   We first examine the legal standard that must be met to establish a freeze-out of minority shareholders. In *Donahue v. Rodd Electrotype Co.* (1975), the Massachusetts Supreme Judicial Court held that shareholders in a close corporation owe one another a fiduciary duty of "utmost good faith and loyalty." Stockholders in a close corporation "may not act out of avarice, expediency or self-interest in derogation of their duty of loyalty to the other stockholders and the corporation."

The court's decision in *Donahue* was premised on the rationale that the corporate form of a close corporation "supplies an opportunity for the majority stockholders to oppress or disadvantage minority stockholders."

Those who employ the freeze-out technique may refuse to declare dividends; they may drain off the corporation's earnings in the form of exorbitant salaries and bonuses to the majority shareholder-officers and perhaps their relatives; they may deprive minority shareholders of corporate offices and of employment by the company; they may cause the corporation to sell its assets at an inadequate price to the majority shareholders. All of these devices are designed to ensure that the minority shareholders do not receive any financial benefits from the corporation. The minority stockholders must either suffer their losses or seek a buyer for their shares. This is often the capstone of the majority plan. Because minority shareholders cannot sell their stock on the open market, as can shareholders in public corporations, the minority shareholders may be compelled to deal with the majority and be vulnerable to low offers for their stock. When the minority stockholder agrees to sell out at less than fair value, the majority has won.

It is not sufficient to allege that the majority shareholder has offered to buy the stock of a minority shareholder at an inadequate price. In a close corporation, a minority shareholder who merely receives an offer from a majority share-

holder to sell stock at an inadequate price, but does not accept that offer, can seek damages if the shareholder can prove that the offer was part of a plan to freeze the minority shareholder out of the corporation. That is, the minority shareholder must first establish that the majority shareholder employed various devices to ensure that the minority shareholder is frozen out of any financial benefits from the corporation through such means as the receipt of dividends or employment, and that the offer to buy stock at a low price is the capstone of the majority plan to freeze out the minority.

The necessary ingredients of a freeze-out of minority shareholders are present in this case. Leonard Sugarman took actions to ensure that Jon and Marjorie would not receive any financial benefits from the corporation. Leonard's overcompensation was designed to freeze out Jon and Marjorie from the company's benefits. Dividends had never been paid by the company. Marjorie had sought and been denied employment and Jon was improperly discharged from employment.

Leonard's offer to buy Jon and Marjorie's stock at an inadequate price was the capstone of a plan to freeze out Jon and Marjorie.

Judgment for Jon and Marjorie affirmed.

Liability of Shareholders of Statutory Close Corporations

Some statutes, such as the Statutory Close Corporation Supplement to the MBCA, permit close corporation shareholders to dispense with a board of directors or to arrange corporate affairs as if the corporation were a partnership. The effect of these statutes is to impose management responsibilities, including the fiduciary duties of directors, on the shareholders. In essence, the shareholders are partners and owe each other fiduciary duties similar to those owed between partners of a partnership.

Dissolution and Termination of Corporations

The MBCA provides that a corporation doing business may be dissolved by action of its directors and

shareholders. The directors must adopt a dissolution resolution, and a majority of the shares outstanding must be cast in favor of dissolution at a shareholders' meeting. For a **voluntary dissolution** to be effective, the corporation must file articles of dissolution with the secretary of state. The dissolution is effective when the articles are filed.

A corporation may be also dissolved **without its consent** by administrative action of the secretary of state or by judicial action of a court. The secretary of state may commence an administrative proceeding to dissolve a corporation that has not filed its annual report, paid its annual franchise tax, appointed or maintained a registered office or agent in the state, or whose period of duration has expired. **Administrative dissolution** requires that the secretary of state give written notice to the corporation of the grounds for dissolution. If, within 60 days, the corporation has not corrected the default or demonstrated that the default does not exist, the secretary dissolves the corporation by signing a certificate of dissolution.

The shareholders, secretary of state, or the creditors of a corporation may ask a court to order the involuntary dissolution of a corporation. Any **shareholder** may obtain judicial dissolution when there is a deadlock of the directors that is harmful to the corporation, when the shareholders are deadlocked and cannot elect directors for two years, or when the directors are acting contrary to the best interests of the corporation. The **secretary of state** may obtain judicial dissolution if it is proved that a corporation obtained its articles of incorporation by fraud or exceeded or abused its legal authority. **Creditors** may request dissolution if the corporation is insolvent.

Under the MBCA, a corporation that has not issued shares or commenced business may be dissolved by the vote of a majority of its incorporators or initial directors.

Many close corporations are nothing more than incorporated partnerships, in which all the shareholders are managers and friends or relatives. Recently, corporation law has reflected the special needs of those shareholders of close corporations who want to arrange their affairs to make the close corporation more like a partnership. The Close Corporation Supplement to the MBCA recognizes that a **close corporation shareholder** should have the same dissolution power as a partner. This section, like similar provisions in many states, permits the articles of incorporation to empower any shareholder to dissolve the corporation at will or upon the occurrence of a specified event such as the death of a shareholder.

Winding Up and Termination

A dissolved corporation continues its corporate existence but may not carry on any business except that appropriate to winding up its affairs. Therefore, winding up (liquidation) must follow dissolution. Winding up is the orderly collection and disposal of the corporation's assets and the distribution of the proceeds of the sale of assets. From these proceeds, the claims of creditors will be paid first. Next, the liquidation preferences of preferred shareholders will be paid. Then, common shareholders receive any proceeds that remain.

After winding up has been completed, the corporation's existence terminates. A person who purports to act on behalf of a terminated corporation has the liability of a person acting for a corporation prior to its incorporation. Some courts, like the court in the next case, impose similar liability on a person acting on behalf of a dissolved corporation, especially when dissolution is obtained by the secretary of state such as for the failure to file an annual report or to pay franchise taxes.

Bodine Aluminum Co., Inc. v. Mitauer

776 S.W.2d 485 (Mo. Ct. App. 1989)

East Side Metals, Inc., a Missouri corporation, failed to file an annual registration statement required by the Missouri corporation statute. Consequently, in November 1984, its corporate charter was forfeited. On East Side's last annual registration statement, Harlin, Louis, and Bernice Mitauer were listed as its officers and directors. Although East Side's charter was forfeited, the Mitauers continued to operate the business. In 1985, the business purchased scrap aluminum from Bodine Aluminum Co., Inc. When the business failed to pay $17,064 of the purchase price, Bodine sued the Mitauers to recover the remainder. The trial court held that the Mitauers individually owed Bodine $17,064. The Mitauers appealed to the Missouri Court of Appeals.

Grimm, Judge The Missouri corporation statute provides:

If any corporation: (1) Fails to comply with the provisions of this chapter with respect to its annual registration the corporate rights and privileges of the corporation shall be forfeited, and the secretary of state shall notify the corporation that its corporate existence and rights in this state have been forfeited and canceled, and the corporation dissolved; and the directors and officers in office when the forfeiture occurs shall be the trustees of the corporation, who shall have full authority to wind up its business and affairs; and the trustees shall be jointly and severally responsible to the creditors and shareholders of the corporation to the extent of its property and effects that shall have come into their hands.

This statute places a limit on the liability of officers and directors as they wind up the affairs of a corporation after its corporate rights and privileges have been forfeited. When, however, the officers

and directors continue to operate the business after forfeiture, individual liability may be imposed on them.

East Side's charter was forfeited on November 1, 1984. The Mitauers then became statutory trustees for the purpose of winding up the affairs of the corporation. When no effort was made to wind up, all post-forfeiture debts became the personal liability of the Mitauers.

Judgment affirmed for Bodine.

CONCEPT REVIEW
ROLES OF SHAREHOLDERS AND THE BOARD OF DIRECTORS

Corporate Action	Board's Role	Shareholders' Role
Day-to-Day Management	Selects officers; supervises management	Elect and remove directors
Issuance of Shares	Issues shares	Protected by preemptive right
Merger and Share Exchange	Adopts articles of merger or share exchange	Vote to approve merger or share exchange; protected by dissenters' rights
Amendment of Articles of Incorporation	Proposes amendment	Vote to approve amendment
Dissolution	Proposes dissolution	Vote to approve dissolution
Dividends	Declares dividends	Receive dividends
Board of Directors Harms Individual Shareholder Rights	Has harmed shareholders	Bring individual or class action against directors or the corporation
Directors Harm Corporation	Sues wrongdoing directors	Bring derivative action against wrongdoing directors

ETHICAL AND PUBLIC POLICY CONCERNS

1. Why should shareholders in a close corporation be permitted to make a long-term voting agreement that permits them to control the corporation? Who benefits from shareholder voting agreements? Does the corporation benefit from such an agreement? Who is harmed by such an agreement? May

such an agreement harm shareholders who are parties to the agreement? Is it possible for persons harmed by such agreements to protect themselves? Should there be a maximum legal time period for such agreements?

2. Are dissenters' rights to seek appraisal of their shares the only protection a shareholder needs when the corporation's board of directors proposes a merger harmful to the corporation? Should the shareholder be content with the fair value of his shares although he would rather stop the merger? How can shareholders use their dissenters' rights to deter the board of directors from effecting a merger harmful to the corporation?

3. Should a corporation be permitted to use a shareholder litigation committee (SLC) to decide the future of a shareholder derivative suit? Should the business judgment rule apply to the decision of a SLC, or should the *Zapata* two-step test apply? Do your answers depend on whether the shareholders are suing the directors or someone outside the corporation? How could it ever be in the best interests of a corporation not to sue directors who have personally profited by mismanaging the corporation?

4. Do you agree with the decision in the *Perlman v. Feldman* case, which is discussed in the next to last section of this chapter? Do you agree that Newport Steel lost its ability to exploit excess demand for steel merely by being acquired by another corporation? After the acquisition, Newport became a subsidiary of the acquiring corporation. Thinking back to the discussion of piercing the corporate veil (Chapter 40, History and Nature of Corporations) and the discussion of conflicts of interests (Chapter 42, Management of Corporations), what price must the parent corporation pay when it buys steel from Newport?

PROBLEMS AND PROBLEM CASES

1. Facing billions of dollars of creditors' claims, Manville Corporation sought a bankruptcy reorganization. In 1985, Manville's management and its creditors agreed to a reorganization plan, but a group of Manville shareholders objected to the plan's intent to eliminate 90 percent of the shareholders' equity in Manville. The shareholders sued to force Manville to have a shareholders' meeting at which shareholders would remove the current directors and replace them with directors who would negotiate a reorganization plan that would better preserve the shareholders' equity. Manville had not held a shareholders' meeting since 1982. Manville claimed that holding a shareholders' meeting would obstruct its reorganization. Should the court grant the shareholders' request for a meeting?

2. Edward Carey owned 109,000 of the 2,700,341 outstanding shares of Pennsylvania Enterprises, Inc. (PEI). Concerned that Carey would attempt to take over PEI, its board of directors announced a proposal to widen the distribution of PEI shares. The proposal required shareholder approval. PEI announced that a special meeting of shareholders would be held on October 12, and its board of directors set the record date as September 2, 1988. Needing 1,350,171 votes to pass, the proposal received 1,373,968 votes in favor, passing with a margin of almost 24,000 votes. However, 79,118 of the shares voted in favor of the proposal were recorded in the names of Loriot & Co. and Cede & Co. but voted by other persons. Loriot and Cede were nominees for Manufacturer's Hanover Trust, which administered PEI's Dividend Reinvestment Plan (DRIP). Under the DRIP, PEI shareholders could opt to reinvest their cash dividends with PEI, which would issue new shares to the shareholders. Instead of registering the new shares in the names of the individual shareholders, however, PEI registered new shares to Loriot or Cede. A provision of the DRIP provided that the individual shareholders (beneficial shareholders), not Loriot and Cede, were able to vote the shares. At the special shareholders' meeting, the election judges permitted the DRIP beneficial shareholders to vote the DRIP shares in favor of the proposal. Did the election judges act properly?

3. Don Sanders owned 2 percent of the shares of Houston Sports Association (HSA). A group of minority shareholders, including Sanders, tried to enter a voting agreement with 51 percent of HSA shares. The purpose of the agreement was to oust from management John McMullen, the largest shareholder (34 percent) of HSA. However, McMullen promised Sanders that McMullen would vote his shares annually to elect Sanders to the HSA board of directors if Sanders agreed to withdraw his support from the minority shareholder group and to vote his shares to retain McMullen in management. Sanders agreed. Their agreement was only oral. Subsequently, McMullen was able to acquire 63 percent ownership of HSA, and Sanders—at McMullen's request—increased his holdings to 13 percent. Two years later, Sanders was not reelected to the board despite McMullen's majority ownership of shares. Sanders sued McMullen for violating their voting agreement. Was McMullen held liable?

4. In July 1981, Amplica, Inc., made a public offering of its shares. David Steinberg bought 75 shares for $10 each. Three months later, Amplica announced that it planned to merge with another company. Under the terms of the merger, Amplica shareholders would receive $13.50 per share, which was $.50 more than the market price of Amplica shares on the day prior to the announcement of the merger. Amplica's shareholders approved the merger. Steinberg did not vote for or against the merger, but he turned in his shares and received $13.50 for each share. One month later, Steinberg discovered facts that he believed proved that Amplica's directors acted improperly in approving the merger. He also believed that the price he and other shareholders received was grossly inadequate. Is Steinberg able to enforce his dissenter's rights or to bring a derivative suit on behalf of Amplica against the directors?

5. In July 1969, Charles Pillsbury discovered that Honeywell, Inc., manufactured munitions used in the Vietnam war. Pillsbury had long opposed the Vietnam war, and he was upset to learn that bombs were produced in his own community. On July 14, Pillsbury's agent purchased 100 Honeywell shares in the name of a Pillsbury family nominee. The sole purpose of Pillsbury's purchase was to permit him to communicate with other Honeywell shareholders in the hope of persuading Honeywell's board of directors to cease producing munitions. Later in July, he learned that he was a contingent beneficiary of 242 shares of Honeywell under the terms of a trust formed for his benefit by his grandmother. On August 11, Pillsbury purchased one share of Honeywell in his own name. Pillsbury demanded to inspect Honeywell's shareholder list and all corporate records dealing with munitions manufacture. Must Honeywell make these records available to Pillsbury?

6. Historically, Liggett Group, Inc., had paid quarterly dividends to its shareholders in March, June, September, and December of each year. On May 14, 1980, the Liggett board of directors recommended that shareholders accept a tender offer by GM Sub Corporation at $69 per share. The tender offer provided that if GM Sub acquired more than 50 percent of the Liggett shares, GM Sub and Liggett would merge; the Liggett shareholders who did not tender during the tender offer would receive $69 per share under the merger. Subsequently, 87.4 percent of Liggett shareholders tendered their shares. The cash-out merger was effected on August 7. Because the Liggett board believed that it would have been unfair to the shareholders who accepted the tender offer, the board skipped the June 1980 dividend. The board believed that the shareholders who did not tender should not be rewarded for refusing to tender their shares to GM Sub knowing that they would receive the same price per share in the merger. Also, the board believed that $69 was a fair price for the shares. Gabelli & Co. surrendered its Liggett shares pursuant to the merger agreement but then sued Liggett to force payment of the June 1980 dividend. Did Gabelli succeed?

7. Fred and Maxine Brandon and their four children owned all the shares of Brandon Construction Co., a family corporation. Fred and Maxine owned a majority of the shares. In 1987, the shareholders agreed that Fred and Maxine each would receive a monthly salary of $12,500. Two months later, daughter Betty Brandon alleged that the salaries were excessive, and that Fred and Maxine were dismantling the corporation and distributing its assets to themselves, without regard for the children's rights as minority shareholders. She initiated a derivative action against her parents, but her siblings responded that Betty did not represent their interests as minority shareholders and that they were content with the salaries paid to their parents. Is Betty a proper person to bring a derivative suit?

8. Robert Orchard and Albert Covelli owned a majority of the shares of six corporations and all the shares of one corporation that operated McDonald's restaurant franchises. Covelli purchased the shares of the minority shareholders of the six corporations, making him the owner of 73 percent of the shares of the corporations and Orchard owner of 27 percent. Covelli owned 85 percent and Orchard 15 percent of the seventh corporation. Since Orchard and Covelli were by then dissatisfied with their relationship, Orchard asked Covelli to repurchase his shares at the same price Covelli paid for the minority shareholders' shares. Covelli agreed to pay Orchard for his shares of the six corporations, but wanted Orchard to give him the shares of the seventh corporation for no consideration. When Orchard refused to do so, Covelli made known his intent to force Orchard into bankruptcy and to remove him from any responsible positions in the corporations. Covelli terminated Orchard's employment with the corporations, removed him as a director, and replaced him with Covelli's son. Orchard remained a minority shareholder of the seven corporations, but the corporations paid no dividends. Does Orchard have any grounds upon which to sue Covelli?

9. H. F. Ahmanson & Co. was the controlling shareholder of United Savings and Loan Association. There was very little trading in the Association's shares, however. To create a public market for their shares, Ahmanson and a few other shareholders of the Association incorporated United Financial Corporation and exchanged each of their Association shares for United shares. United then owned more than 85 percent of the shares of the Association. The minority shareholders of the Association were not given an opportunity to exchange their shares. United made two public offerings of its shares. As a result, trading in United shares was very active, while sales of Association shares decreased to half of the formerly low level, with United as virtually the only purchaser. United offered to purchase Association shares from the minority shareholders for $1,100 per share. Some of the minority shareholders accepted this offer. At that time, the shares held by the majority shareholders were worth $3,700. United also caused the Association to decrease its dividend payments. Has Ahmanson done anything wrong?

10. Albert Martin and Raymond Martin were brothers, each owning 50 percent of Martin's News Service, Inc., a retail store selling newspapers, lottery tickets, and cigarettes. Beginning in 1973, they had difficulty working together, eventually communicating only through their accountant. Directors' and shareholders' meetings ceased. In 1983, Albert fell ill and was unable to work in the store. In December 1983, Albert sued for a judicial dissolution of the corporation. Will the court order dissolution?

SECURITIES

REGULATION

INTRODUCTION

Modern securities regulation arose from the rubble of the great stock market crash of October 1929. After the crash, Congress studied its causes and discovered several common problems in securities transactions, the most important ones being:

1. Investors lacked the necessary information to make intelligent decisions whether to buy, sell, or hold securities.
2. Disreputable sellers of securities made outlandish claims about the expected performance of securities and sold securities in nonexistent companies.

Faced with these perceived problems, Congress chose to require securities sellers to disclose the information that investors need to make intelligent investment decisions. Congress found that investors are able to make intelligent investment decisions if they are given sufficient information about the company whose securities they are to buy. This **disclosure scheme** *assumes that investors need assistance from government in acquiring information but that they need no help in evaluating information.*

PURPOSES OF SECURITIES REGULATION

To implement its disclosure scheme, in the early 1930s Congress passed two major statutes, which are the hub of federal securities regulation in the United States today. These two statutes, the **Securities Act of 1933** and the **Securities Exchange Act of 1934**, have three basic purposes:

1. To require the disclosure of meaningful information about a security and its issuer to allow investors to make intelligent investment decisions.
2. To impose liability on those persons who make inadequate and erroneous disclosures of information.
3. To require the registration of issuers, insiders, professional sellers of securities, securities exchanges, and other self-regulatory securities organizations.

The crux of the securities acts is to impose on issuers of securities, other sellers of securities, and selected buyers of securities the affirmative duty to disclose important information, even if they are not asked by investors to make the disclosures. By requiring disclosure, Congress hoped to restore investor confidence in the securities markets. Congress wanted to bolster investor confidence in the honesty of the stock market and thus encourage more investors to invest in securities. Building investor confidence would increase capital formation and, it was hoped, help the American economy emerge from the Great Depression of the 1930s.

SECURITIES AND EXCHANGE COMMISSION

The Securities and Exchange Commission (SEC) was created by the 1934 Act. Its responsibility is to administer the 1933 Act, 1934 Act, and other securities statutes. Like other federal administrative agencies, the SEC has legislative, executive, and judicial functions. Its legislative branch promulgates rules and regulations; its executive branch brings enforcement actions against alleged violators of the securities statutes and their rules and regulations; its judicial branch decides whether a person has violated the securities laws.

SEC Actions

The SEC is empowered to investigate violations of the 1933 Act and 1934 Act and to hold hearings to determine whether the acts have been violated. Such hearings are held before an administrative law judge (ALJ), who is an employee of the SEC. The administrative law judge is a finder of both fact and law. Decisions of the ALJ are reviewed by the commissioners of the SEC. Decisions of the commissioners are appealed to the U.S. courts of appeals. Most SEC actions are not litigated. Instead, the SEC issues consent orders, by which the defendant promises not to violate the securities laws in the future but does not admit to having violated them in the past.

The SEC has the power to impose civil penalties (fines) up to $500,000 and to issue **cease and desist orders**. A cease and desist order directs a defendant to stop violating the securities laws and to desist from future violations. Nonetheless, the SEC does not have the power to issue injunctions; only courts may issue injunctions. The 1933 Act and the 1934 Act empower the SEC only to ask federal district courts for injunctions against persons who have violated or are about to violate either act. The SEC

may also ask the courts to grant ancillary relief, a remedy in addition to an injunction. Ancillary relief may include, for example, the disgorgement of profits that a defendant has made in a fraudulent sale or in an illegal insider trading transaction.

WHAT IS A SECURITY?

The first issue in securities regulation is the definition of a security. If a transaction involves no security, then the law of securities regulation does not apply. The 1933 Act defines the term **security** broadly:

Unless the context otherwise requires the term "security" means any note, stock, bond, debenture, evidence of indebtedness, certificate of interest of participation in any profit-sharing agreement, . . . preorganization certificate or subscription, . . . investment contract, voting trust certificate, . . . fractional undivided interest in oil, gas, or mineral rights, . . . or, in general, any interest or instrument commonly known as a "security."

The 1934 Act definition of security is similar, but excludes notes and drafts that mature not more than nine months from the date of issuance.

While typical securities like common shares, preferred shares, bonds, and debentures are defined as securities, the definition of a security also includes many contracts that the general public may believe are not securities. This is because the term **investment contract** is broadly defined by the courts. The Supreme Court's three-part test for an investment contract, called the *Howey* test, has been the guiding beacon in the area for the past 45 years.[1] The *Howey* test states that an investment contract is an investment of money in a common enterprise with an expectation of profits solely from the efforts of others.

In the *Howey* case, the sales of plots in an orange grove along with a management contract were held to be sales of securities. The purchasers had investment motives (they intended to make a profit from, not to consume the oranges produced by the trees). There was a common enterprise, because the investors were similarly affected by the efforts of the sellers who grew and sold the oranges for all investors. The sellers, not the buyers, did all of the work needed to make the plots profitable.

---

[1] *SEC v. W. J. Howey Co.,* 328 U.S. 293 (U.S. Sup. Ct. 1946).

In other cases, sales of limited partnership interests, Scotch whisky receipts, and restaurant franchises have been held to constitute investment contracts and, therefore, securities. In the following case, the court applied the *Howey* test to cattle-feeding consulting agreements.

LONG v. SHULTZ CATTLE CO., INC.
881 F.2d 129 (5th Cir. 1989)

Jim Long, Jerome Atchley, and Jon and Linda Coleman invested in a cattle-feeding program offered by Shultz Cattle Company, Inc. (SCCI). They participated in SCCI's individual feeding program, under which investors would purchase and raise their own cattle. Each investor was required to sign a consulting agreement by which SCCI agreed to provide advice regarding the purchase, feeding, and sale of the investor's cattle. SCCI received only a flat-rate consulting fee of $20 per head of cattle for these services and received no share of the investors' profits.

To receive tax benefits from the investment, the tax laws required investors to participate actively in farming. Therefore, SCCI required each investor to represent that "he will exert substantial and significant control over, and will, exercising independent judgment, make all principal and significant management decisions concerning his cattle feeding operations."

Investors could limit any real risk of loss of investment by hedging their cattle: By buying or selling commodities futures they could lock in a price and minimize their potential losses. SCCI arranged for hedging transactions to be conducted through financial institutions, feedyards, and a brokerage firm of which SCCI was a branch office.

Long's, Atchley's, and the Colemans' cattle were fed, along with those of many other SCCI clients, in a feedyard in which the cattle were commingled. The cattle were tagged by pen number and not by individual investor. Each investor therefore owned a percentage of the total pounds of cattle in the pen. If any cattle died, the loss was not attributed to a single investor but was distributed pro rata among the investors.

During the first year, Long, Atchley, and the Colemans hedged all their cattle and lost half of the money they had invested. In the second year, they decided to hedge only half of their 1,450 head of cattle. When beef prices declined drastically, they lost over $100,000. They sued SCCI for selling unregistered securities. The jury found that the consulting agreements were not investment contracts or otherwise securities. Long, Atchley, and the Colemans appealed.

King, Circuit Judge   In *S.E.C. v. W. J. Howey Co.* (1946), the Supreme Court held that to determine whether a scheme is an investment contract, the test is whether the scheme involves (1) an investment of money (2) in a common enterprise (3) with profits to come solely from the efforts of others. The parties do not dispute that the first prong of the *Howey* test is satisfied in this case. Only the latter two elements are contested. Because the controversy centers primarily on the third prong, we will discuss that issue first.

To ensure that the securities laws are not easily circumvented by agreements requiring a "modicum of effort" by investors, the word "solely" in the third prong of the *Howey* test has not been construed literally. The critical inquiry is instead whether the efforts made by those other than the investor are the undeniably significant ones, those essential managerial efforts which affect the failure or success of the enterprise. Even where an investor formally possesses substantial powers, the third prong of the *Howey* test may be met if the investor demonstrates that he is so inexperienced and unknowledgeable in the field of business at issue that he is incapable of intelligently exercising the rights he formally possesses.

Long, Atchley, and the Colemans had a substantial degree of theoretical control over their investments.

They could, theoretically, move their cattle to a different feedyard, decide what to feed them, provide their own veterinary care, or seek buyers on their own. Moreover, the investors were *required* to authorize every management decision involving their cattle. However, at each juncture, the investors relied solely on the advice of SCCI: they followed SCCI's recommendations regarding the purchase of cattle, the choice of a feedyard, the choice of financial institution to provide financing, the choice of commodities brokers, the decision when to sell, and the decision to whom to sell.

Long, Atchley, and the Colemans, who lived in places far removed from their cattle, lacked the experience necessary to care for, feed, and market their cattle. They acquired *from* SCCI all of the knowledge necessary to "actively manage" their "individual" cattle-feeding businesses. We do not believe that the securities laws may be avoided so easily.

SCCI hopes to avoid the securities laws by simply attaching the label "consulting agreement" to a package of services which otherwise would clearly be an investment contract. The label "consulting agreement" cannot bear the meaning SCCI has given it.

Although Long, Atchley, and the Colemans' decision to hedge only half of their cattle was "undeniably significant" in terms of the risks to which the investors were exposed, it does not alter the essential character of the SCCI scheme. An investor may authorize the assumption of particular risks that would create the possibility of greater profits or losses but still depend on a third party for all of the essential managerial efforts without which the risk could not pay off. The fact that Long, Atchley, and the Colemans chose the riskier course cannot, by itself, transform the essential nature of the underlying contract any more than the fact that an individual investor chooses to buy high-risk junk bonds rather than low-risk AAA bonds causes one bond and not the other to be a security.

We conclude that the third prong of the *Howey* test was established as a matter of law. The jury's verdict would nevertheless stand if the evidence could support the conclusion that the second prong of the *Howey* test—the existence of a common enterprise—was not met. The Third, Sixth, and Seventh Circuits hold that a showing of "horizontal commonality"—a pooling of investors—is necessary to meet the common enterprise requirement. Under this standard, investors' fortunes must be tied to one another in order to constitute a common enterprise.

This court, together with the Ninth and Eleventh Circuits, has explicitly rejected the view that horizontal commonality is a prerequisite to establishing a common enterprise and has focused instead on the "vertical commonality" between the investors and the promoter. The critical factor is not the similitude or coincidence of investor input, but rather the uniformity of impact of the promoter's decisions.

While our standard requires interdependence between the investors and the promoter, it does not define that interdependence narrowly in terms of shared profits and losses. Rather, the necessary interdependence may be demonstrated by the investors' collective reliance on the promoter's expertise even where the promoter receives only a flat fee or commission rather than a share in the profits of the venture.

We recognize that under our standard the second and third prongs of the *Howey* test may in some cases overlap and that our standard has been criticized for that reason. We are not convinced that it would be desirable to adopt a rigid requirement that profits and losses be shared on a *pro rata* basis among investors, or that the promoter's fortunes correlate directly to the profits and losses of investors.

Here, all of SCCI's clients were dependent on SCCI's expertise to manage their investments. Moreover, SCCI's fortunes clearly were interwoven with those of their clients. SCCI received substantial "consulting fees" from its clients in exchange for its services in constructing and administering effective tax shelters through the cattle-feeding business. Through the inexorable force of the market, SCCI's success would correspond to that of its clients.

Judgment reversed in favor of Long, Atchley, and the Colemans.

Courts have used the *Howey* test to hold that some contracts with typical security names are not securities. Using an **economic realities test**, the courts point out that some of these contracts possess few of the typical characteristics of a security. For example, in *United Housing Foundation, Inc. v. Forman,*[2] the Supreme Court held that although tenants in a cooperative apartment building purchased contracts labeled as stock, the contracts were not securities. The "stock" possessed few of the typical characteristics of stock and the economic realities of the transaction bore few similarities to those of the typical stock sale: The stock gave tenants no dividend rights or voting rights in proportion to the number of shares owned, it was not negotiable, and it could not appreciate in value. More important, tenants bought the stock not for the purpose of investment but to acquire suitable living space.

However, when investors are misled to believe that the securities laws apply because a seller sold a contract bearing both the name of a typical security and significant characteristics of that security, the securities laws do apply to the sale of the security.

In 1990, the Supreme Court further extended this rationale in *Reves v. Ernst & Young,*[3] adopting the **family resemblance test** to determine whether promissory notes were securities. The Supreme Court held that it is inappropriate to apply the *Howey* test to notes. Instead, applying the family resemblance test, the Court held that notes are presumed to be securities unless they bear a "strong family resemblance" to a type of note that is not a security. Types of notes that are not securities include consumer notes, mortgage notes, short-term notes secured by a lien on a small business, short-term notes secured by accounts receivable, and notes evidencing loans by commercial banks for current operations.

SECURITIES ACT OF 1933

The Securities Act of 1933 (1933 Act) is concerned primarily with public distributions of securities. That is, the 1933 Act regulates the sale of securities while they are passing from the hands of the issuer into the hands of public investors. An issuer selling securities publicly must make necessary disclosures at the time the issuer sells the securities to the public.

The 1933 Act has two principal regulatory components: (1) registration provisions and (2) liability provisions. The registration requirements of the 1933 Act are designed to give investors the information they need to make intelligent decisions whether to purchase securities when an issuer sells its securities to the public. The various liability provisions in the 1933 Act impose liability on sellers of securities for misstating or omitting facts of material significance to investors.

REGISTRATION OF SECURITIES UNDER THE 1933 ACT

The 1933 Act requires that *every* offering of securities be registered with the SEC prior to any offer or sale of the securities, unless the offering or the securities are exempt from registration. That is, an issuer and its underwriters may not offer or sell securities unless the securities are registered with the SEC or exempt from registration. Over the next few pages, we will cover the registration process. Then the exemptions from registration will be addressed.

Mechanics of a Registered Offering

When an issuer makes a decision to raise money by a public offering of securities, the issuer needs to obtain the assistance of securities market professionals. The issuer will contact a managing underwriter, the primary person assisting the issuer in selling the securities. The managing underwriter will review the issuer's operations and financial statements and reach an agreement with the issuer regarding the type of securities to sell, the offering price, and the compensation to be paid to the underwriters. The issuer and the managing underwriter will determine what type of underwriting to use.

In a **stand-by underwriting,** the underwriters obtain subscriptions from prospective investors, but the issuer sells the securities only if there is

---

[2]*United Housing Foundation, Inc. v. Forman,* 421 U.S. 837 (U.S. Sup. Ct. 1975).

[3]494 U.S. 56 (U.S. Sup. Ct. 1990).

sufficient investor interest in the securities. The underwriters receive warrants—options to purchase the issuer's securities at a bargain price—as compensation for their efforts. The stand-by underwriting is typically used only to sell common shares to existing shareholders pursuant to a preemptive rights offering.

With a **best efforts underwriting,** the underwriters are merely agents making their best efforts to sell the issuer's securities. The underwriters receive a commission for their selling efforts. The best efforts underwriting is used when an issuer is not well established and the underwriter is unwilling to risk being unable to sell the securities.

The classic underwriting arrangement is a **firm commitment underwriting.** Here the managing underwriter forms an underwriting group and a selling group. The underwriting group agrees to purchase the securities from the issuer at a discount from the public offering price, for example 25 cents per share below the offering price. The selling group agrees to buy the securities from the underwriters also at a discount, for example 12½ cents per share below the offering price. Consequently, the underwriters and selling group bear much of the risk with a firm commitment underwriting, but they also stand to make the most profit under such an arrangement.

Registration Statement and Prospectus

The 1933 Act requires the issuer of securities to register the securities with the SEC before the issuer or underwriters may offer or sell the securities. Registration requires filing a **registration statement** with the SEC. Historical and current data about the issuer and its business, full details about the securities to be offered, and the use of the proceeds of the issuance, among other information, must be included in the registration statement prepared by the issuer of the securities with the assistance of the managing underwriter, securities lawyers, and independent accountants. Generally, the registration statement must include audited balance sheets as of the end of each of the two most recent fiscal years, in addition to audited income statements and audited statements of changes in financial position for each of the last three fiscal years.

The registration statement becomes effective after it has been reviewed by the SEC. The 1933 Act provides that the registration statement becomes effective automatically on the 20th day after its filing, unless the SEC delays or advances the effective date.

The **prospectus** is the basic selling document of an offering registered under the 1933 Act. Most of the information in the registration statement must be included in the prospectus. It must be furnished to every purchaser of the registered security prior to or concurrently with the sale of the security to the purchaser. The prospectus enables an investor to base his investment decision on all of the relevant data concerning the issuer, not merely on the favorable information that the issuer may be inclined to disclose voluntarily.

Section 5: Timing, Manner, and Content of Offers and Sales

The 1933 Act restricts the issuer's and underwriter's ability to communicate with prospective purchasers of the securities. Section 5 of the 1933 Act states the basic rules regarding the timing, manner, and content of offers and sales. It creates three important periods of time in the life of a securities offering: (1) the pre-filing period, (2) the waiting period, and (3) the post-effective period.

The Pre-Filing Period   Prior to the filing of the registration statement (the pre-filing period), the issuer and any other person may **not offer or sell** the securities to be registered. A prospective issuer, its directors and officers, and its underwriters must avoid publicity about the issuer and the prospective issuance of securities during the prefiling period. Press releases, advertisements, speeches, and press conferences may be deemed offers if their intent or effect is to condition the market to receive the securities.

SEC Rule 135 permits the issuer to publish a notice about a prospective offering during the pre-filing period. The notice may contain only the name of the issuer and a basic description of the securities and the offering. It may not name the underwriters or state the price at which the securities will be offered.

The Waiting Period   The waiting period is the time between the filing date and the effective date of the registration statement, when the issuer is waiting for the SEC to declare the registration statement effective. During the waiting period, Section 5 permits the securities to be **offered but not sold.** However, not all kinds of offers are permitted. Face-to-face oral offers (including personal phone calls) are allowed during the waiting period. However, written offers may be made only by a statutory prospectus, usually a **preliminary prospectus** that often omits the price of the securities. (A final prospectus will be available after the registration statement becomes effective. It will contain the price of the securities.)

General publicity during the waiting period may be construed as an illegal offer because it conditions the market to receive the securities. One type of general advertisement, called the **tombstone ad**, is permitted during the waiting period and thereafter. The tombstone ad, which appears in financial pub-

---

CONCEPT REVIEW

COMMUNICATIONS WITH INVESTORS BY OR ON BEHALF OF ISSUER PERMITTED BY SECTION 5 DURING A 1933 ACT REGISTRATION

Type of Communication	Pre-Filing Period	Filing Date of Registration Statement — Waiting Period	Effective Date of Registration Statement — Post-Effective Period
Annual Reports, Press Releases, and Quarterly Reports	Permitted; unless designed to assist the placement of securities or arouse interest in a prospective sale of securities	Permitted; unless designed to assist the placement of securities or arouse interest in a prospective sale of securities	Permitted; without restriction if used contemporaneously with or after delivery of final prospectus
Notice of Proposed Offering (Rule 135)	Permitted	Permitted	Permitted
Tombstone Ad (Rule 134)	Not permitted	Permitted	Permitted
Offer by Preliminary Prospectus	Not permitted	Permitted	Not permitted
Offer by Final Prospectus	Not permitted	Not permitted	Permitted
Oral Face-to-Face Offers (including telephone calls)	Not permitted	Permitted	Permitted
Oral Offers at Sales Meeting	Not permitted	Permitted; if each investor has an opportunity to ask unlimited questions	Permitted; if each investor has an opportunity to ask unlimited questions, or if each investor has received a final prospectus
Written Offers Other than a Prospectus	Not permitted	Not permitted	Permitted; contemporaneously with or after delivery of final prospectus
Sales	Not permitted	Not permitted	Permitted; contemporaneously with or after delivery of final prospectus

lications, is permitted by SEC Rule 134, which allows disclosure of the same information as is allowed by Rule 135 plus the general business of the issuer, the price of the securities, and the names of the underwriters who are helping the issuer to sell the securities. In addition, Rule 134 requires the tombstone ad to state that it is not an offer.

The waiting period is an important part of the regulatory scheme of the 1933 Act. It provides an investor with adequate time (at least 20 days) to judge the wisdom of buying the security during a period when he cannot be pressured to buy it. Not even a contract to buy the security may be made during the waiting period.

The Post-Effective Period   After the effective date (the date on which the SEC declares the registration effective), Section 5 permits the security to be **offered and also to be sold,** provided that the buyer has received a **final prospectus** (a preliminary prospectus is not acceptable for this purpose). Written offers not previously allowed are permitted during the post-effective period, but only if the offeree has received a final prospectus.

Liability for Violating Section 5   Section 12(1) of the 1933 Act imposes liability on any person who violates the provisions of Section 5. Liability extends to any *purchaser* to whom an illegal offer or sale was made. The purchaser's remedy is *rescission* or damages.

EXEMPTIONS FROM THE REGISTRATION REQUIREMENTS OF THE 1933 ACT

Complying with the registration requirements of the 1933 Act, including the restrictions of Section 5, is a burdensome, time-consuming, and expensive process. Planning and executing an issuer's first public offering may consume six months and cost in excess of $1 million. Consequently, some issuers prefer to avoid registration when they sell securities. There are two types of exemptions from the registration requirements of the 1933 Act: securities exemptions and transaction exemptions.

Securities Exemptions

Exempt securities never need to be registered, regardless who sells the securities, how they are sold,

or to whom they are sold. The following are the most important securities exemptions.[4]

1. Securities issued or guaranteed by any government in the United States and its territories.

2. A note or draft that has a maturity date not more than nine months after its date of issuance.

3. A security issued by a nonprofit religious, charitable, educational, benevolent, or fraternal organization.

4. Securities issued by banks and by savings and loan associations.

5. Securities issued by railroads and trucking companies regulated by the Interstate Commerce Commission.

6. An insurance policy or an annuity contract.

Although the types of securities listed above are exempt from the registration provisions of the 1933 Act, they are not exempt from the liability provisions of the act. For example, any fraud committed in the course of selling such securities can be attacked by the SEC and by the persons who were defrauded.

Transaction Exemptions

The most important 1933 Act registration exemptions are the transaction exemptions. If a security is sold pursuant to a transaction exemption, that sale is exempt from registration. Subsequent sales, however, are not automatically exempt. Future sales must be made pursuant to a registration or another exemption.

The transaction exemptions are exemptions from the registration provisions only. The antifraud provisions of the 1933 Act apply equally to exempted and nonexempted transactions.

---

[4]Excluded from the list of securities exemptions are the intrastate offering and small offering exemptions. Although the 1933 Act denotes them (except for the section 4(6) exemption) as securities exemptions, they are in practice transaction exemptions. An exempt security is exempt from registration forever. But when securities originally sold pursuant to an intrastate or small offering exemption are resold at a later date, the subsequent sales may have to be registered. The exemption of the earlier offering does not exempt a future offering. The SEC treats these two exemptions as transaction exemptions. Consequently, this chapter also treats them as transaction exemptions.

The most important transaction exemptions are those available to issuers of securities. These exemptions are the intrastate offering exemption, the private offering exemption, and the small offering exemptions.

Intrastate Offering Exemption

Under section 3(a)(11), an offering of securities solely to investors in one state by an issuer resident and doing business in that state is exempt from the 1933 Act's registration requirements. The reason for the exemption is that there is little federal government interest in an offering that occurs in only one state. Although the offering may be exempt from SEC regulation, state securities law may require a registration. The expectation is that state securities regulation will adequately protect investors.

The SEC has defined the intrastate offering exemption more precisely in Rule 147. An issuer must have at least 80 percent of its gross revenues and 80 percent of its assets in the state and use at least 80 percent of the proceeds of the offering in the state. Resale of the securities is limited to persons within the state for nine months.

Rule 147, however, is not an exclusive rule. In the following case, the court applied only the statutory standard of section 3(a)(11).

BUSCH V. CARPENTER
827 F.2d 653 (10th Cir. 1987)

Sonic Petroleum, Inc., was incorporated in Utah for the purpose of acquiring, extracting, and marketing natural resources such as oil, gas, and coal. Its corporate office, books, and records were in Utah. During October and November 1980, Sonic publicly offered and sold 25 million shares entirely to residents of Utah. The proceeds were $500,000. Sonic did not file a Securities Act registration statement with the SEC, instead relying on the exemption from registration for intrastate offerings. At the time of the offering, Sonic had not undertaken any business activities in Utah or anywhere else.

Craig Carpenter, Sonic's president, negotiated Sonic's acquisition of an Illinois drilling corporation owned by William Mason. On May 25, 1981, Sonic issued a controlling block of its shares to Mason in exchange for Mason's corporation. Shortly thereafter, Sonic deposited in Illinois $350,000 of the proceeds from the sale of shares to Utah residents. At about the same time, Mason and Carpenter helped create a public market for Sonic shares. As a result, Paul and Linda Busch, who were California residents, purchased Sonic shares from Utah residents who had purchased shares in October and November 1980. When the shares' value dropped, the Busches sued Carpenter for selling unregistered securities. The trial court held that Sonic sold the shares pursuant to the intrastate offering exemption and, therefore, did not need to register the shares. The Busches appealed.

Seymour, Circuit Judge Section 5 of the Securities Act of 1933 prohibits the offer or sale of any security unless a proper registration statement has first been filed with the SEC. However, Congress also recognized that the protections of the 1933 Act were not essential for those securities that could be supervised effectively by the states. Section 3(a)(11) therefore exempts from the Act's registration requirements

Any security which is part of an issue offered and sold only to persons resident within a single State or Territory, where the issuer of such security is a person resident and doing business within or, if a corporation, incorporated by and doing business within, such State or Territory.

In order to fall within the intrastate exemption, initial sales to state residents must be bona fide. The intrastate exemption becomes unavailable whenever sales or purchases by a subsequent purchaser circumvent the federal securities laws. The SEC has consistently maintained that a distribution of securities must have actually come to rest in the hands of the resident investors—persons purchasing for investment intent and not for purpose of resale.

The Busches contend that Sonic had the burden to prove that the original buyers bought with investment intent. We reject this argument. The intrastate offering exemption requires that the issue be "offered and sold only to persons resident within a single state." In face of Sonic's undisputed showing that all of the original buyers were Utah residents, the Busches were therefore required to produce evidence that the stock had not come to rest but had been sold to people who intended to resell it out of state. The interstate purchases of freely trading shares several months after the completion of the intrastate offering do not, without more, impugn the investment intent of the original buyers.

The Busches alternatively contend that Sonic was not entitled to the intrastate exemption because the corporate issuer was not doing business in Utah as required by section 3(a)(11). An issuer cannot claim the exemption simply by opening an office in a particular state. Conducting substantially all income-producing operations elsewhere defeats the exemption, as do the plans of recently organized companies to invest the net proceeds of initial public offerings only in other states.

Here Sonic never did more than maintain its office, books, and records in Utah. Sonic transferred essentially all of its assets to Illinois and made no prior efforts whatever at locating investment opportunities within Utah. Sonic may have been intending all along to invest its assets outside the state. A newly formed company may not claim the exemption while planning covertly to invest the proceeds of a local offering in other states.

Judgment reversed in favor of the Busches; remanded for trial.

Private Offering Exemption

Section 4(2) of the 1933 Act provides that the registration requirements of the 1933 Act "shall not apply to transactions by an issuer not involving any public offering." A private offering is an offering to a small number of purchasers who can protect themselves because they are wealthy or because they are sophisticated in investment matters and have access to the information that they need to make intelligent investment decisions.

To create greater certainty about what a private offering is, the SEC adopted Rule 506. Although an issuer may exempt a private offering under either the courts' interpretation of section 4(2) or Rule 506, the SEC tends to treat Rule 506 as the exclusive way to obtain the exemption.

Rule 506 Under Rule 506, which is part of Securities Act Regulation D, the issuer must reasonably believe that each purchaser is either (a) an accredited investor or (b) an unaccredited investor who "has such knowledge and experience in financial and business matters that he is capable of evaluating the merits and risks of the prospective investment." Accredited investors include institutional investors (such as banks and mutual funds), wealthy investors, and high-level insiders of the issuer (such as executive officers, directors, and partners).

An issuer may sell to no more than 35 unaccredited purchasers who have sufficient investment knowledge and experience; it may sell to an unlimited number of accredited purchasers, regardless of their investment sophistication.

Each purchaser must be given or have access to the information she needs to make an informed investment decision. For a public company making a nonpublic offering under Rule 506, purchasers must receive information in a form required by the 1934 Act, such as a 10-K or annual report. The issuer must provide the following audited financial statements: two years' balance sheets, three years' income statements, and three years' statements of changes in financial position.

For a nonpublic company making a nonpublic offering under Rule 506, the issuer must provide much of the same nonfinancial information required in a registered offering. A nonpublic company may, however, obtain some relief from the burden of providing audited financial statements to investors. When the amount of the issuance is $2 million or less, only one year's balance sheet need be audited. If the amount issued exceeds $2 million but not $7.5

million, only one year's balance sheet, one year's income statement, and one year's statement of changes in financial position need be audited. When the amount issued exceeds $7.5 million, the issuer must provide two years' balance sheets, three years' income statements, and three years' statements of changes in financial position. In any offering of any amount by a nonpublic issuer, when auditing would involve unreasonable effort or expense, only an audited balance sheet is needed. When a limited partnership issuer finds that auditing involves unreasonable effort or expense, the limited partnership may use financial statements prepared by an independent accountant in conformance with the requirements of federal tax law.

Rule 506 prohibits the issuer from making any general public selling effort. This prevents the issuer from using the radio, newspapers, and television. However, offers to an individual one-on-one are permitted.

In addition, the issuer must take reasonable steps to ensure that the purchasers do not resell the securities in a manner that makes the issuance a public distribution rather than a private one. Usually, the investor must hold the security for a minimum of two years.

In the following case, the issuer failed to prove it was entitled to a private offering exemption under Rule 506.

Mark v. FSC Securities Corp.
870 F.2d 331 (6th Cir. 1989)

FSC Securities Corp., a securities brokerage, sold limited partnership interests in Malaga Arabian Limited Partnership to Mr. and Mrs. Mark. A total of 28 investors purchased limited partnership interests in Malaga. All investors were asked to execute subscription documents, including a suitability letter in which the purchaser stated his income level, that he had an opportunity to obtain relevant information, and that he had sufficient knowledge and experience in business affairs to evaluate the risks of the investment.

When the value of the limited partnership interests fell, the Marks sued FSC to rescind their purchase on the grounds that FSC sold unregistered securities in violation of the Securities Act of 1933. The jury held that the offering was exempt as an offering not involving a public offering. The Marks appealed.

Simpson, Judge   Section 4(2) of the Securities Act exempts from registration with the SEC "transactions by an issuer not involving any public offering." There are no hard and fast rules for determining whether a securities offering is exempt from registration under the general language of section 4(2).

However, the "safe harbor" provision of Regulation D, Rule 506, deems certain transactions to be not involving any public offering within the meaning of section 4(2). FSC had to prove that certain objective tests were met. These conditions include the general conditions not in dispute here, and the following specific conditions:

(i) Limitation on number of purchasers. The issuer shall reasonably believe that there are no more than thirty-five purchasers of securities in any offering under this Section.

(ii) Nature of purchasers. The issuer shall reasonably believe immediately prior to making any sale that each purchaser who is not an accredited investor either alone or with his purchaser representative(s) has such knowledge and experience in financial and business matters that he is capable of evaluating the merits and risks of the prospective investment.

In this case, we take the issuer to be the general partners of Malaga. FSC is required to offer evidence of the issuer's reasonable belief as to the nature of each purchaser. The only testimony at trial competent to establish the issuer's belief as to the nature of the purchasers was that of Laurence Leafer, a general partner in Malaga. By his own admission, he had no knowledge about any purchaser, much less any belief, reasonable or not, as to the purchasers' knowledge and experience in financial and business matters.

Q: What was done to determine if investors were, in fact, reasonably sophisticated?

A: Well, there were two things. Number one, we had investor suitability standards that had to be met. You had to have a certain income, be in a certain tax bracket, this kind of thing. Then in the subscription documents themselves, they, when they sign it, supposedly represented that they had received information necessary to make an informed investment decision, and that they were sophisticated. And if they were not, they relied on an offering representative who was.

Q: Did you review the subscription documents that came in for the Malaga offering?

A: No.

Q: So do you know whether all of the investors in the Malaga offering met the suitability and sophistication requirements?

A: I don't.

FSC also offered as evidence the Marks' executed subscription documents, as well as a set of documents in blank, to establish the procedure it followed in the Malaga sales offering. Although the Marks' executed documents may have been sufficient to establish the reasonableness of any belief the issuer may have had as to the Marks' particular qualifications, that does not satisfy Rule 506. The documents offered no evidence from which a jury could conclude the issuer reasonably believed each purchaser was suitable. Instead, all that was proved was the sale of 28 limited partnership interests, and the circumstances under which those sales were intended to have been made. The blank subscriptions documents simply do not amount to probative evidence, when it is the answers and information received from purchasers that determine whether the conditions of Rule 506 have been met.

Having concluded that the Malaga limited-partnership offering did not meet the registration exemption requirement of Rule 506 of Regulation D, we conclude that the Marks are entitled to the remedy of rescission.

Judgment reversed in favor of the Marks; remanded to the trial court.

Small Offering Exemptions

Sections 3(b) and 4(6) of the 1933 Act permit the SEC to exempt from registration any offering by an issuer not exceeding $5 million. Several SEC rules and regulations permit an issuer to sell small amounts of securities and avoid registration. The rationale for these exemptions is that the dollar amount of the securities offered or the number of purchasers is too small for the federal government to be concerned with registration. State securities law may require registration, however.

Rule 504   SEC Rule 504 of Regulation D allows the issuer to sell up to $1 million of securities in a 12-month period and avoid registration. Rule 504 sets no limits on the number of offerees or purchasers. The purchasers need not be sophisticated in investment matters, and the issuer need disclose information only as required by state securities law. Rule 504 permits general selling efforts, and purchasers are free to resell the securities at any time.

Rule 505   Rule 505 of Regulation D allows the issuer to sell up to $5 million of securities in a 12-month period and avoid registration. No general selling efforts are allowed, and purchasers may not resell the securities for at least two years. The issuer may sell to no more than 35 unaccredited purchasers, but there is no limit on the number of accredited purchasers. The purchasers need not be sophisticated in investment matters. Rule 505 has the same disclosure requirements as Rule 506.

Regulation A   Regulation A permits an issuer to sell up to $5 million of securities in a one-year period. There is no limit on the number of purchasers, no purchaser sophistication requirement, and no purchaser resale restriction.

The Regulation A disclosure document is the offering circular, which must be filed with the SEC. Usually, financial statements in the offering circular need not be audited. There is a 20-day waiting period after the filing of the offering circular, during which offers may be made. Oral offers are permitted, as are brief advertisements and written offers by an offering circular. Sales are permitted after the waiting period.

Regulation A also permits issuers to determine investors' interest in a planned offering prior to undertaking the expense of preparing an offering circular.

Sale of Restricted Securities

Restricted securities are securities issued pursuant to Rules 505 and 506. Restricted securities are supposed to be held by the purchaser for at least two years. If they are sold earlier, the investor may be deemed an underwriter who has assisted the issuer in selling the securities to the general public. Consequently, both the issuer and the investor may have violated Section 5 of the 1933 Act by selling nonexempted securities prior to a registration of the securities with the SEC. As a result, all investors who purchased securities from the issuer in the Rule 506 offering may have the remedy of rescission under Section 12(1), resulting in the issuer being required to return to investors all the proceeds of the issuance.

For example, an investor buys 10,000 common shares issued by Arcom Corporation pursuant to a Rule 506 private offering exemption. One month later, the investor sells the securities to 40 other investors. The original investor has acted as an underwriter because he has helped Arcom distribute the shares to the public. The original investor may not use the issuer's private offering exemption because it exempted only the issuer's sale to him. As a result, both the original investor and Arcom have violated Section 5. The 40 investors who purchased the securities from the original investor—and all other investors who purchased common shares from the issuer in the Rule 506 offering—may rescind their purchases under Section 12(1) of the 1933 Act, receiving from their seller the return of their investment.

SEC Rule 144 allows purchasers of restricted securities to resell the securities and not be deemed underwriters. The resellers must hold the securities for at least two years. Investment information concerning the issuer of the securities must be publicly available. In any three-month period, the reseller may sell only a limited amount of securities—the greater of 1 percent of the outstanding securities or the average weekly volume of trading. The reseller must file a notice (Form 144) with the SEC.

If a purchaser who is not an insider of the issuer has held the restricted securities for at least three years, Rule 144 permits her to sell unlimited amounts of the securities. In addition, investment information concerning the issuer need not be publicly available.

Consequence of Obtaining a Securities or Transaction Exemption

When an issuer has obtained an exemption from the registration provisions of the 1933 Act, the Section 5 limits on when and how offers and sales may be made do not apply. Consequently, Section 12(1)'s remedy of rescission is unavailable to an investor who has purchased securities in an exempt offering.

When an issuer has attempted to comply with a registration exemption and has failed to do so, any offer or sale of securities by the issuer may violate Section 5. Because, the issuer has offered or sold nonexempted securities prior to filing a registration statement with the SEC, any purchaser may sue the issuer under Section 12(1) of the 1933 Act.

Although the registration provisions of the 1933 Act do not apply to an exempt offering, the antifraud provisions of the 1933 Act and 1934 Act, which are discussed later, are applicable. For example, when an issuer gives false information to a purchaser in a Rule 504 offering, the issuer may have violated the antifraud provisions of the two acts. The purchaser may obtain damages from the issuer.

LIABILITY PROVISIONS OF THE 1933 ACT

To deter fraud, deception, and manipulation and to provide remedies to the victims of such practices, Congress included a number of liability provisions in the Securities Act of 1933.

Liability for Defective Registration Statements

Section 11 of the 1933 Act provides civil liabilities for damages when a 1933 Act registration statement on its effective date misstates or omits a material fact. A purchaser of securities issued pursuant to the defective registration statement may sue certain classes of persons that are listed in Section 11—the issuer, its chief executive officer, its chief accounting officer, its chief financial officer, the directors,

COMPARISON OF 1933 ACT REGISTRATION EXEMPTIONS

	Type of Issuer that May Use the Rule	Limit of Amount Sold	Limit of Number of Purchasers
Rule 504	Only an issuer that is not a public company	$1 million	No limit
Rule 505	All issuers	$5 million	35 unaccredited purchasers; unlimited number of accredited purchasers
Rule 506	All issuers	No limit	35 unaccredited purchasers; unlimited number of accredited purchasers
Regulation A	Only an issuer that is not a public company	$5 million	No limit
Rule 147	Only an issuer organized and doing business in the same state as the offerees and purchasers (80% of assets, 80% of sales, 80% of proceeds used in that state)	No limit	No limit

other signers of the registration statement, the underwriter, and experts who contributed to the registration statement (such as auditors who certified the financial statements or lawyers who issued an opinion concerning the tax aspects of a limited partnership). The purchaser's remedy under Section 11 is for damages caused by the misstatement or omission. Damages are presumed to be equal to the difference between the purchase price of the securities less the price of the securities at the time of the lawsuit.

Section 11 is a radical liability section for three reasons. First, reliance is usually not required; that is, the purchaser need not show that she relied on the misstatement or omission in the registration statement. In fact, the purchaser need not have read the registration statement or have seen it. Second, privity is not required; that is, the purchaser need not prove that she purchased the securities from the defendant. All she has to prove is that the defendant is in one of the classes of persons liable under Section 11. Third, the purchaser need not prove that

Must Purchasers Meet Any Requirements?	Is Disclosure Required?	Are General Solicitations Permitted?	Is Resale Restricted?	Is a Filing with the SEC Required?
No	No	Yes	No	Yes; Form D must be filed not later than 15 days after the first sale.
No	Yes, unless selling to accredited purchasers only	No	Yes; for at least 2 years	Yes; Form D must be filed not later than 15 days after the first sale.
Yes; each purchaser must either be accredited or have such knowledge and experience in business and financial matters as to be capable of evaluating the merits and risks of the investment.	Yes; unless selling to accredited purchasers only	No	Yes; for at least 2 years	Yes, Form D must be filed not later than 15 days after the first sale.
No	Yes; an offering circular must be given to investors	Yes	No	The offering circular and other offering material must be filed.
Yes; all offerees and purchasers must reside in the issuer's state	No	Yes	Yes; for 9 months sales may not be made outside the state of the issuance	No

the defendant negligently or intentionally misstated or omitted a material fact. Instead, a defendant who otherwise would be liable under Section 11 may escape liability by proving that he exercised due diligence.

Section 11 Defenses   A defendant can escape liability under Section 11 by proving that the purchaser knew of the misstatement or omission when she purchased the security. In addition, a defendant may raise the **due diligence defense**. It is the more important of the two defenses.

Any defendant except the issuer may escape liability under Section 11 by proving that he acted with due diligence in determining the accuracy of the registration statement. The due diligence defense basically requires the defendant to prove that he was not negligent. The exact defense varies, however, according to the class of defendant and the portion of the registration statement that is defective. Most defendants must prove that after a **reasonable investigation** they had **reasonable grounds to believe** and **did believe** that the registration statement was true and contained no omission of material fact.

Experts need to prove due diligence only in respect to the parts that they have contributed. For example, independent auditors must prove due diligence in ascertaining the accuracy of financial statements they certify. Due diligence requires that an auditor at least comply with generally accepted auditing standards (GAAS).

Nonexperts meet their due diligence defense for parts contributed by experts if they had no reason to believe and did not believe that the expertised parts misstated or omitted any material fact. This defense does not require the nonexpert to investigate the accuracy of expertised portions, unless something alerted the nonexpert to problems with the expertised portions.

The following is the most famous case construing the due diligence defense of Section 11.

Escott v. BarChris Construction Corp.
283 F.Supp. 643 (S.D.N.Y. 1968)

BarChris Construction Corporation was in the business of constructing bowling centers. With the introduction of automatic pinsetters in 1952, there was a rapid growth in the popularity of bowling, and BarChris's sales increased from $800,000 in 1956 to over $9 million in 1960. By 1960, it was building about 3 percent of the lanes constructed, while Brunswick Corporation and AMF were building 97 percent. BarChris contracted with its customers to construct and equip bowling alleys for them. Under the contracts, a customer was required to make a small down payment in cash. After the alleys were constructed, customers gave BarChris promissory notes for the balance of the purchase price. BarChris discounted the notes with a factor. The factor kept part of the face value of the notes as a reserve until the customer paid the notes. BarChris was obligated to repurchase the notes if the customer defaulted.

In 1960, BarChris offered its customers an alternative financing method in which BarChris sold the interior of a bowling alley to a factor, James Talcott, Inc. Talcott then leased the alley either to a BarChris customer (Type A financing) or to a BarChris subsidiary that then subleased to the customer (Type B financing). Under Type A financing, BarChris guaranteed 25 percent of the customer's obligation under the lease. With Type B financing, BarChris was liable for 100 percent of its subsidiaries' lease obligations. Under either financing method, BarChris made substantial expenditures before receiving payment from customers and, therefore, experienced a constant need of cash.

In early 1961, BarChris decided to issue debentures and to use part of the proceeds to help its cash position. In March 1961, BarChris filed with the SEC a registration statement covering the debentures. The statement became effective on May 16. The proceeds of the offering were received by BarChris on May 24, 1961. By that time, BarChris had difficulty collecting from some of its customers, and other customers were in arrears on their payments to the factors of the discounted notes. Due to overexpansion in the bowling alley industry, many BarChris customers failed. On October 29, 1962, BarChris filed a petition for bankruptcy. On November 1, it defaulted on the payment of interest on the debentures.

Escott and other purchasers of the debentures sued BarChris and its officers, directors, and auditors, among others, under Section 11 of the Securities Act of 1933. BarChris's registration statement contained material misstatements and omitted material facts. It overstated current assets by $609,689 (15.6 percent), sales by $653,900 (7.7 percent), and earnings per share by 10 cents (15.4 percent) in the 1960 balance sheet and income statement certified by its auditors, Peat, Marwick, Mitchell & Co. The registration statement also understated BarChris's contingent liabilities by $618,853 (42.8 percent) as of April 30, 1961. It overstated gross profit for the first quarter of 1961 by $230,755 (92 percent) and sales for the first quarter of 1961 by $519,810 (32.1 percent). The March 31, 1961, backlog was overstated by $4,490,000 (186 percent). The 1961 figures were not audited by Peat, Marwick.

In addition, the registration statement reported that prior loans from officers had been repaid, but failed to disclose that officers had made new loans to BarChris totaling $386,615. BarChris had used $1,160,000 of the proceeds of the debentures to pay old debts, a use not disclosed in the registration statement. BarChris's potential liability of $1,350,000 to factors due to customer delinquencies on factored notes was not disclosed. The registration statement represented BarChris's contingent liability on Type B financings as 25 percent instead of 100 percent. It misrepresented the nature of BarChris's business by failing to disclose that BarChris was already engaged and was about to become more heavily engaged in the operation of bowling alleys, including one called Capitol Lanes, as a way of minimizing its losses from customer defaults.

Trilling, BarChris's comptroller, signed the registration statement. Auslander, a director, signed the registration statement. Peat, Marwick consented to being named as an expert in the registration statement. All three would be liable to Escott unless they could meet the due diligence defense of Section 11.

McLean, District Judge The question is whether Trilling, Auslander, and Peat, Marwick have proved their due diligence defenses. The position of each defendant will be separately considered.

Trilling

Trilling was BarChris's controller. He signed the registration statement in that capacity. Trilling entered BarChris's employ in October 1960. He was Kircher's [BarChris's treasurer] subordinate. When Kircher asked him for information, he furnished it.

Trilling was not a member of the executive committee. He was a comparatively minor figure in BarChris. The description of BarChris's management in the prospectus does not mention him. He was not considered to be an executive officer.

Trilling may well have been unaware of several of the inaccuracies in the prospectus. But he must have known of some of them. As a financial officer, he was familiar with BarChris's finances and with its books of account. He knew that part of the cash on deposit on December 31, 1960, had been procured temporarily by Russo [BarChris's executive vice president] for window-dressing purposes. He knew that BarChris was operating Capitol Lanes in 1960. He should have known, although perhaps through carelessness he did not know at the time, that BarChris's contingent liability on Type B lease transactions was greater than the prospectus stated. In the light of these facts, I cannot find that Trilling believed the entire prospectus to be true.

But even if he did, he still did not establish his due diligence defenses. He did not prove that as to the parts of the prospectus expertised by Peat, Marwick he had no reasonable ground to believe that it was untrue. He also failed to prove, as to parts of the prospectus not expertised by Peat, Marwick, that he made a reasonable investigation which afforded him a reasonable ground to believe that it was true. As far as appears, he made no investigation. He did what was asked of him and assumed that others would properly take care of supplying accurate data as to the other aspects of the company's business. This would have been well enough but for the fact that he signed the registration statement. As a signer, he could not avoid responsibility by leaving it up to others to make it accurate. Trilling did not sustain the burden of proving his due diligence defenses.

Auslander

Auslander was an outside director, i.e., one who was not an officer of BarChris. He was chairman of the board of Valley Stream National Bank in Valley Stream, Long Island. In February 1961, Vitolo [BarChris's president] asked him to become a director of BarChris. In February and early March 1961, before accepting Vitolo's invitation, Auslander made some investigation of BarChris. He obtained Dun & Bradstreet reports that contained sales and earnings figures for periods earlier than December 31, 1960. He caused inquiry to be made of certain of BarChris's banks and was advised that they regarded BarChris favorably. He was informed that inquiry of Talcott had also produced a favorable response.

On March 3, 1961, Auslander indicated his willingness to accept a place on the board. Shortly thereafter, on March 14, Kircher sent him a copy of BarChris's annual report for 1960. Auslander observed that BarChris's auditors were Peat, Marwick. They were also the auditors for the Valley Stream National Bank. He thought well of them.

Auslander was elected a director on April 17, 1961. The registration statement in its original form had already been filed, of course without his signature. On May 10, 1961, he signed a signature page for the first amendment to the registration statement which was filed on May 11, 1961. This was a separate sheet without any document attached. Auslander did not know that it was a signature page for a registration statement. He vaguely understood that it was something "for the SEC."

At the May 15 directors' meeting, however, Auslander did realize that what he was signing was a signature sheet to a registration statement. This was the first time that he had appreciated the fact. A copy of the registration statement in its earlier form as amended on May 11, 1961, was passed around at the meeting. Auslander glanced at it briefly. He did not read it thoroughly. At the May 15 meeting, Russo and Vitolo stated that everything was in order and that the prospectus was correct. Auslander believed this statement.

In considering Auslander's due diligence defenses, a distinction must be drawn between the expertised and nonexpertised portions of the prospectus. As to the former, Auslander knew that Peat, Marwick had audited the 1960 figures. He believed them to be correct because he had confidence in Peat, Marwick. He had no reasonable ground to believe otherwise.

As to the nonexpertised portions, however, Auslander is in a different position. He seems to have been under the impression that Peat, Marwick was responsible for all the figures. This impression was not correct, as he would have realized if he had read the prospectus carefully. Auslander made no investigation of the accuracy of the prospectus. He relied on the assurance of Vitolo and Russo, and upon the information he had received in answer to his inquiries back in February and early March. These inquiries were general ones, in the nature of a credit check. The information which he received in answer to them was also general, without specific reference to the statements in the prospectus, which was not prepared until some time thereafter.

It is true that Auslander became a director on the eve of the financing. He had little opportunity to familiarize himself with the company's affairs. The question is whether, under such circumstances, Auslander did enough to establish his due diligence.

Section 11 imposes liability upon a director, no matter how new he is. He is presumed to know his responsibility when he becomes a director. He can escape liability only by using that reasonable care to investigate the facts that a prudent man would employ in the management of his own property. In my opinion, a prudent man would not act in an important matter without any knowledge of the relevant facts, in sole reliance upon general information which does not purport to cover the particular case. To say that such minimal conduct measures up to the statutory standard would, to all intents and purposes, absolve new directors from responsibility merely because they are new. This is not a sensible construction of Section 11, when one bears in mind its fundamental purpose of requiring full and truthful disclosure for the protection of investors.

Auslander has not established his due diligence defense with respect to the misstatements and omissions in those portions of the prospectus other than the audited 1960 figures.

Peat, Marwick

The part of the registration statement purporting to be made upon the authority of Peat, Marwick as an expert was the 1960 figures. But because the statute requires the court to determine Peat, Marwick's belief, and the grounds thereof, "at the time such part of the registration statement became effective," for the purposes of this affirmative defense, the matter must be viewed as of May 16, 1961, and the question is whether at that time Peat, Marwick, after reasonable investigation, had reasonable ground to believe and did believe that the 1960 figures were true and that no material fact had been omitted from the registration statement which should have been included in order to make the 1960 figures not misleading. In deciding this issue, the court must consider not only what Peat, Marwick did in its 1960 audit, but also what it did in its subsequent S–1 review. The proper scope of that review must also be determined.

The 1960 Audit

Peat, Marwick's work was in general charge of a member of the firm, Cummings, and more immediately in charge of Peat, Marwick's manager, Logan. Most of the actual work was performed by a senior accountant, Berardi, who had junior assistants, one of whom was Kennedy.

Berardi was then about 30 years old. He was not yet a CPA. He had had no previous experience with the bowling industry. This was his first job as a senior accountant. He could hardly have been given a more difficult assignment.

It is unnecessary to recount everything that Berardi did in the course of the audit. We are concerned only with the evidence relating to what Berardi did or did not do with respect to those items which I have found to have been incorrectly reported in the 1960 figures in the prospectus. More narrowly, we are directly concerned only with such of those items as I have found to be material.

First and foremost is Berardi's failure to discover that Capitol Lanes had not been sold. This error affected both the sales figure and the liability side of the balance sheet. Fundamentally, the error stemmed from the fact that Berardi never realized that Heavenly Lanes and Capitol were two different names for the same alley. Berardi assumed that Heavenly was to be treated like any other completed job.

Berardi read the minutes of the board of directors meeting of November 22, 1960, which recited that "the Chairman recommended that the Corporation operate Capitol Lanes." Berardi knew from various BarChris records that Capitol Lanes, Inc., was paying rentals to Talcott. Also, a Peat, Marwick work paper bearing Kennedy's initials recorded that Capitol Lanes, Inc., held certain insurance policies.

Berardi testified that he inquired of Russo about Capitol Lanes and that Russo told him that Capitol Lanes, Inc., was going to operate an alley someday but as yet it had no alley. Berardi testified that he understood that the alley had not been built and that he believed that the rental payments were on vacant land.

I am not satisfied with this testimony. If Berardi did hold this belief, he should not have held it. The entries as to insurance and as to "operation of alley" should have alerted him to the fact that an alley existed. He should have made further inquiry on the subject. It is apparent that Berardi did not understand this transaction.

He never identified this mysterious Capitol with the Heavenly Lanes which he had included in his sales and profit figures. The vital question is whether he failed to make a reasonable investigation which, if he had made it, would have revealed the truth.

Certain accounting records of BarChris, which Berardi testified he did not see, would have put him on inquiry. One was a job cost ledger card for job no. 6036, the job number which Berardi put on his own sheet for Heavenly Lanes. This card read "Capitol Theatre (Heavenly)." In addition, two accounts receivable cards each showed both names on the same card, Capitol and Heavenly. Berardi testified that he looked at the accounts receivable records but that he did not see these particular cards. He testified that he did not look on the job cost ledger cards because he took the costs from another record, the costs register.

The burden of proof on this issue is on Peat, Marwick. Although the question is a rather close one, I find that Peat, Marwick has not sustained that burden. Peat, Marwick has not proved that Berardi made a reasonable investigation as far as Capitol Lanes was concerned and that his ignorance of the true facts was justified.

I turn now to the errors in the current assets. As to cash, Berardi properly obtained a confirmation from the bank as to BarChris's cash balance on December 31, 1960. He did not know that part of this balance had been temporarily increased by the deposit of reserves returned by Talcott to BarChris conditionally for a limited time. I do not believe that Berardi reasonably should have known this. It would not be reasonable to require Berardi to examine all of BarChris's correspondence files [which contained correspondence indicating that BarChris was to return the cash to Talcott] when he had no reason to suspect any irregularity.

The S–1 Review

The purpose of reviewing events subsequent to the date of a certified balance sheet (referred to as an S–1 review when made with reference to a registration statement) is to ascertain whether any material change has occurred in the company's financial position which should be disclosed in order to prevent the balance sheet figures from being misleading. The scope of such a review, under generally accepted auditing standards, is limited. It does not amount to a complete audit.

Berardi made the S–1 review in May 1961. He devoted a little over two days to it, a total of 20½ hours. He did not discover any of the errors or omissions pertaining to the state of affairs in 1961, all of which were material. The question is whether, despite his failure to find out anything, his investigation was reasonable within the meaning of the statute.

What Berardi did was to look at a consolidating trial balance as of March 31, 1961, which had been prepared by BarChris, compare it with the audited

December 31, 1960 figures, discuss with Trilling certain unfavorable developments which the comparison disclosed, and read certain minutes. He did not examine any important financial records other than the trial balance.

In substance, Berardi asked questions, he got answers which he considered satisfactory, and he did nothing to verify them. Since he never read the prospectus, he was not even aware that there had ever been any problem about loans from officers. He made no inquiry of factors about delinquent notes in his S–1 review. Since he knew nothing about Kircher's notes of the executive committee meetings, he did not learn that the delinquency situation had grown worse. He was content with Trilling's assurance that no liability theretofore contingent had become direct. Apparently the only BarChris officer with whom Berardi communicated was Trilling. He could not recall making any inquiries of Russo, Vitolo, or Pugliese [a BarChris vice-president].

There had been a material change for the worse in BarChris's financial position. That change was sufficiently serious so that the failure to disclose it made the 1960 figures misleading. Berardi did not discover it. As far as results were concerned, his S–1 review was useless.

Accountants should not be held to a standard higher than that recognized in their profession. I do not do so here. Berardi's review did not come up to that standard. He did not take some of the steps which Peat, Marwick's written program prescribed. He did not spend an adequate amount of time on a task of this magnitude. Most important of all, he was too easily satisfied with glib answers to his inquiries.

This is not to say that he should have made a complete audit. But there were enough danger signals in the materials which he did examine to require some further investigation on his part. Generally accepted auditing standards require such further investigation under these circumstances. It is not always sufficient merely to ask questions.

Here again, the burden of proof is on Peat, Marwick. I find that burden has not been satisfied. I conclude that Peat, Marwick has not established its due diligence defense.

Judgment for Escott and the other purchasers.

Due Diligence Meeting Officers, directors, underwriters, accountants, and other experts attempt to reduce their Section 11 liability by holding a due diligence meeting just prior to the effective date of a registration statement. At the due diligence meeting, the participants obtain assurances and demand proof from each other that the registration statement contains no misstatements or omissions of material fact. If it appears from the meeting that there are inadequacies in the investigation of the information in the registration statement, the issuer will delay the effective date until an appropriate investigation is undertaken.

Other Liability Provisions

Section 12(2) of the 1933 Act prohibits misstatements or omissions of material fact in any written or oral communication in connection with the offer or sale of any security (except government-issued or government-guaranteed securities). Section 17(a) prohibits the use of any device or artifice to defraud, or the use of any untrue or misleading statement, in connection with the offer or sale of any security. Two of the subsections of Section 17(a) require that the defendant merely act negligently, while the third subsection requires proof of scienter. Scienter is the intent to deceive, manipulate, or defraud the purchaser. Some courts have held that scienter also includes recklessness.

Since these liability sections are part of federal law, there must be some connection between the illegal activity and interstate commerce for liability to exist. Section 11 merely requires the filing of a registration statement with the SEC. Sections 12(1), 12(2), and 17(a) require the use of the mails or other instrumentality or means of interstate communication or transportation.

Criminal Liability

Section 24 of the 1933 Act provides for criminal liability for any person who willfully violates the Act or its rules and regulations. The maximum penalty is a $10,000 fine and five years' imprisonment. Criminal actions under the 1933 Act are brought by the attorney general of the United States, not by the SEC.

SECURITIES EXCHANGE ACT OF 1934

The Securities Exchange Act of 1934 is chiefly concerned with requiring the disclosure of material information to investors. Unlike the 1933 Act, which is primarily a one-time disclosure statute, the 1934 Act requires **periodic disclosure** by issuers with publicly held equity securities. An issuer with publicly traded equity securities must report annually and quarterly to its shareholders. Also, any material information about the issuer must be disclosed as the issuer obtains it, unless the issuer has a valid business purpose for withholding disclosure.

In addition, the 1934 Act regulates insiders' transactions in securities, proxy solicitations, tender offers, brokers and dealers, and securities exchanges. The 1934 Act also has several sections prohibiting fraud and manipulation in securities transactions. The ultimate purpose of the 1934 Act is to keep investors fully informed to allow them to make intelligent investment decisions at any time.

Registration of Securities under the 1934 Act

Under the 1934 Act, issuers must **register classes of securities**. This is different from the 1933 Act, which requires issuers to register issuances of securities. Under the 1933 Act, securities are registered only for the term of an issuance. Under the 1934 Act, registered classes of securities remain registered until the issuer takes steps to deregister the securities. The chief consequence of having securities registered under the 1934 Act is that the issuer is required to disclose information about itself to its owners and the SEC.

Registration Requirement   Two types of issuers must register securities with the SEC under the 1934 Act.

1. An issuer whose total assets exceed $5 million must register a class of equity securities held by at least 500 shareholders if the securities are traded in interstate commerce.

2. An issuer must register any security traded on a national security exchange, such as common shares traded on the American Stock Exchange.

To register the securities, the issuer must file a 1934 Act **registration statement** with the SEC. The information required in the 1934 Act registration statement is similar to that required in the 1933 Act registration statement, except that offering information is omitted.

Termination of Registration   An issuer may avoid the expense and burden of complying with the periodic disclosure and other requirements of the 1934 Act if the issuer terminates its registration. A 1934 Act registration may be terminated if the issuer has fewer than 300 shareholders. In addition, a registration may be terminated if the issuer has fewer than 500 shareholders of any class of equity securities and assets of no more than $5 million. However, an issuer with securities listed on a national securities exchange would not be able to terminate a registration of the listed securities.

Periodic Reporting Requirement   To maintain a steady flow of material information to investors, the 1934 Act requires public issuers to file periodic reports with the SEC. Three types of issuers must file such reports:

1. An issuer whose total assets exceed $5 million and who has a class of equity securities held by at least 500 shareholders, if the securities are traded in interstate commerce.

2. An issuer whose equity securities are traded on a national securities exchange.

3. An issuer who has made a registered offering under the 1933 Act.

The first two types of issuers—which are issuers that must also register securities under the 1934 Act—must file several periodic reports, including an annual report (Form 10-K) and a quarterly report (Form 10-Q). They must file a monthly report (Form 8-K) when material events occur. Comparable reports must also be sent to their shareholders. The third type of issuer—an issuer who must disclose under the 1934 Act only because it has made a registered offering under the 1933 Act—must file the same reports as the other issuers, except that it need not provide an annual report to its shareholders.

Nineteen thirty-four Act disclosure required of the third type of issuer is in addition to the disclosure required by the 1933 Act.

The 10-K annual report must include audited financial statements plus current information about the conduct of the business, its management, and the status of its securities. The 10-K auditing requirements are the same as for a 1933 Act registration statement—two years' audited balance sheets, three years' audited income statements, and three years' audited statements of changes in financial position.

The quarterly report, the 10-Q, requires only a summarized, unaudited operating statement and unaudited figures on capitalization and shareholders' equity. The 8-K monthly report must be filed within 10 days of the end of any month in which any specified event occurs, such as a change in the amount of securities, an acquisition or disposition of assets, a change in control of the company, a revaluation of assets, or "any materially important event."

The SEC permits issuers to file reports electronically, transmitting them by telephone or by sending computer tapes or disks to the SEC. These electronic filings are made with the SEC's Electronic Data Gathering, Analysis, and Retrieval system: EDGAR.

Suspension of Duty to File Reports An issuer's duty to file periodic reports is suspended if the issuer has fewer than 300 shareholders. In addition, a suspension occurs if the issuer has fewer than 500 shareholders of any class of equity securities and assets of no more than $5 million. However, an issuer with securities traded on a national securities exchange would remain obligated to file periodic reports.

Holdings and Trading by Insiders

Section 16 of the 1934 Act is designed to promote investor confidence in the integrity of the securities markets by limiting the ability of insiders to profit from trading in the shares of their issuers. Section 16(a) requires statutory insiders to disclose their ownership of their company's securities. In addition, statutory insiders must report any transaction in such securities within 10 days following the end of the month in which the transaction occurs. They

must also report purchases and sales made up to six months before and up to six months after becoming an officer, director, or a 10 percent holder.

A statutory insider is a person who falls into any of the following categories:

1. An officer of a corporation having equity securities registered under the 1934 Act.
2. A director of such a corporation.
3. An owner of more than 10 percent of a class of equity securities registered under the 1934 Act.

Section 16(b) prevents an insider from profiting from short-swing trading in his company's shares. Any profit made by a statutory insider is recoverable by the issuer if the profit resulted from the purchase and sale (or the sale and purchase) of any class of the issuer's equity securities within less than a six-month period. This provision was designed to stop speculative insider trading on the basis of information that "may have been obtained by such owner, director, or officer by reason of his relationship to the issuer." The application of the provision is without regard to intent to use or actual use of inside information. However, a few cases have held that sales made by a statutory insider without actual access to inside information do not violate Section 16(b).

Proxy Solicitation Regulation

In a public corporation, shareholders rarely attend and vote at shareholder meetings. Many shareholders are able to vote at shareholder meetings only by **proxy**, a document by which shareholders direct other persons to vote their shares. Just as investors need information to be able to make intelligent investment decisions, shareholders need information to make intelligent voting and proxy decisions.

The 1934 Act regulates the solicitation of proxies. SEC Regulation 14A requires any person soliciting proxies from holders of securities registered under the 1934 Act to furnish each holder with a **proxy statement** containing voting information. Usually, the only party soliciting proxies is the corporation's management, which is seeking proxies from common shareholders to enable it to reelect itself to the board of directors.

If the management of the corporation does not solicit proxies, it must nevertheless inform the shareholders of material information affecting matters that are to be put to a vote of the shareholders. This **information statement**, which contains about the same information as a proxy statement, must be sent to all shareholders that are entitled to vote at the meeting.

The primary purpose of the SEC rules concerning information that must be included in the proxy or information statement is to permit shareholders to make informed decisions while voting for directors and considering any resolutions proposed by the management or shareholders. Information on each director nominee must include the candidate's principal occupation, his shareholdings in the corporation, his previous service as a director of the corporation, his material transactions with the corporation (such as goods or services provided), and his directorships in other corporations. The total remuneration of the five directors or officers who are highest paid, including bonuses, grants under stock option plans, fringe benefits, and other perquisites, must also be included in the proxy statement.

SEC rules regarding the content of proxies ensure that the shareholder understands how his proxy will be voted. The proxy form must indicate in boldface type on whose behalf it is being solicited—for example, the corporation's management. Generally, the proxy must permit the shareholder to vote for or against the proposal or to abstain from voting on any resolutions on the meeting's agenda. The proxy form may ask for discretionary voting authority if the proxy indicates in bold print how the shares will be voted. For directors' elections, the shareholders must be provided with a means for withholding approval for each nominee.

SEC Rule 14a-9 prohibits misstatements or omissions of material fact in the course of a proxy solicitation. If a violation is proved, a court may enjoin the holding of the shareholders' meeting, void the proxies that were illegally obtained, or rescind the action taken at the shareholders' meeting.

Proxy Contests   A shareholder may decide to solicit proxies in competition with management. Such a competition is called a proxy contest, and a solicitation of this kind is also subject to SEC rules. To facilitate proxy contests, the SEC requires the corporation either to furnish a shareholder list to shareholders who desire to wage a proxy contest or to mail the competing proxy material for them.

Shareholder Proposals   In a large public corporation, it is very expensive for a shareholder to solicit proxies in support of a proposal for corporate action that she will offer at a shareholders' meeting. Therefore, she usually asks the management to include her proposal in its proxy statement. SEC Rule 14a-8 covers proposals by shareholders.

Under SEC Rule 14a-8, the corporation must include a shareholder's proposal in its proxy statement if, among other things, the shareholder owns at least 1 percent or $1,000 of the securities to be voted at the shareholders' meeting. A shareholder may submit only one proposal per meeting. The proposal and its supporting statement may not exceed 500 words.

Under Rule 14a-8, a corporation's management may exclude many types of shareholder proposals from its proxy statement. For example, a proposal is excludable if:

1. The proposal deals with the ordinary business operations of the corporation. For example, Pacific Telesis Group was permitted on this ground to omit a proposal that the board consider adding an environmentalist director and designate a vice president for environmental matters for each subsidiary. However, TRW, Inc., was required to include in its proxy statement a proposal that it establish a shareholder advisory committee that would advise the board of directors on the interests of shareholders.

2. The proposal relates to operations that account for less than 5 percent of a corporation's total assets and is not otherwise significantly related to the company's business. For example, Harsco Corp. could not omit a proposal that it sell its 50 percent interest in a South African firm even though the investment was arguably economically insignificant—only 4.5 percent of net earnings—because the issues raised by the proposal were significantly related to Harsco's business.

3. The proposal requires the issuer to violate a state or federal law. For example, one shareholder asked North American Bank to put a lesbian on the board of directors. The proposal was excludable because it may have required the bank to violate antidiscrimination laws.

4. The proposal relates to a personal claim or grievance. A proposal that the corporation pay the shareholder $1 million for damages that she suffered from using one of the corporation's products would be excludable.

In addition, Rule 14a-8 prevents a shareholder from submitting a proposal similar to recent proposals that have been overwhelmingly rejected by shareholders in recent years.

Liability Provisions of the 1934 Act

To prevent fraud, deception, or manipulation and to provide remedies to the victims of such practices, Congress included provisions in the 1934 Act that impose liability on persons who engage in wrongful conduct.

Liability for False Statements in Filed Documents

Section 18 is the 1934 Act counterpart to Section 11 of the 1933 Act. Section 18 imposes liability on any person responsible for a false or misleading statement of material fact in any document filed with the SEC under the 1934 Act. (Filed documents include the 10-K report, 8-K report, and proxy statements, but not the 10-Q report.) Any person who relies on a false or misleading statement in such a filed document may sue for damages. The purchaser need not prove that the defendant was at fault. Instead, the defendant has a defense that he acted in good faith and had no knowledge that the statement was false or misleading. This defense requires only that the defendant prove that he did not act with scienter.

Section 10(b) and Rule 10b-5

The most important liability section in the 1934 Act is Section 10(b), an extremely broad provision prohibiting the use of any manipulative or deceptive device in contravention of any rules that the SEC prescribes as "necessary or appropriate in the public interest or for the protection of investors." Rule 10b-5 was adopted by the SEC under Section 10(b). The rule states:

It shall be unlawful for any person, directly or indirectly, by use of any means or instrumentality of interstate commerce or of the mails, or of any facility of any national securities exchange,

(a) to employ any device, scheme, or artifice to defraud,

(b) to make any untrue statement of a material fact or to omit to state a material fact necessary in order to make the statements made, in the light of the circumstances under which they were made, not misleading, or

(c) to engage in any act, practice, or course of business which operates or would operate as a fraud or deceit upon any person,

in connection with the purchase or sale of any security.

Rule 10b-5 applies to all transactions in all securities, whether or not registered under the 1933 Act or the 1934 Act.

Rule 10b-5 prohibits only *misstatements or omissions of material fact.* A person **misstates** material facts, for example, when a manager of an unprofitable business induces shareholders to sell their stock to him by stating that the business will fail, although he knows that the business has become potentially profitable.

Liability for an **omission of a material fact** arises when a person fails to disclose material facts when he has a duty to disclose. For example, a securities broker is liable to his customer for not disclosing that he owns the shares that he recommends to the customer. As an agent of the customer, he owes a fiduciary duty to his customer to disclose his conflict of interest. In addition, a person is liable for omitting to tell all of the material facts after he has chosen to disclose some of them. His incomplete disclosure creates the duty to disclose all of the material facts.

Under Rule 10b-5, the misstated or omitted fact must be **material**. In essence, material information is any information that is likely to have an impact on the price of a security in the market. A fact is material if there is a substantial likelihood that a reasonable shareholder would consider it important to his decision, that the fact would have assumed actual significance in the deliberations of the reasonable shareholder, and that the disclosure of the fact would have been viewed by the reasonable investor as having significantly altered the total mix of information made available.

Under Rule 10b-5, the defendant is not liable unless he acted with **scienter**. Scienter is an intent to deceive, manipulate, or defraud. Scienter probably includes gross recklessness of the defendant in ascertaining the truth of his statements. Mere negligence is not scienter.

Rule 10b-5 requires that private plaintiffs seeking damages be **actual purchasers or sellers** of securities. Persons who were deterred from purchasing securities by fraudulent statements may not recover lost profits under Rule 10b-5.

Under Rule 10b-5, private plaintiffs alleging damages due to misstatements by the defendant must prove that they **relied** on the misstatement of material fact. The SEC as plaintiff need not prove reliance. For private plaintiffs, reliance is not usually required in omission cases; the investor need merely prove that the omitted fact was material.

Several courts have held that an investor's reliance on the availability of the securities on the market satisfies the reliance requirement of Rule 10b-5 because the securities market is defrauded as to the value of the securities. This **fraud-on-the-market theory** is based on the hypothesis that, in an open and developed securities market, the price of a company's stock is determined by the available material information regarding the company and its business. With the presence of a market, the market is interposed between seller and buyer and, ideally, transmits information to the investor in the processed form of a market price. Thus, the market is performing a substantial part of the valuation process performed by the investor in a face-to-face transaction. The market is acting as the unpaid agent of the investor, informing him that given all the information available to it, the value of the stock is the same as the market price. Misleading statements will therefore defraud purchasers of stock even if the purchasers do not directly rely on the misstatements and even if the defendants never communicated with the plaintiffs.

In *Levinson v. Basic, Inc.*, which follows this section, the Supreme Court held that the fraud-on-the-market theory permits a court to presume an investor's reliance merely from the public availability of material misrepresentations. That presumption, however, is rebuttable, such as by evidence that an investor knew the market price was incorrect.

For Rule 10b-5 to apply, the wrongful action must be accomplished *by the mails, with an instrumentality of interstate commerce,* or *on a national securities exchange*. This element satisfies the federal jurisdiction requirement. Use of the mails or a telephone within one state has been held to meet this element.

The scope of activities proscribed by Rule 10b-5 is not immediately obvious. While it is easy to understand that actual fraud and price manipulation are covered by the rule, two other areas are less easily mastered—the corporation's continuous disclosure obligation and insider trading.

Continuous Disclosure Obligation   The purpose of the 1934 Act is to ensure that investors have the information they need in order to make intelligent investment decisions at all times. The periodic reporting requirements of the 1934 Act are especially designed to accomplish this result. If important developments arise between the disclosure dates of reports, however, investors will not have all of the information they need to make intelligent decisions unless the corporation discloses the material information immediately. Rule 10b-5 requires a corporation to disclose material information immediately, unless the corporation has a valid business purpose for withholding disclosure. When a corporation chooses to disclose information or to comment on information that it has no duty to disclose, it must do so accurately.

Until 1988, courts had disagreed on whether Rule 10b-5 requires disclosure of merger and other acquisition negotiations prior to an agreement in principle. In the following case, the Supreme Court of the United States held that materiality of merger negotiations is to be determined on a case-by-case basis. The Court held that materiality depends on the probability that the transaction will be consummated and its significance to the issuer of the securities. In addition, the Court stated that a corporation that chooses to comment on acquisition negotiations must do so truthfully.

LEVINSON V. BASIC, INC.
485 U.S. 224 (U.S. Sup. Ct. 1988)

For over a decade, Combustion Engineering, Inc. (CEI), had been interested in acquiring Basic, Inc. When antitrust barriers to such an acquisition were eliminated in 1976, CEI's secret strategic plan listed the acquisition of Basic as an objective. Between September 1976 and October 1977, the managements of Basic and CEI privately discussed several times a possible acquisition of Basic by CEI. Throughout 1977 and 1978, despite the secrecy of merger negotiations, there were repeated instances of abnormal trading in Basic's shares on the New York Stock Exchange. On October 19 and 20, 1977, the trading volume in Basic's shares rose from an average of 7,000 shares per day to 29,000 shares. On October 21, 1977, Max Muller, the president of Basic, made a public announcement, reported in a major newspaper, that "the company knew no reason for the stock's activity and that no negotiations were under way with any company for a merger."

Secret contacts between Basic and CEI continued, however. On June 7, 1978, CEI offered $28 per share for Basic, which Basic rejected as too low. CEI stated it would make a better offer, but Muller told CEI to "hold off until we tell you," because Muller wanted to see an investment banker's valuation of Basic before evaluating any CEI offer. Muller and other Basic officials decided to ask CEI for its best offer. On July 10, 1978, Muller and CEI agreed that CEI would make an informal offer to Basic. CEI advised Muller to make no public disclosures about the negotiations.

On July 14, 1978, the price of Basic shares rose more than 12 percent to $27 per share on trading of 18,200 shares. The New York Stock Exchange called Basic and asked it to explain the trading in its shares. Basic denied that any undisclosed merger or acquisition plans or any other significant corporate development existed. On September 24, 1978, the price of Basic shares rose more than 2 points to $30 per share on volume of 31,900 shares. The next day, the price rose almost 3 points to $33 per share on volume of 28,500 shares, even though the Dow Jones Industrial Average fell more than 3 points. Again the Exchange asked Basic whether there were any undisclosed acquisition plans or any other significant corporate developments. Basic flatly denied that there were any corporate developments and issued a press release that stated:

management is unaware of any present or pending corporate development that would result in the abnormally heavy trading activity and price fluctuation in company shares that have been experienced in the past few days.

Secret contacts between Basic and CEI continued. In early November, Basic sent a quarterly report to its shareholders in which it stated:

With regard to the stock market activity in the Company's shares we remain unaware of any present or pending developments that would account for the high volume of trading and price fluctuations in recent months.

On November 27, 1978, CEI secretly offered to buy Basic's outstanding shares for $35 per share. Basic rejected the offer. On December 14, 1978, CEI offered $46 per share. The next day, Friday, December 15, the price of Basic's shares soared. Again Basic answered the Exchange's inquiry with a denial of corporate developments. On Monday, December 18, 1978, Basic asked the Exchange to suspend trading in Basic shares, because it had been "approached" concerning a possible merger. The next day, Basic accepted CEI's offer. On the following day, December 19, Basic announced its acceptance of CEI's offer to buy Basic's outstanding shares for $46 per share.

Max Levinson and several other Basic shareholders sold their Basic shares between October 21, 1977 and December 15, 1978, at a price lower than CEI's offer. They claimed that Basic's statements denying that any merger discussions were occurring violated Section 10(b) and Rule 10b-5 of the Securities Exchange Act of 1934. The district court held that the statements were not material. Levinson appealed to the Sixth Circuit Court of Appeals, which held that Basic possessed no general duty to disclose the merger negotiations. However, the court found that Basic released statements that were so incomplete as to be misleading. Basic appealed to the Supreme Court.

———————————————— ◆ ————————————————

Blackmun, Justice Underlying the adoption of extensive disclosure requirements of the 1934 Act was a legislative philosophy: There cannot be honest markets without honest publicity. Manipulation and dishonest practices of the market place thrive upon mystery and secrecy.

The Court previously has explicitly defined a standard of materiality under the securities laws, concluding in the proxy-solicitation context that "[a]n omitted fact is material if there is a substantial likelihood that a reasonable shareholder would consider it important in deciding how to vote." *TSC*

Industries, Inc. v. Northway, Inc. (1976). The Court was careful not to set too low a standard of materiality; it was concerned that a minimal standard might bring an overabundance of information within its reach, and lead management "simply to bury the shareholders in an avalanche of trivial information—a result that is hardly conducive to informed decisionmaking." To fulfill the materiality requirement "there must be a substantial likelihood that the disclosure of the omitted fact would have been viewed by the reasonable investor as having significantly altered the "total mix" of information made available." We now expressly adopt the *TSC Industries* standard of materiality for the Section 10(b) and Rule 10b-5 context.

The application of this materiality standard to preliminary merger discussions is not self-evident. Where the event is contingent or speculative in nature, it is difficult to ascertain whether the "reasonable investor" would have considered the omitted information significant at the time. Merger negotiations, because of the ever-present possibility that the contemplated transaction will not be effectuated, fall into this category.

Basic urges upon us the Third Circuit test for resolving this difficulty. Under this approach, preliminary merger discussions do not become material until "agreement-in-principle" as to the price and structure of the transaction has been reached between the would-be merger partners. See *Greenfield v. Heublein, Inc.* (3d Cir. 1984). By definition, then, information concerning any negotiations not yet at the agreement-in-principle stage could be withheld or even misrepresented without a violation of Rule 10b-5.

Three rationales have been offered in support of the "agreement-in-principle" test. The first derives from the concern that an investor not be overwhelmed by excessively detailed and trivial information and focuses on the substantial risk that preliminary merger discussions may collapse: because such discussions are inherently tentative, disclosure of their existence itself could mislead investors and foster false optimism. The other two justifications for the agreement-in-principle standard are based on management concerns: because the requirement of "agreement-in-principle" limits the scope of disclosure obligations, it helps preserve the confidentiality of merger discussions where ear-

lier disclosure might prejudice the negotiations; and the test also provides a usable, bright-line rule for determining when disclosure must be made.

None of these policy-based rationales, however, purports to explain why drawing the line at agreement-in-principle reflects the significance of the information upon the investor's decision. The first rationale "assumes that investors are nitwits, unable to appreciate—even when told—that mergers are risky propositions up until the closing." *Flamm v. Eberstadt* (7th Cir. 1987).

The second rationale, the importance of secrecy during the early stages of merger discussions, also seems irrelevant to an assessment whether their existence is significant to the trading decision of a reasonable investor. To avoid a "bidding war" over its target, an acquiring firm often will insist that negotiations remain confidential and at least one Court of Appeals has stated that "silence pending settlement of the price and structure of a deal is beneficial to most investors, most of the time." *Flamm v. Eberstadt.*

We need not ascertain, however, whether secrecy necessarily maximizes shareholder wealth—although we note that the proposition is at least disputed as a matter of theory and empirical research—for this case does not concern the timing of a disclosure; it concerns only its accuracy and completeness. We face here the narrow question whether information concerning the existence and status of preliminary merger discussions is significant to the reasonable investor's trading decision. Arguments based on the premise that some disclosure would be "premature" in a sense are more properly considered under the rubric of an issuer's duty to disclose. The "secrecy" rationale is simply inapposite to the definition of materiality.

The final justification offered in support of the agreement-in-principle test seems to be directed solely at the comfort of corporate managers. A bright-line rule indeed is easier to follow than a standard that requires the exercise of judgment in light of all the circumstances. But ease of application alone is not an excuse for ignoring the purposes of the securities acts and Congress' policy decisions.

We therefore find no valid justification for artificially excluding from the definition of materiality information concerning merger discussions, which would otherwise be considered significant to the trading decision of a reasonable investor, merely because agreement-in-principle as to price and structure has not yet been reached by the parties or their representatives.

Even before this Court's decision in *TSC Industries*, the Second Circuit had explained the role of the materiality requirement of Rule 10b-5, with respect to contingent or speculative information or events. Under such circumstances, materiality "will depend at any given time upon a balancing of both the indicated probability that the event will occur and the anticipated magnitude of the event in light of the totality of the company activity." *SEC v. Texas Gulf Sulphur Co.* (2d Cir. 1968).

The late Judge Friendly applied the Texas Gulf Sulphur probability/magnitude approach in the specific context of preliminary merger negotiations. He stated:

Since a merger in which it is bought out is the most important event that can occur in a small corporation's life, to wit, its death, we think that inside information, as regards a merger of this sort, can become material at an earlier stage than would be the case as regards lesser transactions—and this even though the mortality rate of mergers in such formative stages is doubtless high. *SEC v. Geon Industries, Inc.* (2d Cir. 1976).

We agree with that analysis.

Whether merger discussions in any particular case are material therefore depends on the facts. Generally, in order to assess the probability that the event will occur, a factfinder will need to look to indicia of interest in the transaction at the highest corporate levels. Board resolutions, instructions to investment bankers, and actual negotiations between principals or their intermediaries may serve as indicia of interest. To assess the magnitude of the transaction to the issuer of the securities allegedly manipulated, a factfinder will need to consider such facts as the size of the two corporate entities and of the potential premiums over market value. No particular event or factor short of closing the transaction need be either necessary or sufficient by itself to render merger discussions material.

As we clarify today, materiality depends on the significance the reasonable investor would place on the withheld or misrepresented information. Because the standard of materiality we have adopted differs from that used by both courts below, we remand the case for reconsideration.

Judgment vacated and remanded to the Court of Appeals.

In response to the *Basic* decision, in 1989 the SEC released guidelines to help public companies decide whether they must disclose merger negotiations. A company is not required to disclose merger negotiations if all three of the following requirements are met:

1. The company did not make any prior disclosures about the merger negotiations,
2. Disclosure is not compelled by other SEC rules, and
3. Management determines that disclosure would jeopardize completion of the merger transaction.

Trading on Inside Information   One of the greatest destroyers of public confidence in the integrity of the securities market is the belief that insiders can trade securities while possessing corporate information that is not available to the general public.

Rule 10b-5 prohibits **insider trading** on nonpublic corporate information. A person with nonpublic, confidential, inside information may not use that information when trading with a person who does not possess that information. He must either disclose the information before trading or refrain from trading. The difficult task in the insider trading area is determining when a person is subject to this **disclose-or-refrain** rule.

In *United States v. Chiarella*,[5] the Supreme Court laid down the test for determining an insider's liability for trading on nonpublic, corporate information:

The duty to disclose arises when one party has information that the other party is entitled to know because of a fiduciary or similar relation of trust and confidence between them. A relationship of trust and confidence exists

---

[5]445 U.S. 222 (U.S. Sup. Ct. 1980).

between the shareholders of a corporation and those insiders who have obtained confidential information by reason of their position with that corporation. This relationship gives rise to a duty to disclose because of the necessity of preventing a corporate insider from taking unfair advantage of the uninformed stockholders.

Under this test, **insiders** include not only officers and directors of the corporation, but also anyone who is *entrusted with corporate information for a corporate purpose*. Insiders include outside consultants, lawyers, independent auditors, engineers, investment bankers, public relations advisers, news reporters, and personnel of government agencies who are given confidential corporate information for a corporate purpose.

Tippees are recipients of inside information (tips) from insiders. Tippees of insiders—such as relatives and friends of insiders, stockbrokers, and security analysts—are forbidden to trade on inside information and are subject to recovery of their profits if they do.

In the following case, the Supreme Court stated the applicability of Rule 10b-5 to tippees. The Court held that a tippee has liability if (1) an insider has breached a fiduciary duty of trust and confidence to the shareholders by disclosing to the tippee and (2) the tippee knows or should know of the insider's breach. In addition, the court held that an insider has not breached her fiduciary duty to the shareholders unless she has received a personal benefit by disclosing to the tippee.

SEC v. Dirks
463 U.S. 646 (U.S. Sup. Ct. 1983)

On March 6, 1973, Raymond Dirks, a security analyst in a New York brokerage firm, received nonpublic information from Ronald Secrist, a former officer of Equity Funding of America, a seller of life insurance and mutual funds. Secrist alleged that the assets of Equity Funding were vastly overstated as the result of fraudulent corporate practices. He also stated that the SEC and state insurance departments had failed to act on similar charges of fraud made by Equity Funding employees. Secrist urged Dirks to verify the fraud and to disclose it publicly.

Dirks visited Equity Funding's headquarters in Los Angeles and interviewed several officers and employees of the corporation. The senior management denied any wrongdoing, but certain employees corroborated the charges of fraud. Dirks openly discussed the information he had obtained with a number of his clients and investors. Some of these persons sold their holdings of Equity Funding securities.

Dirks urged a *Wall Street Journal* reporter to write a story on the fraud allegations. The reporter, fearing libel, declined to write the story.

During the two-week period in which Dirks investigated the fraud and spread the word of Secrist's charges, the price of Equity Funding stock fell from $26 per share to less than $15 per share. The New York Stock Exchange halted trading in Equity Funding stock on March 27. On that date, Dirks voluntarily presented his information on the fraud to the SEC. Only then did the SEC bring an action for fraud against Equity Funding. Shortly thereafter, California insurance authorities impounded Equity Funding's records and uncovered evidence of the fraud. On April 2, *The Wall Street Journal* published a front-page story based largely on information assembled by Dirks. Equity Funding immediately went into receivership.

The SEC brought an administrative proceeding against Dirks for violating Rule 10b-5 by passing along confidential inside information to his clients. The SEC found that he had violated Rule 10b-5, but it merely censured him, since he had played an important role in bringing the fraud to light. Dirks appealed to the Court of Appeals, which affirmed the judgment. Dirks then appealed to the Supreme Court.

Powell, Justice In *U.S. v. Chiarella* (1980), we accepted the two elements set out in *In re Cady, Roberts* (1961) for establishing a Rule 10b-5 violation: (i) the existence of a relationship affording access to inside information intended to be available only for a corporate purpose, and (ii) the unfairness of allowing a corporate insider to take advantage of that information by trading without disclosure. The Court found that a duty to disclose under Section 10(b) does not arise from the mere possession of nonpublic market information. Such a duty arises from the existence of a fiduciary relationship.

There can be no duty to disclose when the person who has traded on inside information was not the corporation's agent, was not a fiduciary, or was not a person in whom the sellers of the securities had placed their trust and confidence.

This requirement of a specific relationship between the shareholders and the individual trading on inside information has created analytical difficulties for the SEC and courts in policing tippees who trade on inside information. Unlike insiders who have independent fiduciary duties to both the corporation and its shareholders, the typical tippee has no such relationship. In view of this absence, it has been unclear how a tippee acquires the duty to refrain from trading on inside information.

Not only are insiders forbidden by their fiduciary relationship from personally using undisclosed corporate information to their advantage, but also they may not give such information to an outsider for the same improper purpose of exploiting the information for their personal gain. The transactions of those who knowingly participate with the fiduciary in such a breach are as forbidden as transactions on behalf on the trustee himself. Thus, the tippee's duty to disclose or abstain is derivative from that of the insider's duty. The tippee's obligation has been viewed as arising from his role as a participant after the fact in the insider's breach of a fiduciary duty.

A tippee assumes a fiduciary duty to the shareholders of a corporation not to trade on material nonpublic information only when the insider has breached his fiduciary duty to the shareholders by disclosing the information to the tippee and the tippee knows or should know that there has been a breach.

In determining whether a tippee is under an obligation to disclose or abstain, it thus is necessary to determine whether the insider's tip constituted a breach of the insider's fiduciary duty. Whether disclosure is a breach of duty therefore depends in large part on the purpose of the disclosure. Thus, the test is whether the insider personally will benefit, directly or indirectly, from his disclosure. Absent some personal gain, there has been no breach of duty to stockholders. And absent a breach by the insider, there is no derivative breach.

This requires courts to focus on objective criteria, *i.e.*, whether the insider receives a direct or indirect personal benefit from the disclosure, such as a pecuniary gain or a reputational benefit that will translate into future earnings. For example, there may be a relationship between the insider and the recipient that suggests a *quid pro quo* from the latter, or an intention to benefit the particular recipient. The elements of fiduciary duty and exploitation of nonpublic information also exist when an insider makes a gift of confidential information to a relative or friend who trades. The tip and trade resemble trading by the insider himself followed by a gift of the profits to the recipient.

Under the inside-trading and tipping rules set forth above, we find that there was no violation by Dirks. Dirks was a stranger to Equity Funding, with no pre-existing fiduciary duty to its shareholders. He took no action, directly or indirectly, that induced the shareholders or officers of Equity Funding to repose trust or confidence in him. There was no expectation by Dirks' sources that he would keep their information in confidence. Nor did Dirks misappropriate or illegally obtain the information about Equity Funding. Unless the insiders breached their *Cady, Roberts* duty to shareholders in disclosing the nonpublic information to Dirks, he breached no duty when he passed it on to investors as well as to *The Wall Street Journal.*

It is clear that neither Secrist nor the other Equity Funding employees violated their *Cady, Roberts* duty to the corporation's shareholders by providing information to Dirks. Secrist intended to convey relevant information that management was unlawfully concealing, and he believed that persuading Dirks to investigate was the best way to disclose the fraud. The tippers received no monetary or personal benefit for revealing Equity Funding's secrets, nor was their purpose to make a gift of valuable information to Dirks. The tippers were motivated by a desire to expose the fraud. In the absence of a breach of duty to shareholders by the insiders, there was no derivative breach by Dirks. Dirks therefore could not have been a participant after the fact in an insider's breach of a fiduciary duty.

Judgment reversed in favor of Dirks.

Extent of Liability for Insider Trading   Section 20A of the 1934 Act allows persons who traded in the securities at about the same time as the insider or tippee to recover damages from the insider or tippee. Although there may be several persons trading at about the same time, the insider or tippee's total liability cannot exceed the profit she has made or the loss she has avoided by trading on inside information.

This limitation, which merely requires disgorgement of profits, has been assailed as not adequately deterring insider trading, because the defendant may realize an enormous profit if her trading is not discovered, but lose nothing beyond her profits if it is. In response to this issue of liability, Congress passed an amendment to the 1934 Act permitting the SEC to seek a civil penalty of three times the profit gained or the loss avoided by trading on inside information. This treble penalty is paid to the Treasury of the United States. The penalty applies only to SEC actions; it does not affect the amount of damages that may be recovered by private plaintiffs. The 1934 Act also grants the SEC power to award up to 10 percent of any triple-damage penalty as a bounty to informants who helped the SEC uncover insider trading.

Criminal Liability

Like the 1933 Act, the 1934 Act provides for liability for criminal violations of the Act. Section 32 provides that individuals may be fined up to $1 million and imprisoned up to 10 years for willful violations of the 1934 Act or the related SEC rules. Businesses may be fined up to $2.5 million.

Tender Offer Regulation

Historically, the predominant procedure by which one corporation acquired another was the merger, a transaction requiring the cooperation of the acquired corporation's management. Since the early 1970s, the **tender offer** has become an often used acquisition device. A tender offer is a public offer by a **bidder** to purchase a **subject company's** equity securities directly from its shareholders at a specified price for a fixed period of time. The offering price is usually well above the market price of the shares. Such offers are often made even though there is opposition from the subject company's

management. Opposed offers are called hostile tender offers. The legality of efforts opposing a tender offer is covered in Chapter 42.

The Williams Act amendments to the 1934 Act require bidders and subject companies to provide a shareholder with information on which to base his decision whether to sell his shares to a bidder. The aim of the Williams Act is to protect investors and to give the bidder and the subject company equal opportunities to present their cases to the shareholder. The intent is to encourage an auction of the shares with the highest bidder purchasing the shares. The Williams Act applies only when the subject company's equity securities are registered under the 1934 Act.

The Williams Act does not define a tender offer, but the courts have compiled a list of factors to determine whether a person has made a tender offer. The greater the number of people solicited and the lower their investment sophistication, the more likely it is that the bidder will be held to have made a tender offer. Also, the shorter the offering period, the more rigid the price, and the greater the publicity concerning the offer, the more likely it is that the purchase efforts of the bidder will be treated as a tender offer. Given these factors, a person who offers to purchase shares directly from several shareholders at a set price for only a few days risks having a court treat the offer like a tender offer. The Williams Act clearly states, however, that there is no tender offer unless the bidder intends to become a holder of at least 5 percent of the subject company's shares.

A bidder making a tender offer must file a tender offer statement (Schedule 14D-1) with the SEC when the offer commences. The information in this schedule includes the terms of the offer (for example, the price), the background of the bidder, and the purpose of the tender offer (including whether the bidder intends to control the subject company).

The SEC requires the bidder to keep the tender offer open for at least 20 business days and prohibits any purchase of shares during that time. This rule is to give shareholders adequate time to make informed decisions regarding whether to tender their shares. Tendering shareholders may withdraw their tendered shares during the entire term of the offer. This rules allow the highest bidder to buy the shares, as in an auction.

All tender offers, whether made by the issuer or by a third-party bidder, must be made to all holders of the targeted class of shares. When a bidder increases the offering price during the term of the tender offer, all of the shareholders must be paid the higher price even if they tendered their shares at a lower price. If more shares are tendered than the bidder offered to buy, the bidder must prorate its purchases among all of the shares tendered. This proration rule is designed to foster careful shareholder decisions about whether to sell shares. Shareholders might rush to tender their shares if the bidder could accept shares on a first-come, first-served basis.

The management of the subject company is required to inform the shareholders of its position on the tender offer, with its reasons, within 10 days after the offer has been made. It must also provide the bidder with a list of the holders of the equity securities that the bidder seeks to acquire.

SEC Rule 14e-3 prohibits persons who have knowledge of an impending tender offer from using such information prior to its public disclosure. The rule limits insider trading in the tender offer context.

Private Acquisitions of Shares

The Williams Act regulates private acquisitions of shares differently from tender offers. When the bidder privately seeks a controlling block of the subject company's shares on a stock exchange or in face-to-face negotiations with only a few shareholders, no advance notice to the SEC or disclosure to shareholders is required. However, a person making a private acquisition is required to file a Schedule 13D with the SEC and to send a copy to the subject company within 10 days after he becomes a holder of 5 percent of its shares. A Schedule 13G (which requires less disclosure than a 13D) must be filed when a 5 percent holder has purchased no more than 2 percent of the shares within the past 12 months.

State Regulation of Tender Offers

Statutes that apply to tender offers have been enacted by about two thirds of the states. State statutes have become highly protective of subject companies. For example, the Indiana statute gives shareholders other than the bidder the right to determine whether the shares acquired by the bidder may be voted in directors' elections and other matters. The statute, which essentially gives a subject company the power to require shareholder approval of a hostile tender offer, has been copied by several states.

Other states, such as Delaware, have adopted business combination moratorium statutes. These statutes delay the effectuation of a merger of the corporation with a shareholder owning a large percentage of shares (such as 15 percent) unless the board of director's approval is obtained. Because the typical large shareholder in a public company is a bidder who has made a tender offer, these state statutes primarily affect the ability of a bidder to effectuate a merger after a tender offer and, therefore, may have the effect of deterring hostile acquisitions.

THE FOREIGN CORRUPT PRACTICES ACT

The Foreign Corrupt Practices Act (FCPA) was passed by Congress in 1977 as an amendment to the Securities Exchange Act of 1934. Its passage followed discoveries that more than 400 American corporations had given bribes or made other improper or questionable payments in connection with business abroad and within the United States. Many of these payments were bribes to high-level officials of foreign governments for the purpose of obtaining contracts for the sale of goods or services. Officers of the companies that had made the payments argued that such payments were customary and necessary in business transactions in many countries. This argument was pressed forcefully with regard to facilitating payments. Such payments were said to be essential to get lower-level government officials in a number of countries to perform their nondiscretionary or ministerial tasks, such as preparing or approving necessary import or export documents.

In a significant number of cases, bribes had been accounted for as commission payments, as normal transactions with foreign subsidiaries, or as payments for services rendered by professionals or other firms, or had in other ways been made to appear as normal business expenses. These bribes were then illegally deducted as normal business expenses in income tax returns filed with the Internal Revenue Service.

The Payments Prohibition

The FCPA makes it a crime for any American firm—whether or not it has securities registered under the 1934 Act—to offer, promise, or make payments or gifts of anything of value to foreign officials and certain others. Payments are prohibited if the person making the payment knows or should know that some or all of it will be used for the purpose of influencing a governmental decision, even if the offer is not accepted or the promise is not carried out. The FCPA prohibits offers or payments to foreign political parties and candidates for office as well as offers and payments to government officials. Payments of kickbacks to foreign businesses and their officials are not prohibited unless it is known or should be known that these payments will be passed on to government officials or other illegal recipients.

Facilitating or grease payments are not prohibited by the FCPA. For example, suppose a corporation applies for a radio license in Italy and makes a payment to the government official who issues the licenses. If the official grants licenses to every applicant and the payment merely speeds up the processing of the application, the FCPA is not violated.

Substantial penalties for violations may be imposed. A company may be fined up to $2 million. Directors, officers, employees, or agents participating in violations are liable for fines of up to $100,000 and prison terms of up to five years.

Record-Keeping and Internal Controls Requirements

The FCPA also establishes record-keeping and internal control requirements for firms subject to the periodic disclosure provisions of the Securities Exchange Act of 1934. The purpose of such controls is to prevent unauthorized payments and transactions and unauthorized access to company assets that may result in illegal payments.

The FCPA requires the making and keeping of records and accounts "which, in reasonable detail, accurately, and fairly reflect the transactions and dispositions of the assets of the issuer" of securities. It also requires the establishment and maintenance of a system of internal accounting controls that provides "reasonable assurances" that the firm's transactions are executed in accordance with management's authorization and that the firm's assets are used or disposed of only as authorized by management.

STATE SECURITIES LAW

State securities laws are frequently referred to as blue-sky laws, since the early state securities statutes were designed to protect investors from pro-moters and security salespersons who would "sell building lots in the blue sky." The first state to enact a securities law was Kansas, in 1911. All of the states now have such legislation.

The National Conference of Commissioners on Uniform State Laws has adopted the Uniform Securities Act of 1956. The Act contains antifraud provisions, requires the registration of securities, and demands broker-dealer registration. About two thirds of the states have adopted the Act, but many states have made significant changes in it.

All of the state securities statutes provide penalties for fraudulent sales and permit the issuance of injunctions to protect investors from additional or anticipated fraudulent acts. Most of the statutes grant broad power to investigate fraud to some state official—usually the attorney general or his appointee as securities administrator. All of the statutes provide criminal penalties for selling fraudulent securities and conducting fraudulent transactions.

Registration of Securities

Most of the state securities statutes adopt the philosophy of the 1933 Act that informed investors can make intelligent investment decisions. The states with such statutes have a registration scheme much like the 1933 Act, with required disclosures for public offerings and exemptions from registration for small and private offerings. Other states reject the contention that investors with full information can make intelligent investment decisions. The securities statutes in these states have a **merit registration** requirement, giving a securities administrator power to deny registration on the merits of the security and its issuer. Only securities that are not unduly risky and promise an adequate return to investors may receive administrator approval.

All state statutes have a limited number of exemptions from registration. Most statutes have private offering exemptions that are similar to Securities Act Rule 506 of Regulation D. In addition, a person may avoid the registration requirements of state securities laws by not offering or selling securities. However, as illustrated by the *Capital General* case, which follows, state courts broadly define the term *sale* in order to prevent abusive attempts to circumvent the registration requirements.

Registration by Coordination   The Uniform Securities Act permits an issuer to register its securities by coordination. Instead of filing a registration statement under the Securities Act of 1933 and a different one as required by state law, registration by coordination allows an issuer to file the 1933 Act registration statement with the state securities administrator. Registration by coordination decreases an issuer's expense of complying with state law when making an interstate offering of its securities.

CAPITAL GENERAL CORP. V. UTAH DEPARTMENT OF BUSINESS REGULATION, SECURITIES DIVISION
777 P. 2d 494 (Utah Ct. App. 1989)

On January 7, 1986, Amenity, Inc., was incorporated with capitalization of 100 million shares. On January 8, 1986, 1 million shares of Amenity, Inc., stock were issued to Capital General Corporation (CGC), a financial consulting firm, for $2,000. CGC distributed a total of 90,000 of those shares to approximately 900 of its clients, business associates, and other contacts to create and maintain goodwill among its clients and contacts. CGC did not receive any monetary or other direct financial consideration from those receiving the stock.

Amenity, Inc., had no actual business function at this time, and its sole asset was the $2,000 CGC had paid for the 1 million shares. Through CGC's efforts, Amenity, Inc., was acquired by another company, which paid CGC $25,000 for its efforts.

On June 5, 1986, the Utah Securities Division sought to suspend trading in Amenity, Inc., stock on the grounds that CGC distributed the Amenity, Inc., stock in violation of the Utah Securities Act.

A hearing was held before an administrative law judge, who held that the Act's registration requirements did not apply to CGC's distribution of the Amenity, Inc., stock. The Securities Division obtained a hearing by the Utah Securities Advisory Board. The Board concluded that CGC's distribution of the 90,000 shares was covered by the Act. The Board issued an order of suspension. CGC filed a petition in the district court seeking reversal of the Board's order. The district court affirmed the Board's decision, and CGC appealed.

Orme, Judge   The Utah Securities Act provides, "It is unlawful for any person to offer or sell any security in this state unless it is registered . . . or the security or transaction is exempted." Thus, we must determine if CGC's disposition of the 90,000 shares was an "offer or sale" of Amenity, Inc., securities.

The Act provides that an "offer or sale" includes the "disposition of . . . a security for value."

The Board's determination that CGC's disposition of the Amenity, Inc. stock was "for value" is reasonable and rational. By "giving away" 90,000 shares (or 9 percent of its total holdings), CGC essentially transformed Amenity, Inc., into a publicly held company, ripe for acquisition, in which it held most of the stock. "Value" can include enhanced abilities to borrow, raise capital, and other general benefits associated with publicly held companies, all of which CGC received through the disposition. These economic benefits render the disposition "for value" even though those benefits flowed indirectly from the marketplace rather than directly from the transferees.

CGC additionally argues the disposition was a "good faith gift" under the Act. CGC bears the burden to prove its entitlement to the "good faith gift" exception to the definition of "offer or sale." CGC fails to meet this burden. CGC's veiled but fairly obvious purpose was to advance its own economic objectives rather than to make a gift for reasons of simple generosity.

CGC's actual purpose in making the distribution included an intent to convert a private company into a public company without registration. CGC similarly converted at least thirty other private companies into public companies using the same method employed here. At least three of these companies were then acquired by other companies, resulting in substantial profits for CGC.

Judgment for the Securities Division affirmed.

ETHICAL AND PUBLIC POLICY CONCERNS

1. Should the federal and state governments require disclosure by issuers of securities? Are investors able to protect themselves by insisting that issuers provide relevant information prior to the investors' purchasing securities from issuers? How can current securities owners ensure that they will continue to receive relevant investment information? Could investors have contracted at the time of purchase to receive information as needed in the future?

2. Who are the primary beneficiaries of the securities laws; that is, who primarily buys and sells securities? Nearly all securities are owned by persons whose wealth places them in the top 10 percent of the population. Is securities regulation merely welfare for the wealthy? Does anyone else benefit from securities regulation? Does the benefit to those persons justify the costs of securities regulation?

3. Should insider trading be illegal? Is insider trading unfair? To whom is it unfair? What are the social and economic costs of insider trading? What are the social and economic benefits of insider trading? Does insider trading improve the efficiency of the securities markets? Should shareholders be given the power to authorize insiders to trade on inside information? Why might shareholders want insiders to trade on inside information?

4. Should the payments prohibition part of the Foreign Corrupt Practices Act be repealed? What is unethical about an American corporation making bribes to foreign government officials and political parties? What benefits does the United States receive from the making of such payments? What detriments does the United States suffer from the making of such payments? Does the analysis change if bribery is a standard way of business life in a foreign country?

PROBLEMS AND PROBLEM CASES

1. Beverly Chew and other promoters created 35 general partnerships, each of which purchased 80 acres of land for the purpose of farming jojoba, "the super bean of the future." Each general partner had one operating general partner and several other general partners. The general partners had full and exclusive control of the business of each partnership; however, none of the general partners had any experience in jojoba farming. Most were doctors, dentists, and their relatives. Even the operating general partners made decisions as directed by the promoters. Actual farming was under the control of the promoters. One person farmed all the acreage, because it was not feasible to farm jojoba in 80-acre parcels. The same business plan was followed for all the general partnerships. All the partnerships shared the same field office. When the general partnerships failed, the investors sued the promoters for selling unregistered securities. Were the general partnership interests securities?

2. Attempting to reach as wide an audience as possible, a mutual fund company inserts prospectuses for the issuance of its shares in local newspapers and magazines. In subsequent editions of the newspapers and issues of the magazines, the company distributes additional sales materials. Has the company violated Section 5 of the Securities Act of 1933?

3. King's College is a private college organized under the not-for-profit corporation law of New York. The Internal Revenue Service has issued King's College an exemption from federal income taxation. The college proposes to sell $500,000 of bonds to raise funds for equipment purchases and other capital improvements. The college will sell the bonds in the minimum amount of $500 and will offer them to no more than 1,000 individuals. Only individuals having shown a prior interest in King's College will be solicited. Is the bond offering exempt from the registration requirements of the 1933 Act?

4. Western-Realco Limited Partnership sold $800,000 of its limited partnership interests through the services of securities brokers. Western-Realco did not supervise the brokers and was unaware of whether the brokers solicited their clients in a newsletter or to the public in general. Will Western-Realco be able to use the private offering exemption or Rule 504 to avoid a 1933 Act registration?

5. Capital Sunbelt Securities, Inc. (Sunbelt), and Phoenix Financial Corp. were two brokerages that sold limited partnership interests in Capital: Maple Leaf Estates, Ltd. (Capital) and Maple Leaf Estates, Ltd. (Maple Leaf). Capital was to purchase a mobile home park that would be operated by

Maple Leaf. Sunbelt and Phoenix kept logs reflecting the persons to whom they distributed copies of the limited offering circulars for Capital and Maple Leaf. Ninety-six persons received copies of the Capital offering circular and 34 received the Maple Leaf circular. The circulars contained the same information as a 1933 Act registration statement. In addition, Capital and Maple Leaf promised to make available any additional information requested by investors. All offerees had a prior relationship with Phoenix or Sunbelt, and there were no seminars or meetings attended by the general public. There was no advertising, and each offering circular was addressed to a specific person. All investors were required to state that they were acquiring the limited partnership interests for investment. Proceeds of the offerings were $2,677,000 for Capital and $950,000 for Maple Leaf. Phoenix offered to sell Capital limited partnership interests to 228 persons and sold to 33 investors, 16 of which had a net worth in excess of $1 million. There were 187 offerees of the Maple Leaf limited partnership interests and 13 purchasers, 9 of whom had a net worth over $1 million. At the conclusion of the offerings, no Form D was filed with the SEC. Were the offerings exempt from registration under Section 4(2) or Rule 506 of the Securities Act?

6. Commonwealth Edison Co. registered 3 million common shares with the SEC and sold the shares for about $28 per share. The price of the purchasers' stock dropped to $21 when the Atomic Safety and Licensing Board denied ComEd's application to license one of its reactors. It was the first and only time the Board had denied a license application. ComEd assumed that the license would be granted; therefore, its registration statement failed to disclose the pendency of the license application. Did ComEd violate Section 11 of the Securities Act?

7. Joseph Crotty was a vice president of United Artists Communications, Inc. (UA), a corporation with equity securities registered under the Securities Exchange Act of 1934. Crotty was the head film buyer of UA's western division. He had virtually complete and autonomous control of film buying for the 351 UA theaters in the western United States, including negotiating and signing movie acquisition agreements, supervising movie distribution, and settling contracts after the movies had been shown. Crotty knew how many contracts were being nego-

tiated at any one time and the price UA was paying for the rental of each movie. Crotty was required to consult with higher officers only if he wanted to exceed a certain limit on the amount of the cash advance paid to a distributor for a movie. This occurred no more than two or three times a year. The gross revenue from Crotty's division was about 35 percent of UA's gross revenue from movie exhibitions and around 17 percent of its total gross revenue. During a six-month period, Crotty purchased 7,500 shares of UA and sold 3,500 shares, realizing a large profit. Has Crotty violated Section 16(b) of the 1934 Act?

8. Potlatch Corporation was in the forests products industry, an industry that had experienced a wave of takeovers. The Potlatch board of directors approved a voting rights amendment to the articles of incorporation that granted four votes per share to current shareholders and other specified shareholders. New shareholders would have only one vote per share until they held the shares for four years. The effect of the amendment would be to deter and frustrate a hostile takeover of Potlatch. The board issued a proxy statement in connection with its solicitation of proxies from the shareholders. A letter issued with the proxy statement stated that the intent of the voting rights amendment was to give long-term shareholders a greater voice in the affairs of Potlatch. The voting rights amendment was approved by shareholders. Potlatch shareholders sued the company under Section 14(a) of the 1934 Act, seeking to void the shareholders' approval of the voting rights amendment. They alleged that the shareholders' votes were procured by fraud because the board failed to disclose the real purpose of the voting rights amendment—entrenchment of current management. Should the shareholders succeed?

9. J. C. Harrelson, the president and chief shareholder of Alabama Supply and Equipment Company (ASECo), and Clarence Hamilton conspired to defraud investors. They induced Frisco City, Alabama, to create the Industrial Development Board of Frisco City to issue tax-exempt bonds to investors. The Board offered and sold bonds pursuant to an offering circular, which misstated or omitted several material facts, due to misrepresentations made by Harrelson and Hamilton. The Board used the proceeds of the bond issuance to build a manufacturing plant for ASECo. After the ASECo plant was constructed, ASECo ceased all operations and defaulted on its rental payments to the Board, causing the value of the bonds to drop precipitously. The bondholders received only $373.33 for each $1,000 bond. Clarence Bishop had purchased four of the bonds for $4,096. He never saw the offering circular or knew that one existed. He bought the bonds solely on his broker's oral representations that they were a good investment and that others in the community had purchased them. Can Bishop sue Harrelson and Hamilton under Rule 10b-5 even though he failed to read or even to seek to read the offering circular?

10. James Jordan was a shareholder of Duff & Phelps, Inc., a closely held corporation, and one of its employees in its Chicago office. The transferability of his shares was restricted: If he terminated his employment with Duff & Phelps, he was required to resell his shares to the corporation. Between May and August 1983, Duff & Phelps and Security Pacific Corporation negotiated a merger of the two corporations. The negotiators reached an agreement, but it was vetoed by a high official within Security Pacific on August 11, 1983. During this same time, Jordan was looking for a new job. On November 16, 1983, Jordan told Duff & Phelps that he was going to resign effective at the end of the year in order to accept a job in Houston. Jordan did not ask about any potential merger. Duff & Phelps did not volunteer any information, even though two days earlier its board of directors had decided to seek offers to acquire the company. In December 1983, Duff & Phelps and Security Pacific had serious merger discussions after the high official who vetoed the deal on August 11 changed his mind. On December 30, 1983, Jordan delivered his shares to Duff & Phelps and received a check for $23,225. On January 10, 1984, Duff & Phelps and Security announced their agreement to merge. Jordan would have received at least $452,000 for his shares had he not resigned from Duff & Phelps. Does Jordan have any recourse against Duff & Phelps under Rule 10b-5?

11. In May 1983, Phil Gutter read a report in *The Wall Street Journal* that listed certain corporate bonds as trading with interest. Relying on the report, Gutter purchased $36,000 of the bonds. In reality, the bonds were trading without interest. When *The Wall Street Journal* corrected its error, the price of the bonds fell, resulting in Gutter suffering a loss of $1,692. Is *The Wall Street Journal* liable to Gutter for his loss under Rule 10b-5?

12. When he was the Oklahoma Sooner football coach, Barry Switzer attended a track meet, where he spoke with friends and acquaintances, including G. Platt, a director of Phoenix Corporation and chief executive officer of Texas International Company (TIC), a business that sponsored Switzer's coach's television show. TIC owned more than 50 percent of Phoenix's shares. Switzer moved around the bleachers at the track meet in order to talk to various people. After speaking with Platt and his wife Linda for the last of five times, Switzer lay down to sunbathe on a row of bleachers behind the Platts. G. Platt, unaware that Switzer was behind him, carelessly spoke too loud while talking with his wife about his desire to sell or liquidate Phoenix. He also talked about several companies making bids to buy Phoenix. Switzer also overheard that an announcement of a possible liquidation of Phoenix might be made within a week. Switzer used the information he obtained in deciding to purchase Phoenix shares. Did Switzer trade illegally on inside information?

13. Edper, Inc., identified Brascan, Inc., as a potential takeover target. On behalf of Edper, a securities broker contacted 40 institutional investors and 12 substantial individual holders of Brascan shares who were his clients. The broker told the investors that Edper was interested in buying 3 to 4 million shares. Eventually, Edper bought 6.3 million shares—nearly 25 percent of Brascan's outstanding shares—from these investors at a price that the broker and each individual investor agreed on. Did Edper make a tender offer for Brascan's shares that required it to file a Schedule 14D-1 prior to the making the offers to the investors?

14. First City Financial Corp., a Canadian company controlled by the Belzberg family, was engaged in the business of investing in publicly held American corporations. Marc Belzberg identified Ashland Oil Company as a potential target, and on February 11, 1986, he secretly purchased 61,000 shares of Ashland stock for First City. By February 26, additional secret purchases of Ashland shares pushed First City's holdings to just over 4.9 percent of Ashland's stock. These last two purchases were effected for First City by Alan "Ace" Greenberg, the chief executive officer of Bear Stearns, a large Wall Street brokerage. On March 4, Belzberg called Greenberg and told him, "It wouldn't be a bad idea if you bought Ashland Oil here." Immediately after the phone call, Greenberg purchased 20,500 Ashland shares for about $44 per share. If purchased for

First City, those shares would have increased First City's Ashland holdings above 5 percent. Greenberg believed he was buying the shares for First City under a put and call agreement, under which First City had the right to buy the shares from Bear Stearns and Bear Stearns had the right to require First City to buy the shares from it. Between March 4 and 14, Greenberg purchased an additional 330,700 shares. On March 17, First City and Bear Stearns signed a formal put and call agreement covering all the shares Greenberg purchased. On March 25, First City announced publicly for the first time that it intended to make a tender offer for all of Ashland's shares. First City filed a Schedule 13D on March 26. Has First City violated the Williams Act?

15. Video Case. See "Cafeteria Conversation." Steve has authority to write checks on the account of his employer, a public company under the Securities Exchange Act of 1934. Because Steve is a compulsive gambler and substance abuser, he needs a constant supply of cash to finance his habits. Steve regularly issues checks payable to actual suppliers not currently owed money, steals the checks, signs the names of the payees, and cashes the checks. Because Steve is also in charge of reconciling his employer's bank statements, his embezzlement scheme is not discovered by the employer's independent auditor during a routine audit. Is the independent auditor liable to its client for its losses resulting from Steve's embezzlement?

LEGAL RESPONSIBILITIES OF ACCOUNTANTS

INTRODUCTION

This chapter covers the legal responsibilities of accountants. It considers the professional relationships of accountants with their clients and others who rely on their work. This chapter also covers the criminal and administrative sanctions for wrongful professional conduct by accountants.

GENERAL STANDARD OF PERFORMANCE

The general duty that accountants owe to their clients and to other persons who are affected by their actions is to exercise the skill and care of the ordinarily prudent accountant in the same circumstances. Hence, accountants must act carefully and diligently; they are *not* guarantors of the accuracy of their work. The accountant's duty to exercise reasonable care is a subset of the negligence standard of tort law. Two elements compose the general duty of performance: skill and care.

An accountant must have the **skill of the ordinarily prudent accountant**. This element focuses on the education or knowledge of the accountant, whether acquired formally at school or by self-instruction. For example, to prepare tax returns, an accountant must know the tax laws as well as the ordinarily prudent accountant does. To audit financial records, an accountant must know generally accepted auditing standards (GAAS) and generally accepted accounting principles (GAAP). GAAS and GAAP are standards and principles embodied in the rules, releases, and pronouncements of the Securities and Exchange Commission, the American Institute of Certified Public Accountants (AICPA), and the Financial Accounting Standards Board (FASB).

The care element requires an accountant to act **as carefully as the ordinarily prudent accountant**. For example, in preparing a tax return, he must discover the income exclusions, the deductions, and the tax credits that the reasonably careful accountant would find are available to the client. When auditing financial statements, he must follow the rules of GAAS and GAAP.

Courts and legislatures usually defer to the members of the accounting profession in determining what the ordinarily prudent accountant would do. Such deference recognizes the lawmakers' lack of understanding of the nuances of accounting practice. However, the accounting profession will not be permitted to establish a standard of conduct that is harmful to the interests of clients or other members of society.

Originally, accountants were held to the standard of the ordinarily prudent accountant in his locality. This local standard has given way to a national standard in recent years. Due to improved means of communication in the modern world and the widespread availability of continuing accounting education courses, few accountants today can argue that they are unaware of modern accounting techniques.

ACCOUNTANTS' LIABILITY TO CLIENTS

Acountants are frequently sued by their clients. For example, an accountant may wrongfully claim deductions on a client's tax return. When the IRS discovers the wrongful deduction, the individual will have to pay the extra tax, interest, and perhaps a penalty. The individual may sue his accountant to recover the amount of the penalty. For another example, consider an accountant who prepares an income statement that understates a client's income. The client uses the income statement to apply for a loan, but is denied the loan because her stated net income is inadequate. The client may sue her accountant for damages caused by the erroneous income statement.

There are three principal bases of liability of an accountant to his client: contract, tort, and trust.

Contractual Liability

As a party to a contract with her client, an accountant owes a duty to the client to perform as she has agreed to perform. This includes an implied duty to perform the contract as the ordinarily prudent accountant would perform it. If the accountant fails to perform as agreed, ordinarily an accountant is liable only for those damages that are reasonably contemplated by the client and the accountant.

An accountant is not liable for breach of contract if the client obstructs the accountant's performance of the contract. For example, an accounting firm is not liable for failing to complete an audit on time when the client refuses to give the firm access to needed records and property.

An accountant may not delegate his duty to perform a contract without the consent of the client. Delegation is not permitted because the performance of a contract for accounting services depends on the skill, training, and character of the accountant. As a result, for example, Price Waterhouse & Co., a public accounting firm, may not delegate to Ernst & Young, another public accounting firm, the contractual duty to audit the financial statements of GM, even though both firms are nearly equally skillful and careful.

Tort Liability

Accountants' tort liability to their clients may be based on the common law concepts of negligence and fraud or on the violation of a statute, principally the federal and state securities laws.

Negligence The essence of negligence is the failure of an accountant to exercise the skill and care of the ordinarily prudent accountant. An accountant is negligent when the accountant breaches the duty to act skillfully and carefully and proximately causes damages to the client. For example, a client may recover the interest on excess taxes that he paid as a result of his accountant's lack of due care in claiming allowable deductions on a tax return.

Sometimes, an accountant will audit a company, yet fail to uncover fraud, embezzlement, or other intentional wrongdoing by an employee of the company. Ordinarily, an accountant has no specific duty to uncover employee fraud or embezzlement. Nonetheless, an accountant must uncover employee fraud or embezzlement if an ordinarily prudent accountant would have discovered it. The accountant who fails to uncover such fraud or embezzlement is negligent and liable to his client. In addition, an accountant owes a duty to investigate suspicious circumstances that tend to indicate fraud, regardless of how he became aware of those circumstances. Also, an accountant has a duty to inform a proper party of his suspicions. It is not enough to inform or confront the person suspected of fraud.

When an accountant is hired to perform a fraud audit to investigate suspected fraud or embezzlement, she has a greater duty to investigate. She must be as skillful and careful as the ordinarily prudent auditor performing a fraud audit.

When an accountant negligently fails to discover embezzlement, generally he is liable to his client only for an amount equal to the embezzlement that occurred after he should have discovered the embezzlement. The accountant is usually not liable for any part of the embezzlement that occurred prior to the time he should have uncovered the embezzlement unless his tardy discovery prevented the client from recovering embezzled funds.

In the following case, an accounting firm was held liable to its client for failing to meet the standard of the profession.

DIVERSIFIED GRAPHICS, LTD. V. GROVES
868 F.2d 293 (8th Cir. 1989)

Diversified Graphics, Ltd. (D.G.), hired Ernst & Whinney (E & W) to assist it in obtaining a computer system to fit its data processing needs. D.G. had a longstanding relationship with E & W during which D.G. developed great trust and reliance on E & W's services. Because D.G. lacked computer expertise, it decided to entrust E & W with the selection and implementation of an in-house computer data processing system. E & W had promised to locate a "turnkey" system, which would be fully operational without the need for extensive employee training. D.G. instead received a system that was difficult to operate and failed to meet its needs. D.G. sued E & W and its partners, including Ray Groves, for negligence. The jury found in favor of D.G.; E & W and its partners appealed.

Lay, Chief Judge D.G.'s theory for recovery based on negligence encompasses the notion of a consultant-client relationship and therefore the existence of a professional standard of care.

The degree of skill and care that may be required of a professional is a question of fact for the jury. We find that there was substantial evidence regarding the applicable standard of a professional consultant.

E & W's Guidelines to Practice incorporates the Management Advisory Services Practice Standards which were adopted by the American Institute of Certified Public Accountants, Inc. (AICPA Standards). The AICPA Standards require that "due professional care" is to be exercised in providing management advisory services. These standards in part generally provide:

In performing management advisory services, a practitioner must act with integrity and objectivity and be independent in mental attitude.

Engagements are to be performed by practitioners having competence in the analytical approach and process, and in the technical subject matter under consideration.

Due professional care is to be exercised in the performance of a management advisory services engagement.

Before accepting an engagement, a practitioner is to notify the client of any reservations he has regarding anticipated benefits.

Before undertaking an engagement, a practitioner is to inform his client of all significant matters related to the engagement.

Engagements are to be adequately planned, supervised, and controlled.

Sufficient relevant data is to be obtained, documented, and evaluated in developing conclusions and recommendations.

All significant matters relating to the results of the engagement are to be communicated to the client.

AICPA Standards Nos. 1–8.

D.G. had determined that it required a "turnkey" computer system that would fully perform all of its data processing in-house. The term "turnkey" is intended to describe a self-sufficient system which the purchaser need only "turn the key" to commence operation. The purchaser should not have to hire programmers, and current employees should not have to undergo extensive training to be able to operate the system. To procure this type of customized and fully operational system, great care must be taken to carefully detail a business's needs and to properly develop specifications for the computer system. Potential vendors must be carefully scrutinized to discover all of the inadequacies of their data processing systems. Once a vendor is chosen, proper implementation is imperative to ensure that the purchaser truly need only "turn the key" to commence full operation of the system. A fundamental part of implementation involves testing the system through parallel data processing operation. Finally, the existence of adequate documentation regarding the operation of the system is crucial once the system is up and running. As previously stated,

employees will have had only minimal training and will depend heavily on the instructions for operation. Moreover, documentation is particularly important because this type of system is highly customized and standard instruction sources will have only limited value.

Thus, the jury could conclude that E & W's conduct fell short of adhering to the applicable professional standard of care.

Judgment for Diversified Graphics affirmed.

Contributory Negligence of Client   Courts are reluctant to permit an accountant to escape liability to a client merely because the client was **contributorily negligent**. Since the accountant has skills superior to those of the client, courts generally allow clients to rely on the accountant's duty to discover employee fraud, available tax deductions, and other matters for which the accountant is hired. The client is not required to exercise reasonable care to discover these things himself.

Nonetheless, some courts allow the defense of contributory negligence or the defense of comparative negligence, such as when clients negligently fail to follow an accountant's advice or when clients possess information that makes their reliance on the accountant unwarranted.

Fraud   An accountant is liable to his client for fraud when he misstates or omits facts in communications with his client and acts with **scienter**. An accountant acts with scienter when he knows of the falsity of a statement or he recklessly disregards the truth. Thus, accountants are liable in fraud for their intentional or reckless disregard for accuracy in their work.

For example, an accountant chooses not to examine the current figures in a client's books of account, but relies on last year's figures because he is behind in his work for other clients. As a result, the accountant understates the client's income on an income statement that the client uses to apply for a loan. The client obtains a loan, but he has to pay a higher interest rate because his low stated income

makes the loan a higher risk for the bank. Such misconduct by the accountant proves scienter and, therefore, amounts to fraud.

Scienter also includes recklessly ignoring facts, such as an auditor's finding obvious evidence of embezzlement yet failing to notify a client of the embezzlement.

The chief advantage of establishing fraud is that the client may get a higher damage award than when the accountant is merely negligent. Usually, a client may receive only compensatory damages for a breach of contract or negligence. By proving fraud, a client may be awarded punitive damages as well.

Breach of Trust

An accountant owes a duty of trust to his client. Information and assets that are entrusted to an accountant may be used only to benefit the client. Therefore, an accountant may not disclose sensitive matters such as a client's income and wealth. In addition, an accountant may not use the assets of his client for his own benefit. The duty of trust also requires the accountant to maintain the confidentiality of the client's information entrusted to the accounting firm.

Securities Law

Federal and state securities law creates several rights of action for persons harmed in connection with the purchase or sale of securities. These rights of action are based in tort. Although available to clients of an accountant, they are rarely used for that purpose. Usually, only third parties (nonclients) sue under the securities law. The securities law sections that apply to accountants are discussed later in this chapter.

ACCOUNTANTS' LIABILITY TO THIRD PERSONS: COMMON LAW

Other persons besides an accountant's clients may use her work product. Banks may use financial statements prepared by a loan applicant's accountant in deciding whether to make a loan to the applicant. Investors may use financial statements certified by a company's auditors in deciding whether to buy or sell the company's securities. These documents prepared by an accountant may prove incorrect, resulting in damages to the nonclients who relied on them. For example, banks may lend money to a corporation only because an income statement prepared by an accountant overstated the corporation's income. When the corporation fails to repay the loan, the bank may sue the accountant to recover the damages it suffered.

Nonclients may sue accountants for common law negligence, common law fraud, and violations of the securities laws. In this section, common law negligence and fraud are discussed.

Negligence and Negligent Misrepresentation

When an accountant fails to perform as the ordinarily prudent accountant would perform, she risks having liability for negligence. Many courts have restricted the ability of nonclients to sue an accountant for damages proximately caused by the accountant's negligent conduct. These courts limit nonclient suits on the grounds that nonclient users of an accountant's work product have not contracted with the accountant and, therefore, are not in **privity of contract** with the accountant. Essentially, these courts hold that an accountant owes no duty to nonclients to exercise ordinary skill and care.

This judicial stance conflicts with the usual principles of negligence law under which a negligent person is liable to all persons who are reasonably foreseeably damaged by his negligence. The rationale for the restrictive judicial stance was expressed in the *Ultramares* case,[1] a decision of the highest court in New York. In that case, Judge Benjamin Cardozo refused to hold an auditor liable to third parties for mere negligence. His rationale was stated as follows:

If liability for negligence exists, a thoughtless slip or blunder, the failure to detect a theft or forgery beneath the cover of deceptive entries, may expose accountants to a liability in an indeterminate amount for an indeterminate time to an indeterminate class.

Ultramares dominated the thinking of judges for many years, and its impact is still felt today. However, many courts understand that many nonclients use and reasonably rely on the work product of accountants. To varying degrees, these courts have relaxed the privity requirement and expanded the class of persons who may sue an accountant for negligence conduct. Today, most courts adopt one of the following three tests to determine whether a nonclient may sue an accountant for negligence.

Primary Benefit Test   The *Ultramares* court adopted a primary benefit test for imposing liability for negligence. Under this test, an accountant's duty of care extends only to those persons for whose primary benefit the accountant prepares financial reports and other documents. The accountant must actually foresee the nonclient's use and prepare the document primarily for use by a specified nonclient. That is, the nonclient must be a **foreseen user** of the accountant's work product. The accountant must know two things: (1) the name of the person who will use the accountant's work product and (2) the particular purpose for which that person will use the work product.

Foreseen Users and Foreseen Class of Users Test By 1965, a draft of the *Restatement (Second) of Torts* proposed that the law of professional negligence expand the class of protected persons to **foreseen users** and **users within a foreseen class of users** of reports. Under this test, the accountant must know either the user of the work product or the use to be made of the work product. The protected

---

[1]*Ultramares Corp. v. Touche*, 174 N.E. 441 (N.Y. Ct. App. 1931).

persons are (1) those persons who an accountant knows will use the accountant's work product and (2) those persons who use an accountant's work product in a way the accountant knew the work product would be used.

For example, an accountant prepares an income statement that he knows his client will use to obtain a loan at Bank X. Any bank to which the client supplies the statement to obtain a loan, including Bank Y, may sue the accountant for damages caused by a negligently prepared income statement. Bank X is a foreseen user, and Bank Y is in a foreseen class of users. On the other hand, if an accountant prepares an income statement for a tax return and the client, without the accountant's knowledge, uses the income statement to apply for a loan from a bank, the bank is not among the protected class of persons—the accountant did not know that the tax return would be used for that purpose.

Foreseeable Users Test   A few courts have applied traditional negligence causation principles to accountants' negligence. They have extended liability to **foreseeable users** of an accountant's reports who suffered damages that were proximately caused by the accountant's negligence. To be liable to a nonclient under this test, an accountant need merely be able to expect or foresee the nonclient's use of the accountant's work product. It is not necessary for the nonclient to prove that the accountant actually expected or foresaw the nonclient's use.

In the following case, the court rejected the foreseeable users test as too broad and instead adopted the *Restatement*'s foreseen class of users test in the negligent misrepresentation context.

BILY v. ARTHUR YOUNG & CO.
834 P.2d 745 (Cal. Sup. Ct. 1992)

Founded in 1980 by enterpreneur Adam Osborne, Osborne Computer Company manufactured the first personal computer for the mass market. By fall 1982, sales of the Osborne I computer reached $10 million per month, making Osborne Computer one of the fastest growing businesses in American history.

The company proposed an early 1983 public offering of its common shares. To obtain temporary financing until the company went public, Osborne Computer issued warrants to investors in exchange for the investors making or securing loans to Osborne Computer. The warrants entitled the investors to purchase Osborne Computer shares at a favorable price. It was expected that once the public offering was made, the investors holding warrants would make a substantial profit. The investors were individuals, pension funds, and capital investment firms. Other investors purchased common shares of Osborne Computer. Robert Bily, a director of the company, was one of the investors; he purchased 37,500 shares for $1.5 million from Adam Osborne.

The investors were given and relied on an unqualified audit opinion of Osborne Computer's 1982 financial statements. The audit opinion, issued by Arthur Young & Co., stated that Arthur Young had examined the financial statements in compliance with GAAS, that the statements had been prepared in compliance with GAAP, and that the statements presented fairly Osborne Computer's financial position. The 1982 financial statements revealed that Osborne Computer had a net operating profit of $69,000 on sales of $68 million. Arthur Young delivered 100 sets of the opinion to Osborne Computer.

In the first half of 1983, Osborne Computer's sales declined sharply because of manufacturing problems with its new Executive model computer. In June 1983, the IBM personal computer became a major factor in the small-computer market. Osborne never made a public offering of its shares, and on September 13, 1983, filed for bankruptcy. The investors lost their investments.

The investors sued Arthur Young, alleging professional negligence and negligent misrepresentation. At trial, evidence showed that Arthur Young did not comply with GAAS, resulting in its failure to find that Osborne Computer's liabilities were understated by $3 million. As a result, the supposed operating profit of $69,000 was actually a loss of $3 million. Also, Arthur Young had failed to detect weaknesses in Osborne

Computer's accounting procedures and systems. The jury was instructed that liability for professional negligence extended to those third parties who reasonably and foreseeably relied on the audited financial statements. The court also instructed the jury that for Arthur Young to have liability for negligent misrepresentation, Arthur Young must have intended to induce the plaintiff or a particular class of persons to which the plaintiff belongs to rely on the audit opinion. The jury found Arthur Young liable for professional negligence but not negligent misrepresentation, and it awarded the investors damages of $4.3 million. The California Court of Appeals affirmed, and Arthur Young appealed to the Supreme Court of California.

Lucas, Chief Justice   We decline to permit all merely foreseeable third party users of audit reports to sue the auditor on a theory of professional negligence.

An auditor is a watchdog, not a bloodhound. Audits are performed in a client-controlled environment. The client typically prepares its own financial statements. Because, the auditor cannot in the time available become an expert in the client's business and record-keeping systems, the client necessarily furnishes the information base for the audit. Moreover, an audit report is not a simple statement of verifiable fact that, like the weight of a load of beans, can be easily checked against uniform standards of indisputable accuracy. Rather, an audit report is a professional opinion based on numerous and complex factors, involving discretion and judgment on the part of the auditor at every stage.

Although the auditor's role in the financial reporting process is secondary, the liability it faces is primary and personal and can be massive. The client, its promoters, and its managers have generally left the scene, headed in most cases for bankruptcy. The auditor has now assumed center stage as the remaining solvent defendant and is faced with a claim for all sums of money ever loaned to or invested in the client. Such disproportionate liability cannot fairly be justified on moral, ethical, or economic grounds.

Investors, creditors, and others who read and rely on audit reports and financial statements possess considerable sophistication in analyzing financial information and are aware from training and experience of the limits of an audit report. The third party in an audit negligence case can "privately order" the risk of inaccurate financial reporting by contractual arrangements with the client. For example, a third party might expend its own resources to verify the client's financial statements. It might commission its own audit or investigation, thus establishing privity between itself and an auditor. In addition, it might bargain with the client for special security or improved terms in a credit or investment transaction. Finally, the third party could insist that an audit be conducted on its behalf or establish direct communications with the auditor.

As a matter of economic and social policy, third parties should be encouraged to rely on their own prudence, diligence, and contracting power. This kind of self-reliance promotes sound investment and credit practices and discourages the careless use of monetary resources. If, instead, third parties are simply permitted to recover from the auditor for mistakes in the client's financial statements, the auditor becomes an insurer of not only the financial statements, but also of bad loans and investments in general.

We doubt that a significant and desirable improvement in audit care would result from an expanded rule of liability. In view of the inherent dependence of the auditor on the client and the labor-intensive nature of auditing, we doubt whether audits can be done in ways that would yield significantly greater accuracy without disadvantages. Auditors may rationally respond to increased liability by simply reducing audit services in fledgling industries where the business failure rate is high, reasoning that they will inevitably be singled out and sued when their client goes into bankruptcy regardless of the care or detail of their audits. It might also be doubted whether auditors are the most efficient absorbers of the losses from inaccuracies in financial information. Investors and creditors can limit the impact of losses by diversifying investments and loan portfolios.

A foreseeability rule applied in this context inevitably produces large numbers of expensive and complex lawsuits of questionable merit as scores of investors and lenders seek to recoup business losses. We hold that an auditor's liability for general negligence in the conduct of an audit of its client's financial statements is confined to the client, i.e., the person who contracts for or engages the audit services.

There is, however, a further narrow class of persons who, although not clients, may reasonably come to receive and rely on an audit report and whose existence constitutes a risk of auditing reporting that may fairly be imposed on the auditor. Such persons are specifically intended beneficiaries of the audited report who are known to the auditor and for whose benefit it renders the report. While such persons may not recover on a general negligence theory, we hold they may recover on a theory of negligent misrepresentation. Negligent misrepresentation is a separate and distinct tort. Where the defendant makes false statements, honestly believing that they are true, but without reasonable ground for such belief, he may be liable for negligent misrepresentation, a form of deceit.

Under certain circumstances, expressions of professional opinion are treated as representations of fact. When a party possesses superior knowledge or expertise regarding the subject matter and a plaintiff is so situated that it may reasonably rely on such supposed knowledge or expertise, the defendant's representation may be treated as one of material fact. There is no dispute that Arthur Young's statements in audit opinions fall within these principles.

But the person or class of persons entitled to rely upon the representations is restricted to those to whom or for whom the misrepresentations were made. Restatement Second of Tort section 552 is most consistent with the elements and policy foundations of the tort of negligent misrepresentation. By confining liability to those persons whom the engagement is designed to benefit, the Restatement rule requires that the supplier of information receive notice of potential third party claims,

thereby allowing it to ascertain the potential scope of its liability and make rational decisions regarding the undertaking. Liability should be confined to cases in which the supplier *manifests* an intent to supply the information for the *sort of use* in which the plaintiff's loss occurs.

Having determined that intended beneficiaries of an audit report are entitled to recovery on a theory of negligent misrepresentation, we must consider whether they may also recover on a general negligence theory. We conclude they may not. Because the audit report, not the audit itself, is the foundation of the third person's claim, negligent misrepresentation more precisely captures the gravamen of the cause of action and more clearly conveys the elements essential to a recovery.

Based on our decision, the California standard jury instructions concerning negligent misrepresentation should be amended in future auditor liability cases to permit the jury to determine whether plaintiff belongs to the class of persons to whom or for whom the representations in the audit report were made. The representation must have been made with the intent to induce plaintiff, or a particular class of persons to which plaintiff belongs, to act in reliance upon the representation in a specific transaction, or a specific type of transaction, that defendant intended to influence. Defendant is deemed to have intended to influence its client's transaction with plaintiff whenever defendant knows with substantial certainty that plaintiff, or the particular class of persons to which plaintiff belongs, will rely on the representation in the course of the transaction. If others become aware of the representation and act upon it, there is no liability even though defendant should reasonably have foreseen such a possibility.

Judgment reversed in favor of Arthur Young.

Fraud

Fraud is such reprehensible conduct that all courts have extended an accountant's liability for fraud to all foreseeable users of his work product who suffered damages that were proximately caused by

the accountant's fraud. Privity of contract, therefore, is not required when a person sues an accountant for fraud, even in a state that has adopted the *Ultramares* test for negligence actions. To prove fraud, a nonclient must establish that an accountant acted with scienter.

COMMON LAW BASES OF LIABILITY OF ACCOUNTANT TO NONCLIENTS

Privity Test Adopted by State	Basis of Liability	
	Negligence	**Fraud**
Primary Benefit Test (*Ultramares*)	Accountant liable only to foreseen users (accountant knew name of user and purpose of the user's use)	Regardless of test adopted, accountant liable to all persons whose damages were caused by their reliance on accountant's fraud
Restatement (Second) of Torts Test	Accountant liable to foreseen users and users in a foreseen class of users (accountant knew at least the purpose of the user's use)	
Foreseeable Users Test	Accountant liable to all foreseeable users (accountant can expect or foresee the purpose of the user's use)	

ACCOUNTANT'S LIABILITY TO THIRD PARTIES: SECURITIES LAW

The slow reaction of the common law in creating a negligence remedy for third parties has led to an increased use of securities law by nonclients—that is, persons not in privity with an accountant. Many liability sections in these statutes either eliminate the privity requirement or expansively define privity.

Securities Act of 1933

There are several liability sections under the Securities Act of 1933 (1933 Act). The most important liability section of the Securities Act of 1933 is Section 11, but Sections 12(2) and 17(a) are also important.

Section 11 Liability   Section 11 imposes on auditors liability for misstatements or omissions of material fact in certified financial statements that they provide for Securities Act registration statements. The 1933 Act registration statement must be filed with the Securities and Exchange Commission by an issuer making a public distribution of securities. An auditor is liable to any purchaser of securities issued pursuant to a defective registration statement. The purchaser need not establish privity of contract with the auditor; he need merely prove that the auditor is a person who furnished the certified financial statements for inclusion in the registration statement. Usually, the purchaser need not prove he relied on the misstated or omitted material fact; he need not even have read or seen the defective financial statement.

For example, an auditor certifies a client's income statement that overstates net income by 85 percent. The defective income statement is included in the client's registration statement pursuant to which the client sells its preferred shares. Without reading the registration statement or the income statement, a person buys from the client 100 preferred shares for $105 per share. After the correct income figure is released, the price of the shares drops to $25 per share. The auditor will most likely be liable to the purchaser for $8,000.

Under Section 11, auditors may escape liability by proving that they exercised due diligence. This **due diligence defense** requires that an auditor of certified financial statements prove that she made a reasonable investigation and that she reasonably believed that there were no misstatements or omissions of material fact in the certified financial statements at time the registration statement became effective. Because the effective date is often several

CONCEPT REVIEW

LIABILITY SECTIONS OF THE 1933 ACT AND 1934 ACT

	Wrongful Conduct	Covered Communications	Who May Sue?	Must the Plaintiff Prove Reliance on the Wrongful Conduct?
Securities Act of 1933 Section 11	Misstatement or omission of material fact	1933 Act registration statement only	Any purchaser of securities issued pursuant to the registration statement	No
Securities Act of 1933 Section 12(2)	Misstatement or omission of material fact	Any communication in connection with any offer to sell or a sale of any security (except government issued or guaranteed securities)	Any purchaser of the securities offered or sold	No
Securities Act of 1933 Section 17(a)	Misstatement or omission of material fact	Any communication in connection with any offer to sell or sale of any security	Any purchaser of the securities offered or sold	Yes
Securities Exchange Act of 1934 Section 10(b) and Rule 10b-5	Misstatement or omission of material fact	Any communication in connection with a purchase or sale of any security	Any purchaser or seller of the securities	Yes
Securities Exchange Act of 1934 Section 18	False or misleading statement of material fact	Any document filed with the SEC under the 1934 Act (includes the 1934 Act registration statement, 10-K, 8-K, and proxy statements)	Any purchaser or seller of a security whose price was affected by the statement	Yes

Who May Be Sued?	Must the Plaintiff and Defendant Be in Privity of Contract?	Defendant's Level of Fault	Who Has the Burden of Proving or Disproving Defendant's Level of Fault?	Amount of Defendant's Liability to Plaintiff
Issuer, underwriters, directors, selected officers, and experts who contribute to the registration statement	No	Negligence	Defendant may escape liability by proving he made a reasonable investigation and had reason to believe and did believe there were no misstatements or omissions of material fact	The price the purchaser paid for the securities less the market price of the securities at the time of the suit
Any person who sells a security or actively solicits a sale of a security	Yes (although met by a defendant who has a financial interest in a sale of securities)	Negligence	Defendant may escape liability by proving he did not know and could not reasonably have known of the misstatement or omission of material fact	The price the purchaser paid for the securities (upon the purchaser's return of the securities)
Any person responsible for the misstatement or omission	No	Negligence for some parts of Section 17(a); scienter for one part	Plaintiff must prove the defendant acted negligently or with scienter	Plaintiff's damages caused by his reliance on the misstatement or omission
Any person responsible for the misstatement or omission	No	Scienter	Plaintiff must prove the defendant acted with scienter	Plaintiff's damages caused by his reliance on the misstatement or omission
Any person who made or caused the statement to be made	No	Scienter	Defendant may escape liability by proving he acted in good faith with no knowledge that the statement was false or misleading	Plaintiff's damages caused by his reliance on the false or misleading statement

months after an audit has been completed, an auditor must perform an additional review of the audited statements to ensure that the statements are accurate as of the effective date. In essence, due diligence means that an auditor was not negligent, which is usually proved by showing that she complied with GAAS and GAAP. The due diligence defense is explained more fully in *Escott v. BarChris Construction Corp.*, which appears in Chapter 44, Securities Regulation.

Section 12(2)   Section 12(2) imposes liability on any person who misstates or omits a material fact in connection with an offer or sale of a security. Privity of contract between the plaintiff and the defendant apparently is required, because Section 12(2) states that the defendant is liable to the person *purchasing* the security *from him.*

Until recently, Section 12(2) had been interpreted broadly to impose liability on auditors of financial statements that misstate or omit material facts. Recent decisions of the Supreme Court, including the *Central Bank* case that appears below, suggest that auditors are unlikely to be held liable under Section 12(2) in the future. An accountant must have direct contact with a buyer of a security to be liable. Merely performing professional services, such as drafting or certifying financial statements, is not enough for Section 12(2) liability. The accountant must actively solicit the sale, motivated at least by a desire to serve his own financial interest. Such a financial interest is unlikely to be met by an accountant whose compensation is a fee unconnected to the proceeds of the securities sale. In addition, the *Central Bank* case makes it fairly clear that auditors who merely *aid and abet* a client's Section 12(2) violation will not have liability under Section 12(2).

In the event that an accountant has sufficient contact with a purchaser to incur Section 12(2) liability, the accountant may escape liability by proving that she did not know and could not reasonably have known of the untruth or omission; that is, she must prove that she was not negligent.

Section 17(a)   Under Section 17(a), a purchaser of a security must prove his reliance on a misstatement or omission of material fact for which an accountant is responsible. Under two of the

subsections of Section 17(a), the investor need prove only negligence by the accountant. Under the third, the investor must prove the accountant acted with scienter.

Securities Exchange Act of 1934

Two sections of the 1934 Act—Section 18 and Section 10(b)—especially affect the liability of accountants to nonclients.

Section 18   Section 18 of the 1934 Act imposes liability on accountants who furnish misleading and false statements of material fact in any report or document filed with the Securities and Exchange Commission under the 1934 Act. Such reports or documents include the annual 10-K report, which includes certified financial statements, the monthly 8-K report, and proxy statements.

Under Section 18, a purchaser or seller of a security may sue the accountant if he relied on the defective statement in the filed document and it caused his damages. Usually, this means that a plaintiff must have *read and relied* on the defective statement in the filed document. The purchaser or seller may sue the accountant even if they are not in privity of contract.

An accountant may escape Section 18 liability by proving that she acted in *good faith* and had *no knowledge* that the information was misleading. That is, she must show that she acted *without scienter.*

Section 10(b) and Rule 10b-5   Securities Exchange Act Rule 10b-5, pursuant to Section 10(b), has been the basis for most of the recent suits investors have brought against accountants. Rule 10b-5 prohibits any person from making a misstatement or omission of material fact in connection with the purchase or sale of any security. Rule 10b-5 applies to misstatements or omissions in any communications with investors, covering any use of financial statements certified by accountants resulting in a purchase or sale of a security. The wrongful act must have a connection with interstate commerce, the mails, or a national securities exchange.

A purchaser or seller of a security may sue an accountant who has misstated or omitted a material fact. Privity is not required. The purchaser or seller must rely on the misstatement or omission. In omission cases, reliance may be inferred from materiality.

In addition, the accountant must act with scienter. In this context, scienter is an intent to deceive, manipulate, or defraud. Negligence is not enough.

Aiding and Abetting

Until recently, a common way investors held an accountant liable under Rule 10b-5 was to prove that the accountant aided and abetted a client's fraud. Most courts had recognized accountants' aiding and abetting liability under Rule 10b-5 by requiring (1) a primary violation by another person (such as a client fraudulently overstating its earnings), (2) the accountant's knowledge of the primary violation, and (3) the accountant's substantial assistance in the achievement of the primary violation (such as an accountant's failure to disclose a client's fraud known to the accountant).

In April 1994 in the *Central Bank* case that follows, the Supreme Court of the United States by a 5–4 decision held that those who merely aid and abet Rule 10b-5 violations have no liability to those injured by the fraud. The court drew a distinction between those **primarily** responsible for the fraud—who retain Rule 10b-5 liability—and those **secondarily** responsible—who no longer have liability under Rule 10b-5. The distinction between primary and secondary responsibility is unclear. Intentionally certifying false financial statements is primary fault and would impose Rule 10b-5 liability on the auditor. However, an independent accountant's work in connection with false unaudited statements or other financial information released by a client may be only secondary and may not impose Rule 10b-5 liability on the accountant.

While the defendants in the *Central Bank* case were not accountants, the issue decided is of crucial importance to accountants and other professionals who are not directly involved in a client's fraudulent conduct but either have knowledge of the fraud or recklessly disregard facts indicating fraud. It appears that *Central Bank* substantially reduces an accountant's risk of liability. However, injured parties may attempt to circumvent the limits of *Central Bank* by recharacterizing an accountant as a primary wrongdoer. In addition, the issue is certain to be considered by Congress, which may decide to reinstate aiding and abetting liability under Rule 10b-5.

CENTRAL BANK OF DENVER V. FIRST INTERSTATE BANK OF DENVER
62 U.S.L.W. 4230 (U.S. Sup. Ct. April 19, 1994)

In 1986 and 1988, the Colorado Springs-Stetson Hills Public Building Authority (Authority) issued $26 million in bonds to finance public improvements at Stetson Hills, a planned residential and commercial development in Colorado Springs. Central Bank served as the trustee for the bondholders, undertaking a fiduciary duty to the bondholders to ensure that the Authority complied with indenture provisions protecting bondholders. The bonds were secured by liens against 522 acres of land. The indenture required that the land be worth at least 160 percent of the bonds' outstanding principal and interest.

In January 1988, AmWest Development—the developer of Stetson Hills—gave Central Bank an appraisal of the land. The appraisal showed land values almost unchanged from a 1986 appraisal, even though property values were declining in Colorado Springs. Central Bank's in-house appraiser reviewed the 1988 appraisal and decided that it was optimistic. He suggested that Central Bank use an independent outside appraiser to review the 1988 appraisal. After an exchange of letters between Central Bank and AmWest in early 1988, Central Bank agreed to delay independent review of the appraisal until the end of 1988, six months after the 1988 bonds had been issued to investors. Before the independent review was complete, the Authority defaulted on the 1988 bonds.

First Interstate Bank and others purchased $2.1 million of the 1988 bonds relying on the 1988 appraisal. They sued the Authority, the bond's underwriters, an AmWest director, and Central Bank for violations of section 10(b) of the Securities Exchange Act of 1934. They alleged that Central Bank was secondarily liable under section 10 (b) for aiding and abetting the Authority's fraudulent sale of the bonds by failing to act on its knowledge that the 1988 appraisal may have been wrong. The district court granted judgment in favor of Central Bank. The 10th Circuit Court of Appeals reversed, holding that Central Bank could be liable as an aider and abetter. Central Bank asked the Supreme Court of the United States to review the decision.

Kennedy, Justice   In the wake of the 1929 stock market crash and in response to reports of widespread abuses in the securities industry, Congress enacted two landmark pieces of securities legislation: the Securities Act of 1933 and the Securities Exchange Act of 1934. The 1933 Act regulates initial distributions of securities, and the 1934 Act for the most part regulates post-distribution trading. Together, the Acts embrace a fundamental purpose to substitute a philosophy of full disclosure for the philosophy of *caveat emptor*

The 1933 and 1934 Acts create an extensive scheme of civil liability. The Securities and Exchange Commission (SEC) may bring administrative actions and injunctive proceedings to enforce a variety of statutory prohibitions. Private plaintiffs may sue under the express private rights of action contained in the Acts. They may also sue under private rights of action we have found to be implied by the terms of section 10(b) and section 14(a) of the 1934 Act. This case concerns the most familiar private cause of action: the one we have found to be implied by section 10(b), the general antifraud provision of the 1934 Act. Section 10(b) states:

It shall be unlawful for any person, directly or indirectly, by the use of any means or instrumentality of interstate commerce or of the mails, or of any facility of any national securities exchange—

*   *   *   *   *

(b) To use or employ, in connection with the purchase or sale of any security registered on a national securities exchange or any security not so registered, any manipulative or deceptive device or contrivance in contravention of such rules and regulations as the [SEC] may prescribe.

Rule 10b-5, adopted by the SEC in 1942, casts the proscription in similar terms.

With respect to the scope of conduct prohibited by section 10(b), the text of the statute controls our decision. The private plaintiff may not bring a 10b-5 suit against a defendant for acts not prohibited by the text of section 10(b). That bodes ill for First Interstate, for the language of section 10(b) does not in terms mention aiding and abetting. To overcome this problem, First Interstate and the SEC suggest (or hint at) the novel argument that the use of the phrases "directly or indirectly" in the text of section 10(b) covers aiding and abetting.

There is a basic flaw with the interpretation. The problem, of course, is that aiding and abetting liability extends beyond persons who engage, even indirectly, in a proscribed activity; aiding and abetting liability reaches persons who do not engage in the proscribed activities at all, but who give a degree of aid to those who do. A further problem with First Interstate's interpretation of the "directly or indirectly" language is posed by the numerous provisions of the 1934 Act that use the term in a way that does not impose aiding and abetting liability.

Congress knew how to impose aiding and abetting liability when it chose to do so. If Congress intended to impose aiding and abetting liability, we presume it would have used the words "aid" and "abet" in the statutory text. But it did not.

We reach the uncontroversial conclusion that the text of the 1934 Act does not itself reach those who aid and abet a section 10(b) violation. We think that conclusion resolves the case. We cannot amend the statute to create liability for acts that are not themselves manipulative or deceptive within the meaning of the statute.

The absence of section 10(b) aiding and abetting liability does not mean that secondary actors in the securities markets are always free from liability under the securities Acts. Any person or entity, including a lawyer, accountant, or bank, who employs a manipulative device or makes a material misstatement (or omission) on which a purchaser or seller of securities relies may be liable as a primary violator under 10b-5.

Judgment reversed in favor of Central Bank.

State Securities Law

All states have securities statutes with liability sections. Most of the states have a liability section similar to Section 12(2) of the Securities Act.

LIMITING ACCOUNTANTS' LIABILITY: PROFESSIONAL CORPORATIONS AND LIMITED LIABILITY PARTNERSHIPS

Every state permits professionals to incorporate their business under a professional incorporation statute. Most statutes permit a professional accounting corporation to be owned only by accountants.

While there are significant taxation advantages to incorporation, the principal advantage of incorporation—*limited liability of the shareholders*—does not isolate accountants from liability for professional misconduct. For example, an accountant who injures his client by failing to act as the ordinarily prudent accountant would act has liability to his client, despite the incorporation of the accountant's business.

When two or more accountants conduct an accounting business as co-owners, incorporation may offer them limited liability. While partners in a partnership are jointly and severally liable for each other's negligence, some states permit incorporated accountants to escape liability for their associate's torts, unless the accountant actually supervised the wrongdoing associate or participated in the tort. Other states do not allow incorporated accountants to limit their liability for their associates' torts, making all the shareholder/accountants jointly and severally liable for the professional misconduct of any of its accountants.

Reacting to the large personal liability sometimes imposed on lawyers and accountants for the professional malpractice of their partners, Texas enacted in 1991 the first statute permitting the formation of limited liability partnerships (LLP). An LLP is similar to a partnership, except that a partner's liability for his partners' professional malpractice is limited to the partnership's assets, unless the partner supervised the work of the wrongdoing partner. In addition, a partner retains unlimited liability for his *own* malpractice and for all *non*professional obligations of the partnership.

As of April 1994, seven states and the District of Columbia have passed LLP statutes. Several other states are considering such laws. As more states adopt LLP statutes, the LLP will become the preferred form of business for accountants who do not incorporate.

For more information on the limited liability partnership, see Chapter 36.

QUALIFIED OPINIONS, DISCLAIMERS OF OPINION, ADVERSE OPINIONS, AND UNAUDITED STATEMENTS

After performing an audit of financial statements, an independent auditor **certifies** the financial statements by issuing an opinion letter. The **opinion letter** expresses whether the audit has been performed in compliance with GAAS and whether, in the auditor's opinion, the financial statements fairly present the client's financial position and results of operations in conformity with GAAP. Usually, an auditor issues an **unqualified opinion**—that is, an opinion that there has been compliance with GAAS and GAAP. Sometimes, an auditor issues a qualified opinion, a disclaimer of opinion, or an adverse opinion. Up to this point, you have studied the liability of an auditor who has issued unqualified opinions yet has not complied with GAAS and GAAP.

What liability should be imposed on an auditor who discloses that he has not complied with GAAS and GAAP? An auditor is relieved of responsibility only to the extent that a qualification or disclaimer is specifically expressed in the opinion letter. Therefore, letters that purport to totally disclaim liability for false and misleading financial statements are too general to excuse an accountant from exercising ordinary skill and care.

For example, an auditor qualifies his opinion of the ability of financial statements to present the financial position of a company by indicating that there is uncertainty about how an antitrust suit against the company may be decided. He would not be held liable for damages resulting from an unfavorable verdict in the antitrust suit. He would remain liable, however, for failing to make an examination in compliance with GAAS that would have revealed other serious problems.

For another example, consider an auditor who, due to the limited scope of the audit, disclaims any opinion on the ability of the financial statements to present the financial position of the company. She would nonetheless be liable for the nondiscovery of problems that the limited audit should have revealed.

Likewise, an accountant who issued an adverse opinion that depreciation had not been calculated according to GAAP would not be liable for damages resulting from the wrongful accounting treatment of depreciation, but he would be liable for damages resulting from the wrongful treatment of receivables.

Merely preparing unaudited statements does not create a disclaimer as to their accuracy. The mere fact that the statements are unaudited only permits an accountant to exercise a lower level of inquiry. Even so, an accountant must act as the ordinarily prudent accountant would act under the same circumstances in preparing unaudited financial statements.

CRIMINAL, INJUNCTIVE, AND ADMINISTRATIVE PROCEEDINGS

In addition to being held liable for damages to clients and third parties, an accountant may be found criminally liable for his violations of securities, tax, and other laws. For criminal violations, he may be fined and imprisoned. His wrongful conduct may also result in the issuance of an injunction, which bars him from doing the same acts in the future. In addition, his wrongful conduct may be the subject of administrative proceedings by the Securities and Exchange Commission and state licensing boards. An administrative proceeding may result in the revocation of an accountant's license to practice or the suspension from practice. Finally, disciplinary proceedings may be brought against an accountant by professional societies such as the AICPA.

Criminal Liability under the Securities Laws

Both the Securities Act of 1933 and the Securities Exchange Act of 1934 have criminal provisions that can be applied to accountants. The 1933 Act imposes criminal liability for willful violations of any section of the 1933 Act, including Sections 11, 12(2), and 17(a), or any 1933 Act rule or regulation. For example, willfully making an untrue statement or omitting any material fact in a 1933 Act registration statement imposes criminal liability on an accountant. The maximum penalty for a criminal violation of the 1933 Act is a $10,000 fine and five years' imprisonment.

The 1934 Act imposes criminal penalties for willful violations of any section of the 1934 Act, such as Sections 10(b) and 18, and any 1934 Act rule or regulation, such as Rule 10b-5. For example, willfully making false or misleading statements in reports that are required to be filed under the 1934 Act incurs criminal liability. Such filings include 10-Ks, 8-Ks, and proxy statements. An individual accountant may be fined up to $1 million and imprisoned for up to 10 years for a criminal violation of the 1934 Act; however, an individual accountant who proves that he had no knowledge of an SEC rule or regulation may not be imprisoned for violating that rule or regulation. An accounting firm may be fined up to $2.5 million.

Most of the states have statutes imposing criminal penalties on accountants who willfully falsify financial statements or other reports in filings under the state securities laws and who willfully violate the state securities laws or aid and abet criminal violations of these laws by others.

In the following case, accountants permitting a client to book unbilled sales after the close of the fiscal period subjected the accountants to the criminal penalties of the 1934 Act.

UNITED STATES V. NATELLI
527 F.2d 311 (2d Cir. 1975)

Anthony Natelli was the partner in charge of the Washington, D.C., office of Peat, Marwick, Mitchell & Co., a large CPA firm. In August 1968, Peat, Marwick became the independent public auditor of National Student Marketing Corporation. Natelli was the engagement partner for the audit of Student Marketing. Joseph Scansaroli was Peat, Marwick's audit supervisor on that engagement.

Student Marketing provided its corporate clients with a wide range of marketing services to help them reach the lucrative youth market. In its financial statements for the nine months ended May 31, 1968, Student Marketing had counted as income the entire amount of oral customer commitments to pay fees in Student Marketing's "fixed-fee marketing programs," even though those fees had not yet been paid. They were to be paid for services that Student Marketing would provide over a period of several years. Standard accounting practice required that part of the unpaid fees be considered income in the present year but that part be deferred as income until the years when Student Marketing actually performed the services for which the fees were paid. Therefore, in making the year-end audit, Natelli concluded that he would use a percentage-of-completion approach on these commitments, taking as income in the present year only those fees that were to be paid for services in that year.

The customer fee commitments were oral only, making it difficult to verify whether they really existed. Natelli directed Scansaroli to try to verify the fee commitments by telephoning the customers but not by seeking written verification. However, Scansaroli never called Student Marketing's clients. Instead, Scansaroli accepted a schedule prepared by Student Marketing showing estimates of the percentage of completion of services for each corporate client and the amount of the fee commitment from each client. This resulted in an adjustment of $1.7 million for "unbilled accounts receivable." The adjustment turned a loss for the year into a profit twice that of the year before.

By May 1969, a total of $1 million of the customer fee commitments had been written off as uncollectible. The effect of the write-off was to reduce 1968 income by $209,750. However, Scansaroli, with Natelli's approval, offset this by reversing a deferred tax item of approximately the same amount.

Student Marketing issued a proxy statement in September 1969 in connection with a shareholders' meeting to consider merging six companies into Student Marketing. The proxy statement was filed with the Securities and Exchange Commission. It contained several financial statements, some of which had been audited by Peat, Marwick. Others had not been audited, but Peat, Marwick had aided in their preparation. In the proxy statement, a footnote to the financial statements failed to show that the write-off of customer fee commitments had affected Student Marketing's fiscal 1968 income.

The proxy statement required an unaudited statement of nine months' earnings through May 31, 1969. This statement was prepared by Student Marketing with Peat, Marwick's assistance. Student Marketing produced a $1.2 million commitment from the Pontiac Division of General Motors Corporation two months after the end of May, but it was dated April 28, 1969. At 3 A.M. on the day the proxy statement was to be printed, Natelli informed Randall, the chief executive officer and founder of Student Marketing, that this commitment could not be included because it was not a legally binding contract. Randall responded at once that he had "a commitment from Eastern Airlines" for a somewhat comparable amount attributable to the same period. Such a letter was produced at the printing plant a few hours later, and the Eastern commitment was substituted for the Pontiac sale in the proxy. Shortly thereafter, another Peat, Marwick accountant, Oberlander, discovered $177,547 in "bad" commitments from 1968. These were known to Scansaroli in May 1969 as being doubtful, but they had not been written off. Oberlander suggested to the company that these commitments plus others, for a total of $320,000, be written off, but Scansaroli, after consulting with Natelli, decided against the suggested write-off.

There was no disclosure in the proxy statement that Student Marketing had written off $1 million (20 percent) of its 1968 sales and over $2 million of the $3.3 million of unbilled sales booked in 1968 and 1969. A true disclosure would have shown that Student Marketing had made no profit for the first nine months of 1969.

Subsequently, it was revealed that many of Student Marketing's fee commitments were fictitious. The attorney general of the United States brought a criminal action against Natelli and Scansaroli for violating the Securities Exchange Act of 1934 by willfully and knowingly making false and misleading statements in a proxy statement. The district court jury convicted both Natelli and Scansaroli, and they appealed.

Gurfein, Circuit Judge   The original action of Natelli in permitting the booking of unbilled sales after the close of the fiscal period in an amount sufficient to convert a loss into a profit was contrary to sound accounting practice. When the uncollectibility, and indeed, the nonexistence of these large receivables was established in 1969, the revelation stood to cause Natelli severe criticism and possible liability. He had a motive, therefore, intentionally to conceal the write-offs that had to be made.

Honesty should have impelled Natelli and Scansaroli to disclose in the footnote that annotated their own audited statement for fiscal 1968 that substantial write-offs had been taken, after year-end, to reflect a loss for the year. A simple desire to right the wrong that had been perpetrated on the stockholders and others by the false audited financial statement should have dictated that course.

The accountant owes a duty to the public not to assert a privilege of silence until the next audited annual statement comes around in due time. Since companies were being acquired by Student Marketing for its shares in this period, Natelli had to know that the 1968 audited statement was being used continuously.

Natelli contends that he had no duty to verify the Eastern commitment because the earnings statement within which it was included was unaudited. This raises the issue of the duty of the CPA in relation to an unaudited financial statement contained within a proxy statement where the figures are reviewed and to some extent supplied by the auditors. The auditors were associated with the statement and were required to object to anything they actually knew to be materially false. In the ordinary case involving an unaudited statement, the auditor would not be chargeable simply because he failed to discover the invalidity of booked accounts receivable, inasmuch as he had not undertaken an audit with verification. In this case, however, Natelli knew the history of post-period bookings and the dismal consequences later discovered.

In terms of professional standards, the accountant may not shut his eyes in reckless disregard of his knowledge that highly suspicious figures, known to him to be suspicious, were being included in the unaudited earnings figures in the proxy statement with which he was associated.

There is some merit to Scansaroli's point that he was simply carrying out the judgments of his superior, Natelli. The defense of obedience to higher authority has always been troublesome. There is no sure yardstick to measure criminal responsibility except by measurement of the degree of awareness on the part of a defendant that he is participating in a criminal act, in the absence of physical coercion such as a soldier might face. Here the motivation to conceal undermines Scansaroli's argument that he was merely implementing Natelli's instructions, at least with respect to concealment of matters that were within his own ken. The jury could properly have found him guilty on the specification relating to the footnote.

With respect to the Eastern commitment, Scansaroli stands in a position different from that of Natelli. Natelli was his superior. He was the man to make the judgment whether or not to object to the last-minute inclusion of a new commitment in the nine-months statement. There is insufficient evidence that Scansaroli engaged in any conversations about the Eastern commitment or that he was a participant with Natelli in any check on its authenticity. Since in the hierarchy of the accounting firm it was not his responsibility to decide whether to book the Eastern contract, his mere adjustment of the figures to reflect it under orders was not a matter for his discretion.

Conviction of Natelli affirmed. Conviction of Scansaroli affirmed in part and reversed in part.

Other Criminal Law Violations

Federal tax law imposes on accountants a wide range of penalties for a wide variety of wrongful conduct. At one end of the penalty spectrum is a $25 fine for failing to furnish a client with a copy of his income tax return or failing to sign a client's return. At the other end is a fine of $100,000 and imprisonment of three years for tax fraud. In between is the penalty for promoting abusive tax shelters. The fine is $1,000, or 20 percent of the accountant's income from her partici-

pation in the tax shelter, whichever is greater. In addition, all of the states impose criminal penalties for specified violations of their tax laws.

Several other federal statutes also impose criminal liability on accountants. The most notable of these statutes is the general mail fraud statute, which prohibits the use of the mails to commit fraud. To be held liable, an accountant must know or foresee that the mails will be used to transmit materials containing fraudulent statements provided by her.

In addition, the general false-statement-to-government-personnel statute prohibits fraudulent statements to government personnel. The false-statement-to-bank statute proscribes fraudulent statements on a loan application to a bank or other financial institution.

RICO   The Racketeer Influenced and Corrupt Organizations Act (RICO) makes it a federal crime to engage in a pattern of racketeering activity. Although RICO was designed to attack the activities of organized crime enterprises, it applies to accountants who conduct or participate in the affairs of an enterprise in almost any pattern of business fraud. A pattern of fraud is proved by the commission of two predicate offenses within a 10-year period. Predicate offenses include securities law violations, mail fraud, and bribery. Individuals convicted of a RICO violation may be fined up to $25,000 and imprisoned up to 20 years.

A person who is injured in his business or property by reason of an accountant's conduct or participation, directly or indirectly, in an enterprise's affairs through a pattern of racketeering activity may recover treble damages (three times his actual damages) from the accountant. In *Reves v. Ernst & Young*,[2] the Supreme Court held that merely by auditing financial statements that substantially overvalued a client's assets, an accounting firm was not conducting or participating in the affairs of the client's business. The Court held that the accounting firm must participate in the "operation or management" of the enterprise itself to be liable under RICO.

Injunctions

Adminstrative agencies such as the SEC and the Internal Revenue Service may bring injunctive actions against an accountant in a federal district court. The purpose of such an injunction is to prevent an accountant from committing a future violation of the securities or tax laws.

After an injunction has been issued by a court, violating the injunction may result in serious sanctions. Not only may penalties be imposed for contempt, but a criminal violation may also be more easily proven.

[2]113 S. Ct. 1163 (1993).

Administrative Proceedings

The SEC has the authority to bring administrative proceedings against persons who violate the provisions of the federal securities acts. In recent years, the SEC has stepped up enforcement of SEC Rule of Practice 2(e). Rule 2(e) permits the SEC to bar temporarily or permanently from practicing before the SEC an accountant who has demonstrated a lack of the qualifications required to practice before it, such as an accountant who has prepared financial statements not complying with GAAP. Rule 2(e) also permits the SEC to take action against an accountant who has willfully violated or aided and abetted another's violation of the securities acts. An SEC administrative law judge hears the case and makes an initial determination. The SEC commissioners then issue a final order, which may be appealed to a federal court of appeals.

Rule 2(e) administrative proceedings can impose severe penalties on an accountant. By suspending an accountant from practicing before it, the SEC may take away a substantial part of an accountant's practice. Also, the SEC may impose civil penalties up to $500,000.

In addition, state licensing boards may suspend or revoke an accountant's license to practice if she engages in illegal or unethical conduct. If such action is taken, an accountant may lose her entire ability to practice accounting.

OWNERSHIP OF WORKING PAPERS

The personal records that a client entrusts to an accountant remain the property of the client. An accountant must return these records to his client. Nonetheless, the working papers produced by independent auditors belong to the accountant, not the client.

Working papers are the records made during an audit. They include such items as work programs or plans for the audit, evidence of the testing of accounts, explanations of the handling of unusual matters, data reconciling the accountant's report with the client's records, and comments about the client's internal controls. The client has a right of access to the working papers. The accountant must obtain the client's permission before the working papers can be transferred to another accountant.

ACCOUNTANT–CLIENT PRIVILEGE

An accountant-client privilege of confidentiality protects many of the communications between accountants and their clients from the prying eyes of courts and other government agencies. In addition, it protects an accountant's working papers from the discovery procedures available in a lawsuit.

Although the common law does not recognize an accountant-client privilege, a large number of states have granted such a privilege by statute. The provisions of the statutes vary, but usually the privilege belongs to the client, and an accountant may not refuse to disclose the privileged material in a courtroom if the client consents to its disclosure.

Generally, the state-granted privileges are recognized in both state and federal courts deciding questions of state law. Nonetheless, federal courts do not recognize the privilege in matters involving federal questions, including antitrust and criminal matters.

In federal tax matters, for example, no privilege of confidentiality is recognized on the grounds that an accountant has a duty as a public watchdog to ensure that his client correctly reports his income tax liability. Consequently, an accountant can be required to bring his working papers into court and to testify as to matters involving the client's tax records and discussions with the client regarding tax matters. In addition, an accountant may be required by subpoena to make available his working papers involving a client who is being investigated by the IRS or who has been charged with tax irregularities. The same holds true for SEC investigations.

In the next case, the court held that Pennsylvania's accountant-client privilege did not cover a business appraisal or the communications concerning the appraisal.

GATEWOOD V. U.S. CELLULAR CORP.

124 F.R.D. 504 (D.D.C. 1989)

Robert Gatewood and two other limited partners entered a limited partnership agreement with United States Cellular Corporation (USCC), the sole general partner. The agreement provided that in the event the partners were unable to agree on the value of a cellular phone system in which they had an interest, each would select an appraiser, and the two appraisers would select a third. An impasse arose concerning the selection of this third appraiser, and a federal district court was asked to resolve the dispute.

During litigation, USCC took the deposition of Terry Korn, a Pennsylvania certified public accountant and appraiser selected by the limited partners. USCC sought to inquire about the conduct and results of Korn's appraisal as well as any communications between Korn and the limited partners. The limited partners directed Korn not to respond to any of these questions, asserting that the communications were covered by the Pennsylvania statutory accountant-client privilege.

Attridge, Magistrate   The Pennsylvania accountant-client privilege protects from disclosure ". . . information of which he may have come possessed relative to and in connection with any professional services as a certified public accountant, (or) public accountant. . . ." This statute being in derogation of common law is to be strictly construed. Thus, in order for the statute to be at least prima facially applicable, there must be a showing that an accountant's services were sought in an accounting capacity. In these proceedings, there is nothing to show that Korn was acting in his capacity as an accountant in making his appraisal. Appraisals may be rendered by experts with varying backgrounds who may be otherwise qualified. The appraisal process is not unique to the accounting field. Moreover, the records used to evaluate the financial value of the cellular phone system were not private documents of the limited partners, but rather, records of the system to be evaluated. The purpose of the statute, to foster the free flow of financial data to an accountant by a client in order to obtain financial advice, would not be advanced nor promoted by applying the statute to the events that took place in these proceedings.

The appraisal performed by Korn was not an accounting function and the communications he had with the limited partners were not communications protected by the accountant-client privilege. The fact that Korn is an accountant is merely an accidental circumstance rather than a controlling event.

Judgment for United States Cellular Corporation.

ETHICAL AND PUBLIC POLICY CONCERNS

1. Is it enough that an accountant acts in accordance with the standards of the accounting profession? What risk arises if society entrusts the accounting profession with regulating itself? How great is the risk? Can clients collectively or individually reduce this risk? Is it fair that some clients cannot protect themselves from this risk and yet may have no legal recourse?

2. Should accountants have liability for negligence to persons who are not their clients? What are the social and economic costs of making accountants liable to all users of their work product? What are the social and economic costs of relieving accountants from liability to persons who are not their clients? Is it fair to allow an accountant to be negligent and not have liability to those who relied on the accountant's work product?

3. Should an accountant-client privilege exist? What are the social benefits and costs? In the tax context, why should an accountant be burdened with the public watchdog function when lawyers are not; that is, why must accountants ensure that their clients comply with the tax laws, when a lawyer is permitted to serve the best interests of his client? When a tax accountant is working for a client who also has a lawyer, how can the accountant's work product become privileged? Does the answer to that question suggest a logical or ethical inconsistency in the law?

PROBLEMS AND PROBLEM CASES

1. The 1136 Tenants' Corporation, a cooperative apartment house, hired Max Rothenberg & Co., a firm of certified public accountants, to perform accounting services for it. Rothenberg discovered that several invoices were missing from the financial records of the apartment house. These invoices were needed to prove that payments of $44,000 had been made to creditors of the apartment house and were not embezzled by someone with authority to make payments for the apartment house. Rothenberg noted the missing invoices on his worksheet, but failed to notify the apartment house that there were missing invoices. In fact, there were no invoices. Jerome Riker, the apartment house manager, had embezzled the $44,000 from the apartment house by ordering it to make unauthorized payments to him. Riker embezzled more money after the audit was completed. Is Rothenberg liable to its client for failing to inform it of Riker's embezzlement?

2. O'Connor, Brooks & Co., an accounting firm, negligently failed to discover embezzlements by an officer of its client, American Trust & Savings Bank. O'Connor, Brooks claimed that certain bank directors breached their duty of care to the bank, thereby permitting the embezzlement to occur. Does O'Connor, Brooks have a defense to liability?

3. From 1983 to 1985, Baumann-Furrie & Co. provided accounting services to Halla Nursery, Inc. During this time, Halla's bookkeeper embezzled $135,000. In 1986, Halla sued Baumann-Furrie alleging it negligently failed to detect the embezzlement. Baumann-Furrie claimed that Halla negligently failed to put in place internal financial controls to protect the company from embezzlement. The jury found Halla 80 percent at fault and Baumann-Furrie 20 percent at fault. Is Baumann-Furrie nonetheless liable to Halla?

4. *Video Case.* See "Cafeteria Conversation." Steve has authority to write checks on the account of his employer, a public company under the Securities Exchange Act of 1934. Because Steve is a compulsive gambler and substance abuser, he needs a constant supply of cash to finance his habits.

Steve regularly issues checks payable to actual suppliers not currently owed money, steals the checks, signs the names of the payees, and cashes the checks. Because Steve is also in charge of reconciling his employer's bank statements, his embezzlement scheme is not discovered by the employer's independent auditor during a routine audit. Is the independent auditor liable to its client for damages resulting from Steve's embezzlement?

5. When Robert Hicks offered to sell his shares in Intermountain Merchandising, Inc. (IMI), to Montana Merchandising (MM), IMI hired Alan Bloomgren, a CPA, to audit IMI. Based on Bloomgren's clean opinion on IMI's balance sheet, MM purchased Hicks's shares, advanced funds to IMI, and signed financial guaranties for IMI. Bloomgren knew that MM would rely on the audit and that the audit would be used to aid MM in buying out IMI, including making loans and guaranties. Bloomgren's audit was materially defective, failing to represent that IMI had a negative net worth. MM sued Bloomgren for negligence. Is Bloomgren liable to MM?

6. Max Mitchell & Co., a public accounting firm, performed an audit of the financial statements of C.M. Systems, Inc. At the time Mitchell performed the audit, it was not known that the audited financial statements would be used to obtain a loan from First Florida Bank. However, subsequent to preparing the audited financial statements, Mitchell negotiated a loan with First Florida Bank on behalf of C.M. and personally delivered the financial statements to the bank. Relying on the financial statements, First Florida loaned $500,000 to C.M. After C.M. defaulted on the loan, First Florida discovered that the financial statements materially understated C.M.'s liabilities and materially overstated its assets and net income. Is Mitchell liable to First Florida under the theory of negligence?

7. For the years 1973 to 1976, Timm, Schmidt & Co., an accounting firm, prepared financial statements for Clintonville Fire Apparatus, Inc. (CFA). For every year except 1973, Timm sent an opinion letter to CFA stating that the financial statements fairly presented the financial condition of CFA and that the statements were prepared in accordance with generally accepted accounting principles. In November 1975, CFA obtained a $300,000 loan from Citizens State Bank. Citizens made the loan to CFA after reviewing the financial statements that

Timm had prepared. Citizens made additional loans to CFA in 1976. By the end of 1976, CFA owed Citizens $380,000. In early 1977, Timm employees discovered that the 1974 and 1975 financial statements contained a number of material errors totaling over $400,000. When Timm informed Citizens of the errors, Citizens called all of CFA's loans due. As a result, CFA was liquidated. CFA's assets were insufficient to pay the loans from Citizens. Citizens sued Timm, seeking to recover $152,000, the amount due on its loans to CFA. If Timm failed to comply with generally accepted auditing standards (GAAS) when it first audited the 1974 and 1975 financial statements, is Timm liable to Citizens for negligence?

8. To aid its decision whether to purchase all the shares of Gillespie Furniture Company, DMI Furniture, Inc., hired Arthur Young & Co. to review an audit of Gillespie's financial statements that had been performed by Brown, Kraft & Company. Arthur Young wrote a letter stating that Brown, Kraft had "performed a quality audit." Based on this letter, DMI decided to buy all of Gillespie's shares. When Gillespie became less profitable than DMI expected, DMI sued Arthur Young under Securities Exchange Act Rule 10b-5. DMI alleged that Arthur Young acted recklessly in failing to detect and to disclose that Brown, Kraft's audit report was inaccurate and misleading because it grossly overstated inventory and showed a profit when there was a loss. Do DMI's allegations establish that Arthur Young has violated Rule 10b-5?

9. In early 1984, Arthur Andersen & Co. advised Financial Corporation of America (FCA) that FCA could account for Government National Mortgage Association (Ginny Mae) repurchase transactions as it accounted for financing transactions, thereby recording the purchase liability without recognizing any loss or gain. Following this advice, FCA bought $2 billion of Ginny Maes and resold them to the original holders subject to reverse repurchase agreements. In mid-1984, the Securities and Exchange Commission announced that repurchase transactions must be accounted for as forward commitments with profits or losses recognized as they accrue. As a result, FCA was obliged to report a net loss of $107 million for the quarter ended June 30, 1984, resulting in a drop in the price of FCA's shares. FCA alleged that it would not have purchased the Ginny Maes had not Arthur Andersen knowingly or recklessly disregarded the fact that accounting for the repurchases as financing transactions was wholly inappropriate. Do FCA's allegations establish a Rule 10b-5 violation?

10. John Schulzetenberg was the engagement partner for Touche Ross & Co.'s audit of the financial statements of Inter-Regional Financial Group, Inc. (IRF). The audited financial statements were filed with the Securities and Exchange Commission. From 1981 through 1983, IRF's management misrepresented the delinquency status of its receivables, which accounted for more than 90 percent of its assets. Schulzetenberg's 1981 audit of the receivables was insufficiently planned, supervised, and executed, and did not meet the requirements of GAAS. As a result, he failed to detect that IRF's allowance for uncollectible receivables was materially understated. In 1982, Schulzetenberg failed to correct the 1981 errors, even though it should have been clear to him that the 1981 allowance was materially understated. Is Schulzetenberg subject to penalties under SEC Rule of Practice 2(e)?

11. Bill Thomas, a CPA, was a member of Lawhon, Thomas, Holmes & Co. (LTH), a public accounting firm. When LTH performed accounting services for Xenerex Corp., LTH received 144,000 Xenerex shares instead of cash. LTH continued to hold the Xenerex shares when the three LTH members joined the accounting firm of Oppenheim, Appel, Dixon & Co. (OAD). LTH ceased operations and sold all its assets except the Xenerex shares to OAD. The three former LTH members, including Thomas, retained ownership of LTH. After he joined OAD, Thomas immediately solicited Xenerex as a client for OAD. Thomas, on behalf of OAD, signed a new client acceptance form for Xenerex, giving a negative response to the question, "Are there any known independence problems?" Thomas prepared and signed OAD's report on Xenerex's financial statements and annual report filed on Form 10-K with the SEC. Has Thomas violated SEC Rule of Practice 2(e)?

12. While performing a routine audit of the tax returns of Amerada Hess Corporation, the Internal Revenue Service discovered questionable payments of $7,830. The IRS issued a summons to Arthur Young & Co., the accounting firm that had prepared the tax accrual working papers that might reveal the nature of the payments. The working papers had been prepared in the process of Arthur Young's review of Amerada Hess's financial statements, as required by federal securities law. In the summons, the IRS ordered Arthur Young to make available to the IRS all of its Amerada Hess files, including its tax accrual working papers. Amerada Hess directed Arthur Young not to comply with the summons on the grounds that they were protected by an accountant-client privilege. Is Amerada Hess correct?

CHAPTER

46

ADMINISTRATIVE

AGENCIES

INTRODUCTION

Today's businesses operate in a highly regulated environment. The **administrative agency** *serves as the fundamental vehicle for the creation and enforcement of modern regulation. As governmental bodies that are neither courts nor legislatures, administrative agencies have the legal power to take actions affecting the rights of private individuals and organizations. Supreme Court Justice Robert H. Jackson characterized the sweeping influence of administrative agencies this way:*

The rise of administrative bodies probably has been the most significant legal trend of the last century and perhaps more values today are affected by their decisions than by those of all of the courts, review of administrative decisions apart. They also have begun to have important consequences on personal rights. . . . They have become a veritable fourth branch of the Government, which has deranged our three-branch legal theories as much as the concept of a fourth dimension unsettles our three-dimensional thinking.[1]

    This chapter focuses on federal administrative agencies. It is important to remember, however, that the great growth in federal *regulation during this century has been accompanied by a comparable growth in* state *and* local *regulation by agencies at those levels of government.*

    It is difficult to think of an area of modern individual life that is not somehow touched by the action of administrative agencies. The energy that heats and lights your home and workplace, the clothes you wear, the food you eat, the medicines you take, the design of the car you drive, the programs you watch on television, and the contents of (and label on) the pillow on which you lay your head at night are all shaped in some way by regulation. If anything, this observation is even more appropriate to corporations than to individuals. Virtually every significant aspect of contemporary corporate operations is regulated to the point that the legal *consequences of a corporation's actions are nearly as important to its future success as the* business *consequences of its decisions.*

    Because administrative agencies have enormous power and some novel characteristics, they have always been objects of controversy. Are they protectors of the public or impediments to business effi-

---

[1]*FTC v. Ruberoid Co.*, 343 U.S. 470 (U.S. Sup. Ct. 1952).

ciency? Are they guardians of competitive market structures or a shield behind which noncompetitive firms have sought refuge from more vigorous competitors? Have they been impartial, efficient agents of the public interest or are they more often overzealous, or inept, or "captives" of the industries they supposedly regulate? At various times, and where various agencies are concerned, each of the above allegations has probably been true. Why, then, did we resort to such controversial entities to perform the regulatory function?

Origins of Administrative Agencies

In the latter decades of the 19th century, the United States was in the midst of a dramatic transformation from an agrarian nation to a major industrial power. Improved means of transportation and communication facilitated a dramatic market expansion. Large business organizations acquired unheard of economic power, and new technologies promised additional social transformations.

The tremendous growth that resulted from these developments, however, was not attained without some cost. Large organizations sometimes abused their power at the expense of their customers, distributors, and competitors. New technologies often posed risks of harm to large numbers of citizens. Yet traditional institutions of legal control, such as courts and legislatures, were not particularly well suited to the regulatory needs of an increasingly complex, interdependent society in the throes of rapid change.

Courts, after all, are passive institutions that must await a genuine case or controversy before they can act. Courts may also lack the technical expertise necessary to address many regulatory issues intelligently. In addition, they are constrained by the formalistic rules of procedure and evidence that make litigation a time-consuming and expensive process.

Legislatures, on the other hand, are theoretically able to anticipate social problems and to act in a comprehensive fashion to minimize or avoid social harm. In reality, however, legislatures rarely act until a problem has become severe enough to generate strong political support for a regulatory solution. Legislatures may also lack (as do courts) the expertise necessary to make rational policy regarding highly technical activities.

What was needed, therefore, appeared to be a new type of governmental entity: one that would be exclusively devoted to monitoring a particular area of activity; one that could, by its exclusive focus and specialized hiring practices, develop a reservoir of expertise about the object of its efforts; and one that could provide the continuous attention and constant policy development demanded by a rapidly changing environment. Such new entities, it was thought, could best perform their regulatory tasks if they were given considerable latitude in the procedures they followed and the approaches they took to achieve regulatory goals.

In 1887, the modern regulatory era was born when Congress, in response to complaints about discriminatory ratemaking practices by railroads, passed the Interstate Commerce Act. This statute created the Interstate Commerce Commission and gave it the power to regulate transportation industry ratemaking practices. Thereafter, new administrative agencies have been added whenever *pressing social problems* (such as the threat to competition that led to the creation of the Federal Trade Commission) or *new technologies*, such as aviation (Federal Aviation Administration), communications (Federal Communications Commission), and nuclear power (Nuclear Regulatory Commission), have generated a political consensus in favor of regulation. More recently, developing scientific knowledge about the *dangers that modern technologies and industrial processes pose* to the environment and to industrial workers has led to the creation of new federal agencies empowered to regulate environmental pollution (Environmental Protection Agency) and promote workplace safety (Occupational Safety and Health Administration). The following sections of this chapter examine the legal dimensions of the process by which such administrative agencies are created.

Agency Creation

Enabling Legislation

Administrative agencies are statutorily created when Congress passes **enabling legislation** specifying the name, composition, and powers of the agency. For example, consider the following language from Section 1 of the Federal Trade Commission Act:

A commission is created and established, to be known as the Federal Trade Commission, which shall be composed of five commissioners, who shall be appointed by the President, by and with the advice and consent of the Senate.

This section creates the Federal Trade Commission (FTC). Section 5 of the FTC Act prohibits "unfair methods of competition" and "unfair or deceptive acts or practices in commerce" and empowers the FTC to prevent such practices.[2] Section 5 also describes the procedures the Commission must follow to charge persons or organizations with violations of the act, and provides for judicial review of agency orders. Subsequent portions of the statute give the FTC the power "to make rules and regulations for the purpose of carrying out the provisions of the Act," to conduct investigations of business practices, to require reports from interstate corporations concerning their practices and operations, to investigate possible violations of the antitrust laws,[3] to publish reports concerning its findings and activities, and to recommend new legislation to Congress.

Thus, Congress has given the FTC powers typically associated with the three traditional branches of government. The FTC may, for instance, act in a legislative fashion by *promulgating rules* that have binding legal effect on future behavior. It may also take the executive branch-like actions of *investigating* and *prosecuting* alleged violations. Finally, the FTC may act much as courts do and *adjudicate* disputes concerning alleged violations of the law. Most other federal administrative agencies have a similarly broad mix of governmental powers, making these agencies potentially powerful agents of social control.

But great power to do good can also be great power to do evil. Regulatory bias, zeal, insensitivity, or corruption, if left unchecked, can infringe on the basic freedoms that are the essence of our system of government. Accordingly, the fundamental problem in administrative law, a problem that will surface repeatedly throughout this chapter, is how to design a system of control over agency

action that minimizes the potential for arbitrariness and harm yet preserves the power and flexibility that make administrative agencies uniquely valuable instruments of public policy.

Administrative Agencies and the Constitution

Because administrative agencies are governmental bodies, administrative action is *governmental action* and, as such, is subject to the basic constitutional checks discussed in Chapter 3. As the *Mallen* case, which follows shortly, demonstrates, this "fourth branch of government" is bound by basic constitutional guaranties such as *due process, equal protection,* and *freedom of speech*, just as the three traditional branches are. However, one basic constitutional principle is uniquely important when the creation of administrative agencies is at issue—the principle of **separation of powers**.

One of the fundamental attributes of our Constitution is its allocation of governmental power among the three branches of government. Lawmaking power is given to the legislative branch, law enforcing power to the executive branch, and law interpreting power to the judicial branch. By limiting the powers of each branch, and by giving each branch some checks on the exercise of power by the other branches, the Constitution seeks to ensure that governmental power remains accountable to the public will. (In reality, of course, this separation is never perfectly complete. As you learned in Chapter 1, for instance, courts often "make" law when developing common law doctrines or interpreting broadly worded statutes.)

Administrative agencies, exercising powers resembling those of each of the three branches of government, create obvious concerns about separation of powers. In particular, the congressional delegation of legislative power to an agency in its enabling legislation may be challenged as violating the separation of powers principle if such legislation is so broadly worded as to indicate that Congress has abdicated its lawmaking responsibilities. Early judicial decisions exploring the manner in which Congress could delegate its power tended to require enabling legislation to contain fairly specific guidelines and standards limiting the exercise of agency discretion.

---

[2]Section 5 of the FTC Act is discussed in detail in Chapter 47.

[3]The antitrust laws are discussed in detail in Chapters 48 and 49.

More recently, the courts have tended to sustain quite broad delegations of power to administrative agencies. For example, Section 5 of the FTC Act is a broad delegation of power. A great range of unspecified behavior falls within the statute's prohibition of "unfair methods of competition" and "unfair or deceptive acts or practices." Courts tend to approve broad delegations of power when Congress has expressed an "intelligible principle" to guide the agency's actions.[4]

---

[4]*J. W. Hampton, Jr. & Co. v. United States*, 276 U.S. 394 (U.S. Sup. Ct. 1928).

FEDERAL DEPOSIT INSURANCE CORP. v. MALLEN
486 U.S. 230 (U.S. Sup. Ct. 1988)

On December 10, 1986, James Mallen was indicted by a federal grand jury in Iowa for making false statements to the Federal Deposit Insurance Corporation (FDIC) and for making false statements to Farmers State Bank for the purpose of influencing the actions of the FDIC. At the time of the indictment, Mallen was the president and a director of a federally insured bank. On January 20, 1987, the FDIC issued an *ex parte* order finding that Mallen's continued service might "pose a threat to the interests of the bank's depositors or threaten to impair public confidence in the bank," suspending him as president and as a director of the bank and prohibiting him "from further participation in any manner in the conduct of the affairs of the Bank, or any other bank insured by the FDIC."

In issuing the suspension order without first holding a hearing on the matter, the FDIC was acting pursuant to a section of the Financial Institutions Supervisory Act of 1966 [12 U.S.C. section 1818(g)]. A copy of the order was served on Mallen on January 26, 1987, and four days later Mallen's attorney filed a written request for an "immediate administrative hearing" to commence no later than February 9, 1987. The FDIC set a hearing date for February 18, 1987, but on February 6, 1987, Mallen filed suit against the FDIC in the Federal District Court for the Northern District of Iowa. When the District Court ruled in Mallen's favor, entering a preliminary injunction against the suspension order, the FDIC appealed.

Stevens, Justice   The District Court expressed no opinion on the merits of the suspension; its decision rested entirely on the perceived procedural shortcomings in the post-suspension process. It is undisputed that Mallen's interest in the right to continue to serve as president of the bank and to participate in the conduct of its affairs is a property right protected by the Fifth Amendment Due Process Clause. The FDIC cannot arbitrarily interfere with Mallen's employment relationship with the bank, nor with his interest as a substantial stockholder in the bank's holding company. It is also undisputed that the FDIC's order affected a deprivation of this property interest.

Once it is determined that due process applies, the question remains what process is due. Mallen does not contend that he was entitled to an opportunity to be heard prior to the order of suspension. An important governmental interest, accompanied by a substantial assurance that the deprivation is not baseless or unwarranted, may in limited cases demanding prompt action justify postponing the opportunity to be heard until after the initial deprivation. In this case, the postponement of the hearing is supported by such an interest. The legislation under scrutiny is premised on the congressional finding that prompt suspension of indicted bank officers may be necessary to protect the interests of depositors and to maintain public confidence in our banking institutions.

Moreover, Mallen's suspension was supported by findings that assure that the suspension was not baseless. A grand jury had determined that there was probable cause to believe that he had committed a felony. Such an *ex parte* finding of probable cause provides sufficient basis for an arrest, which of course constitutes a temporary deprivation of liberty. It should certainly be sufficient to support the order entered in this case even though the FDIC did not provide Mallen with a separate pre-suspension hearing.

We cannot agree with the District Court that Mallen was denied a sufficiently prompt post-deprivation hearing. The District Court was properly concerned about the importance of providing prompt post-deprivation procedures in situations in which an agency's discretionary impairment of an individual's property is not preceded by an opportunity for a pre-deprivation hearing. However, the District Court seems to have been improperly concerned with the danger of an interminable delay by the agency, rather than by what would have happened in this case if the proceedings had not been interrupted, or indeed, if the FDIC had been as dilatory as the statute permits. For even though there is a point at which an unjustified delay in completing a post-deprivation proceeding would become a constitutional violation, the significance of such a delay cannot be evaluated in a vacuum.

Section 1818(g)(3) requires the FDIC to hold a hearing within 30 days of a written request for an opportunity to appear before the agency to contest a suspension and requires that it notify the suspended officer of its decision within 60 days of the hearing. Thus, at a maximum, the suspended officer receives a decision within 90 days of his or her request for a hearing. In this case, the agency reported that it would have been able to issue a written decision within 30 days after the hearing. In addition, the initial hearing was scheduled to take place 19 days after it was formally requested.

Mallen's interest in continued employment is without doubt an important interest that ought not be interrupted without substantial justification. Yet, even assuming that the FDIC required the complete 90 days to hear the case and reach its decision, we are not persuaded that this exceeds permissible limits. In fact, a suspended bank officer has an interest in seeing that a decision concerning his or her continued suspension is not made with excessive haste. The statute imposes a permissive stan-dard for continuing a suspension, and presumably, when in doubt, the agency may give greater weight to the public interest and leave the suspension in place, particularly when the suspension does not impose the additional harm of a significant, incremental injury to reputation. Through the return of an indictment, the Government has already accused Mallen of serious wrongdoing. The incidental suspension is not likely to augment this injury to his reputation. We thus conclude that the 90 day period is not so long that it will always violate due process.

In many cases, perhaps most, it will be justified by an important government interest coupled with factors minimizing the risk of an erroneous deprivation. The magnitude of the public interest in a correct decision counsels strongly against any constitutional imperative that might require overly hasty decisionmaking. Congress has determined that the integrity of the banking industry requires that indicted bank officers be suspended until it is determined that they do not pose a threat to the interests of the bank's depositors or threaten to undermine public confidence in the bank. To return these officers to a position of influence in the conduct of the bank's affairs prior to an opportunity to weigh the evidence carefully would threaten these interests in the same way as allowing them to remain in office from the start.

Moreover, there is little likelihood that the deprivation is without basis. The returning of the indictment establishes that an independent body has determined that there is probable cause to believe that the officer has committed a crime. This finding is relevant in at least two important ways. First, the finding of probable cause by an independent body demonstrates that the suspension is not arbitrary. Second, the indictment itself is an objective fact that will in most cases raise serious public concern that the bank is not being managed in a responsible manner.

The post-suspension procedure authorized by section 1818(g)(3) is not unconstitutional on its face; nor do we find any unfairness in the FDIC's use of that procedure in this case.

District Court preliminary injunction reversed.

AGENCY TYPES AND ORGANIZATION

Agency Types

Administrative agencies may be found under a variety of labels. They may be called "administration," "agency," "authority," "board," "bureau," "commission," "department," "division," or "service." They sometimes have a governing body, which may be appointed or elected. They almost invariably have an administrative head (variously called "Chairman," "Commissioner," "Director," etc.), and a staff. Since our focus is on federal administrative agencies, it is important for us to distinguish between the two basic types of federal administrative agencies: executive agencies and independent agencies.

Executive Agencies   Administrative agencies that reside within the Executive Office of the President or within the executive departments of the president's cabinet are called **executive agencies**. Examples of such executive agencies and their cabinet homes are: the Food and Drug Administration (Department of Health and Human Services); the Nuclear Regulatory Agency and the Federal Energy Regulatory Agency (Department of Energy); the Occupational Safety and Health Administration (Department of Labor); and the Internal Revenue Service (Treasury Department). In addition to their executive home, such agencies share one other important attribute. Their administrative heads serve "at the pleasure of the President"—they are appointed and removable at his will.

Independent Agencies   The Interstate Commerce Commission was the first independent administrative agency created by Congress. Much of the most significant regulation businesses face emanates from independent agencies such as the FTC, the National Labor Relations Board, the Consumer Product Safety Commission, the Equal Employment Opportunity Commission, the Environmental Protection Agency, and the Securities and Exchange Commission. Independent agencies are usually headed by a board or a commission (e.g., the FTC has five commissioners) whose members are appointed by the president "with the advice and consent of the Senate." Commissioners or board members are usually appointed for fixed terms (e.g., FTC commissioners serve seven-year, staggered terms) and are removable only for cause (e.g., FTC commissioners may be removed only for "inefficiency, neglect of duty, or malfeasance in office"). Finally, it is quite common for enabling legislation to require political balance in agency appointments (e.g., the FTC Act provides that "[n]ot more than three of the commissioners shall be members of the same political party").

Agency Organization

As the organizational chart of the FTC reproduced in Figure 1 indicates, an agency's organizational structure is largely a function of its regulatory mission. Thus, the operational side of the FTC is divided into three bureaus: the Bureau of Competition, which enforces the antitrust laws and unfair competitive practices; the Bureau of Consumer Protection, which focuses on unfair or deceptive trade practices; and the Bureau of Economics, which gathers data, compiles statistics, and furnishes technical assistance to the other bureaus. The Commission is headquartered in Washington, D.C., but it also maintains regional offices in Atlanta, Boston, Chicago, Cleveland, Dallas, Denver, Los Angeles, New York, San Francisco, and Seattle. This regional office system enhances the Commission's enforcement, investigative, and educational missions by locating Commission staff closer to the public it serves.

AGENCY POWERS AND PROCEDURES

Nature, Types, and Source of Powers

The powers administrative agencies possess may be classified in a variety of ways. Some agencies' powers are largely *ministerial* in nature, concerned primarily with the routine performance of duties imposed by law. The most important administrative agencies, however, have broad *discretionary* powers that necessitate the exercise of significant discretion and judgment when they are employed. The most important formal discretionary powers agencies can possess are **investigative power, rulemaking power,** and **adjudicatory power.**

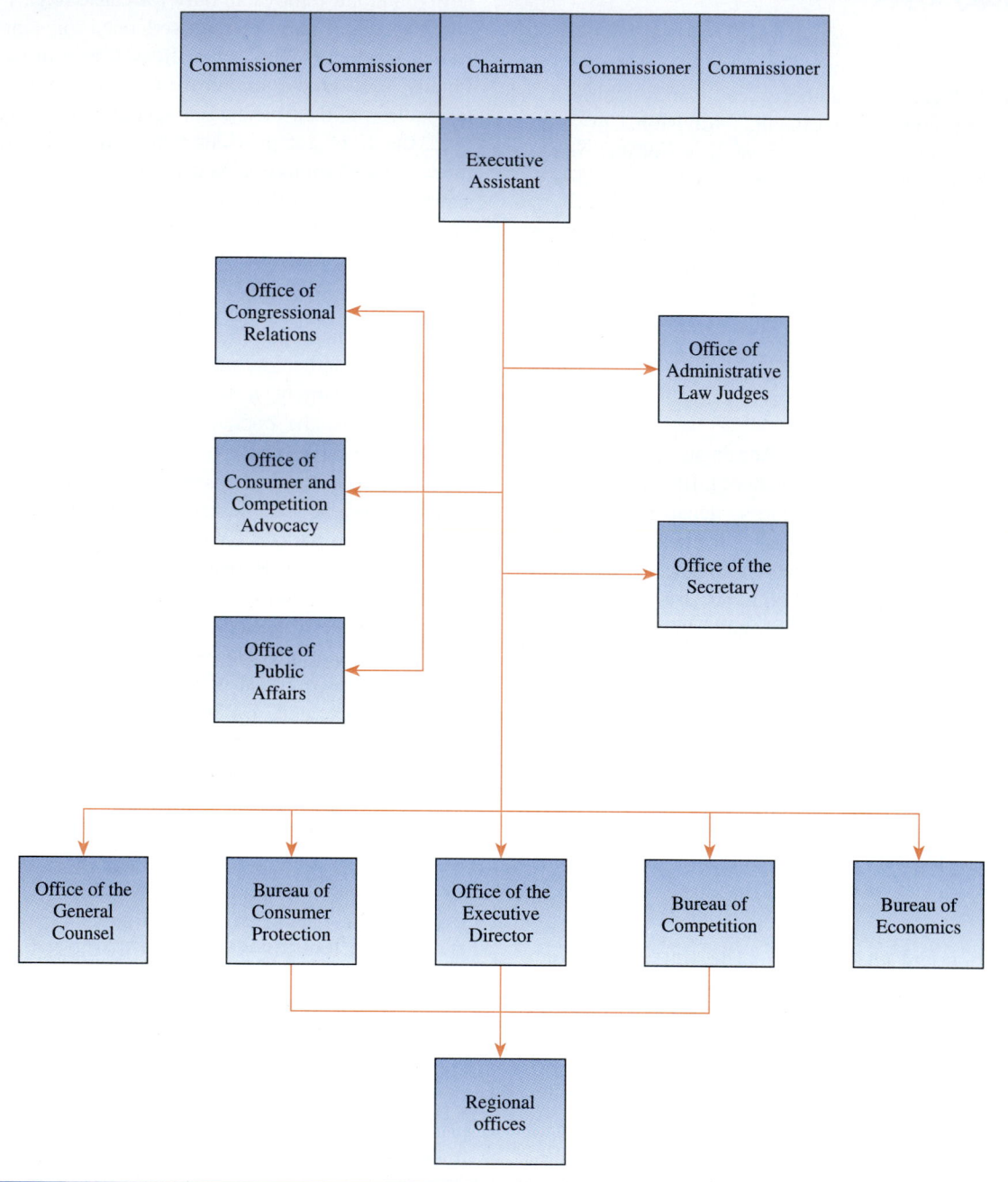

FIGURE 1 **Federal Trade Commission**

Source: *U.S. Government Manual 1989–90* (Washington, D.C.: U.S. Government Printing Office, 1989), p. 603.

The formal powers an agency possesses are those granted by its enabling legislation. Important federal agencies such as the FTC normally enjoy significant levels of each of the formal discretionary powers. As the following sections illustrate, however, even such powerful agencies face significant limitations on the exercise of their powers. In addition to explicit limits on agency proceedings contained in enabling legislation, basic constitutional provisions restrict agency action.

A federal agency's exercise of its rulemaking and adjudicatory powers is also constrained by the *Administrative Procedure Act (APA)*. The APA was enacted by Congress in 1946 in an attempt to standardize federal agency procedures and to respond to critics who said that administrative power was out of control. The APA applies to all federal agencies, although it will not displace stricter procedural requirements contained in a particular agency's enabling legislation. In addition to specifying agency procedures, the APA plays a major role in shaping the conditions under which courts will review agency actions and the standards courts will use when conducting such a review. Most states have adopted "baby APAs" to govern the activities of state administrative agencies.

Finally, as later parts of this chapter will confirm, each of the three traditional branches of government possesses substantial powers to mold and constrain the powers of the "fourth branch." That being said, one final point needs to be made before we turn to a detailed examination of formal agency powers and procedures. An agency's formal powers also confer on it significant *informal* power. Agency "advice," "suggestions," or "guidelines," which technically lack the legal force of formal agency regulations or rulings, may nonetheless play a major role in shaping the behavior of regulated industries because they carry with them the implicit or explicit threat of formal agency action in the event that they are ignored. Such gentle persuasion can be a highly effective regulatory tool, and one that is subject to far fewer constraints than formal agency action.

Investigative Power

Effective regulation is impossible without accurate information. Administrative agencies need information about business practices and activities not only so that they can detect and prosecute regulatory violations, but also to enable them to identify areas in which new rules are needed or existing rules require modification. Much of the information agencies require to do their jobs is readily available. "Public interest" groups, complaints from customers or competitors, and other regulatory agencies are all important sources of information.

However, much of the information necessary to effective agency enforcement can come only from sources that may be strongly disinclined to provide it—the individuals and business organizations who are subject to regulation. This reluctance may be due to the desire to avoid or delay the regulation or regulatory action that disclosure would generate. It might also, however, be the product of more legitimate concerns, such as a desire to protect personal privacy, a desire to prevent competitors from acquiring trade secrets and other sensitive information from agency files, or a reluctance to incur the costs that sometimes can accompany compliance with substantial information demands. Agencies, therefore, need the means to compel unwilling possessors of information to comply with legitimate demands for information. The two most important (and most intrusive) investigative tools employed by administrative agencies are *subpoenas* and *searches and seizures*.

Subpoenas   There are two basic types of subpoena: the subpoena *ad testificandum* and the subpoena *duces tecum*. Subpoenas *ad testificandum* may be used by an agency to compel unwilling witnesses to appear and testify at agency hearings. Subpoenas *duces tecum* may be used by an agency to compel the production of most types of documentary evidence, such as accounting records and office memoranda.

It should be obvious that unlimited agency subpoena power would sacrifice individual liberty and privacy in the name of regulatory efficiency. Accordingly, the courts have formulated a number of limitations that seek to balance an agency's legitimate need to know against an investigatory target's legitimate privacy interests.

Agency investigations must be *authorized by law* and *conducted for a legitimate purpose*. The former requirement means that the agency's enabling legislation must have granted the agency the investigatory power it is seeking to assert. The latter requirement prohibits bad faith investigations pursued for improper motives (e.g., Internal Revenue Service investigations undertaken solely to harass political opponents of an incumbent administration).

Even when the investigation is legally authorized and is undertaken for a legitimate purpose, the information sought must be *relevant to that lawful purpose*. The Fourth Amendment to the Constitution is the source of this limitation on agency powers. However, an agency issuing an administrative subpoena need not possess the "probable cause" that the Fourth Amendment requires in support of regular search warrants.[5] In the words of the Supreme Court, an agency "can investigate merely on the suspicion that the law is being violated, or even just because it wants assurance that it is not."[6] This lesser standard makes sense in the agency context, since the only evidence of many regulatory violations is documentary and "probable cause" might be demonstrable only after inspection of the target's records. In such cases, a probable cause requirement would effectively negate agency enforcement power.

Similarly, agency information demands must be *sufficiently specific* and *not unreasonably burdensome*. This requirement also derives from the Fourth Amendment's prohibition against "unreasonable searches and seizures."[7] It means that agency subpoenas must describe adequately the information the agency seeks. It also means that the cost to the target of complying with the agency's demand (e.g., the cost of assembling and reproducing the data, the disruption of business operations, or the risk that proprietary information will be indirectly disclosed

to competitors) must not be unreasonably disproportionate to the agency's interest in obtaining the information.

Finally, the information sought *must not be privileged*. Various statutory and common law privileges can, at times, limit an agency's power to compel the production of information. However, by far the most important privilege in this respect is the Fifth Amendment *privilege against compelled testimonial self-incrimination*, or "the right to silence." As you learned in Chapter 5, however, this privilege is subject to serious limitations in the business context. The right to silence in the administrative context is further limited by the fact that it is only available in *criminal* proceedings. In some regulatory contexts, the potential sanctions for violation may be labeled "civil penalties" or "forfeitures." Only when such sanctions are essentially punitive in their intent or effect will they be considered "criminal" for the purpose of allowing the invocation of the privilege.

Public policy concerns provide another subpoena power limitation that may apply even if neither the Fifth Amendment nor another privilege bars production of the documents sought by an agency. As indicated in the *Collins* case, which follows, courts may conclude that an agency subpoena should not be enforced if its enforcement would tend to compromise important operations being conducted by another agency or arm of the government.

---

[5]The Fourth Amendment's Warrant Clause is discussed in detail in Chapter 5.

[6]*United States v. Morton Salt*, 338 U.S. 632 (U.S. Sup. Ct. 1950).

[7]The Fourth Amendment's guarantee against unreasonable searches and seizures is discussed in detail in Chapter 5.

COMMODITY FUTURES TRADING COMMISSION V. COLLINS
997 F.2d 1230 (7th Cir. 1993)

The Commodity Futures Trading Commission (CFTC) was investigating Thomas Collins for possible civil violations of the Commodity Exchange Act. Among the violations of which Collins was suspected was the trading of commodities futures contracts other than on a commodities exchange. The CFTC's staff suspected that these trades were spurious trades, which (the staff theorized) were intended to enable Collins to reallocate losses to persons who would reap the maximum tax benefits from the losses. As part of this investigation, the CFTC issued a subpoena directing Collins to produce copies of his federal income tax returns for examination by the CFTC's staff. The staff's reasoning was that the presence of tax motives would be evidence of a likely violation of rules enforced by the CFTC.

Collins resisted the subpoena on the ground that it would force him to incriminate himself. Collins argued that the tax returns contained information that could be evidence—or could lead to evidence—of felony violations of federal law. The CFTC argued that the tax returns were required records and that compelling their disclosure therefore would not violate the Fifth Amendment. (See Chapter 5's discussion of the required-records doctrine, which operates to eliminate Fifth Amendment privilege claims regarding the contents of such records.) The district court agreed with the CFTC and entered an enforcement order requiring Collins to obey the subpoena. Collins appealed.

In a portion of its opinion not set forth here, the Seventh Circuit Court of Appeals concluded that the required-records doctrine was inapplicable because the subpoena sought a taxpayer's *copies* of his tax returns—copies that the taxpayer was not required by law to make—rather than the actual tax returns whose preparation and filing with the Internal Revenue Service were required by law. The Seventh Circuit then (as set forth below) continued its analysis of Collins's Fifth Amendment argument and addressed other policy concerns triggered by the CFTC's subpoena.

Posner, Judge   [The inapplicability of the required-records doctrine] does not end our inquiry. The [required-records] doctrine only comes into play if, were it not for the doctrine, the government would be forcing a person to incriminate himself. *Garner v. United States* (1976) holds that the taxpayer who includes incriminating information on his return is like the witness who blurts out incriminating testimony rather than invoking the Fifth Amendment and keeping mum: he has not been compelled to testify against himself, so he has no Fifth Amendment claim. *Garner . . .* is consistent with the cases which hold that there is no Fifth Amendment privilege in already created documents, because the disclosures in them were not compelled. *Garner* and [the cases dealing with already created documents] make the required-records exception to the Fifth Amendment privilege largely, perhaps entirely, superfluous, because records that are not required are by the same token not privileged. And those decisions suggest another reason for doubting that Collins has any Fifth Amendment claim: Collins created copies of his tax returns voluntarily, so any information in the copies, however incriminating, was not compelled by the government.

In light of all this it is doubtful that Collins has any constitutional leg to stand on. No matter. All constitutional concerns to one side, we think it was an abuse of discretion for the district judge to enforce this subpoena. Income tax returns are highly sensitive documents; that is why [federal law provides that agencies such as the CFTC] cannot get Collins's tax returns directly from the Internal Revenue Service. The self-reporting, self-assessing character of the income tax system would be compromised were they promiscuously disclosed to agencies enforcing regulatory programs unrelated to tax collection itself. The CFTC made no showing that it needed Collins's tax returns. All it legitimately wants to know is whether Collins traded off the exchange and if so, why. It can ask him. If it doubts his answer, it can ask for substantiation. If he refuses to furnish it on the ground that it would compel him to incriminate himself, the CFTC can draw the appropriate inference—for example, that he was trading off the exchange in order to reap tax benefits. No law forbids a regulatory agency to draw the logical inference from a regulated entity's refusing on Fifth Amendment grounds to play ball with the agency. Should the government want to prosecute Collins criminally the Fifth Amendment would be a potential bar—but a very feeble one, in light of our previous discussion.

We are not experts in the investigation of violations of the commodity laws, so we may have overlooked reasons why, despite appearances, the effectiveness of the CFTC's investigation of Collins depends on its having access to his tax returns. The CFTC has not advanced any such reasons. It asked for and obtained the enforcement of the subpoena as a matter of rote, upon its bare representation that the tax returns might contain information germane to the investigation. That is not enough, if an appropriate balance is to be struck between the privacy of income tax returns and the needs of law enforcement. [L]arger interests are at stake than those of the immediate parties—namely the interest, unrepresented by . . . the parties to this case (for the CFTC is not represented by the Department of Justice, which might be assumed to be speaking for the Internal Revenue Service as well), in the effective administration of the federal tax laws.

District court order enforcing subpoena reversed in favor of Collins.

Searches and Seizures Sometimes the evidence necessary to prove a regulatory violation can be obtained only by entering private property such as a home, an office, or a factory. When administrative agencies seek to gather information by such an entry, the Fourth Amendment's prohibition against unreasonable searches and seizures and its warrant requirement come into play. As the *Dow Chemical* case in Chapter 5 indicates, the owners of commercial property, although afforded less Fourth Amendment protection than the owners of private dwellings, do have some legitimate expectations of privacy in their business premises.

Not all agency information-gathering efforts, however, will be considered so intrusive as to amount to a prohibited search and seizure. In *Dow Chemical*, for instance, the Environmental Protection Agency's warrantless aerial photography of one of Dow's plants was upheld. Furthermore, in *State of New York v. Burger*,[8] the Supreme Court upheld the constitutionality of warrantless administrative inspections of the premises of "closely regulated" businesses so long as three criteria are satisfied: (1) there must be a substantial government interest in the regulatory scheme in question, (2) the warrantless inspections must be necessary to further the scheme, and (3) the inspection program must provide a constitutionally adequate substitute for a warrant by giving owners of commercial property adequate notice that their property is subject to inspection and by limiting the discretion of inspecting officers.

Rulemaking Power

An agency's rulemaking power derives from its enabling legislation. For example, the FTC Act gives the FTC the power "to make rules and regulations for the purpose of carrying out the provisions of this Act." The Administrative Procedure Act (APA) defines a rule as "an agency statement of general or particular applicability and future effect designed to complement, interpret or prescribe law or policy." All agency rules are compiled and published in the *Code of Federal Regulations*.

Types of Rules Administrative agencies create three types of rules: procedural rules, interpretive rules, and legislative rules.

Procedural rules specify how the agency will conduct itself. For instance, agencies typically have procedural rules dealing with such matters as the manner in which advance notice of agency rulemaking proceedings will be disseminated.

Interpretive rules are designed to advise regulated individuals and entities of the manner in which an agency interprets the statutes it enforces. For example, the FTC has promulgated a rule interpreting the term *consumer product*, as used in the Magnuson-Moss Warranty Act (a statute the FTC has the legal responsibility to enforce).[9] Interpretive rules technically do not have the force of law. Therefore, they are not binding on businesses and the courts. Courts interpreting regulatory statutes often give agency interpretations substantial weight, however, in deference to the agency's familiarity with the statutes it administers and its presumed expertise in the general area being regulated. Business is also likely to pay attention to agency interpretive rules because such rules indicate the circumstances in which an agency is likely to take formal enforcement action.

If consistent with an agency's enabling legislation and the Constitution, and if created in accordance with the procedures dictated by the APA, *legislative rules* have the full force and effect of law. Legislative rules thus are binding on the courts, the public, and the agency. Federal agencies have promulgated very large numbers of legislative rules, many of which address highly specific matters. For example, an FTC legislative rule states that if a party sells a quick-freeze aerosol spray product designed for the frosting of beverage glasses and the product contains an ingredient known as Fluorocarbon 12, the seller must issue a warning (on the product label) that the product should not be inhaled in concentrated form, due to the risk that such behavior may lead to severe harm or death.[10]

Given the greater relative importance of legislative rules, you should not be surprised to learn that the process by which they are promulgated—unlike the process by which procedural and interpretive

---

[8]482 U.S. 691 (U.S. Sup. Ct. 1987).

[9]16 *Code of Federal Regulations* § 700.1 (1990). The Magnuson-Moss Warranty Act and FTC regulations related to it are discussed in Chapters 20 and 47.

[10]16 *Code of Federal Regulations* § 417.6 (1990).

rules are created—is highly regulated by the APA and closely scrutinized by the courts. At present, there are three basic types of agency rulemaking: informal rulemaking, formal rulemaking, and hybrid rulemaking.

Informal Rulemaking

Informal rulemaking (or "notice and comment" rulemaking) is the method most commonly employed by administrative agencies that are not forced by their enabling legislation to follow the more stringent procedures of formal rulemaking. The informal rulemaking process commences with the publication of a *"Notice of Proposed Rulemaking"* in the *Federal Register*. The APA requires that such notices contain: a statement of the time and place at which the proceedings will be held; a statement of the nature of the proceedings; a statement of the legal authority for the proceedings (usually the agency's enabling legislation); and either a statement of the terms of the proposed rule or a description of the subjects or issues to be addressed by the rule.

Publication of notice must then be followed by a *comment period* during which interested parties may submit to the agency written comments detailing their views about the proposed rule. After comments have been received and considered, the agency must publish the regulation in its final form in the *Federal Register*. As a general rule, the rule cannot become effective until at least 30 days after this final publication. The APA, however, recognizes a "good cause" exception to the 30 day waiting period requirement, and to the notice of rulemaking requirement as well, when notice would be impractical, unnecessary, or contrary to the public interest.

Agencies tend to favor the informal rulemaking process because it allows quick and efficient regulatory action. Such quickness and efficiency, however, are purchased at a significant cost—a relatively minimal opportunity for interested parties to participate in the rule-formation process. Giving interested parties the opportunity to be heard may, in some cases, ultimately further regulatory goals. For example, the vigorous debate about a proposed rule that a public hearing can provide may contribute to the creation of more effective rules. Also, providing interested parties with what they perceive to be an adequate opportunity to participate in the rulemaking process lends credibility to that process and the rules it produces, thereby enhancing the chances of voluntary compliance by the regulated industry.

Formal Rulemaking

Formal rulemaking (or "on the record" rulemaking) is designed to give interested parties a far greater opportunity to make their views heard than that afforded by informal rulemaking. As does informal rulemaking, formal rulemaking begins with publication of a *"Notice of Proposed Rulemaking"* in the *Federal Register*. Unlike the notice employed to announce informal rulemaking procedures, however, this notice must include notice of a time and place at which a public hearing concerning the proposed rule will be held. Such hearings resemble trials in that the agency must produce evidence justifying the proposed regulation, and interested parties are likewise allowed to present evidence in opposition to it. Both sides are entitled to examine each other's exhibits and to cross-examine each other's witnesses. At the conclusion of the proceedings, the agency must prepare a formal, written document detailing its findings based on the evidence presented in the hearing.

Although the formal rulemaking process affords interested parties greatly enhanced opportunities to be heard, this greater access is purchased at significant expense and at the risk that some parties will abuse their access rights to impede the regulatory process. By tireless cross-examination of government witnesses and lengthy presentations of their own, opponents seeking to derail or delay regulation may consume months, or even years, of agency time. The classic example of such behavior would be the Food and Drug Administration's hearings on a proposed rule requiring that the minimum peanut content of peanut butter be set at 90 percent. Industry forces favored an 87 percent minimum and were able to delay regulation for almost 10 years.

Hybrid Rulemaking

Frustration over the lack of access afforded by informal rulemaking and the potential for paralyzing the regulatory process that is inherent in formal rulemaking have led some courts and legislators to attempt the creation of a rulemaking process embodying some of the elements of informal and formal procedures. Although hybrid rulemaking procedures are insufficiently established and standardized at this point to permit a detailed discussion of them, some general tendencies are evident. Hybrid procedures bear some resemblance to those of formal rulemaking in that both involve some sort of hearing. Unlike formal rulemaking procedures, however, hybrid procedures tend to limit the right of interested parties to cross-examine agency witnesses.

Adjudicatory Power

Most major federal agencies possess substantial adjudicatory powers. Besides having the authority to investigate alleged behaviors and to produce regulations that have legal effect, they have the power to instigate and conduct proceedings to determine whether regulatory or statutory violations have occurred. The administrative adjudication process is at once similar to, but substantially different from, the judicial process you studied in Chapter 2.

The administrative adjudication process normally begins with a complaint filed by the agency. The party charged in the complaint (called the *respondent*) files an answer. Respondents are normally entitled to a hearing before the agency. At this hearing, they may confront and cross-examine agency witnesses and present evidence of their own. Respondents may be represented by legal counsel. No juries are present in administrative adjudications, however. The cases are heard by an agency employee usually called an **administrative law judge (ALJ)**. Also, unlike criminal prosecutions, the burden of proof in administrative proceedings is normally the civil *preponderance of the evidence* standard. Constitutional procedural safeguards such as the exclusionary rule do not protect the respondent.[11]

The agency, in effect, functions as police officer, prosecutor, judge, and jury. The APA attempts to deal with the obvious potential for abuse inherent in this combination in a number of ways. First, the APA attempts to ensure that ALJs are as independent as possible by requiring internal separation between an agency's judges and its investigative and prosecutorial functions. (Note, for example, the organizational separation of the FTC's Office of Administrative Law Judges, as depicted in Figure 1.) The APA also prohibits ALJs from having private consultations with anyone who is a party to an agency proceeding and shields them from agency disciplinary action other than for "good cause."

---

[11]*INS v. Lopez-Mendoza*, 468 U.S. 1032 (U.S. Sup. Ct. 1984). The exclusionary rule and the beyond a reasonable doubt standard employed in criminal cases are discussed in Chapter 5. The preponderance of the evidence standard is discussed in Chapter 6.

Finally, insufficient separation between an agency's adjudication function and its other functions can be contrary to basic due process requirements.

After each party to the proceeding has been heard, the ALJ renders a decision stating her findings of fact and conclusions of law, and imposing whatever penalty she deems appropriate within the parameters established by the agency's enabling legislation (e.g., a fine or a cease and desist order). If neither party challenges the ALJ's decision, it becomes final. The losing party, however, may appeal an ALJ's decision, in which case it will be subjected to a **de novo review** by the governing body of the agency (e.g., appeals from FTC ALJ decisions are heard by the five FTC commissioners). *De novo review* means that the agency's governing body may treat the proceedings as if they were occurring for the first time and may totally ignore the ALJ's findings. Often, however, the agency's governing body will adopt the ALJ's findings. In any event, those findings will be part of the record if a disappointed respondent seeks judicial review of an agency's decision.

Finally, when considering agency adjudicatory powers it is important to note that many agency proceedings are settled by a **consent order** before completion of the adjudication process. Consent orders are similar to the nolo contendere pleas discussed in Chapter 5. Respondents who sign consent orders do not admit wrongdoing, but they waive all rights to judicial review, agree to accept a specific sanction imposed by the agency, and commonly agree to discontinue the business practice that triggered the agency action.

Figure 2 depicts the major powers of this "fourth branch" of the government.

CONTROLLING ADMINISTRATIVE AGENCIES

By this point in our discussion of administrative agencies, we have already encountered several legal controls on agency action, such as the terms of an agency's enabling legislation, the procedural requirements imposed by the APA, and the basic constraints that the Constitution places on all governmental action. The following sections continue to focus on the important theme of agency control by examining the various devices, both formal and informal, through which the three traditional branches of government influence and control the actions of administrative agencies.

FIGURE 2   **Administrative Agencies and Separation of Powers**

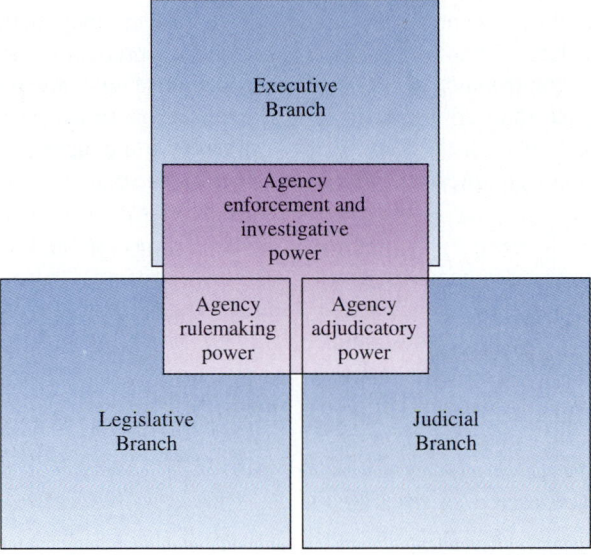

Presidential Controls

The executive branch has at its disposal a number of tools that can be employed to shape agency action. The most obvious among them is the president's power to appoint and remove agency administrators. For example, in Chapters 48 and 49, you will learn that President Reagan's appointees to the Department of Justice and the FTC made major changes in governmental antitrust enforcement policies because of their commitment to "Chicago School" antitrust ideas. This presidential power is obviously more limited in the case of independent agencies than it is where executive agencies are concerned, but the president generally has the power to appoint the heads of independent agencies and demote the prior chairpersons without cause. Skillful use of the new chair's managerial powers, probably the most important of which is the power to influence agency hiring policies, can eventually effect substantial changes in agency policy. Also, significant and sustained policy differences between an independent agency and the executive branch often eventually trigger resignations by agency commissioners, thus providing the president with the opportunity to appoint new members whose philosophies are more congruent with his own.

The executive branch also exercises significant control over agency action through the Office of Management and Budget (OMB). The OMB plays a major role in the creation of the annual executive budget the president presents to Congress. In the process, the OMB reviews, and sometimes modifies, the budgetary requests of executive agencies. In addition, an executive order requires executive agencies to prepare cost-benefit and least-cost analyses for all major proposed rules and to submit this information to the OMB for review prior to seeking public comments. This and a subsequent executive order requiring agencies to give the OMB early warning of possible rule changes have made the OMB a powerful player in the rulemaking process.

Finally, the president's power to *veto* legislation concerning administrative agencies represents another point of executive influence over agency operations.

Congressional Controls

The legislative branch possesses a number of devices, both formal and informal, by which it may influence agency action. Obvious avenues of congressional control include the Senate's "advice and consent" role in agency appointments, the power to amend an agency's enabling legislation (what Congress has given, Congress can take away), and the power to pass legislation that mandates changes in agency practices or procedures. Examples of the latter include the National Environmental Policy Act (NEPA), which dictated that administrative agencies file *environmental impact statements* for every agency action that might significantly affect the quality of the environment, and the Regulatory Flexibility Act of 1980, which ordered changes in agency rulemaking procedures designed to give small businesses improved notice of agency rule-making activities that may have a substantial impact on them. Congress can also pass *sunset legislation* providing for the automatic expiration of an agency's authority unless Congress expressly extends it by a specified date. Such legislation ensures periodic congressional review of the initial decision to delegate legislative authority to an administrative agency.

Congress also enjoys several other less obvious, but no less important, points of influence over agency action. For example, Congress must authorize agency budgetary appropriations. Thus, Congress may limit or deny funding for agency programs with which it disagrees. Also, the Governmental Operations Committees of both houses of Congress exercise significant oversight over agency activities. These committees review agency programs and conduct hearings concerning proposed agency appointments and appropriations. Finally, individual members of Congress may seek to influence agency action through "casework"—informal contacts with an agency on behalf of constituents who are involved with the agency.

Judicial Review

As important as the roles of the executive and legislative branches are in controlling agency action, the courts exercise the greatest amount of control over agency behavior. This may be due, in part, to the fact that they are the branch of government most accessible to members of the public aggrieved by agency action. The APA provides for judicial review of most agency action, which takes place either in one of the U.S. courts of appeals or a U.S. district court, depending on the nature of the agency action at issue. The

Supreme Court, if it chooses to grant certiorari, is the court of last resort for review of agency action.[12]

Not all agency actions are subject to judicial review. Moreover, only certain parties may challenge those that are reviewable. An individual or organization seeking judicial review must demonstrate that the agency action being challenged is *reviewable*, that the challenging party has *standing to sue*, that *necessary administrative remedies have been exhausted*, and that the dispute is *ripe for judicial review*. These requirements are discussed below.

Reviewability   Only reviewable agency actions may be challenged by dissatisfied individuals and organizations. Normally, it is not difficult for aggrieved parties to show that the agency action is reviewable because the APA creates a strong presumption in favor of reviewability. This presumption may be overcome only by a showing that "statutes preclude review" or that the decision in question is "committed to agency discretion by law." These limitations on reviewability come from Congress's power to dictate the jurisdiction of the federal courts and from judicial deference to the proper functions of the other branches of government (e.g., a decision relating to matters of foreign policy is likely to be seen as outside the proper province of the judiciary).

Standing to Sue   Once reviewability of an agency action has been established, the challenging party must demonstrate that he, she, or it has standing to sue. This means that the individual or organization seeking judicial review is "an aggrieved party" whose interests have been substantially affected by the agency action. Initially, courts took a relatively restrictive view of this basic requirement, requiring plaintiffs to show harm to a legally protected interest. More recently, however, courts have liberalized the standing requirement somewhat, requiring plaintiffs to demonstrate that they have suffered an "injury" to an interest that lies within the "zone of interests" protected by the statute or constitutional provision

---

[12]The Supreme Court's certiorari jurisdiction is discussed in Chapter 2.

that serves as the basis of their challenge. Demonstrating an economic loss remains the surest way to satisfy the "injury" requirement, but emotional, aesthetic, and environmental injuries have been found sufficient on occasion.

Lujan v. Defenders of Wildlife, which follows, demonstrates that even though the standing requirement has been liberalized over the years, an asserted injury that is overly abstract, speculative, or tenuous in nature will be insufficient to confer standing on the plaintiff.

LUJAN V. DEFENDERS OF WILDLIFE
112 S. Ct 2130 (U.S. Sup. Ct. 1992)

Section 7(a)(2) of the Endangered Species Act of 1973 divides responsibilities as to protection of endangered species between the Secretary of the Interior and the Secretary of Commerce. The statute also requires each federal agency to consult with the relevant secretary in order to ensure that any action funded by the agency would be unlikely to jeopardize the existence or habitat of an endangered or threatened species. In 1978, the secretaries referred to above promulgated a joint regulation stating that the obligations imposed by Section 7(a)(2) extend not only to actions taken in the United States but also to actions taken in foreign nations. A revised joint regulation, reinterpreting Section 7(a)(2) to require consultation only for actions taken in the United States or on the high seas, was promulgated in 1986. Defenders of Wildlife (DOW), an organization dedicated to wildlife conservation and other environmental causes, sued the Secretary of the Interior, seeking a declaratory judgment that the 1986 regulation erroneously interpreted the geographic scope of Section 7(a)(2). DOW also sought an injunction requiring the secretary to develop a new regulation restoring the interpretation set forth in the 1978 regulation. The district court denied the secretary's motion for summary judgment on the issue of whether DOW had standing to sue, granted DOW's motion for summary judgment on all issues, and ordered the secretary to develop a revised regulation. After the Eighth Circuit Court of Appeals affirmed, the Supreme Court granted certiorari.

Scalia, Justice   The preliminary issue, and the only one we reach, is whether DOW has standing to seek judicial review [of the 1986 regulation]. [Article III of the U.S. Constitution] limits the jurisdiction of federal courts to "Cases" and "Controversies." Though some of its elements express merely prudential considerations that are part of judicial self-government, the core component of standing is an essential and unchanging part of the case-or-controversy requirement of Article III.

Over the years, our cases have established that the irreducible constitutional minimum of standing contains three elements: First, the plaintiff must have suffered an injury in fact—an invasion of a legally-protected interest which is (a) concrete and particularized, and (b) actual or imminent, not conjectural or hypothetical. Second, there must be a causal connection between the injury and the conduct complained of. Third, it must be likely, as opposed to merely speculative, that the injury will be redressed by a favorable decision.

The party invoking federal jurisdiction bears the burden of establishing these elements. When the suit is one challenging the legality of government action or inaction, the nature and extent of facts [necessary] to establish standing depends considerably upon whether the plaintiff is himself an object of the action (or foregone action) at issue. If he is, there is ordinarily little question that the action or inaction has caused him injury, and that a judgment preventing or requiring the action will redress it. When, however, as in this case, a plaintiff's asserted injury arises from the government's allegedly unlawful regulation (or lack of regulation) of *someone else*, . . . standing is not precluded, but it is ordinarily substantially more difficult to establish [the necessary elements outlined above].

DOW's claim to injury is that the lack of consultation with respect to certain funded activities abroad "increases the rate of extinction of endangered and threatened species." Of course, the desire to use or observe an animal species, even for purely aesthetic purposes, is undeniably a cognizable interest for purpose of standing. "But the 'injury in fact' test requires more than an injury to a cognizable interest. It requires that the party seeking review be himself among the injured." *Sierra Club v. Morton* (1972). We shall assume for the sake of argument that [the affidavits of two DOW members, offered by DOW in opposition of the secretary's motion for summary judgment on the standing issue,] contain facts showing that certain agency-funded projects threaten listed species [a variety of crocodile in Egypt and the Asian elephant and the leopard in Sri Lanka]. [The affidavits] plainly contain no facts, however, showing how damage to the species will produce "imminent" injury to [the affiants]. That the affiants "had visited" the areas of the projects before the projects commenced proves nothing. And the affiants' profession of an "intent" to return to the places they had visited before—where they will presumably, this time, be deprived of the opportunity to observe animals of the endangered species—is simply not enough. Such "some day" intentions—without any description of concrete plans, or indeed any specification of *when* the some day will be—do not support a finding of the "actual or imminent" injury that our cases require.

[DOW also asserts theories] called, alas, the "animal nexus" approach, whereby anyone who has an interest in studying or seeing the endangered animals anywhere on the globe has standing; and the "vocational nexus" approach, under which anyone with a professional interest in such animals can sue. Under these theories, anyone who goes to see elephants in the Bronx Zoo, and anyone who is a keeper of Asian elephants in the Bronx Zoo, has standing to sue because the Director of AID did not consult with the Secretary regarding the AID-funded project in Sri Lanka. This is beyond all reason. Standing is not "an ingenious academic exercise in the conceivable." *U.S. v. Students Challenging Regulatory Agency Procedures* (1973). [Instead, standing requires] a factual showing of perceptible harm. It is clear that the person who observes or works with a particular animal threatened by a federal decision is facing perceptible harm, since the very subject of his interest will no longer exist. It is even plausible—though it goes to the outermost limit of plausibility—to think that a person who observes or works with animals of a particular species in the very area of the world where that species is threatened by a federal decision is facing such harm, since some animal that might have been the subject of his interest will no longer exist. It goes beyond the limit, however, and into pure speculation and fantasy, to say that anyone who observes or works with an endangered species, anywhere in the world, is appreciably harmed by a single project affecting some portion of that species with which he has no more specific connection.

The Court of Appeals found that DOW had standing for an additional reason: because it had suffered a "procedural injury" [by virtue of the Endangered Species Act's so-called "citizen-suit" provision stating that "any person" may bring suit to enjoin a violation of the statute]. The court held that . . . the citizen-suit provision [allows] *anyone* [to] file suit in federal court to challenge the Secretary's (or presumably any other official's) failure to follow the assertedly correct consultative procedure, notwithstanding their inability to allege any discrete injury flowing from that failure. The court held that the injury-in-fact requirement [for standing purposes] had been satisfied by congressional conferral upon *all* persons of an abstract, self-contained, noninstrumental "right" to have the Executive [branch] observe the procedures required by law. We reject this view. We have consistently held that a plaintiff raising only a generally available grievance about government— claiming only harm to his and every citizen's interest in proper application of the Constitution and laws, and seeking relief that no more directly and tangibly benefits him than it does the public at large—does not state an Article III case or controversy.

[I]t is clear that in suits against the government, at least, the concrete injury requirement must remain. We hold that DOW lacks standing to bring this action.

Decision of Eighth Circuit Court of Appeals reversed in favor of Secretary of Interior.

Exhaustion and Ripeness   Once standing has been established, two further obstacles—exhaustion and ripeness—confront the party challenging an agency action. Courts do not want to allow regulated parties to short-circuit the regulatory process. They also want to give agencies the chance to correct their own mistakes and to develop fully their positions in disputed matters. Accordingly, they normally insist that aggrieved parties *exhaust necessary administrative remedies* before they will grant judicial review.[13] The requirement that a dispute be *ripe* for judicial review is a general requirement emanating from the Constitution's insistence that only "cases or controversies" are judicially resolvable. In determining ripeness, the courts weigh the hardship to the parties of withholding judicial review against the degree of refinement of the issues still possible (e.g., might further administrative action alter the nature of the issues or eliminate the need for judicial review?).

Legal Bases for Challenging Agency Actions
Assuming that the above prerequisites to judicial review are met, there are several legal theories on which agency action may be attacked. It may be alleged that the agency's action was *ultra vires* (exceeded its authority as granted by its enabling legislation) or that the agency *substantially deviated from procedural requirements* contained in the APA or in the agency's enabling legislation. Agency action may also be challenged as *unconstitutional* or as the product of an *erroneous interpretation of statutes*. (The *American Hospital Association* case, which follows shortly, illustrates the latter line of attack.) Finally, agency action may be overturned if it is *unsubstantiated by the facts* before the agency when it acted.

Standards of Review   The degree of scrutiny that courts will apply to agency action depends on the nature of issues under dispute and the type of agency proceedings that produced the challenged action. Courts are least likely to defer to agency action when *questions of law* are at issue. Although courts afford substantial consideration to an agency's interpretations of the statutes it enforces, the courts are still the ultimate arbiters of the meaning of statutes and constitutional provisions.

When *questions of fact* or *policy* are at issue, however, courts are more likely to defer to the agency because it presumably has superior expertise and because the agency fact finders who heard and viewed the evidence were better situated to judge its merit. When agency factual judgments are at stake, the APA provides for three standards of review, the most rigorous of which is *de novo* review.

When conducting a *de novo* review, courts make an independent finding of the facts after conducting a new hearing. Efficiency considerations plainly favor limited judicial review of the facts. Accordingly, *de novo* review is employed only when required by statute, when inadequate fact-finding proceedings were used in an agency adjudicatory proceeding, or when new factual issues that were not before the agency are raised in a proceeding to enforce a nonadjudicatory agency action.

When courts review formal agency adjudications or formal rulemaking, the APA calls for the application of a **substantial evidence** test. Only agency findings that are "unsupported by substantial evidence" will be overturned. In conducting substantial evidence reviews, courts look at the reasonableness of an agency's actions in relation to the facts before it rather than conducting an independent fact-finding hearing (such as that done in *de novo* reviews). The substantial evidence test also tends to be employed in hybrid rulemaking cases.

The judicial standard of review used in cases involving informal agency adjudications or rulemaking is the **arbitrary and capricious** test. This is the least rigorous standard of judicial review, due to the great degree of deference it accords agency decisions. In deciding whether an agency's action was arbitrary and capricious, a reviewing court theoretically should not substitute its judgment for that of the agency. Instead, it should ask whether there was an adequate factual basis for the agency's action, and should sustain actions that do not amount to a "clear error of judgment." Although the substantial evidence and arbitrary and capricious tests are separate and distinct in theory, the distinctions often tend to blur in actual practice.

---

[13]Necessary administrative remedies are those a statute or regulation establishes as mandatory steps to be completed before judicial review can be sought. In *Darby v. Cisneros*, 113 S. Ct. 2539 (U.S. Sup. Ct. 1993), the Supreme Court held that federal courts do not have the authority to require plaintiffs to exhaust available administrative remedies before seeking judicial review unless the relevant statutes or agency rules specifically mandate exhaustion as a prerequisite to judicial review.

BOWEN V. AMERICAN HOSPITAL ASSOCIATION

476 U.S. 610 (U.S. Sup. Ct. 1986)

In April 1982, the parents of an infant with Down's syndrome and other handicaps refused consent to surgery to remove an obstruction in the infant's esophagus that prevented oral feeding. In May 1982, after the child's death, the Secretary of Health and Human Services promulgated rules that, among other things, required hospitals and other health care providers to post notices that health care should not be withheld from infants on the basis of mental or physical handicap. The rules were adopted pursuant to section 504 of the Rehabilitation Act of 1973, which permits the head of any executive branch agency to promulgate rules prohibiting discrimination against an "otherwise qualified handicapped individual . . . solely by reason of his handicap." The American Hospital Association challenged the validity of the rules. The District Court found the rules invalid, and the Second Circuit Court of Appeals affirmed. The secretary appealed to the Supreme Court of the United States.

Stevens, Justice   It is an axiom of administrative law that an agency's explanation of the basis for its decision must include a rational connection between the facts found and the choice made. Agency deference has not come so far that we will uphold regulations whenever it is possible to conceive a basis for administrative action. The mere fact that there is some rational basis within the knowledge and experience of the agency under which it might have concluded that the regulation was necessary to discharge its statutorily authorized mission will not suffice to validate agency decisionmaking. Our recognition of Congress's need to vest administrative agencies with ample power to assist in the difficult task of governing a vast and complex Nation carries with it the correlative responsibility of the agency to explain the rationale and factual basis for its decision, even though we show respect for the agency's judgment in both.

Before examining the Secretary's reasons for issuing the Rules, it is essential to understand the pre-existing state-law framework governing the provision of medical care to handicapped infants. In broad outline, state law vests decisional responsibility in the parents, subject to review in exceptional cases by the State acting as *parens patriae*. Prior to the regulatory activity culminating in the Rules, the federal government was not a participant in the process of making treatment decisions for newborn infants. We presume that this general framework was familiar to Congress when it enacted section 504 of the Rehabilitation Act.

The Secretary contends that a hospital's refusal to furnish a handicapped infant with medically beneficial treatment solely by reason of its handicap constitutes unlawful discrimination. Yet the preamble to the Rules correctly states that when a non-treatment decision, no matter how discriminatory, is made by parents, rather than by the hospital, section 504 does not mandate that the hospital unilaterally overrule the parental decision and provide treatment notwithstanding the lack of consent by the parents. A hospital's withholding of treatment when no parental consent has been given cannot violate section 504, for without the consent of the parents or a surrogate decisionmaker, the infant is neither "otherwise qualified" for treatment nor has he been denied care "solely by reason of his handicap." Indeed, it would almost certainly be a tort as a matter of state law to operate on an infant without parental consent. This analysis makes clear that the Secretary's heavy reliance on the analogy to race-based refusals is misplaced. If a hospital refused to operate on a black child whose parents had withheld their consent to treatment, the hospital's refusal would not be based on the race of the child even if it were assumed that the parents based *their decision* entirely on a mistaken assumption that the race of the child made the operation inappropriate.

The Rules are not needed to prevent hospitals from denying treatment to handicapped infants. The record contains no evidence that hospitals have ever refused treatment authorized either by the infant's parents or by a court order. In promulgating the

Rules, the Secretary relied upon 49 cases that the Department of Health and Human Services had processed prior to December 1, 1983. Curiously, however, *none* of the 49 cases resulted in a finding of discriminatory withholding of medical care. In fact, in the entire list of 49 cases, there is no finding that a hospital failed or refused to provide treatment to a handicapped infant for which parental consent had been given.

The Secretary has substantial leeway to explore areas in which discrimination against the handicapped poses particularly significant problems and to devise regulations to prohibit such discrimination. Even according the greatest respect to the Secretary's action, however, deference cannot fill the lack of an evidentiary foundation on which the Rules must rest. The history of these Rules exposes the inappropriateness of the extraordinary deference—

virtually a *carte blanche*—requested by the Secretary. The Secretary regards the mission of the Department of Health and Human Services as one principally concerned with the quality of medical care for handicapped infants rather than with the implementation of section 504. But nothing in the Rehabilitation Act authorizes the Secretary to dispense with the law's focus on discrimination and instead to employ federal resources to save the lives of handicapped newborns, without regard to whether they are victims of discrimination. Section 504 does not authorize the Secretary to give unsolicited advice either to parents or to hospitals who are faced with difficult treatment decisions concerning handicapped children.

Judgment for the American Hospital Association affirmed.

INFORMATION CONTROLS

Over the last three decades, Congress has enacted three major statutes aimed at controlling administrative agencies through the regulation of information. Each of these statutes represents a compromise between competing social interests of significant importance. On one hand, we have a strong democratic preference for public disclosure of governmental operations, believing that "government in the dark" is less likely to be consistent with the public interest than is "government in the sunshine." On the other hand, we recognize that some sensitive governmental activities must be shielded from the scrutiny of unfriendly parties, and that disclosure of some information can unjustifiably invade personal privacy, hinder government law enforcement efforts, and provide the competitors of a company about which information is being disclosed with proprietary information that could be used unfairly to the competitors' advantage.

Freedom of Information Act

Congress passed the *Freedom of Information Act* (FOIA) in 1966 and amended it in 1974. The FOIA was designed to enable private citizens to have access to documents in the government's posses-

sion. Agencies must normally respond to public requests for documents within 10 days after such a request has been received. An agency bears the burden of justifying any denial of any FOIA request. Denials are appealable to an appropriate federal district court. Successful plaintiffs may recover their costs and attorney's fees.

Not all government-held documents are obtainable under the FOIA, however. The FOIA exempts from disclosure documents that:

1. Must be kept secret in the interest of national security.
2. Concern an agency's internal personnel practices.
3. Are specifically exempted from disclosure by statute.
4. Contain trade secrets or other confidential or privileged commercial or financial information.
5. Reflect internal agency deliberations on matters of policy or proceedings.
6. Contain individual personnel or medical information if disclosure would constitute an invasion of privacy.
7. Would threaten the integrity of a law enforcement agency's investigations or jeopardize an individual's right to a fair trial.

8. Relate to the supervision or regulation of financial institutions.

9. Contain geological or geophysical data.

Frequent users of the FOIA include the media, industry trade associations, public interest groups, and companies seeking to obtain useful information about their competitors. It is important to note that although the FOIA allows agencies to refuse to disclose exempted documents, it does not impose on them the affirmative duty to do so. The Supreme Court has held that individuals cannot compel an agency to deny an FOIA request for allegedly exempt documents that contain sensitive information about them.[14]

The FOIA has recently been the focus of considerable controversy on two points. First, budgetary cutbacks have combined with growing numbers of requests for information to produce agency delays as long as two years in responding to information requests. Courts tend to tolerate agency delays if the agency can show that it is making a "due diligence" effort to respond. Second, the dramatic increase in computerized information storage that has occurred since the passage of the FOIA has created problems not specifically contemplated by the statute, which focuses on information stored in documentary form. Do interested parties have the same rights of access to data stored in agency computers that they have to government documents? May the government destroy electronic mail messages, or must it save them? Future legislative or judicial action will be necessary to resolve such questions.

Privacy Act of 1974

The *Privacy Act of 1974* allows individuals to inspect files that agencies maintain on them and to request that erroneous or incomplete records be corrected. It also attempts to prevent agencies from gathering unnecessary information about individuals, and forbids the disclosure of an individual's records without his written permission, except in certain specifically exempted circumstances. For example, records may be disclosed to employees of the agency that collected the information if those employees need the records to perform their duties

(the "need to know" exception), to law enforcement agencies, to other agencies' personnel for "routine use" (uses for purposes compatible with the purpose for which the record was collected), and to persons filing legitimate FOIA requests. In addition, records may be disclosed if a court order requires disclosure.

Government in the Sunshine Act

The *Government in the Sunshine Act* of 1976 was designed to ensure that "[e]very portion of every meeting of an agency shall be open to public observation." However, complete public access to all agency meetings could have the same negative consequences that unrestrained public access to agency records can sometimes produce. Accordingly, the Sunshine Act exempts certain agency meetings from public scrutiny under circumstances similar to those under which documents are exempt from disclosure under the FOIA.

ISSUES IN REGULATION

"Old" Regulation versus "New" Regulation

Some interested observers of regulatory developments over roughly the past 30 years have noted significant differences between the regulations that originated during the Progressive (1902 to 1914) and New Deal (1933 to 1938) eras and many regulations promulgated more recently.[15] They argue not only that the number and scope of regulatory controls have increased substantially in recent years, but also that the focus and the impact of regulation have changed significantly.

Whereas earlier regulation often focused on business practices that harmed the economic interests of specific segments of society (e.g., workers, small-business owners, investors), many modern regulations focus on the health and safety of all citizens. Furthermore, whereas earlier regulations often focused on a particular industry or group of industries (e.g., the railroads or the securities

---

[14]*Chrysler Corp. v. Brown*, 441 U.S. 281 (U.S. Sup. Ct. 1980).

[15]See, for example, David Vogel, "The 'New' Social Regulation in Historical and Comparative Perspective," in *Regulation in Perspective*, ed. T. McGraw (Cambridge, Mass.: Harvard University Press, 1981), p. 155.

industry), many modern regulations affect large segments of industry (e.g., Title VII of the Civil Rights Act of 1964 and regulations governing environmental pollution and workplace safety). Finally, whereas earlier congressional delegations of regulatory power tended to be quite broad (e.g., the FTC Act's prohibition of "unfair methods of competition" and "unfair or deceptive acts or practices"), many more recent regulatory statutes (e.g., the Clean Air Acts of 1970 and 1977) have been extremely detailed.

What are the consequences of these changes in the nature of regulation? Far more businesses than ever before feel the impact of federal regulation, and far more areas of internal corporate decisionmaking are affected by regulation. These changes tend to erode the historic distinction between "regulated" and other industries, and to heighten the importance of business-government relations. Detailed regulatory statutes also increase Congress's role in shaping regulatory policy at the expense of administrative discretion, making regulatory policy arguably more vulnerable to legislative lobbying efforts.

"Captive" Agencies and Agencies' "Shadows"

Proponents of regulation have traditionally feared that regulatory agencies would become "captives" of the industries they were charged with regulating. Through "revolving door" appointments by which key figures move back and forth between government and the private sector, and through excessive reliance on "experts" beholden to industry, the independence of administrative agencies may be compromised and their effectiveness as regulators destroyed.

More recently, commentators sympathetic to business have argued that similar dangers to agency independence exist in the form of the nonindustry "shadow" groups that public interest organizations maintain to monitor agency actions (e.g., the Center for Auto Safety, which monitors the work of the Highway Transportation Safety Administration). Agencies may develop dependency relationships with their shadows or at least make decisions based in part on their shadows' anticipated reactions. Such informal means of shaping regulatory policy, when combined with the ability to challenge agency actions in court due to somewhat liberalized standing rules, have made public interest organizations important players in the contemporary regulatory process.

Deregulation versus Reregulation

A useful axiom for understanding the process of social and legal evolution is that *the cost of the status quo is easier to perceive than the cost of change*. Few things are more illustrative of the operation of this axiom than the history of regulation in the United States.

In the latter years of the 19th century, the social costs of living in an unregulated environment were readily apparent. Large business organizations often abused their power at the expense of their customers, suppliers, employees, and distributors, and sought to increase their power by acquiring their competitors or driving them out of business. Market forces, standing alone, were apparently unable to protect the public from defective, and in some cases dangerous, products. As a result of these and numerous other social and historical factors, this century has witnessed a tremendous growth in government, and in government regulation of business.

Regulation, too, has its costs. Regulatory bureaucracies generate their own internal momentum and have their own interests to protect. They may become insensitive to the legitimate concerns of the industries they regulate and the public they supposedly serve. They may continue to seek higher and higher levels of safety, heedless of the fact that life necessarily involves some elements of risk and that the total elimination of risk in a modern technological society may be impossible—or if possible, obtainable at a cost that we cannot afford to pay. At a time when many Americans are legitimately concerned about economic efficiency, as well as the ability of U.S. companies to compete effectively in world markets against competitors who operate in less regulated environments, these and other costs of regulation are readily apparent.

As a result, in the last 10 to 15 years, we have witnessed substantial deregulation in a number of industries such as the airline, banking, railroad, and trucking industries. The results of these efforts are, at best, mixed. The case of airline regulation should suffice to make the point. Proponents of deregulation cite the generally lower fares that deregulation has produced. Opponents tend to point to increased airline overbooking practices, reduced or eliminated services to smaller communities, and increased safety problems, all of which, they argue, are products of deregulation. The costs of deregulation have generated predictable calls for reregulating the airline industry. The ultimate outcome of the deregulation versus reregulation debate will depend on which costs we as a society decide we would prefer to pay.

ETHICAL AND PUBLIC POLICY CONCERNS

1. Earlier in this chapter, you learned that agency formal rulemaking procedures are vulnerable to industry tactics aimed at delaying regulation (e.g., the example concerning the minimum peanut content of peanut butter). Are such industry tactics ethically justifiable?

2. In our discussion of the Freedom of Information Act, you learned that companies seeking to obtain useful information about their competitors frequently seek access to documents covered by the act. Is this an ethical way to gain access to information?

3. Although question 1 in this section focuses on delaying tactics practiced by industry, it is important to note that agencies have also been known to engage in delay and other tactics designed to frustrate citizens and organizations with whom they interact. For example, an agency may delay its response to an FOIA request, untruthfully arguing that staff shortages prevent a timely response, or it may refuse to turn over documents that it knows are not exempt from disclosure, forcing those seeking disclosure to engage in expensive and time-consuming litigation to attain their ends. Are such agency tactics ethically justifiable?

PROBLEMS AND PROBLEM CASES

1. Title X of the Public Health Service Act provides federal funding for family-planning services. Section 1008 of the statute specifies that none of the federal funds provided under Title X are to be "used in programs where abortion is a method of family planning." In 1988, the Secretary of Health and Human Services issued new regulations that, among other things, prohibited family-planning services that receive Title X funds from engaging in counseling concerning the use of abortion as a method of family planning, referrals for abortion as a method of family planning, and activities amounting to encouragement or advocacy of abortion as a method of family planning. Various Title X grantees and physicians supervising Title X funds challenged the validity of the regulations and sought an injunction against their implementation. Were the regulations a permissible interpretation of Section 1008? Did the regulations violate constitutional guarantees?

2. In November 1984, the Federal Election Commission (FEC) began an investigation of the activities of the Lyndon Larouche Campaign for the Democratic Party's presidential nomination. The investigation centered on allegations that the campaign had falsified its records and obtained federal election matching funds by claiming that donations via credit cards had been made by individuals who denied making the donations. In December 1984, the FEC issued a subpoena requiring the campaign to produce records regarding the solicitation of contributions (including the names of solicitors and those solicited), contributions actually received, and all telephone records regarding the solicitation of funds. When the Larouche campaign failed to comply with the subpoena, the FEC brought an action in a federal district court to obtain enforcement. The district court ordered the campaign to comply with the subpoena. The Larouche campaign appealed on First Amendment grounds. Was the district court's compliance order proper?

3. One of the sections in the federal Endangered Species Act makes it a crime for any person to "take" any endangered species of fish or wildlife listed under the statute. A definitional section in the statute states that "take" means "to harass, harm, pursue, hunt, shoot, wound, kill, trap, capture, or collect, or to attempt to engage in any such conduct." The Fish & Wildlife Service promulgated a regulation that purported to define the term "harm" for purposes of the statutory definition quoted above. This regulation stated that "harm," as used in the statute, "means an act which actually kills or injures wildlife" and that "[s]uch act may include significant habitat modification or degradation where it actually kills or injures wildlife by significantly impairing essential behavioral patterns, including breeding, feeding or sheltering." Sweet Home Chapter of Communities for a Great Oregon, along with other organizations, brought suit in federal district court in an effort to have the Fish &

Wildlife Service regulation defining "harm" invalidated as an unreasonable interpretation of the Endangered Species Act. Were Sweet Home and the other plaintiffs correct in their characterization of the regulation?

4. Fenster, president and part owner of Utica Packing Company, was convicted of bribing a federal meat inspector, an employee of the United States Department of Agriculture (USDA). In a hearing before an administrative law judge (ALJ), the USDA sought a withdrawal of meat inspection services from Utica unless Fenster sold his ownership of Utica and withdrew from its management. The ALJ ruled in the USDA's favor, effectively eliminating Utica's ability to conduct its business. Utica appealed the decision to the USDA Judicial Officer, Donald Campbell, who had the power to make final adjudicative orders for the USDA. Campbell affirmed the ALJ's decision, and so did a federal District Court. The Sixth Circuit Court of Appeals, however, held that Campbell erred by not considering mitigating circumstances in the case. Upon reconsideration, Campbell reluctantly held that the mitigating circumstances prevented him from finding that Utica was unfit to receive inspection services. USDA executive officials strongly disagreed with Campbell's decision. They convinced the Secretary of Agriculture to replace Campbell with Deputy Assistant Secretary John Franke, who was not a lawyer and had no adjudicatory experience. Franke then reconsidered Campbell's decision at the USDA's request, finding that the mitigating circumstances were insufficient to justify Fenster's bribing the meat inspector. Utica appealed, arguing that its due process rights had been violated. Is Utica correct?

5. John Doe began work at the Central Intelligence Agency (CIA) in 1973 as a clerk-typist. Periodic fitness reports consistently rated him as an excellent or outstanding employee. By 1977, he had been promoted to covert electronics technician. In January 1982, Doe voluntarily told a CIA security officer that he was a homosexual. Almost immediately, the CIA placed Doe on paid administrative leave and began an investigation of his sexual orientation and conduct. Doe submitted to an extensive polygraph examination during which he denied having sexual relations with foreign nationals and maintained that he had not disclosed classified

information to any of his sexual partners. The polygraph officer told Doe that the test results indicated that his responses had been truthful. Nonetheless, a month later Doe was told that the CIA's Office of Security had determined that his homosexuality posed a threat to security. CIA officials declined, however, to explain the nature of the danger. Doe was asked to resign. When he refused to do so he was dismissed by CIA Director William Webster, who "deemed it necessary and advisable in the interests of the United States to terminate [Doe's] employment with this Agency pursuant to section 102(c) of the National Security Act." The statutory section cited by the director allows termination of a CIA employee whenever the director "shall deem such termination necessary or advisable in the interests of the United States." Doe filed suit against the CIA, arguing that his termination was unlawful under section 102(c) and various constitutional guarantees. The CIA moved to dismiss Doe's complaint, arguing that the director's decision was a decision committed to agency discretion by law and thus was not subject to judicial review. Was the CIA's argument correct?

6. Chaney and other prison inmates were sentenced to death under the laws of Oklahoma and Texas. They were to be executed by lethal injection of drugs. The drugs were approved by the Food and Drug Administration for medical purposes stated on their labels. The FDA had not, however, approved their use for human executions. Chaney claimed that use of the drugs for human executions violated the Food, Drug, and Cosmetic Act (FDCA) as an unapproved use of an approved drug. He argued that under the FDCA, the FDA was required to approve the drugs as "safe and effective" for human execution before they could be distributed. Chaney asked the FDA to investigate these perceived violations of the FDCA and to take enforcement actions, including seizing the drugs from state prisons and recommending the prosecution of those who knowingly distribute or purchase the drugs with the intent to use them for human executions. The FDA refused to take any action on the ground that it had no power to interfere with the use of lethal injections in a state criminal justice system. Chaney sought judicial review of the FDA's refusal to act. The district court held that the FDA's refusal to take enforcement action was not subject to judicial review. Was the district court's decision correct?

7. On August 1, 1982, Larry Morrison, a pilot for Northwest Airlines, piloted a passenger airliner while he was intoxicated. Four days later, Northwest Airlines discharged him as an employee. The next day, Morrison began four weeks of voluntary alcoholism treatment. He attended weekly counseling sessions thereafter. On January 20, 1983, the Federal Aviation Administration (FAA) temporarily suspended his pilot certificate. Without a pilot certificate, Morrison could not pilot airplanes within the United States. On September 2, 1983, Morrison requested recertification, which the FAA granted subject to a few restrictions. Northwest Airlines sought judicial review of the FAA's recertification on the grounds that (1) recertifying Morrison would make the skies unsafe for Northwest airplanes, its crews, and its passengers and (2) the FAA's lenient recertification policy would make it more difficult for Northwest to deter drinking among its pilots and other employees. Were these injuries sufficient to give Northwest standing to seek judicial review of the FAA's decision to recertify Morrison?

8. The federal Clean Water Act provides for two sets of water quality measures: effluent limitations, which are promulgated by the Environmental Protection Agency (EPA), and water quality standards, which are promulgated by the states. The Clean Water Act generally prohibits the discharge of effluent into a navigable body of water unless the party making such a discharge obtains a permit to do so from a state with an EPA-approved permit program or from the EPA itself. The EPA issued a Fayetteville, Arkansas sewage treatment plant a permit to discharge effluent into an Arkansas stream that ultimately reaches the Illinois River upstream from the Oklahoma border. The permit included conditions designed to make the Fayetteville discharge comply with Oklahoma's water quality standards. Oklahoma challenged the permit's issuance and terms. Following a hearing, an EPA administrative law judge affirmed the issuance of the permit. After the EPA's chief judicial officer did the same, Oklahoma sought judicial review in federal court. What standard of review should the court follow?

9. An agent of the Pennsylvania Department of Environmental Resources saw Disposal Service's loaded trash truck backing into a building that was used to compact waste to be loaded onto tractor-trailers for transportation and final disposal. Knowing the building's purpose and that Disposal Service did not have a permit to operate it as a transfer station, as required by the state Solid Waste Management Act (SWMA), the agent entered the property, went into the building, and observed the operation. Disposal Service was later prosecuted for operating a transfer station without a permit. Disposal Service moved to suppress the agent's evidence, arguing that his warrantless entry onto the property violated the Fourth Amendment. The state argued that the SWMA's provisions allowing such warrantless inspections were constitutional. Should the evidence be suppressed?

10. The *New York Times* (the *Times*) filed a Freedom of Information Act (FOIA) request with the National Aeronautics and Space Administration (NASA) for "transcripts of all voice and data communications recorded aboard the space shuttle *Challenger*" on the day when the shuttle self-destructed, killing all seven astronauts on board. The *Times* also requested copies of voice communication tapes. NASA provided a written transcript of the only voice recording made, but refused to turn over a copy of the tape itself, arguing that to do so would violate the privacy of the astronauts' families by exposing them to replays of their loved ones' voices. NASA argued that the tape was exempt from disclosure under Exemption 6 to the FOIA because the human voice, being unique to each individual, "clearly is information about the individual and identifiable as such." Should NASA turn over the tape?

11. Britt, a major in the Marine Corps Reserve, was investigated by the Naval Investigative Service in connection with allegations that one of his Reserve subordinates had improperly stored ordnance in his home. While the investigation was in progress, the Naval Investigative Service contacted Britt's regular employer, the Immigration and Naturalization Service (INS), and provided his INS supervisor with reports and other material from the investigation. After Britt was later cleared of all charges by the Marines, he filed suit against the Naval Investigative Service, arguing that it had violated the Privacy Act by releasing information about the investigation to the INS. Were the Naval Investigative Service's actions proper?

CHAPTER

47

THE FEDERAL TRADE COMMISSION ACT AND CONSUMER PROTECTION LAWS

INTRODUCTION

As Chapter 20 demonstrates, consumers' ability to recover civil damages for defective products increased dramatically during the 1960s and 1970s. But direct government regulation of consumer matters also grew tremendously during those decades. This chapter examines the many kinds of federal consumer protection regulation. It begins with a general discussion of America's main consumer watchdog: the Federal Trade Commission (FTC). After describing how the FTC operates, the chapter examines its regulation of anticompetitive, deceptive, and unfair business practices. Then we examine the many other federal laws that regulate consumer matters, many of which involve consumer credit.

THE FEDERAL TRADE COMMISSION

The Federal Trade Commission was formed shortly after passage of the Federal Trade Commission Act (FTC Act) in 1914.[1] The FTC is an independent federal agency, which means that it is outside the executive branch of the federal government and is less subject to political control than agencies that are executive departments. The FTC is headed by five commissioners appointed by the president and confirmed by the Senate for staggered seven-year terms. The president also designates one of the commissioners as chairman of the FTC. The FTC has a Washington headquarters and several regional offices located throughout the United States. Figure 1 in Chapter 46 sets out the Commission's internal organization.

The FTC's Powers

The FTC's principal missions are to keep the U.S. economy both *free* and *fair.* As Figure 1 suggests, Congress has given the Commission many tools for accomplishing these missions. By far the most important is section 5 of the FTC Act, which empowers the Commission to prevent: (1) unfair methods of competition, and (2) unfair or deceptive

---

[1]See Chapter 46 for further discussion of the FTC's creation, organization, powers, and status as an independent agency.

FIGURE 1 **Some of the Major Acts Enforced by the FTC**

Regulation of Economic Competition

FTC Act Section 5 (including Sherman Act standards)—discussed in this chapter and in Chapter 48

Clayton Act—discussed in Chapter 49

Robinson-Patman Act—also discussed in Chapter 49

Hart-Scott-Rodino Antitrust Improvements Act of 1976—requires that certain companies planning mergers notify and provide information to the FTC and the Justice Department

Consumer Protection Measures Discussed in This Chapter

FTC Act Section 5

Magnuson-Moss Warranty Act

Truth in Lending Act (including 1988 Fair Credit and Charge Card Disclosure Act and Home Equity Loan Consumer Protection Act)

Consumer Leasing Act

Fair Credit Reporting Act

Equal Credit Opportunity Act

Fair Credit Billing Act

Fair Debt Collection Practices Act

Other Measures

Export Trade Act—empowers FTC to supervise registration and operation of associations of American exporters engaged in export trade

Fair Packaging and Labeling Act—regulates packaging and labeling of consumer products to ensure accurate quality and value comparisons

Flammable Fabrics Act—FTC has some enforcement powers under act regulating manufacture, sale, and importation of flammable fabrics

Fur Products Labeling Act—regulates labeling, other identification, and advertising of fur products

Hobby Protection Act—regulates certain imitations of political campaign materials and certain imitation coins and paper money

Lanham Act—empowers FTC to petition for the cancellation of certain trademarks

Smokeless Tobacco Act—empowers FTC to approve manufacturers' plans for rotation and display of statements on smokeless tobacco packages and ads

Textile Fiber Products Identification Act—regulates labeling and other identification of textile fiber products

Wool Products Labeling Act—regulates labeling and other identification of wool products

---

Sources: *1993 United States Government Manual* and various statutes.

---

acts or practices. We examine each of these bases of FTC authority later in this chapter. The Commission also enforces the consumer protection and consumer credit measures discussed in the last half of the chapter. Finally, the FTC enforces various other federal acts, some of which are listed in Figure 1.

FTC Enforcement Procedures

The FTC has many legal tools for ensuring compliance with the statutes it administers. The three most important FTC enforcement devices are its proce-

dures for facilitating voluntary compliance, its issuance of trade regulation rules, and its adjudicative proceedings.

Voluntary Compliance   The FTC promotes voluntary, cooperative business behavior by giving advisory opinions and issuing industry guides. An **advisory opinion** is the Commission's response to a private party's query about the legality of proposed business conduct. The FTC is not obligated to furnish advisory opinions. Even where it does furnish such an opinion, the Commission may rescind it when the public interest requires. But when the FTC does so, it cannot proceed against the opinion's recipient for actions taken in good faith reliance on the opinion without giving the recipient notice of the rescission and an opportunity to discontinue those actions.

Industry guides are FTC interpretations of the laws it administers. Their purpose is to encourage businesses to voluntarily abandon certain unlawful practices. To further this end, industry guides are written in lay language. Industry guides lack the force of law. Often, however, behavior that violates an industry guide also violates one of the statutes or other rules the Commission enforces.

Trade Regulation Rules

Unlike industry guides, FTC **trade regulation rules** are written in legalistic language and have the force of law. Thus, the FTC can proceed directly against practices forbidden by a trade regulation rule. This can occur through the *adjudicative proceedings* discussed immediately below. The Commission can also obtain a federal district court *civil penalty* of up to $10,000 for each knowing violation of a rule. Furthermore, it may institute court proceedings to obtain various forms of *consumer redress,* including the payment of damages, the refund of money, the return of property, and the reformation or rescission of contracts.

FTC Adjudicative Proceedings

Often, the FTC proceeds against violations of its statutes or trade regulation rules by administrative action within the Commission itself. The FTC gets evidence of possible violations from private parties, government bodies, and its own investigations. If, after further investigation and discussion, it decides to proceed against the alleged offender (the *respondent*), it enters a formal complaint. The case itself is heard in a public administrative hearing called an *adjudicative proceeding* before an FTC administrative law judge.[2] The judge's decision can be appealed to the FTC's five commissioners and then to the federal courts of appeals and the U.S. Supreme Court.

The usual penalty resulting from a final decision against the respondent is an FTC **cease-and-desist order.** This is basically a command to the respondent ordering it to stop its illegal behavior. As you

will see later in the chapter, however, courts have upheld FTC orders going beyond the command to cease and desist. The civil penalty for noncompliance with a cease-and-desist order is up to $10,000 per violation. Where there is a continuing failure to obey a final order, each day that the violation continues is considered a separate violation.

Many alleged violations are never adjudicated by the FTC but instead are settled through a **consent order.** This is an order approving a negotiated agreement in which the respondent promises to cease certain activities. Consent orders normally provide that the respondent does not admit any violation of the law. The failure to observe a consent order is punishable by civil penalties.

ANTICOMPETITIVE BEHAVIOR

Section 5 of the FTC Act empowers the Commission to prevent "unfair methods of competition." This language allows the FTC to regulate anticompetitive practices made illegal by the Sherman Act.[3] The Commission also has specific statutory authority to enforce the Clayton and Robinson-Patman acts.[4]

For the most part, section 5's application to anticompetitive behavior involves the orthodox antitrust violations discussed in the following two chapters. But section 5 also reaches anticompetitive behavior *not covered by other antitrust statutes.* Section 5 also enables the FTC to proceed against *potential* or *incipient* antitrust violations.

DECEPTION AND UNFAIRNESS

Section 5 of the FTC Act also prohibits "unfair or deceptive acts or practices." This language enables the FTC to regulate a wide range of activities that disadvantage consumers. In doing so, the Commission may proceed under the theory that the activity is *deceptive,* or that it is *unfair.* Here, we set out the general standards that the FTC now uses to define each of these section 5 violations. Much of this discussion involves FTC regulation of advertising, but the standards we outline apply to many other

---

[2]Chapter 46 describes federal administrative proceedings.

[3]Chapter 48 discusses the Sherman Act.

[4]Chapter 49 discusses the Clayton and Robinson-Patman Acts.

misrepresentations, omissions, and practices. Although their details are beyond the scope of this text, the Commission also has enacted numerous trade regulation rules defining specific deceptive and unfair practices.

Deception

The FTC determines the deceptiveness of advertising and other business practices on a case-by-case basis. Courts usually defer to the Commission's determinations. To be considered deceptive under the FTC's 1983 Policy Statement on Deception, an activity must: (1) involve a *material* misrepresentation, omission, or practice; (2) that is *likely to mislead* a consumer; (3) who acts *reasonably* under the circumstances.

Representation, Omission, or Practice Likely to Mislead
Often, sellers expressly make false or misleading claims in their advertisements or other representations. But as stated in the *International Harvester* case (which follows shortly), false or misleading statements can also be implied from the surrounding circumstances. As that case also states, a seller's *omissions* may be deceptive. Finally, certain deceptive *marketing practices* can violate section 5. In one such case, encyclopedia salespeople gained entry to the homes of potential customers by posing as surveyors engaged in advertising research.

In all of these situations, the statement, omission, or practice must be *likely to mislead* a consumer. Actual deception is not required. Determining whether an ad or practice is likely to mislead requires that the FTC evaluate the accuracy of the seller's claims. In some cases, moreover, the Commission requires that sellers *substantiate* objective claims about their products by showing that they have a reasonable basis for making such claims.

The "Reasonable Consumer" Test
To be deceptive, the representation, omission, or practice must also be likely to mislead *reasonable consumers under the circumstances*. This requirement aims to protect sellers from liability for every foolish, ignorant, or outlandish misconception that some consumer might entertain. As the Commission noted some years ago, advertising an American-made pastry as "Danish Pastry" does not violate section 5 just because "a few misguided souls believe . . . that all Danish Pastry is made in Denmark."[5] Also, section 5 is usually not violated by statements of opinion, sales talk, or "puffing"; statements about matters that consumers can easily evaluate for themselves; and statements regarding subjective matters such as taste or smell. Such statements are unlikely to deceive reasonable consumers.

Materiality
Finally, the representation, omission, or practice must be *material*. Material information is important to reasonable consumers and is likely to affect their choice of a product or service. Examples include statements or omissions regarding a product's cost, safety, effectiveness, performance, durability, quality, and warranty protection. In addition, the Commission presumes that express statements are material.

Unfairness

Section 5's prohibition of *unfair* acts or practices enables the FTC to attack behavior that, while not necessarily deceptive, is objectionable for other reasons. As *International Harvester* demonstrates, the FTC now focuses on *consumer injury* when it attacks unfair acts or practices in its own adjudicative proceedings. To violate section 5, this injury must be:

1. *Substantial.* Monetary loss and unwarranted health and safety risks usually constitute substantial harm, but emotional distress or the perceived offensiveness of certain advertisements generally do not.

2. *Not outweighed by any offsetting consumer or competitive benefits produced by the challenged practice.* This element requires the Commission to balance the harm caused by the act or practice against its benefits to consumers and to competition generally. A seller's failure to give a consumer complex technical data about a product, for example, may disadvantage the consumer, but it may also reduce the product's price. Only when an act or practice is injurious in its *net effects* can it be unfair under section 5.

3. *One that consumers could not reasonably have avoided.* An injury is considered reasonably unavoidable when a seller's actions significantly interfere with a consumer's ability to make informed decisions that would have prevented the injury. For example, a seller may withhold

---

[5]*Heinz v. W. Kirchner,* 63 F.T.C. 1282, 1290 (1963).

otherwise-unavailable information about important product features, or use high-pressure sales tactics on vulnerable consumers.

Remedies

Several types of orders can result from a successful FTC adjudicative proceeding attacking deceptive or unfair behavior.[6] One possibility is an order telling

---

[6]Such orders, and FTC regulation of deceptive and unfair advertising generally, may collide with the First Amendment protection of commercial speech discussed in Chapter 3. For the most part, however, the First Amendment has not been a major obstacle to the Commission. One reason is that the constitutional protection given commercial speech does not extend to false or misleading statements and thus does not protect most deceptive advertising.

the respondent to *cease* engaging in the deceptive or unfair conduct. Another is the *affirmative disclosure* of information whose absence made the advertisement deceptive or unfair. Yet another is *corrective advertising.* This requires the seller's future advertisements to correct false impressions created by its past advertisements. In certain cases, moreover, the FTC may issue an *all-products order* extending beyond the product or service whose advertisements violated section 5, and including future advertisements for other products or services marketed by the seller. Finally, the FTC may sometimes go to court to seek the civil penalties or consumer redress noted earlier or to seek injunctive relief.

IN THE MATTER OF INTERNATIONAL HARVESTER COMPANY
104 F.T.C. 949 (1984)

Since at least the early 1950s, the International Harvester Company's gasoline-powered tractors had been subject to "fuel geysering." This was a phenomenon in which hot liquid gasoline would shoot from the tractor's gas tank when the filler cap was opened. The hot gasoline could cause severe burns and could ignite and cause a fire. Over the years, at least 90 fuel geysering incidents involving International Harvester tractors occurred, at least 12 of these involved significant burn injuries, and at least one caused a death.

International Harvester first discovered the full dimensions of the fuel geysering problem in 1963. In that year, it revised its owner's manuals to warn buyers of new gas-powered tractors not to remove the gas cap from a hot or running tractor. In 1976, it produced a new fuel tank decal with a similar warning. Due to an industrywide shift to diesel-powered tractors, however, this warning had a very limited distribution to buyers of new tractors, and it rarely reached former buyers. International Harvester never specifically warned either new or old buyers about the geysering problem until 1980, when it voluntarily made a mass mailing to 630,000 customers.

In 1980, the FTC issued a complaint against International Harvester, alleging that its failure to warn buyers of the fuel geysering problem for 17 years was both deceptive and unfair under FTC Act section 5. The administrative law judge agreed with the Commission on each charge. Due to International Harvester's notification program, however, he concluded that a cease-and-desist order was unnecessary. Both International Harvester and the FTC's complaint counsel appealed to the full Commission.

Douglas, Commissioner   The basic law of this case is section 5 of the FTC Act. That section states that "unfair or deceptive acts or practices . . . are declared unlawful."

Deception

A deception case requires a showing of three elements: (1) there must be a representation, practice, or omission likely to mislead consumers; (2) consumers must be interpreting the message reasonably

under the circumstances; and (3) the misleading effects must be material. Our deception analysis focuses on risk of consumer harm, and actual injury need not be shown. Deception is harmful to consumers, undermines the rational functioning of the marketplace, and never offers increased efficiency or other countervailing benefits.

Deception theory is not limited to false or misleading statements. Under two general circumstances it can also reach omissions. First, it can be deceptive to tell only half the truth, and to omit the rest. This may occur where a seller fails to disclose qualifying information necessary to prevent his affirmative statements from creating a misleading impression. The Commission has challenged the advertising of baldness cures for failing to disclose that most baldness results from male heredity and cannot be treated. It can also be deceptive for a seller to simply remain silent, if he does so under circumstances that constitute an implied but false representation. Such implied representations may arise from the physical appearance of the product, or from the circumstances of a transaction, or they may be based on ordinary consumer expectations. The Commission has upheld charges against sellers who failed to disclose that an apparently new product was actually used, that land sold for investment purposes was poorly suited to that use due to its remote location, and that a book was an abridged rather than a complete edition. One generalization that emerges from these cases is that by offering goods for sale, the seller impliedly represents that they are reasonably fit for their intended uses. The concept of reasonable fitness includes a further implied representation that the products are free of gross safety hazards.

However, the implied warranty of fitness is not violated by all undisclosed safety problems. Where the risk of mishap is very small, it cannot be said that the product is unfit for normal use. Such a case could therefore not satisfy the first element of the deception test, a misleading representation. Harvester manufactured approximately 1.3 million gasoline-powered tractors in the period after 1939. Of this number, twelve are known to have been involved in geysering incidents involving bodily injury. This is an accident rate of less than .001 percent, over a period of more than 40 years.

Unfairness

Unfairness analysis focuses on three criteria: (1) whether the practice creates a serious consumer injury; (2) whether this injury exceeds any offsetting consumer benefits; and (3) whether the injury was one that consumers could not reasonably have avoided. We find that all three criteria are satisfied in the present case.

There clearly has been serious consumer injury. At least one person has been killed and eleven others burned. Many of the burn injuries have been major

ones. It is true that [these injuries] involve only limited numbers of people, but conduct causing a very severe harm to a small number will be covered.

The second criterion states that the consumer injury must not be outweighed by any countervailing benefits to consumers or to competition that the practice also brings about. The principal tradeoff to be considered in this analysis is that involving compliance costs. More information may be helpful to consumers, but such information can be produced only by incurring costs that are ultimately borne as higher prices by those same consumers. Harvester's program which finally led to an effective warning cost the company approximately $2.8 million. Here, however, Harvester's expenses were not large in relation to the injuries that could have been avoided. We therefore conclude that the costs and benefits in this case satisfy the second unfairness criterion.

Finally, the injury must be one that consumers could not reasonably have avoided. Here, tractor operators could have avoided their injuries if they had refrained from removing the cap from a hot or running tractor—something that both the owner's manuals and common knowledge suggested was a dangerous practice. However, whether some consequence is reasonably avoidable depends, not just on whether people know the steps to take to prevent it, but also on whether they understand the necessity of taking those steps. Farmers may have known that loosening the fuel cap was generally a poor practice, but they did not know the full consequences that might follow. Since fuel geysering was a risk that they were not aware of, they could not reasonably have avoided it. This is so even though they had been informed of measures to prevent it. Such information was not the same thing as an effective warning.

Remedy

Having found that Harvester was engaged in unfair practices, we must now determine what corrective measures the public interest will require. Under the particular circumstances of this case, we will issue no order at all. First, Harvester's voluntary notification program has already provided all the relief that could be expected from a Commission order. Second, Harvester has not made a gasoline tractor since 1978 and does not appear likely to do so again in the future.

Decision of the administrative law judge affirmed in part and reversed in part.

CONSUMER PROTECTION LAWS

The term *consumer protection* can include everything from Chapter 20's product liability law to the packaging and labeling regulations listed earlier in Figure 1. Here, we examine federal regulation of product warranties, consumer credit, and product safety. Our main concern is the collection of federal laws governing consumer credit sales.

The Magnuson-Moss Warranty Act

The Magnuson-Moss Warranty Act of 1975 mainly applies to *written warranties* for *consumer products*. Nothing in the act makes sellers give a written warranty, and sellers who decline to give such a warranty generally escape coverage. A consumer product is personal property that is ordinarily used for personal, family, or household purposes. In addition, many Magnuson-Moss provisions apply only when a written warranty is given in connection with the sale of a consumer product to a *consumer*. A consumer is a buyer or transferee of a consumer product who does not use it either for resale or in his own business.

Chapter 20 discusses Magnuson-Moss's provisions giving consumers minimum warranty protection. Here, we examine its rules requiring that consumer warranties contain certain information and that this information be made available to buyers before the sale. Any failure to comply with these rules violates section 5 of the FTC Act and can trigger Commission action. Also, either the FTC or the attorney general may sue to obtain injunctive relief against such violations.

Required Warranty Information The Magnuson-Moss Act and its regulations require the simple, clear, and conspicuous presentation of certain information in written warranties to consumers for consumer products costing more than $15.[7] That information includes: (1) the persons protected by the warranty when coverage is limited to the original purchaser or is otherwise limited; (2) the products, parts, characteristics, components, or properties covered by the warranty; (3) what the warrantor will do in case of a product defect or other failure to conform to the warranty; (4) the time the warranty

begins (if different from the purchase date) and its duration; and (5) the procedure the consumer should follow to obtain the performance of warranty obligations. The act also requires that a warrantor disclose: (1) any limitations on the duration of implied warranties and (2) any attempt to limit consequential damages or other consumer remedies.[8]

Presale Availability of Warranty Information The regulations accompanying Magnuson-Moss also contain detailed rules requiring that warranty terms be made available to a buyer before the sale. These rules generally govern sales of consumer products costing more than $15 to consumers. They set out certain duties that must be met by sellers (usually retailers) and by warrantors (usually manufacturers) of such products. For example:

1. *Sellers* must make the text of the warranty available for the prospective buyer's review before the sale, either by displaying the warranty in close proximity to the product or by furnishing the warranty upon request after posting signs informing buyers of its availability.

2. *Catalog or mail-order sellers* must clearly and conspicuously disclose in their catalog or solicitation either the full text of the warranty or the address from which a free copy can be obtained.

3. *Door-to-door sales.* To give you a concrete illustration of an FTC trade regulation rule, we include the full text of its door-to-door sales rule in Figure 2. As FTC rules go, this one is fairly short and straightforward.

4. *Warrantors* must give sellers the warranty materials necessary for them to comply with the duties stated in paragraph 1; and must give catalog, mail-order, and door-to-door sellers copies of the warranties they need to meet their duties.

Truth in Lending Act

When Congress passed the Truth in Lending Act (TILA) in 1968, its main aims were to increase consumer knowledge and understanding of credit terms by compelling their *disclosure*, and to help

---

[7]Actually, the act states a $5 figure, while the regulations accompanying it state a $15 figure.

[8]Chapter 20 discusses limitations on an implied warranty's duration and on a consumer's remedies.

FIGURE 2 **The FTC's Door-to-Door Sales Rule: 16 C.F.R. section 702.3(d) (1993)**

(d) *Door-to-door sales.* (1) For purposes of this paragraph:

(i) "Door-to-Door sale" means a sale of consumer products in which the seller or his representative personally solicits the sale, including those in response to or following an invitation by a buyer, and the buyer's agreement to offer to purchase is made at a place other than the place of business of the seller.

(ii) "Prospective buyer" means an individual solicited by a door-to-door seller to buy a consumer product who indicates sufficient interest in that consumer product or maintains sufficient contact with the seller for the seller reasonably to conclude that the person solicited is considering purchasing the product.

(2) Any seller who offers for sale to consumers consumer products with written warranties by means of door-to-door sales shall, prior to the consummation of the sale, disclose the fact that the sales representative has copies of the warranties for the warranted products being offered for sale, which may be inspected by the prospective buyer at any time during the sales presentation. Such disclosure shall be made orally and shall be included in any written materials shown to prospective buyers.

---

consumers better shop for credit by commanding *uniform* disclosures. By now, however, the act protects consumers in other ways as well.

Coverage   The TILA generally applies to creditors who extend consumer credit to a debtor in an amount not exceeding $25,000.[9] A *creditor* is a party who regularly extends consumer credit; examples include banks, credit card issuers, and savings and loan associations. Extending credit need not be a creditor's primary business; for instance, auto dealers and retail stores can be creditors so long as they regularly extend credit. To qualify as a creditor, the party in question must also either impose a finance charge or by agreement require payment in more than four installments. *Consumer credit* is credit enabling the purchase of goods, services, or real estate used primarily for personal, family, or household purposes—not business or agricultural purposes. The TILA *debtor* must be a natural person; the act does not protect business organizations.

Disclosure Provisions   The TILA's detailed disclosure provisions break down into three categories.

---

[9]The $25,000 maximum does not apply where a creditor takes a security interest in a debtor's real property or in personal property, such as a mobile home, used as the debtor's principal dwelling. Here, the disclosure rules differ slightly from the rules for closed-end credit discussed shortly. In certain transactions of this kind, moreover, the debtor has a three-day rescission right whose details are beyond the scope of this text.

1. *Open-end credit.* The TILA defines an open-end credit plan as one that contemplates repeated transactions and that involves a finance charge which may be computed from time to time on the unpaid balance. Examples include credit card plans and revolving charge accounts offered by retail stores. Open-end credit plans require two forms of disclosure: (1) an *initial statement* made before the first transaction under the plan, and (2) a series of *periodic statements* (usually, one for each billing cycle). In each case, the required disclosures must be made clearly, conspicuously, and in meaningful sequence.

Among the disclosures required in the initial statement are: (1) when a finance charge is imposed and how it is determined, (2) the amount of any additional charges and the method for computing them, (3) the fact that the creditor has taken or will acquire a security interest in the debtor's property, and (4) the debtor's billing rights. Periodic statements require an even lengthier set of disclosures. Much of the information contained in a monthly credit card statement, for example, is compelled by the TILA.

2. *Closed-end credit.* The TILA requires a different set of disclosures for other credit plans, which generally involve closed-end credit. Closed-end credit such as a car loan or a consumer loan from a finance company is extended for a specific time period; the total amount financed, number of payments, and due dates are all agreed on at the time of the transaction. Examples of the disclosures necessary before the completion of closed-end credit transaction include: (1) the total finance charge; (2) the annual percentage rate (APR); (3) the amount financed; (4) the total number of payments, their due dates, and the amount of each payment; (5) the total dollar value of all payments; (6) any late charges imposed for past-due payments; and (7) any security interest taken by the creditor and the property that it covers.

3. *Credit card applications and solicitations.* In 1988, Congress amended the TILA to impose disclosure requirements on credit card applications and solicitations. These elaborate requirements differ depending on whether the application or solicitation is made by direct mail, telephone, or other means such as catalogs and magazines. To take just one example, direct mail applications and solicitations must include information about matters such as the APR, annual fees, the grace period for paying without incurring a finance charge, and the method for computing the balance on which the finance charge is based.

Other TILA Provisions   The TILA has provisions dealing with *consumer credit advertising*. For example, the act prevents a creditor from "baiting" customers by advertising loan or down payment amounts that it does not usually make available. To help consumers put advertised terms in perspective, ads for open-end consumer credit plans that state any of the plan's specific terms must state various other terms as well. For instance, an advertisement using such terms as "$100 down payment," "8 percent interest," or "$99 per month" must also state other relevant terms such as the APR.

Due to a 1988 amendment, the TILA now regulates *open-end consumer credit plans involving an extension of credit secured by a consumer's principal dwelling*—basically, the popular home equity loans. The act controls *advertisements* for such plans, requiring certain information such as the APR if the ad states any specific terms and forbidding misleading terms such as "free money." It also imposes elaborate disclosure requirements on *applications* for such plans. These include matters such as interest rates, fees, repayment options, minimum payments, and repayment periods. Finally, the act also controls the *terms* of such a plan and the *actions* a creditor can take under it. For example: (1) if the plan involves a variable interest rate, the

"index rate" to which changes in the APR are pegged must be based on some publicly available rate and must not be under the creditor's control; (2) a creditor cannot unilaterally terminate the plan and require immediate repayment of the outstanding balance unless a consumer has made material misrepresentations, has failed to repay the balance, or has adversely affected the creditor's security; and (3) the plan cannot allow a creditor to unilaterally alter its important terms.

Finally, the TILA has a few rules concerning *credit cards*. The most important such rule limits a cardholder's liability for unauthorized use of the card to a maximum of $50. Unauthorized use is use by a person other than the cardholder, where this person lacks express, implied, or apparent authority for such use.[10]

Enforcement   Various federal agencies enforce the TILA. Except in areas committed to a particular agency, overall enforcement authority rests in the FTC. In addition, those who willfully and knowingly violate the act may face criminal prosecution. Civil actions by private parties, including class actions, are also possible.

Consumer Leasing Act

The Consumer Leasing Act, which was passed in 1976, covers leases of personal property: (1) to natural persons (not organizations), (2) for consumer purposes, (3) for an amount not exceeding $25,000, and (4) for a period exceeding four months.

The act requires that a lessor make numerous written *disclosures* to a lessee before the consummation of the lease transaction. Examples include: a description or identification of the leased property; the number, amount, and due dates of the lease payments; their total amount; any express warranties made by the lessor; and any security interest taken by the lessor. The act also requires that lease *advertisements* include certain additional information if they already state: the amount of any payment, the number of required payments, the amount of the down payment, or that no down payment is required.

---

[10]Express, implied, and apparent authority are discussed in Chapter 34. The *Towers* case in that chapter applies this provision of the TILA.

The Consumer Leasing Act subjects creditors violating its disclosure requirements to the same civil suits that are permitted under the TILA. Also, the FTC enforces the act.

Fair Credit Reporting Act

The reports credit bureaus provide to various users can significantly affect one's ability to obtain credit, insurance, employment, and many of life's other goods. Often, affected individuals are unaware of the influence that credit reports had on such decisions. The Fair Credit Reporting Act (FCRA) was enacted in 1970 to give people some protection against abuses in the process of disseminating information about their creditworthiness.

Duties of Consumer Reporting Agencies   The FCRA imposes certain duties on consumer reporting agencies—agencies that regularly compile credit-related information on individuals for the purpose of furnishing consumer credit reports to users. A consumer reporting agency must adopt *reasonable procedures* to:

1. Ensure that *users employ* the information only for the following purposes: consumer credit sales, employment evaluations, the underwriting of insurance, the granting of a government license or other benefit, or any other business transaction where the user has a legitimate business need for the information.

2. Avoid including in a report *obsolete information* predating the report by more than a stated period. This period usually is 7 years; for a prior bankruptcy, it is 10 years. This duty does not apply to credit reports used in connection with certain life insurance policies, large credit transactions, and applications for employment.

3. Assure *maximum possible accuracy* regarding the personal information in credit reports. The *Grant* case (which follows shortly) discusses this duty. However, the act does little to limit the *types* of data included in credit reports. In fact, all kinds of information about a person's character, reputation, personal traits, and mode of life seemingly are permitted.

Disclosure Duties on Users   The FCRA also imposes disclosure duties on *users* of credit reports—mainly, credit sellers, lenders, employers,

and insurers.[11] One of these duties applies to users who order an *investigative consumer report.* This is a credit report that includes information on a person's character, reputation, personal traits, or mode of living and that is based on interviews with neighbors, friends, associates, and the like. If a user procures such a report on a person, it must inform him that the report has been requested, that the report may contain sensitive information, and that he has a right to obtain further disclosures about the user's investigation. If the person requests such disclosures within a reasonable time, the user must reveal the nature and scope of the investigation.

Another disclosure duty arises when, because of information contained in any credit report, a user: (1) rejects an applicant for consumer credit, insurance, or employment; or (2) charges a higher rate for credit or insurance. Here, the user must maintain *reasonable procedures* for advising the affected individual that it relied on the credit report in making its decision, and for stating the name and address of the consumer reporting agency that supplied the report.

Disclosure and Correction of Credit Report Information   After a request from a properly identified individual, a *consumer reporting agency* must normally disclose to that individual: (1) the nature and substance of all its information about the individual, (2) the sources of this information, and (3) the recipients of any credit reports that it has furnished within certain time periods. Then, a person disputing the completeness or accuracy of the agency's information can compel it to reinvestigate. As *Grant* makes clear, the credit bureau must delete the information from the person's file if it finds the information to be inaccurate or unverifiable. An individual who is not satisfied with the agency's investigation may file a brief statement setting forth the nature of her dispute with the agency. If so, any subsequent credit report containing the disputed information must note that it is disputed and must provide either the individual's statement or a clear and accurate summary of it. Also, an agency may be required to notify certain prior recipients of deleted,

---

[11]In addition to the duties stated here, the FCRA also imposes disclosure duties on users who deny consumer credit, or increase the charge for such credit, because of information obtained from *someone other than a consumer reporting agency.*

unverifiable, or disputed information if the individual requests this. However, there is no duty to investigate or to include the consumer's version of the facts if the credit bureau has reason to believe that the individual's request is frivolous or irrelevant.

Enforcement   Violations of the FCRA are violations of FTC Act section 5, and the Commission may use its normal enforcement procedures in such cases. Other federal agencies may also enforce the FCRA in certain situations. The FCRA establishes criminal penalties for: (1) persons who knowingly and willfully obtain consumer information from a credit bureau under false pretenses and (2) credit bureau officers or employees who knowingly or willfully provide information to unauthorized persons. Violations of the FCRA may also trigger private civil suits against consumer reporting agencies and users.

GRANT v. TRW, INC.
789 F. Supp. 690 (D. Md. 1992)

In 1989, Samuel Grant sued, and was sued by, his landlord in a Maryland trial court. Grant recovered $608 against the landlord, and the landlord recovered $476.10 against Grant, leaving Grant with a net recovery of $131.90. In 1990, Texaco denied Grant's application for a Texaco credit card because a TRW, Inc., credit report obtained by Texaco stated that a judgment of $400 had been entered against Grant. After obtaining a credit report from TRW, Grant informed the credit bureau that the litigation between him and his landlord had resulted in a net judgment in his favor. Eventually, TRW sent Grant an "Updated Credit Profile" showing that the $400 judgment had been deleted from Grant's file.

In May 1991, Grant again applied for a Texaco credit card. His application again was denied because the $400 debt appeared on his credit report. Grant then sued TRW under the FCRA in a Maryland trial court. After the case was removed to federal district court, TRW moved to dismiss Grant's claim.

Motz, District Judge   Grant first alleges that TRW violated the FCRA by failing to follow reasonable procedures assuring "maximum possible accuracy of the information concerning the individual about whom the report relates." In order to make out a prima facie violation of [this provision], a consumer must present evidence that a credit reporting agency prepared a report containing inaccurate information. Here, plaintiff concedes that the notation in the credit report that a judgment had been entered against him was accurate insofar as it went. There may be extreme instances in which a technically accurate statement is so inherently misleading that it would run afoul of the "maximum possible accuracy" requirement. For example, if a consumer were a victim of a credit card scam, it would hardly seem accurate for a consumer reporting agency to report that the person was "involved" in the scam. However, the possibility that such extreme cases might be presented does not justify rewriting the FCRA to render actionable the initial reporting of information which, although accurate, is deemed to be misleading because it is incomplete. "Accuracy" can be tested by verification, whereas a determination of "completeness" requires the exercise of judgment on potentially difficult questions concerning the meaning and effect of contextual information. Adding a "completeness" element substantially expands the duties imposed upon consumer reporting agencies and exposes them to dramatically increased litigation.

That is not the end of the matter, however. [The FCRA also] provides: "If the completeness or accuracy of any item of information contained in his file is disputed by a consumer, . . . the consumer reporting agency shall within a reasonable period of time reinvestigate and record the current status of that information unless it has reasonable grounds to believe that the dispute by the consumer is frivolous or irrelevant." This provision . . . places the burden upon the consumer to challenge incomplete information, but, once the challenge is made, it requires reinvestigation and recording of the information provided by the consumer. Here, Grant did notify TRW of the full circumstances surrounding the Maryland trial court judgment, but, inexplicably, after advising Grant that it would delete the challenged notation from his report, TRW neither ef-

fected the deletion nor recorded the information which Grant had provided. This dereliction is actionable under [the FCRA].

TRW's motion to dismiss denied.

Equal Credit Opportunity Act

The Equal Credit Opportunity Act (ECOA), originally passed in 1974, prohibits credit discrimination on the bases of sex, marital status, age, race, color, national origin, religion, and the obtaining of income from public assistance. The ECOA covers all entities that regularly arrange, extend, renew, or continue credit. Examples include banks; savings and loan associations; credit card issuers; and many retailers, auto dealers, and realtors. The act is not limited to consumer credit, and also covers business and commercial loans.

The ECOA governs all phases of a credit transaction. As authorized by the act, the Federal Reserve Board has promulgated regulations detailing permissible and impermissible creditor behavior at each stage. Even where the regulations do not specifically prohibit certain creditor behavior, that behavior may still violate the act itself. Even credit practices that are perfectly neutral on their face may result in ECOA violations if the practice has an adverse statistical impact on one of the ECOA's protected classes.[12]

The ECOA also requires that creditors notify applicants of the action taken on a credit application within 30 days of its receipt or any longer reasonable time stated in the regulations. If the action is unfavorable, an applicant is entitled to a statement of reasons from the creditor.

The ECOA is enforced by several federal agencies, with overall enforcement resting in the hands of the FTC. Which agency enforces the act depends on the type of creditor or credit involved. Civil actions by aggrieved private parties, including class actions, also are possible.

Fair Credit Billing Act

The Fair Credit Billing Act, effective in 1975, is mainly aimed at credit card issuers. Although the act regulates the credit card business in other ways, its most important provisions involve billing disputes.[13] To trigger these provisions, a cardholder must give the issuer written notice of an alleged error in a billing statement within 60 days of the time that the statement is sent to the cardholder. Then, within two complete billing cycles or 90 days (whichever is less), the issuer must either: (1) correct the cardholder's account, or (2) send the cardholder a written statement justifying the statement's accuracy. Until the issuer takes either of these steps, it may not: (1) restrict or close the cardholder's account because of her failure to pay the disputed amount, (2) try to collect the disputed amount, or (3) report or threaten to report the cardholder's failure to pay the disputed amount to a third party such as a consumer reporting agency.

Once an issuer has met the act's requirements, it must also give a cardholder at least 10 days to pay the disputed amount before making an unfavorable report to a third party. If the cardholder disputes the issuer's justification within the 10-day period allowed for payment, the issuer can make such a report only if it also tells the third party that the debt is disputed and gives the cardholder the third party's name and address. In addition, the issuer must report the final resolution of the dispute to the third party.

An issuer that fails to comply with any of these rules forfeits its right to collect $50 of the disputed amount from the cardholder. Because the issuer may

---

[12]This resembles the adverse impact or disparate impact method of proof used in employment discrimination cases under Title VII of the 1964 Civil Rights Act. See Chapter 50.

[13]The Federal Reserve Board has promulgated regulations regarding the resolution of billing errors, and the FTC has some enforcement authority under the act as well.

still be able to collect the balance on large disputed debts, it is doubtful whether this provision does much to deter violations of the act.

Fair Debt Collection Practices Act

Concern over abusive, deceptive, and unfair practices by debt collectors led Congress to pass the Fair Debt Collection Practices Act (FDCPA) in 1977. The act applies to debts that involve money, property, insurance, or services obtained by a *consumer* for *consumer purposes*. Normally, the act only covers those who are in the business of collecting debts owed to *others*. However, creditors who collect their own debts are covered when by using a name other than their own name they indicate that a third party is collecting the debt.

Communication Rules   Except where necessary to locate a debtor, the FDCPA generally prevents debt collectors from contacting third parties such as the debtor's employer, relatives, or friends. The act also limits a collector's contacts with the debtor himself. Unless the debtor consents, for instance, a collector cannot contact him at unusual or inconvenient times or places, or at his place of employment if the employer forbids such contacts. Also, a collector cannot contact a debtor if it knows that the debtor is represented by an attorney, unless the attorney consents to such contact or fails to respond to the collector's communications. In addition, a collector must cease most communications with a debtor if the debtor gives the creditor written notification that he refuses to pay the debt or that he does not desire further communications from the collector.

The FDCPA also requires a collector to give a debtor certain information about the debt within five days of the collector's first communication with the debtor. If the debtor disputes the debt in writing within 30 days after receiving this information, the collector must cease its collection efforts until it sends verification of the debt to the debtor. The *Miller* case (which follows shortly) applies this provision of the FDCPA.

Specific Forbidden Practices   The FDCPA sets out categories of forbidden collector practices and lists specific examples of each category. The listed examples, however, do not exhaust the ways that debt collectors can violate the act. The categories are:

1. *Harassment, oppression, or abuse.* Examples include threats of violence, obscene or abusive language, and repeated phone calls.

2. *False or misleading misrepresentations.* Among the FDCPA's listed examples are statements that a debtor will be imprisoned for failure to pay, that a collector will take an action it is not legally entitled to take, that a collector is affiliated with the government, or that misstate the amount of the debt.

3. *Unfair practices.* These include: collecting from a debtor an amount not authorized by the agreement creating the debt, getting a debtor to accept a collect call before revealing the call's true purpose, and falsely or unjustifiably threatening to take a debtor's property.

Enforcement   The FTC is the main enforcement agency for the FDCPA, although other agencies enforce it in certain cases. The FDCPA also permits individual civil actions and class actions by the affected debtor or debtors.[14]

---

[14]Also, some debt collection practices might lead to tort liability for invasion of privacy or perhaps even for intentional infliction of emotional distress. Chapter 6 discusses these torts.

MILLER v. PAYCO-GENERAL AMERICAN CREDITS, INC.

943 F.2d 482 (4th Cir. 1991)

Lenvil Miller owed $2,501.61 to the Star Bank of Cincinnati. The bank referred the collection of Miller's account to Payco-General American Credits, Inc., a debt collection agency. Payco sent Miller a one-page collection form whose front side provided information about the creditor, the amount of the debt, and Payco's address. In the middle of the page, in large, red, boldfaced type, was the statement: THIS IS A DEMAND FOR

IMMEDIATE FULL PAYMENT OF YOUR DEBT. After that came the following sentences: YOUR SERIOUSLY PAST DUE ACCOUNT HAS BEEN GIVEN TO US FOR IMMEDIATE ACTION. YOU HAVE HAD AMPLE TIME TO PAY YOUR DEBT, BUT YOU HAVE NOT. IF THERE IS A VALID REASON, PHONE US AT [telephone number] TODAY. IF NOT, PAY US—NOW. The bottom third of the form was almost completely filled by the single word NOW in white letters nearly two inches tall against a red background.

At the very bottom of the page in the smallest type appearing on the form was the statement: NOTICE: SEE REVERSE SIDE FOR IMPORTANT INFORMATION. The reverse side of the form contained the "validation notice" required by the FDCPA—statements informing a consumer how to obtain verification of the debt.

Miller sued in federal district court, alleging that the form did not comply with the FDCPA. After the court granted Payco's motion for summary judgment, Miller appealed.

Wilkinson, Circuit Judge   The FDCPA requires a debt collector to send a consumer, either in its initial communication or within five days of its initial communication, a written notice containing: (1) the debt amount; (2) the name of the current creditor; (3) a statement that if the consumer disputes the debt in writing within thirty days, the collector will send verification of the debt to the consumer; (4) a statement that if the consumer does not dispute the debt within thirty days, the collector will assume the debt to be valid; and (5) a statement that the collector will send the name of the original creditor, upon written request within thirty days. If the consumer, in writing, disputes the debt or requests the name of the original creditor, then the collector must halt all collection efforts until it mails verification of the debt or the creditor's name to the consumer.

In interpreting the FDCPA, we bear in mind that the statute was enacted to eliminate abusive debt collection practices. Congress included the debt validation provisions to guarantee that consumers would receive adequate notice of their legal rights. Thus, a debt collector does not comply with the act merely by inclusion of the required debt validation notice; the notice must be conveyed effectively to the debtor. For example, a validation notice printed on the back of a form letter where the front of the letter contains no reference to the notice does not comply with the act. Furthermore, the notice must not be overshadowed or contradicted by other messages or notices appearing in the initial communication.

We agree with Miller that the form both contradicted and overshadowed the validation notice, preventing the notice's effective communication. The front of the form demands IMMEDIATE FULL PAYMENT, and commands the consumer to PHONE US TODAY, emphasized by the word NOW in white letters nearly two inches tall against a red background. The message conveyed by those statements on the face of the form flatly contradicts the information contained on the back.

A consumer who wished to obtain validation of his debt could lose his rights under the statute if he followed the commands to telephone. The FDCPA guarantees that validation will be sent and collection activities will cease only when the consumer disputes the debt in writing. If a consumer attempted to exercise his statutory rights by making the requested telephone call, Payco would be under no obligation to comply with the act's directives to verify the debt and to cease collection efforts.

The emphasis on immediate action also stands in contradiction to the FDCPA [provision] which provides consumers a thirty-day period to decide to request validation. A consumer who received Payco's form could easily be confused between the commands to respond "immediately," "now," and "today," and the thirty-day response time required by the statute.

Payco responds that [the FDCPA] does not mandate a particular format, type size, location, or conspicuous position for the validation notice, but rather looks entirely to its content. We agree that to prescribe the exact size, color, or method of presentation for the validation notice would be judicial rule-writing in which we shall not indulge. Our role instead is the essentially negative one of examining whether a given notice comports with the statute. There are numerous and ingenious ways of circumventing the act under cover of a technical compliance. Payco has devised one such way, and we think that to uphold it would strip the statute of its meaning.

Judgment reversed in favor of Miller. Case remanded to the district court for further proceedings.

Product Safety Regulation

Yet another facet of consumer protection law is federal regulation of product safety. As discussed in Chapter 20, sellers and manufacturers of dangerously defective products often are civilly liable to those injured by such products. Damage recoveries, however, are at best an after-the-fact remedy for injuries caused by such products. Thus, federal law also seeks to promote product safety by *direct regulation* of consumer products.

The Consumer Product Safety Act The most important federal product safety measure is the Consumer Product Safety Act of 1972 (CPSA). The CPSA established the Consumer Product Safety Commission (CPSC), an independent regulatory agency that is the main federal body concerned with the safety of consumer products. Among the CPSC's activities are the following: (1) issuing *consumer product safety standards* (which normally involve the performance of consumer products or require product warnings or instructions); (2) issuing rules *banning* certain *hazardous products*; (3) bringing suit in federal district court to eliminate the dangers presented by *imminently hazardous* consumer products (products that pose an immediate and unreasonable risk of death, serious illness, or severe personal injury); and (4) *ordering private parties to address "substantial product hazards"* after receiving notice of such hazards. The CPSA's remedies and enforcement devices include injunctions, the seizure of products, civil penalties, criminal penalties, and private damage suits.

Other Federal Product Safety Regulation Other federal statutes besides the CPSA regulate various specific consumer products. Among the subjects so regulated are toys, cigarette labeling and advertising, eggs, meat, poultry, smokeless tobacco, flammable fabrics, drugs, cosmetics, pesticides, and motor vehicles. Some of these laws are enforced by the CPSC and some by other bodies.

ETHICAL AND PUBLIC POLICY CONCERNS

1. In the *International Harvester* case earlier in this chapter, the FTC weighed the consumer injury caused by fuel geysering against the costs of providing effective warnings about it. In this case, 12 people had been seriously burned by fuel geysering over a period of about 40 years, and 1 of these people died. The Commission concluded that the injuries that could have been avoided by a warning outweighed the $2.8 million apparently required for an effective warning. However, its method clearly left open the possibility that in some cases a practice's benefits to consumers or to competition might outweigh the harm it causes.

Is it morally right to balance personal injury and human life against economic gain? Doesn't this amount to putting a dollar value on human life? Isn't each human life infinitely precious? How can decisionmaking processes like the FTC's ever be justified?

On the other hand, if you think that the Commission's balancing exercise *is* justifiable, how is one to strike the balance? How would you have struck the balance in the *International Harvester* case?

2. Over the years, some people have argued that modern mass advertising for consumer products and services is much more *manipulative* than *informative*. The idea is that by playing on unconscious or semiconscious consumer impulses of all kinds, such advertising motivates consumers to buy products for reasons other than those products' innate attributes. Generally speaking, do you think that this charge is accurate or inaccurate? In answering, consider: (1) whether advertisers often try such ploys, and (2) whether they generally are effective when tried.

Assuming for the sake of argument that the charge is generally accurate, does FTC Act section 5's ban on *deceptive* advertising do much to address the problem? What body of law discussed in this chapter might conceivably do so?

Again assuming that the charge is accurate, consider two other questions. First, how would manipulative advertising fare under the *utilitarian* ethical criteria discussed in Chapter 4? *Hint:* If advertising manipulates consumers, what happens to the idea that free competition maximizes consumer welfare by rewarding those who sell superior products and services and weeding out their inferior competitors? Second, how would manipulative advertising fare under the two versions of Kant's *categorical imperative* discussed in Chapter 4?

PROBLEMS AND PROBLEM CASES

1. For a long time, advertisements for Listerine Antiseptic Mouthwash had claimed that Listerine was beneficial in the treatment of colds, cold symptoms, and sore throats. An FTC adjudicative proceeding concluded that these claims were false. Thus, the Commission ordered Warner-Lambert Company, the manufacturer of Listerine, to include the following statement in future Listerine advertisements: "Contrary to prior advertising, Listerine will not help prevent colds or sore throats or lessen their severity." Warner-Lambert argued that this order was invalid because it went beyond a command to simply cease and desist from illegal behavior. Is Warner-Lambert correct?

2. Patriot Alcohol Testers, Inc. marketed a coin-operated blood alcohol measuring device that could be placed in bars and restaurants for use by patrons. Patriot falsely represented that distributors' annual income from the device would be $130 per week per device installed. Make *two* arguments that this representation is material under the deception standard the FTC uses under FTC Act section 5.

3. World Travel Vacation Brokers, Inc., advertised Hawaii vacations by offering $29 certificates that could be redeemed for roundtrip airfare to Hawaii. To get these certificates, consumers had to book hotel reservations through World Travel for a minimum of eight days and seven nights at World Travel's "hotel cost." The ads stated that World Travel could offer this $29 price because it had

purchased excess frequent flyer coupons, its huge purchasing volume had enabled it to obtain big discounts from airlines, and the package was part of a promotional "deregulation special" offered by the airlines.

World Travel sold between 600,000 and 700,000 of the $29 Hawaii vacation certificates. Unfortunately for their purchasers, World Travel had effectively charged them full airfare by jacking up the "hotel cost." Language on the certificates, however, stated that "prices do not reflect actual hotel rates." Under the FTC's section 5 policy statement on deceptive advertising, did the consumers who purchased the certificates act reasonably under the circumstances?

4. Between 1966 and 1975, the Orkin Exterminating Company, the world's largest termite and pest control firm, offered its customers a "lifetime" guarantee that could be renewed each year by paying a definite amount specified in its contracts with the customers. The contracts gave no indication that the fees could be raised for any but narrowly specified reasons. Beginning in 1980, Orkin unilaterally breached these contracts by imposing higher-than-agreed-upon annual renewal fees. About 200,000 contracts were breached in this way, and Orkin realized about $7 million in additional revenues from customers who renewed at the higher fees. The additional fees did not purchase a higher level of service than that originally provided for in the contracts. Also, while some of Orkin's competitors may have been willing to assume Orkin's pre-1975 contracts at the fees stated therein, they would not have offered a fixed, locked-in "lifetime" renewal fee like that Orkin originally provided. Under the three-part test stated in the text, did Orkin's behavior violate FTC Act section 5's prohibition against *unfair* acts or practices?

5. Patron Aviation, Inc., an aviation company, bought an airplane engine from L&M Aircraft. The engine was assembled and shipped to L&M by Teledyne Industries, Inc. L&M installed the engine in one of Patron's airplanes. The engine turned out to be defective, and Patron sued L&M and Teledyne. One of the issues presented by the case was whether the Magnuson-Moss Act was applicable. Does the Magnuson-Moss Act apply to this transaction?

6. John and Marilyn Olson ran their farming business through a corporation. They obtained a number of loans from a local bank. Give *two* reasons why the Truth in Lending Act does *not* apply to these loans.

7. Smith rented a television set from ABC Rental Systems. The rental agreement stated that the lease was a week-to-week arrangement and that it was terminable by either party at any time. The agreement stated the figures "$16.00/55.00" in a space provided for the rental rate. The $16 figure was the weekly rate, and the $55 figure was a reduced monthly rate available to a consumer who wished to pay monthly. Smith was never provided with any of the disclosures required by the Consumer Leasing Act. Does the Consumer Leasing Act apply to this transaction?

8. In 1988, Vincent Mone quit his job at Sawyer of Napa, Inc., a California corporation whose president and CEO was Milton Dranow. When Mone established a competing firm, Dranow sued him for $5 million, alleging unfair competition. Three days before filing suit, Dranow had obtained a credit report on Mone from TRW, Inc., a credit reporting agency. Under the Fair Credit Reporting Act, did TRW act properly in giving Dranow the credit report on Mone?

9. The Credit Bureau, Inc. (CBI), maintains credit records on consumers, among them a Mr. and Mrs. Rush. The Rushes obtained a CBI report on themselves, and found an "R-9" credit rating (the lowest possible) next to the entry for their Macy's account. This poor credit rating caused the Rushes to be denied credit on several occasions. The Rushes sued Macy's under the Fair Credit Reporting Act. Will they win under the FCRA? Assume for purposes of argument that the entry was erroneous and was the fault of Macy's.

10. Sylvia Miller, a married woman, wanted to buy a pair of loveseats from a retail furniture store. The store offered to arrange financing for her through the Public Industrial Loan Company. Public later refused to extend credit to Miller unless her husband cosigned the debt obligation. The reason was a consumer reporting agency's unfavorable credit report on Miller. Was Public's action forbidden sex discrimination under the Equal Credit Opportunity Act? In any event, what other legal remedy might Miller have here?

11. John E. Koerner & Co., Inc. applied for a credit card account with the American Express Company. The application was for a company account designed for business customers. Koerner asked American Express to issue cards bearing the company's name to Louis Koerner and four other officers of the corporation. Koerner was required to sign a company account form, agreeing that he would be jointly and severally liable with the company for all charges incurred through use of the company card. American Express issued the cards requested by the company. Thereafter, the cards were used almost totally for business purposes, although Koerner occasionally used his card for personal expenses. Later, a dispute regarding charges appearing on the company account arose. Does the Fair Credit Billing Act apply to this dispute?

12. In connection with its attempt to collect a debt, Collection Accounts Terminal, Inc., sent Josephine Rutyna a letter stating: "Our field investigator has . . . been instructed to make an investigation in your neighborhood and to personally call on your employer." Does this statement violate the Fair Debt Collection Practices Act? Why or why not?

13. ◖▮▮◗ *Video Case.* See "Henry and Wanda." Henry and Wanda, a married couple, had a joint charge account. After Henry left Wanda following an argument over money, he made many purchases on the account, eventually overdrawing it. As a result, Wanda received numerous phone calls at all hours of the day and night. In one of these calls, the caller referred to Wanda as a "deadbeat" because she would not pay her husband's debts. In another, the caller threatened to contact Wanda's employer. Eventually, one of the callers located Henry by contacting his mother, telling her that Henry's father had been involved in a serious accident, and asserting that it was necessary to contact Henry so that he could donate blood to his father. Assuming that all these actions were taken by a covered debt collector and that Henry and Wanda both are protected debtors, explain how these various practices *may* have violated the Fair Debt Collection Practices Act.

ANTITRUST: THE
SHERMAN ACT

INTRODUCTION

The post–Civil War emergence and growth of large industrial combines and trusts significantly altered the business environment of earlier years. A major feature of this economic phenomenon was the tendency of various large business entities to acquire dominant positions in their industries by buying up smaller competitors or engaging in practices aimed at driving smaller competitors out of business. This behavior led to public demands for legislation to preserve competitive market structures and prevent the accumulation of great economic power in the hands of a few firms.

Although the common law had long held that contracts unreasonably restraining trade violated public policy, courts could implement this rule only by refusing to enforce such a contract if one of the parties objected to it. Legislation was therefore necessary to give the courts greater power to deal with the problem of anticompetitive practices. Congress responded in 1890 with the Sherman Act. It supplemented this response by enacting the Clayton Act in 1914 and the Robinson-Patman Act in 1936.

PRESERVATION OF COMPETITION

In enacting the antitrust statutes, Congress adopted a public policy in favor of preserving and promoting free competition as the most efficient means of allocating social resources. The Supreme Court summarized the rationale for this faith in competition's positive effects when it said:

Basic to faith that a free economy best promotes the public weal is that goods must stand the cold test of competition; that the public, acting through the market's impersonal judgment, shall allocate the nation's resources and thus direct the course its economic development will take.[1]

Congress thus presumed, in enacting the antitrust statutes, that competition was more likely to exist in an industrial structure characterized by a large number of competing firms than in concentrated industries dominated by a few large competitors. As Judge Learned Hand observed:

---

[1]*Times-Picayune Co. v. United States*, 345 U.S. 594 (U.S. Sup. Ct. 1953).

Many people believe that possession of an unchallenged economic power deadens initiative, discourages thrift, and depresses energy; that immunity from competition is a narcotic, and rivalry is a stimulant, to industrial progress; that the spur of constant stress is necessary to counteract an inevitable disposition to let well enough alone.[2]

Despite this longstanding policy in favor of competitive market structures, the antitrust laws have not been very successful in halting the trend toward concentration in American industry. The market structure in many important industries today is highly *oligopolistic*, with the bulk of production accounted for by a few dominant firms. Traditional antitrust concepts are often difficult to apply to the behavior of firms in these highly concentrated markets. Recent years have witnessed the emergence of new ideas that challenge various longstanding antitrust policy assumptions.

THE ANTITRUST POLICY DEBATE

Antitrust enforcement necessarily reflects fundamental public policy judgments about the economic activities to be allowed and the industrial structure best suited to foster desirable economic activity. Given the importance of such judgments to the future of the American economy, it is not surprising that antitrust policy spurs vigorous public debate.

Chicago School Theories

In recent years, traditional antitrust assumptions have faced a highly effective challenge from commentators and courts advocating the application of microeconomic theory to antitrust enforcement. These new methods of antitrust analysis are commonly called **Chicago School theories** because many of their major premises were advanced by scholars associated with the University of Chicago.

Chicago School advocates tend to view *economic efficiency* as the primary, if not the sole, goal of antitrust enforcement. They are far less concerned with the supposed effects of industrial concentration than are traditional antitrust thinkers. Even highly concentrated industries, they argue, may engage in significant forms of nonprice competition, such as competition in advertising, styling, and warranties.

They also point out that concentration in a particular industry does not necessarily preclude *interindustry competition* among related industries. For example, a highly concentrated glass container industry may still face significant competition from the makers of metal, plastic, and fiberboard containers. Chicago School advocates are also quick to point out that many markets today are international in scope, so that highly concentrated domestic industries such as automobiles, steel, and electronics may nonetheless face effective foreign competition. In fact, they argue that the technological developments necessary for American industry to compete more effectively in international markets may require the great capital resources that result from concentration in domestic industry.

According to the Chicago School viewpoint, the traditional antitrust focus on the structure of industry has improperly emphasized protecting *competitors* rather than protecting *competition*. Chicago School theorists argue that the primary thrust of antitrust policy should involve *anticonspiracy* efforts rather than *anticoncentration* efforts. In addition, most of these theorists take a rather lenient view toward various vertically imposed restrictions on price and distribution that have been traditionally seen as undesirable, because they believe that such restrictions can promote efficiencies in distribution. Thus, they tend to be more tolerant of attempts by manufacturers to control resale prices and establish exclusive distribution systems for their products.

Traditional Antitrust Theories

Traditional antitrust thinkers, however, contend that although economic efficiency is *an* important goal of antitrust enforcement, antitrust policy has historically embraced *political* as well as economic values. Concentrated economic power, they argue, is undesirable for a variety of noneconomic reasons. It may lead to antidemocratic concentrations of political power. Moreover, it may stimulate greater governmental intrusions into the economy in the same way that the post–Civil War activities of the trusts led to the passage of the antitrust laws. According to the traditional view, lessening concentration enhances individual freedom by reducing the barriers to entry that confront would-be competitors and by ensuring broader input into economic decisions having important social consequences. Judge Learned Hand summed up this perspective on antitrust policy:

---

[2]*United States v. Aluminum Co. of America, Inc.*, 148 F.2d 416 (2d Cir. 1945).

Great industrial consolidations are inherently undesirable, regardless of their economic results. Throughout the history of [sections 1 and 2 of the Sherman Act] it has been constantly assumed that one of their purposes was to perpetuate and preserve, for its own sake and in spite of possible cost, an organization of industry in small units which can effectively compete with each other.[3]

Effect of Chicago School Notions

Chicago School notions, however, have had a significant impact on the course of antitrust enforcement in recent years. The Supreme Court and many of President Reagan's appointees to the lower federal courts have given credence to Chicago School economic arguments in many cases. Some of President Reagan's appointees to the Department of Justice and the Federal Trade Commission were sympathetic to Chicago School policy views. The Bush administration's agency appointees appeared to be somewhat more inclined toward government enforcement of the antitrust laws than their Reagan administration predecessors had been. Public positions taken by Department of Justice officials during the early portion of the Clinton administration (when this book went to press) revealed the likelihood of a stepped-up government role in policing the marketplace for probable antitrust violations. Nevertheless, the presence on the federal bench of so many judges embracing Chicago School ideas means that those views are likely to continue to have an impact on the shape of antitrust law for the foreseeable future.

JURISDICTION, TYPES OF ANTITRUST CASES, AND STANDING

Jurisdiction

The Sherman Act outlaws monopolization and agreements in restraint of trade. Because the federal government's power to regulate business originates in the Commerce Clause of the U.S. Constitution, the federal antitrust laws apply only to behavior having some significant impact on *interstate* or *foreign* commerce.[4] Given the interdependent nature

of our national economy, it is normally fairly easy to demonstrate that a challenged activity either involves interstate commerce (the "in commerce" jurisdiction test) or has a substantial effect on interstate commerce (the "effect on commerce" jurisdiction test). Various cases indicate that a business activity may have a substantial effect on interstate commerce even though the activity occurs solely within the borders of one state. Activities that are purely *intrastate* in their effects, however, are outside the scope of federal antitrust jurisdiction and must be challenged under state law.

The federal antitrust statutes have been extensively applied to activities affecting the international commerce of the United States. The activities of American firms operating outside U.S. borders may be attacked under our antitrust laws if those activities have an intended effect on our foreign commerce. Likewise, foreign firms "continuously engaged" in our domestic commerce are subject to federal antitrust jurisdiction. Determining the full extent of the extraterritorial reach of our antitrust laws often involves courts in difficult questions of antitrust exemptions and immunities (to be discussed in Chapter 49). The extraterritorial reach issue also suggests a troubling political prospect: Aggressive expansion of antitrust law's applicability may create tension between our antitrust policy and our foreign policy in general.

Types of Cases and the Role of Pretrial Settlements

Sherman Act violations may give rise to criminal prosecutions and civil litigation instituted by the federal government (through the Department of Justice), as well as to civil suits filed by private parties. A significant percentage of the antitrust cases brought by the Department of Justice are settled without trial through the use of *nolo contendere* pleas in criminal cases and *consent decrees* in civil cases. A defendant who pleads nolo contendere technically has not admitted guilt. The sentencing court, however, is free to impose the same penalty that would be appropriate in the case of a guilty plea or a conviction at trial. Consent decrees involve a defendant's consent to remedial measures aimed at remedying the competitive harm resulting from his actions. Because neither a nolo plea nor a consent decree is admissible as proof of a violation of the

---

[3]*United States v. Aluminum Co. of America, Inc.*, 148 F.2d 416 (2d Cir. 1945).

[4]Chapter 3 discusses the Commerce Clause in detail.

Sherman Act in a later civil suit filed by a private plaintiff, both of these devices are often attractive to antitrust defendants.

Criminal Prosecutions

Individuals criminally convicted of Sherman Act violations may receive a fine of up to $350,000 per violation and/or a term of imprisonment of up to three years. Corporations convicted of violating the Sherman Act may be fined up to $10 million per violation. Before an individual may be found criminally responsible under the Sherman Act, however, the government must prove an *anticompetitive effect* flowing from the challenged activity, as well as *criminal intent* on the defendant's part. The level of criminal intent required for a violation is a "knowledge of [the challenged activity's] probable consequences" rather than a specific intent to violate the antitrust laws.[5] Civil violations of the antitrust laws may be proved, however, by evidence of either an unlawful purpose or an anticompetitive effect.

Civil Litigation

The federal courts have broad injunctive powers to remedy civil antitrust violations. Courts may order convicted defendants to *divest* themselves of the stock or assets of acquired companies, to *divorce* themselves from a functional level of their operations (e.g., ordering a manufacturer to sell its captive retail outlets), to refrain from particular conduct in the future, and to cancel existing contracts. In extreme cases, courts may also enter a *dissolution decree* ordering a defendant to liquidate its assets and cease business operations. Private individuals and the federal Department of Justice may seek such injunctive relief regarding antitrust violations.

Treble Damages for Private Plaintiffs   Section 4 of the Clayton Act gives private parties a significant incentive to enforce the antitrust laws by providing that private plaintiffs injured by Sherman Act or Clayton Act violations are entitled to recover *treble damages* plus court costs and attorney's fees from the defendant. This means that once antitrust plaintiffs have demonstrated the amount of their

actual losses (such as lost profits or increased costs) resulting from the challenged violation, this amount is tripled. The potential for treble damage liability plainly presents a significant deterrent threat to potential antitrust violators. For example, a famous antitrust case against General Electric Company and several other electrical equipment manufacturers resulted in treble damage awards in excess of $200 million. Some Chicago School critics have argued unsuccessfully that treble damages should be allowed only for *per se* antitrust violations, with plaintiffs who prove *"rule of reason"* violations being limited to recovering actual damages. (Per se and rule of reason violations are discussed later in this chapter.)

Standing

Private plaintiffs seeking to enforce the antitrust laws must first demonstrate that they have **standing** to sue. This means that they must show a *direct antitrust injury* as a result of the challenged behavior. An antitrust injury results from the unlawful aspects of the challenged behavior and is of the sort Congress sought to prevent by enacting the antitrust laws. For example, in *Brunswick Corp. v. Pueblo Bowl-o-Mat, Inc.*,[6] the operator of a chain of bowling centers (Pueblo) challenged a bowling equipment manufacturer's (Brunswick's) acquisition of various competing bowling centers that had defaulted on payments owed to Brunswick for equipment purchases. In essence, Pueblo asserted that if Brunswick had not acquired them, the failing bowling centers would have gone out of business—in which event Pueblo's profits presumably would have increased. The Supreme Court rejected Pueblo's claim because Pueblo's supposed losses flowed from Brunswick's having *preserved* competition by acquiring the failing centers. Allowing recovery for such losses would be contrary to the antitrust purpose of *promoting* competition. The antitrust injury requirement also plays a major role in the *Atlantic Richfield* case, which appears later in the chapter.

Importance of Direct Injury   Proof that an antitrust injury is *direct* is critical because the Supreme Court has held that *indirect purchasers*

[5]*United States v. U.S. Gypsum Co.*, 438 U.S. 422 (U.S. Sup. Ct. 1978).

[6]429 U.S. 477 (U.S. Sup. Ct. 1977).

lack standing to sue for antitrust violations. In *Illinois Brick Co. v. State of Illinois*,[7] the state of Illinois and several other governmental entities sought treble damages from concrete block suppliers who, they alleged, were guilty of illegally fixing the price of the block used in the construction of public buildings. The plaintiffs acknowledged that the builders hired to construct the buildings in question had actually paid the inflated prices for the blocks, but argued that these illegal costs probably had been passed on to them in the form of higher prices for building construction. The Supreme Court refused to allow recovery, however, holding that granting standing to indirect purchasers would create a risk of "duplicative recoveries" by purchasers at various levels in a product's chain of distribution. The Court also observed that affording standing to indirect purchasers would lead to difficult problems of tracing competitive injuries through several levels of distribution and assessing the extent of an indirect purchaser's actual losses.

A number of state legislatures responded to *Illinois Brick* by enacting statutes allowing indirect purchasers to sue under *state* antitrust statutes. The Supreme Court has held that the *Illinois Brick* holding does not preempt such statutes.[8]

SECTION 1—RESTRAINTS OF TRADE

Concerted Action

Section 1 of the Sherman Act states that "[e]very contract, combination in the form of trust or otherwise, or conspiracy, in restraint of trade or commerce among the several states, or with foreign nations is declared to be illegal." A **contract** is any agreement, express or implied, between *two or more* persons or business entities to restrain competition; a **combination** is a continuing *partnership* in restraint of trade; a **conspiracy** occurs when *two or more* persons or business entities join for the purpose of restraining trade.

The above statutory language makes obvious the conclusion that that section 1 of the Sherman Act is aimed at **concerted action** (i.e., *joint action*) in restraint of trade. *Purely unilateral action* by a competitor, on the other hand, cannot violate section 1.

This statutory section reflects a basic public policy that businesspersons should make important competitive decisions on their own, rather than in conjunction with competitors. In his famous book *The Wealth of Nations* (1776), Adam Smith acknowledged both the danger to competition posed by concerted action and the tendencies of competitors to engage in such action. Smith observed that "[p]eople of the same trade seldom meet together, even for merriment and diversion, [without] the conversation end[ing] in a conspiracy against the public, or in some contrivance to raise prices."

Problems Posed by Concerted Action Requirement

Section 1's concerted action requirement poses two major problems. First, how separate must two business entities be before their joint activities are subject to the act's prohibitions? For example, it has long been held that a corporation cannot conspire with itself or its employees and that a corporation's employees cannot be guilty of a conspiracy in the absence of some independent party. What about conspiracies, however, among related corporate entities? In decisions more than 40 years ago, the Supreme Court appeared to hold that a corporation could violate the Sherman Act by conspiring with a wholly owned subsidiary. More recently, however, in *Copperweld Corp. v. Independence Tube Corp.*,[9] the Court repudiated the "intra-enterprise conspiracy doctrine." The Court held that a parent company is legally incapable of conspiring with a wholly owned subsidiary for Sherman Act purposes, because an agreement between parent and subsidiary does not create the risk to competition that results when two independent entities act in concert. It remains to be seen whether this approach extends to corporate subsidiaries and affiliates that are not wholly owned. *Copperweld*'s logic would appear, however, to cover any subsidiary in which the parent firm has a controlling interest.

A second—and more difficult—problem frequently accompanies attempts to enforce section 1. This problem arises when courts are asked to *infer* (from the relevant circumstances) the existence of an agreement or conspiracy to restrain trade despite the lack of any *overt* agreement by the parties.

---

[7]431 U.S. 720 (U.S. Sup. Ct. 1977).

[8]*California v. ARC America Corp.*, 490 U.S. 93 (U.S. Sup. Ct. 1989).

[9]467 U.S. 752 (U.S. Sup. Ct. 1984).

Should parallel pricing behavior by several firms be enough, for instance, to justify the inference that a price-fixing conspiracy exists? Courts have consistently held that proof of pure *"conscious parallelism,"* standing alone, is **not** enough to establish a section 1 violation. Other evidence must be presented to show that the defendants' actions stemmed from an **agreement**, *express or implied*, rather than from independent business decisions. It therefore becomes quite difficult to attack *oligopolies* (a few large firms sharing one market) under section 1, because such firms may independently elect to follow the pricing policies of the industry "price leader" rather than risk their large market shares by engaging in vigorous price competition.

Per Se Analysis

Although section 1's language condemns "every" contract, combination, and conspiracy in restraint of trade, the Supreme Court has long held that the Sherman Act applies only to behavior that *unreasonably* restrains competition. In addition, the Court has developed two fundamentally different approaches to analyzing behavior challenged under section 1. According to the Court, some actions always have a negative effect on competition— an effect that cannot be excused or justified. Such actions are classified as **per se** unlawful. If a particular behavior falls under the per se heading, it is conclusively presumed to violate section 1. Per se rules are thought to provide reliable guidance to business. They also simplify otherwise lengthy antitrust litigation, because if per se unlawful behavior is proven, the defendant cannot assert any supposed justifications in an attempt to avoid liability.

Per se rules, however, are frequently criticized on the ground that they tend to oversimplify complex economic realities. Recent decisions indicate that for *some* economic activities, the Supreme Court is moving away from per se rules and instead adopting "rule of reason" analysis. This trend is consistent with the Court's increased inclination to consider new economic theories that seek to justify behavior previously held to be per se unlawful.

"Rule of Reason" Analysis

Behavior not classified as per se unlawful is judged under the **"rule of reason."** This approach requires a detailed inquiry into the actual competitive effects of the defendant's actions and includes consideration of any justifications that the defendant may advance. If the court concludes that the challenged activity had a significant anticompetitive effect that was not offset by any positive effect on competition or other social benefit such as enhanced economic efficiency, the activity will be held to violate section 1. On the other hand, if the court concludes that the justifications advanced by the defendant outweigh the harm to competition resulting from the defendant's activity, there is no section 1 violation.

The following subsections of the chapter examine some of the behaviors held to violate section 1 of the Sherman Act. The legal treatment (per se or rule of reason) given to the respective behaviors is also considered.

Horizontal Price-Fixing

An essential attribute of a free market is that the price of goods and services is determined by the free play of the impersonal forces of the marketplace. Attempts by competitors to interfere with market forces and control prices—called **horizontal price-fixing**—have long been held per se unlawful under section 1. Price-fixing may take the form of direct agreements among competitors about the price at which they sell or buy a particular product or service. It may also be accomplished by agreements on the quantity of goods to be produced, offered for sale, or bought. In one famous case, an agreement by major oil refiners to purchase and store the excess production of small independent refiners was held to amount to price-fixing because the purpose of the agreement was to affect the market price for gasoline by artificially limiting the available supply.[10]

Some commentators have suggested that agreements among competitors to fix *maximum* prices should be treated under a rule of reason approach rather than the harsher per se standard because, in some instances, such agreements may result in savings to consumers. In addition, lower courts have occasionally sought to craft exceptions to the rule that horizontal price-fixing triggers per se treatment. It is important to note, however, that the Supreme Court continues to adhere to the longstanding rule

---

[10]*United States v. Socony-Vacuum Oil Co.*, 310 U.S. 150 (U.S. Sup. Ct. 1940).

of per se illegality for any form of horizontal price-fixing. In the *Denny's Marina* case, which follows, a federal court of appeals overturned a district court's attempt to limit the applicability of the per se rule in the horizontal price-fixing context.

DENNY'S MARINA, INC. v. RENFRO PRODUCTIONS, INC.
8 F.3d 1217 (7th Cir. 1993)

Denny's Marina, Inc. filed an antitrust action, described more fully below, against various defendants: the "Renfro Defendants" (Renfro Productions, Inc., Indianapolis Boat, Sport, and Travel Show, Inc., and individuals connected with those firms); "CIMDA" (the Central Indiana Marine Dealers Association); and the "Dealer Defendants" (various boat dealers who competed with Denny's in the sale of fishing boats, motors, trailers, and marine accessories in the central Indiana market). The Renfro Defendants operate two boat shows each year, one in the spring and one in the fall, at the Indiana State Fairgrounds. The spring show has occurred annually for more than 30 years and is one of the top three boat shows in the United States. It attracts between 160,000 and 191,000 consumers each year. The fall show is a smaller operation that has occurred each year since 1987. Numerous boat dealers participate in the two shows.

Denny's participated in the fall show in 1988, 1989, and 1990. It participated in the spring show in 1989 and 1990. According to allegations made by Denny's in its antitrust complaint, Denny's was quite successful at each of these shows, apparently because it urged customers to shop the other dealers and then return to Denny's for a lower price. After the 1989 spring show, some of the Dealer Defendants began to complain (according to Denny's) to the Renfro Defendants about the sales methods used by Denny's. In addition, Denny's alleged, the Dealer Defendants spent a significant part of a CIMDA meeting venting frustration about similar sales tactics used by Denny's at the 1990 spring show. Denny's also asserted that the Dealer Defendants' complaints to the Renfro Defendants escalated, and that as a result, the Renfro Defendants informed Denny's after the 1990 fall show that Denny's could no longer participate in the boat shows.

Denny's claimed that the above-described conduct of the defendants amounted to a conspiracy, prohibited by Sherman Act section 1, to exclude Denny's from participating in the boat shows because its policy was to "meet or beat" its competitors' prices at the shows. When the district court granted the defendants' motions for summary judgment, Denny's appealed to the Seventh Circuit Court of Appeals.

Cummings, Circuit Judge Because summary judgment was granted to the defendants, the facts alleged by Denny's and any inferences therefrom must be construed in its favor. Summary judgment will be denied if a reasonable jury could return a verdict for the plaintiff.

A successful claim under Section 1 of the Sherman Act requires proof of three elements: (1) a contract, combination, or conspiracy; (2) a resultant unreasonable restraint of trade in the relevant market; and (3) an accompanying injury. The district court noted that [for purposes of a ruling on their summary judgment motions] defendants do not dispute the first and third elements of proof. Hence the parties' only argument is whether Denny's has made a sufficient showing of the second element, unreasonable restraint of trade, to withstand defendants' motions for summary judgment.

There are two standards for evaluating whether an alleged restraint of trade is unreasonable: the rule of reason and the per se rule. The nature of the restraint determines which rule will be applied. Because the restraint alleged by Denny's constitutes a horizontal price-fixing conspiracy, it is per se an unreasonable restraint of trade [under a long line of Supreme Court decisions]. The conspiracy in this case was horizontal because it . . . consisted of Denny's competitors and their association. That the conspiracy was joined by the operators of the . . . boat shows does not transform it into a vertical agreement.

Likewise, the conspiracy was to fix prices. Price-fixing agreements need not include "explicit agreement on prices to be charged or that one party have the right to be consulted about the other's prices." *Palmer v. BRG of Georgia, Inc.* (1990). "Under the Sherman Act a combination formed for the purpose and with the effect of raising, depressing, fixing, pegging, or stabilizing the price of a commodity in interstate or foreign commerce is illegal per se." *United States v. Socony Vacuum-Oil Co.* (1940). Concerted action by dealers to protect themselves from price competition by discounters constitutes horizontal price-fixing. Hence the actions of the Dealer Defendants and CIMDA, joined by the Renfro Defendants, to prevent Denny's from participating in the boat shows constitutes a horizontal price-fixing conspiracy notwithstanding the apparent lack of an explicit agreement to set prices.

So far, the position of this court is similar to that of the court below. Nevertheless, having essentially found that Denny's had adduced sufficient evidence of a horizontal price-fixing conspiracy to withstand a motion for summary judgment, the court below refused to apply the per se rule that would allow it to conclude that there had been an unreasonable restraint of trade in the relevant market. Instead, before it would apply the per se rule the court required Denny's to demonstrate a substantial potential for impact on competition in the central Indiana market as a whole. Such an exception to the per se rule against price-fixing is unwarranted by cited precedent . . .

[and] would effectively require plaintiffs to make a rule of reason demonstration in order to invoke the per se rule! [In cases governed by the rule of reason], both parties are likely to present extensive economic analysis of the relevant market. It is in part to avoid such excessive costs of litigation that the per se rule is applied in cases where the anti-competitive effect of certain practices may be presumed.

As far back as 1940, it has been clear that horizontal price-fixing is illegal per se without requiring a showing of actual or likely impact on a market. *See Socony-Vacuum Oil.* This is because joint action by competitors to suppress price-cutting has the requisite "substantial potential for impact on competition" to warrant per se treatment. *Federal Trade Commission v. Superior Court Trial Lawyers Association* (1990). The district court would require Denny's to demonstrate a particular potential for impact on the market, when one of the purposes of the per se rule is that in cases like this such a potential is so well-established as not to require individualized showings. The pernicious effects are conclusively presumed.

Since Denny's presented enough evidence for a court and jury to conclude that the defendants engaged in [per se behavior consisting of] a horizontal conspiracy to suppress price competition at boat shows, . . . the district court's grant of summary judgment to the defendants [was erroneous].

Summary judgment for defendants reversed in favor of Denny's; case remanded for trial.

Vertical Price-Fixing

Attempts by manufacturers to control the resale price of their products may also fall within the scope of section 1. This behavior, called **vertical price-fixing** or *resale price maintenance*, has long been held to be per se illegal. Manufacturers may lawfully state a suggested retail price for their products, because such an action is purely unilateral in nature and does not involve the concerted action necessary for a violation of section 1. Per se illegality is present, however, whenever there is a manufacturer-dealer *agreement* (express or implied) obligating the dealer to resell at a price dictated by the manufacturer. The latter scenario involves prohibited *concerted action*.

Consignment Sales   The section 1 emphasis on concerted action provides the basis for two indirect methods that some manufacturers may lawfully be able to use to control resale prices: *consignment sales* and *unilateral refusals to deal*. Consignments are agreements in which an owner of goods (the consignor) delivers them to another who is to act as the owner's agent in selling them (the consignee).

Because the consignee is effectively the consignor's agent in selling the goods, and because the owners of goods generally have the right to determine the price at which their goods are sold, an early Supreme Court decision established that consignment sales were not covered by Section 1.[11]

More recent cases, however, have cast some doubt on the legality of resale price maintenance achieved by consignment dealing.[12] Consignment selling systems whose primary purpose is resale price maintenance may be held unlawful if they result in restraining price competition among a large number of consignees who would otherwise be in competition with one another. This is especially likely to be true in cases where the consignor has sufficient economic power over his consignees to permit him to refuse to deal with them on any basis other than a consignment. Finally, to have any hope of avoiding liability, the arrangement in question must be a true consignment. The consignor must retain title to the goods and bear the risk of loss of the goods while they are in the consignee's hands. In addition, the consignee must have the right to return unsold goods.

Unilateral Refusals to Deal   In *United States v. Colgate & Co.*,[13] the Supreme Court held that a

manufacturer could *unilaterally refuse to deal* with dealers who failed to follow its suggested resale prices. The rationale underlying this holding was that a single firm may deal or not deal with whomever it chooses without violating section 1, because unilateral action is not the concerted action prohibited by the statute. Subsequent cases, however, have narrowly construed the "*Colgate* doctrine." Manufacturers probably will be held to have violated section 1 if they enlist the aid of dealers who are not price-cutting to help enforce their (the manufacturers') pricing policies, or if they engage in other joint action to further those policies.

Future of Per Se Illegality   Recent events have cast doubt on the long-term future of the rule of per se illegality for all resale price maintenance agreements. Chicago School theorists argue that many of the same reasons that led the Supreme Court to extend rule of reason treatment to vertically imposed *nonprice* restraints on distribution (see the *Sylvania* case, set forth later in this chapter) are equally applicable to vertical price-fixing agreements. In particular, these critics argue that vertical restrictions limiting the maximum price at which a dealer can resell may prevent dealers with dominant market positions from exploiting consumers through price-gouging. The *Atlantic Richfield* case, which follows, contains hints that the Supreme Court may be inclined to reconsider the per se rule for vertically imposed maximum price restraints.

---

[11]*United States v. General Electric Co.*, 272 U.S. 476 (U.S. Sup. Ct. 1926).

[12]See, for instance, *Simpson v. Union Oil Co. of California*, 377 U.S. 13 (U.S. Sup. Ct. 1964).

[13]250 U.S. 300 (U.S. Sup. Ct. 1919).

ATLANTIC RICHFIELD CO. v. USA PETROLEUM CO.
495 U.S. 328 (U.S. Sup. Ct. 1990)

Atlantic Richfield (ARCO) is an integrated oil company that sells gasoline to consumers both directly through its own stations and indirectly through ARCO-brand dealers. USA is an independent retail marketer of gasoline which, like other independents, buys gasoline from major petroleum companies for resale under its own brand name. USA competes directly with ARCO dealers at the retail level. Its outlets typically are low-overhead, high-volume "discount" stations that charge less than stations selling equivalent quality gasoline under major brand names.

In early 1982, ARCO adopted a new marketing strategy in order to compete more effectively with independents such as USA. ARCO encouraged its dealers to match the retail gasoline prices offered by independents in various ways, making available to its dealers and distributors short-term discounts and reducing its dealers' costs by, for example, eliminating credit card sales. ARCO's strategy increased its sales and market share. When USA's sales dropped, it sued ARCO, charging that ARCO and its dealers were engaged in a per se illegal vertical price-fixing scheme.

The district court granted ARCO a summary judgment, holding that USA had not shown an antitrust injury resulting from ARCO's actions. When the Ninth Circuit Court of Appeals reversed, ARCO appealed.

Brennan, Justice   A private plaintiff may not recover damages under section 4 of the Clayton Act merely by showing injury causally linked to an illegal presence in the market. Instead, a plaintiff must prove the existence of *antitrust* injury, injury of the type the antitrust laws were intended to prevent that flows from that which makes defendants' acts unlawful. Injury, although causally related to an antitrust violation, nevertheless will not qualify as "antitrust injury" unless it is attributable to an anticompetitive aspect of the practice under scrutiny, since it is inimical to the antitrust laws to award damages for losses stemming from continued competition.

In *Albrecht v. Herald Co.* (1968) we found that a vertical, maximum price-fixing scheme was unlawful *per se* under section 1 of the Sherman Act. We assume, *arguendo*, that *Albrecht* correctly held that vertical, maximum price-fixing is subject to the *per se* rule.

In holding such a vertical agreement illegal, we analyzed the manner in which it might restrain competition by dealers. First, we noted that such a scheme, by substituting the perhaps erroneous judgment of a seller for the forces of the competitive market, may severely intrude upon the ability of buyers to compete and survive in that market. We further explained that maximum prices may be fixed too low for the dealer to furnish services essential to the value which goods have for the consumer or to furnish services and conveniences which consumers desire and for which they are willing to pay. By limiting the ability of small dealers to engage in nonprice competition, a maximum price-fixing agreement might channel distribution through a few large or specifically advantaged dealers. Finally, we observed that if the actual price charged under a maximum price scheme is nearly always the fixed maximum price, which is increasingly likely as the maximum price approaches the actual cost of the dealer, the scheme tends to acquire all the attributes of an arrangement fixing minimum prices.

USA alleges that it has suffered losses as a result of competition with firms following a vertical, maximum price-fixing agreement. But in *Albrecht* we held such an agreement *per se* unlawful because of its potential effects on dealers and consumers, not because of its effect on *competitors*. USA's asserted injury does not resemble any of the potential dangers described in *Albrecht*. For example, if a vertical agreement fixes maximum prices too low for the dealer to furnish services desired by consumers, or in such a way as to channel business to large distributors, then a firm dealing in a competing brand would not be harmed. USA was *benefitted* rather than harmed if ARCO's pricing policies restricted ARCO sales to a few large dealers or prevented ARCO's dealers from offering services desired by consumers such as credit card sales. Even if the maximum price agreement ultimately had acquired all of the attributes of a minimum price-fixing scheme, USA still would not have suffered antitrust injury because higher ARCO prices would have worked to USA's advantage.

USA argues that even if it was not harmed by any of the anticompetitive effects identified in *Albrecht*, it nonetheless suffered antitrust injury because of the low prices produced by the vertical restraint. We disagree. When a firm, or even a group of firms adhering to a vertical agreement, lowers prices but maintains them above predatory levels, the business lost by rivals cannot be viewed as an "anticompetitive" consequence of the claimed violation. A firm complaining about the harm it suffers from nonpredatory price competition "is really claiming that it [is] unable to raise prices." Blair & Harrison, Rethinking Antitrust Injury, 42 Vand. L. Rev. 1539, 1554 (1989). This is not *antitrust* injury; indeed, cutting prices in order to increase business often is the very essence of competition. The antitrust laws were enacted for the protection of *competition*, not *competitors*. To hold that the antitrust laws protect competitors from the loss of profits due to nonpredatory price competition would, in effect, render illegal any decision by a firm to cut prices in order to increase market share.

We also reject USA's suggestion that no antitrust injury need be shown where a *per se* violation is involved. The *per se* rule is a method of determining whether section 1 of the Sherman Act has been violated, but it does not indicate whether a private plaintiff has suffered antitrust injury and thus whether he may recover damages under section 4 of the Clayton Act. *Per se* and rule-of-reason analysis are but two methods of determining whether a restraint is "unreasonable," i.e., whether its anticompetitive effects outweigh its procompetitive effects. The *per se* rule is a presumption of unreasonableness based on business certainty and litigation efficiency. It represents a long-standing judgment that the prohibited practices by their nature have a substantial potential for impact on competition.

The purpose of the antitrust injury requirement is different. It ensures that the harm claimed by the plaintiff corresponds to the rationale for finding a violation in the first place, and it prevents losses that stem from competition from supporting suits by private plaintiffs for either damages or equitable relief. Actions *per se* unlawful under the antitrust laws may nonetheless have *some* procompetitive effects, and private parties might suffer losses therefrom.

When a manufacturer provides a dealer an exclusive area within which to distribute a product, the manufacturer's decision to fix a maximum resale price may actually protect consumers against exploitation by the dealer acting as a local monopolist. The manufacturer acts not out of altruism, of course, but out of a desire to increase its own sales—whereas the dealer's incentive, like that of any monopolist, is to reduce output and increase price. Vertical, maximum price-fixing thus may have procompetitive interbrand effects even if it is *per se* illegal because of its potential effects on dealers and consumers. The procompetitive potential of a vertical maximum price restraint is more evident now than it was when *Albrecht* was decided, because exclusive territorial arrangements and other nonprice restrictions were unlawful *per se* in 1968. These agreements are currently subject only to rule-of-reason scrutiny, making monopolistic behavior by dealers more likely.

Insofar as the *per se* rule permits the prohibition of efficient practices in the name of simplicity, the need for the antitrust injury requirement is underscored. "[P]rocompetitive or efficiency-enhancing aspects of practices that nominally violate the antitrust laws may cause serious harm to individuals, but this kind of harm is the essence of competition and should play no role in the definition of antitrust damages." Page, The Scope of Liability for Antitrust Violations, 37 Stan. L. Rev. 1445, 1460 (1985). We decline to dilute the antitrust injury requirement here because we find that there is no need to encourage private enforcement by competitors of the rule against vertical, maximum price-fixing. If such a scheme causes the anticompetitive consequences detailed in *Albrecht*, consumers and the manufacturer's own dealers may bring suit.

Judgment reversed in favor of ARCO.

Horizontal Divisions of Markets

It has traditionally been said that **horizontal division of markets** agreements—those agreements among competing firms to divide up the available market by assigning one another certain exclusive territories or certain customers—are illegal per se. Such agreements plainly represent agreements not to compete. They result in each firm being isolated from competition in the affected market.

More than 20 years ago, in *United States v. Topco Associates, Inc.*,[14] the Supreme Court reaffirmed this longstanding principle by striking down a horizontal division of markets agreement among members of a cooperative association of local and regional supermarket chains. The *Topco* decision was widely criticized, however, on the ground that its per se approach ignored an arguably important point—that the defendants' joint activities in promoting Topco brand products were aimed at enabling them to compete more effectively with national supermarket chains. Critics argued that when such horizontal restraints were ancillary to *procompetitive* behavior, they should be judged under the rule of reason.

Naked Restraints and Ancillary Restraints Such criticism evidently has had an impact. Several recent decisions by lower federal courts have distinguished

---

[14]405 U.S. 596 (U.S. Sup. Ct. 1972).

between "naked" horizontal restraints (those having no other purpose or effect except restraining competition) and "ancillary" horizontal restraints (those constituting a necessary part of a larger joint undertaking serving procompetitive ends).[15] Although these courts continue to apply the per se rule to naked horizontal restraints, they give rule of reason treatment to ancillary restraints. In determining whether ancillary restraints are lawful under the rule of reason, courts weigh the harm to competition resulting from such restraints against the alleged offsetting benefits to competition. One factor likely to be of substantial importance in this weighing process is the market strength of the defendants. The idea here is that if an agreement restrains competition among firms lacking market power because they face strong competition from other firms not subject to the agreement, consumers are unlikely to be harmed. This is because the existence of competition limits the ability of the agreeing firms to exploit their agreement by raising prices.

Whether the Supreme Court ultimately will endorse such departures from *Topco* remains to be seen. However, the Court's post-*Topco* tendency to discard per se rules in favor of a rule of reason approach in other areas suggests that *Topco*'s critics may ultimately prevail with their arguments.

Vertical Restraints on Distribution

Vertical restraints on distribution (or *vertical nonprice restraints*) also fall within the scope of the

Sherman Act. A manufacturer has always had the power to *unilaterally* assign exclusive territories to its dealers or to limit the dealerships it grants in a particular geographic area. However, manufacturers may run afoul of section 1 by causing dealers to *agree* not to sell outside their dealership territories or by placing other restrictions on their dealers' right to resell their products.

In *United States v. Arnold, Schwinn & Co.*,[16] a 1967 decision, the Supreme Court held that vertical restraints on distribution were per se illegal when applied to goods that the manufacturer had sold to its dealers (consignment sales being treated under the rule of reason). A decade later, however, the Court changed course. In the *Sylvania* case, which follows shortly, the Court abandoned the per se rule in favor of a rule of reason approach to most vertical restraints on distribution. The Court accepted many Chicago School arguments concerning the potential *economic efficiencies* that could result from vertical restraints on distribution. Most notably, such restraints were alleged to offer a chance for increased *interbrand* competition among the product lines of competing manufacturers at the admitted cost of restraining *intrabrand* competition among dealers in a particular manufacturer's product.

Subsequent decisions on the legality of vertical restraints on distribution have emphasized the importance of the market share of the manufacturer imposing the restraints. Restraints imposed by manufacturers with large market shares are more likely to be found unlawful under the rule of reason because the resultant harm to intrabrand competition is unlikely to be offset by significant positive effects on interbrand competition.

---

[15]See, for example, *Polk Bros. v. Forest City Enterprises*, 776 F.2d 185 (7th Cir. 1985). In this case, two retailers were constructing a new building that they were to share. An agreement by the retailers not to compete in the sale of certain product lines was upheld as ancillary to their agreement to develop the joint facility.

[16]338 U.S. 365 (U.S. Sup. Ct. 1967).

CONTINENTAL T.V., INC. v. GTE SYLVANIA, INC.
433 U.S. 36 (U.S. Sup. Ct. 1977)

In the early 1950s, Sylvania's share of the national TV market had declined to about 1 percent. In an attempt to remedy this situation, Sylvania phased out all wholesalers and limited the retail franchises that it granted for a given area. Sylvania also required that each franchisee sell Sylvania products only from the sales location described in its franchise. This strategy apparently contributed to increasing sales by Sylvania, but it led to friction with some dealers when Sylvania shuffled sales location areas and refused to grant requests for expansion of some sales areas.

Continental, a Sylvania dealer, became unhappy when Sylvania franchised another dealer in part of Continental's market and then refused Continental's request for permission to expand into another market area. As the dispute developed, Sylvania reduced Continental's credit line. In response, Continental withheld all payments owed to the finance company that handled all credit arrangements between Sylvania and its retailers. Shortly thereafter, Sylvania terminated Continental's franchise and the finance company filed suit to recover payments due on merchandise purchased by Continental. Continental cross-claimed against Sylvania, arguing that Sylvania's location restriction was a per se violation of section 1 of the Sherman Act. The jury agreed and awarded Continental $1.7 million in treble damages. The Ninth Circuit Court of Appeals reversed, holding that Sylvania's location restriction should be judged under the rule of reason because it presented less of a threat to competition than did the restrictions held per se illegal in the *Schwinn* case. Continental appealed.

Powell, Justice   Vertical restrictions reduce intrabrand competition by limiting the number of sellers of a particular product competing for the business of a given group of buyers. Location restrictions have this effect because of practical constraints on the effective marketing area of retail outlets. Although intrabrand competition may be reduced, the ability of retailers to exploit the resulting market may be limited both by the ability of consumers to travel to other franchised locations and, perhaps more importantly, to purchase the competing products of other manufacturers. None of these key variables, however, is affected by the form of the transaction by which a manufacturer conveys his products to the retailers.

Vertical restrictions promote interbrand competition by allowing the manufacturer to achieve certain efficiencies in the distribution of his products. New manufacturers and manufacturers entering new markets can use the restrictions in order to induce competent and aggressive retailers to make the kind of investment of capital and labor that is often required in the distribution of products unknown to the consumer. Established manufacturers can use them to induce retailers to engage in promotional activities or to provide service and repair facilities necessary to the efficient marketing of their products. Service and repair are vital for many products, such as automobiles and major household appliances. The availability and quality of such services affect a manufacturer's goodwill and the competitiveness of his product. Because of market imperfections such as the so-called free rider effect, these services might not be provided by retailers in a purely competitive situation, despite the fact that each retailer's benefit would be greater if all provided services than if none did.

Economists also have argued that manufacturers have an economic interest in maintaining as much intrabrand competition as is consistent with the efficient distribution of their products. Although the view that the manufacturer's interest necessarily corresponds with that of the public is not universally shared, even the leading critic of vertical restrictions concedes that *Schwinn*'s distinction between sale and nonsale transactions is essentially unrelated to any relevant economic impact.

We revert to the standard articulated in *Northern Pac. R. Co.* for determining whether vertical restrictions must be "conclusively presumed to be unreasonable and therefore illegal without elaborate inquiry as to the precise harm they have caused or the business excuse for their use." Such restrictions, in varying forms, are widely used in our free market economy. There is substantial scholarly and judicial authority supporting their economic utility. There is relatively no showing in this case, either generally or with respect to Sylvania's agreements, that vertical restrictions have or are likely to have a "pernicious effect on competition" or that they "lack any redeeming virtue." Accordingly, the *per se* rule stated in *Schwinn* must be overruled. In so holding we do not foreclose the possibility that particular applications of vertical restrictions might justify *per se* prohibition under *Northern Pac. R. Co.* But we do make clear that departure from the rule of reason standard must be based upon demonstrable economic effect rather than—as in *Schwinn*—upon formalistic line drawing.

Judgment for Sylvania affirmed.

Group Boycotts and Concerted Refusals to Deal

Under the *Colgate* doctrine, a single firm may lawfully refuse to deal with certain firms. The same is not true, however, of *agreements* by two or more business entities to refuse to deal with others, to deal with others only on certain terms and conditions, or to coerce suppliers or customers not to deal with one of their competitors. Such agreements are *joint* restraints on trade. Historically, they have been per se unlawful under section 1. For example, when a trade association of garment manufacturers agreed not to sell to retailers that sold clothing or fabrics with designs pirated from legitimate manufacturers, the agreement was held to be a per se violation of the Sherman Act.[17]

Vertical Boycotts   Recent antitrust developments, however, indicate that not all concerted refusals to deal will receive per se analysis. If a manufacturer terminated a distributor in response to complaints from other distributors that the terminated distributor was selling to customers outside its prescribed sales territory, the manufacturer will be held to have violated section 1 only if the termination resulted in a significant harm to competition. This result follows logically from the *Sylvania* decision. If vertical restraints on distribution are judged under the rule of reason (as established in *Sylvania*), the same standard should apply to a vertical boycott designed to enforce such restraints.

Even distributors claiming to have been terminated as part of a per se illegal vertical price-fixing scheme have found recovery increasingly difficult to obtain in recent years. In *Monsanto v. Spray-Rite Service Corp.*,[18] a manufacturer had terminated a discounting distributor after receiving complaints from its other distributors. The Supreme Court held that these facts would not trigger per se liability for vertical price-fixing in the absence of additional evidence tending to exclude the possibility that the manufacturer and the nonterminated distributors acted independently. More recently, in *Business Electronics Corp. v. Sharp Electronics Corp.*,[19] the

Court held that even proof of a conspiracy between a manufacturer and nonterminated distributors to terminate a price-cutter would not trigger per se liability unless it was accompanied by proof that the manufacturer and nonterminated dealers were also engaged in a vertical price-fixing conspiracy. *Monsanto* and *Sharp* have generated a substantial controversy, as well as proposals for legislation overruling them and codifying the per se rule for vertical price-fixing. As of the time this book went to press, no such legislation had been enacted.

Horizontal Boycotts   It also appears that the Supreme Court is willing to relax the per se rule for some *horizontal* boycotts. For instance, in *Northwest Wholesale Stationers, Inc. v. Pacific Stationery & Printing Co.*, members of an office supply retailers' purchasing cooperative had expelled a member retailer that engaged in some wholesale operations in addition to retail activities. The Court held that rule of reason treatment should be extended to the alleged boycott at issue, but declined to eliminate the per se rule for all horizontal boycotts. The Court has offered only general guidance for determining which horizontal boycotts trigger rule of reason analysis and which ones amount to per se violations. The appropriate legal treatment in a given case is therefore difficult to predict. Future decisions may resolve the uncertainty.

Tying Agreements

Tying agreements occur when a seller refuses to sell a buyer a certain product (the *tying product*) unless the buyer also agrees to purchase a different product (the *tied product*) from the seller. For example, a fertilizer manufacturer refuses to sell its dealers fertilizer (the tying product) unless they also agree to buy its line of pesticides (the tied product). The potential anticompetitive effect of a tying agreement is that the seller's competitors in the sale of the tied product may be foreclosed from competing with the seller for sales to customers that have entered into tying agreements with the seller. To the extent that tying agreements are coercively imposed, they also deprive buyers of the freedom to make independent decisions concerning their purchases of the tied product. Tying agreements may be

---

[17]*Fashion Originators' Guild v. FTC*, 312 U.S. 457 (U.S. Sup. Ct. 1941).

[18]465 U.S. 752 (U.S. Sup. Ct. 1984).

[19]485 U.S. 108 (U.S. Sup. Ct. 1988).

challenged under both section 1 of the Sherman Act and section 3 of the Clayton Act.[20]

Elements of Prohibited Tying Agreements

Tying agreements are often said to be per se illegal under section 1. However, because a tying agreement must meet certain criteria before it is subjected to per se analysis, and because evidence of certain justifications is sometimes considered in tying cases, the rule against tying agreements is at best a "soft" per se rule. Before a challenged tying agreement is held to violate section 1, these must be demonstrated: (1) the agreement involves *two* separate and distinct items rather than integrated components of a larger product, service, or system of doing business; (2) the tying product cannot be purchased unless the tied product is also purchased; (3) the seller has sufficient economic power in the market for the tying product (such as a patent or a large market share) to appreciably restrain competition in the tied product market; and (4) a "not insubstantial" amount of commerce in the tied product is affected by the seller's tying agreements.[21] The following *Eastman Kodak* case contains a discussion of the elements of prohibited tying arrangements, with a focus on the third element: *market power as to the tying product.*

---

[20]Section 3 of the Clayton Act applies, however, only when both the tying and the tied products are commodities. Chapter 49 discusses Clayton Act standards for tying agreement legality.

[21]*U.S. Steel Corp. v. Fortner Enterprises, Inc.*, 429 U.S. 610 (U.S. Sup. Ct. 1977).

EASTMAN KODAK CO. v. IMAGE TECHNICAL SERVICES, INC.
112 S. Ct. 2072 (U.S. Sup. Ct. 1992)

Eastman Kodak Co. (Kodak) manufactures and sells photocopiers and micrographic equipment. In addition, Kodak provides customers with service and replacement parts for its equipment. Kodak produces some of the parts itself. The other parts are made to order for Kodak by independent original equipment manufacturers (OEMs). Rather than selling a complete system of original equipment, lifetime parts, and lifetime service for a single price, Kodak furnishes service after an initial warranty period either through annual service contracts or on a per-call basis. Kodak provides between 80 and 95 percent of the service for Kodak machines.

In the early 1980s, independent service organizations (ISOs) began repairing and servicing Kodak equipment, as well as selling parts for it. ISOs kept an inventory of parts, purchased either from Kodak or from other sources (primarily OEMs). In 1985, Kodak adopted policies designed to limit ISOs' access to parts and to make it more difficult for ISOs to compete with Kodak in servicing Kodak equipment. Kodak began selling replacement parts only to Kodak equipment buyers who used Kodak service or repaired their own machines (i.e., buyers who did not use ISOs for service). In addition, Kodak sought to limit ISO access to other sources of Kodak parts by working out agreements with OEMs that they would sell parts for Kodak equipment to no one other than Kodak, and by pressuring Kodak equipment owners and independent parts distributors not to sell Kodak parts to ISOs.

Eighteen ISOs sued Kodak, claiming that these policies amounted to (1) unlawful tying of the sale of service for Kodak machines to the sale of parts (in violation of Sherman Act Section 1), and (2) monopolization or attempted monopolization of the sale of service for Kodak machines (in violation of Sherman Act Section 2). The U.S. District Court granted summary judgment in favor of Kodak on each of these claims. The Ninth Circuit Court of Appeals reversed, holding that summary judgment was inappropriate because there were genuine issues of material fact regarding the ISOs' claims. The Supreme Court granted Kodak's petition for a writ of certiorari.

Blackmun, Justice   Because this case comes to us on Kodak's motion for summary judgment, the evidence of the ISOs is to be believed, and all justifiable inferences are to be drawn in the ISOs' favor [for purposes of determining whether Kodak is entitled to summary judgment or whether a trial is instead necessary].

A tying arrangement is "an agreement by a party to sell one product but only on the condition that the buyer also purchases a different (or tied) product, or at least agrees that he will not purchase that product from any other supplier." *Northern Pacific Railway Co. v. United States* (1958). Such an arrangement violates Section 1 of the Sherman Act if the seller has "appreciable economic power" in the tying product market and if the arrangement affects a substantial volume of commerce in the tied market. *Fortner Enterprises, Inc. v. U.S. Steel Corp.* (1969). Kodak did not dispute that its arrangement affects a substantial volume of interstate commerce. It, however, did challenge whether its activities constituted a "tying arrangement" and whether Kodak exercised "appreciable economic power" in the tying market.

For the ISOs to defeat [Kodak's] motion for summary judgment, . . . a reasonable trier of fact must be able to find, first, that service and parts are two distinct products, and second, that Kodak has tied the sale of the two products. For service and parts to be considered two distinct products, there must be sufficient consumer demand so that it is efficient for a firm to provide service separately from parts. Evidence in the record indicates that service and parts have been sold separately in the past and still are sold separately to self-service equipment owners. Kodak insists that because there is no demand for parts separate from service, there cannot be separate markets for service and parts. By that logic, we would be forced to conclude that there can never be separate markets, for example, for cameras and film, computers and software, or automobiles and tires. That is an assumption we are unwilling to make.

Kodak's assertion also appears to be incorrect as a factual matter. At least some consumers would purchase service without parts, because some service does not require parts, and some consumers, those who self-service for example, would purchase parts without service. Enough doubt is cast on Kodak's claim of a unified market that it should be

resolved by the trier of fact. [T]he ISOs have [also] presented sufficient evidence of a tie between service and parts. The record indicates that Kodak would sell parts to third parties only if they agreed not to buy service from ISOs.

[We now] consider the other necessary feature of an illegal tying arrangement: appreciable economic power in the tying market. Market power is the power "to force a purchaser to do something that he would not do in a competitive market." *Jefferson Parish Hospital Dist. No. 2 v. Hyde* (1984). The existence of such power ordinarily is inferred from the seller's possession of a predominant share of the market.

The ISOs contend that Kodak has more than sufficient power in the parts market to force unwanted purchases of the tied market, service. The ISOs [assert or] provide evidence that certain parts are available exclusively through Kodak, . . . that Kodak has control over the availability of parts it does not manufacture, [and that Kodak has both] prohibited independent manufacturers from selling Kodak parts to ISOs [and] pressured Kodak equipment owners and independent parts distributors to deny ISOs the purchase of Kodak parts. The ISOs also allege that Kodak's control over the parts market has excluded service competition, boosted service prices, and forced unwilling consumption of Kodak service. [They] offer evidence that consumers have switched to Kodak service even though they preferred ISO service, that Kodak service was of higher price and lower quality than the preferred ISO service, and that ISOs were driven out of business by Kodak's policies. Under our prior precedents, this evidence would be sufficient to entitle the ISOs to a trial on their claim of market power.

Kodak counters that even if it concedes monopoly *share* of the relevant parts market, it cannot actually exercise the necessary market *power* for a Sherman Act violation. This is so, according to Kodak, because competition exists in the equipment market. Kodak argues that it could not have the ability to raise prices of service and parts above the level that would be charged in a competitive market because any increase in profits from a higher price in the aftermarkets at least would be offset by a corresponding loss in profits from lower equipment sales as consumers began purchasing equipment with more attractive service costs. Kodak does not present any actual data on the equipment, service, or parts markets. Instead, it urges the adoption of a substantive legal rule that equipment competition precludes any finding of monopoly power in derivative aftermarkets. Legal presumptions that rest on formalistic distinctions rather than actual market realities are generally disfavored in antitrust law. This Court has preferred to resolve antitrust claims on a case-by-case basis, focusing on the particular facts disclosed by the record ... and the economic reality of the market at issue.

Even if Kodak could not raise the price of service and parts one cent without losing equipment sales, that fact would not disprove market power in the aftermarkets. Kodak's [theory] is based on the false dichotomy that there are only two prices that can be charged [for parts and service]—a competitive price or a ruinous one. But there could easily be a middle, optimum price at which the increased revenues from the higher-priced sales of service and parts would more than compensate for the lower revenues from lost equipment sales. [Contrary to the assertion in Kodak's brief], there is no immutable physical law—no "basic economic reality"—insisting that competition in the equipment market cannot coexist with market power in the aftermarkets.

[Kodak also overlooks] the existence of significant information and switching costs. These costs could create a less responsive connection between service and parts prices and equipment sales. For the service-market price to affect equipment demand, consumers must inform themselves of the total cost of the "package"—equipment, service, and parts—at the time of purchase; that is, consumers must engage in accurate lifecycle pricing. The necessary information would include data on price, quality, and availability of parts needed to operate, upgrade, or enhance the initial equipment, as well as service and repair costs, including estimates of breakdown frequency, nature of repairs, price of service and parts, length of "down-time," and losses incurred from down-time. Much of this information is difficult—some of it impossible—to acquire at the time of purchase.

Moreover, even if consumers were capable of acquiring and processing the complex body of information, they may choose not to do so. Acquiring the information is expensive. [Consumers] may not find it cost-efficient to compile the information. [It therefore] makes little sense to assume, in the absence of any evidentiary support, that equipment-purchasing decisions are based on an accurate assessment of the total cost of equipment, service, and parts over the lifetime of the machine.

A second factor undermining Kodak's claim that supracompetitive prices in the service market lead to ruinous losses in equipment sales is the cost to current owners of switching to a different product. If the cost of switching is high, consumers who already have purchased the equipment, and are thus "locked-in," will tolerate some level of service-price increases before changing equipment brands. Under this scenario, a seller profitably could maintain supracompetitive prices in the aftermarket if the switching costs were high relative to the increase in service prices, and the number of locked-in customers were high relative to the number of new purchasers. Respondents have offered evidence that the heavy initial outlay for Kodak equipment, combined with the required support material that works only with Kodak equipment, makes switching costs very high for existing Kodak customers.

We conclude, then, that Kodak has failed to demonstrate that the ISOs' inference of market power in the service and parts markets is unreasonable. It is clearly reasonable to infer that Kodak has market power to raise prices and drive out competition in the aftermarkets, since the ISOs offer direct evidence that Kodak did so. It is also plausible ... to infer that Kodak chose to gain immediate profits by exerting that market power where locked-in customers [and] high information costs ... limited and perhaps eliminated any long-term loss.

In this case, ... the balance tips against [granting Kodak's request for] summary judgment.

Denial of Kodak's motion for summary judgment affirmed in favor of the ISOs; case remanded for further proceedings.

Note: In another portion of the opinion not set forth here, the Court held that Kodak was not entitled to summary judgment on the ISOs' Sherman Act section 2 claim.

Possible Justifications for Tying Agreements

The first two of the above elements have been particularly significant in recent cases involving alleged tying agreements among franchisors and their franchised dealers. For example, a suit by a McDonald's franchisee alleged that McDonald's violated section 1 by requiring franchisees to lease their stores from McDonald's as a condition of acquiring a McDonald's franchise. The Eighth Circuit Court of Appeals rejected the franchisee's claim, however, holding that no tying agreement was involved. Instead, the franchise and the lease were integral components of a well-thought-out system of doing business.[22]

The lower federal courts have recognized two other possible justifications for tying agreements. First, tying arrangements that are instrumental in launching a new competitor with an otherwise uncertain future may be lawful until the new business has established itself in the marketplace. The logic of this "new business" exception is obvious: If a tying agreement enables a fledgling firm to become a viable competitor, the agreement's net effect on competition is positive. Second, some courts have recognized that tying agreements sometimes may be necessary to protect the reputation of the seller's product line. For example, one of the seller's products functions properly only if used in conjunction with another of its products. To qualify for this exception, however, the seller must convince the court that a tying arrangement is the only viable means to protect its goodwill.

Chicago School Views on Tying Agreements

Chicago School thinkers have long criticized the traditional judicial approach to tying agreements because they do not believe that most tie-ins result in any significant economic harm. They argue that sellers who try to impose a tie-in in competitive markets gain no increased profits as a result. This is so because instead of participating in a tying agreement, buyers may turn to substitutes for the tying product or may purchase the tying product from competing sellers. The net effect of a tie-in may therefore be that any increase in the seller's sales in the tied product is offset by a loss in sales of the

tying product. Only when the seller has substantial power in the tying product market is there potential that a tie-in may be used to increase the seller's power in the tied product market. However, even when the seller has such market power in the tying product, Chicago School thinkers argue that no harm to competition is likely to result if the seller faces strong competition in the tied product market. For these and other reasons, Chicago School thinkers favor a rule of reason approach to all tying agreements. A majority of the Supreme Court has yet to accept these arguments. Some Justices, however, appear willing to do so. If other members of the Court are similarly persuaded in the future, a substantial change in the legal criteria applied to tying agreements will be the likely result.

Reciprocal Dealing Agreements

Under a **reciprocal dealing agreement**, a buyer attempts to exploit its purchasing power by conditioning its purchases from suppliers on reciprocal purchases of some product or service offered for sale by the buyer. For example, an oil company with a chain of wholly owned gas stations refuses to purchase the tires it sells in those stations unless the tire manufacturer (the would-be supplier of the tires) agrees to purchase, from the oil company, the petrochemicals used in the tire manufacturing process. Reciprocal dealing agreements are quite similar in motivation and effect to tying agreements. Courts therefore tend to treat them in a similar fashion. In seeking to impose the reciprocal dealing agreement on the tire manufacturer, the oil company is attempting to gain a competitive advantage over its competitors in the petrochemical market. A court judging the legality of such an agreement would examine the oil company's economic power as a purchaser of tires and the dollar amount of petrochemical sales involved.

Exclusive Dealing Agreements

Exclusive dealing agreements require buyers of a particular product or service to purchase that product or service exclusively from a particular seller. For example, Standard Lawnmower Corporation requires its retail dealers to sell only Standard brand mowers. A common variation of an exclusive dealing agreement is the *requirements contract*, under

---

[22]*Principe v. McDonald's Corp.*, 631 F.2d 303 (4th Cir. 1980).

which the buyer of a particular product agrees to purchase all of its requirements for that product from a particular supplier. For example, a candy manufacturer agrees to buy all of its sugar requirements from one sugar refiner. Exclusive dealing contracts present a threat to competition similar to that involved in tying contracts—they may reduce interbrand competition by foreclosing a seller's competitors from the opportunity to compete for sales to its customers. Unlike tying contracts, however, exclusive dealing agreements may sometimes enhance efficiencies in distribution and stimulate interbrand competition. Exclusive dealing agreements reduce a manufacturer's sales costs and provide dealers with a secure source of supply. They may also encourage dealer efforts to market the manufacturer's products more effectively, because a dealer selling only one product line has a greater stake in the success of that line than does a dealer who sells the products of several competing manufacturers.

Because many exclusive dealing agreements involve commodities, they may also be challenged under section 3 of the Clayton Act. The legal tests applicable to exclusive dealing agreements under both acts are identical. Therefore, we defer discussing those tests until the next chapter.

Joint Ventures by Competitors

A **joint venture** is a combined effort by two or more business entities for a limited purpose such as research. Because joint ventures may yield enhanced efficiencies by integrating the resources of more than one firm, they are commonly judged under the rule of reason. Under this approach, courts tend to ask whether any competitive restraints that are incidental to the venture are necessary to accomplish its lawful objectives and, if so, whether those restraints are offset by the venture's positive effects. Joint ventures whose primary purpose is illegal per se, however, have often been given per se treatment. An example of such a case would be two competing firms that form a joint sales agency and authorize it to fix the price of their products.

National Cooperative Research and Production Act   Antitrust critics have long argued that the threat of antitrust prosecution seriously inhibits the formation of joint research and development ventures, and that American firms are placed at a competitive disadvantage in world markets as a result. Such arguments have enjoyed more acceptance during roughly the past decade, given concerns about the American economy's performance. In 1984, Congress passed the National Cooperative Research Act (NCRA). This act applies to *"joint research and development ventures"* (JRDVs), which are broadly defined to include basic and applied research and joint activities in the licensing of technologies developed by such research. The NCRA requires the application of a reasonableness standard, rather than a per se rule, when a JRDV's legality is determined. It also requires firms contemplating a JRDV to provide the Department of Justice and the Federal Trade Commission with advance notice of their intent to do so. The NCRA provides that only actual (not treble) damages may be recovered for losses flowing from a JRDV ultimately found to be in violation of section 1. In addition, the NCRA contains a provision allowing the parties to a challenged JRDV to recover attorney's fees from an unsuccessful challenger if the suit is shown to be "frivolous, unreasonable, without foundation, or in bad faith." Congress amended the statute in 1993 to extend its application to joint *production* ventures. In doing so, Congress renamed the statute the National Cooperative Research and Production Act.

Figure 1 summarizes the judicial treatment of potentially illegal practices under section 1 of the Sherman Act.

SECTION 2—MONOPOLIZATION

Introduction

Firms that acquire **monopoly power** in a given market have defeated the antitrust laws' objective of promoting competitive market structures. Monopolists, by definition, have the power to fix prices unilaterally because they have no effective competition. Section 2 of the Sherman Act was designed to prevent the formation of monopoly power. It provides: "Every person who shall monopolize, or attempt to monopolize, or combine or conspire with any other person to monopolize any part of trade or commerce among the several states, or with foreign nations shall be deemed guilty of a felony." Section 2 does not, however, outlaw monopolies. Instead, it outlaws the act of *"monopolizing."* Under section 2, a *single firm* can be guilty of "monopolizing" or "attempting to monopolize" a part of trade or

FIGURE 1   Potentially Illegal Practices and Their Treatment under Sherman Act Section 1

Potentially Illegal Practice	Judicial Treatment	
	Per Se	Rule of Reason
Horizontal price-fixing	*	
Vertical price-fixing	*?	
Horizontal division of markets	*?	*?
Vertical division of markets		*
Horizontal boycotts	*	*
Vertical boycotts	*	*
Tying agreements	*?	*
Reciprocal dealing agreements	*?	*
Exclusive dealing agreements		*
Joint ventures	*	*

Note: an entry with an * in both columns means the facts of the individual case determine the treatment. A ? indicates that future treatment is in question.

commerce. The proof of joint action required for violations of section 1 is required only when two or more firms are charged with a conspiracy to monopolize under section 2.

Monopolization

Monopolization is "the willful acquisition or maintenance of monopoly power in a relevant market as opposed to growth as a consequence of superior product, business acumen, or historical accident."[23] This means that to be guilty of monopolization, a defendant must have possessed not only monopoly power but also an **intent to monopolize**.

Monopoly Power   *Monopoly power* is usually defined for antitrust purposes as the power to *fix*

prices or *exclude competitors* in a given market. Such power is generally inferred from the fact that a firm has captured a predominant share of the relevant market. Although the exact percentage share necessary to support an inference of monopoly power remains unclear and courts often look at other economic factors (such as the existence in the industry of barriers to the entry of new competitors), market shares in excess of 70 percent have historically justified an inference of monopoly power.

Before a court can determine a defendant's market share, it must first define the **relevant market**. This is a crucial issue in section 2 cases because a broad definition of the relevant market normally results in a smaller market share for the defendant and a resulting reduction in the likelihood that the defendant will be found to possess monopoly power. The two components of a relevant market determination are the relevant **geographic market** and the relevant **product market**.

Economic realities prevailing in the industry determine the relevant geographic market. In which parts of the country can the defendant effectively compete with other firms in the sale of the product in question? To whom may buyers turn for alternative sources of supply? Factors such as transportation costs may also play a critical role in relevant market determinations. Thus, the relevant market for coal may be regional in nature, but the relevant market for transistors may be national in scope.

The relevant product market is composed of those products meeting the *functional interchangeability* test, which identifies the products "reasonably interchangeable by consumers for the same purposes." This test recognizes that a firm's ability to fix the price for its products is limited by the availability of competing products that buyers view as acceptable substitutes. In a famous antitrust case, for example, Du Pont was charged with monopolizing the national market for cellophane because it had a 75 percent share. The Supreme Court concluded, however, that the relevant market was all "flexible wrapping materials," including aluminum foil, waxed paper, and polyethylene. Du Pont's 20 percent share of that product market was far too small to amount to monopoly power.[24]

---

[23]*United States v. Grinnell Corp.*, 384 U.S. 563 (U.S. Sup. Ct. 1966).

[24]*United States v. E. I. du Pont de Nemours & Co.*, 351 U.S. 377 (U.S. Sup. Ct. 1956).

May a *single brand* of a product or service ever be a relevant market for section 2 purposes? Although most section 2 cases would logically be expected to involve product markets consisting of more than one brand of a given type of product (and perhaps other products that are reasonably interchangeable for the same purposes), the Supreme Court refused to rule, in the *Eastman Kodak* case, that a single brand cannot be a relevant market. (*Eastman Kodak* involved claims under sections 1 and 2 of the Sherman Act. The case's major facts and the section 1 aspect of the Court's opinion were set forth in this chapter's discussion of tying arrangements.) Because *Eastman Kodak* dealt with allegedly anticompetitive practices regarding parts and service for Kodak equipment, the Court observed that "[t]he relevant market for antitrust purposes is determined by the choices available to Kodak equipment owners." The Court concluded that "[b]ecause service and parts for Kodak equipment are not interchangeable with other manufacturers' service and parts, the relevant market from the Kodak-equipment owner's perspective is composed of only those companies that service Kodak machines." According to the Court, "prior cases support the proposition that in some instances one brand of a product can constitute a separate market." Evidence that Kodak controlled nearly 100 percent of the parts market and 80 to 95 percent of the service market for Kodak brand equipment was held to be sufficient evidence of monopoly power for purposes of the Court's ruling that Kodak was not entitled to summary judgment on the plaintiffs' section 2 claim against it.

Intent to Monopolize Proof of monopoly power standing alone, however, is never sufficient to prove a violation of Section 2. The defendant's **intent to monopolize** must also be shown. Early cases under section 2 required evidence that the defendant either acquired monopoly power by predatory or coercive means that violated antitrust rules (e.g., price-fixing or discriminatory pricing) or abused monopoly power in some way after acquiring it (such as by engaging in price-gouging). Contemporary courts focus on how the defendant acquired monopoly power. If the defendant *intentionally acquired it* or *attempted to maintain it* after acquiring it, the defendant possessed an intent to monopolize. Defendants are not in violation of section 2, however, if their monopoly power resulted from the superiority of their products or business decisions, or from historical accident (e.g., the owner of a professional sports franchise in an area too small to support a competing franchise).

Purposeful acquisition or maintenance of monopoly power may be demonstrated in various ways. A famous monopolization case involved Alcoa, which had a 90 percent market share of the American market for virgin aluminum ingot. Alcoa was found guilty of purposefully maintaining its monopoly power by acquiring every new opportunity relating to the production or marketing of aluminum, thereby excluding potential competitors.[25] As the *Grinnell* case indicates, firms that develop monopoly power by acquiring ownership or control of their competitors are very likely to be held to have demonstrated an intent to monopolize.

---

[25]*United States v. Aluminum Co. of America, Inc.*, 148 F.2d 416 (2d Cir. 1945).

UNITED STATES V. GRINNELL CORP.
384 U.S. 563 (U.S. Sup. Ct. 1966)

Grinnell manufactured plumbing supplies and fire sprinkler systems. It also owned 76 percent of the stock of ADT, 89 percent of the stock of AFA, and 100 percent of the stock of Holmes. ADT provided both burglary and fire protection services; Holmes provided burglary services alone; AFA supplied only fire protection service. Each offered a central station service under which hazard-detecting devices installed on the protected premises automatically transmitted an electrical signal to a central station. There were other forms of protective services. The record indicated, however, that subscribers to an accredited central station service (i.e., one approved by the insurance underwriters) received reductions in their insurance premiums substantially greater than the reductions received by the users of other protection services. In 1961, ADT, Holmes, and AFA were the three largest central station service companies in terms of revenue, with about 87 percent of the business.

In 1907, Grinnell and the other defendants entered into a series of agreements that allocated the major cities and markets for central station alarm services in the United States. Each defendant agreed not to compete outside the market areas allocated. Over the years, the defendants bought 30 other companies providing burglar or fire alarm services. After Grinnell acquired control of the other defendants, the latter continued in their attempts to acquire central station companies. Offers were made to at least eight companies between 1955 and 1961, including four of the five largest remaining companies in the business. When the present suit was filed, each of those defendants had outstanding an offer to purchase one of the four largest nondefendant companies.

Over the years, ADT reduced its minimum basic rates to meet competition and renewed contracts at substantially increased rates in cities where it had a monopoly of accredited central station service. ADT threatened retaliation against firms that contemplated inaugurating central station service.

The government filed suit against Grinnell under section 2 of the Sherman Act, asking that Grinnell be forced to divest itself of ADT, Holmes, and AFA and that other injunctive relief be granted. The district court ruled in favor of the government. Grinnell appealed.

Douglas, Justice   The offense of monopolization under Section 2 of the Sherman Act has two elements: (1) the possession of monopoly power in the relevant market and (2) the willful acquisition or maintenance of that power as distinguished from growth or development as a consequence of a superior product, business acumen, or historic accident. This second ingredient presents no major problem here, as what was done in building the empire was done plainly and explicitly for a single purpose. In *United States v. E. I. du Pont de Nemours & Co.*, we defined monopoly power as "the power to control prices or exclude competition." The existence of such power ordinarily may be inferred from the predominant share of the market. In *American Tobacco Co. v. United States*, we said that "over two thirds of the entire domestic field of cigarettes, and over 80 percent of the field of comparable cigarettes" constituted "a substantial monopoly." In *United States v. Aluminum Co. of America*, 90 percent of the market constituted monopoly power. In the present case, 87 percent of the accredited central station service business leaves no doubt that these defendants have monopoly power—power which they did not hesitate to wield—if that business is the relevant market. The only remaining question therefore is, what is the relevant market?

A product may be of such a character that substitute products must also be considered, as customers may turn to them if there is a slight increase in the price of the main product. That is the teaching of the *Du Pont* case, that commodities reasonably interchangeable make up that "part" of trade or commerce which Section 2 protects against monopoly power. The District Court treated the entire accredited central station service business as a single market and it was justified in so doing. Grinnell argues that the different central station services offered are so diverse that they cannot under *Du Pont* be lumped together to make up the relevant market. For example, burglar alarm services are not interchangeable with fire alarm services. It further urges that *Du Pont* requires that protective services other than those of the central station variety be included in the market definition.

We see no barrier to combining in a single market a number of different products or services where that combination reflects commercial realities. There is here a single basic service—the protection of property through use of a central service station—that must be compared with all other forms of property protection. There are, to be sure, substitutes for the accredited central station service. But none of them appears to operate on the same level as the central station service so as to meet the interchangeability test. What Grinnell overlooks is that the high degree of differentiation between central station protection and the other forms means that for many customers, only central station protection will do.

As the District Court found, the relevant market for determining whether the defendants have monopoly power is not the several local areas which the individual stations serve, but the broader national market that reflects the reality of the way in which they built and conduct their business. We have said enough about the great hold that the defendants have on this market. The percentage is so high as to justify the finding of monopoly. And this monopoly was achieved in large part by unlawful and exclusionary practices. The agreements that pre-empted for each company a segment of the market where it was free of competition of the others were one device. Pricing practices that contained competitors were another. The acquisitions by Grinnell of ADT, AFA, and Holmes were still another. Its control of the three other defendants eliminated any possibility of an outbreak of competition that might have occurred when the 1907 agreements terminated. By those acquisitions it perfected the monopoly power to exclude competitors and fix prices.

Judgment for the government affirmed.

Attempted Monopolization

Firms that have not yet attained monopoly power may nonetheless be liable for an **attempt to monopolize** in violation of section 2 if they are dangerously close to acquiring monopoly power and are employing methods likely to result in monopoly power if left unchecked. The *Spectrum Sports* case (which follows shortly) reveals that as part of the required proof of a dangerous probability that monopoly power will be acquired, plaintiffs in attempted monopolization cases must furnish proof of the relevant market—as in monopolization cases. Unlike monopolization cases, however, attempt cases also require proof that the defendant possessed a specific intent to acquire monopoly power through anticompetitive means.

A controversial issue that surfaces in many attempted monopolization cases concerns the role that *predatory pricing* may play in proving an intent to monopolize. The Supreme Court has recently defined predatory pricing as "pricing below an appropriate measure of cost for the purpose of eliminating competitors in the short run and reducing competition in the long run."[26] What constitutes "an appropriate measure of cost" in predatory pricing cases has long been a subject of debate among antitrust scholars. The Supreme Court has declined to resolve this debate definitively. What the Court's recent opinions do tell us is that the Court is likely to take a skeptical view of predatory pricing claims in the future. The Court has described predatory pricing schemes as "rarely tried, and even more rarely successful."[27] As part of this characterization of predatory pricing schemes, the Court indicated that it agrees with those economists who have argued that predatory pricing is often economically irrational because, to be successful, the predator must maintain monopoly power long enough after it has driven its competitors out of business to recoup the profits it lost through predatory pricing. The predator would be able to sustain monopoly power only if high barriers to entry prevented new competitors from being drawn into the market by the supracompetitive prices the predator would have to charge in order to recoup its losses.

Conspiracy to Monopolize

When two or more business entities **conspire to monopolize** a relevant market, section 2 may be violated. This portion of section 2, however, largely overlaps section 1, because it is difficult to conceive of a conspiracy to monopolize that would not also amount to a conspiracy in restraint of trade. The lower federal courts have differed on the elements necessary to prove a conspiracy to monopolize. In addition to requiring proof of the existence of a conspiracy, some courts insist on proof of the relevant market, a specific intent to acquire monopoly power, and overt action in furtherance of the conspiracy. Other courts do not require extensive

---

[26]*Cargill, Inc. & Excel Corp. v. Monfort of Colorado, Inc.*, 479 U.S. 484 (U.S. Sup. Ct. 1986).

[27]*Matsushita Electric Industrial Co., Ltd. v. Zenith Radio Corp.*, 475 U.S. 574 (U.S. Sup. Ct. 1986).

FIGURE 2	Elements of Section 2 Offenses		
Offense	**Monopoly Power**	**Intent to Monopolize**	**Concerted Action**
Monopolization	Required	Required	Not required
Attempted monopolization	"Dangerously close"	Specific intent required	Not required
Conspiracy to monopolize	Not required	Specific intent required	Required

---

proof of the relevant market. According to these courts, a violation is established through proof that the defendants conspired to exclude competitors from, or acquire control over prices in, some significant area of commerce. The Supreme Court's *Spec-* *trum Sports* decision, however, would seem to cast doubt on the validity of an approach that deemphasizes the requirement of proof of the relevant market.

Figure 2 summarizes the elements of section 2 offenses.

SPECTRUM SPORTS, INC. v. McQUILLAN
113 S. Ct. 884 (U.S. Sup. Ct. 1993)

Sorbothane is a patented elastic polymer whose shock-absorbing characteristics make it useful in a variety of medical, athletic, and equestrian products. BTR, Inc. owns the patent rights to sorbothane. Prior to 1982, a BTR subsidiary, Hamilton-Kent Manufacturing Co. (H-K) produced and distributed sorbothane for BTR. Another BTR subsidiary, Sorbothane, Inc. (SI), was formed in 1982 to replace H-K as the manufacturer of sorbothane and holder of distribution rights regarding it.

H-K and Shirley and Larry McQuillan signed a letter of intent in 1980. This letter of intent granted the McQuillans, who were designing a horseshoe pad that used sorbothane, exclusive rights to purchase sorbothane for use in equestrian products. In 1981, H-K established five regional distributorships for sorbothane. The McQuillans were chosen as distributors of all sorbothane products, including medical products and shoe inserts, for the Southwest. Spectrum Sports, Inc., was selected as distributor for another region of the country. Spectrum's co-owner, Kenneth Leighton, Jr., was the son of Kenneth Leighton, Sr., the president of H-K and later the president of SI.

In January 1982, H-K shifted responsibility for selling medical products from five regional distributors to a single national distributor. Three months later, H-K told the McQuillans that it wanted them to relinquish their athletic shoe distributorship as a condition of being able to retain the right to develop and distribute equestrian products. In May 1982, SI (having succeeded H-K in handling the sorbothane business for BTR) made the same demand to the McQuillans. At a meeting scheduled to discuss a possible sale of the McQuillans' athletic shoe distributorship to Spectrum, Shirley McQuillan was told by Leighton, Jr., that if the McQuillans did not come to agreement with Spectrum, they would be "looking for work." The McQuillans refused to sell and continued to distribute athletic shoe inserts.

Leighton, Sr., informed the McQuillans during the fall of 1982 that another firm had been appointed as the national equestrian distributor, and that the McQuillans were "no longer involved in equestrian products." In January 1983, SI began marketing, through a national distributor, a sorbothane horseshoe pad that, according to the McQuillans, was indistinguishable from the one they had designed. SI named Spectrum as the national distributor of sorbothane athletic shoe inserts in August 1983. At roughly the same time, SI informed the McQuillans that it would no longer accept their sorbothane orders. With the McQuillans thus being unable to obtain sorbothane, their business failed.

The McQuillans sued the other parties referred to above on various legal theories, including a claim of attempted monopolization in violation of section 2 of the Sherman Act. The jury returned a $1,743,000 verdict in favor of the McQuillans on the section 2 count. The district court trebled the jury's compensatory damages award. After the Ninth Circuit Court of Appeals affirmed, the Supreme Court granted the petition for a writ of certiorari filed by Spectrum and Leighton, Jr.

White, Justice   On the Section 2 issue ... present here, the Court of Appeals ... rejected [the] argument that attempted monopolization had not been established because the McQuillans had failed to prove that [the defendants] had a specific intent to monopolize a relevant market. The court also held that in order to show that [an] attempt to monopolize was likely to succeed, it was not necessary to present evidence of the relevant market or of the defendants' market power. In so doing, the Ninth Circuit relied on *Lessig v. Tidewater Oil Co.* (1964) [a Ninth Circuit decision] and its progeny. The Court of Appeals noted that these cases, in dealing with attempt to monopolize claims, had ruled that if evidence of unfair or predatory conduct is presented, [such evidence will also] satisfy both the specific intent and dangerous probability elements of the offense, without any proof of relevant market or the defendant's market power. The court went on to find [that the defendants] engaged in unfair or predatory conduct, [that the jury could therefore infer that the defendants] had the specific intent and the dangerous probability of success, [and that the McQuillans] did not have to prove [the] relevant market or the defendants' market power.

The decision below, and the *Lessig* line of decisions on which it relies, conflicts with holdings of courts in other circuits that proving an attempt to monopolize requires proof of a dangerous probability of monopolization of a relevant market. We granted certiorari to resolve this conflict.

Section 2 does not define the elements of the offense of attempted monopolization. Nor is there much guidance to be had in the scant legislative history of that provision. The legislative history does indicate that much of the interpretation of the necessarily broad principles of the Act was to be left for the courts in particular cases.

This Court first addressed the meaning of attempt to monopolize under Section 2 in *Swift & Co. v. United States* (1905). The Court's opinion [set forth the elements of intent to bring about a monopoly and a dangerous probability that a monopoly would

occur]. The Court went on to explain, however, that not every act done with intent to produce an unlawful result constitutes an attempt: "It is a question of proximity and degree." *Swift* thus indicated that intent is necessary, but alone is not sufficient, to establish the dangerous probability of success that is the object of Section 2's prohibition of attempts.

The Court's decisions since *Swift* have reflected the view that the plaintiff charging attempted monopolization must prove a dangerous probability of actual monopolization, which has generally required a definition of the relevant market and examination of market power. In *Walker Process Equipment, Inc. v. Food Machinery & Chemical Corp.* (1965), we found that enforcement of a fraudulently obtained patent claim could violate the Sherman Act. We stated that, to establish monopolization or attempt to monopolize under Section 2 . . ., it would be necessary to appraise the exclusionary power of the illegal patent claim in terms of the relevant market for the product involved. The reason was that "without a definition of that market there is no way to measure ability to lessen or destroy competition." Similarly, this Court reaffirmed in *Copperweld Corp. v. Independence Tube Corp.* (1984) that . . . the conduct of a single firm [violates Section 2] "only when it threatens actual monopolization."

The Courts of Appeals other than the Ninth Circuit have followed this approach. Consistent with our cases, it is generally required that to demonstrate attempted monopolization a plaintiff must prove (1) that the defendant has engaged in predatory or anticompetitive conduct with (2) a specific intent to monopolize and (3) a dangerous probability of achieving monopoly power. In order to determine whether there is a dangerous probability of monopolization, courts have found it necessary to consider the relevant market and the defendant's ability to lessen or destroy competition in that market.

Notwithstanding the array of authority contrary to *Lessig*, the Court of Appeals in this case reaffirmed its prior holdings. We are not at all inclined to embrace *Lessig*'s interpretation of Section 2, for there is little if any support for it in the statute or the case law, and the notion that proof of unfair or predatory conduct alone is sufficient to make out the offense of attempted monopolization is contrary to the purpose and policy of the Sherman Act. The purpose of the Act is not to protect business from the working of the market; it is to protect the public from the failure of the market. The law directs itself not against conduct which is competitive, even severely so, but against conduct which unfairly tends to destroy competition itself. It does so not out of solicitude for private concerns but out of concern for the public interest.

Thus, this Court and other courts have been careful to avoid constructions of Section 2 which might chill competition, rather than foster it. It is sometimes difficult to distinguish robust competition from conduct with long-term anticompetitive effects; moreover, single-firm activity is unlike concerted activity covered by Section 1, which inher-ently is fraught with anticompetitive risk. For these reasons, Section 2 makes the conduct of a single firm unlawful only when it actually monopolizes or dangerously threatens to do so.

The concern that Section 2 might be applied so as to further anticompetitive ends is plainly not met by inquiring only whether the defendant had engaged in "unfair" or "predatory" tactics. Such conduct may be sufficient to prove the necessary intent to monopolize, which is something more than an intent to compete vigorously, but demonstrating the dangerous probability of monopolization in an attempt case also requires inquiry into the relevant product and geographic market and the defendant's economic power in that market.

Judgment reversed in favor of Spectrum and Leighton; case remanded for further proceedings consistent with Supreme Court's opinion.

ETHICAL AND PUBLIC POLICY CONCERNS

1. Early in this chapter, you read Judge Learned Hand's statement that "[g]reat industrial consolidations are inherently undesirable, regardless of their economic results." Yet you also learned that Chicago School antitrust thinkers, who have very different notions about the effects of industrial concentration, have had an important influence on antitrust policy in recent years. Identify two aspects of the current global business environment that might make today's American policymakers less willing than Judge Hand to "perpetuate and preserve, for its own sake and in spite of possible cost, an organization of industry in small units which can effectively compete with each other."

2. Some of the cases in this chapter recite the statement that antitrust was designed to protect competition, not competitors. How is this statement consistent with the ethical justification of markets as the most efficient form of economic organization? Consider the case of a competitor who is driven out of business by another competitor's ultimately un-successful predatory pricing efforts (unsuccessful because the predator could not maintain monopoly power long enough to recoup the profits lost through predatory pricing). Although competition may not suffer in such a case, does such a competitor have any *ethical* claim to compensation? What public policy argument could be made in favor of compensation?

3. Tying arrangements that do not satisfy the criteria for per se illegality explained earlier in this chapter are judged under the rule of reason. This means that they will be judged lawful unless evidence demonstrates that they unreasonably restrain competition. Is there an *ethical* basis for arguing a seller's imposition of a tie-in is wrong, regardless of its effect on competition?

PROBLEMS AND PROBLEM CASES

1. Syufy Enterprises, a motion picture exhibitor operating theaters in four states, entered the Las Vegas first-run movie exhibition market in 1981 by opening a six-screen cinema complex. Before Syufy's entry there were 17 first-run theaters in Las

Vegas. This situation produced intensive bidding among theater owners regarding first-run film exhibition rights because there were often not enough such films to fill all 17 screens. This meant owners paid substantially more for the right to exhibit such films than they paid in other comparable markets. To reduce this competition, Syufy bought out the owners of six Las Vegas theaters. In late July 1984, Syufy submitted successful bids for the right to show the movie *The Cotton Club* during the Christmas season in Las Vegas and several other locations. On October 18, 1984, Syufy bought out Cragin, the owner of the remaining first-run theaters in Las Vegas. On October 23, 1984, after seeing the first trade screening of *The Cotton Club*, Syufy canceled the guarantees included in its bids for *The Cotton Club*. Syufy maintained that the movie was not as good as its distributor, Orion Pictures, had represented it to be, and that contrary to Orion's representations, a viewable version of the film had been available when the blind bids for exhibition rights were solicited. Orion filed suit against Syufy for breach of contract and for monopolizing and attempting to monopolize the Las Vegas market. Orion sought to recover the difference between the amount guaranteed in its contracts with Syufy and the amount it actually earned renting the film to other theaters. Was it proper for the district court to direct a verdict in Syufy's favor on the Sherman Act claims on the ground that Orion had failed to show an antitrust injury?

2. Co-Operative Theatres (Co-op), a Cleveland area movie theater booking agent, began seeking customers in southern Ohio. Shortly thereafter, Tri-State Theatre Services (Tri-State), a Cincinnati booking agent, began to solicit business in the Cleveland area. Later, however, Co-op and Tri-State allegedly entered into an agreement not to solicit each other's customers. The Justice Department prosecuted them for agreeing to restrain trade in violation of section 1 of the Sherman Act. Under a government grant of immunity, Tri-State's vice president testified that Co-op's vice president had approached him at a trade convention and threatened to start taking Tri-State's accounts if Tri-State did not stop calling on Co-op's accounts. He also testified that at a luncheon meeting he attended with officials from both firms, the presidents of both firms said that it would be in the interests of both firms to stop calling on each other's accounts.

Several Co-op customers testified that Tri-State had refused to accept their business because of the agreement with Co-op. The trial court found both firms guilty of a per se violation of the Sherman Act, rejecting their argument that the rule of reason should have been applied and refusing to allow them to introduce evidence that the agreement did not have a significant anticompetitive effect. Should the rule of reason have been applied?

3. Advanced Health-Care Services (ACHS), a supplier of durable medical equipment (DME) such as wheelchairs, hospital beds, walkers, crutches, and other equipment used by persons convalescing at home after hospitalization, filed a Sherman Act suit against Radford Community Hospital and Radford's holding company owner, Southwest Virginia Health Services Corporation (Southwest). ACHS's complaint alleged, among other things, that Radford, which provided acute health care services to approximately 75 percent of the residents of the greater Radford, Virginia, region, had conspired with another wholly owned subsidiary of Southwest's to prevent Radford patients from dealing with ACHS and to induce them to purchase DME from the Southwest subsidiary instead. ACHS argued that Radford and Southwest were guilty of conspiring to restrain trade in violation of Sherman Act section 1, and of monopolization and conspiracy to monopolize in violation of Sherman Act section 2. Was the district court's summary dismissal of all of ACHS's claims proper?

4. The Maricopa Foundation for Medical Care was a nonprofit organization established by the Maricopa County Medical Society to promote fee-for-service medicine. Roughly 70 percent of the physicians in Maricopa County belonged to the foundation. The foundation's trustees set maximum fees that members could charge for medical services provided to policyholders of approved medical insurance plans. To obtain the foundation's approval, insurers had to agree to pay the fees of member physicians up to the prescribed maximum. Member physicians were free to charge less than the prescribed maximum, but had to agree not to seek additional payments in excess of the maximum from insured patients. The Arizona attorney general filed suit for injunctive relief against the Maricopa County Medical Society and the foundation, arguing that the fee agreement constituted per se illegal horizontal price-fixing. The district court denied the

state's motion for a partial summary judgment. The Ninth Circuit Court of Appeals affirmed on the ground that the per se rule was not applicable to the case. Was the Ninth Circuit correct?

5. In 1986, Market Force, Inc. (MFI), began operating in the Milwaukee real estate market as a buyer's broker. MFI and prospective home buyers entered into exclusive contracts providing that MFI would receive a fee equal to 40 percent of the sales commission if it located a house that the buyer ultimately purchased. This 40 percent commission was the same commission selling brokers (those who ultimately produced a buyer, but whose duty of loyalty was to the seller) earned when they sold property placed on the local multiple listing service (MLS) by other brokers. MFI's contracts anticipated that the buyer would ask the listing broker (the one who had listed the property for sale on behalf of its owners and who received 60 percent of the commission when the property was sold) to pay MFI the commission at the time of the sale. If the listing broker agreed to do so, the buyer had no further obligation to MFI. For some time after MFI began operations, other real estate firms treated it inconsistently; some paid the full 40 percent commission but others paid nothing. In the fall of 1987, Wauwatosa Realty Co. and Coldwell Banker, the top two firms listing high-quality homes in Milwaukee, issued formal policies on splitting commissions with buyer's brokers. Wauwatosa said it would pay 20 percent of the selling agent's 40 percent commission. Coldwell Banker said it would pay 20 percent of the total sales commission. Several other real estate firms followed suit, setting their rates at 10 or 20 percent of the total sales commission, with the result that firms accounting for 31 percent of the annual listings of the MLS adopted policies and disseminated them to other MLS members. MFI filed suit against the brokers who had announced policies, arguing that they had conspired to restrain trade in violation of section 1 of the Sherman Act. At trial, the defendants introduced evidence of numerous business justifications for their policies and argued that their knowingly having adopted similar policies was not enough, standing alone, to justify a conclusion that the Sherman Act was violated. Was this argument correct?

6. When Triple-A Baseball Club Associates was in the process of building the Old Orchard Beach Ballpark, both Gemini Concerts, Inc., and Don Law Co., Inc., expressed interest in promoting concerts at the ballpark. Triple-A, however, had neither the time nor money to make the facility suitable for concerts. Gemini eventually ceased its efforts to use the facility. Law, however, persisted. After several years of discussions, Law and Triple-A signed an agreement giving Law the exclusive right to promote concerts at the ballpark for two years, with an option to renew for another five years. In return, Law paid for many of the capital improvements necessary to equip the ballpark for concerts and shared with Triple-A the cost of others. Gemini filed suit against Triple-A and Law, arguing that their exclusive dealing contract violated section 1 of the Sherman Act. Should the trial court grant the restraining order requested by Gemini?

7. Concerned that its dealers might not have sufficient spare parts to make repairs on recently purchased Subaru cars, Subaru of America (SOA) decided in 1973 to require its dealers to keep certain spare parts kits on hand. Grappone, Inc., a New Hampshire Subaru dealer, also had AMC, Pontiac, Jeep, Toyota, and Peugot franchises. Grappone acquired its cars from Subaru of New England, Inc. (SNE), a regional Subaru distributor. Grappone objected when told by SNE that it needed to purchase two "dealer's kits" containing 88 parts for 1974 cars and two "supplemental kits" containing 44 parts each (the total number of different Subaru parts being somewhere between 4,000 and 5,000). SNE refused to give Grappone its 1974 car allotment until Grappone bought the kits. Grappone went 10 months without cars; it then agreed to take the kits. Grappone later sued SNE, arguing that SNE violated section 1 of the Sherman Act by tying the sale of the parts kits to the sale of cars. The evidence introduced at trial indicated that Subaru's national market share was under 1 percent and that its share of the New Hampshire market was 3.4 percent. Was the trial court correct in granting judgment in favor of Grappone?

8. McClain and others brought a private antitrust action under the Sherman Act against the Real Estate Board of New Orleans. They alleged price-fixing by means of fixed commission rates, fee splitting, and suppression of market information useful to buyers. The trial court granted the board's motion for dismissal on the ground that real estate brokerage activities were wholly local in nature and therefore lacked the effect on interstate commerce necessary to invoke the Sherman Act. Was the trial court correct?

9. In mid-1982, Indiana Grocery (Indiana) owned 28 supermarkets in the Indianapolis area and sold about 13 percent of the area's groceries. Indiana bought Preston-Safeway in 1985. After 1986, all of Indiana's Indianapolis stores operated under the Preston-Safeway name. The Kroger Company (Kroger) operates over 1,400 supermarkets throughout the United States. In 1983, Kroger operated 32 stores in the Indianapolis area and sold about 28 percent of the area's groceries. Super Valu Stores, Inc., is primarily a grocery wholesaler. Since 1980, however, it has owned and franchised "Cub" retail food stores in various states. Cub stores, which are substantially larger than conventional supermarkets, offer a low level of services to customers in exchange for prices that normally are 6 to 10 percent lower than those of conventional stores. Between 1983 and 1986, four Cub stores were opened in the Indianapolis area. This ushered in a period of intense price competition as Kroger and others, realizing that gains by Cub would come at their expense, sought to compete. Cub had captured a 15 percent share of Indianapolis retail grocery sales by early 1985. Nevertheless, as of 1987, Kroger (with 33 stores), Marsh (with 30), Indiana (with 24), O'Malia (with 9), Mr.D's (with 5), Aldi (with 5), and Seven-Eleven (with 4), all remained in the Indianapolis market, as did other firms operating approximately 38 more supermarkets. Indiana filed suit in 1985 against Kroger. Indiana asserted, among other things, that Kroger used predatory pricing as a means of attempting to monopolize the Indianapolis retail grocery market. The district court granted summary judgment in Kroger's favor. Was the district court correct in doing so?

10. In July 1977, anesthesiologist Edwin G. Hyde applied for admission to the medical staff of East Jefferson Hospital in New Orleans. The credentials committee and the medical staff executive committee recommended approval, but the hospital board denied the application because the hospital was a party to a contract providing that all anesthesiological services required by the hospital's patients would be performed by Roux & Associates, a professional medical corporation. Hyde filed suit against the board, arguing that the contract violated section 1 of the Sherman Act. The district court ruled in favor of the board, finding that the anticompetitive effects of the contract were minimal and outweighed by the benefits of improved patient care. It noted that there were at least 20 hospitals in the New Orleans metropolitan area and that about 70 percent of the patients residing in Jefferson Parish went to hospitals other than East Jefferson. It therefore concluded that East Jefferson lacked any significant market power and could not use the contract for anticompetitive ends. The Fifth Circuit Court of Appeals reversed, holding that the relevant market was the East Bank Jefferson Parish rather than the New Orleans metropolitan area. The court therefore concluded that because 30 percent of the parish residents used East Jefferson and "patients tend to choose hospitals by location rather than price or quality," East Jefferson possessed sufficient market power to make the contract a per se illegal tying contract. Was the Fifth Circuit correct?

11. Häagen-Dazs was the first "super premium" ice cream manufacturer to achieve national distribution. Häagen-Dazs refused to sell its products to any distributor who also sold a comparable, competing ice cream brand. Two Count had been a Häagen-Dazs distributor in the San Francisco area since 1976. In 1985, Two Count agreed to become a distributor (in addition to being a Häagen-Dazs distributor) for Double Rainbow, another "super premium" ice cream manufacturer. When informed of this agreement, Häagen-Dazs terminated Two Count's distributorship. Two Count and Double Rainbow subsequently sued Häagen-Dazs, arguing, among other things, that Häagen-Dazs was guilty of monopolizing, or attempting to monopolize, the "super premium" ice cream market. At trial, Häagen-Dazs introduced uncontroverted evidence indicating that all grades of ice cream compete with one another for customer preference and space in retailers' freezers. Häagen-Dazs's share of the San Francisco ice cream market was 4 to 5 percent. Its national market share was in the same range. Should the trial court have granted Häagen-Dazs's motion for summary judgment on the section 2 claims?

CHAPTER
49

THE CLAYTON ACT, THE ROBINSON-PATMAN ACT, AND ANTITRUST EXEMPTIONS AND IMMUNITIES

INTRODUCTION

Concentration in the American economy continued despite the 1890 enactment of the Sherman Act. Early restrictive judicial interpretations of section 2 of the Sherman Act limited its effectiveness against many monopolists. Critics therefore sought legislation to thwart would-be monopolists before they achieved full-blown restraint of trade or monopoly power. In 1914, Congress responded by passing the Clayton Act.

Congress envisioned the Clayton Act as a vehicle for attacking some of the specific practices that monopolists had historically employed to acquire monopoly power. These practices included tying and exclusive dealing arrangements designed to squeeze competitors out of the market, mergers and acquisitions aimed at reducing competition through the elimination of competitors, interlocking corporate directorates designed to reduce competition by placing competitors under common leadership, and predatory or discriminatory pricing designed to force competitors out of business. Each of these practices will be discussed in the following pages.

In view of the congressional intent that the Clayton Act serve as a preventive measure, only a probability of a significant anticompetitive effect must be shown for most Clayton Act violations. Because the Clayton Act focuses on probable harms to competition, there are no criminal penalties for violating its provisions. Private plaintiffs, however, may sue for treble damages or injunctive relief if they are injured, or threatened with injury, by another party's violation of the statute. The Justice Department and the Federal Trade Commission (FTC) share responsibility for enforcing the Clayton Act. Each has the authority to seek injunctive relief to prevent or remedy violations of the statute. In addition, the FTC has the power to enforce the Clayton Act through the use of cease and desist orders, which were discussed in Chapter 47.

CLAYTON ACT SECTION 3

Section 3 of the Clayton Act makes it unlawful for any person engaged in interstate commerce to *lease or sell commodities,* or to *fix a price for commodities,* on the *condition, agreement, or understanding* that the lessee or buyer of the commodities will not use or deal in the commodities of the lessor's or seller's competitors, if the effect of doing so *may be* to *substantially lessen competition* or *tend to create a monopoly* in any line of commerce. Section 3 primarily targets two potentially anticompetitive behaviors: **tying agreements** and **exclusive dealing agreements**. As you learned in the preceding chapter, both of these types of contracts may amount to restraints of trade in violation of Sherman Act section 1. The language of section 3, however, contains limitations on the Clayton Act's application to such agreements.

A major limitation is that section 3 applies only to those tying agreements and exclusive dealing contracts involving *commodities*. Any such agreements involving services, real estate, or intangibles must therefore be attacked under the Sherman Act. In addition, section 3 applies only when there has been a *lease or sale* of commodities. It thus does not apply to true consignment agreements, because no sale or lease occurs in a consignment. Although section 3 speaks of sales and leases on the "condition, agreement, or understanding" that the buyer or lessee not deal in the commodities of the seller's or lessor's competitors, no formal agreement is required. Whenever a seller or lessor uses its economic power to prevent its customers from dealing with its competitors, potential Clayton Act concerns are triggered.

Tying Agreements

Many *tying agreements* plainly fall within at least the first portion of the relevant section 3 language. Any agreement that requires a buyer to purchase one product (the *tied product*) from a seller as a condition of purchasing another product (the *tying product*) from the same seller necessarily prevents the buyer from purchasing the tied product from the seller's competitors.

Only tying agreements that may *"substantially lessen competition or tend to create a monopoly,"* however, violate section 3. The lower federal courts are not in complete agreement on the nature of the proof necessary to demonstrate such a probable anticompetitive effect. More than 40 years ago, the Supreme Court appeared to indicate that a tying agreement would violate the Clayton Act if the seller either had monopoly power over the tying product or restrained a substantial volume of commerce in the tied product.[1]

As the *Mozart* case (which follows shortly) indicates, however, many lower federal courts today require essentially the same elements of proof for a Clayton Act violation that they require for a violation of the Sherman Act: the challenged agreement must involve *two separate products, sale of the tying product must be conditioned* on an accompanying sale of the tied product, the seller must have *sufficient economic power in the market for the tying product* to appreciably restrain competition in the tied product market, and the seller's tying arrangements must restrain a *"not insubstantial"* amount of commerce in the tied product market. A few courts continue to apply a less demanding standard for Clayton Act tying liability by dispensing with proof of the seller's economic power in the market for the tying product as long as the seller's tying arrangements involve a "not insubstantial" amount of commerce in the tied product. The *Mozart* case also reveals that defenses to tying liability under the Sherman Act (discussed in the preceding chapter) are also applicable to tying claims brought under the Clayton Act.

---

[1]*Times-Picayune Publ. Co. v. United States*, 345 U.S. 594 (U.S. Sup. Ct. 1953).

Mozart Co. v. Mercedes-Benz of North America, Inc.

833 F.2d 1342 (9th Cir. 1987)

Mercedes-Benz of North America (MBNA), the exclusive U.S. distributor of Mercedes-Benz (Mercedes) automobiles, is a wholly owned subsidiary of Daimler-Benz Aktiengesellschaft (DBAG), the manufacturer of Mercedes automobiles. MBNA required the approximately 400 franchised Mercedes dealers to agree not to sell or use (in the repair or servicing of Mercedes automobiles) any parts other than genuine Mercedes parts. Mozart, a wholesale automotive parts distributor, filed an antitrust suit against MBNA. Mozart alleged, among other things, that MBNA had violated both section 1 of the Sherman Act and section 3 of the Clayton Act by tying the sale of Mercedes parts to the sale of Mercedes automobiles. When the trial court ruled in favor of MBNA, Mozart appealed.

Sneed, Circuit Judge   In *Jefferson Parish Hospital v. Hyde* (1984), a bare majority reaffirmed the per se rule against tying. The majority opinion concluded that it was "far too late in the history of our antitrust jurisprudence to question the proposition that certain tying arrangements pose an unacceptable risk of stifling competition." Three elements are necessary to establish a per se illegal tying arrangement: (1) a tie-in between two distinct products or services; (2) sufficient economic power in the tying product to impose significant restrictions in the tied product market; and (3) an effect on a non-insubstantial volume of commerce in the tied product market.

The district court determined as a matter of law that the Mercedes passenger car and its replacement parts were separate products tied together by the terms of the MBNA dealer agreement, and that the tying arrangement affected a substantial amount of interstate commerce. The market power issue was submitted to the jury, which found that MBNA possessed the requisite power in the tying product, the Mercedes passenger car.

The instructions employed in submitting this issue to the jury were flawed, however. That flaw pertained to the "market power" that the defendant must possess in the tying product to justify the invocation of the per se standard. The required market power must be sufficient to "force a purchaser to do something he would not do in a competitive market." Such "forcing" is the equivalent of increasing the price of the tying product to increase profits.

In *Hyde*, the Court identified three sources of market power. First, when the government has granted the seller a patent or similar monopoly over a product, it is fair to presume that the inability to buy the product elsewhere gives the seller market power. The second is when the seller's share of the market is high. The third is when the seller offers a unique product that competitors are not able to offer. Mozart's theory of this case is that the Mercedes automobile is sufficiently unique to confer economic power on MBNA in the tying product.

The jury was instructed that "[a] prestigious and desirable trademark can be persuasive evidence of economic power." First, a prestigious trademark is not itself persuasive evidence of economic power. It is true that we have previously held that *copyright* protection may be evidence of market power because it creates barriers to entry for competitors in the tying market. *Digidyne Corp. v. Data General Corp.* (1984). However, unlike a patent or copyright, which is designed to protect the uniqueness of the product itself, a trademark protects only the name or symbol of the product. Market power, if any, is derived from the product, not from the name or symbol as such.

Second, the court's instructions indicate that somehow market power can be proven from the uniqueness of the Mercedes automobile. The difficulty with this is that while many individual purchasers undoubtedly regard a Mercedes as unique, it is by no means clear that dealers view the Mercedes in the same manner. The critical issue is whether MBNA possesses the market power to force dealers to purchase the tied product rather than acquire the franchise to sell a different automobile. Obviously there are costs of surrendering one franchise and acquiring another, but these are costs unrelated to the market power of a unique automobile. These costs will enable the car maker to extract concessions from the dealer, but this power is related to the franchise method of doing business, not to the possible uniqueness of the car.

However, we do not find that the flawed instructions necessitate a reversal of the judgment. The instructions were more favorable to Mozart than would be a proper recasting. This brings us to the heart of this case, whether the tying arrangement was justified by business necessity. A tie-in does not violate the antitrust laws if implemented for a legitimate purpose and if no less restrictive alternative is available. The defendant bears the burden of showing that the case falls within the contours of this affirmative defense.

The justification asserted by MBNA is that the tying arrangement is necessary to assure quality control and to protect its goodwill. The difficulty confronting MBNA is the problem of "freeriding" by Mercedes dealers. To MBNA it is crucial that a dealer offer standardized products. Only then can customers confidently rely on the Mercedes name.

Franchisees, on the other hand, experience a conflict of interest. True, they wish to maintain the goodwill of MBNA, but some will yield to avarice and increase their profits by supplying inferior products while continuing to attract customers at the expense of dealers who conform to quality standards. The cost of these transgressions will be borne by all franchisees in the form of decreased future demand. Although a consumer may realize that a particular franchisee "cut a corner," the adverse reaction of consumers as a group is not confined to that particular franchisee because they are appropriately reacting to the poor job of policing done by the franchisor.

Substantial evidence exists to support MBNA's claim that the tie-in was used to assure quality control. MBNA purchases approximately 80% of its replacement parts from DBAG. Of those parts half are manufactured by DBAG itself, and half are acquired from other original equipment manufacturers (OEMs). These OEMs produce the parts according to DBAG specifications. A selection of each shipment of OEM parts, which has already passed through one round of inspection, is tested a second time by DBAG. If any of the test parts is deficient, the whole lot is rejected. The remaining 20% of the replacement parts purchased by MBNA come directly from OEMs that have met DBAG's standards. Mozart purchased most of the parts it sold from OEMs in the United States.

MBNA introduced evidence showing that DBAG's strict testing standards helped to assure the high quality of replacement parts. MBNA maintains an excellent reputation in the automobile industry for reliable service and quality replacement parts. In fact, 75% of Mercedes automobile owners are repeat purchasers, and over one third of the owners return to the dealer for service and repairs. There was con-

siderable testimony by dealers and employees of MBNA about the inferiority of parts supplied by independent jobbers. Although Mozart introduced evidence to the contrary, the jury was entitled to make credibility determinations in favor of MBNA.

Mozart insists that MBNA could have furnished manufacturing specifications for replacement parts, and that such specifications would eliminate the need for a tie-in. The jury rejected this contention. Mozart is right, of course, when it insists that MBNA could have furnished design specifications for Mercedes replacement parts. That alone, however, does not eliminate the business justification defense. MBNA offered evidence that DBAG's vigorous testing programs could not be replicated by individual dealerships. The evidence further indicates the impracticality of Mozart's suggestion that MBNA could have inspected all replacement products furnished to independents. There was evidence from which the jury could find that the cost of such an undertaking would be prohibitive. We do not believe MBNA was required to make extreme steps to protect its legitimate interest in assuring public confidence in the quality of its trademarked product.

The elements for establishing a Sherman Act section 1 claim and a Clayton Act section 3 claim are virtually the same. There is no reason for allowing a business justification for a section 1 claim and not for a section 3 claim. Courts permit a business justification defense to tying claims because of a frank recognition that a package transaction with substantial justifications and few harmful effects should not be condemned. That recognition applies with equal force to the Sherman Act and the Clayton Act. The section 3 claim falls with the section 1 claim.

Judgment for MBNA affirmed.

Exclusive Dealing Agreements

In the preceding chapter, we discussed the nature of *exclusive dealing agreements*. Such contracts clearly fall under the initial portion of the relevant section 3 language because buyers who agree to handle one seller's product exclusively, or to purchase all of their requirements for a particular commodity from one seller, are by definition agreeing not to purchase simi-

lar items from the seller's competitors. As with tying agreements, however, not all exclusive dealing agreements are unlawful. Section 3 outlaws only those agreements that may "substantially lessen competition or tend to create a monopoly."

Exclusive dealing agreements initially were treated in much the same way as tying agreements. Courts looked at the dollar amount of commerce involved and declared illegal those agreements involving a "not insubstantial" amount of commerce. This *quantitative substantiality* test was employed, for example, by the Supreme Court in *Standard Oil Co. v. United States*.[2] Standard Oil was the largest refiner and supplier of gasoline in several western states, holding approximately 14 percent of the retail market. Roughly half of these sales were made by retail outlets owned by Standard. The other half were made by independent dealers who had entered into exclusive dealing contracts with Standard. Standard's six major competitors had entered into similar contracts with their own independent dealers. The Court recognized that exclusive dealing contracts, unlike tying agreements, could benefit both buyers and sellers, but declared Standard's contracts illegal on the ground that nearly $58 million in commerce was involved.

The Court's decision in the *Standard Oil* case provoked considerable criticism. In *Tampa Electric Co. v. Nashville Coal Co.*, however, the Court applied a broader *qualitative substantiality* test to gauge the legality of a long-term requirements contract for the sale of coal to an electric utility.[3] In *Tampa Electric*, the Court looked at the "area of effective competition," which was the total market for coal in the geographic region from which the utility could reasonably purchase its coal needs. The Court then examined the percentage of this region's total coal sales accounted for by the challenged contract. Because that percentage share was less than 1 percent of the region's total coal sales, the Court upheld the agreement even though it represented more than $100 million in coal sales.

Tampa Electric, however, is distinguishable from *Standard Oil*, which, in any event, the Court has not overruled. Unlike *Standard Oil*, *Tampa Electric* involved parties with relatively equal bargaining power and an individual agreement, rather than an industry-wide practice. In addition, there were obvious reasons why an electric utility such as Tampa Electric might want to lock in its coal costs by using a long-term requirements contract. Although lower court opinions employing each test may be found, the *qualitative* approach employed in *Tampa Electric* is the one more likely to be employed by the current Court.

---

[2]337 U.S. 293 (U.S. Sup. Ct. 1949).
[3]365 U.S. 320 (1961).

CLAYTON ACT SECTION 7

Introduction

Section 7 of the Clayton Act was designed to attack **mergers**—a term used broadly in this chapter to refer to the acquisition of one company by another. Our historical experience indicates that one way in which monopolists acquired monopoly power was by acquiring control of their competitors. Section 7 prohibits any party engaged in commerce or in any activity affecting commerce from *acquiring the stock or assets* of another such party if the effect, in *any line of commerce* or *any activity affecting commerce* in any section of the country, *may be* to *substantially lessen competition* or *tend to create a monopoly*. Rather than adopting the Sherman Act section 2 approach of waiting until a would-be monopolist has acquired monopoly power or is dangerously close to doing so, section 7 attempts to "nip monopolies in the bud" by barring mergers that *may* have an anticompetitive effect.

Although section 7 is plainly an anticoncentration device, it has also been used (as the following text indicates) to attack mergers that have had no direct effect on concentration in a particular industry. As such, its future evolution is in doubt, given the influence of Chicago School economic theories on contemporary antitrust law and the more tolerant stance those theories take toward mergers. During the 1980s, the Justice Department signaled a more permissive approach to merger activity than the government had previously adopted. During roughly the first year of the Clinton presidency (the approximate time this book went to press), however, Justice Department officials offered hints of increased government scrutiny of mergers in some industries, though not necessarily on an across-the-board basis. It remains to be seen whether the Clinton administration will in fact pursue a stepped-up enforcement policy regarding mergers. Regardless of the enforcement approach chosen by the federal government, it should be remembered that private enforcement of section 7 is also possible.

Predictions regarding section 7's ultimate judicial treatment are complicated considerably by the fact that many of the important merger cases in recent years have been settled out of court. This leaves interested observers of antitrust policy with few definitive expressions of the Supreme Court's current thinking on many merger issues. Most of the available indications, however, point to potentially significant revisions of merger policy in the years to come.

Relevant Market Determination

Regardless of the treatment section 7 ultimately receives in the courts, determining the **relevant market** affected by a merger is likely to remain a crucial component of any section 7 case. Before a court can determine whether a particular merger will have the *probable* anticompetitive effect required by the Clayton Act, it must first determine the *line of commerce* (or *relevant product market*) and the *section of the country* (or *relevant geographic market*) that are likely to be affected by the merger. If the court adopts a broad relevant market definition, this will usually enhance the government's or private plaintiff's difficulty in demonstrating a probable anticompetitive effect flowing from a challenged merger.

Relevant Product Market "Line of commerce" determinations under the Clayton Act have traditionally employed *functional interchangeability* tests similar to those employed in relevant product market determinations under section 2 of the Sherman Act. Which products do the acquired and acquiring firms manufacture (assuming a merger between competitors), and which products are reasonably interchangeable by consumers to serve the same purposes? The federal government's merger guidelines indicate that the relevant market includes those products that consumers view as good substitutes at prevailing prices. The guidelines also state that the relevent market includes any products that a significant percentage of current customers would shift to in the event of a "small, but significant and non-transitory increase" in price of the products of the merged firms.

Relevant Geographic Market To determine a particular merger's probable anticompetitive effect on a section of the country, courts have traditionally asked where the effects of the merger will be "direct and immediate."[4] This means that the relevant geographic market may not be as broad as the markets in which the acquiring and acquired firms actually operate or, in the case of a merger between competitors, the markets in which they actually compete. The focus of the relevant market inquiry is on those sections of the country in which competition is most likely to be injured by the merger. As a result, the relevant geographic market in a given case could be drawn as narrowly as one metropolitan area or as broadly as the entire nation. All that is necessary to satisfy this aspect of section 7 is proof that the challenged merger might have a significant negative effect on competition in any economically significant geographic market.

The federal government's merger guidelines adopt a somewhat different approach to determining the relevant geographic market. They define the relevant geographic market as the geographic area in which a sole supplier of the product in question could profitably raise its price without causing outside suppliers to begin selling in the area. The guidelines contemplate beginning with the existing markets in which the parties to a merger compete, and then adding the markets of those suppliers that would enter the market in response to a "small, but significant and non-transitory increase" in price.

Horizontal Mergers

The analytical approach employed to gauge a merger's probable effect on competition varies according to the nature of the merger in question. **Horizontal mergers**—mergers among firms competing in the same product and geographic markets—have traditionally been subjected to the most rigorous scrutiny because they clearly lead to increased concentration in the relevant market.

Market Share of Resulting Firm To determine the legality of such a merger, courts look at the *market share of the resulting firm*. In *United States v. Philadelphia National Bank*, the Supreme Court indicated that a horizontal merger producing a firm with an "undue percentage share" of the relevant market (33 percent in that case) and resulting in a "significant increase in concentration" of the firms in that market would be presumed illegal, absent convincing evidence that the merger would not have an anticompetitive effect.[5]

In the past, mergers involving firms with smaller market shares than those involved in *Philadelphia National Bank* were also enjoined if other economic

---

[4]See, for instance, *United States v. Phillipsburg National Bank*, 399 U.S. 350 (U.S. Sup. Ct. 1970).

[5]374 U.S. 321 (1963).

or historical factors pointed toward a probable anti-competitive effect. Some of the factors that courts have traditionally considered relevant include:

1. *A trend toward concentration in the relevant market*: Has the number of competing firms decreased over time?

2. *The competitive position of the merging firms*: Are the defendants dominant firms despite their relatively small market shares?

3. *A past history of acquisitions by the acquiring firm*: Are we dealing with a would-be empire builder?

4. *The nature of the acquired firm*: Is it an aggressive, innovative competitor despite its small market share?

Recent Assessments of Merger Effects   Recent developments, however, indicate that the courts and federal antitrust enforcement agencies have become increasingly less willing to presume that anticompetitive effects will necessarily result from a merger that produces a firm with a relatively large market share. Instead, a more detailed inquiry is made into the nature of the relevant market and of the merging firms in order to ascertain the likelihood of a probable harm to competition as a result of a challenged merger. The federal government's horizontal merger guidelines indicate that when regulators assess a merger's probable effect, the focus is on the existing concentration in the relevant market, the increase in concentration as a result of the proposed merger, and other nonmarket share factors. The more concentrated the existing market and the greater the increase in concentration that would result from the proposed merger, the more likely the merger is to be challenged by the government.

The nonmarket share factors considered by federal regulators are more traditional. They include: the existence of barriers to the entry of new competitors into the relevant market, the prior conduct of the merging firms, and the probable future competitive strength of the acquired firm. The last factor is particularly important because courts have acknowledged that a firm's current market share may not reflect its ability to compete in the future. For example, courts have long recognized a "failing company" justification for some mergers. If the acquired firm is a failing company and no other purchasers are interested in acquiring it, its acquisition by a competitor may be lawful under section 7. Similarly, if an acquired firm has financial problems that reflect some underlying structural weakness, or if it lacks new technologies that are necessary to compete effectively in the future, its current market share may overstate its future competitive importance.

Finally, given the increased weight being assigned to economic arguments in antitrust cases, two other merger justifications may be granted greater credence in the future. Some lower federal courts have recognized the notion that a merger between two small companies may be justifiable, despite the resulting statistical increase in concentration, if the merger enables them to compete more effectively with larger competitors. In a somewhat similar vein, some commentators have argued that mergers resulting in enhanced economic efficiencies should sometimes be allowed even though they may have some anticompetitive impact. Though Courts have not been very receptive to efficiency arguments in the past, the government's horizontal merger guidelines are flexible enough to allow the Justice Department and FTC to consider efficiency claims in deciding whether to challenge a merger.

UNITED STATES V. WASTE MANAGEMENT, INC.

743 F.2d 976 (2d Cir. 1984)

Waste Management, Inc. (WMI), a company in the solid waste disposal business, acquired the stock of EMW Ventures, Inc. EMW was a diversified holding company, one of whose subsidiaries was Waste Resources. WMI and Waste Resources each had subsidiaries operating in or near Dallas, Texas. The government challenged the merger, arguing that it violated section 7 of the Clayton Act. The trial court (Judge Griesa) agreed, defining the relevant market as including all forms of trash collection (except at single-family or multiple-family residences or small apartment complexes) in Dallas County plus a small fringe area. The combined WMI and Waste Resources subsidiaries had 48.8 percent of the market so defined. The trial court found this market share presumptively illegal. WMI appealed.

Winter, Circuit Judge A post-merger market share of 48.8% is sufficient to establish prima facie illegality under *United States v. Philadelphia National Bank*. That decision held that large market shares are a convenient proxy for appraising the danger of monopoly power resulting from a horizontal merger. Under its rationale, a merger resulting in a large market share is presumptively illegal, rebuttable only by a demonstration that the merger will not have anticompetitive effects. Thus, in *United States v. General Dynamics Corp.* (1974), the Court upheld a merger of two leading coal producers because substantially all of the production of one firm was tied up in long-term contracts and its reserves were insubstantial. Since that firm's future ability to compete was negligible, the Court reasoned that its disappearance as an independent competitor could not affect the market.

WMI does not claim that 48.8% is too small a share to trigger the *Philadelphia National Bank* presumption. Rather, it argues that the presumption is rebutted by the fact that competitors can enter the Dallas waste hauling market with such ease that the finding of a 48.8% market share does not accurately reflect market power. WMI argues that it is unable to raise prices over the competitive level because new firms would quickly enter the market and undercut them.

The Supreme Court has never directly held that ease of entry may rebut a showing of *prima facie* illegality under *Philadelphia National Bank*. However, on several occasions it has held that appraisal of the impact of a proposed merger upon competition must take into account potential competition from firms not presently active in the relevant product and geographic markets. Moreover, under *General Dynamics*, a substantial existing market share is insufficient to void a merger where that share is misleading as to actual future competitive effect. In that case, long-term contracts and declining reserves negated the inference of market power drawn from the existing market share. In the present case, a market definition artificially restricted to existing firms competing at one moment may yield market share statistics that are not an accurate proxy for market power when substantial potential competition able to respond quickly to price increases exists.

Finally, the *Merger Guidelines* issued by the government itself not only recognize the economic principle that ease of entry is relevant to appraising the impact upon competition of a merger but also state that it may override all other factors. Where entry is "so easy that existing competitors could not succeed in raising prices for any significant period of time," the government has announced that it will usually not challenge a merger.

Turning to the evidence in this case, we believe that entry into the relevant product and geographic market by new firms or by existing firms in the Fort Worth area is so easy that any anticompetitive impact of the merger before us would be eliminated more quickly by such competition than by litigation. Judge Griesa specifically found that individuals operating out of their homes can acquire trucks and some containers and compete successfully "with any other company." His conclusion that "there is no showing of any circumstances, related to ease of entry or the trend of the business, which promises in and of itself to materially erode the [defendants'] competitive strength" is consistent with our decision. They may well retain their present market share. However, in view of the findings as to ease of entry, that share can be retained only by competitive pricing. Ease of entry constrains not only WMI, but every firm in the market. Should WMI attempt to exercise market power by raising prices, none of its small competitors would be able to follow the price increases because of the ease with which new competitors would appear. WMI would then face lower prices charged by all existing competitors as well as entry by new ones, a condition fatal to its economic prospects if not rectified.

Judgment reversed in favor of Waste Management, Inc.

Vertical Mergers

A **vertical merger** is a merger between firms that previously had, or could have had, a supplier-customer relationship. For example, a manufacturer may seek to vertically integrate its operations by acquiring a company that controls retail outlets at which the manufacturer's products could be sold. Alternatively, the manufacturer could vertically merge by acquiring a company that makes a product the manufacturer regularly uses in its production processes. Vertical mergers, unlike horizontal mergers, do not directly result in an increase in concentration. Nonetheless, they traditionally have been thought to threaten competition in various ways.

Foreclosing Competitors in Relevant Market

First, vertical mergers may *foreclose competitors* from a share of the relevant market. For example, if a major customer for a particular product acquires a captive supplier of that product, the competitors of the acquired firm are thereafter foreclosed from competing with it for sales to the acquiring firm. Similarly, if a manufacturer acquires a captive retail outlet for its products, the manufacturer's competitors are foreclosed from competing for sales to that retail outlet. A vertical merger in the latter case may also result in reduced competition at the retail level. For instance, a shoe manufacturer acquires a retail shoe store chain that carries the brands of several competing manufacturers and has a dominant share of the retail market in certain geographic areas. If the retail chain carries only the acquiring manufacturer's brands after the merger occurs, competition among the acquiring manufacturer and its competitors is reduced in the retail market for shoes.

Creation of Increased Market Entry Barriers

A second way in which vertical mergers threaten competition is that they may lead to *increased barriers to market entry* for new competitors. For example, if a major purchaser of a product acquires a captive supplier of that product, potential producers of the product may be discouraged from commencing production due to the merger-related contraction of the market for the product.

Elimination of Potential Competition in Acquired Firm's Market

In addition, some vertical mergers threaten competition by *eliminating potential competition* in one of two ways. First, an acquiring firm may be perceived by existing competitors in the acquired firm's market as a likely potential entrant into that market. The threat of such a potential entrant "waiting in the wings" may moderate the behavior of existing competitors because they fear that pursuing pricing policies which exploit their current market position might cause the potential entrant to react by entering the market. The acquiring firm's entry into the market by the acquisition of an existing competitor means the end of its moderating influence as a potential entrant. Second, a vertical merger may deprive the market of the potential benefits that would have resulted if the acquiring firm had entered the market in a more competitive manner, such as by creating its own entrant into the market through internal expansion or by making a toehold acquisition of a small existing competitor and subsequently building it into a more significant competitor.

Historically, courts seeking to determine the legality of vertical mergers have tended to look at the *share of the relevant market foreclosed to competition.* If a more than insignificant market share is foreclosed to competition, courts consider other economic and historical factors. Factors viewed as aggravating the anticompetitive potential of a vertical merger include: a trend toward concentration or vertical integration in the industry, a past history of vertical integration in the industry, a past history of vertical acquisitions by the acquiring company, and significant barriers to entry resulting from the merger. This approach to determining the legality of vertical mergers has been criticized by some commentators. These critics argue that vertical integration may yield certain efficiencies of distribution and that vertical integration by merger may be more economically efficient than vertical integration by internal expansion. The Justice Department generally affords greater weight to efficiency arguments in cases involving vertical mergers than in cases involving horizontal mergers. The department generally applies the same criteria to all nonhorizontal mergers. We discuss these criteria in the following section.

Conglomerate Mergers

A **conglomerate merger** is a merger between two firms that neither compete with each other (because they do business in different product or geographic markets) nor have a supplier-customer relationship with each other. Conglomerate mergers may be either *market extension* mergers or *product extension* mergers. In a market extension merger, the acquiring firm expands into a new geographic market by purchasing a firm already doing business in that market. For example, a conglomerate that owns an east coast grocery chain buys a west coast grocery chain. In a product extension merger, the acquiring firm diversifies its operations by purchasing a company in a new product market. For example, a conglomerate with interests in the aerospace and electronics industries purchases a department store chain.

There is considerable disagreement over the economic effects of conglomerate acquisitions. As later discussion will reveal, conglomerate mergers have been attacked with some degree of success under section 7 if they involve **potential reciprocity**, serve to **eliminate potential competition**, or give an acquired firm an **unfair advantage** over its competitors. Nevertheless, there is significant sentiment that the Clayton Act is not well suited to dealing with conglomerate mergers. This realization has produced calls for specific legislation on the subject. Such legislation is probably desirable if we ultimately conclude that conglomerate merger activity is a proper subject for regulation.

Potential Reciprocity   Conglomerate mergers that involve *potential reciprocity* are among those sometimes held to be prohibited by section 7. A conglomerate merger may create a risk of potential reciprocity if the acquired firm produces a product regularly purchased by the acquiring firm's suppliers. Such suppliers, eager to continue their relationship with the acquiring firm, may thereafter purchase the acquired firm's products rather than those of its competitors.

Elimination of Potential Competition   Some conglomerate mergers may result in *elimination of potential competition* in ways similar to vertical mergers, and thus may be vulnerable to attack under section 7. If existing competitors perceive the acquiring company as a potential entrant in the acquired company's market, the acquiring company's entry by means of a conglomerate acquisition may result in the loss of the moderating influence that it had while waiting in the wings. In addition, when the acquiring company actually enters the new

market by acquiring a well-established competitor rather than by starting a new competitor through internal expansion (a *de novo* entry) or by making a toehold acquisition, the market is deprived of the potential for increased competition flowing from the reduction in concentration that would have accompanied either of the latter strategies.

Relevant Supreme Court decisions suggest, however, that a high degree of proof is required before either of these potential competition arguments will be accepted. Arguments that a conglomerate merger eliminated a *perceived potential entrant* must be accompanied by proof that existing competitors actually perceived the acquiring firm as a potential entrant.[6] Arguments that a conglomerate acquisition eliminated an *actual* potential entrant (and thereby deprived the market of the benefits of reduced concentration) must be accompanied by evidence that the acquiring firm had the ability to enter the market by internal expansion or a toehold acquisition and that doing so would have ultimately yielded a substantial reduction in concentration.[7]

Unfair Advantage to Acquired Firm   Finally, conglomerate mergers may violate section 7 in certain instances when the acquired firm obtains an *unfair advantage* over its competitors. When a large firm acquires a firm that already enjoys a significant position in its market, the acquired firm may gain an unfair advantage over its competitors through its ability to draw on the greater resources and expertise of its new owner. This advantage may entrench the acquired firm in its market by deterring existing competitors from actively competing with it for market share and by causing other potential competitors to be reluctant to enter the market after the acquisition.

Virtually all of the important recent conglomerate merger cases have been settled out of court. As a result, we do not have a clear indication of the Supreme Court's current thinking on conglomerate merger issues. In recent years, the Justice Department has taken the position that the primary theories to be used by the department in attacking all *nonhorizontal* mergers are the *elimination of*

---

[6]*United States v. Falstaff Brewing Corp.*, 410 U.S. 526 (U.S. Sup. Ct. 1973).

[7]*United States v. Marine Bancorporation, Inc.*, 418 U.S. 602 (U.S. Sup. Ct. 1974).

FIGURE 1	Types of Mergers Covered by Section 7	
Category	**Description**	**Example**
Horizontal	Between competitors	One automobile manufacturer merges with another automobile manufacturer
Vertical	Between a supplier and its customer	An oil producer merges with an oil refiner
Conglomerate	Between two largely unrelated businesses	A candy company merges with a greeting card company

perceived and actual potential competition theories. In employing these analytical tools, the department also considers other economic factors. These include: (1) the degree of concentration in the acquired firm's market; (2) the existence of barriers to entry into the market and the presence or absence of other firms with a comparable ability to enter; and (3) the market share of the acquired firm (with challenges being unlikely if this is 5 percent or less and likely if it is 20 percent or more). It remains to be seen whether the Supreme Court will accept this more restrictive view of the scope of section 7.

Figure 1 summarizes the types of mergers covered by section 7.

TENNECO, INC. V. FTC
689 F.2d 346 (2d Cir. 1982)

In 1975, Tenneco, Inc., was the 15th largest industrial corporation in America. Tenneco's Walker Manufacturing Division produced and distributed a wide variety of automotive parts, the most important of which were exhaust system parts. Walker was the nation's leading seller of exhaust system parts in 1975 and 1976. Tenneco acquired control of Monroe Auto Equipment Company, a leading manufacturer of automotive shock absorbers. Monroe was the number two firm in the national market for replacement shock absorbers. Monroe and Gabriel, the industry leader, accounted for over 77 percent of replacement shock absorber sales in 1976. General Motors and Questor Corporation, the third and fourth largest firms, controlled another 15 percent of the market.

The replacement shock absorber market exhibited significant barriers to the entry of new competitors. Economies of scale in the industry dictated manufacturing plants of substantial size. Furthermore, the nature of the industry required would-be entrants to acquire significant new technologies and marketing skills unique to the industry. The Federal Trade Commission (Commission) concluded that Tenneco's acquisition of Monroe violated section 7 of the Clayton Act by eliminating both perceived and actual potential competition in the replacement shock absorber market. The Commission therefore ordered Tenneco to divest itself of Monroe. Tenneco appealed.

Meskill, Circuit Judge   The Supreme Court has described the theory of perceived potential competition, which it has approved for application to cases brought under Section 7 of the Clayton Act, as the principal focus of the potential competition doctrine. The Court has recognized that:

A market extension merger may be unlawful if the target market is substantially concentrated, if the acquiring firm has the characteristics, capabilities, and economic incentive to render it a perceived potential *de novo* entrant, and if the acquiring firm's presence on the fringe of the target market in fact tempered oligopolistic behavior on the part of existing participants in that market. *United States v. Marine Bancorporation, Inc.* (1974).

The actual potential competition theory, which has yet to receive sanction from the Supreme Court, would

proscribe a market extension merger solely on the ground that such a merger eliminates the prospect for long-term deconcentration of an oligopolistic market that in theory might result if the acquiring firm were forbidden to enter except through a *de novo* undertaking or through the acquisition of a small existing entrant.

We reject the Commission's finding that Tenneco was an actual potential entrant likely to increase competition in the market for replacement shock absorbers. Tenneco was actively considering entry into the market and was pursuing all leads to that end at least since the late 1960s or early 1970s. Moreover, Tenneco clearly possessed adequate financial resources to make the large initial investment needed to attempt to penetrate the market. The record, however, is deficient in evidence that there were viable toehold options available to Tenneco or that Tenneco would have entered the market *de novo*.

The Commission conceded that Tenneco never expressed any interest in entering the market for replacement shock absorbers "on a completely *de novo* basis." However, the Commission found that Tenneco had expressed interest in entering the market essentially *de novo*, building the required production facilities from scratch and acquiring the necessary technology via a license from an established foreign shock absorber producer. The Commission concluded that Tenneco would likely have done so absent its acquisition of Monroe.

The Commission's reasoning is flawed. It ignores Tenneco's decision not to enter the market during the 1960s and early 1970s, a period of high profitability for shock absorber manufacturers, because of anticipated inadequate earnings during early years. The record is devoid of evidentiary support for the Commission's assertion that in the period relevant to this case, when industry earnings were in decline, Tenneco would have been willing to suffer the "cost disadvantage" inherent in the building of an efficient scale plant that would remain underutilized "for a number of years."

The Commission's conclusion that Tenneco would likely have entered the replacement shock

absorber market through toehold acquisition is similarly flawed. The Commission identified Armstrong Patents, Ltd. ("Armstrong"), a British shock absorber manufacturer, DeCarbon Shock Absorber Co. ("DeCarbon"), a French company, and Blackstone Manufacturing Corp. ("Blackstone"), a small United States producer of shock absorbers, as potential toeholds. However, Tenneco in fact negotiated unsuccessfully with Armstrong and DeCarbon. Armstrong management indicated that Tenneco would have to offer a 100 percent premium over the market price of its stock to generate its interest. Tenneco's negotiations with DeCarbon, which were conducted through an independent broker, were equally fruitless. DeCarbon had asked a selling price of 100 times its earnings.

As for Blackstone, the Commission itself described that company as "a small, struggling domestic firm burdened with aged equipment, a less than complete product line, declining market share and a mediocre reputation." Since 1974 Blackstone had unsuccessfully sought a buyer for its business, soliciting, among others, Midas International Corp., which operates a chain of muffler installation shops, and Questor. Nevertheless, the Commission remarkably concluded that Blackstone "would have served as a viable method of toehold entry."

We also conclude that the record contains inadequate evidence to support the Commission's conclusion that Tenneco's acquisition of Monroe violated Section 7 by eliminating Tenneco as a perceived potential competitor in the market for replacement shock absorbers. There is abundant evidence that the oligopolists in the market for replacement shock absorbers perceived Tenneco as a potential entrant. Industry executives testified that they considered Tenneco one of very few manufacturers with both the incentive and the capability to enter the market. This perception was based on Tenneco's financial strength and on the compatibility of shock absorbers with exhaust system parts produced by Tenneco's Walker Division.

However, the Commission's conclusion that the perception of Tenneco as a potential entrant actually tempered the conduct of oligopolists in the market must also be supported by substantial evidence. It is not. Tenneco argued that in the years immediately preceding its acquisition of Monroe the market for replacement shock absorbers had become highly competitive. The Commission apparently agrees with this assessment. The rate of increase in advertised retail prices for shock absorbers fell significantly behind inflation, and mass merchandisers such as Sears, Roebuck replaced traditional wholesale distributors as the leading purchasers of replacement shock absorbers from manufacturers. Sears's retail prices for shock absorbers were frequently below the prices that manufacturers charged wholesale distributors, who were several levels above the retail customer in the traditional chain of distribution.

The advent of increased sales by mass merchandisers coincided with aggressive competition among shock absorber manufacturers. Manufacturers offered substantial discounts off their circulated price sheets to traditional wholesalers and implemented "stocklifting," a practice in which a manufacturer buys a wholesaler's inventory of a competing manufacturer's product and replaces it with his own product.

While agreeing that competitive activity increased dramatically in the mid-1970s, the Commission stated:

We disagree with [Tenneco] over the cause of that new competitive vigor. In brief, we find that the source of the improved economic performance lay in industry fears that Tenneco was likely to attempt entry—an actual "edge effect"—rather than in the buyer power supposedly asserted by mass merchants against their suppliers.

The Commission's hypothesis depends almost entirely on inferences drawn from the activity of Maremont [Gabriel's owner]. We have no doubt that

direct evidence of an "edge effect" is not required to support a Commission finding of a Section 7 violation. In this case, however, direct evidence concerning Tenneco's "edge effect" on Maremont was elicited by the Commission, though it does not support the Commission's conclusion. During the testimony of Byron Pond, Senior Vice-President and Director of Maremont, the following colloquy occurred:

Q: [by Commission Counsel]: Did the presence of Walker, IPC or Midas and/or TRW as likely potential entrants into the shock absorber market, have any effect on Maremont's decisions, business decisions?

A: [by Mr. Pond]: I don't think that we looked specifically at competitors on a periodic basis or potential competitors in developing our strategy. I think we developed our strategy and approach to the business based on how we perceive it and how we perceived the opportunities.

Mr. Pond's testimony constitutes direct evidence that Tenneco had no direct effect on Maremont's business decisions or competitive activity. In the face of this contrary and unchallenged direct evidence, the substantiality of circumstantial evidence arguably suggesting an "edge effect" vanishes. Accordingly, we hold that the Commission's finding that Maremont's actions were probably taken in response to its desire to dissuade Tenneco from entering the market is unsupported by substantial evidence in the record.

Commission order set aside in favor of Tenneco.

CLAYTON ACT SECTION 8

If the same individuals control theoretically competing corporations, an obvious potential exists for collusive anticompetitive conduct such as price-fixing or division of markets. Section 8 of the Clayton Act was designed to minimize the risks posed by such interlocks. Initially, section 8 prohibited any person from serving as a *director* of two or more corporations (other than banks or common carriers) if either had "capital, surplus, and undivided profits aggregating more than $1,000,000" and the corporations were, or had been, competitors,

"so that elimination of competition by agreement between them" would violate any of the antitrust laws. The Antitrust Amendments Act of 1990 amended section 8's original language to increase the amount required to trigger the statute from $1 million to $10 million (a figure to be adjusted annually by an amount equal to the percentage increase or decrease in the gross national product).

Section 8 establishes a per se standard of liability in the sense that a violation of the statute may be demonstrated without proof that the interlock harmed competition. Until recently, however, the statute's prohibition against interlocks was quite limited in scope because it barred only interlocking *directorates*. Nothing in the original language of section 8 prohibited a person from serving as an *officer* of two competing corporations, or as an officer of one firm and a director of its competitor. The Antitrust Amendments Act of 1990, however, expanded the scope of the statute by including senior *"officers"* (defined as officers elected or chosen by the board of directors) within its reach.

Although government enforcement of section 8 was historically lax, recent years have witnessed some signs of growing government interest in the statute. The Supreme Court, however, has indicated that section 8 should not be interpreted in an expansive fashion that strains the statutory language. *BankAmerica Corp. v. United States*[8] stemmed from a Justice Department attempt to police interlocking directorates between banks and insurance companies. Never before had an interlock involving a bank been challenged under section 8 because of the specific statutory language prohibiting interlocks between corporations "other than banks." Concerned about the increasing areas in which banks and a variety of other businesses were competing in rapidly changing financial markets, the Justice Department argued that the statutory exception should apply only when both of the companies at issue were banks. Had the department been successful, the consequences for the banking industry could have been significant, given the long history of interlocking directorates between banks and other business corporations. The Supreme Court, however, rejected the government's broad reading of the statute, holding that the "most natural reading" of the statute was that the interlocking corporations must all be corporations "other than banks." The Antitrust Amendments Act of 1990 retained the statutory language exempting banks.

Signs of renewed government interest in section 8 produced significant concern in an era of conglomerate merger activity. Given the wide diversification that characterizes many large corporations, it would be increasingly easy to demonstrate some degree of competitive overlap among a substantial number of large, diversified corporations. Critics alleged that section 8 has operated to discourage qualified persons from serving as directors when no

potential for actual competitive harm exists. In response to such criticism, the Antitrust Amendments Act of 1990 specified that individuals may serve as officers or directors of competing corporations when the "competitive overlap" between them is an insignificant part of either company's total sales.

THE ROBINSON-PATMAN ACT

Background

Section 2 of the Clayton Act originally prohibited *local and territorial price discrimination* by sellers, a practice monopolists frequently used to destroy smaller competitors. A large company operating in a number of geographic markets would sell at or below cost in markets where it faced local competitors, and would then make up its losses by selling at higher prices in areas where it faced no competition. Faced with such tactics, the smaller local competitors might eventually be driven out of business. Section 2 was aimed at such **primary level** (or *first line*) price discrimination.

During the 1930s, Congress was confronted with complaints that large chain stores were using their buying power to induce manufacturers to sell to them at prices lower than those offered to their smaller, independent competitors. Chain stores were also inclined to seek and obtain other payments and services their smaller competitors did not receive. Being able to purchase at lower prices and to obtain discriminatory payments and services arguably gave large firms a competitive advantage over their smaller competitors. Such price discrimination in sales to the competing customers of a particular seller is known as **secondary level** (or *second line*) price discrimination.

In addition, the customers of a manufacturer's favored customer (such as a wholesaler receiving a functional discount) may gain a competitive advantage over *their* competitors (for example, other retailers purchasing directly from the manufacturer at a higher price) if the favored customer passes on all or a portion of its discount to its customers. This form of price discrimination is known as **tertiary level** (or *third line*) price discrimination.

Congress responded to these problems by passing the Robinson-Patman Act in 1936. The Robinson-Patman Act preserved Clayton Act section 2's ban on primary level price discrimination. It

---

[8]462 U.S. 122 (U.S. Sup. Ct. 1983).

FIGURE 2	Levels of Price Discrimination		
Type of Discrimination	**Type of Harm**		**Example**
First Line	Injury to the seller's competitors		A seller subsidizes its low prices in an area of high competition by raising its prices in areas where it has little competition.
Second Line	Injury to the competitors of the favored buyer		A high-volume chain store induces its suppliers to give it discriminatorily low prices, enabling it to undersell its competitors.
Third Line	Injury to the competitors of the favored buyer's buyers		A wholesaler receiving discriminatorily low prices from its manufacturer passes the savings on to its retailers, enabling them to undersell their competitors.

also amended section 2 to outlaw secondary and tertiary level direct price discrimination, as well as indirect price discrimination in the form of discriminatory payments and services to a seller's customers. Since its enactment, the Robinson-Patman Act has been the subject of widespread dissatisfaction and criticism. Critics have long charged that the act often protects competitors at the expense of promoting competition. Government enforcement of the act has been haphazard over the years, with prominent officials in the Justice Department and the Federal Trade Commission sometimes voicing disagreement with the act's underlying policies and assumptions. This government stance, when combined with Supreme Court decisions making private enforcement of the act difficult, raises questions about the act's future usefulness as a component of our antitrust laws.

Figure 2 summarizes the levels of price discrimination addressed by the Robinson-Patman Act.

Jurisdiction

The Robinson-Patman Act applies only to discriminatory acts that occur "in commerce." This test is narrower than the "affecting commerce" test employed under the Sherman Act. At least one of the discriminatory acts complained of must take place in interstate commerce. Thus, the act probably would not apply if a Texas manufacturer discriminated in price in sales to two Texas customers. Some lower federal courts have indicated, however, that even wholly intrastate sales may be deemed sufficiently "in commerce" if the nonfavored buyer bought the goods for resale to out-of-state customers.

Section 2(a)

Section 2(a) of the Robinson-Patman Act prohibits sellers, in certain instances, from *discriminating in price* "between different purchasers of commodities of like grade or quality." Such discrimination is prohibited when its effect may be to (1) "substantially . . . lessen competition or tend to create a monopoly in any line of commerce," or (2) "injure, destroy, or prevent competition with any person who either grants [*primary level*] or knowingly receives [*secondary level*] the benefit of such discrimination, or with the customers of either of them [*tertiary level*]."

Price Discrimination   To violate section 2(a), a seller must have made two or more sales to different purchasers at different prices. Merely quoting a discriminatory price or refusing to sell except at a discriminatory price is not a violation of the statute, because no actual purchase is involved. For the same reason, price discrimination in lease or consignment transactions is not covered by section 2(a). Actual sales at different prices to different purchasers will not be treated as discriminatory unless the sales were fairly close in time.

For purposes of deciding whether discriminatory prices have been charged to two or more purchasers, the degree of control a parent corporation exercises over its subsidiaries sometimes assumes major importance. For example, a parent that sells a product directly to one customer at a low price may be found to have engaged in price discrimination if a wholesaler actively controlled by the parent contemporaneously sells the same product at a higher price to a competitor of the parent's customer. On the other hand, contemporaneous sales by a parent to a wholly owned subsidiary and to an independent competitor at different prices are not treated as price discrimination, because no true sale has been made to the subsidiary.

Finally, section 2(a) does not directly address the legality of *functional discounts*. Such discounts are sometimes granted to buyers at various levels in a product's chain of distribution because of differences in the functions those buyers perform in the distribution system. As indicated in the *Texaco* case, which follows shortly, the legality of such discounts depends on their competitive effect. If a seller charges wholesale customers lower prices than it charges retail customers, the Robinson-Patman Act is not violated unless the lower wholesale prices are somehow passed on to retailers in competition with the seller's retail customers.

TEXACO, INC. V. HASBROUCK
496 U.S. 543 (U.S. Sup. Ct. 1990)

Ricky Hasbrouck and 11 other plaintiffs were Texaco retail service station dealers in the Spokane area. They purchased gasoline directly from Texaco and resold it at retail under the Texaco trademark. Throughout the relevant time period (1972–81), Texaco also supplied gasoline to two gasoline distributors, Dompier Oil Company and Gull Oil Company, at a price that was at various times between 2.5 cents and 5.75 cents per gallon lower than the price Hasbrouck paid.

Dompier and Gull sold the gasoline they purchased from Texaco to independent retail service stations. Dompier sold the gasoline to retailers under the Texaco trademark; Gull marketed it under private brand names. Gull's customers either sold their gasoline on consignment (in which case they set their own prices) or on commission (in which case Gull set their resale prices). Gull retained title until the gas was sold to a retail customer in either case. Some of the retail stations supplied by Dompier were owned and operated by Dompier's salaried employees. Both Dompier and Gull picked up gas at the Texaco bulk plant and delivered it to their retail customers, a service for which Dompier was compensated by Texaco at the common carrier rate.

Hasbrouck and the other dealers filed a price discrimination suit against Texaco under section 2(a) of the Robinson-Patman Act. At trial, Texaco argued that its lower prices to Gull and Dompier were lawful "functional discounts." The jury awarded the plaintiffs $1,349,700 in treble damages. When the Ninth Circuit Court of Appeals affirmed the jury award, Texaco appealed.

Stevens, Justice   Section 2(a) contains no express reference to functional discounts. It does contain two affirmative defenses that provide protection for two categories of discounts—those that are justified by savings in the seller's cost of manufacture, delivery, or sale, and those that represent a good faith response to the equally low prices of a competitor. In order to establish a violation of the Act, plaintiffs had the burden of proving four facts: (1) that Texaco's sales to Gull and Dompier were made in interstate commerce; (2) that the gasoline sold to them was of the same grade and quality as that sold to plaintiffs; (3) that Texaco discriminated in price as between Gull and Dompier on the one hand and plaintiffs on the other; and (4) that the discrimination had a prohibited effect on competition.

The first two elements of plaintiffs' case are not disputed in this Court. Texaco does argue, however, that although it charged different prices, it did not "discriminate in price" within the meaning of the Act, and that, at least to the extent that Gull and Dompier acted as wholesalers, the price differentials did not injure competition. Texaco's first argument would create a blanket exception for all functional discounts. Indeed, carried to its logical conclusion, it would exempt all price differentials except those given to competing purchasers. The primary basis for Texaco's argument is the following comment by Congressman Utterback, an active sponsor of the Act:

In its meaning as simple English, a discrimination is more than a mere difference. Underlying the meaning of the word is the idea that some relationship exists between the parties to the discrimination which entitles them to equal treatment, whereby the difference granted to one casts some burden or disadvantage upon the other. . . . [W]here no such relationship exists, where the goods are sold in different markets and the conditions affecting those markets set different price levels for them, the sale to different customers at . . . different prices would not constitute discrimination within the meaning of this bill.

We have previously considered this excerpt from the legislative history, and have refused to draw from it the conclusion Texaco proposes. Although the excerpt does support Texaco's argument, we remain persuaded that the argument is foreclosed by the text of the Act itself. In a statute that plainly reveals a concern with competitive consequences at different levels of distribution, and carefully defines specific affirmative defenses, it would be anomalous to assume that Congress intended the term "discriminate" to have such a limited meaning. Since we have already decided that a price discrimination within the meaning of section 2(a) "is merely a price difference," we must reject Texaco's first argument.

In *FTC v. Morton Salt Co.* (1948), we held that an injury to competition may be inferred from evidence that some purchasers had to pay their supplier "substantially more for their goods than their competitors had to pay." Texaco, supported by the United States and the Federal Trade Commission as *amici curiae*, argues that this presumption should not apply to differences between prices charged to wholesalers and those charged to retail-

ers. Moreover, they argue that it would be inconsistent with fundamental antitrust policies to construe the Act as requiring a seller to control his customers' resale prices. The seller should not be held liable for the independent pricing decisions of his customers. As the Government correctly notes, this argument endorses the position advocated 35 years ago in the Report of the Attorney General's Nation Committee to Study the Antitrust Laws (1955).

After observing that suppliers ought not to be held liable for the independent pricing decisions of their buyers, and that without functional discounts distributors might go uncompensated for the services they performed, the Committee wrote:

On the other hand, the law should tolerate no subterfuge. For instance, where a wholesaler-retailer *buys* only part of his goods as a wholesaler, he must not claim a functional discount on all. Only to the extent that a buyer *actually* performs certain functions, assuming all the risk, investment, and costs involved, should he legally qualify for a functional discount.

We generally agree with this description of the legal status of functional discounts. A supplier need not satisfy the rigorous requirements of the cost justification defense in order to prove that a particular functional discount is reasonable and accordingly did not cause any substantial lessening of competition between a wholesaler's customers and the supplier's direct customers. The record in this case, however, adequately supports the finding that Texaco violated the Act.

The hypothetical predicate for the Committee's entire discussion of functional discounts is a price differential "that merely accords due recognition and reimbursement for actual marketing functions." Such a discount is not illegal. In this case, however, both the District Court and the Court of Appeals concluded that there was no substantial evidence indicating that the discounts to Gull and Dompier constituted a reasonable reimbursement for the value to Texaco of their actual marketing functions. Indeed, Dompier was separately compensated for its hauling function, and neither Gull nor Dompier maintained any significant storage facilities.

Both Gull and Dompier received the full discount on all their purchases even though most of their volume was resold directly to consumers. The extra margin on those sales obviously enabled them to price aggressively in both their retail and their wholesale marketing. To the extent that Dompier and Gull competed with plaintiffs in the retail market, the presumption of adverse effect on competition recognized in the *Morton Salt* case becomes all the more appropriate. The evidence indicates, moreover, that Texaco affirmatively encouraged Dompier to expand its retail business and was fully informed about the persistent and marketwide consequences of its own pricing policies. Indeed, its own executives recognized that the dramatic impact on the market was almost entirely attributable to the magnitude of the distributor discount and the hauling allowance. The special facts of this case thus make it peculiarly difficult for Texaco to claim that it is being held liable for the independent pricing decisions of Gull or Dompier.

The competitive injury component of a Robinson-Patman Act violation is not limited to the injury to competition between the favored and disfavored purchaser; it also encompasses the injury to competition between their customers. This conclusion is compelled by the statutory language, which specifically encompasses not only the adverse effect of price discrimination on persons who either grant or knowingly receive the benefit of such discrimination, but also to the "customers of either of them." Such indirect competitive effects surely may not be presumed automatically in every functional discount setting, and, indeed, one would expect that most functional discounts will be legitimate discounts that do not harm competition. At the least, a functional discount that constitutes a reasonable reimbursement for the purchasers' actual marketing functions will not violate the Act. Yet it is also true that not every functional discount is entitled to a judgment of legitimacy, and that it will sometimes be possible to produce evidence showing that a particular discount caused a price discrimination of the sort that the Act prohibits. When such anticompetitive effects are proved—as we believe they were in this case—they are covered by the Act.

Judgment for Hasbrouck affirmed.

Commodities of Like Grade and Quality   Section 2(a) applies only to price discrimination in the sale of *commodities*. Price discrimination involving intangibles, real estate, or services must be challenged under the Sherman Act (as a restraint of trade or an attempt to monopolize) or under the FTC Act (as an unfair method of competition).[9] The essence of price discrimination is that two or more buyers are charged differing prices for the *same* commodity. Sales of commodities of varying grades or quality at varying prices, therefore, do not violate section 2(a) so long as uniform prices are charged for commodities of equal quality. Some *physical difference* in the grade or quality of two products must be shown to justify a price differential between them. Differences solely in the brand name or label under which a product is sold—such as the seller's standard brand and a "house" brand sold to a large customer for resale under the customer's label—do not justify discriminatory pricing.

Anticompetitive Effect   Only price discrimination having a *probable* anticompetitive effect is prohibited by section 2(a). Traditionally, courts have required a higher degree of proof of likely competitive injury in cases involving primary level price discrimination (which may damage the seller's competitors) than in cases involving secondary or tertiary level discrimination (which threatens competition among the seller's customers or its customers' customers). To prove a primary level violation, a market analysis must show that competitive harm has occurred as a result of the seller's engaging in significant and sustained price discrimination with the intent of punishing or disciplining a competitor. Proof of predatory pricing is often offered as evidence of a seller's anticompetitive intent. The *Brown & Williamson* case, which follows shortly, addresses predatory pricing claims under the Robinson-Patman Act and emphasizes that likely harm to competition—not merely to a competitor— remains the critical focus.

In secondary or tertiary level cases, courts tend to infer the existence of competitive injury from evidence of substantial price discrimination between

---

[9]The FTC Act was discussed in Chapter 47.

competing purchasers over time. Some qualifications on this point are in order, however. Price discrimination for a short period of time ordinarily does not support an inference of competitive injury. Likewise, if the evidence indicates that nonfavored buyers could have purchased the same goods from other sellers at prices identical to those the defendant seller charged its favored customers, no competitive injury is inferred. Finally, buyers seeking treble damages for secondary or tertiary level harm must still prove that they suffered actual damages as a result of a violation of the act.

BROOKE GROUP LTD. V. BROWN & WILLIAMSON TOBACCO CORP.
113 S. Ct. 2578 (U.S. Sup. Ct. 1993)

Brown & Williamson Tobacco Corp. (BW) and Brooke Group Ltd. (referred to here by its former corporate name, Liggett Corp.) are two of only six firms of significant consequence in the oligopolistic cigarette manufacturing industry. In 1980, BW's share of the national cigarette market was roughly 12 percent. This share placed BW a distant third behind market leaders Philip Morris and R.J. Reynolds. Liggett's share was less than half of BW's. Liggett pioneered the development of the economy segment of the national cigarette market in 1980 by introducing a popular line of "black and white" generic cigarettes (low-priced cigarettes sold in plain white packages with simple black lettering). As Liggett's sales of generic cigarettes became substantial, other cigarette manufacturers started introducing economy-priced cigarettes. In 1984, BW introduced a black and white cigarette whose net price was lower than Liggett's. BW achieved this lower price by offering volume rebates to wholesalers.

Liggett sued BW, claiming that BW's volume rebates amounted to price discrimination having a reasonable probability of injuring competition, in violation of section 2(a) of the Robinson-Patman Act. Specifically, Liggett alleged that BW's rebates were integral to a scheme of predatory pricing, under which BW reduced its net prices for generic cigarettes below average variable costs. Liggett further alleged that this pricing by BW was designed to pressure Liggett to raise its list prices on generic cigarettes, so that the percentage price difference between generic and branded cigarettes would narrow. As a result, according to Liggett, the growth of the economy segment would be restrained and BW would thereby be able to preserve its supracompetitive profits on branded cigarettes. Liggett further asserted that it could not afford to reduce its wholesale rebates without losing market share to BW. Therefore, Liggett claimed that its only choice, if it wished to avoid prolonged losses on the generic line that had become its principal product, was to raise retail prices.

After a 115-day trial, the jury returned a verdict in Liggett's favor for $49.6 million in damages. The district court trebled this amount. After reviewing the trial record, however, the district court concluded that BW was entitled to prevail as a matter of law. The court therefore set aside the jury's verdict and entered judgment in BW's favor. Liggett appealed. The Fourth Circuit Court of Appeals affirmed, holding (apparently) that there cannot be liability for predatory price discrimination that allegedly takes place in the context of an oligopoly such as the cigarette industry. The Supreme Court granted Liggett's petition for a writ of certiorari.

Kennedy, Justice   Liggett contends that BW's discriminatory volume rebates to wholesalers threatened substantial competitive injury by furthering a predatory pricing scheme designed to purge competition from the economy segment of the cigarette market. This type of injury, which harms direct competitors of the discriminating seller, is known as primary-line injury. [P]rimary-line competitive in-jury under the Robinson-Patman Act is of the same general character as the injury inflicted by predatory pricing schemes actionable under section 2 of the Sherman Act. [T]he essence of the claim under either statute is the same.

Accordingly, whether the claim alleges predatory pricing under section 2 of the Sherman Act or primary-line price discrimination under the

Robinson-Patman Act, two prerequisites to recovery [exist]. First, a plaintiff seeking to establish competitive injury resulting from a rival's low prices must prove that the prices complained of are below an appropriate measure of its rival's costs. [Second, the plaintiff must demonstrate] that the competitor had a reasonable prospect [if the claim is brought under the Robinson-Patman Act], or . . . a dangerous probability [if the claim is brought under section 2 of the Sherman Act], of recouping its investment in below-cost prices. Recoupment is the ultimate object of an unlawful predatory-pricing scheme; it is the means by which a predator profits from predation. Without it, predatory pricing produces lower aggregate prices in the market, and consumer welfare is enhanced. That below-cost pricing may impose painful losses on its target is of no moment to the antitrust laws if competition is not injured.

For recoupment to occur, below-cost pricing must be capable . . . of producing the intended effects on the firm's rivals, whether driving them from the market, or, as was alleged to be the goal here, causing them to raise their prices to supracompetitive levels within a disciplined oligopoly. If circumstances indicate that below-cost pricing could likely produce its intended effect on the target, there is still the further question whether it would be likely to injure competition in the relevant market. The plaintiff must demonstrate that there is a likelihood that the predatory scheme alleged would cause a rise in prices above a competitive level that would be sufficient to compensate for the amounts expended on the predation. These prerequisites to recovery are not easy to establish, but . . . they are essential components of real market injury.

Liggett . . . allege[s] . . . that BW sought to preserve supracompetitive profits on branded cigarettes by pressuring Liggett to raise its generic cigarette prices through a process of tacit collusion with the other cigarette companies. Tacit collusion, sometimes called oligopolistic price coordination or conscious parallelism, describes the process, not in itself unlawful, by which firms in a concentrated market might in effect share monopoly power, setting their prices at a profit-maximizing, supracompetitive level by recognizing their shared economic interests and their interdependence with respect to price and output decisions.

In *Matsushita Electric Industrial Co. v. Zenith Radio Corp.* (1986), we remarked upon the general implausibility of predatory pricing. *Matsushita* observed that such schemes are even more improbable when they require coordinated action among several firms. However unlikely predatory pricing by multiple firms may be when they conspire, it is even less likely when, as here, there is no express coordination. Firms that seek to recoup predatory losses through the conscious parallelism of oligopoly must rely on uncertain and ambiguous signals to achieve concerted action. The signals are subject to misinterpretation and are a blunt and imprecise means of ensuring smooth cooperation, especially in the context of changing or unprecedented market circumstances. This anticompetitive minuet is most difficult to compose and to perform, even for a disciplined oligopoly.

[O]n the whole, tacit cooperation among oligopolists must be considered the least likely means of recouping predatory losses. In addition to the difficulty of achieving effective tacit coordination and the high likelihood that any attempt to discipline will produce an outbreak of competition, the predator's present losses in a case like this fall on it alone, while the later supracompetitive profits must be shared with every other oligopolist in proportion to its market share, including the intended victim. In this case, for example, BW, with its 11–12% share of the cigarette market, would have had to generate around $9 in supracompetitive profits for each $1 invested in predation; the remaining $8 would belong to its competitors, who had taken no risk.

[However,] [t]o the extent that the Court of Appeals may have held that the interdependent pricing of an oligopoly may never provide a means for achieving recoupment and so may not form the basis of a primary-line injury claim, we disagree. A predatory pricing scheme designed to preserve or create a stable oligopoly, if successful, can injure consumers in the same way, and to the same extent, as one designed to bring about a monopoly. However unlikely that possibility may be as a general matter, when the realities of the market and the record facts indicate that it has occurred and was likely to have succeeded, theory will not stand in the way of liability. The Robinson-Patman Act . . . suggests no exclusion from coverage when primary-line injury occurs in an oligopoly setting. We decline to create a per se rule of nonliability [under the Robinson-Patman Act] for predatory price discrimination when recoupment is alleged to take place through supracompetitive oligopoly pricing.

Although Liggett's theory of liability, as an abstract matter, is within the reach of the statute, we agree with the [lower courts] that Liggett was not entitled to submit its case to the jury. Liggett . . . failed to demonstrate competitive injury as a matter of law. The evidence is inadequate to show that in pursuing [an alleged below-cost pricing] scheme, BW had a reasonable prospect of recovering its losses from below-cost pricing through slowing the growth of generics.

The only means by which BW is alleged to have established oligopoly pricing . . . is through tacit price coordination with the other cigarette firms. Yet the situation facing the cigarette companies in the 1980s would have made such tacit coordination unmanageable. Tacit coordination is facilitated by a stable market environment, fungible products, and a small number of variables upon which the firms seeking to coordinate their pricing may focus. By 1984, however, the cigarette market was in an obvious state of flux. The introduction of generic cigarettes in 1980 represented the first serious price competition in the cigarette market since the 1930s. This development was bound to unsettle previous expectations and patterns of market conduct and to reduce the cigarette firms' ability to predict each other's behavior. The larger number of product types and pricing variables also decreased the probability of effective parallel pricing.

Even if all the cigarette companies were willing to participate in a scheme to restrain the growth of the generic segment, they would not have been able to coordinate their actions and raise prices above a competitive level unless they understood that BW's entry into the [economy] segment was not a genuine effort to compete with Liggett. If even one other firm misinterpreted BW's entry as an effort to expand share, a chain reaction of competitive responses would almost certainly have resulted, and oligopoly discipline would have broken down, perhaps irretrievably. Liggett argues that [BW's] maintaining existing list prices while offering substantial rebates to wholesalers was a signal to the other cigarette firms that BW did not intend to attract additional smokers to the generic segment by its entry. But a reasonable jury could not conclude that this pricing structure eliminated or rendered insignificant the risk that the other firms might misunderstand BW's entry as a competitive move.

We hold that the evidence cannot support a finding that BW's alleged scheme was likely to result in oligopolistic price coordination and sustained supracompetitive pricing in the generic segment of the national cigarette market. Without this, BW had no reasonable prospect of recouping its predatory losses and could not inflict the injury to competition the antitrust laws prohibit.

Judgment for BW affirmed.

Defenses to Section 2(a) Liability

There are three major statutory defenses to liability under section 2(a): *cost justification, changing conditions,* and *meeting competition in good faith.*

Cost Justification   Section 2(a) specifically legalizes price differentials that do no more than make an appropriate allowance for differences in the "cost of manufacture, sale, or delivery resulting from the differing methods or quantities" in which goods are sold or delivered to buyers. This defense recognizes the reality that it may be less costly for a seller to service some buyers than others. Sales to buyers purchasing large quantities may in some cases be more cost-effective than small-quantity

sales to their competitors. Sellers are allowed to pass on such cost savings to their customers.

Utilizing this *cost justification* defense is quite difficult and expensive for sellers, however, because quantity discounts must be supported by *actual evidence of cost savings.* Sellers are allowed to average their costs and classify their customers into categories based on their average sales costs. The customers included in any particular classification, however, must be sufficiently similar to justify similar treatment.

Changing Conditions   Section 2(a) specifically exempts price discriminations that reflect "changing conditions in the market for or the marketability of the goods." The *changing conditions* defense has been narrowly confined to temporary situations caused by the physical nature of the goods. Examples include the deterioration of perishable goods and a declining market for seasonal goods. This defense also applies to forced judicial sales of the goods (such as during bankruptcy proceedings involving the seller) and to good faith sales by sellers that have decided to cease selling the goods in question.

Meeting Competition   Section 2(b) of the Robinson-Patman Act states that price discrimination may be lawful if the discriminatory lower price was charged "in good faith to meet an equally low price of a competitor." This *meeting competition* defense is necessary to prevent the act from stifling the very competition it was designed to preserve. For example, suppose Sony Corporation has been selling a particular model of video recorder to its customers for $350 per unit. Sony then learns that Sharp Electronics is offering a comparable recorder to Acme Appliance Stores for $300 per unit. Acme, however, competes with Best Buy Video Stores, a Sony customer that has recently been charged the $350 price. Should Sony be forced to refrain from offering the lower competitive price to Acme for fear that Best Buy will charge Sony with price discrimination if it does so? If Sony cannot offer the lower competitive price to Acme, competition between Sony and Sharp will plainly suffer.

Section 2(b) avoids this undesirable result by allowing a seller to charge a lower price to certain customers if the seller has reasonable grounds for believing that the lower price is necessary to meet an equally low price offered by a competitor. Sellers may meet competition *offensively* (to gain a new customer) or *defensively* (to keep an existing customer). The meeting competition defense is subject to significant qualifications, however. First, the lower price must be necessary to meet a lower price charged by a competitor of the *seller*, not to enable a customer of the seller to compete more effectively with that customer's competitors. Second, the seller may lawfully seek only to *meet,* not *beat*, its competitor's price. A seller cannot, however, be held in violation of the act for beating a competitor's price if it did so unknowingly in a good faith attempt to meet competition. Third, the seller may reduce its price only to meet competitors' prices for products of *similar quality*.

Courts also have held that the discriminatory price must be a response to an individual competitive situation rather than the product of a seller's wholesale adoption of a competitor's discriminatory pricing system. However, a seller's competitive response need not be on a customer-by-customer basis, so long as the lower price is offered only to those customers that the seller reasonably believes are being offered a lower price by the seller's competitors.

Indirect Price Discrimination

When Congress passed the Robinson-Patman Act, it also addressed **indirect price discrimination**, which takes the form of a seller's discriminating among competing buyers by making discriminatory payments to selected buyers or by furnishing certain buyers with services not made available to their competitors. Three sections of the act are designed to prevent such practices.

False Brokerage   Section 2(c) prohibits sellers from granting, and buyers from receiving, any "commission, brokerage, or other compensation, or any allowance or discount in lieu thereof, except for services rendered in connection with the sale or purchase of goods." This provision prevents large buyers, either directly or through subsidiary brokerage agents, from receiving phony commissions or brokerage payments from their suppliers. The courts and the FTC originally interpreted section 2(c) as prohibiting any brokerage payments to a buyer or its agent, regardless of whether the buyer or agent had in fact provided sale-related services that would otherwise have been performed by the seller or an independent broker. This narrow interpretation drew heavy criticism, however, because it operated to create a closed shop for independent brokers by denying large buyers any incentive to create their own brokerage services. This interpretation also made it difficult for small, independent retailers to create cooperative buying organizations and thereby match more closely the buying power of their large competitors. More recent decisions have responded to these criticisms by allowing payments that are for services actually performed by buyers and represent actual cost savings to sellers.

Section 2(c), unlike section 2(a), establishes a per se standard of liability. No demonstration of probable anticompetitive effect is required for a violation. Neither the cost justification nor meeting competition defense is available in 2(c) cases. Individual plaintiffs still must prove that they have suffered some injury as a result of a 2(c) violation, however, before they are entitled to recover damages.

Discriminatory Payments and Services   Sellers and their customers benefit from merchandising activities that customers employ to promote the sellers' products. Section 2(d) prohibits sellers from making *discriminatory payments* to competing customers for such customer-performed services as advertising and promotional activities or such customer-provided facilities as shelf space. Section 2(e) prohibits sellers from discriminating in the *services* they provide to competing customers, such as by providing favored customers with a display case or a demonstration kit.

A seller may lawfully make payments or provide services to customers only if the payments or services are made available to all competing customers on *proportionately equal terms*. This means that the seller must inform all customers of the availability of the payments or services and must distribute them on some rational basis, such as the quantity of goods bought by the customer. The seller must also devise a flexible plan that enables its various classes of customers to participate in the payment or services program in an appropriate way.

As does section 2(c), sections 2(d) and 2(e) create a per se liability standard. No proof of probable harm to competition is required for a violation; no cost justification defense is available. The meeting competition defense provided by section 2(b) is applicable, however, to actions under sections 2(d) and 2(e).

Buyer Inducement of Discrimination

Section 2(f) of the Robinson-Patman Act makes it illegal for a buyer *knowingly to induce or receive* a discriminatory price in violation of section 2(a). The logic of the section is that buyers who are successful in demanding discriminatory prices should face liability along with the sellers charging discriminatory prices. To violate section 2(f), the buyer must know that the price the buyer received was unjustifiably discriminatory. This means that the price probably was neither cost-justified nor made in response to changing conditions. Section 2(f) does not apply to buyer inducements of discriminatory

payments or services prohibited by sections 2(d) and 2(e). Such buyer actions may, however, be attacked as unfair methods of competition under section 5 of the FTC Act.

In *Great Atlantic and Pacific Tea Co. v. FTC*,[10] the Supreme Court further narrowed the effective reach of section 2(f) by holding that buyers who knowingly received a discriminatory price do not violate the act if their seller has a valid defense to the charge of violating section 2(a). The seller in *Great Atlantic* had a "meeting competition in good faith" defense under section 2(b). This fact was held to insulate the buyer from liability even though the buyer knew that the seller had beaten, rather than merely met, its competitor's price.

ANTITRUST EXCEPTIONS AND EXEMPTIONS

Introduction

A wide variety of economic activities occur outside the reach of the antitrust laws. This is so either because these activities have been specifically exempted by statute or because courts have carved out nonstatutory exceptions designed to balance our antitrust policy in favor of competition against other social policies. With critics charging that a number of existing exemptions are no longer justifiable, recent years have witnessed a judicial tendency to narrow the scope of many exemptions.

Statutory Exemptions

Labor Unions and Certain Union Activities Sections 6 and 20 of the Clayton Act and the Norris-LaGuardia Act of 1932 provide that *labor unions* are not combinations or conspiracies in restraint of trade and exempt certain union activities, including boycotts and secondary picketing, from antitrust scrutiny. This statutory exemption does not, however, exempt union combinations with nonlabor groups aimed at restraining trade or creating a monopoly. An example of such nonexempted activity would be a labor union's agreement with Employer A to call a strike at Employer B's plants. In an attempt to accommodate the strong public policy in favor of collective bargaining, courts have

---

[10]440 U.S. 69 (U.S. Sup. Ct. 1979).

also created a limited nonstatutory exemption for legitimate union-employer agreements arising from the collective bargaining context.

Agricultural Cooperatives and Certain Cooperative Actions

Section 6 of the Clayton Act and the Capper-Volstead Act exempt the formation and collective marketing activities of *agricultural cooperatives* from antitrust liability. Courts have narrowly construed this exemption, however. Cooperatives including members not engaged in the production of agricultural commodities have been denied exempt status. One such example would be a cooperative including retailers or wholesalers who do not also produce the commodity in question. The agricultural cooperatives exemption extends only to legitimate collective marketing activities. It does not legitimize coercive or predatory practices that are unnecessary to accomplish lawful cooperative goals. For example, this exemption would not prevent the antitrust laws from being applied to a boycott designed to force nonmembers of the cooperative to adopt a pricing policy established by the cooperative.

Joint Export Activities

The Webb-Pomerene Act exempts the *joint export activities* of American companies, so long as those activities do not "artificially or intentionally enhance or depress prices within the United States." The purpose of the act is to encourage export activity by allowing the formation of combinations to enable domestic firms to compete more effectively with foreign cartels. Some critics assert that this exemption is no longer needed because there are fewer foreign cartels today and American firms often play a dominant role in foreign trade. Others question whether any group of American firms enjoying significant domestic market shares in the sale of a particular product could agree on an international marketing strategy, such as the amounts that they will export, without indirectly affecting domestic supplies and prices.

Business of Insurance

The McCarran-Ferguson Act exempts from federal antitrust scrutiny those aspects of the *business of insurance* that are subject to state regulation. The act provides, however, that state law cannot legitimize any agreement to boycott, coerce, or intimidate others. Because the insur-

ance industry is extensively regulated by the states, many practices in the industry are outside the reach of the federal antitrust laws.

In recent years, however, courts have tended to decrease the scope of this exemption by narrowly construing the meaning of "business of insurance." For example, in *Union Labor Life Insurance Co. v. Pireno*,[11] the Supreme Court held that the exemption did not insulate from antitrust scrutiny a peer review system in which an insurance company used a committee established by a state chiropractic association to review the reasonableness of particular chiropractors' charges. The Court stated that to qualify for the business of insurance exemption, a challenged practice must have the effect of transferring or spreading policyholders' risk and must be an integral part of the policy relationship between the insured and the insurer. Therefore, only practices related to traditional functions of the insurance business, such as underwriting and risk-spreading, are likely to be exempt.

Calls from some quarters for repeal of the McCarran-Ferguson Act have led to the introduction of bills in Congress to that effect in recent years. These proposals for legislation typically contemplate, however, that insurers could continue to participate in certain joint activities, such as collecting and exchanging information on fraudulent claims, pooling historical loss data, and developing standardized policy forms. The ultimate fate of the McCarran-Ferguson Act and its business of insurance exemption remained unclear as of the time this book went to press.

Other Regulated Industries

Many other *regulated industries* enjoy various degrees of antitrust immunity. The airline, banking, utility, railroad, shipping, and securities industries traditionally have been regulated in the public interest. The regulatory agencies supervising such industries have frequently been given the power to approve industry practices such as rate-setting and mergers that would otherwise violate antitrust laws. In recent years, there has been a distinct tendency to deregulate many regulated industries. If this trend continues, a greater portion of the economic activity in these industries could be subjected to antitrust scrutiny.

---

[11]458 U.S. 119 (U.S. Sup. Ct. 1982).

State Action Exemption

In *Parker v. Brown*,[12] the Supreme Court held that a California state agency's regulation of the production and price of raisins was a state action exempt from the federal antitrust laws. The **state action exemption** developed in *Parker v. Brown* recognizes states' rights to regulate economic activity in the interest of their citizens. It also, however, may tempt business entities to seek "friendly" state regulation as a way of shielding anticompetitive activity from antitrust supervision. Recognizing this possibility, courts have placed important limitations on the scope of the state action exemption.

First, the exemption extends only to governmental actions by a state or to actions compelled by a state acting in its sovereign capacity. Second, as indicated in the *Ticor Title Insurance* case (which follows shortly), challenged activity cannot qualify for immunity under this exemption unless the activity is "clearly articulated and affirmatively expressed as state policy" and "actively supervised" by the state. In other words, the price of antitrust immunity is real regulation by the state. The Supreme Court placed a further limitation on the state action exemption by holding that it does not automatically confer immunity on the actions of municipalities.[13] Municipal conduct is immune only if it was authorized by the state legislature and its anticompetitive effects were a foreseeable result of the authorization. The Court's decision caused concern that the threat of treble damage liability might inhibit legitimate regulatory action by municipal authorities. As a result, Congress passed the Local Government Antitrust Act of 1984. This statute eliminates damage actions against municipalities and their officers, agents, and employees for antitrust violations and makes injunctive relief the sole remedy in such cases. It does not, however, bar damage suits against private individuals who engage in anticompetitive conduct with local government agencies.

---

[12]317 U.S. 341 (U.S. Sup. Ct. 1943).

[13]*Community Communications Co. v. City of Boulder*, 455 U.S. 40 (U.S. Sup. Ct. 1982).

FEDERAL TRADE COMMISSION V. TICOR TITLE INSURANCE CO.
112 S. Ct. 2169 (U.S. Sup. Ct. 1992)

The Federal Trade Commission filed an administrative complaint against six of the nation's title insurance companies, including Ticor Title Insurance Co. The complaint alleged that the title insurers engaged in horizontal price-fixing in their setting of uniform rates for title searches and title examinations. (According to the FTC, these uniform rates pertained to aspects of the business that did not involve insurance, as opposed to the setting of uniform rates for insurance against risk of loss from defective titles. The latter type of ratesetting, which was not challenged by the FTC in this case, would directly involve insurance and would likely be shielded from antitrust scrutiny by the McCarran-Ferguson Act.)

The challenged uniform ratesetting for title searches and title examinations occurred in various states through rating bureaus organized by the title insurers. These rating bureaus allegedly would set standard rates for search and examination services notwithstanding possible differences in efficiencies and costs as between individual title insurance companies. Though privately organized, these rating bureaus and the rates they set were potentially subject to oversight by the various states in which they operated.

Price-fixing by the title insurers was alleged, in the FTC complaint, to have occurred in four states: Connecticut, Wisconsin, Arizona, and Montana. The administrative law judge (ALJ) held that price-fixing had occurred in each of those four states, but that the requirements of the state action exemption from liability applied to the title insurer's actions in Arizona and Montana. As for the title insurers' actions in Connecticut and Wisconsin, the ALJ concluded that the requirements of the state action exemption were not met and that the title insurers therefore should face legal responsibility for their antitrust violations. The FTC commissioners, reviewing the ALJ's decision, concluded that the state action exemption did not apply to the title insurers' actions in any of the four states. On appeal, the Third Circuit Court of Appeals held that the state action exemption shielded the title insurers' actions in all four of the states.

The Supreme Court granted certiorari. (On the question whether the Third Circuit correctly stated and applied the law regarding the state action exemption, the FTC and the title insurers (referred to below simply as "Ticor") confined their briefing—and the Supreme Court largely confined its discussion—to the regulatory regimes existing under Wisconsin and Montana law.)

Kennedy, Justice   [I]n *Parker v. Brown* (1943), we upheld a state-supervised market sharing scheme against a Sherman Act challenge. We announced the doctrine that federal antitrust laws are subject to supersession by state regulatory programs. Our decision was grounded in principles of federalism.

In *California Retail Liquor Dealers Association v. Midcal Aluminum, Inc.* (1980), we announced a two-part [state action immunity test] applicable to instances where private parties participate [with the state in allegedly anticompetitive conduct]: "First, the challenged restraint must be one clearly articulated and affirmatively expressed as state policy; second, the policy must be actively supervised by the State itself." *Midcal* confirms that while a State may not confer antitrust immunity on private parties by fiat, it may displace competition with active state supervision if the displacement is both intended by the State and implemented in its specific details. Actual state involvement, not deference to private price fixing arrangements under the general auspices of state law, is the precondition of immunity from federal law. Immunity is conferred out of respect for ongoing regulation by the State, not out of respect for the economics of price restraint.

The rationale was further elaborated in *Patrick v. Burget*. [In that case, it was noted that the *active supervision* element of the test set forth in *Midcal*] "mandates that the State exercise ultimate control over the challenged anticompetitive conduct" [and establishes that] "mere presence of some state involvement or monitoring does not suffice." [*Patrick* also contained the observation that the] "active supervision prong of the *Midcal* test requires that state officials have and exercise power to review particular anticompetitive acts of private parties and disapprove those that fail to accord with state policy."

Our decisions emphasize that the purpose of the active supervision inquiry . . . is to determine whether the State has exercised sufficient independent judgment and control so that the details of the rates or prices have been established as a product of deliberate state intervention, not simply by agree-ment among private parties. [T]he analysis asks whether the State has played a substantial role in determining the specifics of the economic policy. The question is not how well the state regulation works but whether the anticompetitive scheme is the State's own.

In the case before us, the Court of Appeals relied upon [an erroneous] formulation of the active supervision requirement [in] rul[ing] that the active supervision requirement was met and in [holding] that the [title insurers'] conduct was entitled to state-action immunity from antitrust liability. Where prices or rates are set as an initial matter by private parties, subject only to a veto if the State chooses to exercise it, the party claiming immunity must show that state officials have undertaken the necessary steps to determine the specifics of the price-fixing or ratesetting scheme. The mere potential for state supervision is not an adequate substitute for a decision by the State. Under these standards, we must conclude that there was no active supervision in either Wisconsin or Montana.

[I]n Wisconsin and Montana, the rating bureaus filed rates with state agencies and . . . the so-called negative option rule prevailed. The rates became effective unless they were rejected within a set time. It is [asserted by Ticor] that as a matter of law in those States inaction signified substantive approval. This proposition cannot be reconciled, however, with the detailed findings, entered by the ALJ and adopted by the Commission[ers], which demonstrate that the potential for state supervision was not realized in fact. The ALJ found, and the Commission[ers] agreed, that at most the rate filings were checked for mathematical accuracy. Some were unchecked altogether. In Montana, a rate filing became effective despite the failure of the rating bureau to provide additional requested information. [There was a similar occurrence in Wisconsin.] These findings are fatal to Ticor's attempts to portray the state regulatory regimes as providing the necessary component of active supervision. The findings demonstrate that whatever the potential for state regulatory review in Wisconsin and Montana, active state supervision did not occur. In the absence of active supervision in fact, there can be no state-action immunity for what were otherwise private price fixing agreements.

This case involves horizontal price fixing under a vague imprimatur in form and agency inaction in fact. No antitrust offense is more pernicious than price fixing. In this context, we decline to formulate a rule that would lead to a finding of active state supervision when in fact there was none.

Judgment of court of appeals reversed in favor of Federal Trade Commission; case remanded for further proceedings and consideration of other issues.

The Noerr-Pennington Doctrine

In the *Noerr* and *Pennington* cases, the Supreme Court held that "the Sherman Act does not prohibit two or more persons from associating together in an attempt to persuade the legislature or the executive to take particular action with respect to a law that would produce a restraint or a monopoly."[14] This exemption recognizes that the right to petition government provided by the Bill of Rights takes precedence over the antitrust policy favoring competition. The exemption does not, however, extend to sham activities that are attempts to interfere with the business activities of competitors rather than legitimate attempts to influence governmental action.[15]

Patent Licensing

There is a basic tension between the antitrust objective of promoting competition and the purpose of the patent law, which seeks to promote innovation by granting a limited monopoly to those who develop new products or processes.[16] In the early case of *United States v. General Electric Company*,[17] the Supreme Court allowed General Electric to control the price at which other manufacturers sold light bulbs they had manufactured under patent licensing agreements with General Electric. The Court recognized that an important part of holding a patent was the right to license others to manufacture the patented item. This right effectively would be negated if licensees were allowed to undercut the prices that patent holders charged for their own sales of patented products.

Patent holders cannot, however, lawfully control the price at which patented items are resold by distributors purchasing them from the patent holder. Nor can patent holders use their patents to impose tying agreements on their customers by conditioning the sale of patented items on the purchase of nonpatented items, unless such agreements are otherwise lawful under the Sherman and Clayton Acts. Finally, firms that seek to monopolize an area by acquiring most or all of the patents related to that area of commerce may face liability for violating Sherman Act section 2 or Clayton Act section 7, because a patent has been held to be an asset within the meaning of section 7.

Foreign Commerce

When foreign governments are involved in commercial activities affecting the domestic or international commerce of the United States, our antitrust policy may be at odds with our foreign policy. Congress and the courts have created a variety of antitrust exemptions aimed at reconciling this potential conflict. The Foreign Sovereign Immunities Act of 1976 (FSIA) provides that the governmental actions of foreign sovereigns and their agents are exempt from antitrust liability. The commercial activities of foreign sovereigns, however, are not included within this **sovereign immunity** exemption. Significant international controversy exists concerning the proper criteria for determining whether a particular governmental act is commercial in nature. Under the FSIA, the courts employ a *nature of the act* test, holding that a commercial activity is one that an individual might customarily carry on for a profit.

---

[14]*Eastern R.R. President's Conference v. Noerr Motor Freight, Inc.*, 365 U.S. 127 (U.S. Sup. Ct. 1961); *United Mine Workers v. Pennington*, 381 U.S. 657 (U.S. Sup. Ct. 1965).

[15]*California Motor Transport v. Trucking Unlimited*, 404 U.S. 508 (U.S. Sup. Ct. 1982).

[16]Chapter 8 discusses patent law in detail.

[17]272 U.S. 476 (U.S. Sup. Ct. 1926).

FIGURE 3	Antitrust Exceptions and Exemptions	
Exception/Exemption	**Activities Covered**	**Source**
Statutory Labor	Legitimate union activities	Clayton Act, Norris-LaGuardia Act
Nonstatutory Labor	Collective bargaining agreements	Judicial decision (policy favoring collective bargaining)
Agricultural Cooperatives	Legitimate cooperative activities	Clayton Act, Capper-Volstead Act
Export Trade Associations	Joint export activities	Webb-Pomerene Act
Insurance	Business of insurance	McCarran-Ferguson Act
Regulated Industries	Anticompetitive activities shielded by federal regulation	Regulatory statutes
State Action	State authorized and supervised anticompetitive activities	Judicial decision (federalism)
***Noerr-Pennington* Doctrine**	Attempts to induce anticompetitive governmental action	Judicial decision (First Amendment)
Patent Licensing	Legitimate activities of patent holders	Judicial decision (patent laws)
Sovereign Immunity	Governmental acts of foreign sovereigns	Foreign Sovereign Immunities Act
Act of State Doctrine	Sovereign acts of foreign sovereigns	Judicial decision (separation of powers)
Sovereign Compulsion Doctrine	Private acts compelled by foreign sovereigns	Judicial decision

The **act of state doctrine** provides that an American court cannot adjudicate a politically sensitive dispute whose resolution would require the court to judge the legality of a foreign government's sovereign act. This doctrine reflects judicial deference to the primary role of the executive and legislative branches in the adoption and execution of our foreign policy. The act of state doctrine recognizes (as does the doctrine of sovereign immunity) the importance of respecting the sovereignty of other nations. Unlike the doctrine of sovereign immunity, however, the act of state doctrine also reflects a fundamental attribute of our system of government—the principle of separation of powers.

Finally, the **sovereign compulsion doctrine** provides private parties a defense if they have been compelled by a foreign sovereign to commit, within

that sovereign's territory, acts that would otherwise violate the antitrust laws due to their negative impact on our international commerce. To employ this defense successfully, a defendant must show that the challenged actions were the product of actual compulsion—as opposed to mere encouragement or approval—by a foreign sovereign.

Figure 3 summarizes the various antitrust exceptions and exemptions.

ETHICAL AND PUBLIC POLICY CONCERNS

1. Refer to the facts of the *Mozart* case in this chapter. Assume that some Mercedes dealers sold their customers nonauthorized parts at the same price that they charged for genuine Mercedes parts, but without telling customers that the parts installed were not genuine Mercedes parts. Is such a practice ethically justifiable? Would your answer change if you were convinced that the nonauthorized parts were equal in quality to genuine Mercedes replacement parts?

2. Refer to the facts of problem case 9 at the end of this chapter. Is paying a disguised bribe to win a contract ethically justifiable under such circumstances? Would your answer change if such bribes were a customary means of doing business in Nigeria rather than a violation of Nigerian law?

PROBLEMS AND PROBLEM CASES

1. Crossland started his own vending machine business in the early 1960s. In 1973, he bid successfully for the vending business at Fort Bliss, Texas. This expansion exacerbated his company's existing financial problems. In 1974, after months of negotiations, Crossland signed a contract under which he agreed to become a franchisee of Canteen Corporation. The agreement called for Canteen to provide Crossland's business with badly needed capital by buying all of Crossland's vending equipment for $350,000 and leasing it back to him. Crossland continued to have financial problems and ultimately reached the point at which his company owed Canteen $420,000. Crossland sued Canteen, arguing that Canteen had violated the Sherman and Clayton Acts by tying the lease-back of the equipment to the sale of the Canteen franchise. Was Canteen correct in arguing that both claims should be dismissed?

2. Sterling Electric manufactured electric motors and replacement parts for them. No one else made parts compatible with Sterling motors. After being acquired by A. O. Smith Corporation, Sterling instituted new distribution programs. Its new agreement with distributors who stocked its parts required that these "stocking" distributors buy and aggressively promote minimum quantities of Sterling motors, in return for their being able to buy parts for less than the prices Sterling charged "referral" distributors who merely passed on orders for Sterling parts. On October 1, 1982, Sterling terminated Parts and Electric Motors, Inc. (P&E), a stocking distributor, for insufficient motor pur-

chases. P&E then filed suit against Sterling, arguing that the motor purchase requirement was a tying arrangement prohibited by the Sherman and Clayton Acts. At trial, P&E introduced evidence that the purchase requirement forced dealers to increase their motor purchases by more than $250,000. Was the jury verdict in P&E's favor proper?

3. In 1961, Ford Motor Company acquired Autolite, a manufacturer of spark plugs, in order to enter the profitable aftermarket for spark plugs sold as replacement parts. Ford and the other major automobile manufacturers had previously purchased original equipment spark plugs (those installed in new cars when they leave the factory) from independent producers such as Autolite and Champion, either at or below the producer's cost. The independents were willing to sell original equipment plugs so cheaply because aftermarket mechanics often replace original equipment plugs with the same brand of spark plug. GM had already moved into the spark plug market by developing its own division. Ford decided to do so by means of a vertical merger under which it acquired Autolite. Prior to the Autolite acquisition, Ford bought 10 percent of the total spark plug output. The merger left Champion as the only major independent spark plug producer. Champion's market share thereafter declined because Chrysler was the only major original equipment spark plug purchaser remaining in the market. The government filed a divestiture suit against Ford, arguing that Ford's acquisition of Autolite violated section 7 of the Clayton Act. Should Ford have been ordered to divest itself of Autolite?

4. Siemens, a diversified firm with interests in the medical equipment field, notified the Justice Department in 1979 that it intended to acquire control of Searle Diagnostics (SD), a manufacturer of nuclear medical equipment. Ten years earlier, Siemens had failed in an attempt to start its own nuclear medical equipment division. In 1972, it had considered trying to reenter the field but concluded that it would not be able to recoup the investment reentry required. The top four firms in the nuclear medical equipment market accounted for 77 percent of total sales in 1979. This figure, however, was down from 1975, when they accounted for 92 percent of total sales. Although SD was still first in 1979, it had seen its market share fall from 50 percent to 22 percent during the same five-year period. These facts, together with the fact that SD had lost money in 1978 and 1979, led SD's parent firm to agree to the sale to Siemens. The Justice Department sought a preliminary injunction against the merger, arguing that it would violate section 7 by eliminating both perceived and actual potential competition. The department, however, presented no evidence that any attractive toehold purchase was available to Siemens or that Siemens, as an acknowledged likely entrant, had had any actual impact on the conduct of existing firms in the market. Was a preliminary injunction appropriate?

5. In 1983, Warner Communications, Inc., the second-largest distributor of prerecorded music (18.9 percent market share) in the United States, agreed to merge part of its record operations and form a joint venture company with Polygram Records, Inc., the sixth largest (7.1 percent market share) distributor. The Federal Trade Commission applied for a preliminary injunction to block the joint venture. The FTC presented evidence that the top four distributors collectively commanded 67 percent of the domestic market and that if the joint venture were completed, their collective market share would increase to 75 percent. In addition, the FTC presented evidence showing a trend toward concentration in the industry and the existence of high barriers to entry by new competitors. The trial court ruled that the FTC had failed to demonstrate the likelihood of ultimate success necessary to justify a preliminary injunction. Was that ruling correct?

6. First Comics, Inc., wanted to enter the comic book publishing business. First hired World Color Press to print its comics because World had a less expensive method of printing than other comic book printers did. World allegedly promised to charge First the same price it charged its larger customers such as Marvel Comics Group and DC Comics. When First discovered it was being charged 4.3 cents per copy more than Marvel, First demanded reimbursement or a future credit. When World refused, First filed a price discrimination suit against World under the Robinson-Patman Act. Does the Robinson-Patman Act apply to this case?

7. Indian Coffee Company, a coffee roaster in Pittsburgh, Pennsylvania, sold its Breakfast Cheer coffee in the Pittsburgh area, where it had an 18 percent market share, and in Cleveland, Ohio, where it had a significant, but smaller, market share. Late in 1971, Folger Coffee Company, then the leading

seller of branded coffee west of the Mississippi, entered the Pittsburgh market for the first time. In its effort to gain market share in Pittsburgh, Folger granted retailers high promotional allowances in the form of coupons. Retail customers could use these coupons to obtain price cuts. Redeeming retailers could use the coupons as credits against invoices from Folger. For a time, Indian tried to retain its market share by matching Folger's price concessions, but because Indian only operated in two areas, it could not subsidize such sales with profits from other areas. Indian, which finally was forced out of business in 1974, later filed a Robinson-Patman suit against Folger. At trial, Indian introduced evidence that Folger's Pittsburgh promotional allowances were far higher than its allowances in other geographic areas, and that Folger's Pittsburgh prices were below green (unroasted) coffee cost, below material and manufacturing costs, below total cost, and below marginal cost or average variable cost. Was the trial court's directed verdict in favor of Folger proper?

8. Peugeot Motors of America, Inc. (PMA), the exclusive domestic importer of Peugeot products, controlled all U.S. Peugeot distributors except EAD, the exclusive distributor for Peugeot cars in the southeastern United States. EAD filed suit against PMA, arguing that PMA had violated sections 2(d) and 2(e) of the Robinson-Patman Act by providing cash incentives, training facilities, and parts repurchase programs (allowing dealers to return for credit a part of their obsolete parts inventory) to PMA's dealers without making such incentives, facilities, and programs available to EAD's dealers. The evidence at trial indicated that Memphis, Tennessee, was the only place in the United States where an EAD dealer was within 50 miles of a PMA dealer, and that less than 1 percent of national Peugeot sales were cross-border sales between PMA and EAD territories. EAD's president testified that he did not know the reason for any of the cross-border sales. He also admitted that some such sales occurred for reasons other than competition between the two sets of dealers. The trial court directed a verdict in favor of PMA. Was the trial court correct in doing so?

9. In 1982, a subsidiary of W. S. Kirkpatrick & Co. won a Nigerian Defense Ministry contract for the construction and equipment of an aeromedical center at a Nigerian Air Force base. Environmental

Tectonics Corporation (Environmental), an unsuccessful bidder for the same contract, filed RICO and Robinson-Patman Act claims against Kirkpatrick. Environmental alleged that Kirkpatrick had won the contract by paying a 20 percent "commission" to bribe certain Nigerian officials. The parties agreed that the bribes, if paid, would violate Nigerian law. Was the trial court correct in holding that the act of state doctrine barred Environmental's claim?

10. Pocahontas Coal Company filed suit against a number of other companies engaged in the mining and production of coal in West Virginia. Pocahontas alleged that the defendants were involved in a conspiracy to control the production and pricing of coal. One of Pocahontas's specific claims was that the defendants had violated section 8 of the Clayton Act by "deputizing" various persons to sit on the boards of competing subsidiaries. The defendants moved for summary judgment on the section 8 claim, noting that Pocahontas's complaint contained no factual allegations that any of the defendants were competitors, failed to name any of the alleged "deputies," and was ambiguous because it alleged that certain persons were "officers and/or directors" of competing companies. The trial court offered Pocahontas the opportunity to clarify the complaint by bringing forth additional information on these points. Did the court properly grant the defendants summary judgment when Pocahontas declined to do so?

EMPLOYMENT LAW

INTRODUCTION

Years ago, it was unusual to see a separate employment law chapter in a business law text. At that time, the rights, duties, and liabilities accompanying employment were usually determined by basic legal institutions such as contract, tort, and agency. These common law principles continue to control employer-employee relations unless displaced by government regulations or by new judge-made rules applying specifically to employment. Today, however, such rules and regulations are so numerous that they touch almost every facet of employment. This chapter discusses the most important of these modern legal controls on employment.

SOME BASIC EMPLOYMENT STATUTES

Modern American employment law is so vast and complex a subject that texts designed for lawyers seldom address it in its entirety. Indeed, specialized subjects like labor law and employment discrimination often get book-length treatment in their own right. This chapter's overview of employment law focuses mainly on three topics that have attracted much recent attention—employment discrimination, employee privacy, and common law claims for wrongful discharge. But no discussion of employment law is complete without outlining certain basic regulations that significantly affect the conditions of employment for most Americans. Figure 1 outlines these regulations and the functions they perform.

Workers' Compensation

Nineteenth-century law made it difficult for employees to recover when they sued their employer in negligence for on-the-job injuries.[1] At that time, employers had an *implied assumption of risk* defense under which an employee was said to assume all the normal and customary risks of his employment simply by taking the job. If an employee's own carelessness played some role in his injury, employers could often avoid negligence liability under the traditional rule that even a slight degree of

---

[1]Chapter 7 discusses negligence law and most of the negligence defenses noted in this section.

FIGURE 1   The Ends and Means of Modern Employment Law

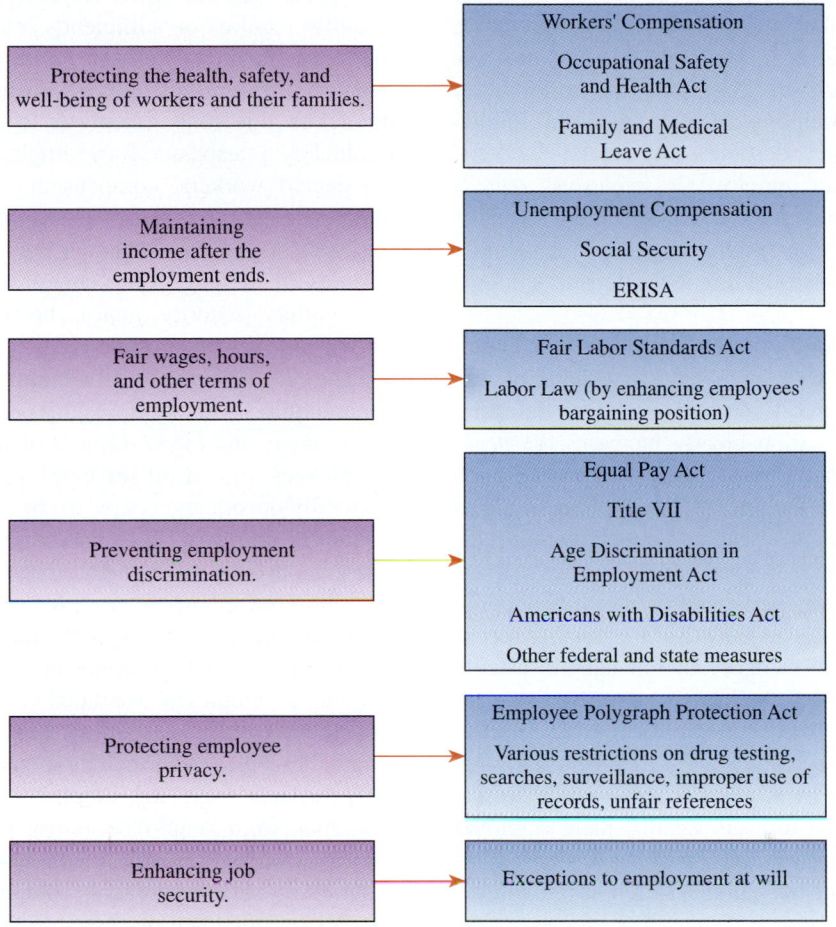

contributory negligence is a complete defense. Another employer defense, the *fellow-servant rule,* said that where an employee's injury resulted from the negligence of a coemployee (or fellow servant), the employer would not be liable. Finally, employees routinely had problems *proving* the employer's negligence. State workers' compensation statutes, which first appeared early in the 20th century, were a response to this situation. Today, all 50 states have such systems.[2]

Basic Features   Workers' compensation only protects *employees*, and not independent contractors.[3] However, many states exempt casual, agricultural, and domestic employees, among others. State and local government employees may be covered by workers' compensation or by some alternative state system. Also, states usually exempt certain *employers*—for example, firms employing fewer than a stated number of employees (often three).

---

[2]In addition, various federal statutes regulate on-the-job injuries suffered by employees of the federal government and other employees such as railroad workers, seamen, longshoremen, and harbor workers.

[3]Chapter 34 discusses the employee–independent contractor distinction.

Where they apply, however, all workers' compensation systems share certain basic features. They allow injured employees to recover under *strict liability,* thus removing any need to prove employer negligence. They also *eliminate the employer's traditional defenses* of contributory negligence, assumption of risk, and the fellow-servant rule. In addition, they make workers' compensation an employee's *exclusive remedy* against her employer for covered injuries. Usually, however, employees injured by their employer's *intentional torts* sue the employer outside workers' compensation.

Workers' compensation is basically a social compromise. Because it involves strict liability and eliminates the three traditional employer defenses, workers' compensation greatly increases the *probability* that an injured employee will recover. Such recoveries usually include: (1) hospital and medical expenses (including vocational rehabilitation), (2) disability benefits, (3) specified recoveries for the loss of certain body parts, and (4) death benefits to survivors and/or dependents. But the *amount* recoverable under each category of damages is usually less than would be obtained in a negligence suit. Thus, as the *Tolbert* case (which follows shortly) illustrates, injured employees sometimes deny that they are covered by workers' compensation so that they can pursue a tort suit against their employer instead.

Although workers' compensation is an injured employee's sole remedy against her employer, she may be able to sue *other parties* whose behavior helped cause her injury. One example is a product liability suit against a manufacturer who supplies an employer with defective machinery or raw materials that cause an on-the-job injury. However, many states immunize coemployees from ordinary tort liability for injuries they inflict on other employees. Complicated questions of contribution, indemnity, and subrogation can arise where an injured employee is able to recover against both an employer and a third party.

The Work-Related Injury Requirement   Another basic feature of workers' compensation is that employees recover only for *work-related* injuries. To be work-related, the injury must: (1) arise out of the employment, and (2) happen in the course of the employment. These tests have been variously interpreted.

The arising-out-of-the-employment requirement usually requires a sufficiently close relationship between the injury and the *nature* of the employment. As *Tolbert* illustrates, courts use different tests to define this requirement. A factory worker assaulted by a trespasser, for example, would probably be denied workers' compensation recovery under the "increased risk" test discussed in *Tolbert* but probably would recover under the "positional risk" test described there. If the same trespasser assaulted an on-duty security guard, however, the guard should recover under either test.

The in-the-course-of-the-employment requirement inquires whether the injury occurred within the *time, place,* and *circumstances* of the employment. Employees injured off the employer's premises are generally outside the course of the employment. For example, injuries suffered while traveling to or from work are usually not compensable. But an employee may be covered where the off-the-premises injury occurred while she was performing employment-related duties such as going on a business trip or running an employment-related errand.

Other work-related injury problems on which courts have disagreed include mental injuries allegedly arising from the employment and injuries resulting from employee horseplay. Virtually all states, however, regard intentionally self-inflicted injuries as outside workers' compensation. Recovery for occupational diseases, on the other hand, is usually allowed today. An employee whose preexisting diseased condition is aggravated by her employment sometimes recovers as well.

Administration and Funding   Workers' compensation systems are usually administered by a state agency that adjudicates workers' claims and administers the system. Its decisions on such claims are normally appealable to the state courts. The states fund workers' compensation by compelling covered employers to: (1) purchase private insurance, (2) self-insure (e.g., by maintaining a contingency fund), or (3) make payments into a state insurance fund. Because employers generally pass on the costs of insurance to their customers, workers' compensation tends to spread the economic risk of workplace injuries throughout society.

TOLBERT V. MARTIN MARIETTA CORPORATION
621 F. Supp. 1099 (D. Colo. 1985)

Deborah Tolbert, a secretary employed by the Martin Marietta Corporation, was raped by a Martin Marietta janitor while on her way to lunch within the secured defense facility where she worked. She sued Martin Marietta, alleging that it had negligently hired the janitor and had negligently failed to make its premises safe for employees. Martin Marietta moved for summary judgment, claiming that Tolbert could not sue in negligence because workers' compensation was her sole remedy.

Carrigan, District Judge   The sole issue is whether the Colorado Workmen's Compensation Act covers Tolbert's injury. If it does, workers' compensation is her exclusive remedy and this tort action is barred. Tolbert asserts that her injury is not covered by workers' compensation, presumably because she expects that a tort action would yield a larger recovery. Martin Marietta, on the other hand, apparently is willing to pay the workers' compensation award to avoid risking a large tort verdict.

Workers' compensation applies where the injury or death is proximately caused by an injury or occupational disease arising out of and in the course of the employee's employment and is not intentionally self-inflicted. Although her injury did arise in the course of her employment, Tolbert contends that it did not "arise out of" the employment. The "arising out of" condition [requires] that there be some causal relationship between the employment and the injury. Courts have interpreted the "arising out of" language in different ways. Unfortunately, Colorado courts have not consistently applied any single test. Martin Marietta argues that positional-risk analysis applies to categorize the case as one [making workers' compensation applicable]. The positional-risk doctrine has been defined thus:

An injury arises out of the employment if it would not have occurred but for the fact that the conditions and obligations of the employment placed claimant in the position where he was injured. . . . This theory supports compensation in cases of stray bullets, roving lunatics and other situations in which the only connection of the employment with the injury is that its obligations placed the employee in the particular place at the particular time when he was injured by some neutral force, meaning by "neutral" neither personal to the claimant nor distinctly associated with the employment.

Invoking this rule, Martin Marietta asserts that Tolbert's injury is covered by workers' compensation because: (1) her employment placed her within the building where she was injured, and (2) the assault was a neutral force.

[However, a 1923 Colorado case] . . . applied the "increased-risk" test of causality. Under the increased-risk test, compensation is awarded only if the employment increases the worker's risk of injury above that to which the general public is exposed. If Colorado presently applies the increased-risk analysis, Tolbert would not be covered by workers' compensation. Certainly her employment as a secretary within a secured defense facility would not be expected to increase her risk of sexual assault above that to which women in the general public are exposed.

Colorado first applied positional risk analysis four years after [the 1923 case] was decided. [In this later positional-risk case,] the court upheld an award to a farmhand who was struck by lightning. It can readily be seen that the positional-risk test provides substantially broader coverage than does the increased-risk test. Unfortunately, the Colorado courts on several more recent occasions have departed from the positional-risk test to impose a higher standard of causal relationship to the employment.

The rape was a nonemployment-motivated act directed at the plaintiff because she was a woman. There is nothing to indicate that any other woman—whether or not a Martin employee—who happened to be in the same area at the time of the attack would not have become the victim. Tolbert was not raped because of the nature of her duties or the nature of her workplace environment, or because of any incident or quarrel growing out of the work.

Both applicable Colorado precedent and sound rationale support holding that the workers' compensation statute has not abolished Tolbert's tort claim. Adopting this position has the additional advantage of providing employers an incentive to make reasonable efforts to screen prospective employees so as to avoid hiring rapists or those having the identifiable characteristics of potential rapists. Tort law does not impose strict liability; Tolbert still has the burden of showing negligence, causation, and damages.

Martin Marietta's motion for summary judgment denied; case proceeds to trial on Tolbert's negligence theories.

The Occupational Safety and Health Act

Although it may stimulate employers to remedy hazardous working conditions, workers' compensation does not directly forbid such conditions. The most important measure directly regulating workplace safety is the federal Occupational Safety and Health Act of 1970. The Occupational Safety and Health Act applies to all employers engaged in a business affecting interstate commerce. Exempted, however, are the U.S. government, the states and their political subdivisions, and certain industries regulated by other federal safety legislation. The Occupational Safety and Health Act is mainly administered by the Occupational Safety and Health Administration (OSHA) of the Labor Department. It does not preempt state workplace safety regulation, and the states can regulate matters subject to federal standards, albeit under federal supervision and control.

The Occupational Safety and Health Act requires employers to provide their employees with employment and a place of employment free from recognized hazards that are likely to cause death or serious physical harm. It also requires employers to comply with the many detailed regulations promulgated by OSHA. OSHA can inspect places of employment for violations of the act and its regulations. If an employer is found to violate the act's general duty provision or any specific standard, OSHA issues a written citation. It must do so with reasonable promptness, and in no event more than six months after the violation. The citation becomes final after 15 workdays following its service on the employer, unless it is contested. Contested citations are reviewed by the Occupational Safety and Health Review Commission, a three-member body composed of presidential appointees. Further review by the federal courts of appeals is possible.

The main sanctions for violations of the act and the regulations are the various civil penalties imposed by OSHA. In addition, any employer who commits a willful violation resulting in death to an employee may suffer a fine, imprisonment, or both. Also, the secretary of labor may seek injunctive relief when an employment hazard presents an imminent danger of death or physical harm that cannot be promptly eliminated by normal citation procedures. Finally, the act imposes various record-keeping and reporting requirements on employers.

Social Security

Today, the law requires that employers help ensure their employees' financial security after the employment ends. One example is the federal social security system, which began in 1935. Social security is mainly financed by the Federal Insurance Contributions Act (FICA). FICA imposes a flat percentage tax on all employee income below a certain base figure and requires employers to pay a matching amount. Self-employed people pay a different rate on a different wage base. FICA revenues finance various forms of financial assistance in addition to the old-age benefits that people usually call social security. These include survivors' benefits to family members of deceased workers, disability benefits, and medical and hospitalization benefits for the elderly (the medicare system).

Unemployment Compensation

Another way that the law protects employees after their employment ends is by providing unemployment compensation for discharged workers. Since 1935, federal law has authorized joint federal-state efforts in this area. Today, each state administers its own unemployment compensation system under federal guidelines. The system's costs are met by subjecting employers to federal and state unemployment compensation taxes.

Unemployment insurance plans vary from state to state but usually share certain features. States often condition the receipt of benefits on the recipient's having worked for a covered employer for a specified time period, and/or having earned a certain minimum income over such a period. Generally, those who voluntarily quit work without good cause, are fired for bad conduct, fail to actively seek suitable new work, or refuse such work are ineligible for benefits. Benefit levels vary from state to state, as do the time periods during which benefits can be received.

ERISA

Many employers voluntarily contribute to their employees' postemployment income by maintaining pension plans. For years, pension plan abuses such as arbitrary termination of participation in the plan, arbitrary benefit reduction, and mismanagement of fund assets were not uncommon. The Employee Retirement Income Security Act of 1974 (ERISA) was a response to these problems. ERISA does not require employers to establish or fund pension plans and does not set benefit levels. Instead, it tries to check abuses and to protect employees' expectations that promised pension benefits will be paid.

ERISA imposes *fiduciary duties* on pension fund managers. For example, it requires that managers diversify the plan's investments to minimize the risk of large losses, unless this is clearly imprudent. ERISA also imposes *record-keeping, reporting,* and *disclosure* requirements. For instance, it requires that covered plans provide annual reports to their participants and specifies the contents of those reports. In addition, the act has a provision restricting an employer's ability to *delay an employee's participation* in the plan. For example, certain employees who complete one year of service with an employer cannot be denied plan participation. Furthermore, ERISA contains *funding* and *plan termination insurance* requirements for protecting plan participants against loss of pension income. Finally, ERISA contains complex *vesting* requirements that determine when an employee's right to receive

pension benefits becomes nonforfeitable. These requirements help prevent employers from using a late vesting date to avoid pension obligations to employees who change jobs or are fired before that date. ERISA's remedies include civil suits by plan participants and beneficiaries, equitable relief, and criminal penalties.

Labor Law

Early in the 19th century, some courts treated labor unions as illegal criminal conspiracies. After this restriction disappeared around mid-century, organized labor began its rise to power. One common explanation for the emergence of unions is that workers had to combine to counter the increasing size and power of their corporate employers. Another is the unfortunate working conditions many 19th-century workers confronted. During the late 19th and early 20th centuries, labor's growing political power and the increasing number of wage earners in the electorate led to the passage of many laws protecting workers. These included statutes outlawing "yellow dog" contracts (under which employees agreed not to join or remain a union member), minimum wage and maximum hours legislation, laws regulating the employment of women and children, factory safety measures, and workers' compensation. Courts, however, tended to represent business interests during this period. Thus, some pro-labor measures were struck down on constitutional grounds. Also, some courts were quick to issue temporary and permanent injunctions to restrain union picketing and boycotts and help quell strikes.

The National Labor Relations Act

Despite the holding actions just mentioned, organized labor's power continued to grow during the first part of the 20th century. In 1926, Congress passed the Railway Labor Act, which regulates labor relations in the railroad industry and which later came to include airlines. This was followed by the Norris-LaGuardia Act of 1932, which limited the circumstances in which federal courts could enjoin strikes and picketing in labor disputes, and also prohibited federal court enforcement of yellow-dog contracts.

The most important 20th-century American labor statute, however, was the National Labor Relations Act of 1935 (the NLRA or Wagner Act). The act gave employees the *right to organize* by enabling them to form, join, and assist labor organizations. It also allowed them to *bargain collectively* through their own representatives and to engage in other activities that would promote collective bargaining. In addition, the Wagner Act prohibited certain *unfair labor practices* that were believed to discourage collective bargaining. These forbidden employer practices include: (1) interfering with employees' exercise of their rights to form, join, and assist labor unions; (2) dominating or interfering with the formation or administration of a labor union, or giving a union financial or other support; (3) discriminating against employees in hiring, tenure, or any term of employment due to their union membership; (4) discriminating against employees because they have filed charges or given testimony under the NLRA; and (5) refusing to bargain collectively with any duly designated employee representative.

The NLRA also established the National Labor Relations Board (NLRB). The NLRB's main functions are: (1) handling representation cases (which involve the process by which a union becomes the certified employee representative within a bargaining unit), and (2) deciding whether challenged employer or union activity is an unfair labor practice.

The Labor Management Relations Act In 1947, Congress amended the NLRA by passing the Labor Management Relations Act (LMRA or Taft-Hartley Act). In part, the Taft-Hartley Act reflected the post–World War II period's revival of business power and its more conservative political climate. It also reflected public concern over frequent strikes, the alleged excessive power of union bosses, and various perceived unfair practices by unions.

Thus, the Taft-Hartley Act declared that certain acts by *unions* are unfair labor practices. These include: (1) restraining or coercing employees in the exercise of their guaranteed bargaining rights (e.g., their right to refrain from joining a union); (2) causing an employer to discriminate against an employee who is not a union member; (3) refusing to bargain collectively with an employer; (4) conducting a secondary strike or a secondary boycott for a specified illegal purpose;[4] (5) requiring employees covered by union-shop contracts to pay

excessive or discriminatory initiation fees or dues; and (6) featherbedding (forcing an employer to pay for work not actually performed).

The LMRA also established an 80-day cooling off period for strikes that the president finds likely to endanger national safety or health. In addition, it created a Federal Mediation and Conciliation Service to assist employers and unions in settling labor disputes.

The Labor Management Reporting and Disclosure Act Congressional investigations during the 1950s uncovered corruption in internal union affairs and also revealed that the internal procedures of many unions were undemocratic. In response to these findings, Congress enacted the Labor Management Reporting and Disclosure Act (or Landrum-Griffin Act) in 1959. The act established a "bill of rights" for union members and attempted to make internal union affairs more democratic. It also amended the NLRA by adding to the LMRA's list of unfair union labor practices.

The Fair Labor Standards Act

Although federal labor law regulates several aspects of labor-management relations, it still permits many terms of employment to be determined by private bargaining. Nonetheless, sometimes the law directly regulates such key terms of employment as wages and hours worked. The most important example is the Fair Labor Standards Act (FLSA) of 1938.

The FLSA regulates *wages and hours* by entitling covered employees to: (1) a specified minimum wage whose amount changes over time, and (2) a time-and-a-half rate for work exceeding 40 hours per week. These provisions basically apply to employees who are engaged in interstate commerce or the production of goods for such commerce, or who are employed by an enterprise that does the same and that has annual gross sales of sufficient size. State and local employees are also covered. The many exemptions from the FLSA's wages-and-hours provisions include executive, administrative, professional, and outside sales personnel.

The FLSA also forbids "oppressive" *child labor* by any employer engaged in interstate commerce or in the production of goods for such commerce, and also forbids the interstate shipment of goods produced in an establishment where oppressive child labor occurs. Oppressive child labor includes:

---

[4]These are strikes or boycotts aimed at a third party with which the union has no real dispute. Their purpose is to coerce that party not to deal with an employer with which the union *does* have a dispute, and thus to gain some leverage over the employer.

(1) most employment of children below the age of 14; (2) employment of children aged 14 to 15, unless they work in an occupation specifically approved by the Department of Labor; and (3) employment of children aged 16 to 17 who work in occupations declared particularly hazardous by the Labor Department. These provisions do not apply to most agricultural employment.

Both affected employees and the Labor Department can recover any unpaid minimum wages or overtime, plus an additional equal amount as liquidated damages, from an employer that has violated the FLSA's wages-and-hours provisions. A suit by the Labor Department terminates an employee's right to sue, but the department pays the amounts it recovers to the employee. Violations of the act's child labor provisions may result in civil penalties. Other FLSA remedies include injunctive relief and criminal liability for willful violations.

The Family and Medical Leave Act

After concluding that proper child-raising, family stability, and job security require that employees get reasonable work leave for family and medical reasons, Congress passed the Family and Medical Leave Act (FMLA) in 1993. In general, the act covers those employed for at least 12 months, and for 1,250 hours during those 12 months, by an employer employing 50 or more employees. In addition to private employers, the act includes federal, state, and local government agencies.

Under the FMLA, covered employees are entitled to a total of 12 workweeks of leave during any 12-month period for one or more of the following reasons: (1) the birth of a child and the need to care for that child; (2) placement of a child with the employee for adoption or foster care; (3) the need to care for a spouse, child, or parent with a serious health condition; and (4) the employee's own serious health condition. Usually, the leave may be without pay. Upon the employee's return from leave, the employer ordinarily must restore her to the position she held when the leave began or to an equivalent position, and not deny her any benefits accrued before the leave began.

Employers who deny any of an employee's FMLA rights are civilly liable to the affected employee for resulting lost wages or, if no wages were lost, for any other resulting monetary losses not exceeding 12 weeks' wages. Employees may also recover an additional equal amount as liquidated damages unless the employer acted in good faith and had reasonable grounds for believing that it was not violating the act. Like the FLSA, the FMLA permits civil actions by the secretary of labor, with any sums recovered distributed to affected employees. Employees may also obtain equitable relief, including reinstatement and promotion.

The Equal Pay Act

The Equal Pay Act (EPA), which forbids *sex* discrimination regarding *pay,* was a 1963 amendment to the FLSA. Its coverage resembles the coverage of the FLSA's minimum wage provisions. Unlike the FLSA, however, the EPA covers executive, administrative, and professional employees.

The Equal Pay Act forbids gender-based pay discrimination against men. But the typical EPA case involves a woman who claims that she has received lower pay than a male employee performing substantially equal work for the same employer. The requirement of substantially equal work is met if the plaintiff's job and the higher-paid male employee's job involve *each* of the following: (1) equal effort, (2) equal skill, (3) equal responsibility, and (4) similar working conditions.

Effort basically means physical or mental exertion. *Skill* refers to the experience, training, education, and ability required for the positions being compared. Here, the issue is not whether the employees being compared have equal skills, but whether *their jobs require or utilize* substantially the same skills. *Responsibility* (or accountability) involves such factors as the degree of supervision each job requires and the importance of each job to the employer. For instance, a retail sales position in which an employee may not approve customer checks is probably not equal to a sales position in which an employee has this authority. *Working conditions* refer to such factors as temperature, weather, fumes, ventilation, toxic conditions, and risk of injury. These need only be *similar,* not equal. As the *Grove* case (which follows shortly) suggests, many courts do not discuss the four equal-work criteria individually.

If the two jobs are substantially equal but they are paid unequally, an employer must prove one of the EPA's four defenses or it will lose the case. To do so, the employer must show that the pay disparity is based on: (1) seniority, (2) merit, (3) quality or quantity of production (e.g., a piecework system), or (4) any factor other than sex. As *Grove* emphasizes in the case of merit, the first three defenses usually require an employer to show some organized, systematic, structured, and communicated rating system with predetermined criteria that apply equally to employees of each sex. The any-factor-other-than-sex defense is a catchall category that may include shift differentials, bonuses paid because the job is part of a training program, and differences in the profitability of the products or services on which employees work.

The EPA's remedial scheme resembles the FLSA's scheme. Under the EPA, however, employee suits are for the amount of *back pay* lost because of an employer's discrimination, not for unpaid minimum wages or overtime. An employee may also recover an equal sum as liquidated damages. The EPA is enforced by the Equal Employment Opportunity Commission (EEOC) rather than the Labor Department.[5] Unlike some of the employment discrimination statutes described later, however, the EPA does not require that private plaintiffs submit their complaints to the EEOC or a state agency before mounting suit.

---

[5]The EEOC is an independent federal agency with a sizable staff and many regional offices. Its functions include: (1) enforcing most of the employment discrimination laws discussed in this chapter through lawsuits that it initiates or in which it intervenes, (2) conciliating employment discrimination charges (e.g., by encouraging their negotiated settlement), (3) investigating discrimination-related matters, and (4) interpreting the statutes it enforces through regulations and guidelines.

GROVE V. FROSTBURG STATE BANK
549 F. Supp. 922 (D. Md. 1982)

Sheila Grove and David Klink were hired as loan tellers by the Frostburg National Bank in 1967. Both were high school graduates at the time, and neither had prior work experience. Each was paid the same yearly starting salary in 1967. Klink was drafted into the army late in 1967, and he returned to the bank in 1969. From that time until 1976, he basically performed a loan teller's duties, although he also took on various miscellaneous tasks. Grove also basically performed loan teller duties during the period 1969 to 76. Throughout that period, Klink's yearly salary exceeded Grove's. Salary and raise determinations were made by David P. Willetts, the bank's vice president, who based these determinations primarily on his own observations of employees. Grove sued the bank in federal district court under the Equal Pay Act.

Jones, District Judge   The burden is on the plaintiff to make a prima facie showing that the employer pays different wages to males and females for equal work requiring equal skill, effort, and responsibility under similar working conditions. Once that showing is made, the employer has the burden of showing that the pay differential is justified under one of the four statutory exceptions. Only substantial equality of work need be proved; the jobs need not be identical. A wage differential is justified by extra tasks only if they create significant variations in skill, effort, and responsibility. If the purported extra tasks are not done; if females also have extra tasks of equal skill, effort, and responsibility; if females are not given the opportunity to do the extra tasks; or if the extra tasks only involve minimal time and are of peripheral importance, they do not justify a wage differential.

Sheila Grove performed work substantially equal to that of David Klink from 1969 through September, 1976. As loan tellers, [each] had basically the same duties. Klink had some extra tasks from time to time. He set up the drive-in branch in 1970. He reviewed the safe deposit box rent records and noted some delinquencies and increases in 1971. After 1971, he arranged for drilling the boxes. Some time in the 1970s, he began shredding paper.

Setting up the drive-in branch was a one-time task, involving taking supplies and equipment to the drive-in installation. To the extent that it involved any different skills or effort than the normal work of the loan tellers, they were largely physical. Moreover, no female loan teller had an opportunity to perform this task, because it was done at the request of Willetts. Although Klink's initiative in bringing the box rents up to date is commendable, the work did not consume a significant amount of time, as compared with his other duties. It was a one-time project. To the extent that he performed extra tasks thereafter in arranging for the drilling, no significant amount of time was involved. Shredding paper is a task involving less skill, effort, and responsibility than the regular work of loan tellers. It did not involve a significant amount of time, only occasional afternoons or Saturdays.

Grove has sustained her burden of demonstrating that her work as loan teller was substantially equal to that of Klink. The bank tried to justify Klink's higher salary on two grounds. It stated that Klink was paid a higher salary when he returned to the bank in 1969, which was perpetuated through yearly increases, as a reward for his patriotism in serving in the Army. The bank also claimed that Klink received higher pay because he was more responsible, conscientious, and harder-working: that is, on merit.

The bank has failed to show that Klink's 1969 salary was based on a factor other than sex. Even assuming that military service could be a proper reason for a wage differential, Klink was drafted into the service. No female worker could have been.

The bank has also failed to show that the wage differential was based on a legitimate merit system. A merit system need not be in writing to be recognized; it must, however, be an organized and structured procedure with systematic evaluations under predetermined criteria. If it is not in writing, employees must be aware of it. The system used by Willetts does not meet this test. It was not organized or structured; Willetts did not recall, for example, whether he had consulted with department supervisors at the end of each year concerning individual employees. A systematic evaluation, using predetermined criteria, was not made. Although Willetts cited a number of factors that influenced his pay decisions, these were not applied uniformly, and he eventually admitted that the primary criterion was his "gut feeling" about the employee. Finally, employees were not aware of the existence of any merit system.

Judgment for Grove.

TITLE VII

Unlike the other laws discussed in the previous section, the EPA is an *employment discrimination* provision. Employment discrimination might be defined as employer behavior that penalizes certain individuals because of personal traits that they cannot control and/or that bear no relation to effective job performance. Such discrimination was common before the law began to attack it during the 1960s and 1970s. Today, however, employers confront a maze of legal rules forbidding various kinds of employment discrimination.

Of the many employment discrimination laws in force today, the most important is Title VII of the 1964 Civil Rights Act. Unlike the Equal Pay Act, which merely forbids sex discrimination regarding pay, Title VII is a wide-ranging employment discrimination provision. It prohibits discrimination based on *race, color, religion, sex,* and *national origin* in hiring, firing, job assignments, pay, access to training and apprenticeship programs, and most other employment decisions.

Basic Features of Title VII

In discussing Title VII,[6] we first examine some general rules that govern all the kinds of discrimination it forbids. Then we examine each forbidden basis of discrimination in detail.

Covered Entities   Title VII covers all employers employing 15 or more employees and engaging in an industry affecting interstate commerce. Employers include individuals, partnerships, corporations, colleges and universities, labor unions and employment agencies (with respect to their own employees),

---

[6]This discussion reflects the state of the law at the conclusion of 1993.

and state and local governments.[7] Also, *referrals* by employment agencies are covered, no matter what the size of the agency, if an employer serviced by the agency has 15 or more employees. In addition, Title VII covers certain unions—mainly those with 15 or more members—in their capacity as *employee representatives.*

Procedures   Although the EEOC sometimes sues to enforce Title VII, the usual Title VII suit is a private claim. The complicated procedures governing private Title VII suits are beyond the scope of this text, but a few points should be kept in mind. Private parties with a Title VII claim have no automatic right to sue. Instead, they first must file a *charge* with the EEOC, or with a state agency in states having suitable fair employment laws and enforcement schemes. This allows the EEOC or the state agency to investigate the claim, attempt conciliation if the claim has substance, or sue the employer itself. If a plaintiff files with a state agency and the state fails to act, the plaintiff can still file a charge with the EEOC. Even if the EEOC fails to act on the claim, a plaintiff may still mount her own suit. Here, the EEOC issues a "right-to-sue letter" enabling the plaintiff to sue.

Proving Discrimination   The permissible methods for *proving* a Title VII violation are critical to its effectiveness against employment discrimination. For this reason, they have been a major political battleground in recent years. Proof of discrimination is easy in cases such as the *Johnson Controls* decision later in the chapter, where the employer had an **express policy** disfavoring one of Title VII's protected classes. **Direct evidence** of a discriminatory motive such as testimony or written evidence is obviously useful to plaintiffs as well. However, employers can discriminate without leaving such obvious tracks. Thus, the courts have devised other methods of proving a Title VII violation. As of late 1993, two such methods predominated. Both are difficult, controversial, and critical in determining Title VII's practical impact. Because each method's many details are beyond the scope of this text, and because each may have changed by the time you read this section, we merely outline them here.

---

[7]Employment discrimination within the federal government is beyond the scope of this text.

Title VII **disparate treatment** suits usually involve an individual plaintiff who alleges some specific instance or instances of discrimination. In such suits, the plaintiff first must show a *prima facie case*—a case strong enough to create a presumption of discrimination and to require a counterargument from the defendant. The proof needed for a prima facie case varies with the nature of the challenged employment decision (e.g., hiring or promotion), but ordinarily it gives plaintiffs few difficulties. Once the plaintiff establishes a prima facie case, the employer must *produce evidence* that the challenged employment decision was taken for *legitimate, nondiscriminatory reasons* or it will lose the lawsuit. In a hiring case, for example, an employer might produce evidence that it rejected the plaintiff because she did not meet its criteria for the position in question. If the employer produces satisfactory reasons, the plaintiff then must *show that discrimination actually occurred.* She might do so by showing that the employer's alleged nondiscriminatory reasons were a *pretext* for a decision that really involved discrimination. For example, she might show that the employer's alleged hiring criteria were not applied to similarly situated male job applicants.

Title VII's **disparate impact** (or adverse impact) proof method is most often used when the alleged discrimination affects many employees. Here, the plaintiffs ordinarily maintain that the employer uses a *particular employment practice* that causes a *disparate impact* on the basis of race, color, religion, sex, or national origin. Often, the practice is an employer rule that is neutral on its face but has a disproportionate adverse effect on one of Title VII's protected groups—for example, a height, weight, or high school diploma requirement for hiring, or a written test for hiring or promotion. If the plaintiffs show a disparate impact, the employer loses unless it demonstrates that the challenged practice is *job-related for the position in question and consistent with business necessity.* For example, the employer might show that its promotion test really predicts effective job performance, and that effective performance in the relevant job is necessary for its operations. Even if the employer makes this demonstration, the plaintiffs have another option—to show that the employer's legitimate business needs can be advanced by an *alternative employment practice* that is *less discriminatory than the challenged practice.* For example, the plaintiffs might show that the employer's legitimate needs can be met by a different promotion test that has less adverse impact on the protected group. If the employer refuses to adopt this practice, the plaintiffs prevail.

Defenses Even if a plaintiff proves a Title VII violation, the employer still prevails if it can establish one of Title VII's defenses. The most important such defenses are:

1. *Seniority.* Title VII is not violated if the employer treats employees differently pursuant to a *bona fide seniority system.* To be bona fide, such a system at least must treat all employees equally on its face, not have been created for discriminatory reasons, and not operate in a discriminatory fashion.

2. *The various "merit" defenses.* An employer also escapes Title VII liability if it acts pursuant to: a *bona fide merit system,* a system basing earnings on *quantity or quality of production,* or the results of a *professionally developed ability test.* Presumably, such systems and tests at least must meet the general standards for seniority systems stated above. Also, the EEOC has promulgated lengthy *Uniform Guidelines on Employee Selection Procedures* that speak to these and other matters.

3. *The BFOQ defense.* Finally, Title VII allows employers to discriminate on the bases of sex, religion, or national origin where one of those traits is a *bona fide occupational qualification (BFOQ) that is reasonably necessary to the business in question.* This BFOQ defense does not protect race or color discrimination. As the following *Johnson Controls* case makes clear, moreover, the defense is a narrow one even where it applies. Generally, it is available only where a certain gender, religion, or national origin is necessary for effective job performance. For example, a BFOQ probably would exist where a female is employed to model women's clothing or to fit women's undergarments, or a French restaurant hires a French chef. But the BFOQ defense is usually unavailable where the discrimination is based on stereotypes (e.g., that women are less aggressive than men) or on the preferences of co-workers or customers (e.g., the preference of airline travelers for female rather than male flight attendants). As *Johnson Controls* suggests, the defense is also unavailable where the employer's discriminatory practice promotes goals such as fetal protection that do not concern effective job performance.

Auto Workers v. Johnson Controls, Inc.
499 U.S. 187 (U.S. Sup. Ct. 1991)

Johnson Controls, Inc. manufactures batteries. Lead is a primary ingredient in that manufacturing process. A female employee's occupational exposure to lead involves a risk of harm to any fetus she carries. For this reason, Johnson Controls excluded women who are pregnant or who are capable of bearing children from jobs that involve exposure to lead. Numerous plaintiffs, including a woman who had chosen to be sterilized to avoid losing her job, entered a federal district court class action alleging that Johnson Controls' policy constituted illegal sex discrimination under Title VII. The district court entered a summary judgment for Johnson Controls and the court of appeals affirmed. The plaintiffs appealed to the U.S. Supreme Court.

Blackmun, Justice Johnson Controls' fetal-protection policy explicitly discriminates against women on the basis of their sex. The policy excludes women with childbearing capacity from lead-exposed jobs and so creates a facial classification based on gender. [But] an employer may discriminate on the basis of "religion, sex, or national origin in those certain instances where religion, sex, or national ori-

gin is a bona fide occupational qualification reasonably necessary to the normal operation of that particular business or enterprise." The BFOQ defense is written narrowly, and this Court has read it narrowly.

Johnson Controls argues that its fetal-protection policy falls within the so-called safety exception [of] the BFOQ. Discrimination on the basis of sex because of safety concerns is allowed only in narrow circumstances. In *Dothard v. Rawlinson* (1977), we allowed the employer to hire only male guards in contact areas of maximum-security male penitentiaries only because more was at stake than the individual woman's decision to weigh and accept the risks of employment. We found sex to be a BFOQ inasmuch as the employment of a female guard would create real risks of safety to others if [rape-related] violence broke out because the guard was a woman. Sex discrimination was tolerated because sex was related to the guard's ability to do the job—maintaining prison security. Similarly, some courts have approved airlines' layoffs of pregnant flight attendants on the ground that the employer's policy was necessary to ensure the safety of passengers. In two of these cases, the courts pointedly indicated that fetal, as opposed to passenger, safety was best left to the mother.

Therefore, the safety exception is limited to instances in which sex or pregnancy actually interferes with the employee's ability to perform the job. . . . [Thus,] Johnson Controls cannot establish a BFOQ. Fertile women, as far as appears in the record, manufacture batteries as efficiently as anyone else. Johnson Controls' professed moral and ethical concerns about the next generation do not suffice to establish a BFOQ of female sterility. Decisions about the welfare of future children must be left to the parents who conceive, bear, support, and raise them rather than to the employers who hire those parents.

Judgment in favor of Johnson Controls reversed; case returned to the lower courts for further proceedings consistent with the Supreme Court's opinion.

Remedies   Various remedies are possible once private plaintiffs or the EEOC win a Title VII suit. If intentional discrimination has caused lost wages, employees can obtain **back pay** accruing from a date two years before the filing of the charge. At the court's discretion, successful private plaintiffs may also recover reasonable **attorney's fees.** Victims of intentional discrimination can also recover **compensatory damages** for harms such as emotional distress, sickness, loss of reputation, or denial of credit. Victims of intentional discrimination can also recover **punitive damages** where the defendant discriminated with malice or with reckless indifference to the plaintiff's rights. However, the sum of the plaintiff's compensatory and punitive damages cannot exceed certain amounts that vary with the size of the employer. For example, they cannot total more than $300,000 for an employer with more than 500 employees.

Intentional discrimination may also entitle successful plaintiffs to **equitable relief.** Examples include orders compelling hiring, reinstatement, or retroactive seniority. On occasion, moreover, the courts have ordered quotalike racial preferences in Title VII cases.[8] After determining that an employer has engaged in a longstanding pattern of hiring discrimi-

nation against racial minorities, for example, a court might order that whites and minorities be hired on a 50–50 basis until minority representation in the employer's work force reaches some specified percentage. Generally speaking, such orders are permissible if: (1) an employer has engaged in severe, widespread, or longstanding discrimination; (2) the order does not unduly restrict the employment interests of white people; and (3) it does not force an employer to hire unqualified workers. Minority preferences may also appear in the **consent decrees** courts issue when approving the terms on which the parties have settled a Title VII case.

Race or Color Discrimination

At this point, we consider each of Title VII's prohibited bases of discrimination in more detail. *Race or color* discrimination includes discrimination against blacks, other racial minorities, Eskimos, and Native Americans, among others. Title VII also prohibits racial discrimination against whites. Nonetheless, voluntary racial preferences that favor minorities survive a Title VII attack if they: (1) are intended to correct a "manifest imbalance" reflecting underrepresentation of minorities in "traditionally segregated job categories," (2) do not "unnecessarily trammel" the rights of white employees or

---

[8] Occasionally, such preferential relief has been awarded in sex discrimination cases as well.

create an absolute bar to their advancement, and (3) are only temporary.[9] Note that here our concern is not the use of minority preferences as a *remedy* for a Title VII violation, but whether such preferences *themselves violate* Title VII when voluntarily established by an employer.

National Origin Discrimination

National origin discrimination includes discrimination based on: (1) the country of one's or one's ancestors' origin; or (2) one's possession of physical, cultural, or linguistic characteristics identified with people of a particular nation. Thus, plaintiffs in national origin discrimination cases need not have been born in the country at issue. In fact, if the discrimination is based on physical, cultural, or linguistic traits identified with a particular nation, even the plaintiff's ancestors need not have been born there. Thus, a person of pure French ancestry may have a Title VII case if she suffers discrimination because she looks like, acts like, or talks like a German.

Certain formally neutral employment practices can also constitute national origin discrimination. Employers who hire only U.S. citizens may violate Title VII if their policy has the purpose or effect of discriminating against one or more national origin groups. This could happen where the employer is located in an area where aliens of a particular nationality are heavily concentrated. Also, employment criteria such as height, weight, and fluency in English may violate Title VII if they have a disparate impact on a national origin group and are not job-related.

Religious Discrimination

For Title VII purposes, the term *religion* is broadly defined. Although all courts may not agree, the EEOC says that it includes any set of moral beliefs that are sincerely held with the same strength as traditional religious views. In fact, Title VII forbids religious discrimination against atheists. It also forbids discrimination based on religious *observances or practices*—for example, grooming, clothing, or

the refusal to work on the Sabbath. But such discrimination is permissible if an employer cannot reasonably accommodate the religious practice without undue hardship. Undue hardship exists when the accommodation imposes more than a minimal cost on an employer.

Sex Discrimination

Title VII's ban on sex discrimination aims at *gender-based* discrimination and does not forbid discrimination on the basis of homosexuality or transsexuality. Just as clearly, it applies to gender discrimination against *both men and women.* Still, voluntary employer programs favoring women in hiring or promotion survive a Title VII attack if they meet the previous tests for voluntary racial preferences (reformulated in terms of gender). Title VII also forbids discrimination on the bases of *pregnancy and childbirth*, and requires employers to treat these conditions like any other condition similarly affecting working ability in their sick leave programs, medical benefit and disability plans, and so forth. Finally, *sexual stereotyping* violates Title VII. This is employer behavior that either: (1) denies a woman employment opportunities by assuming that she must have traditionally "female" traits (e.g., unaggressiveness), or (2) penalizes her for lacking such traits (e.g., for acting aggressively).

Sexual Harassment Unwelcome sexual advances, requests for sexual favors, and other verbal or physical conduct of a sexual nature can violate Title VII under two different theories.[10] The first, called **quid pro quo** sexual harassment, involves some express or implied linkage between an employee's submission to sexually oriented behavior and tangible job consequences. Quid pro quo cases usually arise when, due to an employee's refusal to submit, she suffers a *tangible job detriment* of an economic nature; indeed, courts generally require such a detriment for recovery. For example, suppose that a supervisor fires a secretary because she

---

[9]*United Steelworkers v. Weber*, 443 U.S. 193 (1979), a different portion of which is excerpted in Chapter 1.

[10]The principles stated in this discussion also apply to race, color, religious, and national origin harassment. In addition, men can sue for sexual harassment by women. A few courts have allowed recoveries for homosexually oriented sexual harassment. A few also have allowed recoveries by employees who are passed over for some job benefit in favor of a co-employee who submits to sexual behavior.

refuses to have sexual relations with him or refuses to submit to other sex-related behavior. Such conduct would violate Title VII whether or not the supervisor expressly told the secretary that she would be fired for refusing to submit. Title VII is also violated if a supervisor denies a subordinate a deserved promotion or other job benefit for refusing to submit.

However, no quid pro quo and no tangible job detriment are required when an employee is subjected to **work environment** sexual harassment. As stated in the *Harris* case below, this is unwelcome sex-related behavior that is sufficiently severe or pervasive to change the conditions of the victim's employment and create an abusive working environment. Work environment sexual harassment can be inflicted by both supervisors and co-workers; *Harris* is an example of the former. Because such behavior must be *unwelcome,* however, an em-

ployee may have trouble recovering if she instigated or contributed to the sex-related behavior. Also, the offending behavior must be sufficiently *severe or pervasive* to create an environment that a *reasonable person* would find hostile or abusive. Finally, the victim must *subjectively perceive* the environment as hostile or abusive.

When is an *employer* liable for sexual harassment committed by its employees? Courts try to use agency law to resolve this question.[11] They usually conclude that: (1) employers are strictly liable for quid pro quo harassment, and (2) employers are liable for work environment harassment if they knew or should have known of the harassment and failed to take appropriate corrective action.

---

[11]It is unclear *which* agency law rules courts should apply in sexual harassment cases. Chapter 35 provides some possibilities.

HARRIS V. FORKLIFT SYSTEMS, INC.
114 S. Ct. 367 (U.S. Sup. Ct. 1993)

In April 1985, Theresa Harris started work as a manager for Forklift Systems, Inc. (Forklift). During Harris's two and one-half years with Forklift, she was subjected to gender-based insults and unwanted sexual innuendos from Charles Hardy, the firm's president. Several times, for example, Hardy told Harris: "You're a woman, what do you know?" and "We need a man as the rental manager." Once, he suggested that he and Harris negotiate her raise at the Holiday Inn. Hardy would also ask Harris and other female employees to get coins from his front pants pocket and to pick up objects that he threw on the ground. Most of these incidents occurred with other employees present.

After Harris complained to Hardy in August 1987, he apologized and promised to stop his offensive behavior. In early September, however, he inquired whether Harris had promised sex to a customer with whom she had concluded a deal on Forklift's behalf. On October 1, Harris quit. She then sued Forklift for work environment sexual harassment in federal district court. Although it considered Harris's claim "a close case," the court found for Forklift. It did so in part because it concluded that Hardy's actions were not sufficiently severe to seriously affect Harris's psychological well-being. After the court of appeals affirmed, Harris appealed to the U.S. Supreme Court.

O'Connor, Justice Title VII makes it "an unlawful employment practice for an employer . . . to discriminate against any individual with respect to his compensation, terms, conditions, or privileges of employment, because of such individual's race, color, religion, sex, or national origin." . . . The phrase "terms, conditions, or privileges of employment" evinces a Congressional intent to strike at the entire spectrum of disparate treatment of men and women in employment, which includes requiring people to work in a discriminatorily hostile or abusive environment. When the workplace is permeated with discriminatory intimidation, ridicule, and insult that is sufficiently severe or pervasive to alter the conditions of the victim's employment and create an abusive working environment, Title VII is violated.

This standard ... takes a middle path between making actionable any conduct that is merely offensive and requiring the conduct to cause a tangible psychological injury. ... Conduct that is not severe or pervasive enough to create an environment that a reasonable person would find hostile or abusive is beyond Title VII's purview. Likewise, if the victim does not subjectively perceive the environment to be abusive, there is no Title VII violation.

But Title VII comes into play before the harassing conduct leads to a nervous breakdown. A discriminatorily abusive work environment, even one that does not seriously affect employees' psychological well-being, can and often will detract from employees' job performance, discourage employees from remaining on the job, or keep them from advancing in their careers. We therefore believe the district court erred in relying on whether the conduct seriously affected plaintiff's psychological well-being or led her to suffer injury. Such an inquiry may needlessly focus the fact-finder's attention on concrete psychological harm, an element

Title VII does not require. Certainly Title VII bars conduct that would seriously affect a reasonable person's psychological well-being, but the statute is not limited to such conduct. So long as the environment would reasonably be perceived, and is perceived, as hostile or abusive, there is no need for it also to be psychologically injurious.

This is not, and by its nature cannot be, a mathematically precise test. ... Whether an environment is "hostile" or "abusive" can be determined only by looking at all the circumstances. These may include the frequency of the discriminatory conduct; its severity; whether it is physically threatening or humiliating, or a mere offensive utterance; and whether it unreasonably interferes with an employee's work performance.

Court of appeals decision in Forklift's favor reversed. Case returned to the district court for proceedings consistent with the Supreme Court's opinion.

OTHER IMPORTANT EMPLOYMENT DISCRIMINATION PROVISIONS

Section 1981

Where it applies, a post–Civil War civil rights statute called section 1981 sets employment discrimination standards resembling those of Title VII. Section 1981 apparently applies to public and private employment discrimination against blacks, people of certain racially characterized national origins such as Mexicans, and ethnic groups such as gypsies and Jews. Due to a 1991 amendment, section 1981 now applies to most of the contexts in which an employer might discriminate against an employee.

Section 1981 is important because it gives covered plaintiffs certain advantages that Title VII does not provide. Although courts often use Title VII's methods of proof in section 1981 cases, Title VII's limitations on covered employers and its complex procedural requirements do not apply. Also, damages are apt to be greater under section 1981; in particular, Title VII's limits on compensatory and punitive damages are inapplicable. For these rea-

sons, covered plaintiffs often include a section 1981 claim along with a Title VII claim in their complaint.

Age Discrimination in Employment Act

The 1967 Age Discrimination in Employment Act (ADEA) prohibits age-based employment discrimination against employees who are *at least 40 years of age.* People within this age group are protected against age discrimination in favor of both younger and older individuals, including favored individuals inside the protected age group.

Coverage   The ADEA covers individuals, partnerships, labor organizations and employment agencies (as to their employees), and corporations that: (1) engage in an industry affecting interstate commerce, and (2) employ at least 20 persons. The act also controls state and local governments.[12] *Referrals*

---

[12] Age discrimination in the federal government is beyond the scope of this text.

by an employment agency to a covered employer are within the ADEA's scope regardless of the agency's size. In addition, the ADEA reaches labor union practices affecting *union members;* usually, unions with 25 or more members are covered. The ADEA protects against age discrimination in many employment contexts, including hiring, firing, pay, job assignment, and fringe benefits.

Procedural Requirements   The complex procedural requirements for an ADEA suit are beyond the scope of this text. Before she can sue in her own right, a private plaintiff must file a charge with the EEOC or with an appropriate state agency. The EEOC may also sue to enforce the ADEA; such a suit precludes private suits arising from the same alleged violation. For both government and private suits, the statute of limitations is three years from the date of an alleged *willful* violation and two years from the date of an alleged *nonwillful* violation.

Proof   Proving age discrimination is no problem where an employer uses an explicit age classification, and may be easy where there is direct evidence of discrimination such as testimony or incriminating documents. However, many ADEA cases, such as the following *Biggins* decision, are brought under the Title VII disparate treatment theory discussed earlier. A few courts have used Title VII's disparate impact theory in ADEA cases.

Defenses   The ADEA allows employers to discharge or otherwise discipline an employee for *good cause,* and to use *reasonable factors other than age* in their employment decisions. It also allows employers to observe the terms of a *bona fide seniority system,* except where such a system is used to require or permit the involuntary retirement of anyone 40 or over.

In addition, the ADEA has a bona fide occupational qualification (BFOQ) defense. In general, an employer seeking to use this defense must show that its age classification is reasonably necessary to the proper performance—usually the safe performance—of the job in question. Specifically, the employer must show *either*: (1) that it was reasonable to believe that all or most employees of a certain age cannot perform the job safely, or (2) that it is impossible or highly impractical to test employees on an individualized basis. For example, an employer that refuses to hire anyone over 60 as a helicopter pilot should have a BFOQ defense if it has a reasonable basis for concluding that 60-and-over helicopter pilots pose significant safety risks, or that it is not feasible to test older pilots individually.

Remedies   Remedies available after a successful ADEA suit include unpaid back wages and overtime pay resulting from the discrimination; an additional equal award of liquidated damages where the employer acted willfully; attorney's fees; and equitable relief, including hiring, reinstatement, and promotion. Most courts do not allow punitive damages and recoveries for pain, suffering, mental distress, and so forth.

HAZEN PAPER CO. V. BIGGINS
113 S. Ct. 1701 (U.S. Sup. Ct. 1993)

Walter F. Biggins worked as a technical director for the Hazen Paper Company. In 1986, when Biggins was 62, Hazen fired him. Its justification was that Biggins had been doing business with Hazen's competitors. At the time of the firing, Biggins was within a few weeks of completing the 10-year vesting period for his employer-provided pension. There was also evidence that Hazen offered to retain Biggins as a consultant to the company, in which case he would not have been entitled to pension benefits.

After Biggins sued Hazen under the ADEA, a federal district court jury found in his favor. The court of appeals affirmed, and Hazen appealed to the U.S. Supreme Court.

O'Connor, Justice The courts of appeals repeatedly have faced the question whether an employer violates the ADEA by acting on the basis of a factor, such as an employee's pension status or seniority, that is empirically correlated with age. We now clarify that there is no disparate treatment under the ADEA when the factor motivating the employer is some feature other than the employee's age.

We have long distinguished between disparate treatment and disparate impact theories of employment discrimination. The disparate treatment theory is available under the ADEA. By contrast, we have never decided whether a disparate impact theory of liability is available under the ADEA, and we need not do so here. Biggins claims only that he received disparate treatment.

In a disparate treatment case, liability depends on whether the protected trait (under the ADEA, age) actually motivated the employer's decision. It is the very essence of age discrimination for an older employee to be fired because the employer believes that productivity and competence decline with old age. The employer cannot rely on age as a proxy for an employee's remaining characteristics, such as productivity, but must instead focus on those factors directly.

When the employer's decision *is* wholly motivated by factors other than age, the problem of inaccurate and stigmatizing stereotypes disappears. This is true even if the motivating factor is correlated with age, as pension status typically is. Pension plans typically provide that an employee's accrued benefits will become nonforfeitable, or "vested," once the employee completes a certain number of years of service with the employer. On average, an older employee has had more years in the work force than a younger employee, and thus may well have accumulated more years of service with a particular employer. Yet an employee's age is analytically distinct from his years of service. An employee who is younger than 40, and therefore outside the class of older workers as defined by the ADEA, may have worked for a particular employer his entire career, while an older worker may have been newly hired. Because age and years of service are analytically distinct, an employer can take account of one while ignoring the other, and thus it is incorrect to say that a decision based on years of service is necessarily age-based.

We do not mean to suggest that an employer *lawfully* could fire an employee in order to prevent his pension benefits from vesting. Such conduct is actionable under [ERISA]. But it would not, without more, violate the ADEA.

Besides the evidence of pension interference, the court of appeals cited some additional evidentiary support for ADEA liability. Biggins was asked to sign a confidentiality agreement, even though no other employee had been required to do so, and his replacement was a younger man who was given a less onerous agreement. In the ordinary ADEA case, indirect evidence of this kind may well suffice to support liability if the plaintiff also shows that the employer's explanation for its decision—here, that Biggins had been disloyal to Hazen by doing business with its competitors—is unworthy of credence. But inferring age-motivation from the implausibility of the employer's explanation may be problematic in cases where other unsavory motives, such as pension interference, were present. We therefore remand the case for the court of appeals to reconsider whether the jury had sufficient evidence to find an ADEA violation.

Judgment reversed. Case returned to the court of appeals to consider whether, under the standards outlined in its opinion, there was sufficient evidence to find Hazen liable for age discrimination.

Americans with Disabilities Act

Until recently, federal regulation of employment discrimination against handicapped people was mainly limited to certain federal contractors and recipients of federal financial assistance. By passing Title I of the Americans with Disabilities Act of 1990 (ADA), however, Congress addressed this problem comprehensively. This portion of the ADA is primarily enforced by the EEOC, and its procedures and remedies are the same as for Title VII.

Covered Entities   After mid-1994, Title I of the ADA covers employers who have 15 or more employees and who are engaged in an industry affecting interstate commerce. Employers include individuals, partnerships, corporations, colleges and universities, labor unions and employment agencies (regarding their own employees), and state and local governments. The act also covers certain labor unions in their capacity as employee representatives, as well as employment agencies' treatment of their clients.

Substantive Protections   The ADA forbids covered entities from discriminating against qualified individuals with a disability because of that disability. It covers disability-related discrimination regarding hiring, firing, promotion, pay, and innumerable other employment decisions. The act defines a *disability* as: (1) a physical or mental impairment that substantially limits one or more of an individual's major life activities, (2) a record of such an impairment, or (3) one's being regarded as having such an impairment. (The last two categories protect, among others, those who have previously been misdiagnosed or who have recovered from earlier impairments.) Not protected, however, are those who suffer discrimination for currently engaging in the illegal use of drugs. Furthermore, homosexuality, bisexuality, transvestism, transsexualism, and various other sex-related traits or conditions are not considered disabilities.

A *qualified individual with a disability* is a person who can perform the essential functions of the relevant job either: (1) without reasonable accommodation, or (2) with such accommodation. Thus, the ADA protects both individuals who can perform their job despite their handicap, and individuals who could perform their job if reasonable accommodation is provided. In the latter case, employers illegally discriminate if they do not provide such accommodation. *Reasonable accommodation* includes: making existing facilities readily accessible and usable, acquiring new equipment, restructuring jobs, modifying work schedules, and reassigning workers to vacant positions, among other options. In the following *Harmer* case, the employer provided the employee with reasonable accommodation because it did enough to allow him to perform the essential functions of his job.

In addition, employers need not make reasonable accommodation—and thus can discriminate against handicapped individuals—where such accommodation would cause them to suffer *undue hardship*. Undue hardship is an act requiring significant difficulty or expense. Among the factors used to determine its existence are the cost of the accommodation, the covered entity's overall financial resources, and the accommodation's effect on the covered entity's activities. The ADA also protects employers whose allegedly discriminatory decisions are based on *job-related criteria and business necessity,* so long as proper job performance cannot be accomplished by reasonable accommodation.

HARMER V. VIRGINIA ELECTRIC & POWER CO.
831 F. Supp. 1300 (E.D. Va. 1993)

Robert Harmer was a buyer in the purchasing department at the headquarters of Virginia Electric & Power Company. He worked in an unenclosed cubicle. Harmer suffered from bronchial asthma, and that condition was aggravated by tobacco smoke from nearby workers. Nonetheless, he always received satisfactory performance evaluations for his work.

As early as 1989, Harmer and other workers requested that Virginia Electric eliminate the smoke-filled air in Harmer's working environment. Virginia Electric took various steps to deal with the problem, culminating in a virtual ban on smoking in all its facilities effective August 1, 1993. Nonetheless, Harmer sued Virginia Electric under the ADA for an injunction against all smoking in its facilities (on the theory that the utility could always revoke its new policy). He also sought alleged lost wages, compensatory damages, punitive damages, attorney's fees and costs. Virginia Electric moved for summary judgment.

———————————◾———————————

Williams, District Judge   The ADA forbids discrimination by covered employers against a qualified individual with a disability. Virginia Power, as an employer engaged in an industry affecting commerce who has [15] or more employees, qualifies as a covered employer. Discrimination includes failure to provide reasonable accommodations for the physical and mental limitations of an otherwise qualified individual with a disability, unless the accommodation would impose an undue hardship on the operation of the employer's business. The act defines a qualified individual with a disability as a disabled individual who, with or without reasonable accommodation, can perform the essential functions of his position. [It] defines a disability as a physical or mental impairment that substantially limits one or more of an individual's major life activities, a record of such an impairment, or being regarded as having such an impairment. The court assumes for purposes of Virginia Electric's summary judgment motion that Harmer has a disability as defined by the act.

Therefore, the ADA protects Harmer from discrimination due to his disability. But Harmer still must show that he is entitled to a complete smoking ban as a reasonable accommodation to his disability, and he is unable to do so. The purpose of reasonable accommodation is to allow a disabled employee to perform the essential functions of his job. Harmer is not entitled to absolute accommodation because he can perform the essential functions of his position with the reasonable accommodations made by Virginia Electric, as [is] evidenced by his job performance appraisals, which indicate that he consistently met his job requirements. . . . Therefore, because the evidence established that Harmer could at all times adequately perform his employment duties, Harmer is not entitled to further accommodation under the ADA.

Virginia Electric's motion for summary judgment granted.

Executive Order 11246

Executive Order 11246, issued in 1965 and later amended, forbids race, color, national origin, religion, and sex discrimination by certain federal contractors. The order is enforced by the Labor Department's Office of Federal Contract Compliance Programs (OFCCP). Under the order, each federal contracting agency must insert an "equal opportunity clause" in most of its private-sector contracts for more than $10,000. Among other things, this clause requires that the contractor not discriminate on the grounds mentioned above and that it undertake affirmative action to prevent such discrimination.

State Antidiscrimination Laws

Most states have statutes that parallel Title VII, the EPA, the ADEA, and the ADA. These statutes sometimes provide more extensive protection than their fed-

eral counterparts. In addition, some states prohibit forms of discrimination not barred by federal law. Examples include discrimination on the bases of one's marital status, physical appearance, sexual orientation, political affiliation, AIDS infection, and off-the-job smoking.

Finally, some states and localities have adopted laws that adopt the employment discrimination theory called **comparable worth.** These laws, which typically apply only to public employees, sometimes say that state governments should not discriminate in pay between female-dominated jobs and male-dominated jobs of comparable overall worth to the employer. The worth of different jobs is often determined by giving each job a point rating under factors such as skill, responsibility, effort, and working conditions; adding the ratings; and comparing the totals. It was once believed that comparable worth claims might find favor under Title VII, but that possibility has receded over the years.

THE EMPLOYMENT DISCRIMINATION LAWS COMPARED

	Protected Traits	Covered Employer Decisions	Need to File Charge in Private Suit?
Equal Pay Act	Sex only	Pay only	No
Title VII	Race, color, national origin, religion, sex	Wide range	Yes
Section 1981	Race, racially characterized national origin, perhaps alienage	Wide range	No
Age Discrimination in Employment Act	Age, if victim 40 or over	Wide range	Yes
Americans with Disabilities Act	Existence of disability, if person qualified to perform job with or without reasonable accommodation	Wide range	Yes
Executive Order 11246	Race, color, religion, national origin, sex	Wide range	Not applicable; enforced by OFCCP

EMPLOYEE PRIVACY

The term *employee privacy* describes several employment-related issues that have assumed increasing importance recently. Uniting these issues is a concern with protecting employees' personal dignity and increasing their freedom from intrusions, surveillance, and the revelation of personal matters.

Polygraph Testing

Over the years, employers have made increasing use of polygraph and other lie detector tests—most often, to screen job applicants and to investigate employee thefts. This has led to concerns about the accuracy of such tests; the personal questions examiners sometimes ask; and the tests' impact on workers' job prospects, job security, and personal privacy. Besides provoking various state restrictions on polygraph testing, such worries led Congress to pass the Employee Polygraph Protection Act in 1988.

The Employee Polygraph Protection Act mainly regulates lie detector tests, which include polygraph tests and certain other devices for assessing a person's honesty. Under the act, employers may not: (1) require, suggest, request, or cause employees or prospective employees to take any lie detector test; (2) use, accept, refer to, or inquire about the results of any lie detector test administered to employees or prospective employees; and (3) take or threaten to take almost any unfavorable employment-related action against employees or prospective employees because of the results of any lie detector test, or because such parties failed or refused to take such a test.

However, certain employers and tests are exempt from these provisions. They include: (1) federal, state, and local government employers; (2) certain national defense and security-related tests by the federal government; (3) certain tests by security service firms; and (4) certain tests by firms manufacturing and distributing controlled substances. The act also contains a limited exemption for private employers that use polygraph tests when investigating economic losses caused by theft, embezzlement, industrial espionage, and so forth. Finally, the act restricts the disclosure of test results by examiners and by most employers.

The Polygraph Protection Act is enforced by the Labor Department, which has issued regulations in furtherance of that mission. It does not preempt state laws that prohibit lie detector tests or that set standards stricter than those imposed by federal law. Violations of the act or its regulations can result in civil penalties, suits for equitable relief by the Labor Department, and private suits for damages and equitable relief. Workers and job applicants who succeed in a private suit can obtain employment, reinstatement, promotion, and payment of lost wages and benefits.

Drug and Alcohol Testing

Due to their impact on employees' safe and effective job performance, employers have become increasingly concerned about both on-the-job and off-the-job drug and alcohol use. Thus, employers increasingly require employees and job applicants to undergo urine tests for drugs and/or alcohol. Because those who test positive may be either disciplined or induced to undergo treatment, and because the tests themselves can raise privacy concerns, some legal checks on their use have emerged.

Drug and alcohol testing by *public* employers can be attacked under the Fourth Amendment's search-and-seizure provisions. However, such tests generally are constitutional where there is a reasonable basis for suspecting that an employee is using drugs or alcohol, or drug use in a particular job could threaten the public interest or public safety. Due to the government action requirement discussed in Chapter 3, *private-sector* employees generally have no federal constitutional protection against drug and alcohol testing. Some state constitutions, however, lack a government action requirement. In addition, several states now regulate private drug and/or alcohol testing by statute. Tort suits for invasion of privacy or infliction of emotional distress may also be possible in some cases.[13]

Despite these protections, however, federal law *requires* private-sector drug testing in certain situations.[14] Under a 1988 Defense Department rule, for example, employers who contract with the department must agree to establish a drug-testing program under which employees who work in sensitive positions may sometimes be tested. Also, 1988 Transportation Department regulations require random testing of public and private employees occupying safety-sensitive or security-related positions in industries such as aviation, trucking, railroads, mass transit, and others.

Employer Searches

Employers concerned about thefts, drug use, and other misbehavior by their employees sometimes conduct searches of those employees' offices, desks, lockers, files, briefcases, packages, vehicles, and even bodies to confirm their suspicions. In 1987, the Supreme Court held that public employees sometimes have a reasonable expectation of privacy in areas such as their offices, desks, or files. But it also held that searches of those areas are constitutional under the Fourth Amendment when they are reasonable under the circumstances. Determining reasonableness generally means balancing the employee's legitimate privacy expectations against the government's need for supervision and control of the workplace, with more intrusive searches demanding a higher degree of justification. Finally, the Court also said that neither probable cause nor a warrant is necessary for such searches to proceed.

As noted above, the U.S. Constitution ordinarily does not apply to private employment. Nonetheless, both private and public employees can mount common law invasion of privacy suits against employers who conduct searches. In such cases, courts usually try to weigh the intrusiveness of the search against the purposes justifying it, and consider the availability of less intrusive alternatives that still would satisfy the employer's legitimate needs.

---

[13]Invasion of privacy and intentional infliction of emotional distress are discussed in Chapter 6, and negligent infliction of emotional distress is discussed in Chapter 7.

[14]The ADA, however, is neutral on the subject, saying that nothing in the act should be construed to encourage, prohibit, or authorize drug testing or the making of employment decisions on that basis.

Employer Monitoring

Although employers have always monitored their employees' work, recent technological advances enable such monitoring to occur without those employees' knowledge. Examples include closed-circuit television, video monitoring, telephone monitoring, the monitoring of computer workstations (e.g., by counting keystrokes), and metal detectors at plant entrances. Such monitoring has encountered objections because employees are often unaware that it exists, or may suffer stress when they do know or suspect its existence. Employers counter these objections by stressing that monitoring is highly useful in evaluating employee performance, improving efficiency, and reducing theft.

Telephone monitoring has occasionally been found illegal under federal wiretapping law. Although such claims have been uncommon, invasion of privacy suits may succeed in situations where an employer's need for surveillance is slight and it is conducted in areas, such as restrooms and lounges, in which employees have a reasonable expectation of privacy. Despite various state and federal bills proposing statutes regulating various forms of monitoring, little such legislation had passed as of late 1993.

Records and References

Many states allow both public and private employees at least some access to personnel files maintained by their employers. Also, some states limit third-party access to such records. In addition, employers who transmit such data to third parties may be civilly liable for defamation or invasion of privacy.[15] However, truth is a defense in defamation cases, and in both defamation and invasion of privacy suits the employer's actions may be privileged. These defenses can protect employers who are sued for truthful, good faith statements made in references for former employees.

---

[15]Defamation and invasion of privacy are discussed in Chapter 6, which examines defamation suits against employers by their ex-employees in greater detail.

Wrongful Discharge

The Doctrine of Employment at Will

The traditional employment-at-will rule, which first appeared around 1870, says that either party can terminate an employment contract for an indefinite time period. Indefinite-time contracts include those for "steady," "regular," or "permanent" employment. The termination can occur at any time; and can be for good, bad, or no cause. However, employees may recover for work actually done.

The Common Law Exceptions

Because it gives employers the ability to discharge indefinite-term employees with virtual impunity, employment at will has long been regarded as a boon to business and a threat to workers' interests. Although the doctrine remains important today, it has been eroded by many of the developments described in this chapter. For example, the NLRA forbids dismissal for union affiliation, and labor contracts frequently bar termination without just cause. Also, Title VII prohibits firings based on certain personal traits, the ADEA blocks discharges on the basis of age, and the ADA forbids terminations for covered personal disabilities.

Over the past 20 years, courts have been carving out further exceptions to employment at will. The three most important such exceptions are discussed below. Although a few states have refused to do so, most recognize one or more of these exceptions. In such states, a terminated employee can recover against her employer for **wrongful discharge** or **unjust dismissal**. The remedies in successful wrongful discharge suits depend heavily on whether the plaintiff's suit is a contract or a tort claim, with tort remedies being more advantageous for plaintiffs.

The Public Policy Exception The *public policy* exception to employment at will, which has been recognized by over three fourths of the states, is the most common basis for a wrongful discharge suit. As the *Peterson* case (which follows shortly) suggests, it is usually a tort claim. In public policy cases, the terminated employee argues that his discharge was unlawful because it violated the state's public policy. As *Peterson* makes clear, there is some disagreement about the permissible *sources* of state public policies. Perhaps the most common pattern is to limit public policy to the policies furthered by *existing laws* such as constitutional provisions and statutes. For this reason, employees often fail to recover where they are fired for *ethical* objections to job assignments or employer practices.

Successful suits under the public policy exception usually involve firings motivated by an employee's: (1) refusal to commit an unlawful act (e.g., committing perjury or violating the antitrust laws), (2) performance of an important public obligation (e.g., jury duty or whistle-blowing),[16] or (3) exercise of a legal right or privilege (e.g., making a workers' compensation claim or refusing to take an illegal polygraph test). In each case, the act (or refusal to act) that caused the firing is consistent with some public policy; for this reason, the firing tends to frustrate the policy. For example, firing an employee for filing a workers' compensation claim undermines the public policies underlying state workers' compensation statutes.

---

[16]Whistle-blowers are employees who publicly disclose dangerous, illegal, or improper employer behavior. A few states have passed statutes protecting the employment rights of certain whistle-blowers.

The Implied Covenant of Good Faith and Fair Dealing   A wrongful discharge suit based on the *implied covenant of good faith and fair dealing* is usually a contract claim. Here, the employee argues that her discharge was unlawful because it was not made in good faith or did not amount to fair dealing, thus violating the implied contract term. Only about 25 percent of the states have recognized this exception to employment at will, and most of these give it a narrow scope.

Promises by Employers   Using various legal theories, courts have increasingly made employers liable for breaking *promises* to their employees regarding termination policy. Such promises typically are express statements made by employers during hiring or employee orientation, or in their employee manuals, handbooks, personnel policies, and benefit plans. Occasionally, such promises are implied from business custom and usage as well. If such sources state the reasons for which employees will be fired or the procedures accompanying employee terminations, and if the employer fails to follow those promises, it is liable for breach of contract. At least two thirds of the states recognize this exception to employment at will. As the following *Progress Printing* case suggests, however, employers often succeed in disclaiming liability for their own promises.

PETERSON V. BROWNING
832 P.2d 1280 (Utah Sup. Ct. 1992)

Vern Peterson was a customs officer with Browning, a Utah corporation. After being terminated from that position, Peterson sued Browning in federal district court, alleging that he was fired for refusing to falsify tax documents in violation of Utah and Missouri law and to falsify customs documents in violation of federal law. The district court then certified two questions to the Utah Supreme Court: (1) whether the Utah public policy exception to employment at will includes violations of federal law and the law of states other than Utah; and (2) whether the Utah public policy exception is a tort claim or a contract claim.

Durham, Justice   The public policy exception to employment at will restricts an employer's right to terminate an employee for any reason. Under the exception, the at-will doctrine will not insulate an employer from liability where an employee is fired in a manner or for a reason that contravenes a clear and substantial public policy. Actions falling within the public policy exception typically involve termination of employment for: (1) refusing to commit an illegal or wrongful act, (2) performing a public obligation, or (3) exercising a legal right or privilege. Here, Peterson alleges that he was terminated for refusing to commit an unlawful act.

How a court defines "public policy" is a determining factor in whether it will invoke the public policy exception. Declarations of public policy can be found in our statutes and constitutions. This does not mean that all statements made in a statute are expressions of public policy. Many statutes impose requirements whose fulfillment does not implicate fundamental public policy concerns. A number of courts have refused to recognize a cause of action unless the public policy allegedly violated is clear or substantial. This court will narrowly construe the public policies on which a wrongful termination action may be based. It is not the purpose of the exception to eliminate employer discretion in discharging at-will employees, or to impose a requirement of good cause for discharge. We hold that the public policy exception applies in this state when the statutory language expressing the public conscience is clear and when the affected interests of society are substantial.

We turn to the question whether the public policy exception in this state includes violations of federal law and the laws of other states in addition to Utah law. A number of state courts have recognized that certain federal laws may properly form the basis for a wrongful termination action under a state's public policy exception. We are not prepared to hold, however, that a violation of any federal or other state's law automatically provides the basis for a wrongful termination action based on the Utah public policy exception. Many ancient, anachronistic, and unenforced criminal sanctions remain on the books of local, state, and national governments. Violations of such laws would not necessarily violate Utah public policy. A violation of a state or federal law must contravene the clear and substantial public policy of the state of Utah. A plaintiff must establish the connection between the law violated and the public policies of Utah. That has been done here.

In the present case, it is alleged that the employer discharged the employee because he would not falsify tax and customs documents. Such falsification involves serious misconduct and is in all likelihood a felony. To hold that one's continued employment could be made contingent upon his commission of a felonious act at the instance of his employer would be to encourage criminal conduct [by] both the employee and the employer and would contaminate the honest administration of public affairs. Persons who are terminated from their employment because they refuse to engage in illegal activities that implicate clear and substantial Utah public policy considerations should be protected regardless of whether the applicable law is that of Utah, the federal government, or another state.

The second issue is whether the public policy exception sounds in tort or in contract. Characterizing a case as tort or contract orients the parties to the requisite elements of proof, permits anticipation of potential defenses, and defines the remedies available. Of those courts recognizing the public policy exception, the overwhelming majority adopt the tort theory. We agree with the majority and hold that the exception sounds in tort.

The duty at issue in actions for wrongful termination in violation of public policy does not arise out of the employment contract. It is imposed by law, and thus is properly conceptualized as a tort. Significant consequences flow from this conceptual approach, one of which is the type of damages available. When a contract theory is applied, compensation may be limited to economic losses such as back pay. In contrast, a tort theory will permit a plaintiff [to] recover punitive damages. Potential punitive damages will exert a valuable deterrent effect on employers who might otherwise subject their employees to a choice between violating the law and losing their jobs.

The Utah Supreme Court held that: (1) the Utah public policy exception includes violations of federal law and the laws of other states if those violations contravene the clear and substantial public policies of Utah; and (2) the public policy exception is a tort claim rather than a contract claim.

PROGRESS PRINTING CO. V. NICHOLS
421 S.E.2d 428 (Va. Sup. Ct. 1992)

On January 20, 1987, William H. Nichols began work as a pressman for the Progress Printing Company. At that time, Nichols was provided with a copy of the company's Employees' Handbook. The handbook stated that Progress would not discharge or suspend an employee "without just cause" and that the company "shall give at least one warning notice in writing" before termination, except under certain circumstances not relevant here.

On February 2, 1987, however, the firm's personnel director gave Nichols a form that stated in part:

I have received a copy of the Progress Printing Employee Handbook. I recognize that an udestanding [sic] of this information is important to a successful relationship between Progress Printing and myself. I agree to follow the procedures and guidelines it contains. Any questions concerning Progress Printing's polices will be directed to the Personnel Director.

The employment relationship between Progress Printing and the employee is *at will and may be terminated by either party at any time* [emphasis in original].

Nichols and the personnel director both signed the form.

On March 8, 1989, Nichols became upset over Progress's failure to correct a recurring defect in a print job, and he refused to complete that job assignment as a result. Nichols was fired on the following day, without the prior written notice promised by the Employee Handbook.

Nichols then sued for wrongful discharge in a Virginia trial court. After that court ruled in his favor and awarded him $9,000 in damages, Progress appealed.

Lacy, Justice   In Virginia, as in a majority of jurisdictions, the employment relationship is presumed to be "at will," which means that the employment term extends for an indefinite period and may be terminated for any reason. This presumption may be rebutted if sufficient evidence is produced to show that the employment is for a definite, rather than an indefinite, term. Progress argues that Nichols failed to rebut the presumption because the handbook did not constitute an enforceable employment contract and, even if it did, the subsequent execution of the acknowledgement form created an at-will employment relationship.

A number of jurisdictions have held that the employer can be bound by termination-for-cause provisions contained in employee handbooks where those provisions are communicated to the employee in a sufficiently specific manner. We have held that an employment condition which allows termination only for cause sets a definite term for the duration of the employment. We nevertheless agree with

Progress that the acknowledgement form specifically superseded and replaced that [just cause] provision with the agreement that the employment relationship was at will. We base this holding on a number of grounds.

The termination-for-cause language of the handbook and the employment-at-will relationship agreed to in the subsequent acknowledgement form are in direct conflict and cannot be reconciled in any reasonable way. If the documents are considered a single contract, this conflict fails to provide sufficient evidence to rebut the presumption of employment at will.

[In any event,] the acknowledgement form was not a part of the handbook and was executed thirteen days after Nichols began work. Under these circumstances, the form reflects an understanding between the parties separate from that contained in the handbook. Execution of the form memorialized reciprocal commitments that satisfy the requisites of a contract—there was an offer of employment at will; the employee continued service, which constituted the consideration; and the employee accepted by performance.

We conclude that the employment relationship between Nichols and Progress was at-will employment which either party could terminate at any time.

Therefore, Progress did not breach the employment contract when it terminated Nichols.

Trial court decision on Nichols's employment-at-will claim reversed in favor of Progress.

ETHICAL AND PUBLIC POLICY CONCERNS

1. Do you think that the employer in the preceding *Progress Printing* case behaved ethically? Why or why not?

2. Over the past 150 years, the moral theory known as *utilitarianism* has been very influential. Utilitarianism, which was discussed in Chapter 4, basically asserts that the test for determining the rightness or wrongness of actions (including laws) is their ability to produce the greatest net balance of satisfactions over dissatisfactions throughout society as a whole. Give a utilitarian justification for the traditional employment-at-will rule. You can assume that economic well-being counts as a "satisfaction" for utilitarian purposes. You also can assume that the people fired under the traditional employment-at-will rule suffer from their firing.

PROBLEMS AND PROBLEM CASES

1. A class of male employees sued the American Cast Iron Pipe Company (ACIPCO) under the Equal Pay Act. One of the plaintiffs, James Dollar, argued that the act was violated because he was paid less than certain female employees despite having greater skills and responsibility. Dollar had worked for ACIPCO as a production machinist, radial drill operator, and machinist apprentice. The female employees to whom Dollar compared himself included data entry operators, receptionists, estimators, stenographer-clerks, and a truckload-carload coordinator. Did Dollar's EPA claim succeed?

2. Dianne Rawlinson, a rejected female applicant for employment as a prison guard in the Alabama prison system, challenged certain state rules restricting her employment prospects under

Title VII. They were: (1) requirements that all prison employees be at least 5 feet 2 inches tall and weigh at least 120 pounds, and (2) a rule expressly prohibiting women from assuming close-contact prison guard positions in maximum-security prisons (most of which were all-male). What method of proving a Title VII case should Rawlinson use in attacking the height and weight requirements? Does she need to use one of these methods to attack the second rule? What argument should the state use if Rawlinson establishes a prima facie case against the height and weight requirements? What Title VII defense might the state have for the second rule? With regard to the second rule, assume that at this time Alabama's maximum security prisons housed their male prisoners dormitory-style rather than putting them in cells, and that they did not separate sex offenders from other prisoners.

3. The American Cast Iron Pipe Company (ACIPCO) limits the medical and dental benefits it provides to its employees' dependents. In order for the children of an employee to qualify for coverage, the company requires that the children reside full time with their employee-parent. Because men comprised 397 of the 400 ACIPCO employees who were negatively affected by this policy, a male employee named Ray Beavers mounted a Title VII class action suit against the firm for sex discrimination. Can a male employee like Beavers sue for sex discrimination under Title VII? In any event, what Title VII proof method would Beavers's suit have to involve?

4. Farah Manufacturing Company had a long-standing policy against employing aliens. Cecilia Espinoza, a lawful alien married to an American citizen, applied for employment as a seamstress at Farah. She was rejected, and she sued Farah under Title VII for national origin discrimination. Did Farah's decision violate Title VII? Assume that Espinoza's suit attacks the policy just described and that she is not making either a disparate treatment or a disparate impact argument.

5. Jesse Cook, a Seventh Day Adventist, worked at a Chrysler Corporation plant. Because he lacked sufficient seniority in his job, Cook was assigned to the evening shift, which required him to work on Friday nights. Cook's religion prohibited him from working from sundown Friday until sundown Saturday. Cook was informed that under the relevant collective bargaining agreement, his shift could not be changed. Eventually, Cook was fired for his continuing Friday night absences from work. Accommodating Cook probably would have required Chrysler to make Cook a part-time employee while paying him full-time benefits. Also, it probably would have required Chrysler to use a temporary part-time employee (or floater) to replace Cook every Friday night. This would have meant that Chrysler either had to forgo using a floater elsewhere or hire another floater. Also, more repairs and lower efficiency are likely when a floater is used on the line.

Cook sued Chrysler and the union for religious discrimination under Title VII. Will the defendants succeed if they argue that they were not discriminating against Cook's *religion* as such, but rather against his refusal to work on Friday nights? In any event, what other argument might they use? Will it work here?

6. Ann Hopkins, a senior manager at the accounting firm of Price Waterhouse, was denied partnership in the firm. A persistent theme in existing partners' written comments on Hopkins's candidacy was the belief that Hopkins acted in ways inappropriate for a woman to act. Thus, one partner described her as "macho," another wrote that she "overcompensated for being a woman," yet another advised that she take "a course at charm school," and still others objected to her use of profanity. Also, a partner who tried to help Hopkins through the process told her that to improve her chances, she should walk more femininely, dress more femininely, wear makeup, have her hair styled, and wear jewelry. Assuming that these opinions were the only reason for Hopkins's failure to make partner, was that denial illegal sex discrimination under Title VII?

7. Mechelle Vinson alleged that during her four years with the Meritor Savings Bank, her supervisor Sidney Taylor repeatedly demanded sexual favors from her, and that she had sexual intercourse with him on 40 to 50 separate occasions. She also contended that Taylor fondled her in front of other employees, followed her into the women's restroom, exposed himself to her, and forcibly raped her on several occasions. Despite these allegations, however, Vinson apparently was well treated by her employer in other respects. She received three promotions during her time with the bank, and it was undisputed that her advancement was based solely on merit. Assuming that Vinson's allegations are true and that Taylor's behavior was unwelcome to her, can she recover against the bank for quid pro quo sexual harassment? Can she recover for work environment sexual harassment? Assume that the bank would be liable for Taylor's behavior.

8. William Guthrie managed a J. C. Penney Company store in Meridian, Mississippi. J. C. Penney originally had a policy that all store managers retire at age 60, but this policy was changed after passage of the ADEA. In 1979, just before Guthrie's 60th birthday, various Penney employees made "friendly" inquiries about his retirement plans. Guthrie, however, continued to manage the Meridian store, receiving satisfactory performance ratings and making decent profits for J. C. Penney. In 1982, however, Guthrie's new Penney supervisor reprimanded Guthrie before other store employees, overrode several decisions ordinarily made by Guthrie, lowered Guthrie's performance ratings, and gave him some difficult new performance objectives. Feeling that his discharge was inevitable, Guthrie resigned. Under the younger store manager who succeeded him, the Meridian store did less well in sales and profits, but the new manager received satisfactory performance ratings and was allowed to run the store without interference.

Guthrie sued Penney for constructive discharge under the ADEA. What method of proof would his suit involve? Can that method be used under the ADEA?

9. At the age of 66, Fleming Tullis was discharged from his job as a school bus driver with a private school. He sued the school under the Age Discrimination in Employment Act. Did the school have a BFOQ defense here? Assume that tests for determining the driving ability of individual people are available and reliable. Also, assume that the school failed to produce any evidence showing that people in their 60s cannot safely operate school buses.

10. Catherine Sue Wagenseller was fired from her job as paramedic coordinator in the Scottsdale Memorial Hospital's emergency department. She sued the hospital for wrongful discharge under the public policy exception to the employment-at-will doctrine, alleging that she was fired because of animosity resulting from her refusal to participate in an off-the-job group parody of the song *Moon River* in which group members mooned the audience. A state statute provided that: "A person commits indecent exposure if he or she exposes his or her genitals or anus . . . and another person is present, and the defendant is reckless about whether such other person, as a reasonable person, would be offended or alarmed by the act." Assuming that the audience to the parody enjoyed watching the mooning, would Wagenseller have been criminally liable if she had participated? Does this necessarily defeat her civil claim for wrongful discharge under the public policy exception?

11. [video icon] *Video Case.* See "How Safe is Too Safe?" Mike, a factory worker at XYZ Manufacturing, suffers injury to his fingers while working for XYZ. The injury occurs while Mike is operating a table saw built by ABCO Assembly. The saw was designed with a detachable blade guard assembly. The blade guard assembly would have prevented Mike's injury had it been in place while he was using the saw, but it was detached at that time. Assuming for the sake of argument that Mike was contributorily negligent or that he assumed the risk of the injury he suffered, can XYZ use either of these defenses to prevent Mike from recovering under workers' compensation for his injuries? Suppose that Mike wants to mount a product liability suit against ABCO. Would workers' compensation block such a suit?

Environmental Law

INTRODUCTION

Today's businessperson must be concerned with not only competing effectively against competitors but also complying with a myriad of regulatory requirements. For many businesses, particularly those that manufacture goods or that generate wastes, the environmental laws and regulations loom large in terms of the requirements and costs they impose. They can have a significant effect on the way businesses have to be conducted as well as on their profitability. This area of the law has expanded dramatically over the last two decades, and environmental issues are a major concern of people and governments around the world. This chapter will briefly discuss the development of environmental law and will outline the major federal statutes that have been enacted to control pollution of air, water, and land.

Historical Perspective

Historically, people assumed that the air, water, and land around them would absorb their waste products. In recent times, however, it has become clear that nature's capacity to assimilate people's wastes is not infinite. Burgeoning population, economic growth, and the products of our industrial society can pose risks to human health and the environment. The societal challenge is to accommodate economic activity and growth and at the same time provide reasonable protection of human health and the environment.

Concern about the environment is not a recent phenomenon. In medieval England, Parliament passed smoke control acts making it illegal to burn soft coal at certain times of the year. Where the owner or operator of a piece of property is using it in such a manner as to unreasonably interfere with another owner's (or the public's) health or enjoyment of his property, the courts have long entertained suits to abate the nuisance. Nuisance actions, which are discussed in Chapter 24, Real Property, are frequently not ideal vehicles for dealing with widespread pollution problems. Rather than a hit-or-miss approach, a comprehensive across-the-board approach may be required.

Realizing this, the federal government, as well as many state and local governments, had passed laws to abate air and water pollution by the late 1950s and 1960s. As the 1970s began, concern over the quality and future of the environment produced new laws and fresh public demands for action. During the 1980s, these laws were refined and, in some cases, their coverage was extended. In the 1990s environmental concerns continue to be prominent around the globe, and many countries, both individually and collectively, are taking steps to address these concerns. Accordingly, it is increasingly important that the businessperson be cognizant of the legal requirements and the public's environmental concerns in operating a business. These requirements and concerns not only may pose challenges to businesses but can also provide opportunities for them as well.

The Environmental Protection Agency

In 1970, the Environmental Protection Agency was created to consolidate the federal government's environmental responsibilities. This was an explicit recognition that the problems of air and water pollution, solid waste disposal, water supply, and pesticide and radiation control were interrelated and required a consolidated approach. Congress subsequently passed comprehensive new legislation covering, among other things, air and water pollution, pesticides, ocean dumping, and waste disposal. Among the factors prompting these laws were protection of human health, aesthetics, economic costs of continued pollution, and protection of natural systems.

The initial efforts were aimed at problems that could largely be seen, smelled, or tasted. As control requirements have been put in place, implemented by industry and government, and progress has been noted in the form of cleaner air and water, attention has focused increasingly on problems that are somewhat less visible but potentially more threatening—the problems posed by toxic substances. These problems have come into more prominence as scientific research indicates the risks posed by some substances, as new detection technology has enabled the detection of suspect substances in ever more minute quantities in the world around us, and as increased monitoring and testing is conducted. Determination of the degree of risk posed by any particular substance or proposed action—and deciding the most appropriate control strategy—frequently triggers strong disagreements within the society because of what is at stake in terms of economic costs and protection of health or the environment.

The National Environmental Policy Act

The **National Environmental Policy Act** (NEPA) was signed into law on January 1, 1970. The act required that an environmental impact statement be prepared for every recommendation or report on legislation and for every major federal action significantly affecting the quality of the environment. The environmental impact statement must: (1) describe the environmental impact of the proposed action, (2) discuss impacts that cannot be avoided, (3) discuss the alternatives to the proposed action, (4) indicate differences between short- and long-term impacts, and (5) detail any irreversible commitments of resources.

NEPA requires a federal agency to consider the environmental impact of a project before the project is undertaken. Other federal, state, and local agencies, as well as interested citizens, have an opportunity to comment on the environmental impact of a project before the agency can proceed. Where the process is not followed, citizens can and have gone to court to force compliance with NEPA. A number of states and local governments have passed their own environmental impact laws requiring NEPA-type statements for major public and private developments.

While the federal and state laws requiring the preparation of environmental impact statements appear directed at government actions, it is important to note that the government actions covered often include the granting of permits to private parties. Thus, businesspeople may readily find themselves involved in the preparation of an environmental impact statement—for example, in connection with a marina to be built in a navigable waterway or a resort development that will impact wetlands, both of which require permits from the U.S. Army Corps of Engineers. Similarly, a developer seeking a local zoning change so she can build a major commercial or residential development may find that she is asked to finance a study of the potential environmental impact of her proposed project.

AIR POLLUTION

Background

Fuel combustion, industrial processes, and solid waste disposal are the major contributors to air pollution. People's initial concern with air pollution related to what they could see—visible or smoke pollution. For instance, in the 1880s, Chicago and Cincinnati enacted smoke control ordinances. As the technology became available to deal with smoke and particulate emissions, attention focused on other, less visible gases that could adversely affect human health and vegetation, or that could increase the acidity of lakes, thus making them unsuitable for fish.

Clean Air Act

The first federal legislation came in 1955, when Congress authorized $5 million each year for air pollution research. While the federal role was modestly increased through intervening enactments, the comprehensive legislation enacted in 1970 and known as the **Clean Air Act** provides the basis for our present approach to air pollution control. In 1977, Congress modified the 1970 act and enacted provisions designed to prevent deterioration of the air in areas where its quality currently exceeds that required by federal law. Thirteen years then passed before Congress, in 1990, enacted a major revision to the act to deal with acid rain, air toxics, and urban smog problems that were not satisfactorily dealt with under the existing legislation.

Ambient Air Control Standards

The Clean Air Act established a comprehensive approach for dealing with air pollution. EPA is required to set **national ambient air quality standards** for the major pollutants that have an adverse impact on human health—that is, to regulate the amount of a given pollutant that may be present in the air around us. The ambient air quality standards are set at two levels: (1) **primary standards** are designed to protect the public's health from harm; and (2) **secondary standards** are designed to protect vegetation, materials, climate, visibility, and economic values. Pursuant to this statutory mandate, EPA has set national ambient air quality standards for carbon monoxide, nitrogen oxide, sulfur oxide, ozone, lead, and particulate matter.

Each state is required to develop a **state implementation plan** for meeting national ambient air quality standards. This necessitates an inventory of the various sources of air pollution and their contribution to the total air pollution in the air quality region. The major emitters of pollutants are then required to reduce their emissions to a level that ensures that overall air quality meets the national standards. For example, a factory may be required to limit its emissions of volatile organic compounds (a contributor to ozone or smog) to a certain amount per unit of production or hour of operation; similarly, a power plant might have its emissions of sulfur oxides and nitrogen oxides limited to so many pounds per Btu of energy produced. The states have the responsibility for selecting which activities must be regulated or curtailed so that overall emissions at any point in the state or area do not exceed the national standards.

Because by the late 1980s many of the nation's major urban areas were still not in compliance with the health-based standards for ozone and carbon monoxide, Congress, in its 1990 amendments, imposed an additional set of requirements on the areas that were not in compliance. Thus, citizens living in the areas and existing businesses, as well as prospective businesses seeking to locate in the designated areas, face increasingly stringent control measures designed to bring the areas into attainment with the national standards. These new requirements will mean that businesses such as bakeries that are generally not thought of as major polluters of the air will have to further control their emissions, and that paints and other products that contain solvents may have to be reformulated.

Acid Rain Controls

Responding to the 1970 Clean Air Act, which sought to protect the air in the area near sources of air pollution, many electric generating facilities built tall smokestacks so that the emissions were dispersed over a broader area. Unwittingly, this contributed to long-range transport of some of the pollutants, which changed chemically enroute and fell to earth many miles away in the form of acid rain, snow, fog, or dry deposition. For a number of years, a considerable debate ensued over acid rain, in particular as to whether it was a problem, what kind of damage it caused, whether anything should be done about it, and who should pay for the cost of limiting it. The 1990 amendments address acid deposition by, among other things, placing a cap on the overall emissions of the contributors to it (the oxides of sulfur and nitrogen) and requiring electric utilities to reduce their emissions to specified levels in two steps over the next decade. This will require most electric generating facilities in the country to install large control devices known as scrubbers, to switch to lower sulfur coal, or to install so-called clean coal technologies. The 1990 amendments also provide an innovative system whereby companies whose emissions are cleaner than required by law can sell their rights to emit more sulfur oxide— known as *allowances*—to other companies that may be finding it more difficult to meet the standards.

Control of Air Toxics

The 1970 Clean Air Act also required EPA to regulate the emission of toxic air pollutants. Under this authority, EPA has only set standards for asbestos, beryllium, mercury, vinyl chloride, benzene, and radionuclides. Unhappy with the slow pace of regulation of toxic air pollutants, Congress in 1990 specified a list of 189 chemicals for which EPA is required to issue regulations requiring the installation of the maximum available control technology. The regulations are to be developed and the control technology installed by industry in phases over the next decade. Thus, while many toxic emissions have largely gone unregulated, that situation will change in the next few years. In addition, a number of chemical companies have announced they are voluntarily reducing their emissions of toxic chemicals to levels below those they are required to meet by law.

The case that follows, *United States v. Tzavah Urban Renewal Corp.*, involves the enforcement of an existing EPA regulation that controls the removal and disposal of asbestos and asbestos-containing material from buildings.

UNITED STATES V. TZAVAH URBAN RENEWAL CORP.
696 F. Supp. 1013 (D. N. J. 1988)

In August 1986, Tzavah Urban Renewal Corporation purchased from the city of Newark a building at 16 Park Place formerly known as the Old Military Park Hotel. While the buyer was given an opportunity to inspect the building, it was not informed by the city that the building was permeated with asbestos-containing material. At the time of the purchase, the building was in great disrepair and had been uninhabited for many years. Its proposed renovation was to be a major urban renewal project.

In June 1987, Tzavah contracted with Greer Industrial Corporation to "gut" the building. While the work was going on, an EPA inspector visited the site and concluded that the hotel was contaminated with asbestos. He observed Greer employees throwing asbestos-laced objects out of the windows of the building and noted an uncovered refuse pile next to the hotel that contained asbestos. The workers were not wetting the debris before heaving it out the windows and the refuse pile was also dry. As a result, asbestos dust was being released into the air. Although the hotel was located in a commercial district, there were private homes nearby.

Renovation of buildings contaminated with asbestos is regulated under the Clean Air Act. The EPA regulations require building owners or operators to notify EPA before commencing renovation or demolition and prescribe various procedures for storage and removal of the asbestos. Tzavah failed to provide the required notice or to comply with the procedures required. After being notified by EPA of the violation of the law, Tzavah stopped the demolition work, left the building unsecured, and left the waste piles dry and uncovered. EPA tried informally to get Tzavah to complete the work in accordance with the asbestos regulations; when Tzavah did not take action, EPA brought a lawsuit against Tzavah to do so.

Lechner, District Judge   As the facts reveal, the EPA has attempted to remedy the hazardous conditions at 16 Park Place for almost a year. Thus far, the Agency's efforts to assure full compliance with the National Emission Standard for Hazardous Air Pollutants (NESHAP) regulations have proved ineffective. Asbestos is still present at the facility and continues to pose a significant danger to the health of the community. In order to ensure that this danger is abated, the Government brought this action for injunctive relief pursuant to the Clean Air Act.

Defendants assert that an injunction is unnecessary because there is "no current renovation operation being conducted at 16 Park Place." This argument is based on a fundamental misinterpretation of the asbestos NESHAP. As the Government correctly points out, the NESHAP regulations are activated when demolition or renovation begins and remain in effect until the facility has been rid of the dangers posed by asbestos dust. To permit a building owner to commence renovation and when asbestos is discovered, simply discontinue work with impunity, defies the purpose and logic of the statute. The procedures for asbestos emissions control and the waste disposal provisions of the regulations anticipate that once asbestos is identified, it will be rendered non-hazardous by proper disposal. Defendants cannot circumvent the affirmative obligation imposed upon them by federal law and simply walk away from the Park Place project. Indeed, the defendants' numerous efforts at compliance underscore their awareness of this responsibility.

Motion granted enjoining the defendants to secure the facility, properly dispose of the asbestos containing material, and to comply with the EPA's orders.

New Source Controls

The Clean Air Act requires that new stationary sources such as factories and power plants install the best available technology for reducing air pollution. EPA is required to establish the standards to be met by new stationary sources and has done so for the major stationary sources of air pollution. This means that a new facility covered by the regulations must install state-of-the-art control technology, even if it is locating in an area where the air quality is much better than that required by law. Two major policy objectives underlie this requirement: (1) providing a level playing field for new industry irrespective of where it locates and (2) gradually improving air quality by requiring state-of-the-art controls whenever a new facility is built.

Enforcement

The primary responsibility for enforcing air quality standards lies with the states, but the federal government has the right to enforce the standards where the states fail to do so. The Clean Air Act also provides for suits by citizens to force industry or the government to fully comply with the act's provisions.

Automobile Pollution

The Clean Air Act provides specifically for air pollution controls on transportation sources such as automobiles. The major pollutants from automobiles are carbon monoxide, hydrocarbons, and nitrogen oxides. Carbon monoxide is a colorless, odorless gas that can dull mental performance and even cause death when inhaled in large quantities. Hydrocarbons, in the form of unburned fuel, are part of a category of air pollutants known as volatile organic compounds (VOCs). VOCs combine with nitrogen oxides under the influence of sunlight to become ozone—we know it as smog.

The 1970 Clean Air Act required a reduction of 90 percent of the carbon monoxide and hydrocarbons emitted by automobiles by 1975 and a 90 percent reduction in the nitrogen oxides emitted by 1976. At the time, these requirements were "technology forcing"; that is, the manufacturers could not rely on already existing technology to meet the standards but rather had to develop new technology. Ultimately, most manufacturers had to go beyond simply making changes in engine design and utilize pollution control devices known as catalytic converters.

Subsequently, Congress addressed the question of setting even more stringent limits on automobile emissions while at the same time requiring that the new automobiles get better gas mileage. The 1990 amendments require further limitations on emissions from tailpipes, the development of so-called clean-fueled vehicles (such as electric and natural gas–fueled vehicles) for use in cities with dirty air, and the availability of oxygenated fuels (which are cleaner burning) in specified areas of the country that are having difficulty meeting the air quality limits at least part of the year. These new requirements have significant ramifications for the oil and automobile industries.

Under the Clean Air Act, no manufacturer may sell vehicles subject to emission standards without prior certification from EPA that the vehicles meet the required standards. The tests are performed on prototype vehicles, and if they pass, a certificate of conformity covering that type of engine and vehicle is issued. EPA subsequently can test vehicles on the assembly line to make sure that the production vehicles covered by the certificate are meeting the standards. The manufacturers are required to warrant that the vehicle, if properly maintained, will comply with the emission standards for its useful life. If EPA discovers that vehicles in actual use exceed the emission standards, it may order the manufacturer to recall and repair the defective models; this is a power that EPA has exercised on a number of occasions.

The act also provides for the regulation and registration of fuel additives such as lead. In the 1980s, lead was largely phased out of use as an octane enhancer in gasoline. As indicated previously, the 1990 amendments provide for the availability of alternative fuels based on ethanol and methanol.

International Air Problems

During the late 1970s and 1980s, concern developed that the release of chlorine-containing substances such as chlorofluorocarbons (CFCs) used in air conditioning, refrigeration, and certain foam products was depleting the stratospheric ozone layer. This could lead to more ultraviolet radiation reaching the earth and, in turn, more skin cancer. Subsequently, a number of nations, acting under the aegis of the United Nations, signed a treaty agreeing first to limit any increases in production of chlorine-containing substances and ultimately to significantly phase out their use. The 1990 amendments to the Clean Air Act implement the obligations of the United States under the treaty and provide for the phasedown and phaseout of a number of chlorofluorocarbons; accordingly, many businesses are trying to develop or locate substitutes for those chemicals that will be available only in reduced quantities, if at all.

Other air pollution issues with international dimensions that may result in multinational control efforts are acid rain and global warming/climate change, resulting, in part, from increased emissions of carbon dioxide to the atmosphere.

Indoor Air Pollution

As we increased the insulation and made our buildings airtight to conserve energy, we generally reduced the air exchange and increased the concentrations of pollutants in our homes and workplaces. In recent years, attention has focused on a range of indoor air problems, sometimes known under the term *sick building syndrome,* including radon gas, asbestos, the products of combustion from fireplaces and stoves, molds and pollens, formaldehyde, cigarette smoke, pesticides, and cleaning products. Some of these problems are being dealt with on a problem-by-problem, or product-by-product, basis under various laws. Others are being addressed by providing information to consumers so that they can take appropriate actions to protect themselves. In some cases, Congress and other legislative bodies have required that steps be taken to minimize the risks, such as the federal requirement for schools to inspect for asbestos and to remove it where certain conditions are found.

Radiation Control

In recent years, people have been concerned about radioactivity, particularly radioactivity from nuclear-fueled power plants. Some of these concerns were accentuated by the accident at Chernobyl in the former USSR and the one at Three Mile Island in the United States. Citizens are specifically concerned about the release of radioactivity into the environment during normal operation of the nuclear reactors, accidents through human error or mechanical failure, and disposal of the radioactive wastes generated by the reactors. They are also concerned that the discharge of heated water used to cool the reactor—thermal pollution—may cause damage to the environment. These issues are of particular concern to businesses such as utilites that operate nuclear-powered generating facilities and also to segments of the health industry—such as hospitals and other medical facilities—that may utilize low-level radioactive materials in their diagnostic and treatment activities.

Currently, the problems of reactor safety are under the jurisdiction of the Nuclear Regulatory Commission, which exercises licensing authority over nuclear power plants. EPA is responsible for setting standards for radioactivity in the overall environment and for dealing with the problem of disposal of some radioactive waste. EPA also handles the thermal pollution problem pursuant to its water pollution control authority. In addition, EPA is responsible for regulating emissions from a variety of other sources, such as uranium mill tailing piles and uranium mines.

WATER POLLUTION

Background

History is replete with plagues and epidemics brought on by poor sanitation and polluted water. Indeed, preventing waterborne disease has always been the major reason for combating water pollution. In the early 1970s, fishing and swimming were prohibited in many bodies of water, and game fish could no longer survive in some waters where they had formerly thrived. Lake Erie was becoming choked with algae and considered to be dying. The nation recognized that water pollution could affect public health, recreation, commercial fishing, agriculture, water supplies, and aesthetics. During the 1970s, Congress enacted three major statutes to protect our water resources: the Clean Water Act; the Marine Protection, Research, and Sanctuaries Act; and the Safe Drinking Water Act.

Early Federal Legislation

Federal water pollution legislation dates back to the 19th century when Congress enacted the River and Harbor Act of 1886. In fact, this statute, recodified in the River and Harbor Act of 1899, furnished the legal basis for EPA's initial enforcement actions against polluters. The act provided that people had to obtain a discharge permit from the Army Corps of Engineers to deposit or discharge refuse into a navigable waterway. Under some contemporary court decisions, even hot water discharged from nuclear power plants was considered refuse. The permit system established pursuant to the "Refuse Act" was replaced in 1972 by a more comprehensive permit system now administered by EPA.

Congress passed the initial Federal Water Pollution Control Act (FWPCA) in 1948. Amendments to the FWPCA in 1956, 1965, 1966, and 1970 increased the federal government's role in water pollution abatement and strengthened its enforcement powers.

Clean Water Act

The 1972 amendments to the FWPCA—now known as the **Clean Water Act**—were as comprehensive in the water pollution field as the 1970 Clean Air Act was in the air pollution field. They proclaimed two general goals for this country: (1) to achieve wherever possible by July 1, 1983, water clean enough for swimming and other recreational uses and clean enough for the protection and propagation of fish, shellfish, and wildlife; and (2) to have no discharges of pollutants into the nation's waters by 1985. These goals reflected a national frustration with the lack of progress in dealing with water pollution and a commitment to end such pollution. The new law set out a series of specific actions that federal, state, and local governments and industry were to take by certain dates and also provided strong enforcement provisions to back up the deadlines. In 1977 and again in 1987, Congress modified the 1972 act by adjusting some of the deadlines and otherwise fine-tuning the act.

State Role

Under the Clean Water Act, the states have the primary responsibility for preventing, reducing, and eliminating water pollution. The states have to do this within a national framework, and EPA is empowered to move in if the states do not fulfill their responsibilities.

Controls on Industrial Wastes

The act set a number of deadlines to control water pollution from industrial sources. It required industries discharging wastes into the nation's waterways to install the *best available water pollution control technology;* new sources of industrial pollution must use the best available demonstrated control technology. In each instance, EPA is responsible for issuing guidelines as to the best available technologies. Industries that discharge their wastes into municipal systems are required to *pretreat* the wastes so that they do not interfere with the biological operation of the plant or pass through the plant without treatment.

Water Quality Standards

The act continued and expanded the previously established system of setting *water quality standards* by designating the uses of specific bodies of water for recreation, public water supply, propagation of fish and wildlife, and agricultural and industrial water supply. Then, the maximum daily loads of various pollutants are set so that the water is suitable for the designated use.

Discharge Permits

The act requires all municipal and industrial dischargers to obtain permits—known as an *NPDES permit* or National Pollution Discharge Elimination System permit—that spell out the amounts and specific pollutants that permit holders are allowed to discharge and any steps that they must take to reduce their present or anticipated discharge. Dischargers are also required to keep records, install and maintain monitoring equipment, and sample their discharges.

Enforcement

Both civil and criminal sanctions are included in the act. Criminal penalties for violating the law range from a minimum of $2,500 for a first offense up to $50,000 per day and two years in prison for subsequent violations. The act is enforced by federal and state governments. In addition, any citizen or group of citizens whose interests are adversely affected has the right to bring a court action against anyone violating an effluent standard, limitation, or order issued by EPA or a state. A significant number of cases have been brought by citizen-action groups against firms whose wastewater discharges exceeded the limits of their discharge permits. Citizens also have the right to take court action against EPA if it fails to carry out mandatory provisions of the law.

Wetlands

Another aspect of the Clean Water Act having the potential to affect businesses as well as individual property owners is the wetlands provision. Commonly, wetlands are transition zones between land and open water. Under Section 404 of the act, any *dredging* or *filling* activity in a wetland that is connected to the waters of the United States—as well as in any water of the United States—requires a permit before any activity begins. The permit program is administered by the Army Corps of Engineers, with the involvement of the Environmental Protection Agency.

As can be seen in the *Bersani v. U.S. Environmental Protection Agency* case, which follows, the permit requirement can significantly limit a landowner's use of his property where the fill activity is viewed as injurious to the values protected by the act.

BERSANI V. U.S. ENVIRONMENTAL PROTECTION AGENCY
674 F. Supp. 405 (N.D.N.Y. 1987) aff'd 395 F.2d 36 (2d Cir. 1988)

Pyramid Companies was an association of partnerships that was in the business of developing, constructing, and operating shopping centers; John Bersani was a principal in one of the partnerships. In 1983, Pyramid became interested in developing a shopping mall in the Attleboro, Massachusetts, area and focused its attention on an 82-acre site known as Sweeden's Swamp along an interstate highway in South Attleboro. The project contemplated altering or filling some 32 acres of the 49.6 acres of wetlands on the property. At the same time, Pyramid planned to excavate 9 acres of uplands (nonwetlands) to create new wetlands and to alter some 13 acres of existing wetlands to enhance their value for fish and wildlife.

In 1984, Pyramid applied to the U.S. Army Corps of Engineers for a permit under Section 404 of the Clean Water Act to do the dredge and fill work in the wetlands. As part of its application, it was required to submit information on practicable alternative sites for its shopping mall. One site subsequently focused on by the Corps and the Environmental Protection Agency was about three miles north in North Attleboro. Pyramid relied on several factors in claiming that the site was not a practicable alternative to its proposed site—namely, the site lacked sufficient traffic volume and access from local roads, potential department store tenants had expressed doubts about the feasibility of the site, and previous attempts to develop the site had met with strong resistance from the surrounding community. However, after Pyramid examined the site, another major developer of shopping centers had taken an option to acquire the property.

The New England division engineer of the Corps recommended that the permit be denied because a practicable alternative with a less adverse effect on the environment existed. The chief of engineers directed that the permit be issued, noting that the alternative site was not available to Pyramid because it was owned by a competitor. He also believed that even if it was considered available, Pyramid had made a convincing case that the site would not fulfill its objectives for a successful project. EPA then exercised its prerogative under the Clean Water Act to veto the permit on the grounds that filling Sweeden's Swamp to build the shopping mall would have an unacceptable adverse effect on the environment. In its view, another less environmentally damaging site had been available to Pyramid at the time it made its site selection; thus, any adverse effects on Sweeden's Swamp were avoidable. Bersani and Pyramid then brought suit challenging the denial of its permit application.

McAvo, Judge   Section 404(a) authorizes the Secretary of the Army, acting through the Corps, to issue permits for the discharge of dredged or fill material at specified disposal sites. Criteria developed by the EPA in conjunction with the Corps govern these permitting decisions. Generally, the Corps must employ a "practicable alternative" analysis in determining whether to allow a proposed discharge. Section 230.10 of the regulations provides:

(a) . . . no discharge of dredged or fill material shall be permitted if there is a practicable alternative to the proposed discharge which would have less adverse impact on the aquatic ecosystem, so long as the alternative does not have other significant adverse environmental consequences.

* * * * *

(2) An alternative is practicable if it is available and capable of being done, after taking into account cost, existing technology, and logistics in light of overall project purposes. If it is otherwise a practicable alternative, an area not presently owned by the applicant which could reasonably be obtained, utilized, expanded or managed in order to fulfill the basic purpose of the proposed activity may be considered.

(3) Where the activity associated with a discharge which is proposed for a special aquatic site (including a wetland) does not require access or proximity to or siting within the special aquatic site in question to fulfill its basic purpose (i.e., is not "water dependent"), practicable alternatives that do not involve special aquatic sites are presumed to be available unless clearly demonstrated otherwise. In addition, where a discharge is proposed for a special aquatic site, all

practicable alternatives to the proposed discharge which do not involve a discharge into a special aquatic site are presumed to have less adverse impact on the aquatic ecosystem, unless clearly demonstrated otherwise.

Where the proposed discharge involves a special aquatic site such as wetlands, a more stringent standard is imposed. Indeed Section 230.10(a) (3) creates a presumption that a practicable alternative exists when the discharge involves wetlands and the activity, here a shopping mall, is not "water dependent." Then the applicant must "clearly demonstrate" that no such alternative does in fact exist.

Pyramid argues that EPA's determination of feasibility was based on its erroneous conclusion that the marketplace considered the North Attleboro site suitable for a virtually identical regional shopping mall. Pyramid notes that six other shopping center developers over the past fifteen years have tried and failed to develop the North Attleboro site as a shopping center. It contends that EPA has substituted its own judgment for that of the marketplace in an area in which it cannot claim expertise.

The EPA, however, contends that it did not simply substitute its judgment for that of the developer. Instead, the EPA argues that the evidence on the record demonstrates that the North Attleboro site is suitable in fact for a regional shopping center mall virtually identical to that proposed by Pyramid. In this respect, the fact that a competing developer, the New England Development Company, had found the site suitable for a similar shopping mall, and its own marketing analysis weighed in reaching this decision. The EPA also engaged in a review of the specific features that Pyramid found objectionable; namely, the distance from the primary trade area, lack of visibility from nearby highways, zoning, past failures of prior attempts to develop a shopping mall at the site, and various considerations. Consequently, the court finds that EPA's feasibility determination was not arbitrary.

Summary judgment granted for EPA.

Ocean Dumping

The **Marine Protection, Research, and Sanctuaries Act of 1972** set up a permit system regulating the dumping of all types of materials into ocean waters. EPA has the responsibility for designating disposal sites and for establishing the rules governing ocean disposal. The Ocean Dumping Ban Act of 1987 required that all ocean dumping of municipal sewage sludge and industrial wastes be terminated by December 31, 1991. Thus, the major remaining questions of ocean dumping concern the disposal of dredge spoils from dredging to keep harbors open.

Drinking Water

In 1974, Congress passed, and in 1986 amended, the **Safe Drinking Water Act,** which is designed to protect and enhance the quality of our drinking water. Under the act, EPA sets *primary drinking water standards,* minimum levels of quality for water consumed by humans. The act also establishes a program governing the injection of wastes into wells. The primary responsibility for complying with the federally established standards lies with the states. Where the states fail to enforce the drinking water standards, the federal government has the right to enforce them.

Waste Disposal

Background

Historically, concern about the environment focused on decreasing air and water pollution as well as protecting natural resources and wildlife. People paid relatively little attention to the disposal of wastes on land. Until the early 1970s, much of the solid and hazardous waste generated was disposed of in open dumps and landfills. Although some of the waste we produce can be disposed of without presenting significant health or environmental problems, some industrial, agricultural, and mining wastes—and even some household wastes—are hazardous and can present serious problems. Unless wastes are properly disposed of, they can cause air, water, and land pollution as well as contamination of the underground aquifers from which much of our drinking water is drawn. Once aquifers have been contaminated, they can take a very long time to cleanse themselves of pollutants.

In the 1970s, the discovery of abandoned dump sites such as Love Canal in New York and the Valley of the Drums in Kentucky heightened public concern about the disposal of toxic and hazardous wastes. Congress has enacted several laws regulating the generation and disposal of hazardous waste: The Resource Conservation and Recovery Act mandates proper management and disposal of wastes currently generated; and the Comprehensive Environmental Response, Compensation, and Liability Act focuses on cleaning up past disposal sites threatening public health and the environment.

The Resource Conservation and Recovery Act

Congress originally enacted the **Resource Conservation and Recovery Act** (RCRA) in 1976 and significantly amended it in 1984. RCRA provides the federal government and the states with the authority to regulate facilities that generate, treat, store, and dispose of hazardous waste. Most of the wastes defined as hazardous are subject to a cradle-to-the-grave tracking system and must be handled and disposed of in defined ways. RCRA requires persons who generate, treat, store, or transport specified quantities of hazardous waste to obtain permits, meet certain standards and follow specified procedures in the handling of the wastes, and keep records. In addition, operators of land waste disposal facilities must meet financial responsibility requirements and monitor groundwater quality. EPA determines whether certain wastes should be banned entirely from land disposal; a significant number of wastes must be treated before they can be disposed of in land disposal units.

Underground Storage Tanks

In 1984, Congress directed that EPA also regulate underground product storage tanks such as gasoline tanks to prevent and respond to leaks that might contaminate underground water. The regulations that EPA issued to implement these requirements impose significant costs on many businesses such as gasoline stations that utilize such storage tanks.

State Responsibilities

EPA sets minimum requirements for state RCRA programs and then delegates the responsibility for conducting programs to the states when they have the legal ability and interest to administer them. Until a state assumes partial or complete responsibility for a RCRA program, the federal government administers the program.

Enforcement

Failure to comply with the hazardous waste regulations promulgated under RCRA can subject violators to civil and criminal penalties. In the *United States v. Dean* case, which follows, an employee of a company that disposed of hazardous waste without a RCRA permit was held criminally liable.

UNITED STATES V. DEAN
969 F.2d 187 (6th Cir. 1992)

General Metal Fabricators, Inc. (GMF), owned and operated a facility in Erwin, Tennessee, that was engaged in metal stamping, plating, and painting. The facility utilized hazardous chemicals and generated hazardous waste but did not have a RCRA permit nor did it maintain the required records of the treatment, storage, and disposal of hazardous substances. The hazardous waste disposal practices at GMF were discovered by chance by state waste-management authorities whose attention was caught, while driving to an appointment at another facility, by two 55-gallon drums abandoned among weeds on GMF's property.

The owners of GMF, Joseph and Jean Sanchez, as well as Clyde Griffith, the plant manager, and Gale Dean, the production manager, were indicted for conspiracy to violate RCRA, and, individually, for violations of various sections of RCRA. At his request, Dean's trial was severed from that of the other defendants.

As production manager, Dean had day-to-day supervision of GMF's production process and employees. Among his duties was the instruction of employees on hazardous waste handling and disposal. Numerous practices at GMF violated RCRA. GMF's plating operations utilized rinse baths, contaminated with hazardous chemicals, which were drained through a pipe into an earthen lagoon outside the facility. In addition, Dean instructed employees to shovel various kinds of solid wastes from the tanks into 55-gallon drums. Dean ordered the construction of a pit, concealed behind the facility, into which 38 drums of such hazardous waste were tossed. The contents spilled onto the soil from open or corroded drums. Chemical analyses of soil and solid wastes revealed that the pit and the lagoon were contaminated with chromium. In addition, the pit was contaminated with toluene and xylene solvents. All of these substances are considered hazardous under RCRA. Drums of spent chromic acid solution were also illegally stored on the premises.

Dean was familiar with the chemicals used in each of the tanks on the production line and with the manner in which the contents of the rinse tanks were deposited in the lagoon. Material Safety Data Sheets (MSDS) provided to GMF by the chemical manufacturer clearly stated that the various chemicals in use at GMF were hazardous and were subject to federal pollution control laws. Dean was familiar with the MSDS and knowledgeable about their contents. The MSDS delivered with the chromic acid made specific reference to

RCRA and to related EPA regulations. Dean told investigators that he "had read this RCRA waste code but thought it was a bunch of bullshit."

Dean was convicted of conspiracy to violate RCRA as well as of (1) failure to file documentation of hazardous waste generation, storage, and disposal, (2) storage of spent chromic acid without a permit, (3) disposal of chromic acid rinse water and sludges in a lagoon without a permit, and (4) disposal of paint sludge and solvent wastes in a pit without a permit, all in violation of RCRA. Dean appealed his conviction.

Joiner, Senior District Judge   The first of the issues raised by Dean is that the trial court erred in denying his motion for acquittal on the permit-related counts because there was no evidence that Dean knew of RCRA's permit requirement. Dean's characterization of the evidence is inaccurate, but moreover, we see no basis on the face of the statute for concluding that knowledge of the permit requirement is an element of the crime. The statute penalizes:

Any person who— . . . (2) knowingly treats, stores or disposes of any hazardous waste identified or listed under this subchapter—(A) without a permit under this subchapter . . . ; or (B) in knowing violation of any material condition or requirement of such permit; or (C) in knowing violation of any applicable interim status or regulations. 42 U.S.C. section 6928(d)(2).

Dean was convicted of violating subsection 6928(d)(2)(A).

The question of interpretation presented by this provision is the familiar one of how far the initial "knowingly" travels. Other courts of appeals have divided on this question. We agree with the reasoning of the Court of Appeals for the Ninth Circuit in *United States v. Hoflin.* The "knowingly" which begins section 6928(d)(2) cannot be read as extending to the subsections without rendering nugatory the word "knowing" contained in subsections 6928(d)(2)(B) and (C). Subsection 6928(d)(2)(A) requires knowing treatment (or knowing storage, or knowing disposal) of hazardous waste. It also requires proof that the treatment, storage or disposal was done without a permit. It does not require that the person charged must have known that a permit was required, and that knowledge is not relevant.

Dean also contends that the district court should have granted his motion for acquittal because subsection 6928(d)(2)(A) was not intended to reach employees who are not "owners" or "operators" of facilities. By its terms, the provision applies to "any person." "Person" is a defined term meaning "an individual. . . ." Dean would be hard pressed to convince the court that he is not an "individual." He argues, however, that because only owners and operators of facilities are required to obtain permits, the penalty imposed for hazardous waste handling without a permit must apply only to owners and operators.

This contention is unpersuasive for numerous reasons. Of primary importance is the fact that it is contrary to the unambiguous language of the statute.

Affirmed.

Solid Waste

Mining, commercial, and household activities generate a large volume of waste material that can present problems if not properly disposed. As population density has increased, causing a corresponding increase in the total volume of waste, it has become more difficult to find land or incinerators where the waste material can be disposed of properly. RCRA authorizes EPA to set minimum standards for such disposal, but states and local governments bear the primary responsibility for the siting and regulation of such activity.

As the cost and difficulty of disposing of waste increases, public attention focuses on reducing the waste to be disposed, on looking for opportunities to recycle some of the waste material, and on changing the characteristics of the material that must ultimately be disposed of so that it poses fewer environmental problems. One of the significant challenges faced by tomorrow's businessperson will be in designing products, packaging, and production processes so as to minimize the waste products that result.

A significant problem for both government and industry is the difficulty in trying to site new waste facilities. The NIMBY, or not-in-my-backyard syndrome, is pervasive as people almost universally desire to have the wastes from their everyday lives and from the economic activity in their community disposed of in someone else's neighborhood—any place but their own. As governments try to cope with the reality of finding places to dispose of wastes in an environmentally safe manner and at the same time cope with public opposition to siting new facilities, the temptation is strong to try to bar wastes from other areas from being disposed of in local facilities.

In the landmark case, *City of Philadelphia v. New Jersey,* the U.S. Supreme Court struck down an attempt by the state of New Jersey to prohibit the importation of most solid waste originating outside the state. An ironic twist is that more than a decade later, we find a number of other eastern and midwestern states trying to find ways to block the importation of wastes from New Jersey into their states. In recent years, the Supreme Court has had the occasion to reiterate its holding in *City of Philadelphia v. New Jersey* in a series of new cases involving efforts by states to block or limit the flow of solid and hazardous waste from outside their state to disposal sites within the state. One of the most recent cases in this series of cases, *Fort Gratiot Sanitary Landfill, Inc. v. Michigan Department of Natural Resources,* follows.

FORT GRATIOT SANITARY LANDFILL, INC. v. MICHIGAN DEPARTMENT OF NATURAL RESOURCES
112 S.Ct. 2019 (1992)

In 1978, Michigan enacted its Solid Waste Management Act (SWMA) that required every Michigan county to estimate the amount of solid waste that would be generated in the county in the next 20 years and to adopt a plan providing for its disposal at facilities that comply with state health standards. After holding public hearings, the St. Clair County Board of Commissioners adopted a solid waste plan for the St. Clair County. In 1987, the Michigan Department of Natural Resources issued a permit to Fort Gratiot Sanitary Landfill, Inc., to operate a sanitary landfill as a solid waste disposal area in the county. In December 1988, the Michigan legislature amended the SWMA by adopting two provisions concerning the "acceptance of waste or ash generated outside the county of disposal area." The new provisions, which were effective immediately, prohibited the acceptance of out-of-county wastes unless the acceptance of such waste was explicitly authorized in the approved county solid waste management plan.

In February 1989, Fort Gratiot submitted an application to the St. Clair County Solid Waste Planning Committee for authority to accept up to 1,750 tons per day of out-of-state waste at its landfill. In the application Fort Gratiot promised to reserve sufficient capacity to dispose of all solid waste generated in the county in the next 20 years. The planning committee denied the application. Because the county's management plan did not authorize the acceptance of any out-of-county waste, Fort Gratiot was effectively prevented from receiving any solid waste that did not originate in St. Clair County.

Fort Gratiot then brought a lawsuit seeking a judgment declaring that the waste import restrictions violated the Commerce Clause of the U.S. Constitution and thus were unconstitutional, and enjoining their enforcement. Fort Gratiot contended that requiring a private landfill operator to limit its business to the acceptance of local waste constituted impermissible discrimination against interstate commerce. The District Court dismissed the lawsuit. It concluded, first, that the statute did not discriminate against interstate commerce because the limitation applied equally to Michigan counties outside the county as well as to out-of-state waste. It also noted that each county had discretion to accept out-of-state waste, and that any incidental burden on interstate commerce was not excessive in relation to the public health and environmental benefits derived by Michigan from the statute. The Court of Appeals affirmed the ruling, and Fort Gratiot appealed to the U.S. Supreme Court.

———————————— ■ ————————————

Stevens, Justice   In *Philadelphia v. New Jersey* (1978) we held that a New Jersey law prohibiting the importation of most "solid or liquid waste which originated or was collected outside the territorial limits of the State" violated the Commerce Clause of the United States Constitution. In this case petitioner challenges a Michigan law that prohibits private landfill operators from accepting solid waste that originates outside the county in which their facilities are located. Adhering to our holding in the New Jersey case we conclude that this Michigan statute is also unconstitutional.

Philadelphia v. New Jersey provides the framework for our analysis of this case. Solid waste, even if it has no value, is an article of commerce. Whether the business arrangements between out-of-state generators of waste and the Michigan operator of a waste disposal site are viewed as "sales" of garbage or "purchases" of transportation and disposal services, the commercial transactions unquestionably have an interstate character. The Commerce Clause thus imposes some constraints on Michigan's ability to regulate these transactions.

As we have long recognized, the "negative" or "dormant" aspect of the Commerce Clause prohibits States from advancing their own commercial interests by curtailing the movement of articles or commerce, either into or out of the state. A state statute that clearly discriminates against interstate commerce is therefore unconstitutional unless the discrimination is demonstrably justified by a valid factor unrelated to economic protectionism.

The Waste Import Restrictions enacted by Michigan authorize each of its 83 counties to isolate itself from the national economy. Indeed, unless a county acts affirmatively to permit other waste to enter its jurisdiction, the statute affords local waste producers complete protection from competition from out-of-state waste producers who seek to use local waste disposal areas. In view of the fact that Michigan has not identified any reason, apart from its origin, why solid waste coming from outside the county should be treated differently from solid waste within the county, the foregoing reasoning would appear to control the disposition of this case.

Michigan and St. Clair County assert that the Waste Import Restrictions are necessary because they enable individual counties to make adequate plans for the safe disposal of future waste. Although accurate forecasts about the volume and composition of future waste flows may be an indispensable part of a comprehensive waste disposal plan, Michigan could attain that objective without discriminating between in- and out-of-state waste. Michigan could, for example, limit the amount of waste that landfill operators may accept each year. There is, however, no valid health and safety reason for limiting the amount of waste that a landfill operator may accept from outside the State, but not the amount that the operator may accept from inside the State. Of course our conclusion would be different if the imported waste raised health or other concerns not presented by Michigan waste.

For the foregoing reasons, the Waste Import Restrictions unambiguously discriminate against interstate commerce and are appropriately characterized as protectionist measures that cannot withstand scrutiny under the Commerce Clause.

Judgment of the Court of Appeals is reversed.

Rehnquist, Chief Justice (dissenting)   When confronted with a dormant Commerce Clause challenge, "the crucial inquiry must be directed to determining whether the challenged statute is basically a protectionist measure, or whether it can fairly be viewed as a law directed to legitimate local concerns with effects on interstate commerce that are only incidental. Because I think the Michigan statute is at least arguably directed to legitimate local concerns, rather than improper economic protectionism, I would remand this case for further proceedings.

The substantial environmental, aesthetic, health, and safety problems flowing from this country's waste piles were already apparent at the time we decided *Philadelphia*. Those problems have only risen in the intervening years. In part, this is due to increased waste volumes, volumes that are expected to continue to rise in the foreseeable future. It is no secret why capacity is not expanding sufficiently to meet the demand—the substantial risks attendant to waste sites make them extraordinarily unattractive neighbors. The result, of course, is that while many are willing to generate waste—indeed it is a practical impossibility to solve the waste problem by banning waste production—few are willing to help dispose of it. Those locales that do provide disposal capacity to serve foreign waste effectively are affording reduced environmental and safety risks to the States that will not take charge of their own waste.

The State of Michigan has stepped into this quagmire in order to address waste problems generated by its own populace. It has done so by adopting a comprehensive approach to the disposal of solid wastes generated within its borders. The legislation challenged today is simply one part of a broad package that includes a number of features: a state-mandated state-wide effort to control and plan for waste disposal; requirements that local units of government participate in the planning process; restrictions to assure safe transport; a ban on the operation of a waste disposal facility unless various design and technical requirements are satisfied and appropriate permits obtained; and commitments to promote source separation, composting, and recycling. The Michigan legislation is thus quite unlike the simple outright ban that we confronted in *Philadelphia*.

In adopting this legislation, the Michigan Legislature also appears to have concluded that, like the State, counties should reap as they have sown—hardly a novel proposition. It has accomplished this by prohibiting waste facilities from accepting waste generated from outside the county, unless special permits are obtained. In the process, of course, this facially neutral restriction (i.e., it applies equally to interstate and intrastate waste) also works to ban disposal from out-of-state sources unless appropriate permits are procurred. But I cannot agree that such a requirement, when imposed as one part of a comprehensive approach to regulating in this difficult field is the stuff of which economic protectionism is made.

Michigan has limited the ability of its own population to despoil the environment and to create health and safety risks by excessive and uncontrolled waste disposal. It does not thereby violate the Commerce Clause when it seeks to prevent this resource from being exported—the result if Michigan is forced to accept foreign waste in its disposal facilities.

The Court today penalizes the State of Michigan for what to all appearances are its good-faith efforts, in turn encouraging each State to ignore the waste problem in the hope that another will pick up the slack. The Court's approach fails to recognize that the latter option is quite real and quite attractive for many States—and becomes even more so when the intermediate option of solving its own problems, but only its own problems, is eliminated.

Superfund

In 1980, Congress passed the **Comprehensive Environmental Response Compensation and Liability Act** (CERCLA), commonly known as Superfund, to deal with the problem of uncontrolled or abandoned hazardous waste sites. In 1986, it strengthened and expanded the law. Under the Superfund law, EPA identified and assessed the sites in the United States where hazardous wastes had been spilled, stored, or abandoned.

Eventually, EPA expects to identify 30,000 such sites. The sites are ranked on the basis of the type, quantity, and toxicity of the wastes; the number of people potentially exposed to the wastes; the differ-

ent ways (e.g., in the air or drinking water) in which they might be exposed; the risks to contamination of aquifers; and other factors. The sites with the highest ranking are put on the National Priority List to receive priority federal and/or state attention for cleanup. At these sites, EPA makes careful scientific and engineering studies to determine the most appropriate cleanup plans. Once a site has been cleaned up, the state is responsible for managing it to prevent future environmental problems. EPA also has the authority to quickly initiate actions at hazardous waste sites—whether or not the site is on the priority list—to address imminent hazards such as the risk of fire, explosion, or contamination of drinking water.

The federal cleanup activity is financed primarily by a tax on chemicals and feedstocks. However, EPA is authorized to require that a site be cleaned up by those persons responsible for contaminating it, either as the owner or operator of the site, a transporter of wastes to the site, or the owner of wastes deposited at the site. Where EPA expends money to clean up a site, it has the legal authority to recover its costs from those who were responsible for the problem. The courts have held that such persons are "jointly and severally responsible for the cost of cleanup." Chapter 7, Negligence and Strict Liability, discusses the concept of joint liability.

The *Chem-Dyne* case, which follows, involves a challenge to the concept of joint and several liability by the contributors to a major hazardous waste site. Of concern to many businesspeople is the fact that this stringent and potentially very expensive liability can in some instances be imposed on a current owner of a site who had nothing to do with the contamination, such as a subsequent purchaser of the land or even a bank that financed the purchase of the property and subsequently took it over when the purchaser defaulted on its obligation to the bank.

UNITED STATES V. CHEM-DYNE CORP.
572 F. Supp. 802 (S.D. Ohio 1983)

The United States brought a lawsuit under the Comprehensive Environmental Response, Compensation, and Liability Act (CERCLA) against 24 defendants who had allegedly generated or transported some of the hazardous substances located at the Chem-Dyne treatment facility in Ohio. The government sought to be reimbursed for money that it had spent in cleaning up hazardous wastes at the facility and asserted that each defendant was jointly and severally liable for the entire cost of the cleanup. The defendants contested the claim that they were jointly and severally liable and moved for summary judgment in their favor on this issue.

Rubin, Chief Judge CERCLA was enacted both to provide rapid responses to the nationwide threats posed by the 30,000–50,000 improperly managed hazardous waste sites in this country as well as to induce voluntary responses to those sites. The legislation established a $1.6 billion trust fund ("Superfund"), drawn from industry and federal appropriations, to finance the clean-up and containment efforts. The state or federal government may then pursue rapid recovery of the costs incurred from persons liable to reimburse the Superfund money expended. This recovery task may prove difficult when several companies used a site, when dumped chemicals react with others to form new or more toxic substances, or when records are unavailable. Nevertheless, those responsible for the problems caused by the hazardous wastes were intended to bear the costs and responsibilities for remedying the condition. The House sponsor, Representative Florio, commented at length:

The liability provisions of this bill do not refer to the terms strict, joint and several liability, terms which were contained in the version of H.R. 7020 passed earlier by this body. The standard of liability in these amendments is intended to be strict liability. . . . I have concluded that despite the absence of these specific terms, the strict liability standard already approved by this body is preserved. Issues of joint and several liability not resolved by this bill shall be governed by traditional and evolving principles of common law. The terms "joint and several" have been deleted with the intent that the liability of joint tortfeasors be determined under common or previous statutory law.

Typically, as in this case, there will be numerous hazardous substance generators or transporters who have disposed of wastes at a particular site. The term joint and several liability was deleted from the express language of the statute in order to avoid its universal application to inappropriate circumstances. An examination of the common law reveals that when two or more persons acting independently cause a distinct or single harm for which there is a reasonable basis for division according to the contribution of each, each is subject to liability only for the portion of the total harm that he has himself caused. But where two or more persons cause a single and indivisible harm, each is subject to liability for the entire harm. Restatement (Second) of Torts, § 875. Furthermore, where the conduct of two or more persons liable under CERCLA has combined to violate the statute, and one or more of the defendants seek to limit their liability on the ground that the entire harm is capable of apportionment, the burden of proof as to apportionment is upon each defendant.

The question of whether the defendants are jointly or severally liable for the clean-up costs turns on a fairly complex factual determination. Read in the light most favorable to the United States, the following facts illustrate the nature of the problem. The Chem-Dyne facility contains a variety of hazardous waste from 289 generators or transporters, consisting of about 608,000 pounds of material. Some of the wastes have been commingled, but the identities of the sources of these wastes remain unascertained. The fact of the mixing of the wastes raises an issue as to the divisibility of the harm. Further, a dispute exists over which of the wastes have contaminated the groundwater, the de-

gree of their migration, and the concomitant health hazard. Finally, the volume of waste of a particular generator is not an accurate predictor of the risk associated with the waste because the toxicity or migratory potential of a particular hazardous substance generally varies independently with the volume of the waste.

This case, as do most pollution cases, turns on the issue of whether the harm caused at Chem-Dyne is "divisible" or "indivisible." If the harm is divisible and if there is a reasonable basis for apportionment of damages, each defendant is liable only for the portion of harm he himself caused. In this situation, the burden of proof as to apportionment is upon each defendant. On the other hand, if the defendants caused an indivisible harm, each is subject to liability for the entire harm. The defendants have not carried their burden of demonstrating the divisibility of the harm and the degrees to which each defendant is responsible.

Defendants' motion for summary judgment is denied.

Community Right to Know and Emergency Cleanup

As part of its 1986 amendments to Superfund, Congress enacted a series of requirements for emergency planning, notification of spills and accidents involving hazardous materials, disclosure by industry to the community of the presence of certain listed chemicals, and notification of the amounts of various chemicals being routinely released into the environment in the area of a facility. This legislation was in response to the industrial accident at Bhopal, India, in 1984 and to several similar incidents in the United States. Firms subject to the requirements have to carefully plan how they will communicate with the surrounding community what chemicals are being regularly released and what precautions the facility has taken to protect the community from regular or accidental releases. Mindful of the difficulty of explaining to a community why large emissions of hazardous substances are taking place, a significant number of companies have undertaken to reduce those emissions below levels they are currently required to meet by law.

REGULATION OF CHEMICALS

Background

More than 60,000 chemical substances are manufactured in the United States and used in a variety of products. Although these chemicals contribute much to the standard of living we enjoy, some of them are toxic or have the potential to cause cancer, birth defects, reproductive failures, and other health-related problems. These risks may be posed in the manufacturing process, during the use of a product, or as a result of the manner of disposal of the chemical or product.

EPA has two statutory authorities that give it the ability to prevent or restrict the manufacture and use of new and existing chemicals to remove unreasonable risks to human health or the environment. These authorities are the Federal Insecticide, Fungicide, and Rodenticide Act and the Toxic Substances Control Act.

Regulation of Agricultural Chemicals

The vast increase in the American farmer's productivity over the past few decades has been in large measure attributable to the farmer's use of chemicals to kill the insects, pests, and weeds that have historically competed with the farmer for crops. Some of these chemicals, such as pesticides and herbicides, were a mixed blessing. They enabled people to dramatically increase productivity and to conquer disease. On the other hand, dead fish and birds provided evidence that chemicals were not only building up in the food chain but also proving fatal to some species. Unless such chemicals are carefully used and disposed of, they can present a danger to the applier and to the consumer of food and water.

Gradually, people realized the need to focus on the effects of using such chemicals.

EPA enforces the **Federal Insecticide, Fungicide, and Rodenticide Act** (FIFRA). This act gives EPA the authority to register pesticides before they can be sold, to provide for the certification of appliers of pesticides designated for restricted use, to set limits on the pesticide residue permitted on crops that provide food for people or animals, and to register and inspect pesticide manufacturing establishments. As noted in *King v. E. I. du Pont de Nemours & Co.,* which follows, the FIFRA provides for a relatively small state role in the regulation of pesticides.

King v. E. I. du Pont de Nemours & Co.
35 E.R.C. 1925 (U.S.D.C. Me. 1992)

Ernest King and Edward Higgins were employed by the Maine Department of Transportation (MDOT). As part of their employment duties, King and Higgins seasonally sprayed one or more herbicides manufactured by E. I. du Pont de Nemours & Co. (Du Pont), the Dow Chemical Company (Dow), Velsicol Chemical Company (Velsicol), and Sandoz Corporation (Sandoz). As a result of their exposure to the herbicides, they claimed to have experienced nausea, headaches, loss of appetite, irritability, loss of concentration, muscle pains, joint pain, memory loss, and continued deterioration of vision; in addition, Higgins claimed to suffer from numbness in his extremities.

King and Higgins brought suit against Du Pont, Dow, Velsicol and Sandoz, seeking to impose liability for damages under state tort law theories of negligence and strict liability. They claimed that the chemical companies had failed to warn them about the safe and proper use of the herbicides as well as about the harm and danger of exposure to these products. The chemical companies moved for summary judgment in their favor. One of the key questions was whether the Federal Insecticide, Fungicide, and Rodenticide Act (FIFRA) preempted state tort claims based on failure to warn or inadequate warnings relating to products subject to the Act's labeling requirements. The parties stipulated that all of the product labels in question were submitted to and approved by the EPA in accordance with FIFRA.

Brody, District Judge   Under FIFRA, the EPA cannot approve an herbicide unless it complies with the requirements established in FIFRA, and the EPA labeling regulations promulgated to implement the Act. The EPA regulations detail how warning labels are to be presented and provide specific requirements for the content, placement, type, size and promotion of the warnings. "Label" is defined under FIFRA to include "the written, printed or graphic matter on, or attached to the pesticide or device or any of its containers or wrappers. Required warnings are specified according to the degree to which ingestion or contact with an herbicide is toxic, and these warnings must include precautionary statements about risks posed to humans. The regulations also specify necessary directions on how to use each chemical.

The procedure for registration under FIFRA requires that each applicant file a statement with the Administrator of the EPA which includes the name of the chemical, a statement of all claims to be made for the product, any directions for the product's use and a full description of the tests made and the results thereof upon which the claims are based.

The data required to be submitted to EPA varies with the nature of the chemical and its intended use. On the basis of the information provided by the registrant, the EPA must register the product if it determines that:

(A) Its composition is such as to warrant the proposed claims for it;

(B) Its labeling and other material required to be submitted comply with the requirements of the [Act];

(C) It will perform its intended function without unreasonable adverse effects on the environment; and

(D) When used in accordance with widespread and commonly recognized practice it will not generally cause unreasonable adverse affects on the environment.

An unreasonable adverse effect on the environment is defined under the Act as "any unreasonable risk to man or the environment, taking into account the economic, social, and environmental costs and benefits of the use of any pesticide."

The 1972 Amendments to FIFRA added a section expressly setting forth the states' authority to regulate pesticides. This section states in relevant part:

(a) In general. A state may regulate the sale or use of any federally registered pesticide or device in the state, but only if and to the extent the regulation does not permit any sale or use prohibited by this [Act].

(b) Uniformity. Such state shall not impose or continue in effect any requirements for labeling or packaging different from those required under this [Act].

The statute's language, by itself, is a powerful limit on state power over labeling. A report accompanying the bill, as originally reported out of the House Committee, also indicates the limits on state power due to the division of authority between the federal and state governments: "In dividing the responsibility between the states and the Federal Government for the management of an effective pesticide program, the Commitee [sic] had adopted language which is intended to completely preempt state authority in regard to packaging and labeling." Congress recognized that while the intent of the provision was to leave to the states the authority to impose stricter regulation on pesticide use than that required under the Act, subsection (b) preempted any state labeling or packaging requirements differing from such requirements under the Act.

Although King and Higgins have stipulated that all of the product labels underlying this controversy were submitted to and approved by EPA under FIFRA, they contend that the defendant chemical companies failed to adequately warn them of the dangers inherent [sic] in their products. The chemical companies argue that these claims are expressly preempted under subsection (b) because, if successful, such claims would constitute state-imposed "requirements for labeling or packaging in addition to or different from those required [under FIFRA]." Alternatively, they claim that FIFRA impliedly preempts such claims.

There is a split among the circuit and district courts on the issue of whether FIFRA preempts state failure to warn claims. Prior to the Supreme Court's ruling in *Cippolone v. Liggett Group, Inc.*, courts examining the preemptive scope of FIFRA failed to apply express preemption analysis exclusively. Because *Cippolone* rested on express preemption under a statute containing language almost identical to the relevant statutory language in FIFRA, we are satisfied that under *Cippolone's* standards, the language of FIFRA presents a case of express preemption.

Chemical companies' motion for summary judgment in their favor was granted.

When the EPA administrator has reason to believe that continued use of a particular pesticide poses an "imminent hazard," he may *suspend* its registration and remove the product from the market. When the administrator believes that there is a less than imminent hazard but that the environmental risks of continuing to use a pesticide outweigh its benefits, the administrator may initiate a *cancellation* of registration proceeding. This proceeding affords all interested persons—manufacturers, distributors, users, environmentalists, and scientists—an opportunity to present evidence on the proposed cancellation. Cancellation of the registration occurs when the administrator finds that the product causes unreasonable adverse effects on the environment.

Companion regulations promulgated by EPA and enforced by the Food and Drug Administration control the amount of pesticide residue that can remain on raw and processed food intended for human or animal consumption. These regulations establish what are known as "tolerances."

Those involved in the food production and distribution process must keep a close watch on regulatory developments at EPA concerning the registration, cancellation, and suspension of products as well as actions it takes concerning permissible residues of pesticides on food products. During the 1980s, the agency took highly publicized actions concerning the use of ethylene dibromide (EDB), a fumigant, on citrus and grain products, the use of sulfites on table grapes, the use of alar on apples, and the use of chlordane as a treatment against termite infestation. In each instance, the economic well-being of many businesses was at risk if they did not adequately anticipate and/or deal with the EPA's actions and the publicity that resulted from these actions.

Toxic Substances Control Act

The other major statute regulating chemical use focuses on toxic substances—such as asbestos and PCBs—and on the new chemical compounds that are developed each year. The **Toxic Substances Control Act,** enacted in 1976, requires that chemicals be tested by manufacturers or processors to determine their effect on human health or the environment before the chemicals are introduced into commerce. The act also gives EPA the authority to regulate chemical substances or mixtures that present an unreasonable risk of injury to health or the environment and to take action against any such substances or mixtures that pose an imminent hazard.

This legislation was enacted in response to the concern that thousands of new substances were being released into the environment each year, sometimes without adequate consideration of their potential for harm, and that it was not until damage from a substance occurs that its manufacture or use was properly regulated. At the same time, a goal of the act is not to unduly impede, or create unnecessary economic barriers to, technological innovation.

Biotechnology

The development of techniques to genetically manipulate organisms—often referred to generally as biotechnology—offers considerable promise to aid our ability to provide food and health care and to generate a range of new products and production processes. At the same time, they raise concerns about their potential to adversely affect human health or the environment. Responsiblity for regulating research and use of biotechnology is shared in the federal government between the Food and Drug Administration, the Department of Agriculture, the Environmental Protection Agency, and the National Institutes of Health. Generally, a review is required of such activity before it takes place. This process is of considerable import to companies that are developing genetically engineered organisms for commercial purposes; it can affect both the speed at which they are able to get the products to market and the public's confidence that release of the organisms does not pose an unreasonable risk.

CONCEPT REVIEW

MAJOR ENVIRONMENTAL LAWS

Act	Focus
Clean Air Act	Protects quality of ambient (outdoor) air through national ambient air quality standards, state implementation plans, control of air toxics, new source performance standards, and controls on automobiles and fuels
Clean Water Act	Protects and enhances quality of surface waters by setting water quality standards and limiting discharges by industry and municipalities to those waters through permit system; also regulates dredging and filling of wetlands

Act	Focus
Marine Protection, Research, and Sanctuaries Act	Regulates dumping of all types of material into ocean waters
Safe Drinking Water Act	Protects and enhances quality of our drinking water. Also regulates disposal of wastes in wells
Resource Conservation and Recovery Act (RCRA)	Establishes a cradle-to-the-grave regulatory system for handling and disposal of hazardous wastes; also deals with solid waste
Comprehensive Environmental Response Compensation and Liability Act (Superfund)	Provides a program to deal with hazardous waste that was inadequately disposed of in the past; financed in part by tax on chemicals and feedstocks
Federal Insecticide, Fungicide, and Rodenticide Act (FIFRA)	Regulates the sale and use of chemicals to be used as pesticides and herbicides, including residues permitted on crops intended for use as food
Toxic Substances Control Act (TSCA)	Requires preclearance of new chemicals and provides for regulation of existing chemicals that pose an unreasonable risk to health or the environment

ETHICAL AND PUBLIC POLICY CONCERNS

1. Suppose that a multinational chemical company with its primary manufacturing facilities in the United States plans to build a manufacturing facility in a developing country where there are few, if any, real state-imposed environmental regulations. Is it sufficient for the company to simply meet the environmental requirements of the host country? Is there any ethical obligation to do more—for example, to build the facility to meet the requirements it would have to meet in this country?

2. Suppose a manufacturing facility emits a chemical into the air that it has reason to believe is inadequately regulated by EPA and that poses a significant threat to nearby residents even at levels lower than permitted by EPA. As manager of the facility, would you be satisfied to meet the EPA required level or would you install the additional controls you believe necessary to achieve a reasonably safe level?

3. Suppose that you own some valuable seashore property that contains some marshland and wetlands that are critical to the local ecology. In evaluating whether or not to develop your property, what weight would you give to the value that the marshland and wetlands have as a part of the local ecological system?

PROBLEMS AND PROBLEM CASES

1. The Interstate Commerce Commission (ICC) has the power to approve or set the tariff rates that railroads charge shippers. As a result of past ICC approvals, the railroad tariffs call for higher shipping charges to carry scrap metals and paper than to carry virgin materials. This disparity operates as an economic discrimination against recycled goods. A group of law students has formed an organization known as SCRAP (Students Challenging Regulatory Agency Procedures). SCRAP is concerned that the ICC-approved rate structure discourages the environmentally desirable use of recycled goods. The ICC approved a 2.5 percent across-the-board surcharge in railroad shipping rates and indicated that no environmental impact statement was necessary because there was no environmental impact. SCRAP is concerned that the increase will further the discrimination against used materials and files suit against the ICC to require that an environmental impact statement be prepared. Should the court decide that an environmental impact statement is required?

2. In July 1984, Vanguard Corporation began operating a metal furniture manufacturing plant in Brooklyn, New York. The plant is located in an area that has not attained the national ambient air quality standards for ozone. The plant is a major stationary source (i.e., has the potential to emit more than 100 tons a year) of volatile organic compounds that contribute to the production of ozone in the atmosphere. The New York state implementation plan (SIP) requires that metal-coating facilities use paint that contains less than three pounds of organic solvent (minus water) per gallon at the time of coating. On August 24, 1984, EPA notified Vanguard that it was not in compliance with the SIP provision concerning coatings and issued it a notice of violation. Vanguard sought to defend against the notice of violation on the grounds that it had used its best faith efforts to comply but that full compliance was technologically and economically infeasible. It indicated that it wanted 18 more months to come into compliance. Should Vanguard be held to be in violation of the Clean Air Act?

3. As part of its iron ore processing operations at Silver Bay, Minnesota, Reserve Mining discharges asbestos fibers into the air. Minnesota air pollution control regulations prohibit the operation of an emission source unless it has filtration equipment that collects 99 percent, by weight, of the particulate matter discharged by the plant. The Reserve filtration equipment did not comply with this standard, thus resulting in levels of asbestos in the air that were potentially harmful to public health. The state of Minnesota brought suit to enjoin the asbestos discharges as a public nuisance. Should an injunction be granted?

4. Mall Properties, Inc., was an organization that for many years sought to develop a shopping mall in the Town of North Haven, Connecticut, a suburb of New Haven. Because the proposed development would require the filling of some wetlands, Mall Properties was required to obtain a permit from the Corps of Engineers pursuant to section 404 of the Clean Water Act. The City of New Haven opposed development of the mall—and the granting of the permit—on the grounds it would jeopardize the fragile economy of New Haven. The Corps of Engineers found the net loss of wetlands would be substantially compensated for by a proposed on-site wetland creation. Relying primarily on the socio-economic concerns of the City of New Haven, the District Engineer rejected the proposed permit. Mall Properties then brought suit against the Corps of Engineers, claiming that the decision was arbitrary and capricious. Should the District Engineer have relied on socioeconomic factors unrelated to the project's environmental impacts in making a decision on the permit?

5. Charles Hanson owned land abutting Keith Lake, a freshwater lake that was subject to some tidal flooding as a result of its connection with tidal waters. In order to minimize the detrimental effects from the tidal activities and consequent flooding, Hanson deposited a large quantity of dirt, rock, bricks, sheet metal, and other debris along the shoreline of his property. He did so without obtaining a permit from the U.S. Army Corps of Engineers under section 404 of the Clean Water Act, which controls dumping and filling activities in navigable waters of the United States. Under the law, discharges of pollutants into navigable waters without a permit are forbidden. The term *pollutant* is defined to include "dredged soil, solid waste, incinerator residue, sewage, garbage, sewage sludge, munitions, chemical wastes, biological materials, radioactive materials, heat, wrecked or discarded equipment, rock, sand, cellar dirt, and industrial, municipal and agricultural waste discharged into water." EPA brought an enforcement action against Hanson claiming he had violated the Clean Water Act. Should the court find that Hanson violated the act?

6. Johnson & Towers, Inc., is in the business of overhauling large motor vehicles. It uses degreasers and other industrial chemicals that contain chemicals classified as "hazardous wastes" under the Resource Conservation and Recovery Act (RCRA), for example, methylene chloride and trichloroethylene. For some period of time, waste chemicals from cleaning operations were drained into a holding tank and, when the tank was full, pumped into a trench. The trench flowed from the plant property into Parker's Creek, a tributary of the Delaware River. Under RCRA, generators of such wastes must obtain a permit for disposal from the Environmental Protection Agency (EPA). EPA had neither issued, nor received an application for, a permit for the Johnson & Towers operations. Over a three-day period, federal agents saw workers pump waste from the tank into the trench, and on the third day toxic chemicals flowed into the creek. The company and two of its employees, Jack Hopkins, a foreman, and Peter Angel, the service manager, were indicted for unlawfully disposing of hazardous wastes. The company pled guilty. The federal district court dismissed the criminal charges against the two individuals, holding that RCRA's criminal penalty provisions imposing fines and imprisonment did not apply to employees. The government appealed. Can employees of a corporation be held criminally liable if their actions on behalf of the corporation violate the federal hazardous waste law?

7. In 1979, Anne Arundel County, Maryland, enacted two related ordinances. One absolutely prohibited the disposal in and the transportation through Anne Arundel County of various hazardous wastes not originating in that county. Another ordinance required a license to dispose of hazardous waste in Anne Arundel County; it also requires a license to transport hazardous wastes through the county. Browning-Ferris, Inc., (BFI), is the owner and operator of a landfill located in Anne Arundel County that is licensed by the state of Maryland to receive hazardous wastes. BFI is also a hauler of hazardous wastes within the county. The county notified BFI that it expected BFI to comply with the new regulations, and BFI filed a lawsuit challenging the ordinances and seeking to have them enjoined. How should the court rule?

8. The Royal McBee Corporation manufactured typewriters at a factory in Springfield, Missouri. As a part of the manufacturing process, Royal McBee generated cyanide-based electroplating wastes, sludge from the bottom of electroplating tanks, and spent plating bath solution. As part of their duties, Royal McBee employees dumped the wastes onto the surface of the soil on a vacant lot adjoining the factory. This took place between 1959 and 1962. Over time, the waste materials migrated outward and downward from the original dumping site, contaminating a large area. In 1970, the manufacturing facility and lot were sold to General Electric, which operated the plant but did not engage in the dumping of wastes on the vacant lot. In the mid-1980s, General Electric was required by EPA and the state of Missouri, under the authority of the federal Superfund law, to clean up the contamination at the site. General Electric then brought a lawsuit against the successor corporation of Royal McBee's typewriter business, Litton Business Systems, to recover for the costs incurred in cleaning up the site. Under the Superfund law, "any person who at the time of disposal of any hazardous substance owned or operated any facilities at which such hazardous substances were disposed of, shall be liable for any other necessary costs of response incurred by any other person" consistent with the Superfund law and regulations. Is General Electric entitled to recover its cleanup costs from Litton?

9. Chemlawn sells pesticide products for use on residential lawns. The active ingredients in Chemlawn's products are registered with the Environmental Protection Agency pursuant to the Federal Insecticide, Fungicide, and Rodenticide Act (FIFRA). Deborah Ryan brought a lawsuit against Chemlawn seeking damages in tort for injuries she claimed that she and her son Kevin sustained from the use of Chemlawn products. Ryan claims that the products are unsafe for commercial use and that they have been inadequately tested by the EPA. Chemlawn contends that Ryan should take her complaints to EPA, which has the responsibility for determining whether the products are safe to be sold. How should the court decide?

SPECIAL

TOPICS

THE LEGAL

ENVIRONMENT FOR

INTERNATIONAL

BUSINESS

INTRODUCTION

Since 1945, American businesses have steadily increased the number and size of transactions with people in foreign markets. American businesses export their goods to other countries, import foreign goods into the United States, establish manufacturing, drilling, and other operations on foreign soil, and license their patents and other technology to foreign businesses. With the economic changes that have swept eastern Europe after the December 1989 revolutions, foreign trade by American firms in the 1990s has accelerated.

THE CHALLENGE OF INTERNATIONAL BUSINESS

Each international business transaction faces dozens of legal and practical problems. The answers to the legal problems come from a mix of the laws of our own country, those of the other country or countries involved, and doctrines of international law. For example, American exporters must comply with American laws concerning the export of goods and foreign laws that restrict the importation of goods. While many nations have signed agreements designed to remove importation restrictions, such international law is not binding on a signatory nation unless its legislature has passed a statute to implement the agreement.

When an American business enters a contract to sell goods to a foreign buyer, the buyer and seller may choose to follow American contract law or foreign contract law. They may use international law embodied in the United Nations Convention on Contracts for the International Sale of Goods (CISG). Usually, the CISG will not apply unless the seller's or buyer's nation has adopted the CISG.

When an American firm makes a direct foreign investment by establishing a manufacturing plant abroad, the firm must comply with all of the foreign nation's laws applicable to its operations, such as employee safety and dismissal laws, antitrust laws, and toxic waste disposal regulations. In addition, American firms doing business abroad must comply with other domestic laws of the host country. For example, many Arabic countries prohibit alcohol consumption and forbid women to operate motor vehicles. Many foreign nations require that any firm doing business within their boundaries be owned by their government or by their citizens. In addition, the foreign nation's laws may restrict the American firm's ability to take its profits back to the United States—reinvestment of profits in the foreign nation may be required. Also, several socialist countries have confiscated or expropriated the business assets of U.S. firms doing business in those countries.

Practical problems abound as well. There are language and cultural differences. Contract negotiations may be either more or less formal than in America. In addition, the parties to international transactions are much less likely to know each other well because they are separated by great distances, thereby increasing a seller's risk of nonpayment by the buyer and a buyer's risk of nondelivery by the seller. There are different currencies, some of which—like the Russian ruble—may be nearly worthless on the world market. Other currencies' values may quickly depreciate, increasing the risk that a buyer of goods will underpay for goods, unless the parties designate a stable currency in their sales contract.

The resolution of disputes is troublesome, as each party may seek to have a dispute resolved in his home court, applying law favorable to his side. Disputes between an American seller and a foreign buyer may be resolved in the courts of either nation or in an international arbitration tribunal. The court or tribunal may apply American law, foreign law, or international law.

Only some of the complexities of the law of international business transactions can be explored within the limited scope of this chapter. The intent of this chapter, therefore, is to give you a sense of the legal environment of international business by examining the most important legal questions that arise in connection with international sales, licensing, and investment. Because most international business transactions entered into by an American business must comply with trade restrictions imposed by the United States and other governments, this chapter begins with a consideration of trade limitations.

LIMITATIONS ON TRADE

Many governmentally imposed barriers to trade affect international business transactions. The most important are export and import controls, including tariffs.

Export Controls

For political or economic purposes, most nations place export controls on certain goods and technology leaving their countries. For example, in 1990, most nations placed an embargo on exports to Iraq in response to Iraq's invasion of Kuwait. Another example is the restriction on the sale of militarily sensitive technology by western nations so that it is not obtained by countries whose governments are considered unfriendly. The restrictions are agreed on unanimously by western countries who are members of the Paris-based Coordinating Committee for Multilateral Export Controls (COCOM). The restrictions are then enforced through laws passed in each country. Failure to abide by the restrictions can lead to imprisonment of the sellers of the restricted goods.

The Export Administration Act of 1985   The Export Administration Act of 1985 is the main law controlling **exports** from the United States. The act is enforced by the Office of Export Administration (OEA) of the Department of Commerce. The act is designed to accomplish three purposes:

1. To enhance national security.
2. To aid in the accomplishment of the objectives of American foreign policy.
3. To preserve commodities and technology essential to the protection of the American economy.

The OEA implements the act by administering a licensing procedure and maintaining a **commodity control list** of goods and technical data subject to the act. The OEA generally requires an exporter to obtain a **license** prior to exportation of the good or technology.

Before applying for a license, an exporter must consult the commodity control list to determine whether exports to the country of destination are restricted. For example, exports to Cuba, Cambodia, and North Korea are almost totally prohibited. Libya's role in international terrorism has resulted in heavy restrictions on exports to Libya. Exports to communist countries are restricted as well. Only recently have exports to Vietnam been permitted. Exports to most western hemisphere nations are not restricted.

When the commodity control list indicates that exportation of the good or technology to the destination country is prohibited, the exporter must abandon its attempt to export. When the exportation is legal, the exporter must consult the commodity control list to determine whether it needs a general or a validated license issued by the OEA.

A **general license** is a blanket authorization to export the covered goods or technology without obtaining permission for a specific export. A general license appears in the form of an administrative regulation and authorizes every exporter to export the covered goods or technology. Thus, for example, an exporter need not obtain specific OEA approval when the OEA has issued a general license to export beer to Canada.

A **validated license** authorizes a specific exporter to export a specific good or technology to a specific country. A validated license may validate one export or a series of exports. The OEA's refusal to grant a validated license may be appealed to the assistant secretary of commerce for trade administration. However, his decision is final; there is no judicial review of his administrative decision.

The commodity control list applies not merely to the exportation by an American firm to a foreign country. It also controls the **reexportation** of American goods and technology by the foreign buyer to a second foreign nation. As a result, when American goods are exported to Germany and reexported to Iraq, the OEA would regulate both the America-to-Germany and Germany-to-Iraq transactions.

The OEA does not have authority to issue licenses for all goods and technology. For example, weapons export is usually controlled by the State Department; the export of nuclear materials is licensed by the Nuclear Regulatory Commission.

Import Controls

Countries control the importation of goods and technology primarily to protect domestic industry. These restrictions commonly take the form of quotas, licensing requirements, import restrictions, or tariffs.

Quotas   A quota is a limit on the number or poundage of an item that may be imported into a country. By setting a quota on the importation of Japanese automobiles, the United States has forced Japan to limit the number of automobiles it sells in the United States as a way of opening up the American market for American-made automobiles.

Licensing   A license is a government-granted privilege to conduct a specific business. By requiring the licensing of foreign technology, Japan has improved the ability of its manufacturers to obtain more favorable bargaining terms. Instead of having different Japanese manufacturers compete with one another to get a desirable piece of technology from an American licensor, the Japanese licensing agency in effect tells the licensor that it will be excluded from the Japanese market unless it agrees to accept considerably less favorable terms than would have resulted without the regulation. In developing nations, licensing regulations may ensure that a country's scarce resources are not being used unless the imported technology fits into the country's basic development plans. To protect domestic employees, some nations require technical training of local personnel in return for license approval.

Prohibited Imports   Most countries also maintain a list of prohibited imports. There are a large number of goods that may not be imported into the United States. For example, the American fur industry is protected by a prohibition on the import of furs from Russia. Public morals are protected by the exclusion of obscene materials and lottery tickets. The domestic fishing industry is served by prohibiting the importation of fish from nations that seize American fishing boats.

Tariffs   A tariff is a tax or duty assessed on goods, generally when they are imported into a country. The duty is **ad valorem**—that is, a percentage of the value of the goods, such as 10 percent. Through the use of tariffs, governments can discourage imports and protect domestic industry from foreign competition. A sufficiently high ad valorem duty makes the product so expensive that most consumers will refuse to buy it; consequently, consumers do without the good or buy a domestically produced equivalent.

In the United States, import duties are assessed and collected by the U.S. Customs Service. Imported goods are unloaded under the supervision of the Customs Service and taken to a warehouse, where they are kept until a formal entry into the United States is made. **Entry** is the presentation of documentation necessary to classify the goods and assess the duty. After a bond is posted to ensure payment of the duty, the goods are examined. If importation of the goods is prohibited or the goods are not listed on the invoices, the goods may be seized and criminal charges brought against the importer. If the goods pass examination, a tentative duty is assessed and the goods are released to the importer. The Customs Service has the right to charge an additional duty at a later time. The importer may protest or ask for review of the duty

before an appraisal specialist at the Customs headquarters. Further reviews are heard by the Court of International Trade and the Court of Appeals for the Federal Circuit in Washington, D.C.

In the next case, the Federal Circuit affirmed the decision of the Court of International Trade holding that imported G.I. Joe toys were dutiable as dolls.

HASBRO INDUSTRIES, INC. V. U.S.
879 F.2d 838 (Fed. Cir. 1989)

Hasbro Industries, Inc., imported G.I. Joe Action Figures from Hong Kong. G.I. Joe figures are made of plastic, are approximately 3½ inches tall, and have the appearance of humans dressed and equipped in a manner associated with actual or fictional warfare. They are noticeably lifelike and constructed to permit a range of movements. The head turns and the arms are jointed at the shoulder and elbow. They can turn at the waist and also bend slightly in all directions from the waist. The legs have a wide range of movement.

Each figure is packaged singly in a large plastic blister mounted on a large card that contains specific biographical information for each figure. For example, First Sergeant, Code Name: Duke, has the following personnel card:

File Name: Hauser, Conrad S.
Primary Military Specialty: Airborne Infantryman
Birthplace: St. Louis, MO Grade: E-8 (Master Sergeant)

Duke was fluent in French, German, and English when he enlisted in 1967. Graduated top of his class at airborne school, Fort Benning. Went Special Forces in 1979. Ran four different Special Forces schools. Turned down a commission in 1971. Statement after declining commission: "They tell me that an officer's job is to impel others to take the risks—so that the officer survives to take the blame in the event of total catastrophe. With all due respect, sir . . . if that's what an officer does, I don't want any part of it."

In addition, each figure comes with its own specialized accessories. For example, First Sergeant comes with plastic pieces representing binoculars, a helmet, an assault pack, and an M-32 submachine gun.

In 1982 and 1983, the U.S. Customs Service classified G.I. Joe figures as "other dolls" under the Tariff Schedule of the United States (TSUS) and assessed a duty on the figures. Hasbro claimed that G.I. Joe was not a doll and should be importable free of duty. Hasbro appealed the Custom Service's decision to the Court of International Trade, which affirmed the decision. Hasbro next appealed to the Federal Circuit Court of Appeals.

Michel, Judge   Hasbro argues that these toy figures are excepted from duty because they are properly classifiable as "Toy figures of animate objects (except dolls): Not having a spring mechanism: Not stuffed: Other" under the TSUS. Hasbro contends that G.I. Joe is nothing more than a modern version of a traditional toy soldier.To determine the common meaning of a tariff term like "doll," the court may consult dictionaries, scientific authorities, and other reliable information sources to

ascertain that common meaning. The Court of International Trade referred to a general dictionary defining the word "doll" as a representation of a human being used as a child's plaything. While we conclude that this summary definition is not an all-inclusive definition for the term "doll," we determine that it is suitable for this case.

Given this broad common meaning of the term "doll," we next review whether the Court of International Trade clearly erred when it found that the

G.I. Joe action figure fit within that term. We determine it did not. The evidence includes testimony (including expert testimony), magazine articles referring to G.I. Joe as a doll, letters from purchasers to Hasbro also referring to G.I. Joe as a doll, doll collector books, and the imported articles themselves.

Finally, we turn to Hasbro's argument that the long established practice of the Customs Service is to exclude traditional toy soldiers from the tariff provision for dolls. As the Court of International Trade explained, the individual personality of each of these figures, as evidenced by his biographical file cards and physical characteristics inviting "intimate and manipulative" play, indicates that these figures are not comparable to the identical, immobile faceless soldiers of yesteryear that were sold in groups of a dozen or so in bags.

Although Hasbro has fought valiantly that these figures are not dolls, we are unable to agree. Even though G.I. Joe has lost this battle, hopefully he will not lose his courage for combat, despite being officially designated by the United States Customs Service as a "doll."

Judgment for the United States affirmed.

GATT   Tariffs have been the most common barrier to free trade, and as a result, many governments are cooperating to control or eliminate tariffs. One of the most comprehensive efforts at cooperation has been the rounds of negotiations under the **General Agreement on Tariffs and Trade (GATT),** a treaty subscribed to by more than 80 nations.

Negotiations under GATT have resulted in significant tariff reductions. The focus of GATT is much broader than tariff reduction, however; its purpose is to reduce all trade barriers and promote a stable world trade environment. Among other ways, it attempts to do this through a **most favored nation** clause, which requires a signatory nation (such as the United States) to offer all other signatory nations treatment as favorable as that granted to any individual signatory country. Thus, with some exceptions, this eliminates discrimination among countries on the basis of tariffs and duties.

Regional Trade Associations   Another way that tariffs and trade barriers have been reduced is through the formation of regional associations. Regional trade associations are formed in compliance with treaties signed by participating countries, which treaties foster free trade within the association. The **North American Free Trade Agreement (NAFTA)** is a regional trade association of the United States, Canada, and Mexico. The United States approved NAFTA in 1993. The purpose of NAFTA is to eliminate most trade barriers between the United States, Canada, and Mexico.

One of the best known economic unions is the **European Economic Community (EEC),** also known as the European Union (EU), the European Community (EC), and the Common Market. Formed in 1957, the EEC comprises most of the western European countries. The purpose of the EEC is to establish an economic community by promoting free trade within its boundaries. It does this by eliminating tariffs among its members and establishing common tariffs for outside countries, promoting the free movement of workers, goods, and capital among its members, establishing a common monetary policy with the eventual goal of establishing a single monetary unit, and generally promoting the welfare of individuals within the union through economic development. Through this union, the member countries have created an economic force that is far greater than any individual member could have generated on its own.

The EEC countries hoped to complete the Common Market by 1992. However, squabbling between EEC members concerning national interests, such as France's interest in protecting its farmers, threatens the achievement of the EEC's goal to remove trade barriers between EEC countries.

Dumping and Subsidized Goods   One of the most common reasons the United States and other countries impose tariffs today is to counteract dumping and subsidizing goods. **Dumping** is the selling of goods at unfairly low prices. The selling of imported goods at these low prices means that domestic manufacturers cannot effectively compete with them. Thus, duties are imposed on the goods to offset the difference between the import price and the fair price as determined by the nation of import. In the United States, dumping is regulated by an **antidumping** law, the Trade Agreement Act of 1979. When dumping is alleged, the allegation is investigated by the International Trade Administration (ITA) of the Department of Commerce to determine if the goods are being sold at less than fair value. If such a violation is proved, the International Trade Commission (ITC) determines whether the dumping has injured a domestic industry. If both a violation and injury are proved, an antidumping duty can be assessed.

Subsidized goods are goods that in some way have been economically supported by the government of their country of origin. For example, Spain has subsidized goods by rebating domestic taxes to its manufacturers. Because of this support, subsidized goods can then be sold for less than goods not receiving subsidies. Governments impose **countervailing duties** against subsidized imported goods to protect competing domestic goods. Both the United States and the EEC have imposed duties against Japanese goods because of government subsidies. The Trade Agreement Act of 1979 applies to subsidized goods imported into the United States.

Counterfeit and Grey Market Goods

Piracy and other unauthorized uses of American goods or technology protected by U.S. patent, copyright, and trademark law have become a major problem of American businesses. For example, foreign jeans manufacturers may without authorization place the Levi's label on their jeans, thereby damaging the business of Levi Strauss & Co. by depriving it of some of the jeans' market and damaging the value of the Levi trademark, especially if the imported jeans are of inferior quality. This is an example of **counterfeit goods,** goods unlawfully bearing a trademark. Counterfeit goods may also unlawfully appropriate patented technology or copyrighted material. For example, a foreign musical recording company may pirate the latest Madonna album and import thousands of copies of it into the United States without copyright permission.

American firms harmed by the importation of counterfeit goods may obtain injunctions and damages under the Tariff Act of 1930, the Lanham Trademark Act of 1946, the Copyright Act, and federal patent law. In addition, the Trademark Counterfeiting Act of 1984 establishes criminal penalties for counterfeiting goods. It also allows an American firm to recover from a counterfeiter three times its damages or three times the counterfeiter's profits (whichever is greater).

Patent, copyright, and trademark piracy is increasing in many parts of the world, especially developing nations. Some developing nations believe that technology should be transferred freely to foster their economic growth. Consequently, they either encourage piracy or choose not to oppose it. This trend could be reversed if the proposed GATT Code on Discouraging Trade in Counterfeit Goods becomes international law.

Grey market goods are goods lawfully bearing trademarks or using patents and copyrighted material but entering the American market without authorization. For example, Parker Pen Co. may authorize a Japanese manufacturer to make and sell Parker pens only in Japan. When an American firm imports the Japanese-made Parker pens into the United States, the goods become grey market goods.

While importing grey market goods may violate the contract between the American firm and its foreign licensee, it is not clear in what contexts it violates U.S. importation, trademark, patent, or copyright law. Some courts find a Lanham Act or Tariff Act violation, but other courts do not. The Trademark Counterfeiting Act of 1984 specifically excludes grey market goods from its coverage.

FOREIGN SALES OF DOMESTICALLY MANUFACTURED PRODUCTS

Once an American exporter has determined that the sale of its product to a buyer in a foreign nation is permitted by American export law and the foreign nation's import law, the exporter may enter a contract with the foreign buyer. In addition to the logistical problems of negotiation at long distance perhaps in two languages, the primary legal questions are what contract law applies to the transaction and what terms the contract should include.

Regulation of International Sales Contracts

Countries have attempted to address some of the problems raised by international transactions through their agreement to codes that apply across national boundaries. Typically, countries agree to be bound by international codes, then adjust their internal laws in compliance with the laws laid out in the code.

An example of such an agreement is the United Nations Convention on Contracts for the International Sale of Goods (CISG), which has been adopted by many nations, including the United States and Canada. The CISG is designed to provide a uniform code for international contracts much the same way that the Uniform Commercial Code (UCC) provides uniformity and certainty for transactions among contracting parties from different states in the United States. The Convention provides rules governing the formation of international contracts and regulates the transfer of goods under those contracts.

There are substantial differences between the CISG and the UCC. The CISG does not require any sales contract to be written. Offers easily become irrevocable—the offeree need only reasonably believe that it is irrevocable. An attempted acceptance that changes the terms of the offer is not an acceptance.

Need for Written Sales Contracts

Even when the CISG applies to an international sales contract, the parties should not rely exclusively on its protections. Instead, they should draft a comprehensive contract that carefully addresses the major legal and practical problems that may arise in the performance of the contract. The content of the contract varies according to the manner of relationship between the buyer and the seller: (1) A firm may make direct sales to customers abroad, or (2) it may appoint one or more distributors for a particular country or region, which distributors purchase the product from the American firm and resell it to customers in their territories. These two methods of exploiting the world market can involve different legal problems. The following discussion is based on the typical way these transactions are structured to deal with the international climate.

Direct Sale to a Foreign Buyer

When an American firm contracts to sell its goods to a foreign buyer, the buyer and the seller should execute a written contract to ensure their complete understanding of the basic terms and conditions of the contract. The interpretation and enforcement of most of these terms and conditions—such as price, method of payment, currency of payment, and product warranties—primarily involve contract law. To the extent that the CISG does not apply and there is a difference between the contract law of the seller's jurisdiction and that of the buyer, courts typically respect the choice of the parties as to which law applies if the parties, as is usual, have included a **choice of law clause** in the agreement.

In addition, international sales contracts should include a *force majeure* **clause**, which excuses performance due to conditions beyond the parties' control. For example, a *force majeure* clause may excuse a seller of oil from performing when the outbreak of war threatens shipping lanes in the Persian Gulf. *Force majeure* clauses reflect the risks known to have occurred in the past.

As an alternative or in addition to a *force majeure* clause, the CISG has a frustration defense that is similar to the commercial impracticability defense of the UCC. The CISG excuses nonperformance due to an impediment beyond a party's control that the party could not reasonably have been expected to take into account at the time the contract was made or to avoid or overcome at the time of performance.

An international sales contract should also specify the **currency** in which payment is to be made. American dollars are usually selected because their value is relatively stable, while the currencies of some nations—for example, Brazil—continually fall in value due to high inflation. To illustrate, suppose an American firm contracts to sell five trucks worth $100,000 to a Brazilian firm for 150,000 cruzados. If payment is delayed for three months, Brazilian inflation may cause the 150,000 cruzado payment to be worth only $90,000.

Assurance of Payment

Perhaps the most important provisions in the international sales contract cover the manner by which the buyer pays the seller. Frequently, a foreign buyer's contractual promise to pay when the goods arrive does not provide the seller with sufficient assurance of payment. The seller may not know the overseas buyer well enough to determine the buyer's financial condition or inclination to refuse payment if the buyer no longer wants the goods when they arrive. When the buyer fails to make payment, the seller will find it difficult and expensive to pursue its legal rights under the contract. Even if the seller is assured that the buyer will pay for the goods on arrival, the time required for shipping the goods often means that payment is not received until months after shipment.

To solve these problems, the seller often insists on receiving an **irrevocable letter of credit**. The buyer obtains a letter of credit from a bank in the buyer's country. The letter of credit obligates the buyer's bank to pay the amount of the sales contract to the seller. To obtain payment, the seller must produce a **negotiable bill of lading** and other documents proving that it shipped the goods required by the sales contract in conformity with the terms of the letter of credit.[1] A letter of credit is irrevocable when the buyer's bank cannot withdraw its obligation to pay without the consent of the seller and the buyer.

Letters of credit may be confirmed or advised. Under a **confirmed** letter of credit, the seller's bank agrees to assume liability on the letter of credit. Typically, under a confirmed letter of credit, the buyer's bank issues a letter of credit to the seller; the seller's bank confirms the letter of credit; the seller delivers the goods to a carrier; the carrier issues a negotiable bill of lading to the seller; the seller delivers the bill of lading to the seller's bank and presents a draft[2] drawn on the buyer demanding payment for the goods; the seller's bank pays the seller for the goods; the buyer's bank reimburses the seller's bank; and the buyer reimburses its bank. Figure 1 summarizes the confirmed letter of credit transaction.

With an **advised** letter of credit, the seller's bank merely acts as an agent for collection of the amount owed to the seller. The seller's bank acts as agent for the seller by collecting from the buyer's bank and giving the payment to the seller. The buyer's bank is reimbursed by the buyer.

The confirmed letter of credit is the least risky payment method for sellers. The confirmation is needed because the seller, unlike the confirming bank, may not know any more about the financial integrity of the issuing bank than it knows about that of the buyer. The seller has a promise of immediate payment from an entity it knows to be financially solvent—the confirming bank. If the draft drawn pursuant to the letter of credit is not paid, the seller may sue the confirming bank, which is a bank in his home country.

Under the confirmed letter of credit, payment is made to the seller well before the goods arrive. Thus, the buyer cannot claim that the goods are defective and refuse to pay for them. When the goods are truly defective on arrival, however, the customer can commence an action for damages against the seller based on their original sales contract.

Conforming and Nonconforming Documents

In a letter of credit transaction, the promises made by the buyer's and seller's banks are independent of the underlying sales contract between the seller and the buyer. Therefore, when the seller presents a bill of lading and other documents that *conform* to the terms of the letter of credit, the issuing bank and the confirming bank are required to pay, even if the buyer refuses to pay its bank or even, generally, if the buyer claims to know that the goods are defective. However, if the bill of lading or other required documents do not conform to the terms of the letter of credit, a bank may properly refuse to pay. A bill of lading is *nonconforming* when, for example, it indicates the wrong goods were shipped, states the wrong person to receive the goods, or states a buyer's address differently than the letter of credit.

In the following case, even though the seller shipped nonconforming goods to the buyer, the buyer's bank that issued the irrevocable letter of credit was required to pay when the seller presented a bill of lading and other documents that conformed to the letter of credit.

---

[1] A bill of lading is a document issued by a carrier acknowledging that the seller has delivered particular goods to it and entitling the holder of the bill of lading to receive these goods at the place of destination. Bills of lading are discussed in Chapter 33.

[2] A draft is a negotiable instrument by which the drawer (in this case, the seller) orders the drawee (the buyer) to pay the payee (the seller). Drafts are discussed in Chapter 30.

FIGURE 1 **Confirmed Letter of Credit Transaction**

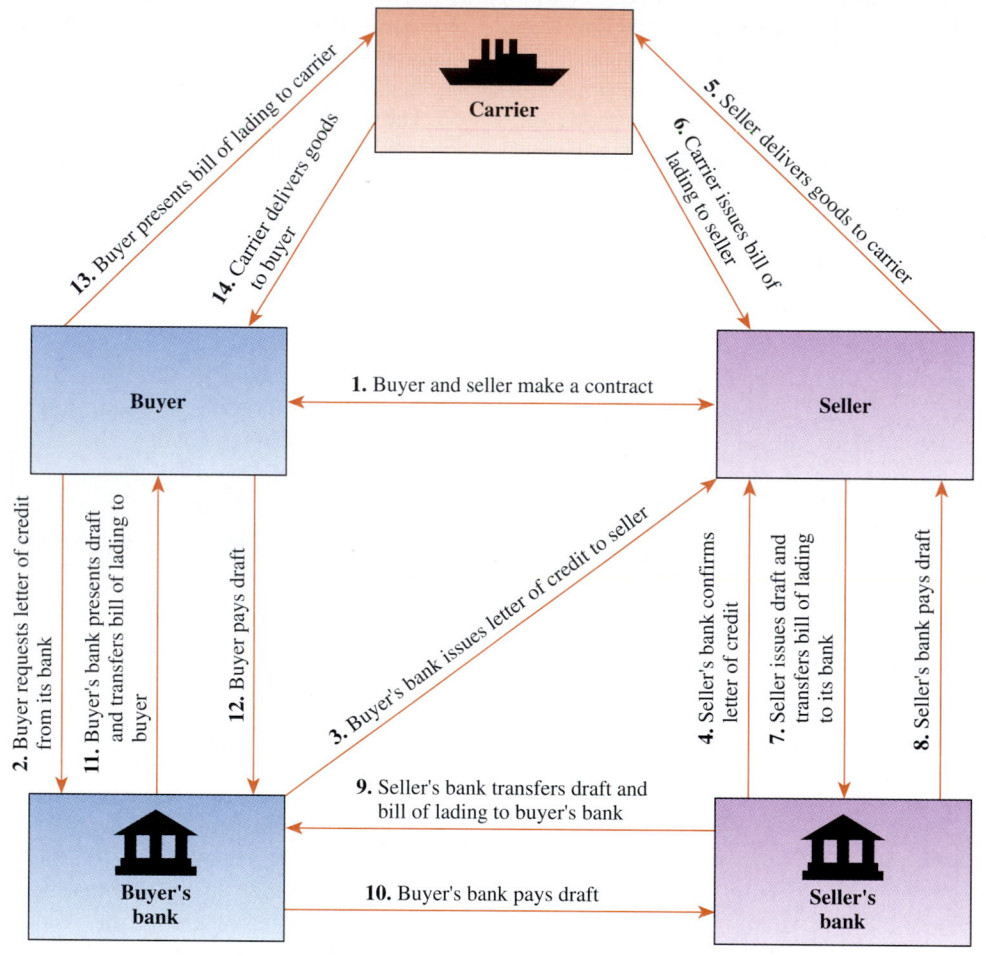

BENETTON SERVICES V. BENEDOT, INC.

551 So.2d 295 (Ala. Sup. Ct. 1989)

Benetton Services Corporation was an Italian clothing manufacturer. Benedot, Inc., was formed for the purpose of selling Benetton clothing at retail outlets in Dothan and Auburn, Alabama. Benedot placed several orders with Benetton over a period of approximately 36 months. All of the orders were delivered late, and all contained some nonconforming merchandise. Benetton told Benedot that Benetton had made changes in personnel, and that future orders would be conforming and would be delivered on time. Relying on this representation, Benedot placed an order with Benetton for spring and summer 1988 clothing.

As a condition to shipping Benedot's order, Benetton required Benedot to pay $20,000, and to have issued to Benetton an irrevocable letter of credit in the amount of $61,000. On behalf of Benedot, Southland Bank of Dothan issued an irrevocable letter of credit for $61,000 to Benetton.

The spring/summer 1988 order was delivered late and it contained nonconforming goods. Benedot accepted the shipment, because it was very difficult and expensive to return the goods to Italy. Nonetheless, to prevent Benetton from collecting for the goods, Benedot obtained a temporary restraining order directing Southland Bank not to pay Benetton. At a hearing, the trial court issued a preliminary injunction enjoining Southland Bank from paying Benetton. Benetton appealed to the Supreme Court of Alabama.

■

Shores, Justice Payment under an irrevocable letter of credit, upon compliance with its terms, is independent of the underlying contract. The issuer of a letter of credit must honor a draft drawn thereunder that complies with the terms of the letter of credit, regardless of whether the goods conform to the underlying contract.

Because the letter of credit represents an independent obligation of the issuer to the beneficiary, payment under an irrevocable letter of credit may not be enjoined absent evidence of forgery or fraud in the issuance of the letter or fraud in the underlying transaction for which the letter of credit was issued.

Benedot has failed to prove fraud. Benetton promised that, upon receipt of the $20,000 and a letter of credit, it would ship conforming goods and that delivery would be timely. This is clearly a promise to do an act in the future; to base a fraud claim on that promise, Benedot had to prove that Benetton, when it made the agreement, did not intend to comply with its terms. Also, Benedot had to prove that, at the time that promise was made, Benetton had an intent to deceive. The record is devoid of any such evidence. The evidence would support, at most, a finding that the promise was recklessly made. A reckless misrepresentation cannot support a fraud action where that misrepresentation relates to a future act. Furthermore, the failure to perform a promised act is not in itself evidence that the defendant, at the time the promise was made, intended to deceive.

The trial court's order granting the preliminary injuction is reversed and the case is remanded with instructions to release the funds due and owing to Benetton pursuant to the letter of credit issued by Southland.

Judgment reversed in favor of Benetton; remanded to the trial court.

Standby Letters of Credit Although an ordinary letter of credit protects the seller, it leaves a buyer at risk if the seller ships defective goods. Therefore, the buyer may insist that the seller obtain a letter of credit from the seller's bank under which the sellers' bank promises to pay the buyer if the seller defaults on the sales contract. Such a **standby letter of credit** operates as a guaranty or insurance for the buyer. The buyer pays the seller, expecting the seller to perform; if the seller defaults on the contract, such as by shipping defective goods, the buyer exercises its rights under the standby letter of credit and obtains payment from the seller's bank. (If the standby letter of credit is confirmed, the buyer would collect from the buyer's confirming bank, which would then collect from the seller's bank.) The seller's bank collects the amount of the payment from the seller, if it has not done so already. Because the seller's bank is in the same city as the seller, it can more easily than the buyer obtain collection from the seller.

Dispute Resolution Disputes between an American seller and a foreign buyer may be resolved in the courts of either nation or in an international arbitration tribunal. The court or tribunal may apply American law, foreign law, or international law.

The international sales contract should include a **choice of forum clause**, which designates which court or arbitration tribunal will resolve disputes between the parties. Of course, each party wants to have the dispute resolved in its national courts applying national or local law. As a compromise, an arbitration panel is often the forum of choice.

Arbitration, the settlement of disputes by a nonjudicial third party, may be cheaper, quicker, and more private than resolving disputes through litigation. Equally important, it can take place in a neutral location. The growing attractiveness of arbitration has resulted in the establishment of arbitration centers in London, Paris, Cairo, Hong Kong, Geneva, and New York.

After an American firm successfully litigates or obtains arbitration against a foreign firm, another problem may arise: enforcement of the judgment or decision. For example, an American firm may obtain a judgment in a U.S. court awarding it $50,000 against an Iranian firm. However, the firm may not have any assets in the United States. Moreover, when the American firm seeks enforcement of the judgment in Iran, an Iranian court may refuse to recognize the judgment or to enforce it. Thus, the firm may find it necessary to relitigate in Iran the issues decided by the American court.

Sales to Nonmarket Economies   The international sales transaction is complicated when an American buyer sells to a buyer in a nation that has a **nonmarket economy (NME)**. NMEs exist in socialist nations, in which a central government owns and controls all significant means of production. This means that a sale by an American seller to a NME will usually be to a buyer that is authorized by its government to enter international sales contracts. Cuba is among the nations having NMEs.

The typical NME buyer is a **foreign trade corporation**. A socialist economy usually has several foreign trade corporations, each empowered to conduct the whole business of exporting or importing a particular good. Contract negotiations with a foreign trade corporation may be slow and costly, due to the unusually high but necessary precision with which the contract is written. Once agreement has been reached, however, foreign trade corporations have an excellent performance record.

Most foreign trade corporations insist that all disputes be resolved by arbitration in their country. This is normally not a great risk for an American seller because most socialist arbitration tribunals have a good record for efficiency and impartiality. When a foreign trade corporation is sued in a court outside its boundaries, it may raise the **doctrine of sovereign immunity**. The doctrine of sovereign immunity is international law; it holds that a nation may not be sued for causing harm. It is founded in the ancient principle that "The King Can Do No Wrong" and, therefore, a king could not be sued by his subjects. Nonetheless, the United States has rejected the doctrine of sovereign immunity in limited circumstances, by allowing actions against foreign governments under the Foreign Sovereign Immunity Act. The United States and other nations deny immunity to the commercial activities of governments, including the international business transactions of foreign trade corporations.

Countertrade   Often, a socialist nation will condition its agreement to buy goods from an American seller on the seller's agreement to purchase NME goods. This is known as a countertrade, of which two kinds are most common: the counterpurchase and the compensation transaction. In a **counterpurchase**, an American firm sells its goods to a NME nation and purchases from the NME nation goods unrelated to the goods it sells. For example, in a counterpurchase agreement with the former Soviet Union, PepsiCo sold bottling rights to Pepsi-Cola and purchased Stolychnaya vodka produced by the Soviet Union.

In a **compensation or buy-back transaction**, an American firm sells equipment or technology to the NME nation and agrees to purchase some of the goods produced with the equipment or technology. For example, Occidental Petroleum sold to the former Soviet Union technology for the construction and operation of ammonia plants and purchased ammonia produced by the plants.

Countertrade is not to be confused with a **barter** transaction, which is a nonmoney transaction in which goods are exchanged. Countertrade involves two reciprocal sales in which each party is paid in money, usually the currency of the NME.

Accepting countertrade may benefit an American seller. It may be the only way an American firm can obtain access to a NME, and it does provide a greater assurance of payment. However, payment is in the NME currency, which either cannot be taken out of the NME nation or has little value on world monetary markets. Also, the goods obtained from the NME nation may not fit into an American firm's normal distribution network and may be of inferior quality. Therefore, an American firm may have difficulty disposing of countertraded goods.

Sales Abroad through a Distributor

If a U.S. firm believes that there is a substantial market for its product in some area abroad, it may find that appointing a distributor located in that area is a more effective and efficient way to exploit the market than selling directly to buyers. If so, it signs a distribution agreement, a contract between the seller and the distributor that sets forth a wide range of terms and conditions of the distributorship. This contract should be written and should contain provisions similar to those in a direct sales contract. However, a distributorship agreement may have additional provisions that cause violations of American and foreign antitrust laws.

Two possible provisions in an international distribution agreement can raise antitrust problems. The first is an exclusive dealing or requirements contract provision whereby the distributor promises not to distribute competing products of any other manufacturer. A seller often wants such a provision because it encourages the distributor to devote its full efforts to sales of the seller's product and not to sales of a competing product. Such an agreement may be illegal under American antitrust laws because it limits the ability of competing firms to export into that territory. The second provision, an exclusive distributorship whereby the seller promises that it will not appoint another distributor in the same territory, is more likely to be challenged under foreign antitrust laws. Distributors frequently want such a provision in order to protect their efforts to build up a base of customers.

The EEC's antitrust laws apply to American firms operating in western Europe. Article 85 of the Treaty of Rome states: "all agreements which . . . may affect trade between member states and which have as their object or effect the prevention, restriction or distortion of competition within the common market" are void, and fines may be imposed on parties entering into such agreements. Article 86 prohibits entities with a dominant market position in a substantial portion of the EEC from taking improper advantage of that position. Exclusive distributorship agreements have been especially susceptible to challenge under Article 85.

Liability of Carriers of Goods

When an American firm ships goods to a foreign buyer, the goods may be shipped by ground, air, or water carrier. The duties and extent of liability of these various carriers is largely determined by domestic statutes and international law.

Ground Carriers   American trucking and railroad companies are regulated by the Interstate Commerce Commission pursuant to the Interstate Commerce Act. American carriers are liable for any loss or damage to the goods with few exceptions—for example, damage caused by acts of God and acts of the shipper (usually the seller of the goods), such as poorly packaging the goods. An American carrier may limit its liability by contract, provided it allows the shipper to obtain full liability by paying a higher shipping charge.

Most European trucking companies are covered by the Convention on the Contract for International Carriage of Goods by Road (CMR); most European railroads are governed by the International Convention Concerning Carriage of Goods by Rail (CIM). These international agreements place liability on carriers for damages to goods they carry with few exceptions—for example, defective packaging by the shipper and circumstances beyond the carrier's control. Each also limits a carrier's liability to an amount stated in the CMR or CIM, unless the shipper agrees to pay for greater liability.

Air Carriers   The Warsaw Convention governs the liability of international air carriers. Most nations have ratified the Warsaw Convention in its original or amended form. Under the Convention, an air carrier is liable to the shipper for damages to goods with few exceptions, including that it was impossible for the carrier to prevent the loss or that the damage was caused by the negligence of the shipper. The Warsaw Convention limits a carrier's liability to a stated amount per pound, unless the shipper pays for greater liability.

Water Carriers   The Hague Rules govern the liability of international water carriers. The Hague Rules were amended in Visby, Sweden, in 1968. The United States codified the Hague Rules in the Carriage of Goods by Sea Act (COGSA), but has not ratified the Visby amendments, which do not substantially change the liability of international water carriers.

The Hague-Visby Rules and the COGSA impose on international water carriers the duties to (1) furnish a seaworthy ship and (2) stow the cargo carefully to prevent it from breaking loose during storms at sea. When these duties are met, a water carrier will not usually be liable for damages to cargo. Water carriers have no liability for damages due to circumstances beyond their control—such as poor packaging, piracy, or acts of war. Under COGSA, liability is limited to $500 per package, unless the shipper agrees to pay a higher shipping fee. Under the Hague-Visby Rules, liability will be the value of the goods declared by the shipper.

Under COGSA or the Hague-Visby Rules, the owner of cargo will be liable for damage his cargo does to other cargo. Also, under the ancient maritime **doctrine of general average**, when a carrier sacrifices an owner's cargo, such as throwing it overboard in order to save the ship and the other cargo, the other owners have liability to the owner whose cargo was sacrificed; liability is pro rated to each owner according to the value of each owner's goods in relation to the value of the voyage (the value of the ship plus the value of the other owners' goods plus the carrier's total shipping fees).

The doctrine of general average is commonly expanded by the contract between the carrier and cargo owners in **New Jason clauses**.[3] Typically, a New Jason clause provides that in *all* cases when goods are damaged and the carrier is not liable under COGSA, the goods owner is entitled to general average contributions from all other cargo owners.

LICENSING FOREIGN MANUFACTURERS

An American firm can also enter the world market by licensing its product or service to a foreign manufacturer. In exchange for granting a license to the foreign licensee, the American licensor will receive royalties from the sale of the licensed product or service. Usually, the licensed product or service or the name under which it is sold will be protected by American intellectual property law, such as patent, trade secret, copyright, or trademark law. Because American intellectual property law does not protect the property outside the boundaries of the United States, a licensor needs to take steps to ensure that its intellectual property will acquire protection in the foreign nation. Otherwise, the licensor risks that a competitor may appropriate the intellectual property without penalty.

Patents and Trade Secrets

A patent filing must be made in each nation in which protection is desired. It is not difficult for a firm to acquire parallel patents in each of the major countries maintaining a patent system, because many countries are parties to the Paris Convention for the Protection of Industrial Property. This convention recognizes the date of the first filing in any nation as the filing date for all, but only if subsequent filings are in fact made within a year of the first filing.

When technology is not patented, either because it is not patentable or because a firm makes a business decision not to patent it, a licensor may control its use abroad under **trade secret** law. For example, an American firm can license its manufacturing know-how to a foreign manufacturer for use in a defined territory in return for promises to pay royalties and to keep the trade secret confidential.

Copyright

An American firm may license a foreign manufacturer to produce literary, artistic, or musical materials for which the firm holds an American copyright. For example, a computer software development firm may grant a license to a foreign manufacturer of software. Also, the American owner of copyrights protecting the Beavis and Butt-head cartoon characters may license a Chinese firm to manufacture Beavis and Butt-head dolls.

International copyright protection is governed by the Berne Convention, which states that a copyright registration in one signatory nation grants the copyright owner rights in all signatory nations. The United States is a signatory of the Berne Convention.

Trademarks

The holder of an American trademark may license the use of its trademark in a foreign nation. For example, McDonald's may license a French firm to use the McDonald's name and golden arches at a restaurant on the Champs-Elysees. Or the holder of the Calvin Klein trademark may license a South Korean firm to manufacture Calvin Klein jeans. In

---

[3]*The Jason*, 225 U.S. 32 (U.S. Sup. Ct. 1912) (upheld the validity of general average clauses in bills of lading).

addition to the grey market goods problem discussed earlier in this chapter, the holder of an American trademark that licenses its product or services abroad runs the risk of losing trademark protection in the foreign market.

Trademark registrations must be made in each nation in which protection is desired. Parallel trademark registrations may be made in compliance with the Paris Convention for the Protection of Industrial Property. Under the Paris Convention, the date of the first filing in any nation is the filing date for all nations, if the subsequent filings are made within six months of the first filing.

The Madrid Agreement permits a firm to register a trademark in all its signatory nations simultaneously by filing an application for registration with the World Intellectual Property Organization in Geneva. The United States is not a signatory of the Madrid Agreement.

Antitrust Problems

International licensing of intellectual property, if done on an exclusive basis, can give rise to the same kinds of antitrust questions as do exclusive distributorships. An exclusive license of a product innovation means that no one other than the licensee, not even the licensor, can manufacture or sell the product or service in the designated territory. Competition among products using the same technology is limited and, therefore, may be illegal.

DIRECT FOREIGN INVESTMENT

An American firm may directly invest in a foreign economy, such as building a manufacturing plant and making its goods near foreign customers. Foreign production may give access to lower-priced labor and raw materials as well as avoid the tariff and other trade barriers erected by foreign nations.

Before an American firm decides to establish a manufacturing operation abroad, its officers must examine a wide variety of legal issues. Some of the issues are ones we have already discussed, such as protection of patents and trademarks. Foreign labor laws may be very different from American law and may impose long-term obligations on the employer. For example, Japanese custom is to hire an employee for life, and in the Netherlands, an employer

must obtain governmental approval to dismiss an employee.

Import license requirements and high tariffs may force the firm to use local sources of supplies and raw materials and to manufacture locally a certain percentage of the parts used in assembling the final product. Some countries—for example, India—prohibit foreigners from having a majority equity interest in any operation within their borders. In socialist nations, direct foreign investment is usually prohibited, although some NME nations—for example, China—allow an American firm to co-own a business with a government-owned entity.

When these legal problems are surmounted and the American firm establishes a successful operation in a foreign nation, two additional problems may arise: (1) restrictions on investment repatriation and (2) expropriation.

Repatriation of Earnings and Investment

Repatriation is bringing back to the United States earnings from a direct foreign investment. Many countries, particularly those in the developing world, have regulations concerning the conversion of their currency into a foreign currency such as dollars, and the removal of the converted currency to another country such as the United States. When an American firm wishes to repatriate some of the earnings from an operation in a country with such regulations, it must obtain permission from the host nation's currency exchange authorities. These authorities operate under rules intended to encourage foreign firms to reinvest their earnings in the country rather than send them home. Some countries place an absolute limit, stated in terms of a set percentage of the amount that a firm has invested, on the amount of earnings that may be repatriated each year. Other countries place a substantial income withholding tax on repatriated earnings, which increases in percentage with the amount repatriated.

When an American firm wants to sell or liquidate its operations, all proceeds in excess of the original investment are usually considered dividends, and their repatriation may be either prohibited or taxed at a very high rate. The existence of such regulations in a country means that an American firm should normally not consider a major investment in that country unless it is prepared to make a long-term commitment.

Expropriation

One of the biggest fears of an American firm investing in a politically unstable country is expropriation, the taking of its facilities by the host government without adequate compensation. Since 1945, expropriations have been common, including the expropriation of hotels and banks in Cuba and oil fields and refineries in Iran, Saudi Arabia, and Libya.

American political leaders take the position that international law requires adequate, effective, and prompt compensation whenever a foreign government takes property belonging to someone who is not a citizen of that country. Although this position, which is consistent with our Constitution, is shared by most western nations, it is rejected by many developing countries and communist countries. Some of these countries contend that international law requires only nondiscriminatory treatment of their citizens and noncitizens. Others recognize the principle that compensation is required, but assert that it may be delayed if immediate payment would frustrate what they view as vital state programs, as would almost always be the case where there is a social revolution that includes a program of massive expropriation of private property.

Regardless, there is difficulty persuading a court to take and listen to such a compensation case. American courts will usually not interfere on the grounds that a foreign government's expropriation action is entitled to deference as an act of state. The **act of state doctrine**, while not international law, is a matter of comity or courtesy between nations. It holds that a nation is not permitted to question the act of another nation committed within its own boundaries. In addition, a court may refuse to allow a foreign government to be sued by an American firm under the doctrine of sovereign immunity. A neutral foreign court is an even less likely forum because it is not anxious to put itself in the middle of a dispute between a citizen of one foreign country and the government of another.

As the following case shows, however, some courts are willing to find a duty to compensate fairly an American firm for the expropriation of its property when a treaty between the United States and the expropriating nation provides for such a remedy. Note, also, that the American court had jurisdiction over funds of the expropriating nation.

KALAMAZOO SPICE EXTRACTION CO. v. PROVISIONAL MILITARY GOVERNMENT OF SOCIALIST ETHIOPIA

729 F.2d 422 (6th Cir. 1984)

In 1966, Kalamazoo Spice Extraction Co. (Kal-Spice), an American corporation, entered a joint venture with Ethiopian citizens. They created the Ethiopian Spice Extraction Co. (ESESCO), an Ethiopian-based corporation that was to engage in the production of spices. Kal-Spice owned approximately 80 percent of the shares of ESESCO, contributed capital, built a production facility, and trained ESESCO's staff, which consisted of Ethiopian citizens. After four years of preparation, construction, and training, production began in 1970.

In 1974, the Provisional Military Government of Socialist Ethiopia (PMGSE) came to power. In February 1975, as part of its program to ensure that Ethiopian industries would "be operated according to the philosophy of Ethiopian socialism," the PMGSE announced the seizure of several businesses, including ESESCO. As a result of the expropriation, Kal-Spice's ownership interest in ESESCO was reduced to 39 percent. In December 1975, the PMGSE established a Compensation Commission, which in October 1981 offered Kal-Spice the equivalent of $450,000 in Ethiopian currency. Believing it was entitled to compensation of $11 million, Kal-Spice rejected the offer and, in retaliation, refused to pay for $1.9 million of spices that ESESCO had shipped to Kal-Spice in Michigan. When ESESCO (controlled by the PMGSE) sued Kal-Spice for payment, Kal-Spice counterclaimed against the PMGSE for damages for expropriating part of its interest in ESESCO. The trial court decided that the act of state doctrine precluded adjudication of the claims against the PMGSE. Kal-Spice appealed.

Keith, Judge   The Act of State doctrine is an exception to the general rule that a court of the United States will decide cases by choosing the rules from among various sources of law, including international law. The roots of the doctrine can be traced to *Underhill v. Hernandez* (1897), where the Supreme Court held:

Every sovereign state is bound to respect the independence of every other sovereign state, and the courts of one country will not sit in judgment on the acts of the government of another done within its own territory.

Kal-Spice requests that this Court recognize a "treaty exception" to the Act of State doctrine. *Banco Nacional de Cuba v. Sabbatino* (1964) provides the basis for a treaty exception:

[T]he Judicial Branch will not examine the validity of a taking of property within its own territory by a foreign sovereign government, extant and recognized by this country at the time of suit, *in the absence of a treaty or other unambiguous agreement regarding controlling legal principles*, even if the complaint alleges that the taking violates customary international law. (Emphasis added.)

This language and the existence of a treaty between the United States and Ethiopia, asserts Kal-Spice, requires a "treaty" exception to the rule that a United States court will not exercise jurisdiction over a foreign sovereign for an act done by that sovereign within its borders. The treaty in existence between the United States and Ethiopia is the 1953 Treaty of Amity and Economic Relations. That treaty provides:

Property of nationals and companies of either High Contracting Party, including interests in property, shall receive the most constant protection and security within the territories of the other High Contracting Party. *Such property shall not be taken except for a public purpose, nor shall it be taken without prompt payment of just and effective compensation.* (Emphasis added.)

The standard of compensation provided for in the Treaty of Amity between Ethiopia and the United States can provide a basis for determining the extent of compensation to which Kal-Spice may be entitled. Numerous treaties employ the standard of compensation used in the 1953 Treaty of Amity between Ethiopia and the United States. Undoubtedly, the widespread use of this compensation standard is evidence that it is an agreed upon principle in international law.

There is a great national interest to be served in this case, i.e., the recognition and execution of treaties that we enter into with foreign nations. The failure of this court to recognize a properly executed treaty would indeed be an egregious error because of the position that treaties occupy in our body of law.

Judgment reversed in favor of Kal-Spice; remanded to the trial court.

The best protection against the risk of expropriation is insurance. To encourage American investment in developing countries, the U.S. government established the Overseas Private Investment Corporation (OPIC). OPIC offers low-cost expropriation insurance for certain investment projects in designated countries.

OFF-SHORE BANKING AND OTHER USES OF TAX HAVENS

Because differences in the business taxation rates of developed nations are minimal, tax shopping among developed nations provides little benefit to an international business. However, small countries in North America and Europe provide significant tax advantages to American firms. These **tax havens**, including the Bahamas, the Cayman Islands, and Bermuda, have no income tax. In addition, some tax havens, such as Switzerland, the Bahamas, and the Cayman Islands, not only have low or no income taxes but also protect the secrecy of banking accounts. Consequently, many American firms have established insurance, banking, and investment company subsidiaries in these tax havens.

Not surprisingly, many persons use tax havens to mask illegal activities, especially drug dealing. During the 1980s, the U.S. government pressured the Swiss government to remove its bank secrecy protections to help the United States prosecute drug dealers and tax defrauders. The United States has not, however, exerted similar pressure against other tax havens that have strong bank secrecy laws.

THE FOREIGN CORRUPT PRACTICES ACT

In 1977, the Congress of the United States passed the Foreign Corrupt Practices Act (FCPA) in response to discoveries that over 400 American firms had made bribes to foreign businesses and government officials in connection with international business transactions. The FCPA makes it a crime for any American firm to offer, promise, or make payments or gifts of anything of value to a foreign official or any other person if the firm knows or should know that it will be used to influence a discretionary governmental decision. An American firm may be fined up to $2 million. Any officer or director who violates the payments prohibition may be fined up to $100,000 and imprisoned up to five years.

ETHICAL AND PUBLIC POLICY CONCERNS

1. Do you think it is right for nations to use export controls for political ends? Consider the 1990 and 1991 world embargo of Iraqi exports in response to its invasion of Kuwait. Did the benefits of such an embargo outweigh its costs? Does it matter that Iraqi citizens were harmed by an embargo that was aimed at Iraq's political leaders?

2. Do you think that foreign governments should restrict the repatriation of earnings and investment? Why do foreign governments restrict repatriation? What are the long-term costs and benefits of restricting repatriation? Would you make a direct foreign investment in a country that has a history of expropriating American investments without adequate compensation? Do you think American firms have given as much to the economies of developing nations as they have taken out of the economies?

3. Do you think it is right for an American firm to establish a banking or other subsidiary in the Cayman Islands? Who benefits from such a decision? Who suffers by such a decision? Would you invest in an American firm that has a banking subsidiary in a tax haven?

PROBLEMS AND PROBLEM CASES

1. Roger Geissler was an exporter of military arms and parts. He exported tires for F-14 fighter jets to Iran for use by the Iranian Air Force. Geissler did not obtain a validated license to export the F-14 tires, even though the Commodity Control List required a validated license for the export of "Other aircraft parts and components, n.e.s. [not elsewhere specified]." The only other federal agency that could regulate the export of F-14 tires—the State Department—explicitly excluded F-14 aircraft tires from its jurisdiction. Has Geissler violated the Export Administration Act?

2. Edward Elkins, an American businessman, was approached about selling Lockheed aircraft to a buyer in Libya. The aircraft had potential military uses. The U.S. Department of State told Elkins the sale would not be approved because of a presidential order prohibiting trade to Libya. Elkins conceived of a plan to obtain validated licenses to sell the aircraft to a German company owned and operated by Libyans and to route the aircraft through Bordeaux, France, to Benin (a small African country), and then to Libya. Is the export of the aircraft in this manner a violation of the Export Administration Act?

3. Holly Stores, Inc., imported into the United States clothing hung on wire or plastic hangers. The Tariff Schedules provided that reusable hangers for clothing were dutiable at a lower rate than nonreusable hangers, which were dutiable at the higher rate for clothing. The hangers were of fairly durable construction and it was physically possible to reuse them. Retailers discarded 99 percent of the hangers; the other 1 percent were given to customers with the clothes on them, used to replace broken hangers, or used to return clothes to a warehouse. Should the hangers be dutied as clothing?

4. To encourage investment and development, the governments of Canada, Alberta, Ontario, and Saskatchewan gave investment tax credits and monetary grants to Canadian producers of tubular steel, including Ipsco Steel, Inc. Ipsco exported tubular steel to the United States. American producers claimed to be harmed by Ipsco's exports. What remedy is available to the American producers?

5. Olympus Corporation (Olympus) was the exclusive American licensee and distributor of the camera products of Olympus Optical Co. (Optical).

Olympus owned the American rights to Optical's trademark. A discount retailer in New York City, 47th Street Photo, Inc., purchased Optical's cameras from Optical's authorized dealers abroad and imported them into the United States. Will Olympus be able to enjoin 47th Street Photo's importations of Optical's cameras on the grounds that it has violated the Tariff Act and the Lanham Act?

6. Asturquimica, S.A., a Spanish company, exported potassium permanganate to the United States in 1985 and 1986. During 1986, the value of the Spanish peso appreciated 13 percent in relation to the American dollar. Asturquimica increased its export price by 6 percent, except to American buyers to whom it was contractually committed to sell at the 1985 price. The result was that Asturquimica sold potassium permanganate in the United States at prices from 7 to 13 percent below the price in Spain. Carus, an American competitor of Asturquimica, asked the International Trade Administration to impose a countervailing duty against Asturquimica. Did the ITA assess the duty?

7. In 1980, National Oil Corporation (NOC), a company owned by the Libyan government, and Libyan Sun Oil Co., a Delaware corporation, agreed to drill for oil in Libya. Their contract contained a *force majeure* clause and provided for arbitration of any dispute by the International Chamber of Commerce (ICC) in Paris. When the United States banned the importation into the United States of Libyan oil, Sun Oil notified NOC that the *force majeure* clause excused its future performance. NOC requested and obtained arbitration before the ICC, which held that the *force majeure* clause did not excuse Sun Oil and found Sun Oil liable to NOC for $20 million. NOC sought to enforce the award of the ICC in a U.S. federal district court. Did the American court enforce the ICC award?

8. Dessaleng Beyene, an American resident, agreed to sell two prefabricated houses to Mohammed Sofan, a resident of Yemen. Sofan obtained a letter of credit from a Yemen bank. The letter of credit was confirmed by Irving Trust Company in New York. Beyene shipped the houses to Sofan and received a bill of lading addressed to "Mohammed So*r*an." When Beyene presented the bill of lading to Irving Trust, it refused to pay Beyene's draft drawn against the letter of credit. Has Irving Trust acted properly?

9. China National Light Industrial Products Import and Export Corp. purchased 25,000 tons of wood pulp from Celulosa Arauco y Constitucion, S.A., a Chilean corporation. Celulosa shipped the wood pulp on the *Damodar Tanaba* from Chile to China. The bill of lading contained a New Jason clause, as did the other bills of lading for goods shipped on the vessel. The wood pulp caught fire; after 75 hours, the fire was extinguished. However, all the wood pulp was ruined, either due to the fire or to water damage from the firefighting efforts. Will China National Light be able to recover a portion of its damages from the other owners of cargo on the vessel?

10. Soon after the Fidel Castro regime came to power in Cuba, the Cuban socialist government expropriated four Cuban branches of the Chase Manhattan Bank. The value of the branches was $6.9 million. The Cuban government made no payment to Chase. At the same time, Chase sold for $17 million collateral it held securing $10 million of loans Chase made to two government-owned Cuban banks. Chase kept the $7 million excess proceeds. In addition, Chase refused to repay $2.5 million that the government-owned Cuban Banks had on deposit at Chase. Banco Nacional de Cuba, a government-owned Cuban bank and the successor of the two government-owned Cuban banks, sued Chase in a U.S. court to recover the $9.5 million. Will the recovery of Banco Nacional be reduced by the value of the Chase bank branches expropriated by the government?

INSURANCE

INTRODUCTION

Insurance serves as a frequent topic of discussion in various contexts in today's society. Advertisements for companies offering life, automobile, and property insurance appear daily on television and in the print media. Journalists report on issues of health insurance coverage and movements for reform. Persons engaged in business publicly and privately lament the excessive (from their perspective) costs of obtaining liability insurance. Insurance companies and insurance industry critics offer differing explanations for why those costs have reached their present levels.

Despite the frequency with which insurance matters receive public discussion and the perceived importance of insurance coverage, major legal aspects of insurance relationships remain largely unfamiliar to many persons. This chapter, therefore, examines important components of insurance law. We begin by discussing the nature of insurance relationships and exploring contract law's application to insurance policies in general. We then discuss other legal concepts and issues associated with specific types of insurance, most notably property insurance, liability insurance, and life insurance.[1] The chapter concludes with an examination of an important judicial trend—allowing insurers to be held liable for compensatory and punitive damages if they refuse in bad faith to perform their policy obligations.

NATURE AND BENEFITS OF INSURANCE RELATIONSHIPS

Insurance relationships arise from an agreement under which a risk of loss that one party (normally the **insured**) otherwise would have to bear is shifted to another party (the **insurer**). The ability to obtain insurance enables the insured to lessen or avoid the adverse financial effects that would be likely if certain happenings were to take place. In return for the insured's payment of necessary consideration

---

[1]This chapter's discussion of health insurance is limited in scope, primarily because at the time this book went to press, differing proposals for potentially sweeping federal legislation governing health insurance availability and coverage were being considered in Congress. Another frequently encountered type of insurance, title insurance, was discussed in Chapter 24.

(the **premium**), the insurer agrees to shoulder the financial consequences stemming from particular risks if those risks should materialize in the form of actual events.

Each party presumably benefits from the insurance relationship. The insured obtains a promise of coverage for losses that, if they materialize, could easily exceed the amounts of the premiums paid. Along with this promise, the insured acquires the supposed "peace of mind" that insurance companies and agents like to emphasize. By collecting premiums from many insureds over a substantial period of time, the insurer stands to profit despite its obligation to make payments covering financial losses that stem from insured-against risks. The insured-against risks, after all, are just that: risks. In some instances, events triggering the insurer's payment obligation to a particular insured may never occur (e.g., the insured's property never sustains damage from a cause contemplated by the property insurance policy). The insurer nonetheless remains entitled to the premiums collected during the policy period. Other times, events that call the insurer's payment obligation into play in a given situation may occur infrequently (e.g., a particular insured under an automobile insurance policy has an accident only every few years) or only after many years of premium collection (e.g., an insured paid premiums on his life insurance policy for 35 years prior to his death).

INSURANCE POLICIES AS CONTRACTS

Interested Parties

Regardless of the type of insurance involved, the insurance relationship is fundamentally contractual. This relationship involves at least two—and frequently more than two—interested parties. As noted earlier, the insurer (usually a corporation), in exchange for the payment of consideration (the premium), agrees to pay for losses caused by specific events (sometimes called *perils*). The insured is the person who acquires insurance on real or personal property or insurance against liability, or, in the case of life or health insurance, the person whose life or health is the focus of the policy. The person to whom the insurance proceeds are payable is the **beneficiary.** Except in the case of life insurance, the insured and the beneficiary will often be the same person. In most but not all instances, the insured

will also be the **owner** of the policy (the person entitled to exercise the contract rights set out in the insurance policy and in applicable law). In view of the contractual nature of the insurance relationship, insurance policies must satisfy all of the elements required for a binding contract.

Offer, Acceptance, and Consideration

The insurance industry's standard practice is to have the potential insured make an offer for an insurance contract by completing and submitting an application (provided by the insurer's agent), along with the appropriate premium, to the insurer. The insurer may then either accept or reject this offer. If the insurer accepts, the parties have an insurance contract under which the insured's initial premium payment and future premium payments furnish consideration for the insurer's promises of coverage for designated risks, and vice versa.

What constitutes acceptance of the offer set forth in the application may vary somewhat, depending on the type of insurance requested and the language of the application. As a general rule, however, acceptance occurs when the insurer (or agent, if authorized to do so) indicates to the insured an intent to accept the application. It is important to know the precise time when an acceptance occurs, because the insurer's contractual obligations to the insured do not commence until acceptance has taken place. If the insured sustains losses after the submission of the application (the making of the offer) but prior to an acceptance by the insurer, those losses normally must be borne by the insured rather than the insurer.

With property insurance and sometimes other types of insurance, the application may be worded so that insurance coverage begins when the insured signs the application. This arrangement provides temporary coverage until the insurer either accepts or rejects the offer contained in the application. The same result may also be achieved by the use of a *binder*, an agreement for temporary insurance pending the insurer's decision to accept or reject the risk.

Figure 1 depicts the formation of an insurance contract.

Insurer's Delay in Acting on Application A common insurance law problem is the effect of the insurer's delay in acting on the application. If the applicant suffers a loss after applying but before a

FIGURE 1 Creation of an Insurance Contract

delaying insurer formally accepts, who must bear the loss? As a general rule, the insurer's delay does not constitute acceptance. Some states, however, have held that an insurer's retention of the premium for an unreasonable time constitutes acceptance and hence obligates the insurer to cover the insured's loss.

Other states have allowed negligence suits against insurers for delaying unreasonably in acting on an application. The theory of these cases is that insurance companies have a public duty to insure qualified applicants and that an unreasonable delay prevents applicants from obtaining insurance protection from another source. A few states have enacted statutes establishing that insurers are bound to the insurance contract unless they reject the prospective insured's application within a specified period of time.

Effect of Insured's Misrepresentation

Applicants for insurance have a duty to reveal to insurers all the material (significant) facts about the nature of the risk so that the insurer may make an intelligent decision about whether to accept the risk. When an insurance application includes a false statement by the insured regarding a material matter, the insured's misrepresentation, if relied on by the insurer, has the same effect produced by misrepresentation in connection with other contracts—the contract becomes voidable at the election of the insurer. This means that the insurer may avoid its obligations under the policy. The same result is possible if the insured failed, in the application, to disclose known material facts to the insurer, which issued a policy it would not have issued if the

disclosures had been made. (As will be seen later in the chapter, however, certain clauses frequently appearing in life insurance policies may limit the ability of issuers of such policies to use the insured's misrepresentation as a way of avoiding all obligations under the policy.)

Warranty/Representation Distinction It sometimes becomes important to distinguish between **warranties** and representations that the insured makes (usually in the application) to induce the insurer to issue an insurance policy. Warranties are *express terms in the insurance policy.* They are intended to operate as conditions on which the insurer's liability is based. The insured's breach of warranty terminates the insurer's duty to perform under the policy. For example, a property insurance policy on a commercial office building specifies that the insured must install and maintain a working sprinkler system in the building, but the insured never installs the sprinkler system. The sprinkler system requirement is a warranty, which the insured breached by failing to install the system. This means that the insurer may not be obligated to perform its obligations under the policy.

Traditionally, an insured's breach of warranty has been seen as terminating the insurer's duty to perform *regardless of whether the condition set forth in the breached warranty was actually material to the insurer's risk* (unlike the treatment given to the insured's misrepresentations, which do not make the insurance policy voidable unless they pertained to a material matter). In view of the potential harshness of the traditional rule concerning the effect of a breach of warranty, some states have refused to allow insurers to escape liability on breach of warranty grounds unless the condition contemplated by the breached warranty was indeed material.

Capacity of Parties

Generally speaking, a contract is not enforceable unless both parties to it had the legal capacity to bind themselves to an agreement. This is seldom a problem in the insurance context, whose typical contracting parties—a corporation and an adult—clearly would have capacity in nearly all instances. An insurance policy taken out by a minor may sometimes be treated differently, due to the usual rule that a minor's lack of capacity makes the minor's contract voidable at the election of the minor.[2] For purposes of the insurance setting, however, many states have departed from the usual rule by enacting statutes that make the insurance contracts of minors enforceable against them.

Legality

The law distinguishes between unlawful wagering contracts and valid insurance contracts. A wagering contract creates a new risk that did not previously exist. Such a contract is contrary to public policy and therefore illegal. An insurance contract, however, *transfers existing risks*—a permissible, even desirable, economic activity. A major means by which insurance law separates insurance contracts from wagering contracts is the typical requirement that the party who purchases a policy of property or life insurance must possess an **insurable interest** in the property or life being insured. Specific discussion of the insurable interest requirement appears in this chapter's later sections on property and life insurance.

Form and Content of Insurance Contracts

Writing
State law governs whether insurance contracts are within the statute of frauds and must be evidenced by a writing. Some states require specific types of insurance contracts to be in writing. Contracts for property insurance are not usually within the statute of frauds, meaning that they may be either written or oral unless they come within some general provision of the statute of frauds—for example, the "one-year" provision.[3] Even when a writing is not legally required, however, wisdom dictates that the parties reduce their agreement to written form whenever possible.

Reformation of Written Policy
As one would expect, insurance companies' customary practice is to issue written policies of insurance regardless of whether the applicable statute of frauds requires a writing. An argument sometimes raised by insureds is that the written policy issued by the insurer did not accurately reflect the content of the parties' actual agreement. For instance, after the occurrence of a loss for which the insured thought there was coverage under the insurance contract, the insured learns that the loss-causing event was excluded from coverage by the terms expressly stated in the written policy. In such a situation, the insured may be inclined to argue that the written policy should be judicially **reformed**, so as to make it conform to the parties' supposed actual agreement.

Although reformation is available in appropriate cases, courts normally presume that the written policy of insurance should be treated as the embodiment of the parties' actual agreement. Courts consider reformation an extreme remedy. Hence, they usually refuse to grant reformation unless either of two circumstances is present. The first reformation-triggering circumstance exists when the insured and the insurer, through its agent or agents, were *mutually mistaken* about a supposedly covered event or other supposed contract term (i.e., both parties believed an event was covered by, or some other term was part of, the parties' insurance agreement but the written policy indicated otherwise). The alternative route to reformation calls for proof that the insurer committed fraud as to the terms contained in the policy or otherwise engaged in inequitable conduct. *Ridenour v. Farm Bureau Insurance Co.*, which follows, illustrates the judicial presumption that the written policy sets forth the parties' true agreement. The case also confirms that the insured's unilateral mistake—as opposed to the parties' mutual mistake—about policy terms will not warrant reformation.

---

[2]An insurance contract taken out on the life of a minor (the insured) *by an adult* (the owner) is not voidable, however. Only when the minor is the owner of the policy does the usual concern over the minor's lack of capacity come into play.

[3]The usual provisions of the statute of frauds are discussed in detail in Chapter 16.

RIDENOUR V. FARM BUREAU INSURANCE COMPANY
377 N.W.2d 101 (Neb. Sup. Ct. 1985)

In August 1982, a hog confinement building owned by Charles Ridenour collapsed and was rendered a total loss. Some of Ridenour's hogs were killed as a further result of the collapse. Ridenour made a claim for these losses with his property insurer, Farm Bureau Insurance Company, whose Country Squire policy had been issued on Ridenour's property in July 1977 and had been renewed on a yearly basis after that. Farm Bureau denied the claim because the policy did not provide coverage for the collapse of farm buildings such as the hog confinement structure. Moreover, though the policy provided coverage for hog deaths resulting from certain designated causes, collapse of a building was not among the causes listed. Asserting that the parties' insurance contract was to have covered the peril of building collapse notwithstanding the terms of the written policy, Ridenour sued Farm Bureau. He asked the court to order reformation of the written policy so that it would conform to the parties' supposed agreement regarding coverage.

At trial, Ridenour testified about a February 1982 meeting in which he, his wife, and their son discussed insurance coverage with Farm Bureau agent Tim Moomey. Ridenour testified that he wanted to be certain there was insurance coverage if the hog confinement building collapsed because he had heard about the collapse of a similar structure owned by someone else. Therefore, he asked Moomey whether the Country Squire policy then in force provided such coverage. According to Ridenour, Moomey said that it did. Ridenour's wife, Thelma, testified that she asked Moomey (during the same meeting) whether there would be coverage if the floor slats of the hog confinement building collapsed and caused hogs to fall into the pit below the building. According to her testimony, Moomey responded affirmatively. The Ridenours' son, Tom, testified to the same effect. Mr. and Mrs. Ridenour both testified that they had not completely read the Country Squire policy and that because they did not understand the wording, they relied on Moomey to interpret the policy for them.

Moomey, who had ended his relationship with Farm Bureau by the time the case came to trial, testified that at no time did the Ridenours request that the hogs and the confinement building be insured so as to provide coverage for losses resulting from collapse of the building. Moomey knew that collapse coverage was not available from Farm Bureau for hog confinement buildings. In addition, Moomey testified that he met with Ridenour in April 1982 and conducted a "farm review" in which he discussed a coverage checklist and the Country Squire policy's declarations pages (which set forth the policy limits). This checklist, which Ridenour signed after Moomey reviewed it with him, made no reference to coverage for collapse losses. (Ridenour admitted in his testimony that he had signed the checklist after Moomey read off the listed items to him.) When Moomey was contacted by the Ridenours on the day the building collapsed, he had his secretary prepare a notice of loss report for submission to Farm Bureau. He also assigned an adjuster to inspect the property. Moomey and the adjuster discussed the fact that the Country Squire policy did not provide coverage for Ridenour's losses. Ridenour further testified that the day after the collapse occurred, Moomey told him he was sorry but that Farm Bureau's home office had said there was no coverage.

The trial court granted reformation, as Ridenour had requested. Farm Bureau appealed.

Caporale, Judge The principle upon which Ridenour relies is that reformation is decreed in order to effectuate the real agreement of the parties when a written instrument does not represent their true intent. In this jurisdiction reformation may be decreed where there has been a mutual mistake or where there has been a unilateral mistake caused by the fraud or in-equitable conduct of the other party. To obtain reformation the evidence must be clear, convincing, and satisfactory. Such evidence is present when there has been produced in the trier of fact a firm belief or conviction that a fact to be proved exists. Moreover, there is a strong presumption that a written instrument correctly expresses the intention of the parties to it.

The record does not produce in us a firm belief or conviction that there was a mutual mistake of fact. Moomey was a trained and experienced insurance agent who, after he had no relationship with Farm Bureau, testified he knew the coverage claimed by Ridenour was not available from Farm Bureau and who denied representing that such coverage existed under the policy. Ridenour argues that Moomey's expression of sorrow over the fact that Farm Bureau's home office said there was no coverage, coupled with the facts that he caused a notice of loss report to be prepared and arranged for an adjuster to inspect the property, establishes that Moomey did think collapse coverage for the hog building existed. We conclude otherwise. Prudence dictated that Ridenour's claim be noted and investigated. Investigation of this claim to determine the facts does not imply a thought that coverage exists. Neither does an expression of regret that the home office said coverage does not exist necessarily imply an earlier belief by Moomey that there was coverage. It may as easily imply regret at the confirmation of what Moomey already knew.

Any mistake which may have existed was therefore one made only by Ridenour. Under such a circumstance he must, in order to recover, clearly, convincingly, and satisfactorily establish that the mistake was either the result of fraud on the part of Farm Bureau or due to Farm Bureau's inequitable conduct. Ridenour concedes in his brief that there was no fraud, but argues that Farm Bureau engaged in inequitable conduct by not delivering the declarations pages until after the loss. The late delivery of the declarations pages is more than adequately explained, however, by the fact that Ridenour was tardy in paying his premium. Moreover, since Ridenour admits that he did not read the policy, he cannot be heard to complain that not having the declarations pages deprived him of an opportunity to discover that he had no collapse coverage on his hog confinement building.

The nature of the conflict in the evidence in this case is not unlike that present in . . . earlier cases which resulted in a denial of reformation. [In addition,] the principal cases relied upon by Ridenour in which reformation was decreed are distinguishable from the case presently before us [because in each of the cases cited by Ridenour, the insured and the insurer's agent both testified that the agent made coverage assumptions and representations that were inconsistent with the terms of the written policy]. Indeed, in [those cases] there was no evidentiary conflict as to what the agent represented; consequently, the only conclusion which could have been reached was that there had been a mutual mistake. In the case before us, however, the evidence falls short of overcoming the presumption that the policy as written correctly expresses the intention of the parties at the time it was renewed.

Judgment and decree of reformation reversed in favor of Farm Bureau.

Interpretation of Insurance Contracts   Modern courts realize that many persons who buy insurance do not have the training or background to fully understand the technical language often contained in insurance policies. As a result, courts tend to interpret insurance policy provisions as they would be understood by an average person. In addition, courts construe ambiguities in an insurance contract against the insurer, the drafter of the contract (and hence the user of the ambiguous language). This rule of construction means that if a word or phrase used in an insurance policy is equally subject to two possible interpretations, one of which favors the insurer and the other of which favors the insured, the court will adopt the interpretation that favors the insured.

A number of states purport to follow the *reasonable expectations of the insured* approach to interpretation of insurance policies. Analysis of judicial decisions reveals, however, that this approach's content and effect vary among the states ostensibly subscribing to it. Some states do little more than attach the reasonable expectations label to the familiar principles of interpretation set forth in the preceding paragraph. A few states give the reasonable expectations approach a much more significant effect by allowing courts to effectively read clauses into or out of an insurance policy, depending on whether reasonable persons in the position of the insured would have expected such clauses to be in a policy of the sort at issue. When applied in the latter manner, the reasonable expectations approach tends to resemble reformation in its effect.

Clauses Required by Law

The insurance business is highly regulated by the states, which recognize the importance of the interests protected by insurance and the difference in bargaining power that often exists between insurers and their insureds. In an attempt to remedy this imbalance, many states' statutes and insurance regulations require the inclusion of certain standard clauses in insurance policies. Many states also regulate such matters as the size and style of the print used in insurance policies. Laws in a growing number of states encourage or require the use of plain, straightforward language (rather than insurance jargon and legal terms of art) in policies whenever such language is possible to use.

Notice and Proof of Loss-Causing Event

The insured (or, in the case of life insurance, the beneficiary) who seeks to obtain the benefits or protection provided by an insurance policy must notify the insurer that an event covered by the policy has occurred. In addition, the insured (or the beneficiary) must furnish reasonable proof of the loss-causing event. Property insurance policies, for instance, ordinarily require the insured to furnish a sworn statement (called a *proof of loss*) in which the covered event and the resulting damage to the insured's property are described. Under life insurance policies, the beneficiary is usually expected to provide suitable documentation of the fact that the insured person has died. Liability insurance policies call for the insured to give the insurer copies of liability claims made against the insured.

Time Limits

Insurance policies commonly specify that notice and proof of loss must be given within a specified time. Policies sometimes state that compliance with these requirements is a condition of the insured's recovery and that failure to comply terminates the insurer's obligation. Other times, policies merely provide that failure to comply suspends the insurer's duty to pay until proper compliance occurs. Some courts require the insurer to prove it was harmed by the insured's failure to give notice before allowing the insurer to avoid liability on the ground of tardy notice.

Cancellation and Lapse

When a party with the power to terminate an insurance policy (extinguish all rights under the policy) exercises that power, **cancellation** has occurred. **Lapse** occurs at the end of the term specified in a policy written for a stated duration, unless the parties take action to renew the policy for an additional period of time. Alternatively, lapse may occur as a result of the insured's failure to pay premiums or some other significant default on the part of the insured. Special issues regarding cancellation and lapse of property and life insurance will be discussed later in the chapter.

Third Parties and Insurance Contracts

As a general rule, contracts are assignable only when the assignment will not materially alter the promisor's burden of performance. The insured's identity, character, and traits are important elements of the risk in property, life, health, and liability insurance policies. Therefore, such policies are generally nonassignable. It is also common for insurance policies to contain express restrictions on assignability. After a loss covered by an insurance policy has occurred, however, the insured may normally assign to another party the right to receive benefits under the policy. Such an assignment is permissible because it involves no change in the insurer's risk.

Performance and Breach by Insurer

The insurer performs its obligations by paying out the sums (and taking other related actions) contemplated by the policy's terms within a reasonable time after the occurrence of an event that calls the duty to perform into play. If the insurer fails or refuses to pay despite the occurrence of a payment-triggering event, the insured of course may sue the insurer for breach of contract. By proving that the insurer's denial of the insured's claim for payment constituted a breach, the insured becomes entitled to recover compensatory damages in at least the amount that the insurer would have had to pay under the policy if the insurer had not breached.

What if the insurer's breach caused the insured to incur consequential damages that, when added to the amount due under the policy, would lead to a damages claim exceeding the dollar limits set forth in the policy? Assume that XYZ Computer Sales, Inc.'s store building is covered by a property insurance policy with Secure Insurance Co., that the building is destroyed by an accidental fire (a covered peril), and that the extent of the destruction makes the full $300,000 policy limit owing from Secure to XYZ. Secure, however, denies payment because it believes—erroneously—that XYZ officials committed arson (a cause, if it had been the actual one, that would have relieved Secure from any duty to pay). Because it needs to rebuild and take other related steps to stay in business but is short on available funds due to Secure's denial of its claim, XYZ borrows the necessary funds from a bank. XYZ thereby incurs substantial interest costs, which are consequential damages XYZ would not have occurred if Secure had performed its obligation under the policy. Assuming that XYZ's consequential damages would have been foreseeable to Secure, most states would allow XYZ to recover the consequential damages in addition to the amount due from Secure under the policy.[4] This is so even though the addition of the consequential damages would cause XYZ's damages recovery to exceed the dollar limit set forth in the parties' insurance policy. The breaching insurer's liability may exceed the policy limits despite the insurer's good faith (though incorrect) basis for denying the claim, because a good faith but erroneous refusal to pay is nonetheless a breach of contract. If the insurer could point to the policy limits as a maximum recovery in this type of situation, it would have an all-too-convenient means of avoiding responsibility for harms that logically flowed from its breach of contract.

Due to similar reasoning, many states' laws provide that if an insured successfully sues her insurer for amounts due under the policy, the insured may recover interest on those amounts (amounts that, after all, should have been paid by the insurer much sooner and without litigation). Some states also have statutes providing that insureds who successfully sue insurers are entitled to

awards of attorney's fees. Punitive damages are *not* allowed, however, when the insurer's breach of contract consisted of a *good faith (though erroneous) denial* of the insured's claim. Later in this chapter, we will explore the recent judicial trend toward allowing punitive damages when the insurer's breach was in *bad faith* and thus amounted to the tort of bad faith breach of contract.

PROPERTY INSURANCE

Owners of residential and commercial property always face the possibility that their property might be damaged or destroyed by any number of causes beyond their control. These causes include, to name a few notable ones, fire, lightning, hail, and wind. Although property owners may not be able to prevent harm to their property, they can secure some protection against resulting financial loss by contracting for property insurance and thereby transferring certain risks of loss to the insurer. Certain persons holding property interests that fall short of ownership may likewise seek to benefit, as will be seen, from the risk-shifting feature of property insurance.

The Insurable Interest Requirement

As noted earlier in this chapter, in order for a property insurance contract not to be considered an illegal wagering contract, the person who purchases the policy (the policy owner) must have an **insurable interest** in the property being insured. One has an insurable interest if he, she, or it possesses a legal or equitable interest in the property and that interest translates into an economic stake in the continued existence of the property and the preservation of its condition. In other words, a person has an insurable interest if he would suffer a financial loss in the event of harm to the subject property. If no insurable interest is present, the policy is void.

Examples of Insurable Interest The legal owner of the insured property would obviously have an insurable interest. So might other parties whose legal or equitable interests in the property do not rise to the level of an ownership interest. For example, mortgagees and other lienholders would have insurable interests in the property on which

---

[4]Even though the terms of the insurance policy almost certainly would state that Secure's payment obligation is limited to costs of repair or replacement or to the property's actual cash value—that is, without any coverage for consequential harms experienced by the insured—Secure cannot invoke this policy language as a defense. If Secure had performed its contract obligation, its payment obligation would have been restricted to what the policy provided in that regard. Having breached the insurance contract, however, Secure stands potentially liable for consequential damages to the full extent provided for by general contract law. For additional discussion of damages for breach of contract, see Chapter 18.

they hold liens.[5] A nonexhaustive list of other examples would also include holders of life estates in real property, buyers under as-yet unperformed contracts for the sale of real property, and lessees of real estate.[6] In the types of situations just noted, the interested party stands to lose financially if the property is damaged or destroyed. *Crowell v. Delafield Farmers Mutual Fire Insurance Company*, which follows shortly, provides a further example of a property interest substantial enough to amount to an insurable interest.

Timing and Extent of Insurable Interest A sensible and important corollary of the insurable interest principle is that the requisite insurable interest must exist *at the time of the loss* (i.e., at the time the subject property was damaged). If an insurable interest existed when the holder thereof purchased the property insurance but the interest was no longer present when the loss occurred, the policy owner is not entitled to payment for the loss. This would mean, for example, that a property owner who purchased property insurance would not be entitled

to collect from the insurer for property damage that occurred after she had transferred ownership to someone else. Similarly, a lienholder who purchased property insurance could not collect under the policy if the loss took place after his lien had been extinguished by payment of the underlying debt or by another means.

The extent of a person's insurable interest in property is limited to the value of that interest. For example, Fidelity Savings & Loan extends Williams a $95,000 loan to purchase a home and takes a mortgage on the home as security. In order to protect this investment, Fidelity obtains a $95,000 insurance policy on the property. Several years later, the house is destroyed by fire, a cause triggering the insurer's payment obligation. At the time of the fire, the balance due on the loan is $84,000. Fidelity's recovery under the insurance policy is limited to $84,000, because that amount is the full extent of its insurable interest. (An alternative way by which mortgagees protect their interest is to insist that the property owner list the mortgagee as the *loss payee* under the property owner's policy. This means that if the property is destroyed, the insurer will pay the policy proceeds to the mortgagee. Once again, however, the mortgagee's entitlement to payment under this approach would be limited to the dollar value of its insurable interest, with surplus proceeds going to the insured property owner.)

---

[5]Chapter 27 contains a detailed discussion of security interests in real property. Chapter 28 addresses security interests in personal property.

[6]Chapter 24 contains a discussion of life estates and an examination of contracts for the sale of real property. Leases of real estate are explored in Chapter 25.

CROWELL V. DELAFIELD FARMERS MUTUAL FIRE INSURANCE COMPANY
453 N.W.2d 724 (Minn. Ct. App. 1990)

Earl and Vonette Crowell owned and operated a farm in Cottonwood County, Minnesota. In 1980, the Crowells took out a mortgage on the property with Farm Credit Services. They also took out a fire insurance policy with Delafield Farmers Mutual Insurance Company. This policy ran from October 1985 until October 1988. The Crowells failed to make their mortgage payments and Farm Credit began foreclosure proceedings. Upon foreclosure, mortgagors such as the Crowells have a right of redemption for a specified time, during which they have the right to buy back their property after it has been sold to another. In November 1987, the Crowells' right of redemption ended. Under Minnesota law, however, farmers who lose their farms to corporate lenders are given an additional opportunity to repurchase their farms under a "right of first refusal." This right meant that Farm Credit was forbidden to sell the farm to anyone else before offering it to the Crowells at a price no higher than the highest price offered by a third party. Farm Credit allowed the Crowells to remain on the farm while they tried to secure financing to buy the property under their right of first refusal.

On November 27, 1987, the farmhouse was substantially destroyed by fire. The Crowells filed a claim for the loss with Delafield. Delafield paid the claim on the Crowells' personal effects inside the house, but denied the claim on the structure itself. It claimed that since the Crowells' period of redemption had expired, they no longer had an insurable interest in the farmhouse. The Crowells brought suit. When the trial court granted summary judgment for the Crowells, Delafield appealed.

Kalitowski, Judge   To be entitled to recovery for a loss, an insured must have an insurable interest in the property covered by the policy. To have an insurable interest, the party must suffer a loss of property interest that is substantial and real. A person has an insurable interest in property when the relationship between him and the property is such that he has a reasonable expectation, based upon a real or legal right, of benefit to be derived from the continued existence of the property and of loss or liability from its destruction. The Minnesota Supreme Court has stated that it is not necessary that the insured should have an absolute right of property, and that he has an insurable interest if, by the destruction of the property, he will suffer a loss, whether he has or has not any title to, lien upon, or possession of the property itself.

Farm Credit foreclosed on the Crowells' farm mortgage. The Crowells remained on and continued to operate the farm. After the redemption period, Farm Credit became the absolute owner of the property. The record indicates Farm Credit allowed the Crowells to remain on the farm after the redemption period expired because it was involved in the Crowells' effort to secure financing to enable them to exercise their statutory right of first refusal. In addition, Farm Credit did not purchase and the Crowells did not cancel fire insurance on the property.

By creating a right of first refusal, the legislature gave financially distressed farmers who had lost their farms to corporate lenders an opportunity to repurchase the farms. The legislative purpose of this right of first refusal is to encourage and protect the family farm as a basic economic unit, to insure it as the most socially desirable mode of agricultural production, and to enhance and promote the stability and well-being of rural society in Minnesota and the nuclear family.

This right of first refusal gives family farmers some additional right or interest in the property they lost to corporate lenders. Based on this legal right in the property, the Crowells had a reasonable expectation to derive a benefit from the continued existence of the farmhouse. Although the Crowells no longer had title to the farm, they were allowed to remain on the land with all parties' knowledge and intention that they would exercise their right of first refusal and regain the farm. Therefore, they expected the benefit of living in the farmhouse until they exercised that right.

It is clear the Crowells suffered a loss from the destruction of the farmhouse. Since the fire the Crowells have been unable to live in the farmhouse. This situation forces the Crowells to live several miles from their farm and commute between their home and the farm, causing additional expenses and inconvenience. The advantage of living on the farm is clearly lost.

Under the facts of this case we hold the trial court was correct in holding this right gave the Crowells an insurable interest in the farm and its structures.

Judgment for the Crowells affirmed.

Covered and Excluded Perils

Property insurers usually do not undertake to provide coverage for losses stemming from any and all causes of harm to property. Instead, property insurers tend to either specify certain causes (**covered perils**) as to which the insured *will* receive payment for resulting losses—meaning that there is no coverage regarding a peril not specified—or set forth a seemingly broad statement of coverage but then specify certain perils concerning which there will be *no* payment for losses (**excluded perils**). (Sometimes, property insurers employ a combination of these two approaches by specifying certain covered perils and certain excluded perils.)

Typical Covered Perils   The effects of these approaches are essentially the same, as most property insurers tend to provide coverage for the same sorts of causes of harm to property. The perils concerning which property insurance policies typically provide benefits include fire, lightning, hail, and wind. In addition, property insurance policies often cover harms to property resulting from causes such as the impact of an automobile or aircraft (e.g., an automobile or aircraft crashes into an insured building), vandalism, certain collapses of buildings, and certain accidental discharges or overflows from pipes or heating and air-conditioning systems.

Fire as a Covered Peril   Historically, the importance of coverage against the peril of fire made *fire insurance* a commonly used term. Various insurance companies incorporated the term into their official firm name; the policies these companies issued came to be called *fire insurance policies* even when they covered perils in addition to fire (as policies increasingly have done in this century). As a result, judges, commentators, and persons affiliated with the insurance industry will sometimes refer to today's policies as fire insurance policies despite the usual property insurer's tendency to cover not only fire but also some combination of the other perils mentioned in the preceding paragraph. Whether the term used is *property insurance* (generally employed in this chapter) or *fire insurance*, reference is being made to the same type of policy.

For purposes of fire coverage, insurance policies are those resulting from accidental fires. An accidental fire is one other than a fire deliberately set by, or at the direction of, the insured for the purpose of damaging the property. In other words, the insured obtains no coverage for losses stemming from the insured's act of arson. This commonsense restriction on an insurer's duty to pay for losses also applies to other harms the insured deliberately caused to his property.

For purposes of fire coverage, insurance contracts often distinguish between *friendly fires*, which are those contained in a place intended for a fire (such as fires in a woodstove or fireplace), and *hostile fires*, which burn where no fire is intended to be (such as fires caused by lightning, outside sources, electrical shorts, or those that began as friendly fires but escaped their boundaries). Losses caused by hostile fires are covered; those stemming from friendly fires tend not to be. As a general rule,

covered fire losses may extend beyond direct damage caused by the fire. Indirect damage caused by smoke and heat is usually covered, as is damage caused by firefighters in their attempts to put out the fire.

"All-Risk" Policies and Property Contamination Claims   A so-called all-risk policy of property insurance takes the previously mentioned approach of setting forth a broad general rule of coverage and then specifying narrowly defined exclusions from that general rule. In recent years, public concern has intensified regarding problems of pollution and contamination of property due to the presence of hazardous wastes, leaking and seepage of toxic chemicals, and the like. The market value of property affected by such problems may be markedly reduced as a result. As Chapter 51 indicates, the federal government sometimes requires the cleanup of contaminated real property. When property owners either are charged with the responsibility of conducting a cleanup or otherwise reach the conclusion that such action will be necessary, they have become increasingly inclined to make claims against their property insurers—particularly those offering all-risk coverage—for recovery of the clean-up costs. Alternatively, affected property owners sometimes make claims against their insurers for payment of a supposed loss that took the form of a reduced property value.

These claims are based on the theory that the release or accumulation of hazardous wastes or other toxic substances on the property constitutes a covered harm within the all-risk policy's broad coverage language (and does not come within an exclusion from coverage). When the pollution problem, hazardous waste accumulation, or toxic chemical contamination did not result from deliberate wrongful actions by the insured, courts sometimes rule that the insured is entitled to recover benefits from the all-risk insurer. Cases of this nature are complicated, however, by various issues that go beyond interpreting a policy's coverage and exclusion provisions. Other difficult issues include determining when the harm to the property took place (when the hazardous substance began accumulating on the property, when the problem first manifested itself, or when the problem became especially acute) and determining whether the harm occurred during the time the insurer at issue was insuring the property. Sometimes, these cases involve various insurers that insured the property at different times and are involved in a dispute as to which one of them must cover the loss. The potential exposure insurers offering all-risk policies may face regarding environmental harms and cleanup costs has caused some property insurers to insert specific "pollution exclusion" or "hazardous waste exclusion" clauses in new policies that they issue.

Typical Excluded Perils Although flood-related harm to property may seem similar to harm stemming from some of the weather-related causes listed earlier among the typical covered perils, it does not usually receive the same treatment. Property insurance policies frequently exclude coverage for flood damage. On this point, however, as with other questions regarding perils covered or excluded, the actual language of the policy at issue must always be consulted before a coverage issue is resolved in any given case.[7] Other typical exclusions include earthquake damage and harm to property stemming from war or nuclear reaction, radiation, or contamination. As previously indicated, property insurance policies exclude coverage for losses caused by the insured's deliberate actions that were intended to cause harm to the property.

Additional Coverages Even as to perils for which there may not be coverage in the typical property insurance policy, the property owner may sometimes be able to purchase a specialized policy (e.g., a flood insurance policy) that does afford coverage for such perils. Other times, even if coverage for a given peril is not provided by the terms of most standard property insurance policies, it may nonetheless be possible for the property owner to have coverage for that peril added to the policy by paying an additional premium. This is sometimes done, for example, by policy owners who desire earthquake coverage.

Personal Property Insurance Although the broad term *property insurance* is what has been employed, the discussion so far in this section has

centered around policies providing coverage for harm to *real* property. Items of *personal* property are, of course, insurable as well. Property insurance policies commonly known as homeowners' policies—because the real property serving as the policy's primary subject is the insured's dwelling—cover not only harm to the dwelling but also to personal property located inside the dwelling or otherwise on the subject real property. (Sometimes, depending on the policy language, there may be coverage even when the item of personal property was not located at the designated real property when the item was damaged.) Property insurance policies covering office buildings and other commercial real estate often provide some level of personal property coverage as well. When personal property coverage is included in a policy primarily concerned with real property coverage, the perils insured against in the personal property coverage tend to be largely the same as, though not necessarily identical to, those applicable to the real property coverage.

Lessees of residential or commercial real estate may obtain insurance policies to cover their items of personal property that are on the leased premises. Such policies are highly advisable, because the apartment or office building owner's insurance policy on the real property is likely to furnish little or no coverage for the tenant's personal property.

Automobile insurance policies are in part personal property insurance policies because they provide coverage (under what are usually called the *comprehensive* and *collision* sections) for car damage resulting from such causes as fire, wind, hail, vandalism, or collision with an animal or tree. (As will be seen, automobile insurance policies also contain significant features of another major type of insurance policy to be discussed later—liability insurance.) Other specialized types of personal property insurance are also available. For example, some farmers purchase crop insurance in order to guard against the adverse financial effects that would result if a hailstorm or other covered peril severely damaged a season's crop.

Nature and Extent of Insurer's Payment Obligation

Property insurance policies are **indemnity** contracts. This means that the insurer is obligated to reimburse the insured for his actual losses associated with a covered harm to the insured property. The insured's

---

[7]It may be that a type of peril frequently excluded in property insurance policies is in fact a covered peril under the language of the policy at issue. Alternatively, losses that at first glance appear to have resulted from an excluded peril may sometimes be characterized as having resulted, at least in part, from a covered peril. In the latter event, there may be some coverage for the losses.

recovery under the policy thus cannot exceed the extent of the loss sustained. Neither may it exceed the extent of the insured's insurable interest (as discussed earlier in this chapter) or the amount of coverage that the insured purchased (the **policy limits**).[8]

Policy provisions other than the policy limits also help define the extent of the insurer's obligation to pay. When covered real property is damaged but not destroyed, the **cost of repair** is normally the relevant measure. Many policies provide that when covered real property is destroyed, the insurer must pay the **actual cash value** (or *fair market value*) of the property. Some policies, however, establish **cost of replacement** as the payment obligation in this situation. The policies that call for payment of the actual cash value frequently give the insurer the option to pay the cost of replacement, however, if that amount would be less than the actual cash value. As to covered personal property, the controlling standard is typically the least of the following: cost of repair, cost of replacement, or actual cash value.[9]

Many property insurance policies supplement the above provisions by obligating the insurer to pay the insured's reasonable costs of temporarily living elsewhere if the insured property was her residence and the damage to the residence made it uninhabitable pending completion of repairs or replacement. Comparable benefits may sometimes be provided in policies covering business property. Lost profits and similar consequential losses resulting from harm to or destruction of one's insured property, however, do not normally fall within the insurer's payment obligation unless a specific provision obligates the insurer along those lines.[10] Regardless of whether

the damaged or destroyed property is real or personal in nature, the particular language of the policy at issue must always be consulted before a definite determination can be made concerning what is and is not within the insurer's duty to pay.

Valued and Open Policies   When insured real property is destroyed as a result of fire or another covered peril, the amount to be paid by the insurer may be further influenced by the type of policy involved. Some property insurance contracts are **valued policies.** If real property insured under a valued policy is destroyed, the insured is entitled to recover the face amount of the policy regardless of the property's fair market value. For example, in 1985, Douglas purchased a home with a fair market value of $90,000. Douglas also purchased a valued policy with a face amount of $90,000 to insure the house against various risks, including fire. The home's fair market value decreased over the next several years because of deterioration in the surrounding neighborhood. In 1994, when the home had a fair market value of only $75,000, it was destroyed by fire. Douglas is entitled to $90,000 (the face amount of the valued policy) despite the reduction in the home's fair market value.

Most property insurance policies, however, are open policies. Open policies allow the insured to recover the fair market value (actual cash value) of the property at the time it was destroyed, up to the limits stated in the policy. Thus, if Douglas had had an open policy in the example presented in the previous paragraph, he would have been entitled to only $75,000 when the home was destroyed by fire. Suppose instead that Douglas's home had increased in value, so that at the time of the fire its fair market value was $105,000. In that event, it would not matter what type of policy (valued or open) Douglas had. Under either type of policy, his recovery would be limited to the $90,000 face amount of the policy.

Coinsurance Clause   Some property insurance policies contain a **coinsurance clause**, which may operate as a further limit on the insurer's payment obligation and the insured's right to recovery. A coinsurance clause provides that in order for the insured to be able to recover the full cost of partial losses, the insured must obtain insurance on the property in an amount equal to a specified percentage (often 80 percent) of the property's fair market value.

---

[8]Some insurers, however, provide (in exchange for a more substantial premium than would be charged for a policy without this feature) a homeowner's policy under which the insurer could become obligated to pay *more* than the policy limits if the insured's home was destroyed and the cost to replace it would actually exceed the policy limits.

[9]Concerning certain designated items of personal property such as furs or jewelry, policies often set forth a maximum insurer payout (such as $1,000) that is less than the general policy limits applicable to personal property. Such a payout limitation would operate as a further restriction on the extent of the insurer's obligation.

[10]Recall, however, that if the insurer violates its payment obligation by wrongfully failing or refusing to pay what the policy contemplates, the insurer has committed a breach of contract. As noted in this chapter's earlier discussion of insurance policies as contracts, fundamental breach of contract principles dictate that the breaching insurer is potentially liable for consequential damages.

FIGURE 2	Operation of Coinsurance Clause			
Fair Market Value at Time of Loss	**Face Value of Policy**	**Amount of Insurance Required**	**Actual Loss**	**Recovery**
$100,000	$60,000	$80,000	$ 40,000	$30,000
100,000	60,000	80,000	100,000	60,000

For example, PDQ Corporation has a fire insurance policy on its warehouse with Cooperative Mutual Insurance Group. The policy has an 80 percent coinsurance clause. The warehouse had a fair market value of $100,000, meaning that PDQ was required to carry at least $80,000 of insurance on the building. PDQ, however, purchased a policy with a face amount of only $60,000. A fire partially destroyed the warehouse, causing $40,000 worth of damage to the structure. Because of the coinsurance clause, PDQ will recover only $30,000 from Cooperative. This figure was arrived at by taking the amount of insurance carried ($60,000) divided by the amount of insurance required ($80,000) times the loss ($40,000).

The coinsurance formula for recovery for partial losses is stated as follows:

$$\frac{\text{Amount of insurance carried}}{\text{Coinsurance percent} \times \text{Fair market value}} \times \text{Loss} = \text{Recovery}$$

Remember that the coinsurance formula applies only to *partial* losses (i.e., damage to, but not complete destruction of, property). If PDQ's warehouse had been totally destroyed by the fire, the formula would not have been used. PDQ would have recovered $60,000—the face amount of the policy—for the total loss. If the formula had been used, it would have indicated that Cooperative owed PDQ $75,000—more than the face amount of the policy. This result would be neither logical nor in keeping with the parties' insurance contract. Whether the loss is total or partial, the insured is not entitled to recover more than the face amount of the policy. The examples just discussed are depicted in Figure 2.

Pro Rata Clause
With the limited exception of the valued policy (discussed above), the insured

cannot recover more than the amount of the actual loss. A rule allowing the insured to recover more than the actual loss could encourage unscrupulous persons to purchase policies from more than one insurer on the same property (thus substantially overinsuring it) and then intentionally destroy the property in a way that appears to be a covered peril (e.g., committing arson but making the fire look accidental). In order to make certain that the insured does not obtain a recovery that exceeds the actual loss, property insurance policies commonly contain a *pro rata clause*, which applies when the insured has purchased insurance policies from more than one insurer. The effect of the pro rata clause is to apportion the loss among the insurance companies. (Applicable state law sometimes contains a rule having this same effect.)

Under the pro rata clause, the amount any particular insurer must pay the insured depends on the percentage of total insurance coverage represented by that insurer's policy. For example, Mumford purchases two insurance policies to cover his home against fire and other risks. His policy from Security Mutual Insurance Corp. has a face amount of $50,000; his policy from Reliable Insurance Co. is for $100,000. Mumford's home is partially destroyed by an accidental fire, with a resulting loss of $30,000. As illustrated in Figure 3, Security Mutual must pay Mumford $10,000, with Reliable having to pay the remaining $20,000 of the loss.

The formula for determining each insurer's liability under a pro rata clause is stated as follows:

$$\frac{\text{Amount of insurer's policy}}{\text{Total coverage by all insurers}} \times \text{Loss} = \text{Liability of insurer}$$

Thus, Security Mutual's payment amount was calculated as follows:

FIGURE 3	**Operation of Pro Rata Clause**				

Policy A	Policy B	Total Insurance (Policy A plus Policy B)	Actual Loss	Liability of Insurer A	Liability of Insurer B
$50,000	$100,000	$150,000	$30,000	$10,000	$20,000

$$\frac{\$50,000 \text{ (Security Mutual's policy)}}{\$150,000 \text{ (Total of both policies)}} \times \$30,000 \text{ (Loss)} = \$10,000$$

Reliable's payment amount could be similarly calculated by substituting $100,000 (Reliable's policy amount) for the $50,000 (Security Mutual's policy amount) in the numerator of the equation. This formula may be used for both partial and total losses. However, each company's payment obligation is limited by the face amount of its policy. Thus, Security Mutual could never be liable for more than $50,000. Similarly, Reliable's liability is limited to a maximum of $100,000.

Right of Subrogation

The insurer may be able in some instances to exercise a **right of subrogation** if it is required to pay for a loss under a property insurance contract. Under the right of subrogation, the insurer obtains all of the insured's rights to pursue legal remedies against anyone who negligently or intentionally caused the harm to the property. For example, Arnett purchased a property insurance policy on her home from Benevolent Insurance Company. Arnett's home was completely destroyed by a fire that spread to her property when her neighbor, Clifton, was burning leaves and negligently failed to control the fire. After Benevolent pays Arnett for her loss, Benevolent's right of subrogation entitles it to sue Clifton to recover the amount Benevolent paid Arnett. Arnett will be obligated to cooperate with Benevolent and furnish assistance to it in connection with the subrogation claim.

If the insured provides the liable third party a general release from liability, the insurer will be released from his payment obligation to the insured. Suppose that in the above scenario, Clifton per-

suaded Arnett to sign an agreement releasing him from liability for the fire. Because this action by Arnett would interfere with Benevolent's right of subrogation, Benevolent would not have to pay Arnett for the loss. A partial release of Clifton by Arnett would relieve Benevolent of responsibility to Arnett to the extent of her release.

Duration and Cancellation of Policy

Property insurance policies are usually effective for a designated period such as six months or a year. They are then extended for consecutive periods of like duration if the insured continues to pay the necessary premium and neither the insured nor the insurer elects to cancel the policy. The insured is normally entitled to cancel the policy at any time by providing the insurer written notice to that effect or by surrendering the policy to the insurer. Although property insurers usually have some right to cancel policies, terms of the policies themselves and/or governing law typically limit the grounds on which property insurers may do so. Permitted grounds for cancellation include the insured's nonpayment of the premium and, as a general rule, the insured's misrepresentation or fraud (see this chapter's discussion of contract law's applicability to insurance policies). Policy provisions and/or applicable law typically provide that if the property insurer intends to cancel the policy, the insured must be given meaningful advance written notice (often 30 days) of this intent before cancellation takes effect.

Another cancellation basis exists by virtue of the **increase of hazard** clauses that appear in many property insurance policies. An increase of hazard clause provides that the insurer's liability will be terminated if the insured takes any action materially increasing the insurer's risk. Some increase of hazard provisions also specify certain types of behavior that will cause termination. Common examples of such behavior include keeping highly explosive material on the property and allowing the premises to remain vacant for a lengthy period of time. *Good v. Continental Insurance Company*, which follows, illustrates the operation of an increase of hazard clause.

Good v. Continental Insurance Company
291 S.E.2d 198 (S.C. Sup. Ct. 1982)

Sims and Dorothy Good purchased a standard fire insurance policy on their home from Continental Insurance Company. The policy contained an "increase of hazard" clause stating that the insurer would not be liable if the risk of fire was increased "by any means within the control or knowledge of the insured." A November 1977 fire almost completely destroyed the house. While putting out the fire, firefighters discovered an illegal liquor still concealed in a false closet under the eaves of the roof. The still, encased by bricks and mortar, consisted of a 90-gallon copper vat over an 8- to 10-inch butane gas burner. Firefighters also discovered 22 half-gallons of "moonshine" and many 55-gallon drums full or partially full of mash. A police department detective who dismantled and examined the still's burner after the fire offered the opinion that the still was in operation when the fire occurred. Good denied this, though he admitted installing the still two years earlier—after his insurance policy became effective. Continental refused to pay for the destruction on the ground that the still was an increased hazard.

The Goods sued Continental to recover proceeds under the policy. When the trial court awarded damages to the Goods, Continental appealed.

Harwell, Justice   In [previous cases], this court held that coverage under an insurance policy was suspended if the increased risk was permanent and continuous even though it did not produce the loss. However, if the increased risk caused the loss, an occasional, temporary increase of risk was sufficient to void a policy.

In addition to these guidelines, to void the policy the increase of hazard must be material and substantial such that the insurer could not reasonably be presumed to have contracted to assume it. Also, according to the policy, increased hazard must be accomplished by means solely within the control and knowledge of Good after the insurance contract was effected.

The evidence leads unmistakably to the following: the distillery was permanently installed; it was regularly used at least during the holiday season; Good installed the still after the insurance policy became effective; and only he operated the still. We conclude that the only reasonable inference from the evidence is that there had been an increase of hazard, thereby voiding the policy.

The use to which the Goods put their dwelling was so foreign to the normal uses of a dwelling as to become beyond the contemplation of the insurer. Surely the insurer did not contemplate providing insurance coverage on a residence which concealed an illegal still and the fruits of its operation.

Judgment reversed in favor of Continental.

Liability Insurance

As its name suggests, liability insurance provides the insured the ability to transfer liability risks to the insurer. Under policies of liability insurance, the insurer agrees, among other things, to pay sums the insured becomes legally obligated to pay to another party. This enables the insured to minimize the troublesome or even devastating financial effects that he could experience in the event of his liability to someone else.

Types of Liability Insurance Policies

Liability insurance policies come in various types. These include, but are not limited to: **personal liability policies** designed to cover a range of liabilities an individual person could face; **business liability policies** (sometimes called *comprehensive general liability policies*) meant to apply to various liabilities that sole proprietors, partnerships, and corporations might encounter in their business operations; **professional liability policies** (sometimes called *malpractice insurance policies*) that cover physicians, attorneys, accountants, and members of other professions against liabilities to clients and sometimes other persons; and **workers' compensation policies** under which insurers agree to cover employers' statutorily required obligation to pay benefits to injured workers.

Some policies combine property insurance features with liability insurance components. Automobile insurance policies, for instance, afford property insurance when they cover designated automobiles owned by the insured against perils such as vandalism, hail, and collisions with animals, telephone poles, and the like. Other sections of automobile insurance policies provide liability insurance to the insured (the policy owner), members of her household, and sometimes other authorized drivers when their use of a covered automobile leads to an accident in which they face liability to another party. Typical homeowners' policies also combine property and liability insurance features. Besides covering the insured's home and contents against perils of the types discussed earlier in this chapter, these policies normally provide the insured coverage for a range of liabilities he may face as an individual.

Liabilities Insured Against

Although the different types of liability insurance policies discussed above contain different terms setting forth the liabilities covered and not covered, liability policies commonly afford coverage against the insured's liability for negligence but not against the insured's liability stemming from deliberate wrongful acts (most intentional torts and most be-

havior constituting a crime).[11] Liability policies tend to reach this common ground in the same sorts of ways property insurance policies define the scope of coverage—by listing particular liabilities that are covered and stating that an unlisted liability is not covered, by setting forth a seemingly broad statement of coverage and then specifying exclusions from coverage, or by employing a combination of the previous approaches (e.g., specifying certain covered liabilities and certain excluded liabilities).

Personal Liability and Homeowners' Policies

Personal liability policies and the liability sections of homeowners' policies often state that coverage is restricted to instances of "bodily injury" and "property damage" experienced by a third party as a result of an "occurrence" for which the insured faces liability. These sorts of policies normally define *occurrence* as an "accident" resulting in bodily injury or property damage. The provisions just noted lead to the conclusion that intentional torts and most criminal behavior, if committed or engaged in by the insured, would fall outside the coverage of the policy at issue because they are not accidents (whereas instances of the insured's negligence would be). This conclusion is underscored by typical clauses purporting to exclude coverage for bodily injury or property damage the insured intended to cause. The occurrence, bodily injury, and property damage references in these policies also indicate that liabilities stemming from, for example, breach of contract would not be covered either (no accident, no bodily injury, no property damage). In addition, personal liability policies and liability sections of homeowners' policies also tend to specify that if bodily injury or property damage results from the insured's business or professional pursuits, it is not covered.

Business Liability Policies   Business liability policies also feature coverage for bodily injury and property damage stemming from the insured's actions. The relevant range of actions, of course, is broadened to include the insured's business pursuits or "conduct of business." A major focus remains on unintentional wrongful conduct (usually negligence)

---

[11]Workers' compensation liability policies are somewhat different, as later discussion in this chapter will reveal.

of the insured, with the insured's deliberate wrongful acts normally being specifically excluded from coverage. These policies also tend to provide the insured coverage in instances where the insured would be liable for certain torts of his employees (normally under the *respondeat superior* doctrine).[12]

In addition, business liability policies sometimes afford coverage broader than instances of tortious conduct producing physical injury or property damage. Some policies, for instance, contain a clause that contemplates coverage for the insured's defa-

mation of another person or invasion of that person's privacy (though other policies specifically exclude coverage for those same torts). Furthermore, the broad "conduct of business" language in certain policies, as well as specialized clauses (in some policies) referring to liability stemming from advertising or unfair competition, may contemplate coverage for the insured's legal wrongs that cause others to experience economic harm. In the end, the particular liabilities covered by a business liability policy cannot be determined without a close examination of the provisions in the policy at issue. It may become necessary for a court to interpret a policy provision whose meaning is unclear or scope is uncertain. In the *Cope* case, which follows, the court addressed the scope of a conduct of business clause through the use of contract interpretation techniques introduced earlier in this chapter.

---

[12]The *respondeat superior* doctrine is discussed in Chapter 35. Although the insured's own intentional torts would not normally be covered, business liability policies sometimes provide that if the insured is liable on *respondeat superior* grounds for an employee's intentional tort such as battery, the insured will be covered unless the insured directed the employee to commit the intentional tort.

PROPERTY OWNERS INSURANCE CO. v. COPE
772 F. Supp. 1096 (N.D. Ind. 1991)

Property Owners Insurance Co. (POI) was the insurer and Thomas Cope was the insured under a liability policy that excluded coverage except in instances of liability "with respect to the conduct of a business" owned by Cope. Cope owned a roofing business. While the policy was in force, Cope traveled to Montana with Edward Urbanski, a person with whom Cope did significant business. While on this trip, Cope snowmobiled with a group of persons that included Gregory Johnson, who died in a snowmobiling accident. Johnson's estate brought a wrongful death suit against Cope in a Montana court. POI then filed a declaratory judgment action against Cope and Johnson's estate in the U.S. District Court for the Northern District of Indiana. In this suit, POI sought a judicial determination that it had no obligations to Cope and Johnson's estate under the liability insurance policy. The parties agreed that Indiana law would control the case, which came before the court on POI's motion for summary judgment.

Moody, District Judge POI maintains that the Montana snowmobiling trip was a recreational event rather than "the conduct of a business" owned by Cope. Thus, argues POI, the Montana trip was not covered by the insurance contract. Cope, however, maintains that he intended the Montana trip to advance both business and pleasure, thus bringing it under the policy.

The parties have not briefed, nor has the court found, any Indiana law interpreting the words "conduct of a business" in the context of an exclusion in a contract to provide liability insurance to a business owner. The closest reported case is apparently *Uni-*

gard Mutual Insurance Co. v. Martin (1982), [an Arizona Court of Appeals case] cited by POI. The evidence before the *Martin* court showed that the object of a large annual fishing trip was both recreation and the advancement of business. The *Martin* court . . . focused on the express terms of the [liability] insurance contract. [Noting that the fishing trip was heavily recreational but only incidentally business-connected, and stressing the policy's exclusion for "personal" activities that were not in "direct conduct of a business," the *Martin* court held that the policy at issue did not afford coverage.]

Applying *Martin* to this case, the court readily distinguishes the Arizona precedent on its facts. The *Martin* court relied heavily on [the] particular wording [of the policy involved there] in making its most important analytical point—namely, that the insurance contract was not ambiguous, but plainly excluded the fishing trip by its express terms. The *Martin* court focused especially on the words "direct conduct" in the exclusion before it, defining each word at length, and with particular emphasis on the word "direct." In the case at bar, the contract language is different, the limitation on coverage arising by negative implication from the words "only with respect to the conduct of a business." The word "direct" does not modify "conduct" in this case, nor does the contract expressly contrast personal and business activities. Accordingly, the *Martin* case does not present a perfect template for dealing with this action.

Whether or not the *Martin* court properly read the contract before it as unambiguous, the policy issue before this court is not resolved by the familiar Indiana rule that where an insurance contract is clear and unambiguous, the language therein must be given its plain meaning. [T]his court holds that the words "with respect to the conduct of a business" are, in this context, not sufficiently self-defining in their plain meaning. Rather, those words are ambiguous and require construction because reasonable persons might well differ on the question of whether they exclude coverage for activities furthering dual purposes of recreation and profit.

[U]nder settled principles for the interpretation of ambiguous insurance contracts . . . , this court construes the policy in favor of the insured. Thus, the court holds that the language of the contract before it does not exclude, as a matter of law, coverage for activities that serve dual purposes of recreation and profit. If insurance companies operating in Indiana desire the benefit of such an exclusion, it is a simple enough matter for them to draft their policies to unambiguously exclude coverage for recreational activities furthering business objectives.

In this case, the record on summary judgment reveals a genuine dispute over the factual nature of the Montana snowmobiling trip. This dispute is certainly material, for the factual nature of the trip will, under the express terms of the contract at issue, determine the applicability of the policy's limit on liability. It remains, however, for the court to further explore the materiality of that dispute by detailing the applicable legal standard for assessing the facts. The *Martin* court, in this regard, paints an alarming picture of insurer liability leaping up in extreme situations, perhaps even with chance meetings at Little League games. On the other hand, if hypotheticals are brought to bear, this court can readily imagine a far different situation at the other extreme, one in which a business executive who enjoys his solitude, loathes the boors to whom he must sell his product, and hopes to retire at the earliest possible moment, must nevertheless occasionally invite customers to cocktails or sporting events for the purely fictional purpose of having fun. The *Martin* court, apparently concerned with the dubious horrors of the slippery slope, seems inclined to create a bright line rule denying coverage in both situations. Given the ambiguity in the contract at issue here, however, this court is prepared to seek out a test in the law capable of discriminating among situations of mixed profit and recreation motives.

Cope advances the workmen's compensation test applied in Indiana law for many years: [whether] the activity at issue was "required by or incidental to" the insured's business. The *Martin* court rejected this type of test because the liberal coverage policy motivating workmen's compensation statutes is not at play in a private insurance contract. In this case, however, the contract is ambiguous, which brings to bear Indiana's policy of construing insurance exclusions against insurers. Thus, a significant policy of Indiana insurance law—already employed in construing the contract to cover mixed motive activities—parallels the expansive coverage policy motivating workmen's compensation, and justifies application of the same test. Accordingly, this court holds that the test for coverage under the "conduct of a business" policy at issue is whether Cope's Montana snowmobiling trip was necessary or incidental to the pursuit of profit through his business.

Of course, nothing in this opinion should be read as establishing that the Montana snowmobiling trip was sufficiently related to the insured's business to support a jury verdict of liability under the policy. Rather, this opinion merely establishes Cope's right to present evidence against exclusion at trial.

POI's motion for summary judgment denied.

Other Liability Policies   Professional liability policies also afford coverage for the insured's tortious conduct, this time in the practice of his or her profession. Negligent professional conduct producing harm to a third party (normally bodily injury in the medical malpractice setting but usually economic harm in the legal or other professional malpractice context) would be a covered liability. Wrongful professional conduct of an intentional nature typically would not be covered.

Automobile liability policies cover liability for physical injury and property damage stemming from the insured's (and certain other drivers') negligent driving. Once again, however, there is no coverage for liability arising from the insured's (or another driver's) deliberate vehicle operation acts of a wrongful nature.

Workers' compensation policies tend to approach coverage questions somewhat differently, primarily because injured employees need not prove negligence on the part of their employer in order to be entitled to benefits. Therefore, the insurer's obligation under a workers' compensation policy is phrased in terms of the liability the insured employer would face under state law.

Insurer's Obligations

Duty to Defend   When another party makes a legal claim against the insured and the nature and allegations of the claim are such that the insurer would be obligated to cover the insured's liability if the claim were proven, the insurer has a **duty to defend** the insured. A commonsense precondition of this duty's being triggered is that the insured must notify the insurer that the claim has been made against her. The duty to defend means that the insurer must furnish, at its expense, an attorney to represent the insured in litigation resulting from the claim against her. If the insurer fails to perform its duty to defend in an instance where the duty arose, the insurer has breached the insurance contract. Depending on the facts, the breaching insurer would at least be liable for compensatory damages (as indicated in this chapter's earlier discussion of insurance policies as contracts)[13]

---

[13]The compensatory damages in such an instance would normally be the reasonable costs incurred by the insured in retaining an attorney and paying him to represent her. Of course, if the insured ended up being held liable in the third party's suit and the insurer wrongfully refused to pay the damages assessed against the insured in that case, the insured's compensatory damages claim against the breaching insurer would be increased substantially.

and potentially for punitive damages as well under the *bad faith* doctrine examined later in this chapter.

Sometimes it is quite clear that the insurer's duty to defend applies or does not apply, given the nature of the claim made against the insured. Other times, however, there may be uncertainty as to whether the claim alleged against the insured would fall within the scope of the liability insurance policy. Such uncertainty, of course, means that it is not clear whether the insurer has a duty to defend. Insurers tend to take one of two approaches in an effort to resolve this uncertainty. Under the first approach, the insurer files a declaratory judgment suit against the insured. In this suit, the insurer asks the court to determine whether the insurer owes obligations to the insured under the policy (including the duty to defend as well as the payment obligation to be discussed shortly) in connection with the particular liability claim made against the insured by the injured third party. The other option insurers often pursue when it is unclear whether the liability policy applies is to retain an attorney to represent the insured in the litigation filed by the third party—thus fulfilling any duty to defend that may be owed—but to do so under a *reservation of rights* notice. By providing the reservation of rights notice to the insured, the insurer indicates that it reserves the right, upon acquisition of additional information, to conclude (or seek a later judicial determination) that it does not have the obligation to pay any damages that may be assessed against the insured as a result of the third party's claim. The insurer's reservation of rights also serves to eliminate an argument that by proceeding to defend the insured, the insurer waived the ability to argue that any actual liability would not be covered.

Duty to Pay Sums Owed by Insured   If a third party's claim against the insured falls within the liabilities covered by the policy, the insurer is obligated to pay the compensatory damages held by a judge or jury to be due and owing from the insured to the third party. In addition, the insured's obligation to pay such expenses as court costs would also be covered. These payment obligations are subject, of course, to the policy limits of the insurance contract involved. For example, if the insured is held liable for compensatory damages and court costs totaling $150,000 but the policy limits of the relevant liability policy are $100,000, the insurer's contractual obligation to pay sums owed by the insured is restricted to $100,000.

Is the insurer also obligated to pay any *punitive damages* assessed against the insured as a result of a covered claim? As a general rule, the insurer will have no such obligation, either because of an insurance contract provision to that effect or because of judicial decisions holding that notions of public policy forbid arrangements by which one could transfer his punitive damages liability to an insurer. Not all courts facing this issue have so held, however, meaning that in occasional instances the insured's punitive damages liability may also be covered if the insurance policy's terms specifically contemplate such a result.

The liability insurer need not wait until litigation has been concluded (and damages are awarded or not awarded) to attempt to dispose of a liability claim made against the insured. Insurance policy provisions, consistent with our legal system's tendency to encourage voluntary settlements of claims, allow insurers to negotiate settlements with third parties who have made liability claims against the insured. These settlements involve payment of an agreed sum of money to the third party, in exchange for the third party's giving up her legal right to proceed with litigation against the insured. Settlements may occur regardless of whether litigation has been formally instituted by the third party or whether the claim against the insured consists of the third party's prelitigation demand for payment by the insured. If settlements are reached—and they are reached much more often than not—the substantial costs involved in taking a case all the way to trial may be avoided. The same is also true, from the insurer's perspective, of the damages that might have been assessed against the insured if the case had been tried. Note, however, that even if the defendant (the insured) wins a suit that does proceed to trial, the costs to the insurer are still substantial even though there is no award of damages to pay. Those costs include a considerable amount for attorney's fees for the insured (the insurer's obligation regardless of the outcome of the case) as well as other substantial expenses associated with protracted litigation. Accordingly, even when the insurer thinks that the insured probably would prevail if the case went to trial, the insurer may be interested in pursuing a settlement with the third party claimant if a reasonable amount (an amount less than what it would cost the insurer to defend the case) can be agreed upon.

Is There a Liability Insurance Crisis?

During roughly the past decade, the necessary premiums for liability insurance policies of various types (particularly business and professional liability policies) have risen considerably. Sometimes, the premiums charged by liability insurers have become so substantial that would-be insureds have concluded that they cannot afford liability insurance and therefore must go without it despite its importance. In addition, some insurers have ceased offering certain types of liability policies and/or have become much more restrictive in their decisions about which persons or firms to insure.

Insurance companies tend to blame the above state of affairs on what they see as a tort law regime under which plaintiffs win lawsuits too frequently and recover very large damage awards too often. As a result, insurers have been among the most outspoken parties calling for tort reform, a subject discussed in earlier chapters in this book. Plaintiffs' attorneys and critics of the insurance industry blame rising liability insurance premiums on, primarily, another alleged cause: questionable investment practices and other unsound business practices supposedly engaged in by insurance companies. The parties making these assertions thus oppose tort reform efforts as being unnecessary and unwise.

Liability insurance premiums in general may not be increasing as rapidly today as they did a few years ago, but they remain substantial in amount. So long as liability insurance remains unaffordable or otherwise difficult to obtain, there is a "crisis," given the adverse financial consequences that could beset an uninsured person. This is so regardless of which of the competing explanations set forth above bears greater legitimacy.

LIFE INSURANCE

Life insurance provides a means of lessening the financial hardships that result from the death of a given person. A few basic life insurance concepts were alluded to in this chapter's section on insurance policies as contracts. This section builds on the earlier discussion by examining specialized legal topics and issues that arise in connection with life insurance.

Parties Other than Insurer

Earlier in the chapter, we noted that in the property and liability insurance contexts, the same person will often be the insured (the purchaser of the insurance), the policy owner (the party entitled to enforce the contract rights set forth in the policy), and the beneficiary (the party entitled to payment under the policy). Life insurance, however, departs from this typical property and liability insurance model. In the life insurance setting, the insured is *the person whose life is insured* under the policy. That person may or may not have been the purchaser of the policy. Although the insured may also be the party entitled to enforce the policy's contract rights (the policy owner), it is not unusual for the policy owner to be someone other than the insured. The policy owner is typically the party who purchased the policy, but this is not always true.

Life insurance also departs from the property and liability model with regard to the identity of the beneficiary (the person entitled to payment when the insured dies). The beneficiary, who is designated by the policy owner, will often be one or more family members or friends of the insured, or sometimes business partners of the insured. Of course, the policy owner may double as the designated beneficiary. It is also possible that the insured's estate could be specified as the beneficiary instead of a particular individual (or individuals) being so designated. Life insurance policies often allow the policy owner to change the designated beneficiary prior to the insured's death. Some policies, however, contain terms under which the designation of a beneficiary is irrevocable, meaning that a different beneficiary cannot be substituted for the one already specified.

Insurable Interest

As discussed earlier in this chapter, an insurable interest is required in order to keep an insurance contract from being an illegal wagering contract. In the life insurance context, the requisite insurable interest *must exist at the time the policy was issued* but need not exist at the time of the insured's death. Persons who stand to suffer a financial loss in the event of the insured's death have the insurable interest necessary to support the purchase of a life insurance policy on the insured. The insured and his or her spouse, parents, children, and other dependents thus possess an insurable interest in the insured's life.

In addition, the business associates of the insured may also have an insurable interest in his or her life. Such persons would include the insured's employer, business partners, or shareholders in a closely held corporation with which the insured is connected. Creditors of the insured also have an insurable interest, but only to the extent of the debt owed by the insured.

Types of Life Insurance Policies

A life insurance contract is a valued policy because, upon the insured's death, the insurer must pay the beneficiary a set amount that equals the **face value** of the policy (the amount of insurance coverage purchased). The policy's face value helps determine the amount of the premiums that must be paid to keep the policy in force. A policy with a large face value will, of course, cost the purchaser of the policy more in premiums than will a policy with a smaller face value.

Two basic types of life insurance, **whole life policies** and **term policies,** merit discussion. Although both types are valued policies, they differ in important respects.

Whole Life Policies   *Whole life policies*— sometimes called *ordinary life* or *straight life* policies—contemplate that the insured (or the owner, if a person other than the insured) will pay a set premium for the remainder of his life or until a specified time when the obligation to pay further premiums will cease. The whole life policy does more than impose on the insurer the obligation to pay the policy's face value upon the insured's death. Such a policy possesses a savings feature, in that it develops a **cash surrender value** as premiums are paid. The insured policy owner may recover this value if the policy is terminated. In addition, whole life policies develop a loan value as premiums are paid. This sometimes enables the policy owner to borrow money from the insurer at favorable interest rates. Because of the investment feature and the potential for borrowing present in whole life policies, premiums that the policy owner must pay for such policies usually tend to be higher than the premiums required for term insurance—at least when the insured is in his 30s and perhaps his 40s.

Term Policies   *Term policies* are so named because they are designed to be in effect for a designated term or duration, such as one year. These policies provide insurance coverage only, without the cash surrender value and loan value features present in whole life insurance. In return for the payment of premiums during the term of the policy, the insurer agrees to pay the face amount of the policy if the insured dies during the term.

For many persons, having a suitable amount of insurance coverage in the event of the insured's death may be much more important than an added investment feature or the prospect of borrowing funds in the future. Term policies may be an economical way of obtaining coverage, because premiums for a term policy of a given face value often start lower than for a whole life policy of the same face value. This tends to be true if the term policy is purchased while the insured is in her 30s or early 40s. Although term policies are typically written for a one-year period, they frequently have a *guaranteed renewability* provision. This provision enables the insured (or the owner, if insured and owner are not one and the same) to renew the policy for successive additional terms up to a specified age, without having to undergo medical examinations designed to show that the insured is still in good health. Those desiring insurance coverage may thus keep the term policy in force.

In keeping a term policy in force year after year, however, they face the downside of term policies—annual premium increases. As the insured gets another year older, the premium necessary to keep the term policy in force rises. Although term insurance premiums typically begin lower than whole life premiums, term insurance premiums eventually will equal or exceed those for a whole life policy of the same face value. Therefore, owners of term policies may eventually face the need to decide whether to convert their term policies to whole life policies and thereby avoid the ever-increasing term premiums (plus acquire the added benefits of whole life policies). Term policies often contain a *guaranteed conversion option,* under which the insured may choose to convert the term policy to a whole life policy.

Other Special Issues and Policy Provisions

Misrepresentation Issues   As explained earlier in this chapter, an insurance applicant's misrepresentations concerning material matters may cause a resulting insurance contract to become voidable at the option of the insurer. In the life insurance setting, misrepresentations regarding the proposed insured's health condition become the focus of considerable attention. Whether the insurer is able to avoid its policy obligations on the basis of the insurance applicant's health-related misstatements or failures to disclose will depend on the seriousness of the matter misstated or not disclosed by the applicant, and on the degree to which knowledge of the truth would have influenced the insurer's decision on whether to issue a policy. If the insurer would not have issued the policy had it known the truth, the insurer is likely to be allowed to avoid its policy obligation.

Misstatement of Age Clauses   Two common provisions in life insurance policies help to offset the potentially harsh effect that might otherwise result from certain false representations by the insurance applicant. These provisions are *misstatement of age clauses* and *incontestability clauses.* Under a misstatement of age clause, the insurer is allowed to reduce the amount it must pay upon the insured's death if the insured's age listed in the application for insurance was lower than the insured's actual age at that time. The amount of the insurer's payment obligation will be lowered to reflect the amount of coverage that the premiums paid would have bought at the correct age's premium rates.

For example, having stated his age as 39, Wingfield purchases a $100,000 face-value policy on himself from Invincible Insurance Co. When Wingfield dies, Invincible learns he was actually 43 when he took out the policy. Because the premium rate for a 43-year-old would have been higher, the total amount of premiums actually paid by Wingfield would have purchased only $85,000 in coverage at the correct premium rate. Therefore, under the misstatement of age clause, Invincible would be obligated to pay Wingfield's beneficiary $85,000 rather than $100,000.

Incontestability Clauses   Under the incontestability clauses commonly seen in life insurance policies, insurers are barred from contesting their liability under the policy on the basis of certain misrepresentations by the insured if the policy has been in force for a specified period of time (frequently, two years). Incontestability clauses do not, however, prevent the insurer from contesting liability on the grounds that the requisite insurable interest was lacking, that an impostor filled in for the insured at the required medical exam, or that the policy purchaser took out the policy with the intent to kill the insured and collect the policy proceeds.

Special Cancellation and Lapse Issues Insurers generally cannot cancel life insurance contracts as long as the necessary premiums are being paid. A contrary rule could tempt insurers to terminate policies covering seriously ill insureds and would thus poorly serve insureds, policy owners, and beneficiaries.

The policy owner may cancel a life insurance policy by surrendering it to the insurer. If the policy is a whole life policy, the owner is usually allowed under the policy provisions to recover the accumulated cash surrender value or to purchase a paid-up or extended policy. Under a paid-up policy, the owner acquires a fully paid-for policy on the insured. The policy's face value is the amount of coverage that the cash surrender value would purchase, in light of the insured's age. An extended policy is a term policy having the same face value as the original policy that was surrendered.

Lapse of a term insurance policy occurs upon the expiration of the stated duration, unless the policy is renewed. Any life insurance policy, whether term or whole life, lapses if the necessary premiums are not paid. When a whole life policy lapses due to nonpayment of premiums, the owner normally has the same rights to cash surrender value and a paid-up or extended policy as are made available to the owner who surrenders a whole life policy. The owner whose term insurance lapses because of nonpayment of premiums, however, has no such remedies.

In order to guard against the potentially harsh consequences stemming from lapsed life insurance policies (particularly lapsed term policies), many states have enacted statutes allowing policy owners a grace period within which they may pay past-due premiums and thereby avoid policy lapse or cancellation. A typical statutory grace period is 30 days. Life insurance policies themselves sometimes contain similarly motivated provisions, under which the owner whose life insurance policy has lapsed is given a limited time within which to pay past-due premiums and furnish proof of insurability (the insured's good health). By doing these things within the specified time, the owner obtains reinstatement of the policy.

HEALTH INSURANCE

With the costs of medical treatment, hospitalization, and medications having increased dramatically in recent years, health insurance has become a critical means by which insureds minimize the adverse financial consequences associated with illness and injury. The costs of serious illness or injury may be financially crippling unless insurance coverage exists.[14] Health insurance has thus become a virtual necessity in today's society, as demonstrated by the fact that a very large percentage of the U.S. population does have some form of health coverage.

Nature of Coverage

Health insurance policies typically provide coverage for medical expenses resulting from a broad range of illnesses and injuries experienced by the insured (or by the insured's family member, if family coverage was procured by the insured). In setting forth the illnesses or injuries covered under the policy, health insurers take approaches similar to the previously discussed methods used by property insurers when they stake out the scope of those policies' coverage. This means that health insurance policies tend to specify an exclusive list of covered illnesses and injuries, set forth a broad general statement of coverage but then specify certain excluded causes, or combine the two approaches by specifying certain covered illnesses and injuries and designating other causes as excluded.

Whichever approach is used, most illnesses and injuries tend to be covered in some fashion. The resulting expenses that stem from medically necessary treatment then become subject to the terms of the insurer's payment obligation, as discussed below. Excluded causes often include preexisting

---

[14]Disability insurance, under which insureds obtain coverage against loss of income resulting from long-term disabilities that interfere with one's ability to perform one's job, addresses the same sorts of financial concerns. Disability insurance will not be discussed further in this chapter.

health conditions—the insured's (or family member's) illnesses or injuries that befell the insured (or family member) before the effective date of the policy.

Insurer's Payment Obligation

As a general rule, health insurance policies require the insured to pay up to a certain amount in medical expenses per year before the insurer's payment obligation is triggered. This amount is known as the **deductible**. The specific amount varies from policy to policy. Once the insured has met his or her deductible, the insurer becomes obligated to pay all or part of the insured's medically necessary expenses that result from a covered illness or injury. If the policy establishes a payment obligation that is a percentage of the medical expenses, 80 percent is fairly typical, though once again this differs from policy to policy. When the health insurer makes payment, it may either pay the insured if the insured has already paid the medical bill or pay the health care provider directly if the insured has not yet paid the bill.

Increasingly, policies tie the insurer's payment obligation to what the insurer establishes as the usual and customary cost of a particular medical procedure or treatment. If the health care provider's charge for a particular procedure or treatment exceeds this usual and customary cost, the excess is not covered. The insurer's payment obligation is then to pay all or the specified percentage (depending on the policy's provisions) of the usual and customary cost.

Health policies tend to make special provisions for covered conditions requiring long-term medical care or hospitalization. These special provisions establish somewhat different payment obligations for the insurer. Often, these provisions specify that the insurer will pay a designated percentage of hospital expenses up to a certain amount, and then all of the hospital expenses once that amount has been reached. The exact percentages and amounts in a given situation are determined by checking the terms of the particular policy at issue.

Special provisions defining the extent of the insurer's obligation to pay for prescription medication costs are not uncommon. In addition, health policies sometimes contain specifications of maximum dollar amounts that the insurer will pay for certain surgical procedures or other medical treat-

ments. Often, policy provisions state that there is no payment obligation regarding experimental medical treatments (treatments that are not yet classifiable as generally accepted medical treatments).

Group Policies

Most persons' health insurance coverage comes through group policies, under which an employer or an organization contracts with a health insurer for coverage to be made available to employees of that employer or members of that organization. From the perspective of insured employees or insured members of organizations, the chief advantage of group policies is that the necessary premiums are significantly lower than the premiums one would have to pay in order to obtain a nongroup policy. The cessation of one's employee or group membership status may lead to a loss of her group insurance benefits and therefore significantly higher costs to her if she is forced to seek nongroup coverage. Sometimes these added costs will simply be prohibitively high. Other times, the typical policy exclusion for preexisting conditions will prove to be a problem when the insured must seek new health insurance coverage because she has lost her group insurance. Congress has attempted to deal with these sorts of problems by establishing limited rights to continued coverage in certain instances where the insured's employee status or organization membership has ended. Nevertheless, the problems persist.

The Health Insurance Debate

Although most U.S. residents have health insurance coverage of some sort, millions do not. Access to affordable coverage has become a major concern in today's society. There has been ongoing debate in the federal and state political arenas concerning how to control spiraling health care costs and increase access to affordable health insurance. As this book went to press, differing proposals for potentially sweeping federal legislation governing health insurance availability and coverage were being proposed and considered in Congress. These competing proposals advocated different approaches on such issues as whether there should be "universal" coverage (for all U.S. residents), whether employers should be required to make health insurance available to their employees, and whether large health insurance purchasing cooperatives should be instituted as a means of attempting to reduce premium costs. Another area of disagreement was the extent to which membership in health maintenance organizations (HMOs) should be encouraged by any federal legislation overhauling the health insurance business. HMOs offer insurance plans under which member patients are treated by HMO-affiliated physicians under arrangements designed to control medical costs and presumably lessen the premiums or fees that HMO members must pay for health care coverage.

Still other debated issues, as of the time this book went to press, included whether Medicare and Medicaid should also be overhauled as part of health care and health insurance reform, and if so, to what extent. Medicare is a government program under which many, but not all, of senior citizens' medical expenses are covered. Medicaid, another government program, handles medical expenses of low-income persons. Some of the proposals for health insurance reform also sought to address insurance access problems stemming from the loss of group insurance and the existence of preexisting health conditions. In addition, the competing proposals addressed whether (and the extent to which) alterations in the law of medical malpractice would be a useful aid in controlling the increases in health care costs and increases in insurance premiums.

As the above discussion suggests, any attempt at legislative reformation of health insurance as we know it is a significant undertaking that necessitates addressing many interrelated issues. If congressionally mandated changes—or even self-imposed changes chosen by the insurance industry—are to occur, they cannot be implemented overnight. Succeeding years will reveal not only the substance of the reform routes chosen but also the effectiveness or ineffectiveness of those routes.

BAD FAITH BREACH OF INSURANCE CONTRACT

Earlier in this chapter, we discussed the liability that an insurer will face if it breaches its policy obligations by means of a good faith but erroneous denial of coverage. That liability is for compensatory damages—damages designed to compensate the insured for the losses stemming from the insurer's breach—just as in breach of contract cases outside the insurance setting. Punitive damages are not available, however, when the insurer's wrongful failure or refusal to perform stemmed from a good faith (though erroneous) coverage denial. What if the insurer's failure or refusal to perform exhibited a lack of good faith? In this section, we examine the recent judicial tendency to go beyond the conventional remedy of compensatory damages and to assess punitive damages against the insurer when the insurer's refusal to perform its policy obligations amounted to the tort of **bad faith breach of contract.**

The special nature of the insurer–insured relationship tends to involve a "we'll take care of you" message that insurers communicate to insureds—at least at the outset of the relationship. Recognizing this, courts have displayed little tolerance in recent years for insurers' unjustifiable refusals to take care of insureds when taking care of them is clearly called for by the relevant policy's terms. When an insurer refuses to perform obvious policy obligations without a plausible, legitimate explanation for the refusal, the insurer risks more than being held liable for compensatory damages. If the facts and circumstances indicate that the insurer's refusal to perform stemmed not from a reasonable argument over coverage but from an intent to "stonewall," deny or unreasonably delay paying a meritorious claim, or otherwise create hardship for the insured, the insurer's breach may be of the bad faith variety. Because bad faith breach is considered an independent tort of a flagrantly wrongful nature, punitive damages—in addition to compensatory damages—have been held to be appropriate. The purposes of punitive damages in this context are the same as in other types of cases that call for punitive damages: to punish the flagrant wrongdoer and to deter the wrongdoer (as well as other potential wrongdoers) from repeating such an action.

The past decade has witnessed bad faith cases in which many millions of dollars in punitive damages have been assessed against insurers. The types of situations in which bad faith liability has been found have included a liability insurer's unjustifiable refusal to defend its insured and/or pay damages awarded against the insured in litigation that clearly triggered the policy obligations. Various cases of very large punitive damages assessments for bad faith liability have stemmed from property insurers' refusals to pay for the insured's destroyed property when the cause was clearly a covered peril and the insurer had no plausible rationale for denying coverage. Still other bad faith cases in which liability was held to exist have included malpractice or other liability insurers' refusals to settle certain probably meritorious claims against the insured within the policy limits. Bad faith liability in these cases tends to involve a situation in which the insured is held legally liable to a plaintiff for an amount well in excess of the dollar limits of the liability policy (meaning that the insured would be personally responsible for the amount of the judgment in excess of the policy limits), after the liability insurer, without reasonable justification, refused the plaintiff's offer to settle the case for an amount less than or equal to the policy limits.

Whether bad faith liability exists in a given case depends, of course, on all of the relevant facts and circumstances. Although bad faith liability is not established in every case in which insureds allege it, cases raising a bad faith claim are of particular concern to insurers.

ETHICAL AND PUBLIC POLICY CONCERNS

1. The law requires that the purchaser of property insurance must have an insurable interest in the property being insured. Why? Does this requirement encourage ethical conduct?

2. Provisions in liability insurance policies often state that the insurer will have no obligation to pay any *punitive* damages assessed against the insured. In addition, controlling legal rules sometimes provide that any agreement to provide insurance coverage for punitive damages liability is unenforceable. Should one be able to insure himself or herself against punitive damages liability? Why or why not?

3. A young parent of two children contacts an insurance agent and indicates that she wishes to purchase a life insurance policy. This parent has a modest income. Her main concern, as stated to the agent, is that her children will be provided for financially if she should die before they reach adulthood. The agent knows that he will make more money if he sells her a *whole life* policy than if he sells her a *term* policy, because his commission is a percentage of the premium (which will be higher

with a whole life policy than with a term policy). What ethical issues does the agent face under these circumstances?

PROBLEMS AND PROBLEM CASES

1. Eighteen-year-old Arthur Smith became intoxicated at a New Year's Eve party. At 11:00 P.M., Smith left the party and began walking home. Police officer Don Czopek saw Smith walking down the center of a road and weaving from side to side. Because Smith was interfering with traffic and placing himself at risk of physical harm, Czopek pulled his patrol car alongside Smith and attempted to talk him into getting off the road. Smith refused, became argumentative, and started shouting. Czopek parked his patrol car, got out, and approached Smith in an effort to calm him down. Smith became increasingly hostile and grabbed Czopek by the lapels of his coat. Officer Herdis Petty then arrived on the scene to assist Czopek. A struggle occurred as the two officers attempted to handcuff Smith and put him into a patrol car. Smith kicked, hit, and bit the officers during this struggle, which continued for a substantial length of time. Czopek suffered frostbite on one of his hands. Petty sustained broken ribs as a result of being kicked by Smith (plus other less serious injuries). Smith was later convicted of assault and battery. He admitted that he intentionally resisted arrest but said that he did not recall hitting or kicking anyone. Officers Czopek and Petty filed a civil suit against Smith's parents, whose homeowners' policy with Group Insurance Company of Michigan (GICOM) provided liability coverage to the insureds—a status that, under the policy's terms, included Arthur Smith—for third parties' personal injury claims resulting from an "occurrence." The policy defined "occurrence" as "an accident, including injurious exposure to conditions, which results . . . in bodily injury or property damage." The policy contained an exclusion from coverage for "bodily injury or property damage which is either expected or intended from the standpoint of the insured." GICOM filed a declaratory judgment suit in which it asked the court to declare that it had no duty to defend or indemnify Arthur Smith and his parents in connection with the litigation brought by Czopek and Petty. Was GICOM entitled to such a ruling by the court?

2. Herbert Prashker was a partner in a law firm. Pursuant to their partnership agreement, the firm's partners purchased two life insurance policies on Prashker's life. The partners were named as beneficiaries. These policies, whose face amounts totaled $1,350,000, were obtained because Prashker was the most significant partner in terms of business generation and size of capital account. Prashker later fell ill with cancer and could no longer practice law. The partners agreed to terminate the partnership business. Five months after the partnership ceased doing business, Prashker died. Prashker's former partners sought to recover the life insurance proceeds. So did Prashker's daughter. She argued that the former partners were not entitled to the insurance proceeds because their insurable interest ended when the partnership was terminated. Were Prashker's former partners entitled to the life insurance proceeds?

3. In a class action suit, the plaintiffs alleged that an automobile loan program instituted by Bank of the West (BOW) violated California's Unfair Business Practices Act. No common law unfair competition claim was made in the suit. The Unfair Business Practices Act did not allow courts to award compensatory or punitive damages, but did authorize courts to order "the disgorgement of money" wrongfully obtained. BOW settled the class action suit by paying $500,000 and agreeing to make changes in the operation of the loan program. BOW contended that the $500,000 payment was covered by the terms of a liability policy issued to BOW by Industrial Indemnity Co. The policy provided coverage for "all sums which the insured shall become legally obligated to pay as damages because of advertising injury to which this insurance applies." The policy went on to define "advertising injury" as "injury arising out of . . . libel, slander, defamation, violation of right of privacy, unfair competition, or infringement of copyright, title or slogan." Industrial filed a declaratory judgment action in which it asked the court to determine that the policy did not cover the $500,000 payment made by BOW to settle the class action suit. The trial court ruled in Industrial's favor, but the intermediate appellate court reversed. It concluded that the policy afforded coverage because the term "unfair competition" was ambiguous and thus could refer to either the common law of unfair competition or statutory claims such as those under the Unfair Business Practices Act. Was the intermediate appellate court correct?

4. Benjamin Born applied for a life insurance policy from Medico Life Insurance Company. The application form called for a health history, which Born provided. In addition, the application form asked specific questions about preexisting medical conditions. Born's wife, Adeline, answered these questions by stating that Born had no preexisting medical problems and was in good health. After issuing the policy, Medico discovered that Born had a history of heart disease, degenerative arthritis, and urinary system disorders. Medico then rescinded the policy and provided Born a check representing a refund of the premiums he had paid. Taking the position that he was still insured, Born refused the refund check. On these facts, was Medico entitled to rescind the policy?

5. The Pecks owned a lawn and garden supply store. Standard Marine was the insurer of the store and its contents. The Pecks placed a fireworks display in the store, where it was subsequently set off by a young boy. A resulting fire damaged or destroyed much of the Pecks' merchandise. Standard Marine refused to reimburse the Pecks for their loss, citing this clause in the policy: "The Company shall not be liable for loss occurring while the hazard is increased by any means within the control or knowledge of the insured." Was Standard Marine obligated to pay the Pecks for their loss?

6. The Plummers owned a commercial building in which they operated two businesses. The building and its contents were insured by Indiana Insurance Company (IIC). After an explosion and fire destroyed the building, the Plummers filed a claim and proof of loss with IIC. After an investigation, IIC denied the claim due to its conclusion that the Plummers had intentionally set the fire. IIC then filed a declaratory judgment action in which it asked for a determination that it had no obligation to cover losses stemming from the fire. The Plummers counterclaimed, seeking damages for breach of contract as well as punitive damages. The jury returned a verdict in favor of the Plummers on all issues. The jury awarded the Plummers approximately $700,000 in compensatory damages (an amount that exceeded the policy limits set forth in the insurance policy at issue), plus $3.5 million in punitive damages. The $700,000 compensatory damages award included not only the value of the destroyed building and its contents (what would have been due under the policy) but also $200,000 in consequential damages allegedly incurred by the Plummers as a result of IIC's lengthy investigation of the fire and ultimate denial of the Plummers' claim. For the most part, the consequential damages represented interest costs and similar expenses incurred by the Plummers—costs and expenses they would not have incurred if IIC had paid their claim. Although the evidence IIC adduced at trial included experts' testimony that the fire had been intentionally set, the jury rejected that testimony and accepted the Plummers' contrary evidence. IIC appealed, arguing that its denial of the Plummers' claim was in good faith, that it therefore should have no liability for consequential damages and punitive damages, and that the damages awarded for breach of an insurance contract cannot exceed the policy limits set forth in the contract. Was IIC correct in these arguments?

7. In 1972, Betty DeWitt and her husband, Joseph, purchased a house. Title was taken in Betty's name. Seven years later, the DeWitts were divorced. Under the 1979 divorce decree, Joseph was given possession of the house and Betty was ordered to sign the deed over to him. Joseph died in January 1980. Soon thereafter, Betty moved into the house and purchased a fire insurance policy from American Family Mutual Insurance Company. The policy had a face value of $38,500. In August 1980, the house was completely destroyed by fire. At that time, American Family learned of her divorce and the decree ordering her to convey title to Joseph. American Family refused to pay on the policy, arguing that Betty did not have an insurable interest. Was American Family correct?

8. Robert Baer and Dareen Dahlstrom had been close friends for more than 20 years. Dahlstrom, who was in the process of separating from her husband, went to visit Baer in July 1988. On various occasions, Baer had used a recreational drug known as Ecstacy. For several years after its discovery, Ecstacy was not an illegal drug. It was, however, designated by federal law as a prohibited controlled substance beginning in March 1988. Baer believed that the use of Ecstacy had certain psychological and emotional benefits, and that using it might help Dahlstrom cope with the personal problems she was experiencing at the time of her July 1988 visit. After she and Baer discussed his beliefs regarding Ecstacy, Dahlstrom told him that she wanted to use the drug. Baer and Dahlstrom went

through various rituals in preparation for use of the drug and recited a prayer that "this [may] bring harm to no one and blessing to all." Baer then removed some Ecstacy from his personal supply, which he had purchased prior to March 1988. Baer dissolved approximately one-half of his usual dose in a glass of water and gave it to Dahlstrom. She drank the mixture. Within approximately 30 minutes, she was dead. Dahlstrom's survivors filed a wrongful death suit against Baer, who asserted that the claim fell within the liability coverage provided to him by State Farm Insurance Company as part of his homeowner's policy. The policy afforded coverage for third parties' claims for physical injury resulting from an "occurrence," which was defined in terms of an "accident" that caused injury. The policy also contained an exclusion from coverage for injury that was either intended or expected by the insured. State Farm filed a declaratory judgment action in which it asked for a judicial determination that in light of the above provisions in the parties' insurance contract as well as public policy considerations, it owed Baer no coverage duties regarding the suit that stemmed from Dahlstrom's death. Was State Farm entitled to the relief it sought?

9. Jeffrey Lane was employed by Memtek, Inc. at its Arby's Restaurant. He was being trained as a cook. After 11:00 one evening, Lane finished work and clocked out. He remained in the restaurant's lobby, however, because he was waiting for the manager to complete her duties. As Lane waited, friends of other restaurant employees came to a door of the restaurant. Lane and the other employees became involved in a conversation with these persons, who included John Taylor. Lane told Taylor that he could not enter the restaurant because it was closed. Taylor did not attempt to force his way into the restaurant. Instead, he "dared" Lane to come outside. Lane left the restaurant "of [his] own will" (according to Lane's deposition) for what he assumed would be a fight with Taylor. In the fight that transpired, Lane broke Taylor's nose and knocked out three of his teeth. Lane later pleaded guilty to a criminal battery charge. Taylor filed a civil suit against Lane and Memtek in an effort to collect damages stemming from the altercation with Lane. American Family Mutual Insurance Company provided liability insurance for Memtek in connection with its restaurant. The policy stated that for purposes of American

Family's duties to defend and indemnify, "the insured" included not only Memtek but also Memtek's "employees, . . . but only for acts within the scope of their employment." American Family filed a declaratory judgment action in which it asked the court to determine that it owed Lane neither a duty to defend nor a duty to indemnify in connection with the incident giving rise to Taylor's lawsuit. American Family's theory was that for purposes of that incident, Lane was not an insured within the above-quoted policy provision. Was American Family correct?

10. In December 1988, Counihan purchased a property insurance policy under which Allstate Insurance Co. insured her house against all risks of loss. In February 1989, the U.S. government seized the house and sought its forfeiture under federal law due to its connection with illegal drug activity that occurred in July 1988. After two trials and an appeal, the Second Circuit Court of Appeals af-

firmed the forfeiture of the property in 1993. A fire had destroyed the house in 1990, while Counihan's policy with Allstate allegedly was in force. Counihan filed a claim with Allstate to recover the value of the destroyed house. The forfeiture statute under which the government had sought forfeiture of Counihan's property stated that "[a]ll right, title, and interest in property [to which the government has been held entitled to forfeiture due to the property's connection with illegal drug activity] shall vest in the United States upon commission of the act giving rise to forfeiture under this section." Arguing that this statute's retroactive effect would mean that Counihan did not possess an insurable interest when she purchased the policy and when the fire destroyed the house, Allstate asserted that its insurance contract with Counihan was void and unenforceable. Did Counihan have the necessary insurable interest at the times in question?

APPENDIXES

APPENDIX A
The Constitution of the
United States of America

APPENDIX B
Uniform Commercial Code
(Excerpts from the Official Text—1990)

THE CONSTITUTION OF THE UNITED STATES OF AMERICA

PREAMBLE

We the People of the United States, in Order to form a more perfect Union, establish Justice, insure domestic Tranquility, provide for the common defense, promote the general Welfare, and secure the Blessings of Liberty to ourselves and our Posterity, do ordain and establish this Constitution for the United States of America.

ARTICLE I

Section 1   All legislative Powers herein granted shall be vested in a Congress of the United States, which shall consist of a Senate and House of Representatives.

Section 2   The House of Representatives shall be composed of Members chosen every second Year by the People of the several States, and the Electors in each State shall have the Qualifications requisite for Electors of the most numerous Branch of the State Legislature.

No Person shall be a Representative who shall not have attained to the age of twenty five Years, and been seven Years a Citizen of the United States, and who shall not, when elected, be an Inhabitant of that State in which he shall be chosen.

Representatives and direct Taxes shall be apportioned among the several States which may be included within this Union, according to their respective Numbers, which shall be determined by adding to the whole Number of free Persons, including those bound to Service for a Term of Years, and excluding Indians not taxed, three fifths of all other Persons.[1] The actual Enumeration shall be made within three Years after the first Meeting of the Congress of the United States, and within every subsequent Term of ten Years, in such Manner as they shall by Law direct. The Number of Representatives shall not exceed one for every thirty Thousand, but each State shall have at Least one Representative, and until such enumeration shall be made, the State of New Hampshire shall be entitled to choose three,

Massachusetts eight, Rhode-Island and Providence Plantations one, Connecticut five, New York six, New Jersey four, Pennsylvania eight, Delaware one, Maryland six, Virginia ten, North Carolina five, South Carolina five, and Georgia three.

When vacancies happen in the Representation from any State, the Executive Authority thereof shall issue Writs of Election to fill such Vacancies.

The House of Representatives shall chuse their Speaker and other Officers; and shall have the sole Power of Impeachment.

Section 3   The Senate of the United States shall be composed of two Senators from each State, chosen by the Legislature thereof,[2] for six Years; and each Senator shall have one Vote.

Immediately after they shall be assembled in Consequence of the first Election, they shall be divided as equally as may be into three Classes. The Seats of the Senators of the first Class shall be vacated at the Expiration of the second Year, of the second Class at the Expiration of the fourth Year, and of the third Class at the Expiration of the sixth Year, so that one third may be chosen every second Year; and if Vacancies happen by Resignation, or otherwise, during the Recess of the Legislature of any State, the Executive thereof may make temporary Appointments until the next Meeting of the Legislature, which shall then fill such Vacancies.[3]

No Person shall be a Senator who shall not have attained to the Age of thirty Years, and been nine Years a Citizen of the United States, and who shall not, when elected, be an Inhabitant of that State for which he shall be chosen.

The Vice President of the United States shall be President of the Senate, but shall have no Vote, unless they be equally divided.

The Senate shall chuse their other Officers, and also a President pro tempore, in the Absence of the Vice President, or when he shall exercise the Office of President of the United States.

---

[1]Changed by the Fourteenth Amendment.

[2]Changed by the Seventeenth Amendment.
[3]Changed by the Seventeenth Amendment.

The Senate shall have the sole Power to try all Impeachments. When sitting for that Purpose, they shall be on Oath or Affirmation. When the President of the United States is tried, the Chief Justice shall preside: And no Person shall be convicted without the Concurrence of two thirds of the Members present.

Judgment in Cases of Impeachment shall not extend further than to removal from Office, and disqualification to hold and enjoy any Office of honor, Trust or Profit under the United States: but the Party convicted shall nevertheless be liable and subject to Indictment, Trial, Judgment and Punishment, according to Law.

Section 4   The Times, Places and Manner of holding Elections for Senators and Representatives, shall be prescribed in each State by the Legislature thereof; but the Congress may at any time by Law make or alter such Regulations, except as to the Places of chusing Senators.

The Congress shall assemble at least once in every Year, and such Meeting shall be on the first Monday in December, unless they shall by Law appoint a different Day.[4]

Section 5   Each House shall be the Judge of the Elections, Returns and Qualifications of its own Members, and a Majority of each shall constitute a Quorum to do Business; but a smaller Number may adjourn from day to day, and may be authorized to compel the Attendance of absent Members, in such Manner, and under such Penalties as each House may provide.

Each House may determine the Rules of its Proceedings, punish its Members for disorderly Behaviour, and with the Concurrence of two thirds, expel a Member.

Each House shall keep a Journal of its Proceedings, and from time to time publish the same, excepting such Parts as may in their Judgment require Secrecy; and the Yeas and Nays of the Members of either House on any question shall, at the Desire of one fifth of those Present, be entered on the Journal.

Neither House, during the Session of Congress, shall, without the Consent of the other, adjourn for more than three days, nor to any other Place than that in which the two Houses shall be sitting.

Section 6   The Senators and Representatives shall receive a Compensation for their Services, to be ascertained by Law, and paid out of the Treasury of the United States. They shall in all Cases, except Treason, Felony and Breach of the Peace, be privileged from Arrest during their Attendance at the Session of their respective Houses, and in going to and returning from the same; and for any Speech or Debate in either House, they shall not be questioned in any other Place.

No Senator or Representative shall, during the Time for which he was elected, be appointed to any civil Office

under the Authority of the United States, which shall have been created, or the Emoluments whereof shall have been encreased during such time; and no Person holding any Office under the United States, shall be a Member of either House during his Continuance in Office.

Section 7   All Bills for raising Revenue shall originate in the House of Representatives; but the Senate may propose or concur with Amendments as on other Bills.

Every Bill which shall have passed the House of Representatives and the Senate, shall, before it becomes a Law, be presented to the President of the United States; If he approves he shall sign it, but if not he shall return it, with his Objections to that House in which it shall have originated, who shall enter the Objections at large on their Journal, and proceed to reconsider it. If after such Reconsideration two thirds of that House shall agree to pass the Bill, it shall be sent, together with the Objections, to the other House, by which it shall likewise be reconsidered, and if approved by two thirds of that House, it shall become a Law. But in all such Cases the Votes of both Houses shall be determined by Yeas and Nays, and the Names of the Persons voting for and against the Bill shall be entered on the Journal of each House respectively. If any Bill shall not be returned by the President within ten Days (Sundays excepted) after it shall have been presented to him, the Same shall be a Law, in like Manner as if he had signed it, unless the Congress by their Adjournment prevent its Return, in which Case it shall not be a Law.

Every Order, Resolution, or Vote to which the Concurrence of the Senate and House of Representatives may be necessary (except on a question of Adjournment) shall be presented to the President of the United States; and before the Same shall take Effect, shall be approved by him, or being disapproved by him, shall be repassed by two thirds of the Senate and House of Representatives, according to the Rules and Limitations prescribed in the Case of a Bill.

Section 8   The Congress shall have Power To lay and collect Taxes, Duties, Imposts and Excises, to pay the Debts and provide for the common Defence and general Welfare of the United States; but all Duties, Imposts and Excises shall be uniform throughout the United States.

To borrow Money on the credit of the United States;

To regulate Commerce with foreign Nations, and among the several States, and with the Indian Tribes;

To establish an uniform Rule of Naturalization, and uniform Laws on the subject of Bankruptcies throughout the United States;

To coin Money, regulate the Value thereof, and of foreign Coin, and fix the Standard of Weights and Measures;

To provide for the Punishment of counterfeiting the Securities and current Coin of the United States;

To establish Post Offices and post Roads;

To promote the Progress of Science and useful Arts, by securing for limited Times to Authors and Inventors

---

[4]Changed by the Twentieth Amendment.

the exclusive Right to their respective Writings and Discoveries;

To constitute Tribunals inferior to the supreme Court;

To define and punish Piracies and Felonies committed on the high Seas, and Offences against the Law of Nations;

To declare War, grant Letters of Marque and Reprisal, and make Rules concerning Captures on Land and Water;

To raise and support Armies, but no Appropriation of Money to that Use shall be for a longer Term than two Years;

To provide and maintain a Navy;

To make Rules for the Government and Regulation of the land and naval Forces;

To provide for calling forth the Militia to execute the Laws of the Union, suppress Insurrections and repel Invasions;

To provide for organizing, arming, and disciplining, the Militia, and for governing such Part of them as may be employed in the Service of the United States, reserving to the States respectively, the Appointment of the Officers, and the Authority of training the Militia according to the discipline prescribed by Congress;

To exercise exclusive Legislation in all Cases whatsoever, over such District (not exceeding ten Miles square) as may, by Cession of particular States, and the Acceptance of Congress, become the Seat of the Government of the United States, and to exercise like Authority over all Places purchased by the Consent of the Legislature of the State in which the Same shall be, for the Erection of Forts, Magazines, Arsenals, dock-Yards, and other needful Buildings;—And

To make all Laws which shall be necessary and proper for carrying into Execution the foregoing Powers, and all other Powers vested by this Constitution in the Government of the United States, or in any Department or Officer thereof.

Section 9   The Migration or Importation of such Persons as any of the States now existing shall think proper to admit, shall not be prohibited by the Congress prior to the Year one thousand eight hundred and eight, but a Tax or duty may be imposed on such Importation, not exceeding ten dollars for each Person.

The Privilege of the Writ of Habeas Corpus shall not be suspended, unless when in Cases of Rebellion or Invasion the public Safety may require it.

No Bill of Attainder or ex post facto Law shall be passed.

No Capitation, or other direct, Tax shall be laid, unless in Proportion to the Census of Enumeration herein before directed to be taken.[5]

No Tax or Duty shall be laid on Articles exported from any State.

_____

[5]Changed by the Sixteenth Amendment.

No Preference shall be given by any Regulation of Commerce or Revenue to the Ports of one State over those of another: nor shall Vessels bound to, or from, one State, be obliged to enter, clear, or pay Duties in another.

No Money shall be drawn from the Treasury, but in Consequence of Appropriations made by Law; and a regular Statement and Account of the Receipts and Expenditures of all public Money shall be published from time to time.

No Title of Nobility shall be granted by the United States: And no Person holding any Office of Profit or Trust under them, shall, without the Consent of the Congress, accept of any present, Emolument, Office, or Title, of any kind whatever, from any King, Prince, or foreign State.

Section 10   No State shall enter into any Treaty, Alliance, or Confederation; grant Letters of Marque and Reprisal; coin Money; emit Bills of Credit; make any Thing but gold and silver coin a Tender in Payment of Debts; pass any Bill of Attainder, ex post facto Law, or Law impairing the Obligation of Contracts, or grant any Title of Nobility.

No State shall, without the Consent of the Congress, lay any Imposts or Duties on Imports or Exports, except what may be absolutely necessary for executing its inspection Laws: and the net Produce of all Duties and Imposts, laid by any State on Imports or Exports, shall be for the Use of the Treasury of the United States; and all such Laws shall be subject to the Revision and Controul of the Congress.

No State shall, without the consent of Congress, lay any Duty of Tonnage, keep Troops, or Ships of War in time of Peace, enter into any Agreement or Compact with another State, or with a foreign Power, or engage in War, unless actually invaded, or in such imminent Danger as will not admit of delay.

ARTICLE II

Section 1   The executive Power shall be vested in a President of the United States of America. He shall hold his Office during the Term of four Years, and, together with the Vice President, chosen for the same Term, be elected, as follows

Each state shall appoint, in such Manner as the Legislature thereof may direct, a Number of Electors, equal to the whole Number of Senators and Representatives to which the State may be entitled in Congress: but no Senator or Representative, or Person holding an Office of Trust or Profit under the United States, shall be appointed an Elector.

The Electors shall meet in their respective States, and vote by Ballot for two Persons, of whom one at least shall not be an inhabitant of the same State with themselves.

And they shall make a List of all the Persons voted for, and of the Number of Votes for each; which List they shall sign and certify, and transmit sealed to the Seat of the Government of the United States, directed to the President of the Senate. The President of the Senate shall, in the Presence of the Senate and House of Representatives, open all the Certificates, and the Votes shall then be counted. The Person having the greatest Number of Votes shall be the President, if such Number be a Majority of the whole Number of Electors appointed; and if there be more than one who have such Majority, and have an equal Number of Votes, then the House of Representatives shall immediately chuse by Ballot one of them for President; and if no Person have a Majority, then from the five highest on the List the said House shall in like Manner chuse the President. But in chusing the President, the Votes shall be taken by States, the Representation from each State having one Vote; A quorum for this purpose shall consist of a Member or Members from two thirds of the States, and a Majority of all the States shall be necessary to a Choice. In every Case, after the Choice of the President, the Person having the greatest Number of Votes of the Electors shall be the Vice President. But if there should remain two or more who have equal Votes, the Senate shall chuse from them by Ballot the Vice President.[6]

The Congress may determine the Time of chusing the Electors, and the Day on which they shall give their Votes; which Day shall be the same throughout the United States.

No Person except a natural born Citizen, or a Citizen of the United States, at the time of the Adoption of this Constitution, shall be eligible to the Office of President; neither shall any Person be eligible to that Office who shall not have attained to the Age of thirty five Years, and been fourteen Years a Resident within the United States.

In Case of the Removal of the President from Office, or of his Death, Resignation, or Inability to discharge the Powers and Duties of the said Office, the Same shall devolve on the Vice President, and the Congress may by Law provide for the Case of Removal, Death, Resignation or Inability, both of the President and Vice President, declaring what Officer shall then act as President, and such Officer shall act accordingly, until the Disability be removed, or a President shall be elected.[7]

The President shall, at stated Times, receive for his Services, a Compensation, which shall neither be encreased nor diminished during the Period for which he shall have been elected, and he shall not receive within that Period any other Emolument from the United States, or any of them.

---

[6]Changed by the Twelfth Amendment.

[7]Changed by the Twenty-fifth Amendment.

Before he enter on the Execution of his Office, he shall take the following Oath or Affirmation:—"I do solemnly swear (or affirm) that I will faithfully execute the Office of President of the United States, and will to the best of my Ability, preserve, protect, and defend the Constitution of the United States."

Section 2   The President shall be Commander in Chief of the Army and Navy of the United States, and of the Militia of the several States, when called into the actual Service of the United States; he may require the Opinion, in writing, of the principal Officer in each of the executive Departments, upon any Subject relating to the Duties of their respective Offices, and he shall have Power to grant Reprieves and Pardons for Offences against the United States, except in Cases of Impeachment.

He shall have Power, by and with the Advice and Consent of the Senate, to make Treaties, provided two thirds of the Senators present concur; and he shall nominate, and by and with the Advice and Consent of the Senate, shall appoint Ambassadors, other public Ministers and Consuls, Judges of the supreme Court, and all other Officers of the United States, whose Appointments are not herein otherwise provided for, and which shall be established by Law; but the Congress may by Law vest the Appointment of such inferior Officers, as they think proper, in the President alone, in the Courts of Law, or in the Heads of Departments.

The President shall have Power to fill up all Vacancies that may happen during the Recess of the Senate, by granting Commissions which shall expire at the End of their next Session.

Section 3   He shall from time to time give to the Congress Information of the State of the Union, and recommend to their Consideration such Measures as he shall judge necessary and expedient; he may, on extraordinary Occasions, convene both Houses, or either of them, and in Case of Disagreement between them, with Respect to the Time of Adjournment, he may adjourn them to such Time as he shall think proper; he shall receive Ambassadors and other public Ministers; he shall take Care that the Laws be faithfully executed, and shall Commission all the Officers of the United States.

Section 4   The President, Vice President and all civil Officers of the United States, shall be removed from Office on Impeachment for, and Conviction of, Treason, Bribery, or other high Crimes and Misdemeanors.

ARTICLE III

Section 1   The judicial Power of the United States, shall be vested in one supreme Court, and in such inferior Courts as the Congress may from time to time ordain and establish. The Judges, both of the supreme and inferior Courts, shall hold their Offices during good Behaviour, and shall, at stated Times, receive for their Services, a Compensation, which shall not be diminished during their Continuance in Office.

Section 2   The judicial Power shall extend to all Cases, in Law and Equity, arising under this Constitution, the Laws of the United States, and Treaties made, or which shall be made, under their Authority;—to all Cases affecting Ambassadors, other public Ministers and Consuls;—to all Cases of admiralty and maritime Jurisdiction;—to Controversies to which the United States shall be a party;—to Controversies between two or more States;—between a State and Citizens of another State;[8]—between Citizens of different States;—between Citizens of the same State claiming Lands under Grants of different States, and between a State, or the Citizens thereof, and foreign States, Citizens or Subjects.

In all Cases affecting Ambassadors, other public Ministers and Consuls, and those in which a State shall be Party, the supreme Court shall have original Jurisdiction. In all the other Cases before mentioned, the supreme Court shall have appellate Jurisdiction, both as to Law and Fact, with such Exceptions, and under such Regulations as the Congress shall make.

The Trial of all Crimes, except in Cases of Impeachment, shall be by Jury: and such Trial shall be held in the State where the said Crimes shall have been committed; but when not committed within any State, the Trial shall be at such Place or Places as the Congress may by Law have directed.

Section 3   Treason against the United States, shall consist only in levying War against them, or in adhering to their Enemies, giving them Aid and Comfort. No Person shall be convicted of Treason unless on the Testimony of two Witnesses to the same overt Act, or on Confession in open Court.

The Congress shall have Power to declare the Punishment of Treason, but no Attainder of Treason shall work Corruption of Blood, or Forfeiture except during the Life of the Person attainted.

ARTICLE IV

Section 1   Full Faith and Credit shall be given in each State to the public Acts, Records, and judicial Proceedings of every other State. And the Congress may by general Laws prescribe the Manner in which such Acts, Records and Proceedings shall be proved, and the Effect thereof.

Section 2   The Citizens of each State shall be entitled to all Privileges and Immunities of Citizens in the several States.

A Person charged in any State with Treason, Felony, or other Crime, who shall flee from Justice, and be found in another State, shall on Demand of the executive Authority of the State from which he fled, be delivered up, to be removed to the State having Jurisdiction of the Crime.

No Person held to Service or Labour in one State, under the Laws thereof, escaping into another, shall, in Consequence of any Law or Regulation therein, be discharged from such Service or Labour, but shall be delivered up on Claim of the Party to whom such Service or Labour may be due.[9]

Section 3   New States may be admitted by the Congress into this Union; but no new State shall be formed or erected within the Jurisdiction of any other State; nor any State be formed by the Junction of two or more States, or Parts of States, without the Consent of the Legislatures of the States concerned as well as of the Congress.

The Congress shall have Power to dispose of and make all needful Rules and Regulations respecting the Territory or other Property belonging to the United States; and nothing in this Constitution shall be so construed as to Prejudice any Claims of the United States, or of any particular State.

Section 4   The United States shall guarantee to every State in this Union a Republican Form of Government, and shall protect each of them against Invasion; and on Application of the Legislature, or of the Executive (when the Legislature cannot be convened) against domestic Violence.

ARTICLE V

The Congress, whenever two thirds of both Houses shall deem it necessary, shall propose Amendments to this Constitution, or, on the Application of the Legislatures of two thirds of the several States, shall call a Convention for proposing Amendments, which, in either Case, shall be valid to all Intents and Purposes, as Part of this Constitution, when ratified by the legislatures of three fourths of the several States, or by Conventions in three fourths thereof, as the one or the other Mode of Ratification may be proposed by the Congress; Provided that no Amendment which may be made prior to the Year One thousand eight hundred and eight shall in any Manner affect the first and fourth Clauses in the Ninth Section of the first Article; and that no State, without its Consent, shall be deprived of its equal Suffrage in the Senate.

ARTICLE VI

All Debts contracted and Engagements entered into, before the Adoption of this Constitution, shall be as valid against the United States under this Constitution, as under the Confederation.

The Constitution, and the Laws of the United States which shall be made in Pursuance thereof; and all Treaties made, or which shall be made, under the Authority of the United States, shall be the supreme Law of the Land; and

---

[8]Changed by the Eleventh Amendment.

[9]Changed by the Thirteenth Amendment.

the Judges in every State shall be bound thereby, any Thing in the Constitution or Laws of any State to the Contrary notwithstanding.

The Senators and Representatives before mentioned, and the Members of the several State Legislatures, and all executive and judicial Officers, both of the United States and of the several States, shall be bound by Oath or Affirmation, to support this Constitution; but no religious Test shall ever be required as a Qualification to any Office or public Trust under the United States.

ARTICLE VII

The Ratification of the Conventions of nine States, shall be sufficient for the Establishment of this Constitution between the States so ratifying the Same.

Done in Convention by the Unanimous Consent of the States present the Seventeenth Day of September in the Year of our Lord one thousand seven hundred and eighty seven and of the Independance of the United States of America the Twelfth. In witness whereof We have hereunto subscribed our Names.

AMENDMENTS

[The first 10 amendments are known as the "Bill of Rights."]

Amendment I (Ratified 1791)

Congress shall make no law respecting an establishment of religion, or prohibiting the free exercise thereof; or abridging the freedom of speech, or of the press; or the right of the people peaceably to assemble, and to petition the Government for a redress of grievances.

Amendment 2 (Ratified 1791)

A well regulated Militia, being necessary to the security of a free State, the right of the people to keep and bear Arms, shall not be infringed.

Amendment 3 (Ratified 1791)

No Soldier shall, in time of peace be quartered in any house, without the consent of the Owner, nor in time of war, but in a manner to be prescribed by law.

Amendment 4 (Ratified 1791)

The right of the people to be secure in their persons, houses, papers, and effects, against unreasonable searches and seizures, shall not be violated, and no Warrants shall issue, but upon probable cause, supported by Oath or affirmation, and particularly describing the place to be searched, and the persons or things to be seized.

Amendment 5 (Ratified 1791)

No person shall be held to answer for a capital, or otherwise infamous crime, unless on a presentment or indictment of a Grand Jury, except in cases arising in the land or naval forces, or in the Militia, when in actual service in time of War or public danger; nor shall any person be subject for the same offence to be twice put in jeopardy of life or limb; nor shall be compelled in any criminal case to be a witness against himself, nor be deprived of life, liberty, or property, without due process of law; nor shall private property be taken for public use, without just compensation.

Amendment 6 (Ratified 1791)

In all criminal prosecutions, the accused shall enjoy the right to a speedy and public trial, by an impartial jury of the State and district wherein the crime shall have been committed, which district shall have been previously ascertained by law, and to be informed of the nature and cause of the accusation; to be confronted with the witnesses against him; to have compulsory process for obtaining Witnesses in his favor, and to have assistance of counsel for his defence.

Amendment 7 (Ratified 1791)

In Suits at common law, where the value in controversy shall exceed twenty dollars, the right of trial by jury shall be preserved, and no fact tried by a jury, shall be otherwise re-examined in any Court of the United States, than according to the rules of the common law.

Amendment 8 (Ratified 1791)

Excessive bail shall not be required, nor excessive fines imposed, nor cruel and unusual punishments inflicted.

Amendment 9 (Ratified 1791)

The enumeration in the Constitution, of certain rights, shall not be construed to deny or disparage others retained by the people.

Amendment 10 (Ratified 1791)

The powers not delegated to the United States by the Constitution, nor prohibited by it to the States, are reserved to the States respectively, or to the people.

Amendment 11 (Ratified 1795)

The Judicial power of the United States shall not be construed to extend to any suit in law or equity, commenced or prosecuted against one of the United States by Citizens of another State, or by Citizens or Subjects of any Foreign State.

Amendment 12 (Ratified 1804)

The Electors shall meet in their respective states, and vote by ballot for President and Vice-President, one of whom, at least, shall not be an inhabitant of the same state with themselves; they shall name in their ballots the person voted for as President, and in distinct ballots the person voted for as Vice-President, and they shall make distinct lists of all persons voted for as President, and of all persons voted for as Vice-President, and of the number of votes for each, which lists they shall sign and certify, and transmit sealed to the seat of the government of the United States, directed to the President of the Senate;— The President of the Senate shall, in the presence of the Senate and House of Representatives, open all the certificates and the votes shall then be counted;—The person having the greatest number of votes for President, shall be the President, if such number be a majority of the whole number of Electors appointed; and if no person have such majority, then from the persons having the highest numbers not exceeding three on the list of those voted for as President, the House of Representatives shall choose immediately, by ballot, the President. But in choosing the President, the votes shall be taken by states, the representation from each state having one vote; a quorum for this purpose shall consist of a member or members from two-thirds of the states, and a majority of all the states shall be necessary to a choice. And if the House of Representatives shall not choose a President whenever the right of choice shall devolve upon them, before the fourth day of March next following, then the Vice-President shall act as president, as in the case of the death or other constitutional disability of the President.[10]—The person having the greatest number of votes as Vice-President, shall be the Vice-President, if such number be a majority of the whole number of Electors appointed, and if no person have a majority, then from the two highest numbers on the list, the Senate shall choose the Vice-President; a quorum for the purpose shall consist of two-thirds of the whole number of Senators, and a majority of the whole number shall be necessary to a choice. But no person constitutionally ineligible to the office of President shall be eligible to that of Vice-President of the United States.

Amendment 13 (Ratified 1865)

Section 1   Neither slavery nor involuntary servitude, except as a punishment for crime whereof the party shall have been duly convicted, shall exist within the United States, or any place subject to their jurisdiction.

Section 2   Congress shall have power to enforce this article by appropriate legislation.

Amendment 14 (Ratified 1868)

Section 1   All persons born or naturalized in the United States, and subject to the jurisdiction thereof, are citizens of the United States and of the State wherein they reside. No State shall make or enforce any law which shall abridge the privileges or immunities of citizens of the United States; nor shall any State deprive any person of life, liberty, or property, without due process of law; nor deny to any person within its jurisdiction the equal protection of the laws.

Section 2   Representatives shall be apportioned among the several States according to their respective numbers, counting the whole number of persons in each State, excluding Indians not taxed. But when the right to vote at any election for the choice of electors for President and Vice President of the United States, Representatives in Congress, the Executive and Judicial officers of a State, or the members of the Legislature thereof, is denied to any of the male inhabitants of such State, being twenty-one[11] years of age, and citizens of the United States, or in any way abridged except for participation in rebellion, or other crime, the basis of representation therein shall be reduced in the proportion which the number of such male citizens shall bear to the whole number of male citizens twenty-one years of age in such State.

Section 3   No person shall be a Senator or Representative in Congress, or elector of President and Vice President, or hold any office, civil or military, under the United States, or under any State, who, having previously taken an oath, as a member of Congress, or as an officer of the United States, or as a member of any State legislature, or as an executive or judicial officer of any State, to support the Constitution of the United States, shall have engaged in insurrection or rebellion against the same, or given aid or comfort to the enemies thereof. But Congress may by a vote of two-thirds of each House, remove such disability.

Section 4   The validity of the public debt of the United States, authorized by law, including debts incurred for payment of pensions and bounties for services in suppressing insurrection or rebellion, shall not be questioned. But neither the United States nor any State shall

---

[10]Changed by the Twentieth Amendment.

[11]Changed by the Twenty-sixth Amendment.

assume or pay any debt or obligation incurred in aid of insurrection or rebellion against the United States, or any claim for the loss or emancipation of any slave; but all such debts, obligations and claims shall be held illegal and void.

Section 5   The Congress shall have power to enforce, by appropriate legislation, the provisions of this article.

Amendment 15 (Ratified 1870)

Section 1   The right of citizens of the United States to vote shall not be denied or abridged by the United States or by any State on account of race, color, or previous condition of servitude.

Section 2   The Congress shall have power to enforce this article by appropriate legislation.

Amendment 16 (Ratified 1913)

The Congress shall have power to lay and collect taxes on incomes, from whatever source derived, without apportionment among the several States, and without regard to any census or enumeration.

Amendment 17 (Ratified 1913)

The Senate of the United States shall be composed of two Senators from each State, elected by the people thereof, for six years; and each Senator shall have one vote. The electors in each State shall have the qualifications requisite for electors of the most numerous branch of the State legislatures.

When vacancies happen in the representation of any State in the Senate, the executive authority of such State shall issue writs of election to fill such vacancies: *Provided,* That the legislature of any State may empower the executive thereof to make temporary appointments until the people fill the vacancies by election as the legislature may direct.

This amendment shall not be so construed as to affect the election or term of any Senator chosen before it becomes valid as part of the Constitution.

Amendment 18 (Ratified 1919; Repealed 1933)

Section 1   After one year from the ratification of this article the manufacture, sale, or transportation of intoxicating liquors within, the importation thereof into, or the exportation thereof from the United States and all territory subject to the jurisdiction thereof for beverage purposes is hereby prohibited.

Section 2   The Congress and the several States shall have concurrent power to enforce this article by appropriate legislation.

Section 3   This article shall be inoperative unless it shall have been ratified as an amendment to the Constitution by the legislatures of the several States, as provided in the Constitution, within seven years from the date of the submission hereof to the States by the Congress.[12]

Amendment 19 (Ratified 1920)

The right of citizens of the United States to vote shall not be denied or abridged by the United States or by any State on account of sex.

Congress shall have power to enforce this article by appropriate legislation.

Amendment 20 (Ratified 1933)

Section 1   The terms of the President and Vice President shall end at noon on the 20th day of January, and the terms of Senators and Representatives at noon on the 3d day of January, of the years in which such terms would have ended if this article had not been ratified; and the terms of their successors shall then begin.

Section 2   The Congress shall assemble at least once in every year, and such meeting shall begin at noon on the 3d day of January, unless they shall by law appoint a different day.

Section 3   If, at the time fixed for the beginning of the term of the President, the President elect shall have died, the Vice President elect shall become President. If a President shall not have been chosen before the time fixed for the beginning of his term, or if the President elect shall have failed to qualify, then the Vice President elect shall act as President until a President shall have qualified; and the Congress may by law provide for the case wherein neither a President elect nor a Vice President elect shall have qualified, declaring who shall then act as President, or the manner in which one who is to act shall be selected, and such person shall act accordingly until a President or Vice President shall have qualified.

Section 4   The Congress may by law provide for the case of the death of any of the persons from whom the House of Representatives may choose a President whenever the right of choice shall have devolved upon them, and for the case of the death of any of the persons from whom the Senate may choose a Vice President whenever the right of choice shall have devolved upon them.

Section 5   Sections 1 and 2 shall take effect on the 15th day of October following the ratification of this article.

---

[12]Repealed by the Twenty-first Amendment.

Section 6   This article shall be inoperative unless it shall have been ratified as an amendment to the Constitution by the legislatures of three-fourths of the several States within seven years from the date of its submission.

Amendment 21 (Ratified 1933)

Section 1   The eighteenth article of amendment to the Constitution of the United States is hereby repealed.

Section 2   The transportation or importation into any State, Territory, or possession of the United States for delivery or use therein of intoxicating liquors, in violation of the laws thereof, is hereby prohibited.

Section 3   This article shall be inoperative unless it shall have been ratified as an amendment to the Constitution by conventions in the several States, as provided in the Constitution, within seven years from the date of the submission hereof to the States by the Congress.

Amendment 22 (Ratified 1951)

Section 1   No person shall be elected to the office of the President more than twice, and no person who has held the office of President, or acted as President, for more than two years of a term to which some other person was elected President shall be elected to the office of the President more than once. But this Article shall not apply to any person holding the office of President when this Article was proposed by the Congress, and shall not prevent any person who may be holding the office of President, or acting as President, during the term within which this Article becomes operative from holding the office of President or acting as President during the remainder of such term.

Section 2   This Article shall be inoperative unless it shall have been ratified as an amendment to the Constitution by the legislatures of three-fourths of the several States within seven years from the date of its submission to the States by the Congress.

Amendment 23 (Ratified 1961)

Section 1   The District constituting the seat of Government of the United States shall appoint in such manner as the Congress may direct:

A number of electors of President and Vice President equal to the whole number of Senators and Representatives in Congress to which the District would be entitled if it were a State, but in no event more than the least populous State; they shall be in addition to those appointed by the States, but they shall be considered, for the purposes of the election of President and Vice President, to be electors appointed by a State; and they shall meet in the District and perform such duties as provided by the twelfth article of amendment.

Section 2   The Congress shall have power to enforce this article by appropriate legislation.

Amendment 24 (Ratified 1964)

Section 1   The right of citizens of the United States to vote in any primary or other election for President or Vice President, for electors for President or Vice President, or for Senator or Representative in Congress, shall not be denied or abridged by the United States or any State by reason of failure to pay any poll tax or other tax.

Section 2   The Congress shall have power to enforce this article by appropriate legislation.

Amendment 25 (Ratified 1967)

Section 1   In case of the removal of the President from office or of his death or resignation, the Vice President shall become President.

Section 2   Whenever there is a vacancy in the office of the Vice President, the President shall nominate a Vice President who shall take office upon confirmation by a majority vote of both Houses of Congress.

Section 3   Whenever the President transmits to the President pro tempore of the Senate and the Speaker of the House of Representatives his written declaration that he is unable to discharge the powers and duties of his office, and until he transmits to them a written declaration to the contrary, such powers and duties shall be discharged by the Vice President as Acting President.

Section 4   Whenever the Vice President and a majority of either the principal officers of the executive departments or of such other body as Congress may by law provide, transmit to the President pro tempore of the Senate and the Speaker of the House of Representatives their written declaration that the President is unable to discharge the powers and duties of his office, the Vice President shall immediately assume the powers and duties of the office as Acting President.

Thereafter, when the President transmits to the President pro tempore of the Senate and the Speaker of the House of Representatives his written declaration that no inability exists, he shall resume the powers and duties of his office unless the Vice President and a majority of either the principal officers of the executive department or of such other body as Congress may by law provide, transmit within four days to the President pro tempore of the Senate and the Speaker of the House of Representatives their written declaration that the President is unable to discharge the powers and duties of his office. Thereupon Congress shall decide the issue, assembling within forty-eight hours for that purpose if not in session. If the Congress, within twenty-one days after receipt of the latter written declaration, or, if Congress is not in session, within twenty-one days after Congress is required to assemble, determines by two-thirds vote of both Houses that the President is unable to discharge the powers and duties of his office, the Vice President shall continue to discharge the same as Acting President; otherwise, the President shall resume the powers and duties of his office.

Amendment 26 (Ratified 1971)

Section 1   The right of citizens of the United States, who are eighteen years of age or older, to vote shall not be denied or abridged by the United States or by any State on account of age.

Section 2   The Congress shall have power to enforce this article by appropriate legislation.

Amendment 27 (Ratified 1992)

No law, varying the compensation for the services of the Senators and Representatives, shall take effect, until an election of Representatives shall have intervened.

Uniform Commercial Code
(Excerpts from the Official Text— 1990)*

Title

An Act

To be known as the Uniform Commercial Code, Relating to Certain Commercial Transactions in or regarding Personal Property and Contracts and other Documents concerning them, including Sales, Commercial Paper, Bank Deposits and Collections, Letters of Credit, Bulk Transfers, Warehouse Receipts, Bills of Lading, other Documents of Title, Investment Securities, and Secured Transactions, including certain Sales of Accounts, Chattel Paper, and Contract Rights; Providing for Public Notice to Third Parties in Certain Circumstances; Regulating Procedure, Evidence and Damages in Certain Court Actions Involving such Transactions, Contracts or Documents; to Make Uniform the Law with Respect Thereto; and Repealing Inconsistent Legislation.

ARTICLE 1 GENERAL PROVISIONS

Part 1 Short Title, Construction, Application and Subject Matter of the Act

§ 1–101. Short Title

This Act shall be known and may be cited as Uniform Commercial Code.

§ 1–102. Purposes; Rules of Construction; Variation by Agreement

(1) This Act shall be liberally construed and applied to promote its underlying purposes and policies.
(2) Underlying purposes and policies of this Act are
    (a) to simplify, clarify and modernize the law governing commercial transactions;
    (b) to permit the continued expansion of commercial practices through custom, usage and agreement of the parties;

    (c) to make uniform the law among the various jurisdictions.
(3) The effect of provisions of this Act may be varied by agreement, except as otherwise provided in this Act and except that the obligations of good faith, diligence, reasonableness and care prescribed by this Act may not be disclaimed by agreement but the parties may by agreement determine the standards by which the performance of such obligations is to be measured if such standards are not manifestly unreasonable.
(4) The presence in certain provisions of this Act of the words "unless otherwise agreed" or words of similar import does not imply that the effect of other provisions may not be varied by agreement under subsection (3).
(5) In this Act unless the context otherwise requires
    (a) words in the singular number include the plural, and in the plural include the singular;
    (b) words of the masculine gender include the feminine and the neuter, and when the sense so indicates words of the neuter gender may refer to any gender.

§ 1–103. Supplementary General Principles of Law Applicable

Unless displaced by the particular provisions of this Act, the principles of law and equity, including the law merchant and the law relative to capacity to contract, principal and agent, estoppel, fraud, misrepresentation, duress, coercion, mistake, bankruptcy, or other validating or invalidating cause shall supplement its provisions.

§ 1–104. Construction Against Implicit Repeal

This Act being a general act intended as a unified coverage of its subject matter, no part of it shall be deemed to be impliedly repealed by subsequent legislation if such construction can reasonably be avoided.

§ 1–105. Territorial Application of the Act; Parties' Power to Choose Applicable Law

(1) Except as provided hereafter in this section, when a transaction bears a reasonable relation to this state and also to another state or nation the parties may agree that

the law either of this state or of such other state or nation shall govern their rights and duties. Failing such agreement this Act applies to transactions bearing an appropriate relation to this state.

(2) Where one of the following provisions of this Act specifies the applicable law, that provision governs and a contrary agreement is effective only to the extent permitted by law (including the conflict of laws rules) so specified:

Rights of creditors against sold goods. Section 2–402.

Applicability of the Article on Leases. Sections 2A–105 and 2A–106.

Applicability of the Article on Bank Deposits and Collections. Section 4–102.

Governing Law in the Article on Funds Transfers. Section 4A–507.

Bulk transfers subject to the Article on Bulk Transfers. Section 6–103.

Applicability of the Article on Investment Securities. Section 8–106.

Perfection provisions of the Article on Secured Transactions. Section 9–103.

§ 1–106. Remedies to Be Liberally Administered

(1) The remedies provided by this Act shall be liberally administered to the end that the aggrieved party may be put in as good a position as if the other party had fully performed but neither consequential or special nor penal damages may be had except as specifically provided in this Act or by other rule of law.

(2) Any right or obligation declared by this Act is enforceable by action unless the provision declaring it specifies a different and limited effect.

§ 1–107. Waiver or Renunciation of Claim or Right After Breach

Any claim or right arising out of an alleged breach can be discharged in whole or in part without consideration by a written waiver or renunciation signed and delivered by the aggrieved party.

§ 1–108. Severability

If any provision or clause of this Act or application thereof to any person or circumstances is held invalid, such invalidity shall not affect other provisions or applications of the Act which can be given effect without the invalid provision or application, and to this end the provisions of this Act are declared to be severable.

§ 1–109. Section Captions

Section captions are parts of this Act.

Part 2 General Definitions and Principles of Interpretation

§ 1–201. General Definitions

Subject to additional definitions contained in the subsequent Articles of this Act which are applicable to specific Articles or Parts thereof, and unless the context otherwise requires, in this Act:

(1) "Action" in the sense of a judicial proceeding includes recoupment, counterclaim, set-off, suit in equity and any other proceedings in which rights are determined.

(2) "Aggrieved party" means a party entitled to resort to a remedy.

(3) "Agreement" means the bargain of the parties in fact as found in their language or by implication from other circumstances including course of dealing or usage of trade or course of performance as provided in this Act (Sections 1–205 and 2–208). Whether an agreement has legal consequences is determined by the provisions of this Act, if applicable; otherwise by the law of contracts (Section 1–103). (Compare "Contract.")

(4) "Bank" means any person engaged in the business of banking.

(5) "Bearer" means the person in possession of an instrument, document of title, or certificated security payable to bearer or indorsed in blank.

(6) "Bill of lading" means a document evidencing the receipt of goods for shipment issued by a person engaged in the business of transporting or forwarding goods, and includes an airbill. "Airbill" means a document serving for air transportation as a bill of lading does for marine or rail transportation, and includes an air consignment note or air waybill.

(7) "Branch" includes a separately incorporated foreign branch of a bank.

(8) "Burden of establishing" a fact means the burden of persuading the triers of fact that the existence of the fact is more probable than its nonexistence.

(9) "Buyer in ordinary course of business" means a person who in good faith and without knowledge that the sale to him is in violation of the ownership rights or security interest of a third party in the goods buys in ordinary course from a person in the business of selling goods of that kind but does not include a pawnbroker. All persons who sell minerals or the like (including oil and gas) at wellhead or minehead shall be deemed to be persons in the business of selling goods of that kind. "Buying" may be for cash or by exchange of other property or on secured or unsecured credit and includes receiving goods or documents of title under a pre-existing contract for sale but does not include a transfer in bulk or as security for or in total or partial satisfaction of a money debt.

(10) "Conspicuous": A term or clause is conspicuous when it is so written that a reasonable person against whom it is to operate ought to have noticed it. A printed heading in capitals (as: NON-NEGOTIABLE BILL OF LADING) is conspicuous. Language in the body of a form is "conspicuous" if it is in larger or other contrasting type or color. But in a telegram any stated term is "conspicuous." Whether a term or clause is "conspicuous" or not is for decision by the court.

(11) "Contract" means the total legal obligation which results from the parties' agreement as affected by this Act and any other applicable rules of law. (Compare "Agreement.")

(12) "Creditor" includes a general creditor, a secured creditor, a lien creditor and any representative of creditors, including an assignee for the benefit of creditors, a trustee in bankruptcy, a receiver in equity and an executor or administrator of an insolvent debtor's or assignor's estate.

(13) "Defendant" includes a person in the position of defendant in a cross-action or counterclaim.

(14) "Delivery" with respect to instruments, documents of title, chattel paper, or certificated securities means voluntary transfer of possession.

(15) "Document of title" includes bill of lading, dock warrant, dock receipt, warehouse receipt or order for the delivery of goods, and also any other document which in the regular course of business or financing is treated as adequately evidencing that the person in possession of it is entitled to receive, hold and dispose of the document and the goods it covers. To be a document of title a document must purport to be issued by or addressed to a bailee and purport to cover goods in the bailee's possession which are either identified or are fungible portions of an identified mass.

(16) "Fault" means wrongful act, omission or breach.

(17) "Fungible" with respect to goods or securities means goods or securities of which any unit is, by nature or usage of trade, the equivalent of any other like unit. Goods which are not fungible shall be deemed fungible for the purposes of this Act to the extent that under a particular agreement or document unlike units are treated as equivalents.

(18) "Genuine" means free of forgery or counterfeiting.

(19) "Good faith" means honesty in fact in the conduct or transaction concerned.

(20) "Holder," with respect to a negotiable instrument, means the person in possession if the instrument is payable to bearer, or in the case of an instrument payable to an identified person, if the identified person is in possession. "Holder" with respect to a document of title means the person in possession of the goods are deliverable to bearer or to the order of the person in possession.

(21) To "honor" is to pay or to accept and pay, or where a credit so engages to purchase or discount a draft complying with the terms of credit.

(22) "Insolvency proceedings" includes any assignment for the benefit of creditors or other proceedings intended to liquidate or rehabilitate the estate of the person involved.

(23) A person is "insolvent" who either has ceased to pay his debts in the ordinary course of business or cannot pay his debts as they become due or is insolvent within the meaning of the federal bankruptcy law.

(24) "Money" means a medium of exchange authorized or adopted by a domestic or foreign government as a part of its currency.

(25) A person has "notice" of a fact when

(a) he has actual knowledge of it; or

(b) he has received a notice or notification of it; or

(c) from all the facts and circumstances known to him at the time in question he has reason to know that it exists.

A person "knows" or has "knowledge" of a fact when he has actual knowledge of it. "Discover" or "learn" or a word or phrase of similar import refers to knowledge rather than to reason to know. The time and circumstances under which a notice or notification may cease to be effective are not determined by this Act.

(26) A person "notifies" or "gives" a notice or notification to another by taking such steps as may be reasonably required to inform the other in ordinary course whether or not such other actually comes to know of it. A person "receives" a notice or notification when

(a) it comes to his attention; or

(b) it is duly delivered at the place of business through which the contract was made or at any other place held out by him as the place for receipt of such communications.

(27) Notice, knowledge or a notice or notification received by an organization is effective for a particular transaction from the time when it is brought to the attention of the individual conducting that transaction, and in any event from the time when it would have been brought to his attention if the organization had exercised due diligence. An organization exercises due diligence if it maintains reasonable routines for communicating significant information to the person conducting the transaction and there is reasonable compliance with the routines. Due diligence does not require an individual acting for the organization to communicate information unless such communication is part of his regular duties or unless he has reason to know of the transaction and that the transaction would be materially affected by the information.

(28) "Organization" includes a corporation, government or governmental subdivision or agency, business trust,

estate, trust, partnership or association, two or more persons having a joint or common interest, or any other legal or commercial entity.

(29) "Party," as distinct from "third party," means a person who has engaged in a transaction or made an agreement within this Act.

(30) "Person" includes an individual or an organization (See Section 1–102).

(31) "Presumption" or "presumed" means that the trier of fact must find the existence of the fact presumed unless and until evidence is introduced which would support a finding of its nonexistence.

(32) "Purchase" includes taking by sale, discount, negotiation, mortgage, pledge, lien, issue or reissue, gift or any other voluntary transaction creating an interest in property.

(33) "Purchaser" means a person who takes by purchase.

(34) "Remedy" means any remedial right to which an aggrieved party is entitled with or without resort to a tribunal.

(35) "Representative" includes an agent, an officer of a corporation or association, and a trustee, executor or administrator of an estate, or any other person empowered to act for another.

(36) "Rights" includes remedies.

(37) "Security interest" means an interest in personal property or fixtures which secures payment or performance of an obligation. The retention or reservation of title by a seller of goods notwithstanding shipment or delivery to the buyer (Section 2–401) is limited in effect to a reservation of a "security interest." The term also includes any interest of a buyer of accounts or chattel paper which is subject to Article 9. The special property interest of a buyer of goods on identification of those goods to a contract for sale under Section 2–401 is not a "security interest," but a buyer may also acquire a "security interest" by complying with Article 9. Unless a consignment is intended as security, reservation of title thereunder is not a "security interest," but a consignment in any event is subject to the provisions on consignment sales (Section 2–326).

Whether a transaction creates a lease or security interest is determined by the facts of each case; however, a transaction creates a security interest if the consideration the lessee is to pay the lessor for the right to possession and use of the goods is an obligation for the term of the lease not subject to termination by the lessee, and

(a) the original term of the lease is equal to or greater than the remaining economic life of the goods,

(b) the lessee is bound to renew the lease for the remaining economic life of the goods or is bound to become the owner of the goods,

(c) the lessee has an option to renew the lease for the remaining economic life of the goods for no additional consideration or nominal additional consideration upon compliance with the lease agreement, or

(d) the lessee has an option to become the owner of the goods for no additional consideration or nominal additional consideration upon compliance with the lease agreement.

A transaction does not create a security interest merely because it provides that

(a) the present value of the consideration the lessee is obligated to pay the lessor for the right to possession and use of the goods is substantially equal to or is greater than the fair market value of the goods at the time the lease is entered into,

(b) the lessee assumes risk of loss of the goods, or agrees to pay taxes, insurance, filing, recording, or registration fees, or service or maintenance costs with respect to the goods,

(c) the lessee has an option to renew the lease or to become the owner of the goods.

(d) the lessee has an option to renew the lease for a fixed rent that is equal to or greater than the reasonably predictable fair market rent for the use of the goods for the term of the renewal at the time the option is to be performed, or

(e) the lessee has an option to become the owner of the goods for a fixed price that is equal to or greater than the reasonably predictable fair market value of the goods at the time the option is to be performed.

For purposes of this subsection (37):

(x) Additional consideration is not nominal if (i) when the option to renew the lease is granted to the lessee the rent is stated to be the fair market rent for the use of the goods for the term of the renewal determined at the time the option is to be performed, or (ii) when the option to become the owner of the goods is granted to the lessee the price is stated to be the fair market value of the goods determined at the time the option is to be performed. Additional consideration is nominal if it is less than the lessee's reasonably predictable cost of performing under the lease agreement if the option is not exercised;

(y) "Reasonably predictable" and "remaining economic life of the goods" are to be determined with reference to the facts and circumstances at the time the transaction is entered into; and

(z) "Present value" means the amount as of a date certain of one or more sums payable in the future, discounted to the date certain. The discount is determined by the interest rate specified by the parties if the rate is not manifestly unreasonable at the time the transaction is entered into; otherwise, the discount is determined by a commercially reasonable rate that takes into account the facts and circumstances of each case at the time the transaction was entered into.

(38) "Send" in connection with any writing or notice means to deposit in the mail or deliver for transmission by any other usual means of communication with postage or cost of transmission provided for and properly addressed and in the case of an instrument to an address specified thereon or otherwise agreed, or if there be none to any address reasonable under the circumstances. The receipt of any writing or notice within the time at which it would have arrived if properly sent has the effect of a proper sending.

(39) "Signed" includes any symbol executed or adopted by a party with present intention to authenticate a writing.

(40) "Surety" includes guarantor.

(41) "Telegram" includes a message transmitted by radio, teletype, cable, any mechanical method of transmission, or the like.

(42) "Term" means that portion of an agreement which relates to a particular matter.

(43) "Unauthorized" signature or indorsement means one made without actual, implied or apparent authority and includes a forgery.

(44) "Value." Except as otherwise provided with respect to negotiable instruments and bank collections (Sections 3–303, 4–208 and 4–209) a person gives "value" for rights if he acquires them

(a) in return for a binding commitment to extend credit or for the extension of immediately available credit whether or not drawn upon and whether or not a chargeback is provided for in the event of difficulties in collection; or

(b) as security for or in total or partial satisfaction of a preexisting claim; or

(c) by accepting delivery pursuant to a preexisting contract for purchase; or

(d) generally, in return for any consideration sufficient to support a simple contract.

(45) "Warehouse receipt" means a receipt issued by a person engaged in the business of storing goods for hire.

(46) "Written" or "writing" includes printing, typewriting or any other intentional reduction to tangible form.

§ 1–202. Prima Facie Evidence by Third Party Documents

A document in due form purporting to be a bill of lading, policy or certificate of insurance, official weigher's or inspector's certificate, consular invoice, or any other document authorized or required by the contract to be issued by a third party shall be prima facie evidence of its own authenticity and genuineness and of the facts stated in the document by the third party.

§ 1–203. Obligation of Good Faith

Every contract or duty within this Act imposes an obligation of good faith in its performance or enforcement.

§ 1–204. Time; Reasonable Time; "Seasonably"

(1) Whenever this Act requires any action to be taken within a reasonable time, any time which is not manifestly unreasonable may be fixed by agreement.

(2) What is a reasonable time for taking any action depends on the nature, purpose and circumstances of such action.

(3) An action is taken "seasonably" when it is taken at or within the time agreed or if no time is agreed at or within a reasonable time.

§ 1–205. Course of Dealing and Usage of Trade

(1) A course of dealing is a sequence of previous conduct between the parties to a particular transaction which is fairly to be regarded as establishing a common basis of understanding for interpreting their expressions and other conduct.

(2) A usage of trade is any practice or method of dealing having such regularity of observance in a place, vocation or trade as to justify an expectation that it will be observed with respect to the transaction in question. The existence and scope of such a usage are to be proved as facts. If it is established that such a usage is embodied in a written trade code or similar writing the interpretation of the writing is for the court.

(3) A course of dealing between parties and any usage of trade in the vocation or trade in which they are engaged or of which they are or should be aware give particular meaning to and supplement or qualify terms of an agreement.

(4) The express terms of an agreement and an applicable course of dealing or usage of trade shall be construed wherever reasonable as consistent with each other; but when such construction is unreasonable express terms control both course of dealing and usage of trade and course of dealing controls usage of trade.

(5) An applicable usage of trade in the place where any part of performance is to occur shall be used in interpreting the agreement as to that part of the performance.

(6) Evidence of a relevant usage of trade offered by one party is not admissible unless and until he has given the other party such notice as the court finds sufficient to prevent unfair surprise to the latter.

§ 1–206. Statute of Frauds for Kinds of Personal Property Not Otherwise Covered

(1) Except in the cases described in subsection (2) of this section a contract for the sale of personal property is not enforceable by way of action or defense beyond five thousand dollars in amount or value of remedy unless there is some writing which indicates that a contract for

sale has been made between the parties at a defined or stated price, reasonably identifies the subject matter, and is signed by the party against whom enforcement is sought or by his authorized agent.

(2) Subsection (1) of this section does not apply to contracts for the sale of goods (Section 2–201) nor of securities (Section 8–319) nor to security agreements (Section 9–203).

§ 1–207. Performance or Acceptance Under Reservation of Rights

(1) A party who with explicit reservation of rights performs or promises performance or assents to performance in a manner demanded or offered by the other party does not thereby prejudice the rights reserved. Such words as "without prejudice," "under protest" or the like are sufficient.

(2) Subsection (1) does not apply to an accord and satisfaction.

§ 1–208. Option to Accelerate at Will

A term providing that one party or his successor in interest may accelerate payment or performance or require collateral or additional collateral "at will" or "when he deems himself insecure" or in words of similar import shall be construed to mean that he shall have power to do so only if he in good faith believes that the prospect of payment or performance is impaired. The burden of establishing lack of good faith is on the party against whom the power has been exercised.

§ 1–209. Subordinated Obligations

An obligation may be issued as subordinated to payment of another obligation of the person obligated, or a creditor may subordinate his right to payment of an obligation by agreement with either the person obligated or another creditor of the person obligated. Such a subordination does not create a security interest as against either the common debtor or a subordinated creditor. This section shall be construed as declaring the law as it existed prior to the enactment of this section and not as modifying it.

Note: This new section is proposed as an optional provision to make it clear that a subordination agreement does not create a security interest unless so intended.

ARTICLE 2 SALES

Part 1 Short Title, General Construction and Subject Matter

§ 2–101. Short Title

This Article shall be known and may be cited as Uniform Commercial Code—Sales.

§ 2–102. Scope; Certain Security and Other Transactions Excluded From This Article

Unless the context otherwise requires, this Article applies to transactions in goods; it does not apply to any transaction which although in the form of an unconditional contract to sell or present sale is intended to operate only as a security transaction nor does this Article impair or repeal any statute regulating sales to consumers, farmers or other specified classes of buyers.

§ 2–103. Definitions and Index of Definitions

(1) In this Article unless the context otherwise requires

(a) "Buyer" means a person who buys or contracts to buy goods.

(b) "Good faith" in the case of a merchant means honesty in fact and the observance of reasonable commercial standards of fair dealing in the trade.

(c) "Receipt" of goods means taking physical possession of them.

(d) "Seller" means a person who sells or contracts to sell goods.

(2) Other definitions applying to this Article or to specified Parts thereof, and the sections in which they appear are:

"Acceptance." Section 2–606.
"Banker's credit." Section 2–325.
"Between merchants." Section 2–104.
"Cancellation." Section 2–106(4).
"Commercial unit." Section 2–105.
"Confirmed credit." Section 2–325.
"Conforming to contract." Section 2–106.
"Contract for sale." Section 2–106.
"Cover." Section 2–712.
"Entrusting." Section 2–403.
"Financing agency." Section 2–104.
"Future goods." Section 2–105.
"Goods." Section 2–105.
"Identification." Section 2–501.
"Installment contract." Section 2–612.
"Letter of Credit." Section 2–325.
"Lot." Section 2–105.
"Merchant." Section 2–104.
"Overseas." Section 2–323.
"Person in position of seller." Section 2–707.
"Present sale." Section 2–106.
"Sale." Section 2–106.
"Sale on approval." Section 2–326.
"Sale or return." Section 2–326.
"Termination." Section 2–106

(3) The following definitions in other Articles apply to this Article:

"Check." Section 3–104.
"Consignee." Section 7–102.

"Consignor." Section 7–102.

"Consumer goods." Section 9–109.

"Dishonor." Section 3–507.

"Draft." Section 3–104.

(4) In addition Article 1 contains general definitions and principles of construction and interpretation applicable throughout this Article.

§ 2–104. Definitions: "Merchant"; "Between Merchants"; "Financing Agency"

(1) "Merchant" means a person who deals in goods of the kind or otherwise by his occupation holds himself out as having knowledge or skill peculiar to the practices or goods involved in the transaction or to whom such knowledge or skill may be attributed by his employment of an agent or broker or other intermediary who by his occupation holds himself out as having such knowledge or skill.

(2) "Financing agency" means a bank, finance company or other person who in the ordinary course of business makes advances against goods or documents of title or who by arrangement with either the seller or the buyer intervenes in ordinary course to make or collect payment due or claimed under the contract for sale, as by purchasing or paying the seller's draft or making advances against it or by merely taking it for collection whether or not documents of title accompany the draft. "Financing agency" includes also a bank or other person who similarly intervenes between persons who are in the position of seller and buyer in respect to the goods (Section 2–707).

(3) "Between merchants" means in any transaction with respect to which both parties are chargeable with the knowledge or skill of merchants.

§ 2–105. Definitions: Transferability; "Goods"; "Future Goods"; "Lot"; "Commercial Unit"

(1) "Goods" means all things (including specially manufactured goods) which are moveable at the time of identification to the contract for sale other than the money in which the price is to be paid, investment securities (Article 8) and things in action. "Goods" also includes the unborn young of animals and growing crops and other identified things attached to realty as described in the section on goods to be severed from realty (Section 2–107).

(2) Goods must be both existing and identified before any interest in them can pass. Goods which are not both existing and identified are "future" goods. A purported present sale of future goods or of any interest therein operates as a contract to sell.

(3) There may be a sale of a part interest in existing identified goods.

(4) An undivided share in an identified bulk of fungible goods is sufficiently identified to be sold although the quantity of the bulk is not determined. Any agreed proportion of such a bulk or any quantity thereof agreed upon by number, weight or other measure may to the extent of the seller's interest in the bulk be sold to the buyer who then becomes an owner in common.

(5) "Lot" means a parcel or a single article which is the subject matter of a separate sale or delivery, whether or not it is sufficient to perform the contract.

(6) "Commercial unit" means such a unit of goods as by commercial usage is a single whole for purposes of sale and division of which materially impairs its character or value on the market or in use. A commercial unit may be a single article (as a machine) or a set of articles (as a suite of furniture or an assortment of sizes) or a quantity (as a bale, gross, or carload) or any other unit treated in use or in the relevant market as a single whole.

§ 2–106. Definitions: "Contract"; "Agreement"; "Contract for Sale"; "Sale"; "Present Sale"; "Conforming to Contract"; "Termination"; "Cancellation"

(1) In this Article unless the context otherwise requires "contract" and "agreement" are limited to those relating to the present or future sale of goods. "Contract for sale" includes both a present sale of goods and a contract to sell goods at a future time. A "sale" consists in the passing of title from the seller to the buyer for a price (Section 2–401). A "present sale" means a sale which is accomplished by the making of the contract.

(2) Goods or conduct including any part of a performance are "conforming" or conform to the contract when they are in accordance with the obligations under the contract.

(3) "Termination" occurs when either party pursuant to a power created by agreement or law puts an end to the contract otherwise than for its breach. On "termination" all obligations which are still executory on both sides are discharged but any right based on prior breach or performance survives.

(4) "Cancellation" occurs when either party puts an end to the contract for breach by the other and its effect is the same as that of "termination" except that the cancelling party also retains any remedy for breach of the whole contract or any unperformed balance.

§ 2–107. Goods to Be Severed From Realty: Recording

(1) A contract for the sale of minerals or the like (including oil and gas) or a structure or its materials to be removed from realty is a contract for the sale of goods within this Article if they are to be severed by the seller but until severance a purported present sale thereof which

is not effective as a transfer of an interest in land is effective only as a contract to sell.

(2) A contract for the sale apart from the land of growing crops or other things attached to realty and capable of severance without material harm thereto but not described in subsection (1) or of timber to be cut is a contract for the sale of goods within this Article whether the subject matter is to be severed by the buyer or by the seller even though it forms part of the realty at the time of contracting, and the parties can by identification effect a present sale before severance.

(3) The provisions of this section are subject to any third party rights provided by the law relating to realty records, and the contract for sale may be executed and recorded as a document transferring an interest in land and shall then constitute notice to third parties of the buyer's rights under the contract for sale.

Part 2 Form, Formation and Readjustment of Contract

§ 2–201. Formal Requirements; Statute of Frauds

(1) Except as otherwise provided in this section a contract for the sale of goods for the price of $500 or more is not enforceable by way of action or defense unless there is some writing sufficient to indicate that a contract for sale has been made between the parties and signed by the party against whom enforcement is sought or by his authorized agent or broker. A writing is not insufficient because it omits or incorrectly states a term agreed upon but the contract is not enforceable under this paragraph beyond the quantity of goods shown in such writing.

(2) Between merchants if within a reasonable time a writing in confirmation of the contract and sufficient against the sender is received and the party receiving it has reason to know its contents, it satisfies the requirements of subsection (1) against such party unless written notice of objection to its contents is given within 10 days after it is received.

(3) A contract which does not satisfy the requirements of subsection (1) but which is valid in other respects is enforceable

(a) if the goods are to be specially manufactured for the buyer and are not suitable for sale to others in the ordinary course of the seller's business and the seller, before notice of repudiation is received and under circumstances which reasonably indicate that the goods are for the buyer, has made either a substantial beginning of their manufacture or commitments for their procurement; or

(b) if the party against whom enforcement is sought admits in his pleading, testimony or otherwise in court that a contract for sale was made, but the contract is not enforceable under this provision beyond the quantity of goods admitted; or

(c) with respect to goods for which payment has been made and accepted or which have been received and accepted (Section 2–606).

§ 2–202. Final Written Expression: Parol or Extrinsic Evidence

Terms with respect to which the confirmatory memoranda of the parties agree or which are otherwise set forth in a writing intended by the parties as a final expression of their agreement with respect to such terms as are included therein may not be contradicted by evidence of any prior agreement or of a contemporaneous oral agreement but may be explained or supplemented

(a) by course of dealing or usage of trade (Section 1–205) or by course of performance (Section 2–208); and

(b) by evidence of consistent additional terms unless the court finds the writing to have been intended also as a complete and exclusive statement of the terms of the agreement.

§ 2–203. Seals Inoperative

The affixing of a seal to a writing evidencing a contract for sale or an offer to buy or sell goods does not constitute the writing of a sealed instrument and the law with respect to sealed instruments does not apply to such a contract or offer.

§ 2–204. Formation in General

(1) A contract for sale of goods may be made in any manner sufficient to show agreement, including conduct by both parties which recognizes the existence of such a contract.

(2) An agreement sufficient to constitute a contract for sale may be found even though the moment of its making is undetermined.

(3) Even though one or more terms are left open a contract for sale does not fail for indefiniteness if the parties have intended to make a contract and there is a reasonably certain basis for giving an appropriate remedy.

§ 2–205. Firm Offers

An offer by a merchant to buy or sell goods in a signed writing which by its terms gives assurance that it will be held open is not revocable, for lack of consideration, during the time stated or if no time is stated for a reasonable time, but in no event may such period of irrevocability exceed three months; but any such term of assurance on a form supplied by the offeree must be separately signed by the offeror.

§ 2–206. Offer and Acceptance in Formation of Contract

(1) Unless otherwise unambiguously indicated by the language or circumstances

(a) an offer to make a contract shall be construed as inviting acceptance in any manner and by any medium reasonable in the circumstances;

(b) an order or other offer to buy goods for prompt or current shipment shall be construed as inviting acceptance either by a prompt promise to ship or by the prompt or current shipment of conforming or nonconforming goods, but such a shipment of nonconforming goods does not constitute an acceptance if the seller seasonably notifies the buyer that the shipment is offered only as an accommodation to the buyer.

(2) Where the beginning of a requested performance is a reasonable mode of acceptance an offeror who is not notified of acceptance within a reasonable time may treat the offer as having lapsed before acceptance.

§ 2–207. Additional Terms in Acceptance or Confirmation

(1) A definite and seasonable expression of acceptance or a written confirmation which is sent within a reasonable time operates as an acceptance even though it states terms additional to or different from those offered or agreed upon, unless acceptance is expressly made conditional on assent to the additional or different terms.

(2) The additional terms are to be construed as proposals for addition to the contract. Between merchants such terms become part of the contract unless:

(a) the offer expressly limits acceptance to the terms of the offer;

(b) they materially alter it; or

(c) notification of objection to them has already been given or is given within a reasonable time after notice of them is received.

(3) Conduct by both parties which recognizes the existence of a contract is sufficient to establish a contract for sale although the writings of the parties do not otherwise establish a contract. In such case the terms of the particular contract consist of those terms on which the writings of the parties agree, together with any supplementary terms incorporated under any other provisions of this Act.

§ 2–208. Course of Performance or Practical Construction

(1) Where the contract for sale involves repeated occasions for performance by either party with knowledge of the nature of the performance and opportunity for objection to it by the other, any course of performance accepted or acquiesced in without objection shall be relevant to determine the meaning of the agreement.

(2) The express terms of the agreement and any such course of performance, as well as any course of dealing and usage of trade, shall be construed whenever reasonable as consistent with each other; but when such construction is unreasonable, express terms shall control

course of performance and course of performance shall control both course of dealing and usage of trade (Section 1–205).

(3) Subject to the provisions of the next section on modification and waiver, such course of performance shall be relevant to show a waiver or modification of any term inconsistent with such course of performance.

§ 2–209. Modification, Rescission and Waiver

(1) An agreement modifying a contract within this Article needs no consideration to be binding.

(2) A signed agreement which excludes modification or rescission except by a signed writing cannot be otherwise modified or rescinded, but except as between merchants such a requirement on a form supplied by the merchant must be separately signed by the other party.

(3) The requirements of the statute of frauds section of this Article (Section 2–201) must be satisfied if the contract as modified is within its provisions.

(4) Although an attempt at modification or rescission does not satisfy the requirements of subsection (2) or (3) it can operate as a waiver.

(5) A party who has made a waiver affecting an executory portion of the contract may retract the waiver by reasonable notification received by the other party that strict performance will be required of any term waived, unless the retraction would be unjust in view of a material change of position in reliance on the waiver.

§ 2–210. Delegation of Performance; Assignment of Rights

(1) A party may perform his duty through a delegate unless otherwise agreed or unless the other party has a substantial interest in having his original promisor perform or control the acts required by the contract. No delegation of performance relieves the party delegating of any duty to perform or any liability for breach.

(2) Unless otherwise agreed all rights of either seller or buyer can be assigned except where the assignment would materially change the duty of the other party, or increase materially the burden or risk imposed on him by his contract, or impair materially his chance of obtaining return performance. A right to damages for breach of the whole contract or a right arising out of the assignor's due performance of his entire obligation can be assigned despite agreement otherwise.

(3) Unless the circumstances indicate the contrary a prohibition of assignment of ''the contract'' is to be construed as barring only the delegation to the assignee of the assignor's performance.

(4) An assignment of ''the contract'' or of ''all my rights under the contract'' or an assignment in similar general terms is an assignment of rights and unless the language or the circumstances (as in an assignment for security) indicate the contrary, it is a delegation of performance of

the duties of the assignor and its acceptance by the assignee constitutes a promise by him to perform those duties. This promise is enforceable by either the assignor or the other party to the original contract.

(5) The other party may treat any assignment which delegates performance as creating reasonable grounds for insecurity and may without prejudice to his rights against the assignor demand assurance from the assignee (Section 2–609).

Part 3 General Obligation and Construction of Contract

§2–301. General Obligations of Parties

The obligation of the seller is to transfer and deliver and that of the buyer is to accept and pay in accordance with the contract.

§ 2–302. Unconscionable Contract or Clause

(1) If the court as a matter of law finds the contract or any clause of the contract to have been unconscionable at the time it was made the court may refuse to enforce the contract, or it may enforce the remainder of the contract without the unconscionable clause, or it may so limit the application of any unconscionable clause as to avoid any unconscionable result.

(2) When it is claimed or appears to the court that the contract or any clause thereof may be unconscionable the parties shall be afforded a reasonable opportunity to present evidence as to its commercial setting, purpose and effect to aid the court in making the determination.

§ 2–303. Allocation or Division of Risks

Where this Article allocates a risk or a burden as between the parties "unless otherwise agreed," the agreement may not only shift the allocation but may also divide the risk or burden.

§ 2–304. Price Payable in Money, Goods, Realty, or Otherwise

(1) The price can be made payable in money or otherwise. If it is payable in whole or in part in goods each party is a seller of the goods which he is to transfer.

(2) Even though all or part of the price is payable in an interest in realty the transfer of the goods and the seller's obligations with reference to them are subject to this Article, but not the transfer of the interest in realty or the transferor's obligations in connection therewith.

§ 2–305. Open Price Term

(1) The parties if they so intend can conclude a contract for sale even though the price is not settled. In such case the price is a reasonable price at the time for delivery if

   (a) nothing is said as to price; or

   (b) the price is left to be agreed by the parties and they fail to agree; or

   (c) the price is to be fixed in terms of some agreed market or other standard as set or recorded by a third person or agency and it is not so set or recorded.

(2) A price to be fixed by the seller or by the buyer means a price for him to fix in good faith.

(3) When a price left to be fixed otherwise than by agreement of the parties fails to be fixed through fault of one party the other may at his option treat the contract as cancelled or himself fix a reasonable price.

(4) Where, however, the parties intend not to be bound unless the price be fixed or agreed and it is not fixed or agreed there is no contract. In such a case the buyer must return any goods already received or if unable so to do must pay their reasonable value at the time of delivery and the seller must return any portion of the price paid on account.

§ 2–306. Output, Requirements and Exclusive Dealings

(1) A term which measures the quantity by the output of the seller or the requirements of the buyer means such actual output or requirements as may occur in good faith, except that no quantity unreasonably disproportionate to any stated estimate or in the absence of a stated estimate to any normal or otherwise comparable prior output or requirements may be tendered or demanded.

(2) A lawful agreement by either the seller or the buyer for exclusive dealing in the kind of goods concerned imposes unless otherwise agreed an obligation by the seller to use best efforts to supply the goods and by the buyer to use best efforts to promote their sale.

§ 2–307. Delivery in Single Lot or Several Lots

Unless otherwise agreed all goods called for by a contract for sale must be tendered in a single delivery and payment is due only on such tender but where the circumstances give either party the right to make or demand delivery in lots the price if it can be apportioned may be demanded for each lot.

§ 2–308. Absence of Specified Place for Delivery

Unless otherwise agreed

   (a) the place for delivery of goods is the seller's place of business or if he has none his residence; but

   (b) in a contract for sale of identified goods which to the knowledge of the parties at the time of contracting are in some other place, that place is the place for their delivery; and

   (c) documents of title may be delivered through customary banking channels.

§ 2–309. Absence of Specific Time Provisions; Notice of Termination

(1) The time for shipment or delivery or any other action under a contract if not provided in this Article or agreed upon shall be a reasonable time.

(2) Where the contract provides for successive performances but is indefinite in duration it is valid for a reasonable time but unless otherwise agreed may be terminated at any time by either party.

(3) Termination of a contract by one party except on the happening of an agreed event requires that reasonable notification be received by the other party and an agreement dispensing with notification is invalid if its operation would be unconscionable.

§ 2–310. Open Time for Payment or Running of Credit: Authority to Ship Under Reservation

Unless otherwise agreed

(a) payment is due at the time and place at which the buyer is to receive the goods even though the place of shipment is the place of delivery; and

(b) if the seller is authorized to send the goods he may ship them under reservation, and may tender the documents of title, but the buyer may inspect the goods after their arrival before payment is due unless such inspection is inconsistent with the terms of the contract (Section 2–513); and

(c) if delivery is authorized and made by way of documents of title otherwise than by subsection (b) then payment is due at the time and place at which the buyer is to receive the documents regardless of where the goods are to be received; and

(d) where the seller is required or authorized to ship the goods on credit the credit period runs from the time of shipment but post-dating the invoice or delaying its dispatch will correspondingly delay the starting of the credit period.

§ 2–311. Options and Cooperation Respecting Performance

(1) An agreement for sale which is otherwise sufficiently definite (subsection (3) of Section 2–204) to be a contract is not made invalid by the fact that it leaves particulars of performance to be specified by one of the parties. Any such specification must be made in good faith and within limits set by commercial reasonableness.

(2) Unless otherwise agreed specifications relating to assortment of the goods are at the buyer's option and except as otherwise provided in subsection (1)(c) and (3) of Section 2–319 specifications or arrangements relating to shipment are at the seller's option.

(3) Where such specification would materially affect the other party's performance but is not seasonably made or where one party's cooperation is necessary to the agreed performance of the other but is not seasonably forthcoming, the other party in addition to all other remedies

(a) is excused for any resulting delay in his own performance; and

(b) may also either proceed to perform in any reasonable manner or after the time for a material part of his own performance treat the failure to specify or to

cooperate as a breach by failure to deliver or accept the goods.

§ 2–312. Warranty of Title and Against Infringement; Buyer's Obligation Against Infringement

(1) Subject to subsection (2) there is in a contract for sale a warranty by the seller that

(a) the title conveyed shall be good, and its transfer rightful; and

(b) the goods shall be delivered free from any security interest or other lien or encumbrance of which the buyer at the time of contracting has no knowledge.

(2) A warranty under subsection (1) will be excluded or modified only by specific language or by circumstances which give the buyer reason to know that the person selling does not claim title in himself or that he is purporting to sell only such right or title as he or a third person may have.

(3) Unless otherwise agreed a seller who is a merchant regularly dealing in goods of the kind warrants that the goods shall be delivered free of the rightful claim of any third person by way of infringement or the like but a buyer who furnishes specifications to the seller must hold the seller harmless against any such claim which arises out of compliance with the specifications.

§ 2–313. Express Warranties by Affirmation, Promise, Description, Sample

(1) Express warranties by the seller are created as follows:

(a) Any affirmation of fact or promise made by the seller to the buyer which relates to the goods and becomes part of the basis of the bargain creates an express warranty that the goods shall conform to the affirmation or promise.

(b) Any description of the goods which is made part of the basis of the bargain creates an express warranty that the goods shall conform to the description.

(c) Any sample or model which is made part of the basis of the bargain creates an express warranty that the whole of the goods shall conform to the sample or model.

(2) It is not necessary to the creation of an express warranty that the seller use formal words such as "warrant" or "guarantee" or that he have a specific intention to make a warranty, but an affirmation merely of the value of the goods or a statement purporting to be merely the seller's opinion or commendation of the goods does not create a warranty.

§ 2–314. Implied Warranty: Merchantability; Usage of Trade

(1) Unless excluded or modified (Section 2–316), a warranty that the goods shall be merchantable is implied in a contract for their sale if the seller is a merchant with respect to goods of that kind. Under this section the serving for value of food or drink to be consumed either on the premises or elsewhere is a sale.

(2) Goods to be merchantable must be at least such as

(a) pass without objection in the trade under the contract description; and

(b) in the case of fungible goods, are of fair average quality within the description; and

(c) are fit for the ordinary purposes for which such goods are used; and

(d) run, within the variations permitted by the agreement, of even kind, quality and quantity within each unit and among all units involved; and

(e) are adequately contained, packaged, and labeled as the agreement may require; and

(f) conform to the promises or affirmations of fact made on the container or label if any.

(3) Unless excluded or modified (Section 2–316) other implied warranties may arise from course of dealing or usage of trade.

§ 2–315. Implied Warranty: Fitness for Particular Purpose

Where the seller at the time of contracting has reason to know any particular purpose for which the goods are required and that the buyer is relying on the seller's skill or judgment to select or furnish suitable goods, there is unless excluded or modified under the next section an implied warranty that the goods shall be fit for such purpose.

§ 2–316. Exclusion or Modification of Warranties

(1) Words or conduct relevant to the creation of an express warranty and words or conduct tending to negate or limit warranty shall be construed wherever reasonable as consistent with each other; but subject to the provisions of this Article on parol or extrinsic evidence (Section 2–202) negation or limitation is inoperative to the extent that such construction is unreasonable.

(2) Subject to subsection (3), to exclude or modify the implied warranty of merchantability or any part of it the language must mention merchantability and in case of a writing must be conspicuous, and to exclude or modify any implied warranty of fitness the exclusion must be by a writing and conspicuous. Language to exclude all implied warranties of fitness is sufficient if it states, for example, that "There are no warranties which extend beyond the description on the face hereof."

(3) Notwithstanding subsection (2)

(a) unless the circumstances indicate otherwise, all implied warranties are excluded by expressions like "as is," "with all faults" or other languages which in common understanding calls the buyer's attention to the exclusion of warranties and makes plain that there is no implied warranty; and

(b) when the buyer before entering into the contract has examined the goods or the sample or model as fully as he desired or has refused to examine the goods there is no implied warranty with regard to defects which an examination ought in the circumstances to have revealed to him; and

(c) an implied warranty can also be excluded or modified by course of dealing or course of performance or usage of trade.

(4) Remedies for breach of warranty can be limited in accordance with the provisions of this Article on liquidation or limitation of damages and on contractual modification of remedy (Section 2–718 and 2–719).

§ 2–317. Cumulation and Conflict of Warranties Express or Implied

Warranties whether express or implied shall be construed as consistent with each other and as cumulative, but if such construction is unreasonable the intention of the parties shall determine which warranty is dominant. In ascertaining that intention the following rules apply:

(a) Exact or technical specifications displace an inconsistent sample or model or general language of description.

(b) A sample from an existing bulk displaces inconsistent general language of description.

(c) Express warranties displace inconsistent implied warranties other than an implied warranty of fitness for a particular purpose.

§ 2–318. Third Party Beneficiaries of Warranties Express or Implied

***Note:** If this Act is introduced in the Congress of the United States this Section should be omitted. (States to select one alternative.)*

Alternative A

A seller's warranty whether express or implied extends to any natural person who is in the family or household of his buyer or who is a guest in his home if it is reasonable to expect that such person may use, consume or be affected by the goods and who is injured in person by breach of the warranty. A seller may not exclude or limit the operation of this section.

Alternative B

A seller's warranty whether express or implied extends to any natural person who may reasonably be expected to use, consume or be affected by the goods and who is injured in person by breach of the warranty. A seller may not exclude or limit the operation of this section.

Alternative C

A seller's warranty whether express or implied extends to any person who may reasonably be expected to use, consume or be affected by the goods and who is injured by breach of the warranty. A seller may not exclude or limit the operation of this section with respect to injury to the person of an individual to whom the warranty extends.

§ 2–319. F.O.B. and F.A.S. Terms

(1) Unless otherwise agreed the term F.O.B. (which means "free on board") at a named place, even though used only in connection with the stated price, is a delivery term under which

(a) when the term is F.O.B. the place of shipment, the seller must at that place ship the goods in the manner provided in this Article (Section 2–504) and bear the expense and risk of putting them into the possession of the carrier; or

(b) when the term is F.O.B. the place of destination, the seller must at his own expense and risk transport the goods to that place and there tender delivery of them in the manner provided in this Article (Section 2–503);

(c) when under either (a) or (b) the term is also F.O.B. vessel, car or other vehicle, the seller must in addition at his own expense and risk load the goods on board. If the term is F.O.B. vessel the buyer must name the vessel and in an appropriate case the seller must comply with the provisions of this Article on the form of bill of lading (Section 2–323).

(2) Unless otherwise agreed the term F.A.S. vessel (which means "free alongside") at a named port, even though used only in connection with the stated price, is a delivery term under which the seller must

(a) at his own expense and risk deliver the goods alongside the vessel in the manner usual in that port or on a dock designated and provided by the buyer; and

(b) obtain and tender a receipt for the goods in exchange for which the carrier is under a duty to issue a bill of lading.

(3) Unless otherwise agreed in any case falling within subsection (1)(a) or (c) or subsection (2) the buyer must seasonably give any needed instructions for making delivery, including when the term is F.A.S. or F.O.B. the loading berth of the vessel and in an appropriate case its name and sailing date. The seller may treat the failure of needed instructions as a failure of cooperation under this Article (Section 2–311). He may also at his option move the goods in any reasonable manner preparatory to delivery or shipment.

(4) Under the term F.O.B. vessel or F.A.S. unless otherwise agreed the buyer must make payment against tender of the required documents and the seller may not tender nor the buyer demand delivery of the goods in substitution for the documents.

§ 2–320. C.I.F. and C. & F. Terms

(1) The term C.I.F. means that the price includes in a lump sum the cost of the goods and the insurance and freight to the named destination. The term C. & F. or C.F. means that the price so includes cost and freight to the named destination.

(2) Unless otherwise agreed and even though used only in connection with the stated price and destination, the term

C.I.F. destination or its equivalent requires the seller at his own expense and risk to

(a) put the goods into the possession of a carrier at the port for shipment and obtain a negotiable bill or bills of lading covering the entire transportation to the named destination; and

(b) load the goods and obtain a receipt from the carrier (which may be contained in the bill of lading) showing that the freight has been paid or provided for; and

(c) obtain a policy or certificate of insurance, including any war risk insurance, of a kind and on terms then current at the port of shipment in the usual amount, in the currency of the contract, shown to cover the same goods covered by the bill of lading and providing for payment of loss to the order of the buyer or for the account of whom it may concern; but the seller may add to the price the amount of the premium for any such war risk insurance; and

(d) prepare an invoice of the goods and procure any other documents required to effect shipment or to comply with the contract; and

(e) forward and tender with commercial promptness all the documents in due form and with any indorsement necessary to perfect the buyer's rights.

(3) Unless otherwise agreed the term C. & F. or its equivalent has the same effect and imposes upon the seller the same obligations and risks as a C.I.F. term except the obligation as to insurance.

(4) Under the term C.I.F. & C. & F. unless otherwise agreed the buyer must make payment against tender of the required documents and the seller may not tender nor the buyer demand delivery of the goods in substitution for the documents.

§ 2–321. C.I.F. or C. & F.: "Net Landed Weights"; "Payment on Arrival"; Warranty of Condition on Arrival

Under a contract containing a term C.I.F. or C. & F.

(1) Where the price is based on or is to be adjusted according to "net landed weights," "delivered weights," "out turn" quantity or quality or the like, unless otherwise agreed the seller must reasonably estimate the price. The payment due on tender of the documents called for by the contract is the amount so estimated, but after final adjustment of the price a settlement must be made with commercial promptness.

(2) An agreement described in subsection (1) or any warranty of quality or condition of the goods on arrival places upon the seller the risk of ordinary deterioration, shrinkage and the like in transportation but has no effect on the place or time of identification to the contract for sale or delivery or on the passing of the risk of loss.

(3) Unless otherwise agreed where the contract provides for payment on or after arrival of the goods the seller must before payment allow such preliminary inspection as is

feasible; but if the goods are lost delivery of the documents and payment are due when the goods should have arrived.

§ 2–322. Delivery "Ex-Ship"

(1) Unless otherwise agreed a term for delivery of goods "ex-ship" (which means from the carrying vessel) or in equivalent language is not restricted to a particular ship and requires delivery from a ship which has reached a place at the named port of destination where goods of the kind are usually discharged.

(2) Under such a term unless otherwise agreed

(a) the seller must discharge all liens arising out of the carriage and furnish the buyer with a direction which puts the carrier under a duty to deliver the goods; and

(b) the risk of loss does not pass to the buyer until the goods leave the ship's tackle or are otherwise properly unloaded.

§ 2–323. Form of Bill of Lading Required in Overseas Shipment; "Overseas"

(1) Where the contract contemplates overseas shipment and contains a term C.I.F. or C. & F. or F.O.B. vessel, the seller unless otherwise agreed must obtain a negotiable bill of lading stating that the goods have been loaded on board or, in the case of a term C.I.F. or C. & F., received for shipment.

(2) Where in a case within subsection (1) a bill of lading has been issued in a set of parts, unless otherwise agreed if the documents are not to be sent from abroad the buyer may demand tender of the full set; otherwise only one part of the bill of lading need be tendered. Even if the agreement expressly requires a full set

(a) due tender of a single part is acceptable within the provisions of this Article on cure of improper delivery (subsection (1) of Section 2–508); and

(b) even though the full set is demanded, if the documents are sent from abroad the person tendering an incomplete set may nevertheless require payment upon furnishing an indemnity which the buyer in good faith deems adequate.

(3) A shipment by water or by air or a contract contemplating such shipment is "overseas" insofar as by usage of trade or agreement it is subject to the commercial, financing or shipping practices characteristic of international deep water commerce.

§ 2–324. "No Arrival, No Sale" Term

Under a term "no arrival, no sale" or terms of like meaning, unless otherwise agreed,

(a) the seller must properly ship conforming goods and if they arrive by any means he must tender them on arrival but he assumes no obligation that the goods will arrive unless he has caused the nonarrival; and

(b) where without fault of the seller the goods are in part lost or have so deteriorated as no longer to conform to the contract or arrive after the contract time, the buyer may proceed as if there had been casualty to identified goods (Section 2–613).

§ 2–325. "Letter of Credit" Term; "Confirmed Credit"

(1) Failure of the buyer seasonably to furnish an agreed letter of credit is a breach of the contract for sale.

(2) The delivery to seller of a proper letter of credit suspends the buyer's obligation to pay. If the letter of credit is dishonored, the seller may on seasonable notification to the buyer require payment directly from him.

(3) Unless otherwise agreed the term "letter of credit" or "banker's credit" in a contract for sale means an irrevocable credit issued by a financing agency of good repute and, where the shipment is overseas, of good international repute. The term "confirmed credit" means that the credit must also carry the direct obligation of such an agency which does business in the seller's financial market.

§ 2–326. Sale on Approval and Sale or Return; Consignment Sales and Rights of Creditors

(1) Unless otherwise agreed, if delivered goods may be returned by the buyer even though they conform to the contract, the transaction is

(a) a "sale on approval" if the goods are delivered primarily for use, and

(b) a "sale or return" if the goods are delivered primarily for resale.

(2) Except as provided in subsection (3), goods held on approval are not subject to the claims of the buyer's creditors until acceptance; goods held on sale or return are subject to such claims while in the buyer's possession.

(3) Where goods are delivered to a person for sale and such person maintains a place of business at which he deals in goods of the kind involved, under a name other than the name of the person making delivery, then with respect to claims of creditors of the person conducting the business the goods are deemed to be on sale or return. The provisions of this subsection are applicable even though an agreement purports to reserve title to the person making delivery until payment or resale or uses such words as "on consignment" or "on memorandum." However, this subsection is not applicable if the person making delivery

(a) complies with an applicable law providing for a consignor's interest or the like to be evidenced by a sign, or

(b) establishes that the person conducting the business is generally known by his creditors to be substantially engaged in selling the goods of others, or

(c) complies with the filing provisions of the Article on Secured Transactions (Article 9).

(4) Any "or return" term of a contract for sale is to be treated as a separate contract for sale within the statute of frauds section of this Article (Section 2–201) and as contradicting the sale aspect of the contract within the provisions of this Article on parol or extrinsic evidence (Section 2–202).

§ 2–327. Special Incidents of Sale on Approval and Sale or Return

(1) Under a sale on approval unless otherwise agreed

(a) although the goods are identified to the contract the risk of loss and the title do not pass to the buyer until acceptance; and

(b) use of the goods consistent with the purpose of trial is not acceptance but failure seasonably to notify the seller of election to return the goods is acceptance, and if the goods conform to the contract acceptance of any part is acceptance of the whole; and

(c) after due notification of election to return, the return is at the seller's risk and expense but a merchant buyer must follow any reasonable instructions.

(2) Under a sale or return unless otherwise agreed

(a) the option to return extends to the whole or any commercial unit of the goods while in substantially their original condition, but must be exercised seasonably; and

(b) the return is at the buyer's risk and expense.

§ 2–328. Sale by Auction

(1) In a sale by auction if goods are put up in lots each lot is the subject of a separate sale.

(2) A sale by auction is complete when the auctioneer so announces by the fall of the hammer or in other customary manner. Where a bid is made while the hammer is falling in acceptance of a prior bid the auctioneer may in his discretion reopen the bidding or declare the goods sold under the bid on which the hammer was falling.

(3) Such a sale is with reserve unless the goods are in explicit terms put up without reserve. In an auction with reserve the auctioneer may withdraw the goods at any time until he announces completion of the sale. In an auction without reserve, after the auctioneer calls for bids on an article or lot, that article or lot cannot be withdrawn unless no bid is made within a reasonable time. In either case a bidder may retract his bid until the auctioneer's announcement of completion of sale, but a bidder's retraction does not revive any previous bid.

(4) If the auctioneer knowingly receives a bid on the seller's behalf or the seller makes or procures such a bid, and notice has not been given that liberty for such bidding is reserved, the buyer may at his option avoid the sale or take the goods at the price of the last good faith bid prior to the completion of the sale. This subsection shall not apply to any bid at a forced sale.

Part 4 Title, Creditors and Good Faith Purchasers

§ 2–401. Passing of Title; Reservation for Security; Limited Application of This Section

Each provision of this Article with regard to the rights, obligations and remedies of the seller, the buyer, purchasers or other third parties applies irrespective of title to the goods except where the provision refers to such title. Insofar as situations are not covered by the other provisions of this Article and matters concerning title become material the following rules apply:

(1) Title to goods cannot pass under a contract for sale prior to their identification to the contract (Section 2–501), and unless otherwise explicitly agreed the buyer acquires by their identification a special property as limited by this Act. Any retention or reservation by the seller of the title (property) in goods shipped or delivered to the buyer is limited in effect to a reservation of a security interest. Subject to these provisions and to the provisions of the Article on Secured Transactions (Article 9), title to goods passes from the seller to the buyer in any manner and on any conditions explicitly agreed on by the parties.

(2) Unless otherwise explicitly agreed title passes to the buyer at the time and place at which the seller completes his performance with reference to the physical delivery of the goods, despite any reservation of a security interest and even though a document of title is to be delivered at a different time or place; and in particular and despite any reservation of a security interest by the bill of lading

(a) if the contract requires or authorizes the seller to send the goods to the buyer but does not require him to deliver them at destination, title passes to the buyer at the time and place of shipment; but

(b) if the contract requires delivery at destination, title passes on tender there.

(3) Unless otherwise explicitly agreed where delivery is to be made without moving the goods,

(a) if the seller is to deliver a document of title, title passes at the time when and the place where he delivers such documents; or

(b) if the goods are at the time of contracting already identified and no documents are to be delivered, title passes at the time and place of contracting.

(4) A rejection or other refusal by the buyer to receive or retain the goods, whether or not justified, or a justified revocation of acceptance revests title to the goods in the seller. Such revesting occurs by operation of law and is not a "sale."

§ 2–402. Rights of Seller's Creditors Against Sold Goods

(1) Except as provided in subsections (2) and (3), rights of unsecured creditors of the seller with respect to goods which have been identified to a contract for sale are

subject to the buyer's rights to recover the goods under this Article (Section 2–502 and 2–716).

(2) A creditor of the seller may treat a sale or an identification of goods to a contract for sale as void if as against him a retention of possession by the seller is fraudulent under any rule of law of the state where the goods are situated, except that retention of possession in good faith and current course of trade by a merchant-seller for a commercially reasonable time after a sale or identification is not fraudulent.

(3) Nothing in this Article shall be deemed to impair the rights of creditors of the seller

(a) under the provisions of the Article on Secured Transactions (Article 9); or

(b) where identification to the contract or delivery is made not in current course of trade but in satisfaction of or as security for a pre-existing claim for money, security or the like and is made under circumstances which under any rule of law of the state where the goods are situated would apart from this Article constitute the transaction a fraudulent transfer or voidable preference.

§ 2–403. Power to Transfer; Good Faith Purchase of Goods; "Entrusting"

(1) A purchaser of goods acquires all title which his transferor had or had power to transfer except that a purchaser of a limited interest acquires rights only to the extent of the interest purchased. A person with voidable title has power to transfer a good title to a good faith purchaser for value. When goods have been delivered under a transaction of purchase the purchaser has such power even though

(a) the transferor was deceived as to the identity of the purchaser, or

(b) the delivery was in exchange for a check which is later dishonored, or

(c) it was agreed that the transaction was to be a "cash sale," or

(d) the delivery was procured through fraud punishable as larcenous under the criminal law.

(2) Any entrusting of possession of goods to a merchant who deals in goods of that kind gives him power to transfer all rights of the entruster to a buyer in ordinary course of business.

(3) "Entrusting" includes any delivery and any acquiescence in retention of possession regardless of any condition expressed between the parties to the delivery or acquiescence and regardless of whether the procurement of the entrusting or the possessor's disposition of the goods have been such as to be larcenous under the criminal law.

(4) The rights of other purchasers of goods and of lien creditors are governed by the Articles on Secured Transactions (Article 9), Bulk Transfers (Article 6) and Documents of Title (Article 7).

Part 5 Performance

§ 2–501. Insurable Interest in Goods; Manner of Identification of Goods

(1) The buyer obtains a special property and an insurable interest in goods by identification of existing goods as goods to which the contract refers even though the goods so identified are nonconforming and he has an option to return or reject them. Such identification can be made at any time and in any manner explicitly agreed to by the parties. In the absence of explicit agreement identification occurs

(a) when the contract is made if it is for the sale of goods already existing and identified;

(b) if the contract is for the sale of future goods other than those described in paragraph (c), when goods are shipped, marked or otherwise designated by the seller as goods to which the contract refers;

(c) when the crops are planted or otherwise become growing crops or the young are conceived if the contract is for the sale of unborn young to be born within twelve months after contracting or for the sale of crops to be harvested within twelve months or the next normal harvest season after contracting whichever is longer.

(2) The seller retains an insurable interest in goods so long as title to or any security interest in the goods remains in him and where the identification is by the seller alone he may until default or insolvency or notification to the buyer that the identification is final substitute other goods for those identified.

(3) Nothing in this section impairs any insurable interest recognized under any other statute or rule or law.

§ 2–502. Buyer's Right to Goods on Seller's Insolvency

(1) Subject to subsection (2) and even though the goods have not been shipped a buyer who has paid a part or all of the price of goods in which he has a special property under the provisions of the immediately preceding section may on making and keeping good a tender of any unpaid portion of their price recover them from the seller if the seller becomes insolvent within ten days after receipt of the first installment on their price.

(2) If the identification creating his special property has been made by the buyer he acquires the right to recover the goods only if they conform to the contract for sale.

§ 2–503. Manner of Seller's Tender of Delivery

(1) Tender of delivery requires that the seller put and hold conforming goods at the buyer's disposition and give the buyer any notification reasonably necessary to enable him to take delivery. The manner, time and place for tender are determined by the agreement and this Article, and in particular

(a) tender must be at a reasonable hour, and if it is of goods they must be kept available for the period reasonably necessary to enable the buyer to take possession; but

(b) unless otherwise agreed the buyer must furnish facilities reasonably suited to the receipt of the goods.

(2) Where the case is within the next section respecting shipment tender requires that the seller comply with its provisions.

(3) Where the seller is required to deliver at a particular destination tender requires that he comply with subsection (1) and also in any appropriate case tender documents as described in subsections (4) and (5) of this section.

(4) Where goods are in the possession of a bailee and are to be delivered without being moved

(a) tender requires that the seller either tender a negotiable document of title covering such goods or procure acknowledgment by the bailee of the buyer's right to possession of the goods; but

(b) tender to the buyer of a non-negotiable document of title or of a written direction to the bailee to deliver is sufficient tender unless the buyer seasonably objects, and receipt by the bailee of notification of the buyer's rights fixes those rights as against the bailee and all third persons; but risk of loss of the goods and of any failure by the bailee to honor the non-negotiable document of title or to obey the direction remains on the seller until the buyer has had a reasonable time to present the document or direction, and a refusal by the bailee to honor the document or to obey the direction defeats the tender.

(5) Where the contract requires the seller to deliver documents

(a) he must tender all such documents in correct form, except as provided in this Article with respect to bills of lading in a set (subsection (2) of Section 2–323); and

(b) tender through customary banking channels is sufficient and dishonor of a draft accompanying the documents constitutes non-acceptance or rejection.

§ 2–504. Shipment by Seller

Where the seller is required or authorized to send the goods to the buyer and the contract does not require him to deliver them at a particular destination, then unless otherwise agreed he must

(a) put the goods in the possession of such a carrier and make such a contract for their transportation as may be reasonable having regard to the nature of the goods and other circumstances of the case; and

(b) obtain and promptly deliver or tender in due form any document necessary to enable the buyer to obtain possession of the goods or otherwise required by the agreement or by usage of trade; and

(c) promptly notify the buyer of the shipment. Failure to notify the buyer under paragraph (c) or to make a proper contract under paragraph (a) is a ground for rejection only if material delay or loss ensues.

§ 2–505. Seller's Shipment Under Reservation

(1) Where the seller has identified goods to the contract by or before shipment:

(a) his procurement of a negotiable bill of lading to his own order or otherwise reserves in him a security interest in the goods. His procurement of the bill to the order of a financing agency or of the buyer indicates in addition only the seller's expectation of transferring that interest to the person named.

(b) a non-negotiable bill of lading to himself or his nominee reserves possession of the goods as security but except in a case of conditional delivery (subsection (2) of Section 2–507) a non-negotiable bill of lading naming the buyer as consignee reserves no security interest even though the seller retains possession of the bill of lading.

(2) When shipment by the seller with reservation of a security interest is in violation of the contract for sale it constitutes an improper contract for transportation within the preceding section but impairs neither the rights given to the buyer by shipment and identification of the goods to the contract nor the seller's powers as a holder of a negotiable document.

§ 2–506. Rights of Financing Agency

(1) A financing agency by paying or purchasing for value a draft which relates to a shipment of goods acquires to the extent of the payment or purchase and in addition to its own rights under the draft and any document of title securing it any rights of the shipper in the goods including the right to stop delivery and the shipper's right to have the draft honored by the buyer.

(2) The right to reimbursement of a financing agency which has in good faith honored or purchased the draft under commitment to or authority from the buyer is not impaired by subsequent discovery of defects with reference to any relevant document which was apparently regular on its face.

§ 2–507. Effect of Seller's Tender; Delivery on Condition

(1) Tender of delivery is a condition to the buyer's duty to accept the goods and, unless otherwise agreed, to his duty to pay for them. Tender entitles the seller to acceptance of the goods and to payment according to the contract.

(2) Where payment is due and demanded on the delivery to the buyer of goods or documents of title, his right as against the seller to retain or dispose of them is conditional upon his making the payment due.

§ 2–508. Cure by Seller of Improper Tender or Delivery; Replacement

(1) Where any tender or delivery by the seller is rejected because non-conforming and the time for performance has not yet expired, the seller may seasonably notify the buyer of his intention to cure and may then within the

contract time make a conforming delivery.

(2) Where the buyer rejects a non-conforming tender which the seller had reasonable grounds to believe would be acceptable with or without money allowance the seller may if he seasonably notifies the buyer have a further reasonable time to substitute a conforming tender.

§ 2–509. Risk of Loss in the Absence of Breach

(1) Where the contract requires or authorizes the seller to ship the good by carrier

(a) if it does not require him to deliver them at a particular destination, the risk of loss passes to the buyer when the goods are duly delivered to the carrier even though the shipment is under reservation (Section 2–505); but

(b) if it does require him to deliver them at a particular destination and the goods are there duly tendered while in the possession of the carrier, the risk of loss passes to the buyer when the goods are there duly so tendered as to enable the buyer to take delivery.

(2) Where the goods are held by a bailee to be delivered without being moved, the risk of loss passes to the buyer.

(a) on his receipt of a negotiable document of title covering the goods; or

(b) on acknowledgment by the bailee of the buyer's right to possession of the goods; or

(c) after his receipt of a non-negotiable document of title or other written direction to deliver, as provided in subsection (4)(b) of Section 2–503.

(3) In any case not within subsection (1) or (2), the risk of loss passes to the buyer on his receipt of the goods if the seller is a merchant; otherwise the risk passes to the buyer on tender of delivery.

(4) The provisions of this section are subject to contrary agreement of the parties and to the provisions of this Article on sale on approval (Section 2–327) and on effect of breach on risk of loss (Section 2–510).

§ 2–510. Effect of Breach on Risk of Loss

(1) Where a tender or delivery of goods so fails to conform to the contract as to give a right of rejection the risk of their loss remains on the seller until cure or acceptance.

(2) Where the buyer rightfully revokes acceptance he may to the extent of any deficiency in his effective insurance coverage treat the risk of loss as having rested on the seller from the beginning.

(3) Where the buyer as to conforming goods already identified to the contract for sale repudiates or is otherwise in breach before risk of their loss has passed to him, the seller may to the extent of any deficiency in his effective insurance coverage treat the risk of loss as resting on the buyer for a commercially reasonable time.

§ 2–511. Tender of Payment by Buyer; Payment by Check

(1) Unless otherwise agreed tender of payment is a condition to the seller's duty to tender and complete any delivery.

(2) Tender of payment is sufficient when made by any means or in any manner current in the ordinary course of business unless the seller demands payment in legal tender and gives any extension of time reasonably necessary to procure it.

(3) Subject to the provisions of this Act on the effect of an instrument on an obligation (Section 3–802), payment by check is conditional and is defeated as between the parties by dishonor of the check on due presentment.

§ 2–512. Payment by Buyer Before Inspection

(1) Where the contract requires payment before inspection non-conformity of the goods does not excuse the buyer from so making payment unless

(a) the non-conformity appears without inspection; or

(b) despite tender of the required documents the circumstances would justify injunction against honor under the provisions of this Act (Section 5–114).

(2) Payment pursuant to subsection (1) does not constitute an acceptance of goods or impair the buyer's right to inspect or any of his remedies.

§ 2–513. Buyer's Right to Inspection of Goods

(1) Unless otherwise agreed and subject to subsection (3), where goods are tendered or delivered or identified to the contract for sale, the buyer has a right before payment or acceptance to inspect them at any reasonable place and time and in any reasonable manner. When the seller is required and authorized to send the goods to the buyer, the inspection may be after their arrival.

(2) Expenses of inspection must be borne by the buyer but may be recovered from the seller if the goods do not conform and are rejected.

(3) Unless otherwise agreed and subject to the provisions of this Article on C.I.F. contracts (subsection (3) of Section 2–321), the buyer is not entitled to inspect the goods before payment of the price when the contract provides

(a) for delivery "C.O.D." or on other like terms; or

(b) for payment against documents of title, except where such payment is due only after the goods are to become available for inspection.

(4) A place or method of inspection fixed by the parties is presumed to be exclusive but unless otherwise expressly agreed it does not postpone identification or shift the place for delivery or for passing the risk of loss. If compliance becomes impossible, inspection shall be as provided in this section unless the place or method fixed was clearly intended as an indispensable condition failure of which avoids the contract.

§ 2–514. When Documents Deliverable on Acceptance; When on Payment

Unless otherwise agreed documents against which a draft is drawn are to be delivered to the drawee on acceptance of the draft if it is payable more than three days after presentment; otherwise, only on payment.

§ 2–515. Preserving Evidence of Goods in Dispute

In furtherance of the adjustment of any claim or dispute

(a) either party on reasonable notification to the other and for the purpose of ascertaining the facts and preserving evidence has the right to inspect, test and sample the goods including such of them as may be in the possession or control of the other; and

(b) the parties may agree to a third party inspection or survey to determine the conformity or condition of the goods and may agree that the findings shall be binding upon them in any subsequent litigation or adjustment.

Part 6 Breach, Repudiation and Excuse

§ 2–601. Buyer's Rights on Improper Delivery

Subject to the provisions of this Article on breach in installment contracts (Section 2–612) and unless otherwise agreed under the sections on contractual limitations of remedy (Sections 2–718 and 2–719), if the goods or the tender of delivery fail in any respect to conform to the contract, the buyer may

(a) reject the whole; or

(b) accept the whole; or

(c) accept any commercial unit or units and reject the rest.

§ 2–602. Manner and Effect of Rightful Rejection

(1) Rejection of goods must be within a reasonable time after their delivery or tender. It is ineffective unless the buyer seasonably notifies the seller.

(2) Subject to the provisions of the two following sections on rejected goods (Sections 2–603 and 2–604),

(a) after rejection any exercise of ownership by the buyer with respect to any commercial unit is wrongful as against the seller; and

(b) if the buyer has before rejection taken physical possession of goods in which he does not have a security interest under the provisions of this Article (subsection (3) of Section 2–711), he is under a duty after rejection to hold them with reasonable care at the seller's disposition for a time sufficient to permit the seller to remove them; but

(c) the buyer has no further obligations with regard to goods rightfully rejected.

(3) The seller's rights with respect to goods wrongfully rejected are governed by the provisions of this Article on Seller's remedies in general (Section 2–703).

§ 2–603. Merchant Buyer's Duties as to Rightfully Rejected Goods

(1) Subject to any security interest in the buyer (subsection (3) of Section 2–711), when the seller has no agent or place of business at the market of rejection a merchant buyer is under a duty after rejection of goods in his possession or control to follow any reasonable instructions received from the seller with respect to the goods and in the absence of such instructions to make reasonable efforts to sell them for the seller's account if they are perishable or threaten to decline in value speedily. Instructions are not reasonable if on demand indemnity for expense is not forthcoming.

(2) When the buyer sells goods under subsection (1), he is entitled to reimbursement from the seller or out of the proceeds for reasonable expenses of caring for and selling them, and if the expenses include no selling commission then to such commission as is usual in the trade or if there is none to a reasonable sum not exceeding ten per cent on the gross proceeds.

(3) In complying with this section the buyer is held only to good faith and good faith conduct hereunder is neither acceptance nor conversion nor the basis of an action for damages.

§ 2–604. Buyer's Options as to Salvage of Rightfully Rejected Goods

Subject to the provisions of the immediately preceding section on perishables if the seller gives no instructions within a reasonable time after notification of rejection the buyer may store the rejected goods for the seller's account or reship them to him or resell them for the seller's account with reimbursement as provided in the preceding section. Such action is not acceptance or conversion.

§ 2–605. Waiver of Buyer's Objections by Failure to Particularize

(1) The buyer's failure to state in connection with rejection a particular defect which is ascertainable by reasonable inspection precludes him from relying on the unstated defect to justify rejection or to establish breach

(a) where the seller could have cured it if stated seasonably; or

(b) between merchants when the seller has after rejection made a request in writing for a full and final written statement of all defects on which the buyer proposes to rely.

(2) Payment against documents made without reservation of rights precludes recovery of the payment for defects apparent on the face of the documents.

§ 2–606. What Constitutes Acceptance of Goods

(1) Acceptance of goods occurs when the buyer

(a) after a reasonable opportunity to inspect the goods signifies to the seller that the goods are conforming or that he will take or retain them in spite of their non-conformity; or

(b) fails to make an effective rejection (subsection (1) of Section 2–602), but such acceptance does not occur until the buyer has had a reasonable opportunity to inspect them; or

(c) does any act inconsistent with the seller's ownership; but if such act is wrongful as against the seller it is an acceptance only if ratified by him.

(2) Acceptance of a part of any commercial unit is acceptance of that entire unit.

§ 2–607. Effect of Acceptance; Notice of Breach; Burden of Establishing Breach After Acceptance; Notice of Claim or Litigation to Person Answerable Over

(1) The buyer must pay at the contract rate for any goods accepted.

(2) Acceptance of goods by the buyer precludes rejection of the goods accepted and if made with knowledge of a nonconformity cannot be revoked because of it unless the acceptance was on the reasonable assumption that the non-conformity would be seasonably cured but acceptance does not of itself impair any other remedy provided by this Article for non-conformity.

(3) Where a tender has been accepted

(a) the buyer must within a reasonable time after he discovers or should have discovered any breach notify the seller of breach or be barred from any remedy; and

(b) if the claim is one for infringement or the like (subsection (3) of Section 2–312) and the buyer is sued as a result of such a breach he must so notify the seller within a reasonable time after he receives notice of the litigation or be barred from any remedy over for liability established by the litigation.

(4) The burden is on the buyer to establish any breach with respect to the goods accepted.

(5) Where the buyer is sued for breach of a warranty or other obligation for which his seller is answerable over

(a) he may give his seller written notice of the litigation. If the notice states that the seller may come in and defend and that if the seller does not do so he will be bound in any action against him by his buyer by any determination of fact common to the two litigations, then unless the seller after seasonable receipt of the notice does come in and defend he is so bound.

(b) if the claim is one for infringement or the like (subsection (3) of Section 2–312) the original seller may demand in writing that his buyer turn over to him control of the litigation including settlement or else be barred from any remedy over and if he also agrees to bear all expense and to satisfy any adverse judgment, then unless the buyer after seasonable receipt of the demand does turn over control the buyer is so barred.

(6) The provisions of subsections (3), (4) and (5) apply to any obligation of a buyer to hold the seller harmless against infringement or the like (subsection (3) of Section 2–312).

§2–608. Revocation of Acceptance in Whole or in Part

(1) The buyer may revoke his acceptance of a lot or commercial unit whose non-conformity substantially impairs its value to him if he has accepted it

(a) on the reasonable assumption that its non-conformity would be cured and it has not been seasonably cured; or

(b) without discovery of such non-conformity if his acceptance was reasonably induced either by the difficulty of discovery before acceptance or by the seller's assurances.

(2) Revocation of acceptance must occur within a reasonable time after the buyer discovers or should have discovered the ground for it and before any substantial change in condition of the goods which is not caused by their own defects. It is not effective until the buyer notifies the seller of it.

(3) A buyer who so revokes has the same rights and duties with regard to the goods involved as if he had rejected them.

§ 2–609. Right to Adequate Assurance of Performance

(1) A contract for sale imposes an obligation on each party that the other's expectation of receiving due performance will not be impaired. When reasonable grounds for insecurity arise with respect to the performance of either party the other may in writing demand adequate assurance of due performance and until he receives such assurance may if commercially reasonable suspend any performance for which he has not already received the agreed return.

(2) Between merchants the reasonableness of grounds for insecurity and the adequacy of any assurance offered shall be determined according to commercial standards.

(3) Acceptance of any improper delivery or payment does not prejudice the aggrieved party's right to demand adequate assurance of future performance.

(4) After receipt of a justified demand failure to provide within a reasonable time not exceeding thirty days such assurance of due performance as is adequate under the circumstances of the particular case is a repudiation of the contract.

§ 2–610. Anticipatory Repudiation

When either party repudiates the contract with respect to a performance not yet due the loss of which will substantially impair the value of the contract to the other, the aggrieved party may

(a) for a commercially reasonable time await performance by the repudiating party; or

(b) resort to any remedy for breach (Section 2–703 or Section 2–711), even though he has notified the repudiating party that he would await the latter's performance and has urged retraction; and

(c) in either case suspend his own performance or proceed in accordance with the provisions of this Article on the seller's right to identify goods to the contract notwithstanding breach or to salvage unfinished goods (Section 2–704).

§ 2–611. Retraction of Anticipatory Repudiation

(1) Until the repudiating party's next performance is due he can retract his repudiation unless the aggrieved party has since the repudiation cancelled or materially changed his position or otherwise indicated that he considers the repudiation final.

(2) Retraction may be by any method which clearly indicates to the aggrieved party that the repudiating party intends to perform, but must include any assurance justifiably demanded under the provisions of this Article (Section 2–609).

(3) Retraction reinstates the repudiating party's right under the contract with due excuse and allowance to the aggrieved party for any delay occasioned by the repudiation.

§ 2–612. "Installment Contract"; Breach

(1) An "installment contract" is one which requires or authorizes the delivery of goods in separate lots to be separately accepted, even though the contract contains a clause "each delivery is a separate contract" or its equivalent.

(2) The buyer may reject any installment which is non-conforming if the non-conformity substantially impairs the value of that installment and cannot be cured or if the non-conformity is a defect in the required documents; but if the non-conformity does not fall within subsection (3) and the seller gives adequate assurance of its cure the buyer must accept that installment.

(3) Whenever non-conformity or default with respect to one or more installments substantially impairs the value of the whole contract there is a breach of the whole. But the aggrieved party reinstates the contract if he accepts a non-conforming installment without seasonably notifying of cancellation or if he brings an action with respect only to past installments or demands performance as to future installments.

§ 2–613. Casualty to Identified Goods

Where the contract requires for its performance goods identified when the contract is made, and the goods suffer casualty without fault of either party before the risk of loss passes to the buyer, or in a proper case under a "no arrival, no sale" term (Section 2–324) then

(a) if the loss is total the contract is avoided; and

(b) if the loss is partial or the goods have so deteriorated as no longer to conform to the contract the buyer may nevertheless demand inspection and at his option either treat the contract as avoided or accept the goods with due allowance from the contract price for the deterioration or the deficiency in quantity but without further right against the seller.

§ 2–614. Substituted Performance

(1) Where without fault of either party the agreed berthing, loading, or unloading facilities fail or an agreed type of carrier becomes unavailable or the agreed manner of delivery otherwise becomes commercially impracticable but a commercially reasonable substitute is available, such substitute performance must be tendered and accepted.

(2) If the agreed means or manner of payment fails because of domestic or foreign governmental regulation, the seller may withhold or stop delivery unless the buyer provides a means or manner of payment which is commercially a substantial equivalent. If delivery has already been taken, payment by the means or in the manner provided by the regulation discharges the buyer's obligation unless the regulation is discriminatory, oppressive or predatory.

§ 2–615. Excuse by Failure of Presupposed Conditions

Except so far as a seller may have assumed a greater obligation and subject to the preceding section on substituted performance:

(a) Delay in delivery or non-delivery in whole or in part by a seller who complies with paragraphs (b) and (c) is not a breach of his duty under a contract for sale if performance as agreed has been made impracticable by the occurrence of a contingency the nonoccurrence of which was a basic assumption on which the contract was made or by compliance in good faith with any applicable foreign or domestic governmental regulation or order whether or not it later proves to be invalid.

(b) Where the causes mentioned in paragraph (a) affect only a part of the seller's capacity to perform, he must allocate production and deliveries among his customers but may at his option include regular customers not then under contract as well as his own requirements for further manufacture. He may so allocate in any manner which is fair and reasonable.

(c) The seller must notify the buyer seasonally that there will be delay or non-delivery and, when allocation is required under paragraph (b), of the estimated quota thus made available for the buyer.

§ 2–616. Procedure on Notice Claiming Excuse

(1) Where the buyer receives notification of a material or indefinite delay or an allocation justified under the preceding section he may by written notification to the seller as to any delivery concerned, and where the prospective deficiency substantially impairs the value of the whole contract under the provisions of this Article relating to breach of installment contracts (Section 2–612), then also as to the whole,

(a) terminate and thereby discharge any unexecuted portion of the contract; or

(b) modify the contract by agreeing to take his available quota in substitution.

(2) If after receipt of such notification from the seller the buyer fails so to modify the contract within a reasonable time not exceeding thirty days the contract lapses with respect to any deliveries affected.

(3) The provisions of this section may not be negated by agreement except in so far as the seller has assumed a greater obligation under the preceding section.

Part 7 Remedies

§ 2–701. Remedies for Breach of Collateral Contracts Not Impaired

Remedies for breach of any obligation or promise collateral or ancillary to a contract for sale are not impaired by the provisions of this Article.

§ 2–702. Seller's Remedies on Discovery of Buyer's Insolvency

(1) Where the seller discovers the buyer to be insolvent he may refuse delivery except for cash including payment for all goods theretofore delivered under the contract, and stop delivery under this Article (Section 2–705).

(2) Where the seller discovers that the buyer has received goods on credit while insolvent he may reclaim the goods upon demand made within ten days after the receipt, but if misrepresentation of solvency has been made to the particular seller in writing within three months before delivery the ten day limitation does not apply. Except as provided in this subsection the seller may not base a right to reclaim goods on the buyer's fraudulent or innocent misrepresentation of solvency or of intent to pay.

(3) The seller's right to reclaim under subsection (2) is subject to the rights of a buyer in ordinary course or other good faith purchaser under this Article (Section 2–403). Successful reclamation of goods excludes all other remedies with respect to them.

§ 2–703. Seller's Remedies in General

Where the buyer wrongfully rejects or revokes acceptance of goods or fails to make a payment due on or before delivery or repudiates with respect to a part or the whole, then with respect to any goods directly affected and, if the breach is of the whole contract (Section 2–612), then also with respect to the whole undelivered balance, the aggrieved seller may

(a) withhold delivery of such goods;

(b) stop delivery by any bailee as hereafter provided (Section 2–705);

(c) proceed under the next section respecting goods still unidentified to the contract;

(d) resell and recover damages as hereafter provided (Section 2–706);

(e) recover damages for non-acceptance (Section 2–708) or in a proper case the price (Section 2–709);

(f) cancel.

§ 2–704. Seller's Right to Identify Goods to the Contract Notwithstanding Breach or to Salvage Unfinished Goods

(1) An aggrieved seller under the preceding section may

(a) identify to the contract conforming goods not already identified if at the time he learned of the breach they are in his possession or control;

(b) treat as the subject of resale goods which have demonstrably been intended for the particular contract even though those goods are unfinished.

(2) Where the goods are unfinished an aggrieved seller may in the exercise of reasonable commercial judgment for the purposes of avoiding loss and of effective realization either complete the manufacture and wholly identify the goods to the contract or cease manufacture and resell for scrap or salvage value or proceed in any other reasonable manner.

§ 2–705. Seller's Stoppage of Delivery in Transit or Otherwise

(1) The seller may stop delivery of goods in the possession of a carrier or other bailee when he discovers the buyer to be insolvent (Section 2–702) and may stop delivery of carload, truckload, planeload or larger shipments of express or freight when the buyer repudiates or fails to make a payment due before delivery or if for any other reason the seller has a right to withhold or reclaim the goods.

(2) As against such buyer the seller may stop delivery until

(a) receipt of the goods by the buyer; or

(b) acknowledgment to the buyer by any bailee of the goods except a carrier that the bailee holds the goods for the buyer; or

(c) such acknowledgment to the buyer by a carrier by reshipment or as warehouseman; or

(d) negotiation to the buyer of any negotiable document of title covering the goods.

(3)(a) To stop delivery the seller must so notify as to enable the bailee by reasonable diligence to prevent delivery of the goods.

(b) After such notification the bailee must hold and deliver the goods according to the directions of the seller but the seller is liable to the bailee for any ensuing charges or damages.

(c) If a negotiable document of title has been issued for goods the bailee is not obliged to obey a notification to stop until surrender of the document.

(d) A carrier who has issued a non-negotiable bill of lading is not obliged to obey a notification to stop received from a person other than the consignor.

§ 2–706. Seller's Resale Including Contract for Resale

(1) Under the conditions stated in Section 2–703 on seller's remedies, the seller may resell the goods concerned or the undelivered balance thereof. Where the resale is made in good faith and in a commercially reasonable manner the seller may recover the difference between the resale price and the contract price together with any incidental damages allowed under the provisions of this Article (Section 2–710), but less expenses saved in consequence of the buyer's breach.

(2) Except as otherwise provided in subsection (3) or unless otherwise agreed resale may be at public or private sale including sale by way of one or more contracts to sell or of identification to an existing contract of the seller. Sale may be as a unit or in parcels and at any time and place and on any terms but every aspect of the sale including the method, manner, time, place and terms must be commercially reasonable. The resale must be reasonably identified as referring to the broken contract, but it is not necessary that the goods be in existence or that any or all of them have been identified to the contract before the breach.

(3) Where the resale is at private sale the seller must give the buyer reasonable notification of his intention to resell.

(4) Where the resale is at public sale

(a) only identified goods can be sold except where there is a recognized market for a public sale of futures in goods of the kind; and

(b) it must be made at a usual place or market for public sale if one is reasonably available and except in the case of goods which are perishable or threaten to decline in value speedily the seller must give the buyer reasonable notice of the time and place of the resale; and

(c) if the goods are not to be within the view of those attending the sale the notification of sale must state the place where the goods are located and provide for their reasonable inspection by prospective bidders; and

(d) the seller may buy.

(5) A purchaser who buys in good faith at a resale takes the goods free of any rights of the original buyer even though the seller fails to comply with one or more of the requirements of this section.

(6) The seller is not accountable to the buyer for any profit made on any resale. A person in the position of a seller (Section 2–707) or a buyer who has rightfully rejected or justifiably revoked acceptance must account for any excess over the amount of his security interest, as hereinafter defined (subsection (3) of Section 2–711).

§ 2–707. "Person in the Position of a Seller"

(1) A "person in the position of a seller" includes as against a principal an agent who has paid or become responsible for the price of goods on behalf of his principal or anyone who otherwise holds a security interest or other right in goods similar to that of a seller.

(2) A person in the position of a seller may as provided in this Article withhold or stop delivery (Section 2–706) and recover incidental damages (Section 2–710).

§ 2–708. Seller's Damages for Non-Acceptance or Repudiation

(1) Subject to subsection (2) and to the provisions of this Article with respect to proof of market price (Section 2–723), the measure of damages for non-acceptance or repudiation by the buyer is the difference between the market price at the time and place for tender and the unpaid contract price together with any incidental damages provided in this Article (Section 2–710), but less expenses saved in consequence of the buyer's breach.

(2) If the measure of damages provided in subsection (1) is inadequate to put the seller in as good a position as performance would have done then the measure of damages is the profit (including reasonable overhead) which the seller would have made from full performance by the buyer, together with any incidental damages provided in this Article (Section 2–710), due allowance for costs reasonably incurred and due credit for payments or proceeds of resale.

§ 2–709. Action for the Price

(1) When the buyer fails to pay the price as it becomes due the seller may recover, together with any incidental damages under the next section, the price

(a) of goods accepted or of conforming goods lost or damaged within a commercially reasonable time after risk of their loss has passed to the buyer; and

(b) of goods identified to the contract if the seller is unable after reasonable effort to resell them at a reasonable price or the circumstances reasonably indicate that such effort will be unavailing.

(2) Where the seller sues for the price he must hold for the buyer any goods which have been identified to the contract and are still in his control except that if resale

becomes possible he may resell them at any time prior to the collection of the judgment. The net proceeds of any such resale must be credited to the buyer and payment of the judgment entitles him to any goods not resold.

(3) After the buyer has wrongfully rejected or revoked acceptance of the goods or has failed to make a payment due or has repudiated (Section 2–610), a seller who is held not entitled to the price under this section shall nevertheless be awarded damages for non-acceptance under the preceding section.

§ 2–710. Seller's Incidental Damages

Incidental damages to an aggrieved seller include any commercially reasonable charges, expenses or commissions incurred in stopping delivery, in the transportation, care and custody of goods after the buyer's breach, in connection with return or resale of the goods or otherwise resulting from the breach.

§ 2–711. Buyer's Remedies in General; Buyer's Security Interest in Rejected Goods

(1) Where the seller fails to make delivery or repudiates or the buyer rightfully rejects or justifiably revokes acceptance then with respect to any goods involved, and with respect to the whole if the breach goes to the whole contract (Section 2–612), the buyer may cancel and whether or not he has done so may in addition to recovering so much of the price as has been paid

    (a) "cover" and have damages under the next section as to all the goods affected whether or not they have been identified to the contract; or

    (b) recover damages for non-delivery as provided in this Article (Section 2–713).

(2) Where the seller fails to deliver or repudiates the buyer may also

    (a) if the goods have been identified recover them as provided in this Article (Section 2–502); or

    (b) in a proper case obtain specific performance or replevy the goods as provided in this Article (Section 2–716).

(3) On rightful rejection or justifiable revocation of acceptance a buyer has a security interest in goods in his possession or control for any payments made on their price and any expenses reasonably incurred in their inspection, receipt, transportation, care and custody and may hold such goods and resell them in like manner as an aggrieved seller (Section 2–706).

§ 2–712. "Cover"; Buyer's Procurement of Substitute Goods

(1) After a breach within the preceding section the buyer may "cover" by making in good faith and without unreasonable delay any reasonable purchase of or contract to purchase goods in substitution for those due from the seller.

(2) The buyer may recover from the seller as damages the difference between the cost of cover and the contract price together with any incidental or consequential damages as hereinafter defined (Section 2–715), but less expenses saved in consequence of the seller's breach.

(3) Failure of the buyer to effect cover within this section does not bar him from any other remedy.

§ 2–713. Buyer's Damages for Non-Delivery or Repudiation

(1) Subject to the provisions of this Article with respect to proof of market price (Section 2–723), the measure of damages for non-delivery or repudiation by the seller is the difference between the market price at the time when the buyer learned of the breach and the contract price together with any incidental and consequential damages provided in this Article (Section 2–715), but less expenses saved in consequence of the seller's breach.

(2) Market price is to be determined as of the place for tender or, in cases of rejection after arrival or revocation of acceptance, as of the place of arrival.

§ 2–714. Buyer's Damages for Breach in Regard to Accepted Goods

(1) Where the buyer has accepted goods and given notification (subsection (3) of Section 2–607) he may recover as damages for any non-conformity of tender the loss resulting in the ordinary course of events from the seller's breach as determined in any manner which is reasonable.

(2) The measure of damages for breach of warranty is the difference at the time and place of acceptance between the value of the goods accepted and the value they would have had if they had been as warranted, unless special circumstances show proximate damages of a different amount.

(3) In a proper case any incidental and consequential damages under the next section may also be recovered.

§ 2–715. Buyer's Incidental and Consequential Damages

(1) Incidental damages resulting from the seller's breach include expenses reasonably incurred in inspection, receipt, transportation and care and custody of goods rightfully rejected, any commercially reasonable charges, expenses or commissions in connection with effecting cover and any other reasonable expense incident to the delay or other breach.

(2) Consequential damages resulting from the seller's breach include

    (a) any loss resulting from general or particular requirements and needs of which the seller at the time of contracting had reason to know and which could not reasonably be prevented by cover or otherwise; and

(b) injury to person or property proximately resulting from any breach of warranty.

§ 2–716. Buyer's Right to Specific Performance or Replevin

(1) Specific performance may be decreed where the goods are unique or in other proper circumstances.

(2) The decree for specific performance may include such terms and conditions as to payment of the price, damages, or other relief as the court may deem just.

(3) The buyer has a right of replevin for goods identified to the contract if after reasonable effort he is unable to effect cover for such goods or the circumstances reasonably indicate that such effort will be unavailing or if the goods have been shipped under reservation and satisfaction of the security interest in them has been made or tendered.

§2–717. Deduction of Damages From the Price

The buyer on notifying the seller of his intention to do so may deduct all or any part of the damages resulting from any breach of the contract from any part of the price still due under the same contract.

§ 2–718. Liquidation or Limitation of Damages; Deposits

(1) Damages for breach by either party may be liquidated in the agreement but only at an amount which is reasonable in the light of the anticipated or actual harm caused by the breach, the difficulties of proof of loss, and the inconvenience or nonfeasibility of otherwise obtaining an adequate remedy. A term fixing unreasonably large liquidated damages is void as a penalty.

(2) Where the seller justifiably withholds delivery of goods because of the buyer's breach, the buyer is entitled to restitution of any amount by which the sum of his payments exceeds

(a) the amount to which the seller is entitled by virtue of terms liquidating the seller's damages in accordance with subsection (1), or

(b) in the absence of such terms, twenty percent of the value of the total performance for which the buyer is obligated under the contract or $500, whichever is smaller.

(3) The buyer's right to restitution under subsection (2) is subject to offset to the extent that the seller establishes

(a) a right to recover damages under the provisions of this Article other than subsection (1), and

(b) the amount or value of any benefits received by the buyer directly or indirectly by reason of the contract.

(4) Where a seller has received payment in goods their reasonable value or the proceeds of their resale shall be treated as payments for the purposes of subsection (2); but if the seller has notice of the buyer's breach before

reselling goods received in part performance, his resale is subject to the conditions laid down in this Article on resale by an aggrieved seller (Section 2–706).

§ 2–719. Contractual Modification or Limitation of Remedy

(1) Subject to the provisions of subsections (2) and (3) of this section and of the preceding section on liquidation and limitation of damages,

(a) the agreement may provide for remedies in addition to or in substitution for those provided in this Article and may limit or alter the measure of damages recoverable under this Article, as by limiting the buyer's remedies to return of the goods and repayment of the price or to repair and replacement of non-conforming goods or parts; and

(b) resort to a remedy as provided is optional unless the remedy is expressly agreed to be exclusive, in which case it is the sole remedy.

(2) Where circumstances cause an exclusive or limited remedy to fail of its essential purpose, remedy may be had as provided in this Act.

(3) Consequential damages may be limited or excluded unless the limitation or exclusion is unconscionable. Limitation of consequential damages for injury to the person in the case of consumer goods is prima facie unconscionable but limitation of damages where the loss is commercial is not.

§ 2–720. Effect of "Cancellation" or "Rescission" on Claims for Antecedent Breach

Unless the contrary intention clearly appears, expressions of "cancellation" or "rescission" of the contract or the like shall not be construed as a renunciation or discharge of any claim in damages for an antecedent breach.

§ 2–721. Remedies for fraud

Remedies for material misrepresentation or fraud include all remedies available under this Article for nonfraudulent breach. Neither rescission or a claim for rescission of the contract for sale nor rejection or return of the goods shall bar or be deemed inconsistent with a claim for damages or other remedy.

§ 2–722. Who Can Sue Third Parties for Injury to Goods

Where a third party so deals with goods which have been identified to a contract for sale as to cause actionable injury to a party to that contract

(a) a right of action against the third party is in either party to the contract for sale who has title to or a security interest or a special property or an insurable interest in the goods; and if the goods have been destroyed or converted a right of action is also in the party who either bore the risk of loss under the contract for sale or has since the injury assumed that risk as against the other;

(b) if at the time of the injury the party plaintiff did not bear the risk of loss as against the other party to the contract for sale and there is no arrangement between them for disposition of the recovery, his suit or settlement is, subject to his own interest, as a fiduciary for the other party to the contract;

(c) either party may with the consent of the other sue for the benefit of whom it may concern.

§ 2–723. Proof of Market Price: Time and Place

(1) If an action based on anticipatory repudiation comes to trial before the time for performance with respect to some or all of the goods, any damages based on market price (Section 2–708 or Section 2–713) shall be determined according to the price of such goods prevailing at the time when the aggrieved party learned of the repudiation.

(2) If evidence of a price prevailing at the times or places described in this Article is not readily available the price prevailing within any reasonable time before or after the time described or at any other place which in commercial judgment or under usage of trade would serve as a reasonable substitute for the one described may be used, making any proper allowance for the cost of transporting the goods to or from such other place.

(3) Evidence of a relevant price prevailing at a time or place other than the one described in this Article offered by one party is not admissible unless and until he has given the other party such notice as the court finds sufficient to prevent unfair surprise.

§ 2–724. Admissibility of Market Quotations

Whenever the prevailing price or value of any goods regularly bought and sold in any established commodity market is in issue, reports in official publications or trade journals or in newspapers or periodicals of general circulation published as the reports of such market shall be admissible in evidence. The circumstances of the preparation of such a report may be shown to affect its weight but not its admissibility.

§ 2–725. Statute of Limitations in Contracts for Sale

(1) An action for breach of any contract for sale must be commenced within four years after the cause of action has accrued. By the original agreement the parties may reduce the period of limitation to not less than one year but may not extend it.

(2) A cause of action accrues when the breach occurs, regardless of the aggrieved party's lack of knowledge of the breach. A breach of warranty occurs when tender of delivery is made, except that where a warranty explicitly extends to future performance of the goods and discovery of the breach must await the time of such performance the cause of action accrues when the breach is or should have been discovered.

(3) Where an action commenced within the time limited by subsection (1) is so terminated as to leave available a remedy by another action for the same breach such other action may be commenced after the expiration of the time limited and within six months after the termination of the first action unless the termination resulted from voluntary discontinuance or from dismissal for failure or neglect to prosecute.

(4) This section does not alter the law on tolling of the statute of limitations nor does it apply to causes of action which have accrued before this Act becomes effective.

ARTICLE 2A LEASES

Part 1 General Provisions

§2A–101. Short Title

This Article shall be known and may be cited as the Uniform Commercial Code—Leases.

§2A–102. Scope

This Article applies to any transaction, regardless of form, that creates a lease.

§2A–103. Definitions and Index of Definitions

(1) In this Article unless the context otherwise requires:

(a) "Buyer in ordinary course of business" means a person who in good faith and without knowledge that the sale to him [or her] is in violation of the ownership rights or security interest or leasehold interest of a third party in the goods buys in ordinary course from a person in the business of selling goods of that kind but does not include a pawnbroker. "Buying" may be for cash or by exchange of other property or on secured or unsecured credit and includes receiving goods or documents of title under a pre-existing contract for sale but does not include a transfer in bulk or as security for or in total or partial satisfaction of a money debt.

(b) "Cancellation" occurs when either party puts an end to the lease contract for default by the other party.

(c) "Commercial unit" means such a unit of goods as by commercial usage is a single whole for purposes of lease and division of which materially impairs its character or value on the market or in use. A commercial unit may be a single article, as a machine, or a set of articles, as a suite of furniture or a line of machinery, or a quantity, as a gross or carload, or any other unit treated in use or in the relevant market as a single whole.

(d) "Conforming" goods or performance under a lease contract means goods or performance that are in accordance with the obligations under the lease contract.

(e) "Consumer lease" means a lease that a lessor regularly engaged in the business of leasing or selling makes to a lessee who is an individual and who takes under the lease primarily for a personal, family, or household purpose [, if the total payments to be made under the lease contract, excluding payments for options to renew or buy, do not exceed $_____].

(f) "Fault" means wrongful act, omission, breach, or default.

(g) "Finance lease" means a lease with respect to which:

    (i) the lessor does not select, manufacture, or supply the goods;

    (ii) the lessor acquires the goods or the right to possession and use of the goods in connection with the lease; and

    (iii) one of the following occurs:

    (A) the lessee receives a copy of the contract by which the lessor acquired the goods or the right to possession and use of the goods before signing the lease contract;

    (B) the lessee's approval of the contract by which the lessor acquired the goods or the right to possession and use of the goods is a condition to effectiveness of the lease contract;

    (C) the lessee, before signing the lease contract, receives an accurate and complete statement designating the promises and warranties, and any disclaimers of warranties, limitations or modifications of remedies, or liquidated damages, including those of a third party, such as the manufacturer of the goods, provided to the lessor by the person supplying the goods in connection with or as part of the contract by which the lessor acquired the goods or the right to possession and use of the goods; or

    (D) if the lease is not a consumer lease, the lessor, before the lessee signs the lease contract, informs the lessee in writing (a) of the identity of the person supplying the goods to the lessor, unless the lessee has selected that person and directed the lessor to acquire the goods or the right to possession and use of the goods from that person, (b) that the lessee is entitled under this Article to the promises and warranties, including those of any third party, provided to the lessor by the person supplying the goods in connection with or as part of the contract by which the lessor acquired the goods or the right to possession and use of the goods, and (c) that the lessee may communicate with the person supplying the goods to the lessor and receive an accurate and complete statement of those promises and warranties, including any disclaimers and limitations of them or of remedies.

(h) "Goods" means all things that are movable at the time of identification to the lease contract, or are fixtures (Section 2A–309), but the term does not include money, documents, instruments, accounts, chattel paper, general intangibles, or minerals or the like, including oil and gas, before extraction. The term also includes the unborn young of animals.

(i) "Installment lease contract" means a lease contract that authorizes or requires the delivery of goods in separate lots to be separately accepted, even though the lease contract contains a clause "each delivery is a separate lease" or its equivalent.

(j) "Lease" means a transfer of the right to possession and use of goods for a term in return for consideration, but a sale, including a sale on approval or a sale or return, or retention or creation of a security interest is not a lease. Unless the context clearly indicates otherwise, the term includes a sublease.

(k) "Lease agreement" means the bargain, with respect to the lease, of the lessor and the lessee in fact as found in their language or by implication from other circumstances including course of dealing or usage of trade or course of performance as provided in this Article. Unless the context clearly indicates otherwise, the term includes a sublease agreement.

(l) "Lease contract" means the total legal obligation that results from the lease agreement as affected by this Article and any other applicable rules of law. Unless the context clearly indicates otherwise, the term includes a sublease contract.

(m) "Leasehold interest" means the interest of the lessor or the lessee under a lease contract.

(n) "Lessee" means a person who acquires the right to possession and use of goods under a lease. Unless the context clearly indicates otherwise, the term includes a sublessee.

(o) "Lessee in ordinary course of business" means a person who in good faith and without knowledge that the lease to him [or her] is in violation of the ownership rights or security interest or leasehold interest of a third party in the goods, leases in ordinary course from a person in the business of selling or leasing goods of that kind but does not include a pawnbroker. "Leasing" may be for cash or by exchange of other property or on secured or unsecured credit and includes receiving goods or documents of title under a pre-existing lease contract but does not include a transfer in bulk or as security for or in total or partial satisfaction of a money debt.

(p) "Lessor" means a person who transfers the right to possession and use of goods under a lease. Unless the context clearly indicates otherwise, the term includes a sublessor.

(q) "Lessor's residual interest" means the lessor's interest in the goods after expiration, termination, or cancellation of the lease contract.

(r) "Lien" means a charge against or interest in goods to secure payment of a debt or performance of an obligation, but the term does not include a security interest.

(s) "Lot" means a parcel or a single article that is the subject matter of a separate lease or delivery, whether or not it is sufficient to perform the lease contract.

(t) "Merchant lessee" means a lessee that is a merchant with respect to goods of the kind subject to the lease.

(u) "Present value" means the amount as of a date certain of one or more sums payable in the future, discounted to the date certain. The discount is determined by the interest rate specified by the parties if the rate was not manifestly unreasonable at the time the transaction was entered into; otherwise, the discount is determined by a commercially reasonable rate that takes into account the facts and circumstances of each case at the time the transaction was entered into.

(v) "Purchase" includes taking by sale, lease, mortgage, security interest, pledge, gift, or any other voluntary transaction creating an interest in goods.

(w) "Sublease" means a lease of goods the right to possession and use of which was acquired by the lessor as a lessee under an existing lease.

(x) "Supplier" means a person from whom a lessor buys or leases goods to be leased under a finance lease.

(y) "Supply contract" means a contract under which a lessor buys or leases goods to be leased.

(z) "Termination" occurs when either party pursuant to a power created by agreement or law puts an end to the lease contract otherwise than for default.

(2) Other definitions applying to this Article and the sections in which they appear are:

"Accessions." Section 2A–310(1).
"Construction mortgage." Section 2A–309(1)(d).
"Encumbrance." Section 2A–309(1)(e).
"Fixtures." Section 2A–309(1)(a).
"Fixture filing." Section 2A–309(1)(b).
"Purchase money lease." Section 2A–309(1)(c).

(3) The following definitions in other Articles apply to this Article:

"Account." Section 9–106.
"Between merchants." Section 2–104(3).
"Buyer." Section 2–103(1)(a).
"Chattel paper." Section 9–105(1)(b).
"Consumer goods." Section 9–109(1).
"Document." Section 9–105(1)(f).
"Entrusting." Section 2–403(3).
"General intangibles." Section 9–106.
"Good faith." Section 2–103(1)(b).
"Instrument." Section 9–105(1)(i).
"Merchant." Section 2–104(1).
"Mortgage." Section 9–105(1)(j).
"Pursuant to commitment." Section 9–105(1)(k).
"Receipt." Section 2–103(1)(c).
"Sale." Section 2–106(1).
"Sale on approval." Section 2–326.
"Sale or return." Section 2–326.
"Seller." Section 2–103(1)(d).

(4) In addition Article 1 contains general definitions and principles of construction and interpretation applicable throughout this Article.

As amended in 1990.

§2A–104. Leases Subject to Other Law

(1) A lease, although subject to this Article, is also subject to any applicable:

(a) certificate of title statute of this State: (list any certificate of title statutes covering automobiles, trailers, mobile homes, boats, farm tractors, and the like);

(b) certificate of title statute of another jurisdiction (Section 2A–105); or

(c) consumer protection statute of this State, or final consumer protection decision of a court of this State existing on the effective date of this Article.

(2) In case of conflict between this Article, other than Sections 2A–105, 2A–304(3), and 2A–305(3), and a statute or decision referred to in subsection (1), the statute or decision controls.

(3) Failure to comply with an applicable law has only the effect specified therein.

As amended in 1990.

§2A–105. Territorial Application of Article to Goods Covered by Certificate of Title

Subject to the provisions of Sections 2A–304(3) and 2A–305(3), with respect to goods covered by a certificate of title issued under a statute of this State or of another jurisdiction, compliance and the effect of compliance or noncompliance with a certificate of title statute are governed by the law (including the conflict of laws rules) of the jurisdiction issuing the certificate until the earlier of (a) surrender of the certificate, or (b) four months after the goods are removed from that jurisdiction and thereafter until a new certificate of title is issued by another jurisdiction.

§2A–106. Limitation on Power of Parties to Consumer Lease to Choose Applicable Law and Judicial Forum

(1) If the law chosen by the parties to a consumer lease is that of a jurisdiction other than a jurisdiction in which the lessee resides at the time the lease agreement becomes enforceable or within 30 days thereafter or in which the goods are to be used, the choice is not enforceable.

(2) If the judicial forum chosen by the parties to a consumer lease is a forum that would not otherwise have jurisdiction over the lessee, the choice is not enforceable.

§2A–107. Waiver or Renunciation of Claim or Right After Default

Any claim or right arising out of an alleged default or breach of warranty may be discharged in whole or in part without consideration by a written waiver or renunciation signed and delivered by the aggrieved party.

§2A–108. Unconscionability

(1) If the court as a matter of law finds a lease contract or any clause of a lease contract to have been unconscionable at the time it was made the court may refuse to enforce the lease contract, or it may enforce the remainder of the lease contract without the unconscionable clause, or it may so limit the application of any unconscionable clause as to avoid any unconscionable result.

(2) With respect to a consumer lease, if the court as a matter of law finds that a lease contract or any clause of a lease contract has been induced by unconscionable conduct or that unconscionable conduct has occurred in the collection of a claim arising from a lease contract, the court may grant appropriate relief.

(3) Before making a finding of unconscionability under subsection (1) or (2), the court, on its own motion or that of a party, shall afford the parties a reasonable opportunity to present evidence as to the setting, purpose, and effect of the lease contract or clause thereof, or of the conduct.

(4) In an action in which the lessee claims unconscionability with respect to a consumer lease:

(a) If the court finds unconscionability under subsection (1) or (2), the court shall award reasonable attorney's fees to the lessee.

(b) If the court does not find unconscionability and the lessee claiming unconscionability has brought or maintained an action he [or she] knew to be groundless, the court shall award reasonable attorney's fees to the party against whom the claim is made.

(c) In determining attorney's fees, the amount of the recovery on behalf of the claimant under subsections (1) and (2) is not controlling.

§2A–109. Option to Accelerate at Will

(1) A term providing that one party or his [or her] successor in interest may accelerate payment or performance or require collateral or additional collateral "at will" or "when he [or she] deems himself [or herself] insecure" or in words of similar import must be construed to mean that he [or she] has power to do so only if he [or she] in good faith believes that the prospect of payment or performance is impaired.

(2) With respect to a consumer lease, the burden of establishing good faith under subsection (1) is on the party who exercised the power; otherwise the burden of establishing lack of good faith is on the party against whom the power has been exercised.

Part 2 Formation and Construction of Lease Contract

§2A–201. Statute of Frauds

(1) A lease contract is not enforceable by way of action or defense unless:

(a) the total payments to be made under the lease contract, excluding payments for options to renew or buy, are less than $1,000; or

(b) there is a writing, signed by the party against whom enforcement is sought or by that party's authorized agent, sufficient to indicate that a lease contract has been made between the parties and to describe the goods leased and the lease term.

(2) Any description of leased goods or of the lease term is sufficient and satisfies subsection (1)(b), whether or not it is specific, if it reasonably identifies what is described.

(3) A writing is not insufficient because it omits or incorrectly states a term agreed upon, but the lease contract is not enforceable under subsection (1)(b) beyond the lease term and the quantity of goods shown in the writing.

(4) A lease contract that does not satisfy the requirements of subsection (1), but which is valid in other respects, is enforceable:

(a) if the goods are to be specially manufactured or obtained for the lessee and are not suitable for lease or sale to others in the ordinary course of the lessor's business, and the lessor, before notice of repudiation is received and under circumstances that reasonably indicate that the goods are for the lessee, has made either a substantial beginning of their manufacture or commitments for their procurement;

(b) if the party against whom enforcement is sought admits in that party's pleading, testimony or otherwise in court that a lease contract was made, but the lease contract is not enforceable under this provision beyond the quantity of goods admitted; or

(c) with respect to goods that have been received and accepted by the lessee.

(5) The lease term under a lease contract referred to in subsection (4) is:

(a) if there is a writing signed by the party against whom enforcement is sought or by that party's authorized agent specifying the lease term, the term so specified;

(b) if the party against whom enforcement is sought admits in that party's pleading, testimony, or otherwise in court a lease term, the term so admitted; or

(c) a reasonable lease term.

§2A–202. Final Written Expression: Parol or Extrinsic Evidence

Terms with respect to which the confirmatory memoranda of the parties agree or which are otherwise set forth in a writing intended by the parties as a final expression of their agreement with respect to such terms as are included therein may not be contradicted by evidence of any prior agreement or of a contemporaneous oral agreement but may be explained or supplemented:

(a) by course of dealing or usage of trade or by course of performance; and

(b) by evidence of consistent additional terms unless the court finds the writing to have been intended also as a complete and exclusive statement of the terms of the agreement.

§2A–203. Seals Inoperative

The affixing of a seal to a writing evidencing a lease contract or an offer to enter into a lease contract does not render the writing a sealed instrument and the law with respect to sealed instruments does not apply to the lease contract or offer.

§2A–204. Formation in General

(1) A lease contract may be made in any manner sufficient to show agreement, including conduct by both parties which recognizes the existence of a lease contract.

(2) An agreement sufficient to constitute a lease contract may be found although the moment of its making is undetermined.

(3) Although one or more terms are left open, a lease contract does not fail for indefiniteness if the parties have intended to make a lease contract and there is a reasonably certain basis for giving an appropriate remedy.

§2A–205. Firm Offers

An offer by a merchant to lease goods to or from another person in a signed writing that by its terms gives assurance it will be held open is not revocable, for lack of consideration, during the time stated or, if no time is stated, for a reasonable time, but in no event may the period of irrevocability exceed 3 months. Any such term of assurance on a form supplied by the offeree must be separately signed by the offeror.

§2A–206. Offer and Acceptance in Formation of Lease Contract

(1) Unless otherwise unambiguously indicated by the language or circumstances, an offer to make a lease contract must be construed as inviting acceptance in any manner and by any medium reasonable in the circumstances.

(2) If the beginning of a requested performance is a reasonable mode of acceptance, an offeror who is not notified of acceptance within a reasonable time may treat the offer as having lapsed before acceptance.

§2A–207. Course of Performance or Practical Construction

(1) If a lease contract involves repeated occasions for performance by either party with knowledge of the nature of the performance and opportunity for objection to it by the other, any course of performance accepted or acquiesced in without objection is relevant to determine the meaning of the lease agreement.

(2) The express terms of a lease agreement and any course of performance, as well as any course of dealing and usage of trade, must be construed whenever reasonable as consistent with each other; but if that construction is unreasonable, express terms control course of performance, course of performance controls both course of dealing and usage of trade, and course of dealing controls usage of trade.

(3) Subject to the provisions of Section 2A–208 on modification and waiver, course of performance is relevant to show a waiver or modification of any term inconsistent with the course of performance.

§2A–208. Modification, Rescission and Waiver

(1) An agreement modifying a lease contract needs no consideration to be binding.

(2) A signed lease agreement that excludes modification or rescission except by a signed writing may not be otherwise modified or rescinded, but, except as between merchants, such a requirement on a form supplied by a merchant must be separately signed by the other party.

(3) Although an attempt at modification or rescission does not satisfy the requirements of subsection (2), it may operate as a waiver.

(4) A party who has made a waiver affecting an executory portion of a lease contract may retract the waiver by reasonable notification received by the other party that strict performance will be required of any term waived, unless the retraction would be unjust in view of a material change of position in reliance on the waiver.

§2A–209. Lessee Under Finance Lease as Beneficiary of Supply Contract

(1) The benefit of a supplier's promises to the lessor under the supply contract and of all warranties, whether express or implied, including those of any third party provided in connection with or as part of the supply contract, extends to the lessee to the extent of the lessee's leasehold interest under a finance lease related to the supply contract, but is subject to the terms of the warranty and of the supply contract and all defenses or claims arising therefrom.

(2) The extension of the benefit of a supplier's promises and of warranties to the lessee (Section 2A–209(1)) does not: (i) modify the rights and obligations of the parties to the supply contract, whether arising therefrom or otherwise, or (ii) impose any duty or liability under the supply contract on the lessee.

(3) Any modification or rescission of the supply contract by the supplier and the lessor is effective between the supplier and the lessee unless, before the modification or rescission, the supplier has received notice that the lessee has entered into a finance lease related to the supply contract. If the modification or rescission is

effective between the supplier and the lessee, the lessor is deemed to have assumed, in addition to the obligations of the lessor to the lessee under the lease contract, promises of the supplier to the lessor and warranties that were so modified or rescinded as they existed and were available to the lessee before modification or rescission.

(4) In addition to the extension of the benefit of the supplier's promises and of warranties to the lessee under subsection (1), the lessee retains all rights that the lessee may have against the supplier which arise from an agreement between the lessee and the supplier or under other law.

As amended in 1990.

§2A–210. Express Warranties

(1) Express warranties by the lessor are created as follows:

(a) Any affirmation of fact or promise made by the lessor to the lessee which relates to the goods and becomes part of the basis of the bargain creates an express warranty that the goods will conform to the affirmation or promise.

(b) Any description of the goods which is made part of the basis of the bargain creates an express warranty that the goods will conform to the description.

(c) Any sample or model that is made part of the basis of the bargain creates an express warranty that the whole of the goods will conform to the sample or model.

(2) It is not necessary to the creation of an express warranty that the lessor use formal words, such as "warrant" or "guarantee," or that the lessor have a specific intention to make a warranty, but an affirmation merely of the value of the goods or a statement purporting to be merely the lessor's opinion or commendation of the goods does not create a warranty.

§2A–211. Warranties Against Interference and Against Infringement; Lessee's Obligation Against Infringement

(1) There is in a lease contract a warranty that for the lease term no person holds a claim to or interest in the goods that arose from an act or omission of the lessor, other than a claim by way of infringement or the like, which will interfere with the lessee's enjoyment of its leasehold interest.

(2) Except in a finance lease there is in a lease contract by a lessor who is a merchant regularly dealing in goods of the kind a warranty that the goods are delivered free of the rightful claim of any person by way of infringement or the like.

(3) A lessee who furnishes specifications to a lessor or a supplier shall hold the lessor and the supplier harmless against any claim by way of infringement or the like that arises out of compliance with the specifications.

§2A–212. Implied Warranty of Merchantability

(1) Except in a finance lease, a warranty that the goods will be merchantable is implied in a lease contract if the lessor is a merchant with respect to goods of that kind.

(2) Goods to be merchantable must be at least such as

(a) pass without objection in the trade under the description in the lease agreement;

(b) in the case of fungible goods, are of fair average quality within the description;

(c) are fit for the ordinary purposes for which goods of that type are used;

(d) run, within the variation permitted by the lease agreement, of even kind, quality, and quantity within each unit and among all units involved;

(e) are adequately contained, packaged, and labeled as the lease agreement may require; and

(f) conform to any promises or affirmations of fact made on the container or label.

(3) Other implied warranties may arise from course of dealing or usage of trade.

§2A–213. Implied Warranty of Fitness for Particular Purpose

Except in a finance lease, if the lessor at the time the lease contract is made has reason to know of any particular purpose for which the goods are required and that the lessee is relying on the lessor's skill or judgment to select or furnish suitable goods, there is in the lease contract an implied warranty that the goods will be fit for that purpose.

§2A–214. Exclusion or Modification of Warranties

(1) Words or conduct relevant to the creation of an express warranty and words or conduct tending to negate or limit a warranty must be construed wherever reasonable as consistent with each other; but, subject to the provisions of Section 2A–202 on parol or extrinsic evidence, negation or limitation is inoperative to the extent that the construction is unreasonable.

(2) Subject to subsection (3), to exclude or modify the implied warranty of merchantability or any part of it the language must mention "merchantability," be by a writing, and be conspicuous. Subject to subsection (3), to exclude or modify any implied warranty of fitness the exclusion must be by a writing and be conspicuous. Language to exclude all implied warranties of fitness is sufficient if it is in writing, is conspicuous and states, for example, "There is no warranty that the goods will be fit for a particular purpose".

(3) Notwithstanding subsection (2), but subject to subsection (4),

(a) unless the circumstances indicate otherwise, all implied warranties are excluded by expressions like "as is," or "with all faults," or by other language that in common understanding calls the lessee's attention to the exclusion of warranties and makes plain that there is no implied warranty, if in writing and conspicuous;

(b) if the lessee before entering into the lease contract has examined the goods or the sample or model as fully as desired or has refused to examine the goods, there is no implied warranty with regard to defects that an examination ought in the circumstances to have revealed; and

(c) an implied warranty may also be excluded or modified by course of dealing, course of performance, or usage of trade.

(4) To exclude or modify a warranty against interference or against infringement (Section 2A–211) or any part of it, the language must be specific, be by a writing, and be conspicuous, unless the circumstances, including course of performance, course of dealing, or usage of trade, give the lessee reason to know that the goods are being leased subject to a claim or interest of any person.

§2A–215. Cumulation and Conflict of Warranties Express or Implied

Warranties, whether express or implied, must be construed as consistent with each other and as cumulative, but if that construction is unreasonable, the intention of the parties determines which warranty is dominant. In ascertaining that intention the following rules apply:

(a) Exact or technical specifications displace an inconsistent sample or model or general language of description.

(b) A sample from an existing bulk displaces inconsistent general language of description.

(c) Express warranties displace inconsistent implied warranties other than an implied warranty of fitness for a particular purpose.

§2A–216. Third-Party Beneficiaries of Express and Implied Warranties

Alternative A

A warranty to or for the benefit of a lessee under this Article, whether express or implied, extends to any natural person who is in the family or household of the lessee or who is a guest in the lessee's home if it is reasonable to expect that such person may use, consume, or be affected by the goods and who is injured in person by breach of the warranty. This section does not displace principles of law and equity that extend a warranty to or for the benefit of a lessee to other persons. The operation of this section may not be excluded, modified, or limited, but an exclusion, modification, or limitation of the warranty, including any with respect to rights and remedies, effective against the lessee is also effective against any beneficiary designated under this section.

Alternative B

A warranty to or for the benefit of a lessee under this Article, whether express or implied, extends to any natural person who may reasonably be expected to use, consume, or be affected by the goods and who is injured in person by breach of the warranty. This section does not displace principles of law and equity that extend a warranty to or for the benefit of a lessee to other persons. The operation of this section may not be excluded, modified, or limited, but an exclusion, modification, or limitation of the warranty, including any with respect to rights and remedies, effective against the lessee is also effective against the beneficiary designated under this section.

Alternative C

A warranty to or for the benefit of a lessee under this Article, whether express or implied, extends to any person who may reasonably be expected to use, consume, or be affected by the goods and who is injured by breach of the warranty. The operation of this section may not be excluded, modified, or limited with respect to injury to the person of an individual to whom the warranty extends, but an exclusion, modification, or limitation of the warranty, including any with respect to rights and remedies, effective against the lessee is also effective against the beneficiary designated under this section.

§2A–217. Identification

Identification of goods as goods to which a lease contract refers may be made at any time and in any manner explicitly agreed to by the parties. In the absence of explicit agreement, identification occurs:

(a) when the lease contract is made if the lease contract is for a lease of goods that are existing and identified;

(b) when the goods are shipped, marked, or otherwise designated by the lessor as goods to which the lease contract refers, if the lease contract is for a lease of goods that are not existing and identified; or

(c) when the young are conceived, if the lease contract is for a lease of unborn young of animals.

§2A–218. Insurance and Proceeds

(1) A lessee obtains an insurable interest when existing goods are identified to the lease contract even though the goods identified are nonconforming and the lessee has an option to reject them.

(2) If a lessee has an insurable interest only by reason of the lessor's identification of the goods, the lessor, until default or insolvency or notification to the lessee that identification is final, may substitute other goods for those identified.

(3) Notwithstanding a lessee's insurable interest under subsections (1) and (2), the lessor retains an insurable

interest until an option to buy has been exercised by the lessee and risk of loss has passed to the lessee.

(4) Nothing in this section impairs any insurable interest recognized under any other statute or rule of law.

(5) The parties by agreement may determine that one or more parties have an obligation to obtain and pay for insurance covering the goods and by agreement may determine the beneficiary of the proceeds of the insurance.

§2A–219. Risk of Loss

(1) Except in the case of a finance lease, risk of loss is retained by the lessor and does not pass to the lessee. In the case of a finance lease, risk of loss passes to the lessee.

(2) Subject to the provisions of this Article on the effect of default on risk of loss (Section 2A–220), if risk of loss is to pass to the lessee and the time of passage is not stated, the following rules apply:

(a) If the lease contract requires or authorizes the goods to be shipped by carrier

   (i) and it does not require delivery at a particular destination, the risk of loss passes to the lessee when the goods are duly delivered to the carrier; but

   (ii) if it does require delivery at a particular destination and the goods are there duly tendered while in the possession of the carrier, the risk of loss passes to the lessee when the goods are there duly so tendered as to enable the lessee to take delivery.

(b) If the goods are held by a bailee to be delivered without being moved, the risk of loss passes to the lessee on acknowledgment by the bailee of the lessee's right to possession of the goods.

(c) In any case not within subsection (a) or (b), the risk of loss passes to the lessee on the lessee's receipt of the goods if the lessor, or, in the case of a finance lease, the supplier, is a merchant; otherwise the risk passes to the lessee on tender of delivery.

§2A–220. Effect of Default on Risk of Loss

(1) Where risk of loss is to pass to the lessee and the time of passage is not stated:

(a) If a tender or delivery of goods so fails to conform to the lease contract as to give a right of rejection, the risk of their loss remains with the lessor, or, in the case of a finance lease, the supplier, until cure or acceptance.

(b) If the lessee rightfully revokes acceptance, he [or she], to the extent of any deficiency in his [or her] effective insurance coverage, may treat the risk of loss as having remained with the lessor from the beginning.

(2) Whether or not risk of loss is to pass to the lessee, if the lessee as to conforming goods already identified to a lease contract repudiates or is otherwise in default under the lease contract, the lessor, or, in the case of a finance lease, the supplier, to the extent of any deficiency in his [or her] effective insurance coverage may treat the risk of loss as resting on the lessee for a commercially reasonable time.

§2A–221. Casualty to Identified Goods

If a lease contract requires goods identified when the lease contract is made, and the goods suffer casualty without fault of the lessee, the lessor or the supplier before delivery, or the goods suffer casualty before risk of loss passes to the lessee pursuant to the lease agreement or Section 2A–219, then:

(a) if the loss is total, the lease contract is avoided; and

(b) if the loss is partial or the goods have so deteriorated as to no longer conform to the lease contract, the lessee may nevertheless demand inspection and at his [or her] option either treat the lease contract as avoided or, except in a finance lease that is not a consumer lease, accept the goods with due allowance from the rent payable for the balance of the lease term for the deterioration or the deficiency in quantity but without further right against the lessor.

Part 3 Effect of Lease Contract

§2A–301. Enforceability of Lease Contract

Except as otherwise provided in this Article, a lease contract is effective and enforceable according to its terms between the parties, against purchasers of the goods and against creditors of the parties.

§2A–302. Title to and Possession of Goods

Except as otherwise provided in this Article, each provision of this Article applies whether the lessor or a third party has title to the goods, and whether the lessor, the lessee, or a third party has possession of the goods, notwithstanding any statute or rule of law that possession or the absence of possession is fraudulent.

§2A–303. Alienability of Party's Interest Under Lease Contract or of Lessor's Residual Interest in Goods; Delegation of Performance; Transfer of Rights

(1) As used in this section, "creation of a security interest" includes the sale of a lease contract that is subject to Article 9, Secured Transactions, by reason of Section 9–102(1)(b).

(2) Except as provided in subsections (3) and (4), a provision in a lease agreement which (i) prohibits the voluntary or involuntary transfer, including a transfer by sale, sublease, creation or enforcement of a security interest, or attachment, levy, or other judicial process, of

an interest of a party under the lease contract or of the lessor's residual interest in the goods, or (ii) makes such a transfer an event of default, gives rise to the rights and remedies provided in subsection (5), but a transfer that is prohibited or is an event of default under the lease agreement is otherwise effective.

(3) A provision in a lease agreement which (i) prohibits the creation or enforcement of a security interest in an interest of a party under the lease contract or in the lessor's residual interest in the goods, or (ii) makes such a transfer an event of default, is not enforceable unless, and then only to the extent that, there is an actual transfer by the lessee of the lessee's right of possession or use of the goods in violation of the provision or an actual delegation of a material performance of either party to the lease contract in violation of the provision. Neither the granting nor the enforcement of a security interest in (i) the lessor's interest under the lease contract or (ii) the lessor's residual interest in the goods is a transfer that materially impairs the prospect of obtaining return performance by, materially changes the duty of, or materially increases the burden or risk imposed on, the lessee within the purview of subsection (5) unless, and then only to the extent that, there is an actual delegation of a material performance of the lessor.

(4) A provision in a lease agreement which (i) prohibits a transfer of a right to damages for default with respect to the whole lease contract or of a right to payment arising out of the transferor's due performance of the transferor's entire obligation, or (ii) makes such a transfer an event of default, is not enforceable, and such a transfer is not a transfer that materially impairs the prospect of obtaining return performance by, materially changes the duty of, or materially increases the burden or risk imposed on, the other party to the lease contract within the purview of subsection (5).

(5) Subject to subsections (3) and (4):

(a) if a transfer is made which is made an event of default under a lease agreement, the party to the lease contract not making the transfer, unless that party waives the default or otherwise agrees, has the rights and remedies described in Section 2A–501(2);

(b) if paragraph (a) is not applicable and if a transfer is made that (i) is prohibited under a lease agreement or (ii) materially impairs the prospect of obtaining return performance by, materially changes the duty of, or materially increases the burden or risk imposed on, the other party to the lease contract, unless the party not making the transfer agrees at any time to the transfer in the lease contract or otherwise, then, except as limited by contract, (i) the transferor is liable to the party not making the transfer for damages caused by the transfer to the extent that the damages could not reasonably be prevented by the party not making the transfer and (ii) a court having jurisdiction may grant other appropriate relief, including cancellation

of the lease contract or an injunction against the transfer.

(6) A transfer of "the lease" or of "all my rights under the lease," or a transfer in similar general terms, is a transfer of rights and, unless the language or the circumstances, as in a transfer for security, indicate the contrary, the transfer is a delegation of duties by the transferor to the transferee. Acceptance by the transferee constitutes a promise by the transferee to perform those duties. The promise is enforceable by either the transferor or the other party to the lease contract.

(7) Unless otherwise agreed by the lessor and the lessee, a delegation of performance does not relieve the transferor as against the other party of any duty to perform or of any liability for default.

(8) In a consumer lease, to prohibit the transfer of an interest of a party under the lease contract or to make a transfer an event of default, the language must be specific, by a writing, and conspicuous.

As amended in 1990.

§2A–304. Subsequent Lease of Goods by Lessor

(1) Subject to Section 2A–303, a subsequent lessee from a lessor of goods under an existing lease contract obtains, to the extent of the leasehold interest transferred, the leasehold interest in the goods that the lessor had or had power to transfer, and except as provided in subsection (2) and Section 2A–527(4), takes subject to the existing lease contract. A lessor with voidable title has power to transfer a good leasehold interest to a good faith subsequent lessee for value, but only to the extent set forth in the preceding sentence. If goods have been delivered under a transaction of purchase, the lessor has that power even though:

(a) the lessor's transferor was deceived as to the identity of the lessor;

(b) the delivery was in exchange for a check which is later dishonored;

(c) it was agreed that the transaction was to be a "cash sale"; or

(d) the delivery was procured through fraud punishable as larcenous under the criminal law.

(2) A subsequent lessee in the ordinary course of business from a lessor who is a merchant dealing in goods of that kind to whom the goods were entrusted by the existing lessee of that lessor before the interest of the subsequent lessee became enforceable against that lessor obtains, to the extent of the leasehold interest transferred, all of that lessor's and the existing lessee's rights to the goods, and takes free of the existing lease contract.

(3) A subsequent lessee from the lessor of goods that are subject to an existing lease contract and are covered by a certificate of title issued under a statute of this State or of another jurisdiction takes no greater rights than those provided both by this section and by the certificate of title statute.

As amended in 1990.

§2A–305. Sale or Sublease of Goods by Lessee

(1) Subject to the provisions of Section 2A–303, a buyer or sublessee from the lessee of goods under an existing lease contract obtains, to the extent of the interest transferred, the leasehold interest in the goods that the lessee had or had power to transfer, and except as provided in subsection (2) and Section 2A–511(4), takes subject to the existing lease contract. A lessee with a voidable leasehold interest has power to transfer a good leasehold interest to a good faith buyer for value or a good faith sublessee for value, but only to the extent set forth in the preceding sentence. When goods have been delivered under a transaction of lease the lessee has that power even though:

(a) the lessor was deceived as to the identity of the lessee;

(b) the delivery was in exchange for a check which is later dishonored; or

(c) the delivery was procured through fraud punishable as larcenous under the criminal law.

(2) A buyer in the ordinary course of business or a sublessee in the ordinary course of business from a lessee who is a merchant dealing in goods of that kind to whom the goods were entrusted by the lessor obtains, to the extent of the interest transferred, all of the lessor's and lessee's rights to the goods, and takes free of the existing lease contract.

(3) A buyer or sublessee from the lessee of goods that are subject to an existing lease contract and are covered by a certificate of title issued under a statute of this State or of another jurisdiction takes no greater rights than those provided both by this section and by the certificate of title statute.

§2A–306. Priority of Certain Liens Arising by Operation of Law

If a person in the ordinary course of his [or her] business furnishes services or materials with respect to goods subject to a lease contract, a lien upon those goods in the possession of that person given by statute or rule of law for those materials or services takes priority over any interest of the lessor or lessee under the lease contract or this Article unless the lien is created by statute and the statute provides otherwise or unless the lien is created by rule of law and the rule of law provides otherwise.

§2A–307. Priority of Liens Arising by Attachment or Levy on, Security Interests in, and Other Claims to Goods

(1) Except as otherwise provided in Section 2A–306, a creditor of a lessee takes subject to the lease contract.

(2) Except as otherwise provided in subsections (3) and (4) and in Sections 2A–306 and 2A–308, a creditor of a lessor takes subject to the lease contract unless:

(a) the creditor holds a lien that attached to the goods before the lease contract became enforceable,

(b) the creditor holds a security interest in the goods and the lessee did not give value and receive delivery of the goods without knowledge of the security interest; or

(c) the creditor holds a security interest in the goods which was perfected (Section 9–303) before the lease contract became enforceable.

(3) A lessee in the ordinary course of business takes the leasehold interest free of a security interest in the goods created by the lessor even though the security interest is perfected (Section 9–303) and the lessee knows of its existence.

(4) A lessee other than a lessee in the ordinary course of business takes the leasehold interest free of a security interest to the extent that it secures future advances made after the secured party acquires knowledge of the lease or more than 45 days after the lease contract becomes enforceable, whichever first occurs, unless the future advances are made pursuant to a commitment entered into without knowledge of the lease and before the expiration of the 45-day period.

As amended in 1990.

§2A–308. Special Rights of Creditors

(1) A creditor of a lessor in possession of goods subject to a lease contract may treat the lease contract as void if as against the creditor retention of possession by the lessor is fraudulent under any statute or rule of law, but retention of possession in good faith and current course of trade by the lessor for a commercially reasonable time after the lease contract becomes enforceable is not fraudulent.

(2) Nothing in this Article impairs the rights of creditors of a lessor if the lease contract (a) becomes enforceable, not in current course of trade but in satisfaction of or as security for a pre-existing claim for money, security, or the like, and (b) is made under circumstances which under any statute or rule of law apart from this Article would constitute the transaction a fraudulent transfer or voidable preference.

(3) A creditor of a seller may treat a sale or an identification of goods to a contract for sale as void if as against the creditor retention of possession by the seller is fraudulent under any statute or rule of law, but retention of possession of the goods pursuant to a lease contract entered into by the seller as lessee and the buyer as lessor in connection with the sale or identification of the goods is not fraudulent if the buyer bought for value and in good faith.

§2A–309. Lessor's and Lessee's Rights When Goods Become Fixtures

(1) In this section:

(a) goods are "fixtures" when they become so related to particular real estate that an interest in them arises under real estate law;

(b) a "fixture filing" is the filing, in the office where a mortgage on the real estate would be filed or recorded, of a financing statement covering goods that are or are to become fixtures and conforming to the requirements of Section 9–402(5);

(c) a lease is a "purchase money lease" unless the lessee has possession or use of the goods or the right to possession or use of the goods before the lease agreement is enforceable;

(d) a mortgage is a "construction mortgage" to the extent it secures an obligation incurred for the construction of an improvement on land including the acquisition cost of the land, if the recorded writing so indicates; and

(e) "encumbrance" includes real estate mortgages and other liens on real estate and all other rights in real estate that are not ownership interests.

(2) Under this Article a lease may be of goods that are fixtures or may continue in goods that become fixtures, but no lease exists under this Article of ordinary building materials incorporated into an improvement on land.

(3) This Article does not prevent creation of a lease of fixtures pursuant to real estate law.

(4) The perfected interest of a lessor of fixtures has priority over a conflicting interest of an encumbrancer or owner of the real estate if:

(a) the lease is a purchase money lease, the conflicting interest of the encumbrancer or owner arises before the goods become fixtures, the interest of the lessor is perfected by a fixture filing before the goods become fixtures or within ten days thereafter, and the lessee has an interest of record in the real estate or is in possession of the real estate; or

(b) the interest of the lessor is perfected by a fixture filing before the interest of the encumbrancer or owner is of record, the lessor's interest has priority over any conflicting interest of a predecessor in title of the encumbrancer or owner, and the lessee has an interest of record in the real estate or is in possession of the real estate.

(5) The interest of a lessor of fixtures, whether or not perfected, has priority over the conflicting interest of an encumbrancer or owner of the real estate if:

(a) the fixtures are readily removable factory or office machines, readily removable equipment that is not primarily used or leased for use in the operation of the real estate, or readily removable replacements of domestic appliances that are goods subject to a consumer lease, and before the goods become fixtures the lease contract is enforceable; or

(b) the conflicting interest is a lien on the real estate obtained by legal or equitable proceedings after the lease contract is enforceable; or

(c) the encumbrancer or owner has consented in writing to the lease or has disclaimed an interest in the goods as fixtures; or

(d) the lessee has a right to remove the goods as against the encumbrancer or owner. If the lessee's right to remove terminates, the priority of the interest of the lessor continues for a reasonable time.

(6) Notwithstanding subsection (4)(a) but otherwise subject to subsections (4) and (5), the interest of a lessor of fixtures, including the lessor's residual interest, is subordinate to the conflicting interest of an encumbrancer of the real estate under a construction mortgage recorded before the goods become fixtures if the goods become fixtures before the completion of the construction. To the extent given to refinance a construction mortgage, the conflicting interest of an encumbrancer of the real estate under a mortgage has this priority to the same extent as the encumbrancer of the real estate under the construction mortgage.

(7) In cases not within the preceding subsections, priority between the interest of a lessor of fixtures, including the lessor's residual interest, and the conflicting interest of an encumbrancer or owner of the real estate who is not the lessee is determined by the priority rules governing conflicting interests in real estate.

(8) If the interest of a lessor of fixtures, including the lessor's residual interest, has priority over all conflicting interests of all owners and encumbrancers of the real estate, the lessor or the lessee may (i) on default, expiration, termination, or cancellation of the lease agreement but subject to the agreement and this Article, or (ii) if necessary to enforce other rights and remedies of the lessor or lessee under this Article, remove the goods from the real estate, free and clear of all conflicting interests of all owners and encumbrancers of the real estate, but the lessor or lessee must reimburse any encumbrancer or owner of the real estate who is not the lessee and who has not otherwise agreed for the cost of repair of any physical injury, but not for any diminution in value of the real estate caused by the absence of the goods removed or by any necessity of replacing them. A person entitled to reimbursement may refuse permission to remove until the party seeking removal gives adequate security for the performance of this obligation.

(9) Even though the lease agreement does not create a security interest, the interest of a lessor of fixtures, including the lessor's residual interest, is perfected by filing a financing statement as a fixture filing for leased goods that are or are to become fixtures in accordance with the relevant provisions of the Article on Secured Transactions (Article 9).

As amended in 1990.

§2A–310. Lessor's and Lessee's Rights When Goods Become Accessions

(1) Goods are "accessions" when they are installed in or affixed to other goods.

(2) The interest of a lessor or a lessee under a lease contract entered into before the goods became accessions is superior to all interests in the whole except as stated in subsection (4).

(3) The interest of a lessor or a lessee under a lease contract entered into at the time or after the goods became accessions is superior to all subsequently acquired interests in the whole except as stated in subsection (4) but is subordinate to interests in the whole existing at the time the lease contract was made unless the holders of such interests in the whole have in writing consented to the lease or disclaimed an interest in the goods as part of the whole.

(4) The interest of a lessor or a lessee under a lease contract described in subsection (2) or (3) is subordinate to the interest of

(a) a buyer in the ordinary course of business or a lessee in the ordinary course of business of any interest in the whole acquired after the goods became accessions; or

(b) a creditor with a security interest in the whole perfected before the lease contract was made to the extent that the creditor makes subsequent advances without knowledge of the lease contract.

(5) When under subsections (2) or (3) and (4) a lessor or a lessee of accessions holds an interest that is superior to all interests in the whole, the lessor or the lessee may (a) on default, expiration, termination, or cancellation of the lease contract by the other party but subject to the provisions of the lease contract and this Article, or (b) if necessary to enforce his [or her] other rights and remedies under this Article, remove the goods from the whole, free and clear of all interests in the whole, but he [or she] must reimburse any holder of an interest in the whole who is not the lessee and who has not otherwise agreed for the cost of repair of any physical injury but not for any diminution in value of the whole caused by the absence of the goods removed or by any necessity for replacing them. A person entitled to reimbursement may refuse permission to remove until the party seeking removal gives adequate security for the performance of this obligation.

§2A–311. Priority Subject to Subordination

Nothing in this Article prevents subordination by agreement by any person entitled to priority.
As added in 1990.

Part 4 Performance of Lease Contract: Repudiated, Substituted and Excused

§2A–401. Insecurity: Adequate Assurance of Performance

(1) A lease contract imposes an obligation on each party that the other's expectation of receiving due performance will not be impaired.

(2) If reasonable grounds for insecurity arise with respect to the performance of either party, the insecure party may demand in writing adequate assurance of due performance. Until the insecure party receives that assurance, if commercially reasonable the insecure party may suspend any performance for which he [or she] has not already received the agreed return.

(3) A repudiation of the lease contract occurs if assurance of due performance adequate under the circumstances of the particular case is not provided to the insecure party within a reasonable time, not to exceed 30 days after receipt of a demand by the other party.

(4) Between merchants, the reasonableness of grounds for insecurity and the adequacy of any assurance offered must be determined according to commercial standards.

(5) Acceptance of any nonconforming delivery or payment does not prejudice the aggrieved party's right to demand adequate assurance of future performance.

§2A–402. Anticipatory Repudiation

If either party repudiates a lease contract with respect to a performance not yet due under the lease contract, the loss of which performance will substantially impair the value of the lease contract to the other, the aggrieved party may:

(a) for a commercially reasonable time, await retraction of repudiation and performance by the repudiating party;

(b) make demand pursuant to Section 2A–401 and await assurance of future performance adequate under the circumstances of the particular case; or

(c) resort to any right or remedy upon default under the lease contract or this Article, even though the aggrieved party has notified the repudiating party that the aggrieved party would await the repudiating party's performance and assurance and has urged retraction. In addition, whether or not the aggrieved party is pursuing one of the foregoing remedies, the aggrieved party may suspend performance or, if the aggrieved party is the lessor, proceed in accordance with the provisions of this Article on the lessor's right to identify goods to the lease contract notwithstanding default or to salvage unfinished goods (Section 2A–524).

§2A–403. Retraction of Anticipatory Repudiation

(1) Until the repudiating party's next performance is due, the repudiating party can retract the repudiation unless, since the repudiation, the aggrieved party has canceled the lease contract or materially changed the aggrieved party's position or otherwise indicated that the aggrieved party considers the repudiation final.

(2) Retraction may be by any method that clearly indicates to the aggrieved party that the repudiating party intends to perform under the lease contract and includes any assurance demanded under Section 2A–401.

(3) Retraction reinstates a repudiating party's rights under a lease contract with due excuse and allowance to the aggrieved party for any delay occasioned by the repudiation.

§2A–404. Substituted Performance

(1) If without fault of the lessee, the lessor and the supplier, the agreed berthing, loading, or unloading facilities fail or the agreed type of carrier becomes unavailable or the agreed manner of delivery otherwise becomes commercially impracticable, but a commercially reasonable substitute is available, the substitute performance must be tendered and accepted.

(2) If the agreed means or manner of payment fails because of domestic or foreign governmental regulation:

(a) the lessor may withhold or stop delivery or cause the supplier to withhold or stop delivery unless the lessee provides a means or manner of payment that is commercially a substantial equivalent; and

(b) if delivery has already been taken, payment by the means or in the manner provided by the regulation discharges the lessee's obligation unless the regulation is discriminatory, oppressive, or predatory.

§2A–405. Excused Performance

Subject to Section 2A–404 on substituted performance, the following rules apply:

(a) Delay in delivery or nondelivery in whole or in part by a lessor or a supplier who complies with paragraphs (b) and (c) is not a default under the lease contract if performance as agreed has been made impracticable by the occurrence of a contingency the nonoccurrence of which was a basic assumption on which the lease contract was made or by compliance in good faith with any applicable foreign or domestic governmental regulation or order, whether or not the regulation or order later proves to be invalid.

(b) If the causes mentioned in paragraph (a) affect only part of the lessor's or the supplier's capacity to perform, he [or she] shall allocate production and deliveries among his [or her] customers but at his [or her] option may include regular customers not then under contract for sale or lease as well as his [or her] own requirements for further manufacture. He [or she] may so allocate in any manner that is fair and reasonable.

(c) The lessor seasonably shall notify the lessee and in the case of a finance lease the supplier seasonably shall notify the lessor and the lessee, if known, that there will be delay or nondelivery and, if allocation is required under paragraph (b), of the estimated quota thus made available for the lessee.

§2A–406. Procedure on Excused Performance

(1) If the lessee receives notification of a material or indefinite delay or an allocation justified under Section 2A–405, the lessee may by written notification to the lessor as to any goods involved, and with respect to all of the goods if under an installment lease contract the value of the whole lease contract is substantially impaired (Section 2A–510):

(a) terminate the lease contract (Section 2A–505(2));or

(b) except in a finance lease that is not a consumer lease, modify the lease contract by accepting the available quota in substitution, with due allowance from the rent payable for the balance of the lease term for the deficiency but without further right against the lessor.

(2) If, after receipt of a notification from the lessor under Section 2A–405, the lessee fails so to modify the lease agreement within a reasonable time not exceeding 30 days, the lease contract lapses with respect to any deliveries affected.

§2A–407. Irrevocable Promises: Finance Leases

(1) In the case of a finance lease that is not a consumer lease the lessee's promises under the lease contract become irrevocable and independent upon the lessee's acceptance of the goods.

(2) A promise that has become irrevocable and independent under subsection (1):

(a) is effective and enforceable between the parties, and by or against third parties including assignees of the parties; and

(b) is not subject to cancellation, termination, modification, repudiation, excuse, or substitution without the consent of the party to whom the promise runs.

(3) This section does not affect the validity under any other law of a covenant in any lease contract making the lessee's promises irrevocable and independent upon the lessee's acceptance of the goods.

As amended in 1990.

Part 5 Default
A. In General

§2A–501. Default: Procedure

(1) Whether the lessor or the lessee is in default under a lease contract is determined by the lease agreement and this Article.

(2) If the lessor or the lessee is in default under the lease contract, the party seeking enforcement has rights and remedies as provided in this Article and, except as limited by this Article, as provided in the lease agreement.

(3) If the lessor or the lessee is in default under the lease contract, the party seeking enforcement may reduce the party's claim to judgment, or otherwise enforce the lease contract by self-help or any available judicial procedure or nonjudicial procedure, including administrative proceeding, arbitration, or the like, in accordance with this Article.

(4) Except as otherwise provided in Section 1–106(1) or this Article or the lease agreement, the rights and remedies referred to in subsections (2) and (3) are cumulative.

(5) If the lease agreement covers both real property and goods, the party seeking enforcement may proceed under this Part as to the goods, or under other applicable law as to both the real property and the goods in accordance with that party's rights and remedies in respect of the real property, in which case this Part does not apply.

As amended in 1990.

§2A–502. Notice After Default

Except as otherwise provided in this Article or the lease agreement, the lessor or lessee in default under the lease contract is not entitled to notice of default or notice of enforcement from the other party to the lease agreement.

§2A–503. Modification or Impairment of Rights and Remedies

(1) Except as otherwise provided in this Article, the lease agreement may include rights and remedies for default in addition to or in substitution for those provided in this Article and may limit or alter the measure of damages recoverable under this Article.

(2) Resort to a remedy provided under this Article or in the lease agreement is optional unless the remedy is expressly agreed to be exclusive. If circumstances cause an exclusive or limited remedy to fail of its essential purpose, or provision for an exclusive remedy is unconscionable, remedy may be had as provided in this Article.

(3) Consequential damages may be liquidated under Section 2A–504, or may otherwise be limited, altered, or excluded unless the limitation, alteration, or exclusion is unconscionable. Limitation, alteration, or exclusion of consequential damages for injury to the person in the case of consumer goods is prima facie unconscionable but limitation, alteration, or exclusion of damages where the loss is commercial is not prima facie unconscionable.

(4) Rights and remedies on default by the lessor or the lessee with respect to any obligation or promise collateral or ancillary to the lease contract are not impaired by this Article.

As amended in 1990.

§2A–504. Liquidation of Damages

(1) Damages payable by either party for default, or any other act or omission, including indemnity for loss or diminution of anticipated tax benefits or loss or damage to lessor's residual interest, may be liquidated in the lease agreement but only at an amount or by a formula that is reasonable in light of the then anticipated harm caused by the default or other act or omission.

(2) If the lease agreement provides for liquidation of damages, and such provision does not comply with subsection (1), or such provision is an exclusive or limited remedy that circumstances cause to fail of its essential purpose, remedy may be had as provided in this Article.

(3) If the lessor justifiably withholds or stops delivery of goods because of the lessee's default or insolvency (Section 2A–525 or 2A–526), the lessee is entitled to restitution of any amount by which the sum of his [or her] payments exceeds:

(a) the amount to which the lessor is entitled by virtue of terms liquidating the lessor's damages in accordance with subsection (1); or

(b) in the absence of those terms, 20 percent of the then present value of the total rent the lessee was obligated to pay for the balance of the lease term, or, in the case of a consumer lease, the lesser of such amount or $500.

(4) A lessee's right to restitution under subsection (3) is subject to offset to the extent the lessor establishes:

(a) a right to recover damages under the provisions of this Article other than subsection (1); and

(b) the amount or value of any benefits received by the lessee directly or indirectly by reason of the lease contract.

§2A–505. Cancellation and Termination and Effect of Cancellation, Termination, Rescission, or Fraud on Rights and Remedies

(1) On cancellation of the lease contract, all obligations that are still executory on both sides are discharged, but any right based on prior default or performance survives, and the cancelling party also retains any remedy for default of the whole lease contract or any unperformed balance.

(2) On termination of the lease contract, all obligations that are still executory on both sides are discharged but any right based on prior default or performance survives.

(3) Unless the contrary intention clearly appears, expressions of "cancellation," "rescission," or the like of the lease contract may not be construed as a renunciation or discharge of any claim in damages for an antecedent default.

(4) Rights and remedies for material misrepresentation or fraud include all rights and remedies available under this Article for default.

(5) Neither rescission nor a claim for rescission of the lease contract nor rejection or return of the goods may bar or be deemed inconsistent with a claim for damages or other right or remedy.

§2A–506. Statute of Limitations

(1) An action for default under a lease contract, including breach of warranty or indemnity, must be commenced within 4 years after the cause of action accrued. By the original lease contract the parties may reduce the period of limitation to not less than one year.

(2) A cause of action for default accrues when the act or omission on which the default or breach of warranty is

based is or should have been discovered by the aggrieved party, or when the default occurs, whichever is later. A cause of action for indemnity accrues when the act or omission on which the claim for indemnity is based is or should have been discovered by the indemnified party, whichever is later.

(3) If an action commenced within the time limited by subsection (1) is so terminated as to leave available a remedy by another action for the same default or breach of warranty or indemnity, the other action may be commenced after the expiration of the time limited and within 6 months after the termination of the first action unless the termination resulted from voluntary discontinuance or from dismissal for failure or neglect to prosecute.

(4) This section does not alter the law on tolling of the statute of limitations nor does it apply to causes of action that have accrued before this Article becomes effective.

§2A–507. Proof of Market Rent: Time and Place

(1) Damages based on market rent (Section 2A–519 or 2A–528) are determined according to the rent for the use of the goods concerned for a lease term identical to the remaining lease term of the original lease agreement and prevailing at the times specified in Sections 2A–519 and 2A–528.

(2) If evidence of rent for the use of the goods concerned for a lease term identical to the remaining lease term of the original lease agreement and prevailing at the times or places described in this Article is not readily available, the rent prevailing within any reasonable time before or after the time described or at any other place or for a different lease term which in commercial judgment or under usage of trade would serve as a reasonable substitute for the one described may be used, making any proper allowance for the difference, including the cost of transporting the goods to or from the other place.

(3) Evidence of a relevant rent prevailing at a time or place or for a lease term other than the one described in this Article offered by one party is not admissible unless and until he [or she] has given the other party notice the court finds sufficient to prevent unfair surprise.

(4) If the prevailing rent or value of any goods regularly leased in any established market is in issue, reports in official publications or trade journals or in newspapers or periodicals of general circulation published as the reports of that market are admissible in evidence. The circumstances of the preparation of the report may be shown to affect its weight but not its admissibility.

As amended in 1990.

B. Default by Lessor

§2A–508. Lessee's Remedies

(1) If a lessor fails to deliver the goods in conformity to the lease contract (Section 2A–509) or repudiates the lease contract (Section 2A–402), or a lessee rightfully rejects the goods (Section 2A–509) or justifiably revokes acceptance of the goods (Section 2A–517), then with respect to any goods involved, and with respect to all of the goods if under an installment lease contract the value of the whole lease contract is substantially impaired (Section 2A–510), the lessor is in default under the lease contract and the lessee may:

(a) cancel the lease contract (Section 2A–505(1));

(b) recover so much of the rent and security as has been paid and is just under the circumstances;

(c) cover and recover damages as to all goods affected whether or not they have been identified to the lease contract (Sections 2A–518 and 2A–520), or recover damages for nondelivery (Sections 2A–519 and 2A–520);

(d) exercise any other rights or pursue any other remedies provided in the lease contract.

(2) If a lessor fails to deliver the goods in conformity to the lease contract or repudiates the lease contract, the lessee may also:

(a) if the goods have been identified, recover them (Section 2A–522); or

(b) in a proper case, obtain specific performance or replevy the goods (Section 2A–521).

(3) If a lessor is otherwise in default under a lease contract, the lessee may exercise the rights and pursue the remedies provided in the lease contract, which may include a right to cancel the lease, and in Section 2A–519(3).

(4) If a lessor has breached a warranty, whether express or implied, the lessee may recover damages (Section 2A–519(4)).

(5) On rightful rejection or justifiable revocation of acceptance, a lessee has a security interest in goods in the lessee's possession or control for any rent and security that has been paid and any expenses reasonably incurred in their inspection, receipt, transportation, and care and custody and may hold those goods and dispose of them in good faith and in a commercially reasonable manner, subject to Section 2A–527(5).

(6) Subject to the provisions of Section 2A–407, a lessee, on notifying the lessor of the lessee's intention to do so, may deduct all or any part of the damages resulting from any default under the lease contract from any part of the rent still due under the same lease contract.

As amended in 1990.

§2A–509. Lessee's Rights on Improper Delivery; Rightful Rejection

(1) Subject to the provisions of Section 2A–510 on default in installment lease contracts, if the goods or the tender or delivery fail in any respect to conform to the lease contract, the lessee may reject or accept the goods or accept any commercial unit or units and reject the rest of the goods.

(2) Rejection of goods is ineffective unless it is within a reasonable time after tender or delivery of the goods and the lessee seasonably notifies the lessor.

§2A–510. Installment Lease Contracts: Rejection and Default

(1) Under an installment lease contract a lessee may reject any delivery that is nonconforming if the nonconformity substantially impairs the value of that delivery and cannot be cured or the nonconformity is a defect in the required documents; but if the nonconformity does not fall within subsection (2) and the lessor or the supplier gives adequate assurance of its cure, the lessee must accept that delivery.

(2) Whenever nonconformity or default with respect to one or more deliveries substantially impairs the value of the installment lease contract as a whole there is a default with respect to the whole. But, the aggrieved party reinstates the installment lease contract as a whole if the aggrieved party accepts a nonconforming delivery without seasonably notifying of cancellation or brings an action with respect only to past deliveries or demands performance as to future deliveries.

§2A–511. Merchant Lessee's Duties as to Rightfully Rejected Goods

(1) Subject to any security interest of a lessee (Section 2A–508(5)), if a lessor or a supplier has no agent or place of business at the market of rejection, a merchant lessee, after rejection of goods in his [or her] possession or control, shall follow any reasonable instructions received from the lessor or the supplier with respect to the goods. In the absence of those instructions, a merchant lessee shall make reasonable efforts to sell, lease, or otherwise dispose of the goods for the lessor's account if they threaten to decline in value speedily. Instructions are not reasonable if on demand indemnity for expenses is not forthcoming.

(2) If a merchant lessee (subsection (1)) or any other lessee (Section 2A–512) disposes of goods, he [or she] is entitled to reimbursement either from the lessor or the supplier or out of the proceeds for reasonable expenses of caring for and disposing of the goods and, if the expenses include no disposition commission, to such commission as is usual in the trade, or if there is none, to a reasonable sum not exceeding 10 percent of the gross proceeds.

(3) In complying with this section or Section 2A–512, the lessee is held only to good faith. Good faith conduct hereunder is neither acceptance or conversion nor the basis of an action for damages.

(4) A purchaser who purchases in good faith from a lessee pursuant to this section or Section 2A–512 takes the goods free of any rights of the lessor and the supplier even though the lessee fails to comply with one or more of the requirements of this Article.

§2A–512. Lessee's Duties as to Rightfully Rejected Goods

(1) Except as otherwise provided with respect to goods that threaten to decline in value speedily (Section 2A–511) and subject to any security interest of a lessee (Section 2A–508(5)):

  (a) the lessee, after rejection of goods in the lessee's possession, shall hold them with reasonable care at the lessor's or the supplier's disposition for a reasonable time after the lessee's seasonable notification of rejection;

  (b) if the lessor or the supplier gives no instructions within a reasonable time after notification of rejection, the lessee may store the rejected goods for the lessor's or the supplier's account or ship them to the lessor or the supplier or dispose of them for the lessor's or the supplier's account with reimbursement in the manner provided in Section 2A–511; but

  (c) the lessee has no further obligations with regard to goods rightfully rejected.

(2) Action by the lessee pursuant to subsection (1) is not acceptance or conversion.

§2A–513. Cure by Lessor of Improper Tender or Delivery; Replacement

(1) If any tender or delivery by the lessor or the supplier is rejected because nonconforming and the time for performance has not yet expired, the lessor or the supplier may seasonably notify the lessee of the lessor's or the supplier's intention to cure and may then make a conforming delivery within the time provided in the lease contract.

(2) If the lessee rejects a nonconforming tender that the lessor or the supplier had reasonable grounds to believe would be acceptable with or without money allowance, the lessor or the supplier may have a further reasonable time to substitute a conforming tender if he [or she] seasonably notifies the lessee.

§2A–514. Waiver of Lessee's Objections

(1) In rejecting goods, a lessee's failure to state a particular defect that is ascertainable by reasonable inspection precludes the lessee from relying on the defect to justify rejection or to establish default:

  (a) if, stated seasonably, the lessor or the supplier could have cured it (Section 2A–513); or

  (b) between merchants if the lessor or the supplier after rejection has made a request in writing for a full and final written statement of all defects on which the lessee proposes to rely.

(2) A lessee's failure to reserve rights when paying rent or other consideration against documents precludes recovery of the payment for defects apparent on the face of the documents.

§2A–515. Acceptance of Goods

(1) Acceptance of goods occurs after the lessee has had a reasonable opportunity to inspect the goods and

(a) the lessee signifies or acts with respect to the goods in a manner that signifies to the lessor or the supplier that the goods are conforming or that the lessee will take or retain them in spite of their nonconformity; or

(b) the lessee fails to make an effective rejection of the goods (Section 2A–509(2)).

(2) Acceptance of a part of any commercial unit is acceptance of that entire unit.

§2A–516. Effect of Acceptance of Goods; Notice of Default; Burden of Establishing Default After Acceptance; Notice of Claim or Litigation to Person Answerable Over

(1) A lessee must pay rent for any goods accepted in accordance with the lease contract, with due allowance for goods rightfully rejected or not delivered.

(2) A lessee's acceptance of goods precludes rejection of the goods accepted. In the case of a finance lease, if made with knowledge of a nonconformity, acceptance cannot be revoked because of it. In any other case, if made with knowledge of a nonconformity, acceptance cannot be revoked because of it unless the acceptance was on the reasonable assumption that the nonconformity would be seasonably cured. Acceptance does not of itself impair any other remedy provided by this Article or the lease agreement for nonconformity.

(3) If a tender has been accepted:

(a) within a reasonable time after the lessee discovers or should have discovered any default, the lessee shall notify the lessor and the supplier, if any, or be barred from any remedy against the party not notified;

(b) except in the case of a consumer lease, within a reasonable time after the lessee receives notice of litigation for infringement or the like (Section 2A–211) the lessee shall notify the lessor or be barred from any remedy over for liability established by the litigation; and

(c) the burden is on the lessee to establish any default.

(4) If a lessee is sued for breach of a warranty or other obligation for which a lessor or a supplier is answerable over the following apply:

(a) The lessee may give the lessor or the supplier, or both, written notice of the litigation. If the notice states that the person notified may come in and defend and that if the person notified does not do so that person will be bound in any action against that person by the lessee by any determination of fact common to the two litigations, then unless the person notified after seasonable receipt of the notice does come in and defend that person is so bound.

(b) The lessor or the supplier may demand in writing that the lessee turn over control of the litigation including settlement if the claim is one for infringement or the like (Section 2A–211) or else be barred from any remedy over. If the demand states that the lessor or the supplier agrees to bear all expense and to satisfy any adverse judgment, then unless the lessee after seasonable receipt of the demand does turn over control the lessee is so barred.

(5) Subsections (3) and (4) apply to any obligation of a lessee to hold the lessor or the supplier harmless against infringement or the like (Section 2A–211).

As amended in 1990.

§2A–517. Revocation of Acceptance of Goods

(1) A lessee may revoke acceptance of a lot or commercial unit whose nonconformity substantially impairs its value to the lessee if the lessee has accepted it:

(a) except in the case of a finance lease, on the reasonable assumption that its nonconformity would be cured and it has not been seasonably cured; or

(b) without discovery of the nonconformity if the lessee's acceptance was reasonably induced either by the lessor's assurances or, except in the case of a finance lease, by the difficulty of discovery before acceptance.

(2) Except in the case of a finance lease that is not a consumer lease, a lessee may revoke acceptance of a lot or commercial unit if the lessor defaults under the lease contract and the default substantially impairs the value of that lot or commercial unit to the lessee.

(3) If the lease agreement so provides, the lessee may revoke acceptance of a lot or commercial unit because of other defaults by the lessor.

(4) Revocation of acceptance must occur within a reasonable time after the lessee discovers or should have discovered the ground for it and before any substantial change in condition of the goods which is not caused by the nonconformity. Revocation is not effective until the lessee notifies the lessor.

(5) A lessee who so revokes has the same rights and duties with regard to the goods involved as if the lessee had rejected them.

As amended in 1990.

§2A–518. Cover; Substitute Goods

(1) After a default by a lessor under the lease contract of the type described in Section 2A–508(1), or, if agreed, after other default by the lessor, the lessee may cover by making any purchase or lease of or contract to purchase or lease goods in substitution for those due from the lessor.

(2) Except as otherwise provided with respect to damages liquidated in the lease agreement (Section 2A–504) or otherwise determined pursuant to agreement of the parties (Sections 1–102(3) and 2A–503), if a lessee's cover is by a lease agreement substantially similar to the original lease agreement and the new lease agreement is made in good faith and in a commercially reasonable manner, the lessee may recover from the lessor as damages (i) the present value, as of the date of the commencement of the term of the new lease agreement, of the rent under the new lease agreement applicable to that period of the new lease term which is comparable to the then remaining

term of the original lease agreement minus the present value as of the same date of the total rent for the then remaining lease term of the original lease agreement, and (ii) any incidental or consequential damages, less expenses saved in consequence of the lessor's default.

(3) If a lessee's cover is by lease agreement that for any reason does not qualify for treatment under subsection (2), or is by purchase or otherwise, the lessee may recover from the lessor as if the lessee had elected not to cover and Section 2A–519 governs.

As amended in 1990.

§2A–519. Lessee's Damages for Non-delivery, Repudiation, Default, and Breach of Warranty in Regard to Accepted Goods

(1) Except as otherwise provided with respect to damages liquidated in the lease agreement (Section 2A–504) or otherwise determined pursuant to agreement of the parties (Sections 1–102(3) and 2A–503), if a lessee elects not to cover or a lessee elects to cover and the cover is by lease agreement that for any reason does not qualify for treatment under Section 2A–518(2), or is by purchase or otherwise, the measure of damages for non-delivery or repudiation by the lessor or for rejection or revocation of acceptance by the lessee is the present value, as of the date of the default, of the then market rent minus the present value as of the same date of the original rent, computed for the remaining lease term of the original lease agreement, together with incidental and consequential damages, less expenses saved in consequence of the lessor's default.

(2) Market rent is to be determined as of the place for tender or, in cases of rejection after arrival or revocation of acceptance, as of the place of arrival.

(3) Except as otherwise agreed, if the lessee has accepted goods and given notification (Section 2A–516(3)), the measure of damages for nonconforming tender or delivery or other default by a lessor is the loss resulting in the ordinary course of events from the lessor's default as determined in any manner that is reasonable together with incidental and consequential damages, less expenses saved in consequence of the lessor's default.

(4) Except as otherwise agreed, the measure of damages for breach of warranty is the present value at the time and place of acceptance of the difference between the value of the use of the goods accepted and the value if they had been as warranted for the lease term, unless special circumstances show proximate damages of a different amount, together with incidental and consequential damages, less expenses saved in consequence of the lessor's default or breach of warranty.

As amended in 1990.

§2A–520. Lessee's Incidental and Consequential Damages

(1) Incidental damages resulting from a lessor's default include expenses reasonably incurred in inspection, receipt, transportation, and care and custody of goods rightfully rejected or goods the acceptance of which is justifiably revoked, any commercially reasonable charges, expenses or commissions in connection with effecting cover, and any other reasonable expense incident to the default.

(2) Consequential damages resulting from a lessor's default include:

(a) any loss resulting from general or particular requirements and needs of which the lessor at the time of contracting had reason to know and which could not reasonably be prevented by cover or otherwise; and

(b) injury to person or property proximately resulting from any breach of warranty.

§2A–521. Lessee's Right to Specific Performance or Replevin

(1) Specific performance may be decreed if the goods are unique or in other proper circumstances.

(2) A decree for specific performance may include any terms and conditions as to payment of the rent, damages, or other relief that the court deems just.

(3) A lessee has a right of replevin, detinue, sequestration, claim and delivery, or the like for goods identified to the lease contract if after reasonable effort the lessee is unable to effect cover for those goods or the circumstances reasonably indicate that the effort will be unavailing.

§2A–522. Lessee's Right to Goods on Lessor's Insolvency

(1) Subject to subsection (2) and even though the goods have not been shipped, a lessee who has paid a part or all of the rent and security for goods identified to a lease contract (Section 2A–217) on making and keeping good a tender of any unpaid portion of the rent and security due under the lease contract may recover the goods identified from the lessor if the lessor becomes insolvent within 10 days after receipt of the first installment of rent and security.

(2) A lessee acquires the right to recover goods identified to a lease contract only if they conform to the lease contract.

C. Default by Lessee

§2A–523. Lessor's Remedies

(1) If a lessee wrongfully rejects or revokes acceptance of goods or fails to make a payment when due or repudiates with respect to a part or the whole, then, with respect to any goods involved, and with respect to all of the goods if under an installment lease contract the value of the whole lease contract is substantially impaired (Section 2A–510), the lessee is in default under the lease contract and the lessor may:

(a) cancel the lease contract (Section 2A–505(1));

(b) proceed respecting goods not identified to the lease contract (Section 2A–524);

(c) withhold delivery of the goods and take possession of goods previously delivered (Section 2A–525);

(d) stop delivery of the goods by any bailee (Section 2A–526);

(e) dispose of the goods and recover damages (Section 2A–527), or retain the goods and recover damages (Section 2A–528), or in a proper case recover rent (Section 2A–529).

(f) exercise any other rights or pursue any other remedies provided in the lease contract.

(2) If a lessor does not fully exercise a right or obtain a remedy to which the lessor is entitled under subsection (1), the lessor may recover the loss resulting in the ordinary course of events from the lessee's default as determined in any reasonable manner, together with incidental damages, less expenses saved in consequence of the lessee's default.

(3) If a lessee is otherwise in default under a lease contract, the lessor may exercise the rights and pursue the remedies provided in the lease contract, which may include a right to cancel the lease. In addition, unless otherwise provided in the lease contract:

(a) if the default substantially impairs the value of the lease contract to the lessor, the lessor may exercise the rights and pursue the remedies provided in subsections (1) or (2); or

(b) if the default does not substantially impair the value of the lease contract to the lessor, the lessor may recover as provided in subsection (2).

As amended in 1990.

§2A–524. Lessor's Right to Identify Goods to Lease Contract

(1) After default by the lessee under the lease contract of the type described in Section 2A–523(1) or 2A–523(3)(a) or, if agreed, after other default by the lessee, the lessor may:

(a) identify to the lease contract conforming goods not already identified if at the time the lessor learned of the default they were in the lessor's or the supplier's possession or control; and

(b) dispose of goods (Section 2A–527(1)) that demonstrably have been intended for the particular lease contract even though those goods are unfinished.

(2) If the goods are unfinished, in the exercise of reasonable commercial judgment for the purposes of avoiding loss and of effective realization, an aggrieved lessor or the supplier may either complete manufacture and wholly identify the goods to the lease contract or cease manufacture and lease, sell, or otherwise dispose of the goods for scrap or salvage value or proceed in any other reasonable manner.

As amended in 1990.

§2A–525. Lessor's Right to Possession of Goods

(1) If a lessor discovers the lessee to be insolvent, the lessor may refuse to deliver the goods.

(2) After a default by the lessee under the lease contract of the type described in Section 2A–523(1) or 2A–523(3)(a) or, if agreed, after other default by the lessee, the lessor has the right to take possession of the goods. If the lease contract so provides, the lessor may require the lessee to assemble the goods and make them available to the lessor at a place to be designated by the lessor which is reasonably convenient to both parties. Without removal, the lessor may render unusable any goods employed in trade or business, and may dispose of goods on the lessee's premises (Section 2A–527).

(3) The lessor may proceed under subsection (2) without judicial process if it can be done without breach of the peace or the lessor may proceed by action.

As amended in 1990.

§2A–526. Lessor's Stoppage of Delivery in Transit or Otherwise

(1) A lessor may stop delivery of goods in the possession of a carrier or other bailee if the lessor discovers the lessee to be insolvent and may stop delivery of carload, truckload, planeload, or larger shipments of express or freight if the lessee repudiates or fails to make a payment due before delivery, whether for rent, security or otherwise under the lease contract, or for any other reason the lessor has a right to withhold or take possession of the goods.

(2) In pursuing its remedies under subsection (1), the lessor may stop delivery until

(a) receipt of the goods by the lessee;

(b) acknowledgment to the lessee by any bailee of the goods, except a carrier, that the bailee holds the goods for the lessee; or

(c) such an acknowledgement to the lessee by a carrier via reshipment or as warehouseman.

(3)(a) To stop delivery, a lessor shall so notify as to enable the bailee by reasonable diligence to prevent delivery of the goods.

(b) After notification, the bailee shall hold and deliver the goods according to the directions of the lessor, but the lessor is liable to the bailee for any ensuing charges or damages.

(c) A carrier who has issued a nonnegotiable bill of lading is not obliged to obey a notification to stop received from a person other than the consignor.

§2A–527. Lessor's Rights to Dispose of Goods

(1) After a default by a lessee under the lease contract of the type described in Section 2A–523(1) or 2A–523(3)(a) or after the lessor refuses to deliver or takes possession of goods (Section 2A–525 or 2A–526), or, if agreed, after other default by a lessee, the lessor may dispose of the goods concerned or the undelivered balance thereof by lease, sale, or otherwise.

(2) Except as otherwise provided with respect to damages liquidated in the lease agreement (Section 2A–504) or

otherwise determined pursuant to agreement of the parties (Sections 1–102(3) and 2A–503), if the disposition is by lease agreement substantially similar to the original lease agreement and the new lease agreement is made in good faith and in a commercially reasonable manner, the lessor may recover from the lessee as damages (i) accrued and unpaid rent as of the date of the commencement of the term of the new lease agreement, (ii) the present value, as of the same date, of the total rent for the then remaining lease term of the original lease agreement minus the present value, as of the same date, of the rent under the new lease agreement applicable to that period of the new lease term which is comparable to the then remaining term of the original lease agreement, and (iii) any incidental damages allowed under Section 2A–530, less expenses saved in consequence of the lessee's default.

(3) If the lessor's disposition is by lease agreement that for any reason does not qualify for treatment under subsection (2), or is by sale or otherwise, the lessor may recover from the lessee as if the lessor had elected not to dispose of the goods and Section 2A–528 governs.

(4) A subsequent buyer or lessee who buys or leases from the lessor in good faith for value as a result of a disposition under this section takes the goods free of the original lease contract and any rights of the original lessee even though the lessor fails to comply with one or more of the requirements of this Article.

(5) The lessor is not accountable to the lessee for any profit made on any disposition. A lessee who has rightfully rejected or justifiably revoked acceptance shall account to the lessor for any excess over the amount of the lessee's security interest (Section 2A–508(5)).

As amended in 1990.

§2A–528. Lessor's Damages for Non-acceptance, Failure to Pay, Repudiation, or Other Default

(1) Except as otherwise provided with respect to damages liquidated in the lease agreement (Section 2A–504) or otherwise determined pursuant to agreement of the parties (Sections 1–102(3) and 2A–503), if a lessor elects to retain the goods or a lessor elects to dispose of the goods and the disposition is by lease agreement that for any reason does not qualify for treatment under Section 2A–527(2), or is by sale or otherwise, the lessor may recover from the lessee as damages for a default of the type described in Section 2A–523(1) or 2A–523(3)(a), or, if agreed, for other default of the lessee, (i) accrued and unpaid rent as of the date of default if the lessee has never taken possession of the goods, or, if the lessee has taken possession of the goods, as of the date the lessor repossesses the goods or an earlier date on which the lessee makes a tender of the goods to the lessor, (ii) the present value as of the date determined under clause (i) of the total rent for the then remaining lease term of the original

lease agreement minus the present value as of the same date of the market rent at the place where the goods are located computed for the same lease term, and (iii) any incidental damages allowed under Section 2A–530, less expenses saved in consequence of the lessee's default.

(2) If the measure of damages provided in subsection (1) is inadequate to put a lessor in as good a position as performance would have, the measure of damages is the present value of the profit, including reasonable overhead, the lessor would have made from full performance by the lessee, together with any incidental damages allowed under Section 2A–530, due allowance for costs reasonably incurred and due credit for payments or proceeds of disposition.

As amended in 1990.

§2A–529. Lessor's Action for the Rent

(1) After default by the lessee under the lease contract of the type described in Section 2A–523(1) or 2A–523(3)(a) or, if agreed, after other default by the lessee, if the lessor complies with subsection (2), the lessor may recover from the lessee as damages:

(a) for goods accepted by the lessee and not repossessed by or tendered to the lessor, and for conforming goods lost or damaged within a commercially reasonable time after risk of loss passes to the lessee (Section 2A–219), (i) accrued and unpaid rent as of the date of entry of judgment in favor of the lessor, (ii) the present value as of the same date of the rent for the then remaining lease term of the lease agreement, and (iii) any incidental damages allowed under Section 2A–530, less expenses saved in consequence of the lessee's default; and

(b) for goods identified to the lease contract if the lessor is unable after reasonable effort to dispose of them at a reasonable price or the circumstances reasonably indicate that effort will be unavailing, (i) accrued and unpaid rent as of the date of entry of judgment in favor of the lessor, (ii) the present value as of the same date of the rent for the then remaining lease term of the lease agreement, and (iii) any incidental damages allowed under Section 2A–530, less expenses saved in consequence of the lessee's default.

(2) Except as provided in subsection (3), the lessor shall hold for the lessee for the remaining lease term of the lease agreement any goods that have been identified to the lease contract and are in the lessor's control.

(3) The lessor may dispose of the goods at any time before collection of the judgment for damages obtained pursuant to subsection (1). If the disposition is before the end of the remaining lease term of the lease agreement, the lessor's recovery against the lessee for damages is governed by Section 2A–527 or Section 2A–528, and the lessor will cause an appropriate credit to be provided against a judgment for damages to the extent that the amount of the judgment exceeds the recovery available

pursuant to Section 2A–527 or 2A–528.

(4) Payment of the judgment for damages obtained pursuant to subsection (1) entitles the lessee to the use and possession of the goods not then disposed of for the remaining lease term of and in accordance with the lease agreement.

(5) After default by the lessee under the lease contract of the type described in Section 2A–523(1) or Section 2A–523(3)(a) or, if agreed, after other default by the lessee, a lessor who is held not entitled to rent under this section must nevertheless be awarded damages for non-acceptance under Section 2A–527 or Section 2A–528.
As amended in 1990.

§2A–530. Lessor's Incidental Damages

Incidental damages to an aggrieved lessor include any commercially reasonable charges, expenses, or commissions incurred in stopping delivery, in the transportation, care and custody of goods after the lessee's default, in connection with return or disposition of the goods, or otherwise resulting from the default.

§2A–531. Standing to Sue Third Parties for Injury to Goods

(1) If a third party so deals with goods that have been identified to a lease contract as to cause actionable injury to a party to the lease contract (a) the lessor has a right of action against the third party, and (b) the lessee also has a right of action against the third party if the lessee:

  (i) has a security interest in the goods;

  (ii) has an insurable interest in the goods; or

  (iii) bears the risk of loss under the lease contract or has since the injury assumed that risk as against the lessor and the goods have been converted or destroyed.

(2) If at the time of the injury the party plaintiff did not bear the risk of loss as against the other party to the lease contract and there is no arrangement between them for disposition of the recovery, his [or her] suit or settlement, subject to his [or her] own interest, is as a fiduciary for the other party to the lease contract.

(3) Either party with the consent of the other may sue for the benefit of whom it may concern.

§2A–532. Lessor's Rights to Residual Interest

In addition to any other recovery permitted by this Article or other law, the lessor may recover from the lessee an amount that will fully compensate the lessor for any loss of or damage to the lessor's residual interest in the goods caused by the default of the lessee.
As added in 1990.

[REVISED] ARTICLE 3 NEGOTIABLE INSTRUMENTS

Part 1 General Provisions and Definitions

§ 3–101. Short Title

This Article may be cited as Uniform Commercial Code—Negotiable Instruments.

§ 3–102. Subject Matter

(a) This Article applies to negotiable instruments. It does not apply to money, to payment orders governed by Article 4A, or to securities governed by Article 8.

(b) If there is conflict between this Article and Article 4 or 9, Articles 4 and 9 govern.

(c) Regulations of the Board of Governors of the Federal Reserve System and operating circulars of the Federal Reserve Banks supersede any inconsistent provision of this Article to the extent of the inconsistency.

§ 3–103. Definitions

(a) In this Article:

  (1) "Acceptor" means a drawee who has accepted a draft.

  (2) "Drawee" means a person ordered in a draft to make payment.

  (3) "Drawer" means a person who signs or is identified in a draft as a person ordering payment.

  (4) "Good faith" means honesty in fact and the observance of reasonable commercial standards of fair dealing.

  (5) "Maker" means a person who signs or is identified in a note as a person undertaking to pay.

  (6) "Order" means a written instruction to pay money signed by the person giving the instruction. The instruction may be addressed to any person, including the person giving the instruction, or to one or more persons jointly or in the alternative but not in succession. An authorization to pay is not an order unless the person authorized to pay is also instructed to pay.

  (7) "Ordinary care" in the case of a person engaged in business means observance of reasonable commercial standards, prevailing in the area in which the person is located, with respect to the business in which the person is engaged. In the case of a bank that takes an instrument for processing for collection or payment by automated means, reasonable commercial standards do not require the bank to examine the instrument if the failure to examine does not violate the bank's prescribed procedures and the bank's

procedures do not vary unreasonably from general banking usage not disapproved by this Article or Article 4.

(8) "Party" means a party to an instrument.

(9) "Promise" means a written undertaking to pay money signed by the person undertaking to pay. An acknowledgement of an obligation by the obligor is not a promise unless the obligor also undertakes to pay the obligation.

(10) "Prove" with respect to a fact means to meet the burden of establishing the fact (Section 1–201(8)).

(11) "Remitter" means a person who purchases an instrument from its issuer if the instrument is payable to an identified person other than the purchaser.

(b) Other definitions applying to this Article and the sections in which they appear are:

"Acceptance"	Section 3–409
"Accommodated party"	Section 3–419
"Accommodation party"	Section 3–419
"Alteration"	Section 3–407
"Anomalous indorsement"	Section 3–205
"Blank indorsement"	Section 3–205
"Cashier's check"	Section 3–104
"Certificate of Deposit"	Section 3–104
"Certified check"	Section 3–409
"Check"	Section 3–104
"Consideration"	Section 3–303
"Draft"	Section 3–104
"Holder in due course"	Section 3–302
"Incomplete instrument"	Section 3–115
"Indorsement"	Section 3–204
"Indorser"	Section 3–204
"Instrument"	Section 3–104
"Issue"	Section 3–105
"Issuer"	Section 3–105
"Negotiable instrument"	Section 3–104
"Negotiation"	Section 3–201
"Note"	Section 3–104
"Payable at a definite time"	Section 3–108
"Payable on demand"	Section 3–108
"Payable to bearer"	Section 3–109
"Payable to order"	Section 3–109
"Payment"	Section 3–602
"Person entitled to enforce"	Section 3–301
"Presentment"	Section 3–501
"Reacquisition"	Section 3–207
"Special indorsement"	Section 3–205
"Teller's check"	Section 3–104
"Transfer of instrument"	Section 3–203
"Traveler's check"	Section 3–104
"Value"	Section 3–303

(c) The following definitions in other Articles apply to this Article:

"Bank"	Section 4–105
"Banking day"	Section 4–104
"Clearing house"	Section 4–104
"Collecting bank"	Section 4–105
"Depositary bank"	Section 4–105
"Documentary draft"	Section 4–104
"Intermediary bank"	Section 4–105
"Item"	Section 4–104
"Payor bank"	Section 4–105
"Suspends payments"	Section 4–104

(d) In addition, Article 1 contains general definitions and principles of construction and interpretation applicable throughout this Article.

§3–104. Negotiable Instrument

(a) Except as provided in subsections (c) and (d), "negotiable instrument" means an unconditional promise or order to pay a fixed amount of money, with or without interest or other charges described in the promise or order, if it:

(1) is payable to bearer or to order at the time it is issued or first comes into possession of a holder;

(2) is payable on demand or at a definite time; and

(3) does not state any other undertaking or instruction by the person promising or ordering payment to do any act in addition to the payment of money, but the promise or order may contain (i) an undertaking or power to give, maintain, or protect collateral to secure payment, (ii) an authorization or power to the holder to confess judgment or realize on or dispose of collateral, or (iii) a waiver of the benefit of any law intended for the advantage or protection of an obligor.

(b) "Instrument" means a negotiable instrument.

(c) An order that meets all of the requirements of subsection (a), except paragraph (1), and otherwise falls within the definition of "check" in subsection (f) is a negotiable instrument and a check.

(d) A promise or order other than a check is not an instrument if, at the time it is issued or first comes into possession of a holder, it contains a conspicuous statement, however expressed, to the effect that the promise or order is not negotiable or is not an instrument governed by this Article.

(e) An instrument is a "note" if it is a promise and is a "draft" if it is an order. If an instrument falls within the definition of both "note" and "draft," a person entitled to enforce the instrument may treat it as either.

(f) "Check" means (i) a draft, other than a documentary draft, payable on demand and drawn on a bank or (ii) a cashier's check or teller's check. An instrument may be a check even though it is described on its face by another term, such as "money order."

(g) "Cashier's check" means a draft with respect to which the drawer and drawee are the same bank or branches of the same bank.

(h) "Teller's check" means a draft drawn by a bank (i) on another bank, or (ii) payable at or through a bank.

(i) "Traveler's check" means an instrument that (i) is payable on demand, (ii) is drawn on or payable at or through a bank, (iii) is designated by the term "traveler's check" or by a substantially similar term, and (iv) requires, as a condition to payment, a countersignature by a person whose specimen signature appears on the instrument.

(j) "Certificate of deposit" means an instrument containing an acknowledgment by a bank that a sum of money has been received by the bank and a promise by the bank to repay the sum of money. A certificate of deposit is a note of the bank.

§3–105. Issue of Instrument

(a) "Issue" means the first delivery of an instrument by the maker or drawer, whether to a holder or nonholder, for the purpose of giving rights on the instrument to any person.

(b) An unissued instrument, or an unissued incomplete instrument that is completed, is binding on the maker or drawer, but nonissuance is a defense. An instrument that is conditionally issued or is issued for a special purpose is binding on the maker or drawer, but failure of the condition or special purpose to be fulfilled is a defense.

(c) "Issuer" applies to issued and unissued instruments and means a maker or drawer of an instrument.

§3–106. Unconditional Promise or Order

(a) Except as provided in this section, for the purposes of Section 3–104(a), a promise or order is unconditional unless it states (i) an express condition to payment, (ii) that the promise or order is subject to or governed by another writing, or (iii) that rights or obligations with respect to the promise or order are stated in another writing. A reference to another writing does not of itself make the promise or order conditional.

(b) A promise or order is not made conditional (i) by a reference to another writing for a statement of rights with respect to collateral, prepayment, or acceleration, or (ii) because payment is limited to resort to a particular fund or source.

(c) If a promise or order requires, as a condition to payment, a countersignature by a person whose specimen signature appears on the promise or order, the condition does not make the promise or order conditional for the purposes of Section 3–104(a). If the person whose specimen signature appears on an instrument fails to countersign the instrument, the failure to countersign is a defense to the obligation of the issuer, but the failure does not prevent a transferee of the instrument from becoming a holder of the instrument.

(d) If a promise or order at the time it is issued or first comes into possession of a holder contains a statement, required by applicable statutory or administrative law, to the effect that the rights of a holder or transferee are subject to claims or defenses that the issuer could assert against the original payee, the promise or order is not thereby made conditional for the purposes of Section 3–104(a); but if the promise or order is an instrument, there cannot be a holder in due course of the instrument.

§3–107. Instrument Payable in Foreign Money

Unless the instrument otherwise provides, an instrument that states the amount payable in foreign money may be paid in the foreign money or in an equivalent amount in dollars calculated by using the current bank-offered spot rate at the place of payment for the purchase of dollars on the day on which the instrument is paid.

§3–108. Payable on Demand or at Definite Time

(a) A promise or order is "payable on demand" if it (i) states that it is payable on demand or at sight, or otherwise indicates that it is payable at the will of the holder, or (ii) does not state any time of payment.

(b) A promise or order is "payable at a definite time" if it is payable on elapse of a definite period of time after sight or acceptance or at a fixed date or dates or at a time or times readily ascertainable at the time the promise or order is issued, subject to rights of (i) prepayment, (ii) acceleration, (iii) extension at the option of the holder, or (iv) extension to a further definite time at the option of the maker or acceptor or automatically upon or after a specified act or event.

(c) If an instrument, payable at a fixed date, is also payable upon demand made before the fixed date, the instrument is payable on demand until the fixed date and, if demand for payment is not made before that date, becomes payable at a definite time on the fixed date.

§3–109. Payable to Bearer or to Order

(a) A promise or order is payable to bearer if it:
(1) states that it is payable to bearer or to the order of bearer or otherwise indicates that the person in possession of the promise or order is entitled to payment;
(2) does not state a payee; or
(3) states that it is payable to or to the order of cash or otherwise indicates that it is not payable to an identified person.

(b) A promise or order that is not payable to bearer is payable to order if it is payable (i) to the order of an identified person or (ii) to an identified person or order. A promise or order that is payable to order is payable to the identified person.

(c) An instrument payable to bearer may become payable to an identified person if it is specially indorsed pursuant to Section 3–205(a). An instrument payable to an identified person may become payable to bearer if it is indorsed in blank pursuant to Section 3–205(b).

§3–110. Identification of Person to Whom Instrument Is Payable

(a) The person to whom an instrument is initially payable is determined by the intent of the person, whether or not authorized, signing as, or in the name or behalf of, the issuer of the instrument. The instrument is payable to the person intended by the signer even if that person is identified in the instrument by a name or other identification that is not that of the intended person. If more than one person signs in the name or behalf of the issuer of an instrument and all the signers do not intend the same person as payee, the instrument is payable to any person intended by one or more of the signers.

(b) If the signature of the issuer of an instrument is made by automated means, such as a check-writing machine, the payee of the instrument is determined by the intent of the person who supplied the name or identification of the payee, whether or not authorized to do so.

(c) A person to whom an instrument is payable may be identified in any way, including by name, identifying number, office, or account number. For the purpose of determining the holder of an instrument, the following rules apply:

(1) If an instrument is payable to an account and the account is identified only by number, the instrument is payable to the person to whom the account is payable. If an instrument is payable to an account identified by number and by the name of a person, the instrument is payable to the named person, whether or not that person is the owner of the account identified by number.

(2) If an instrument is payable to:
  (i) a trust, an estate, or a person described as trustee or representative of a trust or estate, the instrument is payable to the trustee, the representative, or a successor of either, whether or not the beneficiary or estate is also named;
  (ii) a person described as agent or similar representative of a named or identified person, the instrument is payable to the represented person, the representative, or a successor of the representative;
  (iii) a fund or organization that is not a legal entity, the instrument is payable to a representative of the members of the fund or organization; or
  (iv) an office or to a person described as holding an office, the instrument is payable to the named person, the incumbent of the office, or a successor to the incumbent.

(d) If an instrument is payable to two or more persons alternatively, it is payable to any of them and may be negotiated, discharged, or enforced by any or all of them in possession of the instrument. If an instrument is payable to two or more persons not alternatively, it is payable to all of them and may be negotiated, discharged, or enforced only by all of them. If an instrument payable to two or more persons is ambiguous as to whether it is payable to the persons alternatively, the instrument is payable to the persons alternatively.

§3–111. Place of Payment

Except as otherwise provided for items in Article 4, an instrument is payable at the place of payment stated in the instrument. If no place of payment is stated, an instrument is payable at the address of the drawee or maker stated in the instrument. If no address is stated, the place of payment is the place of business of the drawee or maker. If a drawee or maker has more than one place of business, the place of payment is any place of business of the drawee or maker chosen by the person entitled to enforce the instrument. If the drawee or maker has no place of business, the place of payment is the residence of the drawee or maker.

§3–112. Interest

(a) Unless otherwise provided in the instrument, (i) an instrument is not payable with interest, and (ii) interest on an interest-bearing instrument is payable from the date of the instrument.

(b) Interest may be stated in an instrument as a fixed or variable amount of money or it may be expressed as a fixed or variable rate or rates. The amount or rate of interest may be stated or described in the instrument in any manner and may require reference to information not contained in the instrument. If an instrument provides for interest, but the amount of interest payable cannot be ascertained from the description, interest is payable at the judgment rate in effect at the place of payment of the instrument and at the time interest first accrues.

§3–113. Date of Instrument

(a) An instrument may be antedated or postdated. The date stated determines the time of payment if the instrument is payable at a fixed period after date. Except as provided in Section 4–401(c), an instrument payable on demand is not payable before the date of the instrument.

(b) If an instrument is undated, its date is the date of its issue or, in the case of an unissued instrument, the date it first comes into possession of a holder.

§3–114. Contradictory Terms of Instrument

If an instrument contains contradictory terms, typewritten terms prevail over printed terms, handwritten terms prevail over both, and words prevail over numbers.

§3–115. Incomplete Instrument

(a) "Incomplete instrument" means a signed writing, whether or not issued by the signer, the contents of which show at the time of signing that it is incomplete but that the signer intended it to be completed by the addition of words or numbers.

(b) Subject to subsection (c), if an incomplete instrument is an instrument under Section 3–104, it may be enforced according to its terms if it is not completed, or according to its terms as augmented by completion. If an incomplete instrument is not an instrument under Section 3–104, but, after completion, the requirements of Section 3–104 are met, the instrument may be enforced according to its terms as augmented by completion.

(c) If words or numbers are added to an incomplete instrument without authority of the signer, there is an alteration of the incomplete instrument under Section 3–407.

(d) The burden of establishing that words or numbers were added to an incomplete instrument without authority of the signer is on the person asserting the lack of authority.

§3–116. Joint and Several Liability; Contribution

(a) Except as otherwise provided in the instrument, two or more persons who have the same liability on an instrument as makers, drawers, acceptors, indorsers who indorse as joint payees, or anomalous indorsers are jointly and severally liable in the capacity in which they sign.

(b) Except as provided in Section 3–419(e) or by agreement of the affected parties, a party having joint and several liability who pays the instrument is entitled to receive from any party having the same joint and several liability contribution in accordance with applicable law.

(c) Discharge of one party having joint and several liability by a person entitled to enforce the instrument does not affect the right under subsection (b) of a party having the same joint and several liability to receive contribution from the party discharged.

§3–117. Other Agreements Affecting Instrument

Subject to applicable law regarding exclusion of proof of contemporaneous or previous agreements, the obligation of a party to an instrument to pay the instrument may be modified, supplemented, or nullified by a separate agreement of the obligor and a person entitled to enforce the instrument, if the instrument is issued or the obligation is incurred in reliance on the agreement or as part of the same transaction giving rise to the agreement. To the extent an obligation is modified, supplemented, or nullified by an agreement under this section, the agreement is a defense to the obligation.

§3–118. Statute of Limitations

(a) Except as provided in subsection (e), an action to enforce the obligation of a party to pay a note payable at a definite time must be commenced within six years after the due date or dates stated in the note or, if a due date is accelerated, within six years after the accelerated due date.

(b) Except as provided in subsection (d) or (e), if demand for payment is made to the maker of a note payable on demand, an action to enforce the obligation of a party to pay the note must be commenced within six years after the demand. If no demand for payment is made to the maker, an action to enforce the note is barred if neither principal nor interest on the note has been paid for a continuous period of 10 years.

(c) Except as provided in subsection (d), an action to enforce the obligation of a party to an unaccepted draft to pay the draft must be commenced within three years after dishonor of the draft or 10 years after the date of the draft, whichever period expires first.

(d) An action to enforce the obligation of the acceptor of a certified check or the issuer of a teller's check, cashier's check, or traveler's check must be commenced within three years after demand for payment is made to the acceptor or issuer, as the case may be.

(e) An action to enforce the obligation of a party to a certificate of deposit to pay the instrument must be commenced within six years after demand for payment is made to the maker, but if the instrument states a due date and the maker is not required to pay before that date, the six-year period begins when a demand for payment is in effect and the due date has passed.

(f) An action to enforce the obligation of a party to pay an accepted draft, other than a certified check, must be commenced (i) within six years after the due date or dates stated in the draft or acceptance if the obligation of the acceptor is payable at a definite time, or (ii) within six years after the date of the acceptance if the obligation of the acceptor is payable on demand.

(g) Unless governed by other law regarding claims for indemnity or contribution, an action (i) for conversion of an instrument, for money had and received, or like action based on conversion, (ii) for breach of warranty, or (iii) to enforce an obligation, duty, or right arising under this Article and not governed by this section must be commenced within three years after the [cause of action] accrues.

§3–119. Notice of Right to Defend Action

In an action for breach of an obligation for which a third person is answerable over pursuant to this Article or Article 4, the defendant may give the third person written notice of the litigation, and the person notified may then give similar notice to any other person who is answerable over. If the notice states (i) that the person notified may come in and defend and (ii) that failure to do so will bind the person notified in an action later brought by the person giving the notice as to any determination of fact common to the two litigations, the person notified is so bound unless after seasonable receipt of the notice the person notified does come in and defend.

Part 2 Negotiation, Transfer, and Indorsement

§3–201. Negotiation

(a) "Negotiation" means a transfer of possession, whether voluntary or involuntary, of an instrument by a person other than the issuer to a person who thereby becomes its holder.

(b) Except for negotiation by a remitter, if an instrument is payable to an identified person, negotiation requires transfer of possession of the instrument and its indorsement by the holder. If an instrument is payable to bearer, it may be negotiated by transfer of possession alone.

§3–202. Negotiation Subject to Rescission

(a) Negotiation is effective even if obtained (i) from an infant, a corporation exceeding its powers, or a person without capacity, (ii) by fraud, duress, or mistake, or (iii) in breach of duty or as part of an illegal transaction.

(b) To the extent permitted by other law, negotiation may be rescinded or may be subject to other remedies, but those remedies may not be asserted against a subsequent holder in due course or a person paying the instrument in good faith and without knowledge of facts that are a basis for rescission or other remedy.

§3–203. Transfer of Instrument; Rights Acquired by Transfer

(a) An instrument is transferred when it is delivered by a person other than its issuer for the purpose of giving to the person receiving delivery the right to enforce the instrument.

(b) Transfer of an instrument, whether or not the transfer is a negotiation, vests in the transferee any right of the transferor to enforce the instrument, including any right as a holder in due course, but the transferee cannot acquire rights of a holder in due course by a transfer, directly or indirectly, from a holder in due course if the transferee engaged in fraud or illegality affecting the instrument.

(c) Unless otherwise agreed, if an instrument is transferred for value and the transferee does not become a holder because of lack of indorsement by the transferor, the transferee has a specifically enforceable right to the unqualified indorsement of the transferor, but negotiation of the instrument does not occur until the indorsement is made.

(d) If a transfer purports to transfer less than the entire instrument, negotiation of the instrument does not occur. The transferee obtains no rights under this Article and has only the rights of a partial assignee.

§3–204. Indorsement

(a) "Indorsement" means a signature, other than that of a signer as maker, drawer, or acceptor, that alone or accompanied by other words is made on an instrument for the purpose of (i) negotiating the instrument, (ii) restricting payment of the instrument, or (iii) incurring indorser's liability on the instrument, but regardless of the intent of the signer, a signature and its accompanying words is an indorsement unless the accompanying words, terms of the instrument, place of the signature, or other circumstances unambiguously indicate that the signature was made for a purpose other than indorsement. For the purpose of determining whether a signature is made on an instrument, a paper affixed to the instrument is a part of the instrument.

(b) "Indorser" means a person who makes an indorsement.

(c) For the purpose of determining whether the transferee of an instrument is a holder, an indorsement that transfers a security interest in the instrument is effective as an unqualified indorsement of the instrument.

(d) If an instrument is payable to a holder under a name that is not the name of the holder, indorsement may be made by the holder in the name stated in the instrument or in the holder's name or both, but signature in both names may be required by a person paying or taking the instrument for value or collection.

§3–205. Special Indorsement; Blank Indorsement; Anomalous Indorsement

(a) If an indorsement is made by the holder of an instrument, whether payable to an identified person or payable to bearer, and the indorsement identifies a person to whom it makes the instrument payable, it is a "special indorsement." When specially indorsed, an instrument becomes payable to the identified person and may be negotiated only by the indorsement of that person. The principles stated in Section 3–110 apply to special indorsements.

(b) If an indorsement is made by the holder of an instrument and it is not a special indorsement, it is a "blank indorsement." When indorsed in blank, an instrument becomes payable to bearer and may be negotiated by transfer of possession alone until specially indorsed.

(c) The holder may convert a blank indorsement that consists only of a signature into a special indorsement by writing, above the signature of the indorser, words identifying the person to whom the instrument is made payable.

(d) "Anomalous indorsement" means an indorsement made by a person who is not the holder of the instrument. An anomalous indorsement does not affect the manner in which the instrument may be negotiated.

§3–206. Restrictive Indorsement

(a) An indorsement limiting payment to a particular person or otherwise prohibiting further transfer or negotiation of the instrument is not effective to prevent further transfer or negotiation of the instrument.

(b) An indorsement stating a condition to the right of the indorsee to receive payment does not affect the right of the indorsee to enforce the instrument. A person paying the instrument or taking it for value or collection may disregard the condition, and the rights and liabilities of that person are not affected by whether the condition has been fulfilled.

(c) If an instrument bears an indorsement (i) described in Section 4–201(b), or (ii) in blank or to a particular bank using the words "for deposit," "for collection," or other words indicating a purpose of having the instrument collected by a bank for the indorser or for a particular account, the following rules apply:

(1) A person, other than a bank, who purchases the instrument when so indorsed converts the instrument unless the amount paid for the instrument is received by the indorser or applied consistently with the indorsement.

(2) A depositary bank that purchases the instrument or takes it for collection when so indorsed converts the instrument unless the amount paid by the bank with respect to the instrument is received by the indorser or applied consistently with the indorsement.

(3) A payor bank that is also the depositary bank or that takes the instrument for immediate payment over the counter from a person other than a collecting bank converts the instrument unless the proceeds of the instrument are received by the indorser or applied consistently with the indorsement.

(4) Except as otherwise provided in paragraph (3), a payor bank or intermediary bank may disregard the indorsement and is not liable if the proceeds of the instrument are not received by the indorser or applied consistently with the indorsement.

(d) Except for an indorsement covered by subsection (c), if an instrument bears an indorsement using words to the effect that payment is to be made to the indorsee as agent, trustee, or other fiduciary for the benefit of the indorser or another person, the following rules apply:

(1) Unless there is notice of breach of fiduciary duty as provided in Section 3–307, a person who purchases the instrument from the indorsee or takes the instrument from the indorsee for collection or payment may pay the proceeds of payment or the value given for the instrument to the indorsee without regard to whether the indorsee violates a fiduciary duty to the indorser.

(2) A subsequent transferee of the instrument or person who pays the instrument is neither given notice nor otherwise affected by the restriction in the indorsement unless the transferee or payor knows that the fiduciary dealt with the instrument or its proceeds in breach of fiduciary duty.

(e) The presence on an instrument of an indorsement to which this section applies does not prevent a purchaser of the instrument from becoming a holder in due course of the instrument unless the purchaser is a converter under subsection (c) or has notice or knowledge of breach of fiduciary duty as stated in subsection (d).

(f) In an action to enforce the obligation of a party to pay the instrument, the obligor has a defense if payment would violate an indorsement to which this section applies and the payment is not permitted by this section.

§3–207. Reacquisition

Reacquisition of an instrument occurs if it is transferred to a former holder, by negotiation or otherwise. A former holder who reacquires the instrument may cancel indorsements made after the reacquirer first became a holder of the instrument. If the cancellation causes the instrument to be payable to the reacquirer or to bearer, the reacquirer may negotiate the instrument. An indorser whose indorsement is canceled is discharged, and the discharge is effective against any subsequent holder.

Part 3 Enforcement of Instruments

§3–301. Person Entitled to Enforce Instrument

"Person entitled to enforce" an instrument means (i) the holder of the instrument, (ii) a nonholder in possession of the instrument who has the rights of a holder, or (iii) a person not in possession of the instrument who is entitled to enforce the instrument pursuant to Section 3–309 or 3–418(d). A person may be a person entitled to enforce the instrument even though the person is not the owner of the instrument or is in wrongful possession of the instrument.

§3–302. Holder in Due Course

(a) Subject to subsection (c) and Section 3–106(d), "holder in due course" means the holder of an instrument if:

(1) the instrument when issued or negotiated to the holder does not bear such apparent evidence of forgery or alteration or is not otherwise so irregular or incomplete as to call into question its authenticity; and

(2) the holder took the instrument (i) for value, (ii) in good faith, (iii) without notice that the instrument is overdue or has been dishonored or that there is an uncured default with respect to payment of another instrument issued as part of the same series, (iv) without notice that the instrument contains an unauthorized signature or has been altered, (v) without notice of any claim to the instrument described in Section 3–306, and (vi) without notice that any party has a defense or claim in recoupment described in Section 3–305(a).

(b) Notice of discharge of a party, other than discharge in an insolvency proceeding, is not notice of a defense under subsection (a), but discharge is effective against a person who became a holder in due course with notice of the discharge. Public filing or recording of a document does not of itself constitute notice of a defense, claim in recoupment, or claim to the instrument.

(c) Except to the extent a transferor or predecessor in interest has rights as a holder in due course, a person does not acquire rights of a holder in due course of an instrument taken (i) by legal process or by purchase in an execution, bankruptcy, or creditor's sale or similar proceeding, (ii) by purchase as part of a bulk transaction not in ordinary course of business of the transferor, or (iii) as the successor in interest to an estate or other organization.

(d) If, under Section 3–303(a)(1), the promise of performance that is the consideration for an instrument has been partially performed, the holder may assert rights as a holder in due course of the instrument only to the fraction of the amount payable under the instrument equal to the value of the partial performance divided by the value of the promised performance.

(e) If (i) the person entitled to enforce an instrument has only a security interest in the instrument and (ii) the person obliged to pay the instrument has a defense, claim in recoupment, or claim to the instrument that may be asserted against the person who granted the security interest, the person entitled to enforce the instrument may assert rights as a holder in due course only to an amount payable under the instrument which, at the time of enforcement of the instrument, does not exceed the amount of the unpaid obligation secured.

(f) To be effective, notice must be received at a time and in a manner that gives a reasonable opportunity to act on it.

(g) This section is subject to any law limiting status as a holder in due course in particular classes of transactions.

§3–303. Value and Consideration

(a) An instrument is issued or transferred for value if:

(1) the instrument is issued or transferred for a promise of performance, to the extent the promise has been performed;

(2) the transferee acquires a security interest or other lien in the instrument other than a lien obtained by judicial proceeding;

(3) the instrument is issued or transferred as payment of, or as security for, an antecedent claim against any person, whether or not the claim is due;

(4) the instrument is issued or transferred in exchange for a negotiable instrument; or

(5) the instrument is issued or transferred in exchange for the incurring of an irrevocable obligation to a third party by the person taking the instrument.

(b) "Consideration" means any consideration sufficient to support a simple contract. The drawer or maker of an instrument has a defense if the instrument is issued without consideration. If an instrument is issued for a promise of performance, the issuer has a defense to the extent performance of the promise is due and the promise has not been performed. If an instrument is issued for value as stated in subsection (a), the instrument is also issued for consideration.

§3–304. Overdue Instrument

(a) An instrument payable on demand becomes overdue at the earliest of the following times:

(1) on the day after the day demand for payment is duly made;

(2) if the instrument is a check, 90 days after its date; or

(3) if the instrument is not a check, when the instrument has been outstanding for a period of time after its date which is unreasonably long under the circumstances of the particular case in light of the nature of the instrument and usage of the trade.

(b) With respect to an instrument payable at a definite time the following rules apply:

(1) If the principal is payable in installments and a due date has not been accelerated, the instrument becomes overdue upon default under the instrument for nonpayment of an installment, and the instrument remains overdue until the default is cured.

(2) If the principal is not payable in installments and the due date has not been accelerated, the instrument becomes overdue on the day after the due date.

(3) If a due date with respect to principal has been accelerated, the instrument becomes overdue on the day after the accelerated due date.

(c) Unless the due date of principal has been accelerated, an instrument does not become overdue if there is default in payment of interest but no default in payment of principal.

§3–305. Defenses and Claims in Recoupment

(a) Except as stated in subsection (b), the right to enforce the obligation of a party to pay an instrument is subject to the following:

(1) a defense of the obligor based on (i) infancy of the obligor to the extent it is a defense to a simple contract, (ii) duress, lack of legal capacity, or illegality of the transaction which, under other law, nullifies the obligation of the obligor, (iii) fraud that induced the obligor to sign the instrument with neither knowledge nor reasonable opportunity to learn of its character or its essential terms, or (iv) discharge of the obligor in insolvency proceedings;

(2) a defense of the obligor stated in another section of this Article or a defense of the obligor that would be available if the person entitled to enforce the instrument were enforcing a right to payment under a simple contract; and

(3) a claim in recoupment of the obligor against the original payee of the instrument if the claim arose from the transaction that gave rise to the instrument; but the claim of the obligor may be asserted against a transferee of the instrument only to reduce the amount owing on the instrument at the time the action is brought.

(b) The right of a holder in due course to enforce the obligation of a party to pay the instrument is subject to defenses of the obligor stated in subsection (a)(1), but is not subject to defenses of the obligor stated in subsection (a)(2) or claims in recoupment stated in subsection (a)(3) against a person other than the holder.

(c) Except as stated in subsection (d), in an action to enforce the obligation of a party to pay the instrument, the obligor may not assert against the person entitled to enforce the instrument a defense, claim in recoupment, or claim to the instrument (Section 3–306) of another person, but the other person's claim to the instrument may be asserted by the obligor if the other person is joined in the action and personally asserts the claim against the person entitled to enforce the instrument. An obligor is not obliged to pay the instrument if the person seeking enforcement of the instrument does not have rights of a holder in due course and the obligor proves that the instrument is a lost or stolen instrument.

(d) In an action to enforce the obligation of an accommodation party to pay an instrument, the accommodation party may assert against the person entitled to enforce the instrument any defense or claim in recoupment under subsection (a) that the accommodated party could assert against the person entitled to enforce the instrument, except the defenses of discharge in insolvency proceedings, infancy, and lack of legal capacity.

§3–306. Claims to an Instrument

A person taking an instrument, other than a person having rights of a holder in due course, is subject to a claim of a property or possessory right in the instrument or its proceeds, including a claim to rescind a negotiation and to recover the instrument or its proceeds. A person having rights of a holder in due course takes free of the claim to the instrument.

§3–307. Notice of Breach of Fiduciary Duty

(a) In this section:

(1) "Fiduciary" means an agent, trustee, partner, corporate officer or director, or other representative owing a fiduciary duty with respect to an instrument.

(2) "Represented person" means the principal, beneficiary, partnership, corporation, or other person to whom the duty stated in paragraph (1) is owed.

(b) If (i) an instrument is taken from a fiduciary for payment or collection or for value, (ii) the taker has knowledge of the fiduciary status of the fiduciary, and (iii) the represented person makes a claim to the instrument or its proceeds on the basis that the transaction of the fiduciary is a breach of fiduciary duty, the following rules apply:

(1) Notice of breach of fiduciary duty by the fiduciary is notice of the claim of the represented person.

(2) In the case of an instrument payable to the represented person or the fiduciary as such, the taker has notice of the breach of fiduciary duty if the instrument is (i) taken in payment of or as security for a debt known by the taker to be the personal debt of the fiduciary, (ii) taken in a transaction known by the taker to be for the personal benefit of the fiduciary, or (iii) deposited to an account other than an account of the fiduciary, as such, or an account of the represented person.

(3) If an instrument is issued by the represented person or the fiduciary as such, and made payable to the fiduciary personally, the taker does not have notice of the breach of fiduciary duty unless the taker knows of the breach of fiduciary duty.

(4) If an instrument is issued by the represented person or the fiduciary as such, to the taker as payee, the taker has notice of the breach of fiduciary duty if the instrument is (i) taken in payment of or as security for a debt known by the taker to be the personal debt of the fiduciary, (ii) taken in a transaction known by the taker to be for the personal benefit of the fiduciary, or (iii) deposited to an account other than an account of the fiduciary, as such, or an account of the represented person.

§3−308. Proof of Signatures and Status as Holder in Due Course

(a) In an action with respect to an instrument, the authenticity of, and authority to make, each signature on the instrument is admitted unless specifically denied in the pleadings. If the validity of a signature is denied in the pleadings, the burden of establishing validity is on the person claiming validity, but the signature is presumed to be authentic and authorized unless the action is to enforce the liability of the purported signer and the signer is dead or incompetent at the time of trial of the issue of validity of the signature. If an action to enforce the instrument is brought against a person as the undisclosed principal of a person who signed the instrument as a party to the instrument, the plaintiff has the burden of establishing that the defendant is liable on the instrument as a represented person under Section 3−402(a).

(b) If the validity of signatures is admitted or proved and there is compliance with subsection (a), a plaintiff producing the instrument is entitled to payment if the plaintiff proves entitlement to enforce the instrument under Section 3−301, unless the defendant proves a defense or claim in recoupment. If a defense or claim in recoupment is proved, the right to payment of the plaintiff is subject to the defense or claim, except to the extent the plaintiff proves that the plaintiff has rights of a holder in due course which are not subject to the defense or claim.

§3−309. Enforcement of Lost, Destroyed, or Stolen Instrument

(a) A person not in possession of an instrument is entitled to enforce the instrument if (i) the person was in possession of the instrument and entitled to enforce it when loss of possession occurred, (ii) the loss of possession was not the result of a transfer by the person or a lawful seizure, and (iii) the person cannot reasonably obtain possession of the instrument because the instrument was destroyed, its whereabouts cannot be determined, or it is in the wrongful possession of an unknown person or a person that cannot be found or is not amenable to service of process.

(b) A person seeking enforcement of an instrument under subsection (a) must prove the terms of the instru-

ment and the person's right to enforce the instrument. If that proof is made, Section 3−308 applies to the case as if the person seeking enforcement had produced the instrument. The court may not enter judgment in favor of the person seeking enforcement unless it finds that the person required to pay the instrument is adequately protected against loss that might occur by reason of a claim by another person to enforce the instrument. Adequate protection may be provided by any reasonable means.

§3−310. Effect of Instrument on Obligation for Which Taken

(a) Unless otherwise agreed, if a certified check, cashier's check, or teller's check is taken for an obligation, the obligation is discharged to the same extent discharge would result if an amount of money equal to the amount of the instrument were taken in payment of the obligation. Discharge of the obligation does not affect any liability that the obligor may have as an indorser of the instrument.

(b) Unless otherwise agreed and except as provided in subsection (a), if a note or an uncertified check is taken for an obligation, the obligation is suspended to the same extent the obligation would be discharged if an amount of money equal to the amount of the instrument were taken, and the following rules apply:

(1) In the case of an uncertified check, suspension of the obligation continues until dishonor of the check or until it is paid or certified. Payment or certification of the check results in discharge of the obligation to the extent of the amount of the check.

(2) In the case of a note, suspension of the obligation continues until dishonor of the note or until it is paid. Payment of the note results in discharge of the obligation to the extent of the payment.

(3) Except as provided in paragraph (4), if the check or note is dishonored and the obligee of the obligation for which the instrument was taken is the person entitled to enforce the instrument, the obligee may enforce either the instrument or the obligation. In the case of an instrument of a third person which is negotiated to the obligee by the obligor, discharge of the obligor on the instrument also discharges the obligation.

(4) If the person entitled to enforce the instrument taken for an obligation is a person other than the obligee, the obligee may not enforce the obligation to the extent the obligation is suspended. If the obligee is the person entitled to enforce the instrument but no longer has possession of it because it was lost, stolen, or destroyed, the obligation may not be enforced to the extent of the amount payable on the instrument, and to that

extent the obligee's rights against the obligor are limited to enforcement of the instrument.

(c) If an instrument other than one described in subsection (a) or (b) is taken for an obligation, the effect is (i) that stated in subsection (a) if the instrument is one on which a bank is liable as maker or acceptor, or (ii) that stated in subsection (b) in any other case.

§3–311. Accord and Satisfaction by Use of Instrument

(a) If a person against whom a claim is asserted proves that (i) that person in good faith tendered an instrument to the claimant as full satisfaction of the claim, (ii) the amount of the claim was unliquidated or subject to a bona fide dispute, and (iii) the claimant obtained payment of the instrument, the following subsections apply.

(b) Unless subsection (c) applies, the claim is discharged if the person against whom the claim is asserted proves that the instrument or an accompanying written communication contained a conspicuous statement to the effect that the instrument was tendered as full satisfaction of the claim.

(c) Subject to subsection (d), a claim is not discharged under subsection (b) if either of the following applies:

(1) The claimant, if an organization, proves that (i) within a reasonable time before the tender, the claimant sent a conspicuous statement to the person against whom the claim is asserted that communications concerning disputed debts, including an instrument tendered as full satisfaction of a debt, are to be sent to a designated person, office, or place, and (ii) the instrument or accompanying communication was not received by that designated person, office, or place.

(2) The claimant, whether or not an organization, proves that within 90 days after payment of the instrument, the claimant tendered repayment of the amount of the instrument to the person against whom the claim is asserted. This paragraph does not apply if the claimant is an organization that sent a statement complying with paragraph (1)(i).

(d) A claim is discharged if the person against whom the claim is asserted proves that within a reasonable time before collection of the instrument was initiated, the claimant, or an agent of the claimant having direct responsibility with respect to the disputed obligation, knew that the instrument was tendered in full satisfaction of the claim.

§3–312. Lost, Destroyed, or Stolen Cashier's Check, Teller's Check, or Certified Check

(a) In this section:

(1) "Check" means a cashier's check, teller's check, or certified check.

(2) "Claimant" means a person who claims the right to receive the amount of a cashier's check, teller's check, or certified check that was lost, destroyed, or stolen.

(3) "Declaration of loss" means a written statement, made under penalty of perjury, to the effect that (i) the declarer lost possession of a check, (ii) the declarer is the drawer or payee of the check, in the case of a certified check, or the remitter or payee of the check, in the case of a cashier's check or teller's check, (iii) the loss of possession was not the result of a transfer by the declarer or a lawful seizure, and (iv) the declarer cannot reasonably obtain possession of the check because the check was destroyed, its whereabouts cannot be determined, or it is in the wrongful possession of an unknown person or a person that cannot be found or is not amenable to service of process.

(4) "Obligated bank" means the issuer of a cashier's check or teller's check or the acceptor of a certified check.

(b) A claimant may assert a claim to the amount of a check by a communication to the obligated bank describing the check with reasonable certainty and requesting payment of the amount of the check, if (i) the claimant is the drawer or payee of a certified check or the remitter or payee of a cashier's check or teller's check, (ii) the communication contains or is accompanied by a declaration of loss of the claimant with respect to the check, (iii) the communication is received at a time and in a manner affording the bank a reasonable time to act on it before the check is paid, and (iv) the claimant provides reasonable identification if requested by the obligated bank. Delivery of a declaration of loss is a warranty of the truth of the statements made in the declaration. The warranty is made to the obligated bank and any person entitled to enforce the check. If a claim is asserted in compliance with this subsection, the following rules apply:

(1) The claim becomes enforceable at the later of (i) the time the claim is asserted, or (ii) the 90th day following the date of the check, in the case of a cashier's check or teller's check, or the 90th day following the date of the acceptance, in the case of a certified check.

(2) Until the claim becomes enforceable, it has no legal effect and the obligated bank may pay the check or, in the case of a teller's check, may permit the drawee to pay the check. Payment to a person entitled to enforce the check discharges all liability of the obligated bank with respect to the check.

(3) If the claim becomes enforceable before the check is presented for payment, the obligated bank is not obligated to pay the check.

(4) When the claim becomes enforceable, the obligated bank becomes obliged to pay the amount of the check to the claimant if payment of the check has not been made to a person entitled to enforce the check. Subject to Section 4–302(a)(1), payment to the claimant discharges all liability of the obligated bank with respect to the check.

(c) If the obligated bank pays the amount of a check to a claimant under subsection (b)(4) and, after the claim became enforceable, the check is presented for payment by a person having rights of a holder in due course, the claimant is obliged to (i) refund the payment to the obligated bank if the check is paid, or (ii) pay the amount of the check to the person having rights of a holder in due course if the check is dishonored.

(d) If a claimant has the right to assert a claim under subsection (b) and is also a person entitled to enforce a cashier's check, teller's check, or certified check which is lost, destroyed, or stolen, the claimant may assert rights with respect to the check either under this section or Section 3–309.

Part 4 Liability of Parties

§3–401. Signature

(a) A person is not liable on an instrument unless (i) the person signed the instrument, or (ii) the person is represented by an agent or representative who signed the instrument and the signature is binding on the represented person under Section 3–402.

(b) A signature may be made (i) manually or by means of a device or machine, and (ii) by the use of any name, including a trade or assumed name, or by a word, mark, or symbol executed or adopted by a person with present intention to authenticate a writing.

§3–402. Signature by Representative

(a) If a person acting, or purporting to act, as a representative signs an instrument by signing either the name of the represented person or the name of the signer, the represented person is bound by the signature to the same extent the represented person would be bound if the signature were on a simple contract. If the represented person is bound, the signature of the representative is the "authorized signature of the represented person" and the represented person is liable on the instrument, whether or not identified in the instrument.

(b) If a representative signs the name of the representative to an instrument and the signature is an authorized signature of the represented person, the following rules apply:

(1) If the form of the signature shows unambiguously that the signature is made on behalf of the repre-

sented person who is identified in the instrument, the representative is not liable on the instrument.

(2) Subject to subsection (c), if (i) the form of the signature does not show unambiguously that the signature is made in a representative capacity or (ii) the represented person is not identified in the instrument, the representative is liable on the instrument to a holder in due course that took the instrument without notice that the representative was not intended to be liable on the instrument. With respect to any other person, the representative is liable on the instrument unless the representative proves that the original parties did not intend the representative to be liable on the instrument.

(c) If a representative signs the name of the representative as drawer of a check without indication of the representative status and the check is payable from an account of the represented person who is identified on the check, the signer is not liable on the check if the signature is an authorized signature of the represented person.

§3–403. Unauthorized Signature

(a) Unless otherwise provided in this Article or Article 4, an unauthorized signature is ineffective except as the signature of the unauthorized signer in favor of a person who in good faith pays the instrument or takes it for value. An unauthorized signature may be ratified for all purposes of this Article.

(b) If the signature of more than one person is required to constitute the authorized signature of an organization, the signature of the organization is unauthorized if one of the required signatures is lacking.

(c) The civil or criminal liability of a person who makes an unauthorized signature is not affected by any provision of this Article which makes the unauthorized signature effective for the purposes of this Article.

§3–404. Impostors; Fictitious Payees

(a) If an imposter, by use of the mails or otherwise, induces the issuer of an instrument to issue the instrument to the imposter, or to a person acting in concert with the imposter, by impersonating the payee of the instrument or a person authorized to act for the payee, an indorsement of the instrument by any person in the name of the payee is effective as the indorsement of the payee in favor of a person who, in good faith, pays the instrument or takes it for value or for collection.

(b) If (i) a person whose intent determines to whom an instrument is payable (Section 3–110(a) or (b)) does not intend the person identified as payee to have any interest in the instrument, or (ii) the person identified as payee of an instrument is a fictitious person, the following rules apply until the instrument is negotiated by special indorsement:

(1) Any person in possession of the instrument is its holder.

(2) An indorsement by any person in the name of the payee stated in the instrument is effective as the indorsement of the payee in favor of a person who, in good faith, pays the instrument or takes it for value or for collection.

(c) Under subsection (a) or (b), an indorsement is made in the name of a payee if (i) it is made in a name substantially similar to that of the payee or (ii) the instrument, whether or not indorsed, is deposited in a depositary bank to an account in a name substantially similar to that of the payee.

(d) With respect to an instrument to which subsection (a) or (b) applies, if a person paying the instrument or taking it for value or for collection fails to exercise ordinary care in paying or taking the instrument and that failure substantially contributes to loss resulting from payment of the instrument, the person bearing the loss may recover from the person failing to exercise ordinary care to the extent the failure to exercise ordinary care contributed to the loss.

§3–405. Employer's Responsibility for Fraudulent Indorsement by Employee

(a) In this section:

(1) "Employee" includes an independent contractor and employee of an independent contractor retained by the employer.

(2) "Fraudulent indorsement" means (i) in the case of an instrument payable to the employer, a forged indorsement purporting to be that of the employer, or (ii) in the case of an instrument with respect to which the employer is the issuer, a forged indorsement purporting to be that of the person identified as payee.

(3) "Responsibility" with respect to instruments means authority (i) to sign or indorse instruments on behalf of the employer, (ii) to process instruments received by the employer for bookkeeping purposes, for deposit to an account, or for other disposition, (iii) to prepare or process instruments for issue in the name of the employer, (iv) to supply information determining the names or addresses of payees of instruments to be issued in the name of the employer, (v) to control the disposition of instruments to be issued in the name of the employer, or (vi) to act otherwise with respect to instruments in a responsible capacity. "Responsibility" does not include authority that merely allows an employee to have access to instruments or blank or incomplete instrument forms that are being stored or transported or are

part of incoming or outgoing mail, or similar access.

(b) For the purpose of determining the rights and liabilities of a person who, in good faith, pays an instrument or takes it for value or for collection, if an employer entrusted an employee with responsibility with respect to the instrument and the employee or a person acting in concert with the employee makes a fraudulent indorsement of the instrument, the indorsement is effective as the indorsement of the person to whom the instrument is payable if it is made in the name of that person. If the person paying the instrument or taking it for value or for collection fails to exercise ordinary care in paying or taking the instrument and that failure substantially contributes to loss resulting from the fraud, the person bearing the loss may recover from the person failing to exercise ordinary care to the extent the failure to exercise ordinary care contributed to the loss.

(c) Under subsection (b), an indorsement is made in the name of the person to whom an instrument is payable if (i) it is made in a name substantially similar to the name of that person or (ii) the instrument, whether or not indorsed, is deposited in a depositary bank to an account in a name substantially similar to the name of that person.

§3–406. Negligence Contributing to Forged Signature or Alteration of Instrument

(a) A person whose failure to exercise ordinary care substantially contributes to an alteration of an instrument or to the making of a forged signature on an instrument is precluded from asserting the alteration or the forgery against a person who, in good faith, pays the instrument or takes it for value or for collection.

(b) Under subsection (a), if the person asserting the preclusion fails to exercise ordinary care in paying or taking the instrument and that failure substantially contributes to loss, the loss is allocated between the person precluded and the person asserting the preclusion according to the extent to which the failure of each to exercise ordinary care contributed to the loss.

(c) Under subsection (a), the burden of proving failure to exercise ordinary care is on the person asserting the preclusion. Under subsection (b), the burden of proving failure to exercise ordinary care is on the person precluded.

§3–407. Alteration

(a) "Alteration" means (i) an unauthorized change in an instrument that purports to modify in any respect the obligation of a party, or (ii) an unauthorized addition of words or numbers or other change to an incomplete instrument relating to the obligation of a party.

(b) Except as provided in subsection (c), an alteration fraudulently made discharges a party whose obligation is affected by the alteration unless that party assents or is precluded from asserting the alteration. No other alteration discharges a party, and the instrument may be enforced according to its original terms.

(c) A payor bank or drawee paying a fraudulently altered instrument or a person taking it for value, in good faith and without notice of the alteration, may enforce rights with respect to the instrument (i) according to its original terms, or (ii) in the case of an incomplete instrument altered by unauthorized completion, according to its terms as completed.

§3–408. Drawee Not Liable on Unaccepted Draft

A check or other draft does not of itself operate as an assignment of funds in the hands of the drawee available for its payment, and the drawee is not liable on the instrument until the drawee accepts it.

§3–409. Acceptance of Draft; Certified Check

(a) "Acceptance" means the drawee's signed agreement to pay a draft as presented. It must be written on the draft and may consist of the drawee's signature alone. Acceptance may be made at any time and becomes effective when notification pursuant to instructions is given or the accepted draft is delivered for the purpose of giving rights on the acceptance to any person.

(b) A draft may be accepted although it has not been signed by the drawer, is otherwise incomplete, is overdue, or has been dishonored.

(c) If a draft is payable at a fixed period after sight and the acceptor fails to date the acceptance, the holder may complete the acceptance by supplying a date in good faith.

(d) "Certified check" means a check accepted by the bank on which it is drawn. Acceptance may be made as stated in subsection (a) or by a writing on the check which indicates that the check is certified. The drawee of a check has no obligation to certify the check, and refusal to certify is not dishonor of the check.

§3–410. Acceptance Varying Draft

(a) If the terms of a drawee's acceptance vary from the terms of the draft as presented, the holder may refuse the acceptance and treat the draft as dishonored. In that case, the drawee may cancel the acceptance.

(b) The terms of a draft are not varied by an acceptance to pay at a particular bank or place in the United States, unless the acceptance states that the draft is to be paid only at that bank or place.

(c) If the holder assents to an acceptance varying the terms of a draft, the obligation of each drawer and indorser that does not expressly assent to the acceptance is discharged.

§3–411. Refusal to Pay Cashier's Checks, Teller's Checks, and Certified Checks

(a) In this section, "obligated bank" means the acceptor of a certified check or the issuer of a cashier's check or teller's check bought from the issuer.

(b) If the obligated bank wrongfully (i) refuses to pay a cashier's check or certified check, (ii) stops payment of a teller's check, or (iii) refuses to pay a dishonored teller's check, the person asserting the right to enforce the check is entitled to compensation for expenses and loss of interest resulting from the nonpayment and may recover consequential damages if the obligated bank refuses to pay after receiving notice of particular circumstances giving rise to the damages.

(c) Expenses or consequential damages under subsection (b) are not recoverable if the refusal of the obligated bank to pay occurs because (i) the bank suspends payments, (ii) the obligated bank asserts a claim or defense of the bank that it has reasonable grounds to believe is available against the person entitled to enforce the instrument, (iii) the obligated bank has a reasonable doubt whether the person demanding payment is the person entitled to enforce the instrument, or (iv) payment is prohibited by law.

§3–412. Obligation of Issuer of Note or Cashier's Check

The issuer of a note or cashier's check or other draft drawn on the drawer is obliged to pay the instrument (i) according to its terms at the time it was issued or, if not issued, at the time it first came into possession of a holder, or (ii) if the issuer signed an incomplete instrument according to its terms when completed, to the extent stated in Sections 3–115 and 3–407. The obligation is owed to a person entitled to enforce the instrument or to an indorser who paid the instrument under Section 3–415.

§3–413. Obligation of Acceptor

(a) The acceptor of a draft is obliged to pay the draft (i) according to its terms at the time it was accepted, even though the acceptance states that the draft is payable "as originally drawn" or equivalent terms, (ii) if the acceptance varies the terms of the draft, according to the terms of the draft as varied, or (iii) if the acceptance is of a draft that is an incomplete instrument, according to its terms when completed, to the extent stated in Sections 3–115 and 3–407. The obligation is owed to a person entitled to enforce the draft or to the drawer or an indorser who paid the draft under Section 3–414 or 3–415.

(b) If the certification of a check or other acceptance of a draft states the amount certified or accepted, the obligation of the acceptor is that amount. If (i) the certification or acceptance does not state an amount, (ii) the amount of the instrument is subsequently raised, and (iii) the instrument is then negotiated to a holder in due course, the obligation of the acceptor is the amount of the instrument at the time it was taken by the holder in due course.

§3–414. Obligation of Drawer

(a) This section does not apply to cashier's checks or other drafts drawn on the drawer.

(b) If an unaccepted draft is dishonored, the drawer is obliged to pay the draft (i) according to its terms at the time it was issued or, if not issued, at the time it first came into possession of a holder, or (ii) if the drawer signed an incomplete instrument, according to its terms when completed, to the extent stated in Sections 3–115 and 3–407. The obligation is owed to a person entitled to enforce the draft or to an indorser who paid the draft under Section 3–415.

(c) If a draft is accepted by a bank, the drawer is discharged, regardless of when or by whom acceptance was obtained.

(d) If a draft is accepted and the acceptor is not a bank, the obligation of the drawer to pay the draft if the draft is dishonored by the acceptor is the same as the obligation of an indorser under Section 3–415(a) and (c).

(e) If a draft states that it is drawn "without recourse" or otherwise disclaims liability of the drawer to pay the draft, the drawer is not liable under subsection (b) to pay the draft if the draft is not a check. A disclaimer of the liability stated in subsection (b) is not effective if the draft is a check.

(f) If (i) a check is not presented for payment or given to a depositary bank for collection within 30 days after its date, (ii) the drawee suspends payments after expiration of the 30-day period without paying the check, and (iii) because of the suspension of payments, the drawer is deprived of funds maintained with the drawee to cover payment of the check, the drawer to the extent deprived of funds may discharge its obligation to pay the check by assigning to the person entitled to enforce the check the rights of the drawer against the drawee with respect to the funds.

§3–415. Obligation of Indorser

(a) Subject to subsections (b), (c), and (d) and to Section 3–419(d), if an instrument is dishonored, an indorser is obliged to pay the amount due on the instrument (i) according to the terms of the instrument at the time it was indorsed, or (ii) if the indorser indorsed an incomplete instrument, according to its terms when completed, to the extent stated in Section 3–115 and 3–407. The obligation of the indorser is owed to a person entitled to enforce the instrument or to a subsequent indorser who paid the instrument under this section.

(b) If an indorsement states that it is made "without recourse" or otherwise disclaims liability of the indorser, the indorser is not liable under subsection (a) to pay the instrument.

(c) If notice of dishonor of an instrument is required by Section 3–503 and notice of dishonor complying with that section is not given to an indorser, the liability of the indorser under subsection (a) is discharged.

(d) If a draft is accepted by a bank after an indorsement is made, the liability of the indorser under subsection (a) is discharged.

(e) If an indorser of a check is liable under subsection (a) and the check is not presented for payment, or given to a depositary bank for collection, within 30 days after the day the indorsement was made, the liability of the indorser under subsection (a) is discharged.

§3–416. Transfer Warranties

(a) A person who transfers an instrument for consideration warrants to the transferee and, if the transfer is by indorsement, to any subsequent transferee that:

(1) the warrantor is a person entitled to enforce the instrument;
(2) all signatures on the instrument are authentic and authorized;
(3) the instrument has not been altered;
(4) the instrument is not subject to a defense or claim in recoupment of any party which can be asserted against the warrantor; and
(5) the warrantor has no knowledge of any insolvency proceeding commenced with respect to the maker or acceptor or, in the case of an unaccepted draft, the drawer.

(b) A person to whom the warranties under subsection (a) are made and who took the instrument in good faith may recover from the warrantor as damages for breach of warranty an amount equal to the loss suffered as a result of the breach, but not more than the amount of the instrument plus expenses and loss of interest incurred as a result of the breach.

(c) The warranties stated in subsection (a) cannot be disclaimed with respect to checks. Unless notice of a claim for breach of warranty is given to the warrantor within 30 days after the claimant has reason to know of the breach and the identity of the warrantor, the liability of the warrantor under subsection (b) is discharged to the extent of any loss caused by the delay in giving notice of the claim.

(d) A [cause of action] for breach of warranty under this section accrues when the claimant has reason to know of the breach.

§3–417. Presentment Warranties

(a) If an unaccepted draft is presented to the drawee for payment or acceptance and the drawee pays or accepts the draft, (i) the person obtaining payment or acceptance at the time of presentment, and (ii) a previous transferor of the draft, at the time of transfer, warrant to the drawee making payment or accepting the draft in good faith that:

(1) the warrantor is, or was, at the time the warrantor transferred the draft, a person entitled to enforce the draft or authorized to obtain payment or acceptance of the draft on behalf of a person entitled to enforce the draft;

(2) the draft has not been altered; and

(3) the warrantor has no knowledge that the signature of the drawer of the draft is unauthorized.

(b) A drawee making payment may recover from any warrantor damages for breach of warranty equal to the amount paid by the drawee less the amount the drawee received or is entitled to receive from the drawer because of the payment. In addition, the drawee is entitled to compensation for expenses and loss of interest resulting from the breach. The right of the drawee to recover damages under this subsection is not affected by any failure of the drawee to exercise ordinary care in making payment. If the drawee accepts the draft, breach of warranty is a defense to the obligation of the acceptor. If the acceptor makes payment with respect to the draft, the acceptor is entitled to recover from any warrantor for breach of warranty the amounts stated in this subsection.

(c) If a drawee asserts a claim for breach of warranty under subsection (a) based on an unauthorized indorsement of the draft or an alteration of the draft, the warrantor may defend by proving that the indorsement is effective under Section 3–404 or 3–405 or the drawer is precluded under Section 3–406 or 4–406 from asserting against the drawee the unauthorized indorsement or alteration.

(d) If (i) a dishonored draft is presented for payment to the drawer or an indorser or (ii) any other instrument is presented for payment to a party obliged to pay the instrument, and (iii) payment is received, the following rules apply:

(1) The person obtaining payment and a prior transferor of the instrument warrant to the person making payment in good faith that the warrantor is, or was, at the time the warrantor transferred the instrument, a person entitled to enforce the instrument or authorized to obtain payment on behalf of a person entitled to enforce the instrument.

(2) The person making payment may recover from any warrantor for breach of warranty an amount equal to the amount paid plus expenses and loss of interest resulting from the breach.

(e) The warranties stated in subsections (a) and (d) cannot be disclaimed with respect to checks. Unless notice of a claim for breach of warranty is given to the warrantor within 30 days after the claimant has reason to know of the breach and the identity of the warrantor, the liability of the warrantor under subsection (b) or (d) is discharged to the extent of any loss caused by the delay in giving notice of the claim.

(f) A [cause of action] for breach of warranty under this section accrues when the claimant has reason to know of the breach.

§3–418. Payment or Acceptance by Mistake

(a) Except as provided in subsection (c), if the drawee of a draft pays or accepts the draft and the drawee acted on the mistaken belief that (i) payment of the draft had not been stopped pursuant to Section 4–403 or (ii) the signature of the drawer of the draft was authorized, the drawee may recover the amount of the draft from the person to whom or for whose benefit payment was made or, in the case of acceptance, may revoke the acceptance. Rights of the drawee under this subsection are not affected by failure of the drawee to exercise ordinary care in paying or accepting the draft.

(b) Except as provided in subsection (c), if an instrument has been paid or accepted by mistake and the case is not covered by subsection (a), the person paying or accepting may, to the extent permitted by the law governing mistake and restitution, (i) recover the payment from the person to whom or for whose benefit payment was made or (ii) in the case of acceptance, may revoke the acceptance.

(c) The remedies provided by subsection (a) or (b) may not be asserted against a person who took the instrument in good faith and for value or who in good faith changed position in reliance on the payment or acceptance. This subsection does not limit remedies provided by Section 3–417 and 4–407.

(d) Notwithstanding Section 4–215, if an instrument is paid or accepted by mistake and the payor or acceptor recovers payment or revokes acceptance under subsection (a) or (b), the instrument is deemed not to have been paid or accepted and is treated as dishonored, and the person from whom payment is recovered has rights as a person entitled to enforce the dishonored instrument.

§3–419. Instruments Signed for Accommodation

(a) If an instrument is issued for value given for the benefit of a party to the instrument ("accommodated party") and another party to the instrument ("accommodation party") signs the instrument for the purpose of incurring liability on the instrument without being a direct beneficiary of the value given for the instrument, the instrument is signed by the accommodation party "for accommodation."

(b) An accommodation party may sign the instrument as maker, drawer, acceptor, or indorser and, subject to subsection (d), is obliged to pay the instrument in the capacity in which the accommodation party signs. The obligation of an accommodation party may be enforced notwithstanding any statute of frauds and whether or not the accommodation party receives consideration for the accommodation.

(c) A person signing an instrument is presumed to be an accommodation party and there is notice that the instrument is signed for accommodation if the signature is an anomalous indorsement or is accompanied by words indicating that the signer is acting as surety or guarantor with respect to the obligation of another party to the instrument. Except as provided in Section 3–605, the obligation of an accommodation party to pay the instrument is not affected by the fact that the person enforcing the obligation had notice when the instrument was taken by that person that the accommodation party signed the instrument for accommodation.

(d) If the signature of a party to an instrument is accompanied by words indicating unambiguously that the party is guaranteeing collection rather than payment of the obligation of another party to the instrument, the signer is obliged to pay the amount due on the instrument to a person entitled to enforce the instrument only if (i) execution of judgment against the other party has been returned unsatisfied, (ii) the other party is insolvent or in an insolvency proceeding, (iii) the other party cannot be served with process, or (iv) it is otherwise apparent that payment cannot be obtained from the other party.

(e) An accommodation party who pays the instrument is entitled to reimbursement from the accommodated party and is entitled to enforce the instrument against the accommodated party. An accommodated party who pays the instrument has no right of recourse against, and is not entitled to contribution from, an accommodation party.

§3–420. Conversion of Instrument

(a) The law applicable to conversion of personal property applies to instruments. An instrument is also converted if it is taken by transfer, other than a negotiation, from a person not entitled to enforce the instrument or a bank makes or obtains payment with respect to the instrument for a person not entitled to enforce the instrument or receive payment. An action for conversion of an instrument may not be brought by (i) the issuer or acceptor of the instrument or (ii) a payee or indorsee who did not receive delivery of the instrument either directly or through delivery to an agent or a co-payee.

(b) In an action under subsection (a), the measure of liability is presumed to be the amount payable on the instrument, but recovery may not exceed the amount of the plaintiff's interest in the instrument.

(c) A representative, other than a depositary bank, who has in good faith dealt with an instrument or its proceeds on behalf of one who was not the person entitled to enforce the instrument is not liable in conversion to that person beyond the amount of any proceeds that it has not paid out.

Part 5 Dishonor

§3–501. Presentment

(a) "Presentment" means a demand made by or on behalf of a person entitled to enforce an instrument (i) to pay the instrument made to the drawee or a party obliged to pay the instrument or, in the case of a note or accepted draft payable at a bank, to the bank, or (ii) to accept a draft made to the drawee.

(b) The following rules are subject to Article 4, agreement of the parties, and clearing-house rules and the like:

(1) Presentment may be made at the place of payment of the instrument and must be made at the place of payment if the instrument is payable at a bank in the United States; may be made by any commercially reasonable means, including an oral, written, or electronic communication; is effective when the demand for payment or acceptance is received by the person to whom presentment is made; and is effective if made to any one of two or more makers, acceptors, drawees, or other payors.

(2) Upon demand of the person to whom presentment is made, the person making presentment must (i) exhibit the instrument, (ii) give reasonable identification and, if presentment is made on behalf of another person, reasonable evidence of authority to do so, and (. . .) sign a receipt on the instrument for any payment made or surrender the instrument if full payment is made.

(3) Without dishonoring the instrument, the party to whom presentment is made may (i) return the instrument for lack of a necessary indorsement, or (ii) refuse payment or acceptance for failure of the presentment to comply with the terms of the instrument, an agreement of the parties, or other applicable law or rule.

(4) The party to whom presentment is made may treat presentment as occurring on the next business day after the day of presentment if the party to whom presentment is made has established a cut-off hour not earlier than 2 P.M. for the receipt and processing of instruments presented for payment or acceptance and presentment is made after the cut-off hour.

§3–502. Dishonor

(a) Dishonor of a note is governed by the following rules:

(1) If the note is payable on demand, the note is dishonored if presentment is duly made to the maker and the note is not paid on the day of presentment.

(2) If the note is not payable on demand and is payable at or through a bank or the terms of the note require presentment, the note is dishonored if presentment is duly made and the note is not paid on the day it becomes payable or the day of presentment, whichever is later.

(3) If the note is not payable on demand and paragraph (2) does not apply, the note is dishonored if it is not paid on the day it becomes payable.

(b) Dishonor of an unaccepted draft other than a documentary draft is governed by the following rules:

(1) If a check is duly presented for payment to the payor bank otherwise than for immediate payment over the counter, the check is dishonored if the payor bank makes timely return of the check or sends timely notice of dishonor or nonpayment under Section 4–301 or 4–302, or becomes accountable for the amount of the check under Section 4–302.

(2) If a draft is payable on demand and paragraph (1) does not apply, the draft is dishonored if presentment for payment is duly made to the drawee and the draft is not paid on the day of presentment.

(3) If a draft is payable on a date stated in the draft, the draft is dishonored if (i) presentment for payment is duly made to the drawee and payment is not made on the day the draft becomes payable or the day of presentment, whichever is later, or (ii) presentment for acceptance is duly made before the day the draft becomes payable and the draft is not accepted on the day of presentment.

(4) If a draft is payable on elapse of a period of time after sight or acceptance, the draft is dishonored if presentment for acceptance is duly made and the draft is not accepted on the day of presentment.

(c) Dishonor of an unaccepted documentary draft occurs according to the rules stated in subsection (b)(2), (3), and (4), except that payment or acceptance may be delayed without dishonor until no later than the close of the third business day of the drawee following the day on which payment or acceptance is required by those paragraphs.

(d) Dishonor of an accepted draft is governed by the following rules:

(1) If the draft is payable on demand, the draft is dishonored if presentment for payment is duly made to the acceptor and the draft is not paid on the day of presentment.

(2) If the draft is not payable on demand, the draft is dishonored if presentment for payment is duly made to the acceptor and payment is not made on the day it becomes payable or the day of presentment, whichever is later.

(e) In any case in which presentment is otherwise required for dishonor under this section and presentment is excused under Section 3–504, dishonor occurs without presentment if the instrument is not duly accepted or paid.

(f) If a draft is dishonored because timely acceptance of the draft was not made and the person entitled to demand acceptance consents to a late acceptance, from the time of acceptance the draft is treated as never having been dishonored.

§3–503. Notice of Dishonor

(a) The obligation of an indorser stated in Section 3–415(a) and the obligation of a drawer stated in Section 3–414(d) may not be enforced unless (i) the indorser or drawer is given notice of dishonor of the instrument complying with this section or (ii) notice of dishonor is excused under Section 3–504(b).

(b) Notice of dishonor may be given by any person; may be given by any commercially reasonable means, including an oral, written, or electronic communication; and is sufficient if it reasonably identifies the instrument and indicates that the instrument has been dishonored or has not been paid or accepted. Return of an instrument given to a bank for collection is sufficient notice of dishonor.

(c) Subject to Section 3–504(c), with respect to an instrument taken for collection by a collecting bank, notice of dishonor must be given (i) by the bank before midnight of the next banking day following the banking day on which the bank receives notice of dishonor of the instrument, or (ii) by any other person within 30 days following the day on which the person receives notice of dishonor. With respect to any other instrument, notice of dishonor must be given within 30 days following the day on which dishonor occurs.

§3–504. Excused Presentment and Notice of Dishonor

(a) Presentment for payment or acceptance of an instrument is excused if (i) the person entitled to present the instrument cannot with reasonable diligence make presentment, (ii) the maker or acceptor has repudiated an obligation to pay the instrument or is dead or in insolvency proceedings, (iii) by the terms of the instrument presentment is not necessary to enforce the obligation of indorsers or the drawer, (iv) the drawer or indorser whose obligation is being enforced has waived presentment or otherwise has no reason to expect or right to require that the instrument be paid or accepted, or (v) the drawer instructed the drawee not to pay or accept the draft or the drawee was not obligated to the drawer to pay the draft.

(b) Notice of dishonor is excused if (i) by the terms of the instrument notice of dishonor is not necessary to enforce the obligation of a party to pay the instrument, or (ii) the party whose obligation is being enforced waived notice of dishonor. A waiver of presentment is also a waiver of notice of dishonor.

(c) Delay in giving notice of dishonor is excused if the delay was caused by circumstances beyond the control of the person giving the notice and the person giving the notice exercised reasonable diligence after the cause of the delay ceased to operate.

§3–505. Evidence of Dishonor

(a) The following are admissible as evidence and create a presumption of dishonor and of any notice of dishonor stated:

(1) a document regular in form as provided in subsection (b) which purports to be a protest;

(2) a purported stamp or writing of the drawee, payor bank, or presenting bank on or accompanying the instrument stating that acceptance or payment has been refused unless reasons for the refusal are stated and the reasons are not consistent with dishonor;

(3) a book or record of the drawee, payor bank, or collecting bank, kept in the usual course of business which shows dishonor, even if there is no evidence of who made the entry.

(b) A protest is a certificate of dishonor made by a United States consul or vice consul, or a notary public or other person authorized to administer oaths by the law of the place where dishonor occurs. It may be made upon information satisfactory to that person. The protest must identify the instrument and certify either that presentment has been made or, if not made, the reason why it was not made, and that the instrument has been dishonored by nonacceptance or nonpayment. The protest may also certify that notice of dishonor has been given to some or all parties.

Part 6 Discharge and Payment

§3–601. Discharge and Effect of Discharge

(a) The obligation of a party to pay the instrument is discharged as stated in this Article or by an act or agreement with the party which would discharge an obligation to pay money under a simple contract.

(b) Discharge of the obligation of a party is not effective against a person acquiring rights of a holder in due course of the instrument without notice of the discharge.

§3–602. Payment

(a) Subject to subsection (b), an instrument is paid to the extent payment is made (i) by or on behalf of a party obliged to pay the instrument, and (ii) to a person entitled to enforce the instrument. To the extent of the payment, the obligation of the party obliged to pay the instrument is discharged even though payment is made with knowledge of a claim to the instrument under Section 3–306 by another person.

(b) The obligation of a party to pay the instrument is not discharged under subsection (a) if:

(1) a claim to the instrument under Section 3–306 is enforceable against the party receiving payment and (i) payment is made with knowledge by the

payor that payment is prohibited by injunction or similar process of a court of competent jurisdiction, or (ii) in the case of an instrument other than a cashier's check, teller's check, or certified check, the party making payment accepted, from the person having a claim to the instrument, indemnity against loss resulting from refusal to pay the person entitled to enforce the instrument; or

(2) the person making payment knows that the instrument is a stolen instrument and pays a person it knows is in wrongful possession of the instrument.

§3–603. Tender of Payment

(a) If tender of payment of an obligation to pay an instrument is made to a person entitled to enforce the instrument, the effect of tender is governed by principles of law applicable to tender of payment under a simple contract.

(b) If tender of payment of an obligation to pay an instrument is made to a person entitled to enforce the instrument and the tender is refused, there is discharge, to the extent of the amount of the tender, of the obligation of an indorser or accommodation party having a right of recourse with respect to the obligation to which the tender relates.

(c) If tender of payment of an amount due on an instrument is made to a person entitled to enforce the instrument, the obligation of the obligor to pay interest after the due date on the amount tendered is discharged. If presentment is required with respect to an instrument and the obligor is able and ready to pay on the due date at every place of payment stated in the instrument, the obligor is deemed to have made tender of payment on the due date to the person entitled to enforce the instrument.

§3–604. Discharge by Cancellation or Renunciation

(a) A person entitled to enforce an instrument, with or without consideration, may discharge the obligation of a party to pay the instrument (i) by an intentional voluntary act, such as surrender of the instrument to the party, destruction, mutilation, or cancellation of the instrument, cancellation or striking out of the party's signature, or the addition of words to the instrument indicating discharge, or (ii) by agreeing not to sue or otherwise renouncing rights against the party by a signed writing.

(b) Cancellation or striking out of an indorsement pursuant to subsection (a) does not affect the status and rights of a party derived from the indorsement.

§3–605. Discharge of Indorsers and Accommodation Parties

(a) In this section, the term "indorser" includes a drawer having the obligation described in ·Section 3–414(d).

(b) Discharge, under Section 3–604, of the obligation of a party to pay an instrument does not discharge the obligation of an indorser or accommodation party having a right of recourse against the discharged party.

(c) If a person entitled to enforce an instrument agrees, with or without consideration, to an extension of the due date of the obligation of a party to pay the instrument, the extension discharges an indorser or accommodation party having a right of recourse against the party whose obligation is extended to the extent the indorser or accommodation party proves that the extension caused loss to the indorser or accommodation party with respect to the right of recourse.

(d) If a person entitled to enforce an instrument agrees, with or without consideration, to a material modification of the obligation of a party other than an extension of the due date, the modification discharges the obligation of an indorser or accommodation party having a right of recourse against the person whose obligation is modified to the extent the modification causes loss to the indorser or accommodation party with respect to the right of recourse. The loss suffered by the indorser or accommodation party as a result of the modification is equal to the amount of the right of recourse unless the person enforcing the instrument proves that no loss was caused by the modification or that the loss caused by the modification was an amount less than the amount of the right of recourse.

(e) If the obligation of a party to pay an instrument is secured by an interest in collateral and a person entitled to enforce the instrument impairs the value of the interest in collateral, the obligation of an indorser or accommodation party having a right of recourse against the obligor is discharged to the extent of the impairment. The value of an interest in collateral is impaired to the extent (i) the value of the interest is reduced to an amount less than the amount of the right of recourse of the party asserting discharge, or (ii) the reduction in value of the interest causes an increase in the amount by which the amount of the right of recourse exceeds the value of the interest. The burden of proving impairment is on the party asserting discharge.

(f) If the obligation of a party is secured by an interest in collateral not provided by an accommodation party and a person entitled to enforce the instrument impairs the value of the interest in collateral, the obligation of any party who is jointly and severally liable with respect to the secured obligation is discharged to the extent the impairment causes the party asserting discharge to pay more than that party would have been obliged to pay, taking into account rights of contribution, if impairment had not occurred. If the party asserting discharge is an accommodation party not entitled to discharge under subsection (e), the party is deemed to have a right to contribution based on joint and several liability rather than a right to reimbursement. The burden of proving impairment is on the party asserting discharge.

(g) Under subsection (e) or (f), impairing value of an interest in collateral includes (i) failure to obtain or maintain perfection or recordation of the interest in collateral, (ii) release of collateral without substitution of collateral of equal value, (iii) failure to perform a duty to preserve the value of collateral owed, under Article 9 or other law, to a debtor or surety or other person secondarily liable, or (iv) failure to comply with applicable law in disposing of collateral.

(h) An accommodation party is not discharged under subsection (c), (d), or (e) unless the person entitled to enforce the instrument knows of the accommodation or has notice under Section 3–419(c) that the instrument was signed for accommodation.

(i) A party is not discharged under this section if (i) the party asserting discharge consents to the event or conduct that is the basis of the discharge, or (ii) the instrument or a separate agreement of the party provides for waiver of discharge under this section either specifically or by general language indicating that parties waive defenses based on suretyship or impairment of collateral.

ARTICLE 4 BANK DEPOSITS AND COLLECTIONS

Part 1 General Provisions and Definitions

§4–101. Short Title

This Article may be cited as Uniform Commercial Code—Bank Deposits and Collections.
As amended in 1990.

§4–102. Applicability

(a) To the extent that items within this Article are also within Articles 3 and 8, they are subject to those Articles. If there is conflict, this Article governs Article 3, but Article 8 governs this Article.

(b) The liability of a bank for action or non-action with respect to an item handled by it for purposes of presentment, payment, or collection is governed by the law of the place where the bank is located. In the case of action or non-action by or at a branch or separate office of a bank, its liability is governed by the law of the place where the branch or separate office is located.
As amended in 1990.

§4–103. Variation by Agreement; Measure of Damages; Action Constituting Ordinary Care

(a) The effect of the provisions of this Article may be varied by agreement, but the parties to the agreement cannot disclaim a bank's responsibility for its lack of good faith or failure to exercise ordinary care or limit the measure of damages for the lack or failure. However, the parties may determine by agreement the standards by which the bank's responsibility is to be measured if those standards are not manifestly unreasonable.

(b) Federal Reserve regulations and operating circulars, clearing-house rules, and the like have the effect of agreements under subsection (a), whether or not specifically assented to by all parties interested in items handled.

(c) Action or non-action approved by this Article or pursuant to Federal Reserve regulations or operating circulars is the exercise of ordinary care and, in the absence of special instructions, action or non-action consistent with clearing-house rules and the like or with a general banking usage not disapproved by this Article, is prima facie the exercise of ordinary care.

(d) The specification or approval of certain procedures by this Article is not disapproval of other procedures that may be reasonable under the circumstances.

(e) The measure of damages for failure to exercise ordinary care in handling an item is the amount of the item reduced by an amount that could not have been realized by the exercise of ordinary care. If there is also bad faith it includes any other damages the party suffered as a proximate consequence.

As amended in 1990.

§4−104. Definitions and Index of Definitions

(a) In this Article, unless the context otherwise requires:

(1) "Account" means any deposit or credit account with a bank, including a demand, time, savings, passbook, share draft, or like account, other than an account evidenced by a certificate of deposit;

(2) "Afternoon" means the period of day between noon and midnight;

(3) "Banking day" means the part of a day on which a bank is open to the public for carrying on substantially all of its banking functions;

(4) "Clearing house" means an association of banks or other payors regularly clearing items;

(5) "Customer" means a person having an account with a bank or for whom a bank has agreed to collect items, including a bank that maintains an account at another bank;

(6) "Documentary draft" means a draft to be presented for acceptance or payment if specified documents, certificated securities (Section 8−102) or instructions for uncertificated securities (Section 8−308), or other certificates, statements, or the like are to be received by the drawee or other payor before acceptance or payment of the draft;

(7) "Draft" means a draft as defined in Section 3−104 or an item, other than an instrument, that is an order;

(8) "Drawee" means a person ordered in a draft to make payment;

(9) "Item" means an instrument or a promise or order to pay money handled by a bank for collection or payment. The term does not include a payment order governed by Article 4A or a credit or debit card slip;

(10) "Midnight deadline" with respect to a bank is midnight on its next banking day following the banking day on which it receives the relevant item or notice or from which the time for taking action commences to run, whichever is later;

(11) "Settle" means to pay in cash, by clearing-house settlement, in a charge or credit or by remittance, or otherwise as agreed. A settlement may be either provisional or final;

(12) "Suspends payments" with respect to a bank means that it has been closed by order of the supervisory authorities, that a public officer has been appointed to take it over, or that it ceases or refuses to make payments in the ordinary course of business.

(b) Other definitions applying to this Article and the sections in which they appear are:

"Agreement for electronic presentment"	Section 4−110.
"Bank"	Section 4−105.
"Collecting bank"	Section 4−105.
"Depositary bank"	Section 4−105.
"Intermediary bank"	Section 4−105.
"Payor bank"	Section 4−105.
"Presenting bank"	Section 4−105.
"Presentment notice"	Section 4−110.

§4−105. "Bank"; "Depositary Bank"; "Payor Bank"; "Intermediary Bank"; "Collecting Bank"; "Presenting Bank"

In this Article:

(1) "Bank" means a person engaged in the business of banking, including a savings bank, savings and loan association, credit union, or trust company;

(2) "Depositary bank" means the first bank to take an item even though it is also the payor bank, unless the item is presented for immediate payment over the counter;

(3) "Payor bank" means a bank that is the drawee of a draft;

(4) "Intermediary bank" means a bank to which an item is transferred in course of collection except the depositary or payor bank;

(5) "Collecting bank" means a bank handling an item for collection except the payor bank;

(6) "Presenting bank" means a bank presenting an item except a payor bank.

As amended in 1990.

§4–106. Payable Through or Payable at Bank: Collecting Bank

(a) If an item states that it is "payable through" a bank identified in the item, (i) the item designates the bank as a collecting bank and does not by itself authorize the bank to pay the item, and (ii) the item may be presented for payment only by or through the bank.

Alternative A

(b) If an item states that it is "payable at" a bank identified in the item, the item is equivalent to a draft drawn on the bank.

Alternative B

(b) If an item states that it is "payable at" a bank identified in the item, (i) the item designates the bank as a collecting bank and does not by itself authorize the bank to pay the item, and (ii) the item may be presented for payment only by or through the bank.

(c) If a draft means a nonbank drawee and it is unclear whether a bank named in the draft is a co-drawee or a collecting bank, the bank is a collecting bank.
As added in 1990.

§4–107. Separate Office of Bank

A branch or separate office of a bank is a separate bank for the purpose of computing the time within which and determining the place at or to which action may be taken or notices or orders shall be given under this Article and under Article 3.
As amended in 1962 and 1990.

§4–108. Time of Receipt of Items

(a) For the purpose of allowing time to process items, prove balances, and make the necessary entries on its books to determine its position for the day, a bank may fix an afternoon hour of 2 P.M. or later as a cutoff hour for the handling of money and items and the making of entries on its books.

(b) An item or deposit of money received on any day after a cutoff hour so fixed or after the close of the banking day may be treated as being received at the opening of the next banking day.
As amended in 1990.

§4–109. Delays

(a) Unless otherwise instructed, a collecting bank in a good faith effort to secure payment of a specific item drawn on a payor other than a bank, and with or without the approval of any person involved, may waive, modify, or extend time limits imposed or permitted by this [Act] for a period not exceeding two additional banking days without discharge of drawers or indorsers or liability to its transferor or a prior party.

(b) Delay by a collecting bank or payor bank beyond time limits prescribed or permitted by this [Act] or by instructions is excused if (i) the delay is caused by interruption of communication or computer facilities, suspension of payments by another bank, war, emergency conditions, failure of equipment, or other circumstances beyond the control of the bank, and (ii) the bank exercises such diligence as the circumstances require.
As amended in 1990.

§4–110. Electronic Presentment

(a) "Agreement for electronic presentment" means an agreement, clearing-house rule, or Federal Reserve regulation or operating circular, providing that presentment of an item may be made by transmission of an image of an item or information describing the item ("presentment notice") rather than delivery of the item itself. The agreement may provide for procedures governing retention, presentment, payment, dishonor, and other matters concerning items subject to the agreement.

(b) Presentment of an item pursuant to an agreement for presentment is made when the presentment notice is received.

(c) If presentment is made by presentment notice, a reference to "item" or "check" in this Article means the presentment notice unless the context otherwise indicates.
As added in 1990.

§4–111. Statute of Limitations

An action to enforce an obligation, duty, or right arising under this Article must be commenced within three years after the [cause of action] accrues.
As added in 1990.

Part 2 Collection of Items: Depositary and Collecting Banks

§4–201. Status of Collecting Bank as Agent and Provisional Status of Credits; Applicability of Article; Item Indorsed "Pay Any Bank"

(a) Unless a contrary intent clearly appears and before the time that a settlement given by a collecting bank for an item is or becomes final, the bank, with respect to an item, is an agent or sub-agent of the owner of the item and any settlement given for the item is provisional. This provision applies regardless of the form of indorsement or lack of indorsement and even though credit given for the item is subject to immediate withdrawal as of right or is in fact withdrawn; but the continuance of ownership of an item by its owner and any rights of the owner to proceeds of the item are subject to rights of a collecting bank, such as those resulting from outstanding advances on the item and rights of recoupment or setoff. If an item is handled by banks for purposes of presentment, payment, collection, or return, the relevant provisions of this Article apply even though action of the parties clearly establishes that a particular bank has purchased the item and is the owner of it.

(b) After an item has been indorsed with the words "pay any bank" or the like, only a bank may acquire the rights of a holder until the item has been:

(1) returned to the customer initiating collection; or

(2) specially indorsed by a bank to a person who is not a bank.

As amended in 1990.

§4–202. Responsibility for Collection or Return; When Action Timely

(a) A collecting bank must exercise ordinary care in:

(1) presenting an item or sending it for presentment;

(2) sending notice of dishonor or nonpayment or returning an item other than a documentary draft to the bank's transferor after learning that the item has not been paid or accepted, as the case may be;

(3) settling for an item when the bank receives final settlement; and

(4) notifying its transferor of any loss or delay in transit within a reasonable time after discovery thereof.

(b) A collecting bank exercises ordinary care under subsection (a) by taking proper action before its midnight deadline following receipt of an item, notice, or settlement. Taking proper action within a reasonably longer time may constitute the exercise of ordinary care, but the bank has the burden of establishing timeliness.

(c) Subject to subsection (a)(1), a bank is not liable for the insolvency, neglect, misconduct, mistake, or default of another bank or person or for loss or destruction of an item in the possession of others or in transit.

As amended in 1990.

§4–203. Effect of Instructions

Subject to Article 3 concerning conversion of instruments (Section 3–420) and restrictive indorsements (Section 3–206), only a collecting bank's transferor can give instructions that affect the bank or constitute notice to it, and a collecting bank is not liable to prior parties for any action taken pursuant to the instructions or in accordance with any agreement with its transferor.

As amended in 1990.

§4–204. Methods of Sending and Presenting; Sending Directly to Payor Bank

(a) A collecting bank shall send items by a reasonably prompt method, taking into consideration relevant instructions, the nature of the item, the number of those items on hand, the cost of collection involved, and the method generally used by it or others to present those items.

(b) A collecting bank may send:

(1) an item directly to the payor bank;

(2) an item to a nonbank payor if authorized by its transferor; and

(3) an item other than documentary drafts to a nonbank payor, if authorized by Federal Reserve regulation or operating circular, clearing-house rule, or the like.

(c) Presentment may be made by a presenting bank at a place where the payor bank or other payor has requested that presentment be made.

As amended in 1962 and 1990.

§4–205. Depositary Bank Holder of Unindorsed Item

If a customer delivers an item to a depositary bank for collection:

(1) the depositary bank becomes a holder of the item at the time it receives the item for collection if the customer at the time of delivery was a holder of the item, whether or not the customer indorses the item, and, if the bank satisfies the other requirements of Section 3–302, it is a holder in due course; and

(2) the depositary bank warrants to collecting banks, the payor bank or other payor, and the drawer that the amount of the item was paid to the customer or deposited to the customer's account.

As amended in 1990.

§4–206. Transfer Between Banks

Any agreed method that identifies the transferor bank is sufficient for the item's further transfer to another bank.

As amended in 1990.

§4–207. Transfer Warranties

(a) A customer or collecting bank that transfers an item and receives a settlement or other consideration warrants to the transferee and to any subsequent collecting bank that:

(1) the warrantor is a person entitled to enforce the item;

(2) all signatures on the item are authentic and authorized;

(3) the item has not been altered;

(4) the item is not subject to a defense or claim in recoupment (Section 3–305(a)) of any party that can be asserted against the warrantor; and

(5) the warrantor has no knowledge of any insolvency proceeding commenced with respect to the maker or acceptor or, in the case of an unaccepted draft, the drawer.

(b) If an item is dishonored, a customer or collecting bank transferring the item and receiving settlement or other consideration is obliged to pay the amount due on the item (i) according to the terms of the item at the time it was transferred, or (ii) if the transfer was of an incomplete item, according to its terms when completed as stated in Sections 3–115 and 3–407. The obligation of a transferor is owed to the transferee and to any subsequent collecting bank that takes the item in good faith. A transferor cannot disclaim its obligation under this subsection by an indorsement stating that it is made "without recourse" or otherwise disclaiming liability.

(c) A person to whom the warranties under subsection (a) are made and who took the item in good faith may recover from the warrantor as damages for breach of warranty an amount equal to the loss suffered as a result of the breach, but not more than the amount of the item plus expenses and loss of interest incurred as a result of the breach.

(d) The warranties stated in subsection (a) cannot be disclaimed with respect to checks. Unless notice of a claim for breach of warranty is given to the warrantor within 30 days after the claimant has reason to know of the breach and the identity of the warrantor, the warrantor is discharged to the extent of any loss caused by the delay in giving notice of the claim.

(e) A cause of action for breach of warranty under this section accrues when the claimant has reason to know of the breach.
As added in 1990.

§4–208. Presentment Warranties

(a) If an unaccepted draft is presented to the drawee for payment or acceptance and the drawee pays or accepts the draft, (i) the person obtaining payment or acceptance, at the time of presentment, and (ii) a previous transferor of the draft, at the time of transfer, warrant to the drawee that pays or accepts the draft in good faith that:

(1) the warrantor is, or was, at the time the warrantor transferred the draft, a person entitled to enforce the draft or authorized to obtain payment or acceptance of the draft on behalf of a person entitled to enforce the draft;

(2) the draft has not been altered; and

(3) the warrantor has no knowledge that the signature of the purported drawer of the draft is unauthorized.

(b) A drawee making payment may recover from a warrantor damages for breach of warranty equal to the amount paid by the drawee less the amount the drawee received or is entitled to receive from the drawer because of the payment. In addition, the drawee is entitled to compensation for expenses and loss of interest resulting from the breach. The right of the drawee to recover damages under this subsection is not affected by any failure of the drawee to exercise ordinary care in making payment. If the drawee accepts the draft (i) breach of warranty is a defense to the obligation of the acceptor, and (ii) if the acceptor makes payment with respect to the draft, the acceptor is entitled to recover from a warrantor for breach of warranty the amounts stated in this subsection.

(c) If a drawee asserts a claim for breach of warranty under subsection (a) based on an unauthorized indorsement of the draft or an alteration of the draft, the warrantor may defend by proving that the indorsement is effective under Section 3–404 or 3–405 or the drawer is precluded under Section 3–406 or 4–406 from asserting against the drawee the unauthorized indorsement or alteration.

(d) If (i) a dishonored draft is presented for payment to the drawer or an indorser or (ii) any other item is presented for payment to a party obliged to pay the item, and the item is paid, the person obtaining payment and a prior transferor of the item warrant to the person making payment in good faith that the warrantor is, or was, at the time the warrantor transferred the item, a person entitled to enforce the item or authorized to obtain payment on behalf of a person entitled to enforce the item. The person making payment may recover from any warrantor for breach of warranty an amount equal to the amount paid plus expenses and loss of interest resulting from the breach.

(e) The warranties stated in subsections (a) and (d) cannot be disclaimed with respect to checks. Unless notice of a claim for breach of warranty is given to the warrantor within 30 days after the claimant has reason to know of the breach and the identity of the warrantor, the warrantor is discharged to the extent of any loss caused by the delay in giving notice of the claim.

(f) A cause of action for breach of warranty under this section accrues when the claimant has reason to know of the breach.
As added in 1990.

§4–209. Encoding and Retention Warranties

(a) A person who encodes information on or with respect to an item after issue warrants to any subsequent collecting bank and to the payor bank or other payor that the information is correctly encoded. If the customer of a depositary bank encodes, that bank also makes the warranty.

(b) A person who undertakes to retain an item pursuant to an agreement for electronic presentment warrants to any subsequent collecting bank and to the payor bank or other payor that retention and presentment of the item comply with the agreement. If a customer of a depositary bank undertakes to retain an item, that bank also makes this warranty.

(c) A person to whom warranties are made under this section and who took the item in good faith may recover from the warrantor as damages for breach of warranty an amount equal to the loss suffered as a result of the breach, plus expenses and loss of interest incurred as a result of the breach.
As added in 1990.

§4–210. Security Interest of Collecting Bank in Items, Accompanying Documents and Proceeds

(a) A collecting bank has a security interest in an item and any accompanying documents or the proceeds of either:

(1) in case of an item deposited in an account, to the extent to which credit given for the item has been withdrawn or applied;

(2) in case of an item for which it has given credit available for withdrawal as of right, to the extent of the credit given, whether or not the credit is drawn upon or there is a right of charge-back; or

(3) if it makes an advance on or against the item.

(b) If credit given for several items received at one time or pursuant to a single agreement is withdrawn or applied in part, the security interest remains upon all the items, any accompanying documents or the proceeds of either. For the purpose of this section, credits first given are first withdrawn.

(c) Receipt by a collecting bank of a final settlement for an item is a realization on its security interest in the item, accompanying documents, and proceeds. So long as the bank does not receive final settlement for the item or give up possession of the item or accompanying documents for purposes other than collection, the security interest continues to that extent and is subject to Article 9, but:

(1) no security agreement is necessary to make the security interest enforceable (Section 9–203(1)(a));

(2) no filing is required to perfect the security interest; and

(3) the security interest has priority over conflicting perfected security interests in the item, accompanying documents, or proceeds.

As amended in 1990.

§4–211. When Bank Gives Value for Purposes of Holder in Due Course

For purposes of determining its status as a holder in due course, a bank has given value to the extent it has a security interest in an item, if the bank otherwise complies with the requirements of Section 3–302 on what constitutes a holder in due course.

As amended in 1990.

§4–212. Presentment by Notice of Item Not Payable by, Through, or at Bank; Liability of Drawer or Indorser

(a) Unless otherwise instructed, a collecting bank may present an item not payable by, through, or at a bank by sending to the party to accept or pay a written notice that the bank holds the item for acceptance or payment. The notice must be sent in time to be received on or before the day when presentment is due and the bank must meet any requirement of the party to accept or pay under Section 3–501 by the close of the bank's next banking day after it knows of the requirement.

(b) If presentment is made by notice and payment, acceptance, or request for compliance with a requirement under Section 3–501 is not received by the close of business on the day after maturity or, in the case of demand items, by the close of business on the third banking day after notice was sent, the presenting bank may treat the item as dishonored and charge any drawer or indorser by sending it notice of the facts.

As amended in 1990.

§4–213. Medium and Time of Settlement by Bank

(a) With respect to settlement by a bank, the medium and time of settlement may be prescribed by Federal Reserve regulations or circulars, clearing-house rules, and the like, or agreement. In the absence of such prescription:

(1) the medium or settlement is cash or credit to an account in a Federal Reserve bank of or specified by the person to receive settlement; and

(2) the time of settlement is:

(i) with respect to tender of settlement by cash, a cashier's check, or teller's check, when the cash or check is sent or delivered;

(ii) with respect to tender of settlement by credit in an account in a Federal Reserve Bank, when the credit is made;

(iii) with respect to tender of settlement by a credit or debit to an account in a bank, when the credit or debit is made or, in the case of tender of settlement by authority to charge an account, when the authority is sent or delivered; or

(iv) with respect to tender of settlement by a funds transfer, when payment is made pursuant to Section 4–406(a) to the person receiving settlement.

(b) If the tender of settlement is not by a medium authorized by subsection (a) or the time of settlement is not fixed by subsection (a), no settlement occurs until the tender of settlement is accepted by the person receiving settlement.

(c) If settlement for an item is made by cashier's check or teller's check and the person receiving settlement, before its midnight deadline:

(1) presents or forwards the check for collection, settlement is final when the check is finally paid; or

(2) fails to present or forward the check for collection, settlement is final at the midnight deadline of the person receiving settlement.

(d) If settlement for an item is made by giving authority to charge the account of the bank giving settlement in the bank receiving settlement, settlement is final when the charge is made by the bank receiving settlement if there are funds available in the account for the amount of the item.

As amended in 1990.

§4–214. Right of Charge-Back or Refund; Liability of Collecting Bank: Return of Item

(a) If a collecting bank has made provisional settlement with its customer for an item and fails by reason of dishonor, suspension of payments by a bank, or otherwise to receive settlement for the item which is or becomes final, the bank may revoke the settlement given by it, charge back the amount of any credit given for the item to its customer's account, or obtain refund from its customer, whether or not it is able to return the item, if by its midnight deadline or within a longer reasonable time after it learns the facts it returns the item or sends notification of the facts. If the return or notice is delayed beyond the bank's midnight deadline or a longer reasonable time after it learns the facts, the bank may revoke the settlement, charge back the credit, or obtain refund from its customer, but it is liable for any loss resulting from the delay. These rights to revoke, charge back, and obtain refund terminate if and when a settlement for the item received by the bank is or becomes final.

(b) A collecting bank returns an item when it is sent or delivered to the bank's customer or transferor or pursuant to its instructions.

(c) A depositary bank that is also the payor may charge back the amount of an item to its customer's account or obtain refund in accordance with the section governing return of an item received by a payor bank for credit on its books (Section 4–301).

(d) The right to charge back is not affected by:

(1) previous use of a credit given for the item; or

(2) failure by any bank to exercise ordinary care with respect to the item, but a bank so failing remains liable.

(e) A failure to charge back or claim refund does not affect other rights of the bank against the customer or any other party.

(f) If credit is given in dollars as the equivalent of the value of an item payable in foreign money, the dollar amount of any charge-back or refund must be calculated on the basis of the bank-offered spot rate for the foreign money prevailing on the day when the person entitled to the charge-back or refund learns that it will not receive payment in ordinary course.

As amended in 1990.

§4–215. Final Payment of Item by Payor Bank; When Provisional Debits and Credits Become Final; When Certain Credits Become Available for Withdrawal

(a) An item is finally paid by a payor bank when the bank has first done any of the following:

(1) paid the item in cash;

(2) settled for the item without having a right to revoke the settlement under statute, clearing-house rule, or agreement; or

(3) made a provisional settlement for the item and failed to revoke the settlement in the time and manner permitted by statute, clearing-house rule, or agreement.

(b) If provisional settlement for an item does not become final, the item is not finally paid.

(c) If provisional settlement for an item between the presenting and payor banks is made through a clearing house or by debits or credits in an account between them, then to the extent that provisional debits or credits for the item are entered in accounts between the presenting and payor banks or between the presenting and successive prior collecting banks seriatim, they become final upon final payment of the item by the payor bank.

(d) If a collecting bank receives a settlement for an item which is or becomes final, the bank is accountable to its customer for the amount of the item and any provisional credit given for the item in an account with its customer becomes final.

(e) Subject to (i) applicable law stating a time for availability of funds and (ii) any right of the bank to apply the credit to an obligation of the customer, credit given by a bank for an item in a customer's account becomes available for withdrawal as of right:

(1) if the bank has received a provisional settlement for the item, when the settlement becomes final and the bank has had a reasonable time to receive return of the item and the item has not been received within that time;

(2) if the bank is both the depositary bank and the payor bank, and the item is finally paid, at the opening of the bank's second banking day following receipt of the item.

(f) Subject to applicable law stating a time for availability of funds and any right of a bank to apply a deposit to an obligation of the depositor, a deposit of money becomes available for withdrawal as of right at the opening of the bank's next banking day after receipt of the deposit. As amended in 1990.

§4–216. Insolvency and Preferences

(a) If an item is in or comes into the possession of a payor or collecting bank that suspends payment and the item has not been finally paid, the item must be returned by the receiver, trustee, or agent in charge of the closed bank to the presenting bank or the closed bank's customer.

(b) If a payor bank finally pays an item and suspends payments without making a settlement for the item with its customer or the presenting bank which settlement is or becomes final, the owner of the item has a preferred claim against the payor bank.

(c) If a payor bank gives or a collecting bank gives or receives a provisional settlement for an item and thereafter suspends payments, the suspension does not prevent or interfere with the settlement's becoming final if the finality occurs automatically upon the lapse of certain time or the happening of certain events.

(d) If a collecting bank receives from subsequent parties settlement for an item, which settlement is or becomes final and the bank suspends payments without making a settlement for the item with its customer which settlement is or becomes final, the owner of the item has a preferred claim against the collecting bank.

As amended in 1990.

Part 3 Collection of Items: Payor Banks

§4–301. Deferred Posting; Recovery of Payment by Return of Items; Time of Dishonor; Return of Items by Payor Bank

(a) If a payor bank settles for a demand item other than a documentary draft presented otherwise than for immediate payment over the counter before midnight of the banking day of receipt, the payor bank may revoke the settlement and recover the settlement if, before it has made final payment and before its midnight deadline, it

(1) returns the item; or
(2) sends written notice of dishonor or nonpayment if the item is unavailable for return.

(b) If a demand item is received by a payor bank for credit on its books, it may return the item or send notice of dishonor and may revoke any credit given or recover the amount thereof withdrawn by its customer, if it acts within the time limit and in the manner specified in subsection (a).

(c) Unless previous notice of dishonor has been sent, an item is dishonored at the time when for purposes of dishonor it is returned or notice sent in accordance with this section.

(d) An item is returned:

(1) as to an item presented through a clearing house, when it is delivered to the presenting or last collecting bank or to the clearing house or is sent or delivered in accordance with clearing-house rules; or
(2) in all other cases, when it is sent or delivered to the bank's customer or transferor or pursuant to instructions.

As amended in 1990.

§4–302. Payor Bank's Responsibility for Late Return of Item

(a) If an item is presented to and received by a payor bank, the bank is accountable for the amount of:

(1) a demand item, other than a documentary draft, whether properly payable or not, if the bank, in any case in which it is not also the depositary bank, retains the item beyond midnight of the banking day of receipt without settling for it or, whether or not it is also the depositary bank, does not pay or return the item or send notice of dishonor until after its midnight deadline; or
(2) any other properly payable item unless, within the time allowed for acceptance or payment of that item, the bank either accepts or pays the item or returns it and accompanying documents.

(b) The liability of a payor bank to pay an item pursuant to subsection (a) is subject to defenses based on breach of a presentment warranty (Section 4–208) or proof that the person seeking enforcement of the liability presented or transferred the item for the purpose of defrauding the payor bank.

As amended in 1990.

§4–303. When Items Subject to Notice, Stop-Payment Order, Legal Process, or Setoff; Order in Which Items May be Charged or Certified

(a) Any knowledge, notice, or stop-payment order received by, legal process served upon, or setoff exercised by a payor bank comes too late to terminate, suspend, or modify the bank's right or duty to pay an item or to charge its customer's account for the item if the knowledge, notice, stop-payment order, or legal process is received or served and a reasonable time for the bank to act thereon expires or the setoff is exercised after the earliest of the following:

(1) the bank accepts or certifies the item;
(2) the bank pays the item in cash;
(3) the bank settles for the item without having a right to revoke the settlement under statute, clearing-house rule, or agreement;
(4) the bank becomes accountable for the amount of the item under Section 4–302 dealing with the payor bank's responsibility for late return of items; or
(5) with respect to checks, a cutoff hour no earlier than one hour after the opening of the next banking day after the banking day on which the bank received the check and no later than the close of that next banking day or, if no cutoff hour is fixed, the close of the next banking day after the banking day on which the bank received the check.

(b) Subject to subsection (a), items may be accepted, paid, certified, or charged to the indicated account of its customer in any order.

As amended in 1990.

Part 4 Relationship Between Payor Bank and Its Customer

§4–401. When Bank May Charge Customer's Account

(a) A bank may charge against the account of a customer an item that is properly payable from the account even though the charge creates an overdraft. An item is properly payable if it is authorized by the customer and is in accordance with any agreement between the customer and bank.

(b) A customer is not liable for the amount of an overdraft if the customer neither signed the item nor benefited from the proceeds of the item.

(c) A bank may charge against the account of a customer a check that is otherwise properly payable from the account, even though payment was made before the date of the check, unless the customer has given notice to the bank of the postdating describing the check with reasonable certainty. The notice is effective for the period stated in Section 4–403(b) for stop-payment orders, and must be received at such time and in such manner as to afford the bank a reasonable opportunity to act on it before the bank takes any action with respect to the check described in Section 4–303. If a bank charges against the account of a customer a check before the date stated in the notice of postdating, the bank is liable for damages for the loss resulting from its act. The loss may include damages for dishonor of subsequent items under Section 4–402.

(d) A bank that in good faith makes payment to a holder may charge the indicated account of its customer according to:

(1) the original terms of the altered item; or

(2) the terms of the completed item, even though the bank knows the item has been completed unless the bank has notice that the completion was improper.

As amended in 1990.

§4–402. Bank's Liability to Customer for Wrongful Dishonor; Time of Determining Insufficiency of Account

(a) Except as otherwise provided in this Article, a payor bank wrongfully dishonors an item if it dishonors an item that is properly payable, but a bank may dishonor an item that would create an overdraft unless it has agreed to pay the overdraft.

(b) A payor bank is liable to its customer for damages proximately caused by the wrongful dishonor of an item. Liability is limited to actual damages proved and may include damages for an arrest or prosecution of the customer or other consequential damages. Whether any consequential damages are proximately caused by the wrongful dishonor is a question of fact to be determined in each case.

(c) A payor bank's determination of the customer's account balance on which a decision to dishonor for insufficiency of available funds is based may be made at any time between the time the item is received by the payor bank and the time that the payor bank returns the item or gives notice in lieu of return, and no more than one determination need be made. If, at the election of the payor bank, a subsequent balance determination is made for the purpose of reevaluating the bank's decision to dishonor the item, the account balance at that time is determinative of whether a dishonor for insufficiency of available funds is wrongful.

As amended in 1990.

§4–403. Customer's Right to Stop Payment; Burden of Proof of Loss

(a) A customer or any person authorized to draw on the account if there is more than one person may stop payment of any item drawn on the customer's account or close the account by an order to the bank describing the item or account with reasonable certainty received at a time and in a manner that affords the bank a reasonable opportunity to act on it before any action by the bank with respect to the item described in Section 4–303. If the signature of more than one person is required to draw on an account, any of these persons may stop payment or close the account.

(b) A stop-payment order is effective for six months, but it lapses after 14 calendar days if the original order was oral and was not confirmed in writing within that period. A stop-payment order may be renewed for additional six-month periods by a writing given to the bank within a period during which the stop-payment order is effective.

(c) The burden of establishing the fact and amount of loss resulting from the payment of an item contrary to a stop-payment order or order to close an account is on the customer. The loss from payment of an item contrary to a stop-payment order may include damages for dishonor of subsequent items under Section 4–402.

As amended in 1990.

§4–404. Bank Not Obliged to Pay Check More Than Six Months Old

A bank is under no obligation to a customer having a checking account to pay a check, other than a certified check, which is presented more than six months after its date, but it may charge its customer's account for a payment made thereafter in good faith.

§4–405. Death or Incompetence of Customer

(a) A payor or collecting bank's authority to accept, pay, or collect an item or to account for proceeds of its collection, if otherwise effective, is not rendered ineffective by incompetence of a customer of either bank existing at the time the item is issued or its collection is undertaken if the bank does not know of an adjudication of incompetence. Neither death nor incompetence of a customer revokes the authority to accept, pay, collect, or account until the bank knows of the fact of death or of an adjudication of incompetence and has reasonable opportunity to act on it.

(b) Even with knowledge, a bank may for 10 days after the date of death pay or certify checks drawn on or before that date unless ordered to stop payment by a person claiming an interest in the account.

As amended in 1990.

§4–406. Customer's Duty to Discover and Report Unauthorized Signature or Alteration

(a) A bank that sends or makes available to a customer a statement of account showing payment of items for the account shall either return or make available to the customer the items paid or provide information in the statement of account sufficient to allow the customer reasonably to identify the items paid. The statement of account provides sufficient information if the item is described by item number, amount, and date of payment.

(b) If the items are not returned to the customer, the person retaining the items shall either retain the items or, if the items are destroyed, maintain the capacity to furnish legible copies of the items until the expiration of seven years after receipt of the items. A customer may request an item from the bank that paid the item, and that bank must provide in a reasonable time either the item or, if the item has been destroyed or is not otherwise obtainable, a legible copy of the item.

(c) If a bank sends or makes available a statement of account or items pursuant to subsection (a), the customer must exercise reasonable promptness in examining the statement or the items to determine whether any payment was not authorized because of an alteration of an item or because a purported signature by or on behalf of the customer was not authorized. If, based on the statement or items provided, the customer should reasonably have discovered the unauthorized payment, the customer must promptly notify the bank of the relevant facts.

(d) If the bank proves that the customer failed, with respect to an item, to comply with the duties imposed on the customer by subsection (c), the customer is precluded from asserting against the bank:

(1) the customer's unauthorized signature or any alteration on the item, if the bank also proves that it suffered a loss by reason of the failure; and

(2) the customer's unauthorized signature or alteration by the same wrongdoer on any other item paid in good faith by the bank if the payment was made before the bank received notice from the customer of the unauthorized signature or alteration and after the customer had been afforded a

reasonable period of time, not exceeding 30 days, in which to examine the item or statement of account and notify the bank.

(e) If subsection (d) applies and the customer proves that the bank failed to exercise ordinary care in paying the item and that the failure substantially contributed to loss, the loss is allocated between the customer precluded and the bank asserting the preclusion according to the extent to which the failure of the customer to comply with subsection (c) and the failure of the bank to exercise ordinary care contributed to the loss. If the customer proves that the bank did not pay the item in good faith, the preclusion under subsection (d) does not apply.

(f) Without regard to care or lack of care of either the customer or the bank, a customer who does not within one year after the statement or items are made available to the customer (subsection (a)) discover and report the customer's unauthorized signature on or any alteration on the item is precluded from asserting against the bank the unauthorized signature or alteration. If there is a preclusion under this subsection, the payor bank may not recover for breach or warranty under Section 4–208 with respect to the unauthorized signature or alteration to which the preclusion applies.

As amended in 1990.

§4–407. Payor Bank's Right to Subrogation on Improper Payment

If a payor bank has paid an item over the order of the drawer or maker to stop payment, or after an account has been closed, or otherwise under circumstances giving a basis for objection by the drawer or maker, to prevent unjust enrichment and only to the extent necessary to prevent loss to the bank by reason of its payment of the item, the payor bank is subrogated to the rights

(1) of any holder in due course on the item against the drawer or maker;

(2) of the payee or any other holder of the item against the drawer or maker either on the item or under the transaction out of which the item arose; and

(3) of the drawer or maker against the payee or any other holder of the item with respect to the transaction out of which the item arose.

As amended in 1990.

Part 5 Collection of Documentary Drafts

§4–501. Handling of Documentary Drafts; Duty to Send for Presentment and to Notify Customer of Dishonor

A bank that takes a documentary draft for collection shall present or send the draft and accompanying documents for presentment and, upon learning that the draft has not been paid or accepted in due course, shall seasonally notify its customer of the fact even though it may have discounted or bought the draft or extended credit available for withdrawal as of right.

As amended in 1990.

§4–502. Presentment of "On Arrival" Drafts

If a draft or the relevant instructions require presentment "on arrival," "when goods arrive" or the like, the collecting bank need not present until in its judgment a reasonable time for arrival of the goods has expired. Refusal to pay or accept because the goods have not arrived is not dishonor; the bank must notify its transferor of the refusal but need not present the draft again until it is instructed to do so or learns of the arrival of the goods.

As amended in 1990.

§4–503. Responsibility of Presenting Bank for Documents and Goods; Report of Reasons for Dishonor; Referee in Case of Need

Unless otherwise instructed and except as provided in Article 5, a bank presenting a documentary draft:

(1) must deliver the documents to the drawee on acceptance of the draft if it is payable more than three days after presentment; otherwise, only on payment; and

(2) upon dishonor, either in the case of presentment for acceptance or presentment for payment, may seek and follow instructions from any referee in case of need designated in the draft or, if the presenting bank does not choose to utilize the referee's services, it must use diligence and good faith to ascertain the reason for dishonor, must notify its transferor of the dishonor and of the results of its effort to ascertain the reasons therefor, and must request instructions.

However the presenting bank is under no obligation with respect to goods represented by the documents except to follow any reasonable instructions seasonably received; it has a right to reimbursement for any expense incurred in following instructions and to prepayment of or indemnity for those expenses.

As amended in 1990.

§4–504. Privilege of Presenting Bank to Deal With Goods; Security Interest for Expenses

(a) A presenting bank that, following the dishonor of a documentary draft, has seasonably requested instructions but does not receive them within a reasonable time may store, sell, or otherwise deal with the goods in any reasonable manner.

(b) For its reasonable expenses incurred by action under subsection (a) the presenting bank has a lien upon the goods or their proceeds, which may be foreclosed in the same manner as an unpaid seller's lien. As amended in 1990.

ARTICLE 4A FUNDS TRANSFERS

Part 1 Subject Matter and Definitions

§4A–101. Short Title

This Article may be cited as Uniform Commercial Code—Funds Transfers.

§4A–102. Subject Matter

Except as otherwise provided in Section 4A–108, this Article applies to funds transfers defined in Section 4A–104.

§4A–103. Payment Order—Definitions

(a) In this Article:

(1) "Payment order" means an instruction of a sender to a receiving bank, transmitted orally, electronically, or in writing, to pay, or to cause another bank to pay, a fixed or determinable amount of money to a beneficiary if:

(i) the instruction does not state a condition to payment to the beneficiary other than time of payment,

(ii) the receiving bank is to be reimbursed by debiting an account of, or otherwise receiving payment from, the sender, and

(iii) the instruction is transmitted by the sender directly to the receiving bank or to an agent, funds-transfer system, or communication system for transmittal to the receiving bank.

(2) "Beneficiary" means the person to be paid by the beneficiary's bank.

(3) "Beneficiary's bank" means the bank identified in a payment order in which an account of the beneficiary is to be credited pursuant to the order or which otherwise is to make payment to the beneficiary if the order does not provide for payment to an account.

(4) "Receiving bank" means the bank to which the sender's instruction is addressed.

(5) "Sender" means the person giving the instruction to the receiving bank.

(b) If an instruction complying with subsection (a)(1) is to make more than one payment to a beneficiary, the instruction is a separate payment order with respect to each payment.

(c) A payment order is issued when it is sent to the receiving bank.

§4A–104. Funds Transfer—Definitions

In this Article:

(a) "Funds transfer" means the series of transactions, beginning with the originator's payment order, made for the purpose of making payment to the beneficiary of the order. The term includes any payment order issued by the originator's bank or an intermediary bank intended to carry out the originator's payment order. A funds transfer is completed by acceptance by the beneficiary's bank of a payment order for the benefit of the beneficiary of the originator's payment order.

(b) "Intermediary bank" means a receiving bank other than the originator's bank or the beneficiary's bank.

(c) "Originator" means the sender of the first payment order in a funds transfer.

(d) "Originator's bank" means (i) the receiving bank to which the payment order of the originator is issued if the originator is not a bank, or (ii) the originator if the originator is a bank.

§4A–105. Other Definitions

(a) In this Article:

(1) "Authorized account" means a deposit account of a customer in a bank designated by the customer as a source of payment of payment orders issued by the customer to the bank. If a customer does not so designate an account, any account of the customer is an authorized account if payment of a payment order from that account is not inconsistent with a restriction on the use of that account.

(2) "Bank" means a person engaged in the business of banking and includes a savings bank, savings and loan association, credit union, and trust company. A branch or separate office of a bank is a separate bank for purposes of this Article.

(3) "Customer" means a person, including a bank, having an account with a bank or from whom a bank has agreed to receive payment orders.

(4) "Funds-transfer business day" of a receiving bank means the part of a day during which the receiving bank is open for the receipt, processing, and transmittal of payment orders and cancellations and amendments of payment orders.

(5) "Funds-transfer system" means a wire transfer network, automated clearing house, or other communication system of a clearing house or other association of banks through which a payment order by a bank may be transmitted to the bank to which the order is addressed.

(6) "Good faith" means honesty in fact and the observance of reasonable commercial standards of fair dealing.

(7) "Prove" with respect to a fact means to meet the burden of establishing the fact (Section 1–201(8)).

(b) Other definitions applying to this Article and the sections in which they appear are:

"Acceptance"	Section 4A–209
"Beneficiary"	Section 4A–103
"Beneficiary's bank"	Section 4A–103
"Executed"	Section 4A–301
"Execution date"	Section 4A–301
"Funds transfer"	Section 4A–104
"Funds-transfer system rule"	Section 4A–501
"Intermediary bank"	Section 4A–104
"Originator"	Section 4A–104
"Originator's bank"	Section 4A–104
"Payment by beneficiary's bank to beneficiary"	Section 4A–405
"Payment by originator to beneficiary"	Section 4A–406
"Payment by sender to receiving bank"	Section 4A–403
"Payment date"	Section 4A–401
"Payment order"	Section 4A–103
"Receiving bank"	Section 4A–103
"Security procedure"	Section 4A–201
"Sender"	Section 4A–103

(c) The following definitions in Article 4 apply to this Article:

"Clearing house"	Section 4–104
"Item"	Section 4–104
"Suspends payments"	Section 4–104

(d) In addition Article 1 contains general definitions and principles of construction and interpretation applicable throughout this Article.

§4A–106. Time Payment Order Is Received

(a) The time of receipt of a payment order or communication cancelling or amending a payment order is determined by the rules applicable to receipt of a notice stated in Section 1–201(27). A receiving bank may fix a cut-off time or times on a funds-transfer business day for the receipt and processing of payment orders and communications cancelling or amending payment orders. Different cut-off times may apply to payment orders, cancellations, or amendments, or to different categories of payment orders, cancellations, or amendments. A cut-off time may apply to senders generally or different cut-off times may apply to different senders or categories of payment orders. If a payment order or communication cancelling or amending a payment order is received after the close of a funds-transfer business day or after the appropriate cut-off time on a funds-transfer business day, the receiving bank may treat the payment order or communication as received at the opening of the next funds-transfer business day.

(b) If this Article refers to an execution date or payment date or states a day on which a receiving bank is required to take action, and the date or day does not fall on a funds-transfer business day, the next day that is a funds-transfer business day is treated as the date or day stated, unless the contrary is stated in this Article.

§4A–107. Federal Reserve Regulations and Operating Circulars

Regulations of the Board of Governors of the Federal Reserve System and operating circulars of the Federal Reserve Banks supersede any inconsistent provision of this Article to the extent of the inconsistency.

§4A–108. Exclusion of Consumer Transactions Governed by Federal Law

This Article does not apply to a funds transfer any part of which is governed by the Electronic Fund Transfer Act of 1978 (Title XX, Public Law 95-630, 92 Stat. 3728, 15 U.S.C. § 1693 et seq.) as amended from time to time.

Part 2 Issue and Acceptance of Payment Order

§4A–201. Security Procedure

"Security procedure" means a procedure established by agreement of a customer and a receiving bank for the purpose of (i) verifying that a payment order or communication amending or cancelling a payment order is that of the customer, or (ii) detecting error in the transmission or the content of the payment order or communication. A security procedure may require the use of algorithms or other codes, identifying words or numbers, encryption, callback procedures, or similar security devices. Comparison of a signature on a payment order or communication with an authorized specimen signature of the customer is not by itself a security procedure.

§4A–202. Authorized and Verified Payment Orders

(a) A payment order received by the receiving bank is the authorized order of the person identified as sender if that person authorized the order or is otherwise bound by it under the law of agency.

(b) If a bank and its customer have agreed that the authenticity of payment orders issued to the bank in the name of the customer as sender will be verified pursuant to a security procedure, a payment order received by the receiving bank is effective as the order of the customer, whether or not authorized, if (i) the security procedure is a commercially reasonable method of providing security against unauthorized payment orders, and (ii) the bank proves that it accepted the payment order in good faith and in compliance with the security procedure and any written agreement or instruction of the customer restricting acceptance of payment orders issued in the name of the customer. The bank is not required to follow an instruction that violates a written agreement with the customer or notice of which is not received at a time and in a manner affording the bank a reasonable opportunity to act on it before the payment order is accepted.

(c) Commercial reasonableness of a security procedure is a question of law to be determined by considering the wishes of the customer expressed to the bank, the circumstances of the customer known to the bank, including the size, type, and frequency of payment orders normally issued by the customer to the bank, alternative security procedures offered to the customer, and security procedures in general use by customers and receiving banks similarly situated. A security procedure is deemed to be commercially reasonable if (i) the security procedure was chosen by the customer after the bank offered, and the customer refused, a security procedure that was commercially reasonable for that customer, and (ii) the customer expressly agreed in writing to be bound by any payment order, whether or not authorized, issued in its name and accepted by the bank in compliance with the security procedure chosen by the customer.

(d) The term "sender" in this Article includes the customer in whose name a payment order is issued if the order is the authorized order of the customer under subsection (a), or it is effective as the order of the customer under subsection (b).

(e) This section applies to amendments and cancellations of payment orders to the same extent it applies to payment orders.

(f) Except as provided in this section and in Section 4A–203(a)(1), rights and obligations arising under this section or Section 4A–203 may not be varied by agreement.

§4A–203. Unenforceability of Certain Verified Payment Orders

(a) If an accepted payment order is not, under Section 4A–202(a), an authorized order of a customer identified as sender, but is effective as an order of the customer pursuant to Section 4A–202(b), the following rules apply:

(1) By express written agreement, the receiving bank may limit the extent to which it is entitled to enforce or retain payment of the payment order.

(2) The receiving bank is not entitled to enforce or retain payment of the payment order if the customer proves that the order was not caused, directly or indirectly, by a person (i) entrusted at any time with duties to act for the customer with respect to payment orders or the security procedure, or (ii) who obtained access to transmitting facilities of the customer or who obtained, from a source controlled by the customer and without authority of the receiving bank, information facilitating breach of the security procedure, regardless of how the information was obtained or whether the customer was at fault. Information includes any access device, computer software, or the like.

(b) This section applies to amendments of payment orders to the same extent it applies to payment orders.

§4A–204. Refund of Payment and Duty of Customer to Report With Respect to Unauthorized Payment Order

(a) If a receiving bank accepts a payment order issued in the name of its customer as sender which is (i) not authorized and not effective as the order of the customer under Section 4A–202, or (ii) not enforceable, in whole or in part, against the customer under Section 4A–203, the bank shall refund any payment of the payment order received from the customer to the extent the bank is not entitled to enforce payment and shall pay interest on the refundable amount calculated from the date the bank received payment to the date of the refund. However, the customer is not entitled to interest from the bank on the amount to be refunded if the customer fails to exercise ordinary care to determine that the order was not authorized by the customer and to notify the bank of the relevant facts within a reasonable time not exceeding 90 days after the date the customer received notification from the bank that the order was accepted or that the customer's account was debited with respect to the order. The bank is not entitled to any recovery from the customer on account of a failure by the customer to give notification as stated in this section.

(b) Reasonable time under subsection (a) may be fixed by agreement as stated in Section 1–204(1), but the obligation of a receiving bank to refund payment as stated in subsection (a) may not otherwise be varied by agreement.

§4A–205. Erroneous Payment Orders

(a) If an accepted payment order was transmitted pursuant to a security procedure for the detection of error and the payment order (i) erroneously instructed payment to a beneficiary not intended by the sender, (ii) erroneously instructed payment in an amount greater than the amount intended by the sender, or (iii) was an erroneously transmitted duplicate of a payment order previously sent by the sender, the following rules apply:

(1) If the sender proves that the sender or a person acting on behalf of the sender pursuant to Section 4A–206 complied with the security procedure and that the error would have been detected if the receiving bank had also complied, the sender is not obliged to pay the order to the extent stated in paragraphs (2) and (3).

(2) If the funds transfer is completed on the basis of an erroneous payment order described in clause (i) or (iii) of subsection (a), the sender is not obliged to pay the order and the receiving bank is entitled to recover from the beneficiary any amount paid to the beneficiary to the extent allowed by the law governing mistake and restitution.

(3) If the funds transfer is completed on the basis of a payment order described in clause (ii) of subsection (a), the sender is not obliged to pay the order to the extent the amount received by the beneficiary is greater than the amount intended by the sender. In that case, the receiving bank is entitled to recover from the beneficiary the excess amount received to the extent allowed by the law governing mistake and restitution.

(b) If (i) the sender of an erroneous payment order described in subsection (a) is not obliged to pay all or part of the order, and (ii) the sender receives notification from the receiving bank that the order was accepted by the bank or that the sender's account was debited with respect to the order, the sender has a duty to exercise ordinary care, on the basis of information available to the sender, to discover the error with respect to the order and to advise the bank of the relevant facts within a reasonable time, not exceeding 90 days, after the bank's notification was received by the sender. If the bank proves that the sender failed to perform that duty, the sender is liable to the bank for the loss the bank proves it incurred as a result of the failure, but the liability of the sender may not exceed the amount of the sender's order.

(c) This section applies to amendments to payment orders to the same extent it applies to payment orders.

§4A–206. Transmission of Payment Order Through Funds-Transfer or Other Communication System

(a) If a payment order addressed to a receiving bank is transmitted to a funds-transfer system or other third-party communication system for transmittal to the bank, the system is deemed to be an agent of the sender for the purpose of transmitting the payment order to the bank. If there is a discrepancy between the terms of the payment order transmitted to the system and the terms of the payment order transmitted by the system to the bank, the terms of the payment order of the sender are those transmitted by the system. This section does not apply to a funds-transfer system of the Federal Reserve Banks.

(b) This section applies to cancellations and amendments of payment orders to the same extent it applies to payment orders.

§4A–207. Misdescription of Beneficiary

(a) Subject to subsection (b), if, in a payment order received by the beneficiary's bank, the name, bank account number, or other identification of the beneficiary refers to a nonexistent or unidentifiable person or account, no person has rights as a beneficiary of the order and acceptance of the order cannot occur.

(b) If a payment order received by the beneficiary's bank identifies the beneficiary both by name and by an identifying or bank account number and the name and number identify different persons, the following rules apply:

    (1) Except as otherwise provided in subsection (c), if the beneficiary's bank does not know that the name and number refer to different persons, it may rely on the number as the proper identification of the beneficiary of the order. The beneficiary's bank need not determine whether the name and number refer to the same person.

    (2) If the beneficiary's bank pays the person identified by name or knows that the name and number identify different persons, no person has rights as beneficiary except the person paid by the beneficiary's bank if that person was entitled to receive payment from the originator of the funds transfer. If no person has rights as beneficiary, acceptance of the order cannot occur.

(c) If (i) a payment order described in subsection (b) is accepted, (ii) the originator's payment order described the beneficiary inconsistently by name and number, and (iii) the beneficiary's bank pays the person identified by number as permitted by subsection (b)(1), the following rules apply:

    (1) If the originator is a bank, the originator is obliged to pay its order.

    (2) If the originator is not a bank and proves that the person identified by number was not entitled to receive payment from the originator, the originator is not obliged to pay its order unless the originator's bank proves that the originator, before acceptance of the originator's order, had notice that payment of a payment order issued by the originator might be made by the beneficiary's bank on the basis of an identifying or bank account number even if it identifies a person different from the named beneficiary. Proof of notice may be made by any admissible evidence. The originator's bank satisfies the burden of proof if it proves that the originator, before the payment order was accepted, signed a writing stating the information to which the notice relates.

(d) In a case governed by subsection (b)(1), if the beneficiary's bank rightfully pays the person identified by number and that person was not entitled to receive payment from the originator, the amount paid may be recovered from that person to the extent allowed by the law governing mistake and restitution as follows:

    (1) If the originator is obliged to pay its payment order as stated in subsection (c), the originator has the right to recover.

    (2) If the originator is not a bank and is not obliged to pay its payment order, the originator's bank has the right to recover.

§4A–208. Misdescription of Intermediary Bank or Beneficiary's Bank

(a) This subsection applies to a payment order identifying an intermediary bank or the beneficiary's bank only by an identifying number.

    (1) The receiving bank may rely on the number as the proper identification of the intermediary or beneficiary's bank and need not determine whether the number identifies a bank.

    (2) The sender is obliged to compensate the receiving bank for any loss and expenses incurred by the receiving bank as a result of its reliance on the number in executing or attempting to execute the order.

(b) This subsection applies to a payment order identifying an intermediary bank or the beneficiary's bank both by name and an identifying number if the name and number identify different persons.

    (1) If the sender is a bank, the receiving bank may rely on the number as the proper identification of the intermediary or beneficiary's bank if the receiving bank, when it executes the sender's order, does not know that the name and number identify different persons. The receiving bank need not determine whether the name and number refer to the same person or whether the number refers to a bank. The sender is obliged to compensate the receiving bank for any loss and expenses incurred by the receiving bank as a result of its reliance on the number in executing or attempting to execute the order.

    (2) If the sender is not a bank and the receiving bank proves that the sender, before the payment order was accepted, had notice that the receiving bank might rely on the number as the proper identification of the intermediary or beneficiary's bank even if it identifies a person different from the bank identified by name, the rights and obligations of the sender and the receiving bank are governed by subsection (b)(1), as though the sender were a bank. Proof of notice may be made by any admissible evidence. The receiving bank satisfies the burden of proof if it proves that the sender, before the payment order was accepted, signed a writing stating the information to which the notice relates.

    (3) Regardless of whether the sender is a bank, the receiving bank may rely on the name as the proper identification of the intermediary or beneficiary's bank if the receiving bank, at the time it executes the sender's order, does not know that the name and number identify different persons. The receiving bank need not determine whether the name and number refer to the same person.

(4) If the receiving bank knows that the name and number identify different persons, reliance on either the name or the number in executing the sender's payment order is a breach of the obligation stated in Section 4A–302(a)(1).

§4A–209. Acceptance of Payment Order

(a) Subject to subsection (d), a receiving bank other than the beneficiary's bank accepts a payment order when it executes the order.

(b) Subject to subsections (c) and (d), a beneficiary's bank accepts a payment order at the earliest of the following times:

(1) when the bank (i) pays the beneficiary as stated in Section 4A–405(a) or 4A–405(b), or (ii) notifies the beneficiary of receipt of the order or that the account of the beneficiary has been credited with respect to the order unless the notice indicates that the bank is rejecting the order or that funds with respect to the order may not be withdrawn or used until receipt of payment from the sender of the order;

(2) when the bank receives payment of the entire amount of the sender's order pursuant to Section 4A–403(a)(1) or 4A–403(a)(2); or

(3) the opening of the next funds-transfer business day of the bank following the payment date of the order if, at that time, the amount of the sender's order is fully covered by a withdrawable credit balance in an authorized account of the sender or the bank has otherwise received full payment from the sender, unless the order was rejected before that time or is rejected within (i) one hour after that time, or (ii) one hour after the opening of the next business day of the sender following the payment date if that time is later. If notice of rejection is received by the sender after the payment date and the authorized account of the sender does not bear interest, the bank is obliged to pay interest to the sender on the amount of the order for the number of days elapsing after the payment date to the day the sender receives notice or learns that the order was not accepted, counting that day as an elapsed day. If the withdrawable credit balance during that period falls below the amount of the order, the amount of interest payable is reduced accordingly.

(c) Acceptance of a payment order cannot occur before the order is received by the receiving bank. Acceptance does not occur under subsection (b)(2) or (b)(3) if the beneficiary of the payment order does not have an account with the receiving bank, the account has been closed, or the receiving bank is not permitted by law to receive credits for the beneficiary's account.

(d) A payment order issued to the originator's bank cannot be accepted until the payment date if the bank is the beneficiary's bank, or the execution date if the bank is not the beneficiary's bank. If the originator's bank executes the originator's payment order before the execution date or pays the beneficiary of the originator's payment order before the payment date and the payment order is subsequently canceled pursuant to Section 4A–211(b), the bank may recover from the beneficiary any payment received to the extent allowed by the law governing mistake and restitution.

§4A–210. Rejection of Payment Order

(a) A payment order is rejected by the receiving bank by a notice of rejection transmitted to the sender orally, electronically, or in writing. A notice of rejection need not use any particular words and is sufficient if it indicates that the receiving bank is rejecting the order or will not execute or pay the order. Rejection is effective when the notice is given if transmission is by a means that is reasonable in the circumstances. If notice of rejection is given by a means that is not reasonable, rejection is effective when the notice is received. If an agreement of the sender and receiving bank establishes the means to be used to reject a payment order, (i) any means complying with the agreement is reasonable and (ii) any means not complying is not reasonable unless no significant delay in receipt of the notice resulted from the use of the noncomplying means.

(b) This subsection applies if a receiving bank other than the beneficiary's bank fails to execute a payment order despite the existence on the execution date of a withdrawable credit balance in an authorized account of the sender sufficient to cover the order. If the sender does not receive notice of rejection of the order on the execution date and the authorized account of the sender does not bear interest, the bank is obliged to pay interest to the sender on the amount of the order for the number of days elapsing after the execution date to the earlier of the day the order is canceled pursuant to Section 4A–211(d) or the day the sender receives notice or learns that the order was not executed, counting the final day of the period as an elapsed day. If the withdrawable credit balance during that period falls below the amount of the order, the amount of interest is reduced accordingly.

(c) If a receiving bank suspends payments, all unaccepted payment orders issued to it are deemed rejected at the time the bank suspends payments.

(d) Acceptance of a payment order precludes a later rejection of the order. Rejection of a payment order precludes a later acceptance of the order.

§4A–211. Cancellation and Amendment of Payment Order

(a) A communication of the sender of a payment order cancelling or amending the order may be transmitted to the receiving bank orally, electronically, or in writing. If a security procedure is in effect between the sender and the receiving bank, the communication is not effective to cancel or amend the order unless the communication is verified pursuant to the security procedure or the bank agrees to the cancellation or amendment.

(b) Subject to subsection (a), a communication by the sender cancelling or amending a payment order is effective to cancel or amend the order if notice of the communication is received at a time and in a manner affording the receiving bank a reasonable opportunity to act on the communication before the bank accepts the payment order.

(c) After a payment order has been accepted, cancellation or amendment of the order is not effective unless the receiving bank agrees or a funds-transfer system rule allows cancellation or amendment without agreement of the bank.

(1) With respect to a payment order accepted by a receiving bank other than the beneficiary's bank, cancellation or amendment is not effective unless a conforming cancellation or amendment of the payment order issued by the receiving bank is also made.

(2) With respect to a payment order accepted by the beneficiary's bank, cancellation or amendment is not effective unless the order was issued in execution of an unauthorized payment order, or because of a mistake by a sender in the funds transfer which resulted in the issuance of a payment order (i) that is a duplicate of a payment order previously issued by the sender, (ii) that orders payment to a beneficiary not entitled to receive payment from the originator, or (iii) that orders payment in an amount greater than the amount the beneficiary was entitled to receive from the originator. If the payment order is canceled or amended, the beneficiary's bank is entitled to recover from the beneficiary any amount paid to the beneficiary to the extent allowed by the law governing mistake and restitution.

(d) An unaccepted payment order is canceled by operation of law at the close of the fifth funds-transfer business day of the receiving bank after the execution date or payment date of the order.

(e) A canceled payment order cannot be accepted. If an accepted payment order is canceled, the acceptance is nullified and no person has any right or obligation based on the acceptance. Amendment of a payment order is deemed to be cancellation of the original order at the time of amendment and issue of a new payment order in the amended form at the same time.

(f) Unless otherwise provided in an agreement of the parties or in a funds-transfer system rule, if the receiving bank, after accepting a payment order, agrees to cancellation or amendment of the order by the sender or is bound by a funds-transfer system rule allowing cancellation or amendment without the bank's agreement, the sender, whether or not cancellation or amendment is effective, is liable to the bank for any loss and expenses, including reasonable attorney's fees, incurred by the bank as a result of the cancellation or amendment or attempted cancellation or amendment.

(g) A payment order is not revoked by the death or legal incapacity of the sender unless the receiving bank knows of the death or of an adjudication of incapacity by a court of competent jurisdiction and has reasonable opportunity to act before acceptance of the order.

(h) A funds-transfer system rule is not effective to the extent it conflicts with subsection (c)(2).

§4A–212. Liability and Duty of Receiving Bank Regarding Unaccepted Payment Order

If a receiving bank fails to accept a payment order that it is obliged by express agreement to accept, the bank is liable for breach of the agreement to the extent provided in the agreement or in this Article, but does not otherwise have any duty to accept a payment order or, before acceptance, to take any action, or refrain from taking action, with respect to the order except as provided in this Article or by express agreement. Liability based on acceptance arises only when acceptance occurs as stated in Section 4A–209, and liability is limited to that provided in this Article. A receiving bank is not the agent of the sender or beneficiary of the payment order it accepts, or of any other party to the funds transfer, and the bank owes no duty to any party to the funds transfer except as provided in this Article or by express agreement.

Part 3 Execution of Sender's Payment Order by Receiving Bank

§4A–301. Execution and Execution Date

(a) A payment order is "executed" by the receiving bank when it issues a payment order intended to carry out the payment order received by the bank. A payment order received by the beneficiary's bank can be accepted but cannot be executed.

(b) "Execution date" of a payment order means the day on which the receiving bank may properly issue a payment order in execution of the sender's order. The execution date may be determined by instruction of the sender but cannot be earlier than the day the order is received and, unless otherwise determined, is the day the order is received. If the sender's instruction states a payment date, the execution date is the payment date or an earlier date on which execution is reasonably necessary to allow payment to the beneficiary on the payment date.

§4A-302. Obligations of Receiving Bank in Execution of Payment Order

(a) Except as provided in subsections (b) through (d), if the receiving bank accepts a payment order pursuant to Section 4A-209(a), the bank has the following obligations in executing the order:

(1) The receiving bank is obliged to issue, on the execution date, a payment order complying with the sender's order and to follow the sender's instructions concerning (i) any intermediary bank or funds-transfer system to be used in carrying out the funds transfer, or (ii) the means by which payment orders are to be transmitted in the funds transfer. If the originator's bank issues a payment order to an intermediary bank, the originator's bank is obliged to instruct the intermediary bank according to the instruction of the originator. An intermediary bank in the funds transfer is similarly bound by an instruction given to it by the sender of the payment order it accepts.

(2) If the sender's instruction states that the funds transfer is to be carried out telephonically or by wire transfer or otherwise indicates that the funds transfer is to be carried out by the most expeditious means, the receiving bank is obliged to transmit its payment order by the most expeditious available means, and to instruct any intermediary bank accordingly. If a sender's instruction states a payment date, the receiving bank is obliged to transmit its payment order at a time and by means reasonably necessary to allow payment to the beneficiary on the payment date or as soon thereafter as is feasible.

(b) Unless otherwise instructed, a receiving bank executing a payment order may (i) use any funds-transfer system if use of that system is reasonable in the circumstances, and (ii) issue a payment order to the beneficiary's bank or to an intermediary bank through which a payment order conforming to the sender's order can expeditiously be issued to the beneficiary's bank if the receiving bank exercises ordinary care in the selection of the intermediary bank. A receiving bank is not required to follow an instruction of the sender designating a funds-transfer system to be used in carrying out the funds transfer if the receiving bank, in good faith, determines that it is not feasible to follow the instruction or that following the instruction would unduly delay completion of the funds transfer.

(c) Unless subsection (a)(2) applies or the receiving bank is otherwise instructed, the bank may execute a payment order by transmitting its payment order by first class mail or by any means reasonable in the circumstances. If the receiving bank is instructed to execute the sender's order by transmitting its payment order by a particular means, the receiving bank may issue its payment order by the means stated or by any means as expeditious as the means stated.

(d) Unless instructed by the sender, (i) the receiving bank may not obtain payment of its charges for services and expenses in connection with the execution of the sender's order by issuing a payment order in an amount equal to the amount of the sender's order less the amount of the charges, and (ii) may not instruct a subsequent receiving bank to obtain payment of its charges in the same manner.

§4A-303. Erroneous Execution of Payment Order

(a) A receiving bank that (i) executes the payment order of the sender by issuing a payment order in an amount greater than the amount of the sender's order, or (ii) issues a payment order in execution of the sender's order and then issues a duplicate order, is entitled to payment of the amount of the sender's order under Section 4A-402(c) if that subsection is otherwise satisfied. The bank is entitled to recover from the beneficiary of the erroneous order the excess payment received to the extent allowed by the law governing mistake and restitution.

(b) A receiving bank that executes the payment order of the sender by issuing a payment order in an amount less than the amount of the sender's order is entitled to payment of the amount of the sender's order under Section 4A-402(c) if (i) that subsection is otherwise satisfied and (ii) the bank corrects its mistake by issuing an additional payment order for the benefit of the beneficiary of the sender's order. If the error is not corrected, the issuer of the erroneous order is entitled to receive or retain payment from the sender of the order it accepted only to the extent of the amount of the erroneous order. This subsection does not apply if the receiving bank executes the sender's payment order by issuing a payment order in an amount less than the amount of the sender's order for the purpose of obtaining payment of its charges for services and expenses pursuant to instruction of the sender.

(c) If a receiving bank executes the payment order of the sender by issuing a payment order to a beneficiary different from the beneficiary of the sender's order and the funds transfer is completed on the basis of that error, the sender of the payment order that was erroneously executed and all previous senders in the funds transfer are not obliged to pay the payment orders they issued. The issuer of the erroneous order is entitled to recover from the beneficiary of the order the payment received to the extent allowed by the law governing mistake and restitution.

§4A–304. Duty of Sender to Report Erroneously Executed Payment Order

If the sender of a payment order that is erroneously executed as stated in Section 4A–303 receives notification from the receiving bank that the order was executed or that the sender's account was debited with respect to the order, the sender has a duty to exercise ordinary care to determine, on the basis of information available to the sender, that the order was erroneously executed and to notify the bank of the relevant facts within a reasonable time not exceeding 90 days after the notification from the bank was received by the sender. If the sender fails to perform that duty, the bank is not obliged to pay interest on any amount refundable to the sender under Section 4A–402(d) for the period before the bank learns of the execution error. The bank is not entitled to any recovery from the sender on account of a failure by the sender to perform the duty stated in this section.

§4A–305. Liability for Late or Improper Execution or Failure to Execute Payment Order

(a) If a funds transfer is completed but execution of a payment order by the receiving bank in breach of Section 4A–302 results in delay in payment to the beneficiary, the bank is obliged to pay interest to either the originator or the beneficiary of the funds transfer for the period of delay caused by the improper execution. Except as provided in subsection (c), additional damages are not recoverable.

(b) If execution of a payment order by a receiving bank in breach of Section 4A–302 results in (i) non-completion of the funds transfer, (ii) failure to use an intermediary bank designated by the originator, or (iii) issuance of a payment order that does not comply with the terms of the payment order of the originator, the bank is liable to the originator for its expenses in the funds transfer and for incidental expenses and interest losses, to the extent not covered by subsection (a), resulting from the improper execution. Except as provided in subsection (c), additional damages are not recoverable.

(c) In addition to the amounts payable under subsections (a) and (b), damages, including consequential damages, are recoverable to the extent provided in an express written agreement of the receiving bank.

(d) If a receiving bank fails to execute a payment order it was obliged by express agreement to execute, the receiving bank is liable to the sender for its expenses in the transaction and for incidental expenses and interest losses resulting from the failure to execute. Additional damages, including consequential damages, are recoverable to the extent provided in an express written agreement of the receiving bank, but are not otherwise recoverable.

(e) Reasonable attorney's fees are recoverable if demand for compensation under subsection (a) or (b) is made and refused before an action is brought on the claim. If a claim is made for breach of an agreement under subsection (d) and the agreement does not provide for damages, reasonable attorney's fees are recoverable if demand for compensation under subsection (d) is made and refused before an action is brought on the claim.

(f) Except as stated in this section, the liability of a receiving bank under subsections (a) and (b) may not be varied by agreement.

Part 4 Payment

§4A–401. Payment Date

"Payment date" of a payment order means the day on which the amount of the order is payable to the beneficiary by the beneficiary's bank. The payment date may be determined by instruction of the sender but cannot be earlier than the day the order is received by the beneficiary's bank and, unless otherwise determined, is the day the order is received by the beneficiary's bank.

§4A–402. Obligation of Sender to Pay Receiving Bank

(a) This section is subject to Sections 4A–205 and 4A–207.

(b) With respect to a payment order issued to the beneficiary's bank, acceptance of the order by the bank obliges the sender to pay the bank the amount of the order, but payment is not due until the payment date of the order.

(c) This subsection is subject to subsection (e) and to Section 4A–303. With respect to a payment order issued to a receiving bank other than the beneficiary's bank, acceptance of the order by the receiving bank obliges the sender to pay the bank the amount of the sender's order. Payment by the sender is not due until the execution date of the sender's order. The obligation of that sender to pay its payment order is excused if the funds transfer is not completed by acceptance by the beneficiary's bank of a payment order instructing payment to the beneficiary of that sender's payment order.

(d) If the sender of a payment order pays the order and was not obliged to pay all or part of the amount paid, the bank receiving payment is obliged to refund payment to the extent the sender was not obliged to pay. Except as provided in Sections 4A–204 and 4A–304, interest is payable on the refundable amount from the date of payment.

(e) If a funds transfer is not completed as stated in subsection (c) and an intermediary bank is obliged to refund payment as stated in subsection (d) but is unable to do so because not permitted by applicable law or because the bank suspends payments, a sender in the funds transfer that executed a payment order in compliance with an instruction, as stated in Section 4A–302(a)(1), to route the funds transfer through that intermediary bank is entitled to receive or retain payment from the sender of the payment order that is accepted. The first sender in the funds transfer that issued an instruction requiring routing through that intermediary bank is subrogated to the right of the bank that paid the intermediary bank to refund as stated in subsection (d).

(f) The right of the sender of a payment order to be excused from the obligation to pay the order as stated in subsection (c) or to receive refund under subsection (d) may not be varied by agreement.

§4A–403. Payment by Sender to Receiving Bank

(a) Payment of the sender's obligation under Section 4A–402 to pay the receiving bank occurs as follows:

(1) If the sender is a bank, payment occurs when the receiving bank receives final settlement of the obligation through a Federal Reserve Bank or through a funds-transfer system.

(2) If the sender is a bank and the sender (i) credited an account of the receiving bank with the sender, or (ii) caused an account of the receiving bank in another bank to be credited, payment occurs when the credit is withdrawn or, if not withdrawn, at midnight of the day on which the credit is withdrawable and the receiving bank learns of that fact.

(3) If the receiving bank debits an account of the sender with the receiving bank, payment occurs when the debit is made to the extent the debit is covered by a withdrawable credit balance in the account.

(b) If the sender and receiving bank are members of a funds-transfer system that nets obligations multilaterally among participants, the receiving bank receives final settlement when settlement is complete in accordance with the rules of the system. The obligation of the sender to pay the amount of a payment order transmitted through the funds-transfer system may be satisfied, to the extent permitted by the rules of the system, by setting off and applying against the sender's obligation the right of the sender to receive payment from the receiving bank of the amount of any other payment order transmitted to the sender by the receiving bank through the funds-transfer system. The aggregate balance of obligations owed by each sender to each receiving bank in the funds-transfer system may be satisfied, to the extent permitted by the rules of the system, by setting off and applying against that balance the aggregate balance of obligations owed to the sender by other members of the system. The aggregate balance is determined after the right of setoff stated in the second sentence of this subsection has been exercised.

(c) If two banks transmit payment orders to each other under an agreement that settlement of the obligations of each bank to the other under Section 4A–402 will be made at the end of the day or other period, the total amount owed with respect to all orders transmitted by one bank shall be set off against the total amount owed with respect to all orders transmitted by the other bank. To the extent of the setoff, each bank has made payment to the other.

(d) In a case not covered by subsection (a), the time when payment of the sender's obligation under Section 4A–402(b) or 4A–402(c) occurs is governed by applicable principles of law that determine when an obligation is satisfied.

§4A–404. Obligation of Beneficiary's Bank to Pay and Give Notice to Beneficiary

(a) Subject to Sections 4A–211(e), 4A–405(d), and 4A–405(e), if a beneficiary's bank accepts a payment order, the bank is obliged to pay the amount of the order to the beneficiary of the order. Payment is due on the payment date of the order, but if acceptance occurs on the payment date after the close of the funds-transfer business day of the bank, payment is due on the next funds-transfer business day. If the bank refuses to pay after demand by the beneficiary and receipt of notice of particular circumstances that will give rise to consequential damages as a result of nonpayment, the beneficiary may recover damages resulting from the refusal to pay to the extent the bank had notice of the damages, unless the bank proves that it did not pay because of a reasonable doubt concerning the right of the beneficiary to payment.

(b) If a payment order accepted by the beneficiary's bank instructs payment to an account of the beneficiary, the bank is obliged to notify the beneficiary of receipt of the order before midnight of the next funds-transfer business day following the payment date. If the payment order does not instruct payment to an account of the beneficiary, the bank is required to notify the beneficiary only if notice is required by the order. Notice may be given by first class mail or any other means reasonable in the circumstances. If the bank fails to give the required notice, the bank is obliged to pay interest to the beneficiary on the amount of the payment order from the day notice should have been given until the day the beneficiary learned of receipt of the payment order by the bank. No other damages are recoverable. Reasonable attorney's fees are also recoverable if demand for interest is made and refused before an action is brought on the claim.

(c) The right of a beneficiary to receive payment and damages as stated in subsection (a) may not be varied by agreement or a funds-transfer system rule. The right of a beneficiary to be notified as stated in subsection (b) may be varied by agreement of the beneficiary or by a funds-transfer system rule if the beneficiary is notified of the rule before initiation of the funds transfer.

§4A–405. Payment by Beneficiary's Bank to Beneficiary

(a) If the beneficiary's bank credits an account of the beneficiary of a payment order, payment of the bank's obligation under Section 4A–404(a) occurs when and to the extent (i) the beneficiary is notified of the right to withdraw the credit, (ii) the bank lawfully applies the credit to a debt of the beneficiary, or (iii) funds with respect to the order are otherwise made available to the beneficiary by the bank.

(b) If the beneficiary's bank does not credit an account of the beneficiary of a payment order, the time when payment of the bank's obligation under Section 4A–404(a) occurs is governed by principles of law that determine when an obligation is satisfied.

(c) Except as stated in subsection (d) and (e), if the beneficiary's bank pays the beneficiary of a payment order under a condition to payment or agreement of the beneficiary giving the bank the right to recover payment from the beneficiary if the bank does not receive payment of the order, the condition to payment or agreement is not enforceable.

(d) A funds-transfer system rule may provide that payments made to beneficiaries of funds transfers made through the system are provisional until receipt of payment by the beneficiary's bank of the payment order it accepted. A beneficiary's bank that makes a payment that is provisional under the rule is entitled to refund from the beneficiary if (i) the rule requires that both the beneficiary and the originator be given notice of the provisional nature of the payment before the funds transfer is initiated, (ii) the beneficiary, the beneficiary's bank and the originator's bank agreed to be bound by the rule, and (iii) the beneficiary's bank did not receive payment of the payment order that it accepted. If the beneficiary is obliged to refund payment to the beneficiary's bank, acceptance of the payment order by the beneficiary's bank is nullified and no payment by the originator of the funds transfer to the beneficiary occurs under Section 4A–406.

(e) This subsection applies to a funds transfer that includes a payment order transmitted over a funds-transfer system that (i) nets obligations multilaterally among participants, and (ii) has in effect a loss-sharing agreement among participants for the purpose of providing funds necessary to complete settlement of the obligations of one or more participants that do not meet their settlement obligations. If the beneficiary's bank in the funds transfer accepts a payment order and the system fails to complete settlement pursuant to its rules with respect to any payment order in the funds transfer, (i) the acceptance by the beneficiary's bank is nullified and no person has any right or obligation based on the acceptance, (ii) the beneficiary's bank is entitled to recover payment from the beneficiary, (iii) no payment by the originator to the beneficiary occurs under Section 4A–406, and (iv) subject to Section 4A–402(e), each sender in the funds transfer is excused from its obligation to pay its payment order under Section 4A–402(c) because the funds transfer has not been completed.

§4A–406. Payment by Originator to Beneficiary; Discharge of Underlying Obligation

(a) Subject to Sections 4A–211(e), 4A–405(d), and 4A–405(e), the originator of a funds transfer pays the beneficiary of the originator's payment order (i) at the time a payment order for the benefit of the beneficiary is accepted by the beneficiary's bank in the funds transfer and (ii) in an amount equal to the amount of the order accepted by the beneficiary's bank, but not more than the amount of the originator's order.

(b) If payment under subsection (a) is made to satisfy an obligation, the obligation is discharged to the same extent discharge would result from payment to the beneficiary of the same amount in money, unless (i) the payment under subsection (a) was made by a means prohibited by the contract of the beneficiary with respect to the obligation, (ii) the beneficiary, within a reasonable time after receiving notice of receipt of the order by the beneficiary's bank, notified the originator of the beneficiary's refusal of the payment, (iii) funds with respect to the order were not withdrawn by the beneficiary or applied to a debt of the beneficiary, and (iv) the beneficiary would suffer a loss that could reasonably have been avoided if payment had been made by a means complying with the contract. If payment by the originator does not result in discharge under this section, the originator is subrogated to the rights of the beneficiary to receive payment from the beneficiary's bank under Section 4A–404(a).

(c) For the purpose of determining whether discharge of an obligation occurs under subsection (b), if the beneficiary's bank accepts a payment order in an amount equal to the amount of the originator's payment order less charges of one or more receiving banks in the funds transfer, payment to the beneficiary is deemed to be in the amount of the originator's order unless upon demand by the beneficiary the originator does not pay the beneficiary the amount of the deducted charges.

(d) Rights of the originator or of the beneficiary of a funds transfer under this section may be varied only by agreement of the originator and the beneficiary.

Part 5 Miscellaneous Provisions

§4A–501. Variation by Agreement and Effect of Funds-Transfer System Rule

(a) Except as otherwise provided in this Article, the rights and obligations of a party to a funds transfer may be varied by agreement of the affected party.

(b) "Funds-transfer system rule" means a rule of an association of banks (i) governing transmission of payment orders by means of a funds-transfer system of the association or rights and obligations with respect to those orders, or (ii) to the extent the rule governs rights and obligations between banks that are parties to a funds transfer in which a Federal Reserve Bank, acting as an intermediary bank, sends a payment order to the beneficiary's bank. Except as otherwise provided in this Article, a funds-transfer system rule governing rights and obligations between participating banks using the system may be effective even if the rule conflicts with this Article and indirectly affects another party to the funds transfer who does not consent to the rule. A funds-transfer system rule may also govern rights and obligations of parties other than participating banks using the system to the extent stated in Sections 4A–404(c), 4A–405(d), and 4A–507(c).

§4A–502. Creditor Process Served on Receiving Bank; Setoff by Beneficiary's Bank

(a) As used in this section, "creditor process" means levy, attachment, garnishment, notice of lien, sequestration, or similar process issued by or on behalf of a creditor or other claimant with respect to an account.

(b) This subsection applies to creditor process with respect to an authorized account of the sender of a payment order if the creditor process is served on the receiving bank. For the purpose of determining rights with respect to the creditor process, if the receiving bank accepts the payment order the balance in the authorized account is deemed to be reduced by the amount of the payment order to the extent the bank did not otherwise receive payment of the order, unless the creditor process is served at a time and in a manner affording the bank a reasonable opportunity to act on it before the bank accepts the payment order.

(c) If a beneficiary's bank has received a payment order for payment to the beneficiary's account in the bank, the following rules apply:

(1) The bank may credit the beneficiary's account. The amount credited may be set off against an obligation owed by the beneficiary to the bank or may be applied to satisfy creditor process served on the bank with respect to the account.

(2) The bank may credit the beneficiary's account and allow withdrawal of the amount credited unless creditor process with respect to the account is served at a time and in a manner affording the bank a reasonable opportunity to act to prevent withdrawal.

(3) If creditor process with respect to the beneficiary's account has been served and the bank has had a reasonable opportunity to act on it, the bank

may not reject the payment order except for a reason unrelated to the service of process.

(d) Creditor process with respect to a payment by the originator to the beneficiary pursuant to a funds transfer may be served only on the beneficiary's bank with respect to the debt owed by that bank to the beneficiary. Any other bank served with the creditor process is not obliged to act with respect to the process.

§4A–503. Injunction or Restraining Order With Respect to Funds Transfer

For proper cause and in compliance with applicable law, a court may restrain (i) a person from issuing a payment order to initiate a funds transfer, (ii) an originator's bank from executing the payment order of the originator, or (iii) the beneficiary's bank from releasing funds to the beneficiary or the beneficiary from withdrawing the funds. A court may not otherwise restrain a person from issuing a payment order, paying or receiving payment of a payment order, or otherwise acting with respect to a funds transfer.

§4A–504. Order in Which Items and Payment Orders May Be Charged to Account; Order of Withdrawals From Account

(a) If a receiving bank has received more than one payment order of the sender or one or more payment orders and other items that are payable from the sender's account, the bank may charge the sender's account with respect to the various orders and items in any sequence.

(b) In determining whether a credit to an account has been withdrawn by the holder of the account or applied to a debt of the holder of the account, credits first made to the account are first withdrawn or applied.

§4A–505. Preclusion of Objection to Debit of Customer's Account

If a receiving bank has received payment from its customer with respect to a payment order issued in the name of the customer as sender and accepted by the bank, and the customer received notification reasonably identifying the order, the customer is precluded from asserting that the bank is not entitled to retain the payment unless the customer notifies the bank of the customer's objection to the payment within one year after the notification was received by the customer.

§4A–506. Rate of Interest

(a) If, under this Article, a receiving bank is obliged to pay interest with respect to a payment order issued to the bank, the amount payable may be determined (i) by agreement of the sender and receiving bank, or (ii) by a funds-transfer system rule if the payment order is transmitted through a funds-transfer system.

(b) If the amount of interest is not determined by an agreement or rule as stated in subsection (a), the amount is calculated by multiplying the applicable Federal Funds rate by the amount on which interest is payable, and then multiplying the product by the number of days for which interest is payable. The applicable Federal Funds rate is the average of the Federal Funds rates published by the Federal Reserve Bank of New York for each of the days for which interest is payable divided by 360. The Federal Funds rate for any day on which a published rate is not available is the same as the published rate for the next preceding day for which there is a published rate. If a receiving bank that accepted a payment order is required to refund payment to the sender of the order because the funds transfer was not completed, but the failure to complete was not due to any fault by the bank, the interest payable is reduced by a percentage equal to the reserve requirement on deposits of the receiving bank.

§4A–507. Choice of Law

(a) The following rules apply unless the affected parties otherwise agree or subsection (c) applies:

(1) The rights and obligations between the sender of a payment order and the receiving bank are governed by the law of the jurisdiction in which the receiving bank is located.

(2) The rights and obligations between the beneficiary's bank and the beneficiary are governed by the law of the jurisdiction in which the beneficiary's bank is located.

(3) The issue of when payment is made pursuant to a funds transfer by the originator to the beneficiary is governed by the law of the jurisdiction in which the beneficiary's bank is located.

(b) If the parties described in each paragraph of subsection (a) have made an agreement selecting the law of a particular jurisdiction to govern rights and obligations between each other, the law of that jurisdiction governs those rights and obligations, whether or not the payment order or the funds transfer bears a reasonable relation to that jurisdiction.

(c) A funds-transfer system rule may select the law of a particular jurisdiction to govern (i) rights and obligations between participating banks with respect to payment orders transmitted or processed through the system, or (ii) the rights and obligations of some or all parties to a funds transfer any part of which is carried out by means of the system. A choice of law made pursuant to clause (i) is binding on participating banks. A choice of law made pursuant to clause (ii) is binding on the originator, other sender, or a receiving bank having notice that the funds-transfer system might be used in the funds transfer and of the choice of law by the system when the originator, other sender, or receiving bank issued or accepted a payment

order. The beneficiary of a funds transfer is bound by the choice of law if, when the funds transfer is initiated, the beneficiary has notice that the funds-transfer system might be used in the funds transfer and of the choice of law by the system. The law of a jurisdiction selected pursuant to this subsection may govern, whether or not that law bears a reasonable relation to the matter in issue.

(d) In the event of inconsistency between an agreement under subsection (b) and a choice-of-law rule under subsection (c), the agreement under subsection (b) prevails.

(e) If a funds transfer is made by use of more than one funds-transfer system and there is inconsistency between choice-of-law rules of the systems, the matter in issue is governed by the law of the selected jurisdiction that has the most significant relationship to the matter in issue.

ARTICLE 5 LETTERS OF CREDIT

§5–101. Short Title

This Article shall be known and may be cited as Uniform Commercial Code—Letters of Credit

§5–102. Scope

(1) This Article applies

(a) to a credit issued by a bank if the credit requires a documentary draft or a documentary demand for payment; and

(b) to a credit issued by a person other than a bank if the credit requires that the draft or demand for payment be accompanied by a document of title; and

(c) to a credit issued by a bank or other person if the credit is not within subparagraphs (a) or (b) but conspicuously states that it is a letter of credit or is conspicuously so entitled.

(2) Unless the engagement meets the requirements of subsection (1), this Article does not apply to engagements to make advances or to honor drafts or demands for payment, to authorities to pay or purchase, to guarantees or to general agreements.

(3) This Article deals with some but not all of the rules and concepts of letters of credit as such rules or concepts have developed prior to this act or may hereafter develop. The fact that this Article states a rule does not by itself require, imply or negate application of the same or a converse rule to a situation not provided for or to a person not specified by this Article.

§5–103. Definitions

(1) In this Article unless the context otherwise requires

(a) "Credit" or "letter of credit" means an engagement by a bank or other person made at the request of a customer and of a kind within the scope of this Article

(Section 5–102) that the issuer will honor drafts or other demands for payment upon compliance with the conditions specified in the credit. A credit may be either revocable or irrevocable. The engagement may be either an agreement to honor or a statement that the bank or other person is authorized to honor.

(b) A "documentary draft" or a "documentary demand for payment" is one honor of which is conditioned upon the presentation of a document or documents. "Document" means any paper including document of title, security, invoice, certificate, notice of default and the like.

(c) An "issuer" is a bank or other person issuing a credit.

(d) A "beneficiary" of a credit is a person who is entitled under its terms to draw or demand payment.

(e) An "advising bank" is a bank which gives notification of the issuance of a credit by another bank.

(f) A "confirming bank" is a bank which engages either that it will itself honor a credit already issued by another bank or that such a credit will be honored by the issuer or a third bank.

(g) A "customer" is a buyer or other person who causes an issuer to issue a credit. The term also includes a bank which procures issuance or confirmation on behalf of that bank's customer.

(2) Other definitions applying to this Article and the sections in which they appear are:

"Notation of Credit." Section 5–108.

"Presenter." Section 5–112(3).

(3) Definitions in other Articles applying to this Article and the sections in which they appear are:

"Accept" or "Acceptance." Section 3–410.

"Contract for sale." Section 2–106.

"Draft." Section 3–104.

"Holder in due course." Section 3–302.

"Midnight deadline." Section 4–104.

"Security." Section 8–102.

(4) In addition, Article 1 contains general definitions and principles of construction and interpretation applicable throughout this Article.

§5–104. Formal Requirements; Signing

(1) Except as otherwise required in subsection (1)(c) of Section 5–102 on scope, no particular form of phrasing is required for a credit. A credit must be in writing and signed by the issuer and a confirmation must be in writing and signed by the confirming bank. A modification of the terms of a credit or confirmation must be signed by the issuer or confirming bank.

(2) A telegram may be a sufficient signed writing if it identifies its sender by an authorized authentication. The authentication may be in code and the authorized naming of the issuer in an advance of credit is a sufficient signing.

§5–105. Consideration

No consideration is necessary to establish a credit or to enlarge or otherwise modify its terms.

§5–106. Time and Effect of Establishment of Credit

(1) Unless otherwise agreed a credit is established

(a) as regards the customer as soon as a letter of credit is sent to him or the letter of credit or an authorized written advice of its issuance is sent to the beneficiary: and

(b) as regards the beneficiary when he receives a letter of credit or an authorized written advice of its issuance.

(2) Unless otherwise agreed once an irrevocable credit is established as regards the customer it can be modified or revoked only with the consent of the customer and once it is established as regards the beneficiary it can be modified or revoked only with his consent.

(3) Unless otherwise agreed after a revocable credit is established it may be modified or revoked by the issuer without notice to or consent from the customer or beneficiary.

(4) Notwithstanding any modification or revocation of a revocable credit any person authorized to honor or negotiate under the terms of the original credit is entitled to reimbursement for or honor of any draft or demand for payment duly honored or negotiated before receipt of notice of the modification or revocation and the issuer in turn is entitled to reimbursement from its customer.

§5–107. Advice of Credit; Confirmation; Error in Statement of Terms

(1) Unless otherwise specified an advising bank by advising a credit issued by another bank does not assume any obligation to honor drafts drawn or demands for payment made under the credit but it does assume obligation for the accuracy of its own statement.

(2) A confirming bank by confirming a credit becomes directly obligated on the credit to the extent of its confirmation as though it were its issuer and acquires the rights of an issuer.

(3) Even though an advising bank incorrectly advises the terms of a credit it has been authorized to advise the credit is established as against the issuer to the extent of its original terms.

(4) Unless otherwise specified the customer bears as against the issuer all risks of transmissions and reasonable translation or interpretation of any message relating to a credit.

§5–108. "Notation Credit"; Exhaustion of Credit

(1) A credit which specifies that any person purchasing or paying drafts drawn or demands for payment made under it must note the amount of the draft or demand on the

letter or advice of credit is a "notation credit."

(2) Under a notation credit

(a) a person paying the beneficiary or purchasing a draft or demand for payment from him acquires a right to honor only if the appropriate notation is made and by transferring or forwarding for honor the documents under the credit such a person warrants to the issuer that the notation has been made; and

(b) unless the credit or a signed statement that an appropriate notation has been made accompanies the draft or demand for payment the issuer may delay honor until evidence of notation has been procured which is satisfactory to it but its obligation and that of its customer continue for a reasonable time not exceeding thirty days to obtain such evidence.

(3) If the credit is not a notation credit

(a) the issuer may honor complying drafts or demands for payment presented to it in the order in which they are presented and is discharged pro tanto by honor of any such draft or demand;

(b) as between competing good faith purchasers of complying drafts or demands the person first purchasing has priority over a subsequent purchaser even though the later purchased draft or demand has been first honored.

§5–109. Issuer's Obligation to Its Customer

(1) An issuer's obligation to its customer includes good faith and observance of any general banking usage but unless otherwise agreed does not include liability or responsibility

(a) for performance of the underlying contract for sale or other transaction between the customer and the beneficiary; or

(b) for any act or omission of any person other than itself or its own branch or for loss or destruction of a draft, demand or document in transit or in the possession of others; or

(c) based on knowledge or lack of knowledge of any usage of any particular trade.

(2) An issuer must examine documents with care so as to ascertain that on their face they appear to comply with the terms of the credit but unless otherwise agreed assumes no liability or responsibility for the genuineness, falsification or effect of any document which appears on such examination to be regular on its face.

(3) A non-bank issuer is not bound by any banking usage of which it has no knowledge.

§5–110. Availability of Credit in Portions; Presenter's Reservation of Lien or Claim

(1) Unless otherwise specified a credit may be used in portions in the discretion of the beneficiary.

(2) Unless otherwise specified a person by presenting a documentary draft or demand for payment under a credit relinquishes upon its honor all claims to the documents and a person by transferring such draft or demand or causing such presentment authorizes such relinquishment. An explicit reservation of claim makes the draft or demand noncomplying.

§5–111. Warranties on Transfer and Presentment

(1) Unless otherwise agreed the beneficiary by transferring or presenting a documentary draft or demand for payment warrants to all interested parties that the necessary conditions of the credit have been complied with. This is in addition to any warranties arising under Articles 3, 4, 7 and 8.

(2) Unless otherwise agreed a negotiating, advising, confirming, collecting or issuing bank presenting or transferring a draft or demand for payment under a credit warrants only the matters warranted by a collecting bank under Article 4 and any such bank transferring a document warrants only the matters warranted by an intermediary under Articles 7 and 8.

§5–112. Time Allowed for Honor or Rejection; Withholding Honor or Rejection by Consent; "Presenter"

(1) A bank to which a documentary draft or demand for payment is presented under a credit may without dishonor of the draft, demand or credit

(a) defer honor until the close of the third banking day following receipt of the documents; and

(b) further defer honor if the presenter has expressly or impliedly consented thereto. Failure to honor within the time here specified constitutes dishonor of the draft or demand and of the credit [except as otherwise provided in subsection (4) of Section 5–114 on conditional payment].

Note: The bracketed language in the last sentence of subsection (1) should be included only if the optional provisions of Section 5–114(4) and (5) are included.

(2) Upon dishonor the bank may unless otherwise instructed fulfill its duty to return the draft or demand and the documents by holding them at the disposal of the presenter and sending him an advice to that effect.

(3) "Presenter" means any person presenting a draft or demand for payment for honor under a credit even though that person is a confirming bank or other correspondent which is acting under an issuer's authorization.

§5–113. Indemnities

(1) A bank seeking to obtain (whether for itself or another) honor, negotiation or reimbursement under a credit may give an indemnity to induce such honor, negotiation or reimbursement.

(2) An indemnity agreement inducing honor, negotiation or reimbursement

(a) unless otherwise explicitly agreed applies to defects in the documents but not in the goods; and

(b) unless a longer time is explicitly agreed expires at the end of ten business days following receipt of the documents by the ultimate customer unless notice of objection is sent before such expiration date. The ultimate customer may send notice of objection to the person from whom he received the documents and any bank receiving such notice is under a duty to send notice to its transferor before its midnight deadline.

§5–114. Issuer's Duty and Privilege to Honor; Right to Reimbursement

(1) An issuer must honor a draft or demand for payment which complies with the terms of the relevant credit regardless of whether the goods or documents conform to the underlying contract for sale or other contract between the customer and the beneficiary. The issuer is not excused from honor of such a draft or demand by reason of an additional general term that all documents must be satisfactory to the issuer, but an issuer may require that specified documents must be satisfactory to it.

(2) Unless otherwise agreed when documents appear on their face to comply with the terms of a credit but a required document does not in fact conform to the warranties made on negotiations or transfer of a document of title (Section 7–507) or of a certified security (Section 8–306) or is forged or fraudulent or there is fraud in the transaction:

(a) the issuer must honor the draft or demand for payment if honor is demanded by a negotiating bank or other holder of the draft or demand which has taken the draft or demand under the credit and under circumstances which would make it a holder in due course (Section 3–302) and in an appropriate case would make it a person to whom a document of title has been duly negotiated (Section 7–502) or a bona fide purchaser of a certificated security (Section 8–302); and

(b) in all other cases as against its customer, an issuer acting in good faith may honor the draft or demand for payment despite notification from the customer of fraud, forgery or other defect not apparent on the face of the document but a court of appropriate jurisdiction may enjoin such honor.

(3) Unless otherwise agreed an issuer which has duly honored a draft or demand for payment is entitled to immediate reimbursement of any payment made under the credit and to be put in effectively available funds not later than the day before maturity of any acceptance made under the credit.

[(4) When a credit provides for payment by the issuer on receipt of notice that the required documents are in the possession of a correspondent or other agent of the issuer

(a) any payment made on receipt of such notice is conditional; and

(b) the issuer may reject documents which do not comply with the credit if it does so within three banking days following its receipt of the documents; and

(c) in the event of such rejection, the issuer is entitled by charge back or otherwise to return of the payment made.]

[(5) In the case covered by subsection (4) failure to reject documents within the time specified in subparagraph (b) constitutes acceptance of the documents and makes the payment final in favor of the beneficiary.]

Note: Subsections (4) and (5) are bracketed as optional. If they are included the bracketed language in that last sentence of Section 5–112(1) should also be included.

§5–115. Remedy for Improper Dishonor or Anticipatory Repudiation

(1) When an issuer wrongfully dishonors a draft or demand for payment presented under a credit the person entitled to honor has with respect to any documents the rights of a person in the position of a seller (Section 2–707) and may recover from the issuer the face amount of the draft or demand together with incidental damages under Section 7–710 on seller's incidental damages and interest but less any amount realized by resale or other use or disposition of the subject matter of the transaction. In the event no resale or other utilization is made the documents, goods or other subject matter involved in the transaction must be turned over to the issuer on payment of judgment.

(2) When an issuer wrongfully cancels or otherwise repudiates a credit before presentment of a draft or demands for payment drawn under it the beneficiary has the rights of a seller after anticipatory repudiation by the buyer under Section 2–610 if he learns of the repudiation in time reasonably to avoid procurement of the required documents. Otherwise the beneficiary has an immediate right of action for wrongful dishonor.

§5–116. Transfer and Assignment

(1) The right to draw under a credit can be transferred or assigned only when the credit is expressly designated as transferable or assignable.

(2) Even though the credit specifically states that it is nontransferable or nonassignable the beneficiary may before performance of the conditions of the credit assign his right to proceeds. Such an assignment is an assignment of an account under Article 9 on Secured Transactions and is governed by that Article except that

(a) the assignment is ineffective until the letter of credit or advice of credit is delivered to the assignee which delivery constitutes perfection of the security interest under Article 9; and

(b) the issuer may honor drafts or demands for payment drawn under the credit until it receives a notification of the assignment signed by the beneficiary which reasonably identifies the credit involved in the assignment and contains a request to pay the assignee; and

(c) after what reasonably appears to be such a notification has been received the issuer may without dishonor refuse to accept or pay even to a person otherwise entitled to honor until the letter of credit or advice of credit is exhibited to the issuer.

(3) Except where the beneficiary has effectively assigned his right to draw or his right to proceeds, nothing in this section limits his right to transfer or negotiate drafts or demands drawn under the credit.

§5–117. Insolvency of Bank Holding Funds for Documentary Credit

(1) Where an issuer or an advising or confirming bank or a bank which has for a customer produced issuance of a credit by another bank becomes insolvent before final payment under the credit and the credit is one to which this Article is made applicable by paragraphs (a) or (b) of Section 5–102(1) on scope, the receipt or allocation of funds or collateral to secure or meet obligations under the credit shall have the following results:

(a) to the extent of any funds or collateral turned over after or before the insolvency as indemnity against or specifically for the purpose of payment of drafts or demands for payment drawn under the designated credit, the drafts or demands are entitled to payment in preference over depositors or other general creditors of the issuer or bank; and

(b) on expiration of the credit or surrender of the beneficiary's rights under it unused any person who has given such funds or collateral is similarly entitled to return thereof; and

(c) a charge to a general or current account with a bank if specifically consented to for the purpose of indemnity against or payment of drafts or demands for payment drawn under the designated credit falls under the same rules as if the funds had been drawn out in cash and then turned over with specific instructions.

(2) After honor or reimbursement under this section the customer or other person for whose account the insolvent bank has acted is entitled to receive the documents involved.

ARTICLE 6 BULK TRANSFERS

§6–101. Short Title

This Article shall be known and may be cited as Uniform Commercial Code—Bulk Sales.

§6–102. Definitions and Index of Definitions

(1) In this Article, unless the context otherwise requires:

(a) "Assets" means the inventory that is the subject of a bulk sale and any tangible and intangible personal property used or held for use primarily in, or arising from, the seller's business and sold in connection with that inventory, but the term does not include:

(i) fixtures (Section 9–313(1)(a)) other than readily removable factory and office machines;

(ii) the lessee's interest in a lease of real property; or

(iii) property to the extent it is generally exempt from creditor process under nonbankruptcy law.

(b) "Auctioneer" means a person whom the seller engages to direct, conduct, control, or be responsible for a sale by auction.

(c) "Bulk sale" means:

(i) in the case of a sale by auction or a sale or series of sales conducted by a liquidator on the seller's behalf, a sale or series of sales not in the ordinary course of the seller's business of more than half of the seller's inventory, as measured by value on the date of the bulk-sale agreement, if on that date the auctioneer or liquidator has notice, or after reasonable inquiry would have had notice, that the seller will not continue to operate the same or a similar kind of business after the sale or series of sales; and

(ii) in all other cases, a sale not in the ordinary course of the seller's business of more than half the seller's inventory, as measured by value on the date of the bulk-sale agreement, if on that date the buyer has notice, or after reasonable inquiry would have had notice, that the seller will not continue to operate the same or a similar kind of business after the sale.

(d) "Claim" means a right to payment from the seller, whether or not the right is reduced to judgment, liquidated, fixed, matured, disputed, secured, legal, or equitable. The term includes costs of collection and attorney's fees only to the extent that the laws of this state permit the holder of the claim to recover them in an action against the obligor.

(e) "Claimant" means a person holding a claim incurred in the seller's business other than:

(i) an unsecured and unmatured claim for employment compensation and benefits, including commissions and vacation, severance, and sick-leave pay;

(ii) a claim for injury to an individual or to property, or for breach of warranty, unless:

(A) a right of action for the claim has accrued;

(B) the claim has been asserted against the seller; and

(C) the seller knows the identity of the person asserting the claim and the basis upon which the person has asserted it; and

(States To Select One Alternative)

Alternative A

[(iii) a claim for taxes owing to a governmental unit.]

Alternative B

[(iii) a claim for taxes owing to a governmental unit, if:

(A) a statute governing the enforcement of the claim permits or requires notice of the bulk sale to be given to the governmental unit in a manner other than by compliance with the requirements of this Article; and

(B) notice is given in accordance with the statute.]

(f) "Creditor" means a claimant or other person holding a claim.

(g)(i) "Date of the bulk sale" means:

(A) if the sale is by auction or is conducted by a liquidator on the seller's behalf, the date on which more than ten percent of the net proceeds is paid to or for the benefit of the seller; and

(B) in all other cases, the later of the date on which:

(I) more than ten percent of the net contract price is paid to or for the benefit of the seller; or

(II) more than ten percent of the assets, as measured by value, are transferred to the buyer.

(ii) For purposes of this subsection:

(A) Delivery of a negotiable instrument (Section 3–104(1)) to or for the benefit of the seller in exchange for assets constitutes payment of the contract price pro tanto;

(B) To the extent that the contract price is deposited in an escrow, the contract price is paid to or for the benefit of the seller when the seller acquires the unconditional right to receive the deposit or when the deposit is delivered to the seller or for the benefit of the seller, whichever is earlier; and

(C) An asset is transferred when a person holding an unsecured claim can no longer obtain through judicial proceedings rights to the asset that are superior to those of the buyer arising as a result of the bulk sale. A person holding an unsecured claim can obtain those superior rights to a tangible asset at least until the buyer has an unconditional right, under the bulk-sale agreement, to possess the asset, and a person holding an unsecured claim can obtain those superior rights to an intangible asset at least until the buyer has an unconditional right, under the bulk-sale agreement, to use the asset.

(h) "Date of the bulk-sale agreement" means:

(i) in the case of a sale by auction or conducted by a liquidator (subsection (c)(i)), the date on which the seller engages the auctioneer or liquidator; and

(ii) in all other cases, the date on which a bulk-sale agreement becomes enforceable between the buyer and the seller.

(i) "Debt" means liability on a claim.

(j) "Liquidator" means a person who is regularly engaged in the business of disposing of assets for businesses contemplating liquidation or dissolution.

(k) "Net contract price" means the new consideration the buyer is obligated to pay for the assets less:

(i) the amount of any proceeds of the sale of an asset, to the extent the proceeds are applied in partial or total satisfaction of a debt secured by the asset; and

(ii) the amount of any debt to the extent it is secured by a security interest or lien that is enforceable against the asset before and after it has been sold to a buyer. If a debt is secured by an asset and other property of the seller, the amount of the debt secured by a security interest or lien that is enforceable against the asset is determined by multiplying the debt by a fraction, the numerator of which is the value of the new consideration for the asset on the date of the bulk sale and the denominator of which is the value of all property securing the debt on the date of the bulk sale.

(l) "Net proceeds" means the new consideration received for assets sold at a sale by auction or a sale conducted by a liquidator on the seller's behalf less:

(i) commissions and reasonable expenses of the sale;

(ii) the amount of any proceeds of the sale of an asset, to the extent the proceeds are applied in partial or total satisfaction of a debt secured by the asset; and

(iii) the amount of any debt to the extent it is secured by a security interest or lien that is enforceable against the asset before and after it has been sold to a buyer. If a debt is secured by an asset and other property of the seller, the amount of the debt secured by a security interest or lien that is enforceable against the asset is determined by multiplying the debt by a fraction, the numerator of which is the value of the new consideration for the asset on the date of the bulk sale and the denominator of which is the value of all property securing the debt on the date of the bulk sale.

(m) A sale is "in the ordinary course of the seller's business" if the sale comports with usual or customary practices in the kind of business in which the seller is engaged or with the seller's own usual or customary practices.

(n) "United States" includes its territories and possessions and the Commonwealth of Puerto Rico.

(o) "Value" means fair market value.

(p) "Verified" means signed and sworn to or affirmed.

(2) The following definitions in other Articles apply to this Article:

(a) "Buyer."	Section 2–103(1)(a).
(b) "Equipment."	Section 9–109(2).
(c)' 'Inventory."	Section 9–109(4).
(d) "Sale."	Section 2–106(1).
(e) "Seller."	Section 2–103(1)(d).

(3) In addition, Article 1 contains general definitions and principles of construction and interpretation applicable throughout this Article.

§6–103. Applicability of Article

(1) Except as otherwise provided in subsection (3), this Article applies to a bulk sale if:

(a) the seller's principal business is the sale of inventory from stock; and

(b) on the date of the bulk-sale agreement the seller is located in this state or, if the seller is located in a jurisdiction that is not a part of the United States, the seller's major executive office in the United States is in this state.

(2) A seller is deemed to be located at his [or her] place of business. If a seller has more than one place of business, the seller is deemed located at his [or her] chief executive office.

(3) This Article does not apply to:

(a) a transfer made to secure payment or performance of an obligation:

(b) a transfer of collateral to a secured party pursuant to Section 9–503;

(c) a sale of collateral pursuant to Section 9–504;

(d) retention of collateral pursuant to Section 9–505;

(e) a sale of an asset encumbered by a security interest or lien if (i) all the proceeds of the sale are applied in partial or total satisfaction of the debt secured by the security interest or lien or (ii) the security interest or lien is enforceable against the asset after it has been sold to the buyer and the net contract price is zero;

(f) a general assignment for the benefit of creditors or to a subsequent transfer by the assignee;

(g) a sale by an executor, administrator, receiver, trustee in bankruptcy, or any public officer under judicial process;

(h) a sale made in the course of judicial or administrative proceedings for the dissolution or reorganization of an organization;

(i) a sale to a buyer whose principal place of business is in the United States and who:

   (i) not earlier than 21 days before the date of the bulk sale, (A) obtains from the seller a verified and dated list of claimants of whom the seller has notice three days before the seller sends or delivers the list to the buyer or (B) conducts a reasonable inquiry to discover the claimants;

   (ii) assumes in full the debts owed to claimants of whom the buyer has knowledge on the date the buyer receives the list of claimants from the seller or on the date the buyer completes the reasonable inquiry, as the case may be;

   (iii) is not insolvent after the assumption; and

   (iv) gives written notice of the assumption not later than 30 days after the date of the bulk sale by sending or delivering a notice to the claimants identified in subparagraph (ii) or by filing a notice in the office of the [Secretary of State];

(j) a sale to a buyer whose principal place of business is in the United States and who:

   (i) assumes in full the debts that were incurred in the seller's business before the date of the bulk sale;

   (ii) is not insolvent after the assumption; and

   (iii) gives written notice of the assumption not later than 30 days after the date of the bulk sale by sending or delivering a notice to each creditor whose debt is assumed or by filing a notice in the office of the [Secretary of State];

(k) a sale to a new organization that is organized to take over and continue the business of the seller and that has its principal place of business in the United States if:

   (i) the buyer assumes in full the debts that were incurred in the seller's business before the date of the bulk sale;

   (ii) the seller receives nothing from the sale except an interest in the new organization that is subordinate to the claims against the organization arising from the assumption; and

   (iii) the buyer gives written notice of the assumption not later than 30 days after the date of the bulk sale by sending or delivering a notice to each creditor whose debt is assumed or by filing a notice in the office of the [Secretary of State];

(l) a sale of assets having:

 (i) a value, net of liens and security interests, of less than $10,000. If a debt is secured by assets and other property of the seller, the new value of the assets is determined by subtracting from their value an amount equal to the product of the debt multiplied by a fraction, the numerator of which is the value of the assets on the date of the bulk sale and the denominator of which is the value of all property securing the debt on the date of the bulk sale; or

 (ii) a value of more than $25,000,000 on the date of the bulk-sale agreement; or

(m) a sale required by, and made pursuant to, statute.

(4) The notice under subsection (3)(i)(iv) must state: (i) that a sale that may constitute a bulk sale has been or will be made;(ii) the date or prospective date of the bulk sale; (iii) the individual, partnership, or corporate names and the addresses of the seller and buyer; (iv) the address to

which inquiries about the sale may be made, if different from the seller's address; and (v) that the buyer assumed or will assume in full the debts owed to claimants of whom the buyer has knowledge on the date the buyer receives the list of claimants from the seller or completes a reasonable inquiry to discover the claimants.

(5) The notice under subsections (3)(j)(iii) and (3)(k)(iii) must state: (i) that a sale that may constitute a bulk sale has been or will be made; (ii) the date or prospective date of the bulk sale; (iii) the individual, partnership, or corporate names and the addresses of the seller and buyer; (iv) the address to which inquiries about the sale may be made, if different from the seller's address; and (v) that the buyer has assumed or will assume the debts that were incurred in the seller's business before the date of the bulk sale.

(6) For purposes of subsection (3)(l), the value of assets is presumed to be equal to the price the buyer agrees to pay for the assets. However, in a sale by auction or a sale conducted by a liquidator on the seller's behalf, the value of assets is presumed to be the amount the auctioneer or liquidator reasonably estimates the assets will bring at auction or upon liquidation.

§6–104. Obligations of Buyer

(1) In a bulk sale as defined in Section 6–102(1)(c)(ii) the buyer shall:

   (a) obtain from the seller a list of all business names and addresses used by the seller within three years before the date the list is sent or delivered to the buyer;

   (b) unless excused under subsection (2), obtain from the seller a verified and dated list of claimants of whom the seller has notice three days before the seller sends or delivers the list to the buyer and including, to the extent known by the seller, the address of and the amount claimed by each claimant:

   (c) obtain from the seller or prepare a schedule of distribution (Section 6–106(l));

   (d) give notice of the bulk sale in accordance with Section 6–105;

   (e) unless excused under Section 6–106(4), distribute the net contract price in accordance with the undertakings of the buyer in the schedule of distribution; and

   (f) unless excused under subsection (2), make available the list of claimants (subsection (1)(b)) by:

      (i) promptly sending or delivering a copy of the list without charge to any claimant whose written request is received by the buyer no later than six months after the date of the bulk sale;

      (ii) permitting any claimant to inspect and copy the list at any reasonable hour upon request received by the buyer no later than six months after the date of the bulk sale; or

      (iii) filing a copy of the list in the office of the [Secretary of State] no later than the time for giving a notice of the bulk sale (Section

6–105(5)). A list filed in accordance with this subparagraph must state the individual, partnership, or corporate name and a mailing address of the seller.

(2) A buyer who gives notice in accordance with Section 6–105(2) is excused from complying with the requirements of subsections (1)(b) and (1)(f).

§6–105. Notice to Claimants

(1) Except as otherwise provided in subsection (2), to comply with Section 6–104(1)(d), the buyer shall send or deliver a written notice of the bulk sale to each claimant on the list of claimants (Section 6–104(1)(b)) and to any other claimant of whom the buyer has knowledge at the time the notice of the bulk sale is sent or delivered.

(2) A buyer may comply with Section 6–104(1)(d) by filing a written notice of the bulk sale in the office of the [Secretary of State] if:

   (a) on the date of the bulk-sale agreement the seller has 200 or more claimants, exclusive of claimants holding secured or matured claims for employment compensation and benefits, including commissions and vacation, severance, and sick-leave pay; or

   (b) the buyer has received a verified statement from the seller stating that, as of the date of the bulk-sale agreement, the number of claimants, exclusive of claimants holding secured or matured claims for employment compensation and benefits, including commissions and vacation, severance, and sick-leave pay, is 200 or more.

(3) The written notice of the bulk sale must be accompanied by a copy of the schedule of distribution (Section 6–106(1)) and state at least:

   (a) that the seller and buyer have entered into an agreement for a sale that may constitute a bulk sale under the laws of the State of _____;

   (b) the date of the agreement;

   (c) the date on or after which more than ten percent of the assets were or will be transferred;

   (d) the date on or after which more than ten percent of the net contract price was or will be paid, if the date is not stated in the schedule of distribution;

   (e) the name and a mailing address of the seller;

   (f) any other business name and address listed by the seller pursuant to Section 6–104(1)(a);

   (g) the name of the buyer and an address of the buyer from which information concerning the sale can be obtained;

   (h) a statement indicating the type of assets or describing the assets item by item;

   (i) the manner in which the buyer will make available the list of claimants (Section 6–104(1)(f)), if applicable; and

   (j) if the sale is in total or partial satisfaction of an antecedent debt owed by the seller, the amount of the debt to be satisfied and the name of the person to whom it is owed.

(4) For purposes of subsections (3)(e) and (3)(g), the name of a person is the person's individual, partnership, or corporate name.

(5) The buyer shall give notice of the bulk sale not less than 45 days before the date of the bulk sale and, if the buyer gives notice in accordance with subsection (1), not more than 30 days after obtaining the list of claimants.

(6) A written notice substantially complying with the requirements of subsection (3) is effective even though it contains minor errors that are not seriously misleading.

(7) A form substantially as follows is sufficient to comply with subsection (3):

Notice of Sale

(1) _____, whose address is _____, is described in this notice as the "seller."

(2) _____, whose address is _____, is described in this notice as the "buyer."

(3) The seller has disclosed to the buyer that within the past three years the seller has used other business names, operated at other addresses, or both, as follows:_____.

(4) The seller and the buyer have entered into an agreement dated _____, for a sale that may constitute a bulk sale under the laws of the state of _____.

(5) The date on or after which more than ten percent of the assets that are the subject of the sale were or will be transferred is _____, and [if not stated in the schedule of distribution] the date on or after which more than ten percent of the net contract price was or will be paid is _____.

(6) The following assets are the subject of the sale: _____.

(7) [If applicable] The buyer will make available to claimants of the seller a list of the seller's claimants in the following manner: _____.

(8) [If applicable] The sale is to satisfy $_____ of an antecedent debt owed by the seller to _____.

(9) A copy of the schedule of distribution of the net contract price accompanies this notice.

§6–106. Schedule of Distribution

(1) The seller and buyer shall agree on how the net contract price is to be distributed and set forth their agreement in a written schedule of distribution.

(2) The schedule of distribution may provide for distribution to any person at any time, including distribution of the entire net contract price to the seller.

(3) The buyer's undertakings in the schedule of distribution run only to the seller. However, a buyer who fails to distribute the net contract price in accordance with the buyer's undertakings in the schedule of distribution is liable to a creditor only as provided in Section 6–107(1).

(4) If the buyer undertakes in the schedule of distribution to distribute any part of the net contract price to a person other than the seller, and, after the buyer has given notice

in accordance with Section 6–105, some or all of the anticipated net contract price is or becomes unavailable for distribution as a consequence of the buyer's or seller's having complied with an order of court, legal process, statute, or rule of law, the buyer is excused from any obligation arising under this Article or under any contract with the seller to distribute the net contract price in accordance with the buyer's undertakings in the schedule if the buyer:

(a) distributes the net contract price remaining available in accordance with any priorities for payment stated in the schedule of distribution and, to the extent that the price is insufficient to pay all the debts having a given priority, distributes the price pro rata among those debts shown in the schedule as having the same priority;

(b) distributes the net contract price remaining available in accordance with an order of court;

(c) commences a proceeding for interpleader in a court of competent jurisdiction and is discharged from the proceeding; or

(d) reaches a new agreement with the seller for the distribution of the net contract price remaining available, sets forth the new agreement in an amended schedule of distribution, gives notice of the amended schedule, and distributes the net contract price remaining available in accordance with the buyer's undertakings in the amended schedule.

(5) The notice under subsection (4)(d) must identify the buyer and the seller, state the filing number, if any, of the original notice, set forth the amended schedule, and be given in accordance with subsection (1) or (2) of Section 6–105, whichever is applicable, at least 14 days before the buyer distributes any part of the net contract price remaining available.

(6) If the seller undertakes in the schedule of distribution to distribute any part of the net contract price, and, after the buyer has given notice in accordance with Section 6–105, some or all of the anticipated net contract price is or becomes unavailable for distribution as a consequence of the buyer's or seller's having complied with an order of court, legal process, statute, or rule of law, the seller and any person in control of the seller are excused from any obligation arising under this Article or under any agreement with the buyer to distribute the net contract price in accordance with the seller's undertakings in the schedule if the seller:

(a) distributes the net contract price remaining available in accordance with any priorities for payment stated in the schedule of distribution and, to the extent that the price is insufficient to pay all the debts having a given priority, distributes the price pro rata among those debts shown in the schedule as having the same priority;

(b) distributes the net contract price remaining available in accordance with an order of court;

(c) commences a proceeding for interpleader in a court of competent jurisdiction and is discharged from the proceeding; or

(d) prepares a written amended schedule of distribution of the net contract price remaining available for distribution, gives notice of the amended schedule, and distributes the net contract price remaining available in accordance with the amended schedule.

(7) The notice under subsection (6)(d) must identify the buyer and the seller, state the filing number, if any, of the original notice, set forth the amended schedule, and be given in accordance with subsection (1) or (2) of Section 6–105, whichever is applicable, at least 14 days before the seller distributes any part of the net contract price remaining available.

§6–107. Liability for Noncompliance

(1) Except as provided in subsection (3), and subject to the limitation in subsection (4):

(a) a buyer who fails to comply with the requirements of Section 6–104(1)(e) with respect to a creditor is liable to the creditor for damages in the amount of the claim, reduced by any amount that the creditor would not have realized if the buyer had complied; and

(b) a buyer who fails to comply with the requirements of any other subsection of Section 6–104 with respect to a claimant is liable to the claimant for damages in the amount of the claim, reduced by any amount that the claimant would not have realized if the buyer had complied.

(2) In an action under subsection (1), the creditor has the burden of establishing the validity and amount of the claim, and the buyer has the burden of establishing the amount that the creditor would not have realized if the buyer had complied.

(3) A buyer who:

(a) made a good faith and commercially reasonable effort to comply with the requirements of Section 6–104(1) or to exclude the sale from the application of this Article under Section 6–103(3); or

(b) on or after the date of the bulk-sale agreement, but before the date of the bulk sale, held a good faith and commercially reasonable belief that this Article does not apply to the particular sale is not liable to creditors for failure to comply with the requirements of Section 6–104. The buyer has the burden of establishing the good faith and commercial reasonableness of the effort or belief.

(4) In a single bulk sale the cumulative liability of the buyer for failure to comply with the requirements of Section 6–104(1) may not exceed an amount equal to:

(a) if the assets consist only of inventory and equipment, twice the net contract price, less the amount of any part of the net contract price paid to or applied for the benefit of the seller or a creditor; or

(b) if the assets include property other than inventory and equipment, twice the net value of the inventory and equipment less the amount of the portion of any part of the net contract price paid to or applied for the benefit of the seller or a creditor which is allocable to the inventory and equipment.

(5) For the purposes of subsection (4)(b), the "net value" of an asset is the value of the asset less (i) the amount of any proceeds of the sale of an asset, to the extent the proceeds are applied in partial or total satisfaction of a debt secured by the asset and (ii) the amount of any debt to the extent it is secured by a security interest or lien that is enforceable against the asset before and after it has been sold to a buyer. If a debt is secured by an asset and other property of the seller, the amount of the debt secured by a security interest or lien that is enforceable against the asset is determined by multiplying the debt by a fraction, the numerator of which is the value of the asset on the date of the bulk sale and the denominator of which is the value of all property securing the debt on the date of the bulk sale. The portion of a part of the net contract price paid to or applied for the benefit of the seller or a creditor that is "allocable to the inventory and equipment" is the portion that bears the same ratio to that part of the net contract price as the net value of the inventory and equipment bears to the net value of all of the assets.

(6) A payment made by the buyer to a person to whom the buyer is, or believes he [or she] is, liable under subsection (1) reduces pro tanto the buyer's cumulative liability under subsection (4).

(7) No action may be brought under subsection (1)(b) by or on behalf of a claimant whose claim is unliquidated or contingent.

(8) A buyer's failure to comply with the requirements of Section 6–104(1) does not (i) impair the buyer's rights in or title to the assets, (ii) render the sale ineffective, void, or voidable, (iii) entitle a creditor to more than a single satisfaction of his [or her] claim, or (iv) create liability other than as provided in this Article.

(9) Payment of the buyer's liability under subsection (1) discharges pro tanto the seller's debt to the creditor.

(10) Unless otherwise agreed, a buyer has an immediate right of reimbursement from the seller for any amount paid to a creditor in partial or total satisfaction of the buyer's liability under subsection (1).

(11) If the seller is an organization, a person who is in direct or indirect control of the seller, and who knowingly, intentionally, and without legal justification fails, or causes the seller to fail, to distribute the net contract price in accordance with the schedule of distribution is liable to any creditor to whom the seller undertook to make payment under the schedule for damages caused by the failure.

§6–108. Bulk Sales by Auction: Bulk Sales Conducted by Liquidator

(1) Sections 6–104, 6–105, 6–106, and 6–107 apply to a bulk sale by auction and a bulk sale conducted by a liquidator on the seller's behalf with the following modifications:

(a) "buyer" refers to auctioneer or liquidator, as the case may be;

(b) "net contract price" refers to net proceeds of the auction or net proceeds of the sale, as the case may be;

(c) the written notice required under Section 6–105(3) must be accompanied by a copy of the schedule of distribution (Section 6–106(1)) and state at least:

    (i) that the seller and the auctioneer or liquidator have entered into an agreement for auction or liquidation services that may constitute an agreement to make a bulk sale under the laws of the State of _____;

    (ii) the date of the agreement;

    (iii) the date on or after which the auction began or will begin or the date on or after which the liquidator began or will begin to sell assets on the seller's behalf;

    (iv) the date on or after which more than ten percent of the net proceeds of the sale were or will be paid, if the date is not stated in the schedule of distribution;

    (v) the name and a mailing address of the seller;

    (vi) any other business name and address listed by the seller pursuant to Section 6–104(1)(a);

    (vii) the name of the auctioneer or liquidator and an address of the auctioneer or liquidator from which information concerning the sale can be obtained;

    (viii) a statement indicating the type of assets or describing the assets item by item;

    (ix) the manner in which the auctioneer or liquidator will make available the list of claimants (Section 6–104(1)(f)), if applicable; and

    (x) if the sale is in total or partial satisfaction of an antecedent debt owed by the seller, the amount of the debt to be satisfied and the name of the person to whom it is owed; and

(d) in a single bulk sale the cumulative liability of the auctioneer or liquidator for failure to comply with the requirements of this section may not exceed the amount of the net proceeds of the sale allocable to inventory and equipment sold less the amount of the portion of any part of the net proceeds paid to or applied for the benefit of a creditor which is allocable to the inventory and equipment.

(2) A payment made by the auctioneer or liquidator to a person to whom the auctioneer or liquidator is, or believes he [or she] is, liable under this section reduces pro tanto the auctioneer's or liquidator's cumulative liability under subsection (1)(d).

(3) A form substantially as follows is sufficient to comply with subsection (1)(c):

Notice of Sale

(1) _____, whose address is _____, is described in this notice as the "seller."

(2) _____, whose address is _____, is described in this notice as the "auctioneer" or "liquidator."

(3) The seller has disclosed to the auctioneer or liquidator that within the past three years the seller has used other business names, operated at other addresses, or both, as follows: _____.

(4) The seller and the auctioneer or liquidator have entered into an agreement dated _____ for auction or liquidation services that may constitute an agreement to make a bulk sale under the laws of the State of _____.

(5) The date on or after which the auction began or will begin or the date on or after which the liquidator began or will begin to sell assets on the seller's behalf is _____, and [if not stated in the schedule of distribution] the date on or after which more than ten percent of the net proceeds of the sale were or will be paid is _____.

(6) The following assets are the subject of the sale: _____.

(7) [If applicable] The auctioneer or liquidator will make available to claimants of the seller a list of the seller's claimants in the following manner: _____.

(8) [If applicable] The sale is to satisfy $_____ of an antecedent debt owed by the seller to _____.

(9) A copy of the schedule of distribution of the net proceeds accompanies this notice.

    [End of Notice]

(4) A person who buys at a bulk sale by auction or conducted by a liquidator need not comply with the requirements of Section 6–104(1) and is not liable for the failure of an auctioneer or liquidator to comply with the requirements of this section.

§6–109. What Constitutes Filing; Duties of Filing Officer; Information From Filing Officer

(1) Presentation of a notice or list of claimants for filing and tender of the filing fee or acceptance of the notice or list by the filing officer constitutes filing under this Article.

(2) The filing officer shall:

    (a) mark each notice or list with a file number and with the date and hour of filing;

    (b) hold the notice or list or a copy for public inspection;

    (c) index the notice or list according to each name given for the seller and for the buyer; and

    (d) note in the index the file number and the addresses of the seller and buyer given in the notice or list.

(3) If the person filing a notice or list furnishes the filing officer with a copy, the filing officer upon request shall note upon the copy the file number and date and hour of the filing of the original and send or deliver the copy to the person.

(4) The fee for filing and indexing and for stamping a copy furnished by the person filing to show the date and place of filing is $_____ for the first page and $_____ for each additional page. The fee for indexing each name more than two is $_____.

(5) Upon request of any person, the filing officer shall issue a certificate showing whether any notice or list with respect to a particular seller or buyer is on file on the date and hour stated in the certificate. If a notice or list is on file, the certificate must give the date and hour of filing of each notice or list and the name and address of each seller, buyer, auctioneer, or liquidator. The fee for the certificate is $_____ if the request for the certificate is in the standard form prescribed by the [Secretary of State] and otherwise is $_____. Upon request of any person, the filing officer shall furnish a copy of any filed notice or list for a fee of $_____.

(6) The filing officer shall keep each notice or list for two years after it is filed.

§6–110. Limitation of Actions

(1) Except as provided in subsection (2), an action under this Article against a buyer, auctioneer, or liquidator must be commenced within one year after the date of the bulk sale.

(2) If the buyer, auctioneer, or liquidator conceals the fact that the sale has occurred, the limitation is tolled and an action under this Article may be commenced within the earlier of (i) one year after the person bringing the action discovers that the sale has occurred or (ii) one year after the person bringing the action should have discovered that the sale has occurred, but no later than two years after the date of the bulk sale. Complete noncompliance with the requirements of this Article does not of itself constitute concealment.

(3) An action under Section 6–107(11) must be commenced within one year after the alleged violation occurs.

[End of Alternative B]

ARTICLE 7 WAREHOUSE RECEIPTS, BILLS OF LADING AND OTHER DOCUMENTS OF TITLE

Part 1 General

§7–101. Short Title

This article shall be known and may be cited as Uniform Commercial Code—Documents of Title.

§7–102. Definitions and Index of Definitions

(1) In this Article, unless the context otherwise requires:

(a) "Bailee" means the person who by a warehouse receipt, bill of lading or other document of title acknowledges possession of goods and contracts to deliver them.

(b) "Consignee" means the person named in a bill to whom or to whose order the bill promises delivery.

(c) "Consignor" means the person named in a bill as the person from whom the goods have been received for shipment.

(d) "Delivery order" means a written order to deliver goods directed to a warehouseman, carrier or other person who in the ordinary course of business issues warehouse receipts or bills of lading.

(e) "Document" means document of title as defined in the general definitions in Article 1 (Section 1–201).

(f) "Goods" means all things which are treated as movable for the purposes of a contract of storage or transportation.

(g) "Issuer" means a bailee who issues a document except that in relation to an unaccepted delivery order it means the person who orders the possessor of goods to deliver. Issuer includes any person for whom an agent or employee purports to act in issuing a document if the agent or employee has real or apparent authority to issue documents, notwithstanding that the issuer received no goods or that the goods were misdescribed or that in any other respect the agent or employee violated his instructions.

(h) "Warehouseman" is a person engaged in the business of storing goods for hire.

(2) Other definitions applying to this Article or to specified Parts thereof, and the sections in which they appear are:

"Duly negotiate." Section 7–501.

"Person entitled under the document." Section 7–403(4).

(3) Definitions in other Articles applying to this Article and the sections in which they appear are:

"Contract for sale." Section 2–106.

"Overseas." Section 2–323.

"Receipt" of goods. Section 2–103.

(4) In addition Article 1 contains general definitions and principles of construction and interpretation applicable throughout this Article.

§7–103. Relation of Article to Treaty, Statute, Tariff, Classification or Regulation

To the extent that any treaty or statute of the United States, regulatory statute of this State or tariff, classification or regulation filed or issued pursuant thereto is applicable, the provisions of this Article are subject thereto.

§7–104. Negotiable and Non-Negotiable Warehouse Receipt, Bill of Lading or Other Document of Title

(1) A warehouse receipt, bill of lading or other document of title is negotiable

(a) if by its terms the goods are to be delivered to bearer or to the order of a named person; or

(b) where recognized in overseas trade, if it runs to a named person or assigns.

(2) Any other documents are non-negotiable. A bill of lading in which it is stated that the goods are consigned to a named person is not made negotiable by a provision that the goods are to be delivered only against a written order signed by the same or another named person.

§7–105. Construction Against Negative Implication

The omission from either Part 2 or Part 3 of this Article of a provision corresponding to a provision made in the other Part does not imply that a corresponding rule of law is not applicable.

Part 2 Warehouse Receipts: Special Provisions

§7–201. Who May Issue a Warehouse Receipt; Storage Under Government Bond

(1) A warehouse receipt may be issued by any warehouseman.

(2) Where goods including distilled spirits and agricultural commodities are stored under a statute requiring a bond against withdrawal or a license for the issuance of receipts in the nature of warehouse receipts, a receipt issued for the goods has like effect as a warehouse receipt even though issued by a person who is the owner of the goods and is not a warehouseman.

§7–202. Forms of Warehouse Receipt; Essential Terms; Optional Terms

(1) A warehouse receipt need not be in any particular form.

(2) Unless a warehouse receipt embodies within its written or printed terms each of the following, the warehouseman is liable for damages caused by the omission to a person injured thereby:

    (a) the location of the warehouse where the goods are stored;

    (b) the date of issue of the receipt;

    (c) the consecutive number of the receipt;

    (d) a statement whether the goods received will be delivered to the bearer, to a specified person, or to a specified person or his order;

    (e) the rate of storage and handling charges, except that where goods are stored under a field warehousing arrangement a statement of that fact is sufficient on a non-negotiable receipt;

    (f) a description of the goods or of the packages containing them;

    (g) the signature of the warehouseman which may be made by his authorized agent;

    (h) if the receipt is issued for goods of which the warehouseman is owner, either solely or jointly or in common with others, the fact of such ownership; and

    (i) a statement of the amount of advances made and of liabilities incurred for which the warehouseman claims a lien or security interest (Section 7–209). If the precise amount of such advances made or of such liabilities incurred is, at the time of the issue of the receipt, unknown to the warehouseman or to his agent who issues it, a statement of the fact that advances have been made or liabilities incurred and the purpose thereof is sufficient.

(3) A warehouseman may insert in his receipt any other terms which are not contrary to the provisions of this Act and do not impair his obligation of delivery (Section 7–403) or his duty of care (Section 7–204). Any contrary provisions shall be ineffective.

§7–203. Liability for Non-Receipt or Misdescription

A party to or purchaser for value in good faith of a document of title other than a bill of lading relying in either case upon the description therein of the goods may recover from the issuer damages caused by the non-receipt or misdescription of the goods, except to the extent that the document conspicuously indicates that the issuer does not know whether any part or all of the goods in fact were received or conform to the description, as where the description is in terms of marks or labels or kind, quantity or condition, or the receipt or description is qualified by "contents, condition and quality unknown," "said to contain" or the like, if such indication be true, or the party or purchaser otherwise has notice.

§7–204. Duty of Care; Contractual Limitation of Warehouseman's Liability

(1) A warehouseman is liable for damages for loss of or injury to the goods caused by his failure to exercise such care in regard to them as a reasonably careful man would exercise under like circumstances but unless otherwise agreed he is not liable for damages which could not have been avoided by the exercise of such care.

(2) Damages may be limited by a term in the warehouse receipt or storage agreement limiting the amount of liability in case of loss or damage, and setting forth a specific liability per article or item, or value per unit of weight, beyond which the warehouseman shall not be liable; provided, however, that such liability may on written request of the bailor at the time of signing such storage agreement or within a reasonable time after receipt of the warehouse receipt be increased on part or all of the goods thereunder, in which event increased rates may be charged based on such increased valuation, but that no such increase shall be permitted contrary to a lawful limitation of liability contained in the warehouseman's tariff, if any. No such limitation is effective with respect to the warehouseman's liability for conversion to his own use.

(3) Reasonable provisions as to the time and manner of presenting claims and instituting actions based on the bailment may be included in the warehouse receipt or tariff.

(4) This section does not impair or repeal . . .

Note: *Insert in subsection (4) a reference to any statute which imposes a higher responsibility upon the warehouseman or invalidates contractual limitations which would be permissible under this Article.*

§7–205. Title under Warehouse Receipt Defeated in Certain Cases

A buyer in the ordinary course of business of fungible goods sold and delivered by a warehouseman who is also in the business of buying and selling such goods takes free of any claim under a warehouse receipt even though it has been duly negotiated.

§7–206. Termination of Storage at Warehouseman's Option

(1) A warehouseman may on notifying the person on whose account the goods are held and any other person known to claim an interest in the goods require payment of any charges and removal of the goods from the warehouse at the termination of the period of storage fixed by the document, or, if no period is fixed, within a stated period not less than thirty days after the notification. If the goods are not removed before the date specified in the notification, the warehouseman may sell them in accordance with the provisions of the section on enforcement of a warehouseman's lien (Section 7–210).

(2) If a warehouseman in good faith believes that the goods are about to deteriorate or decline in value to less than the amount of his lien within the time prescribed in subsection (1) for notification, advertisement and sale, the warehouseman may specify in the notification any reasonable shorter time for removal of the goods and in case the goods are not removed, may sell them at public sale held not less than one week after a single advertisement or posting.

(3) If as a result of a quality or condition of the goods of which the warehouseman had no notice at the time of deposit the goods are a hazard to other property or to the warehouse or to persons, the warehouseman may sell the goods at public or private sale without advertisement on reasonable notification to all persons known to claim an interest in the goods. If the warehouseman after a reasonable effort is unable to sell the goods he may dispose of them in any lawful manner and shall incur no liability by reason of such disposition.

(4) The warehouseman must deliver the goods to any person entitled to them under this Article upon due demand made at any time prior to sale or other disposition under this section.

(5) The warehouseman may satisfy his lien from the proceeds of any sale or disposition under this section but must hold the balance for delivery on the demand of any person to whom he would have been bound to deliver the goods.

§7–207. Goods Must Be Kept Separate; Fungible Goods

(1) Unless the warehouse receipt otherwise provides, a warehouseman must keep separate the goods covered by each receipt so as to permit at all times identification and delivery of those goods except that different lots of fungible goods may be commingled.

(2) Fungible goods so commingled are owned in common by the persons entitled thereto and the warehouseman is severally liable to each owner for that owner's share. Where because of overissue a mass of fungible goods is insufficient to meet all the receipts which the warehouseman has issued against it, the persons entitled include all holders to whom overissued receipts have been duly negotiated.

§7–208. Altered Warehouse Receipts

Where a blank in a negotiable warehouse receipt has been filled in without authority, a purchaser for value and without notice of the want of authority may treat the insertion as authorized. Any other unauthorized alteration leaves any receipt enforceable against the issuer according to its original tenor.

§7–209. Lien of Warehouseman

(1) A warehouseman has a lien against the bailor on the goods covered by a warehouse receipt or on the proceeds thereof in his possession for charges for storage or transportation (including demurrage and terminal charges), insurance, labor, or charges present or future in relation to the goods, and for expenses necessary for preservation of the goods or reasonably incurred in their sale pursuant to law. If the person on whose account the goods are held is liable for like charges or expenses in relation to other goods whenever deposited and it is stated in the receipt that a lien is claimed for charges and expenses in relation to other goods, the warehouseman also has a lien against him for such charges and expenses whether or not the other goods have been delivered by the warehouseman. But against a person to whom a negotiable warehouse receipt is duly negotiated a warehouseman's lien is limited to charges in an amount or at a rate specified on the receipt or if no charges are so specified then to a reasonable charge for storage of the goods covered by the receipt subsequent to the date of receipt.

(2) The warehouseman may also reserve a security interest against the bailor for a maximum amount specified on the receipt for charges other than those specified in subsection (1), such as for money advanced and interest. Such a security interest is governed by the Article on Secured Transactions (Article 9).

(3)(a) A warehouseman's lien for charges and expenses under subsection (1) or a security interest under subsection (2) is also effective against any person who so entrusted the bailor with possession of the goods that a pledge of them by him to a good faith purchaser for value would have been valid but is not effective against a person as to whom the document confers no right in the goods covered by it under Section 7–503.

(b) A warehouseman's lien on household goods for charges and expenses in relation to the goods under subsection (1) is also effective against all persons if the depositor was the legal possessor of the goods at the time of deposit. "Household goods" means furniture, furnishings, and personal effects used by the depositor in a dwelling.

(4) A warehouseman loses his lien on any goods which he voluntarily delivers or which he unjustifiably refuses to deliver.

§7–210. Enforcement of Warehouseman's Lien

(1) Except as provided in subsection (2), a warehouseman's lien may be enforced by public or private sale of the goods in block or in parcels, at any time or place and on any terms which are commercially reasonable, after notifying all persons known to claim an interest in the goods. Such notification must include a statement of the amount due, the nature of the proposed sale and the time and place of any public sale. The fact that a better price could have been obtained by a sale at a different time or in a different method from that selected by the warehouseman is not of itself sufficient to establish that the sale was not made in a commercially reasonable manner. If the warehouseman either sells the goods in the usual manner in any recognized market therefor, or if he sells at the price current in such market at the time of his sale, or if he has otherwise sold in conformity with commercially reasonable practices among dealers in the type of goods sold, he has sold in a commercially reasonable manner. A sale of more goods than apparently necessary to be offered to insure satisfaction of the obligation is not commercially reasonable except in cases covered by the preceding sentence.

(2) A warehouseman's lien on goods other than goods stored by a merchant in the course of his business may be enforced only as follows:

(a) All persons known to claim an interest in the goods must be notified.

(b) The notification must be delivered in person or sent by registered or certified letter to the last known address of any person to be notified.

(c) The notification must include an itemized statement of the claim, a description of the goods subject to the lien, a demand for payment within a specified time not less than ten days after receipt of the notification, and a conspicuous statement that unless the claim is paid within that time the goods will be advertised for sale and sold by auction at a specified time and place.

(d) The sale must conform to the terms of the notification.

(e) The sale must be held at the nearest suitable place to that where the goods are held or stored.

(f) After the expiration of the time given in the notification, an advertisement of the sale must be pub-

lished once a week for two weeks consecutively in a newspaper of general circulation where the sale is to be held. The advertisement must include a description of the goods, the name of the person on whose account they are being held, and the time and place of the sale. The sale must take place at least fifteen days after the first publication. If there is no newspaper of general circulation where the sale is to be held, the advertisement must be posted at least ten days before the sale in not less than six conspicuous places in the neighborhood of the proposed sale.

(3) Before any sale pursuant to this section any person claiming a right in the goods may pay the amount necessary to satisfy the lien and the reasonable expenses incurred under this section. In that event the goods must not be sold, but must be retained by the warehouseman subject to the terms of the receipt and this Article.

(4) The warehouseman may buy at any public sale pursuant to this section.

(5) A purchaser in good faith of goods sold to enforce a warehouseman's lien takes the goods free of any rights of persons against whom the lien was valid, despite noncompliance by the warehouseman with the requirements of this section.

(6) The warehouseman may satisfy his lien from the proceeds of any sale pursuant to this section but must hold the balance, if any, for delivery on demand to any person to whom he would have been bound to deliver the goods.

(7) The rights provided by this section shall be in addition to all other rights allowed by law to a creditor against his debtor.

(8) Where a lien is on goods stored by a merchant in the course of his business the lien may be enforced in accordance with either subsection (1) or (2).

(9) The warehouseman is liable for damages caused by failure to comply with the requirements for sale under this section and in case of willful violation is liable for conversion.

Part 3 Bills of Lading: Special Provisions

§7–301. Liability for Non-Receipt or Misdescription; "Said to Contain"; "Shipper's Load and Count"; Improper Handling

(1) A consignee of a non-negotiable bill who has given value in good faith or a holder to whom a negotiable bill has been duly negotiated relying in either case upon the description therein of the goods; or upon the date therein shown; may recover from the issuer damages caused by the misdating of the bill or the non-receipt or misdescription of the goods, except to the extent that the document indicates that the issuer does not know whether any part or all of the goods in fact were received or conform to the description, as where the description is in terms of marks or labels or kind, quantity, or condition or the receipt or

description is qualified by "contents or condition of contents of packages unknown," "said to contain," "shipper's weight, load and count" or the like, if such indication be true.

(2) When goods are loaded by an issuer who is a common carrier, the issuer must count the packages of goods if package freight and ascertain the kind and quantity if bulk freight. In such cases "shipper's weight, load and count" or other words indicating that the description was made by the shipper are ineffective except as to freight concealed by packages.

(3) When bulk freight is loaded by a shipper who makes available to the issuer adequate facilities for weighing such freight, an issuer who is a common carrier must ascertain the kind and quantity within a reasonable time after receiving the written request of the shipper to do so. In such cases "shipper's weight" or other words of like purport are ineffective.

(4) The issuer may by inserting in the bill the words "shipper's weight, load and count" or other words of like purport indicate that the goods were loaded by the shipper; and if such statement be true the issuer shall not be liable for damages caused by the improper loading. But their omission does not imply liability for such damages.

(5) The shipper shall be deemed to have guaranteed to the issuer the accuracy at the time of shipment of the description, marks, labels, number, kind, quantity, condition and weight, as furnished by him; and the shipper shall indemnify the issuer against damage caused by inaccuracies in such particulars. The right of the issuer to such indemnity shall in no way limit his responsibility and liability under the contract of carriage to any person other than the shipper.

§7–302. Through Bills of Lading and Similar Documents

(1) The issuer of a through bill of lading or other document embodying an undertaking to be performed in part by persons acting as its agents or by connecting carriers is liable to anyone entitled to recover on the document for any breach by such other persons or by a connecting carrier of its obligation under the document but to the extent that the bill covers an undertaking to be performed overseas or in territory not contiguous to the continental United States or an undertaking including matters other than transportation this liability may be varied by agreement of the parties.

(2) Where goods covered by a through bill of lading or other document embodying an undertaking to be performed in part by persons other than the issuer are received by any such person, he is subject with respect to his own performance while the goods are in his possession to the obligation of the issuer. His obligation is discharged by delivery of the goods to another such person pursuant to the document, and does not include

liability for breach by any other such persons or by the issuer.

(3) The issuer of such through bill of lading or other document shall be entitled to recover from the connecting carrier or such other person in possession of the goods when the breach of the obligation under the document occurred, the amount it may be required to pay to anyone entitled to recover on the document therefor, as may be evidenced by any receipt. judgment, or transcript thereof, and the amount of any expense reasonably incurred by it in defending any action brought by anyone entitled to recover on the document therefor.

§7–303. Diversion; Reconsignment; Change of Instructions

(1) Unless the bill of lading otherwise provides, the carrier may deliver the goods to a person or destination other than that stated in the bill or may otherwise dispose of the goods on instructions from

    (a) the holder of a negotiable bill; or

    (b) the consignor on a non-negotiable bill notwithstanding contrary instructions from the consignee; or

    (c) the consignee on a non-negotiable bill in the absence of contrary instructions from the consignor, if the goods have arrived at the billed destination or if the consignee is in possession of the bill; or

    (d) the consignee on a non-negotiable bill if he is entitled as against the consignor to dispose of them.

(2) Unless such instructions are noted on a negotiable bill of lading, a person to whom the bill is duly negotiated can hold the bailee according to the original terms.

§7–304. Bills of Lading in a Set

(1) Except where customary in overseas transportation, a bill of lading must not be issued in a set of parts. The issuer is liable for damages caused by violation of this subsection.

(2) Where a bill of lading is lawfully drawn in a set of parts, each of which is numbered and expressed to be valid only if the goods have not been delivered against any other part, the whole of the parts constitute one bill.

(3) Where a bill of lading is lawfully issued in a set of parts and different parts are negotiated to different persons, the title of the holder to whom the first due negotiation is made prevails as to both the document and the goods even though any later holder may have received the goods from the carrier in good faith and discharged the carrier's obligation by surrender of his part.

(4) Any person who negotiates or transfers a single part of a bill of lading drawn in a set is liable to holders of that part as if it were the whole set.

(5) The bailee is obliged to deliver in accordance with Part 4 of this Article against the first presented part of a bill of lading lawfully drawn in a set. Such delivery discharges the bailee's obligation on the whole bill.

§7–305. Destination Bills

(1) Instead of issuing a bill of lading to the consignor at the place of shipment a carrier may at the request of the consignor procure the bill to be issued at destination or at any other place designated in the request.

(2) Upon request of anyone entitled as against the carrier to control the goods while in transit and on surrender of any outstanding bill of lading or other receipt covering such goods, the issuer may procure a substitute bill to be issued at any place designated in the request.

§7–306. Altered Bills of Lading

An unauthorized alteration or filling in of a blank in a bill of lading leaves the bill enforceable according to its original tenor.

§7–307. Lien of Carrier

(1) A carrier has a lien on the goods covered by a bill of lading for charges subsequent to the date of its receipt of the goods for storage or transportation (including demurrage and terminal charges) and for expenses necessary for preservation of the goods incident to their transportation or reasonably incurred in their sale pursuant to law. But against a purchaser for value of a negotiable bill of lading a carrier's lien is limited to charges stated in the bill or the applicable tariffs, or if no charges are stated then to a reasonable charge.

(2) A lien for charges and expenses under subsection (1) on goods which the carrier was required by law to receive for transportation is effective against the consignor or any person entitled to the goods unless the carrier had notice that the consignor lacked authority to subject the goods to such charges and expenses. Any other lien under subsection (1) is effective against the consignor and any person who permitted the bailor to have control or possession of the goods unless the carrier had notice that the bailor lacked such authority.

(3) A carrier loses his lien on any goods which he voluntarily delivers or which he unjustifiably refuses to deliver.

§7–308. Enforcement of Carrier's Lien

(1) A carrier's lien may be enforced by public or private sale of the goods, in block or in parcels, at any time or place and on any terms which are commercially reasonable, after notifying all persons known to claim an interest in the goods. Such notification must include a statement of the amount due, the nature of the proposed sale and the time and place of any public sale. The fact that a better price could have been obtained by a sale at a different time or in a different method from that selected by the carrier is not of itself sufficient to establish that the sale was not made in a commercially reasonable manner. If the carrier either sells the goods in the usual manner in any recognized market therefor or if he sells at the price current in such market at the time of his sale or if he has otherwise sold in conformity with commercially reasonable practices among dealers in the type of goods sold he has sold in a commercially reasonable manner. A sale of more goods than apparently necessary to be offered to ensure satisfaction of the obligation is not commercially reasonable except in cases covered by the preceding sentence.

(2) Before any sale pursuant to this section any person claiming a right in the goods may pay the amount necessary to satisfy the lien and the reasonable expenses incurred under this section. In that event the goods must not be sold, but must be retained by the carrier subject to the terms of the bill and this Article.

(3) The carrier may buy at any public sale pursuant to this section.

(4) A purchaser in good faith of goods sold to enforce a carrier's lien takes the goods free of any rights of persons against whom the lien was valid, despite noncompliance by the carrier with the requirements of this section.

(5) The carrier may satisfy his lien from the proceeds of any sale pursuant to this section but must hold the balance, if any, for delivery on demand to any person to whom he would have been bound to deliver the goods.

(6) The rights provided by this section shall be in addition to all other rights allowed by law to a creditor against his debtor.

(7) A carrier's lien may be enforced in accordance with either subsection (1) or the procedure set forth in subsection (2) of Section 7–210.

(8) The carrier is liable for damages caused by failure to comply with the requirements for sale under this section and in case of willful violation is liable for conversion.

§7–309. Duty of Care; Contractual Limitation of Carrier's Liability

(1) A carrier who issues a bill of lading whether negotiable or non-negotiable must exercise the degree of care in relation to the goods which a reasonably careful man would exercise under like circumstances. This subsection does not repeal or change any law or rule of law which imposes liability upon a common carrier for damages not caused by its negligence.

(2) Damages may be limited by a provision that the carrier's liability shall not exceed a value stated in the document if the carrier's rates are dependent upon value and the consignor by the carrier's tariff is afforded an opportunity to declare a higher value or a value as lawfully provided in the tariff, or where no tariff is filed he is otherwise advised of such opportunity; but no such limitation is effective with respect to the carrier's liability for conversion to its own use.

(3) Reasonable provisions as to the time and manner of presenting claims and instituting actions based on the shipment may be included in a bill of lading or tariff.

Part 4 Warehouse Receipts and Bills of Lading: General Obligations

§7–401. Irregularities in Issue of Receipt or Bill or Conduct of Issuer

The obligations imposed by this Article on an issuer apply to a document of title regardless of the fact that

(a) the document may not comply with the requirements of this Article or of any other law or regulation regarding its issue, form or content; or

(b) the issuer may have violated laws regulating the conduct of his business; or

(c) the goods covered by the document were owned by the bailee at the time the document was issued; or

(d) the person issuing the document does not come within the definition of warehouseman if it purports to be a warehouse receipt.

§7–402. Duplicate Receipt or Bill; Overissue

Neither a duplicate nor any other document of title purporting to cover goods already represented by an outstanding document of the same issuer confers any right in the goods, except as provided in the case of bills in a set, overissue of documents for fungible goods and substitutes for lost, stolen or destroyed documents. But the issuer is liable for damages caused by his overissue or failure to identify a duplicate document as such by conspicuous notation on its face.

§7–403. Obligation of Warehouseman or Carrier to Deliver; Excuse

(1) The bailee must deliver the goods to a person entitled under the document who complies with subsections (2) and (3), unless and to the extent that the bailee establishes any of the following:

(a) delivery of the goods to a person whose receipt was rightful as against the claimant;

(b) damage to or delay, loss or destruction of the goods for which the bailee is not liable[, but the burden of establishing negligence in such cases is on the person entitled under the document];

Note: the brackets in(1)(b) indicate that State enactments may differ on this point without serious damage to the principle of uniformity.

(c) previous sale or other disposition of the goods in lawful enforcement of a lien or on warehouseman's lawful termination of storage;

(d) the exercise by a seller of his right to stop delivery pursuant to the provisions of the Article on Sales (Section 2–705);

(e) a diversion, reconsignment or other disposition pursuant to the provisions of this Article (Section 7–303) or tariff regulating such right;

(f) release, satisfaction or any other fact affording a personal defense against the claimant;

(g) any other lawful excuse

(2) A person claiming goods covered by a document of title must satisfy the bailee's lien where the bailee so requests or where the bailee is prohibited by law from delivering the goods until the charges are paid.

(3) Unless the person claiming is one against whom the document confers no right under Sec. 7–503(1), he must surrender for cancellation or notation of partial deliveries any outstanding negotiable document covering the goods, and the bailee must cancel the document or conspicuously note the partial delivery thereon or be liable to any person to whom the document is duly negotiated.

(4) "Person entitled under the document" means holder in the case of a negotiable document, or the person to whom delivery is to be made by the terms of or pursuant to written instructions under a non-negotiable document.

§7–404. No Liability for Good Faith Delivery Pursuant to Receipt or Bill

A bailee who in good faith including observance of reasonable commercial standards has received goods and delivered or otherwise disposed of them according to the terms of the document of title or pursuant to this Article is not liable therefor. This rule applies even though the person from whom he received the goods has no authority to procure the document or to dispose of the goods and even though the person to whom he delivered the goods had no authority to receive them.

Part 5 Warehouse Receipts and Bills of Lading: Negotiation and Transfer

§7–501. Form of Negotiation and Requirements of "Due Negotiation"

(1) A negotiable document of title running to the order of a named person is negotiated by his indorsement and delivery. After his indorsement in blank or to bearer any person can negotiate it by delivery alone.

(2)(a) A negotiable document of title is also negotiated by delivery alone when by its original terms it runs to bearer.

(b) When a document running to the order of a named person is delivered to him the effect is the same as if the document had been negotiated.

(3) Negotiation of a negotiable document of title after it has been indorsed to a specified person requires indorsement by the special indorsee as well as delivery.

(4) A negotiable document of title is "duly negotiated" when it is negotiated in the manner stated in this section to a holder who purchases it in good faith without notice of any defense against or claim to it on the part of any person and for value, unless it is established that the negotiation is not in the regular course of business or

financing or involves receiving the document in settlement or payment of a money obligation.

(5) Indorsement of a non-negotiable document neither makes it negotiable nor adds to the transferee's rights.

(6) The naming in a negotiable bill of a person to be notified of the arrival of the goods does not limit the negotiability of the bill nor constitute notice to a purchaser thereof of any interest of such person in the goods.

§7–502. Rights Acquired by Due Negotiation

(1) Subject to the following section and to the provisions of Section 7–205 on fungible goods, a holder to whom a negotiable document of title has been duly negotiated acquires thereby:

    (a) title to the document;

    (b) title to the goods;

    (c) all rights accruing under the law of agency or estoppel, including rights to goods delivered to the bailee after the document was issued; and

    (d) the direct obligation of the issuer to hold or deliver the goods according to the terms of the document free of any defense or claim by him except those arising under the terms of the document or under this Article. In the case of a delivery order the bailee's obligation accrues only upon acceptance and the obligation acquired by the holder is that the issuer and any indorser will procure the acceptance of the bailee.

(2) Subject to the following section, title and rights so acquired are not defeated by any stoppage of the goods represented by the document or by surrender of such goods by the bailee, and are not impaired even though the negotiation or any prior negotiation constituted a breach of duty or even though any person has been deprived of possession of the document by misrepresentation, fraud, accident, mistake, duress, loss, theft or conversion, or even though a previous sale or other transfer of the goods or document has been made to a third person.

§7–503. Document of Title to Goods Defeated in Certain Cases

(1) A document of title confers no right in goods against a person who before issuance of the document had a legal interest or a perfected security interest in them and who neither

    (a) delivered or entrusted them or any document of title covering them to the bailor or his nominee with actual or apparent authority to ship, store or sell or with power to obtain delivery under this Article (Section 7–403) or with power of disposition under this Act (Section 2–403 and 9–307) or other statute or rule of law; nor

    (b) acquiesced in the procurement by the bailor or his nominee of any document of title.

(2) Title to goods based upon an unaccepted delivery order is subject to the rights of anyone to whom a negotiable warehouse receipt or bill of lading covering the goods has been duly negotiated. Such a title may be defeated under the next section to the same extent as the rights of the issuer or a transferee from the issuer.

(3) Title to goods based upon a bill of lading issued to a freight forwarder is subject to the rights of anyone to whom a bill issued by the freight forwarder is duly negotiated; but delivery by the carrier in accordance with Part 4 of this Article pursuant to its own bill of lading discharges the carrier's obligation to deliver.

§7–504. Rights Acquired in the Absence of Due Negotiation; Effect of Diversion; Seller's Stoppage of Delivery

(1) A transferee of a document, whether negotiable or non-negotiable, to whom the document has been delivered but not duly negotiated, acquires the title and rights which his transferor had or had actual authority to convey.

(2) In the case of a non-negotiable document, until but not after the bailee receives notification of the transfer, the rights of the transferee may be defeated

    (a) by those creditors of the transferor who could treat the sale as void under Section 2–402; or

    (b) by a buyer from the transferor in ordinary course of business if the bailee has delivered the goods to the buyer or received notification of his rights; or

    (c) as against the bailee by good faith dealings of the bailee with the transferor.

(3) A diversion or other change of shipping instructions by the consignor in a non-negotiable bill of lading which causes the bailee not to deliver to the consignee defeats the consignee's title to the goods if they have been delivered to a buyer in ordinary course of business and in any event defeats the consignee's rights against the bailee.

(4) Delivery pursuant to a non-negotiable document may be stopped by a seller under Section 2–705, and subject to the requirement of due notification there provided. A bailee honoring the seller's instructions is entitled to be indemnified by the seller against any resulting loss or expense.

§7–505. Indorser Not a Guarantor for Other Parties

The indorsement of a document of title issued by a bailee does not make the indorser liable for any default by the bailee or by previous indorsers.

§7–506. Delivery Without Indorsement: Right to Compel Indorsement

The transferee of a negotiable document of title has a specifically enforceable right to have his transferor supply any necessary indorsement but the transfer becomes a negotiation only as of the time the indorsement is supplied.

§7–507. Warranties on Negotiation or Transfer of Receipt or Bill

Where a person negotiates or transfers a document of title for value otherwise than as a mere intermediary under the next following section, then unless otherwise agreed he warrants to his immediate purchaser only in addition to any warranty made in selling the goods

    (a) that the document is genuine; and

    (b) that he has no knowledge of any fact which would impair its validity or worth; and

    (c) that his negotiation or transfer is rightful and fully effective with respect to the title to the document and the goods it represents.

§7–508. Warranties of Collecting Bank as to Documents

A collecting bank or other intermediary known to be entrusted with documents on behalf of another or with collection of a draft or other claim against delivery of documents warrants by such delivery of the documents only its own good faith and authority. This rule applies even though the intermediary has purchased or made advances against the claim or draft to be collected.

§7–509. Receipt or Bill: When Adequate Compliance With Commercial Contract

The question whether a document is adequate to fulfill the obligations of a contract for sale or the conditions of a credit is governed by the Articles on Sales (Article 2) and on Letters of Credit (Article 5).

Part 6 Warehouse Receipts and Bills of Lading: Miscellaneous Provisions

§7–601. Lost and Missing Documents

(1) If a document has been lost, stolen or destroyed, a court may order delivery of the goods or issuance of a substitute document and the bailee may without liability to any person comply with such order. If the document was negotiable the claimant must post security approved by the court to indemnify any person who may suffer loss as a result of non-surrender of the document. If the document was not negotiable, such security may be required at the discretion of the court. The court may also in its discretion order payment of the bailee's reasonable costs and counsel fees. (2) A bailee who without court order delivers goods to a person claiming under a missing negotiable document is liable to any person injured thereby, and if the delivery is not in good faith becomes liable for conversion. Delivery in good faith is not conversion if made in accordance with a filed classification or tariff or, where no classification or tariff is filed, if the claimant posts security with the bailee if an amount at least double the value of the goods at the time of posting to indemnify any person injured by the delivery who files a notice of claim within one year after the delivery.

§7–602. Attachment of Goods Covered by a Negotiable Document

Except where the document was originally issued upon delivery of the goods by a person who had no power to dispose of them, no lien attaches by virtue of any judicial process to goods in the possession of a bailee for which a negotiable document of title is outstanding unless the document be first surrendered to the bailee or its negotiation enjoined, and the bailee shall not be compelled to deliver the goods pursuant to process until the document is surrendered to him or impounded by the court. One who purchases the document for value without notice of the process or injunction takes free of the lien imposed by judicial process.

§7–603. Conflicting Claims; Interpleader

If more than one person claims title or possession of the goods, the bailee is excused from delivery until he has had a reasonable time to ascertain the validity of the adverse claims or to bring an action to compel all claimants to interplead and may compel such interpleader, either in defending an action for non-delivery of the goods, or by original action, whichever is appropriate.

ARTICLE 8 INVESTMENT SECURITIES

Part 1 Short Title and General Matters

§8–101. Short Title

This Article shall be known and may be cited as Uniform Commercial Code—Investment Securities

§8–102. Definitions and Index of Definitions

(1) In this Article, unless the context otherwise requires:

    (a) A "certified security" is a share, participation, or other interest in property of or an enterprise of the issuer or an obligation of the issuer which is

    (i) represented by an instrument issued in bearer or registered form;

    (ii) of a type commonly dealt in on securities exchanges or markets or commonly recognized in any area in which it is issued or dealt in as a medium for investment; and

    (iii) either one of a class or series or by its terms divisible into a class or series of shares, participations, interests, or obligations.

    (b) An "uncertificated security" is a share, participation, or other interest in property or an enterprise of the issuer or an obligation of the issuer which is

    (i) not represented by an instrument and the transfer of which is registered upon books maintained for that purpose by or on behalf of the issuer;

    (ii) of a type commonly dealt in on securities exchanges or markets; and

(iii) either one of a class or series or by its terms divisible into a class or series of shares, participations, interests, or obligations.

(c) A "security" is either a certificated or an uncertificated security. If a security is certificated, the terms "security" and "certificated security" may mean either the intangible interest, the instrument representing that interest, or both, as the context requires. A writing that is a certificated security is governed by this Article and not by Article 3, even though it also meets the requirements of that Article. This Article does not apply to money. If a certificated security has been retained by or surrendered to the issuer or its transfer agent for reasons other than registration of transfer, other temporary purpose, payment, exchange, or acquisition by the issuer, that security shall be treated as an uncertificated security for purposes of this Article.

(d) A certificated security is in "registered form" if

(i) it specifies a person entitled to the security or the rights it represents; and

(ii) its transfer may be registered upon books maintained for that purpose by or on behalf of the issuer, or the security so states.

(e) A certificated security is in "bearer form" if it runs to bearer according to its terms and not by reason of any indorsement.

(2) A "subsequent purchaser" is a person who takes other than by original issue.

(3) A "clearing corporation" is a corporation registered as a "clearing agency" under the federal securities laws or a corporation:

(a) at least 90 percent of whose capital stock is held by or for one or more organizations, none of which, other than a national securities exchange or association, holds in excess or 20 percent of the capital stock of the corporation, and each of which is

(i) subject to supervision or regulation pursuant to the provisions of federal or state banking laws or state insurance laws,

(ii) a broker or dealer or investment company registered under the federal securities laws, or

(iii) a national securities exchange or association registered under the federal securities laws; and

(b) any remaining capital stock of which is held by individuals who have purchased it at or prior to the time of their taking office as directors of the corporation and who have purchased only so much of the capital stock as is necessary to permit them to qualify as directors.

(4) A "custodian bank" is a bank or trust company that is supervised and examined by state or federal authority having supervision over banks and is acting as custodian for a clearing corporation.

(5) Other definitions applying to this Article or to specified Parts thereof and the sections in which they appear are:

"Adverse claim." Section 8–302.

"Bona fide purchaser." Section 8–302.

"Broker." Section 8–303.

"Debtor." Section 9–105.

"Financial intermediary." Section 8–313.

"Guarantee of the signature." Section 8–402.

"Initial transaction statement." Section 8–408.

"Instruction." Section 8–308.

"Intermediary bank." Section 4–105.

"Issuer." Section 8–201.

"Overissue." Section 8–104.

"Secured Party." Section 9–105.

"Security Agreement." Section 9–105.

(6) In addition, Article 1 contains general definitions and principles of construction and interpretation applicable throughout this Article.

§8–103. Issuer's Lien

A lien upon a security in favor of an issuer thereof is valid against a purchaser only if:

(a) the security is certificated and the right of the issuer to the lien is noted conspicuously thereon: or

(b) the security is uncertificated and a notation of the right of the issuer to the lien is contained in the initial transaction statement sent to the purchaser or, if his interest is transferred to him other than by registration of transfer, pledge, or release, the initial transaction statement sent to the registered owner or the registered pledgee.

§8–104. Effect of Overissue; "Overissue"

(1) The provisions of this Article which validate a security or compel its issue or reissue do not apply to the extent that validation, issue, or reissue would result in overissue; but if:

(a) an identical security which does not constitute an overissue is reasonably available for purchase, the person entitled to issue or validation may compel the issuer to purchase the security for him and either to deliver a certificated security or to register the transfer of an uncertificated security to him, against surrender of any certificated security he holds; or

(b) a security is not so available for purchase, the person entitled to issue or validation may recover from the issuer the price he or the last purchaser for value paid for it with interest from the date of his demand.

(2) "Overissue" means the issue of securities in excess of the amount the issuer has corporate power to issue.

§8–105. Certificated Securities Negotiable; Statements and Instructions Not Negotiable; Presumptions

(1) Certificated securities governed by this Article are negotiable instruments.

(2) Statements (Section 8–408), notices, or the like, sent by the issuer of uncertificated securities and instructions (Section 8–308) are neither negotiable instruments nor certificated securities.

(3) In any action on a security:

(a) unless specifically denied in the pleadings, each signature on a certificated security, in a necessary indorsement, on an initial transaction statement, or on an instruction, is admitted;

(b) if the effectiveness of a signature is put in issue, the burden of establishing it is on the party claiming under the signature, but the signature is presumed to be genuine or authorized.

(c) if signatures on a certificated security are admitted or established, production of the security entitles a holder to recover on it unless the defendant establishes a defense or a defect going to the validity of the security;

(d) if signatures on an initial transaction statement are admitted or established, the facts stated in the statement are presumed to be true as of the time of its issuance; and

(e) after it is shown that a defense or defect exists, the plaintiff has the burden of establishing that he or some person under whom he claims is a person against whom the defense or defect is ineffective (Section 8–202).

§8–106. Applicability

The law (including the conflict of laws rules) of the jurisdiction of organization of the issuer governs the validity of a security, the effectiveness of registration by the issuer, and the rights and duties of the issuer with respect to:

(a) registration of transfer of a certificated security;

(b) registration of transfer, pledge, or release of an uncertificated security; and

(c) sending of statements of uncertificated securities.

§8–107. Securities Transferable; Action for Price

(1) Unless otherwise agreed and subject to any applicable law or regulation respecting short sales, a person obligated to transfer securities may transfer any certificated security of the specified issue in bearer form or registered in the name of the transferee, or indorsed to him or in blank, or he may transfer an equivalent uncertificated security to the transferee or a person designated by the transferee.

(2) If the buyer fails to pay the price as it comes due under a contract of sale, the seller may recover the price of:

(a) certificated securities accepted by the buyer;

(b) uncertificated securities that have been transferred to the buyer or a person designated by the buyer; and

(c) other securities if efforts at their resale would be unduly burdensome or if there is no readily available market for their resale.

§8–108. Registration of Pledge and Release of Uncertificated Securities

A security interest in an uncertificated security may be evidenced by the registration of pledge to the secured party or a person designated by him. There can be no more than one registered pledge of an uncertificated

security at any time. The registered owner of an uncertified security is the person in whose name the security is registered, even if the security is subject to a registered pledge. The rights of a registered pledgee of an uncertificated security under this Article are terminated by the registration of release.

Part 2 Issue—Issuer

§8–201. Issuer

(1) With respect to obligations on or defenses to security, "issuer" includes a person who:

(a) places or authorizes the placing of his name on a certificated security (otherwise than as authenticating trustee, registrar, transfer agent, or the like) to evidence that it represents a share, participation, or other interest in his property or in an enterprise, or to evidence his duty to perform an obligation represented by the certificated security;

(b) creates shares, participations, or other interests in his property or in an enterprise or undertakes obligations, which shares, participations, interests or obligations are uncertificated securities;

(c) directly or indirectly creates fractional interests in his rights or property, which fractional interests are represented by certificated securities; or

(d) becomes responsible for or in place of any other person described as an issuer in this section.

(2) With respect to obligations on or defenses to a security, a guarantor is an issuer to the extent of his guaranty, whether or not his obligation is noted on a certificated security or on statements of uncertificated securities sent pursuant to Section 8–408.

(3) With respect to registration of transfer, pledge, or release (Part 4 of this Article), "issuer" means a person on whose behalf transfer books are maintained.

§8–202. Issuer's Responsibility and Defenses: Notice of Defect or Defense

(1) Even against a purchaser for value and without notice, the terms of a security include:

(a) if the security is certificated, those stated on the security;

(b) if the security is uncertificated, those contained in the initial transaction statement sent to such purchaser, or, if his interest is transferred to him other than by registration of transfer, pledge, or release, the initial transaction statement sent to the registered owner or registered pledgee; and

(c) those made part of the security by reference, on the certificated security or in the initial transaction statement, to another instrument, indenture or document or to a constitution, statute, ordinance, rule, regulation, order or the like, to the extent that the terms referred to do not conflict with the terms stated on the certificated security or contained in the statement. A reference under this paragraph does not of itself charge a purchaser for value with notice of a defect going to the validity of the security, even though the certificated security or statement expressly states that a person accepting it admits notice.

(2) A certificated security in the hands of a purchaser for value or an uncertificated security as to which an initial transaction statement has been sent to a purchaser for value, other than a security issued by a government or governmental agency or unit, even though issued with a defect going to its validity, is valid with respect to the purchaser if he is without notice of the particular defect unless the defect involves a violation of constitutional provisions, in which case the security is valid with respect to a subsequent purchaser for value and without notice of the defect. This subsection applies to an issuer that is a government or governmental agency or unit only if either there has been substantial compliance with the legal requirements governing the issue or the issuer has received a substantial consideration for the issue as a whole or for the particular security and a stated purpose of the issue is one for which the issuer has power to borrow money or issue the security.

(3) Except as provided in the case of certain unauthorized signatures (Section 8–205), lack of genuineness of a certificated security or an initial transaction statement is a complete defense, even against a purchaser for value and without notice.

(4) All other defenses of the issuer of a certificated or uncertificated security, including nondelivery and conditional delivery of a certificated security, are ineffective against a purchaser for value who has taken without notice of the particular defense.

(5) Nothing in this section shall be construed to affect the right of a party to a "when, as and if issued" or a "when distributed" contract to cancel the contract in the event of a material change in the character of the security that is the subject of the contract or in the plan or arrangement pursuant to which the security is to be issued or distributed.

§8–203. Staleness as Notice of Defects or Defenses

(1) After an act or event creating a right to immediate performance of the principal obligation represented by a certificated security or that sets a date on or after which the security is to be presented or surrendered for redemption or exchange, a purchaser is charged with notice of any defect in its issue or defense of the issuer if:

(a) the act or event is one requiring the payment of money, the delivery of certificated securities, the registration of transfer of uncertificated securities, or any of these on presentation or surrender of the certificated security, the funds or securities are available on the date set for payment or exchange, and he takes the security more than one year after that date; and

(b) the act or event is not covered by paragraph (a) and he takes the security more than 2 years after the date set for surrender or presentation or the date on which performance became due.

(2) A call that has been revoked is not within subsection (1).

§8–204. Effect of Issuer's Restrictions on Transfer

A restriction on transfer of a security imposed by the issuer, even if otherwise lawful, is ineffective against any person without actual knowledge of it unless:

(a) the security is certificated and the restriction is noted conspicuously thereon; or

(b) the security is uncertificated and a notation of the restriction is contained in the initial transaction statement sent to the person or, if his interest is transferred to him other than by registration of transfer, pledge, or release, the initial transaction statement sent to the registered owner or the registered pledgee.

§8–205. Effect of Unauthorized Signature on Certificated Security or Initial Transaction Statement

An unauthorized signature placed on a certificated security prior to or in the course of issue or placed on an initial transaction statement is ineffective, but the signature is effective in favor of a purchaser for value of the certificated security or a purchaser for value of an uncertificated security to whom the initial transaction statement has been sent, if the purchaser is without notice of the lack of authority and the signing has been done by:

(a) an authenticating trustee, registrar, transfer agent, or other person entrusted by the issuer with the signing of the security, or similar securities, or of initial transaction statements or the immediate preparation of signing of any of them; or

(b) an employee of the issuer, or of any of the foregoing, entrusted with responsible handling of the security or initial transaction statement.

§8–206. Completion or Alteration of Certificated Security or Initial Transaction Statement

(1) If a certificated security contains the signatures necessary to its issue or transfer but is incomplete in any other respect:

(a) any person may complete it by filling in the blanks as authorized; and

(b) even though the blanks are incorrectly filled in, the security as completed is enforceable by a purchaser who took it for value and without notice of the incorrectness.

(2) A complete certificated security that has been improperly altered, even though fraudulently, remains enforceable, but only according to its original terms.

(3) If an initial transaction statement contains the signatures necessary to its validity but is incomplete in any other respect:

(a) any person may complete it by filling in the blanks as authorized; and

(b) even though the blanks are incorrectly filled in, the statement as completed is effective in favor of the person to whom it is sent if he purchased the security referred to therein for value and without notice of the incorrectness.

(4) A complete initial transaction statement that has been improperly altered, even though fraudulently, is effective in favor of a purchaser to whom it has been sent, but only according to its original terms

§8–207. Rights and Duties of Issuer With Respect to Registered Owners and Registered Pledges

(1) Prior to due presentment for registration of transfer of a certificated security in registered form, the issuer or indenture trustee may treat the registered owner as the person exclusively entitled to vote, to receive notifications, and otherwise to exercise all rights and powers of an owner.

(2) Subject to the provisions of subsections (3), (4), and (6), the issuer or indenture trustee may treat the registered owner of an uncertificated security as the person exclusively entitled to vote, to receive notifications, and otherwise to exercise all the rights and powers of an owner.

(3) The registered owner of an uncertificated security that is subject to a registered pledge is not entitled to registration of transfer prior to the due presentment to the issuer of a release instruction. The exercise of conversion rights with respect to a convertible uncertificated security is a transfer within the meaning of this section.

(4) Upon due presentment of a transfer instruction from the registered pledgee of an uncertificated security, the issuer shall:

(a) register the transfer of the security to the new owner free of pledge, if the instruction specifies a new owner (who may be the registered pledgee) and does not specify a pledgee;

(b) register the transfer of the security to the new owner subject to the interest of the existing pledgee, if the instruction specifies new owner and the existing pledgee; or

(c) register the release of the security from the existing pledge and register the pledge of the security to the other pledgee, if the instruction specifies the existing owner and another pledgee.

(5) Continuity of perfection of a security interest is not broken by registration of transfer under subsection (4) (b) or by registration of release and pledge under subsection (4) (c), if the security interest is assigned.

(6) If an uncertificated security is subject to a registered pledge:

(a) any uncertificated securities issued in exchange for or distributed with respect to the pledged security shall be registered subject to the pledge;

(b) any certificated securities issued in exchange for or distributed with respect to the pledged security shall be delivered to the registered pledgee; and

(c) any money paid in exchange for or in redemption of part or all of the security shall be paid to the registered pledgee.

(7) Nothing in this Article shall be construed to affect the liability of the registered owner of a security for calls, assessments, or the like.

§8–208. Effect of Signature of Authenticating Trustee, Registrar, or Transfer Agent

(1) A person placing his signature upon a certificated security or an initial transaction statement as authenticating trustee, registrar, transfer agent, or the like, warrants to a purchaser for value of the certificated security or a purchaser for value of an uncertificated security to whom the initial transaction statement has been sent, if the purchaser is without notice of the particular defect, that:

(a) the certificated security or initial transaction statement is genuine;

(b) his own participation in the issue or registration of the transfer, pledge, or release of the security is within his capacity and within the scope of the authority received by him from the issuer; and

(c) he has reasonable grounds to believe the security is in the form and within the amount the issuer is authorized to issue.

(2) Unless otherwise agreed, a person by so placing his signature does not assume responsibility for the validity of the security in other respects.

Part 3 Transfer

§8–301. Rights Acquired by Purchaser

(1) Upon transfer of a security to a purchaser (Section 8–313), the purchaser acquires the rights in the security which his transferor had or had actual authority to convey unless the purchaser's rights are limited by Section 8–302(4).

(2) A transferee of a limited interest acquires rights only to the extent of the interest transferred. The creation or release of a security interest in a security is the transfer of a limited interest in that security.

§8–302. "Bona Fide Purchaser"; "Adverse Claim"; Title Acquired by Bona Fide Purchaser

(1) A "bona fide purchaser" is a purchaser for value in good faith and without notice of any adverse claim:

(a) who takes delivery of a certificated security in bearer form or in registered form, issued or indorsed to him or in blank;

(b) to whom the transfer, pledge, or release of an uncertificated security is registered on the books of the issuer; or

(c) to whom a security is transferred under the provisions of paragraph (c), (d) (i), or (g) of Section 8–313(1).

(2) "Adverse claim" includes a claim that a transfer was or would be wrongful or that a particular adverse person is the owner of or has an interest in the security.

(3) A bona fide purchaser in addition to acquiring the rights of a purchaser (Section 8–301) also acquires his interest in the security free of any adverse claim.

(4) Notwithstanding Section 8–301(1), the transferee of a particular certificated security who has been a party to any fraud or illegality affecting the security, or who as a prior holder of that certificated security had notice of an adverse claim, cannot improve his position by taking from a bona fide purchaser.

§8–303. "Broker"

"Broker" means a person engaged for all or part of his time in the business of buying and selling securities, who in the transaction concerned acts for, buys a security from, or sells a security to, a customer. Nothing in this Article determines the capacity in which a person acts for purposes of any other statute or rule to which the person is subject.

§8–304. Notice to Purchaser of Adverse Claims

(1) A purchaser (including a broker for the seller or buyer, but excluding an intermediary bank) of a certificated security is charged with notice of adverse claims if:

(a) the security, whether in bearer or registered form, has been indorsed "for collection" or "for surrender" or for some other purpose not involving transfer; or

(b) the security is in bearer form and has on it an unambiguous statement that it is the property of a person other than the transferor. The mere writing of a name on a security is not such a statement.

(2) A purchaser (including a broker for the seller or buyer, but excluding an intermediary bank) to whom the transfer, pledge, or release of an uncertificated security is registered is charged with notice of adverse claims as to which the issuer has a duty under Section 8–403(4) at the time of registration and which are noted in the initial transaction statement sent to the purchaser or, if his interest is transferred to him other than by registration of transfer, pledge, or release, the initial transaction statement sent to the registered owner or the registered pledgee.

(3) The fact that the purchaser (including a broker for the seller or buyer) or a certificated or uncertificated security has notice that the security is held for a third person or is registered in the name of or indorsed by a fiduciary does not create a duty of inquiry into the rightfulness of the transfer or constitute constructive notice of adverse claims. However, if the purchaser (excluding an intermediary bank) has knowledge that the proceeds are being used or that the transaction is for the individual benefit of the fiduciary or otherwise in breach of duty, the purchaser is charged with notice of adverse claims.

§8–305. Staleness as Notice of Adverse Claims

An act or event that creates a right to immediate performance of the principal obligation represented by a certificated security or sets a date on or after which a certificated security is to be presented or surrendered for redemption or exchange does not itself constitute any notice of adverse claims except in the case of a transfer:

(a) after one year from any date set for presentment or surrender for redemption or exchange; or

(b) after 6 months from any date set for payment of money against presentation or surrender of the security if funds are available for payment on that date.

§8–306. Warranties on Presentment and Transfer of Certificated Securities; Warranties of Originators of Instructions

(1) A person who presents a certificated security for registration of transfer or for payment or exchange warrants to the issuer that he is entitled to the registration, payment, or exchange. But, a purchaser for value and without notice of adverse claims who receives a new, reissued, or reregistered certificated security on registration of transfer or receives an initial transaction statement confirming the registration of transfer of an equivalent uncertificated security to him warrants only that he has no knowledge of any unauthorized signature (Section 8–311) in a necessary indorsement.

(2) A person by transferring a certificated security to a purchaser for value warrants only that:

(a) his transfer is effective and rightful;

(b) the security is genuine and has not been materially altered; and

(c) he knows of no fact which might impair the validity of the security.

(3) If a certificated security is delivered by an intermediary known to be entrusted with delivery of the security on behalf of another or with collection of a draft or other claim against delivery, the intermediary by delivery warrants only his own good faith and authority even though he has purchased or made advances against the claim to be collected against the delivery.

(4) A pledgee or other holder for security who redelivers a certificated security received, or after payment and on order of the debtor delivers that security to a third person, makes only the warranties of an intermediary under subsection (3).

(5) A person who originates an instruction warrants to the issuer that:

(a) he is an appropriate person to originate the instruction: and

(b) at the time the instruction is presented to the issuer he will be entitled to the registration or transfer, pledge, or release. (6) A person who originates an instruction warrants to any person specially guaranteeing his signature (subsection 8–312(3)) that:

(a) he is an appropriate person to originate the instruction; and

(b) at the time the instruction is presented to the issuer

(i) he will be entitled to the registration of transfer, pledge, or release; and

(ii) the transfer, pledge, or release requested in the instruction will be registered by the issuer free from all liens, security interests, restrictions, and claims other than those specified in the instruction.

(7) A person who originates an instruction warrants to a purchaser for value and to any person guaranteeing the instruction (Section 8–312(6)) that:

(a) he is an appropriate person to originate the instruction:

(b) the uncertificated security referred to therein is valid; and

(c) at the time the instruction is presented to the issuer

(i) the transferor will be entitled to the registration of transfer, pledge, or release;

(ii) the transfer, pledge, or release requested in the instruction will be registered by the issuer free from all liens, security interests, restrictions, and claims other than those specified in the instruction; and

(iii) the requested transfer, pledge, or release will be rightful.

(8) If a secured party is the registered pledgee or the registered owner of an uncertificated security, a person who originates an instruction of release or transfer to the debtor or, after payment and on order of the debtor, a transfer instruction to a third person, warrants to the debtor or the third person only that he is an appropriate person to originate the instruction and, at the time the instruction is presented to the issuer, the transferor will be entitled to the registration of release or transfer. If a transfer instruction to a third person who is a purchaser for value is originated on order of the debtor, the debtor makes to the purchaser the warranties of paragraphs (b), (c), (ii) and (c) (iii) of subsection (7).

(9) A person who transfers an uncertificated security to a purchaser for value and does not originate an instruction in connection with the transfer warrants only that:

(a) his transfer is effective and rightful; and

(b) the uncertificated security is valid.

(10) A broker gives to his customer and to the issuer and a purchaser the applicable warranties provided in this section and has the rights and privileges of a purchaser under this section. The warranties of and in favor of the broker, acting as an agent are in addition to applicable warranties given by and in favor of his customer.

§8–307. Effect of Delivery Without Indorsement; Right to Compel Indorsement

If a certificated security in registered form has been delivered to a purchaser without a necessary indorsement he may become a bona fide purchaser only as of the time the indorsement is supplied; but against the transferor, the transfer is complete upon delivery and the purchaser has a specifically enforceable right to have any necessary indorsement supplied.

§8–308. Indorsements; Instructions

(1) An indorsement of a certificated security in registered form is made when an appropriate person signs on it or on a separate document an assignment or transfer of the security or a power to assign or transfer it or his signature is written without more upon the back of the security.

(2) An indorsement may be in blank or special. An indorsement in blank includes an indorsement to bearer. A special indorsement specifies to whom the security is to be transferred, or who has power to transfer it. A holder may convert a blank indorsement into a special indorsement.

(3) An indorsement purporting to be only of part of a certificated security representing units intended by the issuer to be separately transferable is effective to the extent of the indorsement.

(4) An "instruction" is an order to the issuer of an uncertificated security requesting that the transfer, pledge, or release from pledge of the uncertificated security specified therein be registered.

(5) An instruction originated by an appropriate person is:

(a) a writing signed by an appropriate person; or

(b) a communication to the issuer in any form agreed upon in a writing signed by the issuer and an appropriate person. If an instruction has been originated by an appropriate person but is incomplete in any other respect, any person may complete it as authorized and the issuer may rely on it as completed even though it has been completed incorrectly.

(6) "An appropriate person" in subsection (1) means the person specified by the certificated security or by special indorsement to be entitled to the security.

(7) "An appropriate person" in subsection (5) means:

(a) for an instruction to transfer or pledge an uncertificated security which is then not subject to a registered pledge, the registered owner; or

(b) for an instruction to transfer or release an uncertificated security which is then subject to a registered pledge, the registered pledgee.

(8) In addition to the persons designated in subsections

(6) and (7), "an appropriate person" in subsections (1) and (5) includes:

(a) if the person designated is described as a fiduciary but is no longer serving in the described capacity, either that person or his successor;

(b) if the persons designated are described as more than one person as fiduciaries and one or more are no longer serving in the described capacity, the remaining fiduciary or fiduciaries, whether or not a successor has been appointed or qualified.

(c) if the person designated is an individual and is without capacity to act by virtue of death, incompetence, infancy, or otherwise, his executor, administrator, guardian, or like fiduciary;

(d) if the persons designated are described as more than one person as tenants by the entirety or with right of survivorship and by reason of death all cannot sign, the survivor or survivors;

(e) a person having power to sign under applicable law or controlling instrument; and

(f) to the extent that the person designated or any of the foregoing persons may act through an agent, his authorized agent.

(9) Unless otherwise agreed, the indorser of a certificated security by his indorsement or the originator of an instruction by his origination assumes no obligation that the security will be honored by the issuer but only the obligations provided in Section 8–306.

(10) Whether the person signing is appropriate is determined as of the date of signing and an indorsement made by or an instruction originated by him does not become unauthorized for the purposes of this Article by virtue of any subsequent change of circumstances.

(11) Failure of a fiduciary to comply with a controlling instrument or with the law of the state having jurisdiction of the fiduciary relationship, including any law requiring the fiduciary to obtain court approval of the transfer, pledge, or release, does not render his indorsement or any instruction originated by him unauthorized for the purposes of this Article.

§8–309. Effect of Indorsement Without Delivery

An indorsement of a certificated security, whether special or in blank, does not constitute a transfer until delivery of the certificated security on which it appears or, if the indorsement is on a separate document, until delivery of both the document and the certificated security.

§8–310. Indorsement of Certificated Security in Bearer Form

An indorsement of a certificated security in bearer form may give notice of adverse claims (Section 8–304) but does not otherwise affect any right to registration the holder possesses.

§8–311. Effect of Unauthorized Indorsement or Instruction

Unless the owner or pledgee has ratified an unauthorized indorsement or instruction or is otherwise precluded from asserting its ineffectiveness:

(a) he may assert its ineffectiveness against the issuer or any purchaser, other than a purchaser for value and without notice of adverse claims, who has in good faith received a new, reissued, or reregistered certificated security on registration of transfer or received an initial transaction statement confirming the registration of transfer, pledge, or release of an equivalent uncertificated security to him; and

(b) an issuer who registers the transfer of a certificated security upon the unauthorized indorsement or who registers the transfer, pledge, or release of an uncertificated security upon the unauthorized instruction is subject to liability for improper registration (Section 8–404).

§8–312. Effect of Guaranteeing Signature, Indorsement or Instruction

(1) Any person guaranteeing a signature of an indorser of a certificated security warrants that at the time of signing:

(a) the signature was genuine;

(b) the signer was an appropriate person to indorse (Section 8–308); and

(c) the signer had legal capacity to sign.

(2) Any person guaranteeing a signature of the originator of an instruction warrants that at the time of signing:

(a) the signature was genuine;

(b) the signer was an appropriate person to originate the instruction (Section 8–308) if the person specified in the instruction as the registered owner or registered pledgee of the uncertificated security was, in fact, the registered owner or registered pledgee of the security, as to which fact the signature guarantor makes no warranty;

(c) the signer had legal capacity to sign; and

(d) the taxpayer identification number, if any, appearing on the instruction as that of the registered owner or registered pledgee was the taxpayer identification number of the signer or of the owner or pledgee for whom the signer was acting.

(3) Any person specially guaranteeing the signature of the originator of an instruction makes not only the warranties of a signature guarantor (subsection (2) but also warrants that at the time the instruction is presented to the issuer:

(a) the person specified in the instruction as the registered owner or registered pledgee of the uncertificated security will be the registered owner or registered pledgee; and

(b) the transfer, pledge, or release of the uncertificated security requested in the instruction will be registered by the issuer free from all liens, security interests, restrictions, and claims other than those specified in the instruction.

(4) The guarantor under subsections (1) and (2) or the special guarantor under subsection (3) does not otherwise warrant the rightfulness of the particular transfer, pledge, or release.

(5) Any person guaranteeing an indorsement of a certificated security makes not only the warranties of a signature guarantor under subsection (1) but also warrants the rightfulness of the particular transfer in all respects.

(6) Any person guaranteeing an instruction requesting the transfer, pledge, or release of an uncertificated security makes not only the warranties of a special signature guarantor under subsection (3) but also warrants the rightfulness of the particular transfer, pledge, or release in all respects.

(7) No issuer may require a special guarantee of signature (subsection (3)), a guarantee of indorsement (subsection (5)), or a guarantee of instruction (subsection (6)) as a condition to registration of transfer, pledge, or release.

(8) The foregoing warranties are made to any person taking or dealing with the security in reliance on the guarantee, and the guarantor is liable to the person for any loss resulting from breach of the warranties.

§8–313. When Transfer to Purchaser Occurs; Financial Intermediary as Bona Fide Purchaser; "Financial Intermediary"

(1) Transfer of a security or a limited interest (including a security interest) therein to a purchaser occurs only:

(a) at the time he or a person designated by him acquires possession of a certificated security;

(b) at the time the transfer, pledge, or release of an uncertificated security is registered to him or a person designated by him;

(c) at the time his financial intermediary acquires possession of a certificated security specially indorsed to or issued in the name of the purchaser;

(d) at the time a financial intermediary, not a clearing corporation, sends him confirmation of the purchase and also by book entry or otherwise identifies as belonging to the purchaser

(i) a specific certificated security in the financial intermediary's possession;

(ii) a quantity of securities that constitute or are part of a fungible bulk of certificated securities registered in the name of the financial intermediary; or

(iii) a quantity of securities that constitute or are part of a fungible bulk of securities shown on the account of the financial intermediary on the books of another financial intermediary;

(e) with respect to an identified certificated security to be delivered while still in the possession of a third person, not a financial intermediary, at the time that person acknowledges that he holds for the purchaser;

(f) with respect to a specific uncertificated security the pledge or transfer of which has been registered to a third

person, not a financial intermediary, at the time that person acknowledges that he holds for the purchaser;

(g) at the time appropriate entries to the account of the purchaser or a person designated by him on the books of a clearing corporation are made under Section 8–320;

(h) with respect to the transfer of a security interest where the debtor has signed a security agreement containing a description of the security, at the time a written notification, which, in the case of the creation of the security interest, is signed by the debtor (which may be a copy of the security agreement) or which, in the case of the release or assignment of the security interest created pursuant to this paragraph, is signed by the secured party, is received by

(i) a financial intermediary on whose books the interest of the transferor in the security appears;

(ii) a third person, not a financial intermediary, in possession of the security, if it is certificated;

(iii) a third person, not a financial intermediary, who is the registered owner of the security, if it is uncertificated and not subject to a registered pledge; or

(iv) a third person, not a financial intermediary, who is the registered pledgee of the security, if it is uncertificated and subject to a registered pledge;

(i) with respect to the transfer of a security interest where the transferor has signed a security agreement containing a description of the security, at the time new value is given by the secured party; or

(j) with respect to the transfer of a security interest where the secured party is a financial intermediary and the security has already been transferred to the financial intermediary under paragraphs (a), (b), (c), (d), or (g), at the time the transferor has signed a security agreement containing a description of the security and value is given by the secured party.

(2) The purchaser is the owner of a security held for him by a financial intermediary, but cannot be a bona fide purchaser of a security so held except in the circumstances specified in paragraphs (c), (d)(i), and (g) of subsection (1). If a security so held is part of a fungible bulk, as in the circumstances specified in paragraphs (d)(ii) and (d)(iii) of subsection (1), the purchaser is the owner of a proportionate property interest in the fungible bulk.

(3) Notice of an adverse claim received by the financial intermediary or by the purchaser after the financial intermediary takes delivery of a certificated security as a holder for value or after the transfer, pledge, or release of an uncertificated security has been registered free of the claim to a financial intermediary who has given value is not effective either as to the financial intermediary or as to the purchaser. However, as between the financial intermediary and the purchaser the purchaser may demand transfer of an equivalent security as to which no notice of adverse claim has been received.

(4) A "financial intermediary" is a bank, broker, clearing corporation, or other person (or the nominee of any of them) which in the ordinary course of its business maintains security accounts for its customers and is acting in that capacity. A financial intermediary may have a security interest in securities held in account for its customer.

§8–314. Duty to Transfer, When Completed

(1) Unless otherwise agreed, if a sale of a security is made on an exchange or otherwise through brokers:

(a) the selling customer fulfills his duty to transfer at the time he:

(i) places a certificated security in the possession of the selling broker or a person designated by the broker;

(ii) causes an uncertificated security to be registered in the name of the selling broker or a person designated by the broker;

(iii) if requested, causes an acknowledgment to be made to the selling broker that a certificated or uncertificated security is held for the broker; or

(iv) places in the possession of the selling broker or of a person designated by the broker a transfer instruction for an uncertificated security, providing the issuer does not refuse to register the requested transfer if the instruction is presented to the issuer for registration within 30 days thereafter; and

(b) the selling broker, including a correspondent broker acting for a selling customer, fulfills his duty to transfer at the time he:

(i) places a certificated security in the possession of the buying broker or a person designated by the buying broker;

(ii) causes an uncertificated security to be registered in the name of the buying broker;

(iii) places in the possession of the buying broker or of a person designated by the buying broker a transfer instruction for an uncertificated security, providing the issuer does not refuse to register the requested transfer if the instruction is presented to the issuer for registration within 30 days thereafter; or

(iv) effects clearance of the sale in accordance with the rules of the exchange on which the transaction took place.

(2) Except as provided in this section or unless otherwise agreed, a transferor's duty to transfer a security under a contract of purchase is not fulfilled until he:

(a) places a certificated security in form to be negotiated by the purchaser in the possession of the purchaser or of a person designated by the purchaser;

(b) causes an uncertificated security to be registered in the name of the purchaser or a person designated by the purchaser; or

(c) if the purchaser requests, causes an acknowledgment to be made to the purchaser that a certificated or uncertificated security is held for the purchaser.

(3) Unless made on an exchange, a sale to a broker

purchasing for his own account is within subsection (2) and not within subsection (1).

§8–315. Action Against Transferee Based upon Wrongful Transfer

(1) Any person against whom the transfer of a security is wrongful for any reason, including his incapacity, as against anyone except a bona fide purchaser, may:

(a) reclaim possession of the certificated security wrongfully transferred;

(b) obtain possession of any new certificated security representing all or part of the same rights;

(c) compel the origination of an instruction to transfer to him or a person designated by him an uncertificated security constituting all or part of the same rights; or

(d) have damages.

(2) If the transfer is wrongful because of an unauthorized indorsement of a certificated security, the owner may also reclaim or obtain possession of the security or a new certificated security, even from a bona fide purchaser, if the ineffectiveness of the purported indorsement can be asserted against him under the provisions of this Article on unauthorized indorsements (Section 8–311).

(3) The right to obtain or reclaim possession of a certificated security or to compel the origination of a transfer instruction may be specifically enforced and the transfer of a certificated or uncertificated security enjoined and a certificated security impounded pending the litigation.

§8–316. Purchaser's Right to Requisites for Registration of Transfer, Pledge, or Release on Books

Unless otherwise agreed, the transferor of a certificated security or the transferor, pledgor, or pledgee of an uncertificated security on due demand must supply his purchaser with any proof of his authority to transfer, pledge, or release or with any other requisite necessary to obtain registration of the transfer, pledge, or release of the security; but if the transfer, pledge, or release is not for value, a transferor, pledgor, or pledgee need not do so unless the purchaser furnishes the necessary expenses. Failure within a reasonable time to comply with a demand made gives the purchaser the right to reject or rescind the transfer, pledge, or release.

§8–317. Creditor's Rights

(1) Subject to the exceptions in subsections (3) and (4), no attachment or levy upon a certificated security or any share or other interest represented thereby which is outstanding is valid until the security is actually seized by the officer making the attachment or levy, but a certificated security which has been surrendered to the issuer may be reached by a creditor by legal process at the issuer's chief executive office in the United States.

(2) An uncertificated security registered in the name of the debtor may not be reached by a creditor except by legal process at the issuer's chief executive office in the United States.

(3) The interest of a debtor in a certificated security that is in the possession of a secured party not a financial intermediary or in an uncertificated security registered in the name of a secured party not a financial intermediary (or in the name of a nominee of the secured party) may be reached by a creditor by legal process upon the secured party.

(4) The interest of a debtor in a certificated security that is in the possession of or registered in the name of a financial intermediary may be reached by a creditor by legal process upon the financial intermediary on whose books the interest of the debtor appears.

(5) Unless otherwise provided by law, a creditor's lien upon the interest of a debtor in a security obtained pursuant to subsection (3) or (4) is not a restraint on the transfer of the security, free of the lien, to a third party for new value; but in the event of a transfer, the lien applies to the proceeds of the transfer in the hands of the secured party or financial intermediary, subject to any claims having priority.

(6) A creditor whose debtor is the owner of a security is entitled to aid from courts of appropriate jurisdiction, by injunction or otherwise, in reaching the security or in satisfying the claim by means allowed at law or in equity in regard to property that cannot readily be reached by ordinary legal process.

§8–318. No Conversion by Good Faith Conduct

An agent or bailee who in good faith (including observance of reasonable commercial standards if he is in the business of buying, selling, or otherwise dealing with securities) has received certificated securities and sold, pledged, or delivered them or has sold or caused the transfer or pledge of uncertificated securities over which he had control according to the instructions of his principal, is not liable for conversion or for participation in breach of fiduciary duty although the principal had no right so to deal with the securities.

§8–319. Statute of Frauds

A contract for the sale of securities is not enforceable by way of action or defense unless:

(a) there is some writing signed by the party against whom enforcement is sought or by his authorized agent or broker, sufficient to indicate that a contract has been made for sale of a stated quantity of described securities at a defined or stated price;

(b) delivery of a certificated security or transfer instruction has been accepted, or transfer of an uncertificated security has been registered and the transferee has failed to send written objection to the issuer within 10 days after receipt of the initial transaction statement confirming the registration, or payment has been made, but the contract is enforceable under this provision only to the extent of the delivery, registration, or payment;

(c) within a reasonable time a writing in confirmation of the sale or purchase and sufficient against the sender under paragraph (a) has been received by the party against whom enforcement is sought and he has failed to send written objection to its contents within 10 days after its receipt; or

(d) the party against whom enforcement is sought admits in his pleading, testimony, or otherwise in court that a contract was made for the sale of a stated quantity of described securities at a defined or stated price.

§8–320. Transfer or Pledge Within Central Depositary System

(1) In addition to other methods, a transfer, pledge, or release of a security or any interest therein may be effected by the making of appropriate entries on the books of a clearing corporation reducing the account of the transferor, pledgor, or pledgee and increasing the account of the transferee, pledgee, or pledgor by the amount of the obligation or the number of shares or rights transferred, pledged, or released, if the security is shown on the account of a transferor, pledgor, or pledgee on the books of the clearing corporation; is subject to the control of the clearing corporation; and

(a) if certificated,

(i) is in the custody of the clearing corporation, another clearing corporation, a custodian bank, or a nominee of any of them; and

(ii) is in bearer form or indorsed in blank by an appropriate person or registered in the name of the clearing corporation, a custodian bank, or a nominee of any of them; or

(b) if uncertificated, is registered in the name of the clearing corporation, another clearing corporation, a custodian bank, or a nominee of any of them.

(2) Under this section entries may be made with respect to like securities or interests therein as a part of a fungible bulk and may refer merely to a quantity of a particular security without reference to the name of the registered owner, certificate or bond number, or the like, and, in appropriate cases, may be on a net basis taking into account other transfers, pledges, or releases of the same security.

(3) A transfer under this section is effective (Section 8–313) and the purchaser acquires the rights of the transferor (Section 8–301). A pledge or release under this section is the transfer of a limited interest. If a pledge or the creation of a security interest is intended, the security interest is perfected at the time when both value is given by the pledgee and the appropriate entries are made (Section 8–321). A transferee or pledgee under this

section may be a bona fide purchaser (Section 8–302).

(4) A transfer or pledge under this section is not a registration of transfer under Part 4.

(5) That entries made on the books of the clearing corporation as provided in subsection (1) are not appropriate does not affect the validity or effect of the entries or the liabilities or obligations of the clearing corporation to any person adversely affected thereby.

§8–321. Enforceability, Attachment, Perfection and Termination of Security Interests

(1) A security interest in a security is enforceable and can attach only if it is transferred to the secured party or a person designated by him pursuant to a provision of Section 8–313(1).

(2) A security interest so transferred pursuant to agreement by a transferor who has rights in the security to a transferee who has given value is a perfected security interest, but a security interest that has been transferred solely under paragraph (i) of Section 8–313(1) becomes unperfected after 21 days unless within that time, the requirements for transfer under any other provision of Section 8–313(1) are satisfied.

(3) A security interest in a security is subject to the provisions of Article 9, but:

(a) no filing is required to perfect the security interest; and

(b) no written security agreement signed by the debtor is necessary to make the security interest enforceable, except as provided in paragraph (h), (i), or (j) of Section 8–313(1). The secured party has the rights and duties provided under Section 9–207, to the extent they are applicable, whether or not the security is certificated, and, if certificated, whether or not it is in his possession.

(4) Unless otherwise agreed, a security interest in a security is terminated by transfer to the debtor or a person designated by him pursuant to a provision of Section 8–313(1). If a security is thus transferred, the security interest, if not terminated, becomes unperfected unless the security is certificated and is delivered to the debtor for the purpose of ultimate sale or exchange or presentation, collection, renewal, or registration of transfer. In that case, the security interest becomes unperfected after 21 days unless, within that time the security (or securities for which it has been exchanged) is transferred to the secured party or a person designated by him pursuant to a provision of Section 8–313(1).

Part 4 Registration

§8–401. Duty of Issuer to Register Transfer, Pledge, or Release

(1) If a certificated security in registered form is presented to the issuer with a request to register transfer or an instruction is presented to the issuer with a request to register a transfer, pledge, or release, the issuer shall register the transfer, pledge, or release as requested if:

(a) the security is indorsed or the instruction was originated by the appropriate person or persons (Section 8–308);

(b) reasonable assurance is given that those indorsements or instructions are genuine and effective (Section 8–402);

(c) the issuer has no duty as to adverse claims or has discharged the duty (Section 8–403);

(d) any applicable law relating to the collection of taxes has been complied with; and

(e) the transfer, pledge, or release is in fact rightful or is to a bona fide purchaser.

(2) If an issuer is under a duty to register a transfer, pledge, or release of a security, the issuer is also liable to the person presenting a certificated security or an instruction for registration or his principal for loss resulting from any unreasonable delay in registration or from failure or refusal to register the transfer, pledge, or release.

§8–402. Assurance that Indorsements and Instructions Are Effective

(1) The issuer may require the following assurance that each necessary indorsement of a certificated security or each instruction (Section 8–308) is genuine and effective:

(a) in all cases, a guarantee of the signature (Section 8–312(1) or (2)) of the person indorsing a certificated security or originating an instruction including, in the case of an instruction, a warranty of the taxpayer identification number or, in the absence thereof, other reasonable assurance of identity;

(b) if the indorsement is made or the instruction is originated by an agent, appropriate assurance of authority to sign;

(c) if the indorsement is made or the instruction is originated by a fiduciary, appropriate evidence of appointment or incumbency;

(d) if there is more than one fiduciary, reasonable assurance that all who are required to sign have done so; and

(e) if the indorsement is made or the instruction is originated by a person not covered by any of the foregoing, assurance appropriate to the case corresponding as nearly as may be to the foregoing.

(2) A "guarantee of the signature" in subsection (1) means a guarantee signed by or on behalf of a person reasonably believed by the issuer to be responsible. The issue may adopt standards with respect to responsibility if they are not manifestly unreasonable.

(3) "Appropriate evidence of appointment or incumbency" in subsection (1) means:

(a) in the case of a fiduciary appointed or qualified by a court, a certificate issued by or under the direction or supervision of that court or an officer thereof and dated within 60 days before the date of presentation for transfer, pledge, or release; or

(b) in any other case, a copy of a document showing the appointment or a certificate issued by or on behalf of a person reasonably believed by the issuer to be responsible or, in the absence of that document or certificate, other evidence reasonably deemed by the issuer to be appropriate. The issuer may adopt standards with respect to the evidence if they are not manifestly unreasonable. The issuer is not charged with notice of the contents of any document obtained pursuant to this paragraph (b) except to the extent that the contents relate directly to the appointment or incumbency.

(4) The issuer may elect to require reasonable assurance beyond that specified in this section, but if it does so and, for a purpose other than that specified in subsection (3)(b), both requires and obtains a copy of a will, trust, indenture, articles of co-partnership, by-laws, or other controlling instrument, it is charged with notice of all matters contained therein affecting the transfer, pledge, or release.

§8–403. Issuer's Duty as to Adverse Claims

(1) An issuer to whom a certificated security is presented for registration shall inquire into adverse claims if:

(a) a written notification of an adverse claim is received at a time and in a manner affording the issuer a reasonable opportunity to act on it prior to the issuance of a new, reissued, or reregistered certificated security, and the notification identifies the claimant, the registered owner, and the issue of which the security is a part, and provides an address for communications directed to the claimant; or

(b) the issuer is charged with notice of an adverse claim from a controlling instrument it has elected to require under Section 8–402(4).

(2) The issuer may discharge any duty of inquiry by any reasonable means, including notifying an adverse claimant by registered or certified mail at the address furnished by him or, if there be no such address, at his residence or regular place of business that the certificated security has been presented for registration of transfer by a named person, and that the transfer will be registered unless within 30 days from the date of mailing the notification, either:

(a) an appropriate restraining order, injunction, or other process issues from a court of competent jurisdiction; or

(b) there is filed with the issuer an indemnity bond, sufficient in the issuer's judgment to protect the issuer and any transfer agent, registrar, or other agent of the issuer involved from any loss it or they may suffer by complying with the adverse claim.

(3) Unless an issuer is charged with notice of an adverse claim from a controlling instrument which it has elected to require under Section 8–402(4) or receives notification of an adverse claim under subsection (1), if a certificated security presented for registration is indorsed by the appropriate person or persons the issuer is under no duty to inquire into adverse claims. In particular:

(a) an issuer registering a certificated security in the name of a person who is a fiduciary or who is described as a fiduciary is not bound to inquire into the existence, extent, or correct description of the fiduciary relationship; and thereafter the issuer may assume without inquiry that the newly registered owner continues to be the fiduciary until the issuer receives written notice that the fiduciary is no longer acting as such with respect to the particular security;

(b) an issuer registering transfer on an indorsement by a fiduciary is not bound to inquire whether the transfer is made in compliance with a controlling instrument or with the law of the state having jurisdiction of the fiduciary relationship, including any law requiring the fiduciary to obtain court approval of the transfer; and

(c) the issuer is not charged with notice of the contents of any court record or file or other recorded or unrecorded document even though the document is in its possession and even though the transfer is made on the indorsement of a fiduciary to the fiduciary himself or to his nominee.

(4) An issuer is under no duty as to adverse claims with respect to an uncertificated security except:

(a) claims embodied in a restraining order, injunction, or other legal process served upon the issuer if the process was served at a time and in a manner affording the issuer a reasonable opportunity to act on it in accordance with the requirements of subsection (5);

(b) claims of which the issuer has received a written notification from the registered owner or the registered pledgee if the notification was received at a time and in a manner affording the issuer a reasonable opportunity to act on it in accordance with the requirements of subsection (5);

(c) claims (including restrictions on transfer not imposed by the issuer) to which the registration of transfer to the present registered owner was subject and were so noted in the initial transaction statement sent to him; and

(d) claims as to which an issuer is charged with notice from a controlling instrument it has elected to require under Section 8–402(4).

(5) If the issuer of an uncertificated security is under a duty to an adverse claim, he discharges that duty by:

(a) including a notation of the claim in any statements sent with respect to the security under Sections 8–408(3), (6), and (7), and

(b) refusing to register the transfer or pledge of the security unless the nature of the claim does not preclude transfer or pledge subject thereto.

(6) If the transfer of pledge of the security is registered subject to an adverse claim, a notation of the claim must be included in the initial transaction statement and all subsequent statements sent to the transferee and pledgee under Section 8–408.

(7) Notwithstanding subsections (4) and (5), if an uncertificated security was subject to a registered pledge at the time the issuer first came under a duty as to a particular adverse claim, the issuer has no duty as to that claim if transfer of the security is requested by the registered pledgee or an appropriate person acting for the registered pledgee unless:

(a) the claim embodied in legal process which expressly provides otherwise;

(b) the claim was asserted in a written notification from the registered pledgee;

(c) the claim was one as to which the issuer was charged with notice from a controlling instrument it required under Section 8–402(4) in connection with the pledgee's request for transfer; or

(d) the transfer requested is to the registered owner.

§8–404. Liability and Non-Liability for Registration

(1) Except as provided in any law relating to the collection of taxes, the issuer is not liable to the owner, pledgee, or any other person suffering loss as a result of the registration of a transfer, pledge, or release of a security if:

(a) there were on or with a certificated security the necessary indorsements or the issuer had received an instruction originated by an appropriate person (Section 8–308); and

(b) the issuer had no duty as to adverse claims or has discharged the duty (Section 8–403).

(2) If an issuer has registered a transfer of a certificated security to a person not entitled to it, the issuer on demand shall deliver a like security to the true owner unless:

(a) the registration was pursuant to subsection (1);

(b) the owner is precluded from asserting any claim for registering the transfer under Section 8–405(1); or

(c) the delivery would result in overissue, in which case the issuer's liability is governed by Section 8–104.

(3) If an issuer has improperly registered a transfer, pledge, or release of an uncertificated security, the issuer on demand from the injured party shall restore the records as to the injured party to the condition that would have obtained if the improper registration had not been made unless:

(a) the registration was pursuant to subsection (1); or

(b) the registration would result in overissue, in which case the issuer's liability is governed by Section 8–104.

§8–405. Lost, Destroyed, and Stolen Certificated Securities

(1) If a certificated security has been lost, apparently destroyed, or wrongfully taken, and the owner fails to notify the issuer of that fact within a reasonable time after he has notice of it and the issuer registers a transfer of the security before receiving notification, the owner is precluded from asserting against the issuer any claim for registering the transfer under Section 8–404 or any claim to a new security under this section.

(2) If the owner of a certificated security claims that the security has been lost, destroyed, or wrongfully taken, the issuer shall issue a new certificated security or, at the option of the issuer, an equivalent uncertificated security in place of the original security if the owner:

(a) so requests before the issuer has notice that the security has been acquired by a bona fide purchaser;

(b) files with the issuer a sufficient indemnity bond; and

(c) satisfies any other reasonable requirements imposed by the issuer.

(3) If, after the issue of a new certificated or uncertificated security, a bona fide purchaser of the original certificated security presents it for registration of transfer, the issuer shall register the transfer unless registration would result in overissue, in which event the issuer's liability is governed by Section 8–104. In addition to any rights on the indemnity bond, the issuer may recover the new certificated security from the person to whom it was issued or any person taking under him except a bona fide purchaser or may cancel the uncertificated security unless a bona fide purchaser or any person taking under a bona fide purchaser is then the registered owner or registered pledgee thereof.

§8–406. Duty of Authenticating Trustee, Transfer Agent, or Registrar

(1) If a person acts as authenticating trustee, transfer agent, registrar, or other agent for an issuer in the registration of its certificated securities or in the registration of transfers, pledges, and releases of its uncertificated securities, in the issue of new securities, or in the cancellation of surrendered securities:

(a) he is under a duty to the issuer to exercise good faith and due diligence in performing his functions; and

(b) with regard to the particular functions he performs, he has the same obligation to the holder or owner of a certificated security or to the owner or pledgee of an uncertificated security and has the same rights and privileges as the issuer has in regard to those functions.

(2) Notice to an authenticating trustee, transfer agent, registrar or other agent is notice to the issuer with respect to the functions performed by the agent.

§8–407. Exchangeability of Securities

(1) No issuer is subject to the requirements of this section unless it regularly maintains a system for issuing the class of securities involved under which both certificated and uncertificated securities are regularly issued to the category of owners, which includes the person in whose name the new security is to be registered.

(2) Upon surrender of a certificated security with all necessary indorsements and presentation of a written

request by the person surrendering the security, the issuer, if he has no duty as to adverse claims or has discharged the duty (Section 8–403), shall issue to the person or a person designated by him an equivalent uncertificated security subject to all liens, restrictions, and claims that were noted on the certificated security.

(3) Upon receipt of a transfer instruction originated by an appropriate person who so requests, the issuer of an uncertificated security shall cancel the uncertificated security and issue an equivalent certificated security on which must be noted conspicuously any liens and restrictions of the issuer and any adverse claims (as to which the issuer has a duty under Section 8–403(4)) to which the uncertificated security was subject. The certificated security shall be registered in the name of and delivered to:

(a) the registered owner, if the uncertificated security was not subject to a registered pledge; or

(b) the registered pledgee, if the uncertificated security was subject to a registered pledge.

§8–408. Statements of Uncertificated Securities

(1) Within 2 business days after the transfer of an uncertificated security has been registered, the issuer shall send to the new registered owner and, if the security has been transferred subject to a registered pledge, to the registered pledgee, a written statement containing:

(a) a description of the issue of which the uncertificated security is a part;

(b) the number of shares or units transferred;

(c) the name and address and any taxpayer identification number of the new registered owner and, if the security has been transferred subject to a registered pledge, the name and address and any taxpayer identification number of the registered pledgee;

(d) a notation of any liens and restrictions of the issuer and any adverse claims (as to which the issuer has a duty under Section 8–403(4)) to which the uncertificated security is or may be subject at the time of registration or a statement that there are none of those liens, restrictions, or adverse claims; and

(e) the date the transfer was registered.

(2) Within 2 business days after the pledge of an uncertificated security has been registered, the issuer shall send to the registered owner and the registered pledgee a written statement containing:

(a) a description of the issue of which the uncertificated security is a part;

(b) the number of shares or units pledged;

(c) the name and address and any taxpayer identification number of the registered owner and the registered pledgee;

(d) a notation of any liens and restrictions of the issuer and any adverse claims (as to which the issuer has a duty under Section 8–403(4)) to which the uncertificated security is or may be subject at the time of registration or a statement that there are none of those liens, restrictions, or adverse claims; and

(e) the date the pledge was registered.

(3) Within 2 business days after the release from pledge of an uncertificated security has been registered, the issuer shall send to the registered owner and the pledgee whose interest was released a written statement containing:

(a) a description of the issue of which the uncertificated security is a part;

(b) the number of shares or units released from pledge;

(c) the name and address and any taxpayer identification number of the registered owner and the pledgee whose interest was released;

(d) a notation of any liens and restrictions of the issuer and any adverse claims (as to which the issuer has a duty under Section 8–403(4)) to which the uncertificated security is or may be subject at the time of registration or a statement that there are none of those liens, restrictions, or adverse claims; and

(e) the date the release was registered.

(4) An "initial transaction statement" is the statement sent to:

(a) the new registered owner and, if applicable, to the registered pledgee pursuant to subsection (1);

(b) the registered pledgee pursuant to subsection (2); or

(c) the registered owner pursuant to subsection (3).

Each initial transaction statement shall be signed by or on behalf of the issuer and must be identified as "Initial Transaction Statement."

(5) Within 2 business days after the transfer of an uncertificated security has been registered, the issuer shall send to the former registered owner and the former registered pledgee, if any, a written statement containing:

(a) a description of the issue of which the uncertificated security is a part;

(b) the number of shares or units transferred;

(c) the name and address and any taxpayer identification number of the former registered owner and of any former registered pledgee; and

(d) the date the transfer was registered.

(6) At periodic intervals no less frequent than annually and at any time upon the reasonable written request of the registered owner, the issuer shall send to the registered owner of each uncertificated security a dated written statement containing:

(a) a description of the issue of which the uncertificated security is a part;

(b) the name and address and any taxpayer identification number of the registered owner;

(c) the number of shares or units of the uncertificated security registered in the name of the registered owner on the date of the statement;

(d) the name and address and any taxpayer identification number of any registered pledgee and the number of shares of units subject to the pledge; and

(e) a notation of any liens and restrictions of the issuer and any adverse claims (as to which the issuer has a duty under Section 8–403(4)) to which the uncertificated security is or may be subject or a statement that there are none of those liens, restrictions, or adverse claims.

(7) At periodic intervals no less frequent than annually and at any time upon the reasonable written request of the registered pledgee, the issuer shall send to the registered pledgee of each uncertificated security a dated written statement containing:

(a) a description of the issue of which the uncertificated security is a part;

(b) the name and address and any taxpayer identification number of the registered owner;

(c) the name and address and any taxpayer identification number of the registered pledgee;

(d) the number of shares or units subject to the pledge; and

(e) a notation of any liens and restrictions of the issuer and any adverse claims (as to which the issuer has a duty under Section 8–403(4)) to which the uncertificated security is or may be subject or a statement that there are none of those liens, restrictions, or adverse claims.

(8) If the issuer sends the statements described in subsections (6) and (7) at periodic intervals no less frequent than quarterly, the issuer is not obliged to send additional statements upon request unless the owner or pledgee requesting them pays to the issuer the reasonable cost of furnishing them.

(9) Each statement sent pursuant to this section must bear a conspicuous legend reading substantially as follows: "This statement is merely a record of the rights of the addressee as of the time of its issuance. Delivery of this statement, of itself, confers no rights on the recipient. This statement is neither a negotiable instrument nor a security."

ARTICLE 9 SECURED TRANSACTIONS; SALES OF ACCOUNTS AND CHATTEL PAPER

Part 1 Short Title, Applicability and Definitions

§9–101. Short Title

This Article shall be known and may be cited as Uniform Commercial Code—Secured Transactions.

§9–102. Policy and Subject Matter of Article

(1) Except as otherwise provided in Section 9–104 on excluded transactions, this Article applies

(a) to any transaction (regardless of its form) which is intended to create a security interest in personal property or fixtures including goods, documents, instruments, general intangibles, chattel paper or accounts; and also

(b) to any sale of accounts or chattel paper.

(2) This Article applies to security interests created by contract including pledge, assignment, chattel mortgage, chattel trust, trust deed, factor's lien, equipment trust, conditional sale, trust receipt, other lien or title retention contract and lease or consignment intended as security. This Article does not apply to statutory liens except as provided in Section 9–310.

(3) The application of this Article to a security interest in a secured obligation is not affected by the fact that the obligation is itself secured by a transaction or interest to which this Article does not apply.

§9–103. Perfection of Security Interest in Multiple State Transactions

(1) Documents, instruments and ordinary goods.

(a) This subsection applies to documents and instruments and to goods other than those covered by a certificate of title described in subsection (2), mobile goods described in subsection (3), and minerals described in subsection (5).

(b) Except as otherwise provided in this subsection, perfection and the effect of perfection or non-perfection of a security interest in collateral are governed by the law of the jurisdiction where the collateral is when the last event occurs on which is based the assertion that the security interest is perfected or unperfected.

(c) If the parties to a transaction creating a purchase money security interest in goods in one jurisdiction understand at the time that the security interest attaches that the goods will be kept in another jurisdiction, then the law of the other jurisdiction governs the perfection and the effect of perfection or nonperfection of the security interest from the time it attaches until thirty days after the debtor receives possession of the goods and thereafter if the goods are taken to the other jurisdiction before the end of the thirty-day period.

(d) When collateral is brought into and kept in this state while subject to a security interest perfected under the law of the jurisdiction from which the collateral was removed, the security interest remains perfected, but if action is required by Part 3 of this Article to perfect the security interest.

(i) if the action is not taken before the expiration of the period of perfection in the other jurisdiction or the end of four months after the collateral is brought into this state, whichever period first expires, the security interest becomes unperfected at the end of that period and is thereafter deemed to have been unperfected as against a person who became a purchaser after removal;

(ii) if the action is taken before the expiration of the period specified in subparagraph (i), the security interest continues perfected thereafter;

(iii) for the purpose of priority over a buyer of consumer goods (subsection (2) of Section 9–307), the period of effectiveness of a filing in the jurisdiction from which the collateral is removed is governed by the rules with respect to perfection in subparagraphs (i) and (ii).

(2) Certificate of title.

(a) This subsection applies to goods covered by a certificate of title issued under a statute of this state or of another jurisdiction under the law of which indication of a security interest on the certificate is required as a condition of perfection.

(b) Except as otherwise provided in this subsection, perfection and the effect of perfection or non-perfection of the security interest are governed by the law (including the conflict of law rules) of the jurisdiction issuing the certificate until four months after the goods are removed from that jurisdiction and thereafter until the goods are registered in another jurisdiction, but in any event not beyond surrender of the certificate. After the expiration of that period, the goods are not covered by the certificate of title within the meaning of this section.

(c) Except with respect to the rights of a buyer described in the next paragraph, a security interest, perfected in another jurisdiction otherwise than by notation on a certificate of title, in goods brought into this state and thereafter covered by a certificate of title issued by this state is subject to the rules stated in paragraph (d) of subsection (1).

(d) If goods are brought into this state while a security interest therein is perfected in any manner under the law of the jurisdiction from which the goods are removed and a certificate of title is issued by this state and the certificate does not show that the goods are subject to the security interest or that they may be subject to security interests not shown on the certificate, the security interest is subordinate to the rights of a buyer of the goods who is not in the business of selling goods of that kind to the extent that he gives value and receives delivery of the goods after issuance of the certificate and without knowledge of the security interest.

(3) Accounts, general intangibles and mobile goods.

(a) This subsection applies to accounts (other than an account described in subsection (5) on minerals) and general intangibles (other than uncertificated securities) and to goods which are mobile and which are of a type normally used in more than one jurisdiction, such as motor vehicles, trailers, rolling stock, airplanes, shipping containers, road building and construction machinery and commercial harvesting machinery and the like, if the goods are equipment or are inventory leased or held for lease by the debtor to others, and are not covered by a certificate of title described in subsection (2).

(b) The law (including the conflict of laws rules) of the jurisdiction in which the debtor is located governs the perfection and the effect of perfection or non-perfection of the security interest.

(c) If, however, the debtor is located in a jurisdiction which is not part of the United States, and which does not provide for perfection of the security interest by filing or recording in that jurisdiction, the law of the jurisdiction in the United States in which the debtor has its major executive office governs the perfection and the effect of perfection or non-perfection of the security interest through filing. In the alternative, if the debtor is located in a jurisdiction which is not a part of the United States or Canada and the collateral is accounts or general intangibles for money due or to become due, the security interest may be perfected by notification to the account debtor. As used in this paragraph, "United States" includes its territories and possessions and the Commonwealth of Puerto Rico.

(d) A debtor shall be deemed located at his place of business if he has one, at his chief executive office if he has more than one place of business, otherwise at his residence. If, however, the debtor is a foreign air carrier under the Federal Aviation Act of 1958, as amended, it shall be deemed located at the designated office of the agent upon whom service of process may be made on behalf of the foreign air carrier.

(e) A security interest perfected under the law of the jurisdiction of the location of the debtor is perfected until the expiration of four months after a change of the debtor's location to another jurisdiction, or until perfection would have ceased by the law of the first jurisdiction, whichever period first expires. Unless perfected in the new jurisdiction before the end of that period, it becomes unperfected thereafter and is deemed to have been unperfected as against a person who became a purchaser after the change.

(4) Chattel paper. The rules stated for goods in subsection (1) apply to a possessory security interest in chattel paper. The rules stated for accounts in subsection (3) apply to a non-possessory security interest in chattel paper, but the security interest may not be perfected by notification to the account debtor.

(5) Minerals. Perfection and the effect of perfection or nonperfection of a security interest which is created by a debtor who has an interest in minerals or the like (including oil and gas) before extraction and which attaches thereto as extracted, or which attaches to an account resulting from the sale thereof at the wellhead or minehead are governed by the law (including the conflict of laws rules) of the jurisdiction wherein the wellhead or minehead is located.

(6) Uncertificated securities. The law (including the conflict of laws rules) of the jurisdiction or organization of the issuer governs the perfection and the effect of perfection or nonperfection of a security interest in uncertificated securities.

§9–104. Transactions Excluded From Article

This Article does not apply

(a) to a security interest subject to any statute of the United States, to the extent that such statute governs the rights of parties to and third parties affected by transactions in particular types of property; or

(b) to a landlord's lien; or

(c) to a lien given by statute or other rule of law for services or materials except as provided in Section 9–310 on priority of such liens; or

(d) to a transfer of a claim for wages, salary or other compensation of an employee; or

(e) to a transfer by a government or governmental subdivision or agency; or

(f) to a sale of accounts or chattel paper as part of a sale of the business out of which they arose, or an assignment of accounts or chattel paper which is for the purpose of collection only, or a transfer of a right to payment under a contract to an assignee who is also to do the performance under the contract or a transfer of a single account to an assignee in whole or partial satisfaction of a preexisting indebtedness; or

(g) to a transfer of an interest in or claim in or under any policy of insurance, except as provided with respect to proceeds (Section 9–306) and priorities in proceeds (Section 9–312); or

(h) to a right represented by a judgment (other than a judgment taken on a right to payment which was collateral); or

(i) to any right of set-off; or

(j) except to the extent that provision is made for fixtures to Section 9–313, to the creation or transfer of an interest in or lien on real estate, including a lease or rents thereunder; or

(k) to a transfer in whole or in part of any claim arising out of tort; or

(l) to a transfer of an interest in any deposit account (subsection (1) of Section 9–105), except as provided with respect to proceeds (Section 9–306) and priorities in proceeds (Section 9–312).

§9–105. Definitions and Index of Definitions

(1) In this Article unless the context otherwise requires:

(a) "Account debtor" means the person who is obligated on an account, chattel paper or general intangible;

(b) "Chattel paper" means a writing or writings which evidence both a monetary obligation and a security interest in or a lease of specific goods, but a charter or other contract involving the use or hire of a vessel is not chattel paper. When a transaction is evidenced both by such a security agreement or a lease and by an instrument or a series of instruments, the group of writings taken together constitutes chattel paper;

(c) "Collateral" means the property subject to a security interest, and includes accounts and chattel paper which have been sold;

(d) "Debtor" means the person who owes payment or other performance of the obligation secured, whether or not he owns or has rights in the collateral, and includes the seller of accounts or chattel paper. Where the debtor and the owner of the collateral are not the same person, the term "debtor" means the owner of the collateral in any provision of the Article dealing with the collateral, the obligor in any provision dealing with the obligation, and may include both where the context so requires;

(e) "Deposit account" means a demand, time, savings, passbook or like account maintained with a bank, savings and loan association, credit union or like organization, other than an account evidenced by a certificate of deposit;

(f) "Document" means document of title as defined in the general definitions of Article 1 (Section 1–201), and a receipt of the kind described in subsection (2) of Section 7–201;

(g) "Encumbrance" includes real estate mortgages and other liens on real estate and all other rights in real estate that are not ownership interests;

(h) "Goods" includes all things which are movable at the time the security interest attaches or which are fixtures (Section 9–313), but does not include money, documents, instruments, accounts, chattel paper, general intangibles, or minerals or the like (including oil and gas) before extraction. "Goods" also includes standing timber which is to be cut and removed under a conveyance or contract for sale, the unborn young of animals, and growing crops;

(i) "Instrument" means a negotiable instrument (defined in Section 3–104), or a certificated security (defined in Section 8–102) or any other writing which evidences a right to the payment of money and is not itself a security agreement or lease and is of a type which is in ordinary course of business transferred by delivery with any necessary indorsement or assignment;

(j) "Mortgage" means a consensual interest created by a real estate mortgage, a trust deed on real estate, or the like;

(k) An advance is made "pursuant to commitment" if the secured party has bound himself to make it, whether or not a subsequent event of default or other event not within his control has relieved or may relieve him from his obligation;

(l) "Security agreement" means an agreement which creates or provides for a security interest;

(m) "Secured party" means a lender, seller or other person in whose favor there is a security interest, including a person to whom accounts or chattel paper have been sold. When the holders of obligations issued under an indenture of trust, equipment trust agreement or the like are represented by a trustee or other person, the representative is the secured party;

(n) "Transmitting utility" means any person primarily engaged in the railroad, street railway or trolley bus business, the electric or electronics communications transmission business, the transmission of goods or pipeline, or the transmission or the production and transmission of electricity, steam, gas or water, or the provision of sewer service.

(2) Other definitions applying to this Article and the sections in which they appear are:

"Account."	Section 9–106.
"Attach."	Section 9–203.
"Construction mortgage."	Section 9–313(1).
"Consumer goods."	Section 9–109(1).
"Equipment."	Section 9–109(2).
"Farm products."	Section 9–109(3).
"Fixture."	Section 9–313(1).
"Fixture filing."	Section 9–313(1).
"General intangibles."	Section 9–106.
"Inventory."	Section 9–109(4).
"Lien creditor."	Section 9–301(3).
"Proceeds."	Section 9–306(1).
"Purchase money security interest."	Section 9–107.
"United States."	Section 9–103.

(3) The following definitions in other Articles apply to this Article:

"Check."	Section 3–104.
"Contract for sale."	Section 2–106.
"Holder in due course."	Section 3–302.
"Note."	Section 3–104.
"Sale."	Section 2–106.

(4) In addition Article 1 contains general definitions and principles of construction and interpretation applicable throughout this Article.

§9–106. Definitions: "Account"; "General Intangibles"

"Account" means any right to payment for goods sold or leased or for services rendered which is not evidenced by an instrument or chattel paper, whether or not it has been earned by performance. "General tangibles" means any personal property (including things in action) other than goods, accounts, chattel paper, documents, instruments, and money. All rights to payment earned or unearned under a charter or other contract involving the use or hire of a vessel and all rights incident to the charter or contract are accounts.

§9–107. Definitions: "Purchase Money Security Interest"

A security interest is a "purchase money security interest" to the extent that it is

(a) taken or retained by the seller of the collateral to secure all or part of its price; or

(b) taken by a person who by making advances or incurring an obligation gives value to enable the debtor to acquire rights in or the use of collateral if such value is in fact so used.

§9–108. When After-Acquired Collateral Not Security for Antecedent Debt

Where a secured party makes an advance, incurs an obligation, releases a perfected security interest, or otherwise gives new value which is to be secured in whole or in part by after-acquired property his security interest in the after-acquired collateral shall be deemed to be taken for new value and not as security for an antecedent debt if the debtor acquires his rights in such collateral either in the ordinary course of his business or under a contract of purchase made pursuant to the security agreement within a reasonable time after new value is given.

§9–109. Classification of Goods; "Consumer Goods"; "Equipment"; "Farm Products"; "Inventory"

Goods are

(1) "consumer goods" if they are used or bought for use primarily for personal, family or household purposes;

(2) "equipment" if they are used or bought for use primarily in business (including farming or a profession) or by a debtor who is a non-profit organization or a governmental subdivision or agency or if the goods are not included in the definitions of inventory, farm products or consumer goods;

(3) "farm products" if they are crops or livestock or supplies used or produced in farming operations or if they are products of crops or livestock in their unmanufactured states (such as ginned cotton, wool-clip, maple syrup, milk and eggs), and if they are in the possession of a debtor engaged in raising, fattening, grazing or other farming operations. If goods are farm products they are neither equipment nor inventory;

(4) "inventory" if they are held by a person who holds them for sale or lease or to be furnished under contracts of service or if he has so furnished them, or if they are raw materials, work in process or materials used or consumed in a business. Inventory of a person is not be classified as his equipment.

§9–110. Sufficiency of Description

For the purposes of this Article any description of personal property or real estate is sufficient whether or not it is specific if it reasonably identifies what is described.

§9–111. Applicability of Bulk Transfer Laws

The creation of a security interest is not a bulk transfer under Article 6 (see Section 6–103).

§9–112. Where Collateral Is Not Owned by Debtor

Unless otherwise agreed, when a secured party knows that collateral is owned by a person who is not the debtor, the owner of the collateral is entitled to receive from the secured party any surplus under Section 9–502(2) or under Section 9–504(1), and is not liable for the debt or for any deficiency after resale, and he has the same right as the debtor

(a) to receive statements under Section 9–208;

(b) to receive notice of and to object to a secured party's proposal to retain the collateral in satisfaction of the indebtedness under Section 9–505;

(c) to redeem the collateral under Section 9–506;

(d) to obtain injunctive or other relief under Section 9–507(1); and

(e) to recover losses caused to him under Section 9–208(2).

§9–113. Security Interests Arising under Article on Sales

A security interest arising solely under the Article on Sales (Article 2) or the Article on Leases (Article 2A) is subject to the provisions of this Article except that to the extent that and so long as the debtor does not have or does not lawfully obtain possession of the goods

(a) no security agreement is necessary to make the security interest enforceable; and

(b) no filing is required to perfect the security interest; and

(c) the rights of the secured party on default by the debtor are governed (i) by the Article on Sales (Article 2) in the case of a security interest arising solely under such Article or (ii) by the Article on Leases (Article 2A) in the case of a security interest arising solely under such Article.

§9–114. Consignment

(1) A person who delivers goods under a consignment which is not a security interest and who would be required to file under this Article by paragraph (3)(c) of Section 2–326 has priority over a secured party who is or becomes a creditor of the consignee and who would have a perfected security interest in the goods if they were the property of the consignee, and also has priority with respect to identifiable cash proceeds received on or before delivery of the goods to a buyer, if

(a) the consignor complies with the filing provision of the Article on Sales with respect to consignments (paragraph (3)(c) of Section 2–326) before the consignee receives possession of the goods; and

(b) the consignor gives notification in writing to the holder of the security interest if the holder has filed a financing statement covering the same types of goods before the date of the filing made by the consignor; and

(c) the holder of the security interest receives the notification within five years before the consignee receives possession of the goods; and

(d) the notification states that the consignor expects to deliver goods on consignment to the consignee, describing the goods by item or type.

(2) In the case of a consignment which is not a security interest and in which the requirements of the preceding subsection have not been met, a person who delivers goods to another is subordinate to a person who would have a perfected security interest in the goods if they were the property of the debtor.

Part 2 Validity of Security Agreement and Rights of Parties Thereto

§9–201. General Validity of Security Agreement

Except as otherwise provided by this Act a security agreement is effective according to its terms between the parties, against purchasers of the collateral and against creditors. Nothing in this Article validates any charge or practice illegal under any statute or regulation thereunder governing usury, small loans, retail installment sales, or the like, or extends the application of any such statute or regulation to any transaction not otherwise subject thereto.

§9–202. Title to Collateral Immaterial

Each provision of this Article with regard to rights, obligations and remedies applies whether title to collateral is in the secured party or in the debtor.

§9–203. Attachment and Enforceability of Security Interest; Proceeds; Formal Requisites

(1) Subject to the provisions of Section 4–208 on the security interest of a collecting bank, Section 8–321 on security interests in securities and Section 9–113 on a security interest arising under the Article on Sales, a security interest is not enforceable against the debtor or third parties with respect to the collateral and does not attach unless:

(a) the collateral is in the possession of the secured party pursuant to agreement, or the debtor has signed a security agreement which contains a description of the collateral and in addition, when the security interest covers crops growing or to be grown or timber to be cut, a description of the land concerned;

(b) value has been given; and

(c) the debtor has rights in the collateral.

(2) A security interest attaches when it becomes enforceable against the debtor with respect to the collateral. Attachment occurs as soon as all of the events specified in subsection (1) have taken place unless explicit agreement postpones the time of attaching.

(3) Unless otherwise agreed a security agreement gives the secured party the rights to proceeds provided by Section 9–306.

(4) A transaction, although subject to this Article, is also subject to ....*, and in the case of conflict between the provisions of this Article and any such

statute, the provisions of such statute control. Failure to comply with any applicable statute has only the effect which is specified therein.

Note: At * in subsection (4) insert reference to any local statute regulating small loans, retail installment sales and the like.

The foregoing subsection (4) is designed to make it clear that certain transactions, although subject to this Article, must also comply with other applicable legislation.

This Article is designed to regulate all the "security" aspects of transactions within its scope. There is, however, much regulatory legislation, particularly in the consumer field, which supplements this Article and should not be repealed by its enactment. Examples are small loan acts, retail installment selling acts and the like. Such acts may provide for licensing and rate regulation and may prescribe particular forms of contract. Such provisions should remain in force despite the enactment of this Article. On the other hand if a retail installment selling act contains provisions on filing, rights on default, etc., such provisions should be repealed as inconsistent with this Article except that inconsistent provisions as to deficiencies, penalties, etc., in the Uniform Consumer Credit Code and other recent related legislation should remain because those statutes were drafted after the substantial enactment of the Article and with the intention of modifying certain provisions of this Article as to consumer credit.

§9–204. After-Acquired Property; Future Advances

(1) Except as provided in subsection (2), a security agreement may provide that any or all obligations covered by the security agreement are to be secured by after-acquired collateral.

(2) No security interest attaches under an after-acquired property clause to consumer goods other than accessions (Section 9–314) when given as additional security unless the debtor acquires rights in them within ten days after the secured party gives value.

(3) Obligations covered by a security agreement may include future advances or other value whether or not the advances or value are given pursuant to commitment (subsection (1) of Section 9–105).

§9–205. Use or Disposition of Collateral Without Accounting Permissible

A security interest is not invalid or fraudulent against creditors by reason of liberty in the debtor to use, commingle or dispose of all or part of the collateral (including returned or repossessed goods) or to collect or compromise accounts or chattel paper, or to accept the return of goods or make repossessions, or to use, commingle or dispose of proceeds, or by reason of the failure of the secured party to require the debtor to account for proceeds or replace collateral. This section does not relax the requirements of possession where perfection of a security interest depends upon possession of the collateral by the secured party or by a bailee.

§9–206. Agreement Not to Assert Defenses Against Assignee; Modification of Sales Warranties Where Security Agreement Exists

(1) Subject to any statute or decision which establishes a different rule for buyers or lessees of consumer goods, an agreement by a buyer or lessee that he will not assert against an assignee any claim or defense which he may have against the seller or lessor is enforceable by an assignee who takes his assignment for value, in good faith and without notice of a claim or defense, except as to defenses of a type which may be asserted against a holder in due course of a negotiable instrument under the Article on Commercial Paper (Article 3). A buyer who as part of one transaction signs both a negotiable instrument and a security agreement makes such an agreement.

(2) When a seller retains a purchase money security interest in goods the Article on Sales (Article 2) governs the sale and any disclaimer, limitation or modification of the seller's warranties.

§9–207. Rights and Duties When Collateral Is in Secured Party's Possession

(1) A secured party must use reasonable care in the custody and preservation of collateral in his possession. In the case of an instrument or chattel paper reasonable care includes taking necessary steps to preserve rights against prior parties unless otherwise agreed.

(2) Unless otherwise agreed, when collateral is in the secured party's possession

(a) reasonable expenses (including the cost of any insurance and payment of taxes or other charges) incurred in the custody, preservation, use or operation of the collateral are chargeable to the debtor and are secured by the collateral;

(b) the risk of accidental loss or damage is on the debtor to the extent of any deficiency in any effective insurance coverage;

(c) the secured party may hold as additional security any increase or profits (except money) received from the collateral, but money so received, unless remitted to the debtor, shall be applied in reduction of the secured obligation;

(d) the secured party must keep the collateral identifiable but fungible collateral may be commingled;

(e) the secured party may repledge the collateral upon terms which do not impair the debtor's right to redeem it.

(3) a secured party is liable for any loss caused by his failure to meet any obligation imposed by the preceding subsections but does not lose his security interest.

(4) A secured party may use or operate the collateral for the purpose of preserving the collateral or its value or pursuant to the order of a court of appropriate jurisdiction or, except in the case of consumer goods, in the manner and to the extent provided in the security agreement.

§9–208. Request for Statement of Account or List of Collateral

(1) A debtor may sign a statement indicating what he believes to be the aggregate amount of unpaid indebtedness as of a specified date and may send it to the secured party with a request that the statement be approved or corrected and returned to the debtor. When the security agreement or any other record kept by the secured party identifies the collateral a debtor may similarly request the secured party to approve or correct a list of the collateral.

(2) The secured party must comply with such a request within two weeks after receipt by sending a written correction or approval. If the secured party claims a security interest in all of a particular type of collateral owned by the debtor he may indicate that fact in his reply and need not approve or correct an itemized list of such collateral. If the secured party without reasonable excuse fails to comply he is liable for any loss caused to the debtor thereby; and if the debtor has properly included in his request a good faith statement of the obligation or a list of the collateral or both the secured party may claim a security interest only as shown in the statement against persons misled by his failure to comply. If he no longer has an interest in the obligation or collateral at the time the request is received he must disclose the name and address of any successor in interest known to him and he is liable for any loss caused to the debtor as a result of failure to disclose. A successor in interest is not subject to this section until a request is received by him.

(3) A debtor is entitled to such a statement once every six months without charge. The secured party may require payment of a charge not exceeding $10 for each additional statement furnished.

Part 3 Rights of Third Parties; Perfected and Unperfected Security Interests; Rules of Priority

§9–301. Persons Who Take Priority over Unperfected Security Interests; Rights of "Lien Creditor"

(1) Except as otherwise provided in subsection (2), an unperfected security interest is subordinate to the rights of

(a) persons entitled to priority under Section 9–312;

(b) a person who becomes a lien creditor before the security interest is perfected;

(c) in the case of goods, instruments, documents, and chattel paper, a person who is not a secured party and who is a transferee in bulk or other buyer not in ordinary course of business or is a buyer of farm products in ordinary course of business, to the extent that he gives value and receives delivery of the collateral without knowledge of the security interest and before it is perfected;

(d) in the case of accounts and general intangibles, a person who is not a secured party and who is a transferee to the extent that he gives value without knowledge of the security interest and before it is perfected.

(2) If the secured party files with respect to a purchase money security interest before or within ten days after the debtor receives possession of the collateral, he takes priority over the rights of a transferee in bulk or of a lien creditor which arise between the time the security interest attaches and the time of filing.

(3) A "lien creditor" means a creditor who has acquired a lien on the property involved by attachment, levy or the like and includes an assignee for benefit of creditors from the time of assignment, and a trustee in bankruptcy from the date of the filing of the petition or a receiver in equity from the time of appointment.

(4) A person who becomes a lien creditor while a security interest is perfected takes subject to the security interest only to the extent that it secures advances made before he becomes a lien creditor or within 45 days thereafter or made without knowledge of the lien or pursuant to a commitment entered into without knowledge of the lien.

§9–302. When Filing Is Required to Perfect Security Interest; Security Interests to Which Filing Provisions of This Article Do Not Apply

(1) A financing statement must be filed to perfect all security interests except the following:

(a) a security interest in collateral in possession of the secured party under Section 9–305;

(b) a security interest temporarily perfected in instruments or documents without delivery under Section 9–304 or in proceeds for a 10 day period under Section 9–306;

(c) a security interest created by an assignment of a beneficial interest in a trust or a decedent's estate;

(d) a purchase money security interest in consumer goods; but filing is required for a motor vehicle required to be registered; and fixture filing is required for priority over conflicting interests in fixtures to the extent provided in Section 9–313;

(e) an assignment of accounts which does not alone or in conjunction with other assignments to the same assignee transfer a significant part of the outstanding accounts of the assignor;

(f) a security interest of a collecting bank (Section 4–208) or in securities (Section 8–321) or arising under the Article on Sales (see Section 9–113) or covered in subsection (3) of this section;

(g) an assignment for the benefit of all the creditors of the transferor, and subsequent transfers by the assignee thereunder.

(2) If a secured party assigns a perfected security interest, no filing under this Article is required in order to continue the perfected status of the security interest against creditors of the transferees from the original debtor.

(3) The filing of a financing statement otherwise required by this Article is not necessary or effective to perfect a security interest in property subject to

(a) a statute or treaty of the United States which provides for a national or international registration or a national or international certificate of title or which specifies a place of filing different from that specified in this Article for filing of the security interest; or

(b) the following statutes of this state; [list any certificate of title statute covering automobiles, trailers, mobile homes, boats, farm tractors, or the like, and any central filing statute*]; but during any period in which collateral is inventory held for sale by a person who is in the business of selling goods of that kind, the filing provisions of this Article (Part 4) apply to a security interest in that collateral created by him as debtor; or

(c) a certificate of title statute of another jurisdiction under the law of which indication of a security interest on the certificate is required as a condition of perfection (subsection (2) of Section 9–103).

(4) Compliance with a statute or treaty described in subsection (3) is equivalent to the filing of a financing statement under this Article, and a security interest in property subject to the statute or treaty can be perfected only by compliance therewith except as provided in Section 9–103 on multiple state transactions. Duration and renewal of perfection of a security interest perfected by compliance with the statute or treaty are governed by the provisions of the statute or treaty; in other respects the security interest is subject to this Article.

Note: *It is recommended that the provisions of certificate of title acts for perfection of security interests by notation on the certificates should be amended to exclude coverage of inventory held for sale.*

§9–303. When Security Interest Is Perfected; Continuity of Perfection

(1) A security interest is perfected when it has attached and when all of the applicable steps required for perfection have been taken. Such steps are specified in Section 9–302, 9–304, 9–305 and 9–306. If such steps are taken before the security interest attaches, it is perfected at the time when it attaches.

(2) If a security interest is originally perfected in any way permitted under this Article and is subsequently perfected in some other way under this Article, without an intermediate period when it was unperfected, the security interest shall be deemed to be perfected continuously for the purposes of this Article.

§9–304. Perfection of Security Interest in Instruments, Documents, and Goods Covered by Documents; Perfection by Permissive Filing; Temporary Perfection Without Filing or Transfer of Possession

(1) A security interest in chattel paper or negotiable documents may be perfected by filing. A security interest in money or instruments (other than certificated securities or instruments which constitute part of chattel paper) can be perfected only by the secured party's taking possession, except as provided in subsections (4) and (5) of this section and subsections (2) and (3) of Section 9–306 on proceeds.

(2) During the period that goods are in the possession of the issuer of a negotiable document therefor, a security interest in the goods is perfected by perfecting a security interest in the document, and any security interest in the goods otherwise perfected during such period is subject thereto.

(3) A security interest in goods in the possession of a bailee other than one who has issued a negotiable document therefor is perfected by issuance of a document in the name of the secured party or by the bailee's receipt of notification of the secured party's interest or by filing as to the goods.

(4) A security interest in instruments (other than certificated securities) or negotiable documents is perfected without filing or the taking of possession for a period of 21 days from the time it attaches to the extent that it arises from new value given under a written security agreement.

(5) A security interest remains perfected for a period of 21 days without filing where a secured party having a perfected security interest in an instrument (other than a certificated security), a negotiable document or goods in possession of a bailee other than one who has issued a negotiable document therefor

(a) makes available to the debtor the goods or documents representing the goods for the purpose of ultimate sale or exchange or for the purpose of loading, unloading, storing, shipping, transshipping, manufacturing, processing or otherwise dealing with them in a manner preliminary to their sale or exchange, but priority between conflicting security interests in the goods is subject to subsection (3) of Section 9–312; or

(b) delivers the instrument to the debtor for the purpose of ultimate sale or exchange or of presentation, collection, renewal or registration of transfer.

(6) After the 21 day period in subsections (4) and (5) perfection depends upon compliance with applicable provisions of this Article.

§9–305. When Possession by Secured Party Perfects Security Interest Without Filing

A security interest in letters of credit and advices of credit (subsection (2)(a) of Section 5–116), goods, instruments (other than certificated securities), money, negotiable documents, or chattel paper may be perfected by the secured party's taking possession of the collateral. If such collateral other than goods covered by a negotiable document is held by a bailee, the secured party is deemed to have possession from the time possession is taken without a relation back and continues only so long as possession is retained, unless otherwise specified in this Article. The security interest may be otherwise perfected as provided in this Article before or after the period of possession by the secured party.

§9–306. "Proceeds"; Secured Party's Rights on Disposition of Collateral

(1) "Proceeds" includes whatever is received upon the sale, exchange, collection or other disposition of collateral or proceeds. Insurance payable by reason of loss or damage to the collateral is proceeds, except to the extent that it is payable to a person other than a party to the security agreement. Money, checks, deposit accounts, and the like are "cash proceeds." All other proceeds are "non-cash proceeds."

(2) Except where this Article otherwise provides, a security interest continues in collateral notwithstanding sale, exchange or other disposition thereof unless the disposition was authorized by the secured party in the security agreement or otherwise, and also continues in any identifiable proceeds including collections received by the debtor.

(3) The security interest in proceeds is a continuously perfected security interest if the interest in the original collateral was perfected but it ceases to be a perfected security interest and becomes unperfected ten days after receipt of the proceeds by the debtor unless

(a) a filed financing statement covers the original collateral and the proceeds are collateral in which a security interest may be perfected by filing in the office or offices where the financing statement has been filed and, if the proceeds are acquired with cash proceeds, the description of collateral in the financing statement indicates the types of property constituting the proceeds; or

(b) a filed financing statement covers the original collateral and the proceeds are identifiable cash proceeds; or

(c) the security interest in the proceeds is perfected before the expiration of the ten day period. Except as provided in this section, a security interest in proceeds can be perfected only by the methods or under the circumstances permitted in this Article for original collateral of the same type.

(4) In the event of insolvency proceedings instituted by or against a debtor, a secured party with a perfected security interest in proceeds has a perfected security interest only in the following proceeds:

(a) in identifiable non-cash proceeds and in separate deposit accounts containing only proceeds;

(b) in identifiable proceeds in the form of money which is neither commingled with other money nor deposited in a deposit account prior to the insolvency proceedings;

(c) in identifiable cash proceeds in the form of checks and the like which are not deposited in a deposit account prior to the insolvency proceedings; and

(d) in all cash and deposit accounts of the debtor in which proceeds have been commingled with other funds, but the perfected security interest under this paragraph (d) is

(i) subject to any right to setoff; and

(ii) limited to an amount not greater than the amount of any cash proceeds received by the debtor within ten days before the institution of the insolvency proceedings less the sum of (I) the payments to the secured party on account of cash proceeds received by the debtor during such period and (II) the cash proceeds received by the debtor during such period to which the secured party is entitled under paragraph (a) through (c) of this subsection (4).

(5) If a sale of goods results in an account or chattel paper which is transferred by the seller to a secured party, and if the goods are returned to or are repossessed by the seller or the secured party, the following rules determine priorities:

(a) If the goods are collateral at the time of sale, for an indebtedness of the seller which is still unpaid, the original security interest attaches again to the goods and continues as a perfected security interest if it was perfected at the time when the goods were sold. If the security interest was originally perfected by a filing which is still effective, nothing further is required to continue the perfected status; in any other case, the secured party must take possession of the returned or repossessed goods or must file.

(b) An unpaid transferee of the chattel paper has a security interest in the goods against the transferor. Such security interest is prior to a security interest asserted under paragraph (a) to the extent that the transferee of the chattel paper was entitled to priority under Section 9–308.

(c) An unpaid transferee of the account has a security interest in the goods against the transferor. Such security interest is subordinate to a security interest asserted under paragraph (a).

(d) A security interest of an unpaid transferee asserted under paragraph (b) or (c) must be perfected for protection against creditors of the transferor and purchasers of the returned or repossessed goods.

§9–307. Protection of Buyers of Goods

(1) A buyer in ordinary course of business (subsection (9) of Section 1–201) other than a person buying farm products from a person engaged in farming operations takes free of a security interest created by his seller even though the security interest is perfected and even though the buyer knows of its existence.

(2) In a case of consumer goods, a buyer takes free of a security interest even though perfected if he buys without

knowledge of the security interest, for value and for his own personal, family or household purposes unless prior to the purchase the secured party has filed a financing statement covering such goods.

(3) A buyer other than a buyer in ordinary course of business (subsection (1) of this section) takes free of a security interest to the extent that it secures future advances made after the secured party acquires knowledge of the purchase, or more than 45 days after the purchase, whichever first occurs, unless made pursuant to a commitment entered into without knowledge of the purchase and before the expiration of the 45 day period.

§9–308. Purchase of Chattel Paper and Instruments

A purchaser of chattel paper or an instrument who gives new value and takes possession of it in the ordinary course of his business has priority over a security interest in the chattel paper or instrument

(a) which is perfected under Section 9–304 (permissive filing and temporary perfection) or under Section 9–306 (perfection as to proceeds) if he acts without knowledge that the specific paper or instrument is subject to a security interest; or

(b) which is claimed merely as proceeds of inventory subject to a security interest (Section 9–306) even though he knows that the specific paper or instrument is subject to the security interest.

§9–309. Protection of Purchasers of Instruments, Documents and Securities

Nothing in this Article limits the rights of a holder in due course of a negotiable instrument (Section 3–302) or a holder to whom a negotiable document of title has been duly negotiated (Section 7–501) or a bona fide purchaser of a security (Section 8–302) and the holders or purchasers take priority over an earlier security interest even though perfected. Filing under this Article does not constitute notice of the security interest to such holders or purchasers.

§9–310. Priority of Certain Liens Arising by Operation of Law

When a person in the ordinary course of his business furnishes services or materials with respect to goods subject to a security interest, a lien upon goods in the possession of such person given by statute or rule of law for such materials or services takes priority over a perfected security interest unless the lien is statutory and the statute expressly provides otherwise.

§9–311. Alienability of Debtor's Rights: Judicial Process

The debtor's rights in collateral may be voluntarily or involuntarily transferred (by way of sale, creation of a security interest, attachment, levy, garnishment or other judicial process) notwithstanding a provision in the security agreement prohibiting any transfer or making the transfer constitute a default.

§9–312. Priorities among Conflicting Security Interests in the Same Collateral

(1) The rules of priority stated in other sections of this Part and in the following sections shall govern when applicable; Section 4–208 with respect to the security interests of collecting banks in items being collected, accompanying documents and proceeds; Section 9–103 on security interests related to other jurisdictions; Section 9–114 on consignments.

(2) A perfected security interest in crops for new value given to enable the debtor to produce the crops during the production season and given not more than three months before the crops become growing crops by planting or otherwise takes priority over an earlier perfected security interest to the extent that such earlier interest secures obligations due more than six months before the crops become growing crops by planting or otherwise, even though the person giving new value had knowledge of the earlier security interest.

(3) A perfected purchase money security interest in inventory has priority over a conflicting security interest in the same inventory and also has priority in identifiable cash proceeds received on or before the delivery of the inventory to a buyer if

(a) the purchase money security interest is perfected at the time the debtor receives possession of the inventory; and

(b) the purchase money secured party gives notification in writing to the holder of the conflicting security interest if the holder had filed a financing statement covering the same types of inventory (i) before the date of filing made by the purchase money secured party, or (ii) before the beginning of the 21 day period where the purchase money security interest is temporarily perfected without filing or possession (subsection (5) of Section 9–304); and

(c) the holder of the conflicting security interest receives the notification within five years before the debtor receives possession of the inventory; and

(d) the notification states that the person giving the notice has or expects to acquire a purchase money security interest in inventory of the debtor, describing such inventory by item or type.

(4) A purchase money security interest in collateral other than inventory has priority over a conflicting security interest in the same collateral or its proceeds if the purchase money security interest is perfected at the time the debtor receives possession of the collateral or within ten days thereafter.

(5) In all cases not governed by other rules stated in this section (including cases of purchase money security inter-

ests which do not qualify for the special priorities set forth in subsections (3) and (4) of this section), priority between conflicting security interests in the same collateral shall be determined according to the following rules:

(a) Conflicting security interests rank according to priority in time of filing or perfection. Priority dates from the time a filing is first made covering the collateral or the time the security interest is first perfected, whichever is earlier, provided that there is no period thereafter when there is neither filing nor perfection.

(b) So long as conflicting security interests are unperfected, the first to attach has priority.

(6) For the purposes of subsection (5) a date of filing or perfection as to collateral is also a date of filing or perfection as to proceeds.

(7) If future advances are made while a security interest is perfected by filing, the taking of possession, or under Section 8–321 on securities, the security interest has the same priority for the purposes of subsection (5) with respect to the future advances as it does with respect to first advance. If a commitment is made before or while the security interest is so perfected, the security interest has the same priority with respect to advances made pursuant thereto. In other cases a perfected security interest has priority from the date the advance is made.

§9–313. Priority of Security Interests in Fixtures

(1) In this section and in the provisions of Part 4 of this Article referring to fixture filing, unless the context otherwise requires

(a) goods are "fixtures" when they become so related to particular real estate that an interest in them arises under real estate law

(b) a "fixture filing" is the filing in the office where a mortgage on the real estate would be filed or recorded of a financing statement covering goods which are or are to become fixtures and conforming to the requirements of subsection (5) of Section 9–402

(c) a mortgage is a "construction mortgage" to the extent that it secures an obligation incurred for the construction of an improvement on land including the acquisition cost of the land, if the recorded writing so indicates.

(2) A security interest under this Article may be created in goods which are fixtures or may continue in goods which become fixtures, but no security interest exists under this Article in ordinary building materials incorporated into an improvement on land.

(3) This Article does not prevent creation of an encumbrance upon fixtures pursuant to real estate law.

(4) A perfected security interest in fixtures has priority over the conflicting interest of an encumbrancer or owner of the real estate where

(a) the security interest is a purchase money security interest, the interest of the encumbrancer or owner arises before the goods become fixtures, the security interest is perfected by a fixture filing before the goods become fixtures or within ten days thereafter, and the debtor has an interest of record in the real estate or is in possession of the real estate; or

(b) the security interest is perfected by a fixture filing before the interest of the encumbrancer or owner is of record, the security interest has priority over any conflicting interest of a predecessor in title of the encumbrancer or owner, and the debtor has an interest of record in the real estate or is in possession of the real estate; or

(c) the fixtures are readily removable factory or office machines or readily removable replacements of domestic appliances which are consumer goods, and before the goods become fixtures the security interest is perfected by any method permitted by this Article; or

(d) the conflicting interest is a lien on the real estate obtained by legal or equitable proceedings after the security interest was perfected by any method permitted by this Article.

(5) A security interest in fixtures, whether or not perfected, has priority over the conflicting interest of an encumbrancer or owner of the real estate where

(a) the encumbrancer or owner has consented in writing to the security interest or has disclaimed an interest in the goods as fixtures; or

(b) the debtor has a right to remove the goods as against the encumbrancer or owner. If the debtor's right terminates, the priority of the security interest continues for a reasonable time.

(6) Notwithstanding paragraph (a) of subsection (4) but otherwise subject to subsections (4) and (5), a security interest in fixtures is subordinate to a construction mortgage recorded before the goods become fixtures if the goods become fixtures before the completion of the construction. To the extent that it is given to refinance a construction mortgage, a mortgage has this priority to the same extent as the construction mortgage.

(7) In cases not within the preceding subsections, a security interest in fixtures is subordinate to the conflicting interest of an encumbrancer or owner of the related real estate who is not the debtor.

(8) When the secured party has priority over all owners and encumbrancers of the real estate, he may, on default, subject to the provisions of Part 5, remove his collateral from the real estate but he must reimburse any encumbrancer or owner of the real estate who is not the debtor and who has not otherwise agreed for the cost of repair of any physical injury, but not for any diminution in value of the real estate caused by the absence of the goods removed or by any necessity of replacing them. A person entitled to reimbursement may refuse permission to remove until the secured party gives adequate security for the performance of this obligation.

§9–314. Accessions

(1) A security interest in goods which attaches before they are installed in or affixed to other goods takes priority as to the goods installed or affixed (called in this section "accessions") over the claims of all persons to the whole except as stated in subsection (3) and subject to Section 9–315(1).

(2) A security interest which attaches to goods after they become part of a whole is valid against all persons subsequently acquiring interests in the whole except as stated in subsection (3) but is invalid against any person with an interest in the whole at the time the security interest attaches to the goods who has not in writing consented to the security interest or disclaimed an interest in the goods as part of the whole.

(3) The security interest described in subsections (1) and (2) do not take priority over

(a) a subsequent purchaser for value of any interest in the whole; or

(b) a creditor with a lien on the whole subsequently obtained by judicial proceedings; or

(c) a creditor with a prior perfected security interest in the whole to the extent that he makes subsequent advances if the subsequent purchase is made, the lien by judicial proceedings obtained or the subsequent advance under the prior perfected security interest is made or contracted for without knowledge of the security interest and before it is perfected. A purchaser of the whole at a foreclosure sale other than the holder of a perfected security interest purchasing at his own foreclosure sale is a subsequent purchaser within this section.

(4) When under subsections (1) and (2) and (3) a secured party has an interest in accessions which has priority over the claims of all persons who have interests in the whole, he may on default subject to the provisions of Part 5 remove his collateral from the whole but he must reimburse any encumbrancer or owner of the whole who is not the debtor and who has not otherwise agreed for the cost of repair of any physical injury but not for any diminution in value of the whole caused by the absence of the goods removed or by any necessity for replacing them. A person entitled to reimbursement may refuse permission to remove until the secured party gives adequate security for the performance of this obligation.

§9–315. Priority When Goods Are Commingled or Processed

(1) If a security interest in goods was perfected and subsequently the goods or a part thereof have become part of a product or mass, the security interest continues in the product or mass if

(a) the goods are so manufactured, processed, assembled or commingled that their identity is lost in the product or mass; or

(b) a financing statement covering the original goods also covers the product into which the goods have been manufactured, processed or assembled. In a case to which paragraph (b) applies, no separate security interest in that part of the original goods which have been manufactured, processed or assembled into the product may be claimed under Section 9–314.

(2) When under subsection (1) more than one security interest attaches to the product or mass, they rank equally according to the ratio that the cost of the goods to which each interest originally attached bears to the cost of the total product or mass.

§9–316. Priority Subject to Subordination

Nothing in this Article prevents subordination by agreement by any person entitled to priority.

§9–317. Secured Party Not Obligated on Contract of Debtor

The mere existence of a security interest or authority given to the debtor to dispose of or use collateral does not impose contract or tort liability upon the secured party for the debtor's acts or omissions.

§9–318. Defenses Against Assignee; Modification of Contract After Notification of Assignment; Term Prohibiting Assignment Ineffective; Identification and Proof of Assignment

(1) Unless an account debtor has made an enforceable agreement not to assert defenses or claims arising out of a sale as provided in Section 9–206 the rights of an assignee are subject to

(a) all the terms of the contract between the account debtor and assignor and any defense or claim arising therefrom; and

(b) any other defense or claim of the account debtor against the assignor which accrues before the account debtor receives notification of the assignment.

(2) So far as the right to payment or a part thereof under an assigned contract has not been fully earned by performance, and notwithstanding notification of the assignment, any modification of or substitution for the contract made in good faith and in accordance with reasonable commercial standards is effective against an assignee unless the account debtor has otherwise agreed but the assignee acquires corresponding rights under the modified or substituted contract. The assignment may provide that such modification or substitution is a breach by the assignor.

(3) The account debtor is authorized to pay the assignor until the account debtor receives notification that the amount due or to become due has been assigned and that payment is to be made to the assignee. A notification which does not reasonably identify the rights assigned is

ineffective. If requested by the account debtor, the assignee must seasonably furnish reasonable proof that the assignment has been made and unless he does so the account debtor may pay the assignor.

(4) A term in any contract between an account debtor and an assignor is ineffective if it prohibits assignment of an account or prohibits creation of a security interest in a general intangible for money due or to become due or requires the account debtor's consent to such assignment or security interest.

Part 4 Filing

§9–401. Place of Filing; Erroneous Filing; Removal of Collateral

First Alternative Subsection (1)

(1) The proper place to file in order to perfect a security interest is as follows:

(a) when the collateral is timber to be cut or is minerals or the like (including oil and gas) or accounts subject to subsection (5) of Section 9–103, or when the financing statement is filed as a fixture filing (Section 9–313) and the collateral is goods which are or are to become fixtures, then in the office where a mortgage on the real estate would be filed or recorded;

(b) in all other cases, in the office of the [Secretary of State].

Second Alternative Subsection (1)

(1) The proper place to file in order to perfect a security interest is as follows:

(a) when the collateral is equipment used in farming operations, or farm products, or accounts or general intangibles arising from or relating to the sale of farm products by a farmer, or consumer goods, then in the office of the . . . . in the county of the debtor's residence or if the debtor is not a resident of this state then in the office of the . . . . in the county where the goods are kept, and in addition when the collateral is crops growing or to be grown in the office of the . . . . in the county where the land is located;

(b) when the collateral is timber to be cut or is minerals or the like (including oil and gas) or accounts subject to subsection (5) of Section 9–103, or when the financing statement is filed as a fixture filing (Section 9–313) and the collateral is goods which are or are to become fixtures, then in the office where a mortgage on the real estate would be filed or recorded;

(c) in all other cases, in the office of the [Secretary of State].

Third Alternative Subsection (1)

(1) The proper place to file in order to perfect a security interest is as follows:

(a) when the collateral is equipment used in farming operations, or farm products, or accounts or general intangibles arising from or relating to the sale of farm products by a farmer, or consumer goods, then in the office of the . . . . in the county of the debtor's residence or if the debtor is not a resident of this state then in office of the . . . . in the county where the goods are kept, and in addition when the collateral is crops growing or to be grown in the office of the . . . . in the county where the land is located;

(b) when the collateral is timber to be cut or is minerals or the like (including oil and gas) or accounts subject to subsection (5) of Section 9–103, or when the financing statement is filed as a fixture filing (Section 9–313) and the collateral is goods which are or are to become fixtures, then in the office where a mortgage on the real estate would be filed or recorded;

(c) in all other cases, in the office of the [Secretary of State] and in addition, if the debtor has a place of business in only one county of this state, also in the office of . . . . of such county, or, if the debtor has no place of business in this state, but resides in this state, also in the office of . . . . of the county in which he resides.

Note: One of the three alternatives should be selected as subsection (1).

(2) A filing which is made in good faith in an improper place or not in all of the places required by this section is nevertheless effective with regard to any collateral as to which the filing complied with the requirements of this Article and is also effective with regard to collateral covered by the financing statement against any person who has knowledge of the contents of such financing statement.

(3) A filing which is made in the proper place in this state continues effective even though the debtor's residence or place of business or the location of the collateral or its use, whichever controlled the original filing, is thereafter changed.

Alternative to Subsection (3)

[(3) A filing which is made in the proper county continues effective for four months after a change to another county of the debtor's residence or place of business or the location of the collateral, whichever controlled the original filing. It becomes ineffective thereafter unless a copy of the financing statement signed by the secured party is filed in the new county within said period. The security interest may also be perfected in the new county after the expiration of the four-month period; in such case perfection dates from the time of perfection in the new county. A change in the use of the collateral does not impair the effectiveness of the original filing.]

(4) The rules stated in Section 9–103 determines whether filing is necessary in this state.

(5) Notwithstanding the preceding subsections, and subject to subsection (3) of Section 9–302, the proper place to file in order to perfect a security interest in collateral, including fixtures, of a transmitting utility is the office of the [Secretary of State]. This filing constitutes a fixture filing (Section 9–313) as to the collateral described therein which is or is to become fixtures.

(6) For the purposes of this section, the residence of an organization is its place of business if it has one or its chief executive office if it has more than one place of business.

Note: Subsection (6) should be used if the state chooses the Second or Third Alternative Subsection (1).

§9–402. Formal Requisites of Financing Statement; Amendments; Mortgage as Financing Statement

(1) A financing statement is sufficient if it gives the names of the debtor and the secured party, is signed by the debtor, gives an address of the secured party from which information concerning the security interest may be obtained, gives a mailing address of the debtor and contains a statement indicating the types, or describing the items, of collateral. A financing statement may be filed before a security agreement is made or a security interest otherwise attaches. When the financing statement covers crops growing or to be grown, the statement must also contain a description of the real estate concerned. When the financing statement covers timber to be cut or covers minerals or the like (including oil and gas) or accounts subject to subsection (5) of Section 9–103, or when the financing statement is filed as a fixture filing (Section 9–313) and the collateral is goods which are or are to become fixtures, the statement must also comply with subsection (5). A copy of the security agreement is sufficient as a financing statement if it contains the above information and is signed by the debtor. A carbon, photographic or other reproduction of a security agreement or a financing statement is sufficient as a financing statement if the security agreement so provides or if the original has been filed in this state.

(2) A financing statement which otherwise complies with subsection (1) is sufficient when it is signed by the secured party instead of the debtor if it is filed to perfect a security interest in

(a) collateral already subject to a security interest in another jurisdiction when it is brought into this state, or when the debtor's location is changed to this state. Such a financing statement must state that the collateral was brought into this state or that the debtor's location was changed to this state under such circumstances; or

(b) proceeds under Section 9–306 if the security interest in the original collateral was perfected. Such a financing statement must describe the original collateral; or

(c) collateral as to which the filing has lapsed; or

(d) collateral acquired after a change of name, identity or corporate structure of the debtor (subsection (7)).

(3) A form substantially as follows is sufficient to comply with subsection (1):

Name of debtor (or assignor) ....
Address ....
Name of secured party (or assignee)...................
Address ....

1. This financing statement covers the following types (or items) of property:
   (Describe): ....
2. (If collateral is crops) The above described crops are growing or are to be grown on:
   (Describe Real Estate) ....
3. (If applicable) The above goods are to become fixtures on:*
   (Describe Real Estate) ....
   and this financing statement is to be filed [for record] in the real estate records. (If the debtor does not have an interest of record) The name of a record owner is ....
4. (If products of collateral are claimed) Products of the collateral are also covered.
   (Use whichever is applicable) ....
   Signature of Debtor (or Assignor) ....
   Signature of Secured Party (or Assignee) ....

*Note: *Where appropriate substitute either "The above timber is standing on . . ." or "The above minerals or the like (including oil and gas) or accounts will be financed at the wellhead or minehead of the well or mine located on . . ."*

Language in brackets is optional.

(4) A financing statement may be amended by filing a writing signed by both the debtor and the secured party. An amendment does not extend the period of effectiveness of a financing statement. If any amendment adds collateral, it is effective as to the added collateral only from the filing date of the amendment. In this Article, unless the context otherwise requires, the term "financing statement" means the original financing statement and any amendments.

(5) A financing statement covering timber to be cut or covering minerals or the like (including oil and gas) or accounts subject to subsection (5) of Section 9–103, or a financing statement filed as a fixture filing (Section 9–313) where the debtor is not a transmitting utility, must show that it covers this type of collateral, must recite that it is to be filed [for record] in the real estate records, and the financing statement must contain a description of the real estate [sufficient if it were contained in a mortgage of the real estate to give constructive notice of the mortgage under the law of this state]. If the debtor does not have an interest of record in the real estate, the financing statement must show the name of a record owner.

(6) A mortgage is effective as a financing statement filed as a fixture filing from the date of its recording if

(a) the goods are described in the mortgage by item or type; and

(b) the goods are or are to become fixtures related to the real estate described in the mortgage; and

(c) the mortgage complies with the requirements for a financing statement in this section other than a recital that it is to be filed in the real estate records; and

(d) the mortgage is duly recorded.

No fee with reference to the financing statement is required other than the regular recording and satisfaction fees with respect to the mortgage.

(7) A financing statement sufficiently shows the name of the debtor if it gives the individual, partnership or corporate name of the debtor, whether or not it adds other trade names or names of partners. Where the debtor so changes his name or in the case of an organization its name, identity or corporate structure that a filed financing statement becomes seriously misleading, the filing is not effective to perfect a security interest in collateral acquired by the debtor more than four months after the change, unless a new appropriate financing statement is filed before the expiration of that time. A filed financing statement remains effective with respect to collateral transferred by the debtor even though the secured party knows of or consents to the transfer.

(8) A financing statement substantially complying with the requirements of this section is effective even though it contains minor errors which are not seriously misleading.

Note: Where the state has any special recording system for real estate other than the usual grantor-grantee index (as, for instance, a tract system or a title registration or Torrens system) local adaptations of subsection (5) and Section 9–403(7) may be necessary. See Mass. Gen. Laws Chapter 106, Section 9–409.

§9–403. What Constitutes Filing; Duration of Filing; Effect of Lapsed Filing; Duties of Filing Officer

(1) Presentation for filing of a financing statement and tender of the filing fee or acceptance of the statement by the filing officer constitutes filing under this Article.

(2) Except as provided in subsection (6) a filed financing statement is effective for a period of five years from the date of filing. The effectiveness of a filed financing statement lapses on the expiration of the five year period unless a continuation statement is filed prior to the lapse. If a security interest perfected by filing exists at the time insolvency proceedings are commenced by or against the debtor, the security interest remains perfected until termination of the insolvency proceedings and thereafter for a period of sixty days or until expiration of the five year period, whichever occurs later. Upon lapse the security interest becomes un-

perfected, unless it is perfected without filing. If the security interest becomes unperfected upon lapse, it is deemed to have been unperfected as against a person who became a purchaser or lien creditor before lapse.

(3) A continuation statement may be filed by the secured party within six months prior to the expiration of the five year period specified in subsection (2). Any such continuation statement must be signed by the secured party, identify the original statement by file number and state that the original statement is still effective. A continuation statement signed by a person other than the secured party of record must be accompanied by a separate written statement of assignment signed by the secured party of record and complying with subsection (2) of Section 9–405, including payment of the required fee. Upon timely filing of the continuation statement, the effectiveness of the original statement is continued for five years after the last date to which the filing was effective whereupon it lapses in the same manner as provided in subsection (2) unless another continuation statement is filed prior to such lapse. Succeeding continuation statements may be filed in the same manner to continue the effectiveness of the original statement. Unless a statute on disposition of public records provides otherwise, the filing officer may remove a lapsed statement from the files and destroy it immediately if he has retained a microfilm or other photographic record, or in other cases after one year after the lapse. The filing officer shall so arrange matters by physical annexation of financing statements to continuation statements or other related filings, or by other means, that if he physically destroys the financing statements of a period more than five years past, those which have been continued by a continuation statement or which are still effective under subsection (6) shall be retained.

(4) Except as provided in subsection (7) a filing officer shall mark each statement with a file number and with the date and hour of filing and shall hold the statement or a microfilm or other photographic copy thereof for public inspection. In addition the filing officer shall index the statement according to the name of the debtor and shall note in the index the file number and the address of the debtor given in the statement.

(5) The uniform fee for filing and indexing and for stamping a copy furnished by the secured party to show the date and place of filing for an original financing statement or for a continuation statement shall be $. . . . . . if the statement is in the standard form prescribed by the [Secretary of State] and otherwise shall be $. . . . . ., plus in each case, if the financing statement is subject to subsection (5) of Section 9–402, $. . . . . . The uniform fee for each name more than one required to be indexed shall be $. . . . . . The secured party may at his option show a trade name for any person and an extra uniform indexing fee of $. . . . . . shall be paid with respect thereto.

(6) If the debtor is a transmitting utility (subsection (5) of Section 9–401) and a filed financing statement so states, it is effective until a termination statement is filed. A real estate mortgage which is effective as a fixture filing under subsection (6) of Section 9–402 remains effective as a fixture filing until the mortgage is released or satisfied of record or its effectiveness otherwise terminates as to the real estate.

(7) When a financing statement covers timber to be cut or covers minerals or the like (including oil and gas) or accounts subject to subsection (5) of Section 9–103, or is filed as a fixture filing, [it shall be filed for record and] the filing officer shall index it under the names of the debtor and any owner of record shown on the financing statement in the same fashion as if they were the mortgagors in a mortgage of the real estate described, and, to the extent that the law of this state provides for the indexing of mortgages under the name of the mortgagee, under the name of the secured party as if he were the mortgagee thereunder, or where indexing is by description in the same fashion as if the financing statement were a mortgage of the real estate described.

Note: In states in which writings will not appear in the real estate records and indices unless actually recorded the bracketed language in subsection (7) should be used.

§9–404. Termination Statement

(1) If a financing statement covering consumer goods is filed on or after . . . . . ., then within one month or within ten days following written demand by the debtor after there is no outstanding secured obligation and no commitment to make advances, incur obligations or otherwise give value, the secured party must file with each filing officer with whom the financing statement was filed, a termination statement to the effect that he no longer claims a security interest under the financing statement, which shall be identified by file number. In other cases whenever there is no outstanding secured obligation and no commitment to make advances, incur obligations or otherwise give value, the secured party must on written demand by the debtor send the debtor, for each filing officer with whom the financing statement was filed, a termination statement to the effect that he no longer claims a security interest under the financing statement, which shall be identified by file number. A termination statement signed by a person other than the secured party of record must be accompanied by a separate written statement of assignment signed by the secured party of record complying with subsection (2) of Section 9–405, including payment of the required fee. If the affected secured party fails to file such a termination statement as required by this subsection, or to send such a termination statement within ten days after proper demand therefor, he shall be liable to the debtor for one hundred dollars, and in addition for any loss caused to the debtor by such failure.

(2) On presentation to the filing officer of such a termination statement he must note it in the index. If he has received the termination statement in duplicate, he shall return one copy of the termination statement to the secured party stamped to show the time of receipt thereof. If the filing officer has a microfilm or other photographic record of the financing statement, and of any related continuation statement, statement of assignment and statement of release, he may remove the originals from the files at any time after receipt of the termination statement, or if he has no such record, he may remove them from the files at any time after one year after receipt of the termination statement.

(3) If the termination statement is in the standard form prescribed by the [Secretary of State], the uniform fee for filing and indexing the termination statement shall be $. . . . . ., and otherwise shall be $. . . . . ., plus in each case an additional fee of $. . . . . . for each name more than one against which the termination statement is required to be indexed.

Note: The date to be inserted should be the effective date of the revised Article 9.

§9–405. Assignment of Security Interest; Duties of Filing Officer; Fees

(1) A financing statement may disclose an assignment of a security interest in the collateral described in the financing statement by indication in the financing statement of the name and address of the assignee or by an assignment itself or a copy thereof on the face or back of the statement. On presentation to the filing officer of such a financing statement the filing officer shall mark the same as provided in Section 9–403(4). The uniform fee for filing, indexing and furnishing filing data for a financing statement so indicating an assignment shall be $. . . . . if the statement is in the standard form prescribed by the [Secretary of State] and otherwise shall be $. . . . . ., plus in each case an additional fee of $. . . . . . for each name more than one against which the financing statement is required to be indexed.

(2) A secured party may assign of record all or part of his rights under a financing statement by the filing in the place where the original financing statement was filed of a separate written statement of assignment signed by the secured party of record and setting forth the name of the secured party of record and the debtor, the file number and the date of filing of the financing statement and the name and address of the assignee and containing a description of the collateral assigned. A copy of the assignment is sufficient as a separate statement if it complies with the preceding sentence. On presentation to the filing officer of such a separate statement, the filing officer shall mark such separate statement with the date and hour of the filing. He shall note the assignment on the index of the financing statement, or in the case of a fixture

filing, or a filing covering timber to be cut, or covering minerals or the like (including oil and gas) or accounts subject to subsection (5) of Section 9–103, he shall index the assignment under the name of the assignor as grantor and, to the extent that the law of this state provides for indexing the assignment of a mortgage under the name of the assignee, he shall index the assignment of the financing statement under the name of the assignee. The uniform fee for filing, indexing and furnishing filing data about such a separate statement of assignment shall be $. . . . . if the statement is in the standard form prescribed by the [Secretary of State] and otherwise shall be $. . . . ., plus in each case an additional fee of $. . . . . . for each name more than one against which the statement of assignment is required to be indexed. Notwithstanding the provisions of this subsection, an assignment of record of a security interest in a fixture contained in a mortgage effective as a fixture filing (subsection (6) of Section 9–402) may be made only by an assignment of the mortgage in the manner provided by the law of this state other than this Act.

(3) After the disclosure or filing of an assignment under this section, the assignee is the secured party of record.

§9–406. Release of Collateral; Duties of Filing Officer; Fees

A secured party of record may by his signed statement release all or a part of any collateral described in a filed financing statement. The statement of release is sufficient if it contains a description of the collateral being released, the name and address of the debtor, the name and address of the secured party, and the file number of the financing statement. A statement of release signed by a person other than the secured party of record must be accompanied by a separate written statement of assignment signed by the secured party of record and complying with subsection (2) of Section 9–405, including payment of the required fee. Upon presentation of such a statement of release to the filing officer he shall mark the statement with the hour and date of filing and shall note the same upon the margin of the index of the filing of the financing statement. The uniform fee for filing and noting such a statement of release shall be $. . . . . . if the statement is in the standard form prescribed by the [Secretary of State] and otherwise shall be $. . . . ., plus in each case an additional fee of $. . . . . for each name more than one against which the statement of release is required to be indexed.

[§9–407. Information from Filing Officer]

[(1) If the person filing any financing statement, termination statement, statement of assignment, or statement of release, furnishes the filing officer a copy thereof, the filing officer shall upon request note upon the copy the file number and date and hour of the filing of the original and deliver or send the copy to such person.]

[(2) Upon request of any person, the filing officer shall issue his certificate showing whether there is on file on the date and hour stated therein, any presently effective financing statement naming a particular debtor and any statement of assignment thereof and if there is, giving the date and hour of filing of each such statement and the names and addresses of each secured party therein. The uniform fee for such a certificate shall be $. . . . . if the request for the certificate is in the standard form prescribed by the [Secretary of State] and otherwise shall be $. . . . . Upon request the filing officer shall furnish a copy of any filed financing statement or statement of assignment for a uniform fee of $. . . . . . per page.]

Note: This section is proposed as an optional provision to require filing officers to furnish certificates. Local law and practices should be consulted with regard to the advisability of adoption.

§9–408. Financing Statements Covering Consigned or Leased Goods

A consignor or lessor of goods may file a financing statement using the terms "consignor," "consignee," "lessor," "lessee" or the like instead of the terms specified in Section 9–402. The provisions of this Part shall apply as appropriate to such a financing statement but its filing shall not of itself be a factor in determining whether or not the consignment or lease is intended as security (Section 1–201(37)). However, if it is determined for other reasons that the consignment or lease is so intended, a security interest of the consignor or lessor which attaches to the consigned or leased goods is perfected by such filing.

Part 5 Default

§9–501. Default; Procedure When Security Agreement Covers Both Real and Personal Property

(1) When a debtor is in default under a security agreement, a secured party has the rights and remedies provided in this Part and except as limited by subsection (3) those provided in the security agreement. He may reduce his claim to judgment, foreclose or otherwise enforce the security interest by an available judicial procedure. If the collateral is documents the secured party may proceed either as to the documents or as to the goods covered thereby. A secured party in possession has the rights, remedies and duties provided in Section 9–207. The rights and remedies referred to in this subsection are cumulative.

(2) After default, the debtor has the rights and remedies provided in this Part, those provided in the security agreement and those provided in Section 9–207.

(3) To the extent that they give rights to the debtor and

impose duties on the secured party, the rules stated in the subsections referred to below may not be waived or varied except as provided with respect to compulsory disposition of collateral (subsection (3) of Section 9–504 and Section 9–505) and with respect to redemption of collateral (Section 9–506) but the parties may by agreement determine the standard by which the fulfillment of these rights and duties is to be measured if such standards are not manifestly unreasonable:

(a) subsection (2) of Section 9–502 and subsection (2) of Section 9–504 insofar as they require accounting for surplus proceeds of collateral;

(b) subsection (3) of Section 9–504 and subsection (1) of Section 9–505 which deal with disposition of collateral;

(c) subsection (2) of Section 9–505 which deals with acceptance of collateral as discharge of obligation;

(d) Section 9–506 which deals with redemption of collateral; and

(e) subsection (1) of Section 9–507 which deals with the secured party's liability for failure to comply with this Part.

(4) If the security agreement covers both real and personal property, the secured party may proceed under this Part as to the personal property or he may proceed as to both the real and the personal property in accordance with his rights and remedies in respect of the real property in which case the provisions of this Part do not apply.

(5) When a secured party has reduced his claim to judgment the lien of any levy which may be made upon his collateral by virtue of any execution based upon the judgment shall relate back to the date of the perfection of the security interest in such collateral. A judicial sale, pursuant to such execution, is a foreclosure of the security interest by judicial procedure within the meaning of this section, and the secured party may purchase at the sale and thereafter hold the collateral free of any other requirements of this Article.

§9–502. Collection Rights of Secured Party

(1) When so agreed and in any event on default the secured party is entitled to notify an account debtor or the obligor on an instrument to make payment to him whether or not the assignor was theretofore making collections on the collateral, and also to take control of any proceeds to which he is entitled under Section 9–306.

(2) A secured party who by agreement is entitled to charge back uncollected collateral or otherwise to full or limited recourse against the debtor and who undertakes to collect from the account debtors or obligors must proceed in a commercially reasonable manner and may deduct his reasonable expenses of realization from the collections. If the security agreement secures an indebtedness, the secured party must account to the debtor for any surplus, and unless otherwise agreed, the debtor is liable for any deficiency. But, if the underlying transaction was a sale of accounts or chattel paper, the debtor is entitled to any surplus or is liable for any deficiency only if the security agreement so provides.

§9–503. Secured Party's Rights to Take Possession After Default

Unless otherwise agreed a secured party has on default the right to take possession of the collateral. In taking possession a secured party may proceed without judicial process if this can be done without breach of the peace or may proceed by action. If the security agreement so provides the secured party may require the debtor to assemble the collateral and make it available to the secured party at a place to be designated by the secured party which is reasonably convenient to both parties. Without removal a secured party may render equipment unusable, and may dispose of collateral on the debtor's premises under Section 9–504.

§9–504. Secured Party's Right to Dispose of Collateral After Default; Effect of Disposition

(1) A secured party after default may sell, lease or otherwise dispose of any or all of the collateral in its then condition or following any commercially reasonable preparation or processing. Any sale of goods is subject to the Article on Sales (Article 2). The proceeds of disposition shall be applied in the order following to

(a) the reasonable expenses of retaking, holding, preparing for sale or lease, selling, leasing and the like and, to the extent provided for in the agreement and not prohibited by law, the reasonable attorney's fees and legal expenses incurred by the secured party;

(b) the satisfaction of indebtedness secured by the security interest under which the disposition is made;

(c) the satisfaction of indebtedness secured by any subordinate security interest in the collateral if written notification of demand therefor is received before distribution of the proceeds is completed. If requested by the secured party, the holder of a subordinate security interest must reasonably furnish reasonable proof of his interest, and unless he does so, the secured party need not comply with his demand.

(2) If the security interest secures an indebtedness, the secured party must account to the debtor for any surplus, and, unless otherwise agreed, the debtor is liable for any deficiency. But if the underlying transaction was a sale of accounts or chattel paper, the debtor is entitled to any surplus or is liable for any deficiency only if the security agreement so provides.

(3) Disposition of the collateral may be public or private proceedings and may be made by way of one or more contracts. Sale or other disposition may be as a unit or in parcels and at any time and place and on any terms but every aspect of the disposition including the method,

manner, time, place and terms must be commercially reasonable. Unless collateral is perishable or threatens to decline speedily in value or is of a type customarily sold on a recognized market, reasonable notification of the time and place of any public sale or reasonable notification of the time after which any private sale or other intended disposition is to be made shall be sent by the secured party to the debtor, if he has not signed after default a statement renouncing or modifying his right to notification of sale. In the case of consumer goods no other notification need be sent. In other cases notification shall be sent to any other secured party from whom the secured party has received (before sending his notification to the debtor or before the debtor's renunciation of his rights) written notice of a claim of an interest in the collateral. The secured party may buy at any public sale and if the collateral is of a type customarily sold in a recognized market or is of a type which is the subject of widely distributed standard price quotations he may buy at private sale.

(4) When collateral is disposed of by a secured party after default, the disposition transfers to a purchaser for value all of the debtor's rights therein, discharges the security interest under which it is made and any security interest or lien subordinate thereto. The purchaser takes free of all such rights and interests even though the secured party fails to comply with the requirements of this Part or of any judicial proceedings

(a) in the case of a public sale, if the purchaser has no knowledge of any defects in the sale and if he does not buy in collusion with the secured party, other bidders or the person conducting the sale; or

(b) in any other case, if the purchaser acts in good faith.

(5) A person who is liable to a secured party under a guaranty, indorsement, repurchase agreement or the like and who receives a transfer of collateral from the secured party or is subrogated to his rights has thereafter the rights and duties of the secured party. Such a transfer of collateral is not a sale or disposition of the collateral under this Article.

§9–505. Compulsory Disposition of Collateral; Acceptance of the Collateral as Discharge of Obligation

(1) If the debtor has paid sixty per cent of the case price in the case of a purchase money security interest in consumer goods or sixty per cent of the loan in the case of another security interest in consumer goods, and has not signed after default a statement renouncing or modifying his rights under this Part a secured party who has taken possession of collateral must dispose of it under Section 9–504 and if he fails to do so within ninety days after he takes possession the debtor at his option may recover in conversion or under Section 9–507(1) on secured party's liability.

(2) In any other case involving consumer goods or any other collateral a secured party in possession may, after default, propose to retain the collateral in satisfaction of the obligation. Written notice of such proposal shall be sent to the debtor if he has not signed after default a statement renouncing or modifying his rights under this subsection. In the case of consumer goods no other notice need be given. In other cases notice shall be sent to any other secured party from whom the secured party has received (before sending his notice to the debtor or before the debtor's renunciation of his rights) written notice of a claim of an interest in the collateral. If the secured party receives objection in writing from a person entitled to receive notification within twenty-one days after the notice was sent, the secured party must dispose of the collateral under Section 9–504. In the absence of such written objection the secured party may retain the collateral in satisfaction of the debtor's obligation.

§9–506. Debtor's Right to Redeem Collateral

At any time before the secured party has disposed of collateral or entered into a contract for its disposition under Section 9–504 or before the obligation has been discharged under Section 9–505(2) the debtor or any other secured party may unless otherwise agreed in writing after default redeem the collateral by tendering fulfillment of all obligations secured by the collateral as well as the expenses reasonably incurred by the secured party in retaking, holding and preparing the collateral for disposition, in arranging for the sale, and to the extent provided in the agreement and not prohibited by law, his reasonable attorney's fees and legal expenses.

§9–507. Secured Party's Liability for Failure to Comply With This Part

(1) If it is established that the secured party is not proceeding in accordance with the provisions of this Part disposition may be ordered or restrained on appropriate terms and conditions. If the disposition has occurred the debtor or any person entitled to notification or whose security interest has been made known to the secured party prior to the disposition has a right to recover from the secured party any loss caused by a failure to comply with the provisions of this Part. If the collateral is consumer goods, the debtor has a right to recover in any event an amount not less than the credit service charge plus ten per cent of the principal amount of the debt or the time price differential plus 10 per cent of the cash price.

(2) The fact that a better price could have been obtained by a sale at a different time or in a different method from that selected by the secured party is not of itself sufficient to establish that the sale was not made in a commercially reasonable manner. If the secured party either sells the collateral in the usual manner in any recognized market therefor or if he sells at the price current in such market at the time of his sale or if he has otherwise sold in

conformity with reasonable commercial practices among dealers in the type of property sold he has sold in a commercially reasonable manner. The principles stated in the two preceding sentences with respect to sales also apply as may be appropriate to other types of disposition. A disposition which has been approved in any judicial proceeding or by any bona fide creditors' committee or representative of creditors shall conclusively be deemed to be commercially reasonable, but this sentence does not indicate that any such approval must be obtained in any case nor does it indicate that any disposition not so approved is not commercially reasonable.

Note: Articles 10 and 11 have been omitted as unnecessary for the purposes of this text.

GLOSSARY OF LEGAL TERMS AND DEFINITIONS

A

Abandonment   To intentionally give up possession or claim to property with the intent of relinquishment of any ownership or claim.

Abatement   An action of stopping or removing.

Ab Initio   From the beginning. A contract that is void ab initio is void from its inception.

Abstract of Title   A summary of the conveyances, transfers, and other facts relied on as evidence of title, together with all such facts appearing of record that may impair its validity. It should contain a brief but complete history of the title.

Abuse of Process   An intentional tort designed to protect against the initiation of legal proceedings for a primary purpose other than the one for which such proceedings were designed.

Acceleration   The shortening of the time for the performance of a contract or the payment of a note by the operation of some provision in the contract or note itself.

Acceptance   The actual or implied receipt and retention of that which is tendered or offered.

Accession   The acquisition of property by its incorporation or union with other property.

Accommodation Paper   A negotiable instrument signed without consideration by a party as acceptor, drawer, or indorser for the purpose of enabling the payee to obtain credit.

Accommodation Party   A person who signs a negotiable instrument for the purpose of adding his name and liability to another party to the instrument.

Accord and Satisfaction   A legally binding agreement to settle a disputed claim for a definite amount.

Account Stated   An account that has been rendered by one to another and which purports to state the true balance due and that balance is either expressly or impliedly admitted to be due by the debtor.

Acquit   To set free or judicially to discharge from an accusation; to release from a debt, duty, obligation, charge, or suspicion of guilt.

Actionable   Capable of being remedied by a legal action or claim.

Act of God   An occurrence resulting exclusively from natural forces that could not have been prevented or whose effect could not have been avoided by care or foresight.

Act of State Doctrine   A doctrine of international law that no nation is permitted to judge the act of another nation committed within its own boundaries.

Adjudge   To give judgment; to decide; to sentence.

Adjudicate   To adjudge; to settle by judicial decree, as a court.

Ad Litem   During the pendency of the action or proceeding.

Administrator   The personal representative appointed by a probate court to settle the estate of a deceased person who died intestate (without leaving a valid will).

Adoption   In corporation law, a corporation's acceptance of a preincorporation contract by action of its board of directors, by which the corporation becomes liable on the contract.

Advance Directive   A written document such as a living will or durable power of attorney that directs others how future health care decisions should be made in the event that the individual becomes incapacitated.

Adverse Possession   Open and notorious possession of real property over a given length of time that denies ownership in any other claimant.

Advised Letter of Credit   See *Letter of Credit, Advised*.

Affidavit   A signed writing containing statements of fact to whose accuracy the signing party has sworn. Used in a variety of judicial proceedings, including the motion for summary judgment.

Affirm To confirm or uphold a former judgment or order of a court. Appellate courts, for instance, may affirm the decisions of lower courts.

After-Acquired Property Property of the debtor that is obtained after a security interest in the debtor's property has been created.

Agency A legal relationship in which an agent acts under the direction of a principal for the principal's benefit. Also used to refer to government regulatory bodies of all kinds.

Agent One who acts under the direction of a principal for the principal's benefit in a legal relationship known as agency. See *Principal*.

Aggregate Theory In partnership law, the view that there is no distinction between a partnership and the partners who own it. See *Entity Theory*.

Aggrieved One whose legal rights have been invaded by the act of another is said to be aggrieved. Also, one whose pecuniary interest is directly affected by a judgment, or whose right of property may be divested by an action.

Alienation The voluntary act or acts by which one person transfers his or her own property to another.

Alien Corporation A corporation incorporated in one country that is doing business in another country. See *Foreign Corporation*.

Allegation A statement of a party to an action in a declaration or pleading of what the party intends to prove.

Allege To make a statement of fact; to plead.

Alteration An addition or change in a document.

Alter Ego Other self. In corporation law, a doctrine that permits a court to pierce a corporation's veil and to hold a shareholder liable for the actions of a corporation dominated by the shareholder.

Alternative Dispute Resolution (ADR) A general name applied to the many nonjudicial means of settling private disputes.

Amortize To provide for the payment of a debt by creating a sinking fund or paying in installments.

Ancillary Auxiliary to. An ancillary receiver is a receiver who has been appointed in aid of, and in subordination to, the primary receiver.

Ancillary Covenant Not to Compete A promise that is ancillary to (part of) a valid contract whereby one party to a contract agrees not to compete with the other party for a specified time and within a specified location. Also called *non-competition clause*.

Answer The pleading of a defendant in which he or she may deny any or all the facts set out in the plaintiff's declaration or complaint.

Anticipatory Breach A contracting party's indication before the time for performance that he cannot or will not perform the contract.

Appearance The first act of the defendant in court.

Appellant The party making an appeal.

Appellate Jurisdiction Jurisdiction to revise or correct the work of a subordinate court.

Appellee A party against whom a favorable court decision is appealed. May be called the *respondent* in some jurisdictions.

Applicant A petitioner; one who files a petition or application.

Appraisal, Right of A shareholder's right to receive the fair value of her shares from her corporation when she objects to a corporate transaction that significantly alters her rights in the corporation.

Appurtenance An accessory; something that belongs to another thing.

Arbitrate To submit some disputed matter to selected persons and to accept their decision or award as a substitute for the decision of a judicial tribunal.

Argument The discussion by counsel for the respective parties of their contentions on the law and the facts of the case being tried in order to aid the jury in arriving at a correct and just conclusion.

Articles of Incorporation A document that must be filed with a secretary of state to create a corporation. Usually, it includes the basic rights and responsibilities of the corporation and the shareholders.

Articles of Partnership A formal written contract between the partners of a partnership that states the rights and the responsibilities of the partners.

Artisan's Lien A common law possessory security interest arising out of the improvement of property by one skilled in some mechanical art or craft; the lien entitles the improver of the property to retain possession in order to secure the agreed-on price or the value of the work performed.

Assault An intentional tort that prohibits any attempt or offer to cause harmful or offensive contact with another if it results in a well-grounded apprehension of imminent battery in the mind of the threatened person.

Assent To give or express one's concurrence or approval of something done.

Assignable Capable of being lawfully assigned or transferred; transferable; negotiable. Also, capable of being specified or pointed out as an assignable error.

Assignee A person to whom an assignment is made.

Assignment   A transfer of property or some right or interest.

Assignment of Partnership Interest   A partner's voluntary transfer of her partnership interest to the partner's personal creditor, giving the creditor the right to receive the partner's share of partnership profits.

Assignor   The maker of an assignment.

Assumption of Risk   A traditional defense to negligence liability based on the argument that the plaintiff voluntarily exposed himself to a known danger created by the defendant's negligence.

Assurance   To provide confidence or to inform positively.

Attachment   In general, the process of taking a person's property under an appropriate judicial order by an appropriate officer of the court. Used for a variety of purposes, including the acquisition of jurisdiction over the property seized and the securing of property that may be used to satisfy a debt.

Attest   To bear witness to; to affirm; to be true or genuine.

Attorney-in-Fact   An agent who is given express, written authorization by his principal to do a particular act or series of acts on behalf of the principal.

At Will   See *Employment at Will.*

Audit Committee   In corporation law, a committee of the board that recommends and supervises the public accountant who audits the corporation's financial records.

Authentication   Such official attestation of a written instrument as will render it legally admissible in evidence.

Authority   In agency law, an agent's ability to affect his principal's legal relations with third parties. Also used to refer to an actor's legal power or ability to do something. In addition, sometimes used to refer to a statute, case, or other legal source that justifies a particular result.

Authorized Shares   Shares that a corporation is empowered to issue by its articles of incorporation.

Automatic Stay   Under the Bankruptcy Act, the suspension of all litigation against the debtor and his property, which is triggered by the filing of a bankruptcy petition.

Averment   A positive statement of fact made in a pleading.

Avoid   To nullify a contractual obligation.

B

Bad Faith   A person's actual intent to mislead or deceive another; an intent to take an unfair and unethical advantage of another.

Bailee   The person to whom a bailment is made.

Bailment   The transfer of personal property by its owner to another person with the understanding that the property will be returned to the owner in the future.

Bailor   The owner of bailed property; the one who delivers personal property to another to be held in bailment.

Bankruptcy   The state of a person who is unable to pay his or her debts without respect to time; one whose liabilities exceed his or her assets.

Bar   As a collective noun, those persons who are admitted to practice law, members of the bar. The court itself. A plea or defense asserted by a defendant that is sufficient to destroy a plaintiff's action.

Battery   An intentional tort that prohibits the harmful or offensive touching of another without his consent.

Bearer   A person in possession of a negotiable instrument that is payable to him, his order, or to whoever is in possession of the instrument.

Bench   Generally used as a synonym for the term *court* or the judges of a court.

Beneficiary   The person for whose benefit an insurance policy, trust, will, or contract is established. In the case of a contract, the beneficiary is called a *third party beneficiary.*

Bequest   In a will, a gift of personal property or money. Also called a *legacy.*

Bid   To make an offer at an auction or at a judicial sale. As a noun, an offer.

Bilateral Contract   A contract in which the promise of one of the parties forms the consideration for the promise of the other; a contract formed by an offer requiring a reciprocal promise.

Bill of Exchange   An unconditional order in writing by one person to another, signed by the person giving it, requiring the person to whom it is addressed to pay on demand or at a fixed or determinable future time a sum certain in money to order or to bearer.

Bill of Lading   A written acknowledgment of the receipt of goods to be transported to a designated place and delivery to a named person or to his or her order.

Bill of Sale   A written agreement by which one person assigns or transfers interests or rights in personal property to another.

Binder   Also called a *binding slip.* A brief memorandum or agreement issued by an insurer as a temporary policy for the convenience of all the parties, constituting a present insurance in the amount specified, to continue in force until the execution of a formal policy.

Blue Sky Laws   The popular name for state statutes that regulate securities transactions.

Bona Fide   Made honestly and in good faith; genuine.

Bona Fide Purchaser   An innocent buyer for valuable consideration who purchases goods without notice of any defects in the title of the goods acquired.

Bond   A long-term debt security that is secured by collateral.

Bonus Shares   Also called *bonus stock*. Shares issued for no lawful consideration. See *Discount Shares* and *Watered Shares*.

Breaking Bulk   The division or separation of the contents of a package or container.

Brief   A statement of a party's case or legal arguments, usually prepared by an attorney. Often used to support some of the motions described in Chapter 2, and also used to make legal arguments before appellate courts. Also, an abridgement of a reported case.

Broker   An agent who bargains or carries on negotiations in behalf of the principal as an intermediary between the latter and third persons in transacting business relative to the acquisition of contractual rights, or to the sale or purchase of property the custody of which is not intrusted to him or her for the purpose of discharging the agency.

Bulk Transfer   The sale or transfer of a major part of the stock of goods of a merchant at one time and not in the ordinary course of business.

Burden of Proof   Used to refer both to the necessity or obligation of proving the facts needed to support a party's claim, and the persuasiveness of the evidence used to do so. Regarding the second sense of the term, the usual burden of proof in a civil case is a preponderance of the evidence; in a criminal case, it is proof beyond a reasonable doubt.

Business Judgment Rule   A rule protecting business managers from liability for making bad decisions when they have acted prudently and in good faith.

Buy-and-Sell Agreement   A share transfer restriction compelling a shareholder to sell his shares to the other shareholders or the corporation and obligating the other shareholders or the corporation to buy the shareholder's shares.

Buyer in Ordinary Course of Business   A person who, in good faith and without knowledge that the sale to him is in violation of a third party's ownership rights or security interest in the goods, buys in ordinary course from a person who is in the business of selling goods of that kind.

Bylaws   In corporation law, a document that supplements the articles of incorporation and contains less important rights, powers, and responsibilities of a corporation and its shareholders, officers, and directors.

C

C&F   The price of the goods includes the cost of the goods plus the freight to the named destination.

Call   See *Redemption*. Also, a type of option permitting a person to buy a fixed number of securities at a fixed price at a specified time. See *Put*.

Canceled Shares   Previously outstanding shares repurchased by a corporation and canceled by it; such shares no longer exist.

Cancellation   The act of crossing out a writing. The operation of destroying a written instrument.

Capacity   The ability to incur legal obligations and acquire legal rights.

Capital   Contributions of money and other property to a business made by the owners of the business.

Capital Stock   See *Stated Capital*.

Capital Surplus   Also called *additional paid capital*. A balance sheet account; the portion of shareholders' contributions exceeding the par or stated value of shares.

Case Law   The law extracted from decided cases.

Cashier's Check   A draft (including a check) drawn by a bank on itself and accepted by the act of issuance.

Causa Mortis   In contemplation of approaching death.

Cause of Action   A legal rule giving the plaintiff the right to obtain some legal relief once certain factual elements are proven. Often used synonymously with the terms *claim* or *theory of recovery*.

Caveat Emptor   Let the buyer beware.

Caveat Venditor   Let the seller beware.

Certificate of Deposit   An acknowledgment by a bank of the receipt of money with an engagement to pay it back.

Certificate of Limited Partnership   A document that must be filed with a secretary of state to create a limited partnership.

Certification   The return of a writ; a formal attestation of a matter of fact; the appropriate marking of a certified check.

Certified Check   A check that has been accepted by the drawee bank and has been so marked or certified that it indicates such acceptance.

Chancellor   A judge of a court of chancery.

Chancery   Equity or a court of equity.

Charge   The legal instructions that a judge gives a jury before the jury begins its deliberations. In the prosecution of a crime, to formally accuse the offender or charge him with the crime.

Charging Order   A court's order granting rights in a partner's partnership interest to a personal creditor of the partner; a creditor with a charging order is entitled to the partner's share of partnership profits.

Charter   An instrument or authority from the sovereign power bestowing the right or power to do business under the corporate form of organization. Also, the organic law of a city or town, and representing a portion of the statute law of the state.

Chattel   An article of tangible property other than land.

Chattel Mortgage   An instrument whereby the owner of chattels transfers the title to such property to another as security for the performance of an obligation subject to be defeated on the performance of the obligation. Under the UCC, called merely a *security interest.*

Chattel Paper   Written documents that evidence both an obligation to pay money and a security interest in particular goods.

Check   A written order on a bank or banker payable on demand to the person named or his order or bearer and drawn by virtue of credits due the drawer from the bank created by money deposited with the bank.

Chose in Action   A personal right not reduced to possession but recoverable by a suit at law.

CIF   An abbreviation for cost, freight, and insurance, used in mercantile transactions, especially in import transactions.

Citation of Authorities   The reference to legal authorities such as reported cases or treatises to support propositions advanced.

Civil Action   An action brought to enforce a civil right; in contrast to a criminal action.

Civil Law   The body of law applicable to lawsuits involving two private parties.

Class Action   An action brought on behalf of the plaintiff and others similarly situated.

Close Corporation   A corporation with few shareholders generally having a close personal relationship to each other and participating in the management of the business.

COD   Cash on delivery. When goods are delivered to a carrier for a cash on delivery shipment, the carrier must not deliver without receiving payment of the amount due.

Code   A system of law; a systematic and complete body of law.

Codicil   Some addition to or qualification of one's last will and testament.

Collateral   Property put up to secure the performance of a promise, so that if the promisor fails to perform as promised, the creditor may look to the property to make him whole.

Collateral Attack   An attempt to impeach a decree, a judgment, or other official act in a proceeding that has not been instituted for the express purpose of correcting or annulling or modifying the decree, judgment, or official act.

Collateral Contract   A contract in which one person agrees to pay the debt of another if the principal debtor fails to pay. See *Guaranty.*

Comaker   A person who with another or others signs a negotiable instrument on its face and thereby becomes primarily liable for its payment.

Commercial Impracticability   The standards used by the UCC, replacing the common law doctrine of impossibility, to define when a party is relieved of his or her contract obligations because of the occurrence of unforeseeable, external events beyond his or her control.

Commercial Law   The law that relates to the rights of property and persons engaged in trade or commerce.

Commercial Paper   Negotiable paper such as promissory notes, drafts, and checks that provides for the payment of money and can readily be transferred to other parties.

Commercial Unit   Under the UCC, any unit of goods that is treated by commercial usage as a single whole. It may, for example, be a single article or a set of articles such as a dozen, bale, gross, or carload.

Common Area   In landlord-tenant law, an area over which the landlord retains control but which is often used by or for the benefit of tenants. For example, hallways in an apartment building.

Common Carrier   One who undertakes, for hire or reward, to transport the goods of such of the public as choose to employ him.

Common Law   The law that is made and applied by judges in cases not governed by other forms of positive law.

Common Shareholders   Shareholders who claim the residual profits and assets of a corporation, and usually have the exclusive power and right to elect the directors of the corporation.

Comparative Fault   Often used synonymously with *comparative negligence.* But also sometimes used to refer to a defense that operates like comparative negligence but considers the plaintiff's and the defendant's overall fault rather than either's negligence alone.

Comparative Negligence   The contemporary replacement for the traditional doctrine of contributory negligence. The basic idea is that damages are apportioned between the parties to a negligence action in proportion to their relative fault. The details vary from state to state.

Compensatory Damages   See *Damages, Compensatory.*

Complaint   The pleading in a civil case in which the plaintiff states his claim and requests relief.

Composition with Creditors   An agreement between creditors and their common debtor and between themselves whereby the creditors agree to accept the sum or security stipulated in full payment of their claims.

Concealment   In contract law, taking active steps to prevent another from learning the truth.

Concurrent   Running with; simultaneously with. The word is used in different senses. In contracts, concurrent conditions are conditions that must be performed simultaneously by the mutual acts required by each of the parties.

Condemn   To appropriate land for public use. To adjudge a person guilty; to pass sentence on a person convicted of a crime.

Condition   In contract law, a future, uncertain event that creates or extinguishes a duty of performance; a provision or clause in a contract that operates to suspend or rescind a party's duty to perform.

Conditional Acceptance   An acceptance of a bill of exchange containing some qualification limiting or altering the acceptor's liability on the bill.

Conditional Gift   A gift that does not become absolute or complete until the occurrence of some express or implied condition.

Conditional Sale   The term is most frequently applied to a sale in which the seller reserves the title to the goods, although the possession is delivered to the buyer, until the purchase price is paid in full.

Condition Precedent   A condition that operates to give rise to a contracting party's duty to perform.

Condition Subsequent   A condition that operates to relieve or discharge one from his obligation under a contract.

Confession of Judgment   An entry of judgment on the admission or confession of the debtor without the formality, time, or expense involved in an ordinary proceeding.

Confirmed Letter of Credit   See *Letter of Credit, Confirmed.*

Confusion   The inseparable intermixture of property belonging to different owners.

Consent Decree or **Consent Order**   Used to refer to the order courts or administrative agencies issue when approving the settlement of a lawsuit or administrative action against some party.

Consent Restraint   A security transfer restriction requiring a shareholder to obtain the consent of the corporation or its shareholders prior to the shareholder's sale of her shares.

Consequential Damages   See *Damages, Consequential.*

Conservator (of an incompetent person)   A person appointed by a court to take care of and oversee the person and estate of an incompetent person.

Consideration   In contract law, a basic requirement for an enforceable agreement under traditional contract principles, defined in this text as legal value, bargained for and given in exchange for an act or promise. In corporation law, cash or property contributed to a corporation in exchange for shares, or a promise to contribute such cash or property.

Consignee   A person to whom goods are consigned, shipped, or otherwise transmitted, either for sale or for safekeeping.

Consignment   A bailment for sale. The consignee does not undertake the absolute obligation to sell or pay for the goods.

Consignor   One who sends goods to another on consignment. A shipper or transmitter of goods.

Conspicuous   Noticeable by a reasonable person, such as a term or clause in a contract that is in bold print, in capitals, or a contrasting color or type style.

Constructive Eviction   In landlord-tenant law, a breach of duty by the landlord that makes the premises uninhabitable or otherwise deprives the tenant of the benefit of the lease and gives rise to the tenant's right to vacate the property and terminate the lease.

Construe   To read a statute or document for the purpose of ascertaining its meaning and effect, but in doing so the law must be regarded.

Contempt   Conduct in the presence of a legislative or judicial body tending to disturb its proceedings or impair the respect due to its authority, or a disobedience to the rules or orders of such a body, which interferes with the due administration of law.

Continuation Statement   A document, usually a multicopy form, filed in a public office to indicate the continuing viability of a financing statement. See *Financing Statement.*

Contra   Otherwise; disagreeing with; contrary to.

Contract   A legally enforceable promise or set of promises.

Contract of Adhesion   A contract in which a stronger party is able to dictate terms to a weaker party, leaving the weaker party no practical choice but to adhere to the terms. If the stronger party has exploited its bargaining power to achieve unfair terms, the contract is against public policy.

Contribution　In business organization law, the cash or property contributed to a business by its owners.

Contributory Negligence　A traditional defense to negligence liability based on the plaintiff's failure to exercise reasonable care for his own safety.

Conversion　Any distinct act of dominion wrongfully exerted over another's personal property in denial of or inconsistent with his rights therein. That tort committed by a person who deals with chattels not belonging to him in a manner that is inconsistent with the ownership of the lawful owner.

Convertible Securities　Securities giving their holders the power to exchange those securities for other securities without paying any additional consideration.

Conveyance　A written instrument transferring the title to land or some interest therein from one person to another.

Copartnership　A partnership.

Copyright　A set of exclusive rights, protected by federal law, pertaining to certain creative works such as books, musical compositions, computer programs, works of art, and so forth. The rights are: (1) to reproduce the work in question, (2) to prepare derivative works based on it, (3) to sell or otherwise distribute it, and (4) to perform or display it publicly.

Corporation　A form of business organization that is owned by owners, called shareholders, who have no inherent right to manage the business, and is managed by a board of directors that is elected by the shareholders.

Corporation by Estoppel　A doctrine that prevents persons from denying that a corporation exists when the persons hold themselves out as representing a corporation or believe themselves to be dealing with a corporation.

Corporeal　Possessing physical substance; tangible; perceptible to the senses.

Counterclaim　A legal claim made in response to the plaintiff's initial claim in a civil suit. Unlike a defense, the counterclaim is the defendant's affirmative attempt to obtain legal relief; in effect, it states a cause of action entitling the defendant to such relief. Often, the counterclaim must arise out of the occurrence that forms the basis for the plaintiff's claim.

Counteroffer　A cross-offer made by the offeree to the offeror.

Countertrade　A buyer's purchase of the seller's goods in exchange for the seller's agreement to purchase goods of the buyer or other person; usually required as a condition to selling goods to a foreign trade corporation.

Course of Dealing　A sequence of previous conduct between the parties to a transaction that is fairly to be regarded as establishing a common basis for interpreting their contract.

Covenant　A contract; a promise.

Cover　To obtain substitute or equivalent goods.

Credible　As applied to a witness, competent.

Creditor　A person to whom a debt or legal obligation is owed, and who has the right to enforce payment of that debt or obligation.

Crime　An act prohibited by the state; a public wrong.

Criminal Law　The body of law setting out public wrongs that the government attempts to correct by prosecuting wrongdoers.

Culpable　Blameworthy; denotes breach of legal duty but not necessarily criminal conduct.

Cumulative Voting　A procedure for voting for directors that permits a shareholder to multiply the number of shares he owns by the number of directors to be elected and to cast the resulting total of votes for one or more directors. See *Straight Voting*.

Curtesy　At common law, a husband's right in property owned by his wife during her life.

Custody　The bare control or care of a thing as distinguished from the possession of it.

Cy Pres　As near as possible. In the law of trusts, a doctrine applied to prevent a charitable trust from failing when the application of trust property to the charitable beneficiary designated by the settlor becomes illegal or impossible to carry out; in such a case, cy pres allows the court to redirect the distribution of trust property for some purpose that is as near as possible to the settlor's general charitable intent.

D

Damages　The sum of money recoverable by a plaintiff who has received a judgment in a civil case.

　Compensatory　Damages that will compensate a party for direct losses due to an injury suffered.

　Consequential　Damages that do not flow directly and immediately from an act but rather flow from the results of the act; damages that are indirect consequences of a breach of contract or certain other legal wrongs. Examples include personal injury, damage to property, and lost profits.

　Incidental　Collateral damages that result from a breach of contract, including all reasonable expenses that are incurred because of the breach; damages that compensate a person injured by a breach of contract for reasonable costs he incurs in an attempt to avoid further loss.

Liquidated Damages made certain by the prior agreement of the parties.

Nominal Damages that are recoverable when a legal right is to be vindicated against an invasion that has produced no actual present loss.

Punitive Damages designed to punish flagrant wrongdoers and to deter them and others from engaging in similar conduct in the future.

Special Actual damages that would not necessarily but because of special circumstances do in fact flow from an injury.

Treble Three times provable damages, as may be granted to private parties bringing an action under the antitrust laws.

Date of Issue As applied to notes, bonds, and so on of a series, the arbitrary date fixed as the beginning of the term for which they run, without reference to the precise time when convenience or the state of the market may permit their sale or delivery.

D/B/A Doing business as; indicates the use of a trade name.

Deal To engage in transactions of any kind, to do business with.

Debenture A long-term, unsecured debt security.

Debtor A person who is under a legal obligation to pay a sum of money to another (the creditor).

Decedent A person who has died.

Deceit A tort involving intentional misrepresentation or cheating by means of some device.

Decision The judgment of a court; the opinion merely represents the reasons for that judgment.

Declaratory Judgment One that expresses the opinion of a court on a question of law without ordering anything to be done.

Decree An order or sentence of a court of equity determining some right or adjudicating some matter affecting the merits of the cause.

Deed A writing, sealed and delivered by the parties; an instrument conveying real property.

Deed of Trust A three-party instrument used to create a security interest in real property in which the legal title to the real property is placed in one or more trustees to secure the repayment of a sum of money or the performance of other conditions.

De Facto In fact, actual. Often used in contrast to *de jure* to refer to a real state of affairs.

De Facto Corporation A corporation that has complied substantially with the mandatory conditions precedent to incorporation, taken as a whole.

Defalcation The word includes both embezzlement and misappropriation and is a broader term than either.

Defamation An intentional tort that prohibits the publication of false and defamatory statements concerning another.

Default Fault; neglect; omission; the failure of a party to an action to appear when properly served with process; the failure to perform a duty or obligation; the failure of a person to pay money when due or when lawfully demanded.

Defeasible Regarding title to property, capable of being defeated. A title to property that is open to attack or that may be defeated by the performance of some act.

Defend To oppose a claim or action; to plead in defense of an action; to contest an action suit or proceeding.

Defendant The party who is sued in a civil case, or the party who is prosecuted in a criminal case.

Defendant in Error Any of the parties in whose favor a judgment was rendered that the losing party seeks to have reversed or modified by writ of error and whom he names as adverse parties.

Defense A rule of law entitling the defendant to a judgment in his favor even if the plaintiff proves all elements of his claim or cause of action.

Deficiency That part of a debt that a mortgage was made to secure, not realized by the liquidation of the mortgaged property. Something which is lacking.

Defraud To deprive another of a right by deception or artifice.

De Jure According to the law; legitimate; by legal right.

De Jure Corporation A corporation that has complied substantially with each of the mandatory conditions precedent to incorporation.

Delegation In constitutional law and administrative law, a process whereby a legislature effectively hands over some of its legislative power to an administrative agency that it has created, thus giving the agency power to make law within the limits set by the legislature. In contract law, a transaction whereby a person who owes a legal duty to perform under a contract appoints someone else to carry out his performance.

Deliver To surrender property to another person.

Demand A claim; a legal obligation; a request to perform an alleged obligation; a written statement of a claim. In corporation law, a request that the board of directors sue a person who has harmed the corporation; a prerequisite to a shareholder derivative suit.

Demurrer   A civil motion that attacks the plaintiff's complaint by assuming the truth of the facts stated in the complaint for purposes of the motion, and by arguing that even if these facts are true, there is no rule of law entitling the plaintiff to recovery. Roughly similar to the motion to dismiss for failure to state a claim on which relief can be granted.

De Novo   Anew; over again; a second time. A trial de novo, for example, is a new trial in which the entire case is retried.

Deposition   A form of discovery consisting of the oral examination of a party or a party's witness by the other party's attorney.

Deputy   A person subordinate to a public officer whose business and object is to perform the duties of the principal.

Derivative Suit   Also called *derivative action*. A suit to enforce a corporate right of action brought on behalf of a corporation by one or more of its shareholders.

Descent   Hereditary succession. It is the title whereby, upon the death of an ancestor, the heir acquires the ancestor's estate under state law.

Detriment   Any act or forbearance by a promisee. A loss or harm suffered in person or property.

Devise   In a will, a gift of real property.

Dictum   Language in a judicial opinion that is not necessary for the decision of the case and that, while perhaps persuasive, does not bind subsequent courts. Distinguished from *holding*.

Directed Verdict   A verdict issued by a judge who has, in effect, taken the case away from the jury by directing a verdict for one party. Usually, the motion for a directed verdict is made at trial by one party after the other party has finished presenting his evidence.

Disaffirm   In contract law, a party's exercise of his power to avoid a contract entered before the party reached the age of majority; a minor's cancellation of his contract.

Discharge   Release from liability.

Discharge in Bankruptcy   An order or decree rendered by a court in bankruptcy proceedings, the effect of which is to satisfy all debts provable against the estate of the bankrupt as of the time when the bankruptcy proceedings were initiated.

Disclaimer   A term in a contract whereby a party attempts to relieve itself of some potential liability associated with the contract. The most common example is the seller's attempt to disclaim liability for defects in goods that it sells.

Discount   A loan on an evidence of debt, where the compensation for the use of the money until the maturity of the debt is deducted from the principal and retained by the lender at the time of making the loan.

Discount Shares   Also called *discount stock*. Shares issued for less than their par value or stated value. See *Bonus Shares* and *Watered Shares*.

Discovery   A process of information-gathering that takes place before a civil trial. See *Deposition* and *Interrogatory*.

Dishonor   The failure to pay or accept a negotiable instrument that has been properly presented.

Dismiss   To order a cause, motion, or prosecution to be discontinued or quashed.

Dissolution   In partnership law, the change in the relation of the partners caused by any partner ceasing to be associated with the carrying on of the business.

Distribution   In business organization law, a business's gratuitous transfer of its assets to the owners of the business. Includes cash and property dividends and redemptions.

Divided Court   A court is so described when there has been a division of opinion between its members on a matter that has been submitted to it for decision.

Dividends, Cash or Property   A corporation's distribution of a portion of its assets to its shareholders, usually corresponding to current or historical corporate profits; unlike a redemption, it is not accompanied by a repurchase of shares.

Dividends, Share   Also called *stock dividends*. A corporation's pro rata issuance of shares to existing shareholders for no consideration.

Documents of Title   A classification of personal property that includes bills of lading, warehouse receipts, dock warrants, and dock receipts.

Domain   The ownership of land; immediate or absolute ownership. The public lands of a state are frequently termed the *public domain*.

Domicile   A place where a person lives or has his home; in a strict legal sense, the place where he has his true, fixed, permanent home and principal establishment, and to which place he has, whenever he is absent, the intention of returning.

Donee   A person to whom a gift is made.

Donor   A person who makes a gift.

Double Jeopardy Clause   A constitutional provision designed to protect criminal defendants from multiple prosecutions for the same offense.

Dower   The legal right or interest that a wife has in her husband's real estate by virtue of their marriage.

Draft   A written order drawn on one person by another, requesting him to pay money to a designated third person.

Drawee   A person on whom a draft is drawn by the drawer.

Drawer   The maker of a draft.

Due Bill   An acknowledgment of a debt in writing, not made payable to order.

Dummy   One posing or represented as acting for himself, but in reality acting for another. A tool or "straw man" for the real parties in interest.

Dumping   The selling of goods by a seller in a foreign nation at unfairly low prices.

Durable Power of Attorney   A power of attorney that is not affected by the principal's incapacity. See *Power of Attorney* and *Attorney-in-Fact*.

Durable Power of Attorney for Health Care   A durable power of attorney in which the principal specifically gives the attorney-in-fact the authority to make health care decisions for her in the event that the principal should become incompetent. Also called *health care representative*.

Duress   Overpowering of the will of a person by force or fear.

E

Earned Surplus   Also called *retained earnings*. A balance sheet account; a corporation's profits that have not been distributed to shareholders.

Earnest Money   Something given as part of the purchase price to bind the bargain.

Easement   The right to make certain uses of another person's property or to prevent another person from making certain uses of his own property.

Edict   A command or prohibition promulgated by a sovereign and having the effect of law.

E.g.   For example.

Ejectment   By statute in some states, an action to recover the immediate possession of real property.

Eleemosynary Corporation   A corporation created for a charitable purpose or for charitable purposes.

Emancipate   To release; to set free. In contract law, a parent's waiver of his rights to control and receive the services of his minor child.

Embezzlement   A statutory offense consisting of the fraudulent conversion of another's personal property by one to whom it has been intrusted, with the intention of depriving the owner thereof, the gist of the offense being usually the violation of relations of a fiduciary character.

Eminent Domain   A governmental power whereby the government can take or condemn private property for a public purpose on the payment of just compensation.

Employment at Will   A rule stating that if an employment is not for a definite time period, either party may terminate the employment without liability at any time and for any reason.

Enabling Legislation   The statute by which a legislative body creates an administrative agency.

En Banc (in Banc)   By all the judges of a court, with all the judges of a court sitting.

Encumbrance   A right in a third person that diminishes the value of the land but is consistent with the passing of ownership of the land by deed.

Endorsement   See *Indorsement*.

Entity Theory   In partnership law, the view that a partnership is a legal entity distinct from the partners who own it. See *Aggregate Theory*.

Entry   Recordation; noting in a record; going on land; taking actual possession of land.

Environmental Impact Statement   A document that the National Environmental Policy Act requires federal agencies to prepare in connection with any legislative proposals or proposed actions that will significantly affect the environment.

Equity   A system of justice that developed in England separate from the common law courts. Few states in the United States still maintain separate equity courts, though most apply equity principles and procedures when remedies derived from the equity courts are sought. A broader meaning denotes fairness and justice. In business organization law, the capital contributions of owners plus profits that have not been distributed to the owners; stated capital plus capital surplus plus earned surplus.

Equity of Redemption   The right of a mortgagee to discharge the mortgage when due and to have title to the mortgaged property free and clear of the mortgage debt.

Error   A mistake of law or fact; a mistake of the court in the trial of an action.

Escheat   The reversion of land to the state in the event that a decedent dies leaving no heirs.

Estate   An interest in land. Property owned by a decedent at the time of his death.

Estop   To bar or stop.

Estoppel   That state of affairs that arises when one is forbidden by law from alleging or denying a fact because of his previous action or inaction.

Et Al.   And another or and others. An abbreviation for the Latin *et alius*, meaning and another; also of *et alii*, meaning and others.

Eviction   Depriving the tenant of the possession of leased premises.

Evidence   That which makes clear or ascertains the truth of the fact or point in issue either on the one side or the other; those rules of law whereby we determine what testimony is to be admitted and what rejected in each case and what is the weight to be given to the testimony admitted.

Exception   An objection; a reservation; a contradiction.

Exclusionary Rule   The rule that bars the admissibility in criminal proceedings of evidence seized in violation of the Fourth Amendment's prohibition against unreasonable searches and seizures.

Exculpatory Clause   A clause in a contract or trust instrument that excuses a party from some duty.

Executed   When applied to written instruments, synonymous with the word *signed*; more frequently, it means everything has been done to complete the transaction; that is, the instrument has been signed, sealed, and delivered. An executed contract is one in which the object of the contract is performed.

Execution   A process of enforcing a judgment, usually by having an appropriate officer seize property of the defendant and sell it at a judicial sale. The final consummation of a contract or other instrument, including completion of all the formalities needed to make it binding.

Executive Order   A legal rule issued by a chief executive (e.g., the president or a state governor), usually pursuant to a delegation of power from the legislature.

Executor   The personal representative appointed to administer the estate of a person who died leaving a valid will.

Executory   Not yet executed; not yet fully performed, completed, fulfilled, or carried out; to be performed wholly or in part.

Exemption   A release from some burden, duty, or obligation; a grace; a favor; an immunity; taken out from under the general rule, not to be like others who are not exempt.

Exhibit   A copy of a written instrument on which a pleading is founded, annexed to the pleading and by reference made a part of it. Any paper or thing offered in evidence and marked for identification.

Ex Post Facto   After the fact. The U.S. Constitution prohibits ex post facto criminal laws, meaning those that criminalize behavior that was legal when committed.

Express Warranty   A warranty made in words, either oral or written.

Expropriation   A government's taking of a business's assets, such as a manufacturing facility, usually without just compensation.

Ex Ship   A shipping term that does not specify a particular ship for transportation of goods but does not place the expense and risk of transportation on the seller until the goods are unloaded from whatever ship is used.

F

Face Value   The nominal or par value of an instrument as expressed on its face; in the case of a bond, this is the amount really due, including interest.

Factor   An agent who is employed to sell goods for a principal, usually in his own name, and who is given possession of the goods.

False Imprisonment   An intentional tort that prohibits the unlawful confinement of another for an appreciable time without his consent.

FAS   An abbreviation for the expression free alongside steamer.

Federal Supremacy   The ability of federal laws to defeat inconsistent state laws in case they conflict.

Fee Simple Absolute   The highest form of land ownership, which gives the owner the right to possess and use the land for an unlimited period of time, subject only to governmental or private restrictions, and unconditional power to dispose of the property during his lifetime or upon his death.

Felony   As a general rule, all crimes punishable by death or by imprisonment in a state prison.

Fiction   An assumption made by the law that something is true that is or may be false.

Fiduciary   One who holds goods in trust for another or one who holds a position of trust and confidence.

Field Warehousing   A method of protecting a security interest in the inventory of a debtor whereby the creditor or his agent retains the physical custody of the debtor's inventory, which is released to the debtor as he complies with the underlying security agreement.

Financing Statement   A document, usually a multi-copy form, filed in a public office serving as constructive notice to the world that a creditor claims a security interest in collateral that belongs to a certain named debtor.

Firm Offer   Under the Uniform Commercial Code, a signed, written offer by a merchant containing assurances that it will be held open, and which is not revocable for the time stated in the offer, or for a reasonable time if no such time is stated.

Fixture   A thing that was originally personal property and that has been actually or constructively affixed to the soil itself or to some structure legally a part of the land.

FOB   An abbreviation of free on board.

Force Majeure Clause   A contract provision, commonly encountered in international agreements for the sale of goods, that excuses nonperformance that results from conditions beyond the parties' control.

Foreclosure   To terminate the rights of the mortgagor/owner of property.

Foreign Corporation   A corporation incorporated in one state doing business in another state. See *Alien Corporation.*

Foreign Trade Corporation   A corporation in a NME nation that is empowered by the government to conduct the whole business of exporting or importing a particular product.

Forwarder   A person who, having no interest in goods and no ownership or interest in the means of their carriage, undertakes, for hire, to forward them by a safe carrier to their destination.

Franchise   A special privilege conferred by government on individuals, and which does not belong to the citizens of a country generally, of common right. Also a contractual relationship establishing a means of marketing goods or services giving certain elements of control to the supplier (franchisor) in return for the right of the franchisee to use the supplier's tradename or trademark, usually in a specific marketing area.

Fraud   Misrepresentation made with knowledge of its falsity and intent to deceive. See *Misrepresentation.*

Freeze-Out   In corporation law, a type of oppression by which only minority shareholders are forced to sell their shares.

Fungible Goods   Goods any unit of which is from its nature or by mercantile custom treated as the equivalent of any other unit.

Future Advances   Money or other value provided to a debtor by a creditor subsequent to the time a security interest in the debtor's collateral is taken by that creditor.

Futures   Contracts for the sale and future delivery of stocks or commodities, wherein either party may waive delivery, and receive or pay, as the case may be, the difference in market price at the time set for delivery.

G

Garnishee   Used as a noun, the third party who is subjected to the process of garnishment. Used as a verb, to institute garnishment proceedings; to cause a garnishment to be levied on the garnishee.

Garnishment   A statutory proceeding whereby money, property, wages, or credits of the defendant that are in the hands of a third party are seized to satisfy a judgment or legally valid claim that the plaintiff has against the defendant.

General Partnership   See *Partnership.*

Gift   A voluntary transfer of property for which the donor receives no consideration in return.

Good Faith   Honesty in fact; an honest intention to abstain from taking an unfair advantage of another.

Goodwill   The value of a business due to expected continued public patronage of the business.

Grantee   A person to whom a grant is made.

Grantor   A person who makes a grant.

Gravamen   The gist, essence, or central point of a legal claim or argument.

Grey Market Goods   Goods lawfully bearing trademarks or using patented or copyrighted material, but imported into a foreign market without the authorization of the owner of the trademark, patent, or copyright.

Guarantor   A person who promises to perform the same obligation as another person (called the *principal*), upon the principal's default.

Guaranty   An undertaking by one person to be answerable for the payment of some debt, or the due performance of some contract or duty by another person, who remains liable to pay or perform the same.

Guardian   A person (in some rare cases, a corporation) to whom the law has entrusted the custody and control of the person, or estate, or both, of an incompetent person.

H

Habeas Corpus   Any of several common law writs having as their object to bring a party before the court or judge. The only issue it presents is whether the prisoner is restrained of his liberty by due process.

Hearing   The supporting of one's contentions by argument and if need be, by proof.

Hedging   A market transaction in which a party buys a certain quantity of a given commodity at the price current on the date of the purchase and sells an equal quantity of the same commodity for future delivery for the purpose of getting protection against loss due to fluctuation in the market.

Heirs   Those persons appointed by law to succeed to the estate of a decedent who has died without leaving a valid will.

Holder   A person in possession of a document of title or an instrument payable or indorsed to him, his order, or to bearer.

Holder in Due Course   A person who is a holder of a negotiable instrument who took the instrument for value, in good faith, without notice that it is overdue or has been dishonored or that there is any uncured default with respect to payment of another instrument issued as part of the same series, without notice that the instrument contains an unauthorized signature or has been altered, without notice of any claim of a property or possessory interest in it, and without notice that any party has any defense against it or claim in recoupment to it.

Holding   Language in a judicial opinion that is necessary for the decision the court reached and that is said to be binding on subsequent courts. Distinguished from *dictum.*

Holding Company   A corporation whose purpose or function is to own or otherwise hold the shares of other corporations either for investment or control.

Holographic Will   A will written in the handwriting of the testator.

Homestead   In a legal sense, the real estate occupied as a home and also the right to have it exempt from levy and forced sale. It is the land, not exceeding a prescribed amount, upon which the owner and his family reside, including the house in which they reside as an indispensable part.

I

I.e.   That is.

Illusory   Deceiving or intending to deceive, as by false appearances; fallacious. An illusory promise is a promise that appears to be binding but that in fact does not bind the promisor.

Immunity   A personal favor granted by law, contrary to the general rule.

Impanel   To place the names of the jurors on a panel; to make a list of the names of those persons who have been selected for jury duty; to go through the process of selecting a jury that is to try a cause.

Implied Warranty   A warranty created by operation of law.

Implied Warranty of Habitability   Implied warranty arising in lease or sale of residential real estate that the property will be fit for human habitation.

Impossibility   A doctrine under which a party to a contract is relieved of his or her duty to perform when that performance has become impossible because of the occurrence of an event unforeseen at the time of contracting.

Inalienable   Incapable of being alienated, transferred, or conveyed; nontransferable.

In Camera   In the judge's chambers; in private.

Incapacity   A legal disability, such as infancy or want of authority.

Inception   Initial stage. The word does not refer to a state of actual existence but to a condition of things or circumstances from which the thing may develop.

Inchoate   Imperfect; incipient; not completely formed.

Incidental Damages   See *Damages, Incidental.*

Independent Contractor   A person who contracts with a principal to perform some task according to his own methods, and who is not under the principal's control regarding the physical details of the work. Under the *Restatement (Second) of Agency,* an independent contractor may or may not be an agent.

Indictment   A finding by a grand jury that there is probable cause to believe an accused committed a crime.

Indorsement   Writing on the back of an instrument; the contract whereby the holder of an instrument (such as a draft, check, or note) or a document (such as a warehouse receipt or bill of lading) transfers to another person his right to such instrument and incurs the liabilities incident to the transfer.

Infant   See *Minor.*

Information   A written accusation of crime brought by a public prosecuting officer to a court without the intervention of a grand jury.

Injunction   An equitable remedy whereby the defendant is ordered to perform certain acts or to desist from certain acts.

In Pari Delicto   Equally at fault in tort or crime; in equal fault or guilt.

In Personam   Against a person. For example, in personam jurisdiction.

In Re   In the matter of.

In Rem   Against a thing and not against a person; concerning the condition or status of a thing; for example, in rem jurisdiction.

Inside Information   Confidential information possessed by a person due to his relationship with a business.

Insolvency   In corporation law, the inability of a business to pay its currently maturing obligations.

Instrument   Formal or legal documents in writing, such as contracts, deeds, wills, bonds, leases, and mortgages.

Insurable Interest   Any interest in property such that the owner would experience a benefit from the continued existence of the property or a loss from its destruction.

Inter Alia   Among other things.

Interlocutory   Something not final but deciding only some subsidiary matter raised while a lawsuit is pending.

Interpleader   An equitable remedy applicable where one fears injury from conflicting claims. Where a person does not know which of two or more persons claiming certain property held by him has a right to it, filing a bill of interpleader forces the claimants to litigate the title between themselves.

Interrogatory   Written questions directed to a party, answered in writing, and signed under oath.

Inter Se   Between or among themselves.

Interstate   Between or among two or more states.

Intervening Cause   An intervening force that plays so substantial a role in causing a particular plaintiff's injury that it relieves a negligent defendant of any responsibility for that injury. Also called *superseding cause.*

Intervention   A proceeding by which one not originally made a party to an action or suit is permitted, on his own application, to appear therein and join one of the original parties in maintaining his cause of action or defense, or to assert some cause of action against some or all of the parties to the proceeding as originally instituted.

Inter Vivos   A transaction between living persons.

Intestate   Having died without leaving a valid will.

In Toto   Wholly, completely.

Intrastate   Within a particular state.

Investment Contract   In securities law, a type of security encompassing any contract by which an investor invests in a common enterprise with an expectation of profits solely from the efforts of persons other than the investor.

Invitee   A person who is on private premises for a purpose connected with the business interests of the possessor of those premises, or a member of the public who is lawfully on land open to the public.

Ipso Facto   By the fact itself; by the very fact.

Irrevocable Letter of Credit   See *Letter of Credit, Irrevocable.*

Issue   Lineal descendants such as children and grandchildren. This category of persons includes adopted children.

Issued Shares   A corporation's shares that a corporation has sold to its shareholders. Includes shares repurchased by the corporation and retained as treasury shares, but not shares canceled or returned to unissued status.

Issuer   In securities law, a person who issues or proposes to issue a security; the person whose obligation is represented by a security.

J

Joint and Several Liability   Liability of a group of persons in which the plaintiff may sue any member of the group individually and get a judgment against that person, or may sue all members of the group collectively.

Joint Bank Account   A bank account of two persons so fixed that they shall be joint owners thereof during their mutual lives, and the survivor shall take the whole on the death of other.

Joint Liability   Liability of a group of persons in which, if one of these persons is sued, he can insist that the other liable parties be joined to the suit as codefendants, so that all must be sued collectively.

Jointly   Acting together or in concert or cooperating; holding in common or interdependently, not separately. Persons are jointly bound in a bond or note when both or all must be sued in one action for its enforcement, not either one at the election of the creditor.

Joint Tenancy   An estate held by two or more jointly, with an equal right in all to share in the enjoyments of the land during their lives. An incident of joint tenancy is the right of survivorship.

Joint Venture   A form of business organization identical to a partnership, except that it is engaged in a single project, not carrying on a business.

Judgment   A court's final resolution of a lawsuit or other proceeding submitted to it for decision.

Judgment Lien   The statutory lien on the real property of a judgment debtor that is created by the judgment itself. At common law, a judgment imposes no lien on the real property of the judgment debtor, and to subject the property of the debtor to the judgment, it was necessary to take out a writ called an *elegit.*

Judgment notwithstanding the Verdict   A judgment made by a judge contrary to a prior jury verdict whereby the judge effectively overrules the jury's verdict. Also called the *j.n.o.v.* or the *judgment non obstante veredicto.* Similar to the directed verdict, except that it occurs after the jury has issued its verdict.

Judicial Review   The courts' power to declare the actions of the other branches of government unconstitutional.

Jurisdiction   The power of a court to hear and decide a case.

Jurisprudence   The philosophy of law. Also sometimes used to refer to the collected positive law of some jurisdiction.

Jury   A body of lay persons, selected by lot, or by some other fair and impartial means, to ascertain, under the guidance of the judge, the truth in questions of fact arising either in civil litigation or a criminal process.

K

Kite   To secure the temporary use of money by issuing or negotiating worthless paper and then redeeming such paper with the proceeds of similar paper. The word is also used as a noun, meaning the worthless paper thus employed.

L

Laches   The established doctrine of equity that, apart from any question of statutory limitation, its courts will discourage delay and sloth in the enforcement of rights. Equity demands conscience, good faith, and reasonable diligence.

Land Contract   A conditional agreement for the sale and purchase of real estate in which the legal title to the property is retained by the seller until the purchaser has fulfilled the agreement, usually by completing the payment of the agreed-on purchase price.

Larceny   The unlawful taking and carrying away of personal property with the intent to deprive the owner of his property permanently.

Last Clear Chance   Under traditional tort principles, a doctrine that allowed a contributorily negligent plaintiff to recover despite his failure to exercise reasonable care for his own safety by arguing that the defendant had the superior opportunity (last clear chance) to avoid the harm.

Law Merchant   The custom of merchants, or lex mercatorio, that grew out of the necessity and convenience of business, and that, although different from the general rules of the common law, was engrafted into it and became a part of it. It was founded on the custom and usage of merchants.

Leading Case   The most significant and authoritative case regarded as having settled and determined a point of law. Often, the first case to have done so in a definitive and complete fashion.

Leading Questions   Questions that suggest to the witness the answer desired or those that assume a fact to be proved that is not proved, or that, embodying a material fact, allow the witness to answer by a simple negative or affirmative.

Lease   A contract for the possession and use of land or other property, including goods, on one side, and a recompense of rent or other income on the other; a conveyance to a person for life, or years, or at will in consideration of a return of rent or other recompense.

Legacy   A bequest; a testamentary gift of personal property. Sometimes incorrectly applied to a testamentary gift of real property.

Legal   According to the principles of law; according to the method required by statute; by means of judicial proceedings; not equitable.

Letter of Credit   An instrument containing a request (general or special) to pay to the bearer or person named money, or sell him or her some commodity on credit or give something of value and look to the drawer of the letter for recompense.

> **Advised**   The seller's bank acts as the seller's agent to collect against the letter of credit issued by the buyer's bank.
>
> **Confirmed**   The seller's bank agrees to assume liability on the letter of credit issued by the buyer's bank.
>
> **Irrevocable**   The issuing bank may not revoke the letter of credit issued by the buyer's bank.
>
> **Standby**   The seller's bank promises to pay the buyer if the seller defaults on his contract to deliver conforming goods.

Levy   At common law, a levy on goods consisted of an officer's entering the premises where they were and either leaving an assistant in charge of them or removing them after taking an inventory. Today, courts differ as to what is a valid levy, but by the weight of authority there must be an actual or constructive seizure of the goods. In most states, a levy on land must be made by some unequivocal act of the officer indicating the intention of singling out certain real estate for the satisfaction of the debt.

Libel   The defamation action appropriate to printed or written defamations, or to those that have a physical form.

License   A personal privilege to do some act or series of acts on the land of another, without possessing any ownership interest in the land. A permit or authorization to do something that, without a license, would be unlawful.

Licensee   A person lawfully on land in possession of another for purposes unconnected with the business interests of the possessor.

Lien   In its most extensive meaning, it is a charge on property for the payment or discharge of a debt or duty; a qualified right; a proprietary interest that, in a given case, may be exercised over the property of another.

Life Estate   A property interest that gives a person the right to possess and use property for a time that is measured by his lifetime or that of another person.

Limited Partner   An owner of a limited partnership who has no right to manage the business but who possesses liability limited to his capital contribution to the business.

Limited Partnership A form of business organization that has one or more general partners who manage the business and have unlimited liability for the obligations of the business and one or more limited partners who do not manage and have limited liability.

Liquidated Damages The stipulation by the parties to a contract of the sum of money to be recovered by the aggrieved party in the event of a breach of the contract by the other party.

Liquidated Debt A debt that is due and certain. That is, one that is not the subject of a bona fide dispute either as to its existence or the amount that is owed.

Lis Pendens A pending suit. As applied to the doctrine of lis pendens, it is the jurisdiction, power, or control that courts acquire over property involved in a suit, pending the continuance of the action, and until its final judgment.

Listing Contract A so-called contract whereby an owner of real property employs a broker to procure a purchaser without giving the broker an exclusive right to sell. Under such an agreement, it is generally held that the employment may be terminated by the owner at will, and that a sale of the property by the owner terminates the employment.

Litigant A party to a lawsuit.

Living Will A document executed with specific legal formalities stating a person's preference that heroic life support measures should not be used if there is no hope of the person's recovery.

Long-Arm Statute A state statute that grants to a state's courts broad authority to exercise jurisdiction over out-of-state persons who have contacts with the state.

Looting In corporation law, the transfer of a corporation's assets to its managers or controlling shareholders at less than fair value.

M

Magistrate A word commonly applied to the lower judicial officers such as justices of the peace, police judges, town recorders, and other local judicial functionaries. In a broader sense, a magistrate is a public civil officer invested with some part of the legislative, executive, or judicial power given by the Constitution. The president of the United States is the chief magistrate of the nation.

Maker A person who makes or executes an instrument. The signer of an instrument.

Malfeasance The doing of an act that a person ought not to do at all. It is to be distinguished from misfeas-

ance—the improper doing of an act that a person might lawfully do.

Malicious Prosecution An intentional tort designed to protect against the wrongful initiation of criminal proceedings.

Mandamus We command. It is a command issuing from a competent jurisdiction, in the name of the state or sovereign, directed to some inferior court, officer, corporation, or person, requiring the performance of a particular duty therein specified, which duty results from the official station of the party to whom it is directed, or from operation of law.

Margin A deposit by a buyer in stocks with a seller or a stockbroker, as security to cover fluctuations in the market in reference to stocks that the buyer has purchased, but for which he has not paid. Commodities are also traded on margin.

Marshals Ministerial officers belonging to the executive department of the federal government, who with their deputies have the same powers of executing the laws of the United States in each state as the sheriffs and their deputies in such state may have in executing the laws of that state.

Material Important. In securities law, a fact is material if a reasonable person would consider it important in his decision to purchase shares or to vote shares.

Materialman's Lien A claim created by law for the purpose of securing a priority of payment of the price or value of materials furnished in erecting or repairing a building or other structure.

Mechanic's Lien A claim created by law for the purpose of securing a priority of payment of the price or value of work performed and materials furnished in erecting or repairing a building or other structure; as such, it attaches to the land as well as to the buildings erected therein.

Memorandum A writing.

Mens Rea A guilty mind; criminal intent.

Merchant Under the Uniform Commercial Code, one who regularly deals in goods of the kind sold in the contract at issue, or holds himself out as having special knowledge or skill relevant to such goods, or who makes the sale through an agent who regularly deals in such goods or claims such knowledge or skill.

Merchantable Of good quality and salable, but not necessarily the best. As applied to articles sold, the word requires that the article shall be such as is usually sold in the market, of medium quality, and bringing the average price.

Merger In corporation law, traditionally, a transaction by which one corporation acquires another corporation, with the acquiring corporation being owned by the shareholders of both corporations and the acquired corporation going out of existence. Today, loosely applied to any negotiated acquisition of one corporation by another.

Merger Clause   A contract clause providing that the written contract is the complete expression of the parties' agreement. Also called *integration clause.*

Mining Partnership   A form of business organization used for mining and drilling mineral resources that is identical to a partnership, except that mining partnership interests are freely transferable and the death or bankruptcy of a mining partner does not cause a dissolution.

Minor   A person who has not reached the age at which the law recognizes a general contractual capacity (called *majority*), which is 18 in most states.

Misdemeanor   Any crime that is punishable neither by death nor by imprisonment in a state prison.

Misrepresentation   The assertion of a fact that is not in accord with the truth. A contract can be rescinded on the ground of misrepresentation when the assertion relates to a material fact or is made fraudulently and the other party actually and justifiably relies on the assertion.

Mistrial   An invalid trial due to lack of jurisdiction, error in selection of jurors, or some other fundamental requirement.

Mitigation of Damages   A reduction in the amount of damages due to extenuating circumstances.

Mortgage   A conveyance of property to secure the performance of some obligation, the conveyance to be void on the due performance thereof.

Mortgagee   The creditor to whom property has been mortgaged to secure the performance of an obligation.

Mortgagor   The owner of the property that has been mortgaged or pledged as security for a debt.

Motion to Dismiss   A motion made by the defendant in a civil case to defeat the plaintiff's case, usually after the complaint or all the pleadings have been completed. The most common form of motion to dismiss is the motion to dismiss for failure to state a claim on which relief can be granted, which attacks the legal sufficiency of the plaintiff's complaint. See *Demurrer.*

Motive   The cause or reason that induced a person to commit a crime.

Mutuality   Reciprocal obligations of the parties required to make a contract binding on either party.

N

National Ambient Air Quality Standards   Federally established air pollution standards designed to protect the public health and welfare.

Natural Law   A body of allegedly existing ethical rules or principles that is morally superior to positive law and that prevails over positive law in case of a clash between it and the natural law. See *Positive Law.*

Necessaries   That which is reasonably necessary for a minor's proper and suitable maintenance, in view of the income level and social position of the minor's family.

Negligence   The omission to do something that a reasonable person, guided by those considerations that ordinarily regulate human affairs, would do, or doing something that a prudent and reasonable person would not do.

Negligence Per Se   The doctrine that provides that a conclusive presumption of breach of duty arises when a defendant has violated a statute and thereby caused a harm the statute was designed to prevent to a person the statute was designed to protect.

Negotiable   Capable of being transferred by indorsement or delivery so as to give the holder a right to sue in his or her own name and to avoid certain defenses against the payee.

Negotiable Instrument   An instrument that may be transferred or negotiated, so that the holder may maintain an action thereon in his own name.

Negotiation   The transfer of an instrument in such form that the transferee becomes a holder.

NME   A nonmarket economy; a socialist economy in which a central government owns and controls all significant means of production, thereby setting prices and the levels of production.

Nolo Contendere   A no contest plea by the defendant in a criminal case that has much the same effect as a guilty plea but that cannot be used as an admission of guilt in other legal proceedings.

Nominal Damages   See *Damages, Nominal.*

Non Compos Mentis   Mentally incompetent.

Nonfeasance   In the law of agency, the total omission or failure of an agent to enter on the performance of some distinct duty or undertaking that he or she has agreed with the principal to do.

Non Obstante Veredicto   Notwithstanding the verdict. J.n.o.v. See *Judgment notwithstanding the Verdict.*

No-Par Value Stock   Stock of a corporation having no face or par value.

Novation   A mutual agreement, between all parties concerned, for the discharge of a valid existing obligation by the substitution of a new valid obligation on the part of the debtor or another, or a like agreement for the discharge of a debtor to his creditor by the substitution of a new creditor.

Nudum Pactum A naked promise, a promise for which there is no consideration.

Nuisance That which endangers life or health, gives offense to the senses, violates the laws of decency, or obstructs the reasonable and comfortable use of property.

Nuncupative Will An oral will. Such wills are valid in some states, but only under limited circumstances and to a limited extent.

O

Oath Any form of attestation by which a person signifies that he is bound in conscience to perform an act faithfully and truthfully.

Obiter Dictum That which is said in passing; a rule of law set forth in a court's opinion but not necessary to decide the case. See *Dictum.*

Objection In the trial of a case the formal remonstrance made by counsel to something that has been said or done, in order to obtain the court's ruling thereon.

Obligee A person to whom another is bound by a promise or other obligation; a promisee.

Obligor A person who is bound by a promise or other obligation; a promisor.

Offer A proposal by one person to another that is intended to create legal relations on acceptance by the person to whom it is made.

Offeree A person to whom an offer is made.

Offeror A person who makes an offer.

Opinion The opinion of the court represents merely the reasons for its judgment, while the decision of the court is the judgment itself.

Oppression The officers, directors, or controlling shareholder's isolation of one group of shareholders for disadvantageous treatment to the benefit of another group of shareholders.

Option A separate contract in which an offeror agrees not to revoke her offer for a stated period of time in exchange for some valuable consideration.

Option Agreement A share transfer restriction granting a corporation or its shareholders an option to buy a selling shareholder's shares at a price determined by the agreement.

Ordinance A legislative enactment of a county or an incorporated city or town.

Original Jurisdiction The power to decide a case as a trial court.

Outstanding Shares A corporation's shares currently held by shareholders.

Overdraft The withdrawal from a bank by a depositor of money in excess of the amount of money he or she has on deposit there.

Overdue When an instrument is not paid when due or at maturity.

Overplus That which remains; a balance left over.

Owner's Risk A term employed by common carriers in bills of lading and shipping receipts to signify that the carrier does not assume responsibility for the safety of the goods.

P

Par Par means equal, and par value means a value equal to the face of a bond or a stock certificate.

Parent Corporation A corporation that owns a controlling interest of another corporation, called a *subsidiary corporation.*

Parol Oral; verbal; by word of mouth.

Parol Evidence Where a written contract exists, evidence about promises or statements made prior to or during the execution of the writing that are not contained in the written contract.

Parties All persons who are interested in the subject matter of an action and who have a right to make defense, control the proceedings, examine and cross-examine witnesses, and appeal from the judgment.

Partition A proceeding the object of which is to enable those who own property as joint tenants or tenants in common to put an end to the tenancy so as to vest in each a sole estate in specific property or an allotment of the lands and tenements. If a division of the estate is impracticable, the estate ought to be sold and the proceeds divided.

Partners The owners of a partnership.

Partnership A form of business organization; specifically, an association of two or more persons to carry on as co-owners of a business for profit.

Partnership by Estoppel The appearance of partnership when there is no partnership; it arises when a person misleads a second person into believing that the first person is a partner of a third person; a theory that allows the second person to recover from the first person all reasonable damages the second person has suffered due to his reliance on the appearance of partnership.

Partnership Interest A partner's ownership interest in a partnership.

Party to Be Charged The person against whom enforcement of a contract is sought; the person who is asserting the statute of frauds as a defense.

Par Value   An arbitrary dollar amount assigned to shares by the articles of incorporation, representing the minimum amount of consideration for which the corporation may issue the shares and the portion of consideration that must be allocated to the stated capital amount.

Patent   A patent for land is a conveyance of title to government lands by the government; a patent of an invention is the right of monopoly secured by statute to those who invent or discover new and useful devices and processes.

Patentee   The holder of a patent.

Pawn   A pledge; a bailment of personal property as security for some debt or engagement, redeemable on certain terms, and with an implied power of sale on default.

Payee   A person to whom a payment is made or is made payable.

Pecuniary   Financial; pertaining or relating to money.

Pendente Lite   During the litigation.

Per Capita   A distribution of property in which each member of a group shares equally.

Per Curiam   By the court as a whole, without an opinion signed by a particular judge.

Peremptory Challenge   A challenge to a proposed juror that a defendant may make as an absolute right, and that cannot be questioned by either opposing counsel or the court.

Perfection   The process or method by which a secured party obtains a priority in certain collateral belonging to a debtor against creditors or claimants of a debtor; it usually entails giving notice of the security interest, such as by taking possession or filing a financial statement.

Performance   The fulfillment of a contractual duty.

Periodic Tenancy   The tenancy that exists when the landlord and tenant agree that rent will be paid in regular successive intervals until notice to terminate is given but do not agree on a specific duration of the lease. A typical periodic tenancy is a tenancy from month to month.

Perjury   The willful and corrupt false swearing or affirming, after an oath lawfully administered, in the course of a judicial or quasi-judicial proceeding, as to some matter material to the issue or point in question.

Per Se   In itself or as such.

Personal Property   All objects and rights, other than real property, that can be owned. See *Real Property*.

Per Stirpes   A distribution in which each surviving descendant divides the share that his or her parent would have taken if the parent had survived. Also called *by right of representation*.

Petition   In equity pleading, a petition is in the nature of a pleading (at least when filed by a stranger to the suit) and forms a basis for independent action.

Petition (Bankruptcy)   The document filed with the appropriate federal court that initiates a bankruptcy proceeding. It may be either a voluntary petition (i.e., filed by the debtor) or an involuntary petition (i.e., filed by creditors).

Piercing the Corporate Veil   Holding a shareholder responsible for acts of a corporation due to a shareholder's domination and improper use of the corporation.

Plaintiff   The party who sues in a civil case.

Plaintiff in Error   The unsuccessful party to the action who prosecutes a writ of error in a higher court.

Plea   A plea is an answer to a declaration or complaint or any material allegation of fact therein that, if untrue, would defeat the action. In criminal procedure, a plea is the matter that the accused, on his arraignment, alleges in answer to the charge against him.

Pleadings   The documents the parties file with the court when they state their claims and counterarguments early in a civil case. Examples include the complaint and the answer.

Pledge   A pawn; a bailment of personal property as security for some debt or engagement, redeemable on certain terms, and with an implied power of sale on default.

Pledgee   A person to whom personal property is pledged by a pledgor.

Pledgor   A person who makes a pledge of personal property to a pledgee.

Police Power   The states' power to regulate to promote the public health, safety, morals, and welfare.

Positive Law   Laws actually and specifically enacted or adopted by proper authority for the government of a jural society as distinguished from principles of morality or laws of honor.

Possession   Respecting real property, exclusive dominion and control such as owners of like property usually exercise over it. Manual control of personal property either as owner or as one having a qualified right in it.

Postdated Check   A check dated with a date later than its date of issue.

Power of Attorney   A written authorization by a principal to an agent to perform specified acts on behalf of the principal. See *Attorney-in-Fact*.

Precedent   A past judicial decision relied on as authority in a present case.

Preemptive Right   A shareholder's option to purchase new issuances of shares in proportion to the shareholder's current ownership of the corporation.

Preference   The act of a debtor in paying or securing one or more of his creditors in a manner more favorable to them than to other creditors or to the exclusion of such other creditors. In the absence of statute, a preference is perfectly good, but to be legal it must be bona fide, and not a mere subterfuge of the debtor to secure a future benefit to himself or to prevent the application of his property to his debts.

Preferential   Having priority.

Preferred Shareholders   Shareholders who have dividend and liquidation preferences over other classes of shareholders, usually common shareholders.

Prenuptial Contract   A contract between prospective marriage partners respecting matters such as property ownership and division.

Preponderance   Most; majority; more probable than not.

Prerogative   A special power, privilege, or immunity, usually used in reference to an official or his office.

Presentment   A demand for acceptance or payment of a negotiable instrument made on the maker, acceptor, drawee, or other payor by or on behalf of the holder.

Presumption   A term used to signify that which may be assumed without proof, or taken for granted. It is asserted as a self-evident result of human reason and experience.

Pretermitted   In the law of wills, an heir born after the execution of the testator's will.

Prima Facie   At first sight; a fact that is presumed to be true unless disproved by contrary evidence.

Prima Facie Case   A case sufficiently strong that, unless rebutted by the defendant in some fashion, it entitles the plaintiff to recover against the defendant.

Principal   In agency law, one under whose direction an agent acts and for whose benefit that agent acts.

Priority   Having precedence or the better right.

Privilege   Generally, a legal right to engage in conduct that would otherwise result in legal liability. Privileges are commonly classified as absolute (unqualified) or conditional (qualified). Occasionally, privilege is also used to denote a legal right to refrain from particular behavior (e.g., the constitutional privilege against self-incrimination).

Privity of Contract   The existence of a direct contractual relation between two parties.

Probate   A term used to include all matters of which probate courts have jurisdiction, which in many states are the estates of deceased persons and of persons under guardianship.

Procedural Law   The body of law controlling public bodies such as courts, as they create and enforce rules of substantive law. See *Substantive Law*.

Proceeds   Whatever is received on the sale, exchange, collection, or other disposition of collateral.

Process   Generally, the summons or notice of beginning of suit.

Proffer   To offer for acceptance or to make a tender of.

Profit   An interest in land giving a person the right to enter land owned by another and remove natural resources (e.g., timber) from the land. Also called *profit à prendre*.

Promisee   The person to whom a promise is made.

Promisor   A person who makes a promise to another; a person who promises.

Promissory Estoppel   An equitable doctrine that protects those who foreseeably and reasonably rely on the promises of others by enforcing such promises when enforcement is necessary to avoid injustice, even though one or more of the elements normally required for an enforceable agreement is absent.

Promissory Note   Commercial paper or instrument in which the maker promises to pay a specific sum of money to another person, to his order, or to bearer.

Promoter   A person who incorporates a business, organizes its initial management, and raises its initial capital.

Property   Something that is capable of being owned. A right or interest associated with something that gives the owner the ability to exercise dominion over it.

Pro Rata   Proportionate; in proportion.

Prospectus   In securities law, a document given to prospective purchasers of a security that contains information about an issuer of securities and the securities being issued.

Pro Tanto   For so much; to such an extent.

Proximate Cause   A legal limitation on a negligent wrongdoer's liability for the actual consequences of his actions. Such wrongdoers are said to be relieved of responsibility for consequences that are too remote or not the proximate result of their actions. Various tests for proximate cause are employed by the courts.

Proxy   A person who is authorized to vote the shares of another person. Also, the written authorization empowering a person to vote the shares of another person.

Pseudoforeign Corporation   A corporation incorporated under the laws of a state but doing most of its business in one other state.

Publicly Held Corporation   A corporation owned by a large number of widely dispersed shareholders.

Punitive Damages   See *Damages, Punitive.*

Purchase Money Security Interest   A security interest that is (1) taken or retained by the seller of collateral to secure all or part of its purchase price or (2) taken by a debtor to acquire rights in or the use of the collateral if the value is so used.

Put   A type of option permitting a person to sell a fixed number of securities at a fixed price at a specified time. See *Call.*

Q

Qualified Acceptance   A conditional or modified acceptance. In order to create a contract, an acceptance must accept the offer substantially as made; hence, a qualified acceptance is no acceptance at all, is treated by the courts as a rejection of the offer made, and is in effect an offer by the offeree, which the offeror may, if he chooses, accept and thus create a contract.

Quantum Meruit   As much as is deserved. A part of a common law action in assumpsit for the value of services rendered.

Quash   To vacate or make void.

Quasi-Contract   The doctrine by which courts imply, as a matter of law, a promise to pay the reasonable value of goods or services when the party receiving such goods or services has knowingly done so under circumstances that make it unfair to retain them without paying for them.

Quasi-Judicial   Acts of public officers involving investigation of facts and drawing conclusions from them as a basis of official action.

Quiet Title, Action to   An action to establish a claimant's title in land by requiring adverse claimants to come into court to prove their claim or to be barred from asserting it later.

Quitclaim Deed   A deed conveying only the right, title, and interest of the grantor in the property described, as distinguished from a deed conveying the property itself.

Quorum   That number of persons, shares represented, or officers who may lawfully transact the business of a meeting called for that purpose.

Quo Warranto   By what authority. The name of a writ (and also of the whole pleading) by which the government commences an action to recover an office or franchise from the person or corporation in possession of it.

R

Ratification   The adoption or affirmance by a person of a prior act that did not bind him.

Real Property   The earth's crust and all things firmly attached to it.

Rebuttal   Testimony addressed to evidence produced by the opposite party; rebutting evidence.

Receiver   One appointed by a court to take charge of a business or the property of another during litigation to preserve it and/or to dispose of it as directed by the court.

Recklessness   Behavior that indicates a conscious disregard for a known high risk of probable harm to others.

Recognizance   At common law, an obligation entered into before some court of record or magistrate duly authorized, with a condition to do some particular act, usually to appear and answer to a criminal accusation. Being taken in open court and entered on the order book, it was valid without the signature or seal of any of the obligors.

Recorder   A public officer of a town or county charged with the duty of keeping the record books required by law to be kept in his or her office and of receiving and causing to be copied in such books such instruments as by law are entitled to be recorded.

Redemption   The buying back of one's property after it has been sold. The right to redeem property sold under an order or decree of court is purely a privilege conferred by, and does not exist independently of, statute.

Redemption Right   Also called a call. In corporation law, the right of a corporation to repurchase shares held by existing shareholders.

Redress   Remedy; indemnity; reparation.

Reformation   An equitable remedy in which a court effectively rewrites the terms of a contract.

Rejection   In contract law, an express or implied manifestation of an offeree's unwillingness to contract on the terms of an offer. In sales law, a buyer's refusal to accept goods because they are defective or nonconforming.

Release   The giving up or abandoning of a claim or right to a person against whom the claim exists or the right is to be enforced or exercised. It is the discharge of a debt by the act of the party, in distinction from an extinguishment that is a discharge by operation of law.

Remainderman   One who is entitled to the remainder of the estate after a particular estate carved out of it has expired.

Remand   A process whereby an appellate court returns the case to a lower court (usually a trial court) for proceedings not inconsistent with the appellate court's decision.

Remedy   The appropriate legal form of relief by which a remediable right may be enforced.

Glossary of Legal Terms and Definitions

Remittitur   The certificate of reversal issued by an appellate court upon reversing the order or judgment appealed from.

Repatriation   An investor's removal to the investor's nation of profits from his investment in a foreign nation.

Replevin   A common law action by which the owner recovers possession of his own goods.

Repudiation   Indicating to another party to a contract that the party does not intend to perform his obligations.

Res   The thing; the subject matter of a suit; the property involved in the litigation; a matter; property; the business; the affair; the transaction.

Rescind   As the word is applied to contracts, to terminate the contract as to future transactions or to annul the contract from the beginning.

Rescission   The rescinding or cancellation of a contract or transaction. In general, its effect is to restore the parties to their original precontractual position.

Residue   Residuary; all that portion of the estate of a testator of which no effectual disposition has been made by his will otherwise than in the residuary clause.

Res Ipsa Loquitur   Literally, the thing speaks for itself. A doctrine that, in some circumstances, gives rise to an inference that a defendant was negligent and that his negligence was the cause of the plaintiff's injury.

Res Judicata   A matter that has been adjudicated; that which is definitely settled by a judicial decision.

Respondeat Superior   A legal doctrine making an employer (or master) liable for the torts of an employee (servant) that are committed within the scope of the employee's employment.

Respondent   A term often used to describe the party charged in an administrative proceeding. The party adverse to the appellant in a case appealed to a higher court. In this sense, often synonymous with *appellee*.

Restatement(s)   Collections of legal rules produced by the American Law Institute, covering certain subject matter areas. Although *Restatements* are often persuasive to courts, they are not legally binding unless adopted by the highest court of a particular state.

Restitution   A remedy whereby one is able to obtain the return of that which he has given the other party, or an amount of money equivalent to that which he has given the other party.

Restrictive Covenant   An agreement restricting the use of real property.

Reverse   To reject or overturn a judgment or order of a court. An appellate court, for example, may reverse the decision of a trial court. See *Affirm*.

Revocation   In general, the recalling or voiding of a prior action. In contract law, the withdrawal of an offer by the offeror prior to effective acceptance by the offeree.

Right   An interest given and protected by law. In corporation law, an option to purchase shares given to existing shareholders, permitting them to buy quantities of newly issued securities in proportion to their current ownership.

Right of Appraisal   See *Appraisal, Right of*.

Right of First Refusal   In corporation law, a share transfer restriction granting a corporation or its shareholders an option to match the offer that a selling shareholder receives for her shares. See also *Option Agreement*.

Right of Survivorship   A feature of some types of co-ownership of property causing a co-owner's interest in property to be transferred on his death immediately and by operation of law to his surviving co-owner(s). See *Tenancy by the Entirety*, *Tenant in Partnership,* and *Joint Tenancy*.

Riparian   Pertaining to or situated on the bank of a river.

S

Sale of Goods   The transfer of ownership to tangible personal property in exchange for money, other goods, or the performance of service.

Sale on Approval   A conditional sale that is to become final only in case the buyer, after a trial, approves or is satisfied with the article sold.

Sale or Return   A contract in which the seller delivers a quantity of goods to the buyer on the understanding that if the buyer desires to retain, use, or sell any portion of the goods, he will consider such part as having been sold to him, and that he will return the balance or hold it as bailee for the seller.

Sanction   The penalty that will be incurred by a wrongdoer for the violation of a law.

Satisfaction   A performance of the terms of an accord. If such terms require a payment of a sum of money, then satisfaction means that such payment has been made.

Scienter   In cases of fraud and deceit, the word means knowledge on the part of the person making the representations, at the time when they are made, that they are false. In an action for deceit, scienter must be proved.

S Corporation   Also called *Subchapter S corporation*. A close corporation whose shareholders have elected to be taxed essentially like partners are taxed under federal income tax law.

Seal   At common law, a seal is an impression on wax or some other tenacious material, but in modern practice the letters *l.s.* (locus sigilli) or the word *seal* enclosed in a scroll, either written, or printed, and acknowledged in the body of the instrument to be a seal, are often used as substitutes.

Security   An instrument commonly dealt with in the securities markets or commonly recognized as a medium of investment and evidencing an obligation of an issuer or a share, participation, or other interest in an enterprise.

Security Agreement   An agreement that creates or provides a security interest or lien on personal property. A term used in the UCC including a wide range of transactions in the nature of chattel mortgages, conditional sales, and so on.

Security Interest   A lien given by a debtor to his creditor to secure payment or performance of a debt or obligation.

Service   As applied to a process of courts, the word ordinarily implies something in the nature of an act or proceeding adverse to the party served, or of a notice to him.

Set off   That right that exists between two parties, each of whom, under an independent contract, owes an ascertained amount to the other, to calculate their respective debts by way of mutual deduction, so that, in any action brought for the larger debt, the residue only, after such deduction, shall be recovered.

Settlor   A person who creates a trust. Also called *trustor.*

Severable Contract   A contract that is not entire or indivisible. If the consideration is single, the contract is entire; but if it is expressly or by necessary implication apportioned, the contract is severable. The question is ordinarily determined by inquiring whether the contract embraces one or more subject matters, whether the obligation is due at the same time to the same person, and whether the consideration is entire or apportioned.

Share   An equity security, representing a shareholder's ownership of a corporation.

Share Dividend   See *Dividends, Share.*

Shareholder   Also called *stockholder.* An owner of a corporation, who has no inherent right to manage the corporation but has liability limited to his capital contribution.

Share Split   Also called *stock split.* Traditionally, a corporation's dividing existing shares into two or more shares, thereby increasing the number of authorized, issued, and outstanding shares and reducing their par value. In modern corporation law, treated like a share dividend.

Sight   A term signifying the date of the acceptance or that of protest for the nonacceptance of a bill of exchange; for example, 10 days after sight.

Sinking Fund   A fund established by an issuer of securities to accumulate funds to repurchase the issuer's securities.

Situs   Location; local position; the place where a person or thing is, is his situs. Intangible property has no actual situs, but it may have a legal situs, and for the purpose of taxation, its legal situs is at the place where it is owned and not at the place where it is owed.

Slander   The defamation action appropriate to oral defamation.

Sole Proprietor   The owner of a sole proprietorship.

Sole Proprietorship   A form of business under which one person owns and controls the business.

Sovereign Immunity   Generally, the idea that the sovereign (or state) may not be sued unless it consents to be sued. In antitrust law, the statutory immunity from antitrust liability for governmental actions that foreign governments enjoy under the Foreign Sovereign Immunities Act of 1976.

Special Damages   See *Damages, Special.*

Specific Performance   A contract remedy whereby the defendant is ordered to perform according to the terms of his contract.

Stale Check   A check more than six months past its date of issue.

Standby Letter of Credit   See *Letter of Credit, Standby.*

Standing   The legal requirement that anyone seeking to challenge a particular action in court must demonstrate that such action substantially affects his legitimate interests before he will be entitled to bring suit.

Stare Decisis   A doctrine whereby a court is said to be bound to follow past cases that are like the present case on the facts and on the legal issues it presents, and that are issued by an authoritative court.

Stated Capital   Also called *capital stock.* A balance sheet account; shareholders' capital contributions representing the par value of par shares or stated value of no-par shares.

Stated Value   An arbitrary dollar amount assigned to shares by the board of directors, representing the minimum amount of consideration for which the corporation may issue the shares and the portion of consideration that must be allocated to the stated capital account.

State Implementation Plan A document prepared by states in which the emissions to the air from individual sources are limited legally so that the area will meet the national ambient air quality standards.

Status Quo The existing state of things. In contract law, returning a party to status quo or status quo ante means putting him in the position he was in before entering the contract.

Statute of Frauds A statute that provides that no lawsuit may be brought to enforce certain classes of contracts unless there is a written note or memorandum signed by the party against whom enforcement is sought or by his agent.

Statute of Limitations A statute that requires that certain classes of lawsuits must be brought within defined limits of time after the right to begin them accrued or the right to bring the lawsuit is lost.

Stipulation An agreement between opposing counsel in a pending action, usually required to be made in open court and entered on the minutes of the court, or else to be in writing and filed in the action, ordinarily entered into for the purpose of avoiding delay, trouble, or expense in the conduct of the action.

Stock A business's inventory. Also, as used in corporation and securities law, see *Share*.

Stock Dividend See *Dividends, Share*.

Stockholder See *Shareholder*.

Stock Split See *Share Split*.

Stoppage in Transitu A right that the vendor of goods on credit has to recall them, or retake them, on the discovery of the insolvency of the vendee. It continues so long as the carrier remains in the possession and control of the goods or until there has been an actual or constructive delivery to the vendee, or some third person has acquired a bona fide right in them.

Stop-Payment Order A request made by the drawer of a check to the drawee asking that the order to pay not be followed.

Straight Voting A form of voting for directors that ordinarily permits a shareholder to cast a number of votes equal to the number of shares he owns for as many nominees as there are directors to be elected. See *Cumulative Voting*.

Strict Liability Legal responsibility placed on an individual for the results of his actions irrespective of whether he was culpable or at fault.

Strike Suit In corporation law, a derivative suit motivated primarily by an intent to gain an out-of-court settlement for the suing shareholder personally or to earn large attorney's fees for lawyers, rather than to obtain a recovery for the corporation.

Subchapter S Corporation See *S Corporation*.

Sub Judice Before a court.

Sublease A transfer of some but not all of a tenant's remaining right to possess property under a lease.

Sub Nom. Under the name of.

Subpoena A process for compelling a witness to appear before a court and give testimony.

Subrogation The substitution of one person in the place of another with reference to a lawful claim or right, frequently referred to as the doctrine of substitution. It is a device adopted or invented by equity to compel the ultimate discharge of a debt or obligation by the person who in good conscience ought to pay it.

Subscription In corporation law, a promise by a person to purchase from a corporation a specified number of shares at a specified price.

Subsidiary Corporation A corporation owned and controlled by another corporation, called a *parent corporation*.

Substantive Law The body of law setting out rights and duties that affect how people behave in organized social life. See *Procedural Law*.

Sui Generis Of its own kind, unique, peculiar to itself.

Summary Judgment A method of reaching a judgment in a civil case before trial. The standard for granting a motion for summary judgment is that there be no significant issue of material fact and that the moving party be entitled to judgment as a matter of law.

Summary Proceedings Proceedings, usually statutory, in the course of which many formalities are dispensed with. But such proceedings are not concluded without proper investigation of the facts, or without notice, or an opportunity to be heard by the person alleged to have committed the act, or whose property is sought to be affected.

Summons A writ or process issued and served on a defendant in a civil action for the purpose of securing his appearance in the action.

Superseding Cause See *Intervening Cause*.

Supra Above; above mentioned; in addition to.

Surety A person who promises to perform the same obligation as another person (the principal) and who is jointly liable along with the principal for that obligation's performance. See *Guarantor*.

T

T/A Trading as, indicating the use of a trade name.

Tacking The adding together of successive periods of adverse possession of persons in privity with each other, in order to constitute one continuous adverse possession for the time required by the statute, to establish title.

Takeover   A tender offer; also applied generally to any acquisition of one business by another business.

Tangible   Having a physical existence; real; substantial; evident.

Tariff   A tax or duty imposed on goods by a nation when the goods are imported into that nation.

Tax Haven   A nation that has no or minimal taxation of personal, business, and investment income.

Tenancy   General term indicating a possessory interest in property. In landlord-tenant law, a property owner's conveyance to another person of the right to possess the property exclusively for a period of time.

Tenancy at Sufferance   The leasehold interest that occurs when a tenant remains in possession of property after the expiration of a lease.

Tenancy at Will   A leasehold interest that occurs when property is leased for an indefinite period of time and is terminable at the will of either landlord or tenant.

Tenancy by the Entirety   A form of co-ownership of property by a married couple that gives the owners a right of survivorship and cannot be severed during life by the act of only one of the parties.

Tenancy for a Term   A leasehold interest that results when the landlord and tenant agree on a specific duration for a lease and fix the date on which the tenancy will terminate.

Tenancy in Common   A form of co-ownership of property that is freely disposable both during life and at death, and in which the co-owners have undivided interests in the property and equal rights to possess the property.

Tenancy in Partnership   The manner in which partners co-own partnership property, much like a tenancy in common, except that partners have a right of survivorship.

Tender   An unconditional offer of payment, consisting in the actual production in money or legal tender of a sum not less than the amount due.

Tender Offer   A public offer by a bidder to purchase a subject company's shares directly from its shareholders at a specified price for a fixed period of time.

Testament   A will; the disposition of one's property to take effect after death.

Testator   A deceased person who died leaving a will.

Testimony   In some contexts, the word bears the same import as the word *evidence,* but in most connections it has a much narrower meaning. Testimony is the words heard from the witness in court, and evidence is what the jury considers it worth.

Thin Capitalization   In corporation law, a ground for piercing the corporate veil due to the shareholders' contributing too little capital to the corporation in relation to its needs.

Third Party Beneficiary   A person who is not a party to a contract but who has the right to enforce it because the parties to the contract made the contract with the intent to benefit him.

Title   Legal ownership; also, a document evidencing legal rights to real or personal property.

Tombstone Advertisement   A brief newspaper advertisement alerting prospective shareholders that an issuer is offering to sell the securities described in the advertisement.

Tort   A private (civil) wrong against a person or his property.

Tortfeasor   A person who commits a tort; a wrongdoer.

Tortious   Partaking of the nature of a tort; wrongful; injurious.

Trade Fixtures   Articles of personal property that have been annexed to real property leased by a tenant during the term of the lease and that are necessary to the carrying on of a trade.

Trademark   A distinctive word, name, symbol, device, or combination thereof, which enables consumers to identify favored products or services and which may find protection under state or federal law.

Trade Secret   A secret formula, pattern, process, program, device, method, technique, or compilation of information that is used in its owner's business and affords that owner a competitive advantage. Trade secrets are protected by state law.

Transcript   A copy of a writing.

Transferee   A person to whom a transfer is made.

Transferor   A person who makes a transfer.

Treasury Shares   Previously outstanding shares repurchased by a corporation that are not canceled or restored to unissued status.

Treble Damages   See *Damages, Treble.*

Trespass   An unauthorized entry on another's property.

Trial   An examination before a competent tribunal, according to the law of the land, of the facts or law put in issue in a cause, for the purpose of determining such issue. When the court hears and determines any issue of fact or law for the purpose of determining the rights of the parties, it may be considered a trial.

Trust   A legal relationship in which a person who has legal title to property has the duty to hold it for the use or benefit of another person. The term is also used in a general sense to mean confidence reposed in one person by another.

Trustee   A person in whom property is vested in trust for another.

Trustee in Bankruptcy   The federal bankruptcy act defines the term as an officer, and he is an officer of the courts in a certain restricted sense, but not in any such sense as a receiver. He takes the legal title to the property of the bankrupt and in respect to suits stands in the same general position as a trustee of an express trust or an executor. His duties are fixed by statute. He is to collect and reduce to money the property of the estate of the bankrupt.

U

Ultra Vires   Beyond the powers. In administrative law, it describes an act that is beyond the authority granted to an administrative agency by its enabling legislation. In corporation law, it describes a corporation's performing an act beyond the limits of its purposes as stated in its articles of incorporation.

Unconscionable   In contract law, a contract that is grossly unfair or one-sided; one that "shocks the conscience of the court." The Uniform Commercial Code expressly gives courts the broad discretionary powers to deal with such contracts.

Unilateral Contract   A contract formed by an offer or a promise on one side for an act to be done on the other, and a doing of the act by the other by way of acceptance of the offer or promise; that is, a contract wherein the only acceptance of the offer that is necessary is the performance of the act.

Unliquidated   Undetermined in amount.

Usage of Trade   Customs and practices generally known by people in the business and usually assumed by parties to a contract for goods of that type.

Usurpation   In corporation law, an officer, director, or shareholder's taking to himself a business opportunity that belongs to his corporation.

Usury   The taking of more than the law allows on a loan or for forbearance of a debt. Illegal interest; interest in excess of the rate allowed by law.

V

Valid   Effective; operative; not void; subsisting; sufficient in law.

Value   Under the Code (except for negotiable instruments and bank collections), generally any consideration sufficient to support a simple contract.

Vendee   A purchaser of property. The word is more commonly applied to a purchaser of real property, the word *buyer* being more commonly applied to the purchaser of personal property.

Vendor   A person who sells property to a vendee. The words *vendor* and *vendee* are more commonly applied to the seller and purchaser of real estate, and the words *seller* and *buyer* are more commonly applied to the seller and purchaser of personal property.

Venire   The name of a writ by which a jury is summoned.

Venue   A requirement distinct from jurisdiction that the court be geographically situated so that it is the most appropriate and convenient court to try the case.

Verdict   Usually, the decision made by a jury and reported to the judge on the matters or questions submitted to it at trial. In some situations, however, the judge may be the party issuing a verdict, as, for example, in the motion for a directed verdict. See *Directed Verdict.*

Versus   Against.

Vest   To give an immediate fixed right of present or future enjoyment.

Vicarious Liability   The imposition of liability on one party for the wrongs of another. Also called *imputed liability.* For example, the civil liability of a principal for the wrongs his agent commits when acting within the scope of his employment. See *Respondeat Superior.* Such liability is also occasionally encountered in the criminal context (e.g., the criminal liability that some regulatory statutes impose on managers for the actions of employees under their supervision).

Void   That which is entirely null. A void act is one that is not binding on either party and that is not susceptible of ratification.

Voidable   Capable of being made void; not utterly null, but annullable, and hence that may be either voided or confirmed. See *Avoid.*

Voidable Title   A title that is capable of, or subject to, being judged invalid or void.

Voting Trust   A type of shareholder voting arrangement by which shareholders transfer their voting rights to a voting trustee.

W

Waive   To throw away; to relinquish voluntarily, as a right that one may enforce, if he chooses.

Waiver   The intentional relinquishment of a known right. It is a voluntary act and implies an election by the party to dispense with something of value, or to forgo some advantage that he or she might have demanded and insisted on.

Warehouse Receipt   A receipt issued by a person engaged in the business of storing goods for hire.

Warrant   An order authorizing a payment of money by another person to a third person. Also, an option to purchase a security. As a verb, the word means to defend; to guarantee; to enter into an obligation of warranty.

Warrant of Arrest   A legal process issued by competent authority, usually directed to regular officers of the law, but occasionally issued to private persons named in it, directing the arrest of a person or persons on grounds stated therein.

Warranty   An undertaking relating to characteristics of a thing being sold; a guaranty.

Waste   The material alteration, abuse, or destructive use of property by one in rightful possession of it that results in injury to one having an underlying interest in it.

Watered Shares   Also called *watered stock.* Shares issued in exchange for property that has been overvalued. See *Bonus Shares* and *Discount Shares.*

Will   A document executed with specific legal formalities that contains a person's instructions about the disposition of his property at his death.

Winding Up   In partnership and corporation law, the orderly liquidation of the business's assets.

Writ   A commandment of a court given for the purpose of compelling certain action from the defendant, and usually executed by a sheriff or other judicial officer.

Writ of Certiorari   An order of a court to an inferior court to forward the record of a case for reexamination by the superior court.

Wrongful Use of Civil Proceedings   An intentional tort designed to protect against the wrongful initiation of civil proceedings.

INDEX